The Photo-Journal Guide
to
MARVEL COMICS

VOLUME K-Z (#4)

Author and Photographer: Ernst Gerber

Introduction by: Stan Lee

Data compiled by: Paul Theiss

Library of Congress Catalog Number 91-072308

ISBN   Volume AJ (#3)   0-9623328-4-4
        Volume KZ (#4)   0-9623328-5-2
        Set. Vol. 3 & 4   0-9623328-7-9
        Deluxe Edition   0-9623328-8-7

*Dedicated to the
memory of my father
Eduard A. Gerber*

Reintroduction / Key / RVI

Marvel comics once heralded great Nazi Killers through the war years, like the Human Torch,Sub-Mariner and the Great Captain America, only to slowly sink through the waves of the great super-hero depression of the 1950's. The total circulation of the Famed Marvel comics lagged behind most other publishers in 1961 (see graph on page B3).

Then at the low point of Super hero history a relative unknown with opulent creative talents appeared from the nether world to bring forth a new era in comics entertainment. Stan Lee succeeded where others failed and created a new order for the super hero. We are proud to be able to produce this MARVEL reference book which stands as a memorial to his creativity. If you haven't already, please read his introduction in the first volume. Here we'd like to give you a brief biography of "Stan the Man".

✦ ✦ ✦

Stan Lee, Chairman of Marvel Entertainment, is known to millions as the man whose superheroes propelled Marvel to its preeminent position in the comicbook industry. Hundreds of legendary characters, such as Spider-Man, The Incredible Hulk, The Fantastic Four, Iron Man, Daredevil, and Dr. Strange all grew out of his fertile imagination.

"Stan the Man," as he's known to fans worldwide, first joined Marvel Comics in New York more than three decades ago at age sixteen. During his first twenty-five years at Marvel's helm, as editor, art director and head writer, Stan scripted no fewer than two and sometimes as many as five complete comic books per week. His prodigious output may comprise the largest body of published work by any single writer.

Additionally, Stan wrote newspaper features, radio and television scripts, and screenplays. And, in his "spare time," he lectured at virtually every campus in the United States and Canada on such varied topics as "The Relationship of Comicstrips to Screenplays," "The Art of Story Telling," "Icons in Contemporary American Literature," and "Pop Art vs. The Classics."

Stan Lee's first few years at Marvel were interrupted when he volunteered for service with the Signal Corps during World War II. He was one of only nine men in the U.S. Army to be given the military classification "playwright." During his three years of army service, Stan designed and scripted training films and instructional manuals for various branches of the service.

In the early sixties, Stan ushered in what has come to be known as "The Marvel Age of Comics," creating major new superheroes while breathing new life and style into such old favorites as Captain America, The Human Torch, and The Sub-Mariner. His unique concept of superheroes who possess everyday human foibles and frailities captured the hearts of readers everywhere. His innovative concepts, the first comicbook characters with whom readers could truly empathize, resulted in skyrocketing sales for Marvel, as well as the creation of a new, older audience for the entire comicbook industry.

By the time Stan was named publisher of Marvel Comics in 1972, his comics were the nation's biggest sellers. Today, Marvel continues to be a dominant factor in the marketplace, selling in excess of seven million copies a month in the United States and is published in twenty-six different countries in fifteen languages around the world.

Since 1977 Stan has spread his talents into many new arenas. He launched and produced the SPIDER-MAN newspaper strip, which today is the most successful of all super-hero strips, and he has written more than a dozen best-selling books for major publishers. He became creative head of Marvel Productions Ltd., an animation studio on the west coast where Hulk and Spider-Man became Saturday morning television heros; has ventured successfully onto the silver screen with his creative talents and has produced a line of video-cassettes as well. Additionally, Stan is continually creating new and original concepts specifically for motion pictures and television. Though Stan Lee's almost legendary achievements continue to thrill all of comic book fandom, Stan will continue to bring us thrills with a bonanza of unique and new features in the TV and cinema capitol of the world. ✦ ✦ ✦

KEY: Using this reference book

Which Covers are illustrated?

All Marvel titles between 1961 and 1985 are represented. All Super-hero titles and all serious character titles are shown in their entirety from the first Marvel Comic (MC) company issue in July of 1961 until at least 1986. The illustrations of the most important or hot titles are continued through the McFarlane issues into the 1990's. To give the big boys the necessary room and size, some covers were sacrificed during this period. By popular consensus we thinned Westerns, trimmed reprint titles, and beheaded romance and teen issues.

How do I find a particular title?

Generally everything is listed in alphabetical order. However, we like to keep historic numerical sets together under a single title. Therefore, Captain America is shown right after Tales of Suspense;Power-Man is shown right after Luke Cage, etc. You should have no problem in finding your favorite title; however, should the impossible occur, we did supply a title index of illustrated comics at the back of Volume K-Z (#4).

What is a "reference number"?

Having been an active collector since those predawn years of the early 1970's, one single thing always frustrated me more than anything else (being also a faithful stamp collector and disciple of Scott's stamp catalog): that comics never had a permanent identifying catalog or "reference number". So, starting in Photo-Journal Volumes #1 and #2, we assigned each title with a permanent reference number, followed by the issue number. So that Number 85-16 will *always* be AMAZING SPIDER-MAN #16. Sometimes new titles are created and need to fit between whole numbers. We, therefore, similar to librarians, have created a "Dewey-Decimal" system of our own; all set numbers will maintain their numerical and alphabetical place based on the predominant title of a set, even if the title changes. If I want to buy "Ghost Rider #6, it is unclear as to which of several series I want. However, if I instruct that I wish to purchase #772.4-6; that is specific and irrefutably the exact issue I want.

How do I determine the value of a Comic Book?

Each comic book listed in this reference book has a listed RVI value. This is a "Relative Value Index". Dollar values change all the time; if we were to give each comic a dollar value, then by the time this book is published this value would be erroneous. However, comics generally increase in value at the same rate, their value "relative" to each other stays the same. Certainly some titles spurt and some sag for any given year, but by and by "water" and value seek their own relative value. More is said in the chapter entitled "RVI, Value", but for the sake of brevity, check out the graph in that chapter. The 1991 RVI is approximately 1.4. This means if you multiply any RVI times 1.4 the result will be the dollar value for that comic book in Near Mint grade for 1991. For example the RVI for Spider-Man #16 is 80. Thus for 1991 the value of Spider-Man #16 in Near Mint grade is 1.4 X 80 or $112. Values for lesser grade can be determined by multiplying by the fractions found in the "grading chapter". Estimated RVI values are given through 1996; not that we can predict the future, but comics have been the most reliable investment since the 1970's, and predicting a consistent and modest increase through 1996 does not mark us as a swami.

Artist/Info.

The most important ingredient to a comic book is the art work. Without the artwork, we have "Reader's Digest" and not comic books. Characters are great, stories important, but somehow in the last 15 years of collecting, values seem to migrate upward when certain talented artists show their wares. In the 1940's few signed their work, and few readers cared. As the appreciation for the artwork grew, so did the visual credits, and so did the demand for individual creative work. The more the artists get credited, the more their work is sought after. We are intent on doing our part to give credit to this supremely creative artform. We not only credit the "Hot" artists, but also those cloaked into heretofore anonymity. A handy artist index is located on page B9.

Other information provided is shown in brackets and includes origins, first appearances, special character events, and publication dates (shown as; Publ. 5-16-62). Note that the date a comic book first becomes public (publication date) is generally a couple of months before the issue date. It is the publication date that establishes what origin or first appearance really was first.

How is the information presented?

With the photographs, in white print on black background, we show the reference number of the title set, the title name and then list which issue numbers are illustrated. We did not number each issue, since the numbers are generally visible on every comic book. The text information for each set (black type on a white background) generally is shown at the end of the set, or sometimes before, depending on the availability of space. The title is listed and then the number of comic books that were published for that run. Do note that we don't always illustrate all of the comics that were ever published. Finally, we list the reference number together with issue number, the date that appears on each cover, the RVI, and Artist/Info. Please note that our RVI never is less than 1. Our opinion is that any Near Mint back issue stored and inventoried by a comic book business has a minimum value of RVI = 1. ✦✦✦

Collecting Marvel Comics

This chapter concerns itself with collecting Marvel Comics. Not that I have personal favorites, nor that much of what is said hereinafter doesn't also apply itself to DC Comics, Archie Comics, Harvey, or other publishers. I am neutral and whatever wonderful things I say about Marvel comics could just as well have been said about the "others"; it's just that this whole book *is* about Marvel Comics.

I, personally, am not an expert at the characters or the story lines of the 5,000 or more Marvel comics in the Silver Age to present. I have read many outstanding analyses of the actual content of Marvel comics, in particular the Origin books by Stan Lee. This book offers no analysis, but is intended to be a collector's reference guide. We are not as concerned with what happened in the stories and to the characters, but rather with information that answers: When were they published, who did the artwork and what collecting value do they have? We offer some advice on how to treat this hobby so that it doesn't mistreat you.

We really intend this chapter and this book to make you better informed as to the WHOLE of the Silver Age to present, "Marvel Universe" and how it relates to the collecting community. As is/was/and forever shall be with our Photo-Journal Guide to Comics 1933-1961, we want every serious collector/buyer/seller to have one of our books next to him to refer to when collecting/ buying/selling. Why? Because we are spiritually motivated for the true cause of truth, justice, and the American way? No. Because we like to make money the old fashion way...we want to EARN it (and some truth and justice TOO, I promise).

Collecting Transition

By and large, comics from their inception in 1933 through 1960 were born and nurtured to serve a single purpose: to sell and make a profit. Who were they designed to sell to? Kids, generally from 8 to 13 years of age. These kids influenced what was hot and all the publishers frantically changed their characters and what they did for a living to follow the latest trend. Most of our readers can appreciate the Collecting genre graph from Volume 2 that clearly illustrates the violent jerking of the trend crazes.

Certainly we had dozens of creative artists and storytellers, including the incomparable Stan Lee and Jack Kirby that could have made Stephen King look sane. However, they were bound by the editors to follow the trends of the pre-adolescents. Marvel was locked into 5th or 6th place amongst publishers and was working very hard with their unending, neverending monster stories of the late 1950's. Then it happened. As Stan Lee relates, a startling event took place in 1961: His wife spoke to him!! From this inspiration he decided to place his mark on the industry that had already claimed 22 years of his professional career without leaving an impression.

Taking the lead from the "Distinguished Competition" and their seemingly successful, new direction in "JUSTICE LEAGUE OF AMERICA", Stan fashioned a new trend, nay, a new direction, a rebirth of the Gold age of super-heroes, a SILVER age rebirth by giving origin to the FANTASTIC FOUR. But even more important, for the first time stories and comics were slowly building a deeper following than just pre-adolescents; Stan crept with his characterizations into the adolescent market, then into the teen market, and as the collectors grew older Marvel did not release its grip. Eventually, Marvel and their collectors grew to adulthood and collecting and comic books were changed forever.

Transition was complete by the 1980's; comics now were mostly for young adults (in age as well as spirit). The CIRCULATION GRAPH located bottom left, reports the circulation statistics of the major publishers from 1960 through 1986. The significant one in our lives is the circulation of Marvel Comics. Starting in dead last place in 1960, they colored their way through the competition and have been on top since 1970. The graph is also interesting because it illustrates the obvious problems many publishers were having in the early 1980's when the independents were starting to be felt.

The Comic Revolution

Comic collecting, as we have become accustomed to today, is totally different than it was in 1961. Yes, back in 1961 we actually went to grocery stores and drug stores to buy comic books. Those horse and buggy days rendered fond but frustrating memories. You never knew for sure you'd get a copy of your favorite title, and certainly the way they were manhandled on those famous wire display racks makes it a wonder that any mint copies still exist from the 1960's. Comic book store? What was that? Circulation was virtually, totally through the normal magazine distribution network or direct subscription service.

What really spawned the comic revolution was the dawn of price guides and smart young entrepeneurs who ventured into new territory with stores and mail-order businesses featuring comics as their primary revenue. Even in the mid 1970's there were less than a couple dozen stores. As the stores grew by leaps and bounds, the management of distribution, revolutionized by the formation of several carnivorous competing distribution centers, made life so much easier for the stores. Finally (or what will happen next?) the revolution ended with the present format for buying comics.

(1) you look at the distributor's catalogs of up and coming issues, give your advance order selection to your local comic book store, and order a few hundred investment copies of the latest origin or #1 issues. (2) The store fills out an advance order form to the major distributor, who in turn (3) places an order with the comic book publishing company. The publisher now has a good feeling of how many copies to print and (4) can now send most of the freshly printed comics directly to one address.

100
90
80
70
60
50
40
30
20
10
0
-10
(Percent, %)
X-Men
Avengers
Daredevil
Fantastic Four
Captain America
Incredible Hulk
Thor
Spider-Man
1980
1981
1982
1983
1984
1985
1986
1987
1988
1989
1990
1991
YEAR

Marvel
Charlton
Harvey
Archie
DC
10.0
9.0
8.0
7.0
6.0
5.0
4.0
3.0
2.0
1.0
Reported Monthly Circulation (in millions)
1960
1962
1964
1966
1968
1970
1972
1974
1976
1978
1980
1982
1984
1986
YEAR

Do I think this is comic heaven? It has propelled comics back up into the stratosphere where they justly belong. Not many years ago, the TV generation almost wiped us out. Now creativity, great art and inspirational stores are being rewarded by great sales. So, yea, I think we are approaching comic heaven: but hey! you can't get there without a copy of our Photo-Journal; order from your nearest distributor!

Marvel Fervor

It seems that there is a certain Marvel fervor, or mania if you will. Why is that? I believe Stan Lee started the trademark of Marvel by capturing you with continuing "soap-opera" stories that made you identify with the almost human behavior of their super-heroes. In identifying with the characters, the readers developed a mini-bond. and became life long fans. It started slow, but as the readers were converted, they stayed. Finally after many years Marvel inched its way into the circulation lead, and there they stay; after all that is the name of the game!

Does this mean that Marvel is always the best comic to buy? Does this mean that Marvel comics are the perfect investment because they always will go up in value? This is reality: NO! Take a peek at the GRAPH located just above which illustrates the value trends of the "main sails" of the Marvel Line The graph shows, by year, the percentage increase (or decrease) in the value of back-issues.

As you can see, FERVOR can have positive values as well as negative values. This graph is interesting because it shows the individual fluctuations of the various titles as they reacted to certain key fervor influences. The New X-men created strong demand early in 1980's. Even the McFarlane influence can be

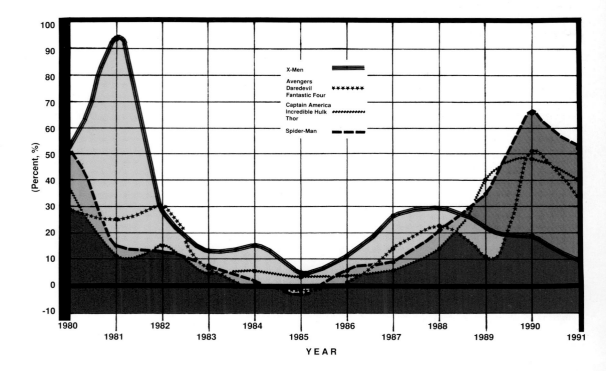

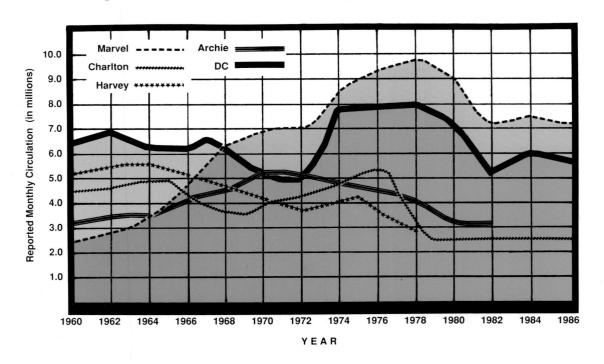

seen on Spider-Man. We can also clearly see the slow and low demand cycle of the Marvels through the weak period of 1981-1986. Certain Marvels were not always hot. Investors should examine this graph very carefully since it is the epitome of what can happen to any "HOT" title.

Collecting FERVOR for Marvels can be divided into two major categories: Short Term Heated Fervor, and Long Term Consistent, Cool but Collected, Fervor. There are anticipatory short term HOT flashes that reverberate throughout the collecting world. With our current advance speculative marketing system, books become HOT before they are published. PAY ATTENTION: this may not be the goose that lays the golden egg. These types of HOT books also produce millions of comics on the supply end of our cycle and after the short term fervor wears off, we might have a scrambled egg rather than gold!

The other half of the Fervor team is the real comic book super-hero: the consistent winner. The success of investments in the consistent demand books like Spider-Man, Fantastic Four or most of the Marvels from the early 1960's has proven over time that these comics are "stable hot". The supply of nice grade comics from the early 1960's is relatively low and the demand will likely always exceed this supply and that is what makes healthy collecting fervor.

Collecting by Genre

No, that isn't a famous french collector; it is a type, or category of collecting. Genre collections could be by the appearing character, by the title, by the artist, or any other category.

In the Marvel collecting world, I've observed that in recent times the contributing artist is one of the single, strongest influences in the demand of a comic book. Spend your collecting dollars on rising, brilliant, young artists and you will do well. A bit riskier option is to go after #1 issues. Certainly, they are a much better risk than going after #2 or #8 issues (if the series lasts that long). New characters are also eagerly snapped up, and so are origin issues. It doesn't take much to look in this Guide or others to come up with the same conclusions as to which comics hold the biggest potential. Every collector/investor's dream is to order 100 mint copies of X-Potato #1 and have it accelerate to fame and triple dollar price guide values. But more often than not, the dreams turns into a nightmare of unsaleable comics that everyone already has.

There are pros and cons to the aspects of heavy investment in new comics. If you can afford it, it is great fun to speculate; almost like working the stock market without a broker. Many great profits have been won in the past, many broken dreams have been the price for misplaced fantasies. My advice to collectors is to buy comics because you want to collect them, because you want to read their stories, because you love the artwork and because you want to save that extra mint copy just in case it booms. but leave the speculating to the speculators. Marvel Comics developed a fervor and a faithful following not because of their investment potential, but because of their unique brand of creative story telling and brilliant artwork. If we continue to support Marvel Comics for those same reasons, we can't lose and they will continue to find ways to give us better stories and better artwork. Support the best, and even they will get better! ◆◆◆

Grading, Buying, Selling and Investment

Grading comic books is more of an art than a science. An art that does not use fine brushes, but rather one that employs the technique of throwing buckets of paint over the canvas; hard to get the same result twice. In volume #3 we discussed grading in somewhat more detail and thusly in this volume we will skim through the basics and get to the meat of the matter; how grading works hand in (or against) hand with buying and selling.

The Skim, or better known as the SAGS Summary

MINT: No flaws visible at arms length, looks and acts like new. Interior pages are near white to very light yellowing.

NEAR MINT: The most important Silver Age grade. Our RVI equates with this grade as 1 (Mint as 1.52, Fine as 0.4). Again appears like new at arms length, but may have one or two faint stress lines along spine or near the staples. Inside pages must be near white or not more than very slight yellowing.

VERY FINE: A cross between Near Mint and Fine. Simply not good enough to be Near Mint, still appears newish (Roberta is going to love that!), but obviously better than Fine.

FINE: A nice flat copy that at arms length appears that it has been read several times, but carefully; a proud copy in any collection. There are, however, multiple minor flaws such as stress lines at staples and spine, and perhaps minor creases, barely noticeable. Yellowing,or if I dare, creaming of the interior pages is acceptable; but no browning pages are permitted in this category.

VERY GOOD: At a glance it has been read, and even re-read by your little brother. But, it is still solid; there are no pieces missing or major rips. A collector's "reading copy".

GOOD, FAIR, POOR: If you are reading this paragraph, you are probably a Gold Age collector, since for the Silver Age readers and recent comic books these categories are a collecting no-no.

The Meat of Grading

Grade to your hearts content, it will mean nothing unless that grading will be accepted by the buyer of your comics; or if you are buying, then by the seller of the comics!

Grading is a form of negotiation, something atuned to buying a car. A car dealer initially sets the price above what he is willing to settle for. You make your initial offer at a price below what you are willing to settle for, then through negotiation you finally agree on a price that on the surface seems to please both parties. When dealers sell, they grade just a tad higher than they truly believe the grade to be. You as a buyer generally grade a lot stricter when buying. Hopefully the two of you will compromise on a grade.

Of course, there is the alter-ego dealer who purports to be Mr. Strict grader, by first grading fairly, but demanding double "Guide" as his starting price. No matter what the method, Grading/pricing is a negotiated vehicle in the matter of exchanging comic books for money.

Another principle applies: "Eyes of the Beholder" as described in detail in Volumes one and two. The principle recognizes that grading is in the eyes of the owner of the comic. No matter how sweet, sincere, and honest you are, there is a genealogical instinct that causes us to grade the comics we buy a lot stricter than those we sell.

For the last 12 years that I have been running comic auctions and selling collections on consignment, 98.6% of the time the collectors whose collections I am selling complain that my grading is too low; whereas a few of the buyers complain that it is too high.

Combine the above understanding of grading and how it is a personal art and not a science. There are no "rights" or "wrongs". What we highly recommend is that you throw away your microscope when buying comics and practice the SAGS approach to arms length grading. When you sell, make an honest evaluation of the grade at which you would be willing to buy. When you buy, before cursing the dealer, think in your mind roughly the grade at which you would sell it.

Dealing With Dealers

I have found that in my dealings with hundreds of sellers, and thousands of buyers, most are reasonable, fair, and honest. That fact has made the buying and selling experience a sincere pleasure.

However, on the other side of the coin (or comic book), there are those dealers and collectors that abuse the word "human". Greed and lust for money has on occasion infiltrated the ranks of comic fandom.

On the dealer side, there are those that intentionally misguide and misrepresent comic books. Fortunately, there are ways to deal with these "subhumans". The CBG, published by Krause Publications, has been scrupulously purging these dealers from the advertising ranks. We commend Krause for that policy.

If you as the buyer are not certain of the credentials of the dealer you are buying from, first check with the Consumer Relations Dept. of Krause Publications, or order your comics by using a major credit card. Generally only the most reputable dealers are authorized by their banks to accept credit charges; and should problems occur, most banks honor your pleas to reverse the charges.

Dealing With Buyers

As I mentioned above, the vast majority of sellers and buyers are pure pleasure to deal with. But this book wouldn't be much help to the reader if all I related were the cherries, blossoms, and rainbows of collecting. We must also look at the dark side. And dealing with buyers, also known as collectors, can also have its downside.

A few collectors practice pure fraud. Among the favorite techniques are check bouncing, stopping payment on money orders after receiving the goods, having friends sign for UPS orders and then declaring they "never received" the comics, and the pet project for these "subhumans": upgrading their collection by returning their known lower grade books and screaming to high heaven that they received overgraded books. The trouble is that for the victims of buyer fraud, we do not have a CBG or Krause that is interested in helping. We have to help ourselves.

Therefore I give the following recommendations to the sellers of comics. On over the counter dealings, all sales should be advertised as final. Accept only payment with verification of identity, address, telephone number, possession of bank card or major credit card. On mail order, allow three weeks for checks *and* money orders to clear the bank before sending the orders (except to known customers). Make xerox copies of the covers of all significant valued comics since they act as a blue print for fraudulent or damaged returns. Insure all orders for full value. Advertise that your delivery responsibility ends with the reception of the goods at the *address* of the buyer, and that all returns must be shipped within five days of receipt.

Another major problem with a very few buyers is that they are predetermined "cherry pickers". That is, they intentionally purchase double or triple the amount of comics they actually wish to purchase and then when they receive them, they pick out the best half or third of the group and return the rest citing "grading discrepancies". This unethical behavior is not fraud, and the only reasonable thing you can do to stop that practice is not to do further business with that party.

I'll finish this sub-chapter by giving the most important tidbit of advice: buyers or sellers will achieve their most optimistic goal plausible by acting, speaking, and writing in a polite and non-accusatory fashion if, in fact, there is a dispute. Aggressive behavior begets an aggressive response and nothing gets accomplished. As sellers, we follow a policy of permitting returns of merchandise within five days of receipt for any reason whatsoever, no questions asked. Even with this policy we average less than two percent returns from our comic book auctions. And yet, there invariably is the buyer that sends the nastiest, coldest and stupidest letter with copy to the CBG. We are all humans, most of us want to be friendly, cooperative and nice. We all are busy surviving in this busy world; we aren't sitting around waiting to service one single fanatic buyer that didn't receive his comics three days after he sent his $14.28 for 17 g/vg comics. Simply practice patience and deliberate professional and courteous communication and we all will be wiser, happier, and profit by the real thrill of this hobby; owning your favorite comics.

Buying Comics

Well, I've already said a mouthful in the previous sub-chapter. In this one I'll limit myself to simply spilling the beans. My advice: (1) Buy a copy of "THE OVERSTREET PRICE GUIDE". Take the estimated values as a *guide* for values, not as a biblical fact. Then write for free catalogs to the major advertisers. (2) Subscribe to Krause publications "The CBG" and Carter's "The Comic Book Market Place" or any new weekly or monthly publications that feature dealer advertisements and check out selling prices and sales lists. (3) Try a few of the dealers with smaller orders and test their service and grading. Go with those that give you the service and quality and prices you find satisfying.

If you prefer that "hands-on" approach and you have the availability of a comic book store, or are able to attend comic book conventions: that is the best. First check out what is available, check out the relative pricing, physically check out each comic you are interested in buying. First attempt to buy the "hot" books that you suspect won't last until the end of the convention and shoot for the best price the dealer is willing to agree to. On books that you can live without, but would enjoy at the right price, wait until the last day of the convention and go for the jugular! Don't be shy about offering a lower than reasonable cash price; you can always go up, but never down. The first law of buying comics: never appear desperate to buy a particular comic book; rather, look disinterested, blase and then snap it up at discount. Be aware, however, that there are Hot comics that will sell at

most any price and the blase look will not work. Be a good judge of what is hot and what is not!

Buying new comics is totally different than what has been alluded to above. It is simple and straight forward. Buy through your local comic book store, preferably one that uses one of the major efficient distribution services. You want speed, reliability and service. If you buy in volume, be sure to get discounts off the retail prices. If you don't have a local comic book store that fits the bill; go for one of the advertised new comic distribution services. What comics should you buy? We'll cover that in the sub-chapter entitled "Investment".

Selling Comics

If you are not planning to go into business selling comic books, if you simply wish to sell your accumulation for the best price with the least hassle, this paragraph is for you. This is not idle chatter, but advice from someone who has sold more than $3,300,000.00 worth of comic books since 1977. We have sold more comics in more different ways than you can shake a stick at. It is not easy, it is not cheap. It takes years to build up an acceptable, effective mailing list and the necessary customers to bring fair market sales.

Here is some advice:

(1) Make a complete list of your comic books in alphabetical order, together with your grading for each. (2) Make about 25 copies of your list and send that list to nationally advertised comic businesses, as well as your local specialty stores. (3) Request offers to buy your collection. If your collection is large, arrange for visits to inspect the goods before arriving at a final price. If small, make arrangements to send prospective buyers the books for inspection with return guarantee if a final price cannot be negotiated. (4) Sell to a professional dealer.

Alternatively you may wish to attempt to sell them yourself through advertisements in the weekly comic industry newspapers. Simply be aware that the hot material will sell immediately and you may need years to sell off the less desirable remaining comics. Finally, if you've got a small accumulation of comics from the 1970's or 1980's don't expect stores or dealers to express any interest in purchase your collection. If you have a large collection with solid, in depth title runs and top quality condition key issues; then yes, you can almost command your price. In comic selling there are comics

that everyone wants and those that nobody wants. Hopefully you invested in the "right" ones.

Investment

Rule of thumb: invest only in what you have expertise. That applies to any investment in any field. Start slowly and spend more time as the collector than the investor. Investing in large doses of new comics is something that most others are also doing and the chance of making a killing is slight; more likely, you will be the victim. If you do, sell when they are hot, even if just weeks after purchase. Generally, the new hot purchases will cool off after a few years. "Strike while the iron is hot" applies very well in the new comic industry. Though I don't profess to be the new comics expert, I'll peel off a few words of advice: Go for new titles with blossoming new and creative artists, go for those with smaller print runs with new characters that you personally find alluring or destined for long and profitable title runs. Don't put major bucks into the blase artist comics or those characters that will produce only test title runs. Whatever you decide to buy, above all, keep those new books MINT by following proper storage practices!

Investment in Back Issues

Keep a strong and watchful eye on the Hot and Cold cycles of the titles you are interested in purchasing. It is not the best time to buy when a title is hot. It is best to buy before it's hot (the swami is at it again!). How is that accomplished? With keeping accurate account of what new artists are going into what feature title runs; by watching if newly introduced characters are hot or not, as they then affect the value of the entire title run; and by watching the relative value increases over the years. If one title was dormant for several years, it may be ready to spring into action. This can be accomplished by noting the clearly underpriced and undervalued older and scarcer title runs from the 1960's. For investment sake, stick to buying Near Mint or Mint comics. Be especially concerned with the tint of the inside pages, the whiter or lighter the pages are, the better your investment will be in the future.

I can't say what others prefer, but for myself I believe back issue comics are the best investments money can buy. Not only have they gained in value, but we derive pleasure out of the stories, the art, and our own collecting frenzy. If it tickles, scratch it! ◆◆◆

Storage/Preservation/Restoration

Now that you know how to use this reference book, know how to grade comics, know what an RVI is, and know the in's and out's of collecting, I bet you wondered if I would finally allow you to just peacefully glance through the pages of brilliantly colorful Marvel Comics; after all, some rest for the weary?

Nay, now that you've spent all that time and money, we need to protect your investment. If you want real detail about this subject, simply review a copy of our PHOTO-JOURNAL GUIDE TO COMIC BOOKS Vol. 1 and the chapter entitled "Preservation and Storage". Not a bad chapter; it was written by a guy who has championed the rights of our decomposing friends since 1979 and who developed patents and many new preservation products and services. The gist of which was:

Preservation Gist

Paper, hence comic books decompose; sometimes faster and sometimes slower. Take it seriously even though it doesn't happen in front of your eyes in minutes, days or months. But if you treat comic books like the pieces of wood pulp fibers they are, they will decompose. yellow, brown, and poof they will be gone. Not that I'm trying to scare you. On the happier side visualize your comics in King Tut's tomb for three or four thousand years, they'd still be in O.K. shape.

In the simplest of terms the number one reason your comics age is your disinterest and genealogical propensity for human procrastination. Why do today that which costs money without it procuring more comic books, that which can be done tomorrow or the next day? Famous last words of the owner of brown, brittle and valueless comic books.

The number two reason for rampant aging is the oxidation of your comic book paper fiber and the conversion of the papers' lignin into paper chewing acids. The primary enemies of your comic books that can be controlled to some degree are: (1) Moisture, (2) oxygen, (3) heat, (4) light, and (5) little brothers. Control these enemies and your comics will be safe for generations. The cheapest and easiest ways to control these enemies is proper storage.

Storage

There are many ways to store comic books, right ways, wrong ways, cheap ways, expensive ways, ways that destroy books, and ways that support the preservation of your books. First a few don'ts: (1) Don't store them in the attic or any other warm or moist area. (2) Don't store them in any vinyl plastic bags or any other relatively volatile plastic. (3) Don't lay them flat in large piles, or loosely stack them vertically in comic boxes. (4) Don't allow

them to be exposed to direct light for prolonged periods of time, such as the bright lights of a convention hall or a comic book store displayed or framed and hanging on your wall.

Do's in the order of increasing expense: (1) Keep them in a cool, dark, and dry area of your home (2) Pack them tightly in comic boxes, vertically with acid free cardboard boards every 10 or so comics to prevent spine roll. (3) Use Mylar* (trademark of Dupont Co.) comic bags, either the thin stuff or the thicker ones for your best books. (4) Use the thickest Mylar bags to offer physical protection, especially against corner damage and spine roll. (5) Store your comics in a temperature and humidity controlled environment. If that is not available, turn one of your closets into the habitat buy putting a small air conditioner in the closet door and keeping the books as consistently cool as possible. (6) Store your comics in an inert, oxygen free, environment such as nitrogen.

Most of the above suggestions are easily obtainable, except perhaps the 6th idea. Whatever you decide to use, try to keep the comics in a *consistent* environment. It hurts them to have changing temperatures, re-exposing them to fresh bursts of oxygen, or repeated exposure to light. Please note that the world's finest preserved collection, the EDGAR CHURCH collection, also known as the MILE HIGH collection, was stored using a number of my suggestions (by coincidence, since I wasn't even born when he started storing them). They were stacked firmly together where oxygen didn't have a chance to get new bites of the paper, they were stored in a cool and dry basement where they never saw the light of day for 40 years; nor were they moved or re-exposed to the negative elements. There is no reason why, with proper storage techniques, you cannot also end up with such a high quality collection 40 years from now!

Restoration

Restoration of comics means that someone physically treats comic books as to change their current natural appearance artificially. This amounts to chemical treatment to reduce the natural acidity of the paper, changing staples, repairing rips, removing tape repairs, redoing artwork, and even replacing missing pieces and pages. For those comics published prior to 1960, this practice is fairly commonplace. However, restoration to comics published since 1960 is far more rare and less of a concern, especially since it is an expensive alternative and reserved for only the most expensive comics. If you are interested in the details of restoration, read the chapter in volume 2 of our Photo-Journal series. Otherwise we will summarize our thoughts and recommendations for the process.

There are acceptable practices that need not be advertised and there are restoration practices that *must* be noticed when attempting to sell valuable comic books. There are acceptable technicians who can do archivally acceptable work, and there are charlatans that represent they can do the same work at half the price. A word to the wise: do not allow anyone to doing anything to your valuable comics unless they have been specifically trained to do archival quality work using strictly archivally acceptable materials and chemicals. One of the biggest problems with "restorers" is that their work may look great after it's done, but how long will it stay that way. Without archivally acceptable chemicals and materials, repairs will deteriorate much faster than the original comic book. I simply caution you to be aware that restoration is only *restoration,* when it lasts for the life of the comic book.

Acceptable Restoration Practices for Silver Age Comics

Cleaning, tape removal (by a professional only), removal of spine roll, cleaning of rusty staples, removal of pencil and ink marks, correction of foxing marks, removal of creases and professional deacidification are all practices which we highly endorse if done correctly.

Practices that are acceptable but only if clearly advertised with the sale of each comic book are: repairs of rips, replacement of missing pieces, chemical strengthening of pages, replacement of missing pages, and other artificial changes in the original integrity of the comic book. A practice that I do not find acceptable is the bleaching of comic book pages to alter their appearance for the purpose of fooling the buyer into thinking that he is buying "white" pages.

Let's face it, not everyone is going to be honest about the comic book they are about to sell you. Certainly thousands of comics have been sold by unwitting sellers that didn't realize their Near Mint issue had actually been restored, but equally certain thousands more have been sold where the seller knew that the book was in fact restored and simply wanted to score big.

Because of this uncertainty, one can't put the burden of proof on the seller (though he must be held accountable and be willing to accept the return). It is really up to the recipient of the comic book to ascertain whether or not it was tampered with. A simple magnifying glass or a smell test will tell tale; if in doubt, there are plenty of experts that will help out for a small fee.

Once upon a time restoration was accepted as the savior for the undernourished valuable comic book. However the trend has been away from the "artificial" restorative techniques. More often than not, those techniques cause your valuable comics to devalue and become unwanted.

The Marvel Trim Fetish

Most Marvel collectors are aware of the Marvel trim fetish, the desire of sellers to trim away the famed "Marvel Chipping", a anomaly of the Silver Aged beauties where the shearing blade of Marvel's cutters was not sharp enough and tended to chip away at the leading edges. Sellers gleefully used their own paper cutters to "straighten" out the problem. Now we have the answer to catch the smaller culprits. In these two volumes are untrimmed unretouched photos of all the most valuable Marvel comics in their untrimmed entirety. Simply compare comics you are buying or ones you own with our photographs. If yours don't have all the artwork as pictured in these books, then they have been the victim of the "Marvel trim fetish".

The Aging/Storage Conditions Graph

The graph, at the bottom of this page, summarizes this chapter by giving some examples of how comic books age in a variety of storage conditions. These are obviously only approximate aging curves for approximate conditions. Each comic book will age individually and that will depend on storage conditions during its entire life. If it had a bad youth, you can't bring back white supple pages. However you can extend its middle age and it can still lead a happy and prosperous life. If your comic book is on its last legs, it may be time to take other measures like chemical restoration, as discussed in other chapters.

Comic book A has been stored under average environmental conditions. B was stored in a warm and humid area. C was stored in a cool and dry area. D was stored in a cool, dry environment, in Mylar* bags tightly stacked. E was stored in a warm and humid area, but deacidified. F was stored in a cool, dry place, in a gas-tight container with nitrogen or other inert non-oxidizing compound. G was stored under normal conditions for the first 20 years and then placed in a cool, dry environment, tightly stacked and inside Mylar* bags. H was stored the same as G, but not until 40 years had elapsed. J was stored under ideal conditions for forty years (such as the Church collection) and then removed to unfavorable conditions.

I believe these are enough samples to get a good idea of how aging works. The better the storage conditions, the flatter the aging line; the less desirable the storage conditions, the steeper the line. The steepness of the line can change any time the storage conditions change. Remember; I've personally seen 10 year old comic books that were brown, brittle and falling apart; I've also seen comic books 50 years old with natural unaged white and supple pages. It is *your* choice how your collection will end up.

If this chapter has worried you enough to prevent you from collecting comic books, then you are worrying too much. Virtually all collectibles are subject to aging effects and you would have to protect them too. If however this chapter has worried you enough for you to correct possible defective storage methods, then we have accomplished what we set out to do, and that is to preserve these treasured collectibles for many generations to come.

The following two pages

...Are sample Marvel Comics or their relatives that we decided would not fly in this set of books. Not that we are prejudiced by race, lack of color, or national origin, but we had to gauge what you, our reader, wanted to see; more black and whites? ...foreigners? ...or instead more and larger pictures of Marvel Comics title runs. We hope you enjoy the following samples of Marvel Magazines, and Marvel licensed Foreign Comics. ✦✦✦

Mylar is a registered trademark of the Dupont Co.

Page Age
White
Off White
Yellowing
Browning
Brown
Brittle
Gone
STORAGE CONDITIONS
Average A
Warm, Humid B, J
Cool/Dry C
Cool/Dry/Mylar/Stacked D,G,H
Warm/Humid/Deacidification E
Cool/Nitrogen F
A
B
C
D
E
F
G
H
J
New
10
20
30
40
50
60
70
80
90
100
Years

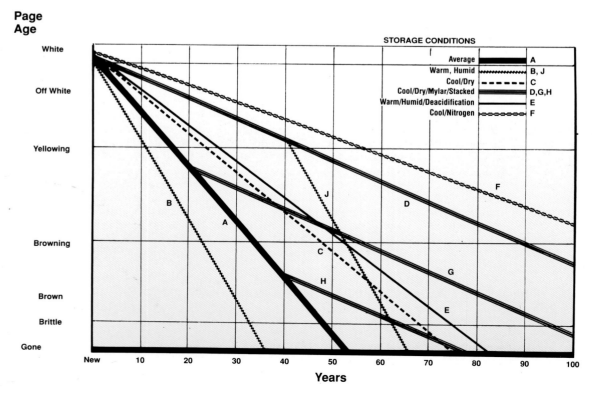

The aging of comic books under a variety of storage conditions.

Pussycat
SEE THE CURVEY CUTIE FROM S.C.O.R.E. VS. THE FOUL FIENDS OF L.U.S.T.
I WANT YOU...
TO JOIN ME IN THE COOL and CUDDLY CAPERS OF A FRIENDLY SECRET AGENT --NAMELY ME!
THE LADY IS A SWINGER!
EXPLODING FROM THE MIGHTY WORLD OF MARVEL...
Captain BRITAIN
50P
No!
WITH BRITAIN'S BEST...
NIGHT RAVEN
ABSLOM DAAK DALEK KILLER
and introducing THE FREE-FALL WARRIORS
NO MAN CAN STAND AGAINST...
THE DEADLY HANDS OF KUNG FU
ACTION STRIPS! PHOTOS! FEATURES!
BRUCE LEE
SECRETS OF KUNG FU REVEALED
DOC SAVAGE
FRENZY IN A FROZEN HELL!
THE MAN OF BRONZE BATTLES THE INFERNO SCHEME!
DRACULA LIVES!
TALES OF TERROR FROM THE COUNT'S OWN CRYPT!
THE WALKING DEAD IN NEW YORK!
WITCHCRAFT IN OLD SALEM!
PLUS: DRACULA CAPTURED ON FILM!
COMICS, FEATURES, AND PHOTOS OF THE MOST FAMOUS, MOST DEADLY VAMPIRE OF ALL!
A MARVEL MAGAZINE / SPRING 1980 / $2.00
epic ILLUSTRATED
Premiere Issue
A new experience in adult fantasy and science-fiction adventure
TALES OF TERROR--BY THE MODERN MASTERS OF FANTASY
THE HAUNT OF HORROR
PLUS: TWO FEAR FEATURES OF SATANA THE DEVIL'S DAUGHTER
MARVEL MAGAZINE GROUP
HOWARD THE DUCK
$1.25
The HULK!
$1.50
KULL AND THE BARBARIANS
FIRST ISSUE COLLECTORS' EDITION
THREE FULL-LENGTH SAGAS FROM THE CREATOR OF CONAN
DRACULA AND THE FRANKENSTEIN MONSTER IN
THE LEGION OF MONSTERS
WORLD PREMIERE ISSUE FEATURING THE ORIGIN OF THE MANPHIBIAN!
IN THIS ISSUE: BRAM STOKER'S DRACULA IN COMICS
MARVEL GRAPHIC NOVEL
THE DEATH OF CAPTAIN MARVEL
by JIM STARLIN
MARVEL PREVIEW PRESENTS
AMERICA'S GREATEST CRIME DESTROYER!
THE PUNISHER
SPECIAL! THE EXECUTIONER SPEAKS OUT!
AN EXCLUSIVE INTERVIEW WITH DON PENDLETON!
MARVEL PREVIEW PRESENTS
STAR LORD
ALL NEW!
ONE MAN AGAINST A GALACTIC EMPIRE!
A MARVEL SUPER SPECIAL!
KISS
Bonus! Full-Color, Four-page, Pull-Out KISS POSTER!
MASTERS OF TERROR
FEATURING: ROBERT E. HOWARD CREATOR OF CONAN
ROBERT BLOCH AUTHOR OF PSYCHO
H.P. LOVECRAFT
IT! A MACABRE MASTERPIECE BY THEODORE STURGEON
MONSTERS UNLEASHED!
THE MONSTER OF FRANKENSTEIN
PLUS: A GHOUL'S GALLERY OF PHOTOS AND FEATURES
WHERE MAN ONCE STOOD SUPREME--NOW RULE THE APES
PLANET OF THE APES
APE AND MAN AT WAR...
CONAN THE BARBARIAN STARRING IN
SAVAGE TALES
KA-ZAR KILLS!
THE COMING OF THE MAN-THING
BEWARE THE SISTERHOOD TOMORROW'S VIOLENT VOLUPTUARIES!
BLACK BROTHER
MORE PAGES SUPER ANNUAL ISSUE MORE THRILLS
SAVAGE TALES FEATURING KA-ZAR
FANTASTIC COLLECTOR'S EDITION!
THE LORD OF THE HIDDEN JUNGLE'S GREATEST ACTION SAGAS!
The SAVAGE SWORD of CONAN THE BARBARIAN
ALL-NEW THRILLS! IRON SHADOWS IN THE MOON
ALSO: BLACKMARK TRIUMPHANT
THE SPECTACULAR SPIDER-MAN
35¢
NOW IN FULL COLOR!
THE SPECTACULAR SPIDER-MAN
HE LIVES! HE STRIKES! NO GRAVE CAN HOLD HIM!
TALES OF THE ZOMBIE
DARE ANY MAN BATTLE BROTHER VOODOO?
ILLUSTRATED TERROR TALES FROM THE UNHOLY HAUNT OF BLACK MAGIC
MORE PAGES SUPER ANNUAL ISSUE MORE THRILLS
NIGHTMARE LEGENDS OF THE LIVING DEAD!
VAMPIRE TALES
A COLLECTOR'S EDITION FEATURING BLOOD DEATH
AND OTHER FRIGHT FEATURES OF THE UNDEAD!

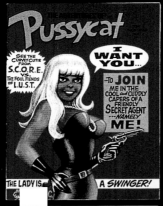

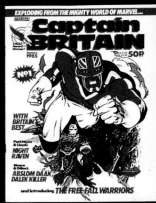

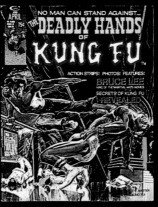

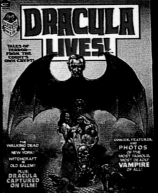

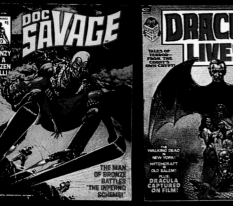

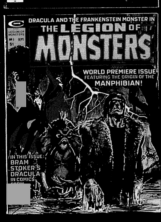

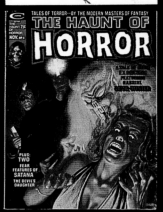

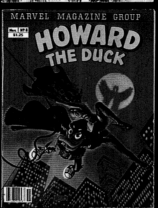

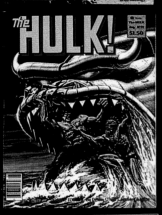

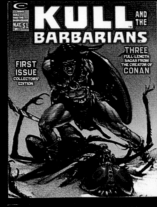

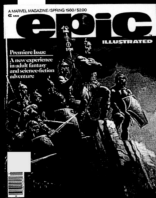

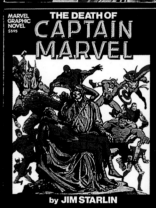

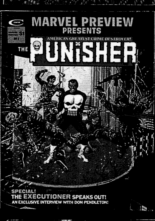

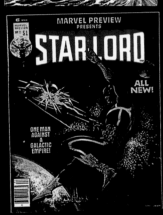

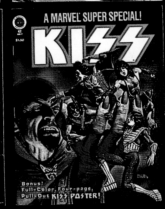

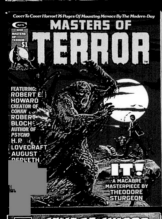

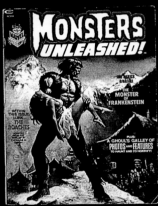

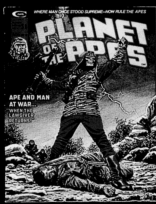

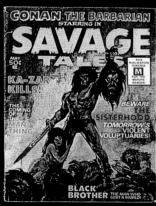

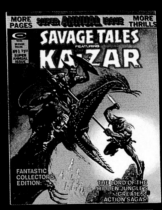

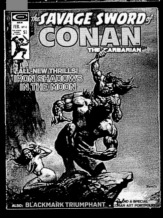

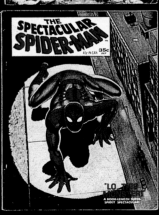

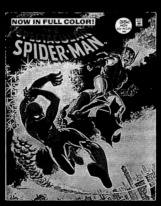

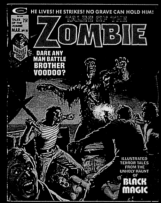

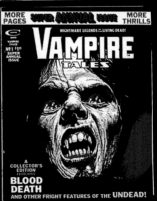

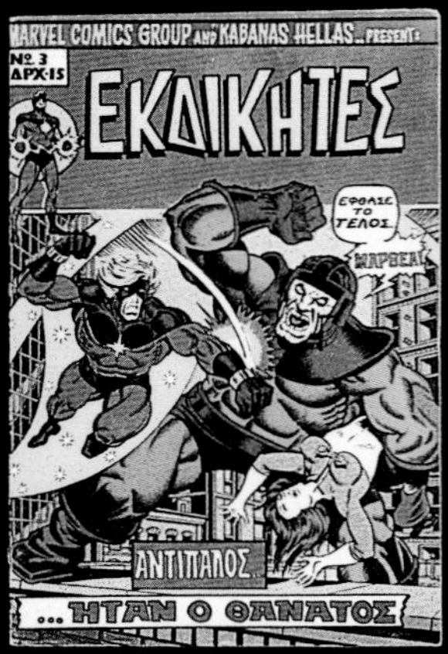
MARVEL COMICS GROUP AND KABANAS HELLAS PRESENT
ΕΚΔΙΚΗΤΕΣ
ΑΝΤΙΠΑΛΟΣ
...ΗΤΑΝ Ο ΘΑΝΑΤΟΣ

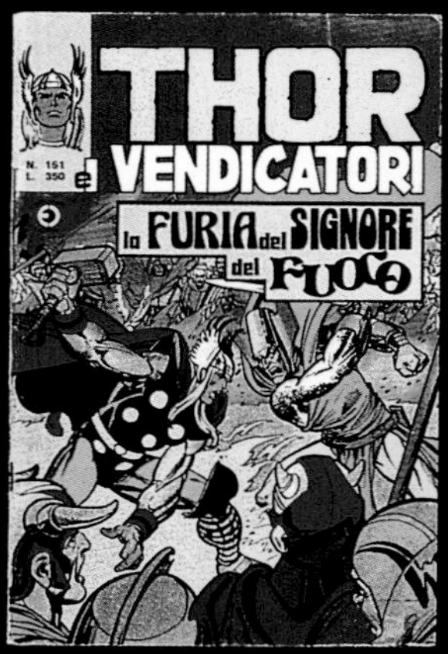
THOR e VENDICATORI
la FURIA del SIGNORE del FUOCO

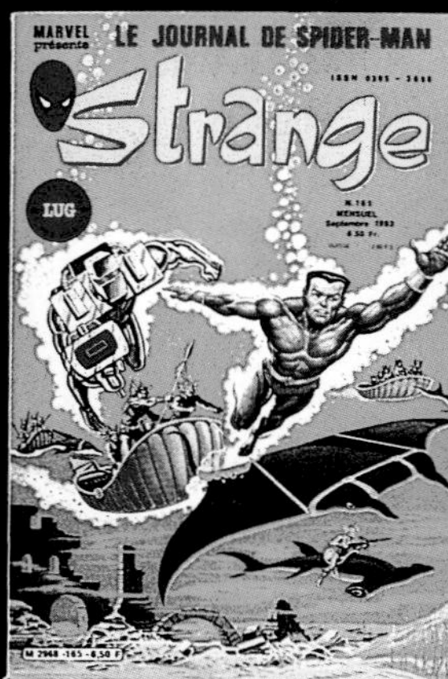
LE JOURNAL DE SPIDER-MAN
Strange
LUG

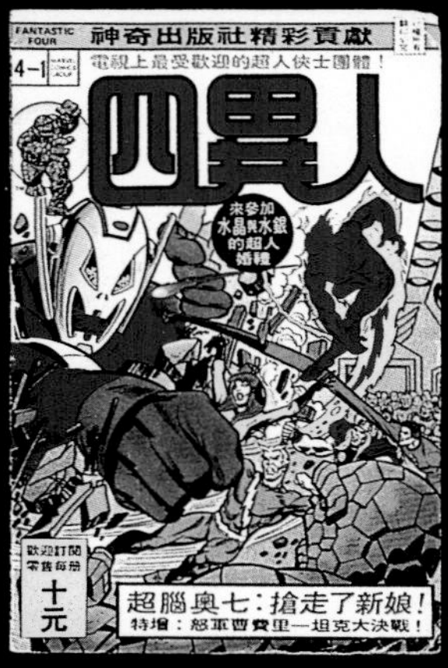
神奇出版社精彩貢獻
四異人
十元

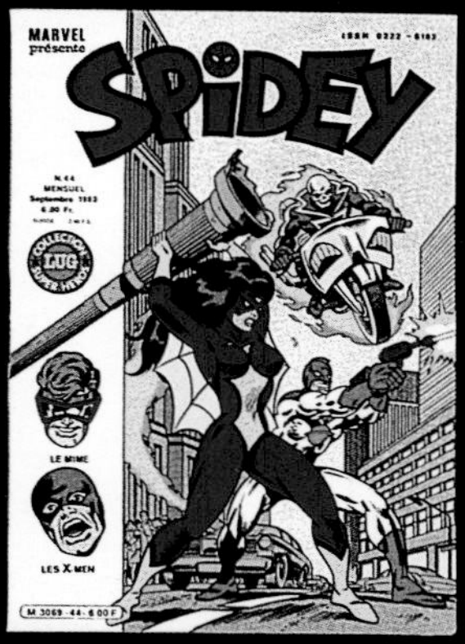
SPIDEY
LUG

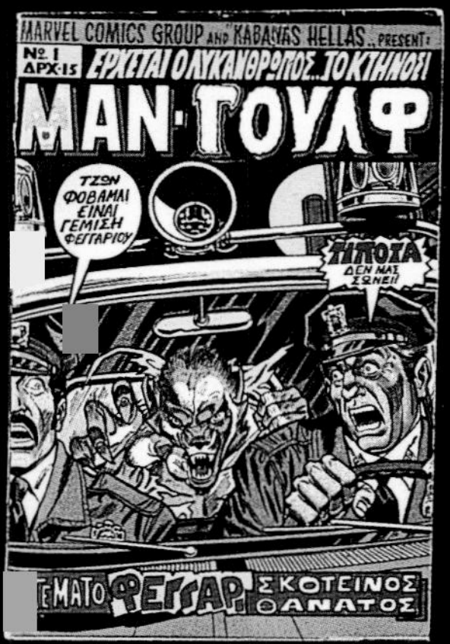
MARVEL COMICS GROUP AND KABANAS HELLAS PRESENT
ΜΑΝ-ΓΟΥΛΦ
ΣΚΟΤΕΙΝΟΣ ΘΑΝΑΤΟΣ

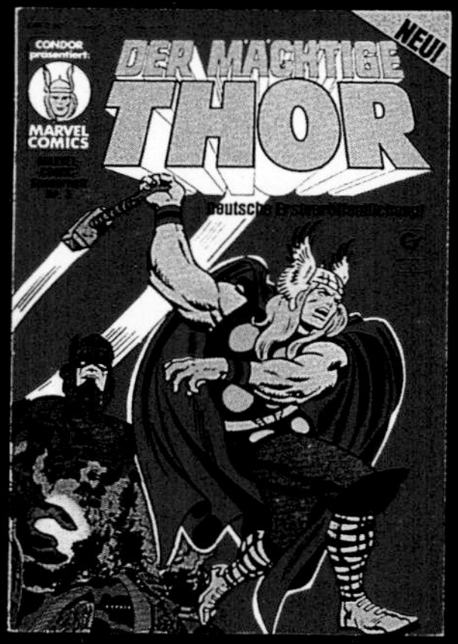
DER MÄCHTIGE THOR
NEU!
MARVEL COMICS

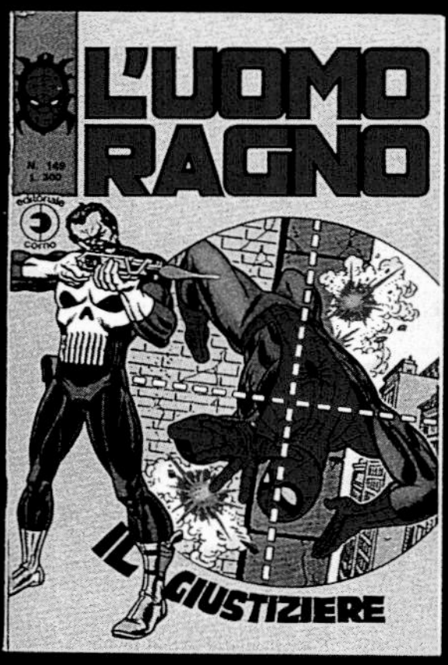
L'UOMO RAGNO
IL GIUSTIZIERE

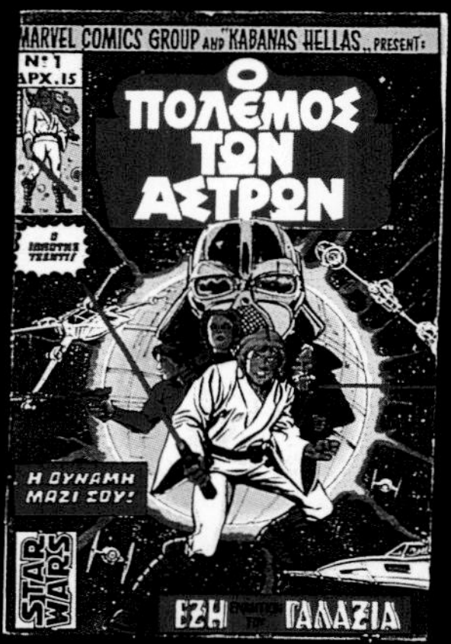
MARVEL COMICS GROUP AND KABANAS HELLAS PRESENT
Ο ΠΟΛΕΜΟΣ ΤΩΝ ΑΣΤΡΩΝ
Η ΔΥΝΑΜΗ ΜΑΖΙ ΣΟΥ!
STAR WARS
ΕΞΗ ΓΑΛΑΞΙΑ

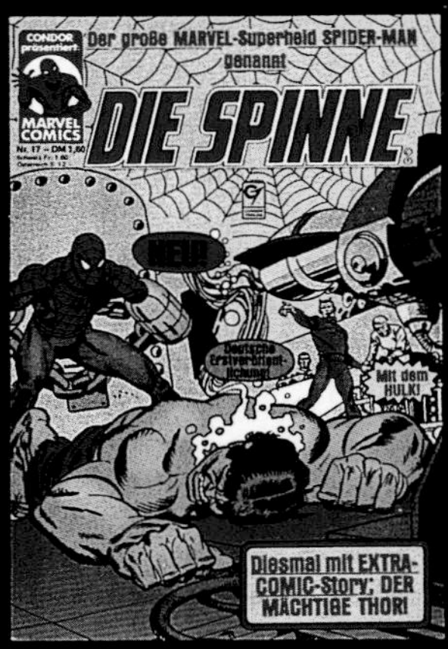
Der große MARVEL-Superheld SPIDER-MAN genannt
DIE SPINNE
MARVEL COMICS
Mit dem HULK!
Diesmal mit EXTRA-COMIC-Story: DER MÄCHTIGE THOR!

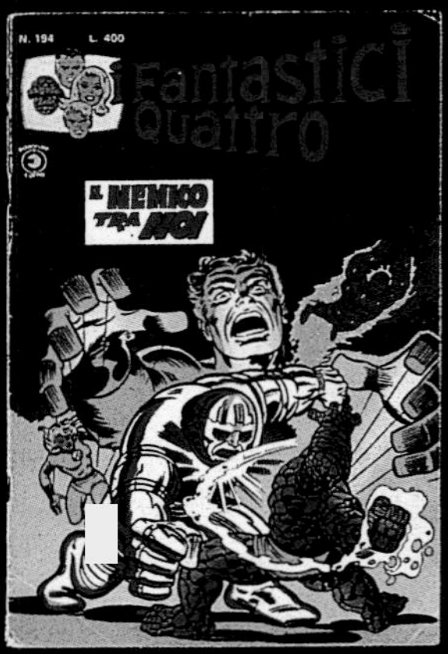
Fantastici Quattro

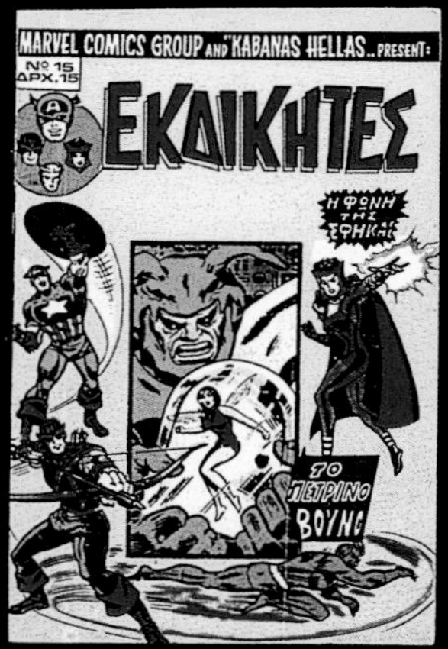
MARVEL COMICS GROUP AND KABANAS HELLAS PRESENT
ΕΚΔΙΚΗΤΕΣ

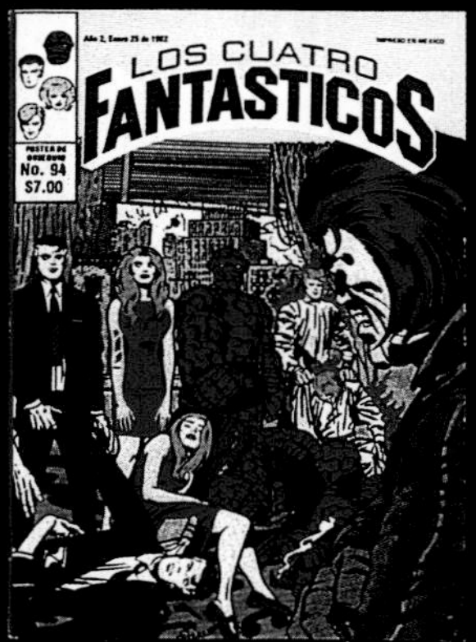
LOS CUATRO FANTASTICOS
No. 94
$7.00

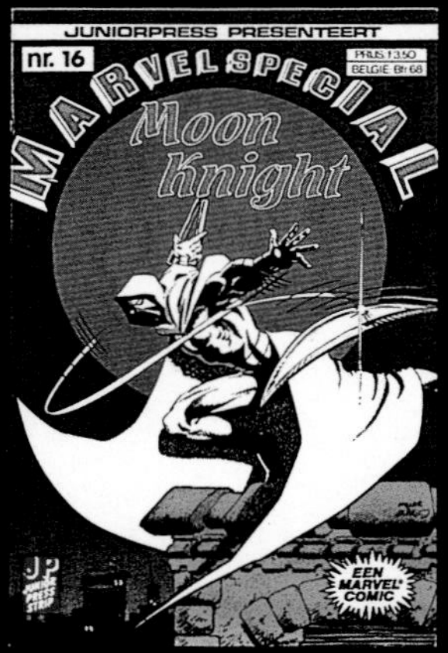
JUNIORPRESS PRESENTEERT
nr. 16
MARVEL SPECIAL
Moon Knight
EEN MARVEL-COMIC

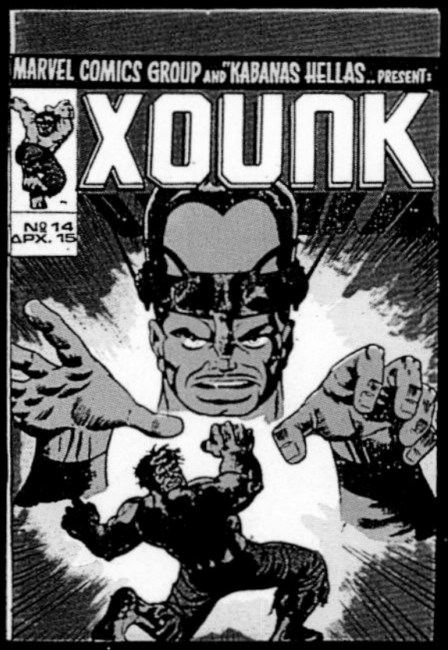
MARVEL COMICS GROUP AND KABANAS HELLAS PRESENT
ΧΟΥΛΚ

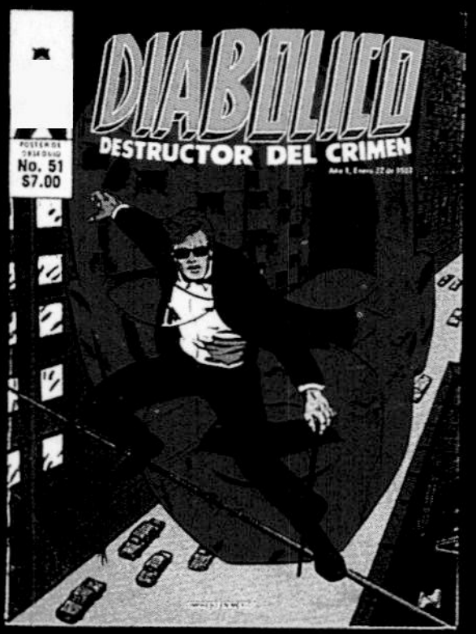
DIABOLICO
DESTRUCTOR DEL CRIMEN
No. 51
$7.00

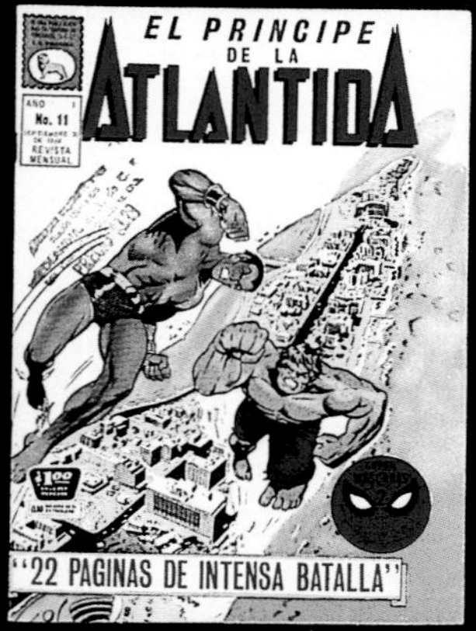
EL PRINCIPE DE LA ATLANTIDA
No. 11
"22 PAGINAS DE INTENSA BATALLA"

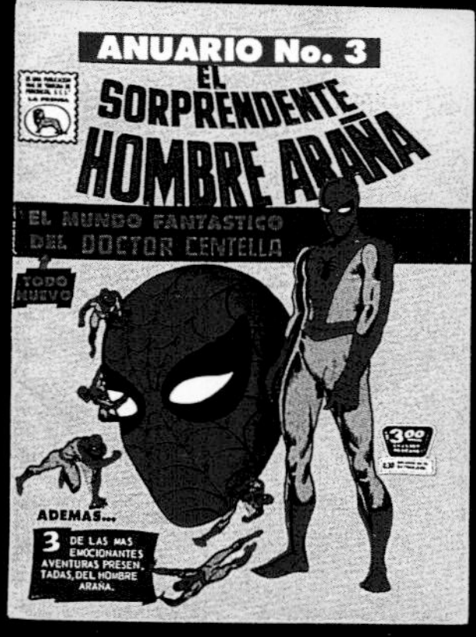
ANUARIO No. 3
EL SORPRENDENTE HOMBRE ARAÑA
EL MUNDO FANTASTICO DEL DOCTOR CENTELLA
ADEMAS...

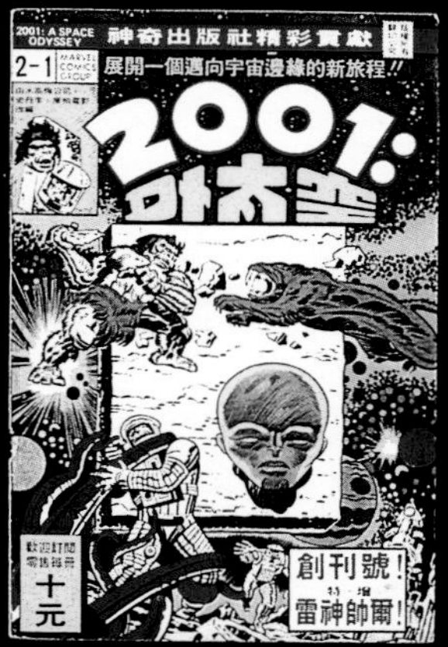
神奇出版社精彩貢獻
2001:
創刊號!
十元

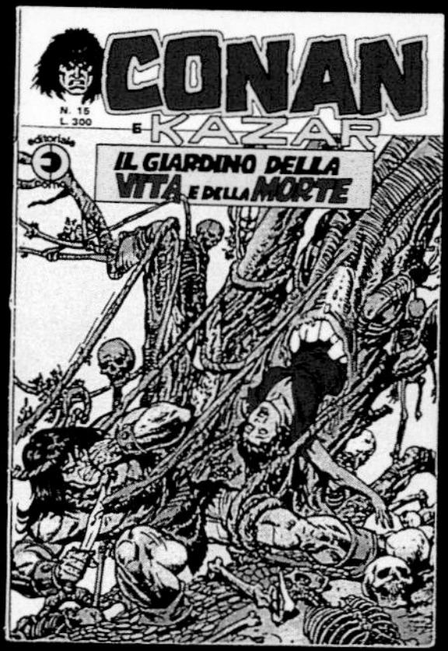
CONAN
KAZAR
IL GIARDINO DELLA VITA E DELLA MORTE

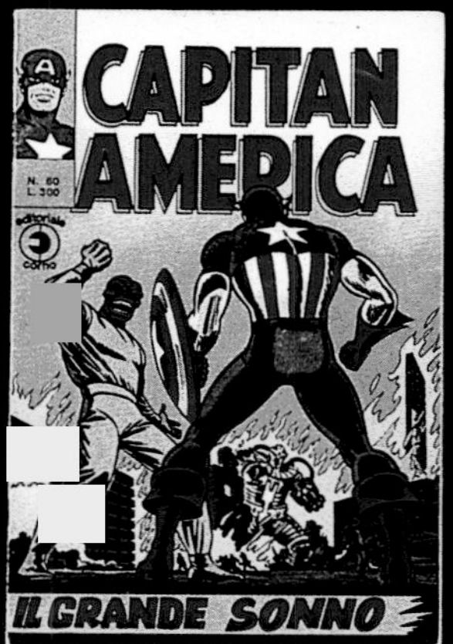
CAPITAN AMERICA
IL GRANDE SONNO

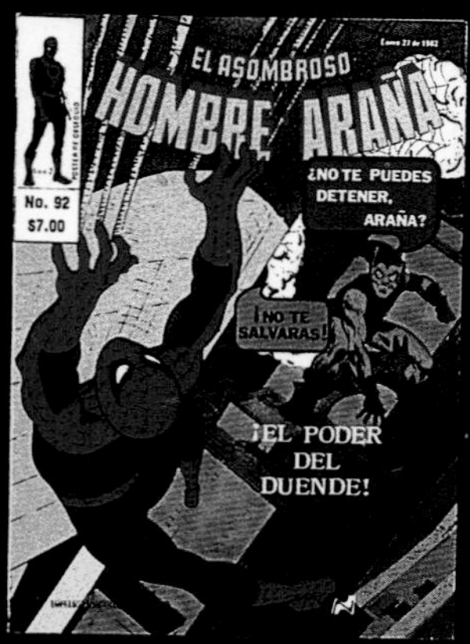
EL ASOMBROSO HOMBRE ARAÑA
No. 92
$7.00
¿NO TE PUEDES DETENER, ARAÑA?
¡NO TE SALVARAS!
¡EL PODER DEL DUENDE!

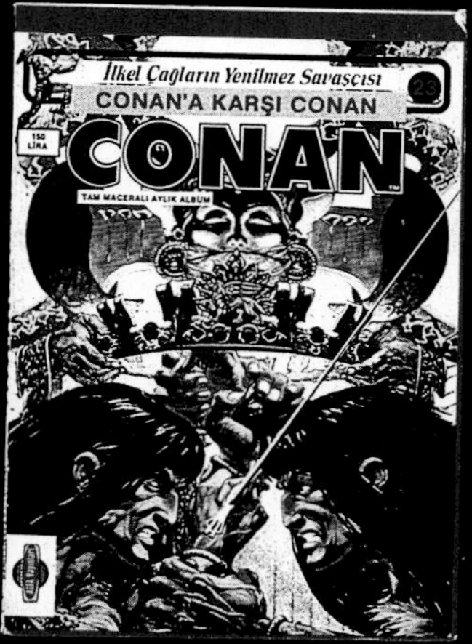
İlkel Çağların Yenilmez Savaşçısı
CONAN'A KARŞI CONAN
CONAN

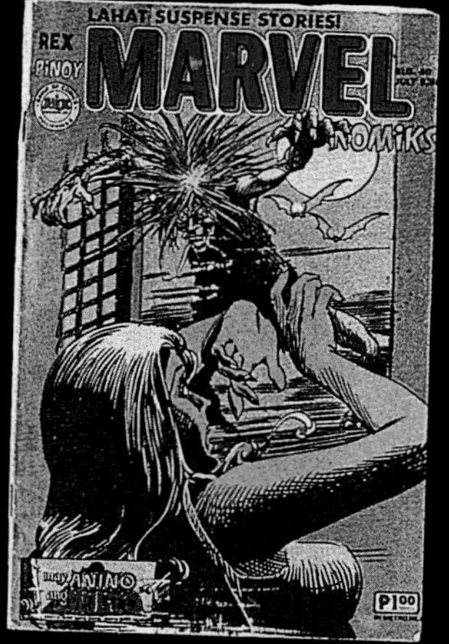
LAHAT SUSPENSE STORIES!
REX
MARVEL
KOMIKS
P1.00

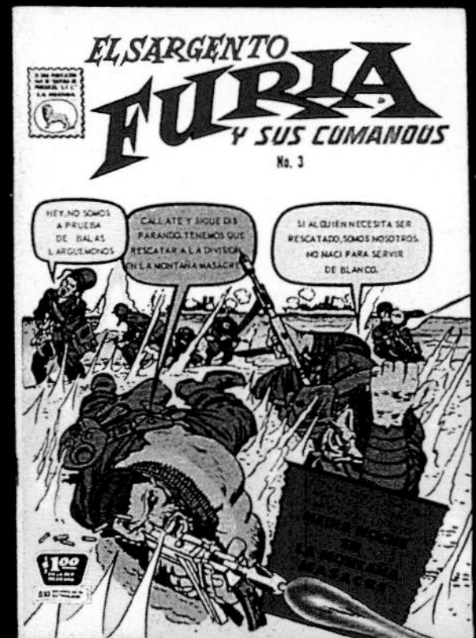
EL SARGENTO FURIA Y SUS COMANDOS
No. 3

1018.4 Ka-Zar 1st Series (1-3)

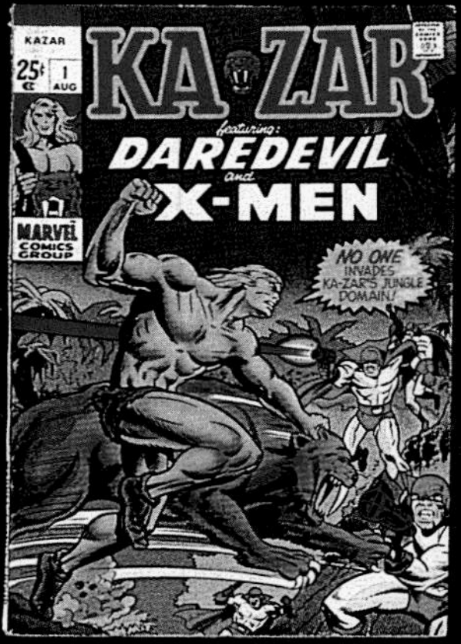
KA-ZAR
featuring DAREDEVIL and X-MEN
NO ONE INVADES KA-ZAR'S JUNGLE DOMAIN!

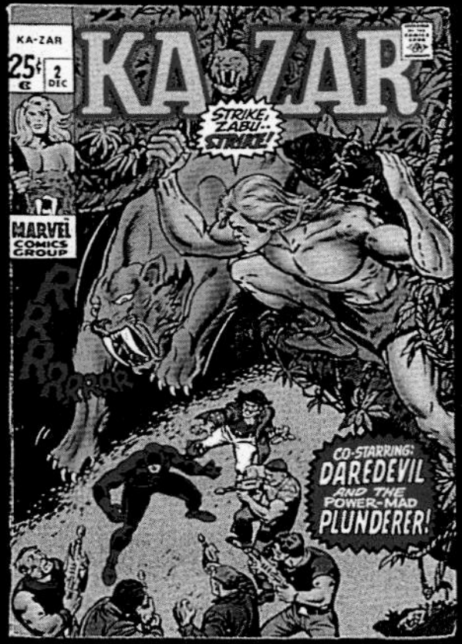
KA-ZAR
STRIKE, ZABU! STRIKE!
CO-STARRING: DAREDEVIL AND THE POWER-MAD PLUNDERER!

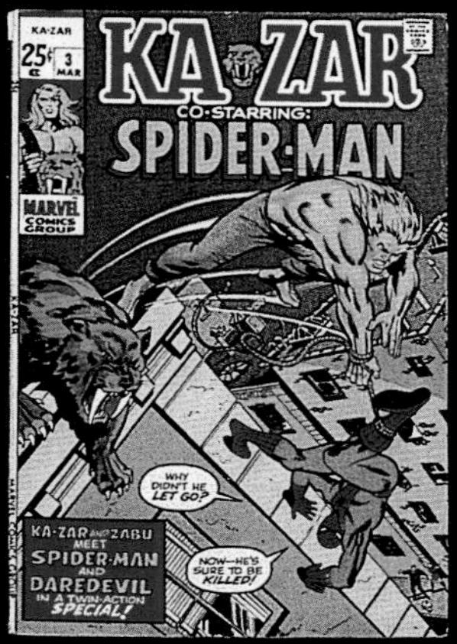
KA-ZAR
CO-STARRING: SPIDER-MAN
KA-ZAR AND ZABU MEET SPIDER-MAN AND DAREDEVIL IN A TWIN-ACTION SPECIAL!
WHY DIDN'T HE LET GO?
NOW--HE'S SURE TO BE KILLED!

1018.6 Ka-Zar 2nd Series (1-20)

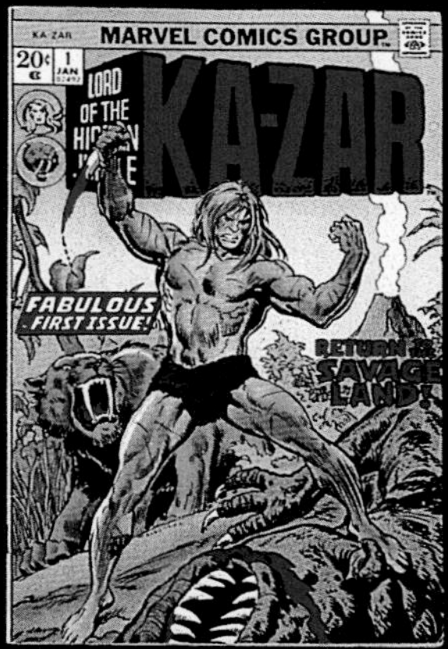
MARVEL COMICS GROUP
LORD OF THE HIDDEN JUNGLE
KA-ZAR
FABULOUS FIRST ISSUE!

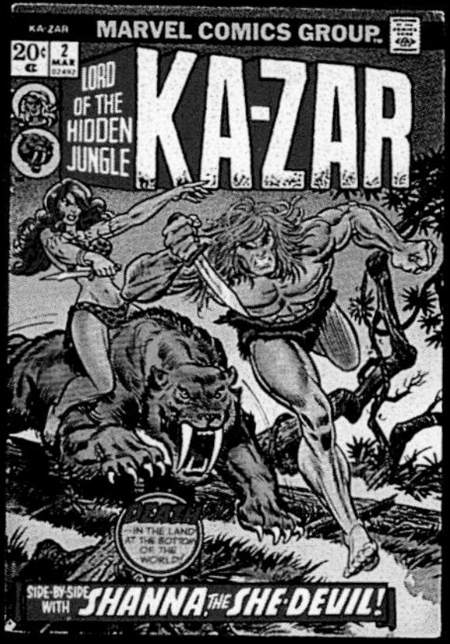
MARVEL COMICS GROUP
LORD OF THE HIDDEN JUNGLE
KA-ZAR
SIDE-BY-SIDE WITH SHANNA THE SHE-DEVIL!

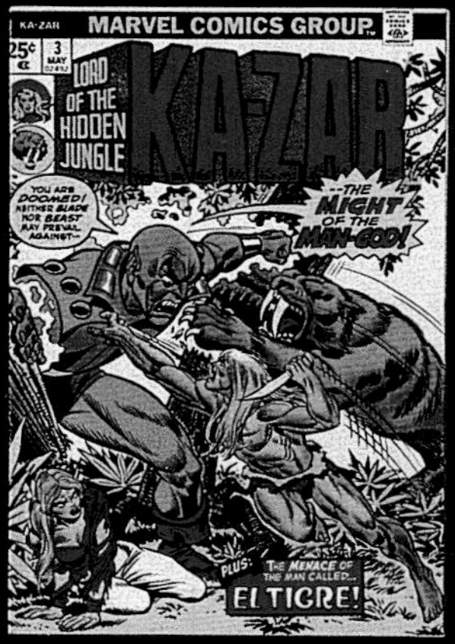
MARVEL COMICS GROUP
LORD OF THE HIDDEN JUNGLE
KA-ZAR
THE NIGHT OF THE MAN-GOD!
PLUS: THE MENACE OF THE MAN CALLED... EL TIGRE!

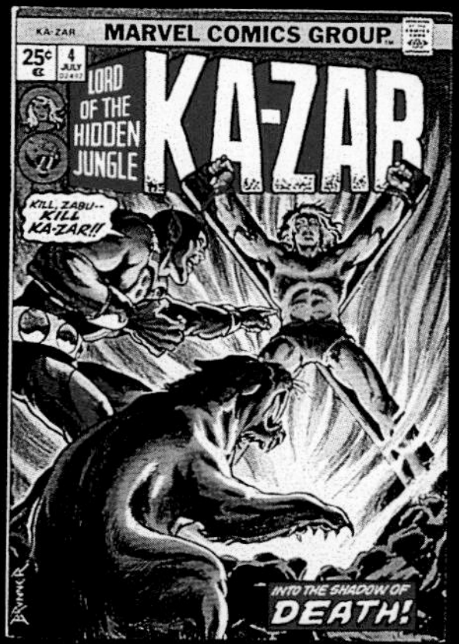
MARVEL COMICS GROUP
LORD OF THE HIDDEN JUNGLE
KA-ZAR
KILL ZABU-- KILL KA-ZAR!!
INTO THE SHADOW OF DEATH!

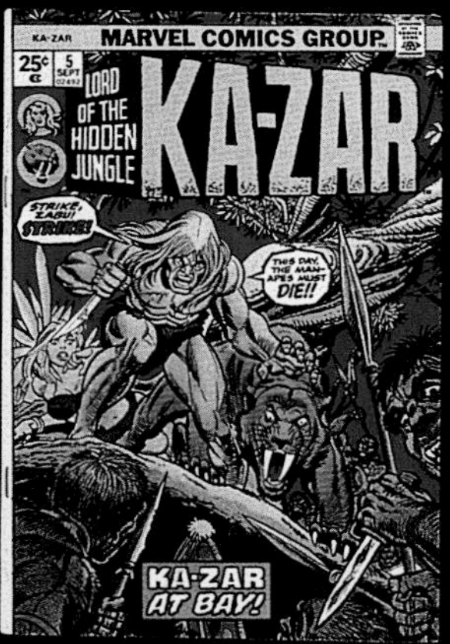
MARVEL COMICS GROUP
LORD OF THE HIDDEN JUNGLE
KA-ZAR
STRIKE, ZABU! STRIKE!
KA-ZAR AT BAY!

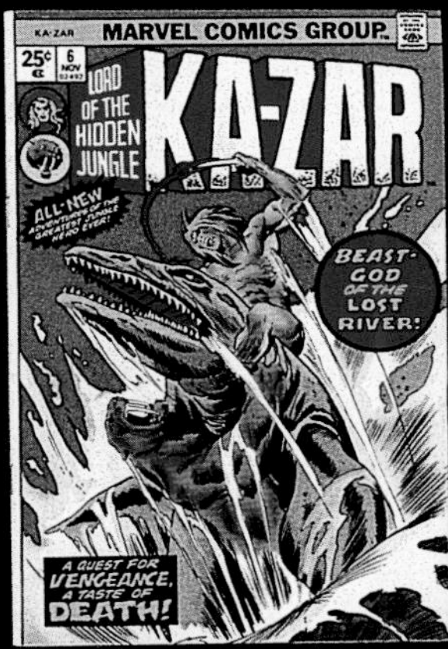
MARVEL COMICS GROUP
LORD OF THE HIDDEN JUNGLE
KA-ZAR
BEAST-GOD OF THE LOST RIVER!
A QUEST FOR VENGEANCE, A TASTE OF DEATH!

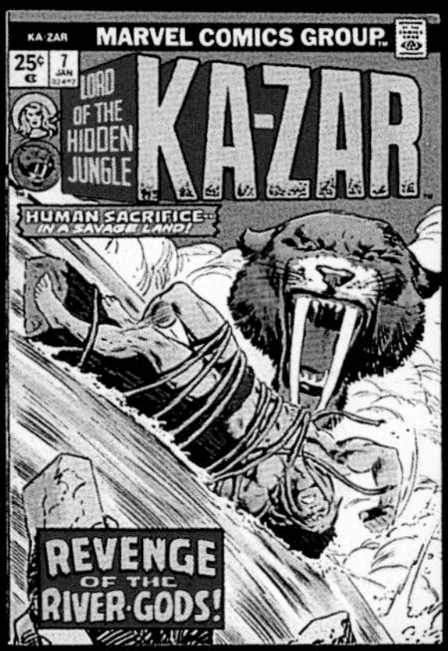
MARVEL COMICS GROUP
LORD OF THE HIDDEN JUNGLE
KA-ZAR
HUMAN SACRIFICE-- IN A SAVAGE LAND!
REVENGE OF THE RIVER-GODS!

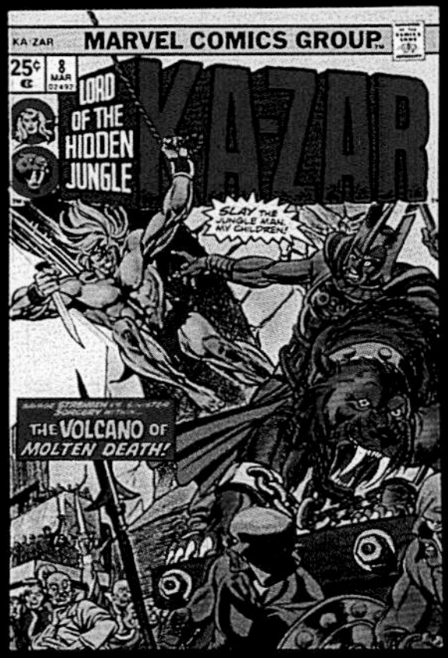
MARVEL COMICS GROUP
LORD OF THE HIDDEN JUNGLE
KA-ZAR
THE VOLCANO OF MOLTEN DEATH!

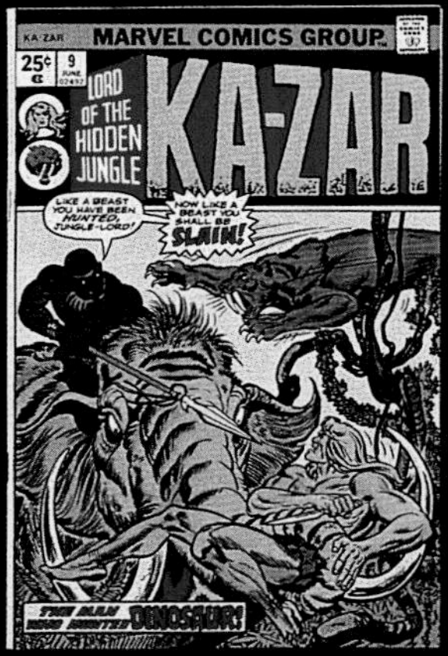
MARVEL COMICS GROUP
LORD OF THE HIDDEN JUNGLE
KA-ZAR
SLAIN!

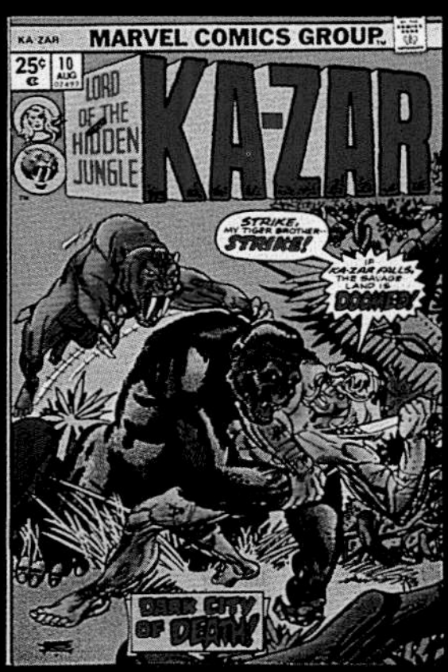
MARVEL COMICS GROUP
LORD OF THE HIDDEN JUNGLE
KA-ZAR
STRIKE!

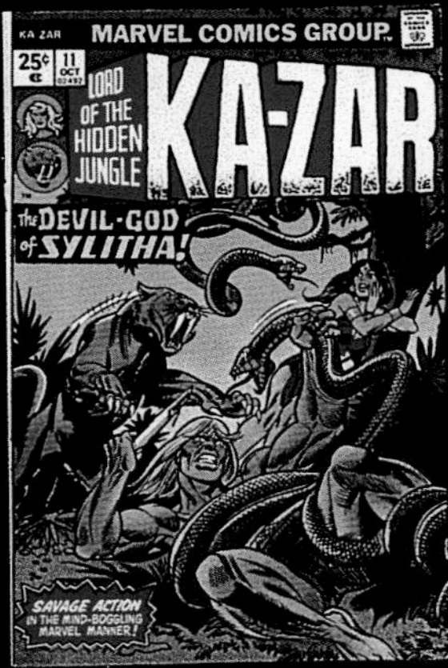
MARVEL COMICS GROUP
LORD OF THE HIDDEN JUNGLE
KA-ZAR
THE DEVIL-GOD OF SYLITHA!
SAVAGE ACTION IN THE MIND-BOGGLING MARVEL MANNER!

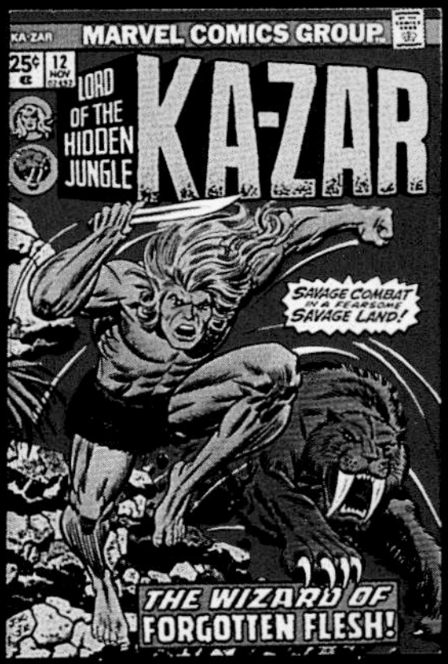
MARVEL COMICS GROUP
LORD OF THE HIDDEN JUNGLE
KA-ZAR
SAVAGE COMBAT IN A FEARSOME SAVAGE LAND!
THE WIZARD OF FORGOTTEN FLESH!

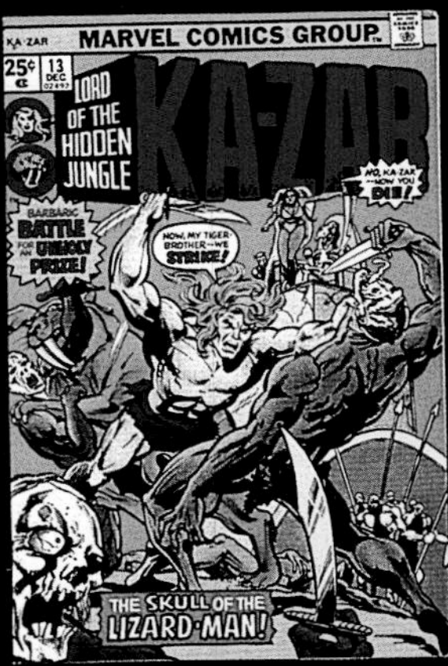
MARVEL COMICS GROUP
LORD OF THE HIDDEN JUNGLE
KA-ZAR
THE SKULL OF THE LIZARD-MAN!

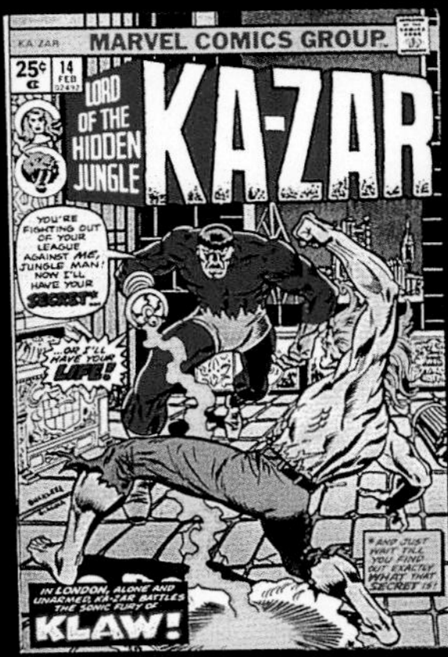
MARVEL COMICS GROUP
LORD OF THE HIDDEN JUNGLE
KA-ZAR
KLAW!

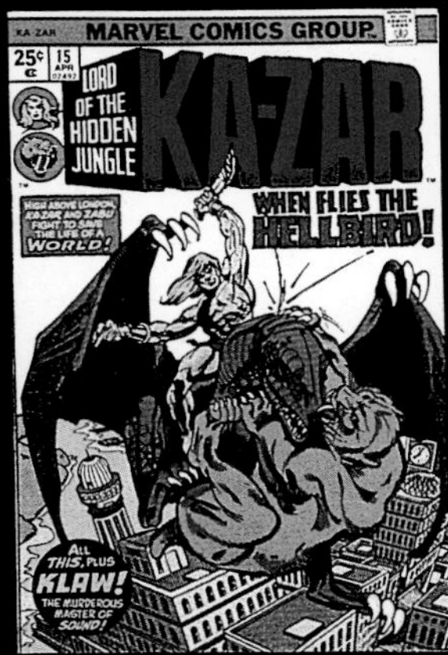
MARVEL COMICS GROUP
LORD OF THE HIDDEN JUNGLE
KA-ZAR
WHEN FLIES THE HELLBIRD!
KLAW!

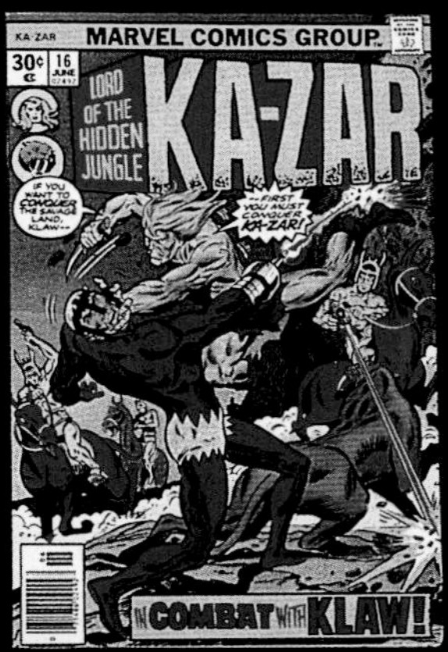
MARVEL COMICS GROUP
LORD OF THE HIDDEN JUNGLE
KA-ZAR
IN COMBAT WITH KLAW!

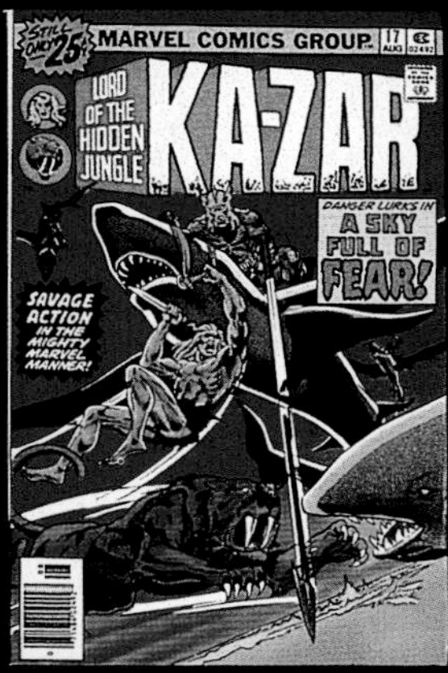
MARVEL COMICS GROUP
LORD OF THE HIDDEN JUNGLE
KA-ZAR
A SKY FULL OF FEAR!
SAVAGE ACTION IN THE MIGHTY MARVEL MANNER!

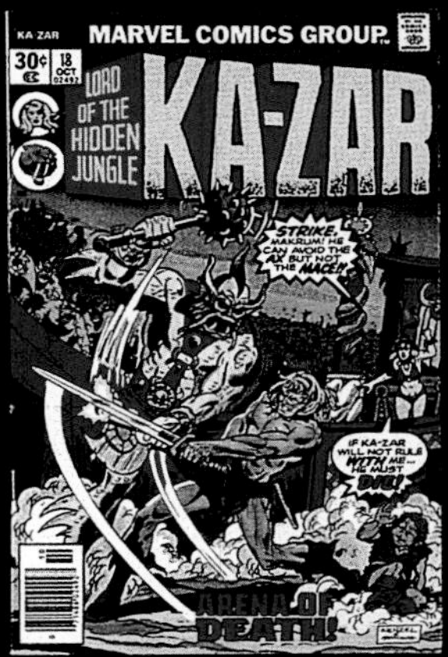
MARVEL COMICS GROUP
LORD OF THE HIDDEN JUNGLE
KA-ZAR
DEATH!

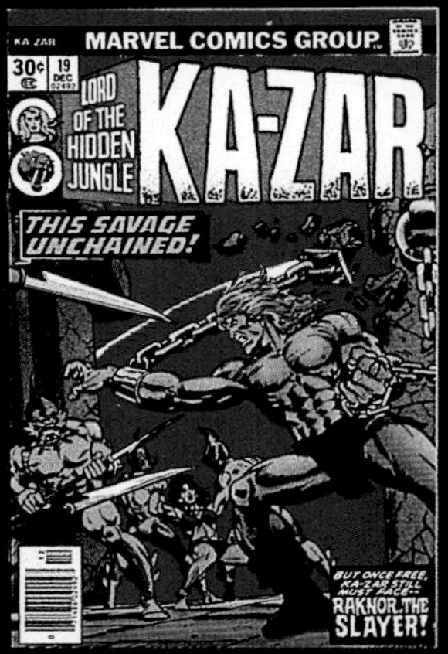
MARVEL COMICS GROUP
LORD OF THE HIDDEN JUNGLE
KA-ZAR
THIS SAVAGE UNCHAINED!
RAKNOR, THE SLAYER!

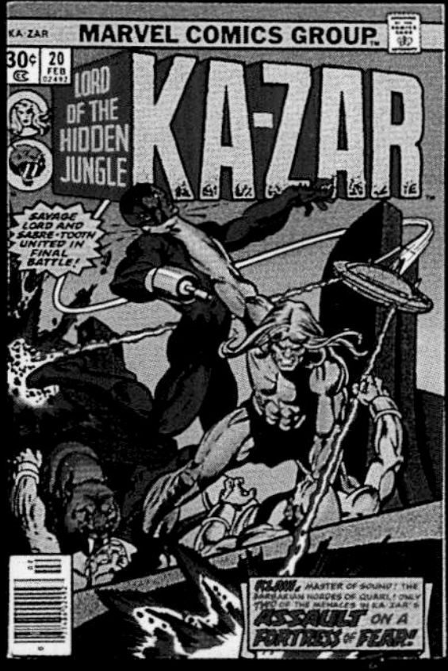
MARVEL COMICS GROUP
LORD OF THE HIDDEN JUNGLE
KA-ZAR

Ka-Zar (1st Series; 1-3) 1018.4

Ref. No.	Date	RVI	Artist/Info.
1018.4-1	Aug. 1970	4	M. Severin/Verpoorten-c, Springer/Ayers-a
1018.4-2	Dec.	2	M. Severin/Everett-c, Tuska/Ayers-a
1018.4-3	Mar. 1971	2	M. Severin/Romita-c, Tuska/Ayers-a

Ka-Zar (2nd Series; 1-20) 1018.6

Ref. No.	Date	RVI	Artist/Info.
1018.6-1	Jan. 1974	1	Buscema-c, Reinman, Royer-a
1018.6-2	Mar.	1	Romita/Giacoia-c, Heck/Abel-a
1018.6-3	May.	1	Kane, Romita/Giacoia-c, Heck/Royer-a
1018.6-4	Jul.	1	Brunner-c, Heck/Royer-a
1018.6-5	Sept.	1	Kane/Giacoia-c, Heck/Esposito-a
1018.6-6	Nov.	1	Buscema-c/a, Alcala-a
1018.6-7	Jan. 1975	1	Buscema-c/a, McLeod-a
1018.6-8	Mar.	1	Kane/Janson-c, Buscema, Alcala-a
1018.6-9	Jun.	1	Kane, Romita/Giacoia-c, Buscema, Trinidad-a
1018.6-10	**Aug.**	**1**	**Kane-c, Buscema/Kida-a**
1018.6-11	Oct.	1	Kane/Giacoia-c, Heck/Springer-a
1018.6-12	Nov.	1	Kirby, Romita-c, Heath-a
1018.6-13	Dec.	1	Kne, Romita/Janson-c, Hama/Kida-a
1018.6-14	Feb. 1976	1	Buckler/Giacoia-c, Hama/Abel, Esposito-a
1018.6-15	Apr.	1	Kane/Janson-c, Mayerik-a
1018.6-16	Jun.	1	
1018.6-17	Aug.	1	
1018.6-18 to 20	Feb. 1977, (#20)	1	

1018.8 Ka-Zar the Savage (1-34)

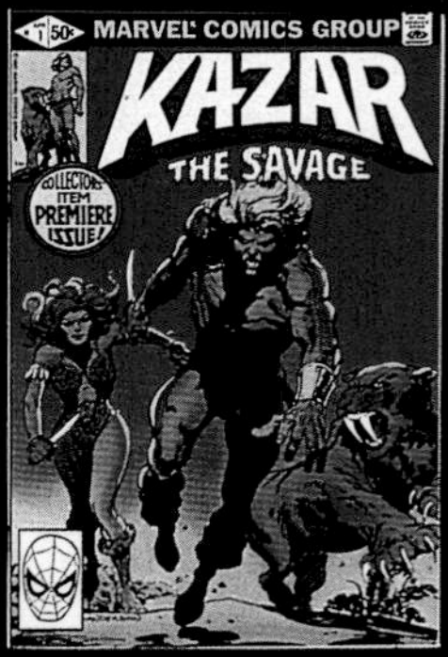
MARVEL COMICS GROUP
KAZAR
THE SAVAGE
COLLECTORS' ITEM PREMIERE ISSUE!
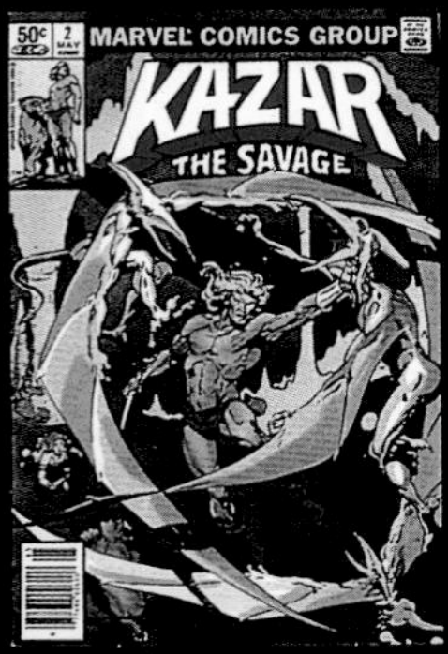
MARVEL COMICS GROUP
KAZAR
THE SAVAGE
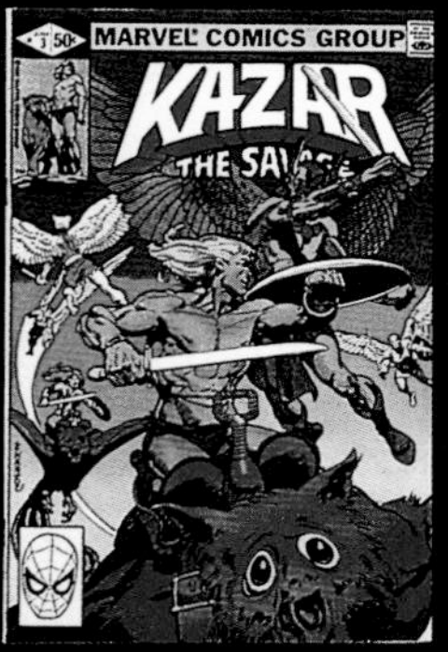
MARVEL COMICS GROUP
KAZAR
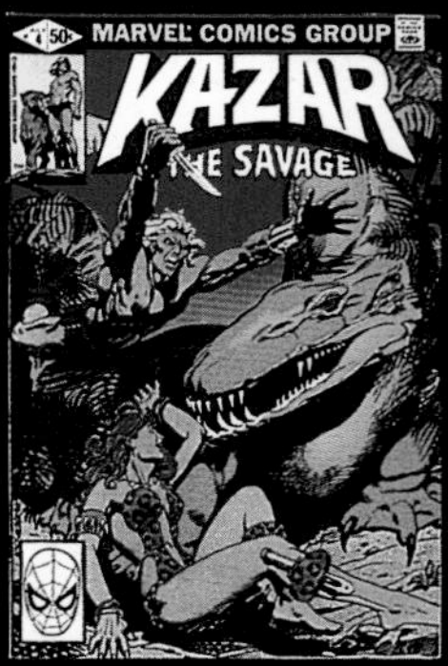
MARVEL COMICS GROUP
KAZAR
THE SAVAGE
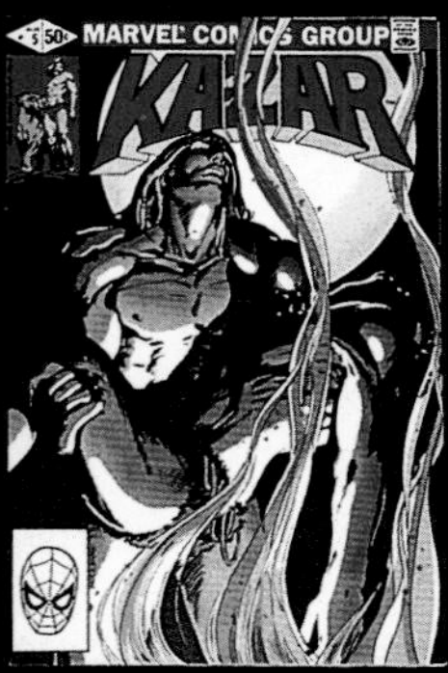
MARVEL COMICS GROUP
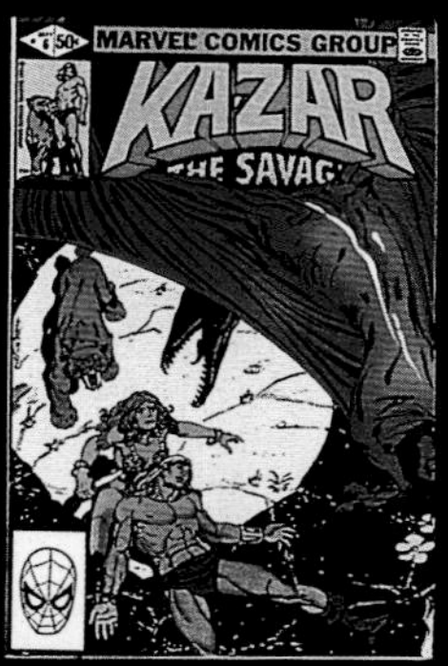
MARVEL COMICS GROUP
KAZAR
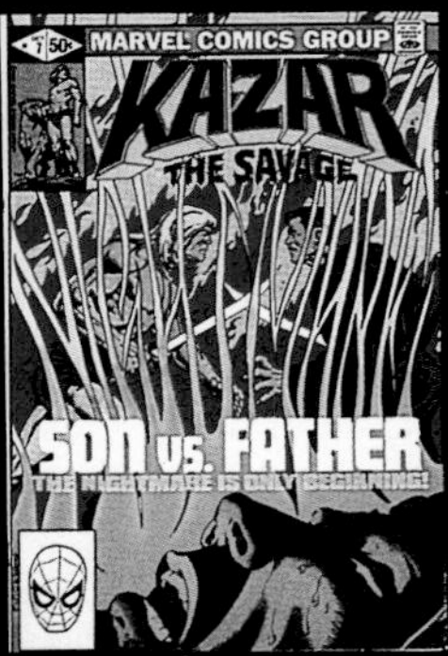
MARVEL COMICS GROUP
KAZAR
THE SAVAGE
SON VS. FATHER
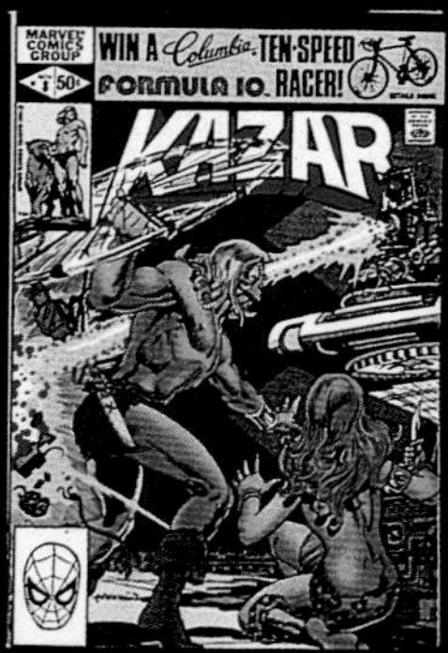
WIN A Columbia TEN-SPEED FORMULA 10 RACER!
KAZAR
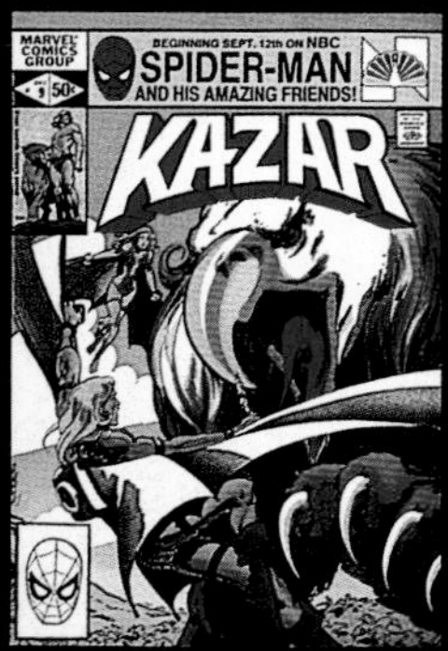
SPIDER-MAN AND HIS AMAZING FRIENDS!
KAZAR
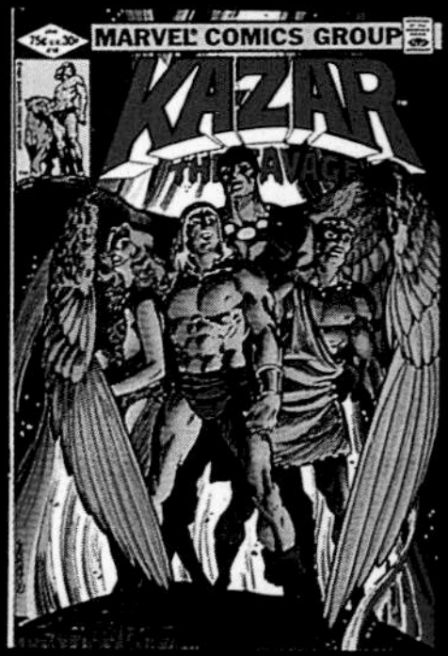
MARVEL COMICS GROUP
KAZAR
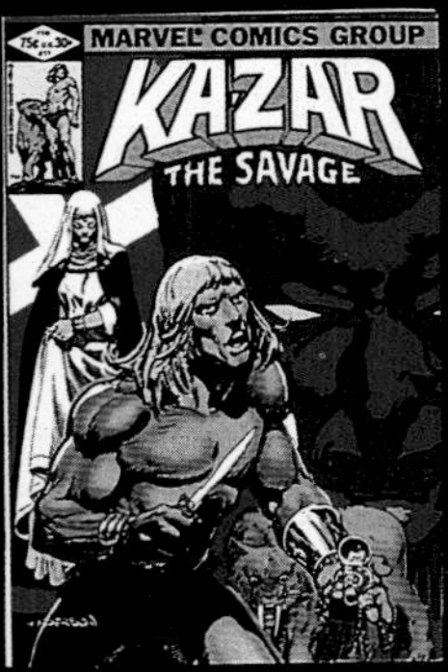
MARVEL COMICS GROUP
KAZAR
THE SAVAGE
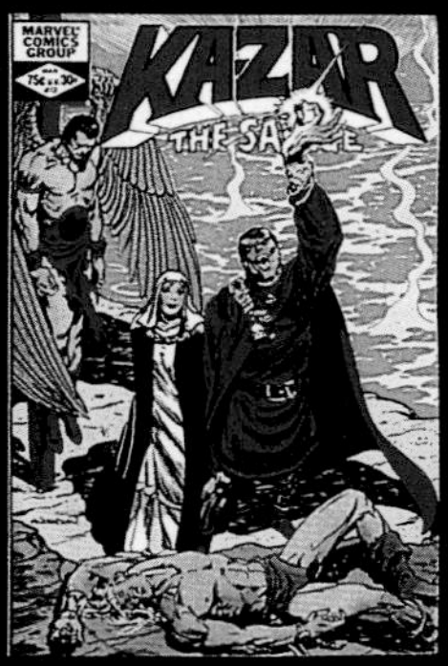
KAZAR
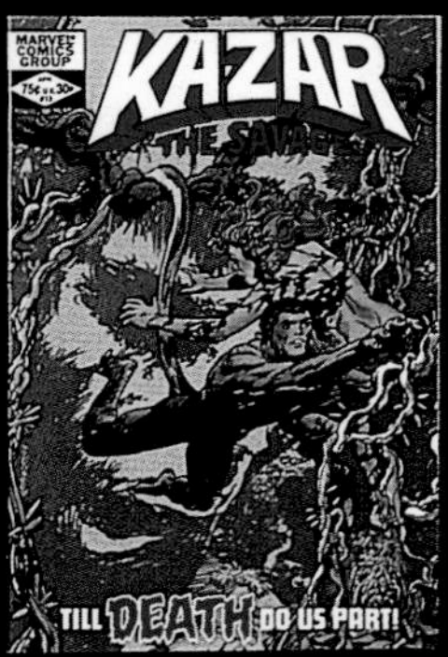
KAZAR
TILL DEATH DO US PART!
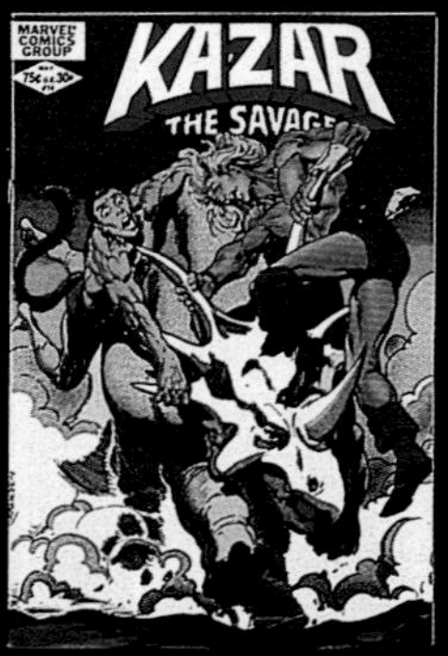
KAZAR
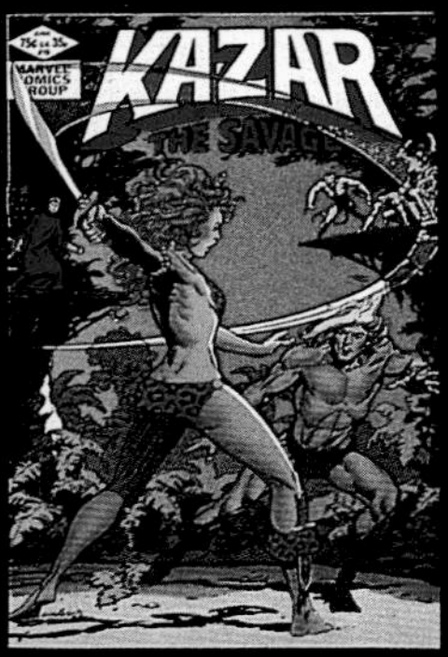
KAZAR
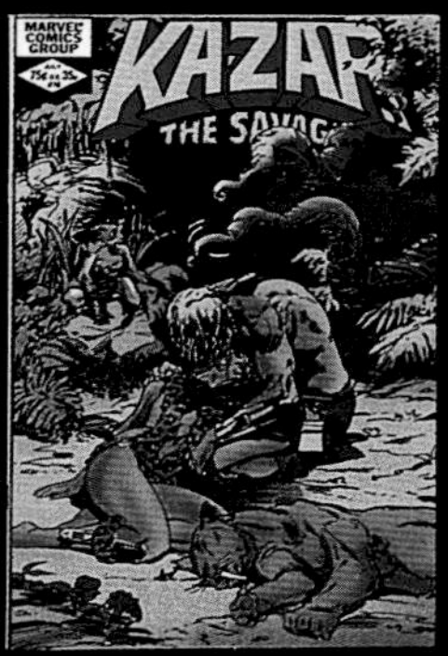
KAZAR
THE SAVAGE
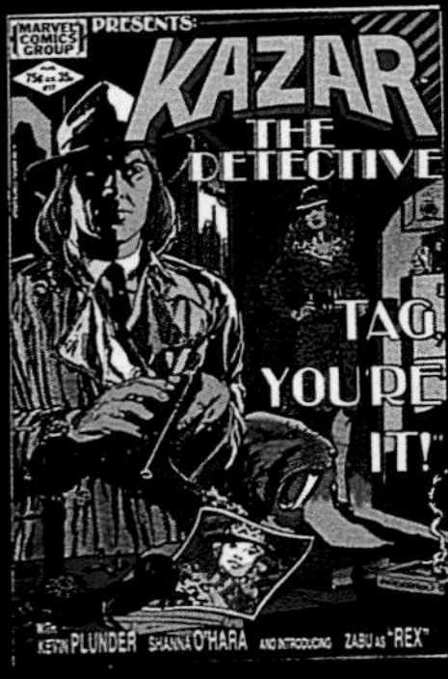
PRESENTS:
KAZAR
THE DETECTIVE
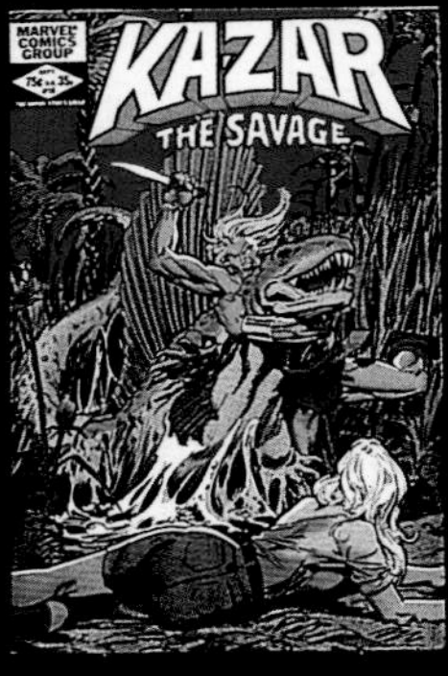
KAZAR
THE SAVAGE
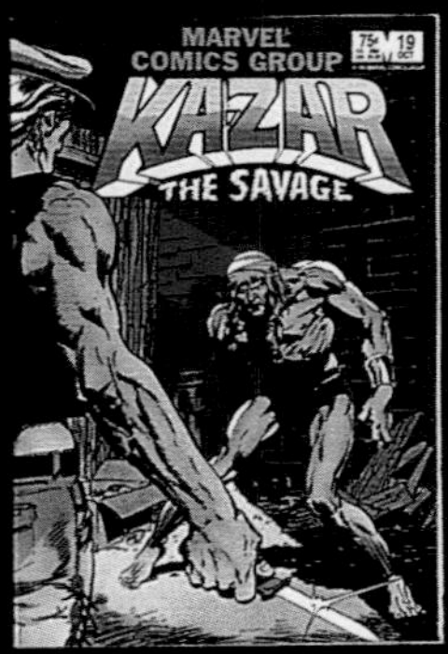
MARVEL COMICS GROUP
KAZAR
THE SAVAGE
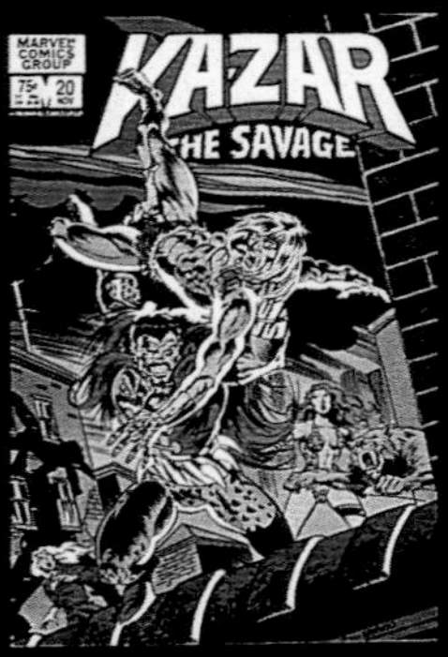
KAZAR
THE SAVAGE
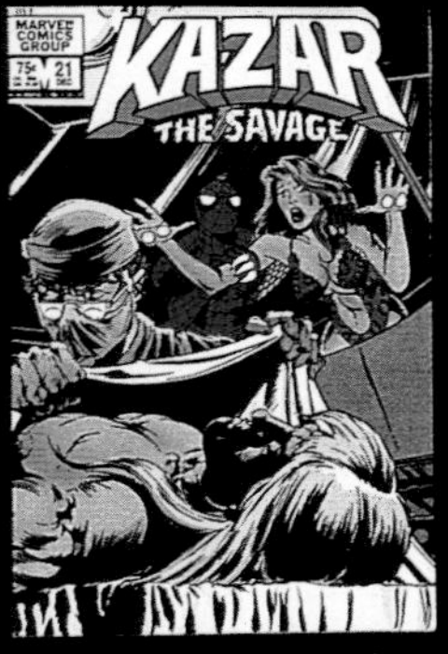
KAZAR
THE SAVAGE
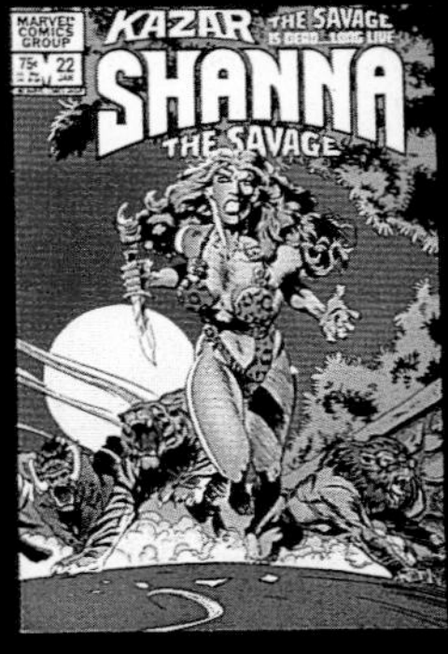
KAZAR
SHANNA
THE SAVAGE
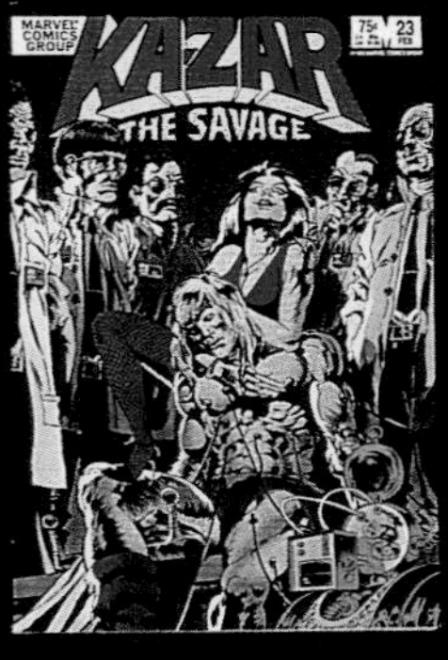
KAZAR
THE SAVAGE
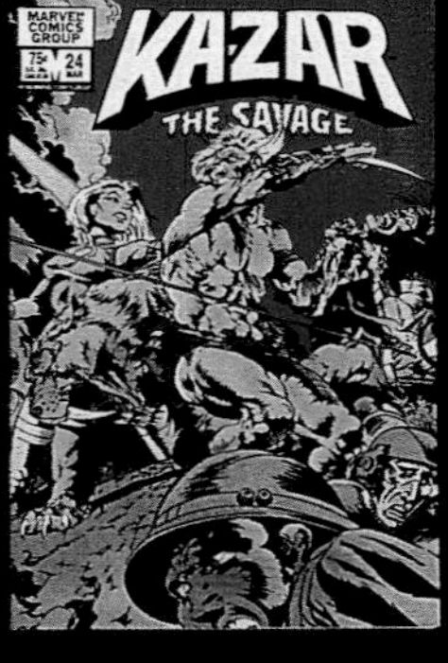
KAZAR
THE SAVAGE
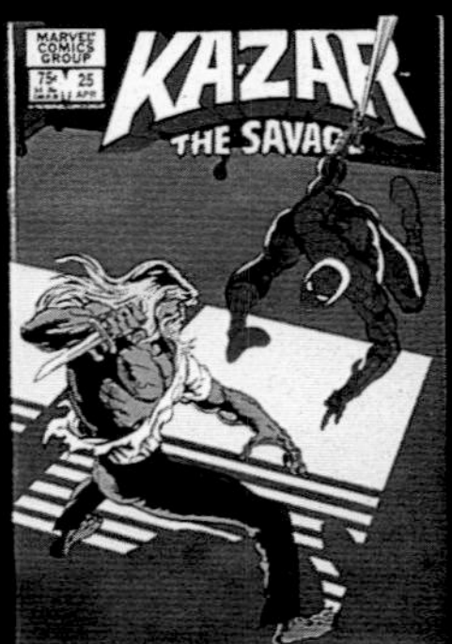
KAZAR
THE SAVAGE
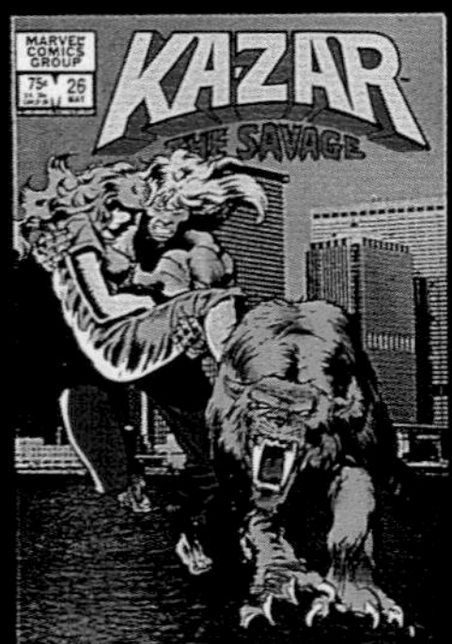
KAZAR
THE SAVAGE
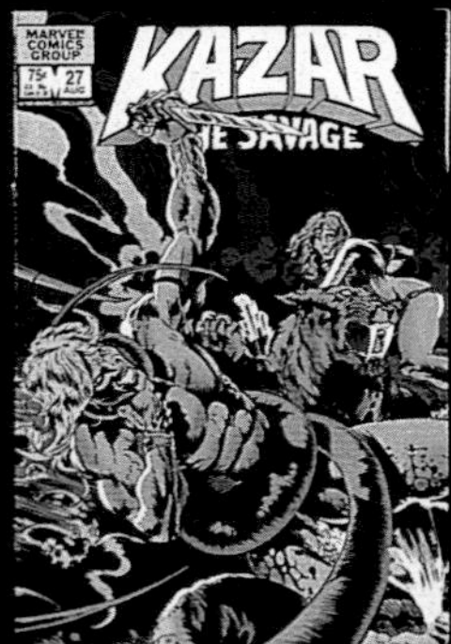
KAZAR
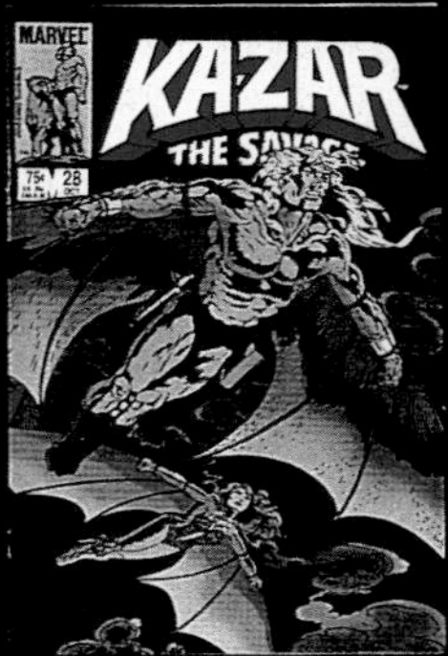
KAZAR
THE SAVAGE
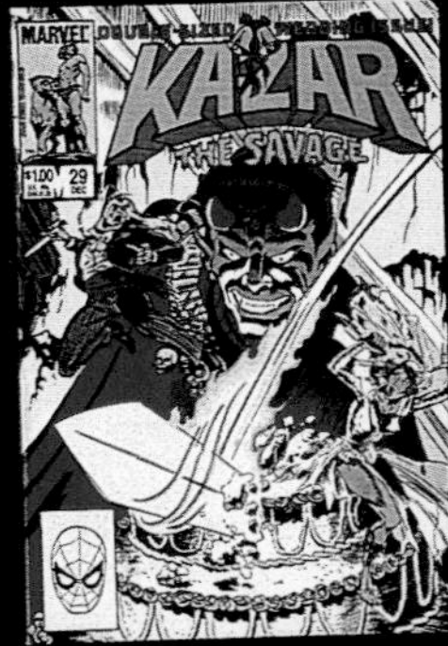
KAZAR
THE SAVAGE
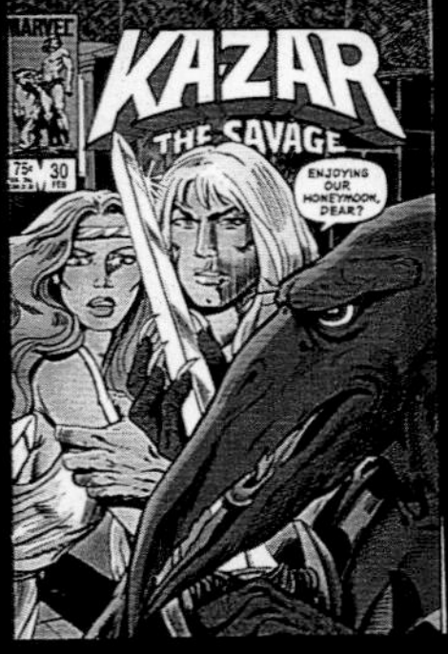
KAZAR
THE SAVAGE
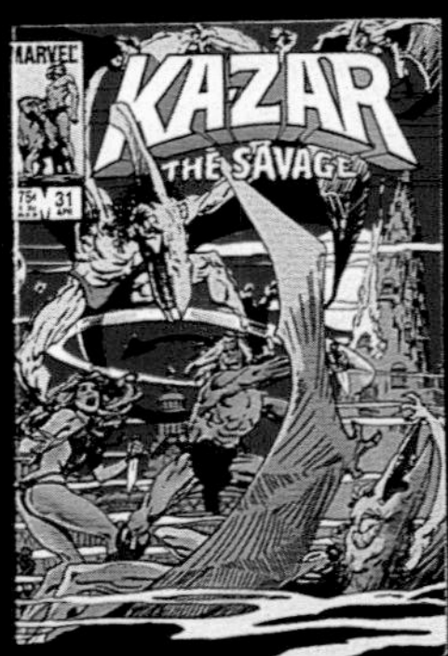
KAZAR
THE SAVAGE
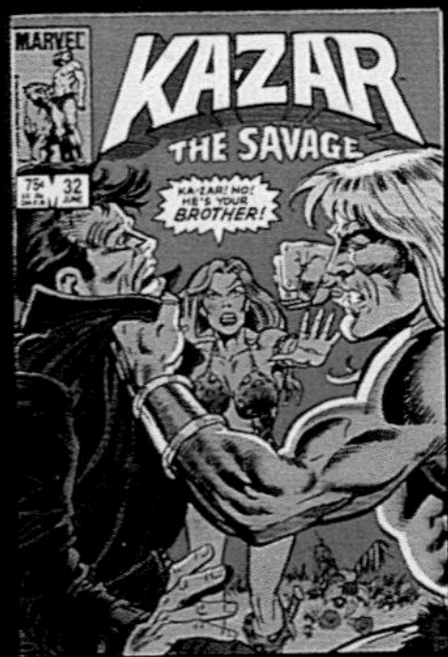
KAZAR
THE SAVAGE
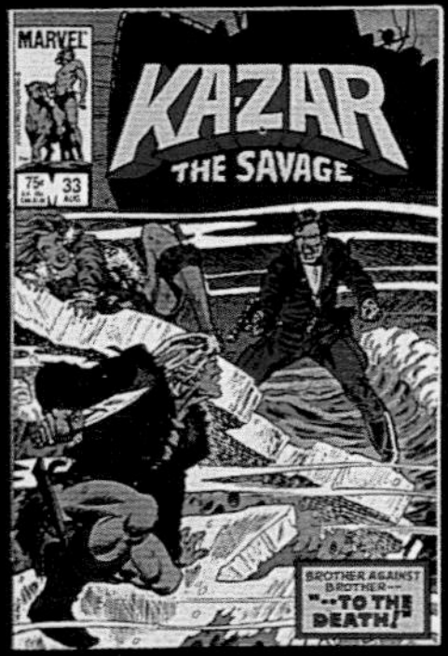
KAZAR
THE SAVAGE
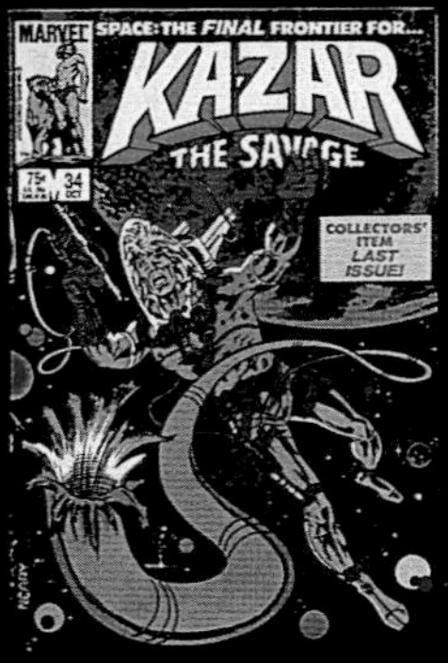
SPACE: THE FINAL FRONTIER FOR...
KAZAR
THE SAVAGE
COLLECTORS' ITEM LAST ISSUE!

Ka-Zar the Savage (1-34) 1018.8

Ref. No.	Date	RVI	Artist/Info.
1018.8-1	Apr. 1981	1	Anderson-c/a, Garzon-a
1018.8-2	May	1	" "
1018.8-3	Jun.	1	" "
1018.8-4	Jul.	1	" "
1018.8-5	Aug.	1	" "
1018.8-6	Sept.	1	" "
1018.8-7	Oct.	1	Anderson-c/a, Bingham/Garzon-a
1018.8-8	Nov.	1	Anderson-c/a, Garzon-a
1018.8-9	Dec.	1	" "
1018.8-10	Jan. 1982	1	" "
1018.8-11	Feb.	1	Anderson-c/a, Rubinstein-a
1018.8-12	Mar.	1	Anderson-c/a, Gil-a
1018.8-13	Apr.	1	" "
1018.8-14	May	1	" "
1018.8-15	Jun.	1	" "
1018.8-16 to 34	Oct. 1984, (#34)	1	(#29, Ka-Zar and Shanna marry)

Kickers, Inc. (1-12) 1031.5

1031.5-1 to 12	Nov. 1986, (#1)	1	

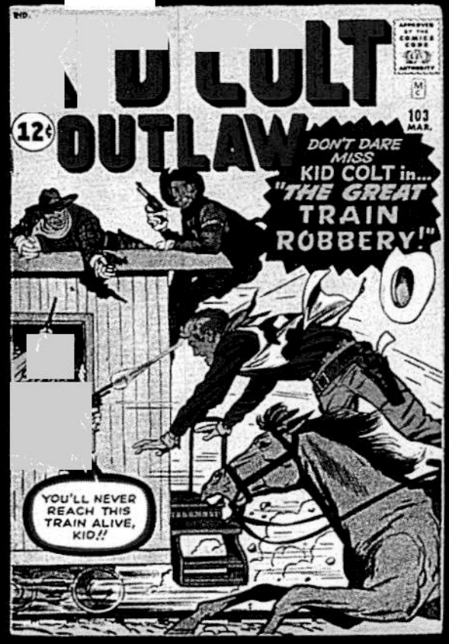
OUTLAW
12¢
DON'T DARE MISS KID COLT in... "THE GREAT TRAIN ROBBERY!"
YOU'LL NEVER REACH THIS TRAIN ALIVE, KID!!

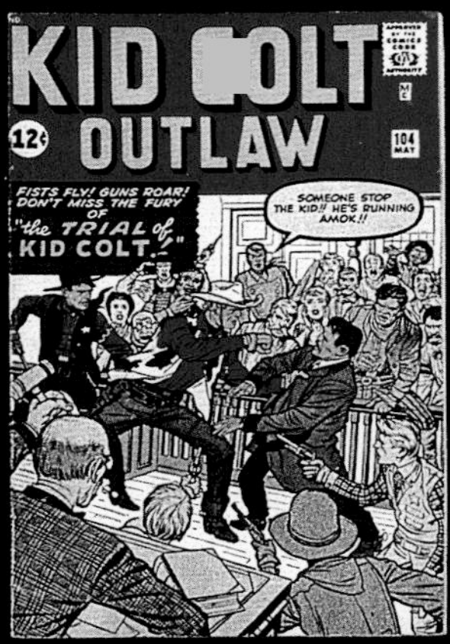
KID OLT
OUTLAW
12¢
FISTS FLY! GUNS ROAR! DON'T MISS THE FURY OF the TRIAL of KID COLT..!
SOMEONE STOP THE KID!! HE'S RUNNING AMOK!!

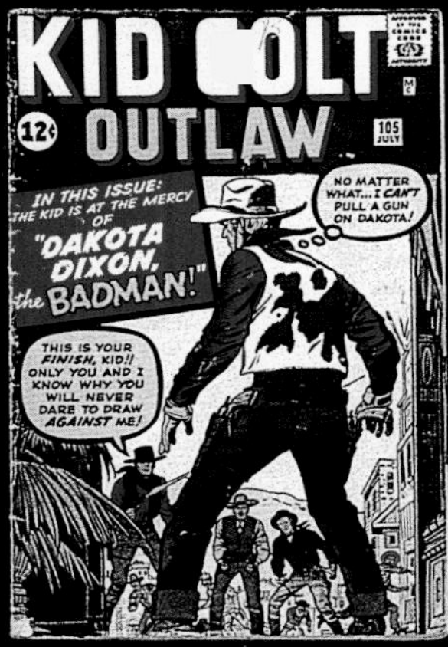
KID OLT
OUTLAW
12¢
IN THIS ISSUE: THE KID IS AT THE MERCY OF "DAKOTA DIXON, the BADMAN!"
NO MATTER WHAT...I CAN'T PULL A GUN ON DAKOTA!
THIS IS YOUR FINISH, KID!! ONLY YOU AND I KNOW WHY YOU WILL NEVER DARE TO DRAW AGAINST ME!

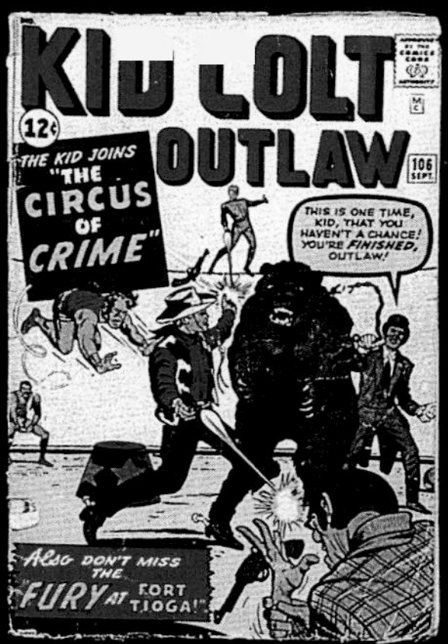
OUTLAW
12¢
THE KID JOINS "THE CIRCUS OF CRIME"
THIS IS ONE TIME, KID, THAT YOU HAVEN'T A CHANCE! YOU'RE FINISHED, OUTLAW!
Also DON'T MISS THE FURY AT FORT TIOGA!

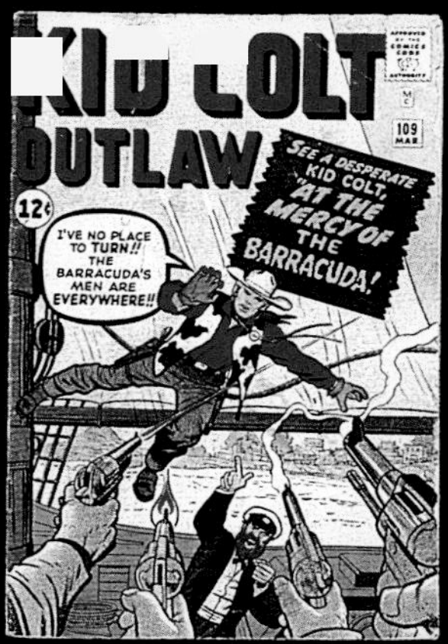
OUTLAW
12¢
SEE A DESPERATE KID COLT "AT THE MERCY OF THE BARRACUDA!"
I'VE NO PLACE TO TURN!! THE BARRACUDA'S MEN ARE EVERYWHERE!!

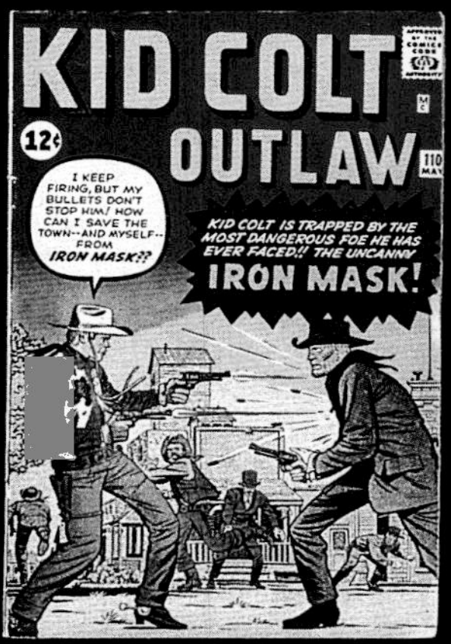
KID COLT
OUTLAW
12¢
I KEEP FIRING, BUT MY BULLETS DON'T STOP HIM! HOW CAN I SAVE THE TOWN--AND MYSELF-- FROM IRON MASK!?
KID COLT IS TRAPPED BY THE MOST DANGEROUS FOE HE HAS EVER FACED!! THE UNCANNY IRON MASK!

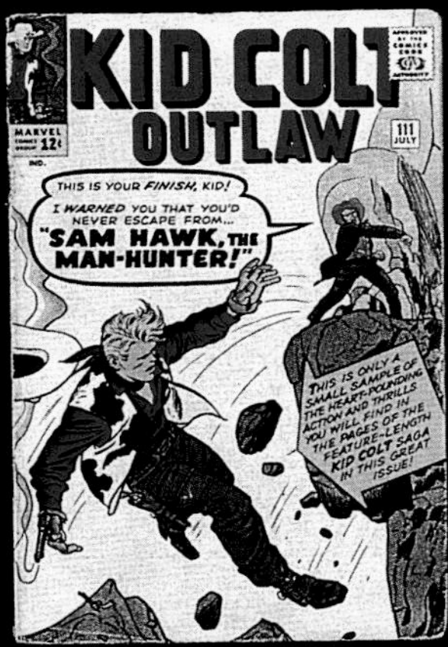
KID COLT
OUTLAW
THIS IS YOUR FINISH, KID!
I WARNED YOU THAT YOU'D NEVER ESCAPE FROM... "SAM HAWK, THE MAN-HUNTER!"

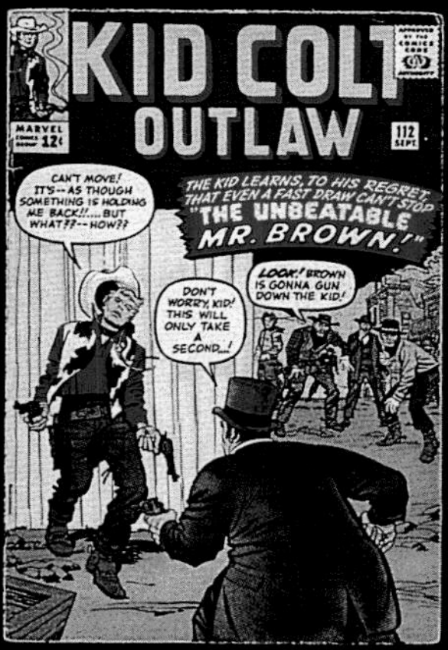
KID COLT
OUTLAW
CAN'T MOVE! IT'S--AS THOUGH SOMETHING IS HOLDING ME BACK!!... BUT WHAT?--HOW??
THE KID LEARNS, TO HIS REGRET, THAT EVEN A FAST DRAW CAN'T STOP THE UNBEATABLE MR. BROWN!
LOOK! BROWN IS GONNA GUN DOWN THE KID!
DON'T WORRY, KID! THIS WILL ONLY TAKE A SECOND...!

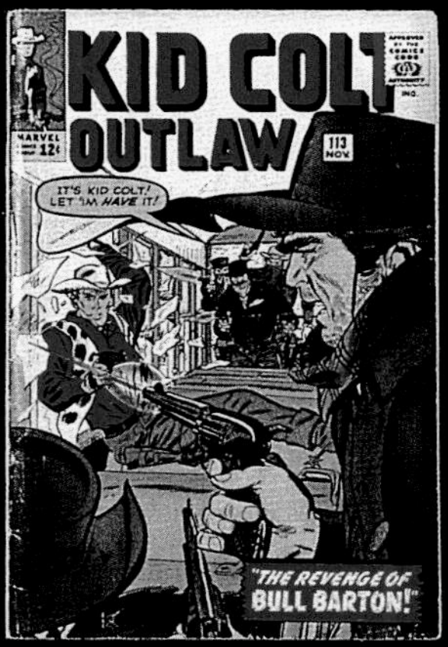
KID COLT
OUTLAW
IT'S KID COLT! LET 'IM HAVE IT!
"THE REVENGE OF BULL BARTON!"

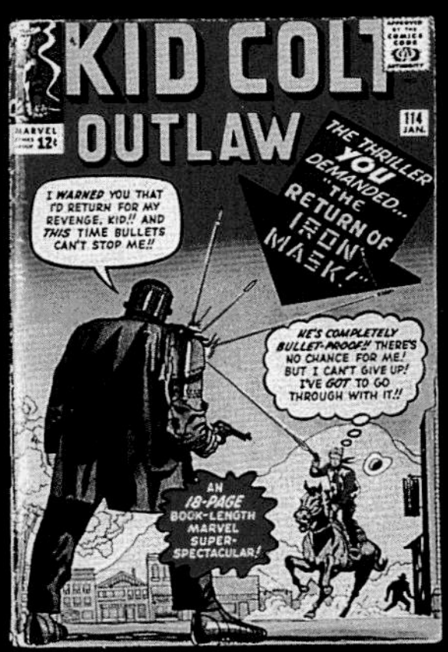
KID COLT
OUTLAW
THE THRILLER YOU DEMANDED... "THE RETURN OF IRON MASK!"
I WARNED YOU THAT I'D RETURN FOR MY REVENGE, KID!! AND THIS TIME BULLETS CAN'T STOP ME!!
HE'S COMPLETELY BULLET-PROOF! THERE'S NO CHANCE FOR ME! BUT I CAN'T GIVE UP! I'VE GOT TO GO THROUGH WITH IT!!
AN 18-PAGE BOOK-LENGTH MARVEL SUPER-SPECTACULAR!

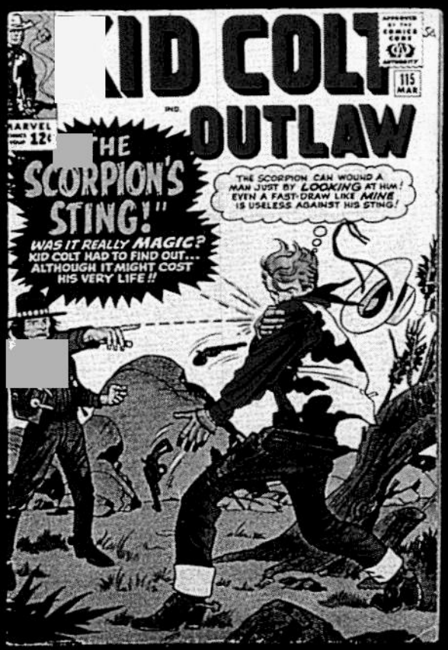
ID COLT
OUTLAW
"THE SCORPION'S STING!"
THE SCORPION CAN WOUND A MAN JUST BY LOOKING AT HIM! EVEN A FAST DRAW LIKE MINE IS USELESS AGAINST HIS STING!
WAS IT REALLY MAGIC? KID COLT HAD TO FIND OUT... ALTHOUGH IT MIGHT COST HIS VERY LIFE!!

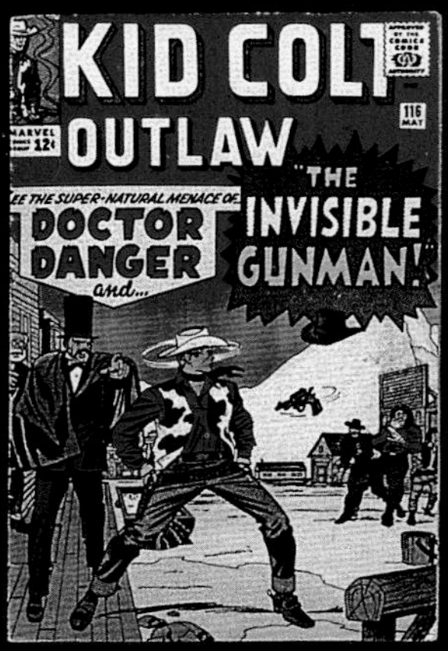
KID COLT
OUTLAW
SEE THE SUPER-NATURAL MENACE OF DOCTOR DANGER and...
"THE INVISIBLE GUNMAN!"

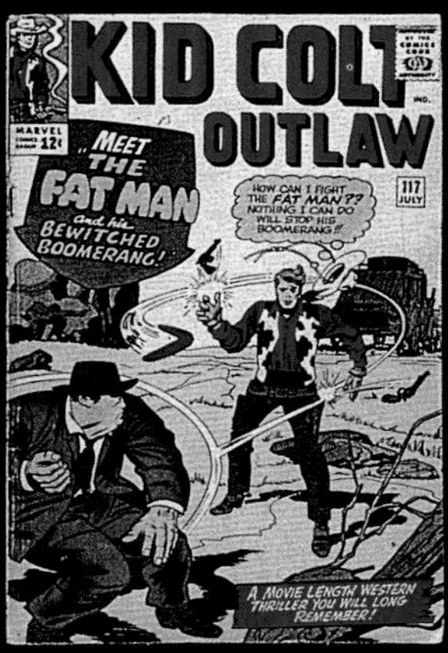
KID COLT
OUTLAW
MEET THE FAT MAN and his BEWITCHED BOOMERANG!
A MOVIE LENGTH WESTERN THRILLER YOU WILL LONG REMEMBER!

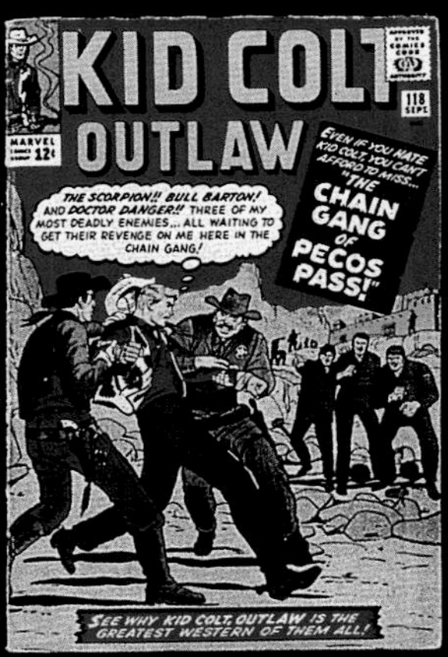
KID COLT
OUTLAW
THE SCORPION!! BULL BARTON! AND DOCTOR DANGER!! THREE OF MY MOST DEADLY ENEMIES... ALL WAITING TO GET THEIR REVENGE ON ME HERE IN THE CHAIN GANG!
"THE CHAIN GANG OF PECOS PASS!"
SEE WHY KID COLT, OUTLAW IS THE GREATEST WESTERN OF THEM ALL!

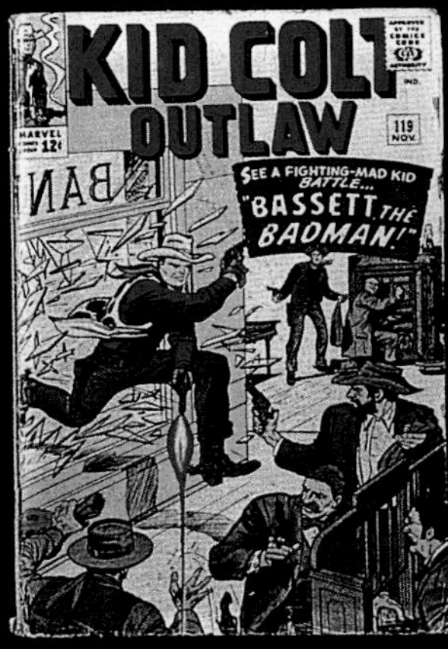
KID COLT
OUTLAW
SEE A FIGHTING-MAD KID BATTLE... "BASSETT THE BADMAN!"

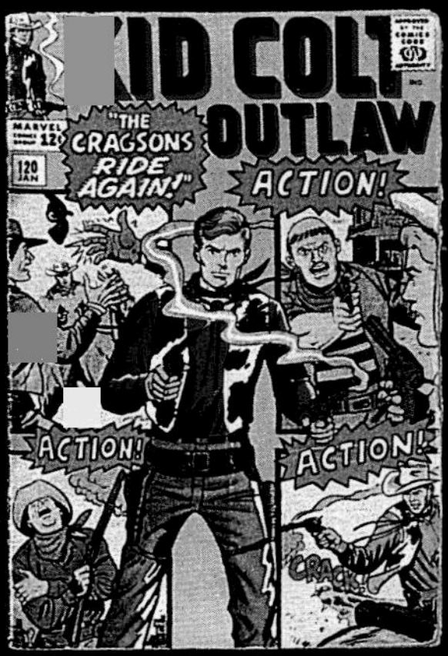
ID COLT
OUTLAW
THE CRAGSONS RIDE AGAIN!
ACTION!
ACTION!
ACTION!

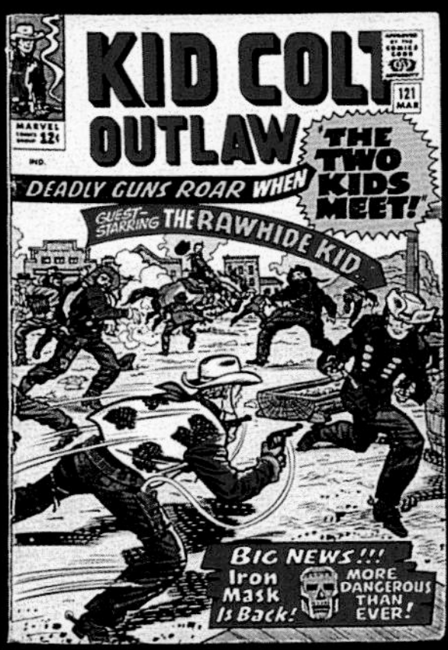
KID COLT
OUTLAW
THE TWO KIDS MEET!
DEADLY GUNS ROAR WHEN
GUEST-STARRING THE RAWHIDE KID
BIG NEWS!!! Iron Mask is Back! MORE DANGEROUS THAN EVER!

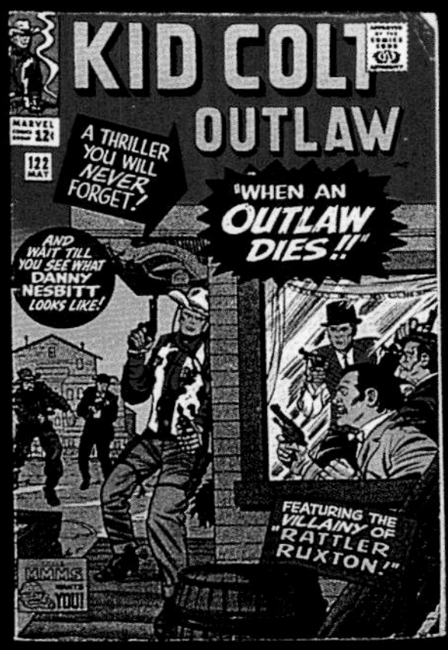
KID COLT
OUTLAW
A THRILLER YOU WILL NEVER FORGET!
"WHEN AN OUTLAW DIES!!"
AND WAIT 'TILL YOU SEE WHAT DANNY NESBITT LOOKS LIKE!
FEATURING THE VILLAINY OF "RATTLER RUXTON!"

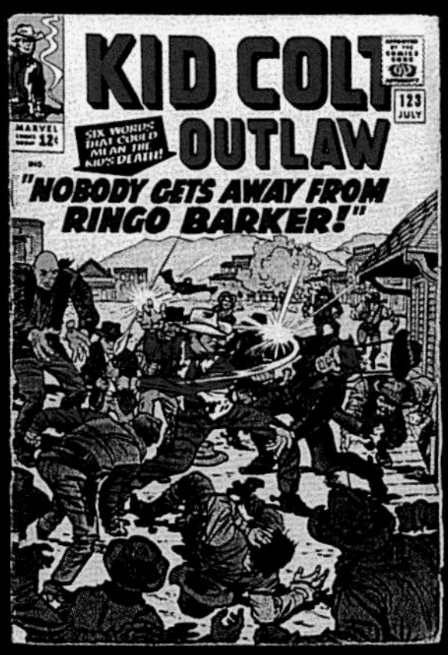
KID COLT
OUTLAW
"NOBODY GETS AWAY FROM RINGO BARKER!"

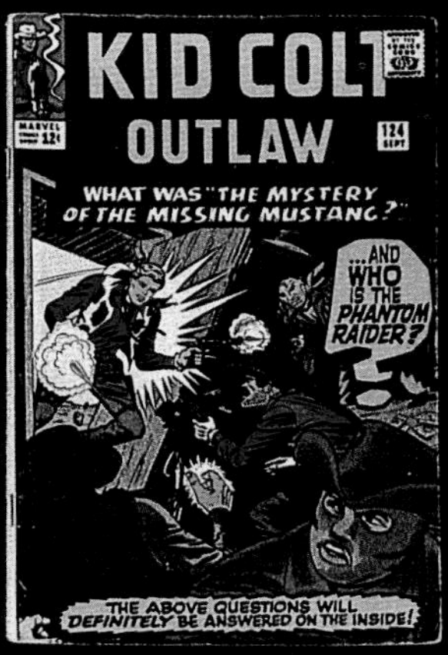
KID COLT
OUTLAW
WHAT WAS "THE MYSTERY OF THE MISSING MUSTANG"...
...AND WHO IS THE PHANTOM RAIDER?
THE ABOVE QUESTIONS WILL DEFINITELY BE ANSWERED ON THE INSIDE!

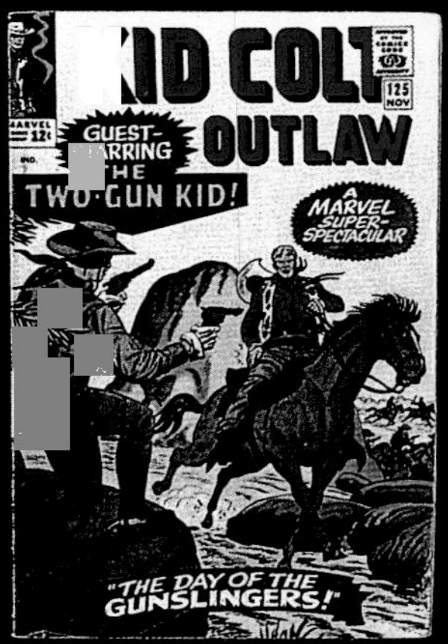
ID COLT
OUTLAW
THE TWO-GUN KID!
MARVEL SUPER-SPECTACULAR
"THE DAY OF THE GUNSLINGERS!"

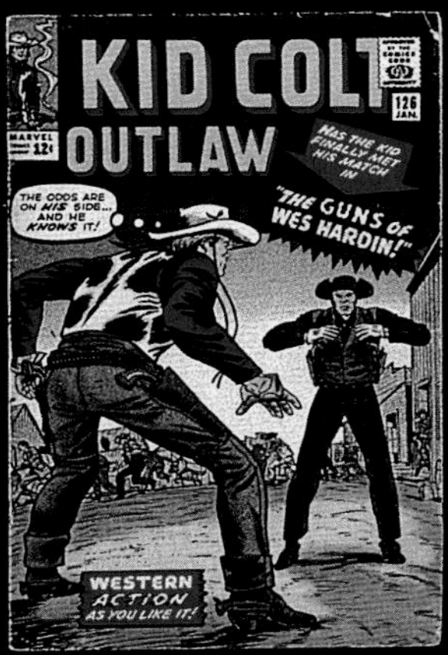
KID COLT
OUTLAW
THE ODDS ARE ON HIS SIDE... AND HE KNOWS IT!
"THE GUNS OF WES HARDIN!"
WESTERN ACTION AS YOU LIKE IT!

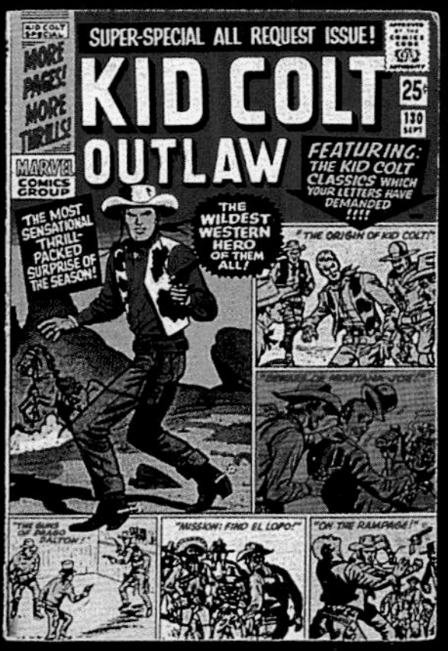
SUPER-SPECIAL ALL REQUEST ISSUE!
KID COLT
OUTLAW
25¢
FEATURING: THE KID COLT CLASSICS WHICH YOUR LETTERS HAVE DEMANDED!!!!
THE WILDEST WESTERN HERO OF THEM ALL!
"THE ORIGIN OF KID COLT!"

Kid Colt Outlaw (103-229) 1033

Ref. No.	Date	RVI	Artist/Info.
1033-103	Mar. 1962	5	Keller-a
1033-104	May	4	Kirby-c, Keller, Heck-a
1033-105	Jul.	4	Keller, Heck-a
1033-106	Sept.	4	Kirby-c, Keller-a
1033-107	Nov.	4	Keller-a
1033-108	Jan. 1963	4	Everett, Keller-a
1033-109	Mar.	4	Brodsky, Ayers, Keller-a
1033-110	**May**	**4**	**Keller, Colan-a**
1033-111	Jul.	4	Kirby-c, Keller-a
1033-112	Sept.	4	" "
1033-113	Nov.	4	Reinman, Keller-a
1033-114	Jan. 1964	4	Kirby-c, Colan, Keller-a
1033-115	Mar.	4	Kirby-c, Keller-a
1033-116	May	4	Kirby-c, Colan, Keller-a
1033-117	Jul.	4	Kirby-c, Lieber, Keller-a
1033-118	Sept.	4	Lieber, Keller-a
1033-119	Nov.	4	Ayers-c, Kirby, Keller-a
1033-120	**Jan. 1965**	**4**	**Keller, Lieber-a**
1033-121 to 129	Jul. 1966, (#129)	2	Keller-a (all) (#25, Two-Gun Kid -app.)
1033-130	Sept.	3	Keller-a (Origin-Kid Colt; 25¢)
1033-131 to 229	Apr. 1979, (#229)	1	(140-229 Reprints)

1044.2 King Conan (1-19)

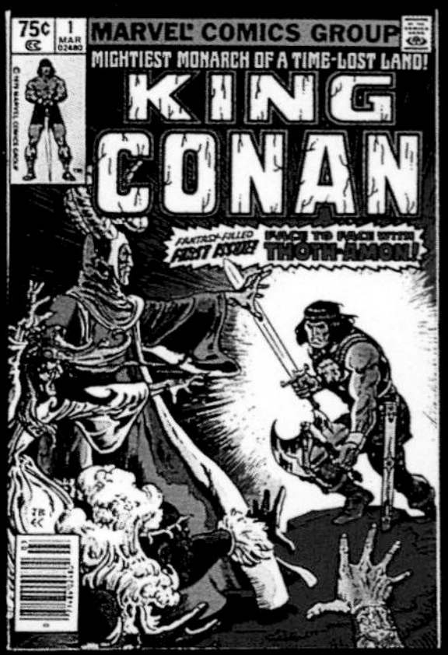
MARVEL COMICS GROUP
MIGHTIEST MONARCH OF A TIME-LOST LAND!
KING CONAN
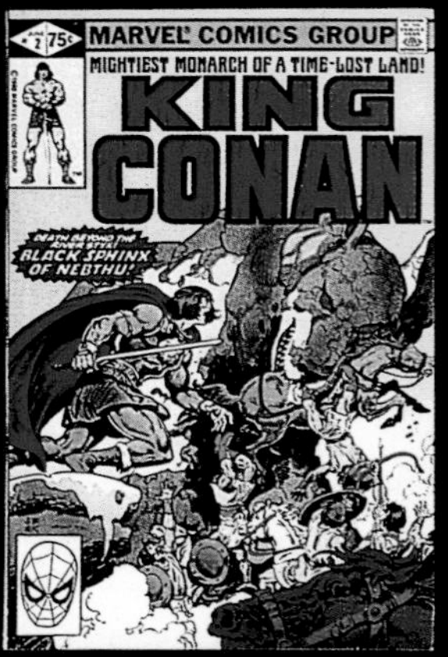
MARVEL COMICS GROUP
MIGHTIEST MONARCH OF A TIME-LOST LAND!
KING CONAN
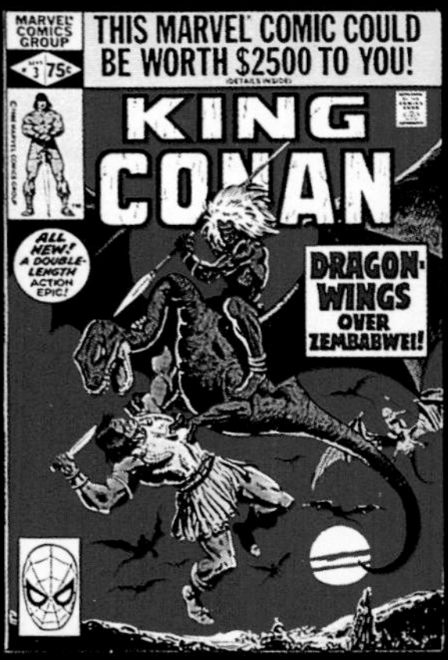
THIS MARVEL COMIC COULD BE WORTH $2500 TO YOU!
KING CONAN
DRAGON-WINGS OVER ZEMBABWEI!
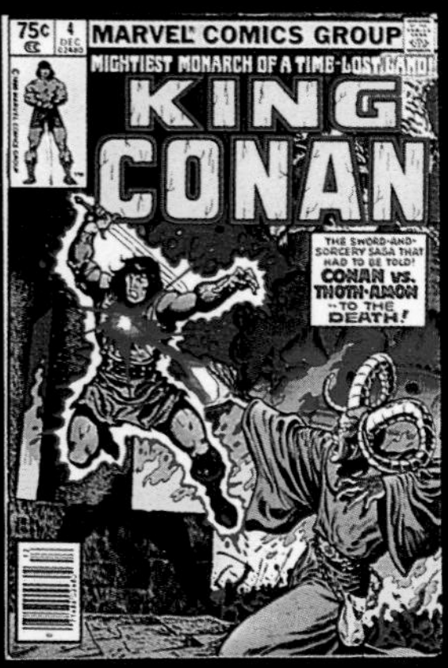
MARVEL COMICS GROUP
MIGHTIEST MONARCH OF A TIME-LOST LAND!
KING CONAN
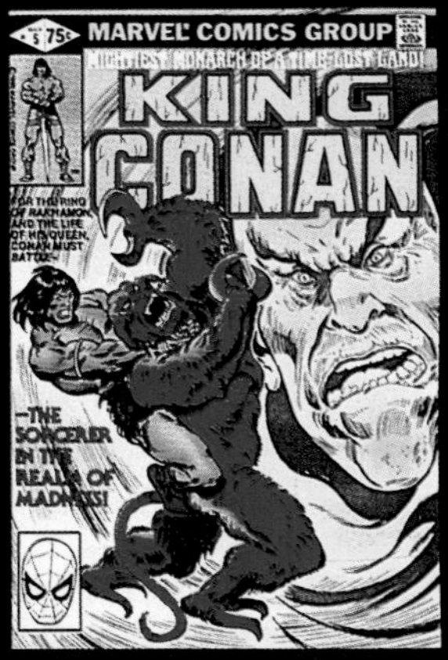
MARVEL COMICS GROUP
MIGHTIEST MONARCH OF A TIME-LOST LAND!
KING CONAN
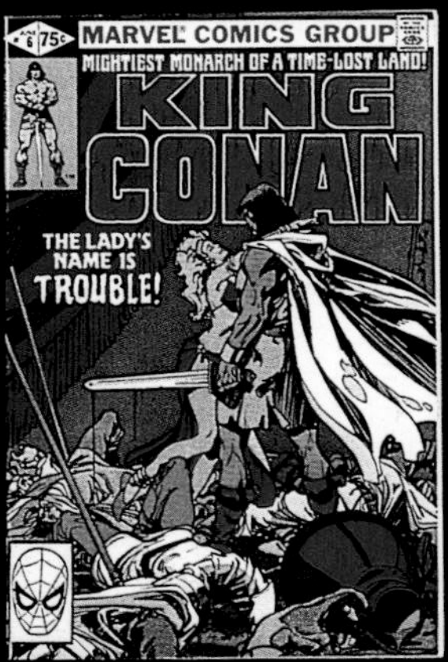
MARVEL COMICS GROUP
MIGHTIEST MONARCH OF A TIME-LOST LAND!
KING CONAN
THE LADY'S NAME IS TROUBLE!
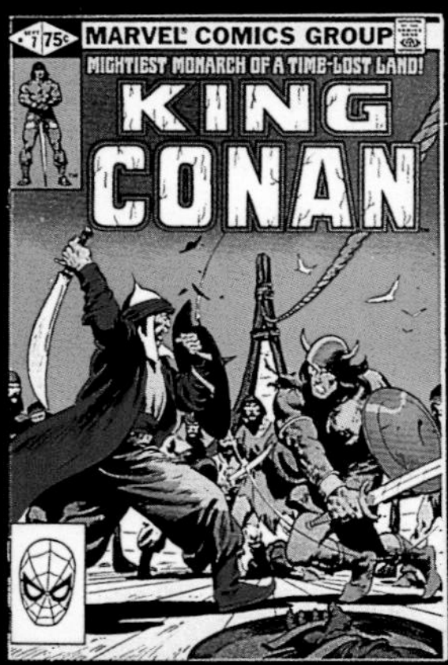
MARVEL COMICS GROUP
MIGHTIEST MONARCH OF A TIME-LOST LAND!
KING CONAN
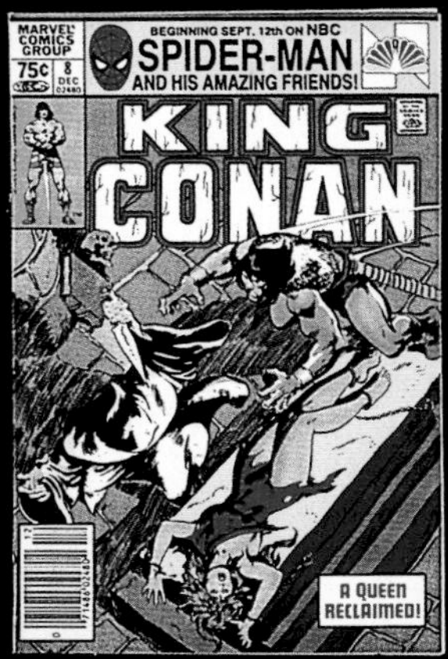
BEGINNING SEPT. 12th ON NBC
SPIDER-MAN AND HIS AMAZING FRIENDS!
KING CONAN
A QUEEN RECLAIMED!
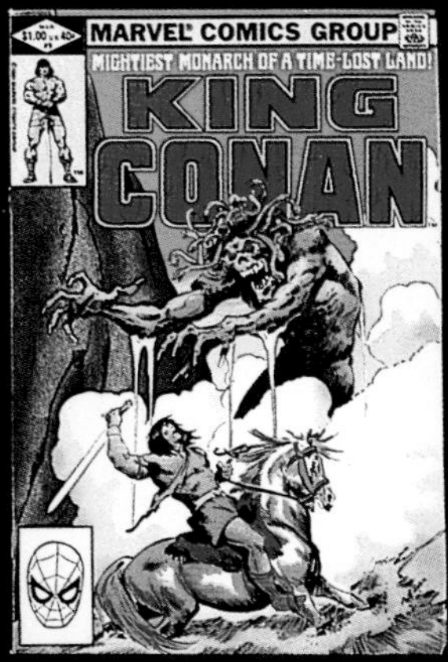
MARVEL COMICS GROUP
MIGHTIEST MONARCH OF A TIME-LOST LAND!
KING CONAN
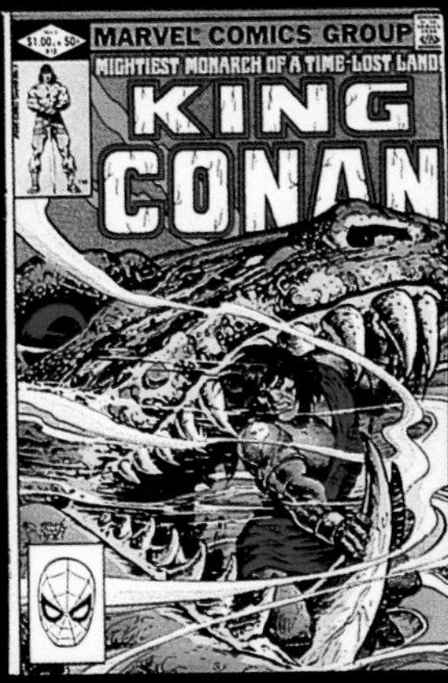
MARVEL COMICS GROUP
MIGHTIEST MONARCH OF A TIME-LOST LAND!
KING CONAN
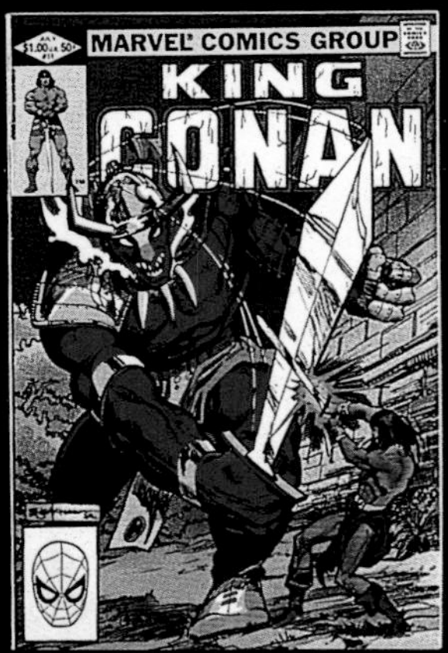
MARVEL COMICS GROUP
KING CONAN
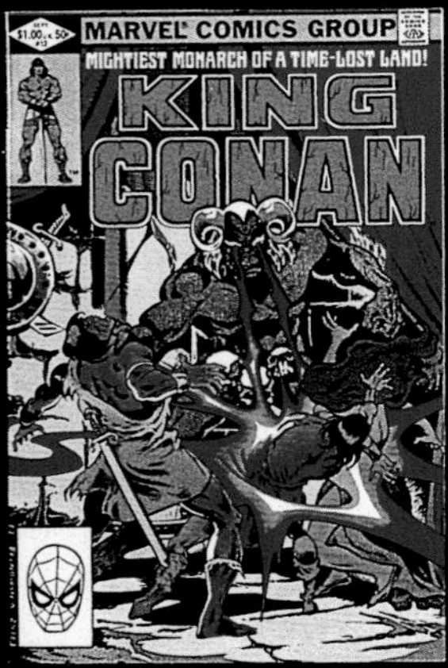
MARVEL COMICS GROUP
MIGHTIEST MONARCH OF A TIME-LOST LAND!
KING CONAN
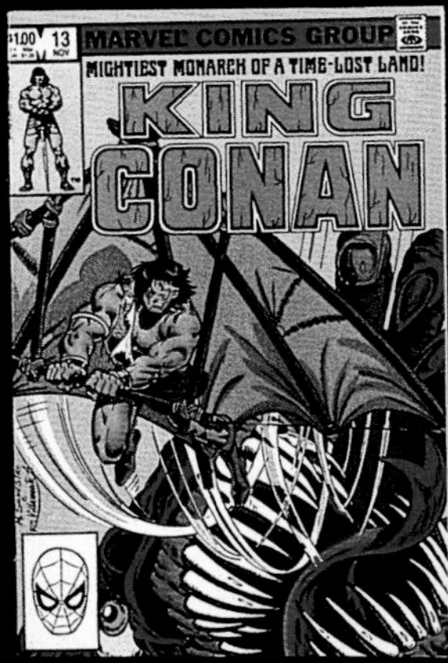
MARVEL COMICS GROUP
MIGHTIEST MONARCH OF A TIME-LOST LAND!
KING CONAN
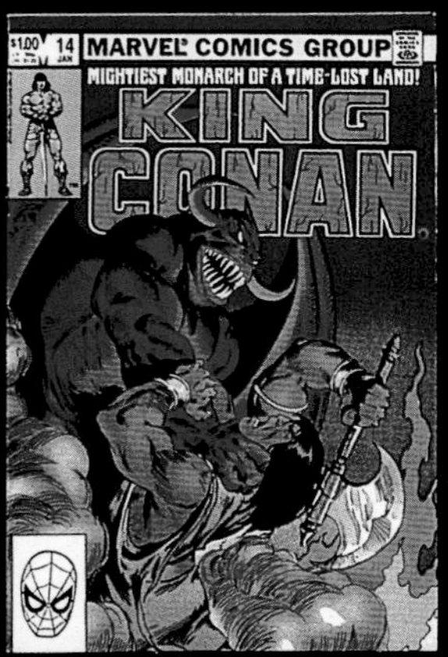
MARVEL COMICS GROUP
MIGHTIEST MONARCH OF A TIME-LOST LAND!
KING CONAN
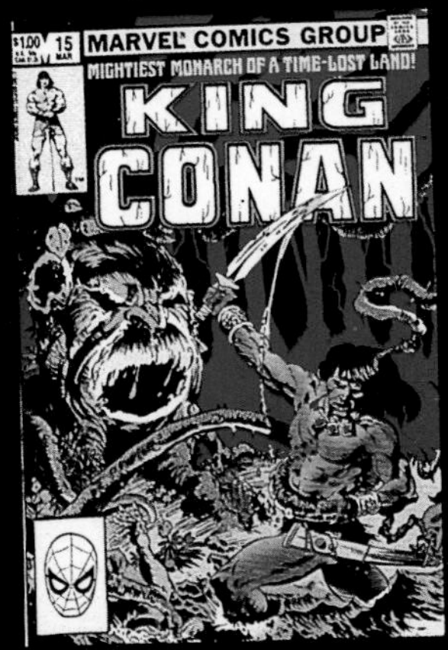
MARVEL COMICS GROUP
KING CONAN

1044.2 Conan the King (20-25)

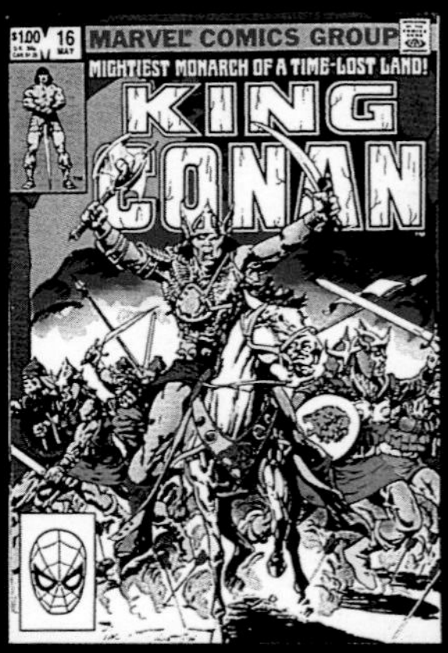
MARVEL COMICS GROUP
MIGHTIEST MONARCH OF A TIME-LOST LAND!
KING CONAN
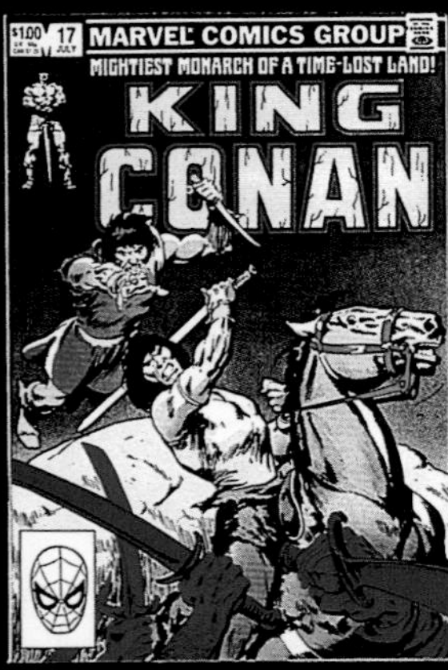
MARVEL COMICS GROUP
MIGHTIEST MONARCH OF A TIME-LOST LAND!
KING CONAN
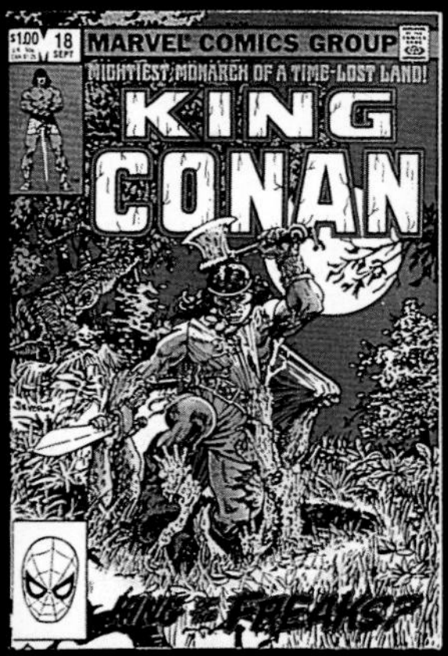
MARVEL COMICS GROUP
MIGHTIEST MONARCH OF A TIME-LOST LAND!
KING CONAN
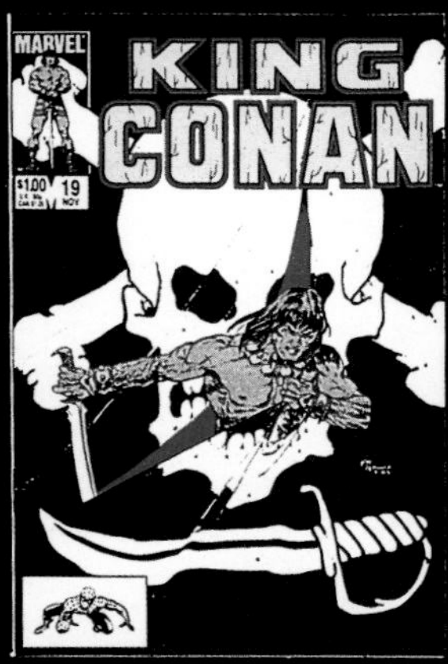
MARVEL
KING CONAN
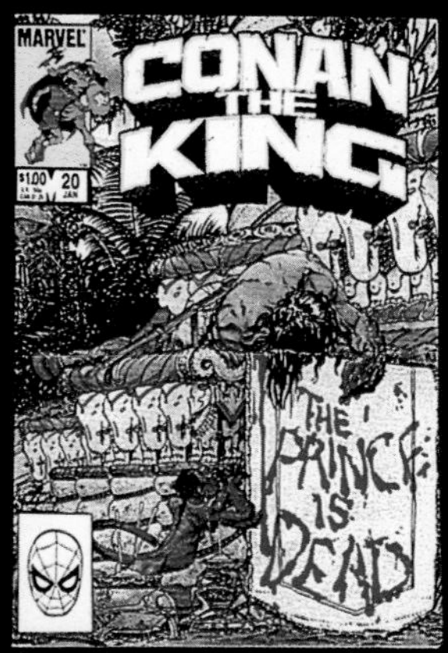
MARVEL
CONAN THE KING
THE PRINCE IS DEAD
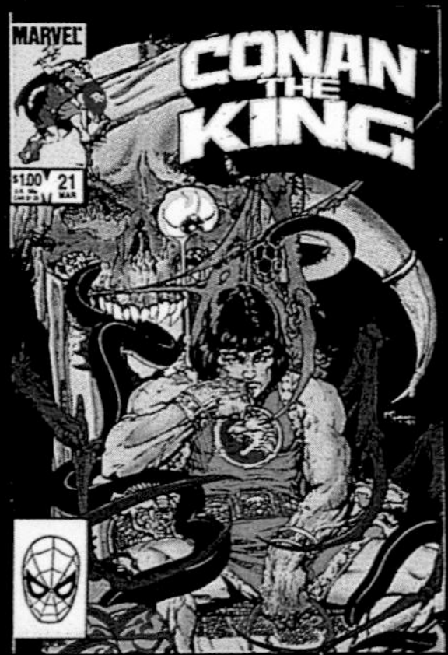
MARVEL
CONAN THE KING
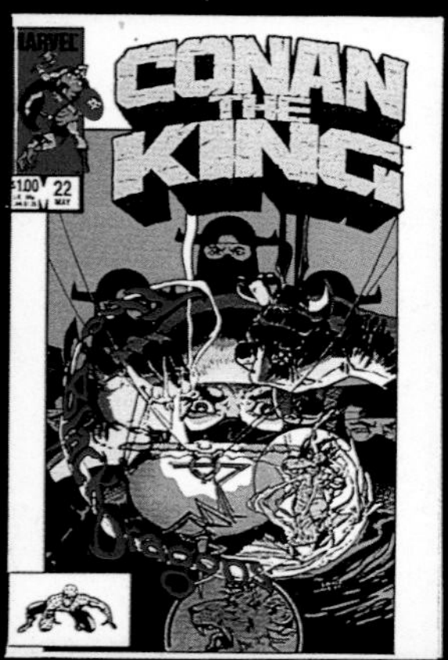
MARVEL
CONAN THE KING
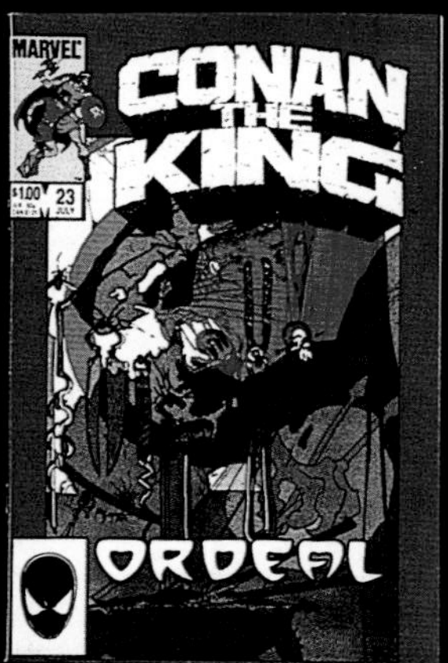
MARVEL
CONAN THE KING
ORDEAL
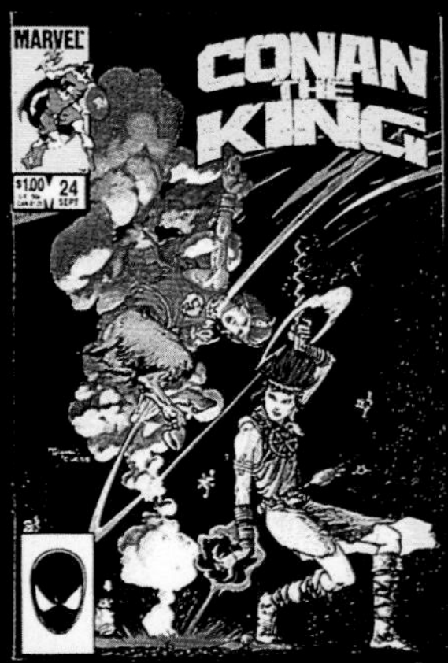
MARVEL
CONAN THE KING
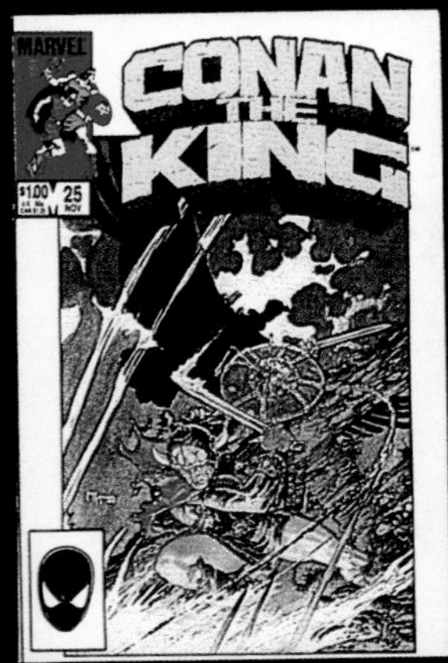
MARVEL
CONAN THE KING

1044.2 Conan the King (26-37)

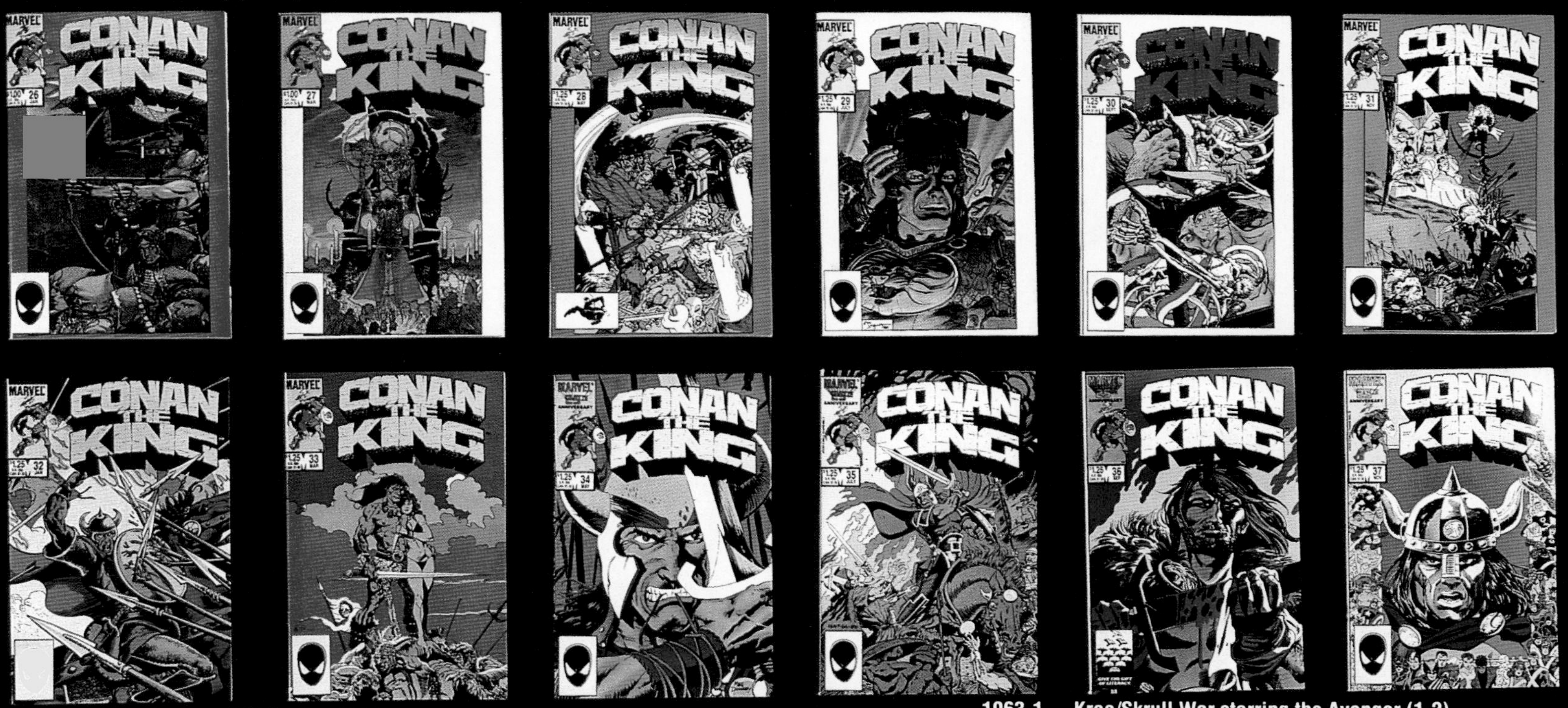
CONAN THE KING

1047.3 Kitty Pryde and Wolverine (1-3)

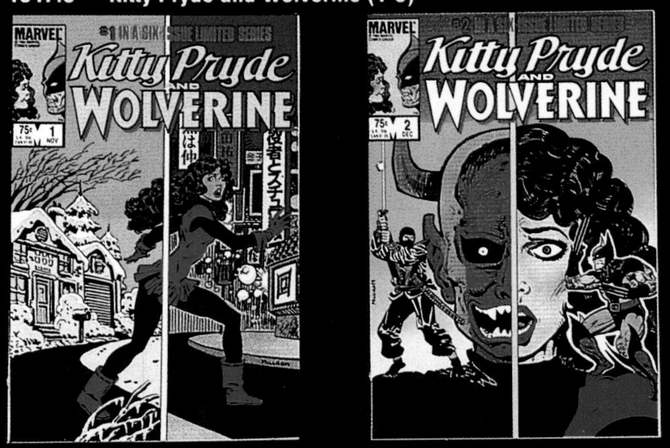
Kitty Pryde and WOLVERINE
#3 IN A SIX-ISSUE LIMITED SERIES

1063.1 Kree/Skrull War starring the Avenger (1-2)

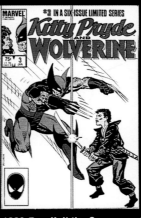

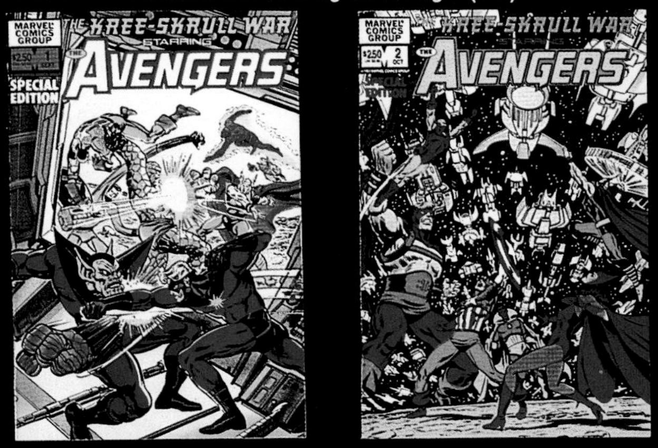
THE KREE-SKRULL WAR STARRING THE AVENGERS
SPECIAL EDITION

1063.4 Krull (1-2)

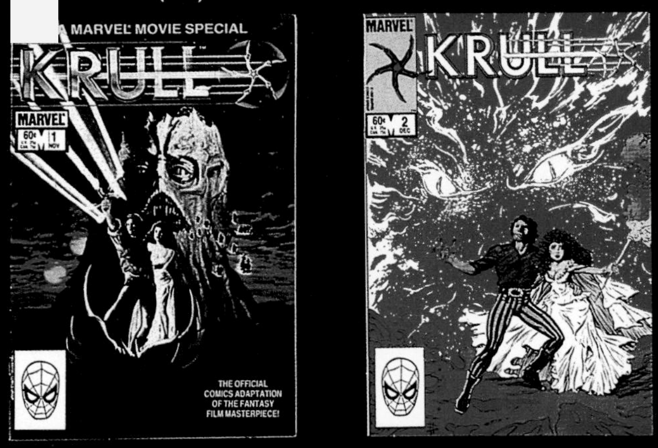
MARVEL MOVIE SPECIAL
KRULL
THE OFFICIAL COMICS ADAPTATION OF THE FANTASY FILM MASTERPIECE!

1063.7 Kull the Conqueror (1-8)

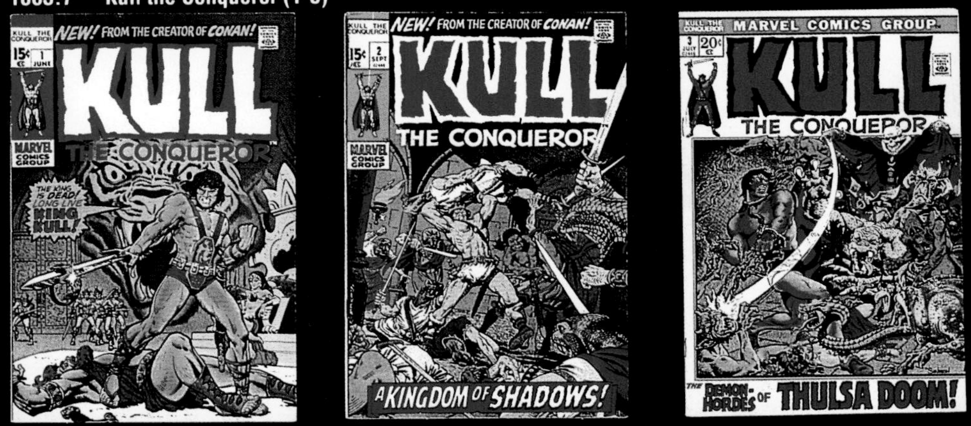
NEW! FROM THE CREATOR OF CONAN!
KULL THE CONQUEROR
A KINGDOM OF SHADOWS!
MARVEL COMICS GROUP
THE DEMON-HORDES OF THULSA DOOM!

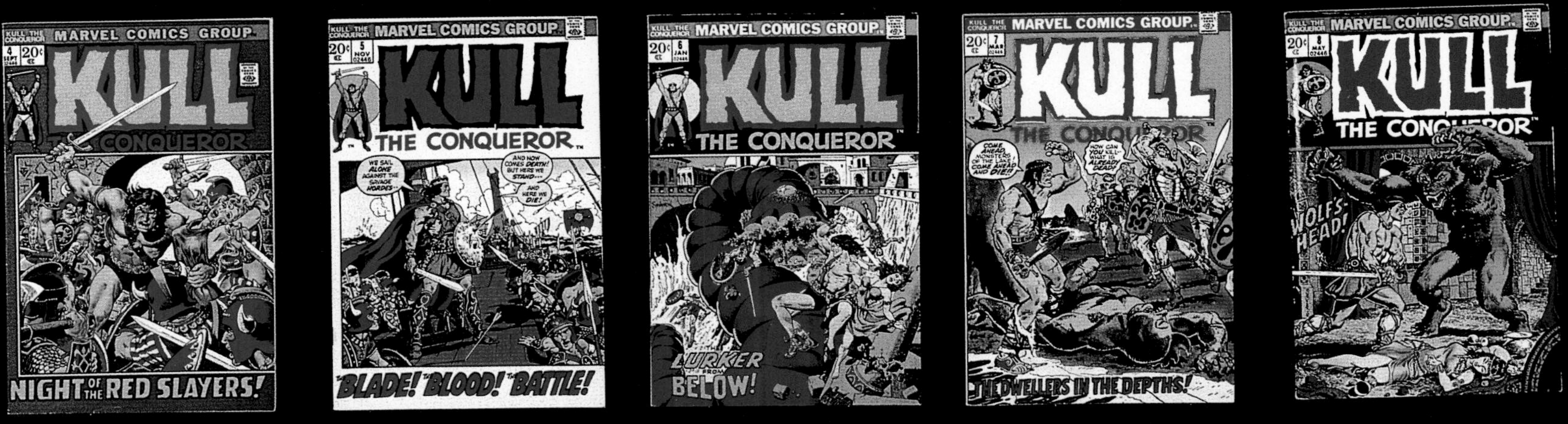
MARVEL COMICS GROUP
KULL THE CONQUEROR
NIGHT OF THE RED SLAYERS!
BLADE! BLOOD! BATTLE!
LURKER FROM BELOW!
THE DWELLERS IN THE DEPTHS!
WOLF'S HEAD!

King Conan (1-19) 1044.2

Ref. No.	Date	RVI	Artist/Info.
1044.2-1	Mar. 1980	2	Buscema/Chan-c/a
1044.2-2 to 19	Nov. 1983, (#19)	1	(#7, 1st Paul Smith art)
Continues as **Conan the King** (20-55)			
1044.2-20	Jan. 1984	1	M. Severin-c/a
1044.2-21 to55	Nov. 1989, (#55)	1	

Kitty Pryde and Wolverine (1-6) 1047.3

1047.3-1	Nov. 1984	4	(6 issue mini-series)
1047.3-2 to 6	Apr. 1985, (#6)	3	Milgrom-c/a

The Kree/Skrull War starring the Avengers (1-2) 1063.1

1063.1-1 to 2	Sept. 1983, (#1)	2	Simonson-c, Adams/Buscema-a

Krull (1-2) 1063.4

1063.4-1 to 2	Nov. 1983, (#1)	1	Blevins/Colletta-a

Kull the Conqueror (1-10) 1063.7

1063.7-1	Jun. 1971	2	Andru/Wood-a (Origin Kull)
1063.7-2	Sept.	1	J. Severin-c, M. Severin-a
1063.7-3	Jul. 1972	1	" "
1063.7-4	Sept.	1	" "

1063.7 Kull the Conqueror (9-29)

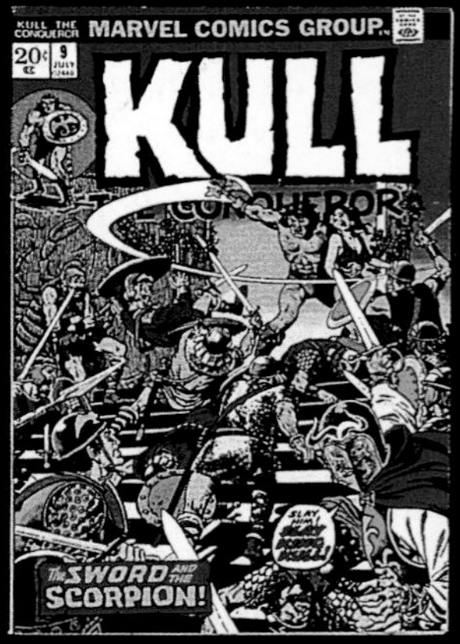
MARVEL COMICS GROUP.
20¢ 9
KULL
THE CONQUEROR
The SWORD and the SCORPION!

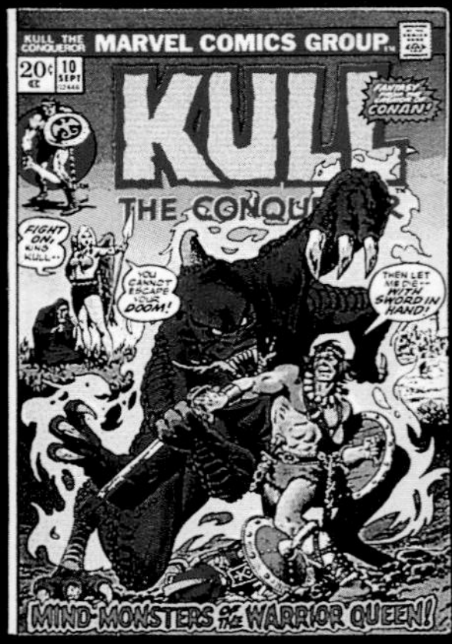
MARVEL COMICS GROUP.
20¢ 10
KULL
THE CONQUEROR
MIND-MONSTERS of the WARRIOR QUEEN!

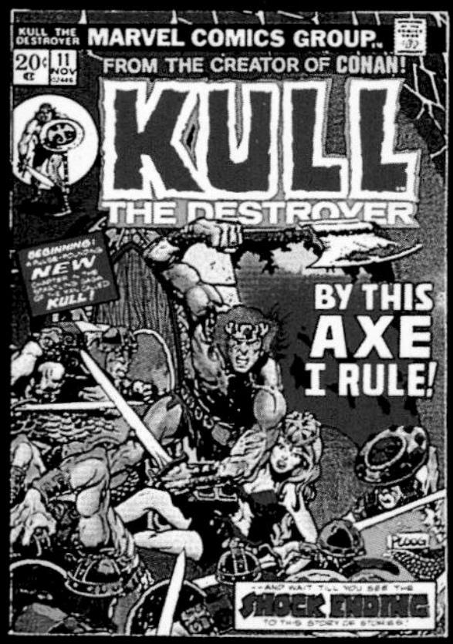
MARVEL COMICS GROUP.
FROM THE CREATOR OF CONAN!
20¢ 11
KULL
THE DESTROYER
BY THIS AXE I RULE!

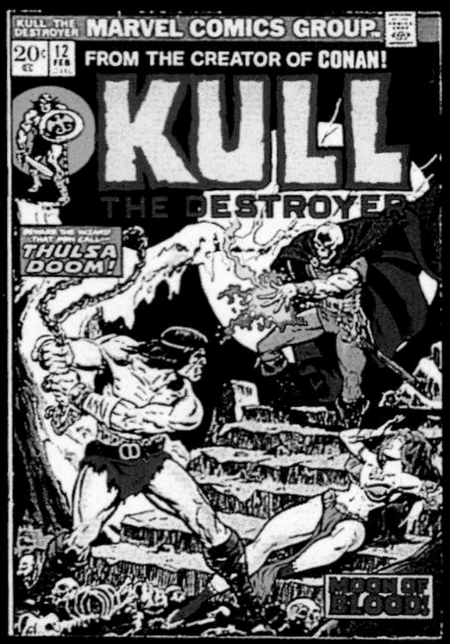
MARVEL COMICS GROUP.
FROM THE CREATOR OF CONAN!
20¢ 12
KULL
THE DESTROYER
THULSA DOOM!
HOUSE OF BLOOD!

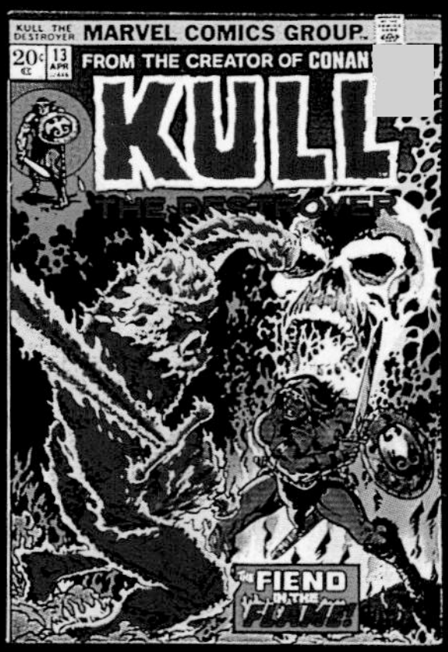
MARVEL COMICS GROUP.
FROM THE CREATOR OF CONAN!
20¢ 13
KULL
THE DESTROYER
FIEND in the FLAME!

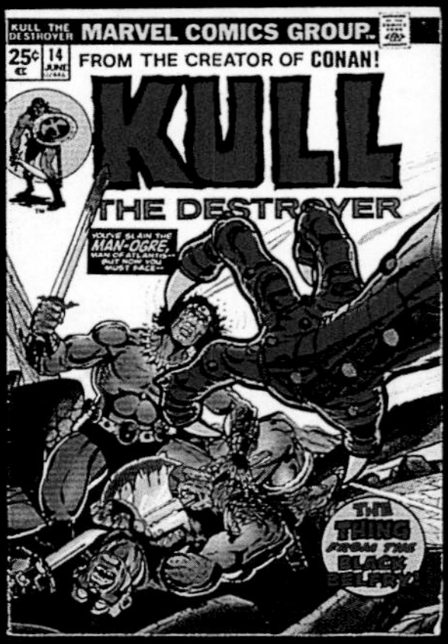
MARVEL COMICS GROUP.
FROM THE CREATOR OF CONAN!
25¢ 14
KULL
THE DESTROYER

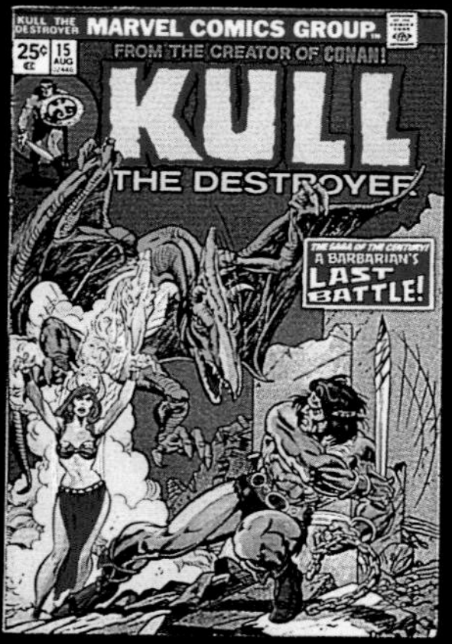
MARVEL COMICS GROUP.
FROM THE CREATOR OF CONAN!
25¢ 15
KULL
THE DESTROYER
LAST BATTLE!

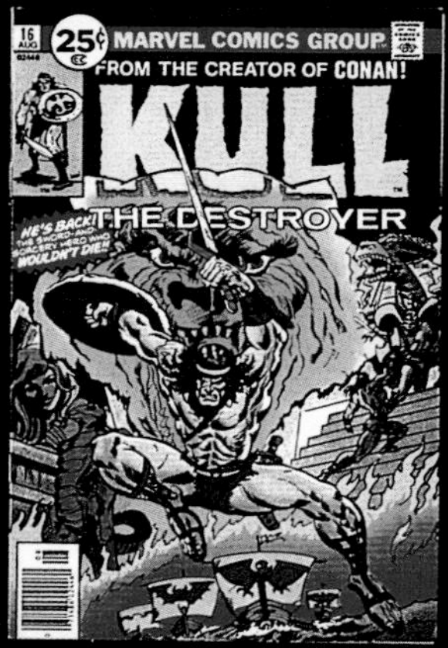
25¢ 16
MARVEL COMICS GROUP
FROM THE CREATOR OF CONAN!
KULL
THE DESTROYER

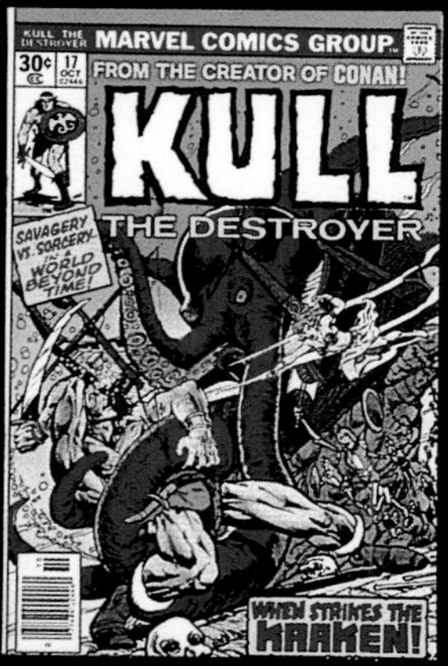
MARVEL COMICS GROUP.
FROM THE CREATOR OF CONAN!
30¢ 17
KULL
THE DESTROYER
WHEN STRIKES THE KRAKEN!

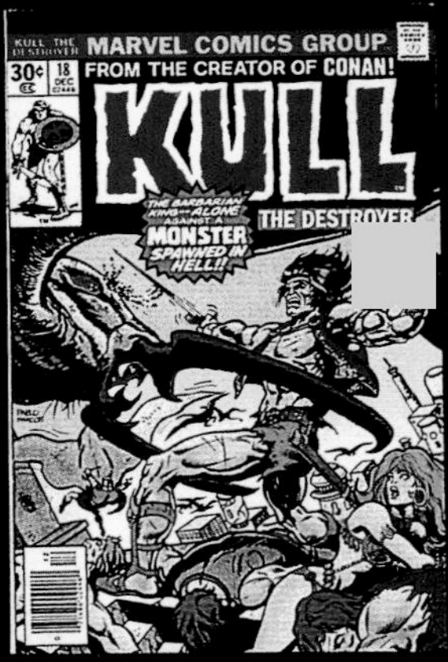
MARVEL COMICS GROUP.
FROM THE CREATOR OF CONAN!
30¢ 18
KULL
THE DESTROYER
MONSTER SPAWNED IN HELL!!

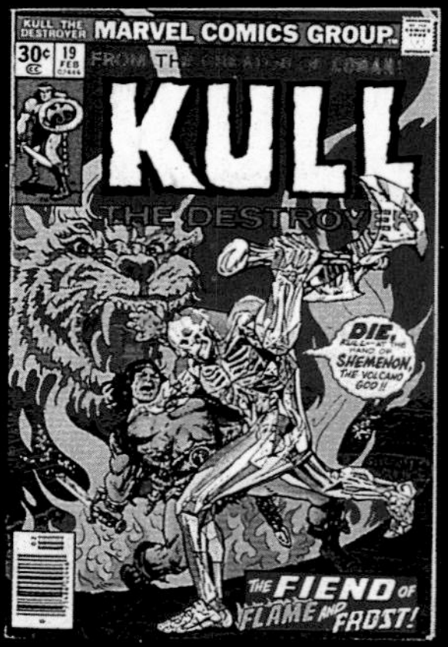
MARVEL COMICS GROUP.
30¢ 19
KULL
THE DESTROYER
DIE
THE FIEND OF FLAME AND FROST!

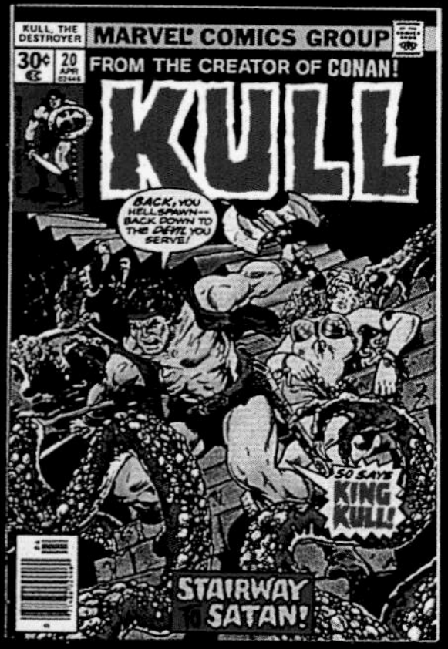
MARVEL COMICS GROUP
FROM THE CREATOR OF CONAN!
30¢ 20
KULL
SO SAYS KING KULL!
STAIRWAY to SATAN!

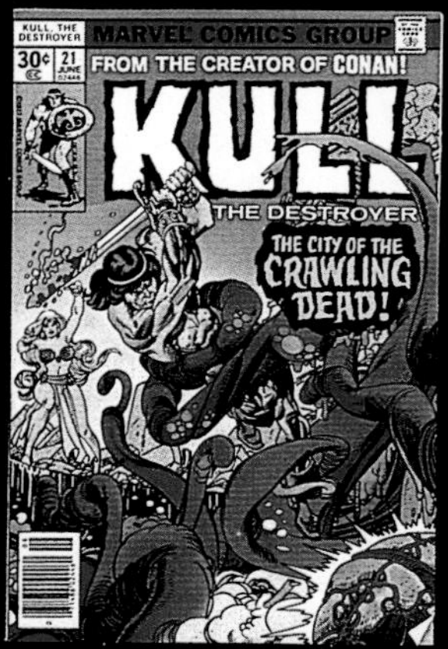
MARVEL COMICS GROUP
FROM THE CREATOR OF CONAN!
30¢ 21
KULL
THE DESTROYER
THE CITY OF THE CRAWLING DEAD!

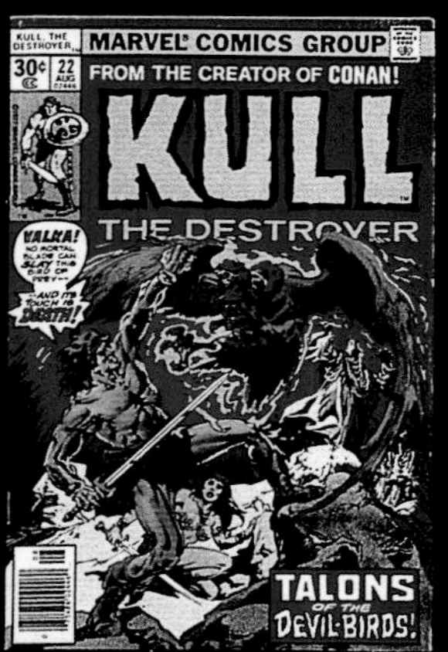
MARVEL COMICS GROUP
FROM THE CREATOR OF CONAN!
30¢ 22
KULL
THE DESTROYER
TALONS OF THE DEVIL-BIRDS!

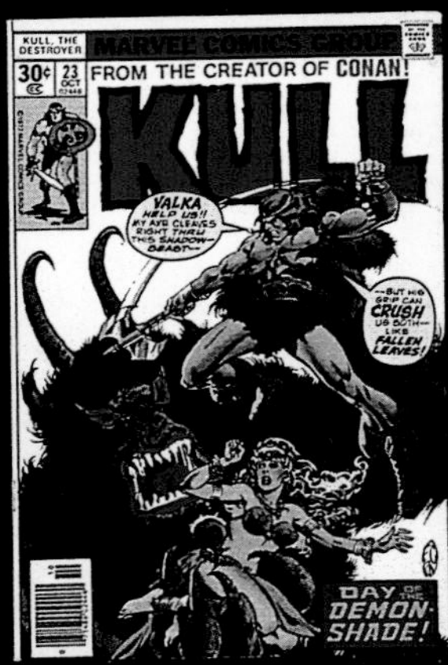
MARVEL COMICS GROUP
FROM THE CREATOR OF CONAN!
30¢ 23
KULL
VALKA
CRUSH
DAY OF DEMON-SHADE!

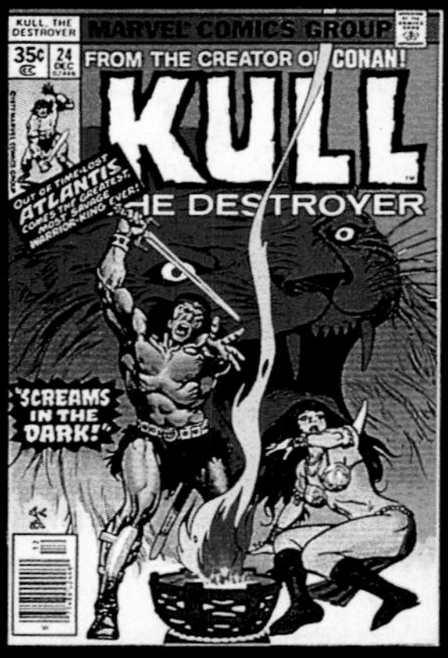
MARVEL COMICS GROUP
FROM THE CREATOR OF CONAN!
35¢ 24
KULL
THE DESTROYER
ATLANTIS
SCREAMS IN THE DARK!

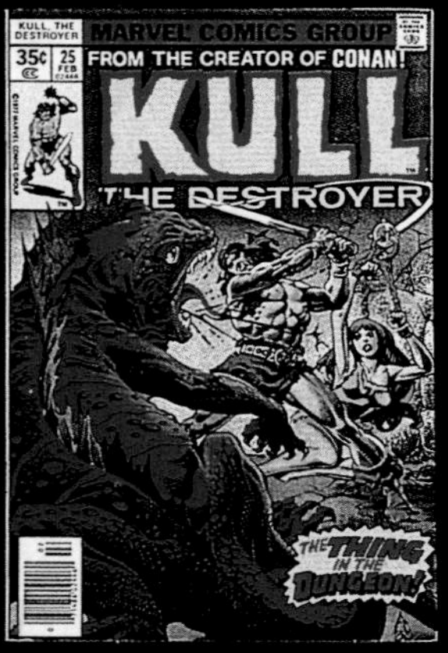
MARVEL COMICS GROUP
FROM THE CREATOR OF CONAN!
35¢ 25
KULL
THE DESTROYER
THE THING IN THE DUNGEON!

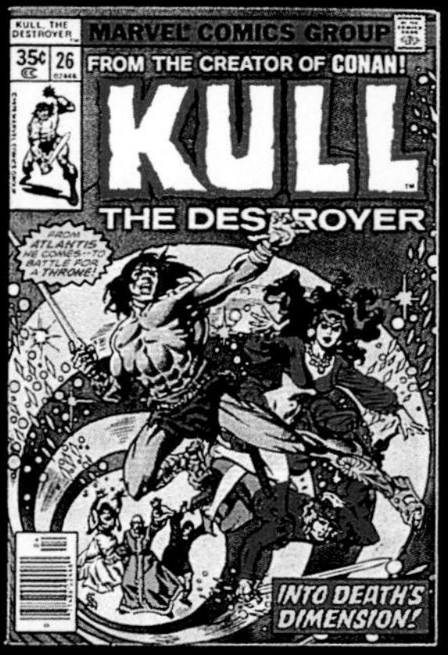
MARVEL COMICS GROUP
FROM THE CREATOR OF CONAN!
35¢ 26
KULL
THE DESTROYER
INTO DEATH'S DIMENSION!

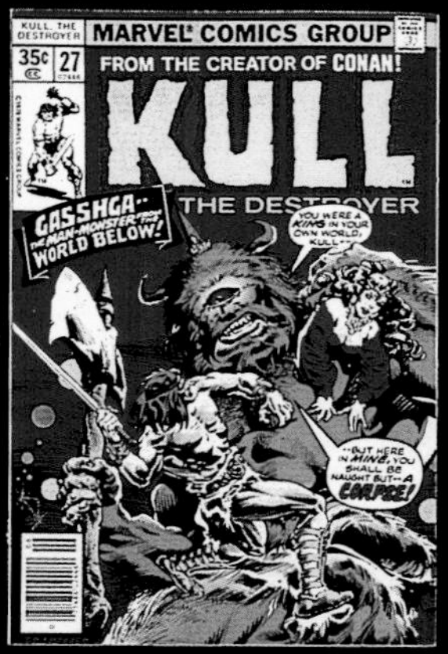
MARVEL COMICS GROUP
FROM THE CREATOR OF CONAN!
35¢ 27
KULL
THE DESTROYER
GASSHGA
WORLD BELOW!
EMPIRE!

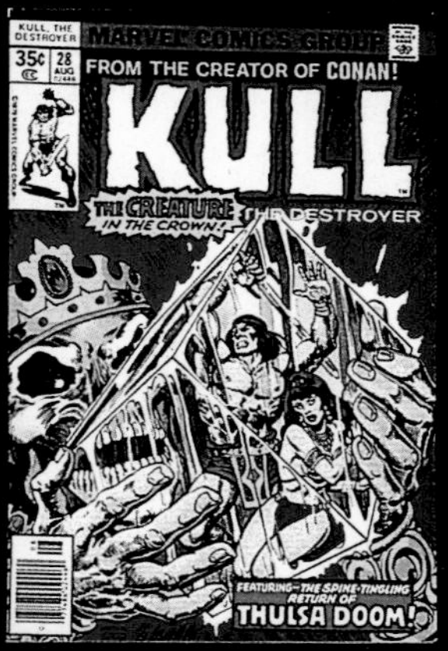
MARVEL COMICS GROUP
FROM THE CREATOR OF CONAN!
35¢ 28
KULL
THE CREATURE IN THE CROWN!
THE DESTROYER
THULSA DOOM!

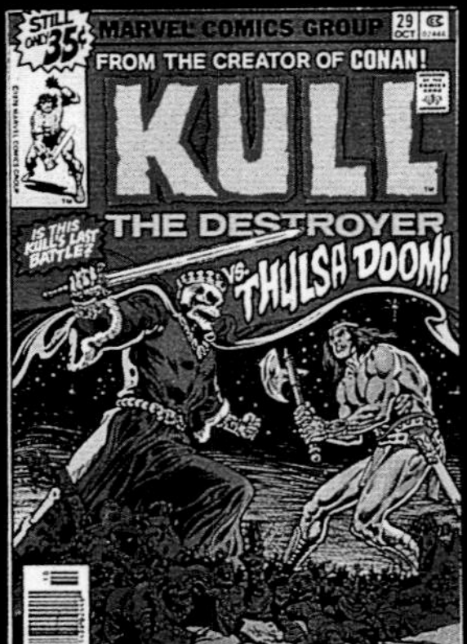
STILL ONLY 35¢
MARVEL COMICS GROUP
29
FROM THE CREATOR OF CONAN!
KULL
THE DESTROYER
VS. THULSA DOOM!

1063.8 Kull the Conqueror (1)

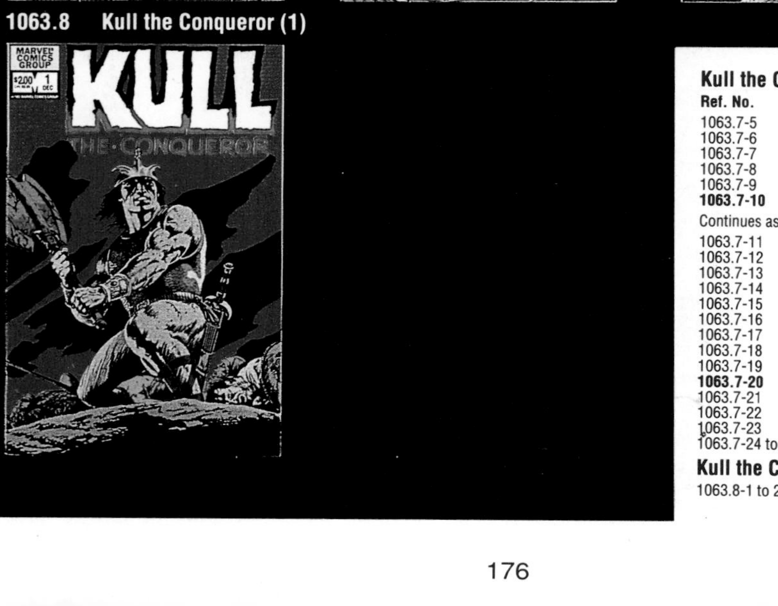
MARVEL COMICS GROUP
$2.00 1 DEC
KULL
THE CONQUEROR

Kull the Conqueror 1063.7

Ref. No.	Date	RVI	Artist/Info.
1063.7-5	Nov. 1972	1	J. Severin-c/a, M. Severin-a
1063.7-6	Jan. 1973	1	" "
1063.7-7	Mar.	1	" "
1063.7-8	May	1	" "
1063.7-9	Jul.	1	" "
1063.7-10	**Sept.**	**1**	**J. & M. Severin-c, M. Severin/Chiaramonte-a**
Continues as **Kull the Destroyer** (11-29) 1063.7			
1063.7-11	Nov. 1973	1	Ploog-c/a (Origin-King Kull retold)
1063.7-12	Feb. 1974	1	Ploog-c/a, Buscema, Romita-a
1063.7-13	Apr.	1	Ploog-c/a, Milgrom-a
1063.7-14	Jun.	1	Starlin-c, Ploog/Abel-a
1063.7-15	Aug.	1	Kane/Palmer-c, Ploog/Chua-a
1063.7-16	Aug. 1976	1	
1063.7-17	Oct.	1	Alcala-a
1063.7-18	Nov.	1	
1063.7-19	Jan. 1977	1	
1063.7-20	**Mar.**	**1**	**Alcala/Hannigan-a**
1063.7-21	May	1	Chan, Hoberg-a
1063.7-22	Jul.	1	Chan, Montano-a
1063.7-23	Sept.	1	" "
1063.7-24 to 29	Oct. 1978, (#29)	1	Chan-c/a

Kull the Conqueror (1-2) 1063.8

Ref. No.	Date	RVI	Artist/Info.
1063.8-1 to 2	Dec. 1982, (#1)	1	Buscema-a

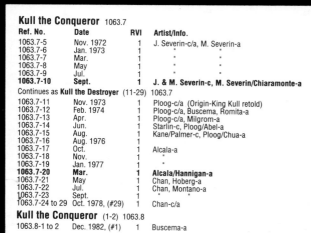

1063.9 Kull the Conqueror (1-7)

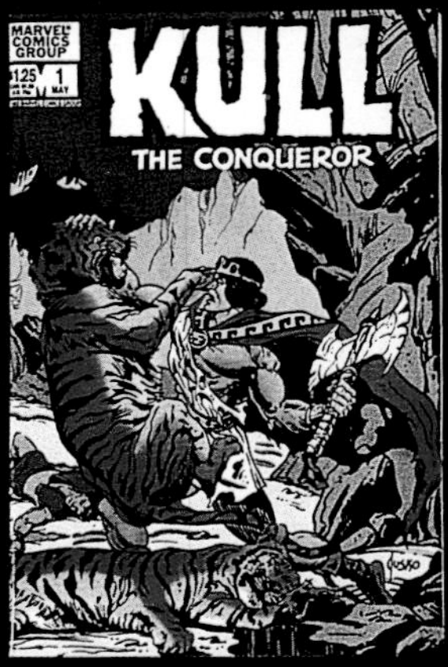
MARVEL COMICS GROUP
KULL
THE CONQUEROR
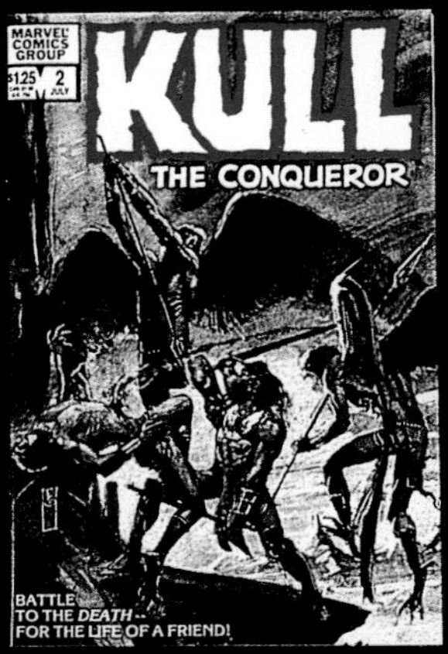
MARVEL COMICS GROUP
KULL
THE CONQUEROR
BATTLE TO THE DEATH— FOR THE LIFE OF A FRIEND!
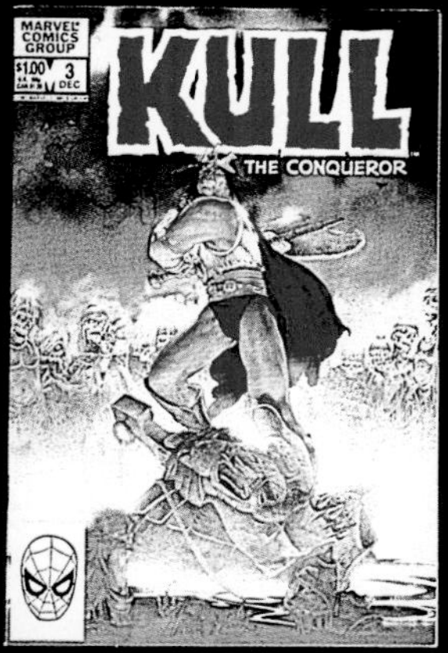
MARVEL COMICS GROUP
KULL
THE CONQUEROR
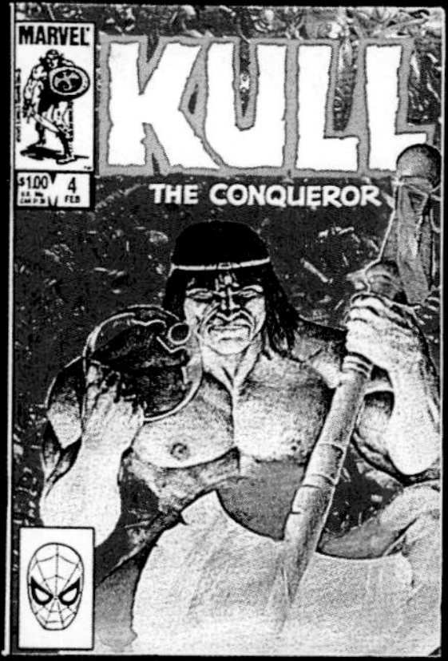
MARVEL
KULL
THE CONQUEROR
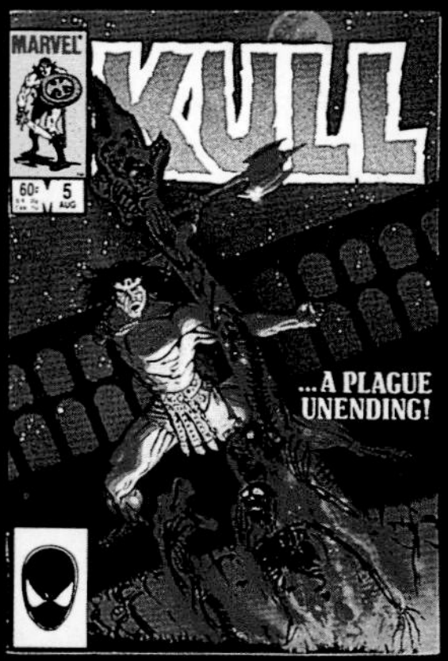
MARVEL
KULL
...A PLAGUE UNENDING!
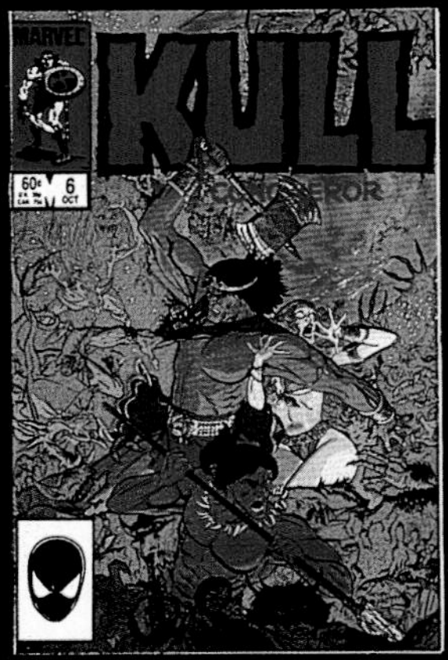
MARVEL
KULL
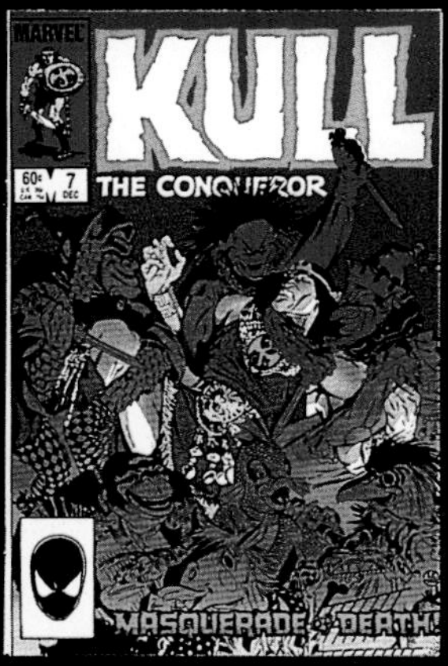
MARVEL
KULL
THE CONQUEROR
MASQUERADE OF DEATH

1075.9 The Last Starfighter (1-3)

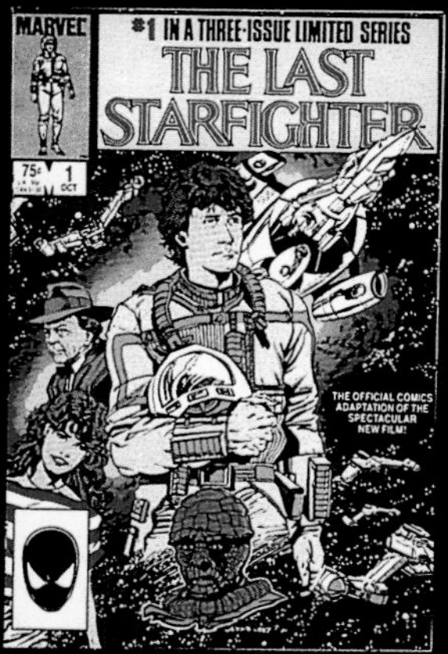
MARVEL
#1 IN A THREE-ISSUE LIMITED SERIES
THE LAST STARFIGHTER
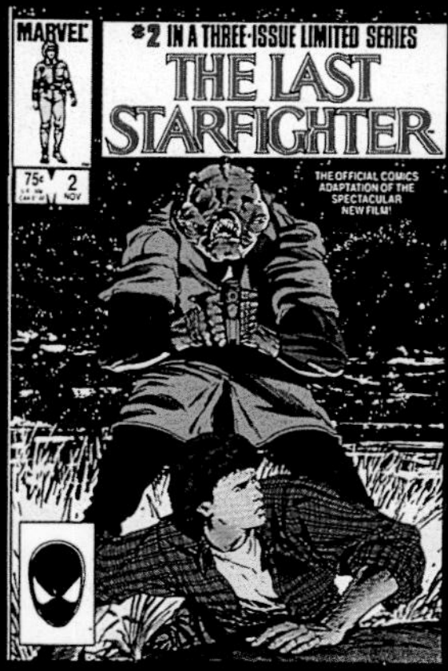
MARVEL
#2 IN A THREE-ISSUE LIMITED SERIES
THE LAST STARFIGHTER
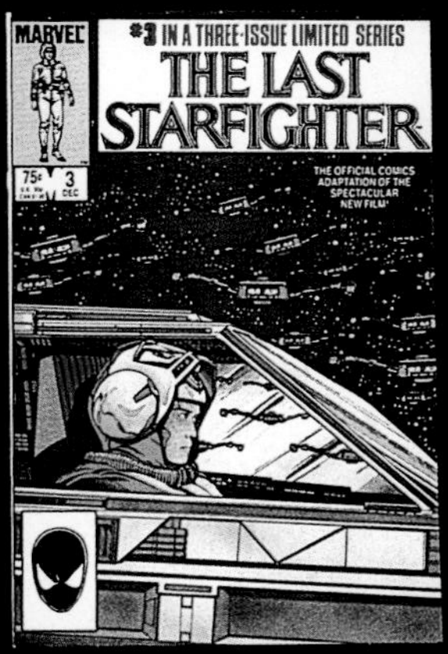
MARVEL
#3 IN A THREE-ISSUE LIMITED SERIES
THE LAST STARFIGHTER

1089 The Life of Captain Marvel (1-5)

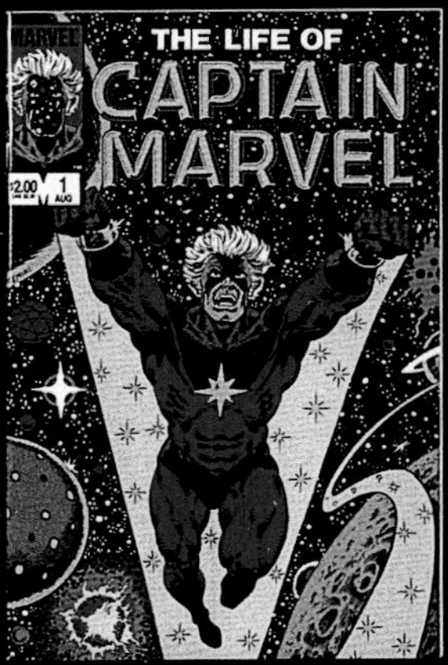
THE LIFE OF
CAPTAIN MARVEL
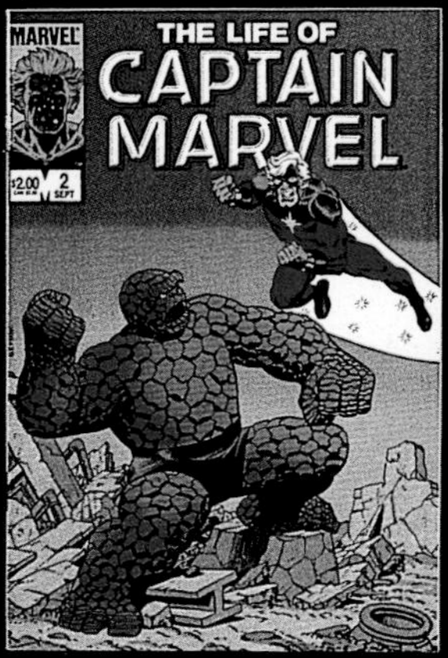
MARVEL
THE LIFE OF
CAPTAIN MARVEL
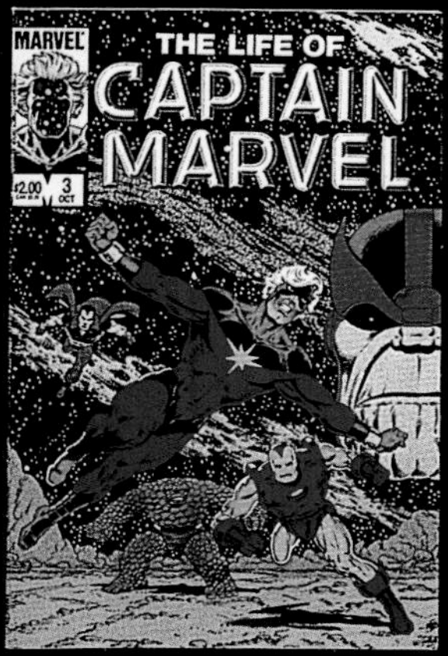
MARVEL
THE LIFE OF
CAPTAIN MARVEL
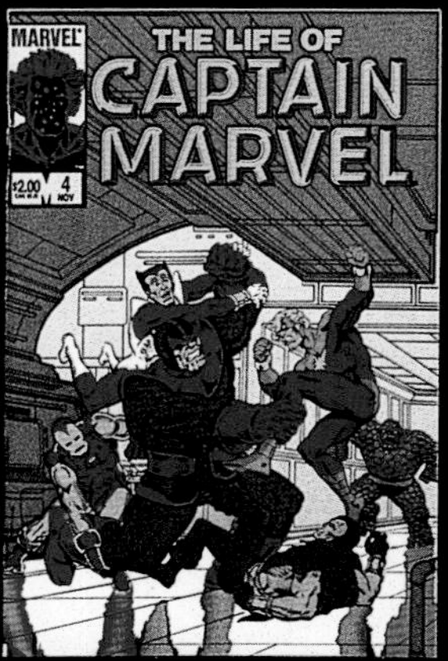
MARVEL
THE LIFE OF
CAPTAIN MARVEL
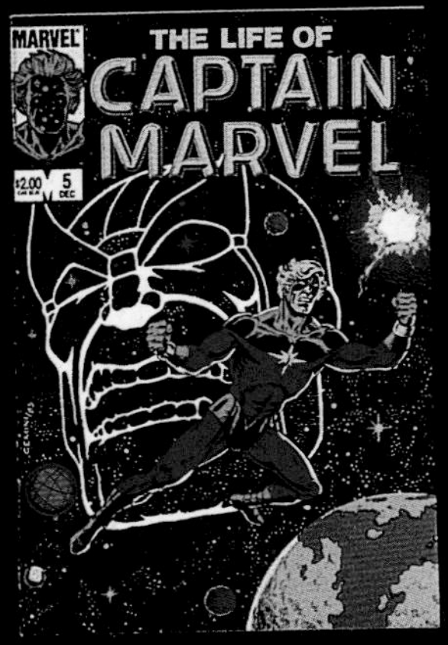
MARVEL
THE LIFE OF
CAPTAIN MARVEL

1138.5 Logan's Run (1-7)

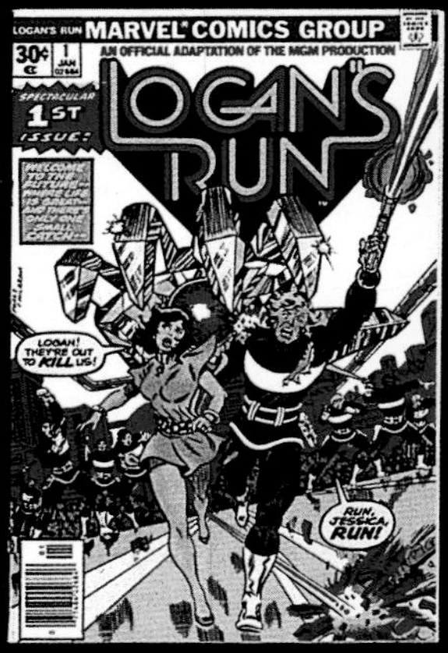
MARVEL COMICS GROUP
LOGAN'S RUN
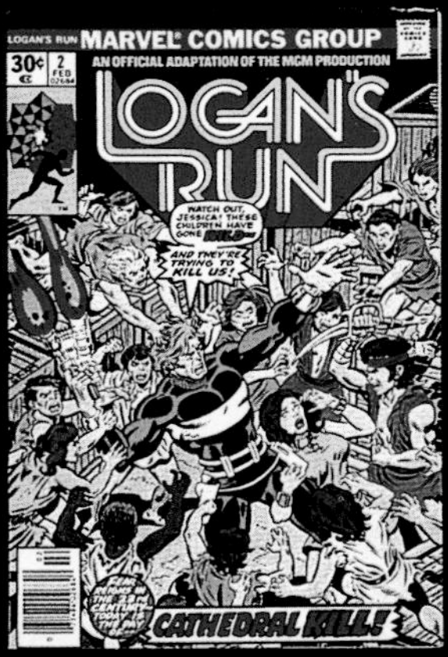
MARVEL COMICS GROUP
LOGAN'S RUN
CATHEDRAL KILL!
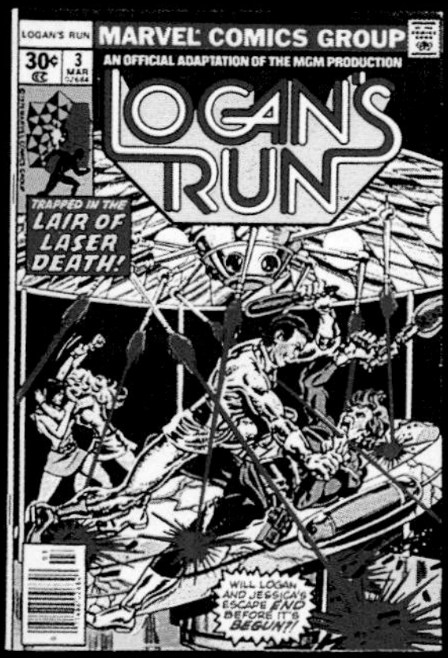
MARVEL COMICS GROUP
LOGAN'S RUN
TRAPPED IN THE LAIR OF LASER DEATH!
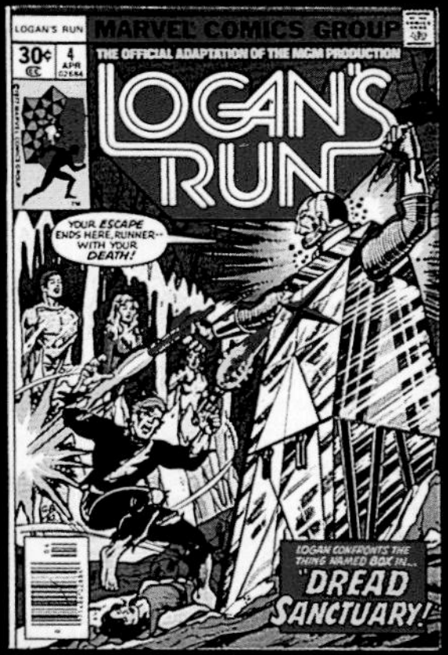
MARVEL COMICS GROUP
LOGAN'S RUN
"DREAD SANCTUARY!"
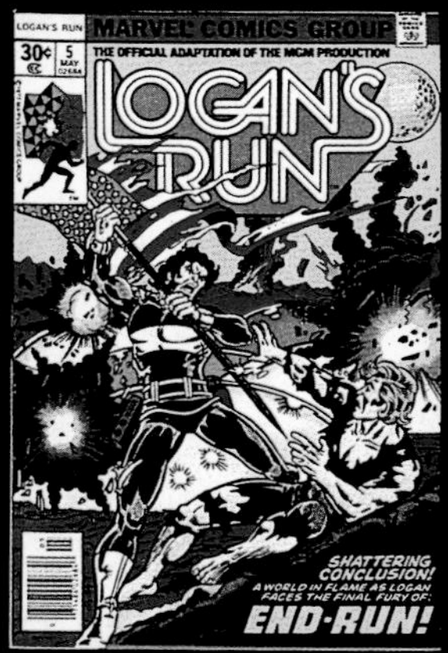
MARVEL COMICS GROUP
LOGAN'S RUN
SHATTERING CONCLUSION!
END-RUN!
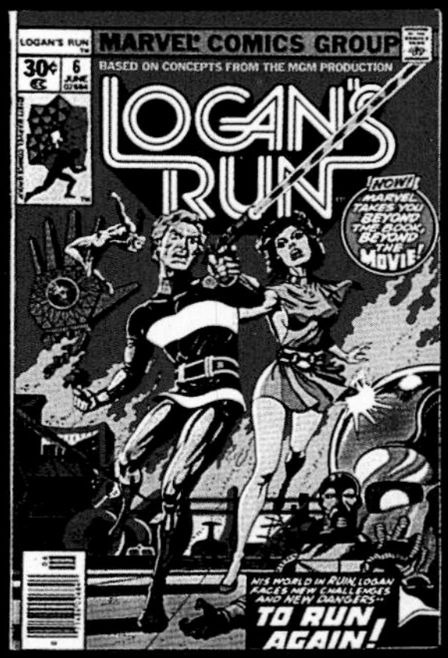
MARVEL COMICS GROUP
LOGAN'S RUN
TO RUN AGAIN!
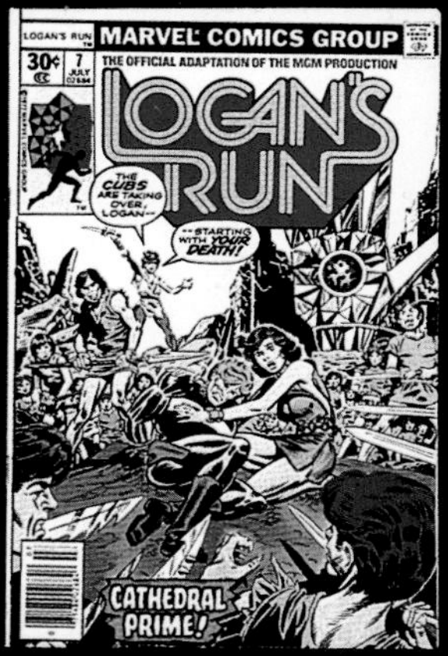
MARVEL COMICS GROUP
LOGAN'S RUN
CATHEDRAL PRIME!

Kull the Conqueror V.3 (1-10) 1063.9

Ref. No.	Date	RVI	Artist/Info.	
1063.9-1	May 1983	1	J. Buscema/Wiacek, Green-a	
1063.9-2 to 10	Jun. 1985, (#10)	1	Buscema (in most)-a	

The Last Starfighter (1-3) 1075.9

Ref. No.	Date	RVI	Artist/Info.	
1075.9-1	Oct. 1984	1	Guice-c, Blevins/Salmons-a	
1075.9-2	Nov.	1	Blevins/Salmons-a	
1075.9-3	Dec. 1984	1	" "	

The Life of Captain Marvel (1-5) 1089

Ref. No.	Date	RVI	Artist/Info.	
1089-1	Aug. 1985	1	Starlin/Esposito-a	Reprints
1089-2	Sept.	1	Starlin/Cockrum-a	"
1089-3	Oct.	1	Starlin/Milgrom-a	"
1089-4	Nov.	1	Starlin/Sinnott-a	"
1089-5	Dec.	1	Starlin/Green-a	"

Logan's Run (1-7) 1138.5

Ref. No.	Date	RVI	Artist/Info.	
1138.5-1	Jan. 1977	1	Perez, Milgrom-c, Perez/Janson-a	
1138.5-2	Feb.	1	" " " "	
1138.5-3	Mar.	1	Perez/Janson-a	
1138.5-4	Apr.	1	Perez/Janson-c/a	
1138.5-5	May	1	Perez/Janson-a	
1138.5-6 to 7	Jul. (#7)	1	Sutton, Janson-a	

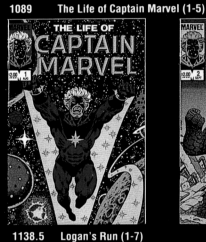

1145.3 Longshot (1-6)

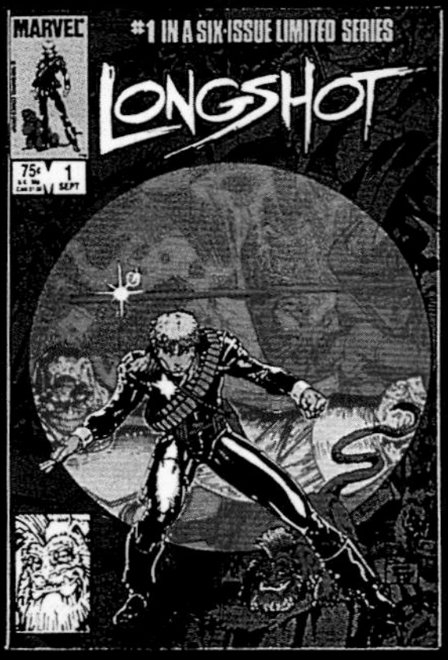

MARVEL
#1 IN A SIX-ISSUE LIMITED SERIES
LONGSHOT

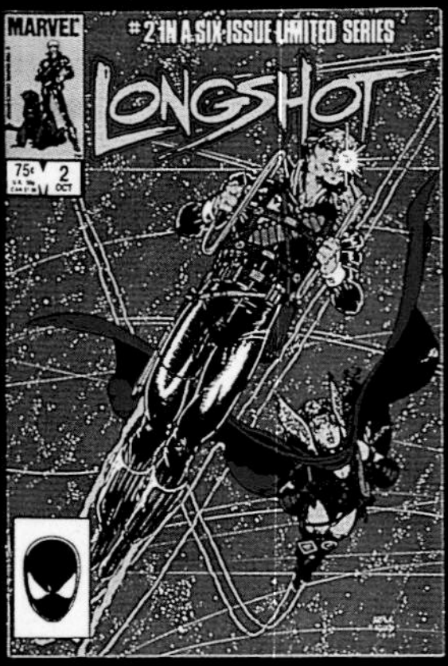

MARVEL
#2 IN A SIX-ISSUE LIMITED SERIES
LONGSHOT

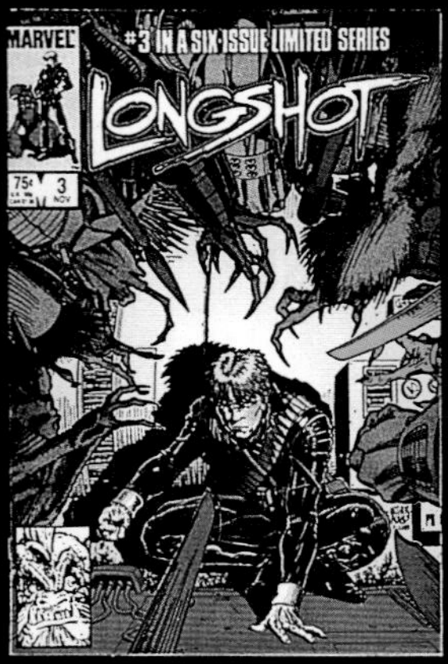

MARVEL
#3 IN A SIX-ISSUE LIMITED SERIES
LONGSHOT

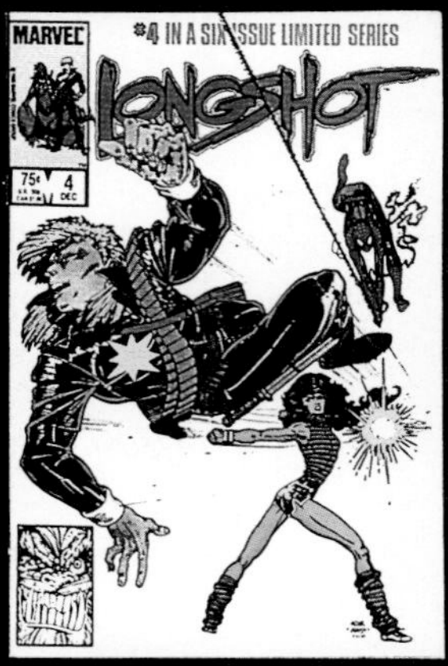

MARVEL
#4 IN A SIX-ISSUE LIMITED SERIES
LONGSHOT

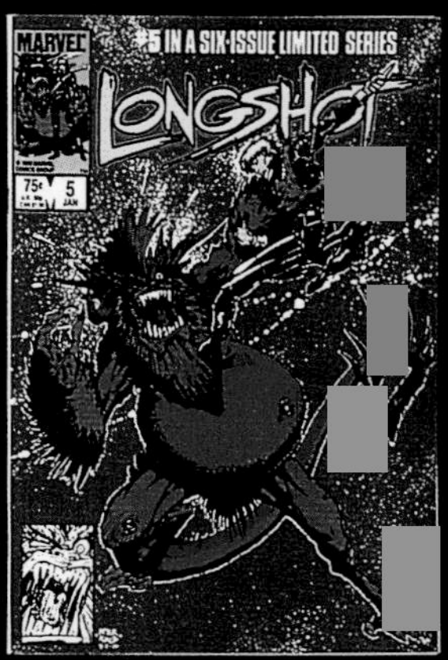

MARVEL
#5 IN A SIX-ISSUE LIMITED SERIES
LONGSHOT

1187 Machine Man (1-19)

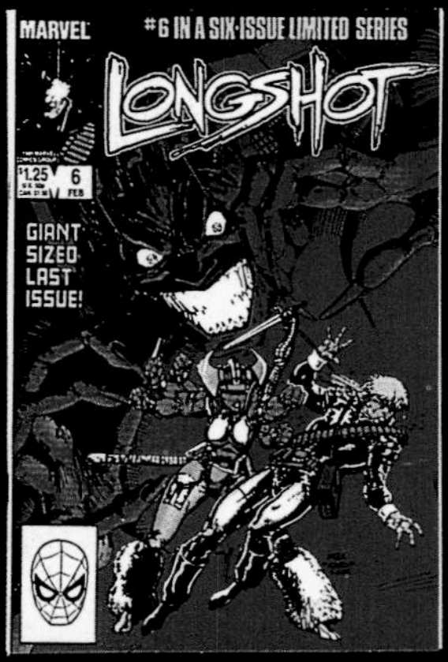

MARVEL
#6 IN A SIX-ISSUE LIMITED SERIES
LONGSHOT
GIANT SIZED LAST ISSUE!

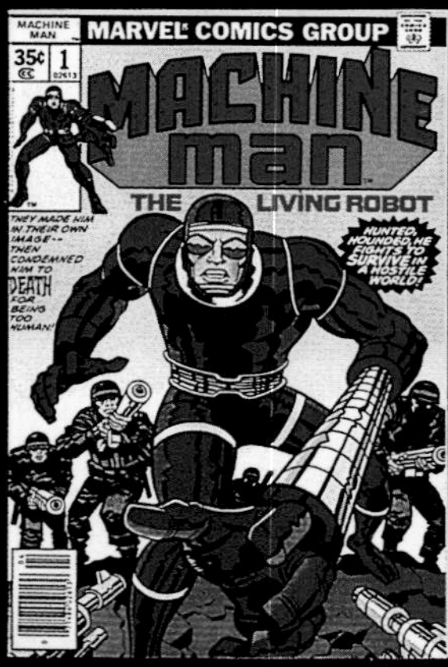

MARVEL COMICS GROUP
MACHINE man
THE LIVING ROBOT

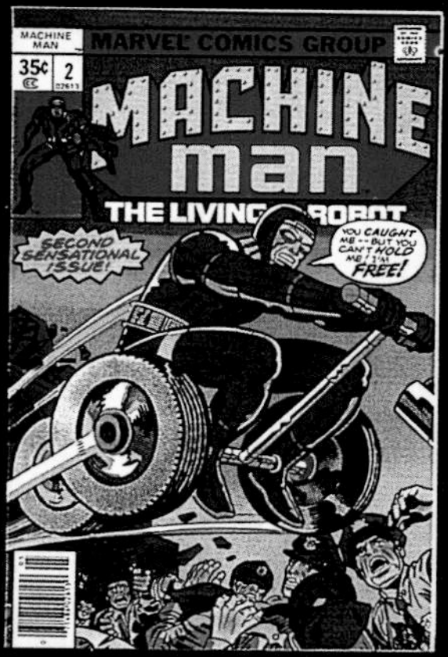

MARVEL COMICS GROUP
MACHINE man
THE LIVING ROBOT
SECOND SENSATIONAL ISSUE!

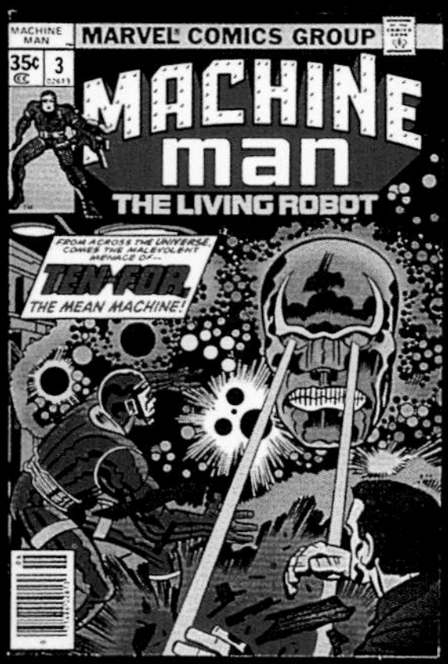

MARVEL COMICS GROUP
MACHINE man
THE LIVING ROBOT
THE MEAN MACHINE!

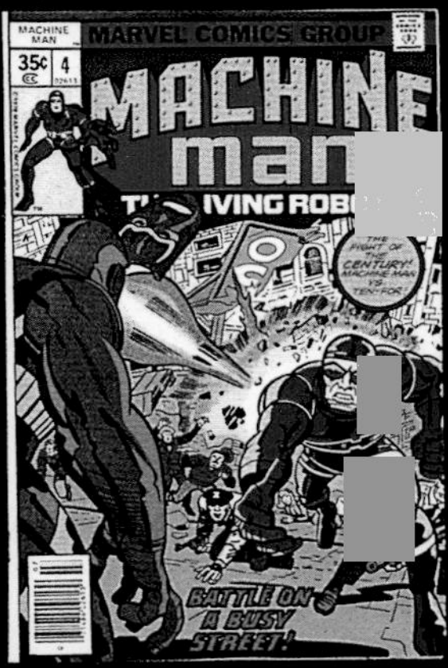

MARVEL COMICS GROUP
MACHINE man
BATTLE ON A BUSY STREET!

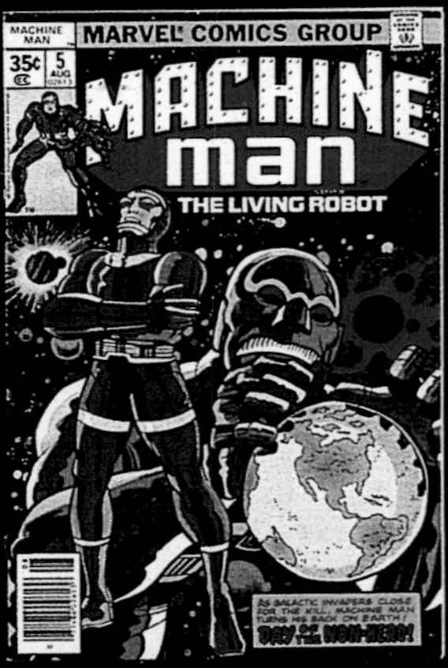

MARVEL COMICS GROUP
MACHINE man
THE LIVING ROBOT

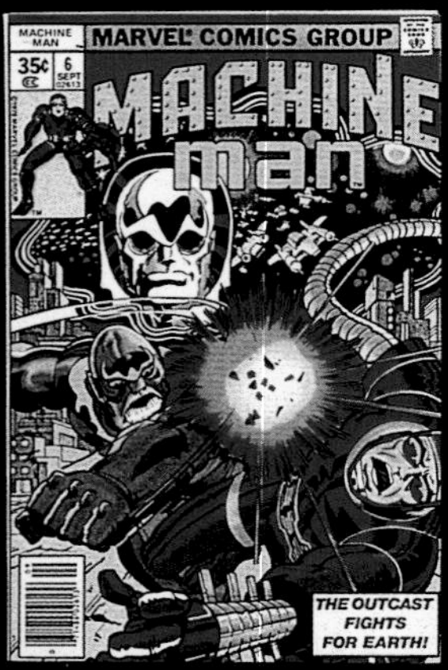

MARVEL COMICS GROUP
MACHINE man

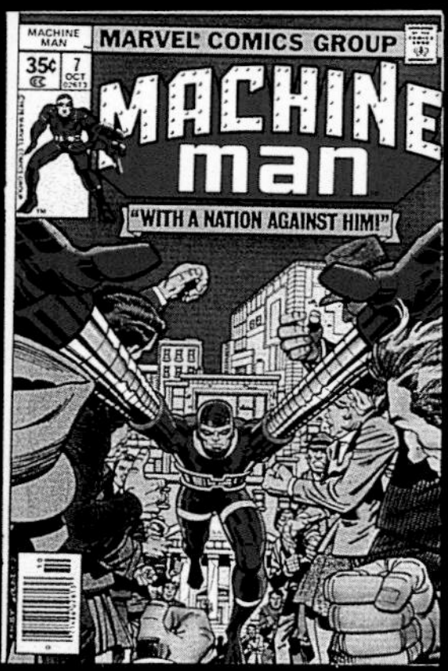

MARVEL COMICS GROUP
MACHINE man
"WITH A NATION AGAINST HIM!"
THE OUTCAST FIGHTS FOR EARTH!

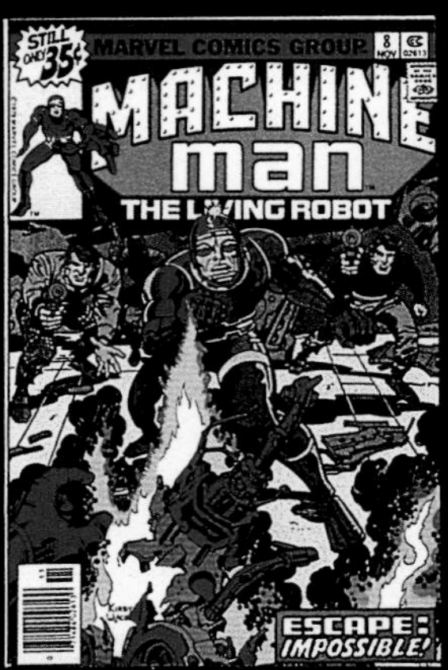

MARVEL COMICS GROUP
MACHINE man
THE LIVING ROBOT
ESCAPE: IMPOSSIBLE!

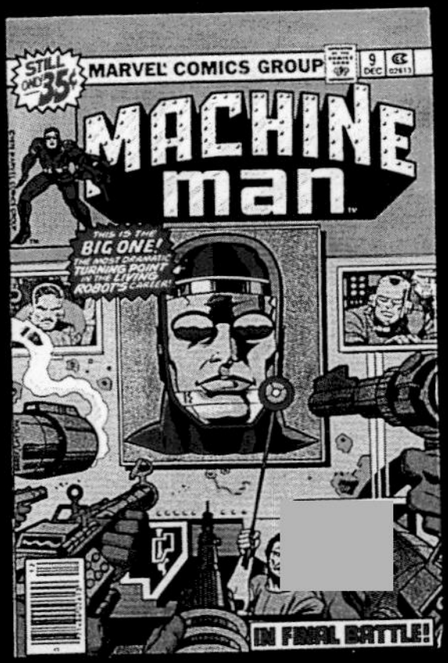

MARVEL COMICS GROUP
MACHINE man
THIS IS THE BIG ONE!
IN FINAL BATTLE!

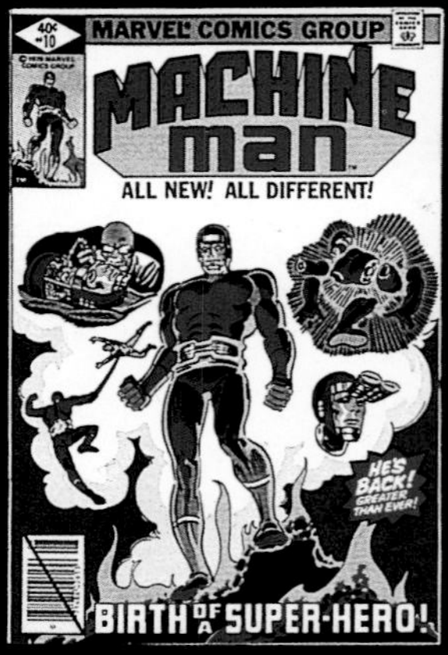

MARVEL COMICS GROUP
MACHINE man
ALL NEW! ALL DIFFERENT!
HE'S BACK!
BIRTH OF A SUPER-HERO!

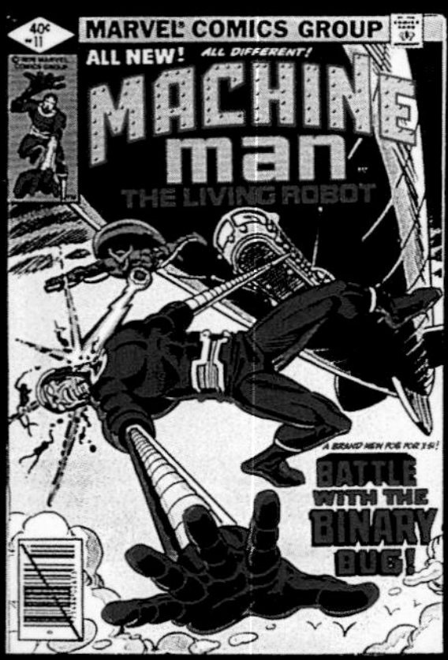

MARVEL COMICS GROUP
ALL NEW! ALL DIFFERENT!
MACHINE man
THE LIVING ROBOT
BATTLE WITH THE BINARY BUG!

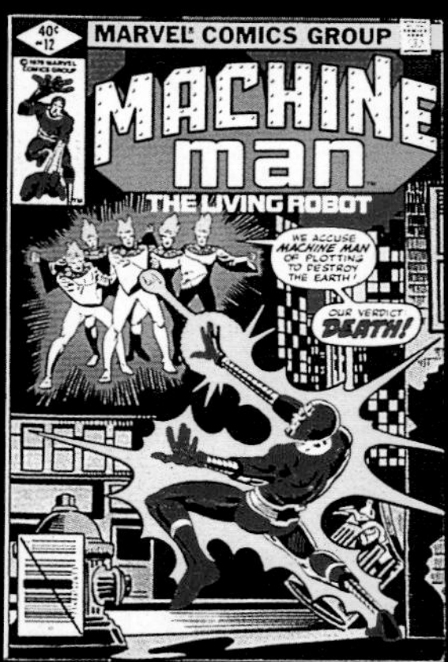

MARVEL COMICS GROUP
MACHINE man
THE LIVING ROBOT
OUR VERDICT DEATH!

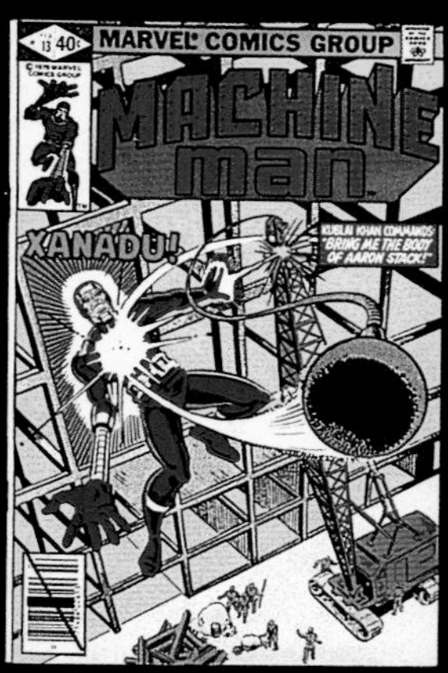

MARVEL COMICS GROUP
MACHINE man
XANADU!

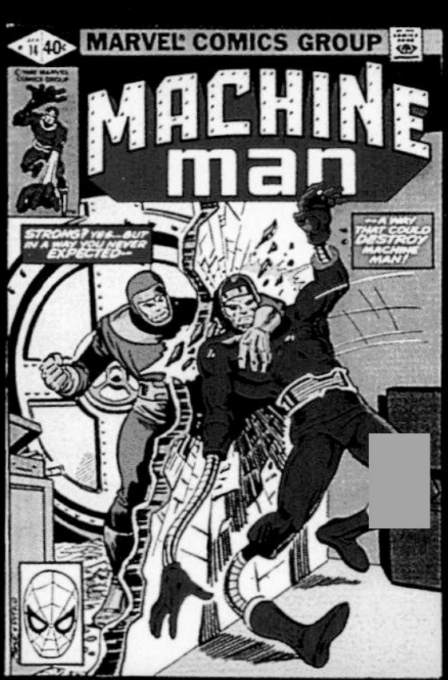

MARVEL COMICS GROUP
MACHINE man

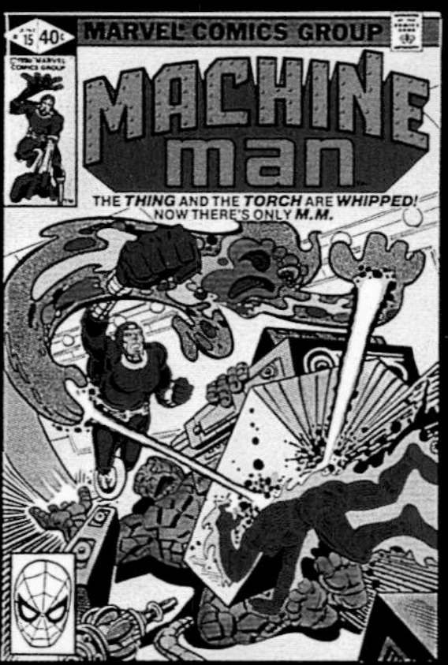

MARVEL COMICS GROUP
MACHINE man
THE THING AND THE TORCH ARE WHIPPED! NOW THERE'S ONLY M.M.

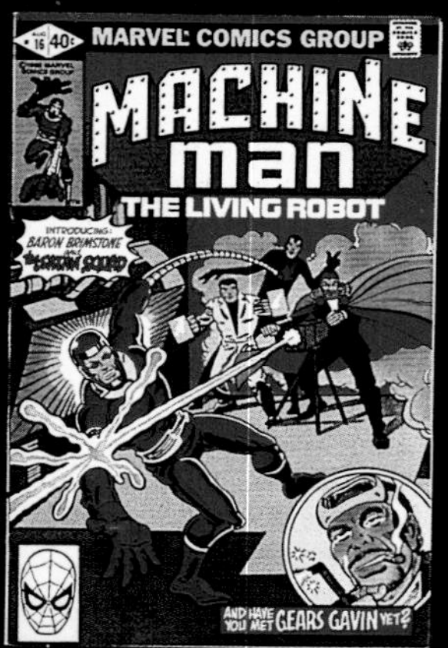

MARVEL COMICS GROUP
MACHINE man
THE LIVING ROBOT
GEARS GAVIN

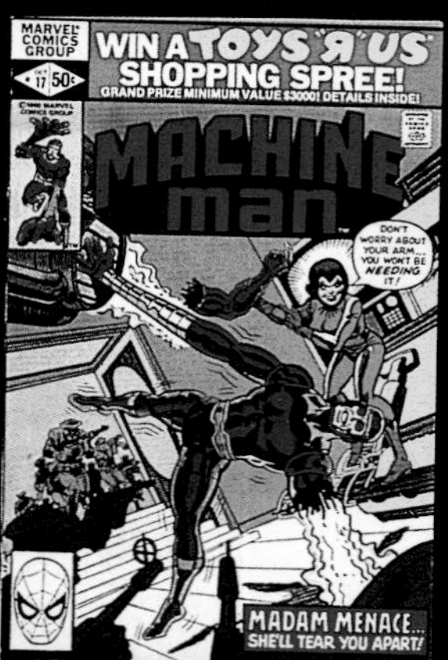

WIN A TOYS R US SHOPPING SPREE!
MACHINE man
MADAM MENACE...
SHE'LL TEAR YOU APART!

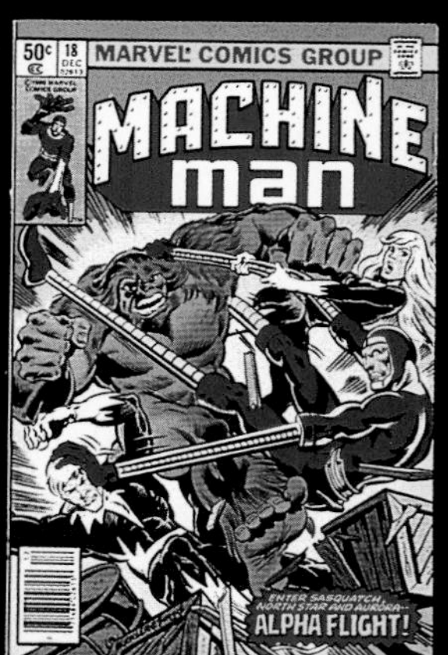

MARVEL COMICS GROUP
MACHINE man
ALPHA FLIGHT!

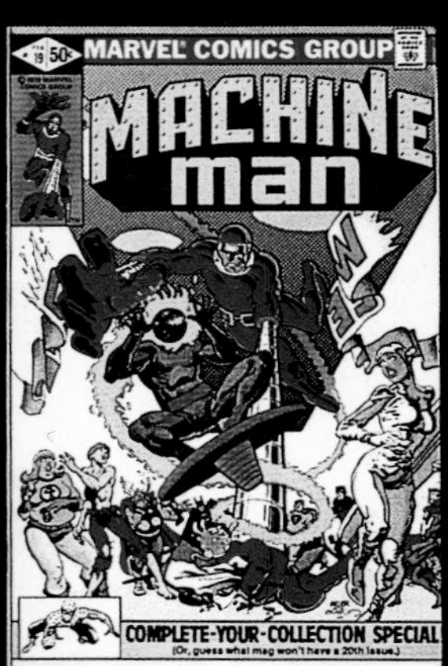

MARVEL COMICS GROUP
MACHINE man
COMPLETE-YOUR-COLLECTION SPECIAL

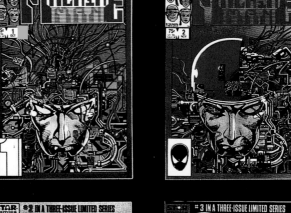

1187.3 Machine Man (1-4)

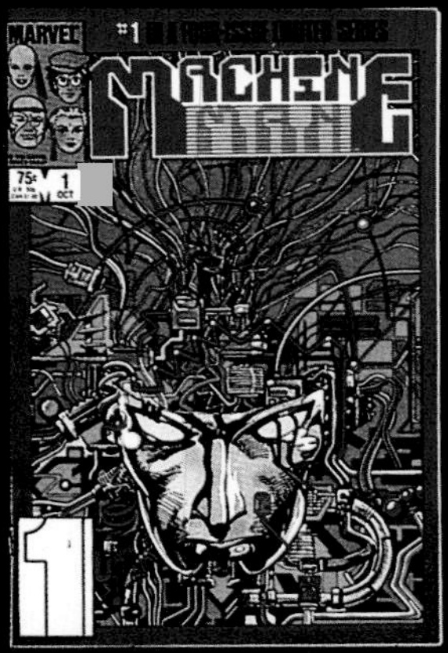
MARVEL
#1 IN A FOUR-ISSUE LIMITED SERIES
MACHINE MAN

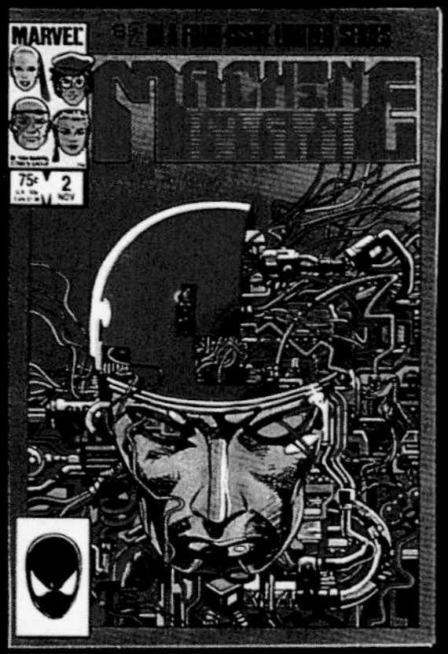
MARVEL
MACHINE MAN

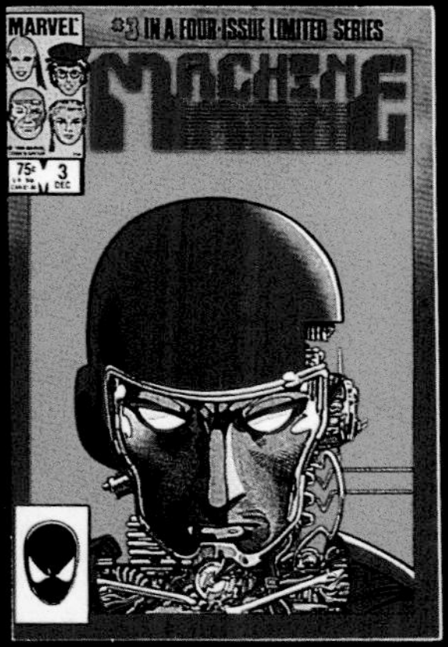
MARVEL
#3 IN A FOUR-ISSUE LIMITED SERIES
MACHINE MAN

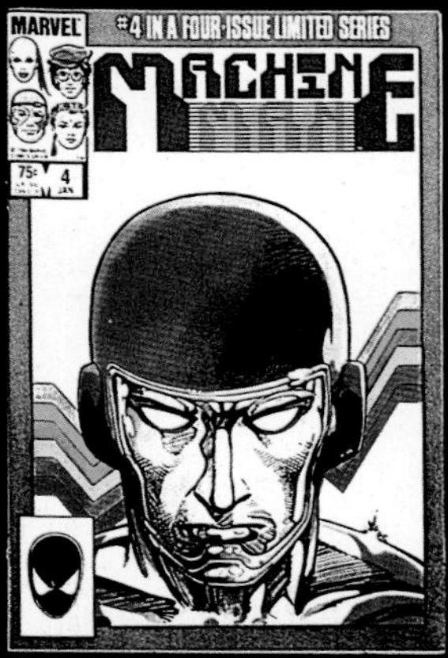
MARVEL
#4 IN A FOUR-ISSUE LIMITED SERIES
MACHINE MAN

1188.6 Madballs (1-6)

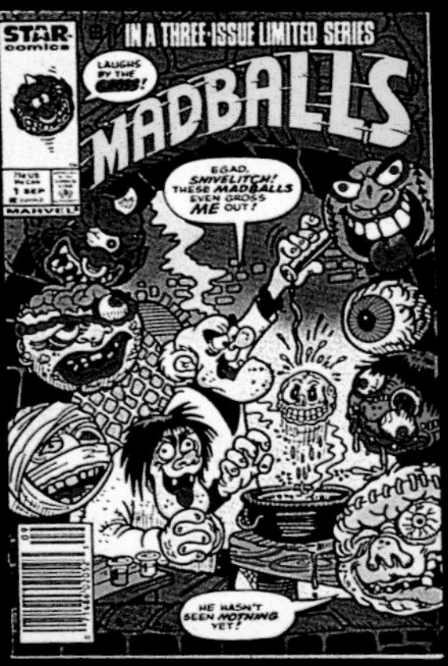
STAR comics
IN A THREE-ISSUE LIMITED SERIES
MADBALLS

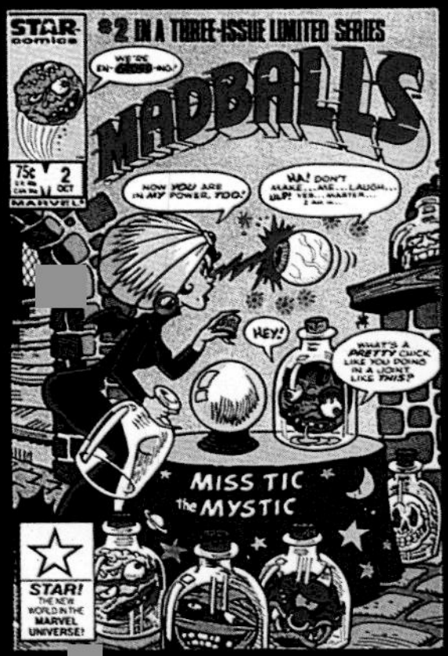
STAR comics
#2 IN A THREE-ISSUE LIMITED SERIES
MADBALLS
MISS TIC the MYSTIC
STAR!

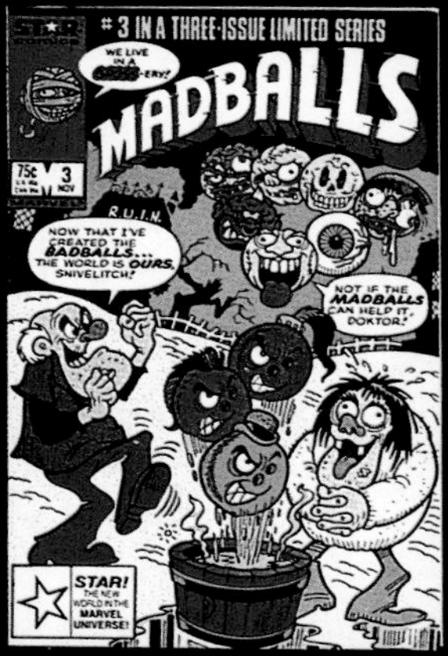
STAR comics
#3 IN A THREE-ISSUE LIMITED SERIES
MADBALLS
STAR!

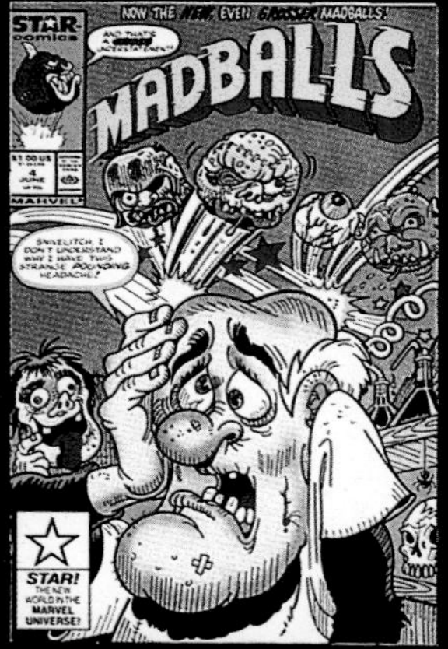
STAR comics
MADBALLS
STAR!

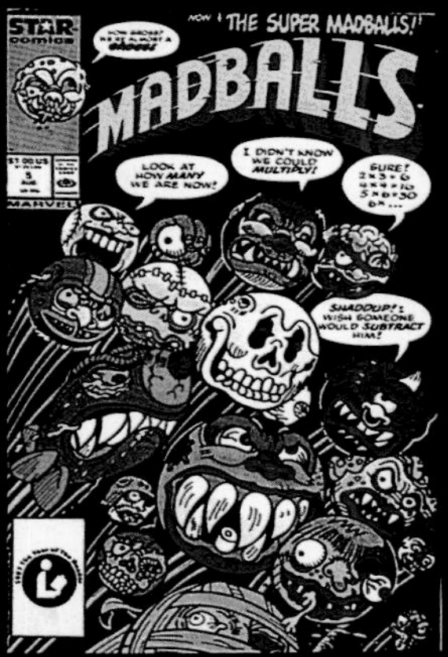
STAR comics
"THE SUPER MADBALLS!"
MADBALLS

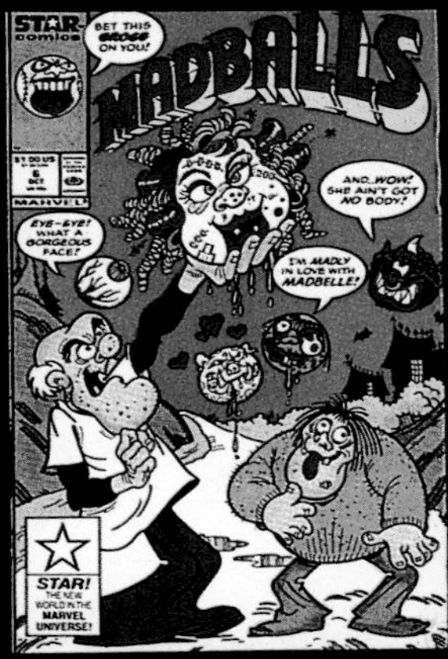
STAR comics
MADBALLS
STAR!

119 Magik (1-4)

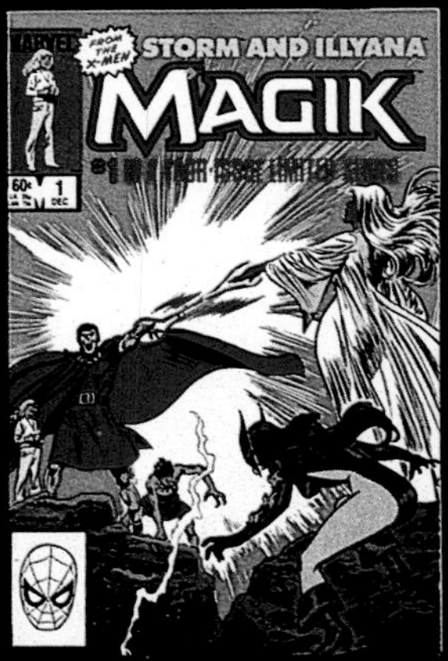
MARVEL
STORM AND ILLYANA
MAGIK

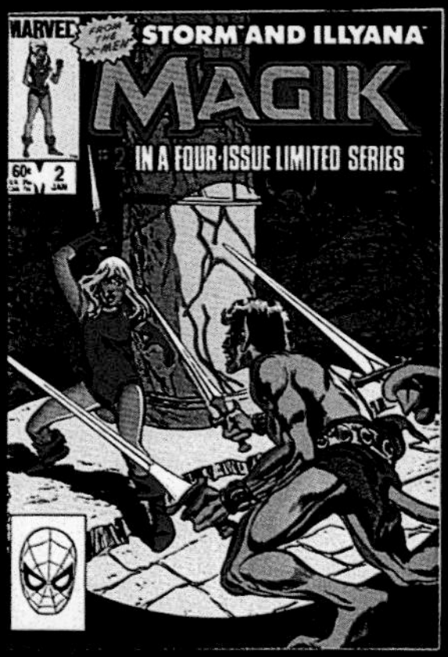
MARVEL
STORM AND ILLYANA
MAGIK
IN A FOUR-ISSUE LIMITED SERIES

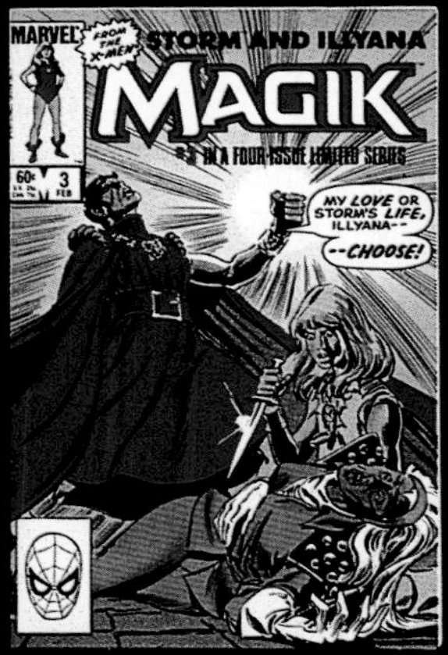
MARVEL
STORM AND ILLYANA
MAGIK
MY LOVE OR STORM'S LIFE, ILLYANA-- --CHOOSE!

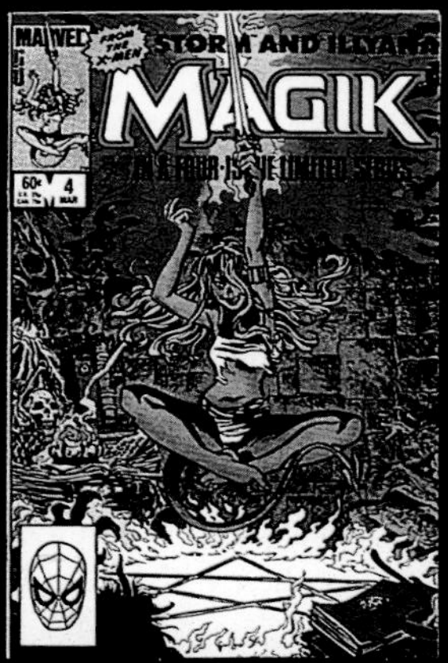
MARVEL
STORM AND ILLYANA
MAGIK

1201.3 Man from Atlantis (1-7)

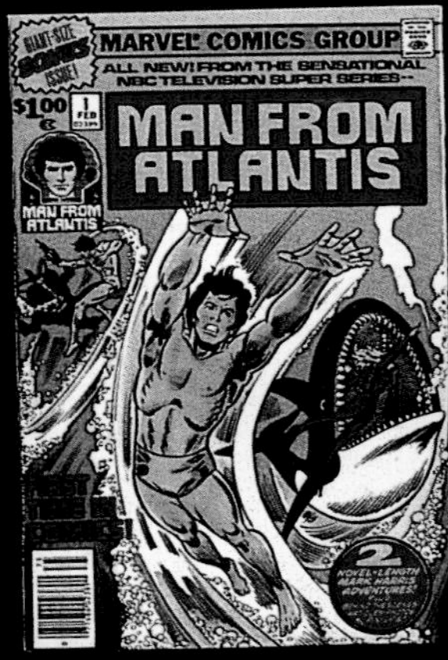
MARVEL COMICS GROUP
ALL NEW! FROM THE SENSATIONAL NBC TELEVISION SUPER SERIES--
MAN FROM ATLANTIS

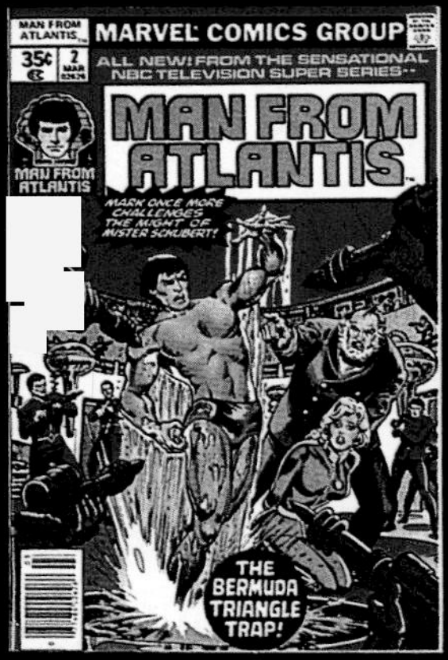
MARVEL COMICS GROUP
ALL NEW! FROM THE SENSATIONAL NBC TELEVISION SUPER SERIES--
MAN FROM ATLANTIS
THE BERMUDA TRIANGLE TRAP!

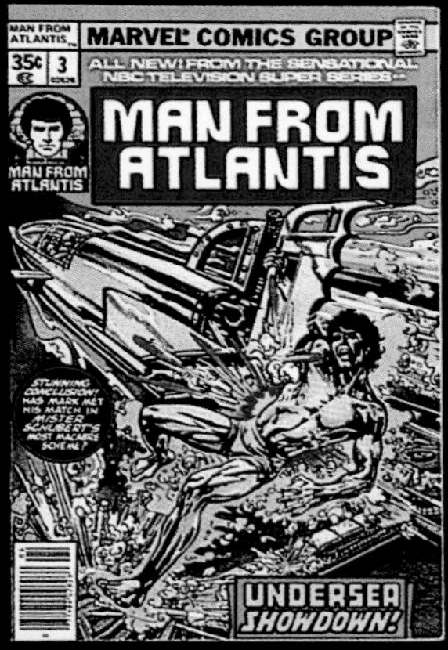
MARVEL COMICS GROUP
ALL NEW! FROM THE SENSATIONAL NBC TELEVISION SUPER SERIES--
MAN FROM ATLANTIS
UNDERSEA SHOWDOWN!

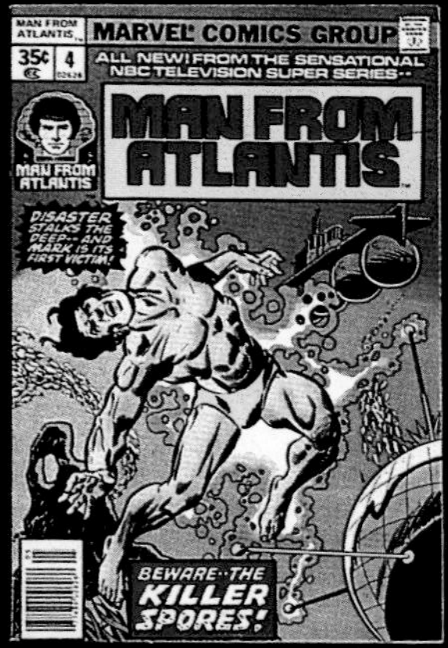
MARVEL COMICS GROUP
ALL NEW! FROM THE SENSATIONAL NBC TELEVISION SUPER SERIES--
MAN FROM ATLANTIS
BEWARE--THE KILLER SPORES!

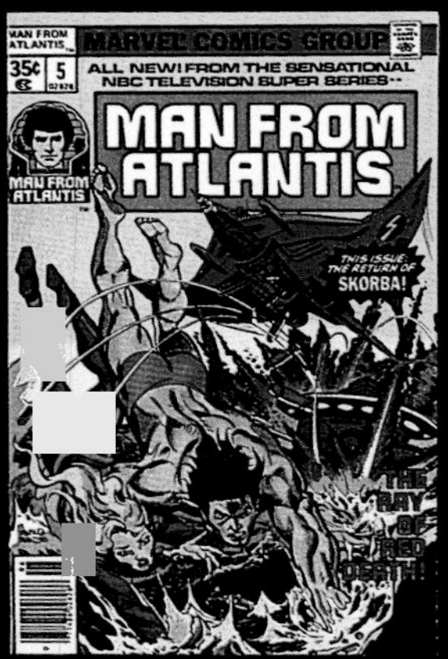
MARVEL COMICS GROUP
ALL NEW! FROM THE SENSATIONAL NBC TELEVISION SUPER SERIES--
MAN FROM ATLANTIS
SKORBA!

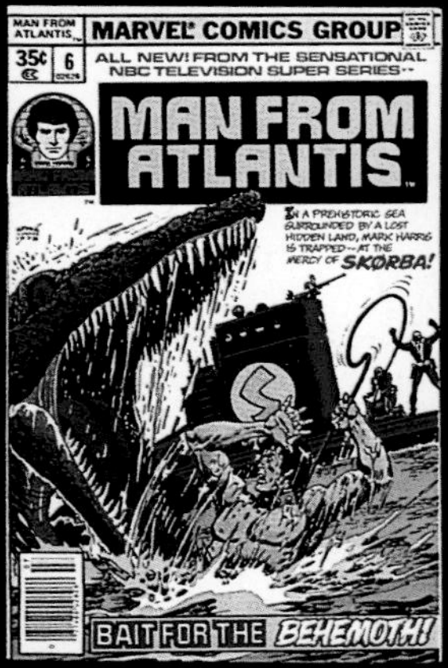
MARVEL COMICS GROUP
ALL NEW! FROM THE SENSATIONAL NBC TELEVISION SUPER SERIES--
MAN FROM ATLANTIS
SKORBA!
BAIT FOR THE BEHEMOTH!

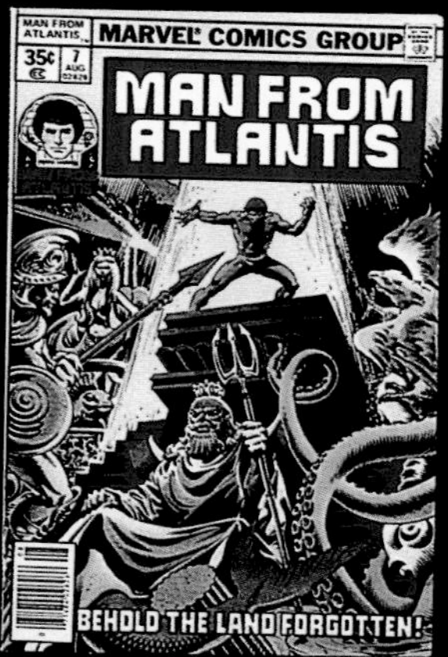
MARVEL COMICS GROUP
MAN FROM ATLANTIS
BEHOLD THE LAND FORGOTTEN!

Longshot (1-6) 1145.3

Ref. No.	Date	RVI	Artist/Info.
1145.3-1	Sept. 1985	17	Adams-c/a, Anderson, Portacio-a
1145.3-2	Oct.	14	Adams-c/a, Portacio-a
1145.3-3	Nov.	10	" "
1145.3-4	Dec.	10	" "
1145.3-5	Jan. 1986	10	" "
1145.3-6	Feb.	12	" "

Machine Man (1-19) 1187

Ref. No.	Date	RVI	Artist/Info.
1187-1	Apr. 1978	2	Kirby/Royer-a
1187-2	May	1	" "
1187-3	Jun.	1	" "
1187-4	Jul.	1	" "
1187-5	Aug.	1	" "
1187-6	Sept.	1	Simonson-c, Kirby/Royer-a
1187-7	Oct.	1	Kirby/Austin-c, Kirby/Royer-a
1187-8	Nov.	1	Kirby/Wiacek-c, Kirby/Royer-a
1187-9	Dec.	1	Kirby/Layton-c, Kirby/Royer-a
1187-10	**Aug. 1979**	**1**	**Ditko/Orzechowsky-a**
1187-11	Oct.	1	Ditko-a
1187-12	Dec.	1	"
1187-13	Feb. 1980	1	"
1187-14	Apr.	1	Byrne/Ditko-c, Ditko-a
1187-15	Jun.	1	Ditko-a
1187-16	Aug.	1	"
1187-17	Oct.	1	Byrne-c, Ditko-a
1187-18	Dec.	3	Buckler/Simons-c, Ditko-a
1187-19	Feb. 1981	1	Miller/Austin-c, Ditko-a

Machine Man (1-4) 1187.3

Ref. No.	Date	RVI	Artist/Info.
1187.3-1	Oct. 1984	1	Trimpe/Smith-a
1187.3-2 to 4	Jan. 1985, (#4)	1	Smith-a

Mad about Millie (1-17) 1188.2

Ref. No.	Date	RVI	Artist/Info.
1188.2-1	Apr. 1969	5	(Giant issue)
1188.2-2 to 17	Dec. 1970, (#17)	3	

Madballs (1-10) 1188.6

Ref. No.	Date	RVI	Artist/Info.
1188.6-1 to 10	Sept. 1986, (#1)	1	Post/Edelman-a (all)

Magik (1-4) 1192.4

Ref. No.	Date	RVI	Artist/Info.
1192.4-1	Dec. 1983	1	Buscema/Palmer-c/a
1192.4-2 to 4	Mar. 1984, (#4)	1	Palmer-c/a (all)

Man from Atlantis (1-7) 1201.3

Ref. No.	Date	RVI	Artist/Info.
1201.3-1	Feb. 1978	1	Sutton, Trinidad-a
1201.3-2	Mar.	1	Robbins/Springer-a
1201.3-3	Apr.	1	" "
1201.3-4 to 7	Aug. 1978, (#7)	1	" " (all)

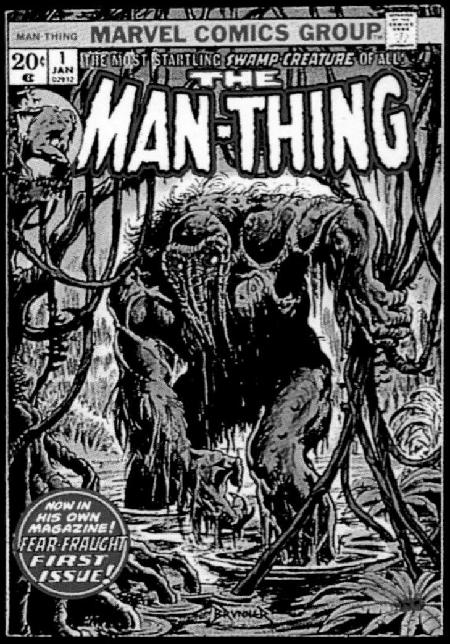
MARVEL COMICS GROUP
20¢ 1 JAN
THE MOST STARTLING SWAMP-CREATURE OF ALL!
THE MAN-THING
NOW IN HIS OWN MAGAZINE! FEAR-FRAUGHT FIRST ISSUE!

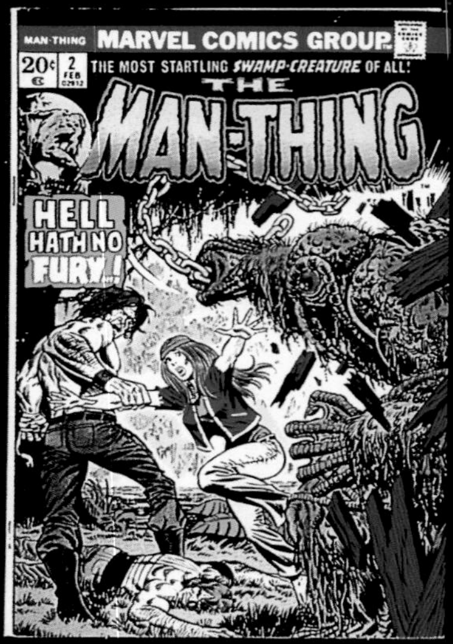
MARVEL COMICS GROUP
20¢ 2 FEB
THE MOST STARTLING SWAMP-CREATURE OF ALL!
THE MAN-THING
HELL HATH NO FURY..!

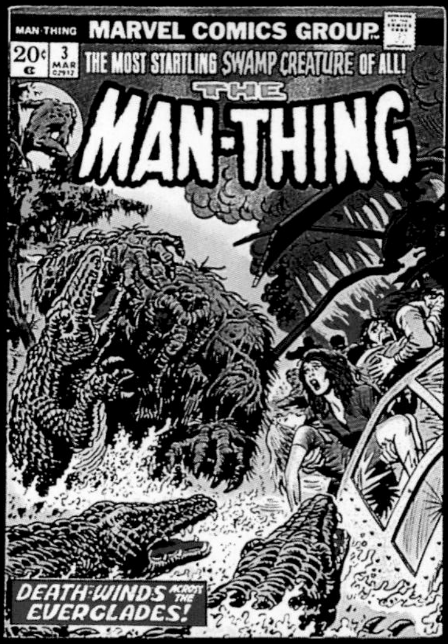
MARVEL COMICS GROUP
20¢ 3 MAR
THE MOST STARTLING SWAMP CREATURE OF ALL!
THE MAN-THING
DEATH-WINDS ACROSS THE EVERGLADES!

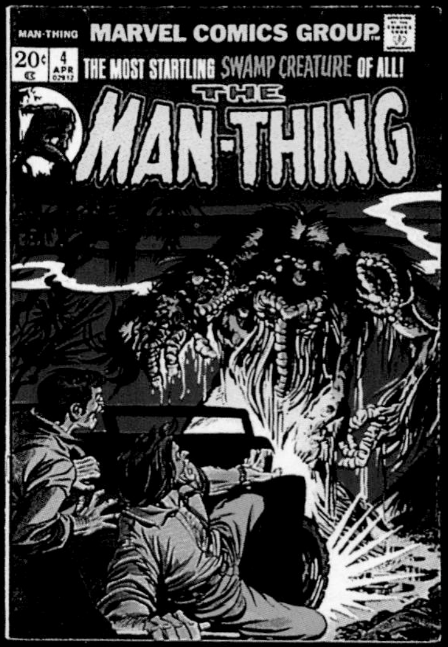
MARVEL COMICS GROUP
20¢ 4 APR
THE MOST STARTLING SWAMP CREATURE OF ALL!
THE MAN-THING

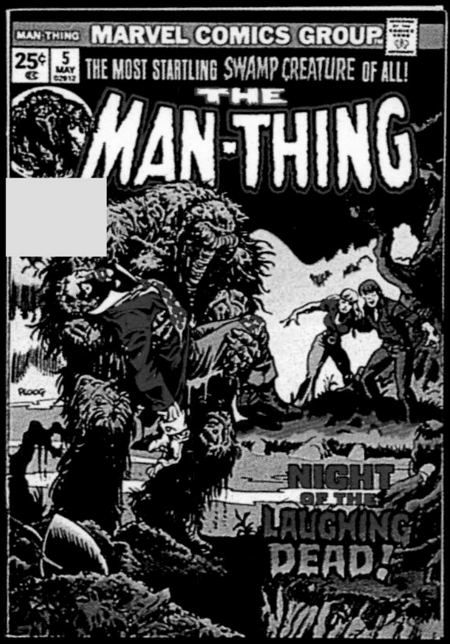
MARVEL COMICS GROUP
25¢ 5 MAY
THE MOST STARTLING SWAMP CREATURE OF ALL!
THE MAN-THING
NIGHT OF THE LAUGHING DEAD!

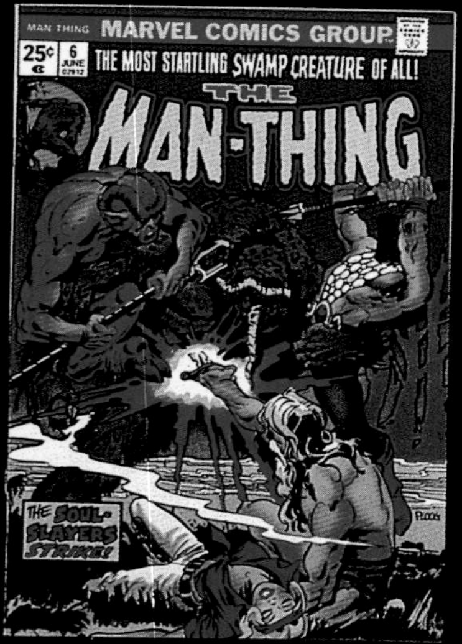
MARVEL COMICS GROUP
25¢ 6 JUNE
THE MOST STARTLING SWAMP CREATURE OF ALL!
THE MAN-THING
THE SOUL-SLAYERS STRIKE!

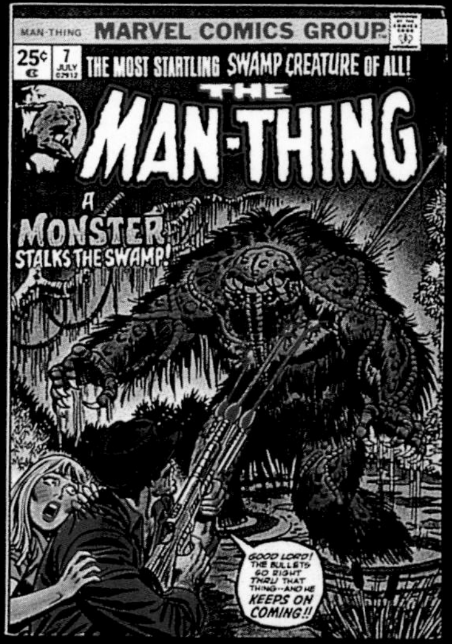
MARVEL COMICS GROUP
25¢ 7 JULY
THE MOST STARTLING SWAMP CREATURE OF ALL!
THE MAN-THING
A MONSTER STALKS THE SWAMP!
GOOD LORD! THE BULLETS GO RIGHT THRU THAT THING--AND HE KEEPS ON COMING!!

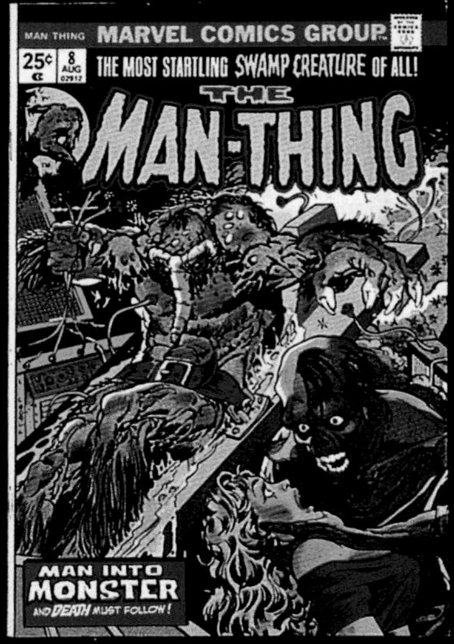
MARVEL COMICS GROUP
25¢ 8 AUG
THE MOST STARTLING SWAMP CREATURE OF ALL!
THE MAN-THING
MAN INTO MONSTER AND DEATH MUST FOLLOW!

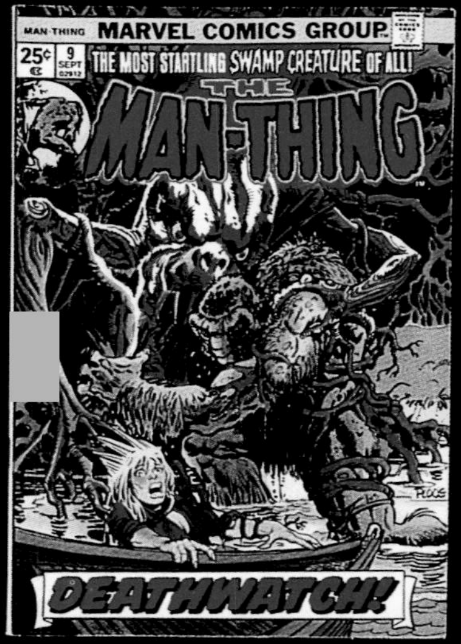
MARVEL COMICS GROUP
25¢ 9 SEPT
THE MOST STARTLING SWAMP CREATURE OF ALL!
THE MAN-THING
DEATHWATCH!

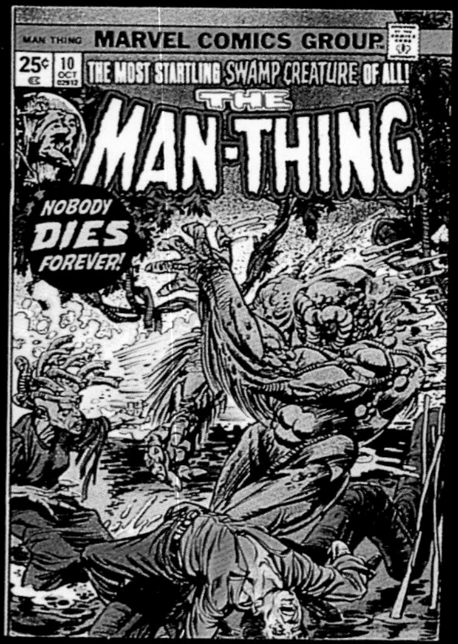
MARVEL COMICS GROUP
25¢ 10 OCT
THE MOST STARTLING SWAMP CREATURE OF ALL!
THE MAN-THING
NOBODY DIES FOREVER!

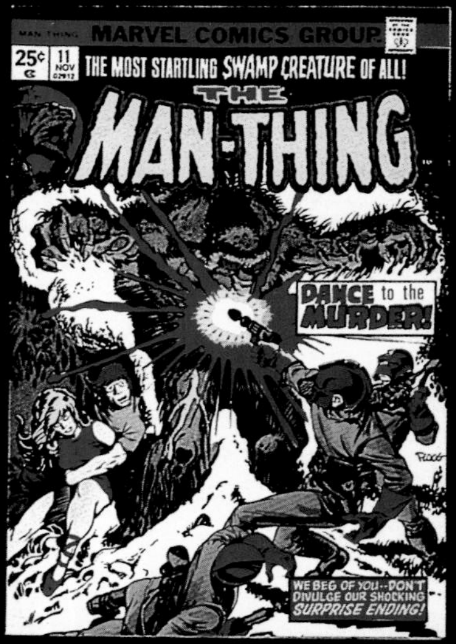
MARVEL COMICS GROUP
25¢ 11 NOV
THE MOST STARTLING SWAMP CREATURE OF ALL!
THE MAN-THING
DANCE to the MURDER!
WE BEG OF YOU--DON'T DIVULGE OUR SHOCKING SURPRISE ENDING!

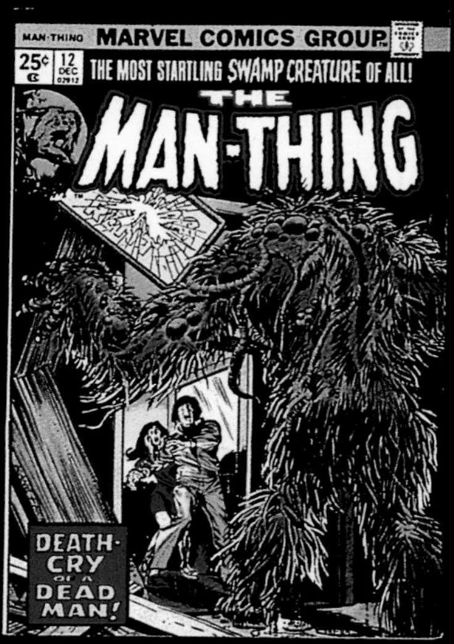
MARVEL COMICS GROUP
25¢ 12 DEC
THE MOST STARTLING SWAMP CREATURE OF ALL!
THE MAN-THING
DEATH-CRY OF A DEAD MAN!

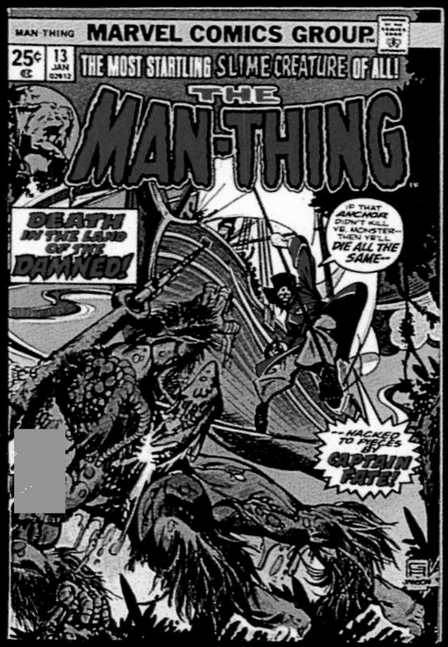
MARVEL COMICS GROUP
25¢ 13 JAN
THE MOST STARTLING SLIME CREATURE OF ALL!
THE MAN-THING
DEATH IN THE LAND OF THE DAMNED!
HACKED TO PIECES BY CAPTAIN FATE!

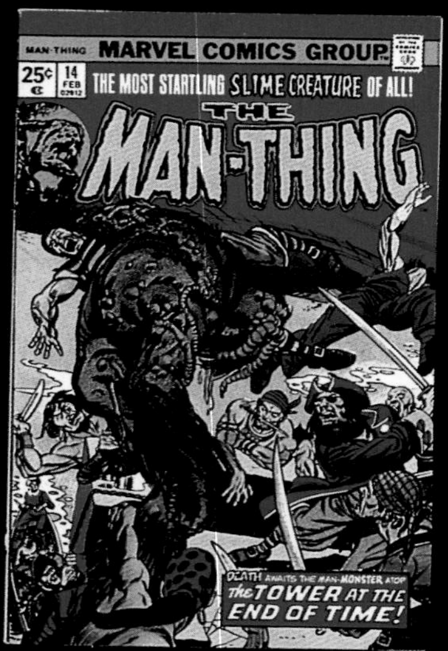
MARVEL COMICS GROUP
25¢ 14 FEB
THE MOST STARTLING SLIME CREATURE OF ALL!
THE MAN-THING
THE TOWER AT THE END OF TIME!

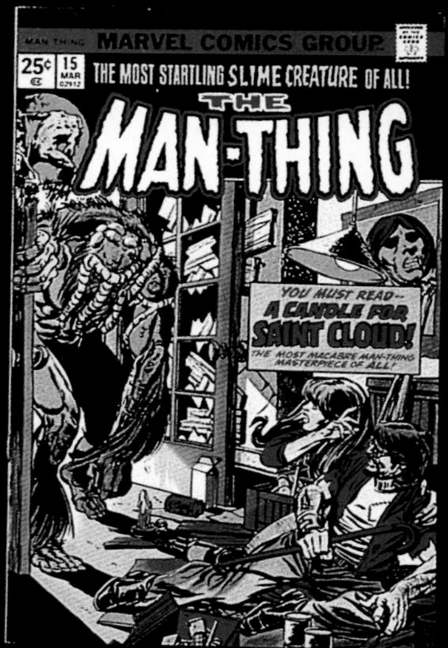
MARVEL COMICS GROUP
25¢ 15 MAR
THE MOST STARTLING SLIME CREATURE OF ALL!
THE MAN-THING
YOU MUST READ-- A CANDLE FOR SAINT CLOUD!
THE MOST MACABRE MAN-THING MASTERPIECE OF ALL!

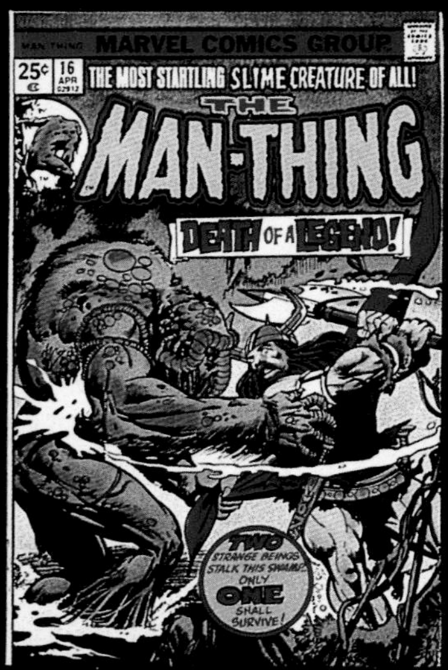
MARVEL COMICS GROUP
25¢ 16 APR
THE MOST STARTLING SLIME CREATURE OF ALL!
THE MAN-THING
DEATH OF A LEGEND!
TWO STRANGE BEINGS STALK THIS SWAMP! ONLY ONE SHALL SURVIVE!

1206 Man-Thing (17-22)

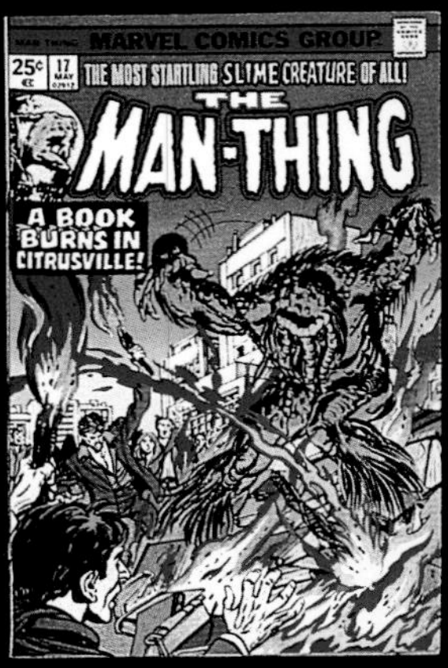
MARVEL COMICS GROUP
THE MOST STARTLING SLIME CREATURE OF ALL!
THE MAN-THING
A BOOK BURNS IN CITRUSVILLE!

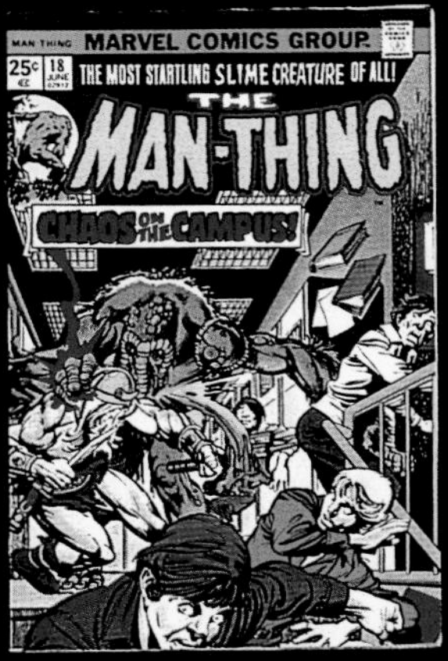
MARVEL COMICS GROUP
THE MOST STARTLING SLIME CREATURE OF ALL!
THE MAN-THING

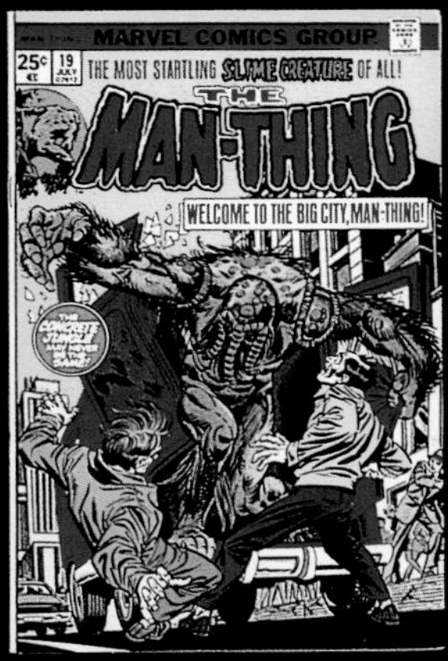
MARVEL COMICS GROUP
THE MOST STARTLING SLIME CREATURE OF ALL!
THE MAN-THING
WELCOME TO THE BIG CITY, MAN-THING!

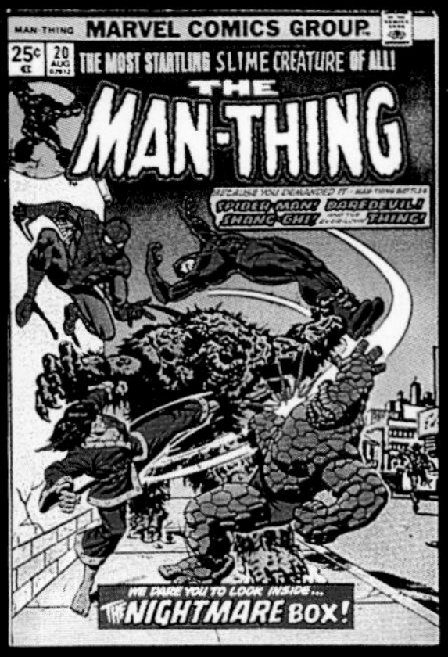
MARVEL COMICS GROUP
THE MOST STARTLING SLIME CREATURE OF ALL!
THE MAN-THING
NIGHTMARE BOX!

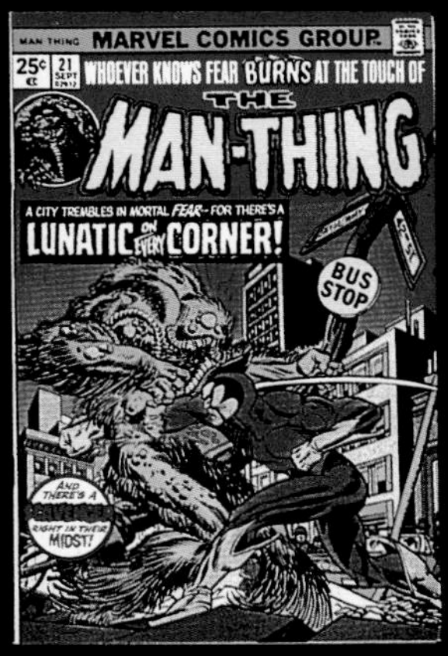
MARVEL COMICS GROUP
WHOEVER KNOWS FEAR BURNS AT THE TOUCH OF
THE MAN-THING
LUNATIC CORNER!
BUS STOP

1206 Man-Thing V.2 (1-10; GS. 1-4)

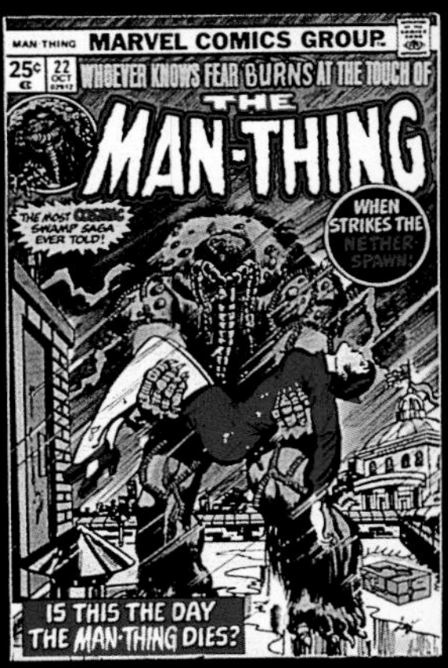
MARVEL COMICS GROUP
WHOEVER KNOWS FEAR BURNS AT THE TOUCH OF
THE MAN-THING
IS THIS THE DAY THE MAN-THING DIES?

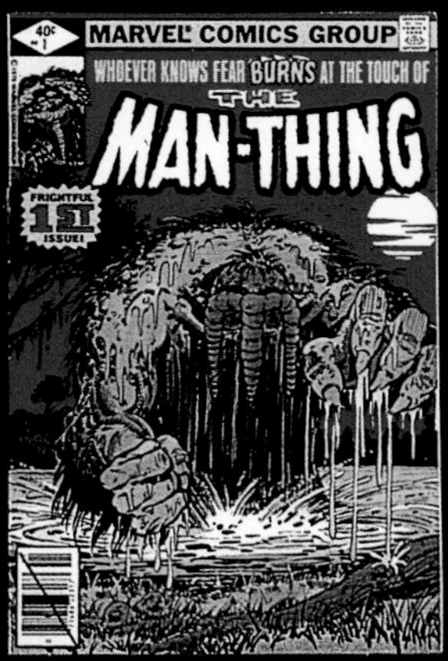
MARVEL COMICS GROUP
WHOEVER KNOWS FEAR BURNS AT THE TOUCH OF
THE MAN-THING

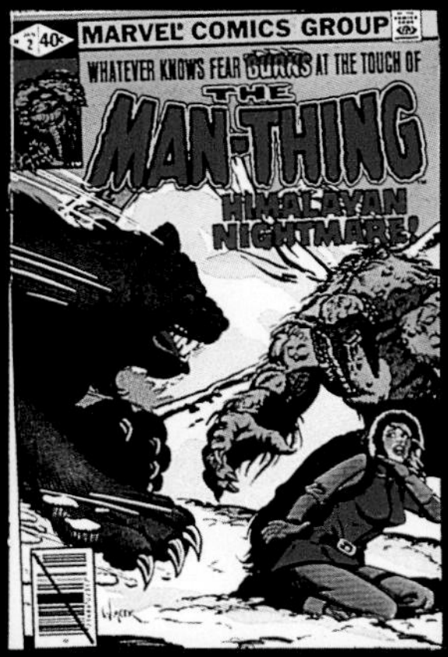
MARVEL COMICS GROUP
WHATEVER KNOWS FEAR BURNS AT THE TOUCH OF
THE MAN-THING

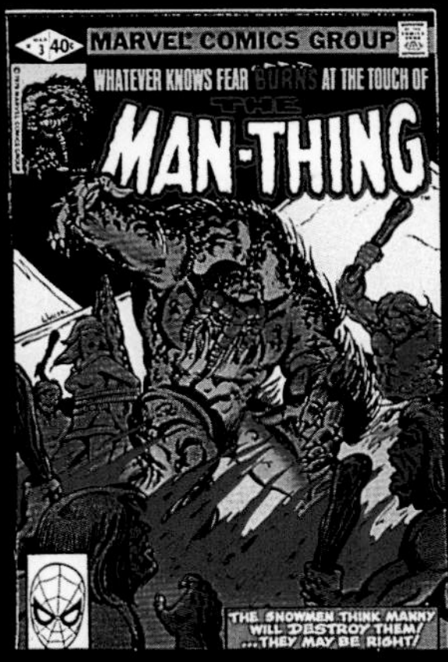
MARVEL COMICS GROUP
WHATEVER KNOWS FEAR BURNS AT THE TOUCH OF
MAN-THING

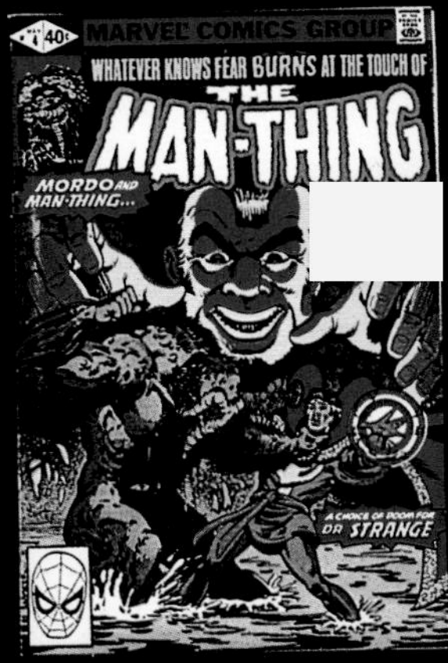
MARVEL COMICS GROUP
WHATEVER KNOWS FEAR BURNS AT THE TOUCH OF
THE MAN-THING

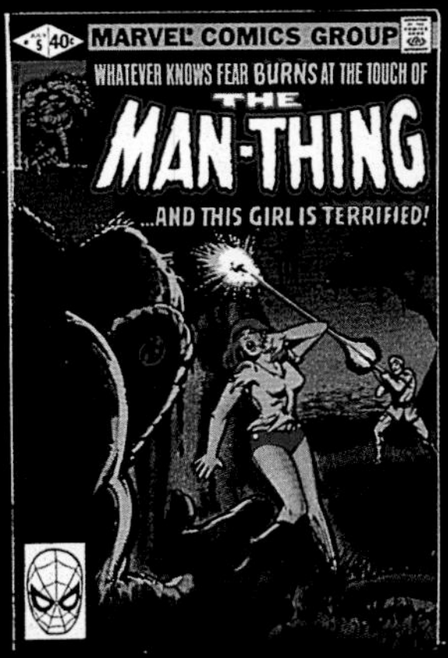
MARVEL COMICS GROUP
WHATEVER KNOWS FEAR BURNS AT THE TOUCH OF
THE MAN-THING
...AND THIS GIRL IS TERRIFIED!

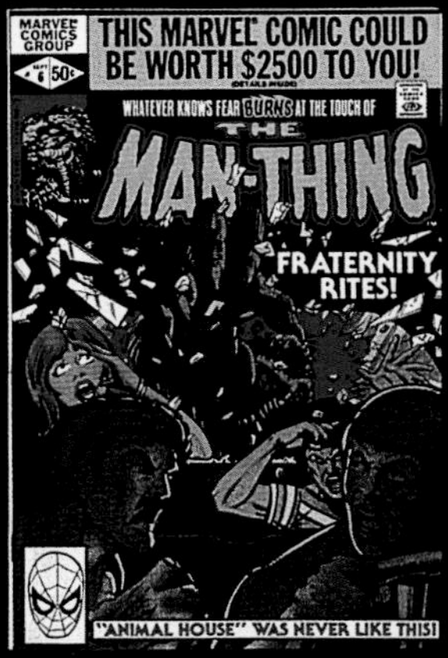
THIS MARVEL COMIC COULD BE WORTH $2500 TO YOU!
MAN-THING
FRATERNITY RITES!
"ANIMAL HOUSE" WAS NEVER LIKE THIS!

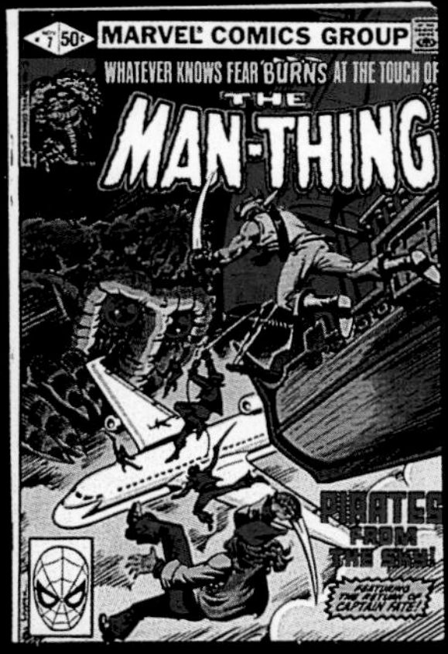
MARVEL COMICS GROUP
WHATEVER KNOWS FEAR BURNS AT THE TOUCH OF
THE MAN-THING

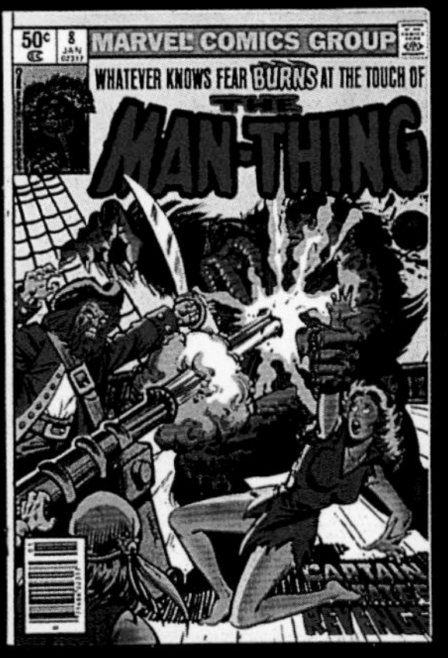
MARVEL COMICS GROUP
WHATEVER KNOWS FEAR BURNS AT THE TOUCH OF
MAN-THING

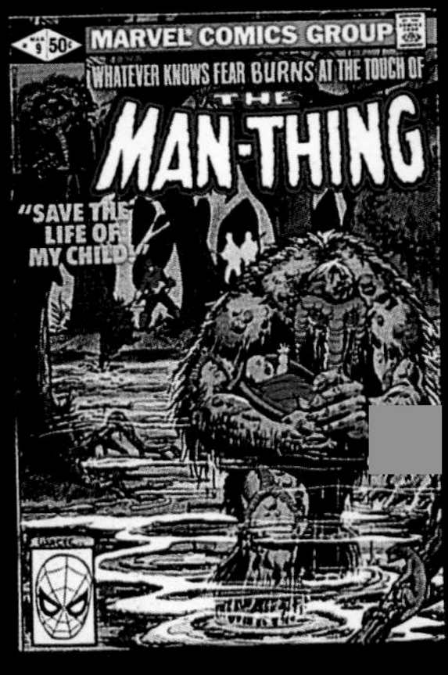
MARVEL COMICS GROUP
WHATEVER KNOWS FEAR BURNS AT THE TOUCH OF
THE MAN-THING

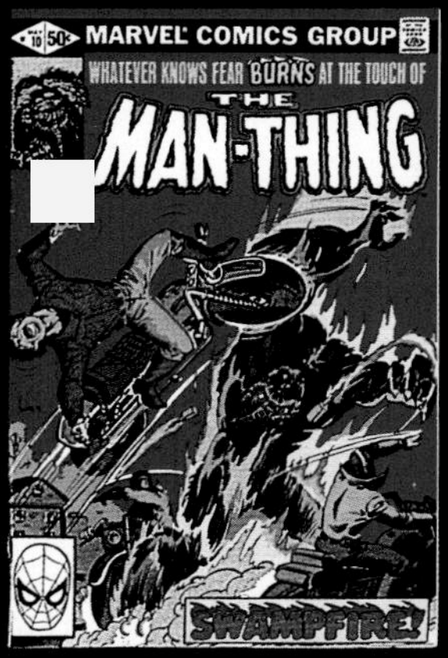
MARVEL COMICS GROUP
WHATEVER KNOWS FEAR BURNS AT THE TOUCH OF
THE MAN-THING
SWAMPFIRE!

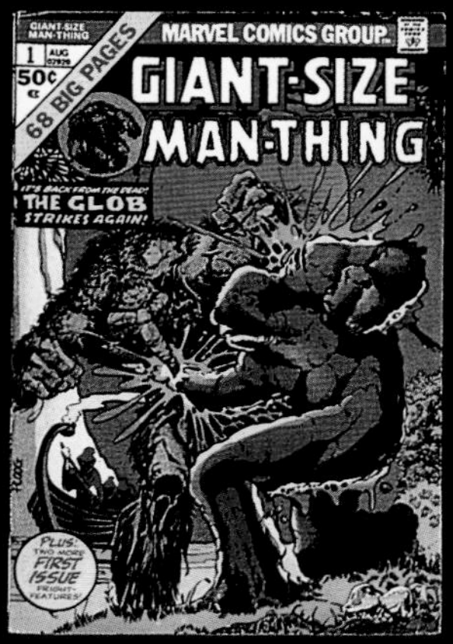
MARVEL COMICS GROUP
GIANT-SIZE MAN-THING
68 BIG PAGES
THE GLOB STRIKES AGAIN!

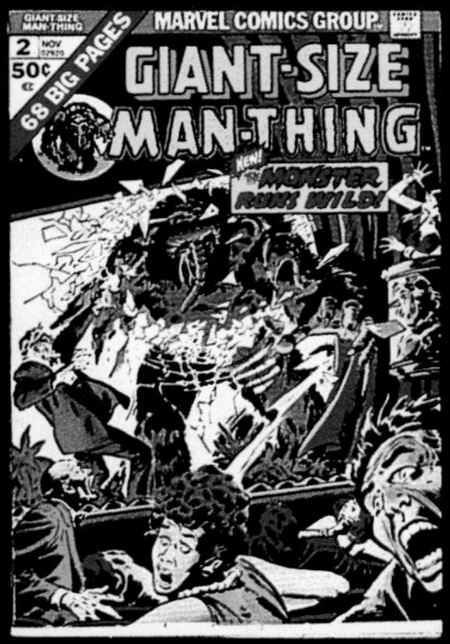
MARVEL COMICS GROUP
GIANT-SIZE MAN-THING
68 BIG PAGES

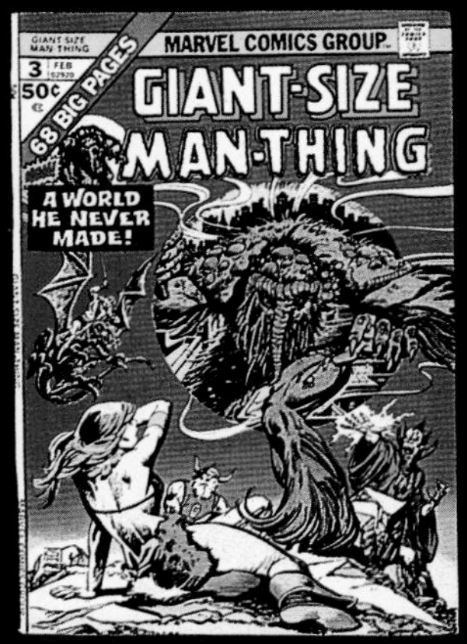
MARVEL COMICS GROUP
GIANT-SIZE MAN-THING
68 BIG PAGES
A WORLD HE NEVER MADE!

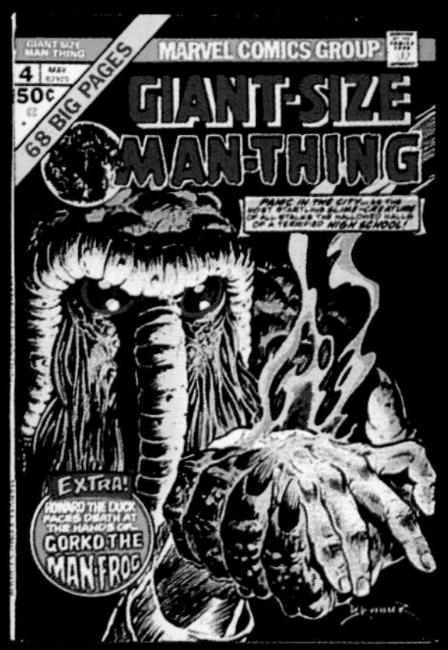
MARVEL COMICS GROUP
GIANT-SIZE MAN-THING
68 BIG PAGES
EXTRA!
GORKO THE MAN-FROG

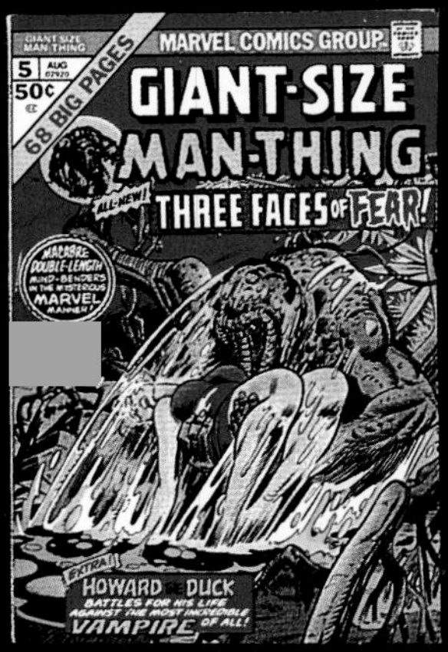
MARVEL COMICS GROUP
GIANT-SIZE MAN-THING
68 BIG PAGES
THREE FACES OF FEAR!
HOWARD THE DUCK
VAMPIRE

Man-Thing (1-22) 1206

Ref. No.	Date	RVI	Artist/Info.
1206-1	Jan. 1974	5	Brunner-c, Mayerik/Trapani-a
1206-2	Feb.	2	Mayerik/Trapani-a
1206-3	Mar.	3	Mayerik/Abel-a
1206-4	Apr.	1	Kane-c, Mayerik/Abel-a
1206-5	May	1	Ploog-c/a, Chiaramonte-a
1206-6	Jun.	1	" "
1206-7	Jul.	1	Ploog-c/a
1206-8	Aug.	1	"
1206-9	Sept.	1	Ploog-c/a, Chiaramonte-a
1206-10	**Oct.**	**1**	**" "**
1206-11	Nov.	1	" "
1206-12	Dec.	1	Kane-c, Janson-a
1206-13	Jan. 1975	1	Janson-c, Sutton-a
1206-14	Feb.	1	Janson-c, Alcala-a
1206-15	Mar.	1	Janson-c, Rival-a
1206-16	Apr.	1	Janson-c, Buscema/Palmer-a
1206-17	May	1	Mooney-a
1206-18	Jun.	1	"
1206-19	Jul.	1	Mooney/Springer-a
1206-20	**Aug.**	**1**	**Mooney-a**
1206-21	Sept.	1	"
1206-22	Oct. 1975	1	"
1206-G.S. 1	Aug. 1974	1	Ploog-c/a, Chiaramonte-a
1206-G.S. 2	Nov. 1974	1	Buscema/Janson-a
1206-G.S. 3	Feb. 1975	1	Alcala-a
1206-G.S. 4	May 1975	3	Brunner-c, Hannigan, Wilson/Springer-a
1206-G.S. 5	Aug. 1975	3	Adkins-c, Hannigan/Adkins-a

Man-Thing V.2 (1-11) 1206.1

Ref. No.	Date	RVI	Artist/Info.
1206.1-1	Nov. 1979	1	Mooney/Wiacek-a
1206.1-2	Jan. 1980	1	Wiacek-c/a, Mooney-a
1206.1-3	Mar.	1	" "
1206.1-4	May	1	Wiacek-c/a, Perlin-a
1206.1-5	Jul.	1	Perlin, Wiacek-a
1206.1-6	Sept.	1	" "
1206.1-7	Nov.	1	Wiacek-c/a, Perlin-a
1206.1-8	Jan. 1981	1	" "
1206.1-9	Mar.	1	Wiacek-c, Hama/Bulanadi-a
1206.1-10	**May**	**1**	**Wiacek-c/a, Perlin-a**
1206.1-11	July	1	

1214.25 Marvel Adventures (1-6)

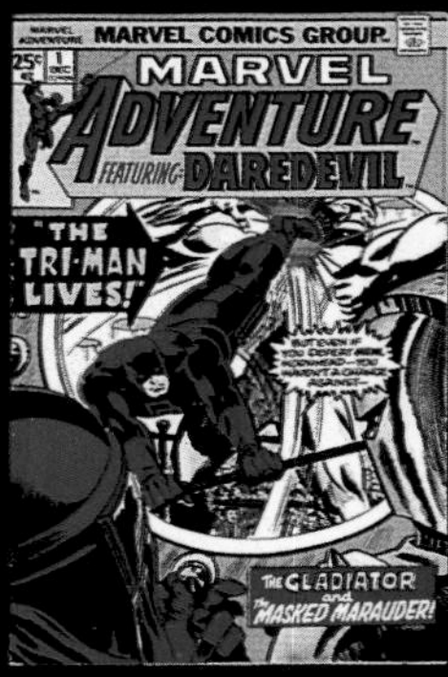
MARVEL COMICS GROUP
MARVEL ADVENTURE FEATURING DAREDEVIL
THE TRI-MAN LIVES!
THE GLADIATOR AND THE MASKED MARAUDER!
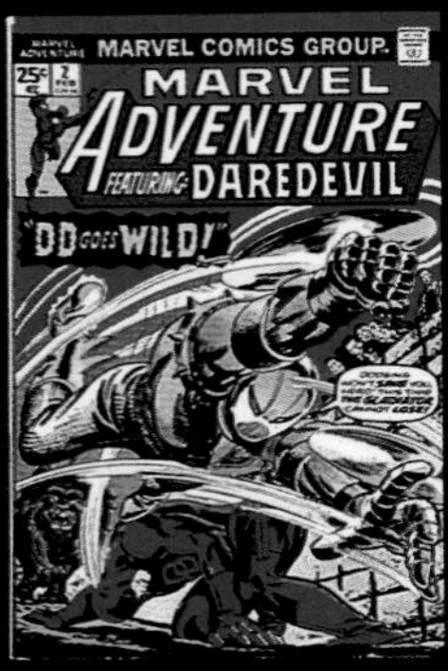
MARVEL COMICS GROUP
MARVEL ADVENTURE FEATURING DAREDEVIL
DD GOES WILD!
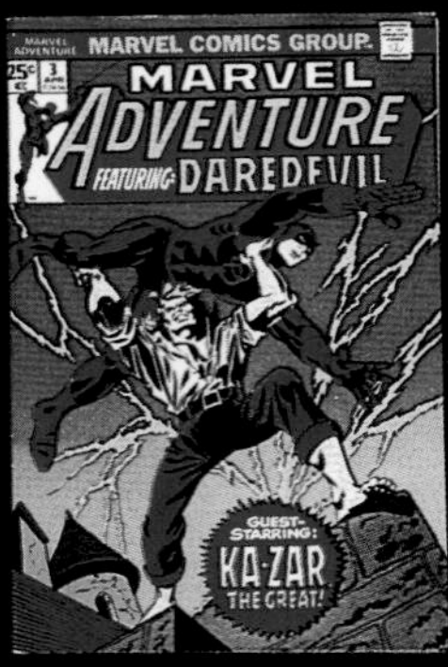
MARVEL COMICS GROUP
MARVEL ADVENTURE FEATURING DAREDEVIL
GUEST-STARRING: KA-ZAR THE GREAT!
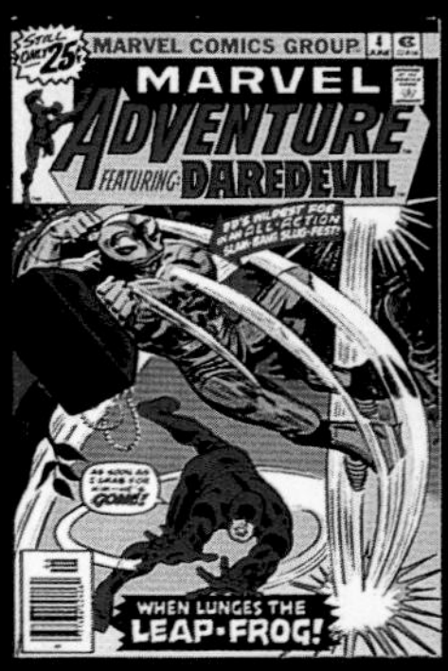
MARVEL COMICS GROUP
MARVEL ADVENTURE FEATURING DAREDEVIL
WHEN LUNGES THE LEAP-FROG!
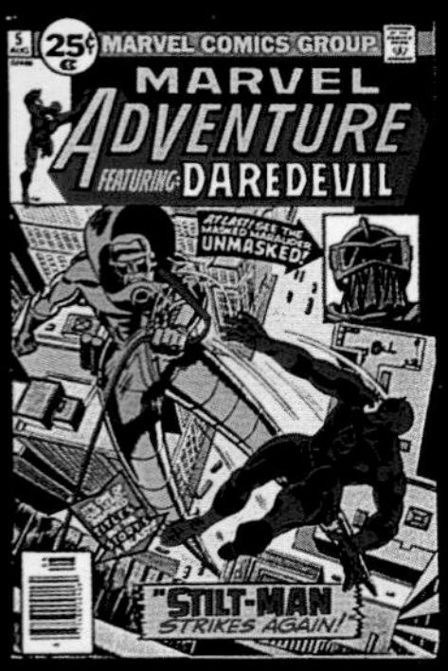
MARVEL COMICS GROUP
MARVEL ADVENTURE FEATURING DAREDEVIL
UNMASKED!
"STILT-MAN STRIKES AGAIN!"
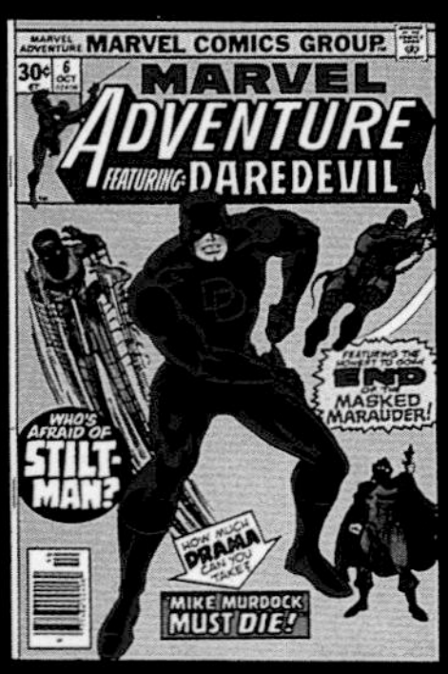
MARVEL COMICS GROUP
MARVEL ADVENTURE FEATURING DAREDEVIL
WHO'S AFRAID OF STILT-MAN?
MIKE MURDOCK MUST DIE!

1214.3 Marvel and DC Present (1) 1214.35 Marvel Chillers (1-7)

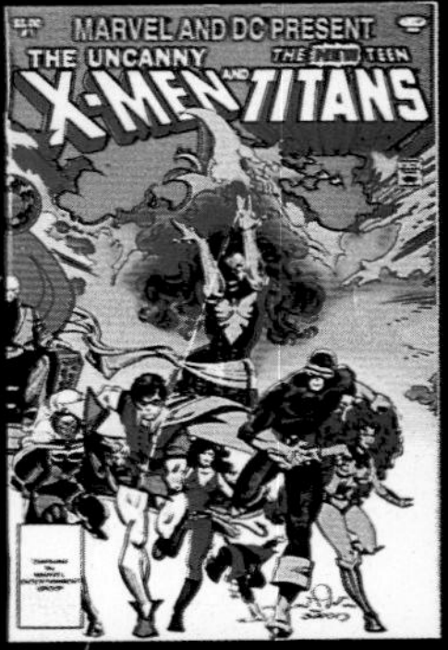
MARVEL AND DC PRESENT
THE UNCANNY X-MEN AND THE NEW TEEN TITANS
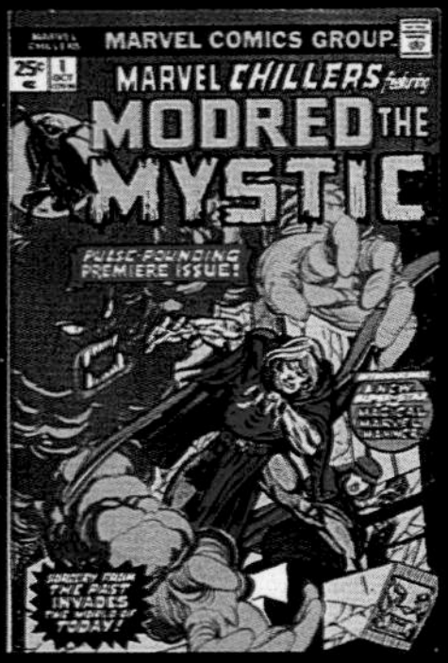
MARVEL COMICS GROUP
MARVEL CHILLERS featuring MODRED THE MYSTIC
PULSE-POUNDING PREMIERE ISSUE!
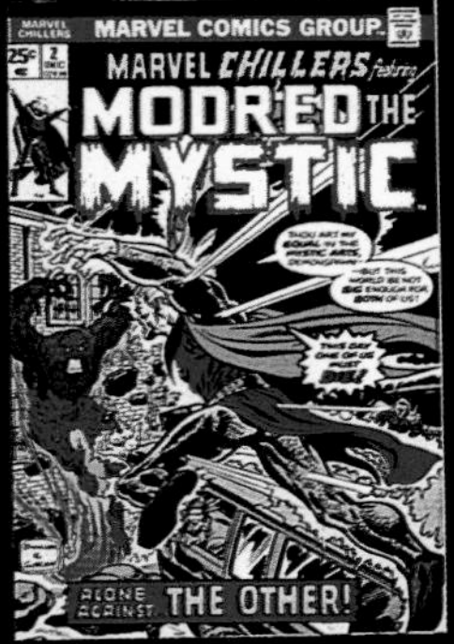
MARVEL COMICS GROUP
MARVEL CHILLERS featuring MODRED THE MYSTIC
ALONE AGAINST THE OTHER!
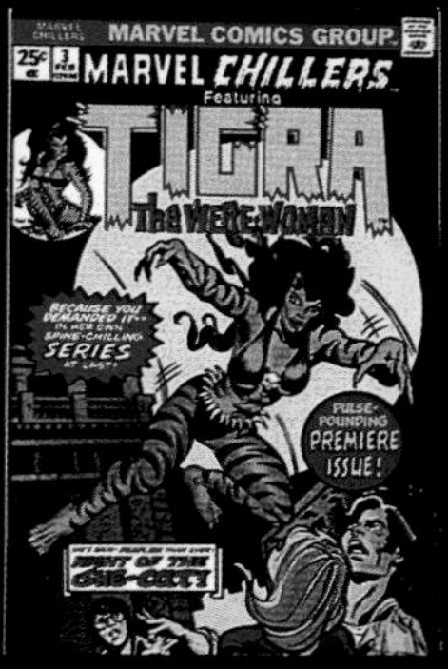
MARVEL COMICS GROUP
MARVEL CHILLERS featuring TIGRA The WERE-WOMAN
PREMIERE ISSUE!
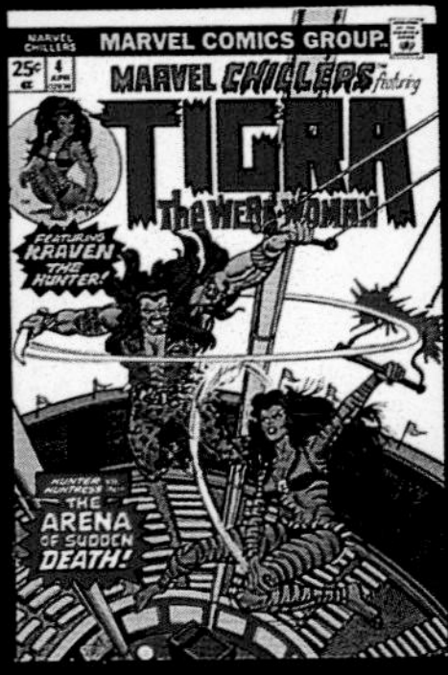
MARVEL COMICS GROUP
MARVEL CHILLERS featuring TIGRA The WERE-WOMAN
ARENA OF SUDDEN DEATH!
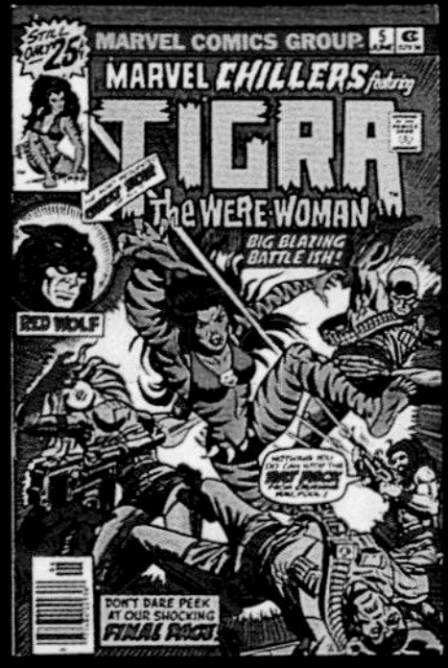
MARVEL COMICS GROUP
MARVEL CHILLERS featuring TIGRA The WERE-WOMAN
RED WOLF
DON'T DARE PEEK AT OUR SHOCKING FINAL PAGE!
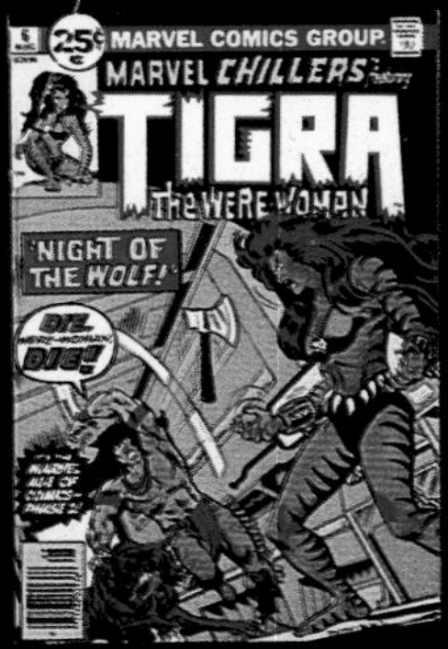
MARVEL COMICS GROUP
MARVEL CHILLERS featuring TIGRA The WERE-WOMAN
NIGHT OF THE WOLF!
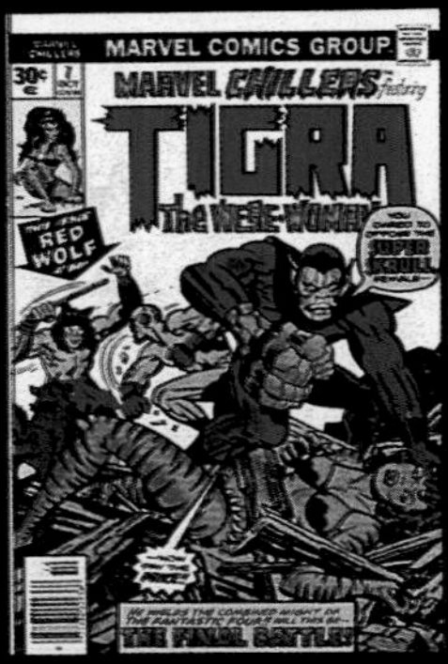
MARVEL COMICS GROUP
MARVEL CHILLERS featuring TIGRA The WERE-WOMAN
RED WOLF

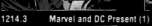

Marvel Adventures (1-6) 1214.25

Ref. No.	Date	RVI	Artist/Info.
1214.25-1	Dec. 1975	1	Colan-a Reprints featuring Daredevil
1214.25.2	Feb. 1976	1	" " " "
1214.25-3	Apr.	1	" " " "
1214.25-4	Jun.	1	" " " "
1214.25-5	Aug.	1	" " " "
1214.25-6	Oct. 1976	1	" " " "

Marvel and DC Present (1) 1214.3

1214.3-1	Nov. 1982	7	Simonson/Austin-c/a, Perez-a

Marvel Chillers (1-7) 1214.35

1214.35-1	Oct. 1975	1	Kane-c
1214.35-2	Dec.	1	
1214.35-3	Feb. 1976	1	Chaykin/Wrightson-c
1214.35-4	Apr.	1	
1214.35-5	Jun.	1	
1214.35-6	Aug.	1	Buckler-c, Byrne-a
1214.35-7	Oct. 1976	1	Kirby-c, Tuska-a

Marvel Classics Comics (1-36) 1214.4

1214.4-1	1976	2	Adkins-c, Redondo-a; Dr. Jekyll and Mr. Hyde
1214.4-2	"	1	A. Nino-a; The Time Machine
1214.4-3	"	1	Janson-c, J. Lo Famia-a; The Hunchback of Notre Dame
1214.4-4	"	1	Adkins-c, Gamboa, Patricia-a; 20,000 Leagues Under the Sea
1214.4-5	"	1	Nebres-a; Black Beauty
1214.4-6	"	1	E.R. Cruz-a; Gulliver's Travels
1214.4-7	"	1	E.R. Cruz-a; Tom Sawyer
1214.4-8	"	1	A. Nono-a; Moby Dick
1214.4-9	"	1	Redondo-a; Dracula
1214.4-10	**"**	**1**	**E.R. Cruz-a; Red Badge of Courage**
1214.4-11	"	1	E.R. Cruz-a; Mysterious Island
1214.4-12	"	1	Kane, Adkins-c, Nino-a; The Three Musketeers
1214.4-13	"	1	Trinidad-a; The Last of the Mohicans
1214.4-14	"	1	Montano, Castrillo-a; War of the Worlds
1214.4-15	"	1	Castrillo-a; Treasure Island
1214.4-16	"	1	Jodloman-a; Ivanhoe
1214.4-17	"	1	Buscema, Chan-c, Castrillo-a; The Count of Monte Cristo
1214.4-18	"	1	Chan-c, Jodloman-a; The Odyssey
1214.4-19 to 36	Dec. 1978, (#38)	1	(#28 RVI 4)

1214.4 Marvel Classics Comics (1-10)

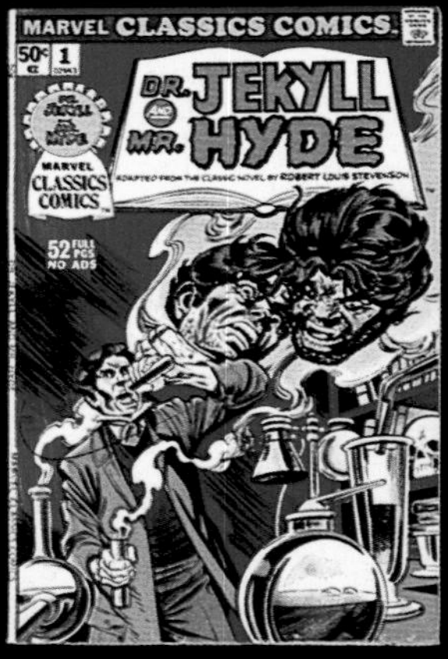
MARVEL CLASSICS COMICS
DR. JEKYLL AND MR. HYDE
52 FULL PGS NO ADS
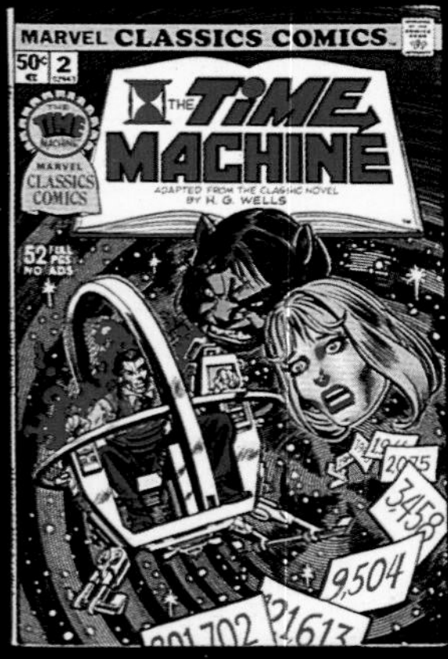
MARVEL CLASSICS COMICS
THE TIME MACHINE
ADAPTED FROM THE CLASSIC NOVEL BY H. G. WELLS
52 FULL PGS NO ADS
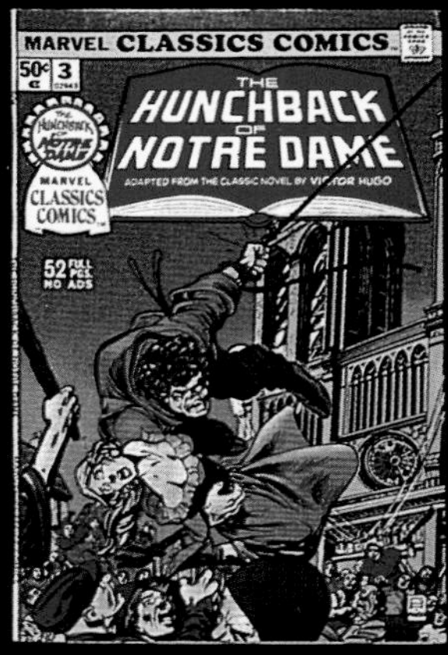
MARVEL CLASSICS COMICS
THE HUNCHBACK OF NOTRE DAME
52 FULL PGS NO ADS
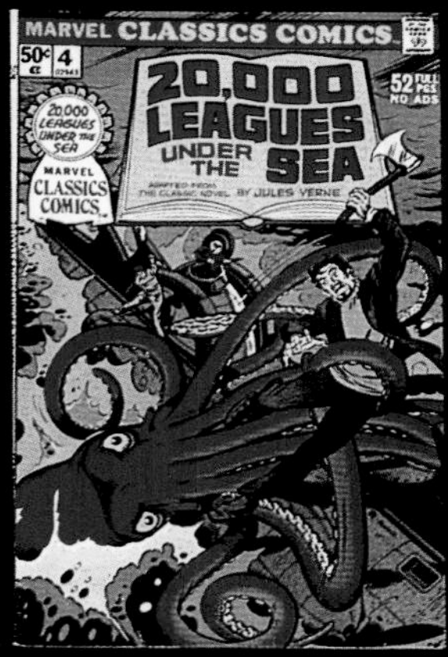
MARVEL CLASSICS COMICS
20,000 LEAGUES UNDER THE SEA
52 FULL PGS NO ADS
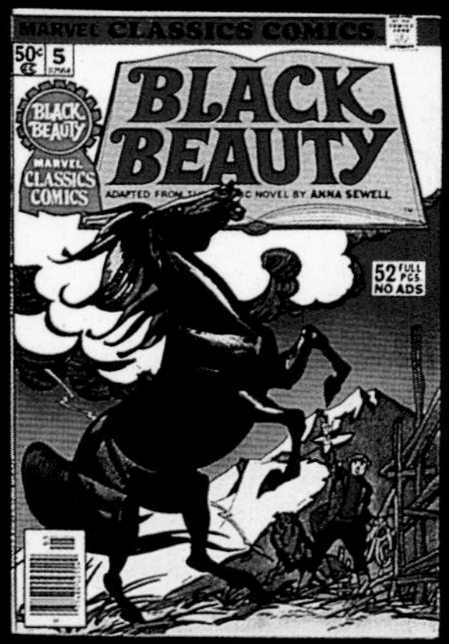
MARVEL CLASSICS COMICS
BLACK BEAUTY
52 FULL PGS NO ADS
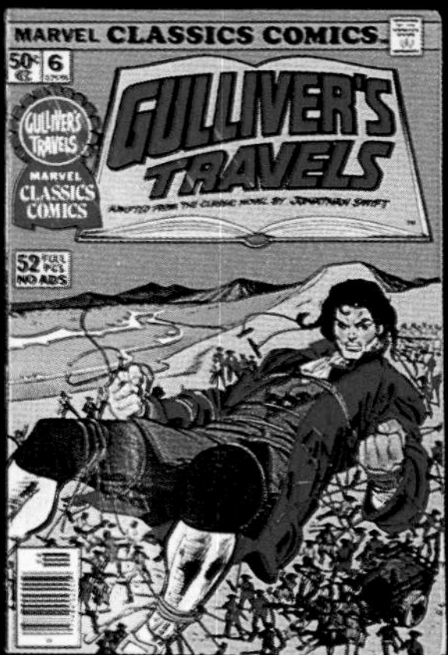
MARVEL CLASSICS COMICS
GULLIVER'S TRAVELS
52 FULL PGS NO ADS
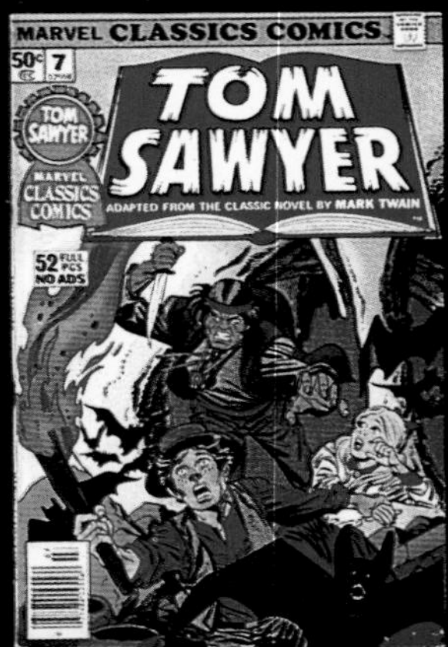
MARVEL CLASSICS COMICS
TOM SAWYER
ADAPTED FROM THE CLASSIC NOVEL BY MARK TWAIN
52 FULL PGS NO ADS
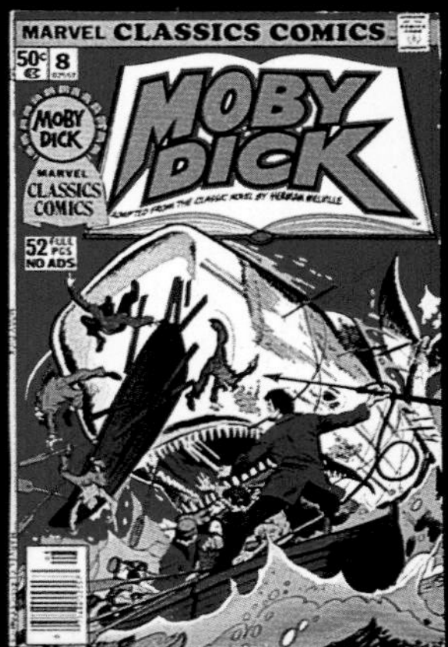
MARVEL CLASSICS COMICS
MOBY DICK
52 FULL PGS NO ADS
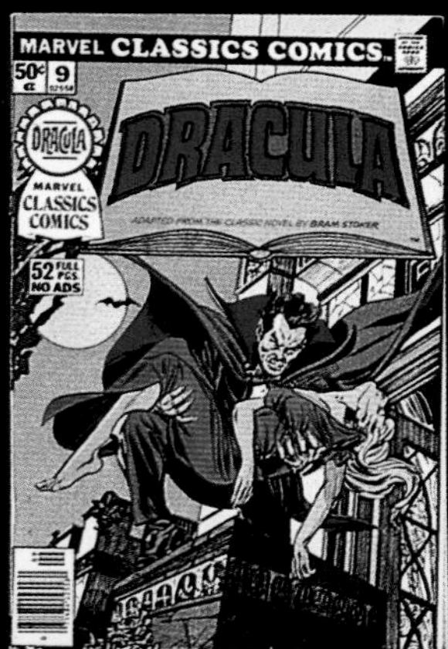
MARVEL CLASSICS COMICS
DRACULA
52 FULL PGS NO ADS
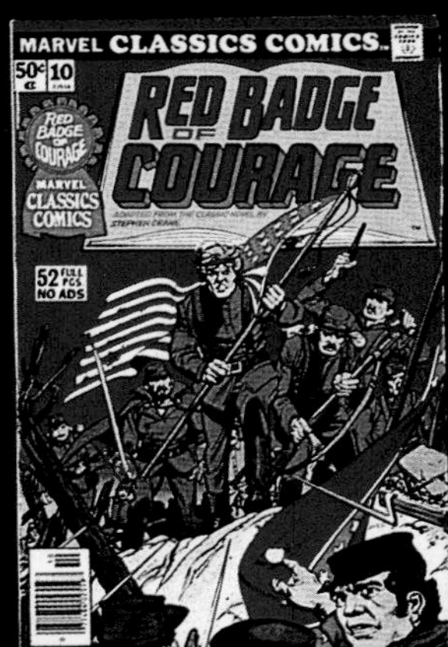
MARVEL CLASSICS COMICS
RED BADGE OF COURAGE
52 FULL PGS NO ADS

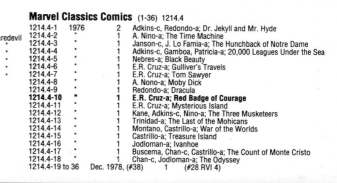

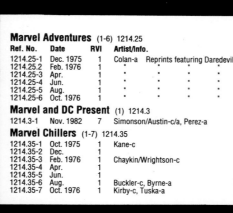

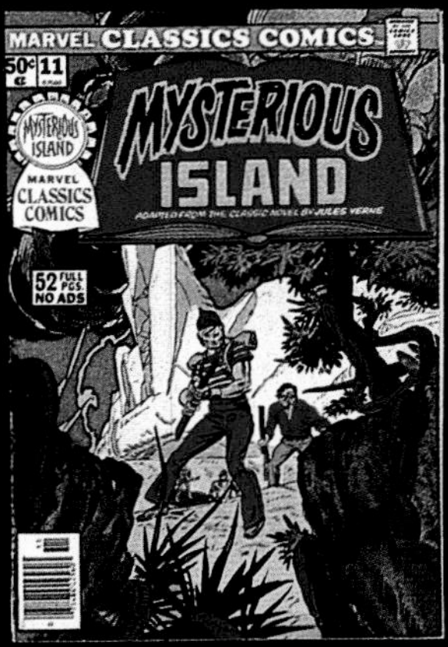
MARVEL CLASSICS COMICS
MYSTERIOUS ISLAND
52 FULL PGS NO ADS

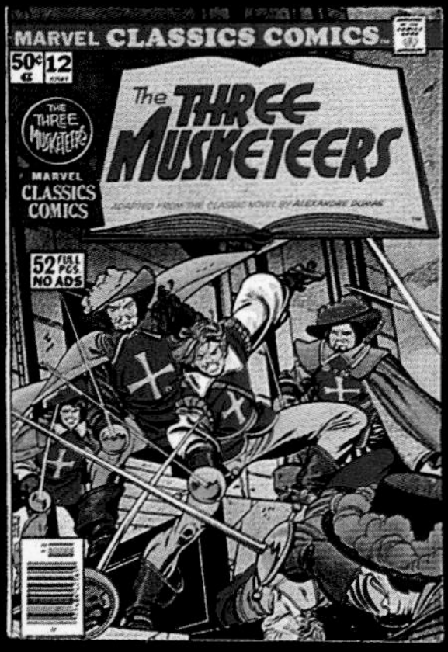
MARVEL CLASSICS COMICS
The THREE MUSKETEERS
52 FULL PGS NO ADS

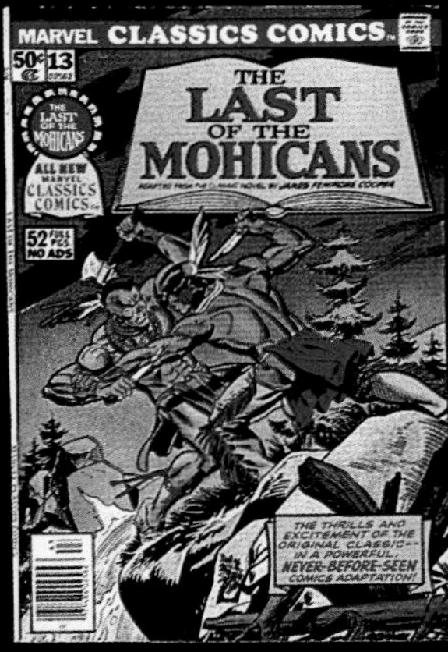
MARVEL CLASSICS COMICS
THE LAST OF THE MOHICANS

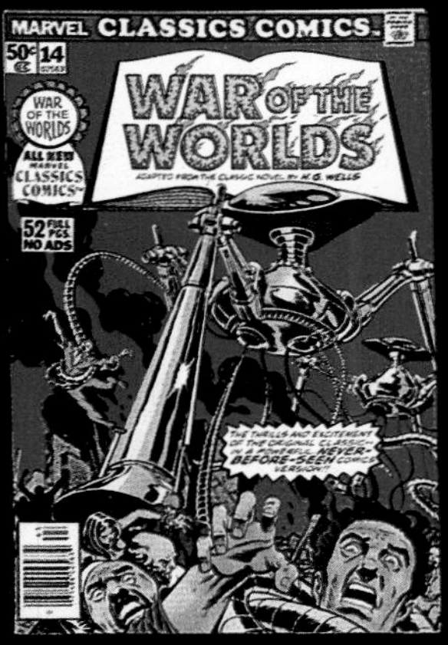
MARVEL CLASSICS COMICS
WAR OF THE WORLDS

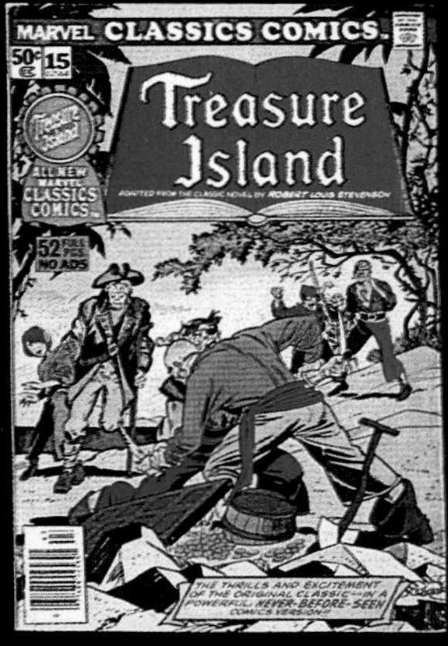
MARVEL CLASSICS COMICS
Treasure Island

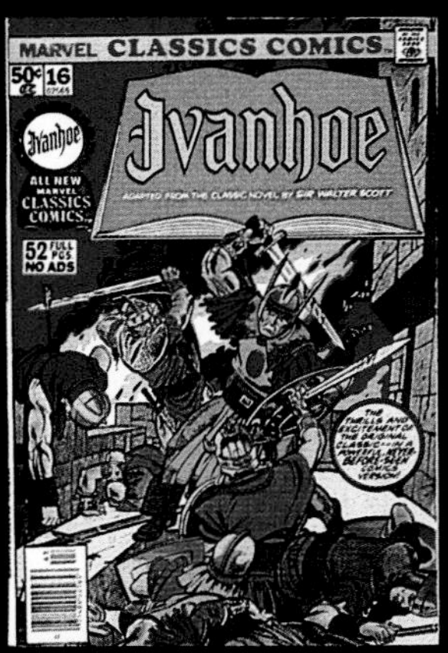
MARVEL CLASSICS COMICS
Ivanhoe

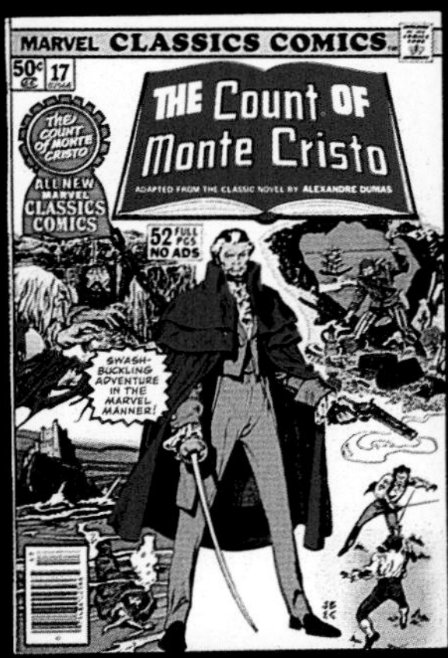
MARVEL CLASSICS COMICS
THE Count OF Monte Cristo

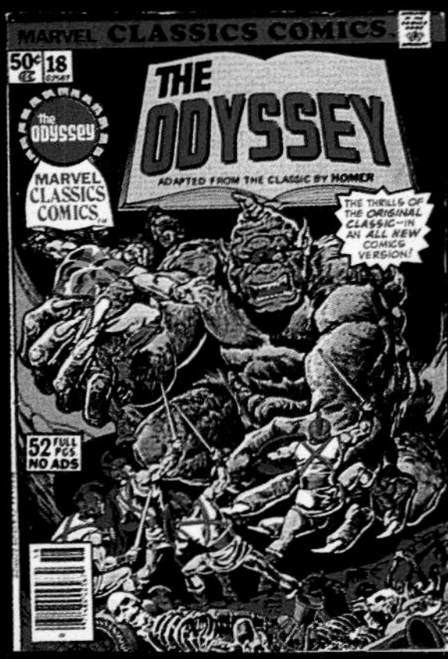
MARVEL CLASSICS COMICS
THE ODYSSEY

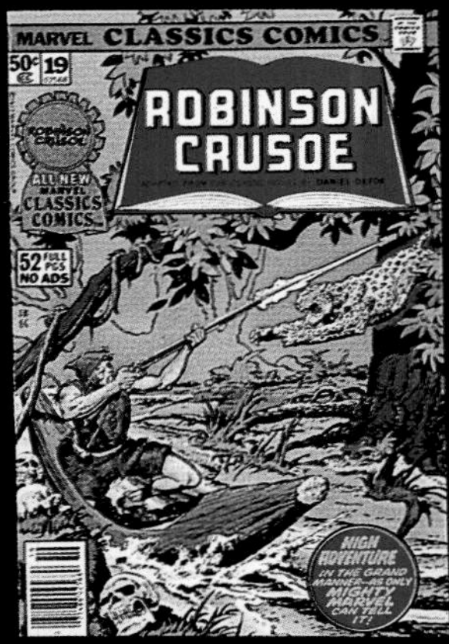
MARVEL CLASSICS COMICS
ROBINSON CRUSOE

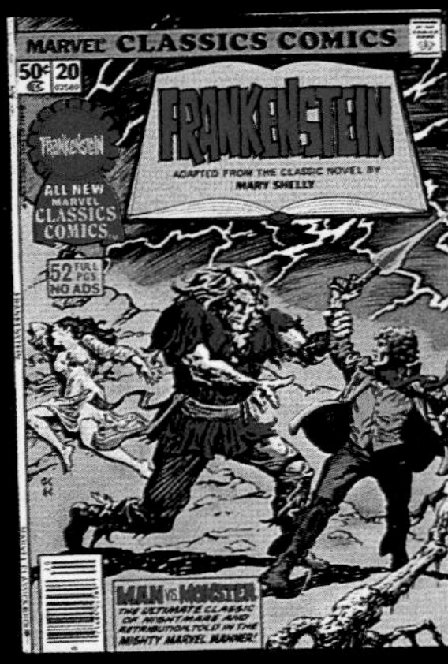
MARVEL CLASSICS COMICS
FRANKENSTEIN

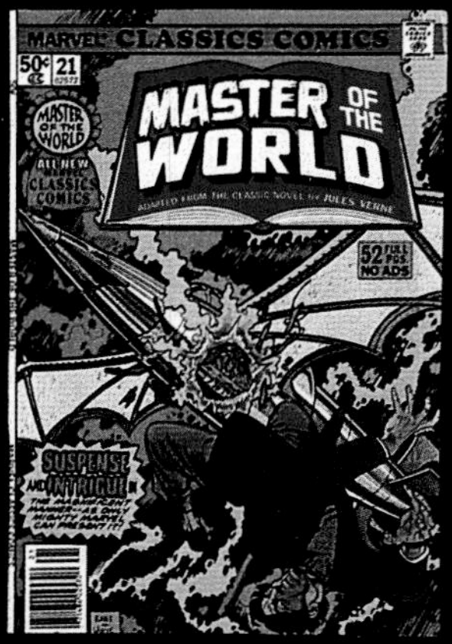
MARVEL CLASSICS COMICS
MASTER OF THE WORLD

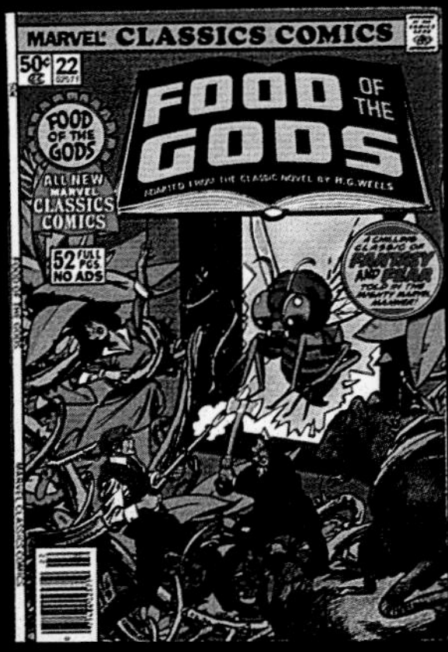
MARVEL CLASSICS COMICS
FOOD OF THE GODS

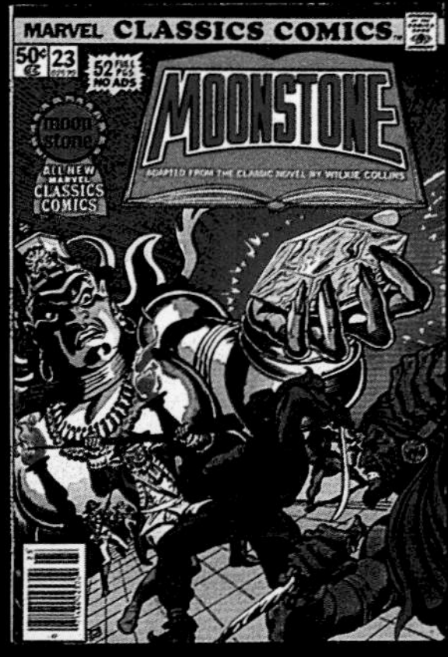
MARVEL CLASSICS COMICS
MOONSTONE

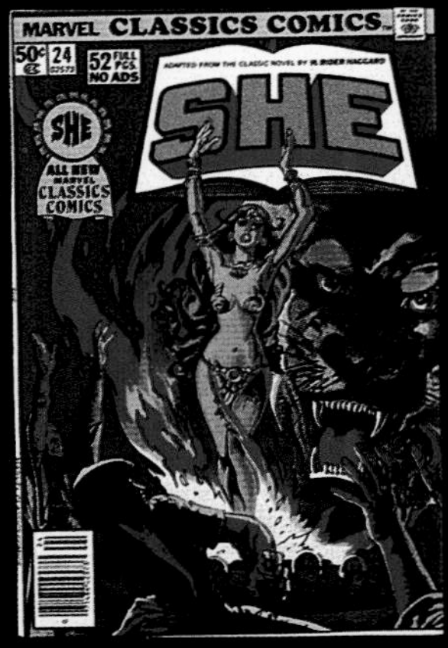
MARVEL CLASSICS COMICS
SHE

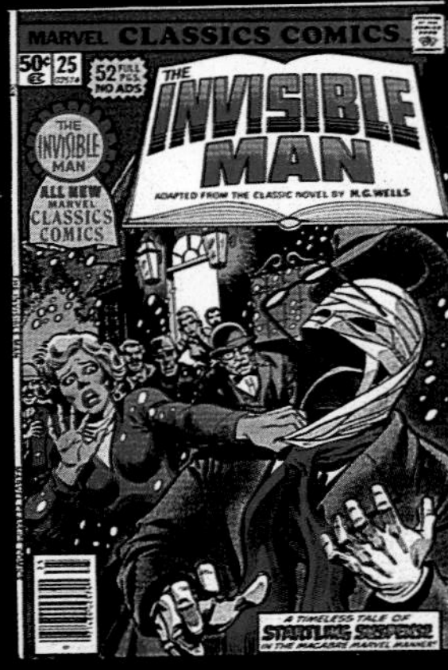
MARVEL CLASSICS COMICS
THE INVISIBLE MAN

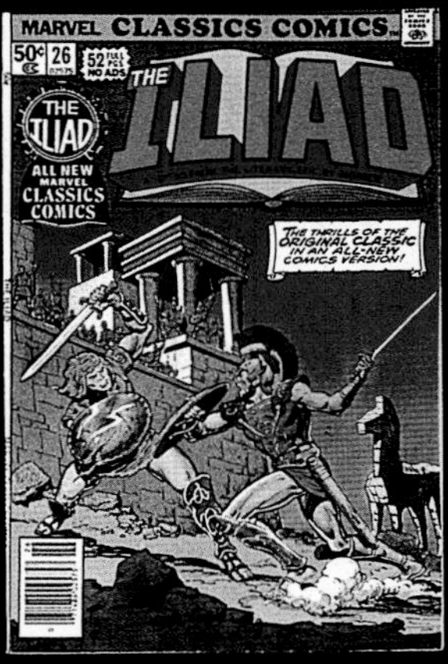
MARVEL CLASSICS COMICS
THE ILIAD

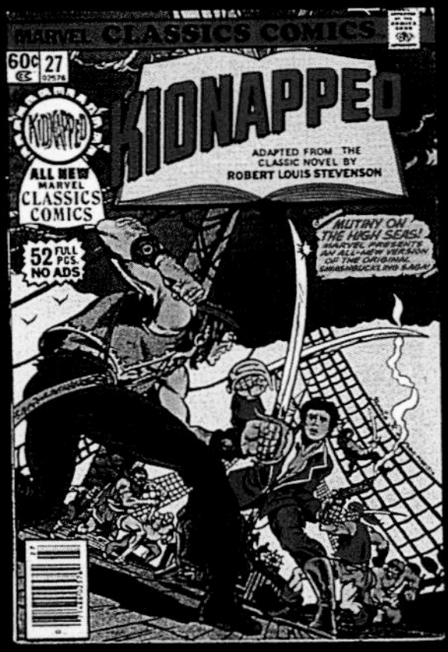
MARVEL CLASSICS COMICS
KIDNAPPED
ADAPTED FROM THE CLASSIC NOVEL BY ROBERT LOUIS STEVENSON

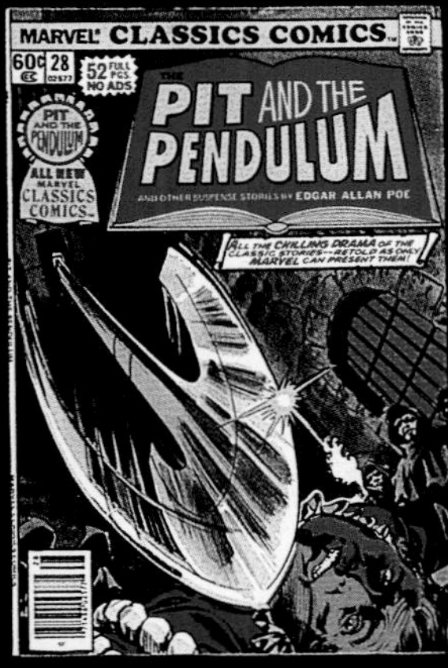
MARVEL CLASSICS COMICS
PIT AND THE PENDULUM

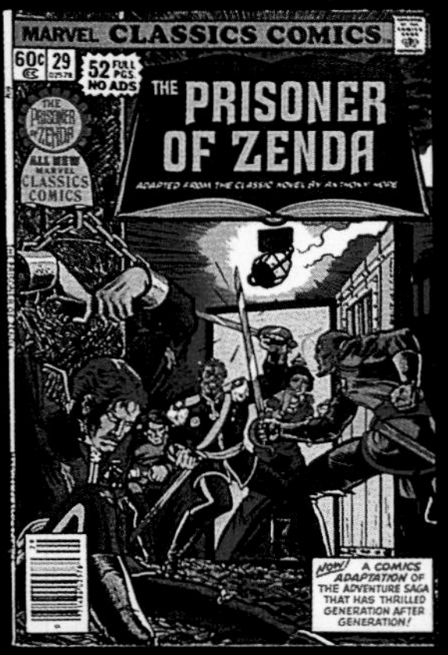
MARVEL CLASSICS COMICS
THE PRISONER OF ZENDA

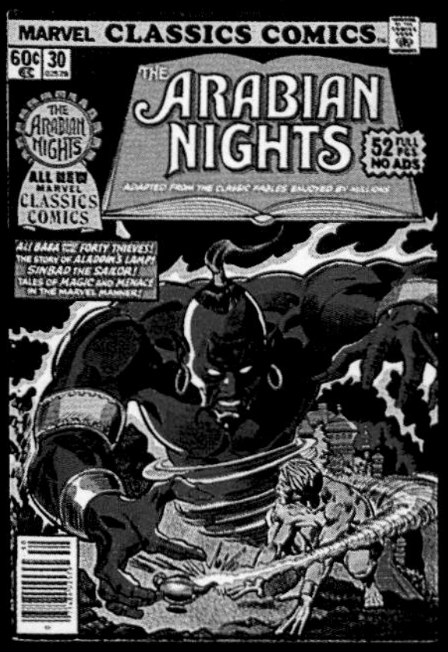
MARVEL CLASSICS COMICS
THE ARABIAN NIGHTS

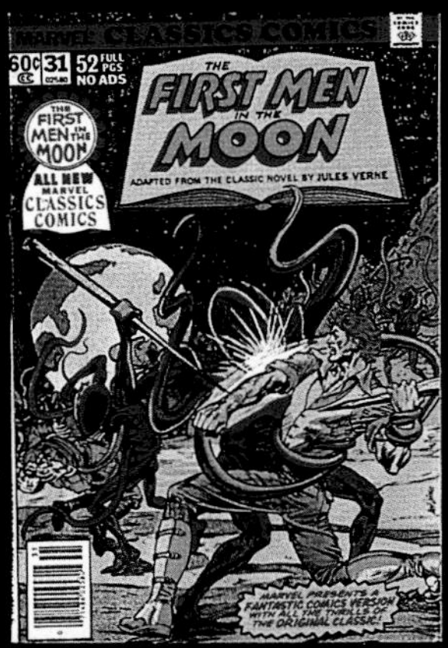
MARVEL CLASSICS COMICS
THE FIRST MEN IN THE MOON

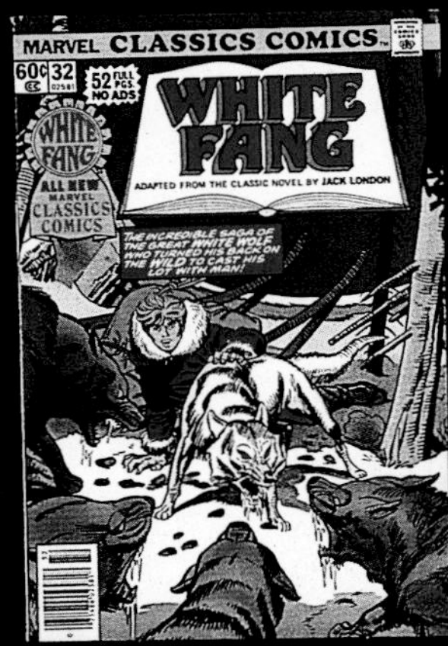
MARVEL CLASSICS COMICS
WHITE FANG
ADAPTED FROM THE CLASSIC NOVEL BY JACK LONDON

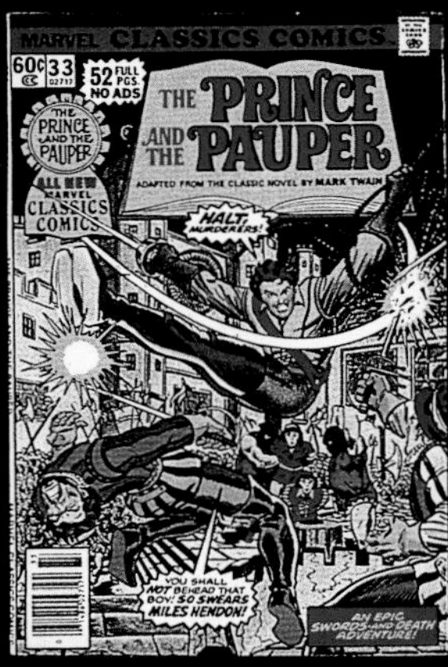
MARVEL CLASSICS COMICS
THE PRINCE AND THE PAUPER

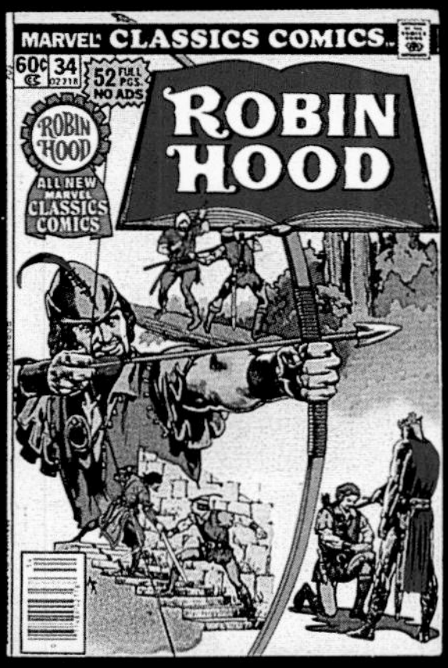
MARVEL CLASSICS COMICS
ROBIN HOOD

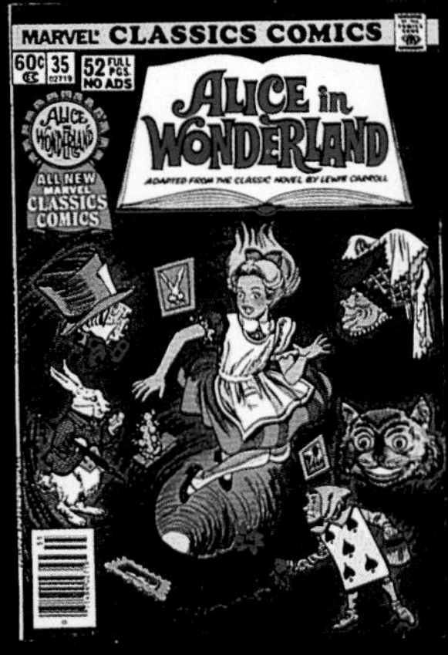
MARVEL CLASSICS COMICS
ALICE in WONDERLAND

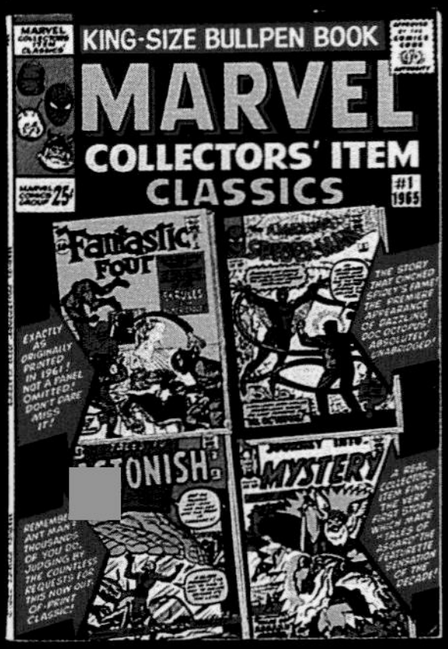
KING-SIZE BULLPEN BOOK
MARVEL
COLLECTORS' ITEM
CLASSICS
#1 1965

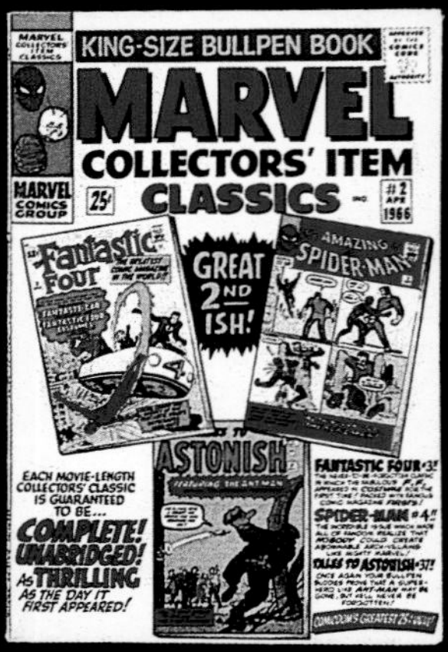
KING-SIZE BULLPEN BOOK
MARVEL
COLLECTORS' ITEM
CLASSICS
#2 1966
GREAT 2ND ISH!

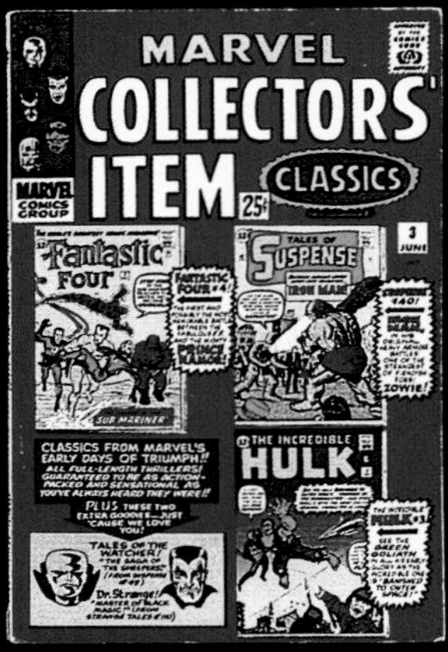
MARVEL
COLLECTORS' ITEM
CLASSICS
25¢
3 JUNE

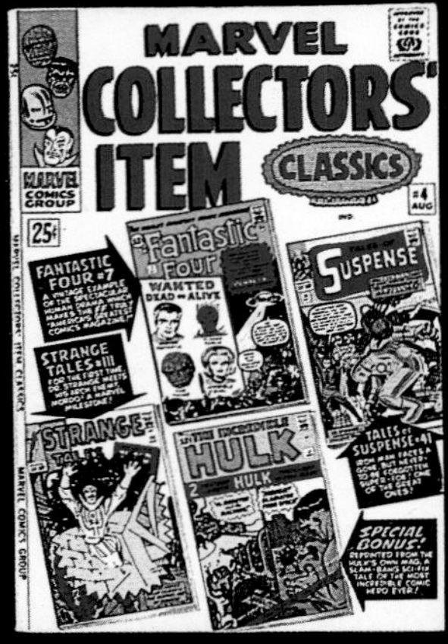
MARVEL
COLLECTORS' ITEM
CLASSICS
25¢
4 AUG

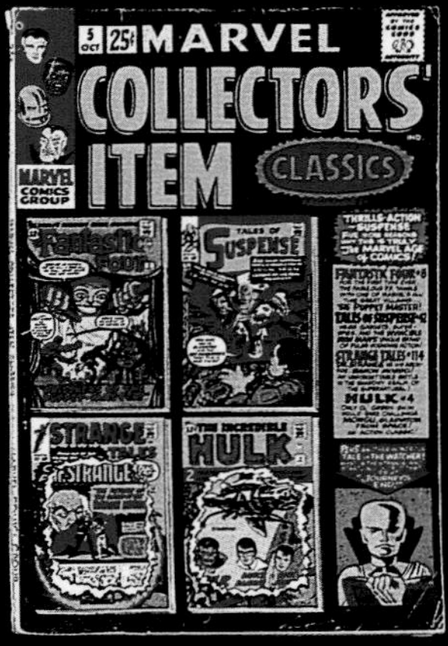
25¢ MARVEL
COLLECTORS' ITEM
CLASSICS

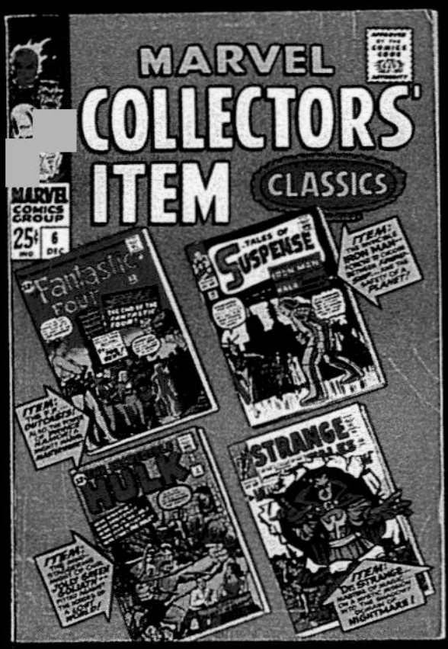
MARVEL
COLLECTORS' ITEM
CLASSICS
25¢

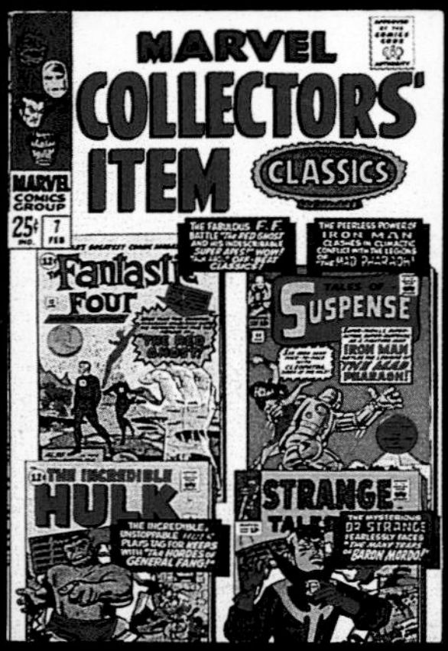
MARVEL
COLLECTORS' ITEM
CLASSICS
25¢
7 FEB

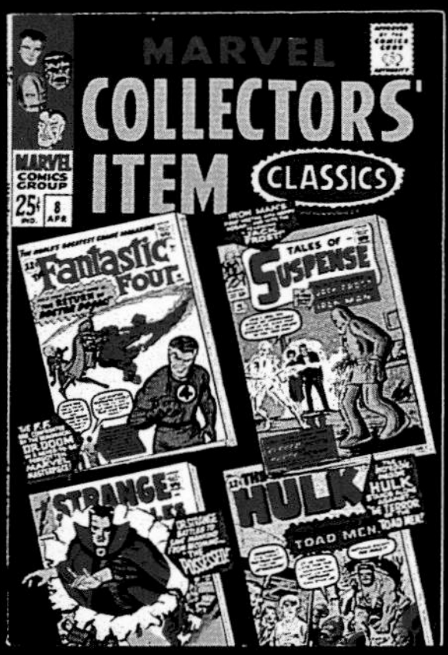
MARVEL
COLLECTORS' ITEM
CLASSICS
25¢
8 APR

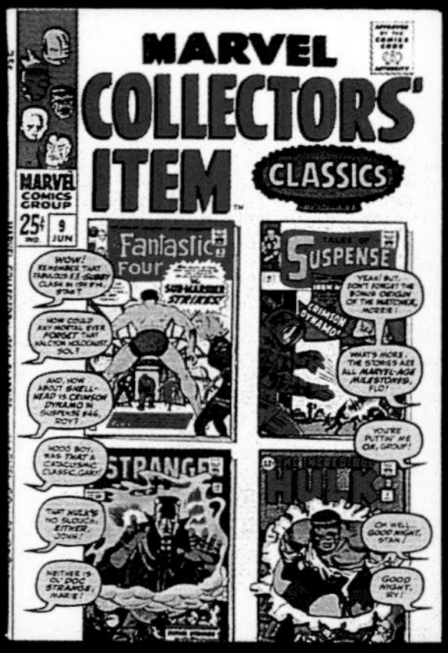
MARVEL
COLLECTORS' ITEM
CLASSICS
25¢
9

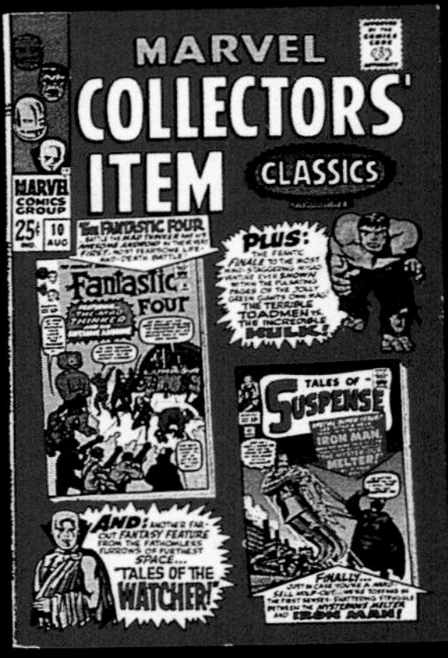
MARVEL
COLLECTORS' ITEM
CLASSICS
25¢
10

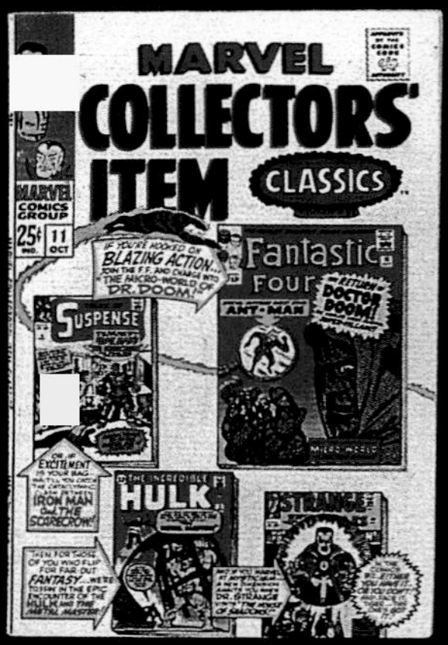
MARVEL
COLLECTORS' ITEM
CLASSICS
25¢
11 OCT

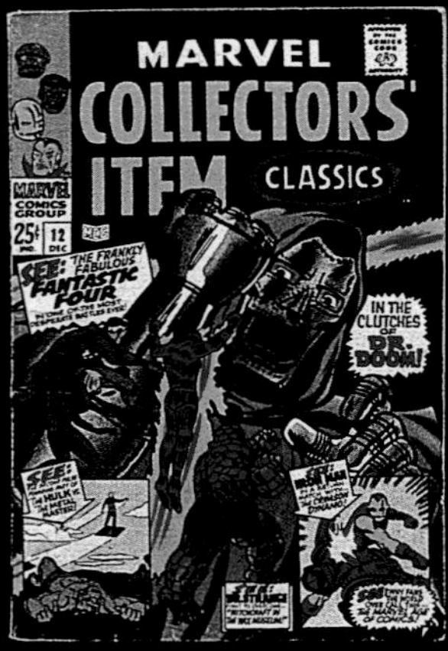
MARVEL
COLLECTORS' ITEM
CLASSICS
25¢
12

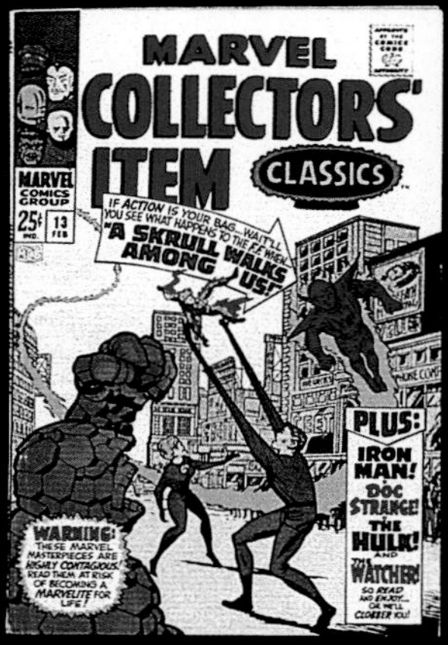
MARVEL
COLLECTORS' ITEM
CLASSICS
25¢
13 FEB
"A SKRULL WALKS AMONG US!"

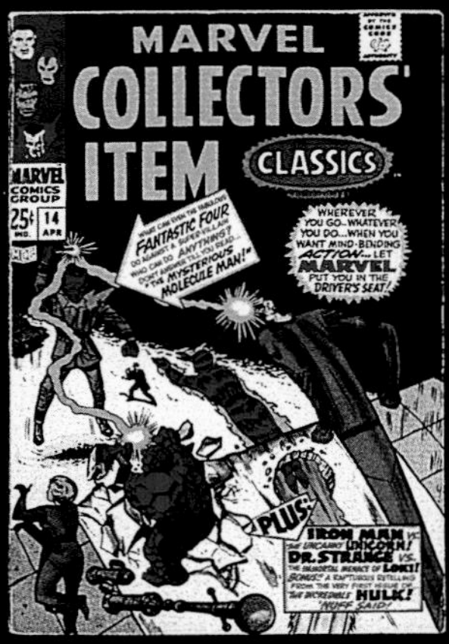
MARVEL
COLLECTORS' ITEM
CLASSICS
25¢
14 APR

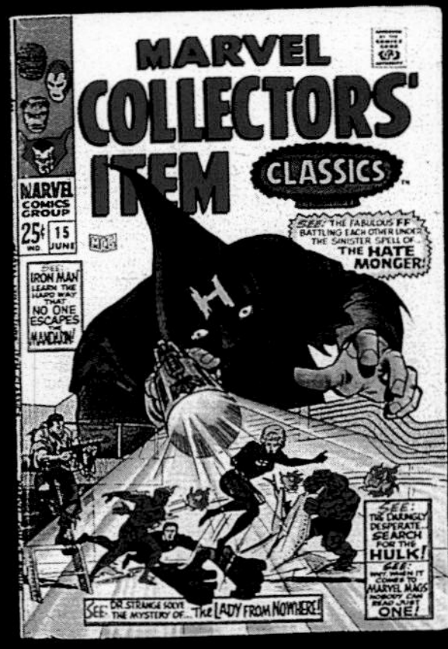
MARVEL
COLLECTORS' ITEM
CLASSICS
25¢
15 JUNE

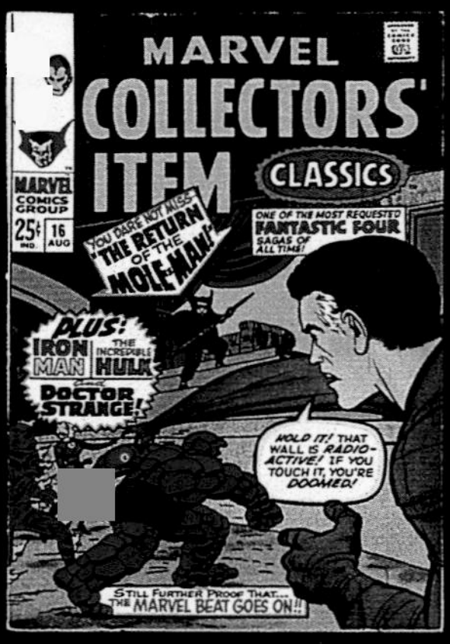
MARVEL
COLLECTORS' ITEM
CLASSICS
25¢
16 AUG
THE RETURN OF THE MOLE-MAN!

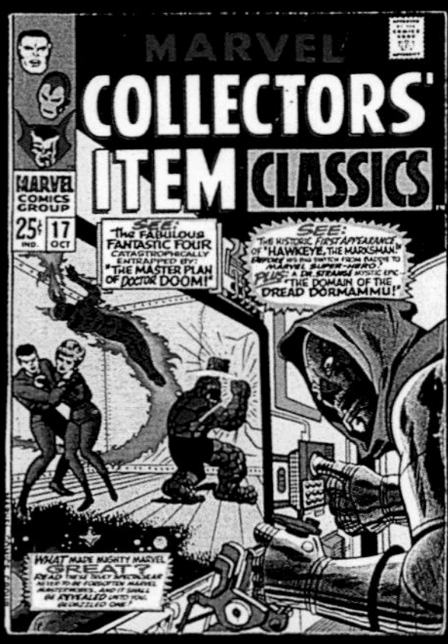
MARVEL
COLLECTORS' ITEM CLASSICS
25¢
17 OCT

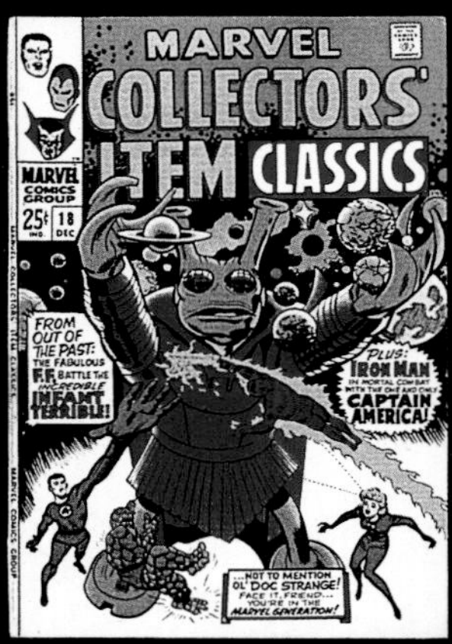
MARVEL
COLLECTORS' ITEM CLASSICS
25¢
18 DEC

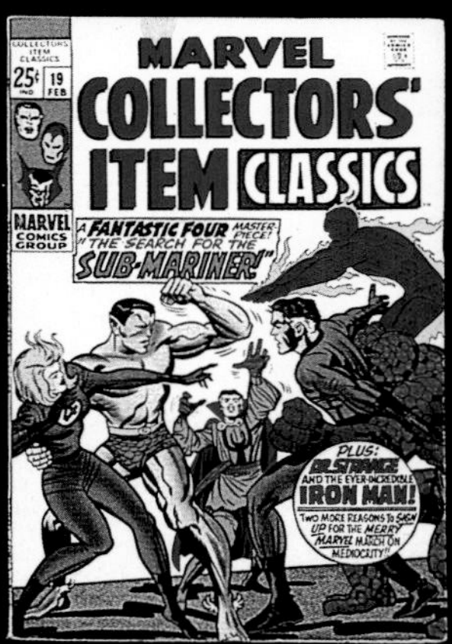
MARVEL
COLLECTORS' ITEM CLASSICS
25¢
19 FEB

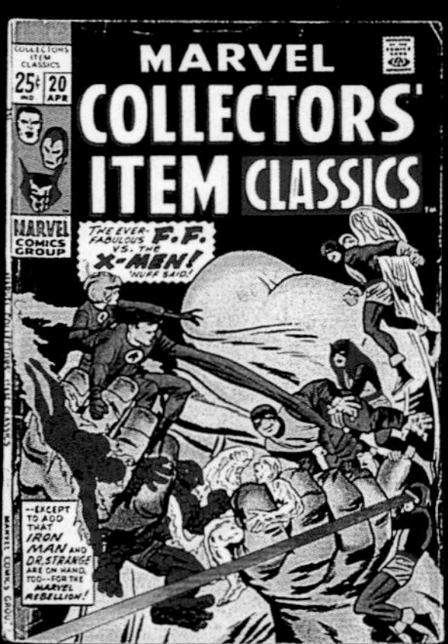
MARVEL
COLLECTORS' ITEM CLASSICS
25¢
20

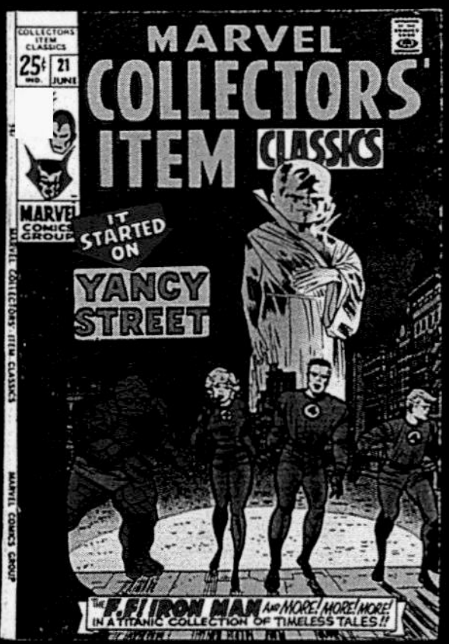
MARVEL
COLLECTORS' ITEM CLASSICS
25¢
21 JUNE
IT STARTED ON YANCY STREET

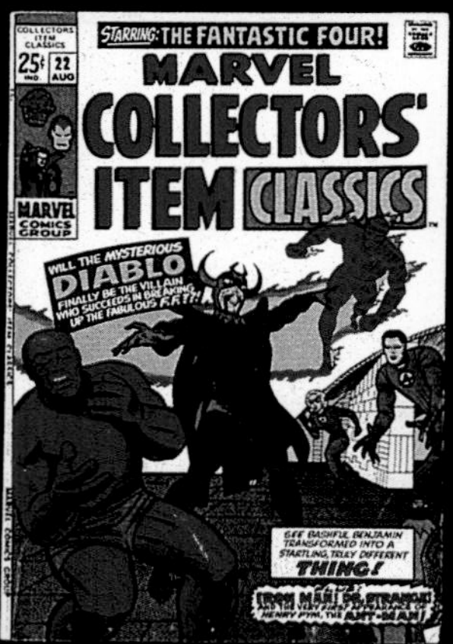
STARRING: THE FANTASTIC FOUR!
MARVEL
COLLECTORS' ITEM CLASSICS
25¢
22 AUG

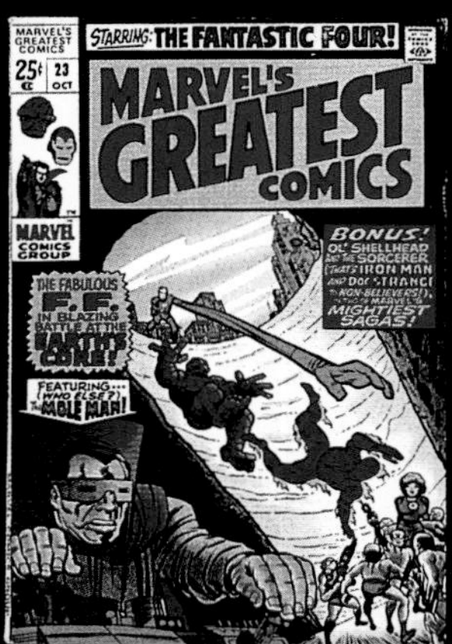
STARRING: THE FANTASTIC FOUR!
MARVEL'S GREATEST COMICS
25¢
23 OCT

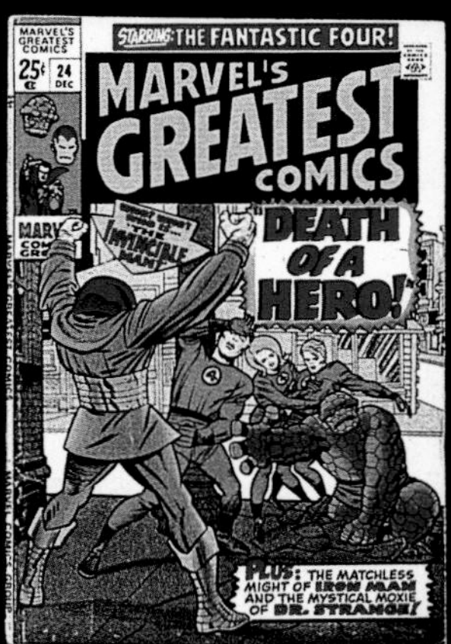
STARRING: THE FANTASTIC FOUR!
MARVEL'S GREATEST COMICS
25¢
24 DEC
"DEATH OF A HERO!"

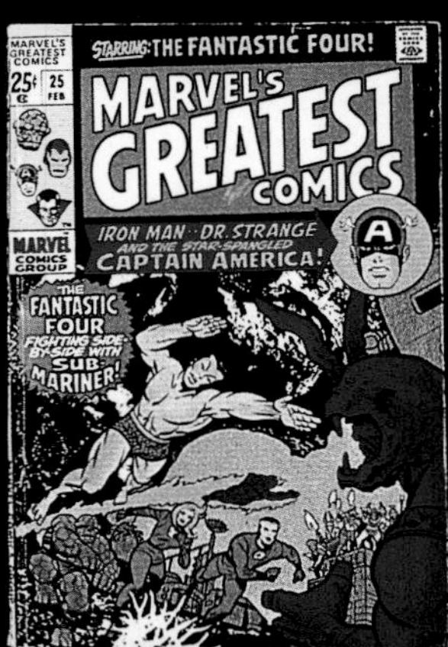
STARRING: THE FANTASTIC FOUR!
MARVEL'S GREATEST COMICS
25¢
25 FEB
IRON MAN · DR STRANGE
CAPTAIN AMERICA!

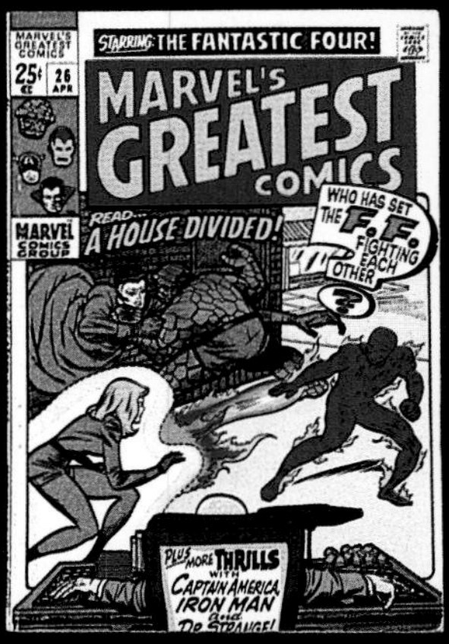
Starring: The Fantastic Four!
Marvel's Greatest Comics
Read... A House Divided!
Who has set the F.F. fighting each other?
Plus more thrills with Captain America, Iron Man and Dr. Strange!

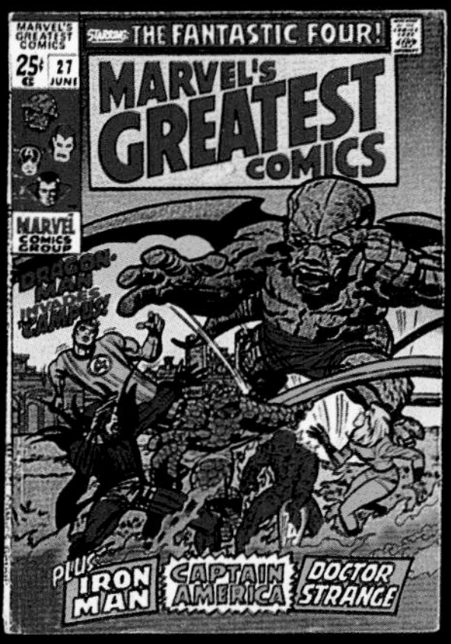
Starring: The Fantastic Four!
Marvel's Greatest Comics
Plus: Iron Man, Captain America, Doctor Strange

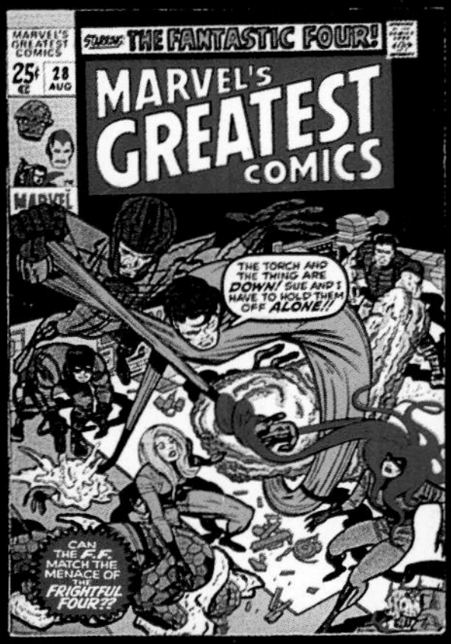
Starring: The Fantastic Four!
Marvel's Greatest Comics
The Torch and the Thing are down! Sue and I have to hold them off alone!
Can they match the menace of the Frightful Four?

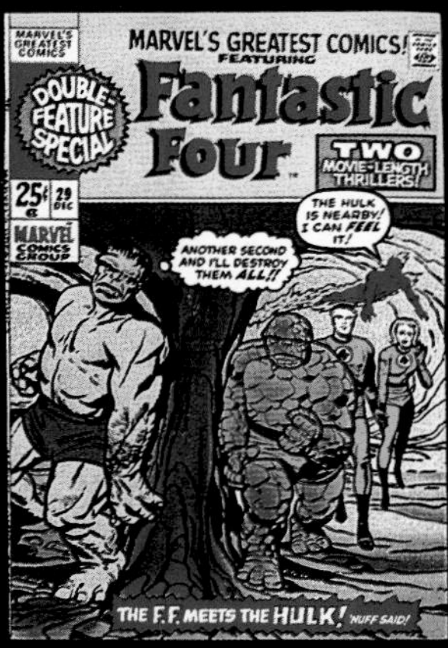
Marvel's Greatest Comics! featuring
Double Feature Special
Fantastic Four
Two movie-length thrillers!
The Hulk is nearby! I can feel it!
Another second and I'll destroy them all!!
The F.F. meets the Hulk! 'Nuff said!

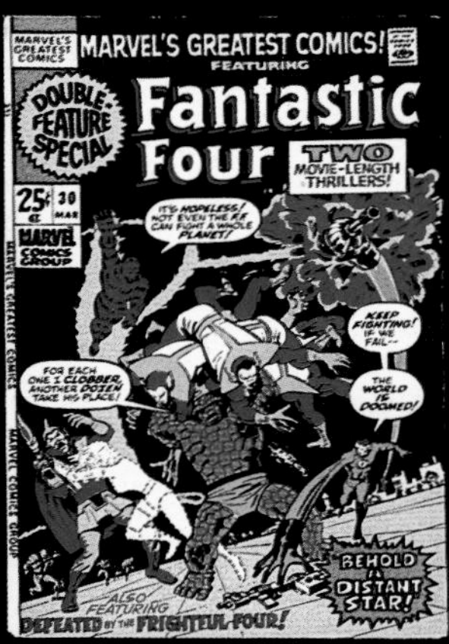
Marvel's Greatest Comics! featuring
Double Feature Special
Fantastic Four
Two movie-length thrillers!
Keep fighting! We can't fail!
Behold a distant star!
Defeated by the Frightful Four!

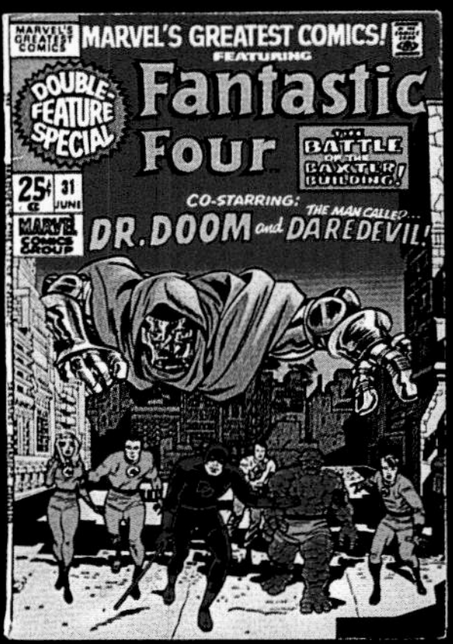
Marvel's Greatest Comics! featuring
Double Feature Special
Fantastic Four
The battle of the Baxter Building!
Co-starring: The man called... Dr. Doom and Daredevil!

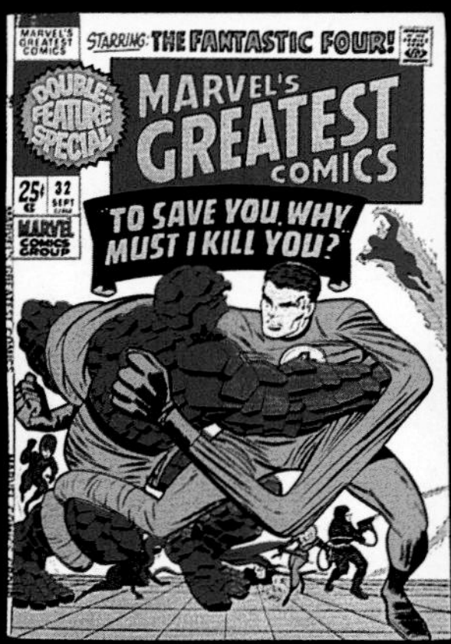
Starring: The Fantastic Four!
Double Feature Special
Marvel's Greatest Comics
To save you, why must I kill you?

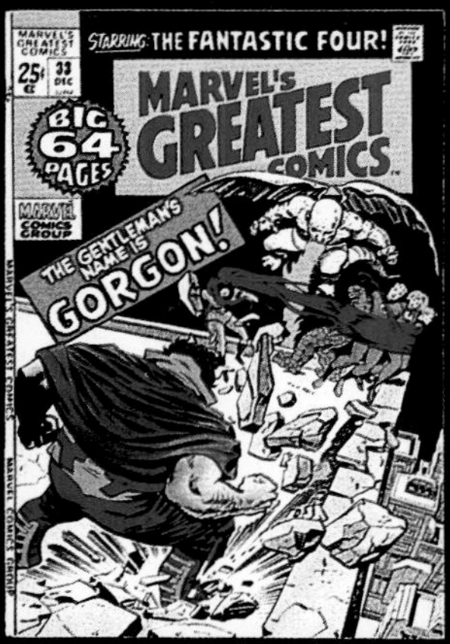
Starring: The Fantastic Four!
Big 64 Pages
Marvel's Greatest Comics
The Gentleman's name is... Gorgon!

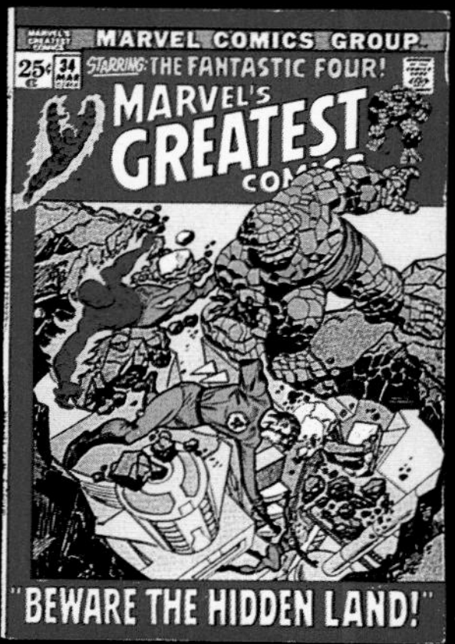
Marvel Comics Group
Starring: The Fantastic Four!
Marvel's Greatest Comics
"Beware the Hidden Land!"

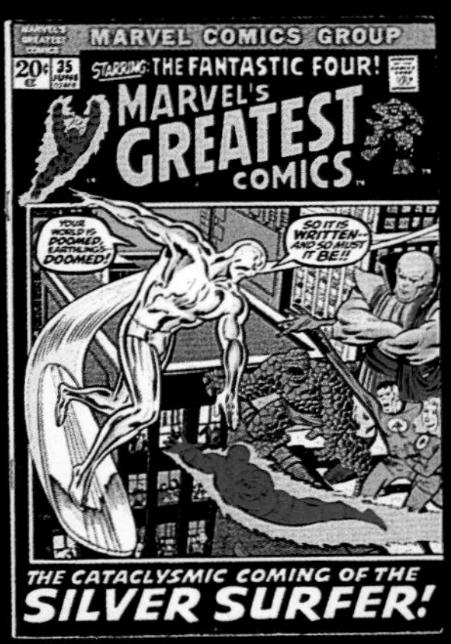
Marvel Comics Group
Starring: The Fantastic Four!
Marvel's Greatest Comics
The cataclysmic coming of the Silver Surfer!

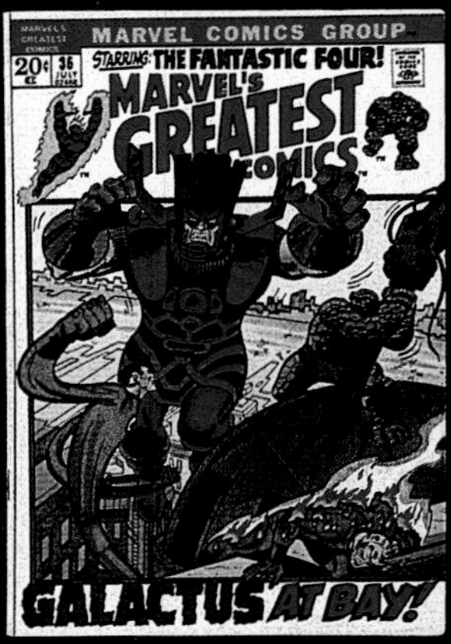
Marvel Comics Group
Starring: The Fantastic Four!
Marvel's Greatest Comics
Galactus at Bay!

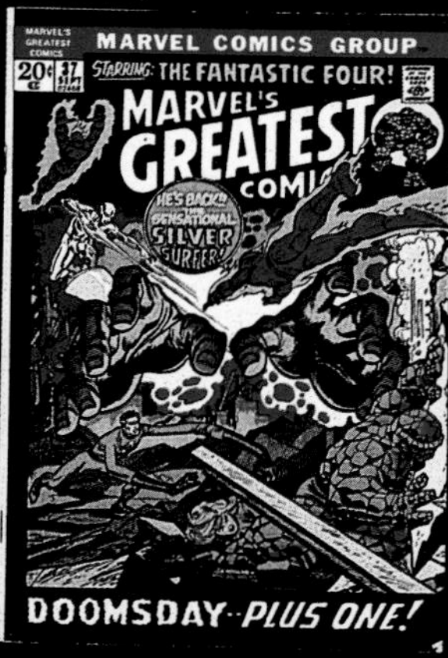
Marvel Comics Group
Starring: The Fantastic Four!
Marvel's Greatest Comics
He's back! The sensational Silver Surfer!
Doomsday Plus One!

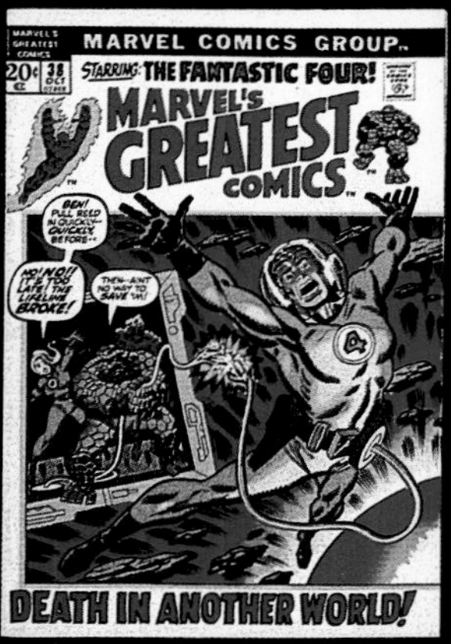
Marvel Comics Group
Starring: The Fantastic Four!
Marvel's Greatest Comics
Death in Another World!

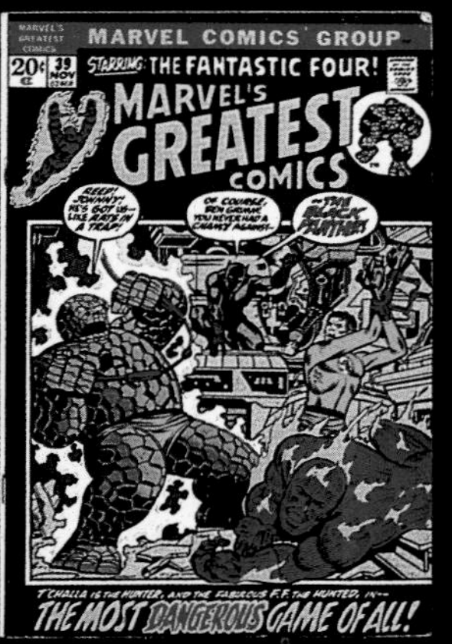
Marvel Comics Group
Starring: The Fantastic Four!
Marvel's Greatest Comics
The Most Dangerous Game of All!

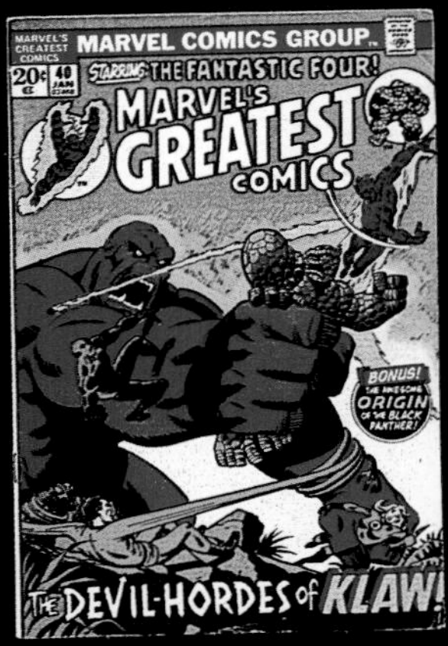
Marvel Comics Group
Starring: The Fantastic Four!
Marvel's Greatest Comics
Bonus! The awesome origin of the Black Panther!
The Devil-Hordes of Klaw!

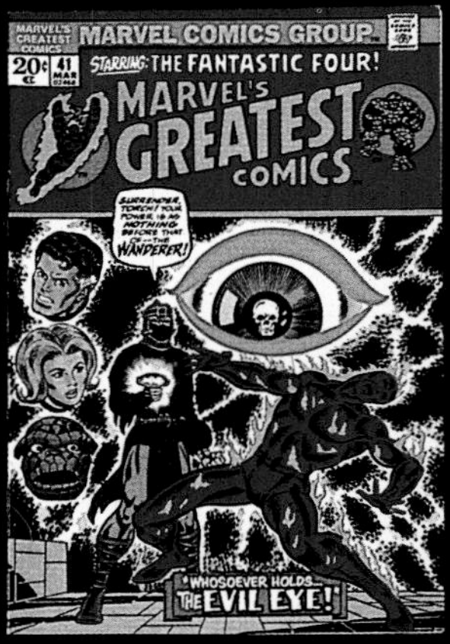
Marvel Comics Group
Starring: The Fantastic Four!
Marvel's Greatest Comics
Whosoever holds... The Evil Eye!

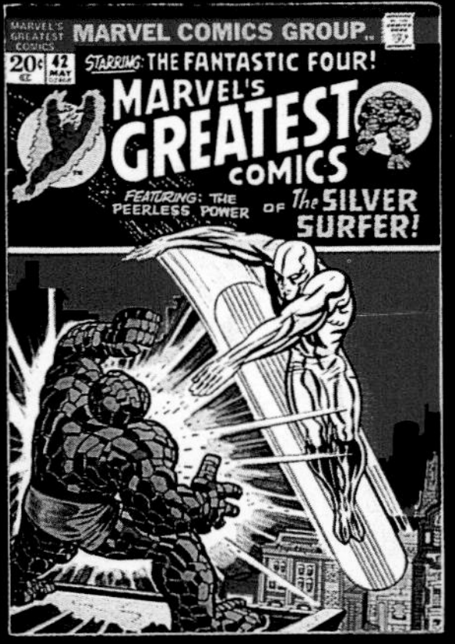
Marvel Comics Group
Starring: The Fantastic Four!
Marvel's Greatest Comics
Featuring: the peerless power of The Silver Surfer!

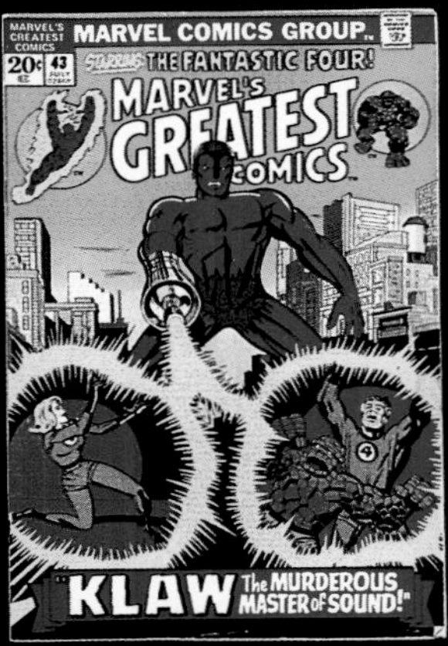
Marvel Comics Group
Starring: The Fantastic Four!
Marvel's Greatest Comics
Klaw The murderous master of sound!

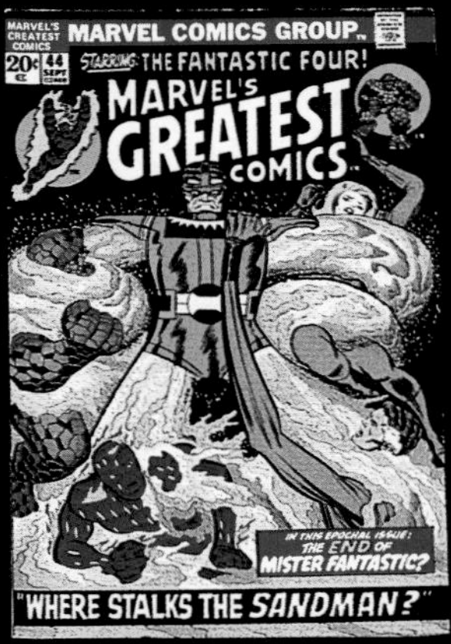
Marvel Comics Group
Starring: The Fantastic Four!
Marvel's Greatest Comics
In this epochal issue: The end of Mister Fantastic?
"Where Stalks the Sandman?"

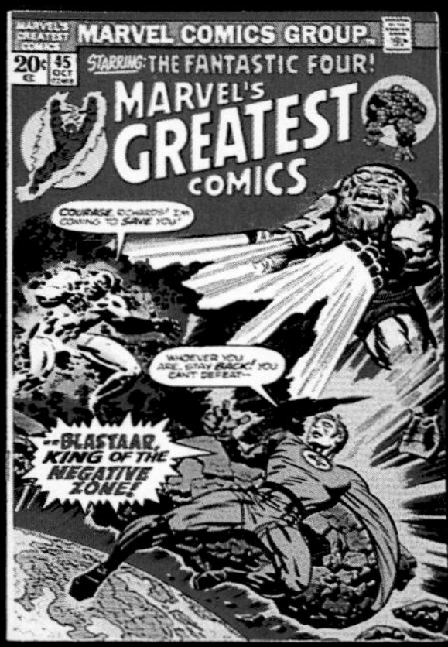
Marvel Comics Group
Starring: The Fantastic Four!
Marvel's Greatest Comics
Blastaar King of the Negative Zone!

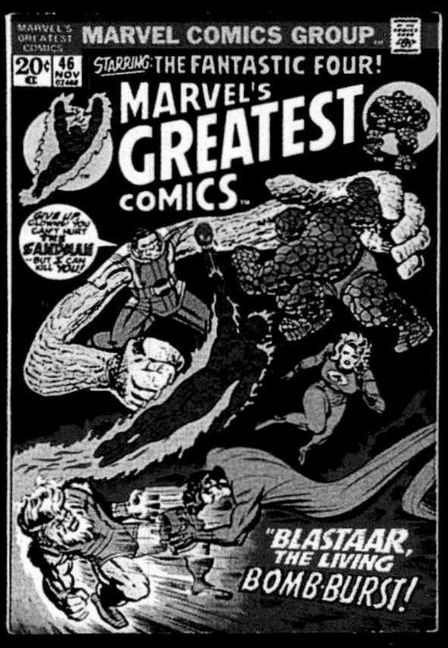
Marvel Comics Group
Starring: The Fantastic Four!
Marvel's Greatest Comics
"Blastaar, the Living Bomb-Burst!"

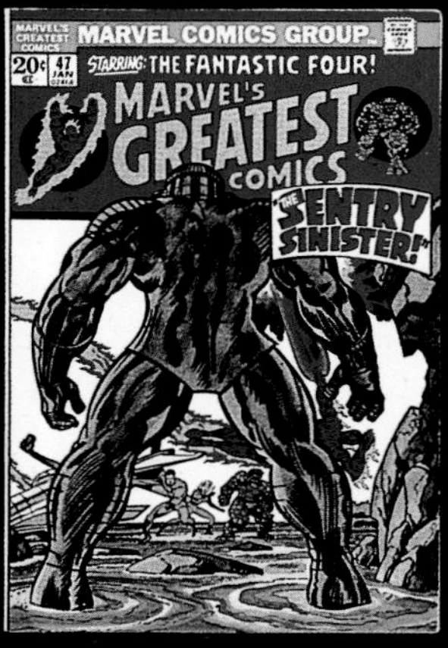
Marvel Comics Group
Starring: The Fantastic Four!
Marvel's Greatest Comics
The Sentry Sinister!

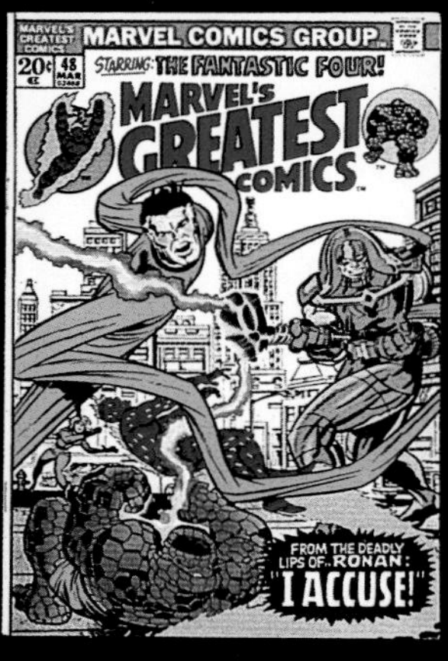
Marvel Comics Group
Starring: The Fantastic Four!
Marvel's Greatest Comics
From the deadly lips of Ronan: I Accuse!

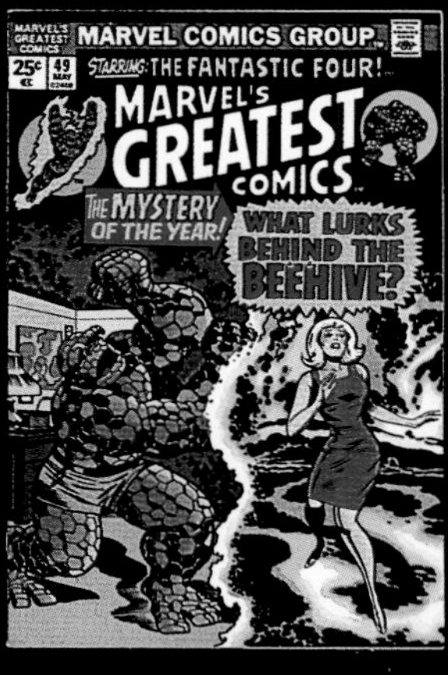
Marvel Comics Group
Starring: The Fantastic Four!
Marvel's Greatest Comics
The Mystery of the Year!
What Lurks Behind the Beehive?

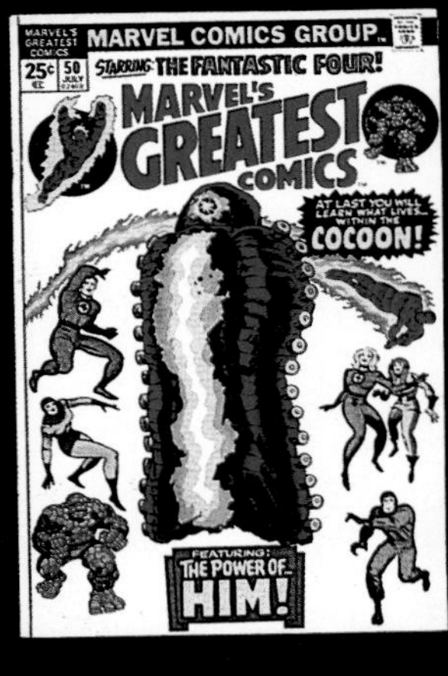
Marvel Comics Group
Starring: The Fantastic Four!
Marvel's Greatest Comics
At last you will learn what lives within the Cocoon!
Featuring: The Power of... Him!

1214.8 Marvel Double Feature (1-21)

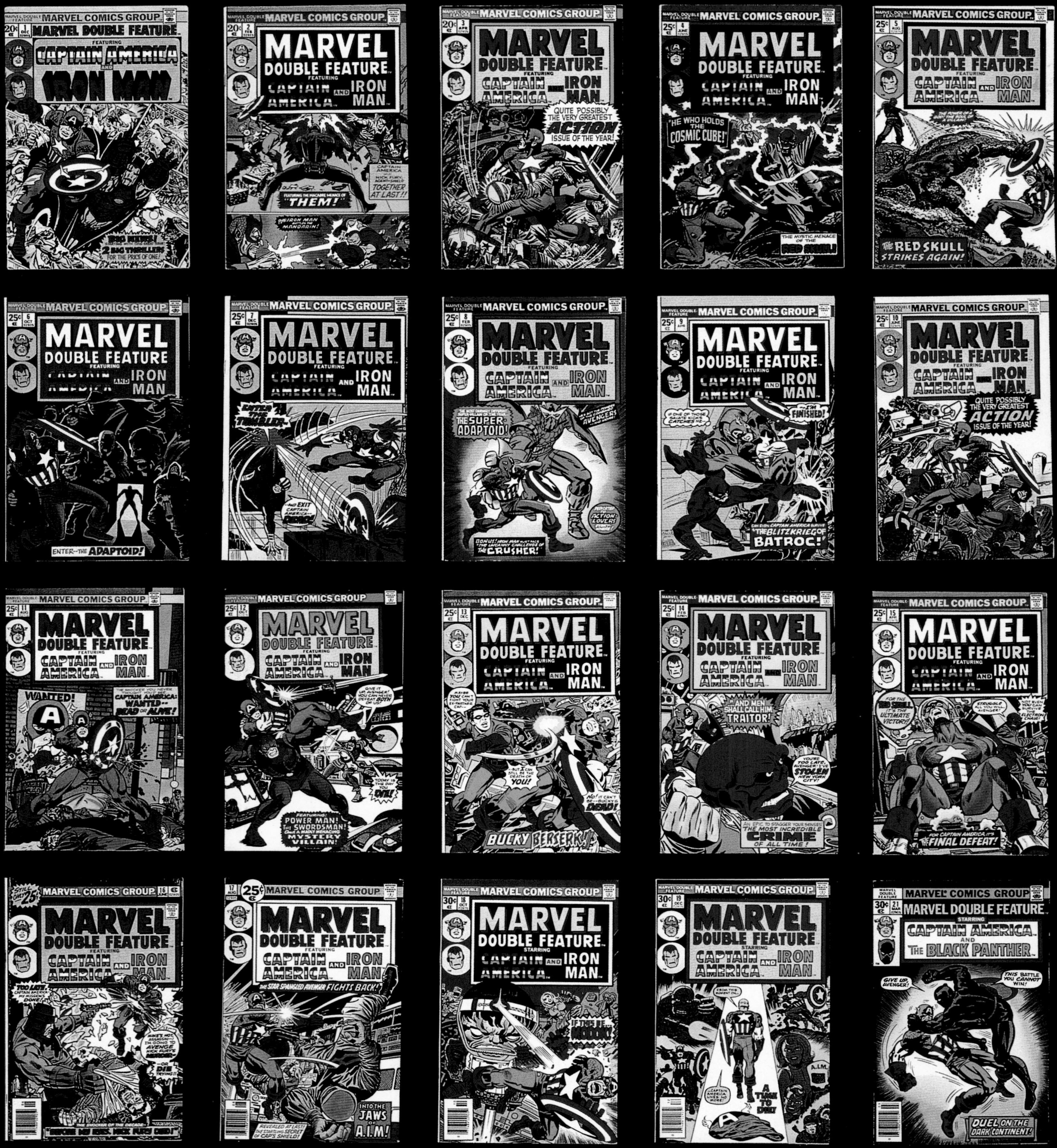
MARVEL COMICS GROUP
MARVEL DOUBLE FEATURE
FEATURING
CAPTAIN AMERICA AND IRON MAN
QUITE POSSIBLY THE VERY GREATEST ACTION ISSUE OF THE YEAR!
"HE WHO HOLDS THE COSMIC CUBE!"
THE MYSTIC MENACE OF THE RED SKULL!
THE RED SKULL STRIKES AGAIN!
ENTER--THE ADAPTOID!
THE SUPER-ADAPTOID!
THE BLITZKRIEG OF BATROC!
FINISHED!
WANTED!
BUCKY BERSERK!
TRAITOR!
FOR CAPTAIN AMERICA, IT'S THE FINAL DEFEAT!
THE STAR SPANGLED AVENGER FIGHTS BACK!
INTO THE JAWS OF A.I.M.!
STARRING
CAPTAIN AMERICA AND THE BLACK PANTHER
THIS BATTLE YOU CANNOT WIN!
GIVE UP, AVENGER!
DUEL ON THE DARK CONTINENT!

Marvel Collectors Item Classics (1-22) 1214.5

Ref. No.	Date	RVI	Artist/Info.	
1214.5-1	Feb. 1965	20	Ditko/Kirby-a	Reprints
1214.5-2	Apr. 1966	10	"	"
1214.5-3	Jun.	9	"	"
1214.5-4	Aug.	8	"	"
1214.5-5	Oct.	5	"	"
1214.5-6	Dec.	4	"	"
1214.5-7	Feb. 1967	4	"	"
1214.5-8	Apr.	4	"	"
1214.5-9	Jun.	4	"	"
1214.5-10	**Aug.**	**4**	**"**	**"**
1214.5-11	Oct.	3	"	"
1214.5-12	Dec.	3	"	"
1214.5-13	Feb. 1968	3	"	"
1214.5-14	Apr.	3	"	"
1214.5-15	Jun.	3	"	"
1214.5-16	Aug.	3	"	"
1214.5-17	Oct.	3	"	"
1214.5-18	Dec.	3	"	"
1214.5-19	Feb. 1969	3	"	"
1214.5-20	**Apr.**	**3**	**"**	**"**
1214.5-21	Jun.	3	"	"
1214.5-22	Aug. 1969	3	"	"

Contunues on as **Marvel's Greatest Comics** (23-96)

Ref. No.	Date	RVI	Artist/Info.	
1214.5-23	Oct. 1969	2	Ditko/Kirby-a	Reprints
1214.5-24	Dec.	2	"	"
1214.5-25	Feb. 1970	2	"	"
1214.5-26	Apr.	2	"	"
1214.5-27	Jun.	2	"	"
1214.5-28	Aug.	2	"	"
1214.5-29	Dec.	2	Kirby-a	"
1214.5-30	**Mar. 1971**	**2**	**"**	**"**
1214.5-31	Jun.	1	"	"
1214.5-32	Sept.	1	"	"
1214.5-33	Dec.	1	"	"
1214.5-34	Mar. 1972	1	"	"
1214.5-35	Jun.	1	"	"
1214.5-36	Jul.	1	"	"
1214.5-37	Sept.	1	"	"
1214.5-38	Oct.	1	"	"
1214.5-39	Nov.	1	"	"
1214.5-40	**Jan. 1973**	**1**	**"**	**"**
1214.5-41	Mar.	1	"	"
1214.5-42	May	1	"	"
1214.5-43	Jul.	1	"	"
1214.5-44	Sept.	1	"	"
1214.5-45	Oct.	1	"	"
1214.5-46 to 96	Jan. 1981, (#96)	1	"	"

Marvel Double Feature (1-21) 1214.8

Ref. No.	Date	RVI	Artist/Info.
1214.8-1	Dec. 1973	2	Kirby, Colan-a
1214.8-2	Feb. 1974	1	" "
1214.8-3	Apr.	1	" "
1214.8-4	Jun.	1	" "
1214.8-5	Aug.	1	" "
1214.8-6	Oct.	1	" "
1214.8-7	Dec.	1	" "
1214.8-8	Feb. 1975	1	" "
1214.8-9	Apr.	1	Colan-a
1214.8-10	**Jun.**	**1**	**"**
1214.8-11	Aug.	1	"
1214.8-12	Oct.	1	"
1214.8-13	Dec.	1	"
1214.8-14	Feb. 1976	1	"
1214.8-15	Apr.	1	Kane, Colan-a
1214.8-16	Jun.	1	Colan-a
1214.8-17	Aug.	1	Kirby-c/a, Colan-a
1214.8-18	Oct.	2	" "
1214.8-19	Dec.	2	" "
1214.8-20	**Feb. 1977**	**1**	**Kirby-c**
1214.8-21	Mar. 1977	1	

1215.1 Marvel Fanfare (1-25)

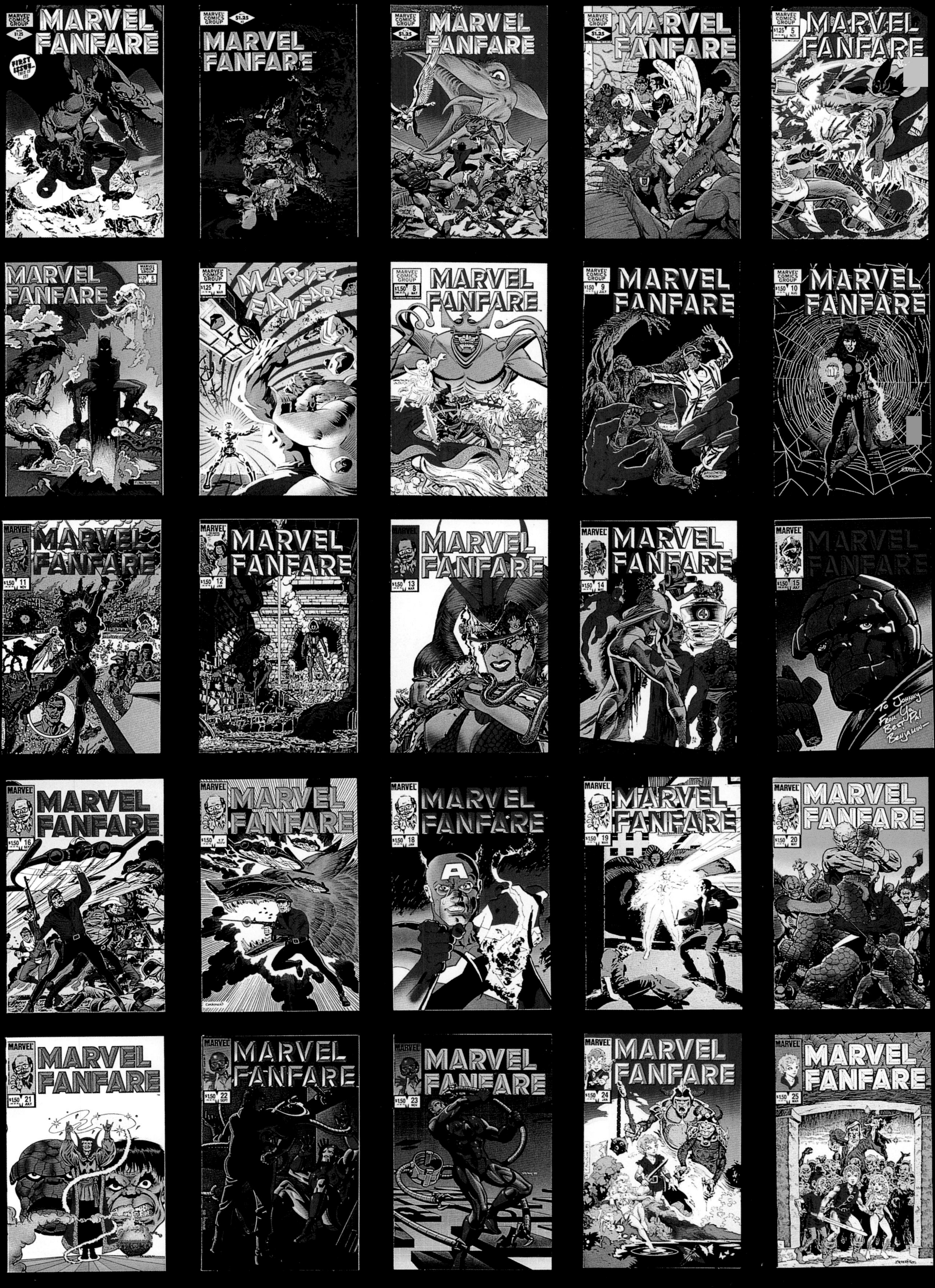

1215.1 Marvel Fanfare (26-35)

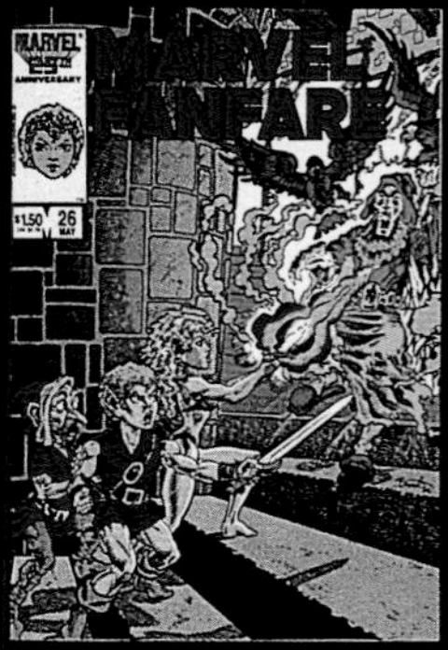

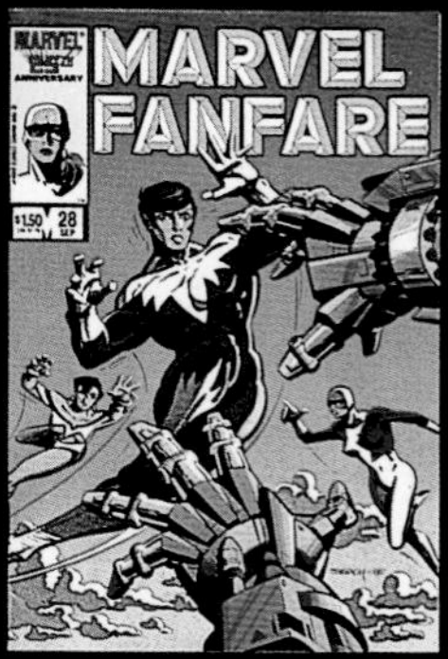

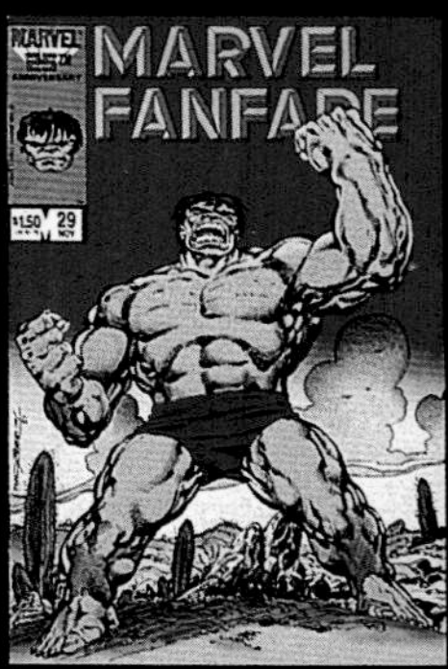

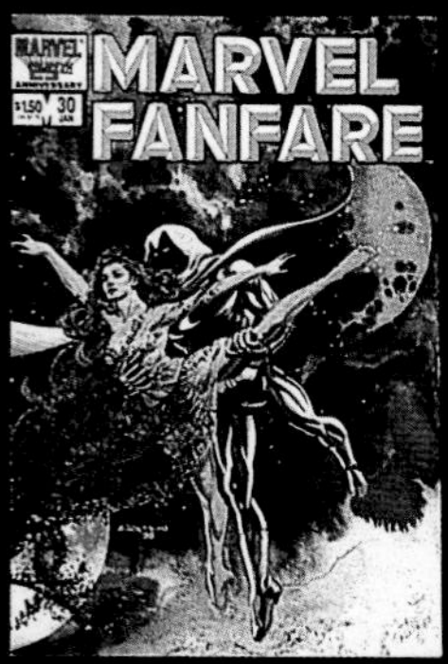

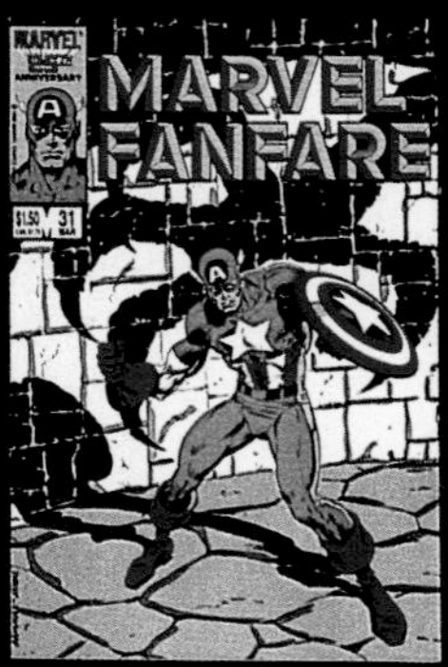

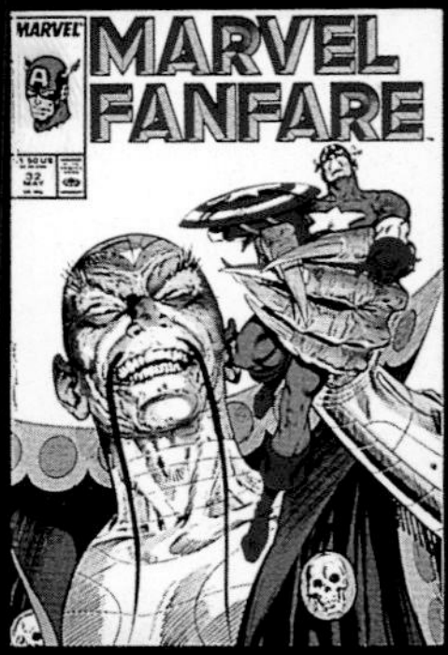

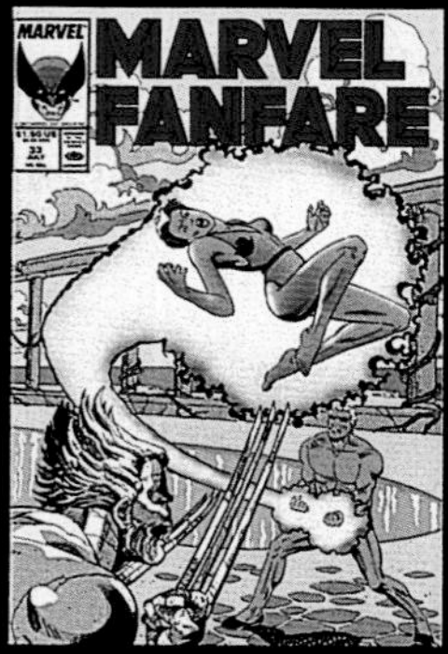

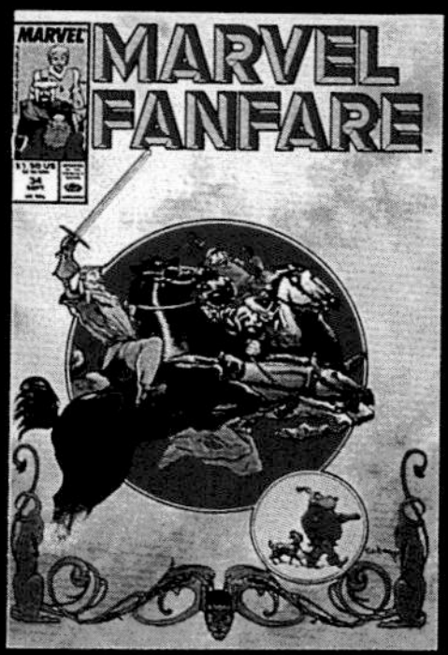

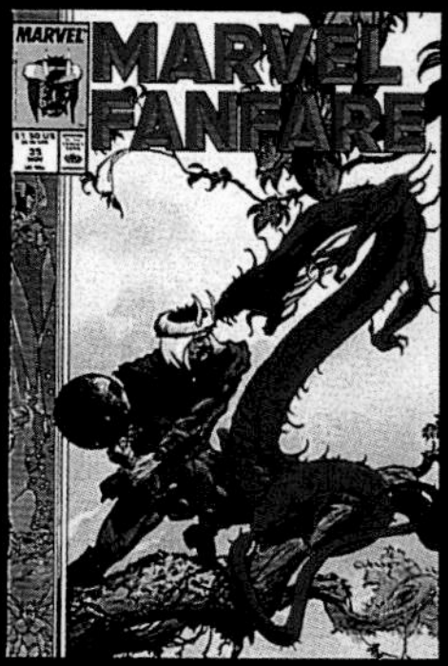

1215.2 Marvel Feature '71 (1-12)

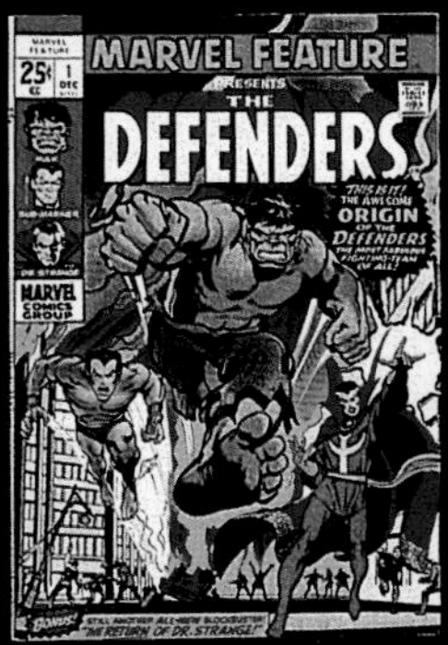

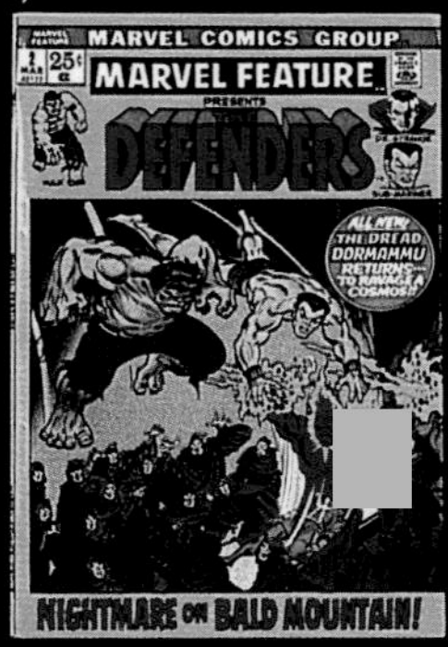

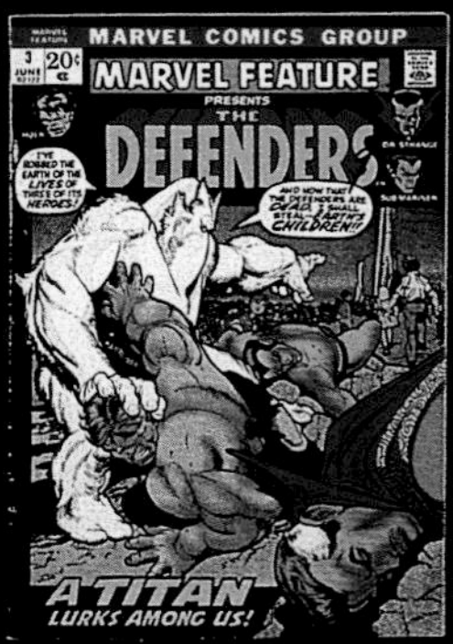

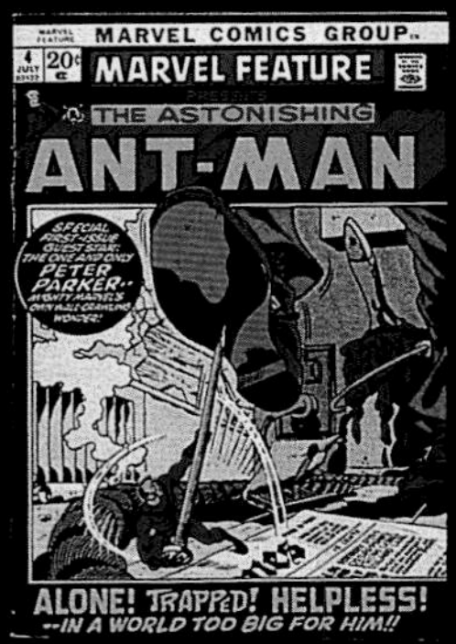

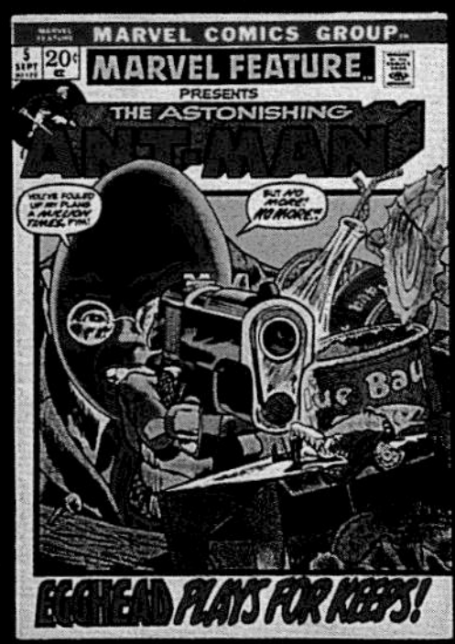

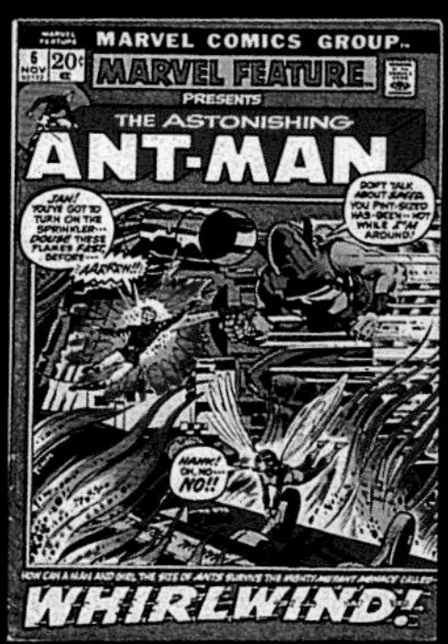

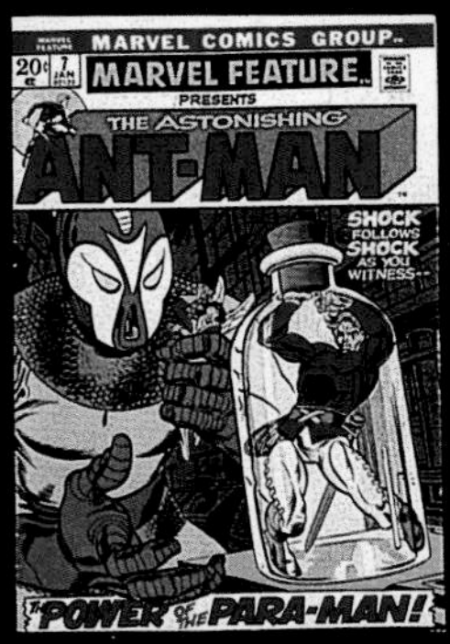

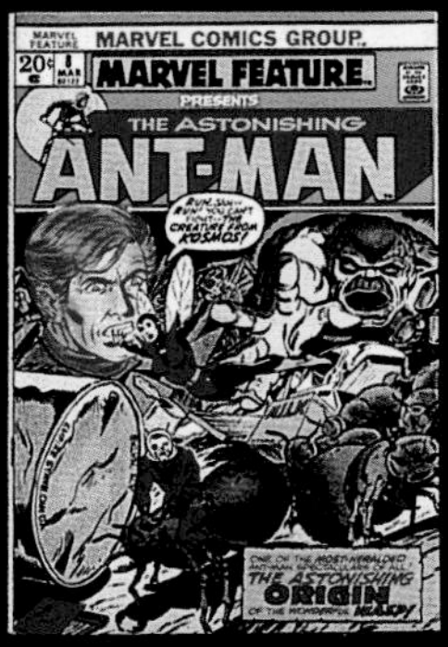

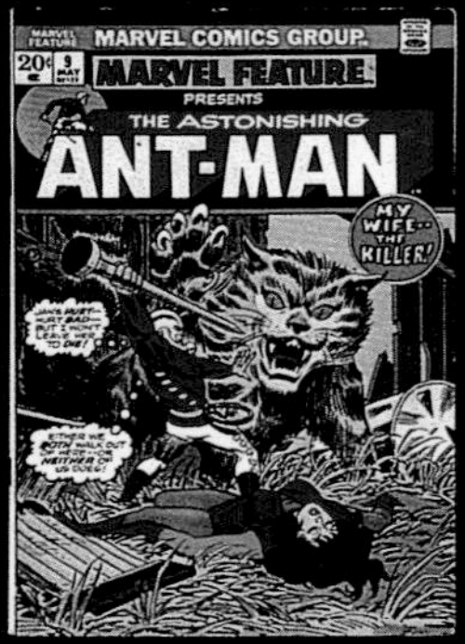

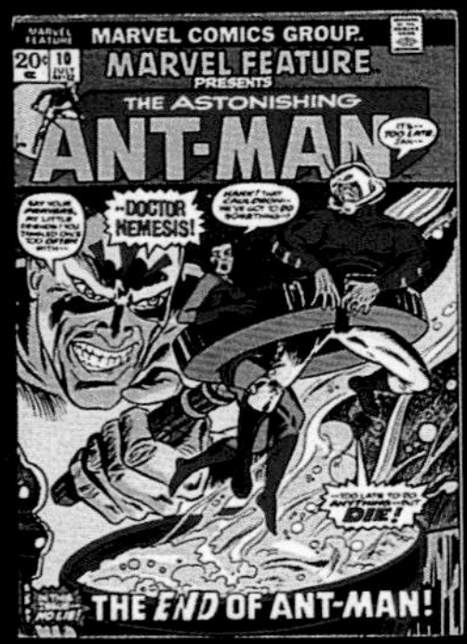

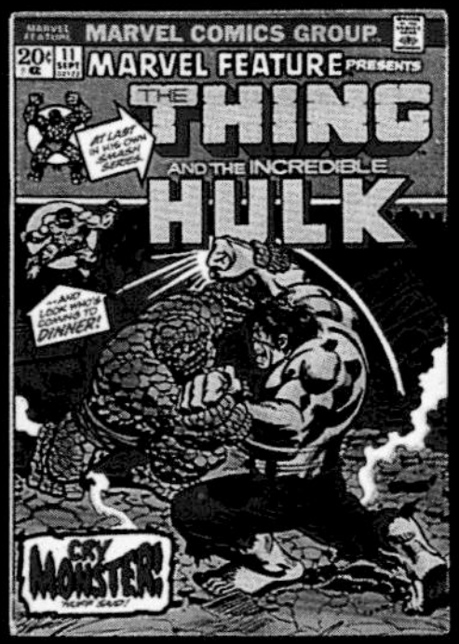

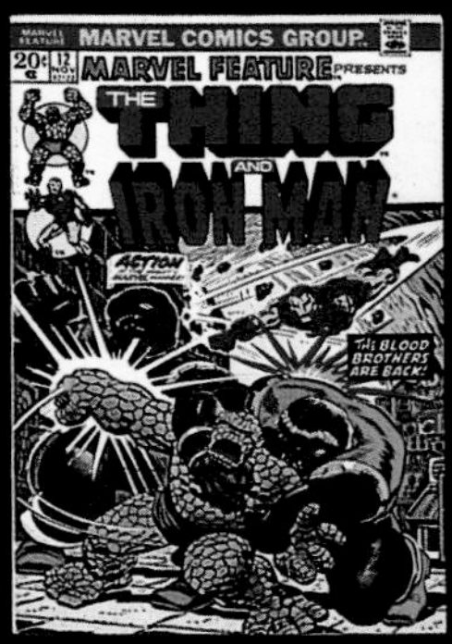

1215.3 Marvel Feature '75 (1-7)

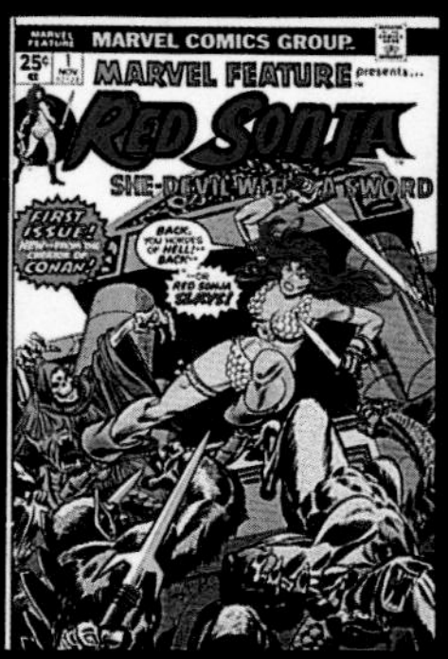

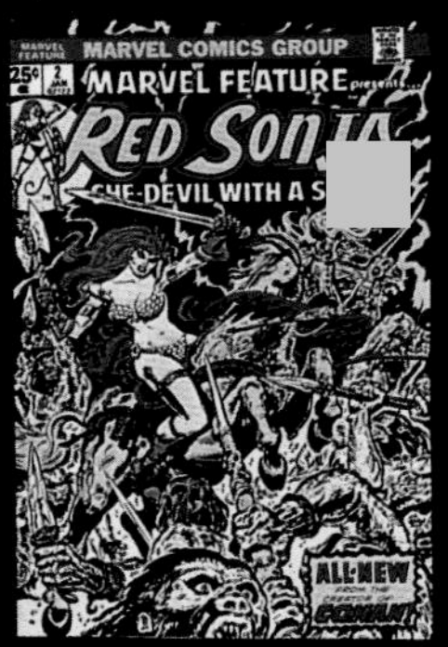

1215.4 Marvel Fumetti Book (1)

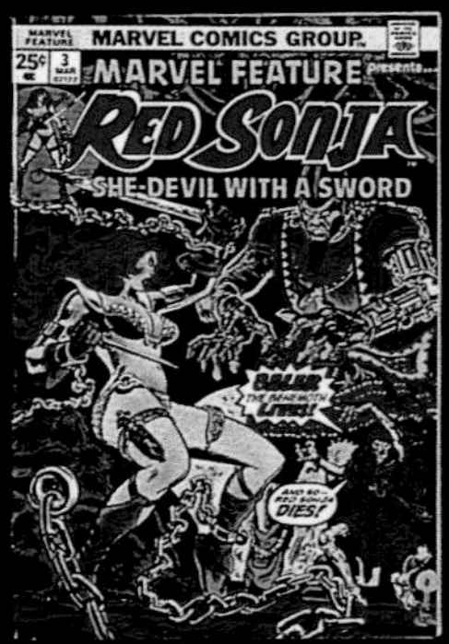

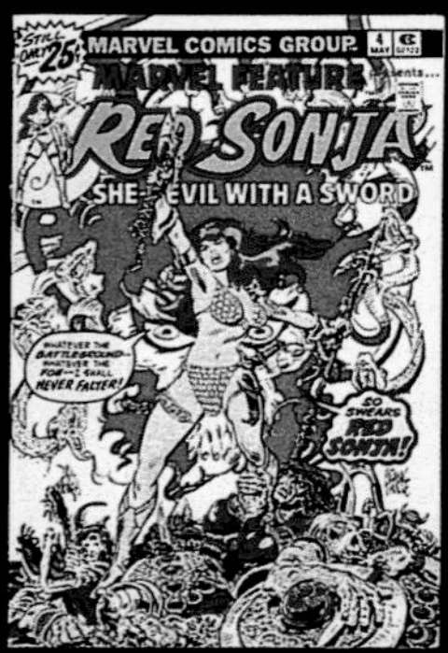

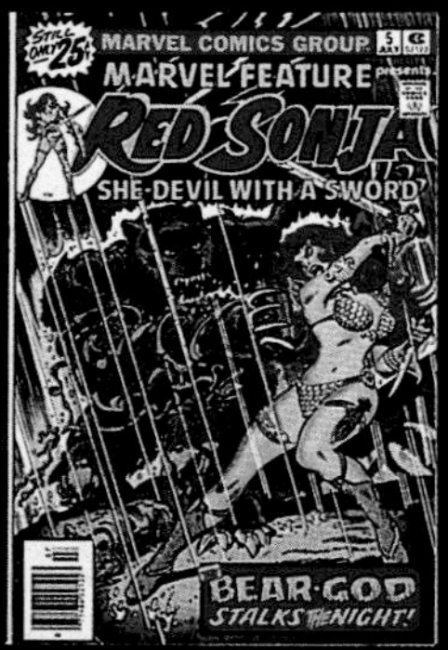

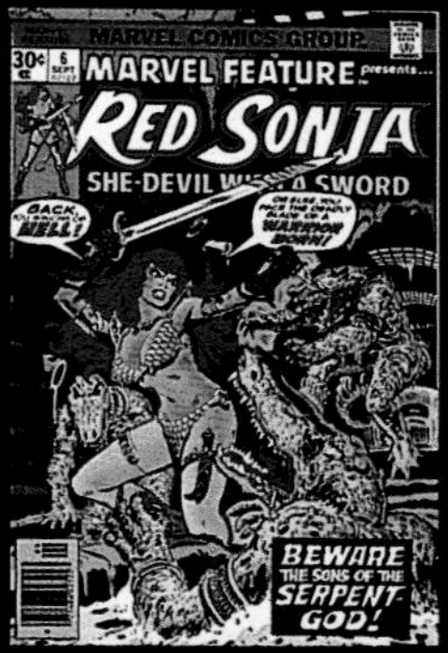

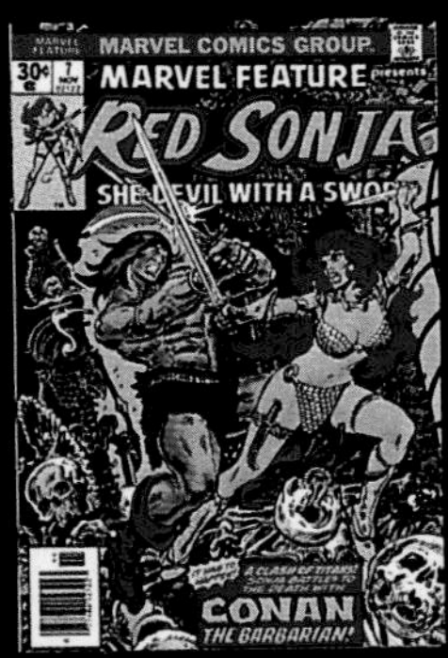

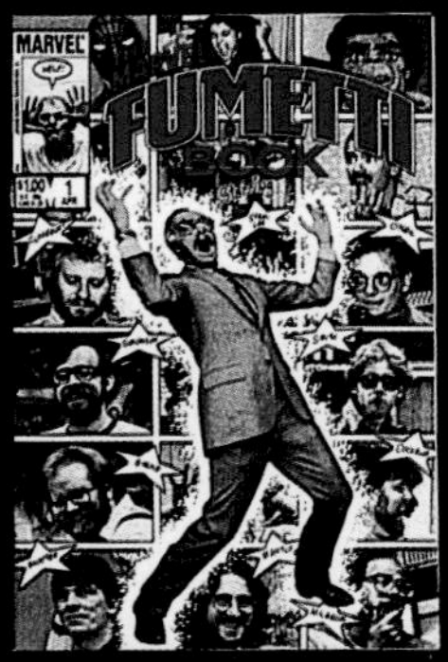

Marvel Movie Showcase (1)

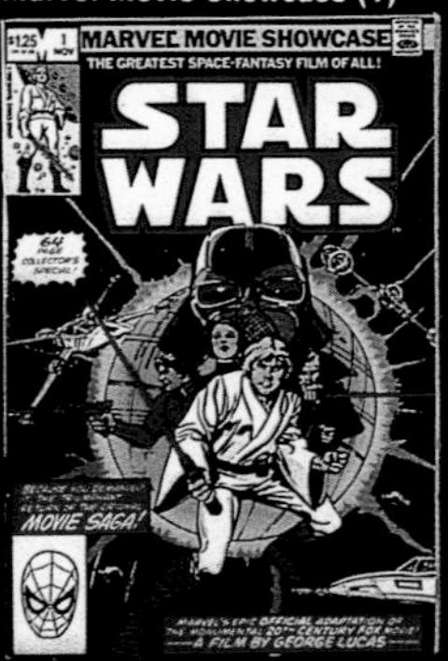

The Marvel No-Prize Book (1)

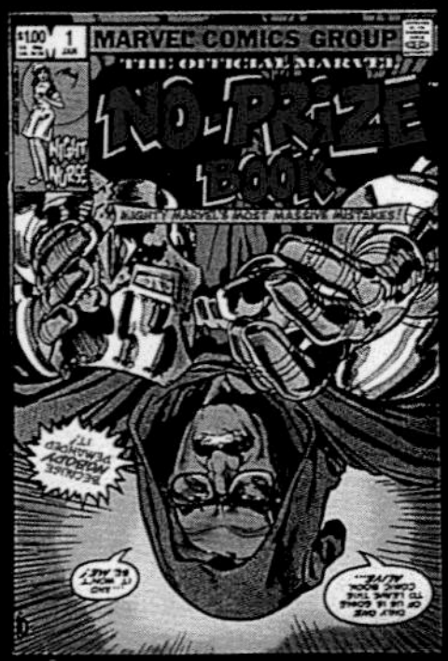

Marvel Fanfare (1-Present) 1215.1

Ref. No.	Date	RVI	Artist/Info.
1215.1-1	Mar. 1982	7	Claremont/Golden-a
1215.1-2	May	8	Von Eeden-c, Claremont/Golden-a
1215.1-3	Jul.	4	Cockrum/McLeod-c/a
1215.1-4	Sept.	4	P. Smith/Austin-a
1215.1-5	Nov.	2	Rogers, Russell-a
1215.1-6	Jan. 1983	1	Plunkett-a, Russell-cs/a
1215.1-7	Mar.	1	Barney/Freeman-a
1215.1-8	May	1	Russell-c/a, Infantino-a
1215.1-9	Jul.	1	Brozowski/Morrow-c/a
1215.1-10	**Aug.**	**1**	**Perez-c/a, Breeding-a**
1215.1-11	Nov.	1	Perez/Layton-c, Perez/Sinnabel-a
1215.1-12	Jan. 1984	1	Milgrom-c/a, Perez-a
1215.1-13	Mar.	1	Adams-c, Perez/Breeding-a
1215.1-14	May	1	Leonardi/Rubinstein-c/a
1215.1-15	Jul.	1	
1215.1-16	Sept.	1	Cockrum-c/a, Sinnott-a
1215.1-17	Nov.	1	" "
1215.1-18 to 55	Feb. 1991 (#55)	1	Doran/Wiacek-c

Marvel Feature (1-12) 1215.2

1215.2-1	Dec. 1971	15	Adams-c, Everett-a
1215.2-2 to 3		7	(#3, Kane-c)
1215.2-4 to 12	Nov. 1973, (#12)	2	

Marvel Feature (2nd Series; 1-7) 1215.3

1215.3-1	Nov. 1975	2	Adams-a (Red Sonja begins)
1215.3-2 to 7	Nov. 1976, (#7)	1	Thorne-c/a (all)

Marvel Fumetti Book (1) 1215.4

1215.4-1	Apr. 1984	1	Adams-c

Marvel Movie Showcase (1-2) 1215.8

1215.8-1 to 2	Nov. 1982, (#1)	1	(Star Wars reprints)

Marvel Movie Spotlight (1) 1215.9

1215.9-1	Nov. 1982	1	Buscema-c/a

The Marvel No-Prize Book (1) 1216.1

1216.1	Jan. 1983	1	Golden-c

1216.2 Marvel Premiere (1-16)

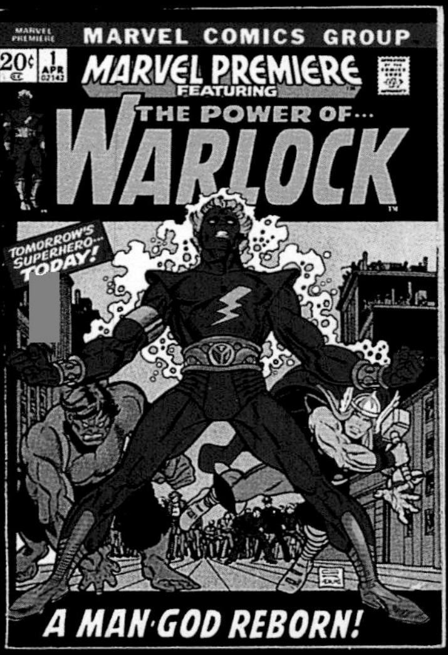
MARVEL COMICS GROUP
MARVEL PREMIERE
FEATURING
THE POWER OF...
WARLOCK
TOMORROW'S SUPERHERO... TODAY!
A MAN-GOD REBORN!

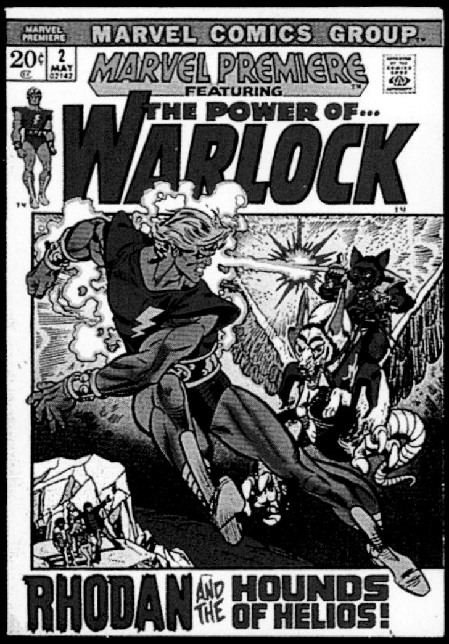
MARVEL COMICS GROUP
MARVEL PREMIERE
FEATURING
THE POWER OF...
WARLOCK
RHODAN AND THE HOUNDS OF HELIOS!

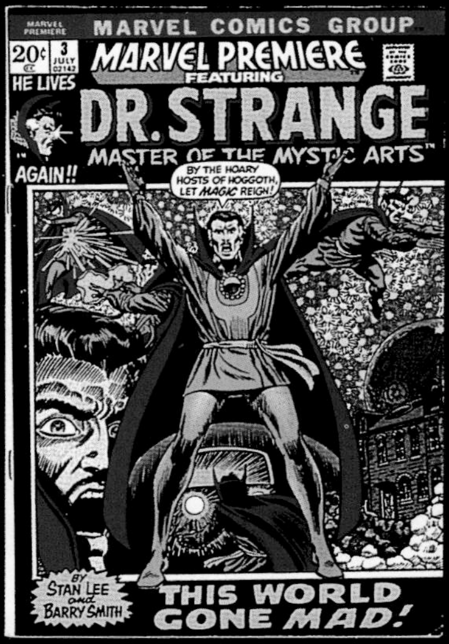
MARVEL COMICS GROUP
MARVEL PREMIERE
FEATURING
HE LIVES
DR. STRANGE
MASTER OF THE MYSTIC ARTS
AGAIN!!
BY THE HOARY HOSTS OF HOGGOTH, LET MAGIC REIGN!
STAN LEE AND BARRY SMITH
THIS WORLD GONE MAD!

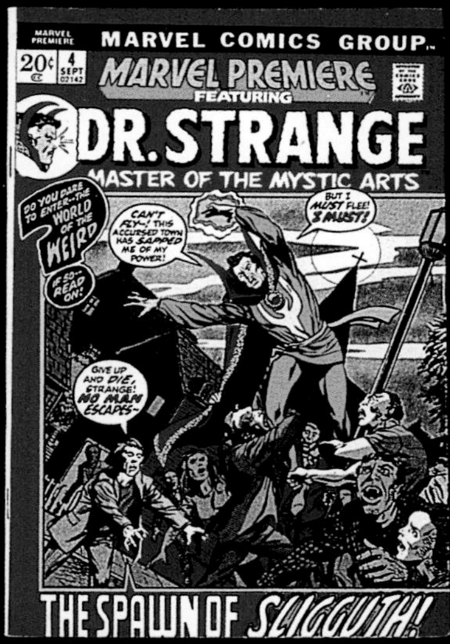
MARVEL COMICS GROUP
MARVEL PREMIERE
FEATURING
DR. STRANGE
MASTER OF THE MYSTIC ARTS
THE SPAWN OF SLIGGUTH!

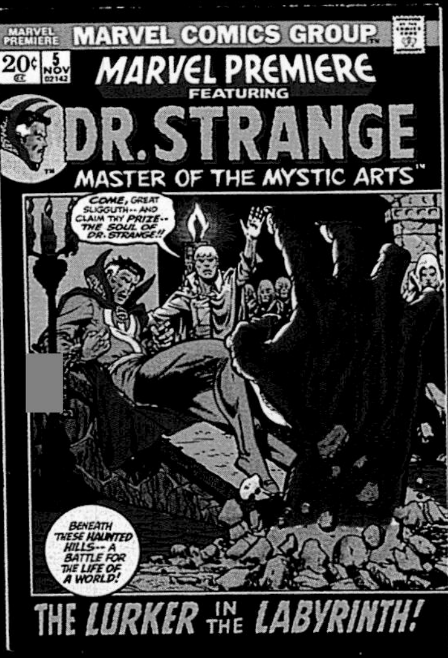
MARVEL COMICS GROUP
MARVEL PREMIERE
FEATURING
DR. STRANGE
MASTER OF THE MYSTIC ARTS
THE LURKER IN THE LABYRINTH!

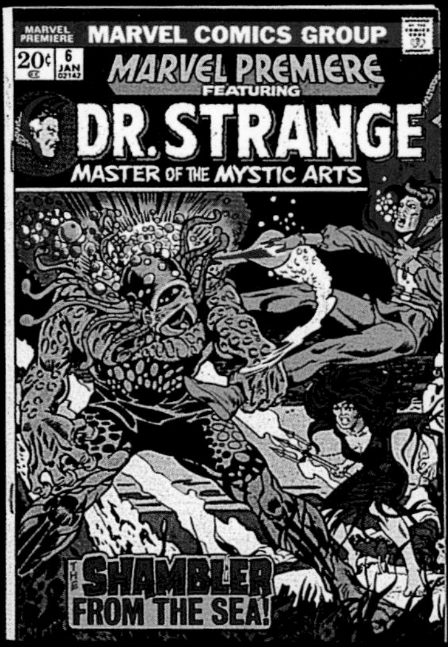
MARVEL COMICS GROUP
MARVEL PREMIERE
FEATURING
DR. STRANGE
MASTER OF THE MYSTIC ARTS
SHAMBLER FROM THE SEA!

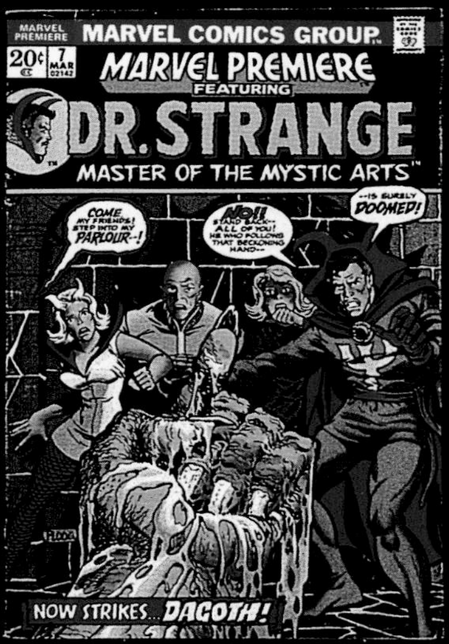
MARVEL COMICS GROUP
MARVEL PREMIERE
FEATURING
DR. STRANGE
MASTER OF THE MYSTIC ARTS
COME INTO MY PARLOUR--!
DOOMED!
NOW STRIKES... DAGOTH!

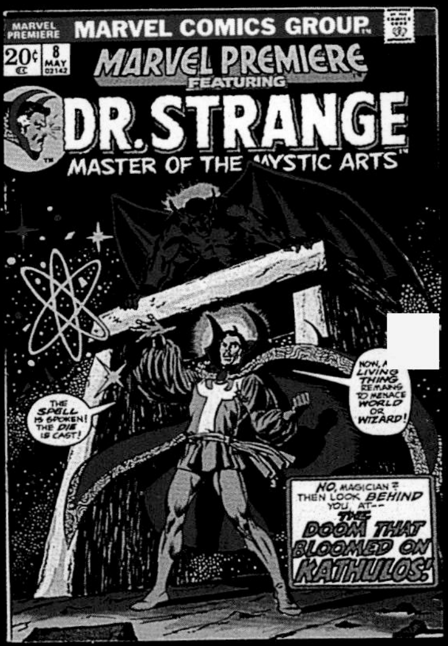
MARVEL COMICS GROUP
MARVEL PREMIERE
FEATURING
DR. STRANGE
MASTER OF THE MYSTIC ARTS
THE DOOM THAT BLOOMED ON KATHULOS!

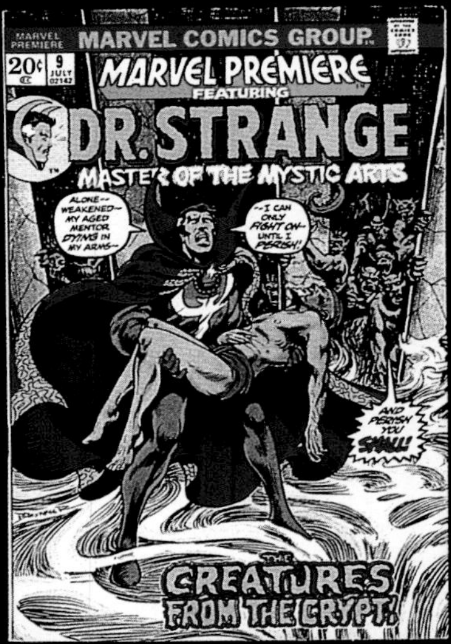
MARVEL COMICS GROUP
MARVEL PREMIERE
FEATURING
DR. STRANGE
MASTER OF THE MYSTIC ARTS
CREATURES FROM THE CRYPT!

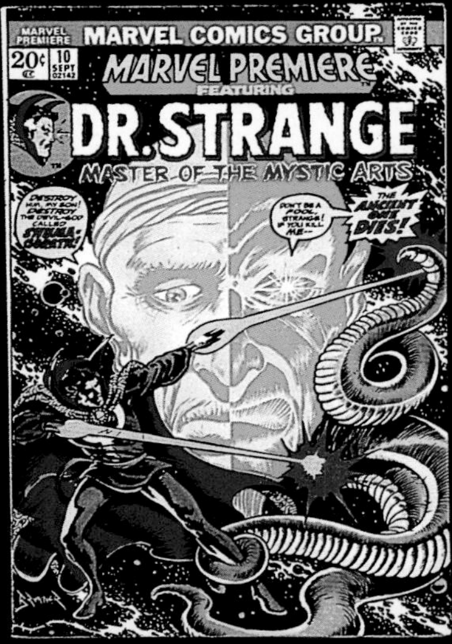
MARVEL COMICS GROUP
MARVEL PREMIERE
FEATURING
DR. STRANGE
MASTER OF THE MYSTIC ARTS

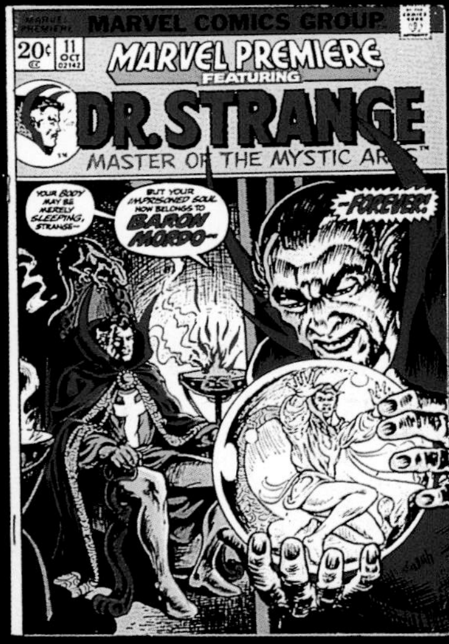
MARVEL COMICS GROUP
MARVEL PREMIERE
FEATURING
DR. STRANGE
MASTER OF THE MYSTIC ARTS
BARON MORDO
--FOREVER!

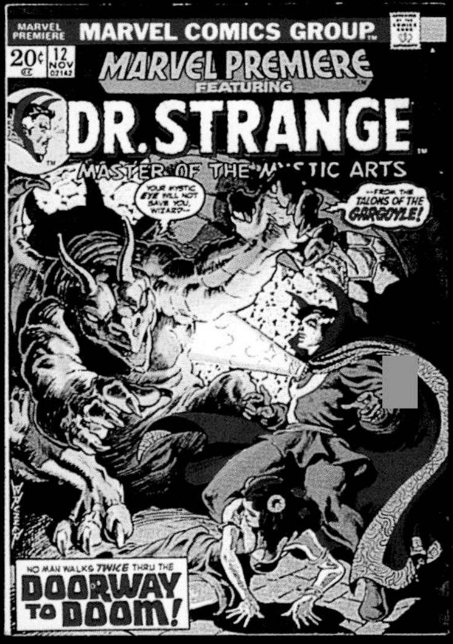
MARVEL COMICS GROUP
MARVEL PREMIERE
FEATURING
DR. STRANGE
MASTER OF THE MYSTIC ARTS
DOORWAY TO DOOM!

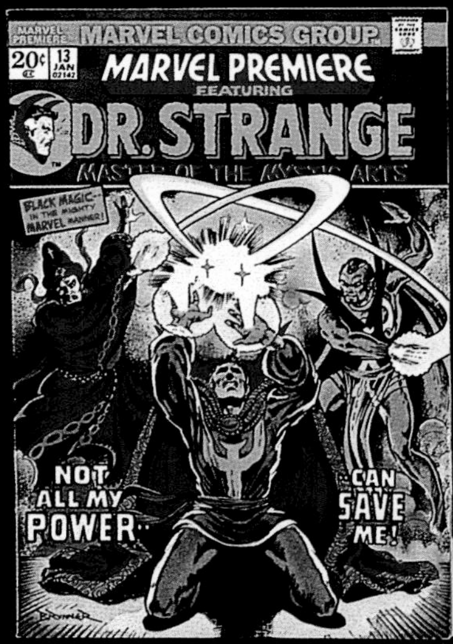
MARVEL COMICS GROUP
MARVEL PREMIERE
FEATURING
DR. STRANGE
MASTER OF THE MYSTIC ARTS
NOT ALL MY POWER
CAN SAVE ME!

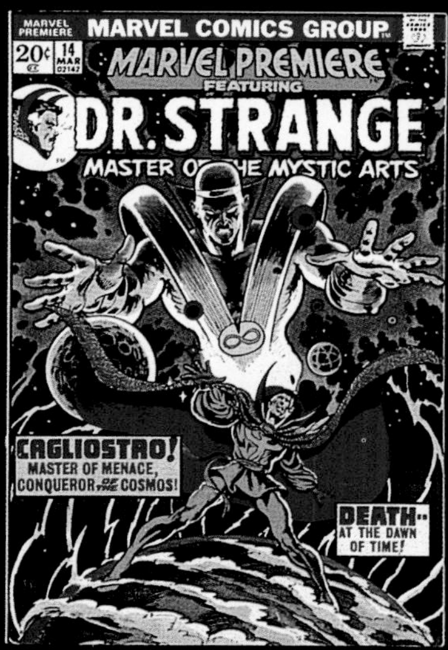
MARVEL COMICS GROUP
MARVEL PREMIERE
FEATURING
DR. STRANGE
MASTER OF THE MYSTIC ARTS
CAGLIOSTRO! MASTER OF MENACE, CONQUEROR OF THE COSMOS!
DEATH AT THE DAWN OF TIME!

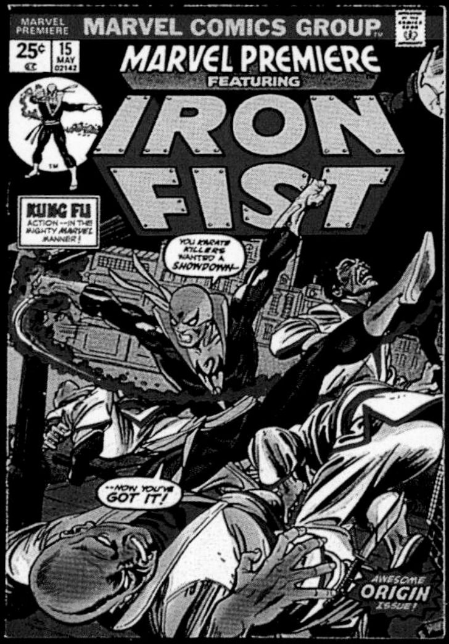
MARVEL COMICS GROUP
MARVEL PREMIERE
FEATURING
IRON FIST
KUNG FU
AWESOME ORIGIN ISSUE!

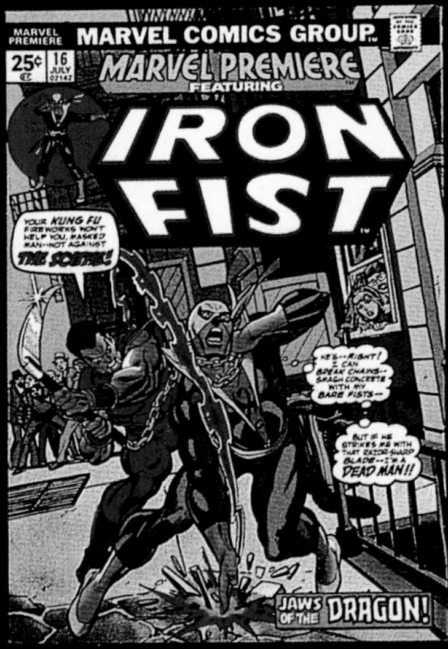
MARVEL COMICS GROUP
MARVEL PREMIERE
FEATURING
IRON FIST
JAWS OF THE DRAGON!

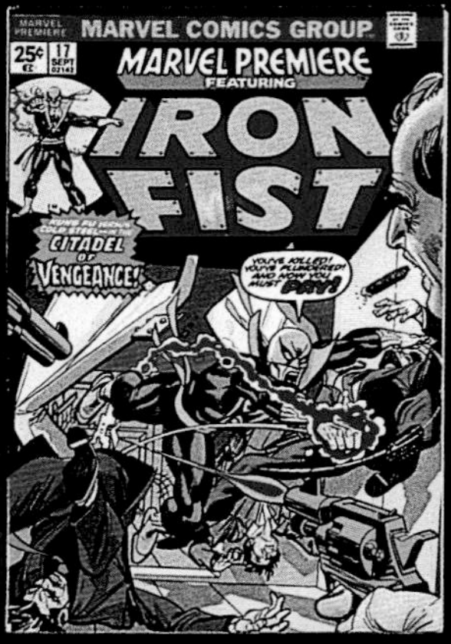
MARVEL COMICS GROUP
MARVEL PREMIERE
FEATURING
IRON FIST
CITADEL
VENGEANCE!

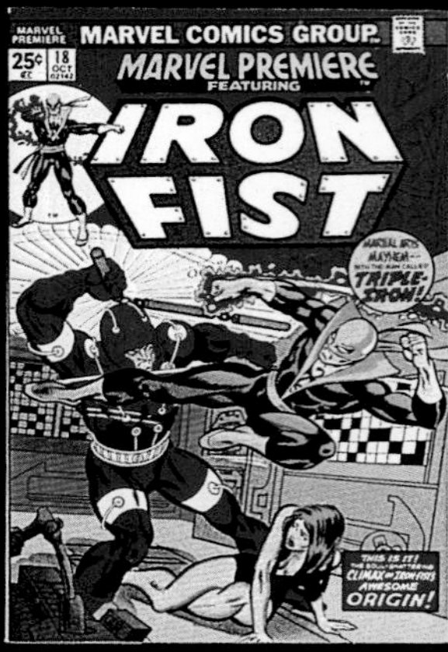
MARVEL COMICS GROUP
MARVEL PREMIERE
FEATURING
IRON FIST
ORIGIN!

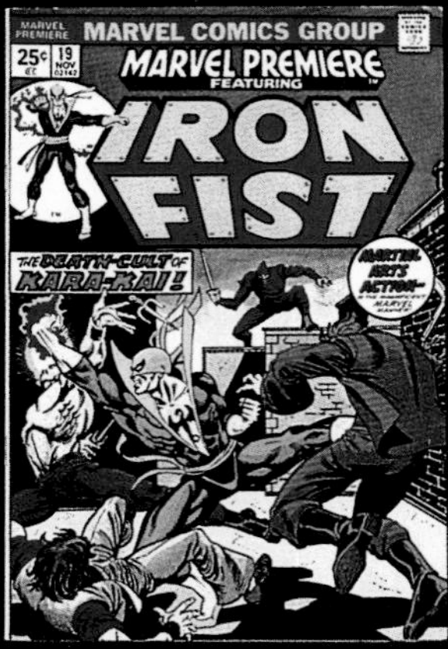
MARVEL COMICS GROUP
MARVEL PREMIERE
FEATURING
IRON FIST

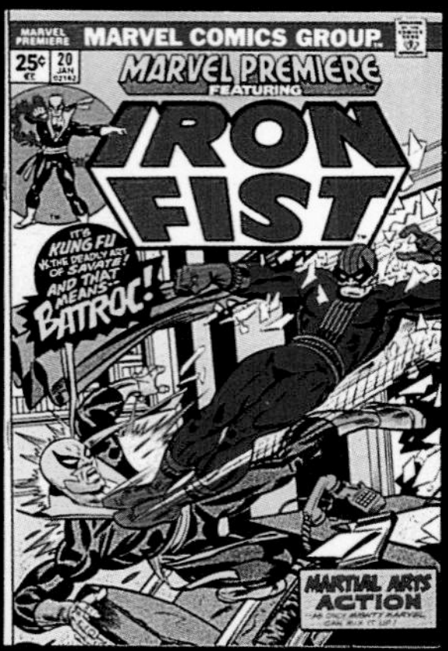
MARVEL COMICS GROUP
MARVEL PREMIERE
FEATURING
IRON FIST
BATROC!
MARTIAL ARTS ACTION

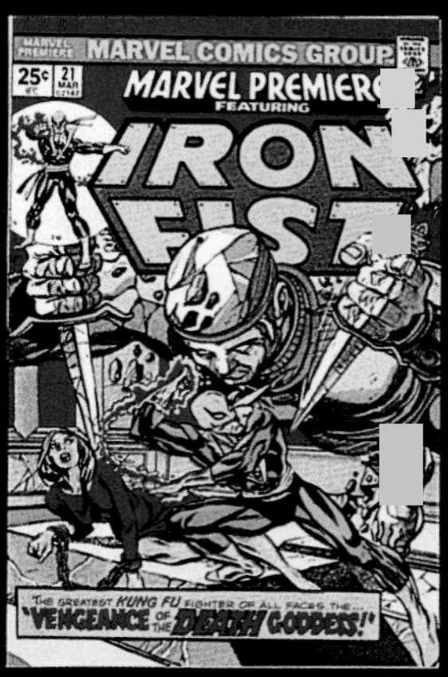
MARVEL COMICS GROUP
MARVEL PREMIERE
FEATURING
IRON FIST

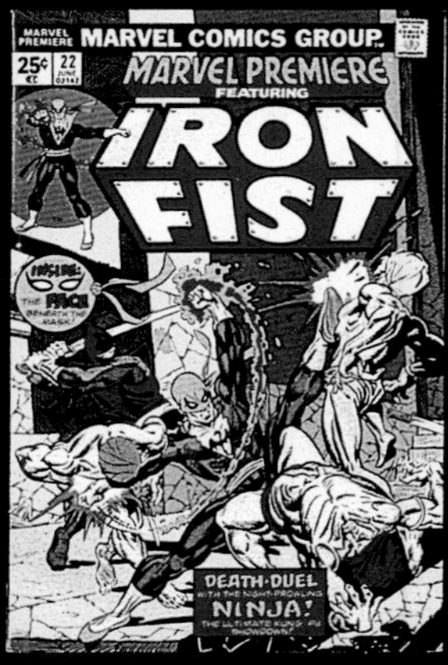
MARVEL COMICS GROUP
MARVEL PREMIERE
FEATURING
IRON FIST
DEATH-DUEL
NINJA!

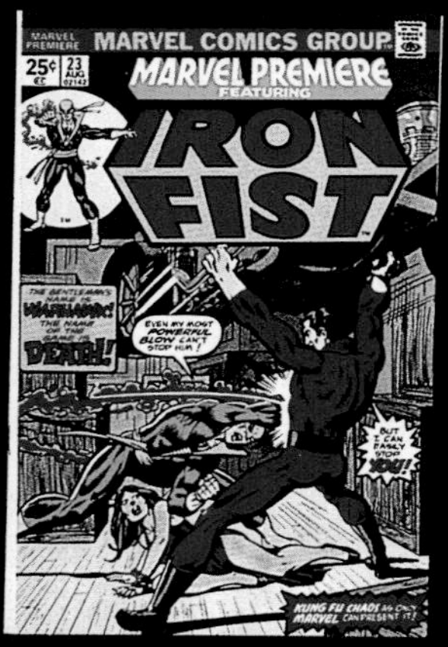
MARVEL COMICS GROUP
MARVEL PREMIERE
FEATURING
IRON FIST

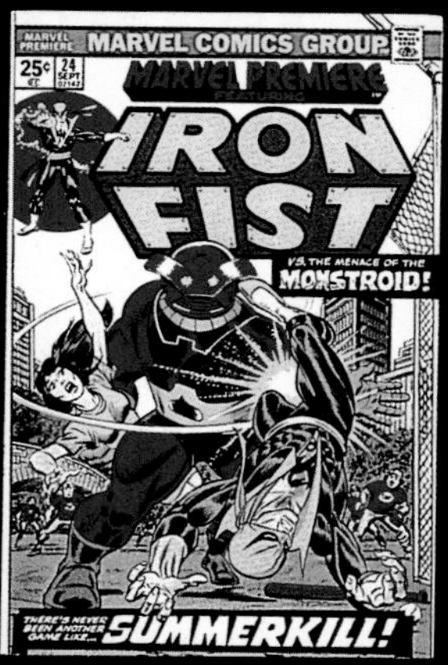
MARVEL COMICS GROUP
MARVEL PREMIERE
FEATURING
IRON FIST
MONSTROID!
SUMMERKILL!

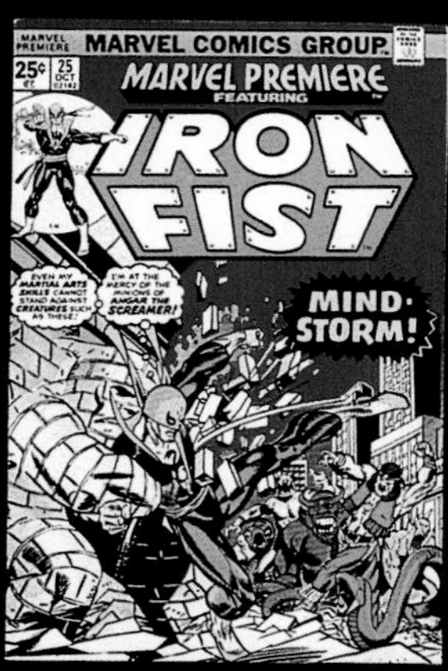
MARVEL COMICS GROUP
MARVEL PREMIERE
FEATURING
IRON FIST
MIND-STORM!

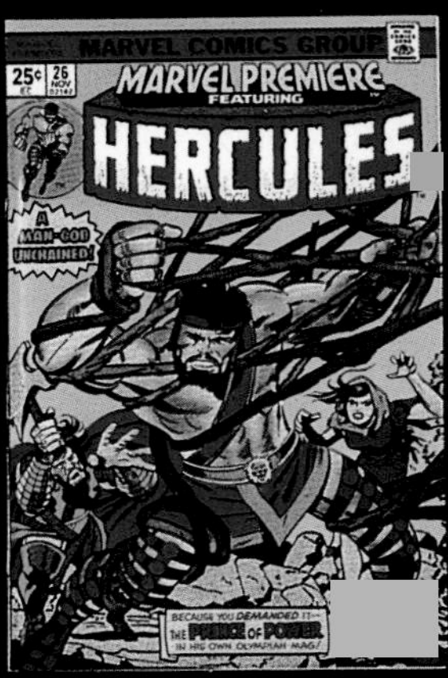
MARVEL COMICS GROUP
MARVEL PREMIERE
FEATURING
HERCULES

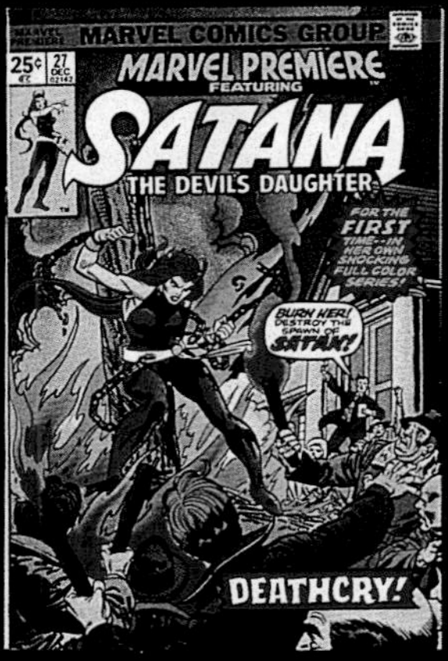
MARVEL COMICS GROUP
MARVEL PREMIERE
FEATURING
SATANA
THE DEVIL'S DAUGHTER
DEATHCRY!

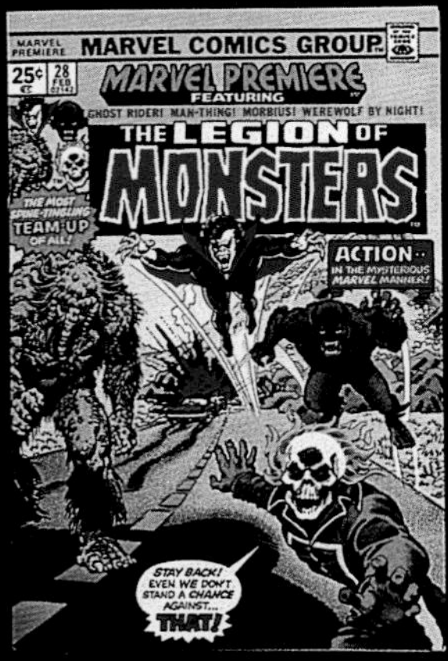
MARVEL COMICS GROUP
MARVEL PREMIERE
FEATURING
GHOST RIDER! MAN-THING! MORBIUS! WEREWOLF BY NIGHT!
THE LEGION OF MONSTERS
ACTION

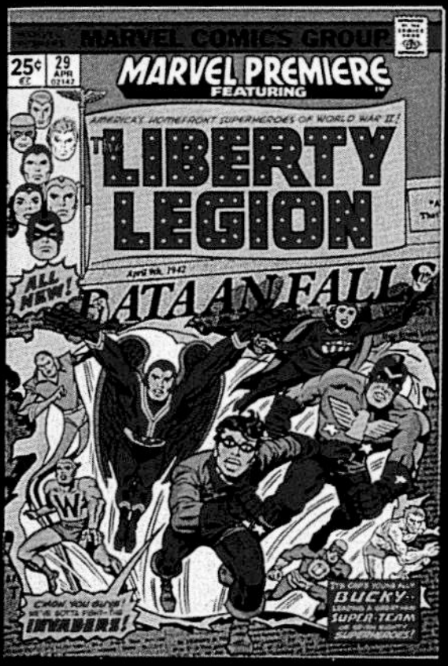
MARVEL COMICS GROUP
MARVEL PREMIERE
FEATURING
LIBERTY LEGION

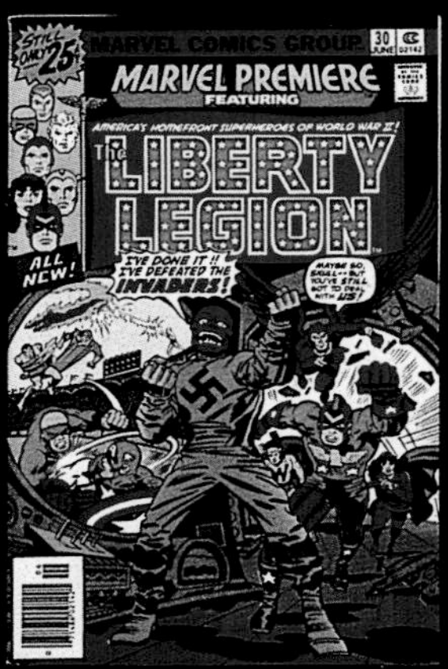
MARVEL COMICS GROUP
MARVEL PREMIERE
FEATURING
LIBERTY LEGION

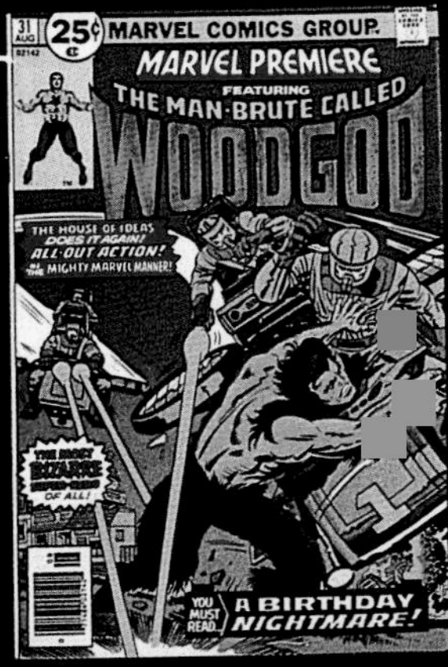
MARVEL COMICS GROUP
MARVEL PREMIERE
FEATURING
THE MAN-BRUTE CALLED
WOODGOD
A BIRTHDAY NIGHTMARE!

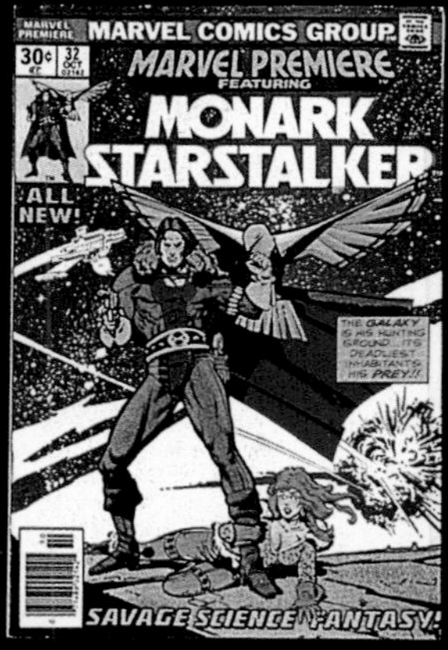
MARVEL COMICS GROUP
MARVEL PREMIERE
FEATURING
MONARK STARSTALKER
SAVAGE SCIENCE FANTASY!

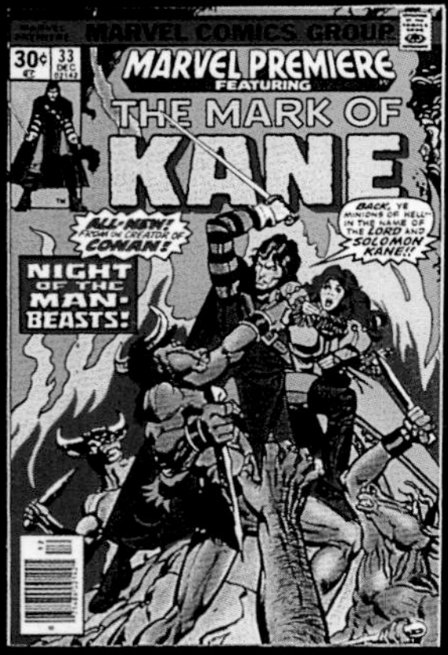
MARVEL COMICS GROUP
MARVEL PREMIERE
FEATURING
THE MARK OF KANE
NIGHT OF THE MAN-BEASTS!

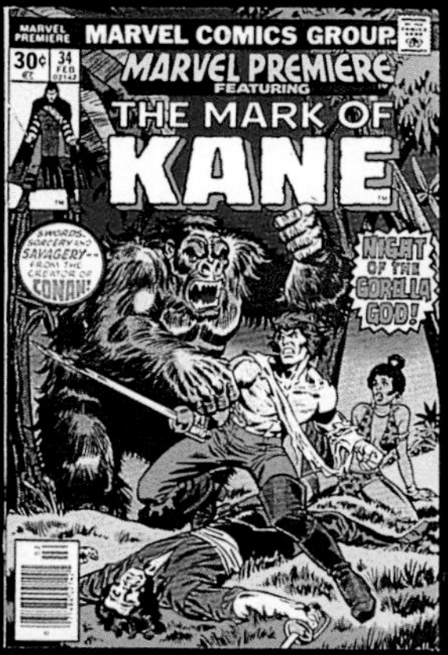
MARVEL COMICS GROUP
MARVEL PREMIERE
FEATURING
THE MARK OF KANE

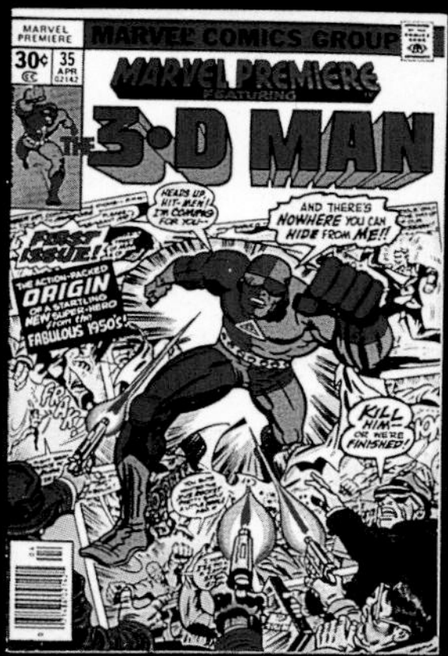
MARVEL COMICS GROUP
MARVEL PREMIERE
FEATURING
THE 3-D MAN
ORIGIN

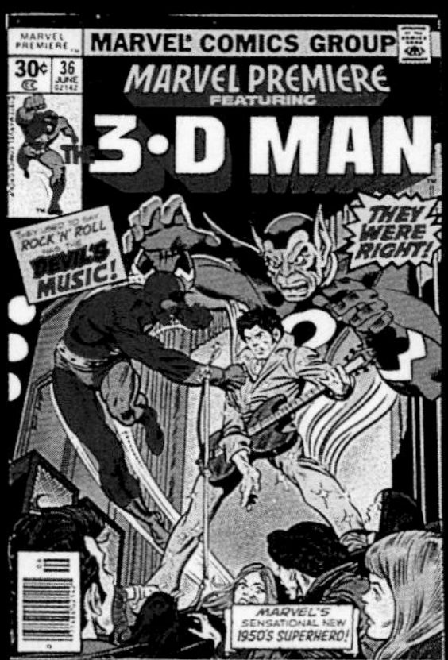
MARVEL COMICS GROUP
MARVEL PREMIERE
FEATURING
3-D MAN

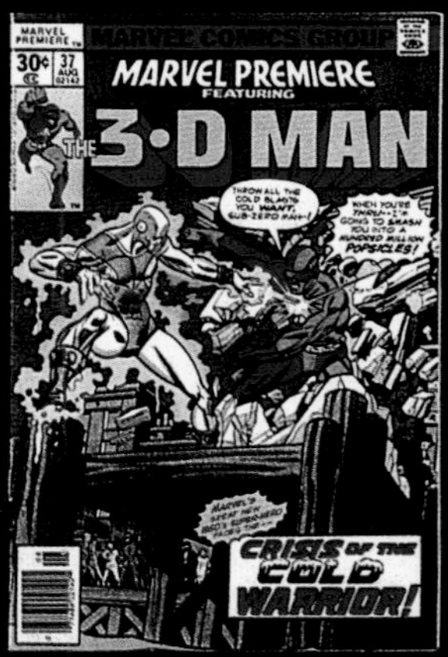
MARVEL COMICS GROUP
MARVEL PREMIERE
FEATURING
THE 3-D MAN
CRISIS OF THE COLD WARRIOR!

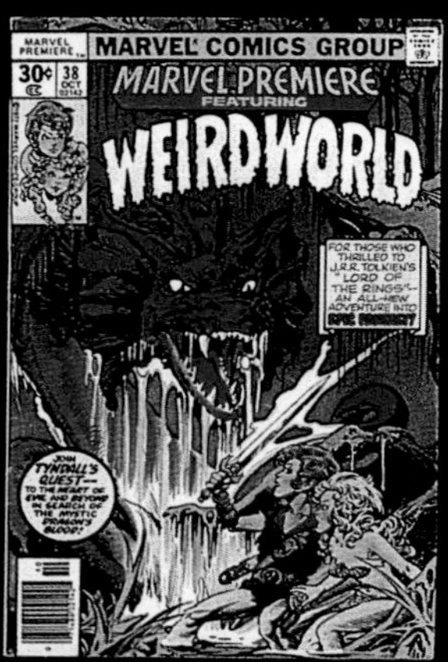
MARVEL COMICS GROUP
MARVEL PREMIERE
FEATURING
WEIRDWORLD

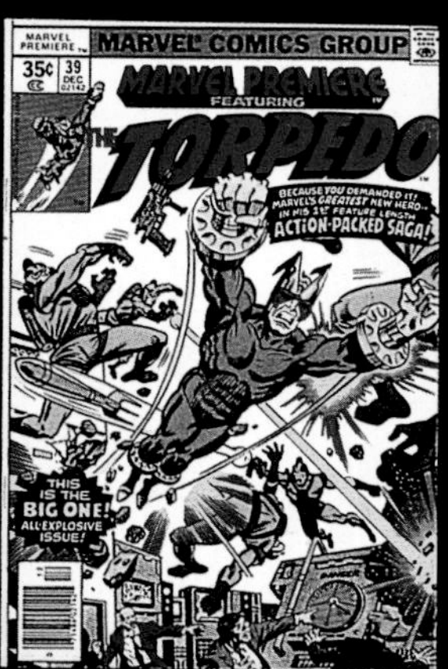
MARVEL COMICS GROUP
MARVEL PREMIERE
FEATURING
THE TORPEDO
ACTION-PACKED SAGA!

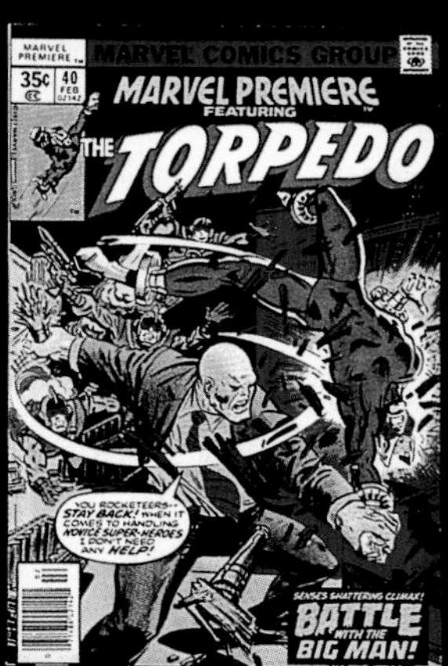
MARVEL COMICS GROUP
MARVEL PREMIERE
FEATURING
THE TORPEDO
BATTLE WITH THE BIG MAN!

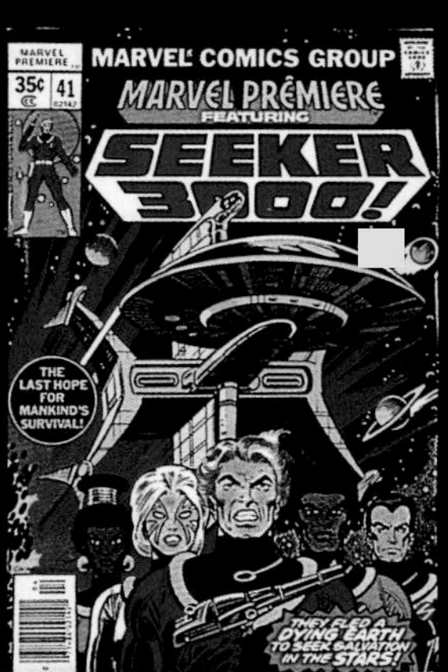
MARVEL COMICS GROUP
MARVEL PREMIERE
FEATURING
SEEKER 3000!

1216.2 Marvel Premiere (42-61)

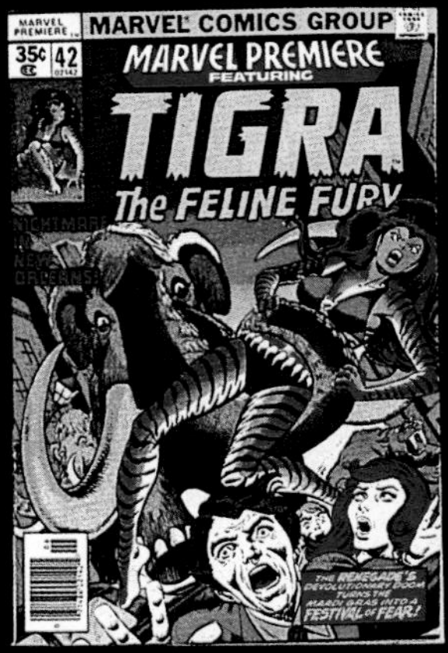
MARVEL COMICS GROUP
MARVEL PREMIERE
TIGRA
The FELINE FURY
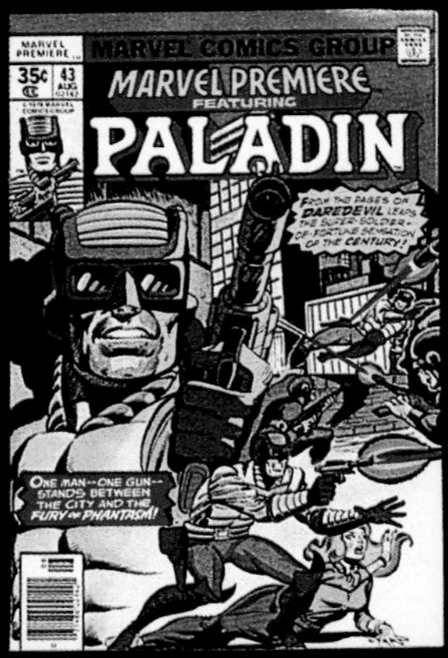
MARVEL COMICS GROUP
MARVEL PREMIERE
PALADIN
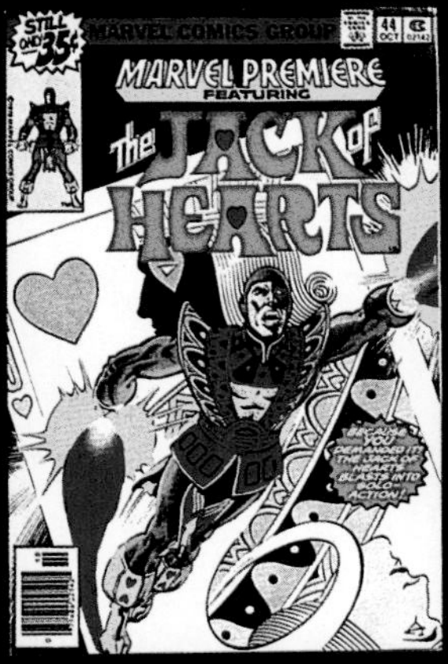
MARVEL COMICS GROUP
MARVEL PREMIERE
The JACK of HEARTS
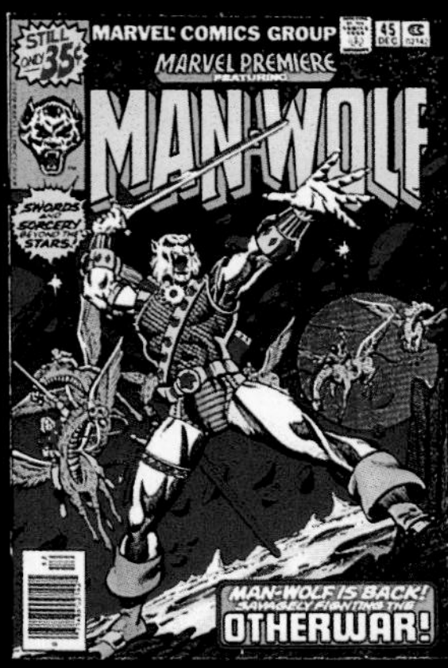
MARVEL COMICS GROUP
MARVEL PREMIERE
MAN-WOLF
OTHERWAR!
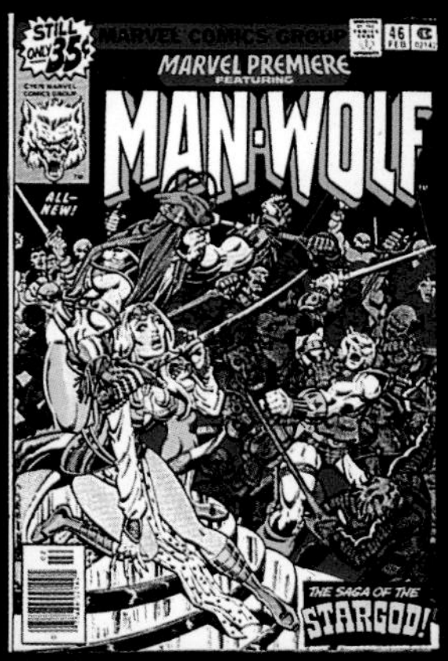
MARVEL COMICS GROUP
MARVEL PREMIERE
MAN-WOLF
STARGOD!
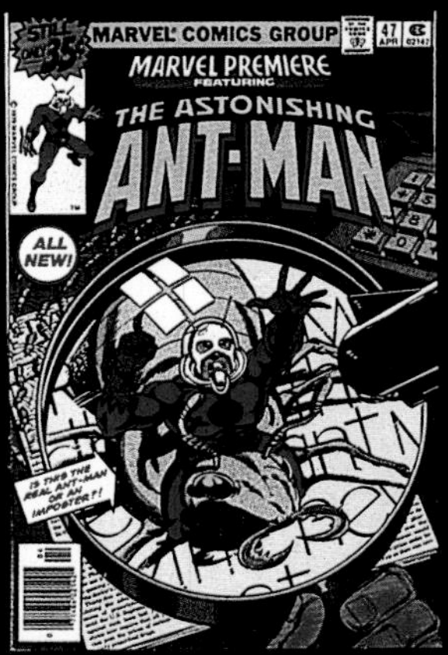
MARVEL COMICS GROUP
MARVEL PREMIERE
THE ASTONISHING
ANT-MAN
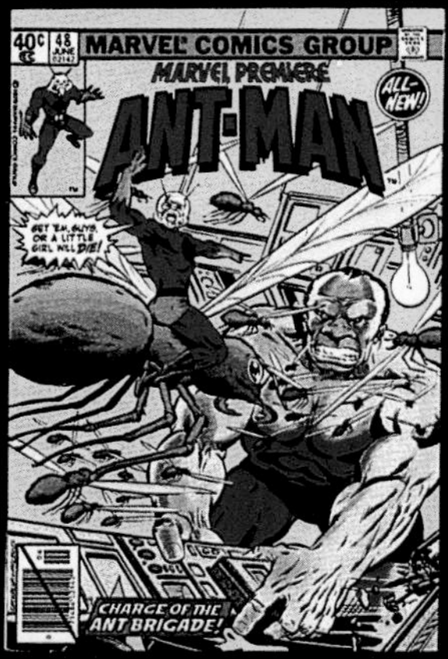
MARVEL COMICS GROUP
ANT-MAN
CHARGE OF THE ANT-BRIGADE!
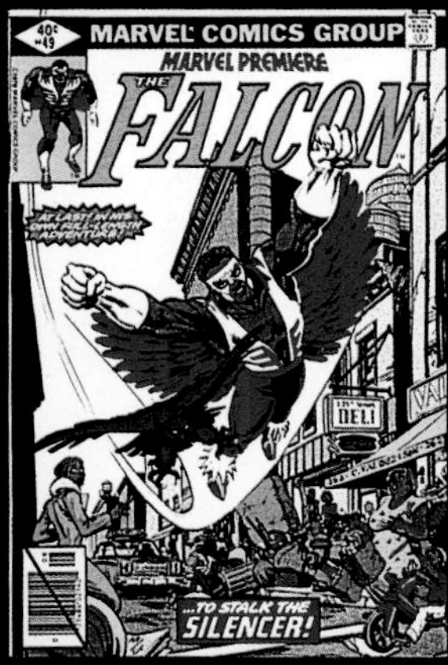
MARVEL COMICS GROUP
MARVEL PREMIERE
FALCON
...TO STALK THE SILENCER!
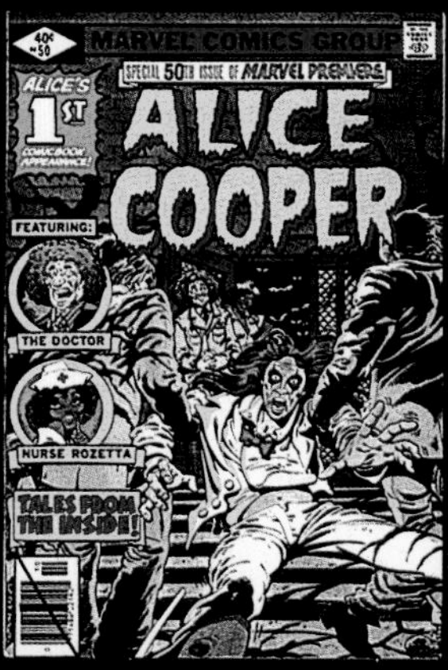
ALICE COOPER
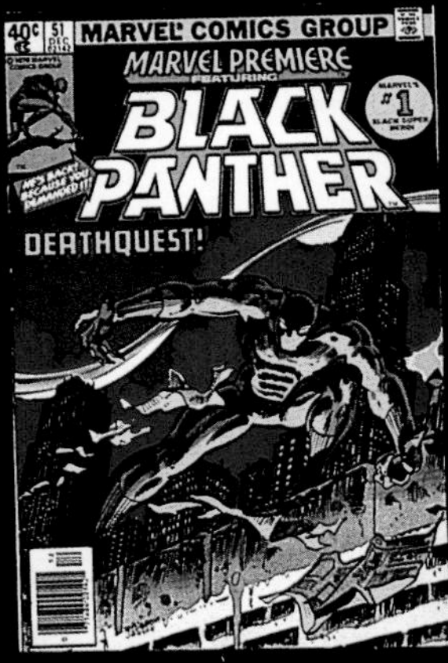
MARVEL COMICS GROUP
MARVEL PREMIERE
BLACK PANTHER
DEATHQUEST!
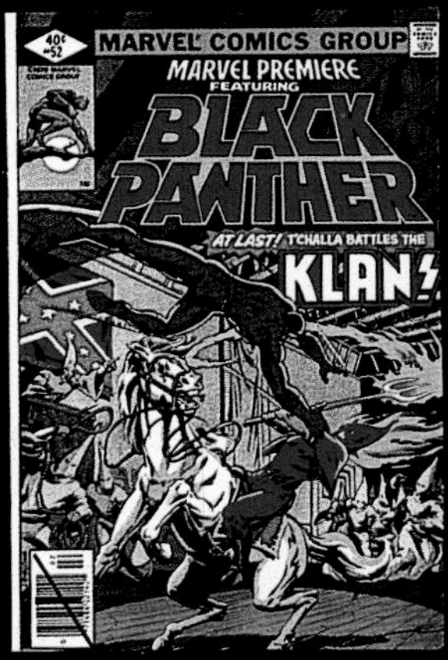
MARVEL COMICS GROUP
MARVEL PREMIERE
BLACK PANTHER
KLAN
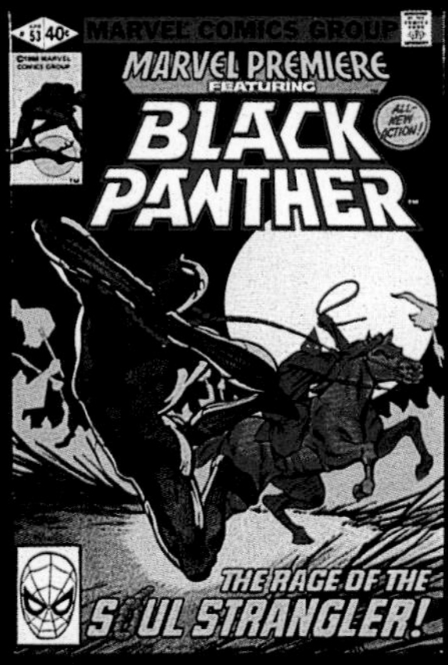
MARVEL PREMIERE
BLACK PANTHER
THE RAGE OF THE SOUL STRANGLER!
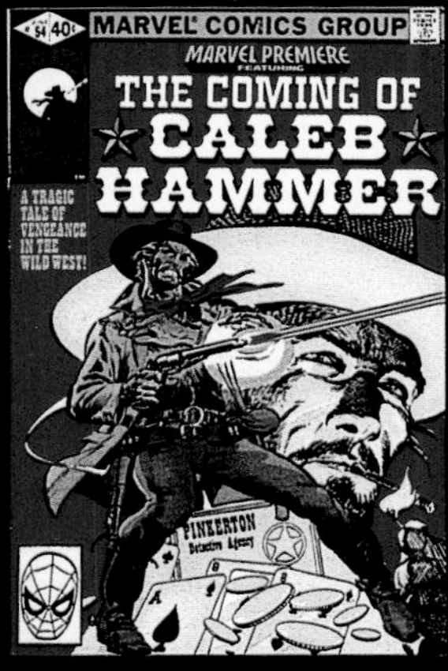
MARVEL COMICS GROUP
MARVEL PREMIERE
THE COMING OF
CALEB HAMMER
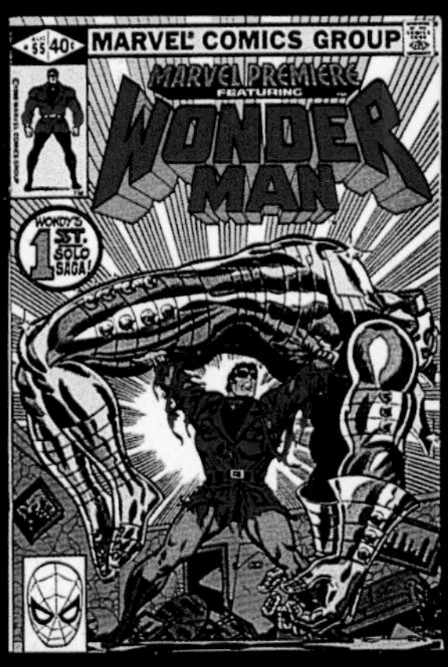
MARVEL COMICS GROUP
MARVEL PREMIERE
WONDER MAN
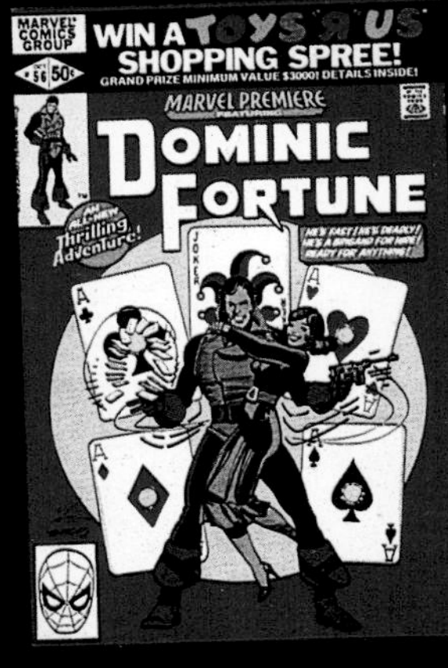
WIN A TOYS R US SHOPPING SPREE!
MARVEL PREMIERE
DOMINIC FORTUNE
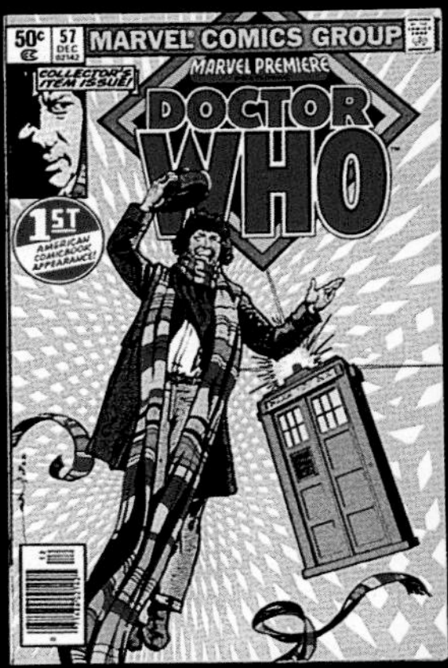
MARVEL COMICS GROUP
MARVEL PREMIERE
DOCTOR WHO
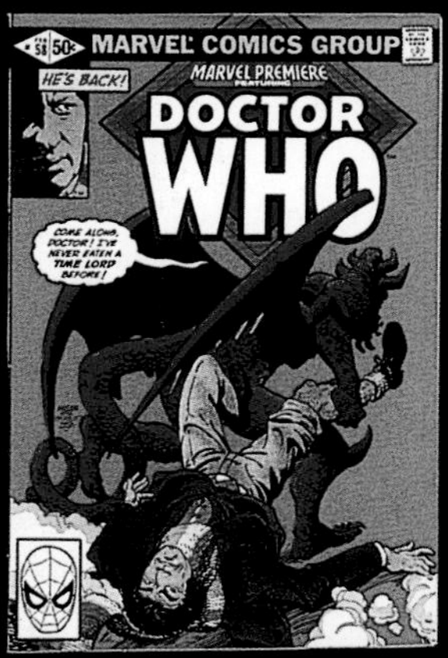
MARVEL COMICS GROUP
MARVEL PREMIERE
DOCTOR WHO
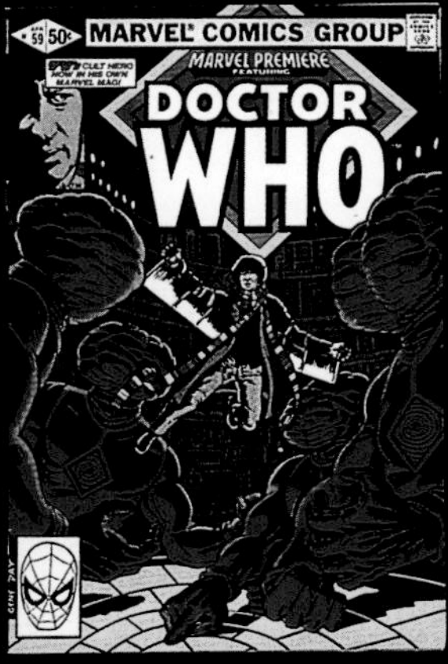
MARVEL COMICS GROUP
MARVEL PREMIERE
DOCTOR WHO
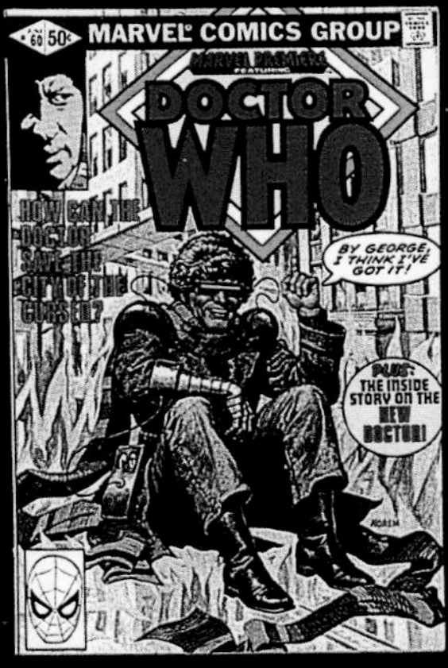
MARVEL COMICS GROUP
DOCTOR WHO
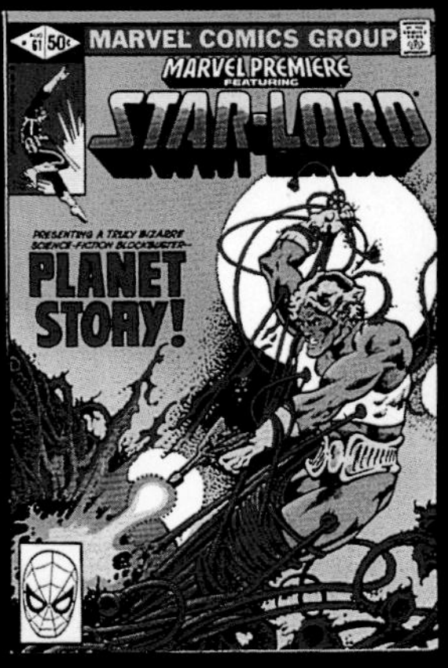
MARVEL COMICS GROUP
MARVEL PREMIERE
STAR-LORD
PLANET STORY!

1216.3 Marvel Presents (1-2)

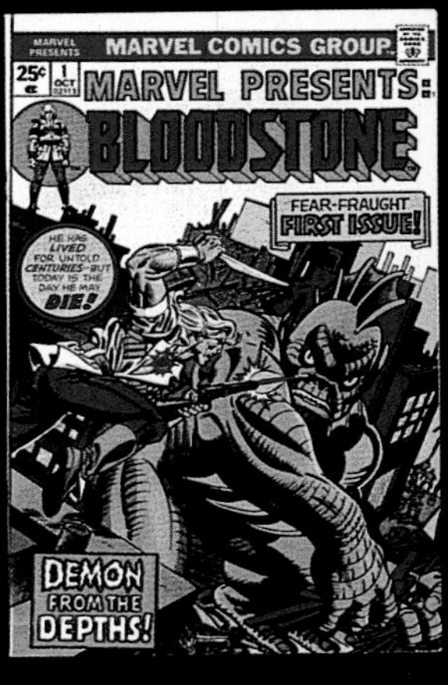
MARVEL COMICS GROUP
MARVEL PRESENTS:
BLOODSTONE
FEAR-FRAUGHT FIRST ISSUE!
DEMON FROM THE DEPTHS!
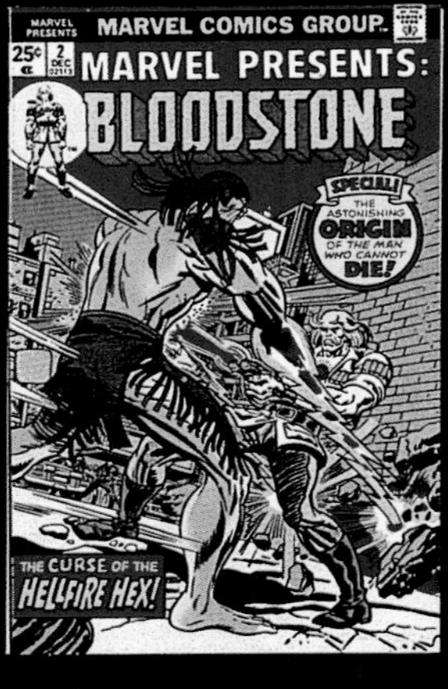
MARVEL COMICS GROUP
MARVEL PRESENTS:
BLOODSTONE
THE CURSE OF THE HELLFIRE HEX!

Marvel Premiere (1-61) 1216.2

Ref. No.	Date	RVI	Artist/Info.
1216.2-1	Apr. 1972	6	Adkins-c, Kane-a (Origin-Warlock)
1216.2-2	May	4	" "
1216.2-3	Jul.	7	B. Smith-a
1216.2-4	Sept.	4	Brunner/Smith-a
1216.2-5	Nov.	2	Wesley/Perlin-a
1216.2-6	Jan. 1973	2	Buscema/Brunner-a
1216.2-7	Mar.	2	Ploog-c, Russell/Giacoia/Hunt-a
1216.2-8	May	2	Starlin/Giacoia/Hunt-a
1216.2-9	Jul.	2	Brunner-c/a, Chua-a
1216.2-10	**Sept.**	**2**	**Brunner-c/a, Crusty Bunkers-a**
1216.2-11	Oct.	1	Ditko-a
1216.2-12	Nov.	1	Brunner-c/a, Crusty Bunkers-a
1216.2-13	Jan. 1974	1	" " "
1216.2-14	Mar.	1	Brunner-c/a, Giordano-a
1216.2-15	May	8	Kane/Giordano-a (First Iron Fist)
1216.2-16	Jul.	2	Hama/Giordano-a
1216.2-17	Sept.	2	" "
1216.2-18	Oct.	2	" "
1216.2-19	Nov.	2	" "
1216.2-20	**Jan. 1975**	**2**	**Jones/Green-a**
1216.2-21	Mar.	1	Jones/Colletta-a
1216.2-22	Jun.	1	Jones/Bradford-a
1216.2-23	Aug.	1	Broderick/McLeod-a
1216.2-24	Sept.	1	Broderick/Colletta-a
1216.2-25	Oct.	5	Byrne/McWilliams-a
1216.2-26	Nov.	1	Tuska/Colletta-a
1216.2-27	Dec.	1	
1216.2-28	Feb. 1976	4	Robbins/Gan-a
1216.2-29	Apr.	1	Heck/Colletta-a
1216.2-30	**Jun.**	**1**	**" "**
1216.2-31	Aug.	1	Giffen/Janson-a
1216.2-32	Oct.	1	Chaykin-a
1216.2-33	Dec.	1	"
1216.2-34	Feb. 1977	1	"
1216.2-35	Apr.	1	Craig/Hunt-a
1216.2-36	Jun.	1	" "
1216.2-37	Aug.	1	" "
1216.2-38	Oct.	1	Ploog, Nino-a
1216.2-39	Dec.	1	Brown, Milgrom-a
1216.2-40	**Feb. 1978**	**1**	**" "**
1216.2-41	Apr.	1	Sutton/Denise, Rick-a
1216.2-42	Jun.	1	Vosburg, Chan-a
1216.2-43	Aug.	1	Sutton-a
1216.2-44	Oct.	1	Giffen, Nebres-a
1216.2-45	Dec.	1	Perez, Giacoia-a
1216.2-46 to 61	Aug. 1981, (#61)	1	

Marvel Presents (1-12) 1216.3

Ref. No.	Date	RVI	Artist/Info.
1216.3-1	Oct. 1975	2	Vosburg/McLeod-a

1216.3 Marvel Presents (3-12)

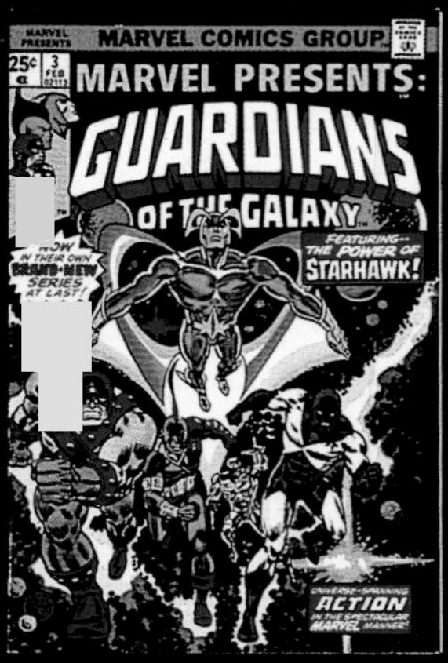
MARVEL COMICS GROUP
MARVEL PRESENTS:
GUARDIANS OF THE GALAXY
FEATURING— THE POWER OF STARHAWK!
ACTION

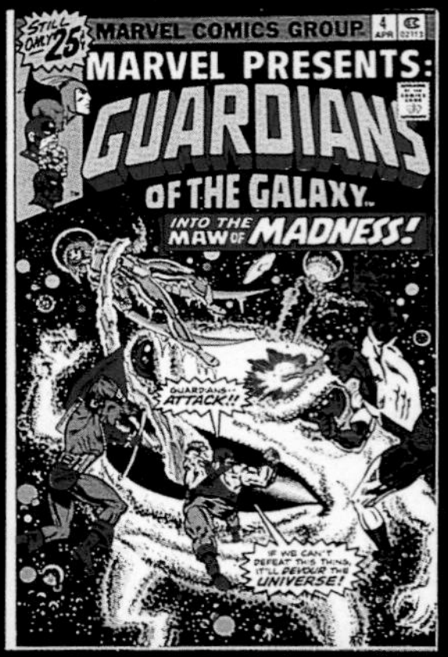
MARVEL COMICS GROUP
MARVEL PRESENTS:
GUARDIANS OF THE GALAXY
INTO THE MAW OF MADNESS!

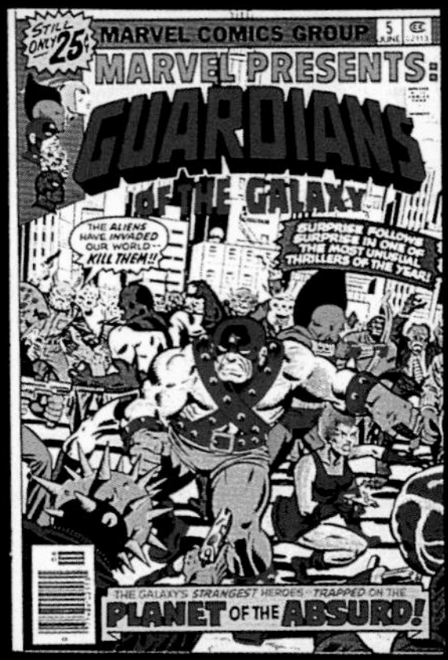
MARVEL COMICS GROUP
MARVEL PRESENTS:
GUARDIANS OF THE GALAXY
PLANET OF THE ABSURD!

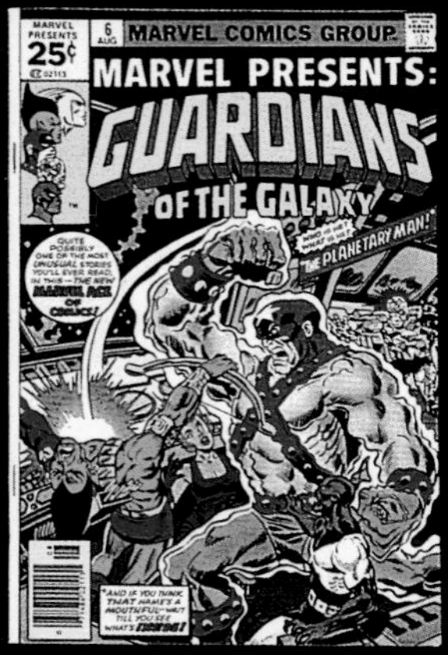
MARVEL COMICS GROUP
MARVEL PRESENTS:
GUARDIANS OF THE GALAXY

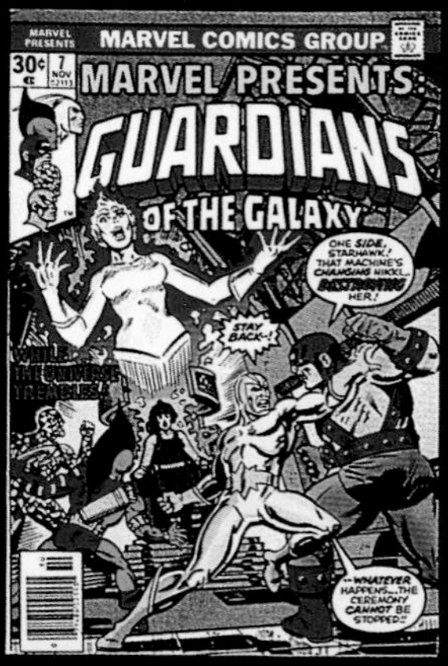
MARVEL COMICS GROUP
MARVEL PRESENTS:
GUARDIANS OF THE GALAXY

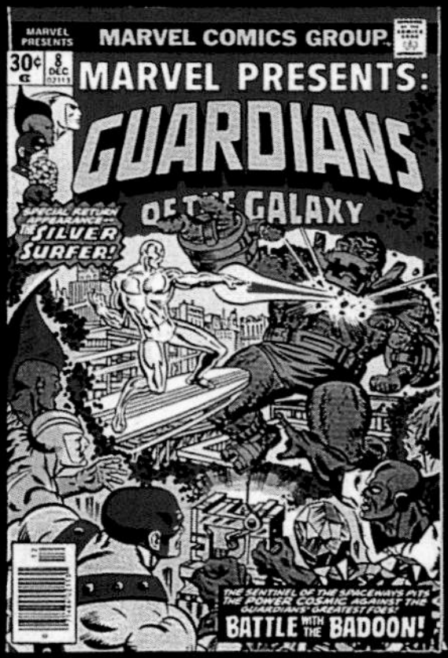
MARVEL COMICS GROUP
MARVEL PRESENTS:
GUARDIANS OF THE GALAXY
SILVER SURFER!
BATTLE THE BADOON!

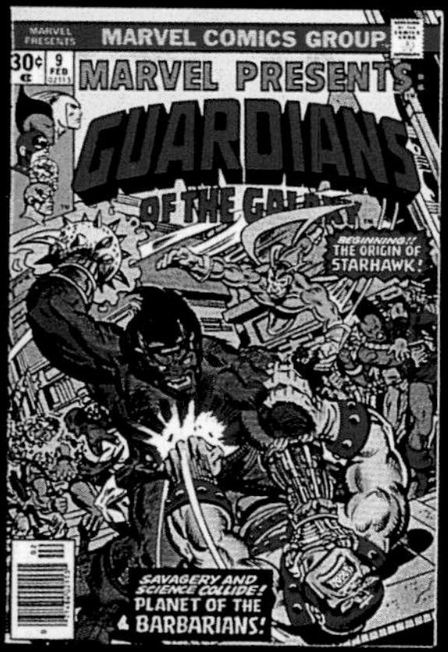
MARVEL COMICS GROUP
MARVEL PRESENTS
GUARDIANS OF THE GALAXY
THE ORIGIN OF STARHAWK!
PLANET OF THE BARBARIANS!

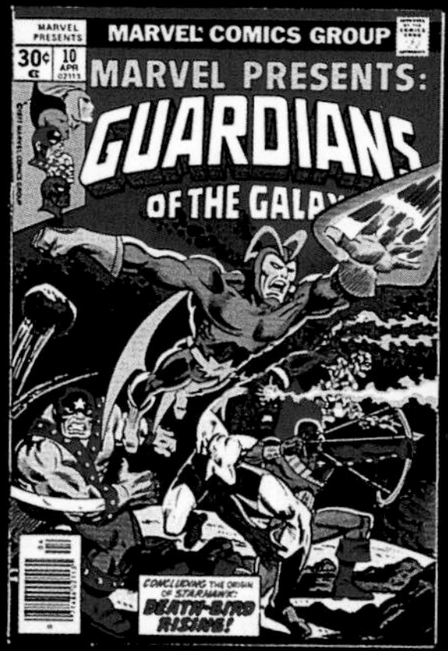
MARVEL COMICS GROUP
MARVEL PRESENTS:
GUARDIANS OF THE GALAXY

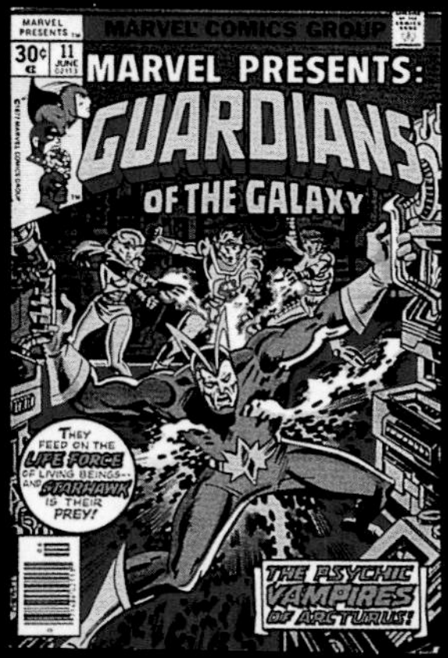
MARVEL COMICS GROUP
MARVEL PRESENTS:
GUARDIANS OF THE GALAXY

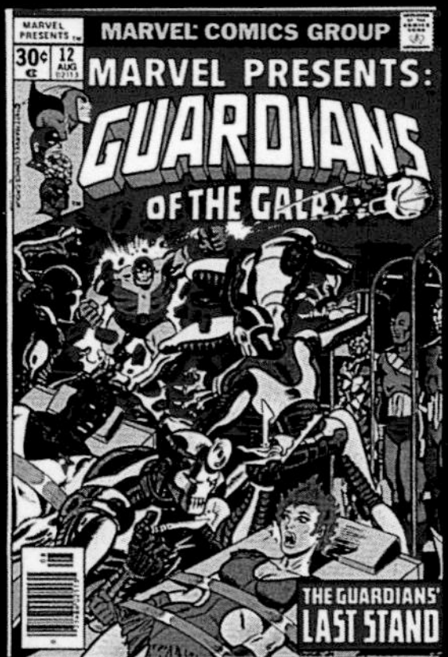
MARVEL COMICS GROUP
MARVEL PRESENTS:
GUARDIANS OF THE GALAXY
THE GUARDIANS' LAST STAND

1216.5 Marvel Saga (1-4)

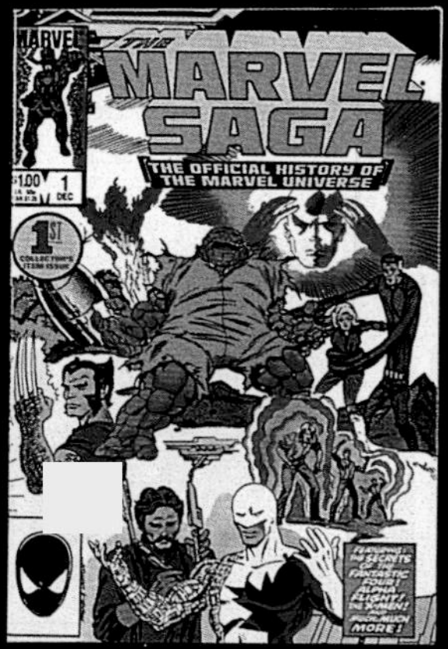
THE MARVEL SAGA
THE OFFICIAL HISTORY OF THE MARVEL UNIVERSE

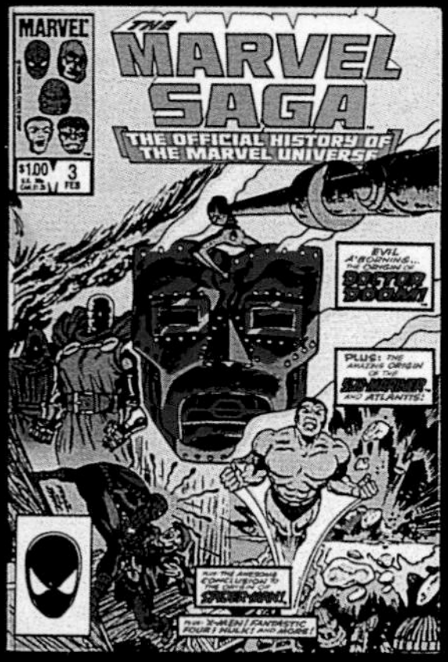
THE MARVEL SAGA
THE OFFICIAL HISTORY OF THE MARVEL UNIVERSE

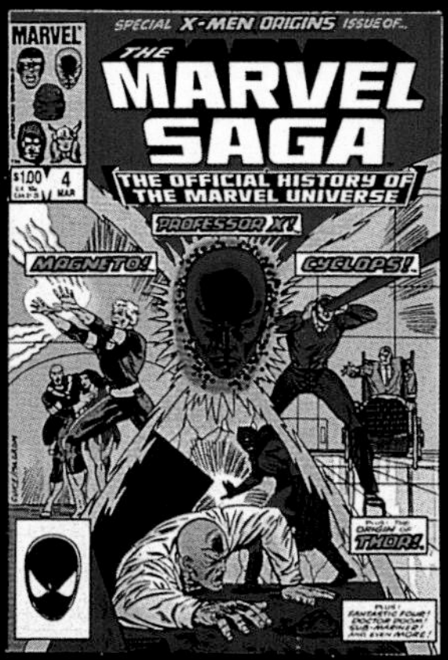
SPECIAL X-MEN ORIGINS ISSUE OF...
THE MARVEL SAGA
THE OFFICIAL HISTORY OF THE MARVEL UNIVERSE
PROFESSOR X!
MAGNETO!
CYCLOPS!

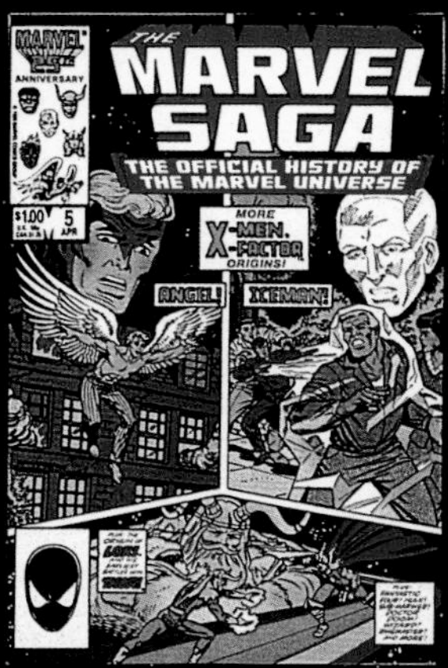
THE MARVEL SAGA
THE OFFICIAL HISTORY OF THE MARVEL UNIVERSE
ANGEL!
ICEMAN!

1217.15 Marvel Spectacular (1-9)

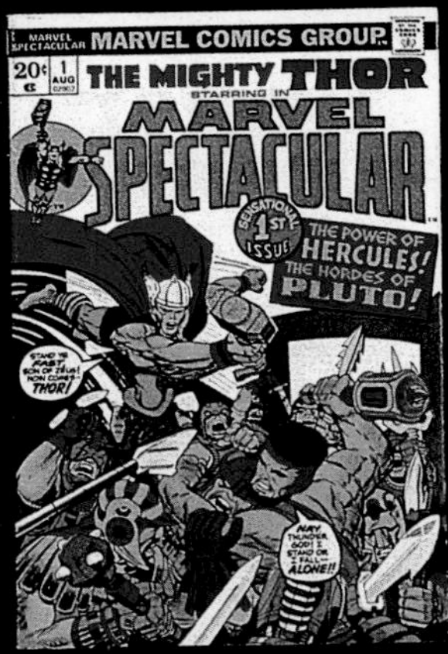
MARVEL COMICS GROUP
THE MIGHTY THOR
STARRING IN
MARVEL SPECTACULAR
THE POWER OF HERCULES! THE HORDES OF PLUTO!

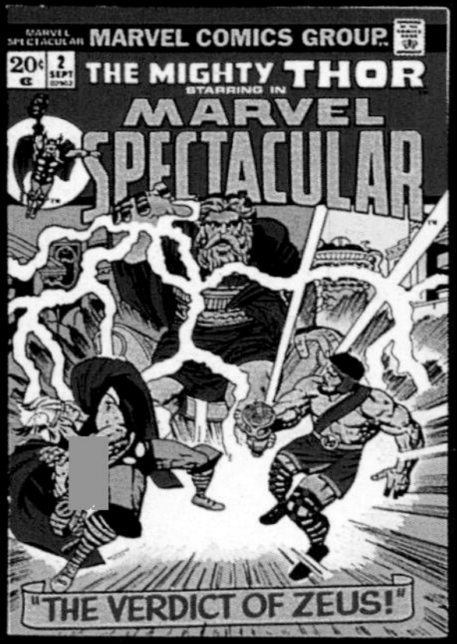
MARVEL COMICS GROUP
THE MIGHTY THOR
MARVEL SPECTACULAR
"THE VERDICT OF ZEUS!"

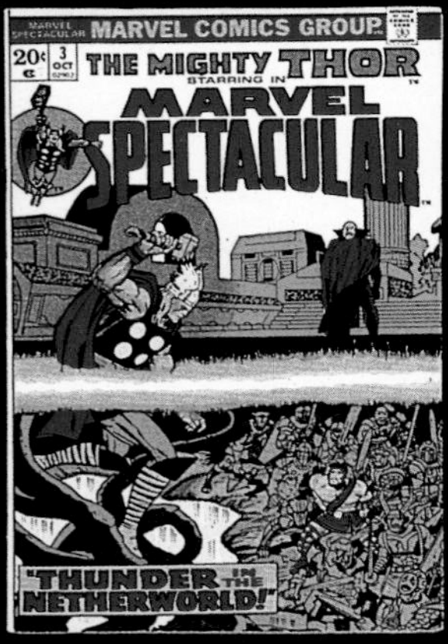
MARVEL COMICS GROUP
THE MIGHTY THOR
MARVEL SPECTACULAR

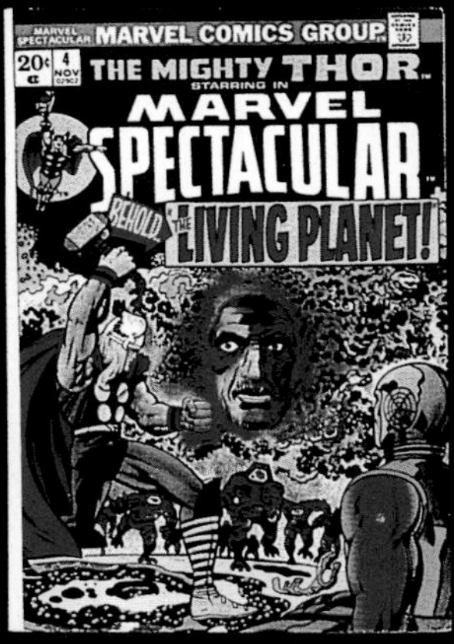
MARVEL COMICS GROUP
THE MIGHTY THOR
MARVEL SPECTACULAR
LIVING PLANET!

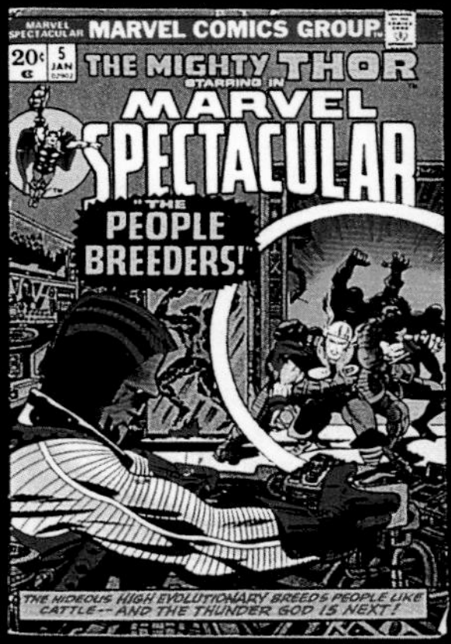
MARVEL COMICS GROUP
THE MIGHTY THOR
MARVEL SPECTACULAR
"THE PEOPLE BREEDERS!"
THE HIDEOUS HIGH EVOLUTIONARY BREEDS PEOPLE LIKE CATTLE-- AND THE THUNDER GOD IS NEXT!

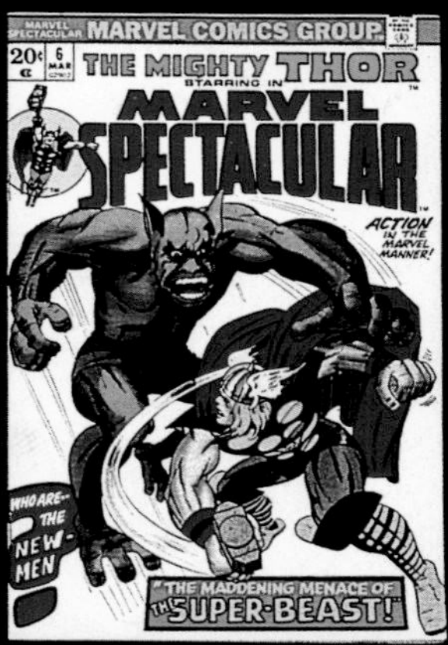
MARVEL COMICS GROUP
THE MIGHTY THOR
MARVEL SPECTACULAR
"THE MADDENING MENACE OF THE SUPER-BEAST!"

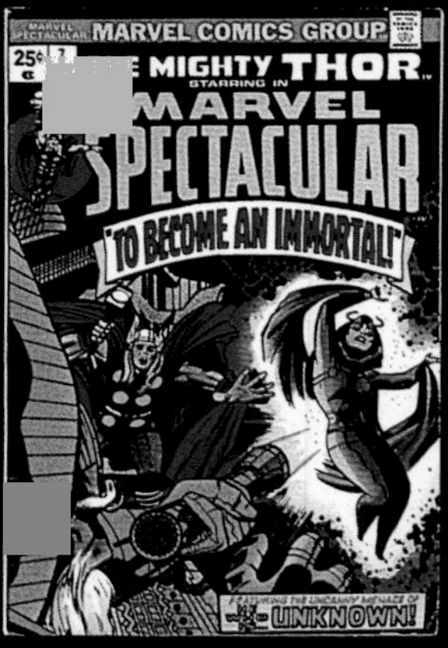
MARVEL COMICS GROUP
THE MIGHTY THOR
MARVEL SPECTACULAR
"TO BECOME AN IMMORTAL!"
UNKNOWN!

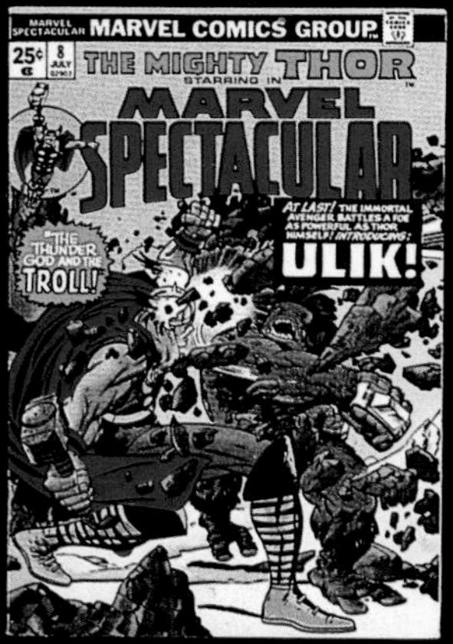
MARVEL COMICS GROUP
THE MIGHTY THOR
MARVEL SPECTACULAR
ULIK!

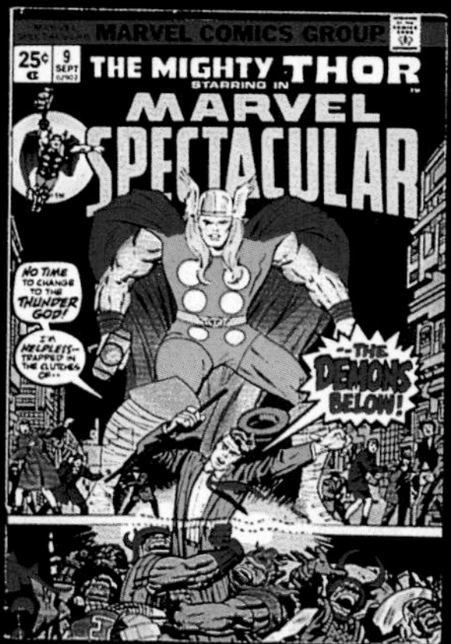
MARVEL COMICS GROUP
THE MIGHTY THOR
MARVEL SPECTACULAR

Marvel Presents (Cont. from Pg. 191)

Ref. No.	Date	RVI	Artist/Info.
1216.3-2	Dec. 1975	1	Trinidad-a (Bloodstone)
1216.3-3	Feb. 1976	4	Milgrom/Marcos-a (Guardian of the Galaxy)
1216.3-4	Apr.	3	Milgrom-a "
1216.3-5	Jun.	3	Milgrom, Chaykin-a "
1216.3-6	Aug.	3	Milgrom/Austin-a "
1216.3-7	Nov.	3	Milgrom/Wiacek-a "
1216.3-8	Dec.	3	" " "
1216.3-9	Feb. 1977	3	" " "
1216.3-10	Apr.	3	" " "
1216.3-11	Jun.	3	Milgrom-c/a, Wiacek-a "
1216.3-12	Aug. 1977	3	Milgrom/Wiacek-a "

The Marvel Saga (1-25) 1216.5

Ref. No.	Date	RVI	Artist/Info.
1216.5-1	Dec. 1985	2	Frenz/Layton-c
1216.5-2 to 25	Dec. 1987, (#25)	1	

Marvel Spectacular (1-19) 1217.15

Ref. No.	Date	RVI	Artist/Info.
1217.15-1	Aug. 1973	1	Reprints
1217.15-2	Sept.	1	"
1217.15-3	Oct.	1	"
1217.15-4	Nov.	1	"
1217.15-5	Jan. 1974	1	"
1217.15-6	Mar.	1	"
1217.15-7 to19	Nov. 1975, (#19)	1	"

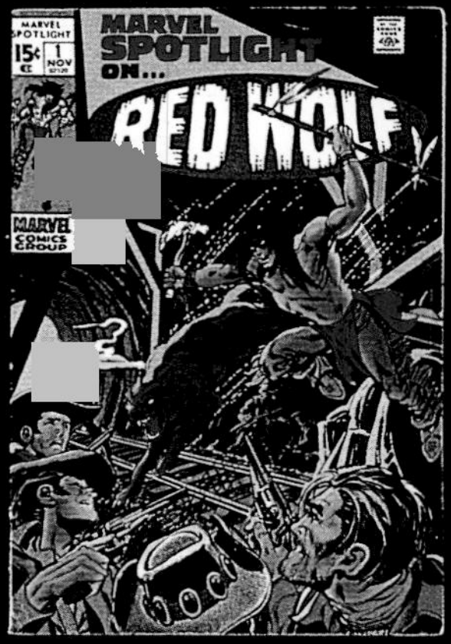
MARVEL SPOTLIGHT ON...
RED WOLF

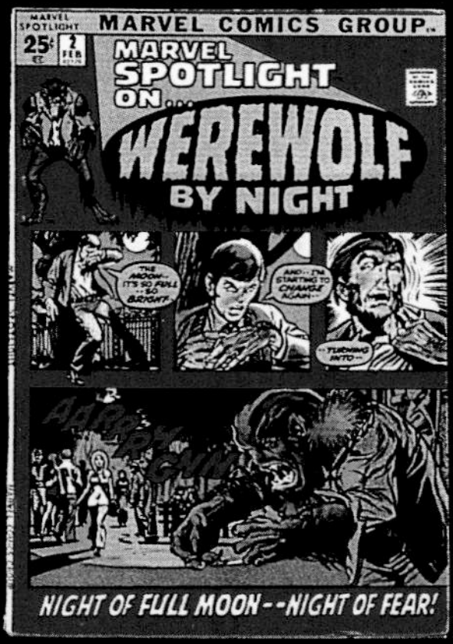
MARVEL COMICS GROUP
MARVEL SPOTLIGHT ON...
WEREWOLF BY NIGHT
NIGHT OF FULL MOON--NIGHT OF FEAR!

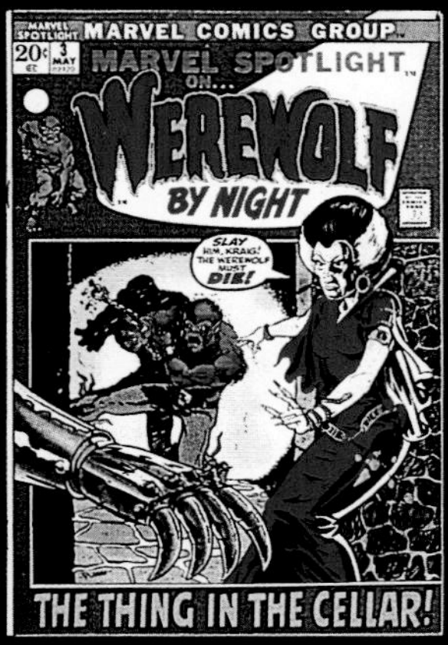
MARVEL COMICS GROUP
MARVEL SPOTLIGHT ON...
WEREWOLF BY NIGHT
THE THING IN THE CELLAR!

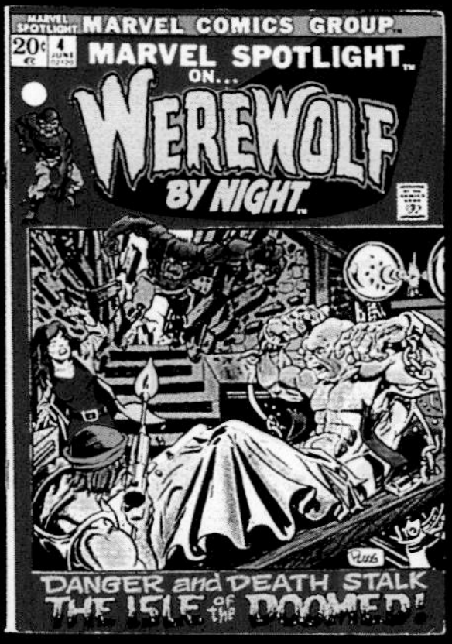
MARVEL COMICS GROUP
MARVEL SPOTLIGHT ON...
WEREWOLF BY NIGHT
DANGER and DEATH STALK
THE ISLE of the DOOMED!

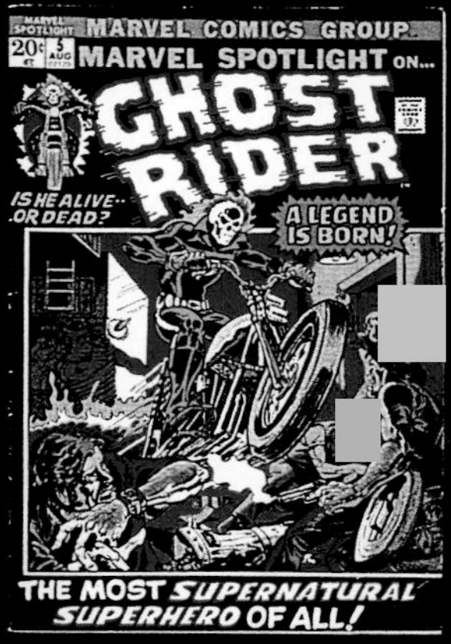
MARVEL COMICS GROUP
MARVEL SPOTLIGHT ON...
GHOST RIDER
IS HE ALIVE--OR DEAD?
A LEGEND IS BORN!
THE MOST SUPERNATURAL SUPERHERO OF ALL!

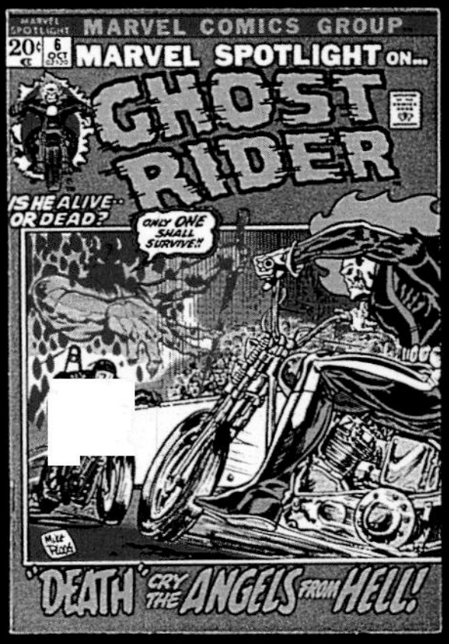
MARVEL COMICS GROUP
MARVEL SPOTLIGHT ON...
GHOST RIDER
IS HE ALIVE-OR DEAD?
'DEATH' CRY THE ANGELS FROM HELL!

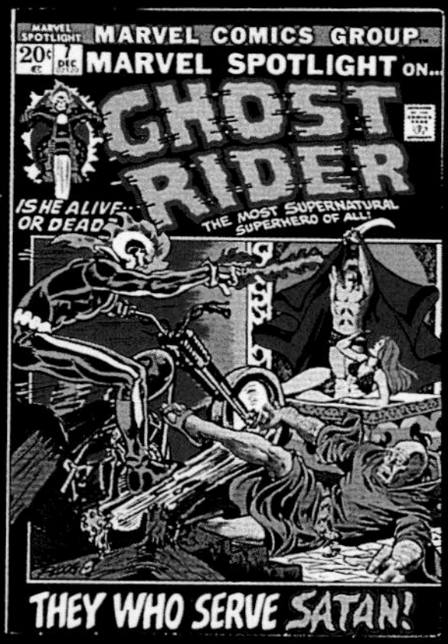
MARVEL COMICS GROUP
MARVEL SPOTLIGHT ON...
GHOST RIDER
IS HE ALIVE-OR DEAD?
THE MOST SUPERNATURAL SUPERHERO OF ALL!
THEY WHO SERVE SATAN!

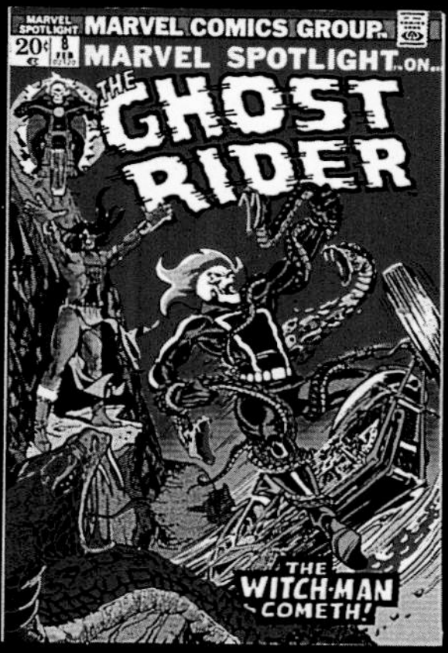
MARVEL COMICS GROUP
MARVEL SPOTLIGHT ON...
THE GHOST RIDER
THE WITCH-MAN COMETH!

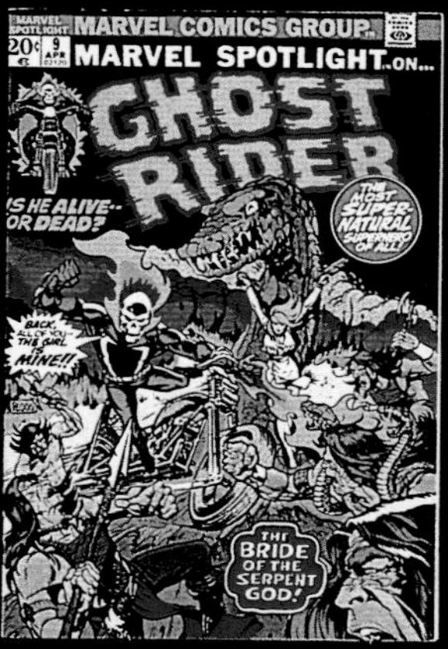
MARVEL COMICS GROUP
MARVEL SPOTLIGHT ON...
GHOST RIDER
IS HE ALIVE-OR DEAD?
THE BRIDE OF THE SERPENT GOD!

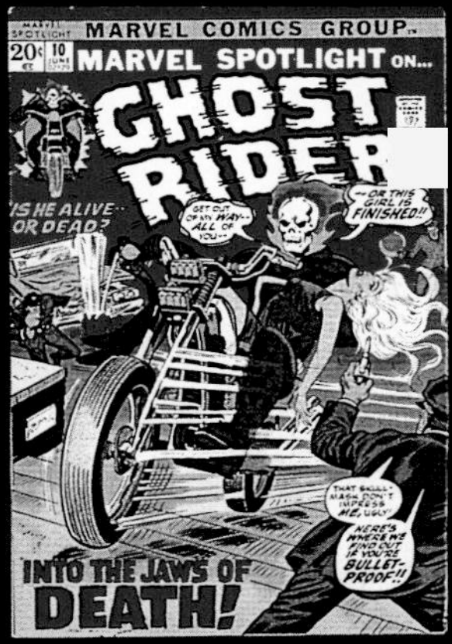
MARVEL COMICS GROUP
MARVEL SPOTLIGHT ON...
GHOST RIDER
IS HE ALIVE-OR DEAD?
INTO THE JAWS OF DEATH!

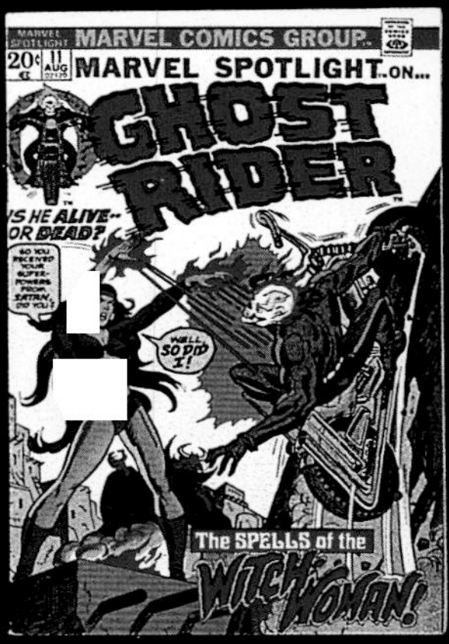
MARVEL COMICS GROUP
MARVEL SPOTLIGHT ON...
GHOST RIDER
IS HE ALIVE-OR DEAD?
The SPELLS of the WITCH-WOMAN!

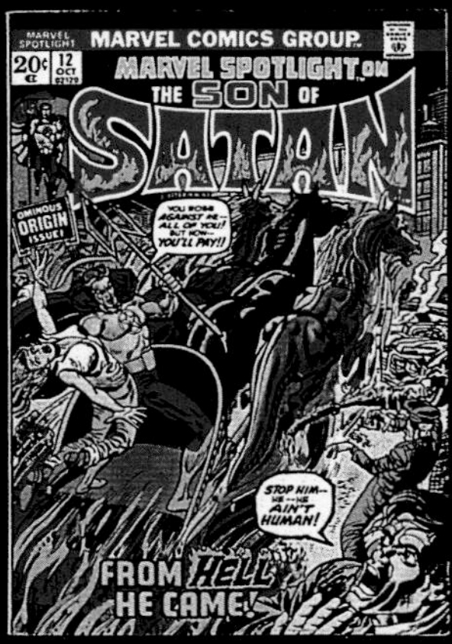
MARVEL COMICS GROUP
MARVEL SPOTLIGHT ON
THE SON OF SATAN
FROM HELL HE CAME!

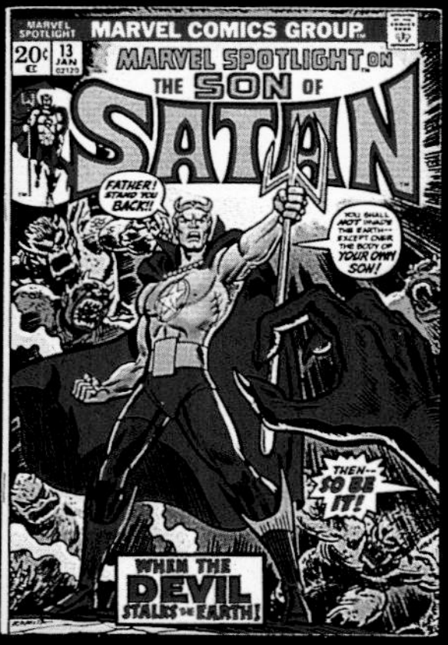
MARVEL COMICS GROUP
MARVEL SPOTLIGHT ON
THE SON OF SATAN
WHEN THE DEVIL STALKS the EARTH!

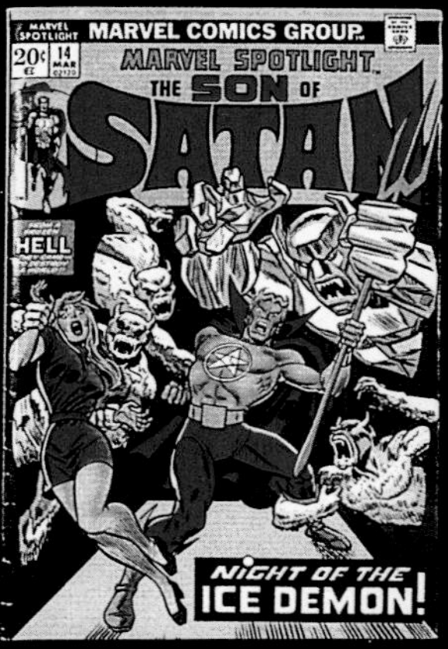
MARVEL COMICS GROUP
MARVEL SPOTLIGHT
THE SON OF SATAN
NIGHT OF THE ICE DEMON!

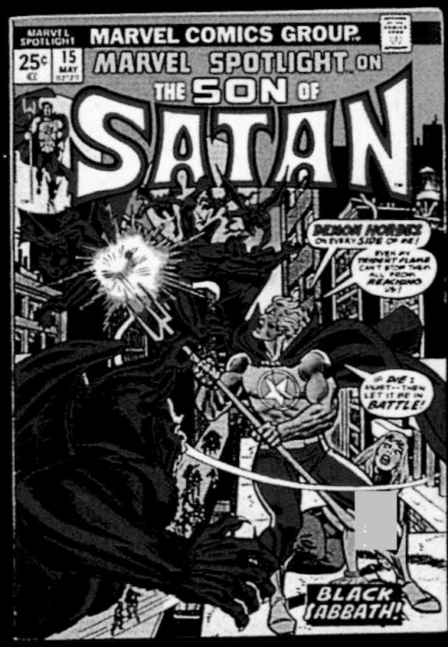
MARVEL COMICS GROUP
MARVEL SPOTLIGHT ON
THE SON OF SATAN
BLACK SABBATH!

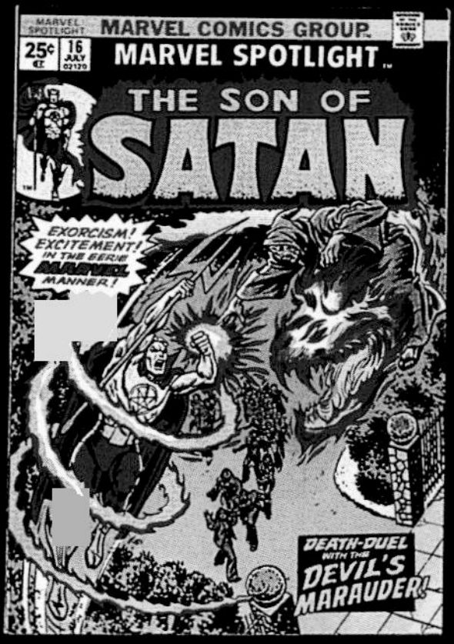
MARVEL COMICS GROUP
MARVEL SPOTLIGHT
THE SON OF SATAN
DEATH-DUEL WITH THE DEVIL'S MARAUDER!

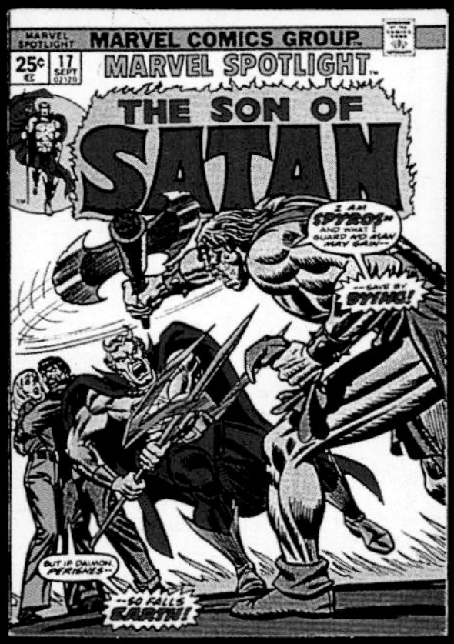
MARVEL COMICS GROUP
MARVEL SPOTLIGHT
THE SON OF SATAN

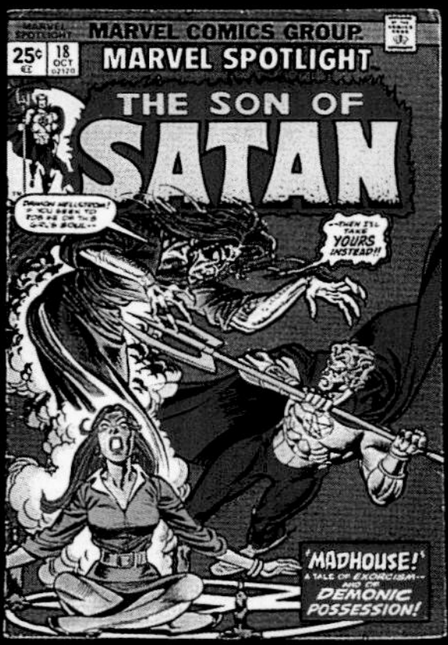
MARVEL COMICS GROUP
MARVEL SPOTLIGHT
THE SON OF SATAN
'MADHOUSE!'
DEMONIC POSSESSION!

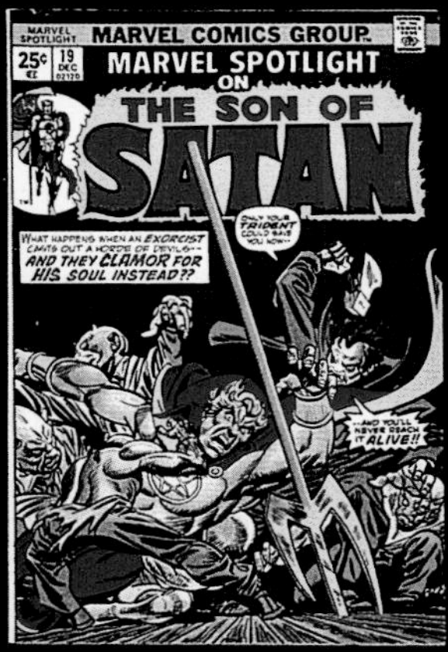
MARVEL COMICS GROUP
MARVEL SPOTLIGHT ON
THE SON OF SATAN
AND THEY CLAMOR FOR HIS SOUL INSTEAD??

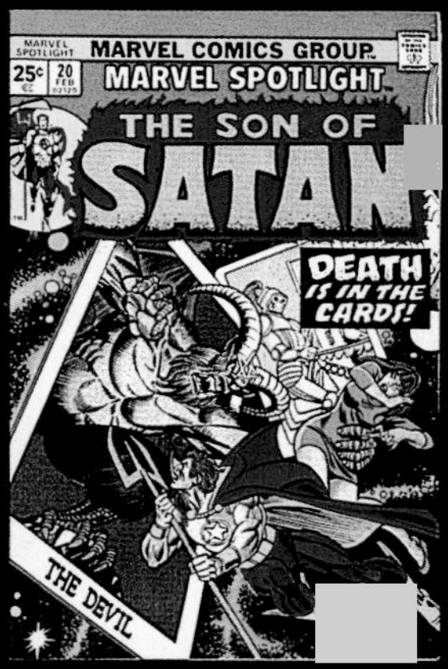
MARVEL COMICS GROUP
MARVEL SPOTLIGHT
THE SON OF SATAN
DEATH IS IN THE CARDS!
THE DEVIL

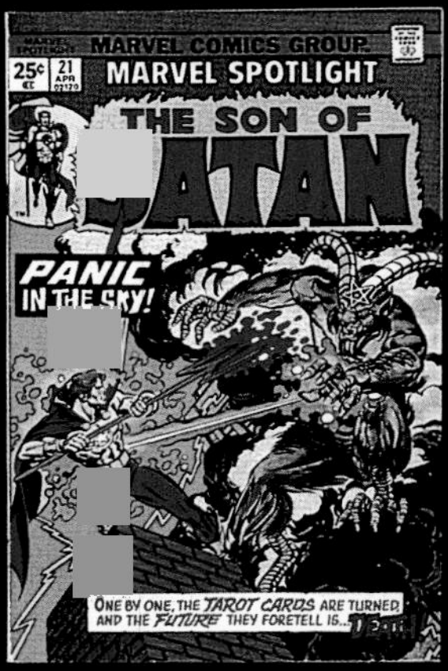
MARVEL COMICS GROUP
MARVEL SPOTLIGHT
THE SON OF
PANIC IN THE SKY!
ONE BY ONE, THE TAROT CARDS ARE TURNED AND THE FUTURE THEY FORETELL IS...

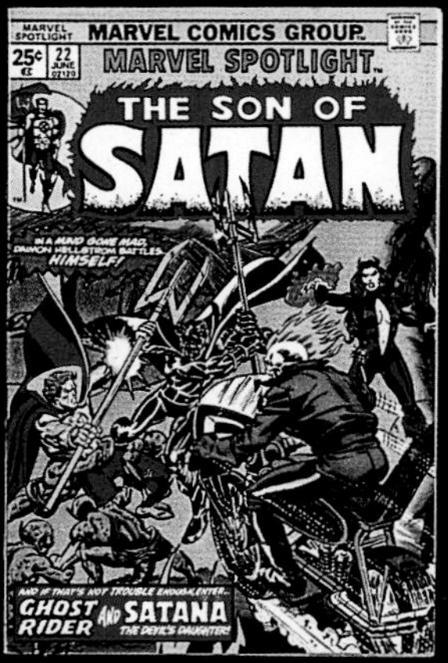
MARVEL COMICS GROUP
MARVEL SPOTLIGHT
THE SON OF SATAN
GHOST RIDER
SATANA

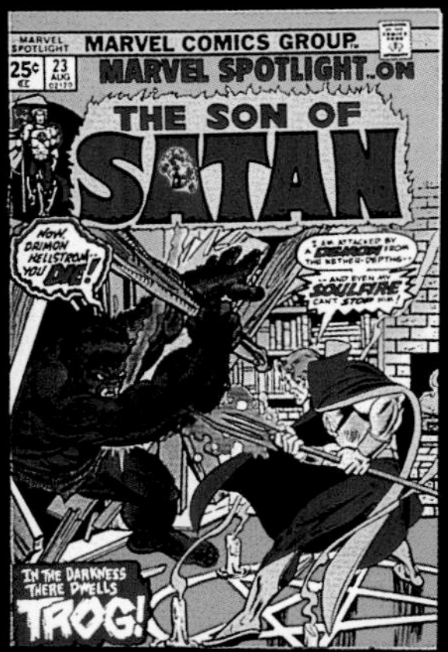
MARVEL COMICS GROUP
MARVEL SPOTLIGHT ON
THE SON OF SATAN
IN THE DARKNESS THERE DWELLS TROG!

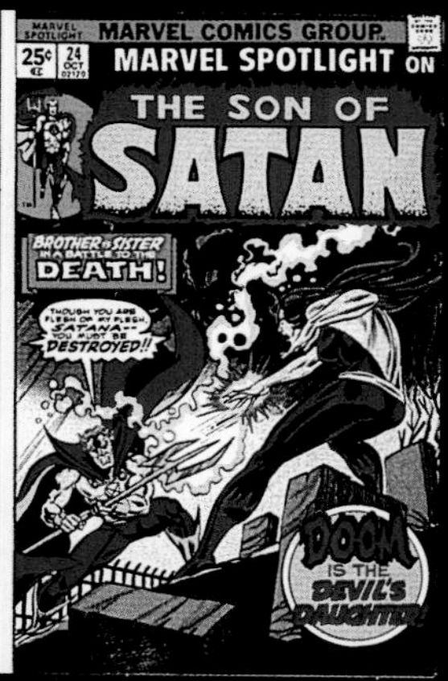
MARVEL COMICS GROUP
MARVEL SPOTLIGHT ON
THE SON OF SATAN
DEATH!
DOOM IS THE DEVIL'S DAUGHTER!

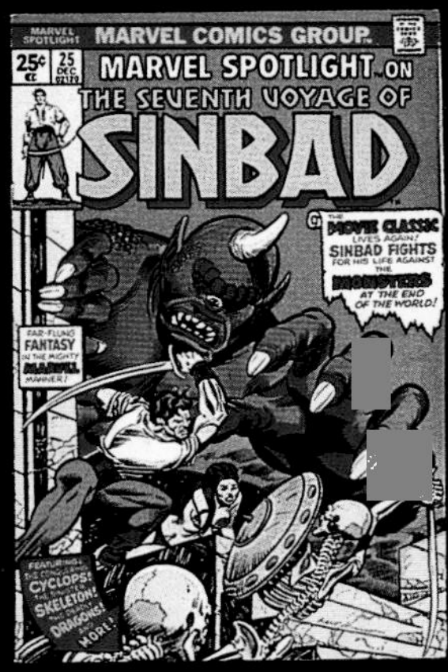
MARVEL COMICS GROUP
MARVEL SPOTLIGHT ON
THE SEVENTH VOYAGE OF SINBAD
MOVIE CLASSIC

1217.2 **Marvel Spotlight (26-33)**

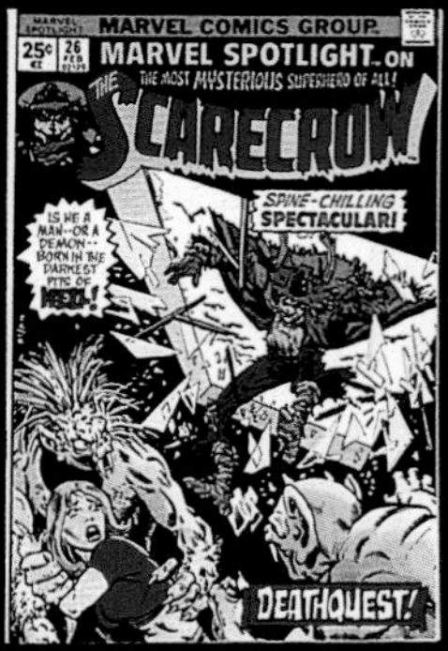
MARVEL COMICS GROUP
MARVEL SPOTLIGHT ON
THE SCARECROW!
SPINE-CHILLING SPECTACULAR!
DEATHQUEST!
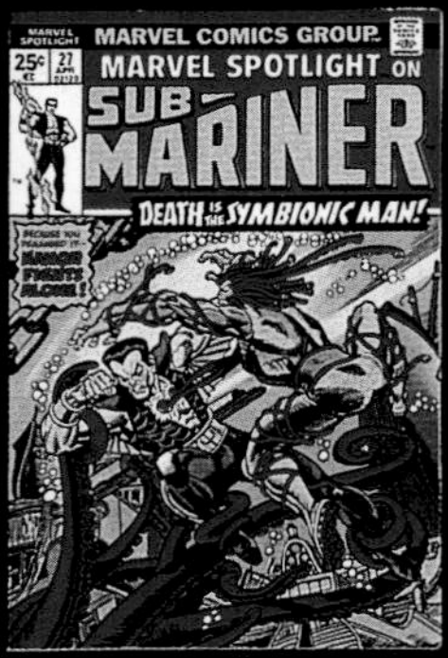
MARVEL COMICS GROUP
MARVEL SPOTLIGHT ON
SUB-MARINER
DEATH IS THE SYMBIONIC MAN!
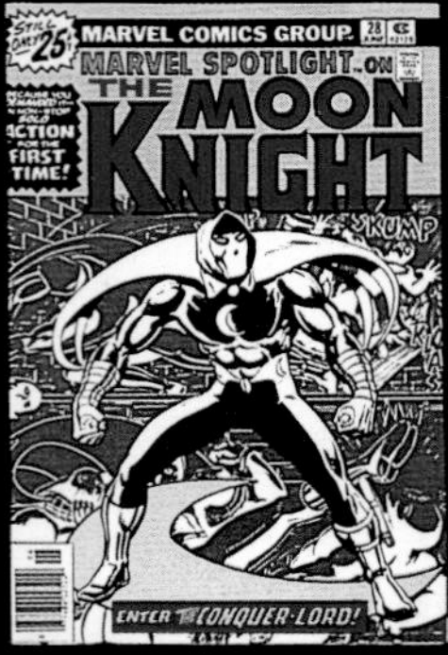
MARVEL COMICS GROUP
MARVEL SPOTLIGHT ON
THE MOON KNIGHT
ENTER THE CONQUER-LORD!
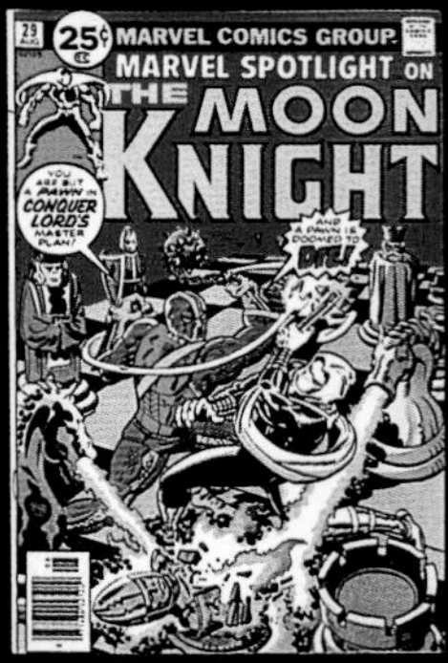
MARVEL COMICS GROUP
MARVEL SPOTLIGHT ON
THE MOON KNIGHT
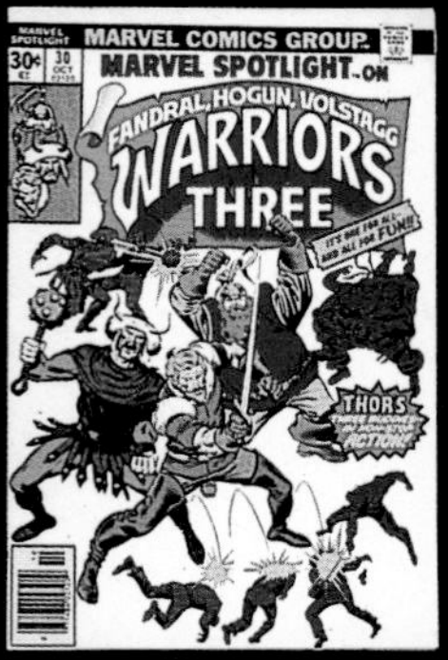
MARVEL COMICS GROUP
MARVEL SPOTLIGHT ON
FANDRAL, HOGUN, VOLSTAGG
WARRIORS THREE
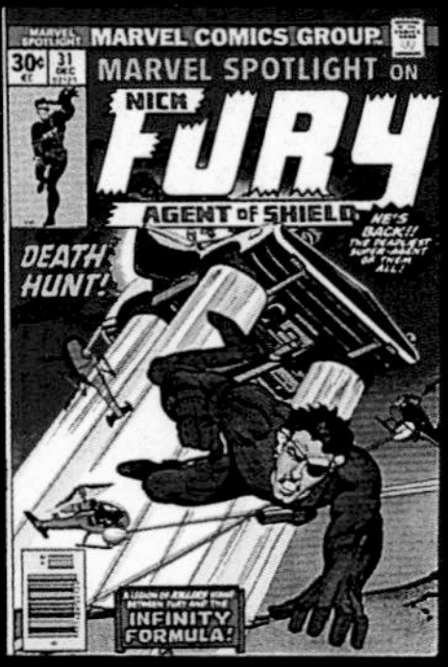
MARVEL COMICS GROUP
MARVEL SPOTLIGHT ON
NICK FURY
AGENT of SHIELD
DEATH HUNT!
INFINITY FORMULA!
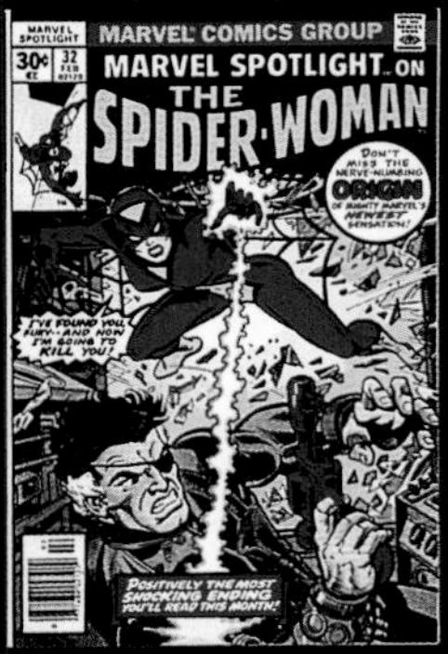
MARVEL COMICS GROUP
MARVEL SPOTLIGHT ON
THE SPIDER-WOMAN
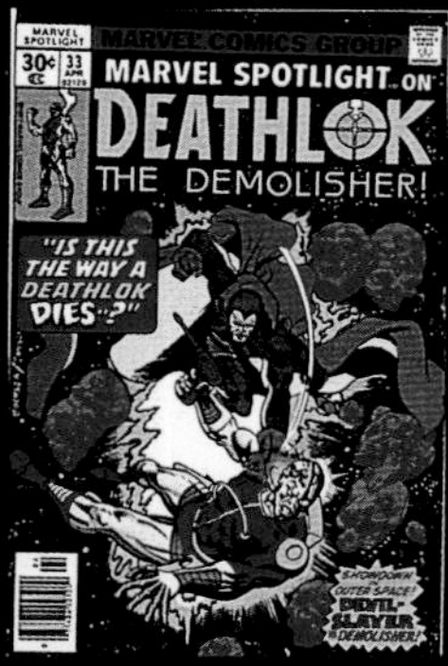
MARVEL COMICS GROUP
MARVEL SPOTLIGHT ON
DEATHLOK
THE DEMOLISHER!
"IS THIS THE WAY A DEATHLOK DIES--?"

1217.25 **Marvel Spotlight (V2, 1-11)**

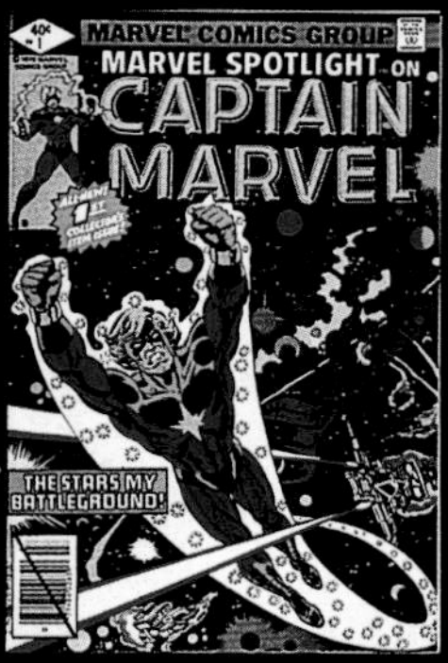
MARVEL COMICS GROUP
MARVEL SPOTLIGHT ON
CAPTAIN MARVEL
THE STARS MY BATTLEGROUND!
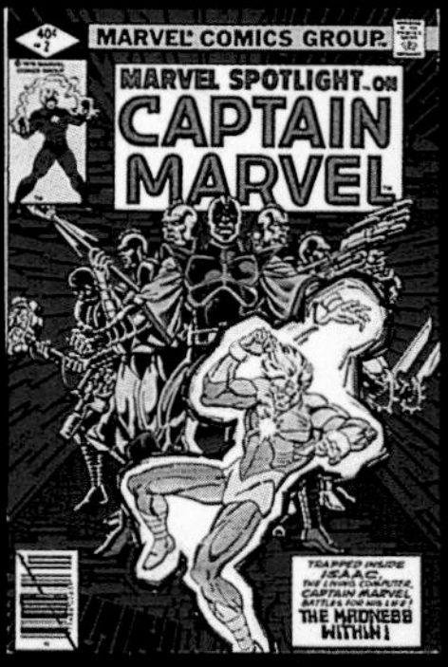
MARVEL COMICS GROUP
MARVEL SPOTLIGHT ON
CAPTAIN MARVEL
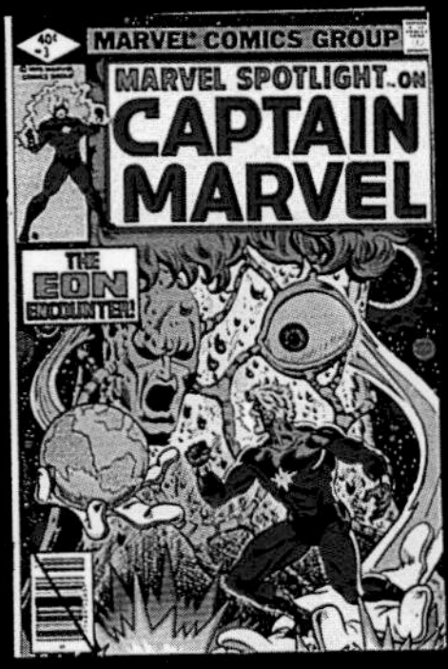
MARVEL COMICS GROUP
MARVEL SPOTLIGHT ON
CAPTAIN MARVEL
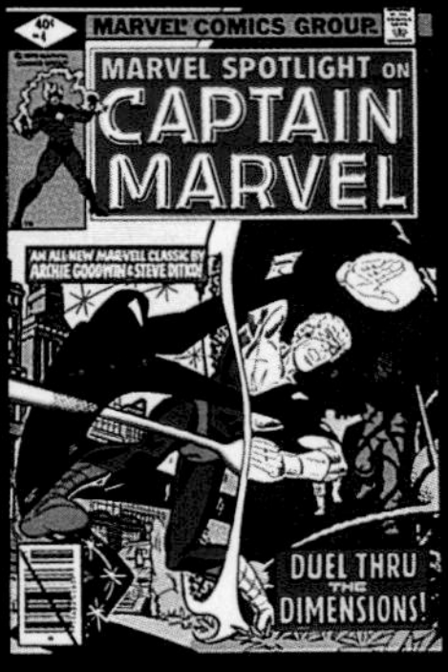
MARVEL COMICS GROUP
MARVEL SPOTLIGHT ON
CAPTAIN MARVEL
DUEL THRU THE DIMENSIONS!
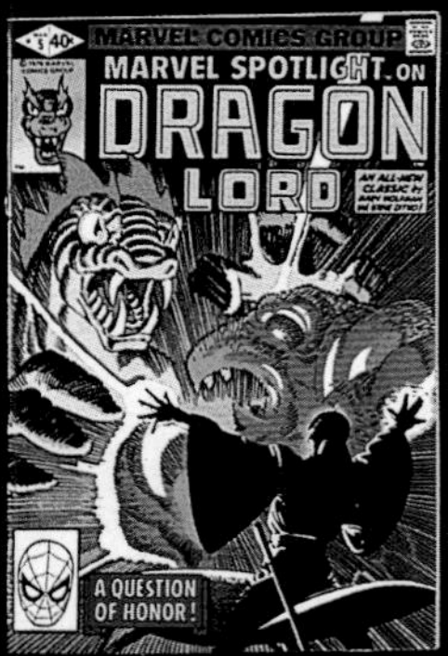
MARVEL COMICS GROUP
MARVEL SPOTLIGHT ON
DRAGON LORD
A QUESTION OF HONOR!
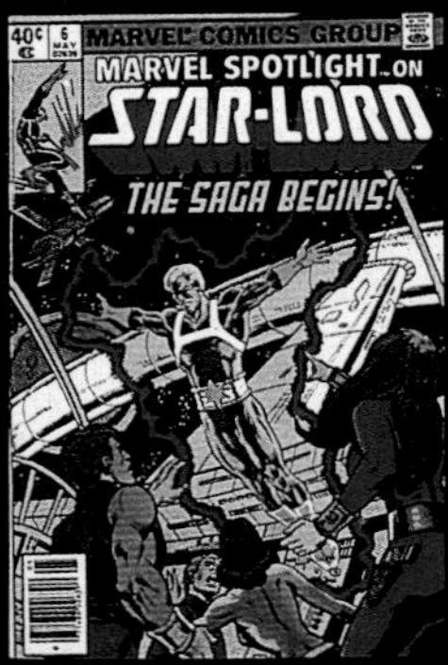
MARVEL COMICS GROUP
MARVEL SPOTLIGHT ON
STAR-LORD
THE SAGA BEGINS!
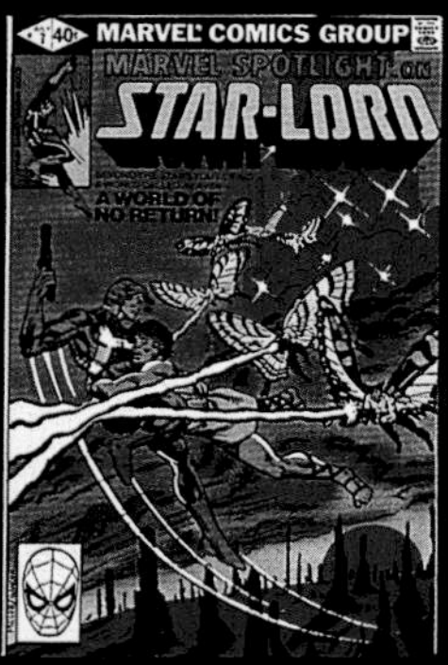
MARVEL COMICS GROUP
MARVEL SPOTLIGHT ON
STAR-LORD
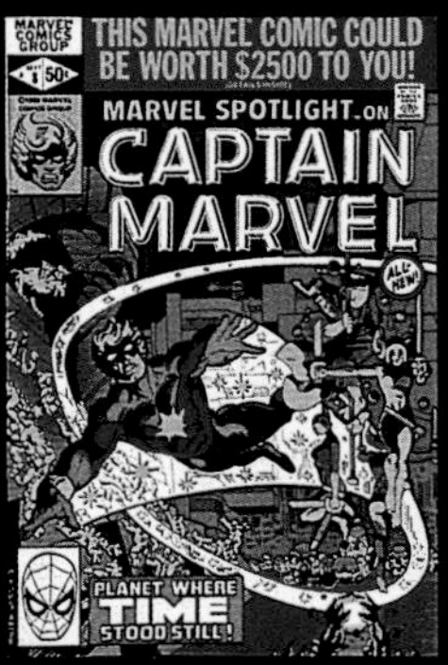
THIS MARVEL COMIC COULD BE WORTH $2500 TO YOU!
MARVEL SPOTLIGHT ON
CAPTAIN MARVEL
PLANET WHERE TIME STOOD STILL!
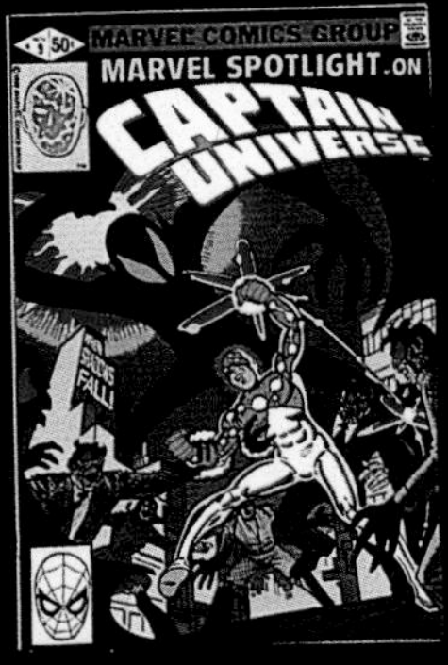
MARVEL COMICS GROUP
MARVEL SPOTLIGHT ON
CAPTAIN UNIVERSE
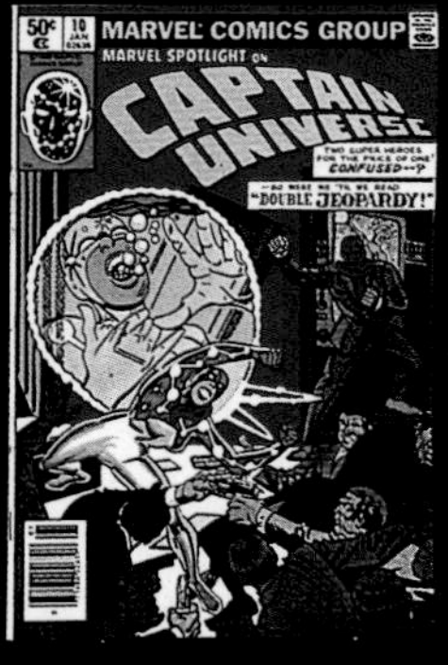
MARVEL COMICS GROUP
MARVEL SPOTLIGHT ON
CAPTAIN UNIVERSE

1217.35 **Marvel Super Hero Contest of Champions (1-3)**

1217.4 **Marvel Super Heroes (1) Marvel Super Heroes Secret Wars (1-12)**

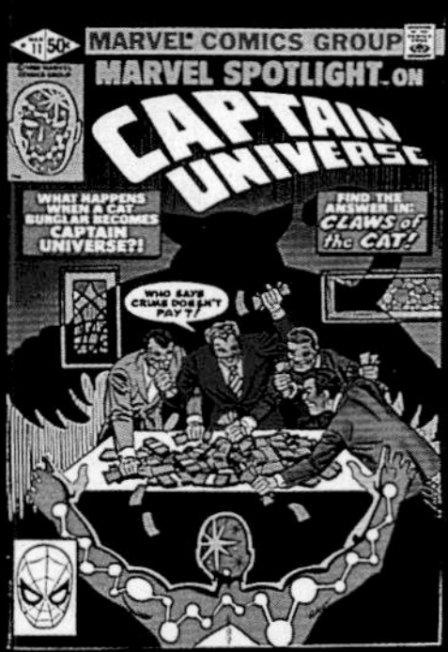
MARVEL COMICS GROUP
MARVEL SPOTLIGHT ON
CAPTAIN UNIVERSE
CLAWS OF THE CAT!
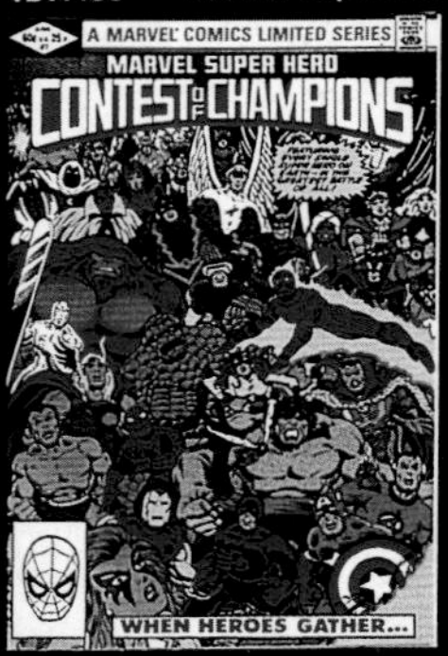
A MARVEL COMICS LIMITED SERIES
MARVEL SUPER HERO
CONTEST OF CHAMPIONS
WHEN HEROES GATHER...
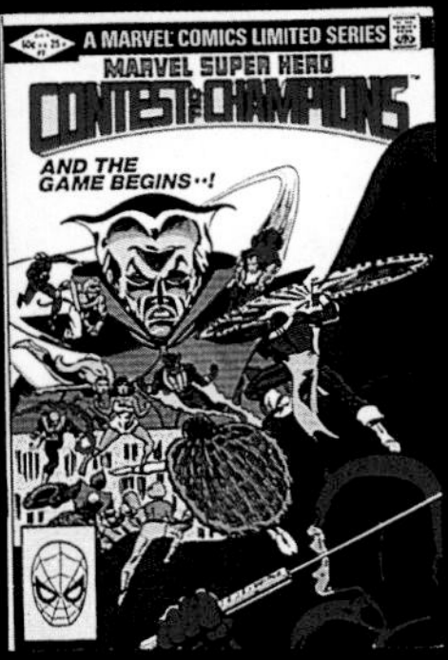
A MARVEL COMICS LIMITED SERIES
MARVEL SUPER HERO
CONTEST OF CHAMPIONS
AND THE GAME BEGINS--!
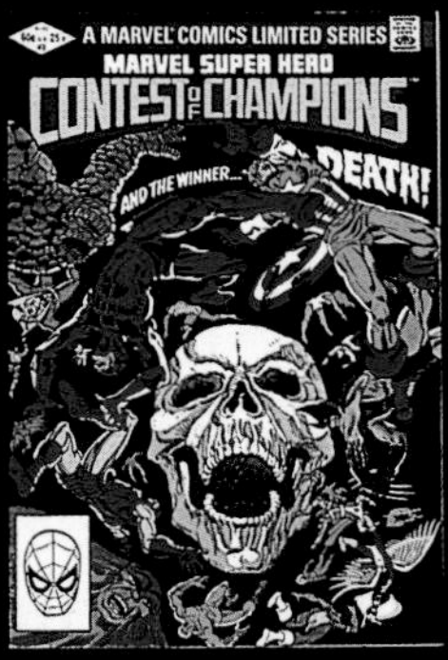
A MARVEL COMICS LIMITED SERIES
MARVEL SUPER HERO
CONTEST OF CHAMPIONS
AND THE WINNER... DEATH!
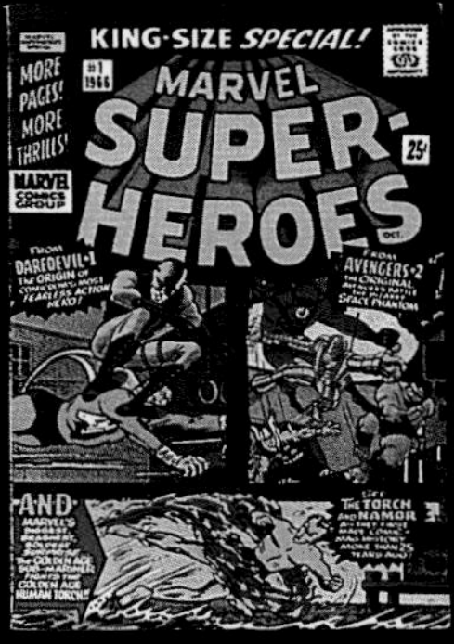
KING-SIZE SPECIAL!
MARVEL SUPER-HEROES
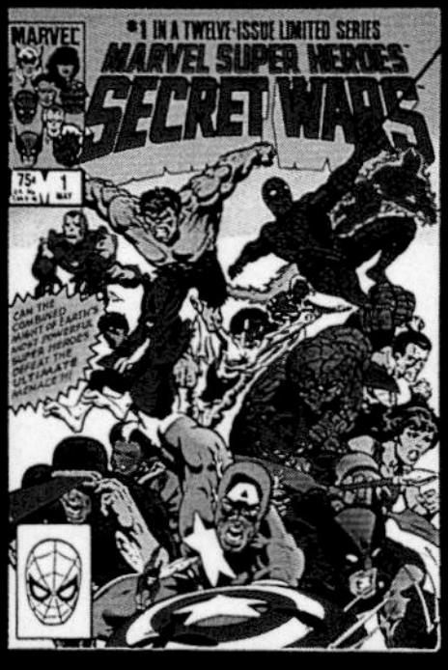
MARVEL SUPER HEROES
SECRET WARS
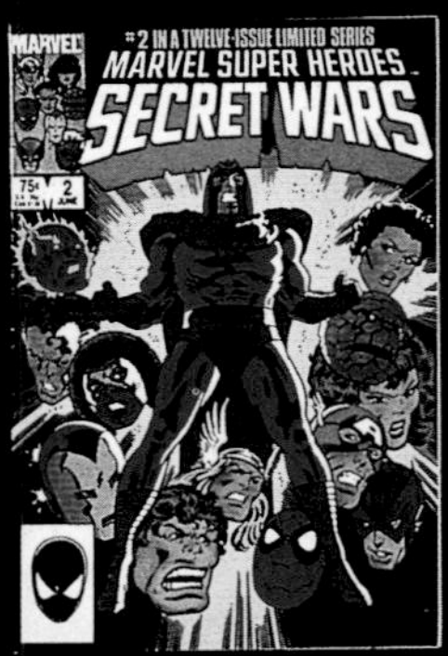
#2 IN A TWELVE-ISSUE LIMITED SERIES
MARVEL SUPER HEROES
SECRET WARS
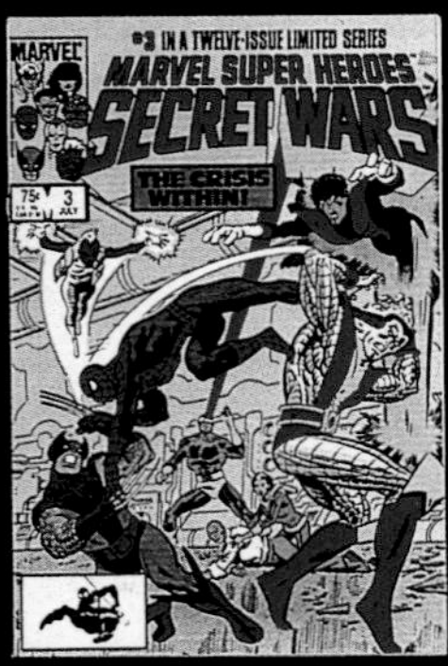
#3 IN A TWELVE-ISSUE LIMITED SERIES
MARVEL SUPER HEROES
SECRET WARS
THE CRISIS WITHIN!
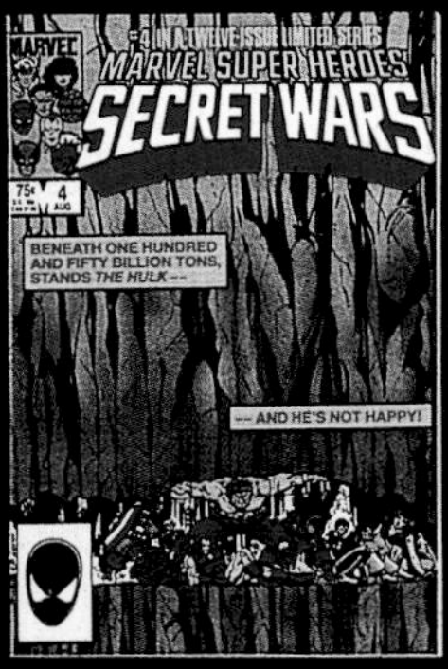
MARVEL SUPER HEROES
SECRET WARS
BENEATH ONE HUNDRED AND FIFTY BILLION TONS STANDS THE HULK--
--AND HE'S NOT HAPPY!
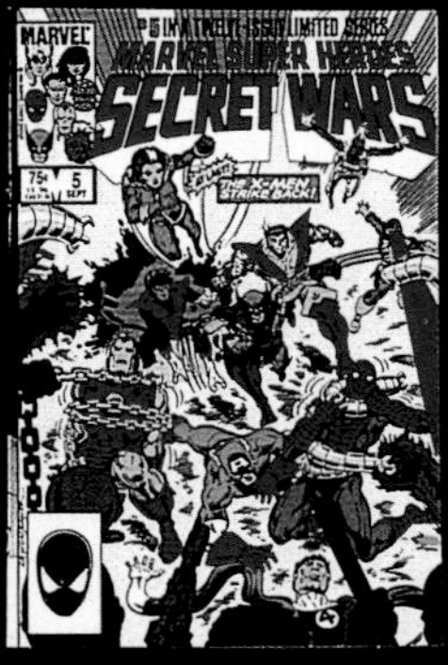
MARVEL SUPER HEROES
SECRET WARS
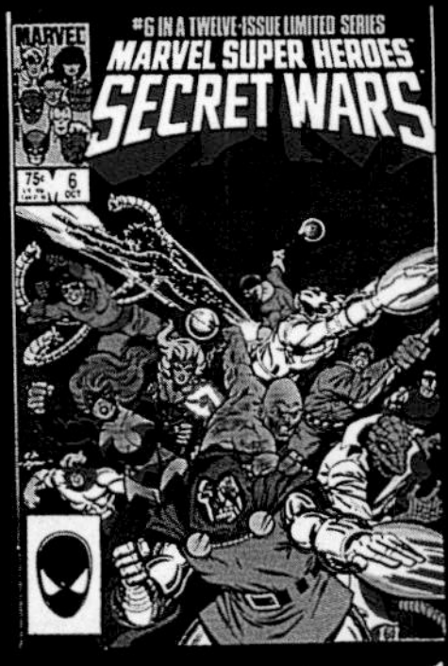
#6 IN A TWELVE-ISSUE LIMITED SERIES
MARVEL SUPER HEROES
SECRET WARS
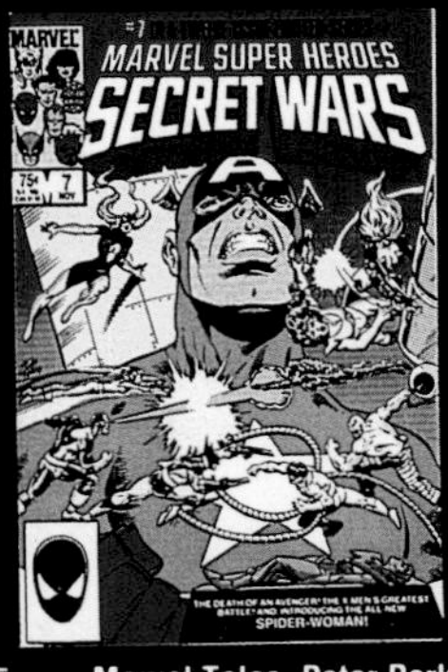
MARVEL SUPER HEROES
SECRET WARS

1217.5 **Marvel Tales, Peter Porker**

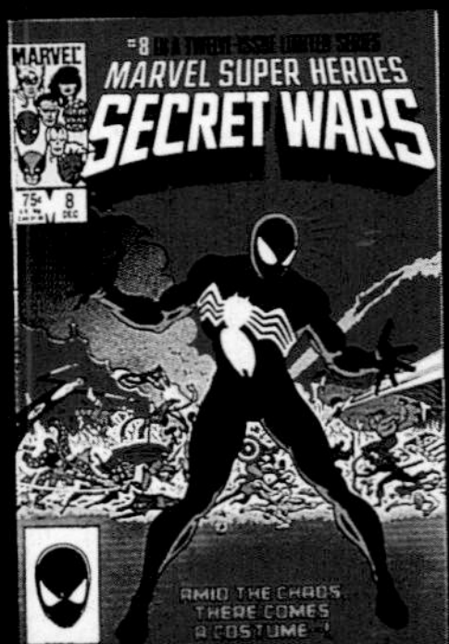
MARVEL SUPER HEROES
SECRET WARS
AMID THE CHAOS THERE COMES A COSTUME!
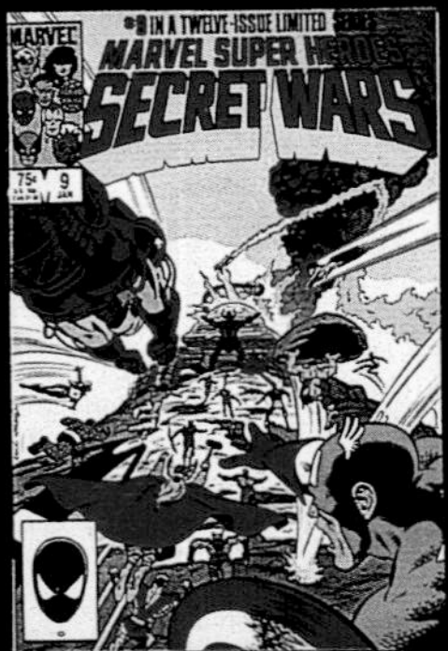
#9 IN A TWELVE-ISSUE LIMITED SERIES
MARVEL SUPER HEROES
SECRET WARS
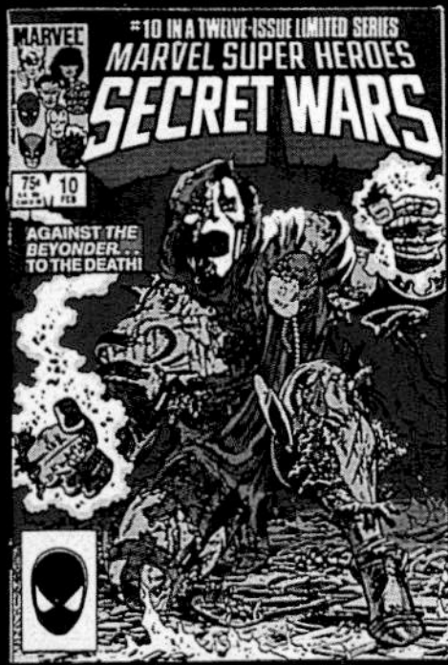
#10 IN A TWELVE-ISSUE LIMITED SERIES
MARVEL SUPER HEROES
SECRET WARS
AGAINST THE BEYONDER TO THE DEATH!
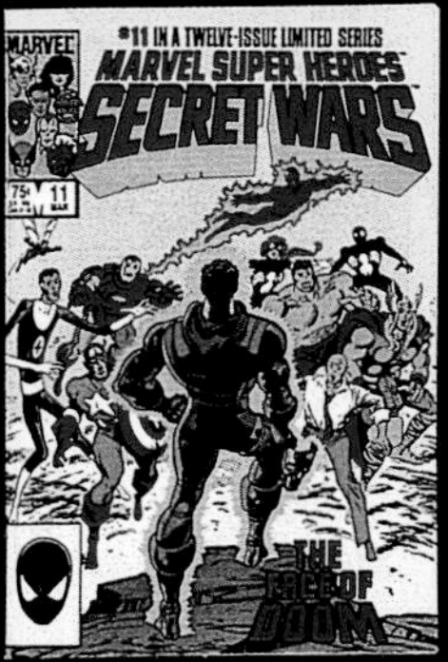
#11 IN A TWELVE-ISSUE LIMITED SERIES
MARVEL SUPER HEROES
SECRET WARS
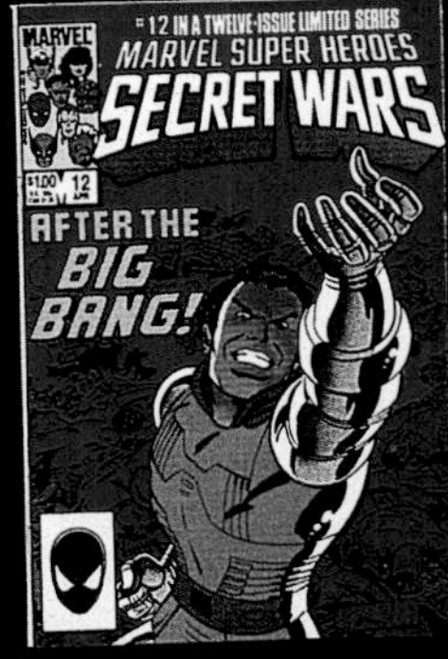
#12 IN A TWELVE-ISSUE LIMITED SERIES
MARVEL SUPER HEROES
SECRET WARS
AFTER THE BIG BANG!
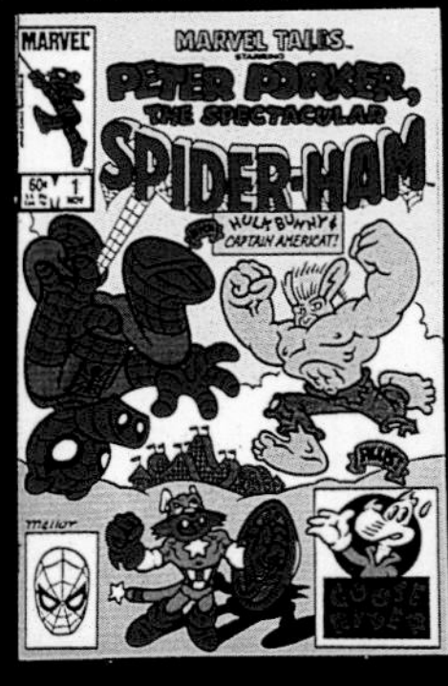
MARVEL TALES
PETER PORKER, THE SPECTACULAR SPIDER-HAM

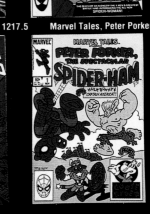

1217.3 Marvel Super-Action (1-34)

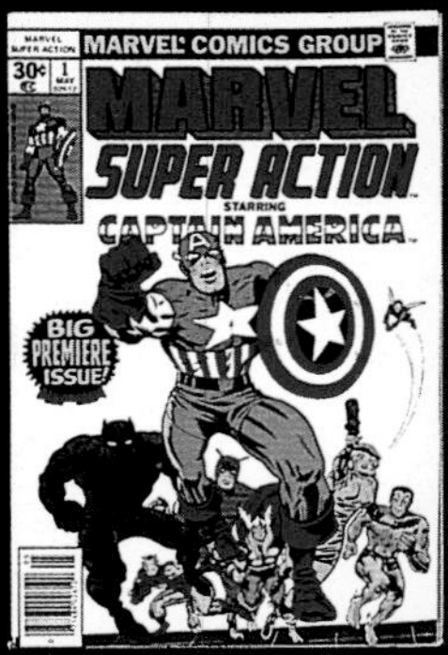
MARVEL COMICS GROUP
MARVEL SUPER ACTION
STARRING CAPTAIN AMERICA
BIG PREMIERE ISSUE!
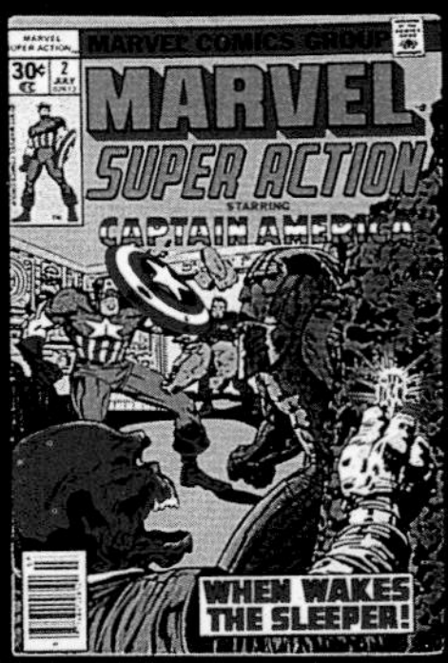
MARVEL COMICS GROUP
MARVEL SUPER ACTION
STARRING CAPTAIN AMERICA
WHEN WAKES THE SLEEPER!
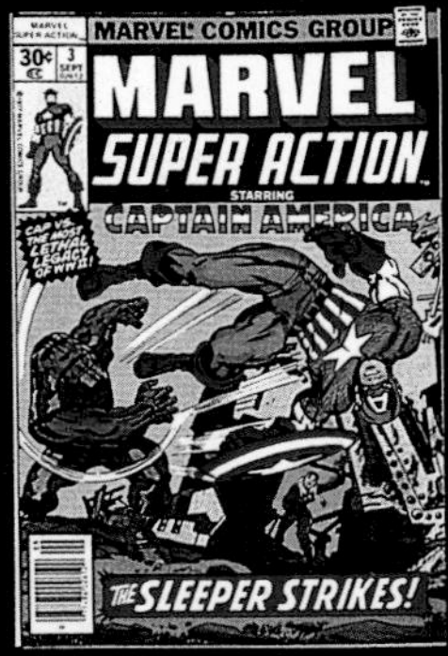
MARVEL COMICS GROUP
MARVEL SUPER ACTION
STARRING CAPTAIN AMERICA
THE SLEEPER STRIKES!
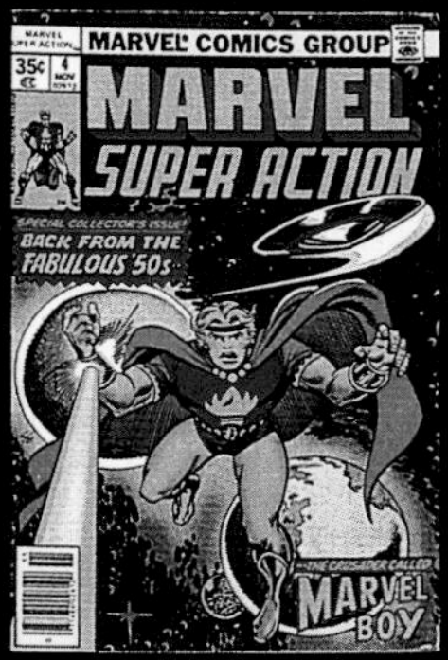
MARVEL COMICS GROUP
MARVEL SUPER ACTION
BACK FROM THE FABULOUS '50s
MARVEL BOY
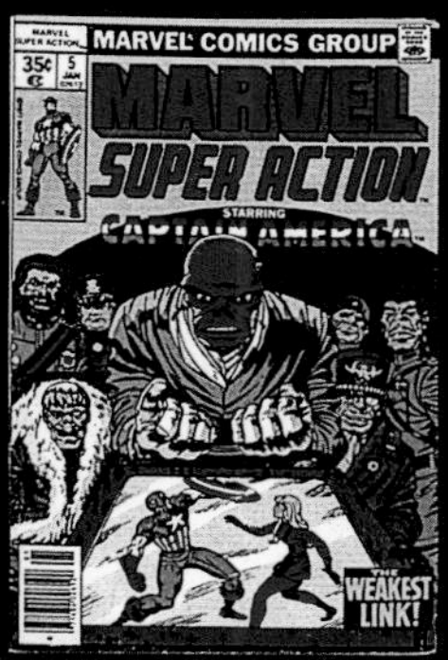
MARVEL COMICS GROUP
MARVEL SUPER ACTION
STARRING CAPTAIN AMERICA
WEAKEST LINK!
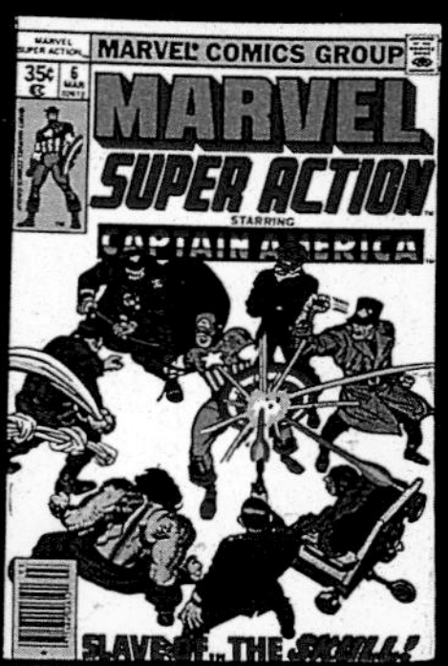
MARVEL COMICS GROUP
MARVEL SUPER ACTION
STARRING CAPTAIN AMERICA
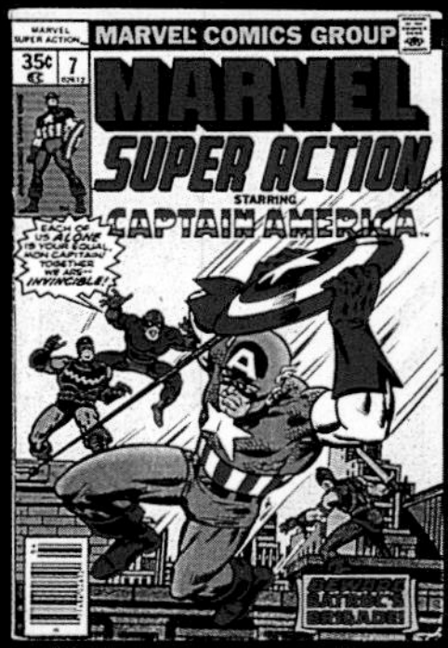
MARVEL COMICS GROUP
MARVEL SUPER ACTION
STARRING CAPTAIN AMERICA
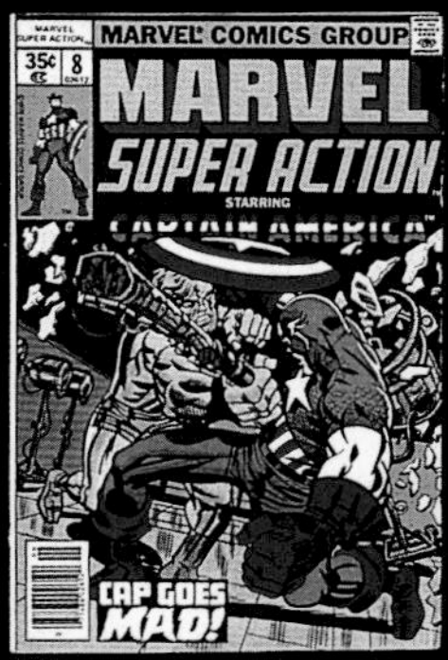
MARVEL COMICS GROUP
MARVEL SUPER ACTION
STARRING CAPTAIN AMERICA
CAP GOES MAD!
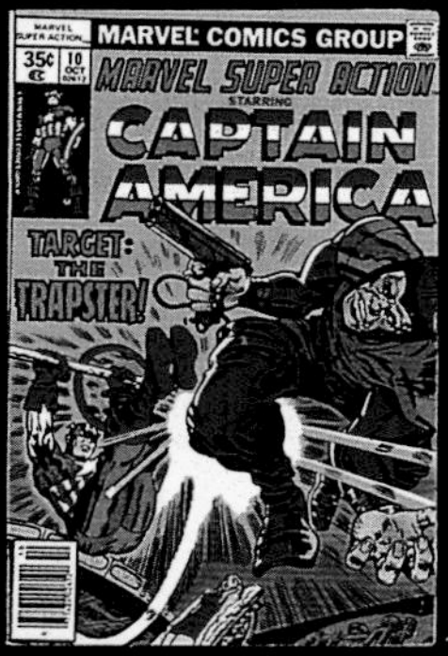
MARVEL COMICS GROUP
MARVEL SUPER ACTION
STARRING CAPTAIN AMERICA
TARGET: THE TRAPSTER!
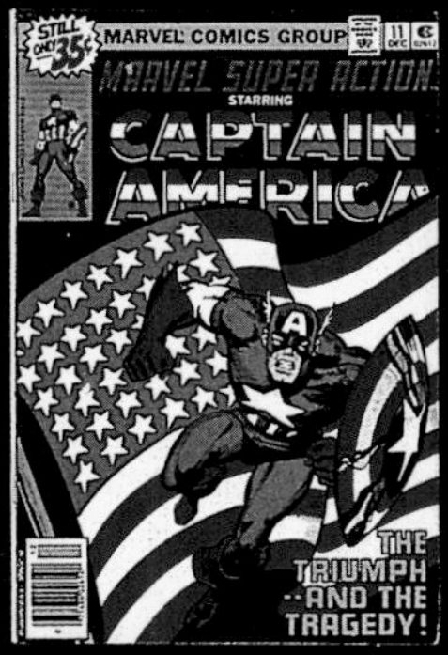
MARVEL COMICS GROUP
MARVEL SUPER ACTION
STARRING CAPTAIN AMERICA
THE TRIUMPH AND THE TRAGEDY!
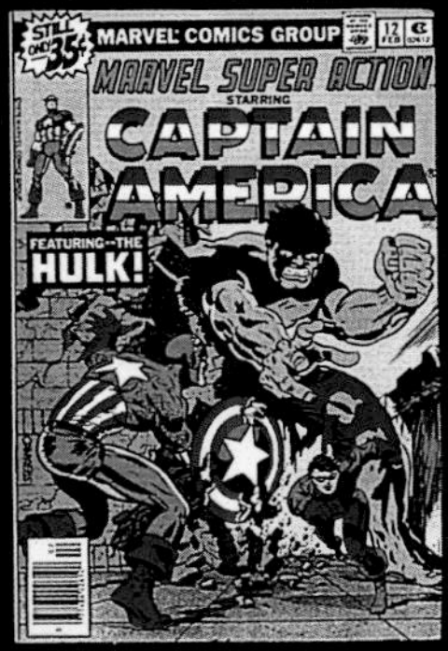
MARVEL COMICS GROUP
MARVEL SUPER ACTION
STARRING CAPTAIN AMERICA
FEATURING THE HULK!
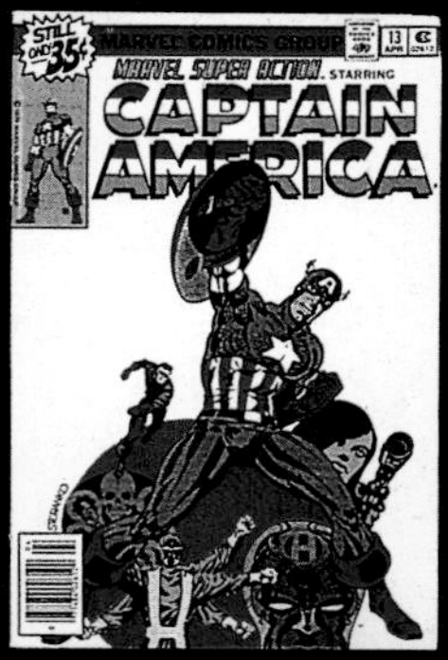
MARVEL COMICS GROUP
MARVEL SUPER ACTION
STARRING CAPTAIN AMERICA
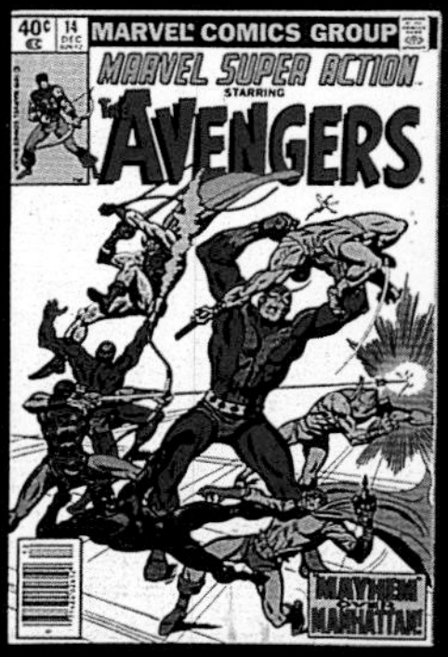
MARVEL COMICS GROUP
MARVEL SUPER ACTION
STARRING THE AVENGERS
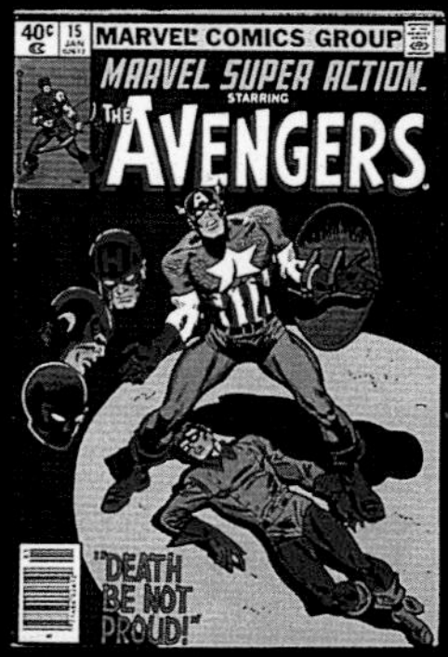
MARVEL COMICS GROUP
MARVEL SUPER ACTION
STARRING THE AVENGERS
"DEATH BE NOT PROUD!"
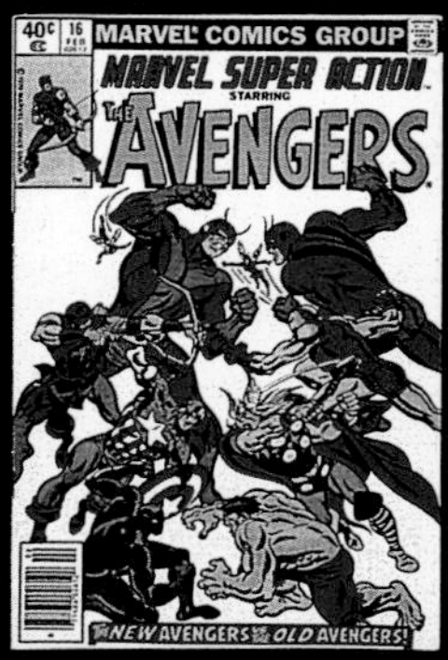
MARVEL COMICS GROUP
MARVEL SUPER ACTION
STARRING THE AVENGERS
NEW AVENGERS OLD AVENGERS!
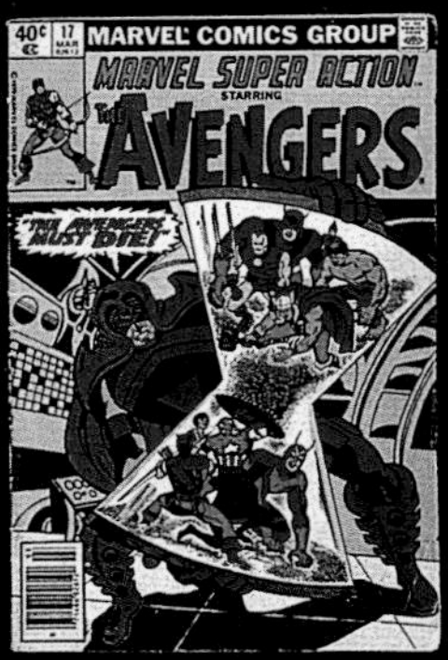
MARVEL COMICS GROUP
MARVEL SUPER ACTION
STARRING THE AVENGERS
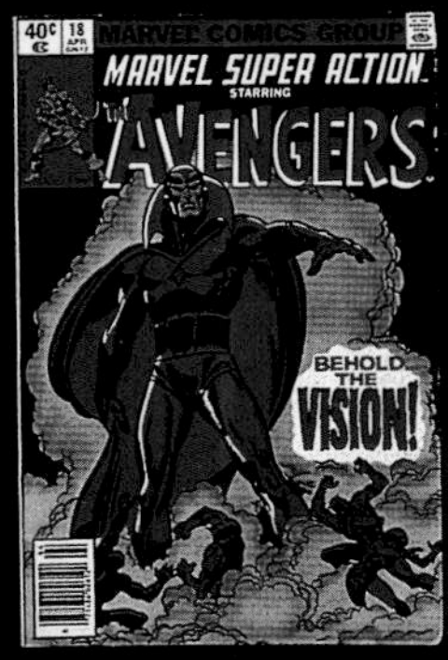
MARVEL COMICS GROUP
MARVEL SUPER ACTION
STARRING THE AVENGERS
BEHOLD THE VISION!
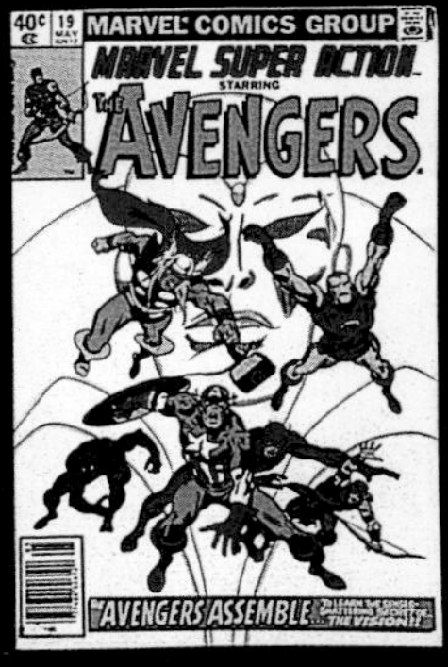
MARVEL COMICS GROUP
MARVEL SUPER ACTION
STARRING THE AVENGERS
AVENGERS ASSEMBLE
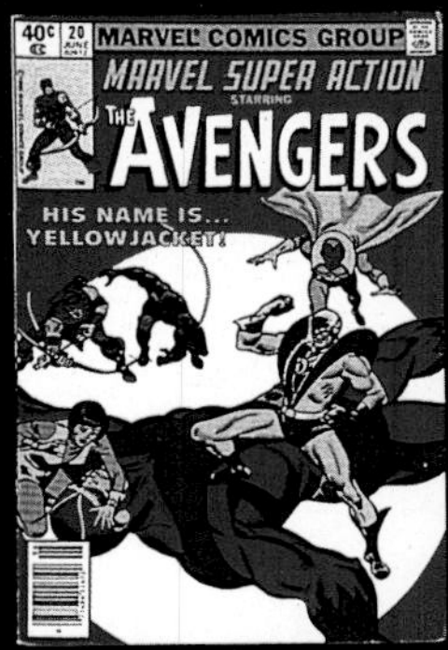
MARVEL COMICS GROUP
MARVEL SUPER ACTION
STARRING THE AVENGERS
HIS NAME IS... YELLOWJACKET!
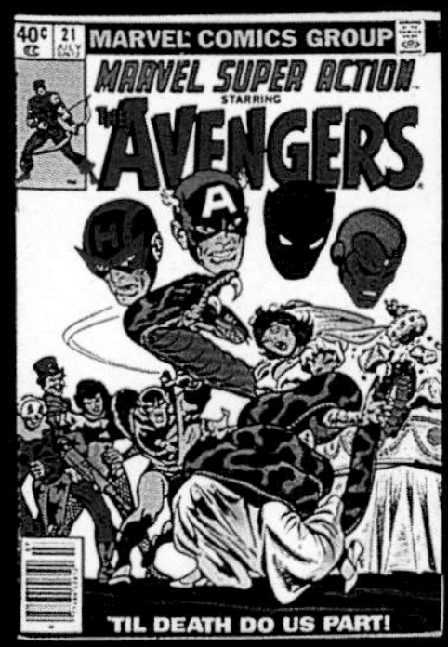
MARVEL COMICS GROUP
MARVEL SUPER ACTION
STARRING THE AVENGERS
'TIL DEATH DO US PART!
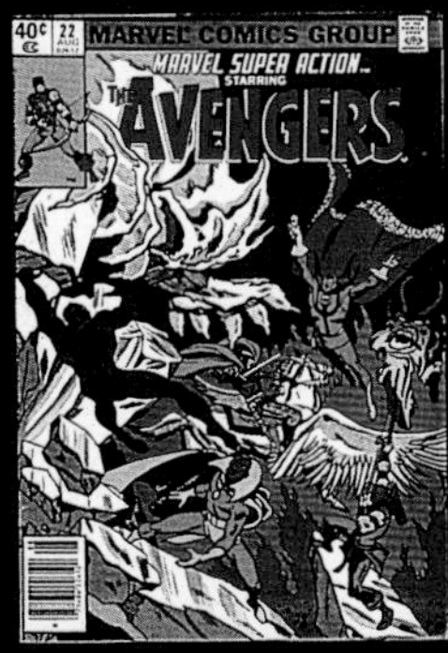
MARVEL COMICS GROUP
MARVEL SUPER ACTION...
STARRING THE AVENGERS
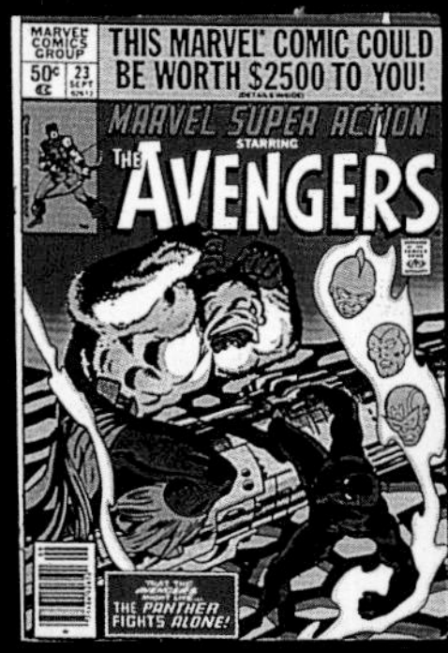
THIS MARVEL COMIC COULD BE WORTH $2500 TO YOU!
MARVEL SUPER ACTION
STARRING THE AVENGERS
THE PANTHER FIGHTS ALONE!
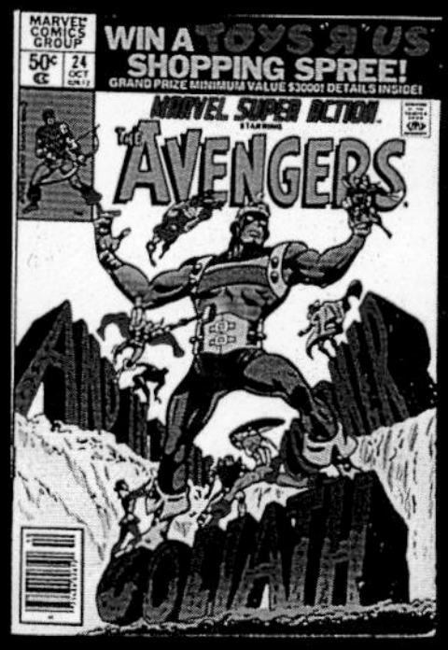
WIN A TOYS 'R' US SHOPPING SPREE!
MARVEL SUPER ACTION
THE AVENGERS
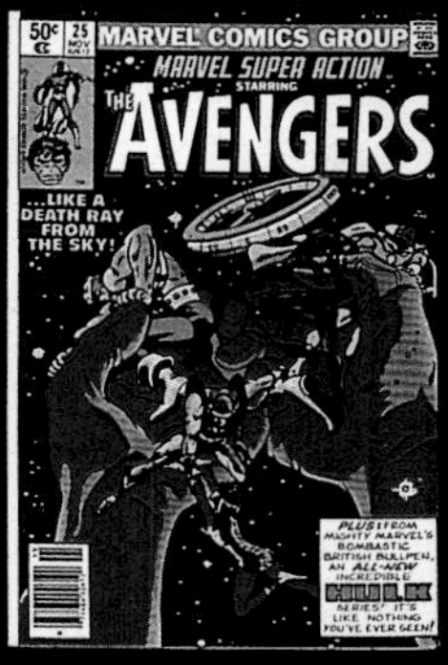
MARVEL COMICS GROUP
MARVEL SUPER ACTION
STARRING THE AVENGERS
...LIKE A DEATH RAY FROM THE SKY!
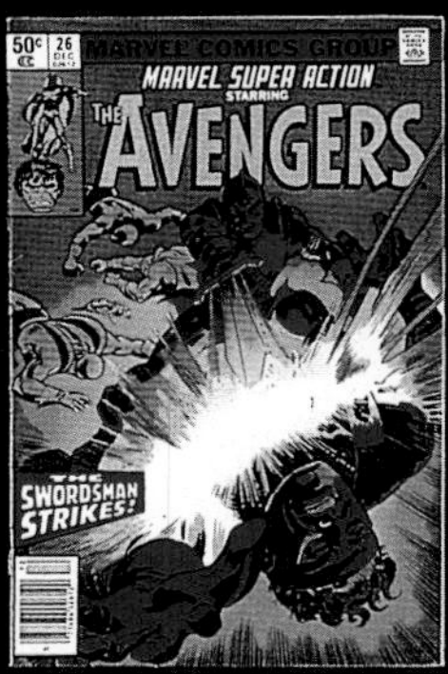
MARVEL COMICS GROUP
MARVEL SUPER ACTION
STARRING THE AVENGERS
SWORDSMAN STRIKES!
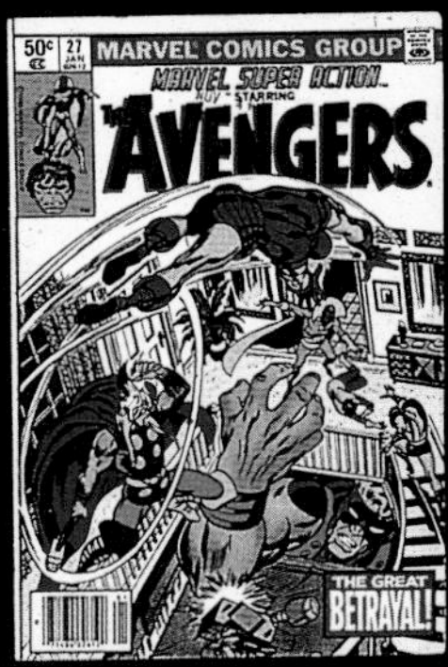
MARVEL COMICS GROUP
MARVEL SUPER ACTION
STARRING THE AVENGERS
THE GREAT BETRAYAL!
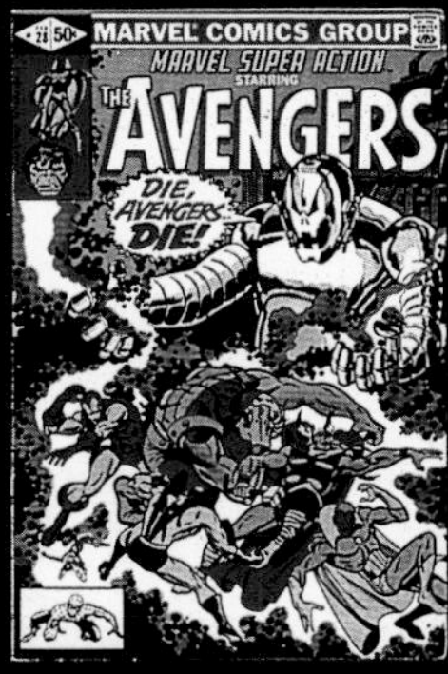
MARVEL COMICS GROUP
MARVEL SUPER ACTION
STARRING THE AVENGERS
DIE, AVENGERS DIE!
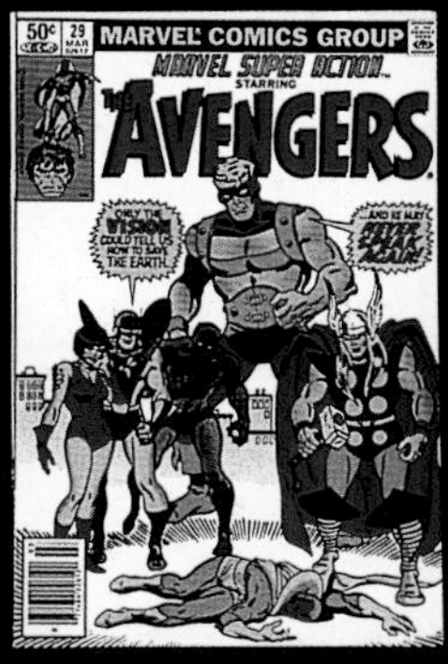
MARVEL COMICS GROUP
MARVEL SUPER ACTION
STARRING THE AVENGERS
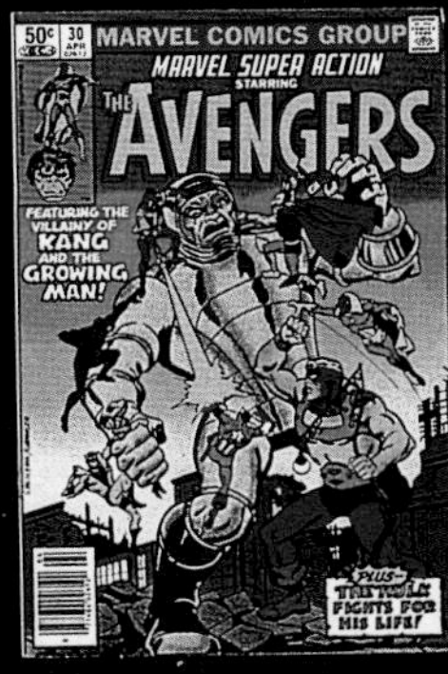
MARVEL COMICS GROUP
MARVEL SUPER ACTION
STARRING THE AVENGERS
FEATURING THE VILLAINY OF KANG AND THE GROWING MAN!
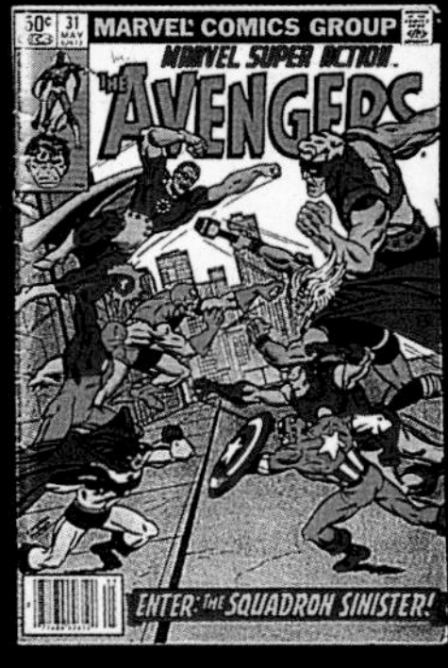
MARVEL COMICS GROUP
MARVEL SUPER ACTION
STARRING THE AVENGERS
ENTER: THE SQUADRON SINISTER!
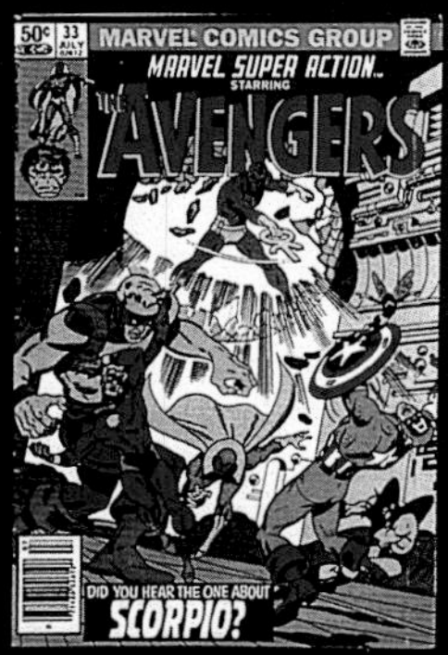
MARVEL COMICS GROUP
MARVEL SUPER ACTION...
STARRING THE AVENGERS
DID YOU HEAR THE ONE ABOUT SCORPIO?

Marvel Super Action (1-37) 1217.3

Ref. No.	Date	RVI	Artist/Info. (All Reprints)
1217.3-1	May 1977	2	Kirby/Shores-a
1217.3-2	Jul.	1	" "
1217.3-3	Sept.	1	" "
1217.3-4	Nov.	1	Cockrum/Sinnott-c/a
1217.3-5	Jan. 1978	1	Kirby/Shores-a
1217.3-6	Mar.	1	Kirby/Adkins-a
1217.3-7	Apr.	1	" "
1217.3-8	Jun.	1	Kirby/Giacoia-a
1217.3-9	Aug.	1	Kirby/Shores-a
1217.3-10	**Oct.**	**1**	**" "**
1217.3-11	Dec.	1	Budiansky/Janson-c, Kirby/Shores-a
1217.3-12	Feb. 1979	1	Steranko-c/a, Sinnott, Zeck-a
1217.3-13	Apr.	1	Steranko-c/a, Sinnott-1
1217.3-14	Dec.	1	Buscema/Klein-a
1217.3-15	Jan. 1980	1	" "
1217.3-16	Feb.	1	Buscema, Heck, Roth/Colletta-a
1217.3-17	Mar.	1	Heck, Roth/Colletta-a
1217.3-18	Apr.	1	Buscema/Klein-a
1217.3-19	May	1	" "
1217.3-20	**Jun.**	**1**	**" "**
1217.3-21	Jul.	1	Buscema/Esposito-a
1217.3-22	Aug.	1	Buscema/Klein-a
1217.3-23	Sept.	1	
1217.3-24	Oct.	1	Colan/Klein-a
1217.3-25	Nov.	1	" "
1217.3-26	Dec.	1	Colan/Grainger, Dillon-a
1217.3-27	Jan. 1981	1	B. Smith/Shores-a
1217.3-28	Feb.	1	B. Smith/Klein-a
1217.3-29	Mar.	1	Buscema/Grainger-a
1217.3-30	**Apr.**	**1**	**Buscema/Grainger-c/a**
1217.3-31	May	1	Buscema/Grainger-c/a, Neary, Richardson-a
1217.3-32 to 37	Nov. (#37)	1	

1217.55 Marvel Tales (1-16)

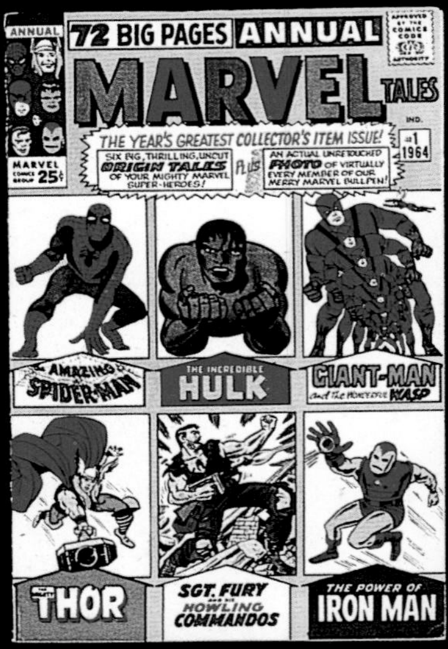

ANNUAL
72 BIG PAGES ANNUAL
MARVEL TALES
THE YEAR'S GREATEST COLLECTOR'S ITEM ISSUE!
#1 1964
MARVEL 25¢
The Amazing SPIDER-MAN
THE INCREDIBLE HULK
GIANT-MAN and the Wonderful WASP
THOR
SGT. FURY and his HOWLING COMMANDOS
THE POWER OF IRON MAN

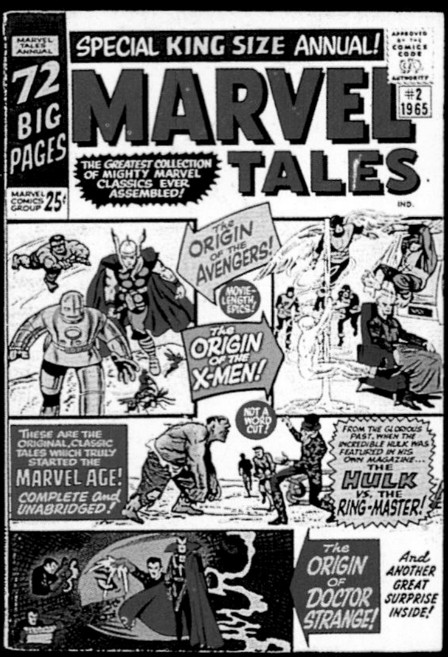

SPECIAL KING SIZE ANNUAL!
72 BIG PAGES
MARVEL TALES
#2 1965
MARVEL COMICS GROUP 25¢
THE GREATEST COLLECTION OF MIGHTY MARVEL CLASSICS EVER ASSEMBLED!
The ORIGIN of the AVENGERS!
The ORIGIN of the X-MEN!
THESE ARE THE ORIGINAL, CLASSIC TALES WHICH TRULY STARTED THE MARVEL AGE! COMPLETE and UNABRIDGED!
The HULK VS. THE RING-MASTER!
The ORIGIN of DOCTOR STRANGE!
And ANOTHER GREAT SURPRISE INSIDE!

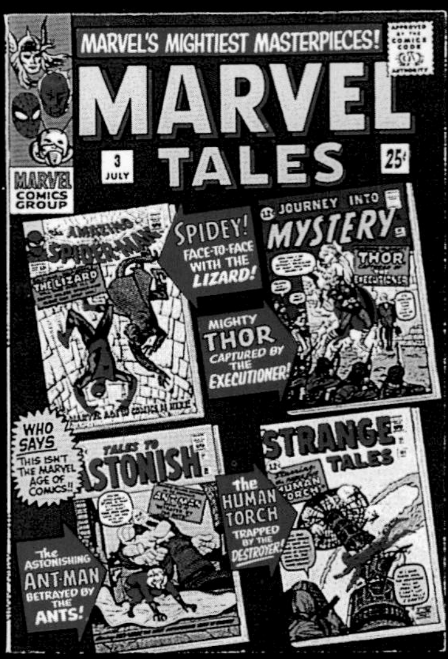

MARVEL'S MIGHTIEST MASTERPIECES!
MARVEL TALES
3 JULY 25¢
MARVEL COMICS GROUP
SPIDEY! FACE-TO-FACE WITH THE LIZARD!
JOURNEY INTO MYSTERY
MIGHTY THOR CAPTURED BY THE EXECUTIONER!
WHO SAYS THIS ISN'T THE MARVEL AGE OF COMICS?
TALES TO ASTONISH
STRANGE TALES
The HUMAN TORCH TRAPPED BY THE DESTROYER!
The Astonishing ANT-MAN BETRAYED BY THE ANTS!

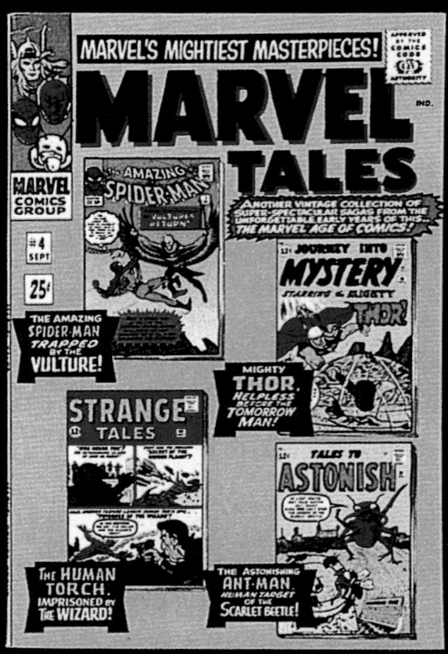

MARVEL'S MIGHTIEST MASTERPIECES!
MARVEL TALES
MARVEL COMICS GROUP
#4 SEPT
25¢
ANOTHER VINTAGE COLLECTION OF SUPER-SPECTACULAR SAGAS FROM THE UNFORGETTABLE EARLY YEARS OF THIS THE MARVEL AGE OF COMICS!
JOURNEY INTO MYSTERY
THE AMAZING SPIDER-MAN TRAPPED BY THE VULTURE!
MIGHTY THOR HELPLESS BEFORE THE TOMORROW MAN!
STRANGE TALES
TALES TO ASTONISH
THE HUMAN TORCH, IMPRISONED BY THE WIZARD!
The Astonishing ANT-MAN VS. THE SCARLET BEETLE!

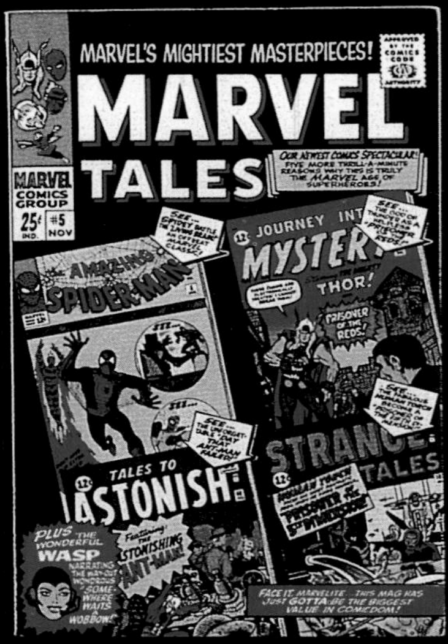

MARVEL'S MIGHTIEST MASTERPIECES!
MARVEL TALES
MARVEL COMICS GROUP
25¢ #5 NOV
JOURNEY INTO MYSTERY
THOR
STRANGE TALES
TALES TO ASTONISH
PLUS THE WONDERFUL WASP
FACE IT, MARVELITE--THIS MAG HAS JUST GOTTA BE THE BIGGEST VALUE IN COMICDOM!

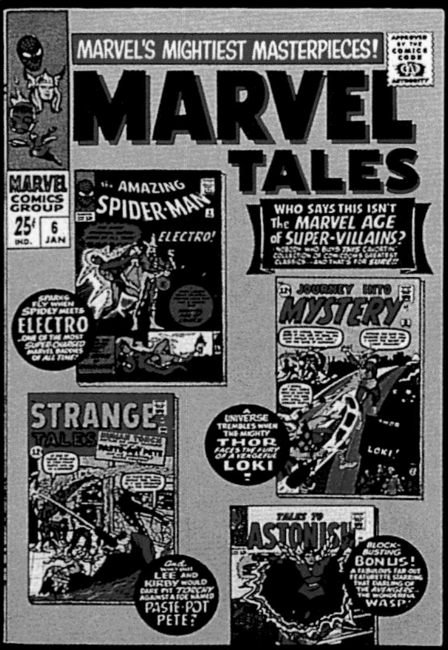

MARVEL'S MIGHTIEST MASTERPIECES!
MARVEL TALES
MARVEL COMICS GROUP
25¢ 6 JAN
WHO SAYS THIS ISN'T THE MARVEL AGE OF SUPER-VILLAINS?
ELECTRO!
JOURNEY INTO MYSTERY
LOKI!
STRANGE TALES
TALES TO ASTONISH
BLOCK-BUSTING BONUS!

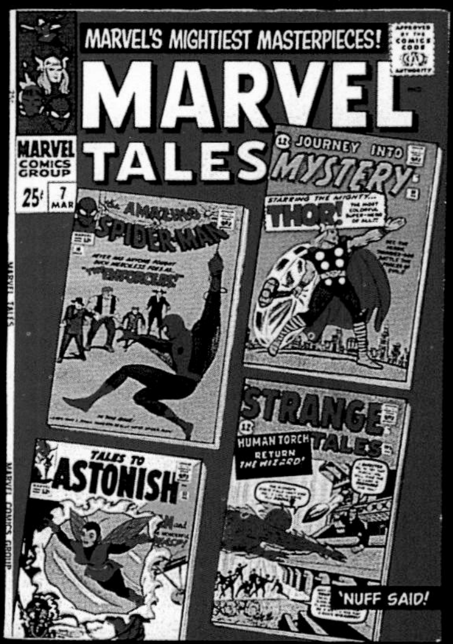

MARVEL'S MIGHTIEST MASTERPIECES!
MARVEL TALES
MARVEL COMICS GROUP
25¢ 7 MAR
JOURNEY INTO MYSTERY
THOR!
STRANGE TALES
HUMAN TORCH
RETURN OF THE WIZARD!
TALES TO ASTONISH
'NUFF SAID!

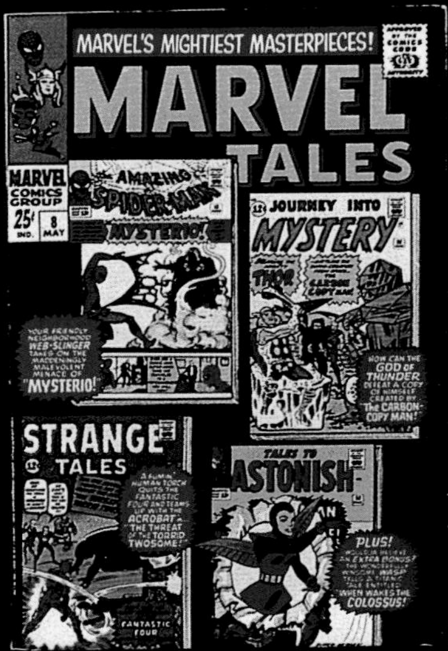

MARVEL'S MIGHTIEST MASTERPIECES!
MARVEL TALES
MARVEL COMICS GROUP
25¢ 8 MAY
JOURNEY INTO MYSTERY
MYSTERIO!
STRANGE TALES
TALES TO ASTONISH
PLUS!

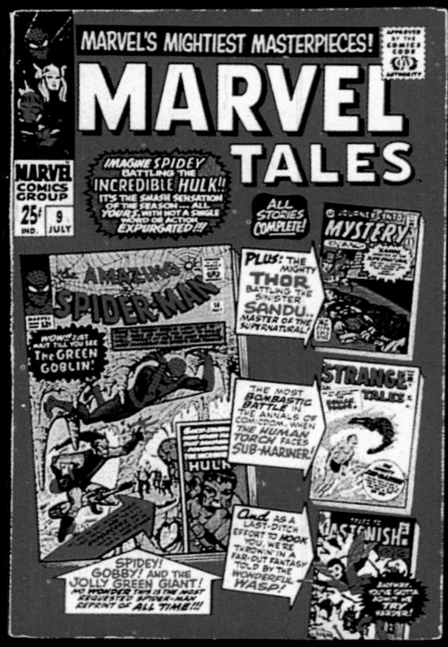

MARVEL'S MIGHTIEST MASTERPIECES!
MARVEL TALES
MARVEL COMICS GROUP
25¢ 9 JULY
IMAGINE SPIDEY BATTLING THE INCREDIBLE HULK!!
ALL STORIES COMPLETE!
JOURNEY INTO MYSTERY
PLUS:
STRANGE TALES
HULK
ASTONISH

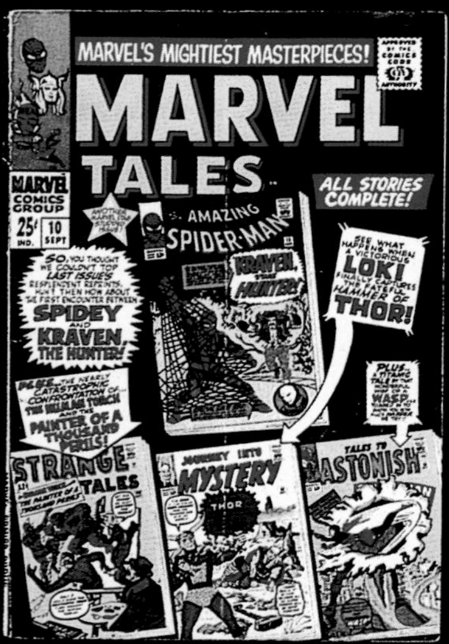

MARVEL'S MIGHTIEST MASTERPIECES!
MARVEL TALES
MARVEL COMICS GROUP
25¢ 10 SEPT
ALL STORIES COMPLETE!
SPIDEY and KRAVEN THE HUNTER!
LOKI
THOR!
STRANGE TALES
JOURNEY INTO MYSTERY
TALES TO ASTONISH

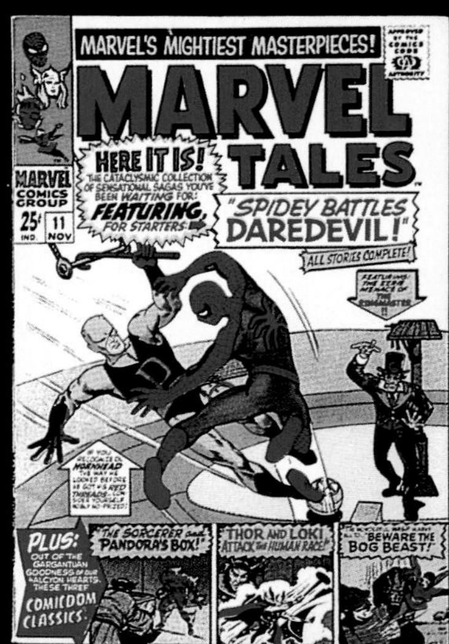

MARVEL'S MIGHTIEST MASTERPIECES!
MARVEL TALES
MARVEL COMICS GROUP
25¢ 11 NOV
HERE IT IS!
FEATURING, FOR STARTERS
"SPIDEY BATTLES DAREDEVIL!"
ALL STORIES COMPLETE!
PLUS:
THE SORCERER and PANDORA'S BOX!
THOR AND LOKI
BEWARE THE BOG BEAST!
COMICDOM CLASSICS!

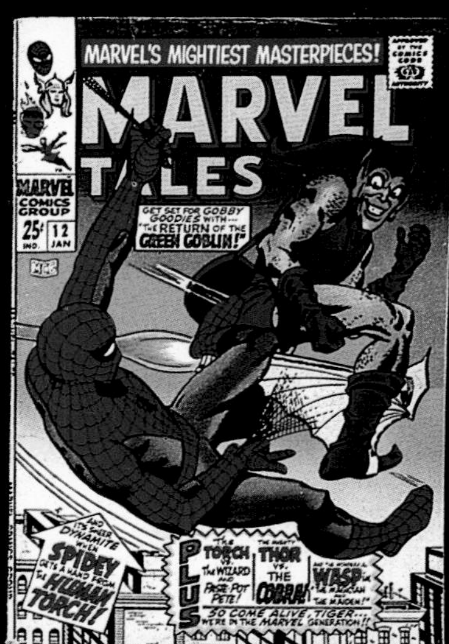

MARVEL'S MIGHTIEST MASTERPIECES!
MARVEL TALES
MARVEL COMICS GROUP
25¢ 12 JAN
GET SET FOR GOBBY GOODIES WITH "THE RETURN OF THE GREEN GOBLIN!"
PLUS
HUMAN TORCH!
THOR
WASP
SO COME ALIVE TIGER--WE'RE IN THE MARVEL GENERATION!

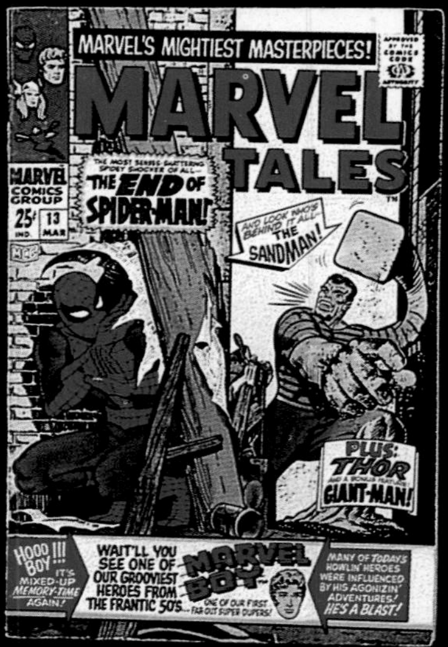

MARVEL'S MIGHTIEST MASTERPIECES!
MARVEL TALES
MARVEL COMICS GROUP
25¢ 13 MAR
"THE END of SPIDER-MAN!"
SANDMAN!
PLUS: THOR
GIANT-MAN!
HOO BOY!!!
WAIT'LL YOU SEE ONE OF OUR GROOVIEST HEROES FROM THE FRANTIC 50'S...
MARVEL BOY

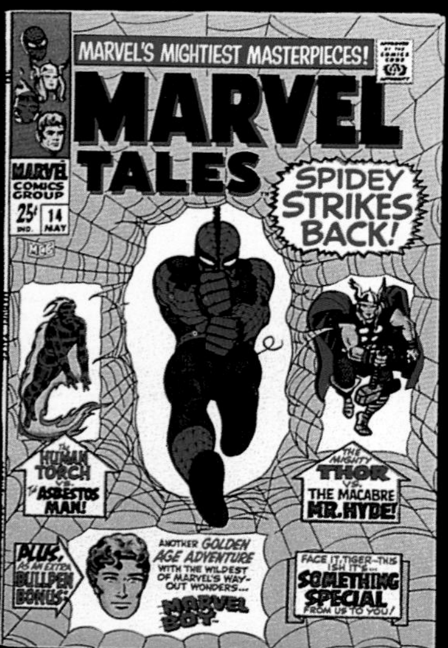

MARVEL'S MIGHTIEST MASTERPIECES!
MARVEL TALES
MARVEL COMICS GROUP
25¢ 14 MAY
SPIDEY STRIKES BACK!
HUMAN TORCH
THE ASBESTOS MAN!
THOR
THE MACABRE MR. HYDE!
PLUS
MARVEL BOY
SOMETHING SPECIAL

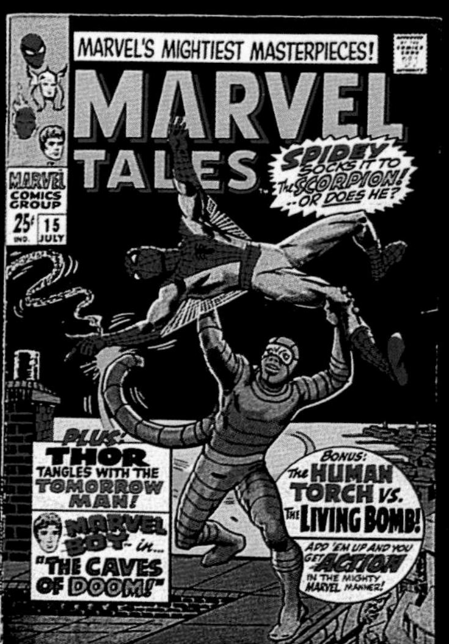

MARVEL'S MIGHTIEST MASTERPIECES!
MARVEL TALES
MARVEL COMICS GROUP
25¢ 15 JULY
SPIDEY SOCKS IT TO The SCORPION! ...OR DOES HE?
PLUS: THOR TANGLES WITH THE TOMORROW MAN!
MARVEL BOY in... "THE CAVES OF DOOM!"
Bonus: The HUMAN TORCH VS. The LIVING BOMB!

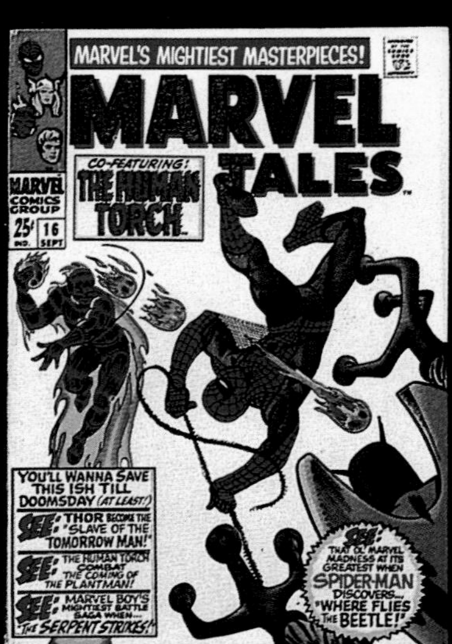

MARVEL'S MIGHTIEST MASTERPIECES!
MARVEL TALES
MARVEL COMICS GROUP
25¢ 16 SEPT
CO-FEATURING! THE HUMAN TORCH
YOU'LL WANNA SAVE THIS ISH TILL DOOMSDAY (AT LEAST)!
SEE: THOR BECOME THE SLAVE OF THE TOMORROW MAN!
SEE: THE HUMAN TORCH AND THE PLANTMAN!
SEE: MARVEL BOY'S ... THE SERPENT STRIKES!
SPIDER-MAN ... "WHERE FLIES THE BEETLE!"

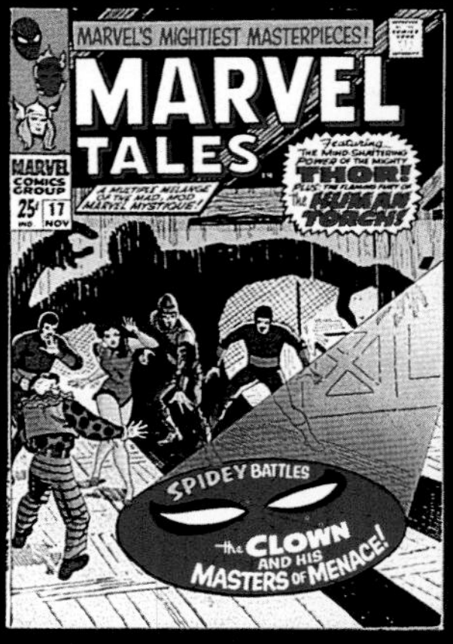
MARVEL'S MIGHTIEST MASTERPIECES!
MARVEL TALES
SPIDEY BATTLES
the CLOWN AND HIS MASTERS OF MENACE!

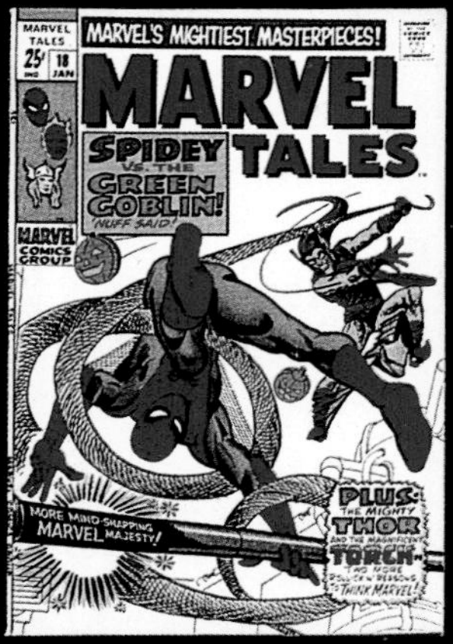
MARVEL'S MIGHTIEST MASTERPIECES!
MARVEL TALES
SPIDEY VS. THE GREEN GOBLIN!
PLUS: THE MIGHTY THOR AND THE TORCH
MORE MIND-SHATTERING MARVEL MAJESTY!

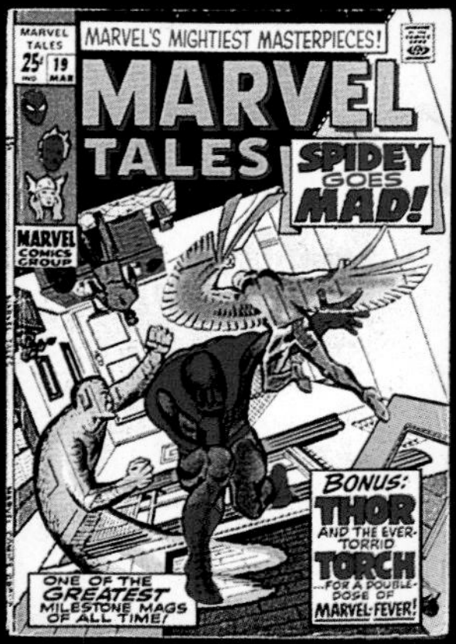
MARVEL'S MIGHTIEST MASTERPIECES!
MARVEL TALES
SPIDEY GOES MAD!
BONUS: THOR AND THE EVER-TORRID TORCH
ONE OF THE GREATEST MILESTONE MAGS OF ALL TIME!

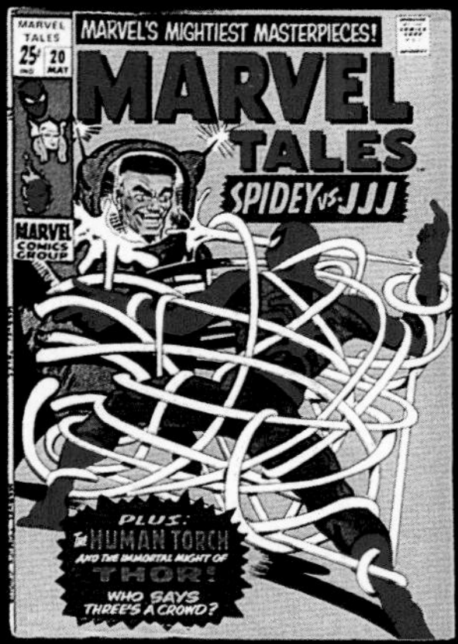
MARVEL'S MIGHTIEST MASTERPIECES!
MARVEL TALES
SPIDEY vs. JJJ
PLUS: THE HUMAN TORCH
THOR!
WHO SAYS THREE'S A CROWD?

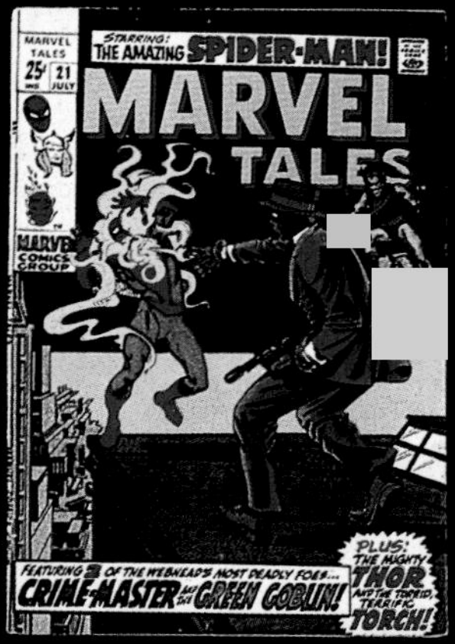
STARRING: THE AMAZING SPIDER-MAN!
MARVEL TALES
CRIME-MASTER and GREEN GOBLIN!
PLUS: THOR TORCH!

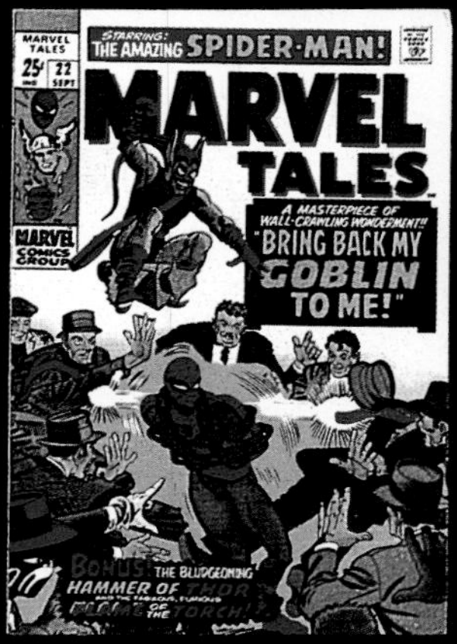
STARRING: THE AMAZING SPIDER-MAN!
MARVEL TALES
A MASTERPIECE OF WALL-CRAWLING WONDERMENT!!
"BRING BACK MY GOBLIN TO ME!"

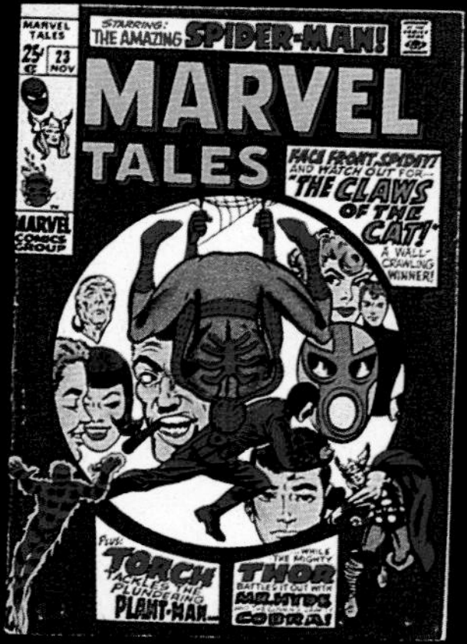
STARRING: THE AMAZING SPIDER-MAN!
MARVEL TALES
THE CLAWS OF THE CAT!
TORCH
PLANT-MAN
COBRA!

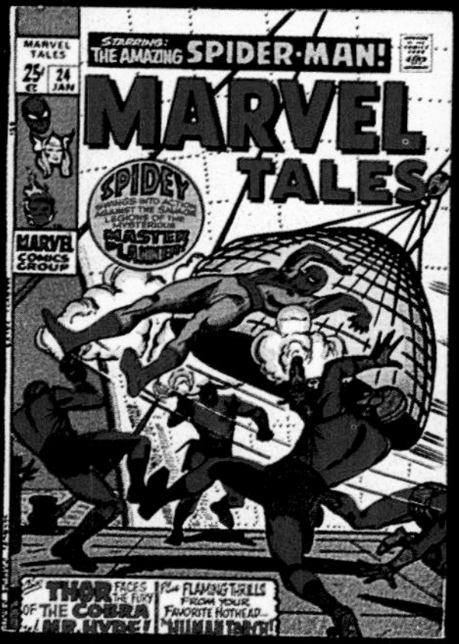
STARRING: THE AMAZING SPIDER-MAN!
MARVEL TALES
SPIDEY
MASTER PLANNER!
THOR
HUMAN TORCH

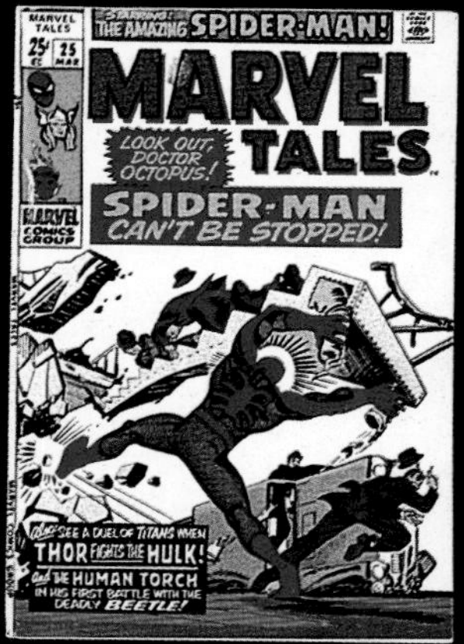
STARRING: THE AMAZING SPIDER-MAN!
MARVEL TALES
LOOK OUT, DOCTOR OCTOPUS!
SPIDER-MAN CAN'T BE STOPPED!
SEE A DUEL OF TITANS WHEN THOR FIGHTS THE HULK!
THE HUMAN TORCH
BEETLE!

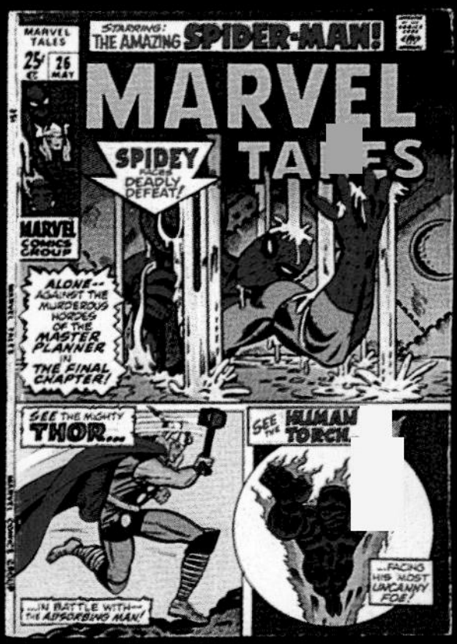
STARRING: THE AMAZING SPIDER-MAN!
MARVEL TALES
SPIDEY DEFEAT!
SEE THE MIGHTY THOR
SEE HUMAN TORCH
THE ABSORBING MAN!

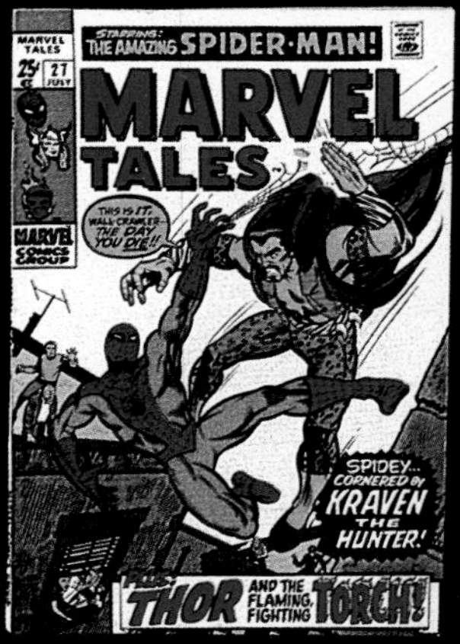
STARRING: THE AMAZING SPIDER-MAN!
MARVEL TALES
SPIDEY... CORNERED BY KRAVEN THE HUNTER!
THOR AND THE FLAMING, FIGHTING TORCH!

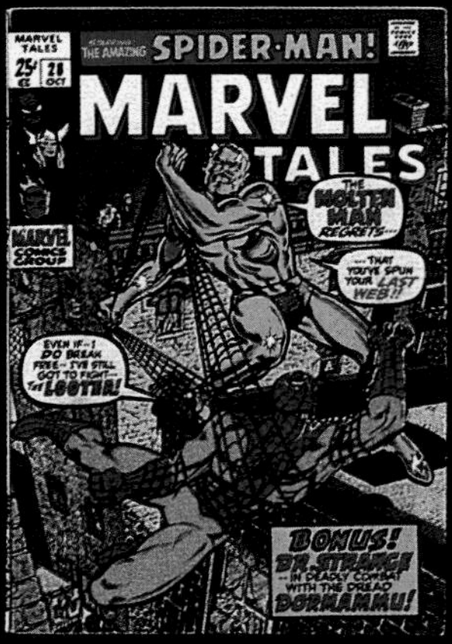
THE AMAZING SPIDER-MAN!
MARVEL TALES
BONUS!
DORMAMMU!

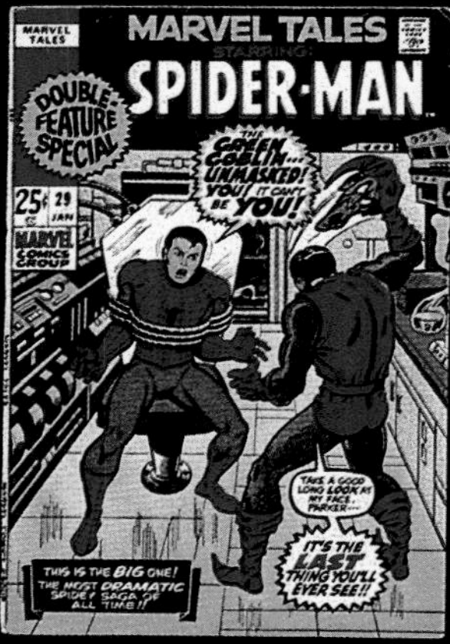
MARVEL TALES
SPIDER-MAN
DOUBLE FEATURE SPECIAL
IT'S THE LAST THING YOU'LL EVER SEE!!
THIS IS THE BIG ONE!

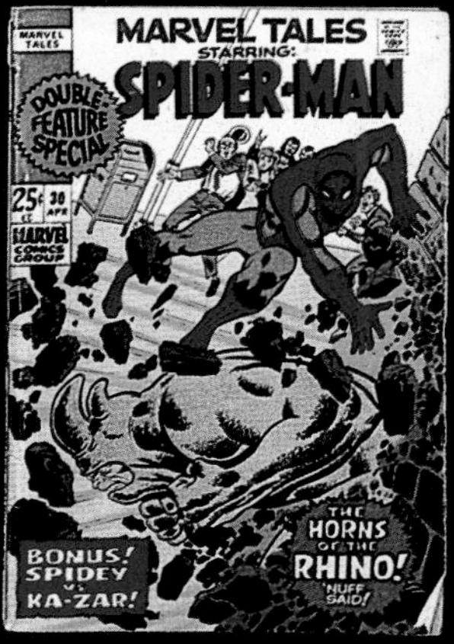
MARVEL TALES
STARRING:
SPIDER-MAN
DOUBLE FEATURE SPECIAL
BONUS! SPIDEY KA-ZAR!
THE HORNS OF THE RHINO!
'NUFF SAID!

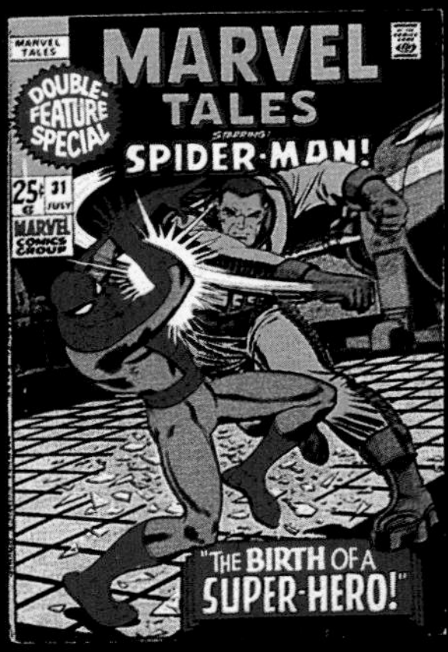
MARVEL TALES
STARRING: SPIDER-MAN!
DOUBLE FEATURE SPECIAL
"THE BIRTH OF A SUPER-HERO!"

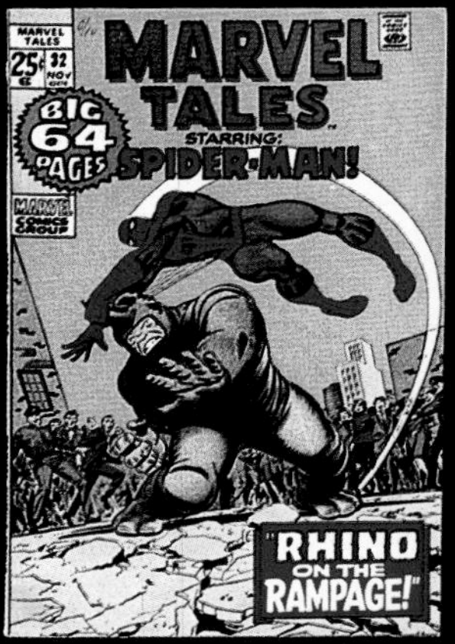
MARVEL TALES
BIG 64 PAGES
STARRING: SPIDER-MAN!
"RHINO ON THE RAMPAGE!"

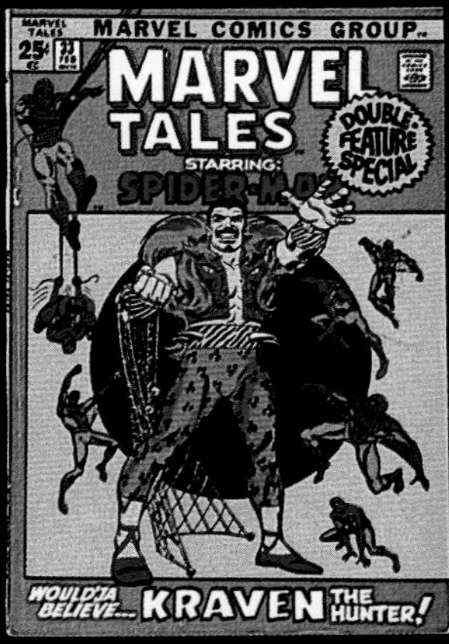
MARVEL COMICS GROUP
MARVEL TALES
DOUBLE FEATURE SPECIAL
STARRING: SPIDER-MAN
KRAVEN THE HUNTER!

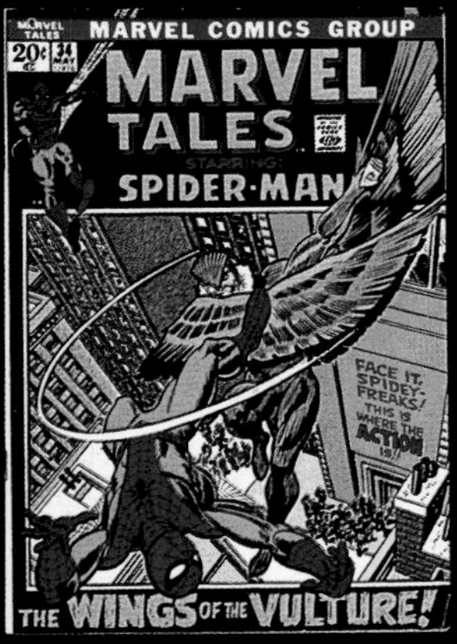
MARVEL COMICS GROUP
MARVEL TALES
SPIDER-MAN
THE WINGS OF THE VULTURE!

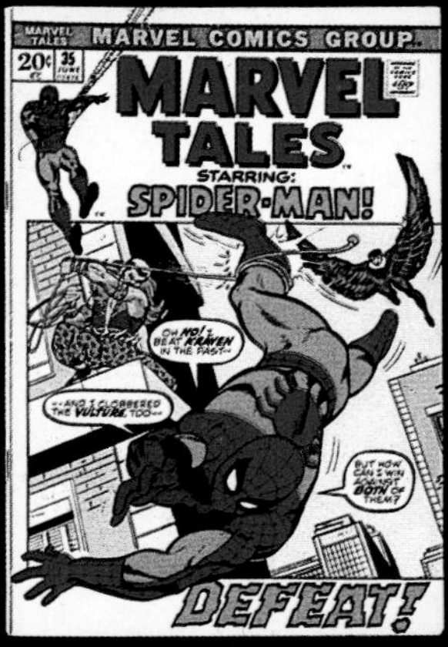
MARVEL COMICS GROUP
MARVEL TALES
STARRING:
SPIDER-MAN!
DEFEAT!

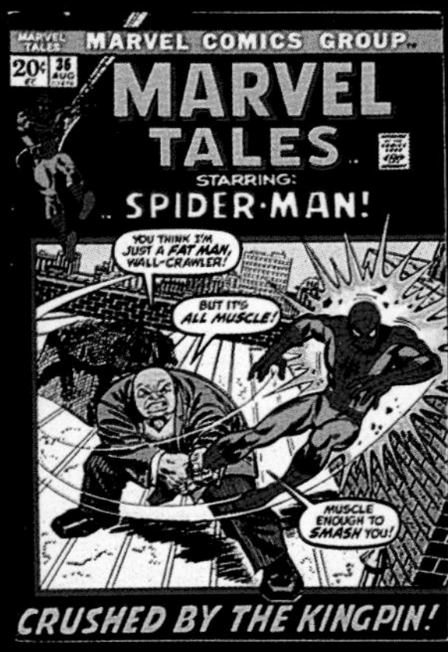
MARVEL COMICS GROUP
MARVEL TALES
STARRING:
SPIDER-MAN!
YOU THINK I'M JUST A FAT MAN, WALL-CRAWLER!
BUT IT'S ALL MUSCLE!
CRUSHED BY THE KINGPIN!

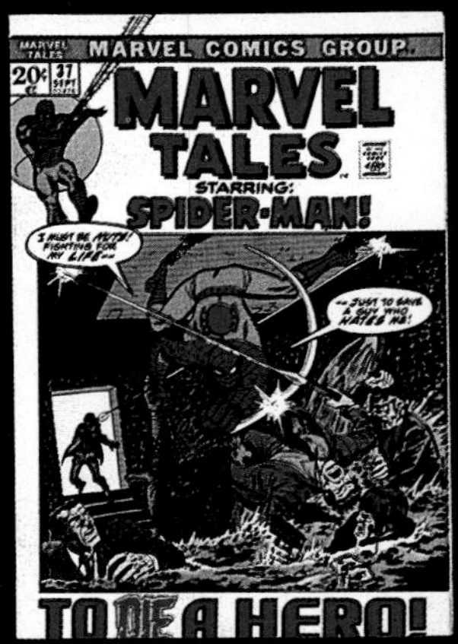
MARVEL COMICS GROUP
MARVEL TALES
STARRING:
SPIDER-MAN!
TO DIE A HERO!

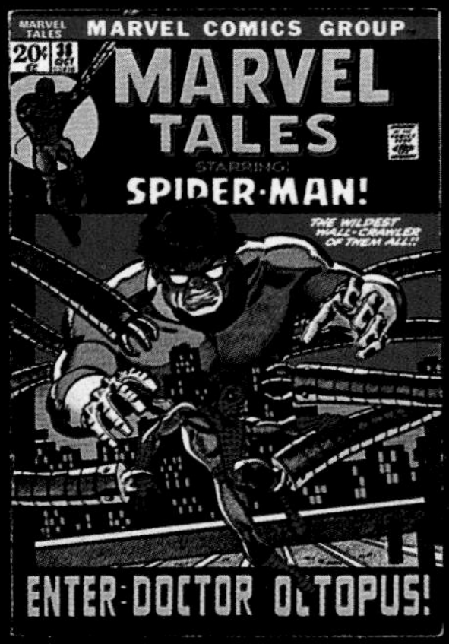
MARVEL COMICS GROUP
MARVEL TALES
SPIDER-MAN!
ENTER DOCTOR OCTOPUS!

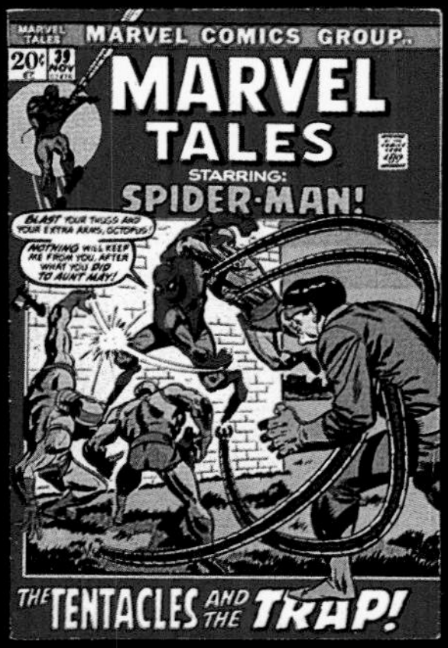
MARVEL COMICS GROUP
MARVEL TALES
STARRING:
SPIDER-MAN!
THE TENTACLES AND THE TRAP!

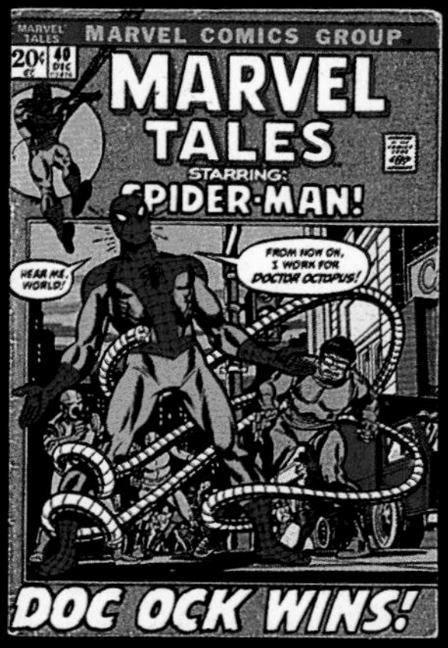
MARVEL COMICS GROUP
MARVEL TALES
STARRING:
SPIDER-MAN!
FROM NOW ON, I WORK FOR DOCTOR OCTOPUS!
DOC OCK WINS!

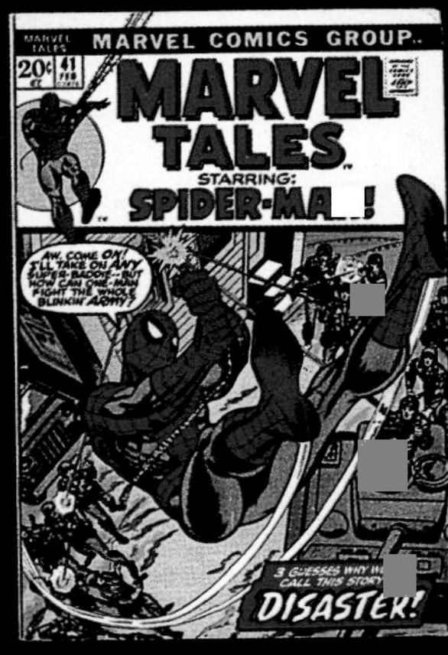
MARVEL COMICS GROUP
MARVEL TALES
STARRING:
DISASTER!

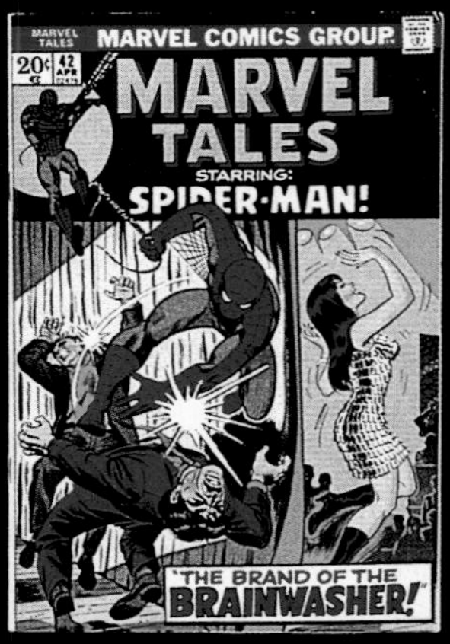
MARVEL COMICS GROUP
MARVEL TALES
STARRING: SPIDER-MAN!
"THE BRAND OF THE BRAINWASHER!"

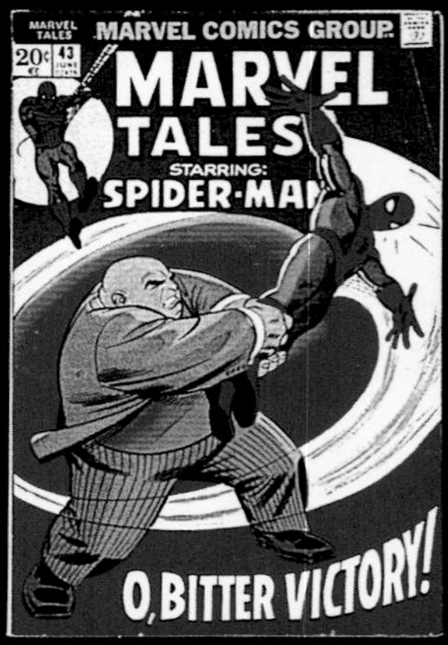
MARVEL COMICS GROUP
MARVEL TALES
STARRING: SPIDER-MAN!
O, BITTER VICTORY!

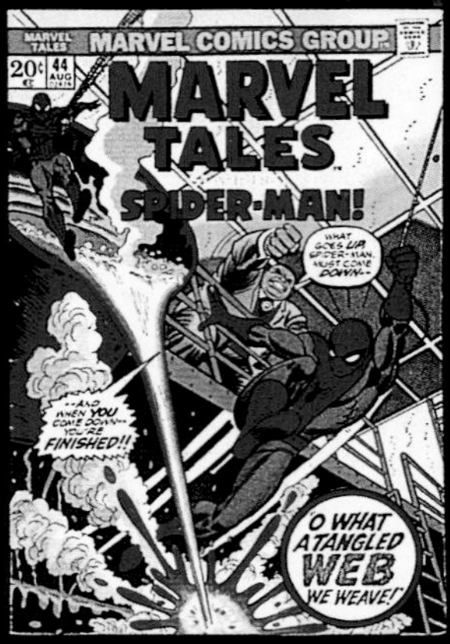
MARVEL COMICS GROUP
MARVEL TALES
SPIDER-MAN!
O WHAT A TANGLED WEB WE WEAVE!

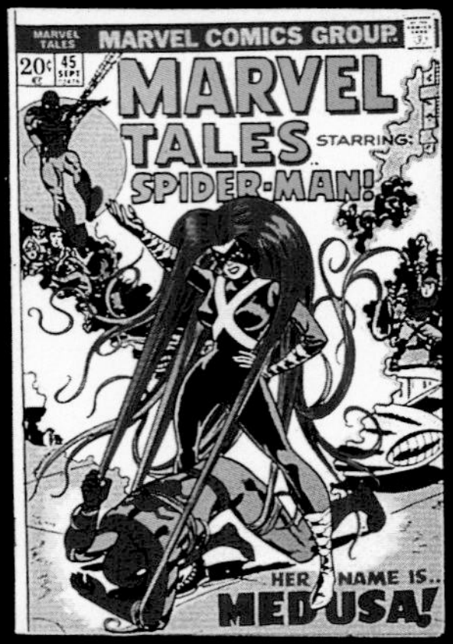
MARVEL COMICS GROUP
MARVEL TALES STARRING: SPIDER-MAN!
HER NAME IS... MEDUSA!

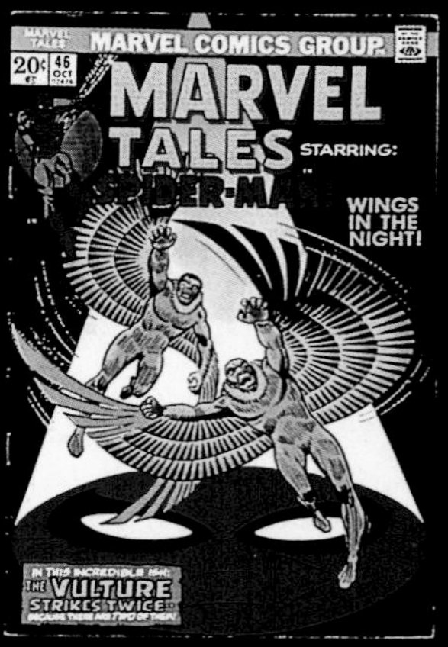
MARVEL COMICS GROUP
MARVEL TALES STARRING:
WINGS IN THE NIGHT!
THE VULTURE STRIKES TWICE!

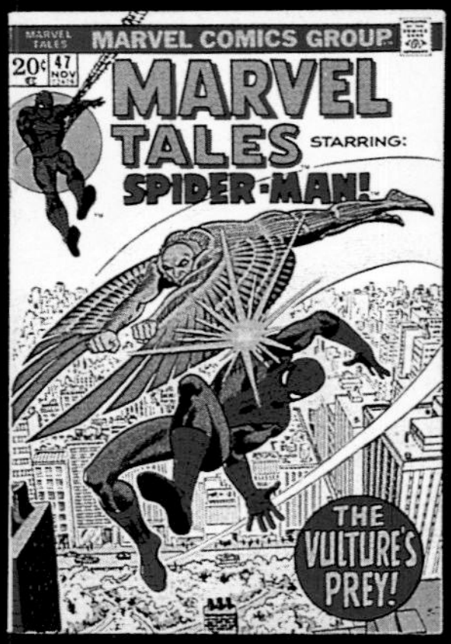
MARVEL COMICS GROUP
MARVEL TALES STARRING: SPIDER-MAN!
THE VULTURE'S PREY!

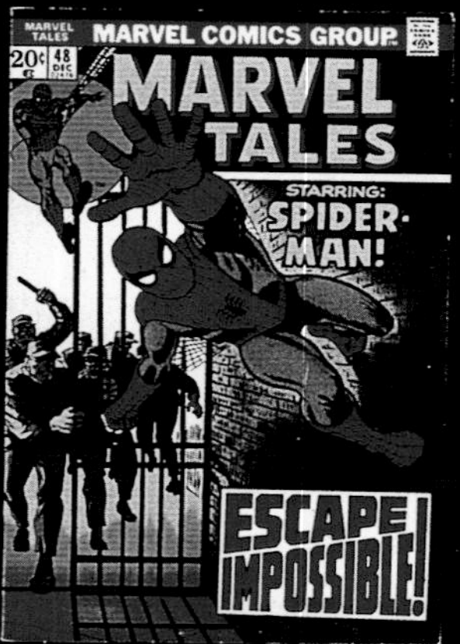
MARVEL COMICS GROUP
MARVEL TALES
STARRING: SPIDER-MAN!
ESCAPE IMPOSSIBLE!

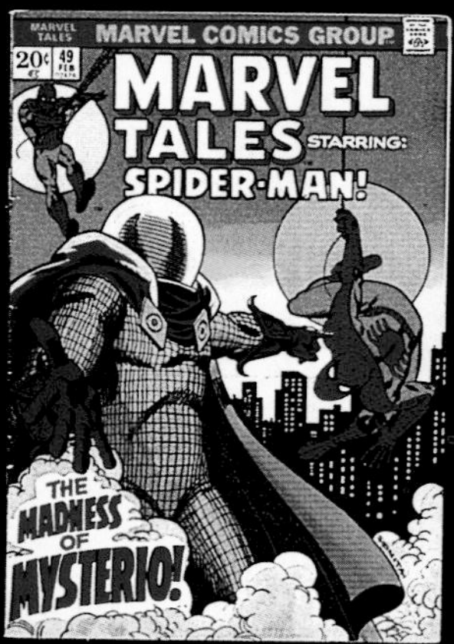
MARVEL COMICS GROUP
MARVEL TALES STARRING: SPIDER-MAN!
THE MADNESS OF MYSTERIO!

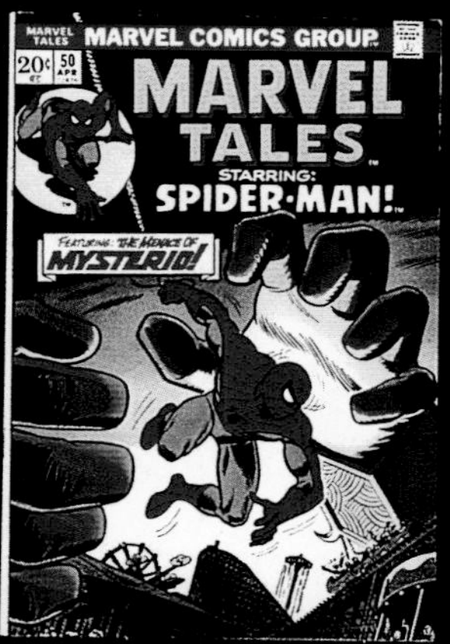
MARVEL COMICS GROUP
MARVEL TALES
STARRING: SPIDER-MAN!
FEATURING: THE MENACE OF MYSTERIO!

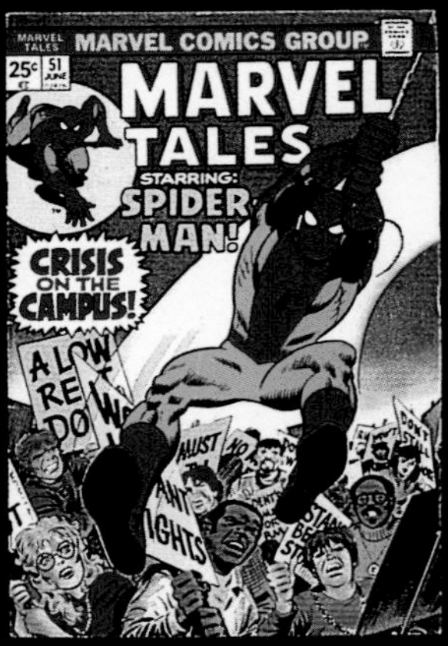
MARVEL COMICS GROUP
MARVEL TALES
STARRING: SPIDER-MAN!
CRISIS ON THE CAMPUS!

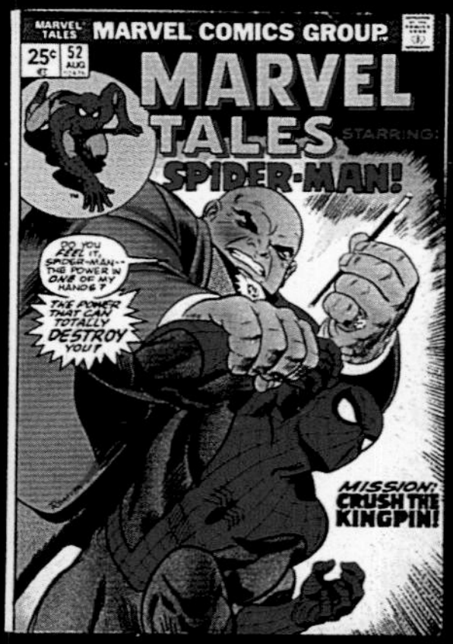
MARVEL COMICS GROUP
MARVEL TALES STARRING: SPIDER-MAN!
MISSION: CRUSH THE KINGPIN!

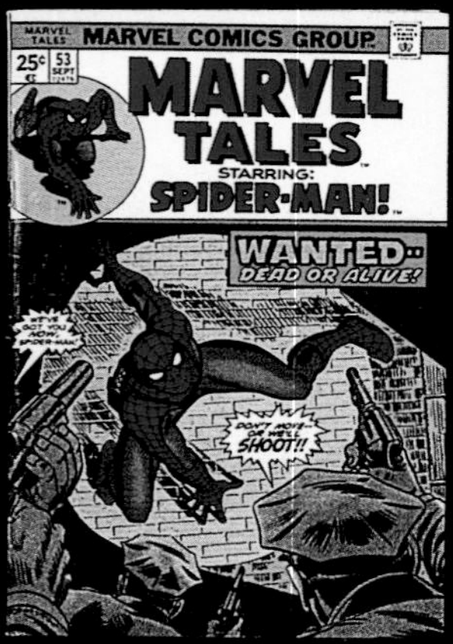
MARVEL COMICS GROUP
MARVEL TALES
STARRING: SPIDER-MAN!
WANTED-- DEAD OR ALIVE!

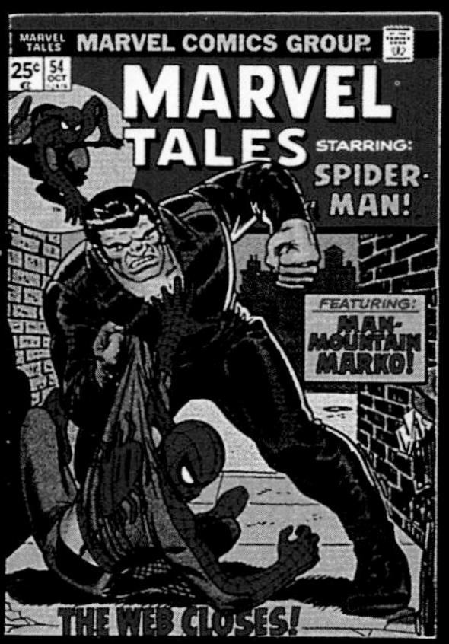
MARVEL COMICS GROUP
MARVEL TALES STARRING: SPIDER-MAN!
FEATURING: MAN-MOUNTAIN MARKO!
THE WEB CLOSES!

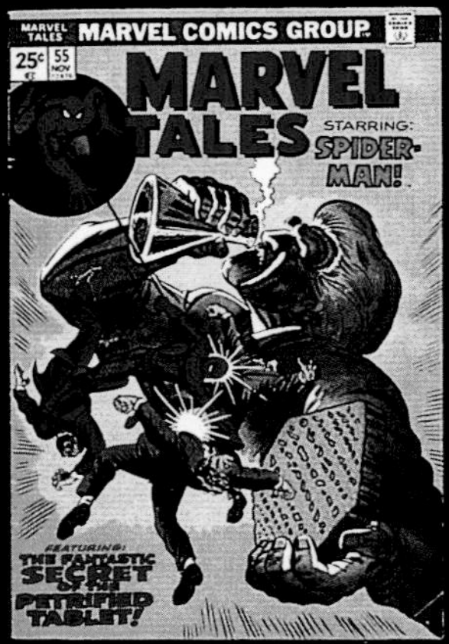
MARVEL COMICS GROUP
MARVEL TALES STARRING: SPIDER-MAN!
FEATURING: THE FANTASTIC SECRET OF THE PETRIFIED TABLET!

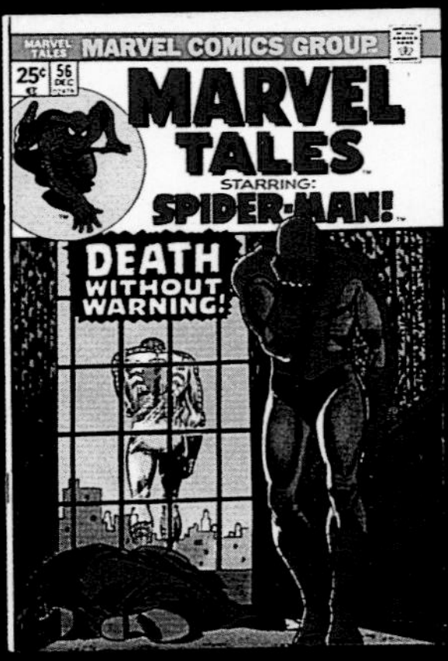
MARVEL COMICS GROUP
MARVEL TALES
STARRING: SPIDER-MAN!
DEATH WITHOUT WARNING!

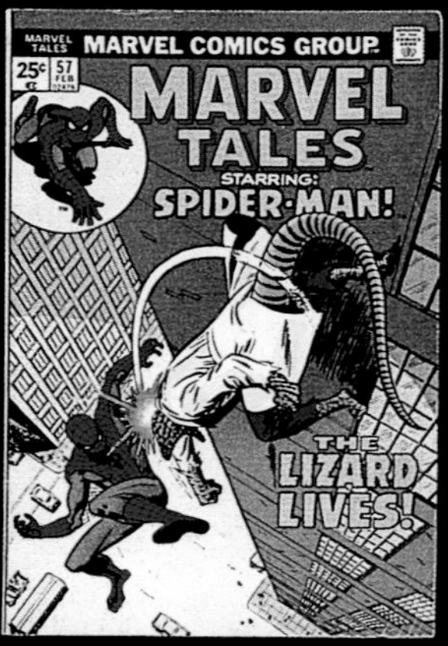
MARVEL COMICS GROUP
MARVEL TALES
STARRING: SPIDER-MAN!
THE LIZARD LIVES!

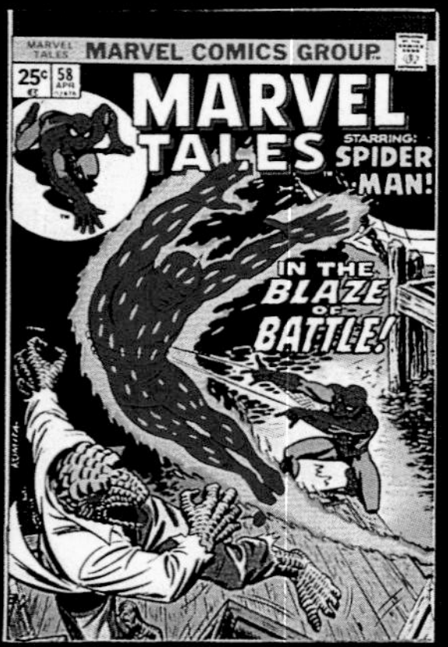
MARVEL COMICS GROUP
MARVEL TALES STARRING: SPIDER-MAN!
IN THE BLAZE OF BATTLE!

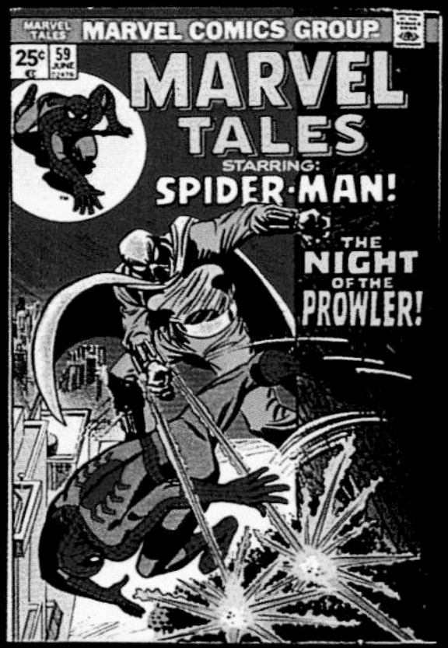
MARVEL COMICS GROUP
MARVEL TALES
STARRING: SPIDER-MAN!
THE NIGHT OF THE PROWLER!

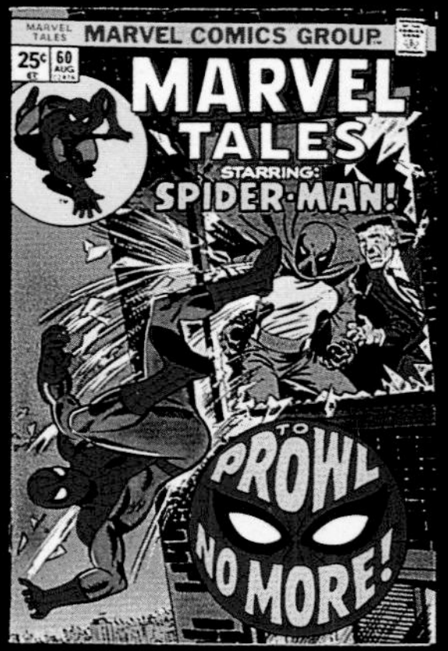
MARVEL COMICS GROUP
MARVEL TALES
STARRING: SPIDER-MAN!
PROWL NO MORE!

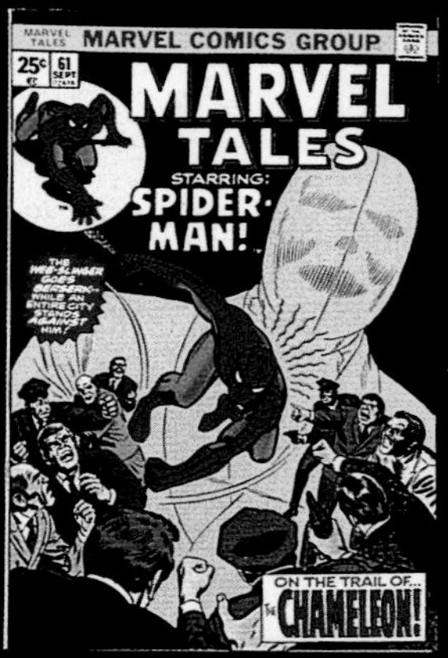
MARVEL COMICS GROUP
MARVEL TALES
STARRING: SPIDER-MAN!
ON THE TRAIL OF THE CHAMELEON!

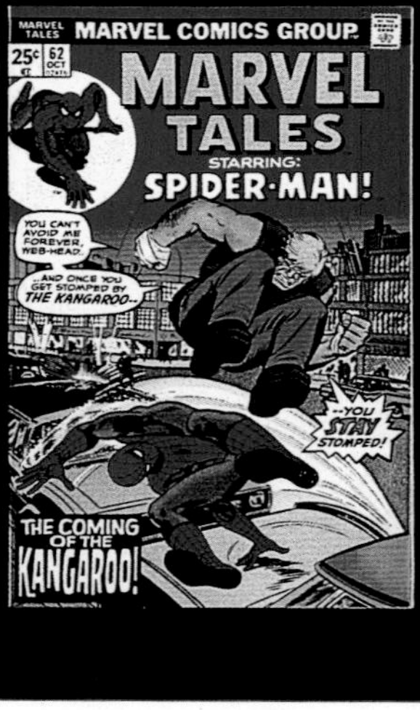
MARVEL COMICS GROUP
MARVEL TALES
STARRING: SPIDER-MAN!
THE COMING OF THE KANGAROO!

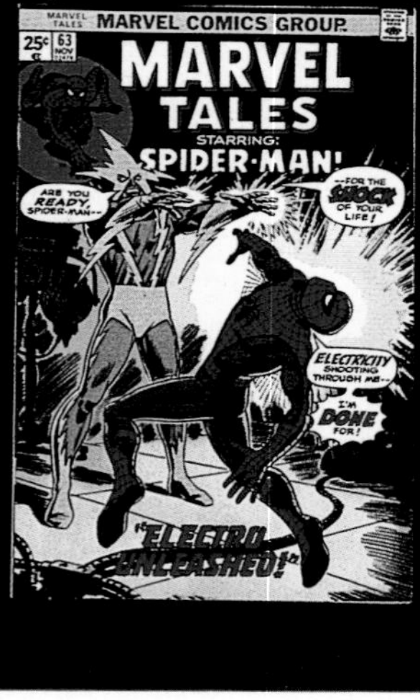
MARVEL COMICS GROUP
MARVEL TALES
STARRING: SPIDER-MAN!
"ELECTRO UNLEASHED!"

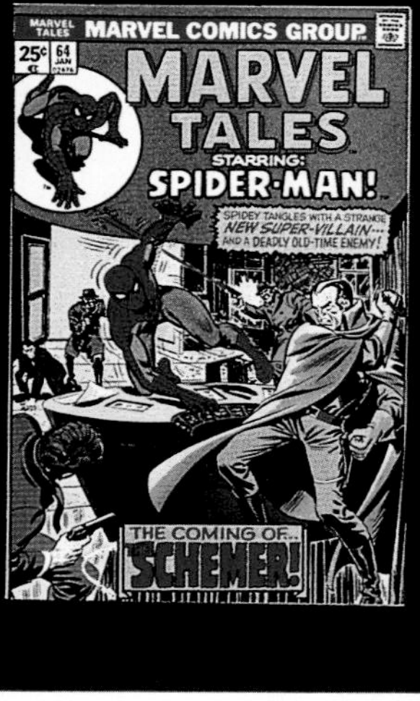
MARVEL COMICS GROUP
MARVEL TALES
STARRING: SPIDER-MAN!
THE COMING OF... SCHEMER!

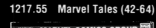

Marvel Tales (1-Present) 1217.55

Ref. No.	Date	RVI	Artist/Info.	
1217.55-1	1964	95	Ditko-a	Reprints
1217.55-2	1965	37	Kirby/Reinman-a	"
1217.55-3	Jul. 1966	18	Ditko-a	"
1217.55-4	Sept.	8	"	"
1217.55-5	Nov.	7	"	"
1217.55-6	Jan. 1967	5	"	"
1217.55-7	Mar.	5	Severin-a	"
1217.55-8	May	5	Ditko-a	"
1217.55-9	Jul.	6	"	"
1217.55-10	**Sept.**	**3**	**"**	**"**
1217.55-11	Nov.	3	"	"
1217.55-12	Jan. 1968	3	"	"
1217.55-13	Mar.	3	" (Origin-Marvel Boy)	"
1217.55-14	May	3	"	"
1217.55-15	Jul.	2	"	"
1217.55-16	Sept.	2	"	"
1217.55-17 to 105		1		"
1217.55-106		6	(Intro. Punisher)	"
1217.55-107 to 244		1	(#223, McFarlane covers begin	"

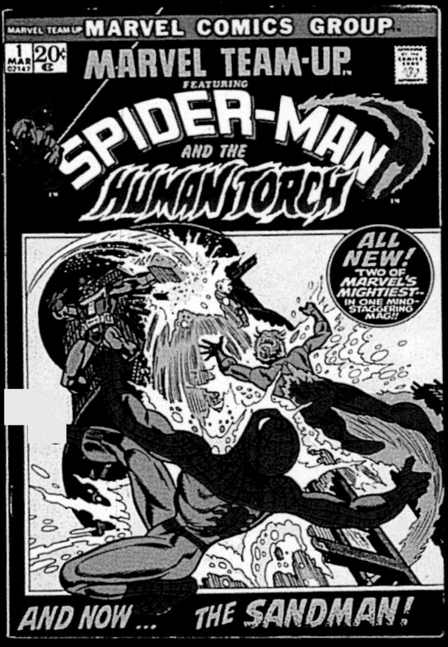
MARVEL COMICS GROUP
MARVEL TEAM-UP
SPIDER-MAN AND THE HUMAN TORCH
ALL NEW! TWO OF MARVEL'S MIGHTIEST IN ONE MIND-STAGGERING MAG!!
AND NOW... THE SANDMAN!

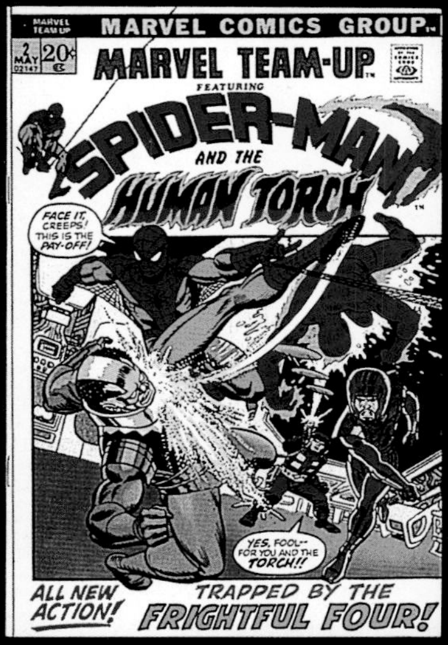
MARVEL COMICS GROUP
MARVEL TEAM-UP
SPIDER-MAN AND THE HUMAN TORCH
FACE IT, CREEPS! THIS IS THE PAY-OFF!
YES, FOOL-- FOR YOU AND THE TORCH!!
ALL NEW ACTION!
TRAPPED BY THE FRIGHTFUL FOUR!

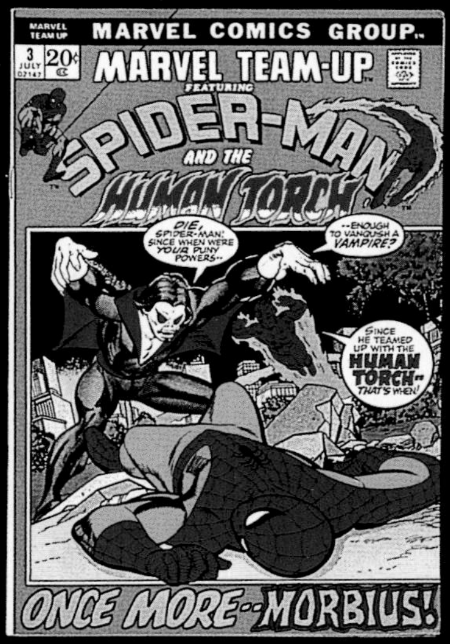
MARVEL COMICS GROUP
MARVEL TEAM-UP
SPIDER-MAN AND THE HUMAN TORCH
DIE, SPIDER-MAN! SINCE WHEN WERE YOUR PUNY POWERS--
--ENOUGH TO VANQUISH A VAMPIRE?
SINCE HE TEAMED UP WITH THE HUMAN TORCH-- THAT'S WHEN!
ONCE MORE--MORBIUS!

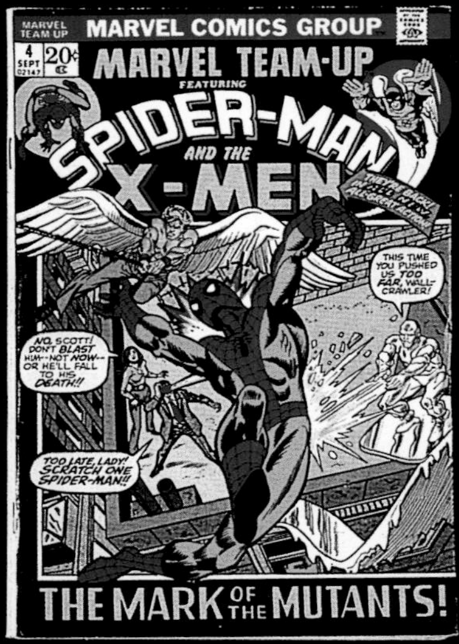
MARVEL COMICS GROUP
MARVEL TEAM-UP
SPIDER-MAN AND THE X-MEN
THIS TIME YOU PUSHED US TOO FAR, WALL-CRAWLER!
NO, SCOTT! DON'T BLAST HIM--NOT NOW-- OR HE'LL FALL TO HIS DEATH!!
TOO LATE, LADY! SCRATCH ONE SPIDER-MAN!!
THE MARK OF THE MUTANTS!

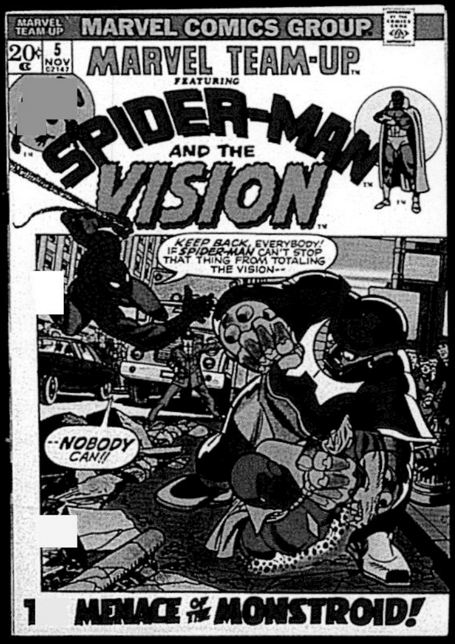
MARVEL COMICS GROUP
MARVEL TEAM-UP
SPIDER-MAN AND THE VISION
KEEP BACK, EVERYBODY! IF SPIDER-MAN CAN'T STOP THAT THING FROM TOTALING THE VISION--
--NOBODY CAN!!
MENACE OF THE MONSTROID!

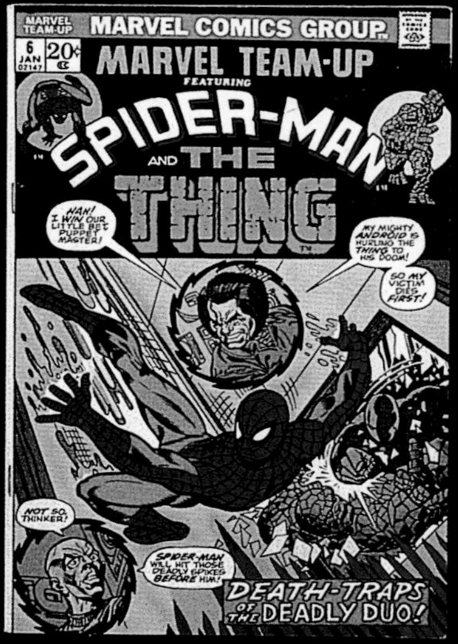
MARVEL COMICS GROUP
MARVEL TEAM-UP
SPIDER-MAN AND THE THING
MY MIGHTY ANDROID IS HURLING THE THING TO HIS DOOM!
SO, MY VICTIM DIES FIRST!
NOT SO, THINKER!
DEATH-TRAPS OF THE DEADLY DUO!

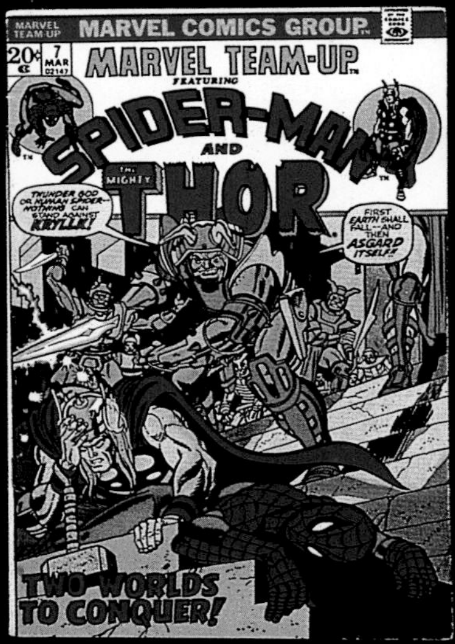
MARVEL COMICS GROUP
MARVEL TEAM-UP
SPIDER-MAN AND THE MIGHTY THOR
FIRST EARTH SHALL FALL--AND THEN ASGARD ITSELF!
TWO WORLDS TO CONQUER!

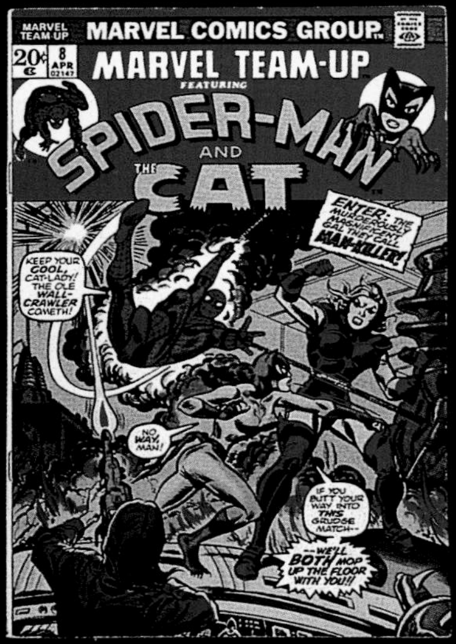
MARVEL COMICS GROUP
MARVEL TEAM-UP
SPIDER-MAN AND THE CAT
MAN-KILLER!

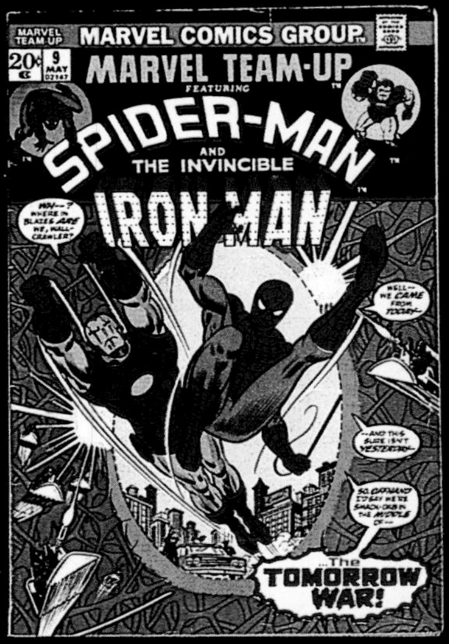
MARVEL COMICS GROUP
MARVEL TEAM-UP
SPIDER-MAN AND THE INVINCIBLE IRON MAN
THE TOMORROW WAR!

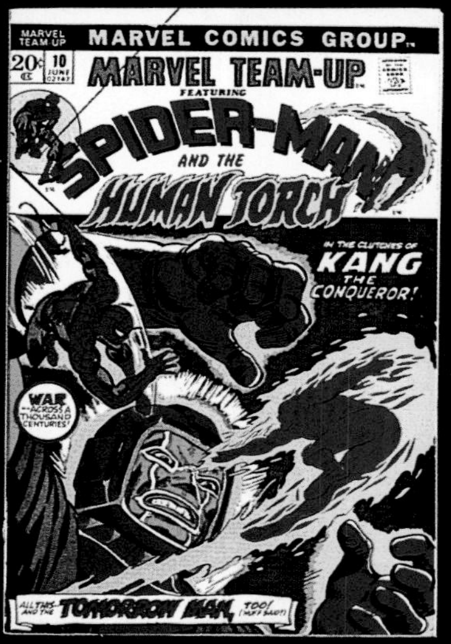
MARVEL COMICS GROUP
MARVEL TEAM-UP
SPIDER-MAN AND THE HUMAN TORCH
IN THE CLUTCHES OF KANG THE CONQUEROR!
WAR ACROSS A THOUSAND CENTURIES!

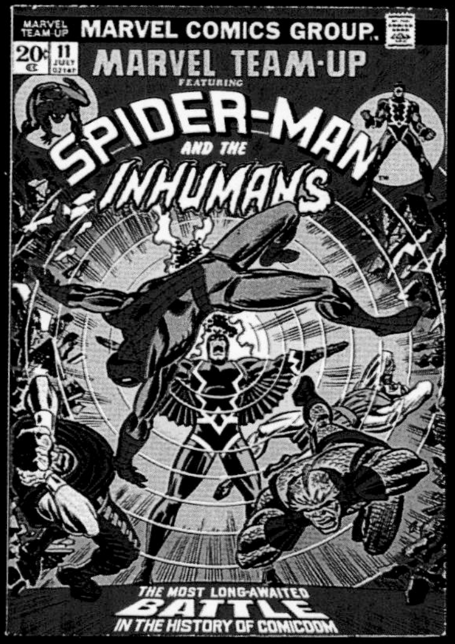
MARVEL COMICS GROUP
MARVEL TEAM-UP
SPIDER-MAN AND THE INHUMANS
THE MOST LONG-AWAITED BATTLE IN THE HISTORY OF COMICDOM

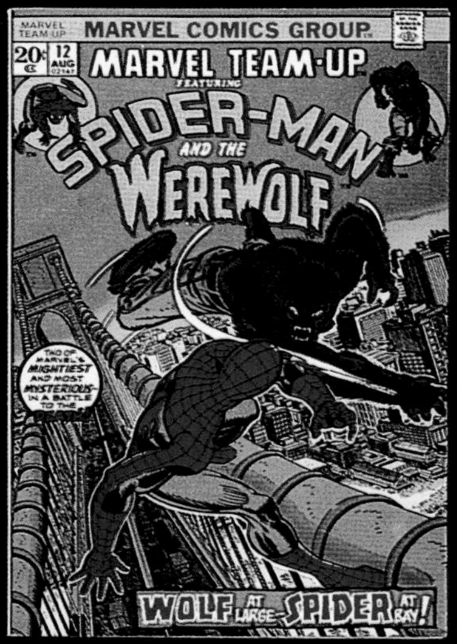
MARVEL COMICS GROUP
MARVEL TEAM-UP
SPIDER-MAN AND THE WEREWOLF
WOLF AT LARGE SPIDER AT BAY!

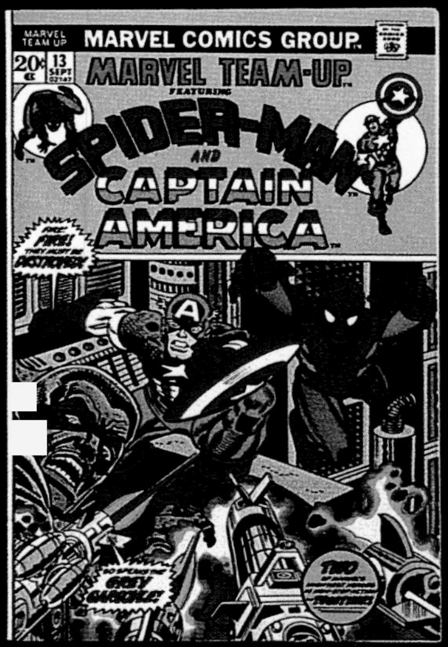
MARVEL COMICS GROUP
MARVEL TEAM-UP
SPIDER-MAN AND CAPTAIN AMERICA

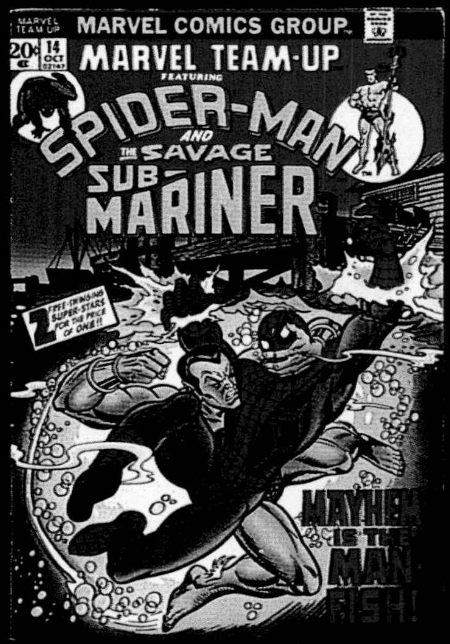
MARVEL COMICS GROUP
MARVEL TEAM-UP
SPIDER-MAN AND THE SAVAGE SUB-MARINER
MAYHEM IS THE MAN-FISH!

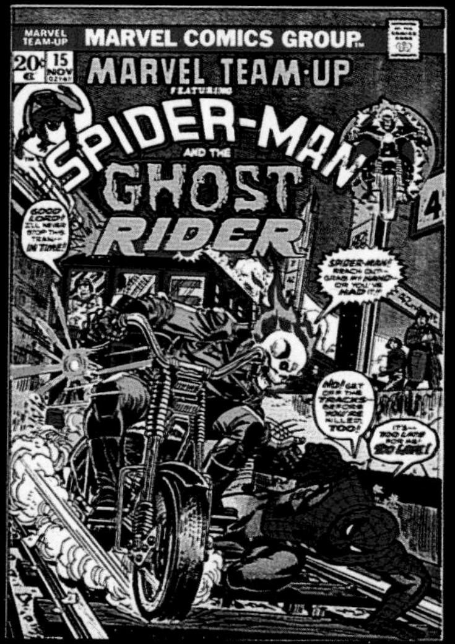
MARVEL COMICS GROUP
MARVEL TEAM-UP
SPIDER-MAN AND THE GHOST RIDER

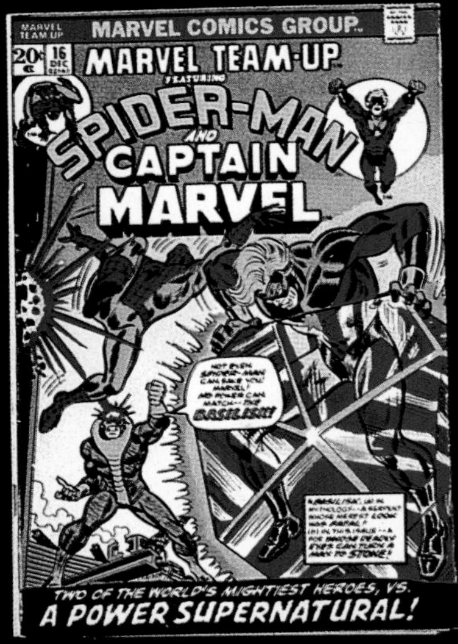
MARVEL COMICS GROUP
MARVEL TEAM-UP
SPIDER-MAN AND CAPTAIN MARVEL
TWO OF THE WORLD'S MIGHTIEST HEROES, VS. A POWER SUPERNATURAL!

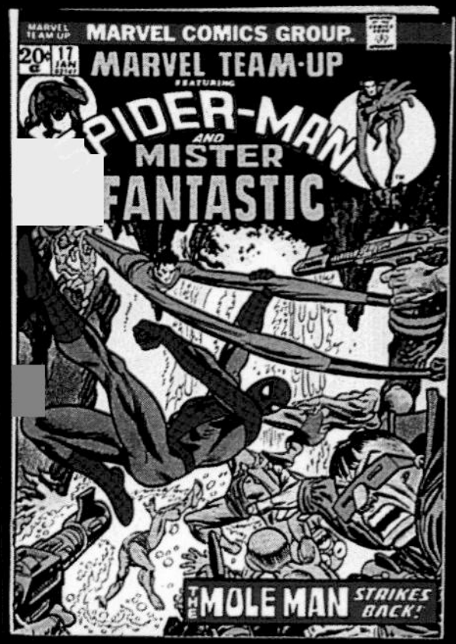
MARVEL COMICS GROUP
MARVEL TEAM-UP
SPIDER-MAN
AND
MISTER FANTASTIC
MOLE MAN STRIKES BACK!

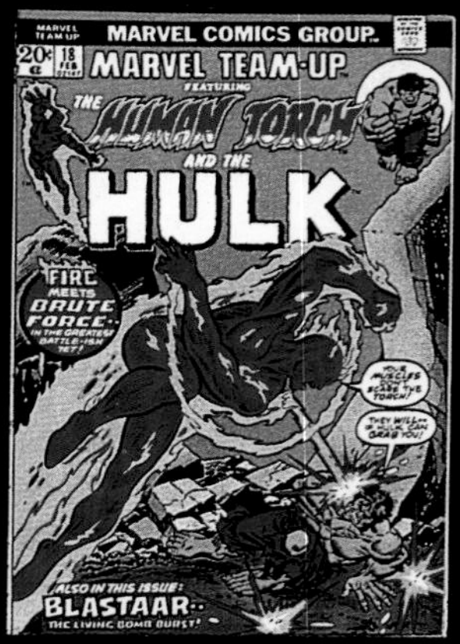
MARVEL COMICS GROUP
MARVEL TEAM-UP
THE HUMAN TORCH
AND THE
HULK
ALSO IN THIS ISSUE BLASTAAR

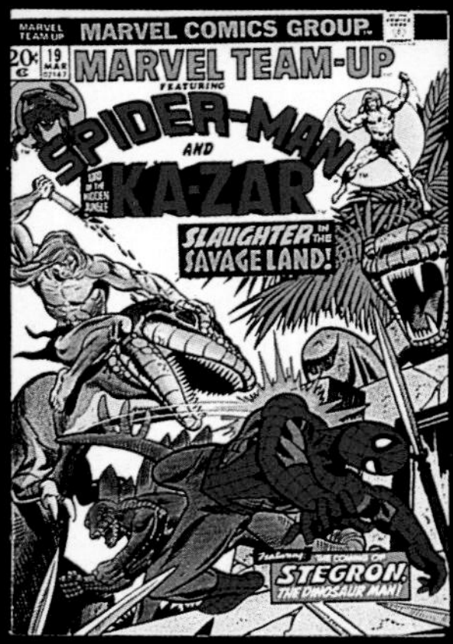
MARVEL COMICS GROUP
MARVEL TEAM-UP
SPIDER-MAN
AND
KA-ZAR
SLAUGHTER IN THE SAVAGE LAND!
STEGRON THE DINOSAUR MAN!

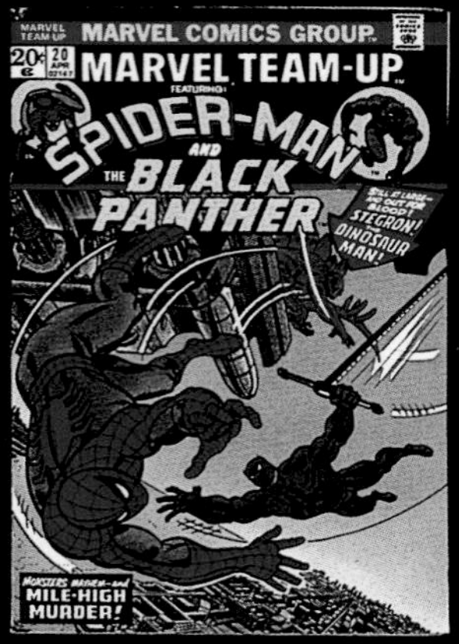
MARVEL COMICS GROUP
MARVEL TEAM-UP
SPIDER-MAN
AND
THE BLACK PANTHER
MONSTERS, MAYHEM and MILE-HIGH MURDER!

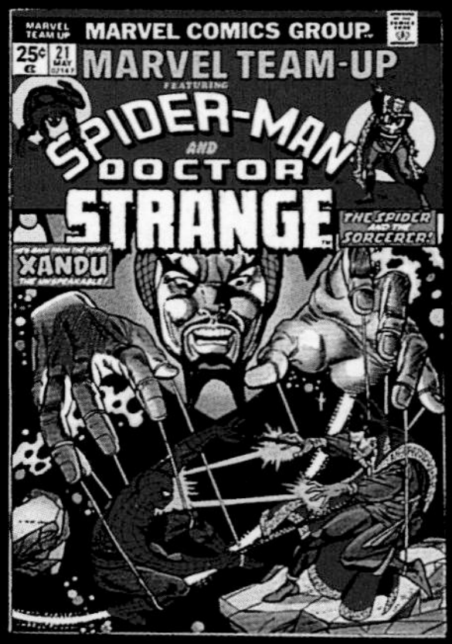
MARVEL COMICS GROUP
MARVEL TEAM-UP
SPIDER-MAN
AND
DOCTOR STRANGE
XANDU
THE SPIDER AND THE SORCERERS

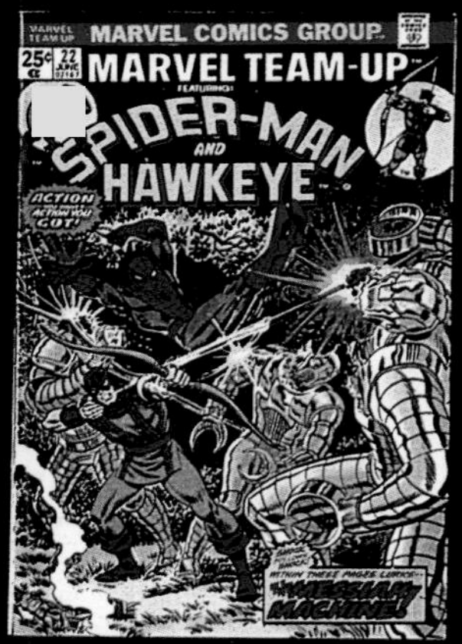
MARVEL COMICS GROUP
MARVEL TEAM-UP
SPIDER-MAN
AND
HAWKEYE

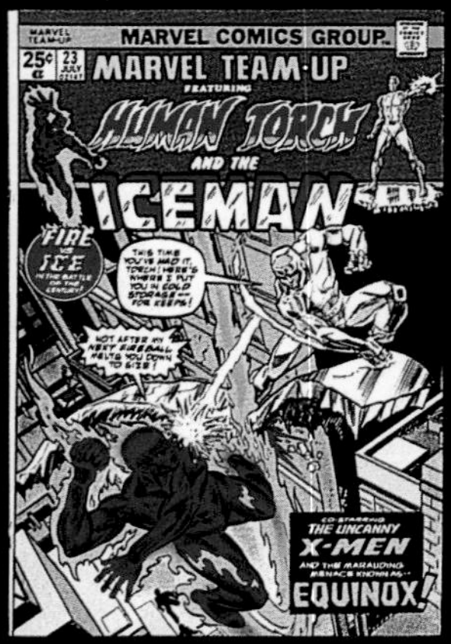
MARVEL COMICS GROUP
MARVEL TEAM-UP
HUMAN TORCH
AND THE
ICEMAN
CO-STARRING THE UNCANNY X-MEN
EQUINOX

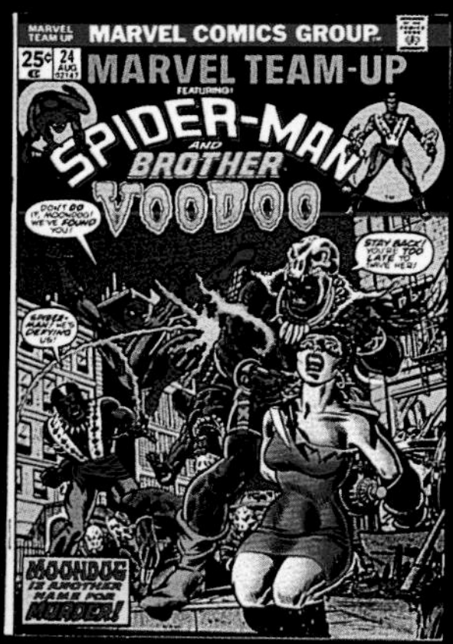
MARVEL COMICS GROUP
MARVEL TEAM-UP
SPIDER-MAN
AND
BROTHER VOODOO

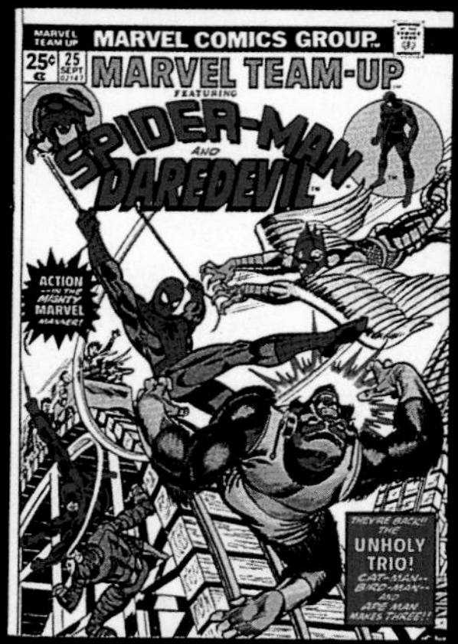
MARVEL COMICS GROUP
MARVEL TEAM-UP
SPIDER-MAN
AND
DAREDEVIL
UNHOLY TRIO!

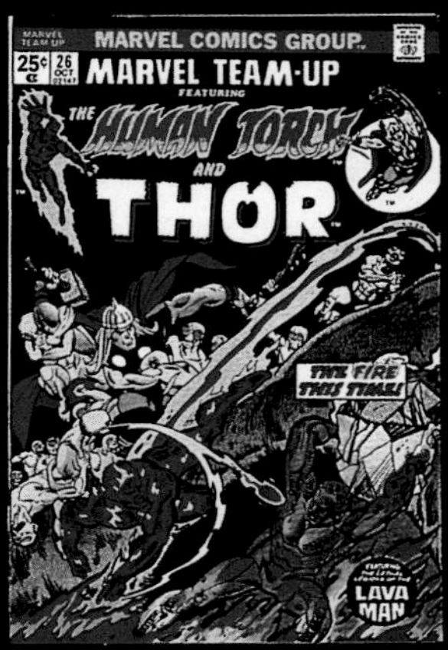
MARVEL COMICS GROUP
MARVEL TEAM-UP
THE HUMAN TORCH
AND
THOR
LAVA MAN

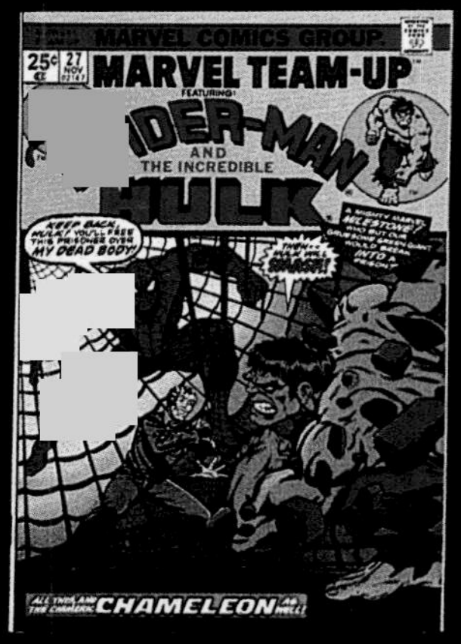
MARVEL COMICS GROUP
MARVEL TEAM-UP
AND
THE INCREDIBLE
HULK
CHAMELEON

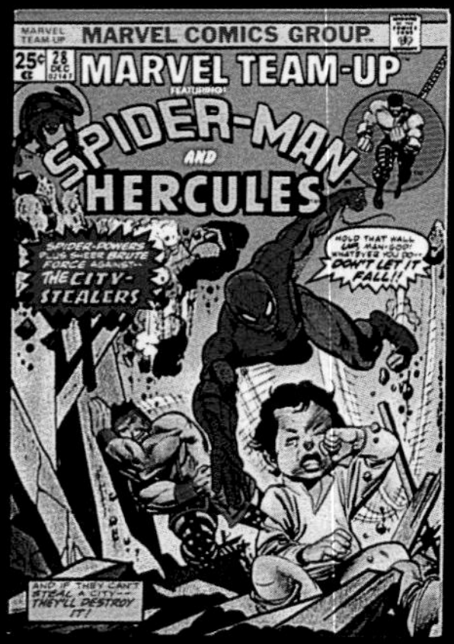
MARVEL COMICS GROUP
MARVEL TEAM-UP
SPIDER-MAN
AND
HERCULES
THE CITY-STEALERS

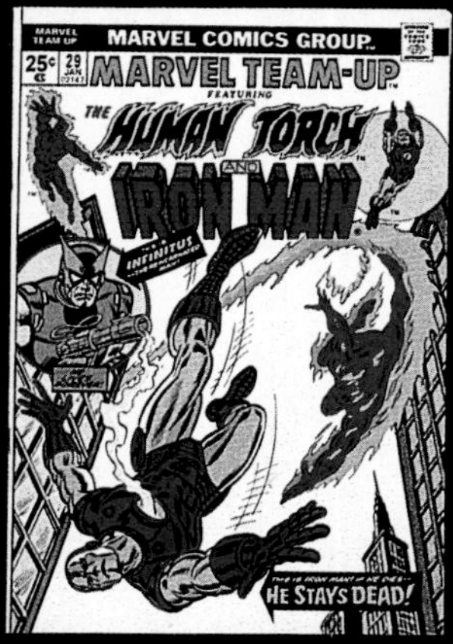
MARVEL COMICS GROUP
MARVEL TEAM-UP
THE HUMAN TORCH
AND
IRON MAN
HE STAYS DEAD!

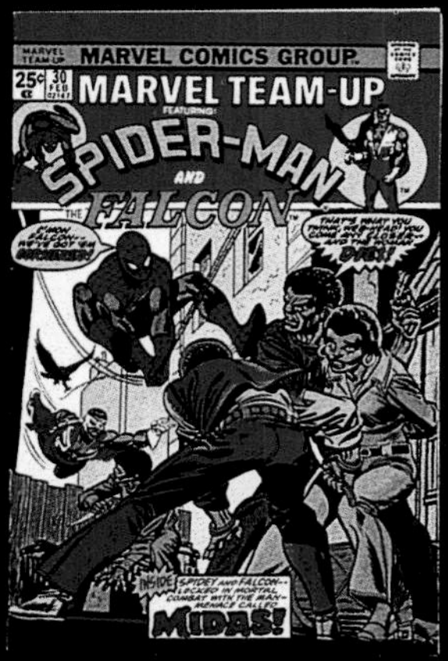
MARVEL COMICS GROUP
MARVEL TEAM-UP
SPIDER-MAN
AND
FALCON
MIDAS!

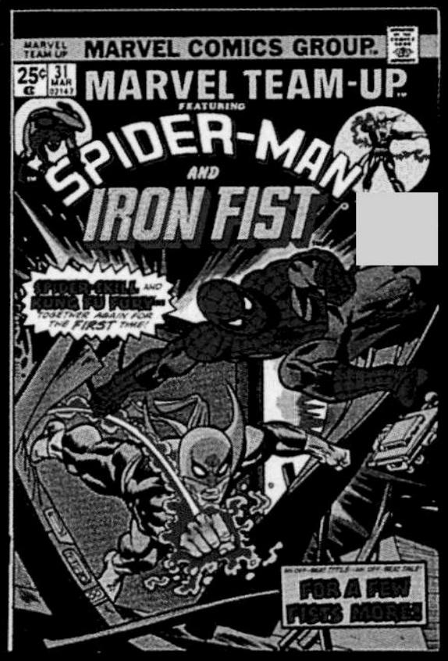
MARVEL COMICS GROUP
MARVEL TEAM-UP
SPIDER-MAN
AND
IRON FIST

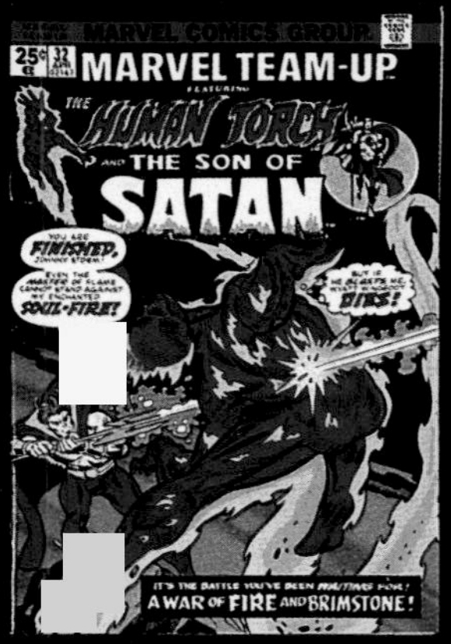
MARVEL TEAM-UP
THE HUMAN TORCH
AND THE SON OF
SATAN
A WAR OF FIRE AND BRIMSTONE!

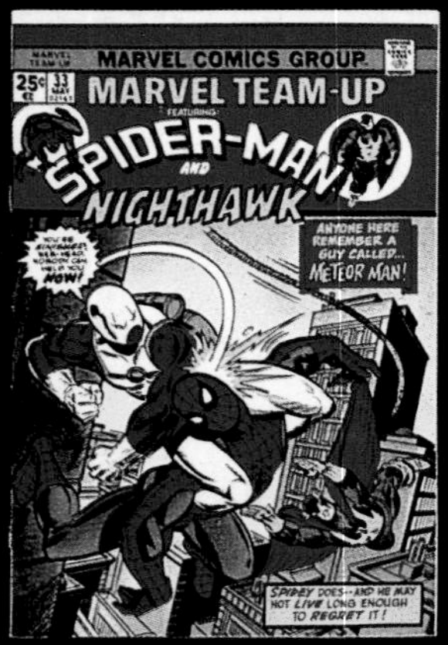
MARVEL COMICS GROUP
MARVEL TEAM-UP
SPIDER-MAN
AND
NIGHTHAWK
METEOR MAN!

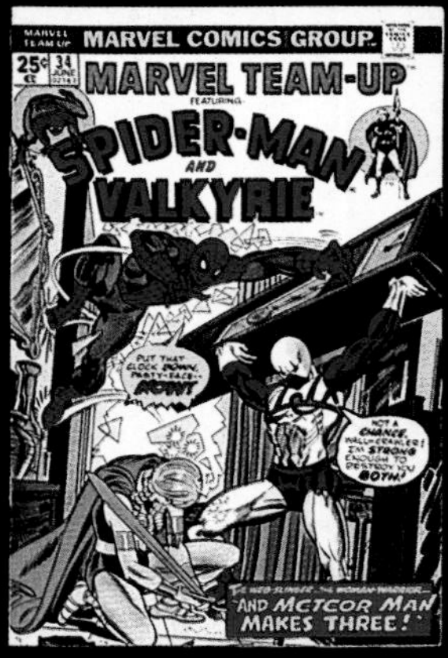
MARVEL COMICS GROUP
MARVEL TEAM-UP
SPIDER-MAN
AND
VALKYRIE
AND METEOR MAN MAKES THREE!

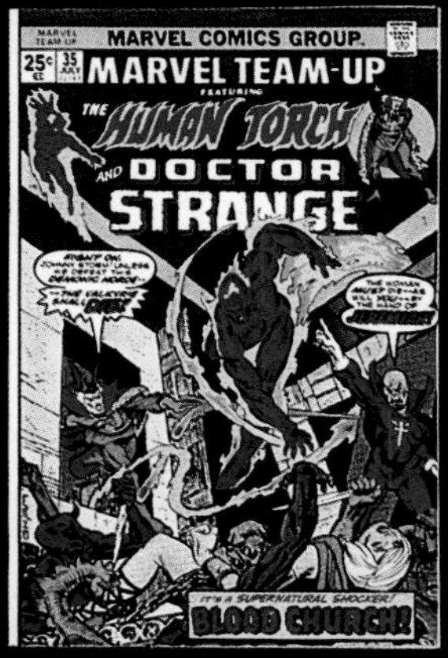
MARVEL COMICS GROUP
MARVEL TEAM-UP
THE HUMAN TORCH
AND
DOCTOR STRANGE
BLOOD CHURCH

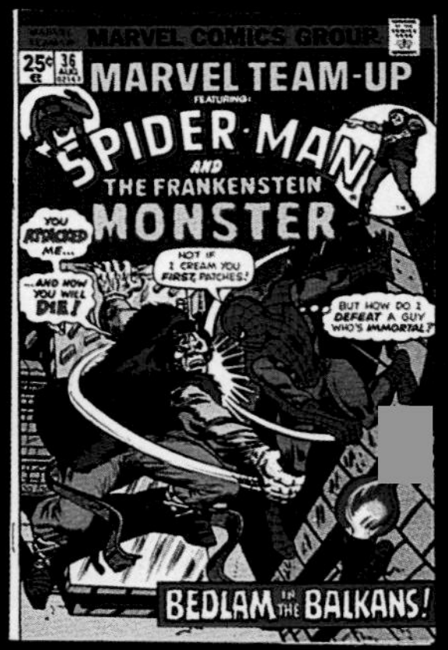
MARVEL COMICS GROUP
MARVEL TEAM-UP
SPIDER-MAN
AND
THE FRANKENSTEIN MONSTER
BEDLAM IN THE BALKANS!

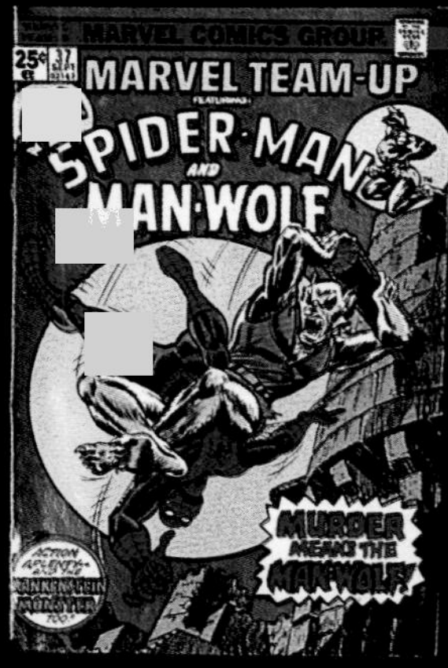
MARVEL COMICS GROUP
MARVEL TEAM-UP
SPIDER-MAN
AND
MAN-WOLF
MURDER MEANS THE MAN-WOLF!

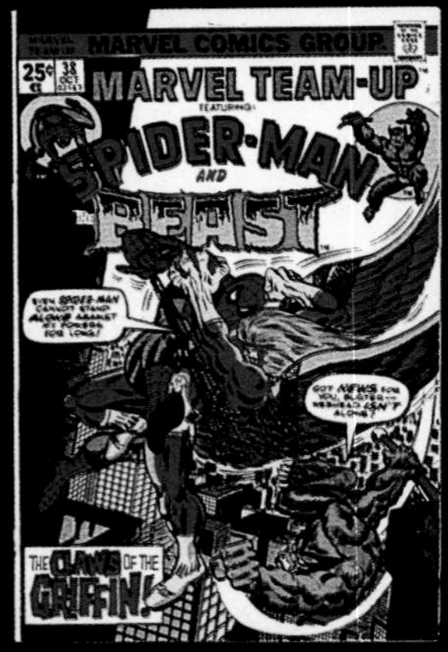
MARVEL TEAM-UP
SPIDER-MAN
AND
BEAST
THE CLAWS OF THE GRIFFIN!

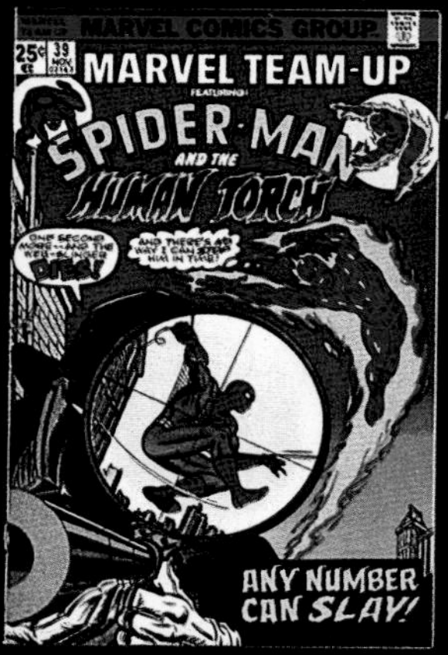
MARVEL TEAM-UP
SPIDER-MAN
AND THE
HUMAN TORCH
ANY NUMBER CAN SLAY!

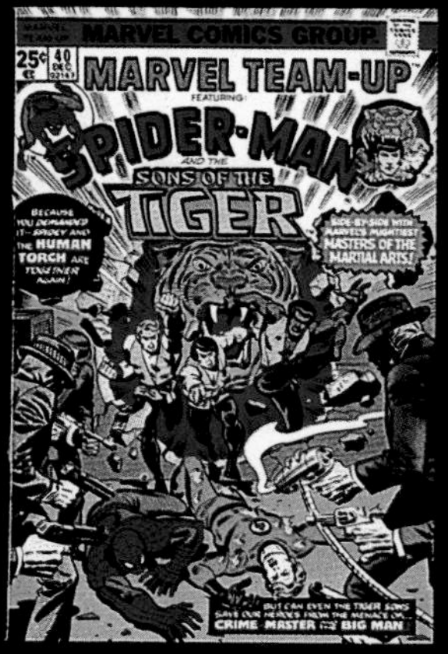
MARVEL TEAM-UP
SPIDER-MAN
SONS OF THE TIGER
CRIME MASTER AND BIG MAN

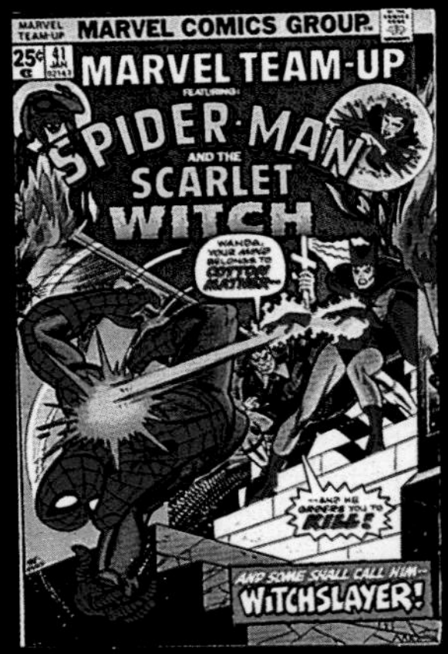
MARVEL COMICS GROUP
MARVEL TEAM-UP
SPIDER-MAN
AND THE
SCARLET WITCH
WITCHSLAYER!

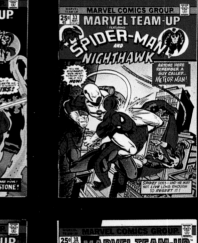

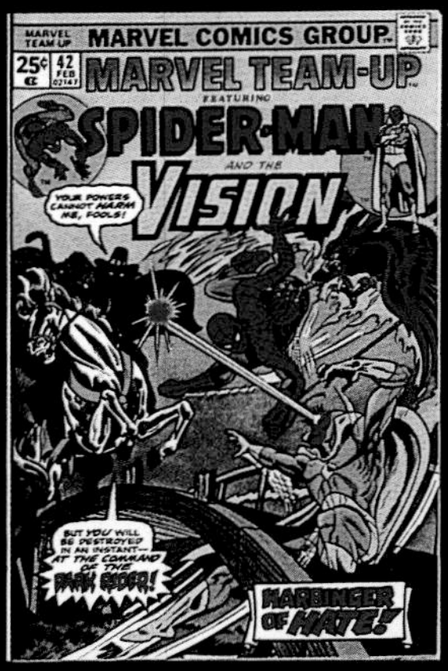
MARVEL COMICS GROUP
MARVEL TEAM-UP
SPIDER-MAN
VISION

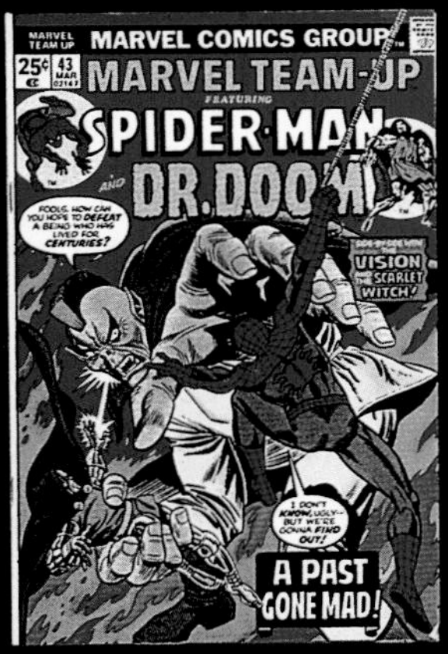
MARVEL COMICS GROUP
MARVEL TEAM-UP
SPIDER-MAN
DR. DOOM
VISION
A PAST GONE MAD!

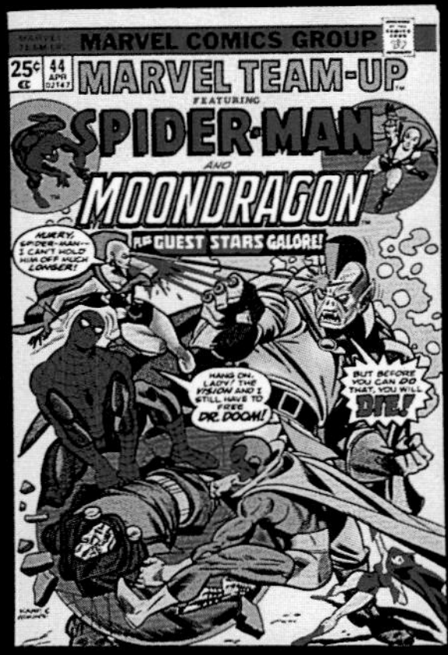
MARVEL COMICS GROUP
MARVEL TEAM-UP
SPIDER-MAN
MOONDRAGON
GUEST STARS GALORE!

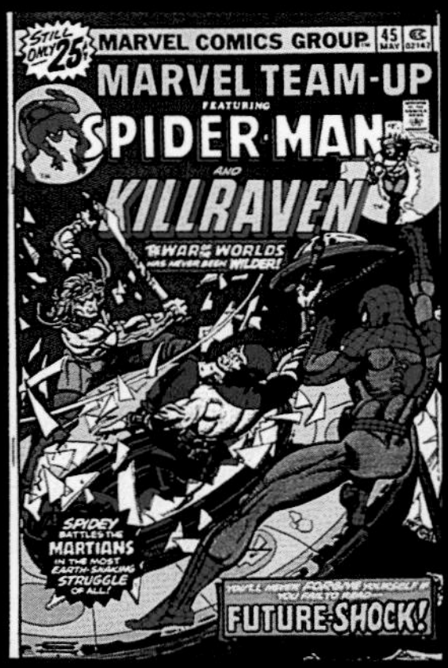
MARVEL COMICS GROUP
MARVEL TEAM-UP
SPIDER-MAN
KILLRAVEN
FUTURE SHOCK!

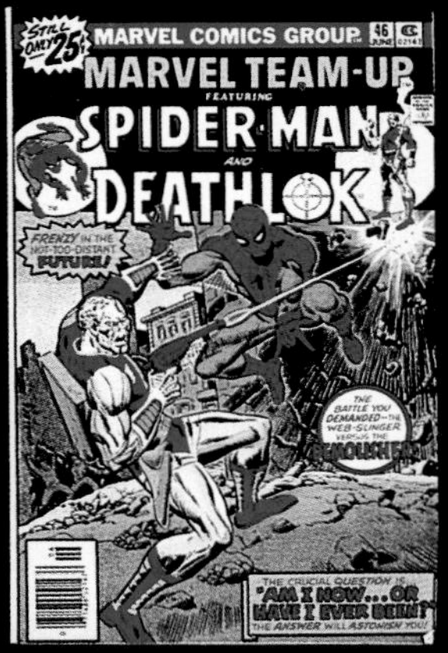
MARVEL COMICS GROUP
MARVEL TEAM-UP
SPIDER-MAN
DEATHLOK

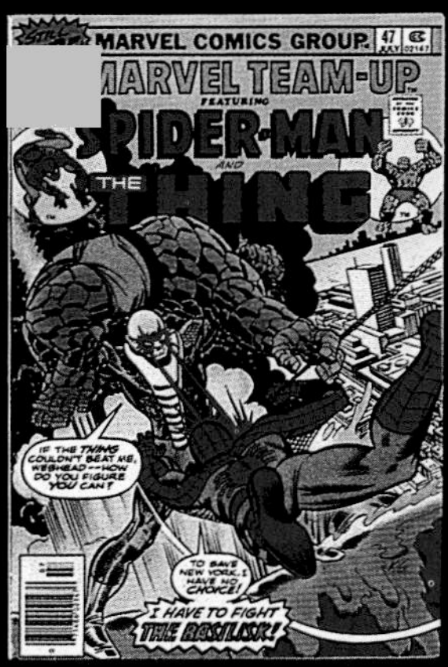
MARVEL COMICS GROUP
MARVEL TEAM-UP
SPIDER-MAN
THING

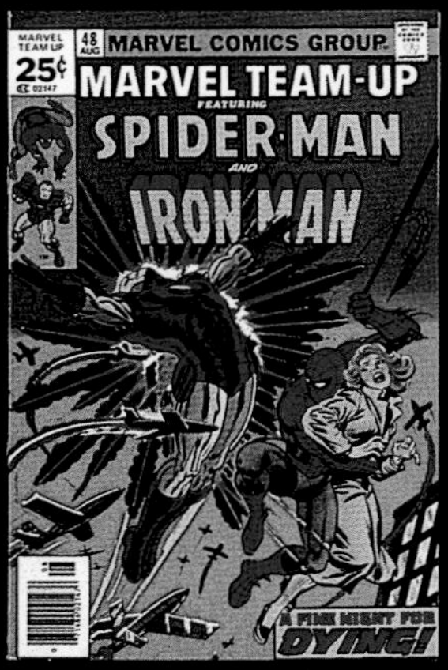
MARVEL COMICS GROUP
MARVEL TEAM-UP
SPIDER-MAN
IRON MAN

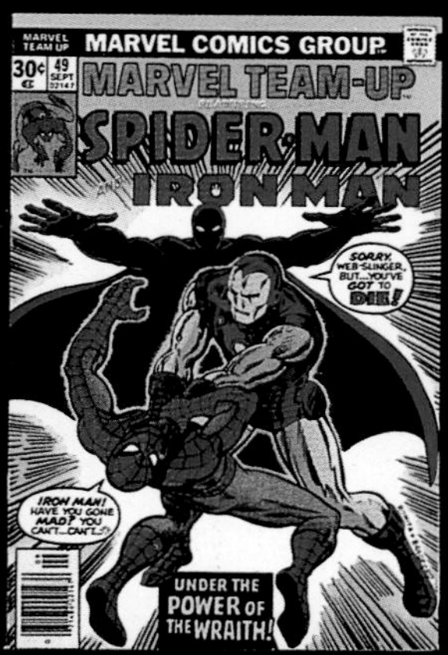
MARVEL COMICS GROUP
MARVEL TEAM-UP
SPIDER-MAN
IRON MAN
UNDER THE POWER OF THE WRAITH!

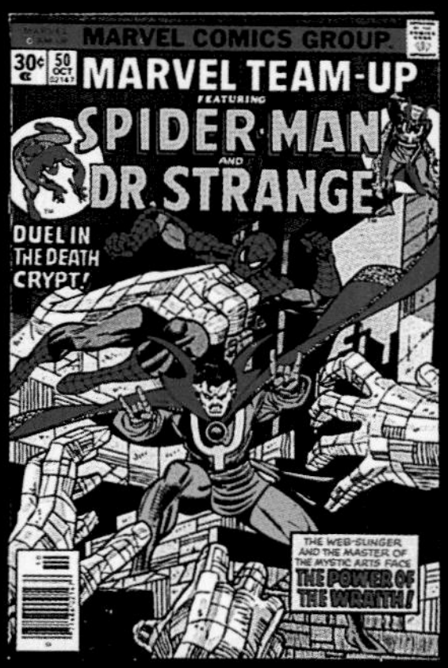
MARVEL COMICS GROUP
MARVEL TEAM-UP
SPIDER-MAN
DR. STRANGE
DUEL IN THE DEATH CRYPT!

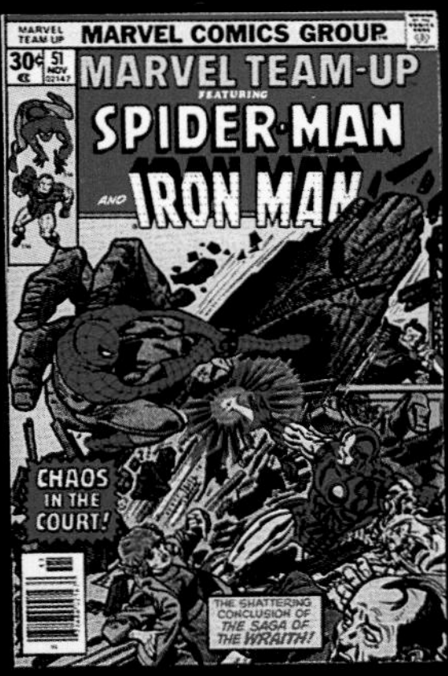
MARVEL COMICS GROUP
MARVEL TEAM-UP
SPIDER-MAN
IRON MAN
CHAOS IN THE COURT!

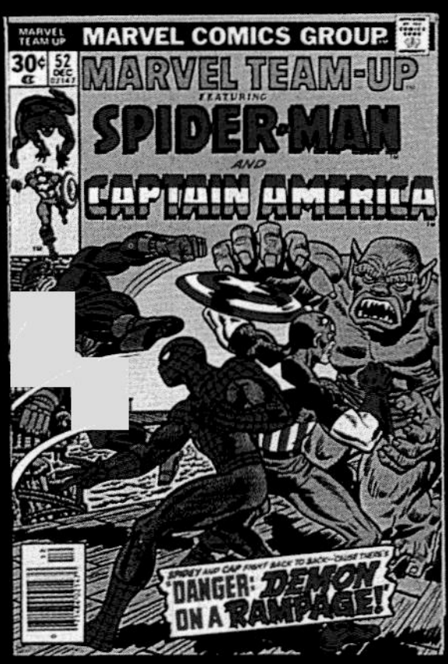
MARVEL COMICS GROUP
MARVEL TEAM-UP
SPIDER-MAN
CAPTAIN AMERICA
DANGER: DEMON ON A RAMPAGE!

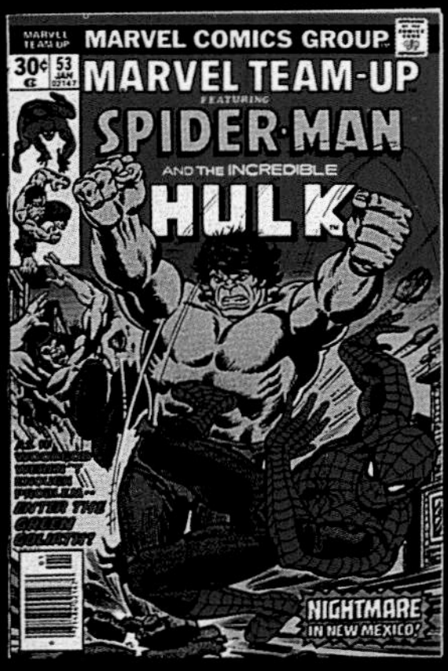
MARVEL COMICS GROUP
MARVEL TEAM-UP
SPIDER-MAN
AND THE INCREDIBLE
HULK
NIGHTMARE IN NEW MEXICO!

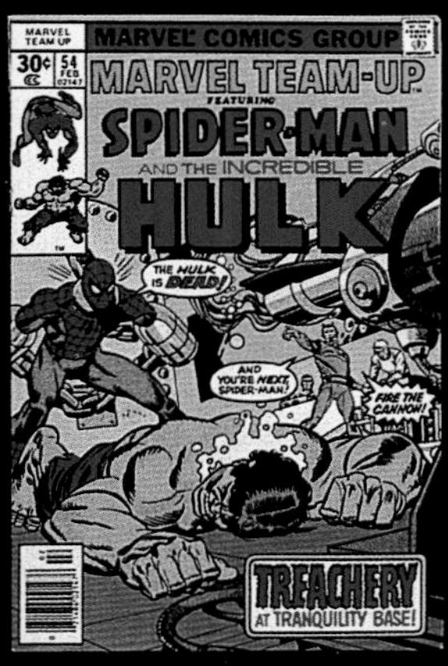
MARVEL COMICS GROUP
MARVEL TEAM-UP
SPIDER-MAN
AND THE INCREDIBLE
HULK
TREACHERY AT TRANQUILITY BASE!

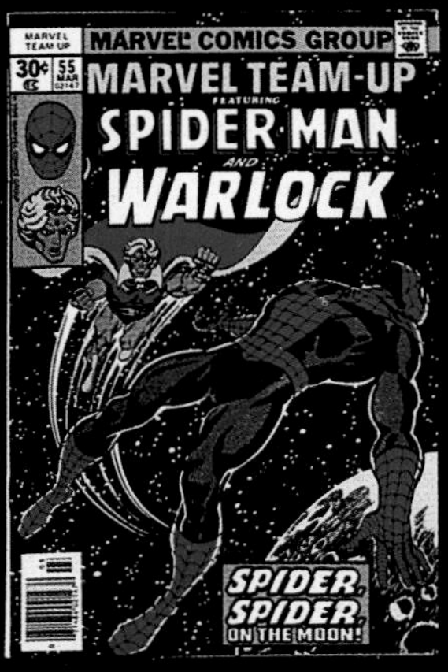
MARVEL COMICS GROUP
MARVEL TEAM-UP
SPIDER-MAN
WARLOCK
SPIDER, SPIDER ON THE MOON!

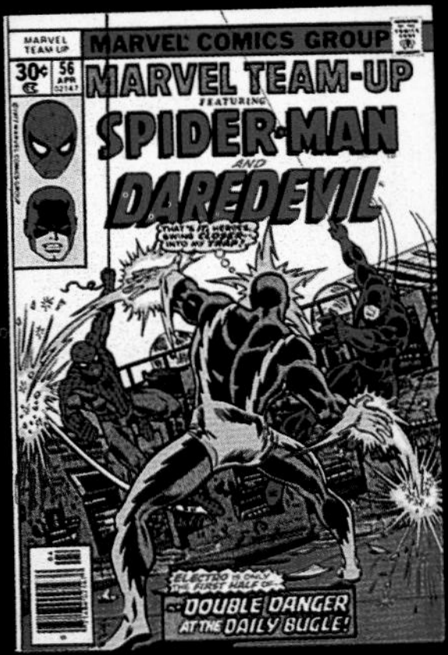
MARVEL COMICS GROUP
MARVEL TEAM-UP
SPIDER-MAN
DAREDEVIL
DOUBLE DANGER AT THE DAILY BUGLE!

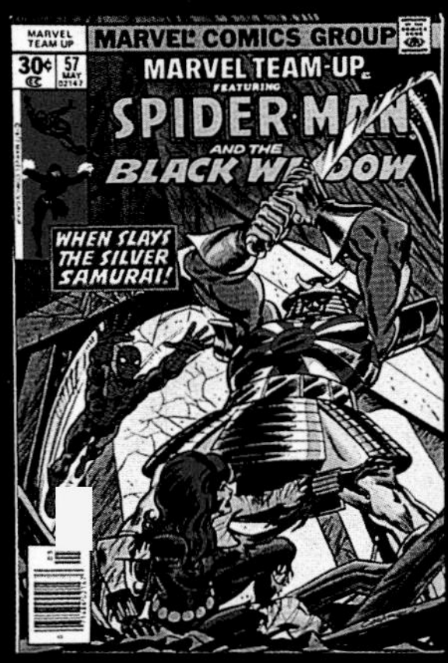
MARVEL COMICS GROUP
MARVEL TEAM-UP
SPIDER-MAN
AND THE BLACK WIDOW
WHEN SLAYS THE SILVER SAMURAI!

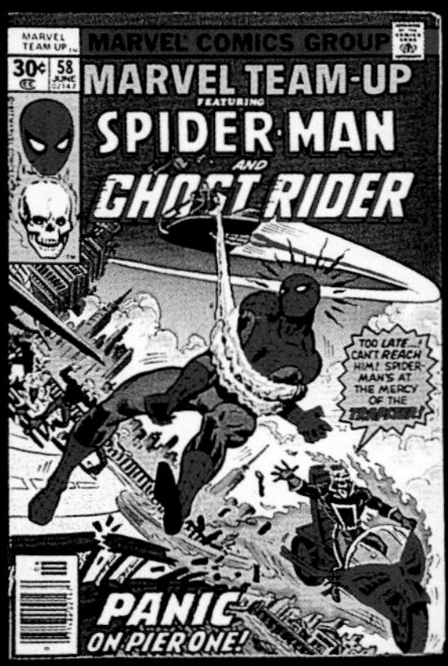
MARVEL COMICS GROUP
MARVEL TEAM-UP
SPIDER-MAN
GHOST RIDER
PANIC ON PIER ONE!

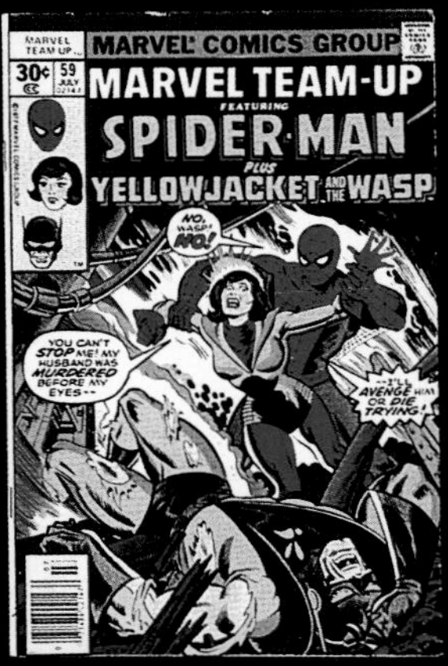
MARVEL COMICS GROUP
MARVEL TEAM-UP
SPIDER-MAN
YELLOWJACKET AND THE WASP

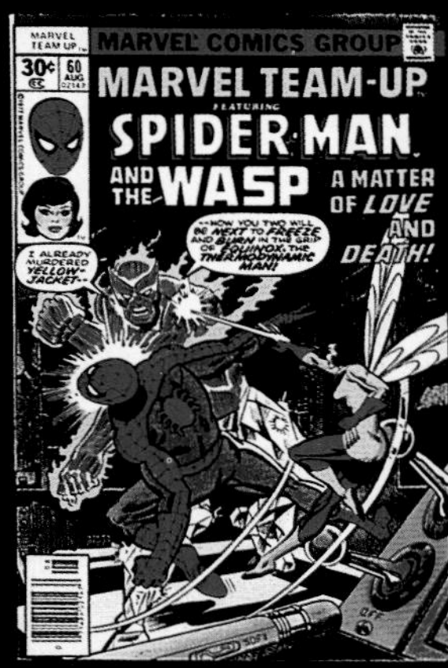
MARVEL COMICS GROUP
MARVEL TEAM-UP
SPIDER-MAN
AND THE WASP
A MATTER OF LOVE AND DEATH!

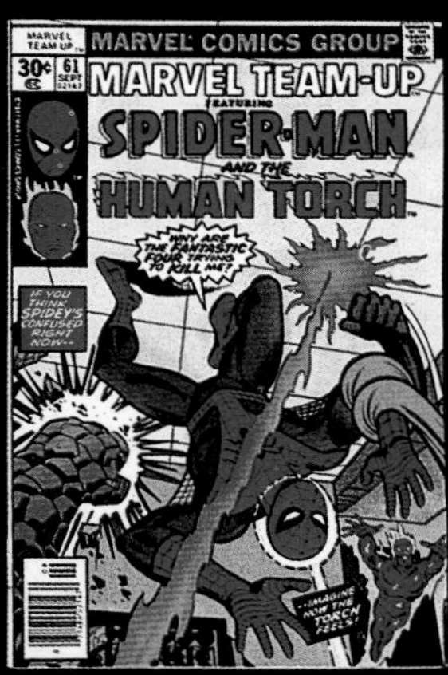
MARVEL COMICS GROUP
MARVEL TEAM-UP
SPIDER-MAN
AND THE HUMAN TORCH

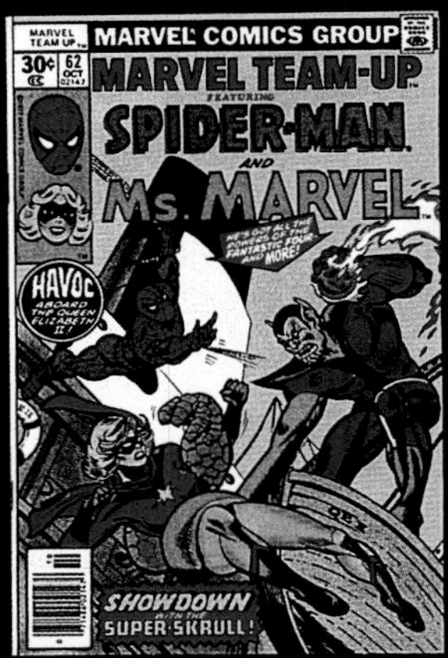
MARVEL COMICS GROUP
MARVEL TEAM-UP
SPIDER-MAN
Ms. MARVEL
HAVOC
SHOWDOWN WITH THE SUPER-SKRULL!

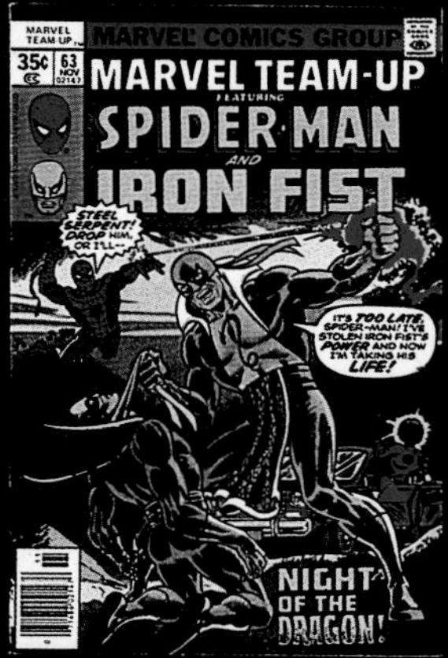
MARVEL COMICS GROUP
MARVEL TEAM-UP
SPIDER-MAN
IRON FIST
NIGHT OF THE DRAGON!

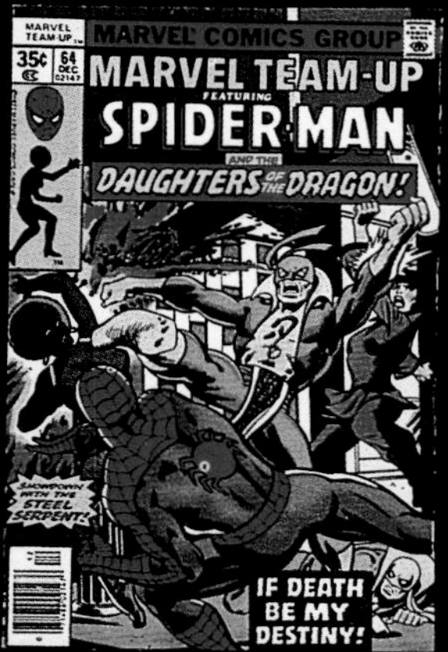
MARVEL COMICS GROUP
MARVEL TEAM-UP
SPIDER-MAN
DAUGHTERS OF THE DRAGON!
IF DEATH BE MY DESTINY!

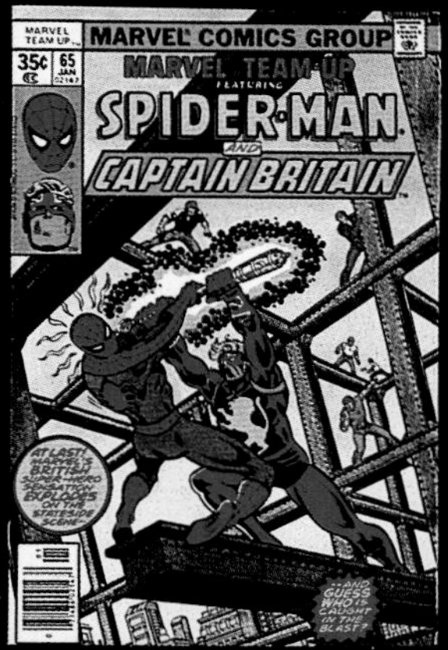
MARVEL COMICS GROUP
MARVEL TEAM-UP
SPIDER-MAN
CAPTAIN BRITAIN

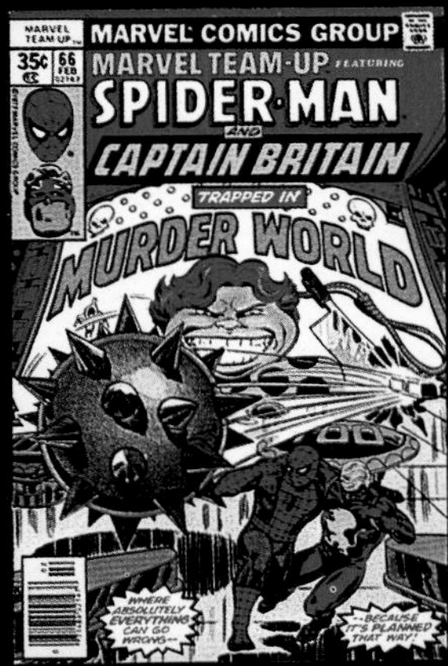
MARVEL COMICS GROUP
MARVEL TEAM-UP
SPIDER-MAN
CAPTAIN BRITAIN
TRAPPED IN
MURDER WORLD

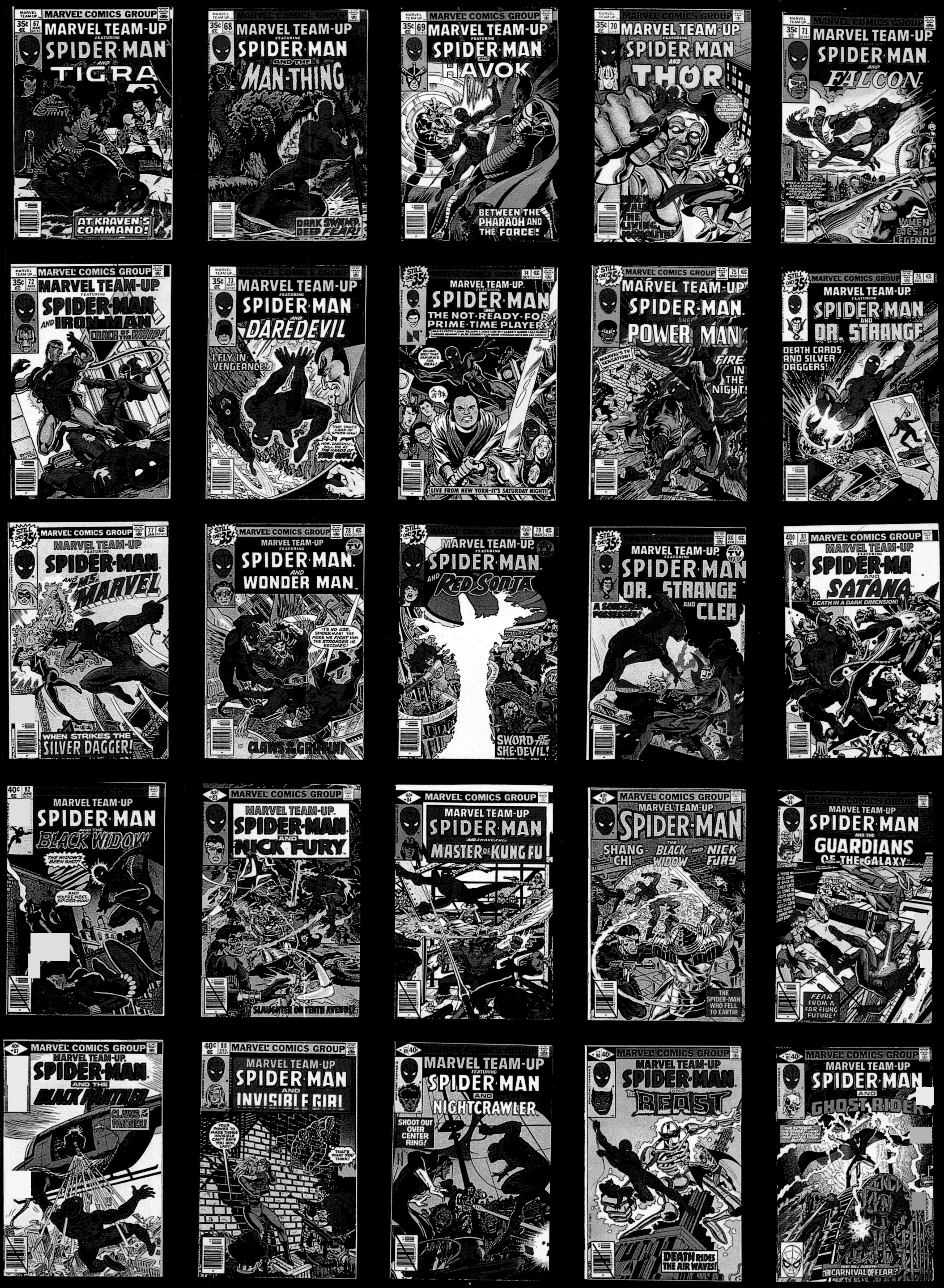
MARVEL COMICS GROUP
MARVEL TEAM-UP
SPIDER-MAN AND TIGRA
AT KRAVEN'S COMMAND!
MARVEL COMICS GROUP
MARVEL TEAM-UP
SPIDER-MAN AND THE MAN-THING
DARK SWAMP DEEP FEAR!
MARVEL COMICS GROUP
MARVEL TEAM-UP
SPIDER-MAN AND HAVOK
BETWEEN THE PHARAOH AND THE FORCE!
MARVEL COMICS GROUP
MARVEL TEAM-UP
SPIDER-MAN AND THOR
MARVEL COMICS GROUP
MARVEL TEAM-UP
SPIDER-MAN AND FALCON
WHEN DIES A LEGEND!
MARVEL COMICS GROUP
MARVEL TEAM-UP
SPIDER-MAN AND IRON MAN
CRACK OF THE WHIP!
MARVEL COMICS GROUP
MARVEL TEAM-UP
SPIDER-MAN AND DAREDEVIL
I FLY IN VENGEANCE!
MARVEL COMICS GROUP
SPIDER-MAN AND THE NOT-READY-FOR PRIME-TIME PLAYERS
LIVE FROM NEW YORK-IT'S SATURDAY NIGHT!
MARVEL COMICS GROUP
MARVEL TEAM-UP
SPIDER-MAN AND POWER MAN
FIRE IN THE NIGHT!
MARVEL COMICS GROUP
MARVEL TEAM-UP
SPIDER-MAN DR. STRANGE
DEATH CARDS AND SILVER DAGGERS!
MARVEL COMICS GROUP
MARVEL TEAM-UP
SPIDER-MAN AND MS. MARVEL
WHEN STRIKES THE SILVER DAGGER!
MARVEL COMICS GROUP
MARVEL TEAM-UP
SPIDER-MAN AND WONDER MAN
CLAWS OF THE GRIFFIN!
MARVEL COMICS GROUP
MARVEL TEAM-UP
SPIDER-MAN AND RED SONJA
SWORD OF THE SHE-DEVIL!
MARVEL COMICS GROUP
MARVEL TEAM-UP
SPIDER-MAN DR. STRANGE AND CLEA
MARVEL COMICS GROUP
MARVEL TEAM-UP
SPIDER-MA AND SATANA
DEATH IN A DARK DIMENSION!
MARVEL COMICS GROUP
MARVEL TEAM-UP
SPIDER-MAN AND THE BLACK WIDOW
MARVEL COMICS GROUP
MARVEL TEAM-UP
SPIDER-MAN AND NICK FURY
SLAUGHTER ON TENTH AVENUE!
MARVEL COMICS GROUP
MARVEL TEAM-UP
SPIDER-MAN AND SHANG-CHI MASTER OF KUNG FU
MARVEL COMICS GROUP
MARVEL TEAM-UP
SPIDER-MAN
SHANG-CHI THE BLACK WIDOW AND NICK FURY
THE SPIDER-MAN WHO FELL TO EARTH!
MARVEL COMICS GROUP
MARVEL TEAM-UP
SPIDER-MAN AND THE GUARDIANS OF THE GALAXY
FEAR FROM A FAR FLUNG FUTURE!
MARVEL COMICS GROUP
MARVEL TEAM-UP
SPIDER-MAN AND THE BLACK PANTHER
CLAWS OF THE PANTHER!
MARVEL COMICS GROUP
MARVEL TEAM-UP
SPIDER-MAN AND INVISIBLE GIRL
MARVEL COMICS GROUP
MARVEL TEAM-UP
SPIDER-MAN AND NIGHTCRAWLER
SHOOT OUT OVER CENTER RING!
MARVEL COMICS GROUP
MARVEL TEAM-UP
SPIDER-MAN AND THE BEAST
DEATH RIDES THE AIR WAVES!
MARVEL COMICS GROUP
MARVEL TEAM-UP
SPIDER-MAN AND GHOST RIDER
THE CARNIVAL OF FEAR!

MARVEL COMICS GROUP
MARVEL TEAM-UP SPIDER-MAN AND HAWKEYE
CALL THEM HEROES? NO, CALL THEM COWARDS!
MISTER FEAR... HE CAN SCARE ANYBODY!
MARVEL COMICS GROUP
MARVEL TEAM-UP SPIDER-MAN AND WEREWOLF
NO VILLAIN IS MORE VILE THAN... TATTERDEMALION!
MARVEL COMICS GROUP
MARVEL TEAM-UP SPIDER-MAN AND THE SHROUD
MASTER of DARKNESS
MARVEL COMICS GROUP
MARVEL TEAM-UP SPIDER-MAN
AND INTRODUCING MARVEL'S NEWEST SENSATION
MOCKINGBIRD
MARVEL COMICS GROUP
MARVEL TEAM-UP SPIDER-MAN AND HOWARD the DUCK
THIS MARVEL COMIC COULD BE WORTH $2500 TO YOU!
MARVEL TEAM-UP HULK AND SPIDER-WOMAN
WIN A TOYS "R" US SHOPPING SPREE!
MARVEL TEAM-UP SPIDER-MAN AND THE BLACK WIDOW
SUDDEN, SWIFT AND VERY VERY DEADLY BUT WHO IS HE?
SPIDEY AND THE WIDOW TOGETHER AGAIN... MAYBE FOR THE LAST TIME!
MARVEL COMICS GROUP
MARVEL TEAM-UP SPIDER-MAN AND MACHINE MAN
BARON BRIMSTONE
PLUS THE SANDMAN
EQUAL THE WORST POSSIBLE KIND OF TROUBLE!
MARVEL COMICS GROUP
MARVEL TEAM-UP SPIDER-MAN AND THE Fantastic Four
SPECIAL DOUBLE-SIZE 100th ISSUE!
THE REASON IS KARMA!
MARVEL COMICS GROUP
MARVEL TEAM-UP SPIDER-MAN AND NIGHTHAWK
THE SPECTERS OF THE SIXTIES ARE BACK
SCREAMING FOR NIGHTHAWK'S BLOOD!
MARVEL COMICS GROUP
MARVEL TEAM-UP SPIDER-MAN AND DOC SAMSON
A BATTLE THEY MUST WIN OR SEE EVERYTHING!
MARVEL COMICS GROUP
MARVEL TEAM-UP SPIDER-MAN AND ANT-MAN
HE'S A WHOLE SWARM OF VILLAINS ROLLED INTO ONE... The TASKMASTER!
MARVEL COMICS GROUP
MARVEL TEAM-UP HULK AND KA-ZAR
MODOK MUST TRIUMPH!
MARVEL COMICS GROUP
MARVEL TEAM-UP THE HULK AND POWER MAN IRON FIST
WHEN THIS BATTLE HAS ENDED THE TROUBLE WILL HAVE ONLY BEGUN!
MARVEL COMICS GROUP
MARVEL TEAM-UP SPIDER-MAN AND CAPTAIN AMERICA
...DEFINITELY NOT A GOOD PLACE TO MEET... THE SCORPION
MARVEL COMICS GROUP
MARVEL TEAM-UP SPIDER-MAN AND SHE-HULK
THIS RUMOR OF REVOLUTION!
MARVEL COMICS GROUP
MARVEL TEAM-UP SPIDER-MAN AND PALADIN
MARVEL COMICS GROUP
MARVEL TEAM-UP SPIDER-MAN AND DAZZLER
MARVEL COMICS GROUP
MARVEL TEAM-UP SPIDER-MAN AND IRON MAN
THE MENACE OF MAGMA!
WIN A Columbia TEN-SPEED FORMULA 10 RACER!
MARVEL TEAM-UP SPIDER-MAN AND DEVIL-SLAYER
TRAPPED IN THE TEMPLE OF THE SPIDER-GOD!
BEGINNING SEPT. 12th ON NBC SPIDER-MAN AND HIS AMAZING FRIENDS!
MARVEL TEAM-UP SPIDER-MAN AND KING KULL
WIN A Columbia TEN-SPEED FORMULA 10 RACER!
MARVEL TEAM-UP SPIDER-MAN AND QUASAR
WIN A Columbia TEN-SPEED FORMULA 10 RACER!
MARVEL TEAM-UP SPIDER-MAN AND THE FALCON
MARVEL COMICS GROUP
SPIDER-MAN AND THOR
MARVEL COMICS GROUP
MARVEL TEAM-UP SPIDER-MAN AND VALKYRIE
HAVE SWORD... WILL TRAVEL!

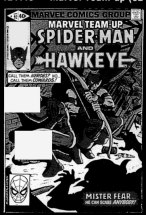

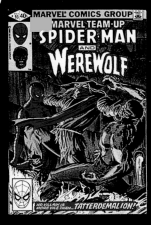

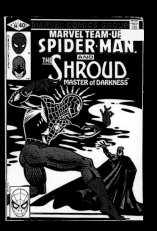

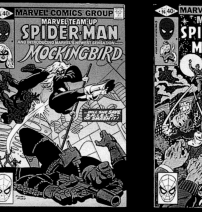

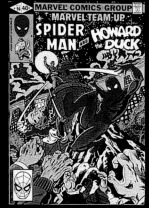

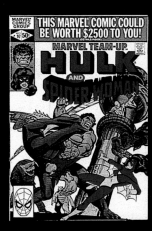

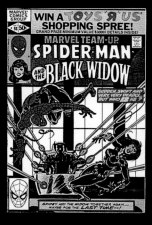

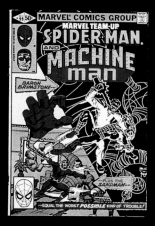

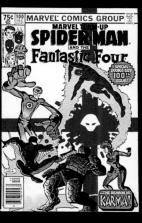

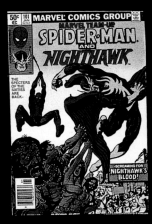

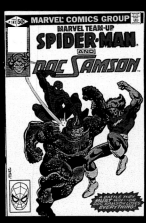

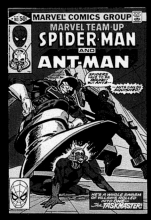

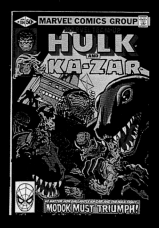

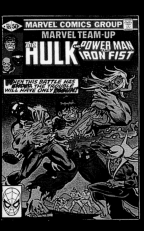

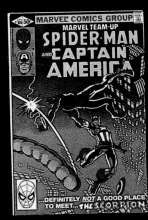

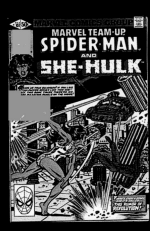

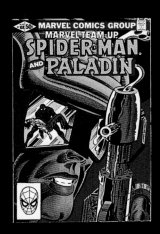

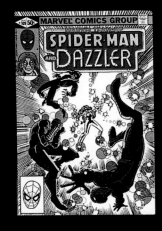

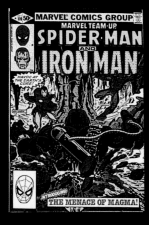

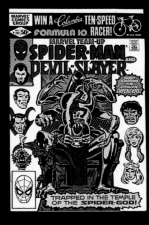

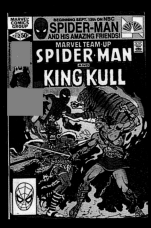

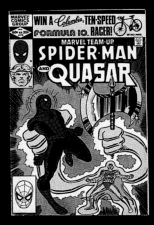

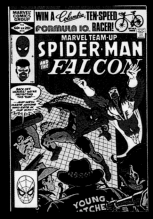

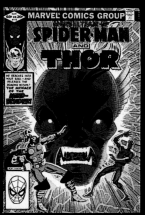

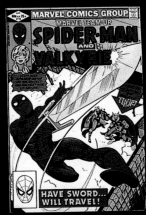

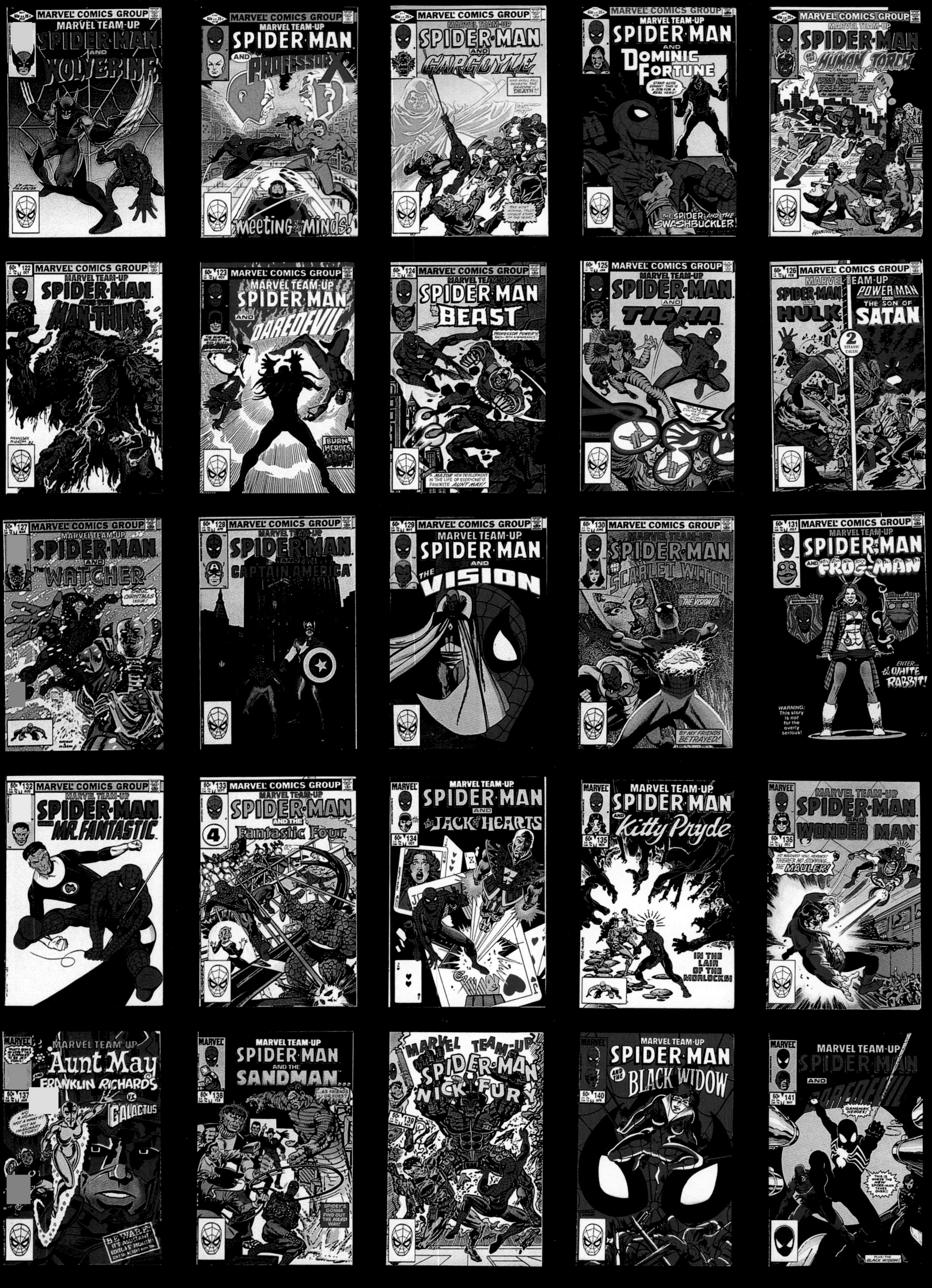
MARVEL COMICS GROUP
MARVEL TEAM-UP
SPIDER-MAN AND WOLVERINE
MARVEL COMICS GROUP
MARVEL TEAM-UP
SPIDER-MAN AND PROFESSOR X
meeting of the minds!
MARVEL COMICS GROUP
MARVEL TEAM-UP
SPIDER-MAN AND GARGOYLE
MARVEL COMICS GROUP
MARVEL TEAM-UP
SPIDER-MAN AND DOMINIC FORTUNE
THE SPIDER AND THE SWASHBUCKLER!
MARVEL COMICS GROUP
MARVEL TEAM-UP
SPIDER-MAN AND THE HUMAN TORCH
MARVEL COMICS GROUP
MARVEL TEAM-UP
SPIDER-MAN AND THE MAN-THING
MARVEL COMICS GROUP
MARVEL TEAM-UP
SPIDER-MAN AND DAREDEVIL
MARVEL COMICS GROUP
MARVEL TEAM-UP
SPIDER-MAN THE BEAST
MAJOR NEW DEVELOPMENT IN THE LIFE OF EVERYONE'S FAVORITE AUNT MAY!
MARVEL COMICS GROUP
MARVEL TEAM-UP
SPIDER-MAN AND TIGRA
MARVEL COMICS GROUP
MARVEL TEAM-UP
SPIDER-MAN AND HULK
POWER MAN AND THE SON OF SATAN
2 TITANIC TALES!
MARVEL COMICS GROUP
MARVEL TEAM-UP
SPIDER-MAN AND The WATCHER
SPECIAL CHRISTMAS ISSUE!
MARVEL COMICS GROUP
MARVEL TEAM-UP
SPIDER-MAN AND CAPTAIN AMERICA
MARVEL COMICS GROUP
MARVEL TEAM-UP
SPIDER-MAN AND THE VISION
MARVEL COMICS GROUP
MARVEL TEAM-UP
SPIDER-MAN AND THE SCARLET WITCH
GUEST-STARRING THE VISION!
BY MY FRIENDS BETRAYED!
MARVEL COMICS GROUP
MARVEL TEAM-UP
SPIDER-MAN AND FROG-MAN
ENTER... the WHITE RABBIT!
WARNING: This story is not for the overly serious!
MARVEL COMICS GROUP
MARVEL TEAM-UP
SPIDER-MAN AND MR. FANTASTIC
MARVEL COMICS GROUP
MARVEL TEAM-UP
SPIDER-MAN AND THE Fantastic Four
MARVEL TEAM-UP
SPIDER-MAN AND the JACK of HEARTS
MARVEL TEAM-UP
SPIDER-MAN AND Kitty Pryde
IN THE LAIR OF THE MORLOCKS!
MARVEL TEAM-UP
SPIDER-MAN AND WONDER MAN
THE MAULER!
MARVEL TEAM-UP
Aunt May AND FRANKLIN RICHARDS VS. GALACTUS
BEWARE! IT'S ASSISTANT EDITOR'S MONTH!
MARVEL TEAM-UP
SPIDER-MAN AND THE SANDMAN...
SPIDEY'S GONNA FIND OUT THE HARD WAY!
MARVEL TEAM-UP
SPIDER-MAN NICK FURY
MARVEL TEAM-UP
SPIDER-MAN AND THE BLACK WIDOW
MARVEL TEAM-UP
SPIDER-MAN AND DAREDEVIL
PLUS: THE BLACK WIDOW!

1217.6 Marvel Team-up (142-149; AN. 1-7)

MARVEL TEAM-UP
SPIDER-MAN AND CAPTAIN MARVEL
MARVEL TEAM-UP
SPIDER-MAN AND STARFOX
MARVEL TEAM-UP
SPIDER-MAN AND MOON KNIGHT
DON'T MESS WITH THE WHITE DRAGON!
MARVEL TEAM-UP
SPIDER-MAN AND IRON MAN
MARVEL TEAM-UP
SPIDER-MAN AND NOMAD
MARVEL TEAM-UP
SPIDER-MAN AND HUMAN TORCH
"PAWNS OF THE BLACK ABBOTT!"
MARVEL TEAM-UP
SPIDER-MAN AND the mighty THOR
MARVEL TEAM-UP
SPIDER-MAN AND CANNONBALL
KING-SIZE ANNUAL!
MARVEL TEAM-UP
SPIDER-MAN AND THE X-MEN
MARVEL COMICS GROUP
KING-SIZE MARVEL TEAM-UP ANNUAL!
SPIDER-MAN AND THE HULK
MARVEL COMICS GROUP
MARVEL TEAM-UP ANNUAL!
HULK AND POWER MAN AND IRON FIST
MAYHEM IN MIDDLE AMERICA!
MARVEL COMICS GROUP
MARVEL TEAM-UP ANNUAL!
SPIDER-MAN AND MOON KNIGHT IRON FIST POWER MAN DAREDEVIL
PAWNS OF THE PURPLE MAN!
MARVEL COMICS GROUP
KING-SIZE ANNUAL!
MARVEL TEAM-UP
SPIDER-MAN AND THE THING SCARLET WITCH DR. STRANGE QUASAR
MARVEL TEAM-UP ANNUAL
SPIDER-MAN
CLOAK AND DAGGER
THE NEW MUTANTS
MARVEL TEAM-UP ANNUAL
SPIDER-MAN AND ALPHA FLIGHT

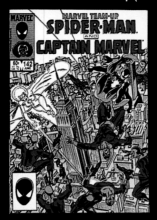

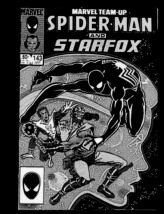

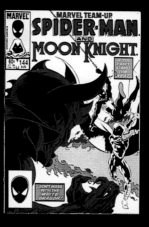

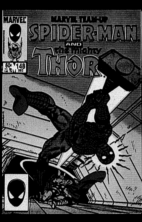

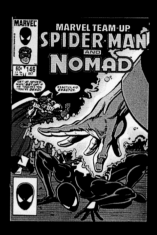

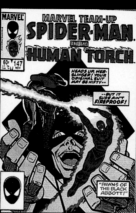

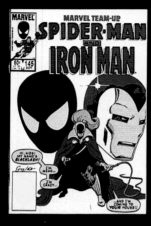

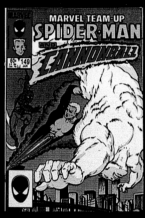

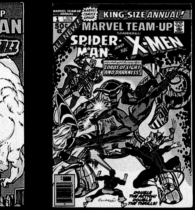

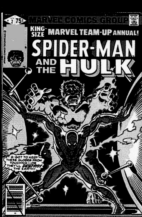

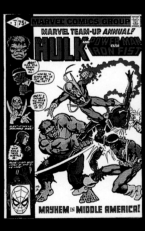

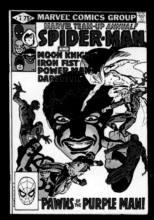

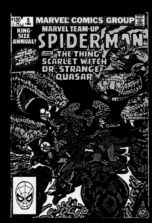

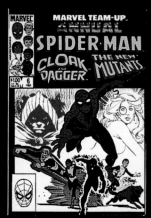

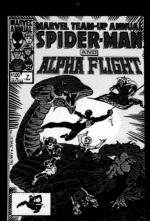

Marvel Team-up (1-150) 1217.6

1217.6-1	Mar. 1972	20	Andru-a; Publ. 11/23/71
1217.6-2	May	7	Andru/Mooney-a
1217.6-3	Jul.	7	Andru/Giacoia-a
1217.6-4	Sept.	12	Kane/Michell-a (X-Men)
1217.6-5	Nov.	3	Kane/Esposito-a
1217.6-6	Jan. 1973	3	" "
1217.6-7	Mar.	3	Andru/Mooney-a
1217.6-8	Apr.	3	Mooney-a
1217.6-9	May	3	Andru/Bolle-a
1217.6-10	**Jun.**	**3**	**Mooney/Giacoia-a**
1217.6-11	Jul.	3	Mooney/Esposito-a
1217.6-12	Aug.	3	Andru/Perlin-a
1217.6-13	Sept.	3	Kane/Giacoia-a
1217.6-14	Oct.	3	Kane/Howard-a
1217.6-15	Nov.	5	Andru/Perlin-a (Ghost Rider)
1217.6-16	Dec.	3	Kane/Mooney-a
1217.6-17	Jan. 1974	3	Kane-a
1217.6-18	Feb.	3	Kane/Giacoia, Esposito-a
1217.6-19	Mar.	3	Kane/Giacoia-a
1217.6-20	**Apr.**	**3**	**Buscema/Giacoia, Esposito-a**
1217.6-21	May	2	Buscema/Giacoia, Hunt-a
1217.6-22	Jun.	2	Buscema/Giacoia-a
1217.6-23	Jul.	2	Kane/Esposito-a
1217.6-24	Aug.	2	Mooney, Trapani-a
1217.6-25	Sept.	2	Mooney, Giacoia-a
1217.6-26	Oct.	2	Mooney, Giacoia, kHunt-a
1217.6-27	Nov.	2	Mooney, Giacoia-a
1217.6-28	Dec.	2	Mooney/Colletta-a
1217.6-29	Jan. 1975	2	" "
1217.6-30	**Feb.**	**2**	**" "**
1217.6-31	Mar.	2	" "
1217.6-32	Apr.	2	Buscema/Colletta-a
1217.6-33	May	2	" "
1217.6-34	Jun.	2	" "
1217.6-35	Jul.	2	Mooney-c, Buscema/Colletta-a
1217.6-36	Aug.	2	Buscema/Colletta-a
1217.6-37	Sept.	2	" "
1217.6-38	Oct.	2	Buscema/Esposito-a
1217.6-35	Nov.	2	" "
1217.6-40	**Dec.**	**2**	**" "**
1217.6-41	Jan. 1976	2	Kane/Adkins-c, Buscema, Esposito-a
1217.6-42	Feb.	2	Buscema, Esposito-a
1217.6-43	Mar.	2	" "
1217.6-44	Apr.	2	Kane/Adkins-c, Buscema, Esposito-a
1217.6-45	May	2	Buscema, Esposito-a
1217.6-46	Jun.	2	Buckler/Esposito-c, Buscema, Esposito-a
1217.6-47	Jul.	2	Wilson/Adkins-a
1217.6-48	Aug.	2	Romita-c, Buscema, Esposito-a
1217.6-49	Sept.	2	Romita/Bradford-c, Buscema, Esposito-a
1217.6-50	**Oct.**	**2**	**Buscema, Esposito-a**
1217.6-51	Nov.	2	" "
1217.6-52	Dec.	2	" "
1217.6-53	Jan. 1977	5	Byrne/Giacoia-a; (New X-Men -app.)
1217.6-54	Feb.	3	Byrne/Esposito-a
1217.6-55	Mar.	3	Cockrum-c, Byrne/Hunt-a
1217.6-56	Apr.	3	Romita/Giacoia-c, Byrne/Hunt-a
1217.6-57	May	3	Cockrum-c, Byrne/Hunt-a
1217.6-58	Jun.	3	Byrne, Marcos-a
1217.6-59	Jul.	3	Byrne/Hunt-a
1217.6-60	**Aug.**	**3**	**" "**
1217.6-61	Sept.	1	" "
1217.6-62	Oct.	1	" "
1217.6-63	Nov.	1	" "
1217.6-64	Dec.	1	" "
1217.6-65	Jan. 1978	1	" "
1217.6-66	Feb.	1	" "
1217.6-67	Mar.	1	" "
1217.6-68	Apr.	1	Byrne/Rubinstein-c, Byrne/Wiacek-a
1217.6-69	May	1	Cockrum-c, Byrne/Villamonte-a
1217.6-70	**Jun.**	**1**	**Byrne/DeZuniga-a**
1217.6-71	Jul.	1	Wenzel/Green-a
1217.6-72	Aug.	1	Byrne/Layton-c, Mooney-a
1217.6-73	Sept.	1	Pollard/McLeod-c, Gammil, Perlin-a
1217.6-74	Oct.	1	Hall/M. Severin-a
1217.6-75	Nov.	1	Byrne/Gordon-a
1217.6-76	Dec.	1	Byrne/Austin-c, Chaykin, Aclin, Ortiz-a
1217.6-77	Jan. 1979	1	Romita, Jr.-c, Chaykin, Aclin, Ortiz-a
1217.6-78	Feb.	1	Milgrom-c, Perlin/Giacoia-a
1217.6-79	Mar.	1	Byrne/Austin-c/a
1217.6-80	**Apr.**	**1**	**Validar/McLeod-c, Vosburg/Day-a**
1217.6-81	May	1	Milgrom/Leialoha-c, Vosburg/Leialoha-a
1217.6-82	Jun.	1	Buckler/McLeod-c, Buscema,Leialoha-a
1217.6-83	Jul.	1	Buckler/Leialoha-c, Buscema, Leialoha-a
1217.6-84	Aug.	1	Leialoha-c, Buscema, Leialoha-a
1217.6-85	Sept.	1	Milgrom-c, Buscema, Leialoha-a
1217.6-86	Oct.	1	McLeod-c/a
1217.6-87	Nov.	1	Colan/Springer-a
1217.6-88	Dec.	1	Buscema, Barreto-a
1217.6-89	Jan. 1980	1	Buckler/Rubinstein-c, Nasser, Buckler/Rubinstein-a
1217.6-90	**Feb.**	**1**	**Milgrom/Abel-c, Vosburg, McLeod-a**
1217.6-91	Mar.	1	Buckler/Milgrom-c, Brokerick/Patterson-a
1217.6-92	Apr.	1	Rubinstein/Milgrom-c, Infantino/Marcos-a
1217.6-93	May	1	Infantino/Mooney-a
1217.6-94	Jun.	1	Milgrom-c, Zeck/Esposito-a
1217.6-95	Jul.	1	Miller/McLeod-c, J. James, Patterson-a
1217.6-96	Aug.	1	Kupperberg/Austin-c, Kupperberg-a
1217.6-97	Sept.	1	Infantino/Gordon-a
1217.6-98	Oct.	1	Milgrom-c, Meugniot/Patterson-a
1217.6-99	Nov.	1	Miller/Simons-c, Bingham/Esposito-a
1217.6-100	**Dec.**	**4**	**Miller/Janson-c, Miller, Wiacek-a**
1217.6-101	Jan. 1981	1	Binham/Esposito-a
1217.6-102	Feb.	1	Miller/Milgrom-c, Springer, Esposito-a
1217.6-103	Mar.	1	Bingham/Esposito-a
1217.6-104	Apr.	1	Milgrom-c, Bingham/Esposito-a
1217.6-105	May	1	Infantino/Esposito-a
1217.6-106	Jun.	1	Trimpe/Esposito-a
1217.6-107	Jul.	1	" "
1217.6-108	Aug.	1	" "
1217.6-109	Sept.	1	" "
1217.6-110	**Oct.**	**1**	**Layton-c, Esposito-a**
1217.6-111	Nov.	1	Trimpe/Esposito-a
1217.6-112	Dec.	1	Severin/Austin-c, Trimpe-a
1217.6-113	Jan. 1982	1	Romita, Jr./Giacoia-c, Trimpe/Esposito-a
1217.6-114	Feb.	1	Zeck/McLeod-c, Trimpe/Esposito-a
1217.6-115	Mar.	1	Layton-c, Trimpe/Esposito-a
1217.6-116	Apr.	1	" " "
1217.6-117	May	5	Layton/Rubinstein-c (Wolverine)
1217.6-118 to 150	Feb. 1985, (#150)	1	(#144, Moon Knight)
1217.6-A1	1976	5	(New X-Men app.)
1217.6-A2	Dec. 1979	1	Milgrom-c, Buscema/Abel-a
1217.6-A3	Nov. 1980	1	Milgrom-c, Trimpe/Esposito-a
1217.6-A4	Oct. 1981	1	" " "
1217.6-A5	1982	1	Milgrom-c, Mooney-a
1217.6-A6	Oct. 1983	1	Frenz/Dzuban-a
1217.6-A7	Oct. 1984	1	Neary-c/a, De la Rosa-a

1217.65 Marvel Treasury Edition (1-16)

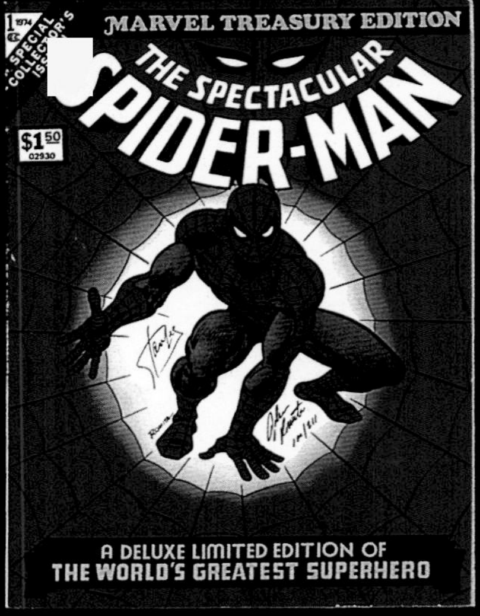

MARVEL TREASURY EDITION
THE SPECTACULAR SPIDER-MAN
$1.50
A DELUXE LIMITED EDITION OF THE WORLD'S GREATEST SUPERHERO

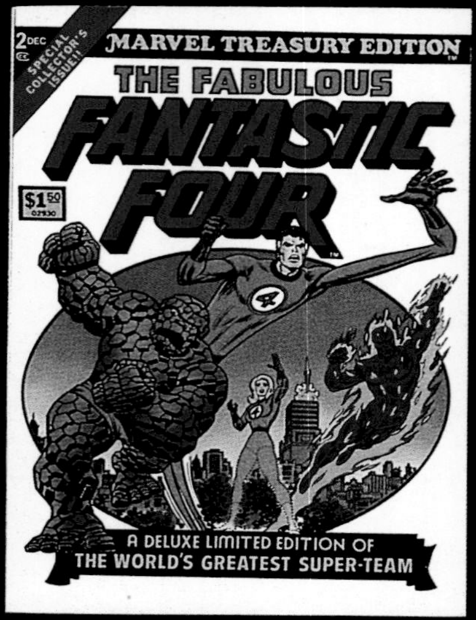

MARVEL TREASURY EDITION
THE FABULOUS FANTASTIC FOUR
$1.50
A DELUXE LIMITED EDITION OF THE WORLD'S GREATEST SUPER-TEAM

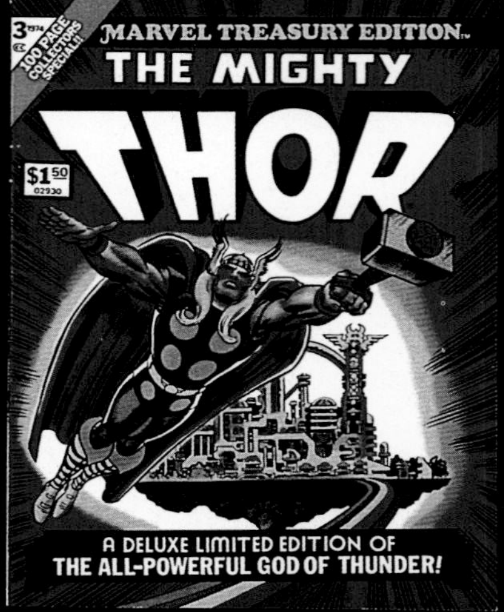

MARVEL TREASURY EDITION
THE MIGHTY THOR
$1.50
A DELUXE LIMITED EDITION OF THE ALL-POWERFUL GOD OF THUNDER!

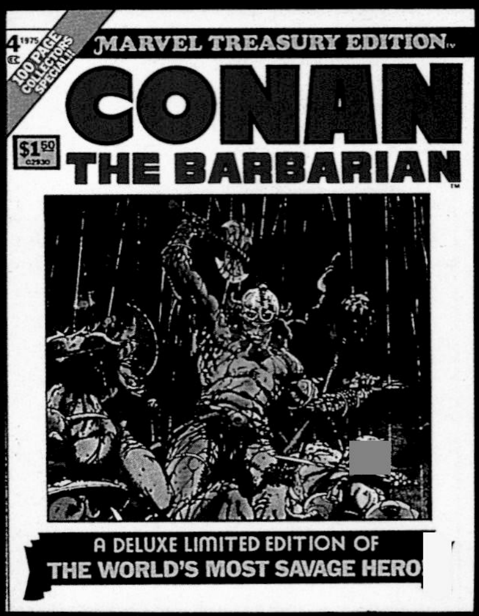

MARVEL TREASURY EDITION
CONAN THE BARBARIAN
$1.50
A DELUXE LIMITED EDITION OF THE WORLD'S MOST SAVAGE HERO

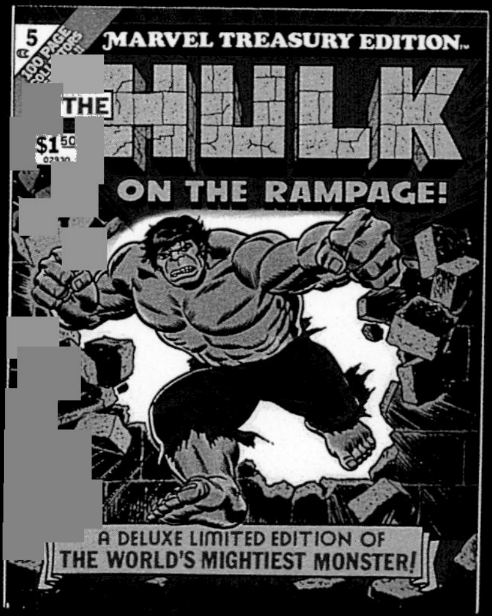

MARVEL TREASURY EDITION
THE HULK ON THE RAMPAGE!
A DELUXE LIMITED EDITION OF THE WORLD'S MIGHTIEST MONSTER!

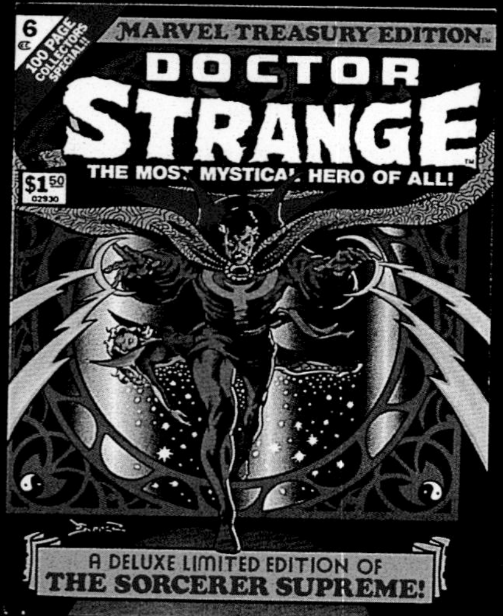

MARVEL TREASURY EDITION
DOCTOR STRANGE
THE MOST MYSTICAL HERO OF ALL!
$1.50
A DELUXE LIMITED EDITION OF THE SORCERER SUPREME!

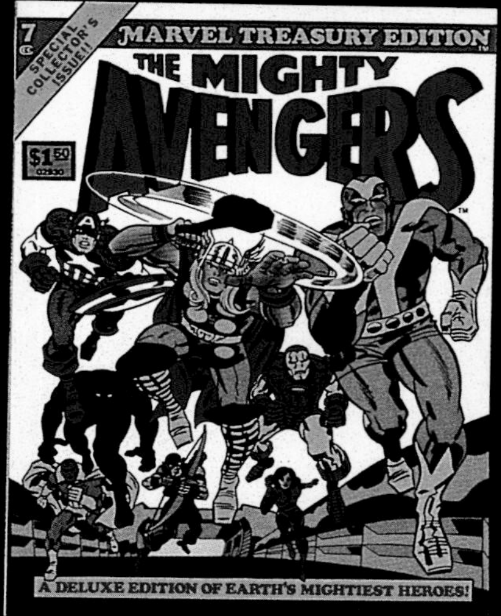

MARVEL TREASURY EDITION
THE MIGHTY AVENGERS
$1.50
A DELUXE EDITION OF EARTH'S MIGHTIEST HEROES!

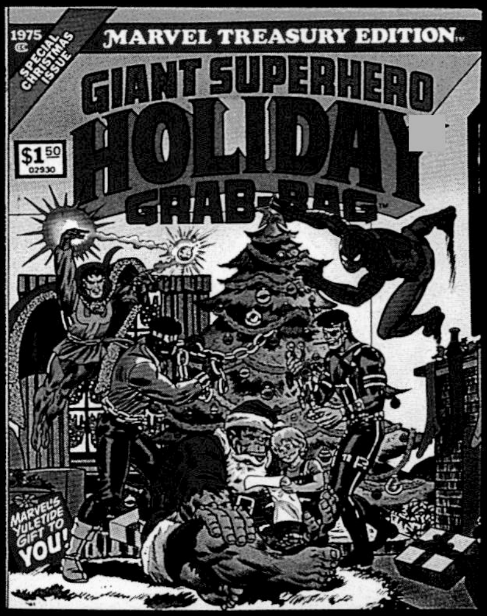

MARVEL TREASURY EDITION
GIANT SUPERHERO HOLIDAY GRAB-BAG
$1.50

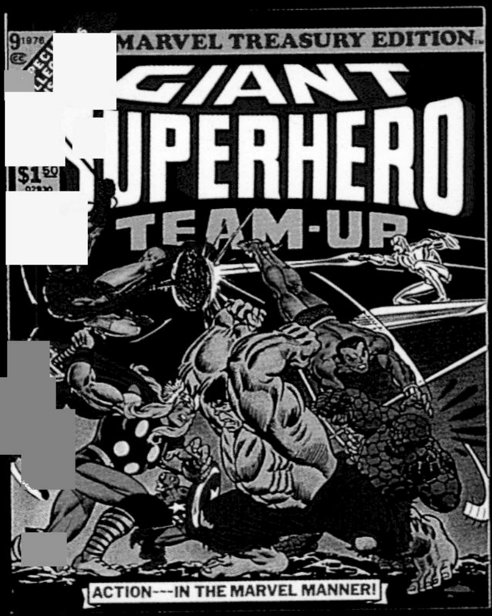

MARVEL TREASURY EDITION
GIANT SUPERHERO TEAM-UP
ACTION---IN THE MARVEL MANNER!

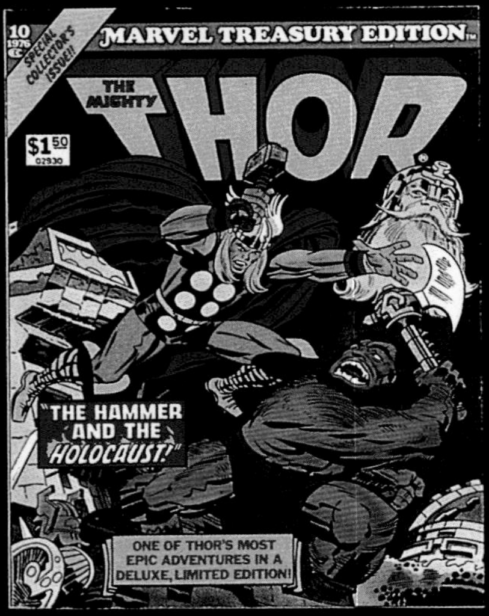

MARVEL TREASURY EDITION
THE MIGHTY THOR
$1.50
"THE HAMMER AND THE HOLOCAUST!"
ONE OF THOR'S MOST EPIC ADVENTURES IN A DELUXE, LIMITED EDITION!

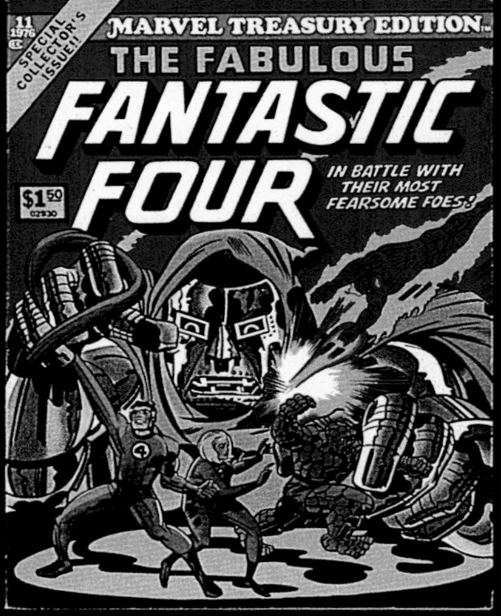

MARVEL TREASURY EDITION
THE FABULOUS FANTASTIC FOUR
IN BATTLE WITH THEIR MOST FEARSOME FOES!
$1.50

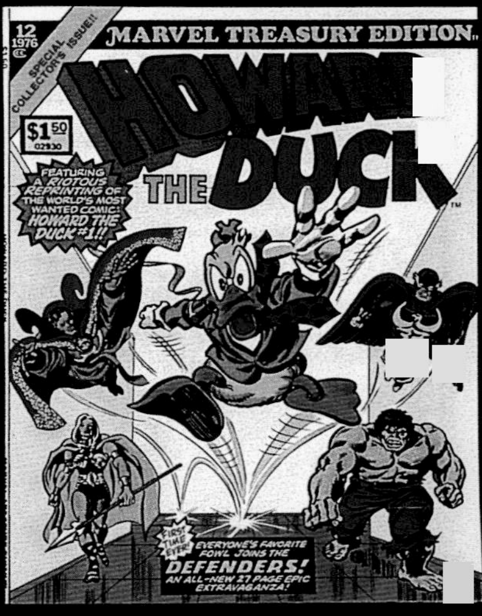

MARVEL TREASURY EDITION
HOWARD THE DUCK
$1.50
DEFENDERS!

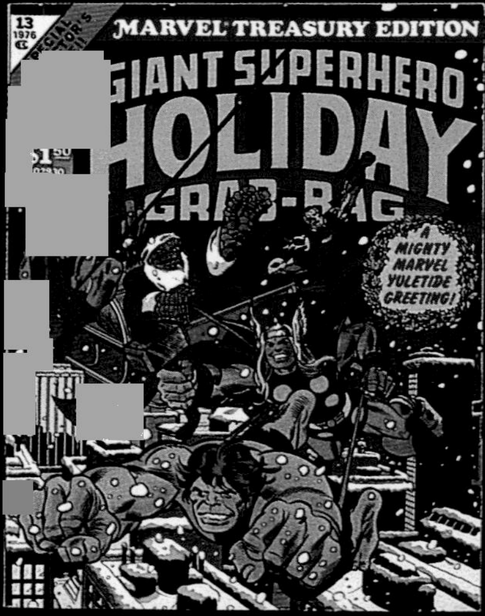

MARVEL TREASURY EDITION
GIANT SUPERHERO HOLIDAY GRAB-BAG
A MIGHTY MARVEL YULETIDE GREETING!

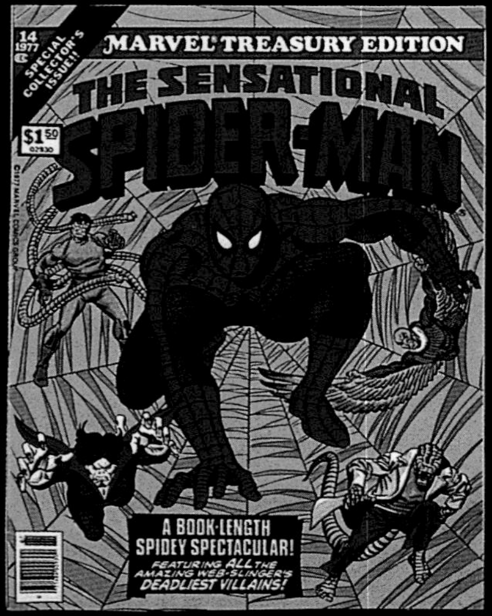

MARVEL TREASURY EDITION
THE SENSATIONAL SPIDER-MAN
$1.50
A BOOK-LENGTH SPIDEY SPECTACULAR!
FEATURING ALL THE AMAZING WEB-SLINGER'S DEADLIEST VILLAINS!

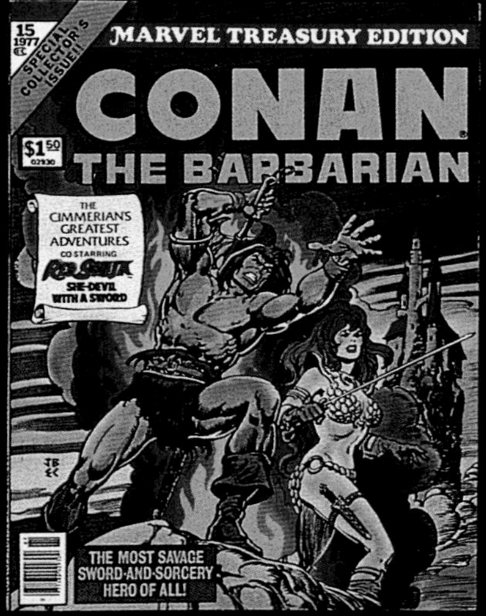

MARVEL TREASURY EDITION
CONAN THE BARBARIAN
$1.50
THE CIMMERIAN'S GREATEST ADVENTURES
RED SONJA SHE-DEVIL WITH A SWORD
THE MOST SAVAGE SWORD-AND-SORCERY HERO OF ALL!

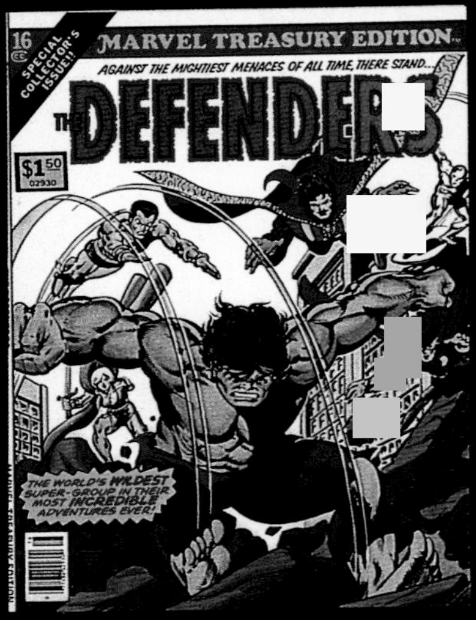

MARVEL TREASURY EDITION
AGAINST THE MIGHTIEST MENACES OF ALL TIME, THERE STAND...
THE DEFENDERS
$1.50

1217.65 Marvel Treasury Edition (17-28)

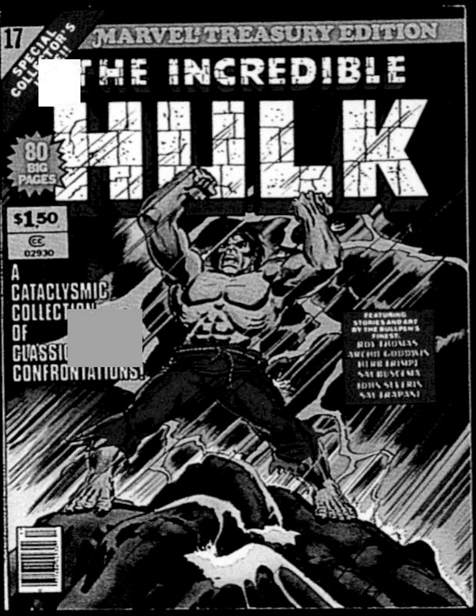
MARVEL TREASURY EDITION
THE INCREDIBLE
HULK
$1.50
A CATACLYSMIC COLLECTION OF CLASSIC CONFRONTATIONS!

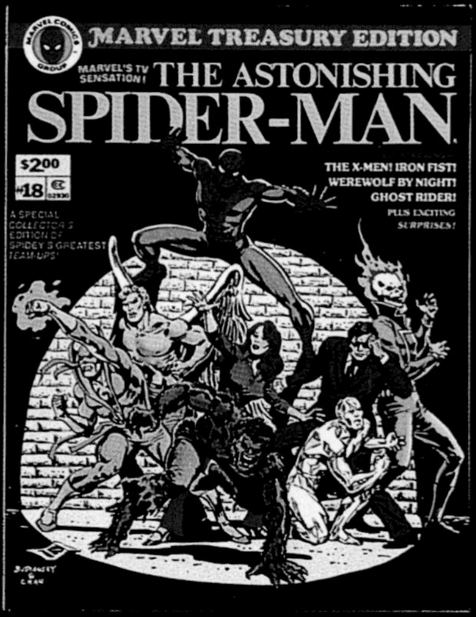
MARVEL TREASURY EDITION
MARVEL'S TV SENSATION! THE ASTONISHING
SPIDER-MAN
$2.00
THE X-MEN! IRON FIST! WEREWOLF BY NIGHT! GHOST RIDER!
PLUS EXCITING SURPRISES!

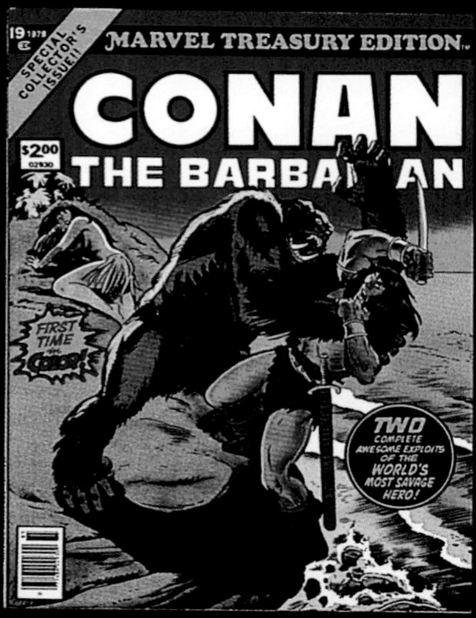
SPECIAL COLLECTOR'S ISSUE!
MARVEL TREASURY EDITION
CONAN
$2.00
FIRST TIME IN COLOR!
TWO COMPLETE AWESOME EXPLOITS OF THE WORLD'S MOST SAVAGE HERO!

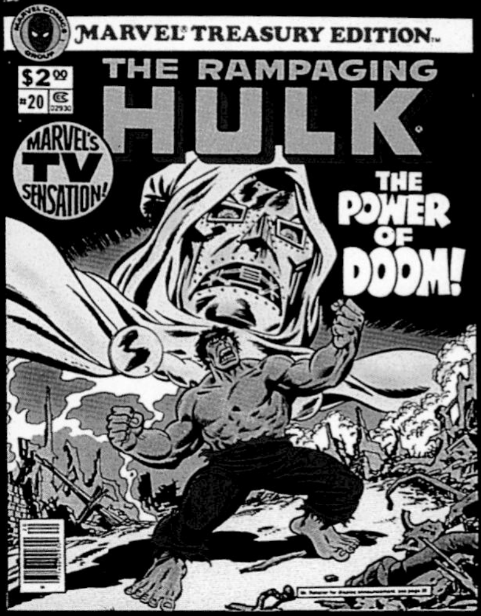
MARVEL TREASURY EDITION
$2.00
THE RAMPAGING
HULK
MARVEL'S TV SENSATION!
THE POWER OF DOOM!

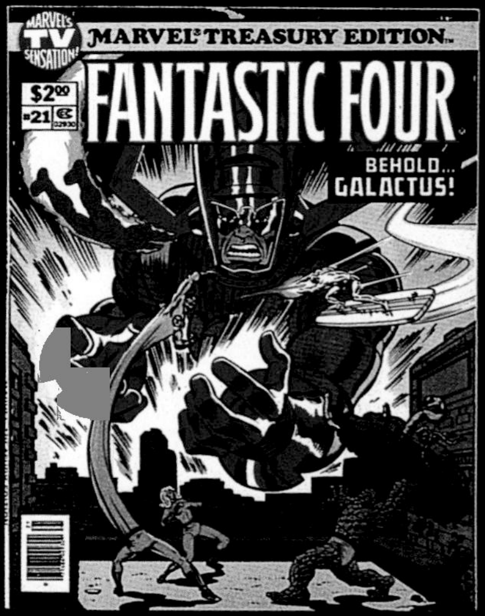
MARVEL'S TV SENSATION!
MARVEL TREASURY EDITION
$2.00
FANTASTIC FOUR
BEHOLD... GALACTUS!

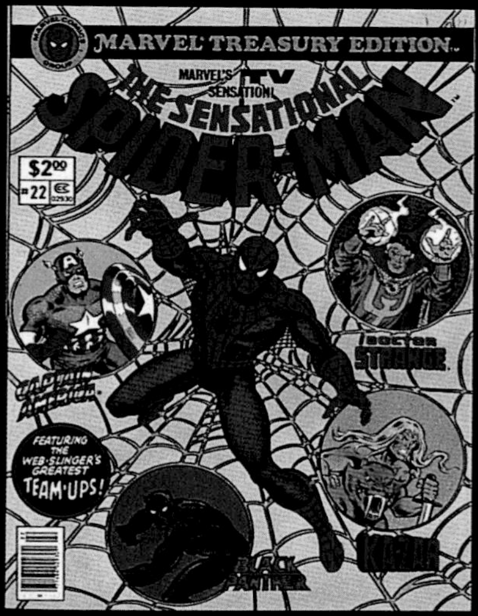
MARVEL TREASURY EDITION
MARVEL'S TV SENSATION!
THE SENSATIONAL
SPIDER-MAN
$2.00
FEATURING THE WEB-SLINGER'S GREATEST TEAM-UPS!

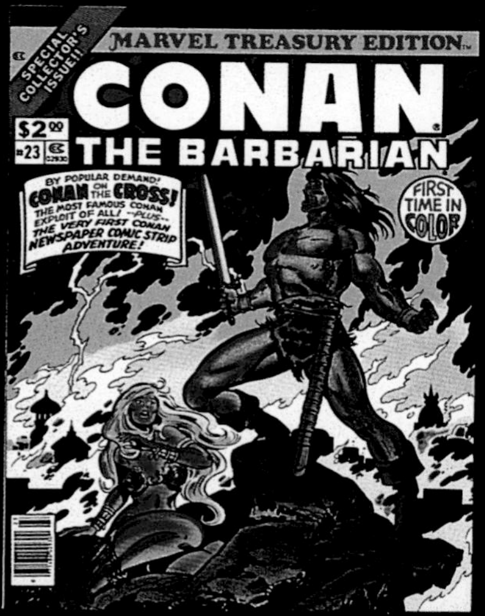
SPECIAL COLLECTOR'S ISSUE!
MARVEL TREASURY EDITION
CONAN
$2.00
THE BARBARIAN
FIRST TIME IN COLOR

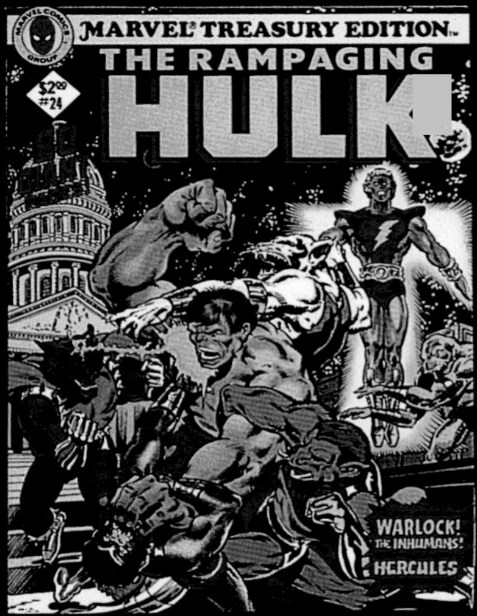
MARVEL TREASURY EDITION
THE RAMPAGING
$2.00
WARLOCK!
THE INHUMANS!
HERCULES

1217.7 Marvel Treasury of Oz (1)

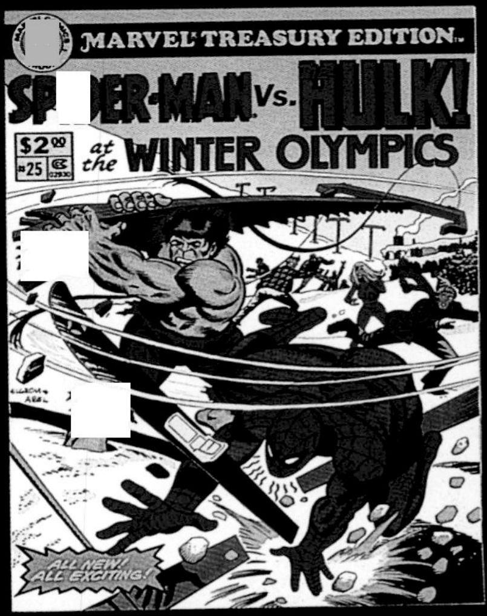
MARVEL TREASURY EDITION
VS.
$2.00
at the WINTER OLYMPICS
ALL NEW! ALL EXCITING!

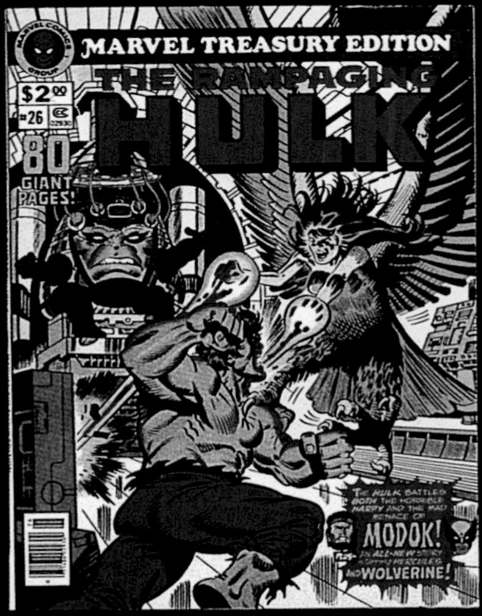
MARVEL TREASURY EDITION
$2.00
THE RAMPAGING
HULK
MODOK!
WOLVERINE!

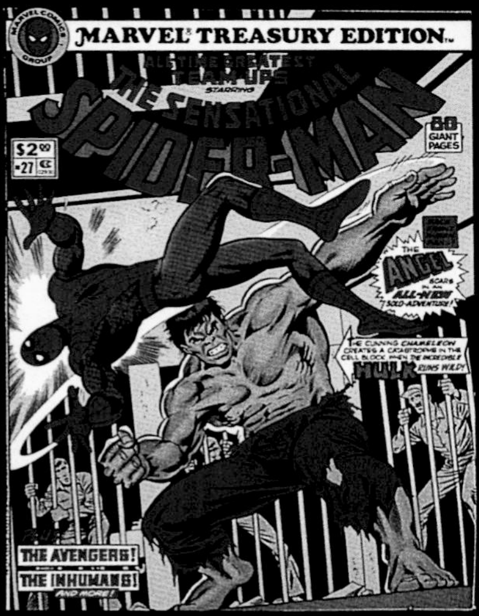
MARVEL TREASURY EDITION
THE SENSATIONAL
SPIDER-MAN
$2.00
THE AVENGERS!
THE INHUMANS!

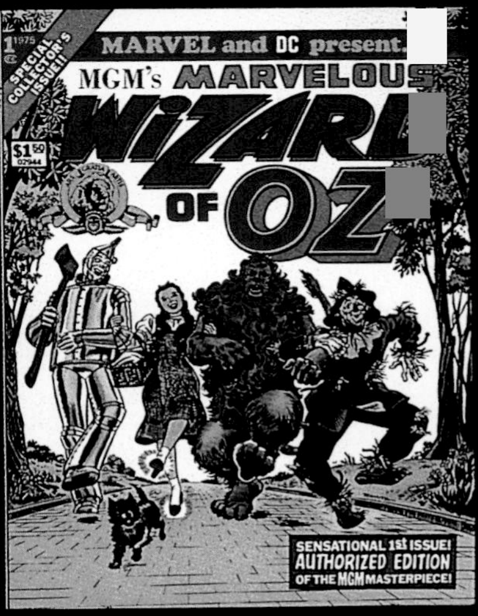
SPECIAL COLLECTOR'S ISSUE!
MARVEL and DC present
MGM's
OF
$1.50
SENSATIONAL 1st ISSUE!
AUTHORIZED EDITION
OF THE MGM MASTERPIECE!

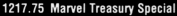

1217.75 Marvel Treasury Special

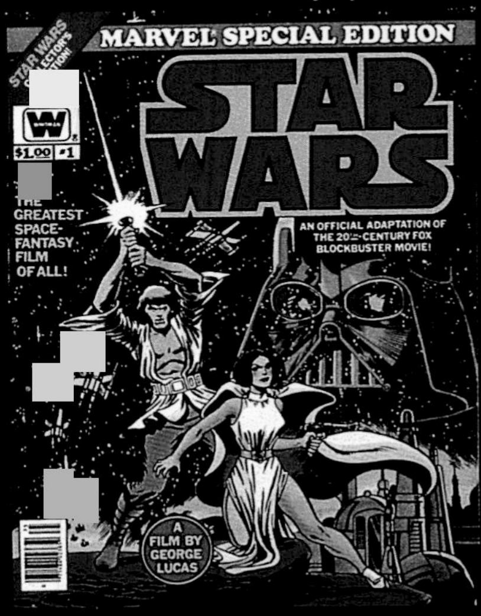
MARVEL SPECIAL EDITION
STAR
WARS
#1
THE GREATEST SPACE-FANTASY FILM OF ALL!
AN OFFICIAL ADAPTATION OF THE 20th CENTURY FOX BLOCKBUSTER MOVIE!
A FILM BY GEORGE LUCAS

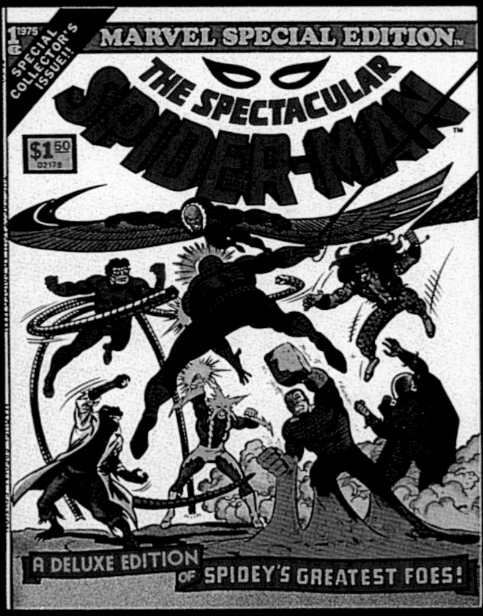
SPECIAL COLLECTOR'S ISSUE!
MARVEL SPECIAL EDITION
THE SPECTACULAR
SPIDER-MAN
$1.50
A DELUXE EDITION OF SPIDEY'S GREATEST FOES!

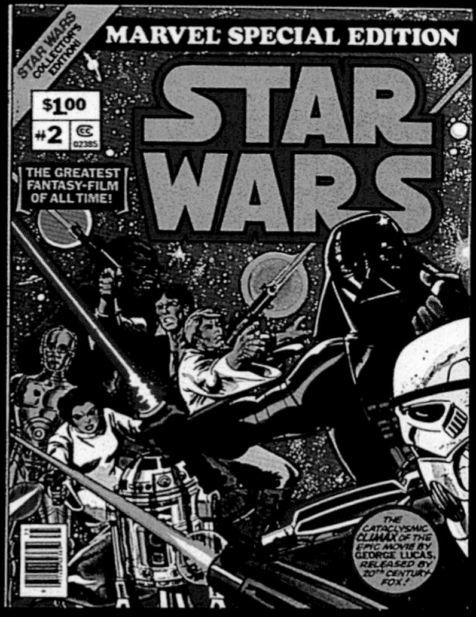
MARVEL SPECIAL EDITION
$1.00
#2
STAR
WARS
THE GREATEST FANTASY-FILM OF ALL TIME!

Marvel Treasury Edition (1-28) 1217.65

Ref. No.	Date	RVI	Artist/Info.
1217.65-1	Sept. 1974	3	(Spectacular Spider-Man)
1217.65-2	Dec.	2	(F.F., Silver Surfer)
1217.65-3	1974	1	(Thor)
1217.65-4	1975	1	Smith-c/a (Conan)
1217.65-5	1975	1	(Hulk)
1217.65-6	1975	1	(Dr. Strange)
1217.65-7	1975	1	(Avengers)
1217.65-8	1975	1	(Christmas stories)
1217.65-9	1976	1	(Superhero Team-up)
1217.65-10	**1976**	**1**	**(Thor)**
1217.65-11	1976	1	(F.F.)
1217.65-12	1976	1	(Howard the Duck)
1217.65-13	1976	1	(Holiday Grab-Bag)
1217.65-14	1977	1	(Spider-Man)
1217.65-15	1977	2	Smith/Adams-a (Conan)
1217.65-16	1977	1	(Defenders)
1217.65-17	1977	1	(Hulk)
1217.65-18	1977	1	(Ghost Rider, X-Men)
1217.65-19	1978	1	(Conan)
1217.65-20 to 28	1981, (#28)	1	(#26, Wolverine -app)

Marvel Treasury of Oz (1) 1217.7

1217.7-1	1975	1	Buscema-a

Marvel Treasury Special (1) 1217.75

1217.75-1	1974	1	
1217.75-1a	Jun. 1976	1	Kirby/Smith-a

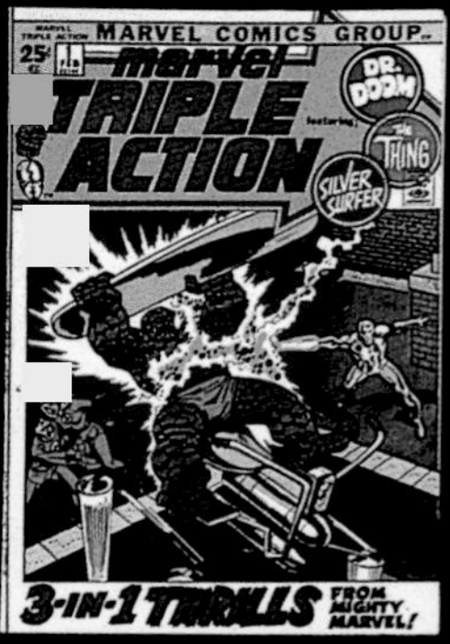
MARVEL COMICS GROUP
marvel TRIPLE ACTION
DR. DOOM
THE THING
SILVER SURFER
3-IN-1 THRILLS FROM MIGHTY MARVEL!
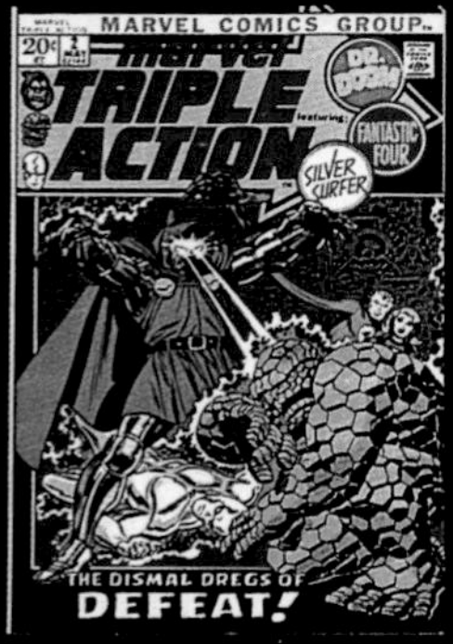
MARVEL COMICS GROUP
marvel TRIPLE ACTION
DR. DOOM
FANTASTIC FOUR
SILVER SURFER
THE DISMAL DREGS OF DEFEAT!
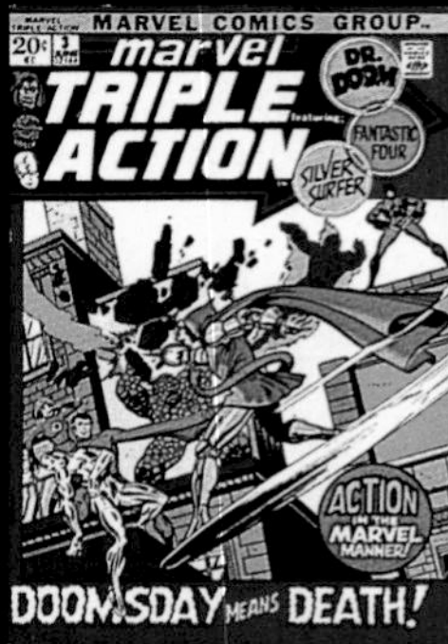
MARVEL COMICS GROUP
marvel TRIPLE ACTION
DR. DOOM
SILVER SURFER
DOOMSDAY MEANS DEATH!
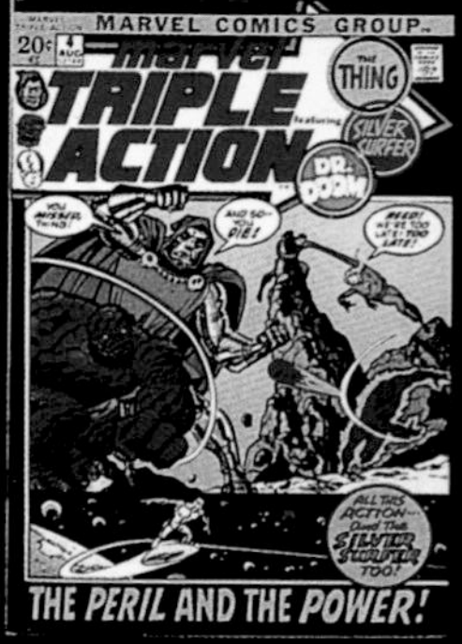
MARVEL COMICS GROUP
marvel TRIPLE ACTION
THE THING
SILVER SURFER
DR. DOOM
THE PERIL AND THE POWER!
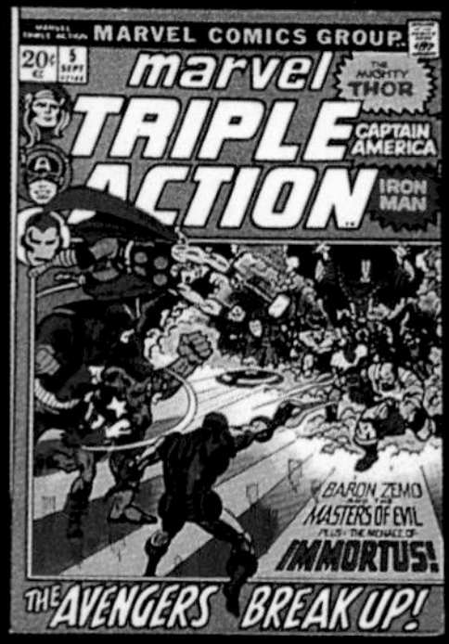
MARVEL COMICS GROUP
marvel TRIPLE ACTION
THOR
CAPTAIN AMERICA
IRON MAN
IMMORTUS!
THE AVENGERS BREAK UP!
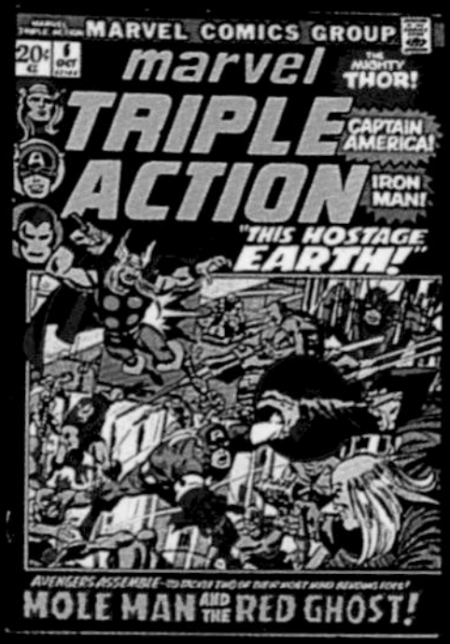
MARVEL COMICS GROUP
marvel TRIPLE ACTION
THOR!
CAPTAIN AMERICA!
IRON MAN!
"THIS HOSTAGE EARTH!"
MOLE MAN AND THE RED GHOST!
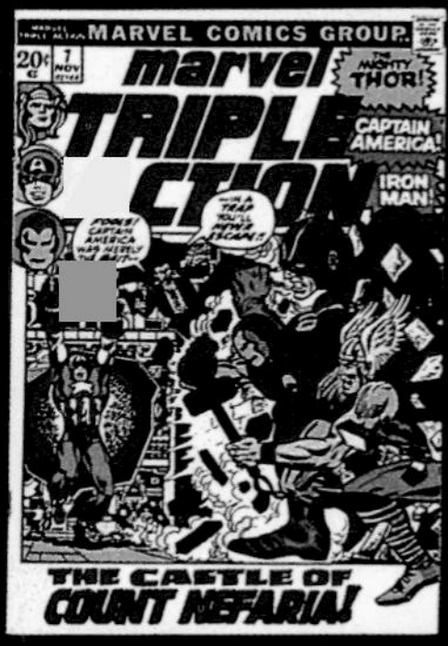
MARVEL COMICS GROUP
marvel TRIPLE ACTION
THOR!
CAPTAIN AMERICA
IRON MAN!
THE CASTLE OF COUNT NEFARIA!
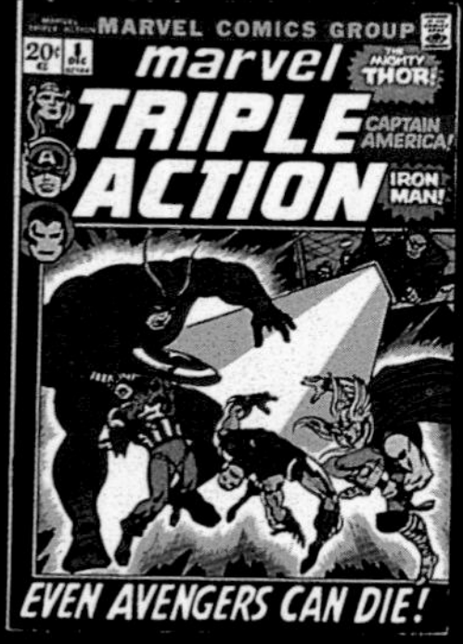
MARVEL COMICS GROUP
marvel TRIPLE ACTION
THOR!
CAPTAIN AMERICA!
IRON MAN!
EVEN AVENGERS CAN DIE!
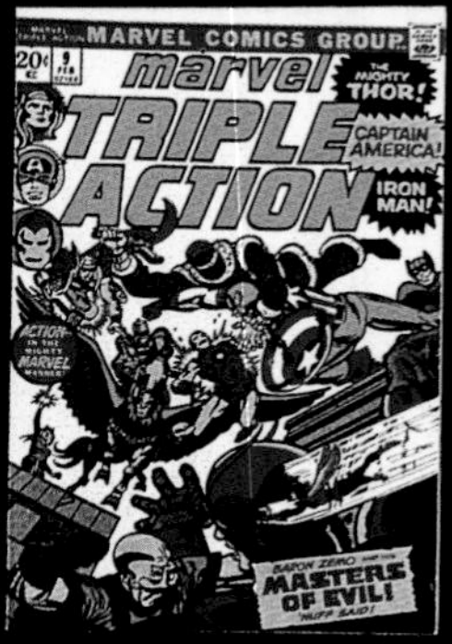
MARVEL COMICS GROUP
marvel TRIPLE ACTION
THOR!
CAPTAIN AMERICA!
IRON MAN!
MASTERS OF EVIL!
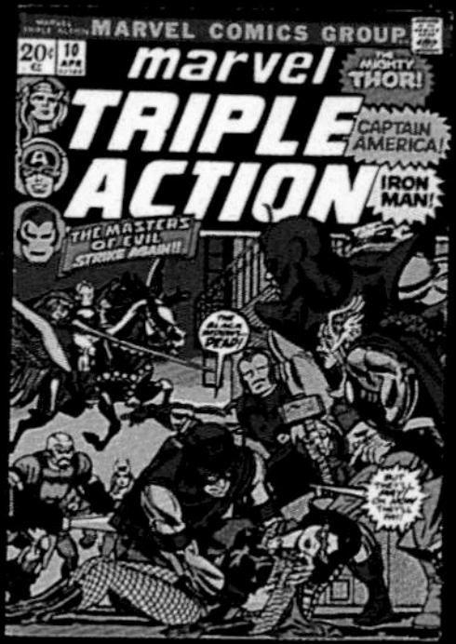
MARVEL COMICS GROUP
marvel TRIPLE ACTION
THOR!
CAPTAIN AMERICA!
IRON MAN!
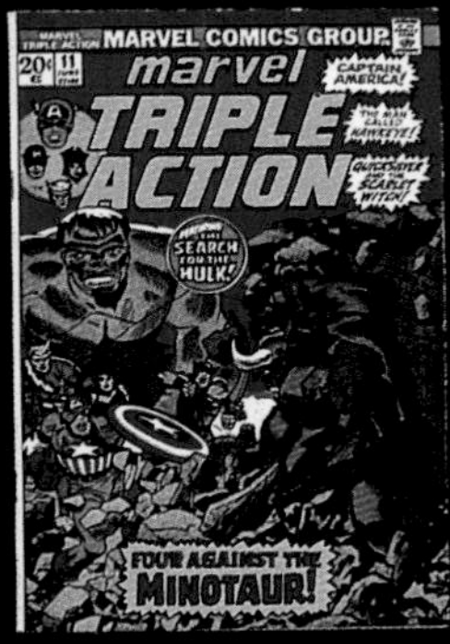
MARVEL COMICS GROUP
marvel TRIPLE ACTION
CAPTAIN AMERICA
FOUR AGAINST THE MINOTAUR!
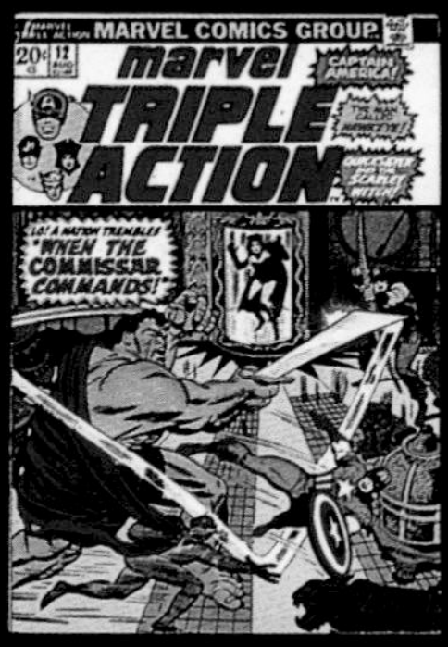
MARVEL COMICS GROUP
marvel TRIPLE ACTION
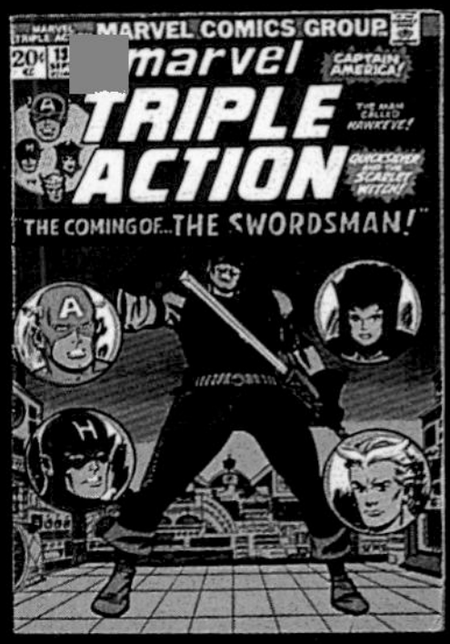
MARVEL COMICS GROUP
marvel TRIPLE ACTION
CAPTAIN AMERICA!
THE COMING OF...THE SWORDSMAN!
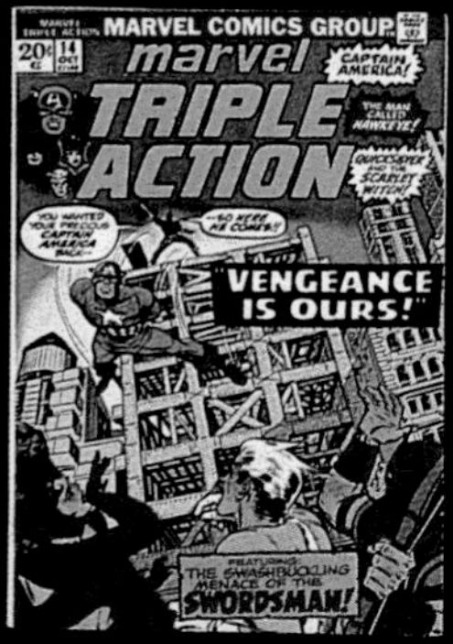
MARVEL COMICS GROUP
marvel TRIPLE ACTION
CAPTAIN AMERICA!
VENGEANCE IS OURS!
SWORDSMAN!
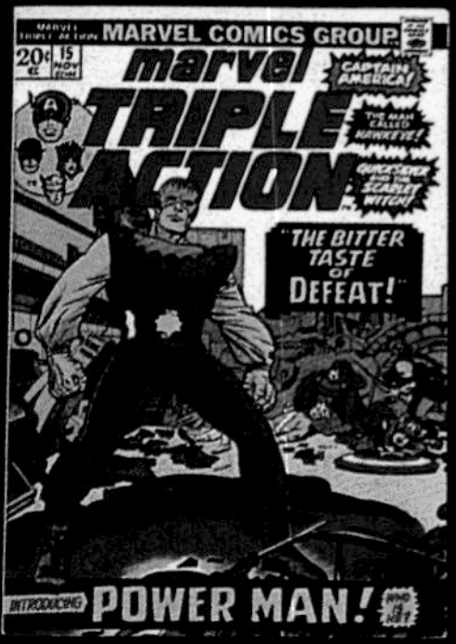
MARVEL COMICS GROUP
marvel TRIPLE ACTION
CAPTAIN AMERICA!
THE BITTER TASTE OF DEFEAT!
POWER MAN!
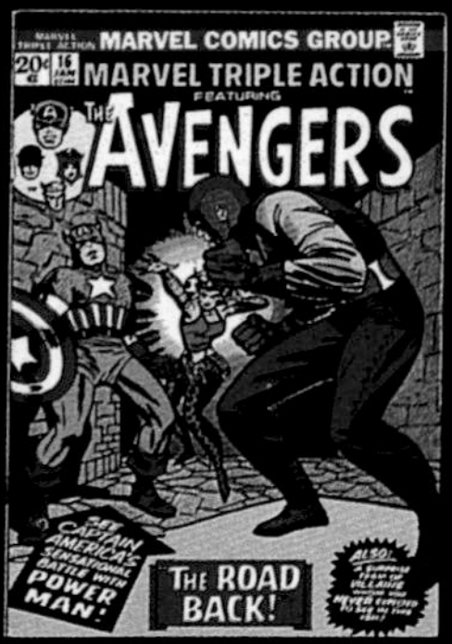
MARVEL COMICS GROUP
MARVEL TRIPLE ACTION
FEATURING
THE AVENGERS
THE ROAD BACK!
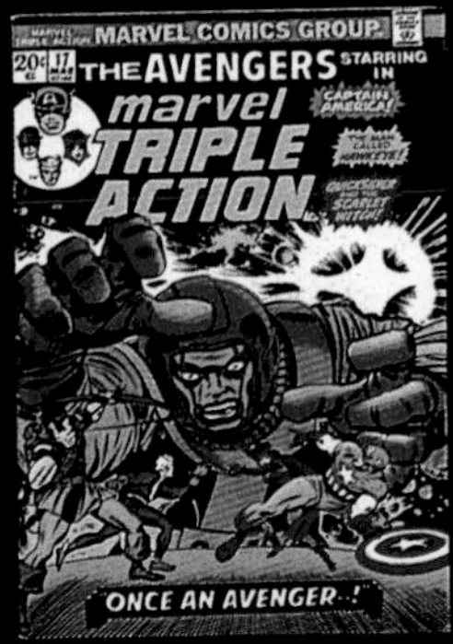
MARVEL COMICS GROUP
THE AVENGERS STARRING IN
marvel TRIPLE ACTION
CAPTAIN AMERICA!
ONCE AN AVENGER
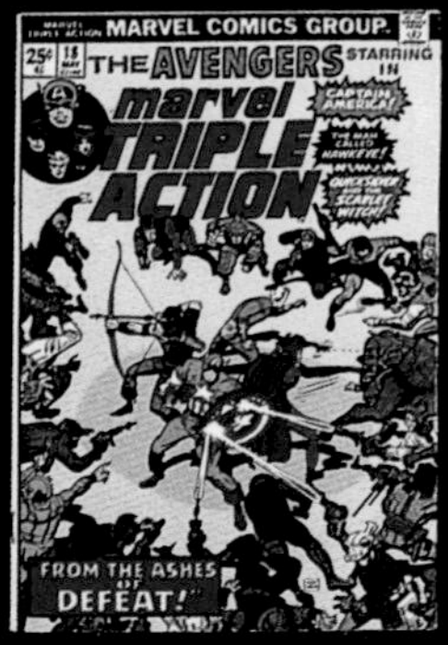
MARVEL COMICS GROUP
THE AVENGERS STARRING IN
marvel TRIPLE ACTION
FROM THE ASHES OF DEFEAT!
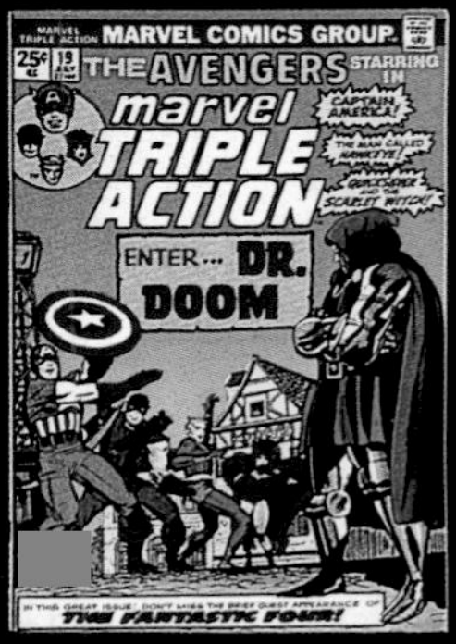
MARVEL COMICS GROUP
THE AVENGERS STARRING IN
marvel TRIPLE ACTION
CAPTAIN AMERICA!
SCARLET WITCH!
ENTER... DR. DOOM
THE FANTASTIC FOUR!
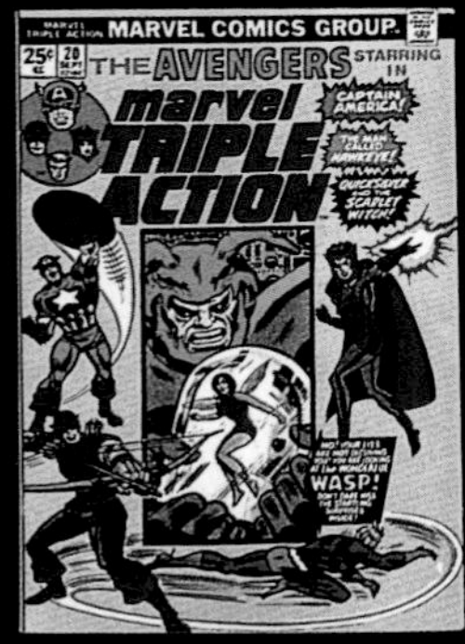
MARVEL COMICS GROUP
THE AVENGERS STARRING IN
marvel TRIPLE ACTION
CAPTAIN AMERICA!
WASP!
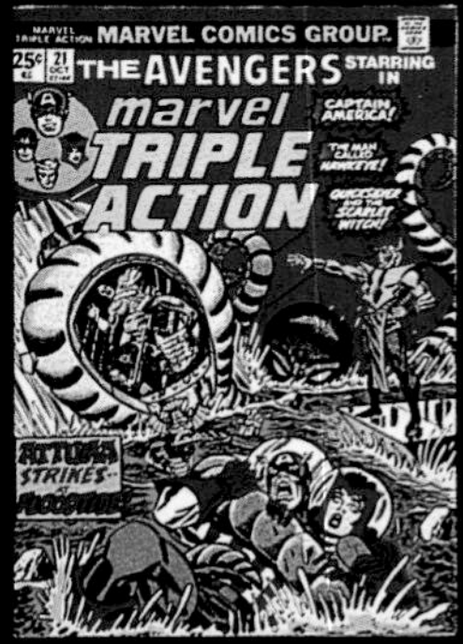
MARVEL COMICS GROUP
THE AVENGERS STARRING IN
marvel TRIPLE ACTION
CAPTAIN AMERICA!
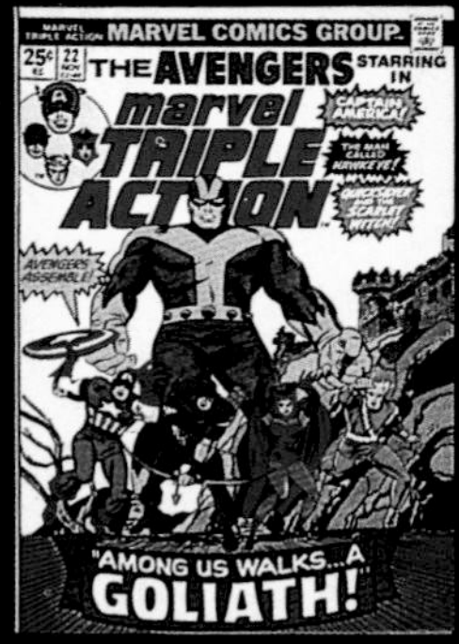
MARVEL COMICS GROUP
THE AVENGERS STARRING IN
marvel TRIPLE ACTION
CAPTAIN AMERICA!
"AMONG US WALKS...A GOLIATH!"
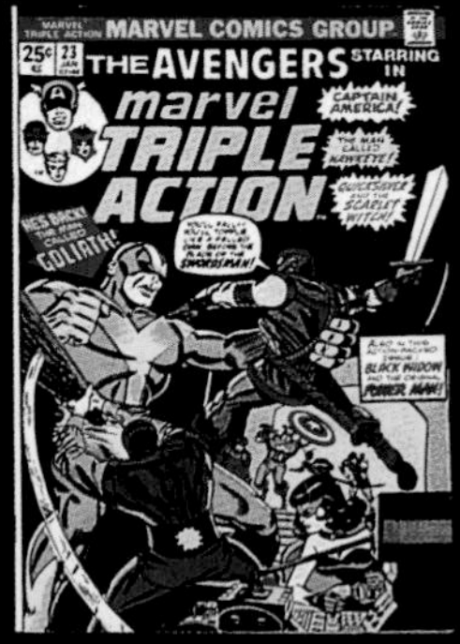
MARVEL COMICS GROUP
THE AVENGERS STARRING IN
marvel TRIPLE ACTION
CAPTAIN AMERICA!
POWER MAN!
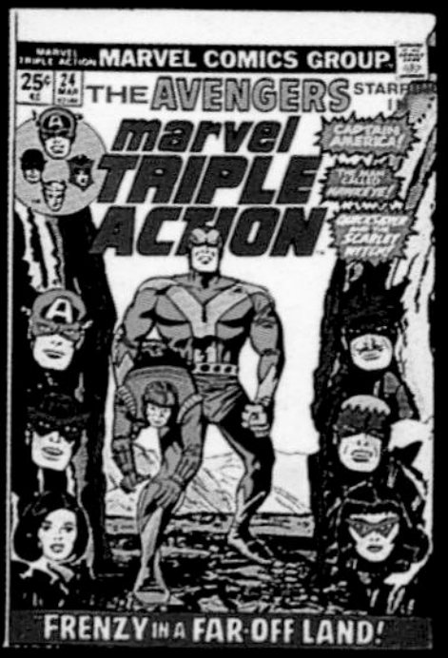
MARVEL COMICS GROUP
THE AVENGERS
marvel TRIPLE ACTION
FRENZY IN A FAR-OFF LAND!
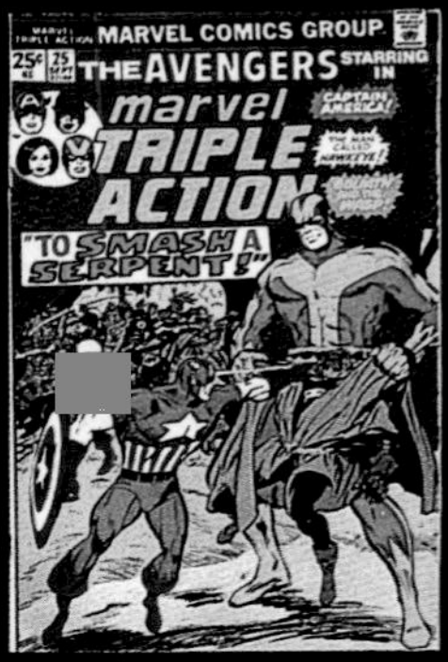
MARVEL COMICS GROUP
THE AVENGERS STARRING IN
marvel TRIPLE ACTION
CAPTAIN AMERICA!
"TO SMASH A SERPENT!"
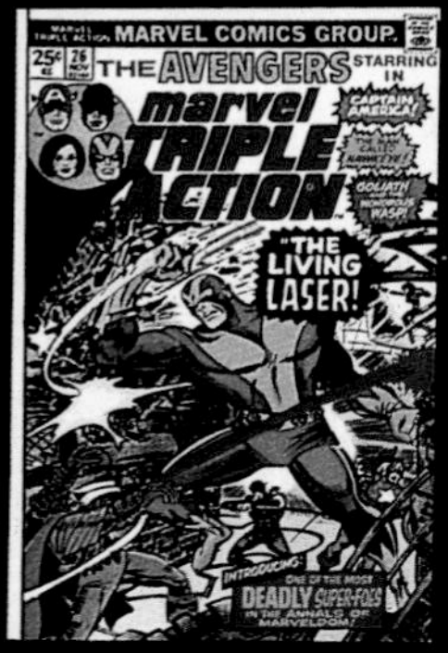
MARVEL COMICS GROUP
THE AVENGERS STARRING IN
marvel TRIPLE ACTION
THE LIVING LASER!
DEADLY
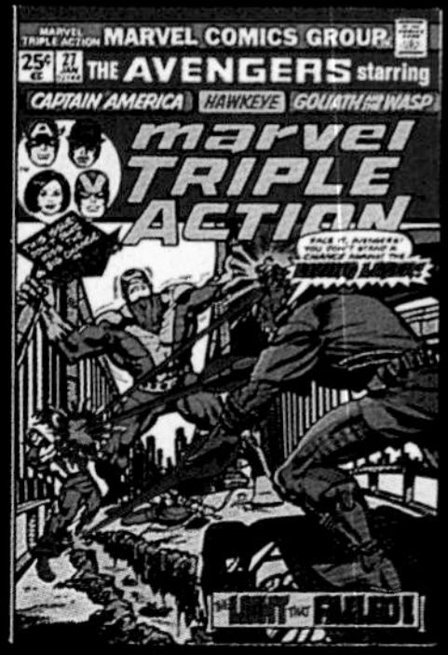
MARVEL COMICS GROUP
THE AVENGERS starring
CAPTAIN AMERICA HAWKEYE GOLIATH AND THE WASP
marvel TRIPLE ACTION
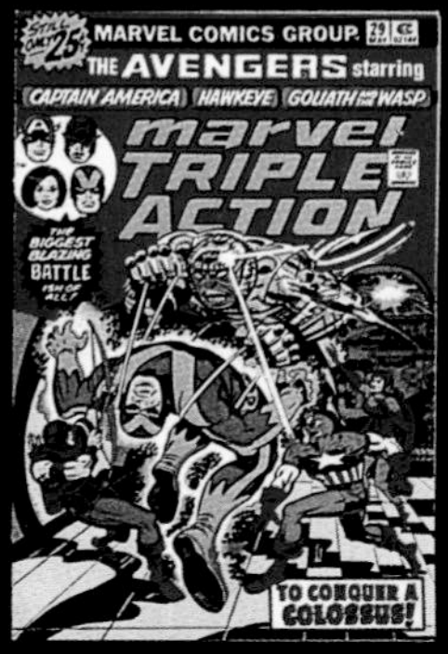
MARVEL COMICS GROUP
THE AVENGERS starring
CAPTAIN AMERICA HAWKEYE GOLIATH AND THE WASP
marvel TRIPLE ACTION
BATTLE
TO CONQUER A COLOSSUS!
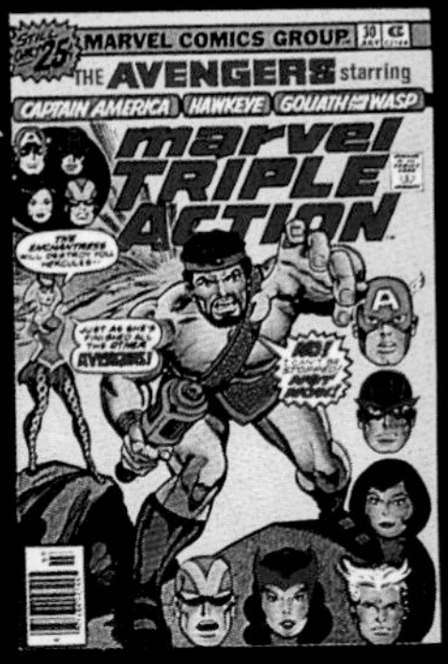
MARVEL COMICS GROUP
THE AVENGERS starring
CAPTAIN AMERICA HAWKEYE GOLIATH AND THE WASP
marvel TRIPLE ACTION
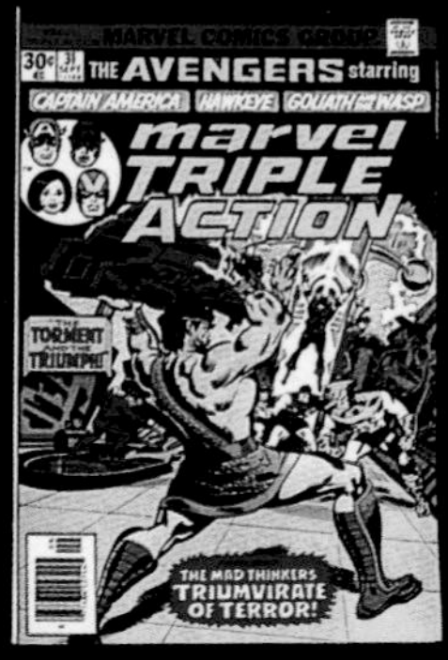
MARVEL COMICS GROUP
THE AVENGERS starring
CAPTAIN AMERICA HAWKEYE GOLIATH AND THE WASP
marvel TRIPLE ACTION
TORMENT TRIUMPH
THE MAD THINKER'S TRIUMVIRATE OF TERROR!
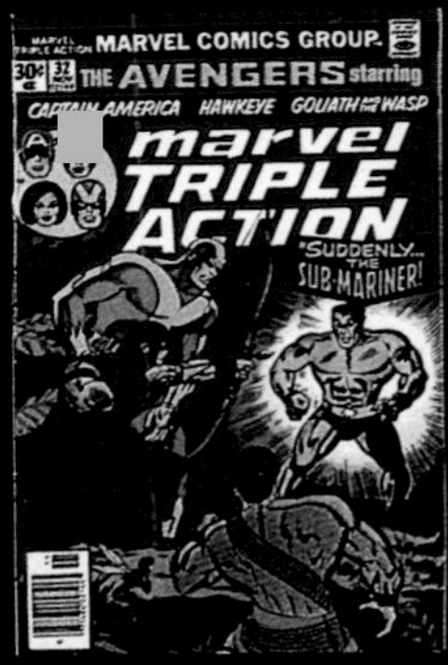
MARVEL COMICS GROUP
THE AVENGERS starring
CAPTAIN AMERICA HAWKEYE GOLIATH AND THE WASP
marvel TRIPLE ACTION
"SUDDENLY... THE SUB-MARINER!"
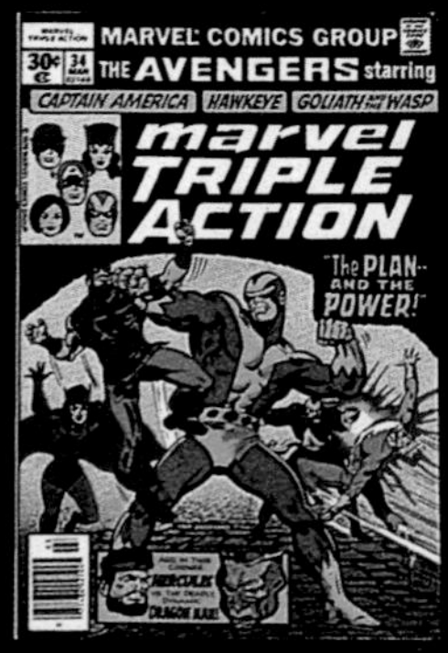
MARVEL COMICS GROUP
THE AVENGERS starring
CAPTAIN AMERICA HAWKEYE GOLIATH AND THE WASP
marvel TRIPLE ACTION
"The PLAN- AND THE POWER!"
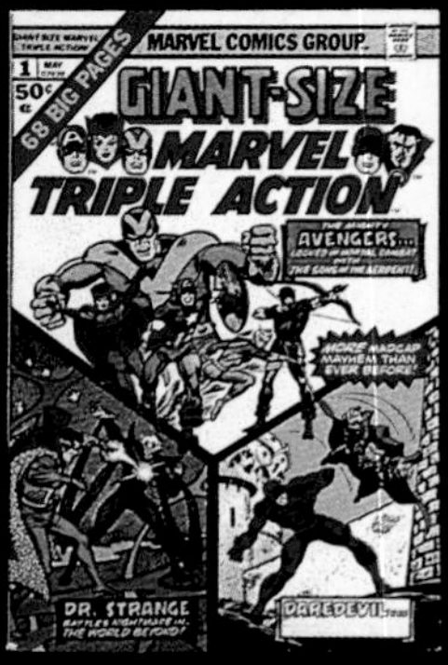
MARVEL COMICS GROUP
68 BIG PAGES
GIANT-SIZE MARVEL TRIPLE ACTION
AVENGERS
DR. STRANGE
DAREDEVIL
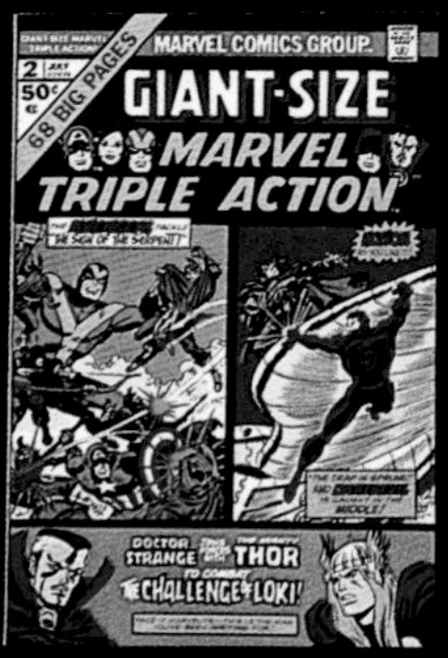
MARVEL COMICS GROUP
68 BIG PAGES
GIANT-SIZE MARVEL TRIPLE ACTION
DOCTOR STRANGE
THOR
CHALLENGE LOKI!

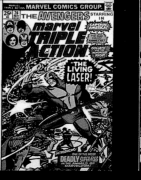

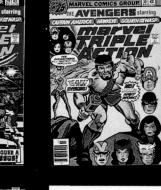

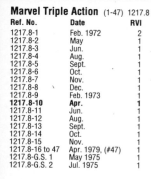

Marvel Triple Action (1-47) 1217.8

Ref. No.	Date	RVI	Artist/Info.	
1217.8-1	Feb. 1972	2	Kirby-a	Reprints
1217.8-2	May	1	Ditko/Kirby-a	"
1217.8-3	Jun.	1	Kirby-a	"
1217.8-4	Aug.	1	"	"
1217.8-5	Sept.	1		"
1217.8-6	Oct.	1		"
1217.8-7	Nov.	1	Starlin-c	"
1217.8-8	Dec.	1		"
1217.8-9	Feb. 1973	1		"
1217.8-10	**Apr.**	**1**		**"**
1217.8-11	Jun.	1		"
1217.8-12	Aug.	1		"
1217.8-13	Sept.	1		"
1217.8-14	Oct.	1		"
1217.8-15	Nov.	1		"
1217.8-16 to 47	Apr. 1979, (#47)	1		"
1217.8-G.S. 1	May 1975	1		"
1217.8-G.S. 2	Jul. 1975	1		"

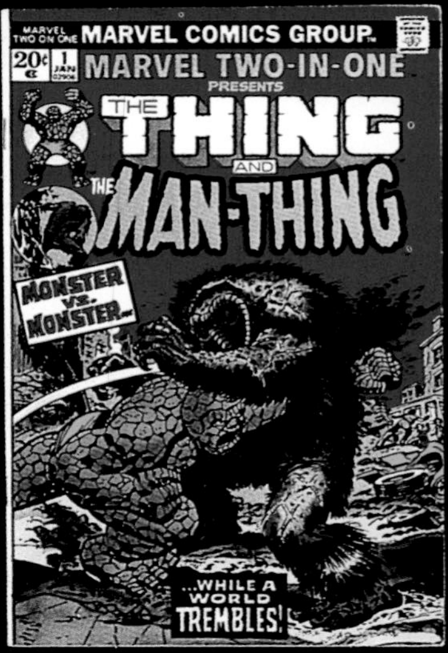
MARVEL COMICS GROUP.
MARVEL TWO-IN-ONE
PRESENTS
THE THING
AND
THE MAN-THING
MONSTER VS. MONSTER...
...WHILE A WORLD TREMBLES!

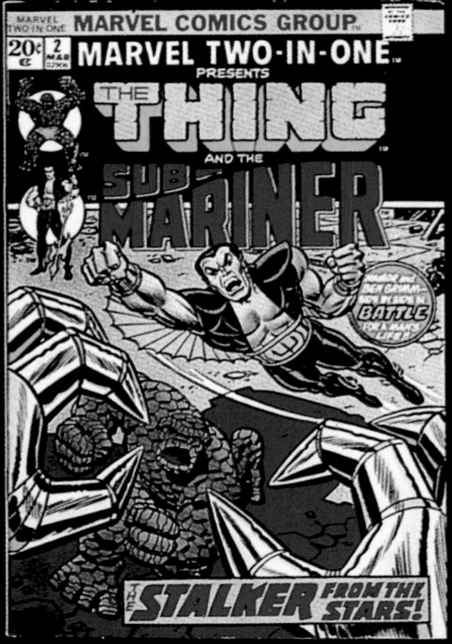
MARVEL COMICS GROUP.
MARVEL TWO-IN-ONE
PRESENTS
THE THING
AND THE
SUB-MARINER
THE STALKER FROM THE STARS!

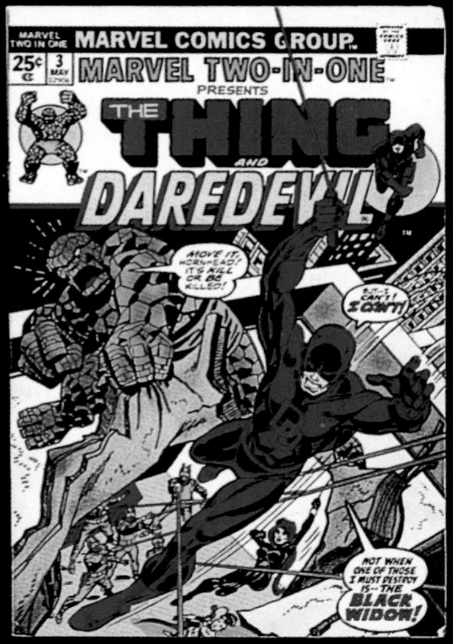
MARVEL COMICS GROUP.
MARVEL TWO-IN-ONE
PRESENTS
THE THING
AND
DAREDEVIL
NOT WHEN ONE OF THOSE I MUST DESTROY IS-- THE BLACK WIDOW!

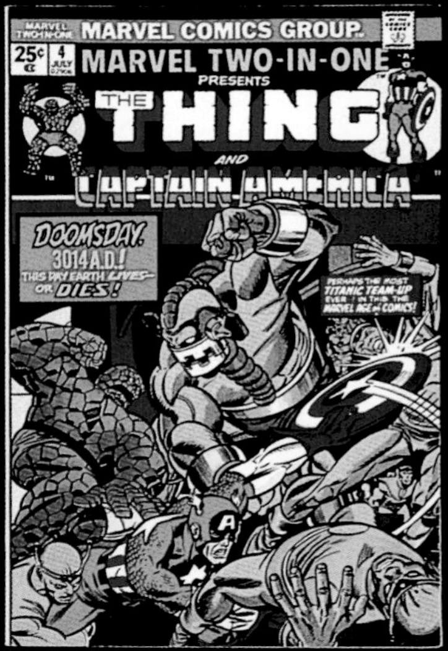
MARVEL COMICS GROUP.
MARVEL TWO-IN-ONE
PRESENTS
THE THING
AND
CAPTAIN AMERICA
DOOMSDAY. 3014 A.D.!

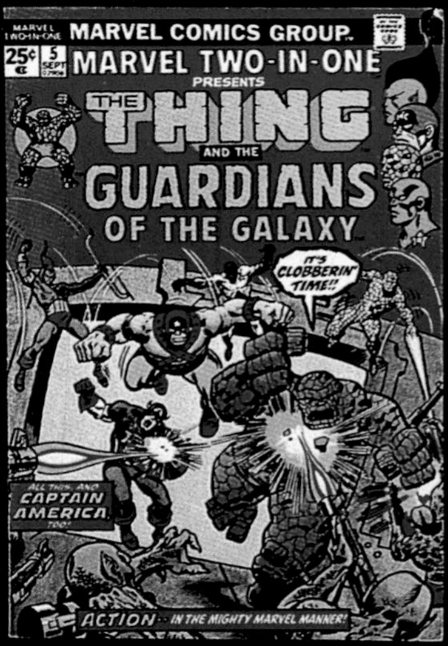
MARVEL COMICS GROUP.
MARVEL TWO-IN-ONE
PRESENTS
THE THING
AND THE
GUARDIANS
OF THE GALAXY
IT'S CLOBBERIN' TIME!!
CAPTAIN AMERICA
ACTION IN THE MIGHTY MARVEL MANNER!

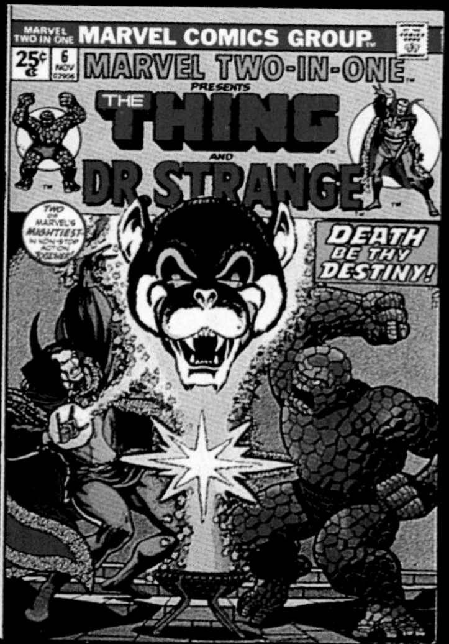
MARVEL COMICS GROUP.
MARVEL TWO-IN-ONE
PRESENTS
THE THING
AND
DR. STRANGE
DEATH BET THY DESTINY!

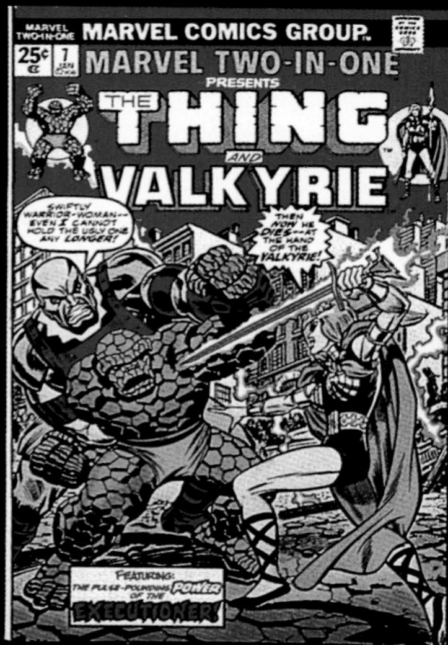
MARVEL COMICS GROUP.
MARVEL TWO-IN-ONE
PRESENTS
THE THING
AND
VALKYRIE
EXECUTIONER!

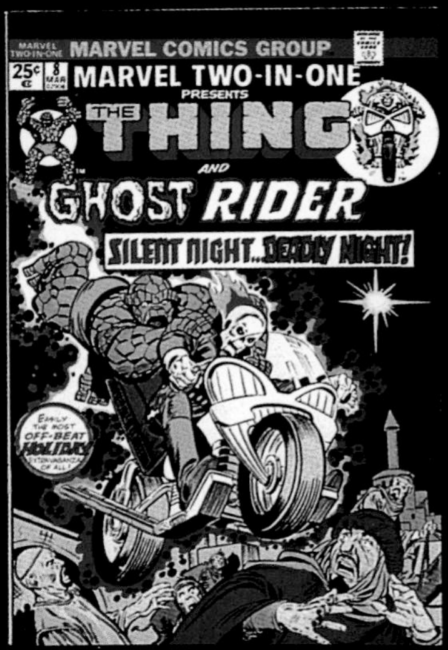
MARVEL COMICS GROUP
MARVEL TWO-IN-ONE
PRESENTS
THE THING
AND
GHOST RIDER
SILENT NIGHT...DEADLY NIGHT!

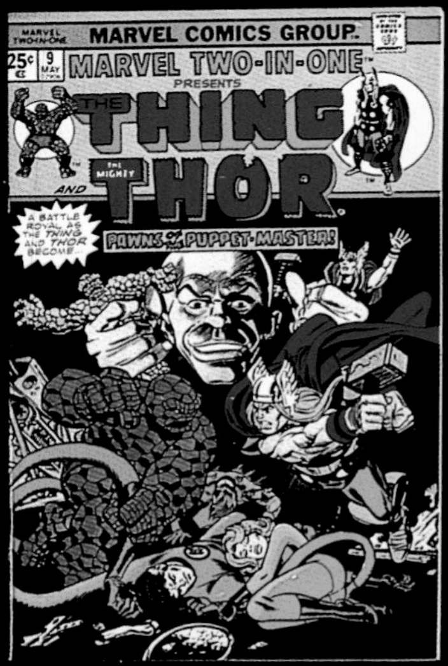
MARVEL COMICS GROUP.
MARVEL TWO-IN-ONE
PRESENTS
THE THING
THOR
PAWNS OF THE PUPPET-MASTER!

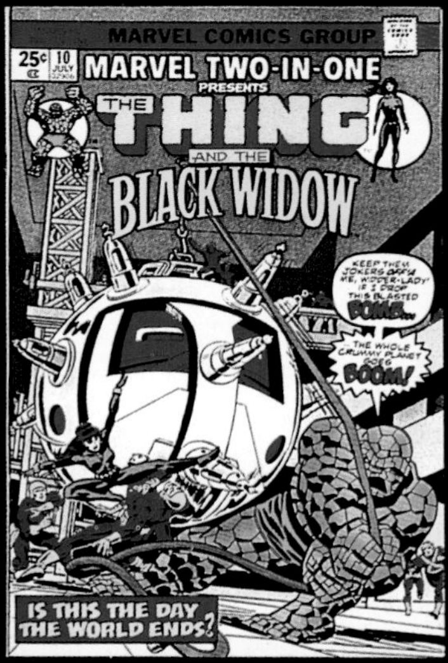
MARVEL COMICS GROUP
MARVEL TWO-IN-ONE
PRESENTS
THE THING
AND THE
BLACK WIDOW
IS THIS THE DAY THE WORLD ENDS?

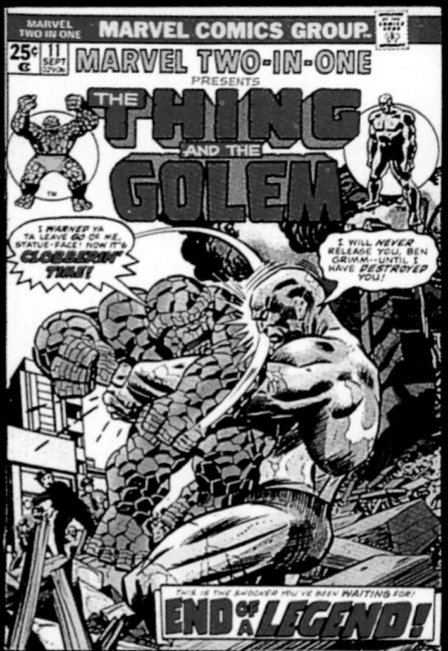
MARVEL COMICS GROUP.
MARVEL TWO-IN-ONE
PRESENTS
THE THING
AND THE
GOLEM
END OF A LEGEND!

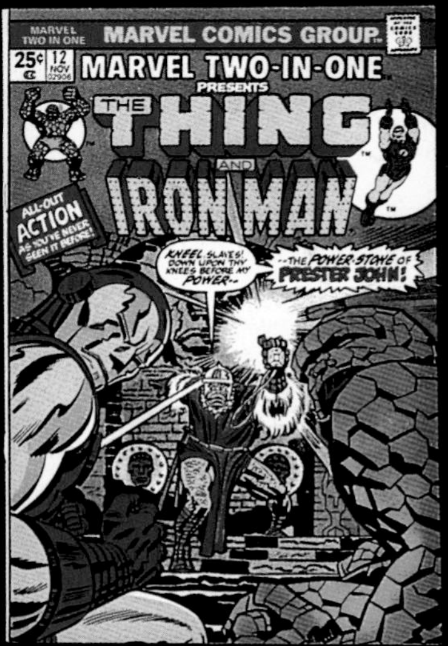
MARVEL COMICS GROUP.
MARVEL TWO-IN-ONE
PRESENTS
THE THING
AND
IRON MAN
ALL-OUT ACTION
PRESTER JOHN!

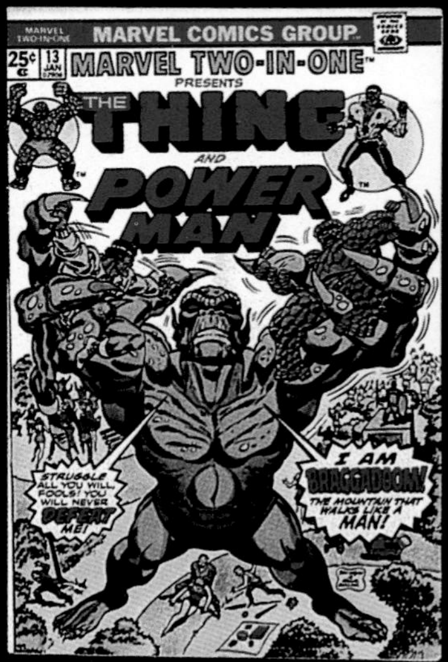
MARVEL COMICS GROUP.
MARVEL TWO-IN-ONE
PRESENTS
THE THING
AND
POWER MAN
I AM BRAGGADOOM! THE MOUNTAIN THAT WALKS LIKE A MAN!

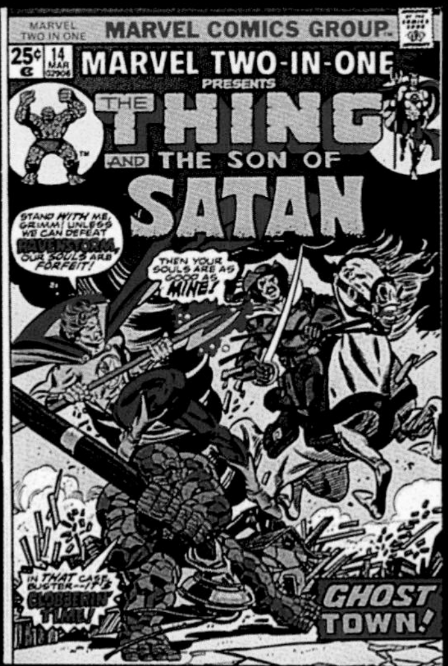
MARVEL COMICS GROUP.
MARVEL TWO-IN-ONE
PRESENTS
THE THING
AND THE SON OF
SATAN
GHOST TOWN!

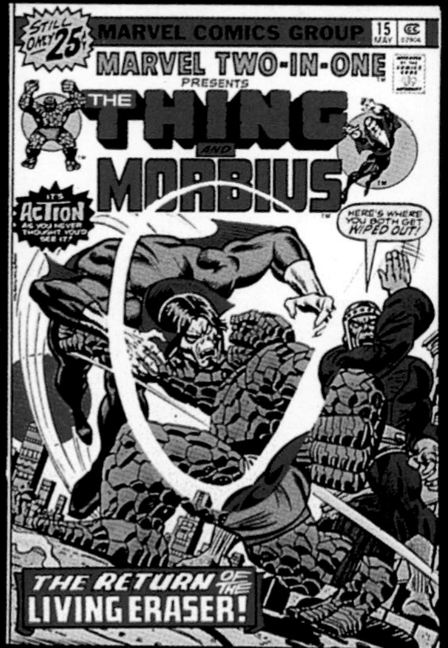
STILL ONLY 25¢
MARVEL COMICS GROUP
MARVEL TWO-IN-ONE
PRESENTS
THE THING
AND
MORBIUS
IT'S ACTION
THE RETURN OF THE LIVING ERASER!

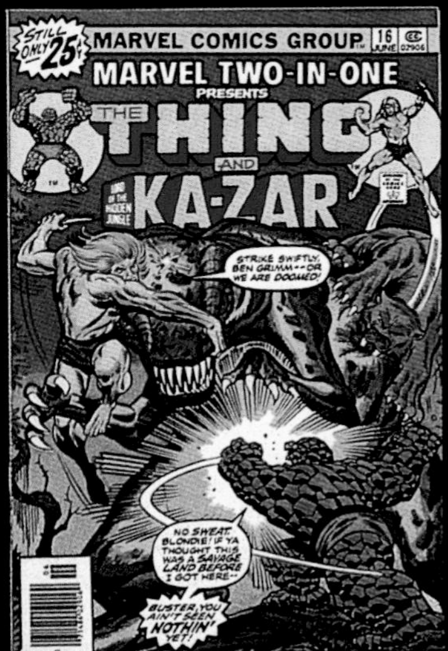
STILL ONLY 25¢
MARVEL COMICS GROUP.
MARVEL TWO-IN-ONE
PRESENTS
THE THING
AND
KA-ZAR

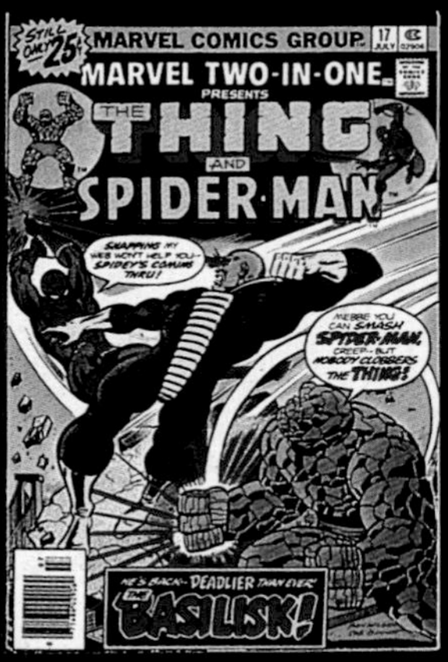
MARVEL COMICS GROUP
MARVEL TWO-IN-ONE
PRESENTS
THE THING
AND
SPIDER-MAN
BASILISK!

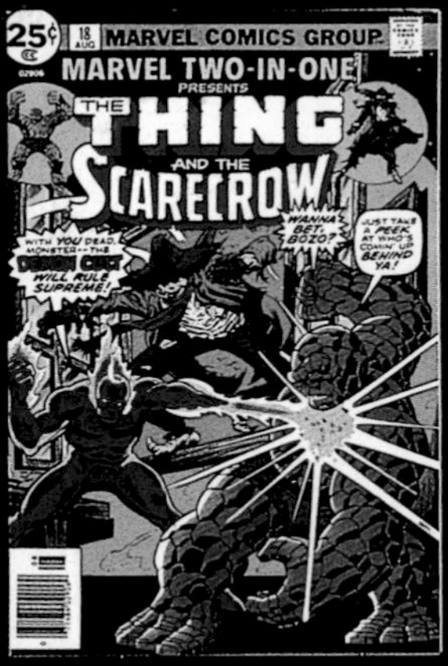
25¢
MARVEL COMICS GROUP
MARVEL TWO-IN-ONE
PRESENTS
THE THING
AND THE
SCARECROW!

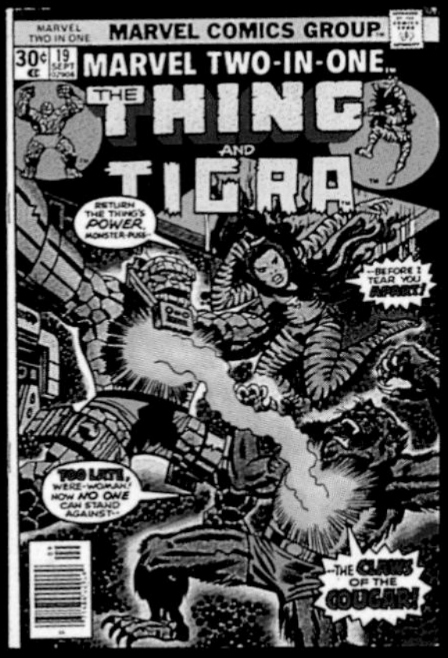
MARVEL COMICS GROUP
MARVEL TWO-IN-ONE
THE THING
AND
TIGRA

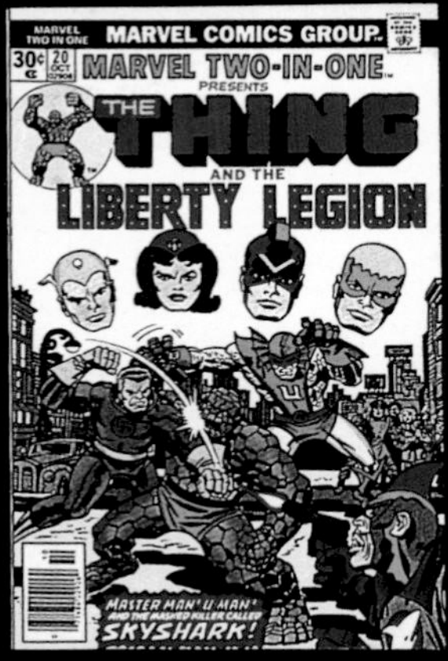
MARVEL COMICS GROUP
MARVEL TWO-IN-ONE
PRESENTS
THE THING
AND THE
LIBERTY LEGION
SKYSHARK!

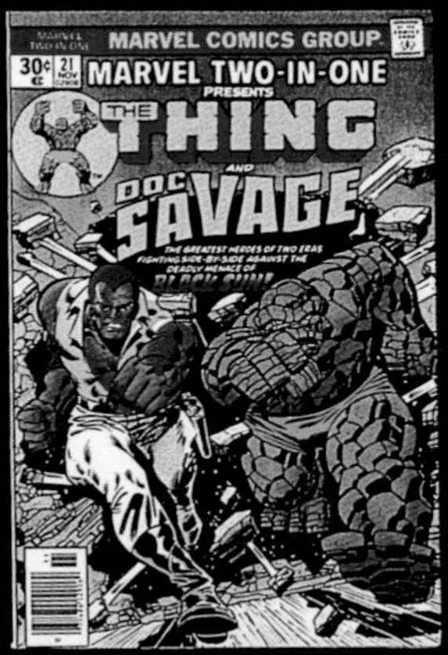
MARVEL COMICS GROUP
MARVEL TWO-IN-ONE
PRESENTS
THE THING
AND
DOC SAVAGE

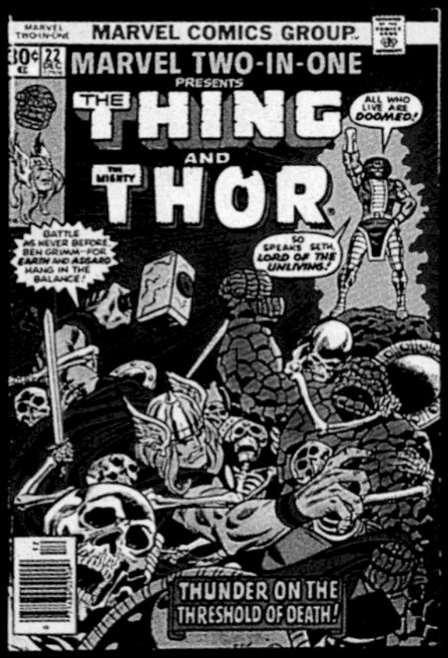
MARVEL COMICS GROUP
MARVEL TWO-IN-ONE
PRESENTS
THE THING
AND
THOR
THUNDER ON THE THRESHOLD OF DEATH!

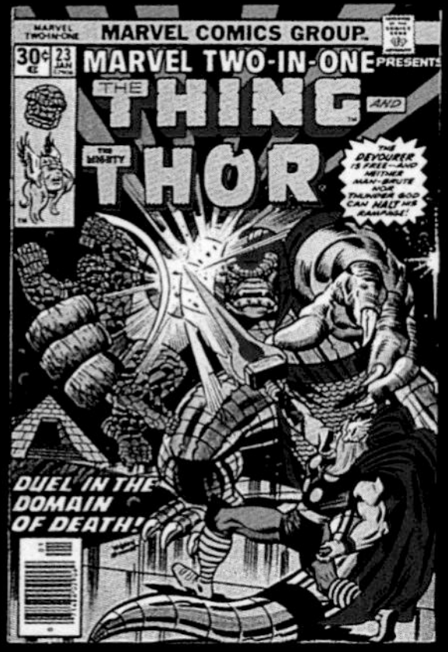
MARVEL COMICS GROUP
MARVEL TWO-IN-ONE
PRESENTS
THE THING
AND
THOR
DUEL IN THE DOMAIN OF DEATH!

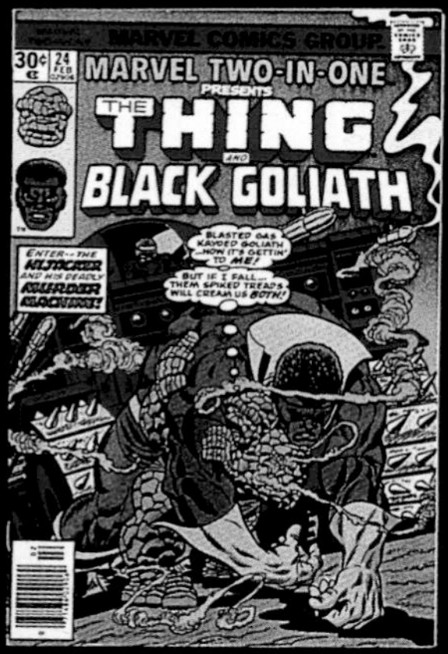
MARVEL TWO-IN-ONE
PRESENTS
THE THING
AND
BLACK GOLIATH

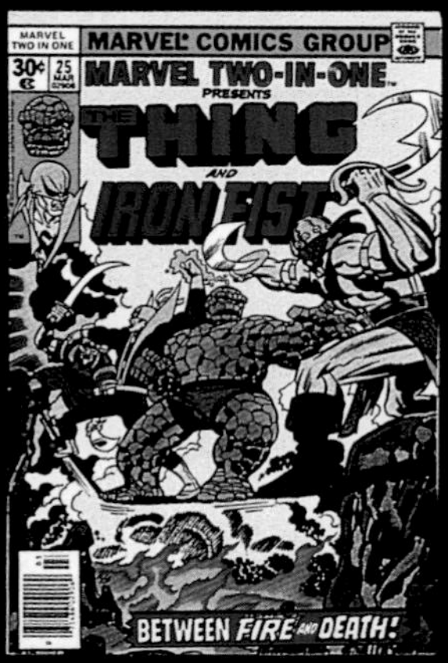
MARVEL COMICS GROUP
MARVEL TWO-IN-ONE
PRESENTS
THE THING
AND
IRON FIST
BETWEEN FIRE AND DEATH!

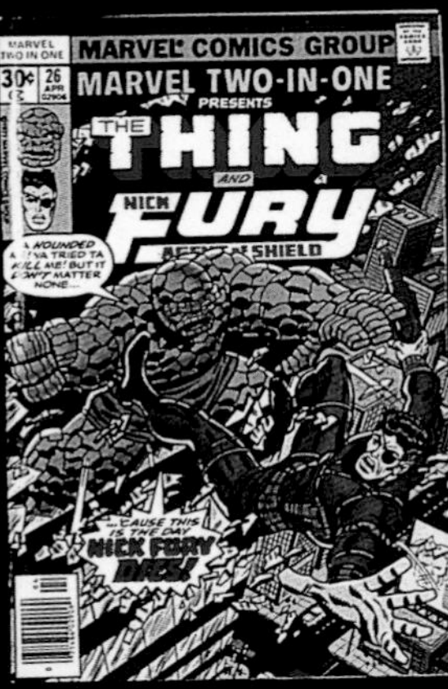
MARVEL COMICS GROUP
MARVEL TWO-IN-ONE
PRESENTS
THE THING
AND
NICK FURY

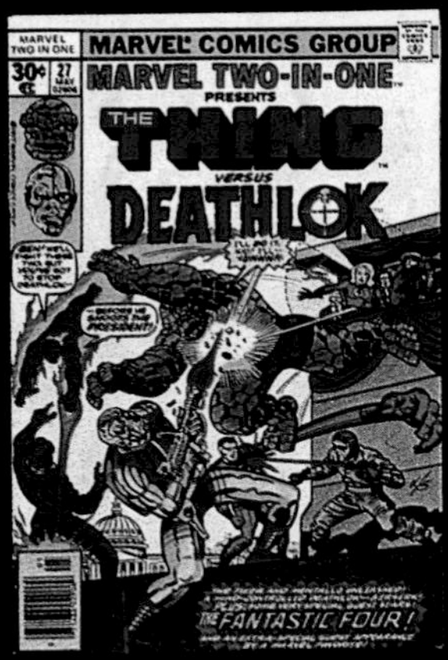
MARVEL COMICS GROUP
MARVEL TWO-IN-ONE
PRESENTS
THE THING
VERSUS
DEATHLOK

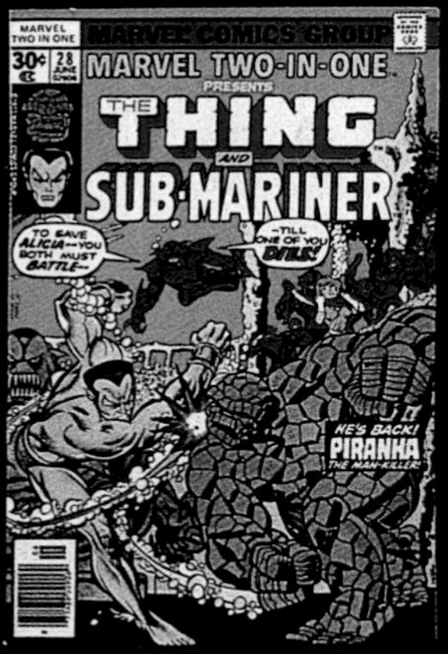
MARVEL COMICS GROUP
MARVEL TWO-IN-ONE
PRESENTS
THE THING
AND
SUB-MARINER
HE'S BACK! PIRANHA

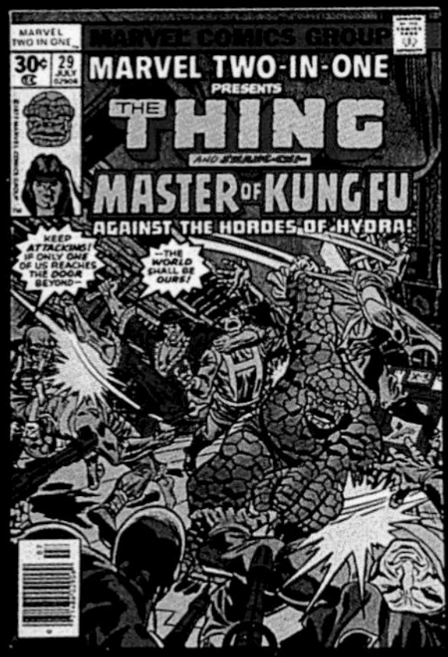
MARVEL COMICS GROUP
MARVEL TWO-IN-ONE
PRESENTS
THE THING
AND
MASTER OF KUNG FU
AGAINST THE HORDES OF HYDRA!

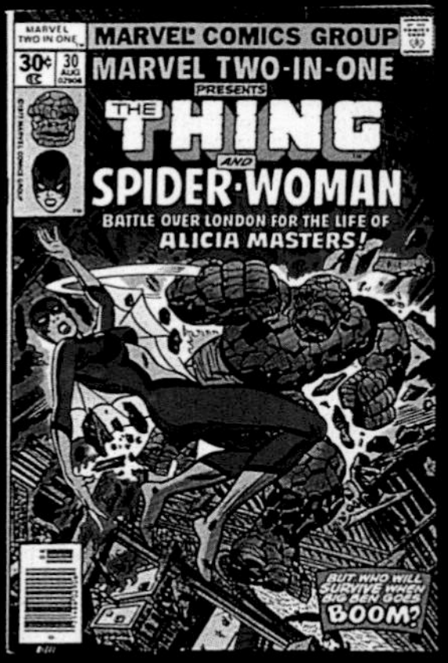
MARVEL COMICS GROUP
MARVEL TWO-IN-ONE
PRESENTS
THE THING
AND
SPIDER-WOMAN
BATTLE OVER LONDON FOR THE LIFE OF ALICIA MASTERS!
BOOM?

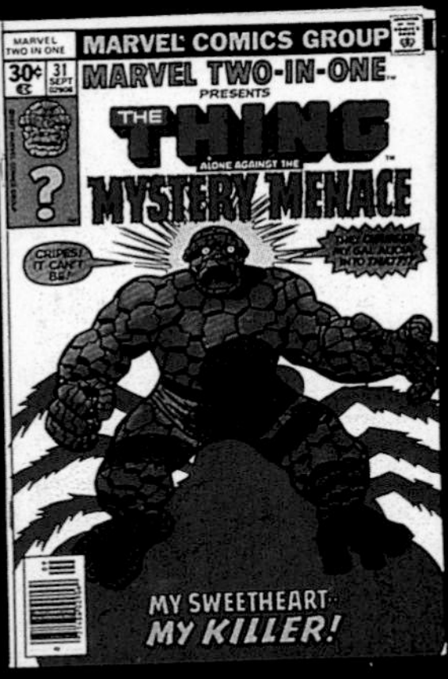
MARVEL COMICS GROUP
MARVEL TWO-IN-ONE
PRESENTS
THE THING
MYSTERY MENACE
MY SWEETHEART MY KILLER!

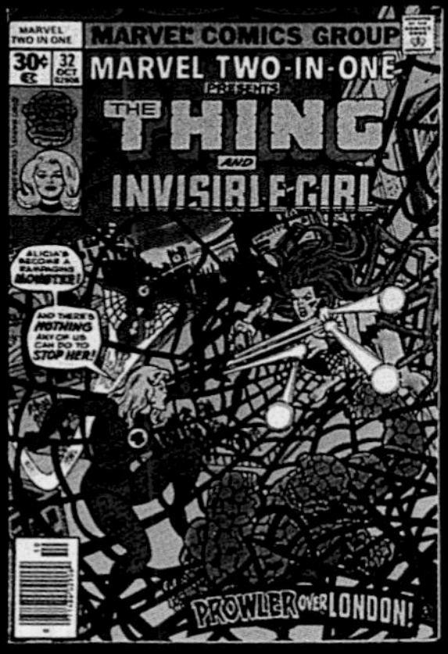
MARVEL COMICS GROUP
MARVEL TWO-IN-ONE
PRESENTS
THE THING
AND
INVISIBLE GIRL
PROWLER OVER LONDON!

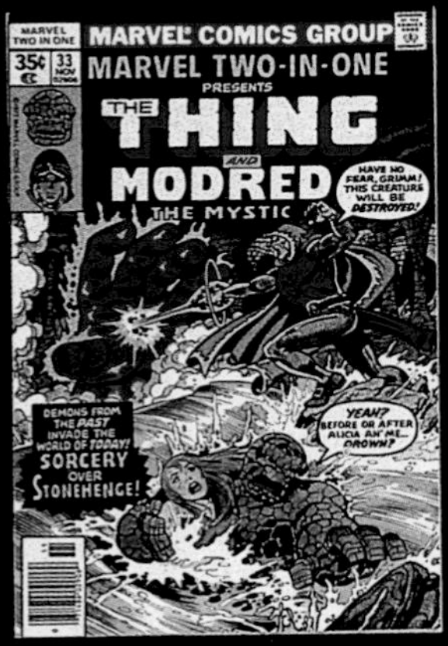
MARVEL COMICS GROUP
MARVEL TWO-IN-ONE
PRESENTS
THE THING
AND
MODRED
THE MYSTIC
SORCERY OVER STONEHENGE!

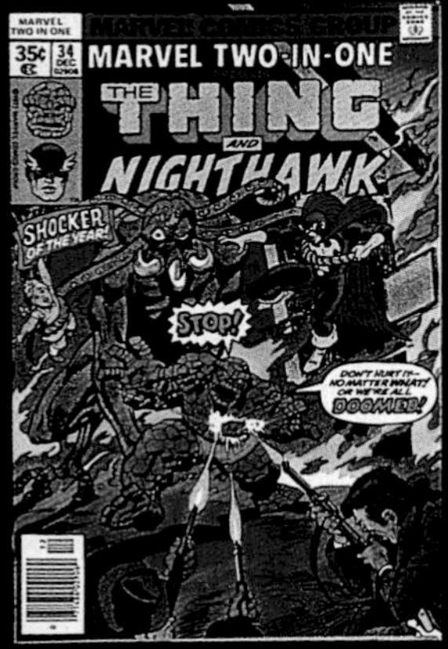
MARVEL COMICS GROUP
MARVEL TWO-IN-ONE
THE THING
AND
NIGHTHAWK
STOP!

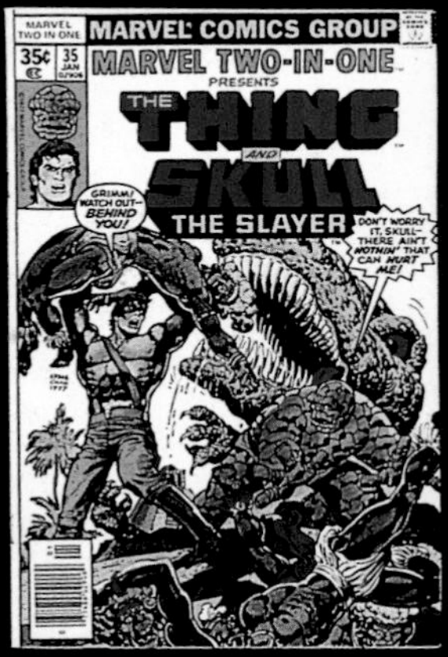
MARVEL COMICS GROUP
MARVEL TWO-IN-ONE
PRESENTS
THE THING
AND
SKULL
THE SLAYER

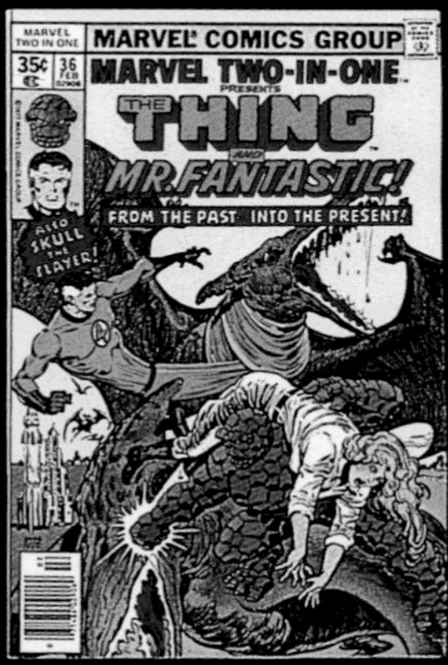
MARVEL COMICS GROUP
MARVEL TWO-IN-ONE
PRESENTS
THE THING
AND
MR. FANTASTIC!
FROM THE PAST INTO THE PRESENT!

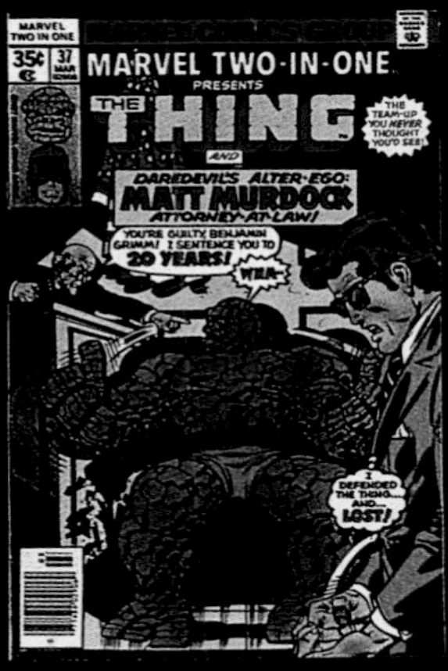
MARVEL TWO-IN-ONE
PRESENTS
THE THING
AND
DAREDEVIL'S ALTER-EGO:
MATT MURDOCK

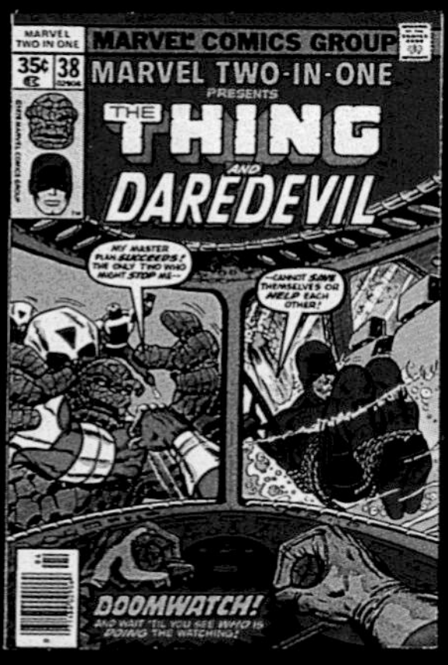
MARVEL COMICS GROUP
MARVEL TWO-IN-ONE
PRESENTS
THE THING
AND
DAREDEVIL
DOOMWATCH!

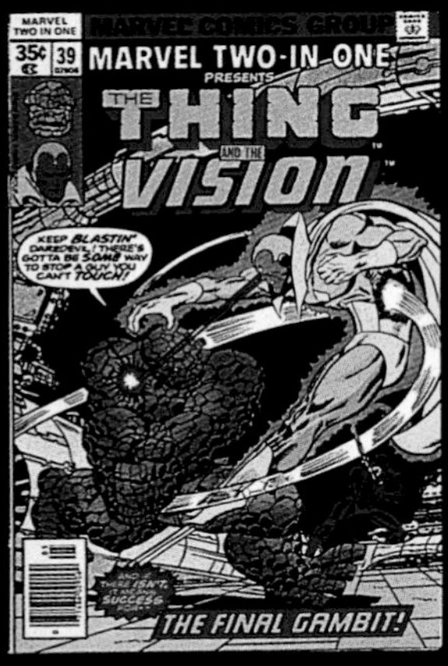
MARVEL TWO-IN-ONE
PRESENTS
THE THING
AND THE
VISION
THE FINAL GAMBIT!

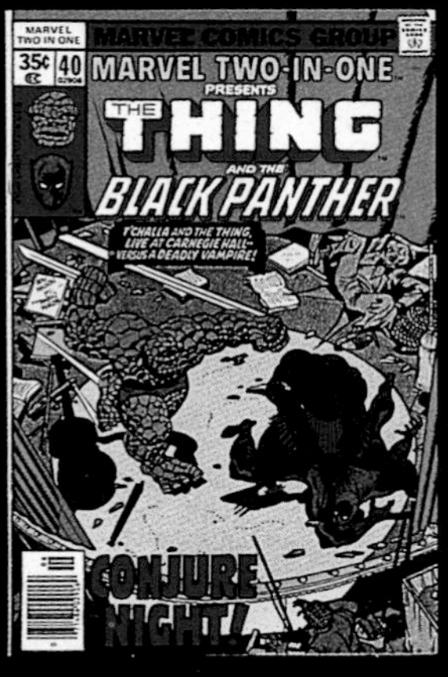
MARVEL COMICS GROUP
MARVEL TWO-IN-ONE
PRESENTS
THE THING
AND THE
BLACK PANTHER
CONJURE NIGHT!

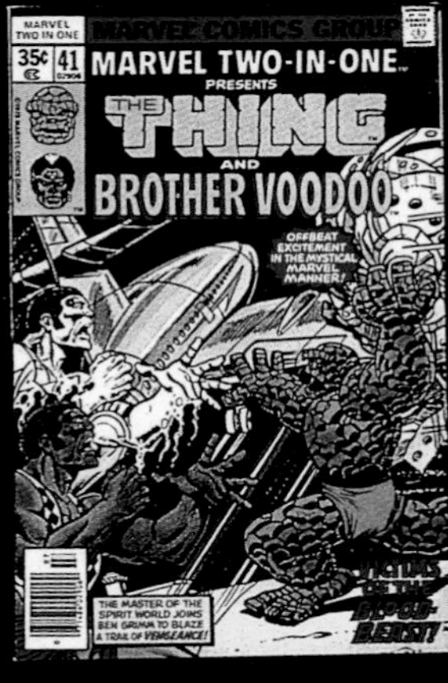
MARVEL COMICS GROUP
MARVEL TWO-IN-ONE
PRESENTS
THE THING
AND
BROTHER VOODOO

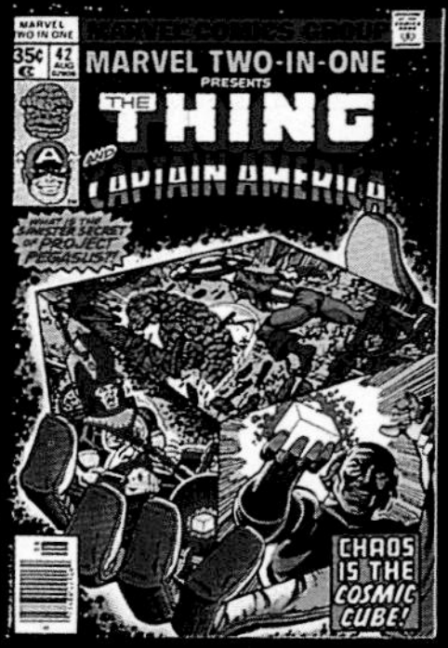
MARVEL COMICS GROUP
MARVEL TWO-IN-ONE
PRESENTS
THE THING
AND CAPTAIN AMERICA
CHAOS IS THE COSMIC CUBE!

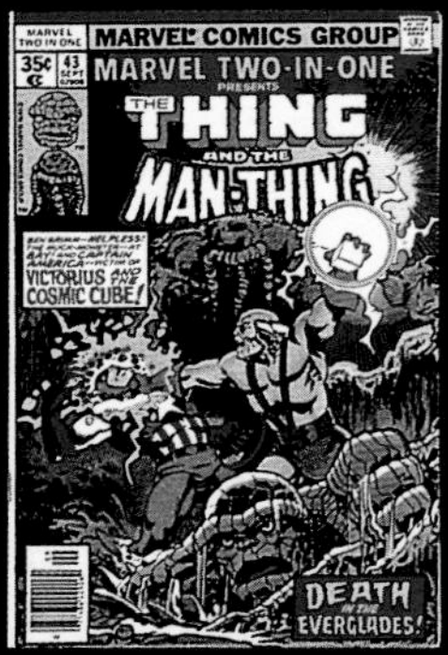
MARVEL COMICS GROUP
MARVEL TWO-IN-ONE
PRESENTS
THE THING
AND THE MAN-THING
VICTORIOUS IS THE COSMIC CUBE!
DEATH IN THE EVERGLADES!

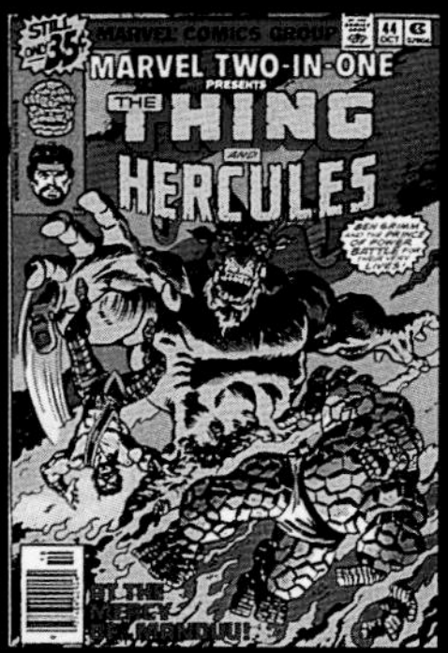
MARVEL COMICS GROUP
MARVEL TWO-IN-ONE
PRESENTS
THE THING
HERCULES

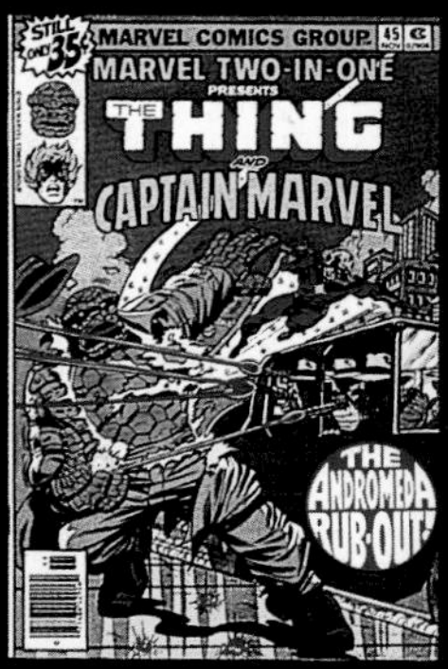
MARVEL COMICS GROUP
MARVEL TWO-IN-ONE
THE THING
AND CAPTAIN MARVEL
THE ANDROMEDA RUB-OUT!

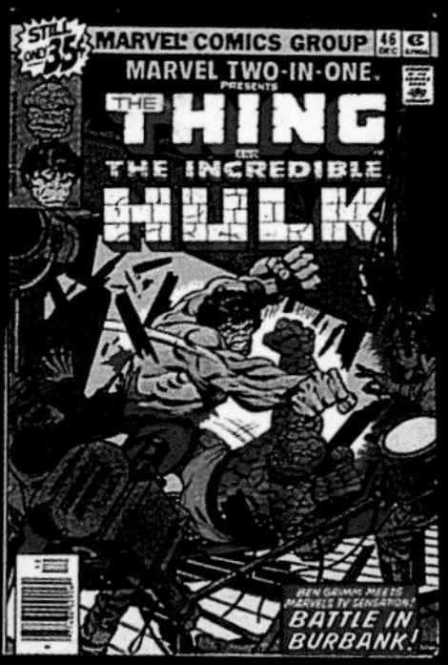
MARVEL COMICS GROUP
MARVEL TWO-IN-ONE
PRESENTS
THE THING
THE INCREDIBLE HULK
BATTLE IN BURBANK!

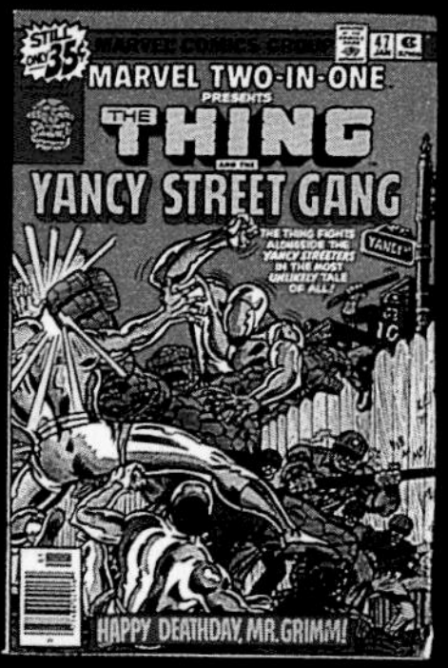
MARVEL COMICS GROUP
MARVEL TWO-IN-ONE
PRESENTS
THE THING
YANCY STREET GANG
HAPPY DEATHDAY, MR. GRIMM!

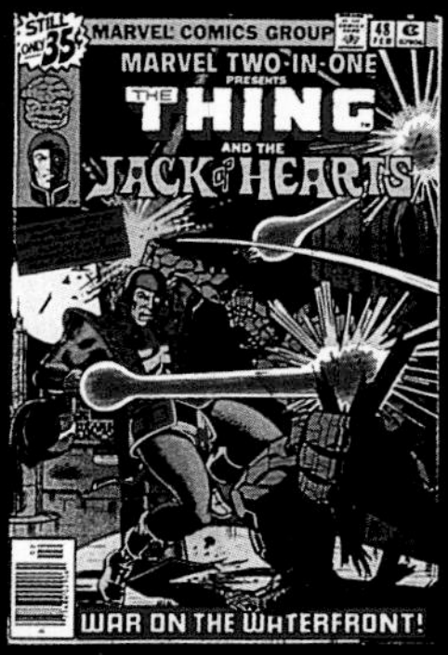
MARVEL COMICS GROUP
MARVEL TWO-IN-ONE
PRESENTS
THE THING
AND THE JACK OF HEARTS
WAR ON THE WATERFRONT!

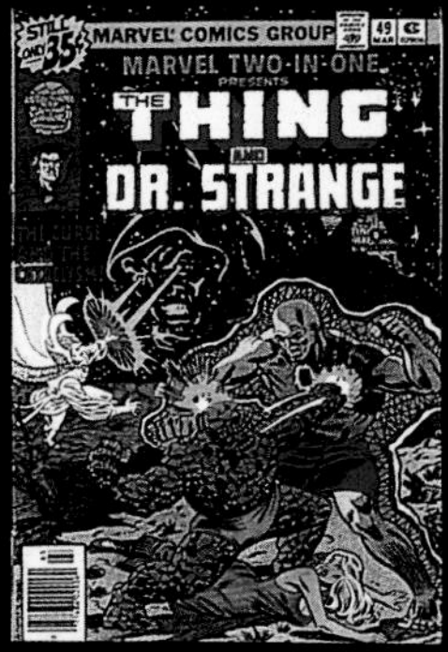
MARVEL COMICS GROUP
MARVEL TWO-IN-ONE
PRESENTS
THE THING
AND DR. STRANGE

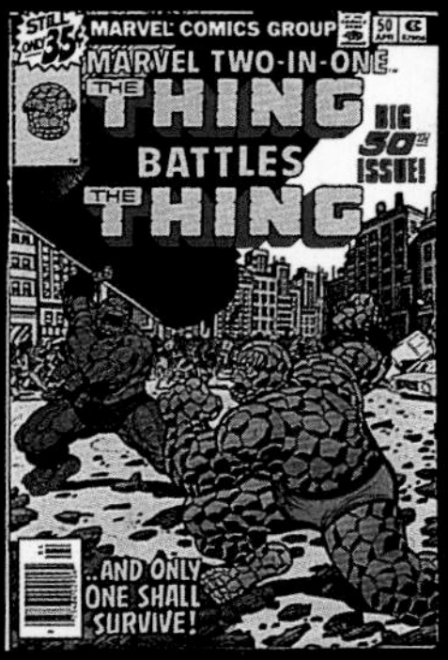
MARVEL COMICS GROUP
MARVEL TWO-IN-ONE
THE THING
BATTLES
THE THING
BIG 50TH ISSUE!
AND ONLY ONE SHALL SURVIVE!

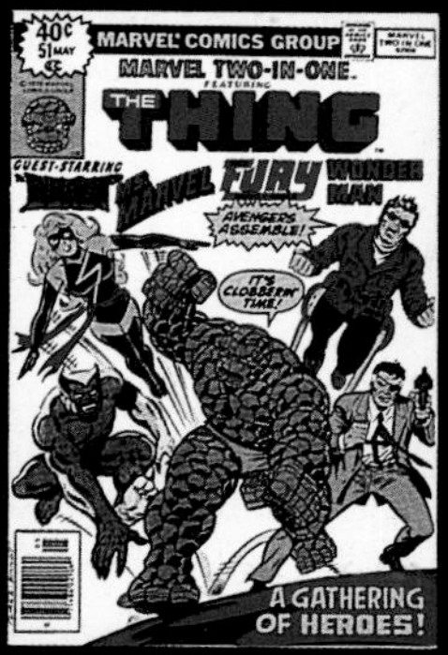
MARVEL COMICS GROUP
THE THING
FURY
A GATHERING OF HEROES!

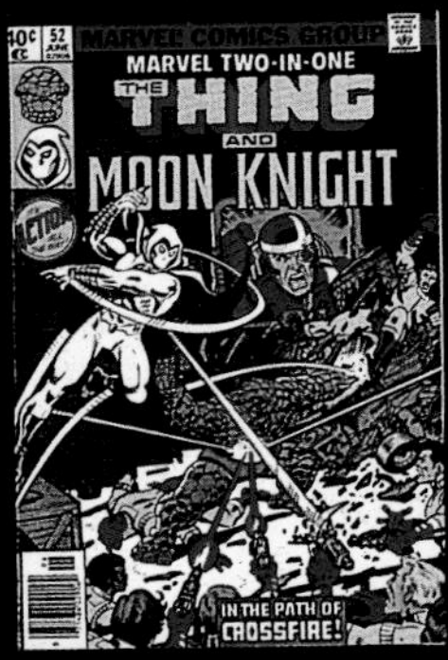
MARVEL COMICS GROUP
MARVEL TWO-IN-ONE
THE THING
AND MOON KNIGHT
IN THE PATH OF CROSSFIRE!

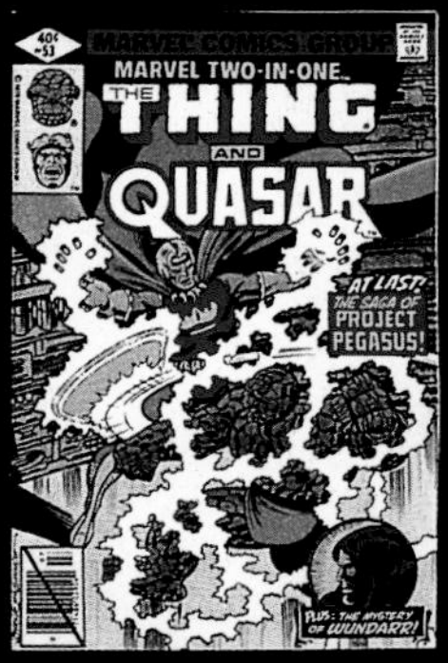
MARVEL COMICS GROUP
MARVEL TWO-IN-ONE
THE THING
AND QUASAR
AT LAST! THE SAGA OF PROJECT PEGASUS!

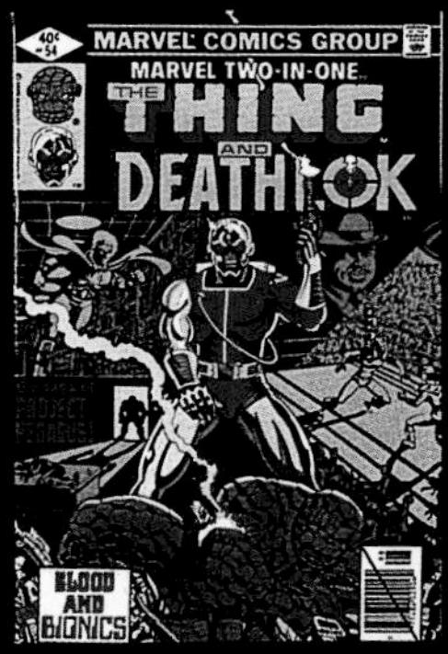
MARVEL COMICS GROUP
MARVEL TWO-IN-ONE
THE THING
DEATHLOK
BLOOD AND BIONICS

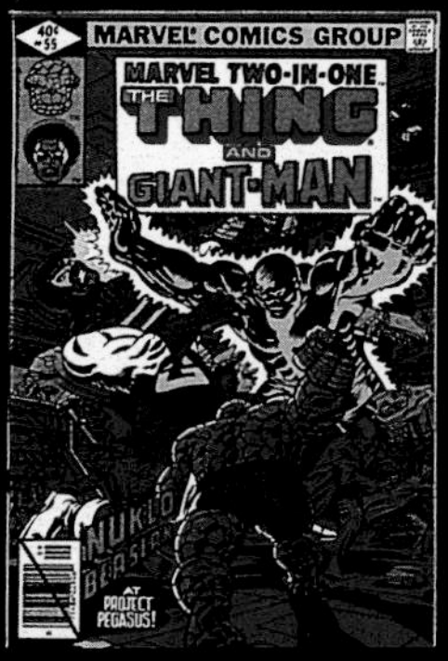
MARVEL COMICS GROUP
MARVEL TWO-IN-ONE
THE THING
AND GIANT-MAN

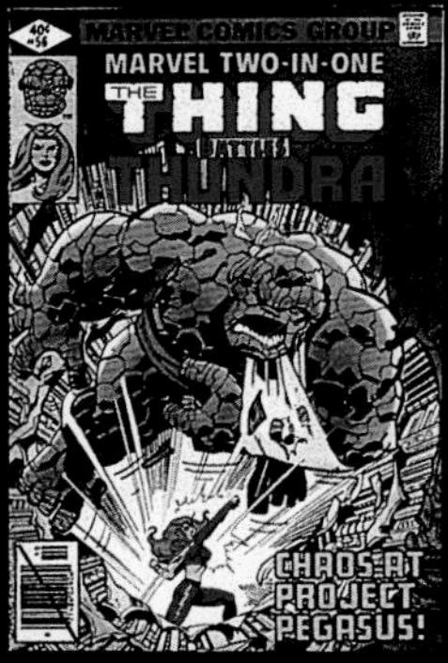
MARVEL COMICS GROUP
MARVEL TWO-IN-ONE
THE THING
THUNDRA
CHAOS AT PROJECT PEGASUS!

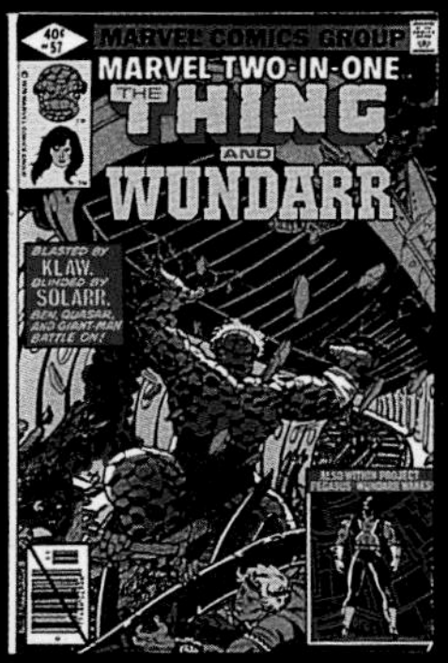
MARVEL COMICS GROUP
MARVEL TWO-IN-ONE
THE THING
AND WUNDARR

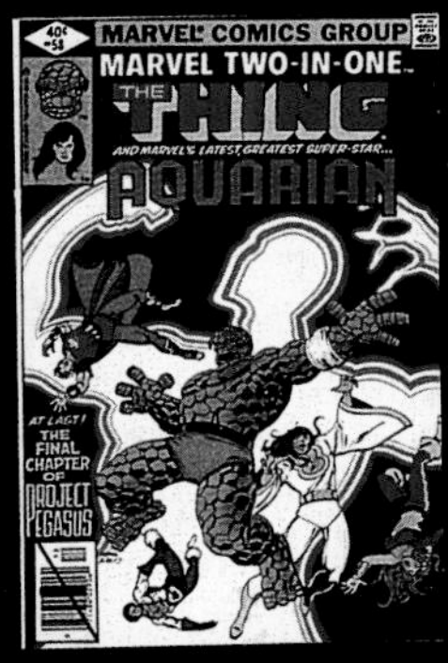
MARVEL COMICS GROUP
MARVEL TWO-IN-ONE
THE THING
AQUARIAN

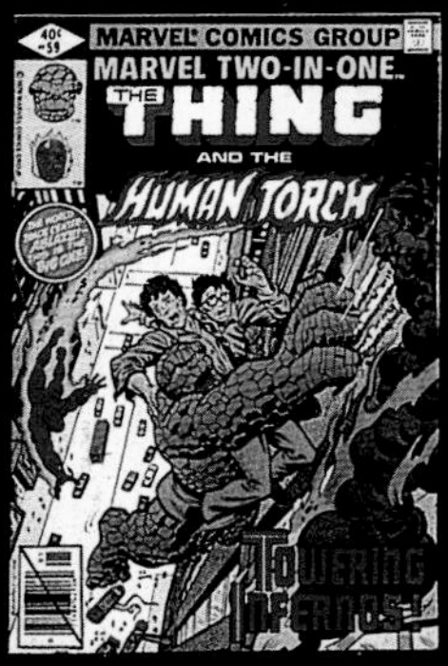
MARVEL COMICS GROUP
MARVEL TWO-IN-ONE
THE THING
AND THE HUMAN TORCH

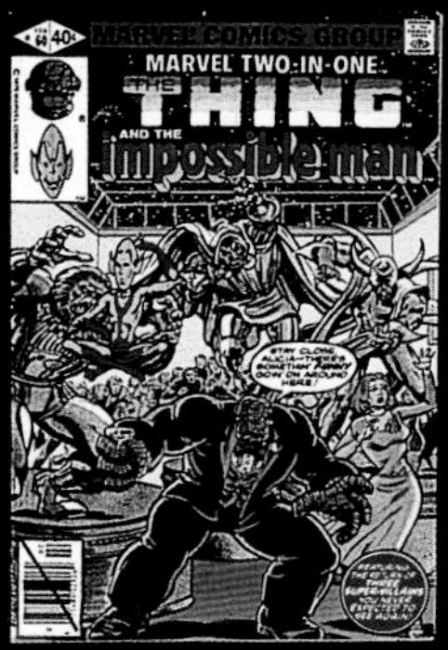
MARVEL COMICS GROUP
MARVEL TWO-IN-ONE
THE THING
AND THE IMPOSSIBLE MAN

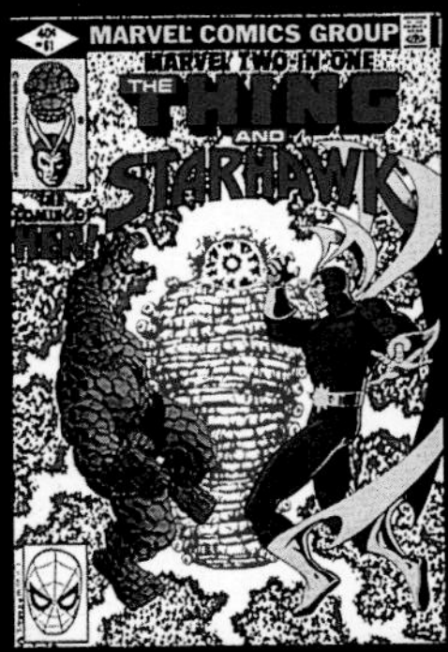
MARVEL COMICS GROUP
MARVEL TWO-IN-ONE
THE THING
STARHAWK

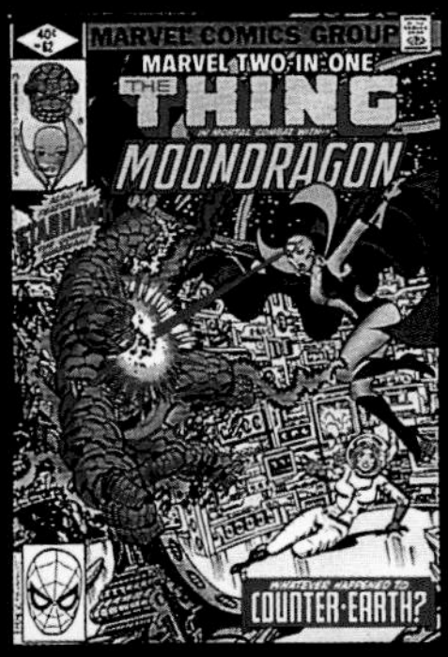
MARVEL COMICS GROUP
MARVEL TWO-IN-ONE
THE THING
MOONDRAGON
COUNTER-EARTH?

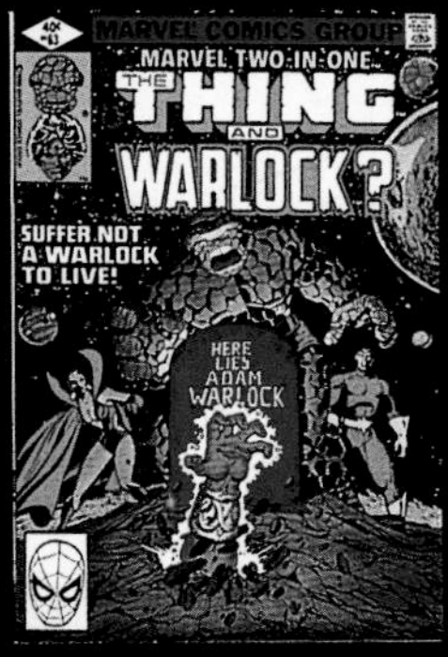
MARVEL COMICS GROUP
MARVEL TWO-IN-ONE
THE THING
WARLOCK?
SUFFER NOT A WARLOCK TO LIVE!
HERE LIES ADAM WARLOCK

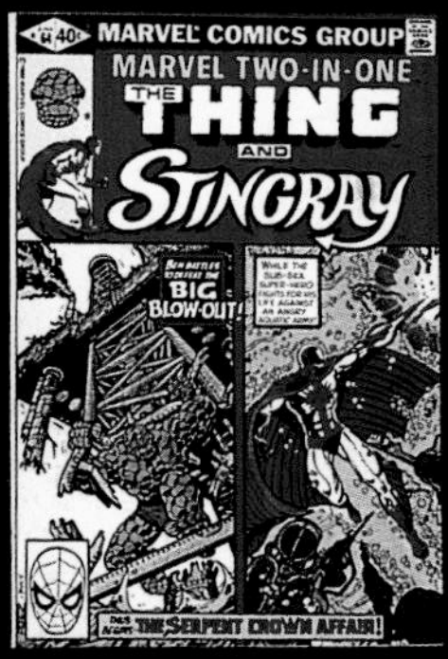
MARVEL COMICS GROUP
MARVEL TWO-IN-ONE
THE THING
AND STINGRAY
BIG BLOW-OUT!
THE SERPENT CROWN AFFAIR!

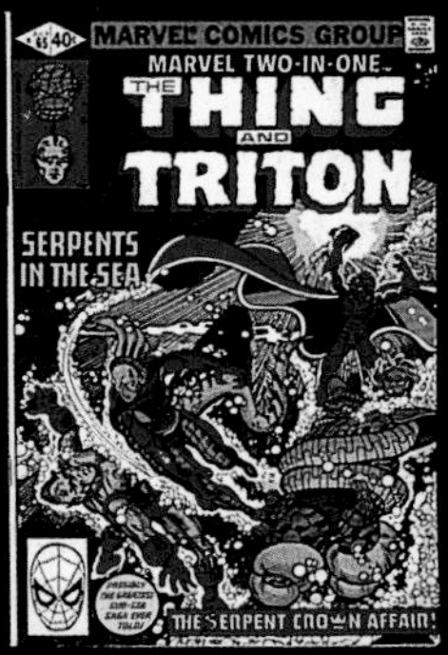
MARVEL COMICS GROUP
MARVEL TWO-IN-ONE
THE THING
AND TRITON
SERPENTS IN THE SEA
THE SERPENT CROWN AFFAIR!

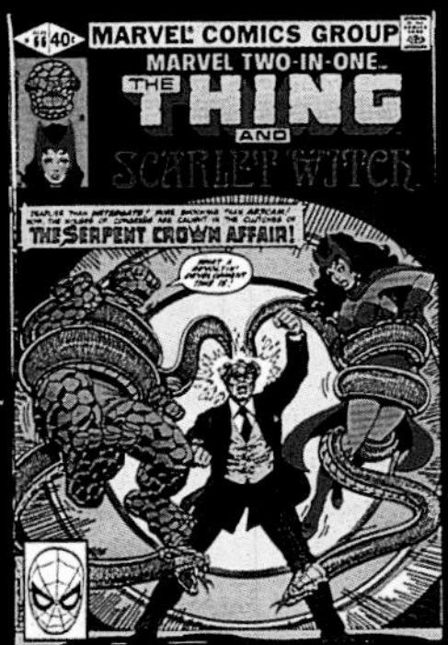
MARVEL COMICS GROUP
MARVEL TWO-IN-ONE
THE THING
AND SCARLET WITCH
THE SERPENT CROWN AFFAIR!

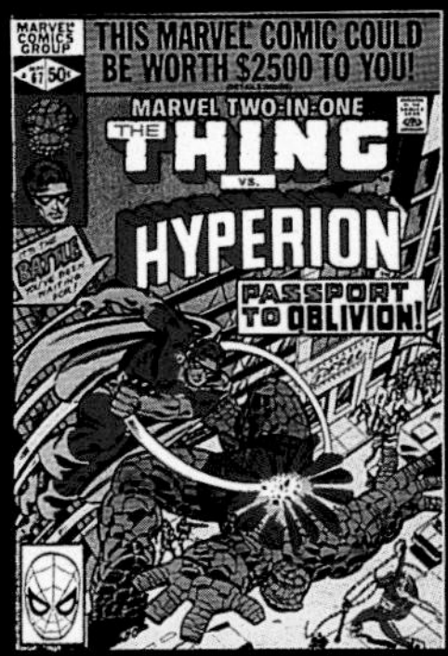
THIS MARVEL COMIC COULD BE WORTH $2500 TO YOU!
MARVEL TWO-IN-ONE
THE THING
VS.
HYPERION
PASSPORT TO OBLIVION!

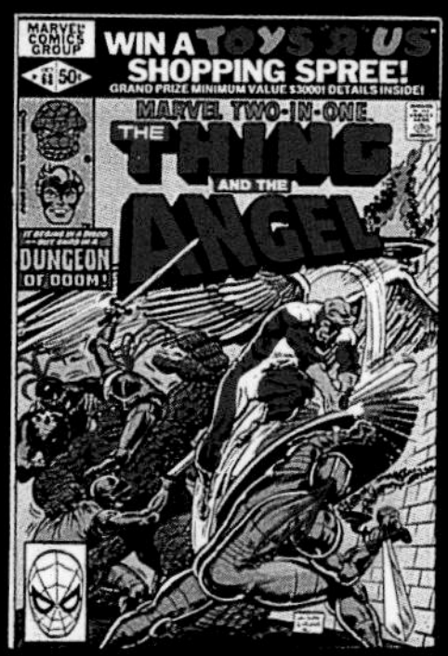
WIN A TOYS R US SHOPPING SPREE!
MARVEL TWO-IN-ONE
THE THING
AND THE ANGEL
DUNGEON OF DOOM!

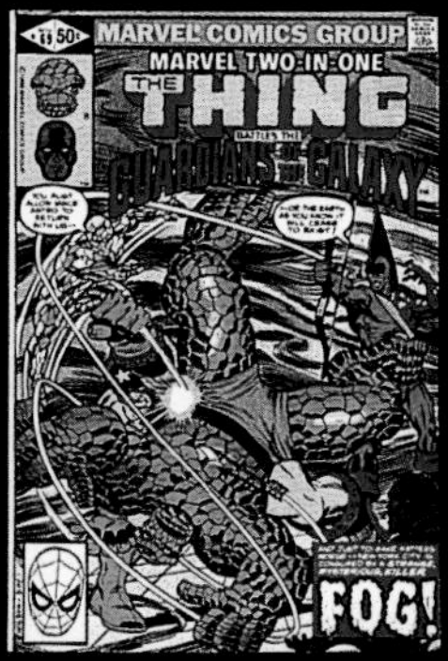
MARVEL COMICS GROUP
MARVEL TWO-IN-ONE
THE THING
FOG!

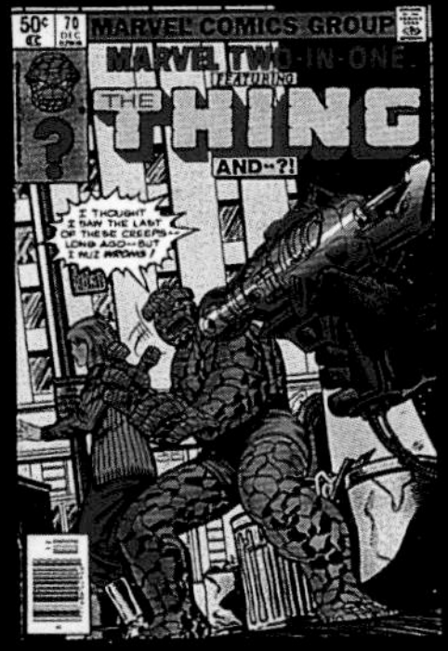
MARVEL COMICS GROUP
MARVEL TWO-IN-ONE
THE THING
AND--?

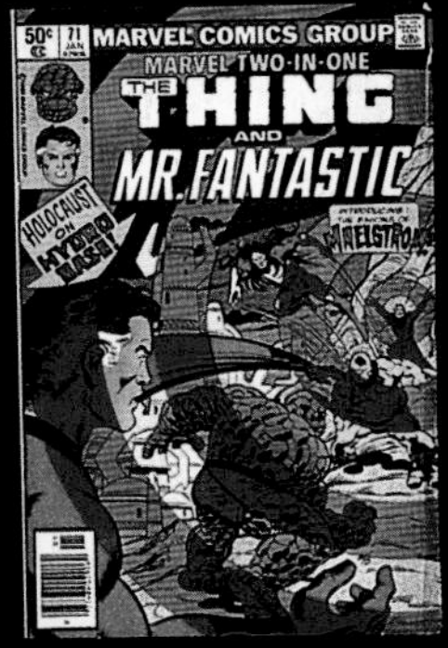
MARVEL COMICS GROUP
MARVEL TWO-IN-ONE
THE THING
AND MR. FANTASTIC

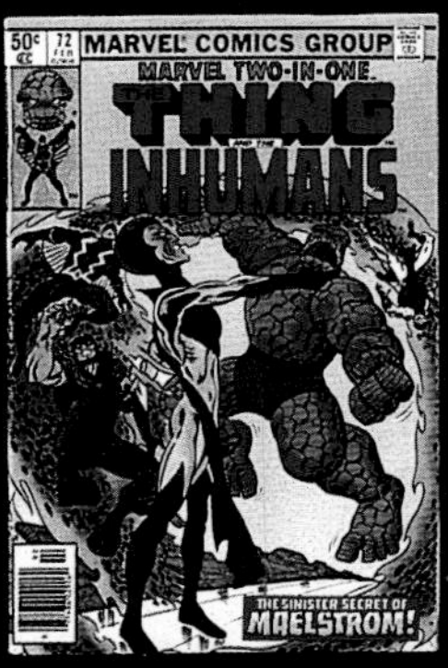
MARVEL COMICS GROUP
MARVEL TWO-IN-ONE
INHUMANS
THE SINISTER SECRET OF MAELSTROM!

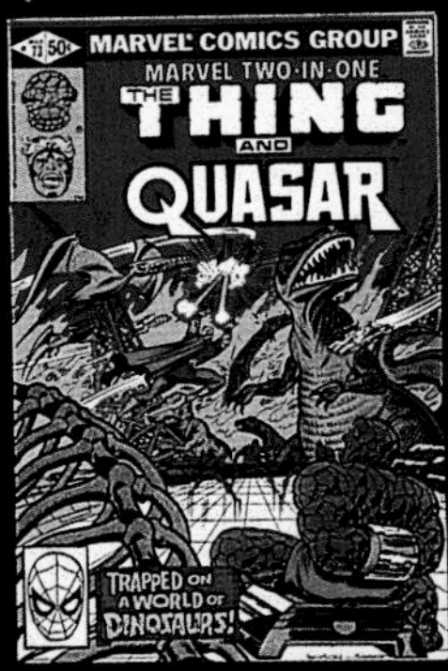
MARVEL COMICS GROUP
MARVEL TWO-IN-ONE
THE THING
AND QUASAR
TRAPPED ON A WORLD OF DINOSAURS!

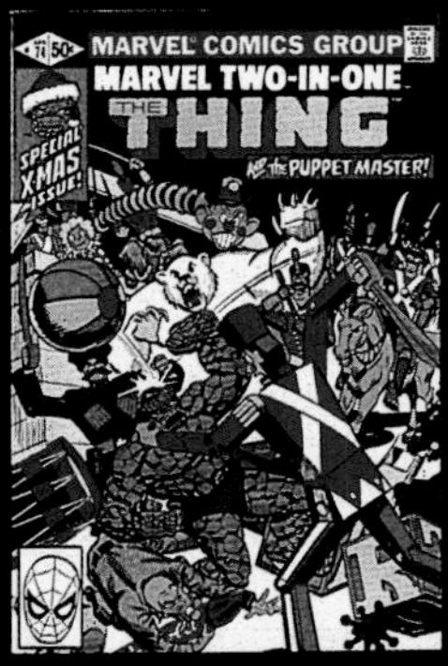
MARVEL COMICS GROUP
MARVEL TWO-IN-ONE
THE THING
SPECIAL XMAS ISSUE
PUPPET MASTER!

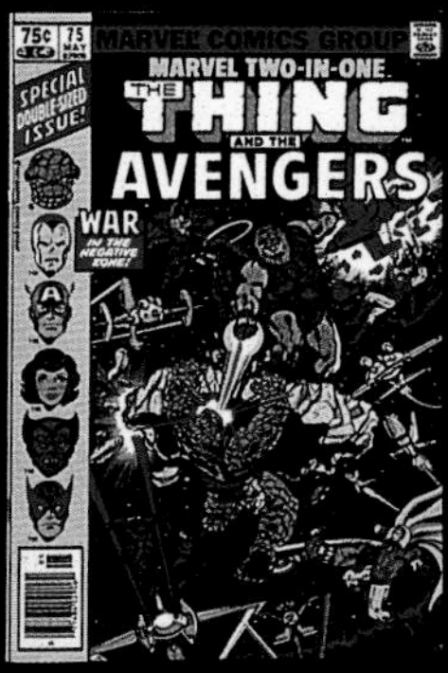
MARVEL COMICS GROUP
MARVEL TWO-IN-ONE
THE THING
AVENGERS
WAR
SPECIAL ISSUE

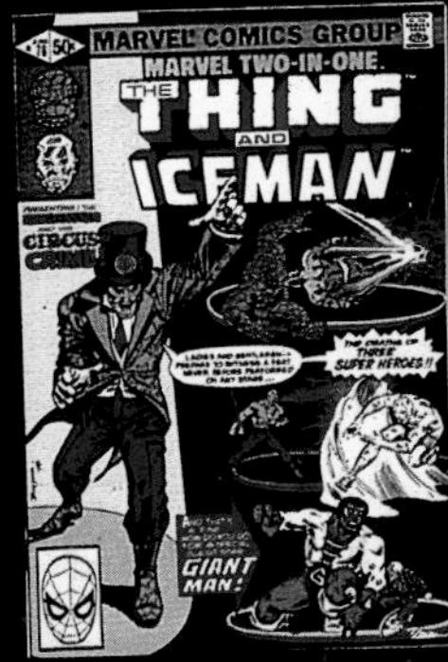
MARVEL COMICS GROUP
MARVEL TWO-IN-ONE
THE THING
ICEMAN
SUPER-HEROES!
GIANT-MAN

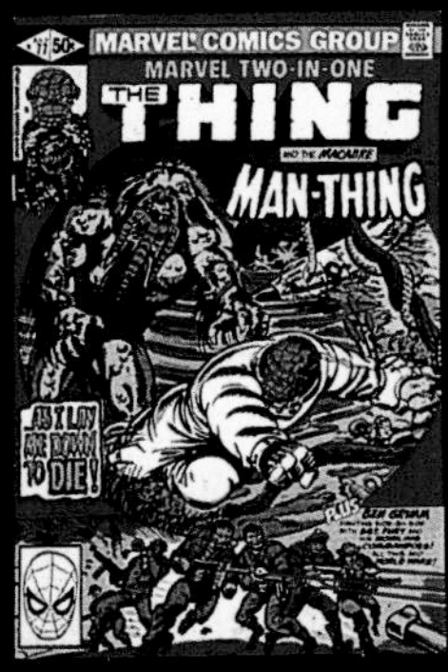
MARVEL COMICS GROUP
MARVEL TWO-IN-ONE
THE THING
MAN-THING
DIE!

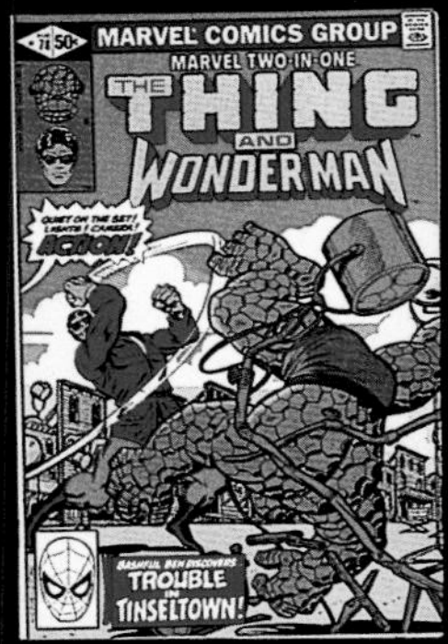
MARVEL COMICS GROUP
MARVEL TWO-IN-ONE
THE THING AND WONDER MAN
TROUBLE IN TINSELTOWN!
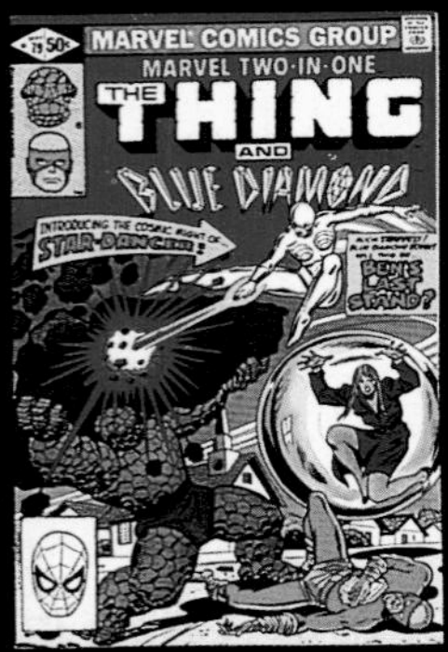
MARVEL COMICS GROUP
MARVEL TWO-IN-ONE
THE THING AND BLUE DIAMOND
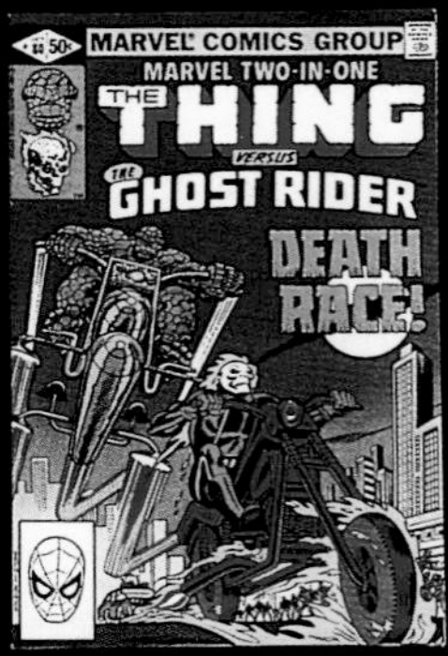
MARVEL COMICS GROUP
MARVEL TWO-IN-ONE
THE THING VERSUS GHOST RIDER
DEATH RACE!
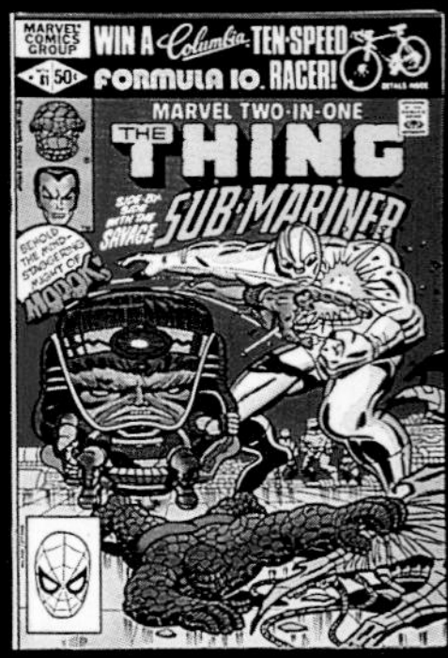
WIN A Columbia TEN-SPEED FORMULA 10. RACER!
MARVEL TWO-IN-ONE
THE THING AND SUB-MARINER
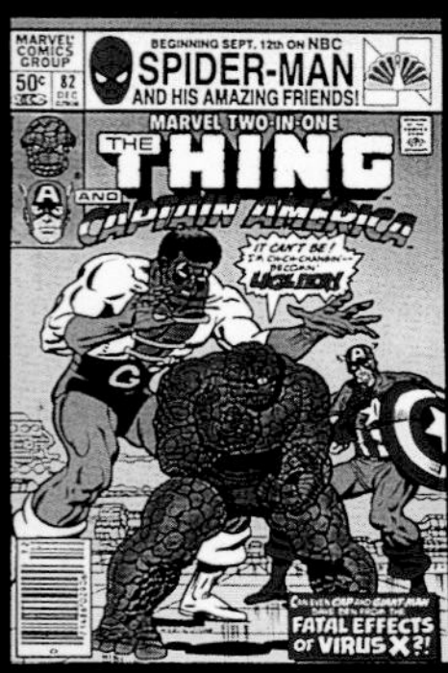
SPIDER-MAN AND HIS AMAZING FRIENDS!
MARVEL TWO-IN-ONE
THE THING AND CAPTAIN AMERICA
FATAL EFFECTS OF VIRUS X?!
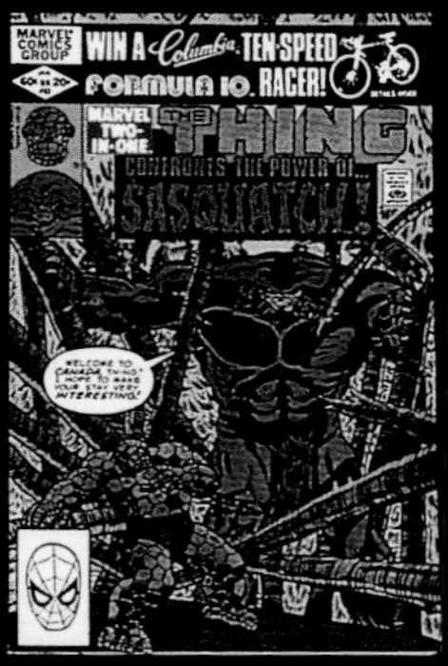
WIN A Columbia TEN-SPEED FORMULA 10. RACER!
THE THING
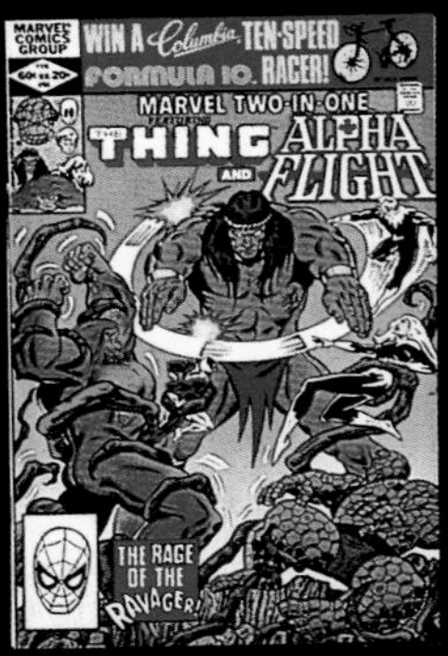
WIN A Columbia TEN-SPEED FORMULA 10. RACER!
MARVEL TWO-IN-ONE
THING AND ALPHA FLIGHT
THE RAGE OF THE RAVAGER!
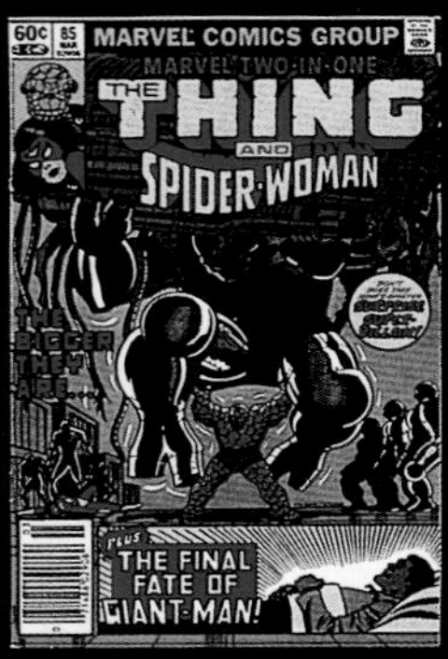
MARVEL COMICS GROUP
MARVEL TWO-IN-ONE
THE THING AND SPIDER-WOMAN
THE FINAL FATE OF GIANT-MAN!
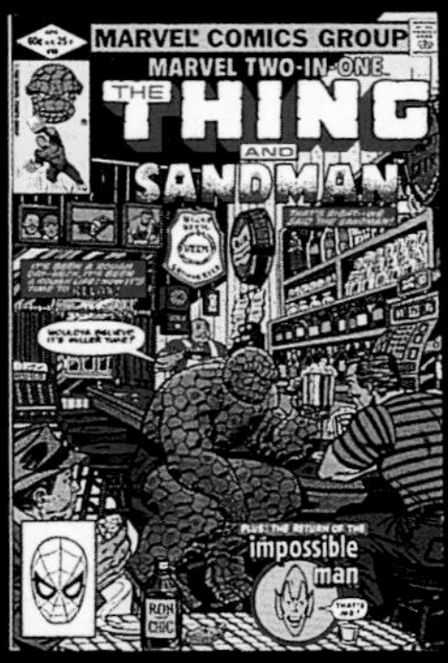
MARVEL COMICS GROUP
MARVEL TWO-IN-ONE
THE THING AND SANDMAN
impossible man
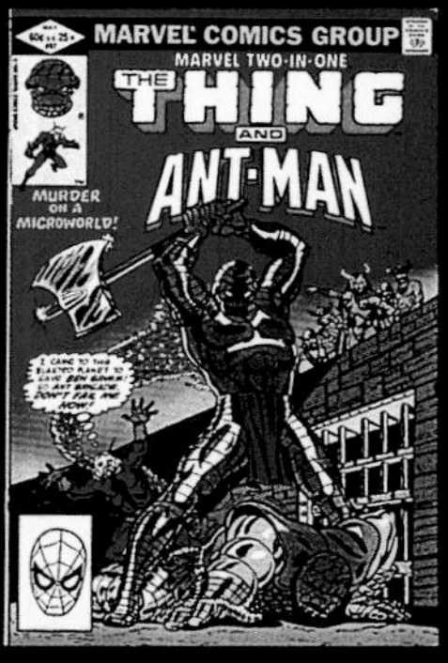
MARVEL COMICS GROUP
MARVEL TWO-IN-ONE
THE THING AND ANT-MAN
MURDER ON A MICROWORLD!
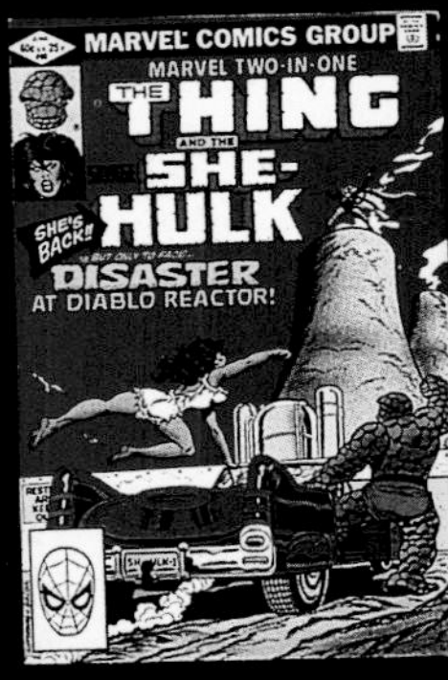
MARVEL COMICS GROUP
MARVEL TWO-IN-ONE
THE THING AND SHE-HULK
DISASTER AT DIABLO REACTOR!
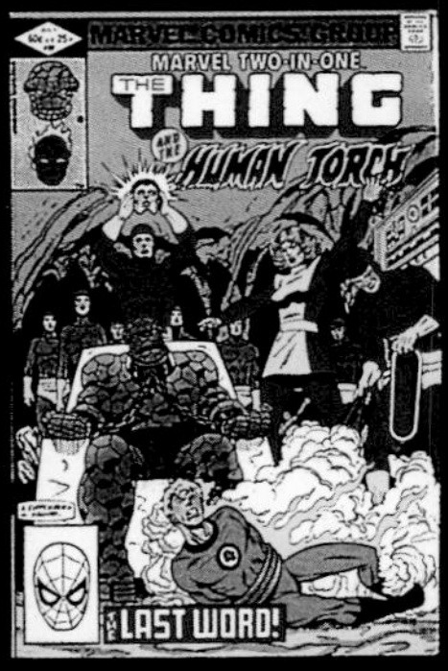
MARVEL COMICS GROUP
MARVEL TWO-IN-ONE
THE THING AND HUMAN TORCH
LAST WORD!
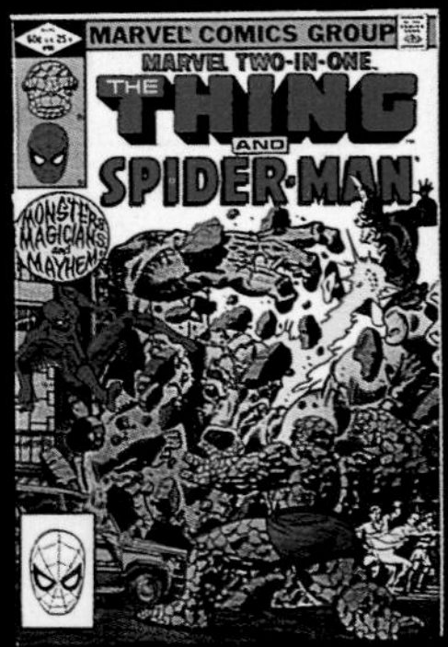
MARVEL COMICS GROUP
MARVEL TWO-IN-ONE
THE THING AND SPIDER-MAN
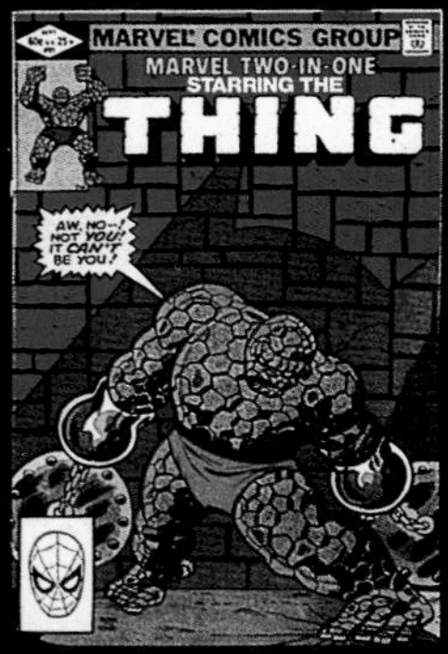
MARVEL COMICS GROUP
MARVEL TWO-IN-ONE
STARRING THE THING
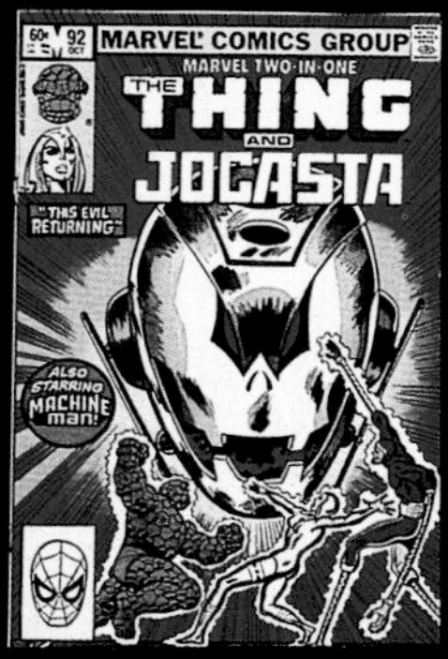
MARVEL COMICS GROUP
MARVEL TWO-IN-ONE
THE THING AND JOCASTA
MACHINE MAN
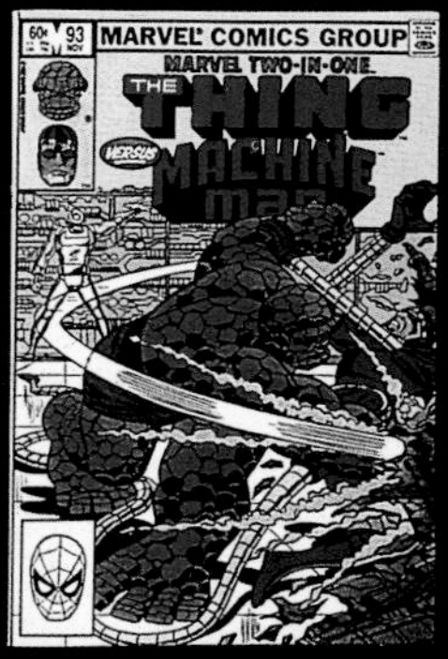
MARVEL COMICS GROUP
MARVEL TWO-IN-ONE
THE THING
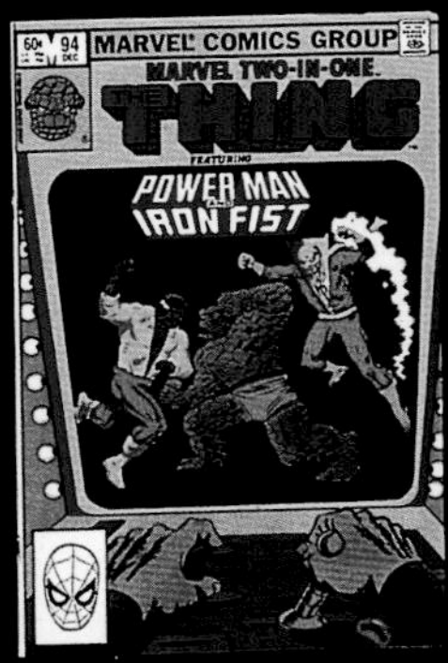
MARVEL COMICS GROUP
MARVEL TWO-IN-ONE
THE THING
POWER MAN IRON FIST
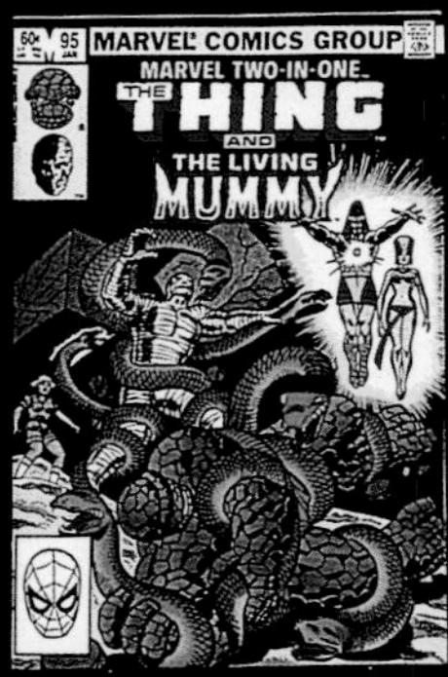
MARVEL COMICS GROUP
MARVEL TWO-IN-ONE
THE THING AND THE LIVING MUMMY
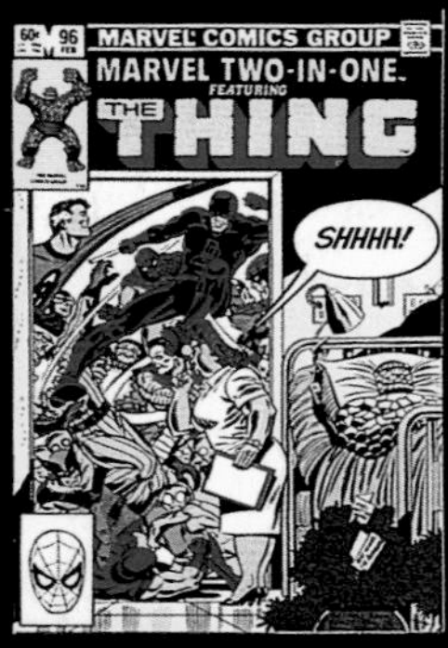
MARVEL COMICS GROUP
MARVEL TWO-IN-ONE
THE THING
SHHHH!
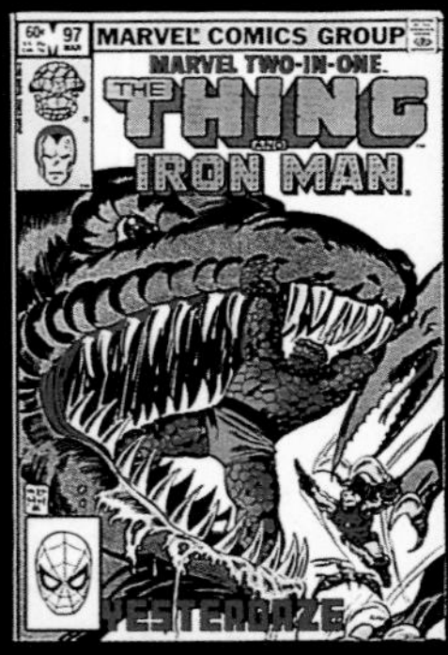
MARVEL COMICS GROUP
MARVEL TWO-IN-ONE
THE THING AND IRON MAN
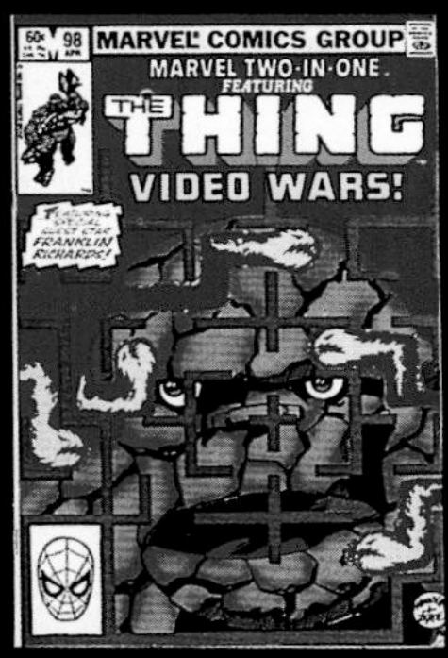
MARVEL COMICS GROUP
MARVEL TWO-IN-ONE
THE THING
VIDEO WARS!
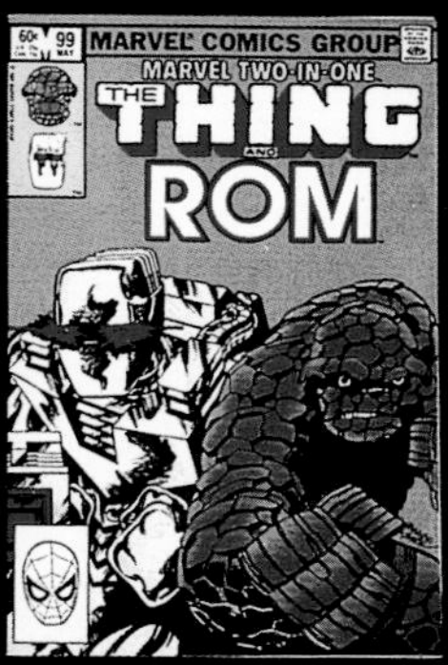
MARVEL COMICS GROUP
MARVEL TWO-IN-ONE
THE THING AND ROM
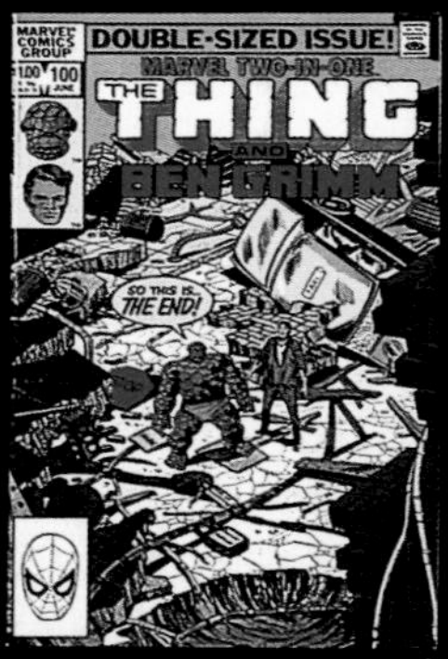
DOUBLE-SIZED ISSUE!
MARVEL TWO-IN-ONE
THE THING
THE END!
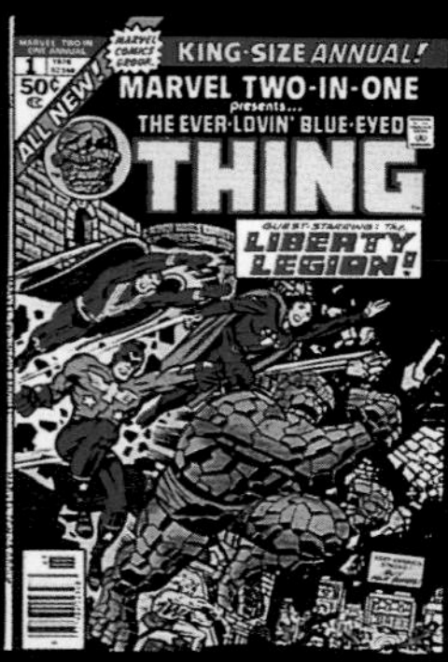
KING-SIZE ANNUAL!
MARVEL TWO-IN-ONE
THE EVER-LOVIN' BLUE-EYED THING
LIBERTY LEGION!
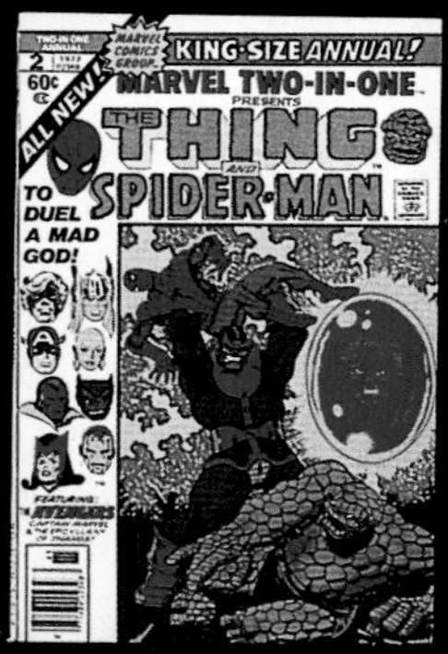
KING-SIZE ANNUAL!
MARVEL TWO-IN-ONE
THE THING AND SPIDER-MAN
TO DUEL A MAD GOD!
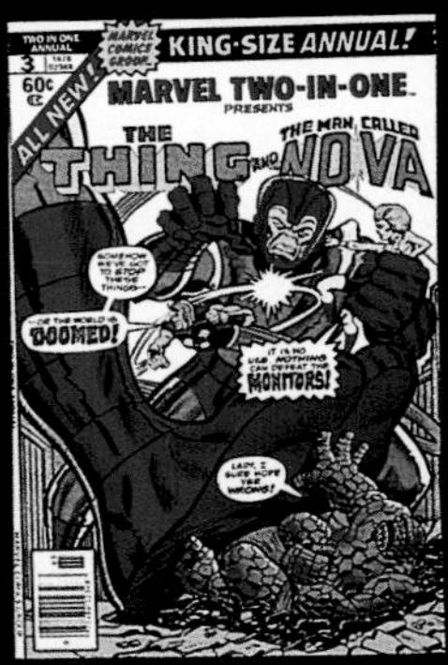
KING-SIZE ANNUAL!
MARVEL TWO-IN-ONE
THE THING AND THE MAN CALLED NOVA
DOOMED!
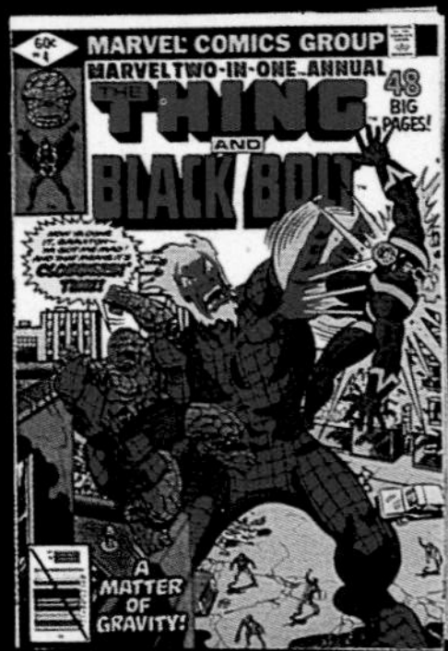
MARVEL COMICS GROUP
MARVEL TWO-IN-ONE ANNUAL
THING AND BLACK BOLT
A MATTER OF GRAVITY!
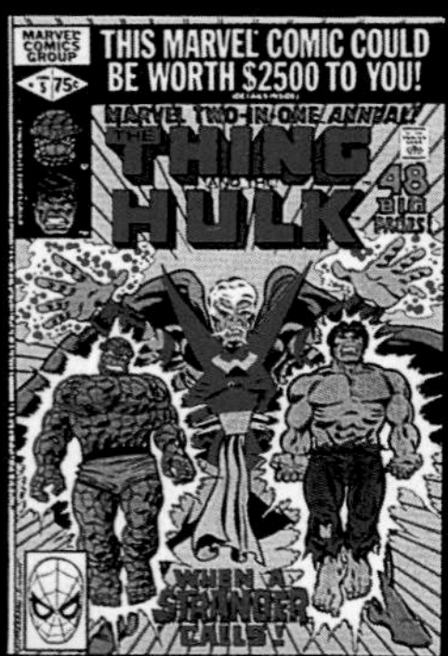
THIS MARVEL COMIC COULD BE WORTH $2500 TO YOU!
THING AND HULK
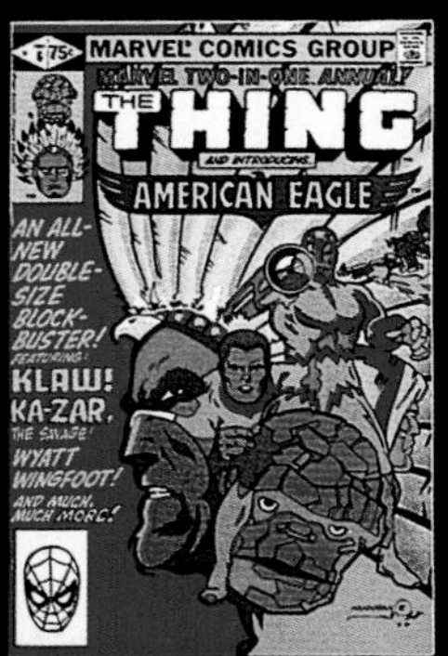
MARVEL COMICS GROUP
THE THING AND INTRODUCING AMERICAN EAGLE
AN ALL-NEW DOUBLE-SIZE BLOCK-BUSTER!
KLAW! KA-ZAR
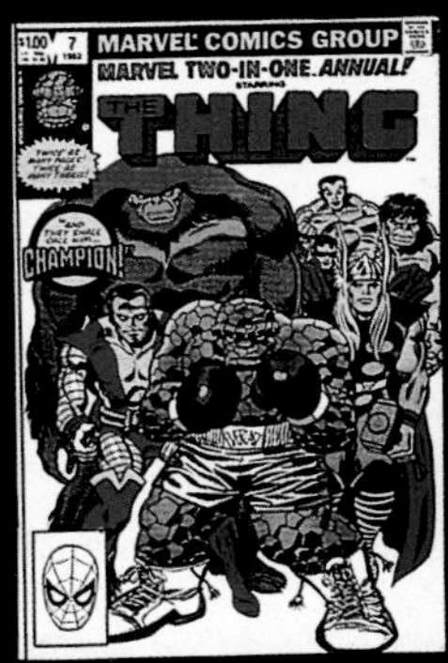
MARVEL COMICS GROUP
MARVEL TWO-IN-ONE ANNUAL!
THE THING
CHAMPION!

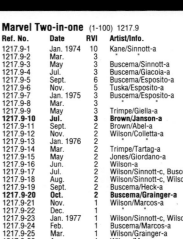

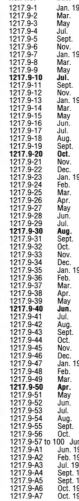

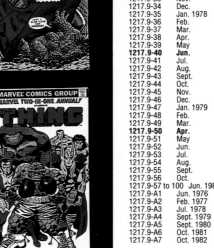

Marvel Two-in-one (1-100) 1217.9

Ref. No.	Date	RVI	Artist/Info.
1217.9-1	Jan. 1974	10	Kane/Sinnott-a
1217.9-2	Mar.	3	" "
1217.9-3	May	3	Buscema/Sinnott-a
1217.9-4	Jul.	3	Buscema/Giacoia-a
1217.9-5	Sept.	6	Buscema/Esposito-a
1217.9-6	Nov.	5	Tuska/Esposito-a
1217.9-7	Jan. 1975	3	Buscema/Esposito-a
1217.9-8	Mar.	3	" "
1217.9-9	May	3	Trimpe/Giella-a
1217.9-10	**Jul.**	**3**	**Brown/Janson-a**
1217.9-11	Sept.	2	Brown/Abel-a
1217.9-12	Nov.	2	Wilson/Colletta-a
1217.9-13	Jan. 1976	2	" "
1217.9-14	Mar.	2	Trimpe/Tartag-a
1217.9-15	May	2	Jones/Giordano-a
1217.9-16	Jun.	2	Wilson-a
1217.9-17	Jul.	2	Wilson/Sinnott-c, Buscema/Esposito-a
1217.9-18	Aug.	2	Wilson/Sinnott-c, Wilson/Mooney-a
1217.9-19	Sept.	2	Buscema/Heck-a
1217.9-20	**Oct.**	**2**	**Buscema/Grainger-a**
1217.9-21	Nov.	1	Wilson/Marcos-a
1217.9-22	Dec.	1	" "
1217.9-23	Jan. 1977	1	Wilson/Sinnott-c, Wilson/Marcos-a
1217.9-24	Feb.	1	Buscema/Marcos-a
1217.9-25	Mar.	1	Wilson/Grainger-a
1217.9-26	Apr.	1	Wilson/Marcos-a
1217.9-27	May	1	" "
1217.9-28	Jun.	1	Kane/Marcos, Wilson/Tartag-a
1217.9-29	Jul.	1	Wilson/Grainger-a
1217.9-30	**Aug.**	**1**	**Buckler/Milgrom-c, Buscema/Marcos-a**
1217.9-31	Sept.	1	Wilson/Grainger-a
1217.9-32	Oct.	1	Wilson/Marcos-a
1217.9-33	Nov.	1	" "
1217.9-34	Dec.	1	" "
1217.9-35	Jan. 1978	1	Chan-c/a
1217.9-36	Feb.	1	"
1217.9-37	Mar.	1	Wilson/Sinnott-c, Wilson/Marcos-a
1217.9-38	Apr.	1	Wilson/Mooney-a
1217.9-39	May	1	Marcos-c/a, Wilson-a
1217.9-40	**Jun.**	**1**	**Wilson/Marcos-c/a**
1217.9-41	Jul.	1	" "
1217.9-42	Aug.	1	Austin-c
1217.9-43	Sept.	1	Byrne-c/a
1217.9-44	Oct.	1	Kay-a
1217.9-45	Nov.	1	Buscema-a
1217.9-46	Dec.	1	(Hulk)
1217.9-47	Jan. 1979	1	(Yancy Street Gang)
1217.9-48	Feb.	1	(Jack of Hearts)
1217.9-49	Mar.	1	Day-a (Dr. Strange)
1217.9-50	**Apr.**	**1**	**Perez-c, Byrne-a**
1217.9-51	May	2	Perez-c, Miller-a
1217.9-52	Jun.	1	Perez-c
1217.9-53	Jul.	1	Byrne-c/a
1217.9-54	Aug.	1	Austin/Perez-c, Byrne-a
1217.9-55	Sept.	1	Perez-c, Byrne-a
1217.9-56	Oct.	1	Byrne/Austin-c, Perez-a
1217.9-57 to 100	Jun. 1983, (#100)	1	
1217.9-A1	Jun. 1976	1	Starlin-c, Roussos-a
1217.9-A2	Feb. 1977	5	Starlin-c/a
1217.9-A3	Jul. 1978	1	
1217.9-A4	Sept. 1979	1	
1217.9-A5	Sept. 1980	1	
1217.9-A6	Oct. 1981	1	Simonson-c
1217.9-A7	Oct. 1982	1	

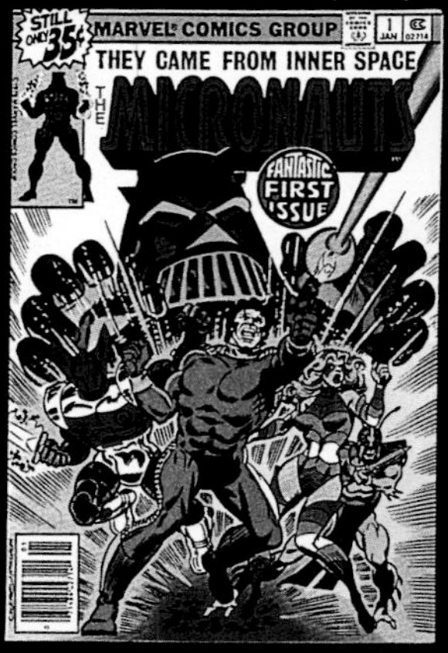
STILL ONLY 35¢
MARVEL COMICS GROUP
THEY CAME FROM INNER SPACE
THE MICRONAUTS
FANTASTIC FIRST ISSUE

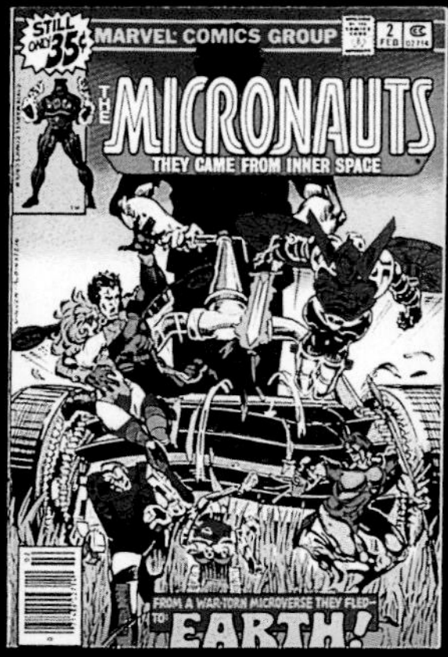
STILL ONLY 35¢
MARVEL COMICS GROUP
THE MICRONAUTS
THEY CAME FROM INNER SPACE
FROM A WAR-TORN MICROVERSE THEY FLED— TO EARTH!

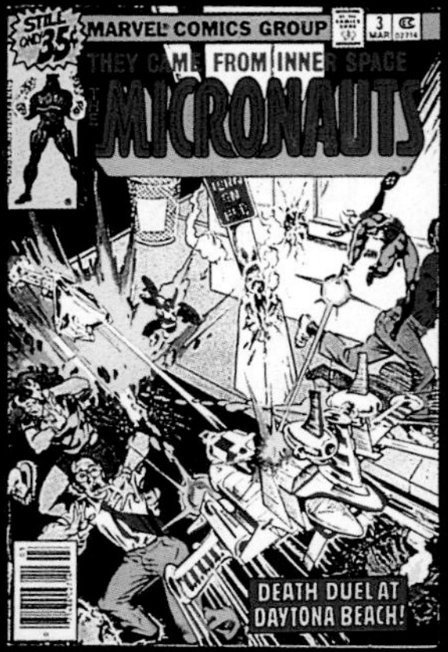
STILL ONLY 35¢
MARVEL COMICS GROUP
THEY CAME FROM INNER SPACE
THE MICRONAUTS
DEATH DUEL AT DAYTONA BEACH!

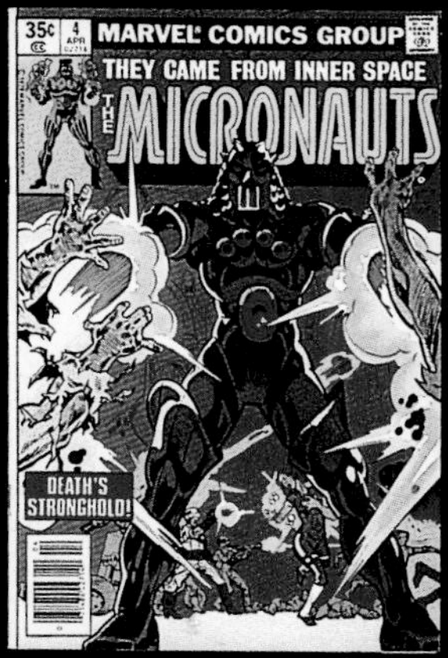
35¢
MARVEL COMICS GROUP
THEY CAME FROM INNER SPACE
THE MICRONAUTS
DEATH'S STRONGHOLD!

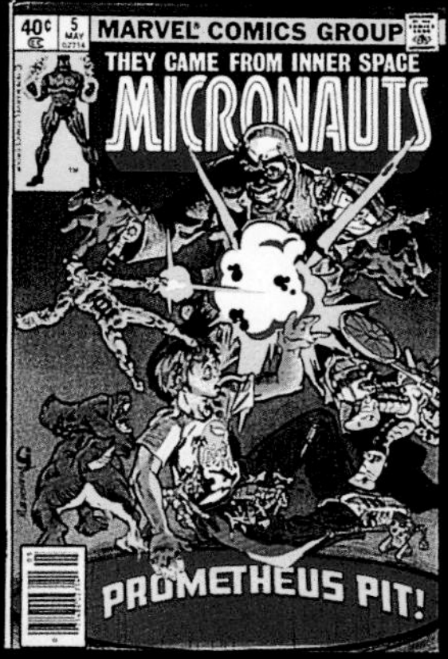
40¢
MARVEL COMICS GROUP
THEY CAME FROM INNER SPACE
MICRONAUTS
PROMETHEUS PIT!

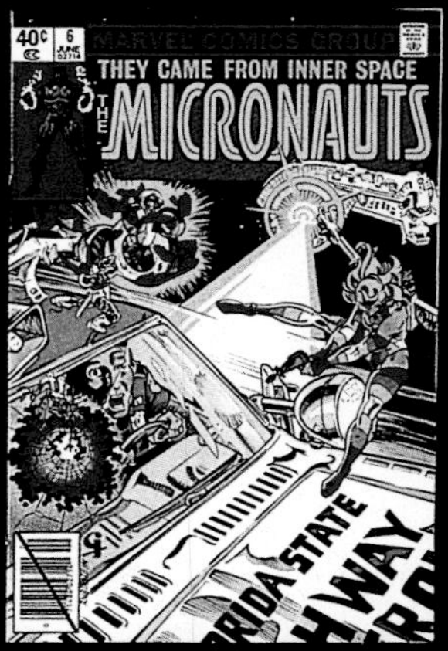
40¢
MARVEL COMICS GROUP
THEY CAME FROM INNER SPACE
THE MICRONAUTS

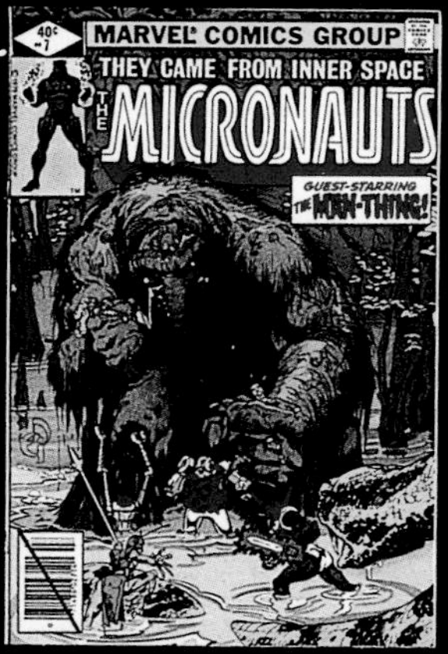
MARVEL COMICS GROUP
THEY CAME FROM INNER SPACE
THE MICRONAUTS
GUEST-STARRING THE MAN-THING!

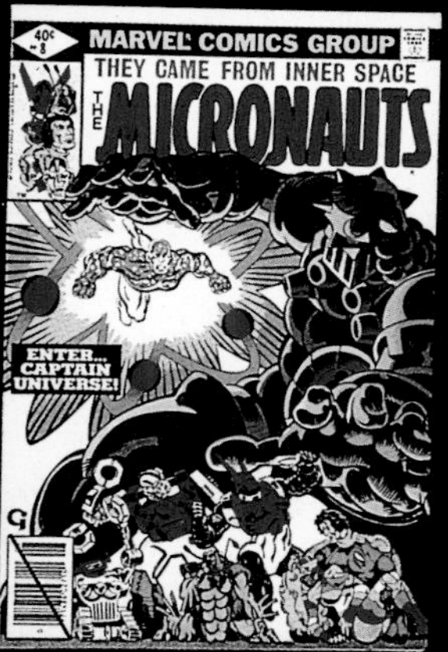
MARVEL COMICS GROUP
THEY CAME FROM INNER SPACE
MICRONAUTS
ENTER... CAPTAIN UNIVERSE!

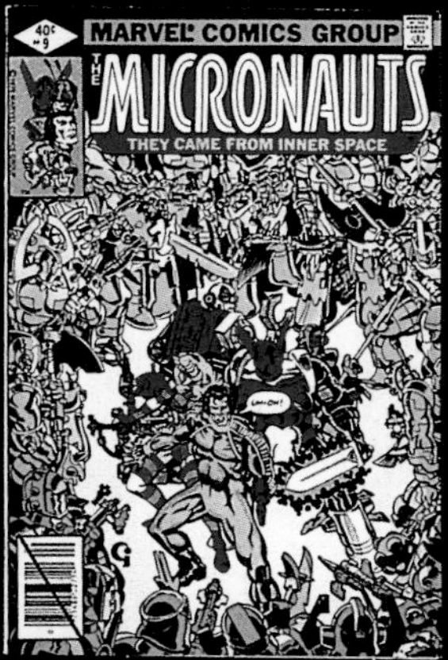
MARVEL COMICS GROUP
THE MICRONAUTS
THEY CAME FROM INNER SPACE

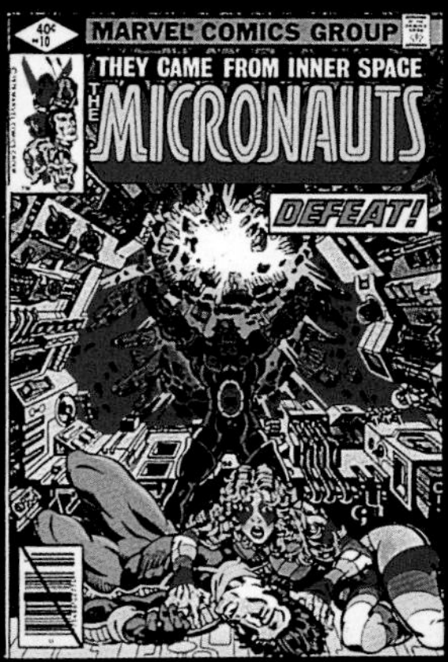
MARVEL COMICS GROUP
THEY CAME FROM INNER SPACE
THE MICRONAUTS
DEFEAT!

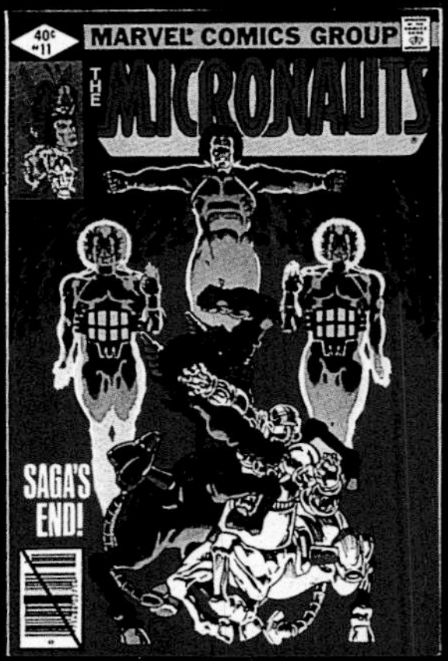
MARVEL COMICS GROUP
THE MICRONAUTS
SAGA'S END!

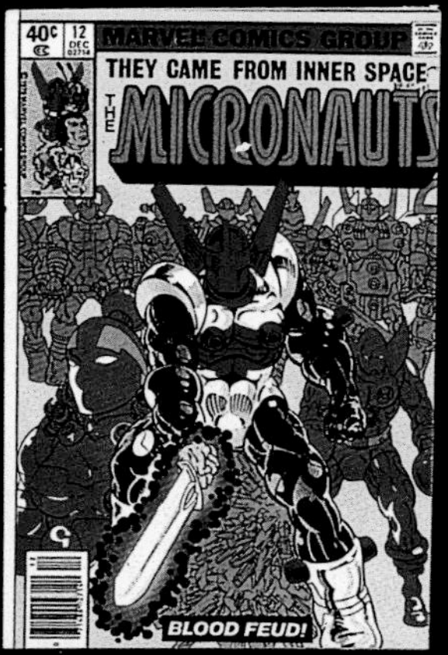
40¢
MARVEL COMICS GROUP
THEY CAME FROM INNER SPACE
THE MICRONAUTS
BLOOD FEUD!

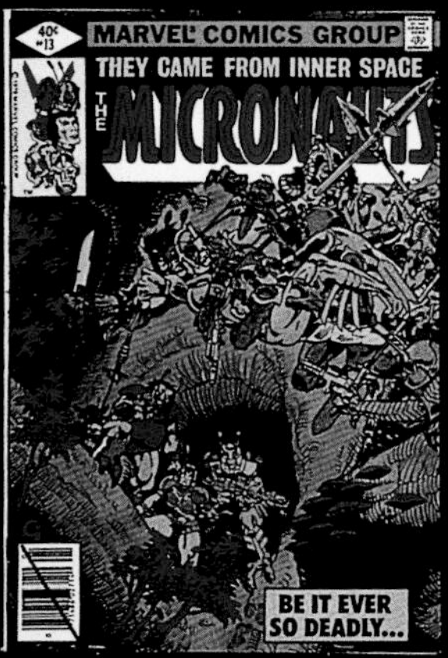
MARVEL COMICS GROUP
THEY CAME FROM INNER SPACE
THE MICRONAUTS
BE IT EVER SO DEADLY...

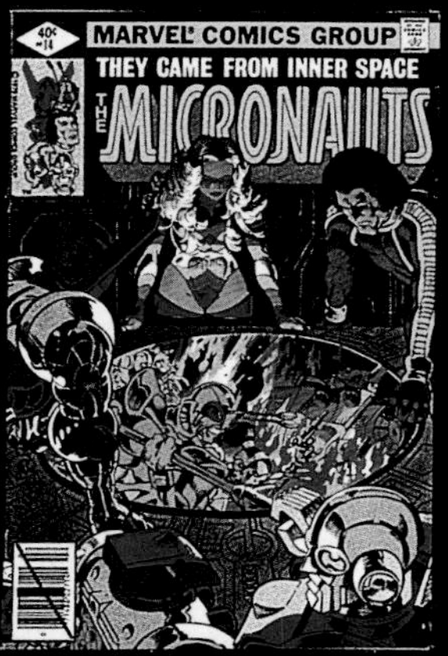
MARVEL COMICS GROUP
THEY CAME FROM INNER SPACE
THE MICRONAUTS

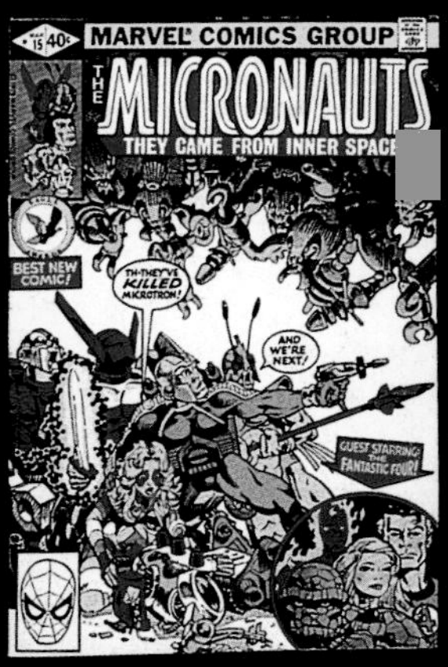
40¢
MARVEL COMICS GROUP
THE MICRONAUTS
THEY CAME FROM INNER SPACE
BEST NEW COMIC!
GUEST STARRING FANTASTIC FOUR

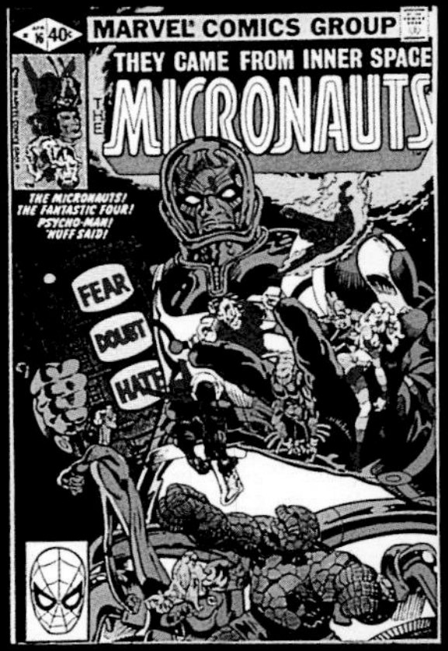
MARVEL COMICS GROUP
THEY CAME FROM INNER SPACE
THE MICRONAUTS
FEAR
DOUBT
HATE

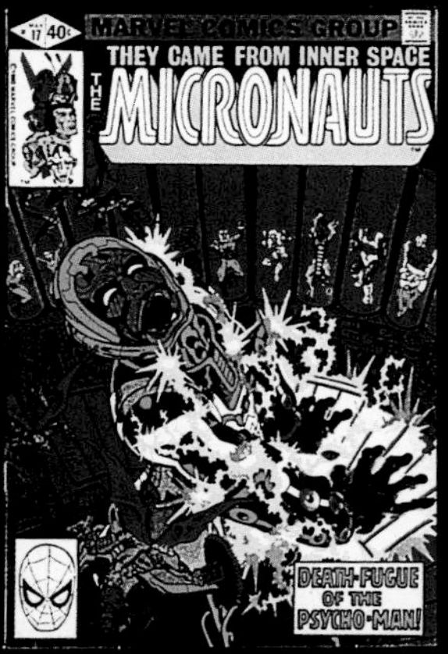
40¢
MARVEL COMICS GROUP
THEY CAME FROM INNER SPACE
THE MICRONAUTS
DEATH-FUGUE OF THE PSYCHO-MAN!

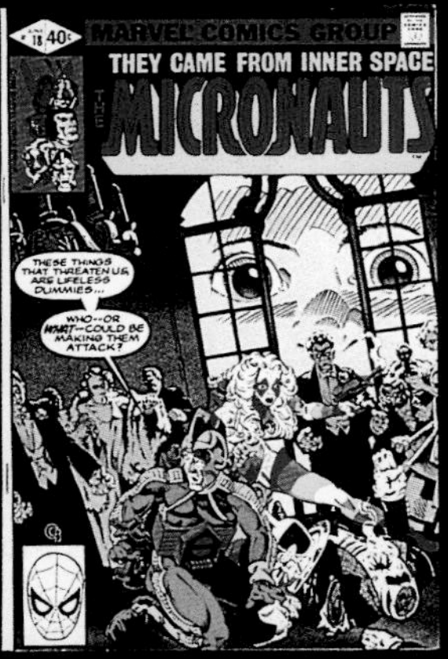
40¢
MARVEL COMICS GROUP
THEY CAME FROM INNER SPACE
THE MICRONAUTS

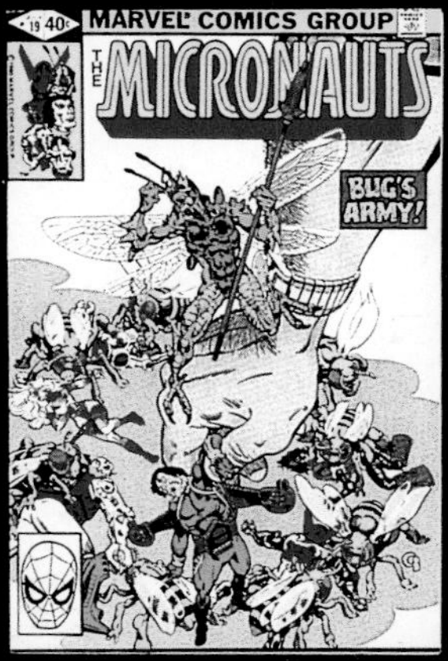
40¢
MARVEL COMICS GROUP
THE MICRONAUTS
BUG'S ARMY!

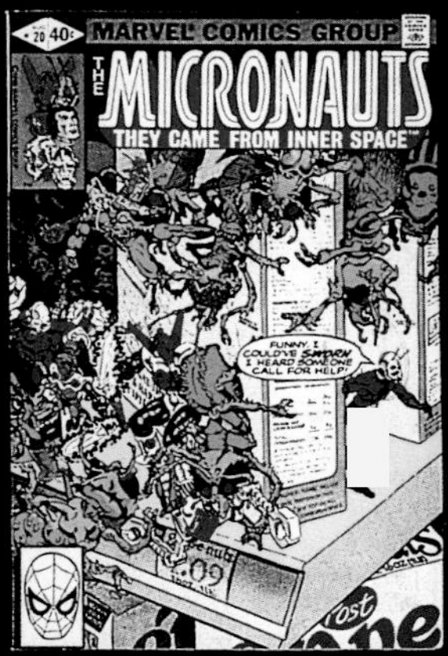
40¢
MARVEL COMICS GROUP
THE MICRONAUTS
THEY CAME FROM INNER SPACE

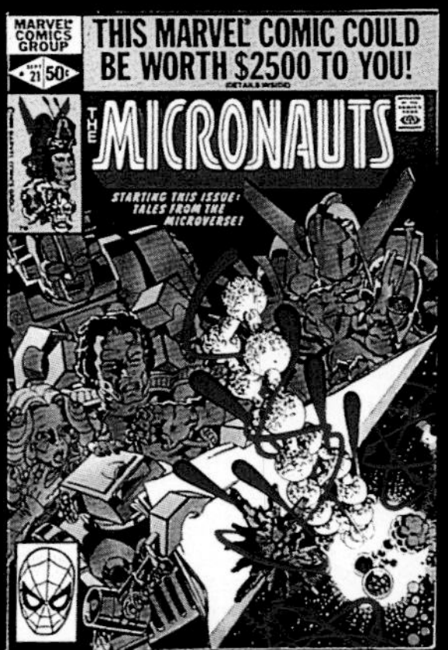
MARVEL COMICS GROUP
THIS MARVEL COMIC COULD BE WORTH $2500 TO YOU!
50¢
THE MICRONAUTS

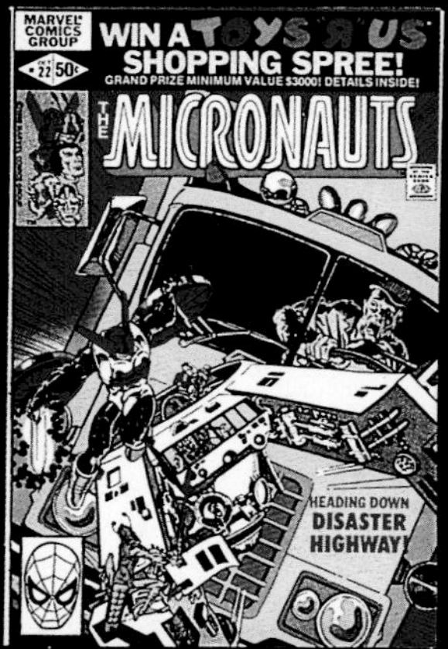
MARVEL COMICS GROUP
WIN A TOYS R US SHOPPING SPREE!
50¢
THE MICRONAUTS
HEADING DOWN DISASTER HIGHWAY!

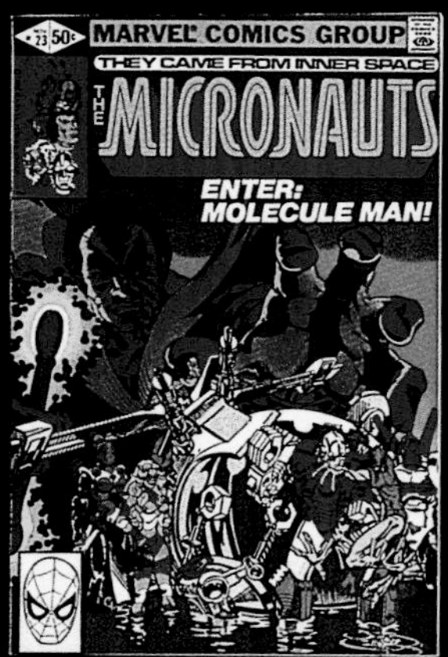
50¢
MARVEL COMICS GROUP
THEY CAME FROM INNER SPACE
THE MICRONAUTS
ENTER: MOLECULE MAN!

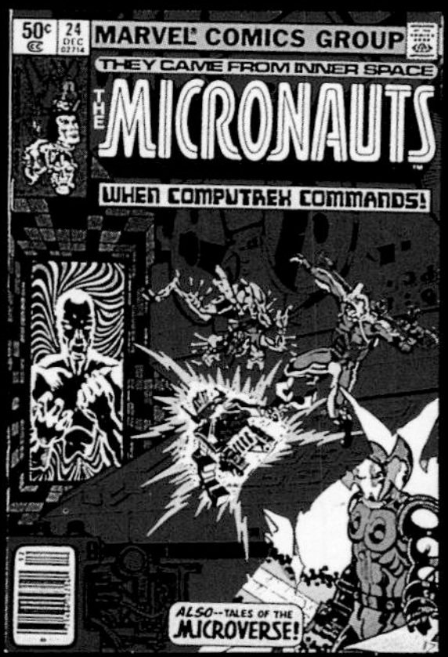
50¢
MARVEL COMICS GROUP
THEY CAME FROM INNER SPACE
THE MICRONAUTS
WHEN COMPUTREX COMMANDS!
ALSO—TALES OF THE MICROVERSE!

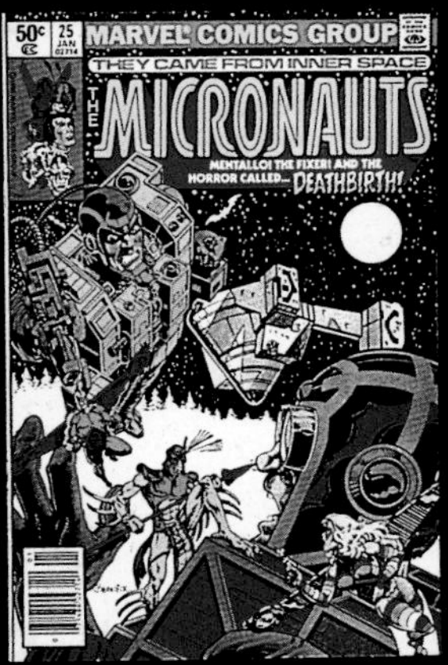
50¢
MARVEL COMICS GROUP
THEY CAME FROM INNER SPACE
THE MICRONAUTS
DEATHBIRTH!

1255.6 Micronauts (26-50)

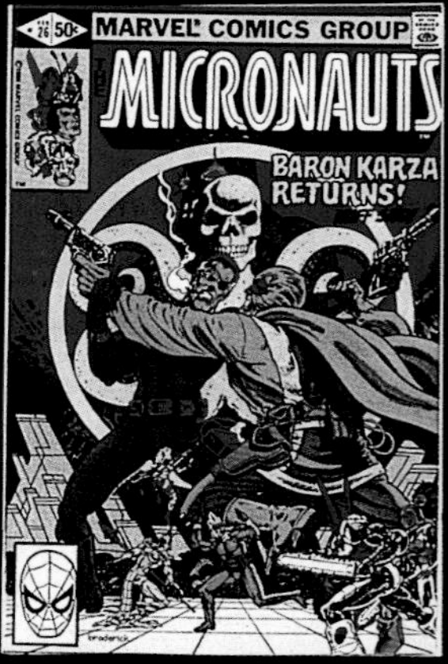
MARVEL COMICS GROUP
MICRONAUTS
BARON KARZA RETURNS!

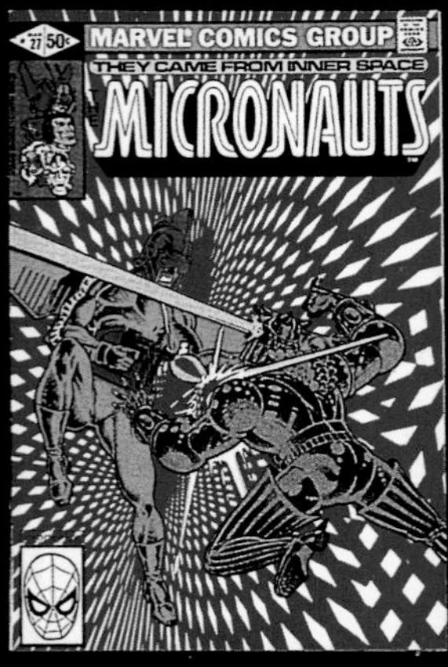
MARVEL COMICS GROUP
THEY CAME FROM INNER SPACE
MICRONAUTS

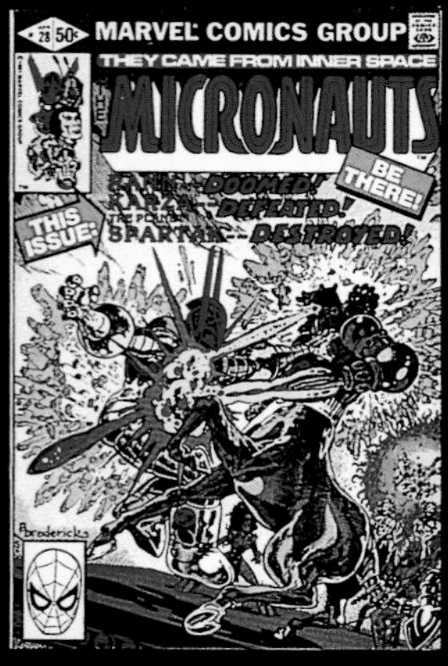
MARVEL COMICS GROUP
THEY CAME FROM INNER SPACE
MICRONAUTS

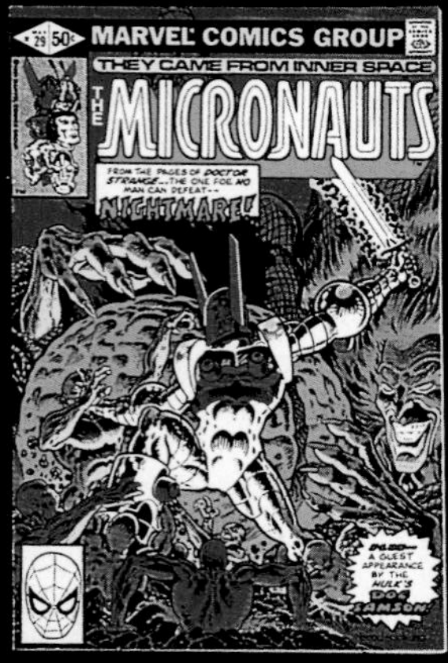
MARVEL COMICS GROUP
THEY CAME FROM INNER SPACE
MICRONAUTS

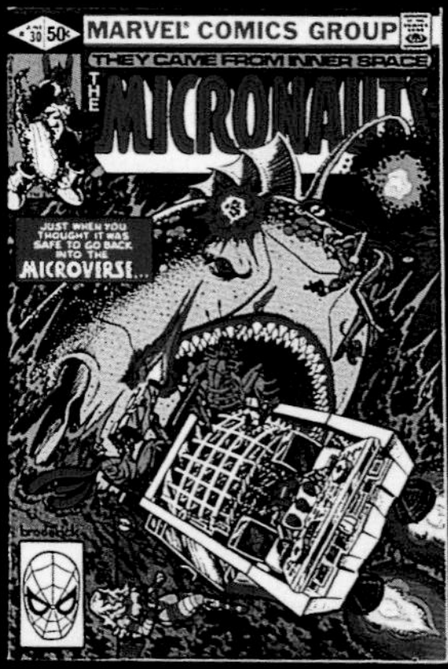
MARVEL COMICS GROUP
THEY CAME FROM INNER SPACE
MICRONAUTS
JUST WHEN YOU THOUGHT IT WAS SAFE TO GO BACK INTO THE MICROVERSE!

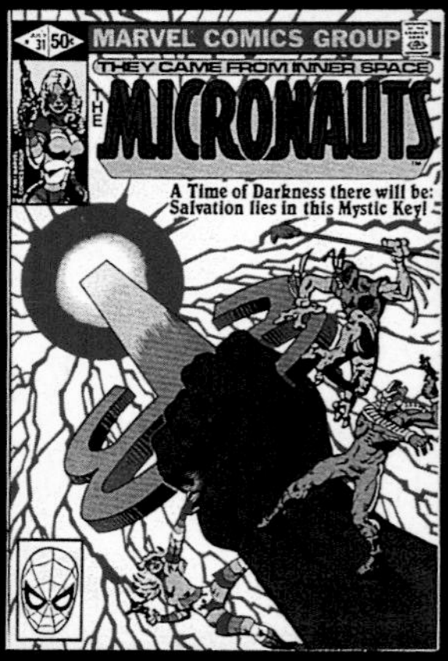
MARVEL COMICS GROUP
THEY CAME FROM INNER SPACE
MICRONAUTS
A Time of Darkness there will be: Salvation lies in this Mystic Key!

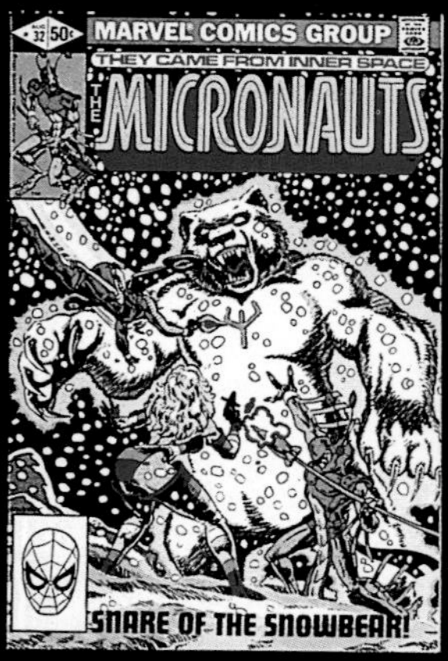
MARVEL COMICS GROUP
THEY CAME FROM INNER SPACE
MICRONAUTS
SNARE OF THE SNOWBEAR!

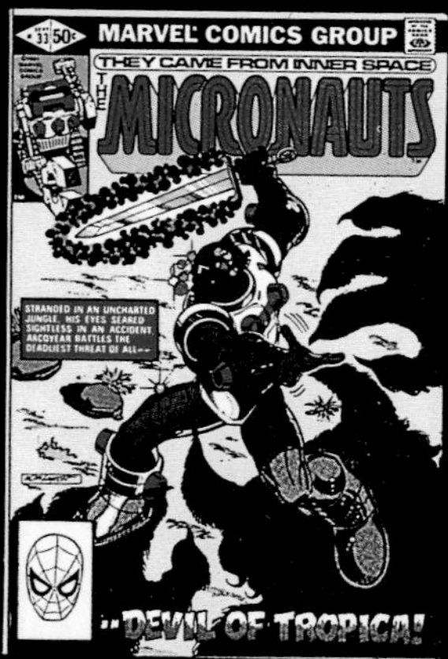
MARVEL COMICS GROUP
THEY CAME FROM INNER SPACE
MICRONAUTS
DEVIL OF TROPICA!

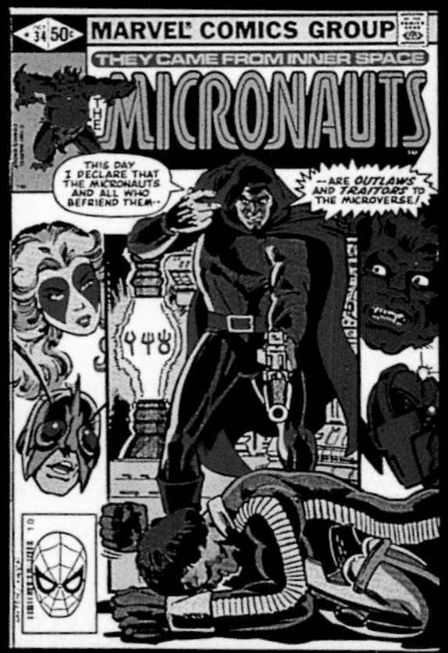
MARVEL COMICS GROUP
THEY CAME FROM INNER SPACE
MICRONAUTS

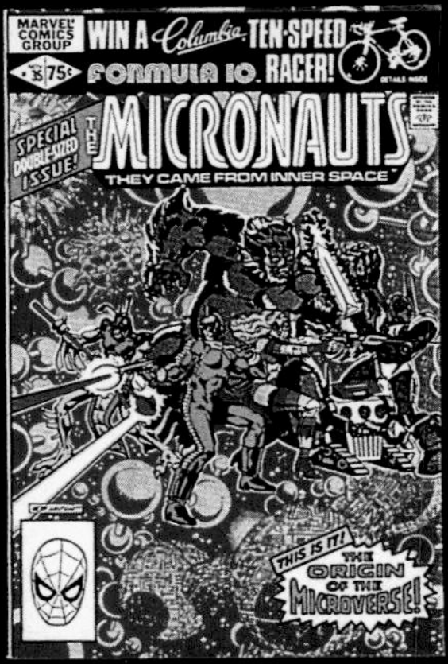
WIN A Columbia TEN-SPEED FORMULA 10. RACER!
MICRONAUTS
THEY CAME FROM INNER SPACE
THE ORIGIN OF THE MICROVERSE!

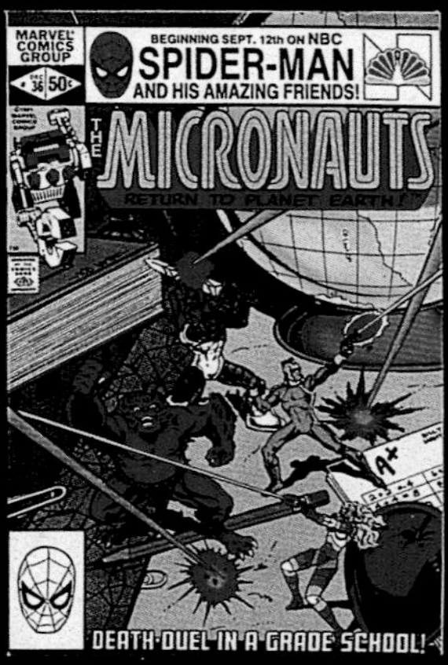
BEGINNING SEPT. 12th ON NBC
SPIDER-MAN AND HIS AMAZING FRIENDS!
MICRONAUTS
RETURN TO PLANET EARTH!
DEATH-DUEL IN A GRADE SCHOOL!

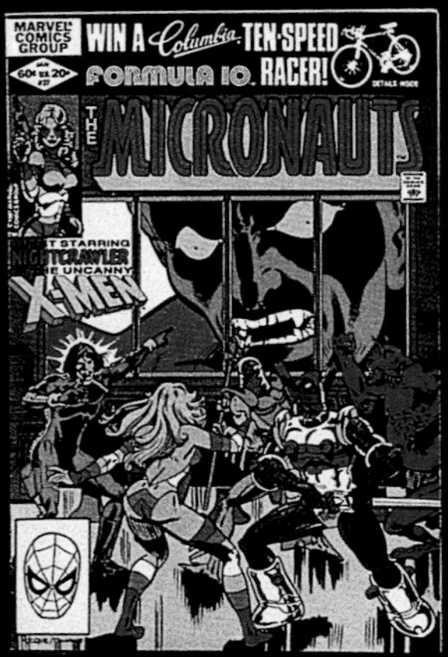
WIN A Columbia TEN-SPEED FORMULA 10. RACER!
MICRONAUTS
X-MEN

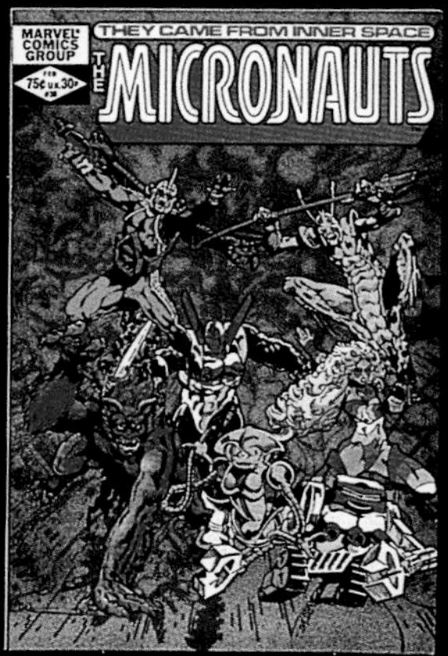
THEY CAME FROM INNER SPACE
MICRONAUTS

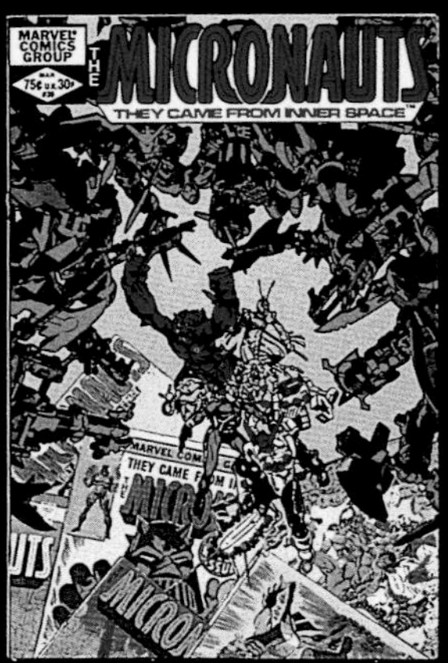
MICRONAUTS
THEY CAME FROM INNER SPACE

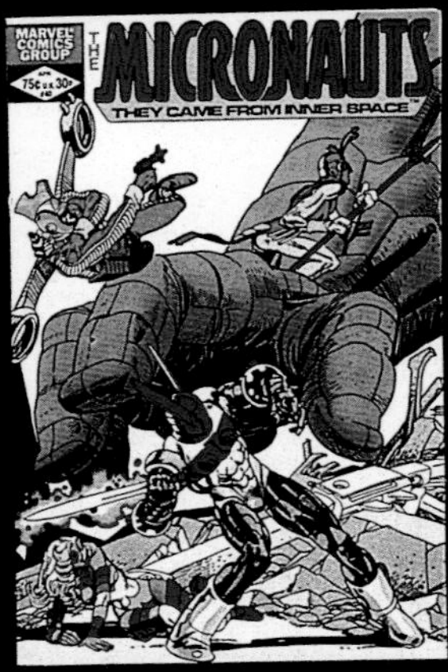
MICRONAUTS
THEY CAME FROM INNER SPACE

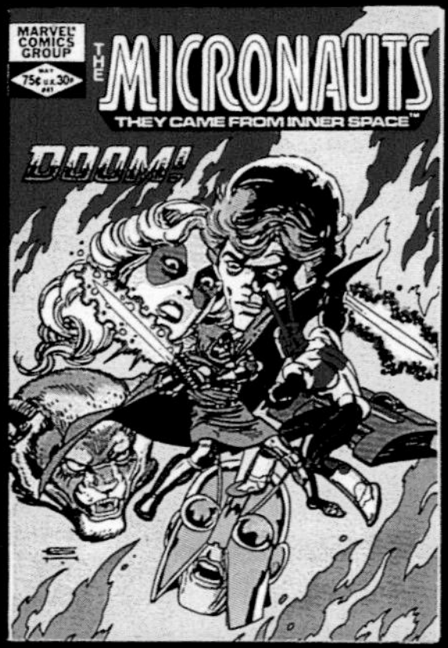
MICRONAUTS
THEY CAME FROM INNER SPACE
DOOM!

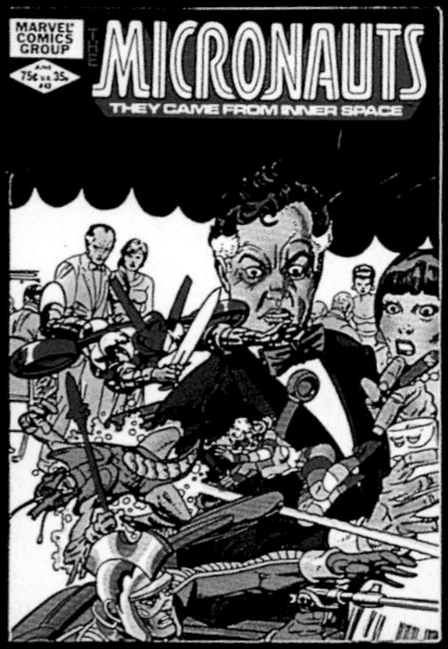
MICRONAUTS
THEY CAME FROM INNER SPACE

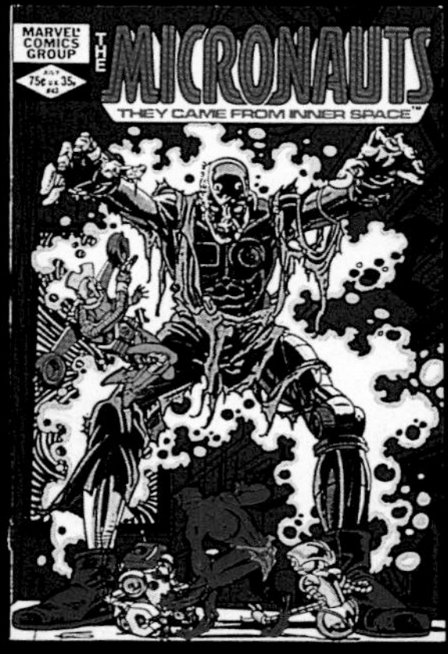
MICRONAUTS
THEY CAME FROM INNER SPACE

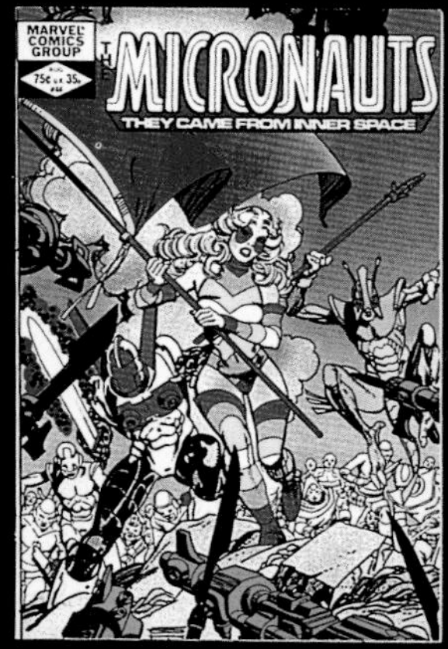
MICRONAUTS
THEY CAME FROM INNER SPACE

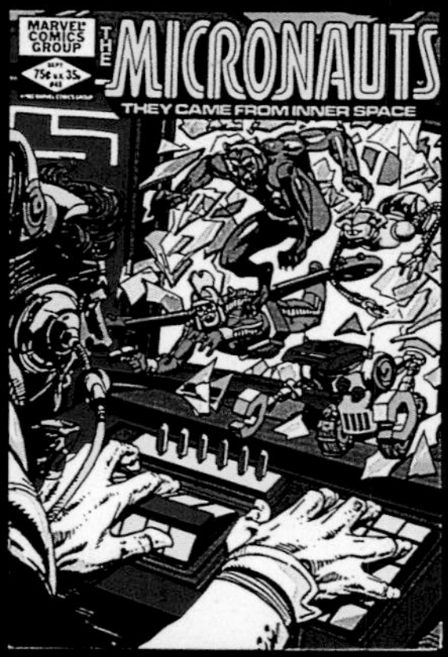
MICRONAUTS
THEY CAME FROM INNER SPACE

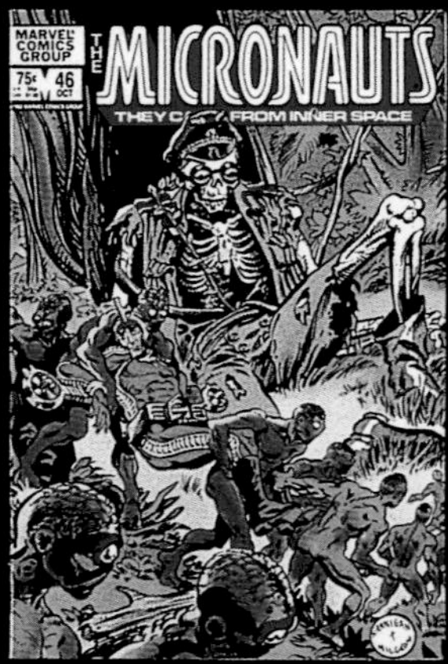
MICRONAUTS

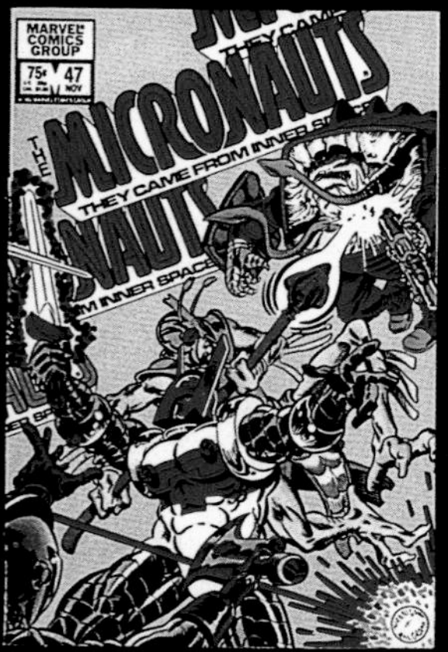
MICRONAUTS

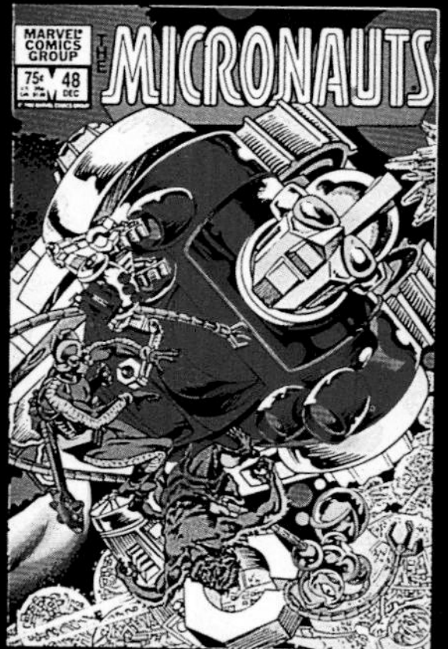
MICRONAUTS

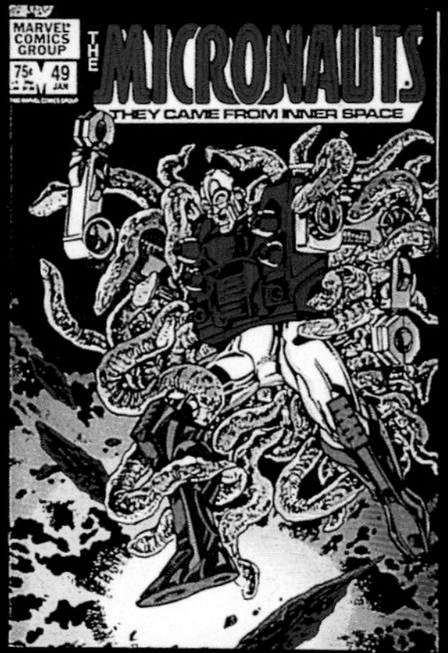
MICRONAUTS
THEY CAME FROM INNER SPACE

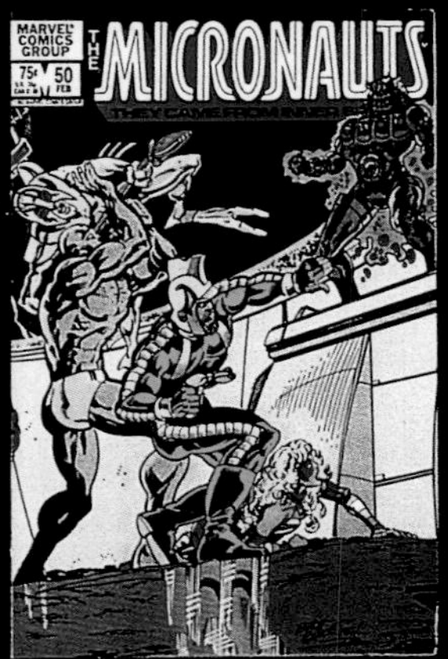
MICRONAUTS

1255.6 Micronauts (51-59; AN. 1-2; Sp. 1-5)

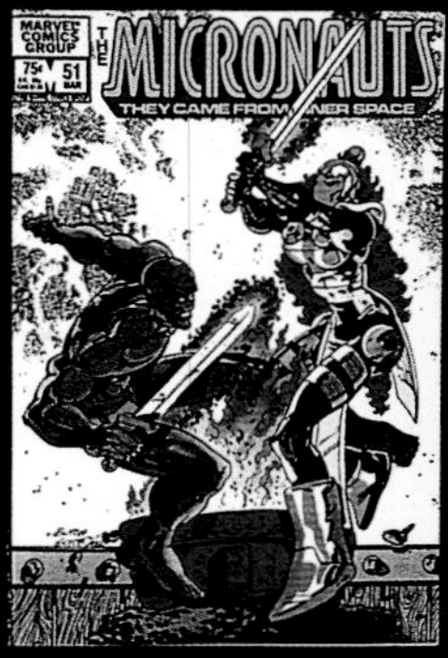
MARVEL COMICS GROUP
THE MICRONAUTS
THEY CAME FROM INNER SPACE
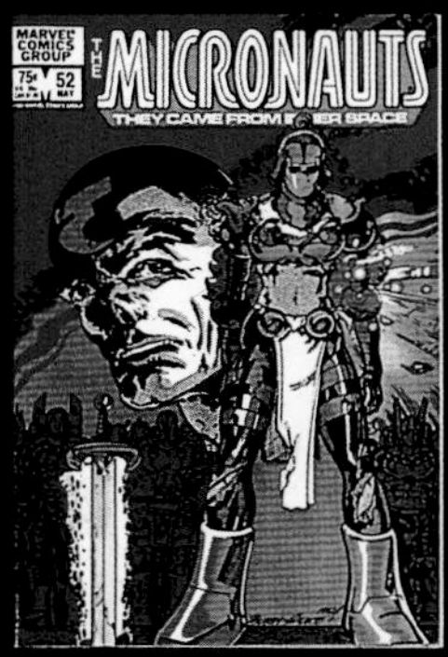
MARVEL COMICS GROUP
THE MICRONAUTS
THEY CAME FROM INNER SPACE
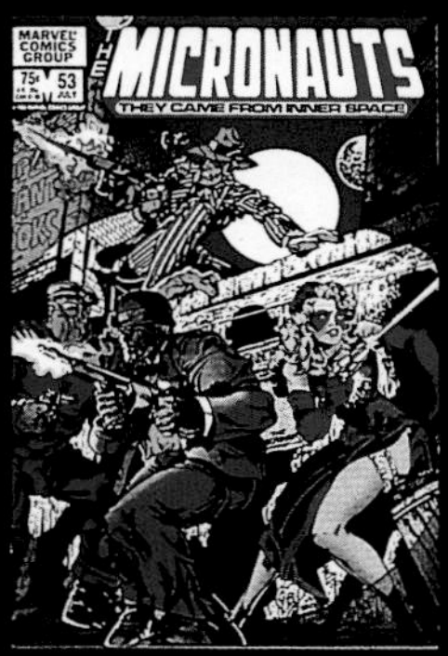
MARVEL COMICS GROUP
THE MICRONAUTS
THEY CAME FROM INNER SPACE
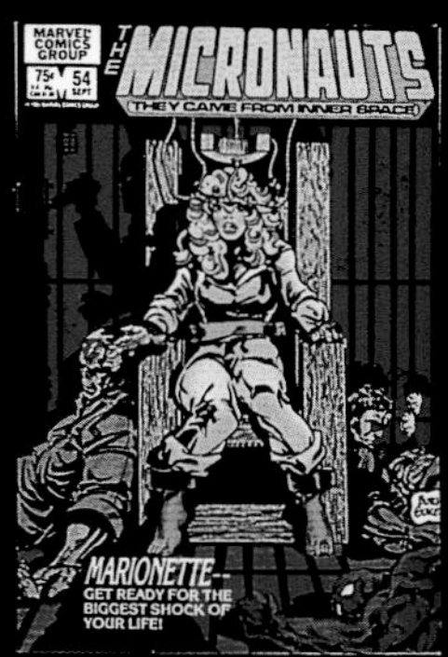
MARVEL COMICS GROUP
THE MICRONAUTS
THEY CAME FROM INNER SPACE
MARIONETTE—
GET READY FOR THE BIGGEST SHOCK OF YOUR LIFE!
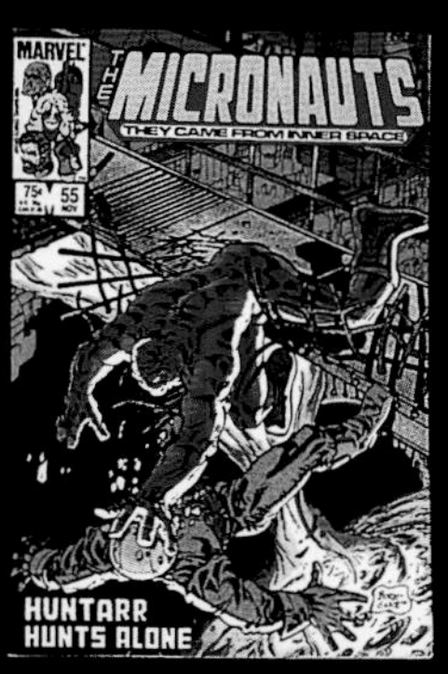
MARVEL
THE MICRONAUTS
THEY CAME FROM INNER SPACE
HUNTARR HUNTS ALONE
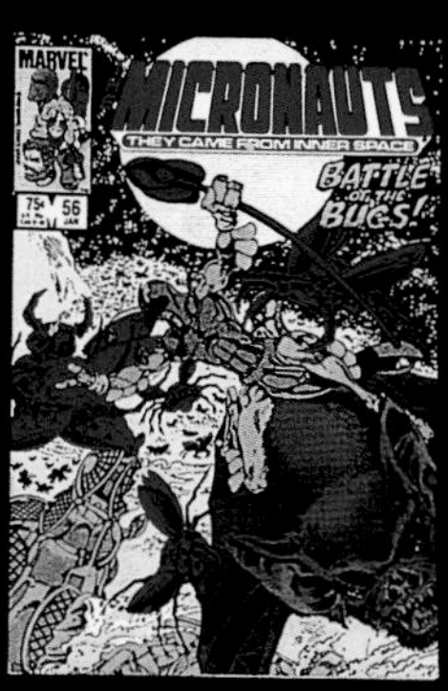
MARVEL
MICRONAUTS
THEY CAME FROM INNER SPACE
BATTLE OF THE BUGS!
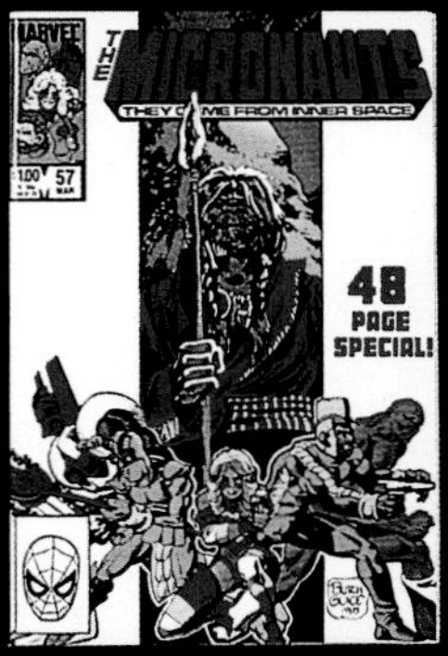
MARVEL
THE MICRONAUTS
THEY CAME FROM INNER SPACE
48 PAGE SPECIAL!
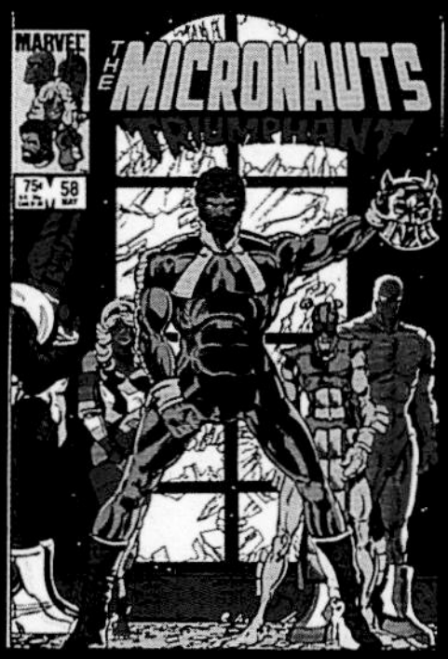
MARVEL
THE MICRONAUTS
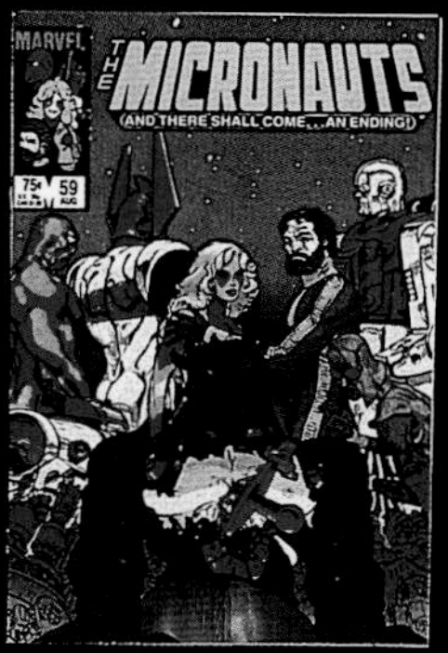
MARVEL
THE MICRONAUTS
(AND THERE SHALL COME ... AN ENDING!)
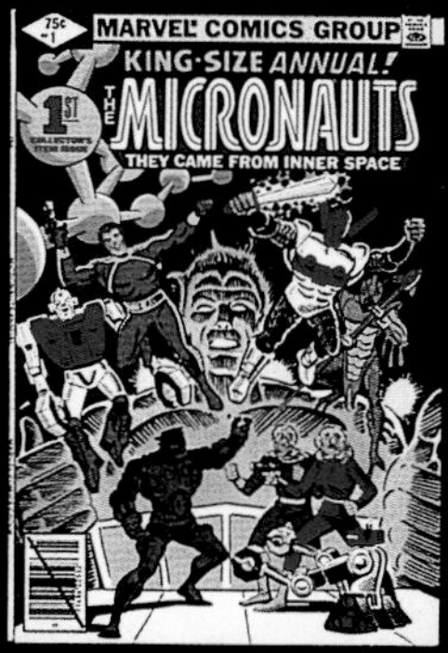
MARVEL COMICS GROUP
KING-SIZE ANNUAL!
THE MICRONAUTS
THEY CAME FROM INNER SPACE
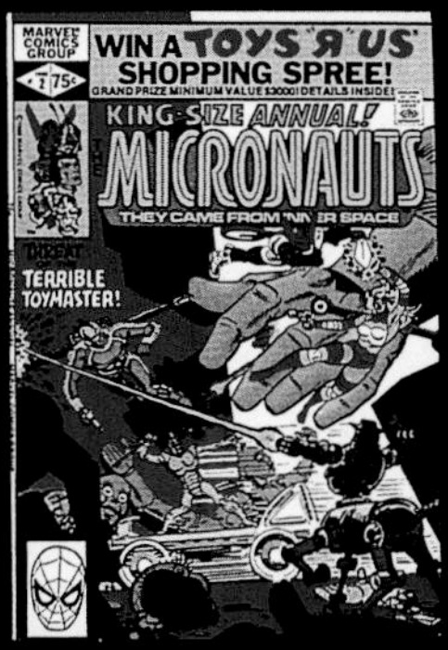
MARVEL COMICS GROUP
WIN A TOYS 'R US SHOPPING SPREE!
KING-SIZE ANNUAL!
MICRONAUTS
THEY CAME FROM INNER SPACE
TERRIBLE TOYMASTER!
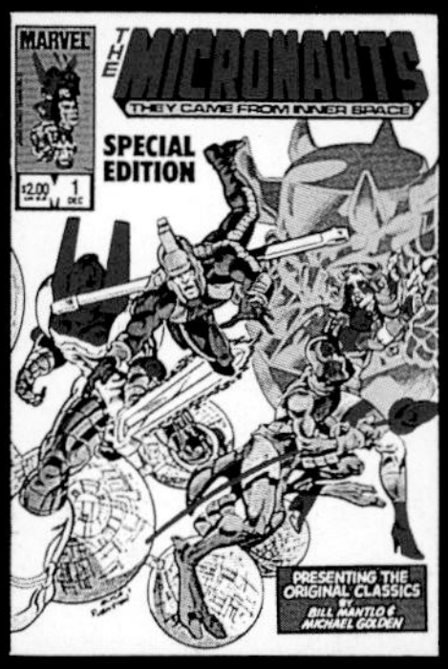
MARVEL
THE MICRONAUTS
THEY CAME FROM INNER SPACE
SPECIAL EDITION
PRESENTING THE ORIGINAL CLASSICS
BY BILL MANTLO & MICHAEL GOLDEN
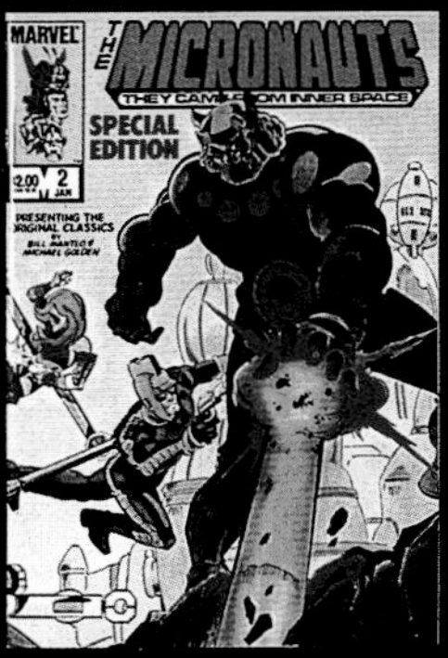
MARVEL
THE MICRONAUTS
THEY CAME FROM INNER SPACE
SPECIAL EDITION
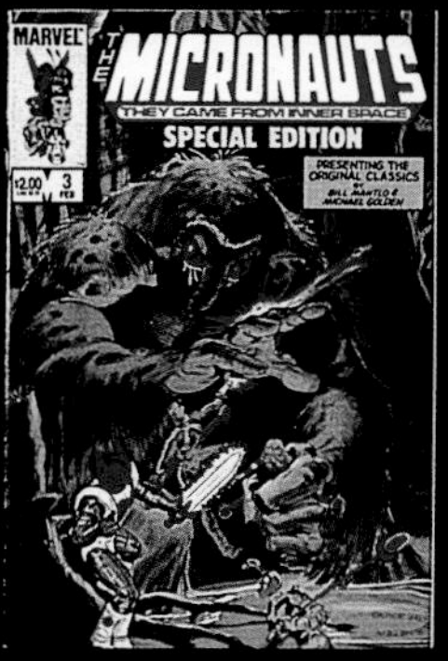
MARVEL
THE MICRONAUTS
THEY CAME FROM INNER SPACE
SPECIAL EDITION
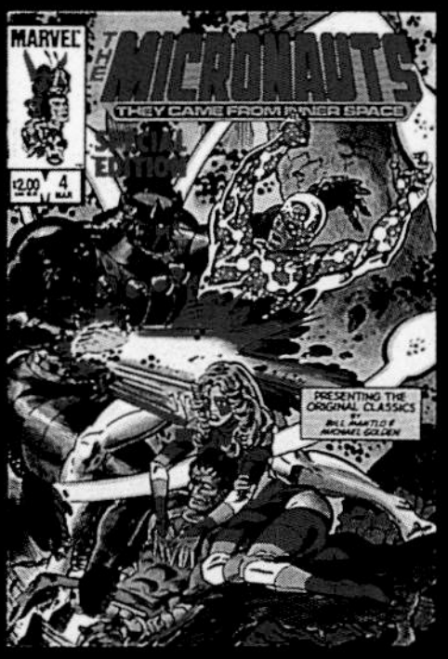
MARVEL
THE MICRONAUTS
THEY CAME FROM INNER SPACE
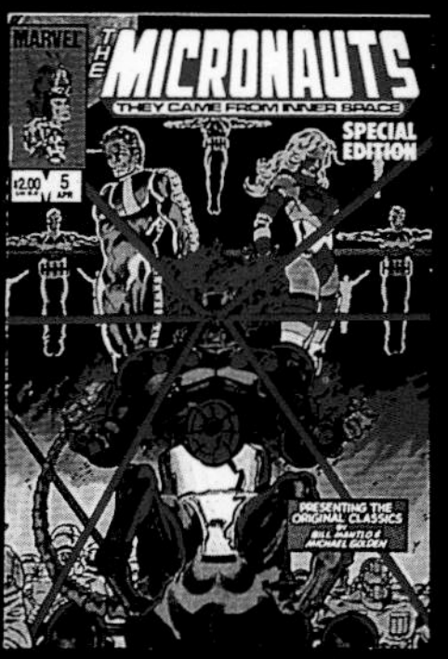
MARVEL
THE MICRONAUTS
THEY CAME FROM INNER SPACE
SPECIAL EDITION

1255.8 Micronauts V.2 (1-16)

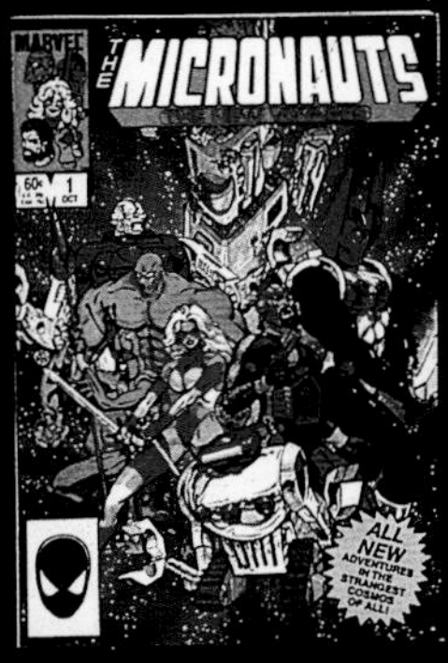
MARVEL
THE MICRONAUTS
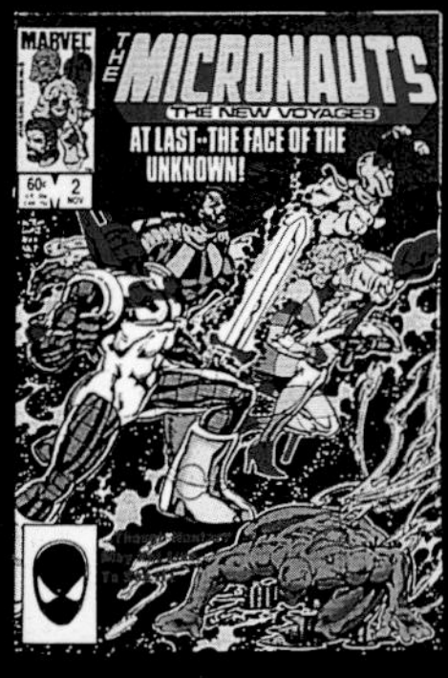
MARVEL
THE MICRONAUTS
THE NEW VOYAGES
AT LAST—THE FACE OF THE UNKNOWN!
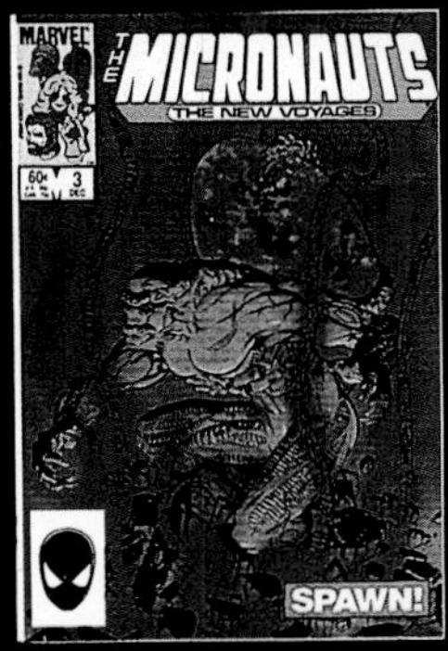
MARVEL
THE MICRONAUTS
THE NEW VOYAGES
SPAWN!
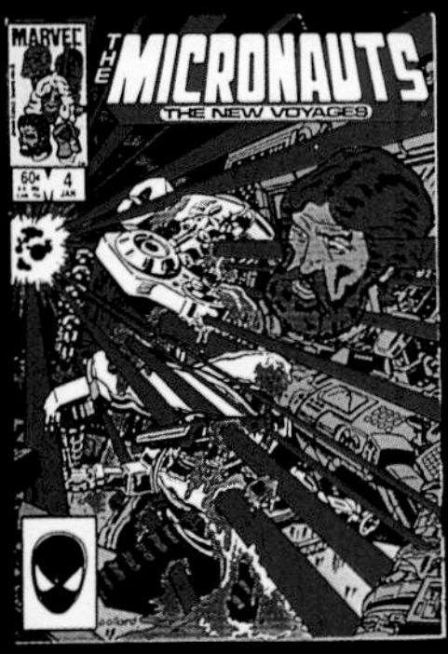
MARVEL
THE MICRONAUTS
THE NEW VOYAGES
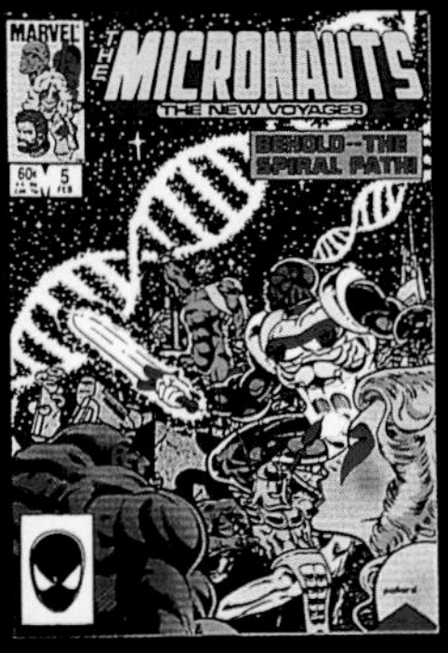
MARVEL
THE MICRONAUTS
THE NEW VOYAGES
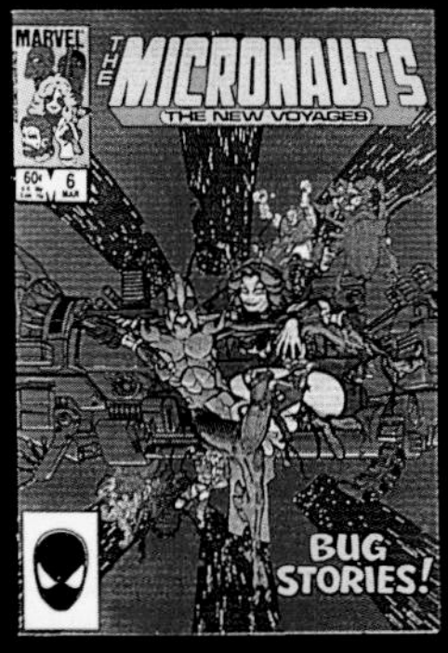
MARVEL
THE MICRONAUTS
THE NEW VOYAGES
BUG STORIES!
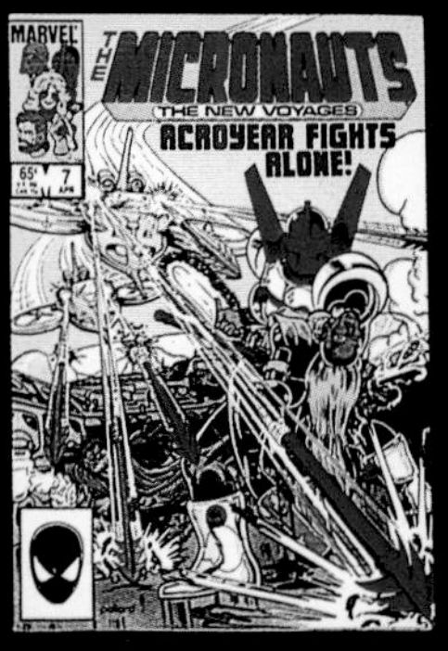
MARVEL
THE MICRONAUTS
THE NEW VOYAGES
ACROYEAR FIGHTS ALONE!
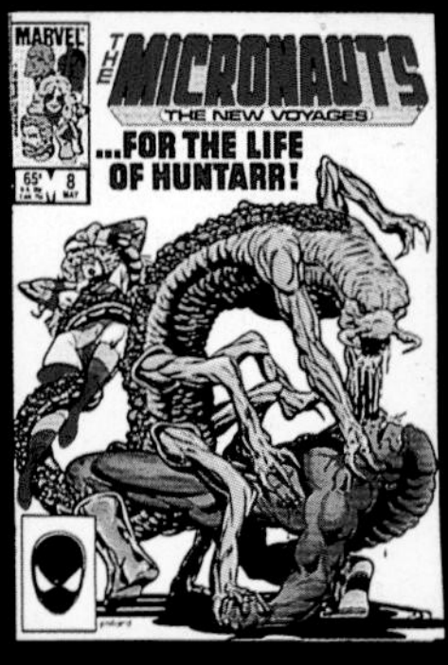
MARVEL
THE MICRONAUTS
THE NEW VOYAGES
...FOR THE LIFE OF HUNTARR!
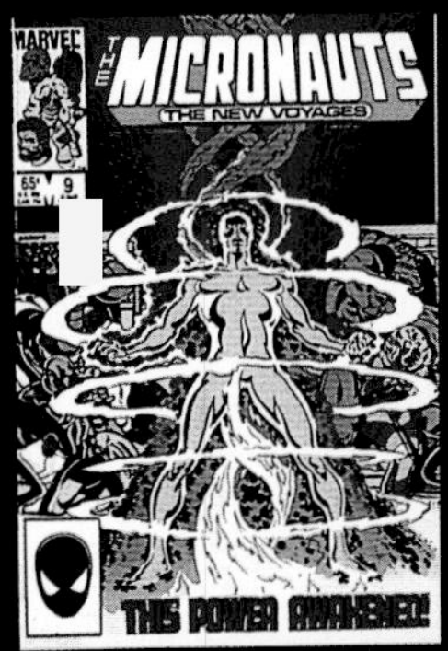
MARVEL
THE MICRONAUTS
THE NEW VOYAGES
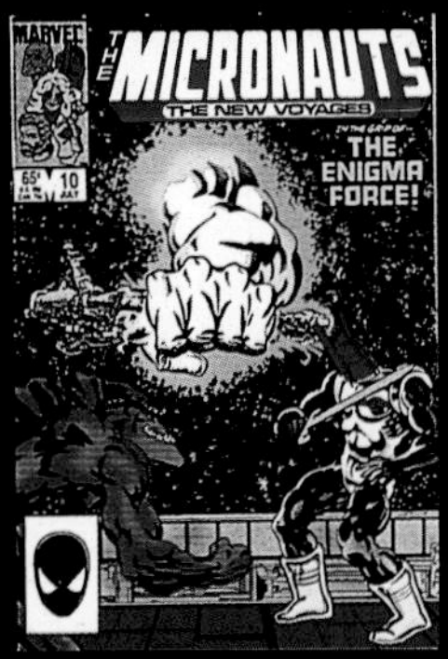
MARVEL
THE MICRONAUTS
THE NEW VOYAGES
THE ENIGMA FORCE!
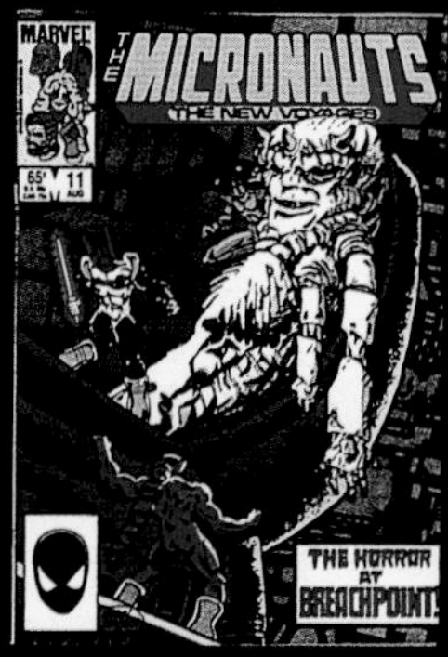
MARVEL
THE MICRONAUTS
THE NEW VOYAGES
THE HORROR AT BREACHPOINT!
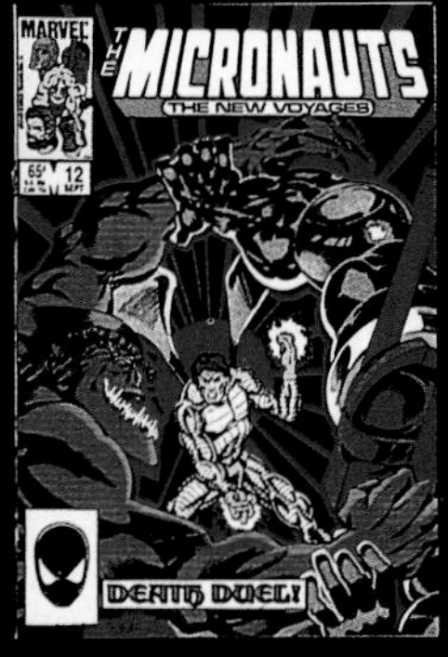
MARVEL
THE MICRONAUTS
THE NEW VOYAGES
DEATH DUEL!
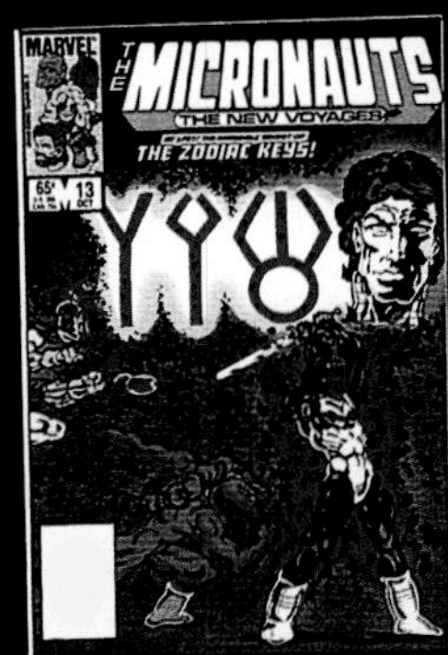
MARVEL
THE MICRONAUTS
THE NEW VOYAGES
THE ZODIAC KEYS!
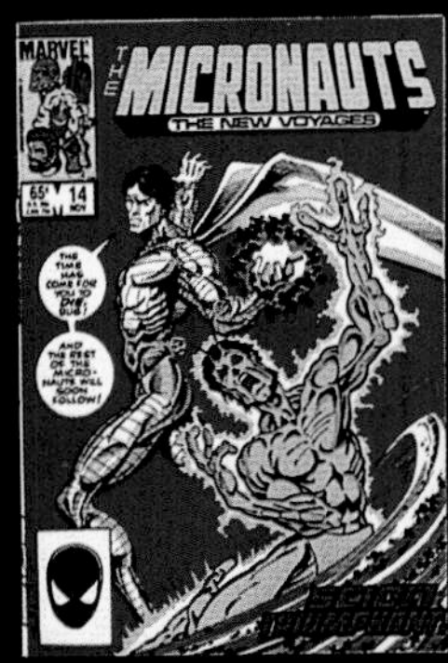
MARVEL
THE MICRONAUTS
THE NEW VOYAGES
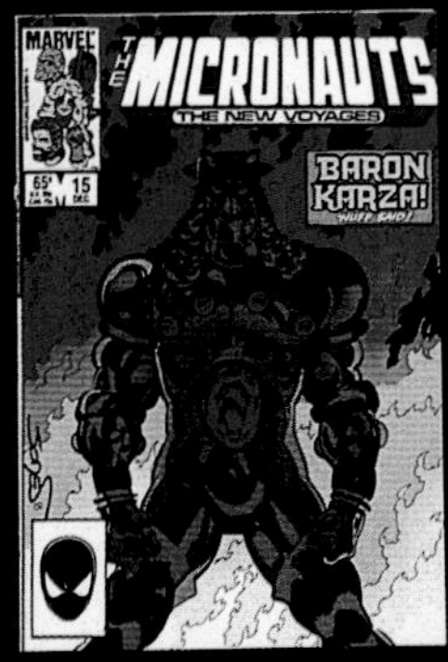
MARVEL
THE MICRONAUTS
THE NEW VOYAGES
BARON KARZA!
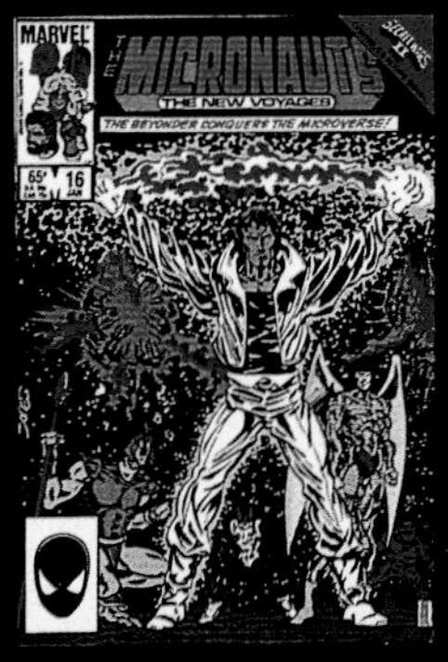
MARVEL
THE MICRONAUTS
THE NEW VOYAGES

Micronauts (1-59) 1255.6

Ref. No.	Date	RVI	Artist/Info.
1255.6-1	Jan. 1979	2	Cockrum/Milgrom-c, Golden/Rubinstein-a
1255.6-2	Feb.	1	Golden/Rubinstein-c/a
1255.6-3	Mar.	1	" "
1255.6-4	Apr.	1	" "
1255.6-5	May	1	Rubinstein-c/a, Golden-a
1255.6-6	Jun.	1	" "
1255.6-7	Jul.	1	Golden/Rubinstein-a
1255.6-8	Aug.	1	Golden/McLeod-a
1255.6-9	Sept.	1	Golden/Milgrom-a
1255.6-10	**Oct.**	**1**	**" "**
1255.6-11	Nov.	1	" "
1255.6-12	Dec.	1	" "
1255.6-13	Jan. 1980	1	Chaykin/Milgrom-a
1255.6-14	Feb.	1	Chaykin/Sharen-a
1255.6-15	Mar.	1	Chaykin/Milgrom-a
1255.6-16	Apr.	1	" "
1255.6-17	May	1	" "
1255.6-18	Jun.	1	" "
1255.6-19	Jul.	1	Broderick/Gil-a
1255.6-20	**Aug.**	**1**	**" "**
1255.6-21 to 59	Aug. 1984, (#50)	1	Chaykin/Sharen-a
1255.6-A1	Dec. 1979	1	Ditko-c/a
1255.6-A2	Oct. 1980	1	"

Micronauts (V.2) (1-20) 1255.8

Ref. No.	Date	RVI	Artist/Info.
1255.8-1	Oct. 1984	1	Jones/Patterson-a
1255.8-2	Nov.	1	Guice/Adams-c, Jones/Patterson-a
1255.8-3	Dec.	1	Jones/Patterson-a
1255.8-4	Jan. 1985	1	Pollard-c, Jones/Patterson, Akin, Garvey-a
1255.8-5	Feb.	1	Pollard-c, Jones/Redding-a
1255.8-6	Mar.	1	Jones/Patterson-a
1255.8-7	Apr.	1	Pollard-c, Whigham/Akin, Garvey-a
1255.8-8	May	1	Pollard-c, Jones/Patterson-a
1255.8-9	Jun.	1	Jones/Patterson-a
1255.8-10	**Jul.**	**1**	**Jones-c/a, Patterson-a**
1255.8-11	Aug.	1	
1255.8-12	Sept.	1	
1255.8-13	Oct.	1	
1255.8-14 to 20	May 1986, (#20)	1	

Micronauts Special Edition (1-5) 1255.9

Ref. No.	Date	RVI	Artist/Info.
1255.9-1	Dec. 1983	1	Guice/Rubinstein-c, Golden/Rubinstein-a
1255.9-2	Jan. 1984	1	" " " "
1255.9-3	Feb.	1	" " " "
1255.9-4	Mar.	1	Guice/Milgrom-c, Golden/McLeod-a
1255.5-9	Apr.	1	Guice/Milgrom-c, Golden/Milgrom-a

1258.8 The Mighty Marvel Western (2-18)

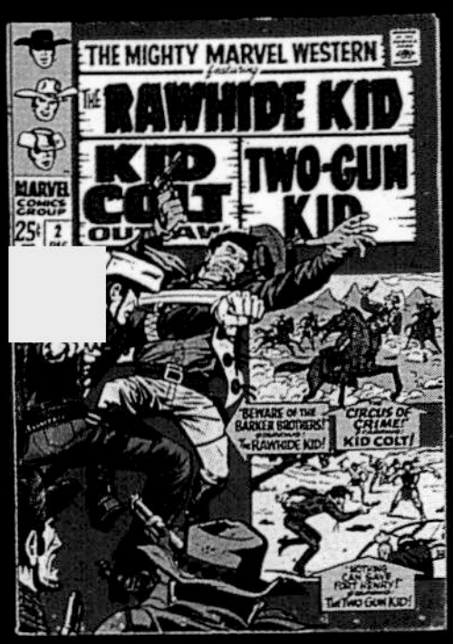
THE MIGHTY MARVEL WESTERN
THE RAWHIDE KID
KID COLT OUTLAW
TWO-GUN KID
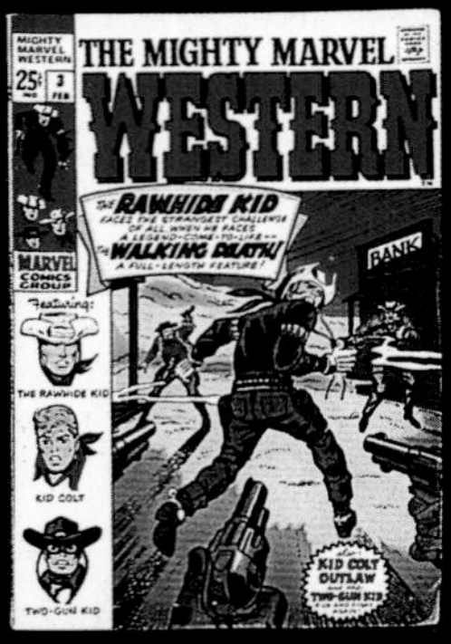
THE MIGHTY MARVEL WESTERN
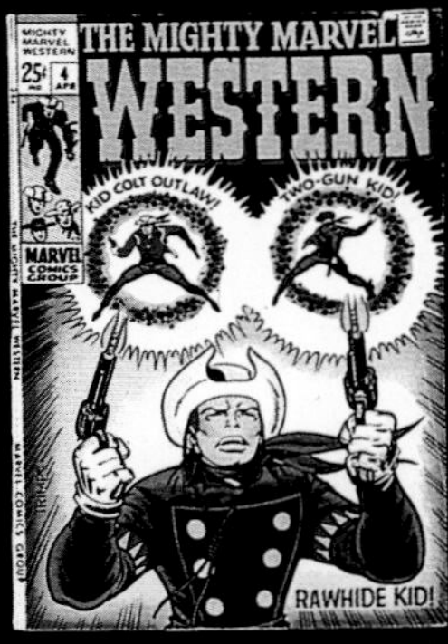
THE MIGHTY MARVEL WESTERN
RAWHIDE KID!
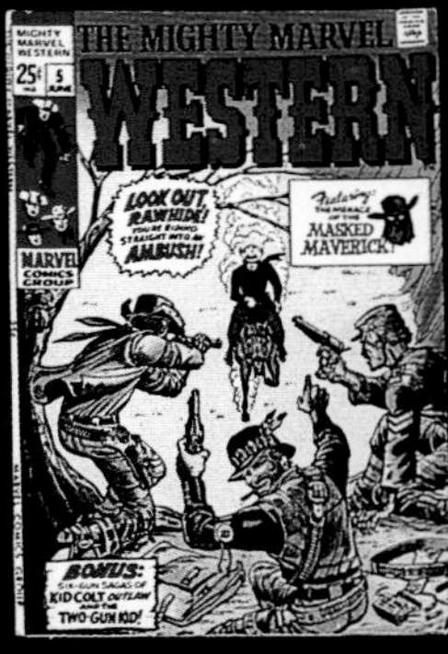
THE MIGHTY MARVEL WESTERN
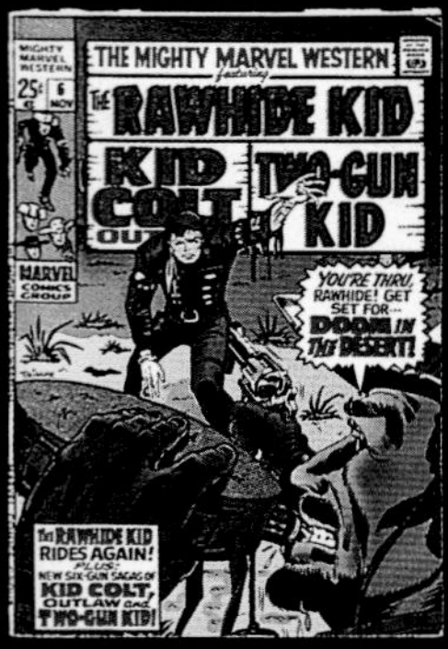
THE MIGHTY MARVEL WESTERN
THE RAWHIDE KID
KID COLT
TWO-GUN KID
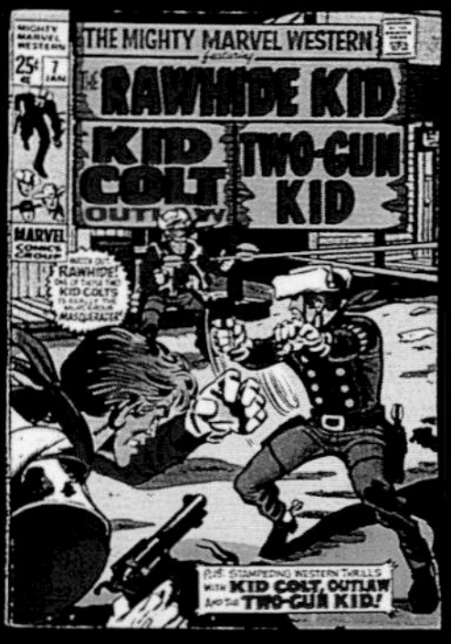
THE MIGHTY MARVEL WESTERN
RAWHIDE KID
KID COLT
TWO-GUN KID
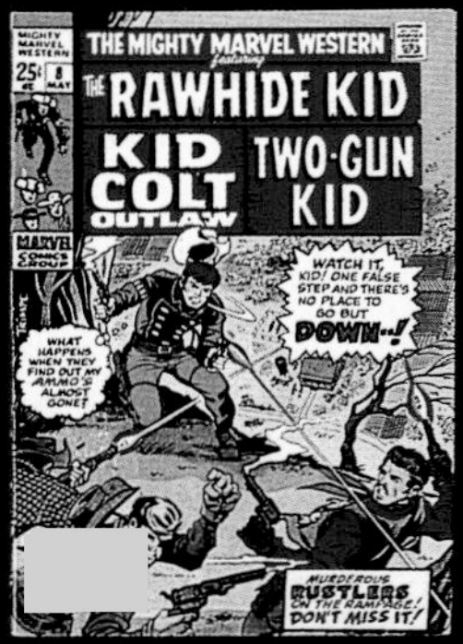
THE MIGHTY MARVEL WESTERN
THE RAWHIDE KID
KID COLT OUTLAW
TWO-GUN KID
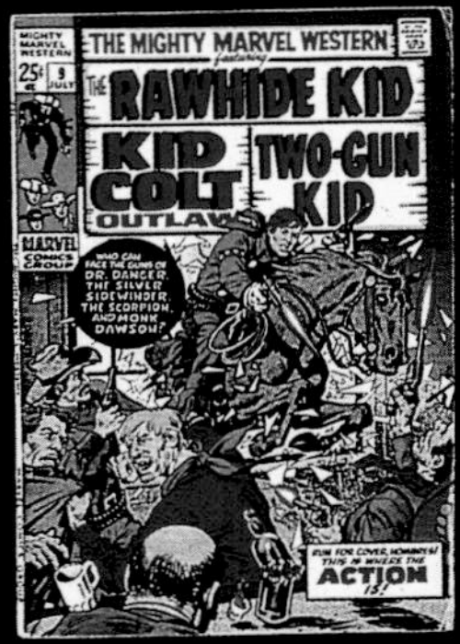
THE MIGHTY MARVEL WESTERN
THE RAWHIDE KID
KID COLT OUTLAW
TWO-GUN KID
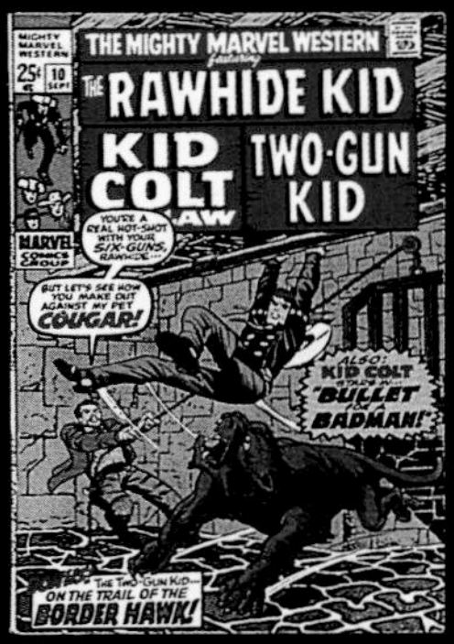
THE MIGHTY MARVEL WESTERN
THE RAWHIDE KID
KID COLT
TWO-GUN KID
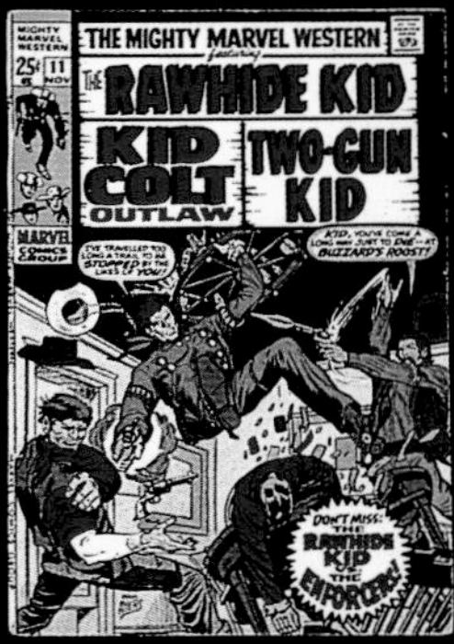
THE MIGHTY MARVEL WESTERN
THE RAWHIDE KID
KID COLT OUTLAW
TWO-GUN KID
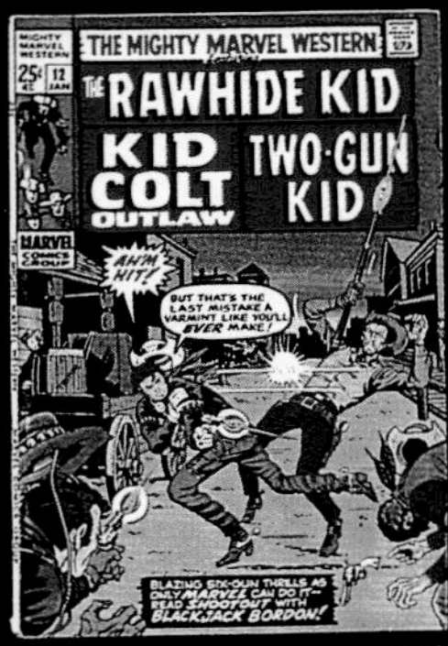
THE MIGHTY MARVEL WESTERN
THE RAWHIDE KID
KID COLT OUTLAW
TWO-GUN KID
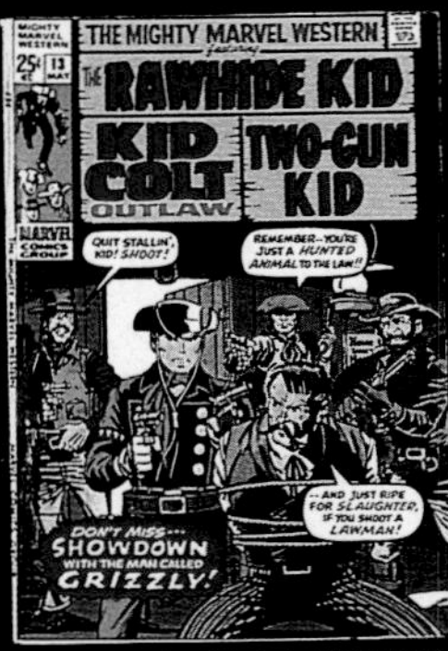
THE MIGHTY MARVEL WESTERN
THE RAWHIDE KID
KID COLT OUTLAW
TWO-GUN KID
SHOWDOWN WITH THE MAN CALLED GRIZZLY!

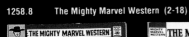

1266 Millie the Model (122-130)

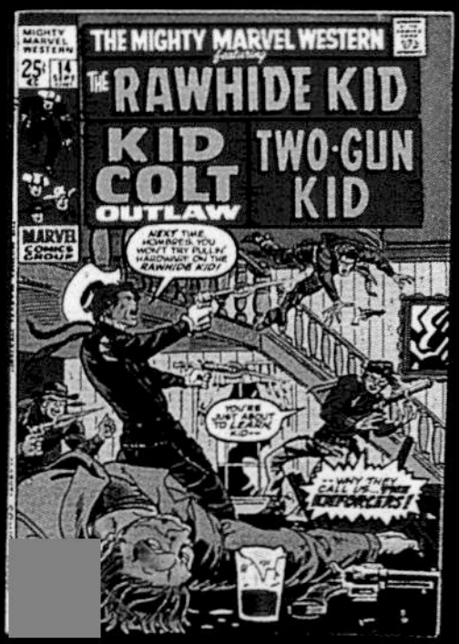
THE MIGHTY MARVEL WESTERN
THE RAWHIDE KID
KID COLT OUTLAW
TWO-GUN KID
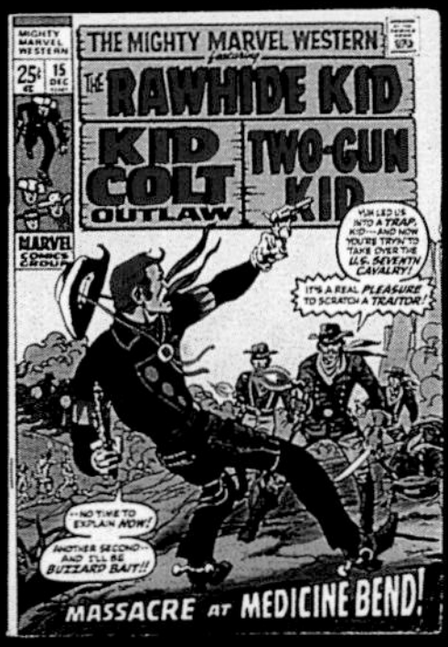
THE MIGHTY MARVEL WESTERN
THE RAWHIDE KID
KID COLT OUTLAW
TWO-GUN KID
MASSACRE AT MEDICINE BEND!
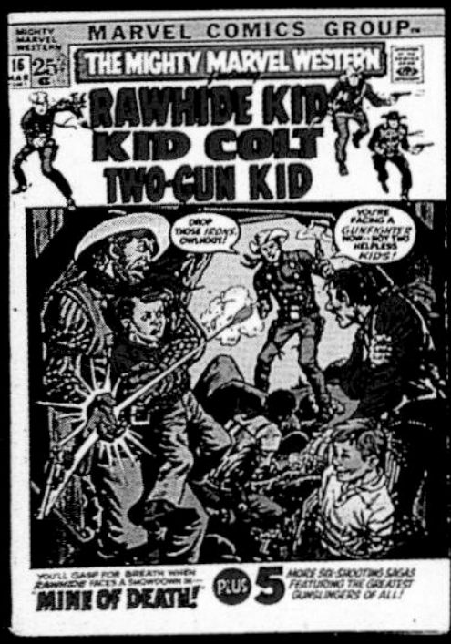
MARVEL COMICS GROUP
THE MIGHTY MARVEL WESTERN
RAWHIDE KID
KID COLT
TWO-GUN KID
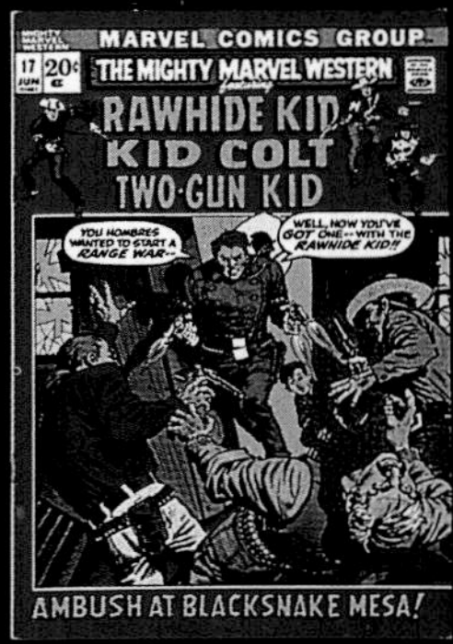
MARVEL COMICS GROUP
THE MIGHTY MARVEL WESTERN
RAWHIDE KID
KID COLT
TWO-GUN KID
AMBUSH AT BLACKSNAKE MESA!
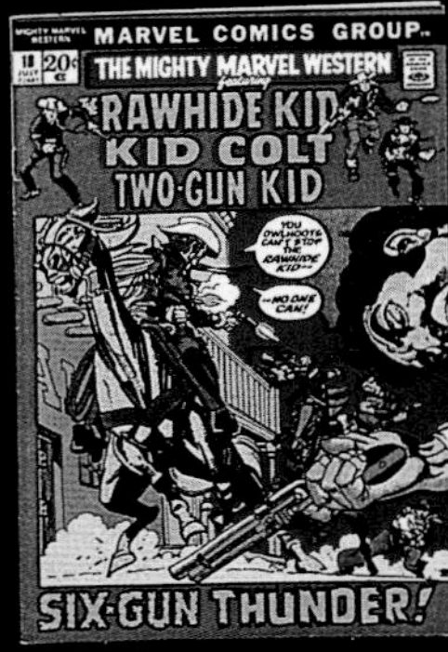
MARVEL COMICS GROUP
THE MIGHTY MARVEL WESTERN
RAWHIDE KID
KID COLT
TWO-GUN KID
SIX-GUN THUNDER!
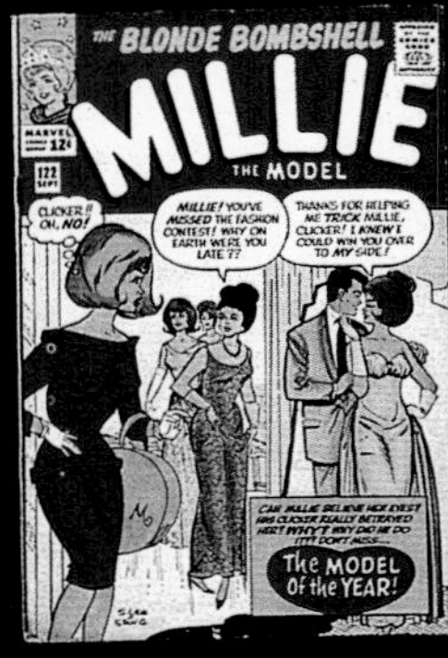
THE BLONDE BOMBSHELL
MILLIE THE MODEL
The MODEL of the YEAR!
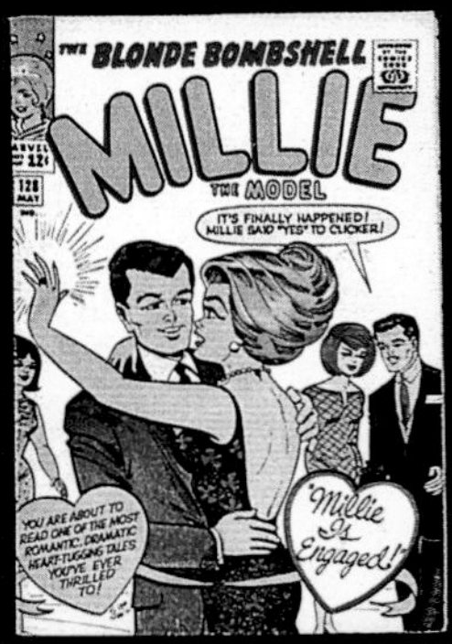
THE BLONDE BOMBSHELL
MILLIE THE MODEL
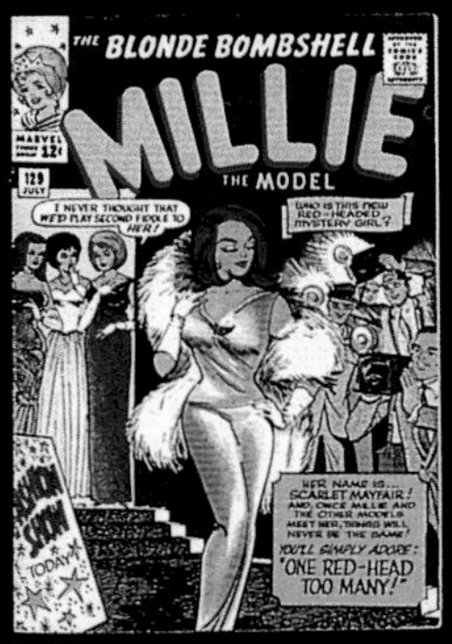
THE BLONDE BOMBSHELL
MILLIE THE MODEL
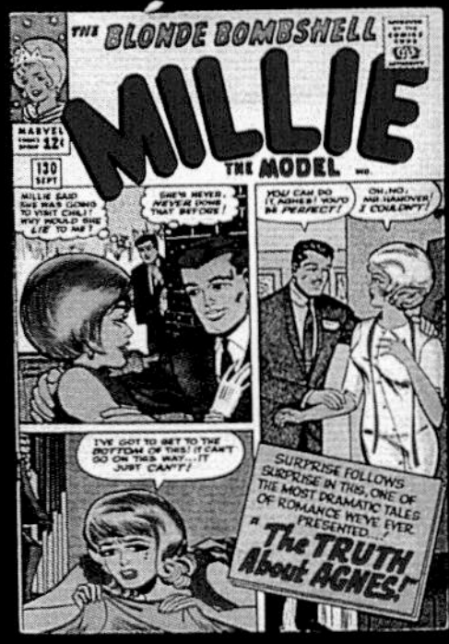
THE BLONDE BOMBSHELL
MILLIE THE MODEL
"The TRUTH About AGNES!"
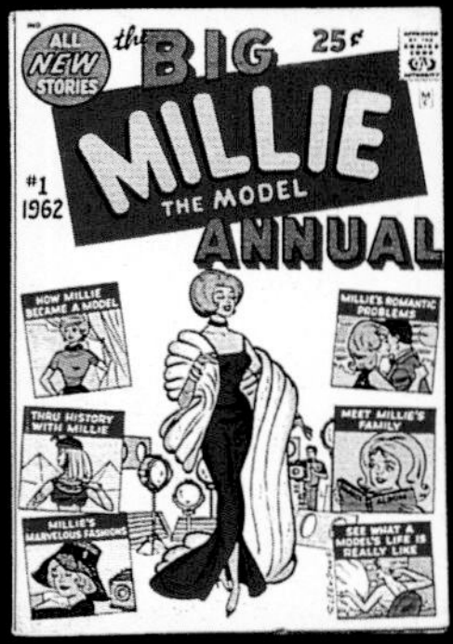
ALL NEW STORIES
the BIG 25¢
MILLIE THE MODEL ANNUAL
#1 1962
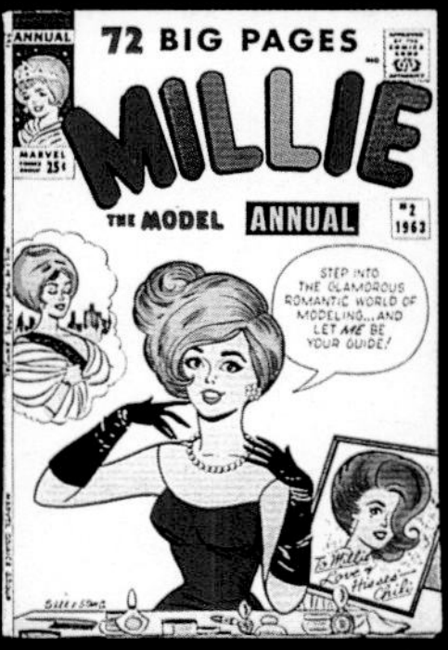
ANNUAL
72 BIG PAGES
MILLIE THE MODEL ANNUAL
#2 1963
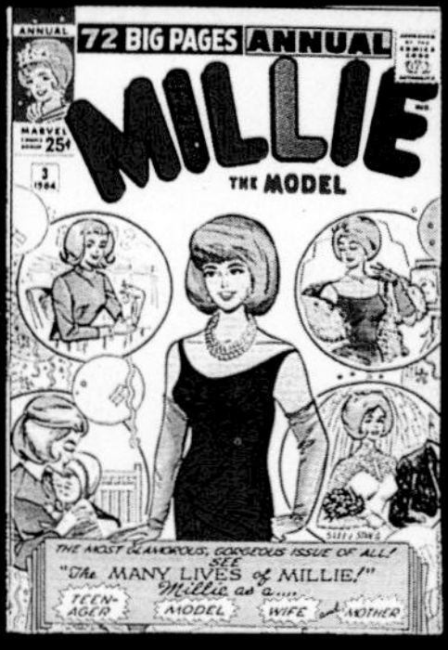
ANNUAL
72 BIG PAGES
MILLIE THE MODEL

1283.5 Modeling with Millie (21-48)

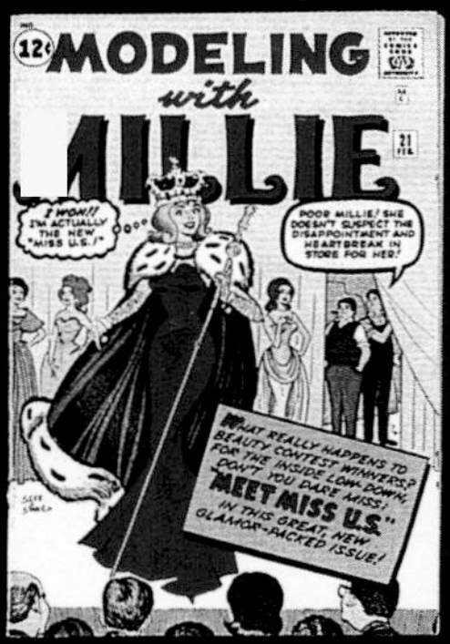
MODELING with MILLIE
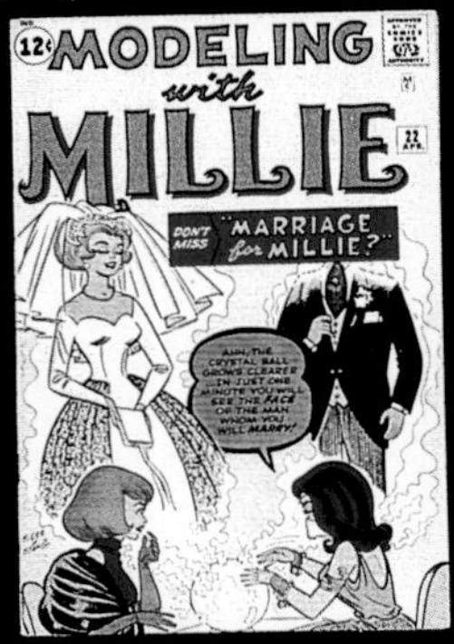
MODELING with MILLIE
"MARRIAGE for MILLIE?"
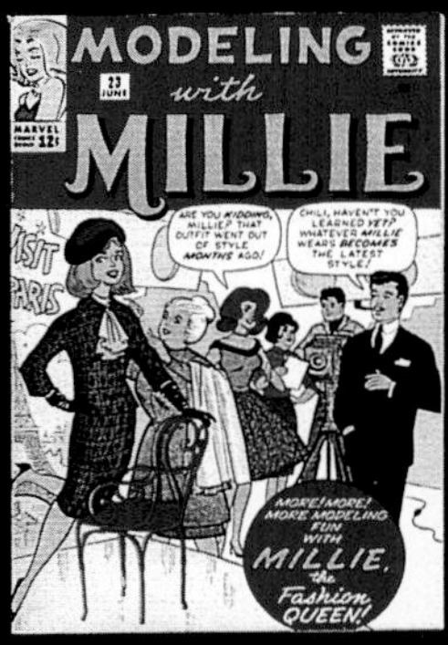
MODELING with MILLIE
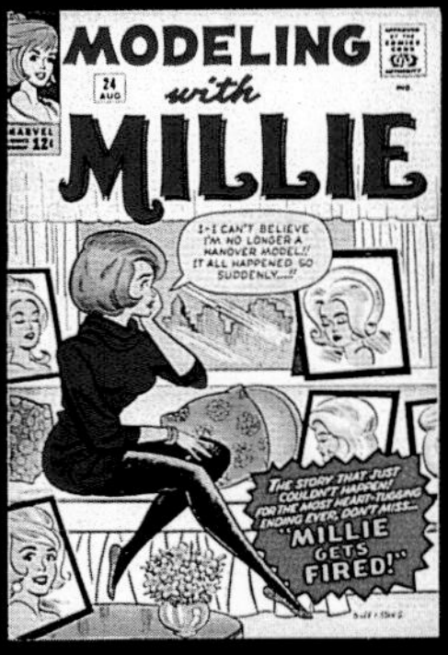
MODELING with MILLIE
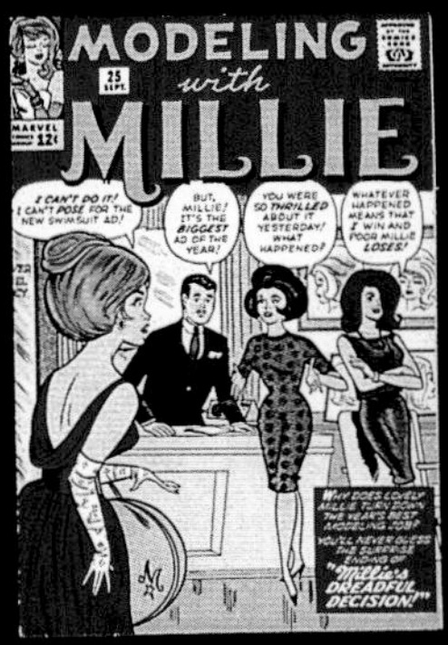
MODELING with MILLIE
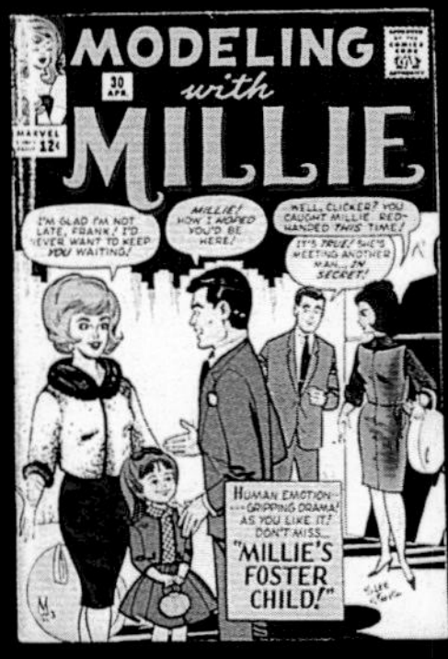
MODELING with MILLIE
"MILLIE'S FOSTER CHILD!"
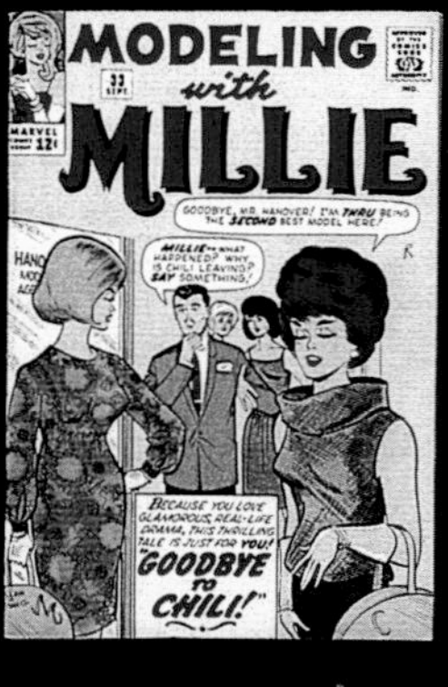
MODELING with MILLIE
GOODBYE TO CHILI!
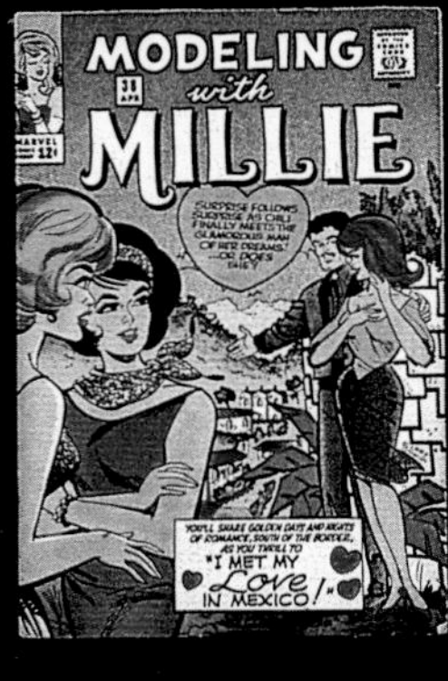
MODELING with MILLIE
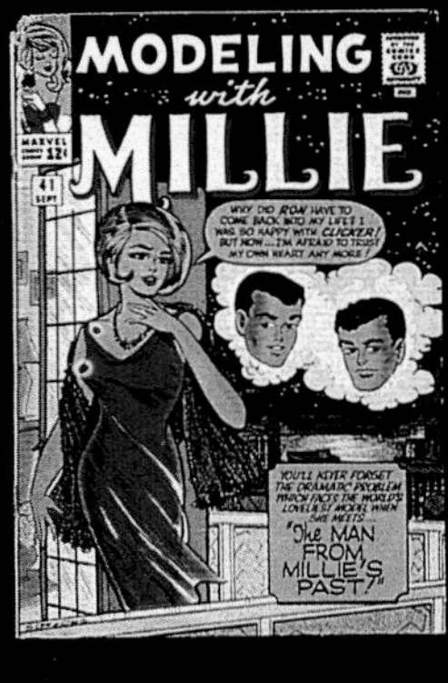
MODELING with MILLIE
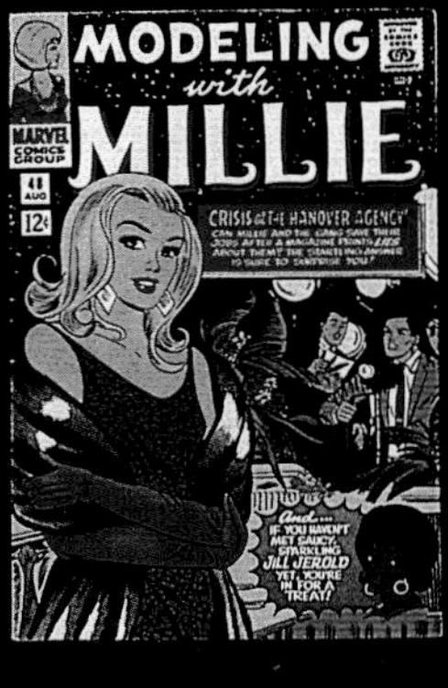
MODELING with MILLIE

Mighty Marvel Western (1-46) 1258.8

Ref. No.	Date	RVI	Artist/Info. (All Reprints)
1258.8-1	Oct. 1968	2	Kirby-a (Kid Colt series begins)
1258.8-2	Dec.	1	Kirby/Ayers-a
1258.8-3	Feb. 1969	1	Trimpe-c, Kirby/Ayers-a
1258.8-4	Apr.	1	Trimpe-c, Lieber, Ayers/Hubbell-a
1258.8-5	Jun.	1	Trimpe-c, Kirby, Lieber, Ayers;/Ray-a
1258.8-6	Nov.	1	Timpe-c, Kirby, Keller, Ayers-a
1258.8-7	Jan. 1970	1	Lieber, Keller, Ayers/Demeo-a
1258.8-8	May	1	Trimpe-c, Lieber, Keller, Ayers/Hubbell-a
1258.8-9	Jul.	1	Severin-c, Lieber, Keller, Kirby/Ayers-a
1258.8-10	Sept.	1	Lieber, Whitney, Heck/Colletta, Bee-a
1258.8-11 to 46	Sept. 1976, (#46)	1	

Millie the Model (101-207) 1266

1266-101 to 105	1963, (#101)	2	Stan-G.-a
1266-106 to 207	Dec. 1973, (#207)	1	Stan-G.-a (#154, New Millie begins)

Modeling with Millie (21-54) 1283.5

1283.5-21	Feb. 1963	6	Stan-G.-c/a
1283.5-22 to 26	Dec. (#26)	4	"
1283.5-27 to 54	Jun. 1967, (#54)	3	"

1293.1 Moon Knight (1-25)

MARVEL COMICS GROUP
MOON KNIGHT
THEY BECOME ONE... TO DO WHAT THEY MUST!
HOW MANY MORE MUST DIE
MIDNIGHT MEANS MURDER!
GENTLEMEN: THE COMMITTEE HAS SUCCEEDED
THERE ARE SOME THINGS YOU CAN'T FIGHT...
IT IS COLD AND BARREN HERE AND HE CAN NOT FIGHT THEM
ONE MINUTE AGO MOON KNIGHT WAS DESTROYED.
HE DOESN'T KNOW IT YET.
THE FIGHT CONTINUES—BUT IT IS ALREADY LOST!
MOON KNIGHT'S GREATEST SECRET DESTROYED!
MARDI GRAS
...HAVING A GOOD TIME DOWN SOUTH!
ONCE HE WAS HUMAN... MORPHEUS!
WIN A Columbia TEN-SPEED FORMULA 10 RACER!
DAREDEVIL & MOON KNIGHT PLAY... A DEADLY GAME THAT NOBODY CAN WIN!
BEGINNING SEPT. 12th ON NBC SPIDER-MAN AND HIS AMAZING FRIENDS!
IF BLACKSMITH WINS... KISS NEW YORK GOODBYE!!
GUEST-STARRING... EVERYBODY'S FAVORITE BLUE-EYED THING!
ALONE AGAINST THE SLAYERS!
OKAY ARSENAL, LET'S START ROUND TWO!
SPECIAL DOUBLE-SIZE ISSUE!

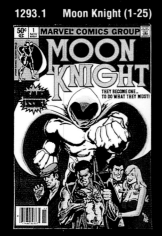

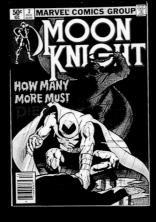

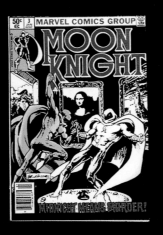

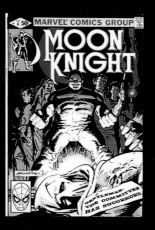

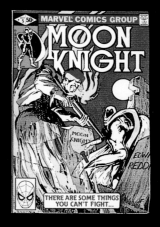

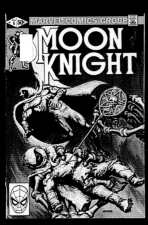

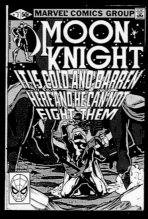

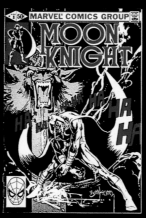

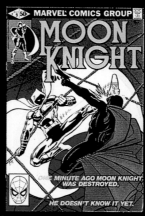

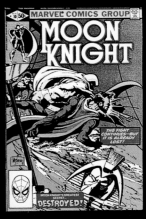

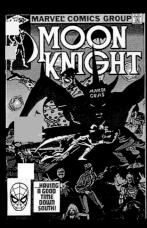

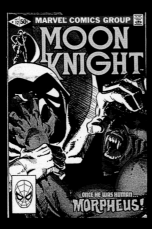

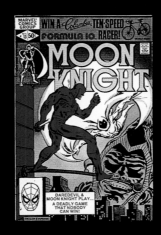

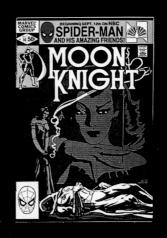

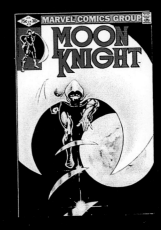

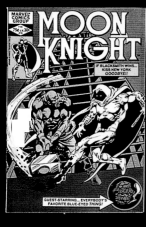

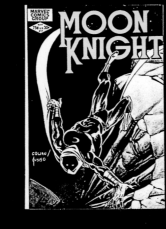

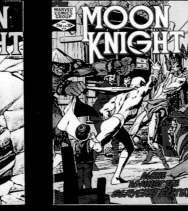

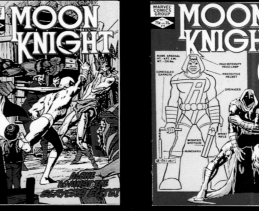

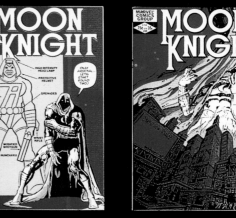

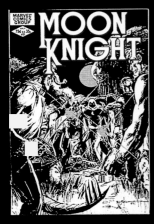

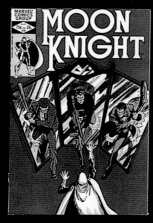

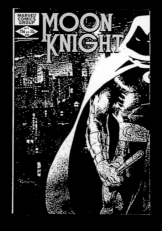

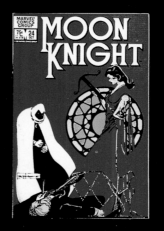

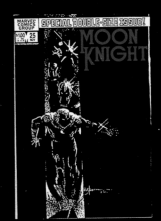

129 Moon Knight (26-38)

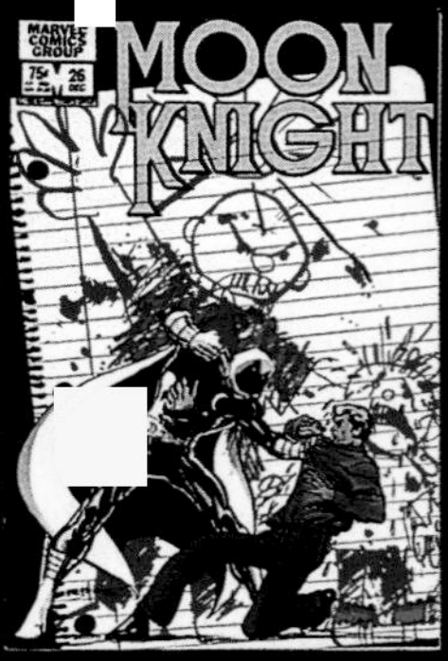
MOON KNIGHT
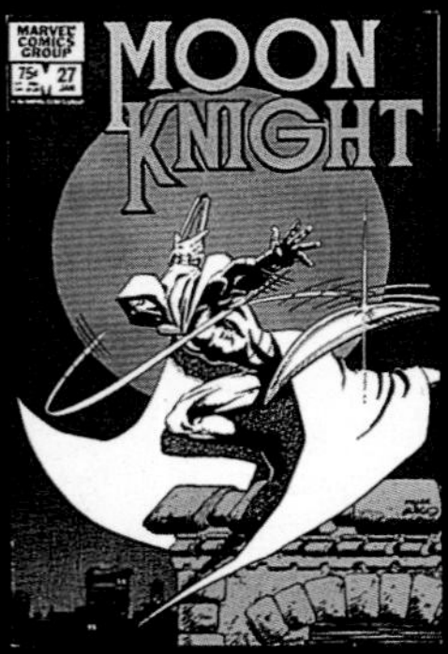
MOON KNIGHT
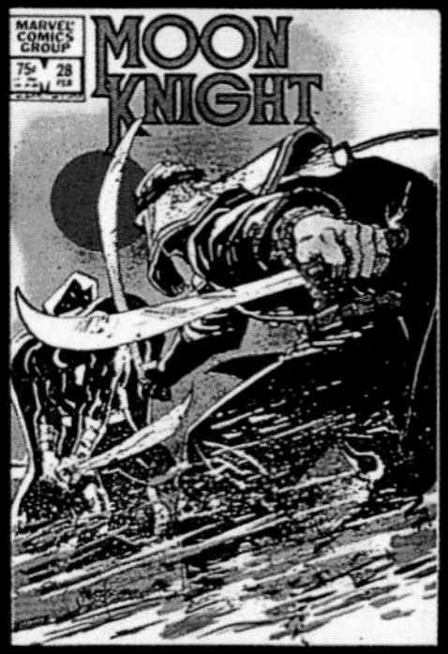
MOON KNIGHT
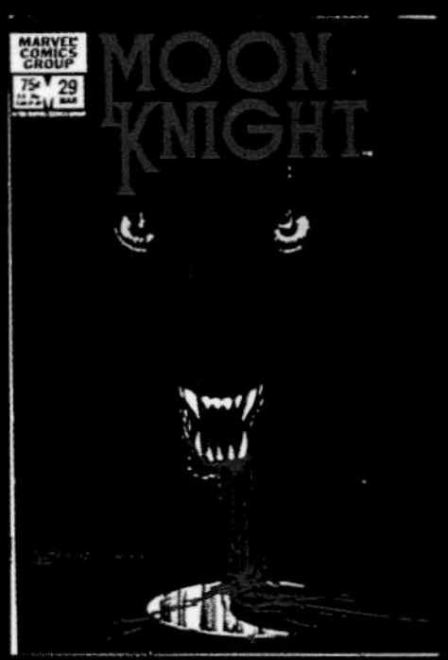
MOON KNIGHT
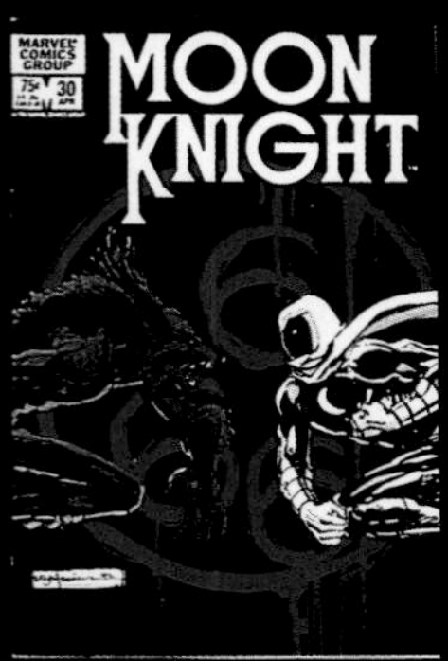
MOON KNIGHT
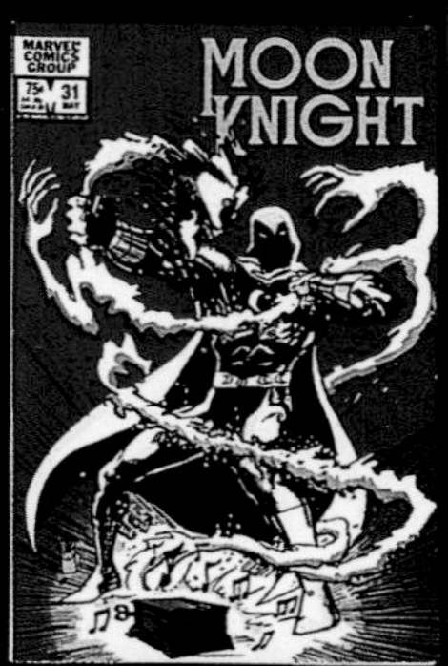
MOON KNIGHT
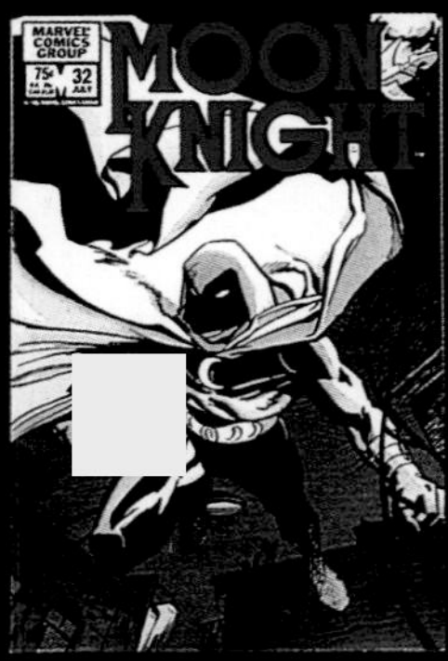
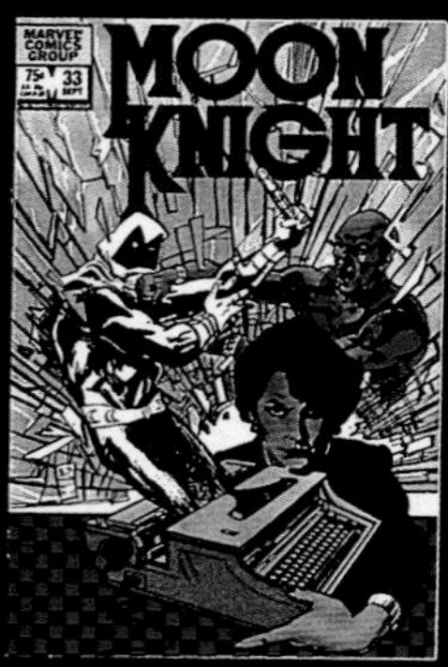
MOON KNIGHT
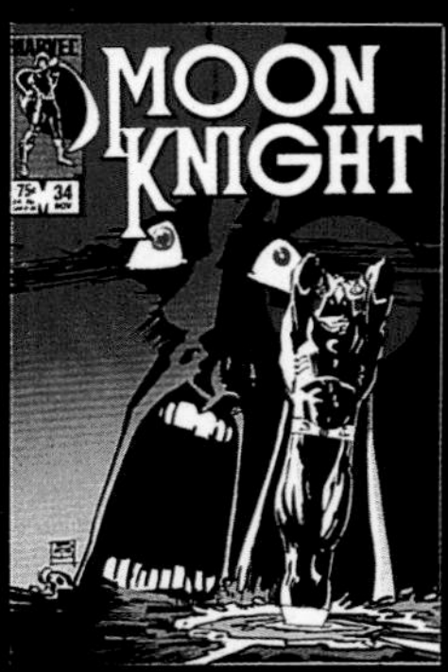
MOON KNIGHT
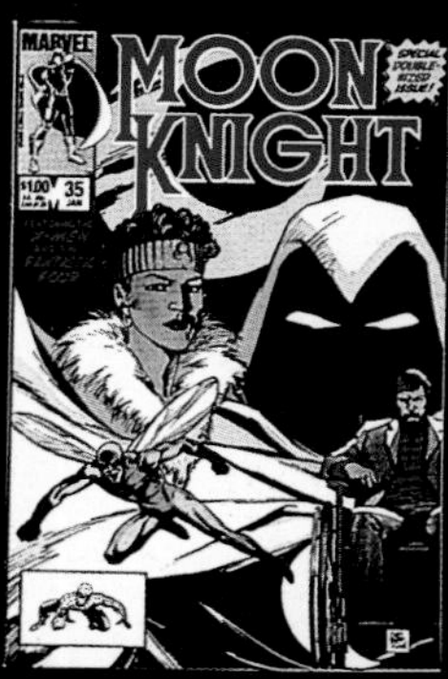
MOON KNIGHT
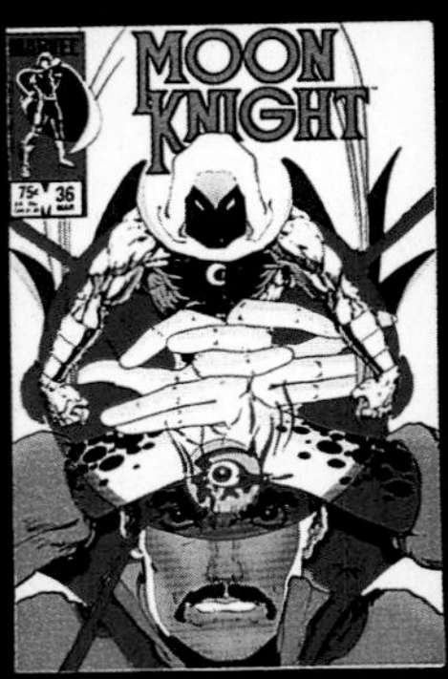
MOON KNIGHT
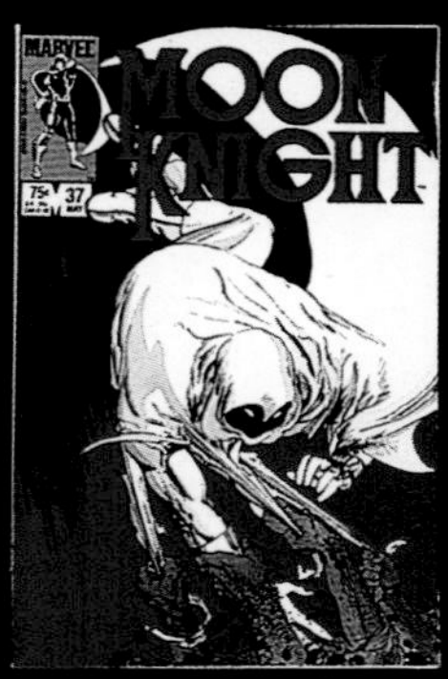

1292.2 Moon Knight (1-6)

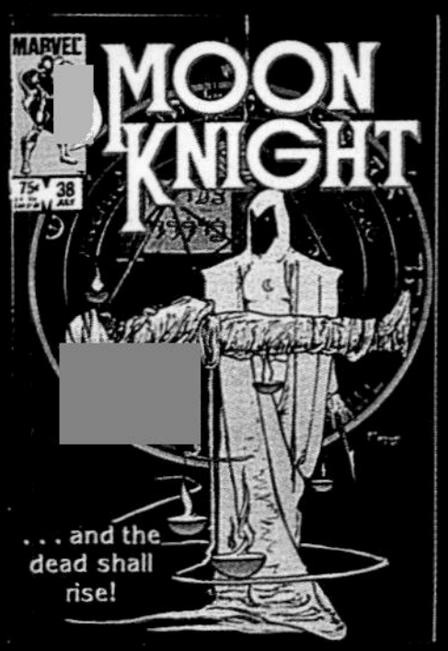
MOON KNIGHT
. . . and the dead shall rise!
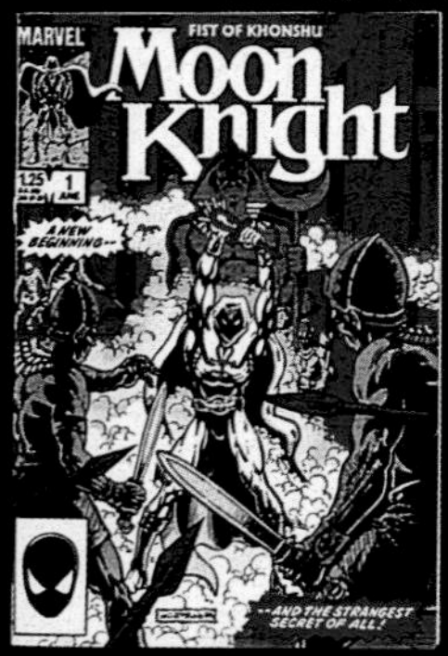
FIST OF KHONSHU
Moon Knight
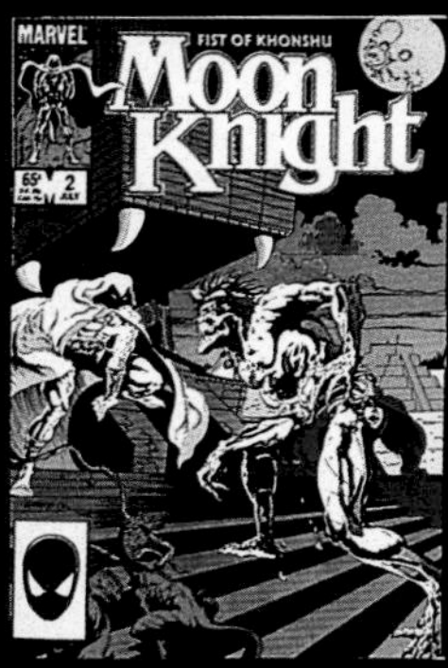
Moon Knight
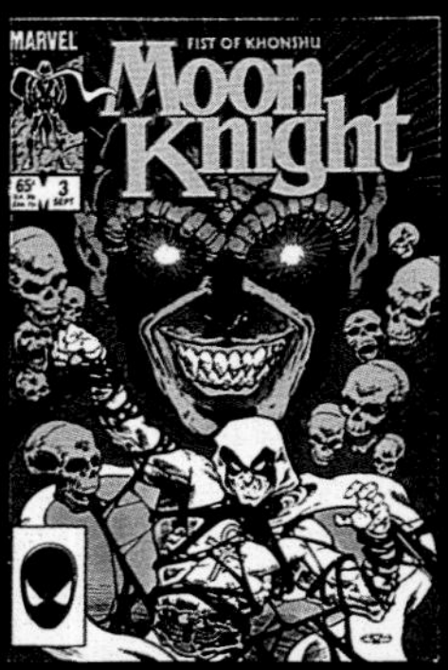
FIST OF KHONSHU
Moon Knight
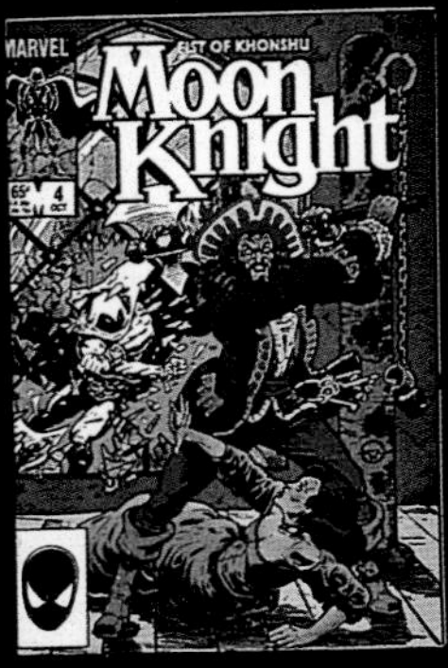
FIST OF KHONSHU
Moon Knight
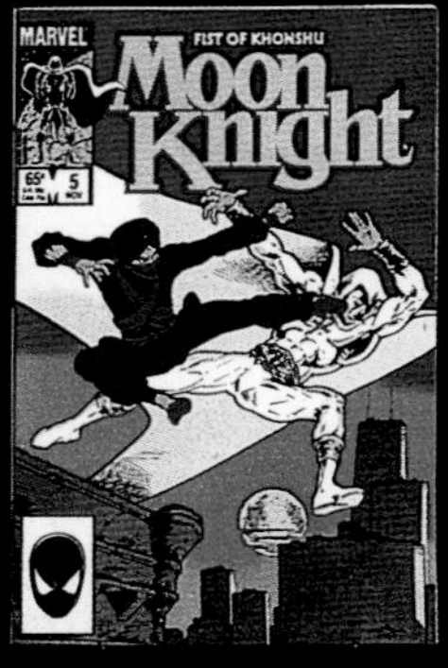
FIST OF KHONSHU
Moon Knight

1292.3 Moon Knight Special Edition (1-3)

1292.4 Moon Knight, Marc Spector (1-12)

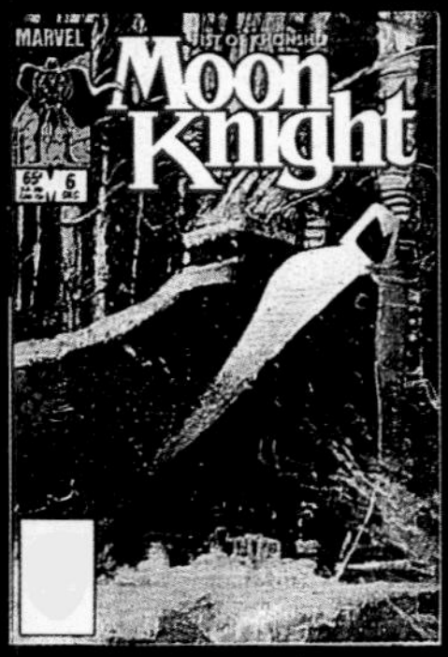
Moon Knight
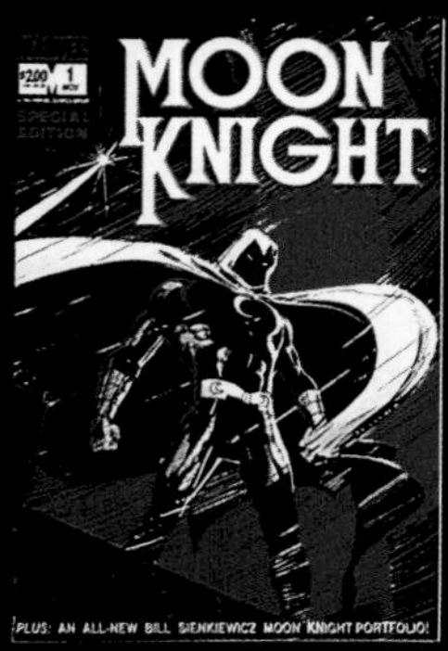
MOON KNIGHT
PLUS: AN ALL-NEW BILL SIENKIEWICZ MOON KNIGHT PORTFOLIO!
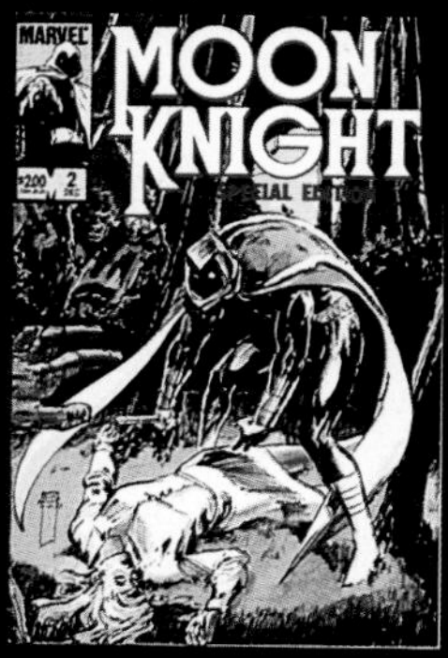
MOON KNIGHT
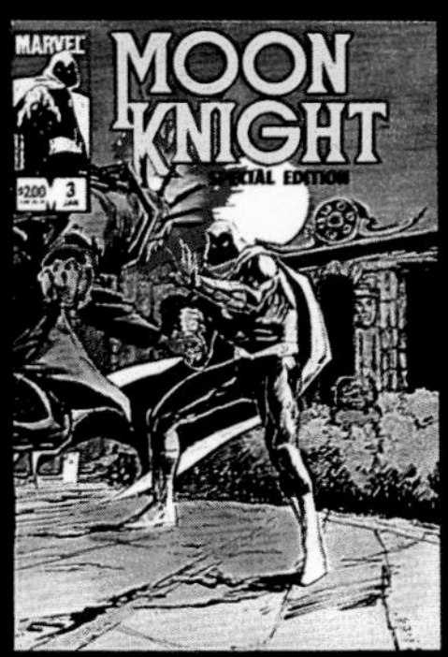
MOON KNIGHT
SPECIAL EDITION
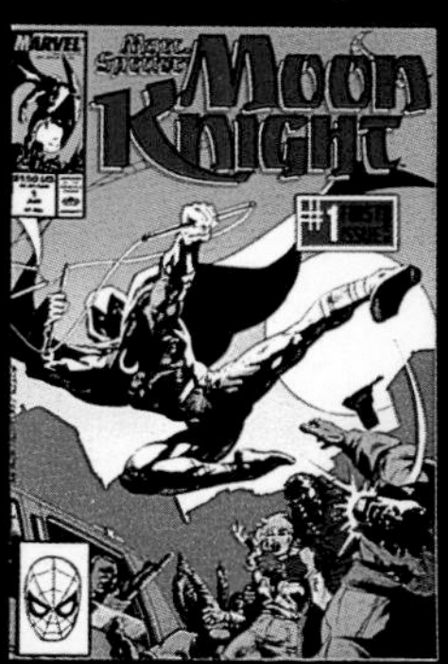
Moon Knight
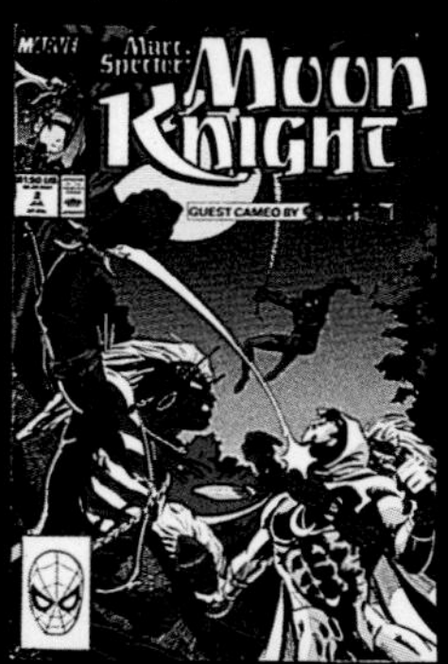
Moon Knight
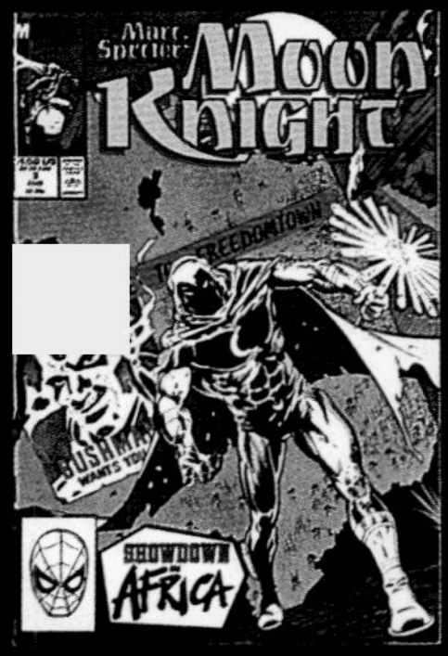
Moon Knight
AFRICA
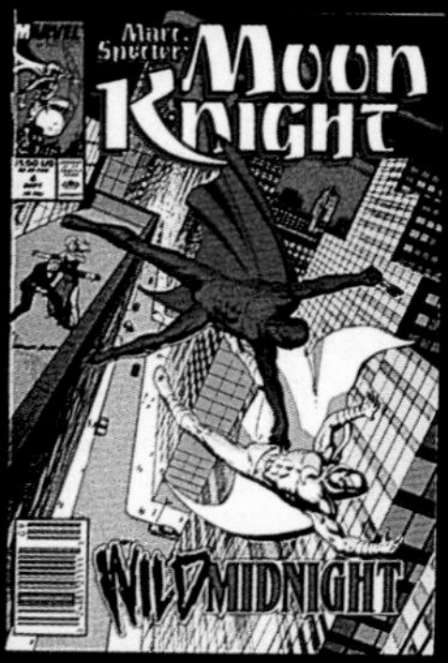
Moon Knight
WILD MIDNIGHT
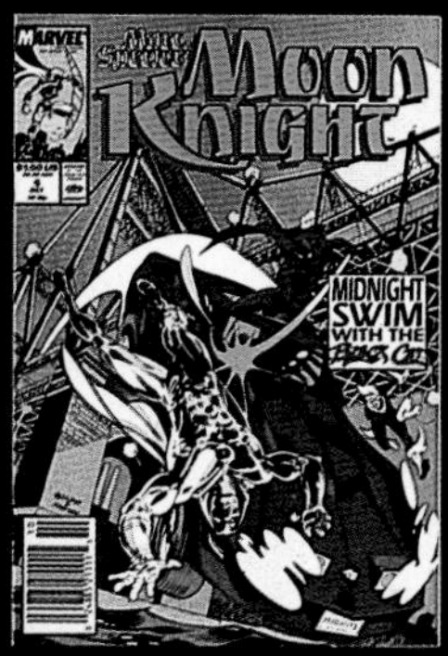
Moon Knight
MIDNIGHT SWIM
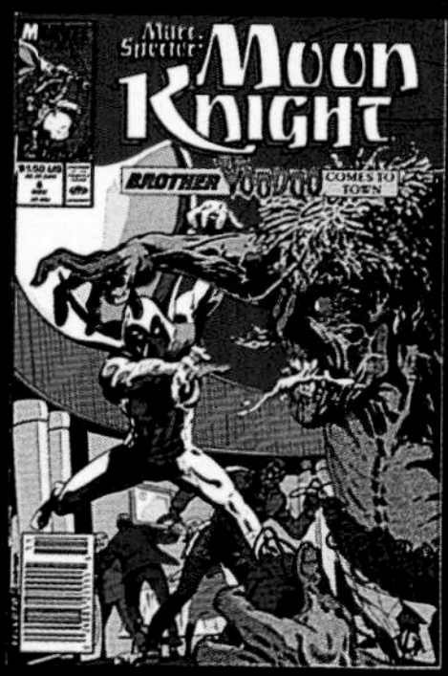
Moon Knight
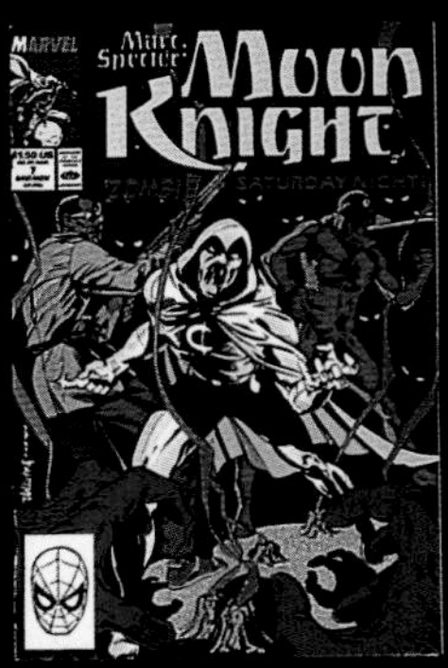
Moon Knight
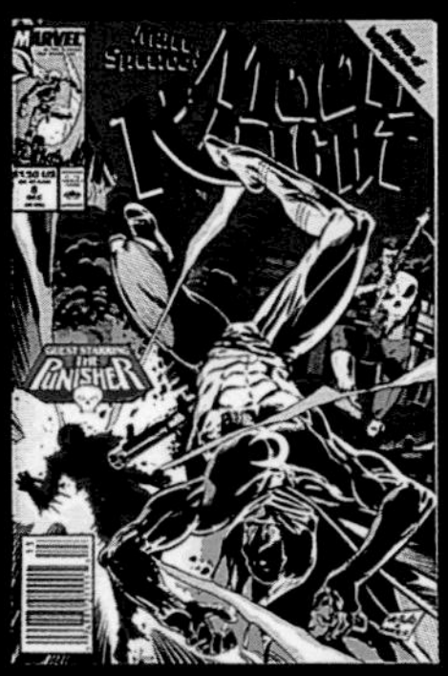
Moon Knight
PUNISHER
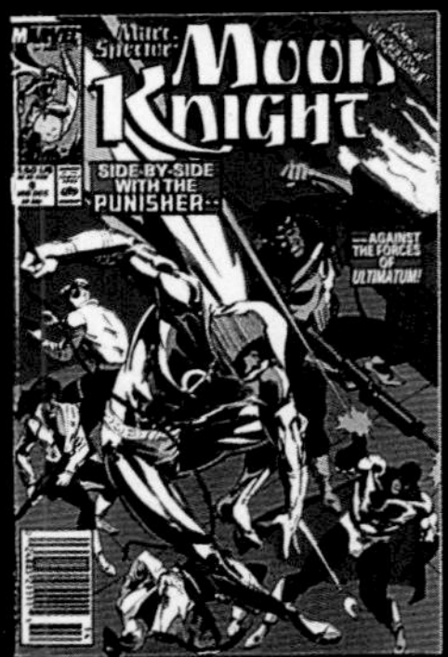
Moon Knight
SIDE-BY-SIDE WITH THE PUNISHER
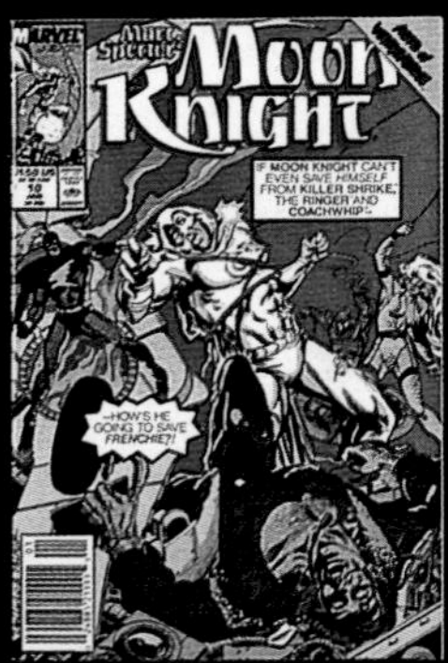
Moon Knight
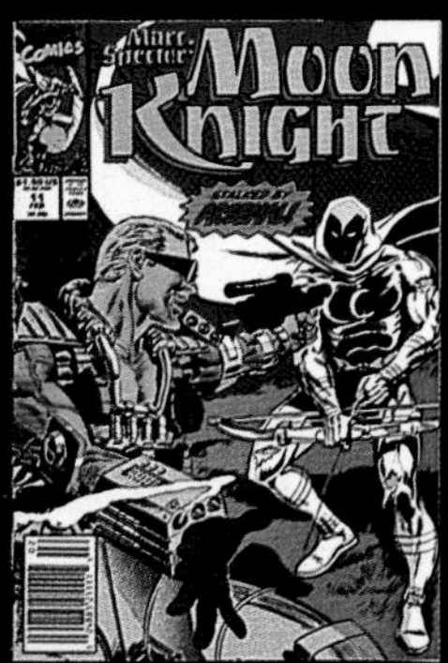
Moon Knight
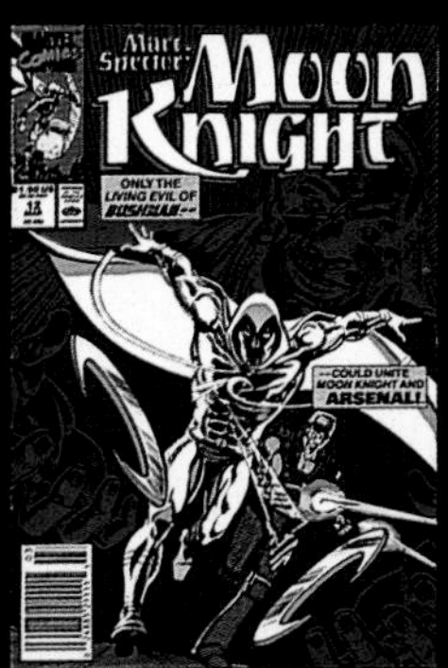
Moon Knight

Moon Knight (1-38) 1292.1

Ref. No.	Date	RVI	Artist/Info.
1293.1-1	Nov. 1980	2	Sienkiewicz/B & F. "S"-a
1293.1-2	Dec.	1	Moench/Sienkiewicz-a
1293.1-3	Jan. 1981	1	Sienkiewicz-c/a
1293.1-4	Feb.	1	Sienkiewicz-c/a, Janson-a
1293.1-5 to 38	Jul. 1984, (#38)	1	(#25, Double-size)

Moon Knight V.2 (1-6) 1292.2

1292.2-1	Jun. 1985	1	(First of Khanshu)
1292.2-2	Jul.	1	"
1292.2-3 to 6	Dec. 1985, (#6)	1	"

Moon Knight Special Edition (1-3) 1292.3

1292.3-1	Nov. 1983	1	(Sienkiewicz Portfolio)
1292.3-2 to 3	Jan. 1984, (#3)	1	

Marc Spector: Moon Knight (1-Present) 1292.4

1292.4-1	Jun. 1989	2	
1292.4-2 to 12	Mar. 1990, (#12)	1	(8,9 Punisher -app., RVI 5)

1297.7 Mother Teresa of Calcutta (1) 1305.2 Ms. Marvel (1-23)

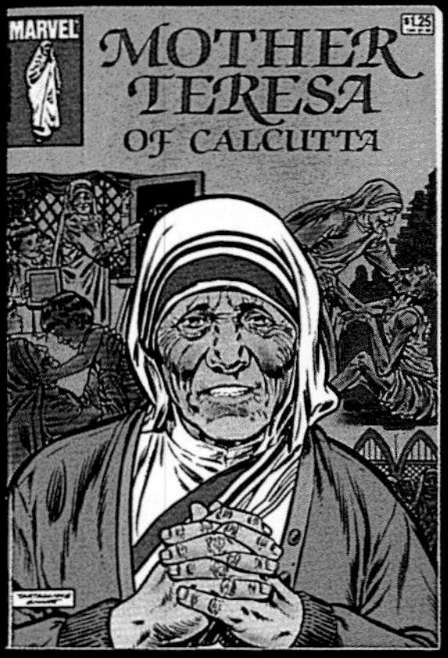
MARVEL
MOTHER TERESA
OF CALCUTTA

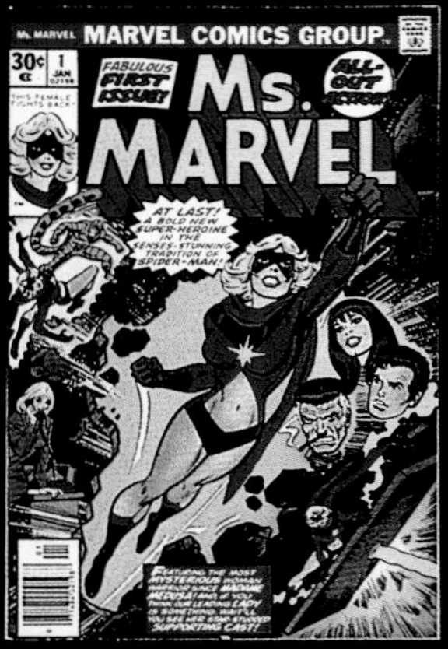
MARVEL COMICS GROUP
Ms. MARVEL
FABULOUS FIRST ISSUE!
ALL-OUT ACTION!

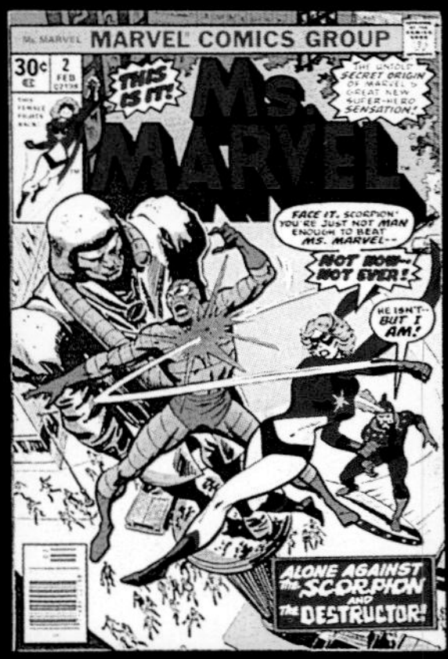
MARVEL COMICS GROUP
Ms. MARVEL
THIS IS IT!
NOT NOW-- NOT EVER!
ALONE AGAINST SCORPION AND THE DESTRUCTOR!

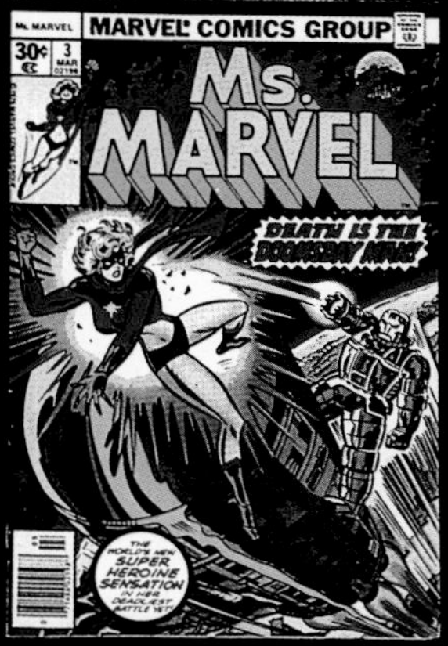
MARVEL COMICS GROUP
Ms. MARVEL
DEATH IS THE DOOMSDAY MAN!
THE WORLD'S NEW SUPER HEROINE SENSATION

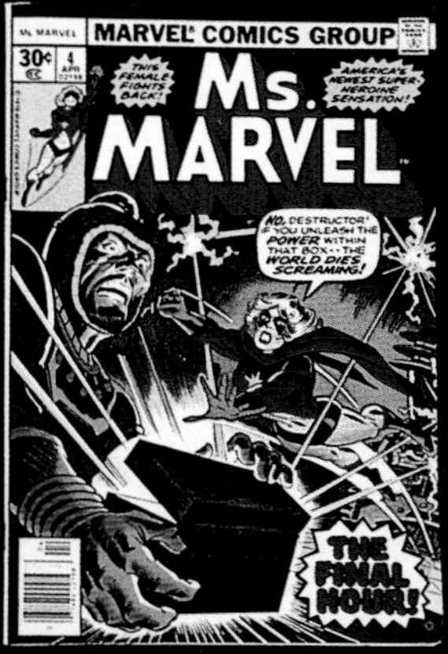
MARVEL COMICS GROUP
Ms. MARVEL
THE FINAL HOUR!

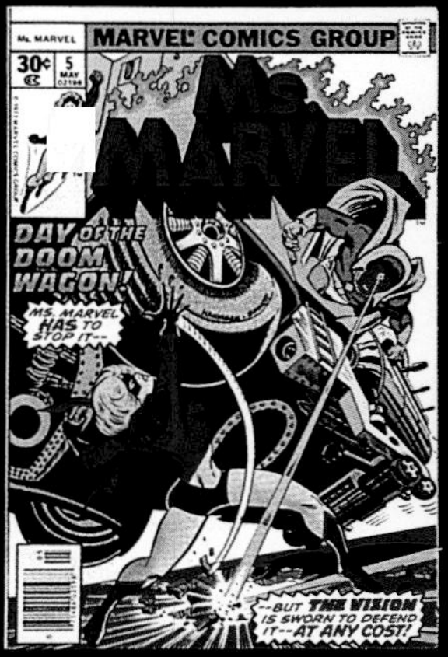
MARVEL COMICS GROUP
Ms. MARVEL
DAY OF THE DOOM WAGON!

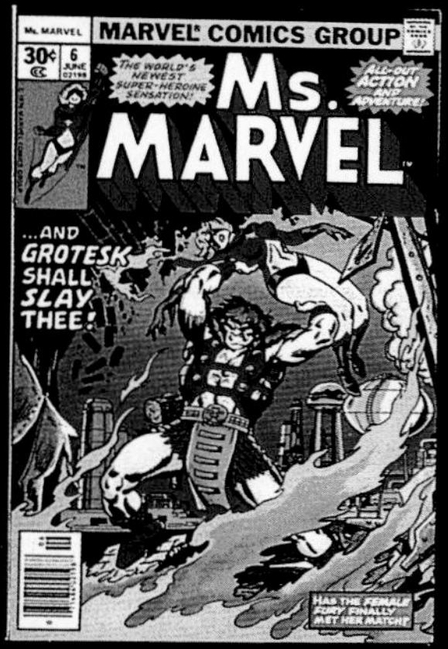
MARVEL COMICS GROUP
Ms. MARVEL
...AND GROTESK SHALL SLAY THEE!

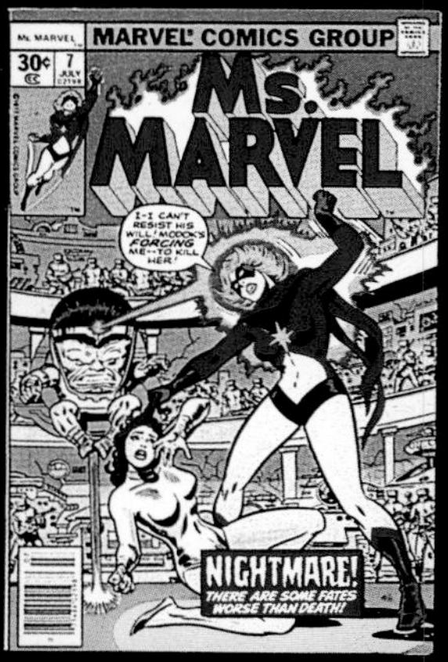
MARVEL COMICS GROUP
Ms. MARVEL
NIGHTMARE!
THERE ARE SOME FATES WORSE THAN DEATH!

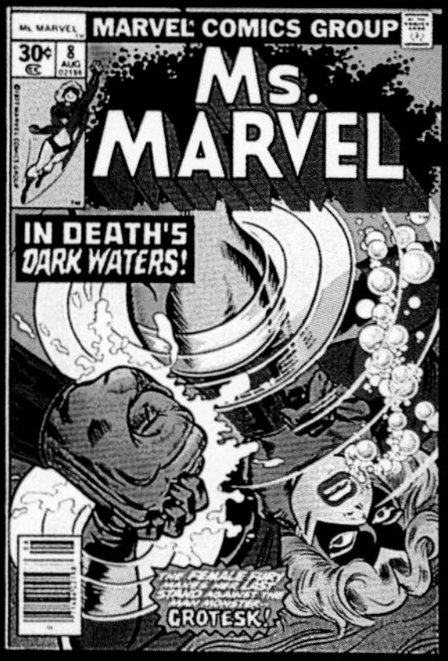
MARVEL COMICS GROUP
Ms. MARVEL
IN DEATH'S DARK WATERS!
GROTESK!

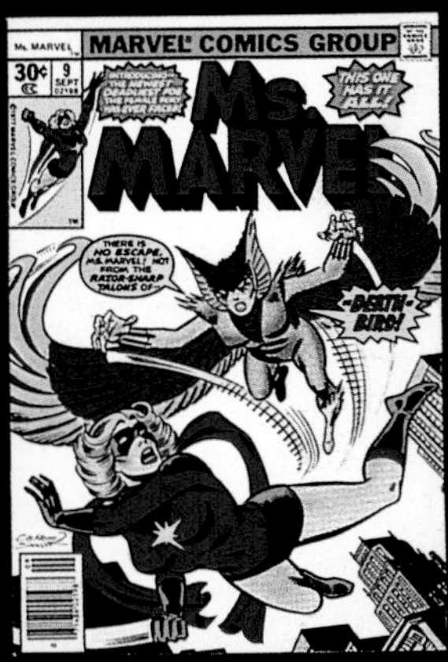
MARVEL COMICS GROUP
Ms. MARVEL
DEATH-BIRD

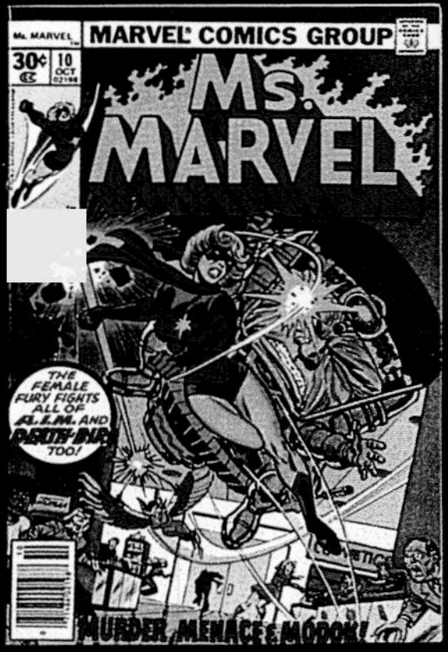
MARVEL COMICS GROUP
Ms. MARVEL

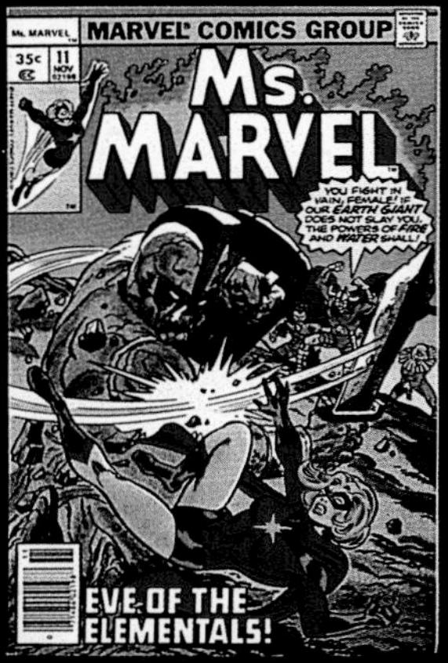
MARVEL COMICS GROUP
Ms. MARVEL
EVE OF THE ELEMENTALS!

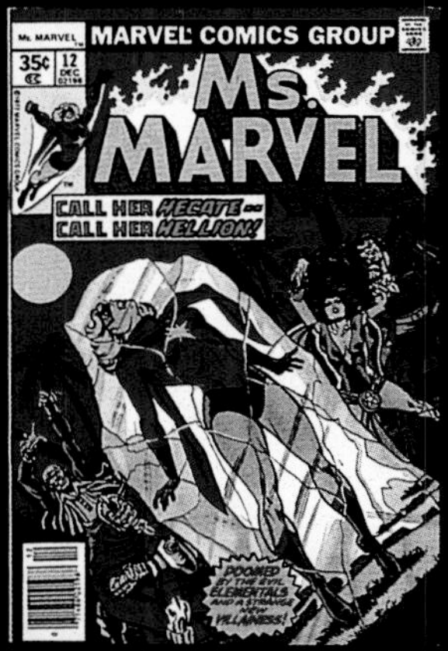
MARVEL COMICS GROUP
Ms. MARVEL

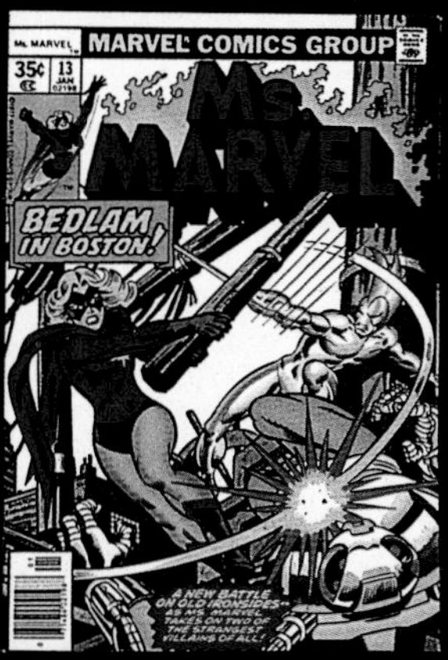
MARVEL COMICS GROUP
Ms. MARVEL
BEDLAM IN BOSTON!

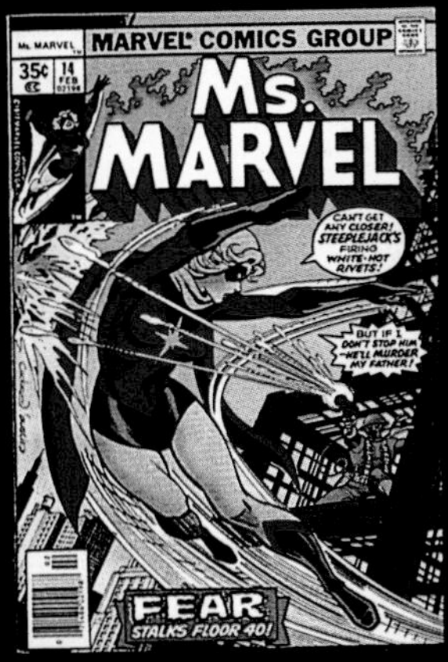
MARVEL COMICS GROUP
Ms. MARVEL
FEAR STALKS FLOOR 40!

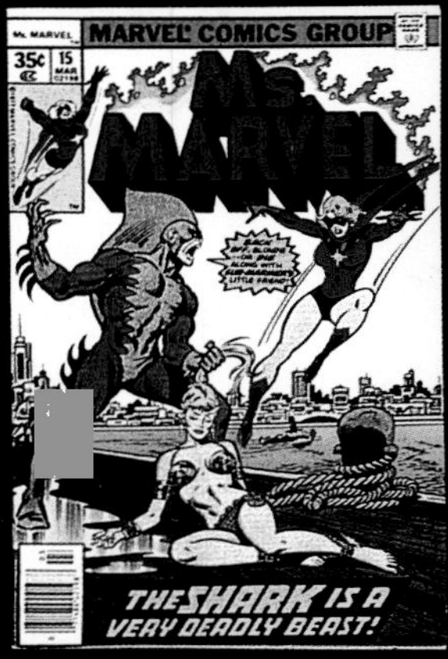
MARVEL COMICS GROUP
Ms. MARVEL
THE SHARK IS A VERY DEADLY BEAST!

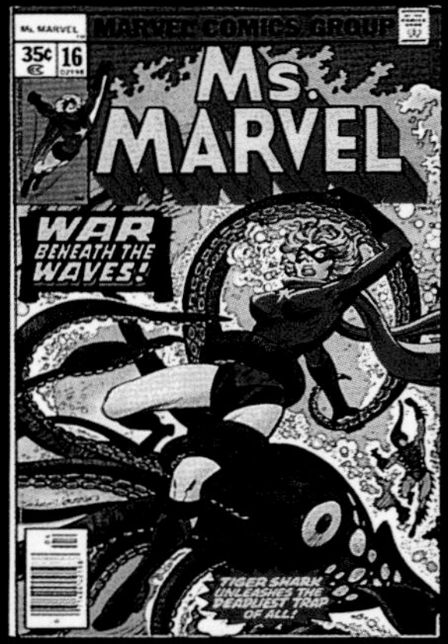
MARVEL COMICS GROUP
Ms. MARVEL
WAR BENEATH THE WAVES!

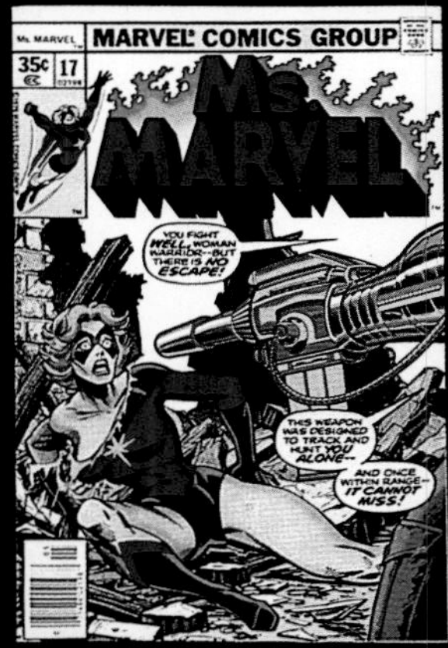
MARVEL COMICS GROUP
Ms. MARVEL

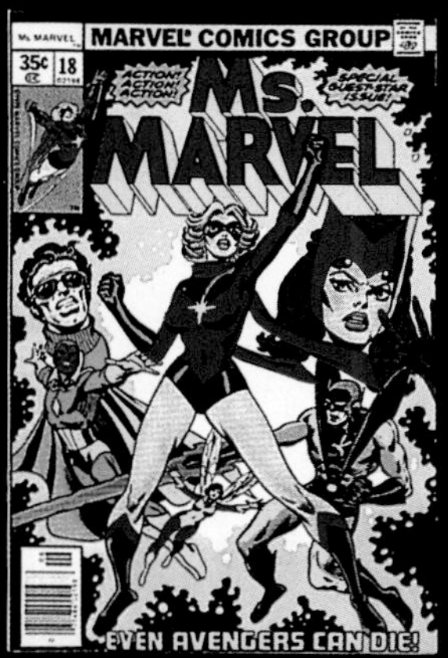
MARVEL COMICS GROUP
Ms. MARVEL
EVEN AVENGERS CAN DIE!

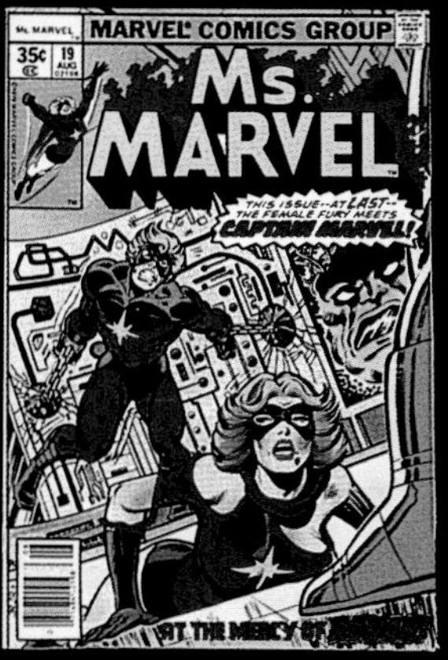
MARVEL COMICS GROUP
Ms. MARVEL

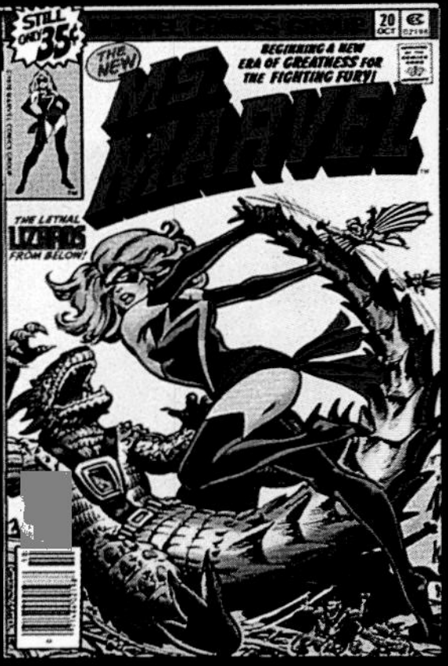
MS. MARVEL

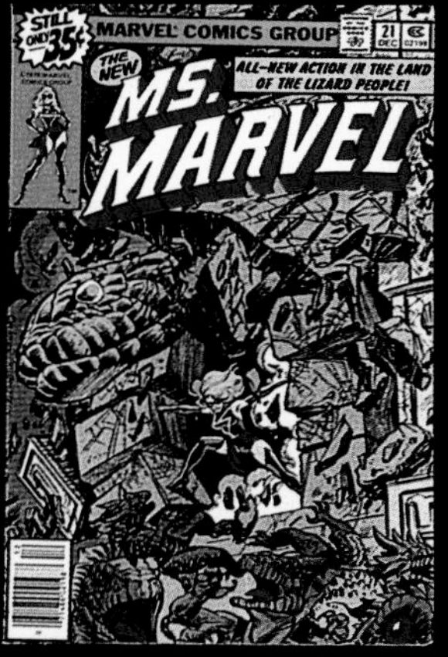
MARVEL COMICS GROUP
MS. MARVEL

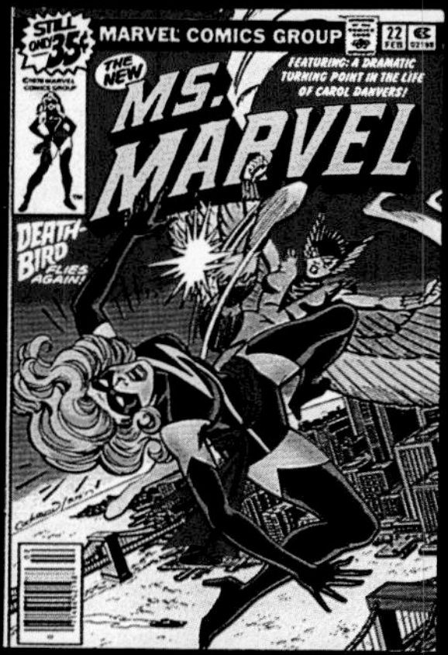
MARVEL COMICS GROUP
MS. MARVEL

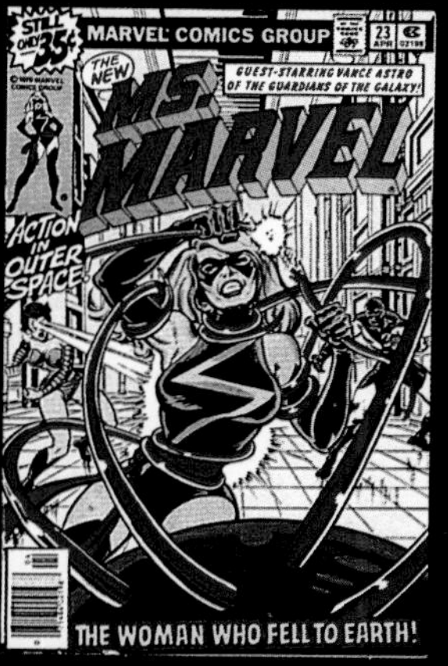
MARVEL COMICS GROUP
MS. MARVEL
THE WOMAN WHO FELL TO EARTH!

1306.8 The Muppets take Manhattan (1)

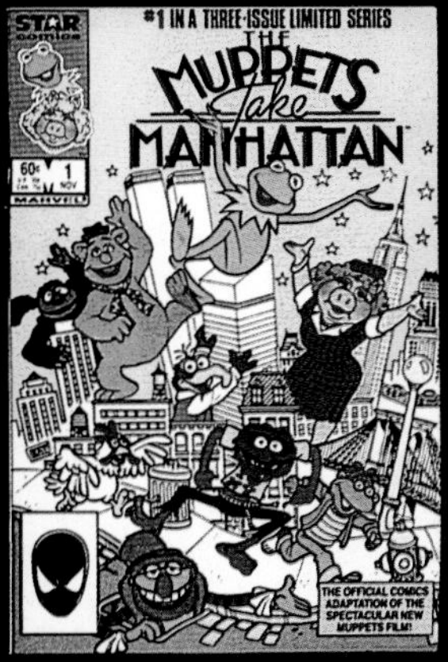
#1 IN A THREE-ISSUE LIMITED SERIES
MUPPETS take MANHATTAN

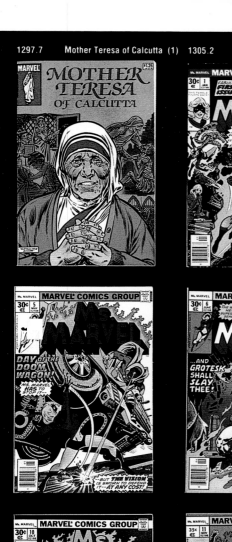

1354.3 The 'Nam (1-10)

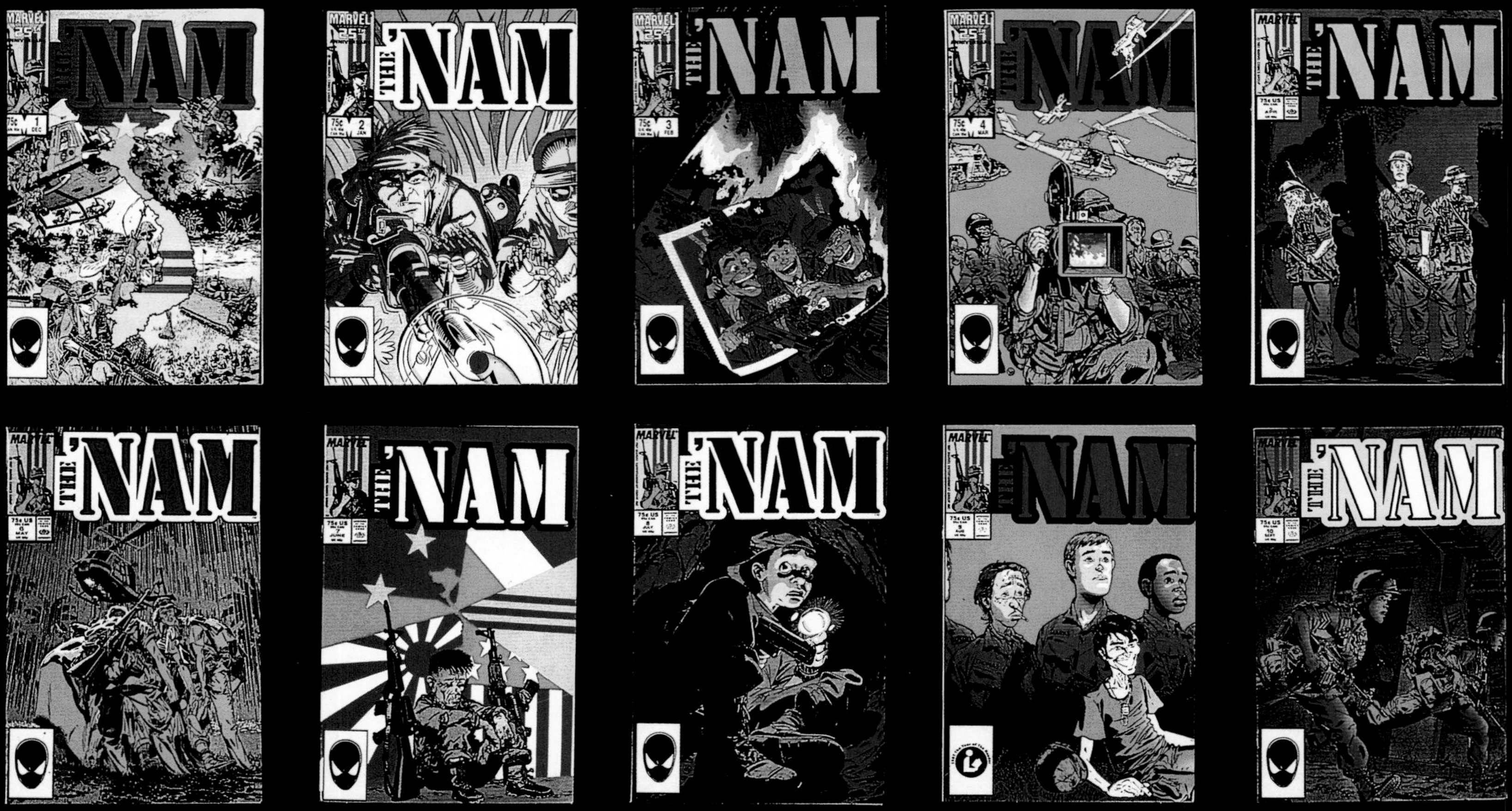
THE 'NAM

1372.8 The New Mutants (1-15)

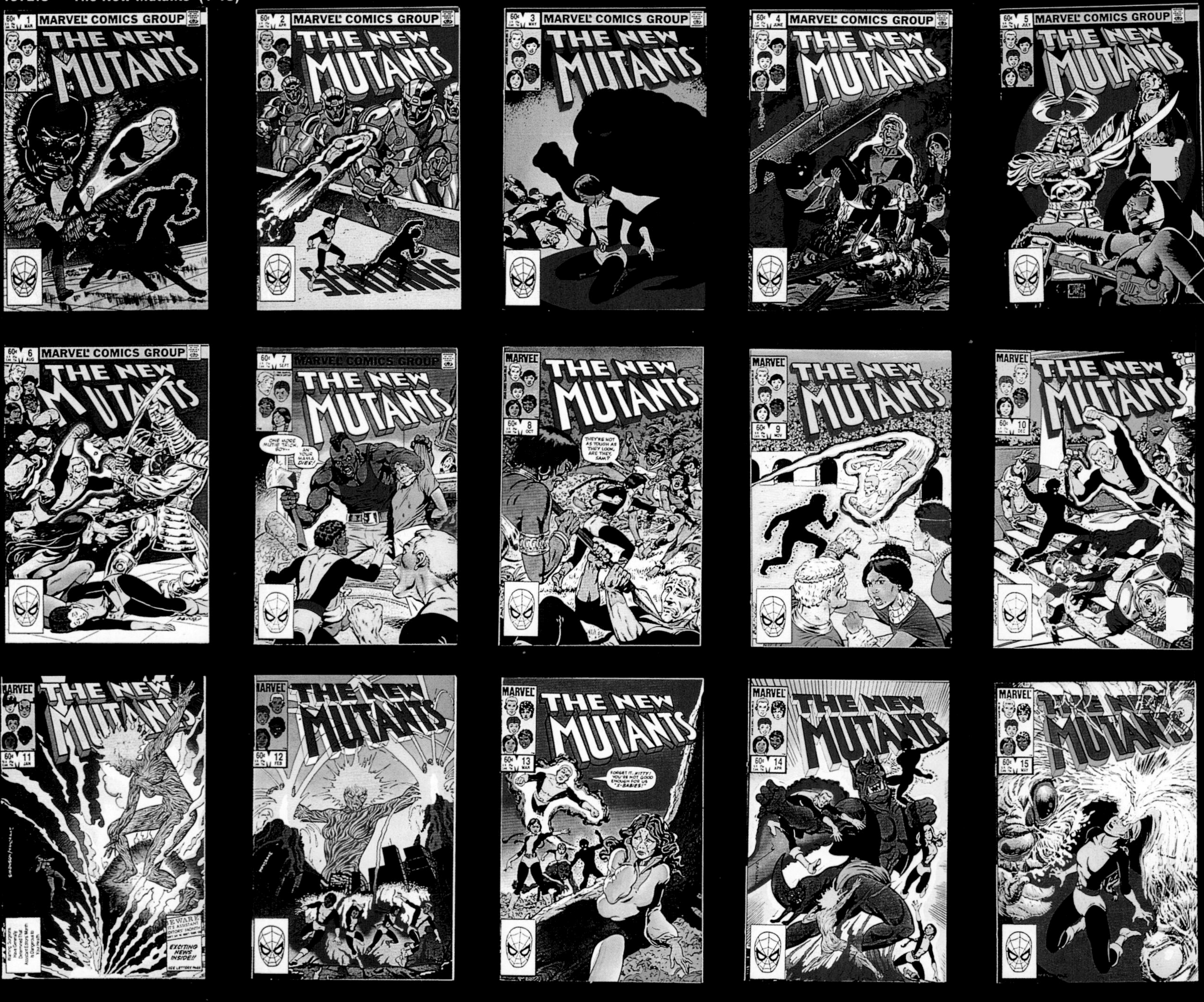
MARVEL COMICS GROUP
THE NEW MUTANTS

1372.8 The New Mutants (16-42, 59, 60)

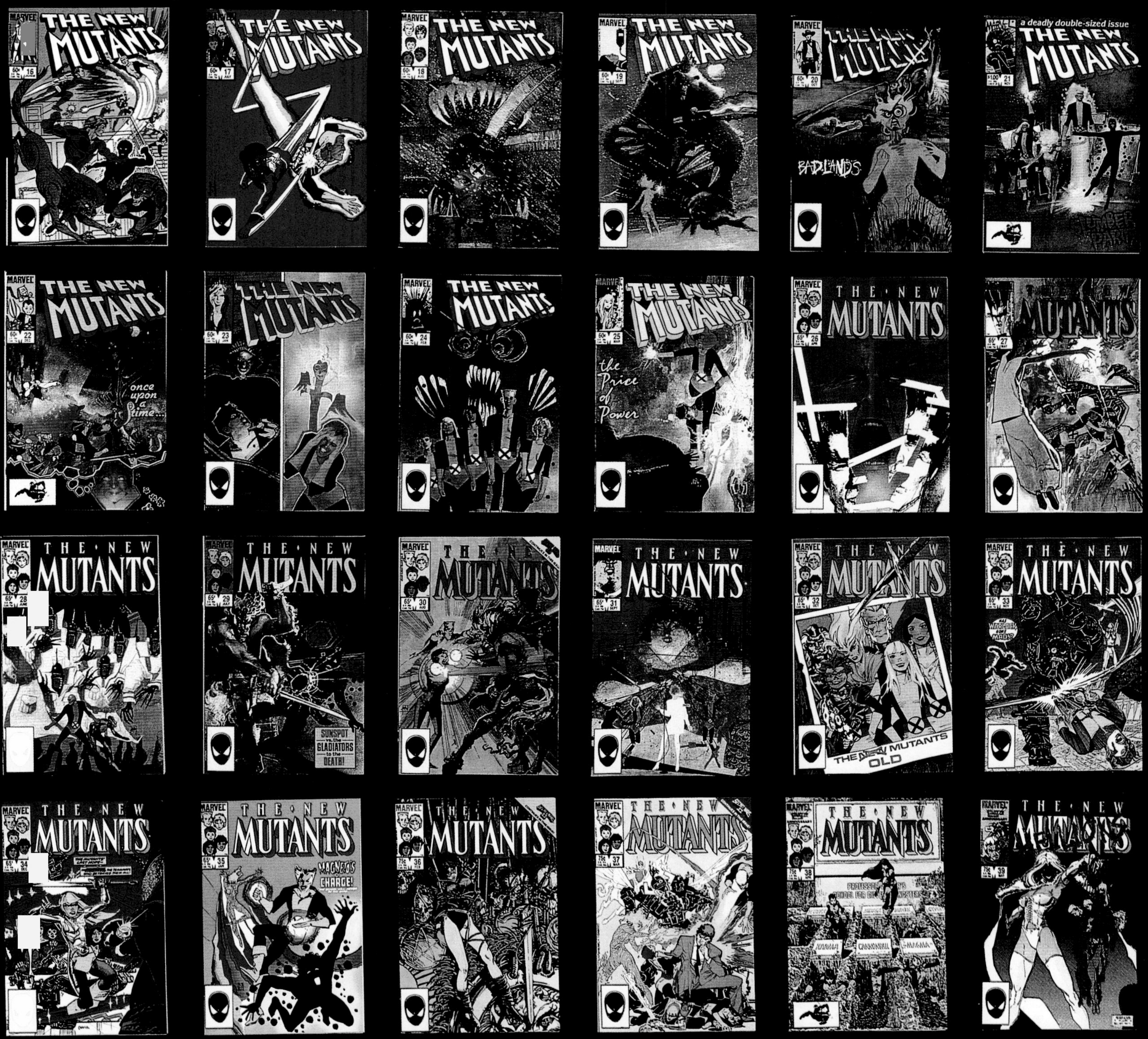
a deadly double-sized issue
BADLANDS
once upon a time...
the Price of Power
SUNSPOT vs. the GLADIATORS to the DEATH!
MAGNETO'S CHARGE!

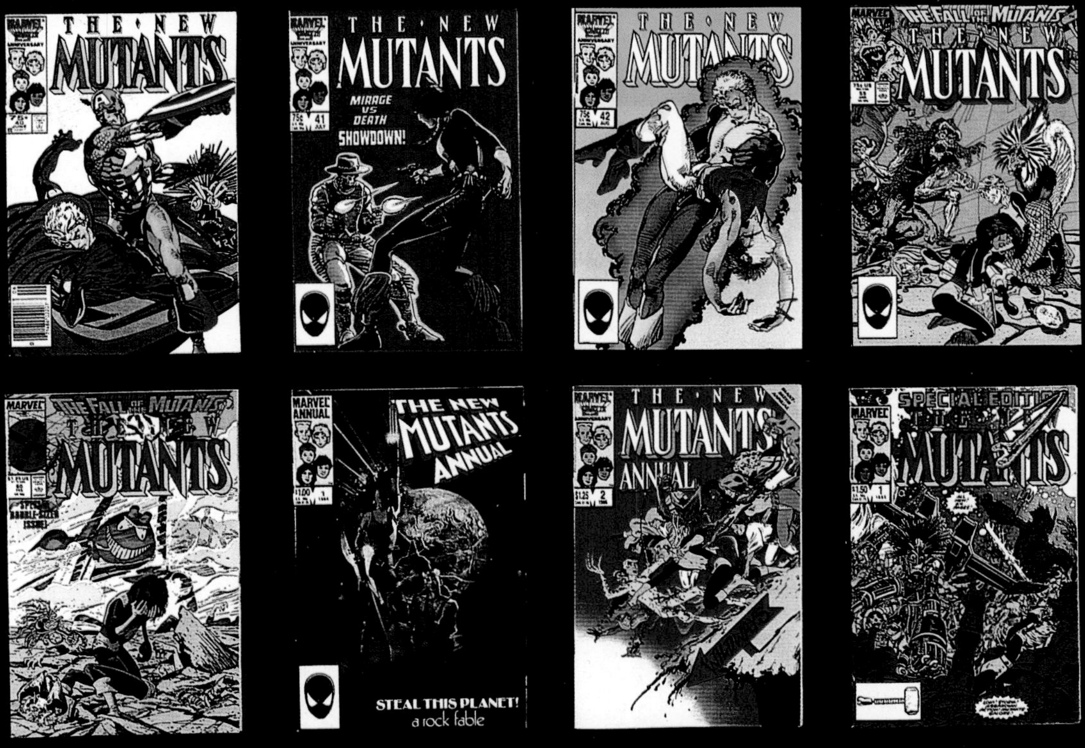
MIRAGE VS DEATH SHOWDOWN!
STEAL THIS PLANET! a rock fable

Mother Teresa of Calcutta (1) 1297.7

Ref. No.	Date	RVI	Artist/Info.
1297.7-1	1984	1	Tartaglione/Sinnott-c

Ms. Marvel (1-23) 1305.2

1305.2-1	Jan. 1977	1	Romita/Giordano-c, Buscema/Smith
1305.2-2	Feb.	1	Buscema/Giordano-c, Buscema/Sinnott-a
1305.2-3	Mar.	1	Milgrom/Sinnott-c, Buscema/Sinnott-a
1305.2-4	Apr.	1	Hannigan/Giacoia-c, Mooney/Sinnott-a
1305.2-5	May	1	Hannigan/Sinnott-c, Mooney/Sinnott-a
1305.2-6	Jun.	1	M. Severin/Giacoia-c, Mooney/Sinnott-a
1305.2-7	Jul.	1	Buscema/Sinnott-c, Mooney/Sinnott-a
1305.2-8	Aug.	1	Wilson/Sinnott-c, Mooney/Sinnott-a
1305.2-9	Sept.	1	Cockrum/Sinnott-c, Pollard/Sinnott, Grainger-a
1305.2-10	Oct.	1	Buscema/Palmer-c/a
1305.2-11 to 23	Apr. 1979, (#23)	1	(#20, New Costume)

Muppets take Manhattan (1-3) 1306.8

1306.8-1 to 3	Nov. 1984, (#1)	1	Reprints

My Love (1-39) 1326.5

1326.5-1	Sept. 1969	2	
1326.5-2		1	
1326.5-3			
1326.5-4 to 39	Mar. 1976, (#39)	1	
1326.5-SP. 1	Dec. 1971	1	

The 'Nam (1-Present) 1354.3

1354.3-1	Dec. 1986	12	(1st P.) Golden/Gil-a
1354.3-2	Jan. 1987	7	Golden/Gil-a
1354.3-3	Feb.	4	" "
1354.3-4	Mar.	4	Golden/Moreno-a
1354.3-5 to 50	Jan. 1991, (#50)	2	(#32, Death of R.F. Kennedy)

The New Mutants (1-Present) 1372.8

1372.8-1	Mar. 1983	6	McLeod-c/a, Gustovich-a
1372.8-2	Apr.	3	Reg. Ed. McLeod-c/a, Gustovich-a
1372.8-3	May	2	McLeod-c, Gustovich-a
1372.8-4 to 30		2	(#18, Intro. Warlock)
1372.8-31 to 90		1	(#50, Double-size; #63, X-Men, Wolverine -app.)
1372.8-A1	1984	3	
1372.8-A2 to A6	Oct. 1986 (A1)	2	
1372.8-SP 1	1985	4	

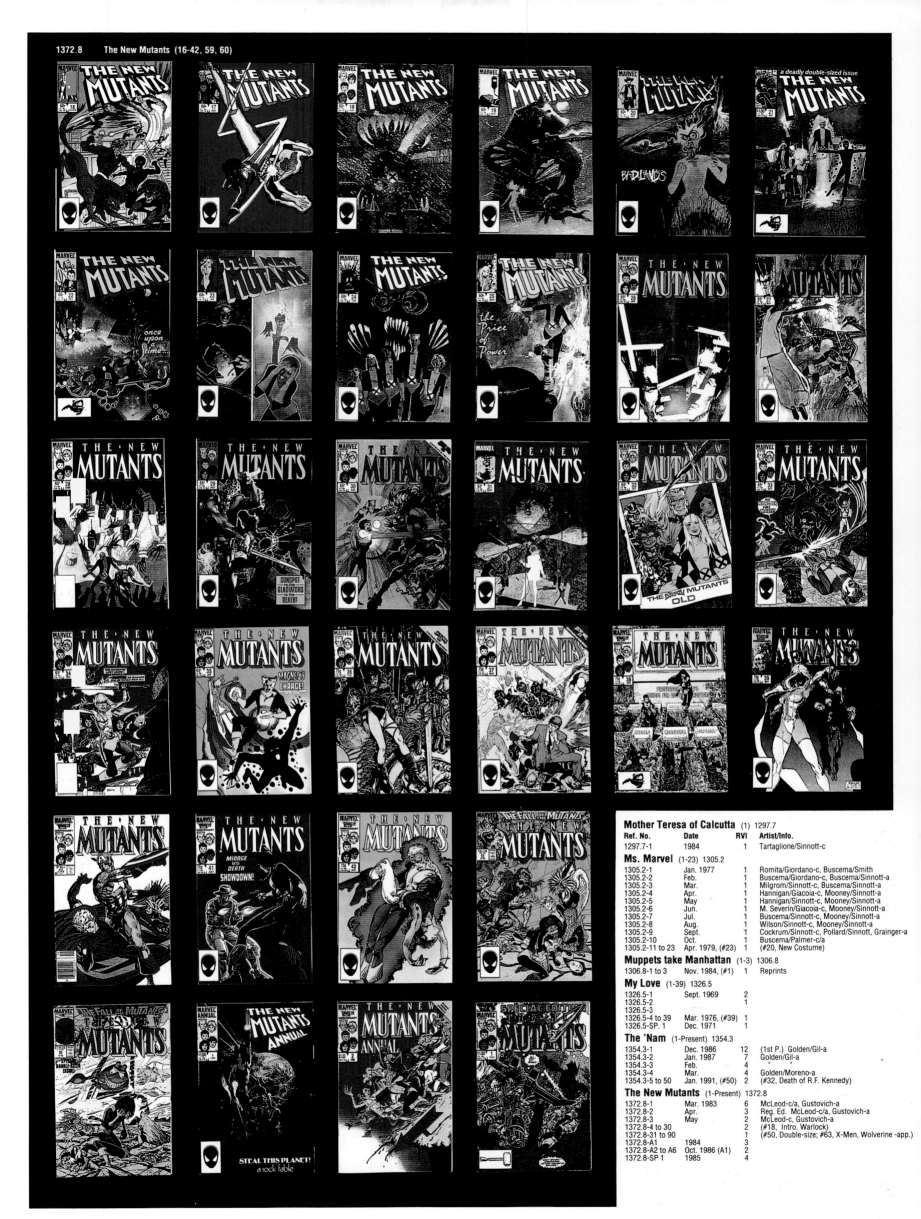

1376.2 Nick Fury, Agent of SHIELD (1-18)

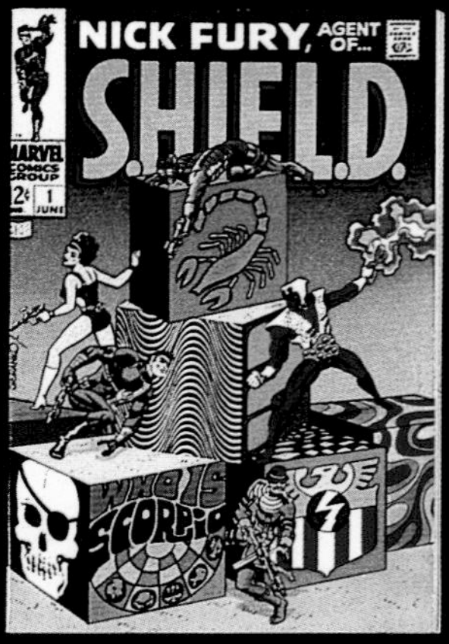
NICK FURY, AGENT OF...
S.H.I.E.L.D.
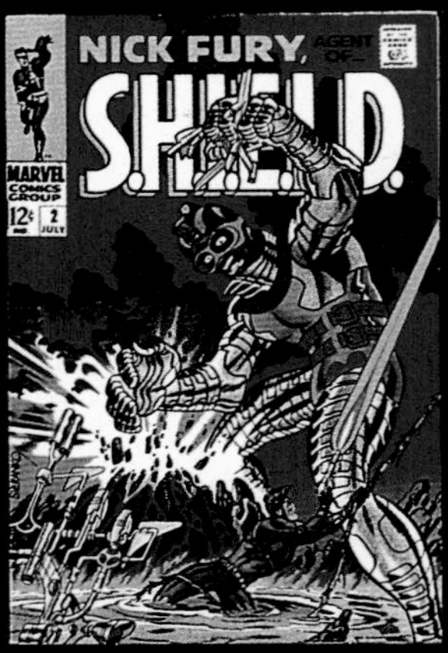
NICK FURY, AGENT OF...
S.H.I.E.L.D.
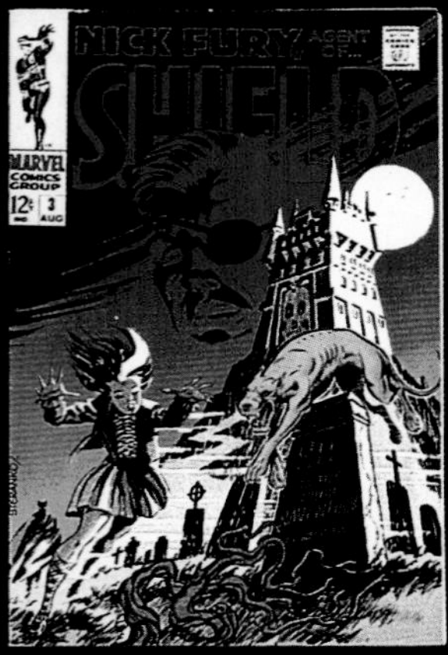
NICK FURY, AGENT OF...
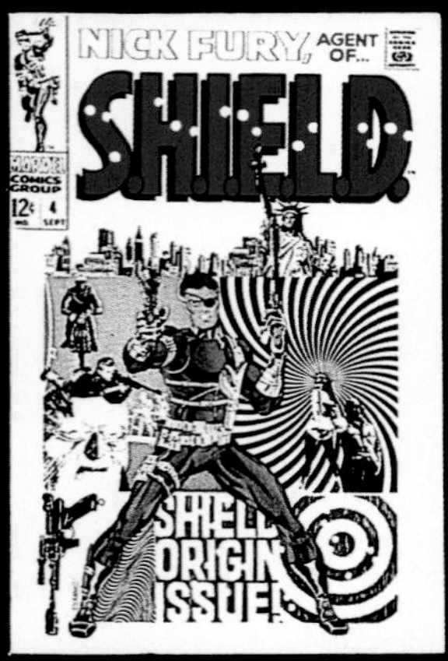
NICK FURY, AGENT OF...
S.H.I.E.L.D.
SHIELD ORIGIN ISSUE!
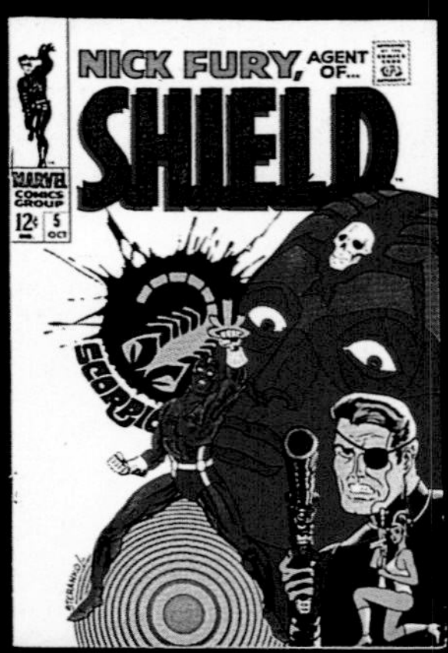
NICK FURY, AGENT OF...
SHIELD
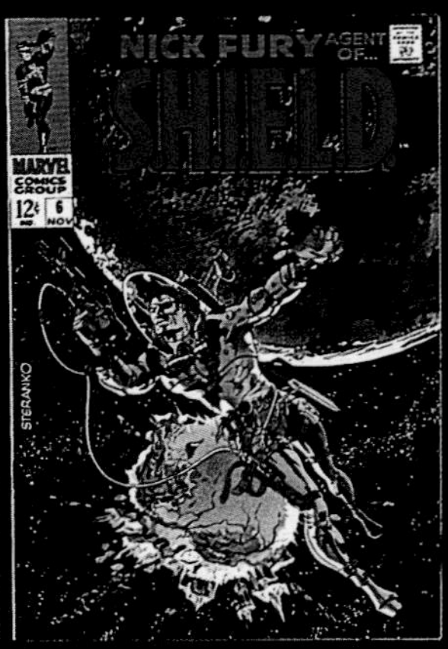
NICK FURY, AGENT OF...
SHIELD
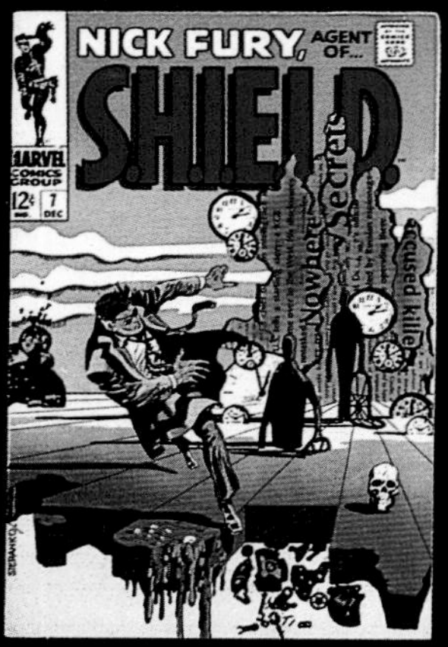
NICK FURY, AGENT OF...
S.H.I.E.L.D.
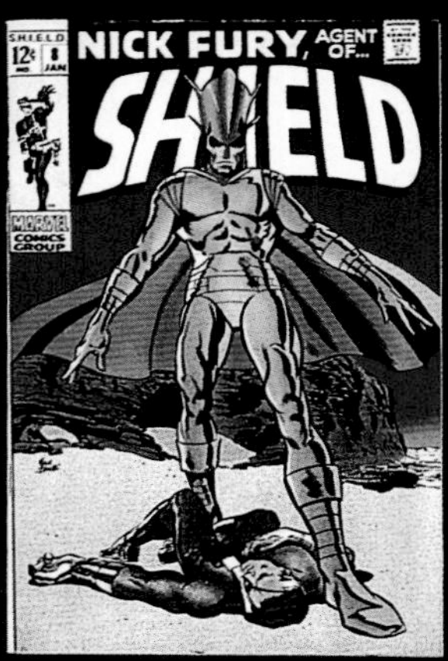
NICK FURY, AGENT OF...
SHIELD
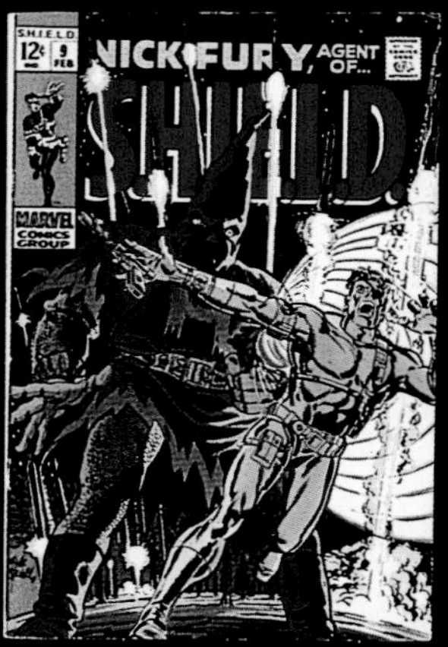
NICK FURY, AGENT OF...
SHIELD
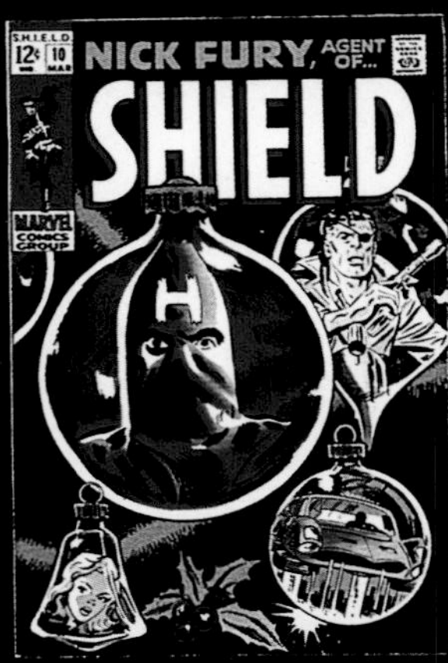
NICK FURY, AGENT OF...
SHIELD
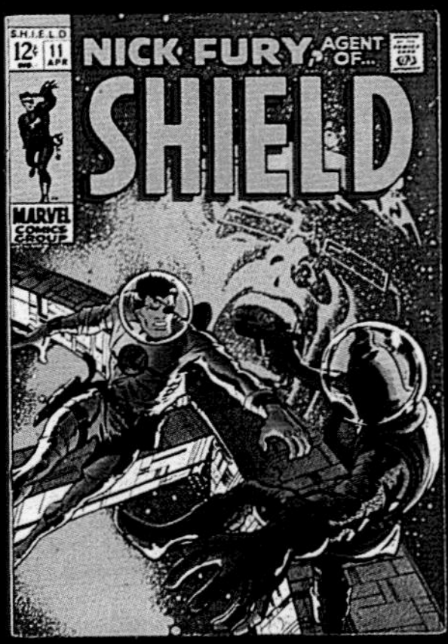
NICK FURY, AGENT OF...
SHIELD
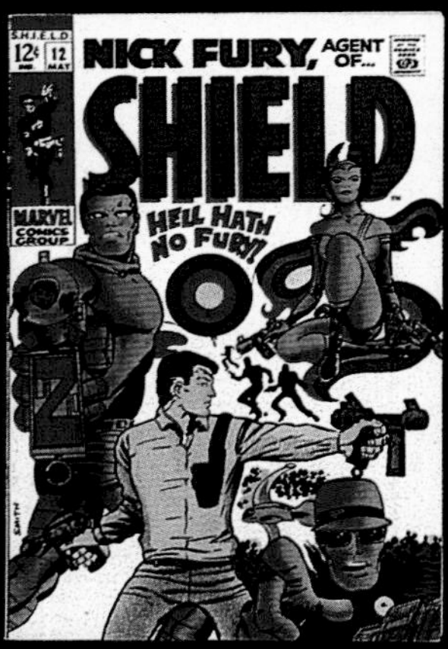
NICK FURY, AGENT OF...
SHIELD
HELL HATH NO FURY!
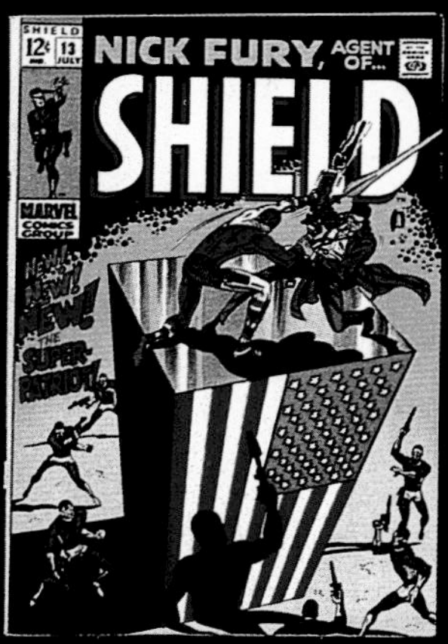
NICK FURY, AGENT OF...
SHIELD
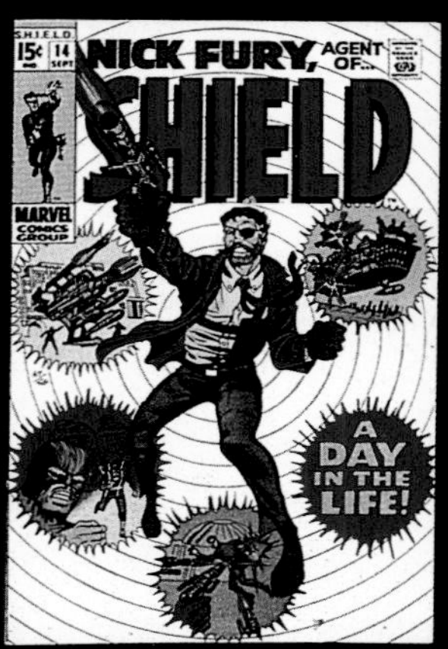
NICK FURY, AGENT OF...
SHIELD
A DAY IN THE LIFE!
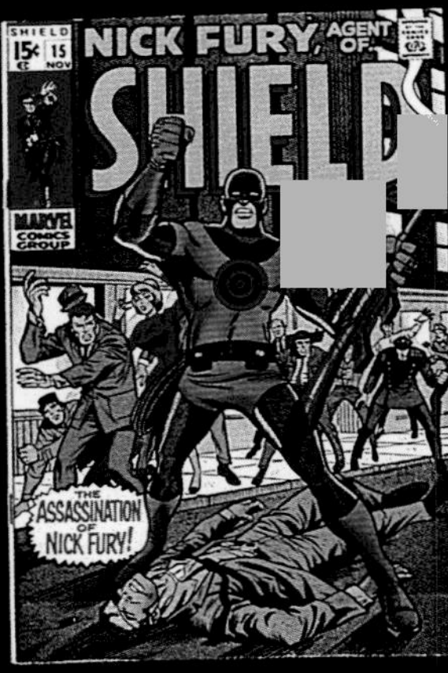
NICK FURY, AGENT OF...
SHIELD
THE ASSASSINATION OF NICK FURY!

1376.4 Nick Fury, Agent of SHIELD (1-2)

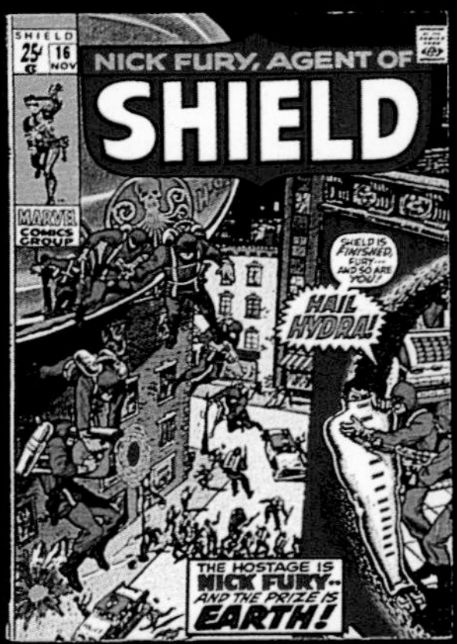
NICK FURY, AGENT OF
SHIELD
THE HOSTAGE IS NICK FURY-- AND THE PRIZE IS EARTH!
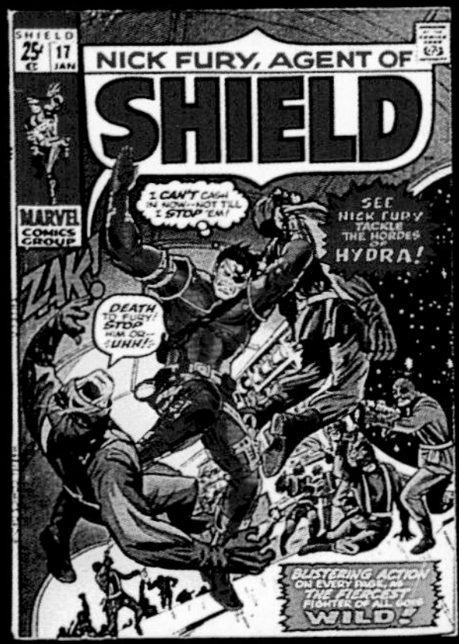
NICK FURY, AGENT OF
SHIELD
SEE NICK FURY TACKLE THE HORDES OF HYDRA!
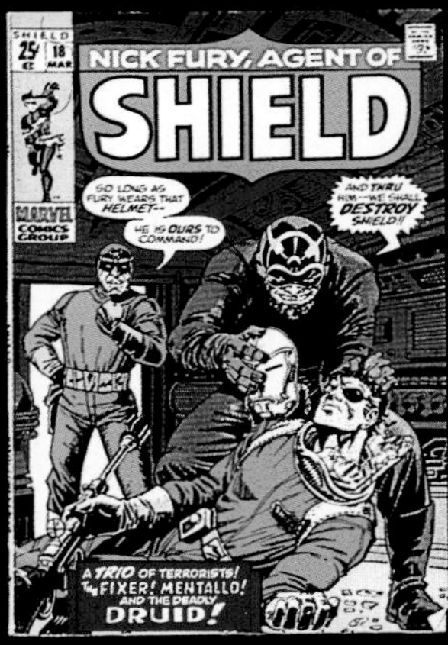
NICK FURY, AGENT OF
SHIELD
A TRIO OF TERRORISTS! FIXER! MENTALLO! AND THE DEADLY DRUID!
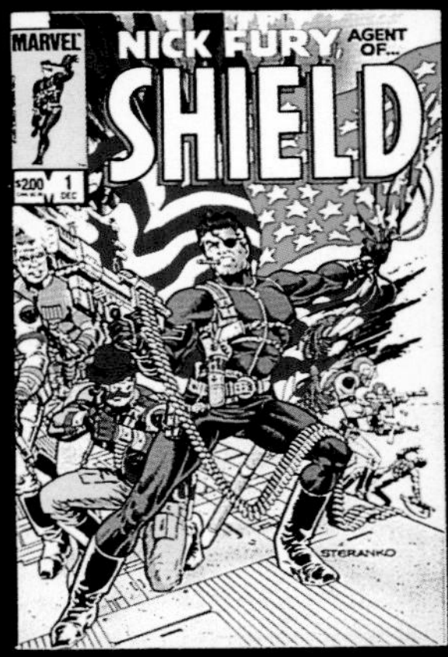
NICK FURY, AGENT OF
SHIELD
STERANKO
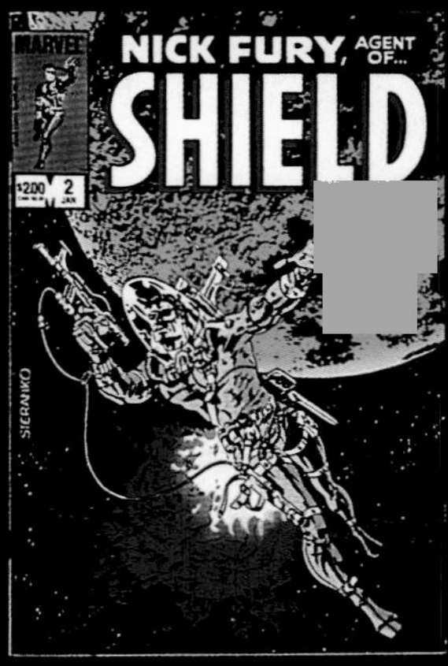
NICK FURY, AGENT OF
SHIELD

1376.6 Nick Fury, Agent of SHIELD (1-3)

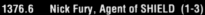

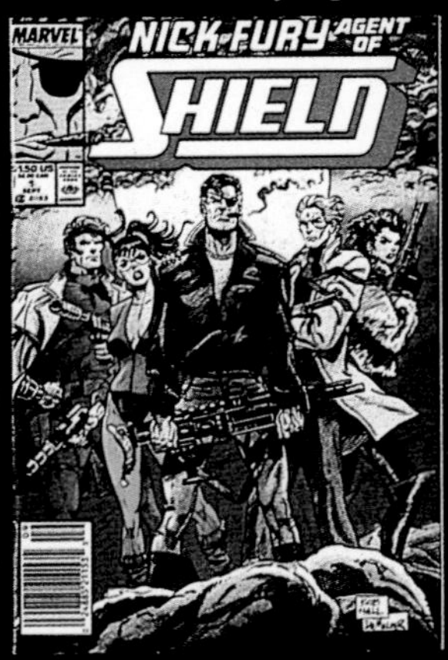
NICK FURY AGENT OF
SHIELD
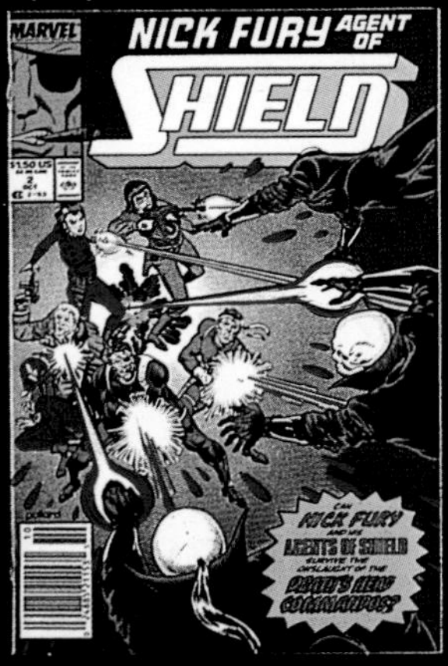
NICK FURY AGENT OF
SHIELD
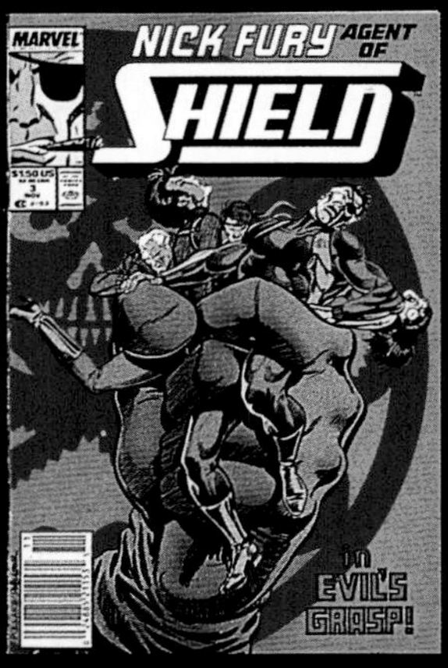
NICK FURY AGENT OF
SHIELD
EVIL'S GRASP!

Nick Fury, Agent of SHIELD (1-18) 1376.2

Ref. No.	Date	RVI	Artist/Info.
1376.2-1	Jun. 1968	22	Steranko-c/a, Sinnott-a
1376.2-2	Jul.	13	Steranko-c/a, Sinnott, Adkins, Tartag-a
1376.2-3	Aug.	13	Steranko/Adkins-a
1376.2-4	Sept.	13	Steranko-c, Springer-a
1376.2-5	Oct.	13	Steranko-c/a
1376.2-6	Nov.	6	Steranko-c, Springer-a
1376.2-7	Dec.	6	" "
1376.2-8 to 13	May 1969, (#12)	4	(#9, Intro. Hate Monger)
1376.2-14 to 18	Mar. 1971, (#18)	1	(RVI #15; 8) (Reprints)

Nick Fury, Agent of SHIELD (1-2) 1376.4

1376.4-1 to 2	Dec. 1983	1	Steranko-c/a Reprints

Nick Fury, Agent of SHIELD V.2 (1-22) 1376.6

1376.6-1	Sept. 1989	1	Hall/DeMulder-c/a
1376.6-2	Oct.	1	Pollard-c/a, DeMulder-a
1376.6-3	Nov.	1	Pollard/DeMulder-c/a
1376.6-4	Dec.	1	
1376.6-5	Jan. 1990	1	
1376.6-6	Feb.	1	
1376.6-7	Mar.	1	
1376.6-8	Apr.	1	
1376.6-9 to 22		1	

Nick Fury vs. SHIELD (1-6) 1376.8

1376.8-1	Jun. 1988	10	Steranko-c
1376.8-2	Jul.	12	Sienkiewicz-c
1376.8-3	Aug.	7	
1376.8-4 to 6	Nov. 1988, (#6)	3	

1376.9 Nick Fury vs. SHIELD (1-6)

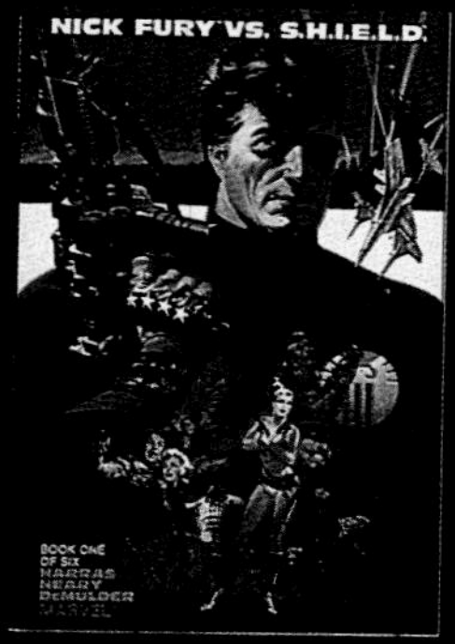
NICK FURY VS. S.H.I.E.L.D.
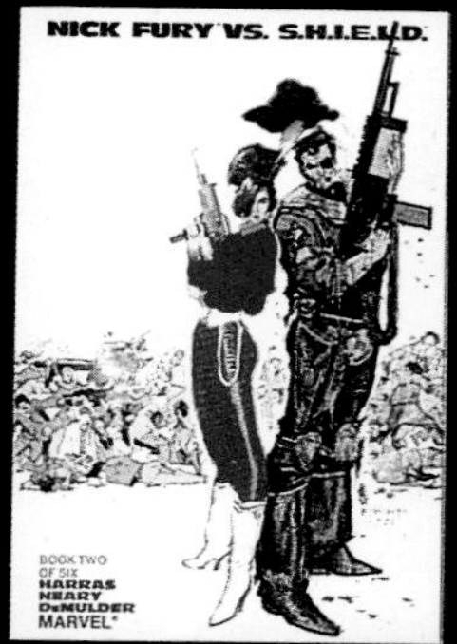
NICK FURY VS. S.H.I.E.L.D.
BOOK TWO OF SIX HARRAS HEARY DeMULDER
MARVEL
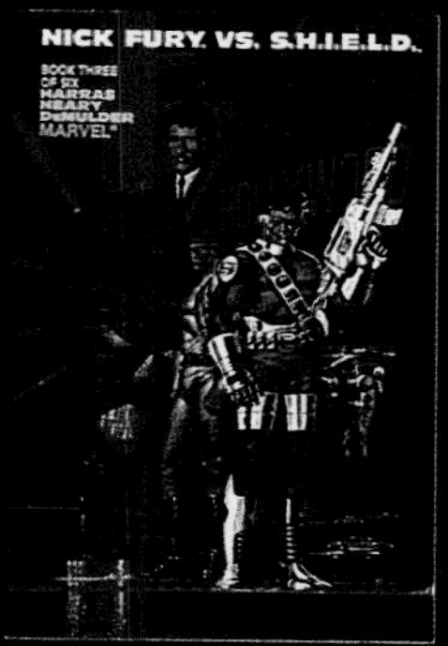
NICK FURY VS. S.H.I.E.L.D.
MARVEL
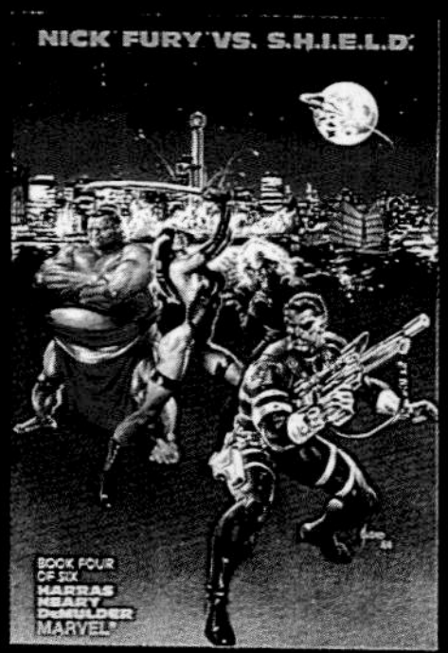
NICK FURY VS. S.H.I.E.L.D.
BOOK FOUR OF SIX HARRAS HEARY DeMULDER
MARVEL
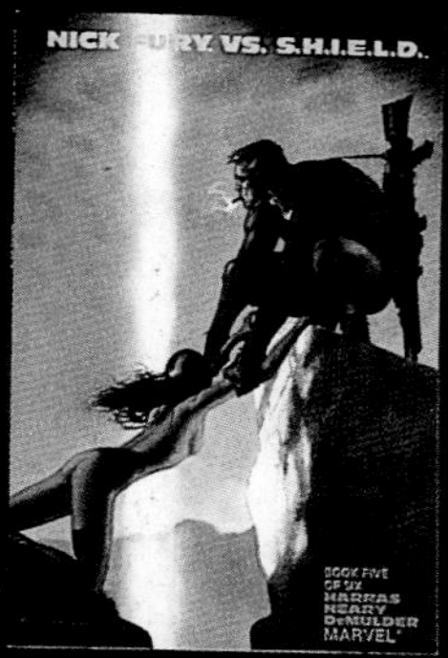
NICK FURY VS. S.H.I.E.L.D.
BOOK FIVE OF SIX HARRAS HEARY DeMULDER
MARVEL
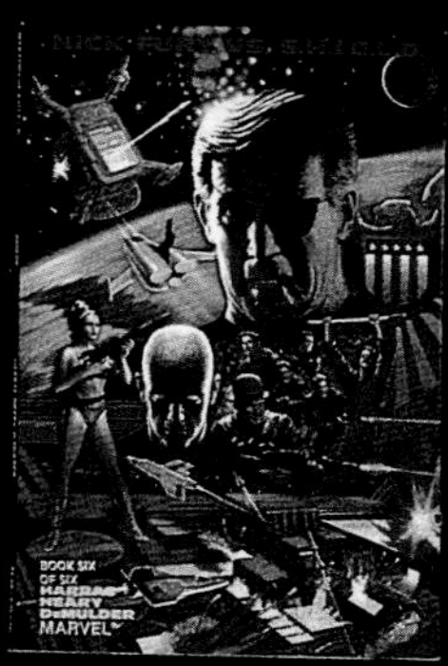
BOOK SIX OF SIX HARRAS HEARY DeMULDER
MARVEL

1378 Nightcrawler (1-4)

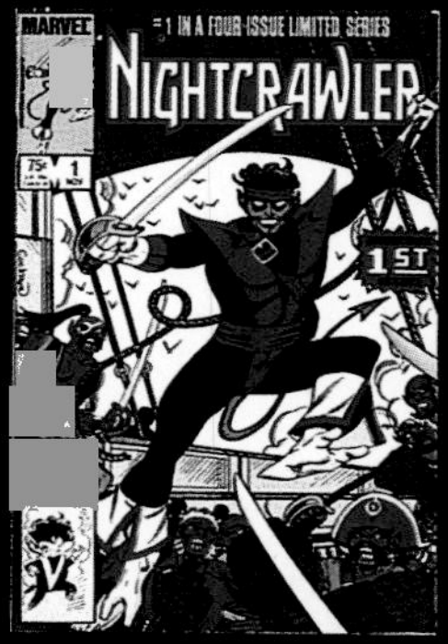
NIGHTCRAWLER
1ST
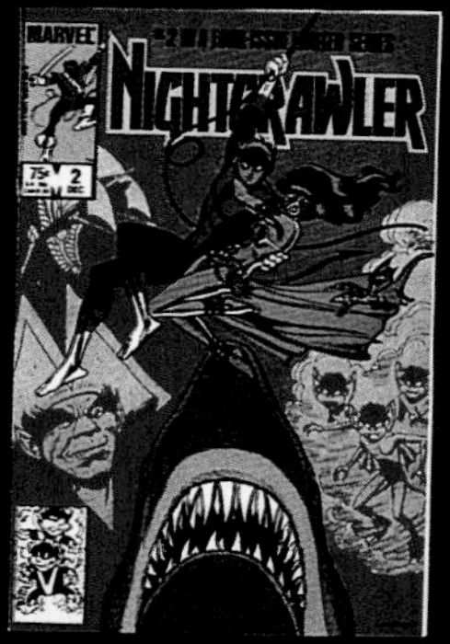
NIGHTCRAWLER
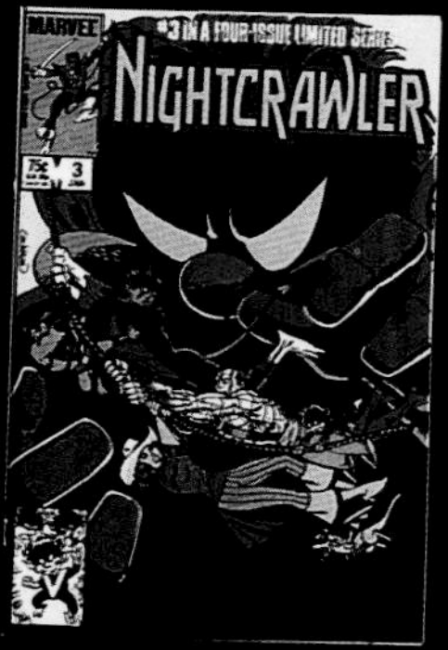
NIGHTCRAWLER
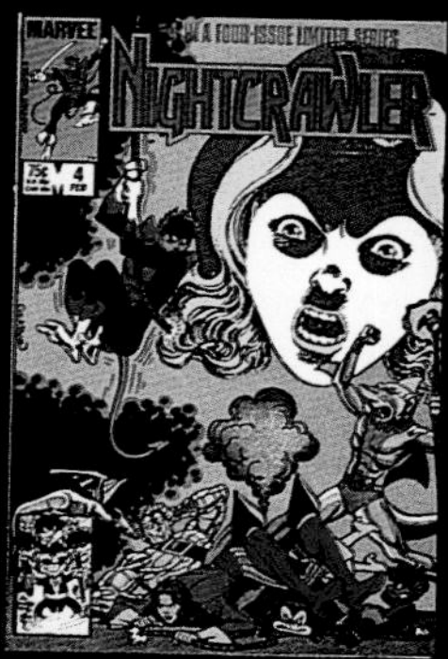
NIGHTCRAWLER

1380.4 Night Nurse (1-2)

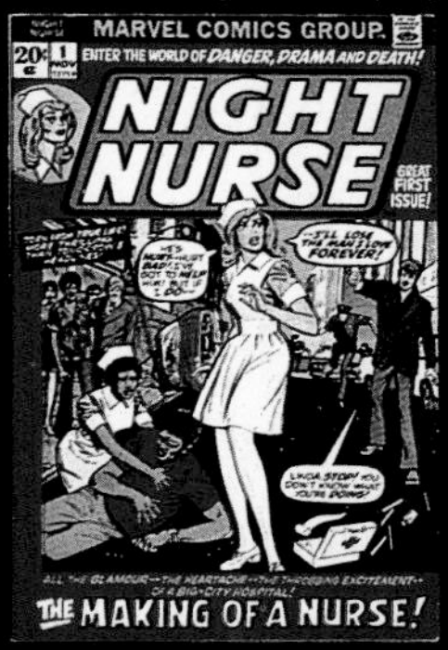
MARVEL COMICS GROUP
ENTER THE WORLD OF DANGER, DRAMA AND DEATH!
NIGHT NURSE
THE MAKING OF A NURSE!
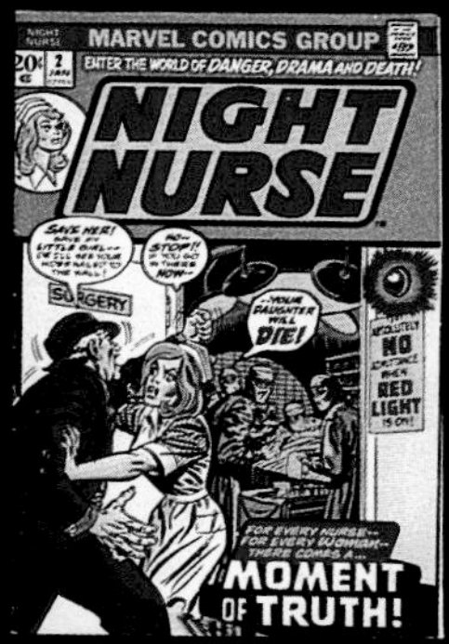
MARVEL COMICS GROUP
ENTER THE WORLD OF DANGER, DRAMA AND DEATH!
NIGHT NURSE
MOMENT OF TRUTH!

1380.35 Nightmask (1-6)

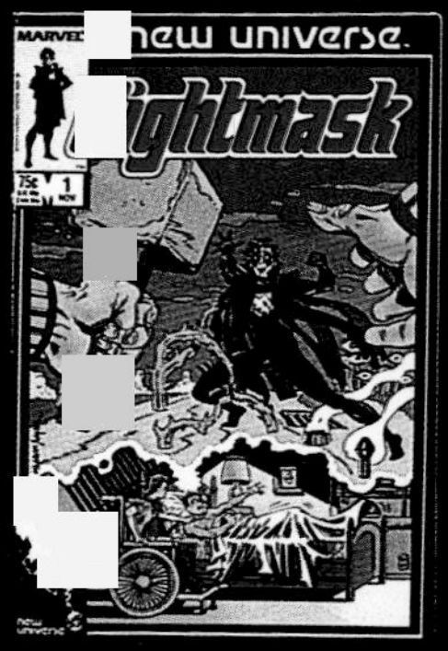
new universe.
Nightmask
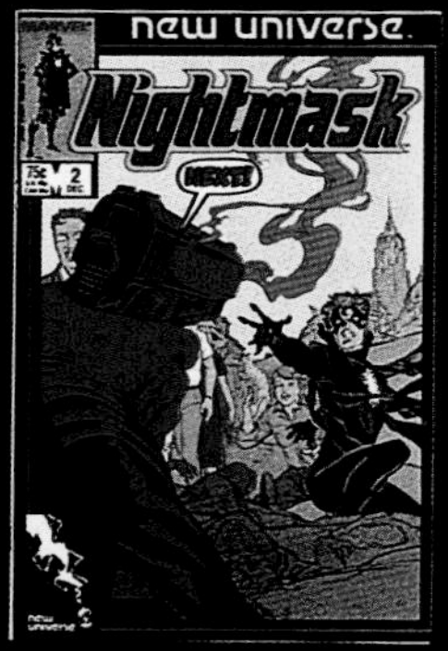
new universe.
Nightmask
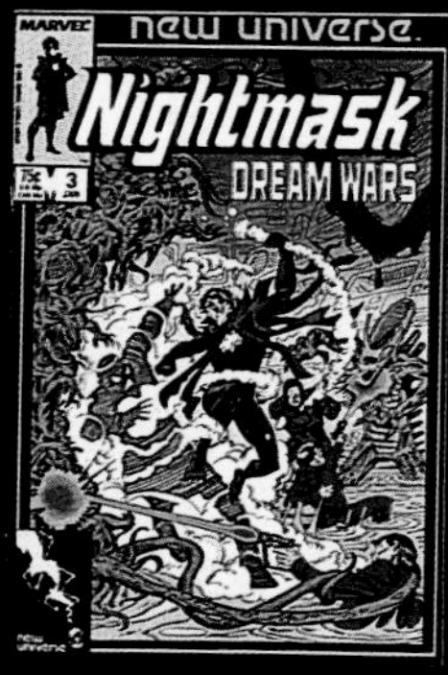
new universe.
Nightmask
DREAM WARS
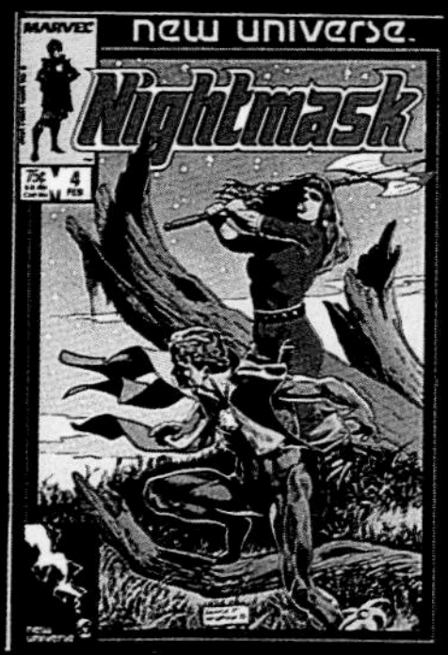
new universe.
Nightmask
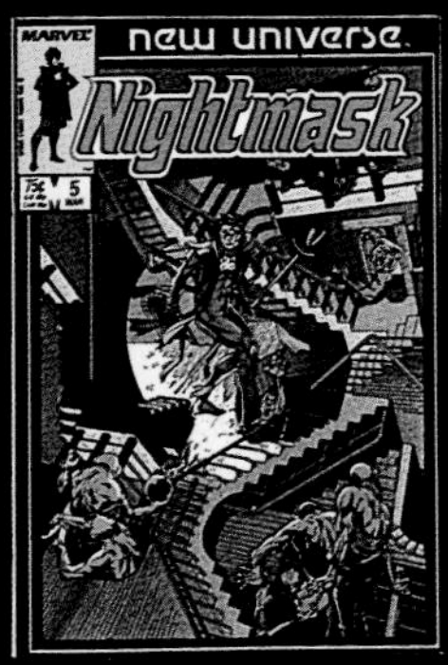
new universe.
Nightmask
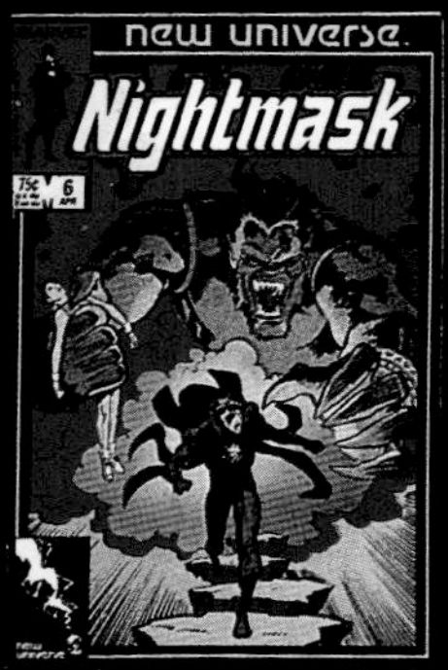
new universe.
Nightmask

1381.1 Not Brand Echh (1-13)

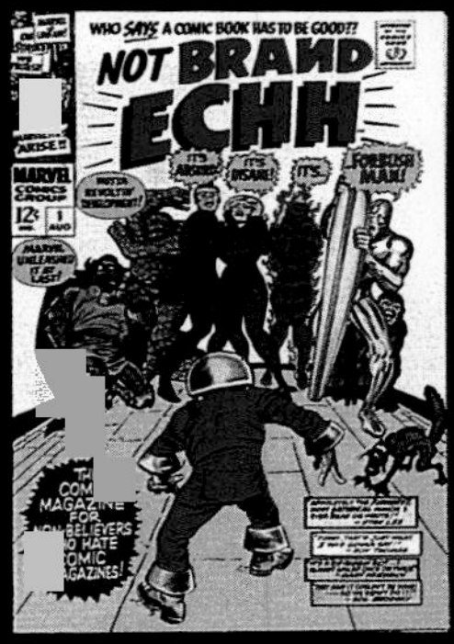
WHO SAYS A COMIC BOOK HAS TO BE GOOD??
NOT BRAND ECHH
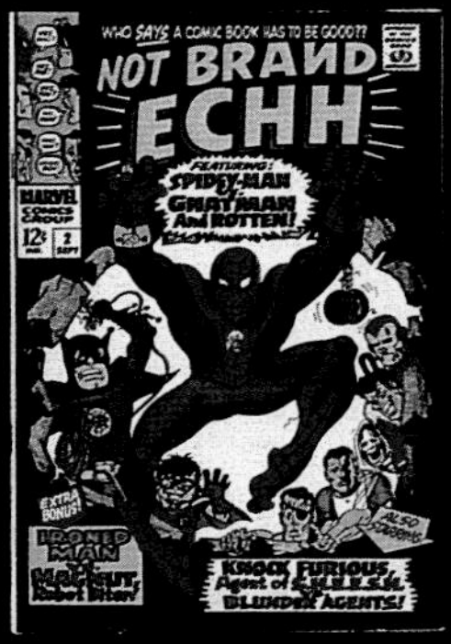
WHO SAYS A COMIC BOOK HAS TO BE GOOD??
NOT BRAND ECHH
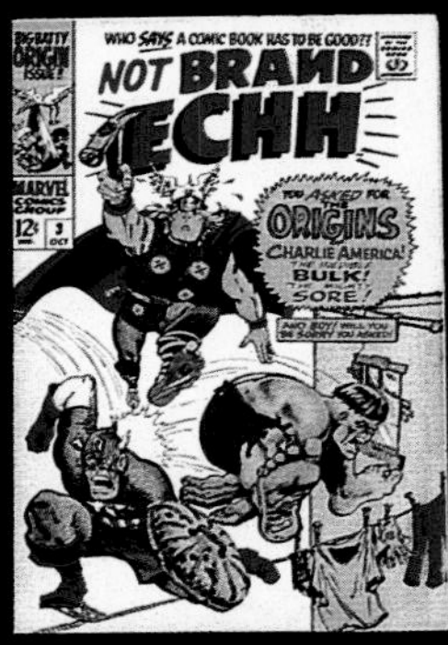
WHO SAYS A COMIC BOOK HAS TO BE GOOD??
NOT BRAND ECHH
ORIGINS
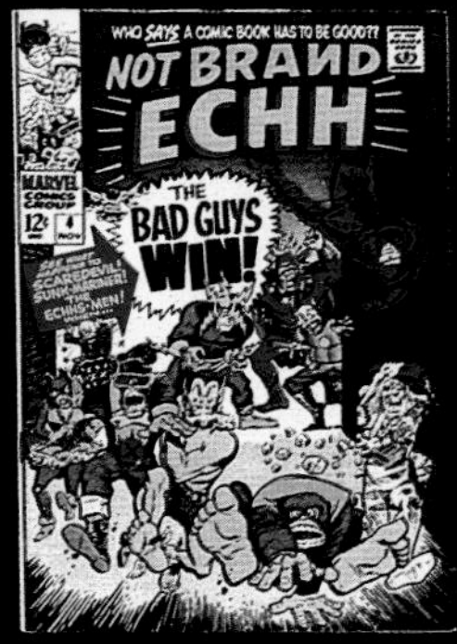
WHO SAYS A COMIC BOOK HAS TO BE GOOD??
NOT BRAND ECHH
THE BAD GUYS WIN!
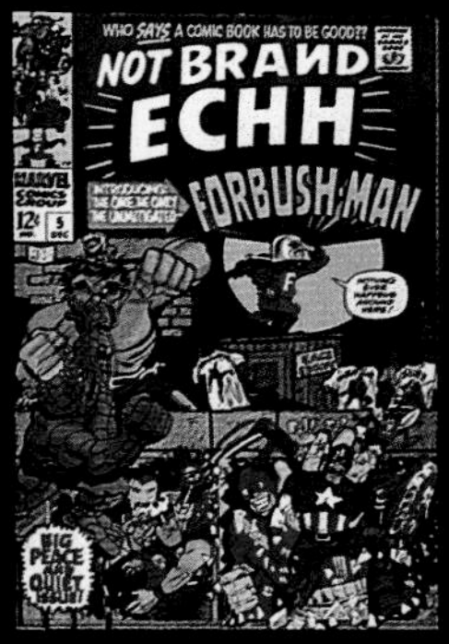
WHO SAYS A COMIC BOOK HAS TO BE GOOD??
NOT BRAND ECHH
FORBUSH-MAN
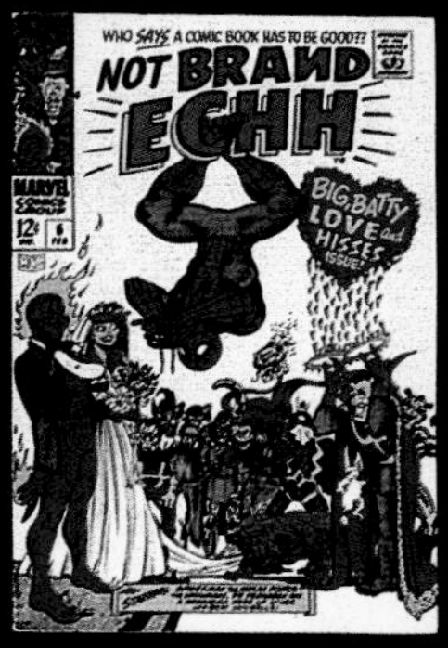
WHO SAYS A COMIC BOOK HAS TO BE GOOD??
NOT BRAND ECHH
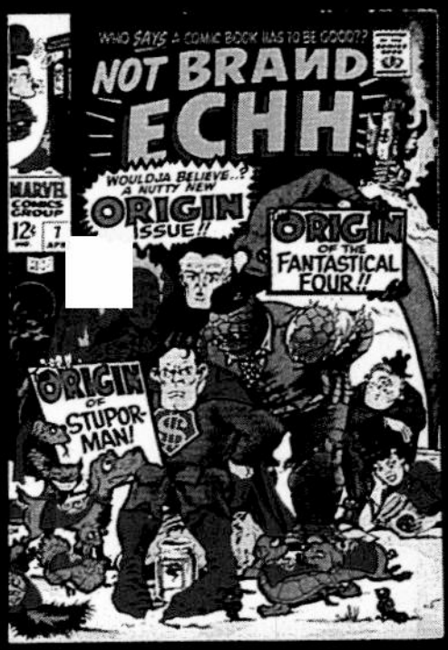
WHO SAYS A COMIC BOOK HAS TO BE GOOD??
NOT BRAND ECHH
ORIGIN ISSUE
ORIGIN OF STUPOR-MAN
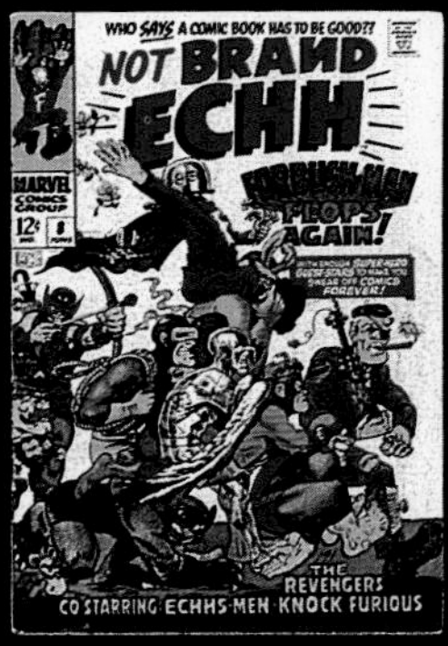
WHO SAYS A COMIC BOOK HAS TO BE GOOD??
NOT BRAND ECHH
THE REVENGERS
CO-STARRING ECHHS-MEN KNOCK FURIOUS
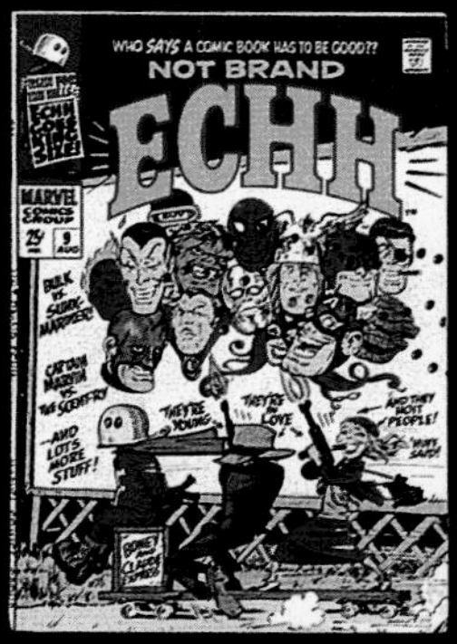
WHO SAYS A COMIC BOOK HAS TO BE GOOD??
NOT BRAND ECHH
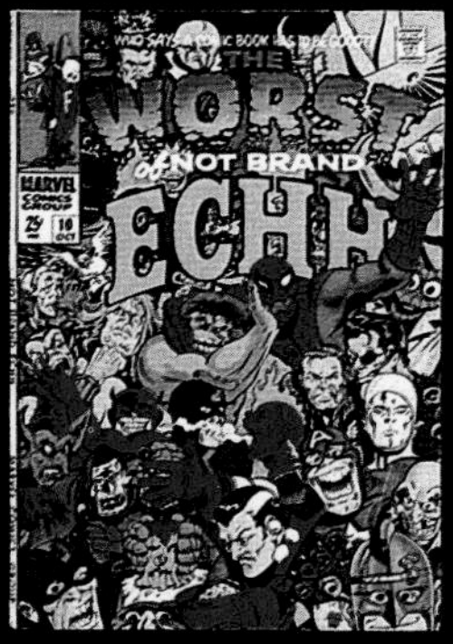
WORST of NOT BRAND ECHH
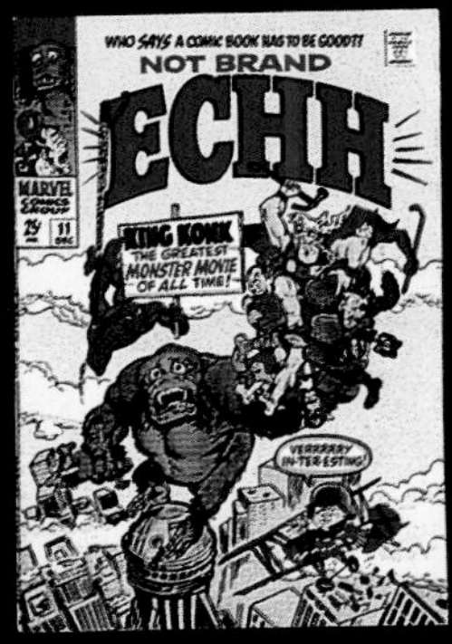
WHO SAYS A COMIC BOOK HAS TO BE GOOD??
NOT BRAND ECHH
KING KONK
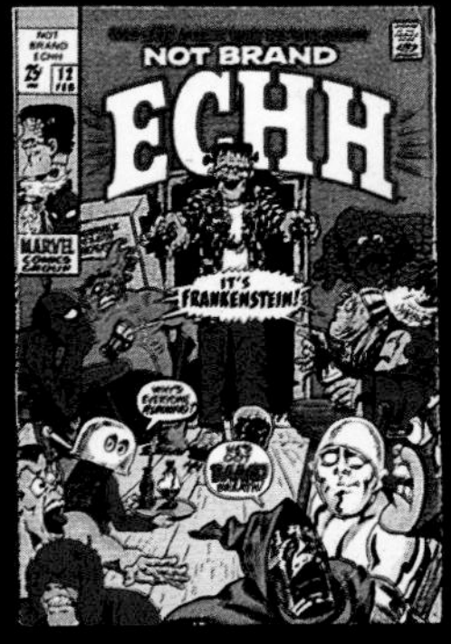
NOT BRAND ECHH
IT'S FRANKENSTEIN!
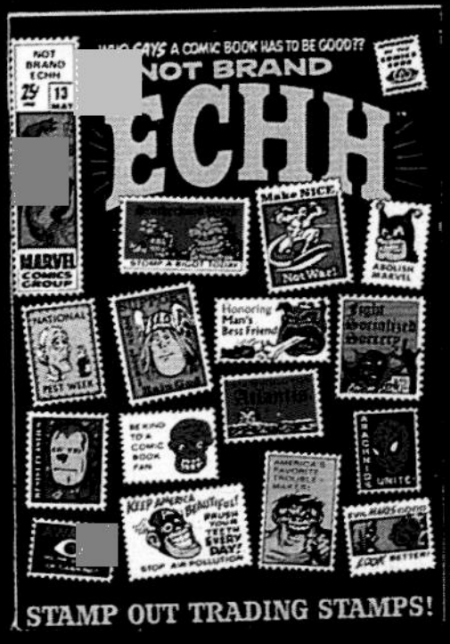
NOT BRAND ECHH
STAMP OUT TRADING STAMPS!

Nightcrawler (1-4) 1378

Ref. No.	Date	RVI	Artist/Info.
1378-1	Nov. 1985	3	Cockrum-c/a
1378-2	Dec.	2	"
1378-3	Jan. 1986	2	"
1378-4	Feb. 1986	2	Cockrum-c/a, Rubinstein-a

Night Nurse (1-4) 1380.4

1380.4-1	Nov. 1972	1	Mortimer-a
1380.4-2	Jan. 1973	1	"
1380.4-3 to 4	May 1973, (#4)	1	" (all)

Night Rider (1-6) 1380.5

1380.5-1	Oct. 1974	1	Reprints of Ghost Rider 1-6
1380.5-2	Dec.	1	"
1380.5-3	Feb. 1975	1	"
1380.5-4	Apr.	1	"
1380.5-5 to 6	Aug. 1975, (#6)	1	"

Not Brand Echh (1-13) 1381.1

1381.1-1	Aug. 1967	12	Kirby-c, Thomas-a
1381.1-2	Sept.	6	M. Severin-c/a, Giacoia-a
1381.1-3	Oct.	7	M. Severin-c, Kirby/Giacoia-a (Origin-Thor, Hulk)
1381.1-4	Nov.	6	Colan/Tartaglione-a
1381.1-5	Dec.	6	Kirby/Sutton-a (Origin-Forbush Man)
1381.1-6	Feb. 1968	6	Severin-c, Kirby/Sutton-a
1381.1-7	Apr.	6	" "
1381.1-8 to 13	May 1969, (#13)	6	(9-13, All Giant-size)

Nova (1-25) 1381.5

1381.5-1	Sept. 1976	2	Buscema/Sinnott-a (Origin-Nova)
1381.5-2	Oct.	1	" "
1381.5-3	Nov.	1	Buscema/Palmer-a
1381.5-4	Dec.	1	" "
1381.5-5	Jan. 1977	1	" "
1381.5-6	Feb.	1	Buscema, Giacoia-a
1381.5-7	Mar.	1	" "
1381.5-8 to 25	May 1979, (#25)	1	

MARVEL COMICS GROUP
THE MAN CALLED NOVA
FABULOUS FIRST ISSUE!
POWER-PACKED ORIGIN!
MARVEL'S NEWEST BOMBSHELL!
HE'S HERE! THE ULTIMATE SUPER-HERO!
FIRST NIGHT OF THE CONDOR!
ENTER DIAMONDHEAD...
THOR
CORRUPTOR!
WHY IS NOVA ON A RAMPAGE?
YOU MUST READ WAR IN SPACE
FEAR IN THE FUN HOUSE!
AND THE SPHINX SHALL INHERIT THE EARTH!
FACE-TO-FACE WITH SPIDER-MAN
PHOTON
THE CRIME BUSTER!
THE SANDMAN RETURNS!
DEATH TRAP FOR NOVA!
OUR GREATEST ISSUE--EVER!
TIDAL WAVE
OUT OF YOUR MIND!
NIGHTMARE!
TRAPPED!
HE'S HERE! THE HUMAN ROCKET!
BLAZING INTO BATTLE ACTION! COMET!
DIAMONDHEAD!
DR. SUN
THE MAN-MACHINE LIVES AGAIN!
ATTACK FROM SPACE!
HE'S GONE! THE HUMAN ROCKET
IN FINAL BATTLE!

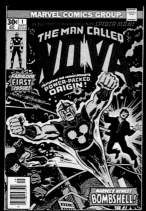

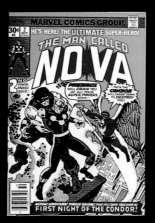

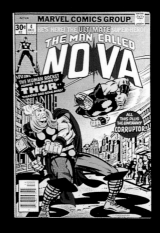

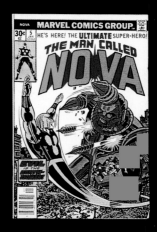

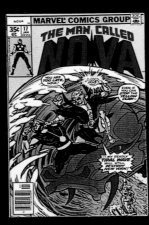

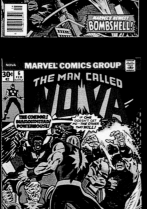

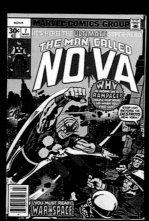

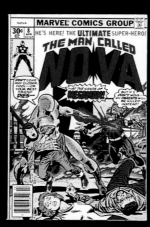

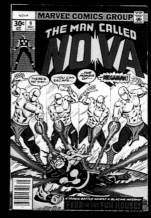

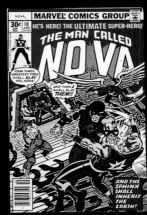

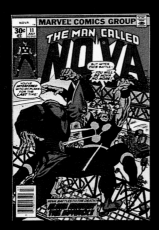

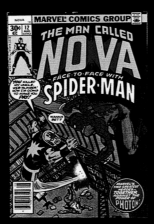

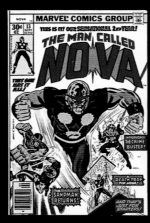

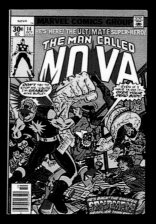

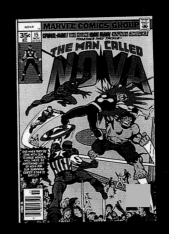

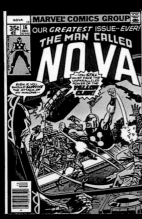

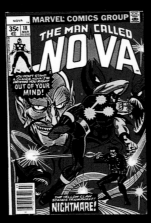

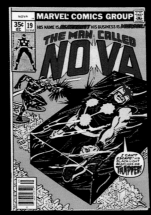

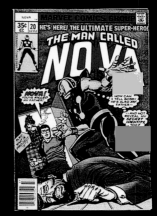

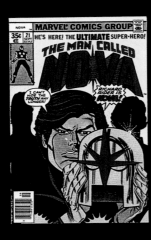

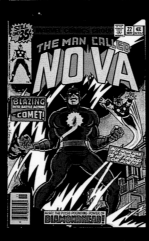

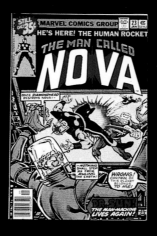

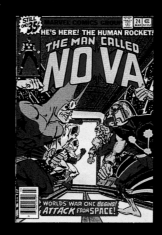

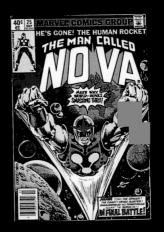

1391.1 Obnoxio the Clown (1) 1391.5 Official Handbook of the Marvel Universe (1-15)

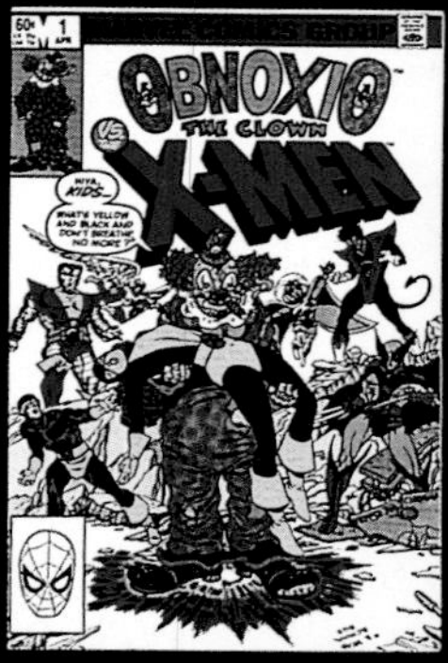
OBNOXIO THE CLOWN
X-MEN
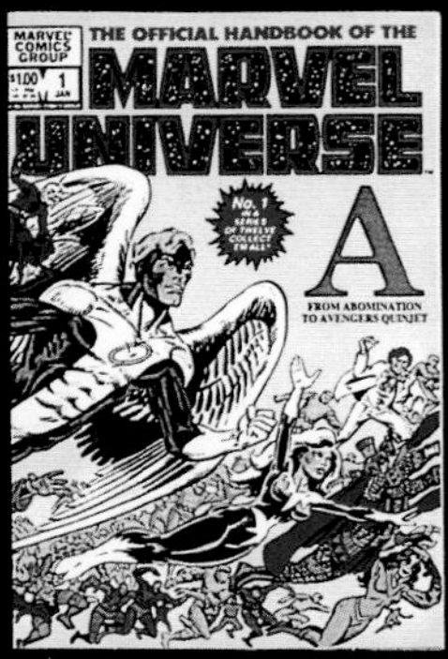
THE OFFICIAL HANDBOOK OF THE
MARVEL UNIVERSE
A
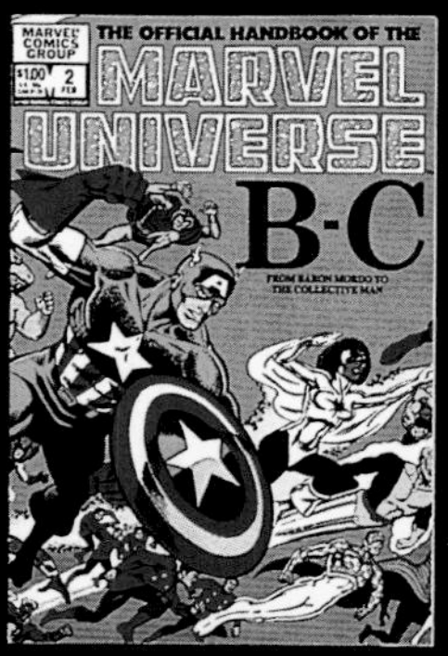
THE OFFICIAL HANDBOOK OF THE
MARVEL UNIVERSE
B-C
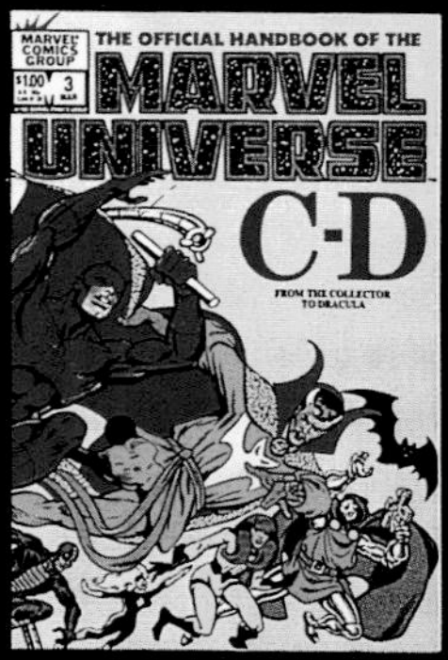
THE OFFICIAL HANDBOOK OF THE
MARVEL UNIVERSE
C-D
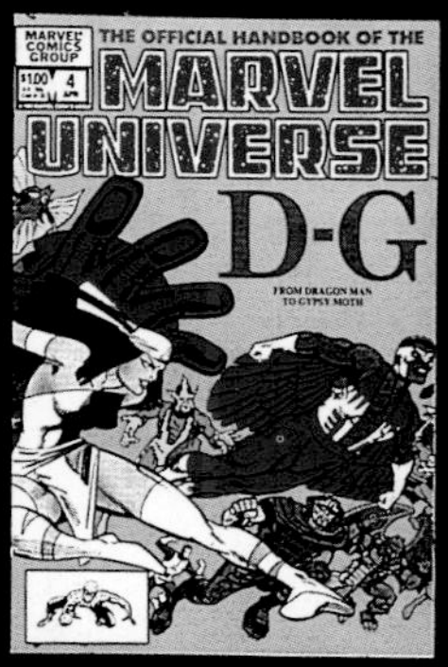
THE OFFICIAL HANDBOOK OF THE
MARVEL UNIVERSE
D-G
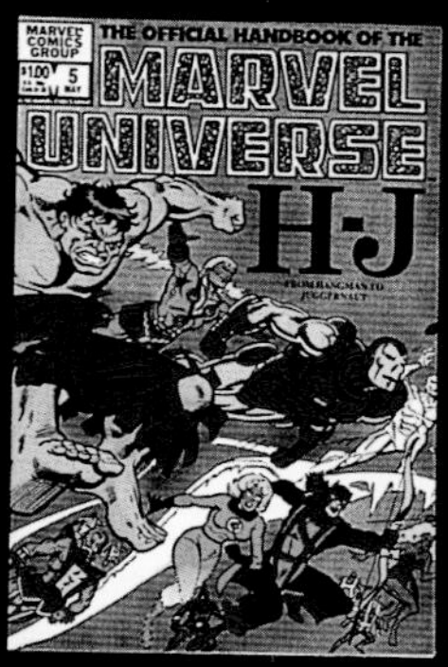
THE OFFICIAL HANDBOOK OF THE
MARVEL UNIVERSE
H-J
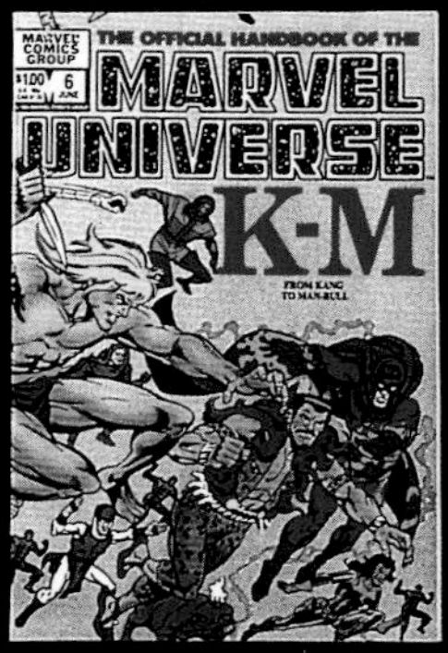
THE OFFICIAL HANDBOOK OF THE
MARVEL UNIVERSE
K-M
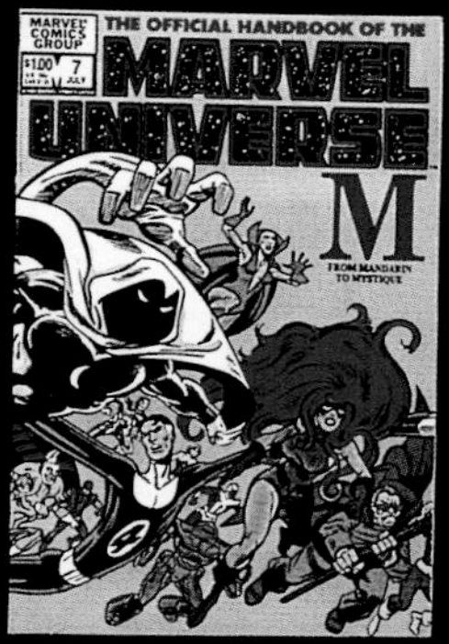
THE OFFICIAL HANDBOOK OF THE
MARVEL UNIVERSE
M
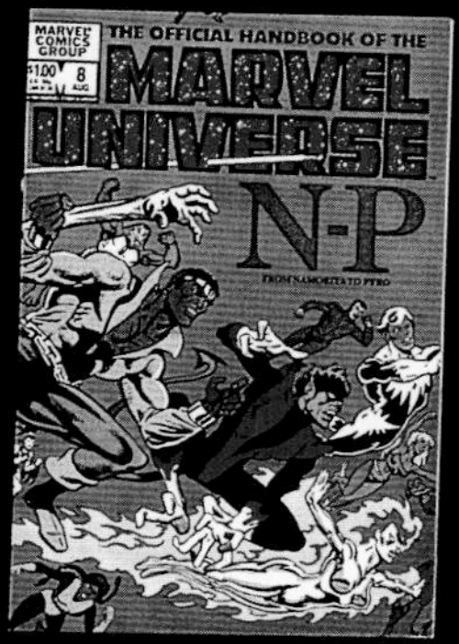
THE OFFICIAL HANDBOOK OF THE
MARVEL UNIVERSE
N-P
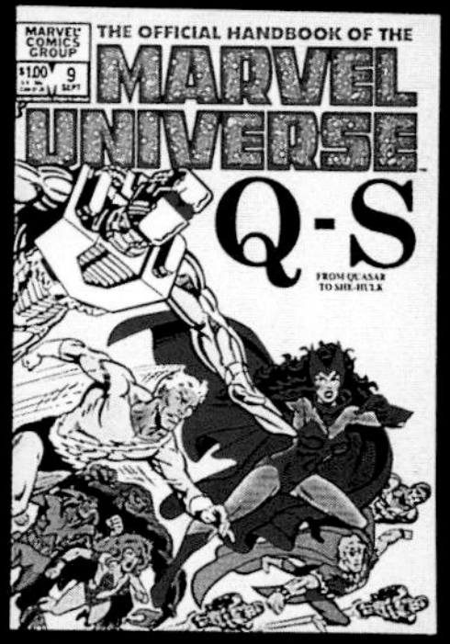
THE OFFICIAL HANDBOOK OF THE
MARVEL UNIVERSE
Q-S
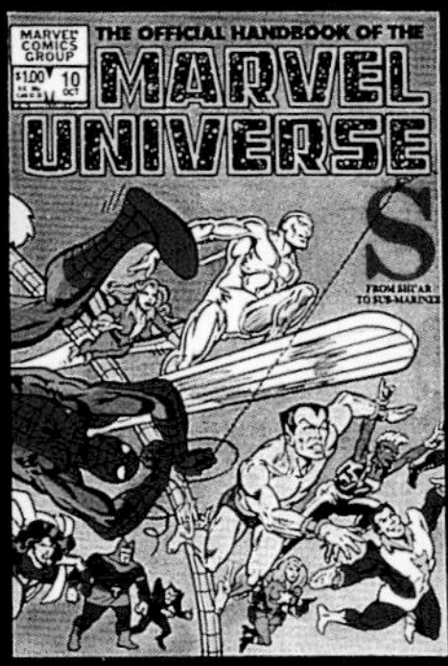
THE OFFICIAL HANDBOOK OF THE
MARVEL UNIVERSE
S
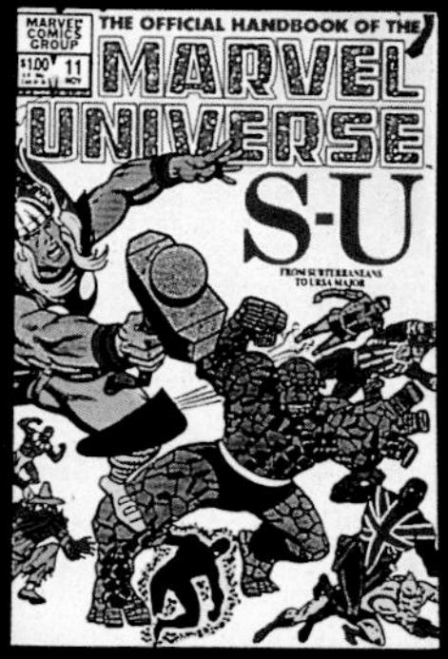
THE OFFICIAL HANDBOOK OF THE
MARVEL UNIVERSE
S-U

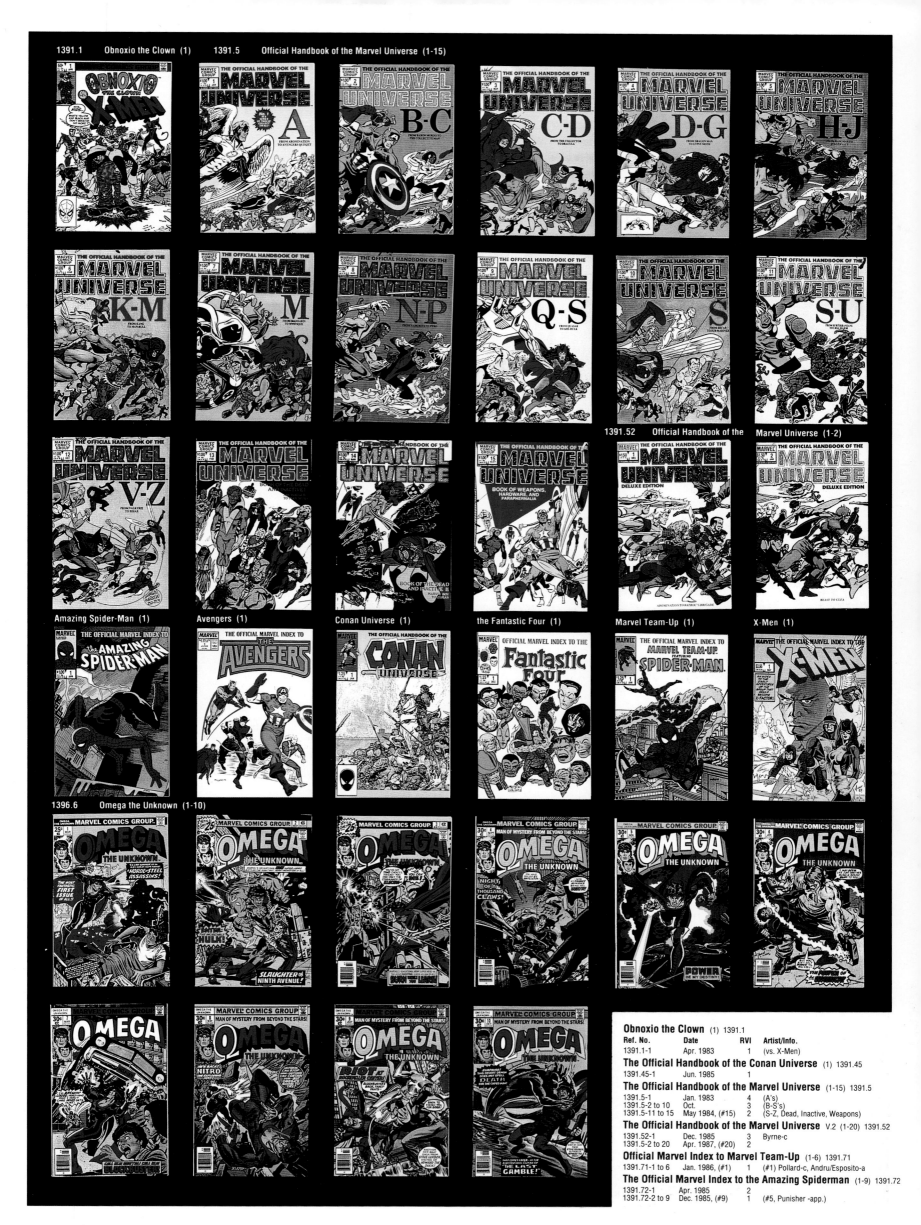

1391.52 Official Handbook of the Marvel Universe (1-2)

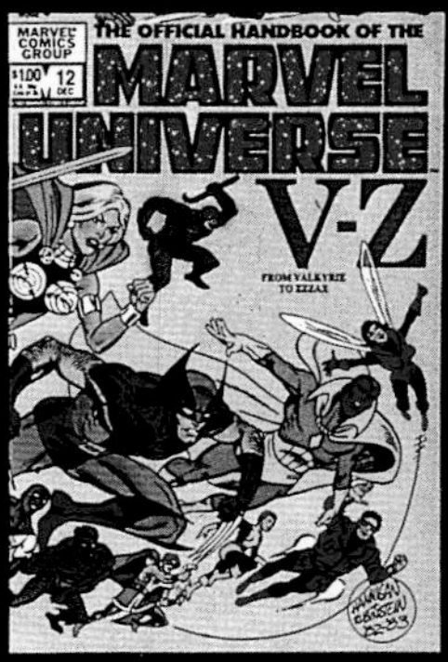
THE OFFICIAL HANDBOOK OF THE
MARVEL UNIVERSE
V-Z
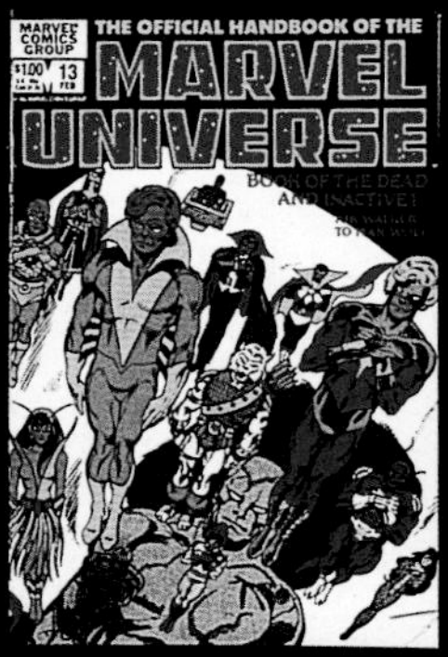
THE OFFICIAL HANDBOOK OF THE
MARVEL UNIVERSE
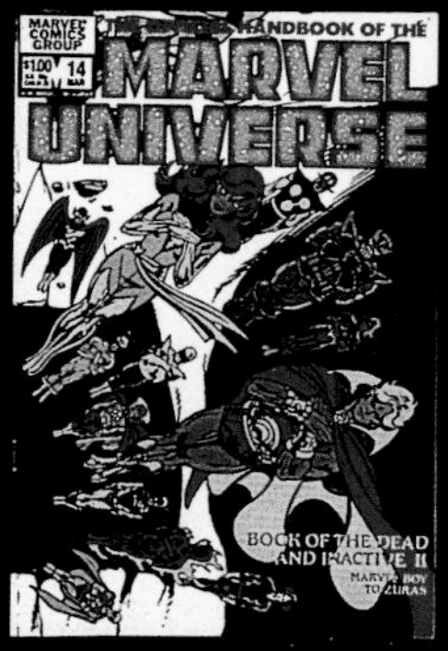
MARVEL UNIVERSE
BOOK OF THE DEAD AND INACTIVE II
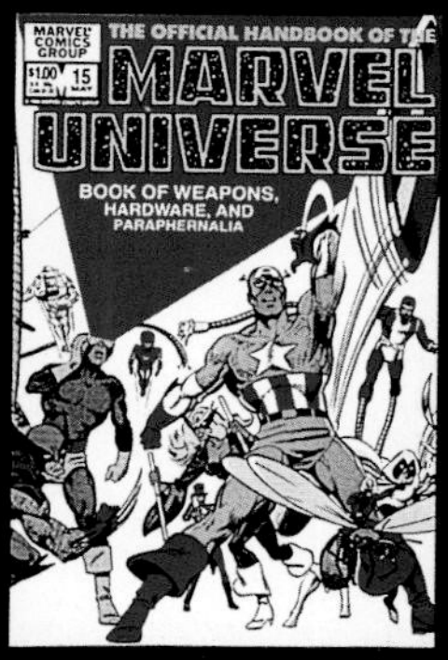
THE OFFICIAL HANDBOOK OF THE
MARVEL UNIVERSE
BOOK OF WEAPONS, HARDWARE, AND PARAPHERNALIA
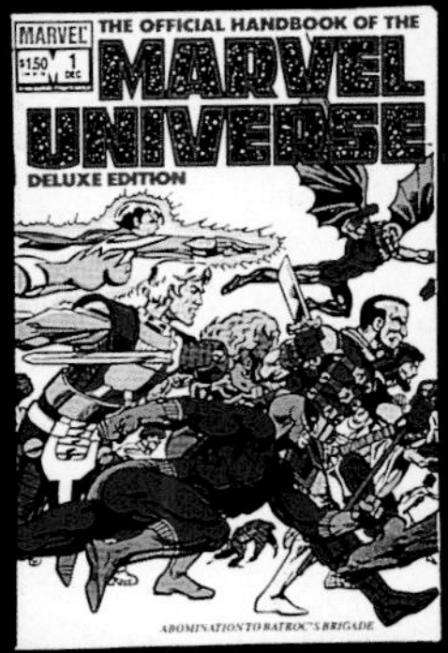
THE OFFICIAL HANDBOOK OF THE
MARVEL UNIVERSE
DELUXE EDITION
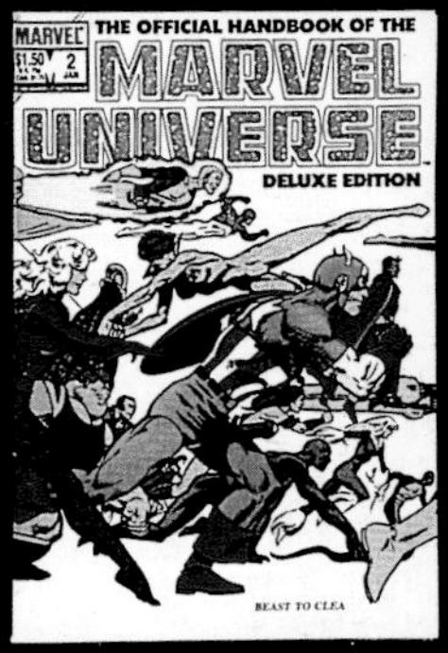
THE OFFICIAL HANDBOOK OF THE
MARVEL UNIVERSE
DELUXE EDITION

Amazing Spider-Man (1) Avengers (1) Conan Universe (1) the Fantastic Four (1) Marvel Team-Up (1) X-Men (1)

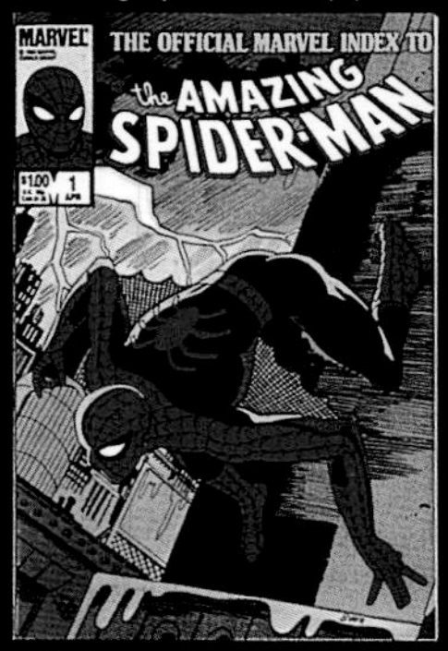
THE OFFICIAL MARVEL INDEX TO
the AMAZING SPIDER-MAN
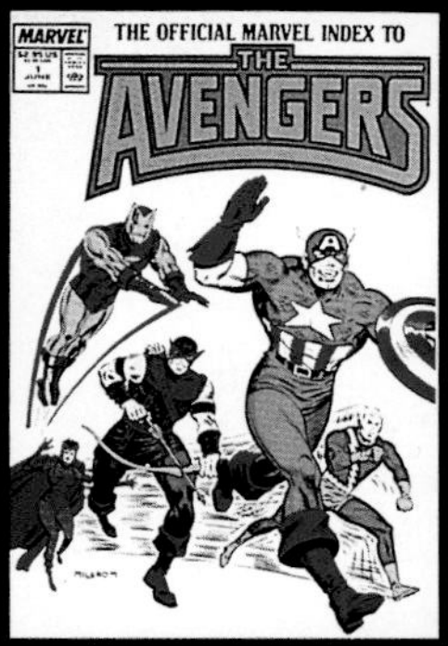
THE OFFICIAL MARVEL INDEX TO
THE AVENGERS
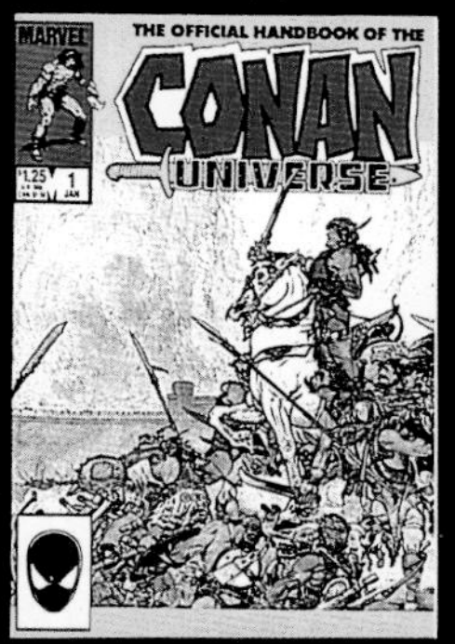
THE OFFICIAL HANDBOOK OF THE
CONAN UNIVERSE
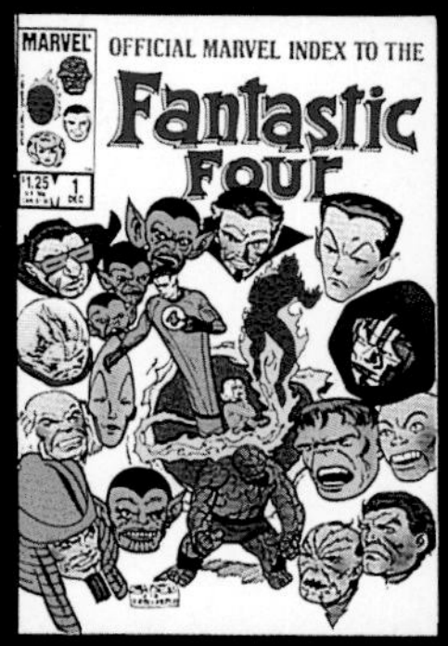
OFFICIAL MARVEL INDEX TO THE
Fantastic Four
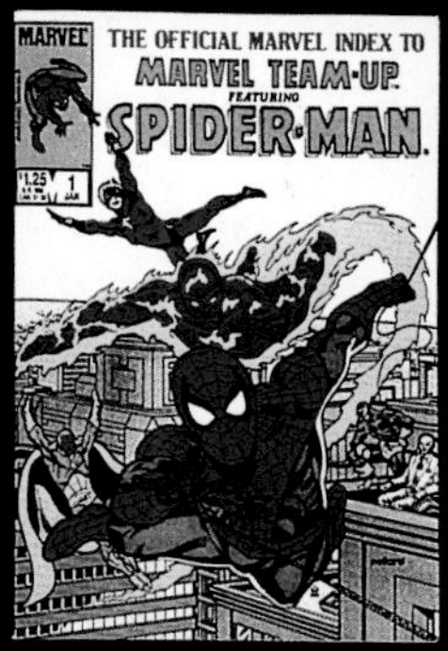
THE OFFICIAL MARVEL INDEX TO
MARVEL TEAM-UP
SPIDER-MAN
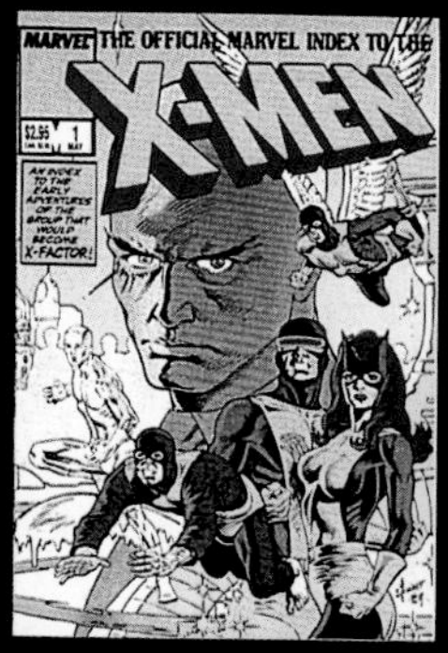
THE OFFICIAL MARVEL INDEX TO THE
X-MEN

1396.6 Omega the Unknown (1-10)

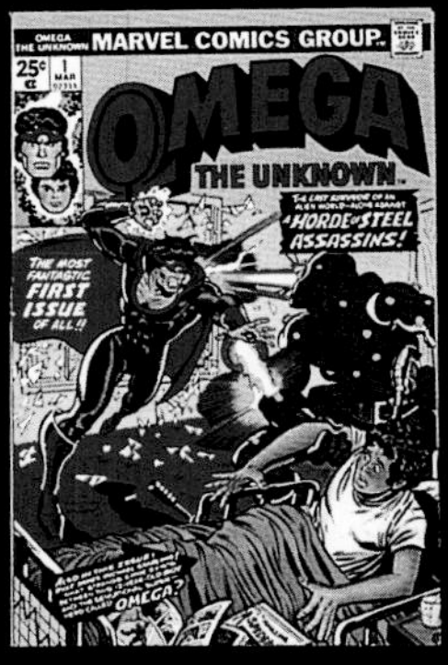
MARVEL COMICS GROUP
OMEGA
THE UNKNOWN
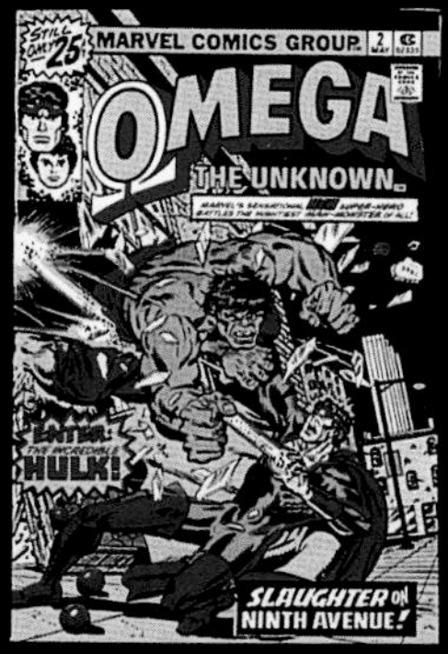
MARVEL COMICS GROUP
OMEGA
THE UNKNOWN
SLAUGHTER ON NINTH AVENUE!
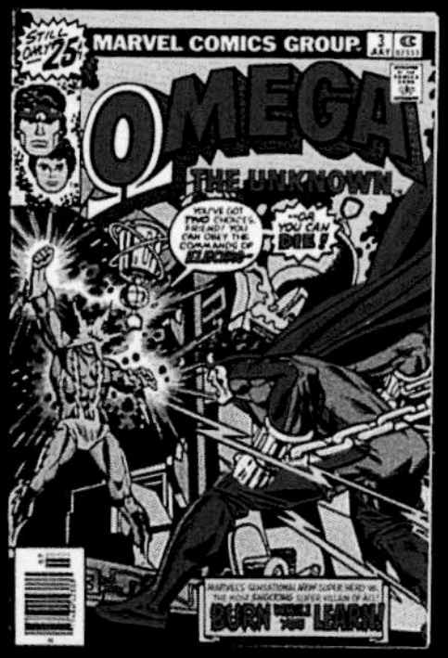
MARVEL COMICS GROUP
OMEGA
THE UNKNOWN
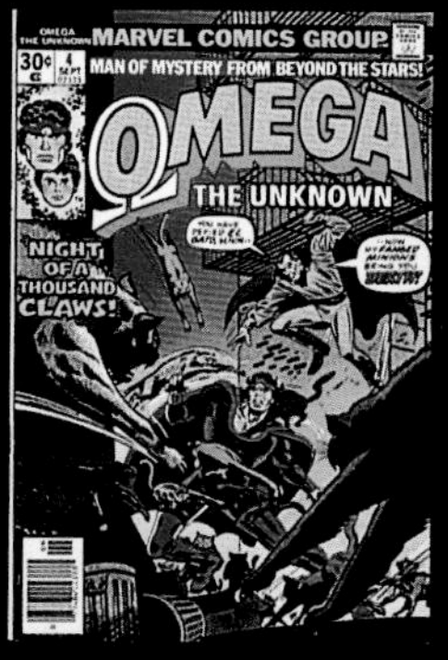
MARVEL COMICS GROUP
MAN OF MYSTERY FROM BEYOND THE STARS!
OMEGA
THE UNKNOWN
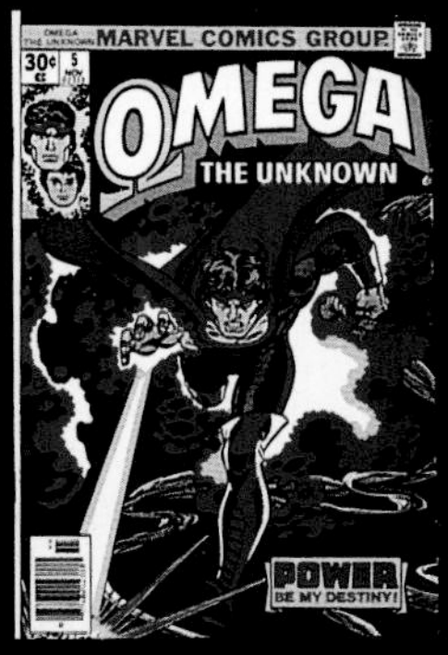
MARVEL COMICS GROUP
OMEGA
THE UNKNOWN
POWER
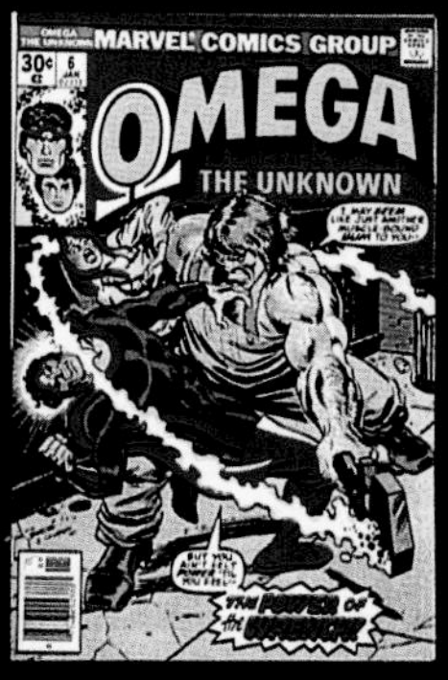
MARVEL COMICS GROUP
OMEGA
THE UNKNOWN
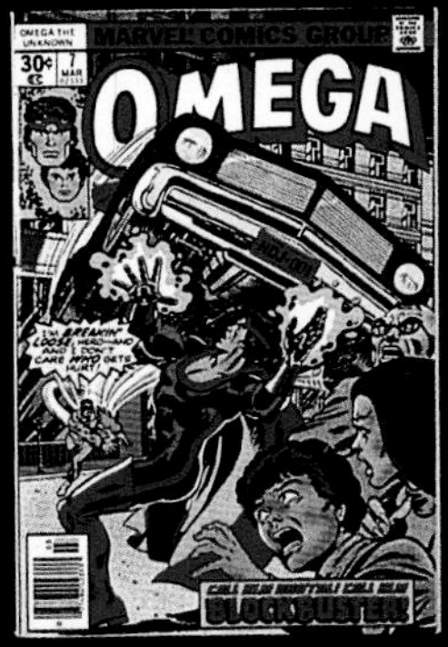
MARVEL COMICS GROUP
OMEGA
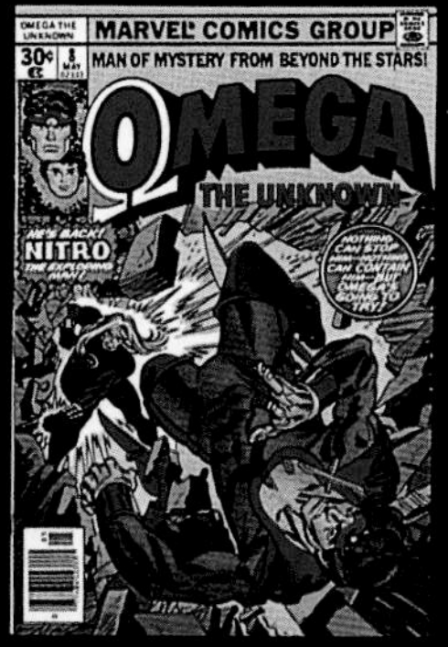
MARVEL COMICS GROUP
MAN OF MYSTERY FROM BEYOND THE STARS!
OMEGA
THE UNKNOWN
NITRO
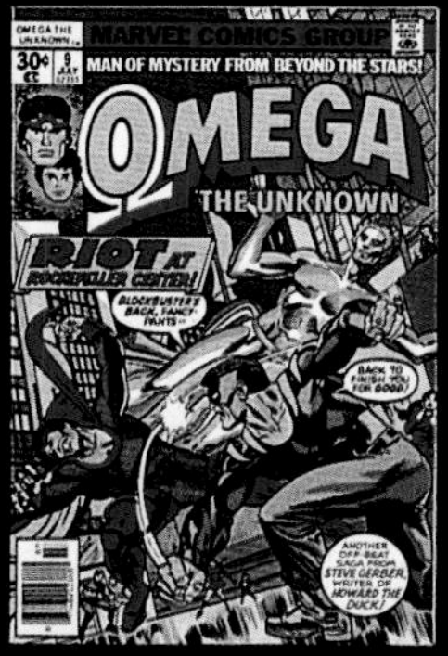
MARVEL COMICS GROUP
MAN OF MYSTERY FROM BEYOND THE STARS!
OMEGA
THE UNKNOWN
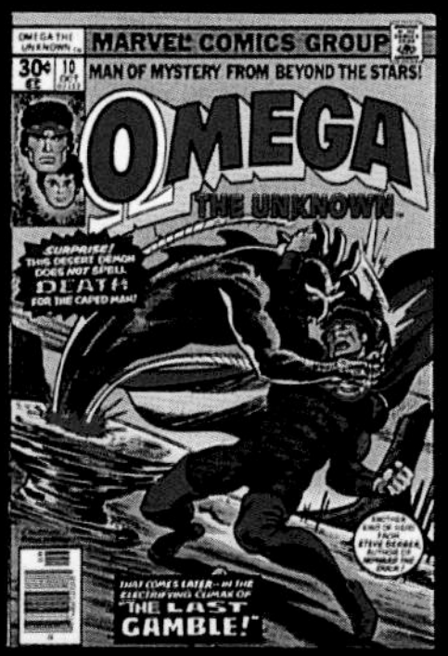
MARVEL COMICS GROUP
MAN OF MYSTERY FROM BEYOND THE STARS!
OMEGA
THE UNKNOWN
THE LAST GAMBLE!

Obnoxio the Clown (1) 1391.1

Ref. No.	Date	RVI	Artist/Info.
1391.1-1	Apr. 1983	1	(vs. X-Men)

The Official Handbook of the Conan Universe (1) 1391.45

1391.45-1	Jun. 1985	1	

The Official Handbook of the Marvel Universe (1-15) 1391.5

1391.5-1	Jan. 1983	4	(A's)
1391.5-2 to 10	Oct.	3	(B-S's)
1391.5-11 to 15	May 1984, (#15)	2	(S-Z, Dead, Inactive, Weapons)

The Official Handbook of the Marvel Universe V.2 (1-20) 1391.52

1391.52-1	Dec. 1985	3	Byrne-c
1391.52-2 to 20	Apr. 1987, (#20)	2	

Official Marvel Index to Marvel Team-Up (1-6) 1391.71

1391.71-1 to 6	Jan. 1986, (#1)	1	(#1) Pollard-c, Andru/Esposito-a

The Official Marvel Index to the Amazing Spiderman (1-9) 1391.72

1391.72-1	Apr. 1985	2	
1391.72-2 to 9	Dec. 1985, (#9)	1	(#5, Punisher -app.)

1411.5 The Outlaw Kid (1-16)

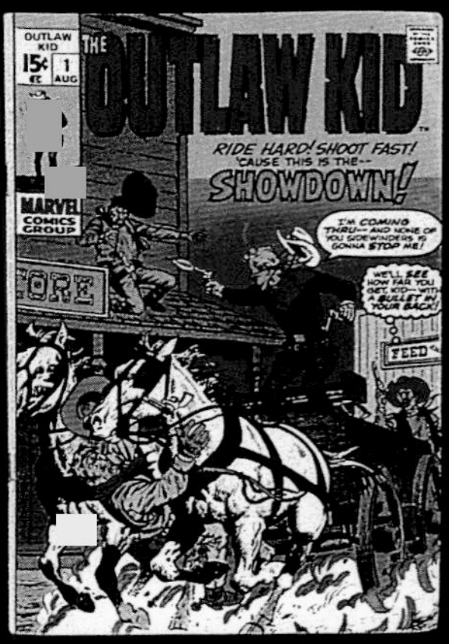
THE OUTLAW KID
RIDE HARD! SHOOT FAST! 'CAUSE THIS IS THE-- SHOWDOWN!
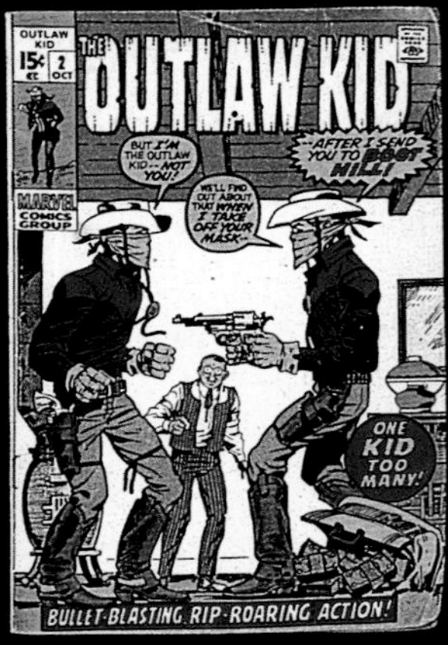
THE OUTLAW KID
ONE KID TOO MANY!
BULLET-BLASTING RIP-ROARING ACTION!
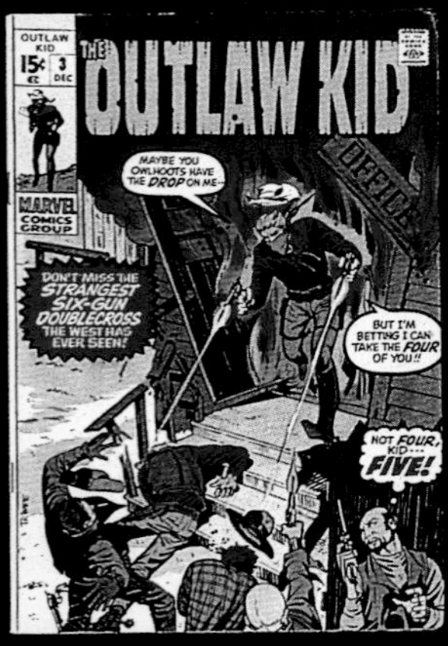
THE OUTLAW KID
DON'T MISS THE STRANGEST SIX-GUN DOUBLECROSS THE WEST HAS EVER SEEN!
NOT FOUR, KID-- FIVE!
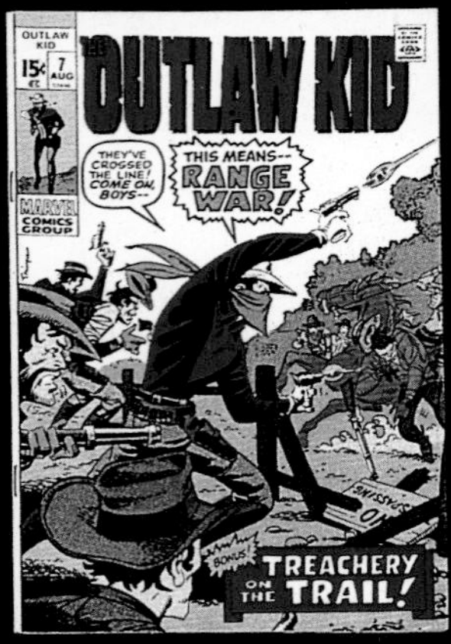
THE OUTLAW KID
THIS MEANS-- RANGE WAR!
TREACHERY ON THE TRAIL!
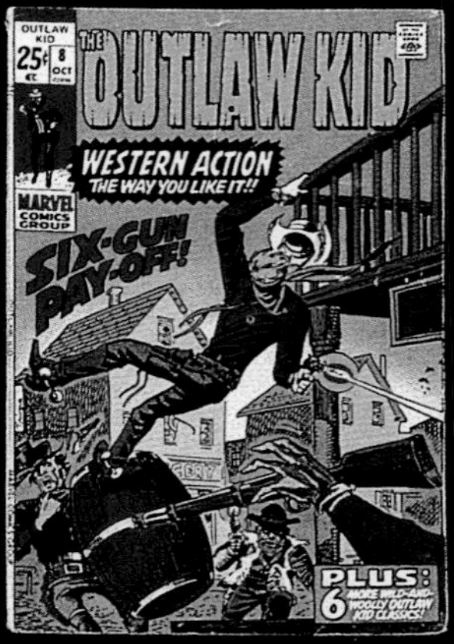
THE OUTLAW KID
WESTERN ACTION THE WAY YOU LIKE IT!!
SIX-GUN PAY-OFF!
PLUS:
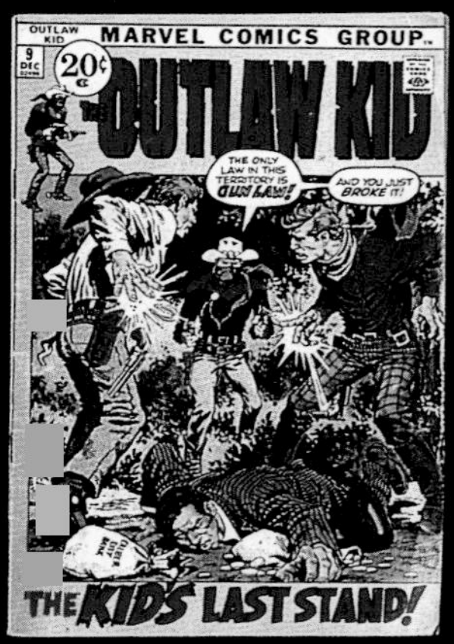
MARVEL COMICS GROUP
THE OUTLAW KID
THE KID'S LAST STAND!
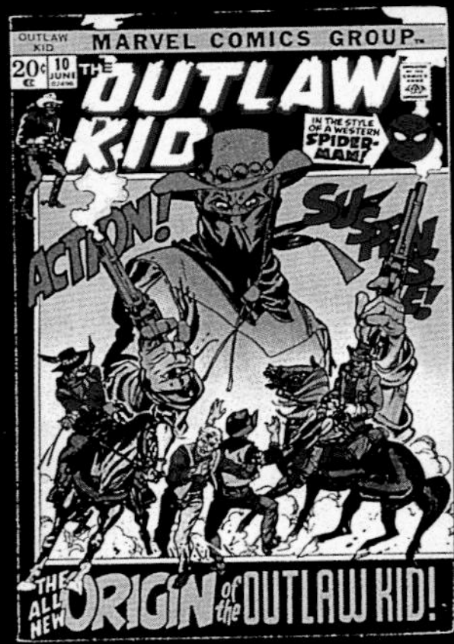
MARVEL COMICS GROUP
THE OUTLAW KID
THE ALL NEW ORIGIN of the OUTLAW KID!
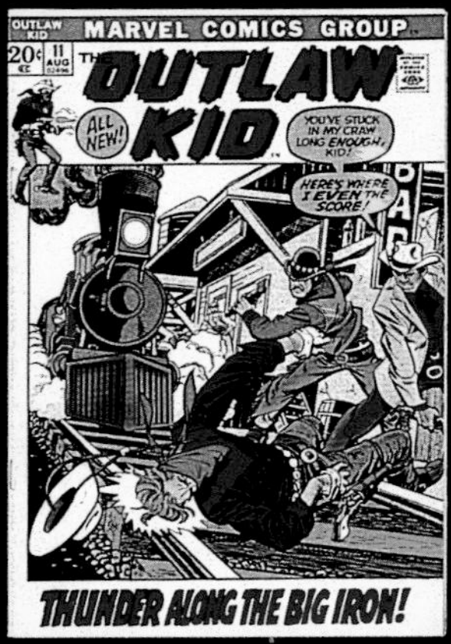
MARVEL COMICS GROUP
THE OUTLAW KID
ALL NEW!
THUNDER ALONG THE BIG IRON!
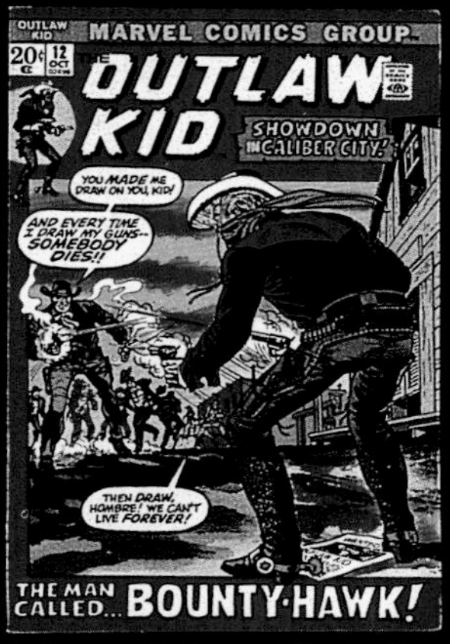
MARVEL COMICS GROUP
THE OUTLAW KID
SHOWDOWN IN CALIBER CITY!
THE MAN CALLED... BOUNTY-HAWK!
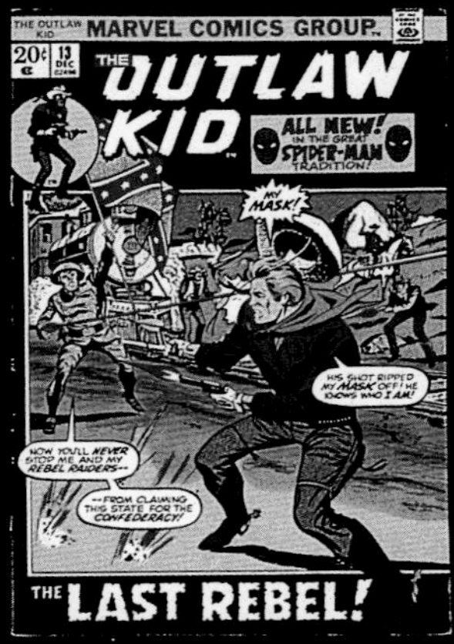
MARVEL COMICS GROUP
THE OUTLAW KID
ALL NEW!
THE LAST REBEL!

1431 Patsy and Hedy (61, 62, 64, A1)

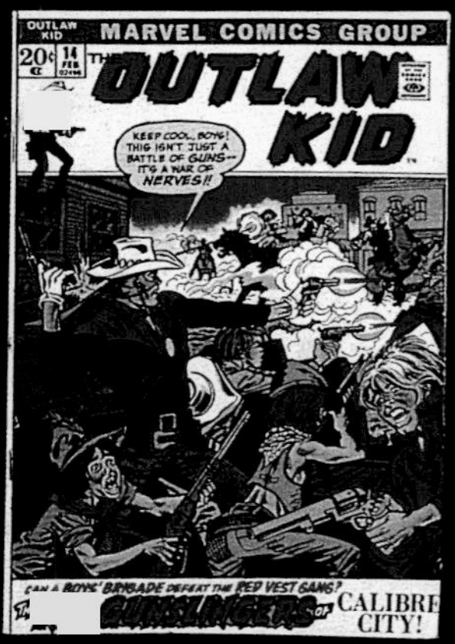
MARVEL COMICS GROUP
THE OUTLAW KID
CALIBRE CITY!
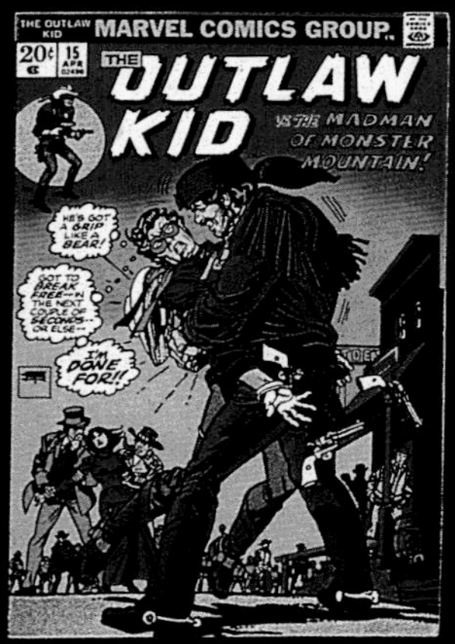
MARVEL COMICS GROUP
THE OUTLAW KID
THE MADMAN OF MONSTER MOUNTAIN!
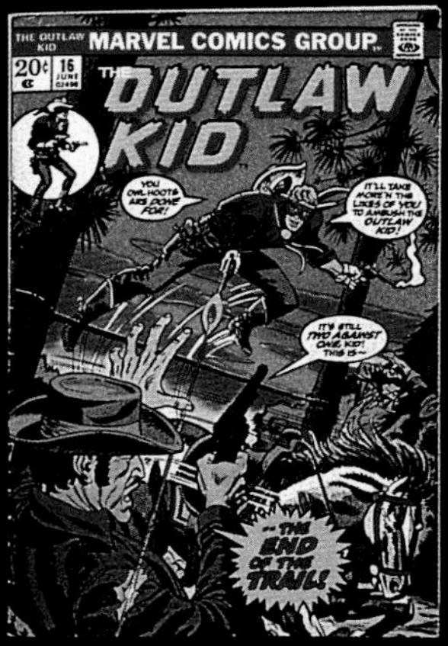
MARVEL COMICS GROUP
THE OUTLAW KID
THE END OF THE TRAIL!
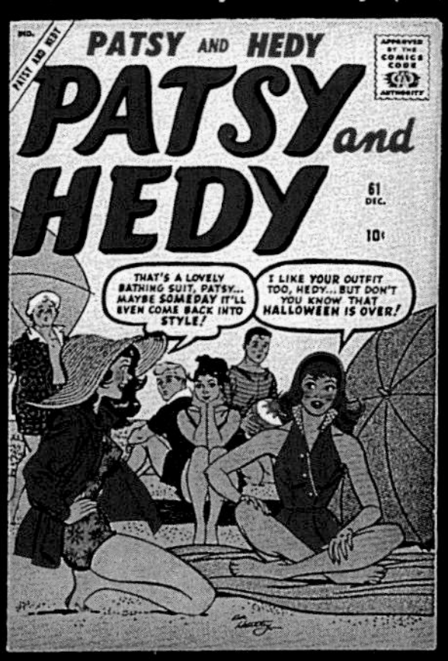
PATSY AND HEDY
PATSY and HEDY
THAT'S A LOVELY BATHING SUIT, PATSY... MAYBE SOMEDAY IT'LL EVEN COME BACK INTO STYLE!
I LIKE YOUR OUTFIT TOO, HEDY... BUT DON'T YOU KNOW THAT HALLOWEEN IS OVER!
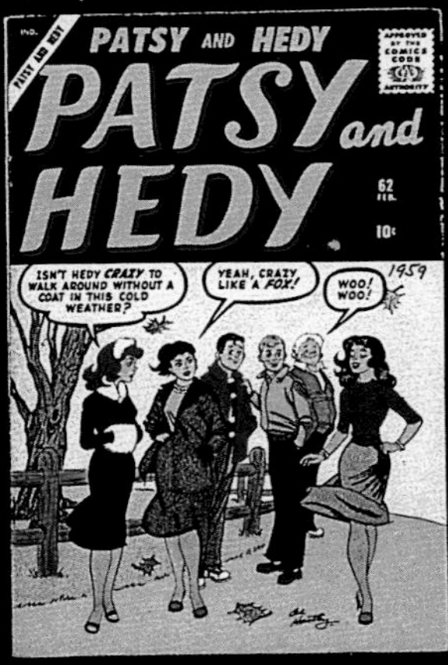
PATSY AND HEDY
PATSY and HEDY
ISN'T HEDY CRAZY TO WALK AROUND WITHOUT A COAT IN THIS COLD WEATHER?
YEAH, CRAZY LIKE A FOX!
WOO!
WOO!

1433 Patsy Walker (81, 83, 84, 102)

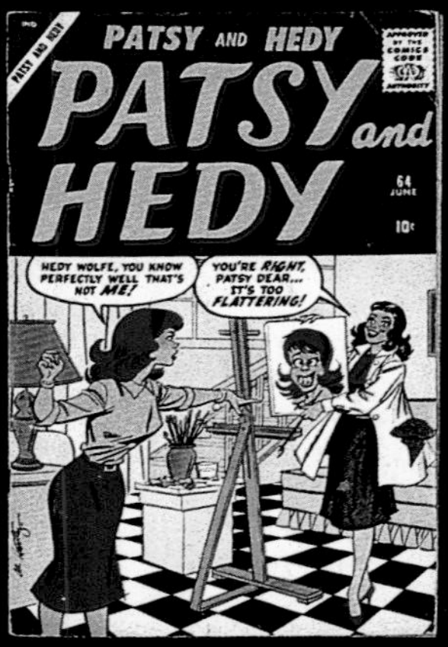
PATSY AND HEDY
PATSY and HEDY
HEDY WOLFE, YOU KNOW PERFECTLY WELL THAT'S NOT ME!
YOU'RE RIGHT, PATSY DEAR... IT'S TOO FLATTERING!
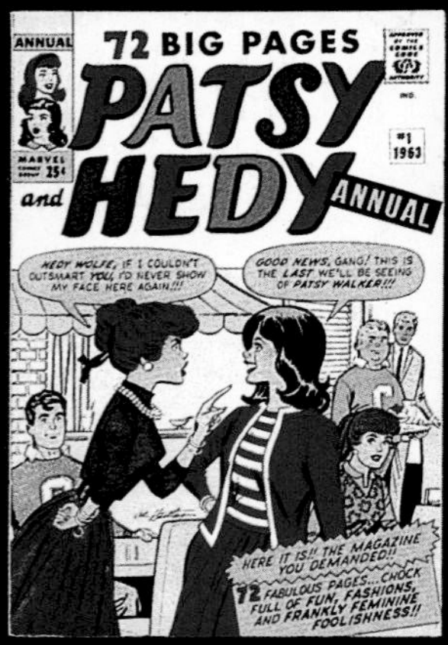
72 BIG PAGES
PATSY and HEDY ANNUAL
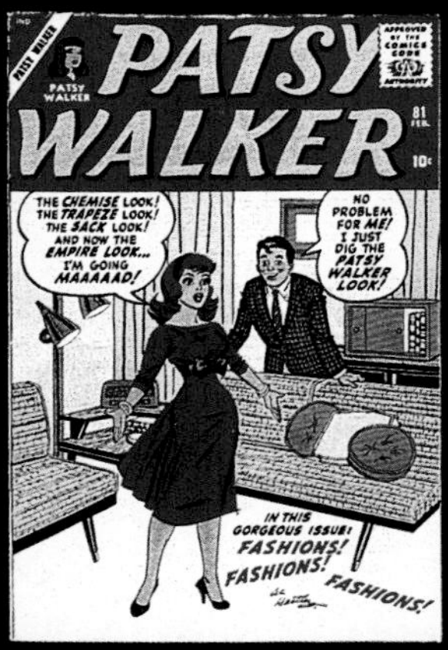
PATSY WALKER
IN THIS GORGEOUS ISSUE: FASHIONS! FASHIONS! FASHIONS!
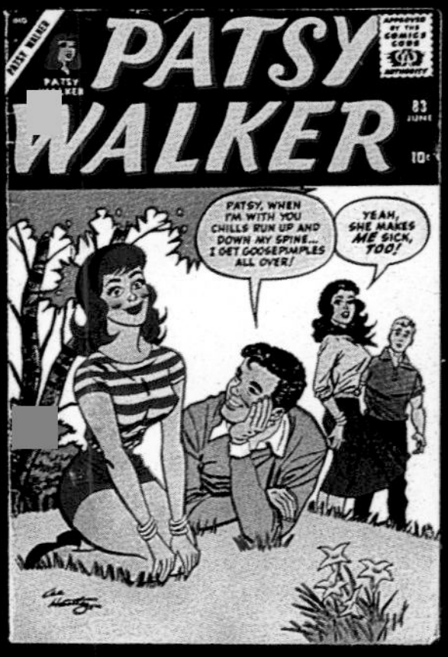
PATSY WALKER
YEAH, SHE MAKES ME SICK, TOO!
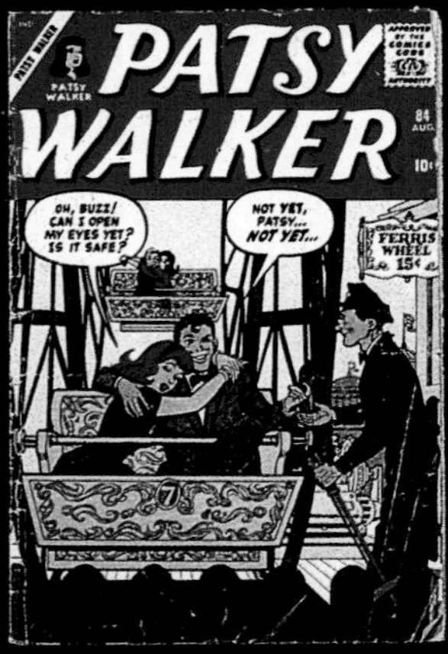
PATSY WALKER
OH, BUZZ! CAN I OPEN MY EYES YET? IS IT SAFE?
NOT YET, PATSY... NOT YET...
FERRIS WHEEL
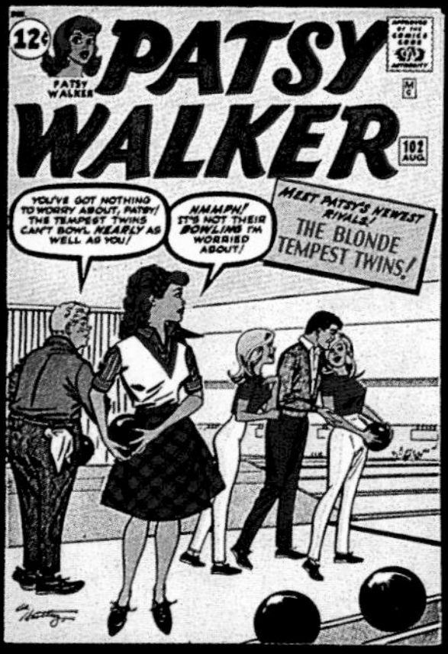
PATSY WALKER
MEET PATSY'S NEWEST RIVALS... THE BLONDE TEMPEST TWINS!

The Official Marvel Index to the Avengers (1-7) 1391.73

Ref. No.	Date	RVI	Artist/Info.
1391.73-1 to 7	Jun. 1987, (#1)	2	

The Official Marvel Index to the Fantastic Four (1-5) 1391.74

Ref. No.	Date	RVI	Artist/Info.
1391.74-1 to 5	Dec. 1985, (#1)	1	Byrne-c (#1)

The Official Marvel Index to the X-Men (1-8) 1391.75

Ref. No.	Date	RVI	Artist/Info.
1391.75-1 to 8	May 1987, (#1)	2	

Omega the Unknown (1-10) 1396.6

Ref. No.	Date	RVI	Artist/Info.
1396.6-1	Mar. 1976	1	Hannigan/Sinnott-c, Mooney-a
1396.6-2 to 7	May 1976, (#2)	1	Mooney-a (all)
1396.7-8	May 1977	4	(1st Fool Killer)
1396.7-9	Jul.	5	(Fool Killer)
1396.7-10	Oct. 1977	1	Mooney-a

Our Love Story (1-38) 1408.5

Ref. No.	Date	RVI	Artist/Info.
1408.5-1	Oct. 1969	3	
1408.5-2 to 4		2	Buscema-a
1408.5-5		5	Steranko-a
1408.5-6 to 38	Feb. 1976, (#38)	1	

The Outlaw Kid (1-30) 1411.5

Ref. No.	Date	RVI	Artist/Info.
1411.5-1	Aug. 1970	2	Severin-c, Wildey-a
1411.5-2	Oct.	1	Wildey-a
1411.5-3	Dec.	1	Trimpe-c, Wildey-a
1411.5-4	Feb. 1971	1	Wildey-a
1411.5-5	Apr.	1	"
1411.5-6	Jun.	1	Wildey, Pakula-a
1411.5-7	Aug.	1	Trimpe-c, Wildey-a
1411.5-8	Oct.	1	" "
1411.5-9	Dec.	1	Severin-c, Wildey-a
1411.5-10	Jun. 1972	1	Kane-c, Ayers/Roussos-a (Origin-)
1411.5-11 to 30	Oct. 1975, (#30)	1	

Patsy and Hedy (91-110) 1431

Ref. No.	Date	RVI	Artist/Info.
1431-91 to 110	Feb. 1967, (#110)	2	Hartley-a
1431.5-A1	1963	10	Hartley-a

Patsy Walker (111 to 124) 1433

Ref. No.	Date	RVI	Artist/Info.
1433-111 to 124	Dec. 1965, (#124)	2	Hartley-a

Peter Porker, The Spectacular Spider-Ham (1-17) 1451.3

Ref. No.	Date	RVI	Artist/Info.
1451.3-1	May 1985	2	
1451.3-2 to 17	Sept. 1987, (#17)	1	

Peter, the Little Pest (1-4) 1453

Ref. No.	Date	RVI	Artist/Info.
1453-1 to 4	Nov. 1969, (#1)	2	(Dexter the Demon, Melvin the Monster reprints)

Phoenix (1) 1460.7

Ref. No.	Date	RVI	Artist/Info.
1460.7-1	Apr. 1984	6	Byrne/Austin-a

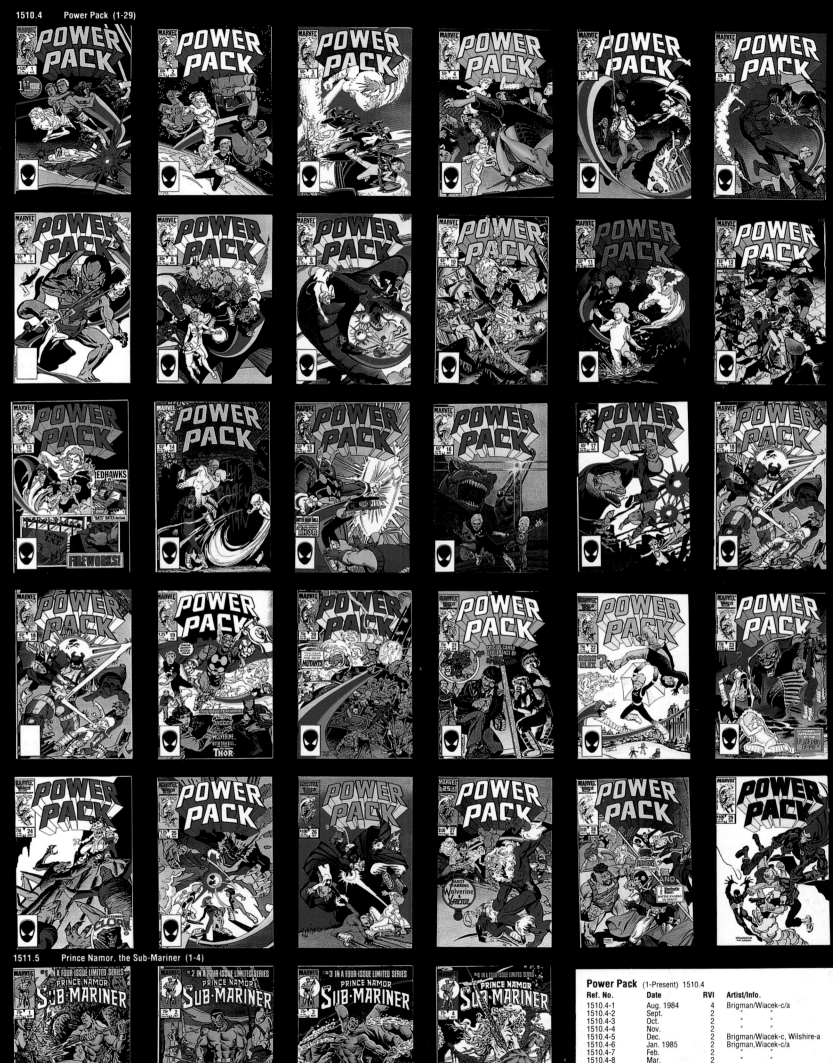

1510.4 Power Pack (1-29)

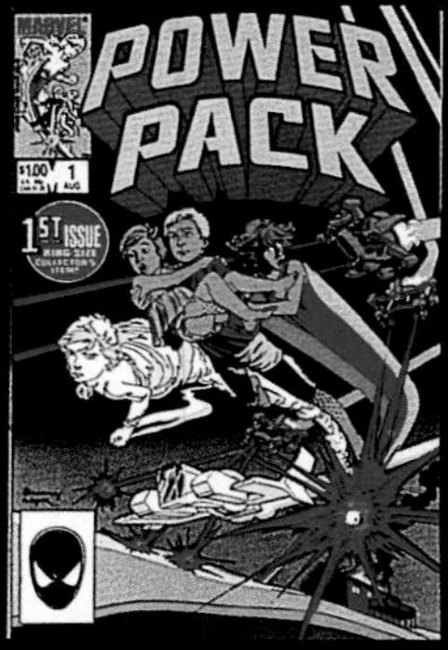
POWER PACK
1ST ISSUE
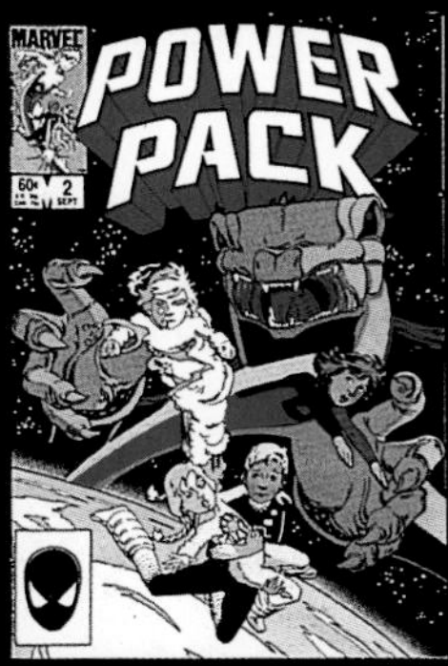
POWER PACK
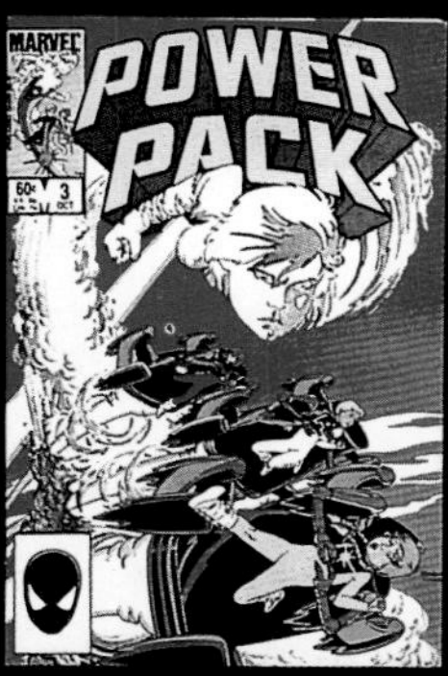
POWER PACK
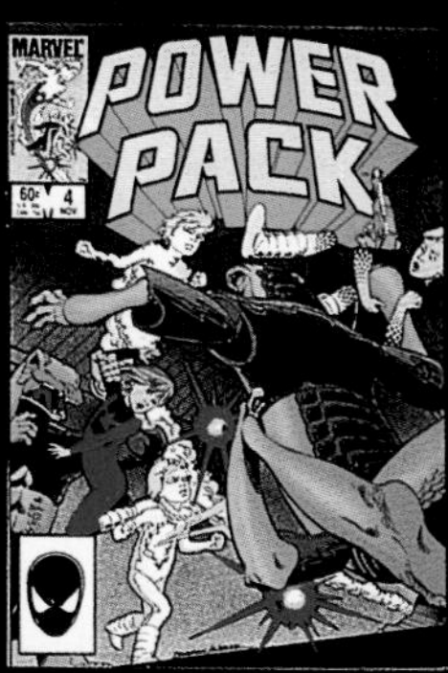
POWER PACK
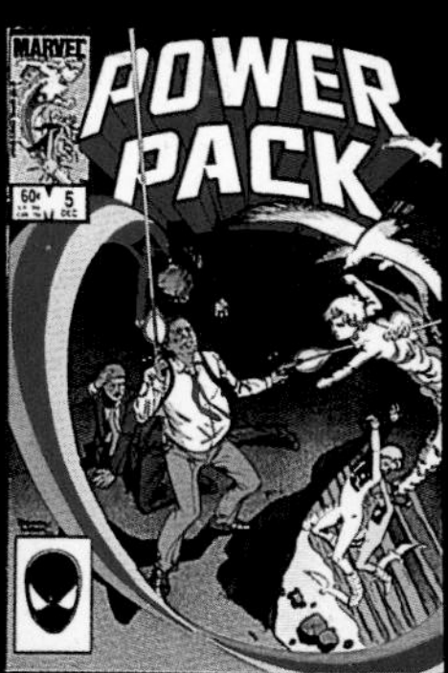
POWER PACK
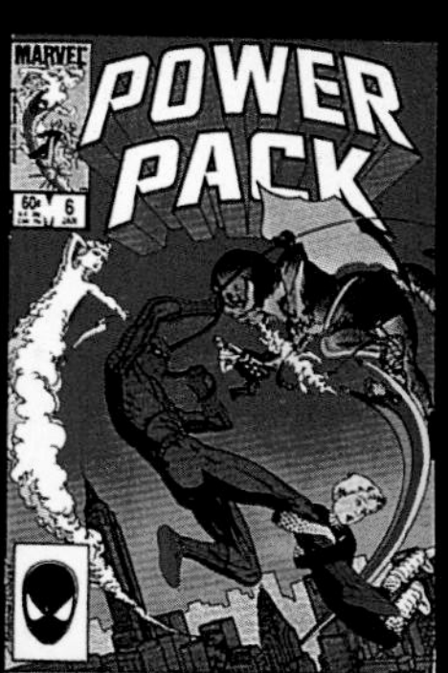
POWER PACK
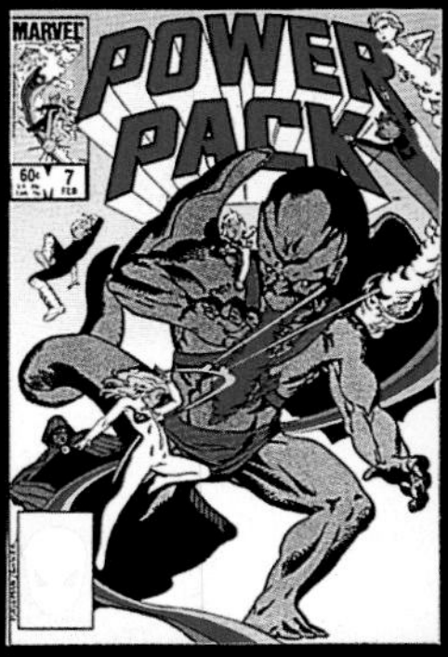
POWER PACK
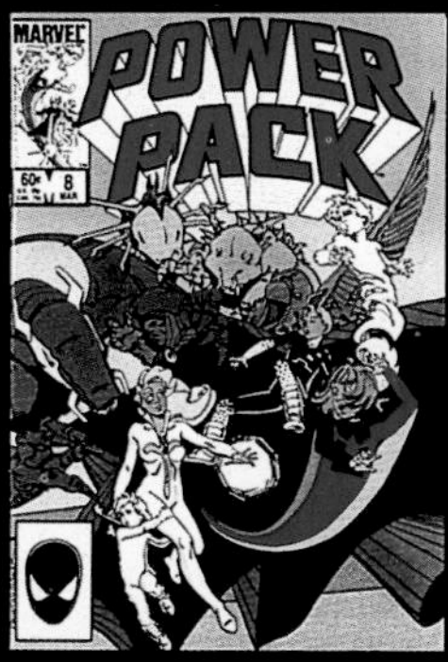
POWER PACK
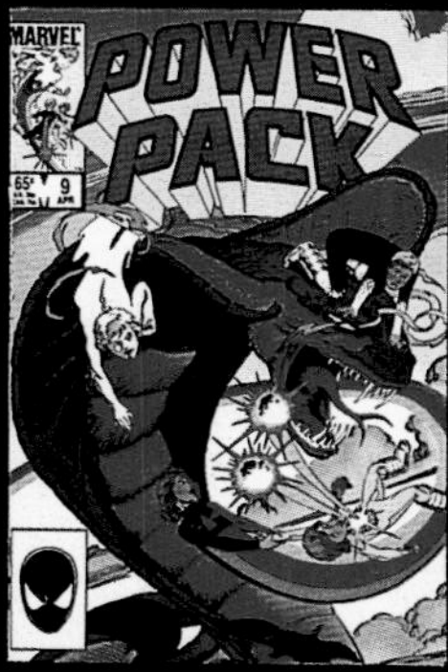
POWER PACK
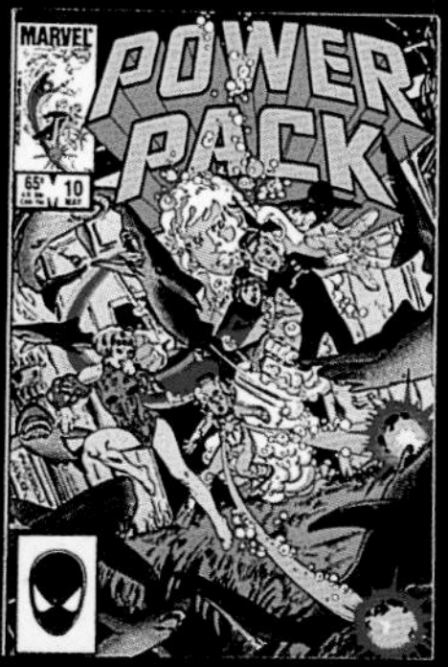
POWER PACK
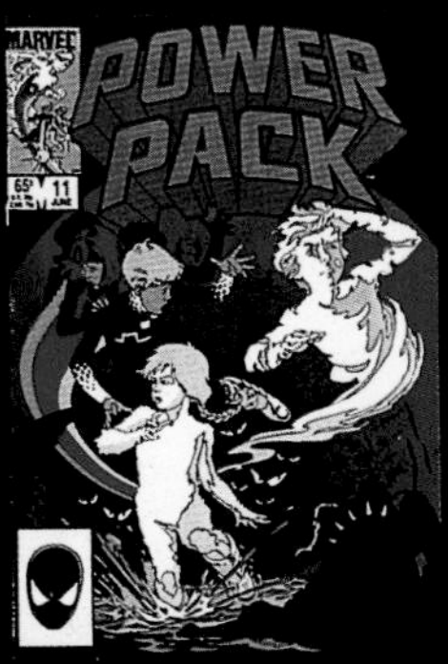
POWER PACK
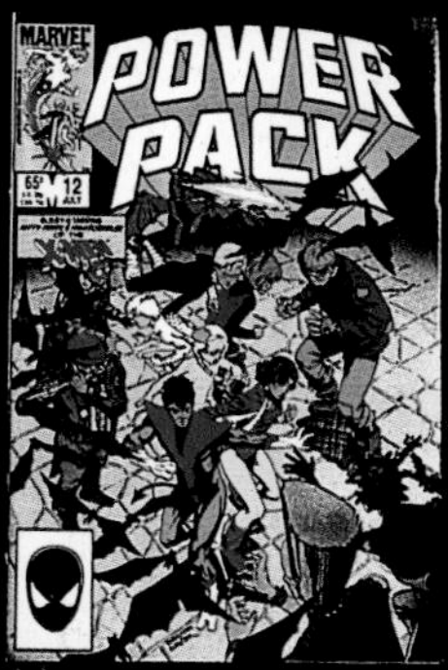
POWER PACK
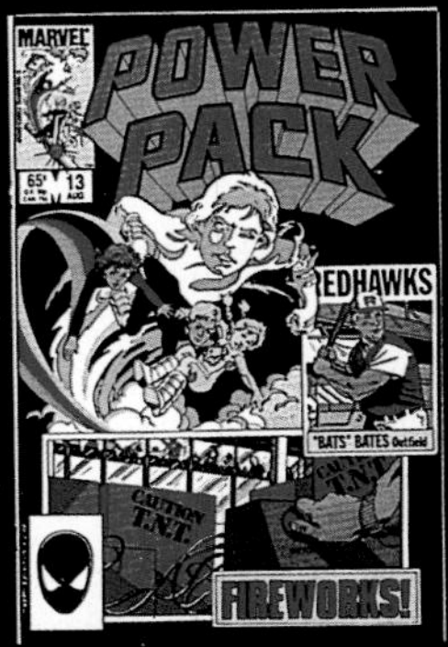
POWER PACK
REDHAWKS
"BATS" BATES OutSide!
FIREWORKS!
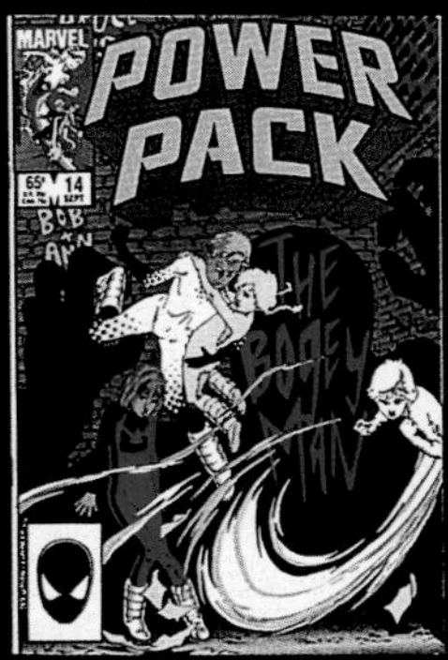
POWER PACK
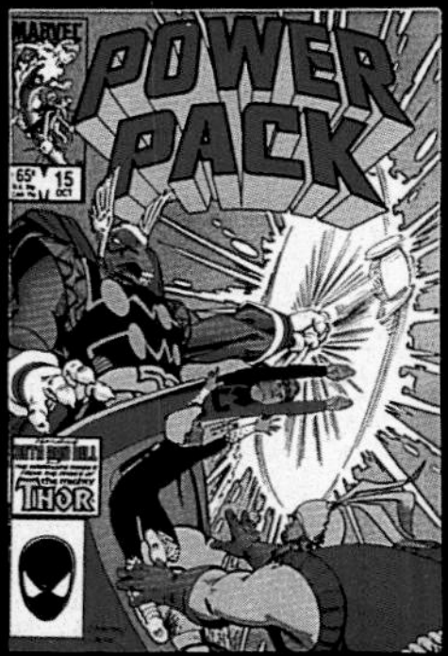
POWER PACK
THOR
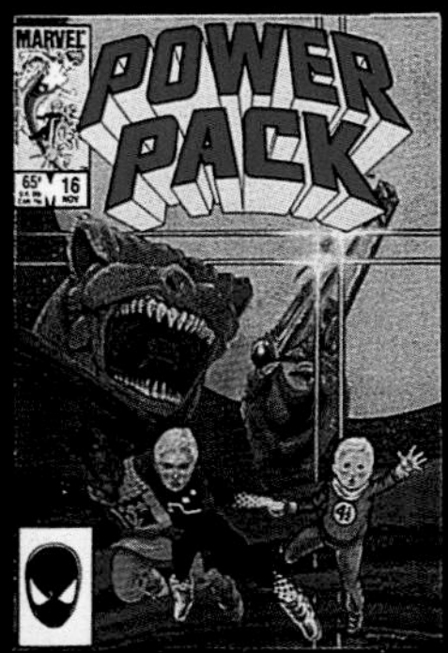
POWER PACK
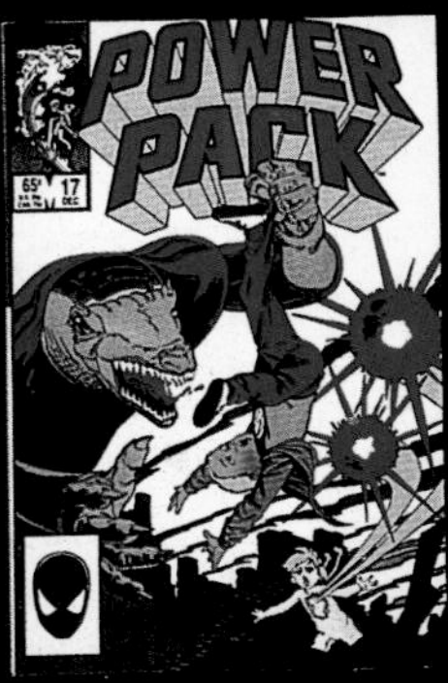
POWER PACK
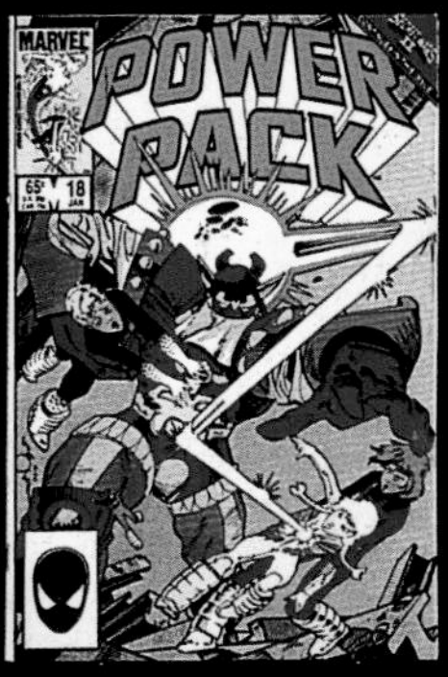
POWER PACK
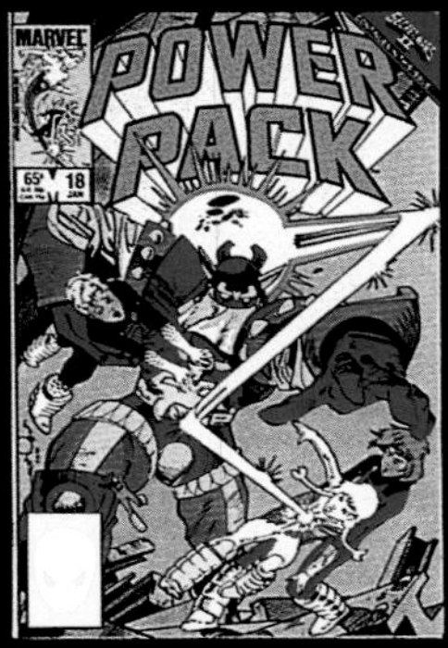
POWER PACK
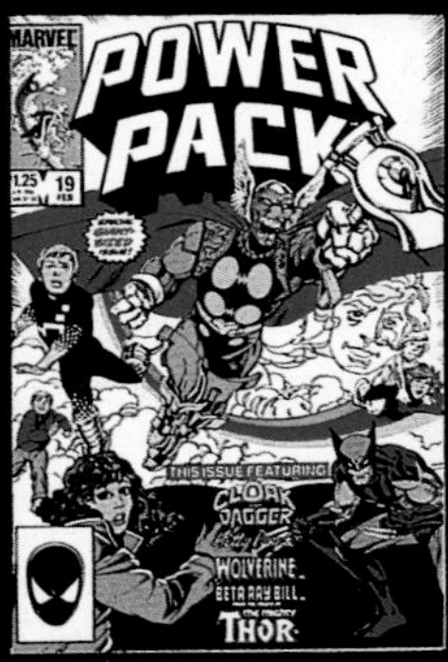
POWER PACK
THIS ISSUE FEATURING
CLOAK
DAGGER
WOLVERINE
THOR
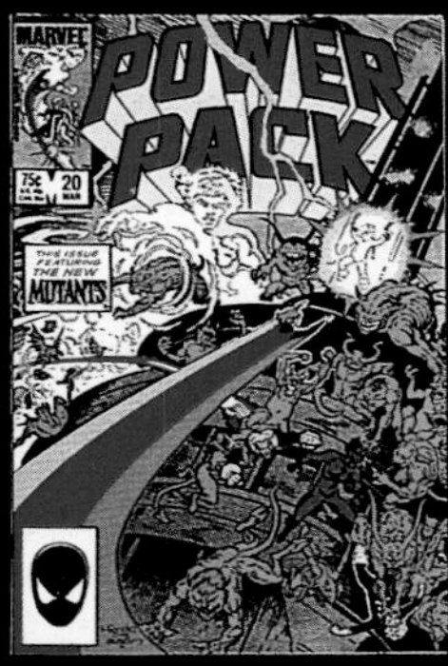
POWER PACK
MUTANTS
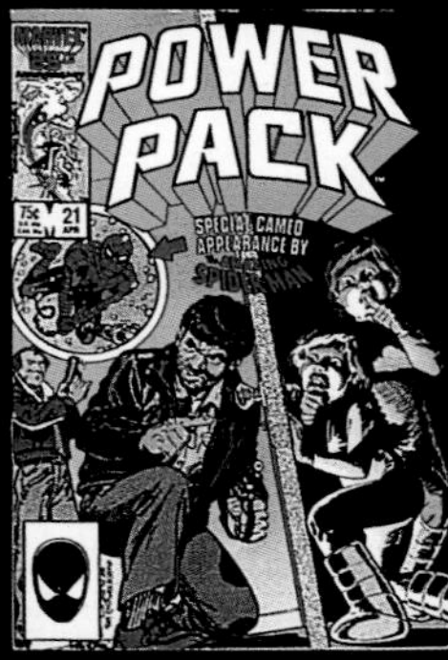
POWER PACK
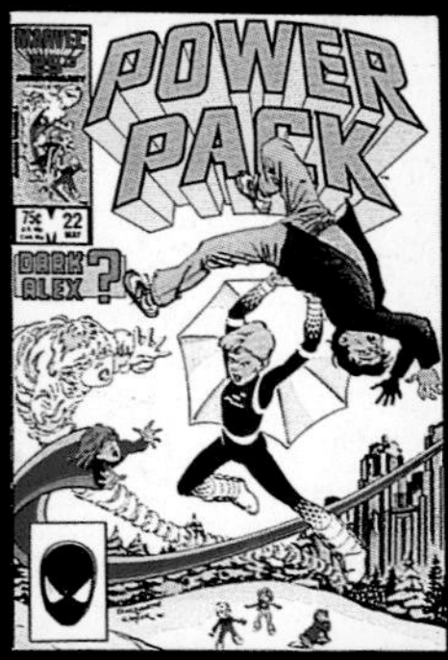
POWER PACK
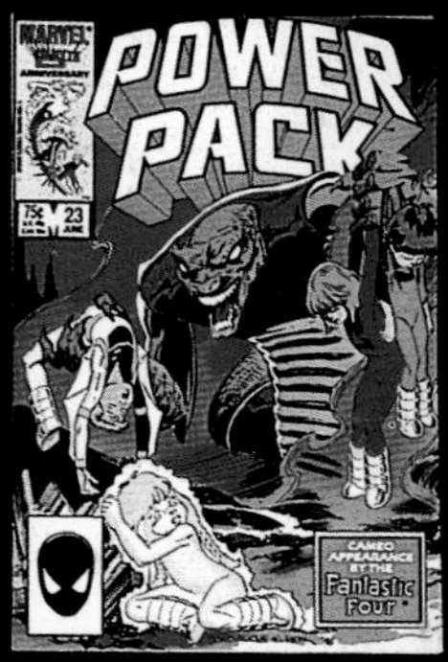
POWER PACK
Fantastic Four
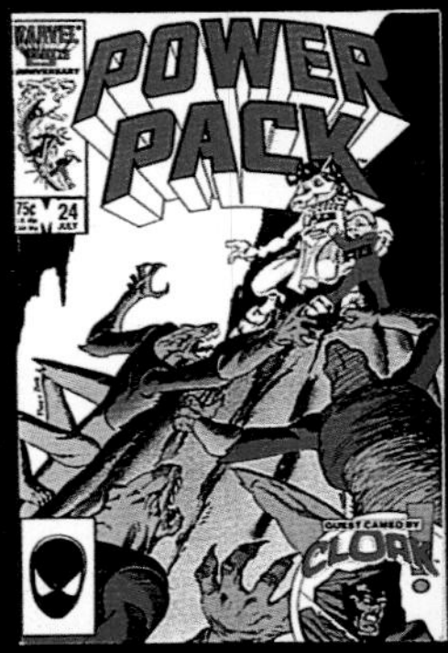
POWER PACK
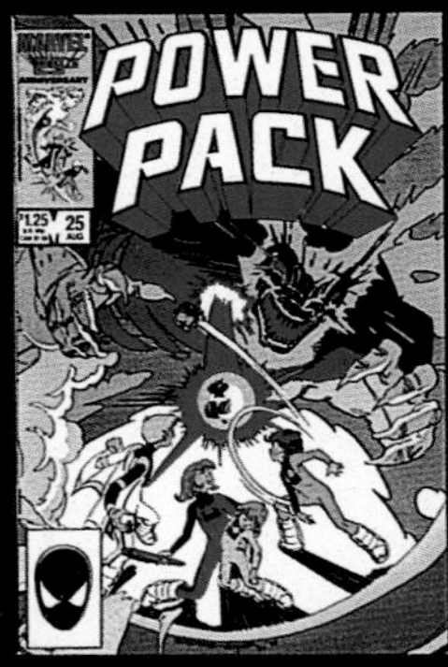
POWER PACK
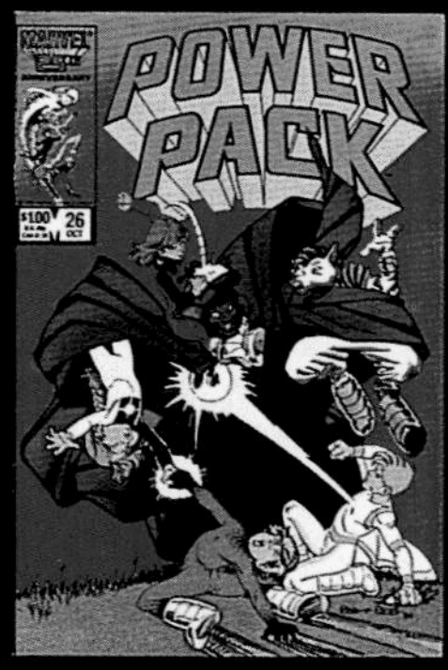
POWER PACK
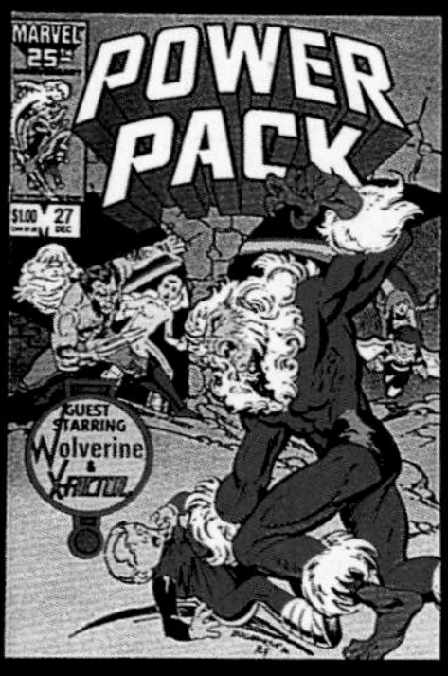
POWER PACK
GUEST STARRING
Wolverine
X-FACTOR
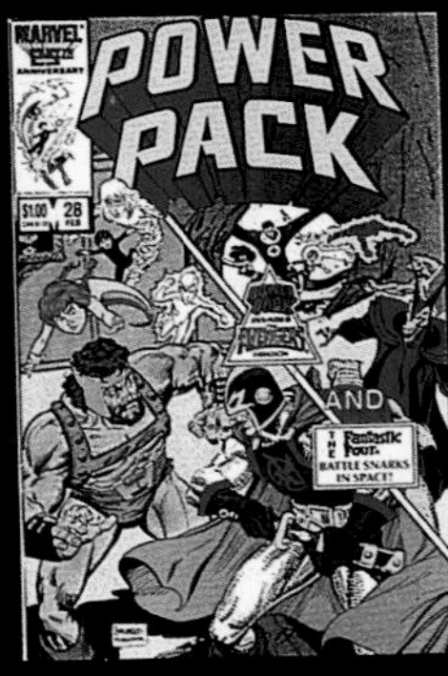
POWER PACK
BATTLE SNARKS IN SPACE!
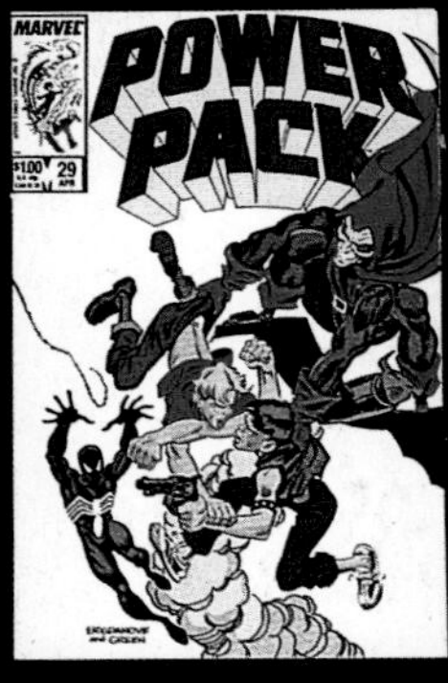
POWER PACK

1511.5 Prince Namor, the Sub-Mariner (1-4)

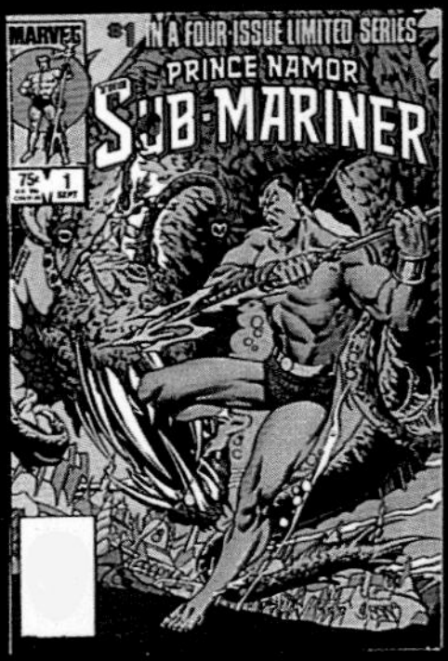
#1 IN A FOUR-ISSUE LIMITED SERIES
PRINCE NAMOR
SUB-MARINER
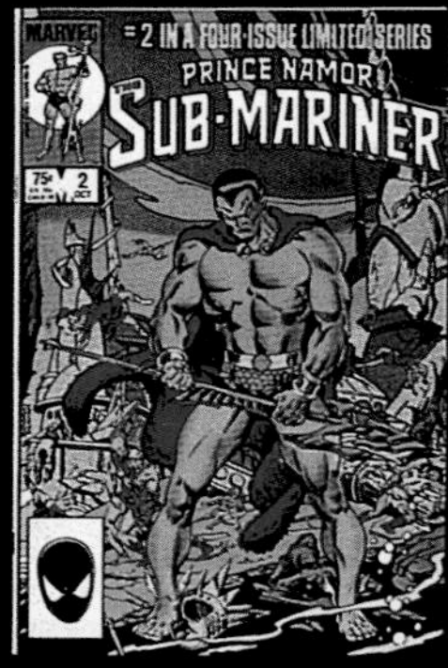
#2 IN A FOUR-ISSUE LIMITED SERIES
PRINCE NAMOR
SUB-MARINER
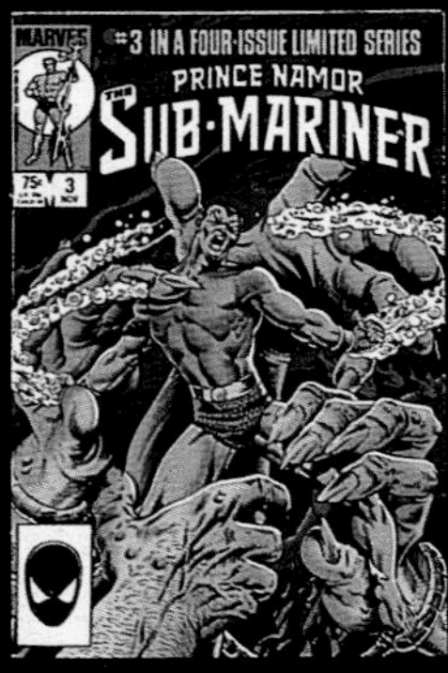
#3 IN A FOUR-ISSUE LIMITED SERIES
PRINCE NAMOR
SUB-MARINER
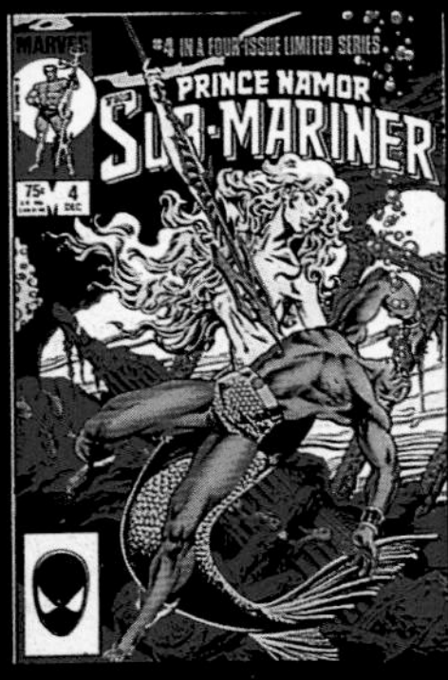
#4 IN A FOUR-ISSUE LIMITED SERIES
PRINCE NAMOR
SUB-MARINER

Power Pack (1-Present) 1510.4

Ref. No.	Date	RVI	Artist/Info.
1510.4-1	Aug. 1984	4	Brigman/Wiacek-c/a
1510.4-2	Sept.	2	" "
1510.4-3	Oct.	2	" "
1510.4-4	Nov.	2	" "
1510.4-5	Dec.	2	Brigman/Wiacek-c, Wilshire-a
1510.4-6	Jan. 1985	2	Brigman,Wiacek-c/a
1510.4-7	Feb.	2	" "
1510.4-8	Mar.	2	" "
1510.4-9	Apr.	2	Anderson/Wiacek-c/a
1510.4-10	**May**	**2**	**" "**
1510.4-11 to 18	Jan. 1986	2	
1510.4-19	Feb.	5	(Wolverine -app.)
1510.4-20 to 26	Sept.	1	(#25, Double-size)
1510.4-27	Oct.	6	(Wolverine -app.)
1510.4-28 to 60		1	(#46, Punisher -app.)

Prince Namor, The Sub-Mariner (1-4) 1511.5

1511.5-1 to 4	Sept. 1984, (#1)	1	

1520.5 Punisher (1-5)

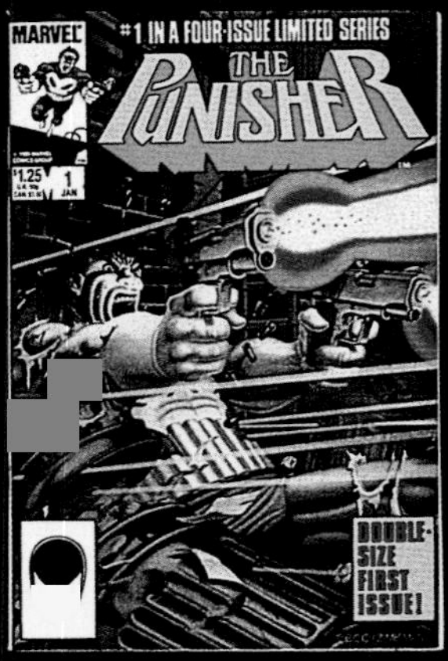

#1 IN A FOUR-ISSUE LIMITED SERIES
THE PUNISHER
DOUBLE-SIZE FIRST ISSUE!

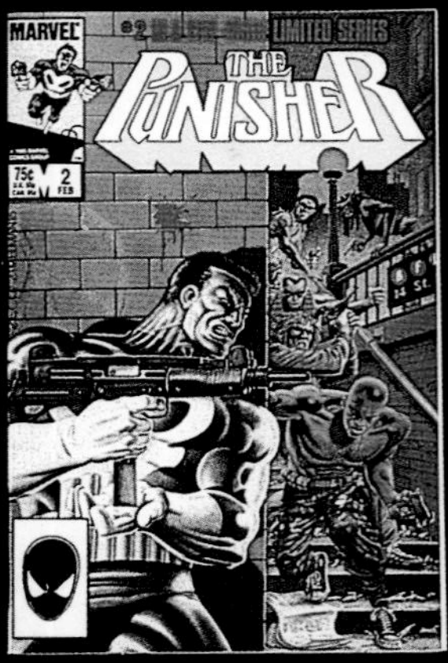

LIMITED SERIES
THE PUNISHER

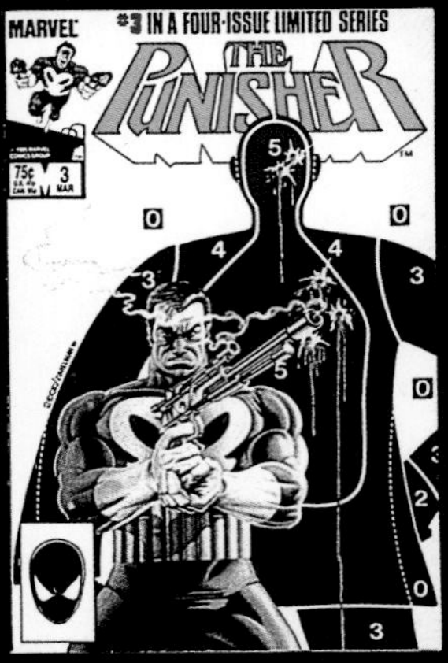

#3 IN A FOUR-ISSUE LIMITED SERIES
THE PUNISHER

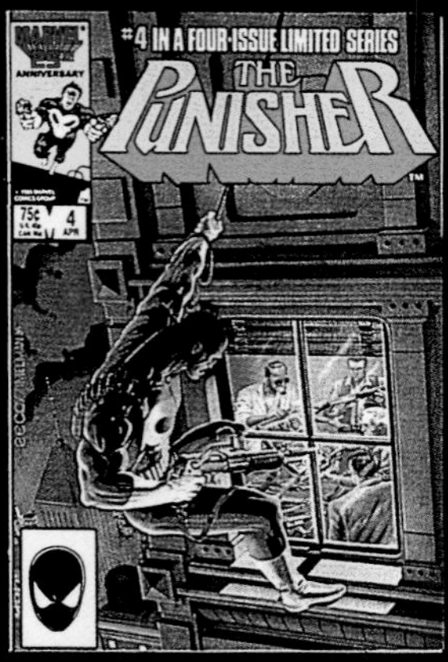

#4 IN A FOUR-ISSUE LIMITED SERIES
THE PUNISHER

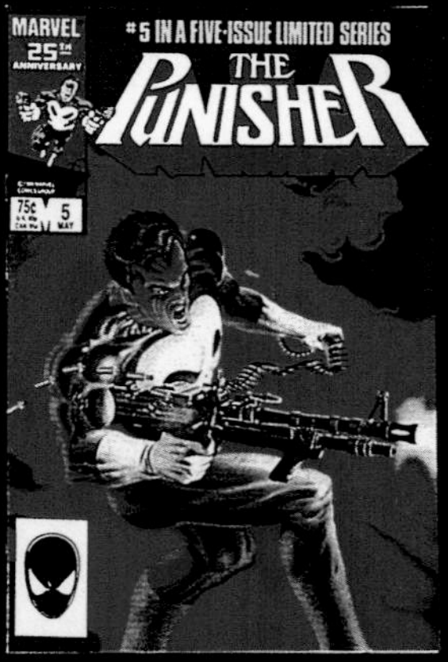

25th ANNIVERSARY
#5 IN A FIVE-ISSUE LIMITED SERIES
THE PUNISHER

1520.6 Punisher (1-20)

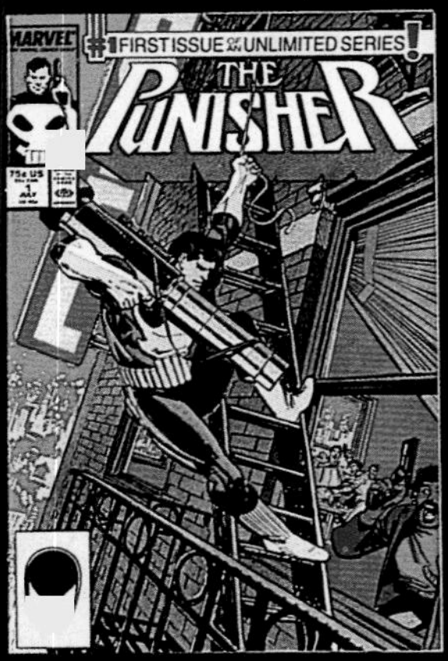

#1 FIRST ISSUE of an UNLIMITED SERIES!
THE PUNISHER

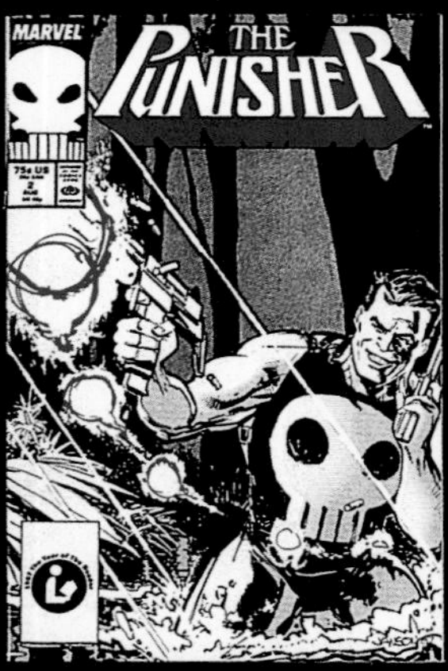

THE PUNISHER

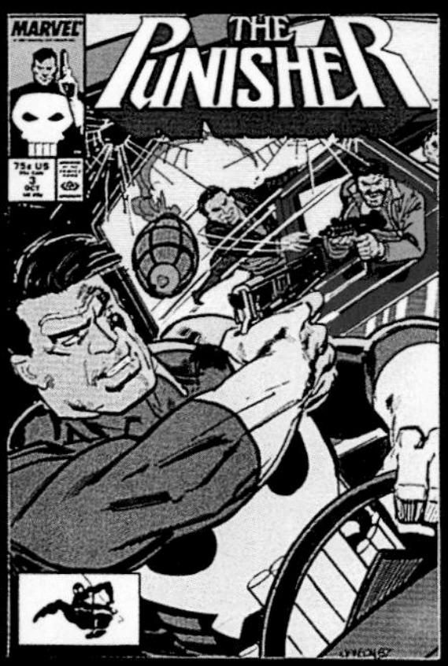

THE PUNISHER

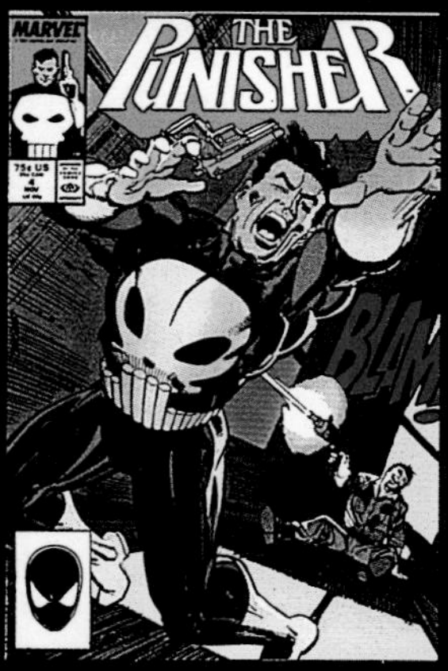

THE PUNISHER

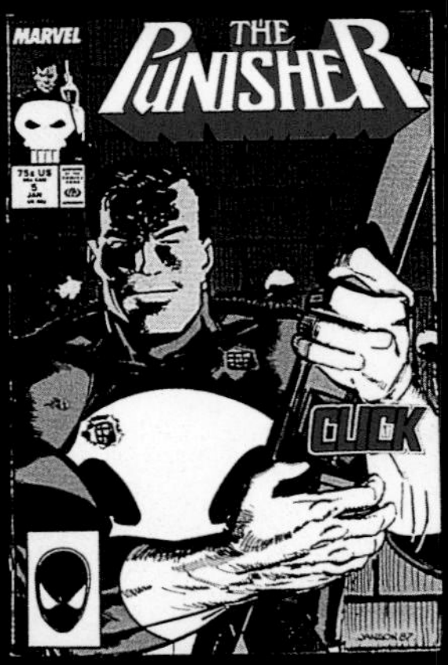

THE PUNISHER
CLICK

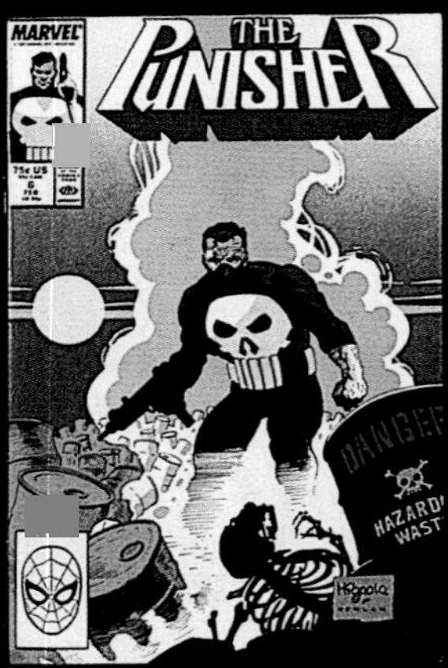

THE PUNISHER

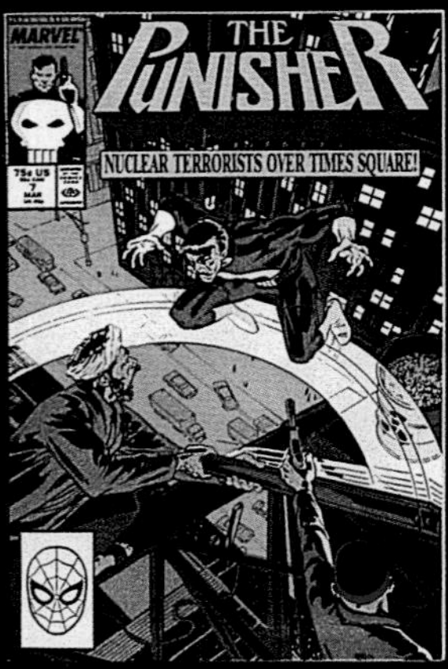

THE PUNISHER
NUCLEAR TERRORISTS OVER TIMES SQUARE!

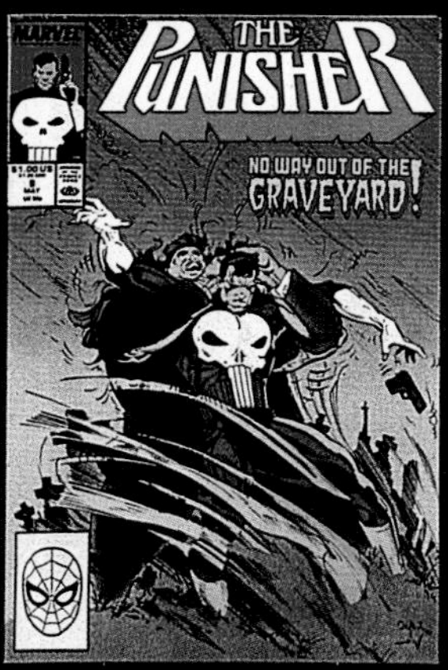

THE PUNISHER
NO WAY OUT OF THE GRAVEYARD!

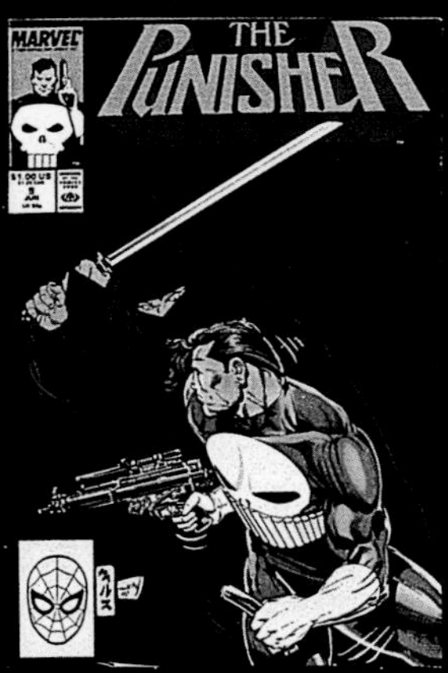

THE PUNISHER

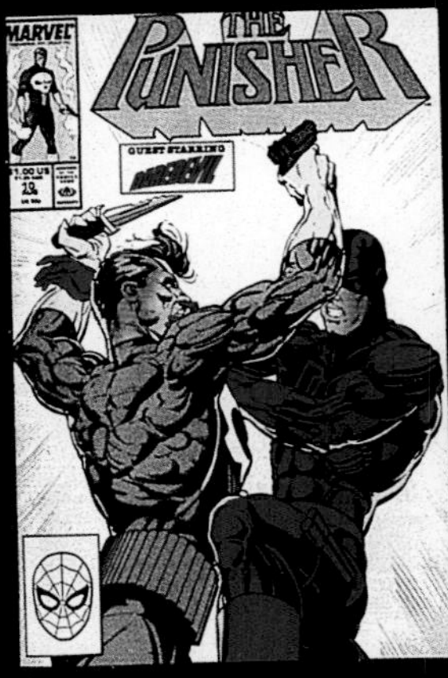

THE PUNISHER

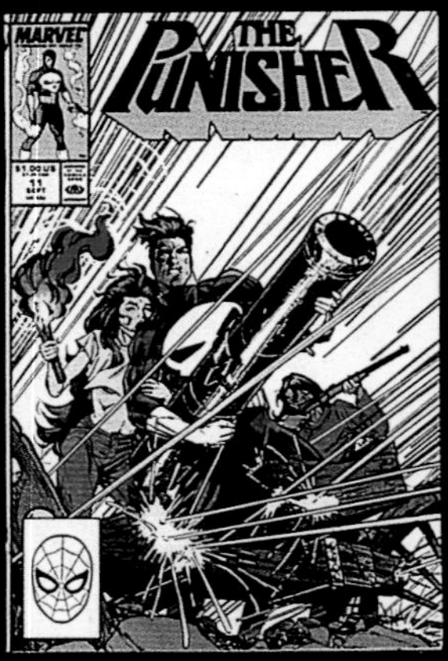

THE PUNISHER

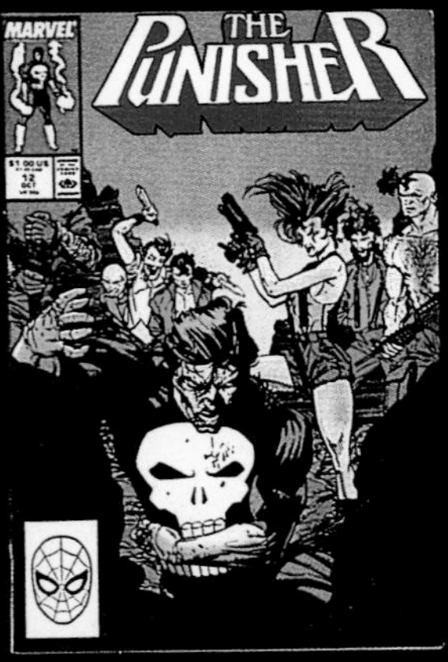

THE PUNISHER

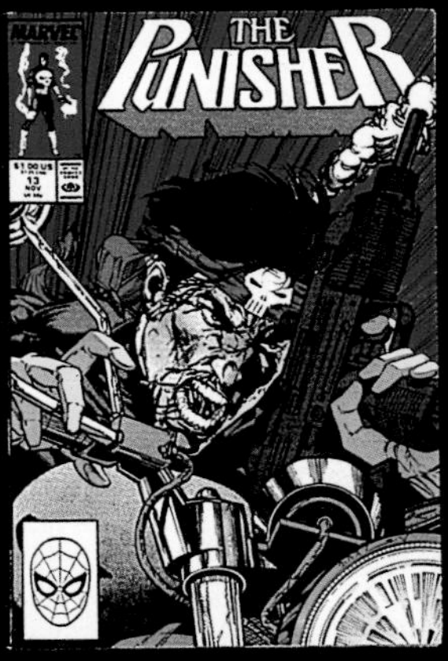

THE PUNISHER

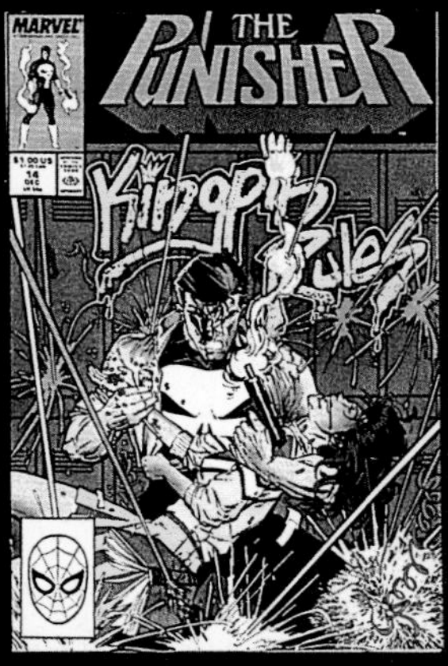

THE PUNISHER
Kingpin Rules

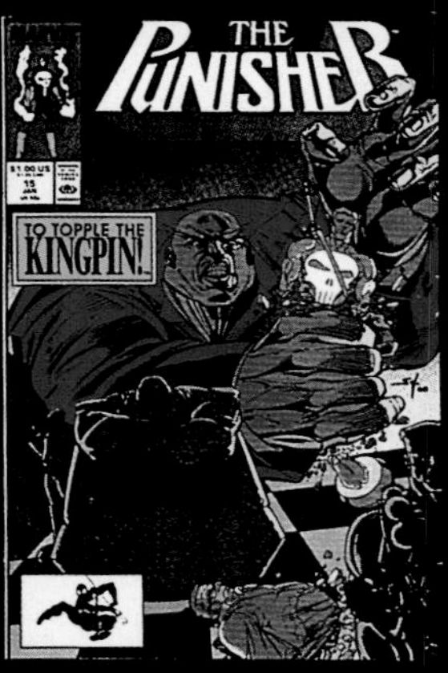

THE PUNISHER
TO TOPPLE THE KINGPIN!

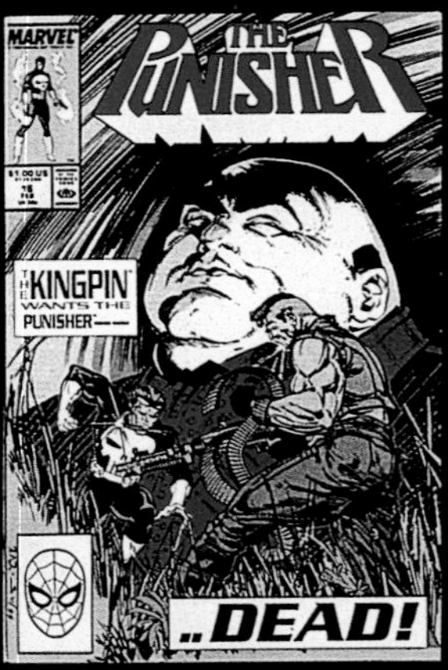

THE PUNISHER
THE KINGPIN WANTS THE PUNISHER
..DEAD!

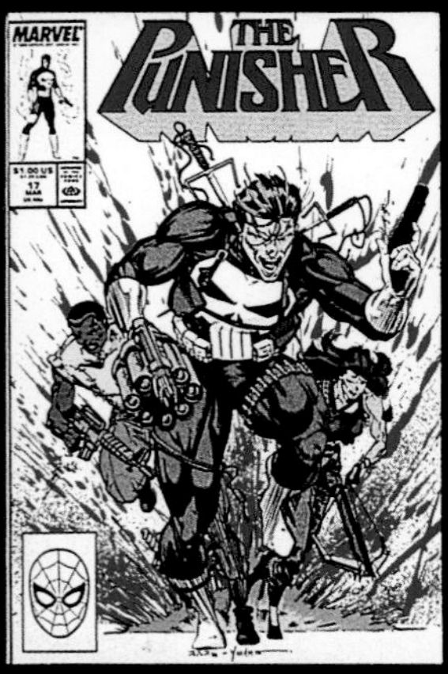

THE PUNISHER

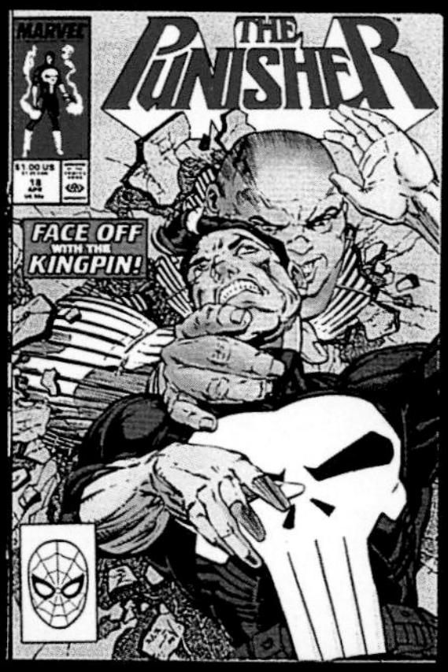

THE PUNISHER
FACE OFF WITH THE KINGPIN!

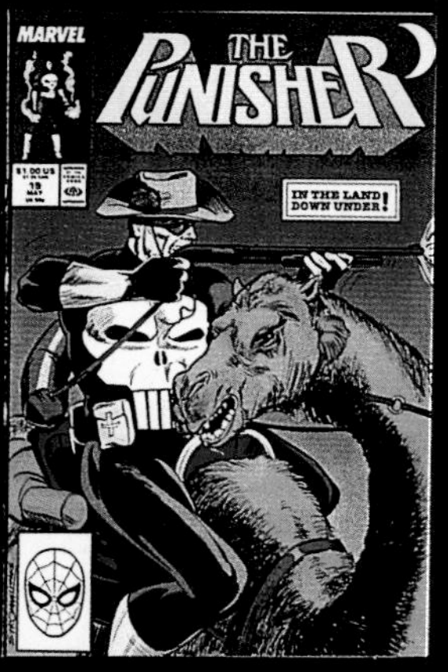

THE PUNISHER
IN THE LAND DOWN UNDER!

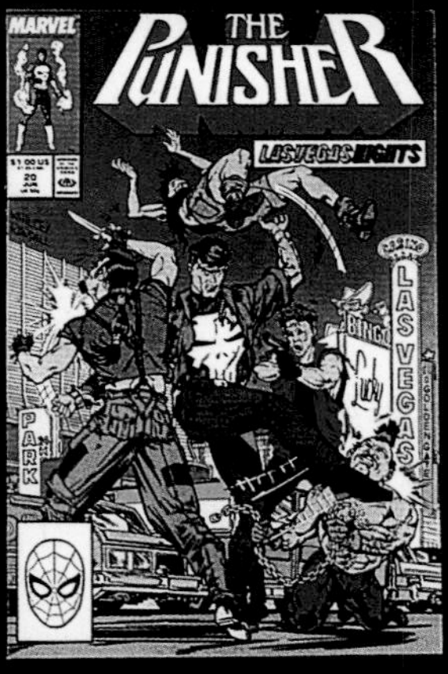

THE PUNISHER
LAS VEGAS NIGHTS
LAS VEGAS

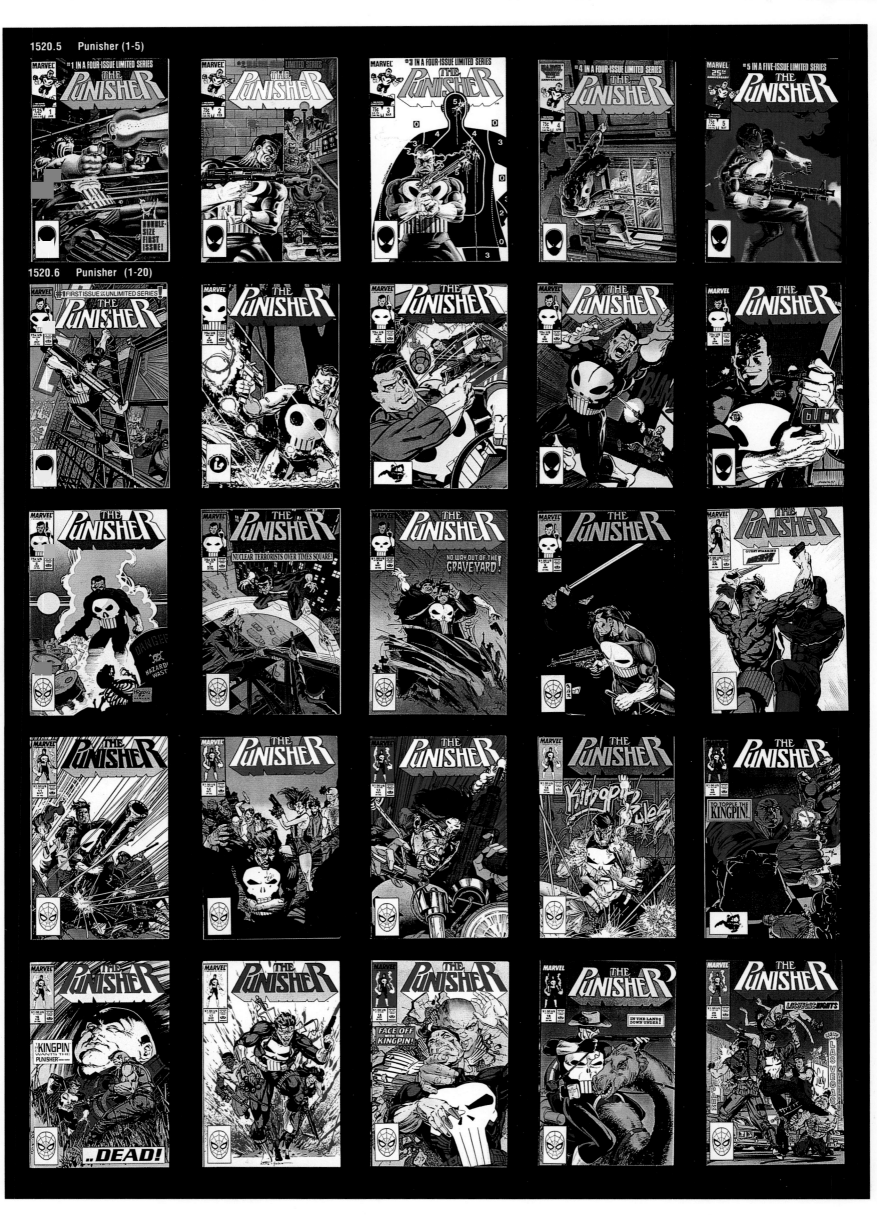

1520.6 Punisher (21-25)

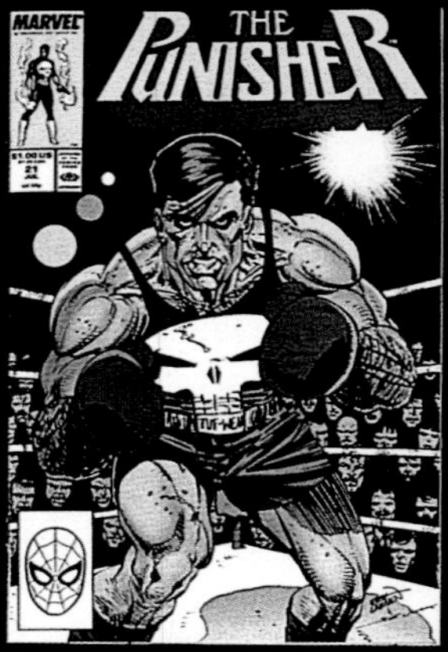
MARVEL
THE PUNISHER

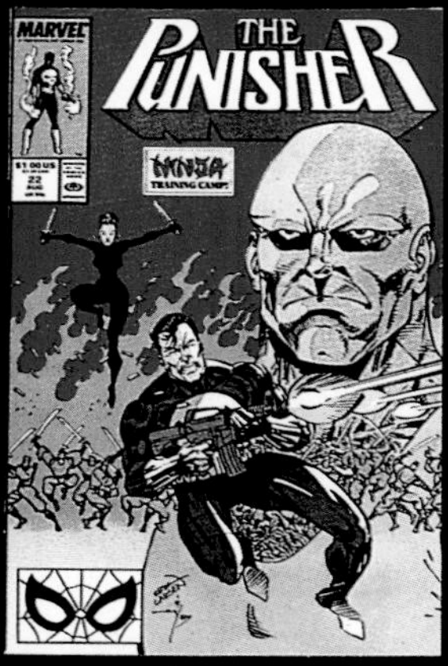
MARVEL
THE PUNISHER

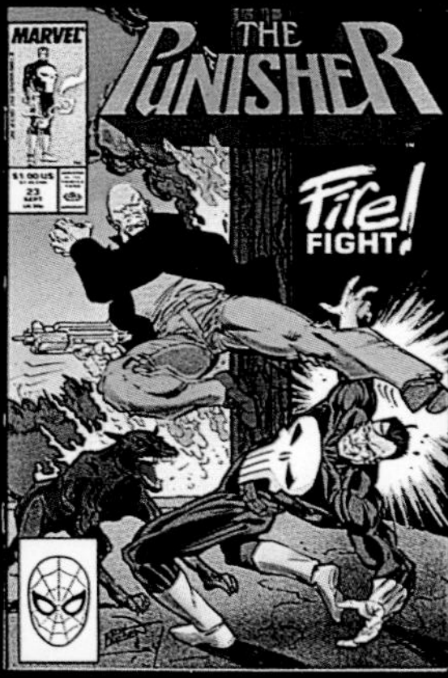
MARVEL
THE PUNISHER
Fire! FIGHT!

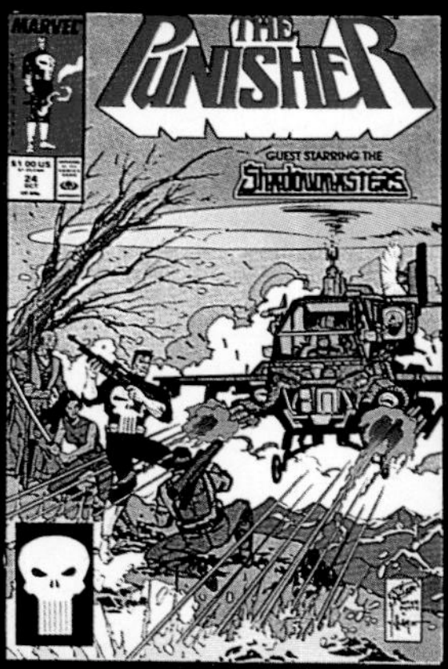
MARVEL
THE PUNISHER
GUEST STARRING THE
SHADOWMASTERS

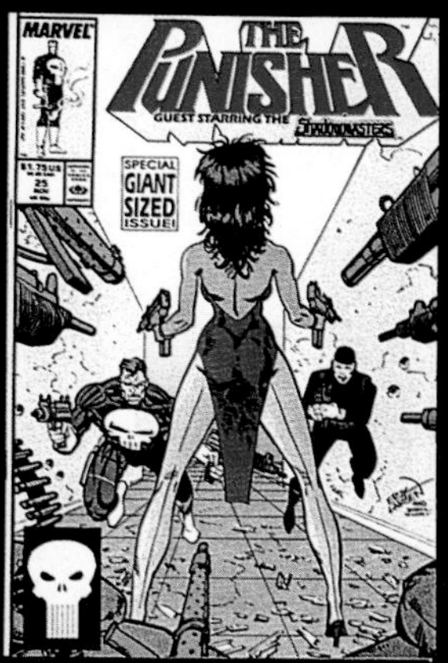
MARVEL
THE PUNISHER
GUEST STARRING THE SHADOWMASTERS
SPECIAL GIANT SIZED ISSUE!

1520.75 Punisher War Journal (1-15)

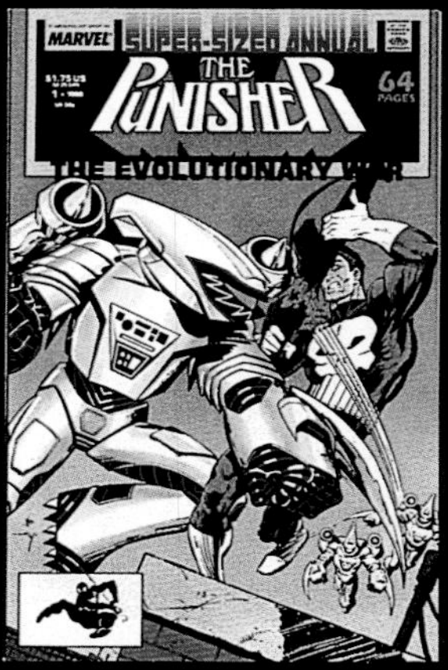
MARVEL
SUPER-SIZED ANNUAL
THE PUNISHER
64 PAGES
THE EVOLUTIONARY WAR

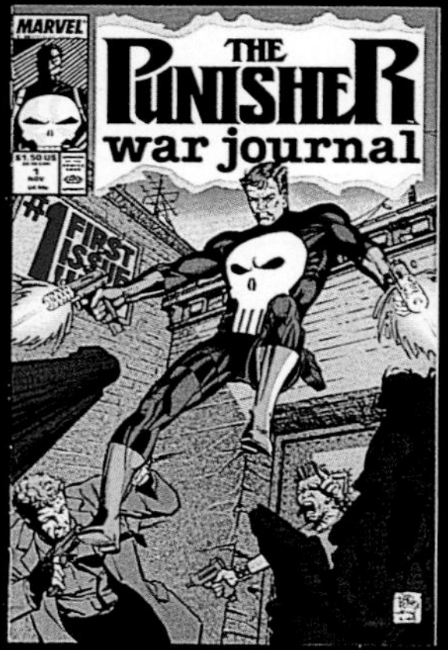
MARVEL
THE PUNISHER
war journal
FIRST ISSUE

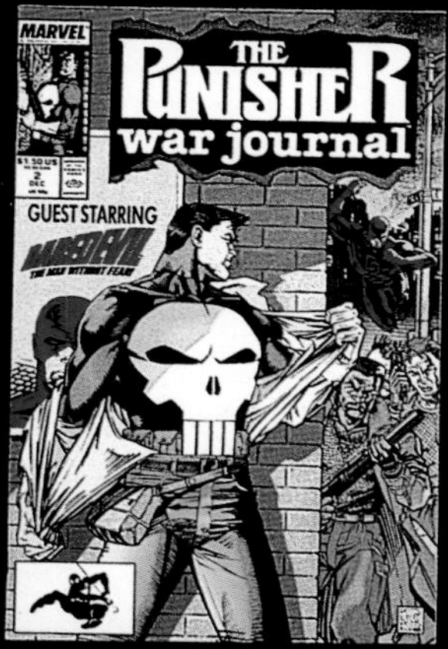
MARVEL
THE PUNISHER
war journal
GUEST STARRING
DAREDEVIL

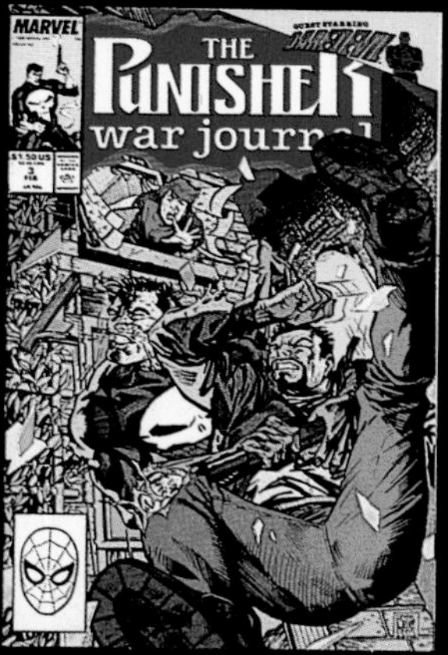
MARVEL
THE PUNISHER
war journal

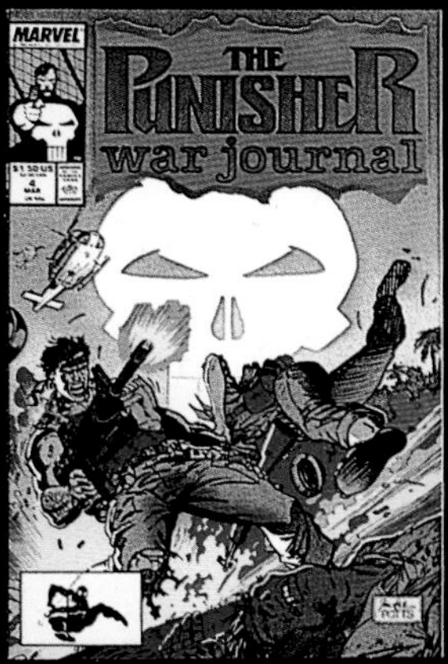
MARVEL
THE PUNISHER
war journal

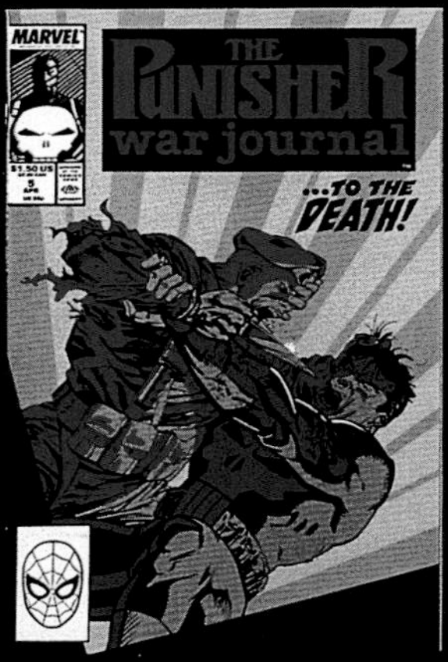
MARVEL
THE PUNISHER
war journal
...TO THE DEATH!

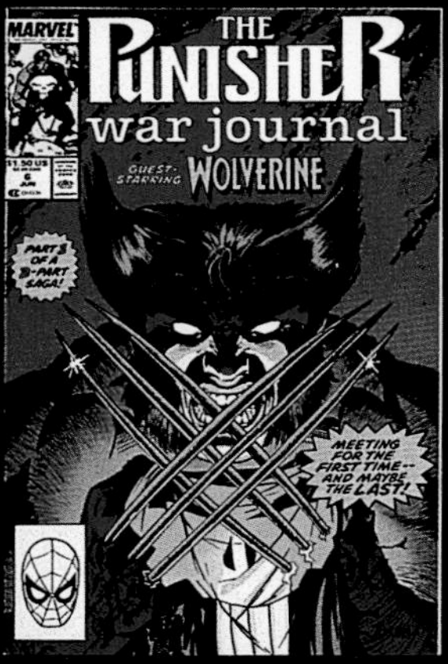
MARVEL
THE PUNISHER
war journal
GUEST-STARRING WOLVERINE

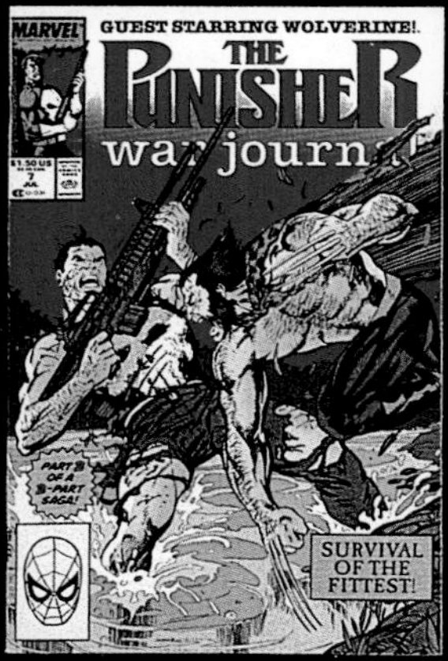
MARVEL
GUEST STARRING WOLVERINE!
THE PUNISHER
war journal
SURVIVAL OF THE FITTEST!

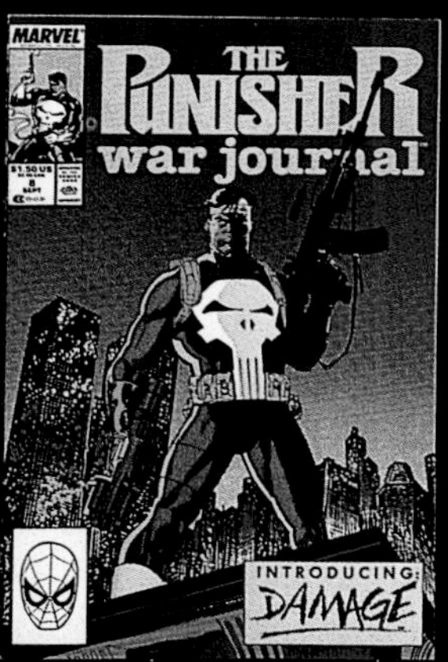
MARVEL
THE PUNISHER
war journal
INTRODUCING: DAMAGE

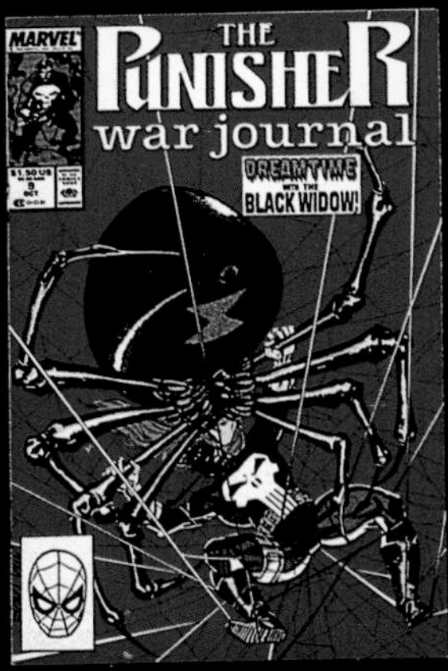
MARVEL
THE PUNISHER
war journal
WITH THE BLACK WIDOW!

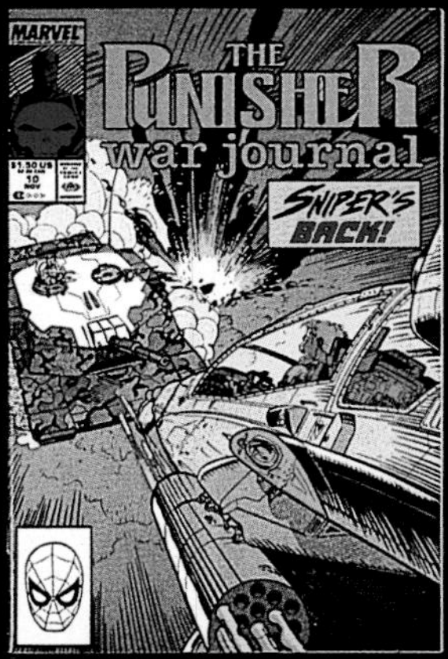
MARVEL
THE PUNISHER
war journal
SNIPER'S BACK!

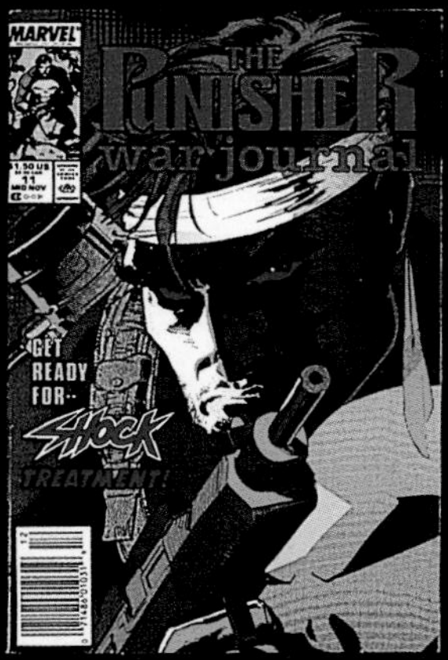
MARVEL
THE PUNISHER
war journal
GET READY FOR...
SHOCK TREATMENT

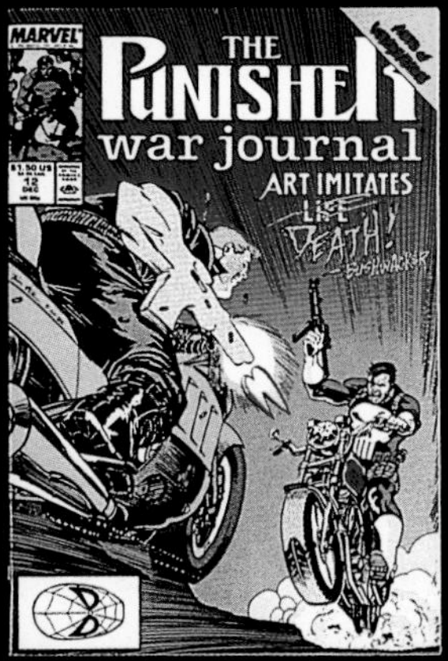
MARVEL
THE PUNISHER
war journal
ART IMITATES LIFE DEATH!

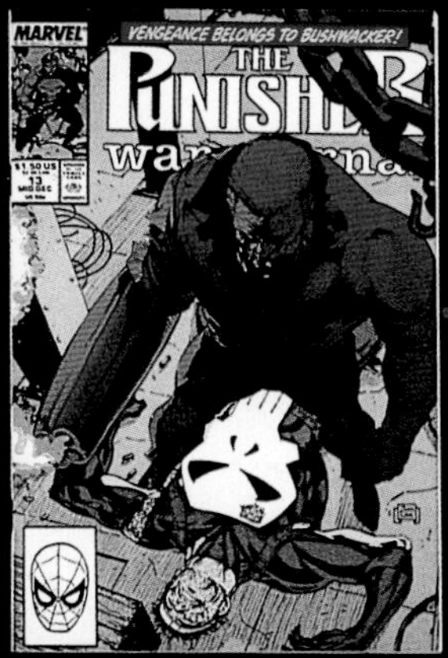
MARVEL
VENGEANCE BELONGS TO BUSHWACKER!
THE PUNISHER

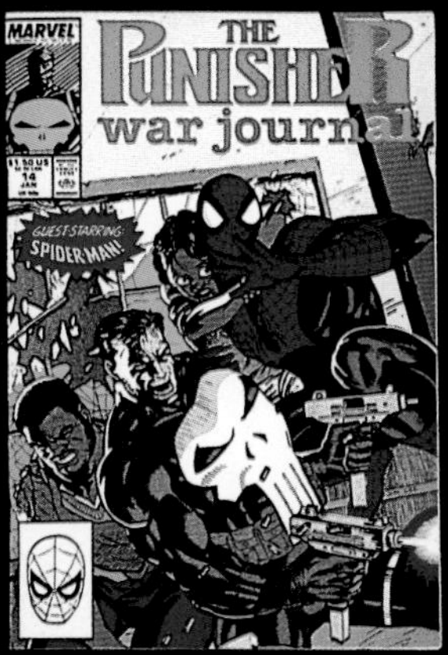
MARVEL
THE PUNISHER
war journal
SPIDER-MAN

1524.5 Questprobe (1)

Raiders of the Lost Ark (1)

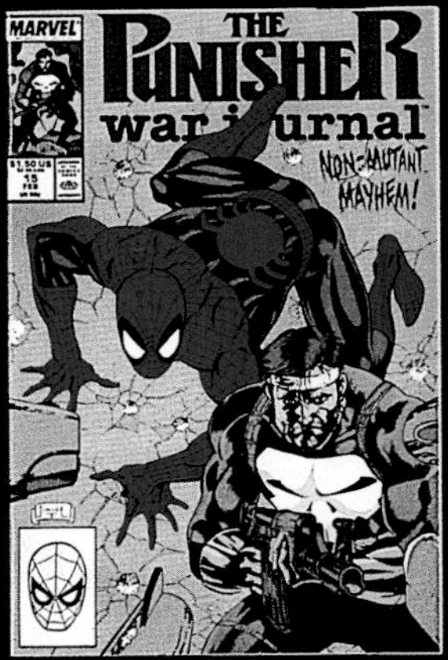
MARVEL
THE PUNISHER
war journal
NON-MUTANT MAYHEM!

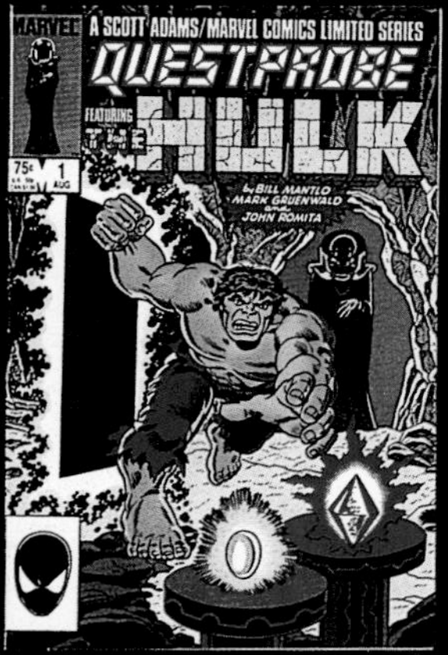
MARVEL
A SCOTT ADAMS/MARVEL COMICS LIMITED SERIES
QUESTPROBE
FEATURING THE HULK

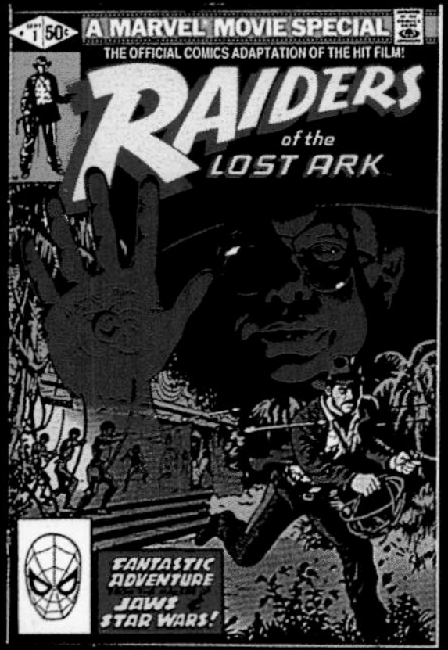
A MARVEL MOVIE SPECIAL
THE OFFICIAL COMICS ADAPTATION OF THE HIT FILM!
RAIDERS of the LOST ARK
FANTASTIC ADVENTURE FROM JAWS TO STAR WARS!

Punisher (1-5) 1520.6

Ref. No.	Date	RVI	Artist/Info.
1520.6-1	Jan. 1986	30	Zech/Zimelman-c, Zech/Beatty-a
1520.6-2	Feb.	15	" " " "
1520.6-3	Mar.	10	" " " "
1520.6-4	Apr.	7	" " " "
1520.6-5	May	7	" " " "

Punisher V.2 (1-Present) 1520.6

1520.6-1	Jul. 1987	11	Janson-c/a
1520.6-2	Aug.	6	"
1520.6-3	Oct.	4	"
1520.6-4	Nov.	4	"
1520.6-5	Jan. 1988	4	"
1520.6-6 to 10	Aug. 1988, (#10)	4	(#10 RVI 10)
1520.6-11 to 20		3	(#24, Intro. Shadowmasters)
1520.6-21 to 48		1	
1520.6-A1	Aug. 1988	4	(Evolutionary Warr -app.)

Punisher War Journal (1-Present) 1520.75

1520.75-1	Nov. 1988	3	Potts-c/a, Lee-a
1520.75-2 to 25		2	(6, 7, Wolverine Story)

Questprobe (1-4) 1524.5

1524.5-1	Aug. 1984	1	Gruenwald/Romita-a
1524.5-2	Jan. 1985	1	Milgrom/Mooney-a
1524.5-3	Nov.	1	Wilson/Sinnott-a
1524.5-4	Dec. 1985, (#4)	1	

Raiders of the Lost Ark (1-3) 1528.3

1528.3-1 to 3	Sept. 1981, (#1)	1	Buscema-a

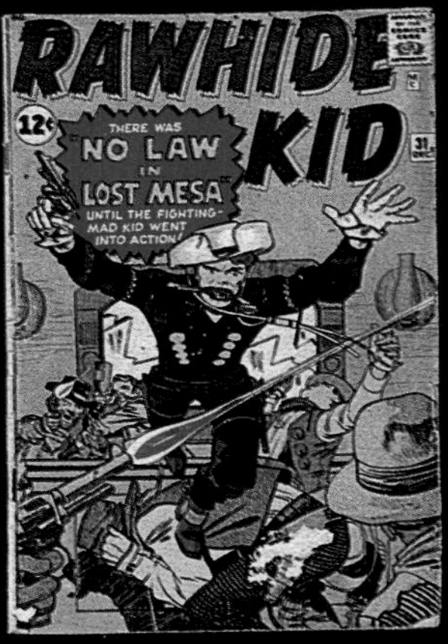
RAWHIDE KID
12¢
31
THERE WAS NO LAW IN LOST MESA UNTIL THE FIGHTING-MAD KID WENT INTO ACTION!

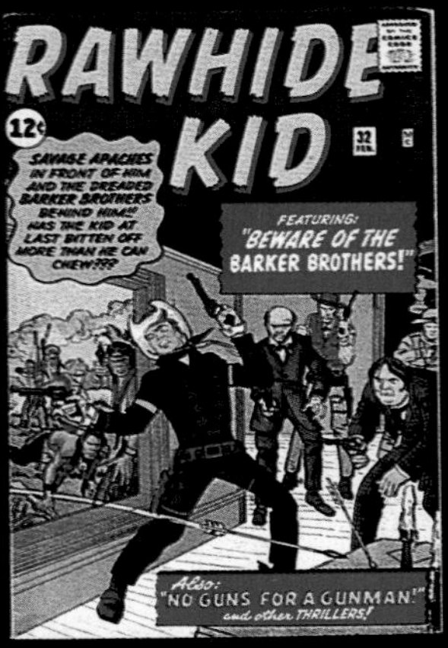
RAWHIDE KID
12¢
32
FEATURING: "BEWARE OF THE BARKER BROTHERS!"
Also: "NO GUNS FOR A GUNMAN" and other THRILLERS!

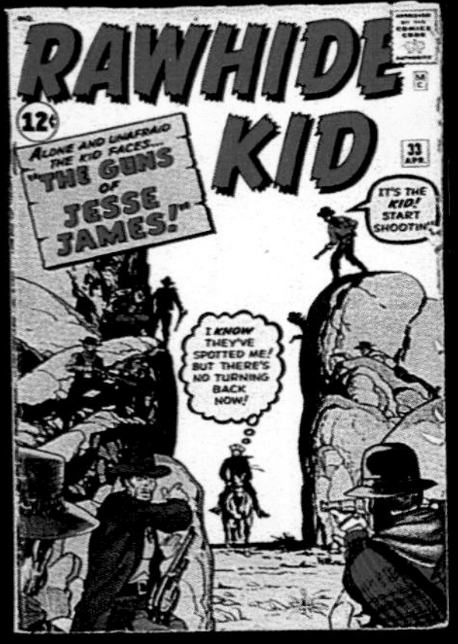
RAWHIDE KID
12¢
33
"THE GUNS OF JESSE JAMES!"
IT'S THE KID! START SHOOTIN'!
I KNOW THEY'VE SPOTTED ME! BUT THERE'S NO TURNING BACK NOW!

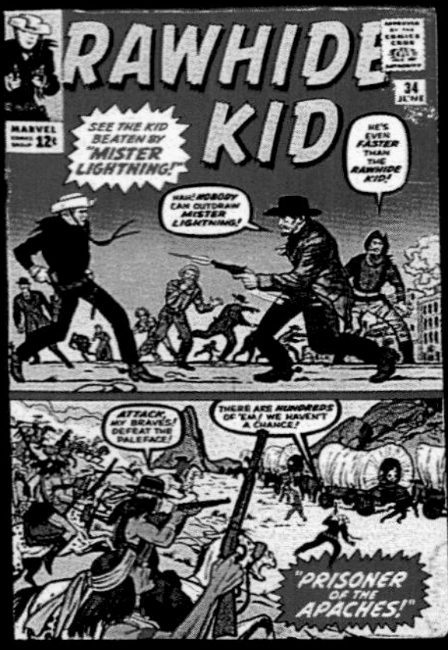
RAWHIDE KID
34
SEE THE KID BEATEN BY "MISTER LIGHTNING!"
"PRISONER OF THE APACHES!"

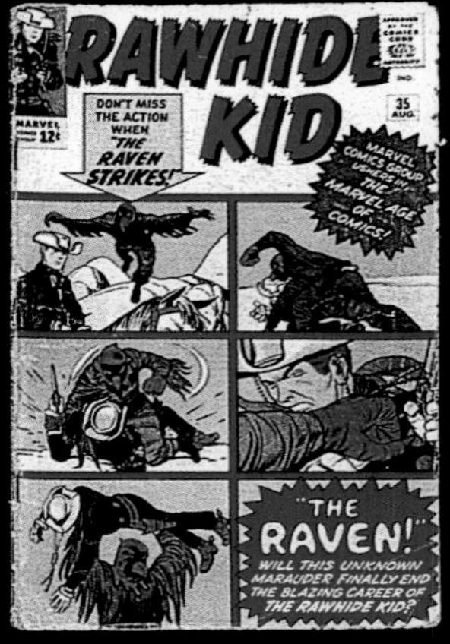
RAWHIDE KID
35
DON'T MISS THE ACTION WHEN "THE RAVEN STRIKES!"
"THE RAVEN!"
WILL THIS UNKNOWN MARAUDER FINALLY END THE BLAZING CAREER OF THE RAWHIDE KID?

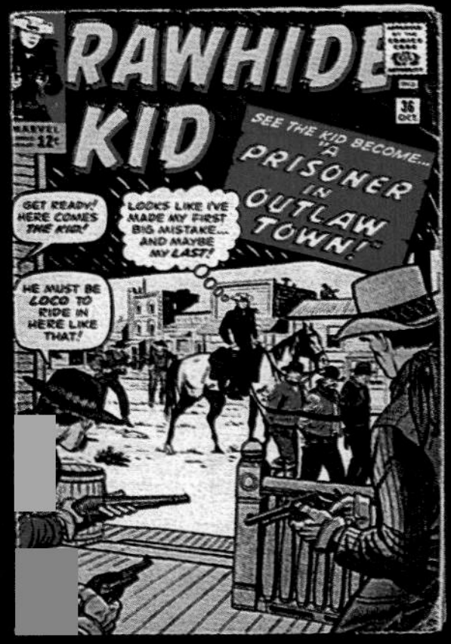
RAWHIDE KID
36
SEE THE KID BECOME A PRISONER IN OUTLAW TOWN!

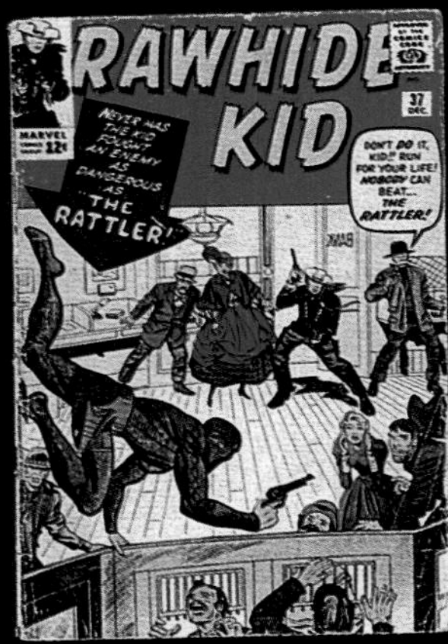
RAWHIDE KID
37
"THE RATTLER!"

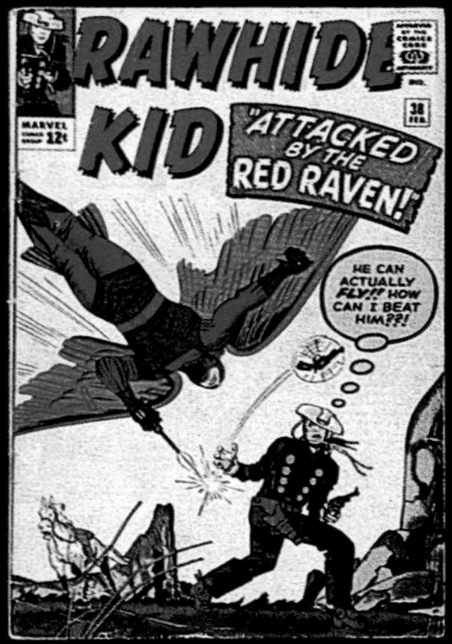
RAWHIDE KID
38
"ATTACKED BY THE RED RAVEN!"

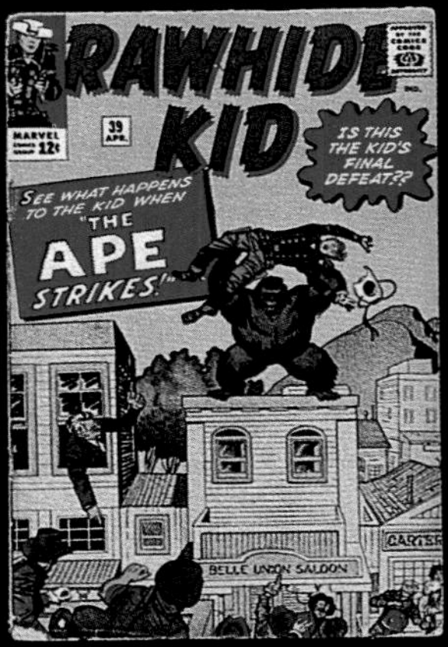
RAWHIDE KID
39
IS THIS THE KID'S FINAL DEFEAT??
SEE WHAT HAPPENS TO THE KID WHEN THE APE STRIKES!
BELLE UNION SALOON

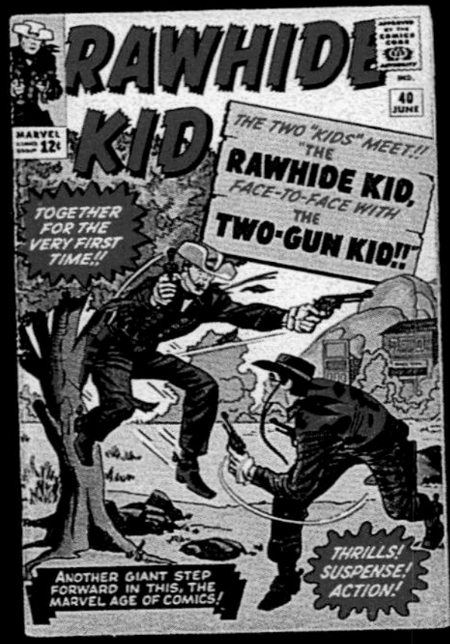
RAWHIDE KID
40
THE TWO "KIDS" MEET!! "THE RAWHIDE KID, FACE-TO-FACE WITH THE TWO-GUN KID!!"
TOGETHER FOR THE VERY FIRST TIME!!
ANOTHER GIANT STEP FORWARD IN THIS, THE MARVEL AGE OF COMICS!
THRILLS! SUSPENSE! ACTION!

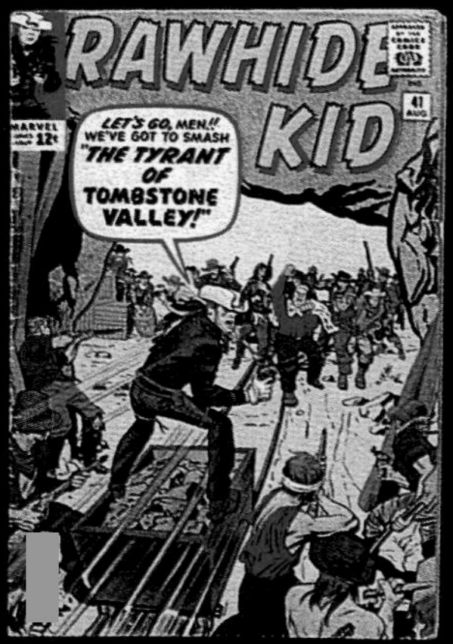
RAWHIDE KID
41
LET'S GO, MEN!! WE'VE GOT TO SMASH "THE TYRANT OF TOMBSTONE VALLEY!"

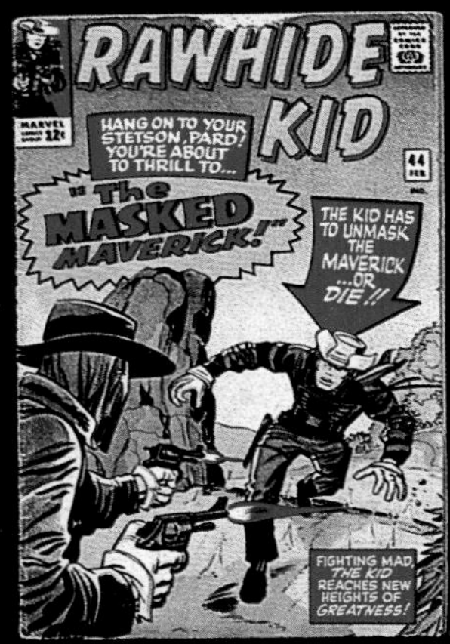
RAWHIDE KID
44
HANG ON TO YOUR STETSON, PARD! YOU'RE ABOUT TO THRILL TO... "The MASKED MAVERICK!"

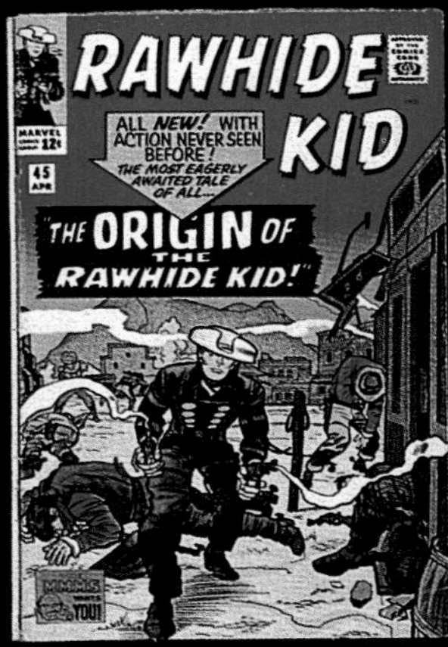
RAWHIDE KID
45
ALL NEW! WITH ACTION NEVER SEEN BEFORE THE MOST EAGERLY AWAITED TALE OF ALL!
THE ORIGIN OF THE RAWHIDE KID!

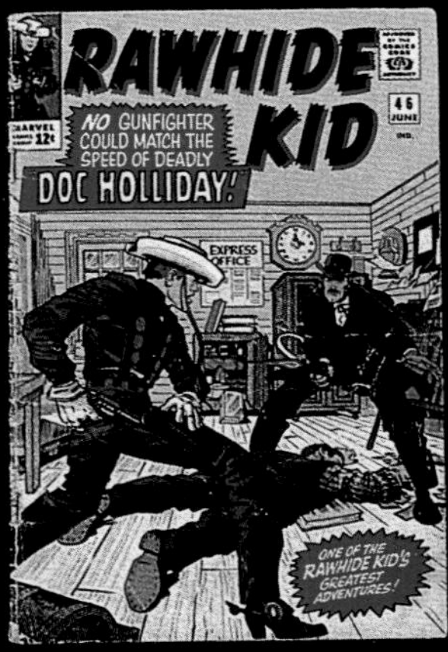
RAWHIDE KID
46
NO GUNFIGHTER COULD MATCH THE SPEED OF DEADLY DOC HOLLIDAY!

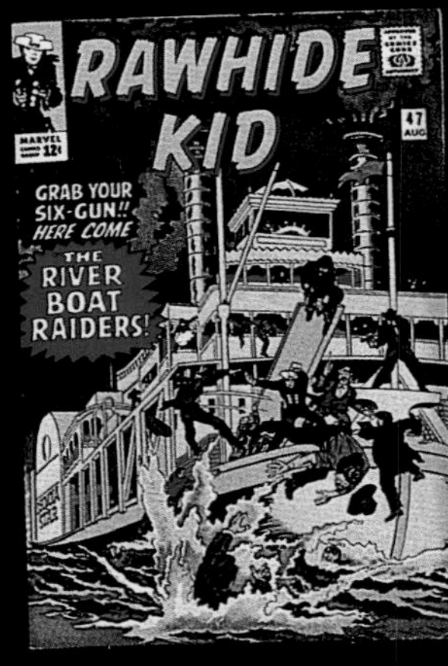
RAWHIDE KID
47
GRAB YOUR SIX-GUN!! HERE COME THE RIVER BOAT RAIDERS!

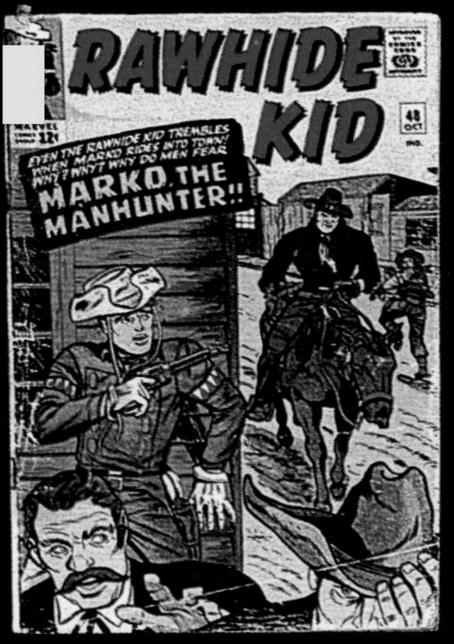
RAWHIDE KID
48
MARKO, THE MANHUNTER!!

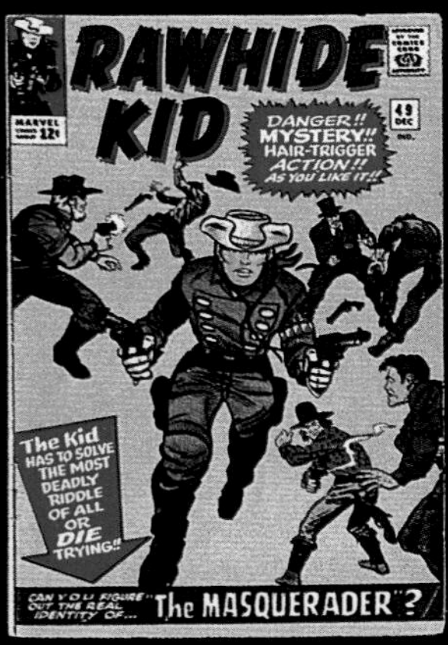
RAWHIDE KID
49
DANGER!! MYSTERY!! HAIR-TRIGGER ACTION!!
The Kid HAS TO SOLVE THE MOST DEADLY RIDDLE OF ALL OR DIE TRYING!
The MASQUERADER"?

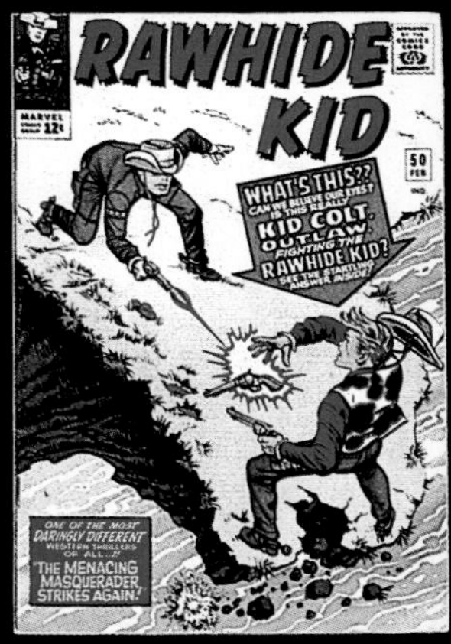
RAWHIDE KID
50
WHAT'S THIS?
KID COLT OUTLAW
RAWHIDE KID
THE MENACING MASQUERADER STRIKES AGAIN!

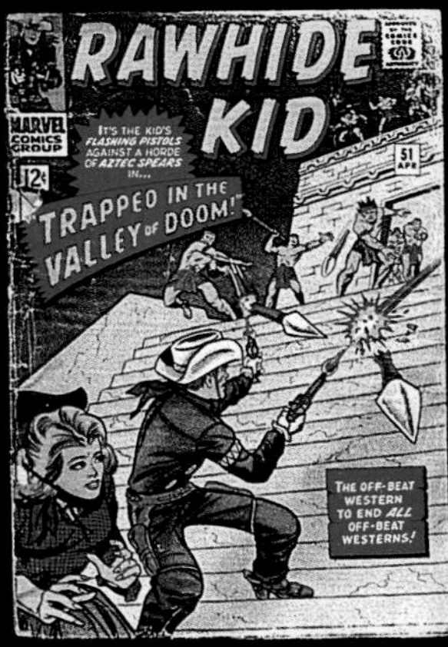
RAWHIDE KID
51
TRAPPED IN THE VALLEY of DOOM!
THE OFF-BEAT WESTERN TO END ALL OFF-BEAT WESTERNS!

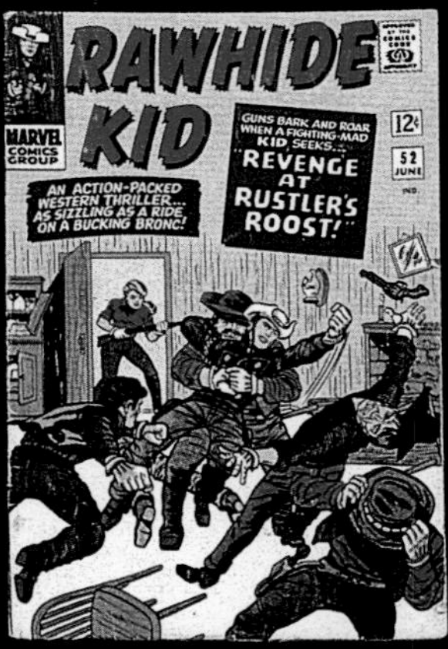
RAWHIDE KID
52
"REVENGE AT RUSTLER'S ROOST!"

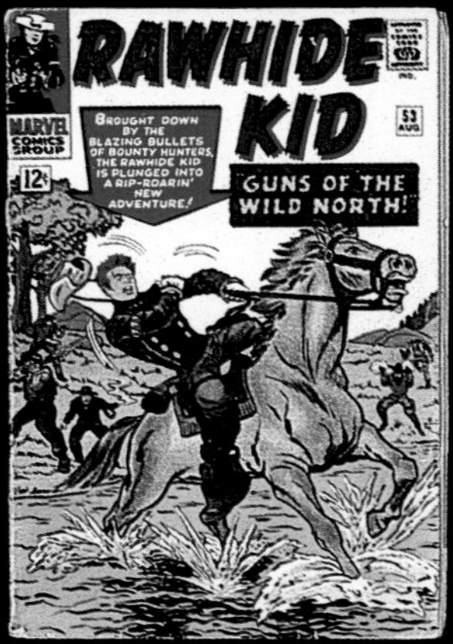
RAWHIDE KID
53
GUNS OF THE WILD NORTH!

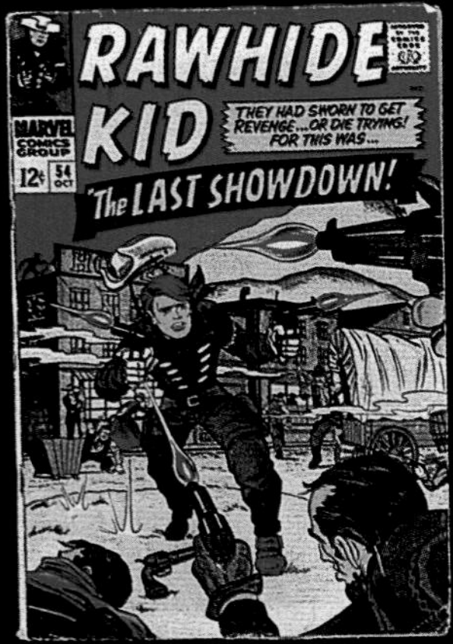
RAWHIDE KID
54
THEY HAD SWORN TO GET REVENGE...OR DIE TRYING! FOR THIS WAS-
"The LAST SHOWDOWN!"

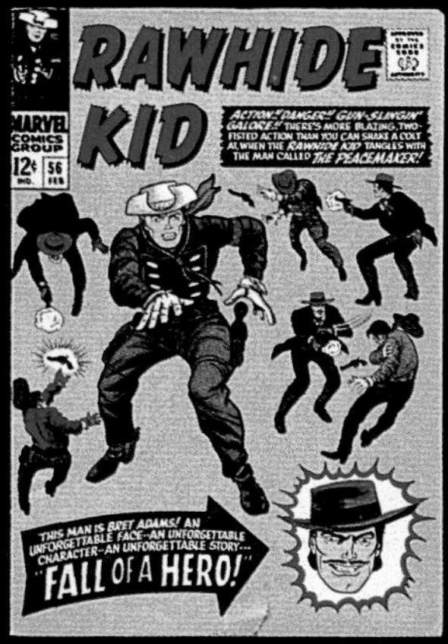
RAWHIDE KID
56
"FALL OF A HERO!"

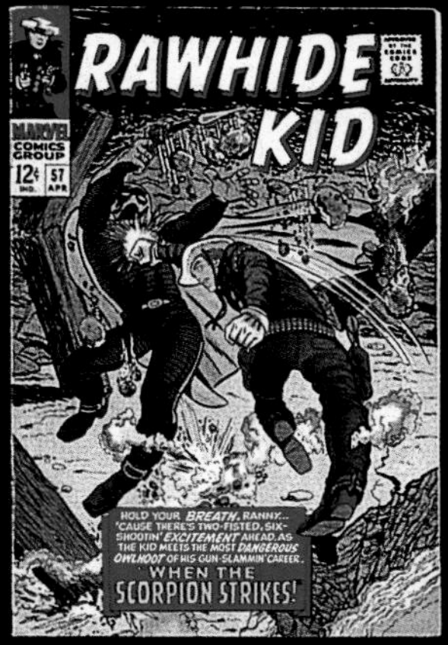
RAWHIDE KID
57
WHEN THE SCORPION STRIKES!

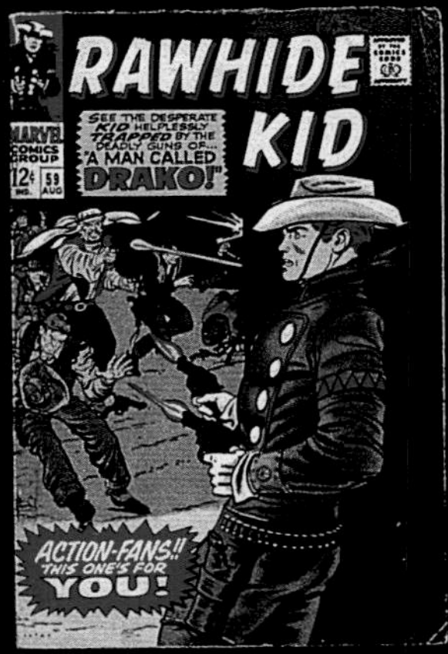
RAWHIDE KID
58
A MAN CALLED DRAKO!
ACTION-FANS!! THIS ONE'S FOR YOU!

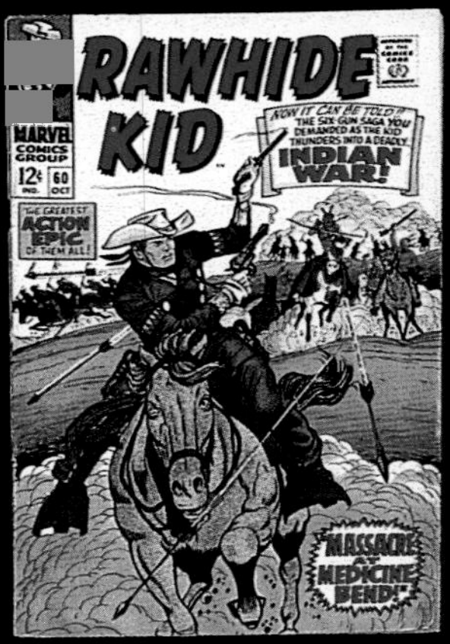
RAWHIDE KID
INDIAN WAR!
MASSACRE AT MEDICINE BEND!

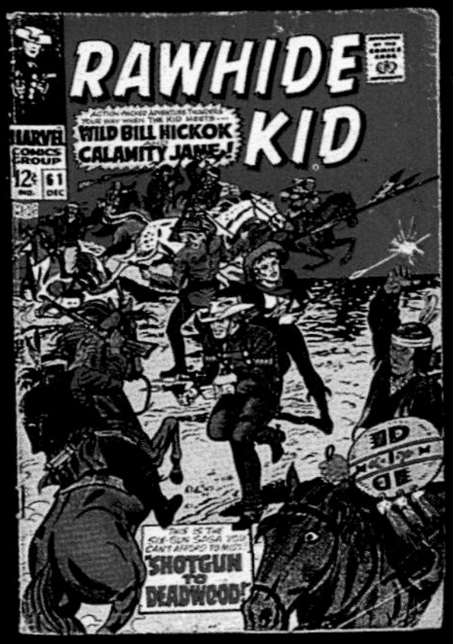
RAWHIDE KID
WILD BILL HICKOK
CALAMITY JANE!
SHOTGUN TO DEADWOOD!

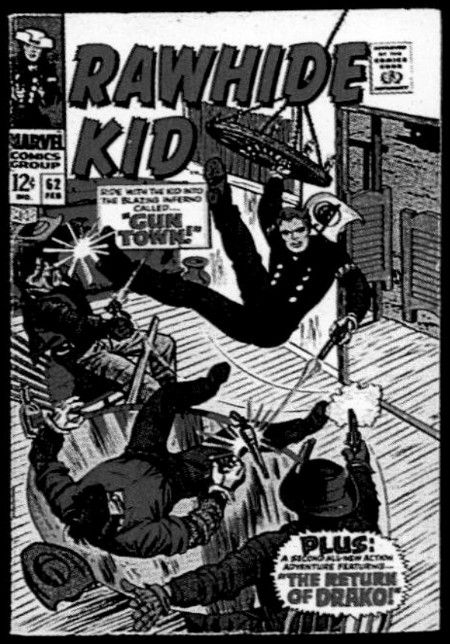
RAWHIDE KID
GUN TOWN
PLUS:
THE RETURN OF DRAKO!

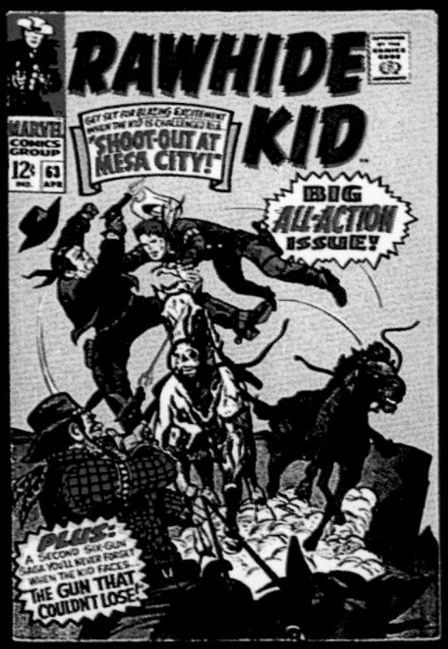
RAWHIDE KID
SHOOT-OUT AT MESA CITY!
BIG ALL-ACTION ISSUE!
THE GUN THAT COULDN'T LOSE!

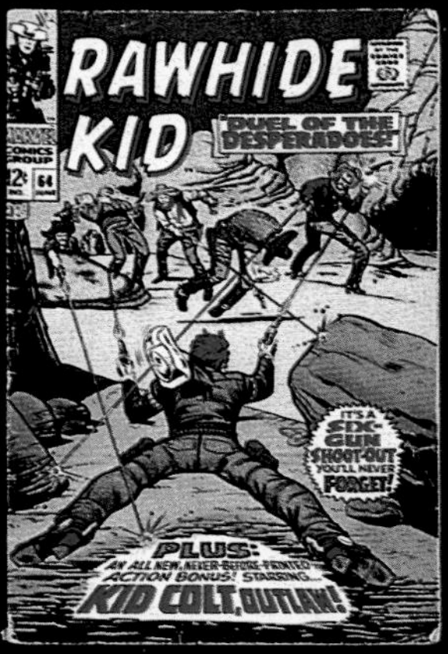
RAWHIDE KID
DUEL OF THE DESPERADOES!
PLUS:
KID COLT, OUTLAW!

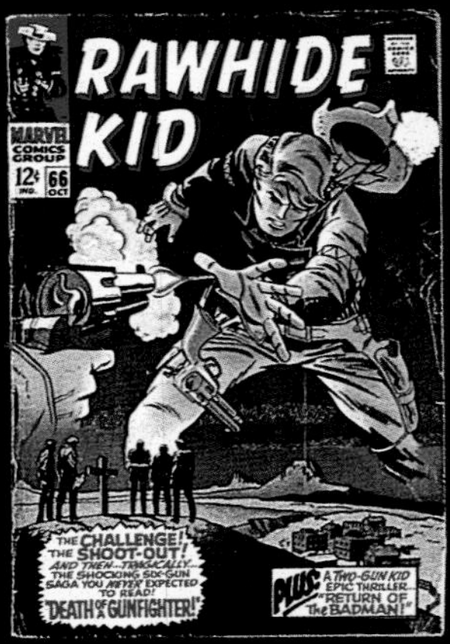
RAWHIDE KID
THE CHALLENGE! THE SHOOT-OUT!
DEATH OF A GUNFIGHTER!
RETURN OF THE BADMAN!

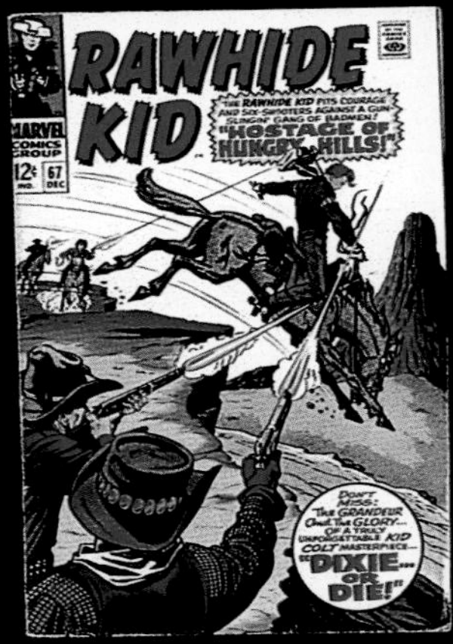
RAWHIDE KID
HOSTAGE OF HUNGRY HILLS!
DUEL OR DIE!

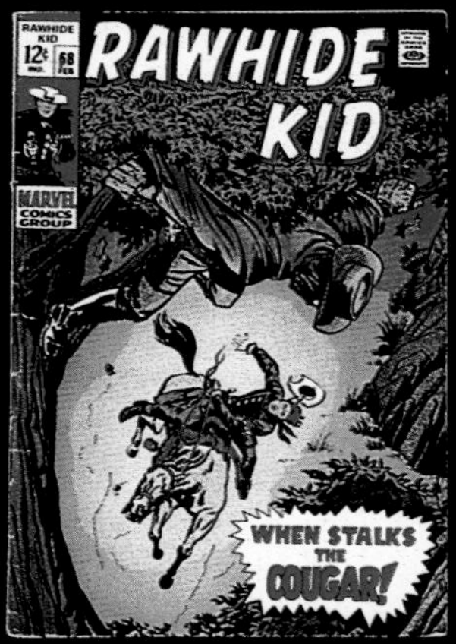
RAWHIDE KID
WHEN STALKS THE COUGAR!

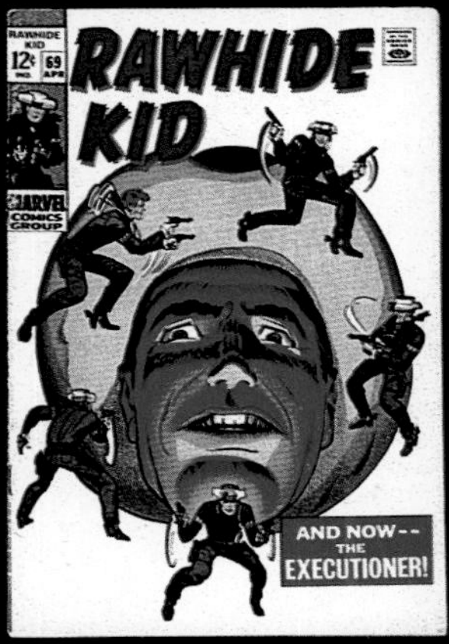
RAWHIDE KID
AND NOW-- THE EXECUTIONER!

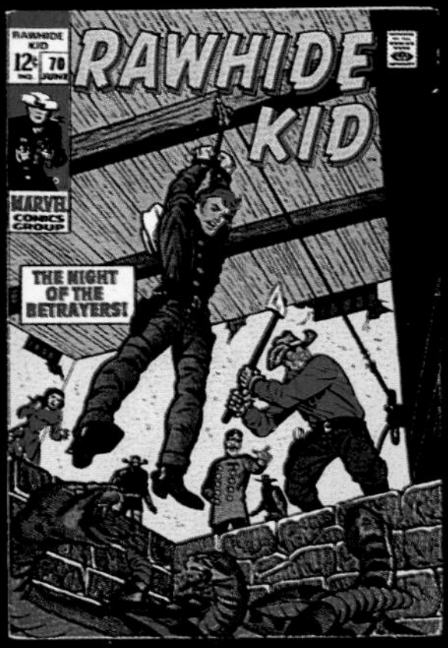
RAWHIDE KID
THE NIGHT OF THE BETRAYERS!

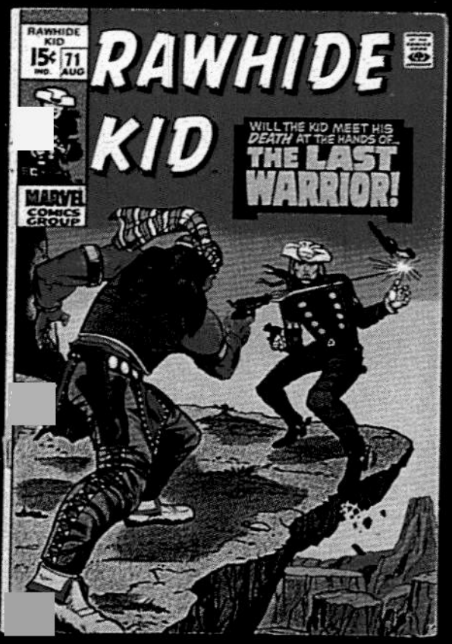
RAWHIDE KID
THE LAST WARRIOR!

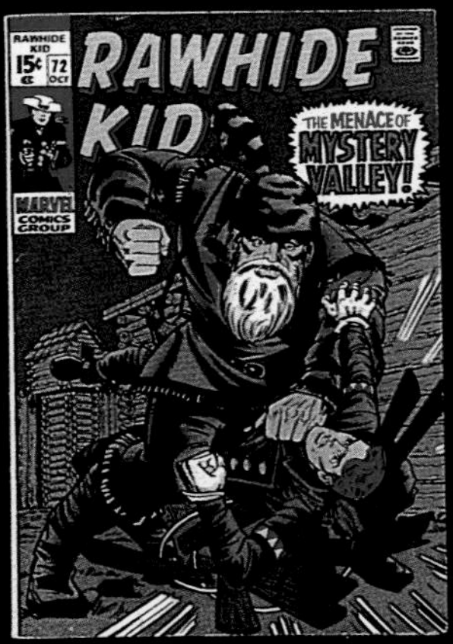
RAWHIDE KID
THE MENACE OF MYSTERY VALLEY!

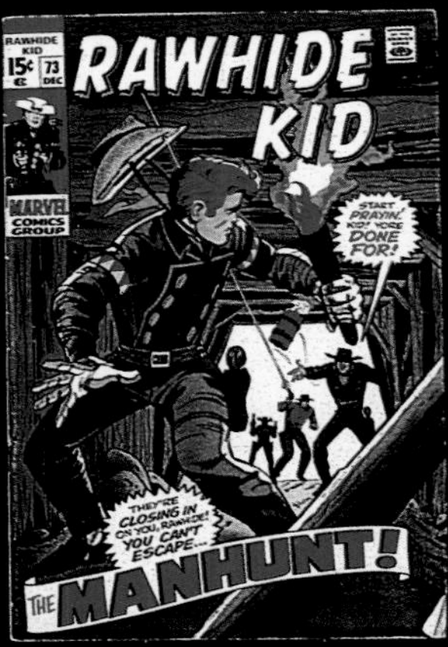
RAWHIDE KID
THE MANHUNT!

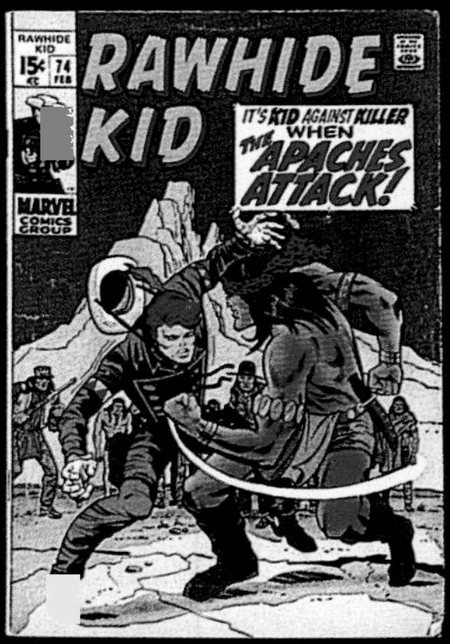
RAWHIDE KID
IT'S KID AGAINST KILLER WHEN THE APACHES ATTACK!

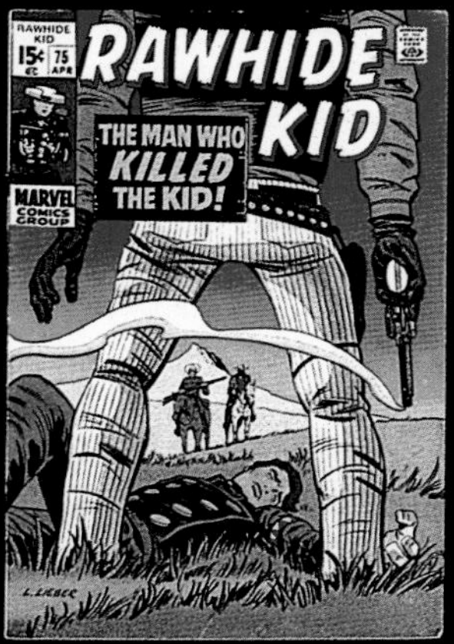
RAWHIDE KID
THE MAN WHO KILLED THE KID!

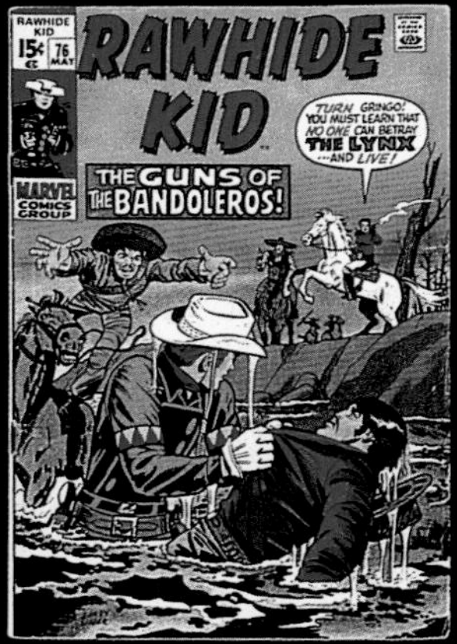
RAWHIDE KID
THE GUNS OF THE BANDOLEROS!

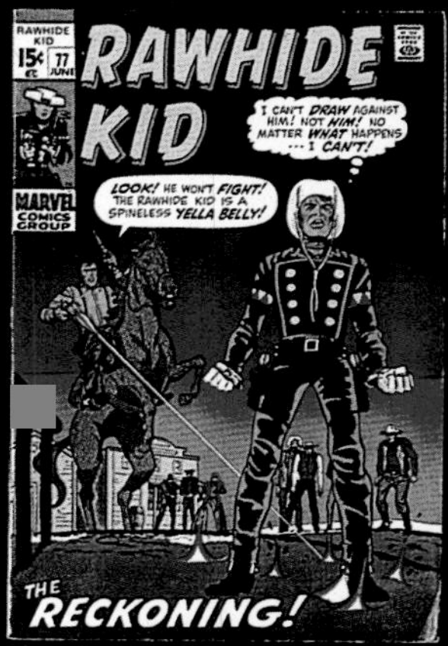
RAWHIDE KID
THE RECKONING!

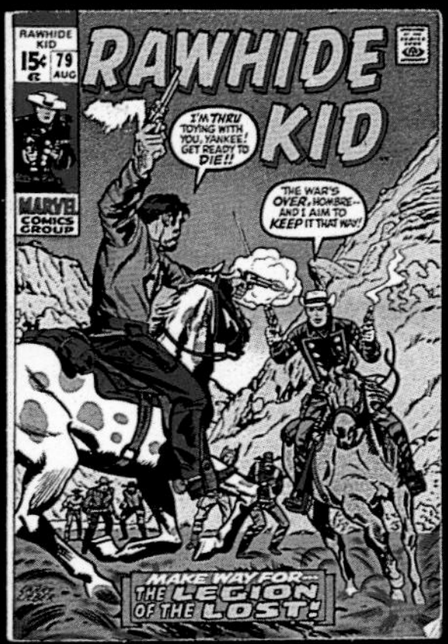
RAWHIDE KID
MAKE WAY FOR-- THE LEGION OF THE LOST!

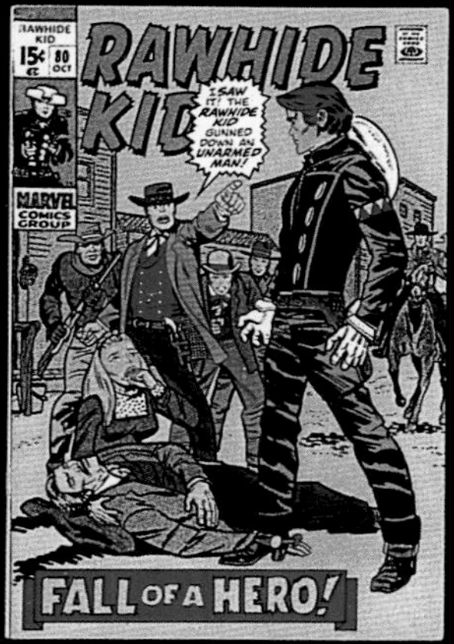
RAWHIDE KID
FALL OF A HERO!

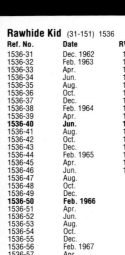

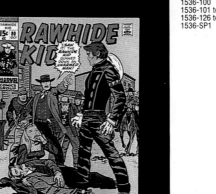

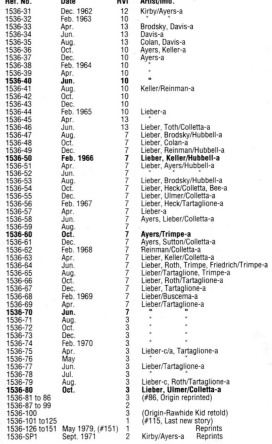

Rawhide Kid (31-151) 1536

Ref. No.	Date	RVI	Artist/Info.
1536-31	Dec. 1962	12	Kirby/Ayers-a
1536-32	Feb. 1963	10	" "
1536-33	Apr.	13	Brodsky, Davis-a
1536-34	Jun.	13	Davis-a
1536-35	Aug.	13	Colan, Davis-a
1536-36	Oct.	10	Ayers, Keller-a
1536-37	Dec.	10	Ayers-a
1536-38	Feb. 1964	10	"
1536-39	Apr.	10	"
1536-40	**Jun.**	**10**	**"**
1536-41	Aug.	10	Keller/Reinman-a
1536-42	Oct.	10	
1536-43	Dec.	10	
1536-44	Feb. 1965	10	Lieber-a
1536-45	Apr.	13	"
1536-46	Jun.	13	Lieber, Toth/Colletta-a
1536-47	Aug.	7	Lieber, Brodsky/Hubbell-a
1536-48	Oct.	7	Lieber, Colan-a
1536-49	Dec.	7	Lieber, Reinman/Hubbell-a
1536-50	**Feb. 1966**	**7**	**Lieber, Keller/Hubbell-a**
1536-51	Apr.	7	Lieber, Ayers/Hubbell-a
1536-52	Jun.	7	" " "
1536-53	Aug.	7	Lieber, Brodsky/Hubbell-a
1536-54	Oct.	7	Lieber, Heck/Colletta, Bee-a
1536-55	Dec.	7	Lieber, Ulmer/Colletta-a
1536-56	Feb. 1967	7	Lieber, Heck/Tartaglione-a
1536-57	Apr.	7	Lieber-a
1536-58	Jun.	7	Ayers, Lieber/Colletta-a
1536-59	Aug.	7	
1536-60	**Oct.**	**7**	**Ayers/Trimpe-a**
1536-61	Dec.	7	Ayers, Sutton/Colletta-a
1536-62	Feb. 1968	7	Reinman/Colletta-a
1536-63	Apr.	7	Lieber, Keller/Colletta-a
1536-64	Jun.	7	Lieber, Roth, Trimpe, Friedrich/Trimpe-a
1536-65	Aug.	7	Lieber/Tartaglione, Trimpe-a
1536-66	Oct.	7	Lieber, Roth/Tartaglione-a
1536-67	Dec.	7	Lieber, Tartaglione-a
1536-68	Feb. 1969	7	Lieber/Buscema-a
1536-69	Apr.	7	Lieber/Tartaglione-a
1536-70	**Jun.**	**7**	**" "**
1536-71	Aug.	3	" "
1536-72	Oct.	3	" "
1536-73	Dec.	3	" "
1536-74	Feb. 1970	3	" "
1536-75	Apr.	3	Lieber-c/a, Tartaglione-a
1536-76	May	3	" "
1536-77	Jun.	3	Lieber/Tartaglione-a
1536-78	Jul.	3	" "
1536-79	Aug.	3	Lieber-c, Roth/Tartaglione-a
1536-80	**Oct.**	**3**	**Lieber, Ulmer/Colletta-a**
1536-81 to 86		3	(#86, Origin reprinted)
1536-87 to 99		2	
1536-100		3	(Origin-Rawhide Kid retold)
1536-101 to125		1	(#115, Last new story)
1536-126 to151	May 1979, (#151)	1	Reprints
1536-SP1	Sept. 1971	2	Kirby/Ayers-a Reprints

1559.3 Red Sonja (1-15)

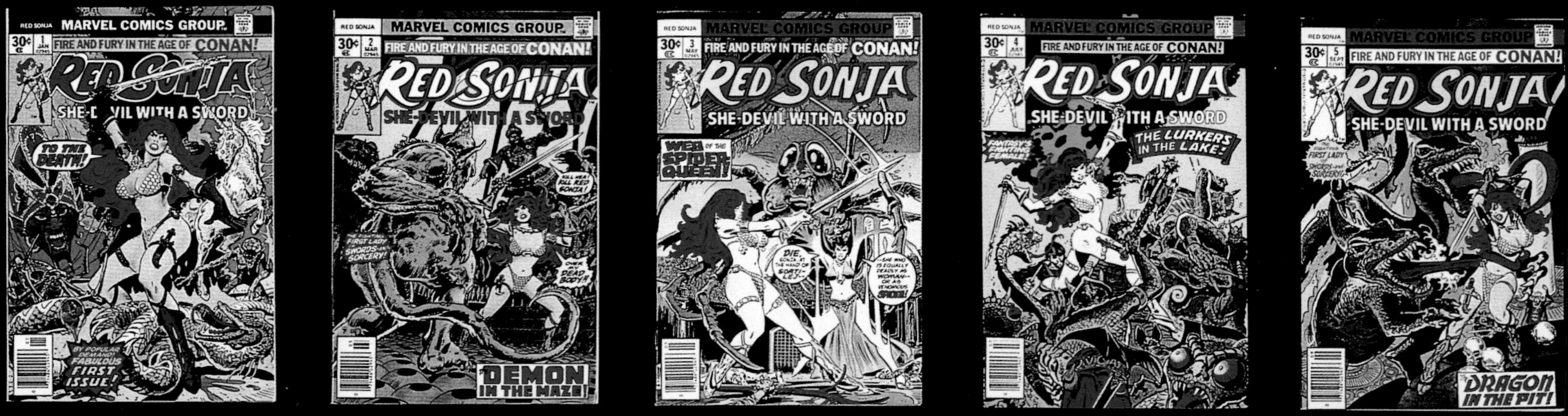
MARVEL COMICS GROUP
FIRE AND FURY IN THE AGE OF CONAN!
RED SONJA
SHE-DEVIL WITH A SWORD
TO THE DEATH!
DEMON IN THE MAZE!
WEB OF THE SPIDER QUEEN!
THE LURKERS IN THE LAKE!
DRAGON IN THE PIT!

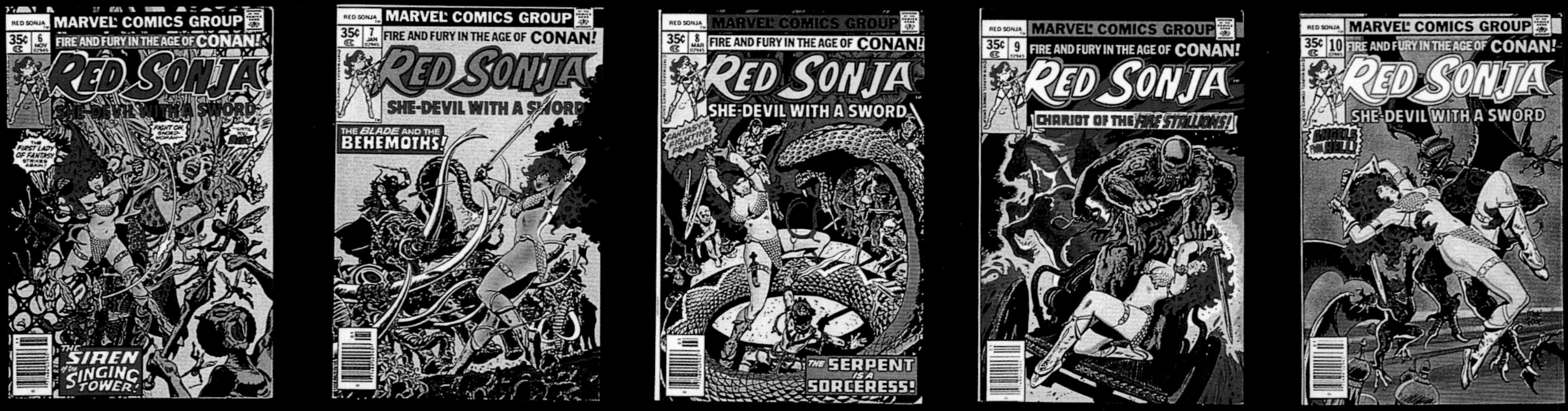
MARVEL COMICS GROUP
FIRE AND FURY IN THE AGE OF CONAN!
RED SONJA
SHE-DEVIL WITH A SWORD
THE SIREN OF THE SINGING TOWER!
THE BLADE AND THE BEHEMOTHS!
THE SERPENT IS A SORCERESS!
CHARIOT OF THE FIRE STALLIONS!

1559.3 Red Sonja

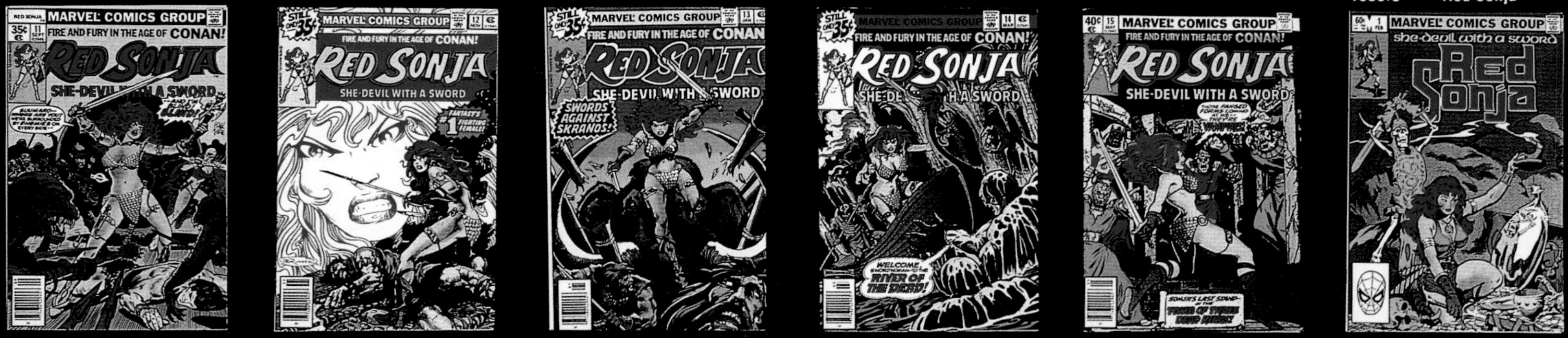
MARVEL COMICS GROUP
FIRE AND FURY IN THE AGE OF CONAN!
RED SONJA
SHE-DEVIL WITH A SWORD
SWORDS AGAINST SKRANOS!

1559.4 Red Sonja V.3 (1-11)

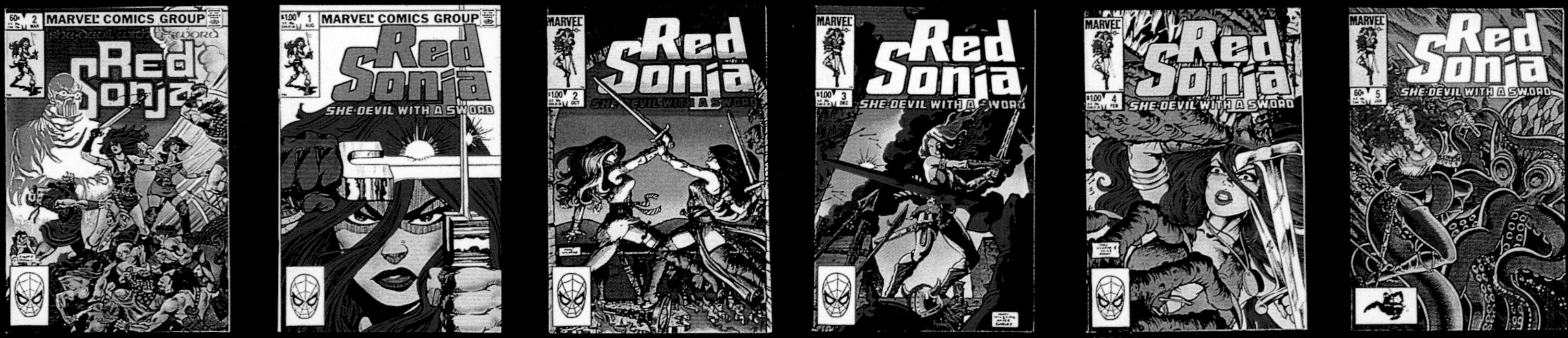
MARVEL COMICS GROUP
Red Sonja
SHE-DEVIL WITH A SWORD

1559.5 Red Sonja, The Movie (1-2)

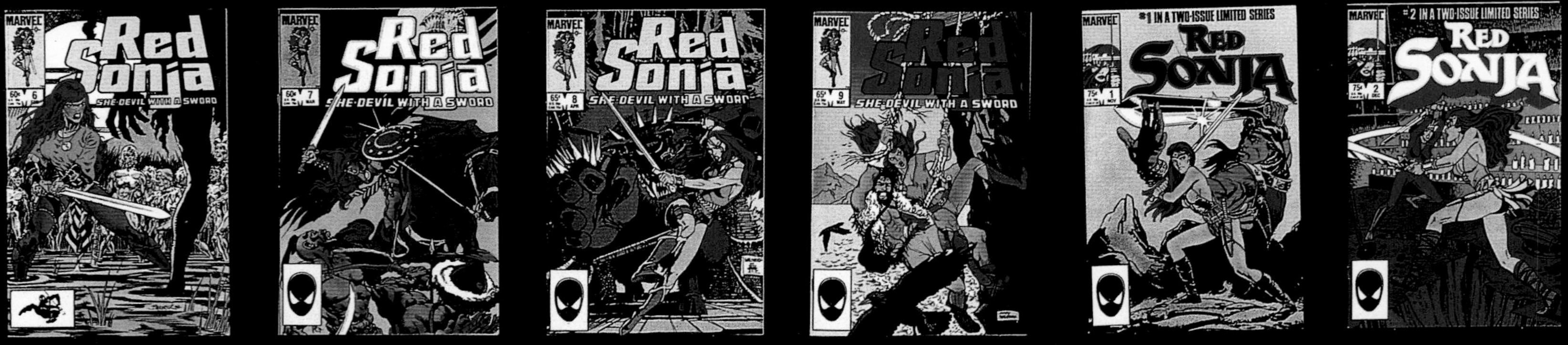
Red Sonja
SHE-DEVIL WITH A SWORD
#1 IN A TWO-ISSUE LIMITED SERIES
#2 IN A TWO-ISSUE LIMITED SERIES
RED SONJA

Red Sonja (1-15) 1559.3

Ref. No.	Date	RVI	Artist/Info.
1559.3-1	Jan. 1977	2	Thorne-a
1559.3-2	Mar.	1	Thorne-c/a
1559.3-3	May	1	"
1559.3-4	Jul.	1	"
1559.3-5	Sept.	1	"
1559.3-6	Nov.	1	"
1559.3-7	Jan. 1978	1	"
1559.3-8	Mar.	1	"
1559.3-9	May	1	"
1559.3-10	**Jul.**	**1**	**"**
1559.3-11	Sept.	1	
1559.3-12	Nov.	1	Brunner-c
1559.3-13	Jan. 1979	1	"
1559.3-14	Mar.	1	"
1559.3-15	May	1	

Red Sonja V.2 (1-2) 1559.3

1559.3-1	Feb. 1983	1	DeZuniga, Colan, Kupperburg-a
1559.3-2	Mar. 1983	1	Simons/Mitchell-c, Colan/Kupperburg-a

Red Sonja V.3 (1-13) 1559.4

1559.4-1	Aug. 1983	1	Simons/Colletta-a
1559.4-2	Oct.	1	Wilshire-c, Redondo-a
1559.4-3	Dec.	1	Wilshire/Garvey-c/a
1559.4-4	Feb. 1984	1	
1559.4-5	Jan. 1985	1	
1559.4-6	Feb.	1	
1559.4-7	Mar.	1	
1559.4-8	Apr.	1	
1559.4-9	May	1	
1559.4-10	**Jun.**	**1**	
1559.4-11	Jul.	1	
1559.4-12	Aug.	1	
1559.4-13	Sept.	1	

Red Sonja: the Movie (1-2) 1559.5

1559.5-1	Nov. 1985	1	Wilshire/Colletta-a
1559.5-2	Dec. 1985	1	" "

1560.1 Red Wolf (1-9)

1580.7 Ringo the Kid (1-19)

RED WOLF
MASKED AVENGER OF THE WESTERN PLAINS!
RED WOLF AND LOBO FIGHT ALONE AGAINST THE GUNS OF FORT RANGO!
DAY OF THE DYNAMITE DOOM!
WAR OF THE WOLF BROTHERS!
INDIAN AVENGER OF THE WESTERN PLAINS!
THE WRATH OF...MAN-BEAR!
'CAUSE I'M THE MAN WHO GUNNED DOWN RED WOLF!
RIDE, DEVIL, RIDE!
NOW! SET IN THE HOLOCAUST OF TODAY!
ECHOES FROM A GOLDEN GRAVE!
HELL ON WHEELS!
TO DIE AGAIN?
EXCITING WESTERN ACTION!
THE RINGO KID
RINGO! THE FASTEST GUN ALIVE!
RINGO! HIS NAME MAKES BADMEN TREMBLE!
RINGO CRASHES INTO A MAN TRAP!
IS THIS THE END OF THE TRAIL!
BAD DAY AT BLACK CREEK!
BULLET FOR A BANDIT!
A BADGE TO DIE FOR!
HOSTAGE AT FORT CHEYENNE!
SHOWDOWN AT THE SILVER CARTWHEEL!
FANG, CLAW AND SIX-GUN!
BATTLE OF CATTLEMAN'S BANK!
GUNDOWN AT THE HACIENDA!

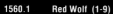

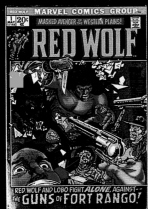

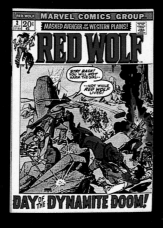

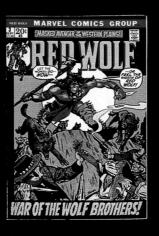

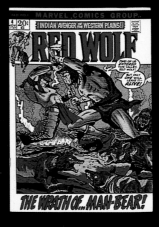

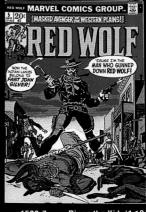

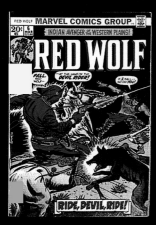

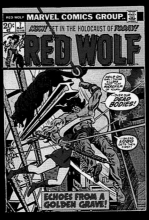

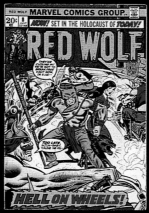

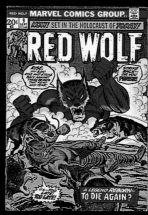

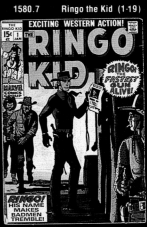

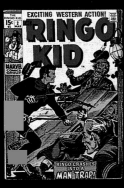

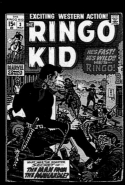

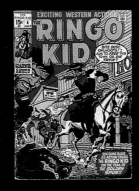

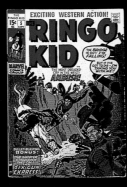

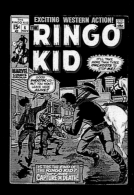

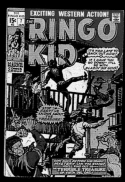

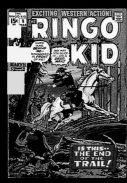

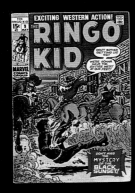

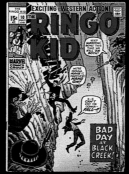

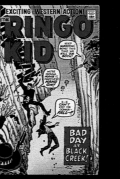

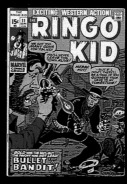

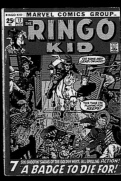

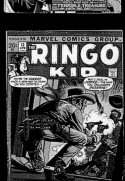

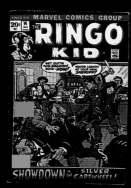

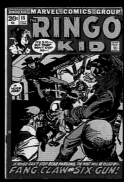

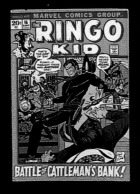

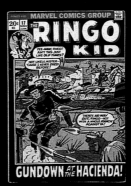

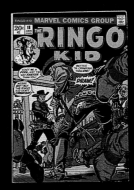

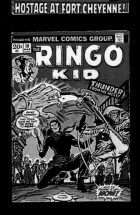

Red Wolf (1-9) 1560.1

Ref. No.	Date	RVI	Artist/Info.
1560.1-1	May 1972	1	Kane/Severin-c, Shores-a
1560.1-2	Jul.	1	Kane-c, Shores-a
1560.1-3	Sept.	1	Shores-c/a, Colletta-a
1560.1-4	Nov.	1	" "
1560.1-5	Jan. 1973	1	Kane-c, Shores/Stone-a
1560.1-6	Mar.	1	Shores-c/a, Abel-a
1560.1-7	May	1	Shores/Abel-a
1560.1-8	Jul.	1	Shores/Stone-a
1560.1-9	Sept. 1973	1	Ayers/Colletta-a (Origin-Lobo)

The Ringo Kid (1-30) 1580.7 (Reprints)

1580.7-1	Jan. 1970	1	Williamson-a
1580.7-2	Mar.	1	Severin-a
1580.7-3	May	1	Romita-a
1580.7-4	Jul.	1	Trimpe-c
1580.7-5	Sept.	1	Maneely-a
1580.7-6	Nov.	1	
1580.7-7	Jan. 1971	1	Trimpe-c, Severin, Forgione/Abel-a
1580.7-8	Mar.	1	
1580.7-9	May	1	Severin, Carrabetta-a
1580.7-10	Jul.	1	
1580.7-11	Sept.	1	
1580.7-12	Nov.	1	Maneely, Kubert/Moskowitz-a
1580.7-13	Apr. 1972	1	Wildey, Maneely-a
1580.7-14	May	1	Maneely, Forgione/Abel-a
1580.7-15	Jul.	1	Colan-a
1580.7-16	Sept.	1	Ayers/Colletta-c, Maneely-a
1580.7-17	Nov.	1	Maneely-a
1580.7-18	Jan. 1973	1	"
1580.7-19	Mar.	1	Forgione, Maneely-a
1580.7-20		1	Williamson-a
1580.7-21 to 30	Nov. 1976, (#30)	1	

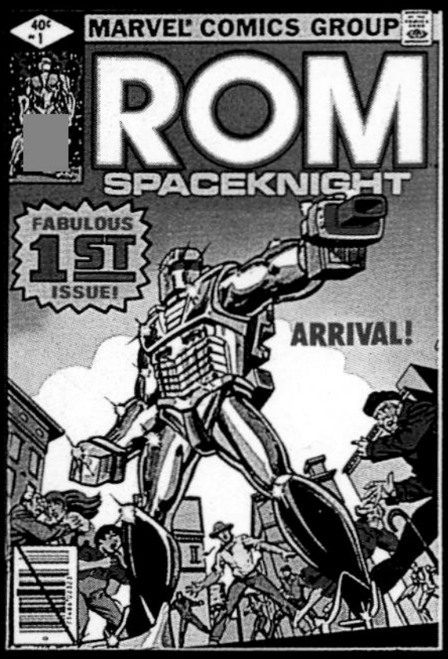
MARVEL COMICS GROUP
ROM
SPACEKNIGHT
FABULOUS 1ST ISSUE!
ARRIVAL!
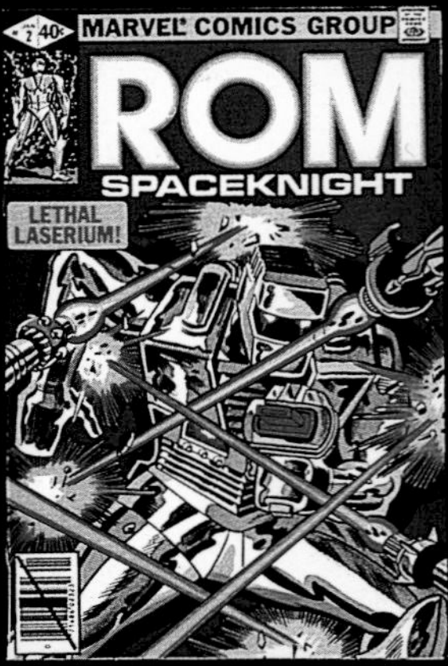
MARVEL COMICS GROUP
ROM
SPACEKNIGHT
LETHAL LASERIUM!
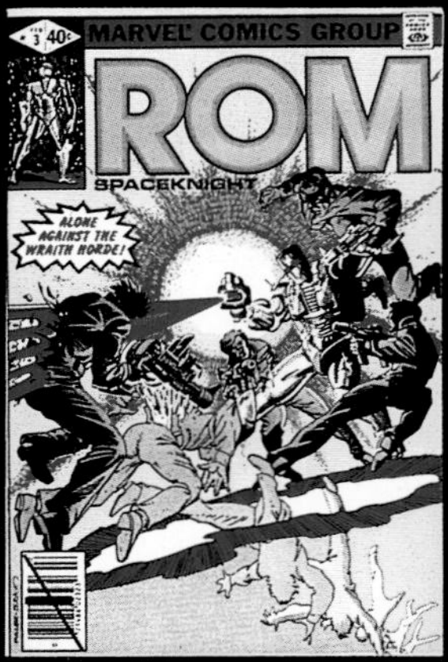
MARVEL COMICS GROUP
ROM
SPACEKNIGHT
ALONE AGAINST THE WRAITH HORDE!
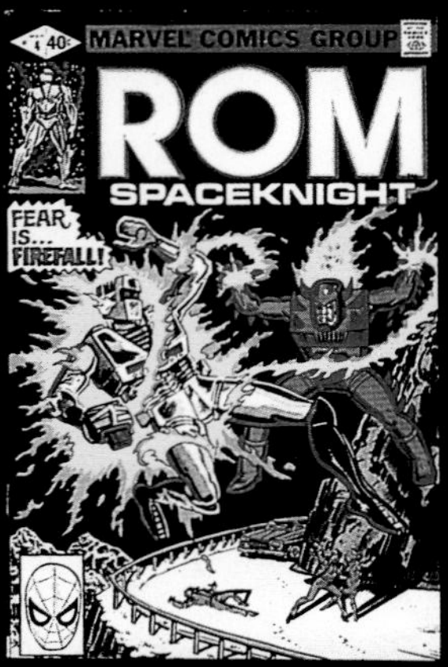
MARVEL COMICS GROUP
ROM
SPACEKNIGHT
FEAR IS... FIREFALL!
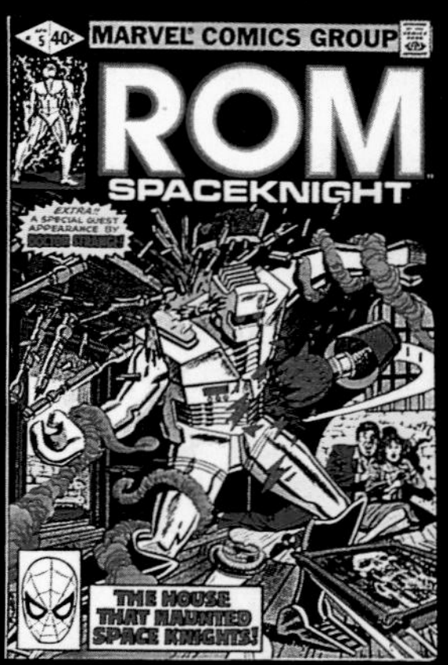
MARVEL COMICS GROUP
ROM
SPACEKNIGHT
THE HOUSE THAT HAUNTED SPACE KNIGHTS!
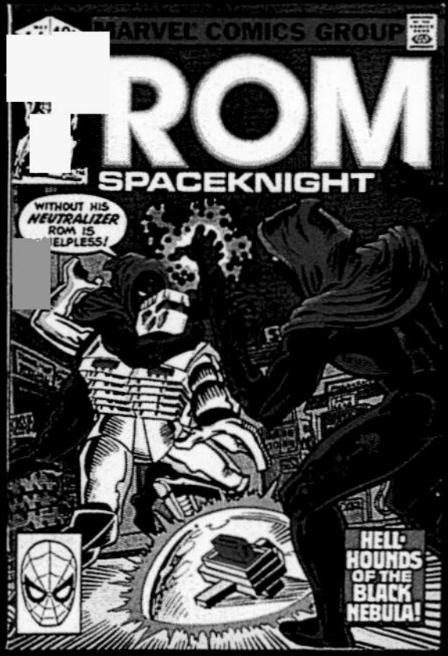
MARVEL COMICS GROUP
ROM
SPACEKNIGHT
HELL-HOUNDS OF THE BLACK NEBULA!
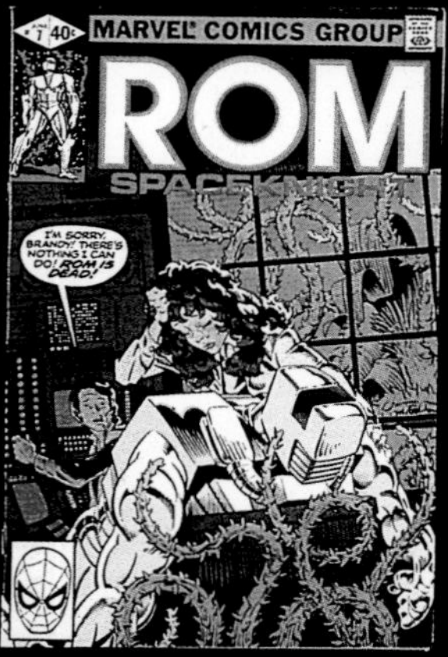
MARVEL COMICS GROUP
ROM
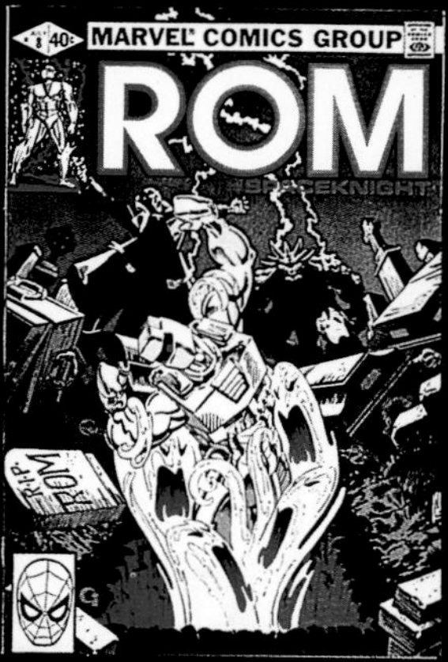
MARVEL COMICS GROUP
ROM
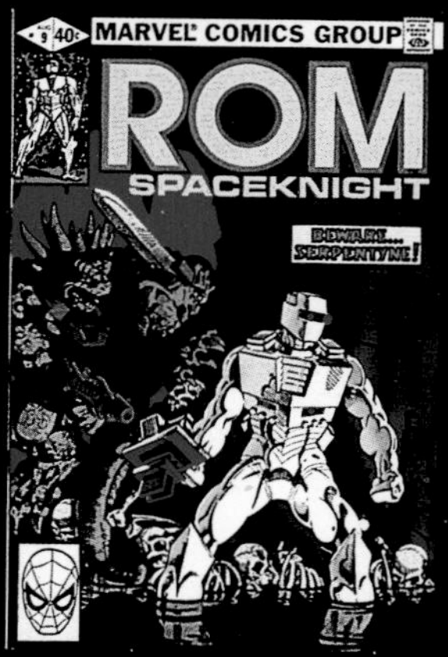
MARVEL COMICS GROUP
ROM
SPACEKNIGHT
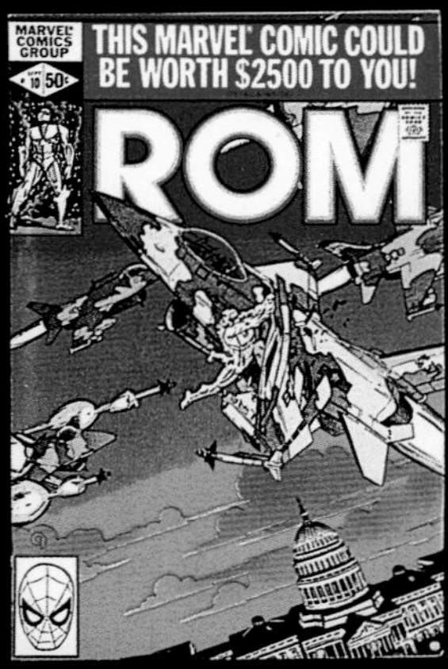
THIS MARVEL COMIC COULD BE WORTH $2500 TO YOU!
ROM
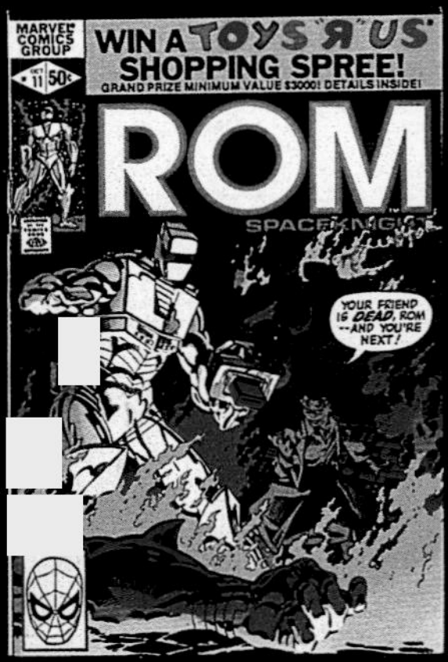
WIN A TOYS R US SHOPPING SPREE!
ROM
YOUR FRIEND IS DEAD, ROM! --AND YOU'RE NEXT!
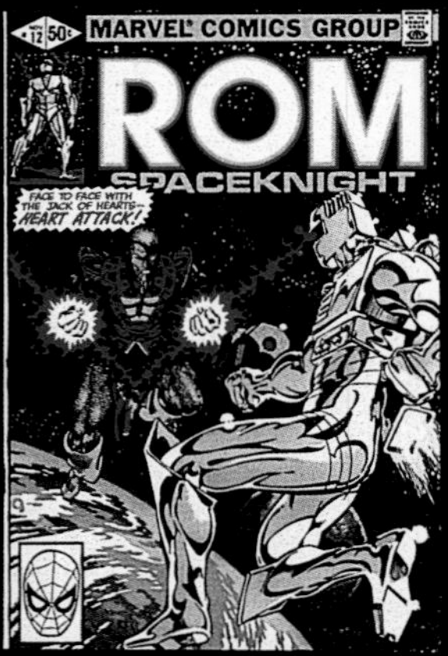
MARVEL COMICS GROUP
ROM
SPACEKNIGHT
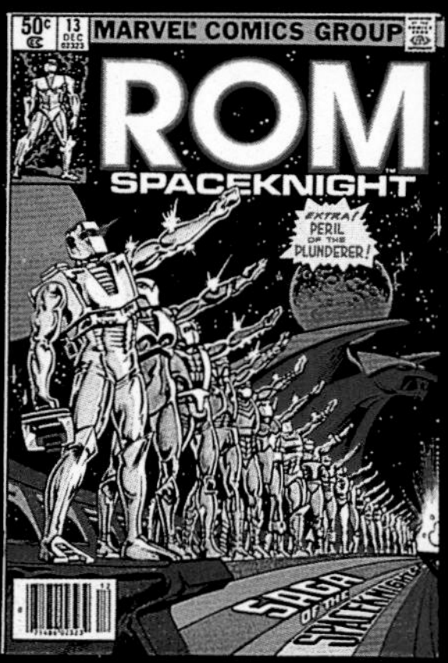
MARVEL COMICS GROUP
ROM
SPACEKNIGHT
EXTRA! PERIL OF THE PLUNDERER!
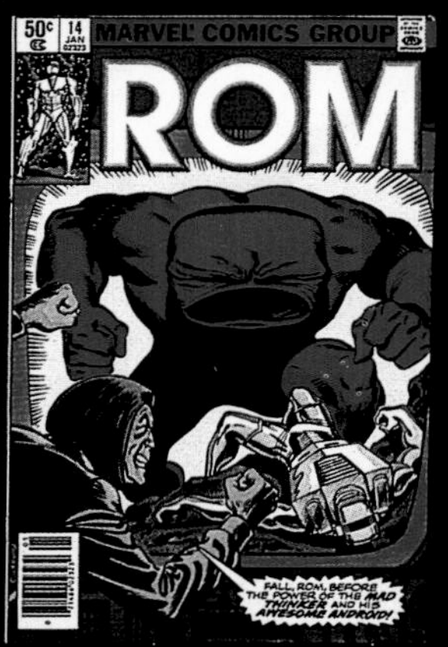
MARVEL COMICS GROUP
ROM
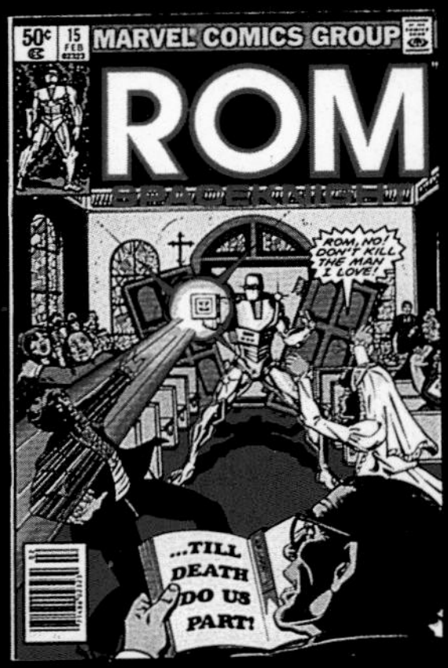
MARVEL COMICS GROUP
ROM
...TILL DEATH DO US PART!
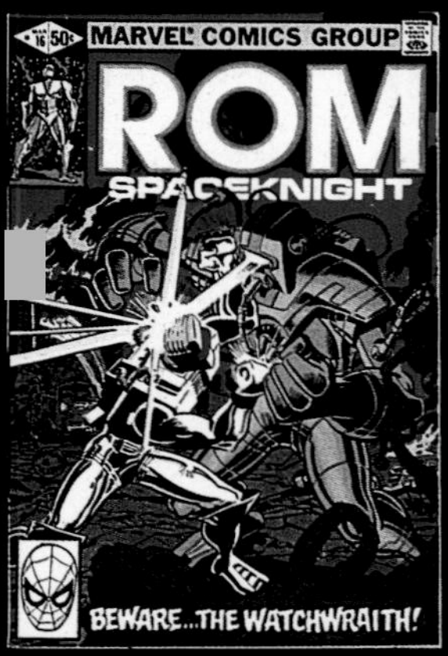
MARVEL COMICS GROUP
ROM
SPACEKNIGHT
BEWARE...THE WATCHWRAITH!
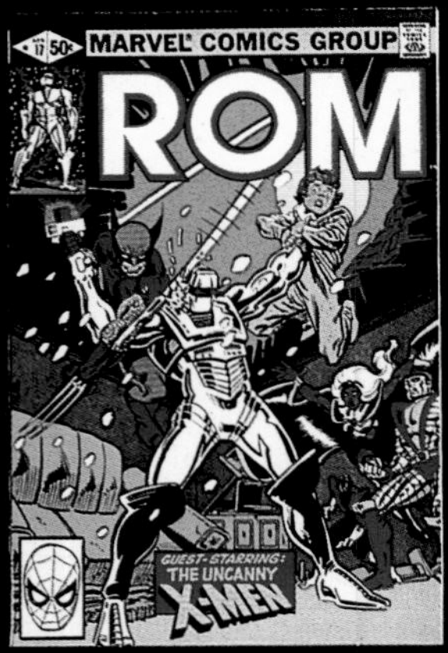
MARVEL COMICS GROUP
ROM
GUEST-STARRING: THE UNCANNY X-MEN
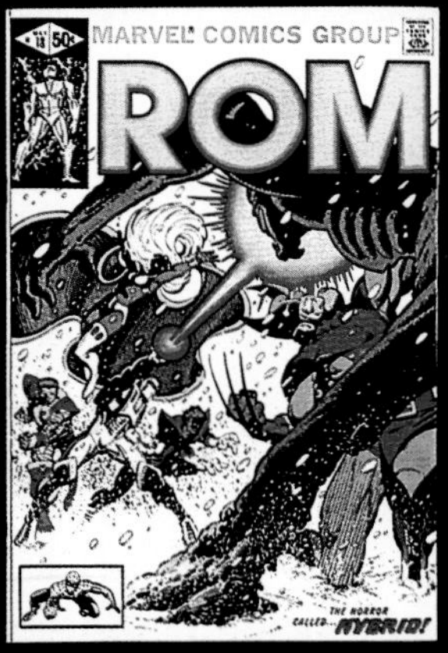
MARVEL COMICS GROUP
ROM
THE HORROR CALLED... HYBRID!
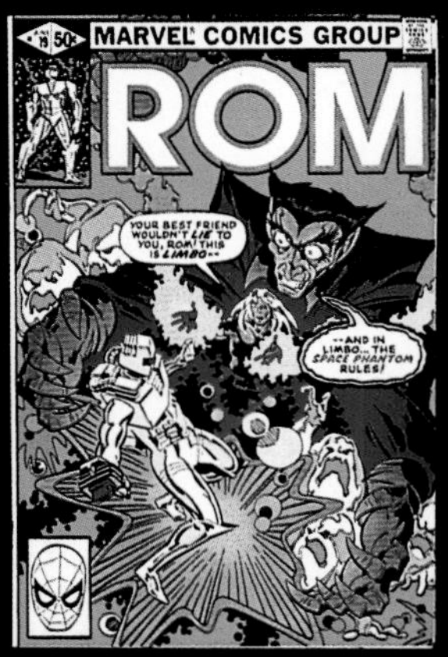
MARVEL COMICS GROUP
ROM
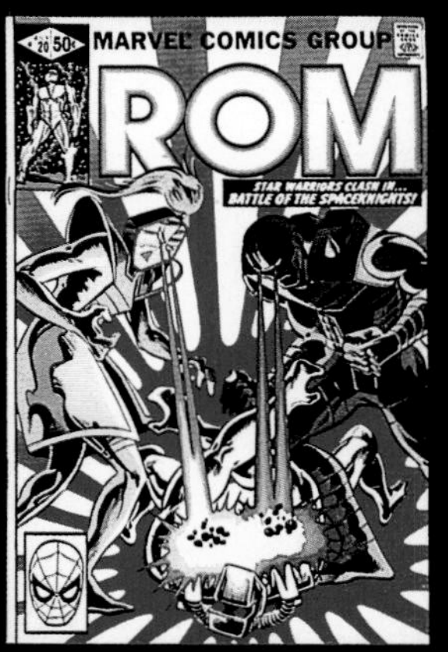
MARVEL COMICS GROUP
ROM
STAR WARRIORS CLASH IN... BATTLE OF THE SPACEKNIGHTS!
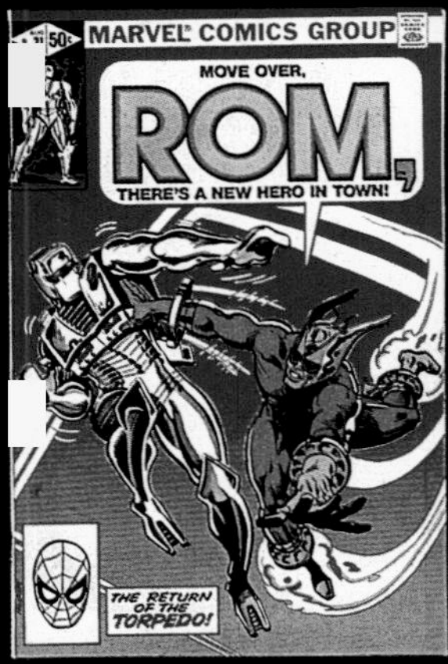
MARVEL COMICS GROUP
MOVE OVER, ROM, THERE'S A NEW HERO IN TOWN!
THE RETURN OF THE TORPEDO!
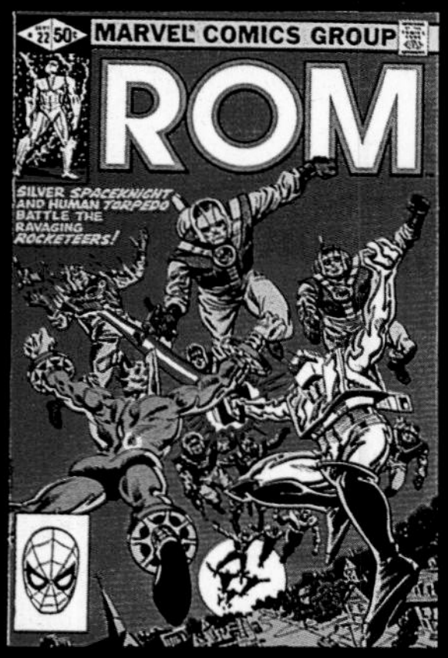
MARVEL COMICS GROUP
ROM
SILVER SPACEKNIGHT AND HUMAN TORPEDO BATTLE THE RAVAGING ROCKETEERS!
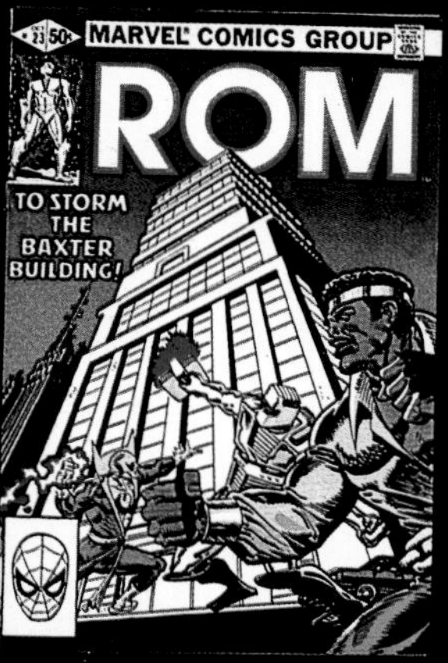
MARVEL COMICS GROUP
ROM
TO STORM THE BAXTER BUILDING!
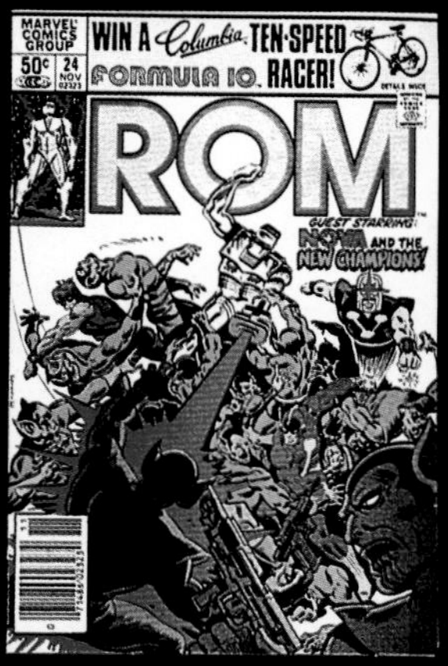
WIN A Columbia TEN-SPEED FORMULA 10 RACER!
ROM
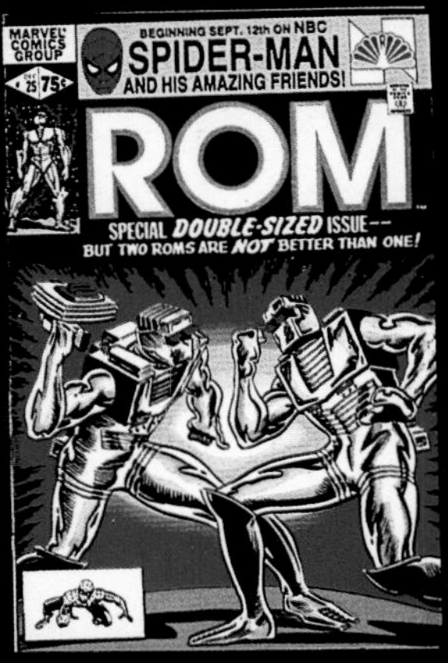
SPIDER-MAN AND HIS AMAZING FRIENDS!
ROM
SPECIAL DOUBLE-SIZED ISSUE-- BUT TWO ROMS ARE NOT BETTER THAN ONE!

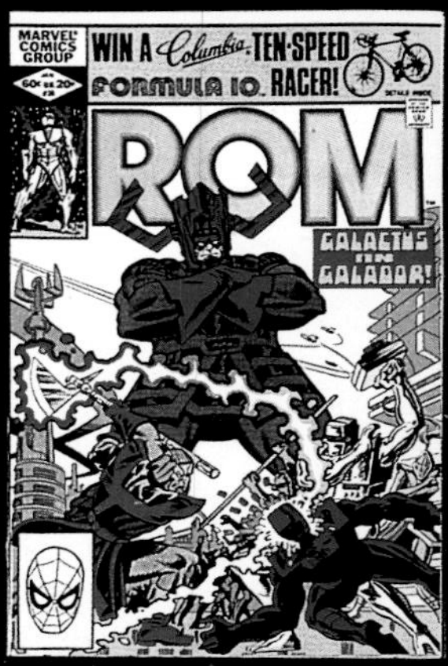
MARVEL COMICS GROUP
WIN A Columbia TEN-SPEED FORMULA 10. RACER!
ROM
GALACTUS ON GALADOR!

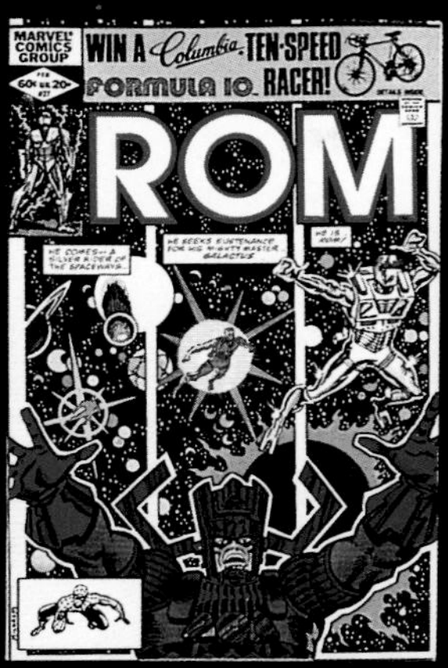
MARVEL COMICS GROUP
WIN A Columbia TEN-SPEED FORMULA 10. RACER!
ROM

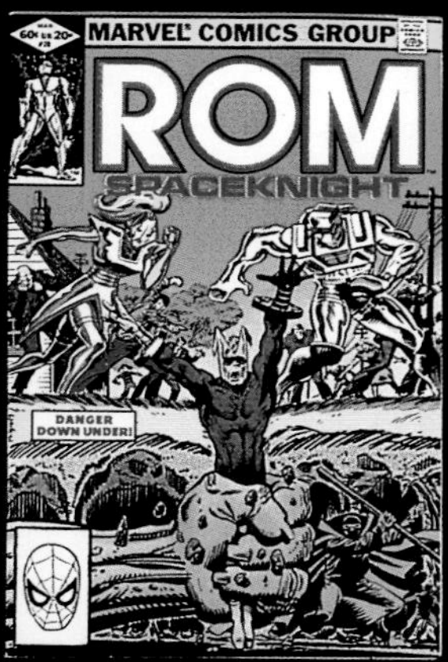
MARVEL COMICS GROUP
ROM
SPACEKNIGHT
DANGER DOWN UNDER!

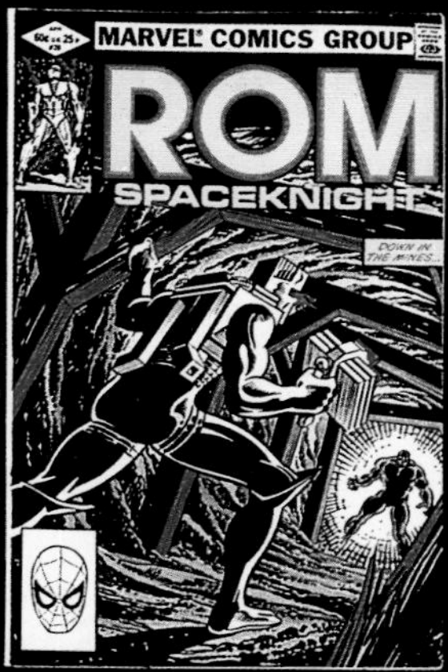
MARVEL COMICS GROUP
ROM
SPACEKNIGHT
DOWN IN THE MINES

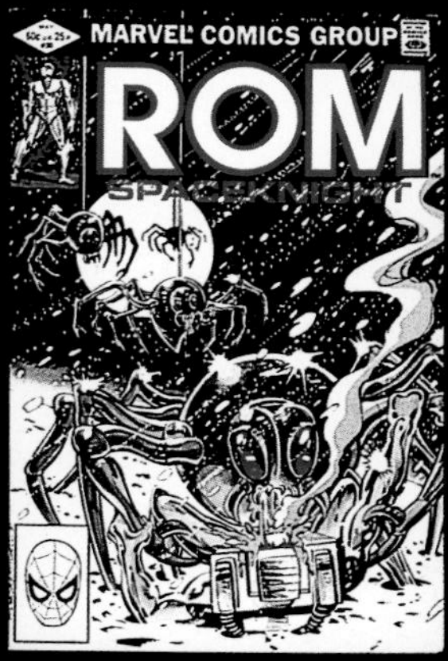
MARVEL COMICS GROUP
ROM

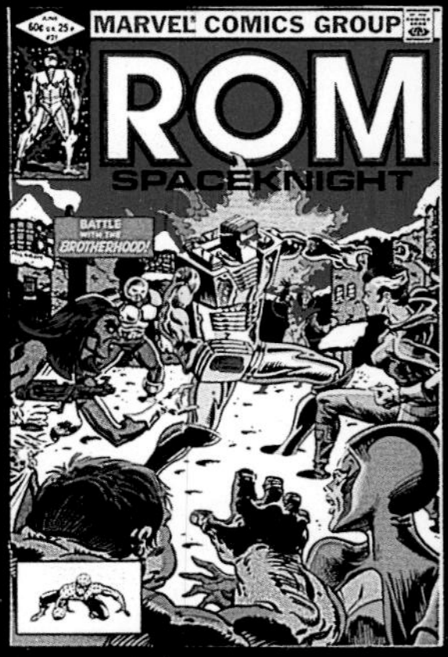
MARVEL COMICS GROUP
ROM
SPACEKNIGHT
BATTLE WITH THE BROTHERHOOD!

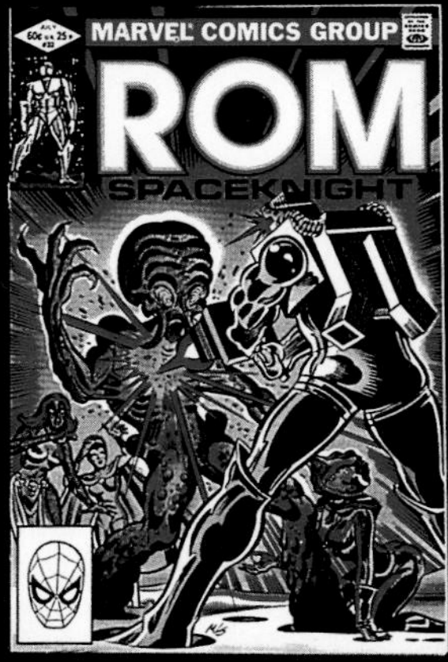
MARVEL COMICS GROUP
ROM
SPACEKNIGHT

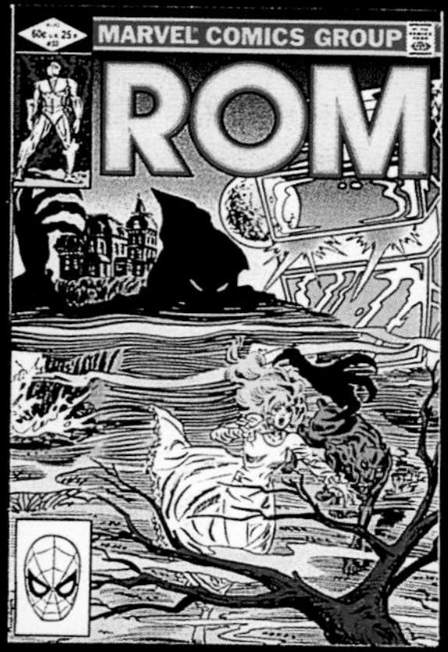
MARVEL COMICS GROUP
ROM

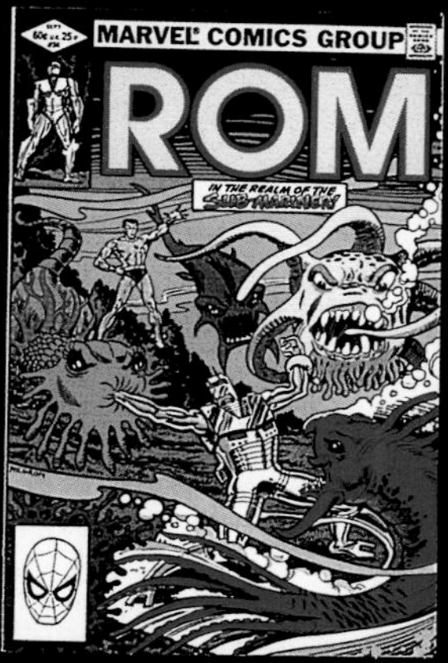
MARVEL COMICS GROUP
ROM

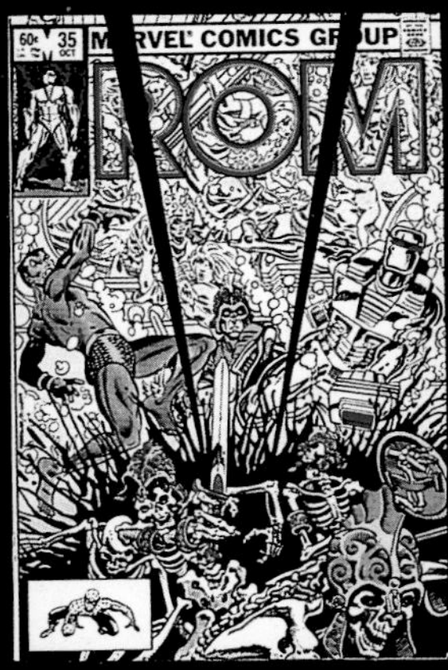
35
MARVEL COMICS GROUP
ROM

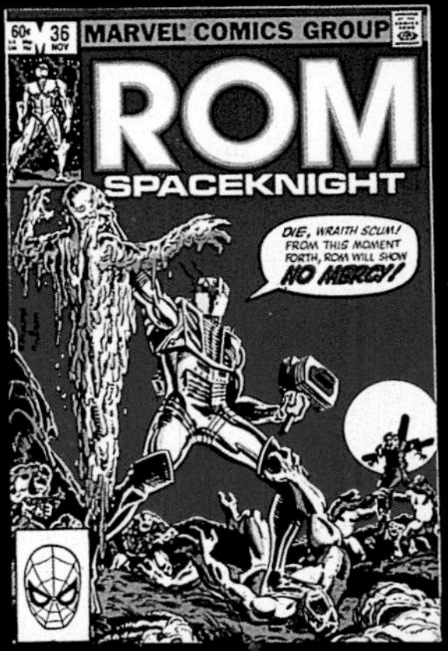
36
MARVEL COMICS GROUP
ROM
SPACEKNIGHT
DIE, WRAITH SCUM! FROM THIS MOMENT FORTH, ROM WILL SHOW NO MERCY!

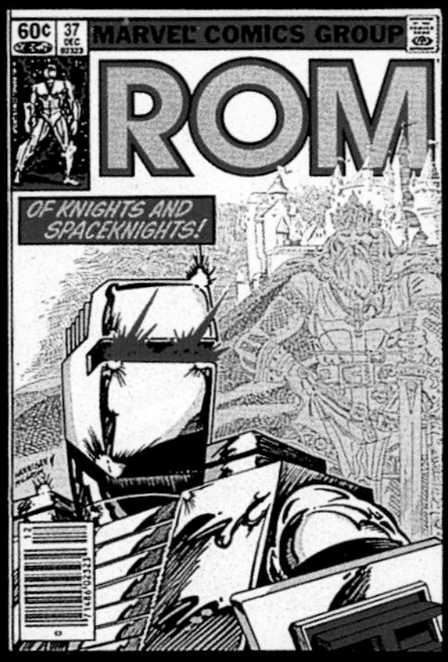
37
MARVEL COMICS GROUP
ROM
OF KNIGHTS AND SPACEKNIGHTS!

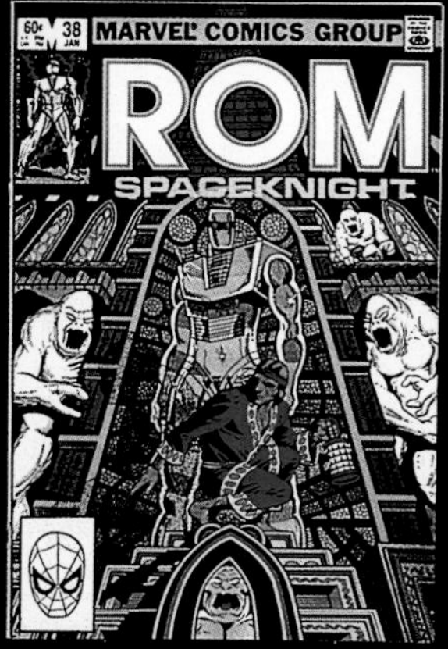
38
MARVEL COMICS GROUP
ROM
SPACEKNIGHT

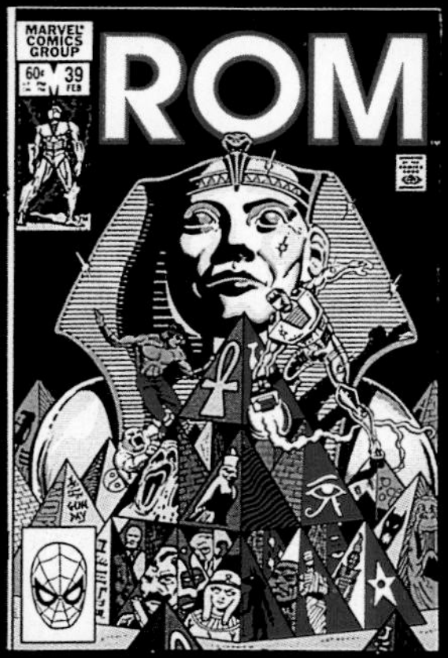
MARVEL COMICS GROUP
39
ROM

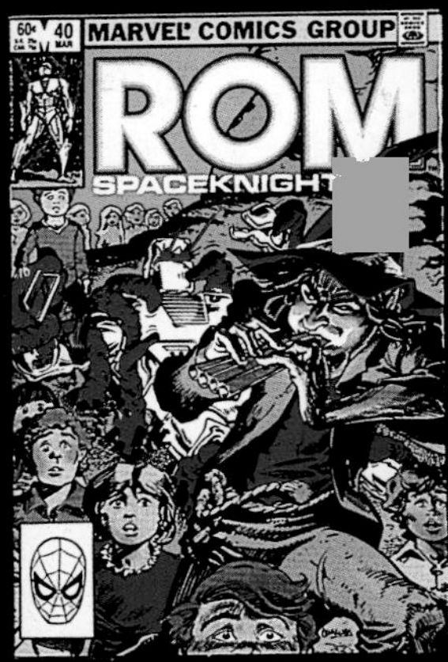
40
MARVEL COMICS GROUP
ROM
SPACEKNIGHT

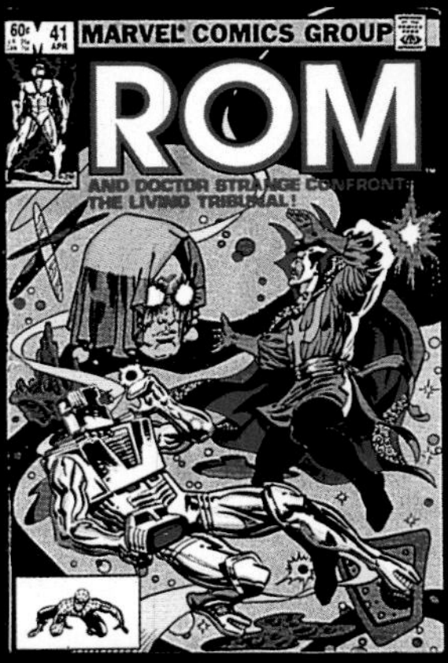
41
MARVEL COMICS GROUP
ROM
AND DOCTOR STRANGE CONFRONT THE LIVING TRIBUNAL!

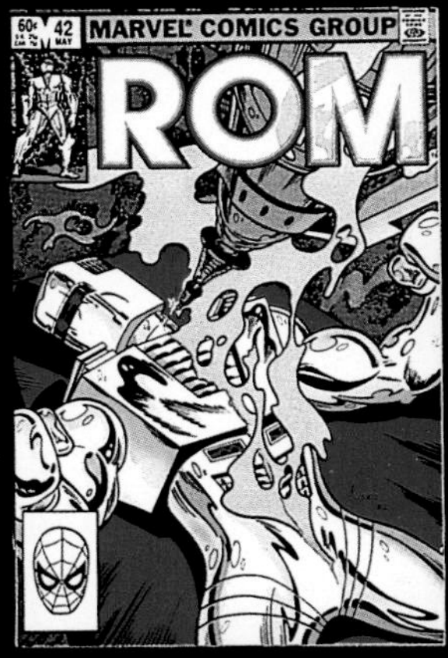
42
MARVEL COMICS GROUP
ROM

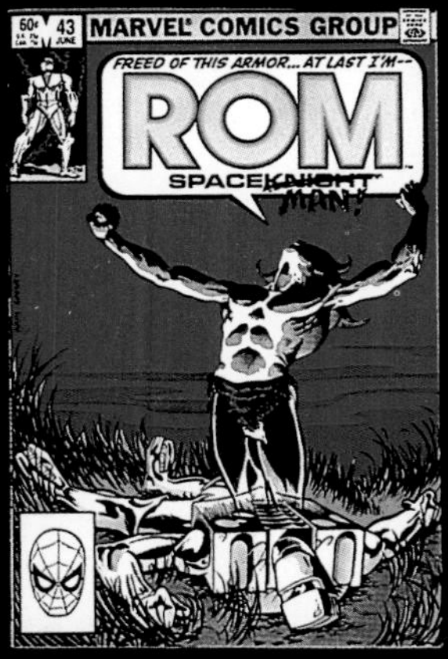
43
MARVEL COMICS GROUP
FREED OF THIS ARMOR... AT LAST I'M--
ROM
SPACEKNIGHT MAN!

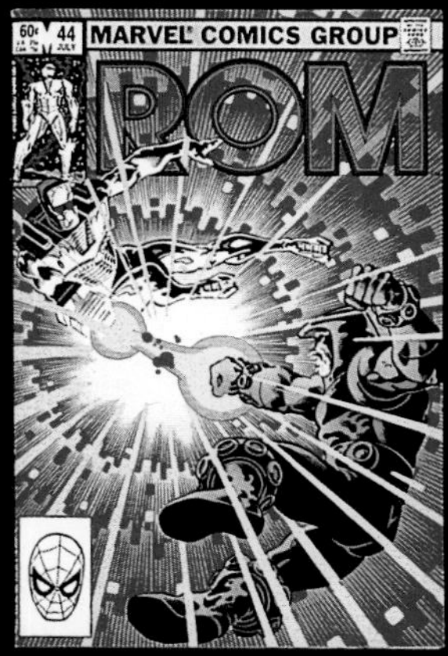
44
MARVEL COMICS GROUP
ROM

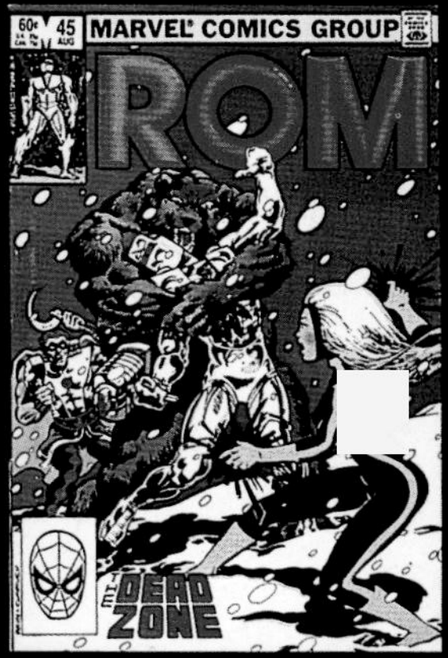
45
MARVEL COMICS GROUP
ROM
DEAD ZONE

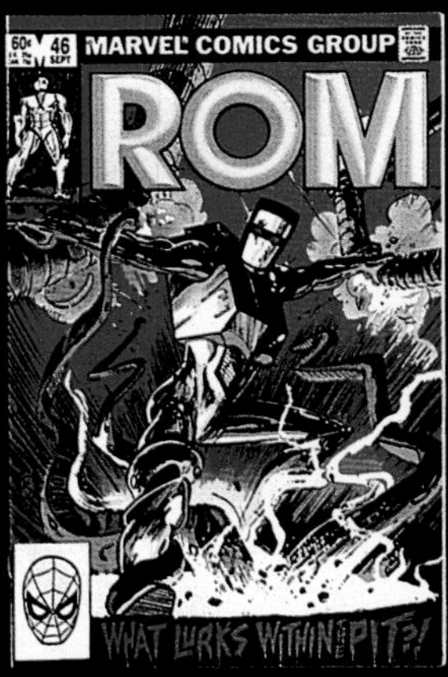
46
MARVEL COMICS GROUP
ROM
WHAT LURKS WITHIN THE PIT?!

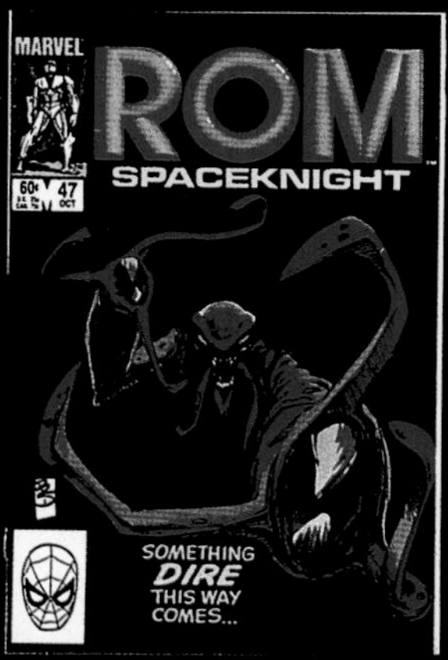
MARVEL
ROM
SPACEKNIGHT
47
SOMETHING DIRE THIS WAY COMES...

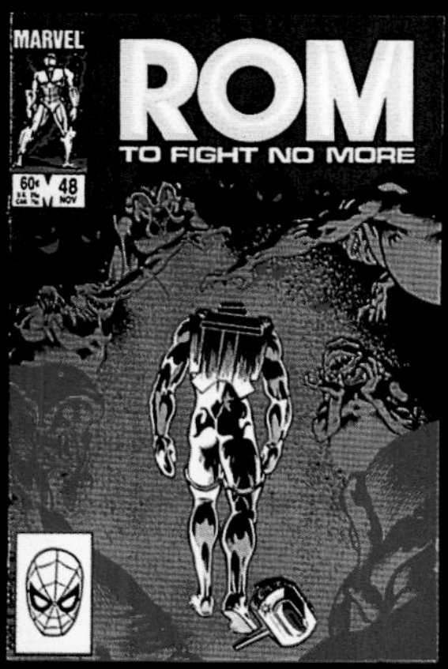
MARVEL
ROM
TO FIGHT NO MORE
48

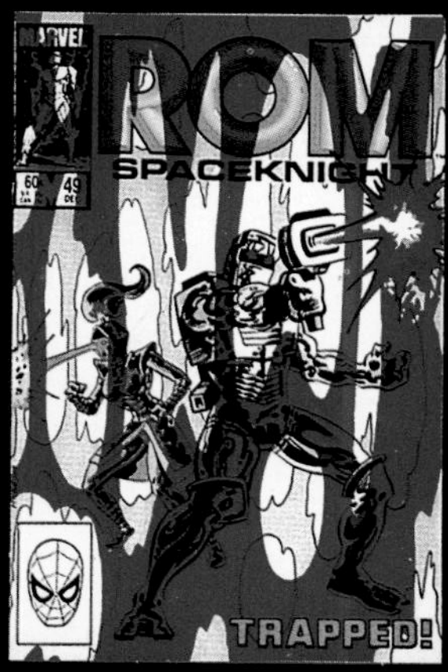
ROM
SPACEKNIGHT
TRAPPED!

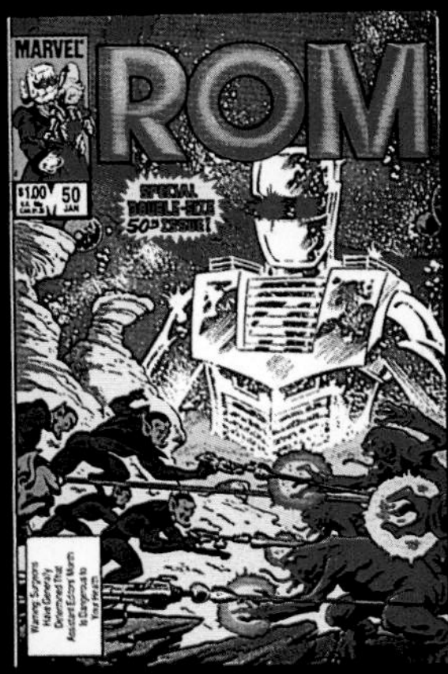
MARVEL
ROM
50

1597.5 ROM (51-75 · AN. 1-4)

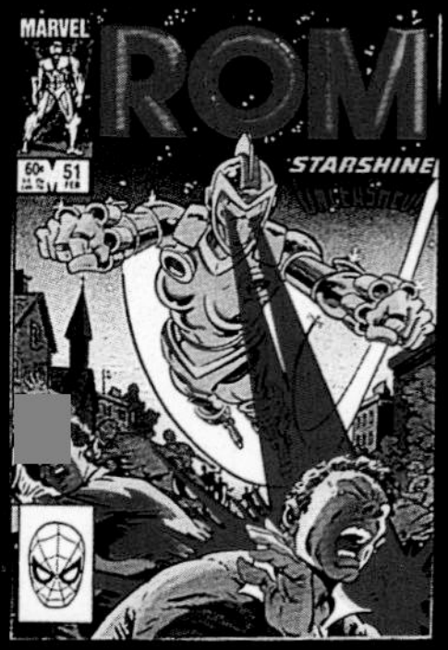
MARVEL
ROM
STARSHINE

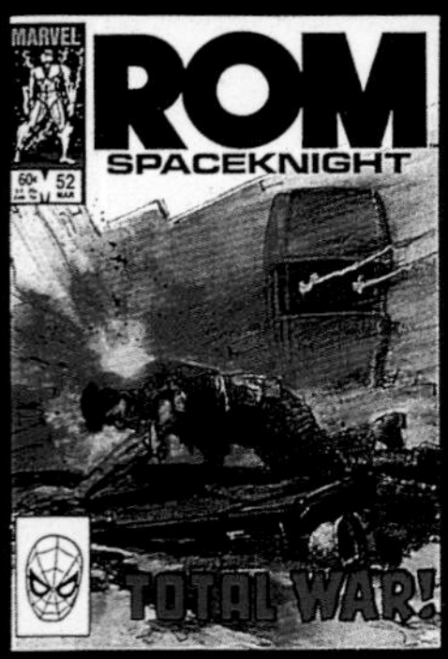
MARVEL
ROM
SPACEKNIGHT
TOTAL WAR!

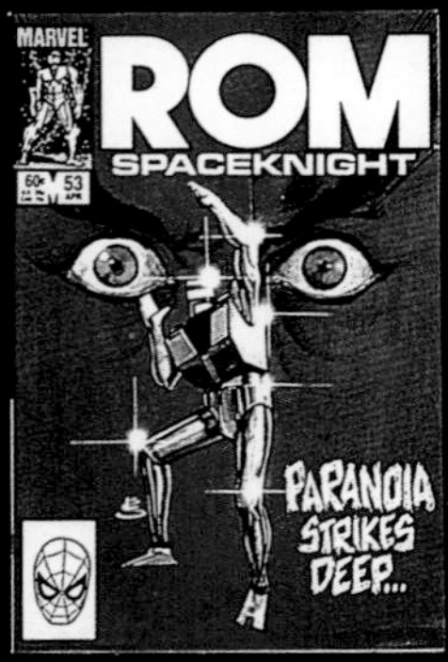
MARVEL
ROM
SPACEKNIGHT
PARANOIA STRIKES DEEP...

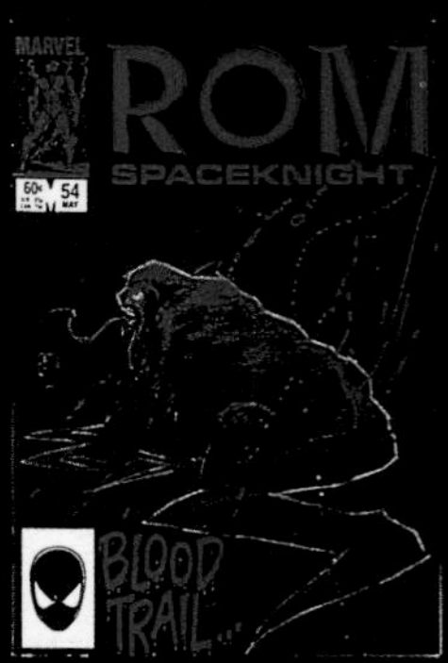
MARVEL
ROM
SPACEKNIGHT
BLOOD TRAIL

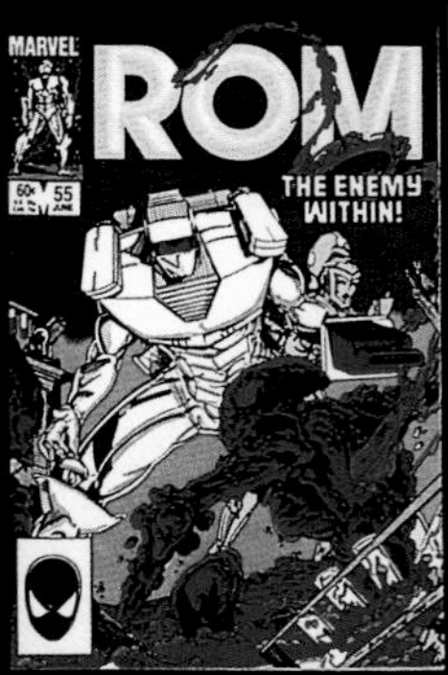
MARVEL
ROM
THE ENEMY WITHIN!

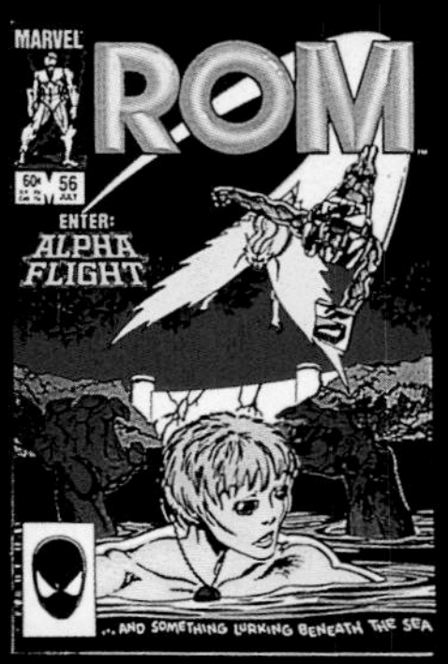
MARVEL
ROM
ENTER: ALPHA FLIGHT
...AND SOMETHING LURKING BENEATH THE SEA

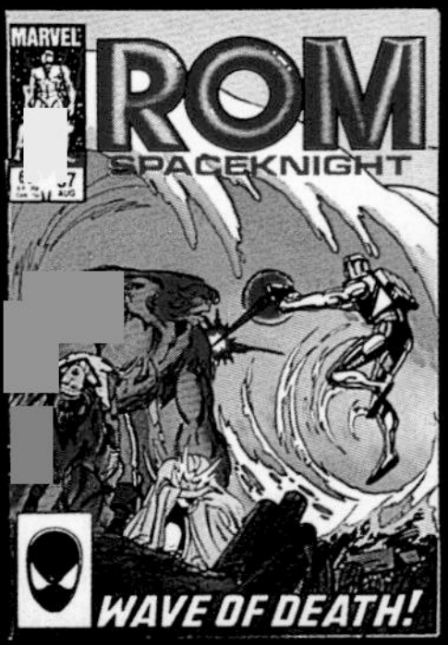
MARVEL
ROM
SPACEKNIGHT
WAVE OF DEATH!

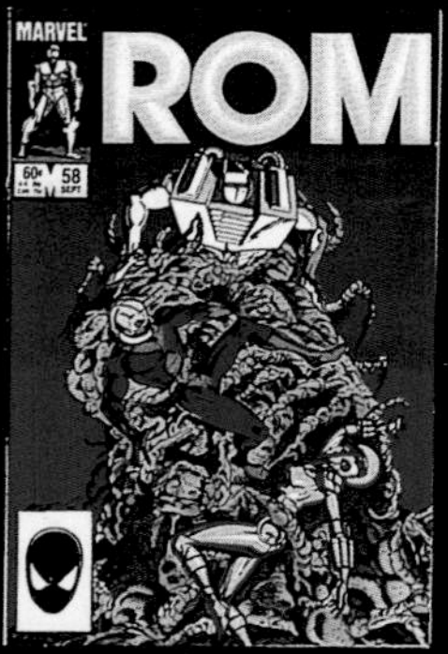
MARVEL
ROM

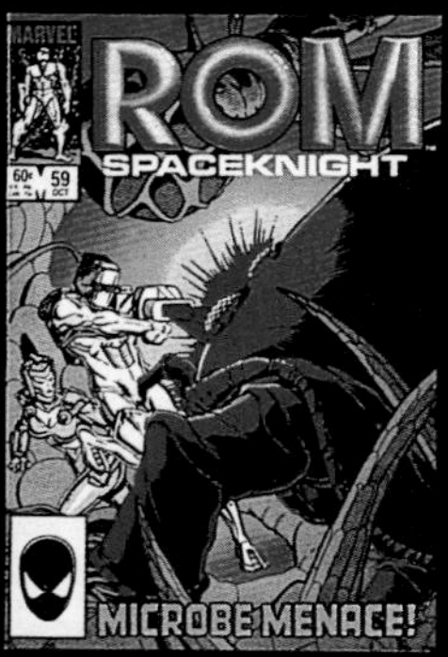
MARVEL
ROM
SPACEKNIGHT
MICROBE MENACE!

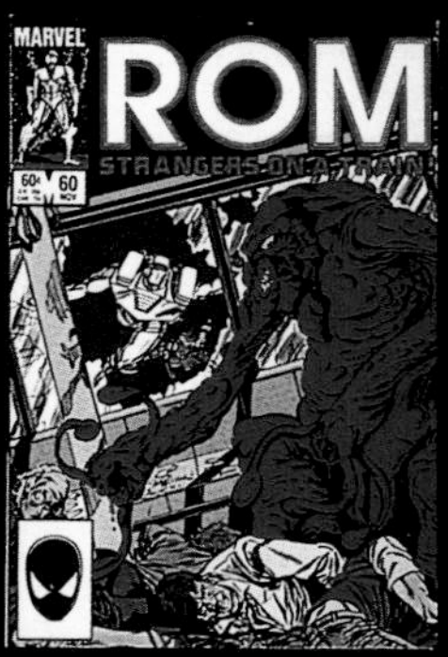
MARVEL
ROM

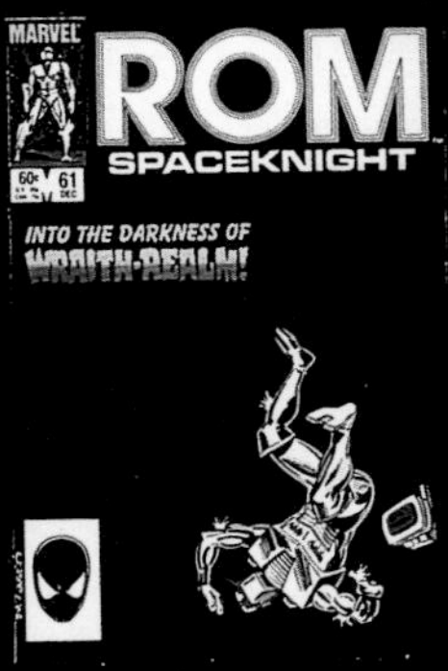
MARVEL
ROM
SPACEKNIGHT
INTO THE DARKNESS OF
WRAITH-REALM!

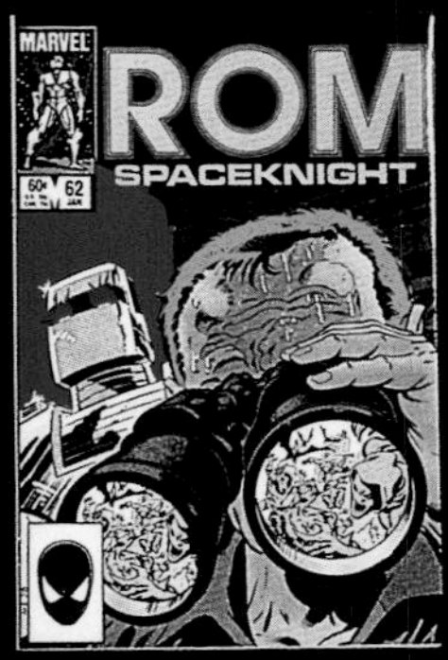
MARVEL
ROM
SPACEKNIGHT

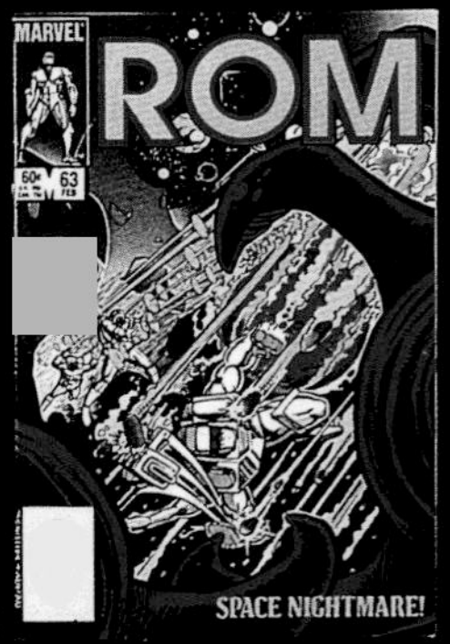
MARVEL
R.O.M.
SPACE NIGHTMARE!

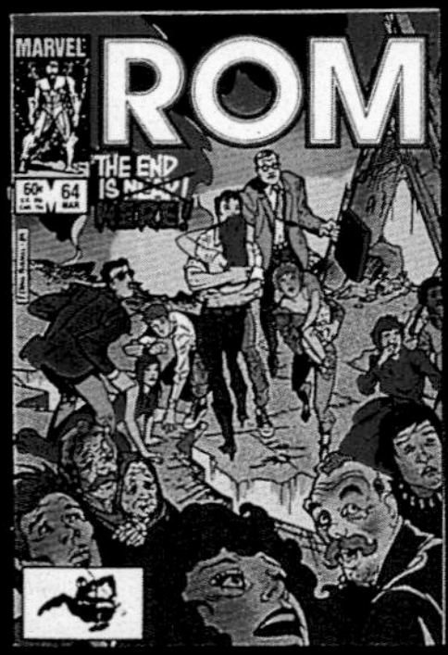
MARVEL
ROM

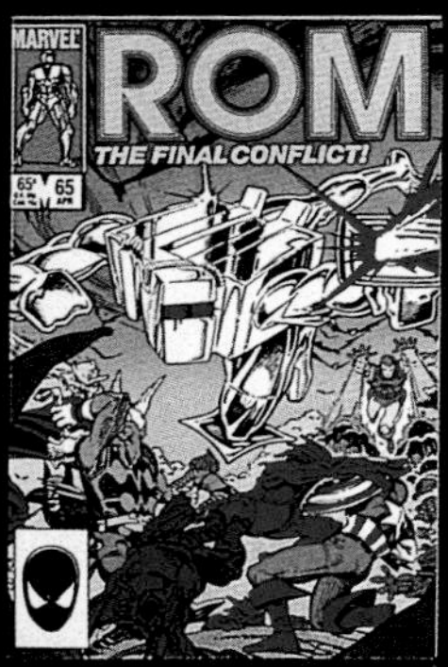
MARVEL
ROM
THE FINAL CONFLICT!

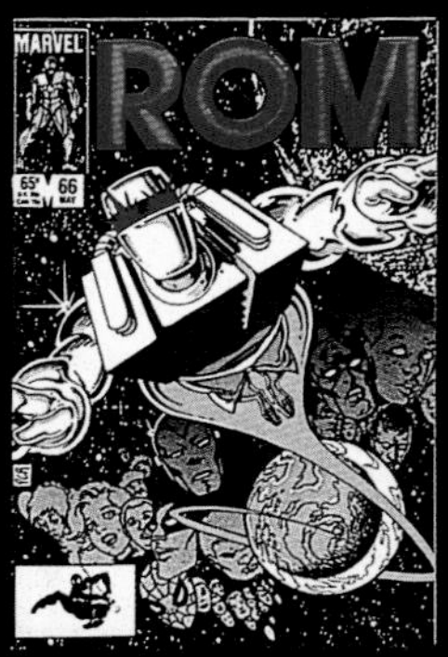
MARVEL
ROM

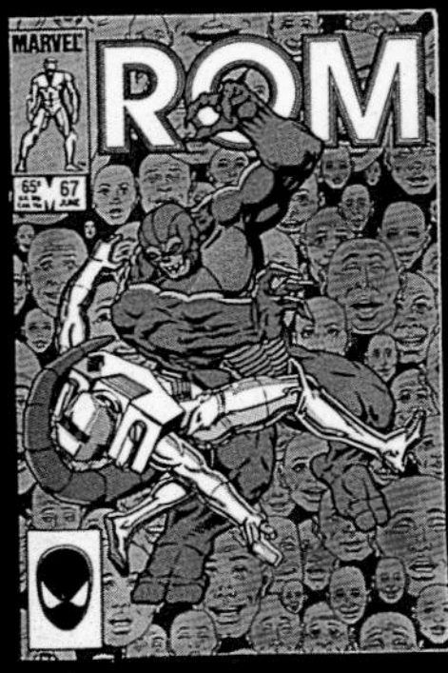
MARVEL
ROM

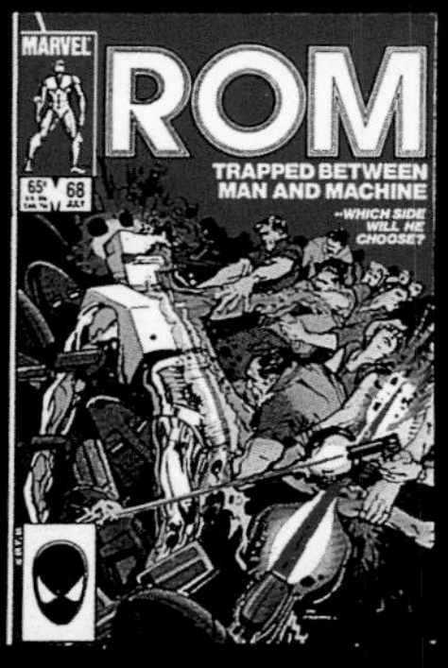
MARVEL
ROM
TRAPPED BETWEEN MAN AND MACHINE
--WHICH SIDE WILL HE CHOOSE?

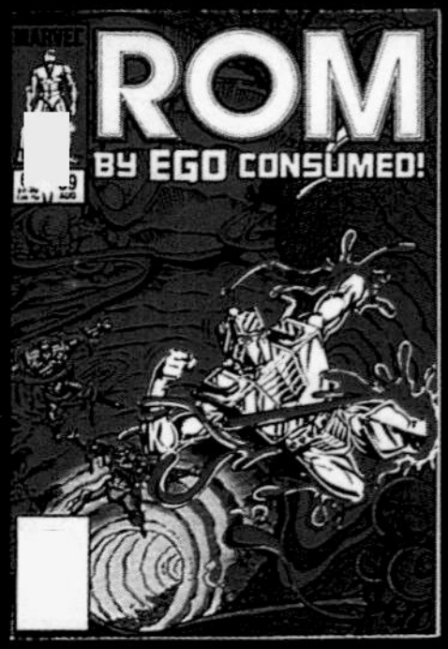
ROM
BY EGO CONSUMED!

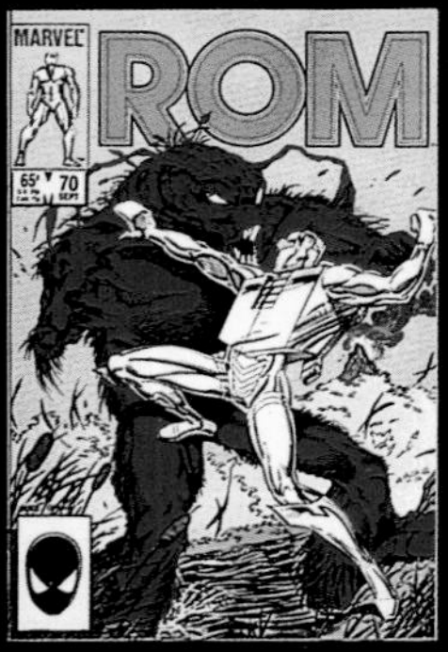
ROM

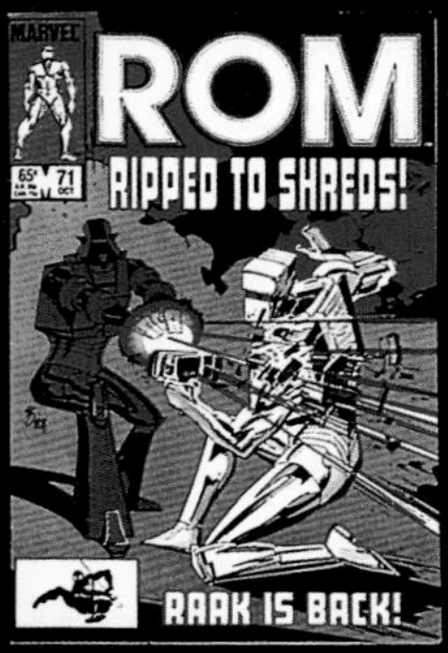
MARVEL
ROM
RIPPED TO SHREDS!
RAAK IS BACK!

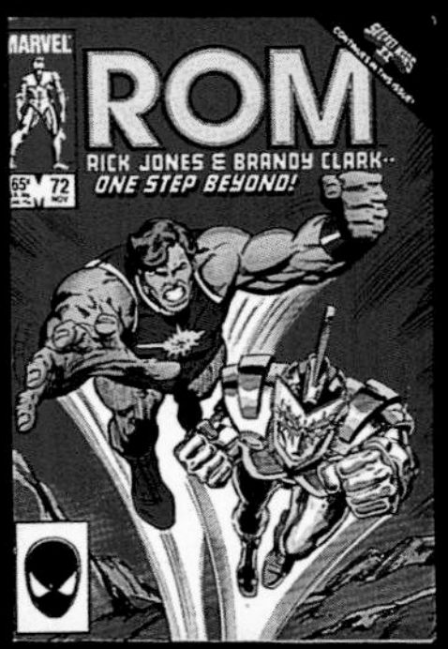
MARVEL
ROM
RICK JONES & BRANDY CLARK--
ONE STEP BEYOND!

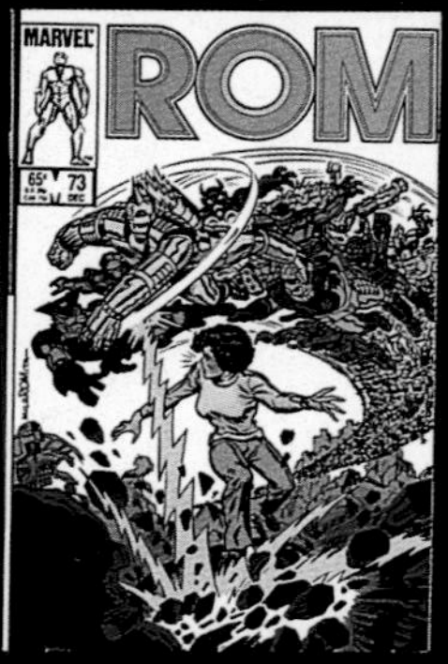
MARVEL
ROM

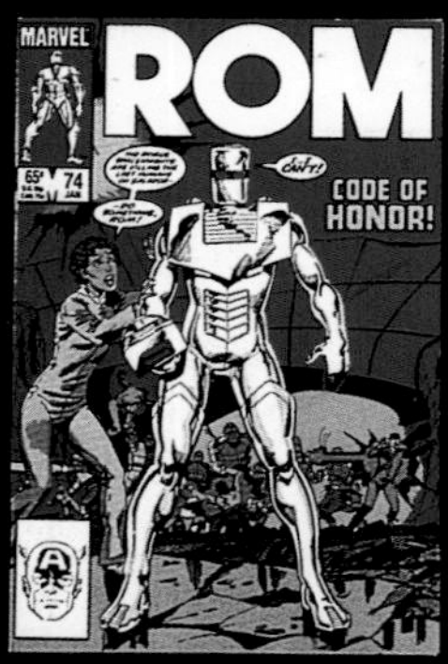
MARVEL
ROM
CODE OF HONOR!

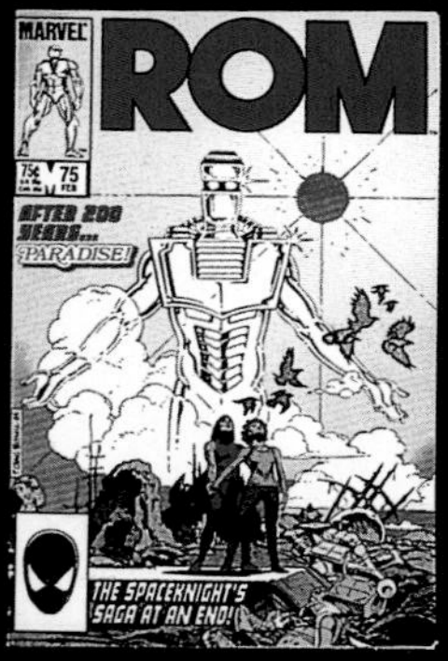
MARVEL
ROM
THE SPACEKNIGHT'S SAGA AT AN END!

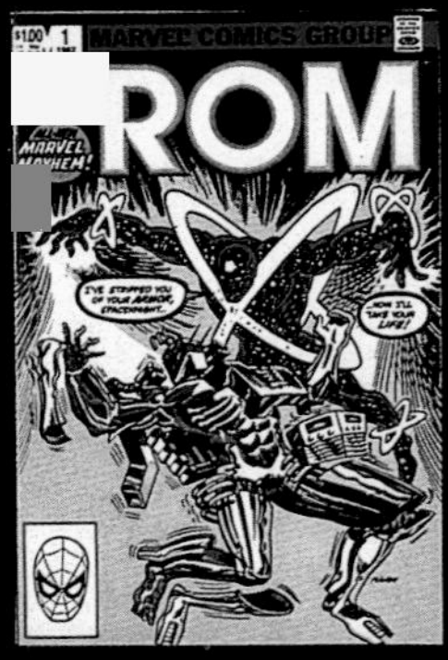
MARVEL COMICS GROUP
ROM

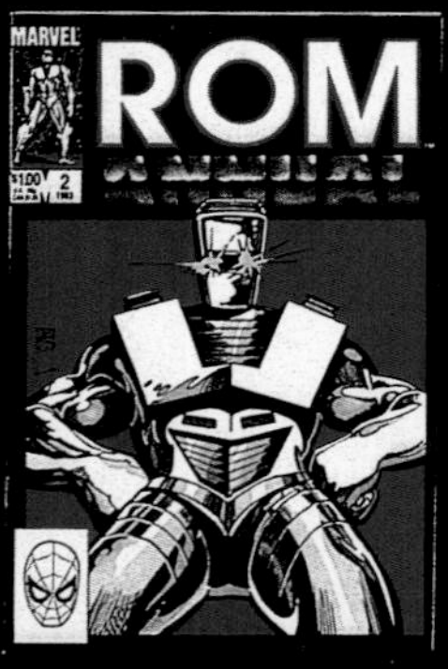
MARVEL
ROM

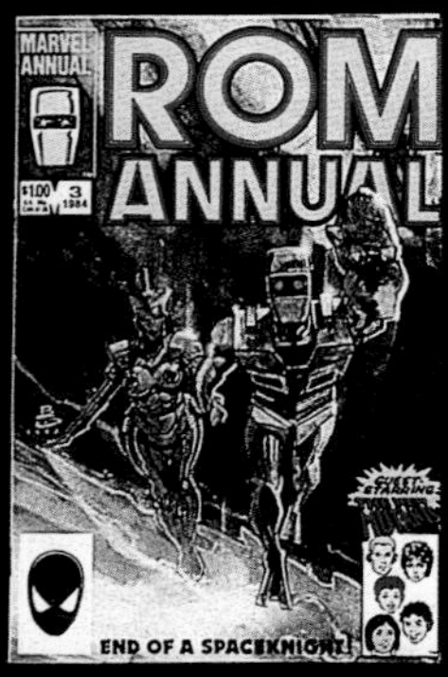
MARVEL ANNUAL
ROM
ANNUAL
END OF A SPACEKNIGHT!

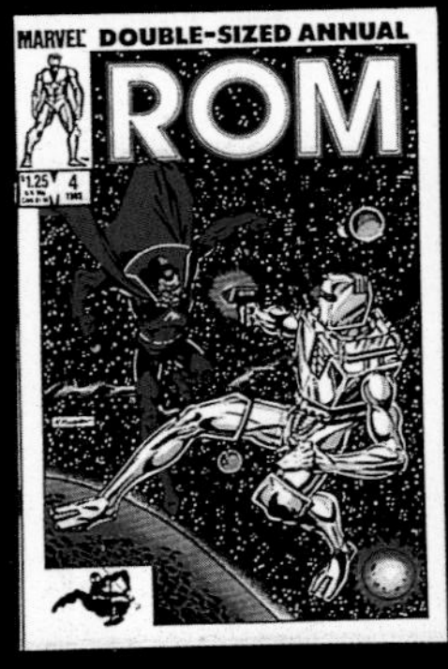
MARVEL
DOUBLE-SIZED ANNUAL
ROM

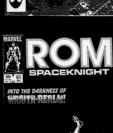

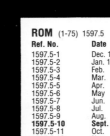

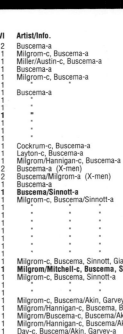

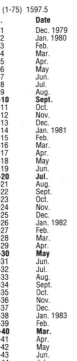

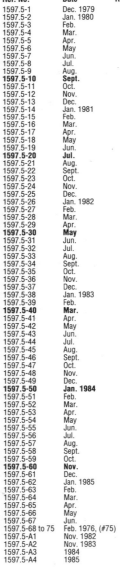

ROM (1-75) 1597.5

Ref. No.	Date	RVI	Artist/Info.
1597.5-1	Dec. 1979	2	Buscema-a
1597.5-2	Jan. 1980	1	Milgrom-c, Buscema-a
1597.5-3	Feb.	1	Miller/Austin-c, Buscema-a
1597.5-4	Mar.	1	Buscema-a
1597.5-5	Apr.	1	Milgrom-c, Buscema-a
1597.5-6	May	1	" "
1597.5-7	Jun.	1	Buscema-a
1597.5-8	Jul.	1	"
1597.5-9	Aug.	1	"
1597.5-10	**Sept.**	**1**	**"**
1597.5-11	Oct.	1	"
1597.5-12	Nov.	1	"
1597.5-13	Dec.	1	"
1597.5-14	Jan. 1981	1	Cockrum-c, Buscema-a
1597.5-15	Feb.	1	Layton-c, Buscema-a
1597.5-16	Mar.	1	Milgrom/Hannigan-c, Buscema-a
1597.5-17	Apr.	2	Buscema-a (X-men)
1597.5-18	May	2	Buscema/Milgrom-a (X-men)
1597.5-19	Jun.	1	Buscema-a
1597.5-20	**Jul.**	**1**	**Buscema/Sinnott-a**
1597.5-21	Aug.	1	Milgrom-c, Buscema/Sinnott-a
1597.5-22	Sept.	1	" " "
1597.5-23	Oct.	1	" " "
1597.5-24	Nov.	1	" " "
1597.5-25	Dec.	1	" " "
1597.5-26	Jan. 1982	1	" " "
1597.5-27	Feb.	1	" " "
1597.5-28	Mar.	1	" " "
1597.5-29	Apr.	1	Milgrom-c, Buscema, Sinnott, Giacoia, Esposito-a
1597.5-30	**May**	**1**	**Milgrom/Mitchell-c, Buscema, Sinnott-a**
1597.5-31	Jun.	1	Milgrom-c, Buscema, Sinnott-a
1597.5-32	Jul.	1	" " "
1597.5-33	Aug.	1	" " "
1597.5-34	Sept.	1	Milgrom-c, Buscema/Akin, Garvey-a
1597.5-35	Oct.	1	Milgrom/Hannigan-c, Buscema, Bulanadi-a
1597.5-36	Nov.	1	Milgrom/Buscema-c, Buscema/Akin, Garvey-a
1597.5-37	Dec.	1	Milgrom/Hannigan-c, Buscema/Akin, Garvey-a
1597.5-38	Jan. 1983	1	Day-c, Buscema/Akin, Garvey-a
1597.5-39	Feb.	1	" " " "
1597.5-40	**Mar.**	**1**	**Leialoha-c, Buscema/Akin, Garvey-a**
1597.5-41	Apr.	1	Severin/Milgrom-c, Buscema/Akin, Garvey-a
1597.5-42	May	1	Jusko-c, Buscema/Akin, Garvey-a
1597.5-43	Jun.	1	Akin/Garvey-c, Buscema/Akin, Garvey-a
1597.5-44	Jul.	1	" " " " "
1597.5-45	Aug.	1	" " " " "
1597.5-46	Sept.	1	Buscema/Akin, Garvey-a
1597.5-47	Oct.	1	" "
1597.5-48	Nov.	1	Akin/Garvey-c, Buscema/Akin, Garvey-a
1597.5-49	Dec.	1	Milgrom-c, Buscema/Akin, Garvey-a
1597.5-50	**Jan. 1984**	**1**	**Double-size**
1597.5-51	Feb.	1	
1597.5-52	Mar.	1	
1597.5-53	Apr.	1	
1597.5-54	May	1	
1597.5-55	Jun.	1	Guice-c
1597.5-56	Jul.	1	Byrne-c
1597.5-57	Aug.	1	Byrne-c (Alpha Flight -app.)
1597.5-58	Sept.	1	Guice-c
1597.5-59	Oct.	1	Ditko/Layton-a
1597.5-60	**Nov.**	**1**	**Guice-c, Ditko-a**
1597.5-61	Dec.	1	Ditko-a
1597.5-62	Jan. 1985	1	"
1597.5-63	Feb.	1	"
1597.5-64	Mar.	1	Russell-c, Ditko-a
1597.5-65	Apr.	1	" "
1597.5-66	May	1	" "
1597.5-67	Jun.	1	Starlin-c, Ditko-a
1597.5-68 to 75	Feb. 1976, (#75)	1	Ditko-a
1597.5-A1	Nov. 1982	1	
1597.5-A2	Nov. 1983	1	
1597.5-A3	1984	1	
1597.5-A4	1985	1	

1631.5 Saga of Crystar (1-11)

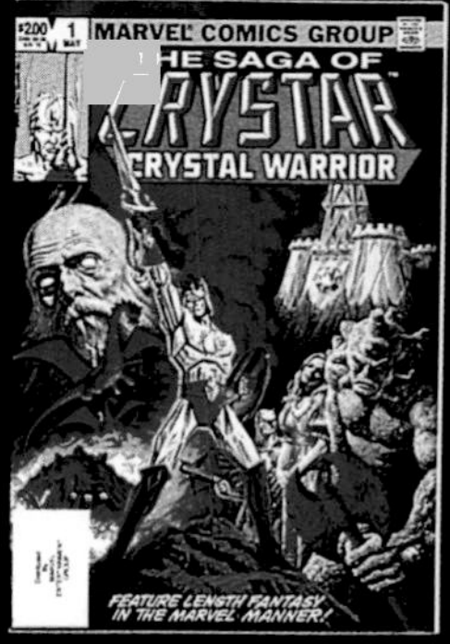
MARVEL COMICS GROUP
THE SAGA OF CRYSTAR
CRYSTAL WARRIOR
FEATURE LENGTH FANTASY IN THE MARVEL MANNER!
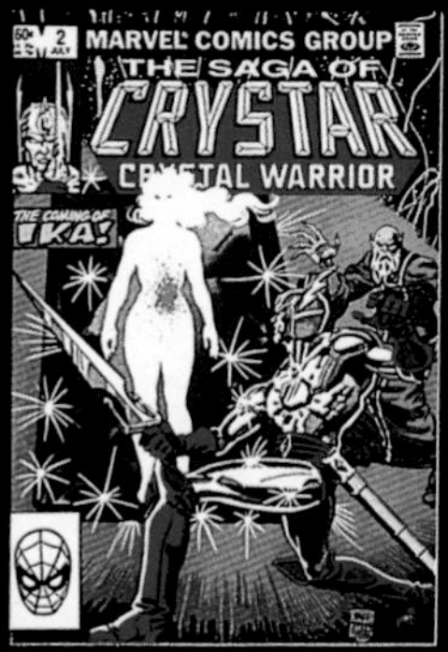
MARVEL COMICS GROUP
THE SAGA OF CRYSTAR
CRYSTAL WARRIOR
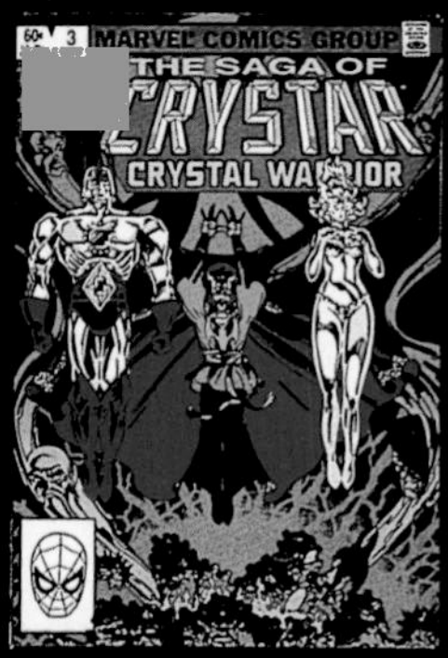
MARVEL COMICS GROUP
THE SAGA OF CRYSTAR
CRYSTAL WARRIOR
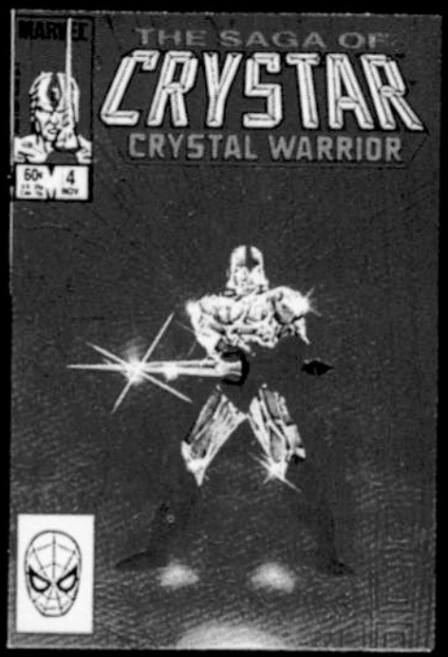
THE SAGA OF CRYSTAR
CRYSTAL WARRIOR
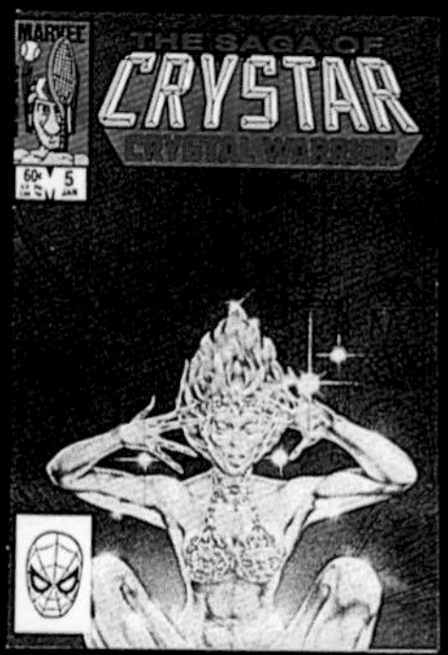
THE SAGA OF CRYSTAR
CRYSTAL WARRIOR
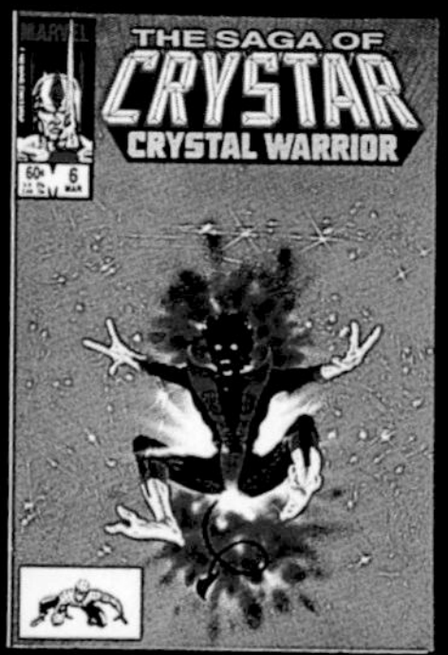
THE SAGA OF CRYSTAR
CRYSTAL WARRIOR
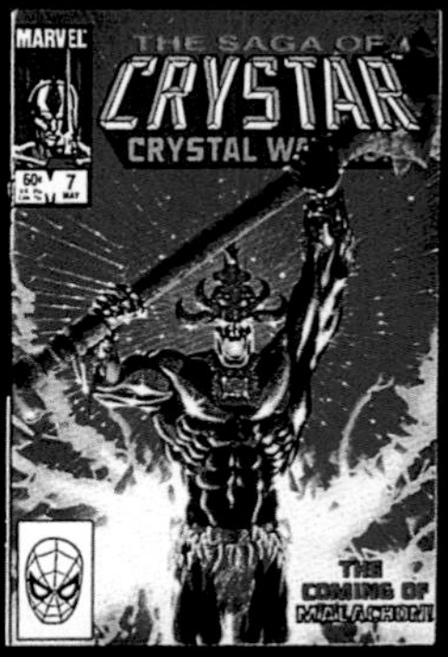
THE SAGA OF CRYSTAR
CRYSTAL WARRIOR
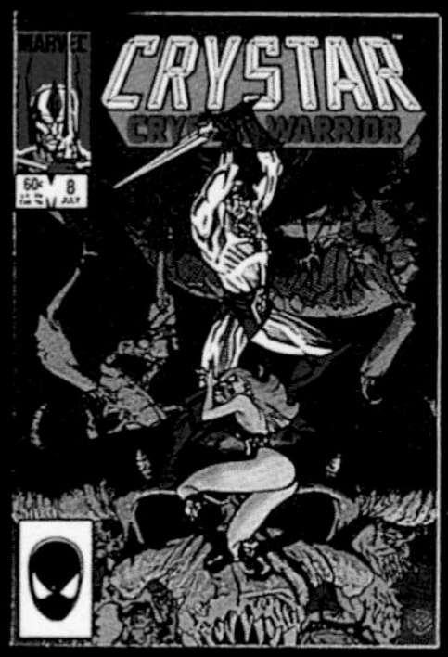
CRYSTAR
CRYSTAL WARRIOR
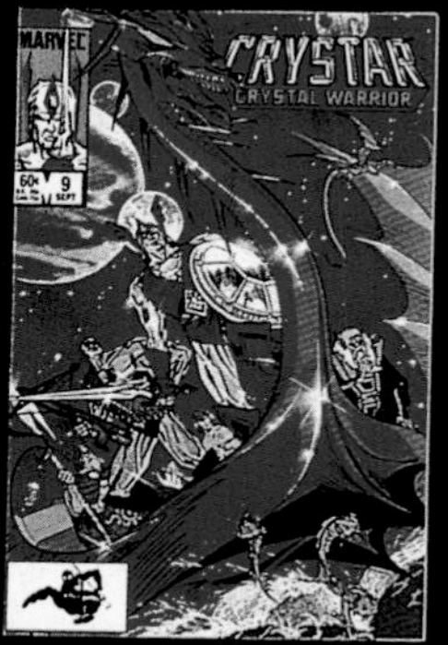
CRYSTAR
CRYSTAL WARRIOR
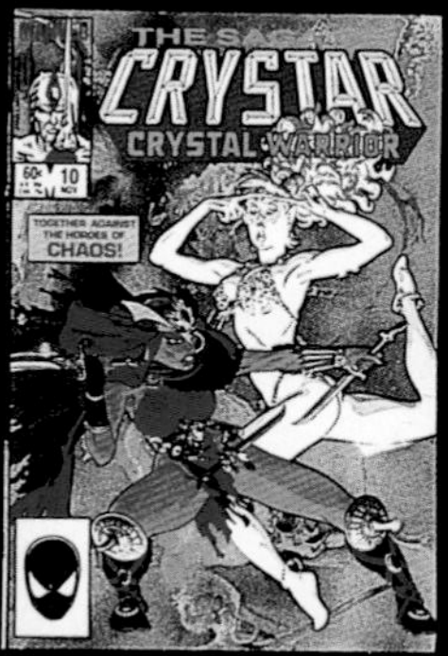
CRYSTAR
CRYSTAL WARRIOR
CHAOS!
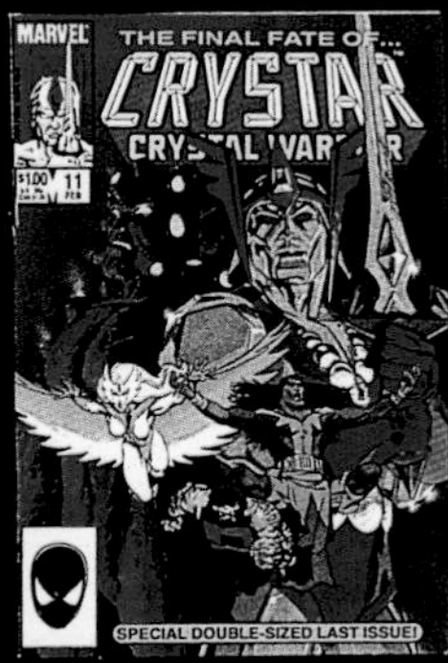
THE FINAL FATE OF...
CRYSTAR
SPECIAL DOUBLE-SIZED LAST ISSUE!

1668.7 Sectaurs (1)

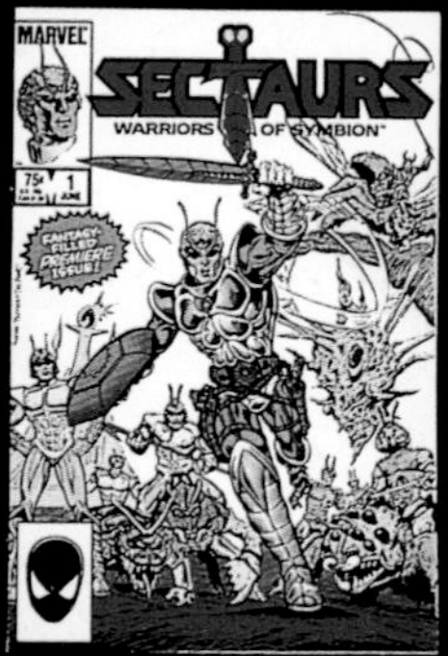
SECTAURS
WARRIORS OF SYMBION
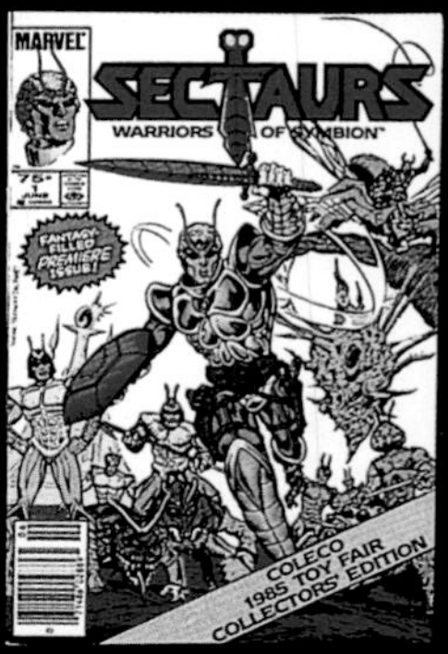
SECTAURS
WARRIORS OF SYMBION
COLECO 1985 TOY FAIR COLLECTORS' EDITION

1645.9 The Savage She-Hulk (1-25)

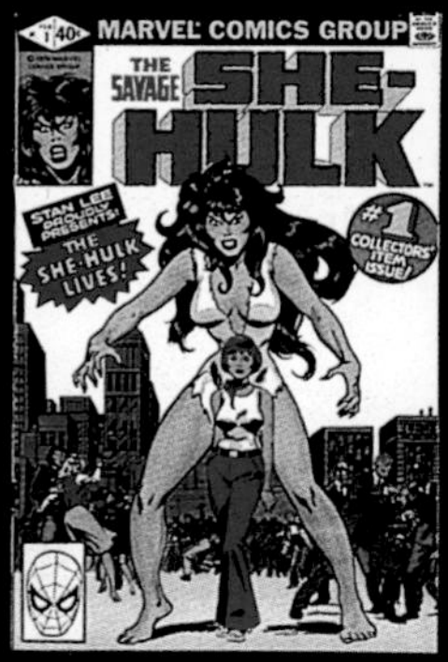
MARVEL COMICS GROUP
THE SAVAGE SHE-HULK
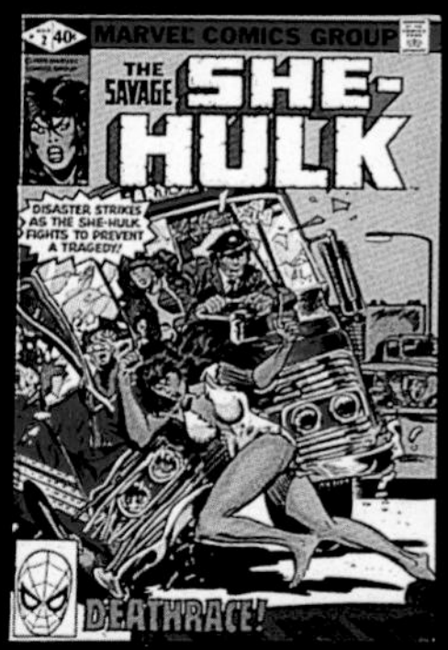
MARVEL COMICS GROUP
THE SAVAGE SHE-HULK
DEATHRACE!
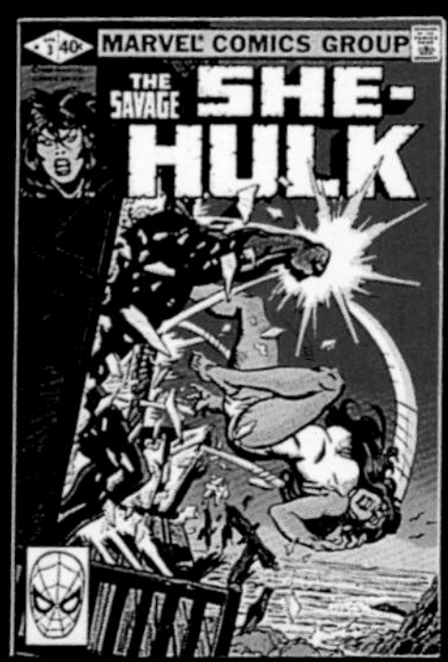
MARVEL COMICS GROUP
THE SAVAGE SHE-HULK
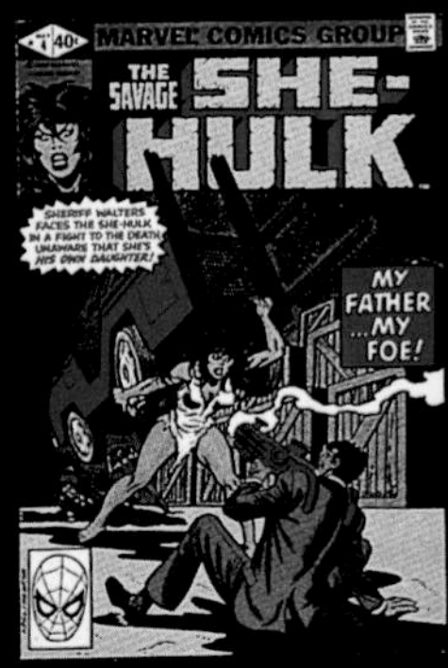
MARVEL COMICS GROUP
THE SAVAGE SHE-HULK
MY FATHER ...MY FOE!
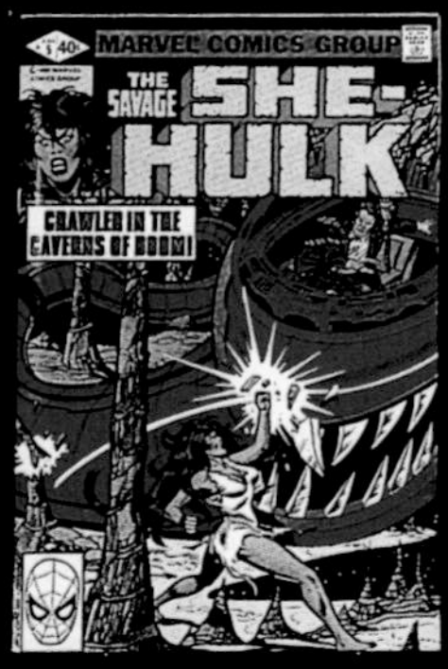
MARVEL COMICS GROUP
THE SAVAGE SHE-HULK
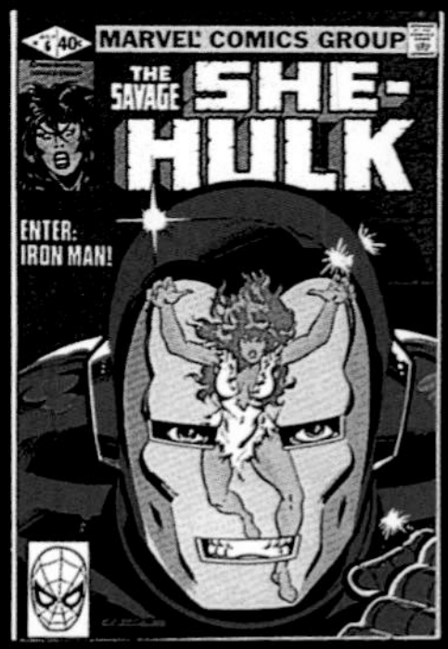
MARVEL COMICS GROUP
THE SAVAGE SHE-HULK
ENTER: IRON MAN!
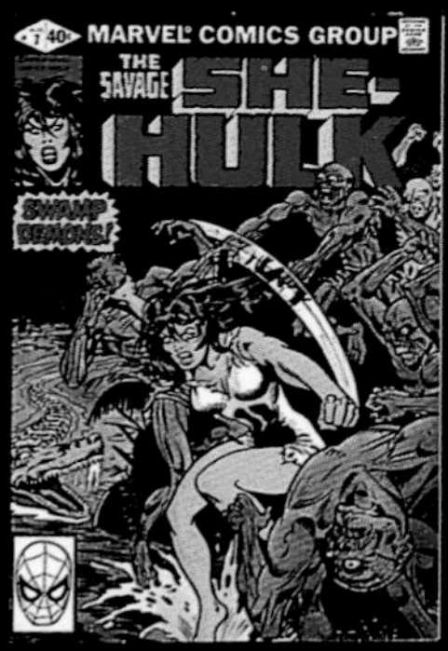
MARVEL COMICS GROUP
THE SHE-HULK
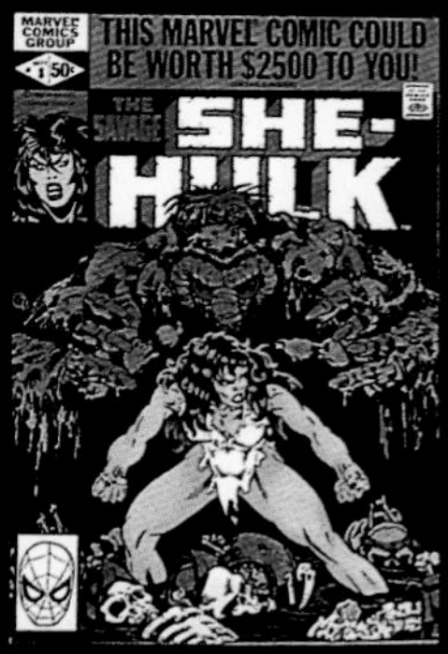
THIS MARVEL COMIC COULD BE WORTH $2500 TO YOU!
THE SAVAGE SHE-HULK
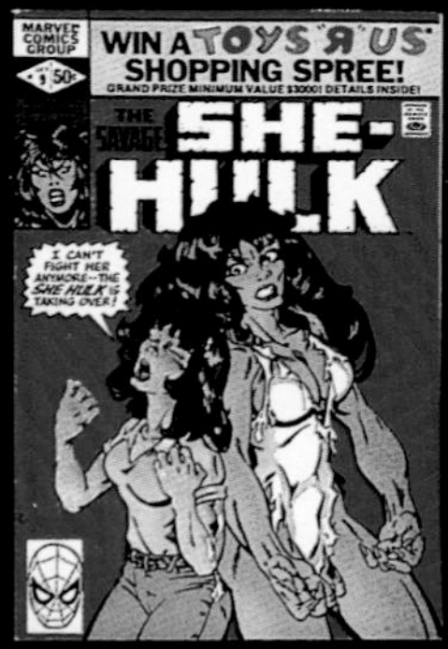
WIN A TOYS R US SHOPPING SPREE!
THE SAVAGE SHE-HULK
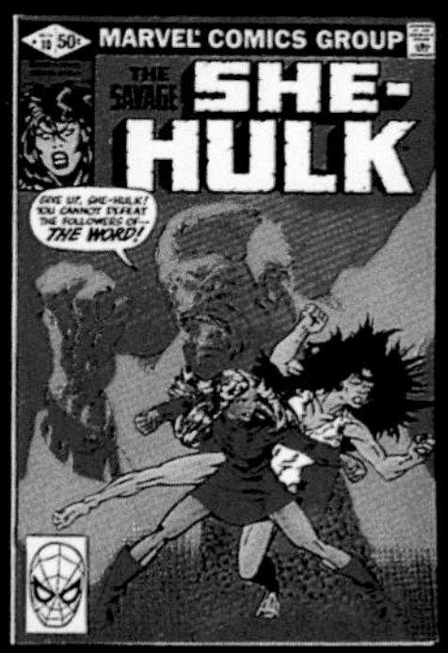
MARVEL COMICS GROUP
THE SAVAGE SHE-HULK
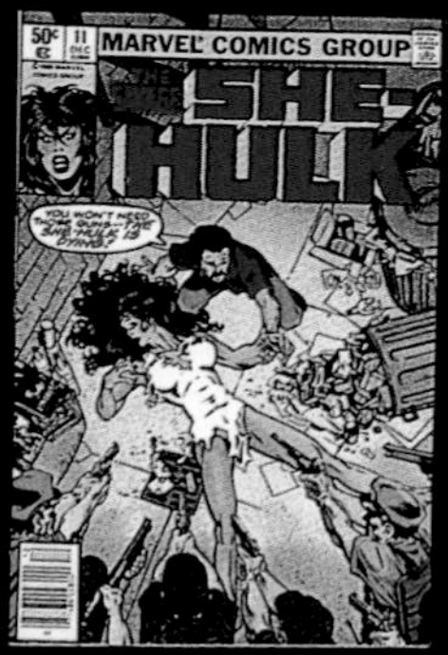
MARVEL COMICS GROUP
SHE-HULK
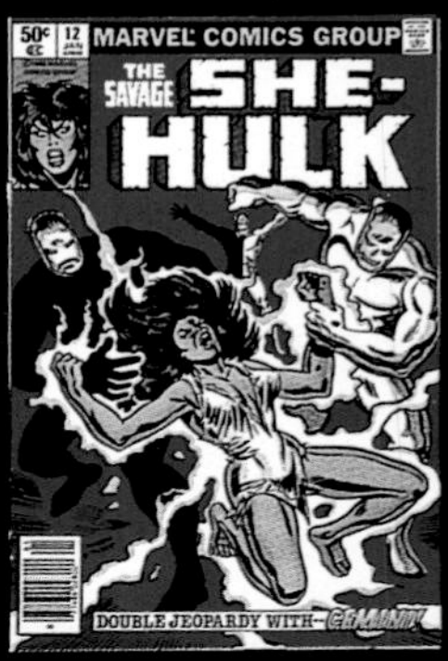
MARVEL COMICS GROUP
THE SAVAGE SHE-HULK
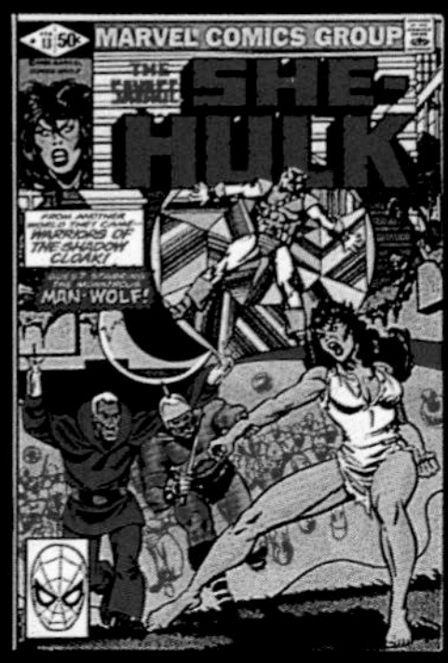
MARVEL COMICS GROUP
SHE-HULK
MAN-WOLF!
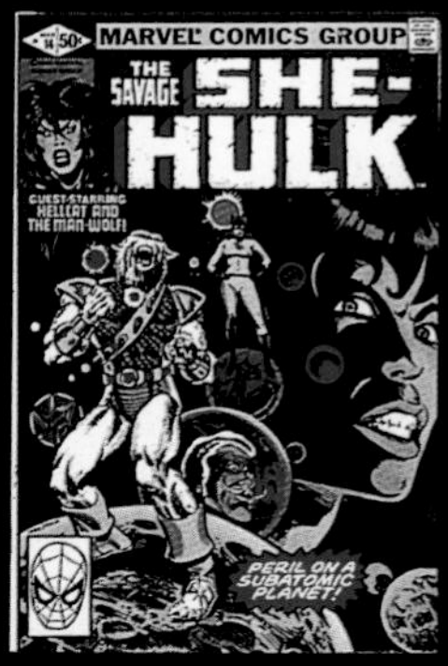
MARVEL COMICS GROUP
THE SAVAGE SHE-HULK
PERIL ON A SUBATOMIC PLANET!
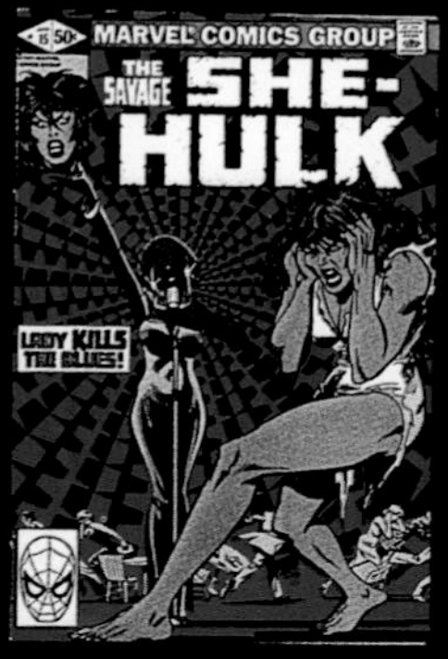
MARVEL COMICS GROUP
THE SAVAGE SHE-HULK
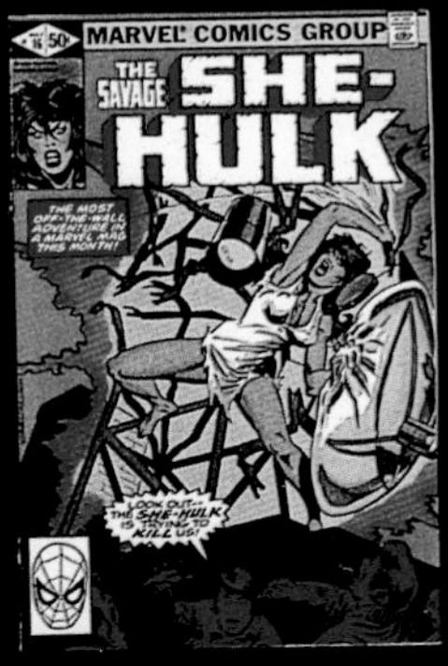
MARVEL COMICS GROUP
THE SAVAGE SHE-HULK
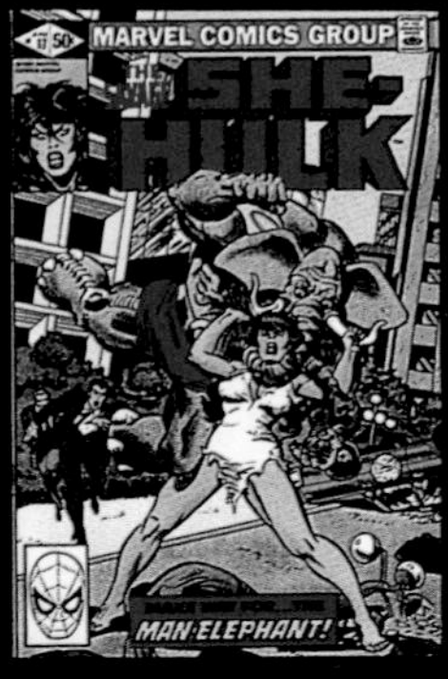
MARVEL COMICS GROUP
SHE-HULK
MAN-ELEPHANT!
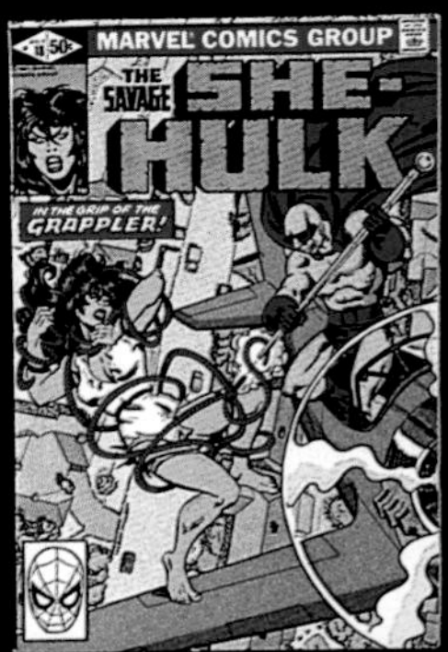
MARVEL COMICS GROUP
THE SAVAGE SHE-HULK
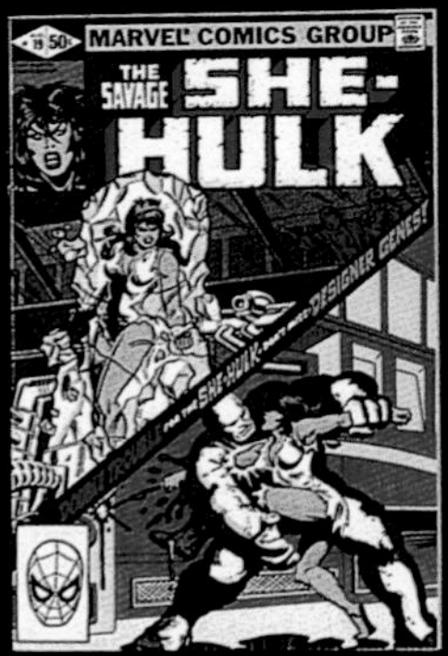
MARVEL COMICS GROUP
THE SAVAGE SHE-HULK
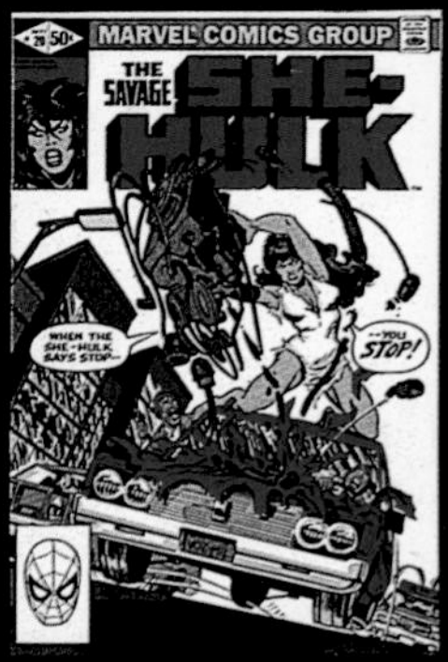
MARVEL COMICS GROUP
THE SAVAGE SHE-HULK
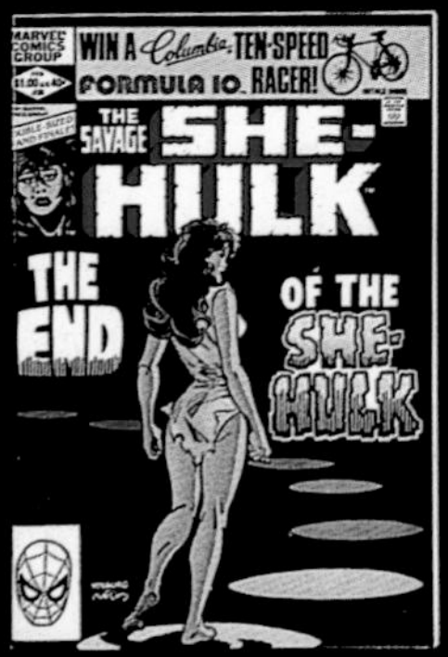
WIN A Columbia TEN-SPEED FORMULA 10 RACER!
THE SAVAGE SHE-HULK
THE END OF THE SHE-HULK

The Saga of Crystar, Crystal Warrior (1-11) 1631.5

Ref. No.	Date	RVI	Artist/Info.
1631.5-1	May 1983	2	(Origin-Crystar)
1631.5-2	Jul.	1	Blevins-a
1631.5-3	Sept.	1	Bulanadi-a
1631.5-4	Nov.	1	Villamonte/Simons-a
1631.5-5	Jan. 1984	1	" "
1631.5-6	Mar.	1	Golden-c (Nightcrawler -app.)
1631.5-7 to 11	Feb. 1985	1	(#11, Alpha flight -app.)

Sectaurs (1-10) 1668.7

1668.7-1	Jun. 1985	2	(Stories based of Coleco toys)
1668.7-2 to 10	1986	1	
1668.71-1	1985	1	(1985 Toy fair giveaway)

The Savage She-Hulk (1-25) 1645.9

1645.9-1	Feb. 1980	2	Buscema-c (Intro. She-Hulk)
1645.9-2 to 25	Feb. 1982, (#25)	1	(#4, Blonde Phantom -app.)

Scooby Do (1-9) 1650.7

1650.7-1 to 9	Oct. 1977, (#1)	1	(Dyno-Mutt)

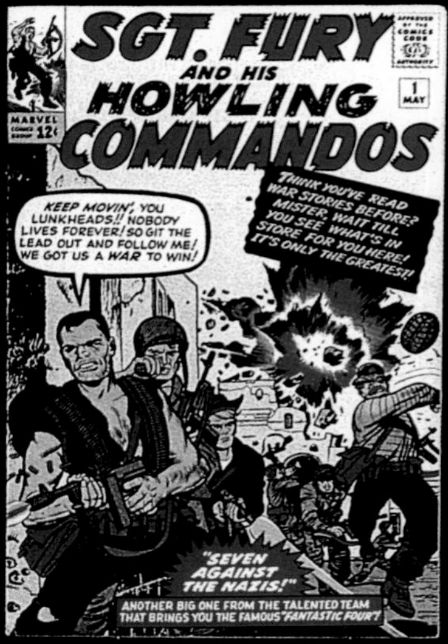
SGT. FURY
AND HIS
HOWLING
COMMANDOS
KEEP MOVIN', YOU LUNKHEADS!! NOBODY LIVES FOREVER! SO GIT THE LEAD OUT AND FOLLOW ME! WE GOT US A WAR TO WIN!
"SEVEN AGAINST THE NAZIS!"
ANOTHER BIG ONE FROM THE TALENTED TEAM THAT BRINGS YOU THE FAMOUS FANTASTIC FOUR!

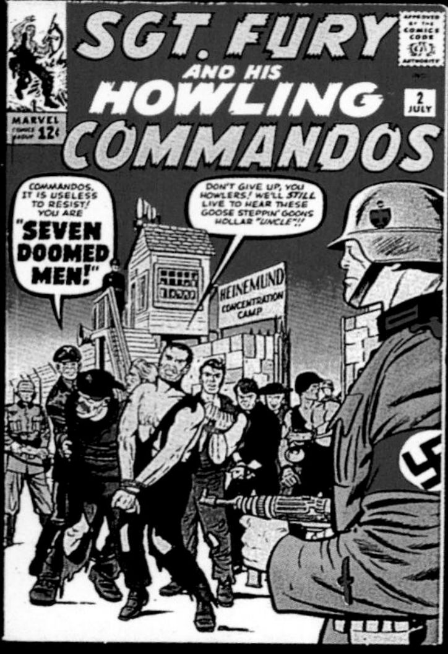
SGT. FURY
AND HIS
HOWLING
COMMANDOS
COMMANDOS, IT IS USELESS TO RESIST! YOU ARE
"SEVEN DOOMED MEN!"
DON'T GIVE UP, YOU HOWLERS! WE'LL STILL LIVE TO HEAR THESE GOOSE STEPPIN' GOONS HOLLAR "UNCLE"!!
HEINEMUND CONCENTRATION CAMP

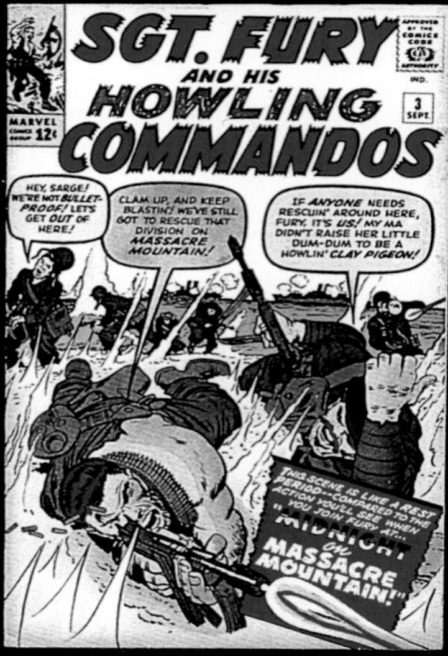
SGT. FURY
AND HIS
HOWLING
COMMANDOS
HEY SARGE! WE'RE NOT BULLET-PROOF! LET'S GET OUT OF HERE!
CLAM UP, AND KEEP BLASTIN'! WE'VE STILL GOT TO RESCUE THAT DIVISION ON MASSACRE MOUNTAIN!
IF ANYONE NEEDS RESCUIN' AROUND HERE, FURY, IT'S US! MY MA DIDN'T RAISE HER LITTLE DUM-DUM TO BE A HOWLIN' CLAY PIGEON!
MIDNIGHT ON MASSACRE MOUNTAIN!

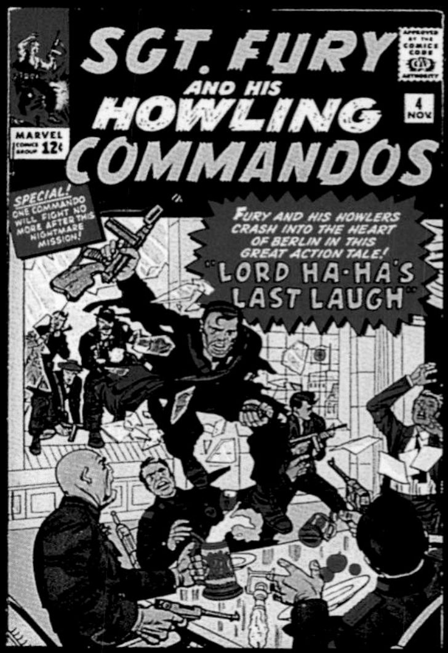
SGT. FURY
AND HIS
HOWLING
COMMANDOS
SPECIAL!
FURY AND HIS HOWLERS CRASH INTO THE HEART OF BERLIN IN THIS GREAT ACTION TALE!
LORD HA-HA'S LAST LAUGH

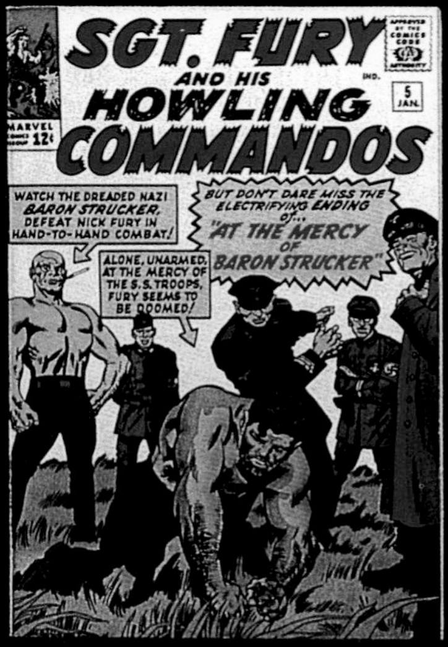
SGT. FURY
AND HIS
HOWLING
COMMANDOS
WATCH THE DREADED NAZI BARON STRUCKER, DEFEAT NICK FURY IN HAND-TO-HAND COMBAT!
BUT DON'T DARE MISS THE ELECTRIFYING ENDING
"AT THE MERCY OF BARON STRUCKER"
ALONE, UNARMED, AT THE MERCY OF THE S.S. TROOPS, FURY SEEMS TO BE DOOMED!

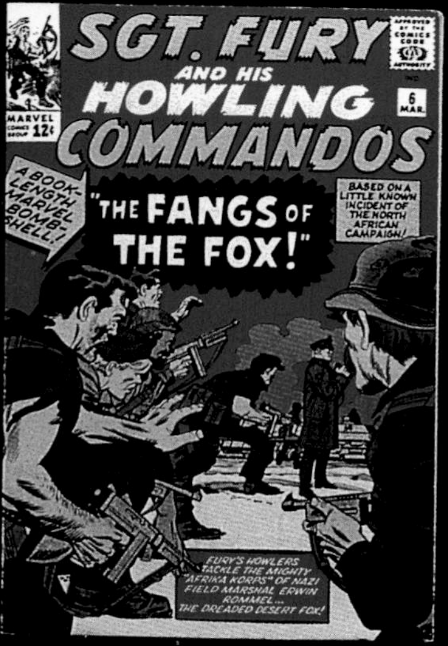
SGT. FURY
AND HIS
HOWLING
COMMANDOS
"THE FANGS OF THE FOX!"
BASED ON A LITTLE KNOWN INCIDENT OF THE NORTH AFRICAN CAMPAIGN!
FURY'S HOWLERS TACKLE THE MIGHTY AFRIKA KORPS OF NAZI FIELD MARSHAL ERWIN ROMMEL... THE DREADED DESERT FOX!

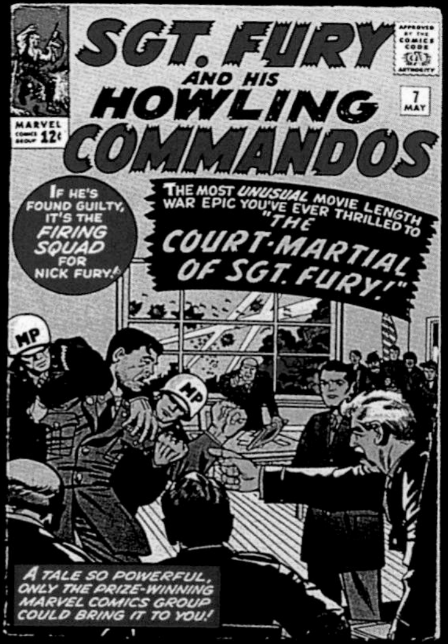
SGT. FURY
AND HIS
HOWLING
COMMANDOS
IF HE'S FOUND GUILTY, IT'S THE FIRING SQUAD FOR NICK FURY!
THE MOST UNUSUAL MOVIE LENGTH WAR EPIC YOU'VE EVER THRILLED TO
"THE COURT-MARTIAL OF SGT. FURY!"
MP
A TALE SO POWERFUL ONLY THE PRIZE-WINNING MARVEL COMICS GROUP COULD BRING IT TO YOU!

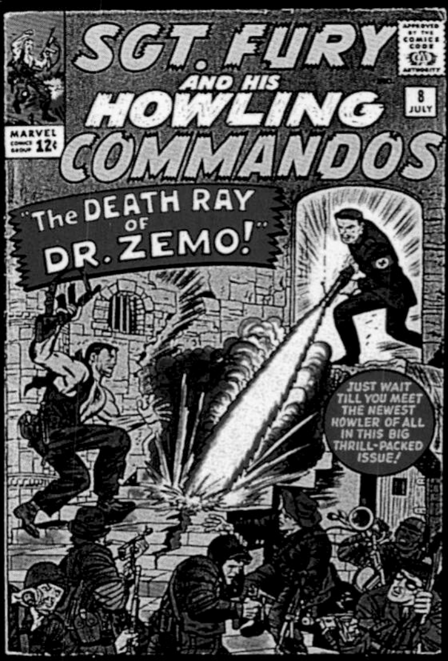
SGT. FURY
AND HIS
HOWLING
COMMANDOS
"The DEATH RAY OF DR. ZEMO!"
JUST WAIT TILL YOU MEET THE NEWEST HOWLER OF ALL IN THIS BIG THRILL-PACKED ISSUE!

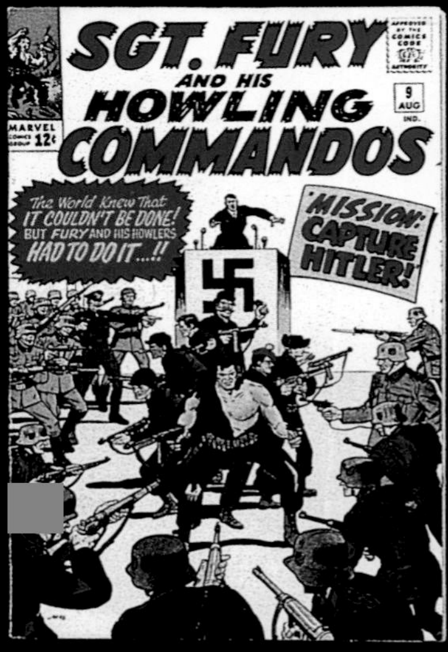
SGT. FURY
AND HIS
HOWLING
COMMANDOS
The World Knew That IT COULDN'T BE DONE! BUT FURY AND HIS HOWLERS HAD TO DO IT...!!
MISSION: CAPTURE HITLER!

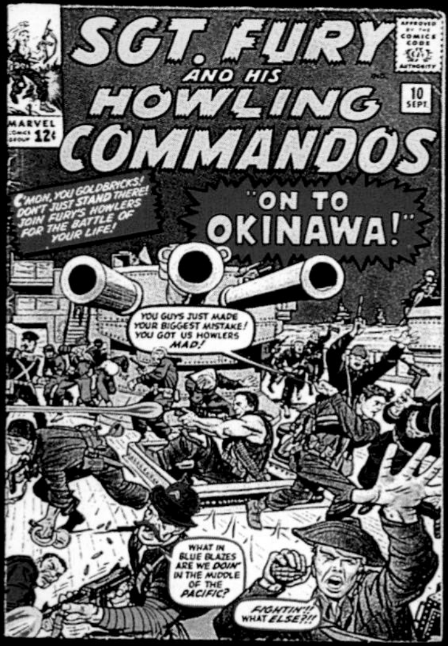
SGT. FURY
AND HIS
HOWLING
COMMANDOS
"ON TO OKINAWA!"
YOU GUYS JUST MADE YOUR BIGGEST MISTAKE! YOU GOT US HOWLERS MAD!
FIGHTIN'!! WHAT ELSE?!!

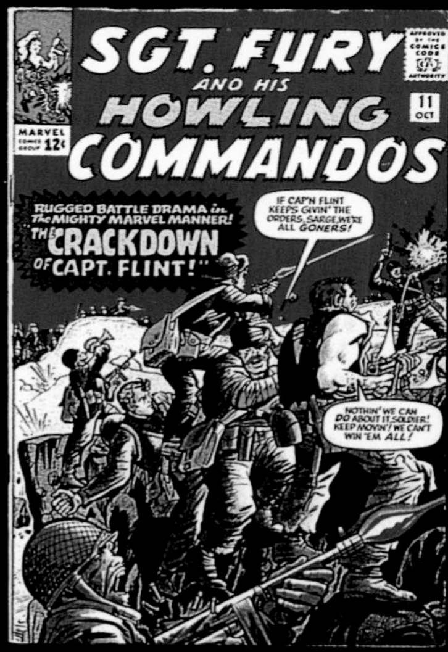
SGT. FURY
AND HIS
HOWLING
COMMANDOS
RUGGED BATTLE DRAMA in the MIGHTY MARVEL MANNER!
"The CRACKDOWN of CAPT. FLINT!"

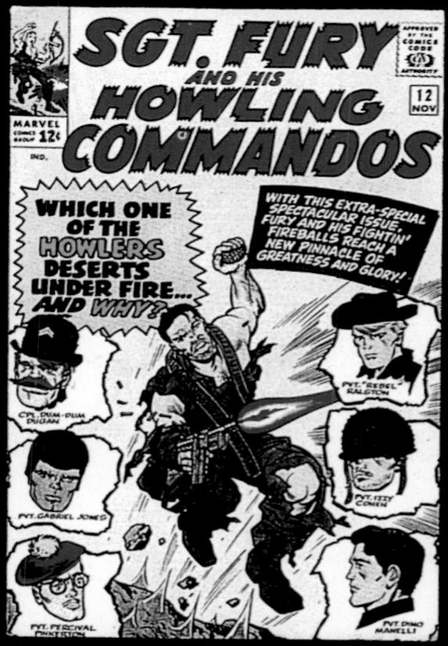
SGT. FURY
AND HIS
HOWLING
COMMANDOS
WHICH ONE OF THE HOWLERS DESERTS UNDER FIRE... AND WHY?
WITH THIS EXTRA-SPECIAL SPECTACULAR ISSUE, FURY AND HIS FIGHTIN' FIREBALLS REACH A NEW PINNACLE OF GREATNESS AND GLORY!

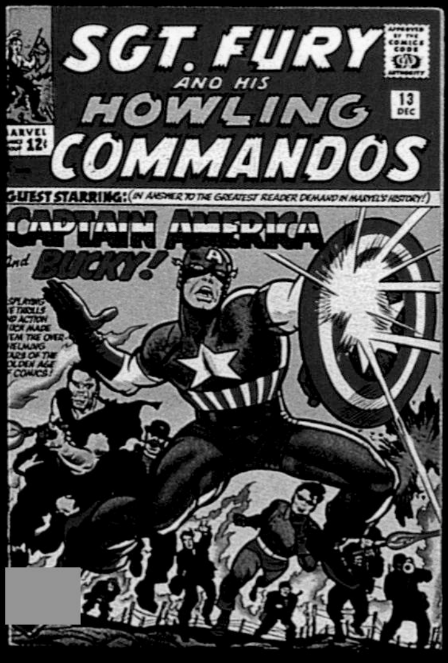
SGT. FURY
AND HIS
HOWLING
COMMANDOS
GUEST STARRING: (IN ANSWER TO THE GREATEST READER DEMAND IN MARVEL'S HISTORY!)
CAPTAIN AMERICA and BUCKY!

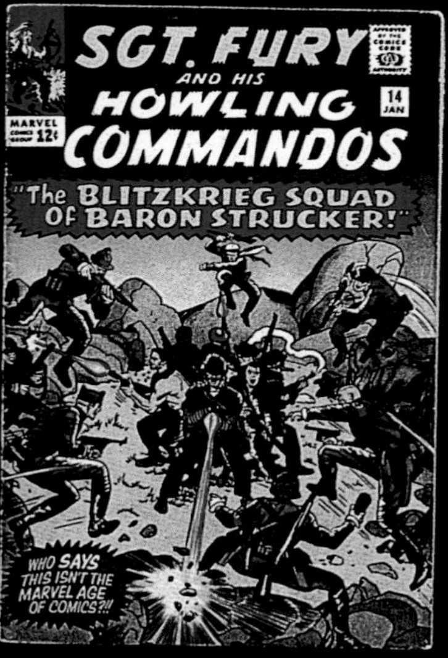
SGT. FURY
AND HIS
HOWLING
COMMANDOS
"The BLITZKRIEG SQUAD OF BARON STRUCKER!"
WHO SAYS THIS ISN'T THE MARVEL AGE OF COMICS?!!

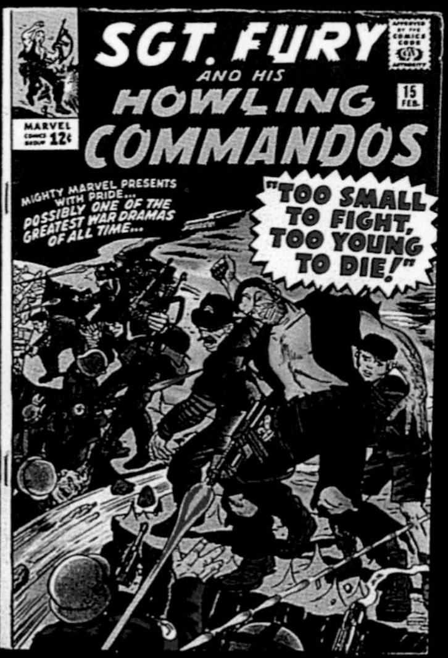
SGT. FURY
AND HIS
HOWLING
COMMANDOS
MIGHTY MARVEL PRESENTS WITH PRIDE... POSSIBLY ONE OF THE GREATEST WAR DRAMAS OF ALL TIME...
"TOO SMALL TO FIGHT, TOO YOUNG TO DIE!"

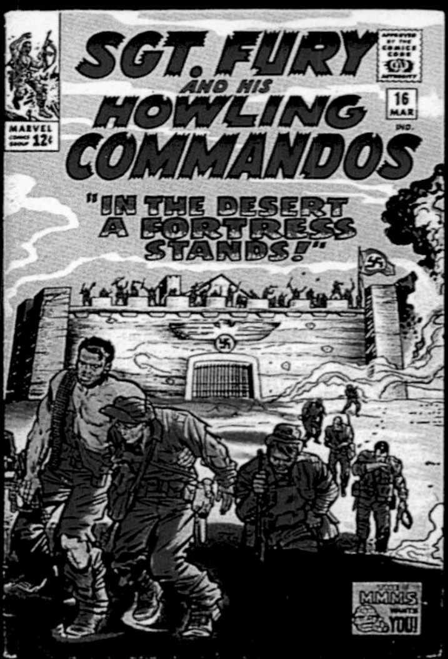
SGT. FURY
AND HIS
HOWLING
COMMANDOS
"IN THE DESERT A FORTRESS STANDS!"

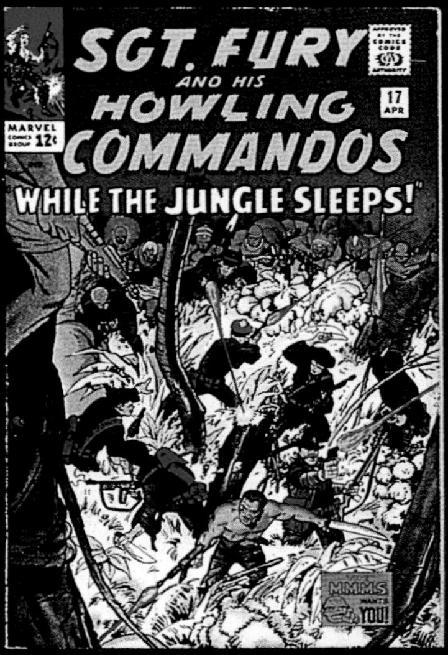
SGT. FURY
AND HIS
HOWLING
COMMANDOS
17 APR
MARVEL COMICS GROUP 12¢
WHILE THE JUNGLE SLEEPS!

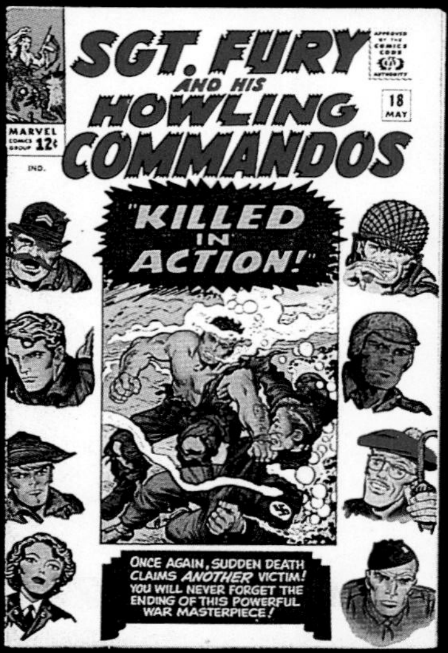
SGT. FURY
AND HIS
HOWLING
COMMANDOS
18 MAY
MARVEL COMICS GROUP 12¢
"KILLED IN ACTION!"
ONCE AGAIN, SUDDEN DEATH CLAIMS ANOTHER VICTIM! YOU WILL NEVER FORGET THE ENDING OF THIS POWERFUL WAR MASTERPIECE!

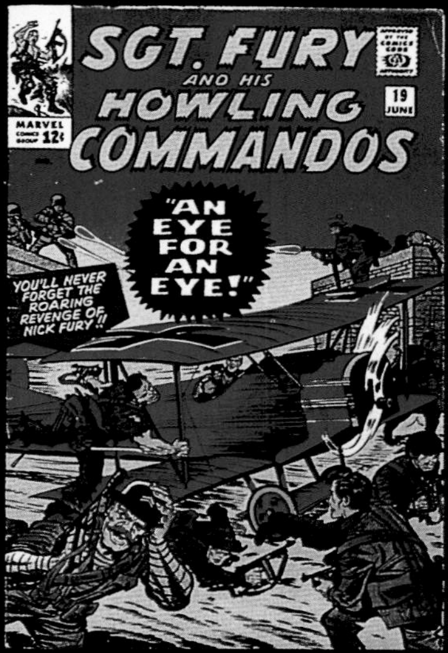
SGT. FURY
AND HIS
HOWLING
COMMANDOS
19 JUNE
MARVEL COMICS GROUP 12¢
"AN EYE FOR AN EYE!"
YOU'LL NEVER FORGET THE ROARING REVENGE OF NICK FURY!!

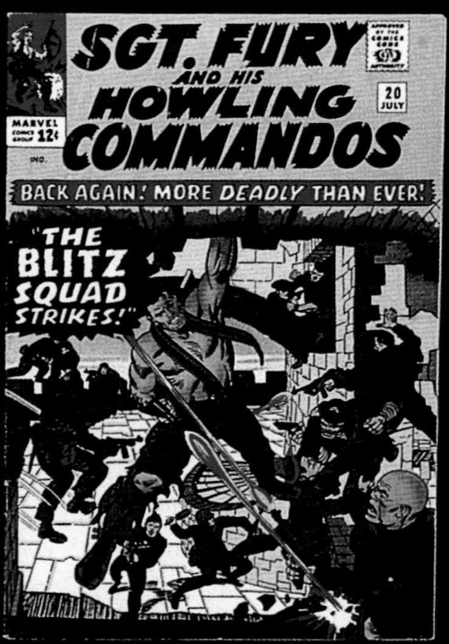
SGT. FURY
AND HIS
HOWLING
COMMANDOS
20 JULY
MARVEL COMICS GROUP 12¢
BACK AGAIN! MORE DEADLY THAN EVER!
"THE BLITZ SQUAD STRIKES!"

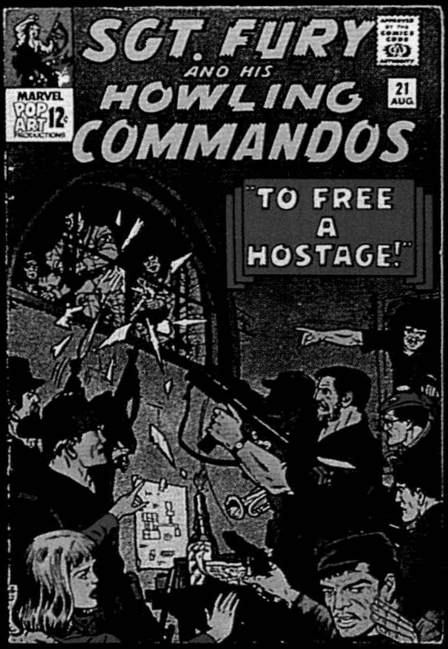
SGT. FURY
AND HIS
HOWLING
COMMANDOS
21 AUG
MARVEL POP ART 12¢
"TO FREE A HOSTAGE!"

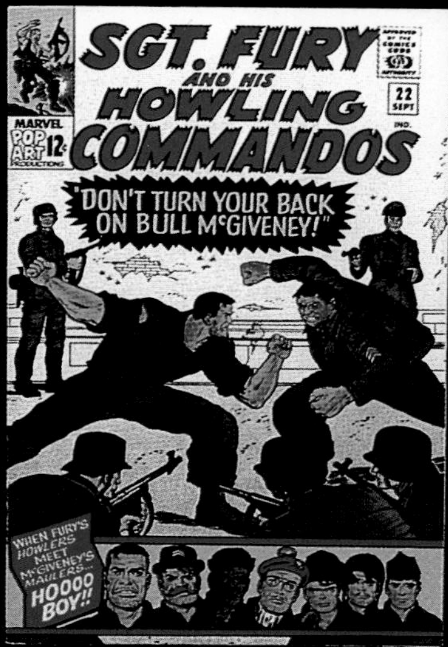
SGT. FURY
AND HIS
HOWLING
COMMANDOS
22 SEPT
MARVEL POP ART 12¢
"DON'T TURN YOUR BACK ON BULL McGIVENEY!"
HOOOO BOY!!

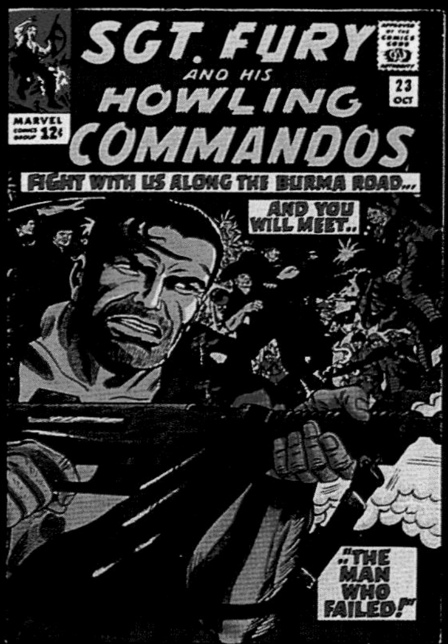
SGT. FURY
AND HIS
HOWLING
COMMANDOS
23 OCT
MARVEL COMICS GROUP 12¢
FIGHT WITH US ALONG THE BURMA ROAD...
AND YOU WILL MEET...
"THE MAN WHO FAILED!"

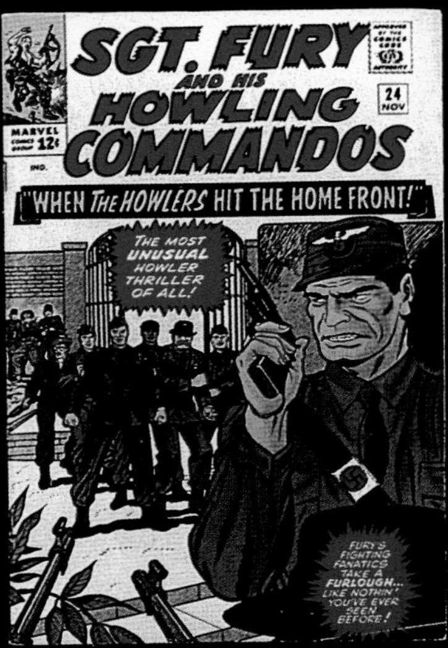
SGT. FURY
AND HIS
HOWLING
COMMANDOS
24 NOV
MARVEL COMICS GROUP 12¢
"WHEN THE HOWLERS HIT THE HOME FRONT!"
THE MOST UNUSUAL HOWLER THRILLER OF ALL!

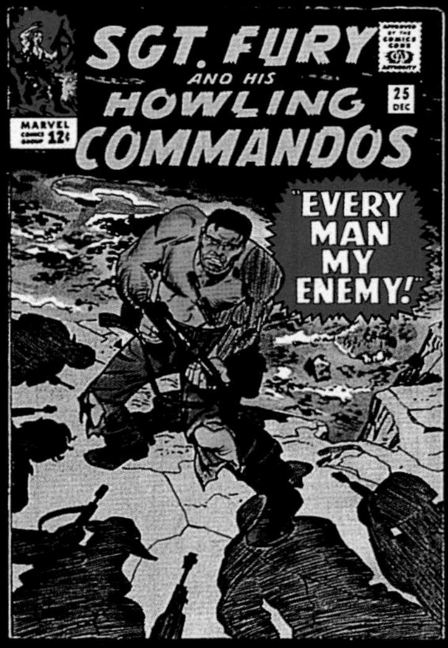
SGT. FURY
AND HIS
HOWLING
COMMANDOS
25 DEC
MARVEL COMICS GROUP 12¢
"EVERY MAN MY ENEMY!"

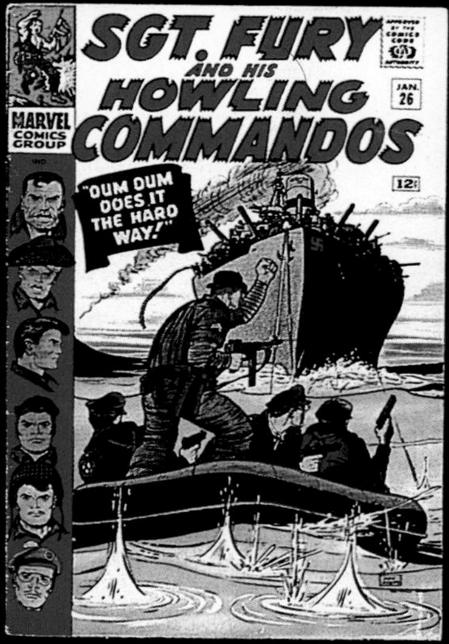
SGT. FURY
AND HIS
HOWLING
COMMANDOS
JAN. 26
MARVEL COMICS GROUP
12¢
"DUM DUM DOES IT THE HARD WAY!"

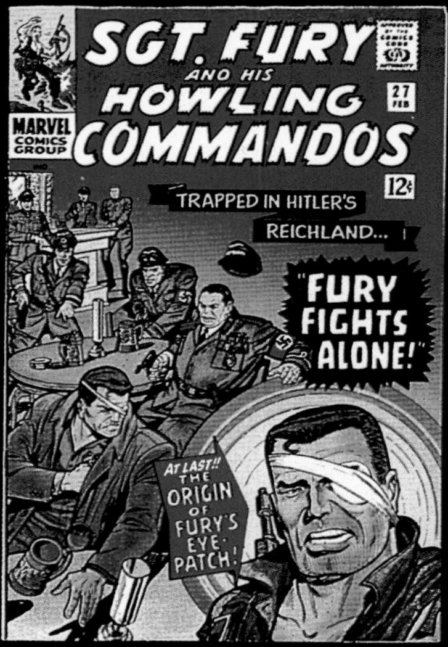
SGT. FURY
AND HIS
HOWLING
COMMANDOS
27 FEB
MARVEL COMICS GROUP
12¢
TRAPPED IN HITLER'S REICHLAND...
"FURY FIGHTS ALONE!"
AT LAST!! THE ORIGIN OF FURY'S EYE-PATCH!

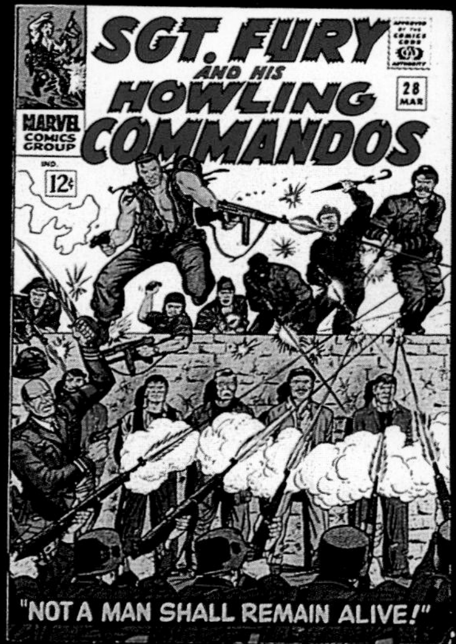
SGT. FURY
AND HIS
HOWLING
COMMANDOS
28 MAR
MARVEL COMICS GROUP
12¢
"NOT A MAN SHALL REMAIN ALIVE!"

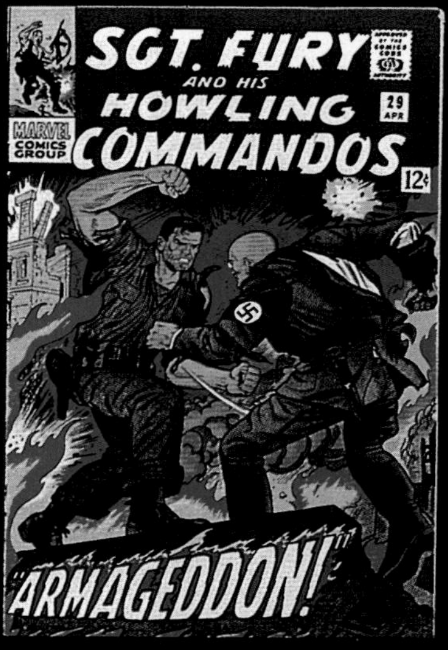
SGT. FURY
AND HIS
HOWLING
COMMANDOS
29 APR
MARVEL COMICS GROUP
12¢
ARMAGEDDON!

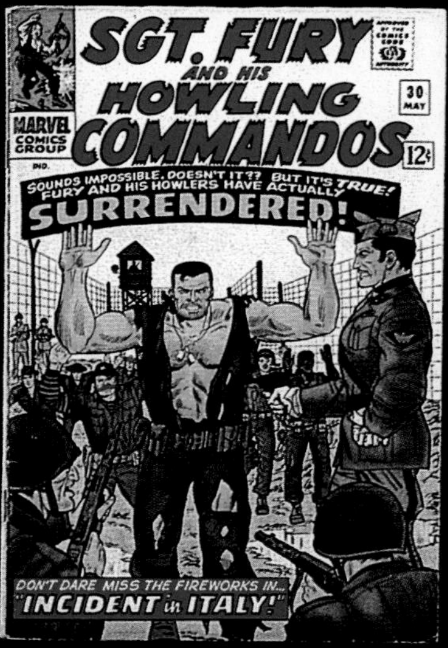
SGT. FURY
AND HIS
HOWLING
COMMANDOS
30 MAY
MARVEL COMICS GROUP
12¢
SOUNDS IMPOSSIBLE, DOESN'T IT? BUT IT'S TRUE! FURY AND HIS HOWLERS HAVE ACTUALLY...
SURRENDERED!
DON'T DARE MISS THE FIREWORKS IN...
"INCIDENT in ITALY!"

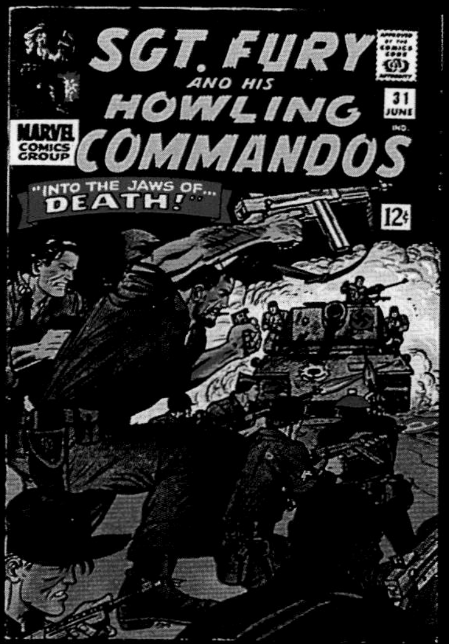
SGT. FURY
AND HIS
HOWLING
COMMANDOS
31 JUNE
MARVEL COMICS GROUP
12¢
"INTO THE JAWS OF... DEATH!"

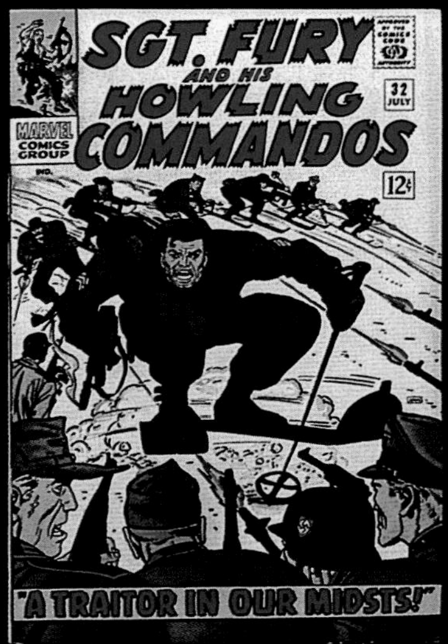
SGT. FURY
AND HIS
HOWLING
COMMANDOS
32 JULY
MARVEL COMICS GROUP
12¢
"A TRAITOR IN OUR MIDSTS!"

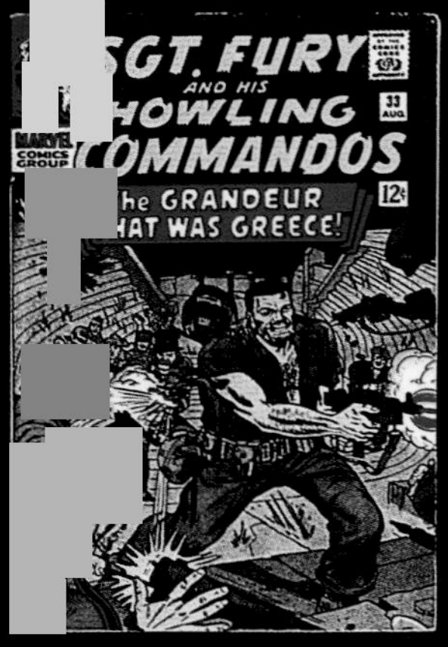
HOWLING
COMMANDOS

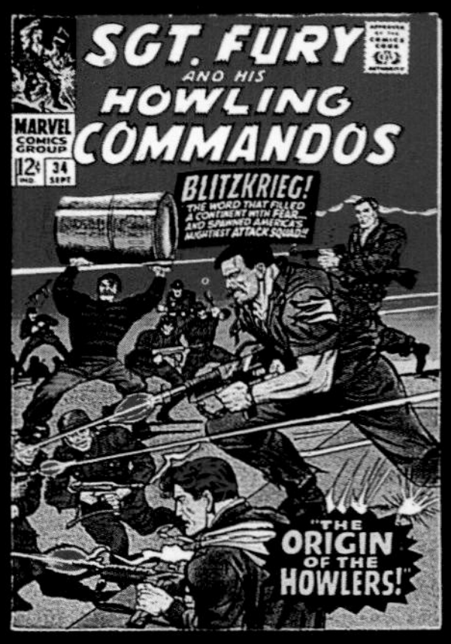
SGT. FURY AND HIS HOWLING COMMANDOS
BLITZKRIEG!
THE ORIGIN OF THE HOWLERS!

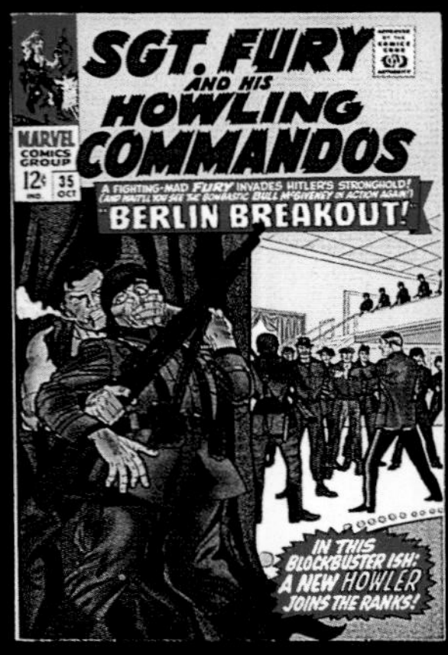
SGT. FURY AND HIS HOWLING COMMANDOS
BERLIN BREAKOUT!
IN THIS BLOCKBUSTER ISH: A NEW HOWLER JOINS THE RANKS!

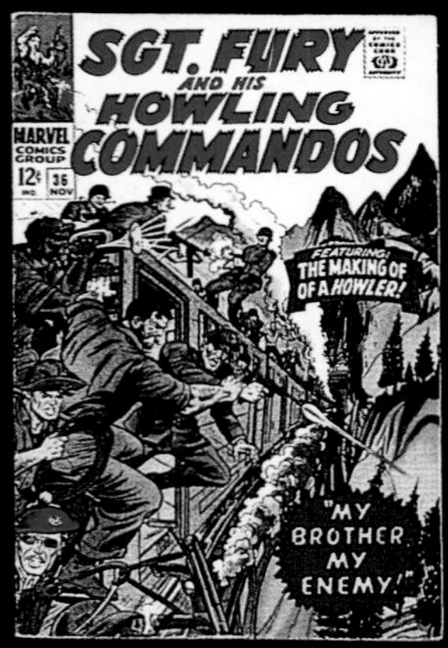
SGT. FURY AND HIS HOWLING COMMANDOS
FEATURING: THE MAKING OF A HOWLER!
MY BROTHER, MY ENEMY!

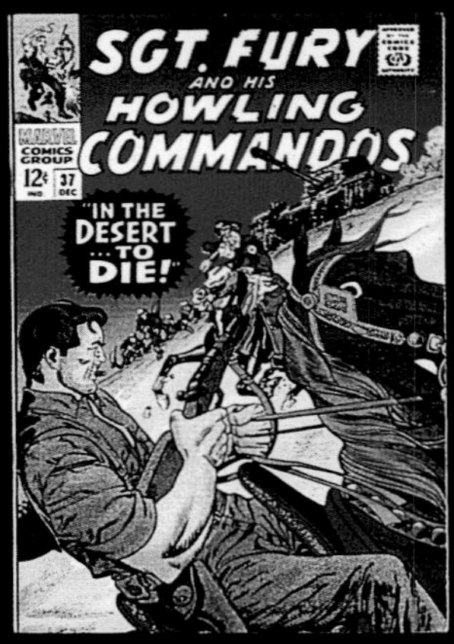
SGT. FURY AND HIS HOWLING COMMANDOS
IN THE DESERT ...TO DIE!

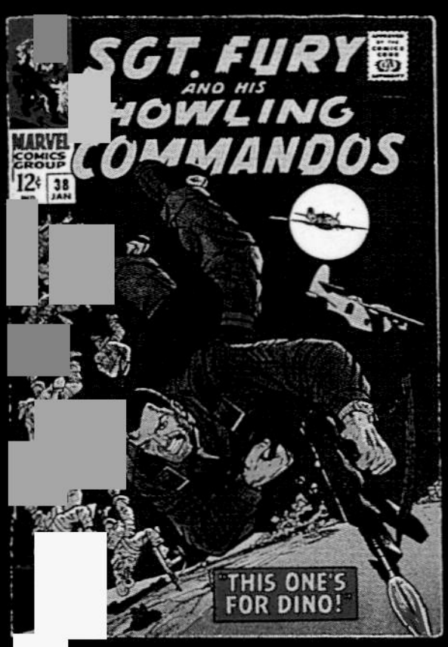
THIS ONE'S FOR DINO!

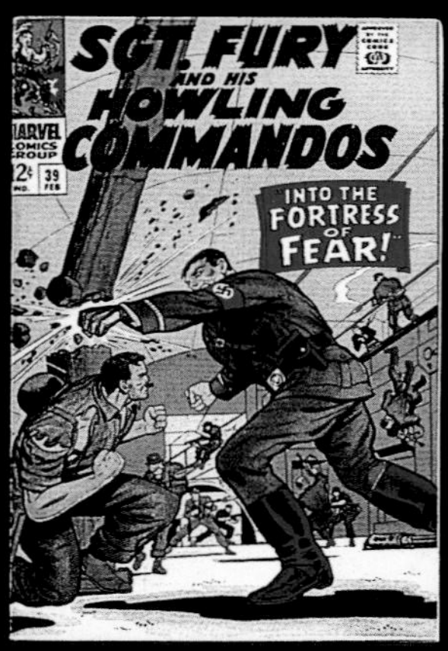
SGT. FURY AND HIS HOWLING COMMANDOS
INTO THE FORTRESS OF FEAR!

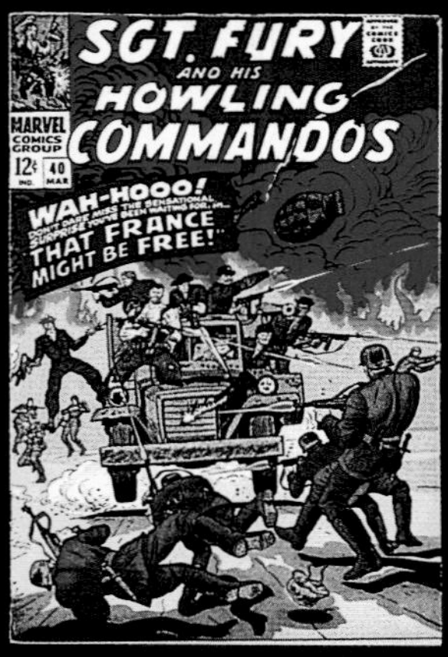
SGT. FURY AND HIS HOWLING COMMANDOS
WAH-HOOO!
THAT FRANCE MIGHT BE FREE!

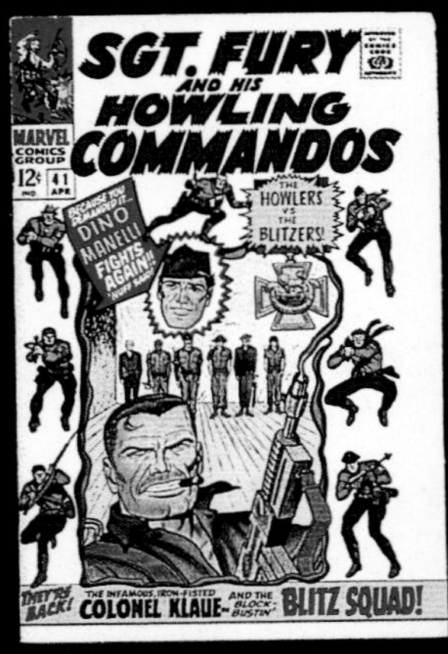
SGT. FURY AND HIS HOWLING COMMANDOS
THE HOWLERS VS. THE BLITZERS!
DINO MANELLI FIGHTS AGAIN!
THEY'RE BACK!
COLONEL KLAUE
BLITZ SQUAD!

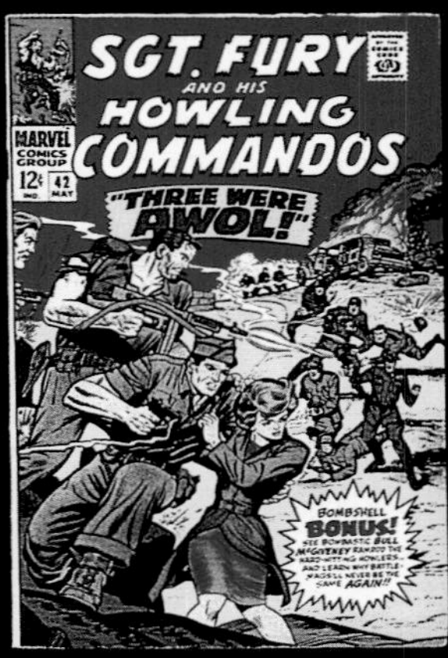
SGT. FURY AND HIS HOWLING COMMANDOS
"THREE WERE AWOL!"
BOMBSHELL BONUS!

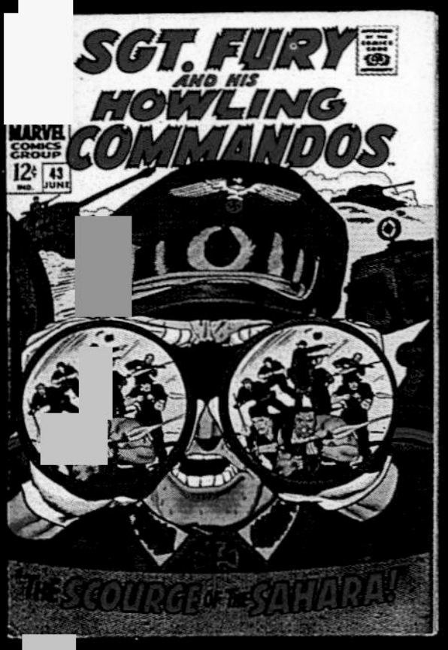
SGT. FURY AND HIS HOWLING COMMANDOS
THE SCOURGE of the SAHARA!

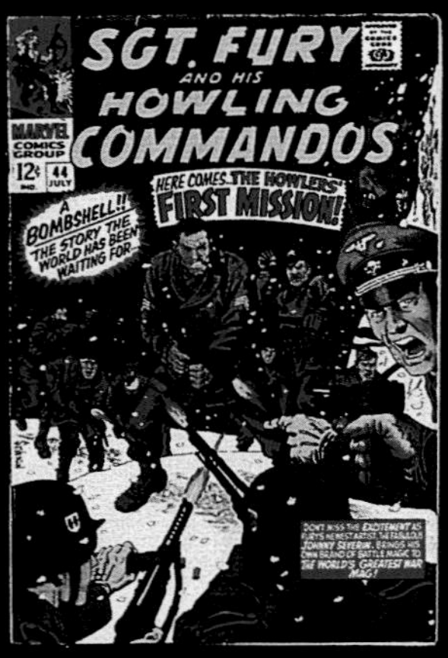
SGT. FURY AND HIS HOWLING COMMANDOS
BOMBSHELL!! THE STORY THE WORLD HAS BEEN WAITING FOR!
HERE COMES...THE HOWLERS' FIRST MISSION!

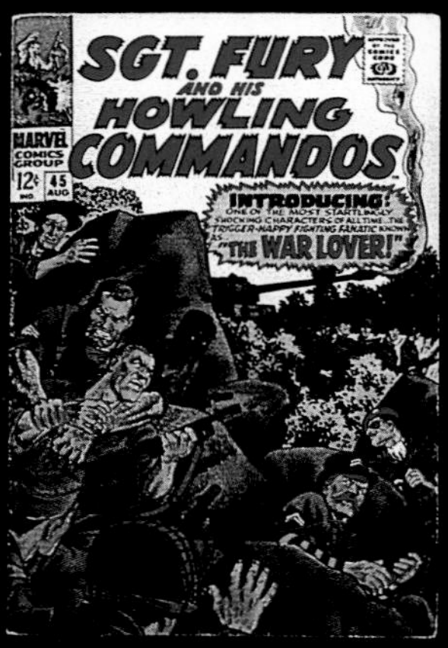
SGT. FURY AND HIS HOWLING COMMANDOS
INTRODUCING!
THE WAR LOVER!

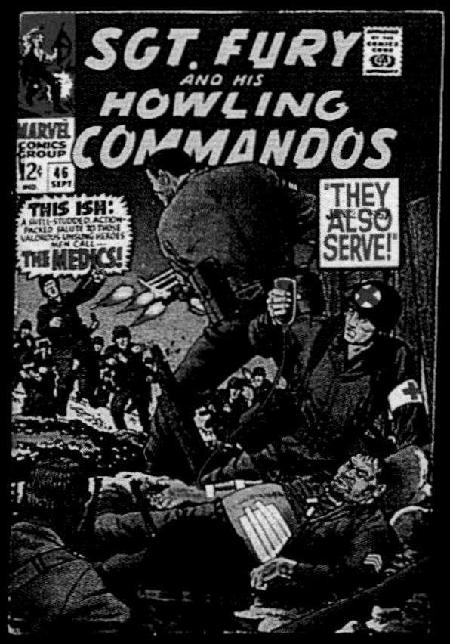
SGT. FURY AND HIS HOWLING COMMANDOS
THIS ISH:
THE MEDICS!
THEY ALSO SERVE!

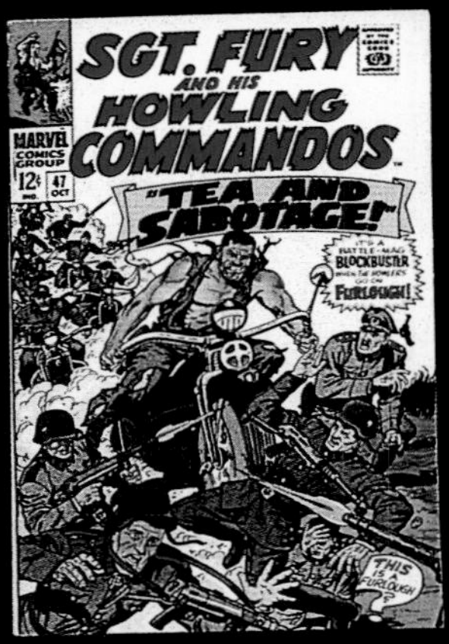
SGT. FURY AND HIS HOWLING COMMANDOS
"TEA AND SABOTAGE!"

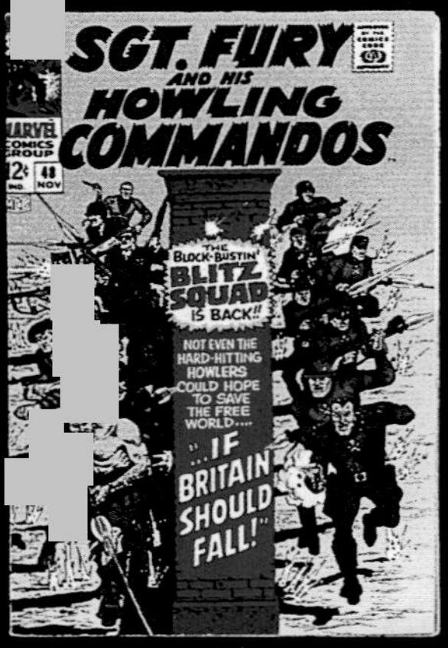
SGT. FURY AND HIS HOWLING COMMANDOS
THE BLOCK-BUSTIN' BLITZ SQUAD IS BACK!!
NOT EVEN THE HARD-HITTING HOWLERS COULD HOPE TO SAVE THE FREE WORLD... IF BRITAIN SHOULD FALL!

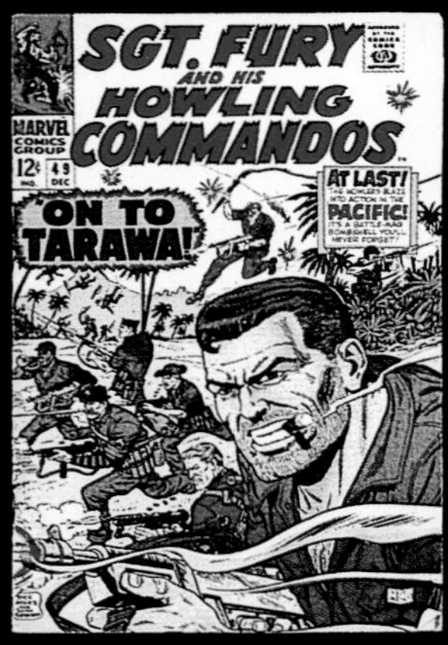
SGT. FURY AND HIS HOWLING COMMANDOS
ON TO TARAWA!
AT LAST!
PACIFIC!

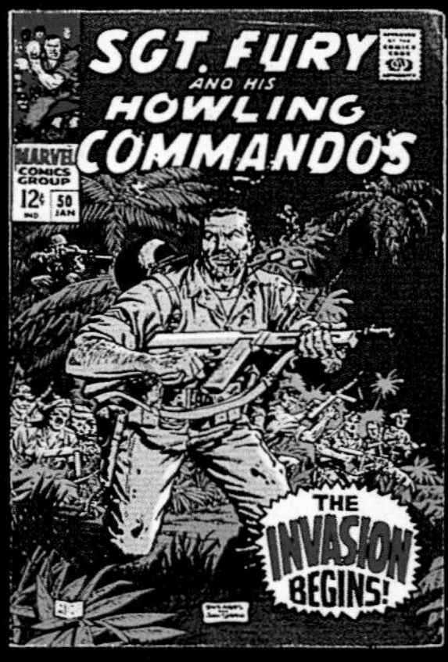
SGT. FURY AND HIS HOWLING COMMANDOS
THE INVASION BEGINS!

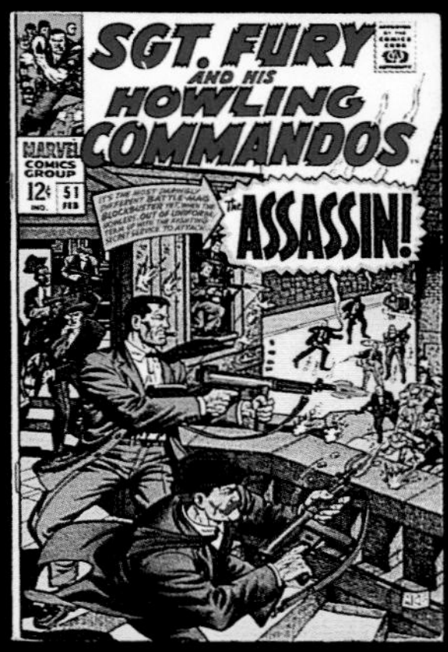
SGT. FURY AND HIS HOWLING COMMANDOS
THE ASSASSIN!

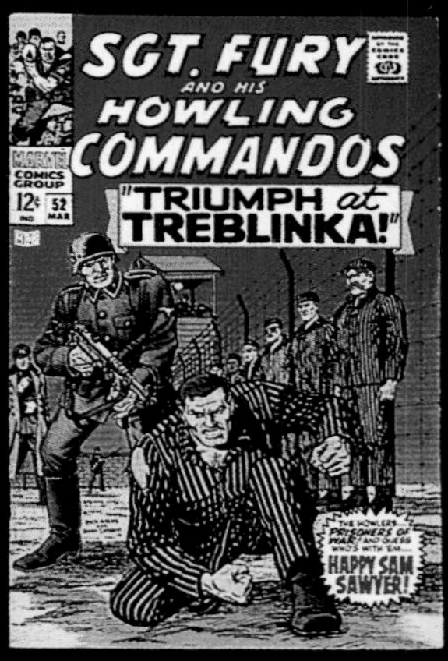
SGT. FURY AND HIS HOWLING COMMANDOS
"TRIUMPH at TREBLINKA!"
HAPPY SAM SAWYER!

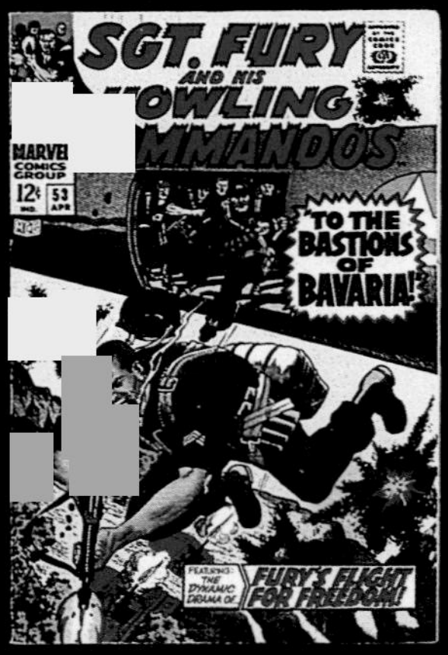
SGT. FURY AND HIS
TO THE BASTIONS OF BAVARIA!
FURY'S FLIGHT FOR FREEDOM!

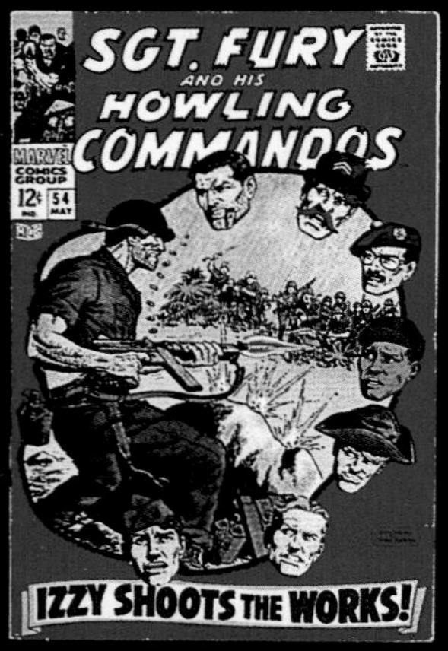
SGT. FURY AND HIS HOWLING COMMANDOS
IZZY SHOOTS THE WORKS!

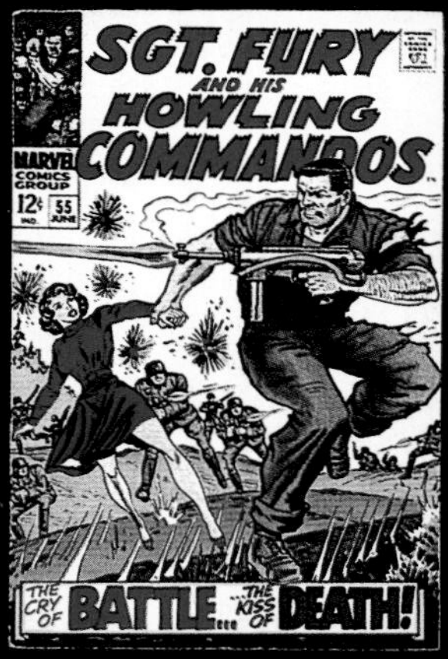
SGT. FURY AND HIS HOWLING COMMANDOS
THE CRY OF BATTLE... THE KISS OF DEATH!

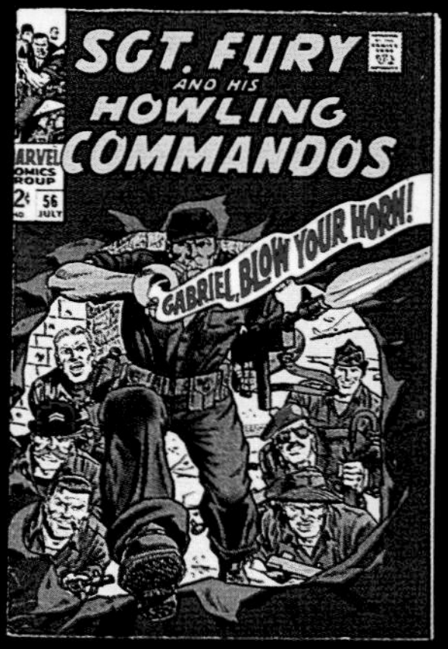
SGT. FURY AND HIS HOWLING COMMANDOS
GABRIEL, BLOW YOUR HORN!

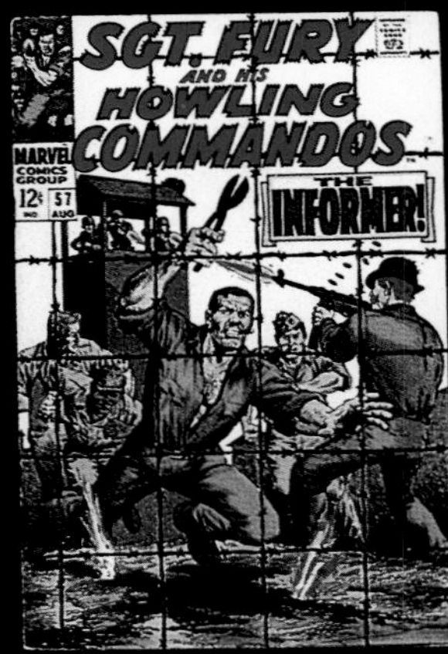
SGT. FURY AND HIS HOWLING COMMANDOS
THE INFORMER!

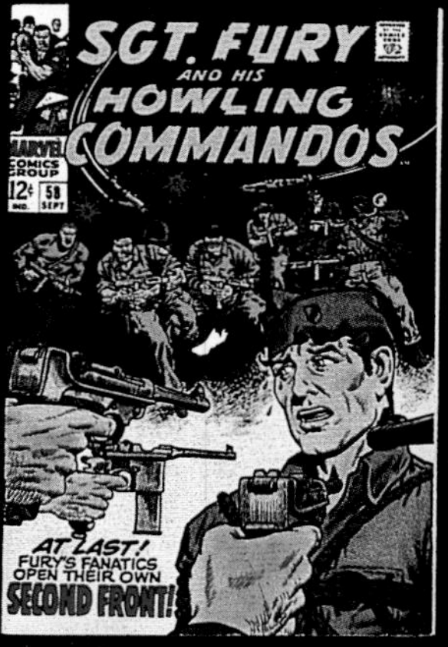
SGT. FURY AND HIS HOWLING COMMANDOS
MARVEL COMICS GROUP
AT LAST! FURY'S FANATICS OPEN THEIR OWN SECOND FRONT!

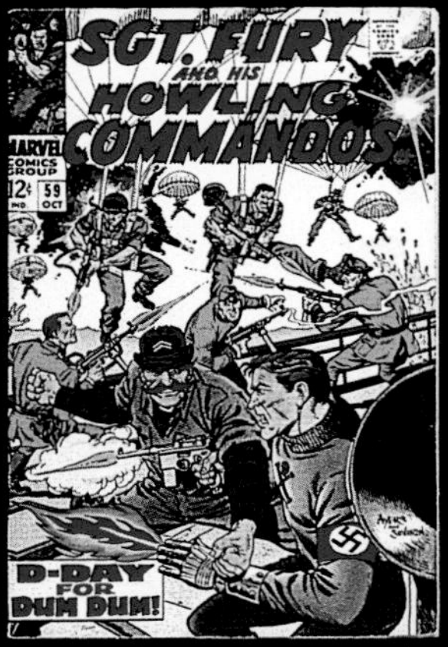
SGT. FURY AND HIS HOWLING COMMANDOS
MARVEL COMICS GROUP
D-DAY FOR DUM DUM!

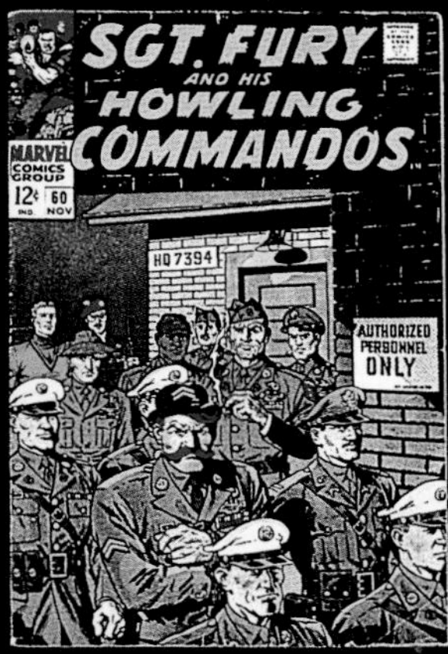
SGT. FURY AND HIS HOWLING COMMANDOS
MARVEL COMICS GROUP
AUTHORIZED PERSONNEL ONLY

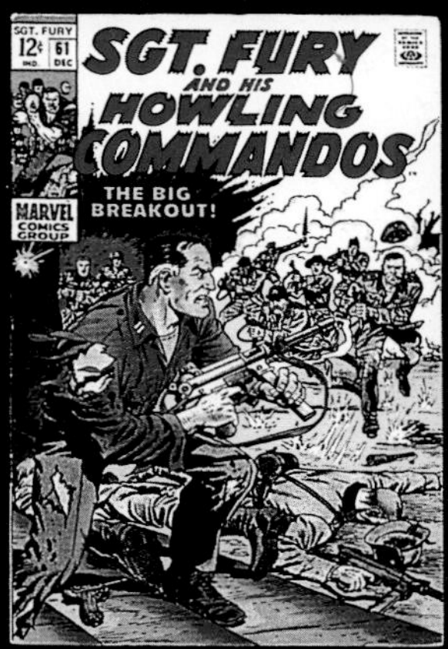
SGT. FURY AND HIS HOWLING COMMANDOS
THE BIG BREAKOUT!
MARVEL COMICS GROUP

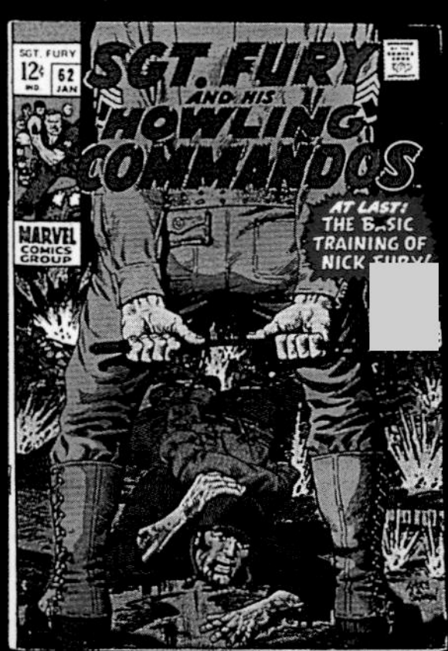
SGT. FURY AND HIS HOWLING COMMANDOS
MARVEL COMICS GROUP

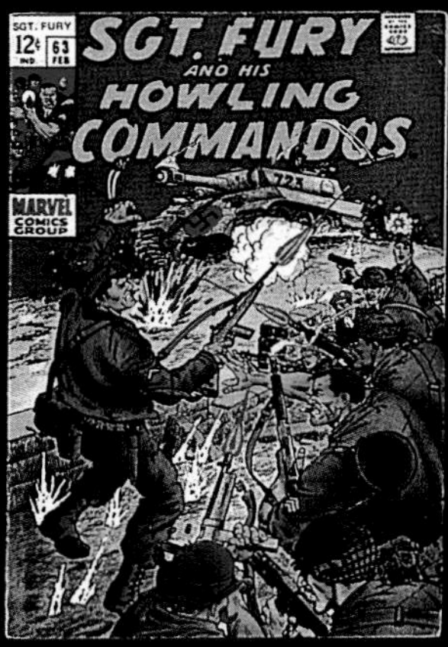
SGT. FURY AND HIS HOWLING COMMANDOS
MARVEL COMICS GROUP

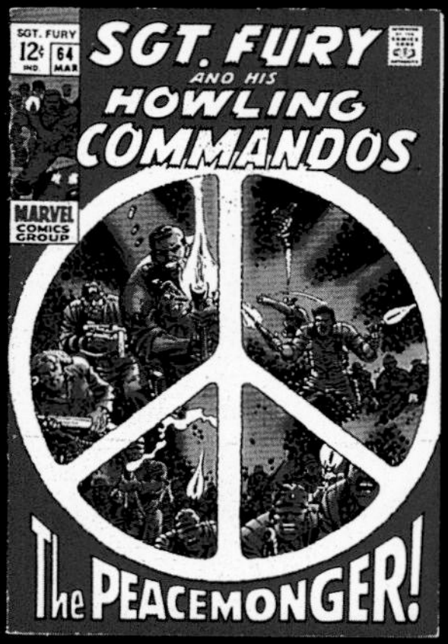
SGT. FURY AND HIS HOWLING COMMANDOS
MARVEL COMICS GROUP
The PEACEMONGER!

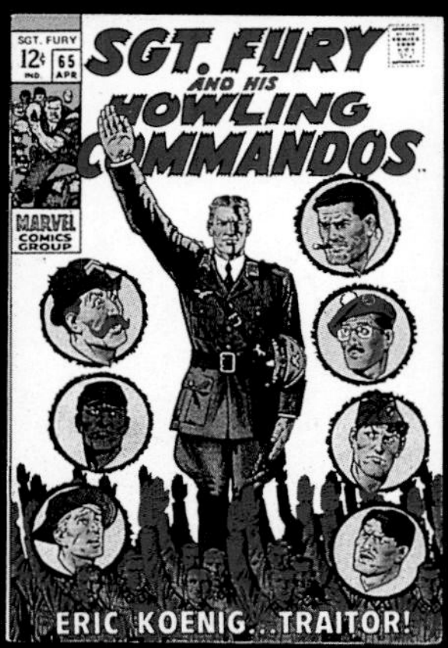
SGT. FURY AND HIS HOWLING COMMANDOS
MARVEL COMICS GROUP
ERIC KOENIG...TRAITOR!

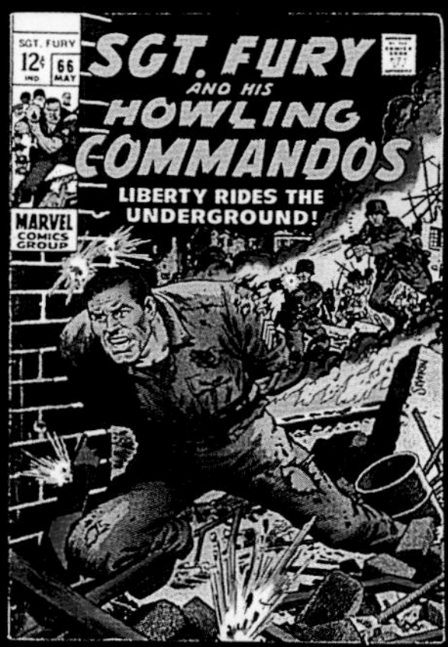
SGT. FURY AND HIS HOWLING COMMANDOS
MARVEL COMICS GROUP
LIBERTY RIDES THE UNDERGROUND!

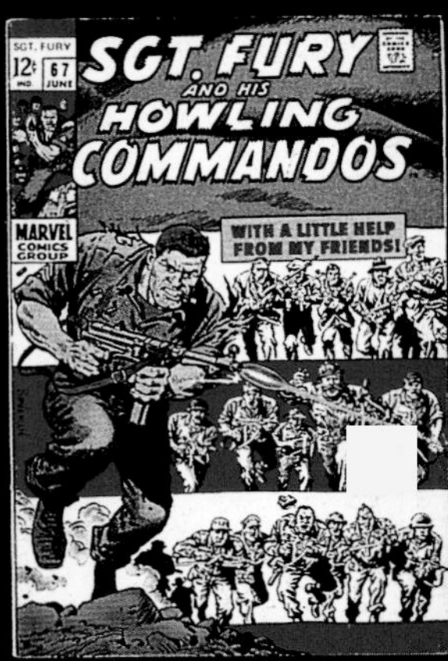
SGT. FURY AND HIS HOWLING COMMANDOS
MARVEL COMICS GROUP
WITH A LITTLE HELP FROM MY FRIENDS!

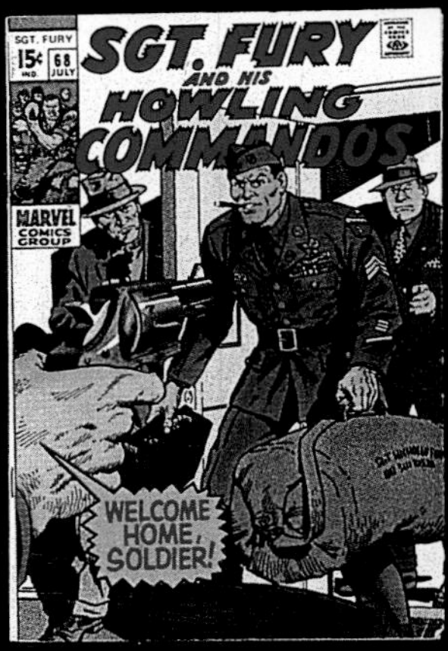
SGT. FURY AND HIS HOWLING COMMANDOS
MARVEL COMICS GROUP
WELCOME HOME, SOLDIER!

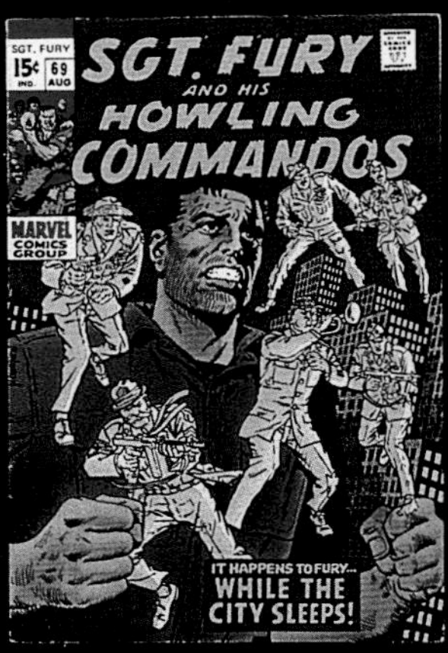
SGT. FURY AND HIS HOWLING COMMANDOS
MARVEL COMICS GROUP
IT HAPPENS TO FURY... WHILE THE CITY SLEEPS!

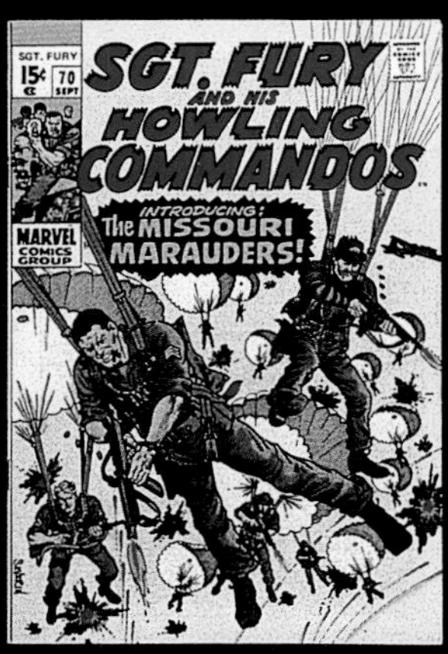
SGT. FURY AND HIS HOWLING COMMANDOS
MARVEL COMICS GROUP
INTRODUCING: The MISSOURI MARAUDERS!

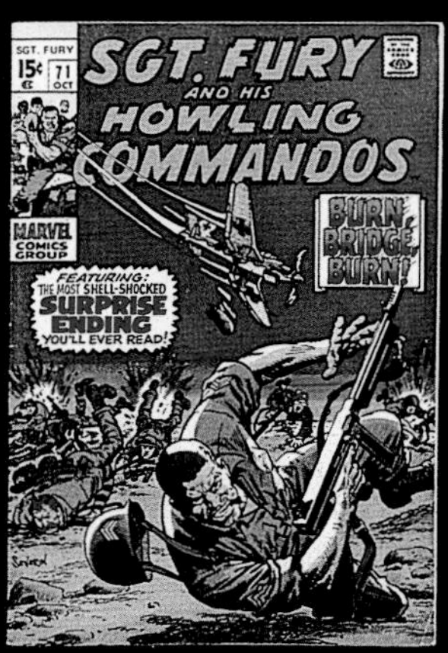
SGT. FURY AND HIS HOWLING COMMANDOS
MARVEL COMICS GROUP
BURN, BRIDGE, BURN!
FEATURING: THE MOST SHELL-SHOCKED SURPRISE ENDING YOU'LL EVER READ!

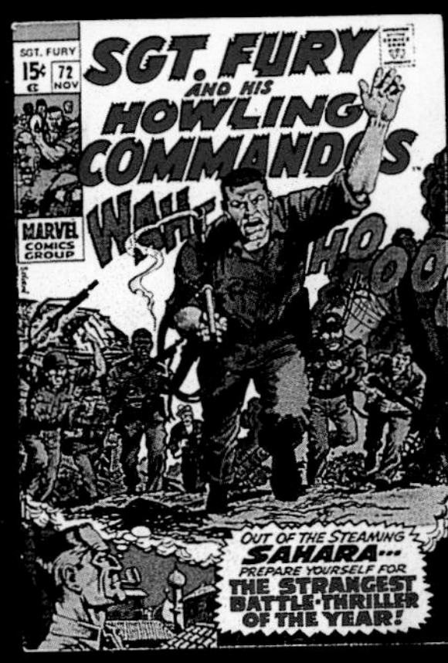
SGT. FURY AND HIS HOWLING COMMANDOS
MARVEL COMICS GROUP
OUT OF THE STEAMING SAHARA-- PREPARE YOURSELF FOR THE STRANGEST BATTLE-THRILLER OF THE YEAR!

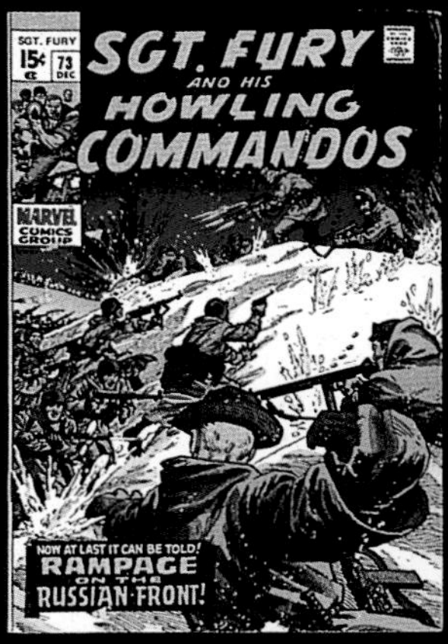
SGT. FURY AND HIS HOWLING COMMANDOS
MARVEL COMICS GROUP
NOW AT LAST IT CAN BE TOLD! RAMPAGE ON THE RUSSIAN FRONT!

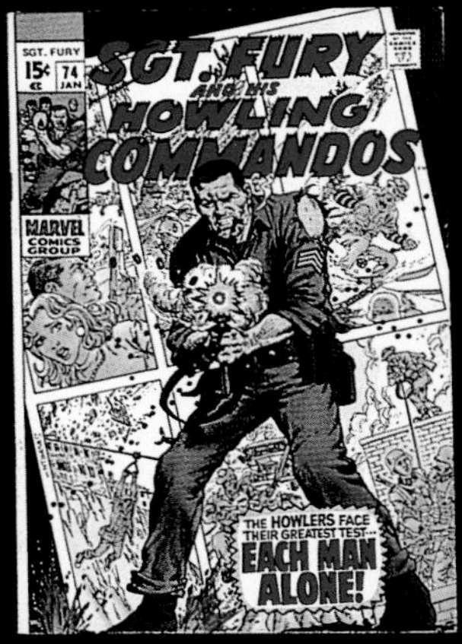
SGT. FURY AND HIS HOWLING COMMANDOS
MARVEL COMICS GROUP
THE HOWLERS FACE THEIR GREATEST TEST-- EACH MAN ALONE!

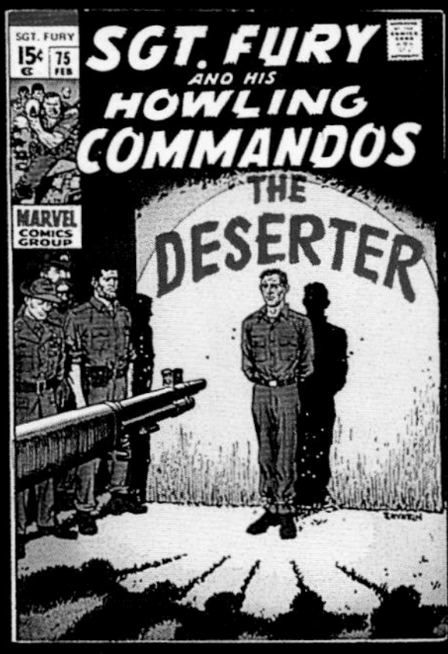
SGT. FURY AND HIS HOWLING COMMANDOS
MARVEL COMICS GROUP
THE DESERTER

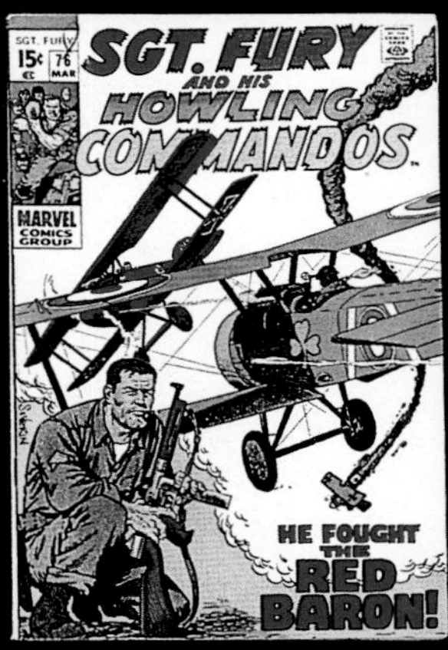
SGT. FURY AND HIS HOWLING COMMANDOS
MARVEL COMICS GROUP
HE FOUGHT THE RED BARON!

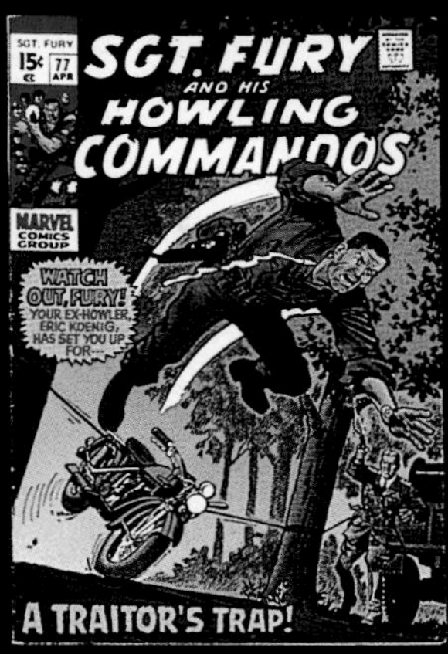
SGT. FURY AND HIS HOWLING COMMANDOS
MARVEL COMICS GROUP
A TRAITOR'S TRAP!

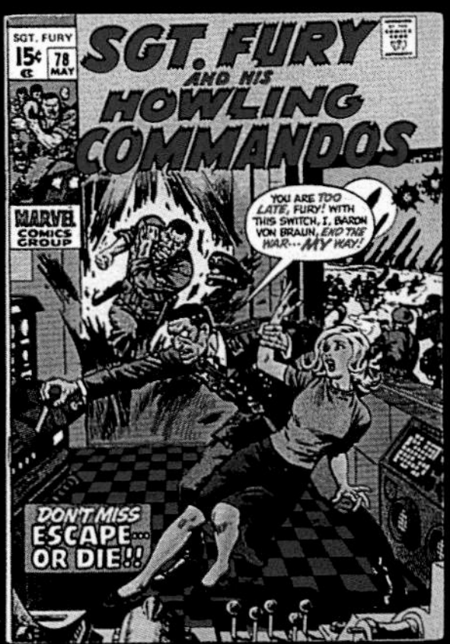
SGT. FURY AND HIS HOWLING COMMANDOS
MARVEL COMICS GROUP
DON'T MISS ESCAPE-- OR DIE!!

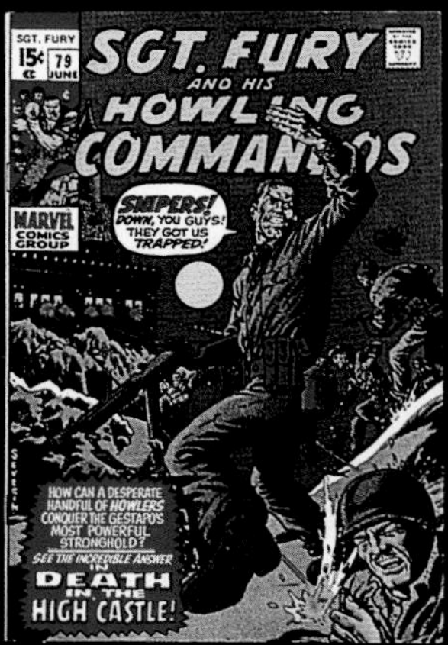
SGT. FURY AND HIS HOWLING COMMANDOS
MARVEL COMICS GROUP
SNIPERS! DOWN, YOU GUYS! THEY GOT US TRAPPED!
DEATH IN THE HIGH CASTLE!

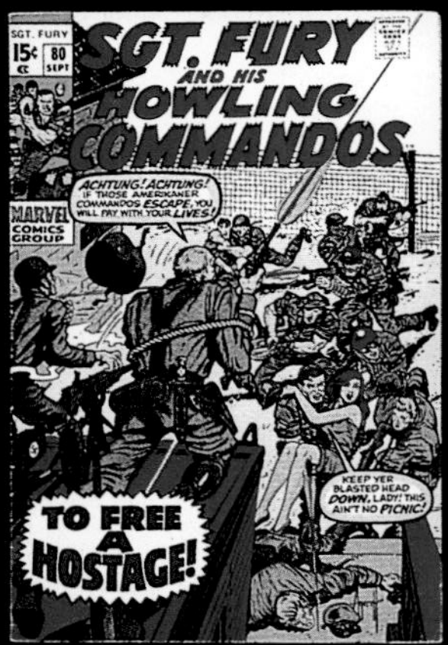
SGT. FURY AND HIS HOWLING COMMANDOS
MARVEL COMICS GROUP
TO FREE A HOSTAGE!

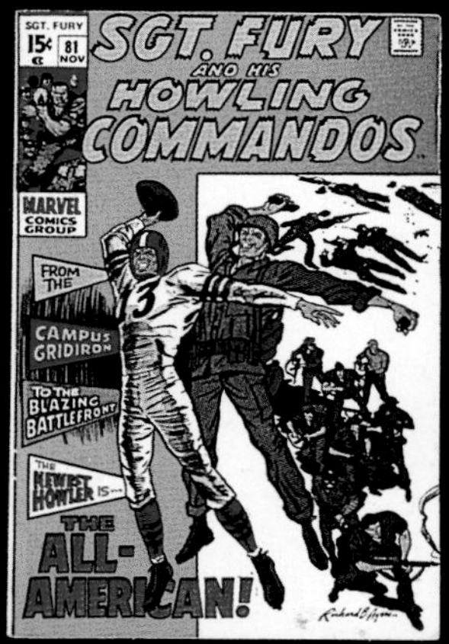
SGT. FURY AND HIS HOWLING COMMANDOS
MARVEL COMICS GROUP
FROM THE CAMPUS GRIDIRON TO THE BLAZING BATTLEFRONT!
THE ALL-AMERICAN!

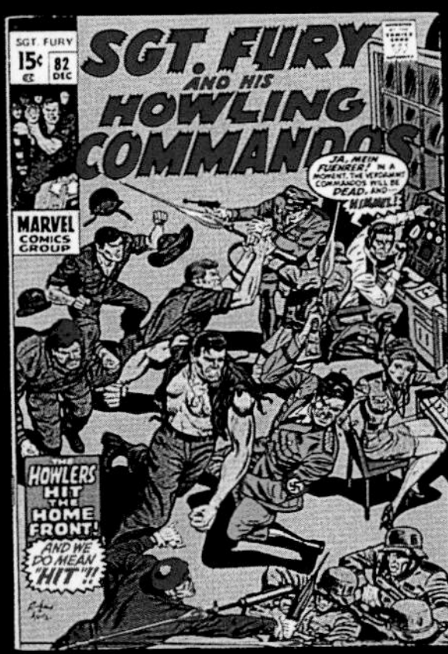
SGT. FURY AND HIS HOWLING COMMANDOS
MARVEL COMICS GROUP
HOWLERS HIT THE HOME FRONT!

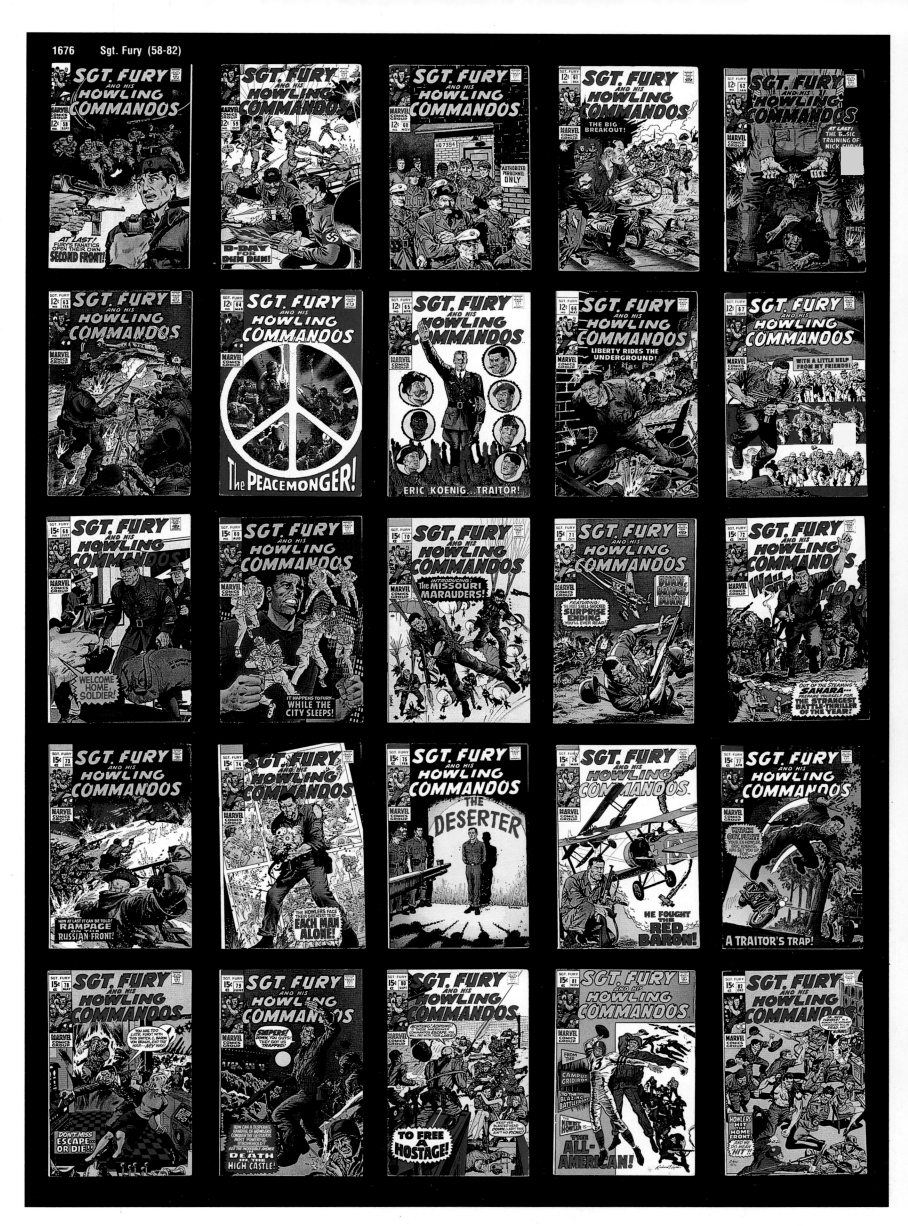

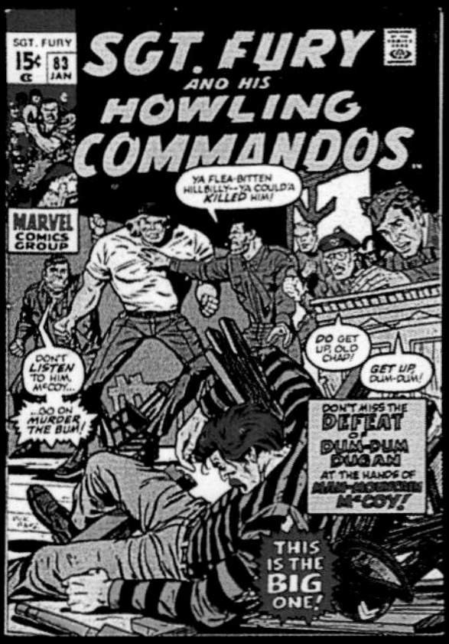
SGT. FURY
AND HIS HOWLING COMMANDOS
YA FLEA-BITTEN HILLBILLY—YA COULDA KILLED HIM!
THIS IS THE BIG ONE!

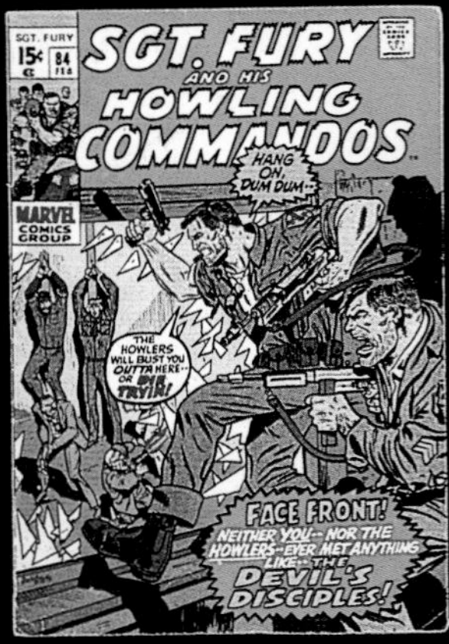
SGT. FURY
AND HIS HOWLING COMMANDOS
FACE FRONT!
DEVIL'S DISCIPLES!

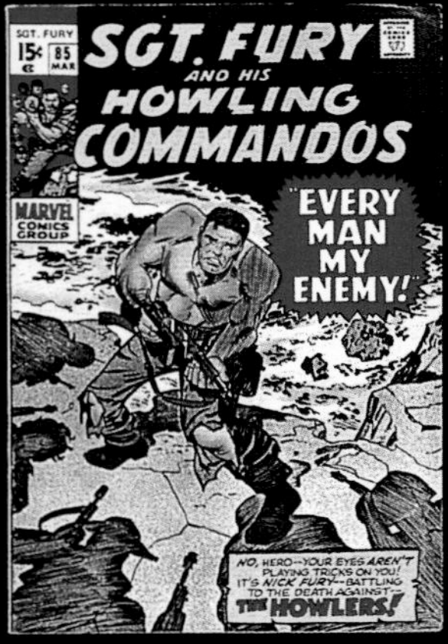
SGT. FURY
AND HIS HOWLING COMMANDOS
EVERY MAN MY ENEMY!
THE HOWLERS!

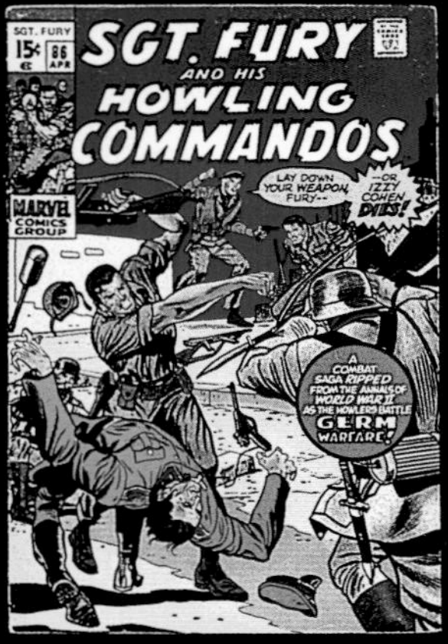
SGT. FURY
AND HIS HOWLING COMMANDOS
GERM WARFARE!

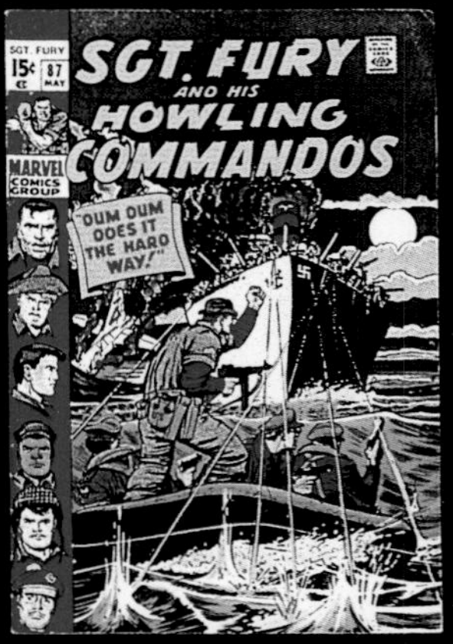
SGT. FURY
AND HIS HOWLING COMMANDOS
DUM DUM DOES IT THE HARD WAY!

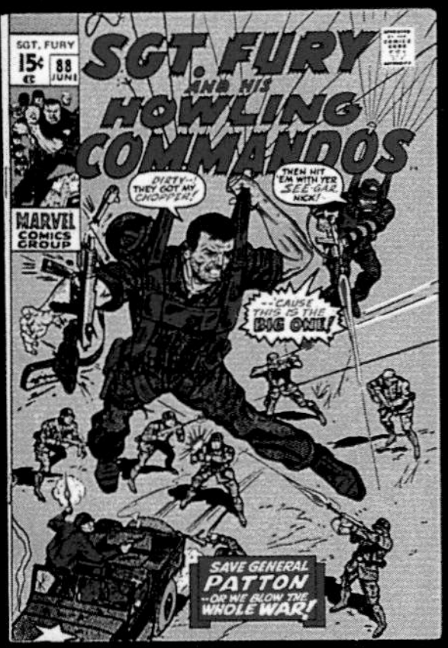
SGT. FURY
AND HIS HOWLING COMMANDOS
SAVE GENERAL PATTON OR LOSE THE WHOLE WAR!

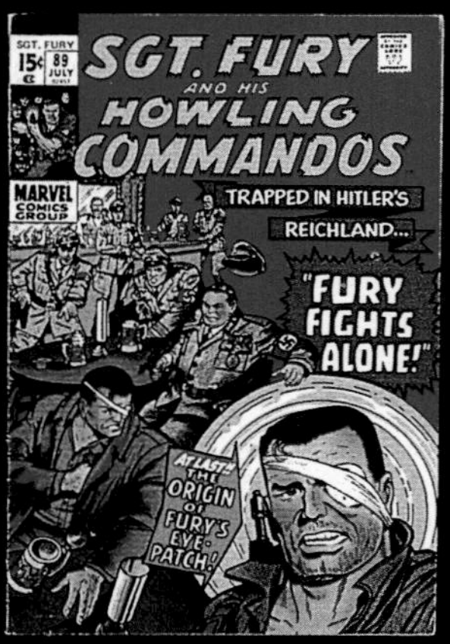
SGT. FURY
AND HIS HOWLING COMMANDOS
TRAPPED IN HITLER'S REICHLAND...
"FURY FIGHTS ALONE!"
AT LAST! THE ORIGIN OF FURY'S EYE PATCH

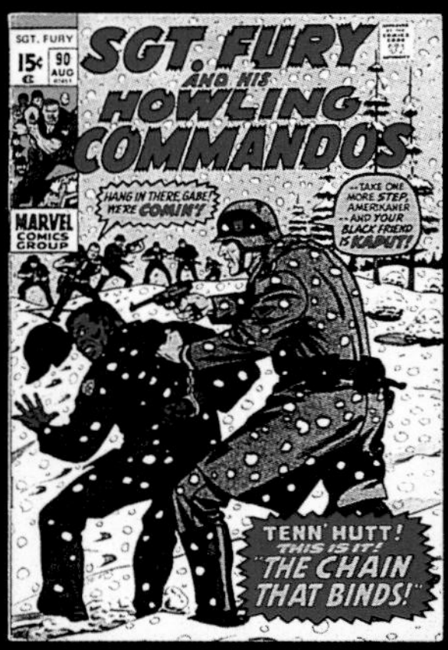
SGT. FURY
AND HIS HOWLING COMMANDOS
TENN' HUTT! THIS IS IT! THE CHAIN THAT BINDS!

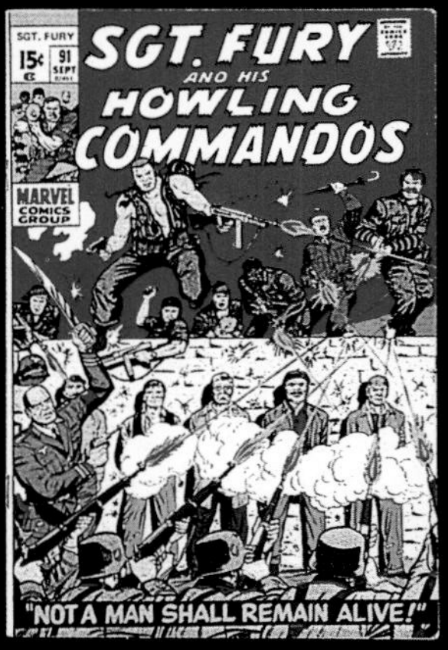
SGT. FURY
AND HIS HOWLING COMMANDOS
"NOT A MAN SHALL REMAIN ALIVE!"

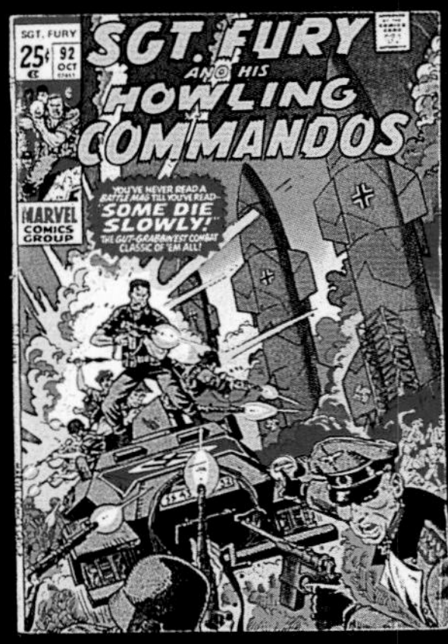
SGT. FURY
AND HIS HOWLING COMMANDOS
SOME DIE SLOWLY!

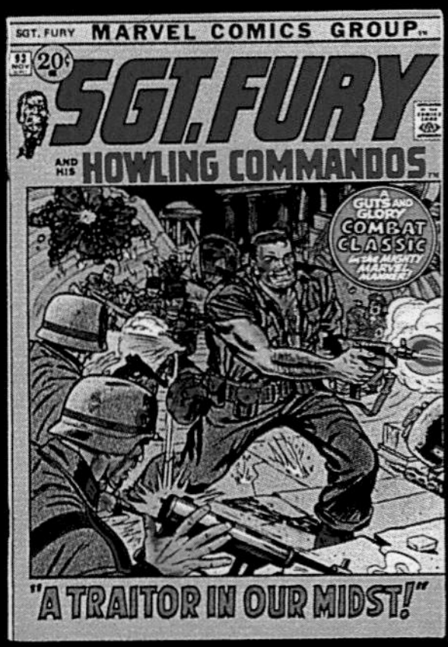
MARVEL COMICS GROUP
SGT. FURY
AND HIS HOWLING COMMANDOS
"A TRAITOR IN OUR MIDST!"

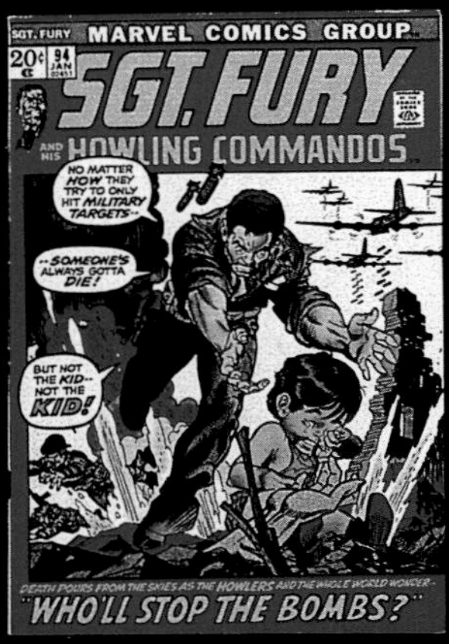
MARVEL COMICS GROUP
SGT. FURY
AND HIS HOWLING COMMANDOS
"WHO'LL STOP THE BOMBS?"

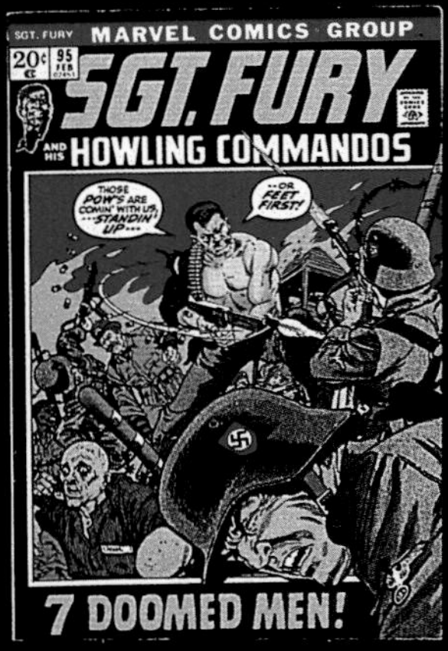
MARVEL COMICS GROUP
SGT. FURY
AND HIS HOWLING COMMANDOS
7 DOOMED MEN!

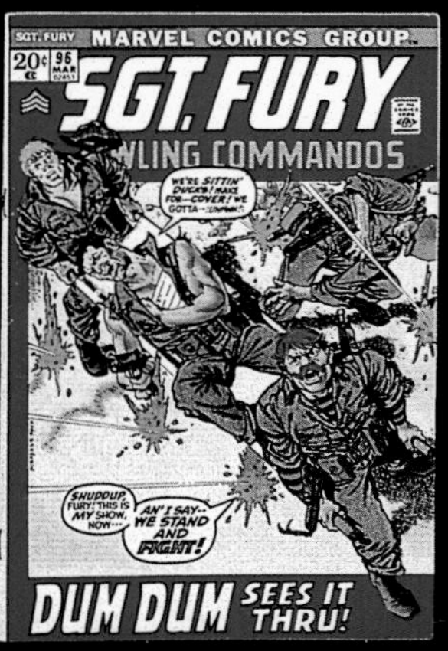
MARVEL COMICS GROUP
SGT. FURY
AND HIS HOWLING COMMANDOS
DUM DUM SEES IT THRU!

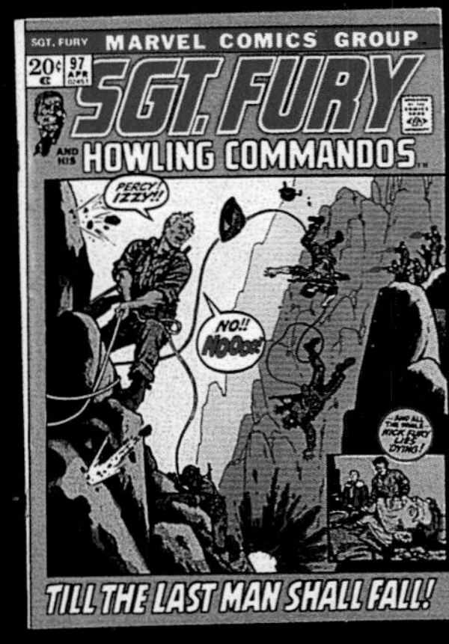
MARVEL COMICS GROUP
SGT. FURY
AND HIS HOWLING COMMANDOS
TILL THE LAST MAN SHALL FALL!

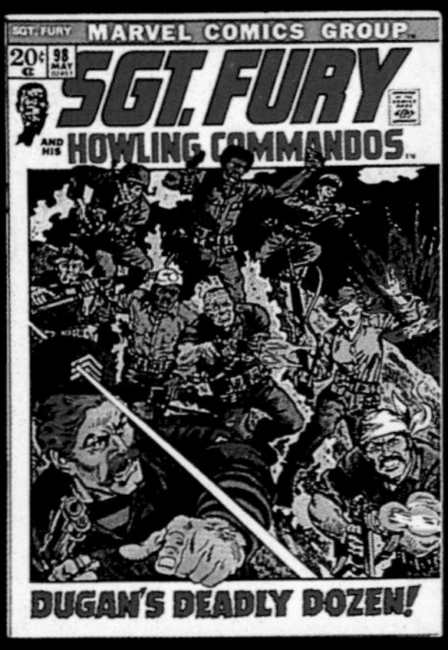
MARVEL COMICS GROUP
SGT. FURY
AND HIS HOWLING COMMANDOS
DUGAN'S DEADLY DOZEN!

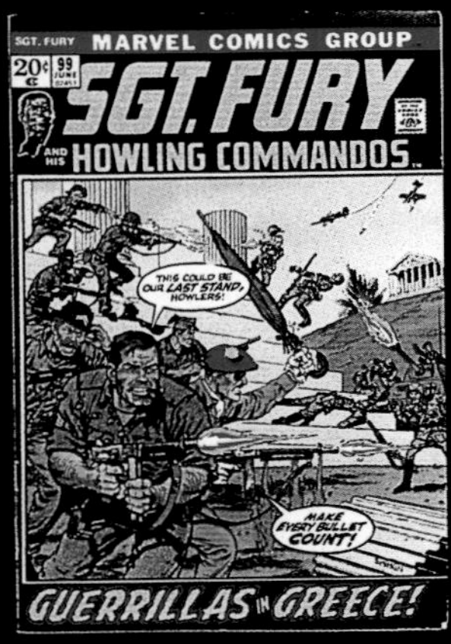
MARVEL COMICS GROUP
SGT. FURY
AND HIS HOWLING COMMANDOS
GUERRILLAS IN GREECE!

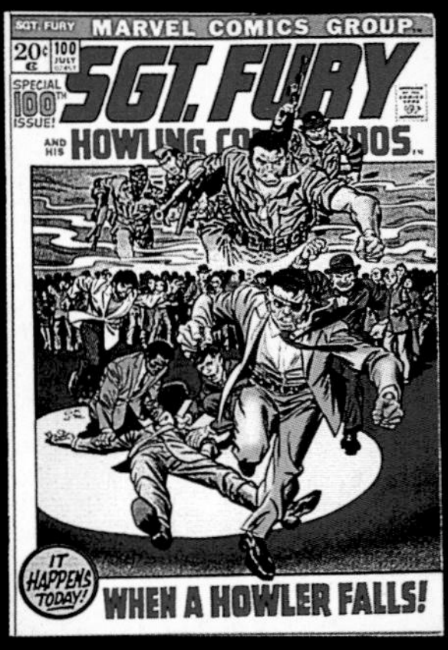
MARVEL COMICS GROUP
SPECIAL 100th ISSUE!
SGT. FURY
AND HIS HOWLING COMMANDOS
IT HAPPENS TODAY!
WHEN A HOWLER FALLS!

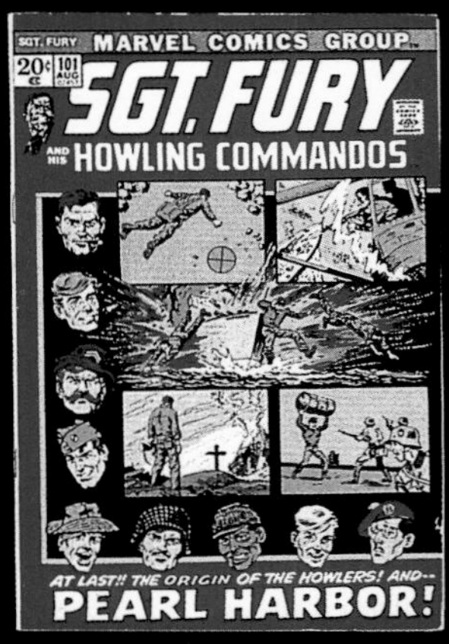
MARVEL COMICS GROUP
SGT. FURY
AND HIS HOWLING COMMANDOS
AT LAST!! THE ORIGIN OF THE HOWLERS! AND—
PEARL HARBOR!

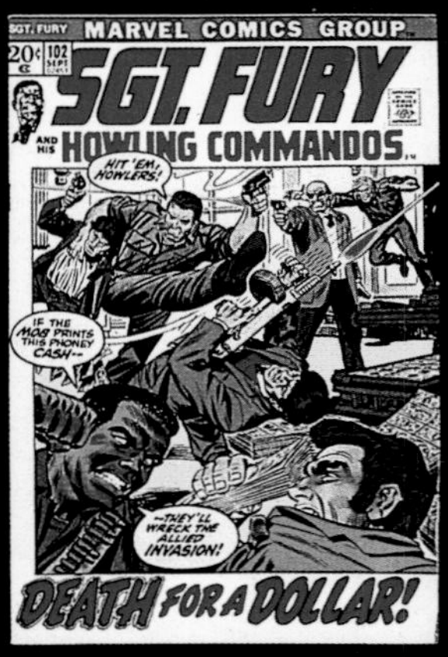
MARVEL COMICS GROUP
SGT. FURY
AND HIS HOWLING COMMANDOS
HIT 'EM, HOWLERS!
DEATH FOR A DOLLAR!

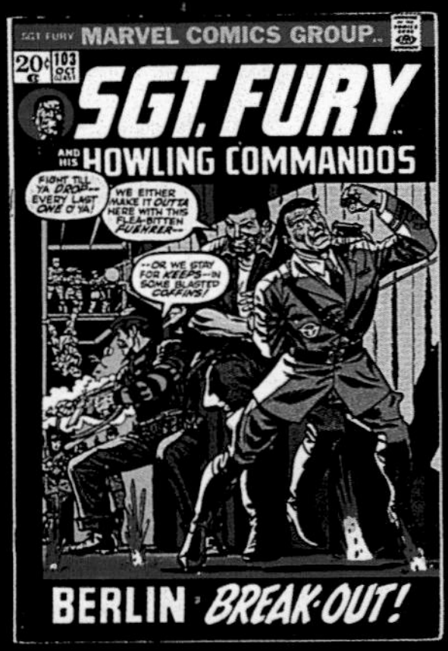
MARVEL COMICS GROUP
SGT. FURY
AND HIS HOWLING COMMANDOS
BERLIN BREAK-OUT!

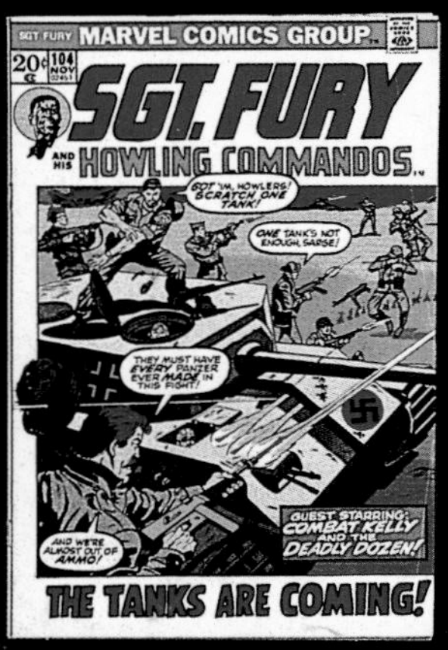
MARVEL COMICS GROUP
SGT. FURY
AND HIS HOWLING COMMANDOS
GUEST STARRING: COMBAT KELLY AND THE DEADLY DOZEN!
THE TANKS ARE COMING!

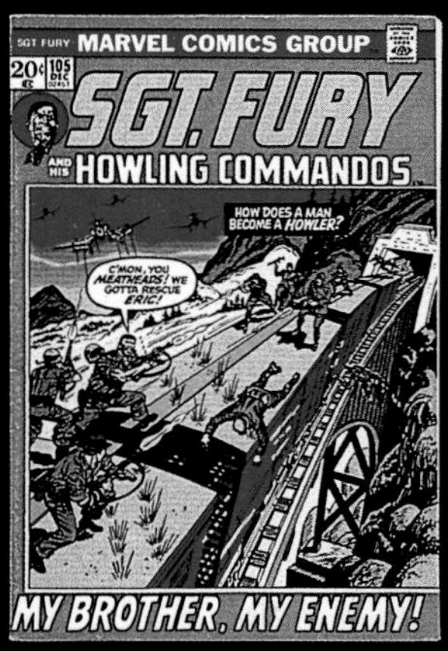
MARVEL COMICS GROUP
SGT. FURY
AND HIS HOWLING COMMANDOS
HOW DOES A MAN BECOME A HOWLER?
MY BROTHER, MY ENEMY!

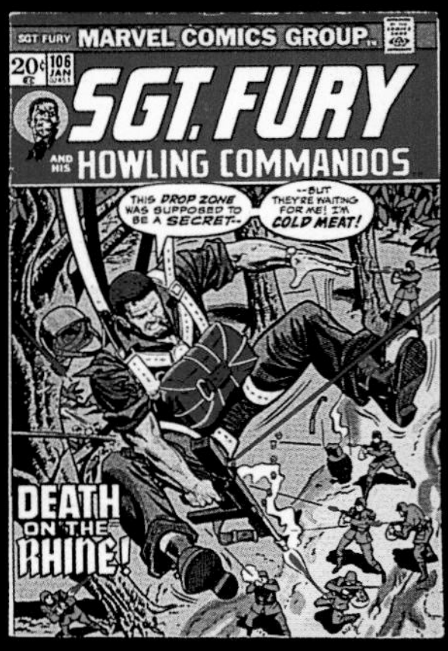
MARVEL COMICS GROUP
SGT. FURY
AND HIS HOWLING COMMANDOS
DEATH ON THE RHINE!

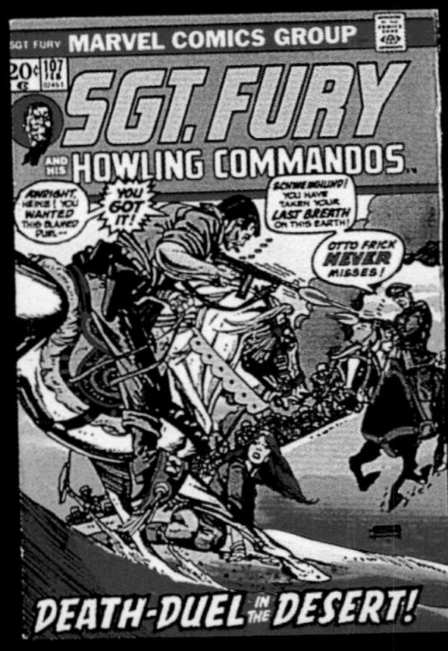
MARVEL COMICS GROUP
SGT. FURY
AND HIS HOWLING COMMANDOS
DEATH-DUEL IN THE DESERT!

1676 Sgt. Fury (108-132, AN. 1-7)

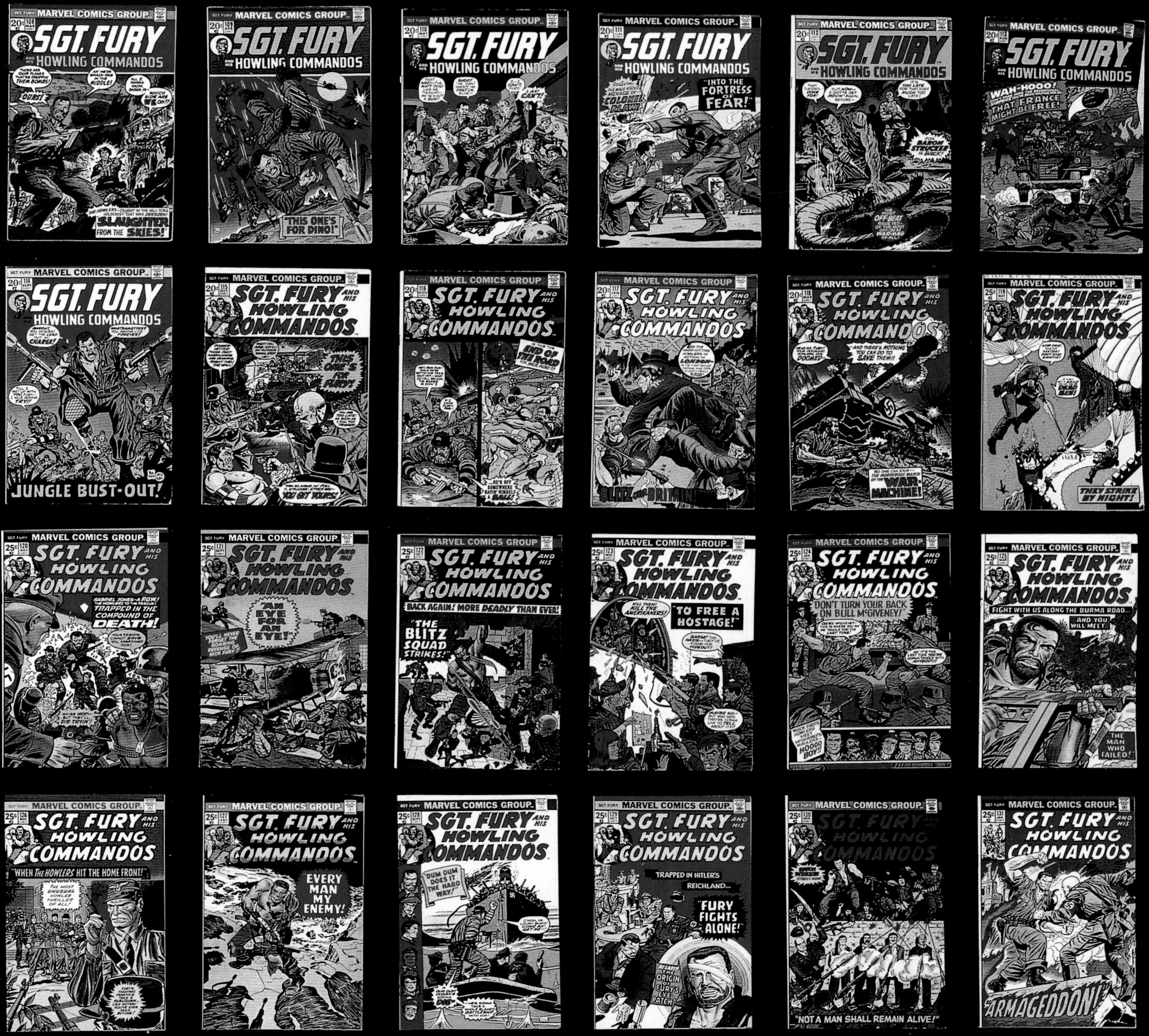
SLAUGHTER FROM THE SKIES!
"THIS ONE'S FOR DINO!"
INTO THE FORTRESS OF FEAR!
JUNGLE BUST-OUT!
BLITZ OVER BRITAIN
THEY STRIKE BY NIGHT!
BACK AGAIN! MORE DEADLY THAN EVER!
"TO FREE A HOSTAGE!"
DON'T TURN YOUR BACK ON BULL McGIVENEY!
FIGHT WITH US ALONG THE BURMA ROAD...
"WHEN THE HOWLERS HIT THE HOME FRONT!"
EVERY MAN MY ENEMY!
THIS WAS... D-DAY!
FURY FIGHTS ALONE!
"NOT A MAN SHALL REMAIN ALIVE!"
ARMAGEDDON!

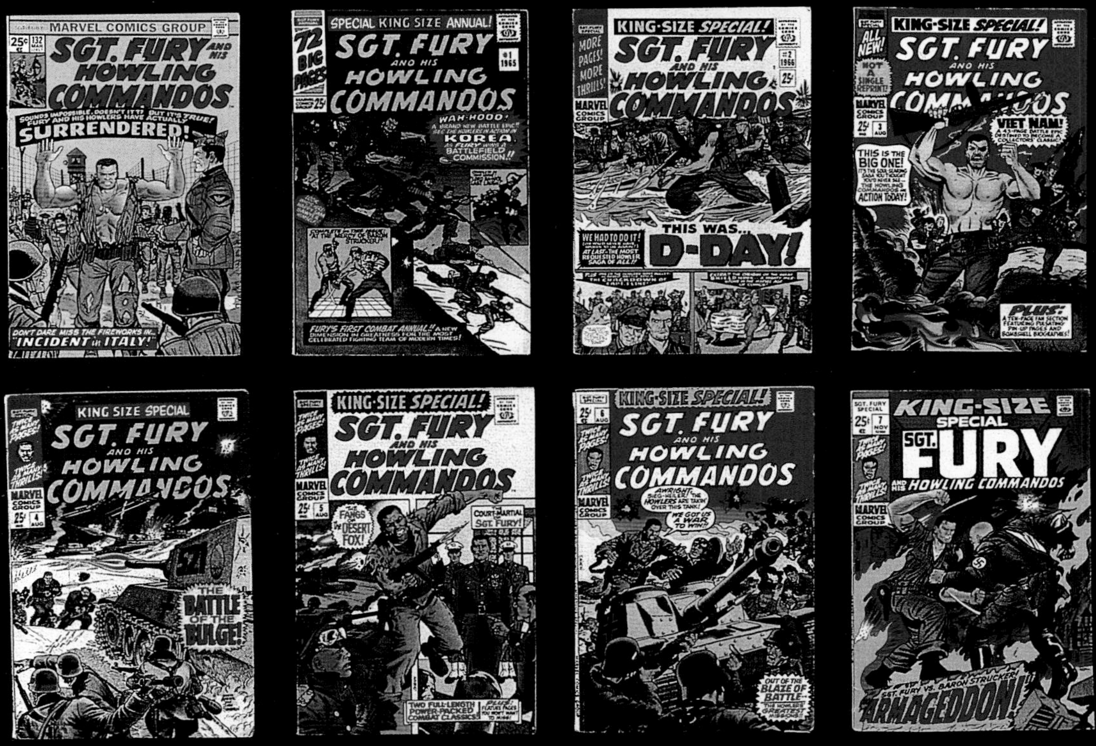
SURRENDERED!
INCIDENT IN ITALY!
SPECIAL KING SIZE ANNUAL!
KOREA
KING-SIZE SPECIAL!
D-DAY!
VIET NAM!
KING SIZE SPECIAL
THE BATTLE OF THE BULGE!
ARMAGEDDON!

Sgt. Fury (1-167) 1676

Ref. No.	Date	RVI	Artist/Info.
1676-1	May 1963	175	Kirby/Ayers-c/a; Publ. 3/5/63
1676-2	Jul.	60	Kirby/Ayers-c/a; Publ. 5/2/63
1676-3	Sept.	35	Kirby/ayers-c/a; Publ. 7/2/63
1676-4	Nov.	35	Kirby/Bell-a; Publ. 9/3/63
1676-5	Jan. 1964	35	Kirby/Bell-a; Publ. 11/5/63
1676-6	Mar.	25	Kirby/Bell-a
1676-7	May	25	" "
1676-8	Jul.	25	Ayers/Bell-c/a; Publ. 5/5/64
1676-9	Aug.	25	" "
1676-10	**Sept.**	**25**	**Ayers/Bell-c/a; Publ. 7/9/64**
1676-11	Oct.	10	" "
1676-12	Nov.	10	" "
1676-13	Dec.	40	Kirby/Ayers-c/a
1676-14	Jan. 1965	10	Ayers/Bell-c/a; Publ. 11/10/64
1676-15	Feb.	10	Kirby/Ayers-c, Ayers/Ditko-a
1676-16	Mar.	10	Ayers/Ray-a
1676-17	Apr.	10	Ayers/Colletta-a
1676-18	May	10	Ayers/Stone-a
1676-19	Jun.	10	Ayers/Ray-a
1676-20	**Jul.**	**10**	**" "**
1676-21	Aug.	6	Ayers/Hubbell-a
1676-22	Sept.	6	" "
1676-23	Oct.	6	Ayers/Ray-a
1676-24	Nov.	6	" "
1676-25	Dec.	6	Ayers/Tartaglione-a
1676-26	Jan. 1966	6	Ayers-c/a, Hubbell-a
1676-27	Feb.	6	Ayers/Tartaglione-a; Publ. 12/9/65
1676-28	Mar.	6	" "
1676-29	Apr.	6	" "
1676-30	**May**	**6**	**" "**
1676-31	Jun.	6	" "
1676-32	Jul.	6	Ayers-c, Tartaglione-a
1676-33	Aug.	6	" "
1676-34	Sept.	6	(Origin-Howling Comandos)
1676-35	Oct.	6	Ayers/Tartaglione-a
1676-36	Nov.	6	" "
1676-37	Dec.	6	Kane-c, Ayers/Tartaglione-a
1676-38 to 50	Jan. 1968, (#50)	6	(#43, Bob Hope, Glen Miller -app.)
1676-51 to 101	Aug.	3	(#100, Captain America -app.)
1676-102 to 167	Dec. 1981, (#167)	2	
1676-A1	1965	20	
1676-A2	1966	6	
1676-A3	Aug. 1966	5	
1676-A4	Aug. 1966	4	
1676-A5	Aug. 1966	3	Kirby-a
1676-A6	Aug. 1966	3	
1676-A7	Nov. 1966	3	

1680.7 Shanna, The She-Devil (1-5)

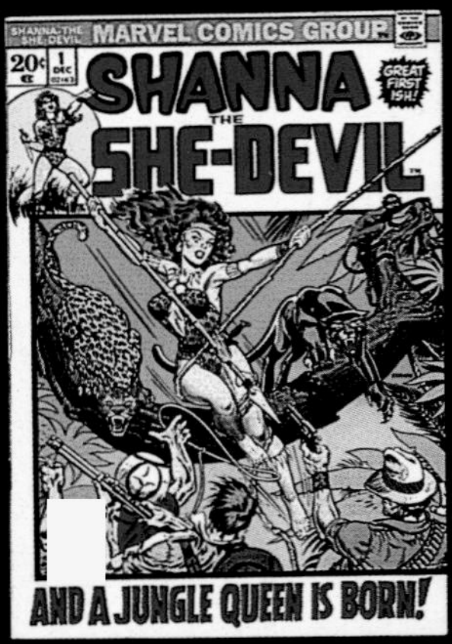
MARVEL COMICS GROUP
SHANNA THE SHE-DEVIL
GREAT FIRST ISH!
AND A JUNGLE QUEEN IS BORN!
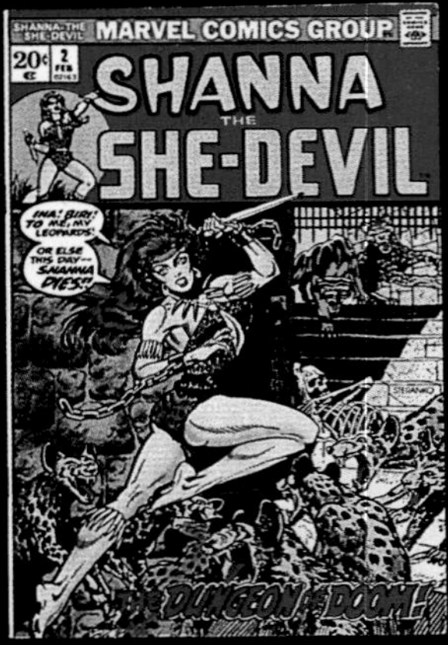
MARVEL COMICS GROUP
SHANNA THE SHE-DEVIL
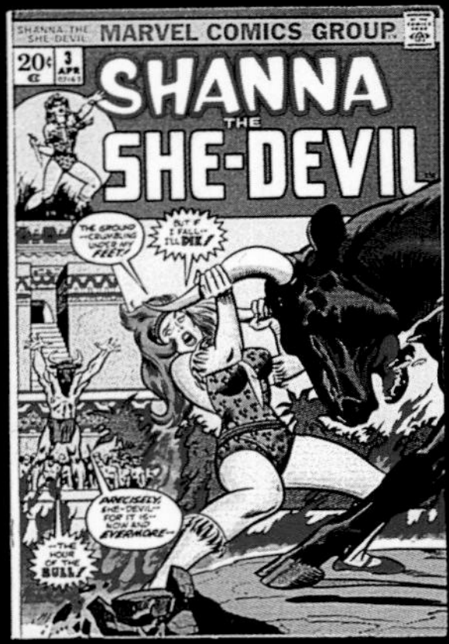
MARVEL COMICS GROUP
SHANNA THE SHE-DEVIL
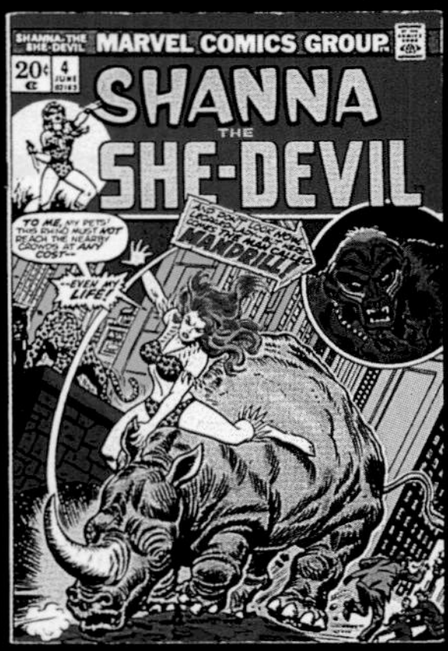
MARVEL COMICS GROUP
SHANNA THE SHE-DEVIL
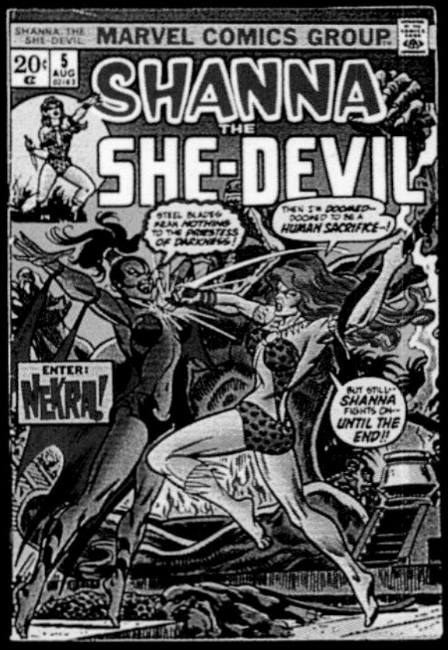
MARVEL COMICS GROUP
SHANNA THE SHE-DEVIL
ENTER! NEKRA!

1681.7 Sheena (1-2)

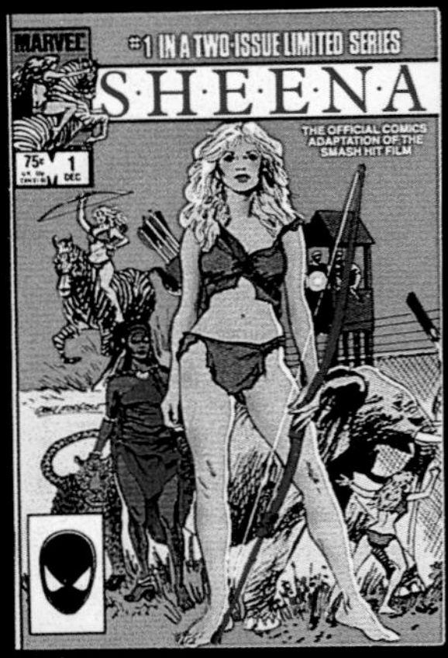
#1 IN A TWO-ISSUE LIMITED SERIES
SHEENA
THE OFFICIAL COMICS ADAPTATION OF THE SMASH HIT FILM
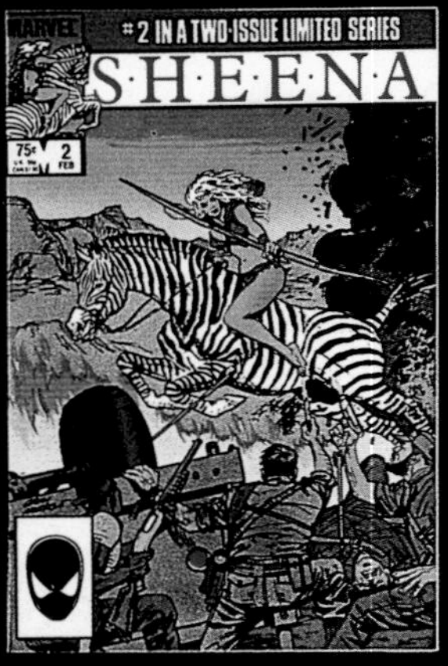
#2 IN A TWO-ISSUE LIMITED SERIES
SHEENA

1686 SHIELD (1-5)

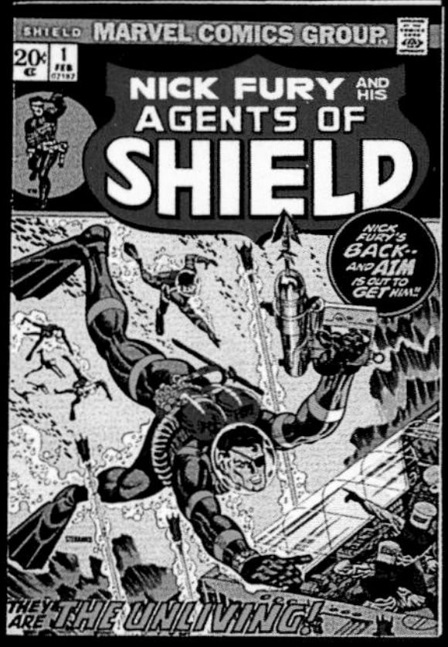
MARVEL COMICS GROUP
NICK FURY AND HIS AGENTS OF SHIELD
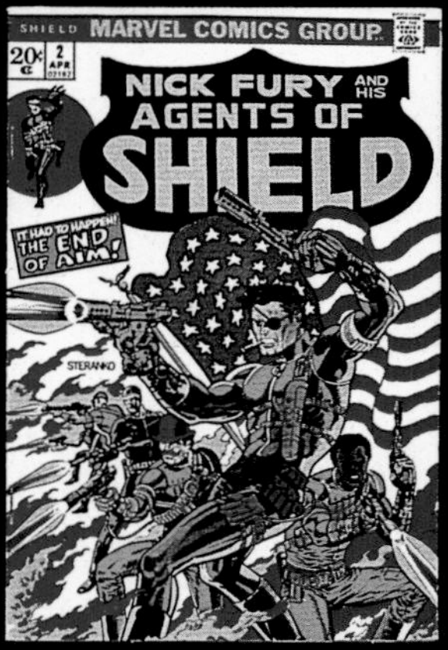
MARVEL COMICS GROUP
NICK FURY AND HIS AGENTS OF SHIELD
IT HAD TO HAPPEN! THE END OF AIM!
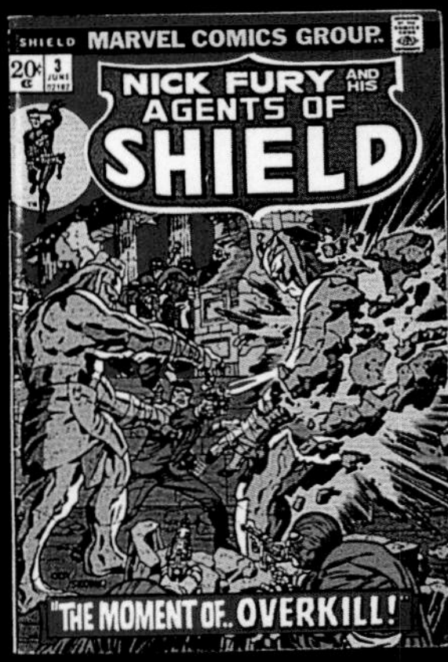
MARVEL COMICS GROUP
NICK FURY AND HIS AGENTS OF SHIELD
"THE MOMENT OF... OVERKILL!"
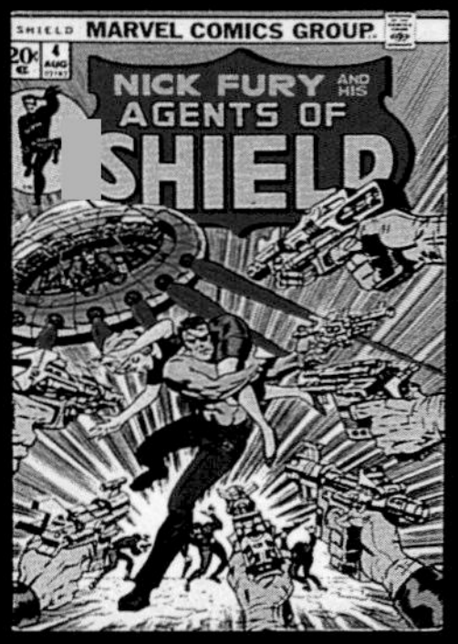
MARVEL COMICS GROUP
NICK FURY AND HIS AGENTS OF SHIELD
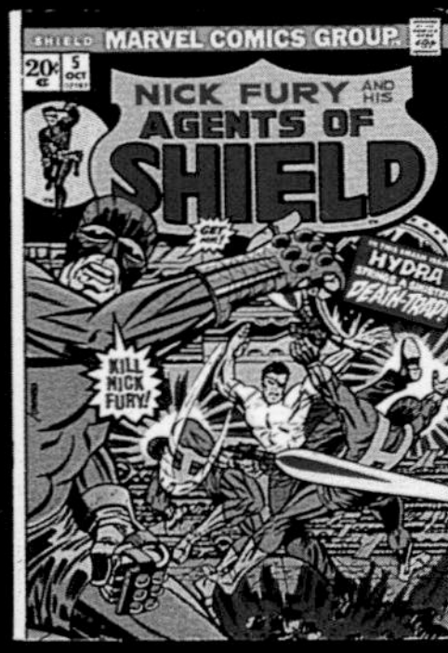
MARVEL COMICS GROUP
NICK FURY AND HIS AGENTS OF SHIELD

1690.3 Shogun Warriors (1-15, 19)

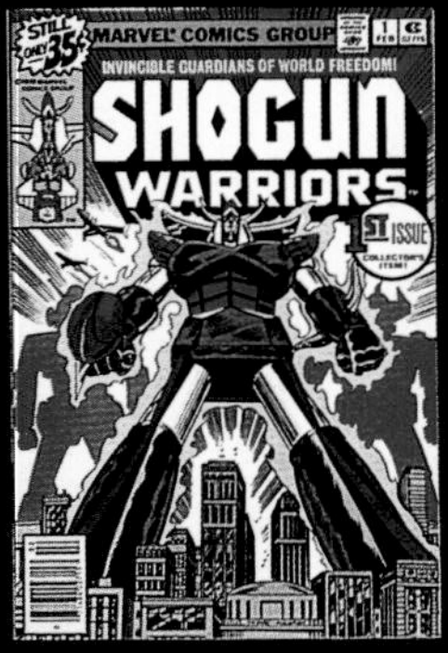
MARVEL COMICS GROUP
INVINCIBLE GUARDIANS OF WORLD FREEDOM!
SHOGUN WARRIORS
1ST ISSUE
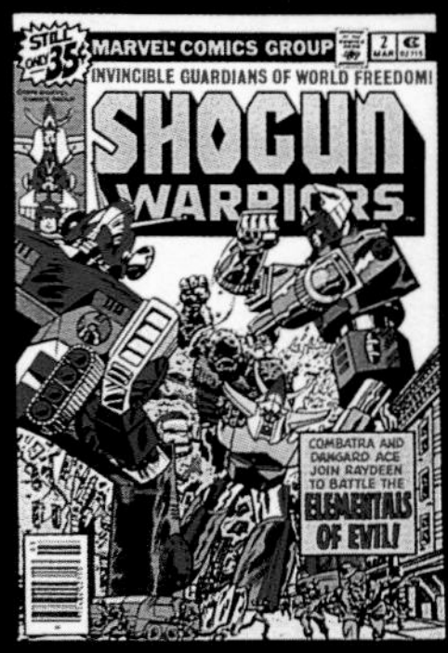
MARVEL COMICS GROUP
INVINCIBLE GUARDIANS OF WORLD FREEDOM!
SHOGUN WARRIORS
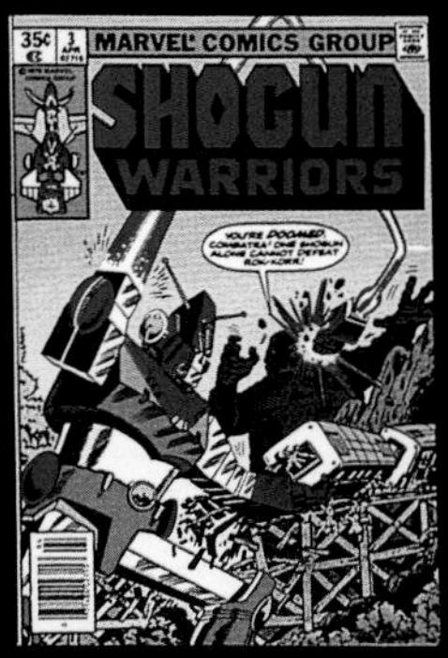
MARVEL COMICS GROUP
SHOGUN WARRIORS
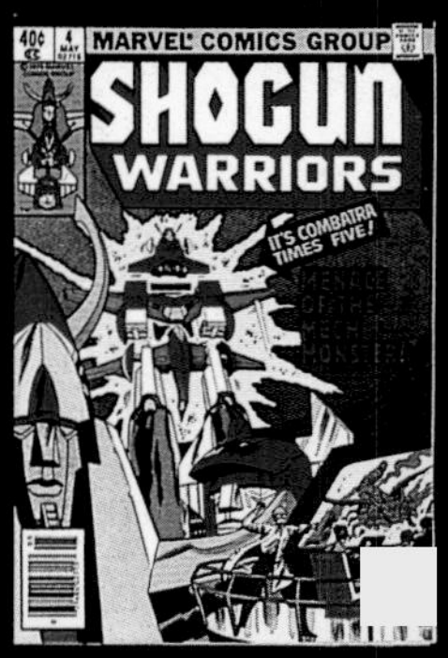
MARVEL COMICS GROUP
SHOGUN WARRIORS
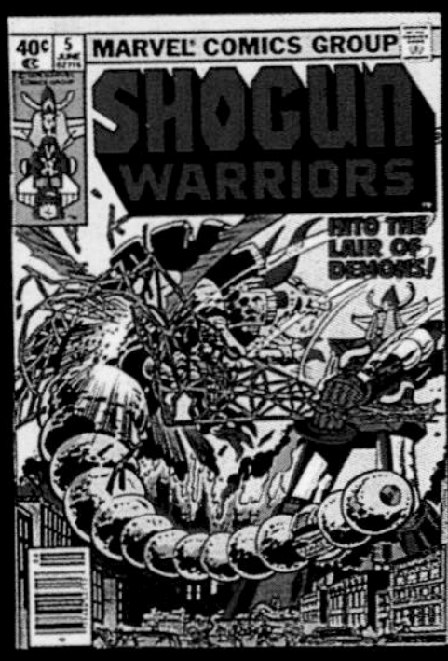
MARVEL COMICS GROUP
SHOGUN WARRIORS
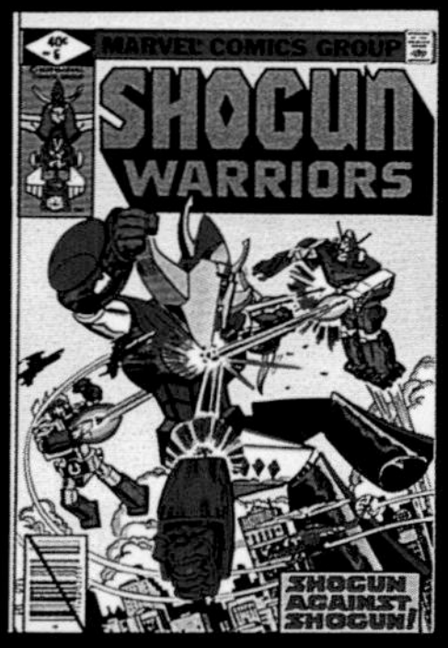
MARVEL COMICS GROUP
SHOGUN WARRIORS
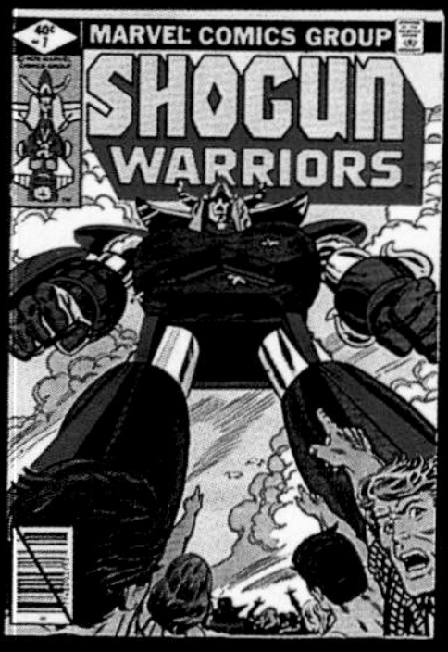
MARVEL COMICS GROUP
SHOGUN WARRIORS
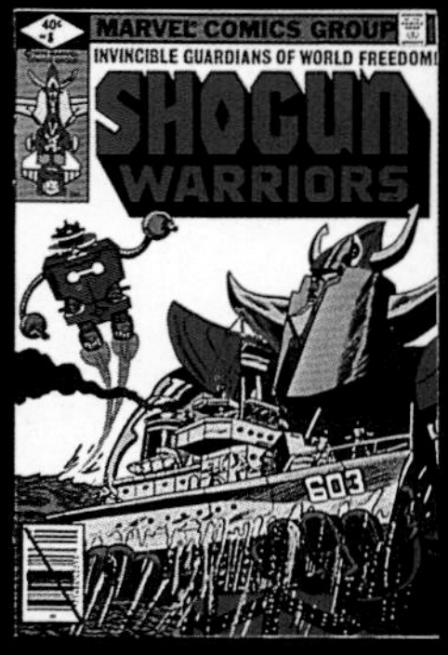
MARVEL COMICS GROUP
INVINCIBLE GUARDIANS OF WORLD FREEDOM!
SHOGUN WARRIORS
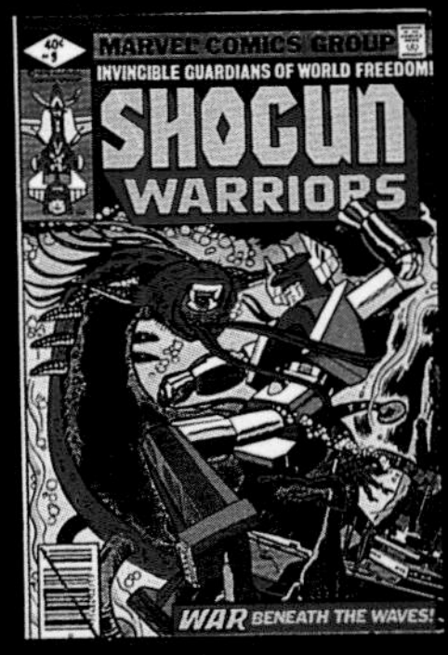
MARVEL COMICS GROUP
INVINCIBLE GUARDIANS OF WORLD FREEDOM!
SHOGUN WARRIORS
WAR BENEATH THE WAVES!
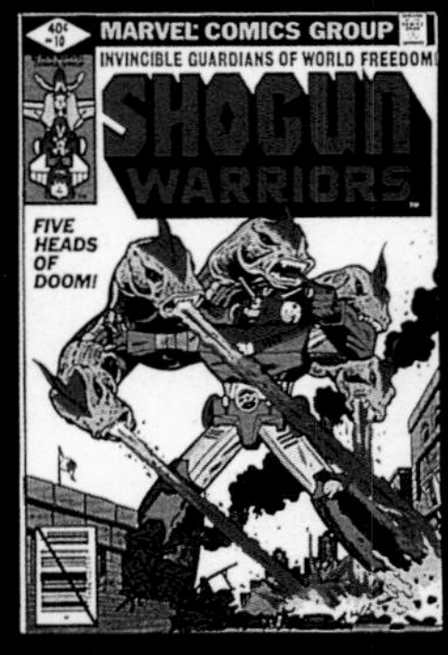
MARVEL COMICS GROUP
INVINCIBLE GUARDIANS OF WORLD FREEDOM!
SHOGUN WARRIORS
FIVE HEADS OF DOOM!
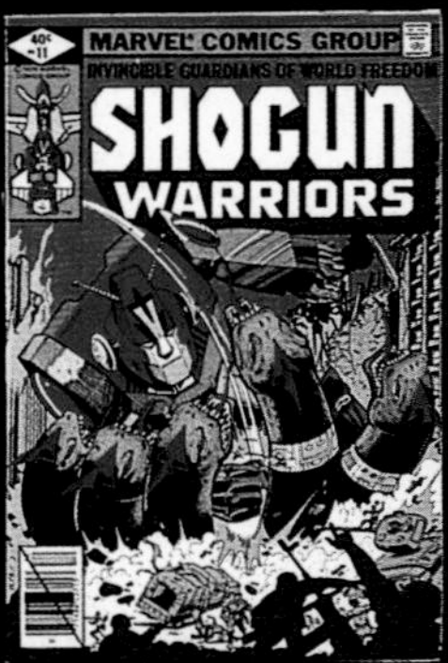
MARVEL COMICS GROUP
INVINCIBLE GUARDIANS OF WORLD FREEDOM!
SHOGUN WARRIORS
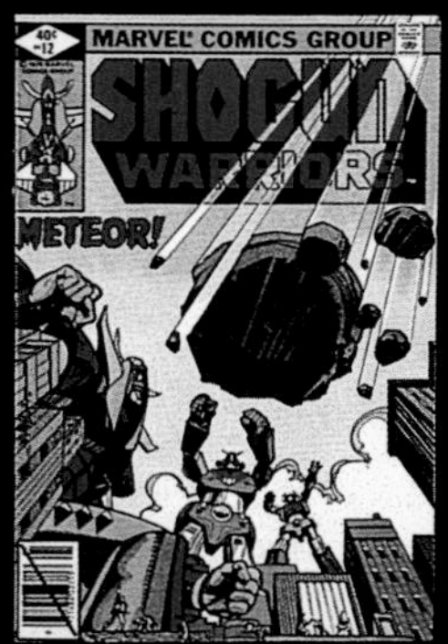
MARVEL COMICS GROUP
SHOGUN WARRIORS
METEOR!
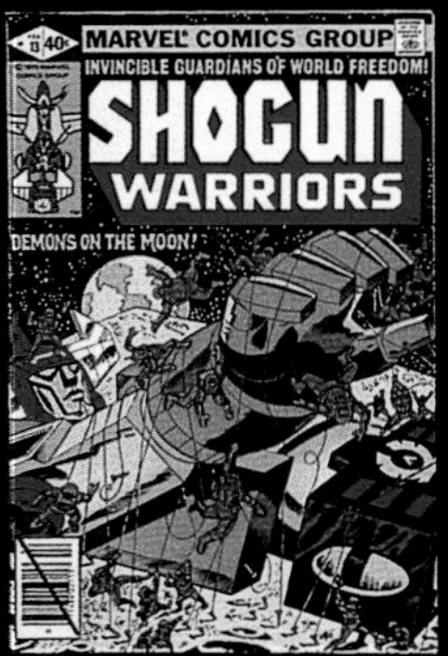
MARVEL COMICS GROUP
INVINCIBLE GUARDIANS OF WORLD FREEDOM!
SHOGUN WARRIORS
DEMONS ON THE MOON!
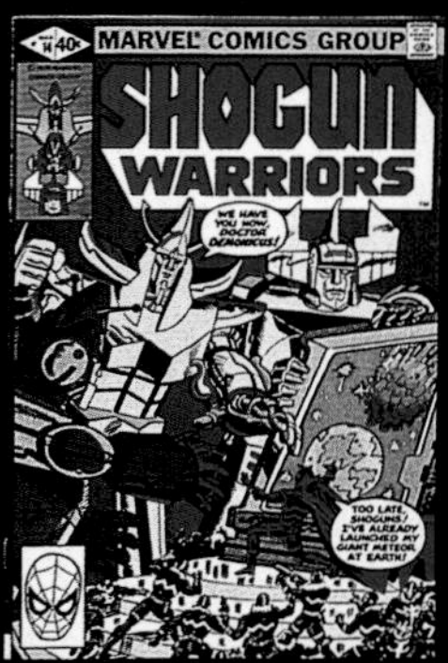
MARVEL COMICS GROUP
SHOGUN WARRIORS
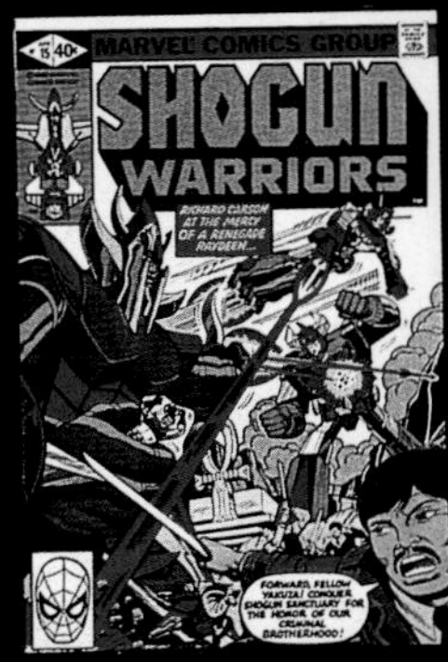
MARVEL COMICS GROUP
SHOGUN WARRIORS
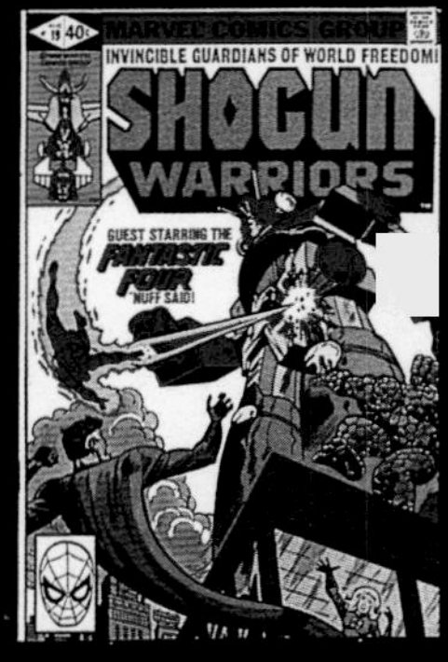
MARVEL COMICS GROUP
INVINCIBLE GUARDIANS OF WORLD FREEDOM!
SHOGUN WARRIORS

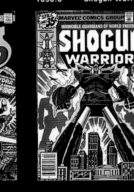

Shanna, The She Devil (1-5) 1680.7

Ref. No.	Date	RVI	Artist/Info.
1680.7-1	Dec. 1972	1	Tuska/Colletta-a
1680.7-2	Feb.	1	Andru/Colletta-a
1680.7-3	Apr.	1	" "
1680.7-4	Jun.	1	" "
1680.7-5	Aug.	1	Romita-c, Andru/Colletta-a

Sheena (1-2) 1681.7

1681.7-1	Dec. 1984	1	Morrow-c/a
1681.7-2	Feb. 1985	1	"

Shield (1-5) 1686

1686-1	Feb. 1973	2	Steranko-c, Kirby-a
1686-2	Apr.	1	"
1686-3	Jun.	1	Steranko/Kirby-c, Buscema-a
1686-4	Aug.	1	Steranko-c, Kirby-a
1686-5	Oct. 1973	1	Kirby-a

Shogun Warriors (1-20) 1690.3

1690.3-1	Feb. 1979	2	Trimpe/Green-a
1690.3-2	Mar.	1	" "
1690.3-3	Apr.	1	Milgrom-c, Trimpe/Green-a
1690.3-4	May	1	Trimpe/Green-a
1690.3-5	Jun.	1	" "
1690.3-6	Jul.	1	Trimpe/Esposito-a
1690.3-7	Aug.	1	" "
1690.3-8	Sept.	1	" "
1690.3-9 to 20	Sept. 1980	1	(#19, Fantastic Four -app.)

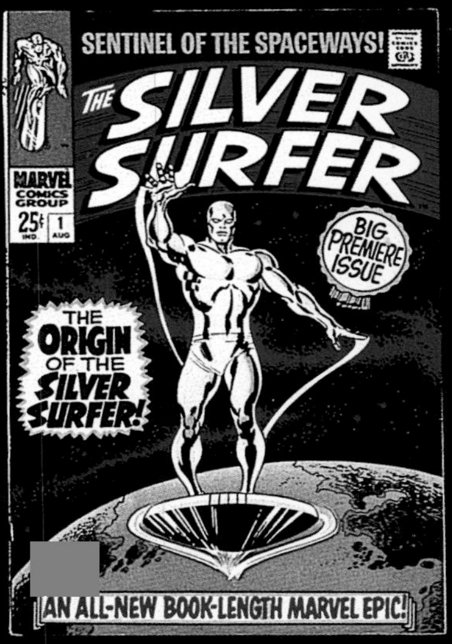
SENTINEL OF THE SPACEWAYS!
THE SILVER SURFER
MARVEL COMICS GROUP
25¢ 1 AUG
BIG PREMIERE ISSUE
THE ORIGIN OF THE SILVER SURFER!
AN ALL-NEW BOOK-LENGTH MARVEL EPIC!

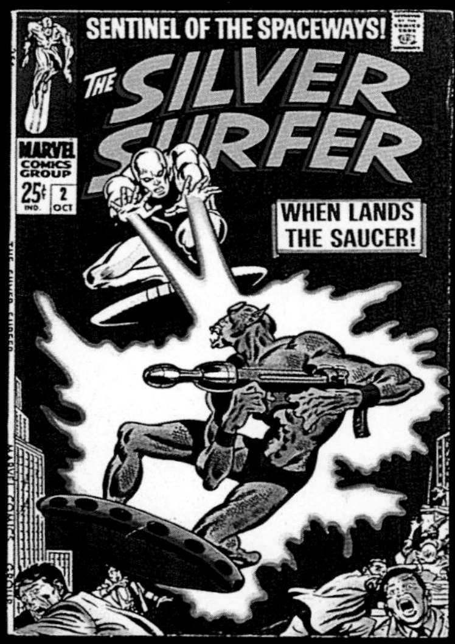
SENTINEL OF THE SPACEWAYS!
THE SILVER SURFER
MARVEL COMICS GROUP
25¢ 2 OCT
WHEN LANDS THE SAUCER!

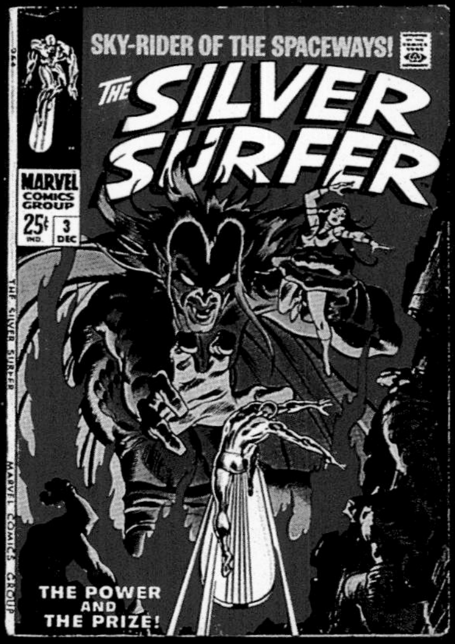
SKY-RIDER OF THE SPACEWAYS!
THE SILVER SURFER
MARVEL COMICS GROUP
25¢ 3 DEC
THE POWER AND THE PRIZE!

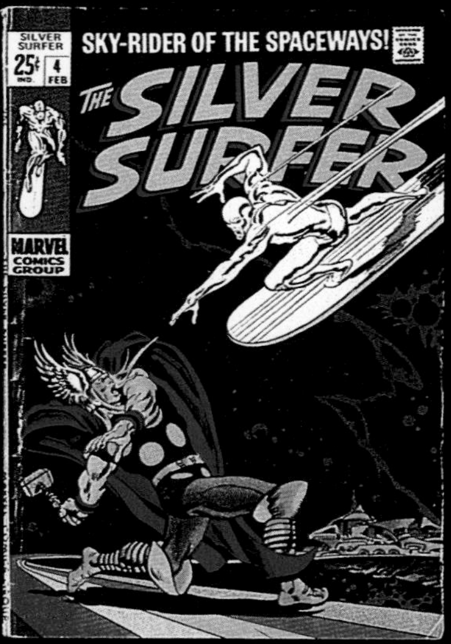
SKY-RIDER OF THE SPACEWAYS!
THE SILVER SURFER
SILVER SURFER 25¢ 4 FEB
MARVEL COMICS GROUP

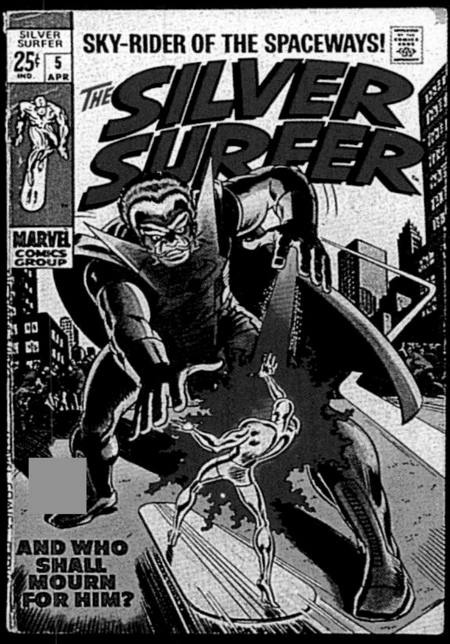
SKY-RIDER OF THE SPACEWAYS!
THE SILVER SURFER
SILVER SURFER 25¢ 5 APR
MARVEL COMICS GROUP
AND WHO SHALL MOURN FOR HIM?

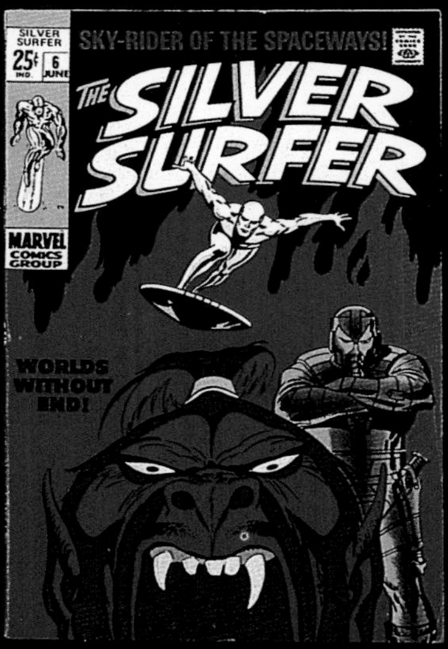
SKY-RIDER OF THE SPACEWAYS!
THE SILVER SURFER
SILVER SURFER 25¢ 6 JUNE
MARVEL COMICS GROUP
WORLDS WITHOUT END!

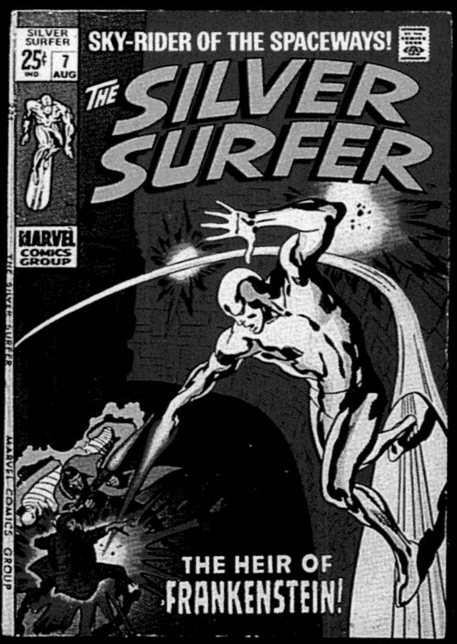
SKY-RIDER OF THE SPACEWAYS!
THE SILVER SURFER
SILVER SURFER 25¢ 7 AUG
MARVEL COMICS GROUP
THE HEIR OF FRANKENSTEIN!

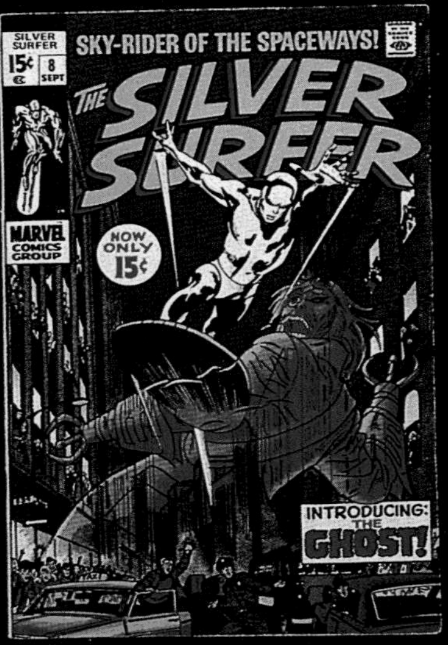
SKY-RIDER OF THE SPACEWAYS!
THE SILVER SURFER
SILVER SURFER 15¢ 8 SEPT
MARVEL COMICS GROUP
NOW ONLY 15¢
INTRODUCING: THE GHOST!

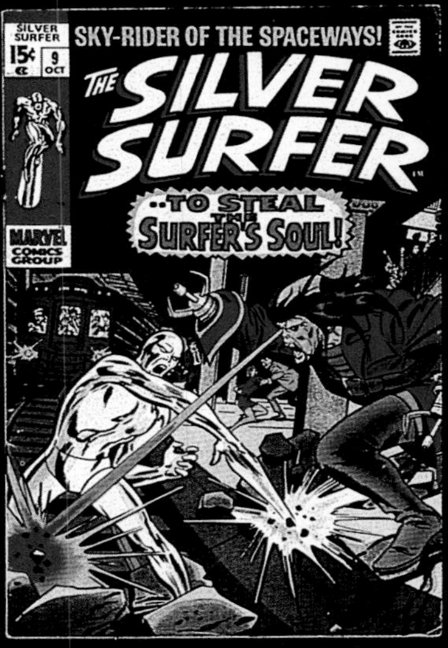
SKY-RIDER OF THE SPACEWAYS!
THE SILVER SURFER
SILVER SURFER 15¢ 9 OCT
MARVEL COMICS GROUP
TO STEAL THE SURFER'S SOUL!

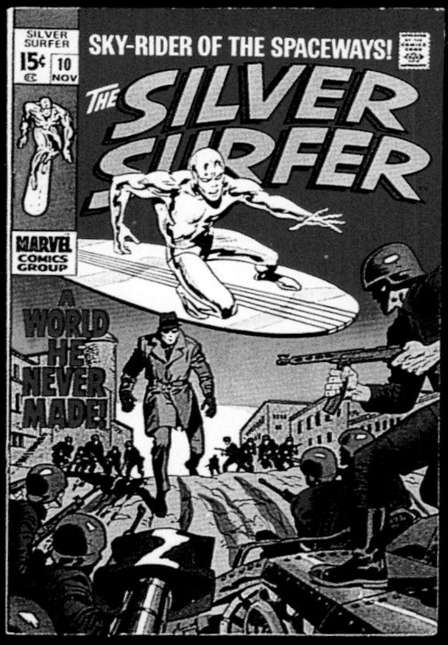
SKY-RIDER OF THE SPACEWAYS!
THE SILVER SURFER
SILVER SURFER 15¢ 10 NOV
MARVEL COMICS GROUP
A WORLD HE NEVER MADE!

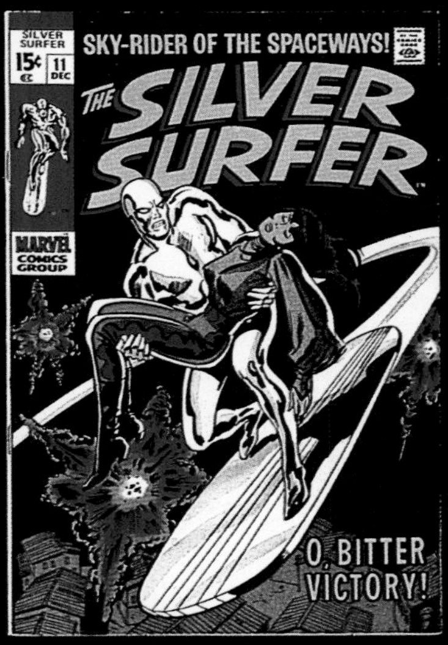
SKY-RIDER OF THE SPACEWAYS!
THE SILVER SURFER
SILVER SURFER 15¢ 11 DEC
MARVEL COMICS GROUP
O, BITTER VICTORY!

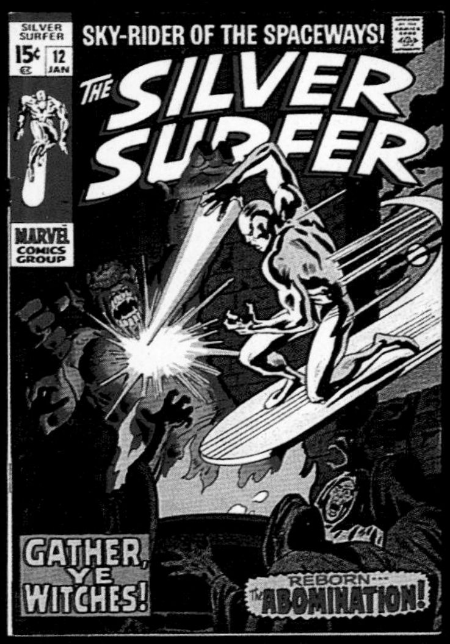
SKY-RIDER OF THE SPACEWAYS!
THE SILVER SURFER
SILVER SURFER 15¢ 12 JAN
MARVEL COMICS GROUP
GATHER, YE WITCHES!
REBORN... THE ABOMINATION!

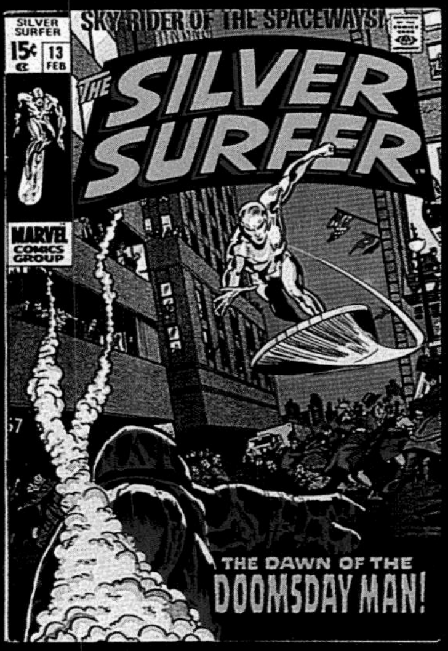
SKY-RIDER OF THE SPACEWAYS!
THE SILVER SURFER
SILVER SURFER 15¢ 13 FEB
MARVEL COMICS GROUP
THE DAWN OF THE DOOMSDAY MAN!

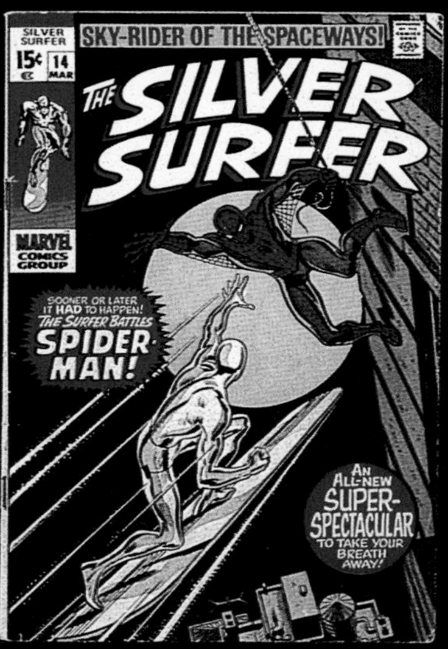
SKY-RIDER OF THE SPACEWAYS!
THE SILVER SURFER
SILVER SURFER 15¢ 14 MAR
MARVEL COMICS GROUP
SOONER OR LATER IT HAD TO HAPPEN! THE SURFER BATTLES SPIDER-MAN!
AN ALL-NEW SUPER-SPECTACULAR TO TAKE YOUR BREATH AWAY!

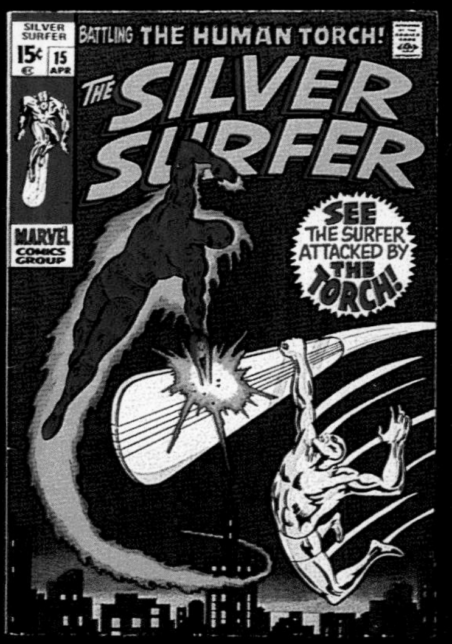
BATTLING THE HUMAN TORCH!
THE SILVER SURFER
SILVER SURFER 15¢ 15 APR
MARVEL COMICS GROUP
SEE THE SURFER ATTACKED BY THE TORCH!

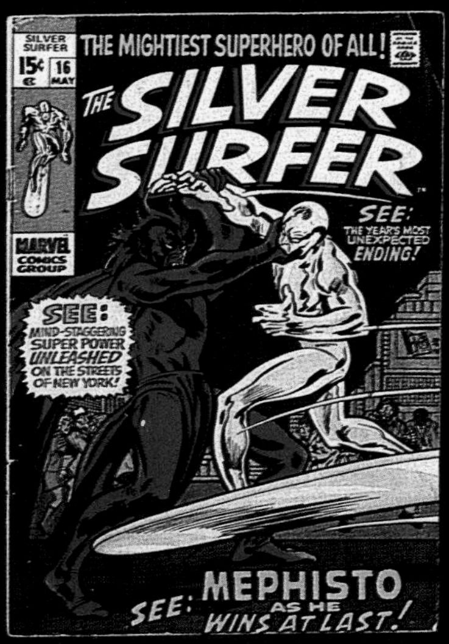
THE MIGHTIEST SUPERHERO OF ALL!
THE SILVER SURFER
SILVER SURFER 15¢ 16 MAY
MARVEL COMICS GROUP
SEE: THE YEAR'S MOST UNEXPECTED ENDING!
SEE: MIND-STAGGERING SUPER POWER UNLEASHED ON THE STREETS OF NEW YORK!
SEE: MEPHISTO AS HE WINS AT LAST!

1696.2 Silver Surfer (17-18, V.2/1)

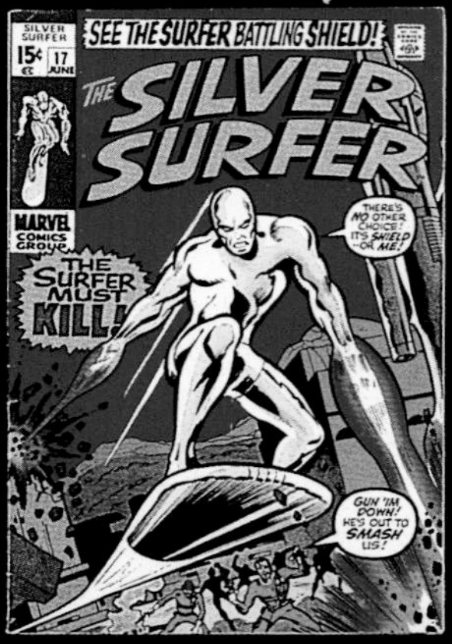
SEE THE SURFER BATTLING SHIELD!
THE SILVER SURFER
THE SURFER MUST KILL!

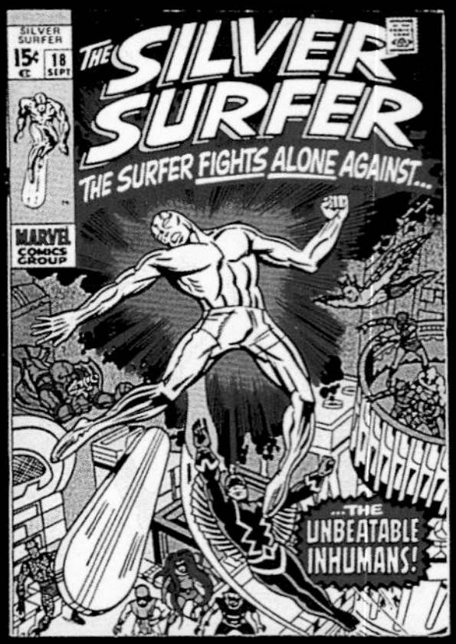
THE SILVER SURFER
THE SURFER FIGHTS ALONE AGAINST...
...THE UNBEATABLE INHUMANS!

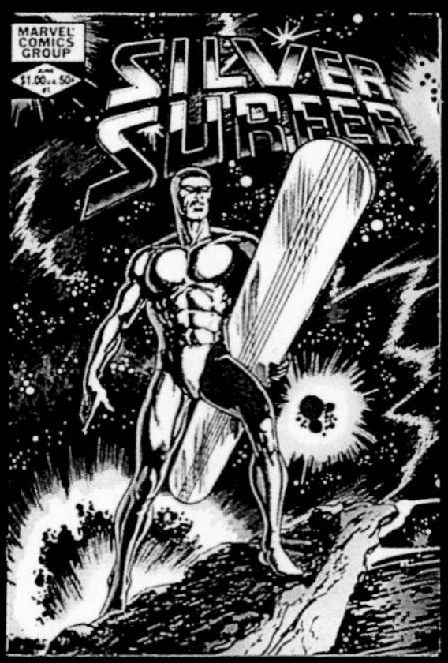
SILVER SURFER

1696.3 Silver Surfer (1-13, 15, 20 AN.1-3)

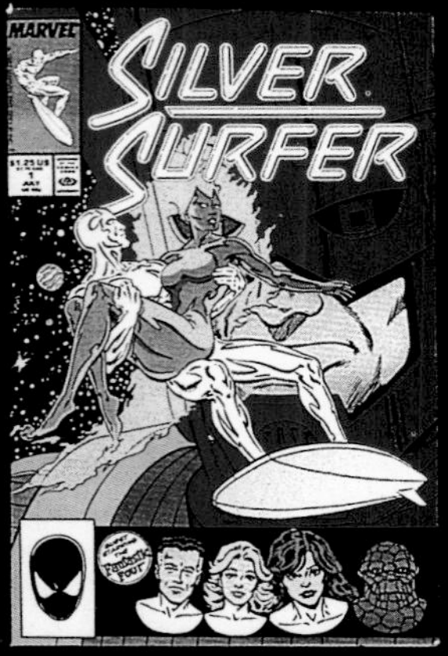
SILVER SURFER

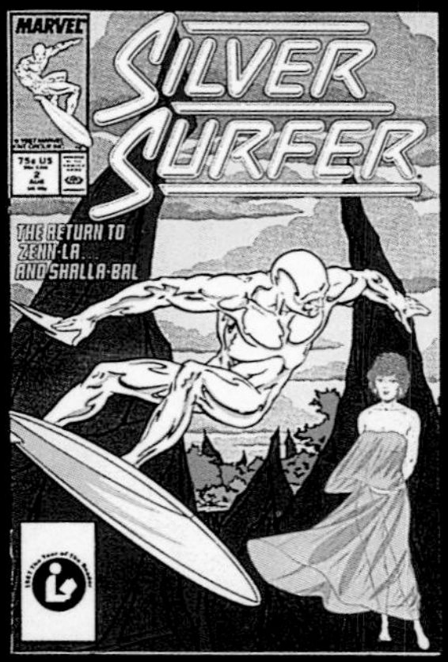
SILVER SURFER
THE RETURN TO ZENN-LA AND SHALLA-BAL

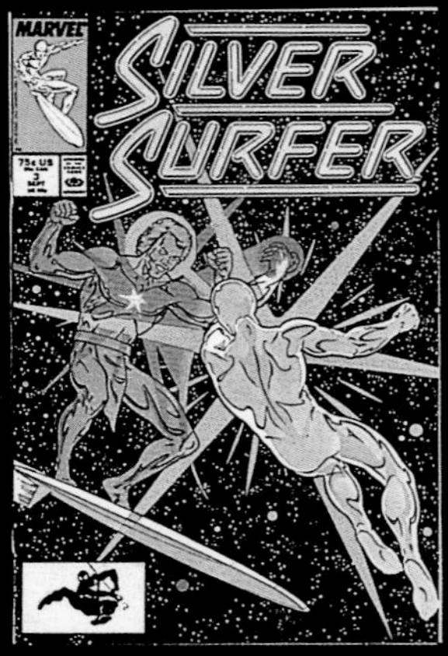
SILVER SURFER

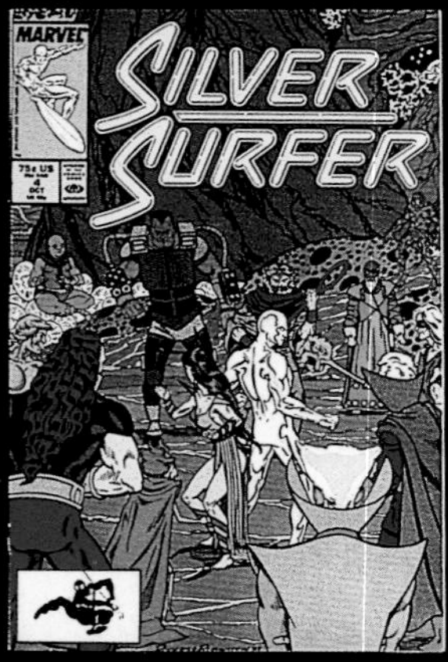
SILVER SURFER

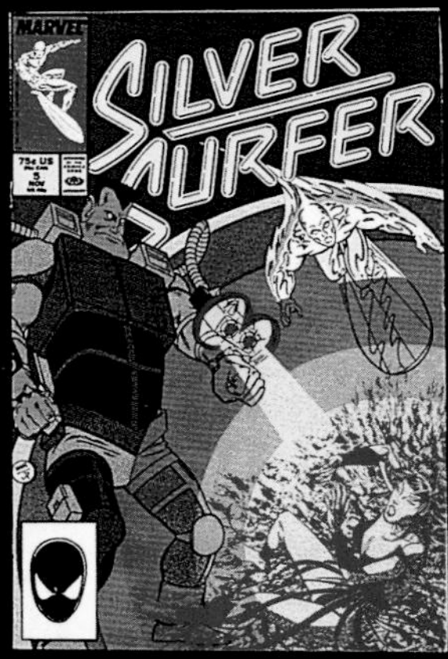
SILVER SURFER

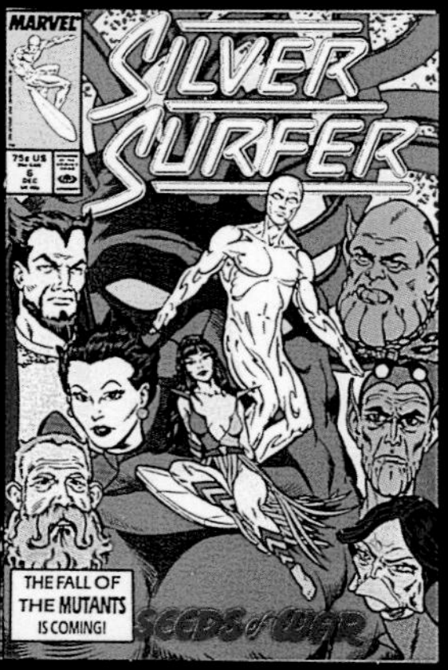
SILVER SURFER
THE FALL OF THE MUTANTS IS COMING!
SEEDS of WAR

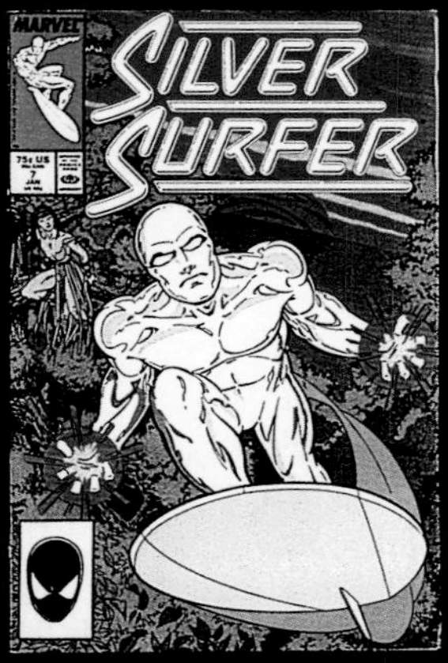
SILVER SURFER

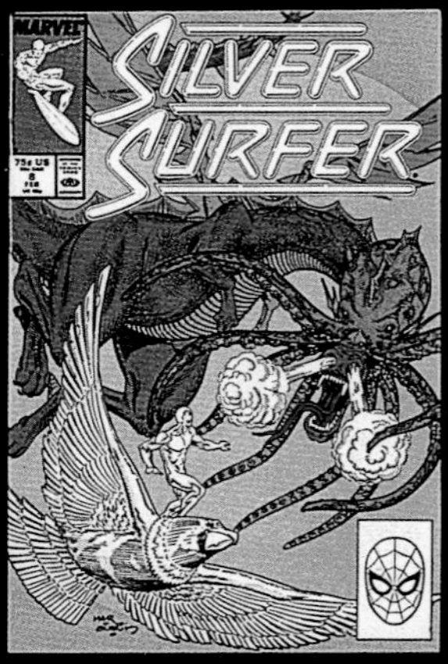
SILVER SURFER

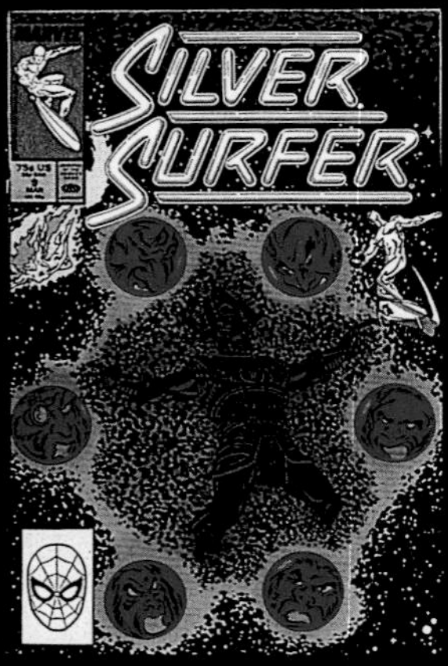
SILVER SURFER

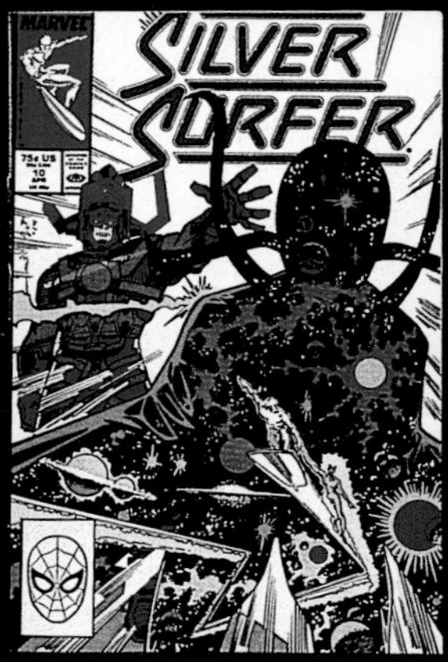
SILVER SURFER

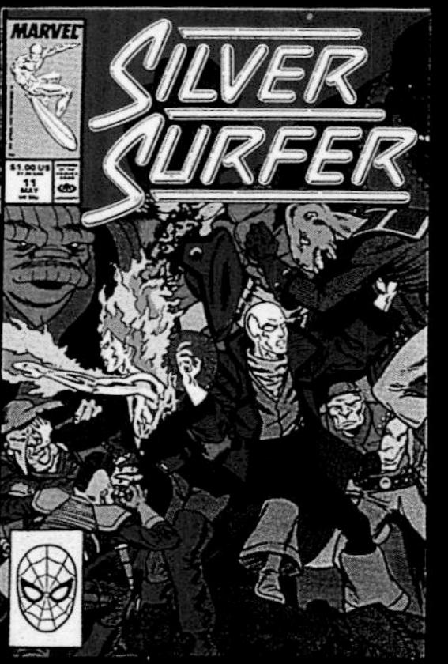
SILVER SURFER

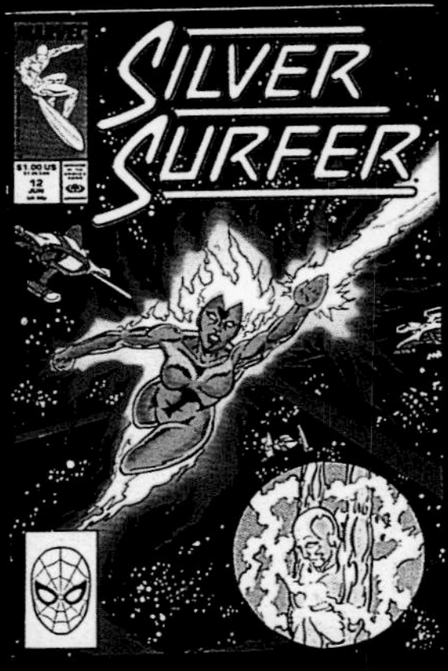
SILVER SURFER

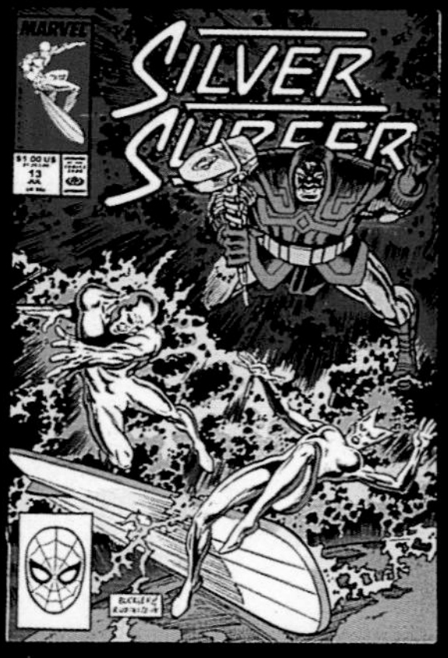
SILVER SURFER

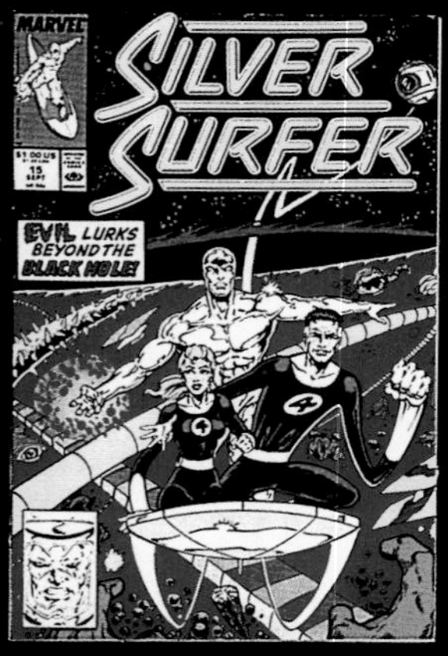
SILVER SURFER
EVIL LURKS BEYOND THE BLACK HOLE!

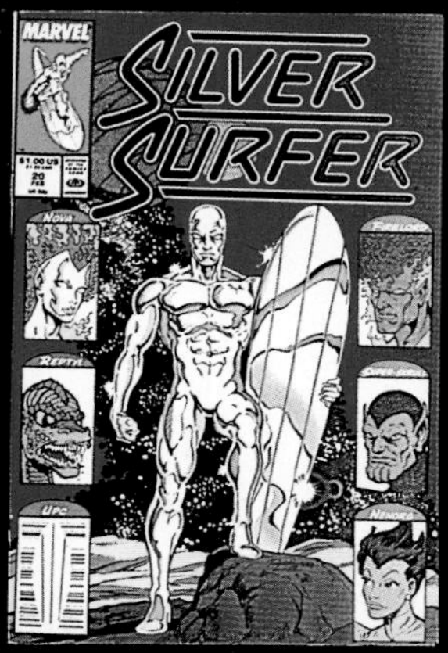
SILVER SURFER

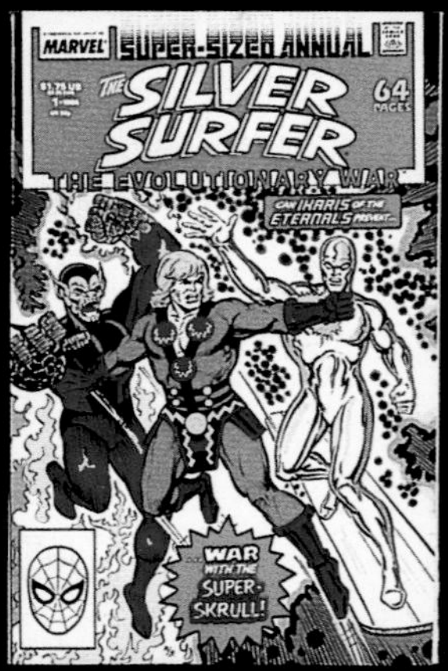
SUPER-SIZED ANNUAL
THE SILVER SURFER
64 PAGES
THE EVOLUTIONARY WAR
WAR WITH THE SUPER-SKRULL!

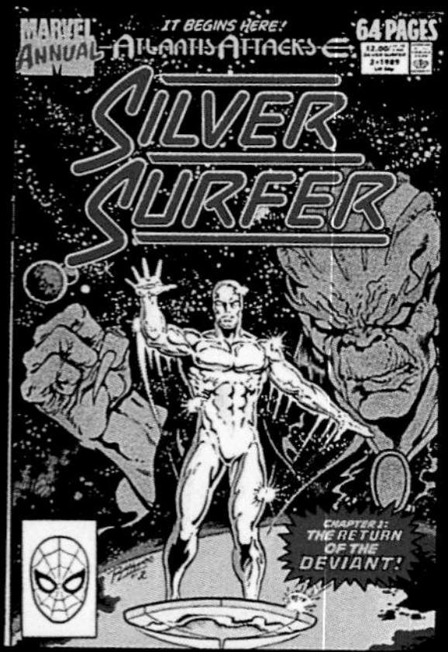
IT BEGINS HERE!
ATLANTIS ATTACKS
64 PAGES
SILVER SURFER
CHAPTER 1: THE RETURN OF THE DEVIANT!

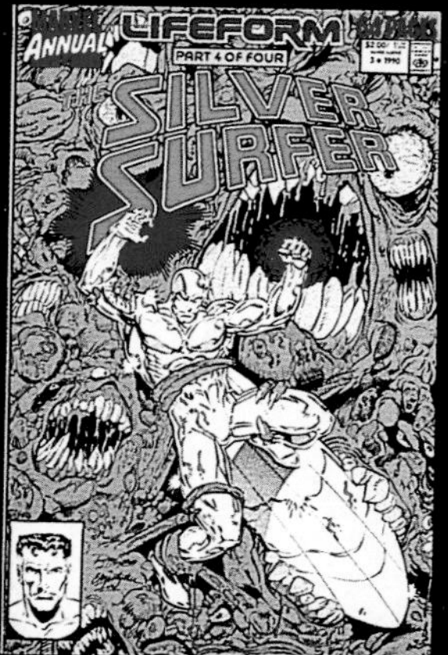
LIFEFORM
PART 4 OF FOUR
SILVER SURFER

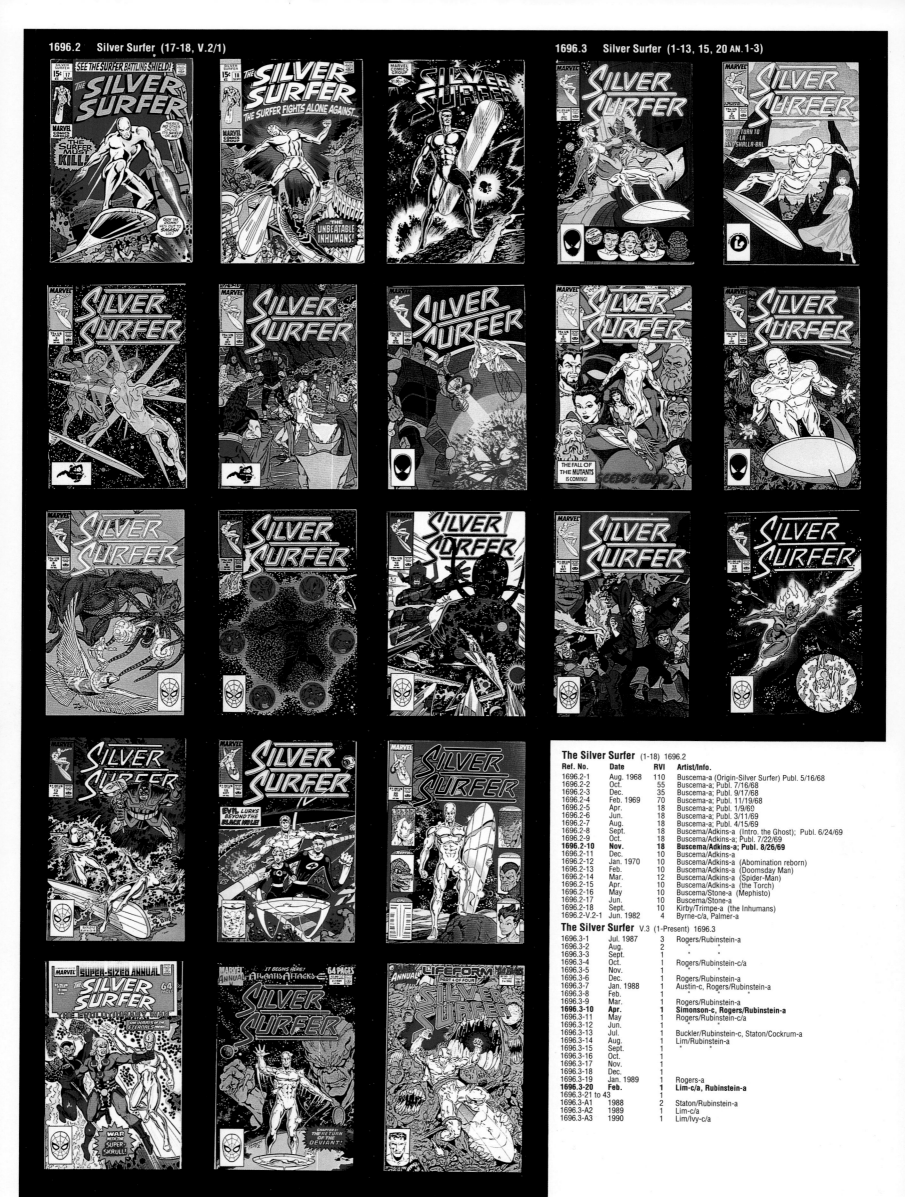

The Silver Surfer (1-18) 1696.2

Ref. No.	Date	RVI	Artist/Info.
1696.2-1	Aug. 1968	110	Buscema-a (Origin-Silver Surfer) Publ. 5/16/68
1696.2-2	Oct.	55	Buscema-a; Publ. 7/16/68
1696.2-3	Dec.	35	Buscema-a; Publ. 9/17/68
1696.2-4	Feb. 1969	70	Buscema-a; Publ. 11/19/68
1696.2-5	Apr.	18	Buscema-a; Publ. 1/9/69
1696.2-6	Jun.	18	Buscema-a; Publ. 3/11/69
1696.2-7	Aug.	18	Buscema-a; Publ. 4/15/69
1696.2-8	Sept.	18	Buscema/Adkins-a (Intro. the Ghost); Publ. 6/24/69
1696.2-9	Oct.	18	Buscema/Adkins-a; Publ. 7/22/69
1696.2-10	**Nov.**	**18**	**Buscema/Adkins-a; Publ. 8/26/69**
1696.2-11	Dec.	10	Buscema/Adkins-a
1696.2-12	Jan. 1970	10	Buscema/Adkins-a (Abomination reborn)
1696.2-13	Feb.	10	Buscema/Adkins-a (Doomsday Man)
1696.2-14	Mar.	12	Buscema/Adkins-a (Spider-Man)
1696.2-15	Apr.	10	Buscema/Adkins-a (the Torch)
1696.2-16	May	10	Buscema/Stone-a (Mephisto)
1696.2-17	Jun.	10	Buscema/Stone-a
1696.2-18	Sept.	10	Kirby/Trimpe-a (the Inhumans)
1696.2-V.2-1	Jun. 1982	4	Byrne-c/a, Palmer-a

The Silver Surfer V.3 (1-Present) 1696.3

1696.3-1	Jul. 1987	3	Rogers/Rubinstein-a
1696.3-2	Aug.	2	" "
1696.3-3	Sept.	1	" "
1696.3-4	Oct.	1	Rogers/Rubinstein-c/a
1696.3-5	Nov.	1	" "
1696.3-6	Dec.	1	Rogers/Rubinstein-a
1696.3-7	Jan. 1988	1	Austin-c, Rogers/Rubinstein-a
1696.3-8	Feb.	1	" " "
1696.3-9	Mar.	1	Rogers/Rubinstein-a
1696.3-10	**Apr.**	**1**	**Simonson-c, Rogers/Rubinstein-a**
1696.3-11	May	1	Rogers/Rubinstein-c/a
1696.3-12	Jun.	1	" "
1696.3-13	Jul.	1	Buckler/Rubinstein-c, Staton/Cockrum-a
1696.3-14	Aug.	1	Lim/Rubinstein-a
1696.3-15	Sept.	1	" "
1696.3-16	Oct.	1	
1696.3-17	Nov.	1	
1696.3-18	Dec.	1	
1696.3-19	Jan. 1989	1	Rogers-a
1696.3-20	**Feb.**	**1**	**Lim-c/a, Rubinstein-a**
1696.3-21 to 43		1	
1696.3-A1	1988	2	Staton/Rubinstein-a
1696.3-A2	1989	1	Lim-c/a
1696.3-A3	1990	1	Lim/Ivy-c/a

1697.6 Sisterhood of Steel (1-8)

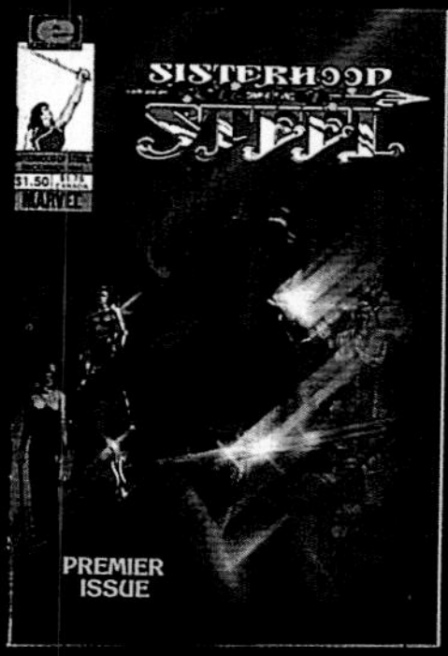
SISTERHOOD
STEEL
PREMIER ISSUE

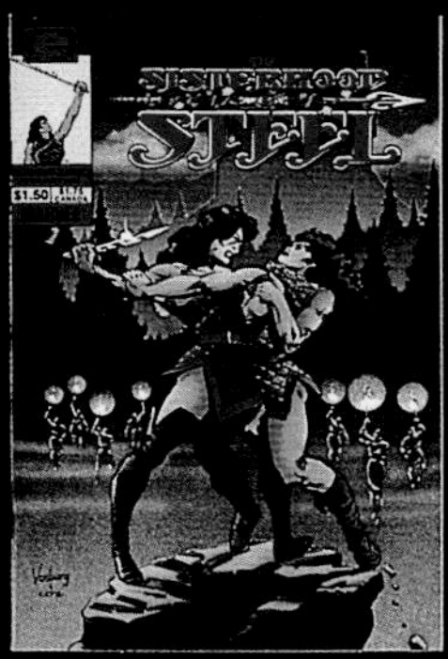
STEEL

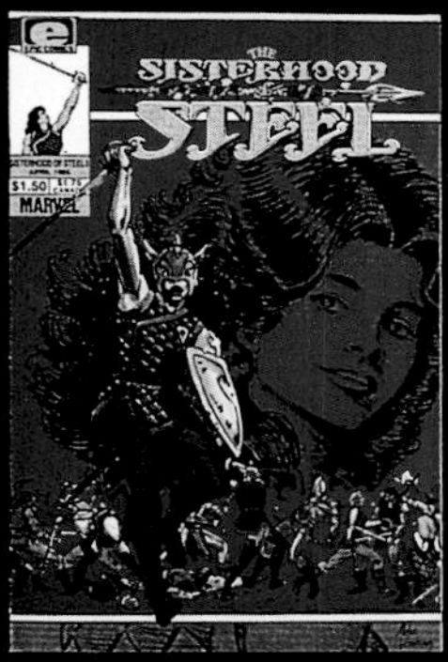
SISTERHOOD
STEEL

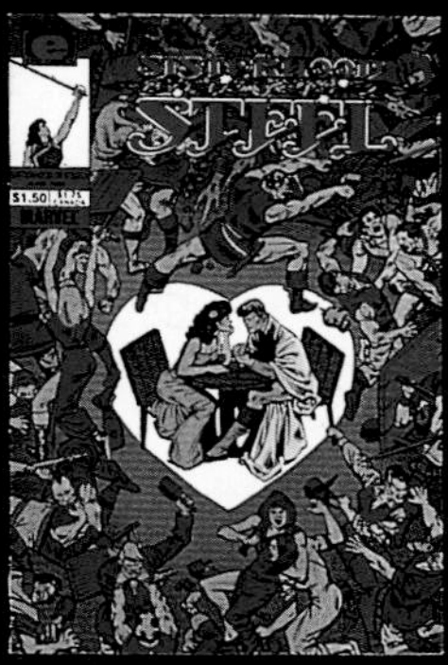
STEEL

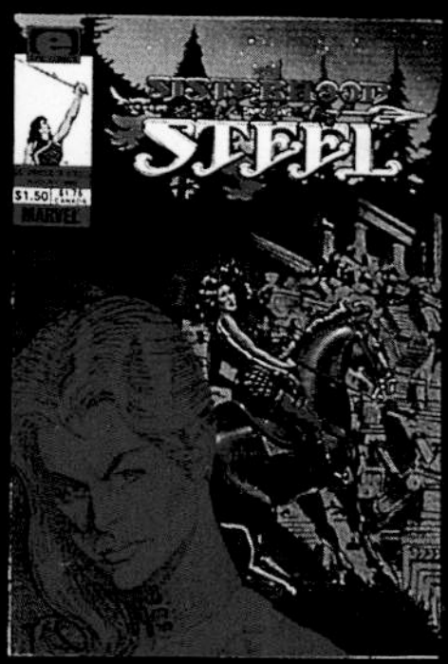
STEEL

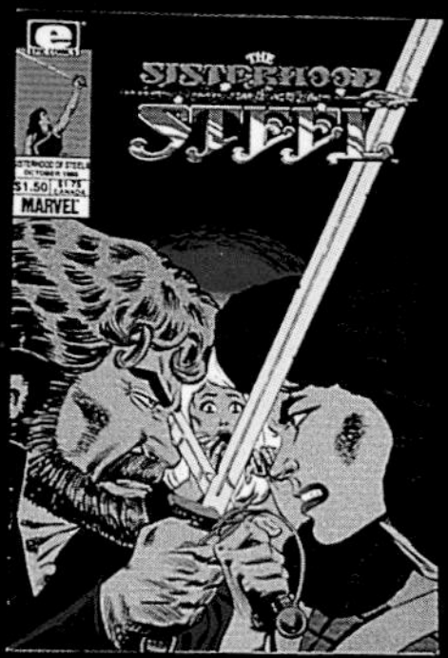
SISTERHOOD
STEEL

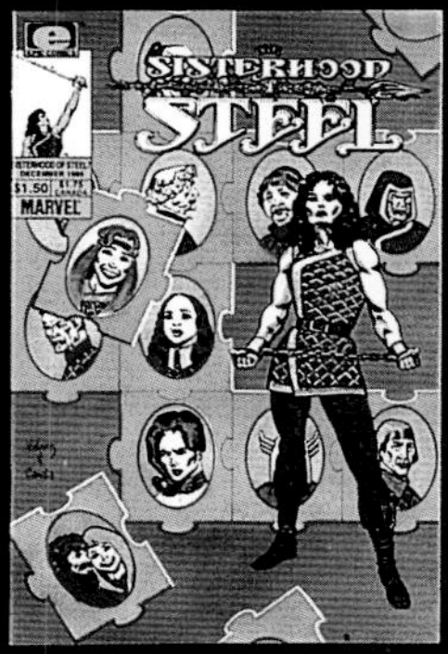
SISTERHOOD
STEEL

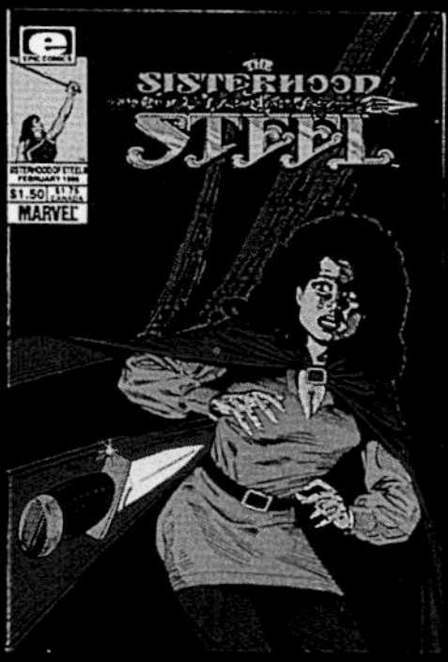
SISTERHOOD
STEEL

1697.8 Six from Sirius (1-4)

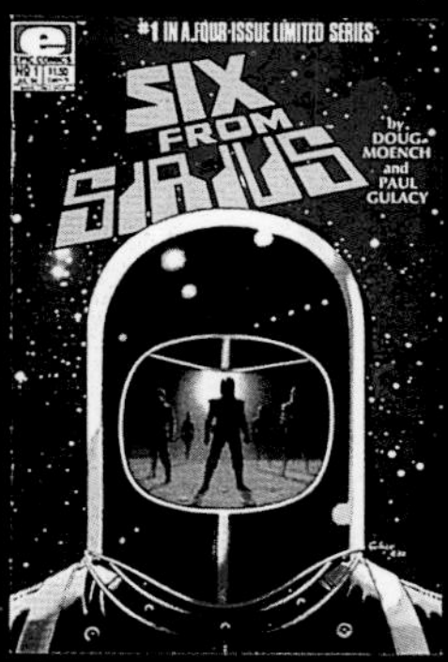
#1 IN A FOUR-ISSUE LIMITED SERIES
SIX FROM SIRIUS
by DOUG MOENCH and PAUL GULACY

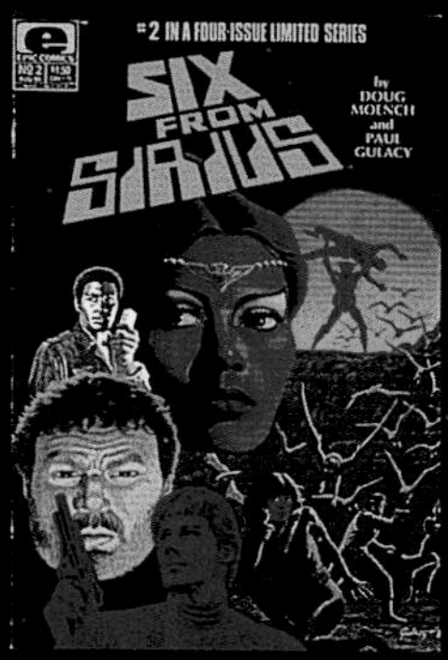
#2 IN A FOUR-ISSUE LIMITED SERIES
SIX FROM SIRIUS
by DOUG MOENCH and PAUL GULACY

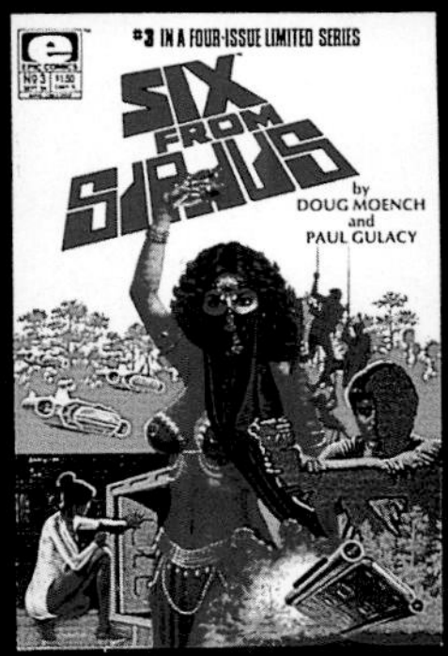
#3 IN A FOUR-ISSUE LIMITED SERIES
SIX FROM SIRIUS
by DOUG MOENCH and PAUL GULACY

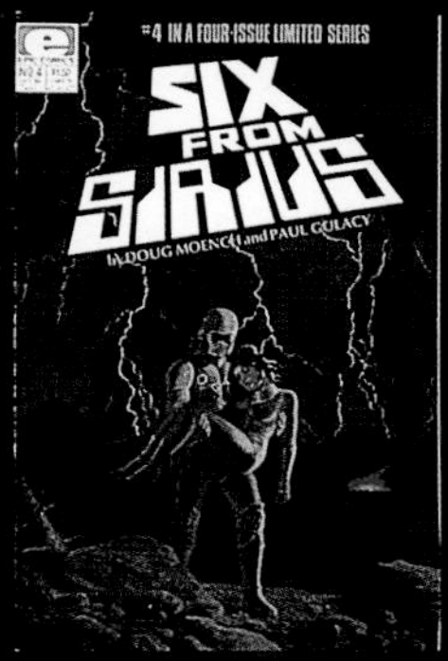
#4 IN A FOUR-ISSUE LIMITED SERIES
SIX FROM SIRIUS
by DOUG MOENCH and PAUL GULACY

1697.85 Six from Sirius II (1-4)

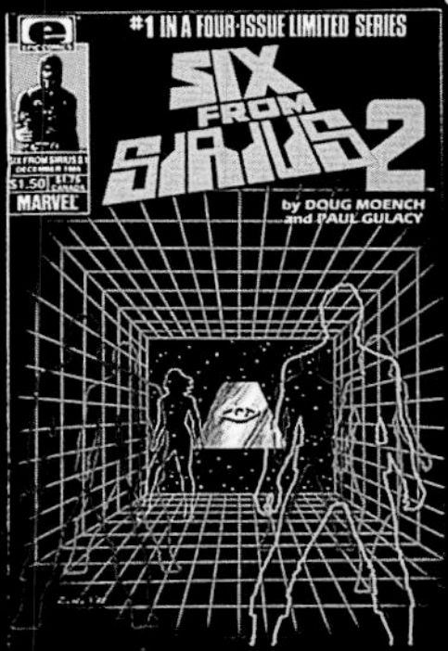
#1 IN A FOUR-ISSUE LIMITED SERIES
SIX FROM SIRIUS 2
by DOUG MOENCH and PAUL GULACY

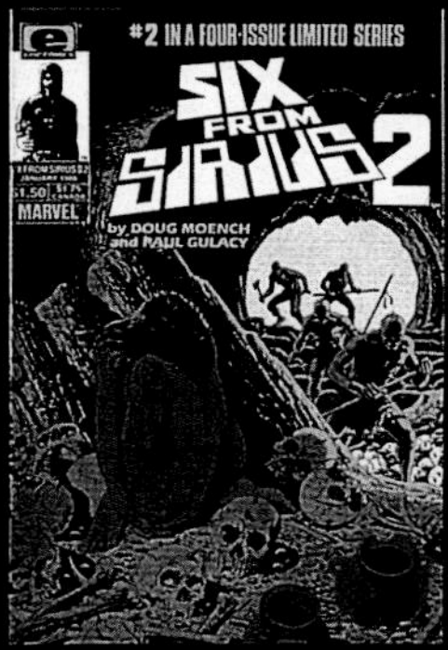
#2 IN A FOUR-ISSUE LIMITED SERIES
SIX FROM SIRIUS 2
by DOUG MOENCH and PAUL GULACY

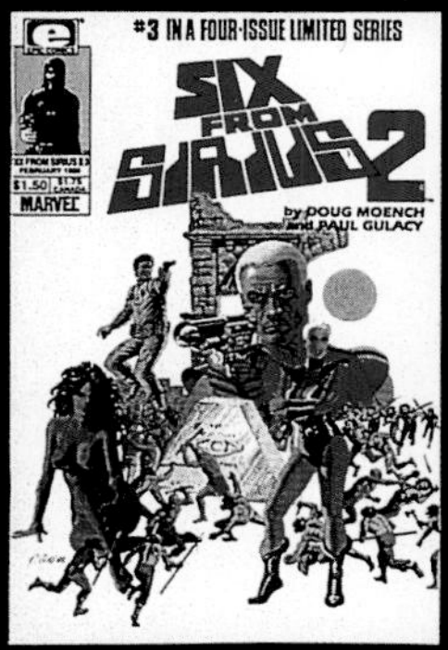
#3 IN A FOUR-ISSUE LIMITED SERIES
SIX FROM SIRIUS 2
by DOUG MOENCH and PAUL GULACY

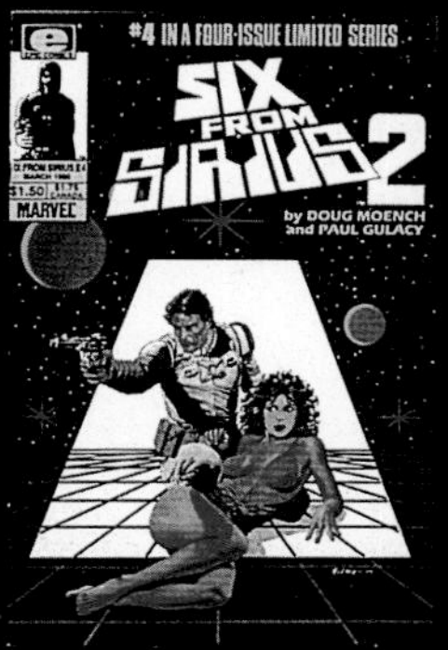
#4 IN A FOUR-ISSUE LIMITED SERIES
SIX FROM SIRIUS 2
by DOUG MOENCH and PAUL GULACY

1701.7 Skull, The Slayer (1-8)

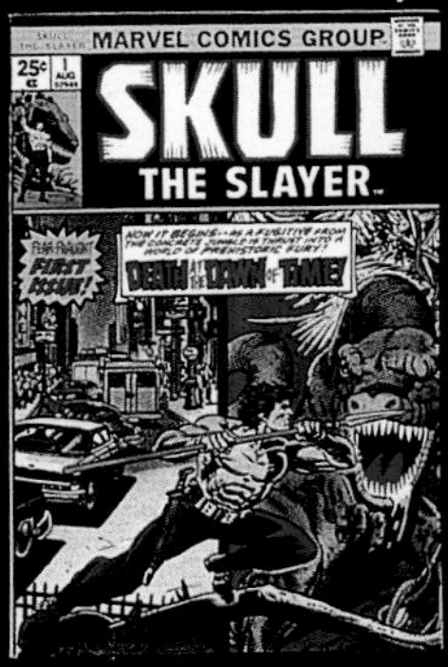
MARVEL COMICS GROUP
SKULL THE SLAYER

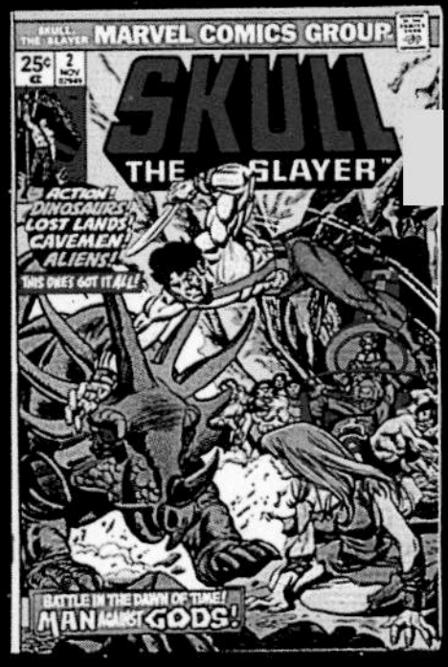
MARVEL COMICS GROUP
SKULL THE SLAYER
BATTLE IN THE DAWN OF TIME! MAN AGAINST GODS!

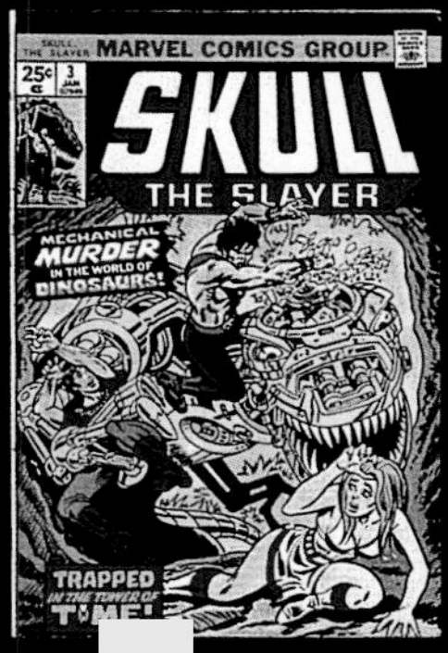
MARVEL COMICS GROUP
SKULL THE SLAYER
MURDER IN THE WORLD OF DINOSAURS!
TRAPPED

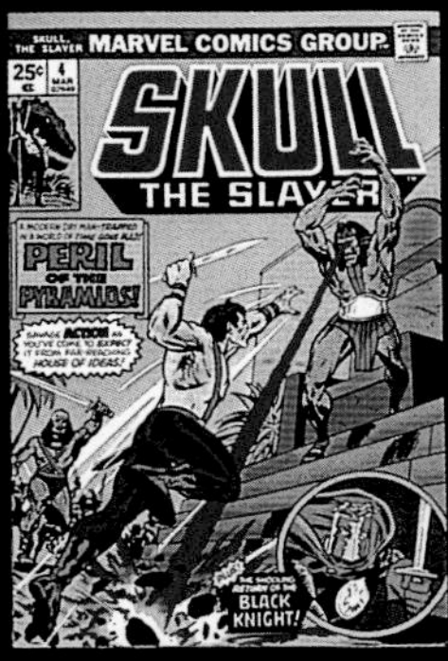
MARVEL COMICS GROUP
SKULL THE SLAYER
PERIL OF THE PYRAMIDS!

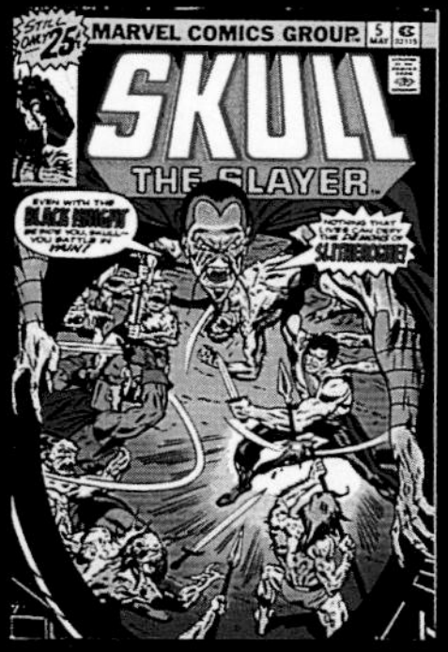
MARVEL COMICS GROUP
SKULL THE SLAYER

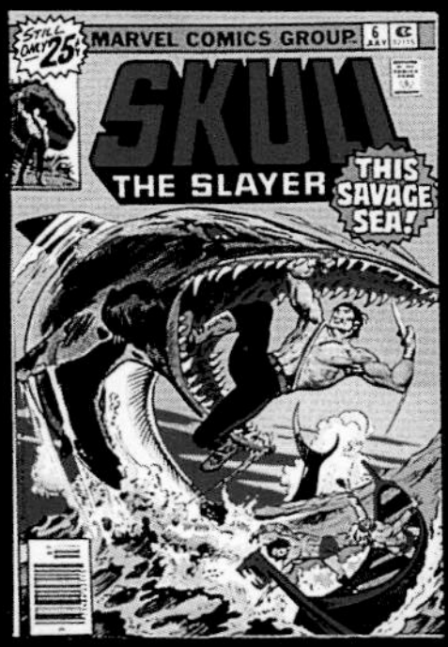
MARVEL COMICS GROUP
SKULL THE SLAYER
THIS SAVAGE SEA!

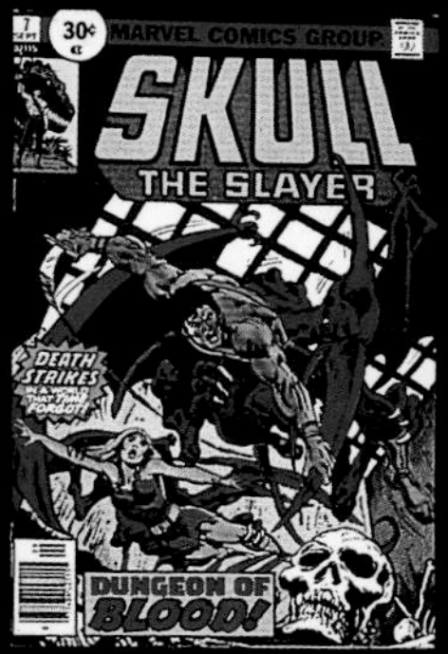
MARVEL COMICS GROUP
SKULL THE SLAYER
DUNGEON OF BLOOD!

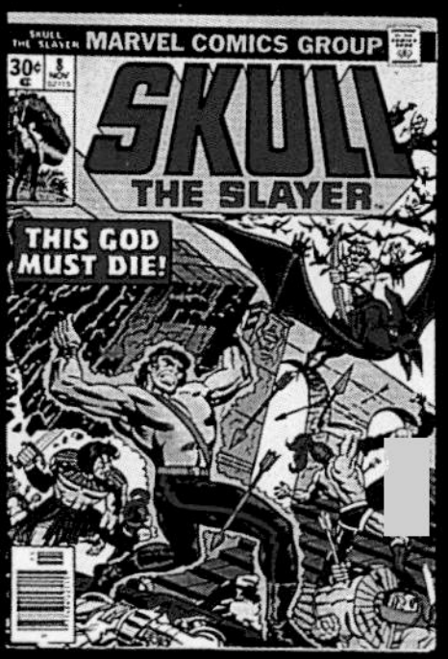
MARVEL COMICS GROUP
SKULL THE SLAYER
THIS GOD MUST DIE!

1717.7 Smurfs (1-2)

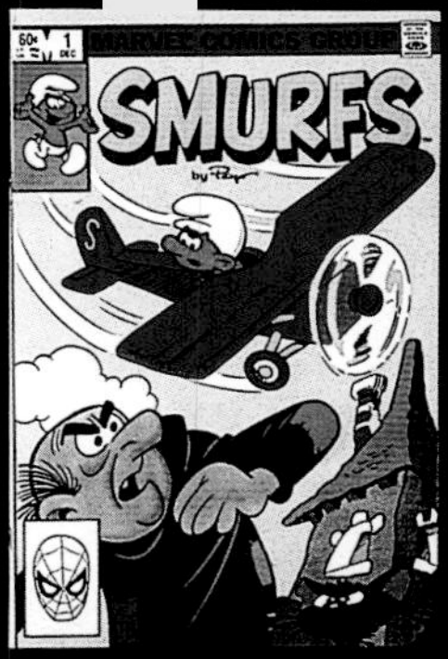
MARVEL COMICS GROUP
SMURFS

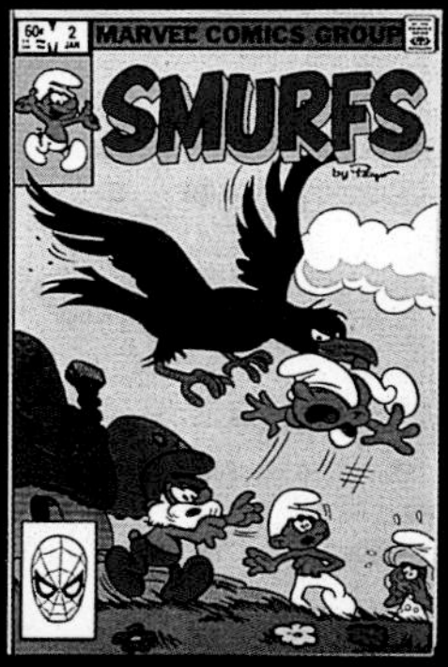
MARVEL COMICS GROUP
SMURFS

1728.8 Son of Satan (1-8)

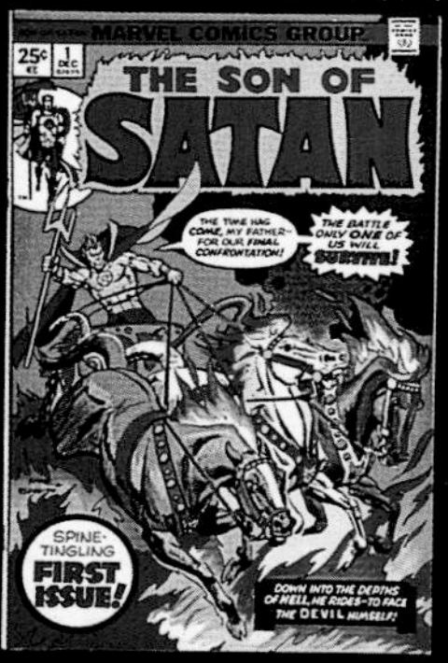
MARVEL COMICS GROUP
THE SON OF SATAN
FIRST ISSUE!

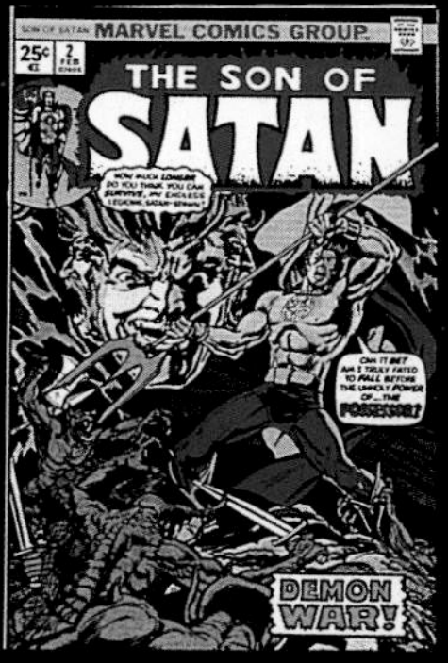
MARVEL COMICS GROUP
THE SON OF SATAN
DEMON WAR!

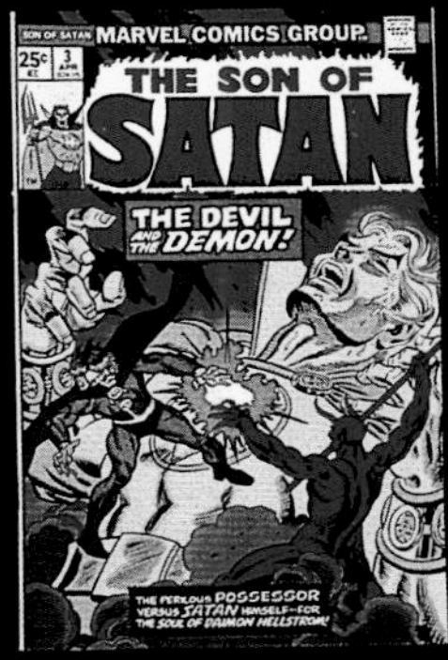
MARVEL COMICS GROUP
THE SON OF SATAN
THE DEVIL AND THE DEMON!

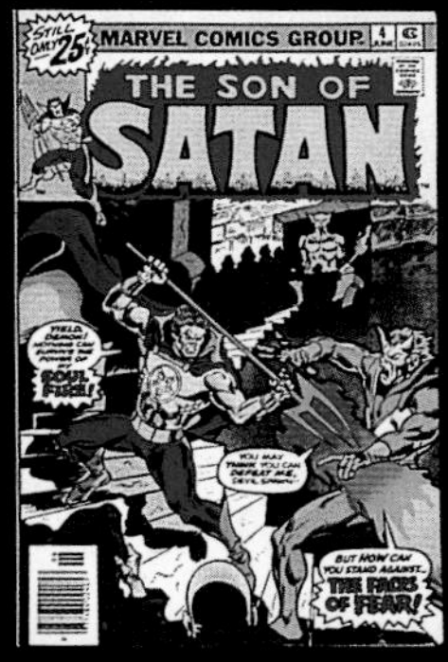
MARVEL COMICS GROUP
THE SON OF SATAN

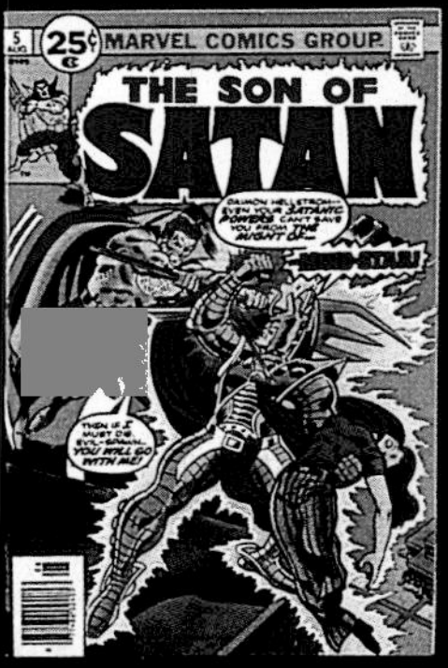
MARVEL COMICS GROUP
THE SON OF SATAN

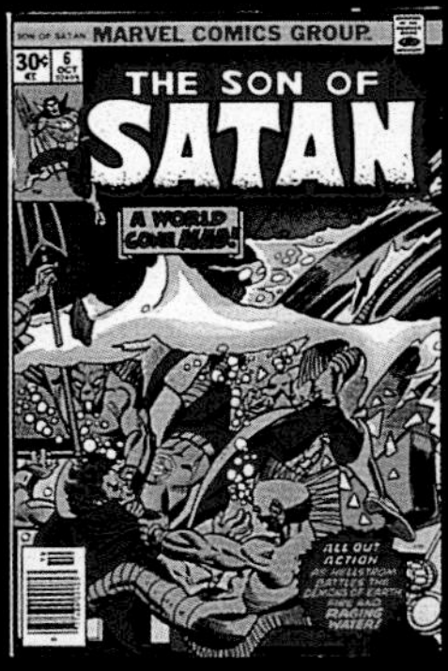
MARVEL COMICS GROUP
THE SON OF SATAN

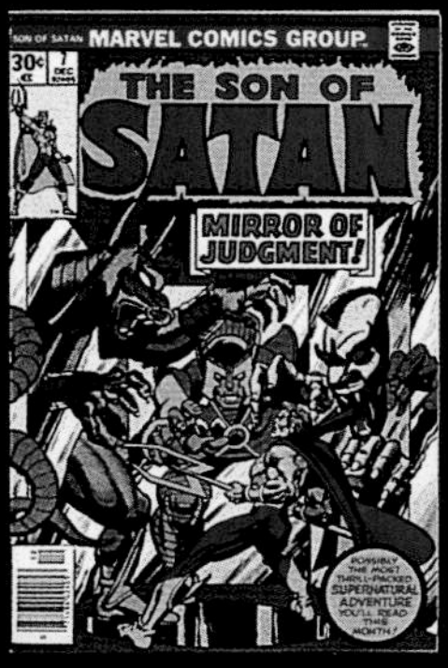
MARVEL COMICS GROUP
THE SON OF SATAN
MIRROR OF JUDGMENT!

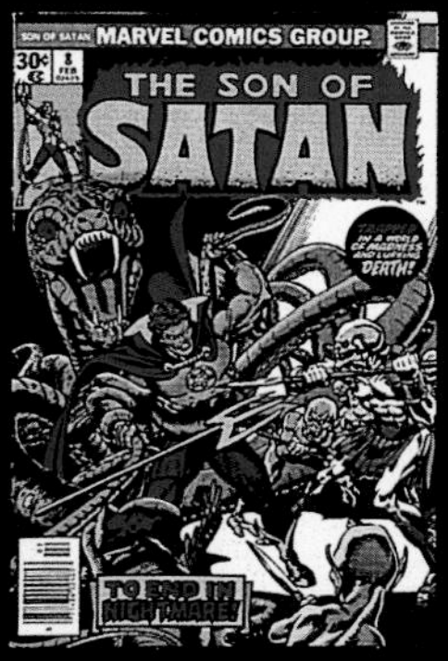
MARVEL COMICS GROUP
THE SON OF SATAN

Sisterhood of Steel (1-8) 1697.6

Ref. No.	Date	RVI	Artist/Info.
1697.6-1	Dec. 1984	2	(Women Mercenaries)
1697.6-2	Feb. 1985	1	
1697.6-3	Apr.	1	
1697.6-4 to 8	Feb. 1986, (#8)	1	

Six from Sirius (1-4) 1697.8

1697.8-1	Jul. 1984	1	Gulacy-c/a
1697.8-2 to 4	Oct. 1984, (#4)	1	Gulacy-c/a (all)

Six from Sirius II 1697.85

1697.85	Dec. 1985	1	Gulacy-c/a
1697.85-2 to 4	May 1986 (#4)	1	Gulacy-c/a (all)

Skull, The Slayer (1-8) 1701.7

1701.7-1	Aug. 1975	1	Kane-c; (Origin-Skull, the Slayer)
1701.7-2 to 8	Nov. 1976, (#8)	1	

Smurfs (1-3) 1718.7

1718.7-1 to 3	Dec. 1982	1	Peyo-a

Son of Satan (1-8) 1728.8

1728.8-1 to 8	Dec. 1975, (#1)	1	Mooney

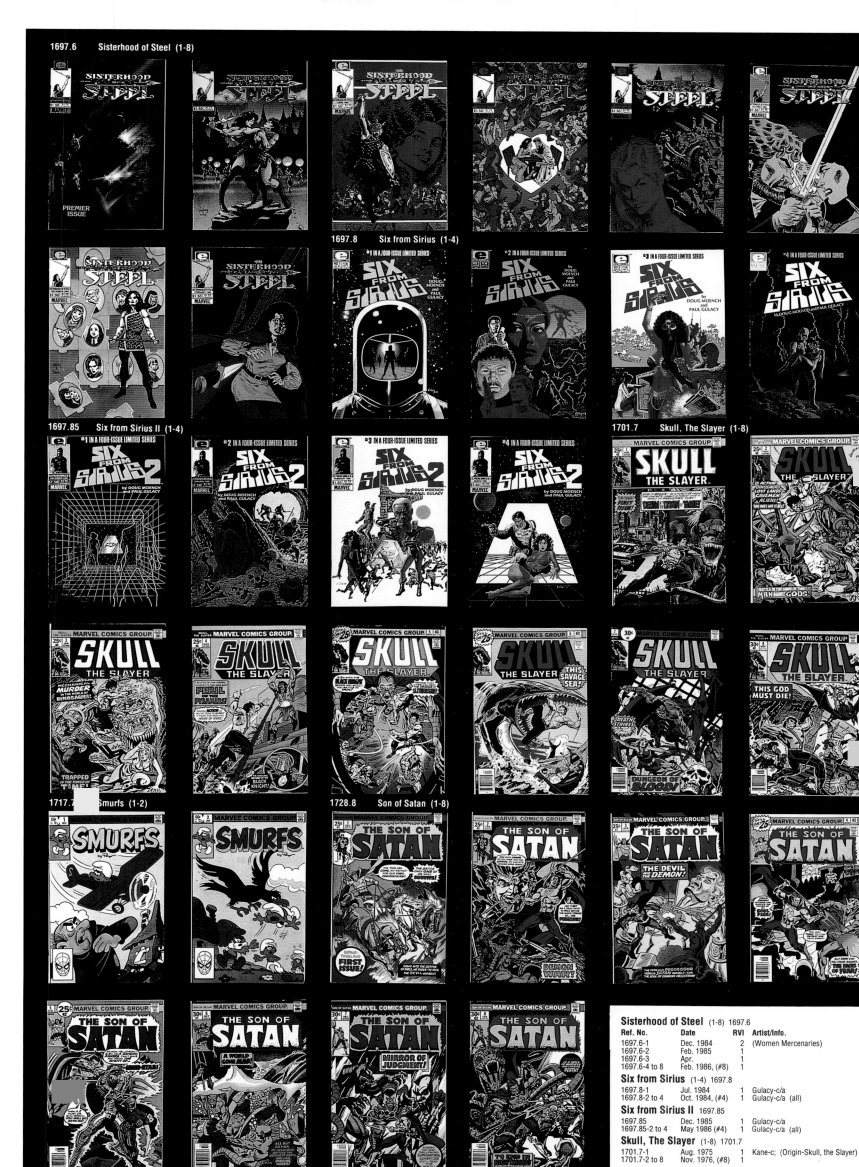

1752.5 Special Marvel Edition (1-16)

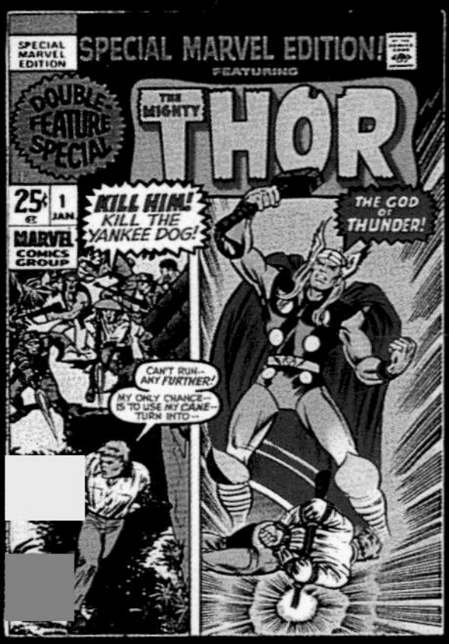
SPECIAL MARVEL EDITION!
DOUBLE FEATURE SPECIAL
THE MIGHTY THOR
KILL HIM! KILL THE YANKEE DOG!
THE GOD OF THUNDER!

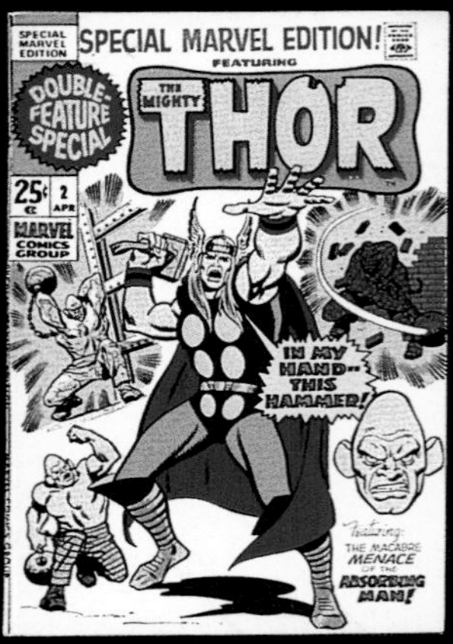
SPECIAL MARVEL EDITION!
DOUBLE FEATURE SPECIAL
THE MIGHTY THOR
IN MY HAND-- THIS HAMMER!

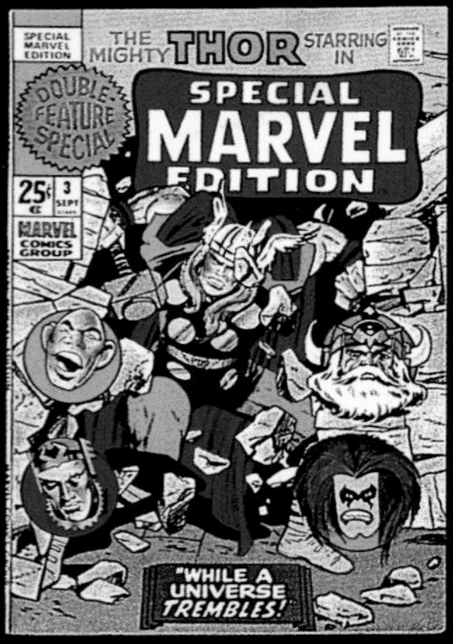
THE MIGHTY THOR STARRING IN
SPECIAL MARVEL EDITION
"WHILE A UNIVERSE TREMBLES!"

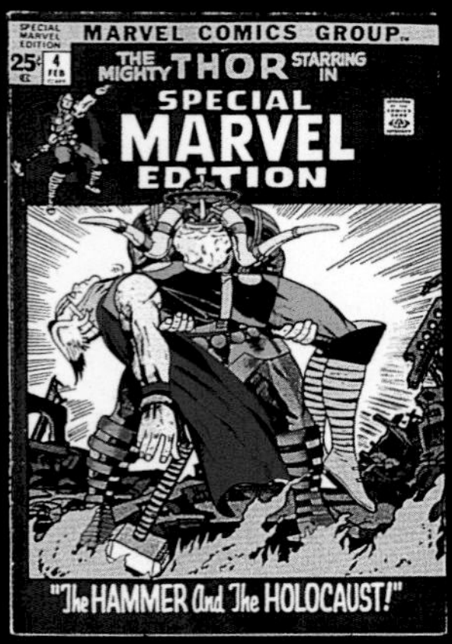
MARVEL COMICS GROUP
THE MIGHTY THOR STARRING IN
SPECIAL MARVEL EDITION
"The HAMMER And The HOLOCAUST!"

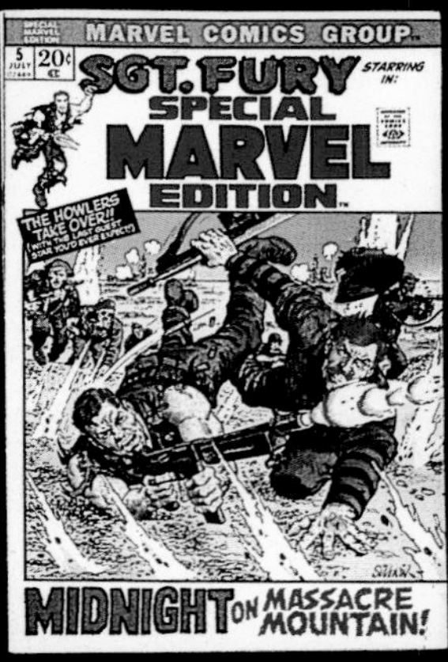
MARVEL COMICS GROUP
SGT. FURY STARRING IN:
SPECIAL MARVEL EDITION
MIDNIGHT ON MASSACRE MOUNTAIN!

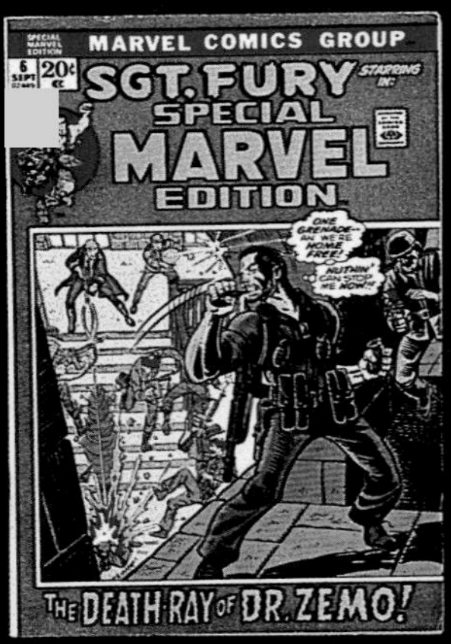
MARVEL COMICS GROUP
SGT. FURY STARRING IN:
SPECIAL MARVEL EDITION
THE DEATH-RAY OF DR. ZEMO!

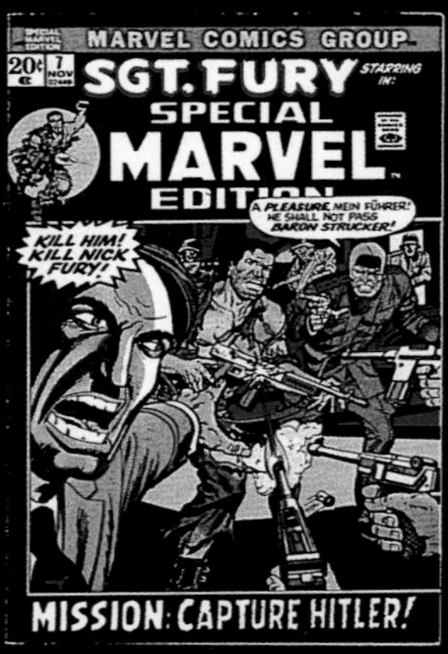
MARVEL COMICS GROUP
SGT. FURY STARRING IN:
SPECIAL MARVEL EDITION
KILL HIM! KILL NICK FURY!
MISSION: CAPTURE HITLER!

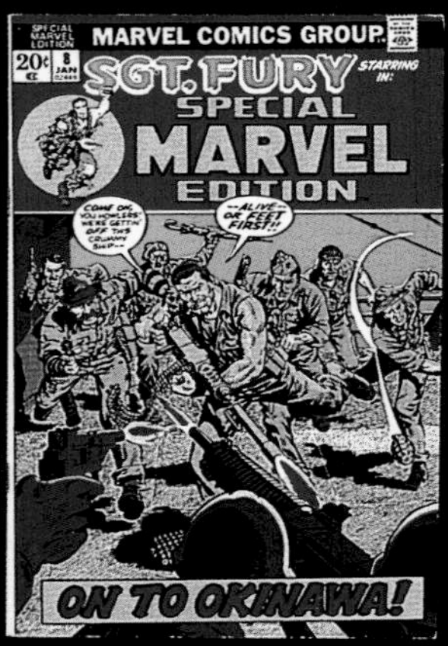
MARVEL COMICS GROUP
SGT. FURY STARRING IN:
SPECIAL MARVEL EDITION
ON TO OKINAWA!

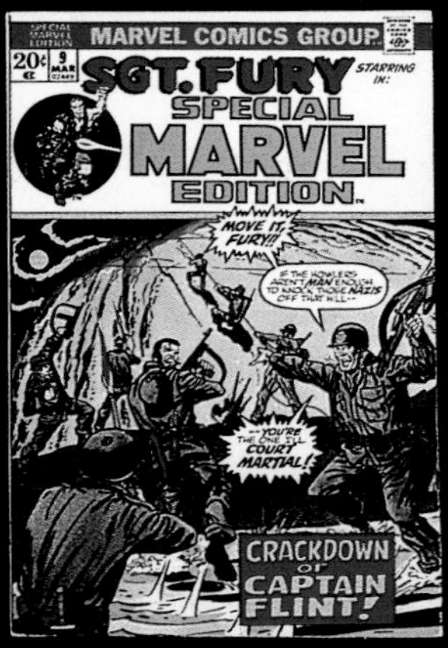
MARVEL COMICS GROUP
SGT. FURY STARRING IN:
SPECIAL MARVEL EDITION
MOVE IT, FURY!
CRACKDOWN OF CAPTAIN FLINT!

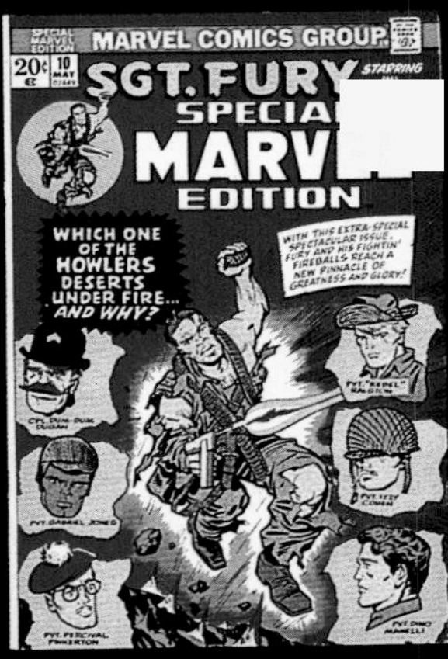
MARVEL COMICS GROUP
SGT. FURY STARRING IN:
SPECIAL
EDITION
WHICH ONE OF THE HOWLERS DESERTS UNDER FIRE... AND WHY?

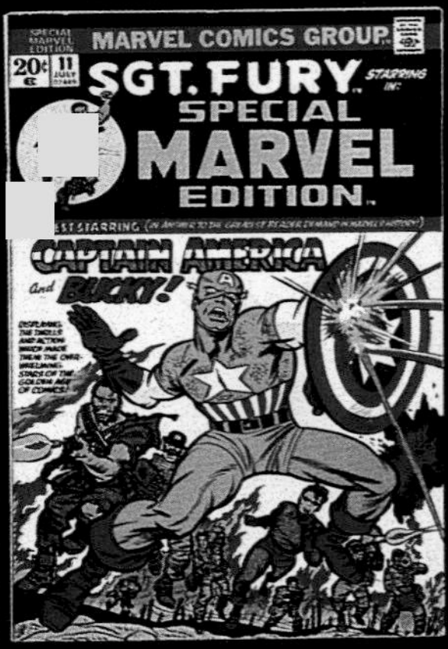
MARVEL COMICS GROUP
SGT. FURY STARRING IN:
SPECIAL MARVEL EDITION
CAPTAIN AMERICA and BUCKY!

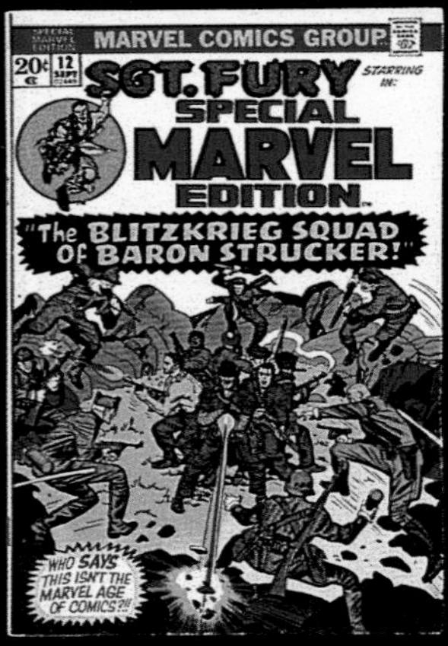
MARVEL COMICS GROUP
SGT. FURY STARRING IN:
SPECIAL MARVEL EDITION
"The BLITZKRIEG SQUAD of BARON STRUCKER!"

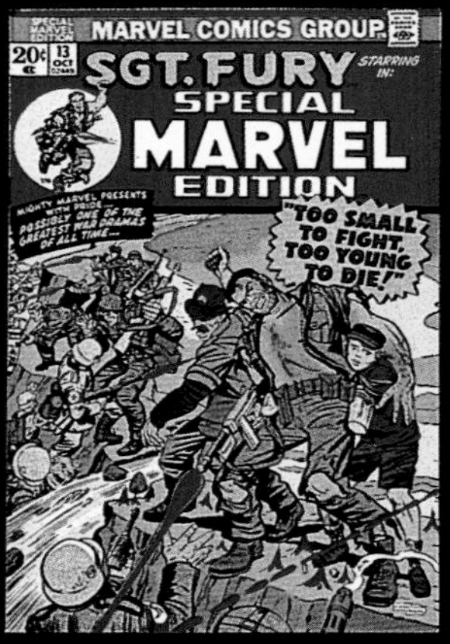
MARVEL COMICS GROUP
SGT. FURY STARRING IN:
SPECIAL MARVEL EDITION
"TOO SMALL TO FIGHT, TOO YOUNG TO DIE!"

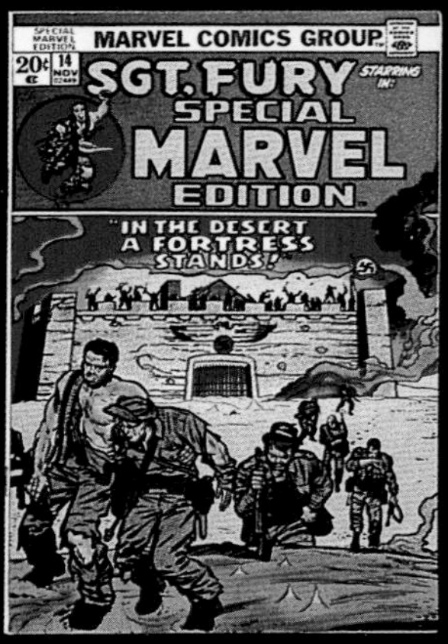
MARVEL COMICS GROUP
SGT. FURY STARRING IN:
SPECIAL MARVEL EDITION
"IN THE DESERT A FORTRESS STANDS!"

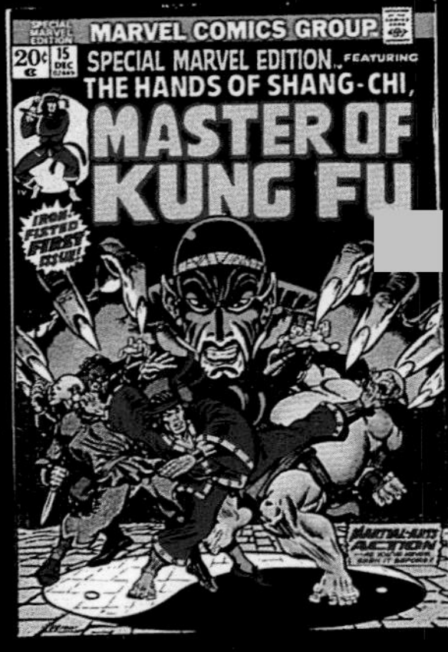
MARVEL COMICS GROUP
SPECIAL MARVEL EDITION FEATURING
THE HANDS OF SHANG-CHI, MASTER OF KUNG FU

1752.5 Master of Kung Fu (17-25)

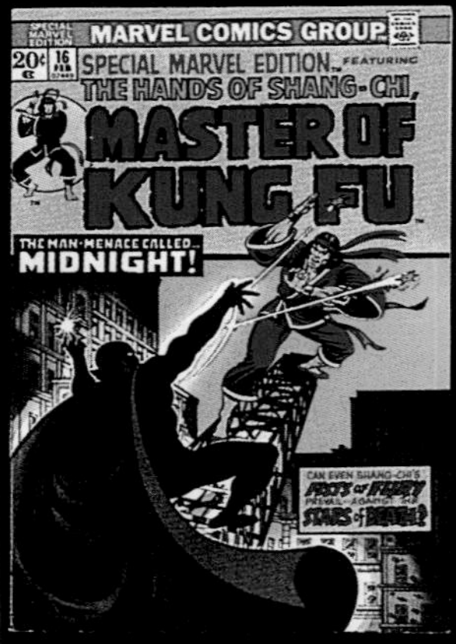
MARVEL COMICS GROUP
SPECIAL MARVEL EDITION FEATURING
THE HANDS OF SHANG-CHI, MASTER OF KUNG FU
THE MAN-MENACE CALLED MIDNIGHT!

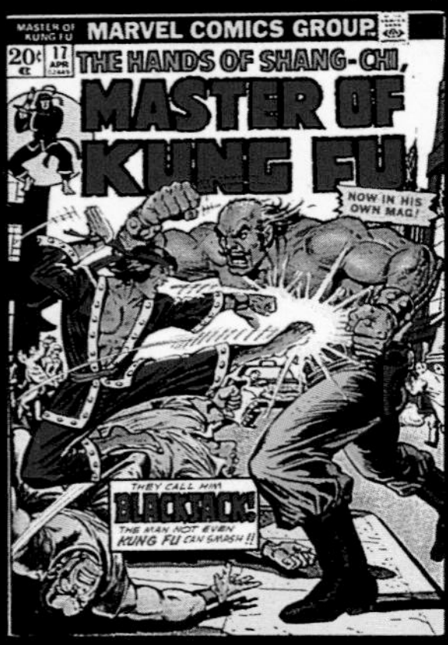
MARVEL COMICS GROUP
THE HANDS OF SHANG-CHI, MASTER OF KUNG FU
NOW IN HIS OWN MAG!
THEY CALL HIM BLACKJACK

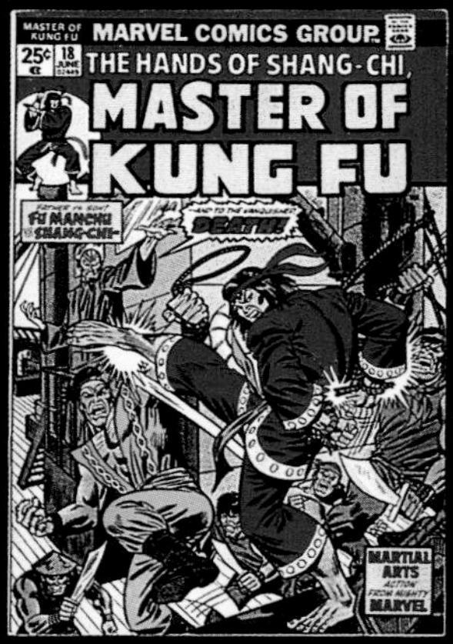
MARVEL COMICS GROUP
THE HANDS OF SHANG-CHI, MASTER OF KUNG FU
MARTIAL ARTS

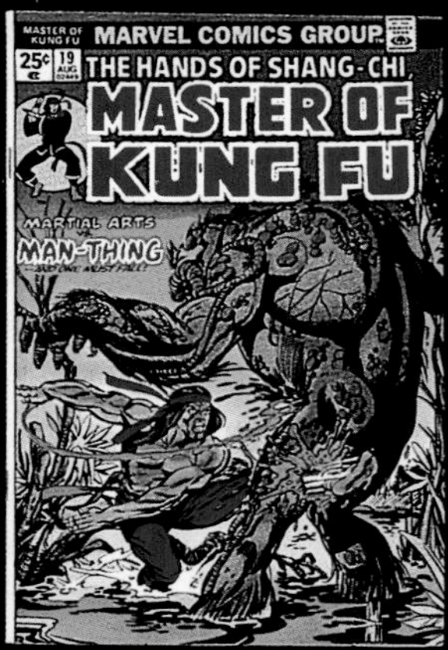
MARVEL COMICS GROUP
THE HANDS OF SHANG-CHI, MASTER OF KUNG FU
MARTIAL ARTS
MAN-THING

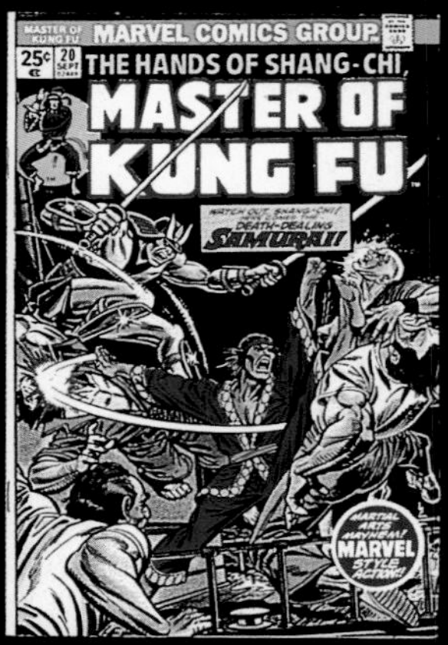
MARVEL COMICS GROUP
THE HANDS OF SHANG-CHI, MASTER OF KUNG FU
SAMURAI!

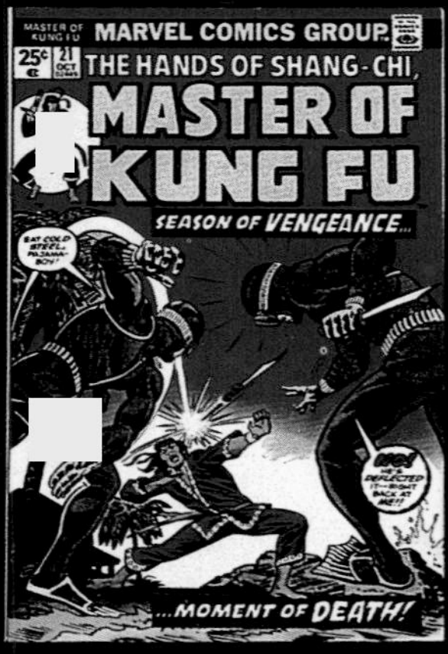
MARVEL COMICS GROUP
THE HANDS OF SHANG-CHI, MASTER OF KUNG FU
SEASON OF VENGEANCE...
...MOMENT OF DEATH!

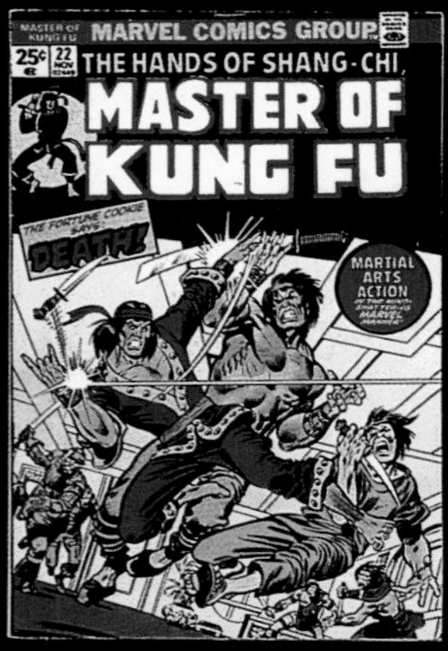
MARVEL COMICS GROUP
MASTER OF KUNG FU
DEATH!
MARTIAL ARTS ACTION

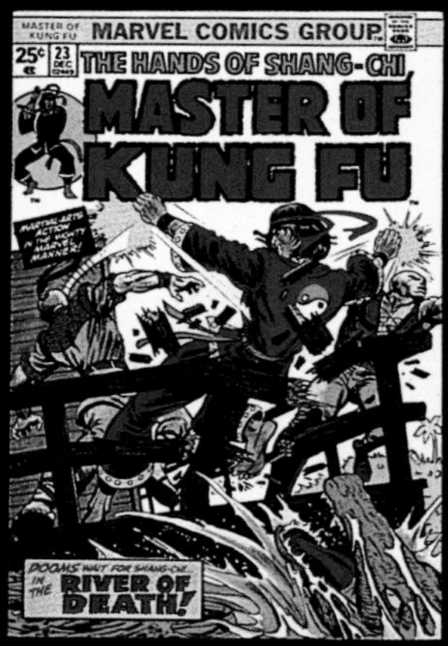
MARVEL COMICS GROUP
THE HANDS OF SHANG-CHI, MASTER OF KUNG FU
RIVER OF DEATH!

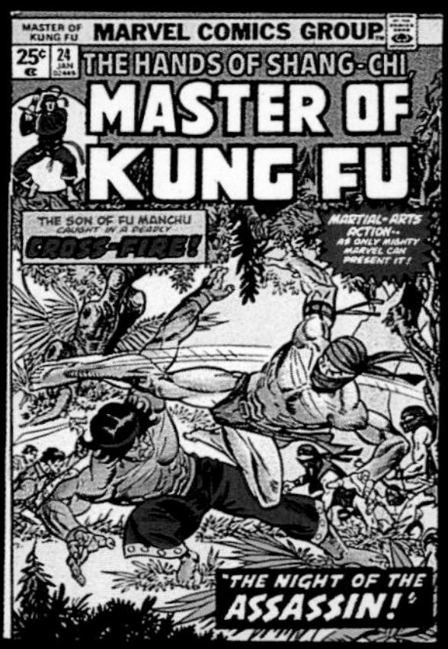
MARVEL COMICS GROUP
THE HANDS OF SHANG-CHI, MASTER OF KUNG FU
CROSS-FIRE!
"THE NIGHT OF THE ASSASSIN!"

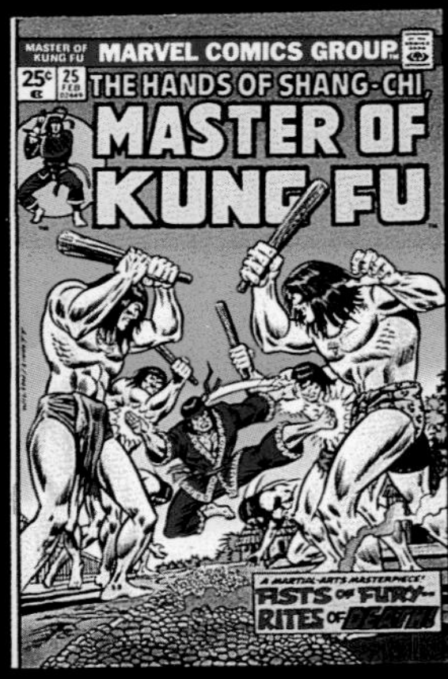
MARVEL COMICS GROUP
THE HANDS OF SHANG-CHI, MASTER OF KUNG FU
FISTS OF FURY-- RITES OF DEATH

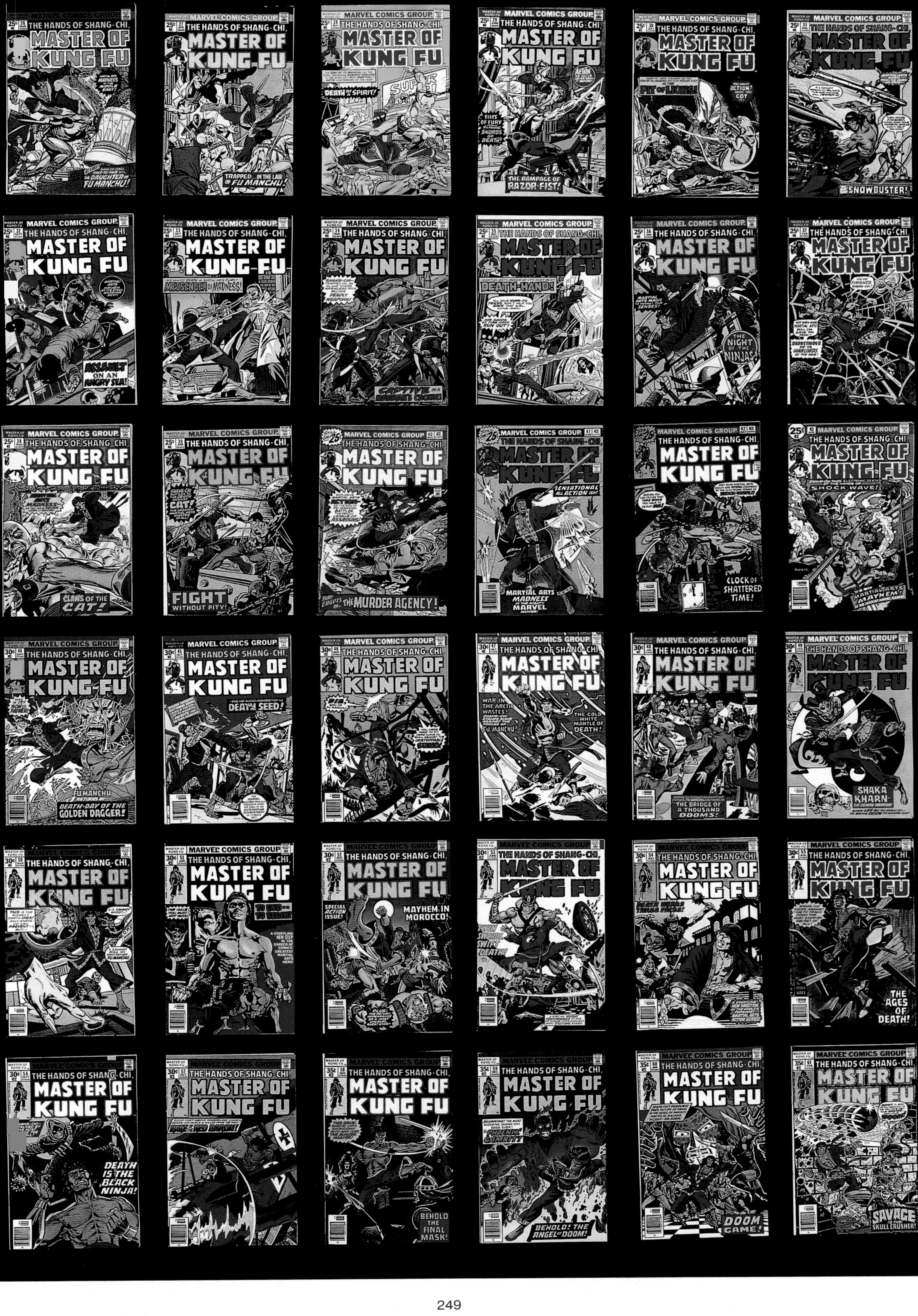
MARVEL COMICS GROUP
THE HANDS OF SHANG-CHI, MASTER OF KUNG FU
THE DAUGHTER OF FU MANCHU!
TRAPPED...IN THE LAIR OF FU MANCHU!
DEATH SPIRIT!
THE RAMPAGE OF RAZOR-FIST!
PIT OF LIONS!
SNOWBUSTER!
ASSAULT ON AN ANGRY SEA!
MESSENGER OF MADNESS!
DEATH-HAND!
THE NIGHT OF THE NINJAS
CLAWS OF THE CAT!
FIGHT WITHOUT PITY!
THE MURDER AGENCY!
SENSATIONAL ALL ACTION ISSUE
MARTIAL ARTS MADNESS
CLOCK OF SHATTERED TIME!
SHOCK WAVE!
FU MANCHU RETURNS IN--
DEATH-DAY OF THE GOLDEN DAGGER!
DEATH SEED!
WAR IN THE ARCTIC WASTES!
THE COLD WHITE MANTLE OF DEATH!
THE BRIDGE OF A THOUSAND DOOMS!
SHAKA KHARN
MAYHEM IN MOROCCO!
SPECIAL ACTION ISSUE!
THE AGES OF DEATH!
DEATH IS THE BLACK NINJA!
BEHOLD THE FINAL MASK!
BEHOLD! THE ANGEL OF DOOM!
DOOM GAME!
SAVAGE IS THE SKULLCRUSHER!

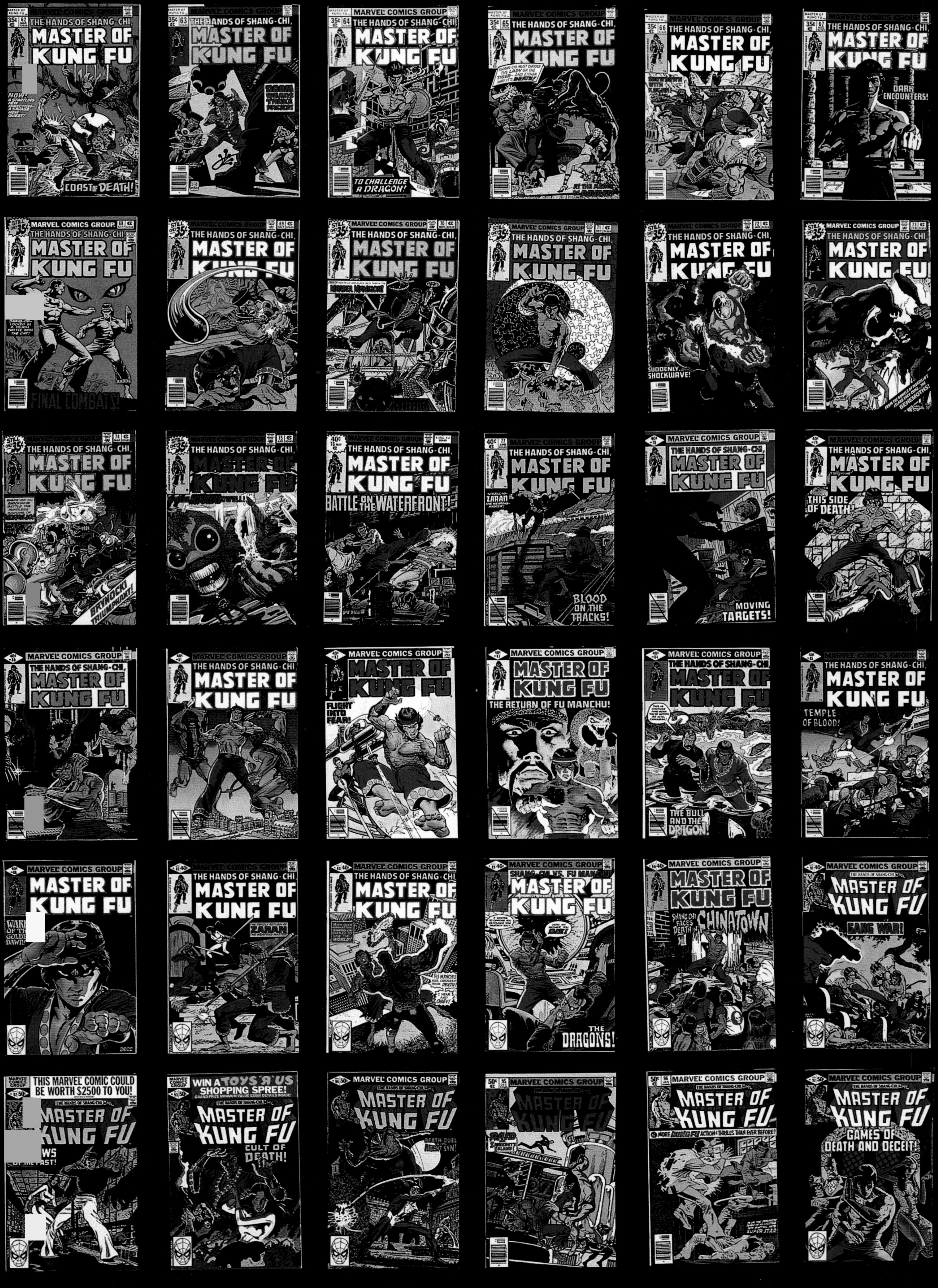
MARVEL COMICS GROUP
THE HANDS OF SHANG-CHI, MASTER OF KUNG FU
COAST OF DEATH!
THE HANDS OF SHANG-CHI, MASTER OF KUNG FU
MARVEL COMICS GROUP
THE HANDS OF SHANG-CHI, MASTER OF KUNG FU
TO CHALLENGE A DRAGON!
MARVEL COMICS GROUP
THE HANDS OF SHANG-CHI, MASTER OF KUNG FU
SHANG-CHI MUST CHOOSE THE LADY OR THE TIGER—AND EITHER WAY IT'S DEATH!
MARVEL COMICS GROUP
THE HANDS OF SHANG-CHI, MASTER OF KUNG FU
MARVEL COMICS GROUP
THE HANDS OF SHANG-CHI, MASTER OF KUNG FU
DARK ENCOUNTERS!
MARVEL COMICS GROUP
THE HANDS OF SHANG-CHI, MASTER OF KUNG FU
FINAL COMBATS!
MARVEL COMICS GROUP
THE HANDS OF SHANG-CHI, MASTER OF KUNG FU
MARVEL COMICS GROUP
THE HANDS OF SHANG-CHI, MASTER OF KUNG FU
MARVEL COMICS GROUP
THE HANDS OF SHANG-CHI, MASTER OF KUNG FU
MARVEL COMICS GROUP
THE HANDS OF SHANG-CHI, MASTER OF KUNG FU
SUDDENLY... SHOCKWAVE!
MARVEL COMICS GROUP
THE HANDS OF SHANG-CHI, MASTER OF KUNG FU
BEHEMOTHS!
MARVEL COMICS GROUP
THE HANDS OF SHANG-CHI, MASTER OF KUNG FU
MARVEL COMICS GROUP
THE HANDS OF SHANG-CHI, MASTER OF KUNG FU
MARVEL COMICS GROUP
THE HANDS OF SHANG-CHI, MASTER OF KUNG FU
BATTLE ON THE WATERFRONT!
MARVEL COMICS GROUP
THE HANDS OF SHANG-CHI, MASTER OF KUNG FU
BLOOD ON THE TRACKS!
MARVEL COMICS GROUP
THE HANDS OF SHANG-CHI, MASTER OF KUNG FU
MOVING TARGETS!
MARVEL COMICS GROUP
THE HANDS OF SHANG-CHI, MASTER OF KUNG FU
THIS SIDE OF DEATH!
MARVEL COMICS GROUP
THE HANDS OF SHANG-CHI, MASTER OF KUNG FU
MARVEL COMICS GROUP
THE HANDS OF SHANG-CHI, MASTER OF KUNG FU
MARVEL COMICS GROUP
MASTER OF KUNG FU
FLIGHT INTO FEAR!
MARVEL COMICS GROUP
MASTER OF KUNG FU
THE RETURN OF FU MANCHU!
MARVEL COMICS GROUP
THE HANDS OF SHANG-CHI, MASTER OF KUNG FU
THE BULL AND THE DRAGON!
MARVEL COMICS GROUP
THE HANDS OF SHANG-CHI, MASTER OF KUNG FU
TEMPLE OF BLOOD!
MARVEL COMICS GROUP
MASTER OF KUNG FU
MARVEL COMICS GROUP
THE HANDS OF SHANG-CHI, MASTER OF KUNG FU
ZARAN
MARVEL COMICS GROUP
THE HANDS OF SHANG-CHI, MASTER OF KUNG FU
MARVEL COMICS GROUP
SHANG-CHI VS. FU MANCHU
MASTER OF KUNG FU
THE DRAGONS!
MARVEL COMICS GROUP
MASTER OF KUNG FU
CHINATOWN
MARVEL COMICS GROUP
MASTER OF KUNG FU
GANG WAR!
THIS MARVEL COMIC COULD BE WORTH $2500 TO YOU!
MASTER OF KUNG FU
WIN A TOYS "R" US SHOPPING SPREE!
MASTER OF KUNG FU
CULT OF DEATH!
MARVEL COMICS GROUP
MASTER OF KUNG FU
MARVEL COMICS GROUP
MASTER OF KUNG FU
MARVEL COMICS GROUP
MASTER OF KUNG FU
MARVEL COMICS GROUP
MASTER OF KUNG FU
GAMES OF DEATH AND DECEIT!

1752.5 Master of Kung Fu (98-125)

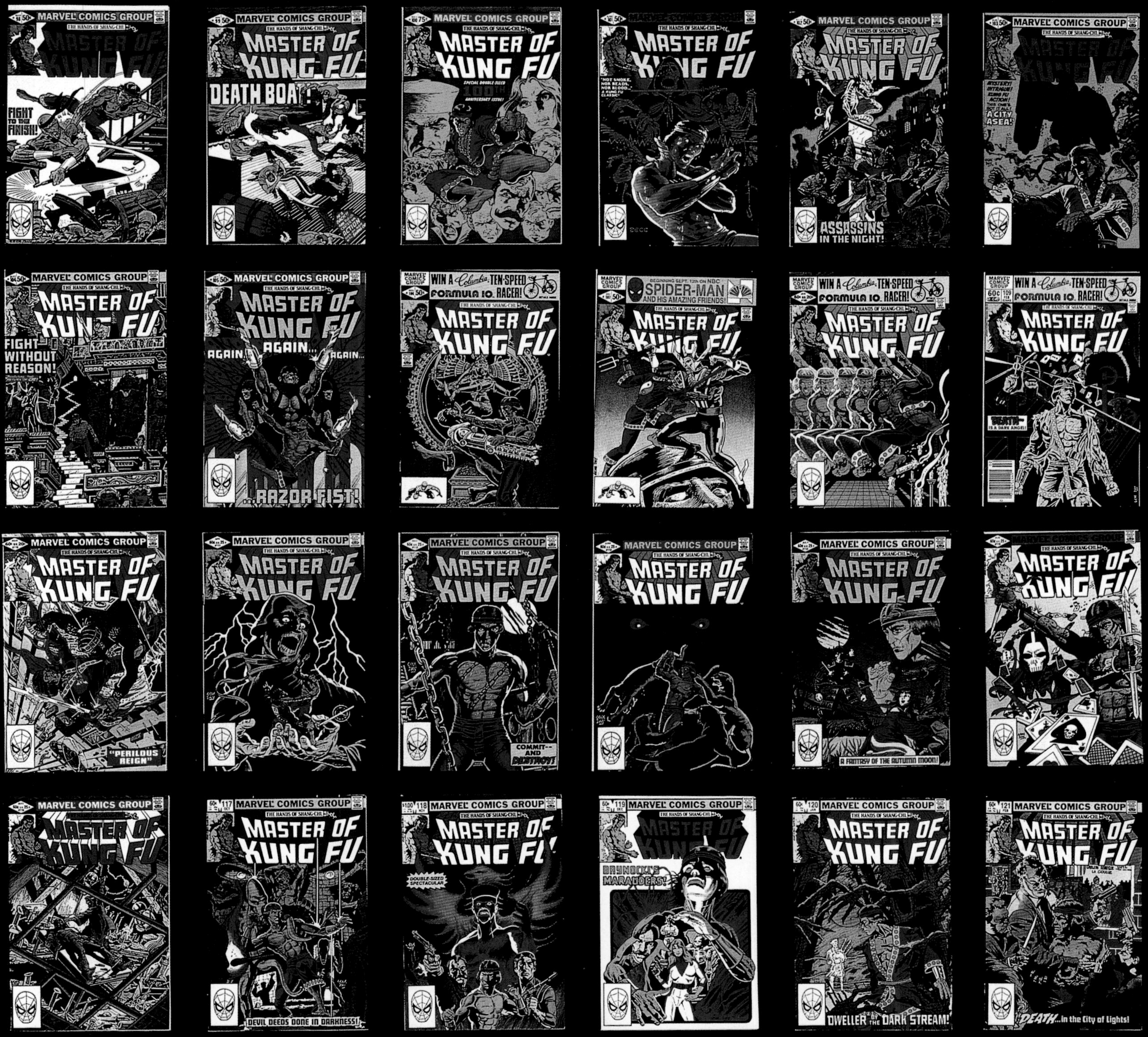
MARVEL COMICS GROUP
MASTER OF KUNG FU
FIGHT TO THE FINISH!
DEATH BOAT!
ASSASSINS IN THE NIGHT!
FIGHT WITHOUT REASON!
AGAIN... AGAIN... AGAIN...
...RAZOR FIST!
WIN A Columbia TEN-SPEED FORMULA 10 RACER!
SPIDER-MAN AND HIS AMAZING FRIENDS!
"PERILOUS REIGN"
COMMIT--AND DESTROY!
A FANTASY OF THE AUTUMN MOON!
DEVIL DEEDS DONE IN DARKNESS!
DWELLER BY THE DARK STREAM!
DEATH...in the City of Lights!

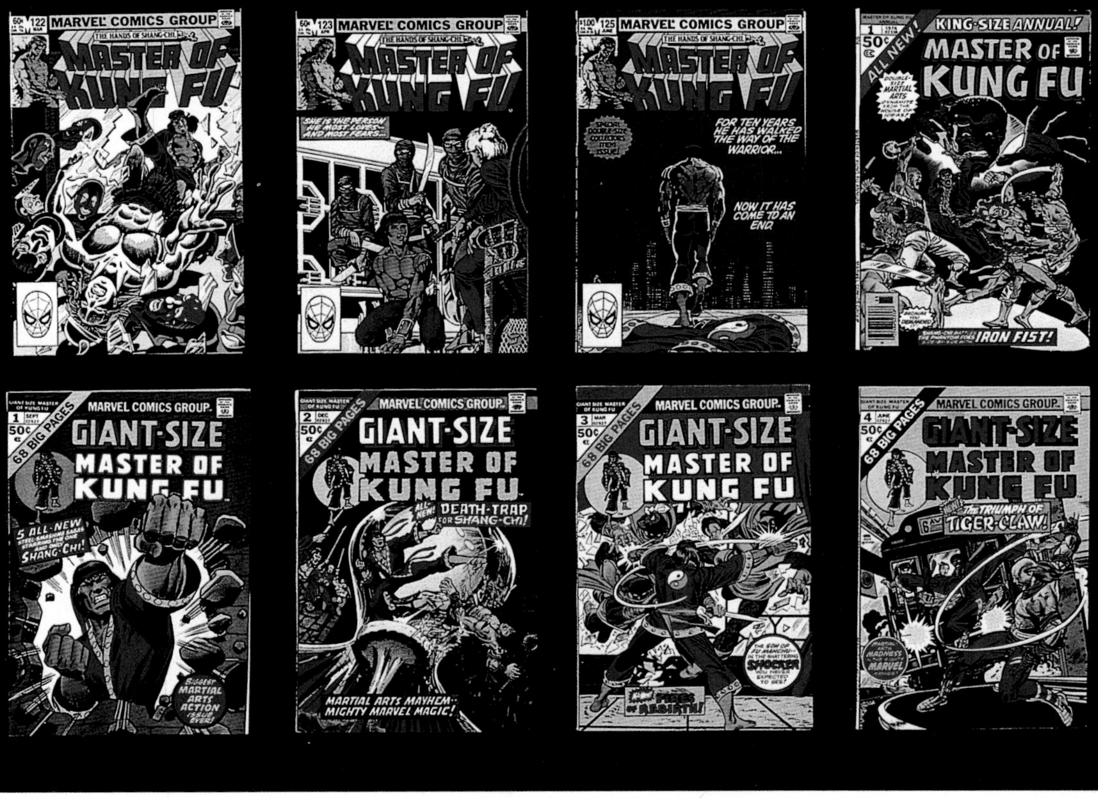
MARVEL COMICS GROUP
MASTER OF KUNG FU
KING-SIZE ANNUAL!
IRON FIST!
GIANT-SIZE MASTER OF KUNG FU
68 BIG PAGES
DEATH-TRAP FOR SHANG-CHI!
MARTIAL ARTS MAYHEM-MIGHTY MARVEL MAGIC!
THE TRIUMPH OF TIGER-CLAW!

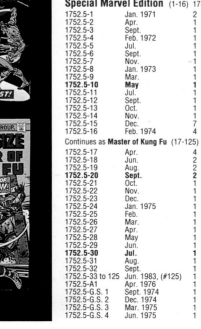

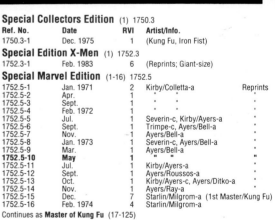

Special Collectors Edition (1) 1750.3

Ref. No.	Date	RVI	Artist/Info.
1750.3-1	Dec. 1975	1	(Kung Fu, Iron Fist)

Special Edition X-Men (1) 1752.3

Ref. No.	Date	RVI	Artist/Info.
1752.3-1	Feb. 1983	6	(Reprints; Giant-size)

Special Marvel Edition (1-16) 1752.5

Ref. No.	Date	RVI	Artist/Info.	
1752.5-1	Jan. 1971	2	Kirby/Colletta-a	Reprints
1752.5-2	Apr.	1	" "	"
1752.5-3	Sept.	1	" "	"
1752.5-4	Feb. 1972	1	" "	"
1752.5-5	Jul.	1	Severin-c, Kirby/Ayers-a	"
1752.5-6	Sept.	1	Trimpe-c, Ayers/Bell-a	"
1752.5-7	Nov.	1	Ayers/Bell-a	"
1752.5-8	Jan. 1973	1	Severin-c, Ayers/Bell-a	"
1752.5-9	Mar.	1	Ayers/Bell-a	"
1752.5-10	**May**	**1**	**" "**	**"**
1752.5-11	Jul.	1	Kirby/Ayers-a	"
1752.5-12	Sept.	1	Ayers/Roussos-a	"
1752.5-13	Oct.	1	Kirby/Ayers-c, Ayers/Ditko-a	"
1752.5-14	Nov.	1	Ayers/Ray-a	"
1752.5-15	Dec.	7	Starlin/Milgrom-a (1st Master/Kung Fu)	
1752.5-16	Feb. 1974	4	Starlin/Milgrom-a	

Continues as **Master of Kung Fu** (17-125)

Ref. No.	Date	RVI	Artist/Info.	
1752.5-17	Apr.	4	Starlin/Milgrom-a	
1752.5-18	Jun.	2	Gulacy/Milgrom-a	
1752.5-19	Aug.	2	" "	
1752.5-20	**Sept.**	**2**	**" "**	
1752.5-21	Oct.	1	Wilson, Milgrom-a	
1752.5-22	Nov.	1	Gulacy, Adkins-a	
1752.5-23	Dec.	1	Milgrom, Janson-a	
1752.5-24	Jan. 1975	1	Starlin, Weiss, Simonson, Milgrom/Trapani-a	
1752.5-25	Feb.	1	Wilson/Sinnott-c, Gulacy/Trapani-a	
1752.5-26	Mar.	1	Pollard/Trapani-a	
1752.5-27	Apr.	1	Buscema/Springer-a	
1752.5-28	May	1	Wilson, Hannigan, Bradford/Trapani-a	
1752.5-29	Jun.	1	Gulacy-a	
1752.5-30	**Jul.**	**1**	**Gulacy, Adkins-a**	
1752.5-31	Aug.	1	Kane/Adkins-c, Gulacy/Adkins-a	
1752.5-32	Sept.	1	Kane/Esposito-c, Buscema/Esposito-a	
1752.5-33 to 125	Jun. 1983, (#125)	1		
1752.5-A1	Apr. 1976	1	(Iron Fist)	
1752.5-G.S. 1	Sept. 1974	1	Russell-a	Reprints
1752.5-G.S. 2	Dec. 1974	1		"
1752.5-G.S. 3	Mar. 1975	1		"
1752.5-G.S. 4	Jun. 1975	1		"

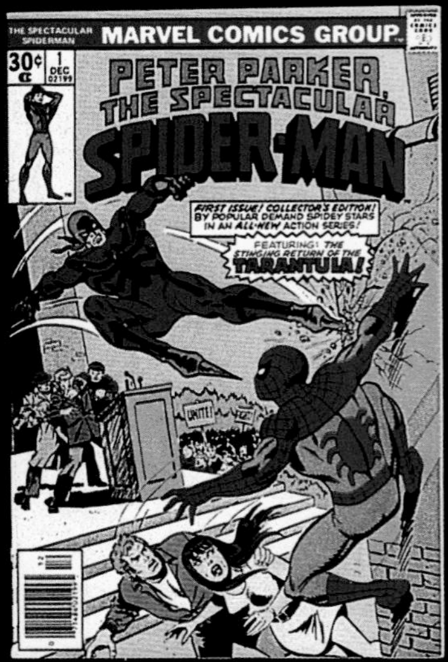
MARVEL COMICS GROUP
30¢ 1 DEC
PETER PARKER, THE SPECTACULAR SPIDER-MAN
FIRST ISSUE! COLLECTOR'S EDITION! BY POPULAR DEMAND SPIDEY STARS IN AN ALL-NEW ACTION SERIES! FEATURING: THE STINGING RETURN OF THE TARANTULA!

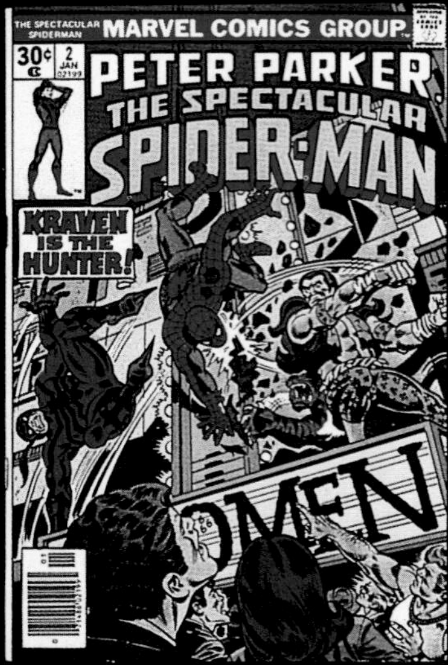
MARVEL COMICS GROUP
30¢ 2 JAN
PETER PARKER THE SPECTACULAR SPIDER-MAN
KRAVEN IS THE HUNTER!

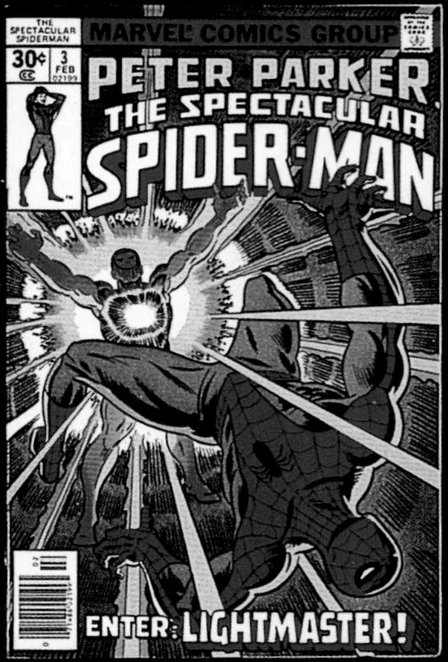
MARVEL COMICS GROUP
30¢ 3 FEB
PETER PARKER THE SPECTACULAR SPIDER-MAN
ENTER: LIGHTMASTER!

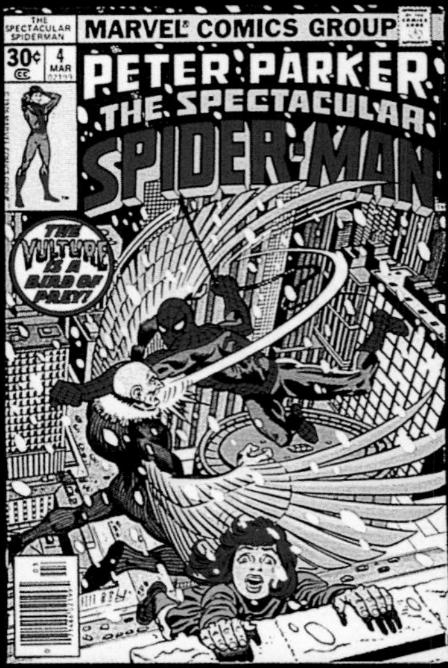
MARVEL COMICS GROUP
30¢ 4 MAR
PETER PARKER THE SPECTACULAR SPIDER-MAN
THE VULTURE IS A BIRD OF PREY!

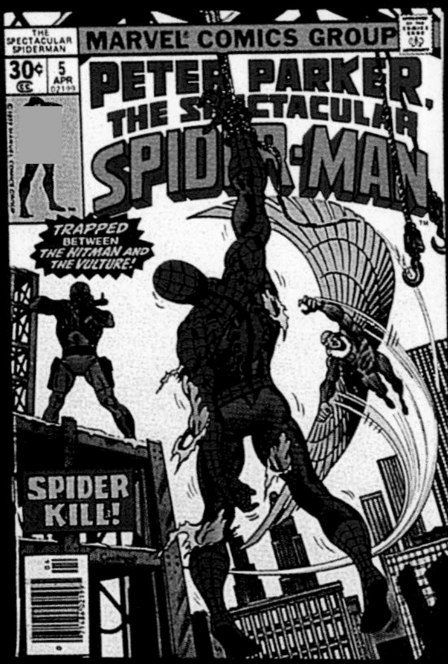
MARVEL COMICS GROUP
30¢ 5 APR
PETER PARKER, THE SPECTACULAR SPIDER-MAN
TRAPPED BETWEEN THE HITMAN AND THE VULTURE!
SPIDER KILL!

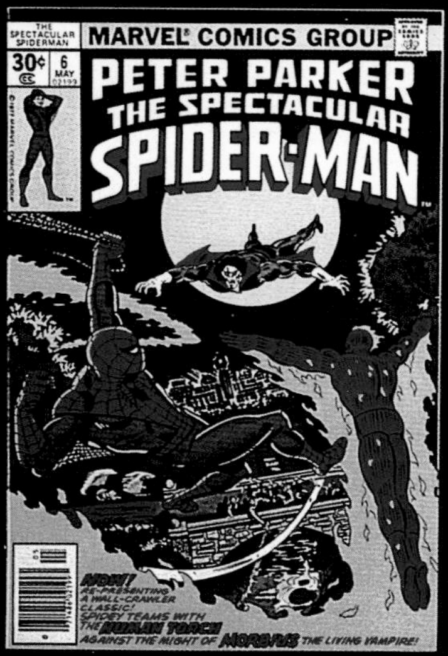
MARVEL COMICS GROUP
30¢ 6 MAY
PETER PARKER THE SPECTACULAR SPIDER-MAN
AGAINST THE MIGHT OF MORBIUS THE LIVING VAMPIRE!

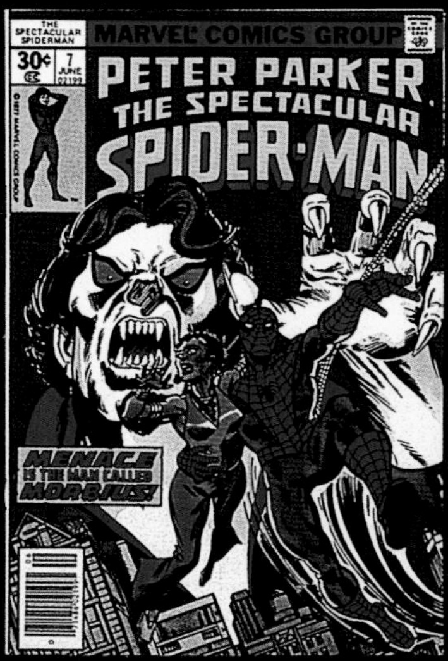
MARVEL COMICS GROUP
30¢ 7 JUNE
PETER PARKER THE SPECTACULAR SPIDER-MAN
MENACE IS THE MAN CALLED MORBIUS!

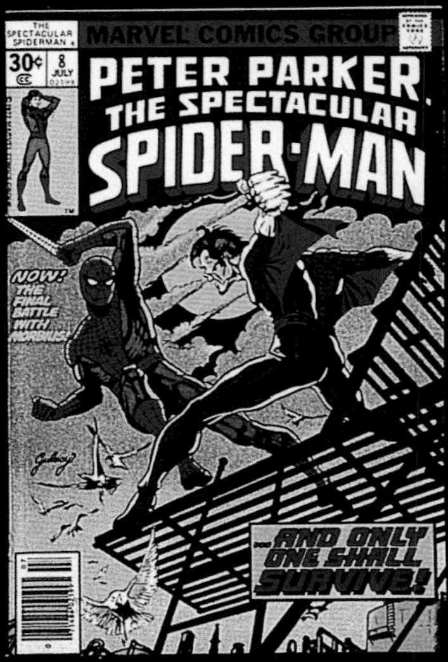
MARVEL COMICS GROUP
30¢ 8 JULY
PETER PARKER THE SPECTACULAR SPIDER-MAN
NOW! THE FINAL BATTLE WITH MORBIUS!
AND ONLY ONE SHALL SURVIVE!

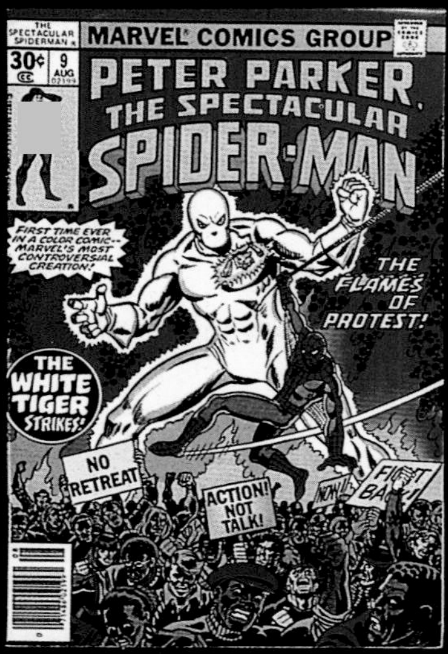
MARVEL COMICS GROUP
30¢ 9 AUG
PETER PARKER, THE SPECTACULAR SPIDER-MAN
FIRST TIME EVER IN A COLOR COMIC: MARVEL'S MOST CONTROVERSIAL CREATION!
THE FLAMES OF PROTEST!
THE WHITE TIGER STRIKES!
NO RETREAT
ACTION! NOT TALK!

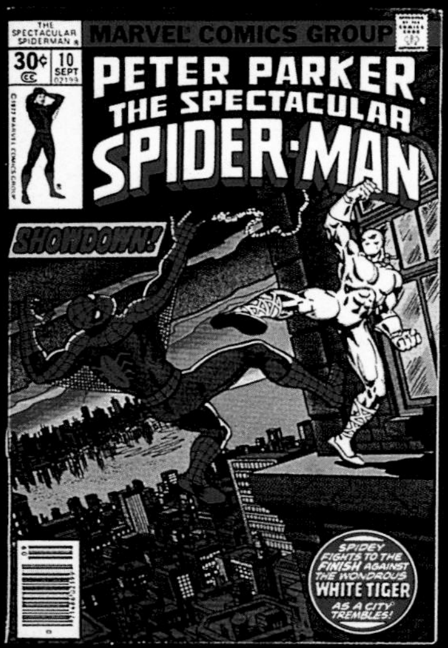
MARVEL COMICS GROUP
30¢ 10 SEPT
PETER PARKER THE SPECTACULAR SPIDER-MAN
SHOWDOWN!
SPIDEY FIGHTS TO THE FINISH AGAINST THE WONDROUS WHITE TIGER AS A CITY TREMBLES!

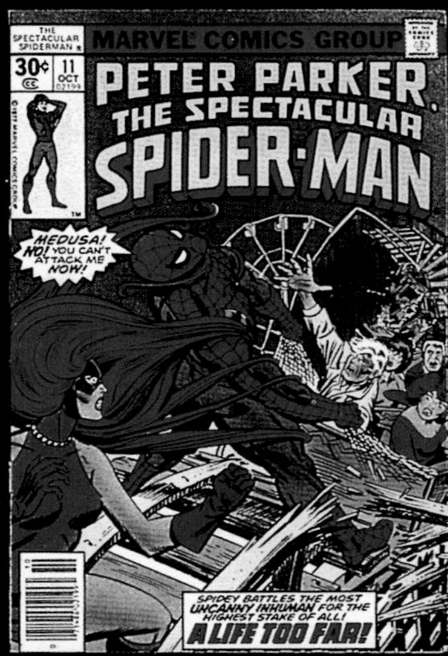
MARVEL COMICS GROUP
30¢ 11 OCT
PETER PARKER THE SPECTACULAR SPIDER-MAN
MEDUSA! NO! YOU CAN'T ATTACK ME NOW!
SPIDEY BATTLES THE MOST UNCANNY INHUMAN FOR THE HIGHEST STAKE OF ALL!
A LIFE TOO FAR!

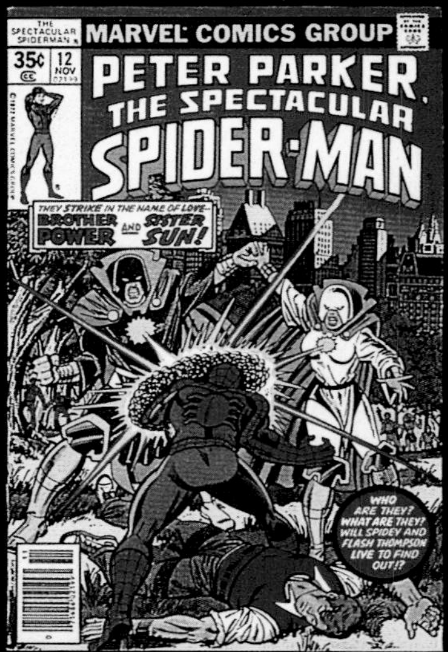
MARVEL COMICS GROUP
35¢ 12 NOV
PETER PARKER THE SPECTACULAR SPIDER-MAN
THEY STRIKE IN THE NAME OF LOVE--
BROTHER POWER AND SISTER SUN!
WHO ARE THEY? WHAT ARE THEY? WILL SPIDEY AND FLASH THOMPSON LIVE TO FIND OUT?!

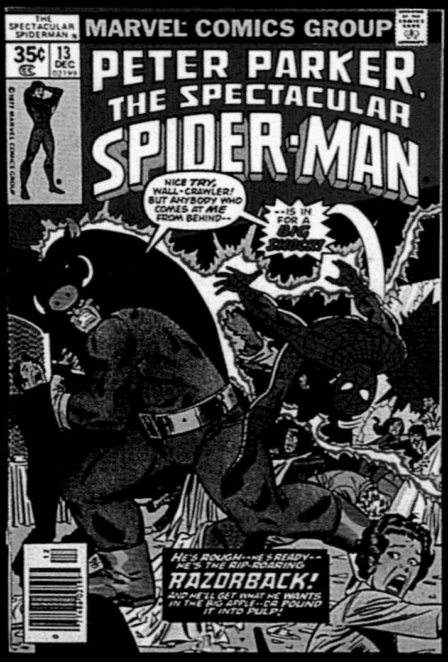
MARVEL COMICS GROUP
35¢ 13 DEC
PETER PARKER, THE SPECTACULAR SPIDER-MAN
NICE TRY, WALL-CRAWLER! BUT ANYBODY WHO COMES AT ME FROM BEHIND--
RAZORBACK!

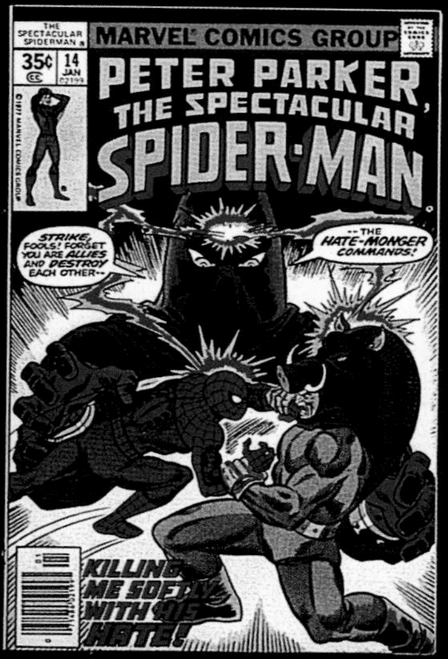
MARVEL COMICS GROUP
35¢ 14 JAN
PETER PARKER, THE SPECTACULAR SPIDER-MAN
STRIKE, FOOLS! FORGET YOU ARE ALLIES AND DESTROY EACH OTHER--
--THE HATE-MONGER COMMANDS!

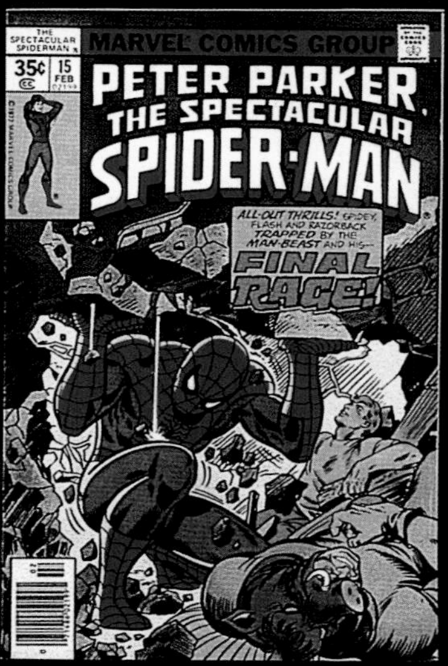
MARVEL COMICS GROUP
35¢ 15 FEB
PETER PARKER, THE SPECTACULAR SPIDER-MAN
FINAL RAGE!

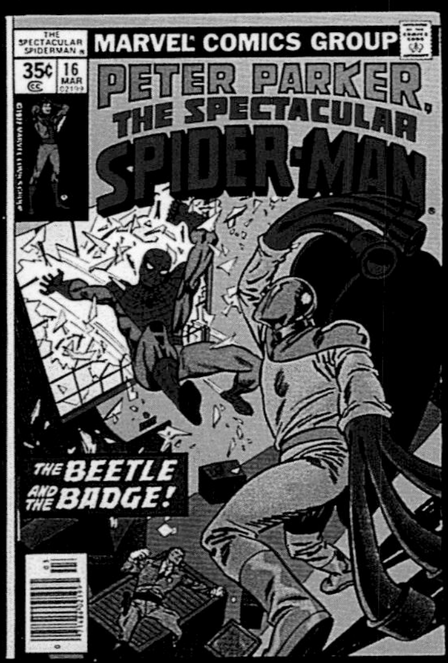
MARVEL COMICS GROUP
35¢ 16 MAR
PETER PARKER, THE SPECTACULAR SPIDER-MAN
THE BEETLE AND THE BADGE!

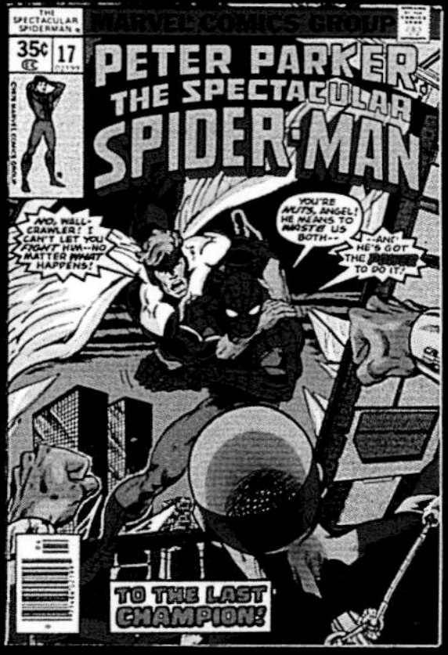
MARVEL COMICS GROUP
35¢ 17
PETER PARKER THE SPECTACULAR SPIDER-MAN
TO THE LAST CHAMPION!

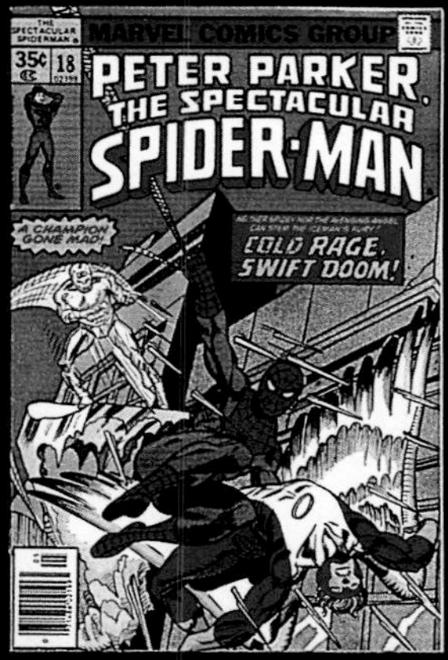
MARVEL COMICS GROUP
35¢ 18
PETER PARKER THE SPECTACULAR SPIDER-MAN
COLD RAGE, SWIFT DOOM!

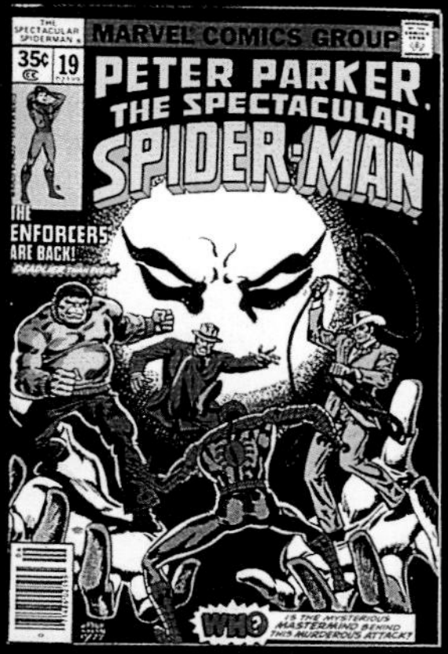
MARVEL COMICS GROUP
35¢ 19
PETER PARKER THE SPECTACULAR SPIDER-MAN
ENFORCERS ARE BACK!
WHO

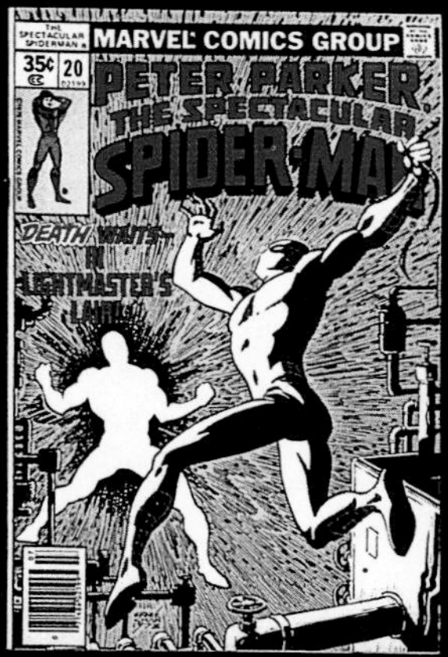
MARVEL COMICS GROUP
35¢ 20
PETER PARKER THE SPECTACULAR SPIDER-MAN
LIGHTMASTER'S

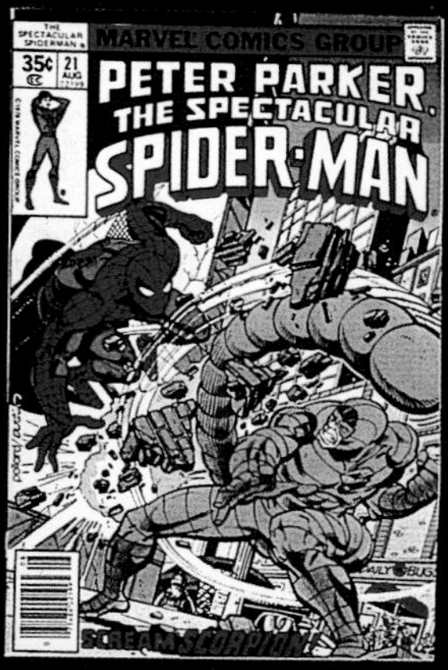
MARVEL COMICS GROUP
35¢ 21
PETER PARKER THE SPECTACULAR SPIDER-MAN

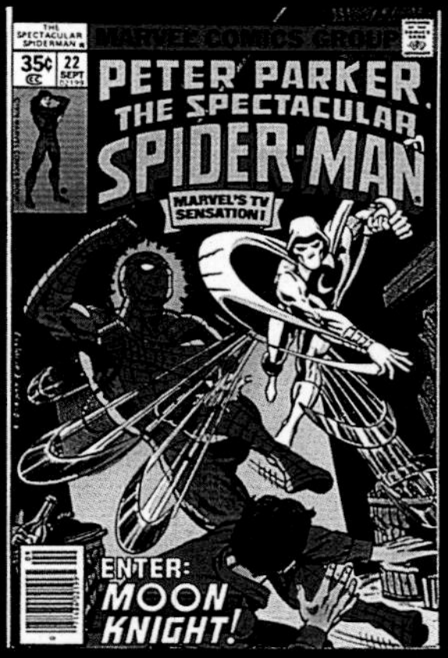
MARVEL COMICS GROUP
35¢ 22
PETER PARKER THE SPECTACULAR SPIDER-MAN
MARVEL'S TV SENSATION!
ENTER: MOON KNIGHT!

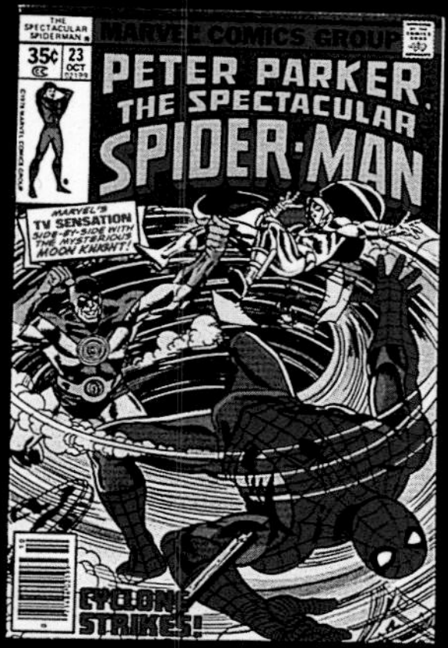
MARVEL COMICS GROUP
35¢ 23
PETER PARKER THE SPECTACULAR SPIDER-MAN
MARVEL'S TV SENSATION
CYCLONE STRIKES!

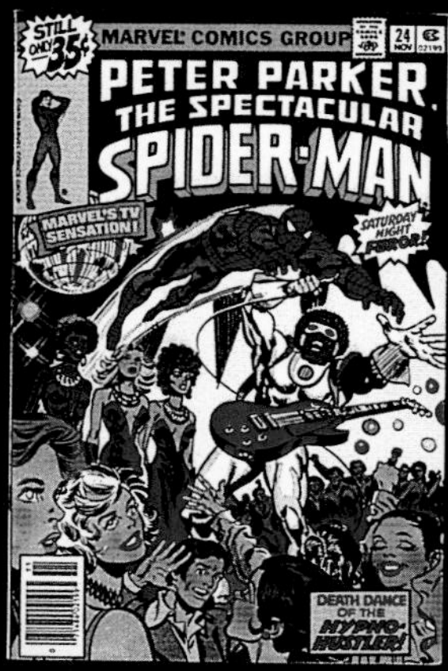
STILL ONLY 35¢
MARVEL COMICS GROUP
24
PETER PARKER THE SPECTACULAR SPIDER-MAN
MARVEL'S TV SENSATION!
DEATH DANCE OF THE

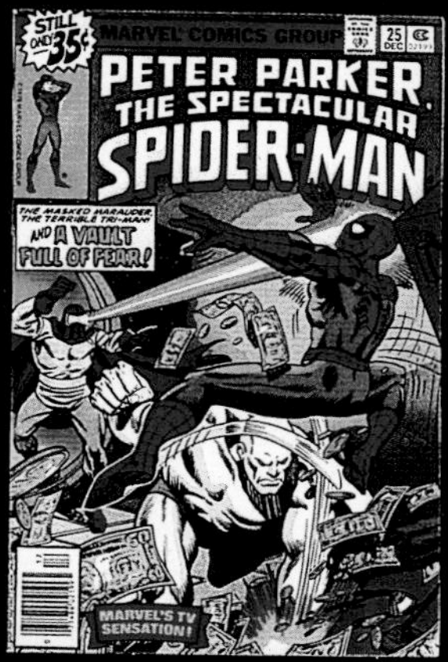
STILL ONLY 35¢
MARVEL COMICS GROUP
25
PETER PARKER THE SPECTACULAR SPIDER-MAN
THE MASKED MARAUDER AND THE TERRIBLE TRI-MAN
AND A VAULT FULL OF FEAR!
MARVEL'S TV SENSATION!

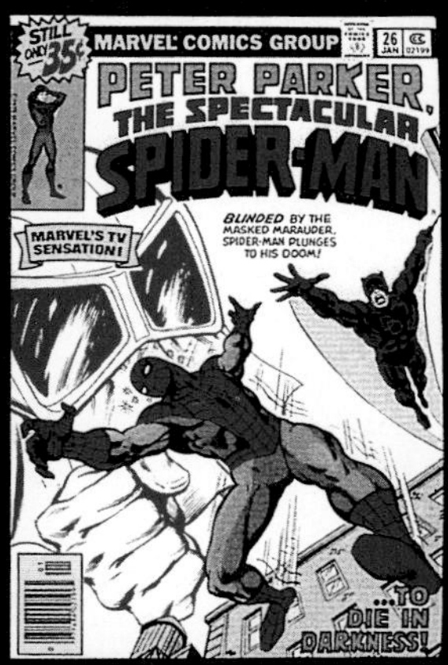
STILL ONLY 35¢
MARVEL COMICS GROUP
26
PETER PARKER, THE SPECTACULAR SPIDER-MAN
MARVEL'S TV SENSATION!
BLINDED BY THE MASKED MARAUDER, SPIDER-MAN PLUNGES TO HIS DOOM!
...TO DIE IN DARKNESS!

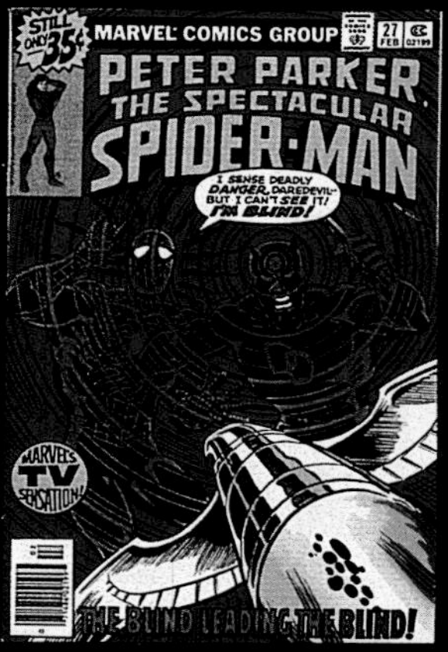
STILL ONLY 35¢
MARVEL COMICS GROUP
27
PETER PARKER THE SPECTACULAR SPIDER-MAN
I SENSE DEADLY DANGER, DAREDEVIL-- BUT I CAN'T SEE IT! I'M BLIND!
MARVEL'S TV SENSATION
THE BLIND LEADING THE BLIND!

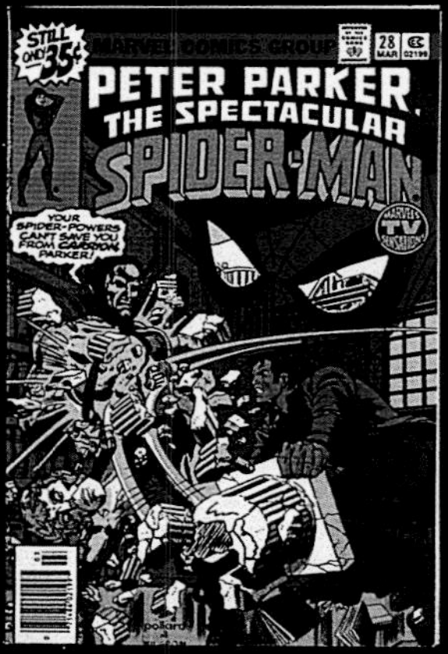
STILL ONLY 35¢
MARVEL COMICS GROUP
28
PETER PARKER THE SPECTACULAR SPIDER-MAN

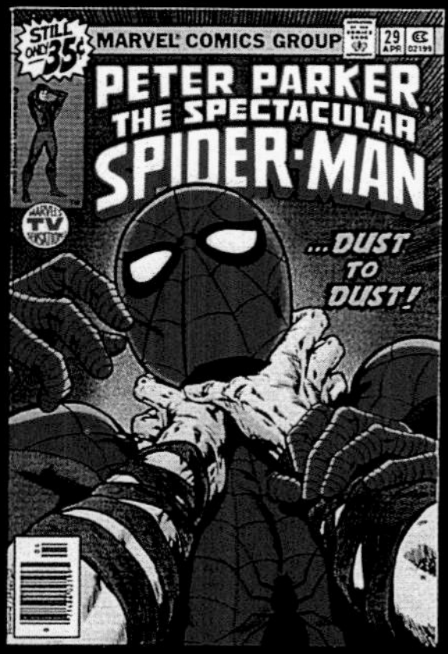
STILL ONLY 35¢
MARVEL COMICS GROUP
29
PETER PARKER THE SPECTACULAR SPIDER-MAN
...DUST TO DUST!

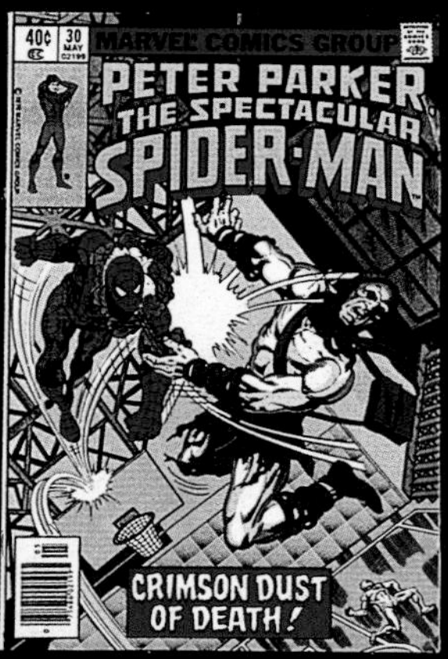
MARVEL COMICS GROUP
40¢ 30
PETER PARKER THE SPECTACULAR SPIDER-MAN
CRIMSON DUST OF DEATH!

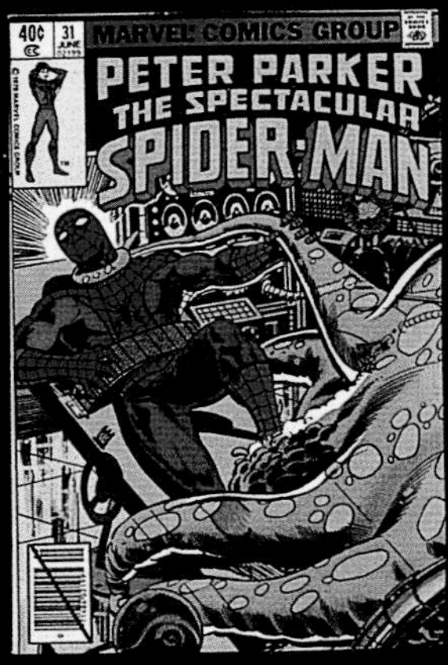
MARVEL COMICS GROUP
40¢ 31
PETER PARKER THE SPECTACULAR SPIDER-MAN

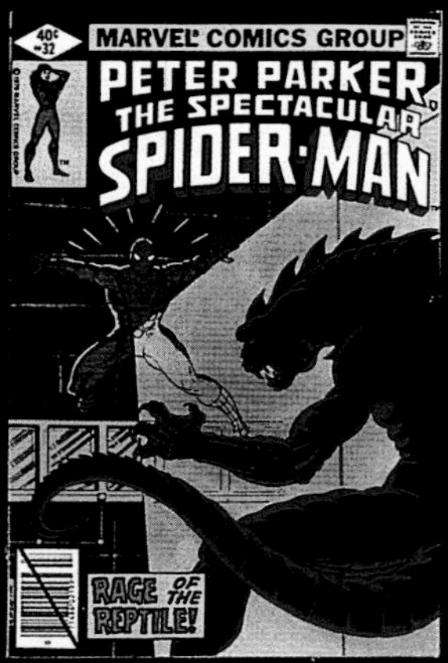
MARVEL COMICS GROUP
PETER PARKER THE SPECTACULAR SPIDER-MAN
RAGE OF THE REPTILE!

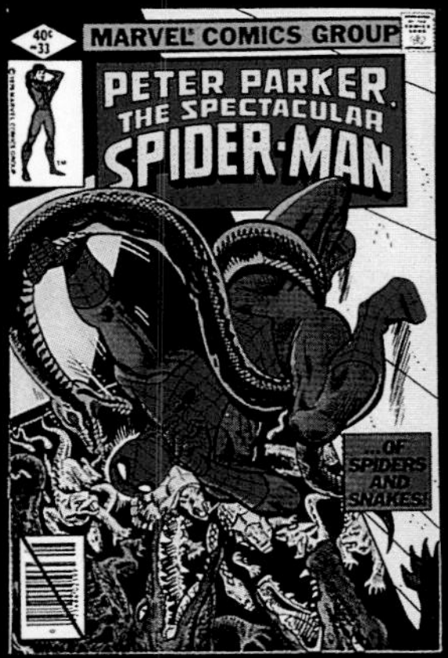
MARVEL COMICS GROUP
PETER PARKER THE SPECTACULAR SPIDER-MAN
OF SPIDERS AND SNAKES!

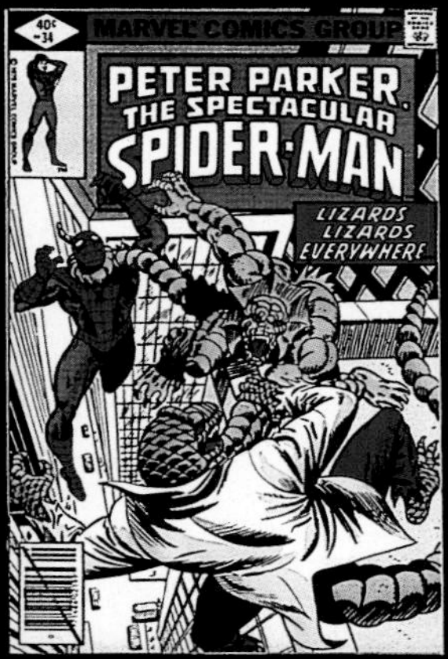
MARVEL COMICS GROUP
PETER PARKER THE SPECTACULAR SPIDER-MAN
LIZARDS LIZARDS EVERYWHERE!

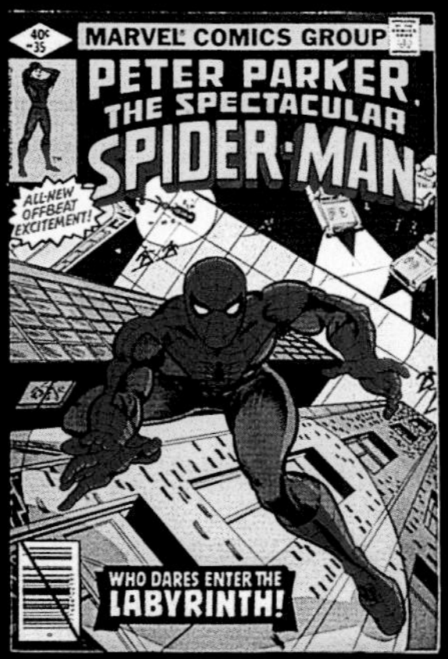
MARVEL COMICS GROUP
PETER PARKER THE SPECTACULAR SPIDER-MAN
ALL-NEW OFFBEAT EXCITEMENT!
WHO DARES ENTER THE LABYRINTH!

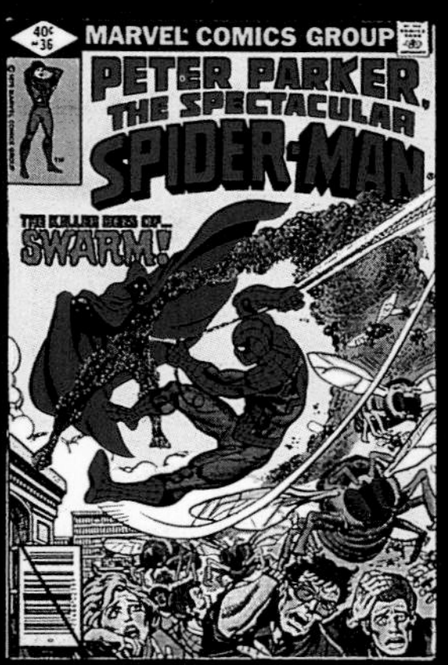
MARVEL COMICS GROUP
PETER PARKER, THE SPECTACULAR SPIDER-MAN
SWARM!

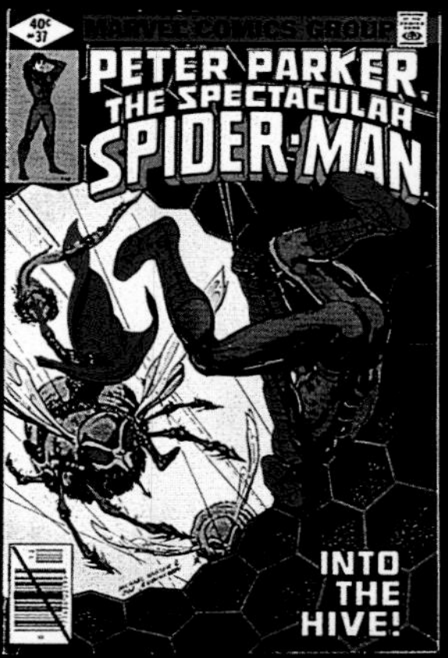
MARVEL COMICS GROUP
PETER PARKER THE SPECTACULAR SPIDER-MAN
INTO THE HIVE!

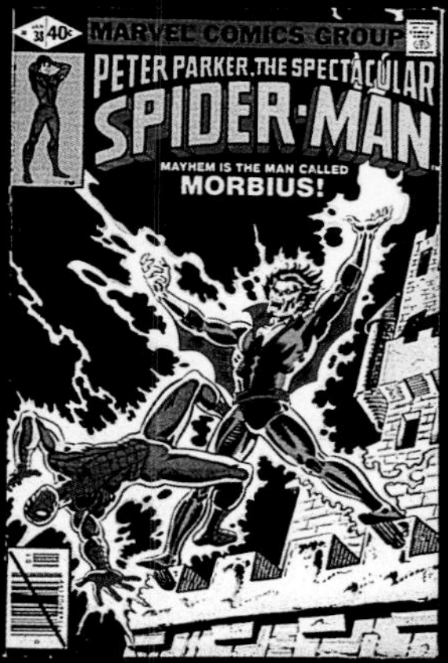
MARVEL COMICS GROUP
PETER PARKER, THE SPECTACULAR SPIDER-MAN
MAYHEM IS THE MAN CALLED MORBIUS!

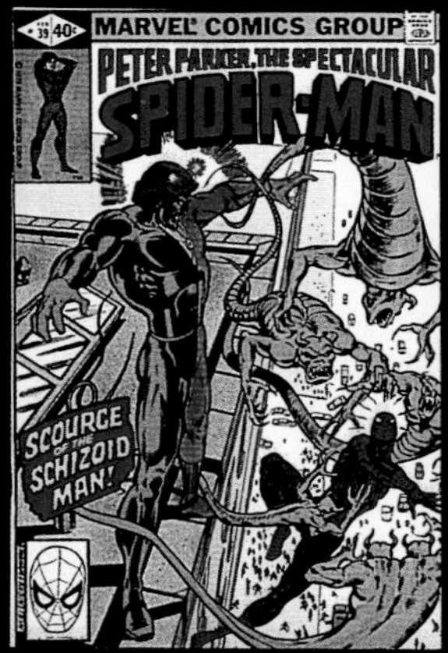
MARVEL COMICS GROUP
PETER PARKER, THE SPECTACULAR SPIDER-MAN
SCOURGE OF THE SCHIZOID MAN!

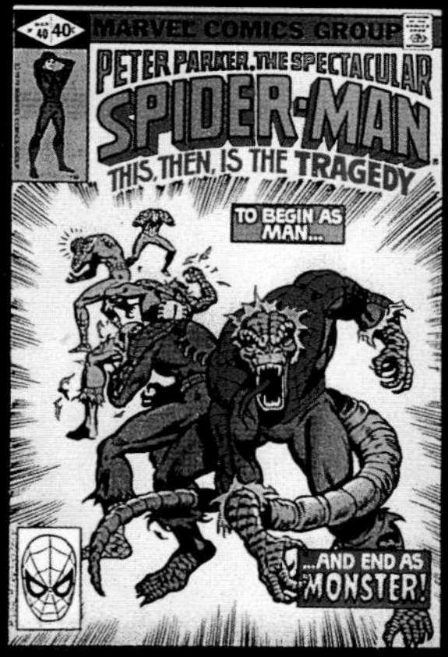
MARVEL COMICS GROUP
PETER PARKER, THE SPECTACULAR SPIDER-MAN
THIS, THEN, IS THE TRAGEDY
TO BEGIN AS MAN...
...AND END AS MONSTER!

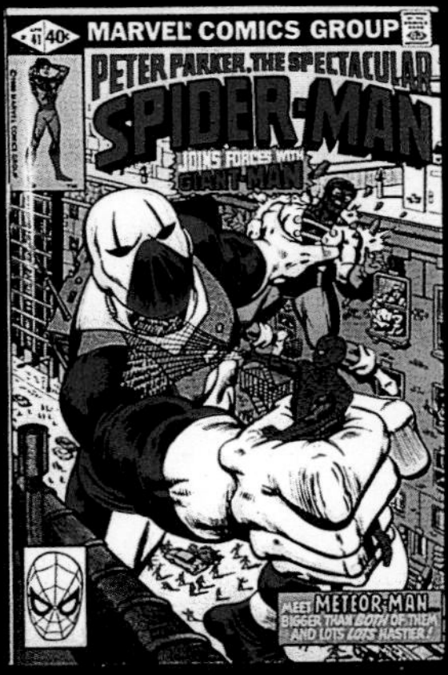
MARVEL COMICS GROUP
PETER PARKER, THE SPECTACULAR SPIDER-MAN
METEOR MAN

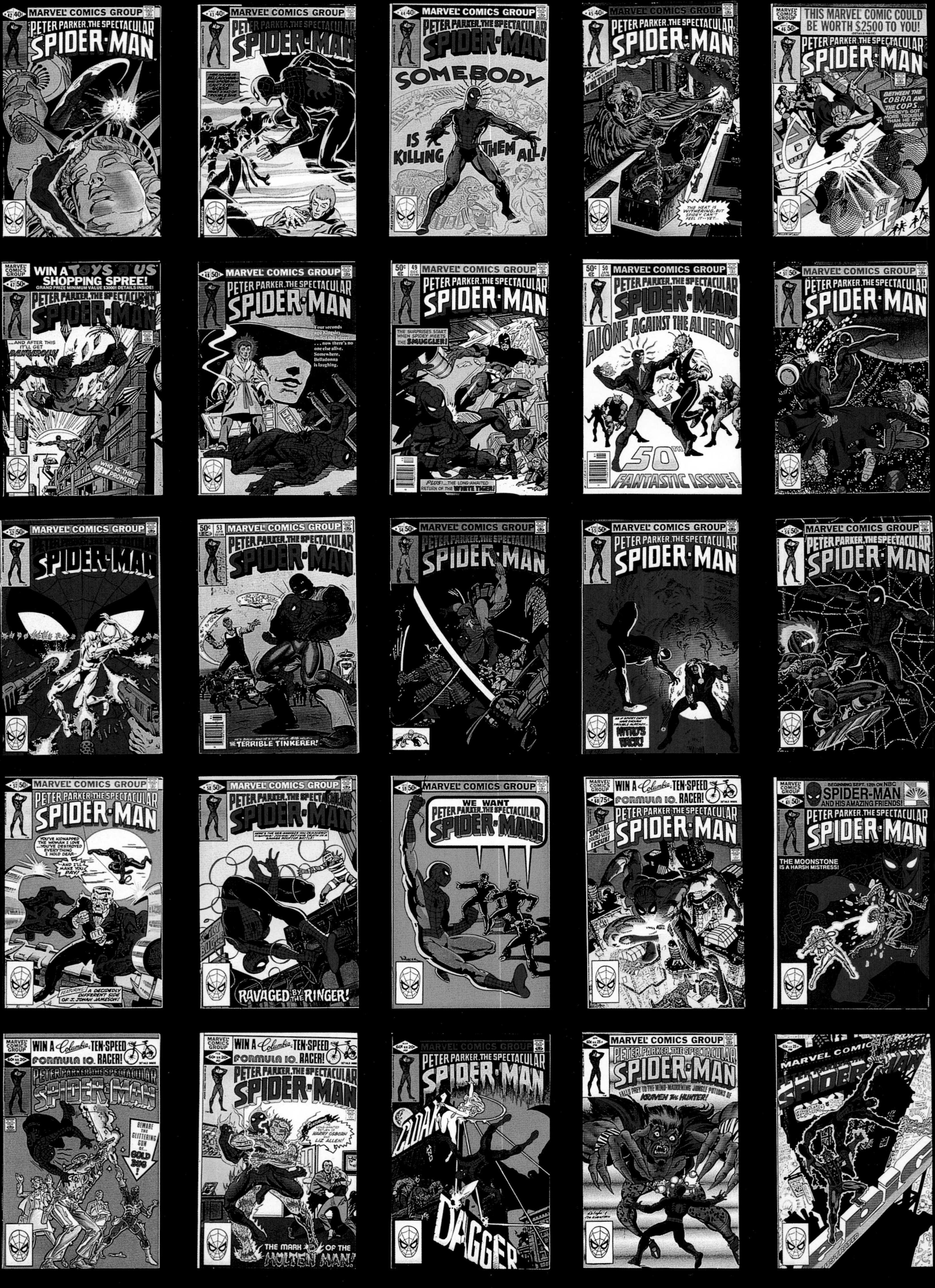
MARVEL COMICS GROUP
PETER PARKER, THE SPECTACULAR SPIDER-MAN
MARVEL COMICS GROUP
PETER PARKER, THE SPECTACULAR SPIDER-MAN
MARVEL COMICS GROUP
PETER PARKER, THE SPECTACULAR SPIDER-MAN
SOMEBODY IS KILLING THEM ALL!
MARVEL COMICS GROUP
PETER PARKER, THE SPECTACULAR SPIDER-MAN
THE HEAT IS WITHERING, BUT SPIDEY CAN'T FEEL IT--YET...
THIS MARVEL COMIC COULD BE WORTH $2500 TO YOU!
PETER PARKER, THE SPECTACULAR SPIDER-MAN
BETWEEN THE COBRA AND THE COPS, SPIDEY'S GOT MORE TROUBLE THAN HE CAN HANDLE!
WIN A TOYS R US SHOPPING SPREE!
GRAND PRIZE MINIMUM VALUE $3000! DETAILS INSIDE!
PETER PARKER, THE SPECTACULAR SPIDER-MAN
...AND AFTER THIS IT'LL GET DANGEROUS!
WHO IS THE NEW PROWLER?
MARVEL COMICS GROUP
PETER PARKER, THE SPECTACULAR SPIDER-MAN
Four seconds ago Kingsley pulled the trigger... now there's no one else alive. Somewhere, Belladonna is laughing.
MARVEL COMICS GROUP
PETER PARKER, THE SPECTACULAR SPIDER-MAN
THE SURPRISES START WHEN SPIDEY MEETS THE SMUGGLER!
PLUS!...THE LONG-AWAITED RETURN OF THE WHITE TIGER!
MARVEL COMICS GROUP
PETER PARKER, THE SPECTACULAR SPIDER-MAN
ALONE AGAINST THE ALIENS!
50TH FANTASTIC ISSUE!
MARVEL COMICS GROUP
PETER PARKER, THE SPECTACULAR SPIDER-MAN
MARVEL COMICS GROUP
PETER PARKER, THE SPECTACULAR SPIDER-MAN
MARVEL COMICS GROUP
PETER PARKER, THE SPECTACULAR SPIDER-MAN
THE TERRIBLE TINKERER!
MARVEL COMICS GROUP
PETER PARKER, THE SPECTACULAR SPIDER-MAN
MARVEL COMICS GROUP
PETER PARKER, THE SPECTACULAR SPIDER-MAN
NITRO'S BACK!
MARVEL COMICS GROUP
PETER PARKER, THE SPECTACULAR SPIDER-MAN
MARVEL COMICS GROUP
PETER PARKER, THE SPECTACULAR SPIDER-MAN
YOU'VE KIDNAPPED THE WOMAN I LOVE ...YOU'VE DESTROYED EVERYTHING I HOLD DEAR--
--AND I'LL MAKE YOU PAY!
FEATURING: A DECIDEDLY DIFFERENT SIDE OF J. JONAH JAMESON!
MARVEL COMICS GROUP
PETER PARKER, THE SPECTACULAR SPIDER-MAN
RAVAGED BY THE RINGER!
MARVEL COMICS GROUP
WE WANT PETER PARKER, THE SPECTACULAR SPIDER-MAN!
WIN A Columbia TEN-SPEED FORMULA 10. RACER!
PETER PARKER, THE SPECTACULAR SPIDER-MAN
SPECIAL DOUBLE-SIZED ISSUE!
BEGINNING SEPT. 12th ON NBC
SPIDER-MAN AND HIS AMAZING FRIENDS!
PETER PARKER, THE SPECTACULAR SPIDER-MAN
THE MOONSTONE IS A HARSH MISTRESS!
WIN A Columbia TEN-SPEED FORMULA 10. RACER!
PETER PARKER, THE SPECTACULAR SPIDER-MAN
BEWARE THE GLITTERING GUN OF GOLD BUG!
WIN A Columbia TEN-SPEED FORMULA 10. RACER!
PETER PARKER, THE SPECTACULAR SPIDER-MAN
THE MARK OF THE MOLTEN MAN!
MARVEL COMICS GROUP
PETER PARKER, THE SPECTACULAR SPIDER-MAN
CLOAK
DAGGER
MARVEL COMICS GROUP
PETER PARKER, THE SPECTACULAR SPIDER-MAN
FALLS PREY TO THE MIND-MADDENING JUNGLE POTIONS OF KRAVEN THE HUNTER!
MARVEL COMICS
SPIDER-MAN

1753.5 The Spectacular Spider-Man (67-102)

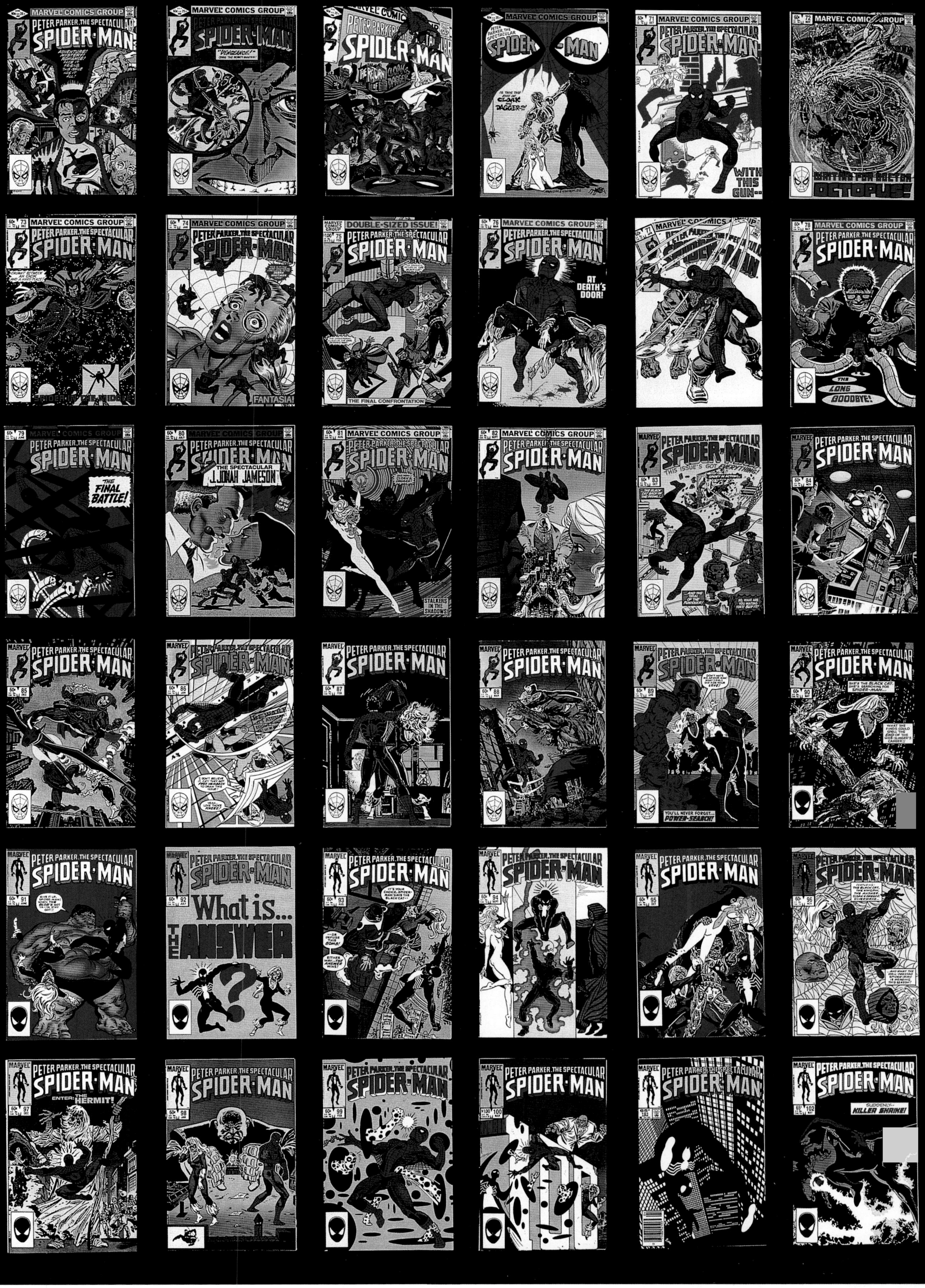
MARVEL COMICS GROUP
PETER PARKER, THE SPECTACULAR SPIDER-MAN
"VENGEANCE!"
THE RETURN OF CLOAK & DAGGER
WITH THIS GUN--
WAITING FOR DOCTOR OCTOPUS!
DOUBLE-SIZED ISSUE!
FANTASIA!
THE FINAL CONFRONTATION
AT DEATH'S DOOR!
THE LONG GOODBYE!
THE FINAL BATTLE!
THE SPECTACULAR J. JONAH JAMESON
STALKERS IN THE SHADOWS!
THIS ISSUE'S GOT EVERYTHING!
YOU'LL NEVER FORGET... POWER-SEARCH!
What is... THE ANSWER
ENTER: THE HERMIT!
SUDDENLY-- KILLER SHRIKE!

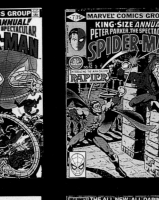

1753.5 The Spectacular Spider-Man (103-120, AN. 1-8)

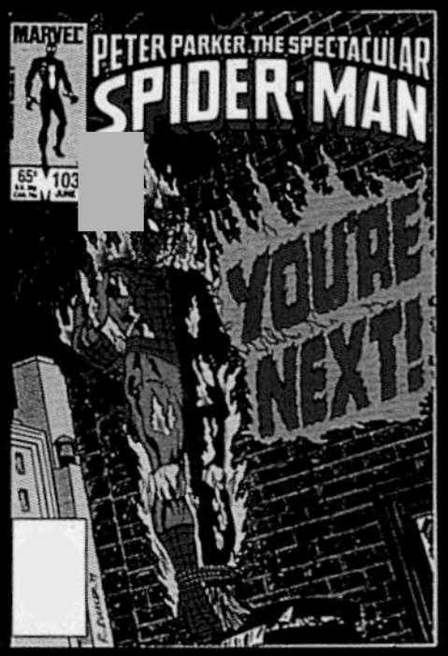
PETER PARKER, THE SPECTACULAR SPIDER-MAN
YOU'RE NEXT!
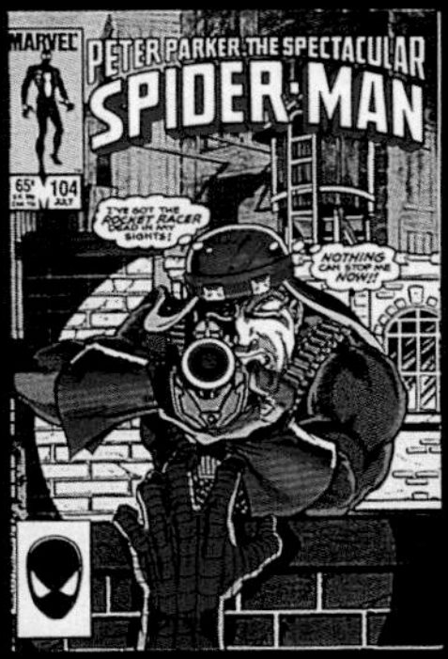
PETER PARKER, THE SPECTACULAR SPIDER-MAN
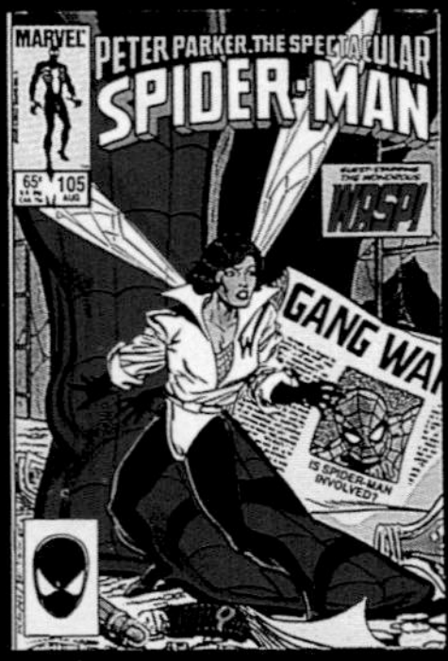
PETER PARKER, THE SPECTACULAR SPIDER-MAN
WASP!
GANG WAR
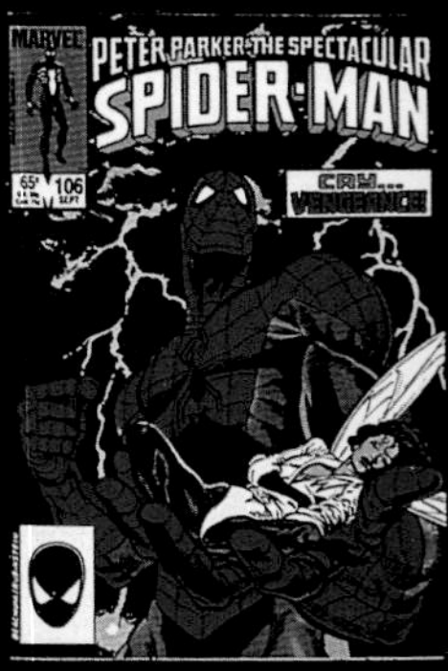
PETER PARKER, THE SPECTACULAR SPIDER-MAN
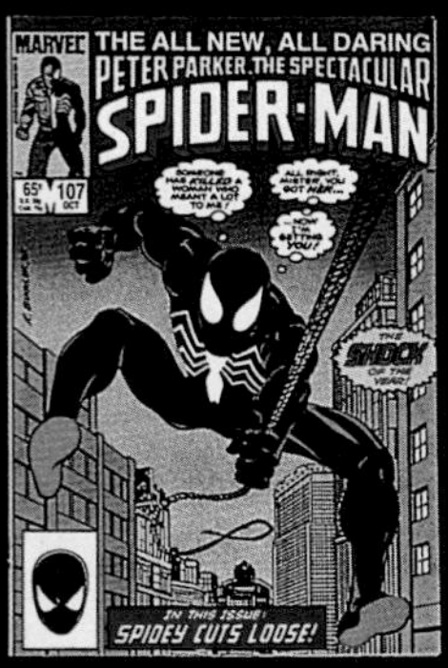
THE ALL NEW, ALL DARING
PETER PARKER, THE SPECTACULAR SPIDER-MAN
SPIDEY CUTS LOOSE!
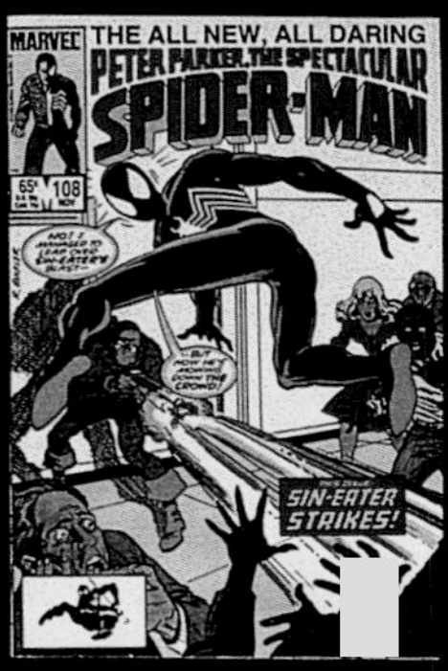
THE ALL NEW, ALL DARING
PETER PARKER, THE SPECTACULAR SPIDER-MAN
SIN-EATER STRIKES!
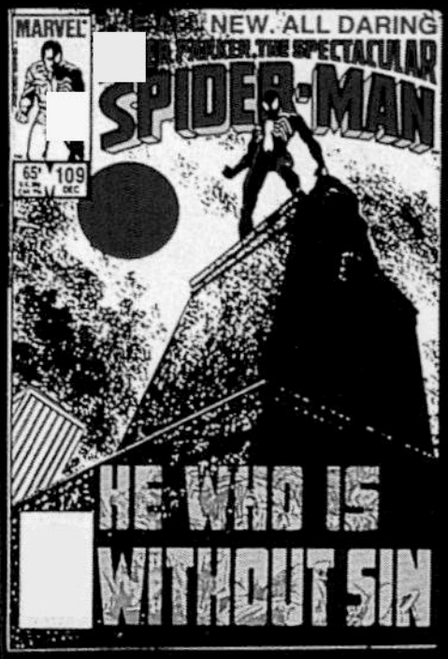
SPIDER-MAN
HE WHO IS WITHOUT SIN
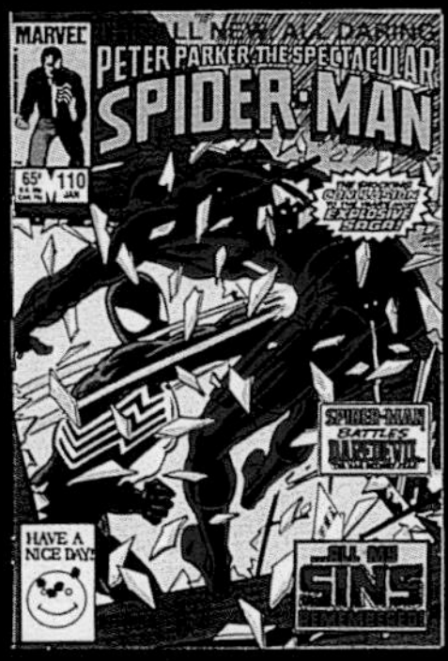
PETER PARKER, THE SPECTACULAR SPIDER-MAN
HAVE A NICE DAY!
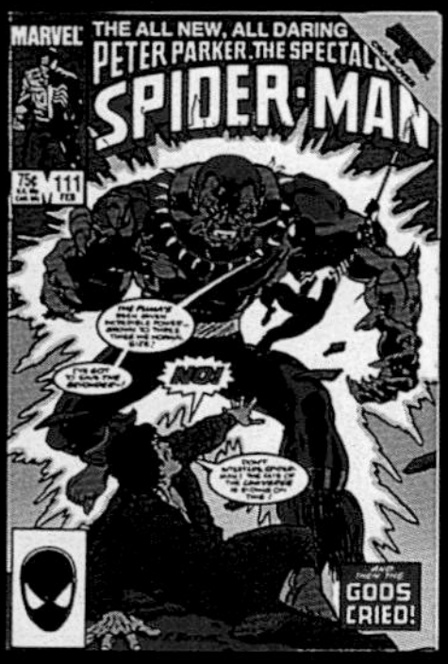
THE ALL NEW, ALL DARING
PETER PARKER, THE SPECTACULAR SPIDER-MAN
GODS CRIED!
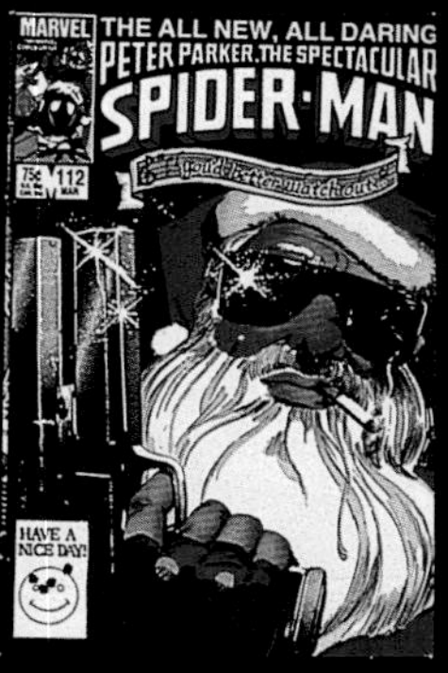
THE ALL NEW, ALL DARING
PETER PARKER, THE SPECTACULAR SPIDER-MAN
HAVE A NICE DAY!
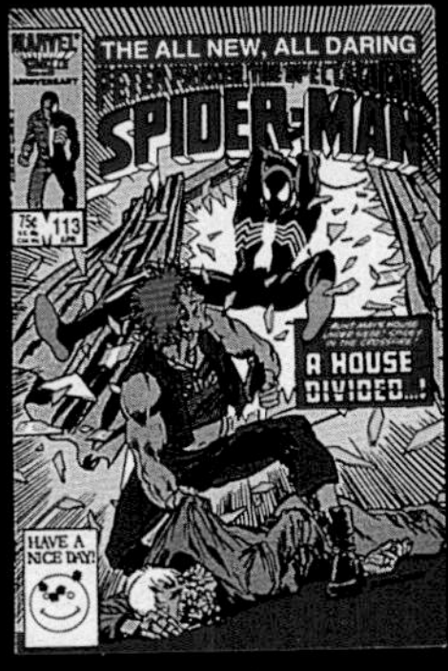
THE ALL NEW, ALL DARING
SPIDER-MAN
A HOUSE DIVIDED...!
HAVE A NICE DAY!
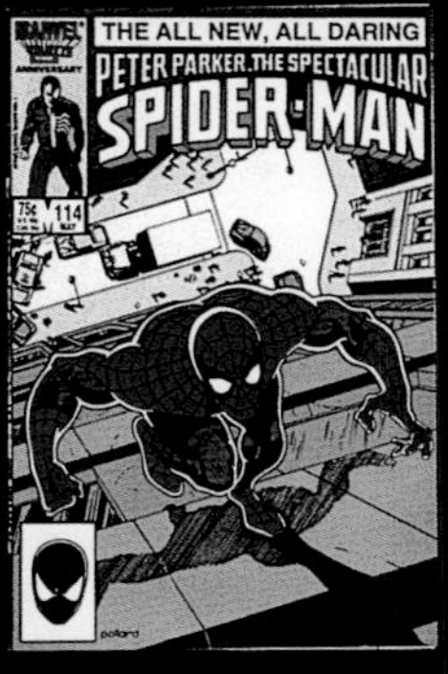
THE ALL NEW, ALL DARING
PETER PARKER, THE SPECTACULAR SPIDER-MAN
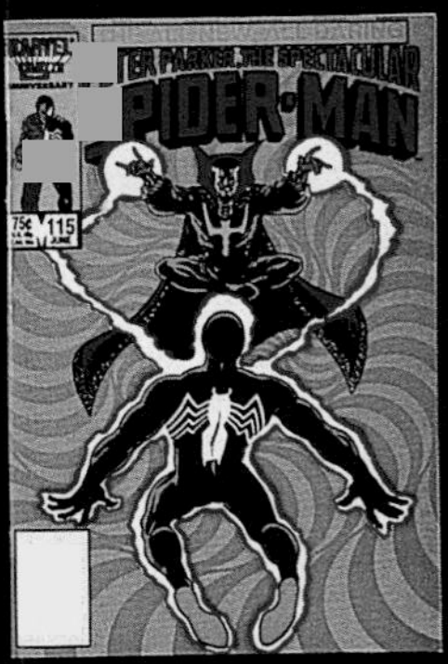
SPIDER-MAN
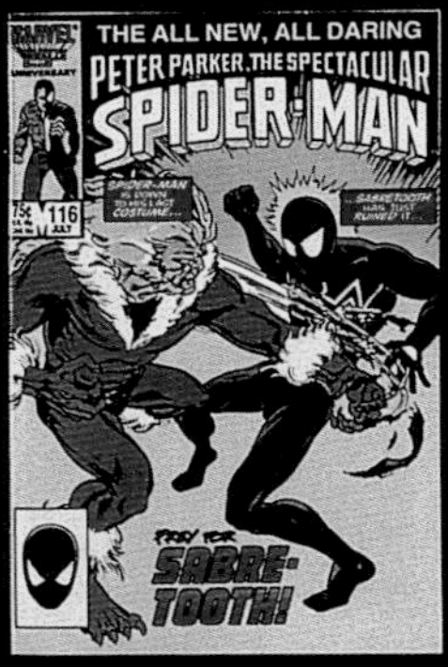
THE ALL NEW, ALL DARING
PETER PARKER, THE SPECTACULAR SPIDER-MAN
SABRE-TOOTH!
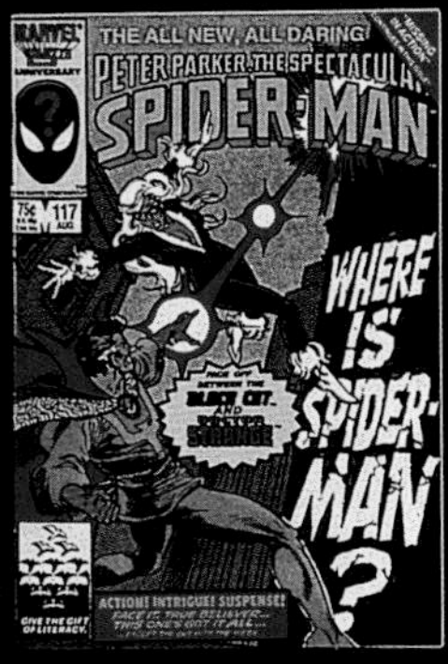
THE ALL NEW, ALL DARING
PETER PARKER, THE SPECTACULAR SPIDER-MAN
WHERE IS SPIDER-MAN?
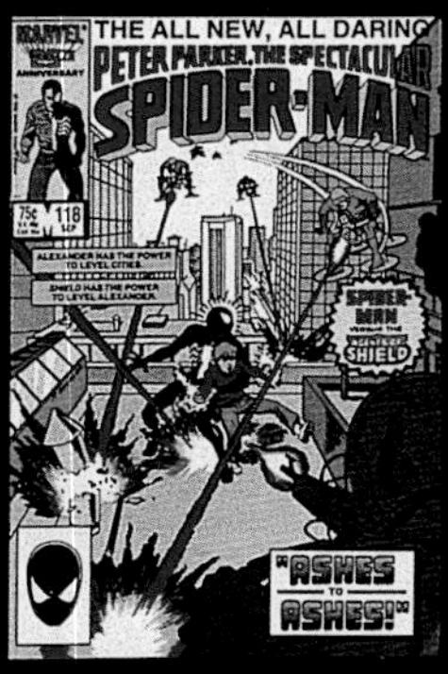
THE ALL NEW, ALL DARING
PETER PARKER, THE SPECTACULAR SPIDER-MAN
"ASHES TO ASHES!"
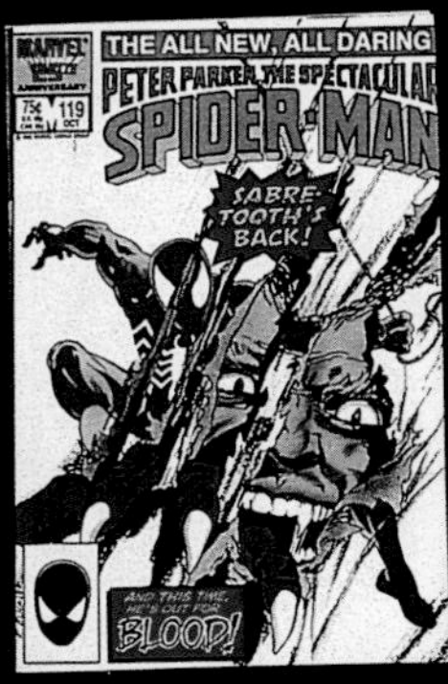
THE ALL NEW, ALL DARING
PETER PARKER, THE SPECTACULAR SPIDER-MAN
SABRE-TOOTH'S BACK!
BLOOD!
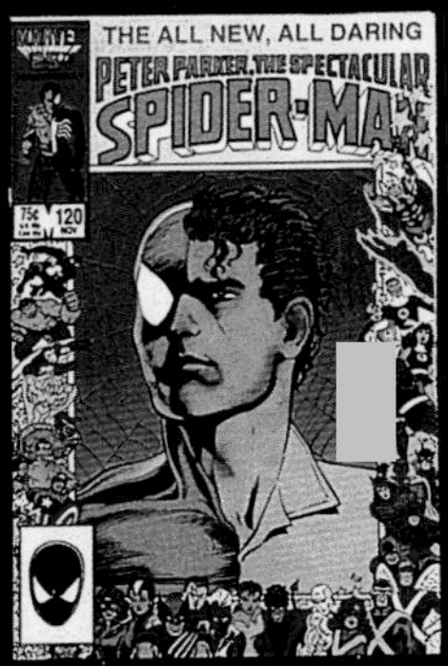
THE ALL NEW, ALL DARING
PETER PARKER, THE SPECTACULAR SPIDER-MAN
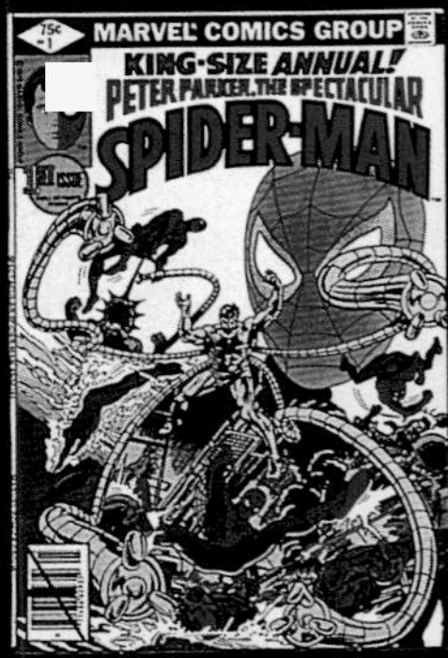
MARVEL COMICS GROUP
KING-SIZE ANNUAL!
PETER PARKER, THE SPECTACULAR SPIDER-MAN
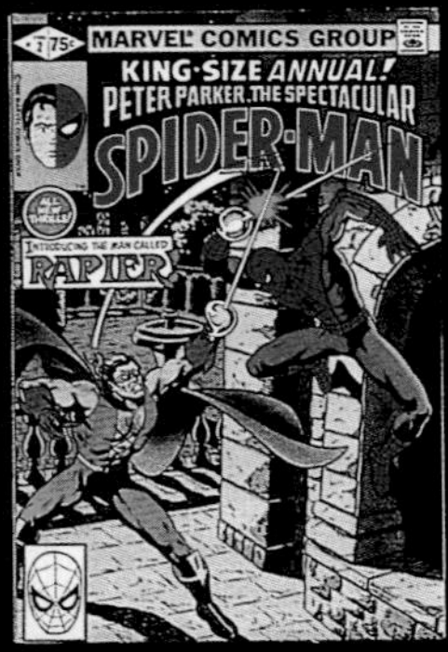
MARVEL COMICS GROUP
KING-SIZE ANNUAL!
PETER PARKER, THE SPECTACULAR SPIDER-MAN
RAPIER
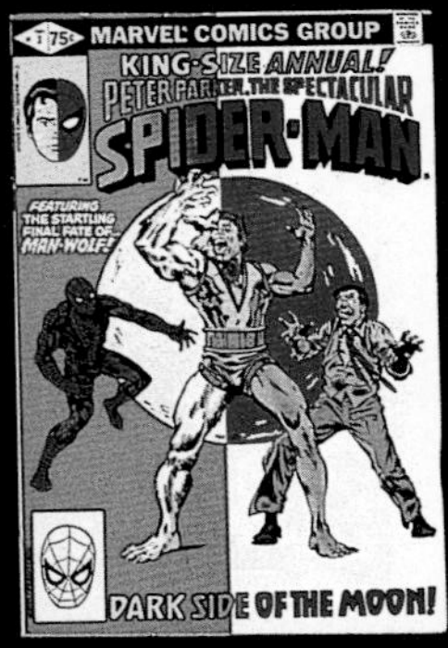
MARVEL COMICS GROUP
KING-SIZE ANNUAL!
SPIDER-MAN
DARK SIDE OF THE MOON!
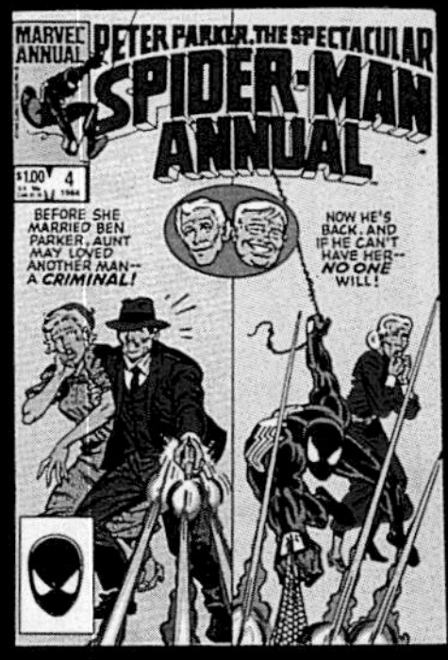
PETER PARKER, THE SPECTACULAR SPIDER-MAN ANNUAL
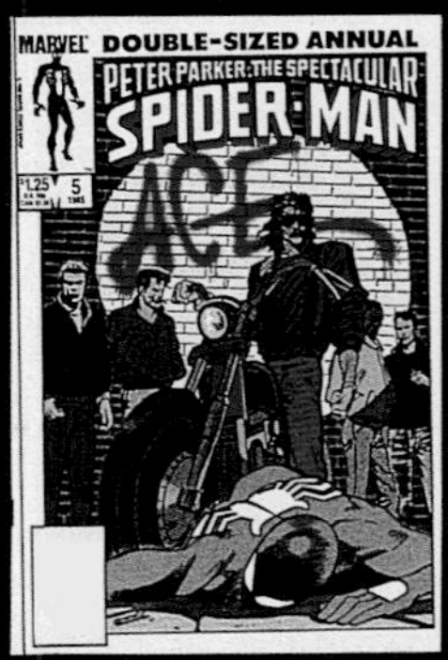
DOUBLE-SIZED ANNUAL
PETER PARKER, THE SPECTACULAR SPIDER-MAN
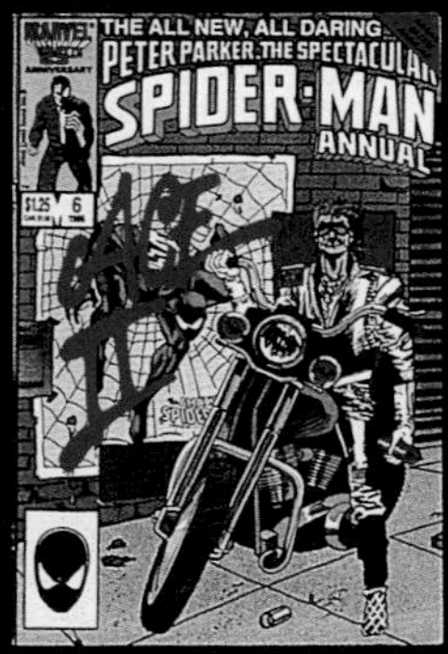
THE ALL NEW, ALL DARING
PETER PARKER, THE SPECTACULAR SPIDER-MAN ANNUAL
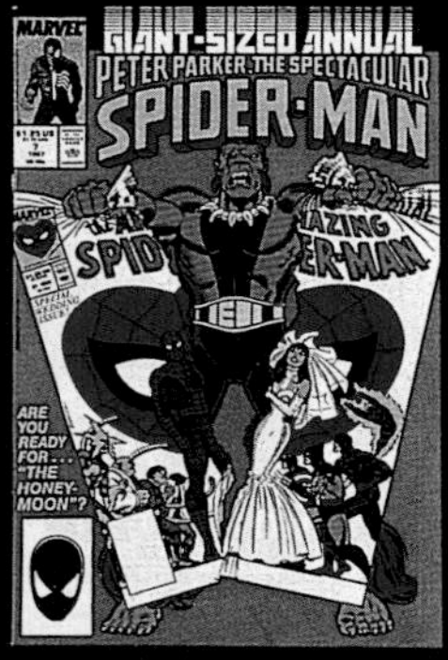
GIANT-SIZED ANNUAL
PETER PARKER, THE SPECTACULAR SPIDER-MAN
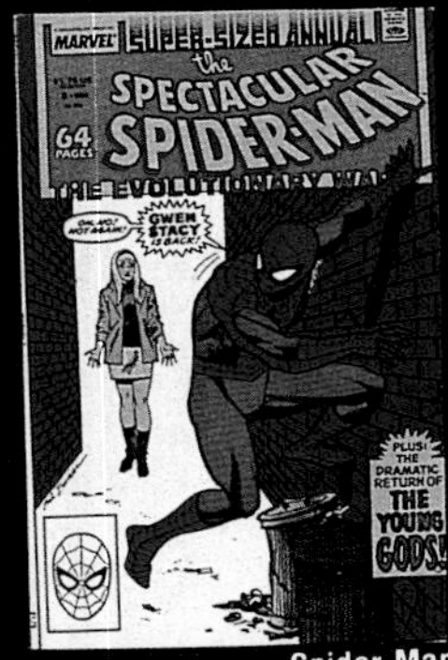
SUPER-SIZED ANNUAL
the SPECTACULAR SPIDER-MAN
THE DRAMATIC RETURN OF THE YOUNG GODS!

1757.2 Spider-Man and

1757.3 Spider-Man and

1757.4 Spider-Man vs.

Spider-Man

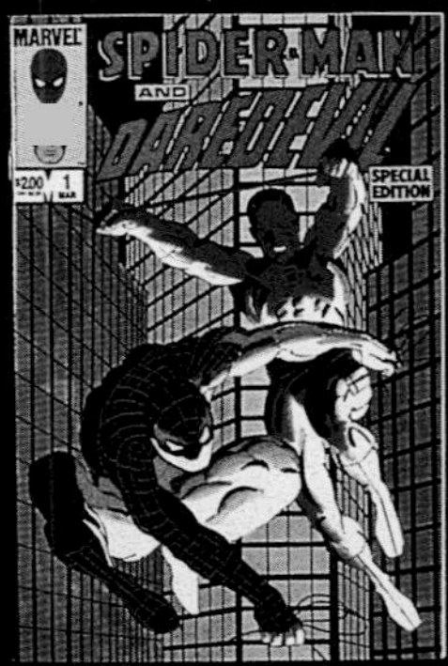
SPIDER-MAN AND DAREDEVIL
SPECIAL EDITION
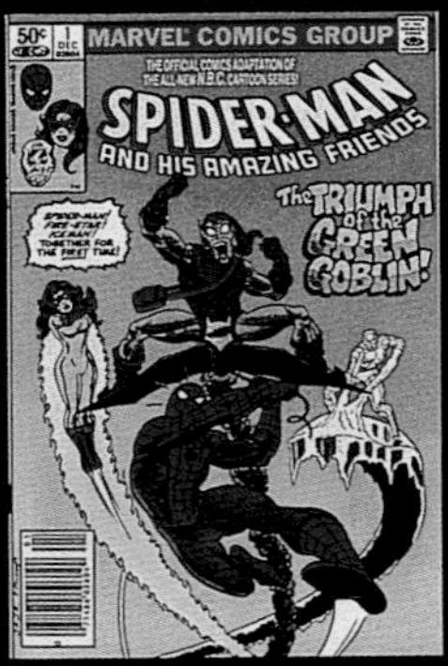
MARVEL COMICS GROUP
SPIDER-MAN AND HIS AMAZING FRIENDS
The TRIUMPH of the GREEN GOBLIN!
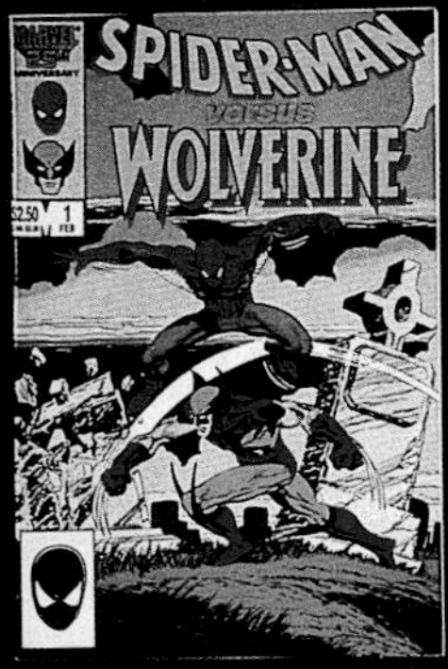
SPIDER-MAN VERSUS WOLVERINE
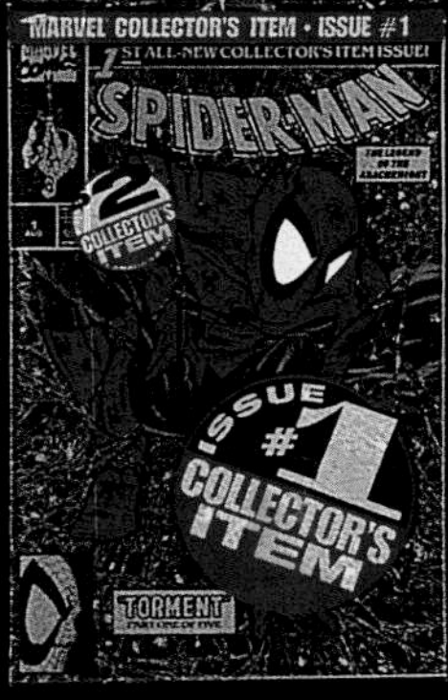
MARVEL COLLECTOR'S ITEM · ISSUE #1
SPIDER-MAN
ISSUE #1 COLLECTOR'S ITEM
TORMENT

The Spectacular Spider-Man (1-Present) 1753.5

Ref. No.	Date	RVI	Artist/Info.
1753.5-1	Dec. 1976	20	Buscema/Esposito-a
1753.5-2	Jan. 1977	10	" "
1753.5-3	Feb.	7	" "
1753.5-4	Mar.	7	" "
1753.5-5	Apr.	7	Cockrum-c, Buscema/Esposito-a
1753.5-6	May	3	Andru/Giacoia-a
1753.5-7	Jun.	3	Cockrum-c, Buscema/Mooney-a
1753.5-8	Jul.	3	Gulacy-c, Buscema/Esposito-a
1753.5-9	Aug.	3	Buscema/Esposito-a
1753.5-10	**Sept.**	**3**	**" "**
1753.5-11	Oct.	3	Mooney/Esposito-a
1753.5-12	Nov.	3	Buscema/Esposito-a
1753.5-13	Dec.	3	" "
1753.5-14	Jan. 1978	3	" "
1753.5-15	Feb.	3	Buscema/Chan-a
1753.5-16	Mar.	3	Buscema/Esposito-a
1753.5-17	Apr.	3	Buscema-c/a, Hunt-a
1753.5-18	May	3	Buscema-a, Hunt-a
1753.5-19	Jun.	3	Chan-c, Buscema/Esposito-a
1753.5-20	**Jul.**	**3**	**" " "**
1753.5-21	Aug.	3	Pollard/Austin-c, Mooney, Esposito-a
1753.5-22	Sept.	4	Cockrum/Rubinstein-c, Zeck/Patterson-a
1753.5-23	Oct.	4	Mooney/Esposito-a
1753.5-24	Nov.	3	Springer-a
1753.5-25	Dec.	3	Pollard/Patterson-c, Mooney/Springer-a
1753.5-26	Jan. 1979	3	Mooney/Springer-a
1753.5-27	Feb.	10	Miller/Springer-a (1st Miller Daredevil)
1753.5-28	Mar.	9	Pollard/Milgrom-c, Miller/Springer-a
1753.5-29	Apr.	2	Pollard/McLeod-c, Mooney/Springer-a
1753.5-30	**May**	**2**	**" " "**
1753.5-31 to 63	Feb. 1981, (#63)	2	(#60, Origin retold; Double-size)
1753.5-64	Mar. 1981	8	(Intro. Cloak and Dagger)
1753.5-65 to 81		1	(#75, Double-size)
1753.5-82		7	(Punisher -app.)
1753.5-83		7	"
1753.5-84 to 130		1	(#130, Hobgoblin -app.)
1753.5-131 to 168		1	(#141, Punisher -app. RVI, 4)
1753.5-A1	Dec. 1979	2	
1753.5-A2	Aug. 1980	2	(Intro. Rapies)
1753.5-A3	Nov. 1981	2	(Manwolf finishes)
1753.5-A4	Nov. 1984	2	
1753.5-A5	Oct. 1985	2	
1753.5-A6	1985	2	

Spider-Man and Daredevil (1) 1757.2

1757.2-1	Mar. 1984	2	Miller-a	Reprints

Spider-Man and his Amazing Friends (1) 1757.3

1757.3	Dec. 1981	1	Spiegle-a

Spider-Man vs. Wolverine (1) 1757.4

1757.4-1	Feb. 1987	7	Williamson-a

Spider-Woman (1-50) 1757.5

1757.5-1	Apr. 1978	2	Infantino/DeZuniga-a
1757.5-2	May	1	Cockrum-c, Infantino/DeZuniga-a
1757.5-3	Jun.	1	" " "
1757.5-4	Jul.	1	Wiacek/Cockrum-c, Infantino/DeZuniga-a
1757.5-5	Aug.	1	Infantino/DeZuniga-a
1757.5-6	Sept.	1	Infantino/Leialoha-c, Infantino/Brant-a
1757.5-7	Oct.	1	Infantino/Leialoha-c/a, Gordon-a
1757.5-8	Nov.	1	Infantino/Leialoha-c, Infantino/Gordon-a
1757.5-9	Dec.	1	Infantino/Wiacek-c, Infantino/Gordon-a
1757.5-10	**Jan. 1979**	**1**	**Infantino/McLeod-c, Infantino/Gordon-a**
1757.5-11	Feb.	1	Infantino/Gordon-a
1757.5-12	Mar.	1	Infantino/McLeod-c, Infantino/Gordon-a
1757.5-13	Apr.	1	Cockrum/McLeod-c, Infantino/Gordon-a
1757.5-14	May	1	Infantino/Gordon-a
1757.5-15 to 50	Jun. 1983, (#50)	1	(#20, Spider-Man -app.)

1757.5   Spider-Woman (1-25)

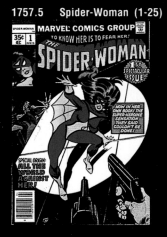
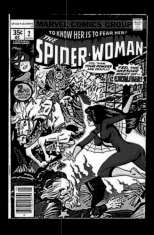
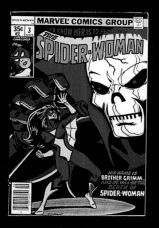
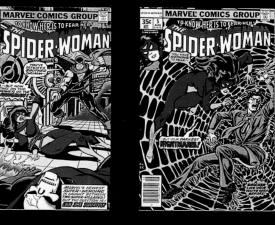

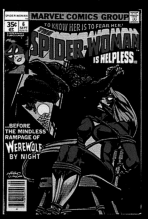
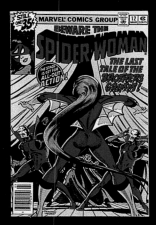
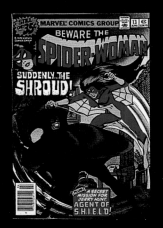
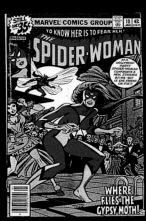

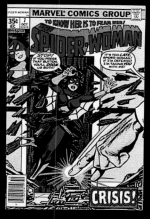
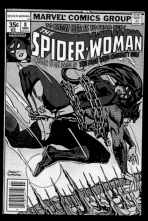
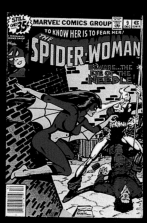
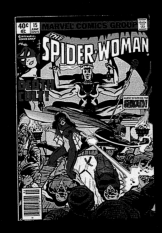

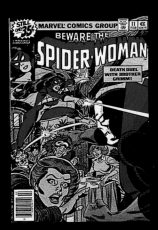
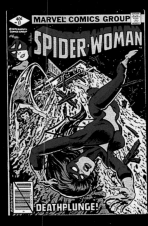
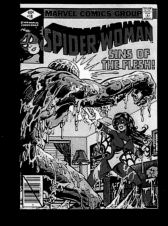
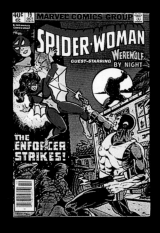
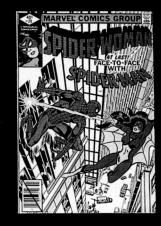

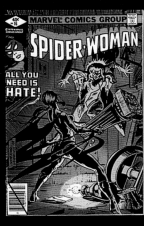
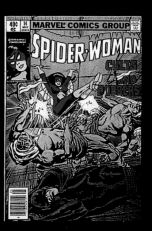

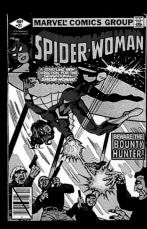
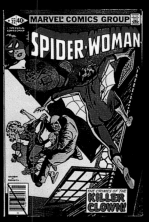
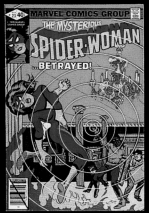
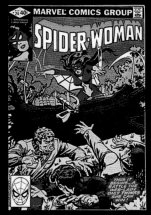
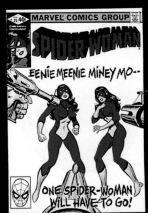

257

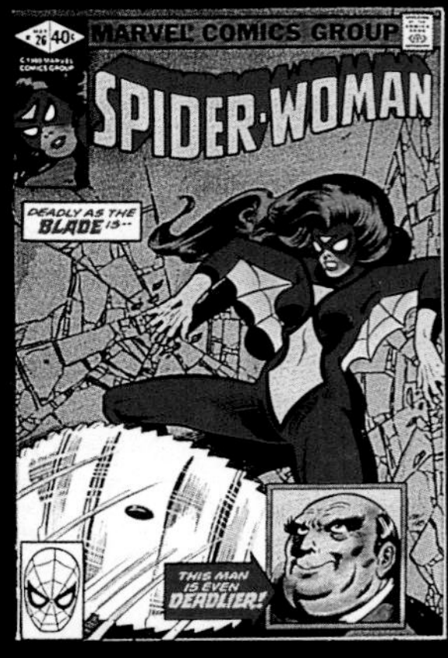
MARVEL COMICS GROUP
SPIDER-WOMAN
DEADLY AS THE BLADE IS—
THIS MAN IS EVEN DEADLIER!

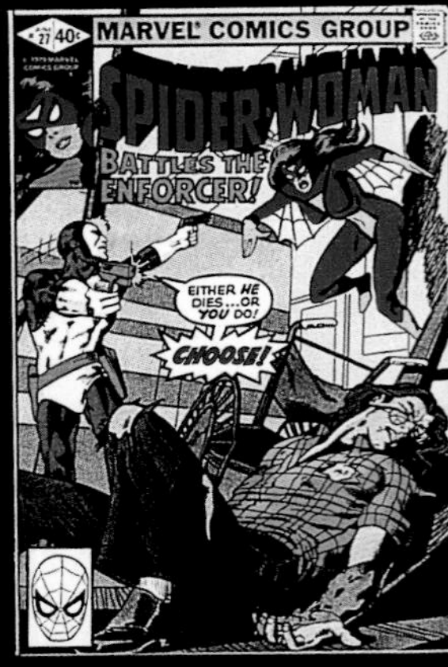
MARVEL COMICS GROUP
SPIDER-WOMAN
BATTLES THE ENFORCER!
EITHER HE DIES...OR YOU DO!
CHOOSE!

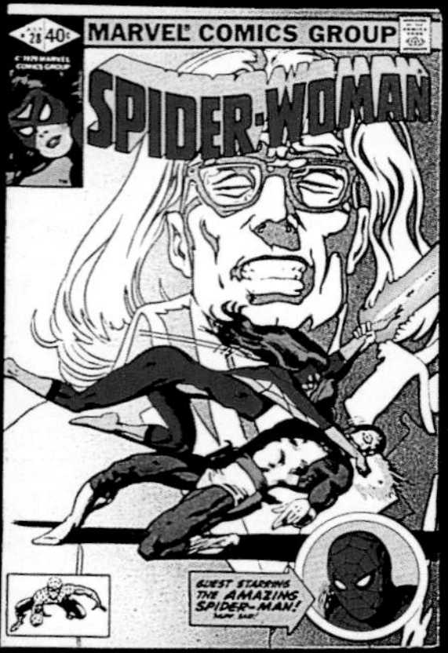
MARVEL COMICS GROUP
SPIDER-WOMAN
GUEST STARRING THE AMAZING SPIDER-MAN!

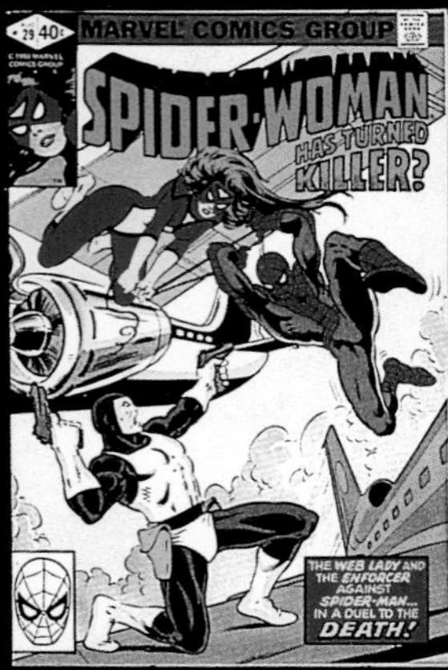
MARVEL COMICS GROUP
SPIDER-WOMAN
HAS TURNED KILLER?
THE WEB LADY AND THE ENFORCER AGAINST SPIDER-MAN... IN A DUEL TO THE DEATH!

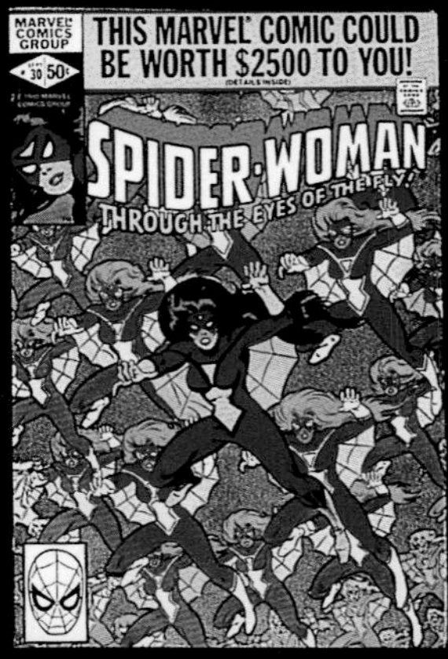
THIS MARVEL COMIC COULD BE WORTH $2500 TO YOU!
SPIDER-WOMAN
THROUGH THE EYES OF THE FLY!

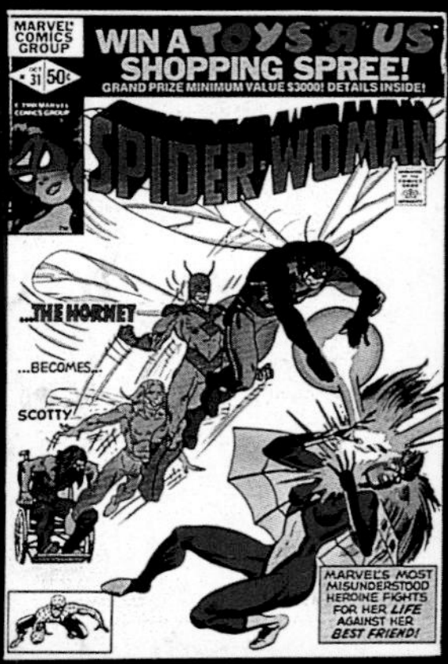
WIN A TOYS "R" US SHOPPING SPREE!
SPIDER-WOMAN
...THE HORNET
...BECOMES...
SCOTTY
MARVEL'S MOST MISUNDERSTOOD HEROINE FIGHTS FOR HER LIFE AGAINST HER BEST FRIEND!

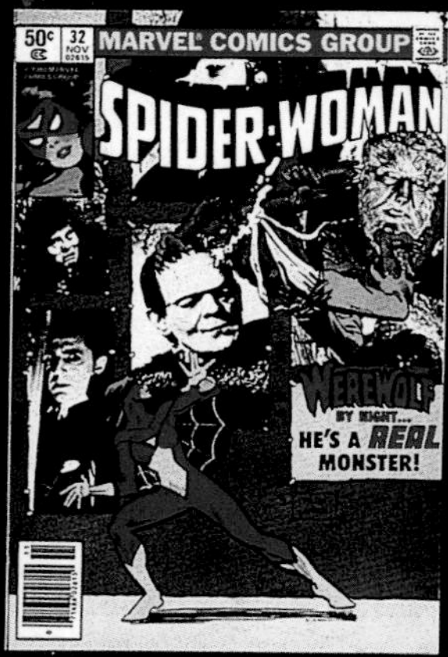
MARVEL COMICS GROUP
SPIDER-WOMAN
WEREWOLF BY NIGHT... HE'S A REAL MONSTER!

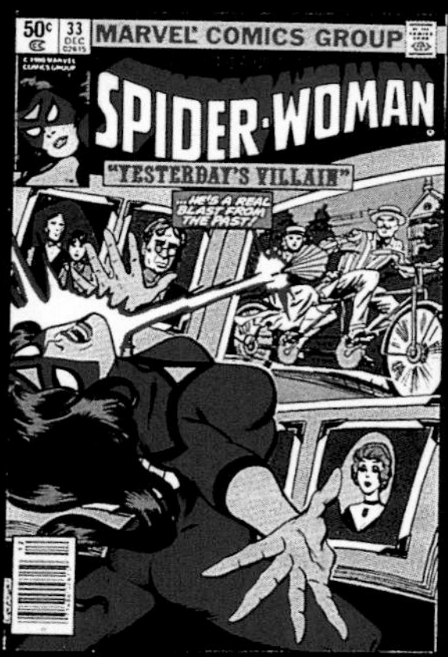
MARVEL COMICS GROUP
SPIDER-WOMAN
"YESTERDAY'S VILLAIN"

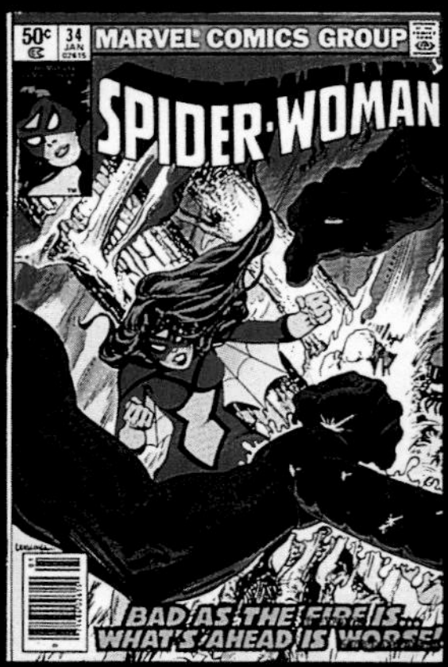
MARVEL COMICS GROUP
SPIDER-WOMAN
BAD AS THE FIRE IS... WHAT'S AHEAD IS WORSE!

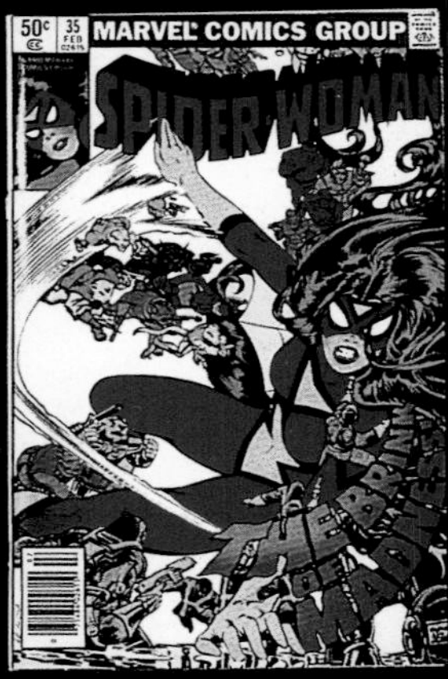
MARVEL COMICS GROUP
SPIDER-WOMAN

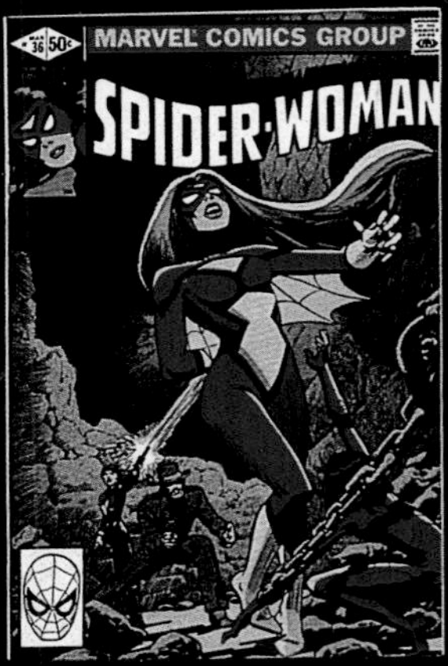
MARVEL COMICS GROUP
SPIDER-WOMAN

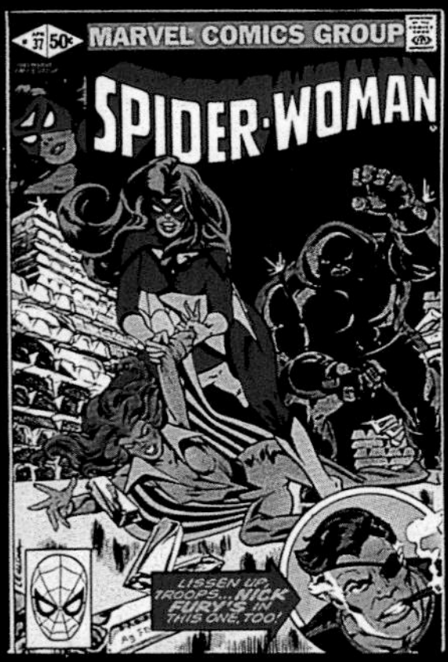
MARVEL COMICS GROUP
SPIDER-WOMAN
LISSEN UP, TROOPS... NICK FURY'S IN THIS ONE, TOO!

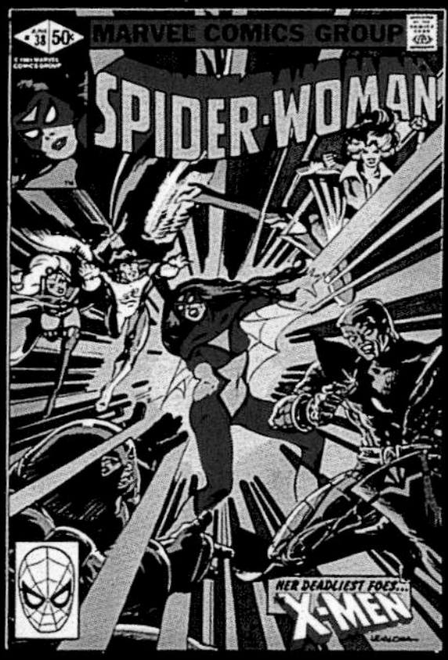
MARVEL COMICS GROUP
SPIDER-WOMAN
HER DEADLIEST FOE... X-MEN

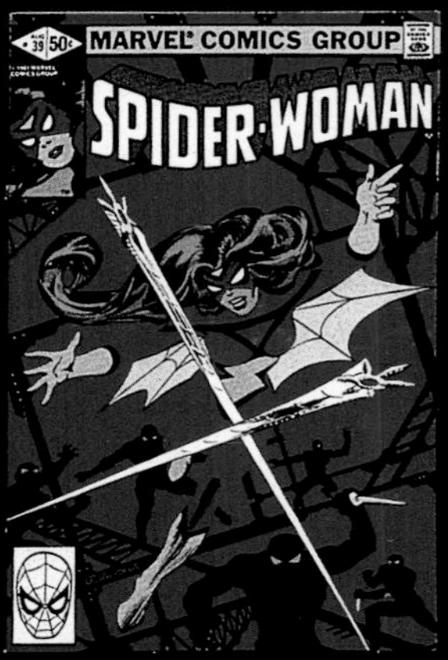
MARVEL COMICS GROUP
SPIDER-WOMAN

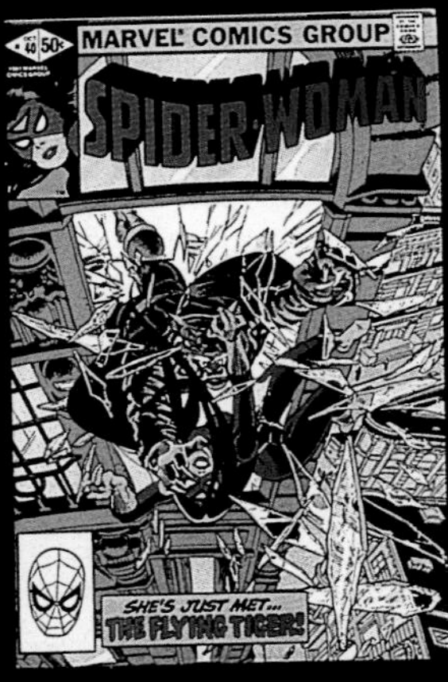
MARVEL COMICS GROUP
SPIDER-WOMAN
SHE'S JUST MET... THE FLYING TIGER!

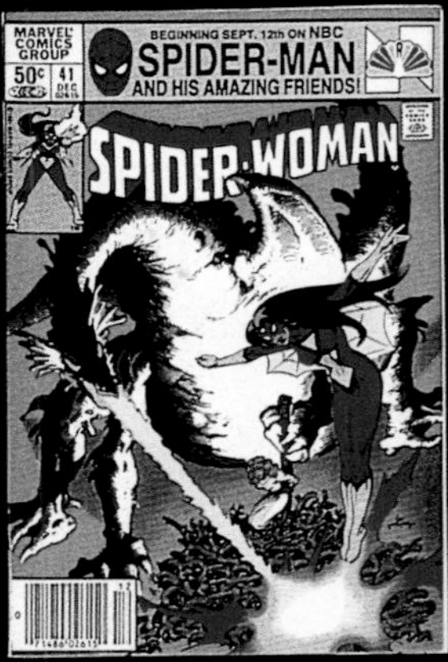
BEGINNING SEPT. 12th ON NBC
SPIDER-MAN AND HIS AMAZING FRIENDS!
SPIDER-WOMAN

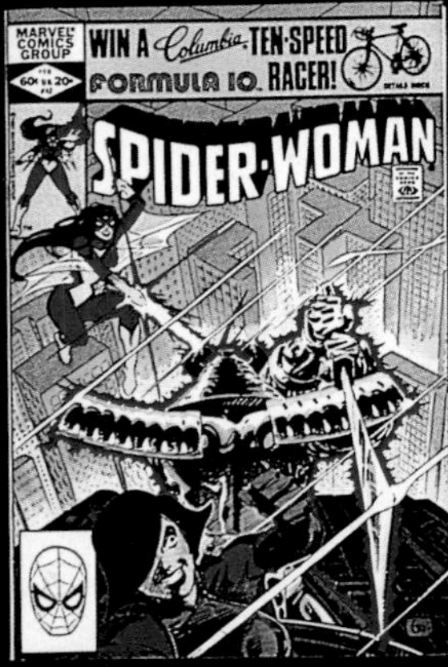
WIN A Columbia TEN-SPEED FORMULA 10 RACER!
SPIDER-WOMAN

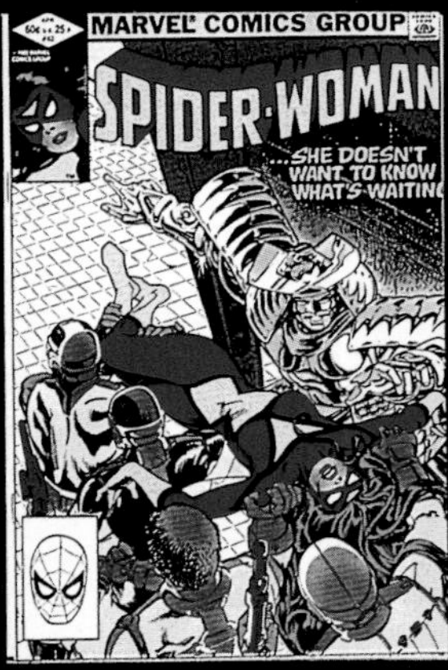
MARVEL COMICS GROUP
SPIDER-WOMAN
SHE DOESN'T WANT TO KNOW WHAT'S WAITING

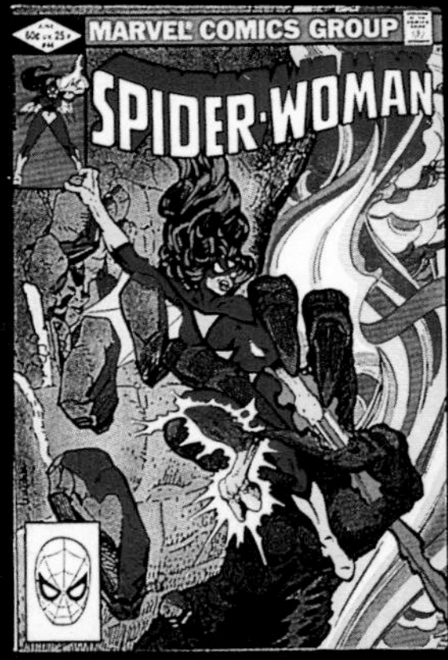
MARVEL COMICS GROUP
SPIDER-WOMAN

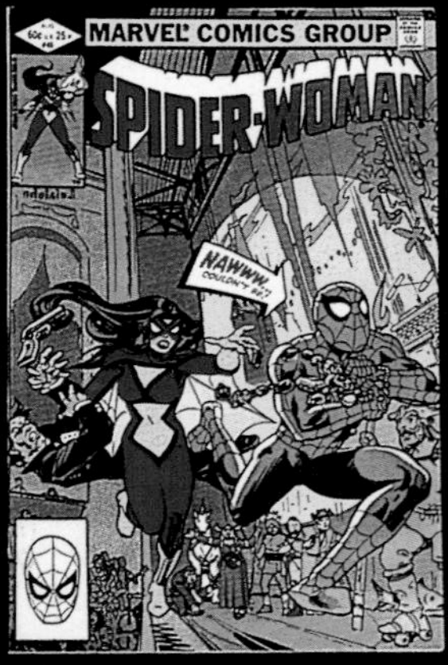
MARVEL COMICS GROUP
SPIDER-WOMAN

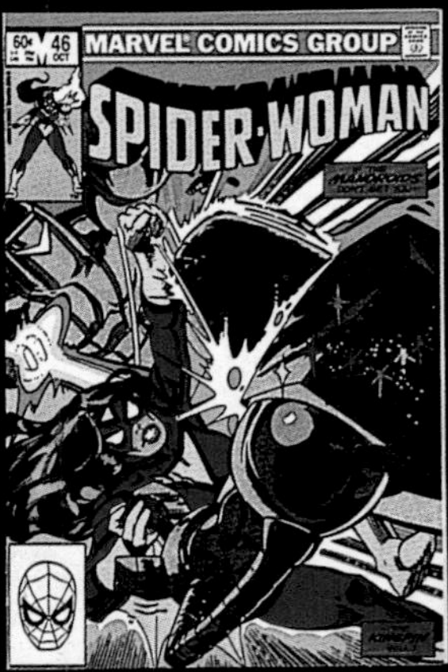
MARVEL COMICS GROUP
SPIDER-WOMAN

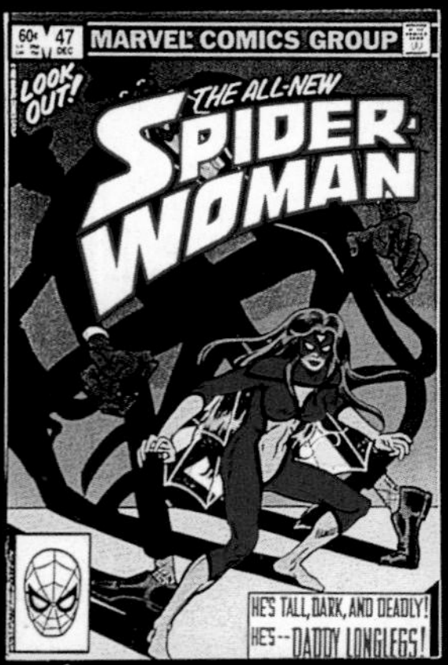
MARVEL COMICS GROUP
LOOK OUT!
THE ALL-NEW SPIDER-WOMAN
HE'S TALL, DARK, AND DEADLY! HE'S—DADDY LONGLEGS!

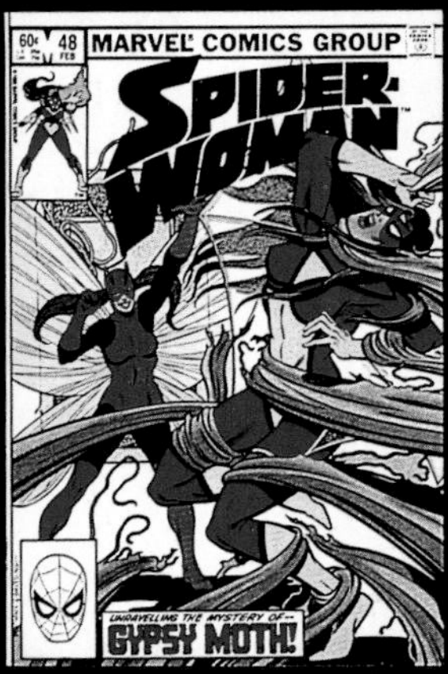
MARVEL COMICS GROUP
SPIDER-WOMAN
GYPSY MOTH!

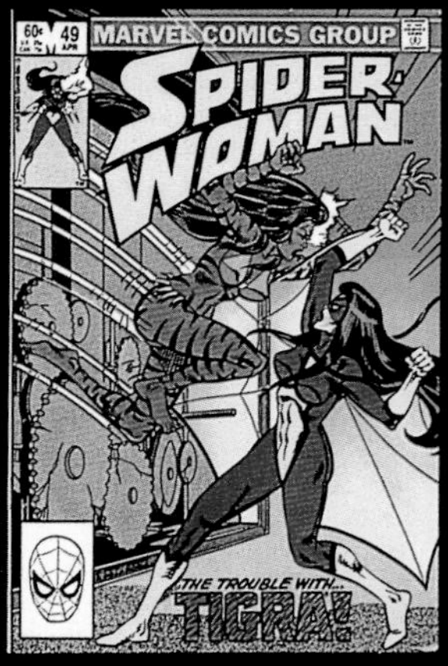
MARVEL COMICS GROUP
SPIDER-WOMAN
THE TROUBLE WITH... TIGRA!

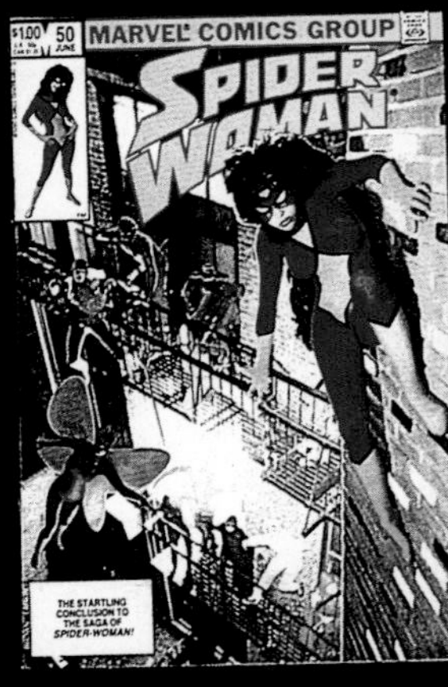
MARVEL COMICS GROUP
SPIDER-WOMAN
THE STARTLING CONCLUSION TO THE SAGA OF SPIDER-WOMAN!

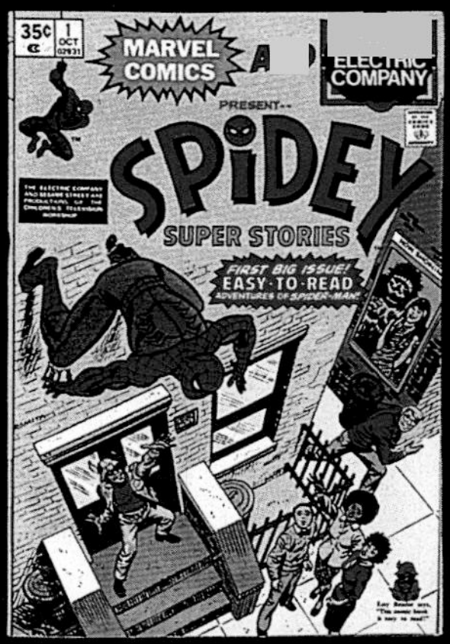
MARVEL COMICS
PRESENT
SPIDEY
SUPER STORIES
FIRST BIG ISSUE! EASY-TO-READ ADVENTURES OF SPIDER-MAN!

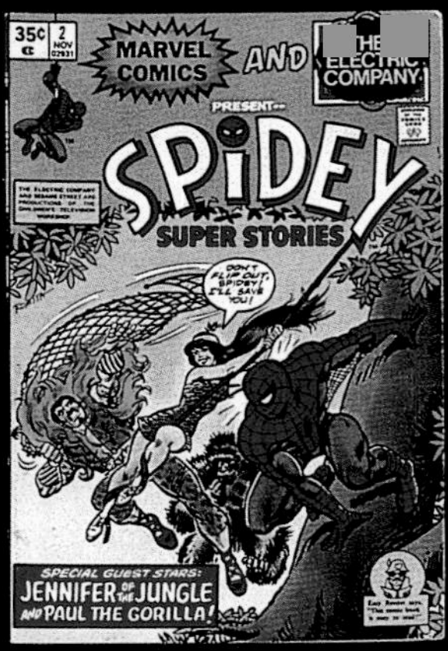
MARVEL COMICS AND
PRESENT
SPIDEY
SUPER STORIES
SPECIAL GUEST STARS: JENNIFER OF THE JUNGLE AND PAUL THE GORILLA!

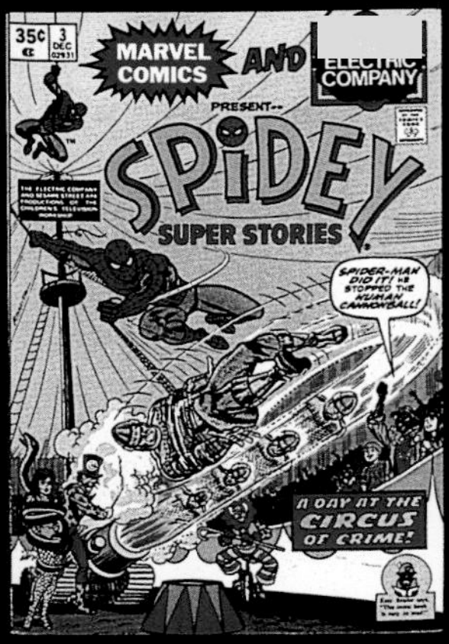
MARVEL COMICS AND
PRESENT
SPIDEY
SUPER STORIES
A DAY AT THE CIRCUS OF CRIME!

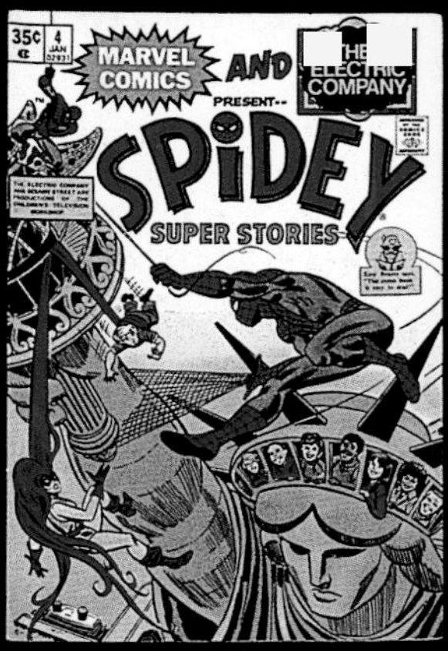
MARVEL COMICS AND
PRESENT
SPIDEY
SUPER STORIES

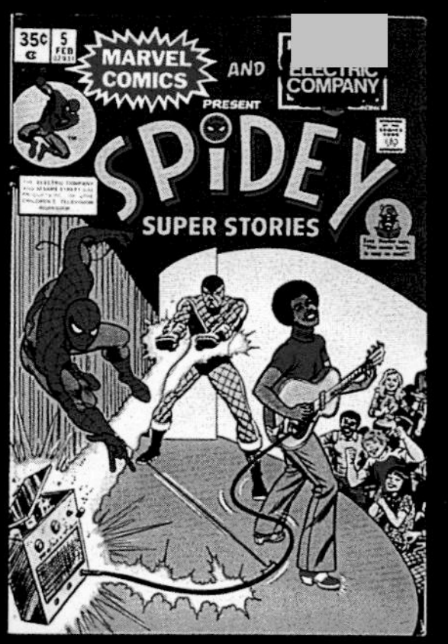
MARVEL COMICS AND
PRESENT
SPIDEY
SUPER STORIES

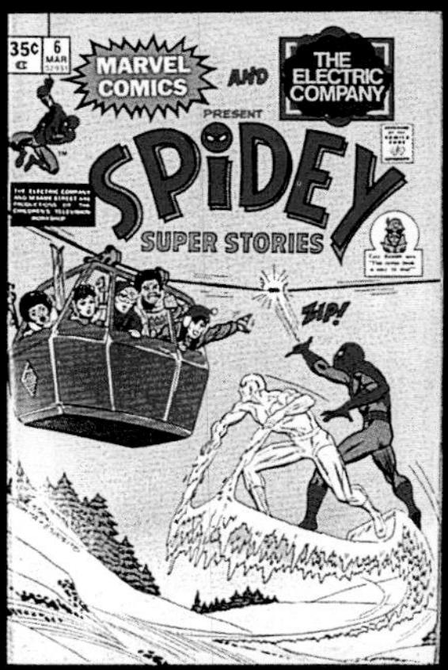
MARVEL COMICS AND THE ELECTRIC COMPANY
PRESENT
SPIDEY
SUPER STORIES
ZIP!

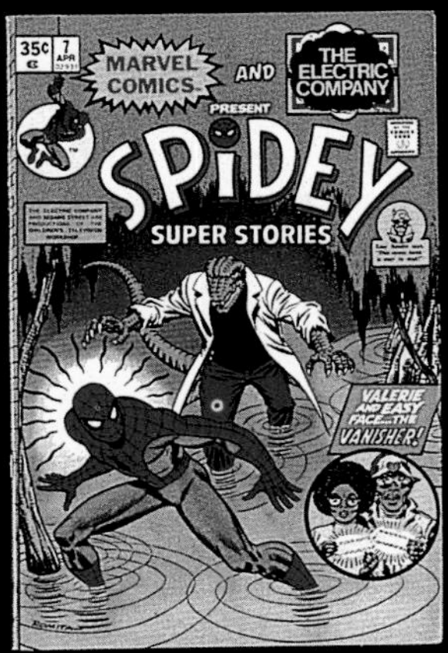
MARVEL COMICS AND THE ELECTRIC COMPANY
PRESENT
SPIDEY
SUPER STORIES
VALERIE AND EASY FACE THE VANISHER!

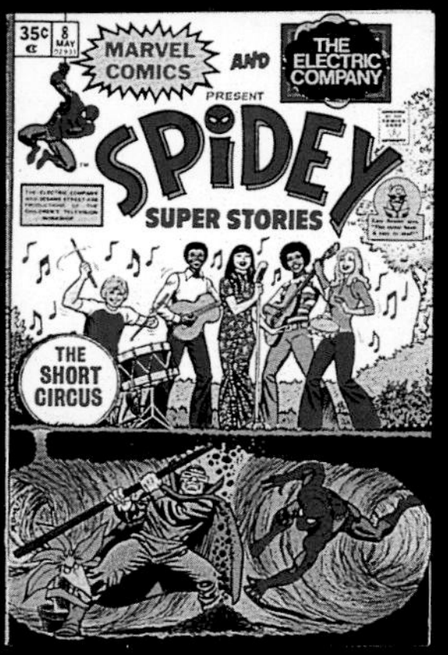
MARVEL COMICS AND THE ELECTRIC COMPANY
PRESENT
SPIDEY
SUPER STORIES
THE SHORT CIRCUS

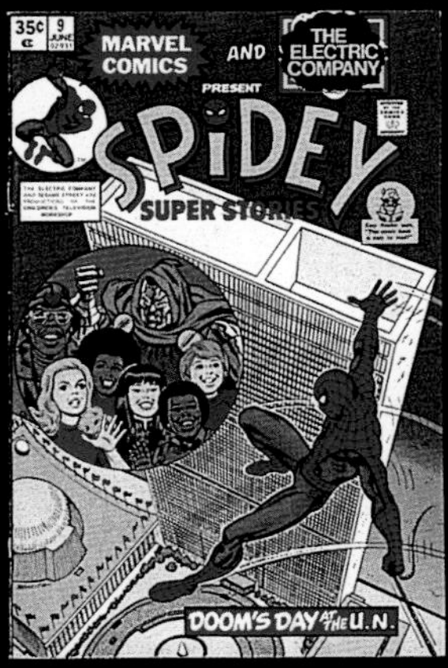
MARVEL COMICS AND THE ELECTRIC COMPANY
PRESENT
SPIDEY
SUPER STORIES
DOOM'S DAY AT THE U.N.

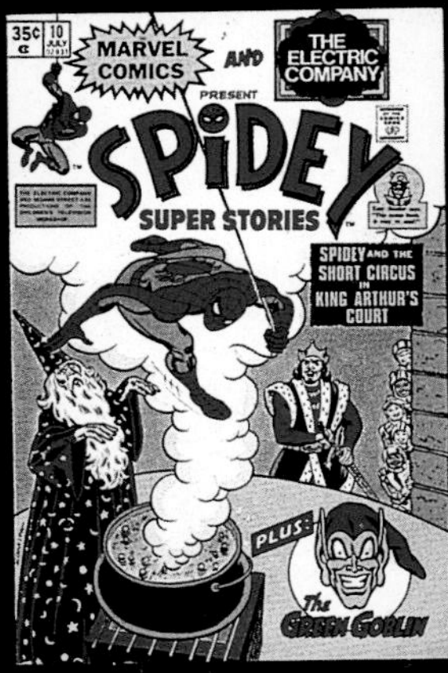
MARVEL COMICS AND THE ELECTRIC COMPANY
PRESENT
SPIDEY
SUPER STORIES
SPIDEY AND THE SHORT CIRCUS IN KING ARTHUR'S COURT
PLUS: The GREEN GOBLIN

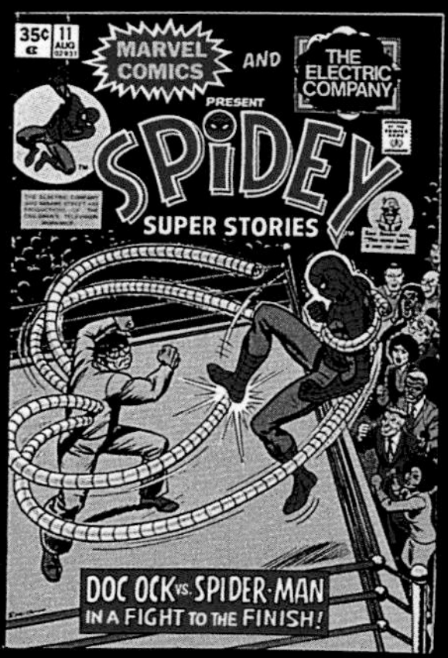
MARVEL COMICS AND THE ELECTRIC COMPANY
PRESENT
SPIDEY
SUPER STORIES
DOC OCK VS. SPIDER-MAN IN A FIGHT TO THE FINISH!

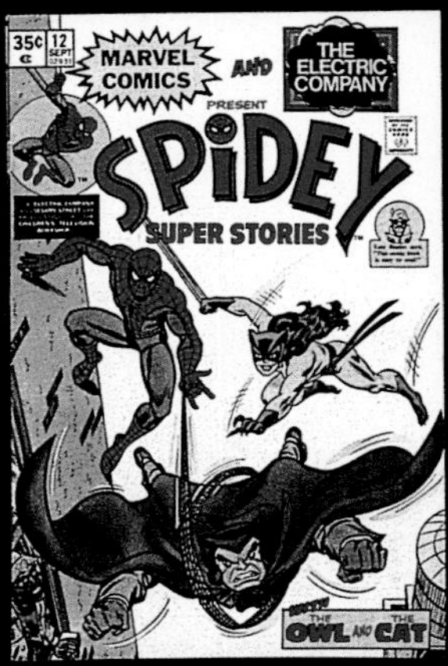
MARVEL COMICS AND THE ELECTRIC COMPANY
PRESENT
SPIDEY
SUPER STORIES
THE OWL AND THE CAT

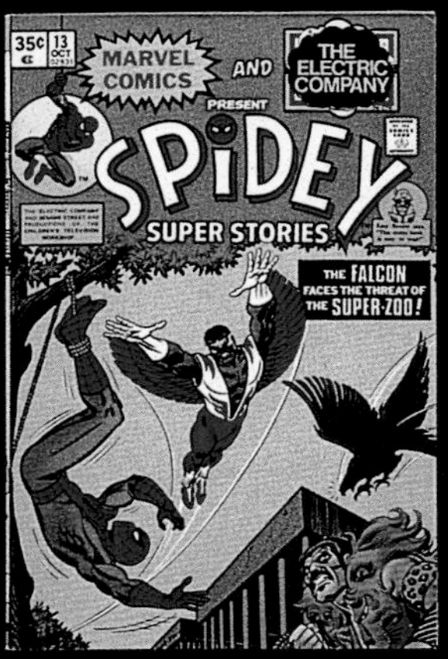
MARVEL COMICS AND THE ELECTRIC COMPANY
PRESENT
SPIDEY
SUPER STORIES
THE FALCON FACES THE THREAT OF THE SUPER-ZOO!

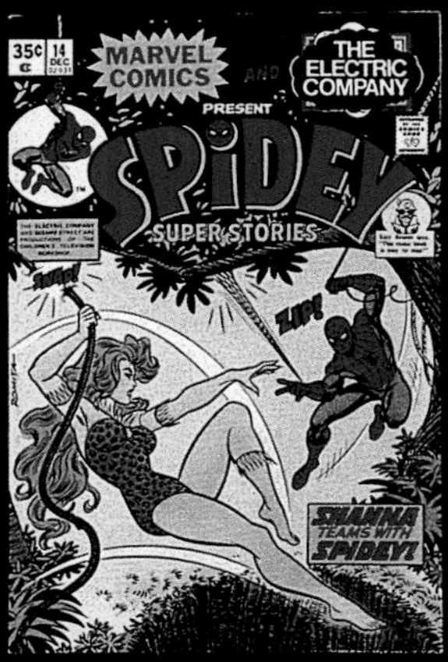
MARVEL COMICS AND THE ELECTRIC COMPANY
PRESENT
SPIDEY
SUPER STORIES

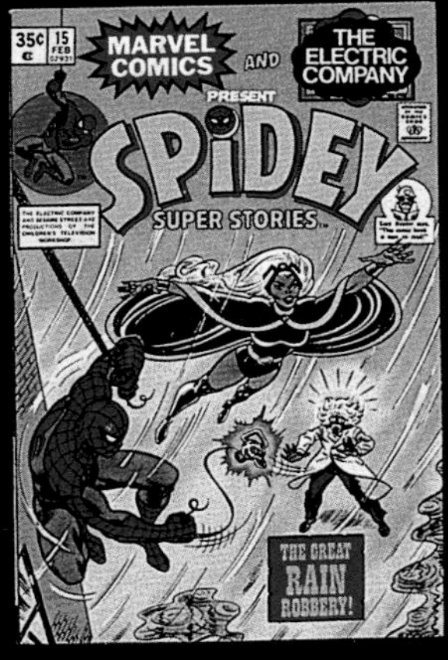
MARVEL COMICS AND THE ELECTRIC COMPANY
PRESENT
SPIDEY
SUPER STORIES
THE GREAT RAIN ROBBERY!

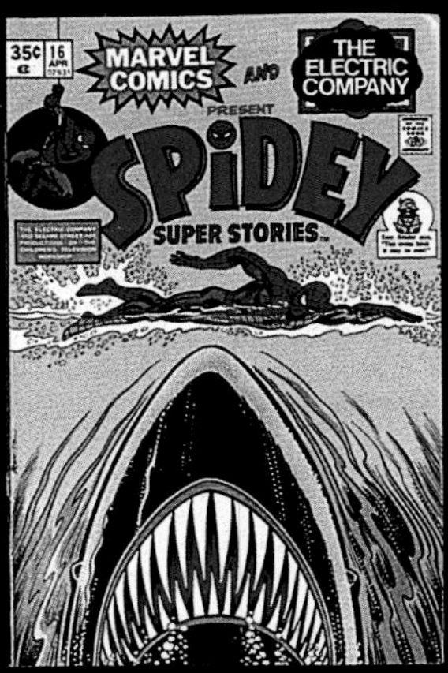
MARVEL COMICS AND THE ELECTRIC COMPANY
PRESENT
SPIDEY
SUPER STORIES

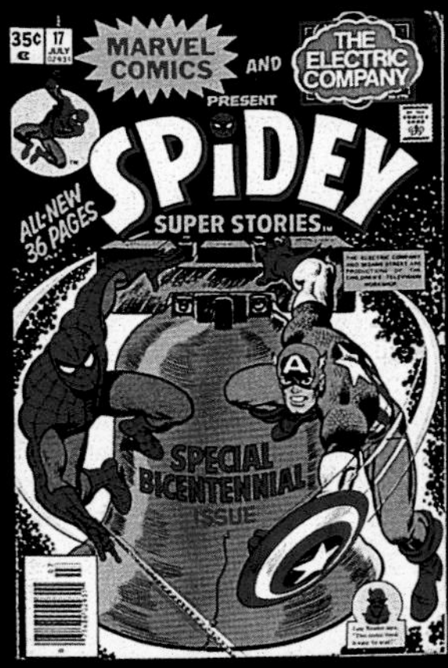
MARVEL COMICS AND THE ELECTRIC COMPANY
PRESENT
SPIDEY
SUPER STORIES
ALL-NEW 36 PAGES
SPECIAL BICENTENNIAL ISSUE

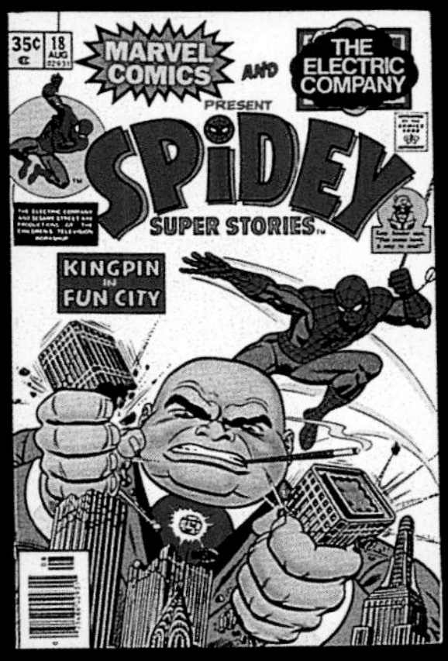
MARVEL COMICS AND THE ELECTRIC COMPANY
PRESENT
SPIDEY
SUPER STORIES
KINGPIN FUN CITY

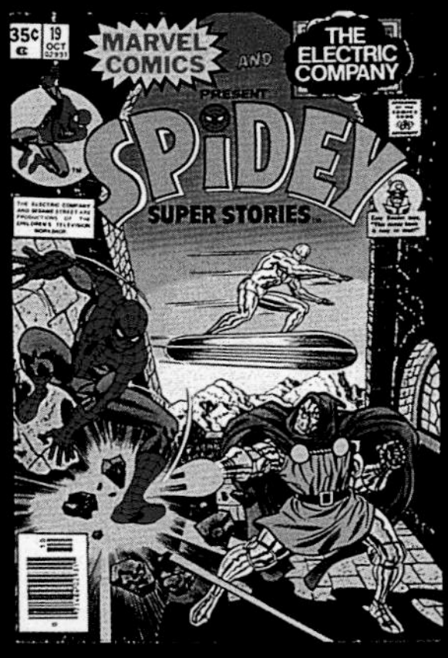
MARVEL COMICS AND THE ELECTRIC COMPANY
PRESENT
SPIDEY
SUPER STORIES

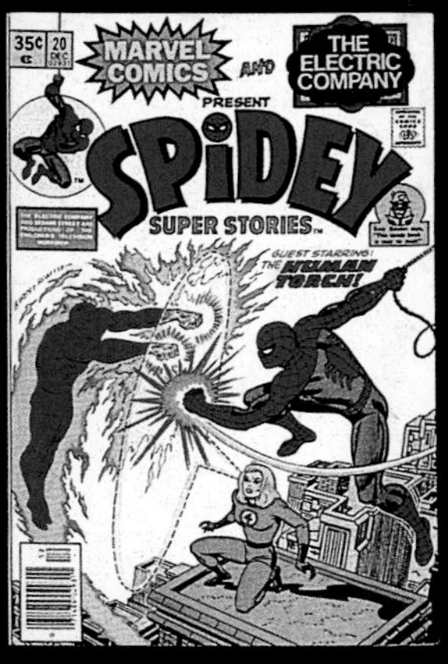
MARVEL COMICS AND THE ELECTRIC COMPANY
PRESENT
SPIDEY
SUPER STORIES

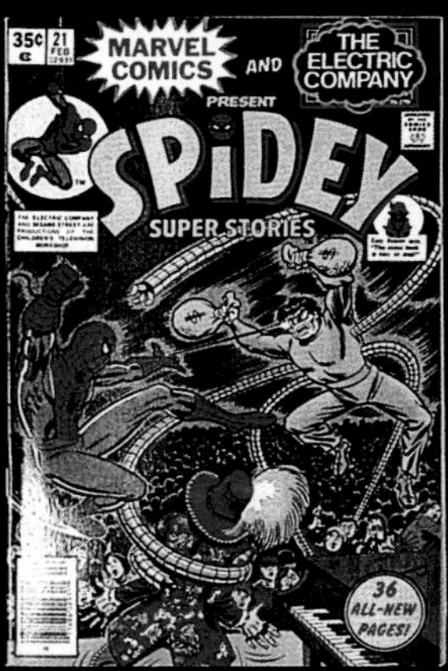
MARVEL COMICS AND THE ELECTRIC COMPANY
PRESENT
SPIDEY
SUPER STORIES
36 ALL-NEW PAGES!

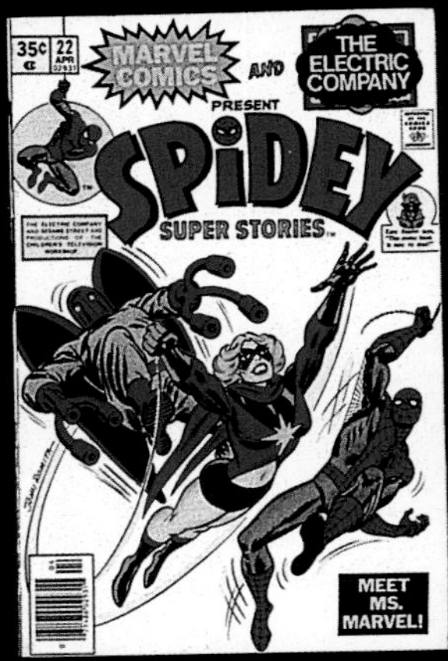
MARVEL COMICS AND THE ELECTRIC COMPANY
PRESENT
SPIDEY
SUPER STORIES
MEET MS. MARVEL!

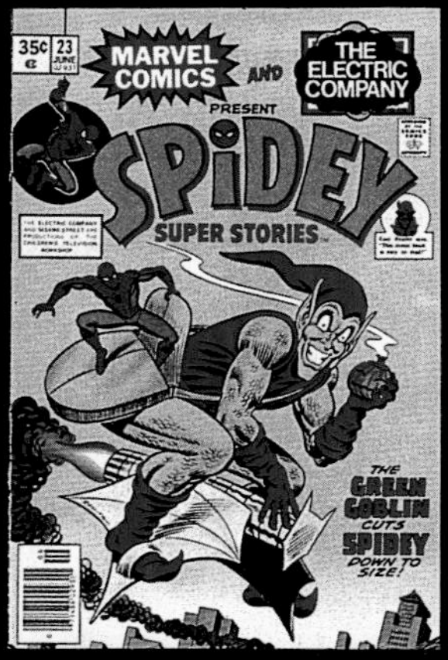
MARVEL COMICS AND THE ELECTRIC COMPANY
PRESENT
SPIDEY
SUPER STORIES
THE GREEN GOBLIN CUTS SPIDEY DOWN TO SIZE!

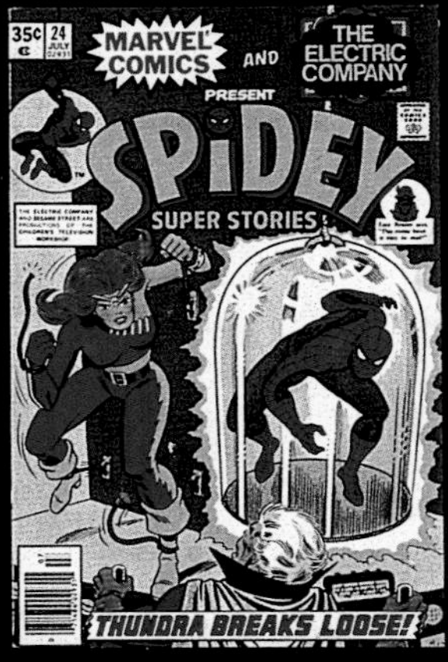
MARVEL COMICS AND THE ELECTRIC COMPANY
PRESENT
SPIDEY
SUPER STORIES
THUNDRA BREAKS LOOSE!

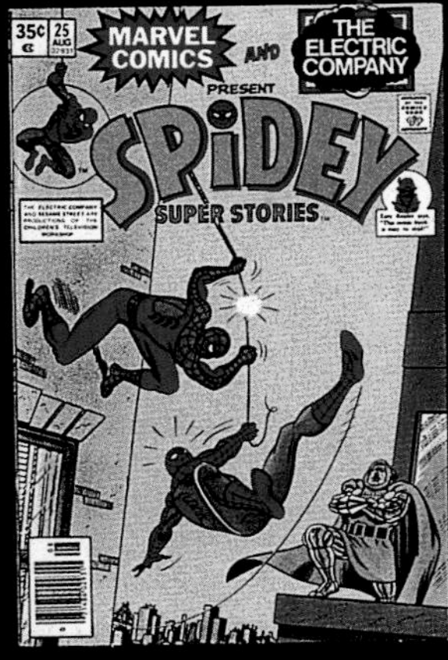
MARVEL COMICS AND THE ELECTRIC COMPANY
PRESENT
SPIDEY
SUPER STORIES

1757.6 Spidey Super Stories (26-57)

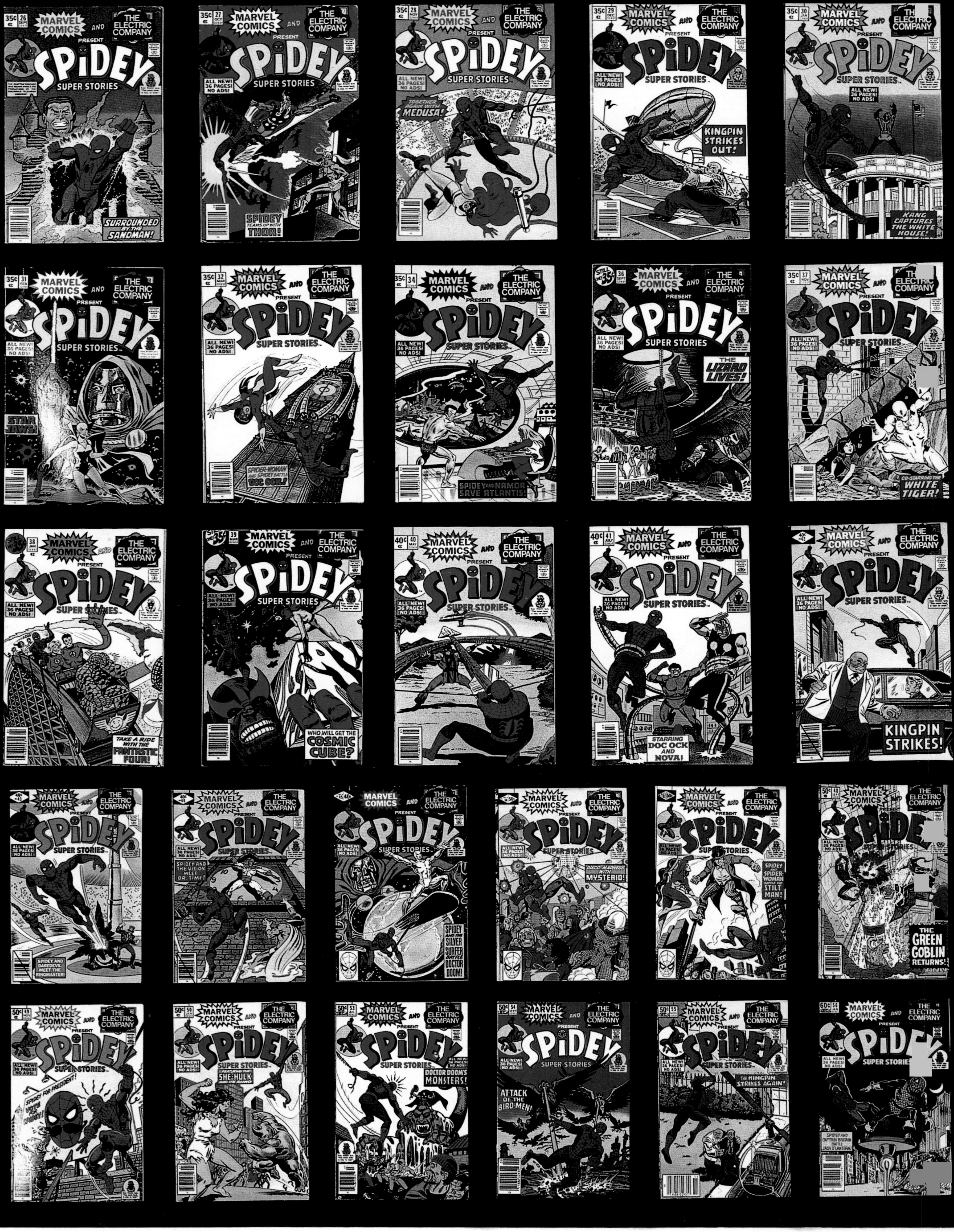

SURROUNDED BY THE SANDMAN!
SPIDEY TEAMS UP WITH THOR!
TOGETHER AGAIN WITH MEDUSA!
KINGPIN STRIKES OUT!
KANG CAPTURES THE WHITE HOUSE!
STAR JAWS!
THE LIZARD LIVES!
SPIDEY AND NAMOR SAVE ATLANTIS!
CO-STARRING THE WHITE TIGER!
TAKE A RIDE WITH THE FANTASTIC FOUR!
WHO WILL GET THE COSMIC CUBE?
STARRING DOC OCK AND NOVA!
KINGPIN STRIKES!
SPIDEY AND DAREDEVIL MEET THE RINGMASTER!
SPIDEY AND THE VISION MEET OR TIME!
SPIDEY AND SILVER SURFER VS. DOCTOR DOOM!
DISCO MADNESS WITH MYSTERIO!
SPIDEY AND SPIDER-WOMAN BATTLE THE STILT MAN!
THE GREEN GOBLIN RETURNS!
SPIDEY FOR PRESIDENT!
SHE-HULK
DOCTOR DOOM'S MONSTERS!
ATTACK OF THE BIRD-MEN!
THE KINGPIN STRIKES AGAIN!

Spidey Super Stories (1-57) 1757.6

Ref. No.	Date	RVI	Artist/Info.
1757.6-1	Oct. 1974	2	Romita-c (Simplified Spider-Man stories, all)
1757.6-2	Nov.	1	Romita-c, Heck, Esposito, Mortimer-a
1757.6-3	Dec.	1	Mortimer, Esposito-a
1757.6-4	Jan. 1975	1	" "
1757.6-5	Feb.	1	Romita-c, Mortimer/Esposito-a
1757.6-6	Mar.	1	Romita, Esposito-c, Mortimer, Esposito-a
1757.6-7	Apr.	1	Romita-c, Mortimer/Esposito-a
1757.6-8	May	1	" " "
1757.6-9	Jun.	1	" " "
1757.6-10	**Jul.**	**1**	**Romita-c, Mortimer-a**
1757.6-11	Aug.	1	Romita-c, Mortimer/Esposito-a
1757.6-12	Sept.	1	Romita-c, Mortimer--a
1757.6-13	Oct.	1	Romita-c, Mortimer/Esposito-a
1757.6-14	Dec.	1	" " "
1757.6-15	Feb. 1976	1	" " "
1757.6-16	Apr.	1	" " "
1757.6-17	Jun.	1	" " "
1757.6-18	Aug.	1	Mortimer/Esposito-a
1757.6-19	Oct.	1	" "
1757.6-20	**Dec.**	**1**	**Kirby, Romita-c, Mortimer/Esposito-a**
1757.6-21	Feb. 1977	1	Mortimer/Esposito-a
1757.6-22	Apr.	1	Romita-c, Mortimer/Esposito-a
1757.6-23	Jun.	1	" " "
1757.6-24 to 57	Jul. (#57)	1	Mortimer/Esposito-a (most)

1764.5 Spoof (1-5)

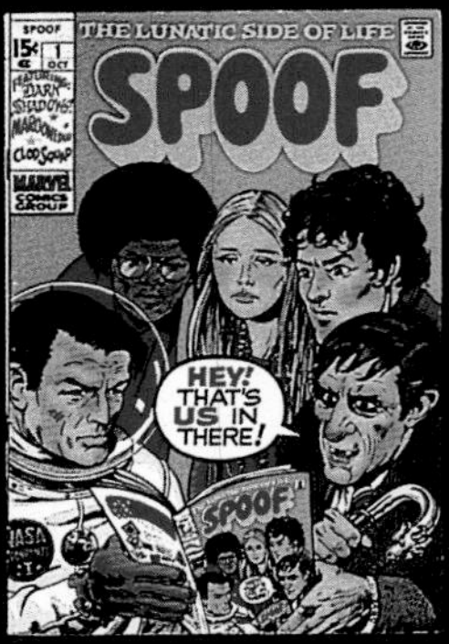
THE LUNATIC SIDE OF LIFE
SPOOF
HEY! THAT'S US IN THERE!

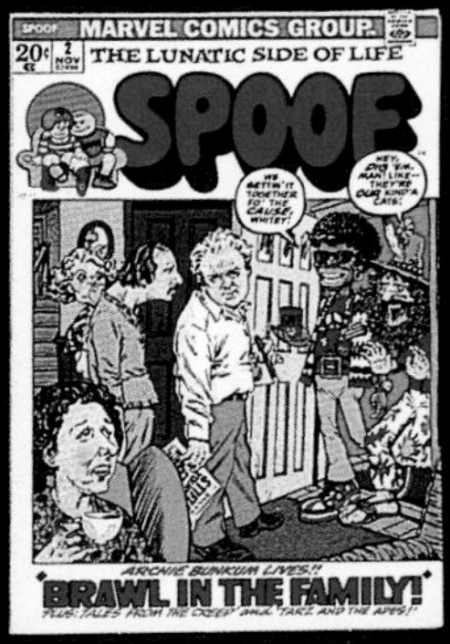
MARVEL COMICS GROUP
THE LUNATIC SIDE OF LIFE
SPOOF
BRAWL IN THE FAMILY!

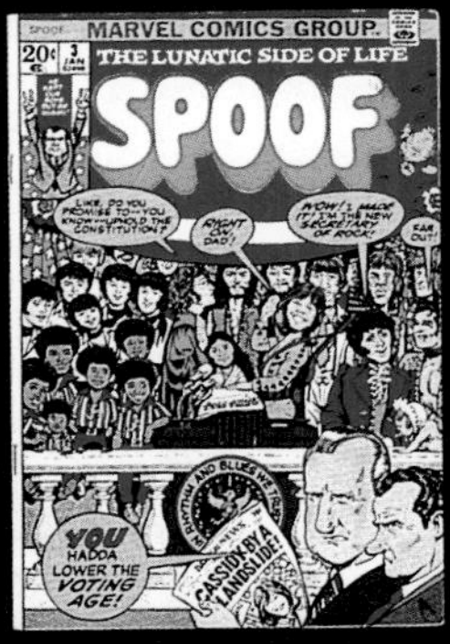
MARVEL COMICS GROUP
THE LUNATIC SIDE OF LIFE
SPOOF

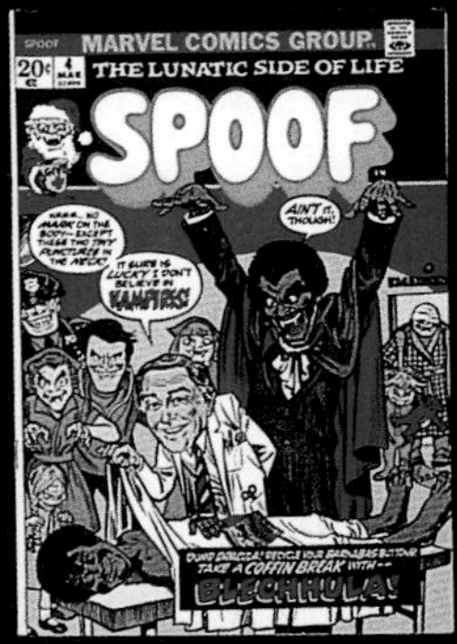
MARVEL COMICS GROUP
THE LUNATIC SIDE OF LIFE
SPOOF

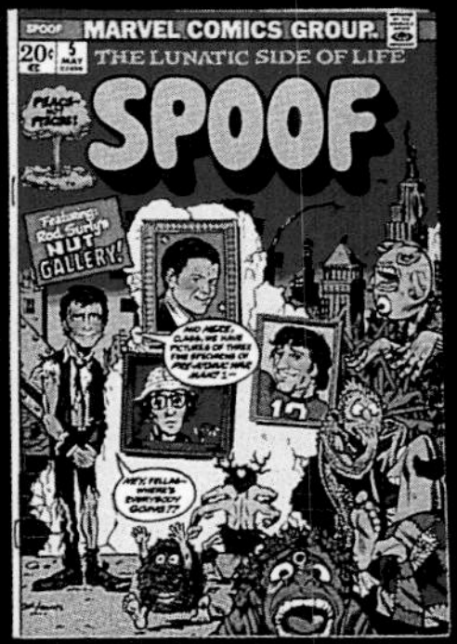
MARVEL COMICS GROUP
THE LUNATIC SIDE OF LIFE
SPOOF

1780.3 Squadron Supreme (1-4)

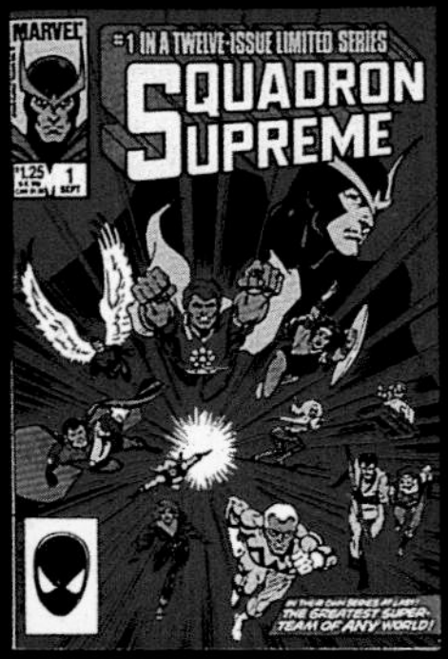
#1 IN A TWELVE-ISSUE LIMITED SERIES
SQUADRON SUPREME

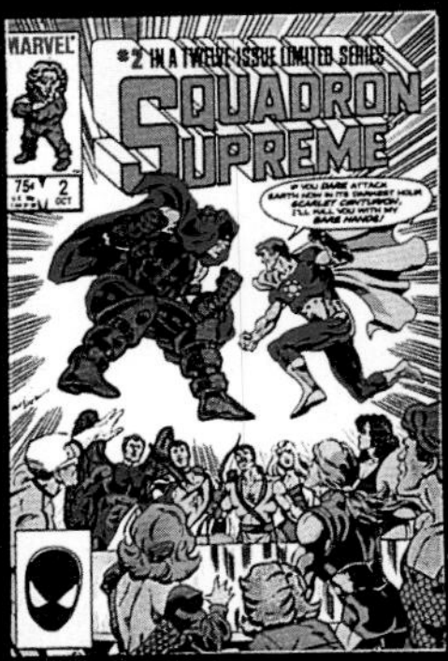
#2 IN A TWELVE-ISSUE LIMITED SERIES
SQUADRON SUPREME

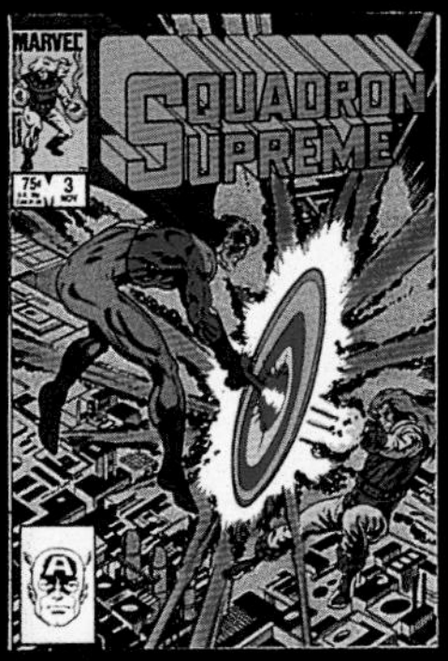
SQUADRON SUPREME

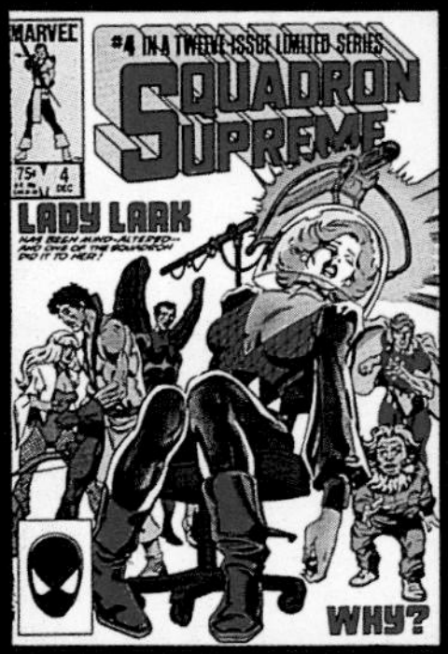
#4 IN A TWELVE-ISSUE LIMITED SERIES
SQUADRON SUPREME
LADY LARK
WHY?

1784.2 Star Lord Special

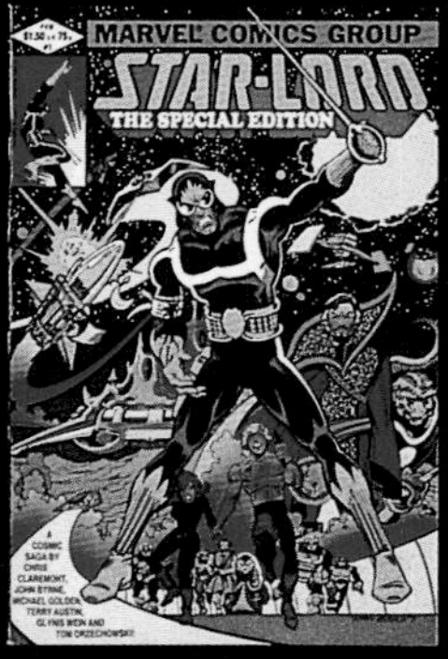
MARVEL COMICS GROUP
STAR-LORD
THE SPECIAL EDITION

1785.7 Starriors (1-4)

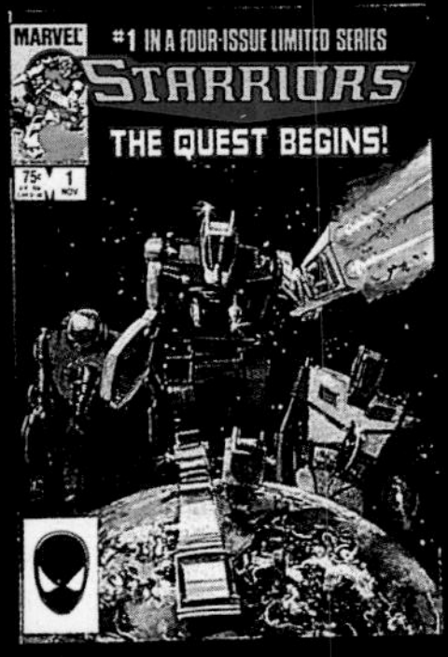
#1 IN A FOUR-ISSUE LIMITED SERIES
STARRIORS
THE QUEST BEGINS!

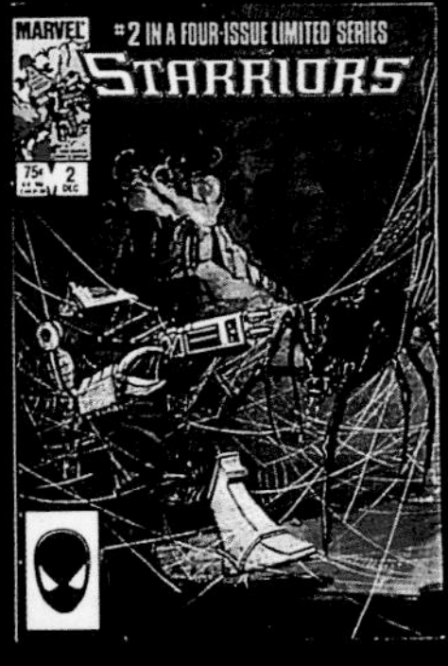
#2 IN A FOUR-ISSUE LIMITED SERIES
STARRIORS

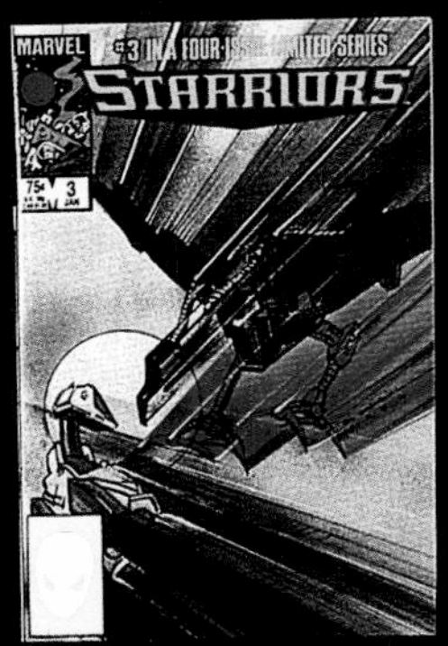
#3 IN A FOUR-ISSUE LIMITED SERIES
STARRIORS

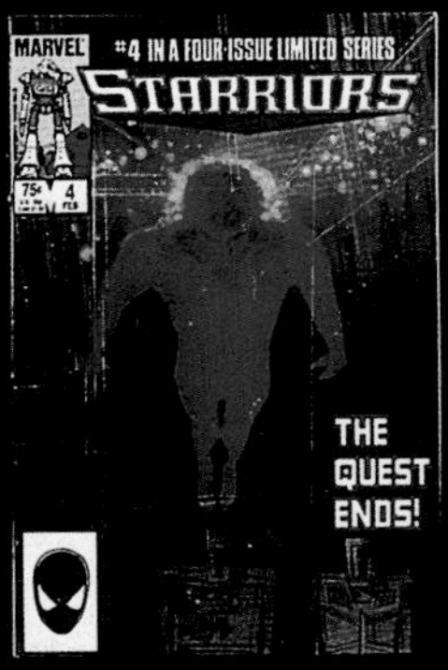
#4 IN A FOUR-ISSUE LIMITED SERIES
STARRIORS
THE QUEST ENDS!

1791.2 Star Trek (1-18)

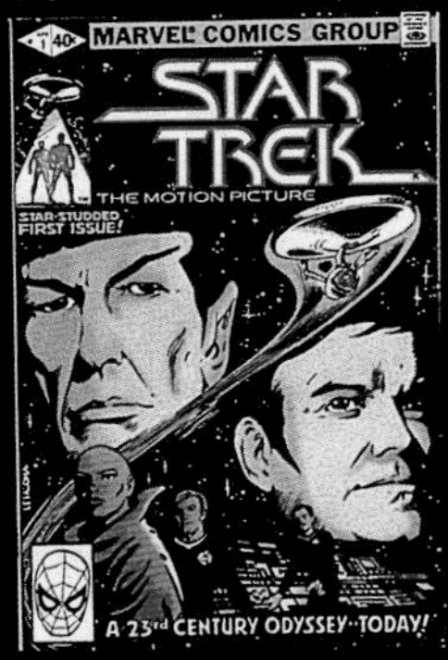
MARVEL COMICS GROUP
STAR TREK
THE MOTION PICTURE
A 23rd CENTURY ODYSSEY--TODAY!

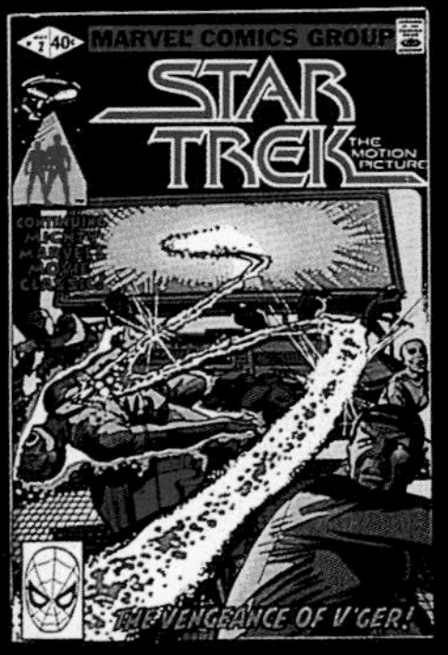
MARVEL COMICS GROUP
STAR TREK
THE MOTION PICTURE
THE VENGEANCE OF V'GER!

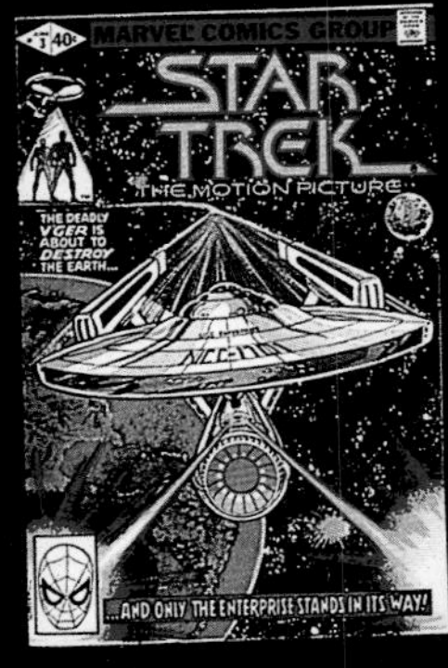
MARVEL COMICS GROUP
STAR TREK
THE MOTION PICTURE
...AND ONLY THE ENTERPRISE STANDS IN ITS WAY!

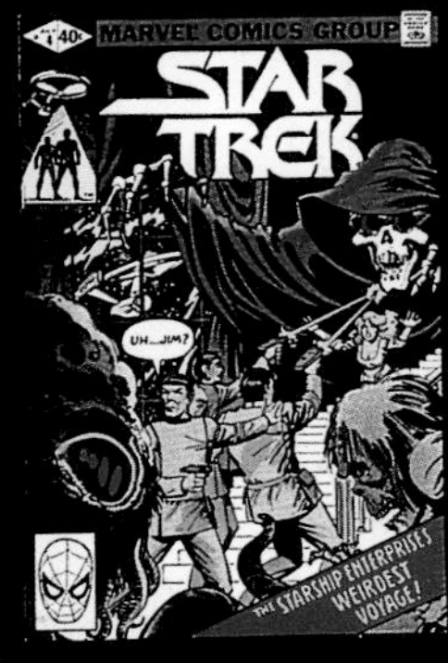
MARVEL COMICS GROUP
STAR TREK

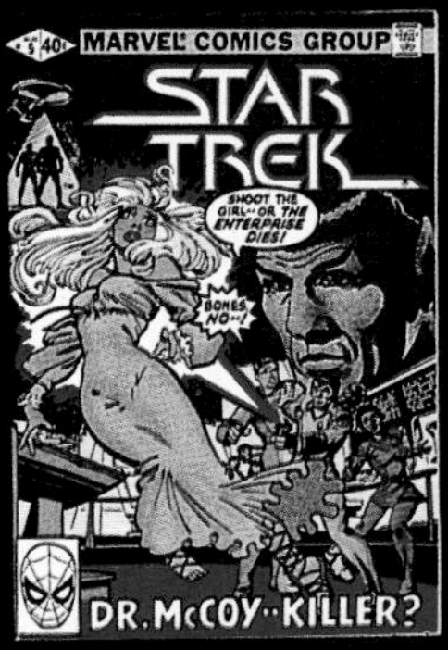
MARVEL COMICS GROUP
STAR TREK
DR. McCOY--KILLER?

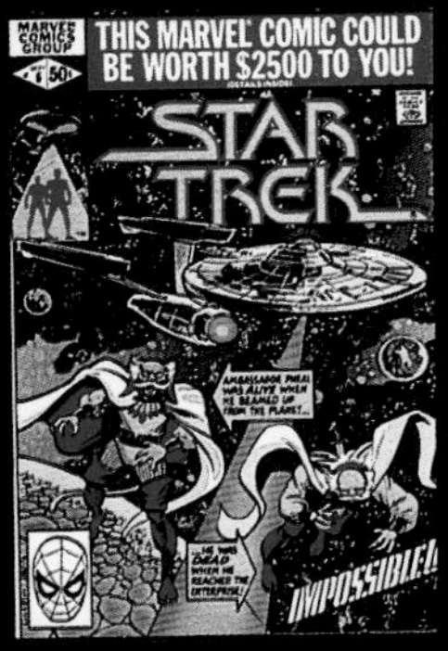
THIS MARVEL COMIC COULD BE WORTH $2500 TO YOU!
STAR TREK

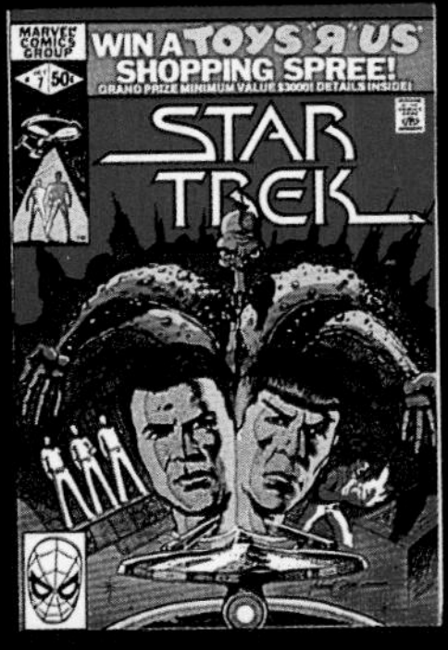
WIN A TOYS R US SHOPPING SPREE!
STAR TREK

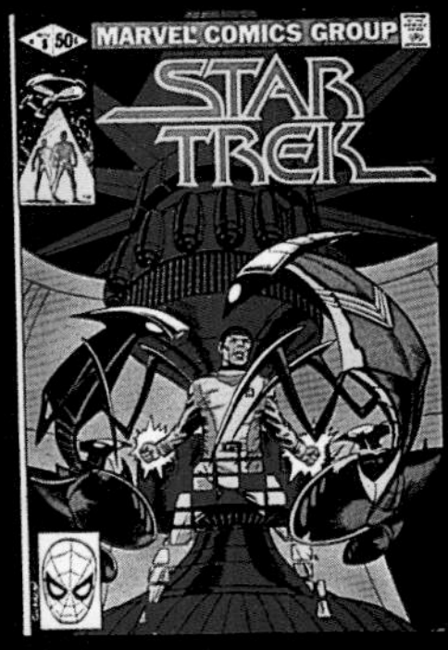
MARVEL COMICS GROUP
STAR TREK

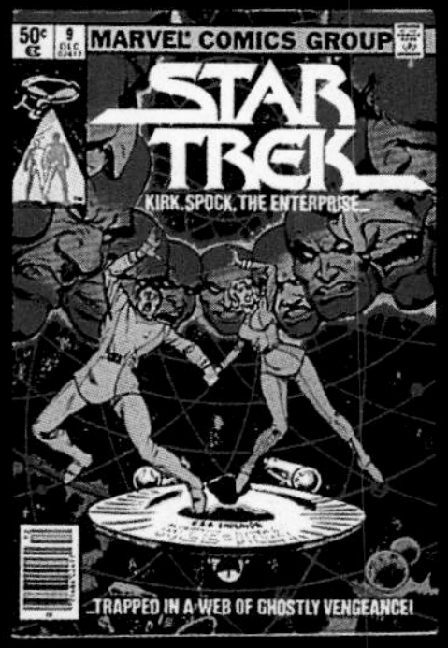
MARVEL COMICS GROUP
STAR TREK
TRAPPED IN A WEB OF GHOSTLY VENGEANCE!

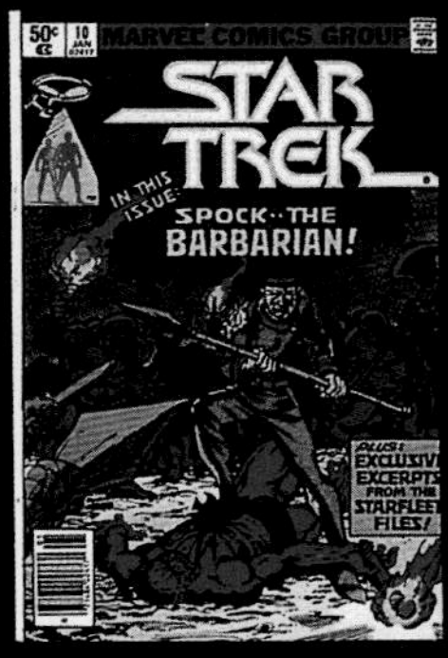
MARVEL COMICS GROUP
STAR TREK
SPOCK--THE BARBARIAN!

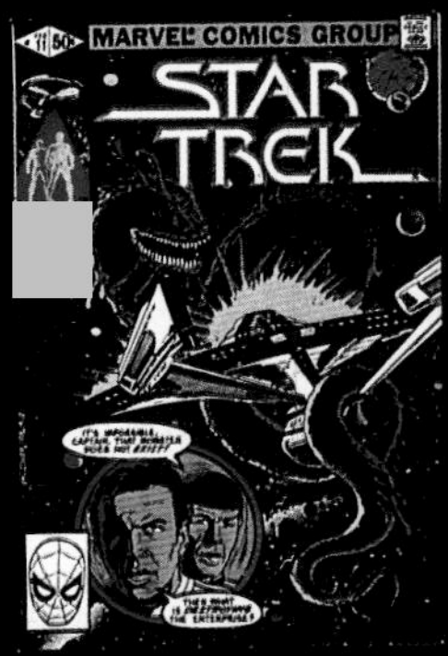
MARVEL COMICS GROUP
STAR TREK

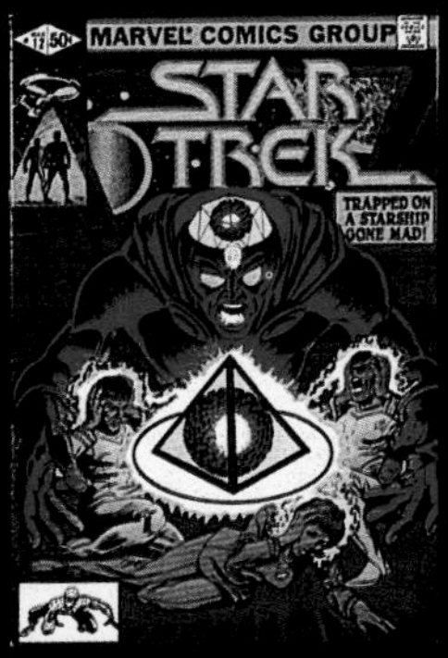
MARVEL COMICS GROUP
STAR TREK

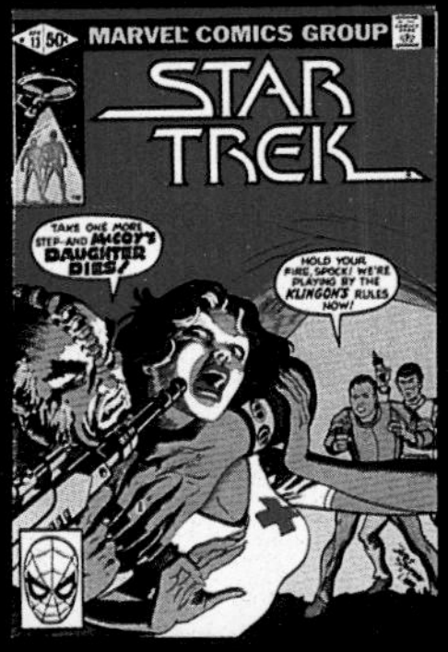
MARVEL COMICS GROUP
STAR TREK

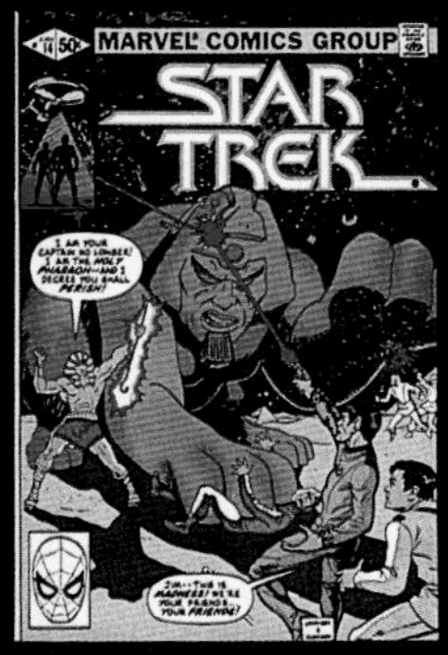
MARVEL COMICS GROUP
STAR TREK

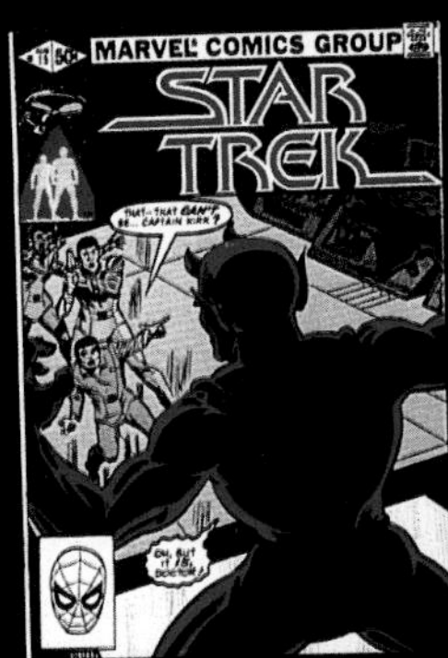
MARVEL COMICS GROUP
STAR TREK

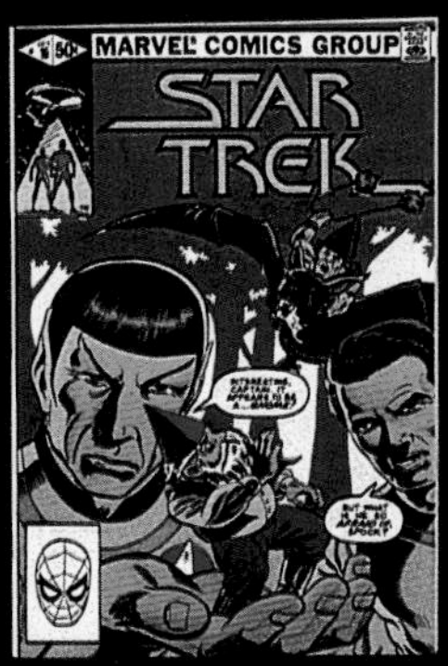
MARVEL COMICS GROUP
STAR TREK

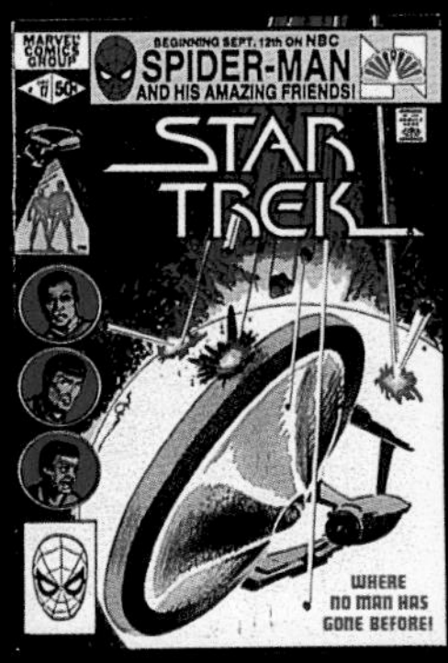
SPIDER-MAN AND HIS AMAZING FRIENDS!
STAR TREK
WHERE NO MAN HAS GONE BEFORE!

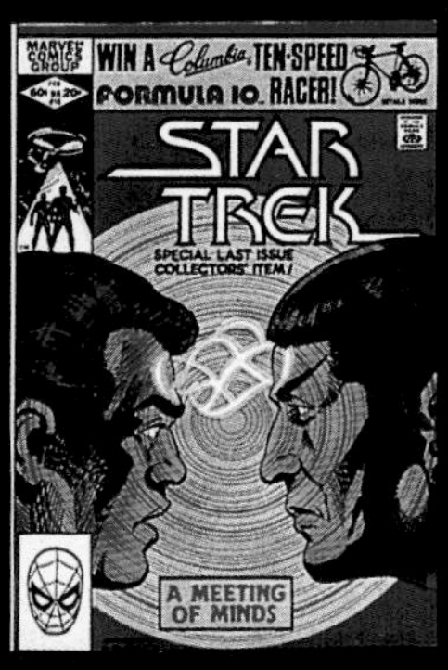
WIN A Columbia TEN-SPEED FORMULA 10 RACER!
STAR TREK
A MEETING OF MINDS

Spoof! (1-5) 1764.5

Ref. No.	Date	RVI	Artist/Info.
1764.5-1	Oct. 1970	1	M. Severin-c/a
1764.5-2	Nov. 1972	1	"
1764.5-3	Jan. 1973	1	"
1764.5-4	Mar.	1	"
1764.5-5	May 1973	1	"

Spotlight (1-4) 1770

1770-1	Sept. 1978	1	(Huckleberry Hound)
1770-2	Nov.	1	(Quick Draw McGraw)
1770-3	Jan. 1979	1	(The Jetsons)
1770-4	Mar. 1979	1	(Migilla the Gorilla)

Squadron Supreme (1-12) 1780.3

1780.3-1	Sept. 1985	1	Hall/Rubinstein-c, Hall/Beatty-a
1780.3-2 to 12	Aug. 1986 (#12)	1	Hay/Layton-c

Star Lord Special Edition (1) 1784.2

1784.2-1	Feb. 1982	2	Terry/Austin-c

Starriors (1-4) 1785.7

1785.7-1 to 4	Aug. 1984, (#1)	1	Chen/Akin/Garvey-a (Tomy toy robots)

Starstruck (1-6) 1788.7

1788.7-1 to 6	Mar. 1985, (#1)	1	Kaluta-c/a

Star Team (nn) 1289.5

1289.5-nn	1977	1	(Toy Giveaway)

Star Trek (1-18) 1791.2

1791.2-1	Apr. 1980	3	Leialoha-c, Cockrum, Janson-a
1791.2-2	May	2	Cockrum, Janson-a
1791.2-3	Jun.	2	Wiacek-c, Cockrum, Janson-a
1791.2-4	Jul.	2	Cockru,-c, Cockrum, Janson-a
1791.2-5	Aug.	2	Cockrum, Janson-a
1791.2-6	Sept.	1	Cockrum, Janson-c/a
1791.2-7	Oct.	1	Nasser-c/a, Janson-a
1791.2-8	Nov.	1	Cockrum-c/a, Villamonte-a
1791.2-9	Dec.	1	Cockrum/Springer-a
1791.2-10	**Jan. 1981**	**1**	**Duramona/Janson-a**
1791.2-11	Feb.	1	Brozowski/Palmer-c/a
1791.2-12 to 18		1	

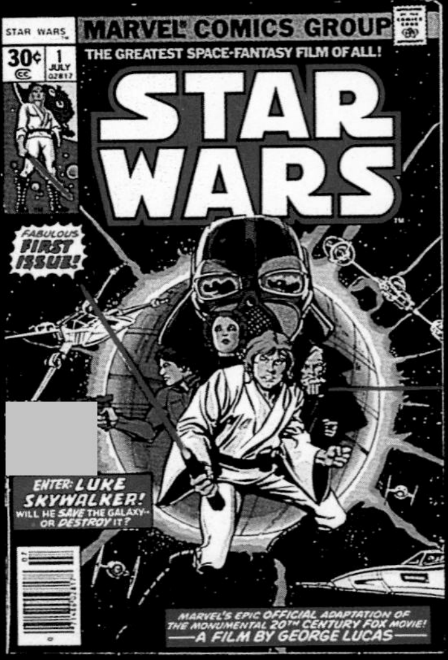
STAR WARS
MARVEL COMICS GROUP
30¢ 1 JULY 02817
THE GREATEST SPACE-FANTASY FILM OF ALL!
STAR WARS
FABULOUS FIRST ISSUE!
ENTER: LUKE SKYWALKER! WILL HE SAVE THE GALAXY-- OR DESTROY IT?
MARVEL'S EPIC OFFICIAL ADAPTATION OF THE MONUMENTAL 20TH CENTURY FOX MOVIE!
--A FILM BY GEORGE LUCAS--

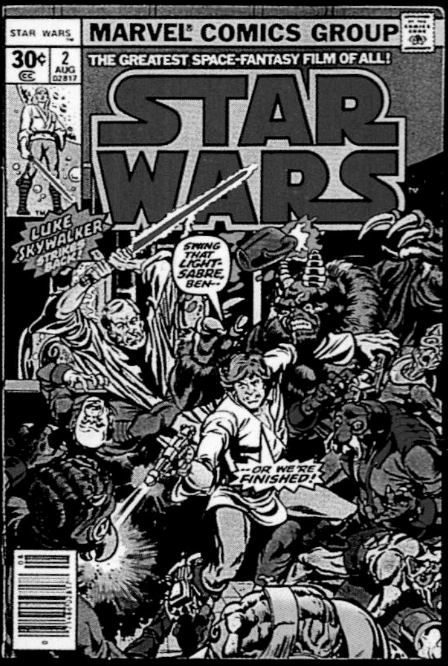
STAR WARS
MARVEL COMICS GROUP
30¢ 2 AUG 02817
THE GREATEST SPACE-FANTASY FILM OF ALL!
STAR WARS
SWING THAT LIGHT-SABRE, BEN--
--OR WE'RE FINISHED!

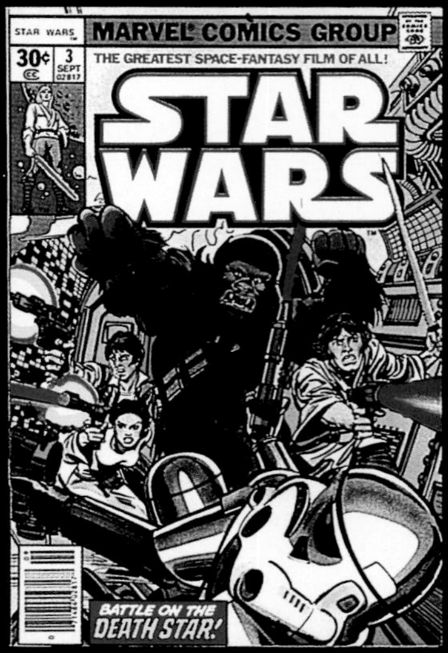
STAR WARS
MARVEL COMICS GROUP
30¢ 3 SEPT 02817
THE GREATEST SPACE-FANTASY FILM OF ALL!
STAR WARS
BATTLE ON THE DEATH STAR!

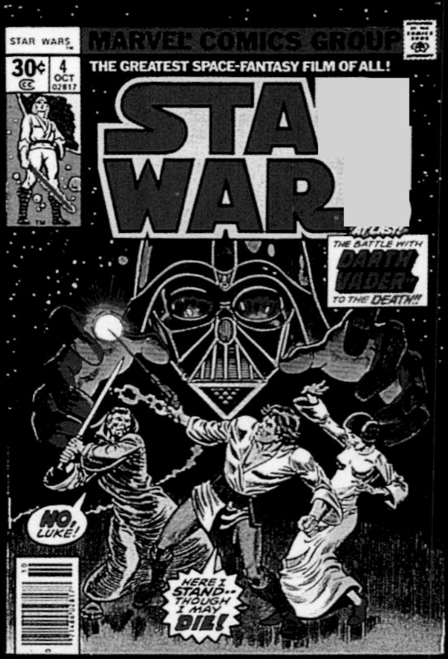
STAR WARS
MARVEL COMICS GROUP
30¢ 4 OCT 02817
THE GREATEST SPACE-FANTASY FILM OF ALL!
THE BATTLE WITH
TO THE DEATH!!
NO, LUKE!

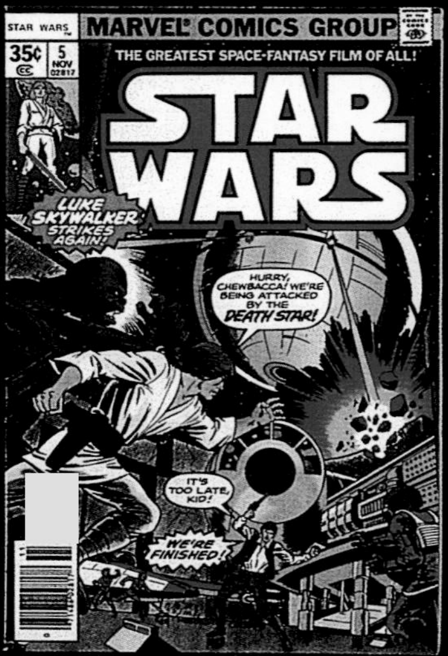
STAR WARS
MARVEL COMICS GROUP
35¢ 5 NOV 02817
THE GREATEST SPACE-FANTASY FILM OF ALL!
STAR WARS
LUKE SKYWALKER STRIKES AGAIN!
HURRY, CHEWBACCA! WE'RE BEING ATTACKED BY THE DEATH STAR!
IT'S TOO LATE, KID!
WE'RE FINISHED!

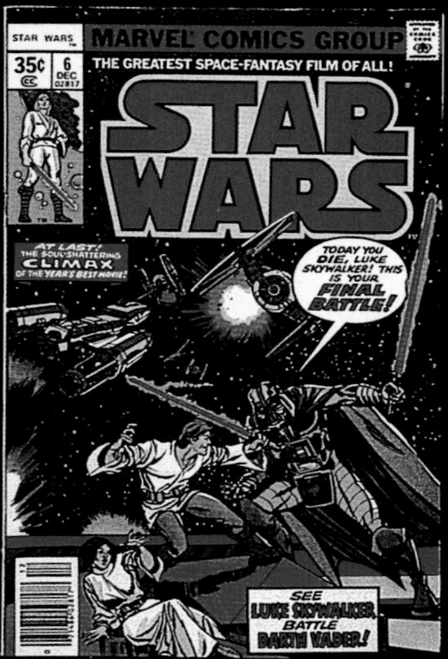
STAR WARS
MARVEL COMICS GROUP
35¢ 6 DEC 02817
THE GREATEST SPACE-FANTASY FILM OF ALL!
STAR WARS
AT LAST! THE SOUL-SHATTERING CLIMAX OF THE YEAR'S BEST MOVIE!
TODAY YOU DIE, LUKE SKYWALKER! THIS IS YOUR FINAL BATTLE!
SEE LUKE SKYWALKER BATTLE DARTH VADER!

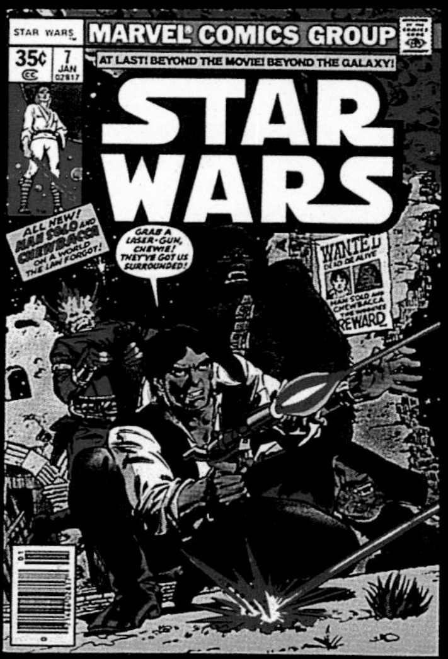
STAR WARS
MARVEL COMICS GROUP
35¢ 7 JAN 02817
AT LAST! BEYOND THE MOVIE! BEYOND THE GALAXY!
STAR WARS
GRAB A LASER-GUN, CHEWIE! THEY'VE GOT US SURROUNDED!
WANTED
REWARD

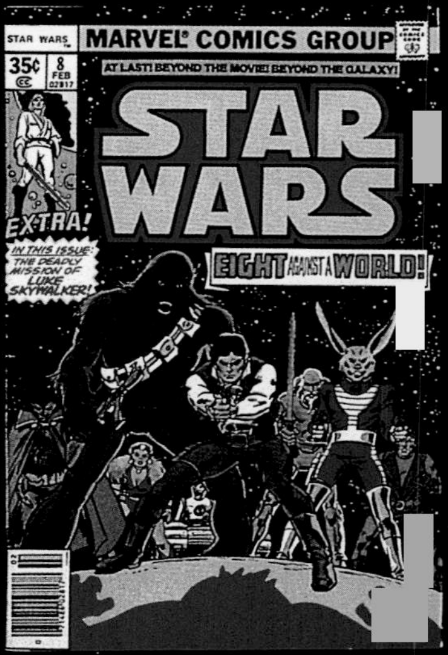
STAR WARS
MARVEL COMICS GROUP
35¢ 8 FEB 02817
AT LAST! BEYOND THE MOVIE! BEYOND THE GALAXY!
STAR WARS
EXTRA!
EIGHT AGAINST A WORLD!

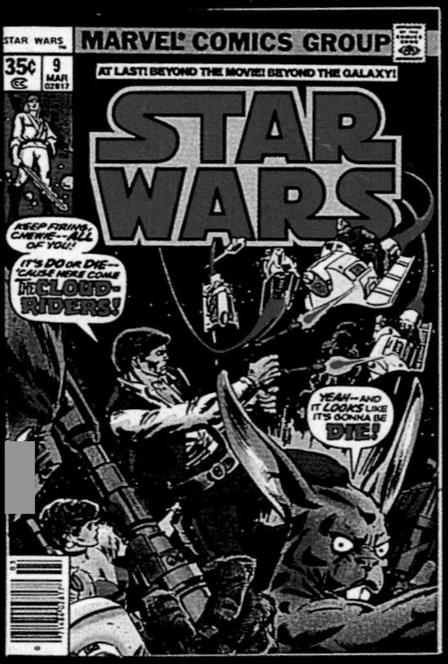
STAR WARS
MARVEL COMICS GROUP
35¢ 9 MAR 02817
AT LAST! BEYOND THE MOVIE! BEYOND THE GALAXY!
STAR WARS
KEEP FIRING, CHEWIE--ALL OF YOU!
YEAH--AND IT LOOKS LIKE IT'S GONNA BE DIE!

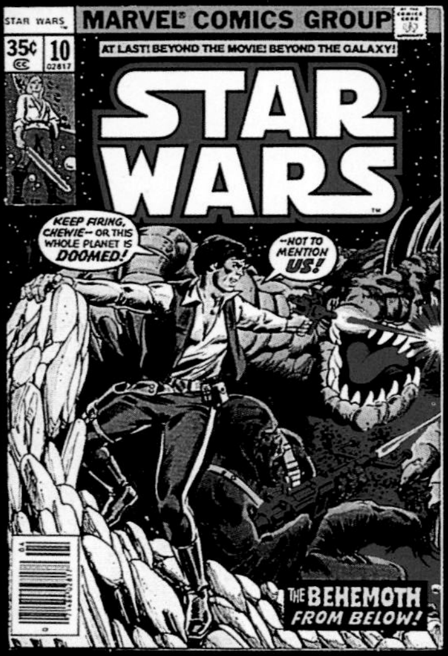
STAR WARS
MARVEL COMICS GROUP
35¢ 10 02817
AT LAST! BEYOND THE MOVIE! BEYOND THE GALAXY!
STAR WARS
KEEP FIRING, CHEWIE-- OR THIS WHOLE PLANET IS DOOMED!
--NOT TO MENTION US!
THE BEHEMOTH FROM BELOW!

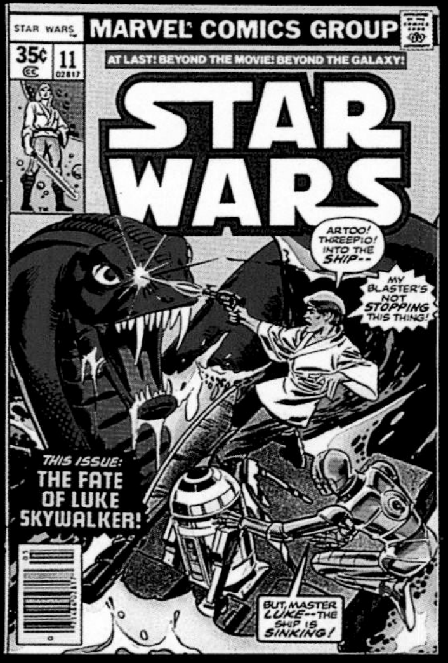
STAR WARS
MARVEL COMICS GROUP
35¢ 11 02817
AT LAST! BEYOND THE MOVIE! BEYOND THE GALAXY!
STAR WARS
ARTOO! THREEPIO! INTO THE SHIP--
MY BLASTER'S NOT STOPPING THIS THING!
THIS ISSUE: THE FATE OF LUKE SKYWALKER!
BUT, MASTER LUKE--THE SHIP IS SINKING!

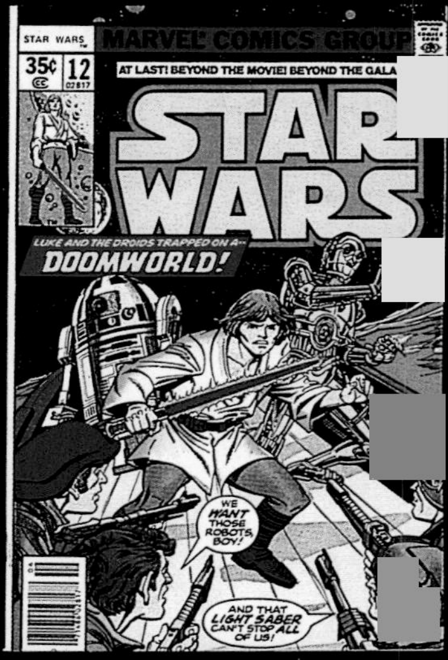
STAR WARS
MARVEL COMICS GROUP
35¢ 12 02817
AT LAST! BEYOND THE MOVIE! BEYOND THE GALAXY!
STAR WARS
DOOMWORLD!
WE WANT THOSE ROBOTS, BOY!
AND THAT LIGHT SABER

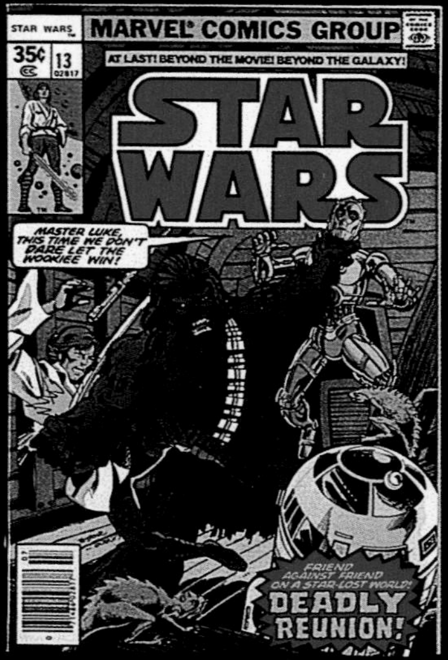
STAR WARS
MARVEL COMICS GROUP
35¢ 13 02817
AT LAST! BEYOND THE MOVIE! BEYOND THE GALAXY!
STAR WARS
DEADLY REUNION!

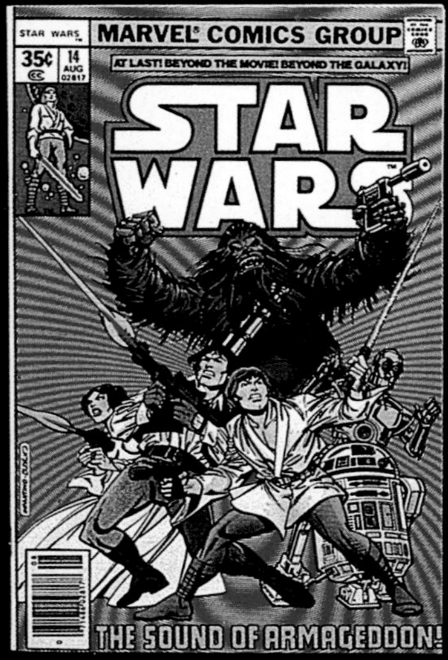
STAR WARS
MARVEL COMICS GROUP
35¢ 14 AUG 02817
AT LAST! BEYOND THE MOVIE! BEYOND THE GALAXY!
STAR WARS
THE SOUND OF ARMAGEDDON!

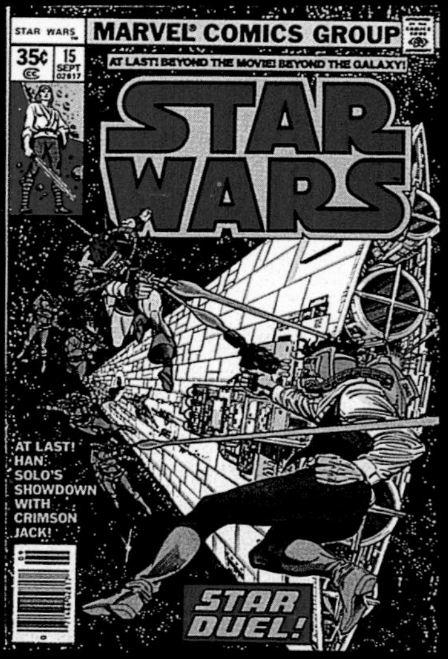
STAR WARS
MARVEL COMICS GROUP
35¢ 15 SEPT 02817
AT LAST! BEYOND THE MOVIE! BEYOND THE GALAXY!
STAR WARS
AT LAST! HAN SOLO'S SHOWDOWN WITH CRIMSON JACK!
STAR DUEL!

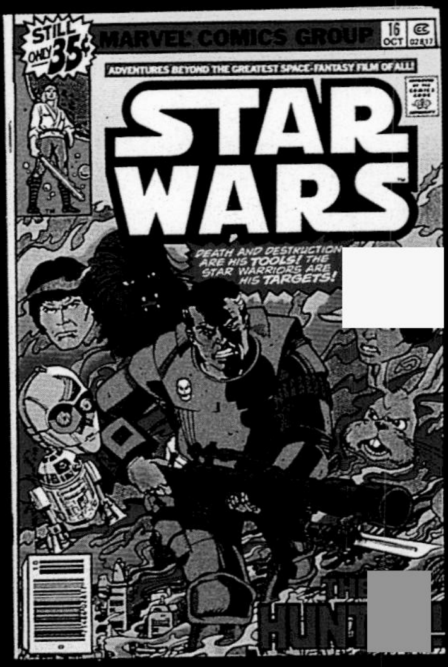
STILL ONLY 35¢
MARVEL COMICS GROUP
16 OCT 02817
STAR WARS
DEATH AND DESTRUCTION ARE HIS TOOLS! STAR WARRIORS ARE HIS TARGETS!

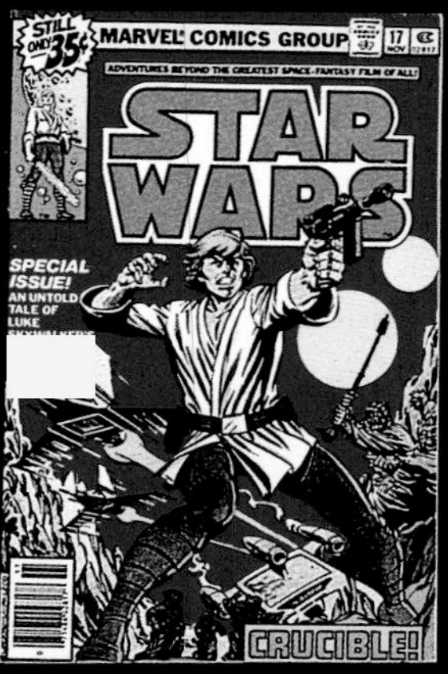
STILL ONLY 35¢
MARVEL COMICS GROUP
17
STAR WARS
SPECIAL ISSUE! AN UNTOLD TALE OF LUKE
CRUCIBLE!

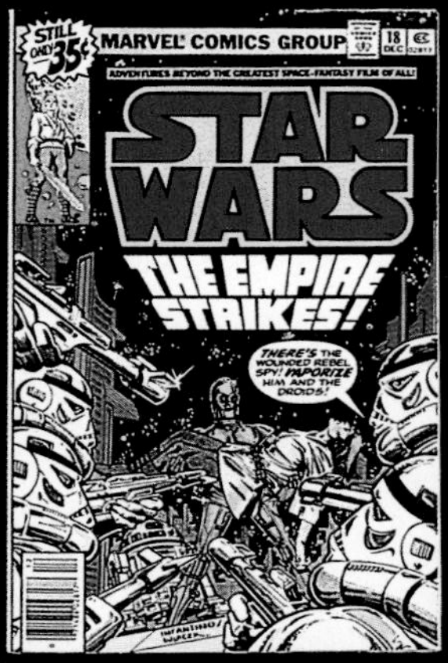
STILL ONLY 35¢
MARVEL COMICS GROUP
18
STAR WARS
THE EMPIRE STRIKES!
THERE'S THE WOUNDED REBEL SPY! VAPORIZE HIM AND THE DROIDS!

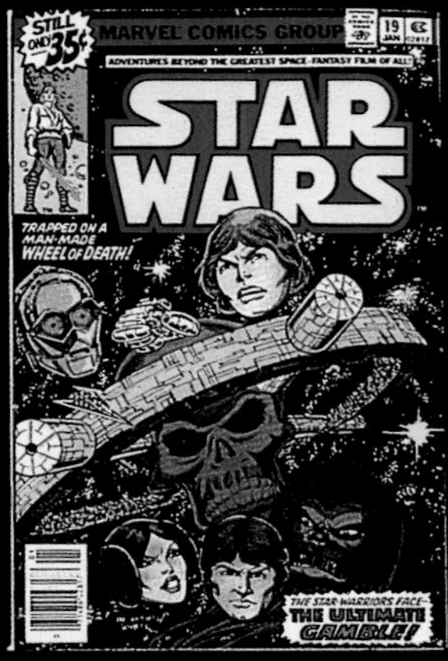
STILL ONLY 35¢
MARVEL COMICS GROUP
19
STAR WARS
TRAPPED ON A MAN-MADE WHEEL OF DEATH!
THE STAR WARRIORS FACE-- THE ULTIMATE GAMBLE!

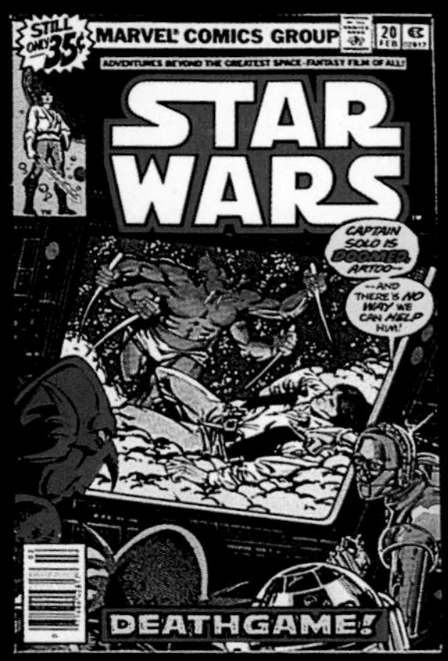
STILL ONLY 35¢
MARVEL COMICS GROUP
20
STAR WARS
DEATHGAME!

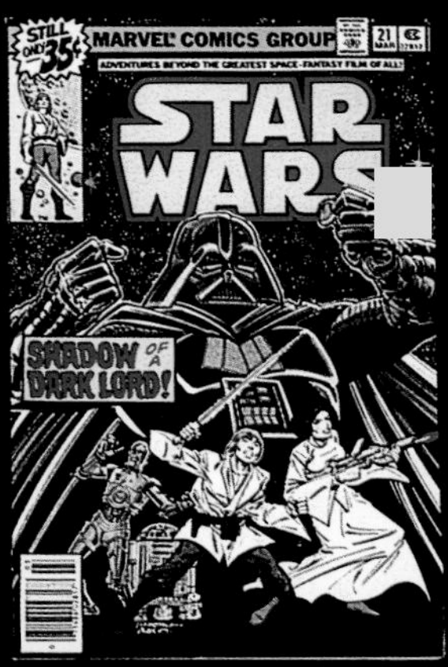
STILL ONLY 35¢
MARVEL COMICS GROUP
21
STAR WARS
SHADOW OF A DARK LORD!

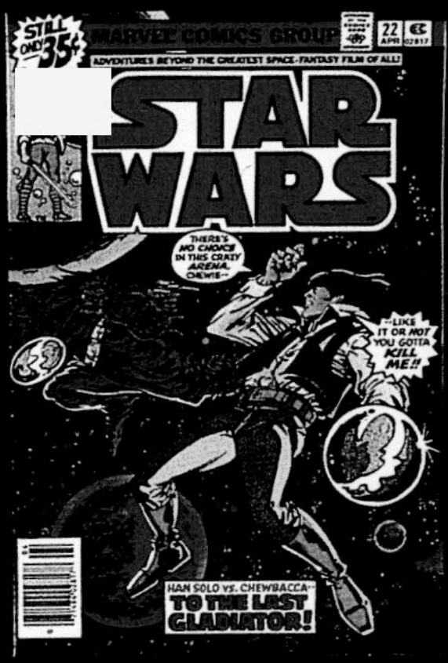
STILL ONLY 35¢
MARVEL COMICS GROUP
22
STAR WARS
HAN SOLO VS. CHEWBACCA! TO THE LAST GLADIATOR!

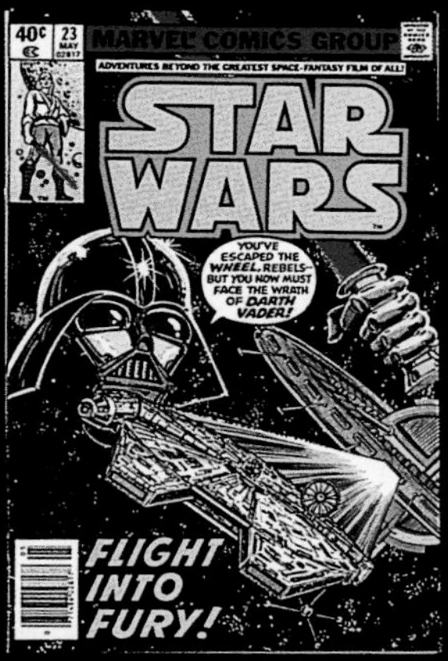
40¢
23
MARVEL COMICS GROUP
STAR WARS
YOU'VE ESCAPED THE WHEEL, REBELS-- BUT YOU NOW MUST FACE THE WRATH OF DARTH VADER!
FLIGHT INTO FURY!

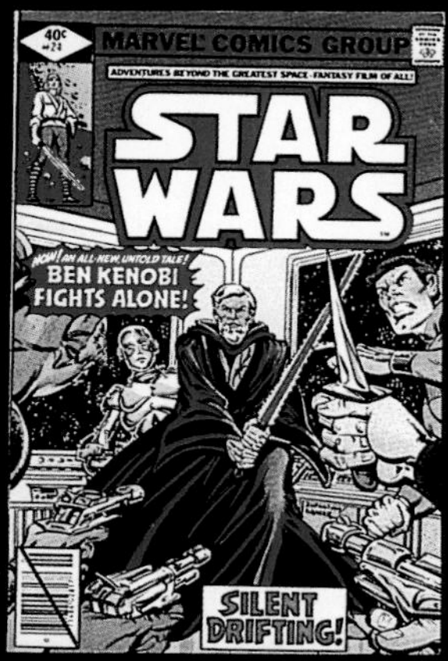
40¢
24
MARVEL COMICS GROUP
STAR WARS
NOW! AN ALL-NEW UNTOLD TALE! BEN KENOBI FIGHTS ALONE!
SILENT DRIFTING!

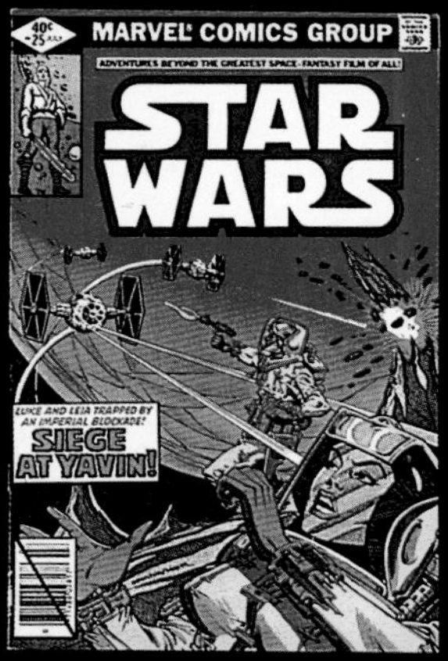
40¢
25
MARVEL COMICS GROUP
STAR WARS
LUKE AND LEIA TRAPPED BY AN IMPERIAL BLOCKADE!
SIEGE AT YAVIN!

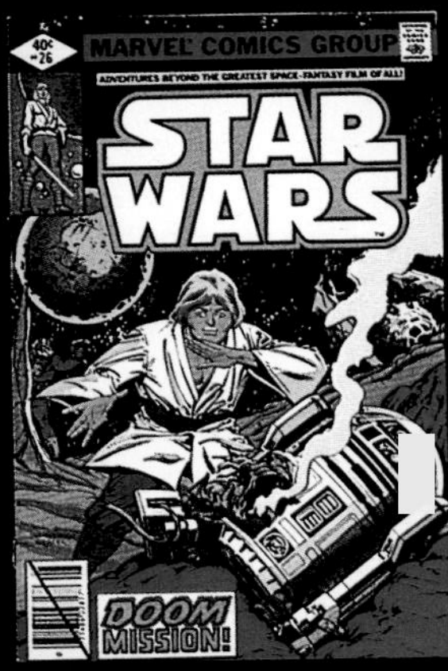
40¢
26
MARVEL COMICS GROUP
STAR WARS
DOOM MISSION!

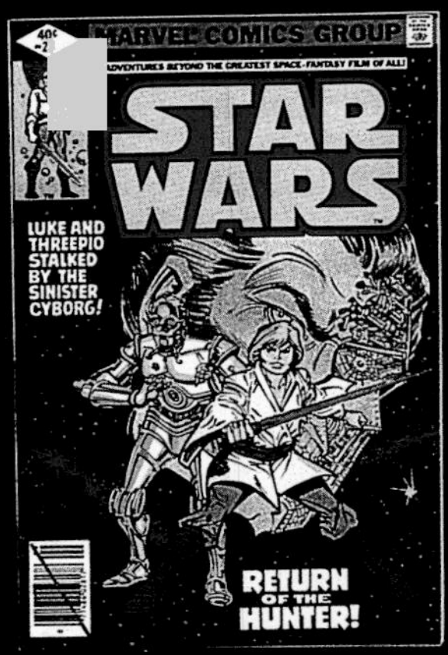
MARVEL COMICS GROUP
STAR WARS
LUKE AND THREEPIO STALKED BY THE SINISTER CYBORG!
RETURN OF THE HUNTER!

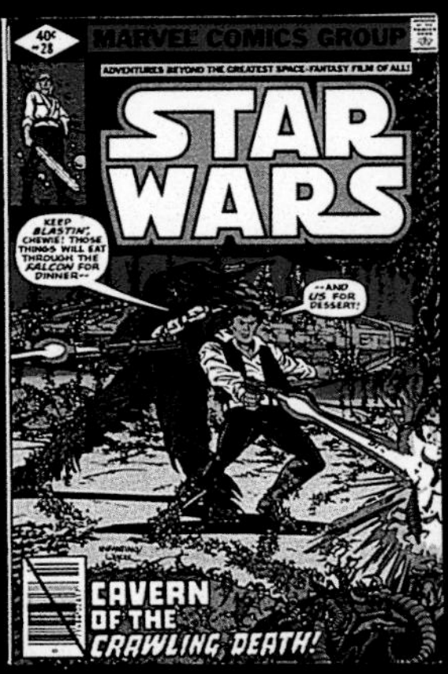
40¢
28
MARVEL COMICS GROUP
STAR WARS
CAVERN OF THE CRAWLING DEATH!

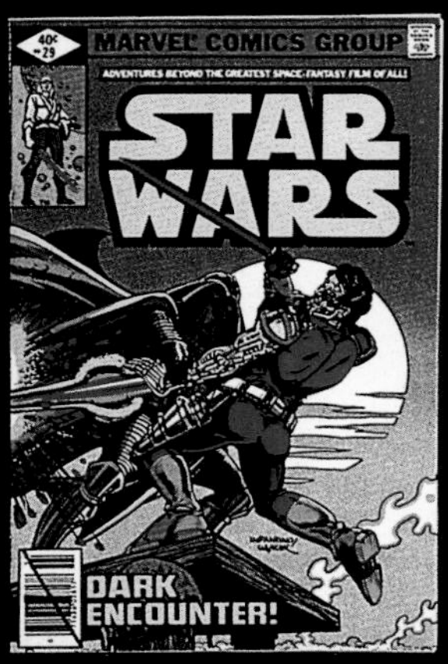
40¢
29
MARVEL COMICS GROUP
STAR WARS
DARK ENCOUNTER!

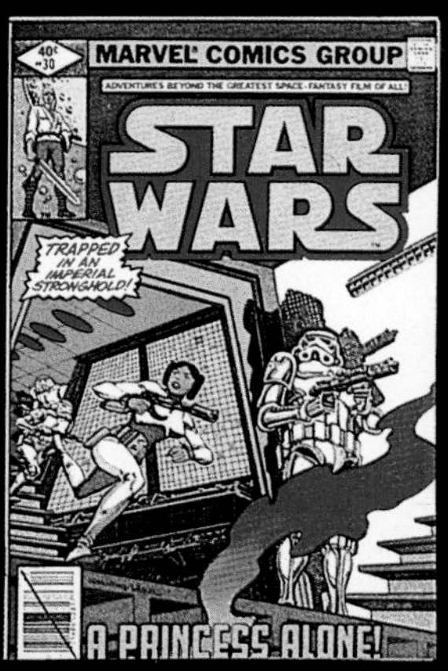
40¢
30
MARVEL COMICS GROUP
STAR WARS
TRAPPED IN AN IMPERIAL STRONGHOLD!
A PRINCESS ALONE!

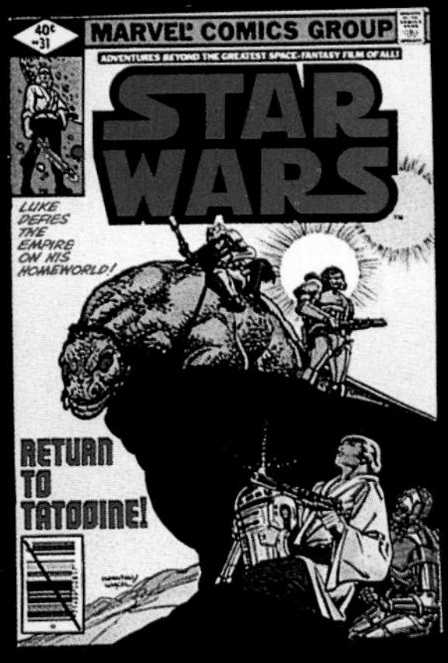
40¢
31
MARVEL COMICS GROUP
STAR WARS
LUKE DEFIES THE EMPIRE ON HIS HOMEWORLD!
RETURN TO TATOOINE!

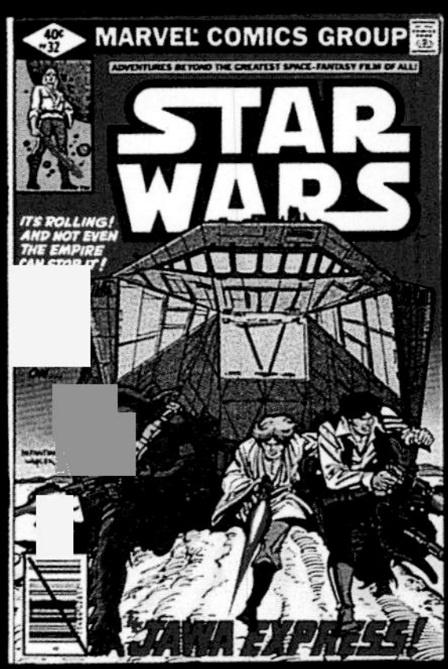
40¢
32
MARVEL COMICS GROUP
STAR WARS
IT'S ROLLING! AND NOT EVEN THE EMPIRE
JAWA EXPRESS!

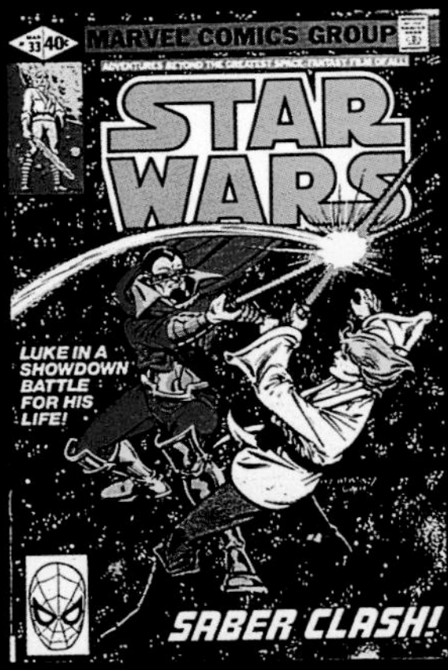
33
40¢
MARVEL COMICS GROUP
STAR WARS
LUKE IN A SHOWDOWN BATTLE FOR HIS LIFE!
SABER CLASH!

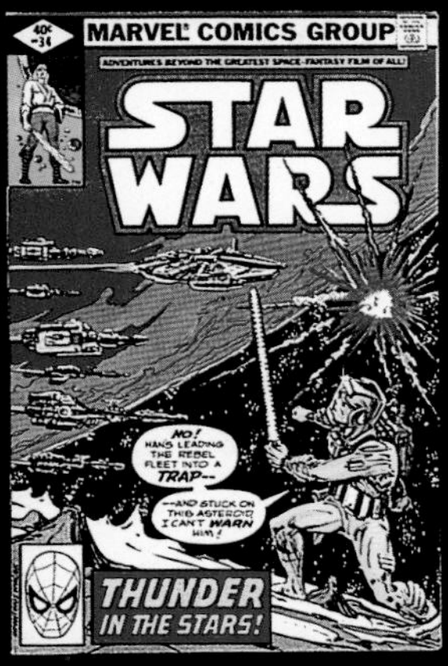
40¢
34
MARVEL COMICS GROUP
STAR WARS
THUNDER IN THE STARS!

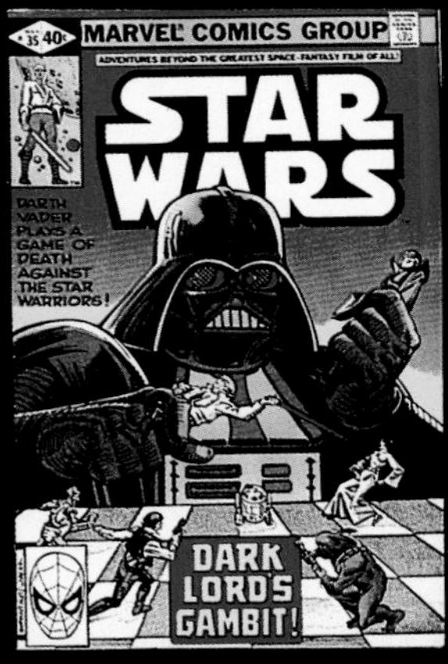
35
40¢
MARVEL COMICS GROUP
STAR WARS
DARTH VADER PLAYS A GAME OF DEATH AGAINST THE STAR WARRIORS!
DARK LORD'S GAMBIT!

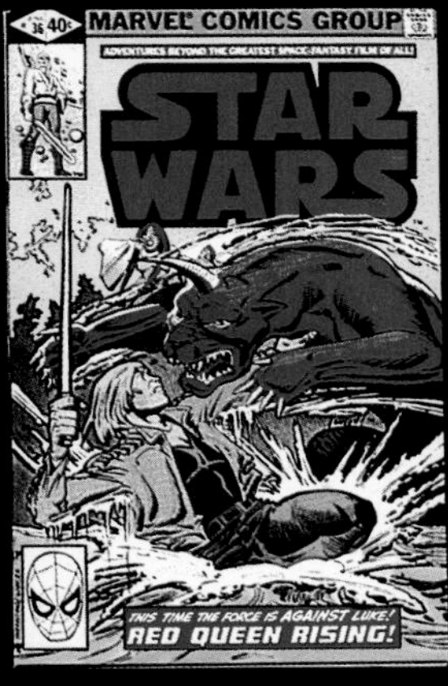
36
40¢
MARVEL COMICS GROUP
STAR WARS
THIS TIME THE FORCE IS AGAINST LUKE!
RED QUEEN RISING!

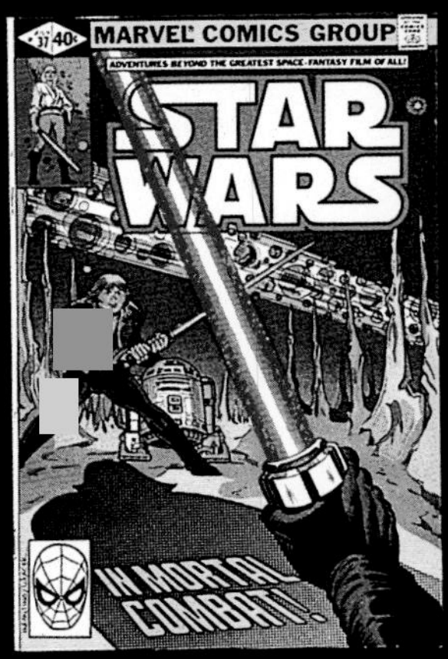
37
40¢
MARVEL COMICS GROUP
STAR WARS
IN MORTAL COMBAT!

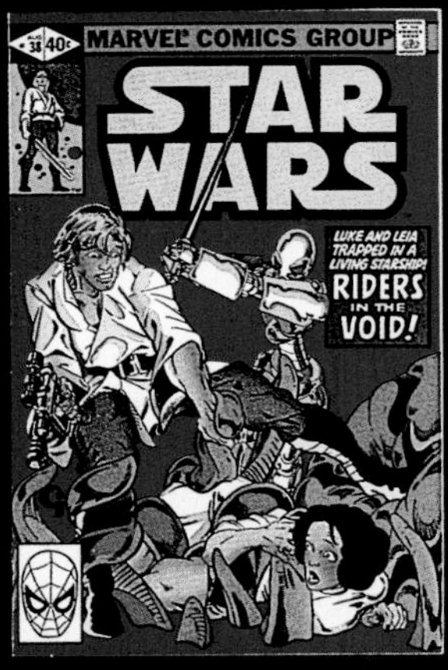
38
40¢
MARVEL COMICS GROUP
STAR WARS
LUKE AND LEIA TRAPPED IN A LIVING STARSHIP! RIDERS IN THE VOID!

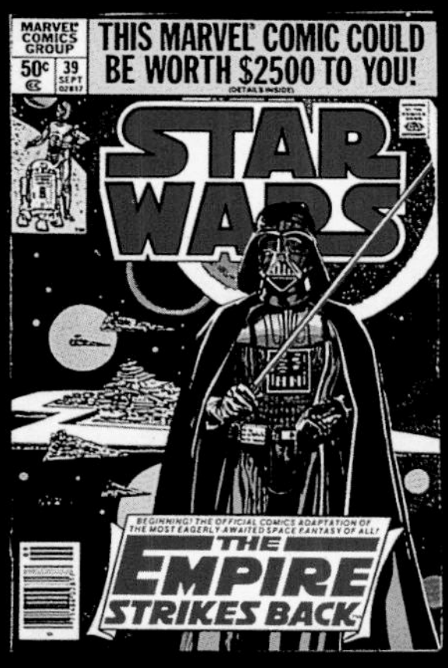
MARVEL COMICS GROUP
50¢
39
THIS MARVEL COMIC COULD BE WORTH $2500 TO YOU!
STAR WARS
THE EMPIRE STRIKES BACK

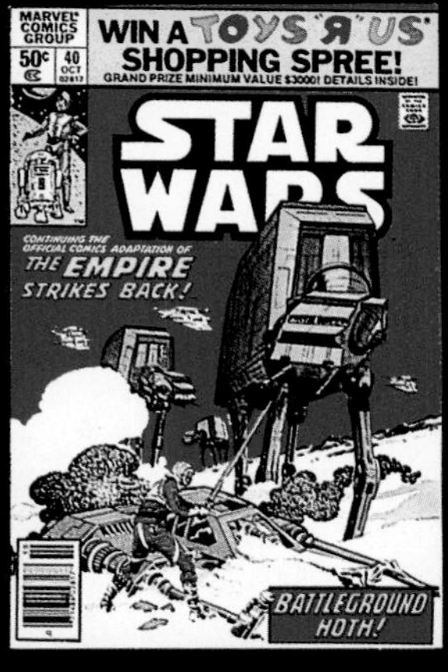
MARVEL COMICS GROUP
50¢
40
WIN A TOYS 'R' US SHOPPING SPREE!
STAR WARS
CONTINUING THE OFFICIAL COMICS ADAPTATION OF THE EMPIRE STRIKES BACK!
BATTLEGROUND HOTH!

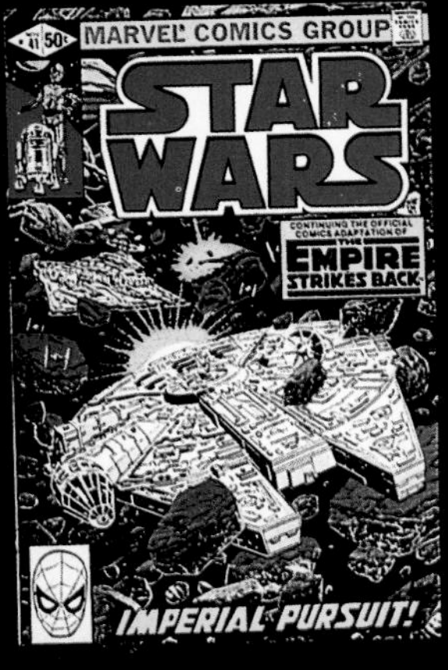
41
50¢
MARVEL COMICS GROUP
STAR WARS
THE EMPIRE STRIKES BACK
IMPERIAL PURSUIT!

MARVEL COMICS GROUP
STAR WARS
BOUNTY HUNTERS!
EMPIRE STRIKES BACK
BETRAYAL AT BESPIN!
EMPIRE STRIKES BACK
DUEL A DARK LORD!
DEATH PROBE!
A LIVING NIGHTMARE STALKS THE UNIVERSE...
DROID WORLD!
THE THIRD LAW!
THE LAST JEDI!
A SUPER-SIZED STAR WARS SAGA! GIANT 50th COLLECTORS' ISSUE!
RESURRECTION OF EVIL!
WIN A Columbia TEN-SPEED FORMULA 10. RACER!
BEGINNING SEPT. 12th ON NBC SPIDER-MAN AND HIS AMAZING FRIENDS!
BATTLE ON BESPIN!
LUKE SKYWALKER: PARIAH!
ALL NEW!
"SERPHIDIAN EYES"
GOLRATH NEVER FORGETS!
YOU FIRST!
MARVEL

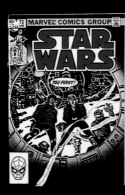

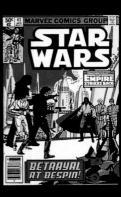

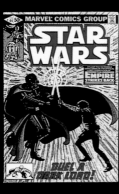

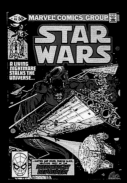

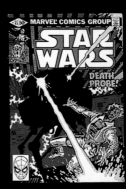

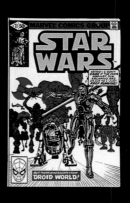

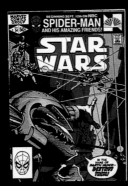

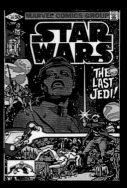

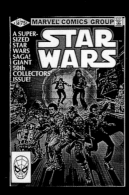

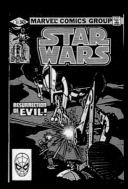

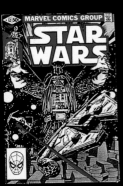

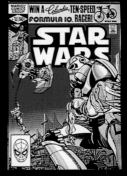

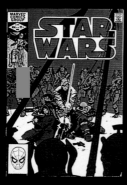

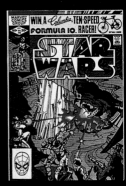

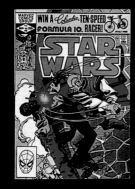

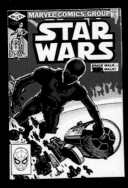

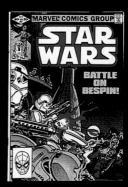

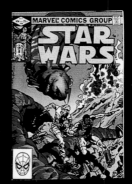

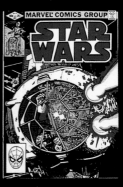

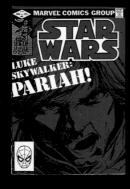

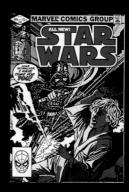

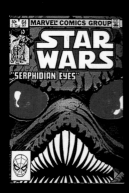

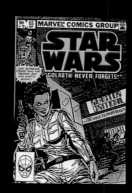

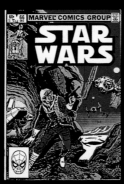

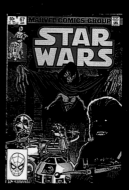

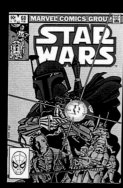

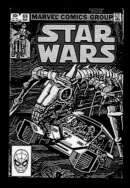

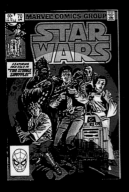

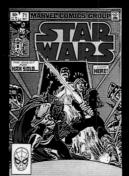

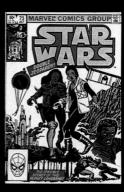

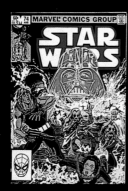

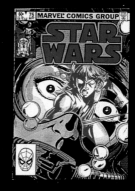

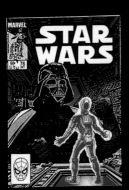

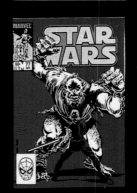

1792 Star Wars (78-103, 107; AN. 1-3)

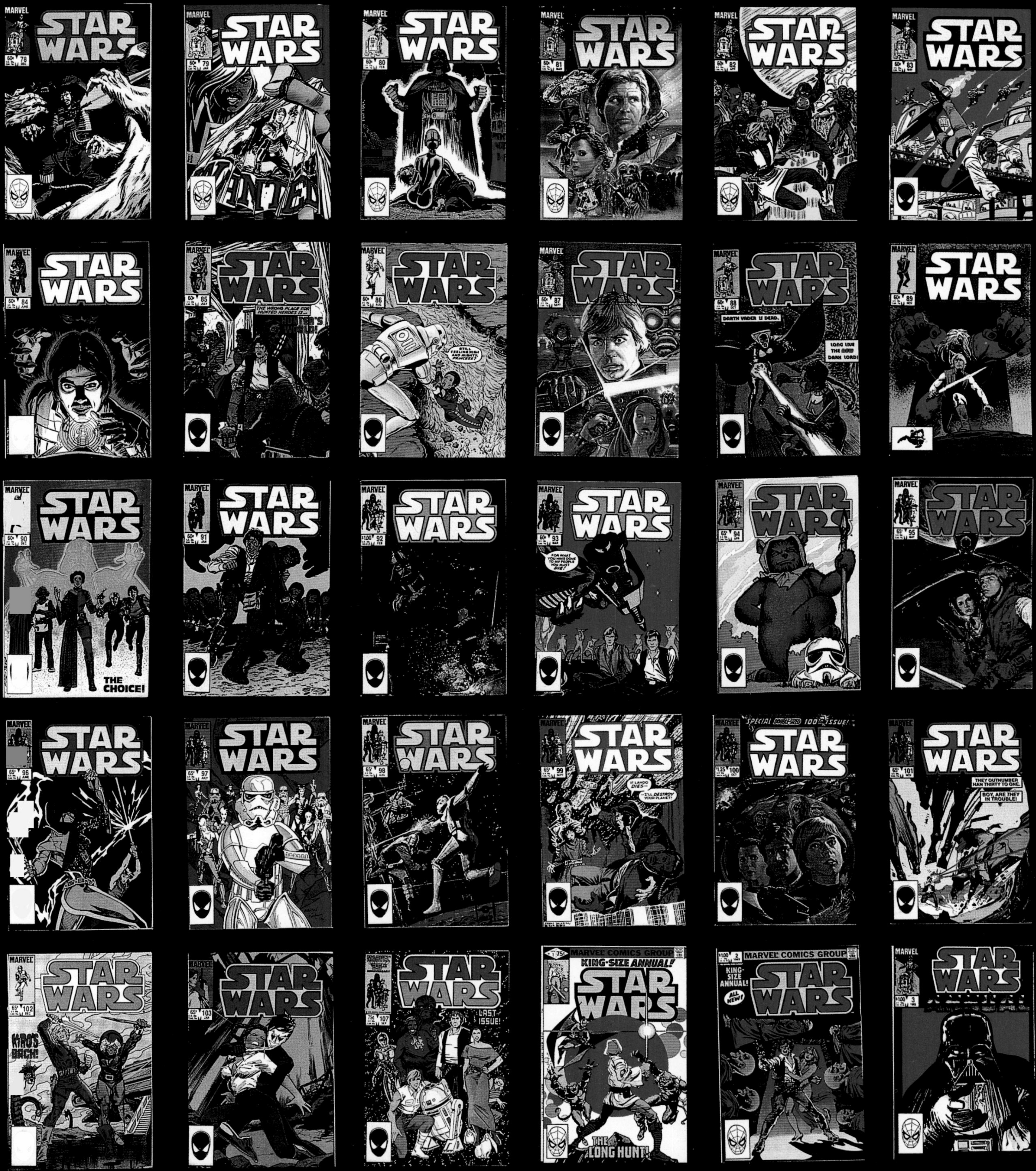
STAR WARS
THE WRONG PLACE FOR HUNTED HEROES IS...
STILL FEELING HIGH AND MIGHTY, PRINCESS?
DARTH VADER IS DEAD.
LONG LIVE THE NEW DARK LORD!
THE CHOICE!
FOR WHAT YOU HAVE DONE TO MY PEOPLE YOU MUST DIE!
SPECIAL DOUBLE-SIZED 100TH ISSUE!
IF LANDO DIES—
—I'LL DESTROY YOUR PLANET!
THEY OUTNUMBER HAN THIRTY TO ONE.
BOY, ARE THEY IN TROUBLE!
KIRO'S BIRCH!
LAST ISSUE!
MARVEL COMICS GROUP
KING-SIZE ANNUAL!
THE LONG HUNT!
KING-SIZE ANNUAL!
ALL NEW!

1792.1 Star Wars: Return of the Jedi (1-4)

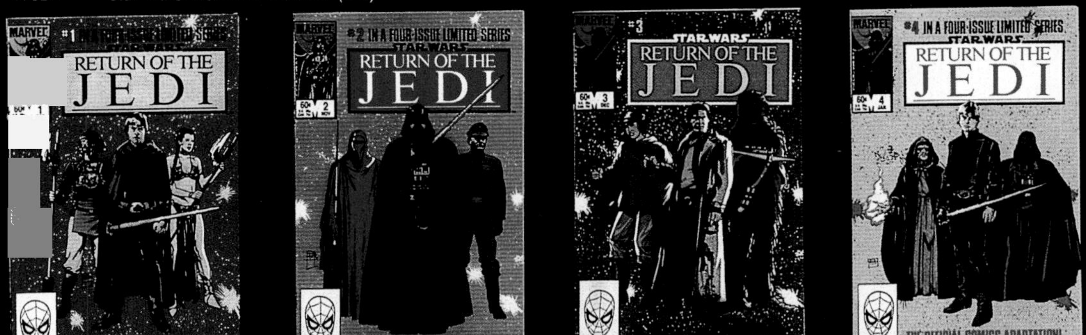
#2 IN A FOUR-ISSUE LIMITED SERIES
#4 IN A FOUR-ISSUE LIMITED SERIES
STAR WARS
RETURN OF THE JEDI
THE OFFICIAL COMICS ADAPTATION!

Star Wars (1-107) 1792

Ref. No.	Date	RVI	Artist/Info.
1792-1	Jul. 1977	10	Chaykin/M. Severin-a (35¢ cover-RVI 250)
1792-2	Aug.	5	Chaykin/Leialoha-a
1792-3	Sept.	3	" "
1792-4	Oct.	3	" "
1792-5	Nov.	3	" "
1792-6	Dec.	2	Chaykin-a
1792-7	Jan. 1978	2	"
1792-8	Feb.	2	Chaykin/Palmer-a (1st Palmer issue)
1792-9	Mar.	2	" "
1792-10	**Apr.**	**2**	**" "**
1792-11	May	1	Infantino/Austin-a
1792-12	Jun.	1	" "
1792-13	Jul.	1	" "
1792-14 to 107	Sept. 1986, (#107)	1	(#39, The Empire Strikes Back Replrints begin)
1792-A1	Dec. 1979	1	Simonson-c
1792-A2	Nov. 1982	1	Nebres-c/a
1792-A3	Dec. 1983	1	

Star Wars: Return of the Jedi (1-4) 1792.1

1792.1-1 to 4	Oct. 1983, (#1)	1	Williamson-a (all)

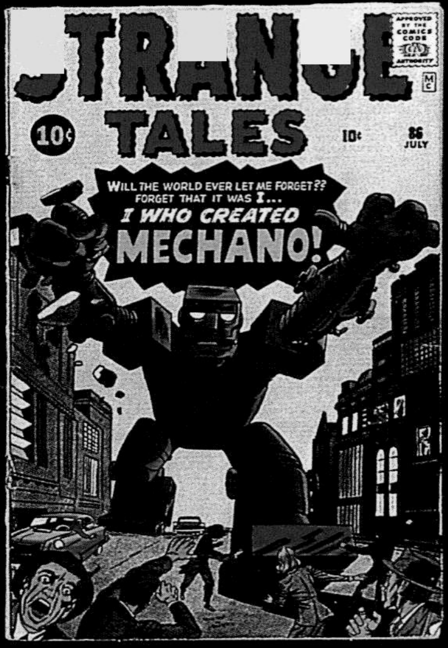
TALES
10¢
86 JULY
WILL THE WORLD EVER LET ME FORGET?? FORGET THAT IT WAS I... I WHO CREATED MECHANO!

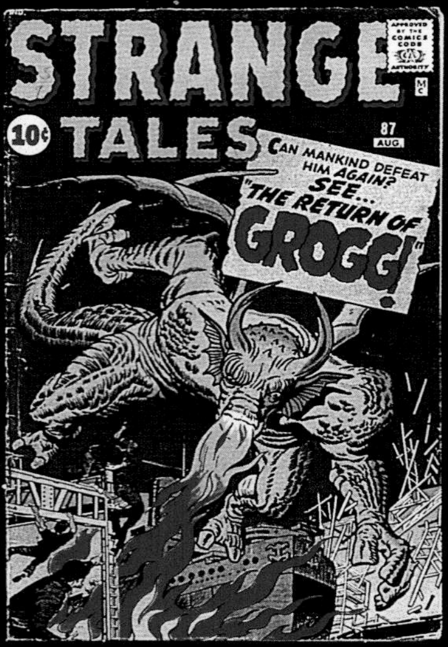
STRANGE TALES
10¢
87 AUG
CAN MANKIND DEFEAT HIM AGAIN? SEE... "THE RETURN OF GROGG!"

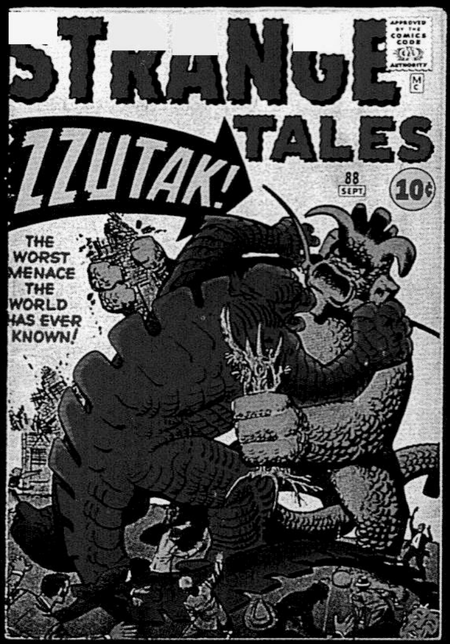
TALES
ZZUTAK!
88 SEPT
10¢
THE WORST MENACE THE WORLD HAS EVER KNOWN!

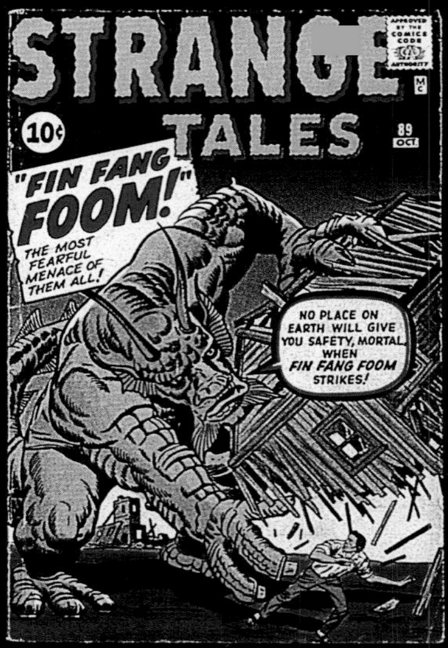
STRANGE TALES
10¢
89 OCT
"FIN FANG FOOM!"
THE MOST FEARFUL MENACE OF THEM ALL!
NO PLACE ON EARTH WILL GIVE YOU SAFETY, MORTAL, WHEN FIN FANG FOOM STRIKES!

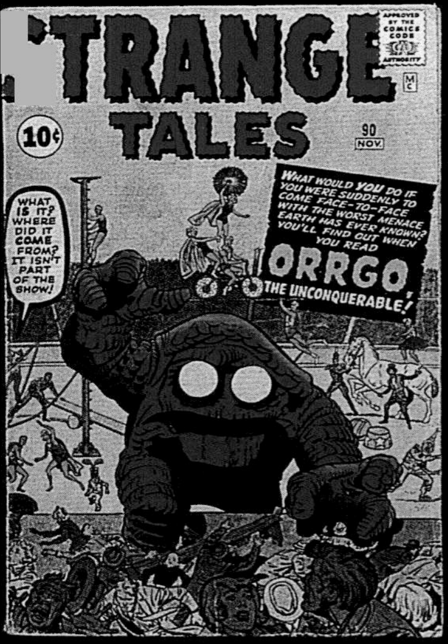
TALES
10¢
90 NOV
WHAT IS IT? WHERE DID IT COME FROM? IT ISN'T PART OF THE SHOW!
WHAT WOULD YOU DO IF YOU WERE SUDDENLY TO COME FACE-TO-FACE WITH THE WORST MENACE EARTH HAS EVER KNOWN? YOU'LL FIND OUT WHEN YOU READ ORRGO, THE UNCONQUERABLE!

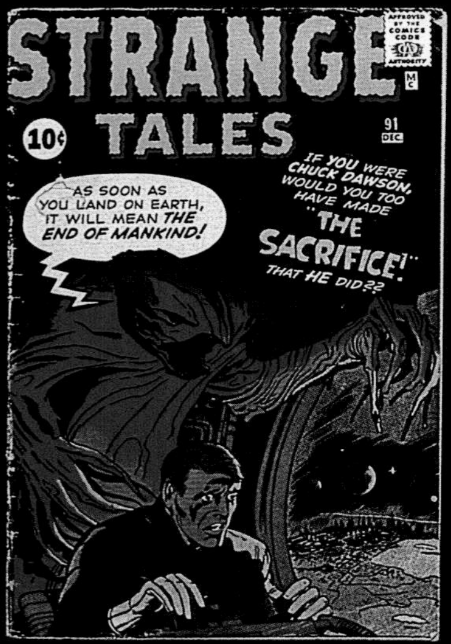
STRANGE TALES
10¢
91 DEC
AS SOON AS YOU LAND ON EARTH, IT WILL MEAN THE END OF MANKIND!
IF YOU WERE CHUCK DAWSON, WOULD YOU TOO HAVE MADE "THE SACRIFICE!" THAT HE DID??

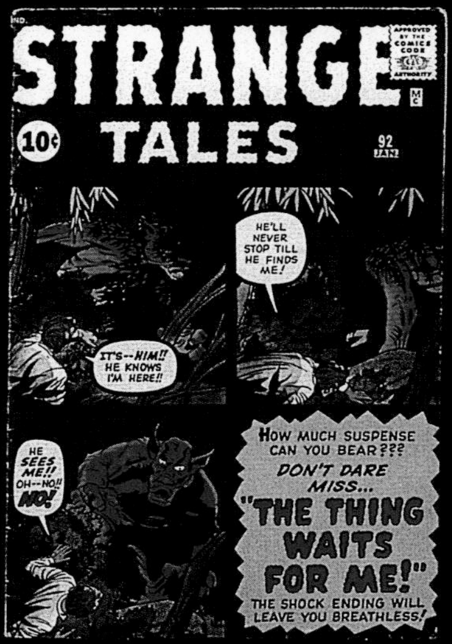
STRANGE TALES
10¢
92 JAN
HE'LL NEVER STOP TILL HE FINDS ME!
IT'S--HIM!! HE KNOWS I'M HERE!!
HE SEES ME!! OH--NO!! NO!
HOW MUCH SUSPENSE CAN YOU BEAR??? DON'T DARE MISS... "THE THING WAITS FOR ME!"
THE SHOCK ENDING WILL LEAVE YOU BREATHLESS!

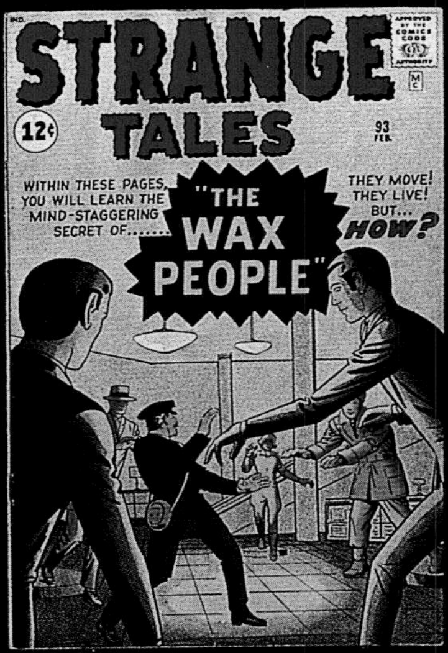
STRANGE TALES
12¢
93 FEB
WITHIN THESE PAGES, YOU WILL LEARN THE MIND-STAGGERING SECRET OF...... "THE WAX PEOPLE"
THEY MOVE! THEY LIVE! BUT... HOW?

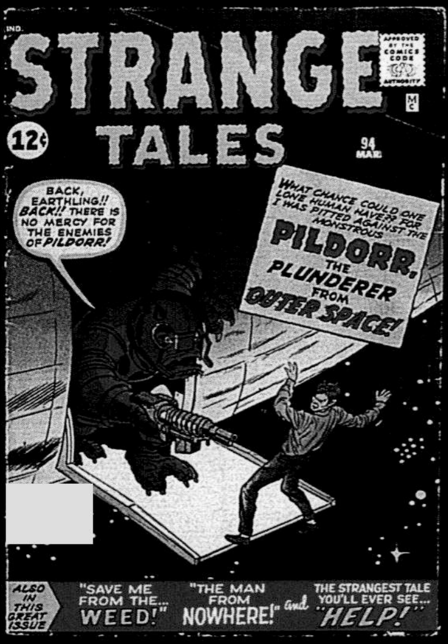
STRANGE TALES
12¢
94 MAR
BACK, EARTHLING!! BACK!! THERE IS NO MERCY FOR THE ENEMIES OF PILDORR!
PILDORR, THE PLUNDERER FROM OUTER SPACE!
ALSO IN THIS GREAT ISSUE
"SAVE ME FROM THE... WEED!"
"THE MAN FROM NOWHERE!"
THE STRANGEST TALE YOU'LL EVER SEE... "HELP!"

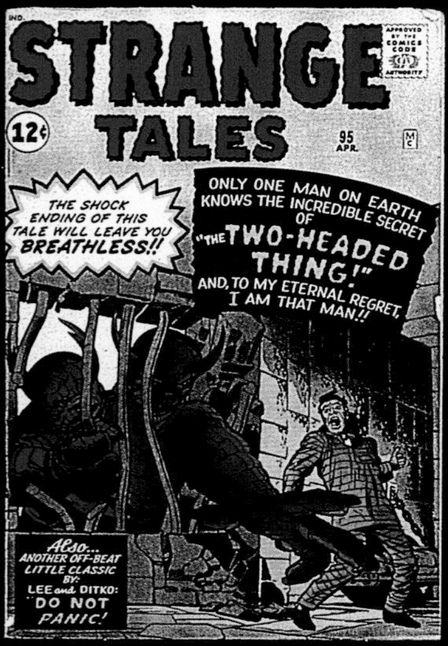
STRANGE TALES
12¢
95 APR
THE SHOCK ENDING OF THIS TALE WILL LEAVE YOU BREATHLESS!!
ONLY ONE MAN ON EARTH KNOWS THE INCREDIBLE SECRET OF "THE TWO-HEADED THING!" AND, TO MY ETERNAL REGRET, I AM THAT MAN!!
Also... ANOTHER OFF-BEAT LITTLE CLASSIC BY: LEE and DITKO: "DO NOT PANIC!"

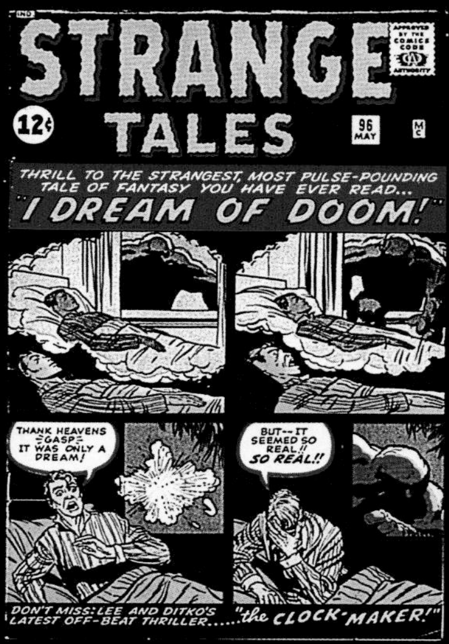
STRANGE TALES
12¢
96 MAY
THRILL TO THE STRANGEST, MOST PULSE-POUNDING TALE OF FANTASY YOU HAVE EVER READ... "I DREAM OF DOOM!"
THANK HEAVENS *GASP* IT WAS ONLY A DREAM!
BUT--IT SEEMED SO SO REAL!!
DON'T MISS: LEE AND DITKO'S LATEST OFF-BEAT THRILLER...... "the CLOCK-MAKER!"

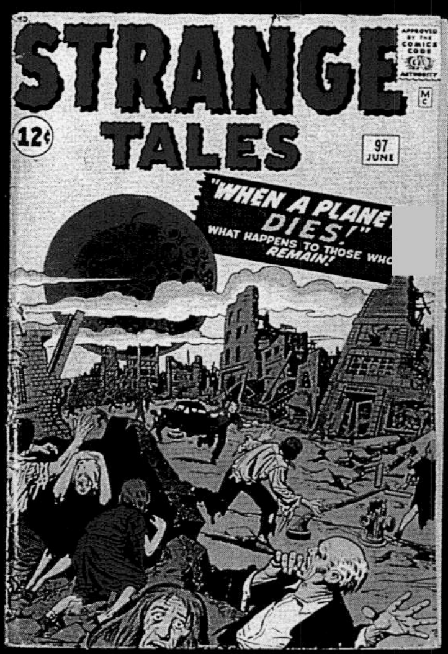
STRANGE TALES
12¢
97 JUNE
"WHEN A PLANET DIES!"

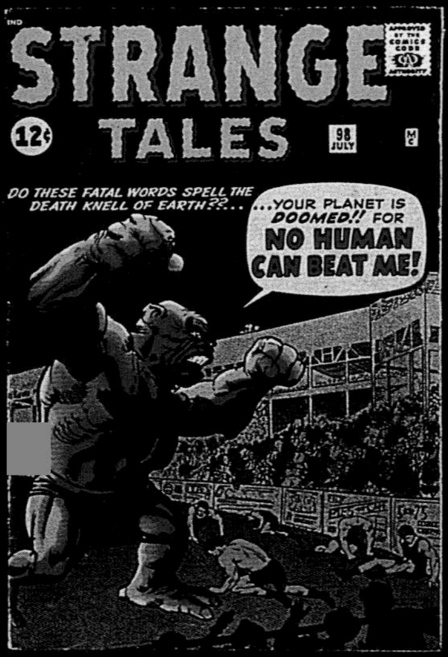
STRANGE TALES
12¢
98 JULY
DO THESE FATAL WORDS SPELL THE DEATH KNELL OF EARTH???...
...YOUR PLANET IS DOOMED!! FOR NO HUMAN CAN BEAT ME!

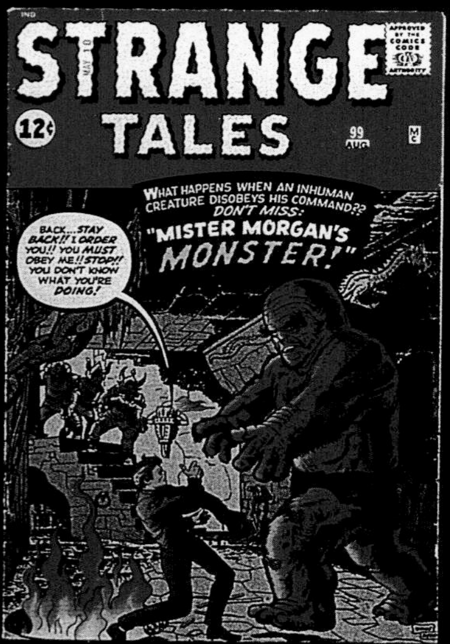
STRANGE TALES
12¢
99 AUG
WHAT HAPPENS WHEN AN INHUMAN CREATURE DISOBEYS HIS COMMAND?? DON'T MISS: "MISTER MORGAN'S MONSTER!"
BACK... STAY BACK!! I ORDER YOU!! YOU MUST OBEY ME!! STOP!! YOU DON'T KNOW WHAT YOU'RE DOING!

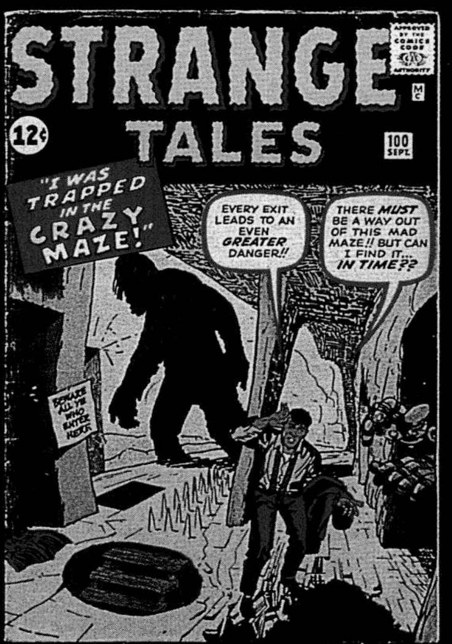
STRANGE TALES
12¢
100 SEPT
"I WAS TRAPPED IN THE CRAZY MAZE!"
EVERY EXIT LEADS TO AN EVEN GREATER DANGER!!
THERE MUST BE A WAY OUT OF THIS MAD MAZE!! BUT CAN I FIND IT... IN TIME??

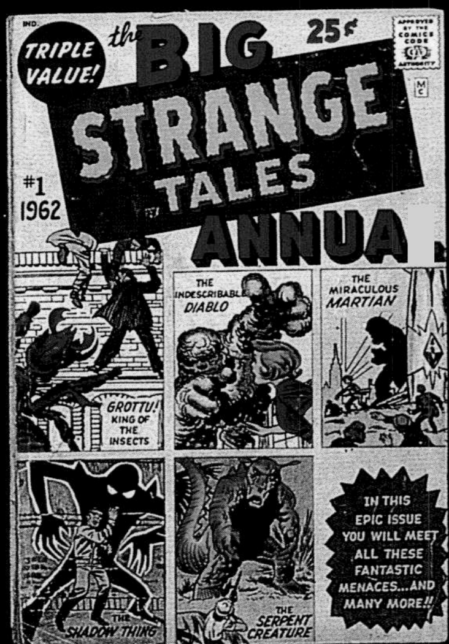
TRIPLE VALUE!
the BIG STRANGE TALES ANNUA
25¢
#1 1962
THE INDESCRIBABLE DIABLO
THE MIRACULOUS MARTIAN
GROTTU! KING OF THE INSECTS
IN THIS EPIC ISSUE YOU WILL MEET ALL THESE FANTASTIC MENACES...AND MANY MORE!!
THE SHADOW THING
THE SERPENT CREATURE

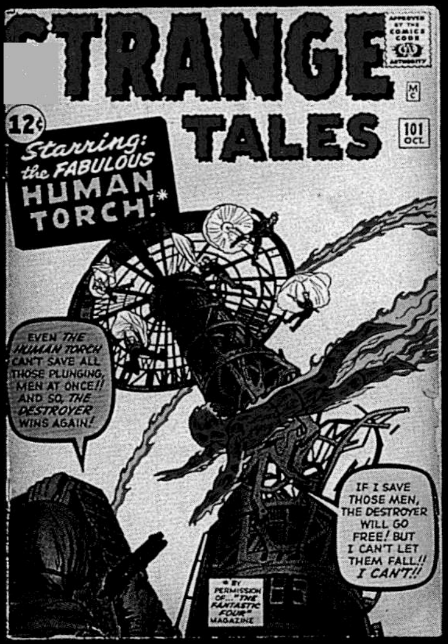
STRANGE TALES
12¢
101 OCT.
Starring: the FABULOUS HUMAN TORCH!*
EVEN THE HUMAN TORCH CAN'T SAVE ALL THOSE PLUNGING MEN AT ONCE!! AND SO, THE DESTROYER WINS AGAIN!
IF I SAVE THOSE MEN, THE DESTROYER WILL GO FREE! BUT I CAN'T LET THEM FALL!! I CAN'T!!
*BY PERMISSION OF "THE FANTASTIC FOUR" MAGAZINE

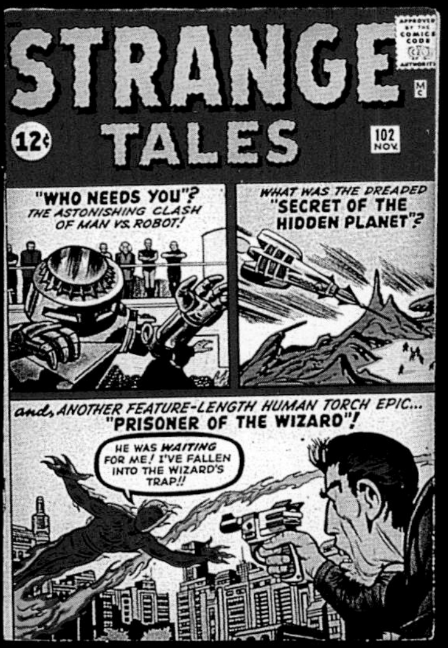
STRANGE TALES
12¢
102 NOV.
"WHO NEEDS YOU"? THE ASTONISHING CLASH OF MAN VS. ROBOT!
WHAT WAS THE DREADED "SECRET OF THE HIDDEN PLANET"?
and, ANOTHER FEATURE-LENGTH HUMAN TORCH EPIC... "PRISONER OF THE WIZARD"!
HE WAS WAITING FOR ME! I'VE FALLEN INTO THE WIZARD'S TRAP!!

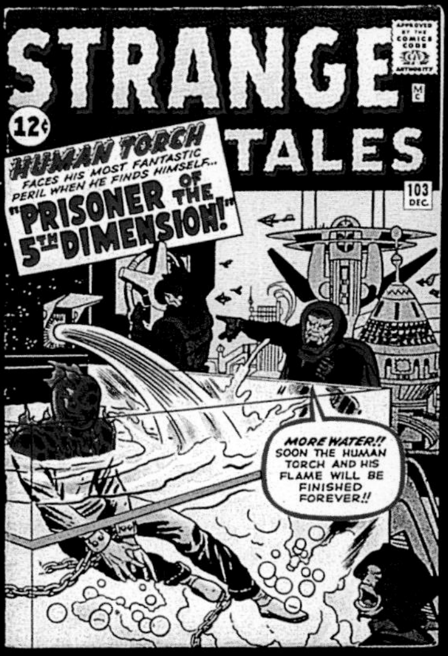
STRANGE TALES
12¢
103 DEC.
HUMAN TORCH FACES HIS MOST FANTASTIC PERIL WHEN HE FINDS HIMSELF... "PRISONER OF THE 5TH DIMENSION!"
MORE WATER!! SOON THE HUMAN TORCH AND HIS FLAME WILL BE FINISHED FOREVER!!

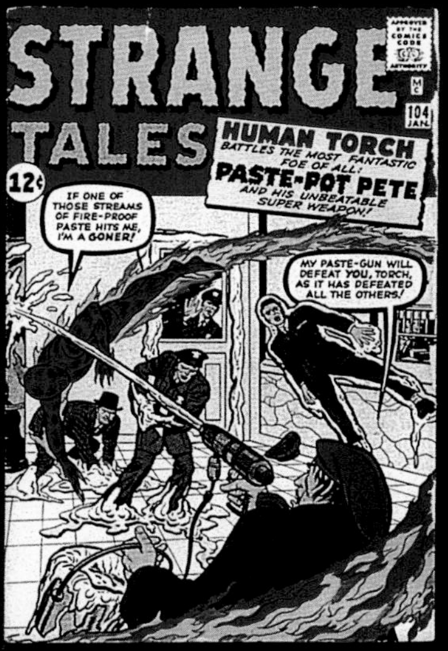
STRANGE TALES
104 JAN.
12¢
HUMAN TORCH BATTLES THE MOST FANTASTIC FOE OF ALL: PASTE-POT PETE AND HIS UNBEATABLE SUPER WEAPON!
IF ONE OF THOSE STREAMS OF FIRE-PROOF PASTE HITS ME, I'M A GONER!
MY PASTE-GUN WILL DEFEAT YOU, TORCH, AS IT HAS DEFEATED ALL THE OTHERS!

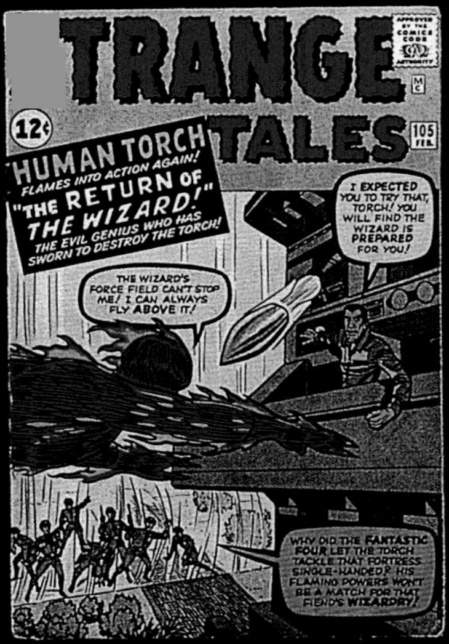
TRANGE TALES
12¢
105 FEB.
HUMAN TORCH FLAMES INTO ACTION AGAIN! "THE RETURN OF THE WIZARD!" THE EVIL GENIUS WHO HAS SWORN TO DESTROY THE TORCH!
I EXPECTED YOU TO TRY THAT, TORCH! YOU WILL FIND THE WIZARD IS PREPARED FOR YOU!
THE WIZARD'S FORCE FIELD CAN'T STOP ME! I CAN ALWAYS FLY ABOVE IT!
WHY DID THE FANTASTIC FOUR LET THE TORCH TACKLE THAT FORTRESS SINGLE-HANDED? HIS FLAMING POWERS WON'T BE A MATCH FOR THAT FIEND'S WIZARDRY!

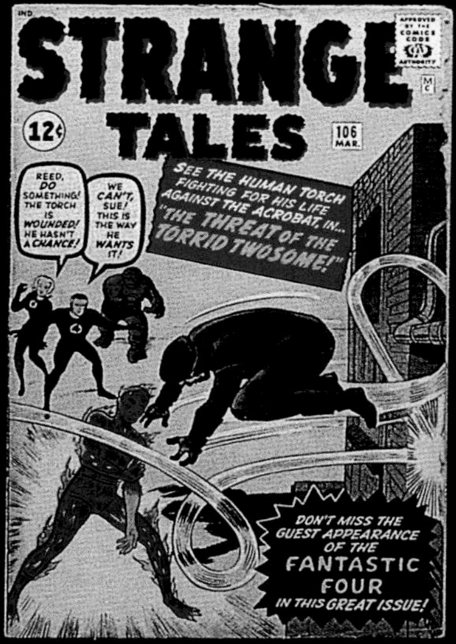
STRANGE TALES
12¢
106 MAR.
REED, DO SOMETHING! THE TORCH IS WOUNDED! HE HASN'T A CHANCE!
WE CAN'T, SUE! THIS IS THE WAY HE WANTS IT!
SEE THE HUMAN TORCH FIGHTING FOR HIS LIFE AGAINST THE ACROBAT, IN... "THE THREAT OF THE TORRID TWOSOME!"
DON'T MISS THE GUEST APPEARANCE OF THE FANTASTIC FOUR IN THIS GREAT ISSUE!

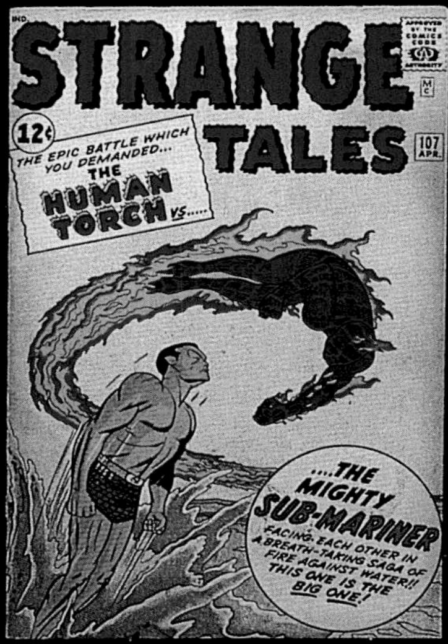
STRANGE TALES
12¢
107 APR.
THE EPIC BATTLE WHICH YOU DEMANDED... THE HUMAN TORCH VS....
...THE MIGHTY SUB-MARINER
FACING EACH OTHER IN A BREATH-TAKING SAGA OF FIRE AGAINST WATER!! THIS ONE IS THE BIG ONE!

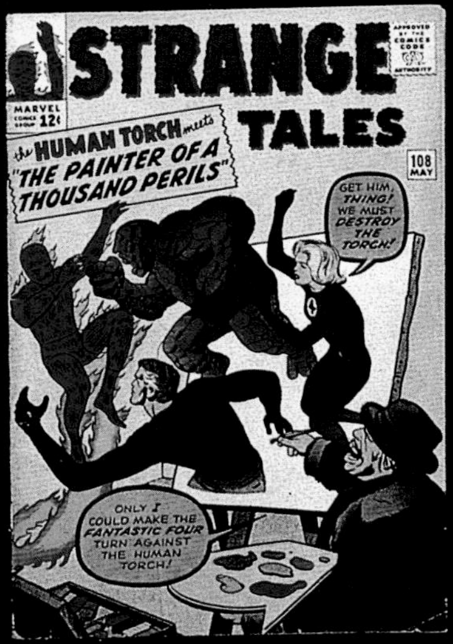
STRANGE TALES
MARVEL COMICS GROUP 12¢
108 MAY
the HUMAN TORCH meets "THE PAINTER OF A THOUSAND PERILS"
GET HIM, THING! WE MUST DESTROY THE TORCH!
ONLY I COULD MAKE THE FANTASTIC FOUR TURN AGAINST THE HUMAN TORCH!

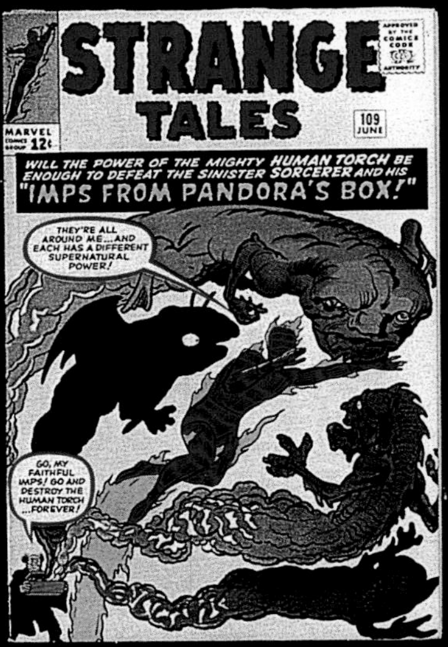
STRANGE TALES
MARVEL COMICS GROUP 12¢
109 JUNE
WILL THE POWER OF THE MIGHTY HUMAN TORCH BE ENOUGH TO DEFEAT THE SINISTER SORCERER AND HIS "IMPS FROM PANDORA'S BOX!"
THEY'RE ALL AROUND ME... AND EACH HAS A DIFFERENT SUPERNATURAL POWER!
GO, MY FAITHFUL IMPS! GO AND DESTROY THE HUMAN TORCH ...FOREVER!

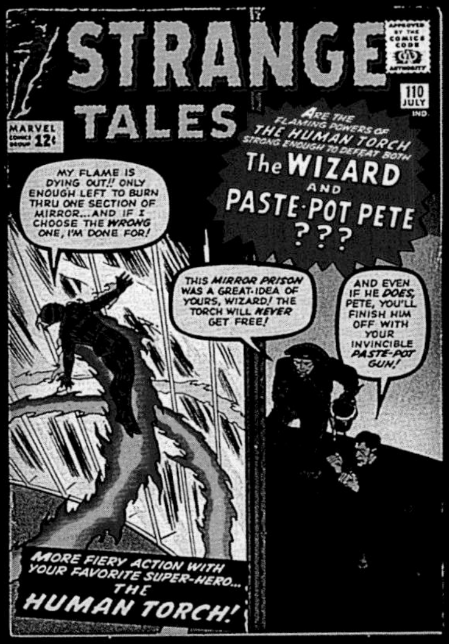
STRANGE TALES
MARVEL COMICS GROUP 12¢
110 JULY
ARE THE FLAMING POWERS OF THE HUMAN TORCH STRONG ENOUGH TO DEFEAT BOTH The WIZARD AND PASTE-POT PETE ???
MY FLAME IS DYING OUT!! ONLY ENOUGH LEFT TO BURN THRU ONE SECTION OF MIRROR... AND IF I CHOOSE THE WRONG ONE, I'M DONE FOR!
THIS MIRROR PRISON WAS A GREAT IDEA OF YOURS, WIZARD! THE TORCH WILL NEVER GET FREE!
AND EVEN IF HE DOES, PETE, YOU'LL FINISH HIM OFF WITH YOUR INVINCIBLE PASTE-POT GUN!
MORE FIERY ACTION WITH YOUR FAVORITE SUPER-HERO... THE HUMAN TORCH!

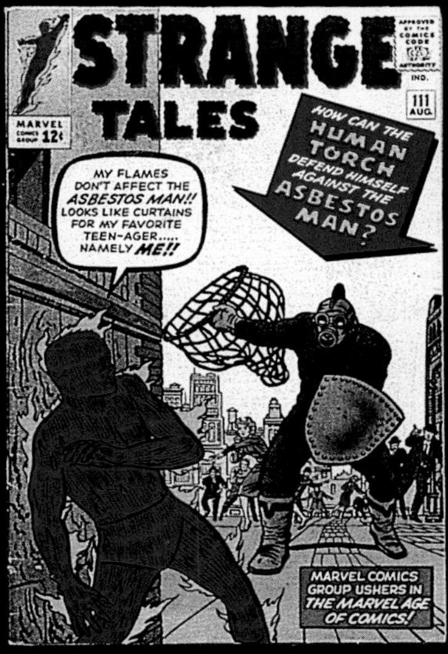
STRANGE TALES
MARVEL COMICS GROUP 12¢
111 AUG.
HOW CAN THE HUMAN TORCH DEFEND HIMSELF AGAINST THE ASBESTOS MAN?
MY FLAMES DON'T AFFECT THE ASBESTOS MAN!! LOOKS LIKE CURTAINS FOR MY FAVORITE TEEN-AGER... NAMELY ME!!
MARVEL COMICS GROUP USHERS IN THE MARVEL AGE OF COMICS!

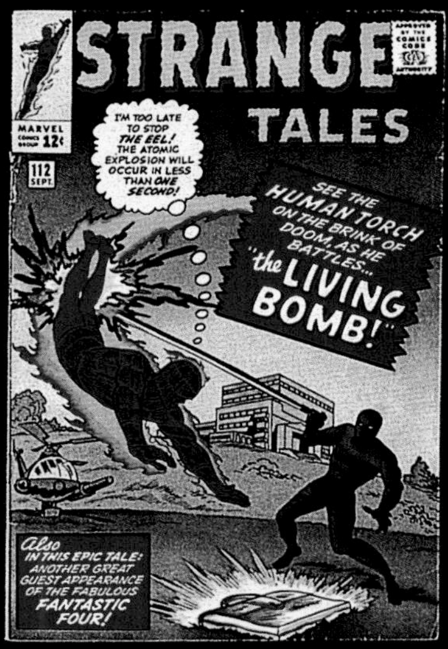
STRANGE TALES
MARVEL COMICS GROUP 12¢
112 SEPT.
I'M TOO LATE TO STOP THE EEL! THE ATOMIC EXPLOSION WILL OCCUR IN LESS THAN ONE SECOND!
SEE THE HUMAN TORCH ON THE BRINK OF DOOM AS HE BATTLES... "the LIVING BOMB!"
Also IN THIS EPIC TALE: ANOTHER GREAT GUEST APPEARANCE OF THE FABULOUS FANTASTIC FOUR!

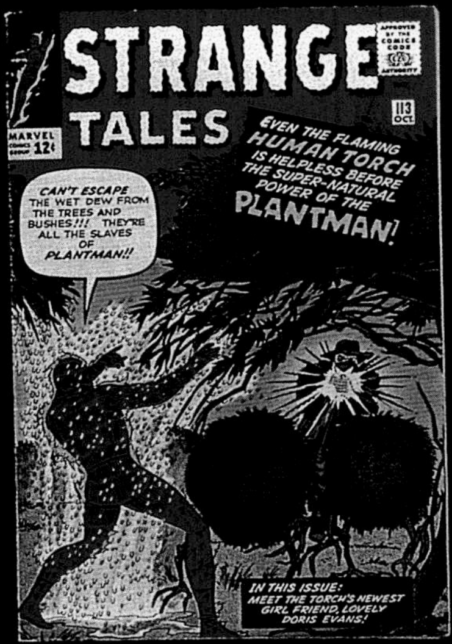
STRANGE TALES
MARVEL COMICS GROUP 12¢
113 OCT.
EVEN THE FLAMING HUMAN TORCH IS HELPLESS BEFORE THE SUPER-NATURAL POWER OF THE PLANTMAN!
CAN'T ESCAPE THE WET DEW FROM THE TREES AND BUSHES!!! THEY'RE ALL THE SLAVES OF PLANTMAN!!
IN THIS ISSUE: MEET THE TORCH'S NEWEST GIRL FRIEND, LOVELY DORIS EVANS!

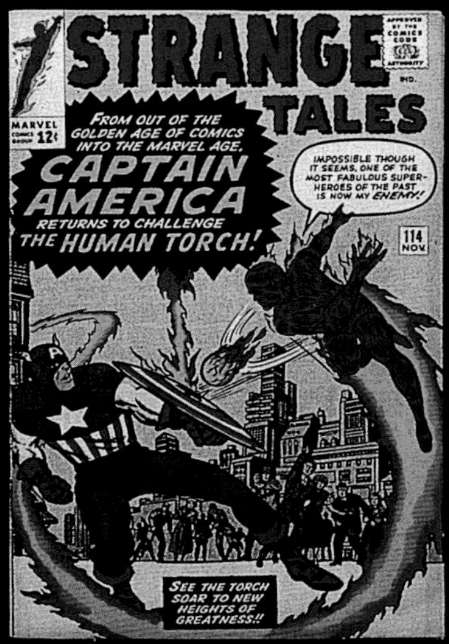
STRANGE TALES
MARVEL COMICS GROUP 12¢
FROM OUT OF THE GOLDEN AGE OF COMICS INTO THE MARVEL AGE, CAPTAIN AMERICA RETURNS TO CHALLENGE THE HUMAN TORCH!
IMPOSSIBLE THOUGH IT SEEMS, ONE OF THE MOST FABULOUS SUPER-HEROES OF THE PAST IS NOW MY ENEMY!
114 NOV.
SEE THE TORCH SOAR TO NEW HEIGHTS OF GREATNESS!!

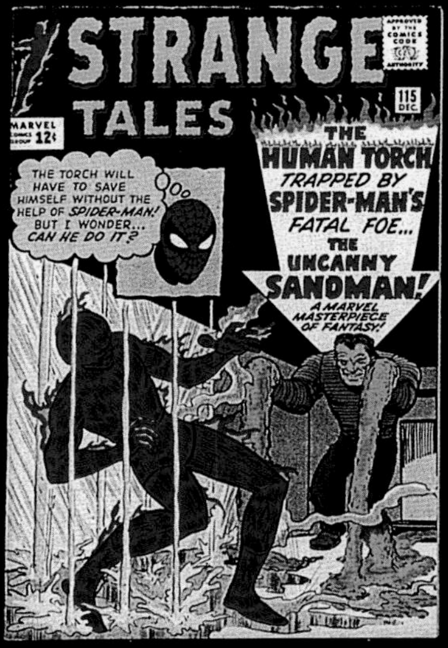
STRANGE TALES
MARVEL COMICS GROUP 12¢
115 DEC.
THE TORCH WILL HAVE TO SAVE HIMSELF WITHOUT THE HELP OF SPIDER-MAN! BUT I WONDER... CAN HE DO IT?
THE HUMAN TORCH TRAPPED BY SPIDER-MAN'S FATAL FOE... THE UNCANNY SANDMAN! A MARVEL MASTERPIECE OF FANTASY!

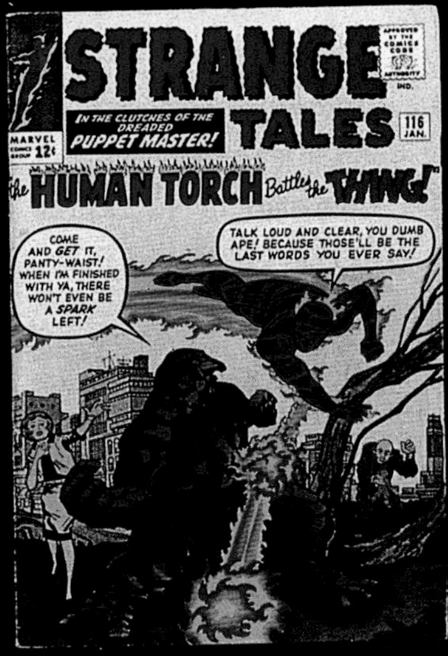
STRANGE TALES
MARVEL COMICS GROUP 12¢
116 JAN.
IN THE CLUTCHES OF THE DREADED PUPPET MASTER!
the HUMAN TORCH Battles the THING!
COME AND GET IT, PANTY-WAIST! WHEN I'M FINISHED WITH YA, THERE WON'T EVEN BE A SPARK LEFT!
TALK LOUD AND CLEAR, YOU DUMB APE! BECAUSE THOSE'LL BE THE LAST WORDS YOU EVER SAY!

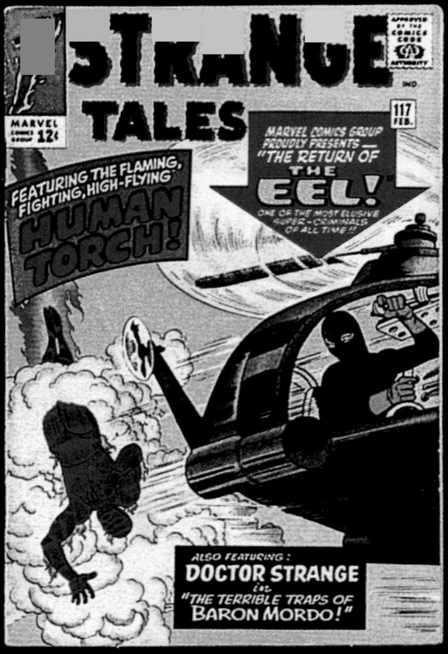
STRANGE TALES
117 FEB.
MARVEL COMICS GROUP PROUDLY PRESENTS "THE RETURN OF THE EEL!"
FEATURING THE FLAMING, FIGHTING, HIGH-FLYING HUMAN TORCH!
ALSO FEATURING: DOCTOR STRANGE in "THE TERRIBLE TRAPS OF BARON MORDO!"

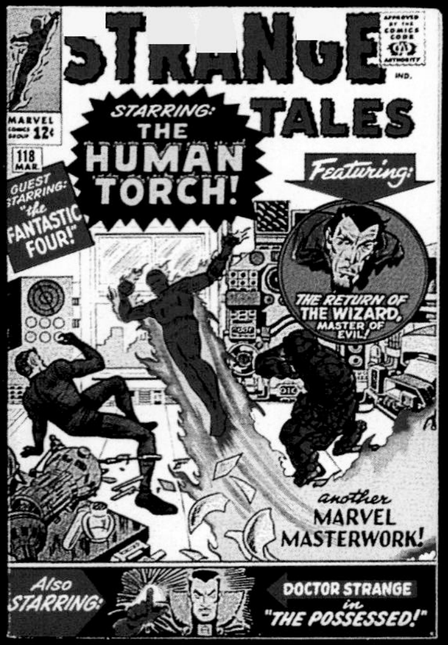
STRANGE TALES
118 MAR
STARRING: THE HUMAN TORCH!
GUEST STARRING: the FANTASTIC FOUR!
Featuring: THE RETURN OF THE WIZARD, MASTER OF EVIL!
another MARVEL MASTERWORK!
Also STARRING: DOCTOR STRANGE in "THE POSSESSED!"

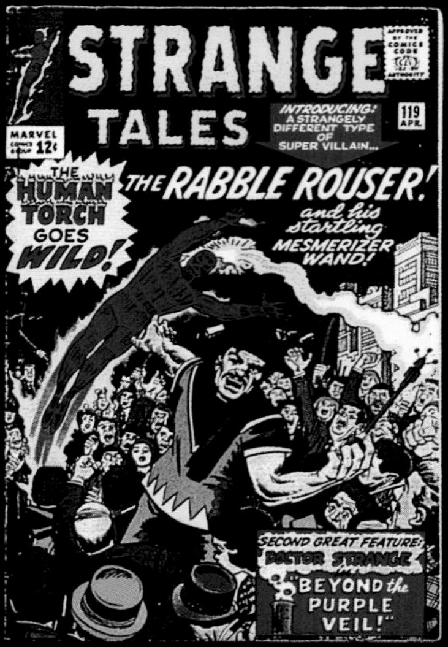
STRANGE TALES
119 APR.
INTRODUCING: A STRANGELY DIFFERENT TYPE OF SUPER VILLAIN...
THE RABBLE ROUSER! and his startling MESMERIZER WAND!
THE HUMAN TORCH GOES WILD!
SECOND GREAT FEATURE: DOCTOR STRANGE BEYOND the PURPLE VEIL!

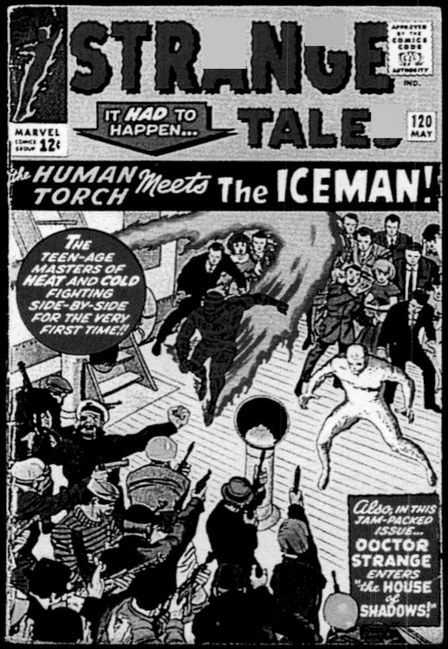
STRANGE TALES
120 MAY
IT HAD TO HAPPEN...
the HUMAN TORCH Meets The ICEMAN!
THE TEEN-AGE MASTERS OF HEAT AND COLD FIGHTING SIDE-BY-SIDE FOR THE VERY FIRST TIME!
Also, in this issue... DOCTOR STRANGE enters "the HOUSE of SHADOWS!"

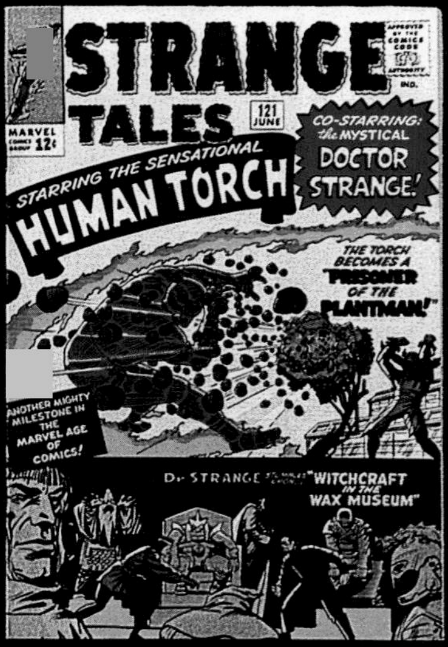
STRANGE TALES
121 JUNE
CO-STARRING: the MYSTICAL DOCTOR STRANGE!
STARRING THE SENSATIONAL HUMAN TORCH!
THE TORCH BECOMES A "PRISONER OF THE PLANTMAN!"
ANOTHER MIGHTY MILESTONE IN THE MARVEL AGE OF COMICS!
Dr. STRANGE "WITCHCRAFT IN THE WAX MUSEUM"

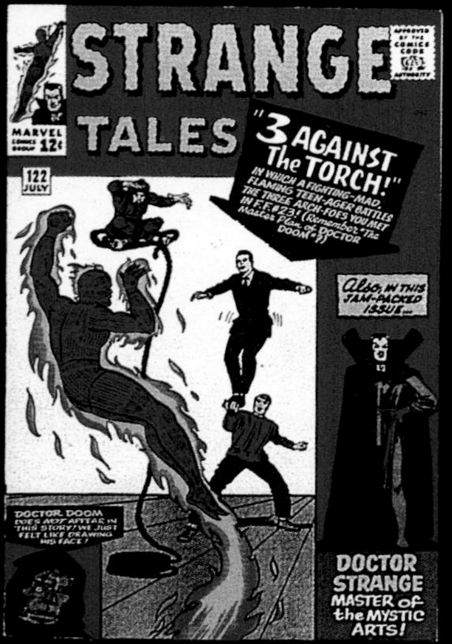
STRANGE TALES
122 JULY
"3 AGAINST The TORCH!"
Also in this jam-packed issue...
DOCTOR STRANGE MASTER of the MYSTIC ARTS!

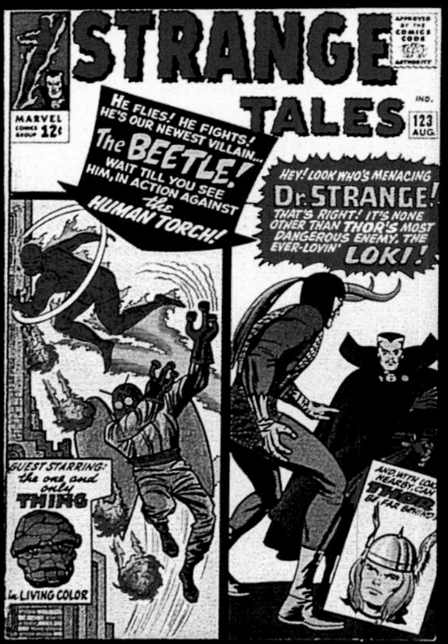
STRANGE TALES
123 AUG.
HE FLIES! HE FIGHTS! HE'S OUR NEWEST VILLAIN... The BEETLE! WAIT TILL YOU SEE HIM, IN ACTION AGAINST the HUMAN TORCH!
HEY! LOOK WHO'S MENACING Dr. STRANGE! THAT'S RIGHT! IT'S NONE OTHER THAN THOR'S MOST DANGEROUS ENEMY, THE EVER-LOVIN' LOKI!
GUEST STARRING: the one and only THING
in LIVING COLOR

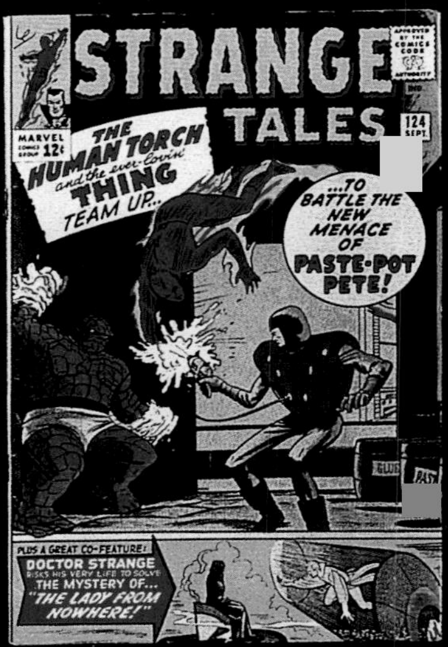
STRANGE TALES
124 SEPT.
THE HUMAN TORCH and the ever-lovin' THING TEAM UP...
...TO BATTLE THE NEW MENACE OF PASTE-POT PETE!
PLUS A GREAT CO-FEATURE: DOCTOR STRANGE RISKS HIS VERY LIFE TO SOLVE THE MYSTERY OF... "THE LADY FROM NOWHERE!"

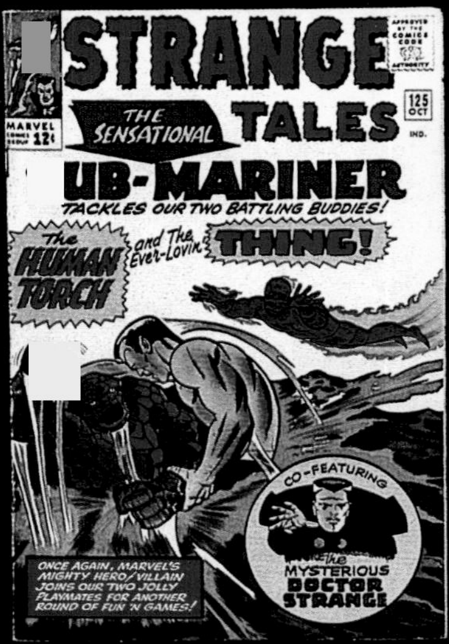
STRANGE TALES
125 OCT
THE SENSATIONAL UB-MARINER TACKLES OUR TWO BATTLING BUDDIES!
The HUMAN TORCH and The Ever-Lovin' THING!
CO-FEATURING The MYSTERIOUS DOCTOR STRANGE
ONCE AGAIN, MARVEL'S MIGHTY HERO/VILLAIN JOINS OUR TWO JOLLY PLAYMATES FOR ANOTHER ROUND OF FUN 'N GAMES!

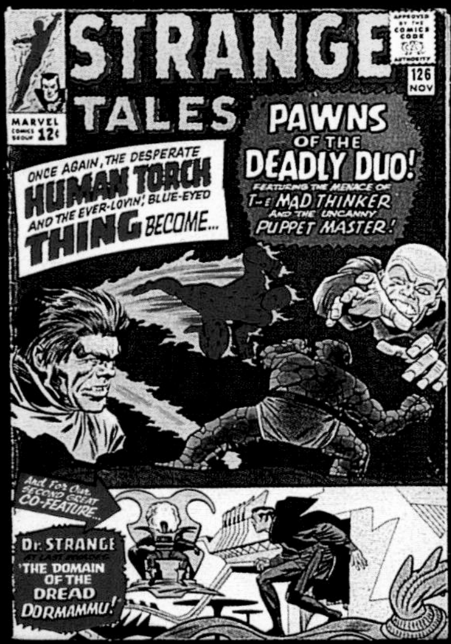
STRANGE TALES
126 NOV
ONCE AGAIN, THE DESPERATE HUMAN TORCH AND THE EVER-LOVIN', BLUE-EYED THING BECOME...
PAWNS OF THE DEADLY DUO! FEATURING THE MENACE OF THE MAD THINKER AND THE UNCANNY PUPPET MASTER!
Dr. STRANGE "THE DOMAIN OF THE DREAD DORMAMMU!"

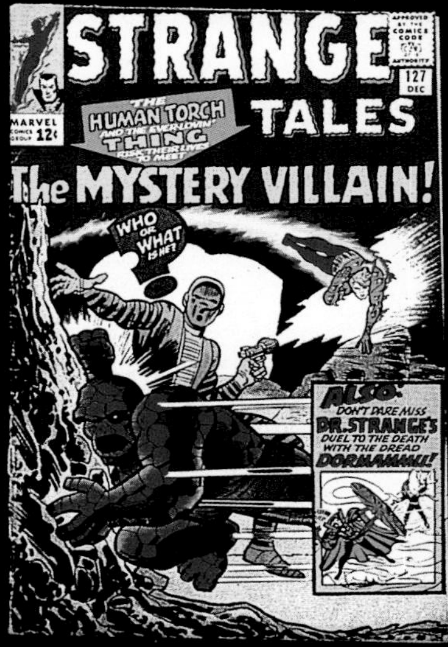
STRANGE TALES
127 DEC
THE HUMAN TORCH AND THE EVER-LOVIN' THING
The MYSTERY VILLAIN!
WHO OR WHAT IS HE?
ALSO: DON'T DARE MISS DR. STRANGE'S DUEL TO THE DEATH WITH THE DREAD DORMAMMU!

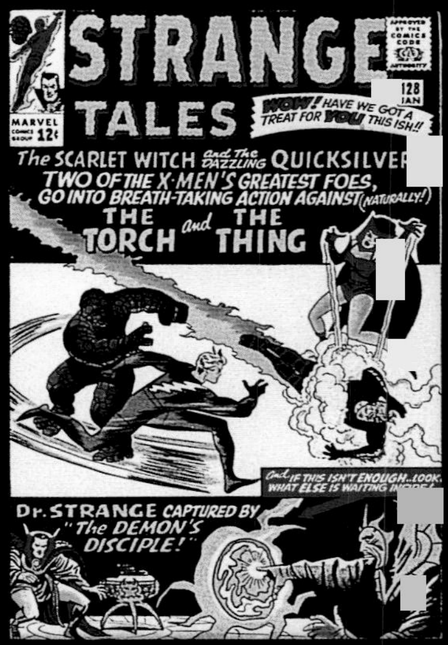
STRANGE TALES
128 JAN
WOW! HAVE WE GOT A TREAT FOR YOU THIS ISH!!
The SCARLET WITCH and the DAZZLING QUICKSILVER TWO OF THE X-MEN'S GREATEST FOES, GO INTO BREATH-TAKING ACTION AGAINST (NATURALLY!) THE TORCH and THE THING
Dr. STRANGE CAPTURED BY "THE DEMON'S DISCIPLE!"

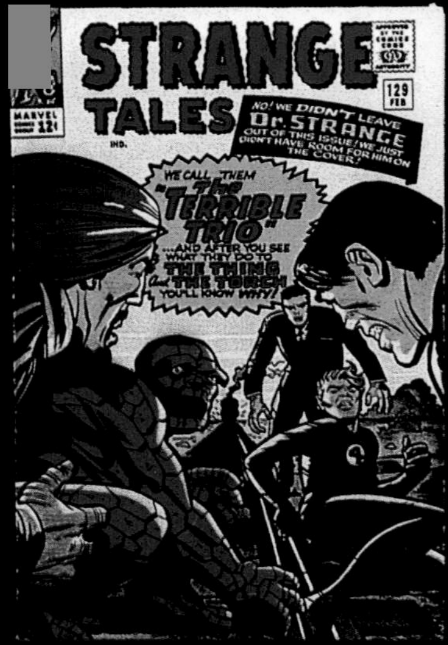
STRANGE TALES
129 FEB
NO! WE DIDN'T LEAVE Dr. STRANGE OUT OF THIS ISSUE! WE JUST DIDN'T HAVE ROOM FOR HIM ON THE COVER!
WE CALL THEM THE TERRIBLE TRIO
THE THING AND THE TORCH

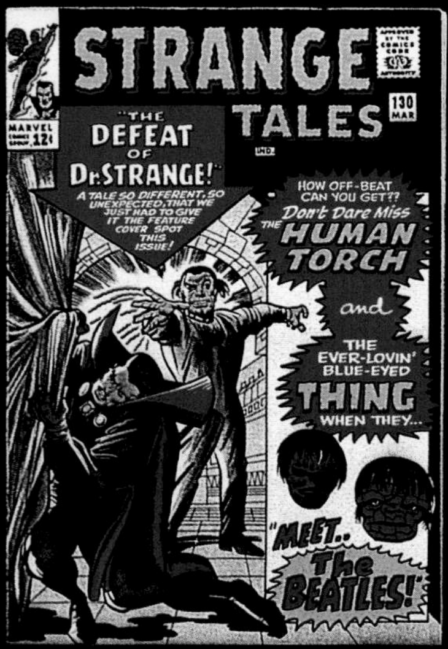
STRANGE TALES
130 MAR
"THE DEFEAT OF Dr. STRANGE!"
HOW OFF-BEAT CAN YOU GET?? Don't Dare Miss the HUMAN TORCH and THE EVER-LOVIN' BLUE-EYED THING WHEN THEY... "MEET... The BEATLES!"

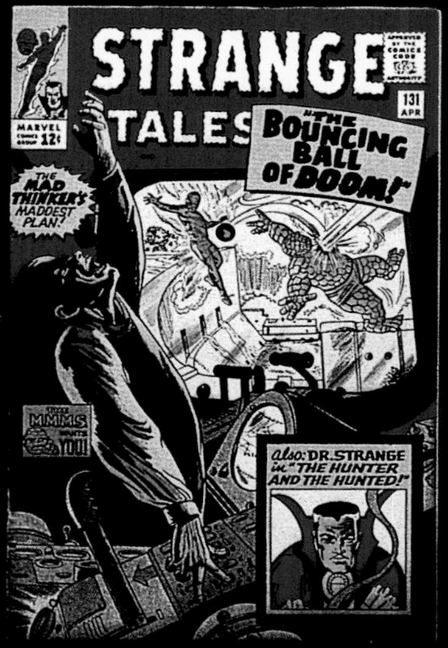
STRANGE TALES
131 APR
BOUNCING BALL OF DOOM!
THE MAD THINKER'S MADDEST PLAN!
also: DR. STRANGE in "THE HUNTER AND THE HUNTED!"

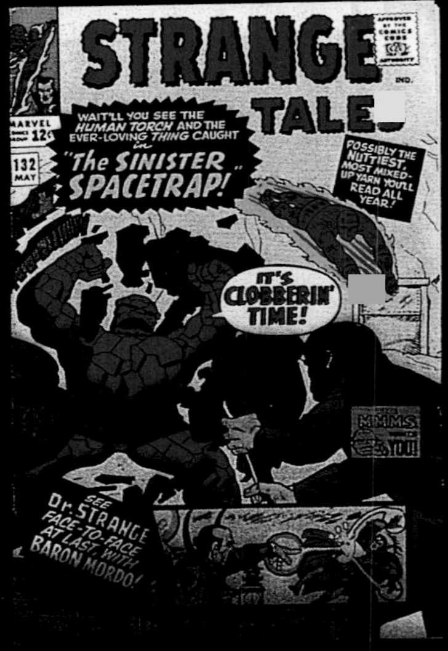
STRANGE TALES
132 MAY
WAIT'LL YOU SEE THE HUMAN TORCH AND THE EVER-LOVING THING CAUGHT in "The SINISTER SPACETRAP!"
POSSIBLY THE NUTTIEST, MOST MIXED-UP YARN YOU'LL READ ALL YEAR!
IT'S CLOBBERIN' TIME!
SEE Dr. STRANGE FACE TO FACE AT LAST WITH BARON MORDO!

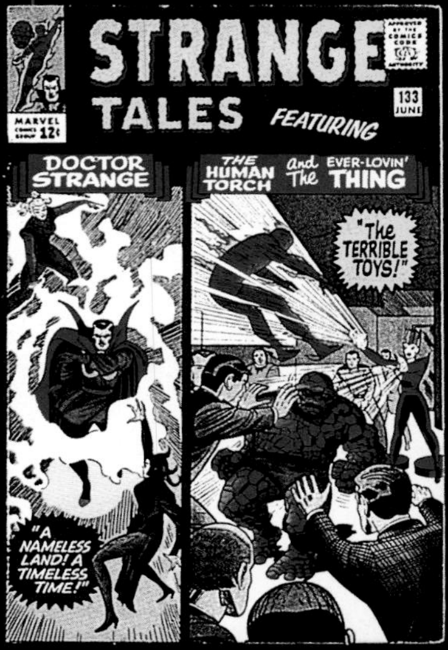
STRANGE TALES
FEATURING
133 JUNE
MARVEL 12¢
DOCTOR STRANGE
THE HUMAN TORCH and The EVER-LOVIN' THING
"The TERRIBLE TOYS!"
"A NAMELESS LAND! A TIMELESS TIME!"

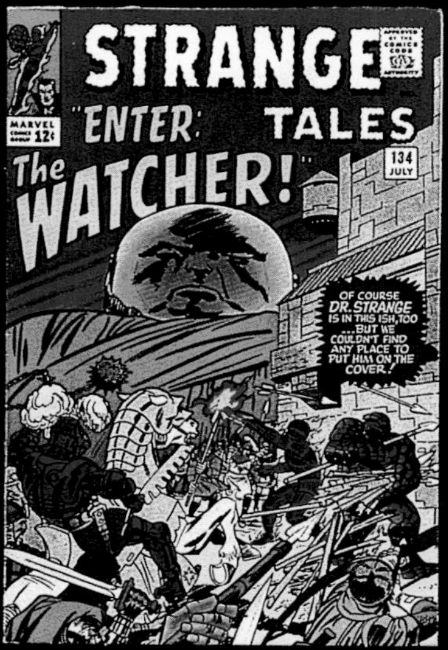
STRANGE TALES
134 JULY
MARVEL 12¢
ENTER: The WATCHER!
OF COURSE DR. STRANGE IS IN THIS ISH, TOO ...BUT WE COULDN'T FIND ANY PLACE TO PUT HIM ON THE COVER.

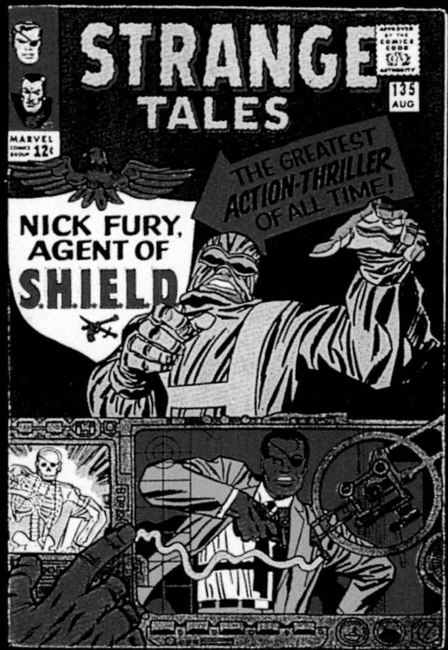
STRANGE TALES
135 AUG
MARVEL 12¢
THE GREATEST ACTION-THRILLER OF ALL TIME!
NICK FURY, AGENT OF S.H.I.E.L.D.

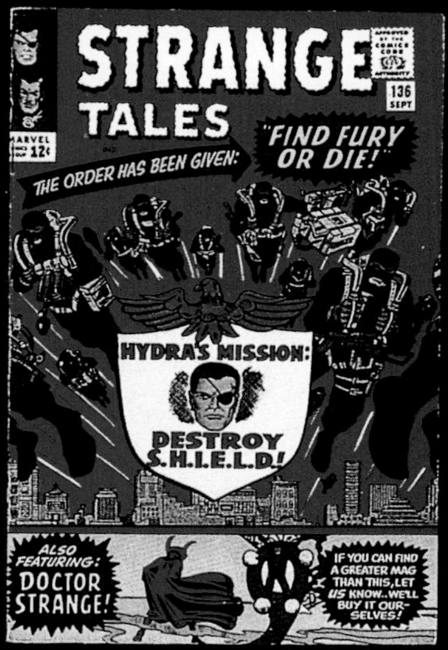
STRANGE TALES
136 SEPT
MARVEL 12¢
THE ORDER HAS BEEN GIVEN: "FIND FURY OR DIE!"
HYDRA'S MISSION:
DESTROY S.H.I.E.L.D.!
ALSO FEATURING: DOCTOR STRANGE!
IF YOU CAN FIND A GREATER MAG THAN THIS, LET US KNOW... WE'LL BUY IT OUR-SELVES!

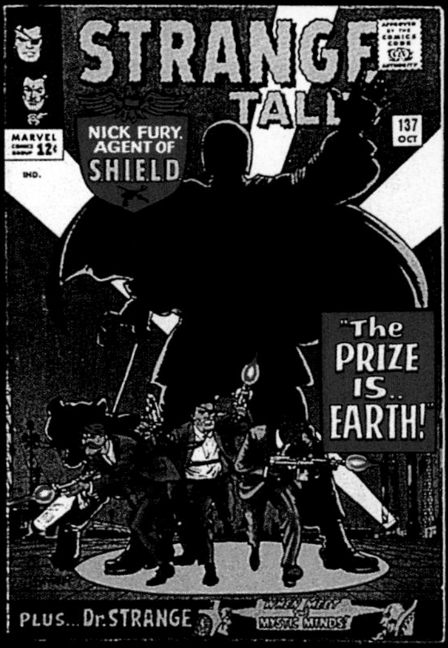
STRANGE TALES
137 OCT
MARVEL 12¢
NICK FURY, AGENT OF SHIELD
"The PRIZE IS.. EARTH!
PLUS... Dr. STRANGE

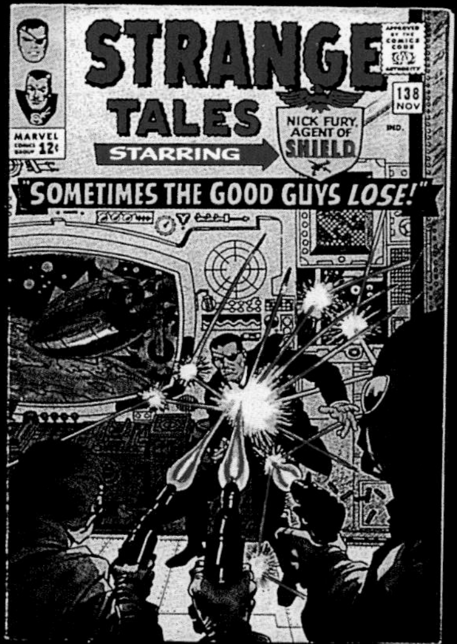
STRANGE TALES
138 NOV
MARVEL 12¢
STARRING
NICK FURY, AGENT OF SHIELD
"SOMETIMES THE GOOD GUYS LOSE!"

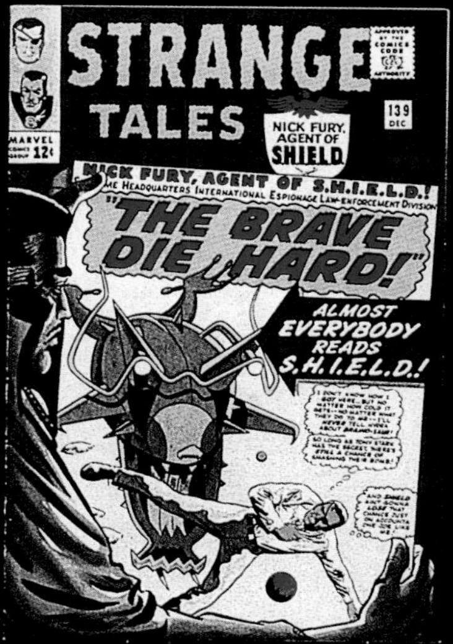
STRANGE TALES
139 DEC
MARVEL 12¢
NICK FURY, AGENT OF SHIELD
NICK FURY, AGENT OF S.H.I.E.L.D.!
THE BRAVE DIE HARD!
ALMOST EVERYBODY READS S.H.I.E.L.D.!

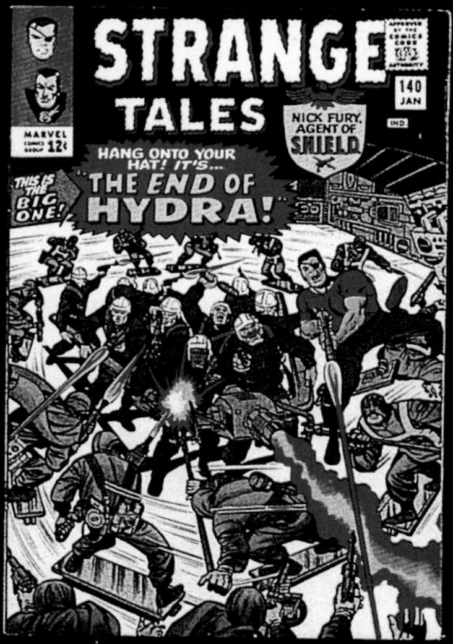
STRANGE TALES
140 JAN
MARVEL 12¢
NICK FURY, AGENT OF SHIELD
HANG ONTO YOUR HAT! IT'S...
THIS IS THE BIG ONE!
THE END OF HYDRA!

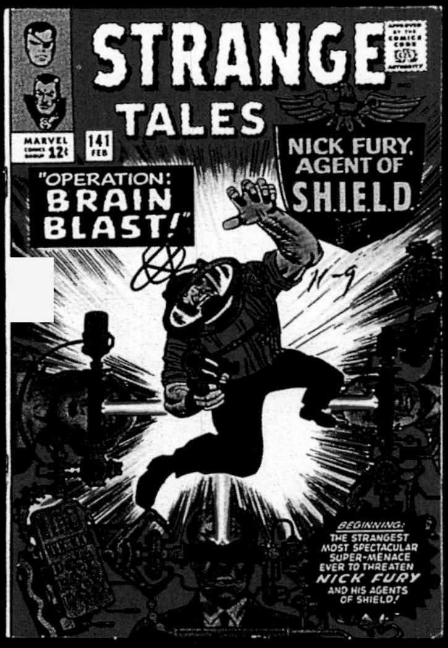
STRANGE TALES
141 FEB
MARVEL 12¢
NICK FURY, AGENT OF S.H.I.E.L.D.
"OPERATION: BRAIN BLAST!"
BEGINNING: THE STRANGEST MOST SPECTACULAR SUPER-MENACE EVER TO THREATEN NICK FURY AND HIS AGENTS OF SHIELD!

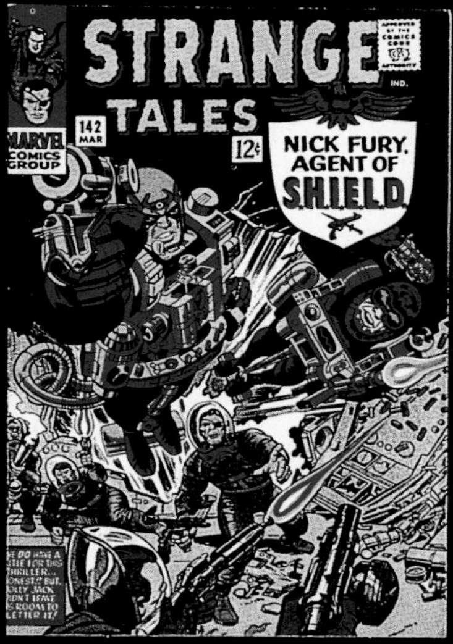
STRANGE TALES
142 MAR
MARVEL COMICS GROUP
12¢
NICK FURY, AGENT OF S.H.I.E.L.D.

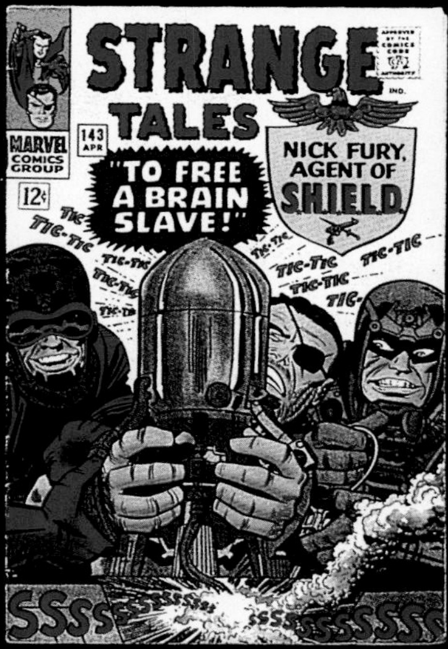
STRANGE TALES
143 APR
MARVEL COMICS GROUP
12¢
NICK FURY, AGENT OF S.H.I.E.L.D.
"TO FREE A BRAIN SLAVE!"
TIC-TIC
SSSSS

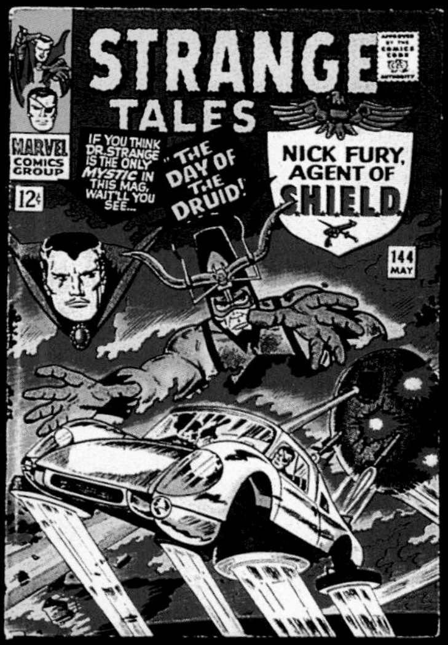
STRANGE TALES
MARVEL COMICS GROUP
12¢
IF YOU THINK DR. STRANGE IS THE ONLY MYSTIC IN THIS MAG, WAIT'LL YOU SEE...
"THE DAY OF THE DRUID!"
NICK FURY, AGENT OF S.H.I.E.L.D.
144 MAY

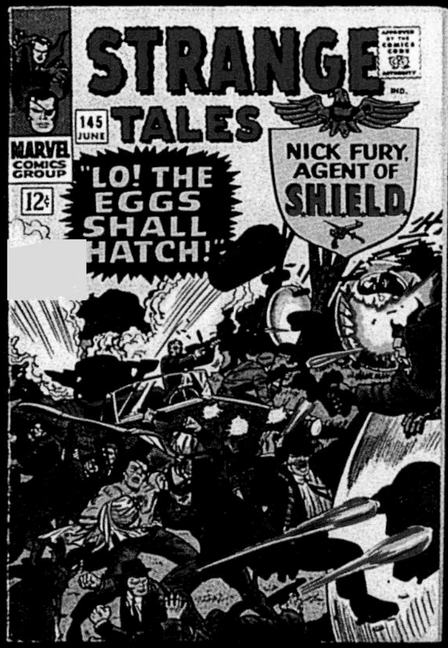
STRANGE TALES
145 JUNE
MARVEL COMICS GROUP
12¢
NICK FURY, AGENT OF S.H.I.E.L.D.
"LO! THE EGGS SHALL HATCH!"

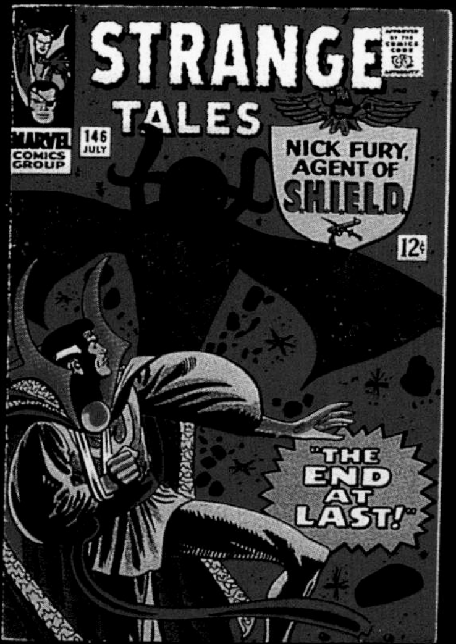
STRANGE TALES
146 JULY
MARVEL COMICS GROUP
NICK FURY, AGENT OF S.H.I.E.L.D.
12¢
"THE END AT LAST!"

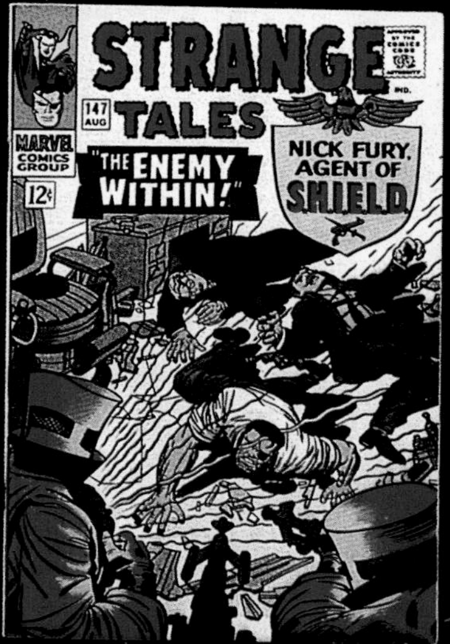
STRANGE TALES
147 AUG
MARVEL COMICS GROUP
12¢
"THE ENEMY WITHIN!"
NICK FURY, AGENT OF S.H.I.E.L.D.

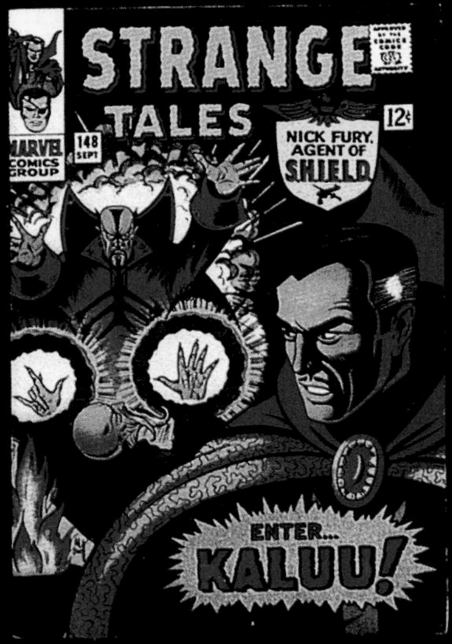
STRANGE TALES
12¢
148 SEPT
MARVEL COMICS GROUP
NICK FURY, AGENT OF S.H.I.E.L.D.
ENTER... KALUU!

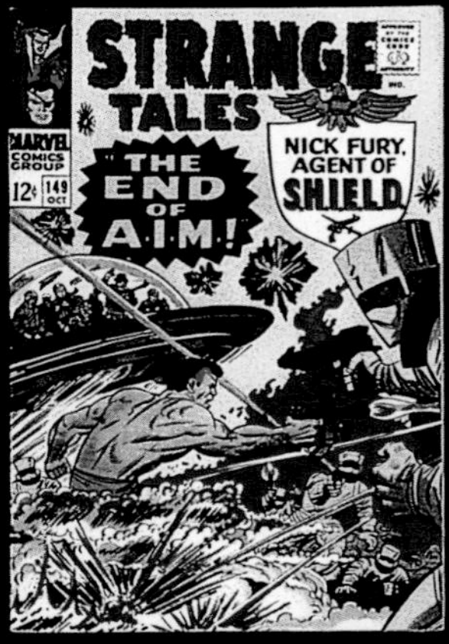
STRANGE TALES
NICK FURY, AGENT OF SHIELD
THE END OF A.I.M.!

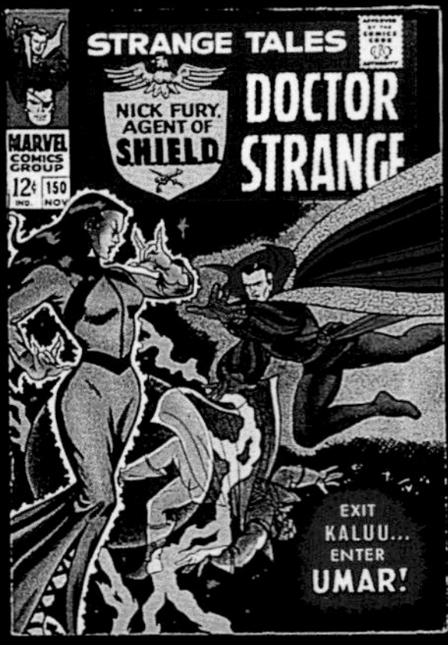
STRANGE TALES
NICK FURY, AGENT OF SHIELD
DOCTOR STRANGE
EXIT KALUU... ENTER UMAR!

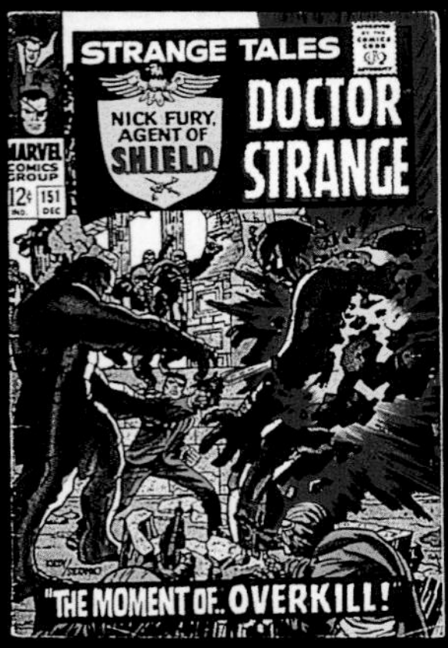
STRANGE TALES
NICK FURY, AGENT OF SHIELD
DOCTOR STRANGE
"THE MOMENT OF... OVERKILL!"

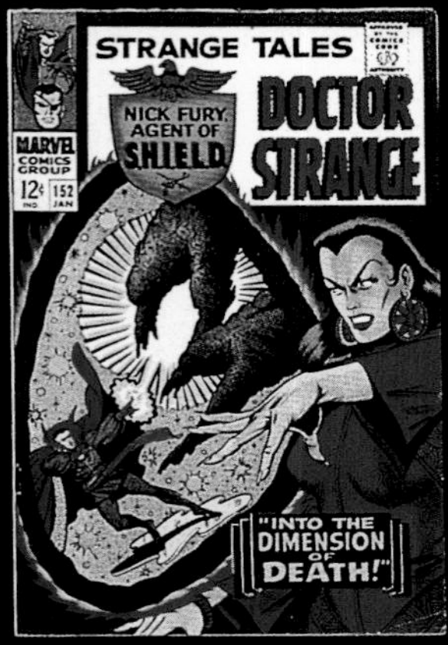
STRANGE TALES
NICK FURY, AGENT OF SHIELD
DOCTOR STRANGE
"INTO THE DIMENSION OF DEATH!"

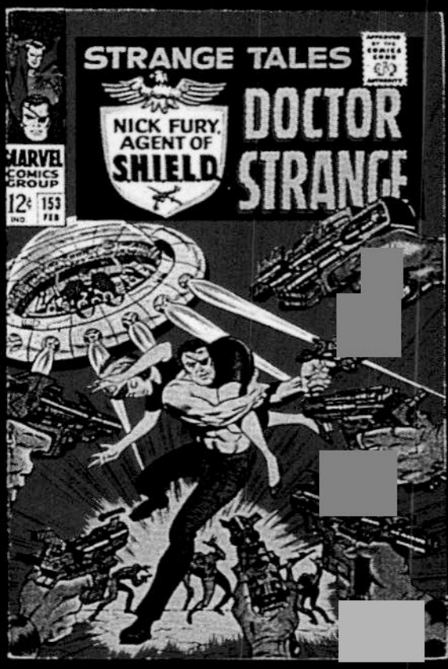
STRANGE TALES
NICK FURY, AGENT OF SHIELD
DOCTOR STRANGE

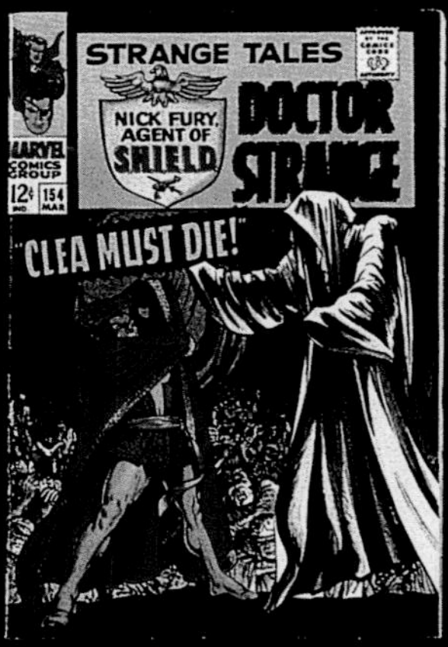
STRANGE TALES
NICK FURY, AGENT OF SHIELD
DOCTOR STRANGE
"CLEA MUST DIE!"

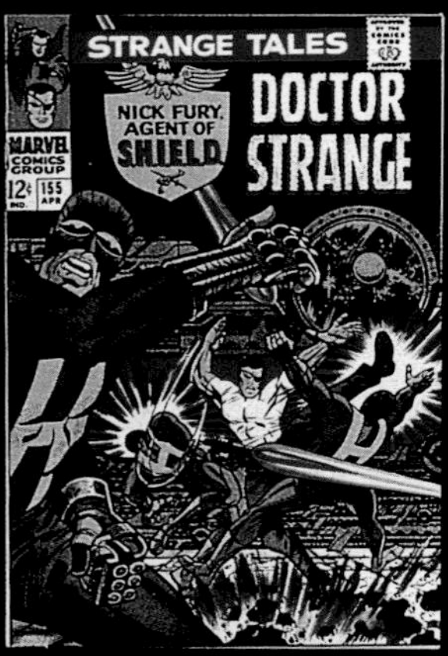
STRANGE TALES
NICK FURY, AGENT OF SHIELD
DOCTOR STRANGE

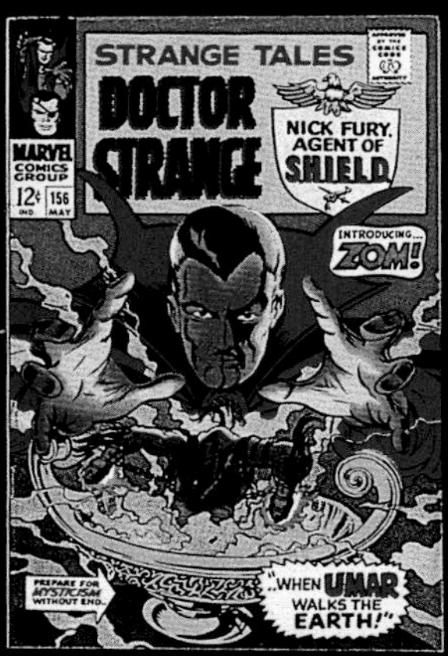
STRANGE TALES
DOCTOR STRANGE
NICK FURY, AGENT OF SHIELD
INTRODUCING... ZOM!
...WHEN UMAR WALKS THE EARTH!

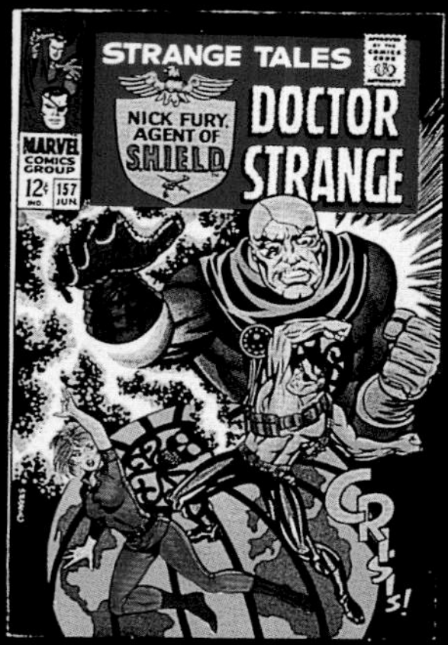
STRANGE TALES
NICK FURY, AGENT OF SHIELD
DOCTOR STRANGE

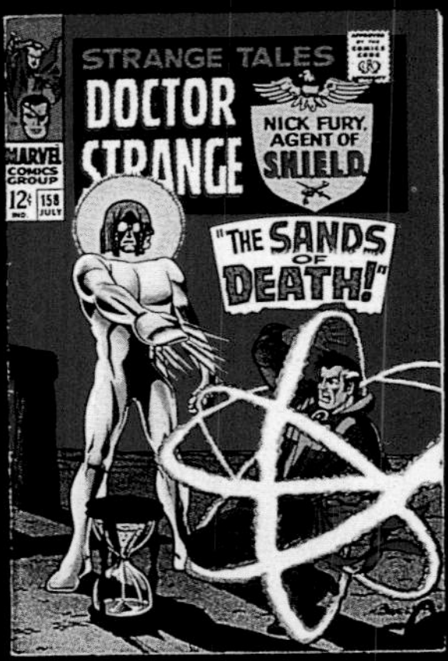
STRANGE TALES
DOCTOR STRANGE
NICK FURY, AGENT OF SHIELD
"THE SANDS OF DEATH!"

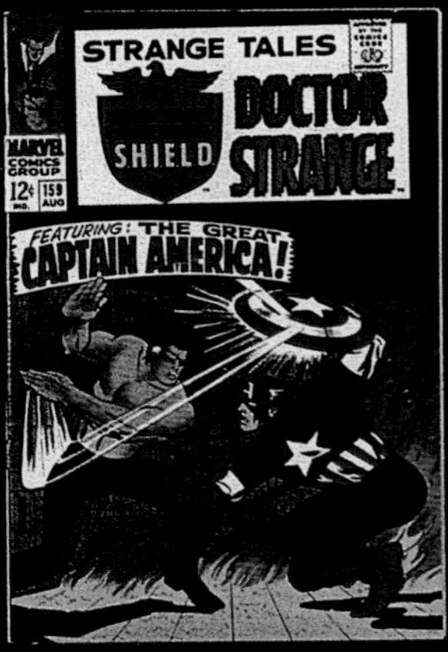
STRANGE TALES
SHIELD
DOCTOR STRANGE
FEATURING: THE GREAT CAPTAIN AMERICA!

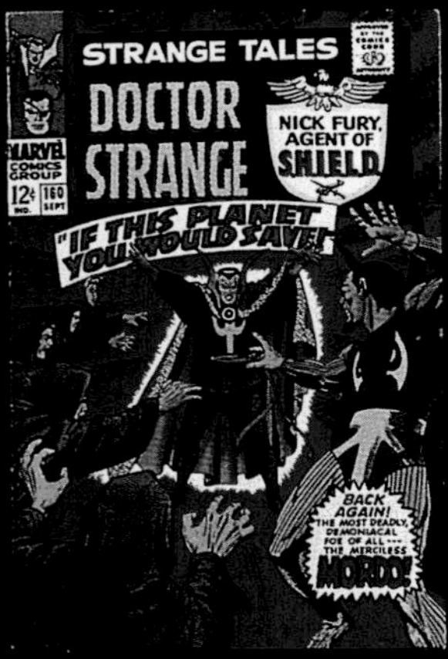
STRANGE TALES
DOCTOR STRANGE
NICK FURY, AGENT OF SHIELD
"IF THIS PLANET YOU WOULD SAVE!"
BACK AGAIN!
MORDO!

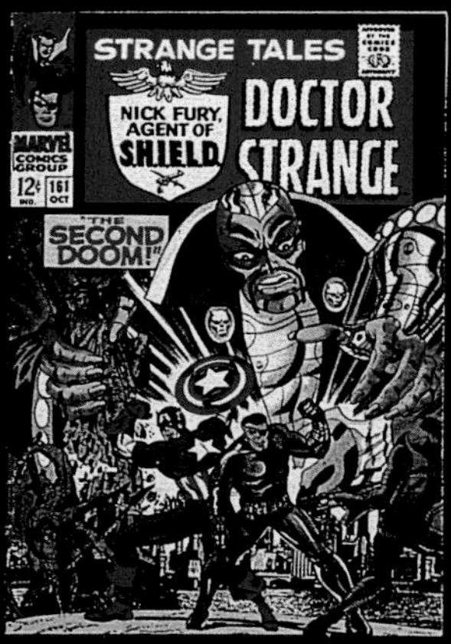
STRANGE TALES
NICK FURY, AGENT OF SHIELD
DOCTOR STRANGE
"THE SECOND DOOM!"

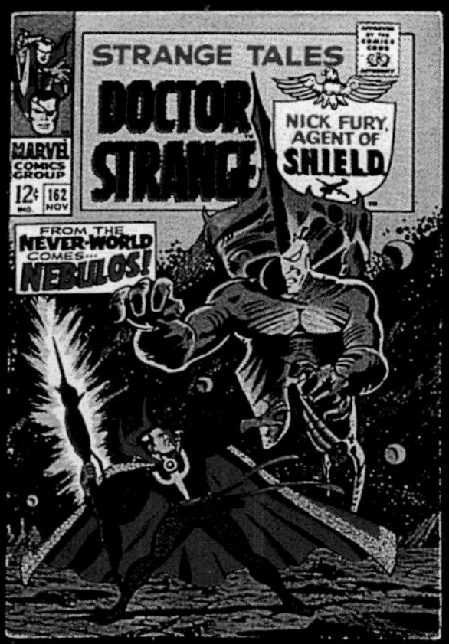
STRANGE TALES
DOCTOR STRANGE
NICK FURY, AGENT OF SHIELD
FROM THE NEVER-WORLD COMES... NEBULOS!

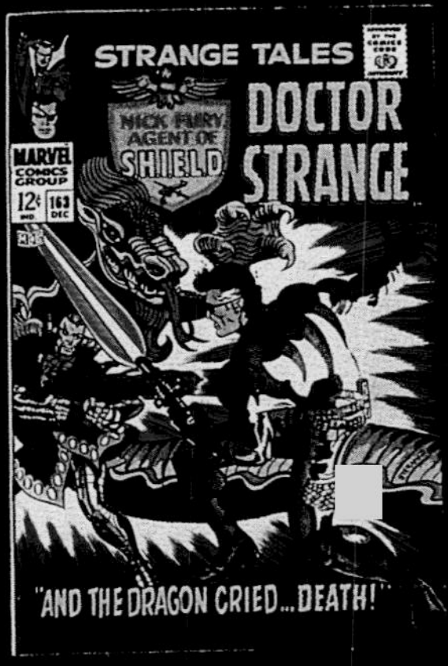
STRANGE TALES
NICK FURY, AGENT OF SHIELD
DOCTOR STRANGE
"AND THE DRAGON CRIED...DEATH!"

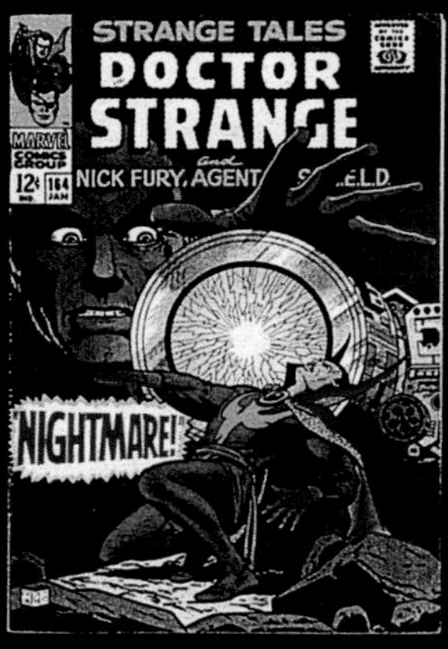
STRANGE TALES
DOCTOR STRANGE
"NIGHTMARE!"

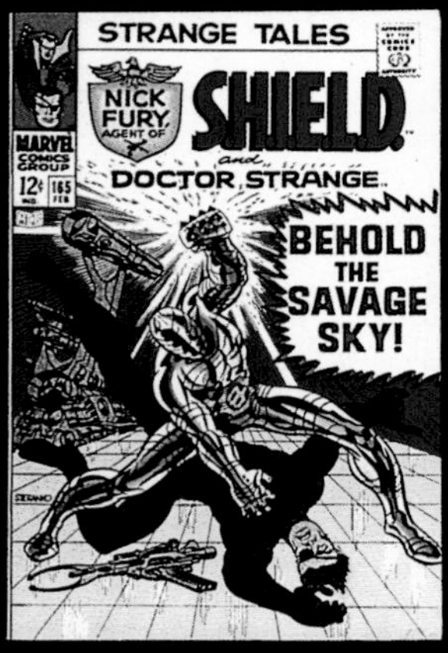
STRANGE TALES
NICK FURY, AGENT OF SHIELD
DOCTOR STRANGE
BEHOLD THE SAVAGE SKY!

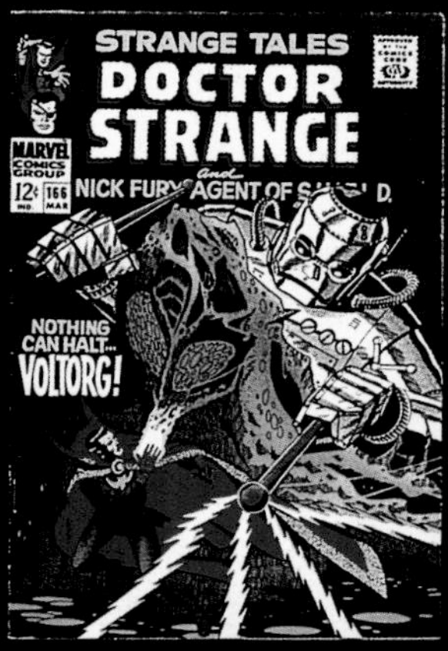
STRANGE TALES
DOCTOR STRANGE
NOTHING CAN HALT... VOLTORG!

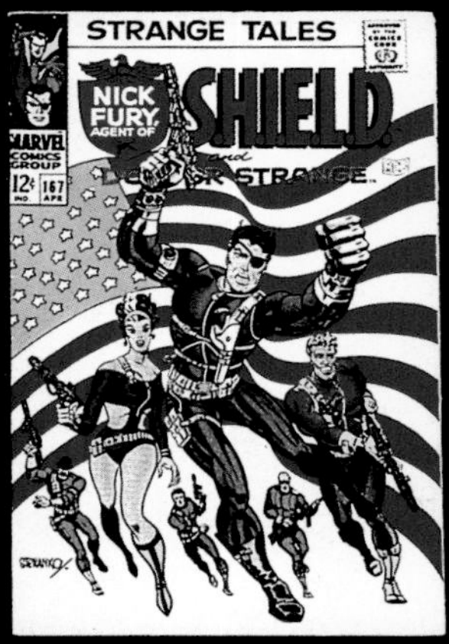
STRANGE TALES
NICK FURY, AGENT OF SHIELD

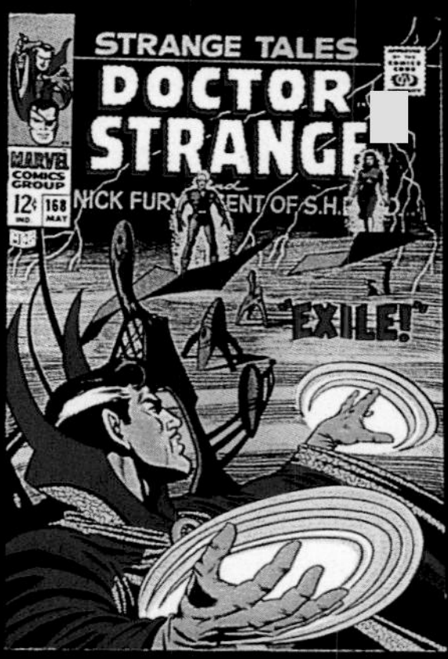
STRANGE TALES
DOCTOR STRANGE
"EXILE!"

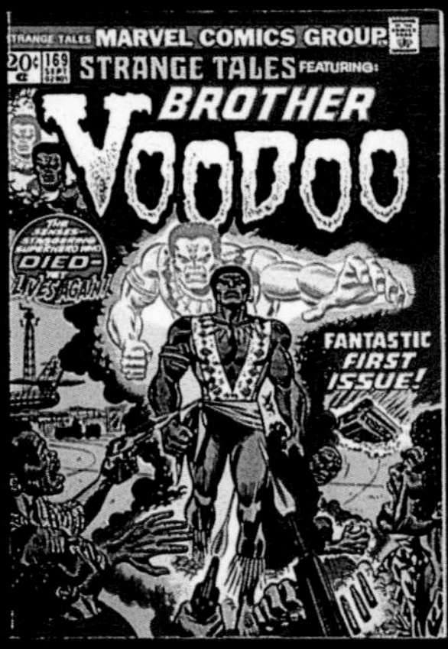
MARVEL COMICS GROUP
STRANGE TALES FEATURING:
BROTHER VOODOO
FANTASTIC FIRST ISSUE!

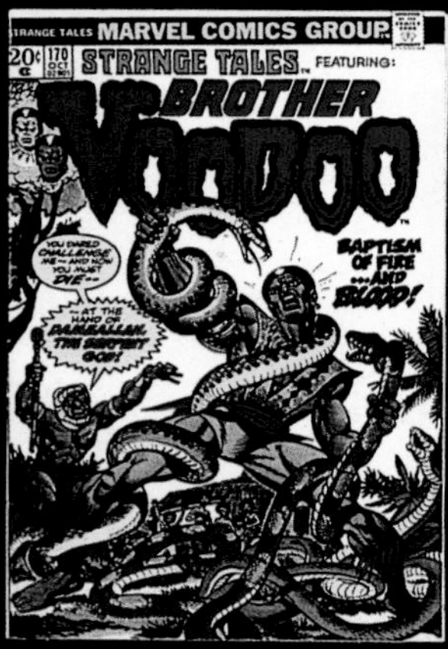
MARVEL COMICS GROUP
STRANGE TALES FEATURING:
BROTHER VOODOO
BAPTISM OF FIRE AND BLOOD!

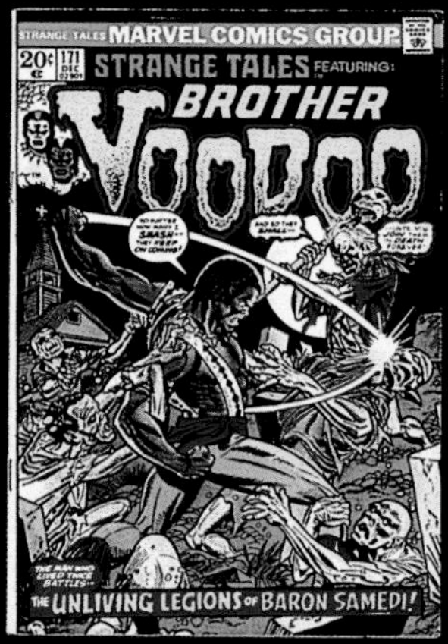
MARVEL COMICS GROUP
STRANGE TALES FEATURING:
BROTHER VOODOO
THE UNLIVING LEGIONS of BARON SAMEDI!

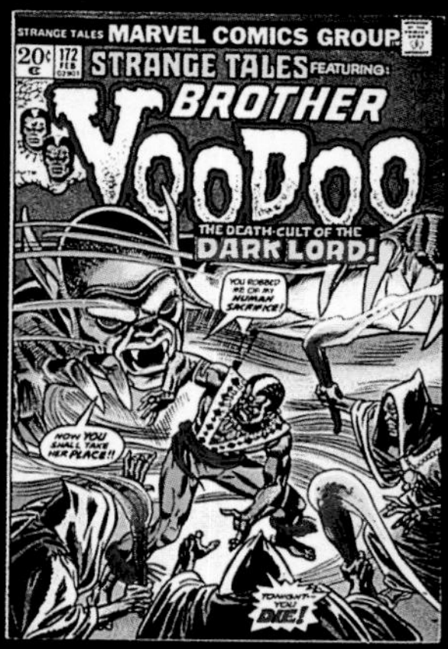
MARVEL COMICS GROUP
STRANGE TALES FEATURING:
BROTHER VOODOO
THE DEATH-CULT OF THE DARK LORD!

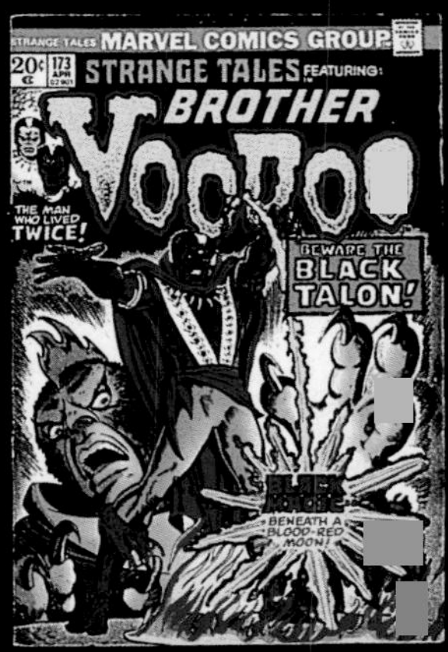
MARVEL COMICS GROUP
STRANGE TALES FEATURING:
BROTHER VOODOO
THE MAN WHO LIVED TWICE!
BEWARE THE BLACK TALON!

1813 Strange Tales (174-188)

MARVEL COMICS GROUP
STRANGE TALES
THE GOLEM
THE THING THAT WALKS LIKE A MAN!
FOR CENTURIES HE HAS WAITED—NOW, HE ATTACKS!

MARVEL COMICS GROUP
STRANGE TALES

MARVEL COMICS GROUP
STRANGE TALES
THE GOLEM
THE THING THAT WALKS LIKE A MAN!
KABALLA!

MARVEL COMICS GROUP
STRANGE TALES
GOLEM
DOOMS-DAY FOR THE DEMI-GOD!

MARVEL COMICS GROUP
STRANGE TALES
WARLOCK

MARVEL COMICS GROUP
STRANGE TALES
WARLOCK
DEATH SHIP!

MARVEL COMICS GROUP
STRANGE TALES
WARLOCK
JUDGMENT DAY

MARVEL COMICS GROUP
STRANGE TALES
WARLOCK
MADNESS MONSTER

MARVEL COMICS GROUP
STRANGE TALES
Dr. STRANGE
THOR

MARVEL COMICS GROUP
STRANGE TALES
Dr. STRANGE
THE DEFEAT OF DOCTOR STRANGE!

MARVEL COMICS GROUP
STRANGE TALES
Dr. STRANGE
FACE-TO-FACE WITH BARON MORDO!

MARVEL COMICS GROUP
STRANGE TALES
Dr. STRANGE

MARVEL COMICS GROUP
STRANGE TALES
Dr. STRANGE
ANCIENT ONE!

MARVEL COMICS GROUP
STRANGE TALES
Dr. STRANGE

MARVEL COMICS GROUP
STRANGE TALES
Dr. STRANGE

ANNUAL
72 BIG PAGES
STRANGE TALES ANNUAL
SPIDER-MAN
HUMAN TORCH

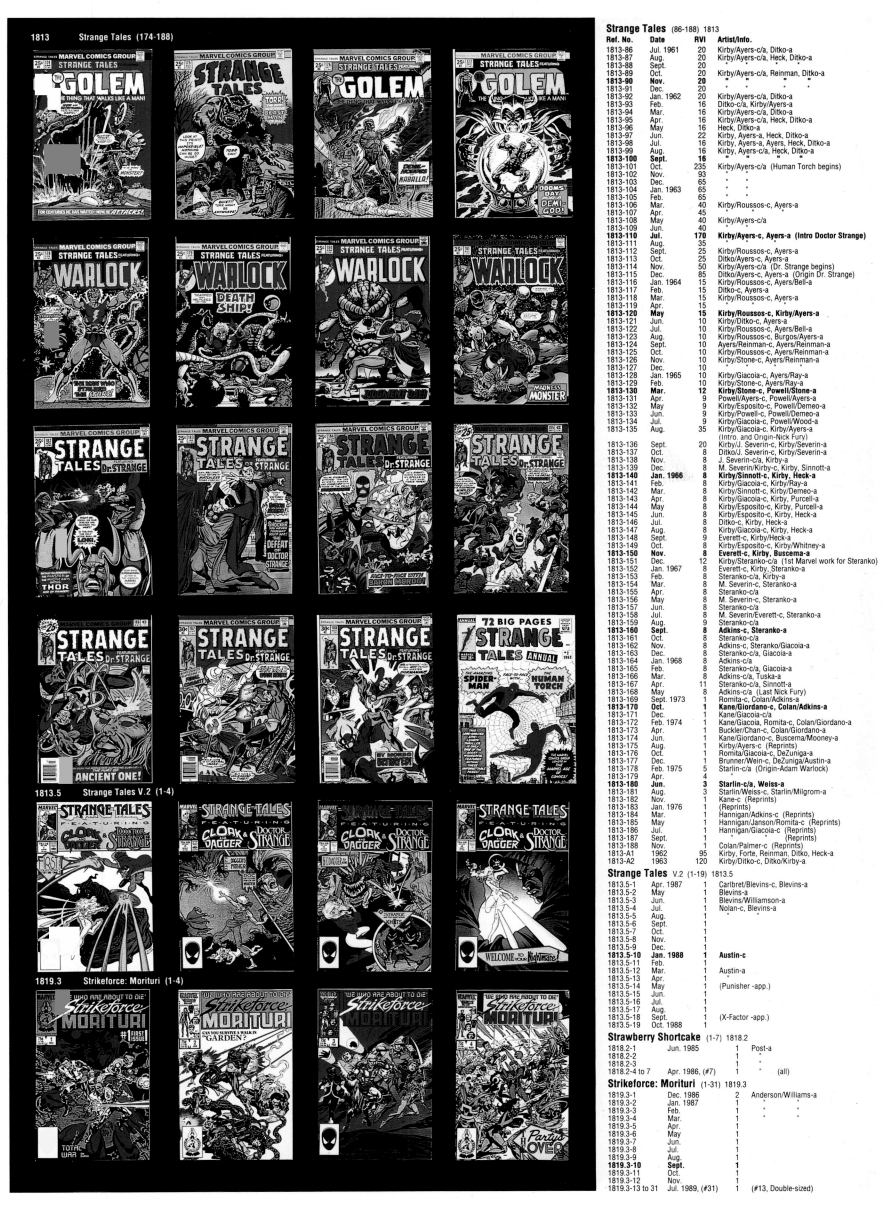

1813.5 Strange Tales V.2 (1-4)

STRANGE TALES
FEATURING
CLOAK & DAGGER
DOCTOR STRANGE

STRANGE TALES
FEATURING
CLOAK & DAGGER
DOCTOR STRANGE

STRANGE TALES
FEATURING
CLOAK & DAGGER
DOCTOR STRANGE

STRANGE TALES
FEATURING
CLOAK & DAGGER
DOCTOR STRANGE
WELCOME TO YOUR Nightmare!

1819.3 Strikeforce: Morituri (1-4)

WE WHO ARE ABOUT TO DIE
Strikeforce MORITURI
#1 FIRST ISSUE!

WE WHO ARE ABOUT TO DIE
Strikeforce MORITURI

WE WHO ARE ABOUT TO DIE
Strikeforce MORITURI

WE WHO ARE ABOUT TO DIE
Strikeforce MORITURI
Party's OVER

Strange Tales (86-188) 1813

Ref. No.	Date	RVI	Artist/Info.
1813-86	Jul. 1961	20	Kirby/Ayers-c/a, Ditko-a
1813-87	Aug.	20	Kirby/Ayers-c/a, Heck, Ditko-a
1813-88	Sept.	20	" " " "
1813-89	Oct.	20	Kirby/Ayers-c/a, Reinman, Ditko-a
1813-90	**Nov.**	**20**	" " " "
1813-91	Dec.	20	" " " "
1813-92	Jan. 1962	20	Kirby/Ayers-c/a, Ditko-a
1813-93	Feb.	16	Ditko-c/a, Kirby/Ayers-a
1813-94	Mar.	16	Kirby/Ayers-c/a, Ditko-a
1813-95	Apr.	16	Kirby/Ayers-c/a, Heck, Ditko-a
1813-96	May	16	Heck, Ditko-a
1813-97	Jun.	22	Kirby, Ayers-a, Heck, Ditko-a
1813-98	Jul.	16	Kirby, Ayers-a, Ayers, Heck, Ditko-a
1813-99	Aug.	16	Kirby, Ayers-c/a, Heck, Ditko-a
1813-100	**Sept.**	**16**	" " " "
1813-101	Oct.	235	Kirby/Ayers-c/a (Human Torch begins)
1813-102	Nov.	93	" "
1813-103	Dec.	65	" "
1813-104	Jan. 1963	65	" "
1813-105	Feb.	65	" "
1813-106	Mar.	40	Kirby/Roussos-c, Ayers-a
1813-107	Apr.	45	" " "
1813-108	May	40	Kirby/Ayers-c/a
1813-109	Jun.	40	" "
1813-110	**Jul.**	**170**	**Kirby/Ayers-c, Ayers-a (Intro Doctor Strange)**
1813-111	Aug.	35	" " "
1813-112	Sept.	25	Kirby/Roussos-c, Ayers-a
1813-113	Oct.	25	Ditko/Ayers-c, Ayers-a
1813-114	Nov.	50	Kirby/Ayers-c/a (Dr. Strange begins)
1813-115	Dec.	85	Ditko/Ayers-c, Ayers-a (Origin Dr. Strange)
1813-116	Jan. 1964	15	Kirby/Roussos-c, Ayers/Bell-a
1813-117	Feb.	15	Ditko-c, Ayers-a
1813-118	Mar.	15	Kirby/Roussos-c, Ayers-a
1813-119	Apr.	15	" " "
1813-120	**May**	**15**	**Kirby/Roussos-c, Kirby/Ayers-a**
1813-121	Jun.	10	Kirby/Ditko-c, Ayers-a
1813-122	Jul.	10	Kirby/Roussos-c, Ayers/Bell-a
1813-123	Aug.	10	Kirby/Roussos-c, Burgos/Ayers-a
1813-124	Sept.	10	Ayers/Reinman-c, Ayers/Reinman-a
1813-125	Oct.	10	Kirby/Roussos-c, Ayers/Reinman-a
1813-126	Nov.	10	Kirby/Stone-c, Ayers/Reinman-a
1813-127	Dec.	10	" " " "
1813-128	Jan. 1965	10	Kirby/Giacoia-c, Ayers/Ray-a
1813-129	Feb.	10	Kirby/Stone-c, Ayers/Ray-a
1813-130	**Mar.**	**12**	**Kirby/Stone-c, Powell/Stone-a**
1813-131	Apr.	9	Powell/Ayers-c, Powell/Ayers-a
1813-132	May	9	Kirby/Esposito-c, Powell/Demeo-a
1813-133	Jun.	9	Kirby/Powell-c, Powell/Demeo-a
1813-134	Jul.	9	Kirby/Giacoia-c, Powell/Wood-a
1813-135	Aug.	35	Kirby/Giacoia-c. Kirby/Ayers-a (Intro. and Origin-Nick Fury)
1813-136	Sept.	20	Kirby/J. Severin-c, Kirby/Severin-a
1813-137	Oct.	8	Ditko/J. Severin-c, Kirby/Severin-a
1813-138	Nov.	8	J. Severin-c/a, Kirby-a
1813-139	Dec.	8	M. Severin/Kirby-c, Kirby, Sinnott-a
1813-140	**Jan. 1966**	**8**	**Kirby/Sinnott-c, Kirby, Heck-a**
1813-141	Feb.	8	Kirby/Giacoia-c, Kirby/Ray-a
1813-142	Mar.	8	Kirby/Sinnott-c, Kirby/Demeo-a
1813-143	Apr.	8	Kirby/Giacoia-c, Kirby, Purcell-a
1813-144	May	8	Kirby/Esposito-c, Kirby, Purcell-a
1813-145	Jun.	8	Kirby/Esposito-c, Kirby, Heck-a
1813-146	Jul.	8	Ditko-c, Kirby, Heck-a
1813-147	Aug.	8	Kirby/Giacoia-c, Kirby, Heck-a
1813-148	Sept.	9	Everett-c, Kirby/Heck-a
1813-149	Oct.	8	Kirby/Esposito-c, Kirby/Whitney-a
1813-150	**Nov.**	**8**	**Everett-c, Kirby, Buscema-a**
1813-151	Dec.	12	Kirby/Steranko-c/a (1st Marvel work for Steranko)
1813-152	Jan. 1967	8	Everett-c, Kirby, Steranko-a
1813-153	Feb.	8	Steranko-c/a, Kirby-a
1813-154	Mar.	8	M. Severin-c, Steranko-a
1813-155	Apr.	8	Steranko-c/a
1813-156	May	8	M. Severin-c, Steranko-a
1813-157	Jun.	8	Steranko-c/a
1813-158	Jul.	8	M. Severin/Everett-c, Steranko-a
1813-159	Aug.	9	Steranko-c/a
1813-160	**Sept.**	**8**	**Adkins-c, Steranko-a**
1813-161	Oct.	8	Steranko-c/a
1813-162	Nov.	8	Adkins-c, Steranko/Giacoia-a
1813-163	Dec.	8	Steranko-c/a, Giacoia-a
1813-164	Jan. 1968	8	Adkins-c/a
1813-165	Feb.	8	Steranko-c/a, Giacoia-a
1813-166	Mar.	8	Adkins-c/a, Tuska-a
1813-167	Apr.	11	Steranko-c/a, Sinnott-a
1813-168	May	8	Adkins-c/a (Last Nick Fury)
1813-169	Sept. 1973	1	Romita-c, Colan/Adkins-a
1813-170	**Oct.**	**1**	**Kane/Giordano-c, Colan/Adkins-a**
1813-171	Dec.	1	Kane/Giacoia-c/a
1813-172	Feb. 1974	1	Kane/Giacoia, Romita-c, Colan/Giordano-a
1813-173	Apr.	1	Buckler/Chan-c, Colan/Giordano-a
1813-174	Jun.	1	Kane/Giordano-c, Buscema/Mooney-a
1813-175	Aug.	1	Kirby/Ayers-c (Reprints)
1813-176	Oct.	1	Romita/Giacoia-c, DeZuniga-a
1813-177	Dec.	1	Brunner/Wein-c, DeZuniga/Austin-a
1813-178	Feb. 1975	5	Starlin-c/a (Origin-Adam Warlock)
1813-179	Apr.	4	"
1813-180	**Jun.**	**3**	**Starlin-c/a, Weiss-a**
1813-181	Aug.	3	Starlin/Weiss-c, Starlin/Milgrom-a
1813-182	Nov.	1	Kane-c (Reprints)
1813-183	Jan. 1976	1	(Reprints)
1813-184	Mar.	1	Hannigan/Adkins-c (Reprints)
1813-185	May	1	Hannigan/Janson/Romita-c (Reprints)
1813-186	Jul.	1	Hannigan/Giacoia-c (Reprints)
1813-187	Sept.	1	" " (Reprints)
1813-188	Nov.	1	Colan/Palmer-c (Reprints)
1813-A1	1962	95	Kirby, Forte, Reinman, Ditko, Heck-a
1813-A2	1963	120	Kirby/Ditko-c, Ditko/Kirby-a

Strange Tales V.2 (1-19) 1813.5

1813.5-1	Apr. 1987	1	Carlbret/Blevins-c, Blevins-a
1813.5-2	May	1	Blevins-a
1813.5-3	Jun.	1	Blevins/Williamson-a
1813.5-4	Jul.	1	Nolan-c, Blevins-a
1813.5-5	Aug.	1	" "
1813.5-6	Sept.	1	
1813.5-7	Oct.	1	
1813.5-8	Nov.	1	
1813.5-9	Dec.	1	
1813.5-10	**Jan. 1988**	**1**	**Austin-c**
1813.5-11	Feb.	1	
1813.5-12	Mar.	1	Austin-a
1813.5-13	Apr.	1	"
1813.5-14	May	1	(Punisher -app.)
1813.5-15	Jun.	1	
1813.5-16	Jul.	1	
1813.5-17	Aug.	1	
1813.5-18	Sept.	1	(X-Factor -app.)
1813.5-19	Oct. 1988	1	

Strawberry Shortcake (1-7) 1818.2

1818.2-1	Jun. 1985	1	Post-a
1818.2-2		1	"
1818.2-3		1	"
1818.2-4 to 7	Apr. 1986, (#7)	1	" (all)

Strikeforce: Morituri (1-31) 1819.3

1819.3-1	Dec. 1986	2	Anderson/Williams-a
1819.3-2	Jan. 1987	1	" "
1819.3-3	Feb.	1	" "
1819.3-4	Mar.	1	" "
1819.3-5	Apr.	1	
1819.3-6	May	1	
1819.3-7	Jun.	1	
1819.3-8	Jul.	1	
1819.3-9	Aug.	1	
1819.3-10	**Sept.**	**1**	
1819.3-11	Oct.	1	
1819.3-12	Nov.	1	
1819.3-13 to 31	Jul. 1989, (#31)	1	(#13, Double-sized)

1821.7 The Sub-Mariner (1-16)

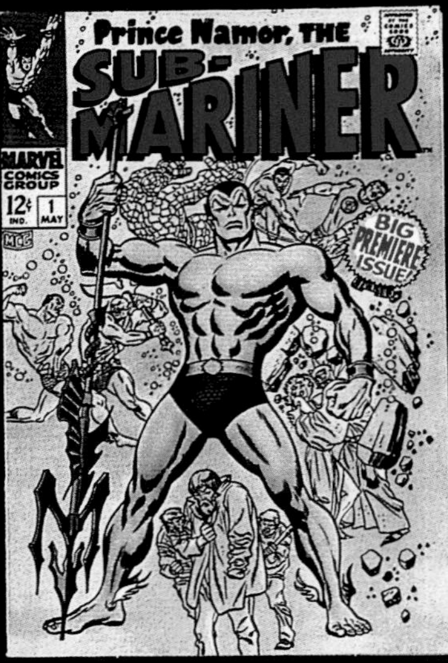
Prince Namor, THE
SUB-MARINER
MARVEL COMICS GROUP
12¢ 1 MAY
BIG PREMIERE ISSUE

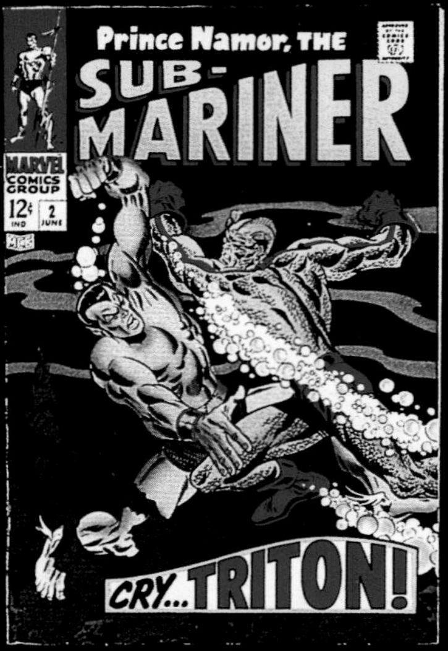
Prince Namor, THE
SUB-MARINER
MARVEL COMICS GROUP
12¢ 2 JUNE
CRY...TRITON!

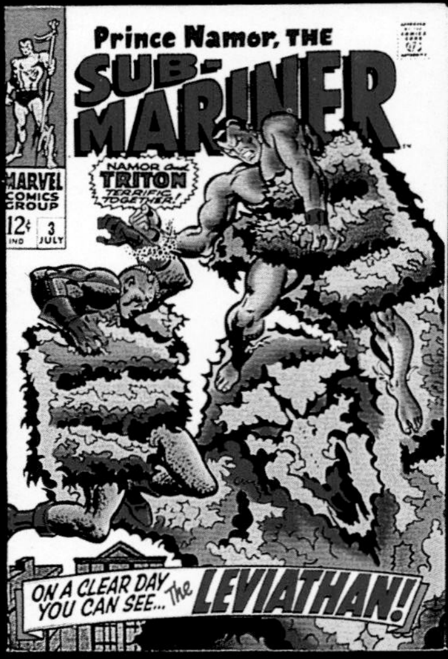
Prince Namor, THE
SUB-MARINER
MARVEL COMICS GROUP
12¢ 3 JULY
ON A CLEAR DAY YOU CAN SEE... THE LEVIATHAN!

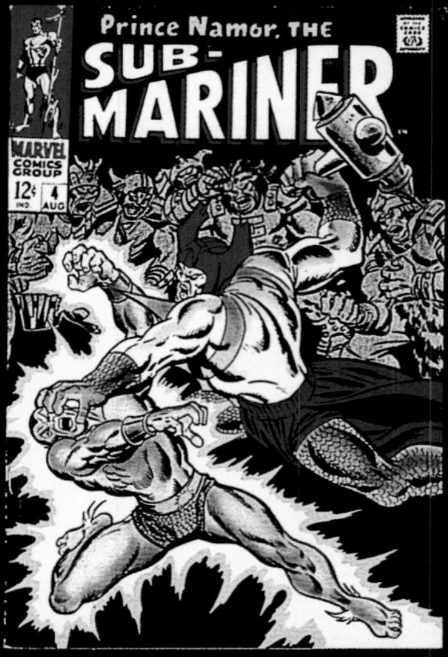
Prince Namor, THE
SUB-MARINER
MARVEL COMICS GROUP
12¢ 4 AUG

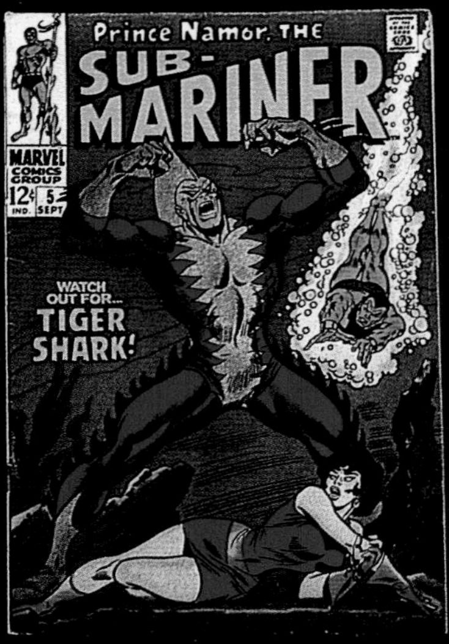
Prince Namor, THE
SUB-MARINER
MARVEL COMICS GROUP
12¢ 5 SEPT
WATCH OUT FOR... TIGER SHARK!

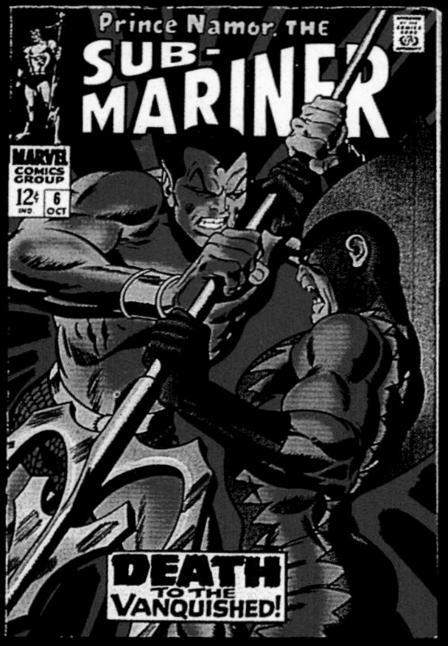
Prince Namor, THE
SUB-MARINER
MARVEL COMICS GROUP
12¢ 6 OCT
DEATH TO THE VANQUISHED!

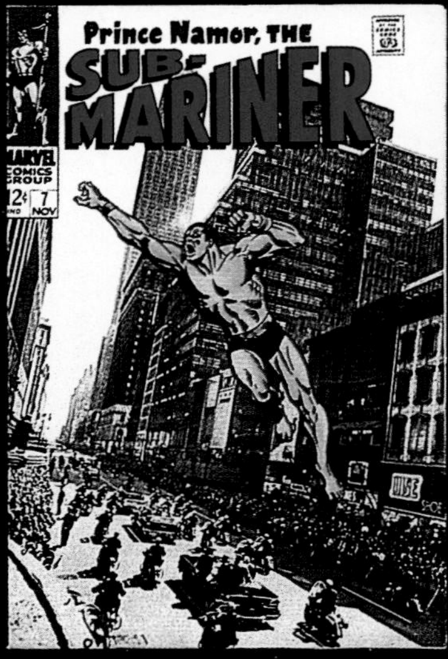
Prince Namor, THE
SUB-MARINER
MARVEL COMICS GROUP
12¢ 7 NOV

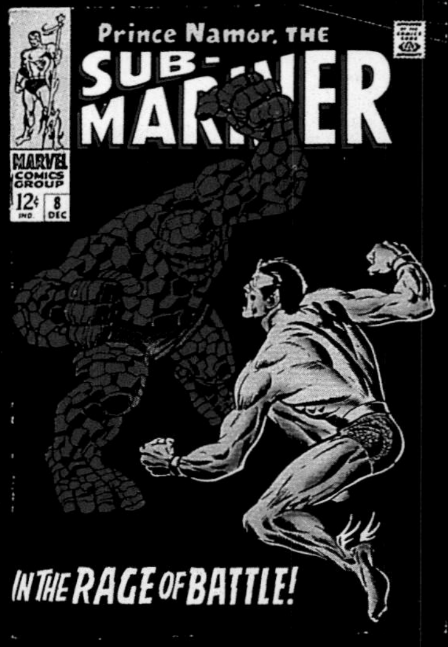
Prince Namor, THE
SUB-MARINER
MARVEL COMICS GROUP
12¢ 8 DEC
IN THE RAGE OF BATTLE!

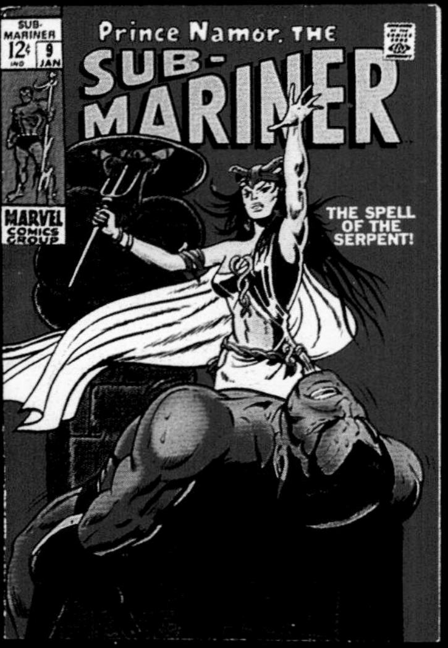
SUB-MARINER 12¢ 9 JAN
Prince Namor, THE
SUB-MARINER
MARVEL COMICS GROUP
THE SPELL OF THE SERPENT!

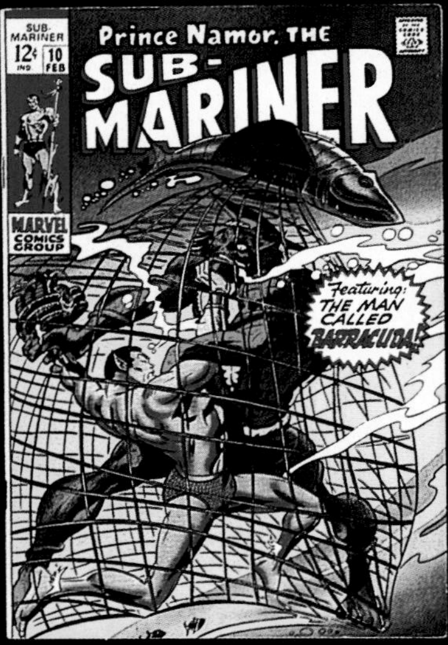
SUB-MARINER 12¢ 10 FEB
Prince Namor, THE
SUB-MARINER
MARVEL COMICS GROUP
featuring: THE MAN CALLED BARRACUDA!

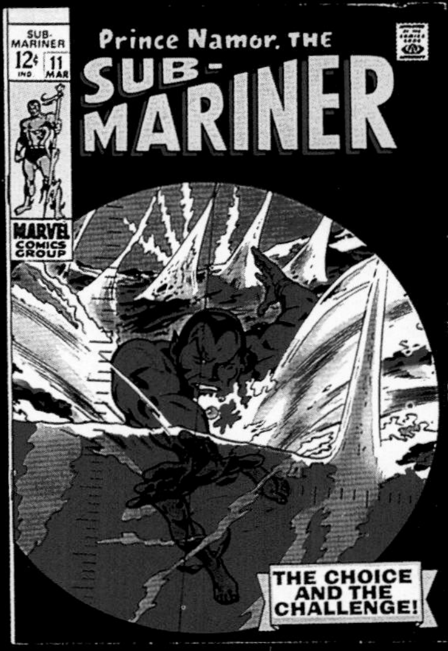
SUB-MARINER 12¢ 11 MAR
Prince Namor, THE
SUB-MARINER
MARVEL COMICS GROUP
THE CHOICE AND THE CHALLENGE!

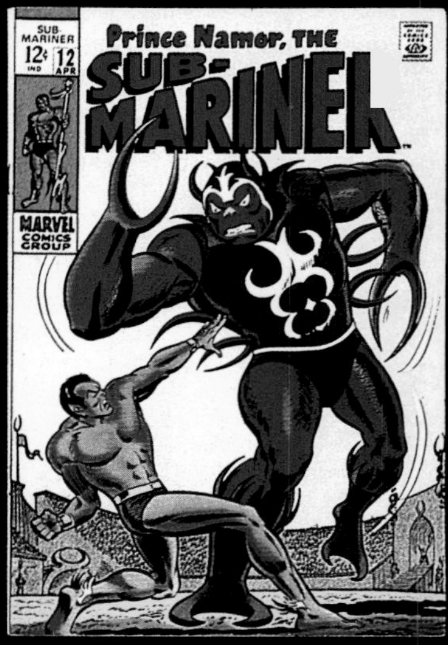
SUB-MARINER 12¢ 12 APR
Prince Namor, THE
SUB-MARINER
MARVEL COMICS GROUP

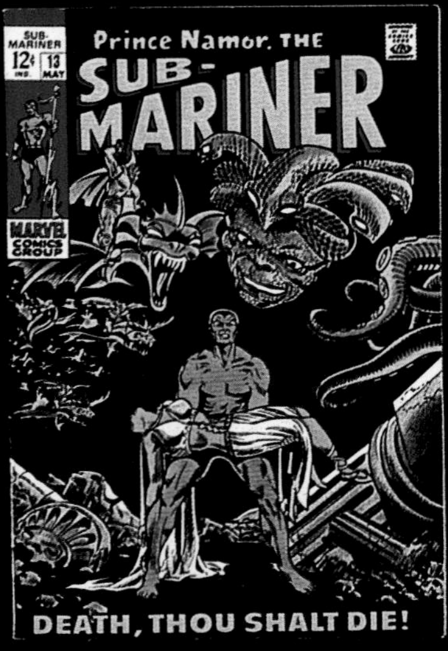
SUB-MARINER 12¢ 13 MAY
Prince Namor, THE
SUB-MARINER
MARVEL COMICS GROUP
DEATH, THOU SHALT DIE!

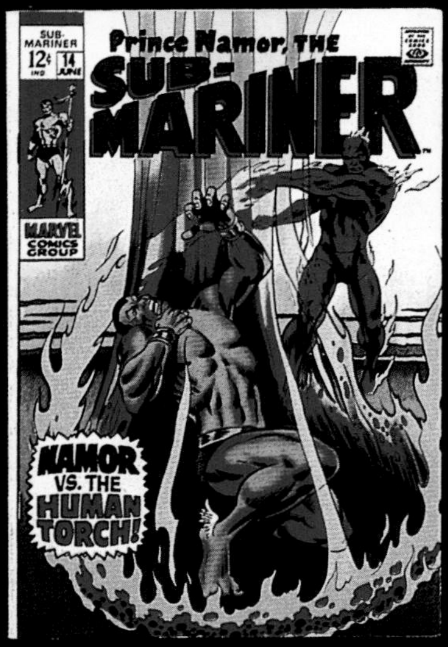
SUB-MARINER 12¢ 14 JUNE
Prince Namor, THE
SUB-MARINER
MARVEL COMICS GROUP
NAMOR VS. THE HUMAN TORCH!

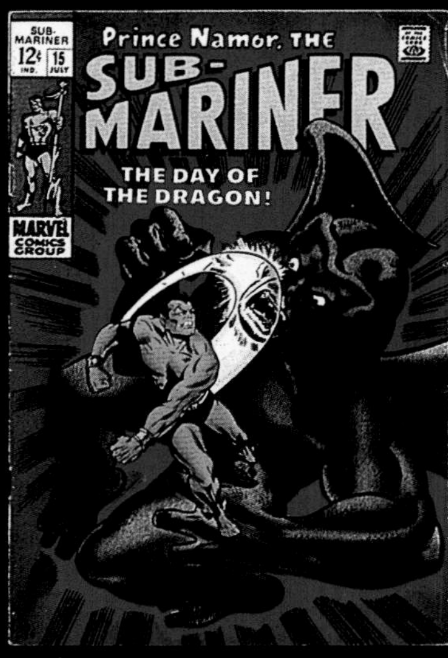
SUB-MARINER 12¢ 15 JULY
Prince Namor, THE
SUB-MARINER
THE DAY OF THE DRAGON!
MARVEL COMICS GROUP

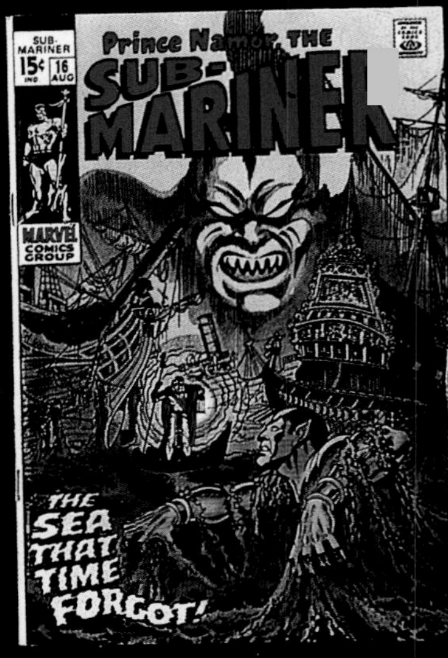
SUB-MARINER 15¢ 16 AUG
Prince Namor, THE
SUB-MARINER
MARVEL COMICS GROUP
THE SEA THAT TIME FORGOT!

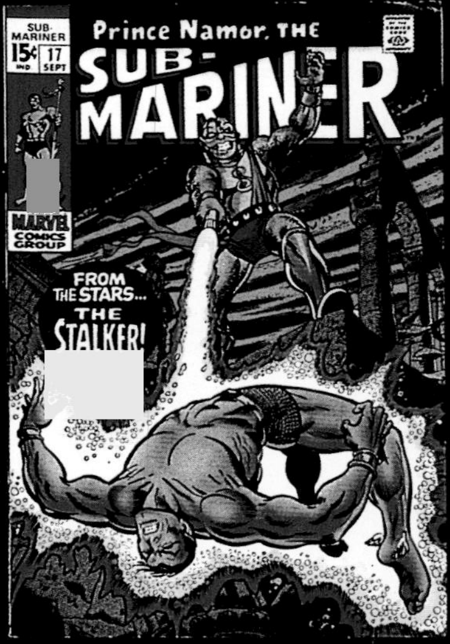
Prince Namor, THE
SUB-MARINER
15¢ 17 SEPT
MARVEL COMICS GROUP
FROM THE STARS... THE STALKER!

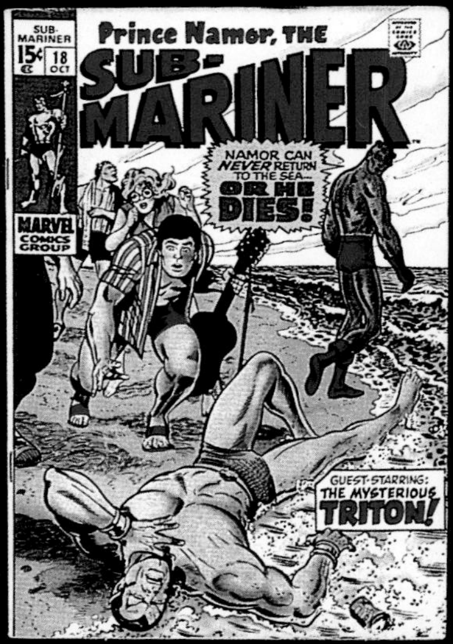
Prince Namor, THE
SUB-MARINER
15¢ 18 OCT
MARVEL COMICS GROUP
NAMOR CAN NEVER RETURN TO THE SEA -- OR HE DIES!
GUEST-STARRING: THE MYSTERIOUS TRITON!

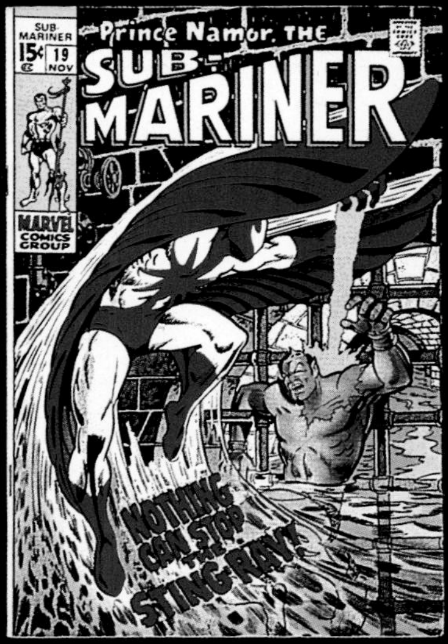
Prince Namor, THE
SUB-MARINER
15¢ 19 NOV
MARVEL COMICS GROUP
NOTHING CAN STOP STING-RAY!

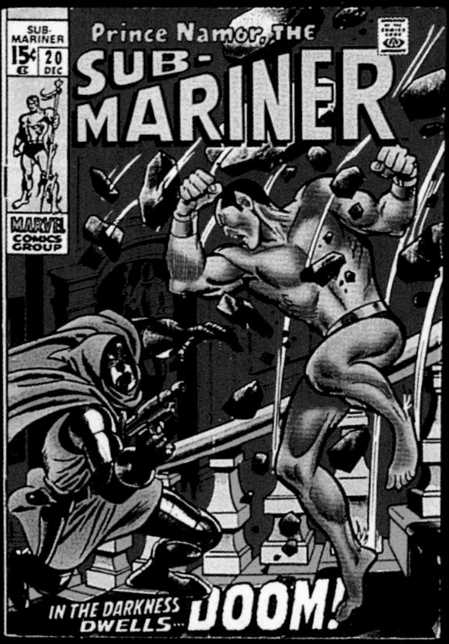
Prince Namor, THE
SUB-MARINER
15¢ 20 DEC
MARVEL COMICS GROUP
IN THE DARKNESS DWELLS... DOOM!

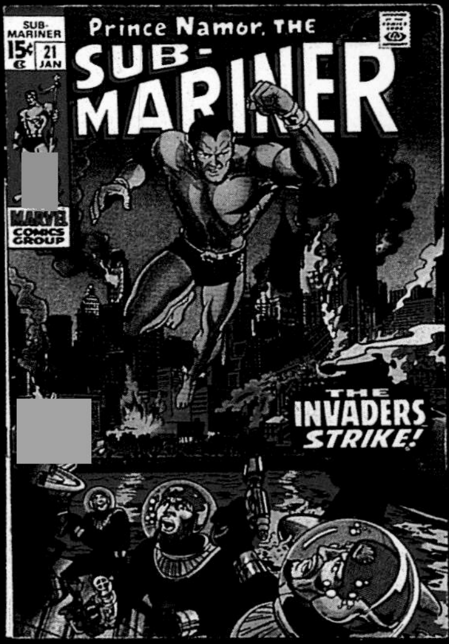
Prince Namor, THE
SUB-MARINER
15¢ 21 JAN
MARVEL COMICS GROUP
THE INVADERS STRIKE!

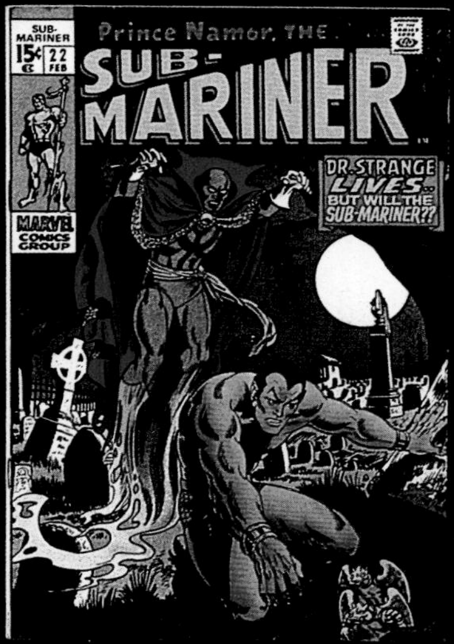
Prince Namor, THE
SUB-MARINER
15¢ 22 FEB
MARVEL COMICS GROUP
DR. STRANGE LIVES-- BUT WILL THE SUB-MARINER??

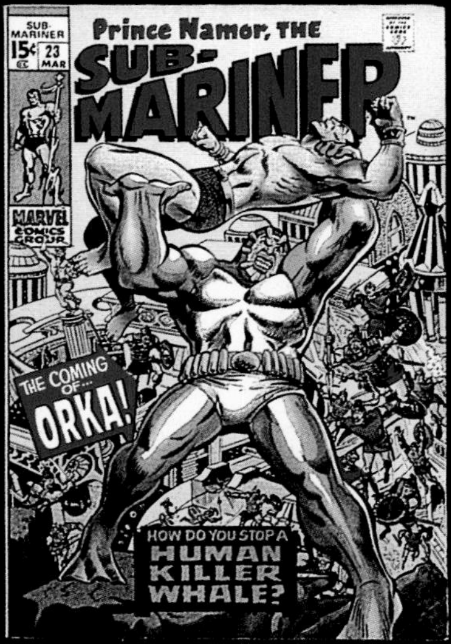
Prince Namor, THE
SUB-MARINER
15¢ 23 MAR
MARVEL COMICS GROUP
THE COMING OF... ORKA!
HOW DO YOU STOP A HUMAN KILLER WHALE?

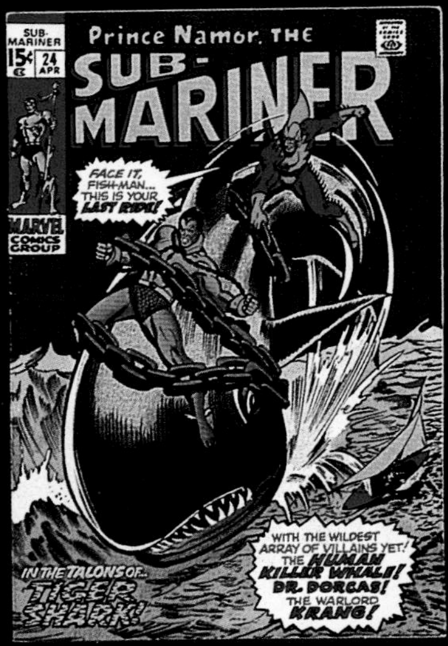
Prince Namor, THE
SUB-MARINER
15¢ 24 APR
MARVEL COMICS GROUP
FACE IT, FISH-MAN... THIS IS YOUR LAST RIDE!
WITH THE WILDEST ARRAY OF VILLAINS YET! THE HUMAN KILLER WHALE!! DR. DORCAS! THE WARLORD KRANG!
IN THE TALONS OF... TIGER SHARK!

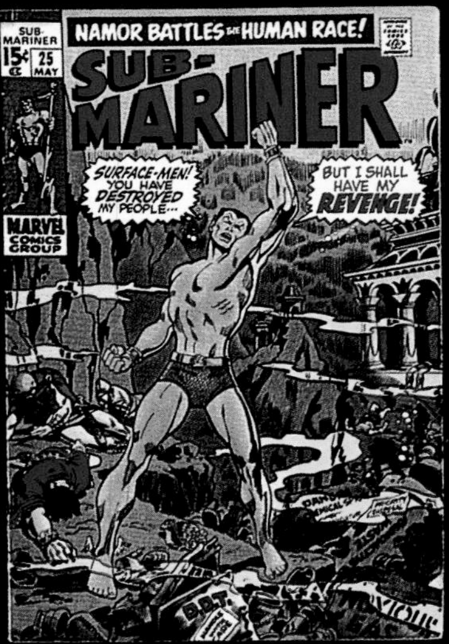
NAMOR BATTLES the HUMAN RACE!
SUB-MARINER
15¢ 25 MAY
MARVEL COMICS GROUP
SURFACE-MEN! YOU HAVE DESTROYED MY PEOPLE...
BUT I SHALL HAVE MY REVENGE!

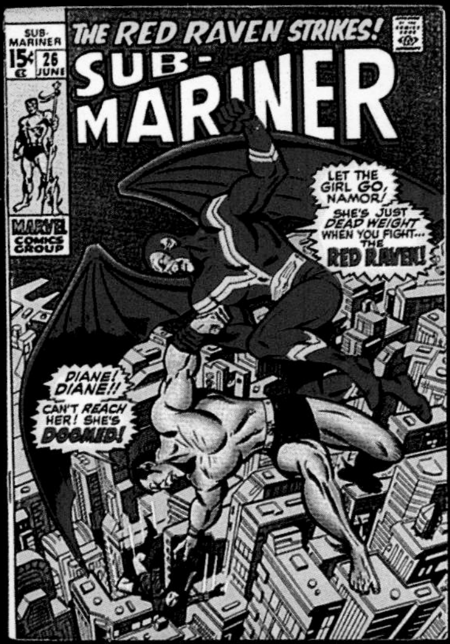
THE RED RAVEN STRIKES!
SUB-MARINER
15¢ 26 JUNE
MARVEL COMICS GROUP
LET THE GIRL GO, NAMOR! SHE'S JUST DEAD WEIGHT WHEN YOU FIGHT-- THE RED RAVEN!
DIANE! DIANE!! CAN'T REACH HER! SHE'S DOOMED!

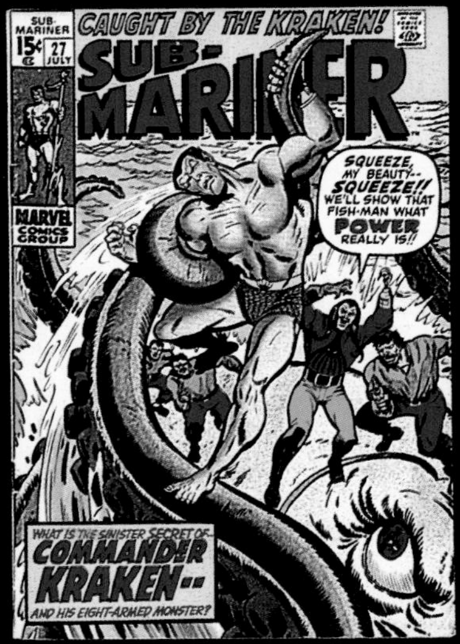
CAUGHT BY THE KRAKEN!
SUB-MARINER
15¢ 27 JULY
MARVEL COMICS GROUP
SQUEEZE, MY BEAUTY-- SQUEEZE!! WE'LL SHOW THAT FISH-MAN WHAT POWER REALLY IS!!
WHAT IS THE SINISTER SECRET OF COMMANDER KRAKEN--
AND HIS EIGHT-ARMED MONSTER?

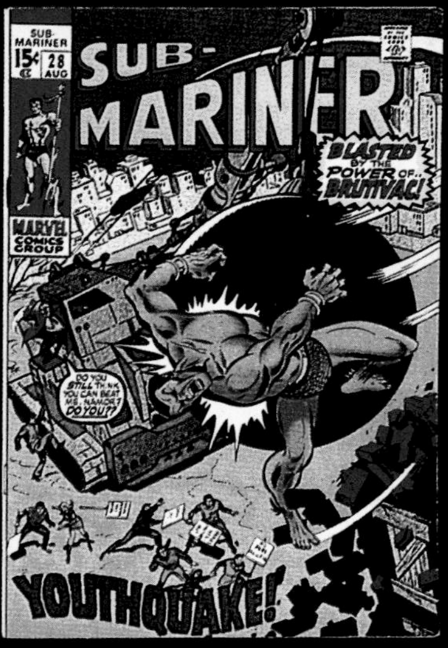
SUB-MARINER
15¢ 28 AUG
MARVEL COMICS GROUP
BLASTED BY THE POWER OF... BRUTIVAC!
DO YOU STILL THINK YOU CAN BEAT US, NAMOR? DO YOU?
YOUTHQUAKE!

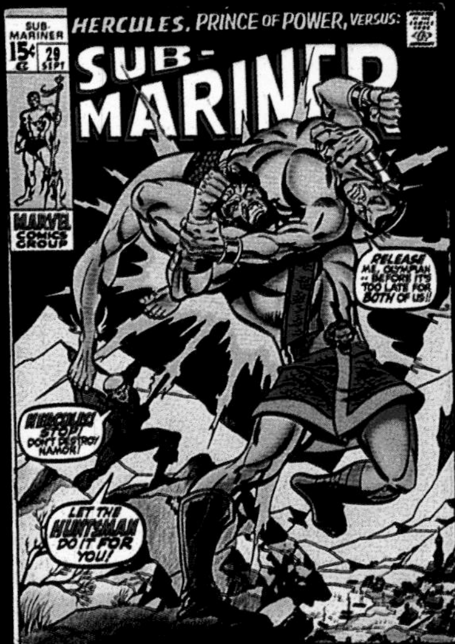
HERCULES, PRINCE OF POWER, VERSUS:
SUB-MARINER
15¢ 29 SEPT
MARVEL COMICS GROUP
RELEASE ME, OLYMPIAN BLOWHARD! TOO LATE FOR BOTH OF US!
LET THE HUMAN DO IT FOR YOU!

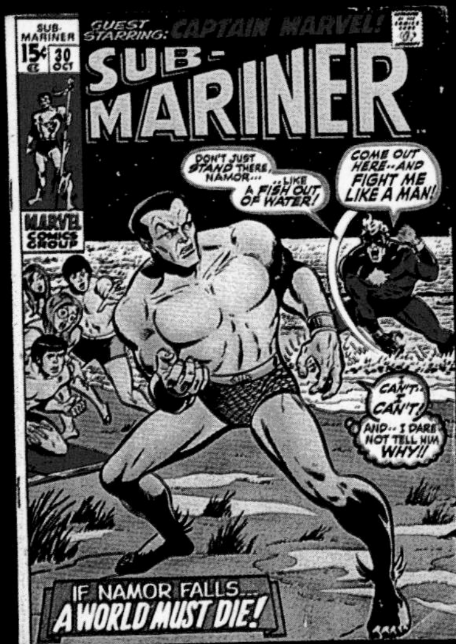
GUEST STARRING: CAPTAIN MARVEL!
SUB-MARINER
15¢ 30
MARVEL COMICS GROUP
DON'T JUST STAND THERE, NAMOR-- ...LIKE A FISH OUT OF WATER!
COME OUT HERE-- AND FIGHT ME LIKE A MAN!
CAN'T... CAN'T! AND-- I DARE NOT TELL HIM WHY!!
IF NAMOR FALLS... A WORLD MUST DIE!

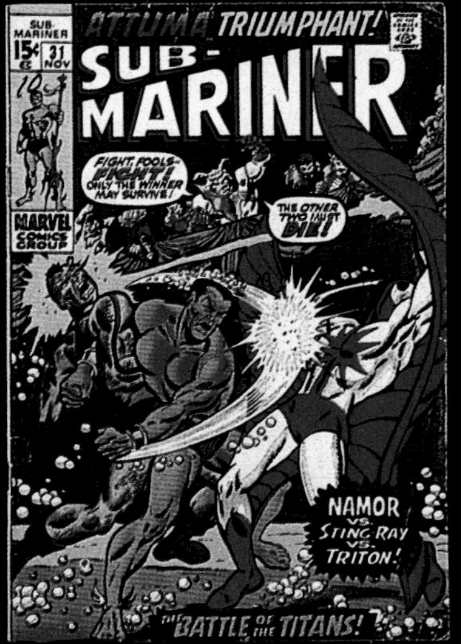
ATTUMA TRIUMPHANT!
SUB-MARINER
15¢ 31
MARVEL COMICS GROUP
FIGHT, FOOLS-- ONLY THE WINNER MAY SURVIVE!
THE OTHER TWO MUST DIE!
NAMOR vs. STING RAY vs. TRITON!
THE BATTLE OF THE TITANS!

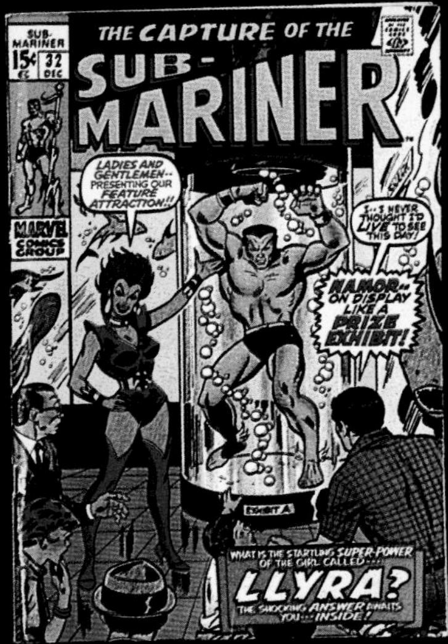
THE CAPTURE OF THE
SUB-MARINER
15¢ 32
MARVEL COMICS GROUP
LADIES AND GENTLEMEN-- PRESENTING OUR FEATURE ATTRACTION!!
WHAT IS THE STARTLING SUPER-POWER OF THE GIRL CALLED... LLYRA?
THE SHOCKING ANSWER WAITS YOU... INSIDE!

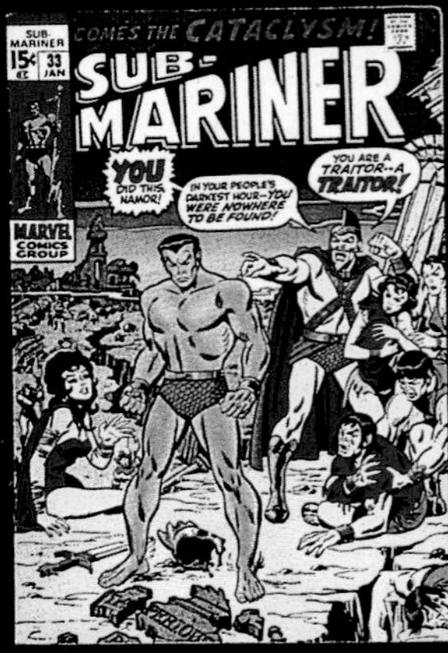
COMES THE CATACLYSM!
SUB-MARINER
YOU ARE A TRAITOR-- A TRAITOR!
MARVEL COMICS GROUP

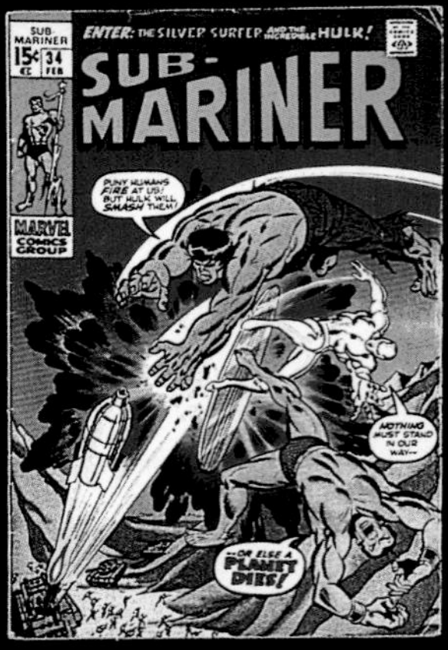
ENTER: THE SILVER SURFER AND THE INCREDIBLE HULK!
SUB-MARINER
MARVEL COMICS GROUP
NOTHING MUST STAND IN OUR WAY!
...OR ELSE A PLANET DIES!

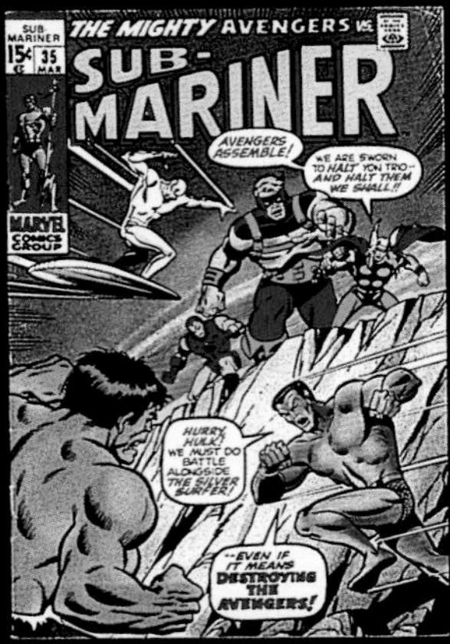
THE MIGHTY AVENGERS vs
SUB-MARINER
AVENGERS ASSEMBLE!
MARVEL COMICS GROUP
...EVEN IF IT MEANS DESTROYING THE AVENGERS!

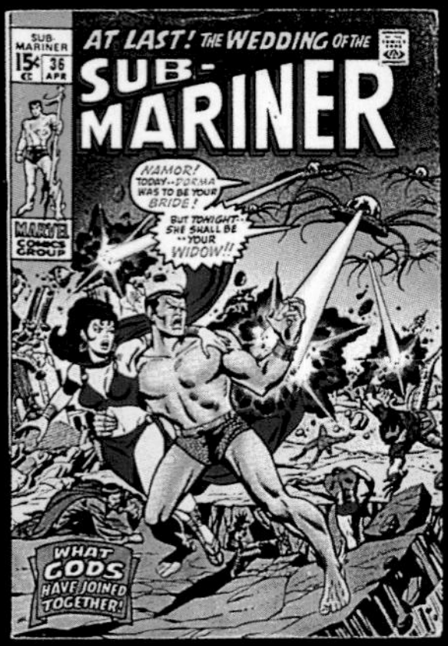
AT LAST! THE WEDDING OF THE
SUB-MARINER
MARVEL COMICS GROUP
WHAT GODS HAVE JOINED TOGETHER

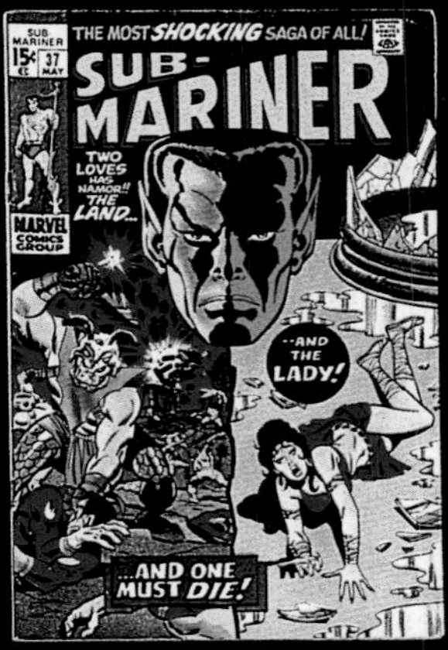
THE MOST SHOCKING SAGA OF ALL!
SUB-MARINER
TWO LOVES HAS NAMOR! THE LAND...
MARVEL COMICS GROUP
--AND THE LADY!
...AND ONE MUST DIE!

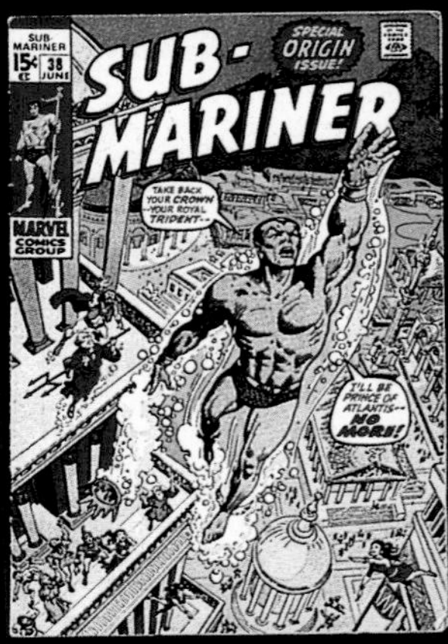
SPECIAL ORIGIN ISSUE!
SUB-MARINER
MARVEL COMICS GROUP
NO MORE!

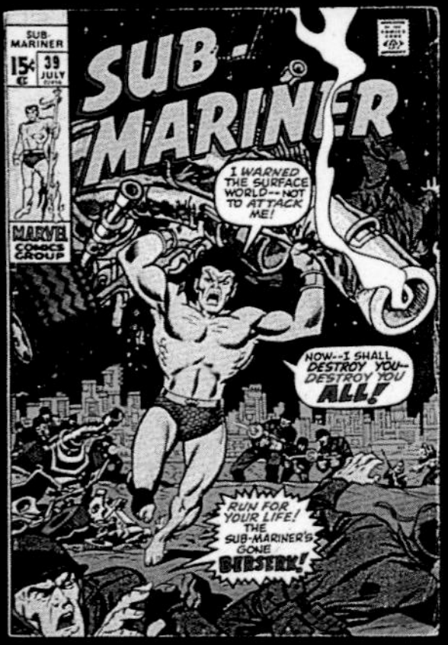
SUB-MARINER
I WARNED THE SURFACE WORLD--NOT TO ATTACK ME!
MARVEL COMICS GROUP
ALL!
BERSERK!

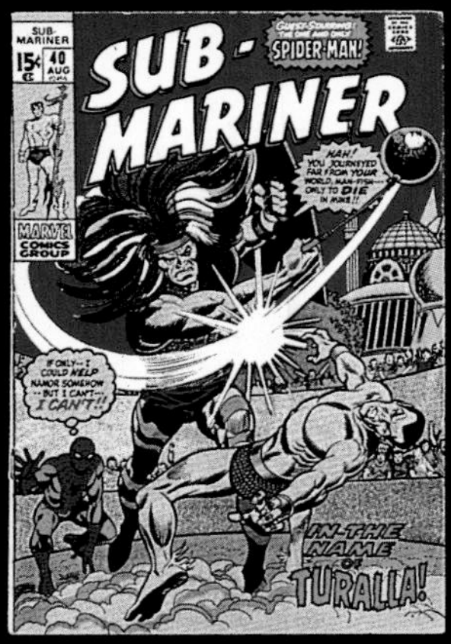
SPIDER-MAN!
SUB-MARINER
MARVEL COMICS GROUP
I CAN'T!
TURALLA!

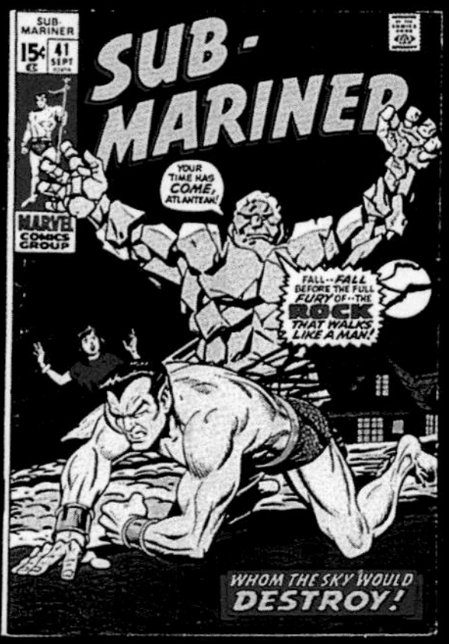
SUB-MARINER
YOUR TIME HAS COME, ATLANTEAN!
MARVEL COMICS GROUP
ROCK
WHOM THE SKY WOULD DESTROY!

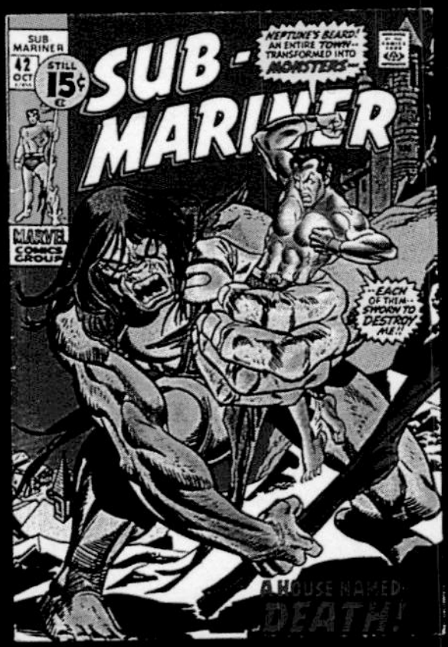
MONSTERS!
SUB-MARINER
DEATH!

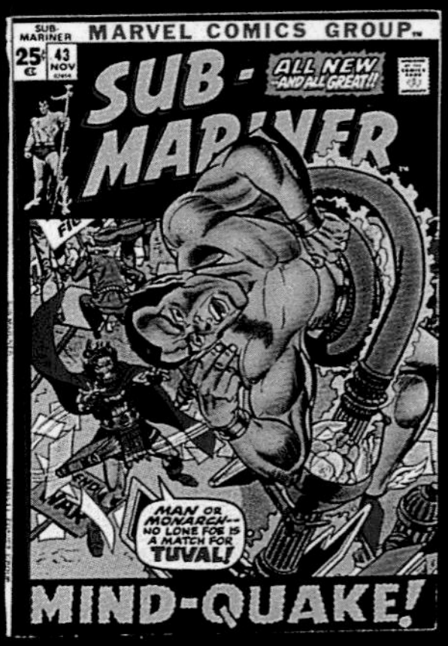
MARVEL COMICS GROUP
ALL NEW AND ALL GREAT!!
SUB-MARINER
TUVAL!
MIND-QUAKE!

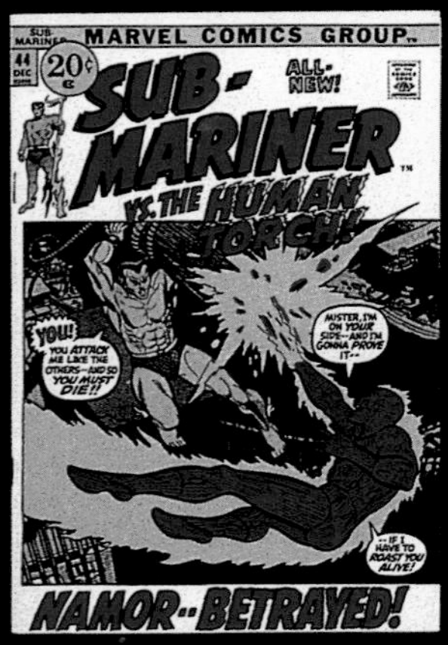
MARVEL COMICS GROUP
ALL-NEW!
SUB-MARINER
VS. THE HUMAN TORCH!
YOU!
NAMOR--BETRAYED!

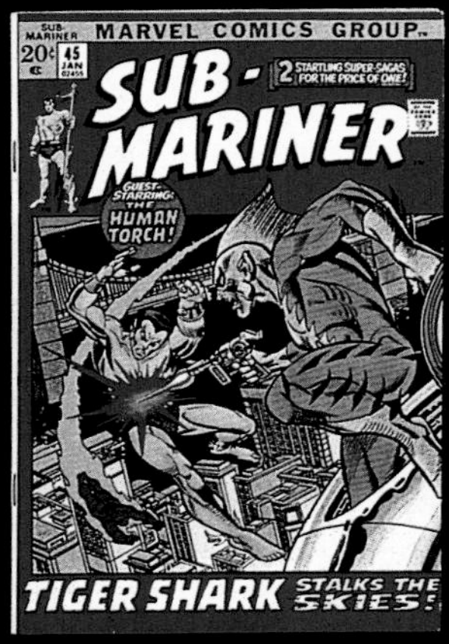
MARVEL COMICS GROUP
2 STARTLING SUPER SAGAS FOR THE PRICE OF ONE!
SUB-MARINER
GUEST-STARRING: THE HUMAN TORCH!
TIGER SHARK STALKS THE SKIES!

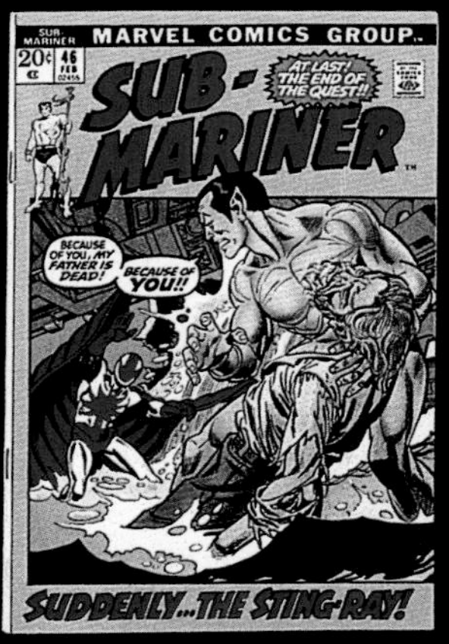
MARVEL COMICS GROUP
AT LAST! THE END OF THE QUEST!
SUB-MARINER
BECAUSE OF YOU!!
SUDDENLY...THE STING-RAY!

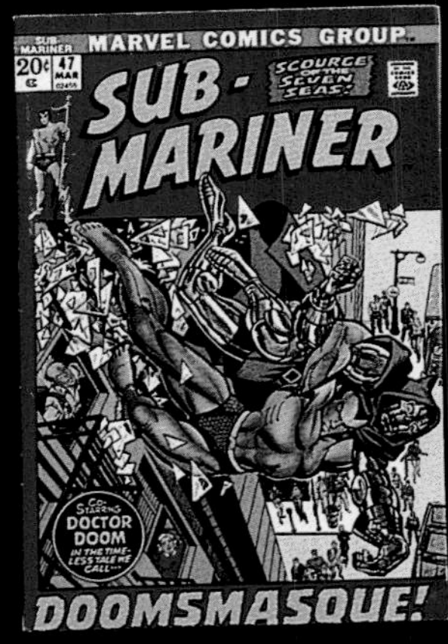
MARVEL COMICS GROUP
SCOURGE OF THE SEVEN SEAS
SUB-MARINER
DOCTOR DOOM
DOOMSMASQUE!

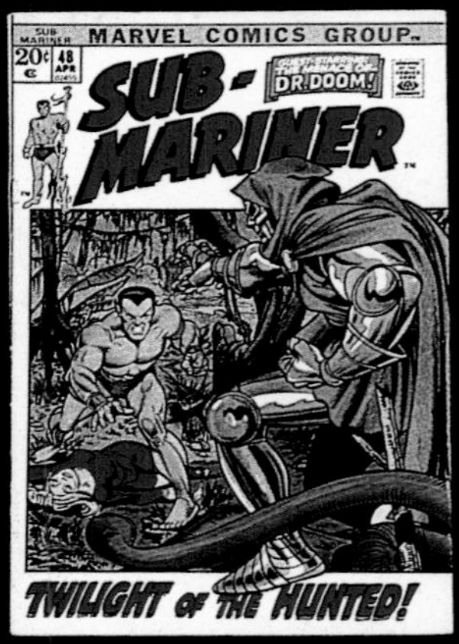
MARVEL COMICS GROUP
DR. DOOM!
SUB-MARINER
TWILIGHT OF THE HUNTED!

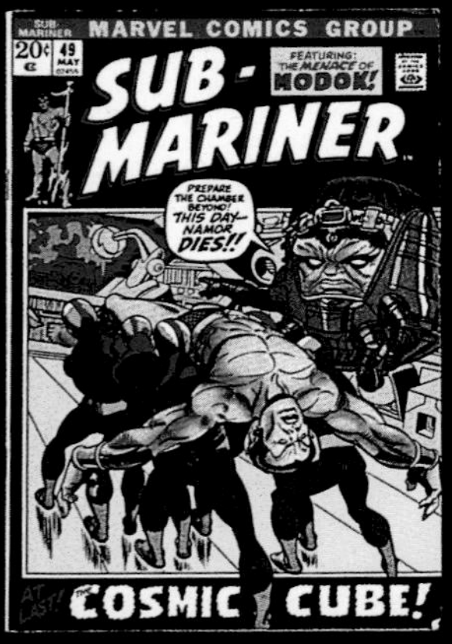
MARVEL COMICS GROUP
FEATURING: THE MENACE OF MODOK!
SUB-MARINER
THIS DAY-- NAMOR DIES!!
COSMIC CUBE!

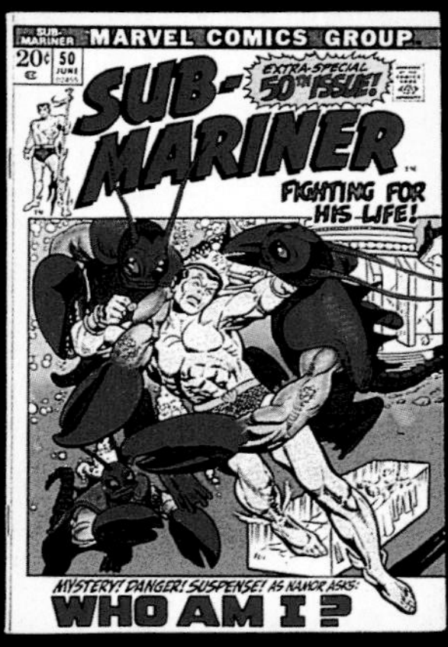
MARVEL COMICS GROUP
EXTRA-SPECIAL 50TH ISSUE!
SUB-MARINER
FIGHTING FOR HIS LIFE!
MYSTERY! DANGER! SUSPENSE! AS NAMOR ASKS:
WHO AM I?

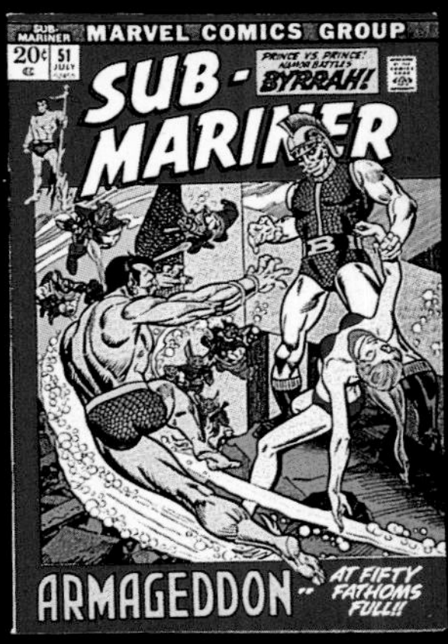
MARVEL COMICS GROUP
PRINCE VS PRINCE!
BYRRAH!
SUB-MARINER
ARMAGEDDON-- AT FIFTY FATHOMS FULL!!

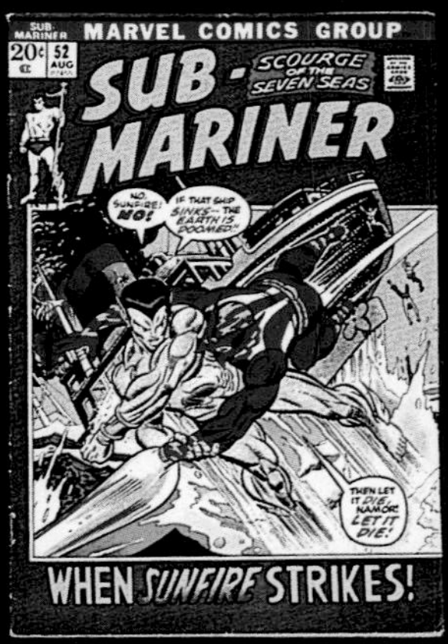
MARVEL COMICS GROUP
SCOURGE OF THE SEVEN SEAS
SUB-MARINER
NO!
WHEN SUNFIRE STRIKES!

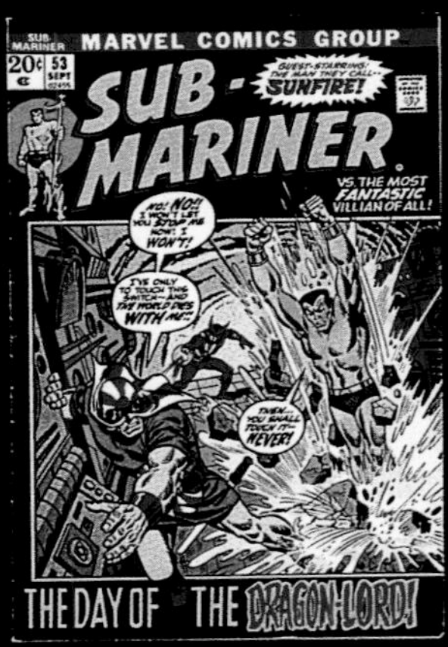
MARVEL COMICS GROUP
SUNFIRE!
SUB-MARINER
VS THE MOST FANTASTIC VILLIAN OF ALL!
NEVER!
THE DAY OF THE DRAGON-LORD!

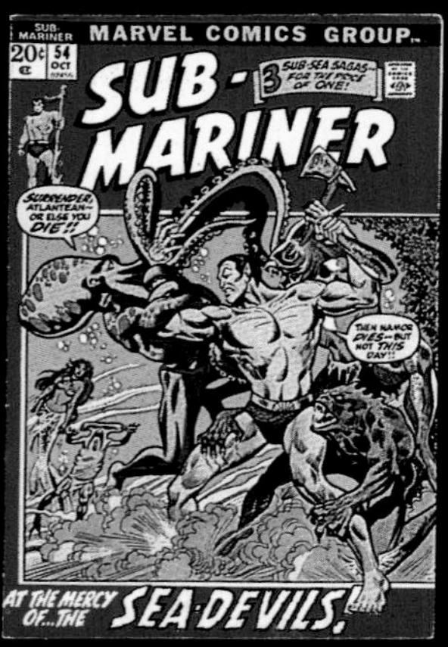
MARVEL COMICS GROUP
SUB-MARINER
DIE!
AT THE MERCY OF... THE SEA-DEVILS!

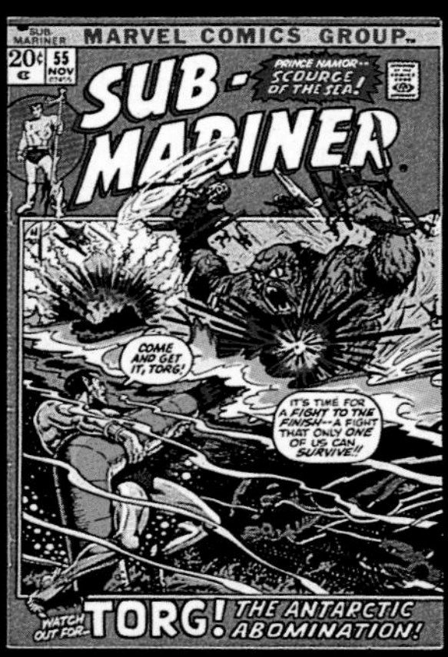
MARVEL COMICS GROUP
PRINCE NAMOR-- SCOURGE OF THE SEA!
SUB-MARINER
COME AND GET IT, TORG!
WATCH OUT FOR... TORG! THE ANTARCTIC ABOMINATION!

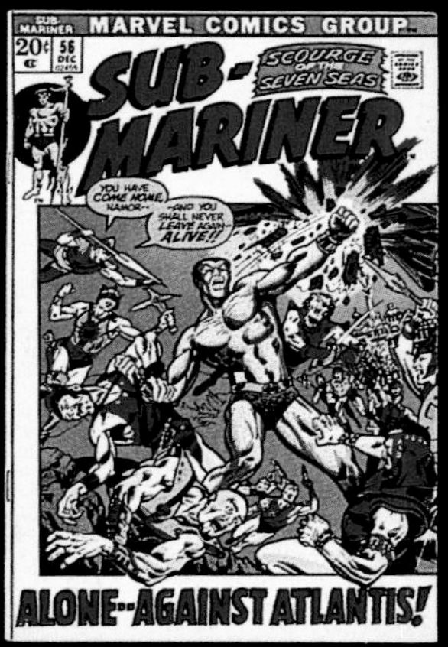
MARVEL COMICS GROUP
SCOURGE OF THE SEVEN SEAS
SUB-MARINER
ALIVE!
ALONE--AGAINST ATLANTIS!

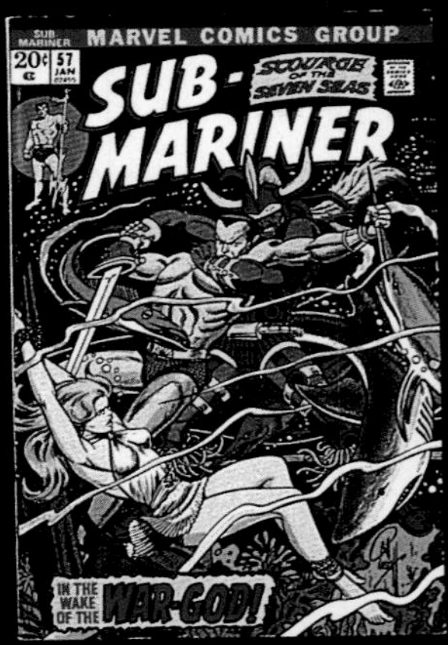
MARVEL COMICS GROUP
SCOURGE OF THE SEVEN SEAS
SUB-MARINER
IN THE WAKE OF THE WAR-GOD!

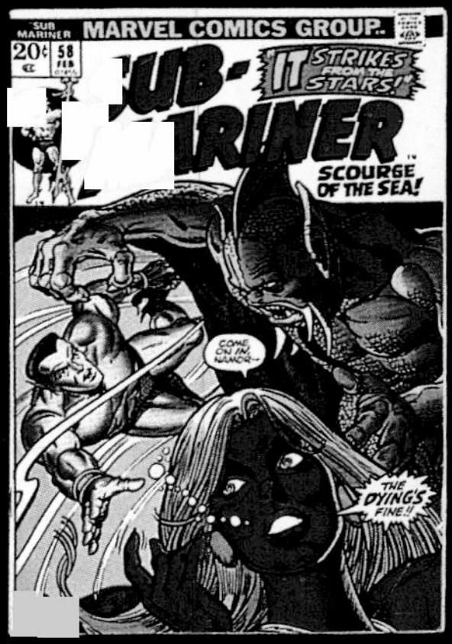
MARVEL COMICS GROUP
SUB-MARINER
IT STRIKES FROM THE STARS!
SCOURGE OF THE SEA!

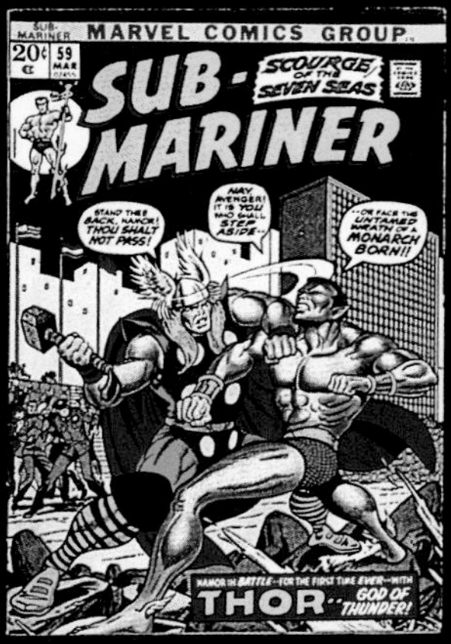
MARVEL COMICS GROUP
SUB-MARINER
SCOURGE OF THE SEVEN SEAS
THOR
GOD OF THUNDER!

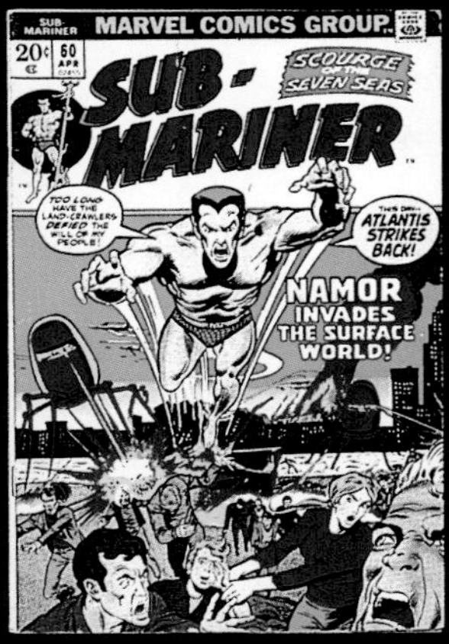
MARVEL COMICS GROUP
SUB-MARINER
SCOURGE OF THE SEVEN SEAS
ATLANTIS STRIKES BACK!
NAMOR INVADES THE SURFACE WORLD!

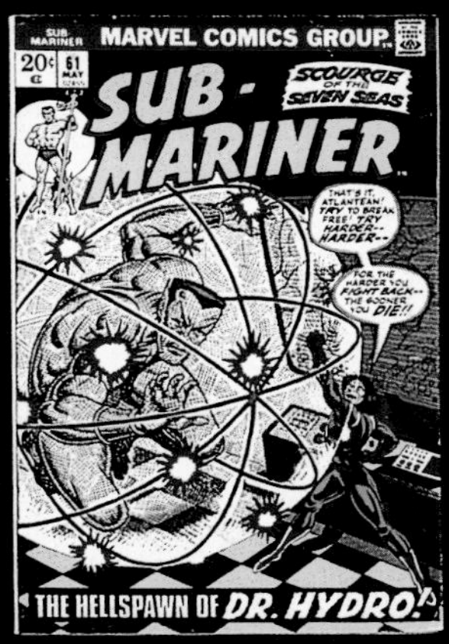
MARVEL COMICS GROUP
SUB-MARINER
SCOURGE OF THE SEVEN SEAS
THE HELLSPAWN OF DR. HYDRO!

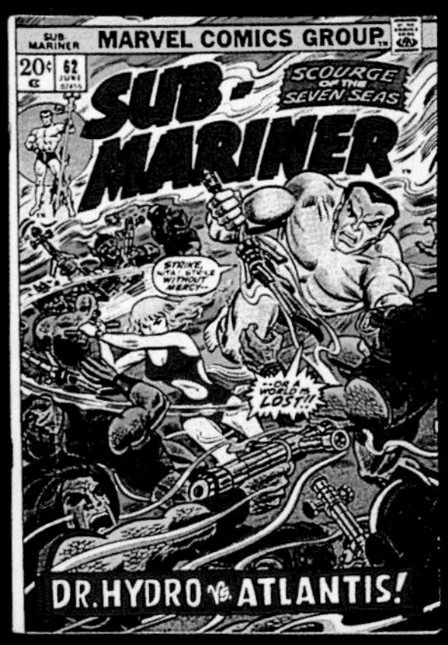
MARVEL COMICS GROUP
SUB-MARINER
SCOURGE OF THE SEVEN SEAS
DR. HYDRO vs ATLANTIS!

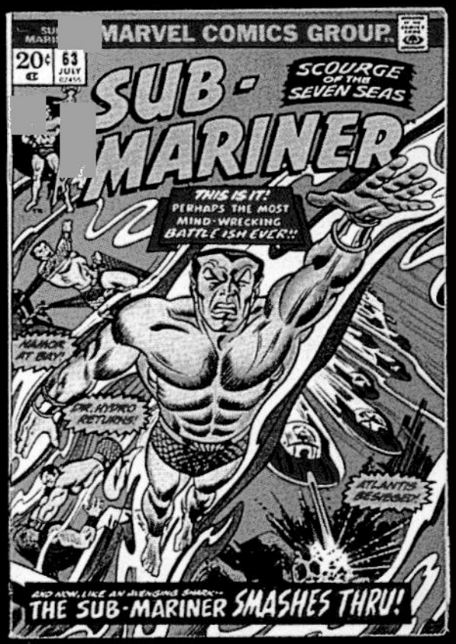
MARVEL COMICS GROUP
SUB-MARINER
SCOURGE OF THE SEVEN SEAS
THE SUB-MARINER SMASHES THRU!

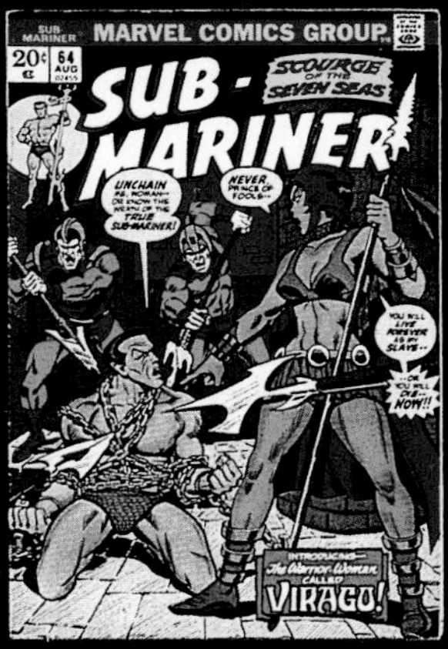
MARVEL COMICS GROUP
SUB-MARINER
SCOURGE OF THE SEVEN SEAS
VIRAGO!

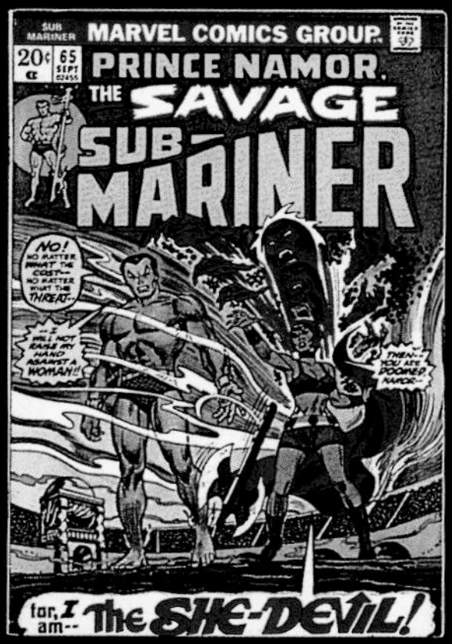
MARVEL COMICS GROUP
PRINCE NAMOR
THE SAVAGE
SUB-MARINER
The SHE-DEVIL!

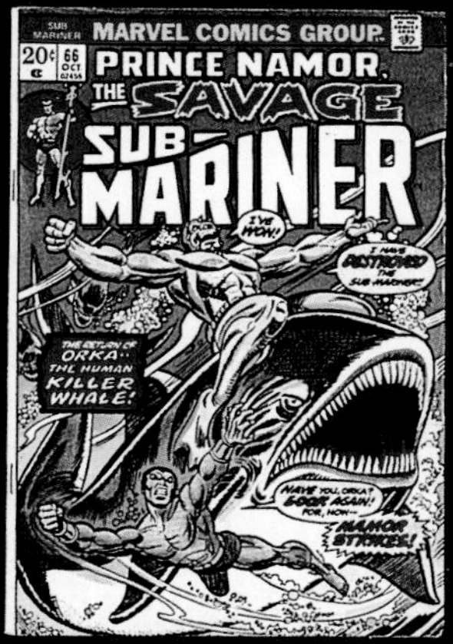
MARVEL COMICS GROUP
PRINCE NAMOR
THE SAVAGE
SUB-MARINER

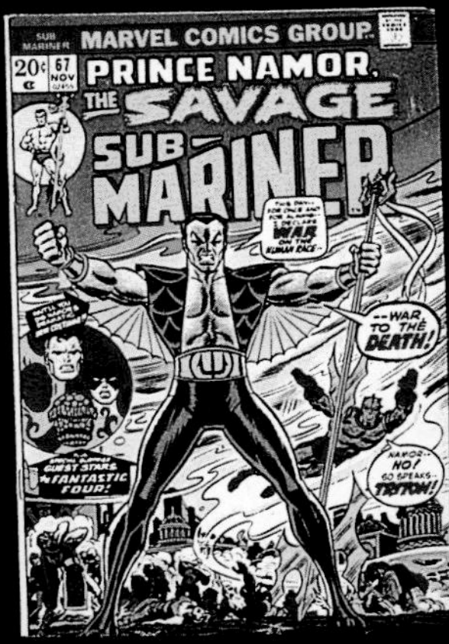
MARVEL COMICS GROUP
PRINCE NAMOR
THE SAVAGE
SUB-MARINER
TRITON!

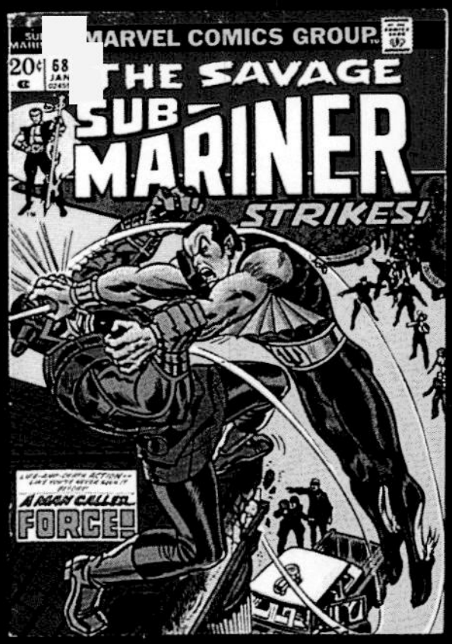
MARVEL COMICS GROUP
THE SAVAGE
SUB-MARINER
STRIKES!
FORCE!

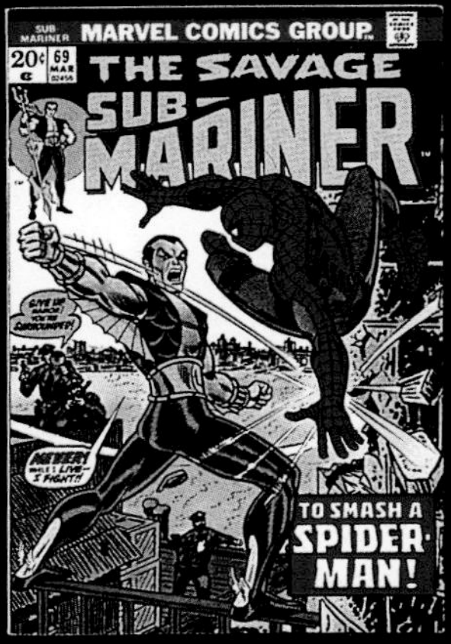
MARVEL COMICS GROUP
THE SAVAGE
SUB-MARINER
TO SMASH A SPIDER-MAN!

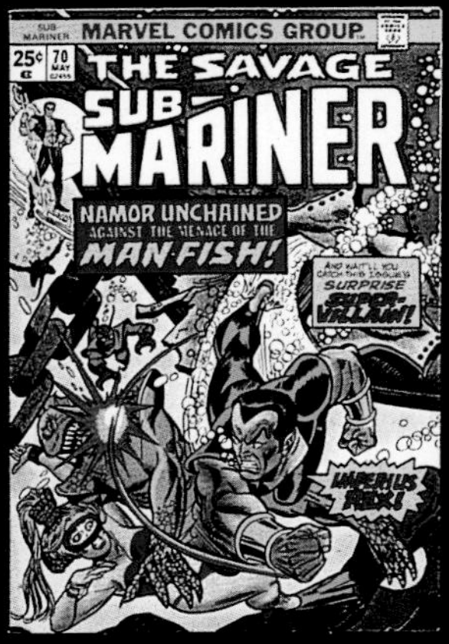
MARVEL COMICS GROUP
THE SAVAGE
SUB-MARINER
NAMOR UNCHAINED AGAINST THE MENACE OF THE MAN-FISH!

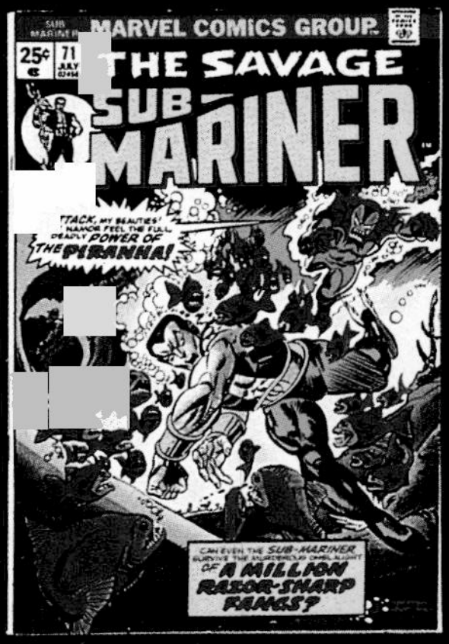
MARVEL COMICS GROUP
THE SAVAGE
SUB-MARINER

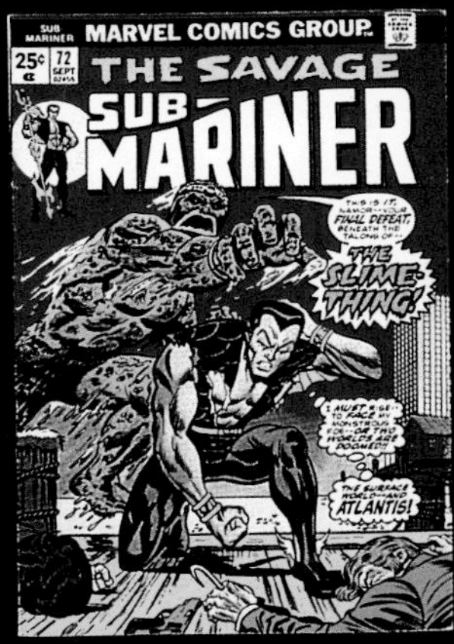
MARVEL COMICS GROUP
THE SAVAGE
SUB-MARINER
SLIME-THING!
ATLANTIS!

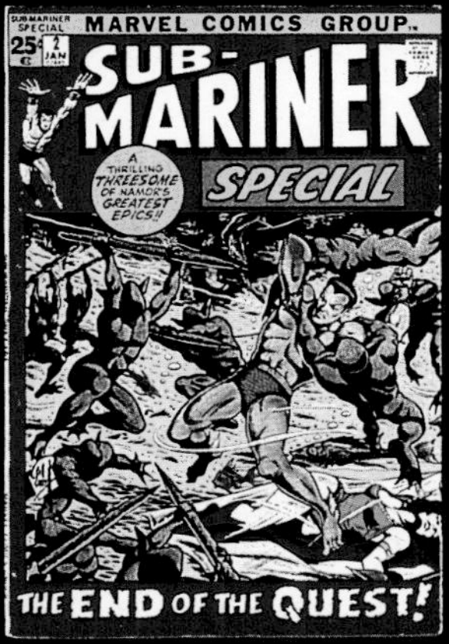
MARVEL COMICS GROUP
SUB-MARINER
SPECIAL
THE END OF THE QUEST!

1511.5 Prince Namor, the Sub-Mariner (1-2)

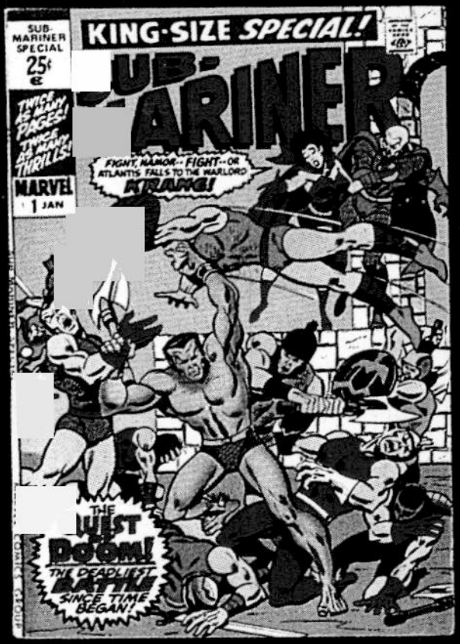
KING-SIZE SPECIAL!
SUB-MARINER

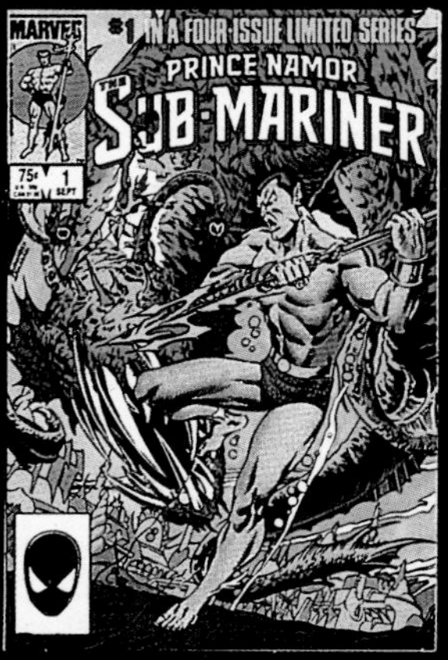
#1 IN A FOUR-ISSUE LIMITED SERIES
PRINCE NAMOR
SUB-MARINER

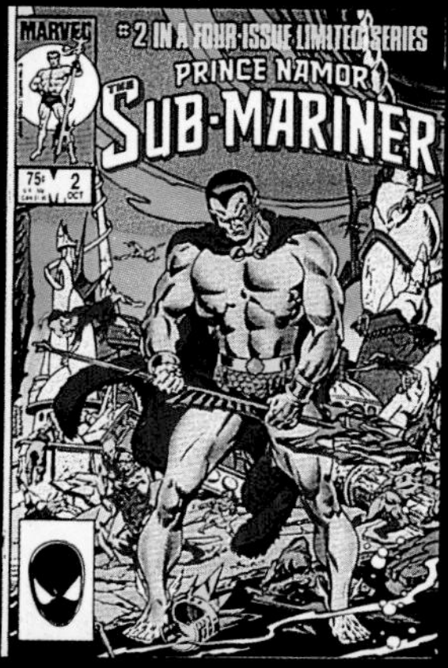
#2 IN A FOUR-ISSUE LIMITED SERIES
PRINCE NAMOR
SUB-MARINER

The Sub-Mariner (2nd Series; 1-72) 1821.7

Ref. No.	Date	RVI	Artist/Info.
1821.7-1	May 1968	70	Buscema/Brodsky-c, Buscema/Giacoia-a Publ. 1/2/68 (Origin)
1821.7-2	Jun.	18	Buscema/Giacoia-c, Buscema/Giacoia-a Publ. 2/29/68
1821.7-3	Jul.	10	Buscema/Giacoia-c/a Publ. 4/2/68
1821.7-4	Aug.	10	" " Publ. 5/2/68
1821.7-5	Sept.	10	" " Publ. 6/4/68
1821.7-6	Oct.	8	Buscema/Adkins-c/a
1821.7-7	Nov.	8	" "
1821.7-8	Dec.	8	" "
1821.7-9	Jan. 1969	8	M. Severin/Adkins-c/a
1821.7-10	**Feb.**	**8**	**Colan/Adkins-c/a**
1821.7-11	Mar.	6	Colan/Adkins-c, Colan/Klein-a
1821.7-12	Apr.	6	M. Severin/Giacoia-c, M. Severin-a
1821.7-13	May	6	M. Severin-c/a, Sinnott-a
1821.7-14	Jun.	10	M. Severin/Gaudioso-a (Submariner vs. Human Torch)
1821.7-15	Jul.	4	M. Severin/Sinnott-c, M. Severin/Colletta-a
1821.7-16	Aug.	4	M. Severin/Giacoia-c, Severin/Gaudioso-a
1821.7-17	Sept.	4	M Severin-c/a, Hawk/Gaudioso-a
1821.7-18	Oct.	4	M. Severin/Esposito-c, Severin/Gaudioso-a
1821.7-19	Nov.	4	M. Severin/Esposito-c, Severin/Craig-a Publ. 7/8/69
1821.7-20	**Dec.**	**4**	**Buscema/Esposito-c, Buscema/Craig-a**
1821.7-21	Jan. 1970	4	Severin/Craig-c/a
1821.7-22	Feb.	3	Severin/Giacoia-c, Severin/Craig-a
1821.7-23	Mar.	3	Severin/Esposito-c, Severin/Craig-a
1821.7-24	Apr.	3	Buscema/Esposito-c, Buscema/Mooney-a
1821.7-25	May	3	Buscema, Severin/Esposito-c, Buscema/Mooney-a
1821.7-26	Jun.	3	Buscema/Esposito-c, Buscema/Gaudioso-a
1821.7-27	Jul.	3	" " " "
1821.7-28	Aug.	3	" " " "
1821.7-29	Sept.	3	" " " "
1821.7-30	**Oct.**	**3**	**" " " "**
1821.7-31	Nov.	3	Buscema-c, Buscema/Gaudioso-a
1821.7-32	Dec.	3	Buscema-c, Buscema/Mooney-a
1821.7-33	Jan. 1971	3	Buscema/Mooney-c/a
1821.7-34	Feb.	3	Buscema-c/a, Mooney-a
1821.7-35	Mar.	3	" " (Silver Surfer -app.)
1821.7-36	Apr.	3	Buscema-c/a, Wrightson-a
1821.7-37	May	3	Buscema-c, Andru/Esposito-a
1821.7-38	Jun.	3	J. & M. Severin-c, Andru/J. Severin-a
1821.7-39	Jul.	3	M. Severin/Buscema-c, Andru/Mooney-a
1821.7-40	**Aug.**	**3**	**Buscema/Giacoia-c, Colan/Grainger-a**
1821.7-41	Sept.	2	Tuska/Esposito-c, Tuska/Grainger-a
1821.7-42	Oct.	2	Kane/Giacoia-c, Tuska/Mooney-a
1821.7-43	Nov.	2	Kane/Giacoia-c, Colan/Esposito-a
1821.7-44	Dec.	2	Kane/Esposito-c, M. Severin/Mooney-a
1821.7-45	Jan. 1972	2	Kane/Giacoia-c, M. Severin/Mooney-a
1821.7-46	Feb.	2	Kane/Esposito-c, Colan/Esposito-a
1821.7-47	Mar.	2	Kane/Everett-c, Colan/Esposito-a
1821.7-48	Apr.	2	" " " "
1821.7-49	May	2	Kane/Giacoia-c, Colan/Giacoia-a
1821.7-50	**Jun.**	**2**	**Kane/Colletta-c, Everett-a**
1821.7-51	Jul.	2	Kane/Giacoia-c, Everett-a
1821.7-52	Aug.	2	Kane/Sinnott-c, Everett-a
1821.7-53	Sept.	2	Buscema/Giacoia-c, Everett-a
1821.7-54	Oct.	2	Weiss/Giacoia-c, Everett-a
1821.7-55	Nov.	2	Everett-c/a
1821.7-56	Dec.	-2	Weiss-c, Adkins-a
1821.7-57	Jan. 1973	2	Everett-c/a
1821.7-58	Feb.	2	Kane/Everett-c, Everett-a
1821.7-59	Mar.	2	Everett-c, Kweskin, Tartaglione-a
1821.7-60	**Apr.**	**2**	**Buckler/Sinnott-c, Kweskin, Mooney-a**
1821.7-61	May	2	Everett-c/a, Mooney-a
1821.7-62	Jun.	2	Romita-c, Kweskin, kGiacoia-a
1821.7-63	Jul.	2	Romita/Sinnott-c, Kweskin, Shores-a
1821.7-64	Aug.	2	Buckler/Everett-c, Heck/Perlin-a
1821.7-65	Sept.	2	Romita, Heck-c, Heck/Perlin-a
1821.7-66	Oct.	2	Kane/Esposito-c, Heck/Perlin-a
1821.7-67	Nov.	2	Romita/Esposito-c, Heck/Bolle-a
1821.7-68	Jan. 1974	2	Romita/Esposito-c, Heck/Mooney-a
1821.7-69	Mar.	2	Romita-c, Tuska/Colletta-a
1821.7-70	**May**	**2**	**Kane/Esposito-c, Tuska/Colletta-a**
1821.7-71	Jul.	2	" " " "
1821.7-72	Sept.	2	Romita/Esposito-c, Adkins/Colletta-a
1821.7-SP1	Jan. 1971	2	Buscema-c
1821.7-SP2	Jan. 1972	1	Everett-c

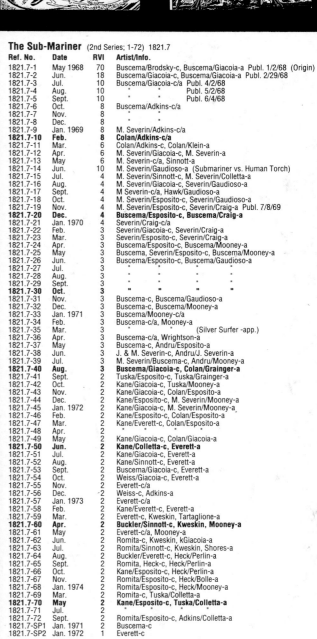

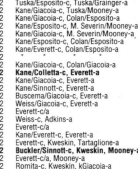

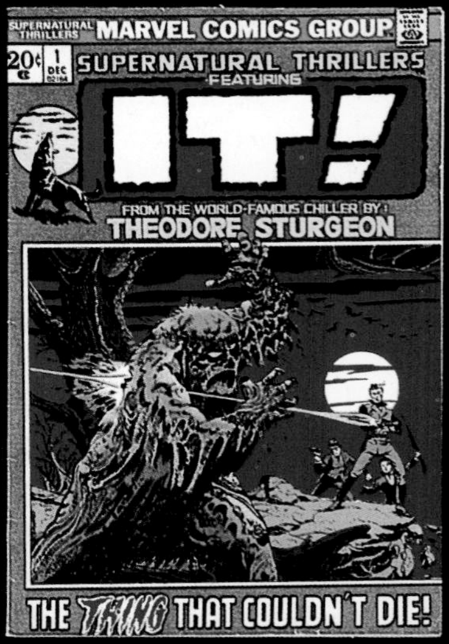
MARVEL COMICS GROUP
SUPERNATURAL THRILLERS
FEATURING
IT!
FROM THE WORLD-FAMOUS CHILLER BY
THEODORE STURGEON
THE THING THAT COULDN'T DIE!

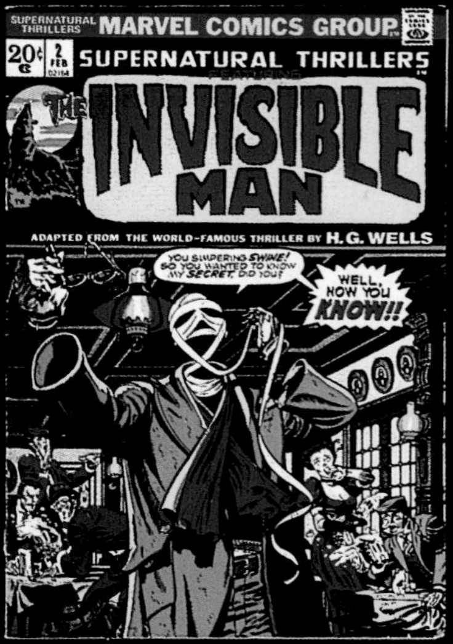
MARVEL COMICS GROUP
SUPERNATURAL THRILLERS
THE INVISIBLE MAN
ADAPTED FROM THE WORLD-FAMOUS THRILLER BY H.G. WELLS
WELL, NOW YOU KNOW!!

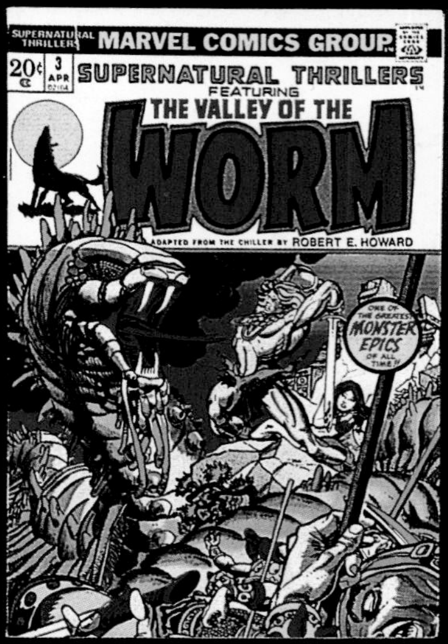
MARVEL COMICS GROUP
SUPERNATURAL THRILLERS
FEATURING
THE VALLEY OF THE WORM
ADAPTED FROM THE CHILLER BY ROBERT E. HOWARD
ONE OF THE GREATEST MONSTER EPICS OF ALL TIME!

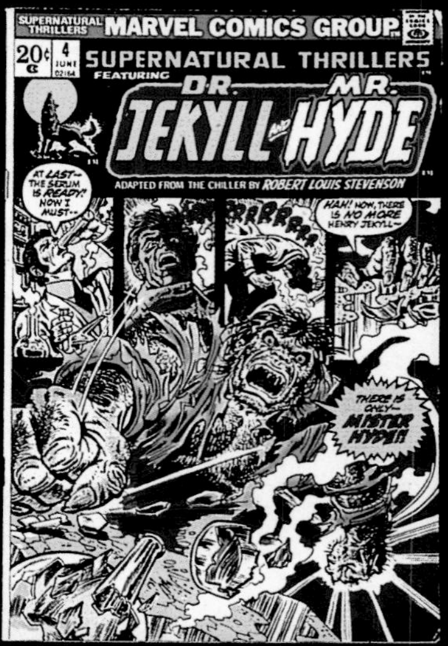
MARVEL COMICS GROUP
SUPERNATURAL THRILLERS
FEATURING
DR. JEKYLL MR. HYDE
ADAPTED FROM THE CHILLER BY ROBERT LOUIS STEVENSON

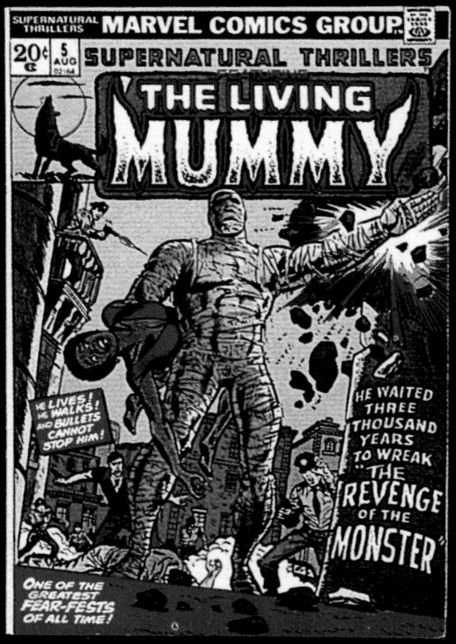
MARVEL COMICS GROUP
SUPERNATURAL THRILLERS
THE LIVING MUMMY
HE WAITED THREE THOUSAND YEARS TO WREAK THE REVENGE OF THE MONSTER
ONE OF THE GREATEST FEAR-FESTS OF ALL TIME!

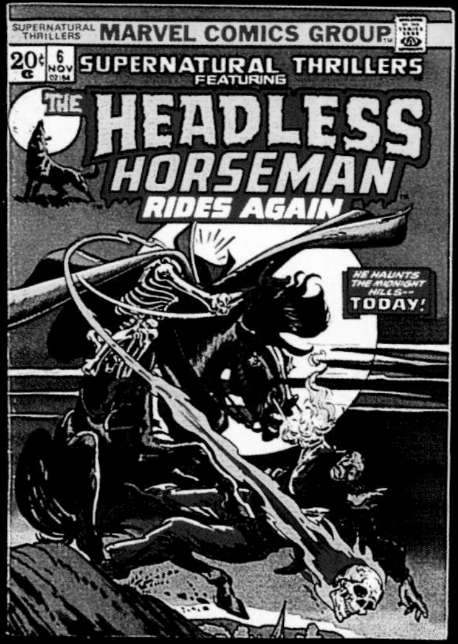
MARVEL COMICS GROUP
SUPERNATURAL THRILLERS
FEATURING
THE HEADLESS HORSEMAN RIDES AGAIN
HE HAUNTS THE MIDNIGHT HILLS -- TODAY!

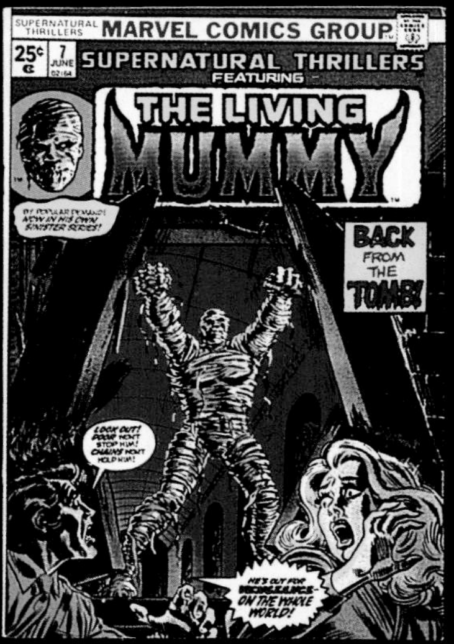
MARVEL COMICS GROUP
SUPERNATURAL THRILLERS
FEATURING
THE LIVING MUMMY
BACK FROM THE TOMB!

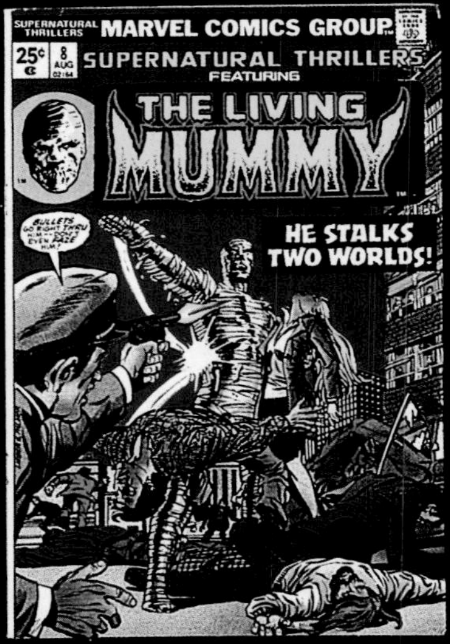
MARVEL COMICS GROUP
SUPERNATURAL THRILLERS
FEATURING
THE LIVING MUMMY
HE STALKS TWO WORLDS!

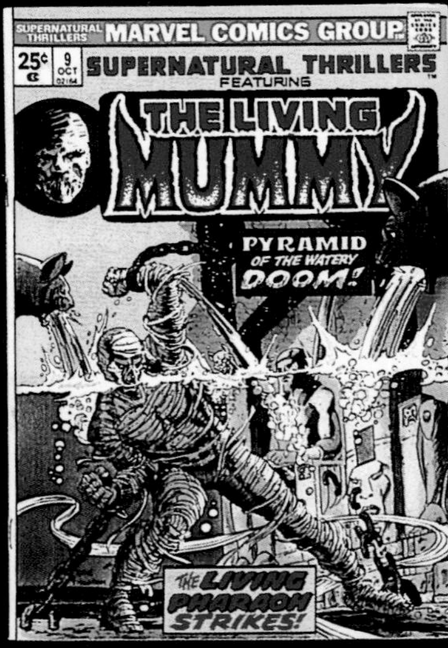
MARVEL COMICS GROUP
SUPERNATURAL THRILLERS
FEATURING
THE LIVING MUMMY
PYRAMID OF THE WATERY DOOM!
THE LIVING PHARAOH STRIKES!

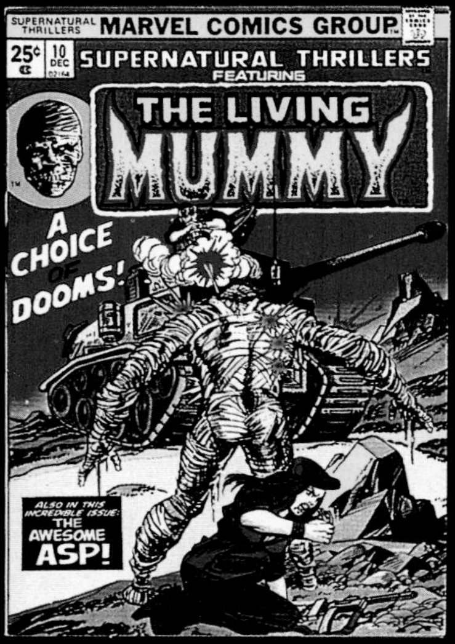
MARVEL COMICS GROUP
SUPERNATURAL THRILLERS
FEATURING
THE LIVING MUMMY
A CHOICE OF DOOMS!
ALSO IN THIS INCREDIBLE ISSUE: THE AWESOME ASP!

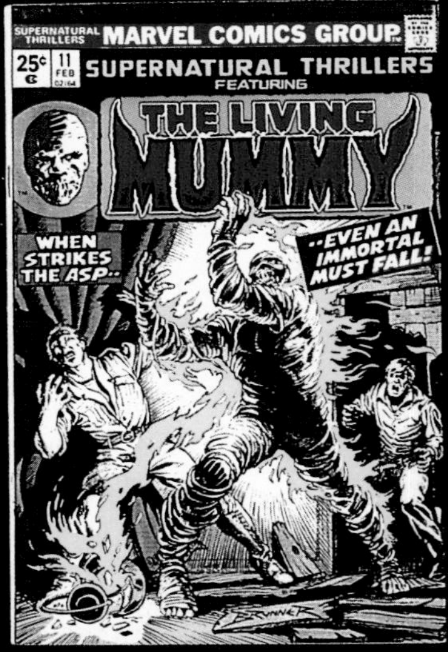
MARVEL COMICS GROUP
SUPERNATURAL THRILLERS
FEATURING
THE LIVING MUMMY
WHEN STRIKES THE ASP--
--EVEN AN IMMORTAL MUST FALL!

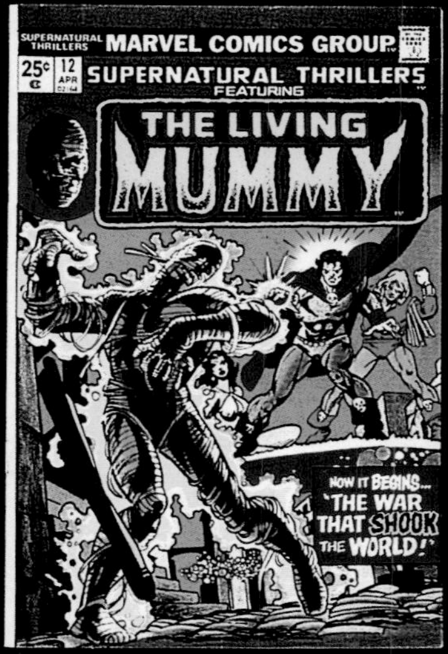
MARVEL COMICS GROUP
SUPERNATURAL THRILLERS
FEATURING
THE LIVING MUMMY
NOW IT BEGINS... THE WAR THAT SHOOK THE WORLD!

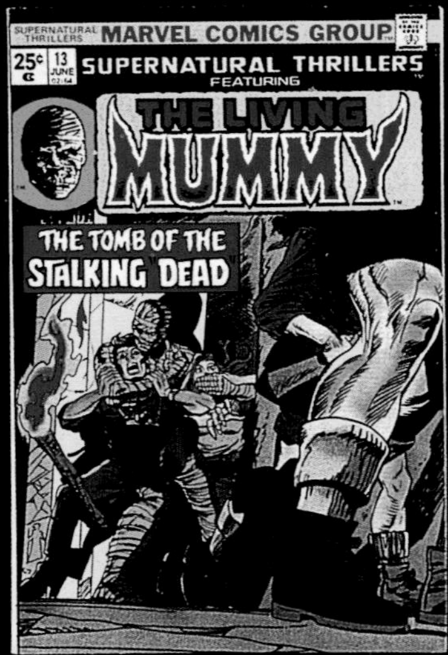
MARVEL COMICS GROUP
SUPERNATURAL THRILLERS
FEATURING
THE LIVING MUMMY
THE TOMB OF THE STALKING DEAD

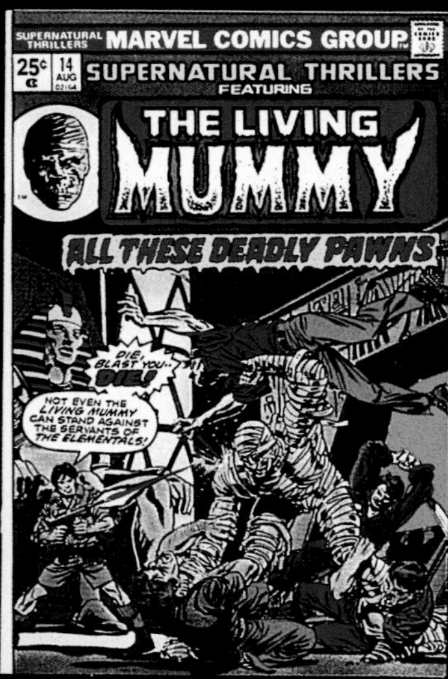
MARVEL COMICS GROUP
SUPERNATURAL THRILLERS
FEATURING
THE LIVING MUMMY
ALL THESE DEADLY PAWNS

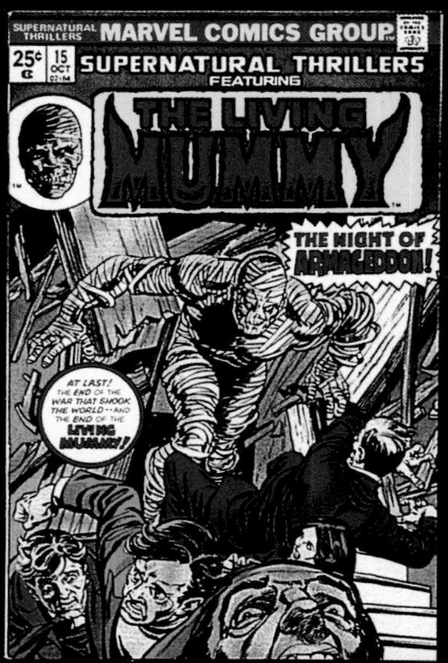
MARVEL COMICS GROUP
SUPERNATURAL THRILLERS
FEATURING
THE LIVING MUMMY
THE NIGHT OF ARMAGEDDON!

Supernatural Thrillers (1-15) 1852.3

Ref. No.	Date	RVI	Artist/Info.
1852.3-1	Dec. 1972	1	Steranko-c, Severin/Giacoia-a (It!)
1852.3-2	Feb. 1973	1	Mayerik/Adkins-a (Invisible Man)
1852.3-3	Apr.	1	Kane/Chua-a
1852.3-4	Jun.	1	Martimer-a (Dr. Jekyll and Mr. Hyc
1852.3-5	Aug.	1	Buckler/Chiaramonte-a
1852.3-6	Nov.	1	Tuska/Abel-a
1852.3-7	Jun. 1974	1	Mayerik-a
1852.3-8	Aug.	1	Lieber/Palmer-c, Mayerik-a
1852.3-9	Oct.	1	Kane/Milgrom-c, Mayerik/Adkins-a
1852.3-10	**Dec.**	**1**	**Mayerik/Adkins-a**
1852.3-11	Feb. 1975	1	Mayerik-a
1852.3-12	Apr.	1	Mayerik/Janson-a
1852.3-13	Jun.	1	Mayerik/Green-a
1852.3-14	Aug.	1	Mayerik/McWilliams-a
1852.3-15	Oct.	1	Sutton-a

1856.5 Super-Villain Classics (1)

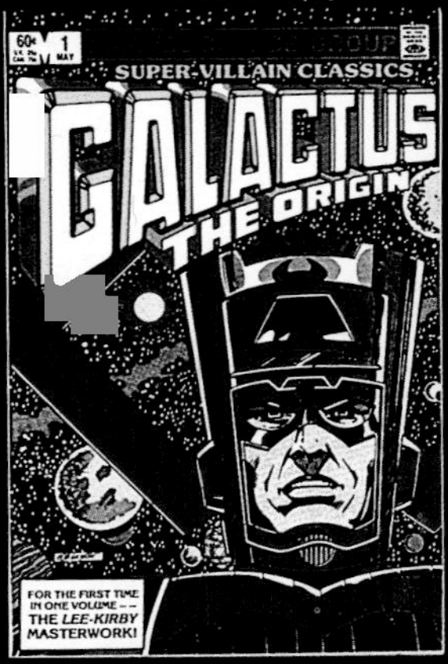
SUPER-VILLAIN CLASSICS
GALACTUS
THE ORIGIN
FOR THE FIRST TIME IN ONE VOLUME -- THE LEE-KIRBY MASTERWORK!

1856.7 Super-Villain Team-Up (1-17, GS. 1-2)

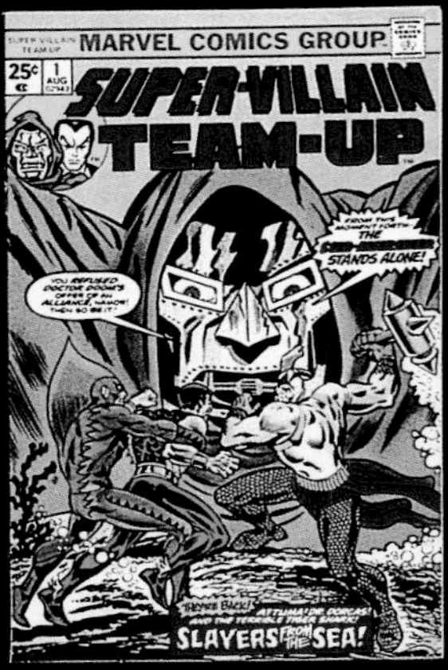
MARVEL COMICS GROUP
SUPER-VILLAIN TEAM-UP
SLAYERS FROM THE SEA!

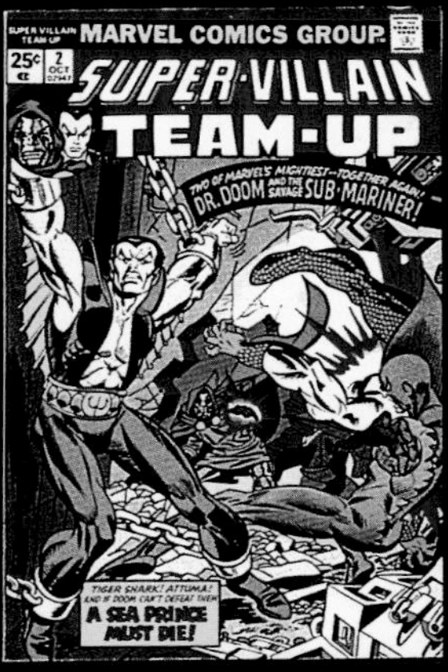
MARVEL COMICS GROUP
SUPER-VILLAIN TEAM-UP
DR. DOOM AND THE SAVAGE SUB-MARINER!
A SEA PRINCE MUST DIE!

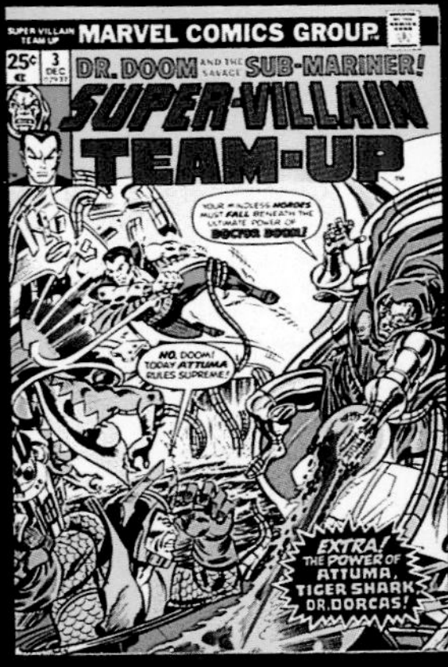
MARVEL COMICS GROUP
DR. DOOM AND THE SAVAGE SUB-MARINER!
SUPER-VILLAIN TEAM-UP
EXTRA! THE POWER OF ATTUMA TIGER SHARK DR. DORCAS!

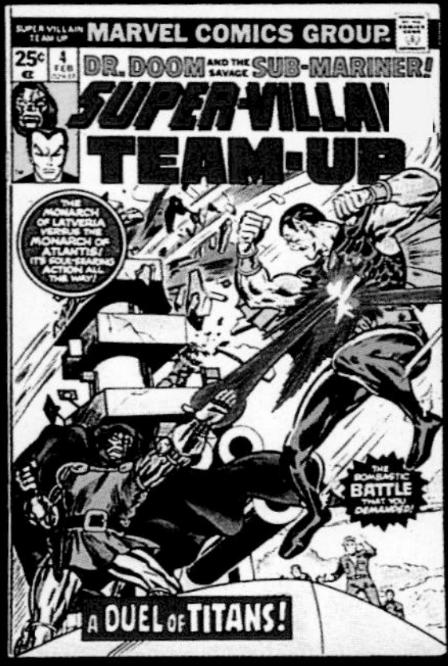
MARVEL COMICS GROUP
DR. DOOM AND THE SAVAGE SUB-MARINER!
SUPER-VILLAIN TEAM-UP
A DUEL OF TITANS!

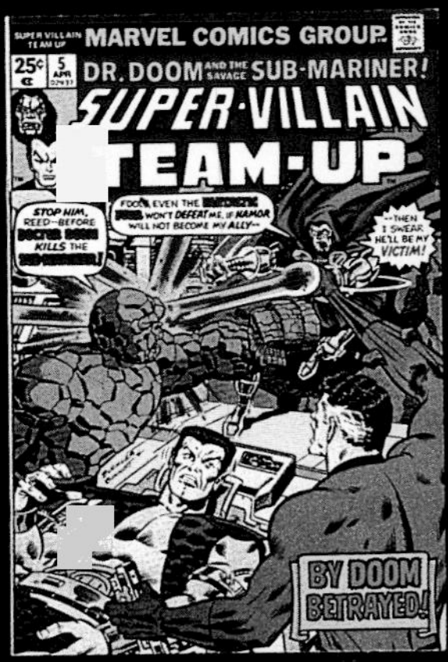
MARVEL COMICS GROUP
DR. DOOM AND THE SAVAGE SUB-MARINER!
SUPER-VILLAIN TEAM-UP
BY DOOM BETRAYED!

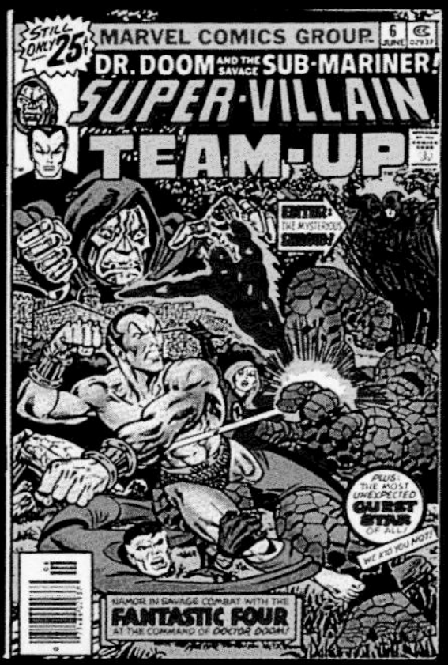
MARVEL COMICS GROUP
DR. DOOM AND THE SAVAGE SUB-MARINER!
SUPER-VILLAIN TEAM-UP
FANTASTIC FOUR

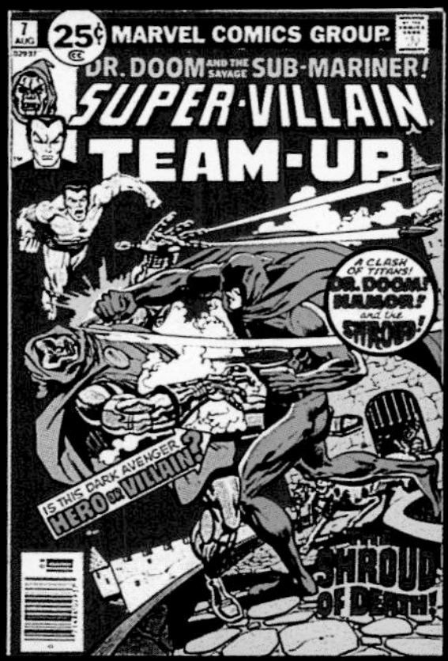
MARVEL COMICS GROUP
DR. DOOM AND THE SAVAGE SUB-MARINER!
SUPER-VILLAIN TEAM-UP
SHROUD OF DEATH!

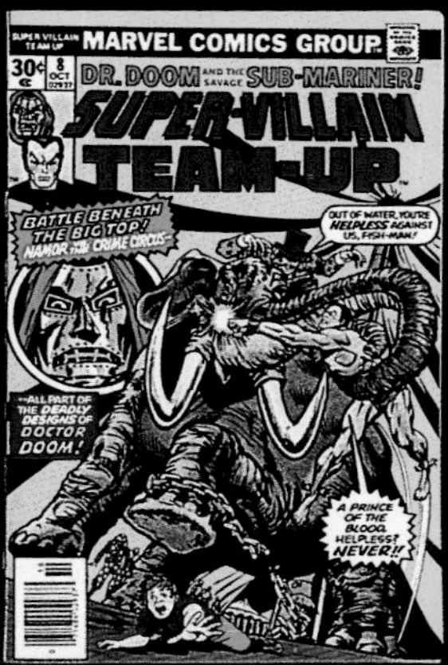
MARVEL COMICS GROUP
DR. DOOM AND THE SAVAGE SUB-MARINER!
SUPER-VILLAIN TEAM-UP

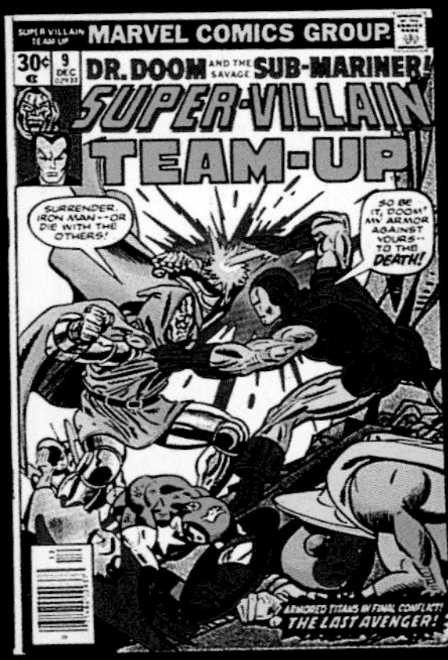
MARVEL COMICS GROUP
DR. DOOM AND THE SAVAGE SUB-MARINER!
SUPER-VILLAIN TEAM-UP
THE LAST AVENGER!

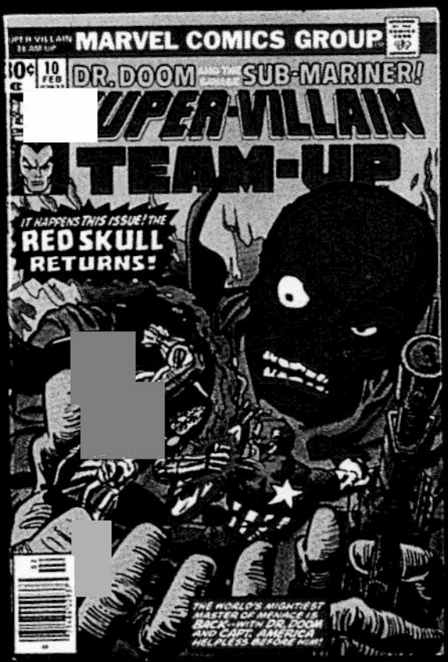
MARVEL COMICS GROUP
SUPER-VILLAIN TEAM-UP
RED SKULL RETURNS!

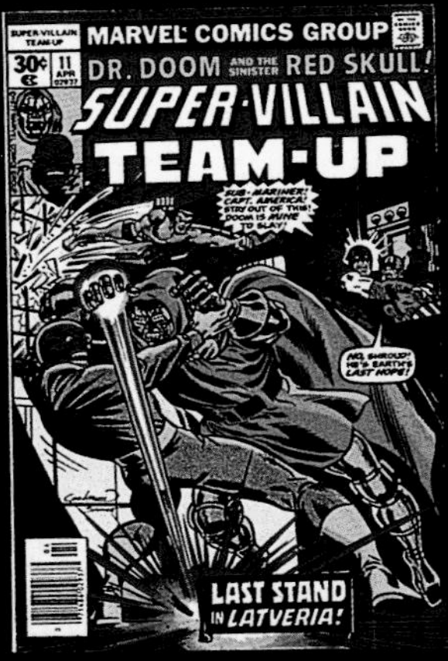
MARVEL COMICS GROUP
DR. DOOM AND THE SINISTER RED SKULL!
SUPER-VILLAIN TEAM-UP
LAST STAND IN LATVERIA!

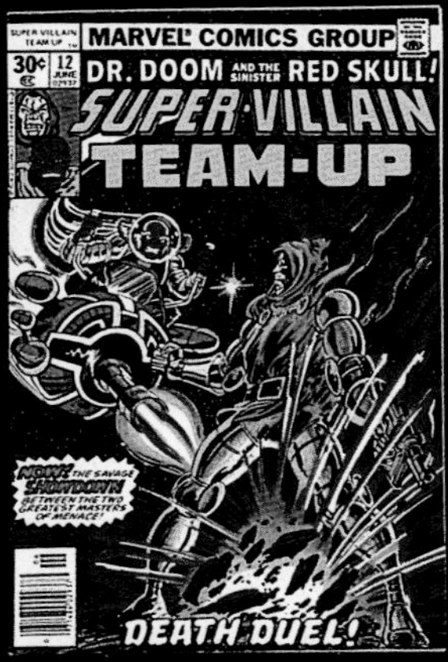
MARVEL COMICS GROUP
DR. DOOM AND THE SINISTER RED SKULL!
SUPER-VILLAIN TEAM-UP
DEATH DUEL!

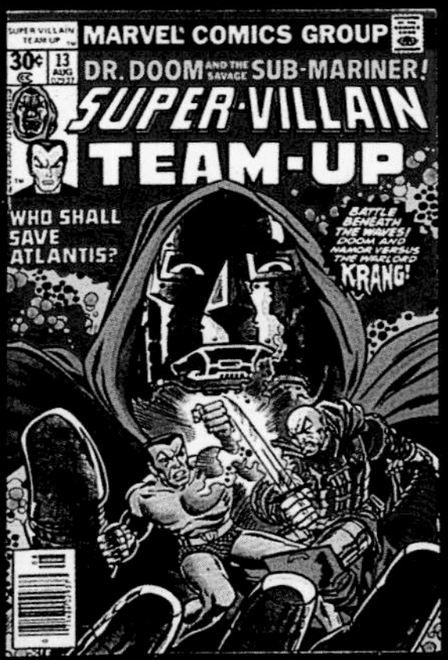
MARVEL COMICS GROUP
DR. DOOM AND THE SAVAGE SUB-MARINER!
SUPER-VILLAIN TEAM-UP
WHO SHALL SAVE ATLANTIS?
KRANG!

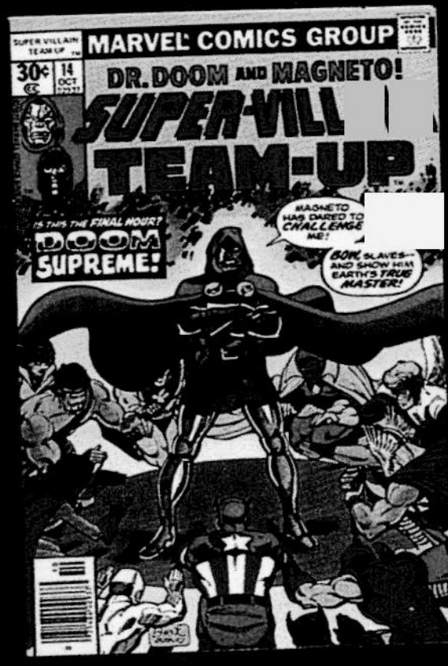
MARVEL COMICS GROUP
DR. DOOM AND MAGNETO!
DOOM SUPREME!

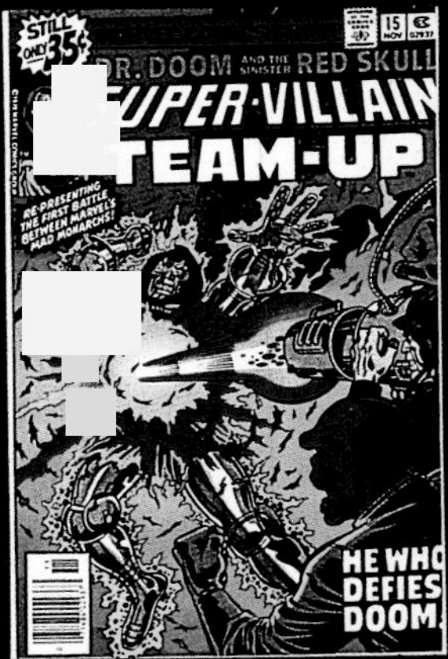
SUPER-VILLAIN TEAM-UP
HE WHO DEFIES DOOM!

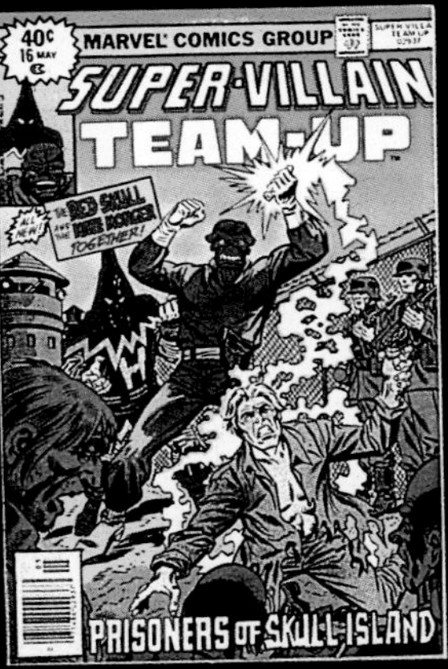
MARVEL COMICS GROUP
SUPER-VILLAIN TEAM-UP
PRISONERS OF SKULL ISLAND

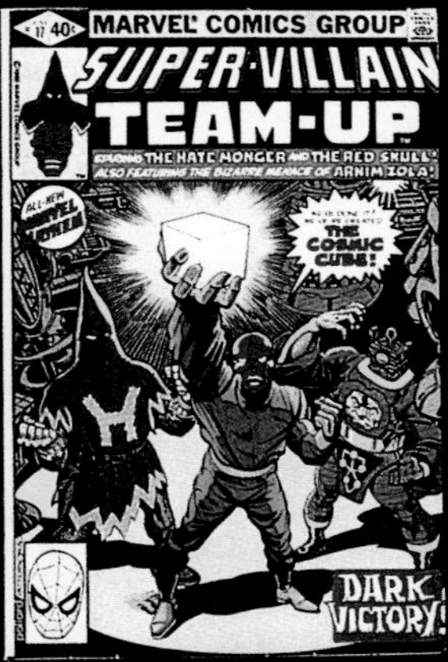
MARVEL COMICS GROUP
SUPER-VILLAIN TEAM-UP
THE COSMIC CUBE!
DARK VICTORY!

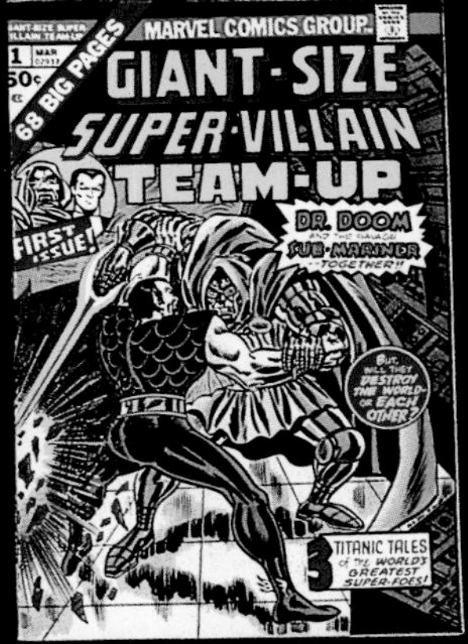
MARVEL COMICS GROUP
68 BIG PAGES
GIANT-SIZE SUPER-VILLAIN TEAM-UP
DR. DOOM
SUB-MARINER
TITANIC TALES OF THE WORLD'S GREATEST SUPER-FOES!

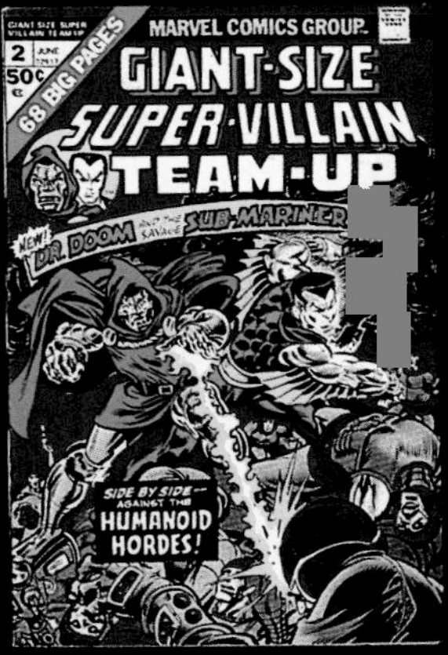
MARVEL COMICS GROUP
68 BIG PAGES
GIANT-SIZE SUPER-VILLAIN TEAM-UP
HUMANOID HORDES!

1877.3 Tales of Asgard (1, V.2/1)

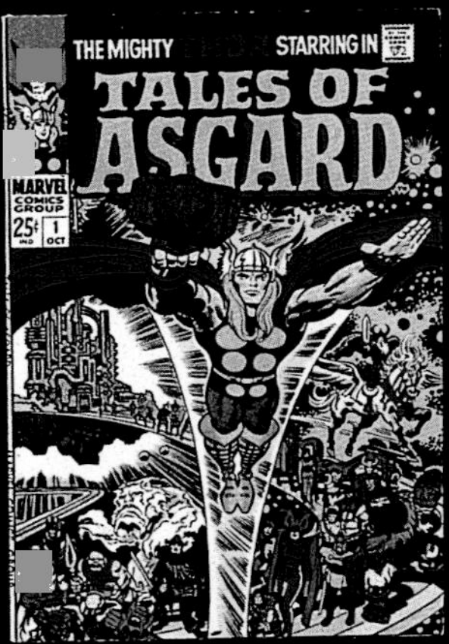
THE MIGHTY
STARRING IN
TALES OF ASGARD

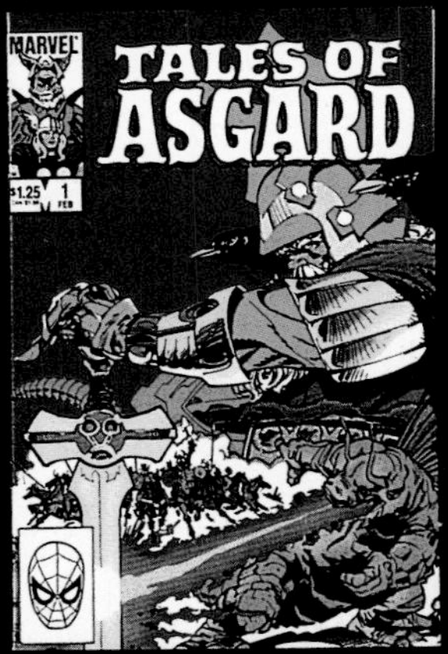
TALES OF ASGARD

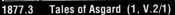

Super Heroes Puzzles and Games (1) 1843.7

Ref. No.	Date	RVI	Artist/Info.
1843.7-1	1979	2	(Origin-Spider-Man, Captain America, Hulk)

Super-Villain Classics (1) 1856.5

1856.5-1	May 1983	1	Layton-c, Kirby/Colletta-a (Galactus the Origin)

Super-Villain Team-up (1-17) 1856.7

1856.7-1	Aug.	2	Tuska, Everett-c, Kida-a
1856.7-2	Oct.	1	Buscema/Kida-a
1856.7-3	Dec.	1	Hannigan-c, Evans/Abel-a
1856.7-4	Feb. 1976	1	Trimpe, Mooney-a
1856.7-5	Apr.	1	Buckler/Sinnott-c, Trimpe/Perlin-a
1856.7-6	Jun.	1	Trimpe/Abel-a
1856.7-7	Aug.	1	Buckler/Janson-c, Trimpe/Marcos-a
1856.7-8	Oct.	1	Giffen, McCarran-a
1856.7-9	Dec.	1	Shooter, Trapani-a
1856.7-10	**Feb. 1976**	**1**	**Hall/Perlin-a**
1856.7-11	Apr.	1	Cockrum/Sinnott-c, Hall/Perlin-a
1856.7-12	Jun.	1	Cockrum/Milgrom-c, Hall/Perlin-a
1856.7-13	Aug.	1	Giffen/Perlin-a
1856.7-14	Oct.	1	Byrne/Austin-c, Hall/Perlin-a
1856.7-15	Nov.	1	Tuska, Esposito-a
1856.7-16	May	1	Infantino/Patterson-a
1856.7-17	Jun.	1	Pollard/Patterson-c, Jones,
1856.7-G.S. 1	Mar. 1975	1	Buscema, Sinnott-a
1856.7-G.S. 2	Jun. 1975	1	Sekowsky, Grainger-a

Tales of Asgard (1) 1877.3

1877.3-1	Oct. 1968	10	Kirby/Bell-c
1877.3-(V.2)-1	Feb. 1984	1	Simonson-c, Kirby/Colletta-a

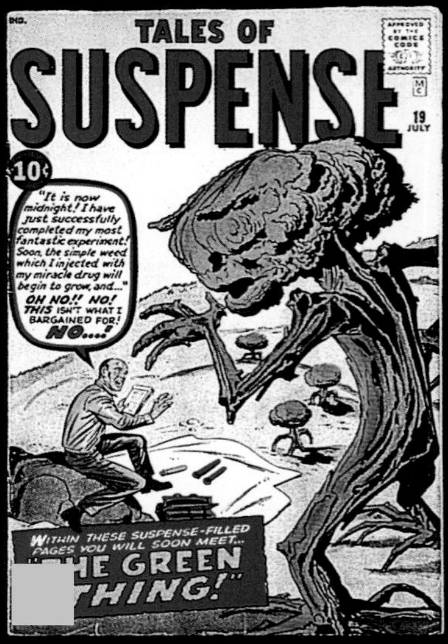
TALES OF
SUSPENSE
19 JULY
10¢
"It is now midnight! I have just successfully completed my most fantastic experiment! Soon, the simple weed which I injected with my miracle drug will begin to grow, and..." OH NO!! NO! THIS ISN'T WHAT I BARGAINED FOR! NO....
WITHIN THESE SUSPENSE-FILLED PAGES YOU WILL SOON MEET... THE GREEN THING!"

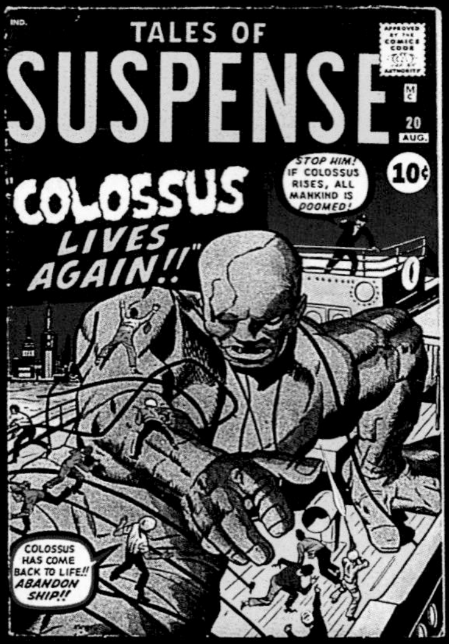
TALES OF
SUSPENSE
20 AUG.
10¢
COLOSSUS LIVES AGAIN!!"
STOP HIM! IF COLOSSUS RISES, ALL MANKIND IS DOOMED!
COLOSSUS HAS COME BACK TO LIFE!! ABANDON SHIP!!

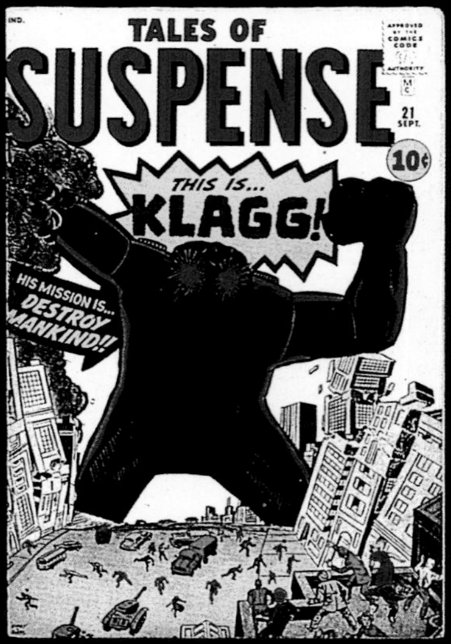
TALES OF
SUSPENSE
21 SEPT.
10¢
THIS IS... KLAGG!
HIS MISSION IS... DESTROY MANKIND!!

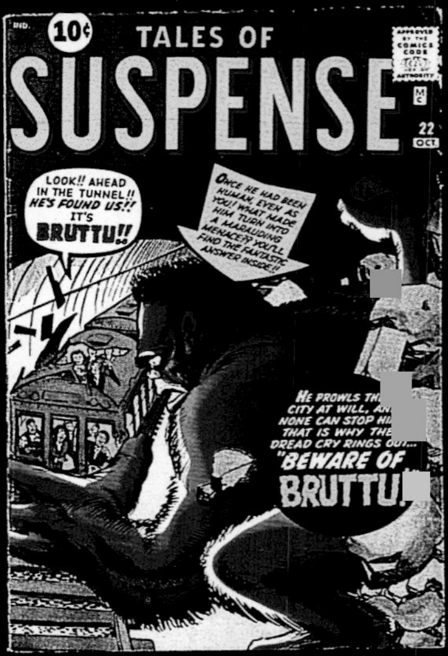
10¢
TALES OF
SUSPENSE
22 OCT.
LOOK!! AHEAD IN THE TUNNEL!! HE'S FOUND US!! IT'S BRUTTU!!
HE PROWLS THE CITY AT WILL... NONE CAN STOP HIM! THAT IS WHY THE DREAD CRY RINGS OUT... "BEWARE OF BRUTTU!

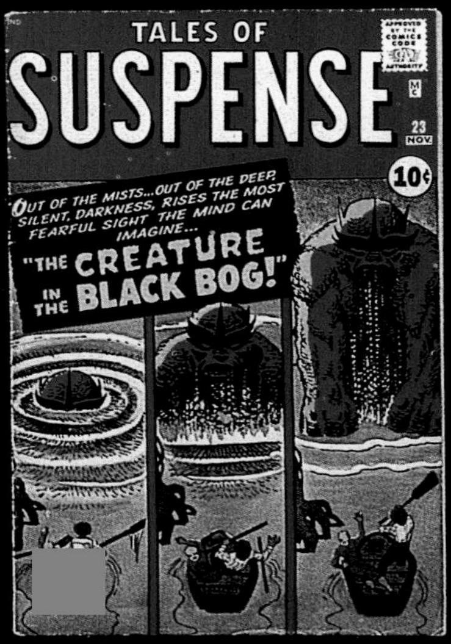
TALES OF
SUSPENSE
23 NOV.
10¢
OUT OF THE MISTS...OUT OF THE DEEP, SILENT, DARKNESS, RISES THE MOST FEARFUL SIGHT THE MIND CAN IMAGINE...
"THE CREATURE IN THE BLACK BOG!"

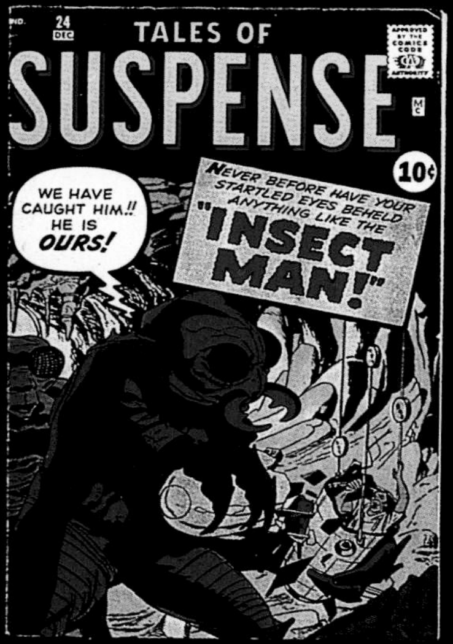
24 DEC.
TALES OF
SUSPENSE
10¢
WE HAVE CAUGHT HIM!! HE IS OURS!
NEVER BEFORE HAVE YOUR STARTLED EYES BEHELD ANYTHING LIKE THE "INSECT MAN!"

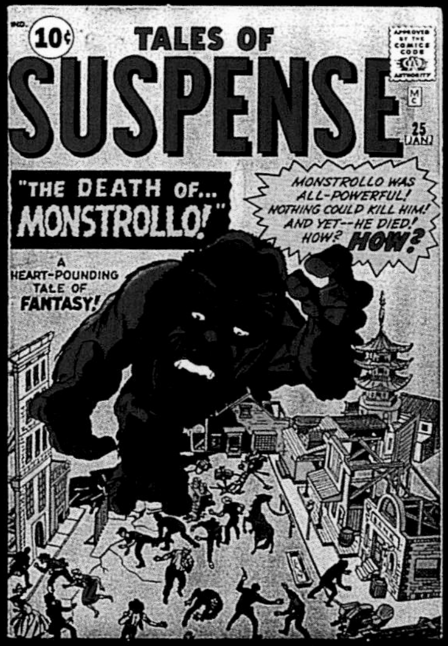
10¢
TALES OF
SUSPENSE
25 JAN.
"THE DEATH OF... MONSTROLLO!"
MONSTROLLO WAS ALL-POWERFUL! NOTHING COULD KILL HIM! AND YET—HE DIED! HOW? HOW?
A HEART-POUNDING TALE OF FANTASY!

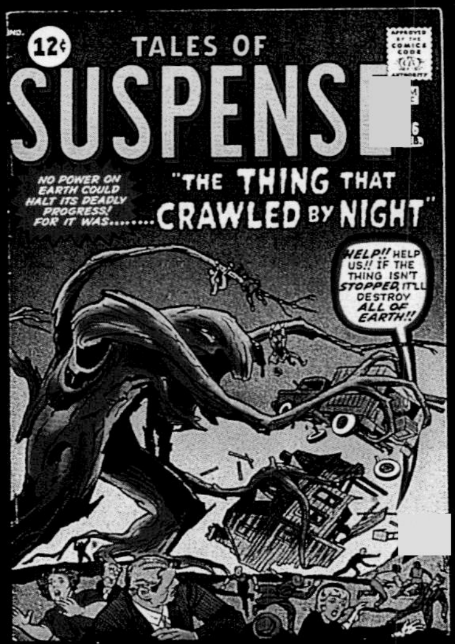
12¢
TALES OF
SUSPENS
NO POWER ON EARTH COULD HALT ITS DEADLY PROGRESS! FOR IT WAS........
"THE THING THAT CRAWLED BY NIGHT"
HELP!! HELP US!! IF THE THING ISN'T STOPPED IT'LL DESTROY ALL OF EARTH!!

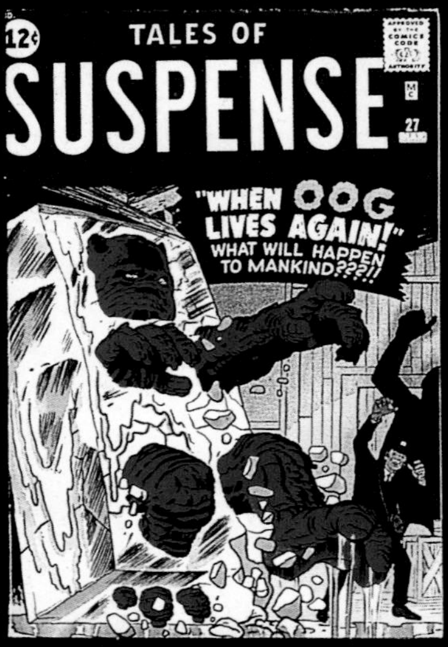
12¢
TALES OF
SUSPENSE
27
"WHEN OOG LIVES AGAIN!" WHAT WILL HAPPEN TO MANKIND???!

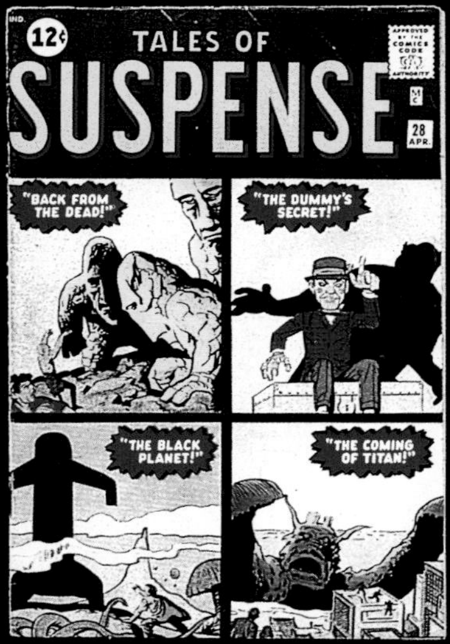
12¢
TALES OF
SUSPENSE
28 APR.
"BACK FROM THE DEAD!"
"THE DUMMY'S SECRET!"
"THE BLACK PLANET!"
"THE COMING OF TITAN!"

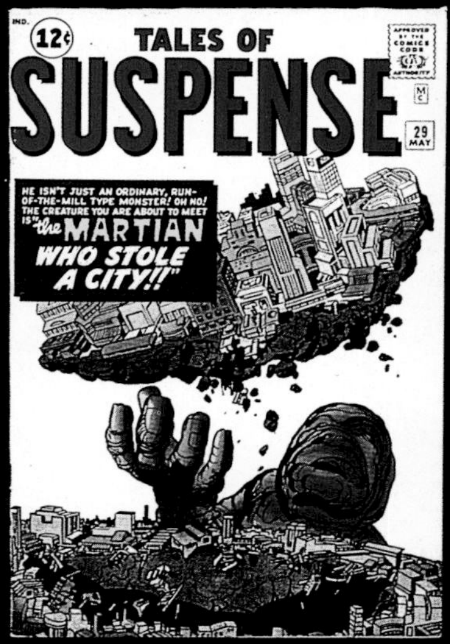
12¢
TALES OF
SUSPENSE
29 MAY
HE ISN'T JUST AN ORDINARY, RUN-OF-THE-MILL TYPE MONSTER! OH NO! THE CREATURE YOU ARE ABOUT TO MEET IS the MARTIAN WHO STOLE A CITY!!"

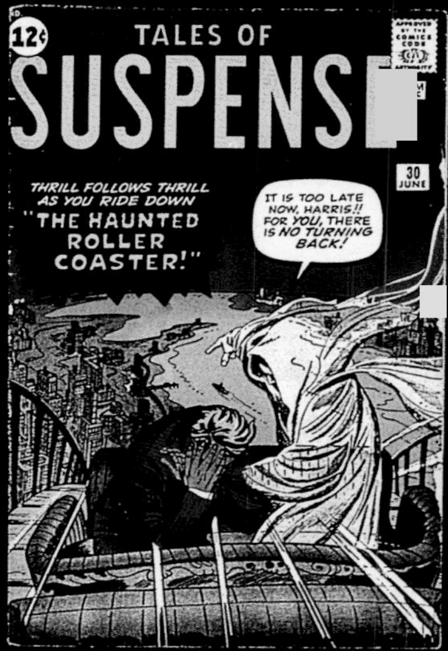
12¢
TALES OF
SUSPENS
30 JUNE
THRILL FOLLOWS THRILL AS YOU RIDE DOWN "THE HAUNTED ROLLER COASTER!"
IT IS TOO LATE NOW, HARRIS!! FOR YOU, THERE IS NO TURNING BACK!

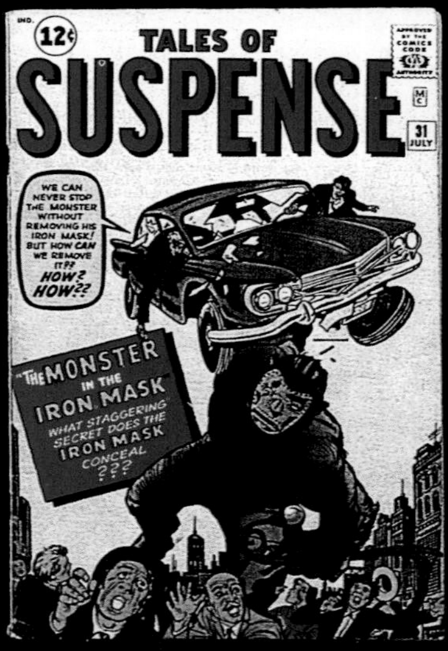
12¢
TALES OF
SUSPENSE
31 JULY
WE CAN NEVER STOP THE MONSTER WITHOUT REMOVING HIS IRON MASK! BUT HOW CAN WE REMOVE IT? HOW? HOW??
THE MONSTER IN THE IRON MASK
WHAT STAGGERING SECRET DOES THE IRON MASK CONCEAL ???

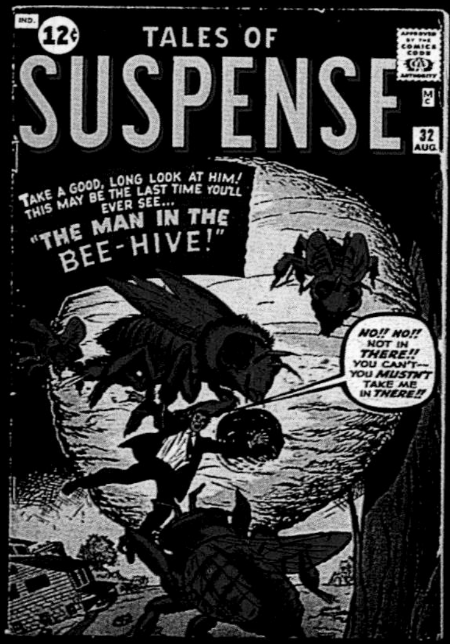
12¢
TALES OF
SUSPENSE
32 AUG.
TAKE A GOOD, LONG LOOK AT HIM! THIS MAY BE THE LAST TIME YOU'LL EVER SEE... "THE MAN IN THE BEE-HIVE!"
NO!! NO!! NOT IN THERE!! YOU CAN'T— YOU MUSTN'T TAKE ME IN THERE!!

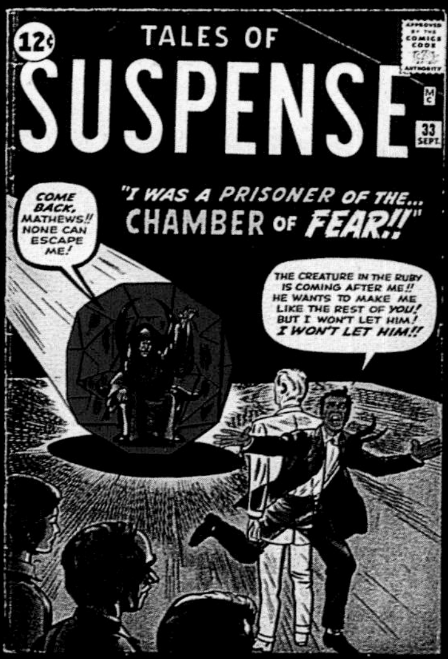
12¢
TALES OF
SUSPENSE
33 SEPT.
COME BACK, MATHEWS!! NONE CAN ESCAPE ME!
"I WAS A PRISONER OF THE... CHAMBER OF FEAR!!"
THE CREATURE IN THE RUBY IS COMING AFTER ME!! HE WANTS TO MAKE ME LIKE THE REST OF YOU! BUT I WON'T LET HIM! I WON'T LET HIM!!

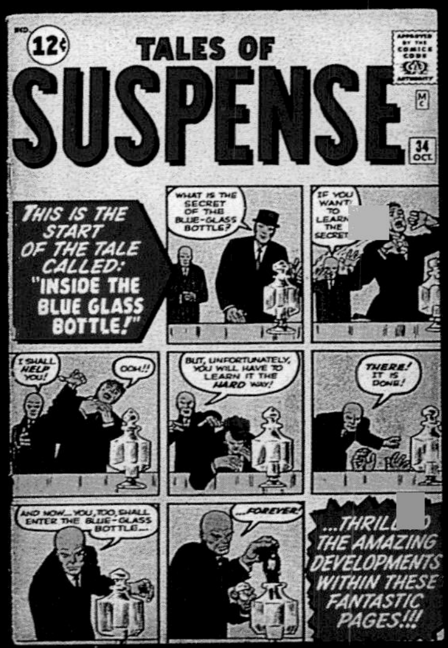
12¢
TALES OF
SUSPENSE
34 OCT.
THIS IS THE START OF THE TALE CALLED: "INSIDE THE BLUE GLASS BOTTLE!"
WHAT IS THE SECRET OF THE BLUE-GLASS BOTTLE?
BUT, UNFORTUNATELY, YOU WILL HAVE TO LEARN IT THE HARD WAY!
THERE! IT IS DONE!
FOREVER!
...THRILL TO THE AMAZING DEVELOPMENTS WITHIN THESE FANTASTIC PAGES!!!

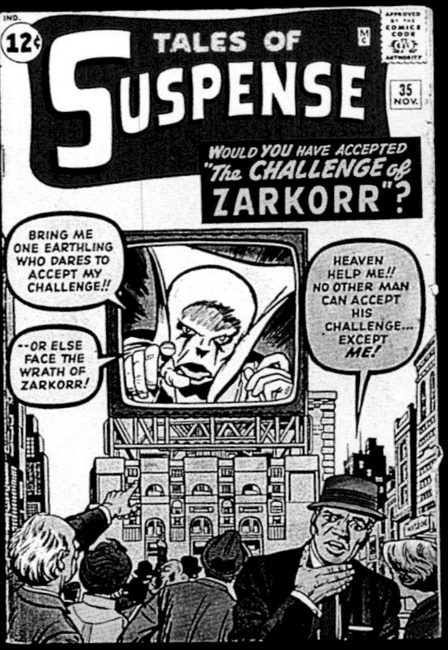
12¢
TALES OF
SUSPENSE
35 NOV.
WOULD YOU HAVE ACCEPTED "The CHALLENGE of ZARKORR"?
BRING ME ONE EARTHLING WHO DARES TO ACCEPT MY CHALLENGE!!
HEAVEN HELP ME!! NO OTHER MAN CAN ACCEPT HIS CHALLENGE... EXCEPT ME!
--OR ELSE FACE THE WRATH OF ZARKORR!

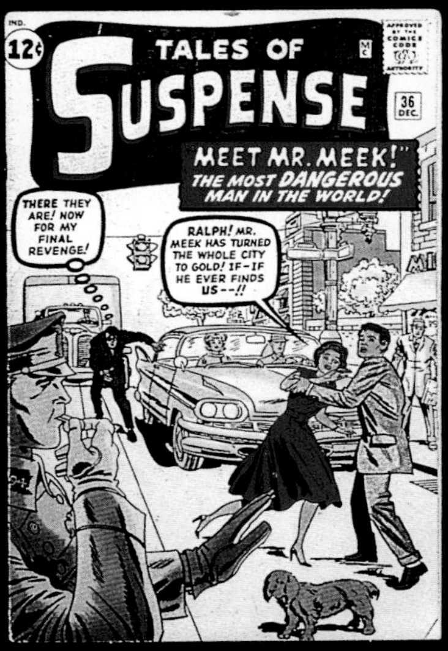
12¢
TALES OF
SUSPENSE
36 DEC.
MEET MR. MEEK! THE MOST DANGEROUS MAN IN THE WORLD!
THERE THEY ARE! NOW FOR MY FINAL REVENGE!
RALPH! MR. MEEK HAS TURNED THE WHOLE CITY TO GOLD! IF-IF HE EVER FINDS US--!!

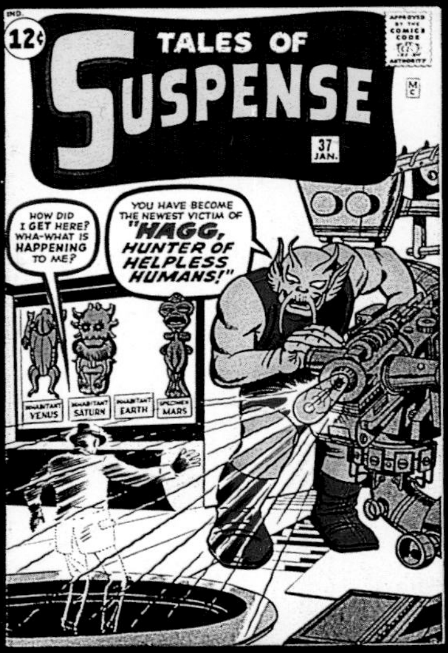
12¢
TALES OF
SUSPENSE
37 JAN.
HOW DID I GET HERE? WHA-WHAT IS HAPPENING TO ME?
YOU HAVE BECOME THE NEWEST VICTIM OF "HAGG, HUNTER OF HELPLESS HUMANS!"
VENUS
SATURN
EARTH
MARS

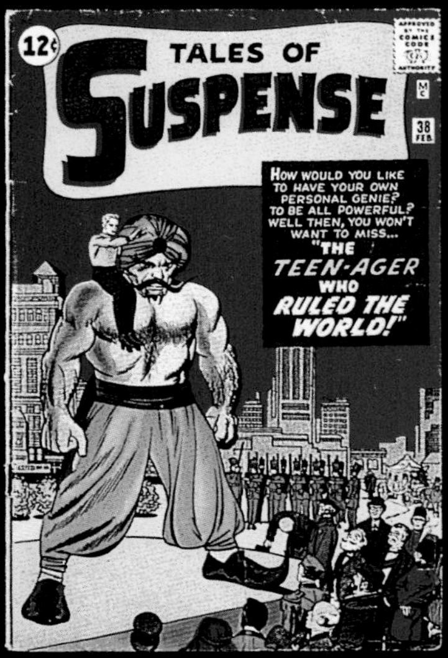
12¢
TALES OF
SUSPENSE
38 FEB.
HOW WOULD YOU LIKE TO HAVE YOUR OWN PERSONAL GENIE? TO BE ALL POWERFUL? WELL THEN, YOU WON'T WANT TO MISS... "THE TEEN-AGER WHO RULED THE WORLD!"

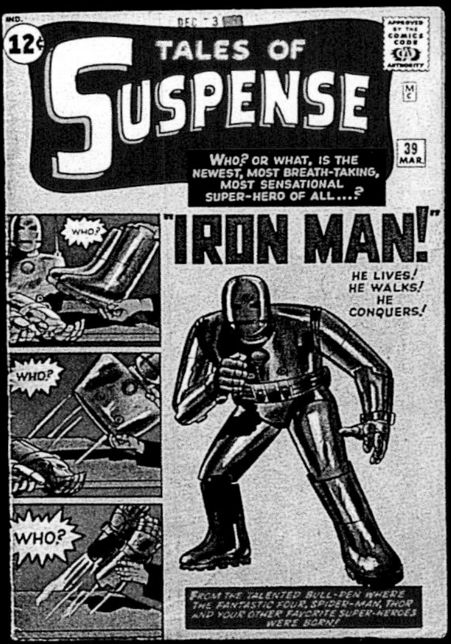
12¢
TALES OF
SUSPENSE
39 MAR.
WHO? OR WHAT, IS THE NEWEST, MOST BREATH-TAKING, MOST SENSATIONAL SUPER-HERO OF ALL...?
"IRON MAN!"
HE LIVES! HE WALKS! HE CONQUERS!
WHO?
WHO?
WHO?
FROM THE TALENTED BULL-PEN WHERE THE FANTASTIC FOUR, SPIDER-MAN, THOR AND YOUR OTHER FAVORITE SUPER-HEROES WERE BORN!

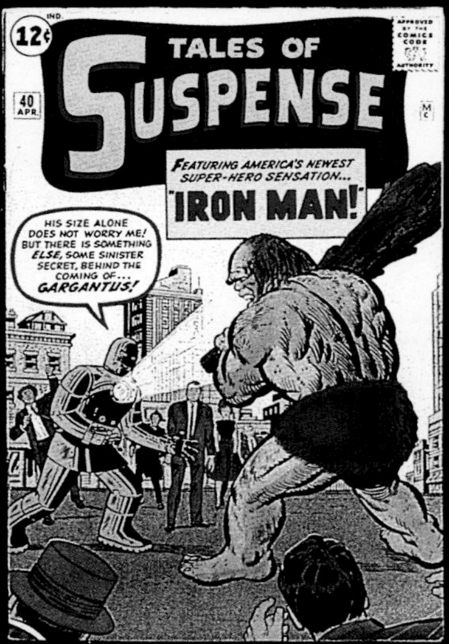
12¢
40 APR.
TALES OF
SUSPENSE
FEATURING AMERICA'S NEWEST SUPER-HERO SENSATION... "IRON MAN!"
HIS SIZE ALONE DOES NOT WORRY ME! BUT THERE IS SOMETHING ELSE, SOME SINISTER SECRET, BEHIND THE COMING OF... GARGANTUS!

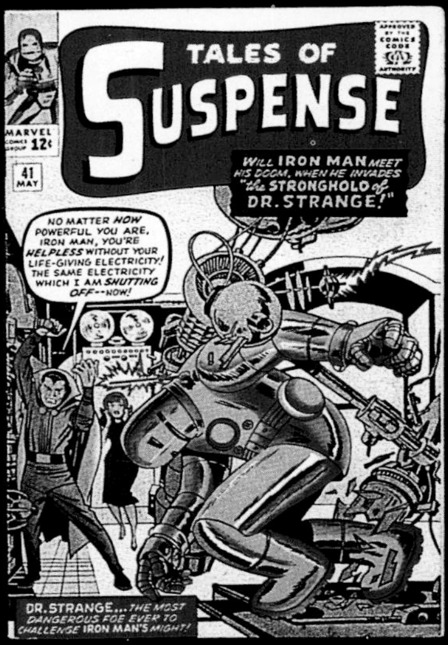
MARVEL COMICS GROUP 12¢
41 MAY
TALES OF
SUSPENSE
WILL IRON MAN MEET HIS DOOM, WHEN HE INVADES "the STRONGHOLD of DR. STRANGE!"
NO MATTER HOW POWERFUL YOU ARE, IRON MAN, YOU'RE HELPLESS WITHOUT YOUR LIFE-GIVING ELECTRICITY! THE SAME ELECTRICITY WHICH I AM SHUTTING OFF--NOW!
DR. STRANGE... THE MOST DANGEROUS FOE EVER TO CHALLENGE IRON MAN'S MIGHT!

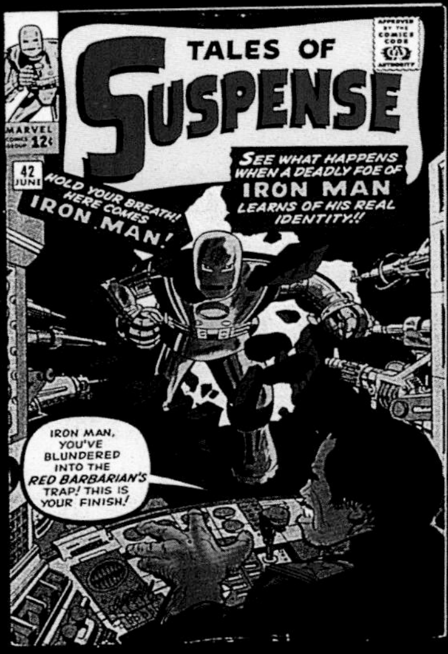
MARVEL COMICS GROUP 12¢
42 JUNE
TALES OF
SUSPENSE
SEE WHAT HAPPENS WHEN A DEADLY FOE OF IRON MAN LEARNS OF HIS REAL IDENTITY!!
HOLD YOUR BREATH! HERE COMES IRON MAN!
IRON MAN, YOU'VE BLUNDERED INTO THE RED BARBARIAN'S TRAP! THIS IS YOUR FINISH!

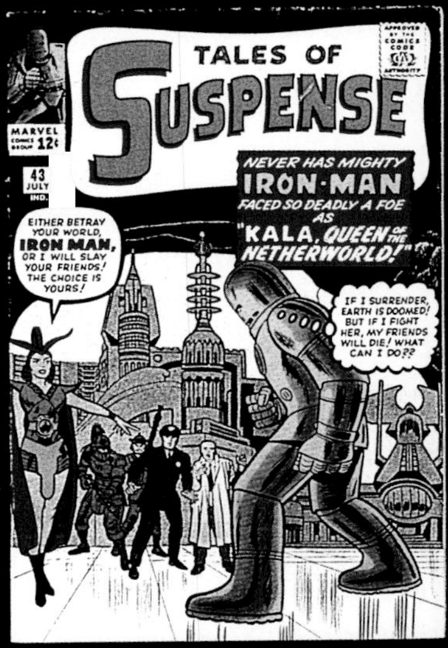
MARVEL COMICS GROUP 12¢
43 JULY
TALES OF
SUSPENSE
NEVER HAS MIGHTY IRON-MAN FACED SO DEADLY A FOE AS "KALA, QUEEN of the NETHERWORLD!"
EITHER BETRAY YOUR WORLD, IRON MAN, OR I WILL SLAY YOUR FRIENDS! THE CHOICE IS YOURS!
IF I SURRENDER, EARTH IS DOOMED! BUT IF I FIGHT HER, MY FRIENDS WILL DIE! WHAT CAN I DO??

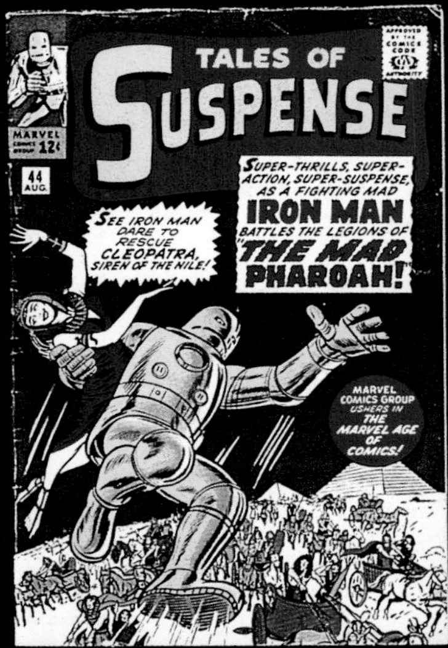
MARVEL COMICS GROUP 12¢
44 AUG.
TALES OF
SUSPENSE
SUPER-THRILLS, SUPER-ACTION, SUPER-SUSPENSE, AS A FIGHTING MAD IRON MAN BATTLES THE LEGIONS OF "THE MAD PHAROAH!"
SEE IRON MAN DARE TO RESCUE CLEOPATRA, SIREN OF THE NILE!
MARVEL COMICS GROUP USHERS IN THE MARVEL AGE OF COMICS!

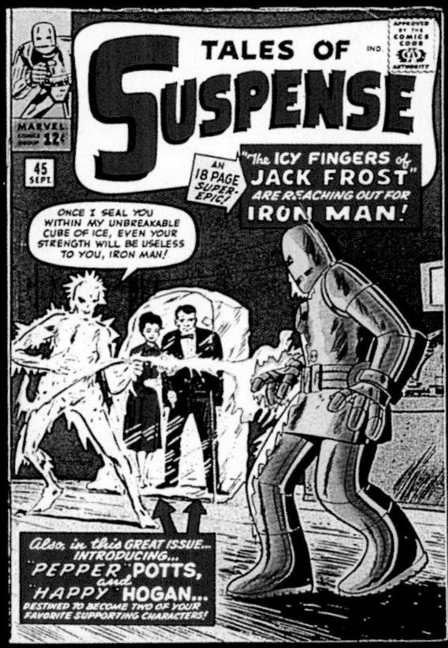
MARVEL COMICS GROUP 12¢
45 SEPT.
TALES OF
SUSPENSE
AN 18 PAGE SUPER EPIC!
"The ICY FINGERS of JACK FROST ARE REACHING OUT FOR IRON MAN!"
ONCE I SEAL YOU WITHIN MY UNBREAKABLE CUBE OF ICE, EVEN YOUR STRENGTH WILL BE USELESS TO YOU, IRON MAN!
Also, in this GREAT ISSUE... INTRODUCING... PEPPER POTTS, and HAPPY HOGAN... DESTINED TO BECOME TWO OF YOUR FAVORITE SUPPORTING CHARACTERS!

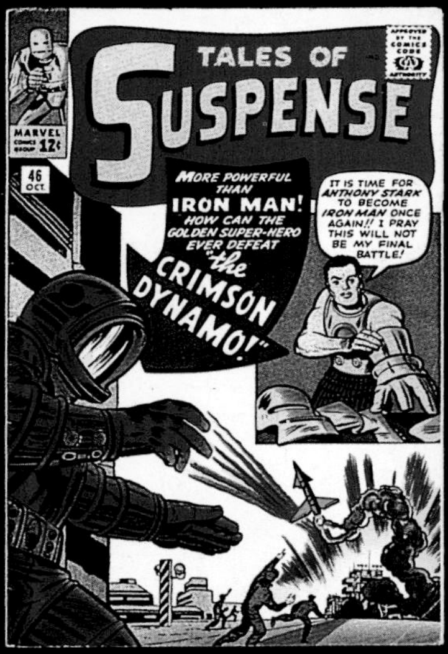
MARVEL COMICS GROUP 12¢
46 OCT.
TALES OF
SUSPENSE
MORE POWERFUL THAN IRON MAN! HOW CAN THE GOLDEN SUPER-HERO EVER DEFEAT "the CRIMSON DYNAMO!"
IT IS TIME FOR ANTHONY STARK TO BECOME IRON MAN ONCE AGAIN!! I PRAY THIS WILL NOT BE MY FINAL BATTLE!

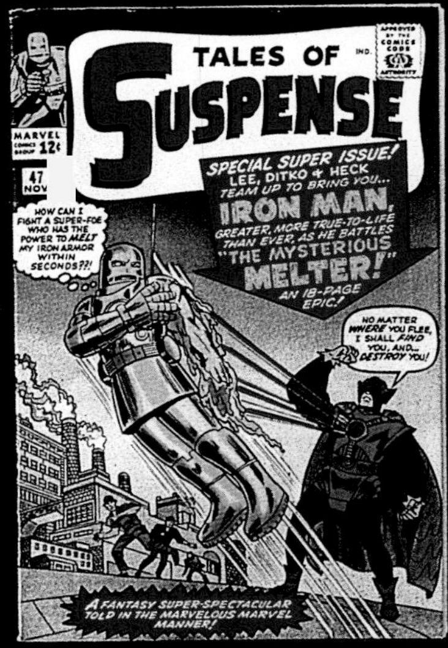
MARVEL COMICS GROUP 12¢
47 NOV.
TALES OF
SUSPENSE
SPECIAL SUPER ISSUE! LEE, DITKO & HECK TEAM UP TO BRING YOU... IRON MAN, GREATER, MORE TRUE-TO-LIFE THAN EVER, AS HE BATTLES "THE MYSTERIOUS MELTER!" AN 18-PAGE EPIC!
HOW CAN I FIGHT A SUPER-FOE WHO HAS THE POWER TO MELT MY IRON ARMOR WITHIN SECONDS??
NO MATTER WHERE YOU FLEE, I SHALL FIND YOU AND... DESTROY YOU!
A FANTASY SUPER-SPECTACULAR TOLD IN THE MARVELOUS MARVEL MANNER!

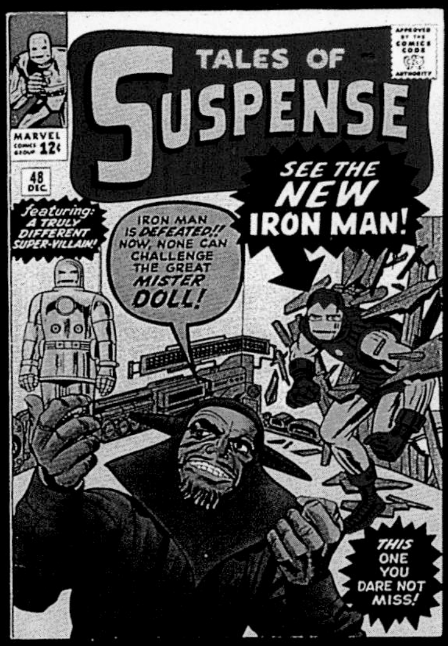
MARVEL COMICS GROUP 12¢
48 DEC.
TALES OF
SUSPENSE
SEE THE NEW IRON MAN!
featuring: A TRULY DIFFERENT SUPER-VILLAIN!
IRON MAN IS DEFEATED!! NOW, NONE CAN CHALLENGE THE GREAT MISTER DOLL!
THIS ONE YOU DARE NOT MISS!

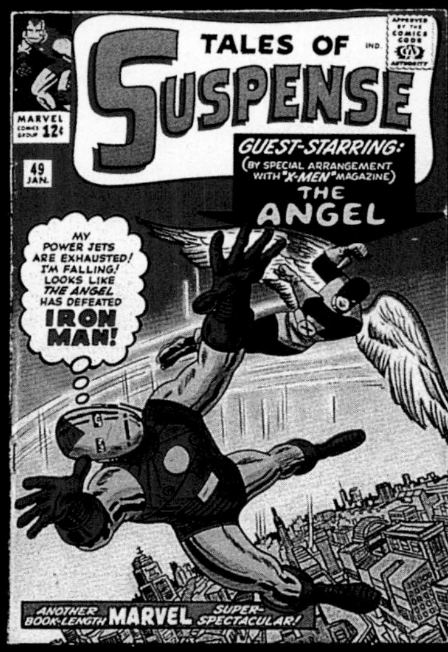
MARVEL COMICS GROUP 12¢
49 JAN.
TALES OF
SUSPENSE
GUEST-STARRING: (BY SPECIAL ARRANGEMENT WITH "X-MEN" MAGAZINE) THE ANGEL
MY POWER JETS ARE EXHAUSTED! I'M FALLING! LOOKS LIKE THE ANGEL HAS DEFEATED IRON MAN!
ANOTHER BOOK-LENGTH MARVEL SUPER SPECTACULAR!

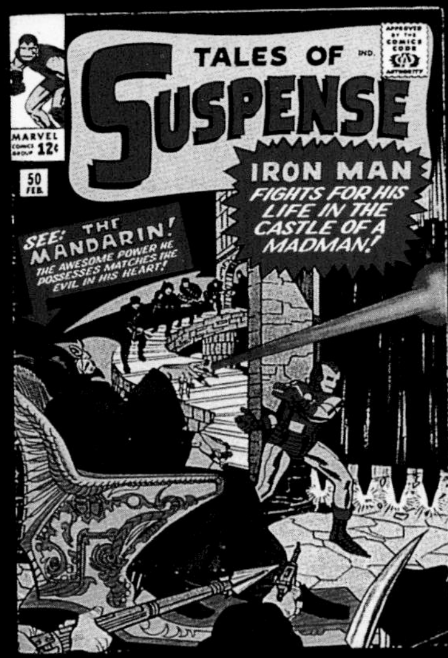
MARVEL COMICS GROUP 12¢
50 FEB.
TALES OF
SUSPENSE
IRON MAN FIGHTS FOR HIS LIFE IN THE CASTLE OF A MADMAN!
SEE: THE MANDARIN! THE AWESOME POWER HE POSSESSES MATCHES THE EVIL IN HIS HEART!

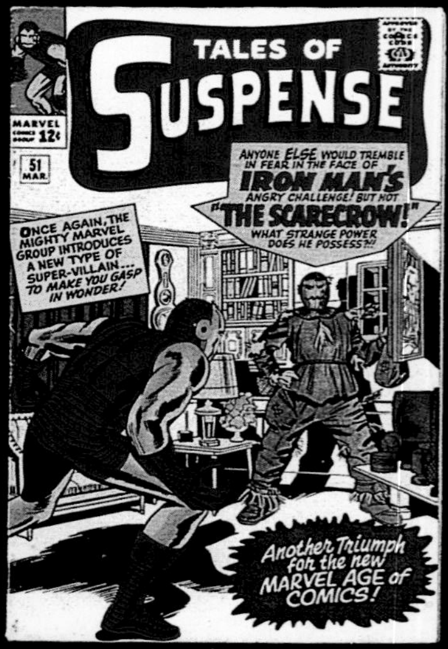
TALES OF SUSPENSE
51 MAR.
ANYONE ELSE WOULD TREMBLE IN FEAR IN THE FACE OF IRON MAN'S ANGRIEST CHALLENGE! BUT NOT "THE SCARECROW!"
WHAT STRANGE POWER DOES HE POSSESS?!
ONCE AGAIN, THE MIGHTY MARVEL GROUP INTRODUCES A NEW TYPE OF SUPER-VILLAIN... TO MAKE YOU GASP IN WONDER!
Another Triumph for the new MARVEL AGE of COMICS!

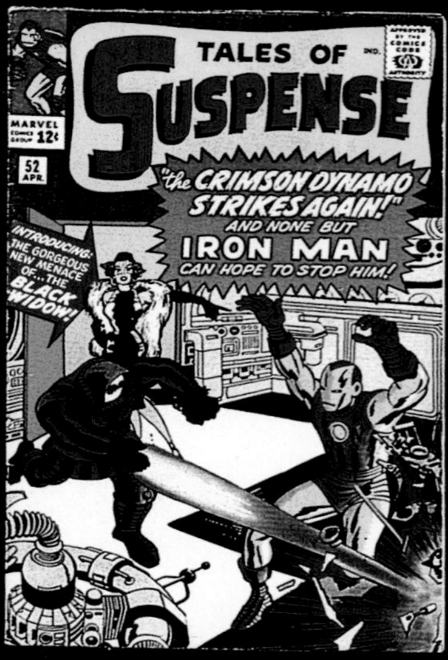
TALES OF SUSPENSE
52 APR.
"the CRIMSON DYNAMO STRIKES AGAIN!"
AND NONE BUT IRON MAN CAN HOPE TO STOP HIM!
INTRODUCING THE GORGEOUS NEW MENACE OF... THE BLACK WIDOW!

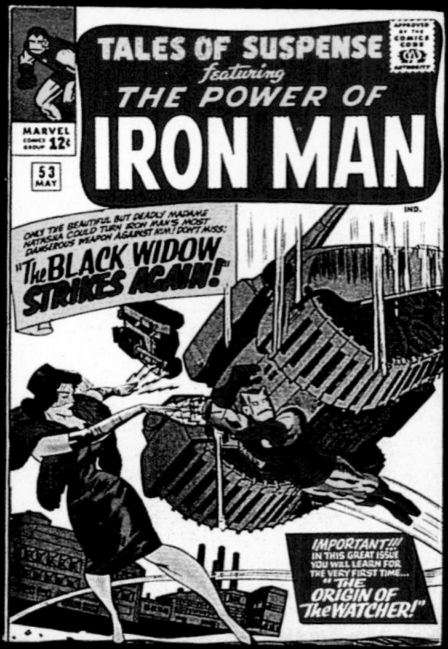
TALES OF SUSPENSE featuring THE POWER OF IRON MAN
53 MAY
"The BLACK WIDOW STRIKES AGAIN!"
IMPORTANT!!! IN THIS GREAT ISSUE YOU WILL LEARN FOR THE VERY FIRST TIME... "THE ORIGIN OF The WATCHER!"

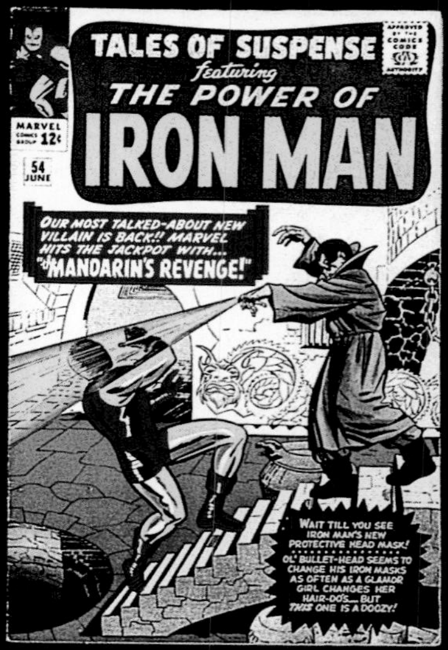
TALES OF SUSPENSE featuring THE POWER OF IRON MAN
54 JUNE
OUR MOST TALKED-ABOUT NEW VILLAIN IS BACK!! MARVEL HITS THE JACKPOT WITH... "MANDARIN'S REVENGE!"
WAIT TILL YOU SEE IRON MAN'S NEW PROTECTIVE HEAD MASK!

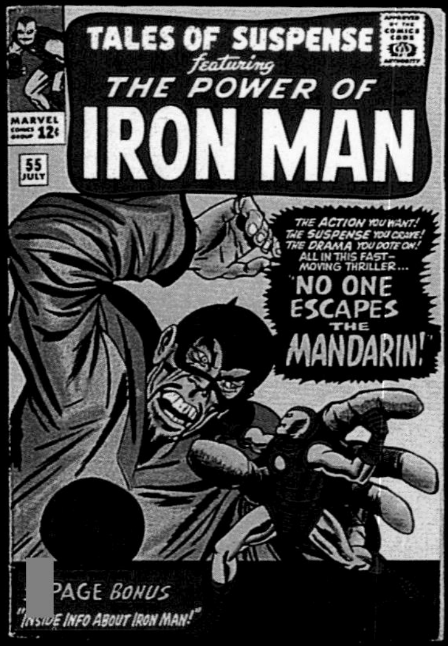
TALES OF SUSPENSE featuring THE POWER OF IRON MAN
55 JULY
THE ACTION YOU WANT! THE SUSPENSE YOU CRAVE! THE DRAMA YOU DOTE ON! ALL IN THIS FAST-MOVING THRILLER...
"NO ONE ESCAPES THE MANDARIN!"
PAGE BONUS
"INSIDE INFO ABOUT IRON MAN!"

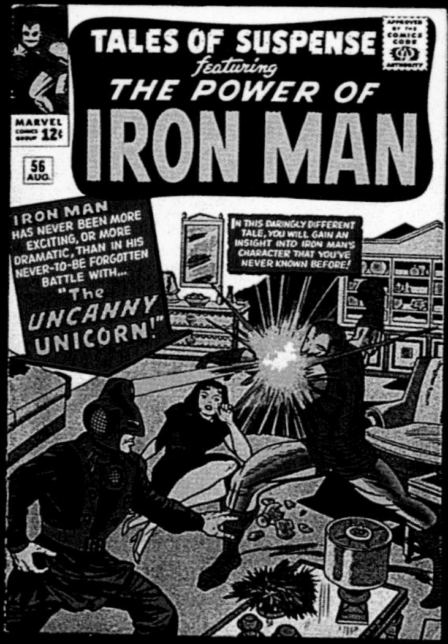
TALES OF SUSPENSE featuring THE POWER OF IRON MAN
56 AUG.
IRON MAN HAS NEVER BEEN MORE EXCITING, OR MORE DRAMATIC, THAN IN HIS NEVER-TO-BE-FORGOTTEN BATTLE WITH... "The UNCANNY UNICORN!"
IN THIS DARINGLY DIFFERENT TALE, YOU WILL GAIN AN INSIGHT INTO IRON MAN'S CHARACTER THAT YOU'VE NEVER KNOWN BEFORE!

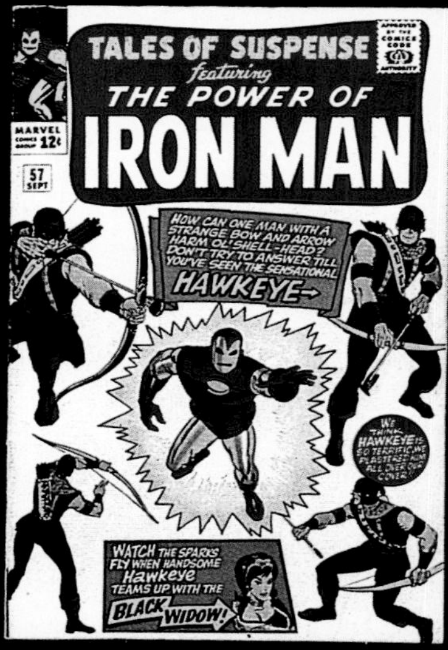
TALES OF SUSPENSE featuring THE POWER OF IRON MAN
57 SEPT
HOW CAN ONE MAN WITH A STRANGE BOW AND ARROW HARM OL' SHELL-HEAD? DON'T TRY TO ANSWER TILL YOU'VE SEEN THE SENSATIONAL HAWKEYE
WATCH THE SPARKS FLY WHEN HANDSOME Hawkeye TEAMS UP WITH THE BLACK WIDOW!

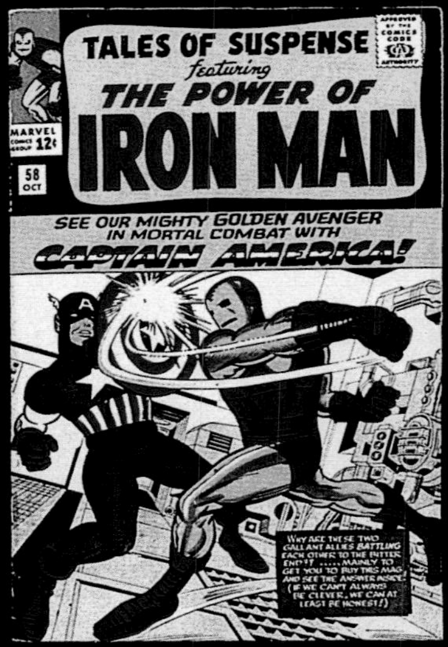
TALES OF SUSPENSE featuring THE POWER OF IRON MAN
58 OCT
SEE OUR MIGHTY GOLDEN AVENGER IN MORTAL COMBAT WITH CAPTAIN AMERICA!

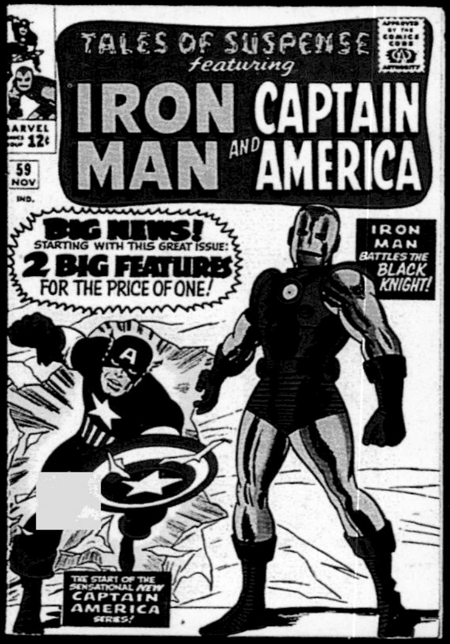
TALES OF SUSPENSE featuring IRON MAN AND CAPTAIN AMERICA
59 NOV
BIG NEWS! STARTING WITH THIS GREAT ISSUE: 2 BIG FEATURES FOR THE PRICE OF ONE!
IRON MAN BATTLES THE BLACK KNIGHT!
THE START OF THE SENSATIONAL NEW CAPTAIN AMERICA SERIES!

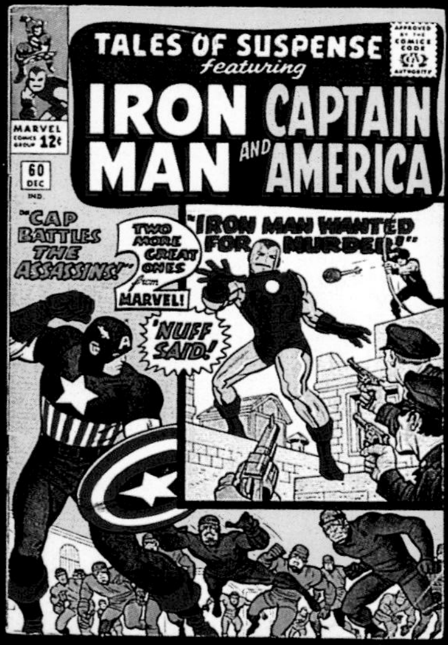
TALES OF SUSPENSE featuring IRON MAN AND CAPTAIN AMERICA
60 DEC
"CAP BATTLES THE ASSASSINS!"
TWO MORE GREAT ONES FROM MARVEL!
"IRON MAN WANTED FOR MURDER!"
'NUFF SAID!

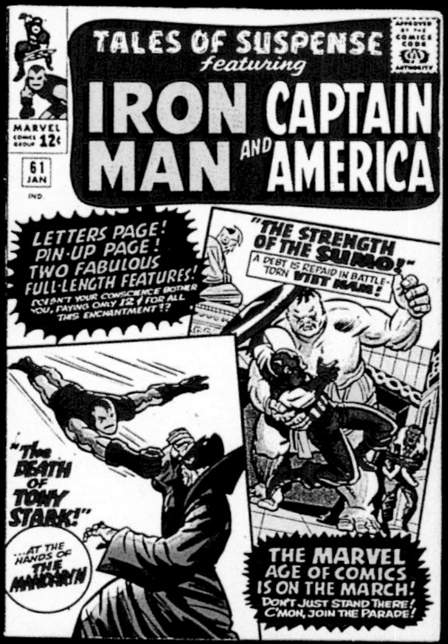
TALES OF SUSPENSE featuring IRON MAN AND CAPTAIN AMERICA
61 JAN
LETTERS PAGE! PIN-UP PAGE! TWO FABULOUS FULL-LENGTH FEATURES!
"THE STRENGTH OF THE SUMO!"
"The DEATH OF TONY STARK!" AT THE HANDS OF THE MANDARIN
THE MARVEL AGE OF COMICS IS ON THE MARCH! DON'T JUST STAND THERE! C'MON, JOIN THE PARADE!

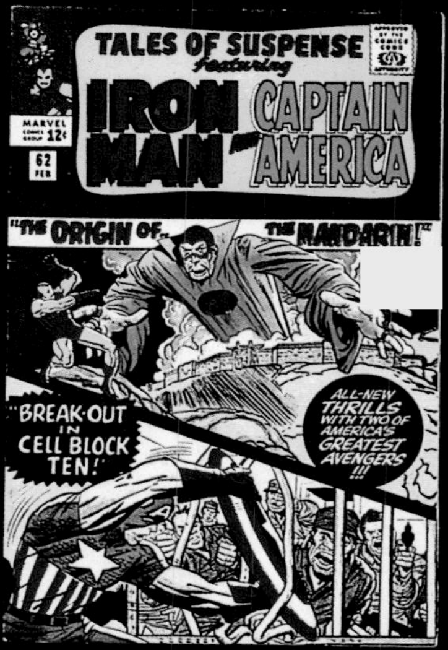
TALES OF SUSPENSE featuring IRON MAN AND CAPTAIN AMERICA
62 FEB
"THE ORIGIN OF... THE MANDARIN!"
"BREAK-OUT IN CELL BLOCK TEN!"
ALL-NEW THRILLS WITH TWO OF AMERICA'S GREATEST AVENGERS!!!

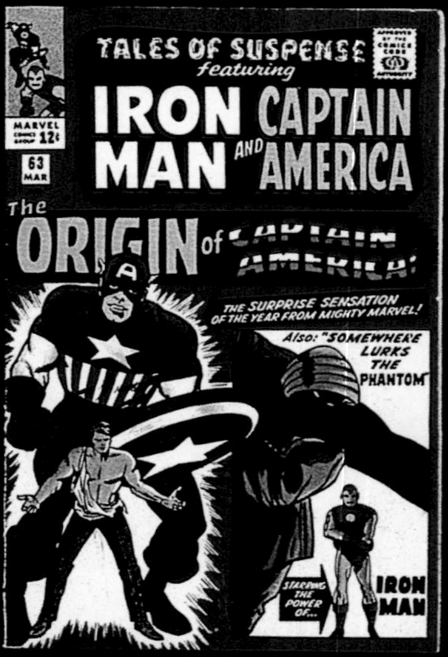
TALES OF SUSPENSE featuring IRON MAN AND CAPTAIN AMERICA
63 MAR
The ORIGIN of CAPTAIN AMERICA!
THE SURPRISE SENSATION OF THE YEAR FROM MIGHTY MARVEL!
Also: "SOMEWHERE LURKS THE PHANTOM"
STARRING THE POWER OF... IRON MAN

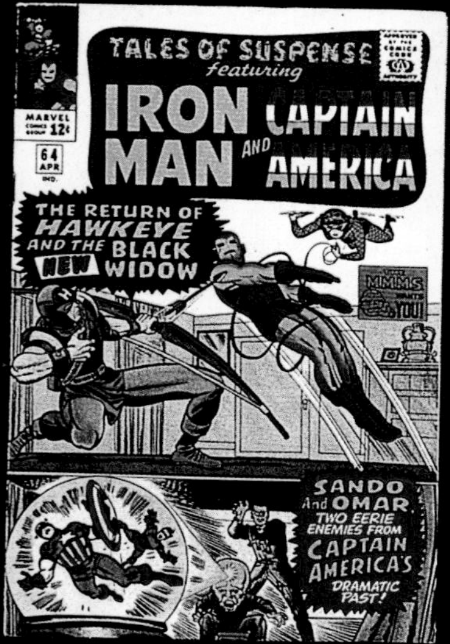
TALES OF SUSPENSE featuring IRON MAN AND CAPTAIN AMERICA
64 APR
THE RETURN OF HAWKEYE AND THE NEW BLACK WIDOW
SANDO AND OMAR TWO EERIE ENEMIES FROM CAPTAIN AMERICA'S DRAMATIC PAST!

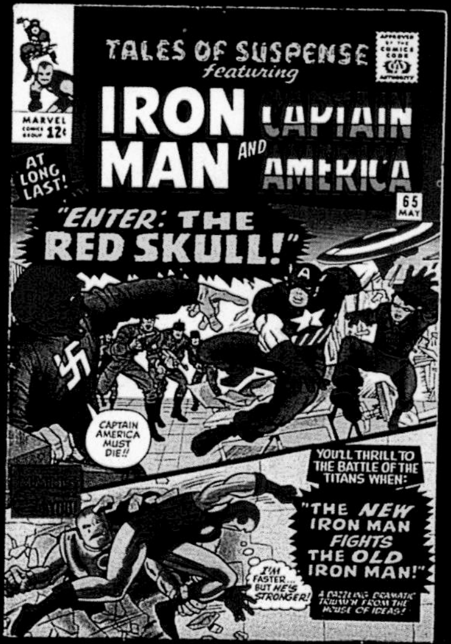
TALES OF SUSPENSE featuring IRON MAN AND CAPTAIN AMERICA
65 MAY
AT LONG LAST!
"ENTER: THE RED SKULL!"
CAPTAIN AMERICA MUST DIE!!
YOU'LL THRILL TO THE BATTLE OF THE TITANS WHEN:
"THE NEW IRON MAN FIGHTS THE OLD IRON MAN!"

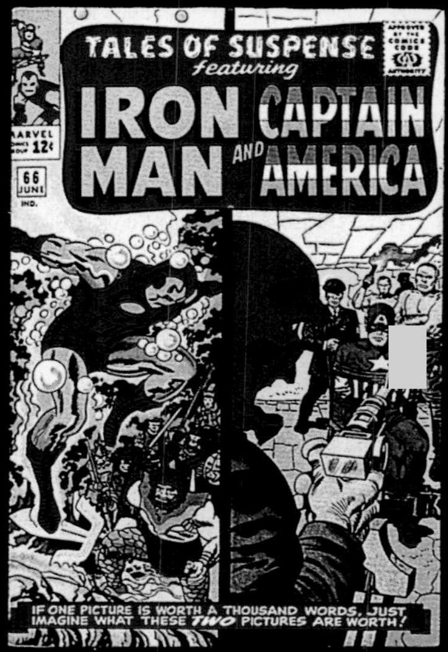
TALES OF SUSPENSE featuring IRON MAN AND CAPTAIN AMERICA
66 JUNE
IF ONE PICTURE IS WORTH A THOUSAND WORDS, JUST IMAGINE WHAT THESE TWO PICTURES ARE WORTH!

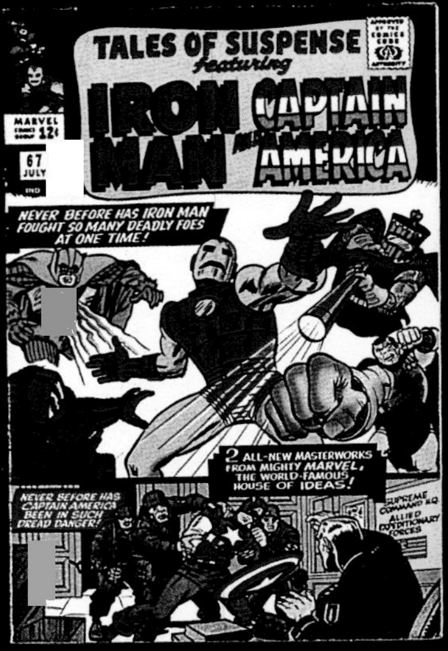
TALES OF SUSPENSE
featuring
IRON MAN AND CAPTAIN AMERICA
67
JULY
NEVER BEFORE HAS IRON MAN FOUGHT SO MANY DEADLY FOES AT ONE TIME!
2 ALL-NEW MASTERWORKS FROM MIGHTY MARVEL, THE WORLD-FAMOUS HOUSE OF IDEAS!
NEVER BEFORE HAS CAPTAIN AMERICA BEEN IN SUCH DREAD DANGER!

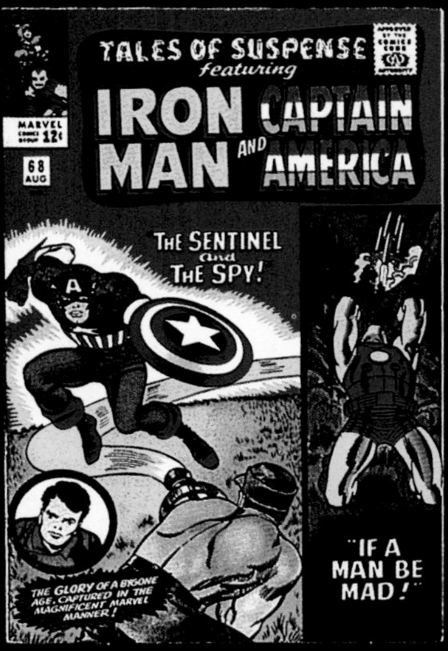
TALES OF SUSPENSE
featuring
IRON MAN AND CAPTAIN AMERICA
68
AUG
THE SENTINEL and THE SPY!
THE GLORY OF A BYGONE AGE, CAPTURED IN THE MAGNIFICENT MARVEL MANNER!
"IF A MAN BE MAD!"

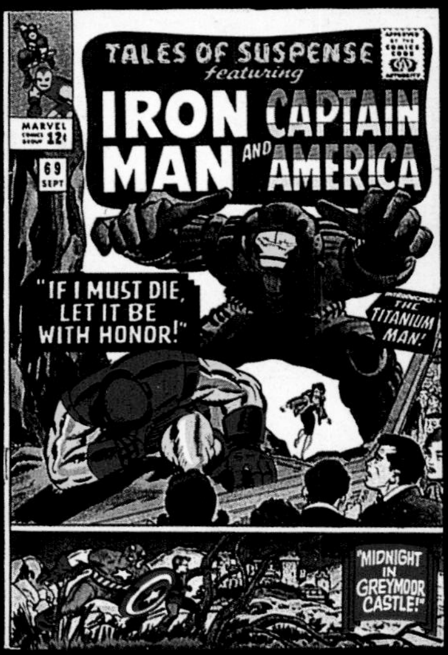
TALES OF SUSPENSE
featuring
IRON MAN AND CAPTAIN AMERICA
69
SEPT
"IF I MUST DIE, LET IT BE WITH HONOR!"
THE TITANIUM MAN!
"MIDNIGHT IN GREYMOOR CASTLE!"

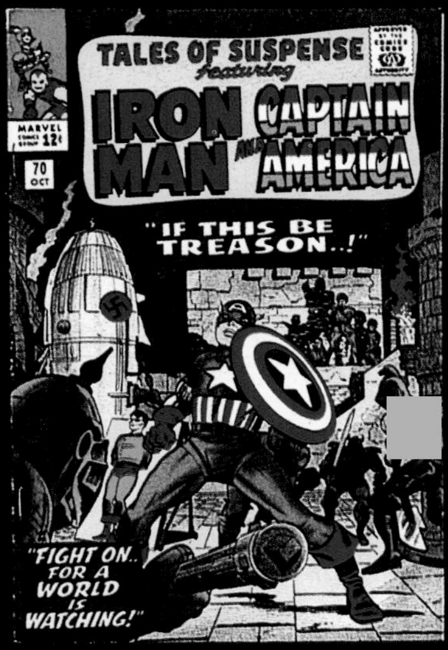
TALES OF SUSPENSE
featuring
IRON MAN AND CAPTAIN AMERICA
70
OCT
"IF THIS BE TREASON..!"
"FIGHT ON, FOR A WORLD IS WATCHING!"

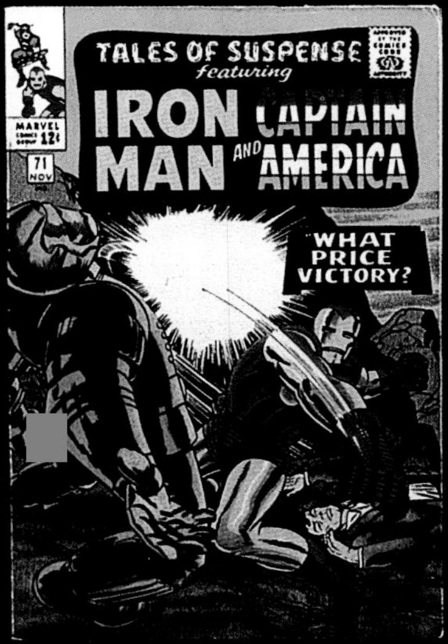
TALES OF SUSPENSE
featuring
IRON MAN AND CAPTAIN AMERICA
71
NOV
"WHAT PRICE VICTORY?"

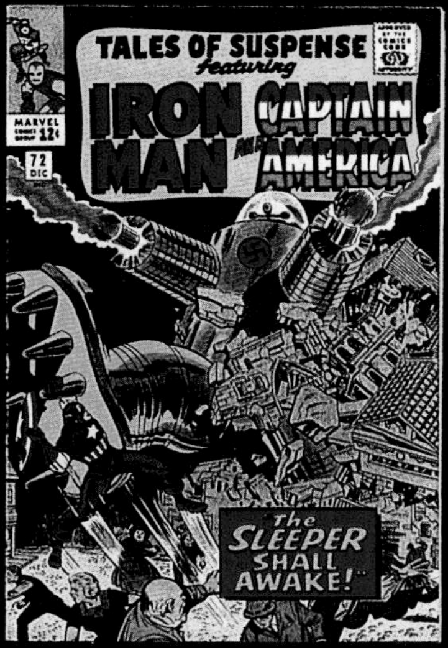
TALES OF SUSPENSE
featuring
IRON MAN AND CAPTAIN AMERICA
72
DEC
"The SLEEPER SHALL AWAKE!"

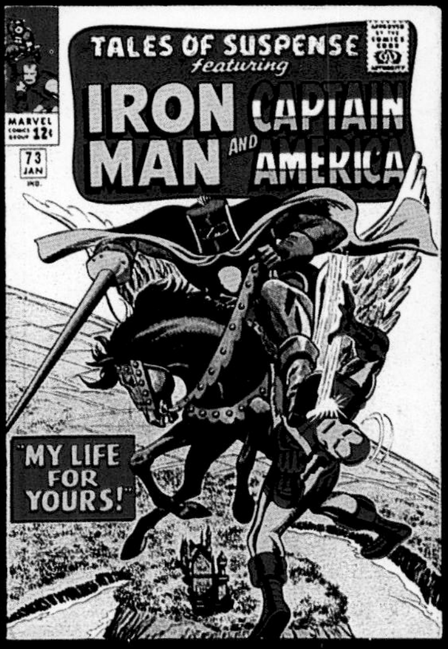
TALES OF SUSPENSE
featuring
IRON MAN AND CAPTAIN AMERICA
73
JAN
"MY LIFE FOR YOURS!"

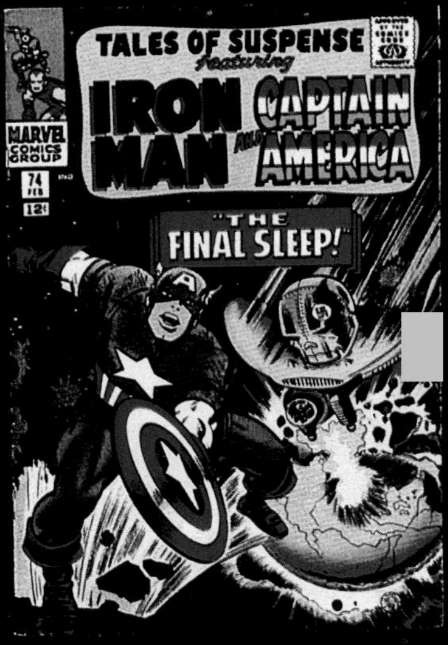
TALES OF SUSPENSE
featuring
IRON MAN AND CAPTAIN AMERICA
MARVEL COMICS GROUP
74
FEB
12¢
"THE FINAL SLEEP!"

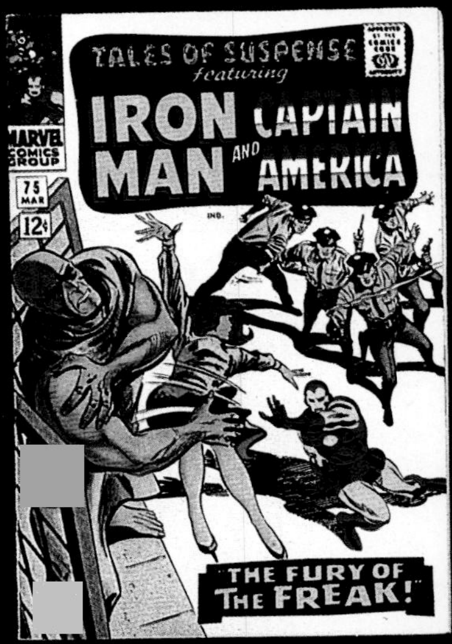
TALES OF SUSPENSE
featuring
IRON MAN AND CAPTAIN AMERICA
MARVEL COMICS GROUP
75
MAR
12¢
THE FURY OF THE FREAK!

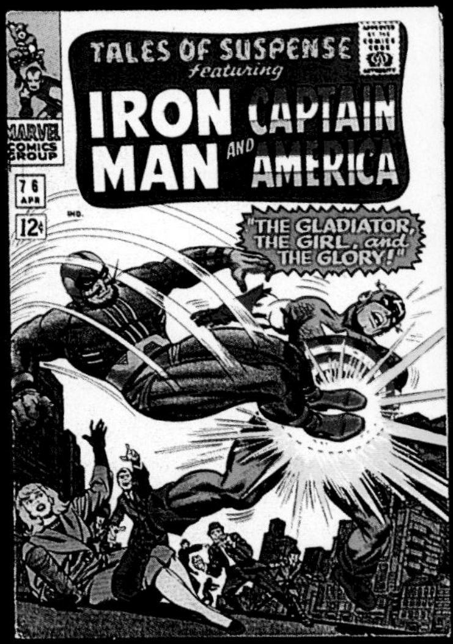
TALES OF SUSPENSE
featuring
IRON MAN AND CAPTAIN AMERICA
MARVEL COMICS GROUP
76
APR
12¢
THE GLADIATOR, THE GIRL, and THE GLORY!

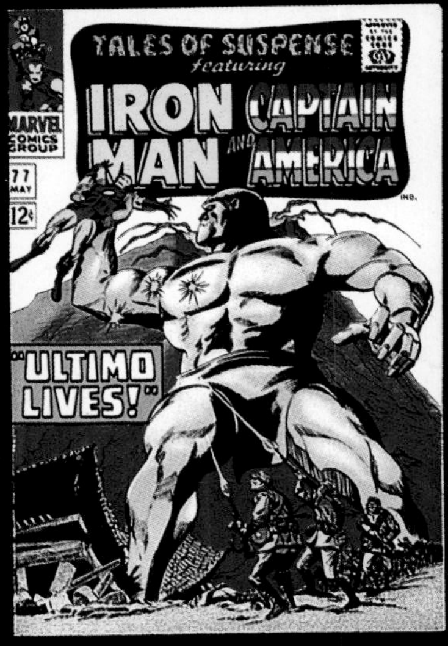
TALES OF SUSPENSE
featuring
IRON MAN AND CAPTAIN AMERICA
MARVEL COMICS GROUP
77
MAY
12¢
"ULTIMO LIVES!"

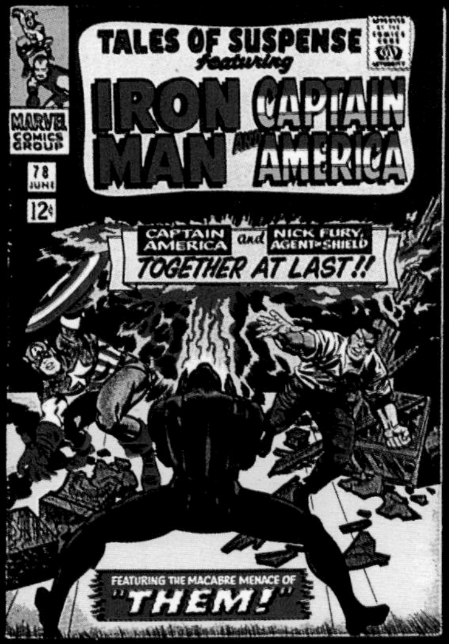
TALES OF SUSPENSE
featuring
IRON MAN AND CAPTAIN AMERICA
MARVEL COMICS GROUP
78
JUNE
12¢
CAPTAIN AMERICA and NICK FURY, AGENT of SHIELD
TOGETHER AT LAST!!
FEATURING THE MACABRE MENACE OF "THEM!"

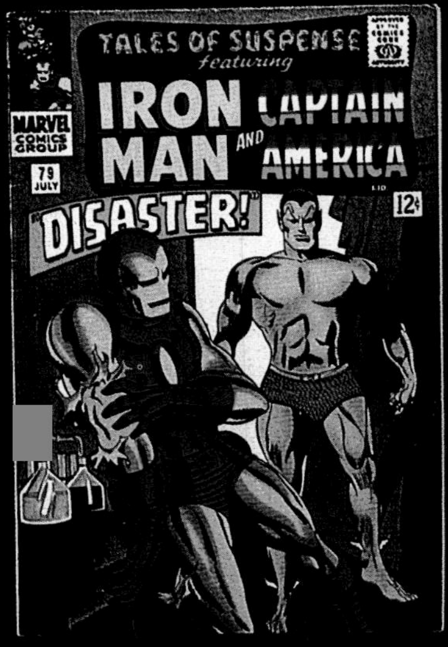
TALES OF SUSPENSE
featuring
IRON MAN AND CAPTAIN AMERICA
MARVEL COMICS GROUP
79
JULY
12¢
DISASTER!

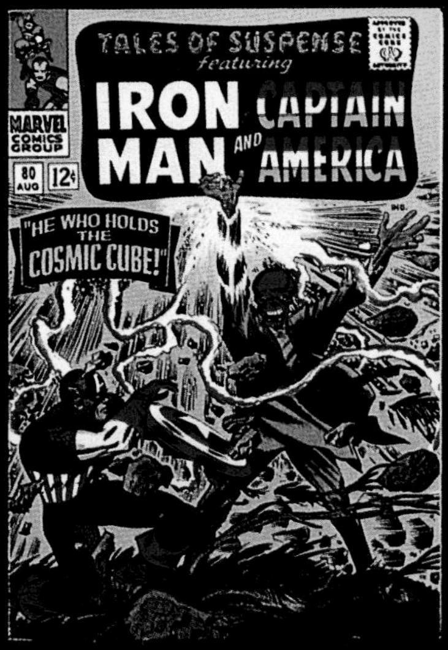
TALES OF SUSPENSE
featuring
IRON MAN AND CAPTAIN AMERICA
MARVEL COMICS GROUP
80
AUG
12¢
"HE WHO HOLDS THE COSMIC CUBE!"

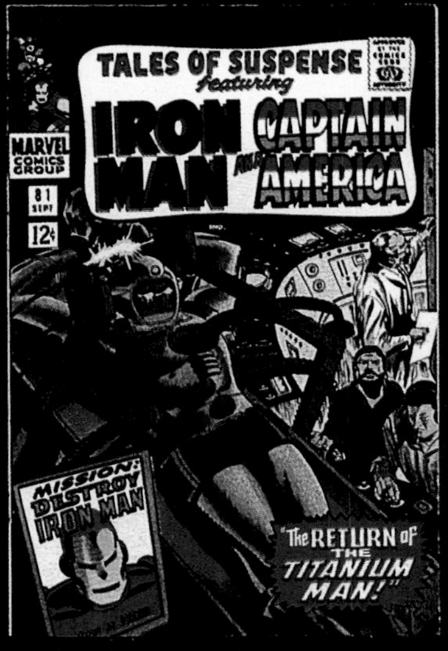
TALES OF SUSPENSE
featuring
IRON MAN AND CAPTAIN AMERICA
MARVEL COMICS GROUP
81
SEPT
12¢
MISSION: DESTROY IRON MAN
"The RETURN of THE TITANIUM MAN!"

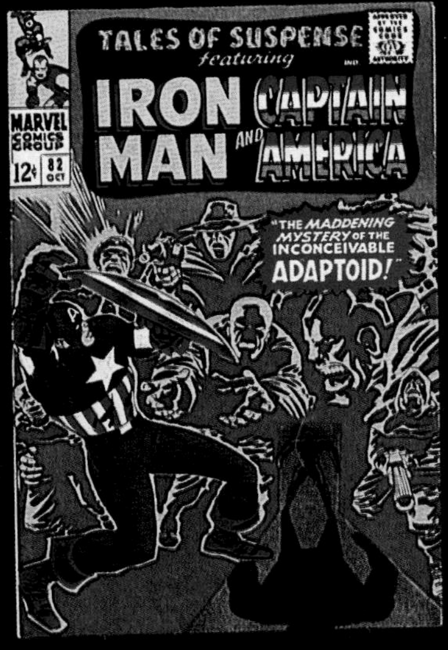
TALES OF SUSPENSE
featuring
IRON MAN AND CAPTAIN AMERICA
MARVEL COMICS GROUP
12¢
82
OCT
"THE MADDENING MYSTERY of the INCONCEIVABLE ADAPTOID!"

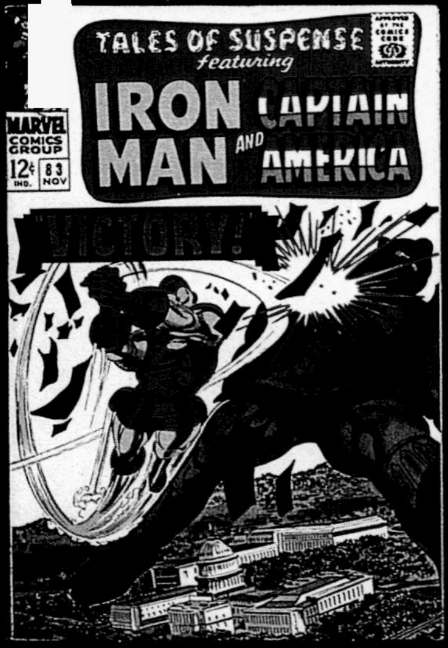
TALES OF SUSPENSE featuring
IRON MAN AND CAPTAIN AMERICA
MARVEL COMICS GROUP
12¢ 83 NOV
VICTORY!

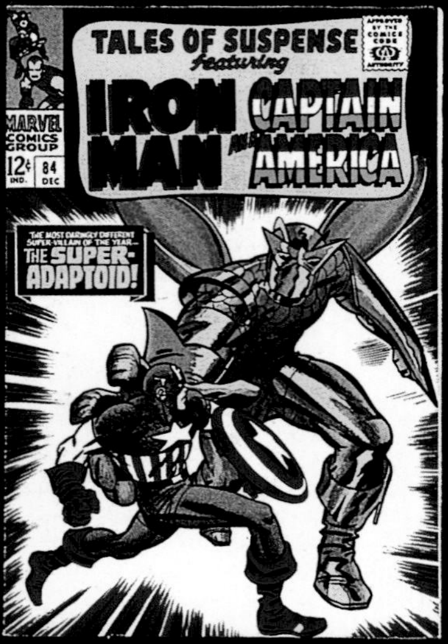
TALES OF SUSPENSE featuring
IRON MAN AND CAPTAIN AMERICA
MARVEL COMICS GROUP
12¢ 84 DEC
THE SUPER-ADAPTOID!

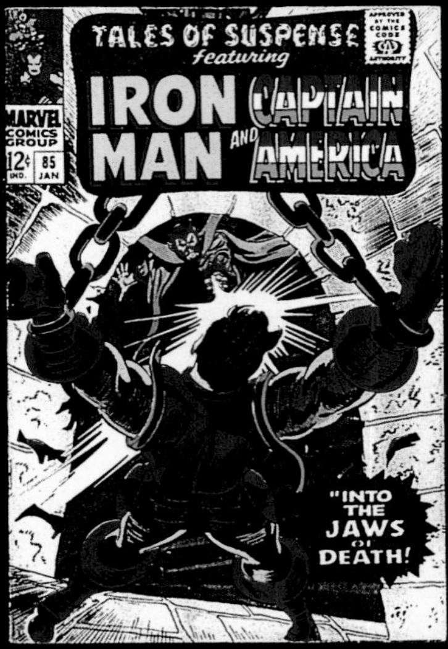
TALES OF SUSPENSE featuring
IRON MAN AND CAPTAIN AMERICA
MARVEL COMICS GROUP
12¢ 85 JAN
"INTO THE JAWS OF DEATH!"

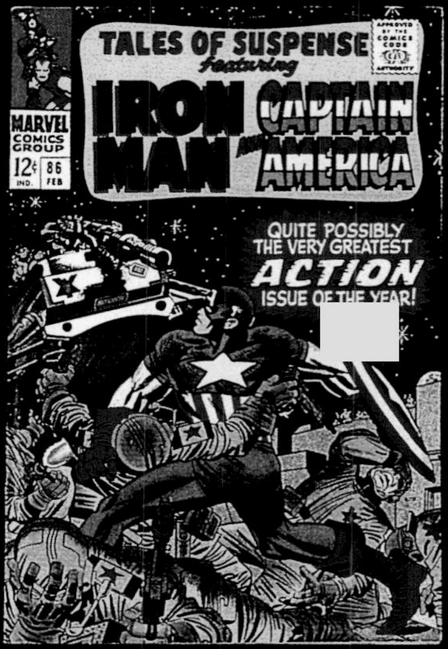
TALES OF SUSPENSE featuring
IRON MAN AND CAPTAIN AMERICA
MARVEL COMICS GROUP
12¢ 86 FEB
QUITE POSSIBLY THE VERY GREATEST ACTION ISSUE OF THE YEAR!

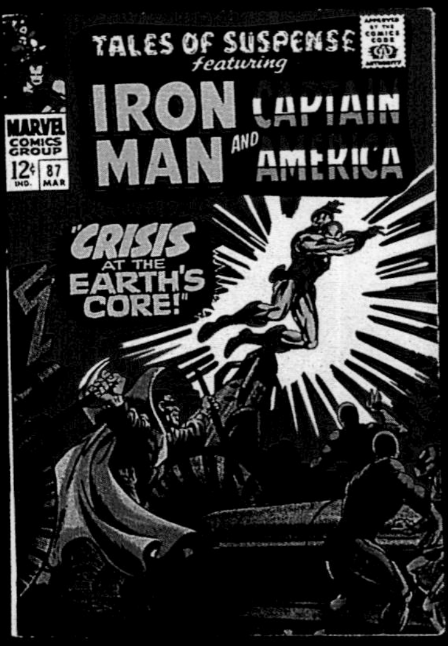
TALES OF SUSPENSE featuring
IRON MAN AND CAPTAIN AMERICA
MARVEL COMICS GROUP
12¢ 87 MAR
"CRISIS AT THE EARTH'S CORE!"

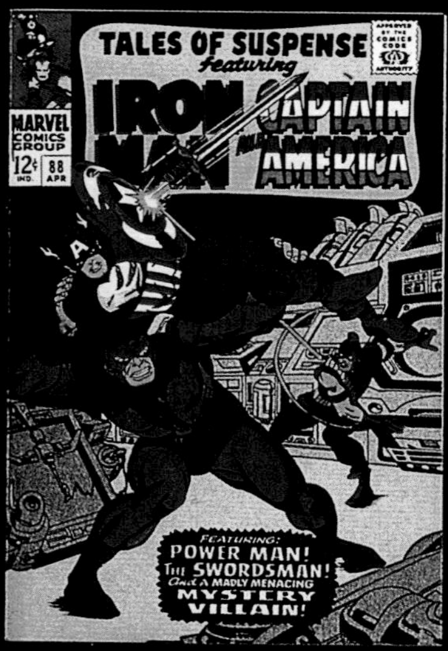
TALES OF SUSPENSE featuring
IRON MAN AND CAPTAIN AMERICA
MARVEL COMICS GROUP
12¢ 88 APR
FEATURING: POWER MAN! THE SWORDSMAN! AND A MADLY MENACING MYSTERY VILLAIN!

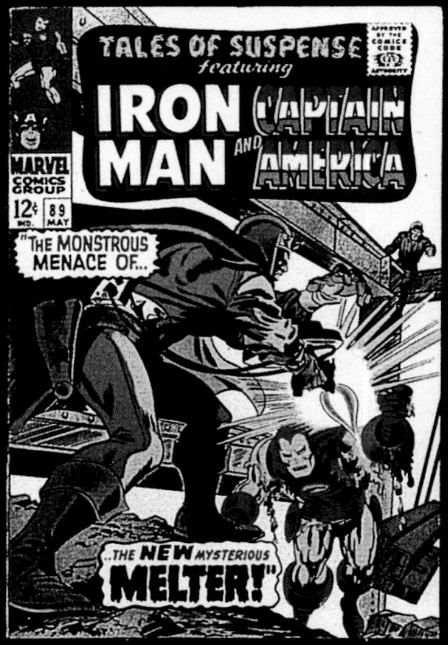
TALES OF SUSPENSE featuring
IRON MAN AND CAPTAIN AMERICA
MARVEL COMICS GROUP
12¢ 89 MAY
"THE MONSTROUS MENACE OF...
...THE NEW MYSTERIOUS MELTER!"

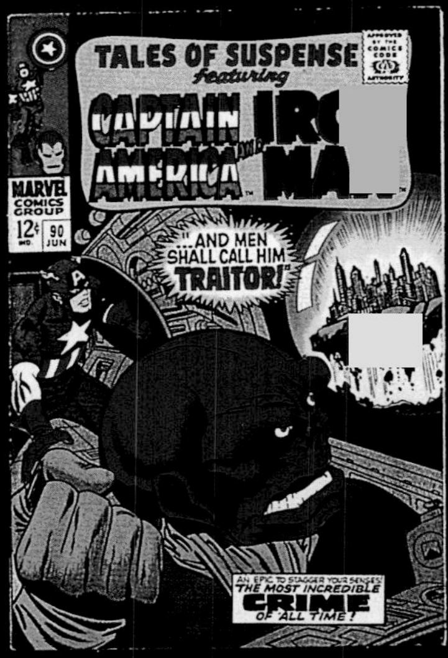
TALES OF SUSPENSE featuring
CAPTAIN AMERICA AND
MARVEL COMICS GROUP
12¢ 90 JUN
...AND MEN SHALL CALL HIM TRAITOR!
AN EPIC TO STAGGER YOUR SENSES! THE MOST INCREDIBLE CRIME OF ALL TIME!

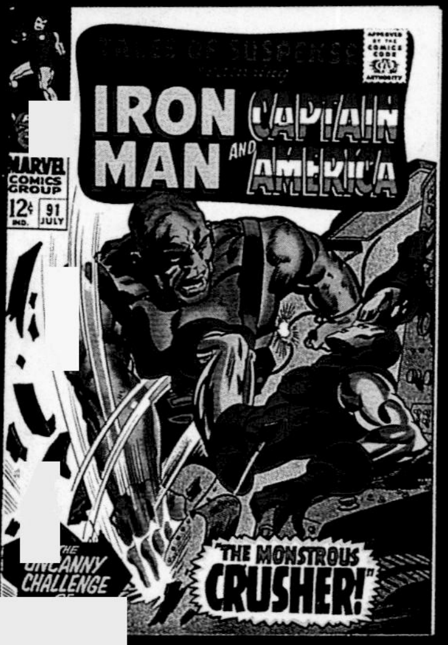
IRON MAN AND CAPTAIN AMERICA
MARVEL COMICS GROUP
12¢ 91 JULY
UNCANNY CHALLENGE
"THE MONSTROUS CRUSHER!"

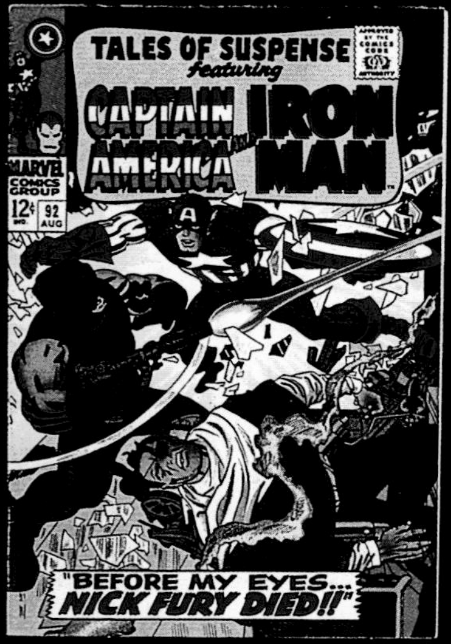
TALES OF SUSPENSE featuring
CAPTAIN AMERICA AND IRON MAN
MARVEL COMICS GROUP
12¢ 92 AUG
"BEFORE MY EYES... NICK FURY DIED!!"

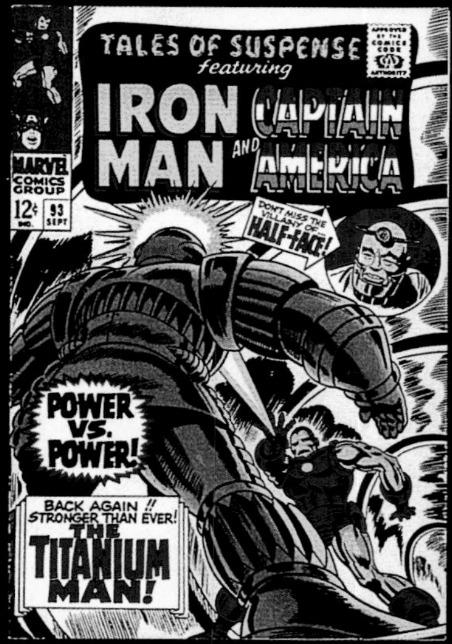
TALES OF SUSPENSE featuring
IRON MAN AND CAPTAIN AMERICA
MARVEL COMICS GROUP
12¢ 93 SEPT
HALF-FACE!
POWER VS. POWER!
BACK AGAIN !! STRONGER THAN EVER! THE TITANIUM MAN!

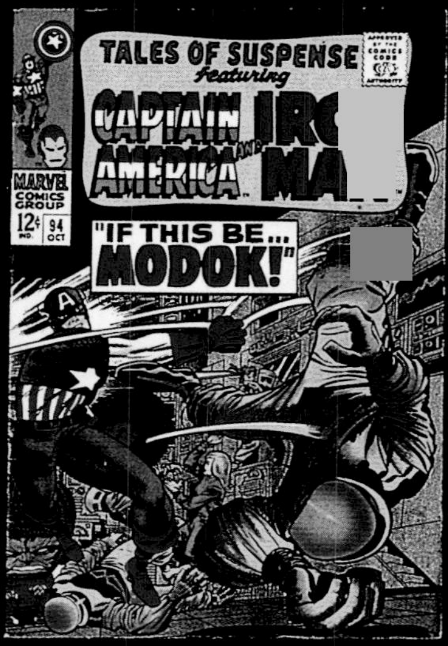
TALES OF SUSPENSE featuring
CAPTAIN AMERICA AND
MARVEL COMICS GROUP
12¢ 94 OCT
"IF THIS BE... MODOK!"

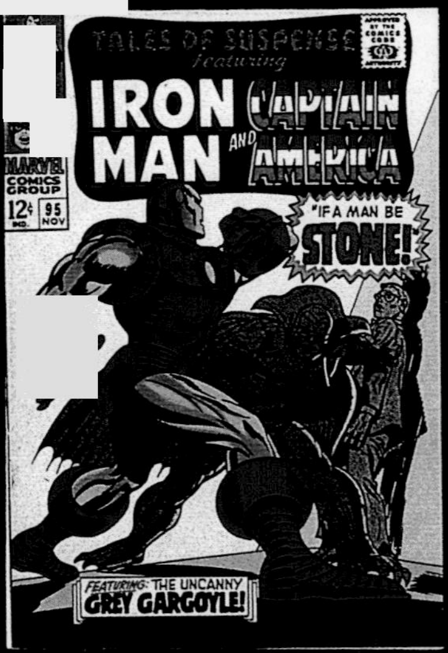
TALES OF SUSPENSE featuring
IRON MAN AND CAPTAIN AMERICA
MARVEL COMICS GROUP
12¢ 95 NOV
"IF A MAN BE STONE!"
FEATURING: THE UNCANNY GREY GARGOYLE!

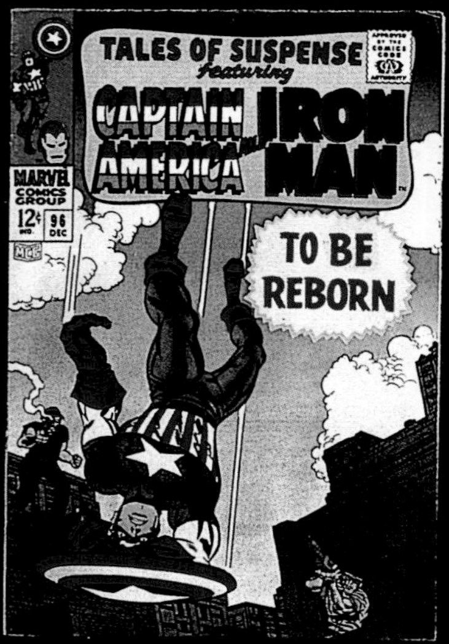
TALES OF SUSPENSE featuring
CAPTAIN AMERICA AND IRON MAN
MARVEL COMICS GROUP
12¢ 96 DEC
TO BE REBORN

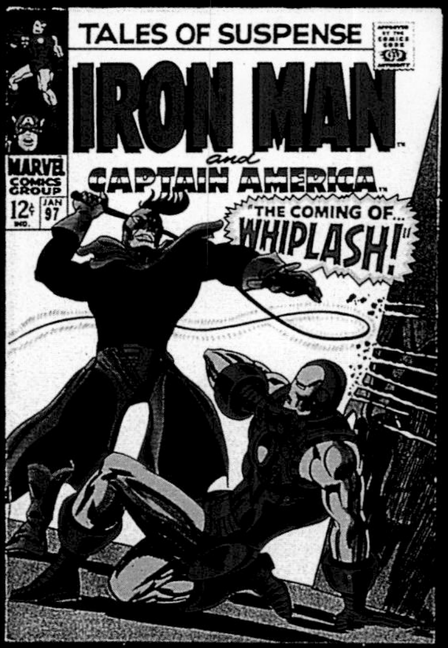
TALES OF SUSPENSE
IRON MAN and CAPTAIN AMERICA
MARVEL COMICS GROUP
12¢ 97 JAN
"THE COMING OF... WHIPLASH!"

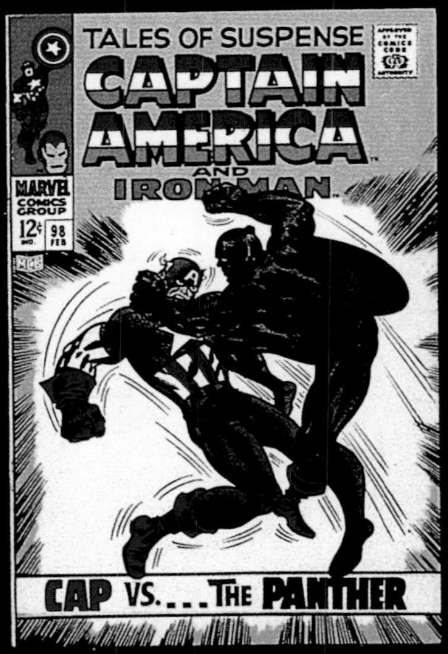
TALES OF SUSPENSE
CAPTAIN AMERICA AND IRON MAN
MARVEL COMICS GROUP
12¢ 98 FEB
CAP VS.... THE PANTHER

1879 Tales of Suspense (99)

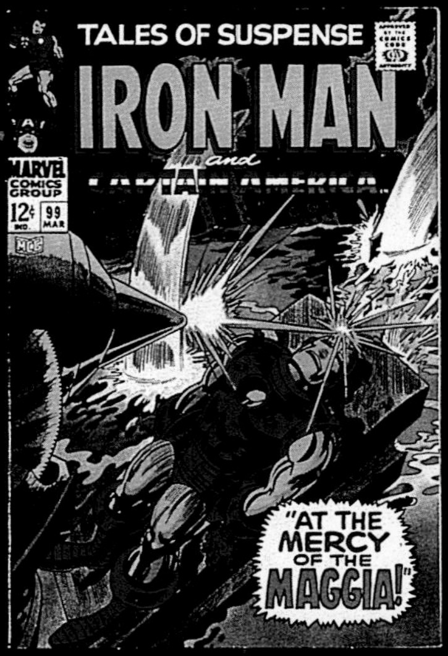
TALES OF SUSPENSE
IRON MAN
and
MARVEL COMICS GROUP
12¢ 99 MAR
"AT THE MERCY OF THE MAGGIA!"

1879 Captain America (100-114)

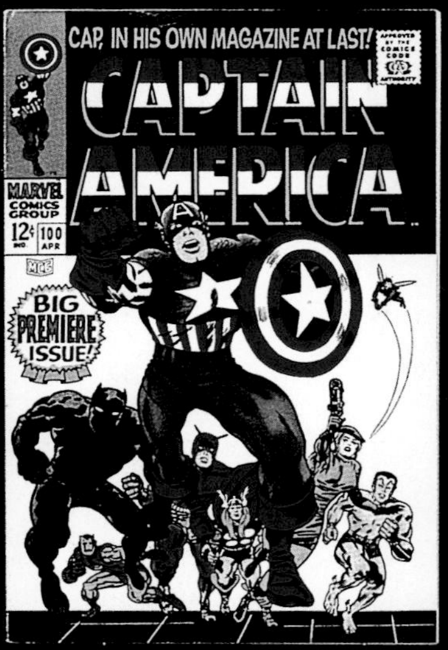
CAP, IN HIS OWN MAGAZINE AT LAST!
CAPTAIN AMERICA
MARVEL COMICS GROUP
12¢ 100 APR
BIG PREMIERE ISSUE

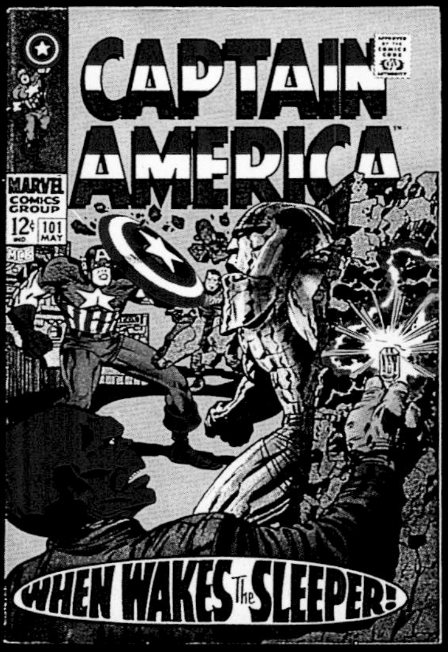
CAPTAIN AMERICA
MARVEL COMICS GROUP
12¢ 101 MAY
WHEN WAKES The SLEEPER!

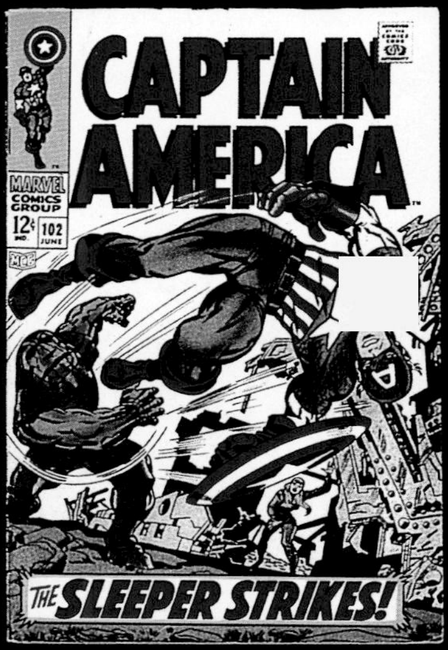
CAPTAIN AMERICA
MARVEL COMICS GROUP
12¢ 102 JUNE
THE SLEEPER STRIKES!

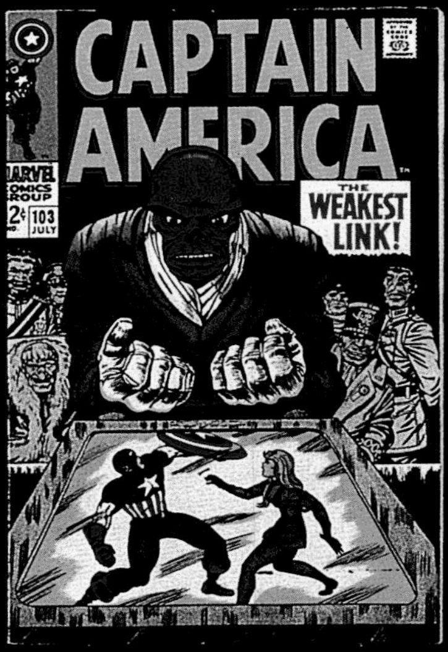
CAPTAIN AMERICA
MARVEL COMICS GROUP
12¢ 103 JULY
THE WEAKEST LINK!

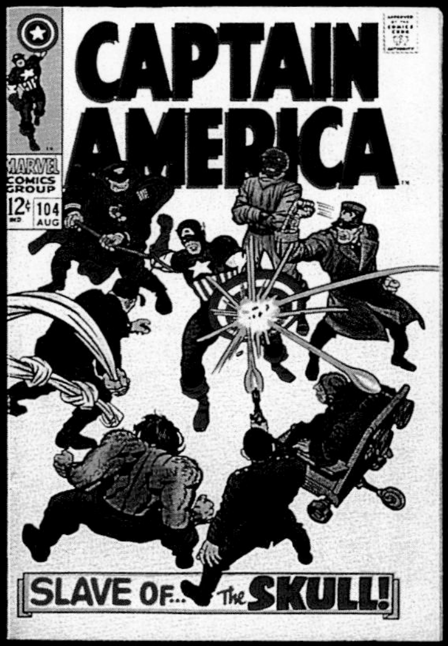
CAPTAIN AMERICA
MARVEL COMICS GROUP
12¢ 104 AUG
SLAVE OF... The SKULL!

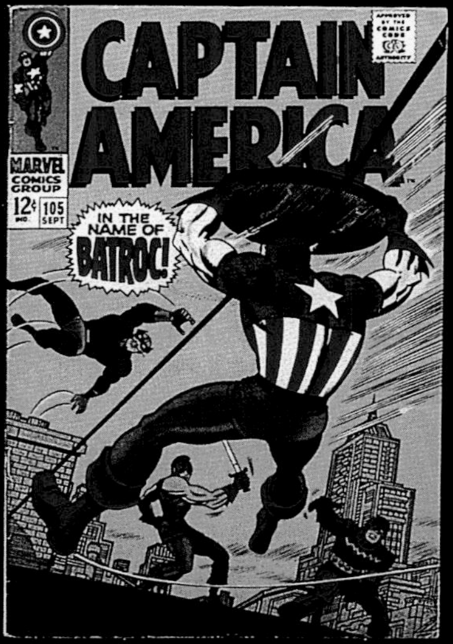
CAPTAIN AMERICA
MARVEL COMICS GROUP
12¢ 105 SEPT
IN THE NAME OF BATROC!

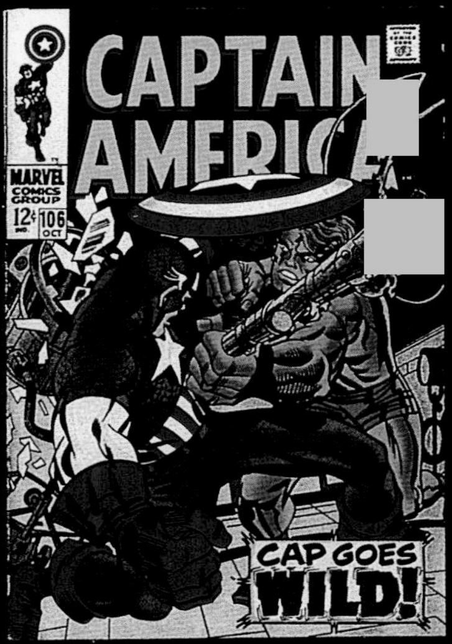
CAPTAIN AMERICA
MARVEL COMICS GROUP
12¢ 106
CAP GOES WILD!

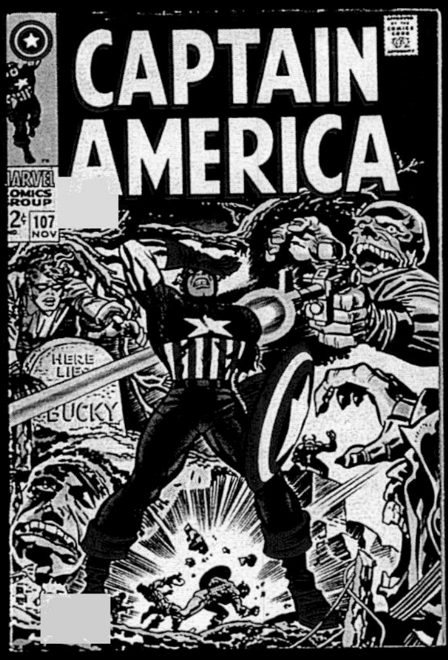
CAPTAIN AMERICA
MARVEL COMICS GROUP
12¢ 107 NOV
BUCKY

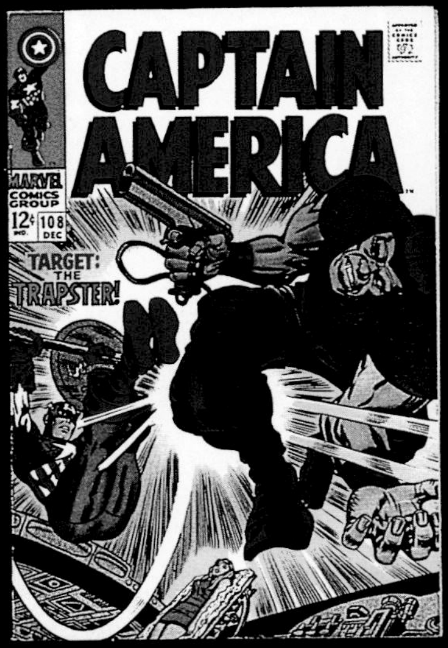
CAPTAIN AMERICA
MARVEL COMICS GROUP
12¢ 108 DEC
TARGET: THE TRAPSTER!

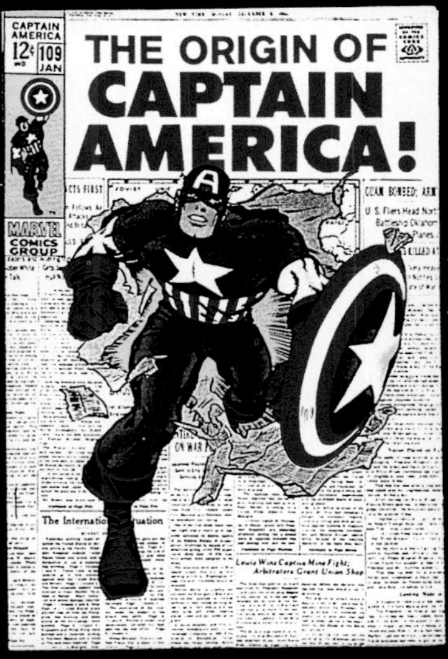
CAPTAIN AMERICA
12¢ 109 JAN
THE ORIGIN OF CAPTAIN AMERICA!
MARVEL COMICS GROUP

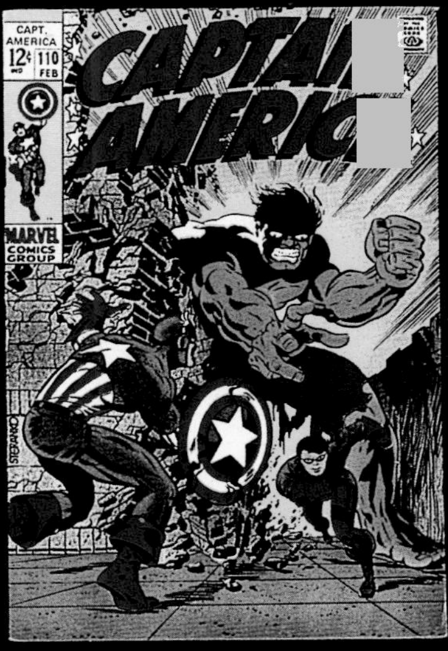
CAPT. AMERICA
12¢ 110 FEB
CAPTAIN AMERICA
MARVEL COMICS GROUP

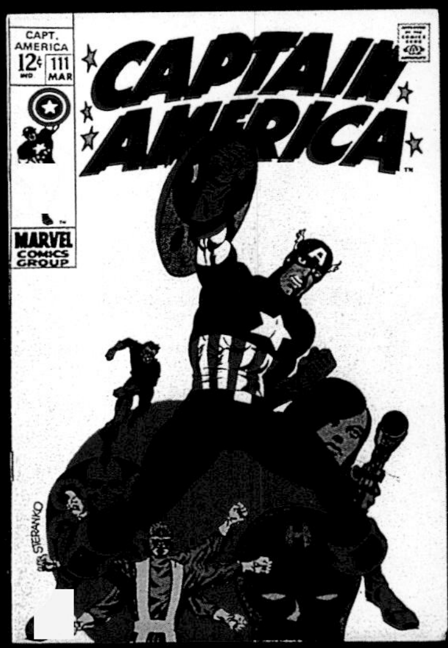
CAPT. AMERICA
12¢ 111 MAR
CAPTAIN AMERICA
MARVEL COMICS GROUP

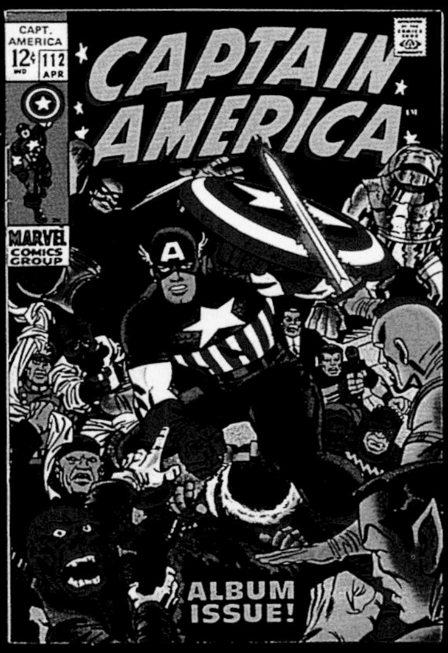
CAPT. AMERICA
12¢ 112 APR
CAPTAIN AMERICA
MARVEL COMICS GROUP
ALBUM ISSUE!

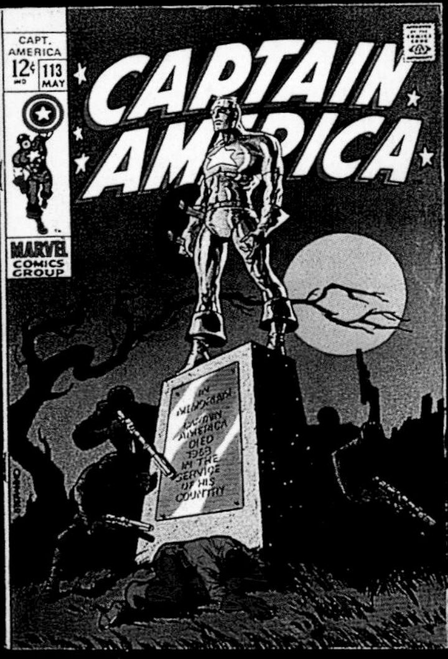
CAPT. AMERICA
12¢ 113 MAY
CAPTAIN AMERICA
MARVEL COMICS GROUP

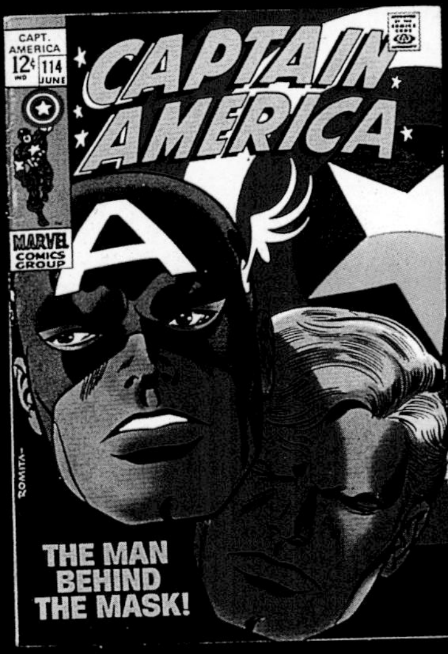
CAPT. AMERICA
12¢ 114 JUNE
CAPTAIN AMERICA
MARVEL COMICS GROUP
THE MAN BEHIND THE MASK!

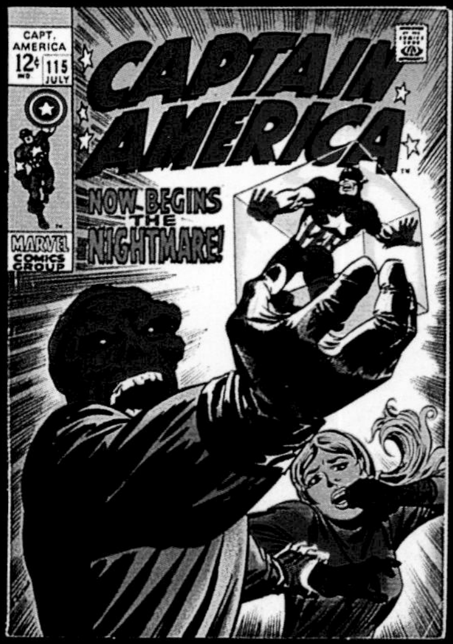
CAPT. AMERICA 12¢ 115 JULY
CAPTAIN AMERICA
MARVEL COMICS GROUP
NOW BEGINS THE NIGHTMARE!

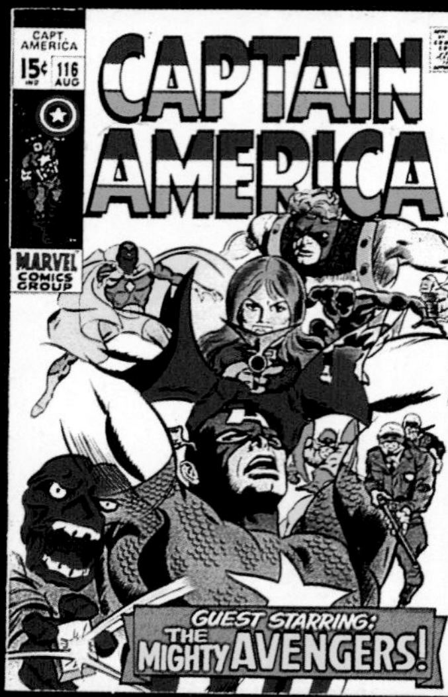
CAPT. AMERICA 15¢ 116 AUG
CAPTAIN AMERICA
MARVEL COMICS GROUP
GUEST STARRING: THE MIGHTY AVENGERS!

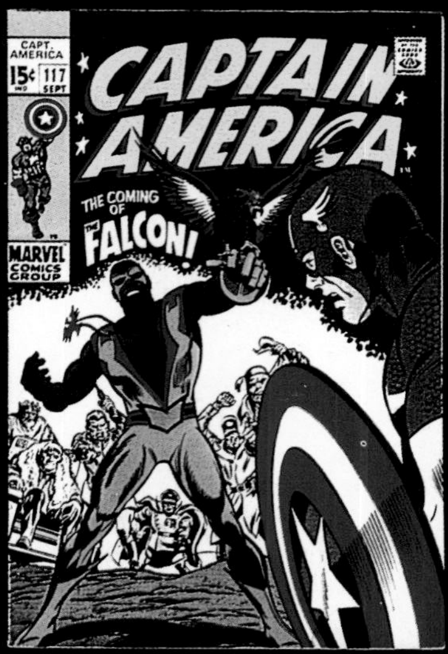
CAPT. AMERICA 15¢ 117 SEPT
CAPTAIN AMERICA
THE COMING OF THE FALCON!
MARVEL COMICS GROUP

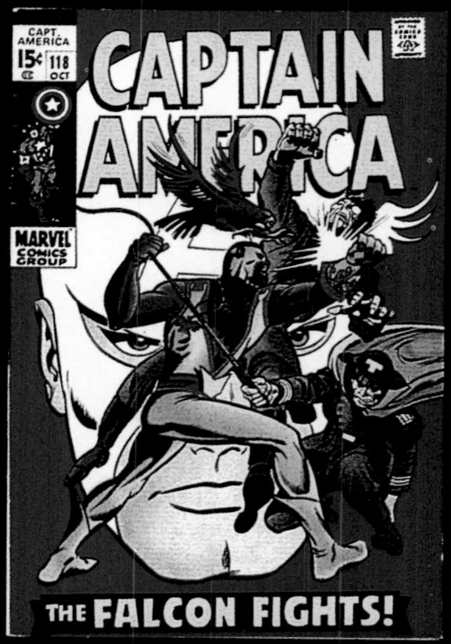
CAPT. AMERICA 15¢ 118 OCT
CAPTAIN AMERICA
MARVEL COMICS GROUP
THE FALCON FIGHTS!

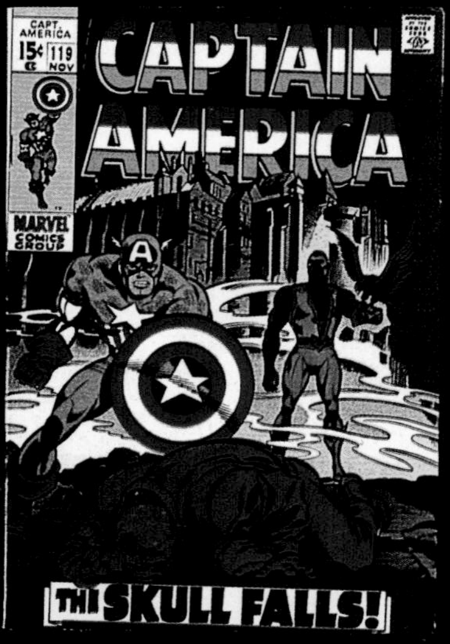
CAPT. AMERICA 15¢ 119 NOV
CAPTAIN AMERICA
MARVEL COMICS GROUP
THE SKULL FALLS!

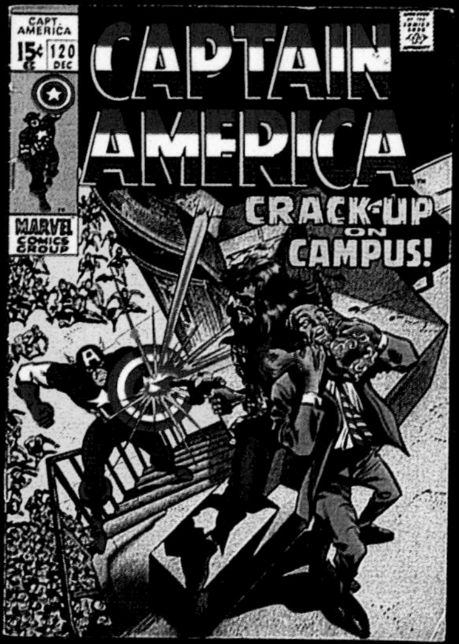
CAPT. AMERICA 15¢ 120 DEC
CAPTAIN AMERICA
MARVEL COMICS GROUP
CRACK-UP ON CAMPUS!

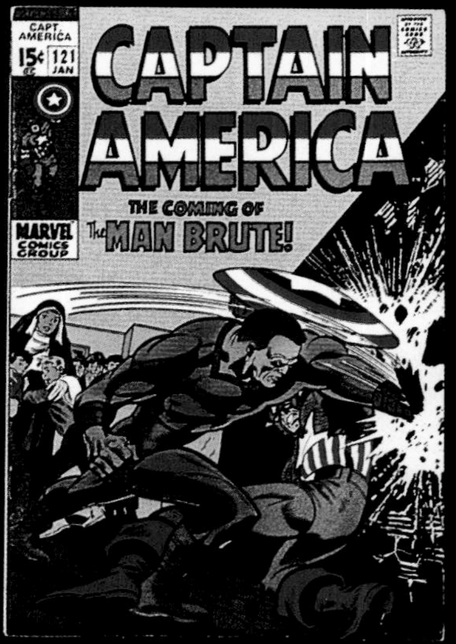
CAPT. AMERICA 15¢ 121 JAN
CAPTAIN AMERICA
MARVEL COMICS GROUP
THE COMING OF THE MAN BRUTE!

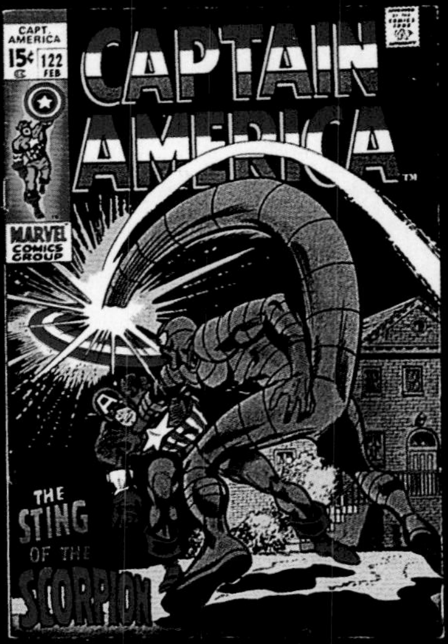
CAPT. AMERICA 15¢ 122 FEB
CAPTAIN AMERICA
MARVEL COMICS GROUP
THE STING OF THE SCORPION

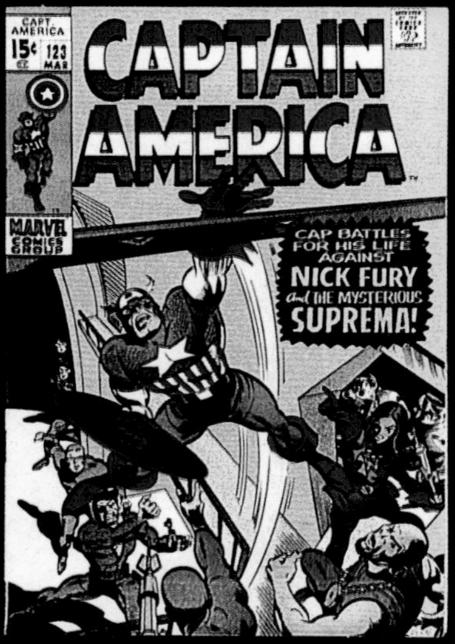
CAPT. AMERICA 15¢ 123 MAR
CAPTAIN AMERICA
MARVEL COMICS GROUP
CAP BATTLES FOR HIS LIFE AGAINST NICK FURY and THE MYSTERIOUS SUPREMA!

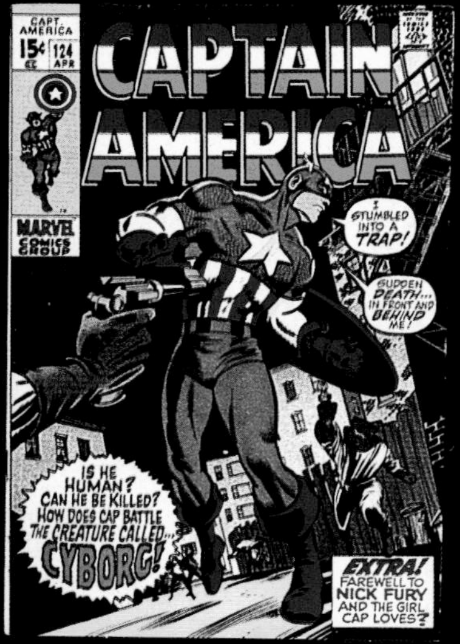
CAPT. AMERICA 15¢ 124 APR
CAPTAIN AMERICA
MARVEL COMICS GROUP
I STUMBLED INTO A TRAP!
SUDDEN DEATH... IN FRONT AND BEHIND ME!
IS HE HUMAN? CAN HE BE KILLED? HOW DOES CAP BATTLE THE CREATURE CALLED CYBORG!
EXTRA! FAREWELL TO NICK FURY AND THE GIRL CAP LOVES!

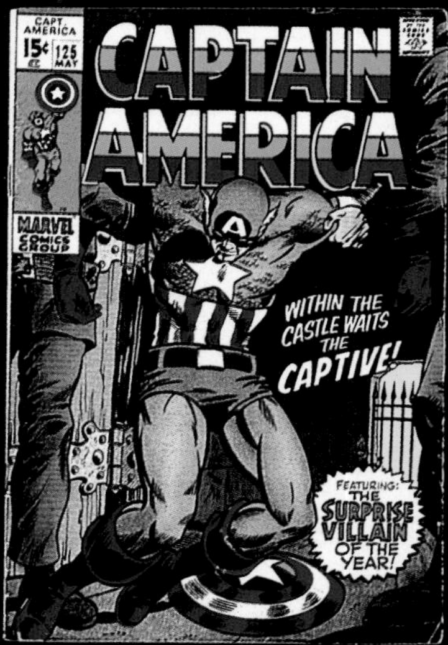
CAPT. AMERICA 15¢ 125 MAY
CAPTAIN AMERICA
MARVEL COMICS GROUP
WITHIN THE CASTLE WAITS THE CAPTIVE!
FEATURING: THE SURPRISE VILLAIN OF THE YEAR!

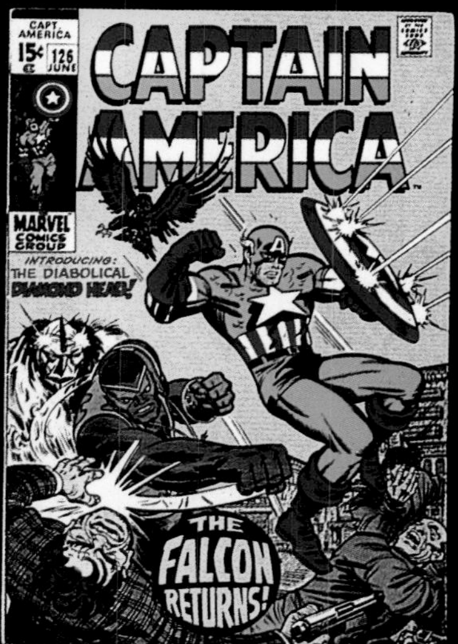
CAPT. AMERICA 15¢ 126 JUNE
CAPTAIN AMERICA
MARVEL COMICS GROUP
INTRODUCING: THE DIABOLICAL DIAMOND HEAD!
THE FALCON RETURNS!

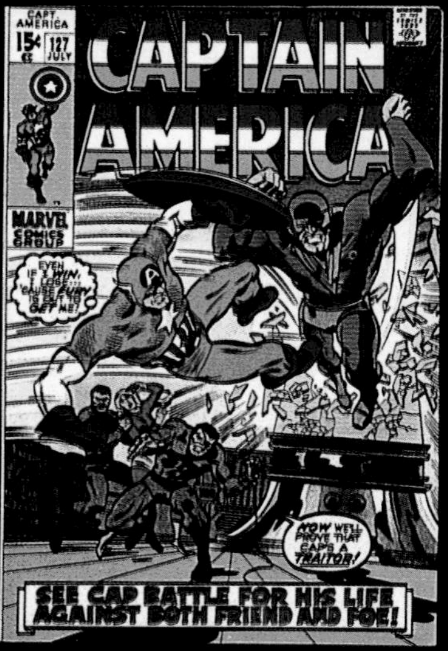
CAPT. AMERICA 15¢ 127 JULY
CAPTAIN AMERICA
MARVEL COMICS GROUP
SEE CAP BATTLE FOR HIS LIFE AGAINST BOTH FRIEND AND FOE!

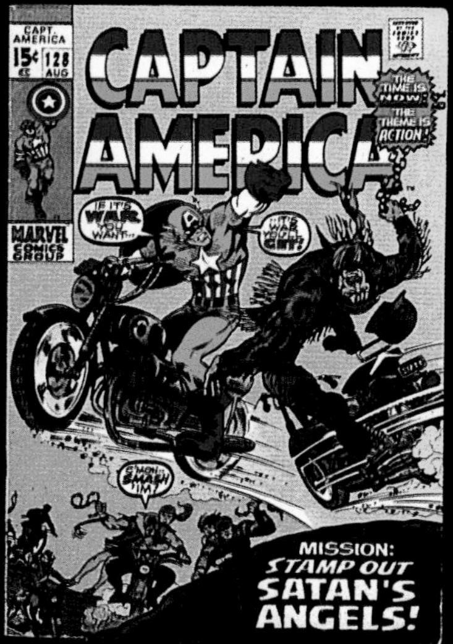
CAPT. AMERICA 15¢ 128 AUG
CAPTAIN AMERICA
MARVEL COMICS GROUP
MISSION: STAMP OUT SATAN'S ANGELS!

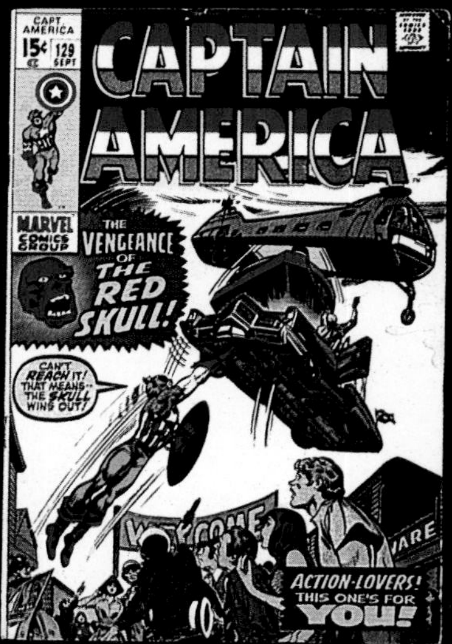
CAPT. AMERICA 15¢ 129 SEPT
CAPTAIN AMERICA
MARVEL COMICS GROUP
THE VENGEANCE OF THE RED SKULL!
ACTION-LOVERS! THIS ONE'S FOR YOU!

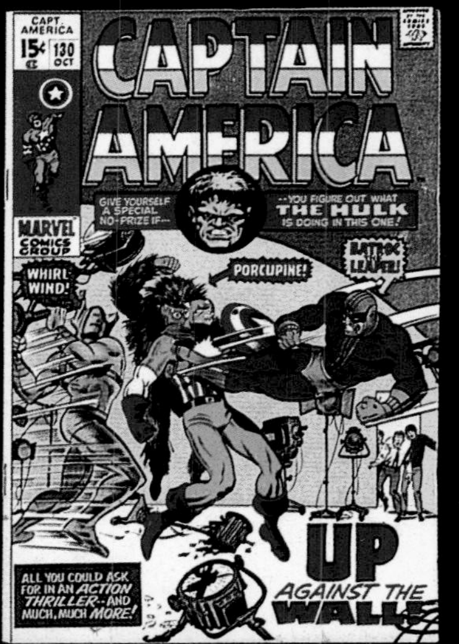
CAPT. AMERICA 15¢ 130 OCT
CAPTAIN AMERICA
MARVEL COMICS GROUP
THE HULK
PORCUPINE!
UP AGAINST THE WALL
ALL YOU COULD ASK FOR IN AN ACTION THRILLER-AND MUCH, MUCH MORE!

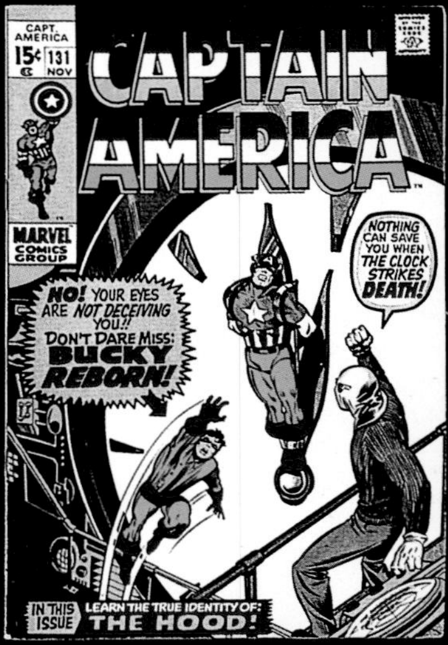
CAPT AMERICA
15¢ 131 NOV
CAPTAIN AMERICA
MARVEL COMICS GROUP
NO! YOUR EYES ARE NOT DECEIVING YOU!! DON'T DARE MISS: BUCKY REBORN!
NOTHING CAN SAVE YOU WHEN THE CLOCK STRIKES DEATH!
IN THIS ISSUE LEARN THE TRUE IDENTITY OF: THE HOOD!

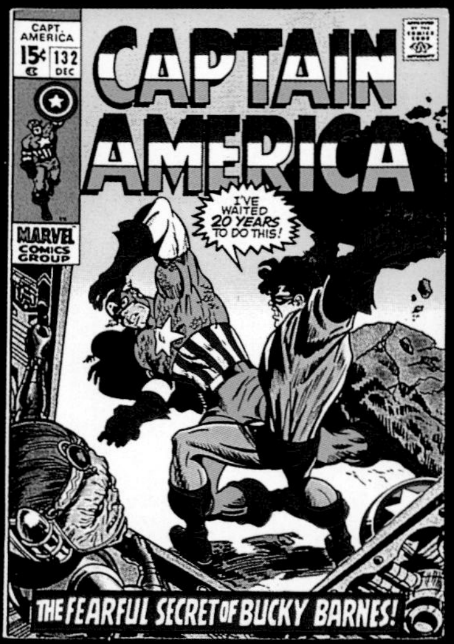
CAPT AMERICA
15¢ 132 DEC
CAPTAIN AMERICA
I'VE WAITED 20 YEARS TO DO THIS!
MARVEL COMICS GROUP
THE FEARFUL SECRET OF BUCKY BARNES!

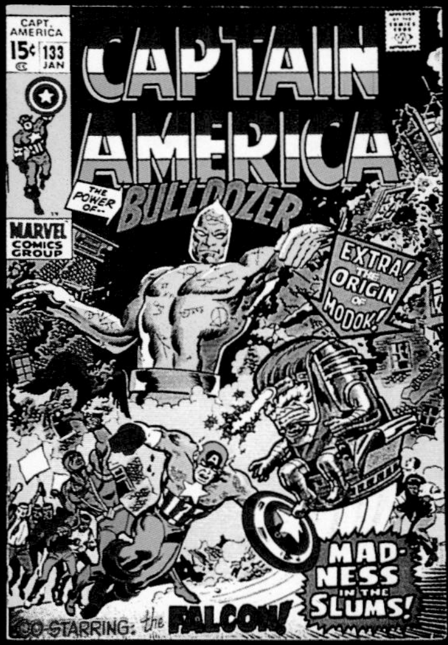
CAPT AMERICA
15¢ 133 JAN
CAPTAIN AMERICA
THE POWER OF... BULLDOZER
MARVEL COMICS GROUP
EXTRA! ORIGIN OF MODOK!
MAD-NESS IN THE SLUMS!
CO-STARRING: the FALCON!

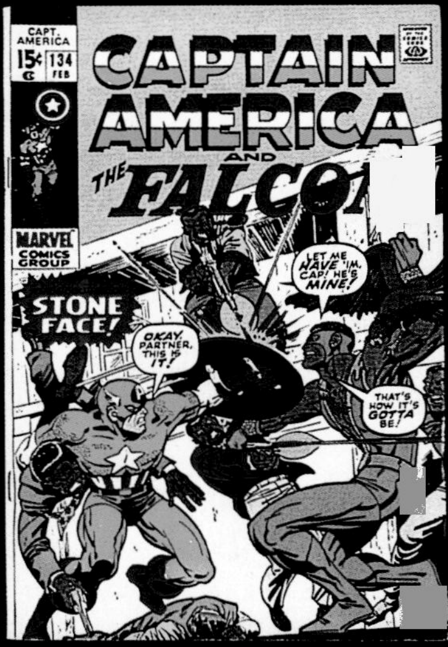
CAPT AMERICA
15¢ 134 FEB
CAPTAIN AMERICA AND THE FALCO
MARVEL COMICS GROUP
LET ME HAVE 'IM, CAP! HE'S MINE!
STONE FACE!
OKAY, PARTNER. THIS IS IT!
THAT'S HOW IT'S GOTTA BE!

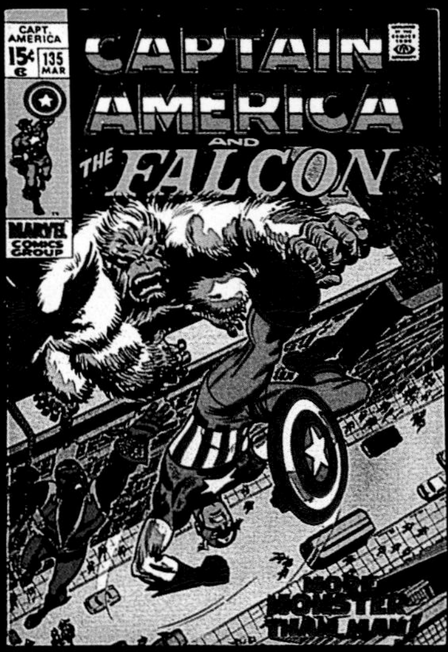
CAPT AMERICA
15¢ 135 MAR
CAPTAIN AMERICA AND THE FALCON
MARVEL COMICS GROUP

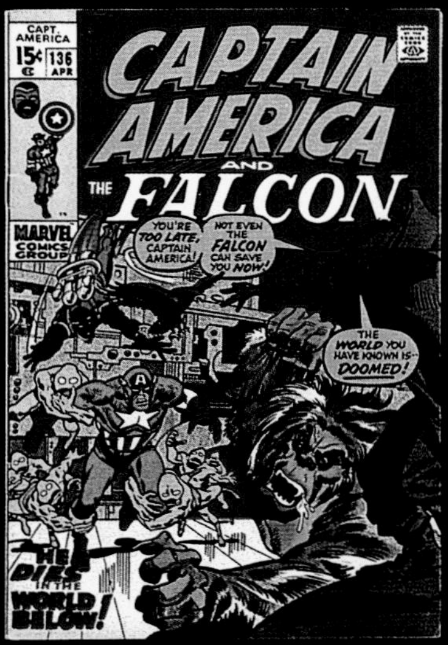
CAPT AMERICA
15¢ 136 APR
CAPTAIN AMERICA AND THE FALCON
MARVEL COMICS GROUP
YOU'RE TOO LATE, CAPTAIN AMERICA!
NOT EVEN THE FALCON CAN SAVE YOU NOW!
THE WORLD YOU HAVE KNOWN IS DOOMED!
WORLD BELOW!

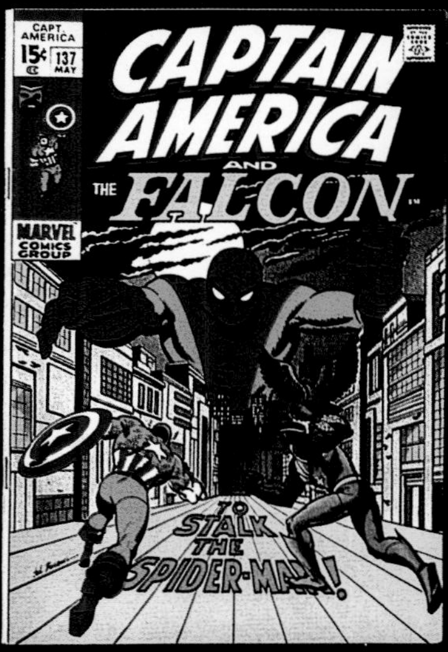
CAPT AMERICA
15¢ 137 MAY
CAPTAIN AMERICA AND THE FALCON
MARVEL COMICS GROUP
TO STALK THE SPIDER-MAN!

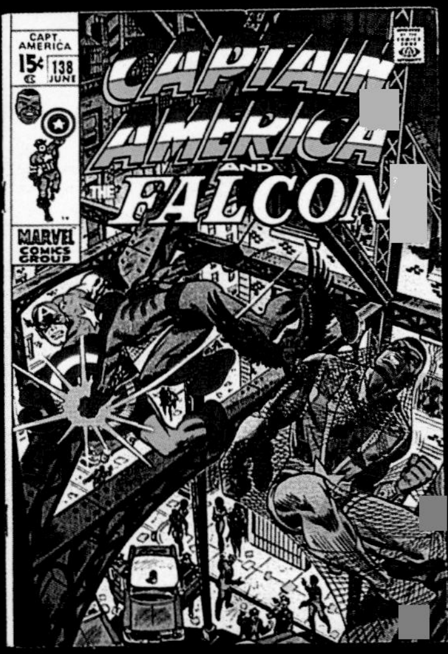
CAPT AMERICA
15¢ 138 JUNE
CAPTAIN AMERICA AND THE FALCON
MARVEL COMICS GROUP

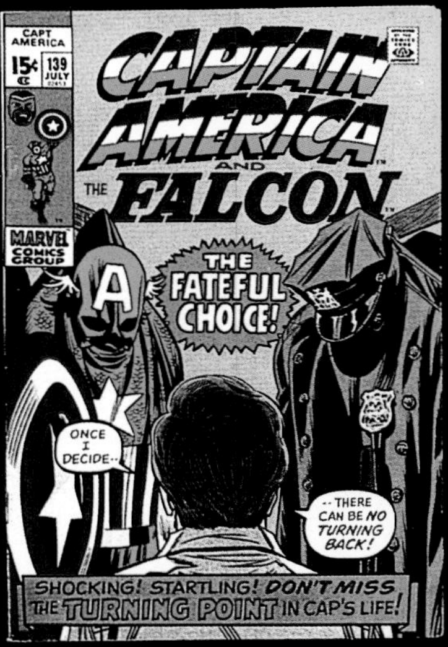
CAPT AMERICA
15¢ 139 JULY
CAPTAIN AMERICA AND THE FALCON
MARVEL COMICS GROUP
THE FATEFUL CHOICE!
ONCE I DECIDE..
-- THERE CAN BE NO TURNING BACK!
SHOCKING! STARTLING! DON'T MISS THE TURNING POINT IN CAP'S LIFE!

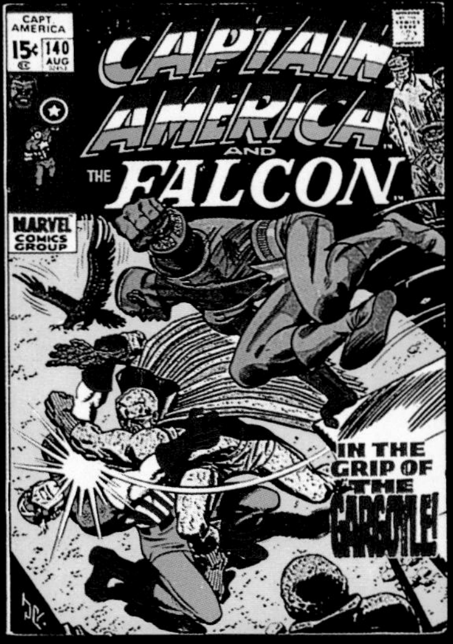
CAPT AMERICA
15¢ 140 AUG
CAPTAIN AMERICA AND THE FALCON
MARVEL COMICS GROUP
IN THE GRIP OF THE GARGOYLE!

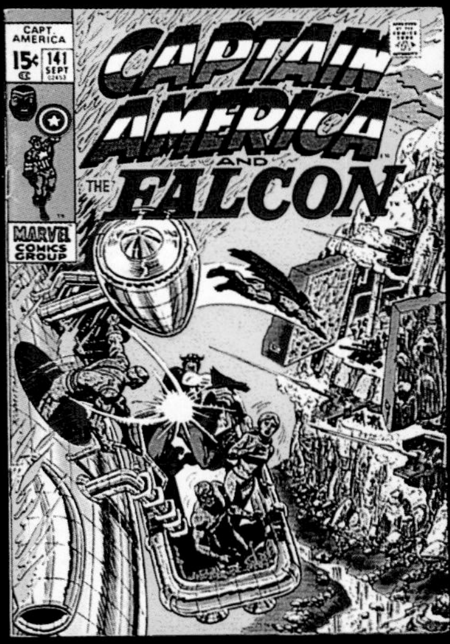
CAPT AMERICA
15¢ 141 SEPT
CAPTAIN AMERICA AND THE FALCON
MARVEL COMICS GROUP

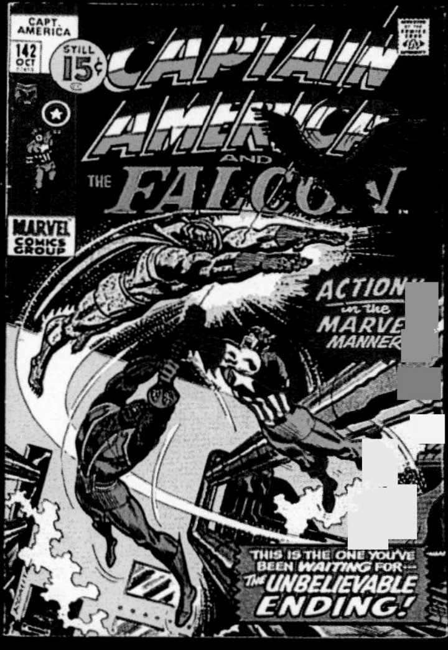
CAPT AMERICA
142 OCT
STILL 15¢
CAPTAIN AMERICA AND THE FALCON
MARVEL COMICS GROUP
ACTION in the MARVEL MANNER
THIS IS THE ONE YOU'VE BEEN WAITING FOR-- THE UNBELIEVABLE ENDING!

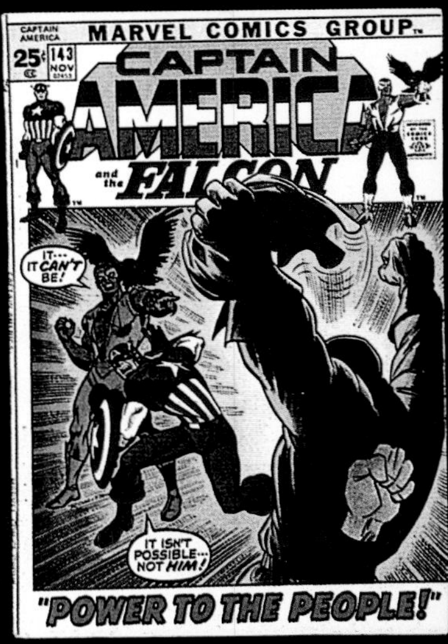
CAPTAIN AMERICA
MARVEL COMICS GROUP
25¢ 143 NOV
CAPTAIN AMERICA and the FALCON
IT... IT CAN'T BE!
IT ISN'T POSSIBLE... NOT HIM!
"POWER TO THE PEOPLE!"

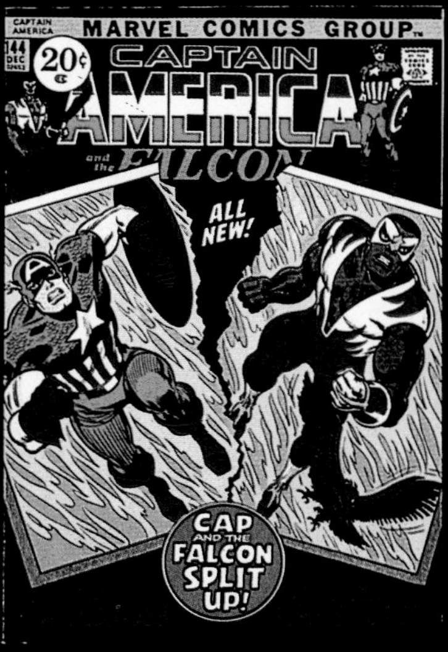
CAPTAIN AMERICA
MARVEL COMICS GROUP
144 DEC
20¢
CAPTAIN AMERICA and the FALCON
ALL NEW!
CAP AND THE FALCON SPLIT UP!

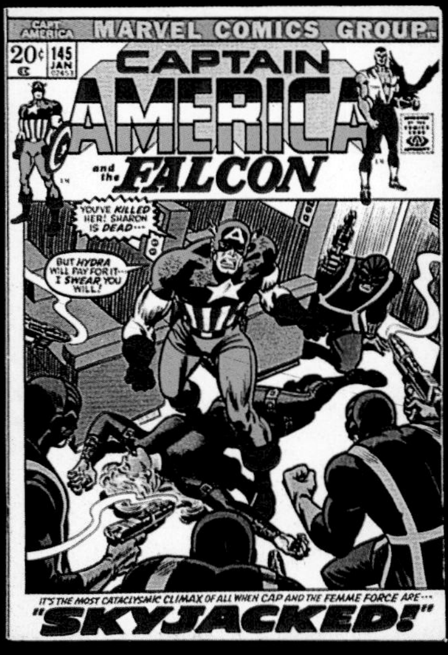
CAPT AMERICA
MARVEL COMICS GROUP
20¢ 145 JAN
CAPTAIN AMERICA and the FALCON
YOU'VE KILLED HER! SHARON IS DEAD--
BUT HYDRA WILL PAY FOR IT-- I SWEAR YOU WILL!
IT'S THE MOST CATACLYSMIC CLIMAX OF ALL WHEN CAP AND THE FEMME FORCE ARE--
SKYJACKED!

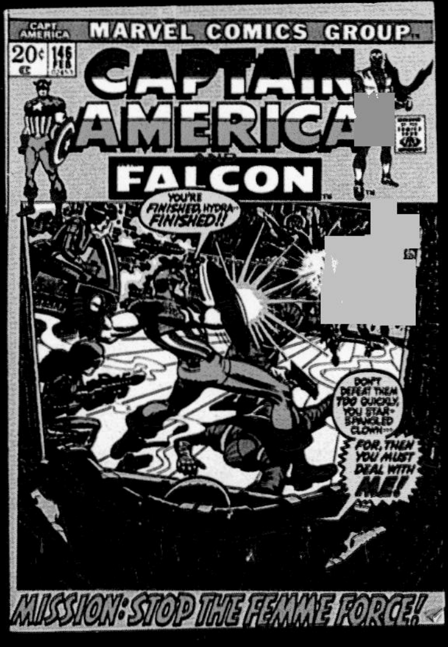
CAPTAIN AMERICA
MARVEL COMICS GROUP
20¢ 146 FEB
CAPTAIN AMERICA
FALCON
YOU'RE FINISHED HYDRA-- FINISHED!
MISSION: STOP THE FEMME FORCE!

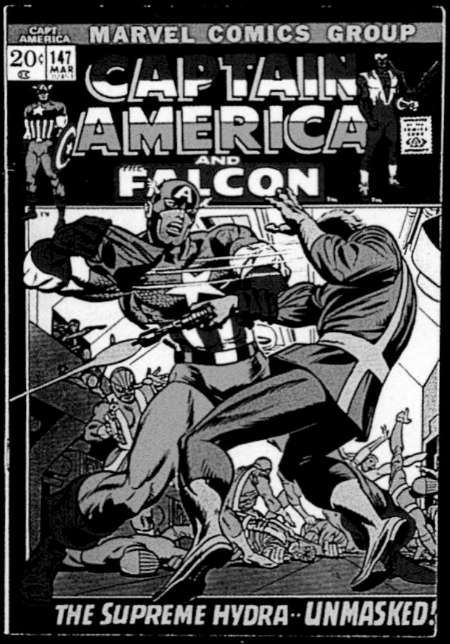
MARVEL COMICS GROUP
CAPTAIN AMERICA AND FALCON
THE SUPREME HYDRA··UNMASKED!

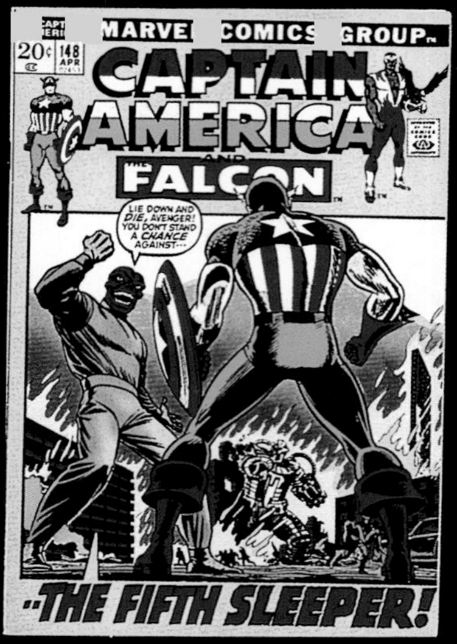
MARVEL COMICS GROUP
CAPTAIN AMERICA AND FALCON
LIE DOWN AND DIE, AVENGER! YOU DON'T STAND A CHANCE AGAINST--
--THE FIFTH SLEEPER!

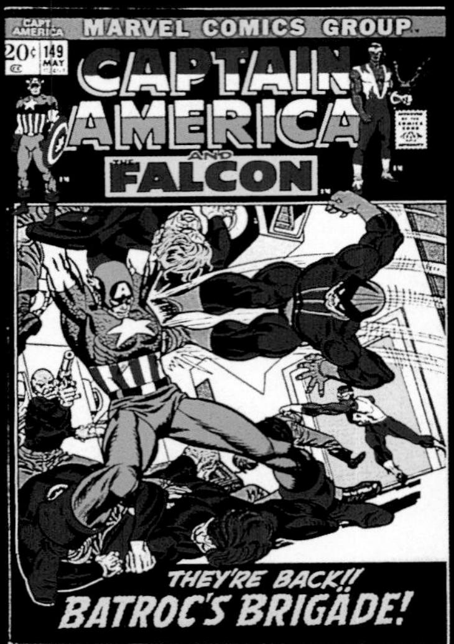
MARVEL COMICS GROUP
CAPTAIN AMERICA AND FALCON
THEY'RE BACK!!
BATROC'S BRIGADE!

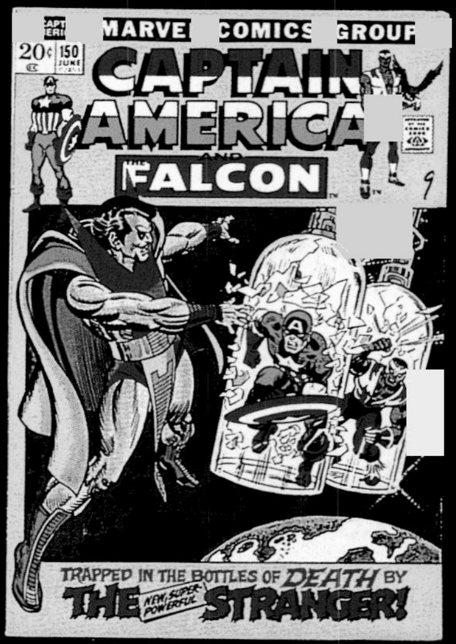
MARVEL COMICS GROUP
CAPTAIN AMERICA AND FALCON
TRAPPED IN THE BOTTLES OF DEATH BY THE STRANGER!

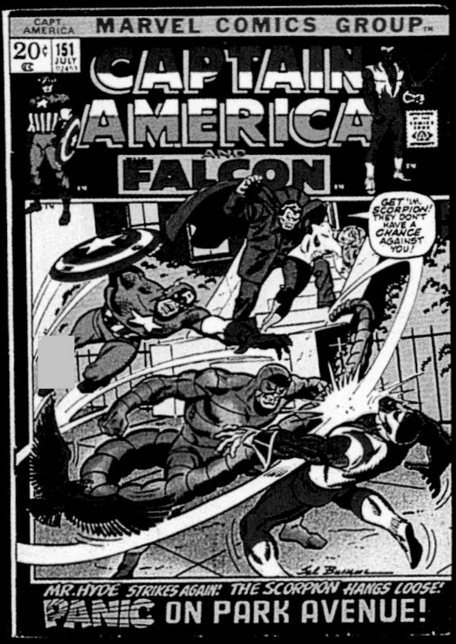
MARVEL COMICS GROUP
CAPTAIN AMERICA AND FALCON
MR. HYDE STRIKES AGAIN! THE SCORPION HANGS LOOSE!
PANIC ON PARK AVENUE!

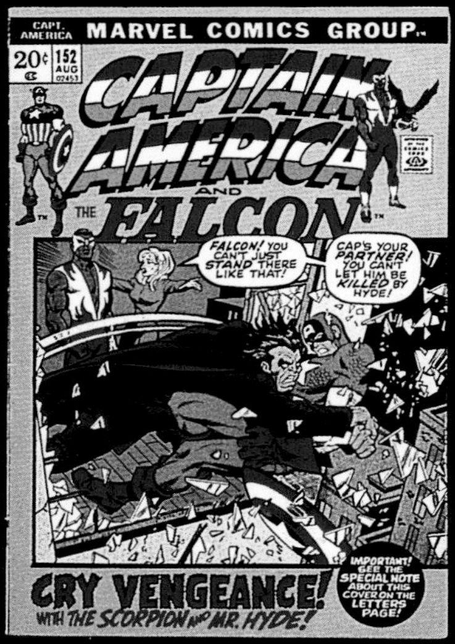
MARVEL COMICS GROUP
CAPTAIN AMERICA AND THE FALCON
FALCON! YOU CAN'T JUST STAND THERE LIKE THAT!
CAP'S YOUR PARTNER! YOU CAN'T LET HIM BE KILLED BY HYDE!
IMPORTANT! SEE THE SPECIAL NOTE ABOUT THIS COVER ON THE LETTERS PAGE!
CRY VENGEANCE! WITH THE SCORPION AND MR. HYDE!

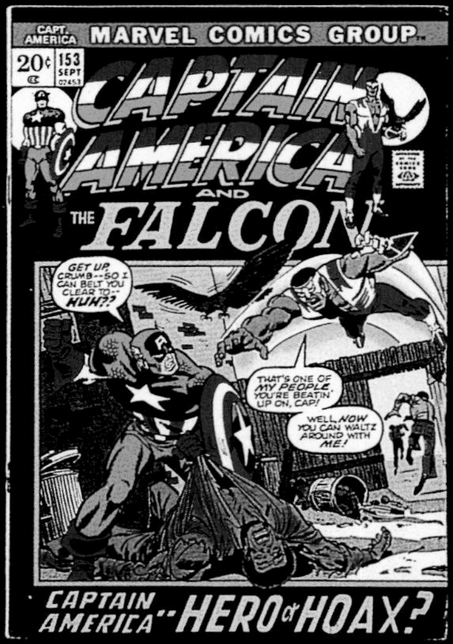
MARVEL COMICS GROUP
CAPTAIN AMERICA AND THE FALCON
CAPTAIN AMERICA··HERO or HOAX?

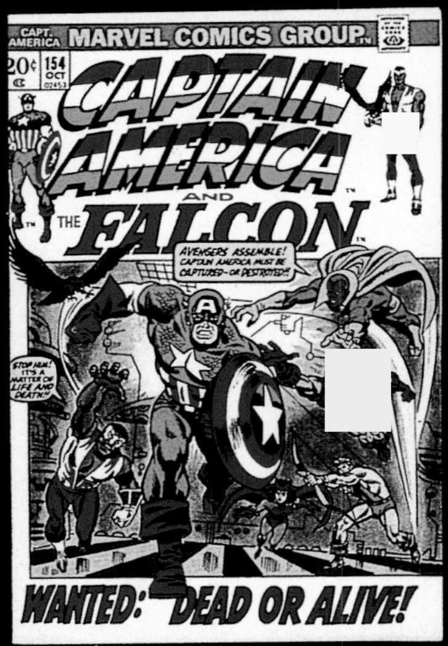
MARVEL COMICS GROUP
CAPTAIN AMERICA AND THE FALCON
AVENGERS ASSEMBLE! CAPTAIN AMERICA MUST BE CAPTURED--OR DESTROYED!
WANTED: DEAD OR ALIVE!

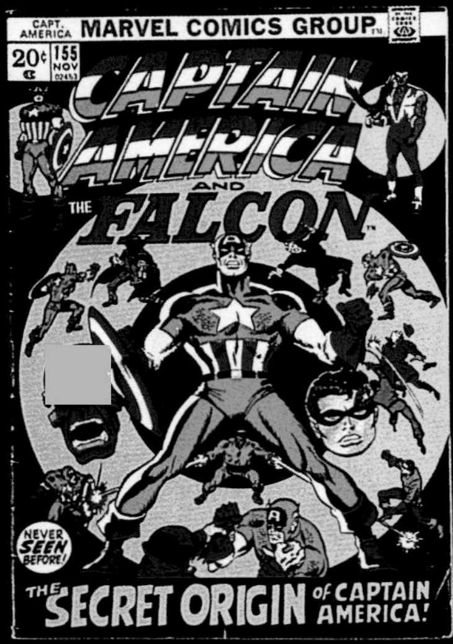
MARVEL COMICS GROUP
CAPTAIN AMERICA AND THE FALCON
NEVER SEEN BEFORE!
THE SECRET ORIGIN of CAPTAIN AMERICA!

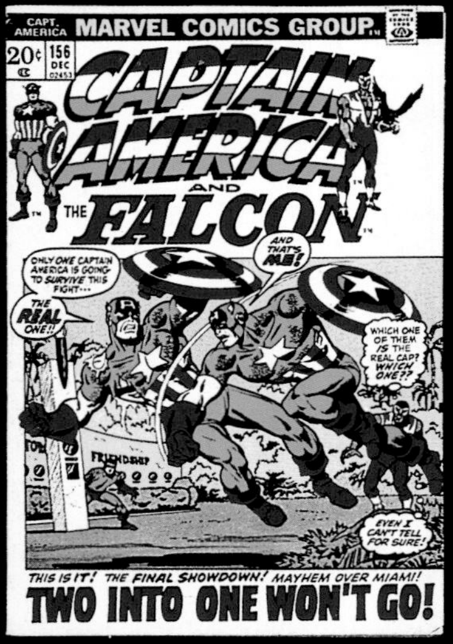
MARVEL COMICS GROUP
CAPTAIN AMERICA AND THE FALCON
THIS IS IT! THE FINAL SHOWDOWN! MAYHEM OVER MIAMI!!
TWO INTO ONE WON'T GO!

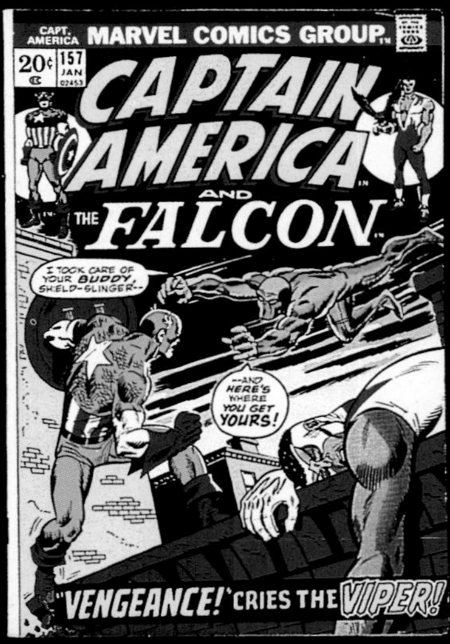
MARVEL COMICS GROUP
CAPTAIN AMERICA AND THE FALCON
"VENGEANCE!" CRIES THE VIPER!

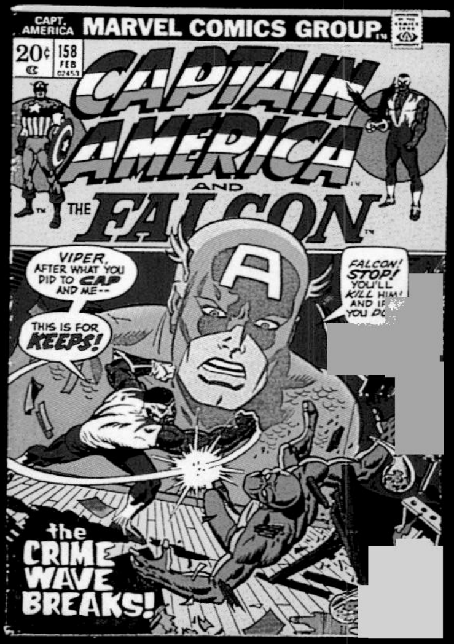
MARVEL COMICS GROUP
CAPTAIN AMERICA AND THE FALCON
THIS IS FOR KEEPS!
the CRIME WAVE BREAKS!

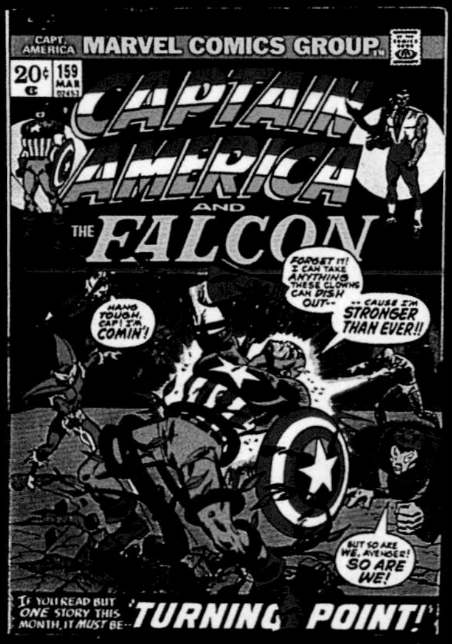
MARVEL COMICS GROUP
CAPTAIN AMERICA AND THE FALCON
--CAUSE I'M STRONGER THAN EVER!!
TURNING POINT!

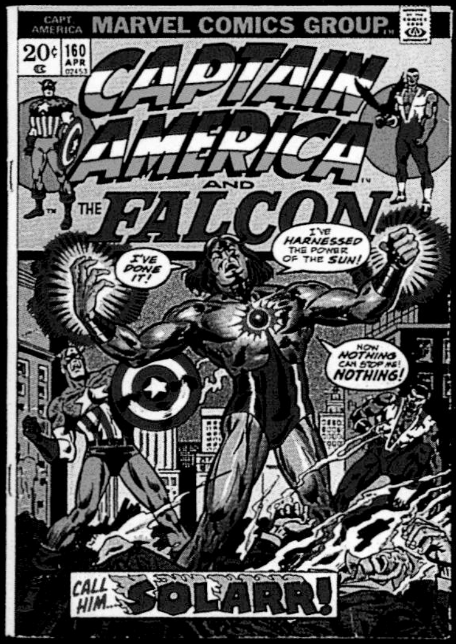
MARVEL COMICS GROUP
CAPTAIN AMERICA AND THE FALCON
I'VE DONE IT!
CALL HIM... SOLARR!

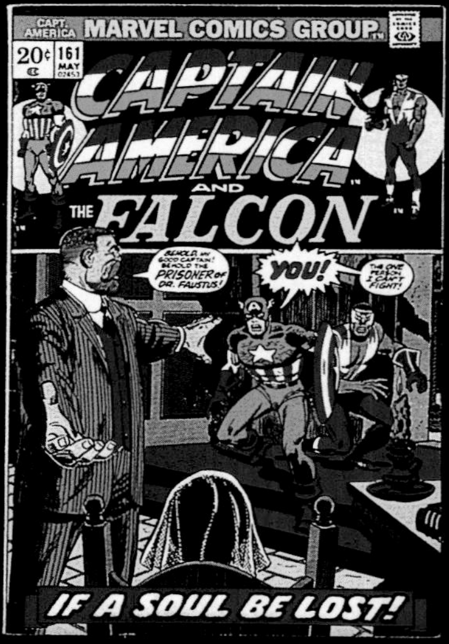
MARVEL COMICS GROUP
CAPTAIN AMERICA AND THE FALCON
YOU!
IF A SOUL BE LOST!

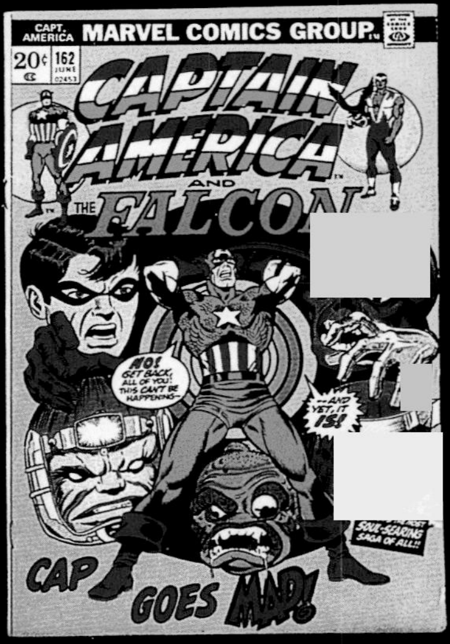
MARVEL COMICS GROUP
CAPTAIN AMERICA AND THE FALCON
CAP GOES MAD!

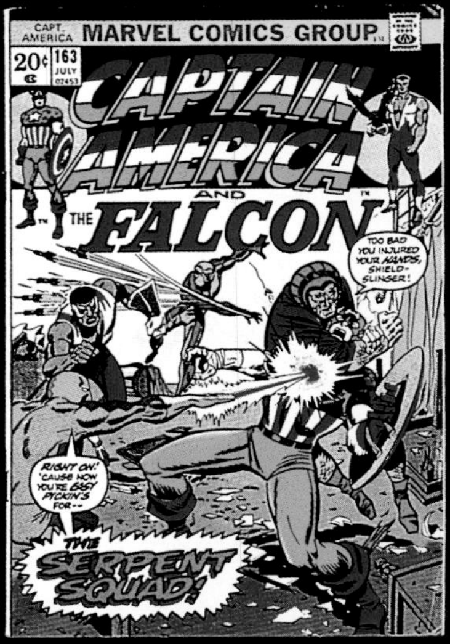
CAPT. AMERICA
MARVEL COMICS GROUP
20¢ 163 JULY
CAPTAIN AMERICA AND THE FALCON
TOO BAD YOU INJURED YOU AGAINST SHIELD-SLINGER!
RIGHT ON! 'CAUSE NOW YOU'RE EASY PICKIN'S FOR--
THE SERPENT SQUAD!

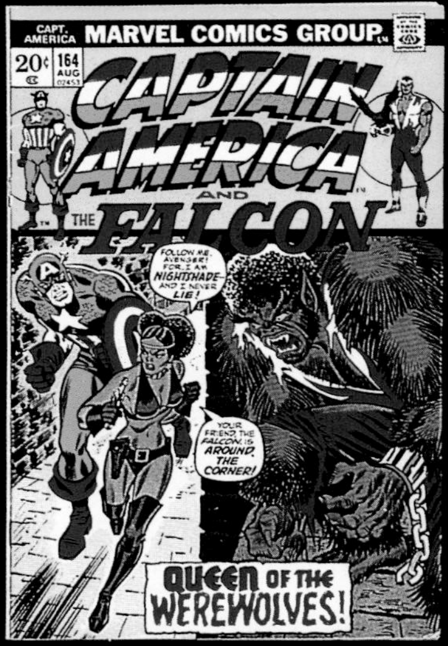
CAPT. AMERICA
MARVEL COMICS GROUP
20¢ 164 AUG
CAPTAIN AMERICA AND THE FALCON
FOLLOW ME AVENGER! FOR I AM NIGHTSHADE-- AND I NEVER LIE!
YOUR FRIEND, THE FALCON IS AROUND THE CORNER!
QUEEN OF THE WEREWOLVES!

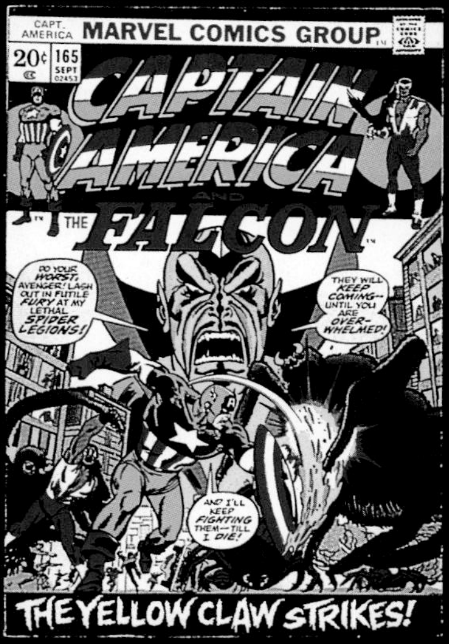
CAPT. AMERICA
MARVEL COMICS GROUP
20¢ 165 SEPT
CAPTAIN AMERICA AND THE FALCON
THEY WILL KEEP COMING-- UNTIL YOU ARE OVER-WHELMED!
AND I'LL KEEP FIGHTING THEM-- TILL I DIE!
THE YELLOW CLAW STRIKES!

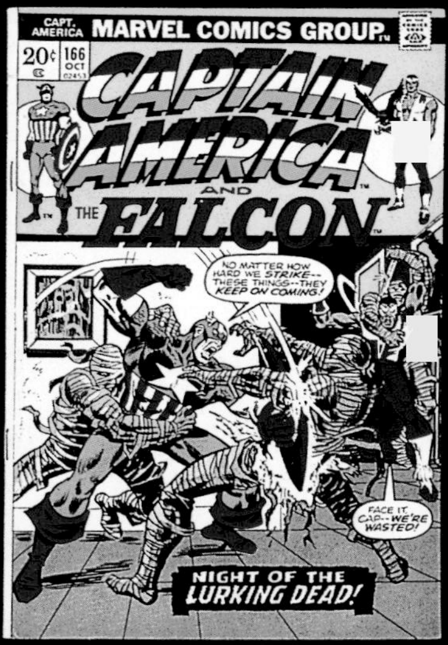
CAPT. AMERICA
MARVEL COMICS GROUP
20¢ 166 OCT
CAPTAIN AMERICA AND THE FALCON
NO MATTER HOW HARD WE STRIKE-- THESE THINGS-- THEY KEEP ON COMING!
FACE IT CAP-- WE'RE WASTED!
NIGHT OF THE LURKING DEAD!

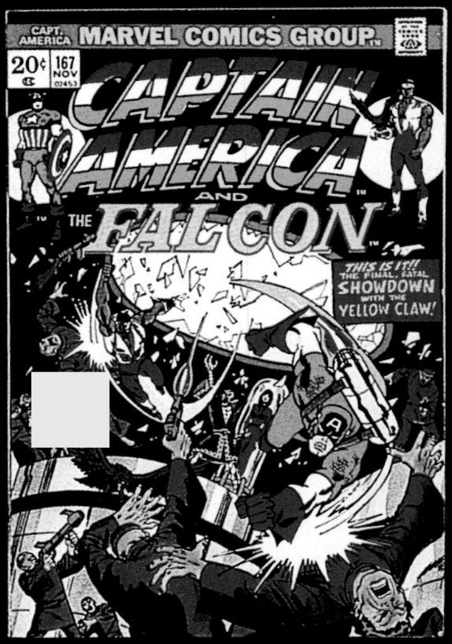
CAPT. AMERICA
MARVEL COMICS GROUP
20¢ 167 NOV
CAPTAIN AMERICA AND THE FALCON
THIS IS IT!! THE FINAL, FATAL SHOWDOWN WITH THE YELLOW CLAW!

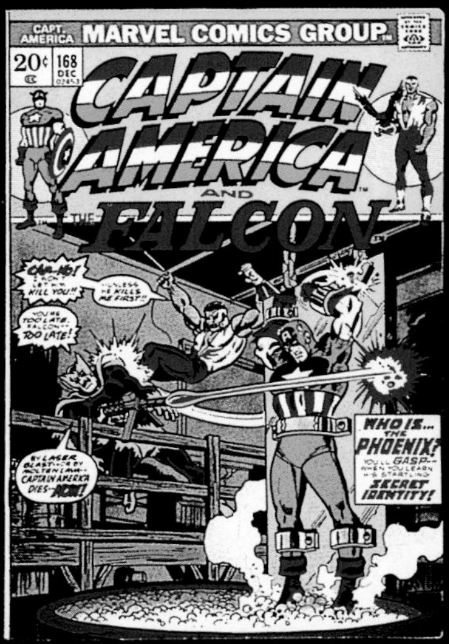
CAPT. AMERICA
MARVEL COMICS GROUP
20¢ 168 DEC
CAPTAIN AMERICA AND THE FALCON
WHO IS... THE PHOENIX? SECRET IDENTITY!!

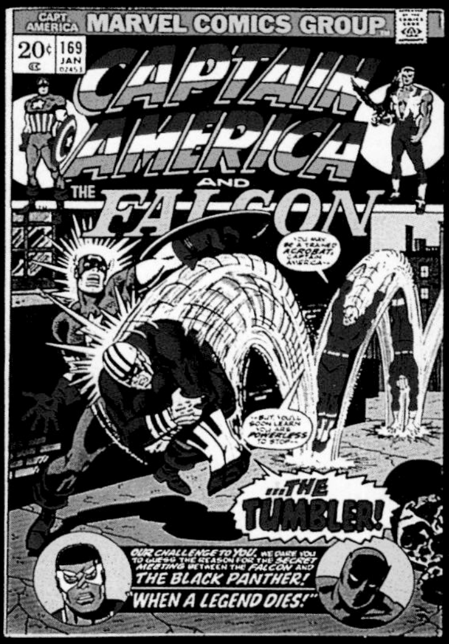
CAPT. AMERICA
MARVEL COMICS GROUP
20¢ 169 JAN
CAPTAIN AMERICA AND THE FALCON
...THE TUMBLER!
THE BLACK PANTHER!
"WHEN A LEGEND DIES!"

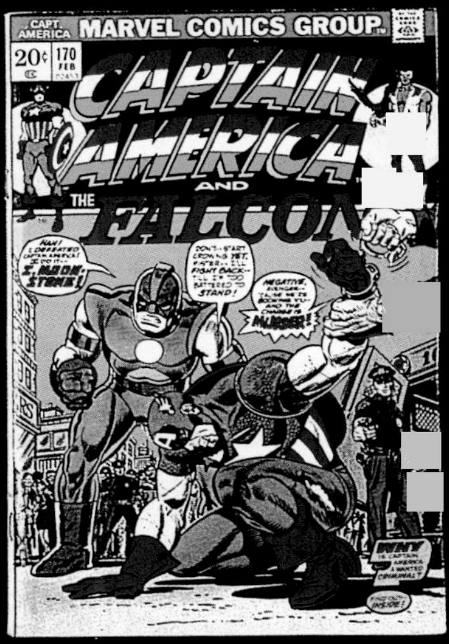
CAPT. AMERICA
MARVEL COMICS GROUP
20¢ 170 FEB
CAPTAIN AMERICA AND THE FALCON

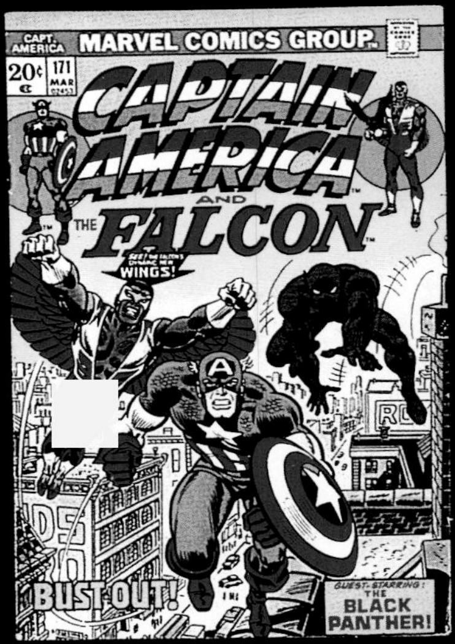
CAPT. AMERICA
MARVEL COMICS GROUP
20¢ 171 MAR
CAPTAIN AMERICA AND THE FALCON
WINGS!
BUST OUT!
GUEST-STARRING: THE BLACK PANTHER!

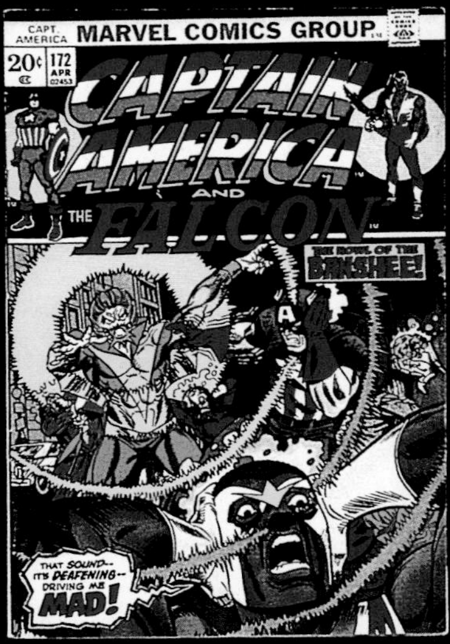
CAPT. AMERICA
MARVEL COMICS GROUP
20¢ 172 APR
CAPTAIN AMERICA AND THE FALCON
BANSHEE!
THAT SOUND-- IT'S DEAFENING-- DRIVING ME MAD!

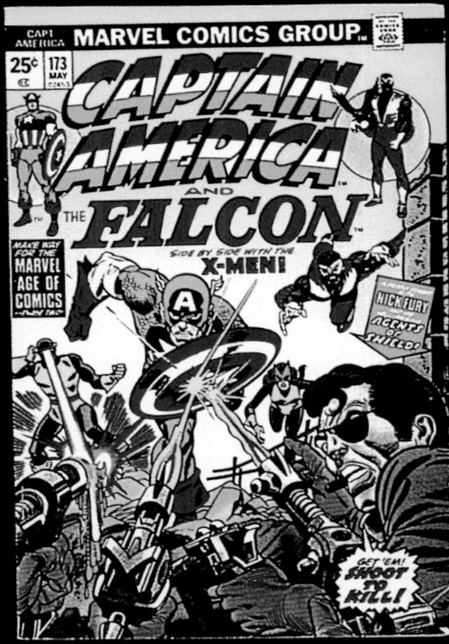
CAPT. AMERICA
MARVEL COMICS GROUP
25¢ 173 MAY
CAPTAIN AMERICA AND THE FALCON
SIDE BY SIDE WITH THE X-MEN!
MARVEL AGE OF COMICS
NICK FURY
GET 'EM! SHOOT TO KILL!

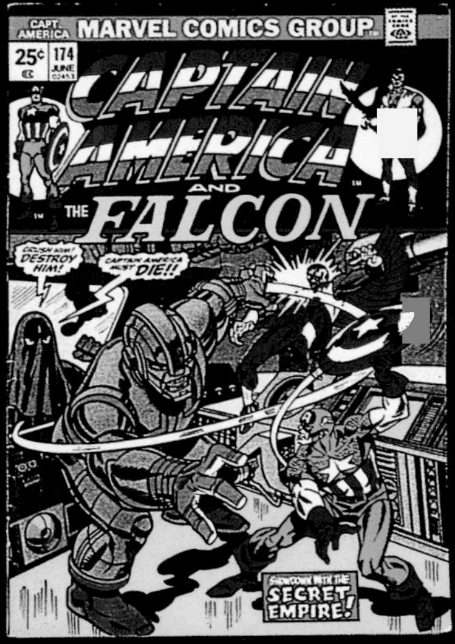
CAPT. AMERICA
MARVEL COMICS GROUP
25¢ 174 JUNE
CAPTAIN AMERICA AND THE FALCON
SECRET EMPIRE!

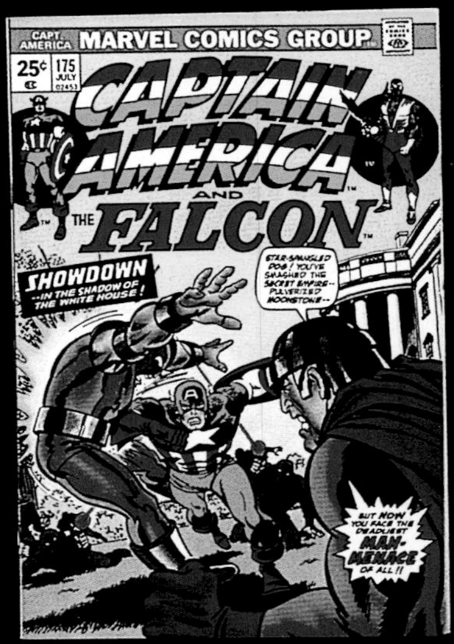
CAPT. AMERICA
MARVEL COMICS GROUP
25¢ 175 JULY
CAPTAIN AMERICA AND THE FALCON
SHOWDOWN --IN THE SHADOW OF THE WHITE HOUSE!
MENACE

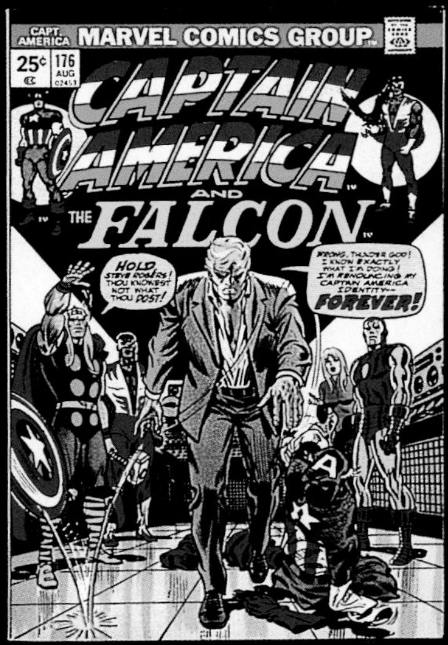
CAPT. AMERICA
MARVEL COMICS GROUP
25¢ 176 AUG
CAPTAIN AMERICA AND THE FALCON
FOREVER!

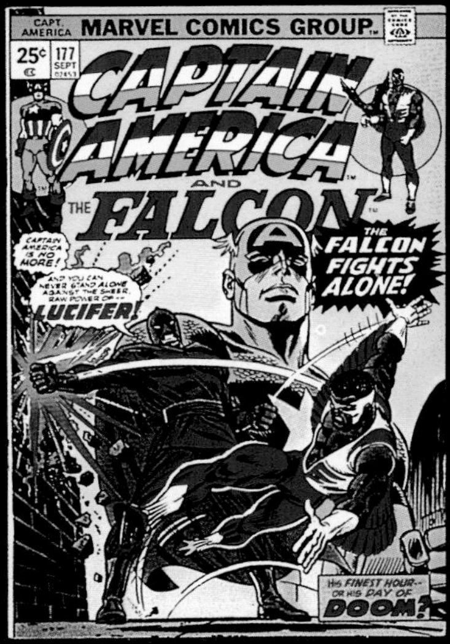
CAPT. AMERICA
MARVEL COMICS GROUP
25¢ 177 SEPT
CAPTAIN AMERICA AND THE FALCON
THE FALCON FIGHTS ALONE!
LUCIFER!
DOOM?

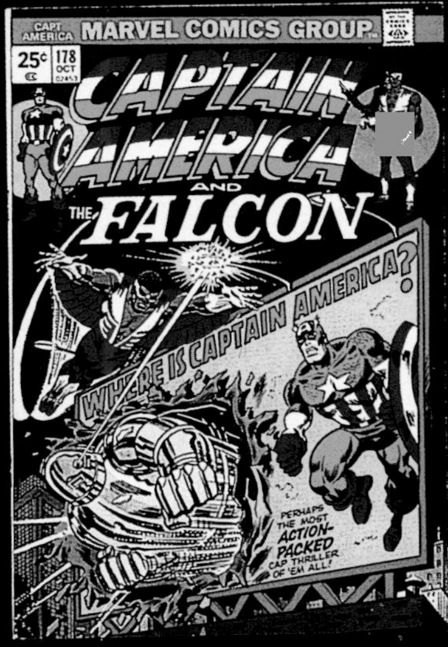
CAPT. AMERICA
MARVEL COMICS GROUP
25¢ 178 OCT
CAPTAIN AMERICA AND THE FALCON
WHERE IS CAPTAIN AMERICA?

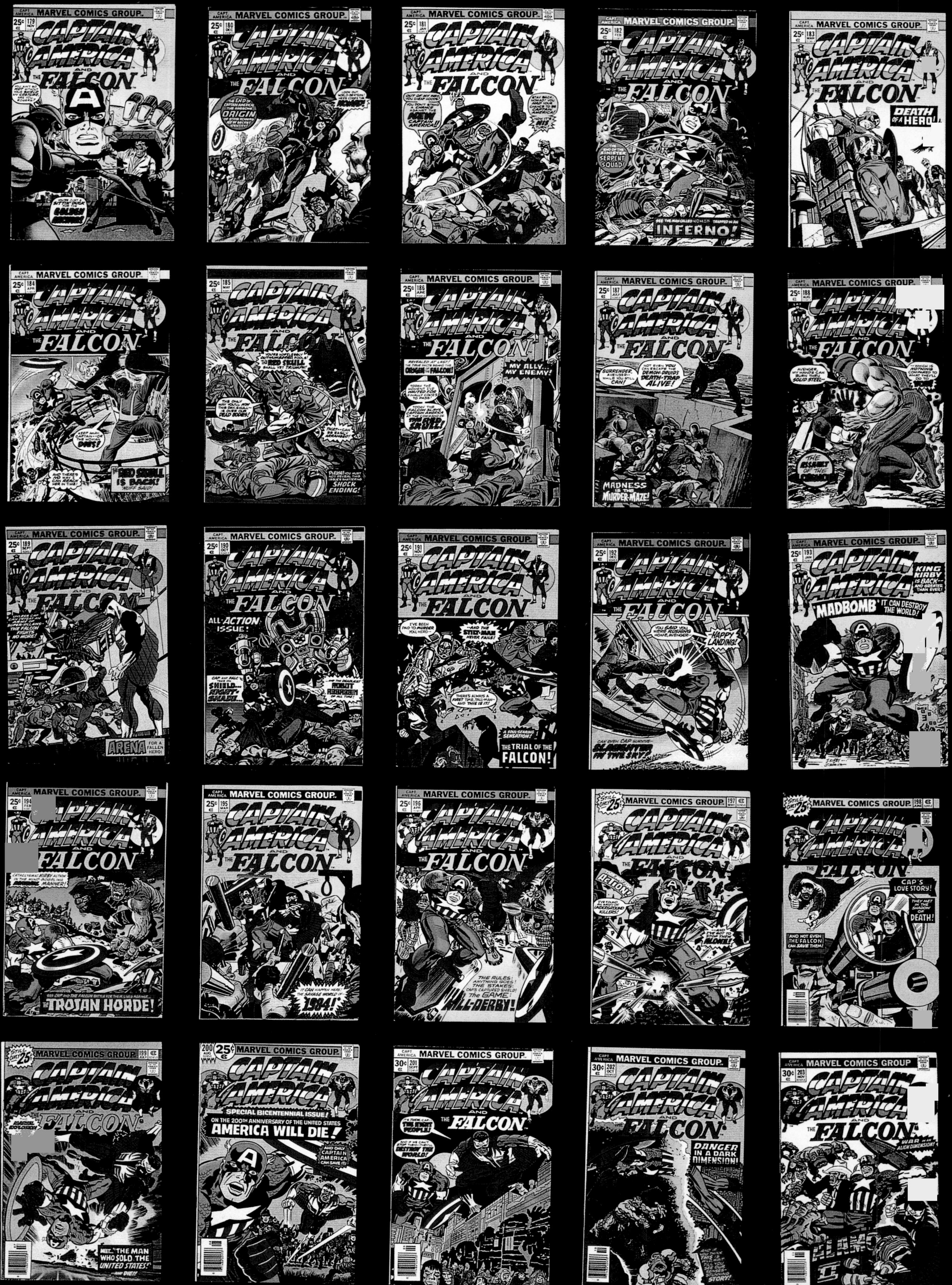
MARVEL COMICS GROUP
CAPTAIN AMERICA AND THE FALCON
DEATH OF A HERO
INFERNO!
SERPENT SQUAD!
RED SKULL IS BACK! 'NUFF SAID!
MY ALLY... MY ENEMY!
SHOCK ENDING!
MADNESS IN THE MURDER-MAZE!
ARENA FOR A FALLEN HERO!
ALL-ACTION ISSUE!
THE TRIAL OF THE FALCON!
HAPPY LANDING!
KING KIRBY IS BACK—AND GREATER THAN EVER!
MADBOMB IT CAN DESTROY THE WORLD!
TROJAN HORDE!
1984!
KILL-DERBY!
CAP'S LOVE STORY!
DEATH!
NEXT: "THE MAN WHO SOLD THE UNITED STATES!"
SPECIAL BICENTENNIAL ISSUE!
ON THE 200TH ANNIVERSARY OF THE UNITED STATES AMERICA WILL DIE!
AND ONLY CAPTAIN AMERICA CAN SAVE IT!
DANGER IN A DARK DIMENSION!

1879 Captain America (204-228)

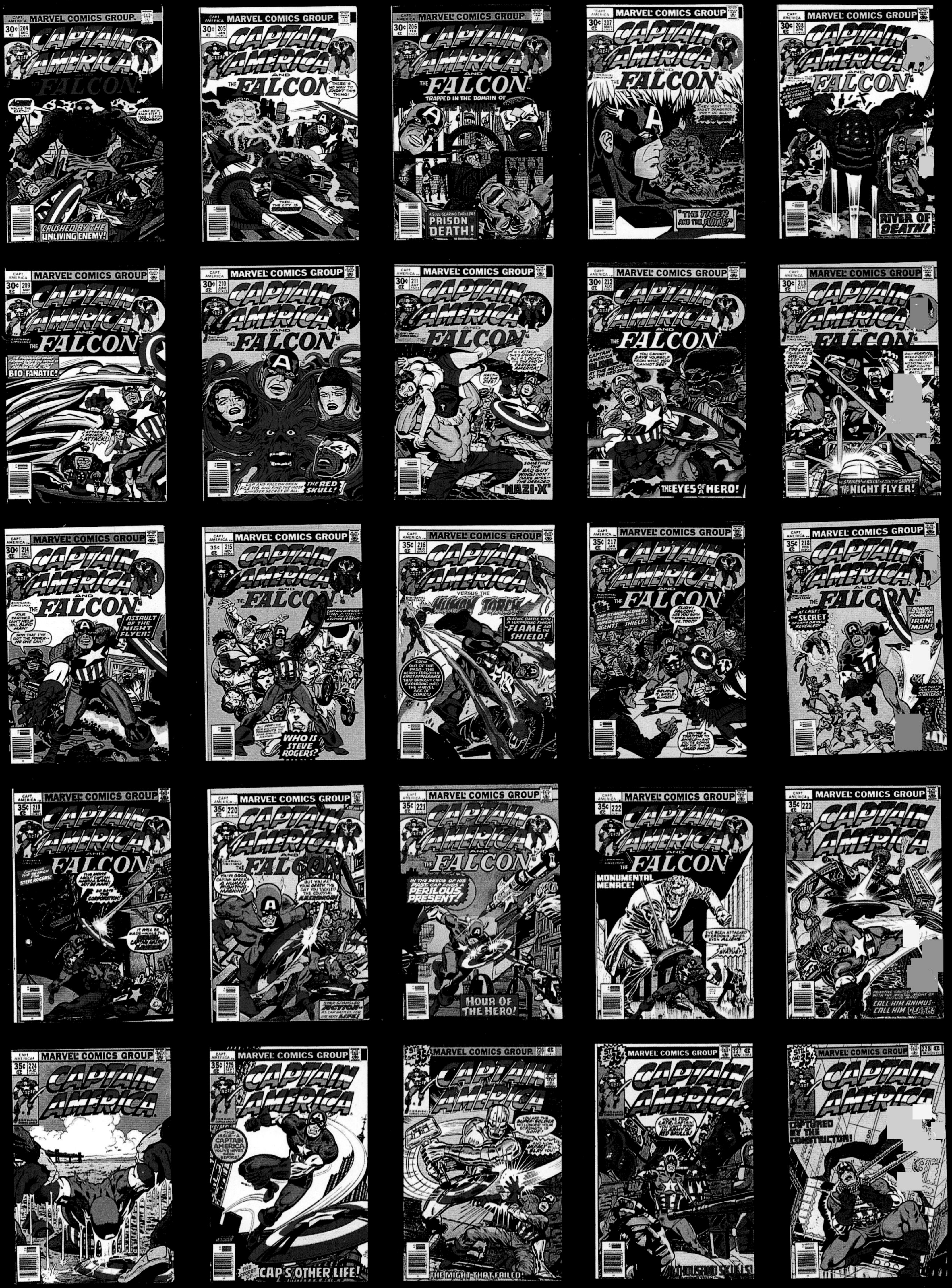

MARVEL COMICS GROUP
CAPTAIN AMERICA
FALCON
CRUSHED BY THE UNLIVING ENEMY!
MARVEL COMICS GROUP
CAPTAIN AMERICA AND THE FALCON
MARVEL COMICS GROUP
CAPTAIN AMERICA AND THE FALCON
PRISON DEATH!
MARVEL COMICS GROUP
CAPTAIN AMERICA AND FALCON
"THE TIGER AND THE FUNKY"
MARVEL COMICS GROUP
CAPTAIN AMERICA AND THE FALCON
RIVER OF DEATH!
MARVEL COMICS GROUP
CAPTAIN AMERICA AND THE FALCON
BIO-FANATIC!
MARVEL COMICS GROUP
CAPTAIN AMERICA AND THE FALCON
THE RED SKULL!
MARVEL COMICS GROUP
CAPTAIN AMERICA AND THE FALCON
"NAZI-X"
MARVEL COMICS GROUP
CAPTAIN AMERICA AND THE FALCON
THE EYES OF A HERO!
MARVEL COMICS GROUP
CAPTAIN AMERICA AND THE FALCON
THE NIGHT FLYER!
MARVEL COMICS GROUP
CAPTAIN AMERICA AND THE FALCON
ASSAULT OF THE NIGHT FLYER!
MARVEL COMICS GROUP
CAPTAIN AMERICA AND THE FALCON
WHO IS STEVE ROGERS?
MARVEL COMICS GROUP
CAPTAIN AMERICA VERSUS THE HUMAN TORCH
FLAME AND SHIELD!
MARVEL COMICS GROUP
CAPTAIN AMERICA AND THE FALCON
MARVEL COMICS GROUP
CAPTAIN AMERICA AND THE FALCON
IRON MAN!
MARVEL COMICS GROUP
CAPTAIN AMERICA AND THE FALCON
MARVEL COMICS GROUP
CAPTAIN AMERICA AND THE FALCON
MARVEL COMICS GROUP
CAPTAIN AMERICA AND THE FALCON
PERILOUS PRESENT!
HOUR OF THE HERO!
MARVEL COMICS GROUP
CAPTAIN AMERICA AND THE FALCON
MONUMENTAL MENACE!
MARVEL COMICS GROUP
CAPTAIN AMERICA
CALL HIM ANIMUS — CALL HIM DEATH!
MARVEL COMICS GROUP
CAPTAIN AMERICA
MARVEL COMICS GROUP
CAPTAIN AMERICA
CAP'S OTHER LIFE!
MARVEL COMICS GROUP
CAPTAIN AMERICA
THE MIGHT THAT FAILED!
MARVEL COMICS GROUP
CAPTAIN AMERICA
A THOUSAND SKULLS!
MARVEL COMICS GROUP
CAPTAIN AMERICA
CAPTURED BY THE CONSTRICTOR!

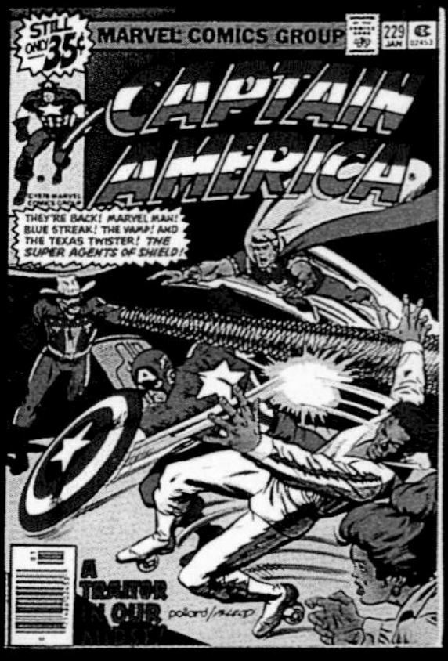
STILL ONLY 35¢
MARVEL COMICS GROUP
229
CAPTAIN AMERICA
THEY'RE BACK! MARVEL MAN! BLUE STREAK! THE VAMP! AND THE TEXAS TWISTER! THE SUPER AGENTS OF SHIELD!
A TRAITOR IN OUR MIDST!

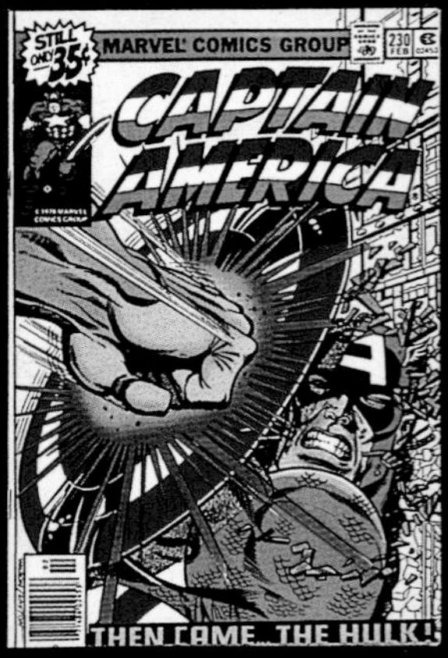
STILL ONLY 35¢
MARVEL COMICS GROUP
230
CAPTAIN AMERICA
THEN CAME...THE HULK!

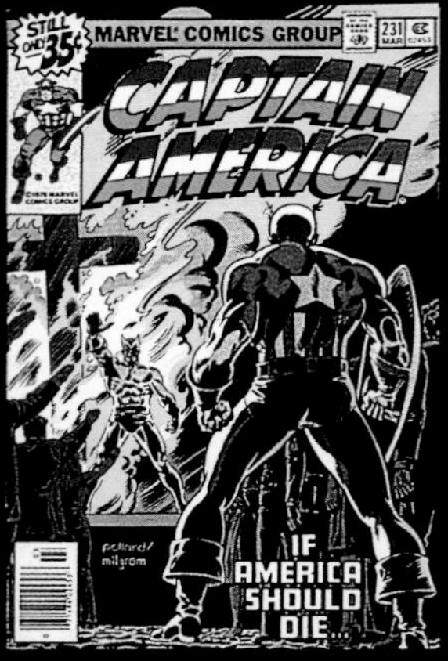
STILL ONLY 35¢
MARVEL COMICS GROUP
231
CAPTAIN AMERICA
IF AMERICA SHOULD DIE...

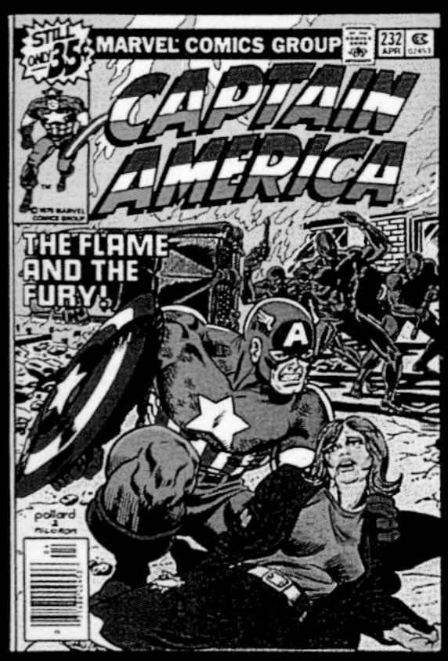
STILL ONLY 35¢
MARVEL COMICS GROUP
232
CAPTAIN AMERICA
THE FLAME AND THE FURY!

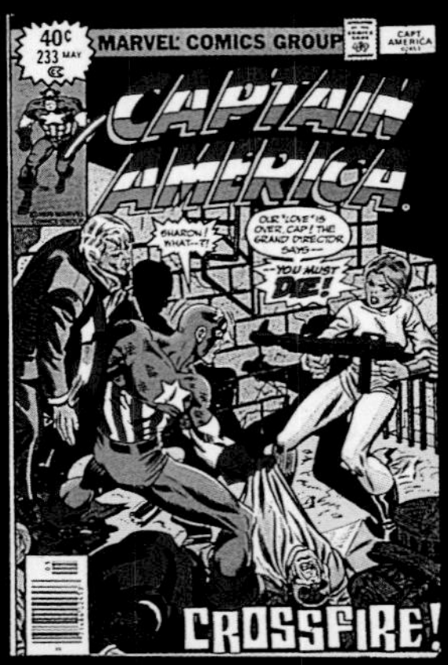
40¢
233
MARVEL COMICS GROUP
CAPTAIN AMERICA
YOU MUST DIE!
CROSSFIRE!

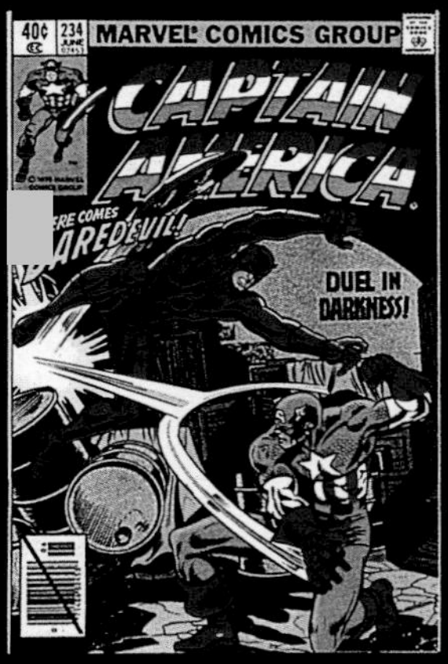
40¢
234
MARVEL COMICS GROUP
CAPTAIN AMERICA
DUEL IN DARKNESS!

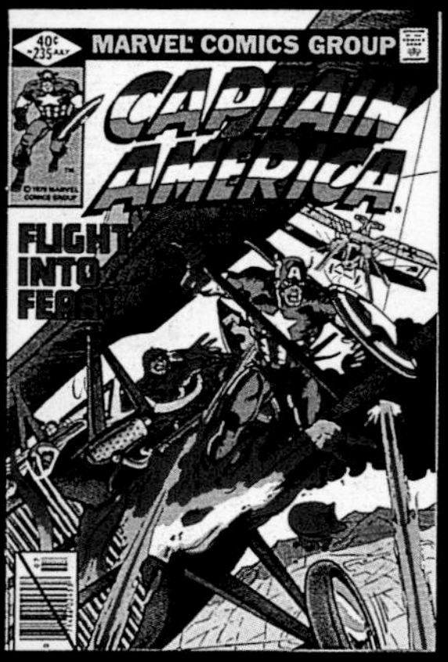
40¢
235
MARVEL COMICS GROUP
CAPTAIN AMERICA

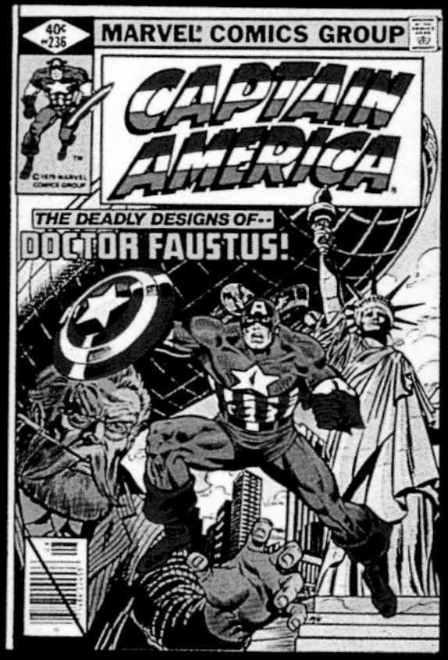
40¢
236
MARVEL COMICS GROUP
CAPTAIN AMERICA
THE DEADLY DESIGNS OF--
DOCTOR FAUSTUS!

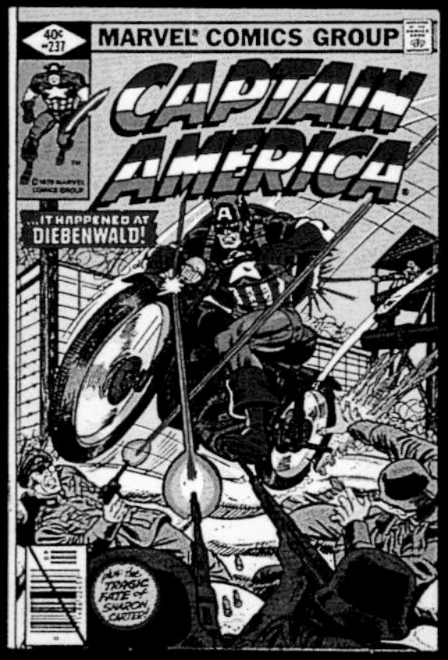
40¢
237
MARVEL COMICS GROUP
CAPTAIN AMERICA
IT HAPPENED AT DIEBENWALD!

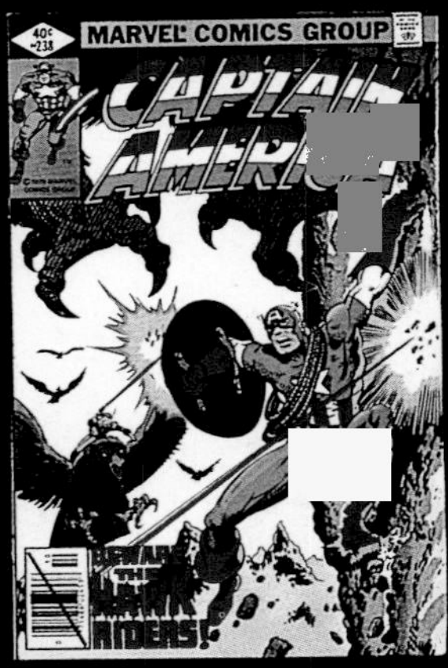
40¢
238
MARVEL COMICS GROUP

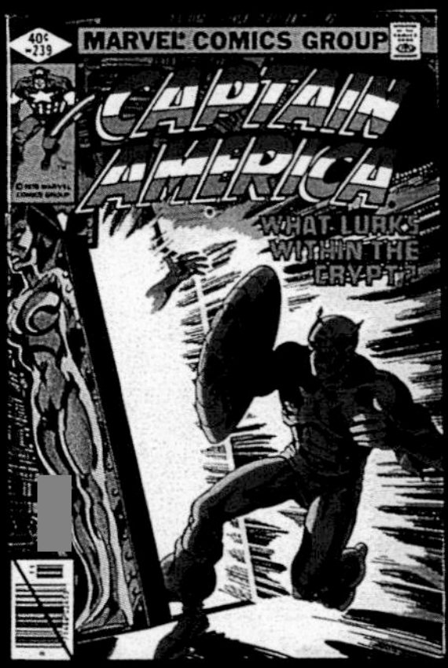
40¢
239
MARVEL COMICS GROUP
CAPTAIN AMERICA

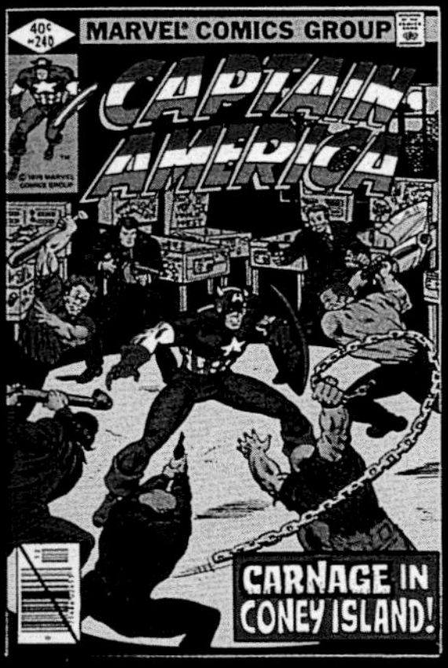
40¢
240
MARVEL COMICS GROUP
CAPTAIN AMERICA
CARNAGE IN CONEY ISLAND!

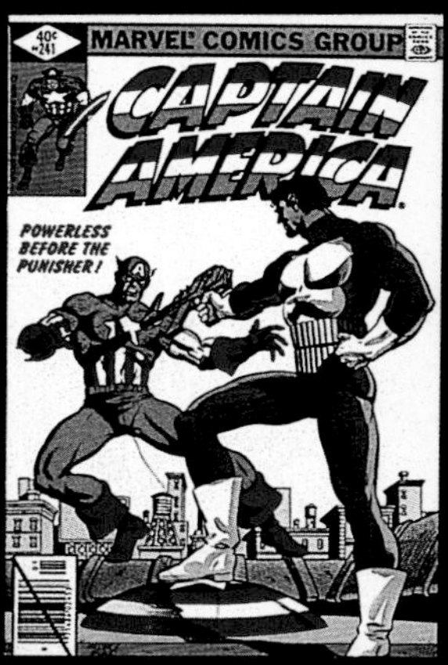
40¢
241
MARVEL COMICS GROUP
CAPTAIN AMERICA
POWERLESS BEFORE THE PUNISHER!

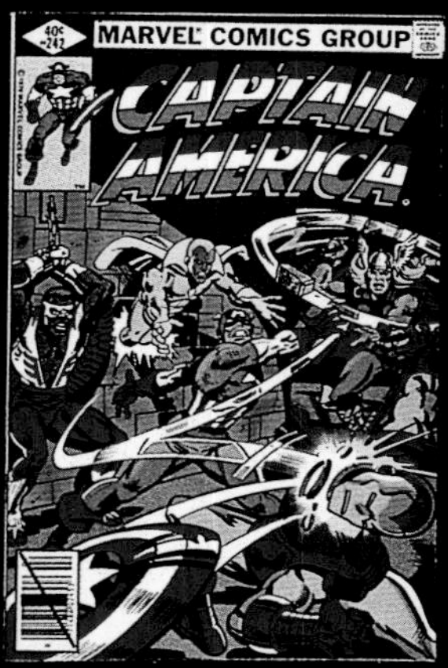
40¢
242
MARVEL COMICS GROUP
CAPTAIN AMERICA

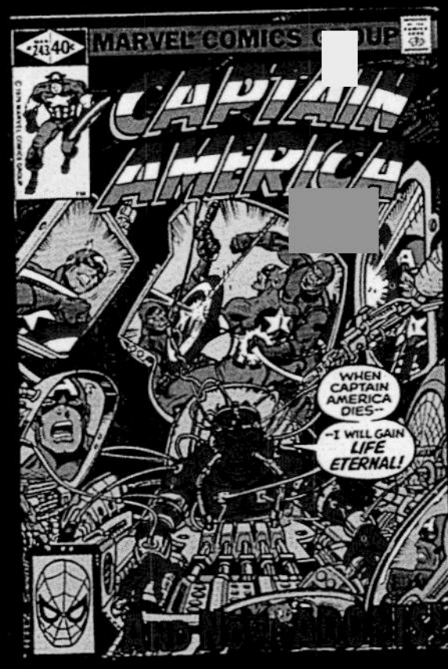
243
40¢
MARVEL COMICS GROUP
CAPTAIN AMERICA
WHEN CAPTAIN AMERICA DIES--
--I WILL GAIN LIFE ETERNAL!

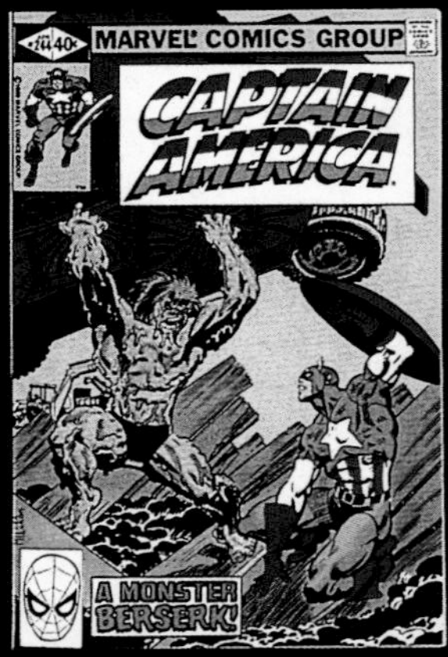
244
40¢
MARVEL COMICS GROUP
CAPTAIN AMERICA
A MONSTER BERSERK!

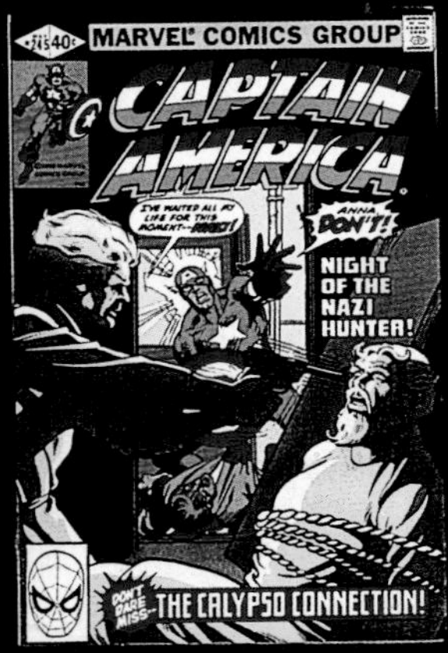
245
50¢
MARVEL COMICS GROUP
CAPTAIN AMERICA
DON'T!
NIGHT OF THE NAZI HUNTER!
THE CALYPSO CONNECTION!

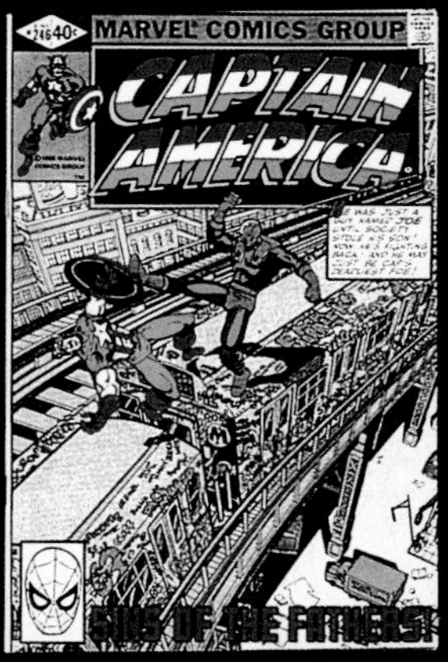
246
40¢
MARVEL COMICS GROUP
CAPTAIN AMERICA

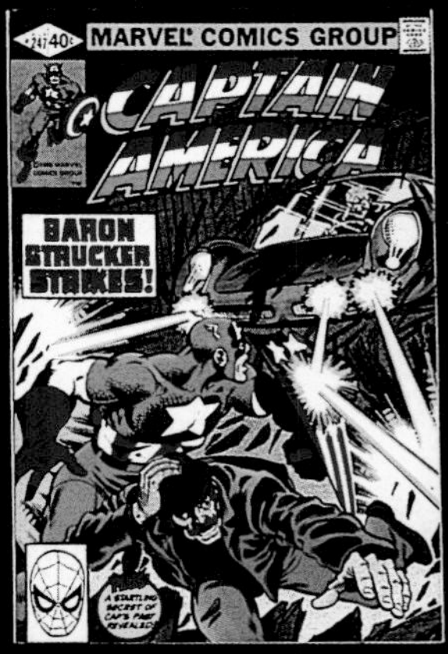
247
40¢
MARVEL COMICS GROUP
CAPTAIN AMERICA
BARON STRUCKER STRIKES!

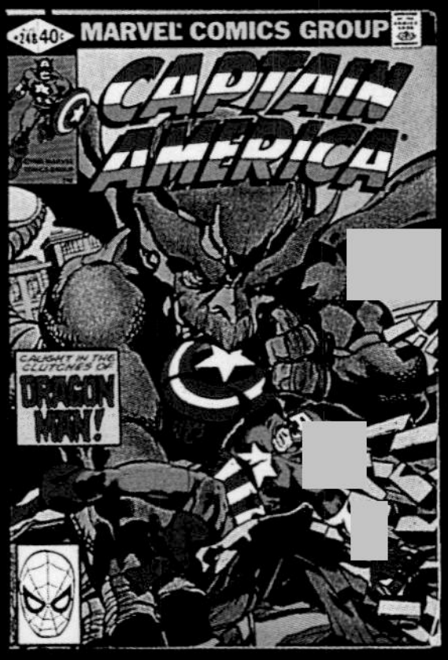
248
40¢
MARVEL COMICS GROUP
CAPTAIN AMERICA
DRAGON MAN!

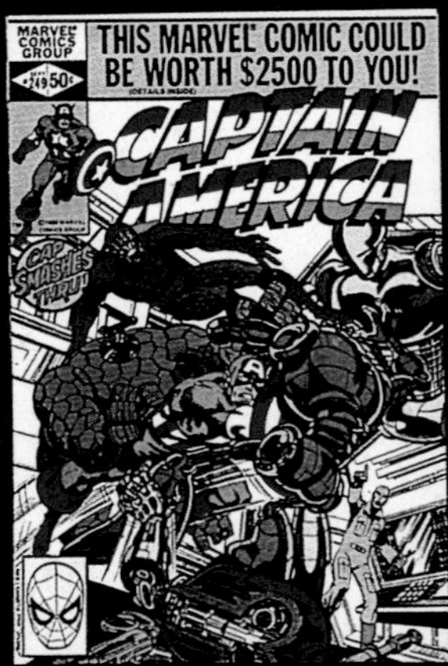
MARVEL COMICS GROUP
THIS MARVEL COMIC COULD BE WORTH $2500 TO YOU!
249
50¢
CAPTAIN AMERICA

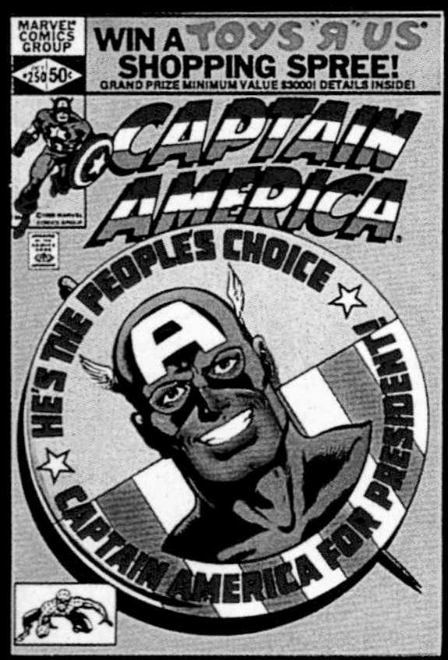
MARVEL COMICS GROUP
WIN A TOYS "R" US SHOPPING SPREE!
250
50¢
CAPTAIN AMERICA
HE'S THE PEOPLE'S CHOICE
CAPTAIN AMERICA FOR PRESIDENT!

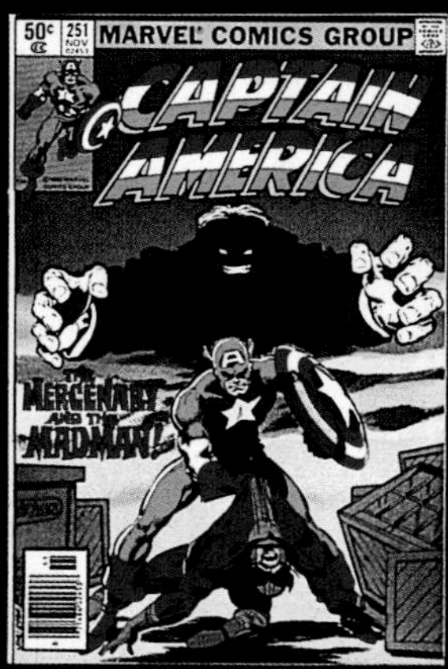
50¢
251
MARVEL COMICS GROUP
CAPTAIN AMERICA
MERCENARY AND THE MADMAN!

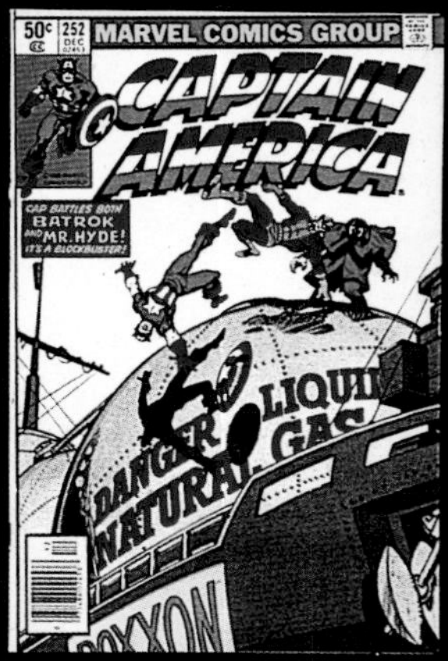
50¢
252
MARVEL COMICS GROUP
CAPTAIN AMERICA
CAP BATTLES BOTH BATROK AND MR. HYDE! IT'S A BLOCKBUSTER!
LIQUID GAS
DANGER NATURAL

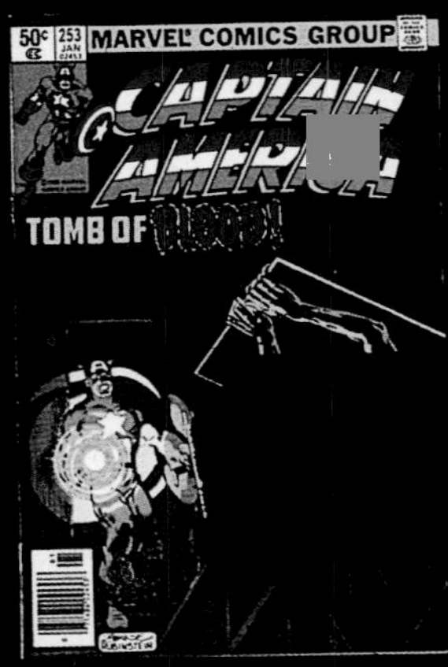
50¢
253
MARVEL COMICS GROUP
TOMB OF

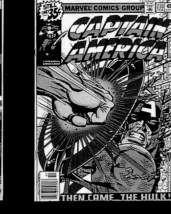

1879 Captain America (254-278)

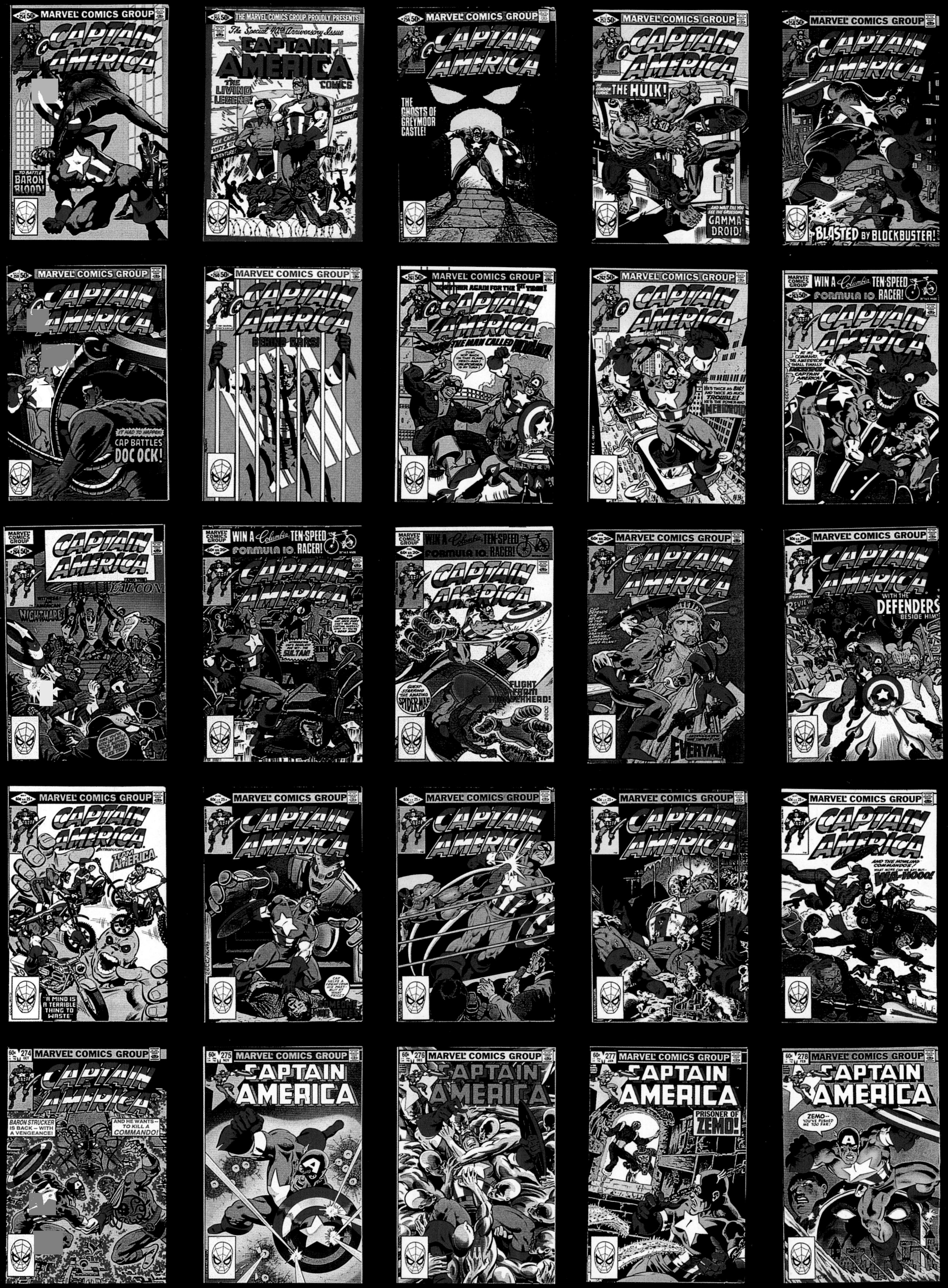
MARVEL COMICS GROUP
CAPTAIN AMERICA
TO BATTLE BARON BLOOD!
THE MARVEL COMICS GROUP PROUDLY PRESENTS:
The Special 40th Anniversary Issue
CAPTAIN AMERICA COMICS
THE LIVING LEGEND!
MARVEL COMICS GROUP
CAPTAIN AMERICA
THE GHOSTS OF GREYMOOR CASTLE!
MARVEL COMICS GROUP
CAPTAIN AMERICA
THE HULK!
...AND WAIT TILL YOU SEE THE GRUESOME GAMMA DROID!
MARVEL COMICS GROUP
CAPTAIN AMERICA
BLASTED BY BLOCKBUSTER!
MARVEL COMICS GROUP
CAPTAIN AMERICA
IT HAD TO HAPPEN! CAP BATTLES DOC OCK!
MARVEL COMICS GROUP
CAPTAIN AMERICA
BEHIND BARS!
MARVEL COMICS GROUP
TOGETHER AGAIN FOR THE 1st TIME!
CAPTAIN AMERICA
MARVEL COMICS GROUP
CAPTAIN AMERICA
MERIDIUS
WIN A Columbia TEN-SPEED FORMULA 10 RACER!
CAPTAIN AMERICA
CAPTAIN AMERICA
FALCON
NIGHTMARE!
WIN A Columbia TEN-SPEED FORMULA 10 RACER!
CAPTAIN AMERICA
SULTAN!
WIN A Columbia TEN-SPEED FORMULA 10 RACER!
CAPTAIN AMERICA
SPIDER-MAN
FLIGHT FROM THUNDERHEAD!
MARVEL COMICS GROUP
CAPTAIN AMERICA
EVERYMAN
MARVEL COMICS GROUP
CAPTAIN AMERICA
WITH THE DEFENDERS BESIDE HIM!
MARVEL COMICS GROUP
CAPTAIN AMERICA
TEAM AMERICA
"A MIND IS A TERRIBLE THING TO WASTE"
MARVEL COMICS GROUP
CAPTAIN AMERICA
MARVEL COMICS GROUP
CAPTAIN AMERICA
MARVEL COMICS GROUP
CAPTAIN AMERICA
MARVEL COMICS GROUP
CAPTAIN AMERICA
AND THE HOWLING COMMANDOS!
WA-HOOO!
MARVEL COMICS GROUP
CAPTAIN AMERICA
BARON STRUCKER IS BACK -- WITH A VENGEANCE!
AND HE WANTS -- TO KILL A COMMANDO!
MARVEL COMICS GROUP
CAPTAIN AMERICA
MARVEL COMICS GROUP
CAPTAIN AMERICA
MARVEL COMICS GROUP
CAPTAIN AMERICA
PRISONER OF ZEMO!
MARVEL COMICS GROUP
CAPTAIN AMERICA
ZEMO-- YOU'VE PUSHED ME TOO FAR!

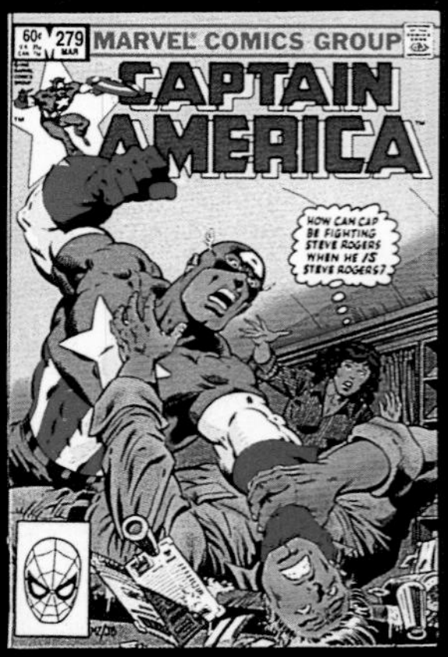
60¢ 279 MAR
MARVEL COMICS GROUP
CAPTAIN AMERICA
HOW CAN CAP BE FIGHTING STEVE ROGERS WHEN HE IS STEVE ROGERS?

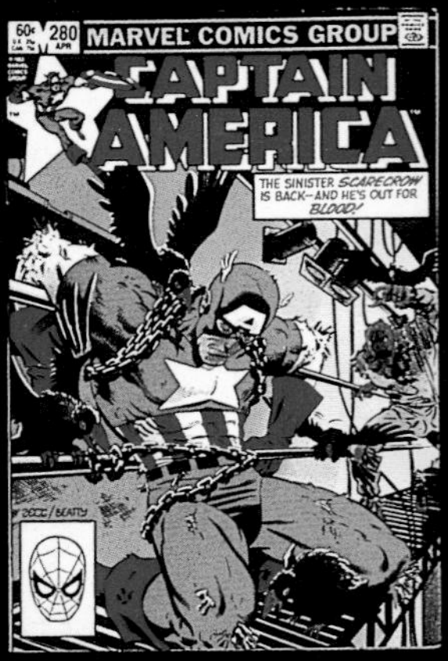
60¢ 280 APR
MARVEL COMICS GROUP
CAPTAIN AMERICA
THE SINISTER SCARECROW IS BACK—AND HE'S OUT FOR BLOOD!

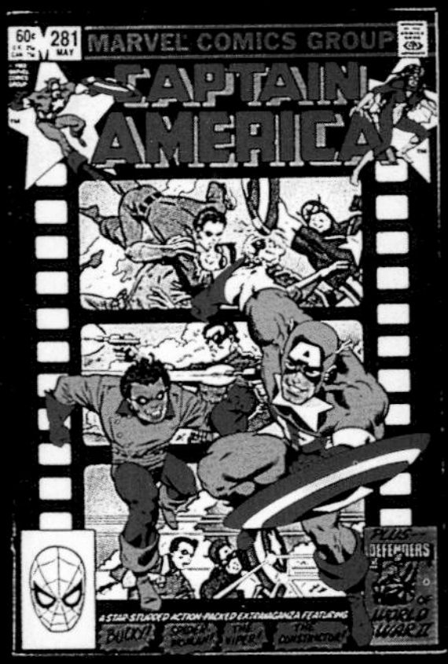
60¢ 281 MAY
MARVEL COMICS GROUP
CAPTAIN AMERICA

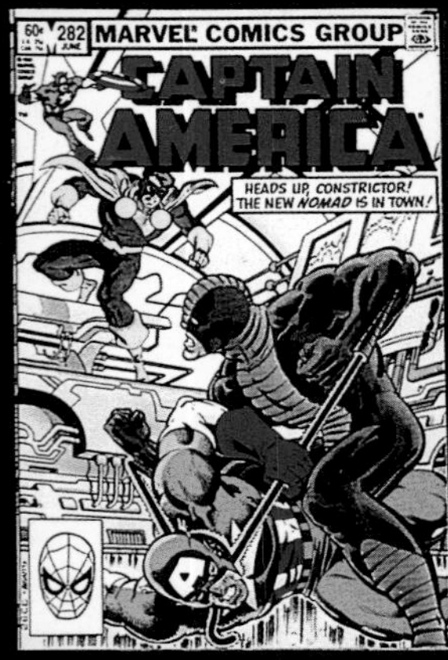
60¢ 282 JUNE
MARVEL COMICS GROUP
CAPTAIN AMERICA
HEADS UP, CONSTRICTOR! THE NEW NOMAD IS IN TOWN!

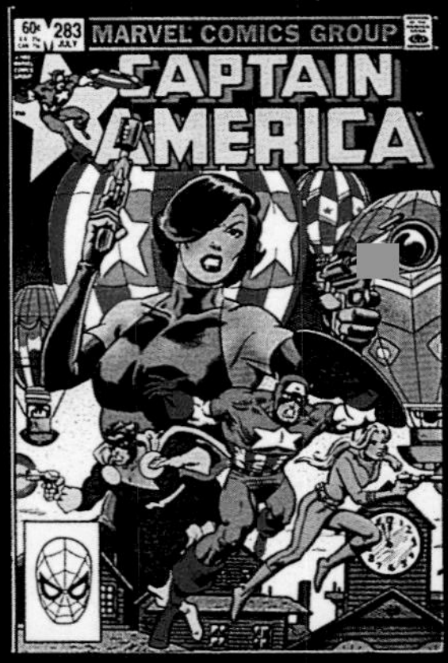
60¢ 283 JULY
MARVEL COMICS GROUP
CAPTAIN AMERICA

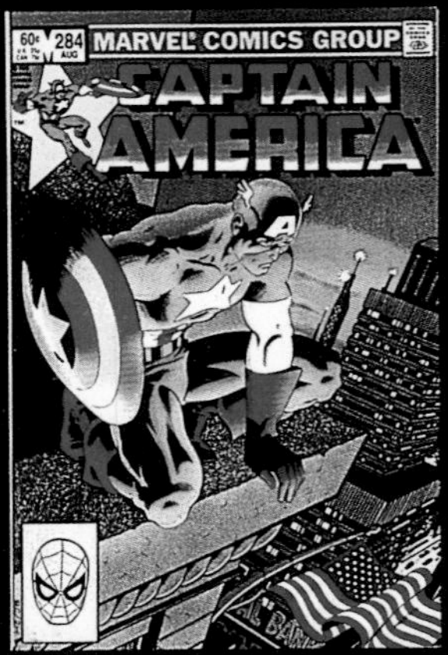
60¢ 284 AUG
MARVEL COMICS GROUP
CAPTAIN AMERICA

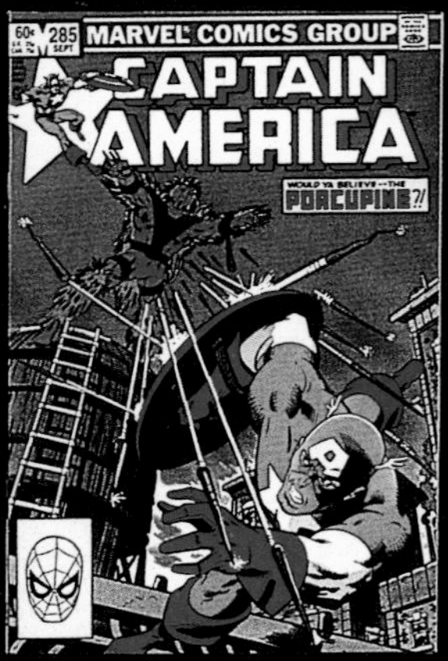
60¢ 285 SEPT
MARVEL COMICS GROUP
CAPTAIN AMERICA
WOULD YOU BELIEVE—THE PORCUPINE?!

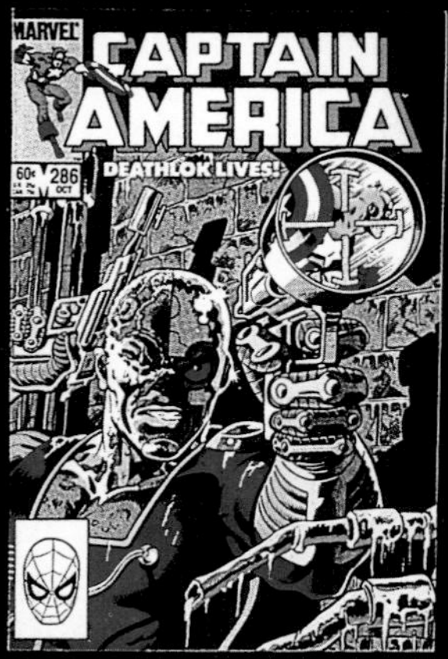
MARVEL
CAPTAIN AMERICA
60¢ 286 OCT
DEATHLOK LIVES!

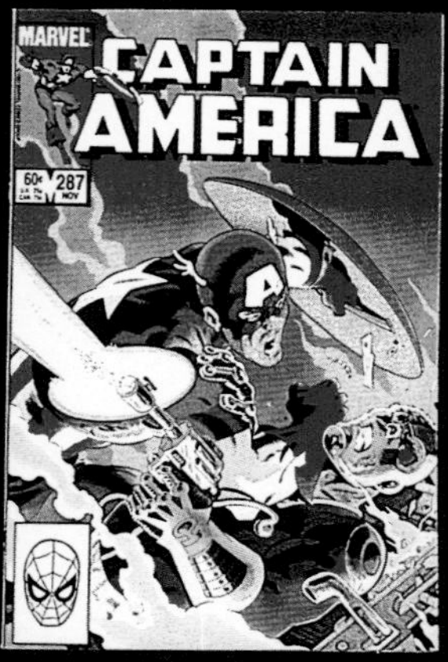
MARVEL
CAPTAIN AMERICA
60¢ 287 NOV

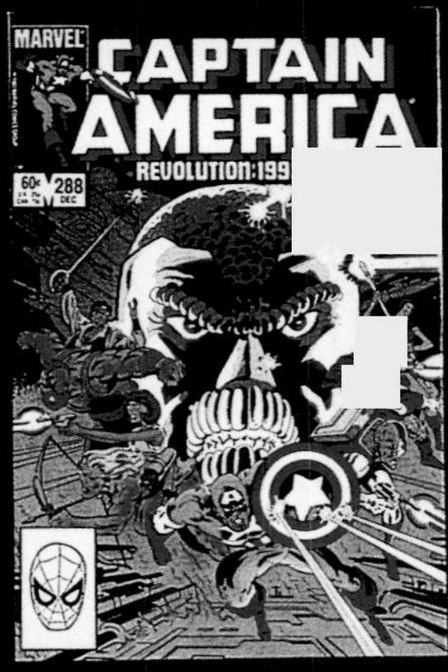
MARVEL
CAPTAIN AMERICA
60¢ 288 DEC

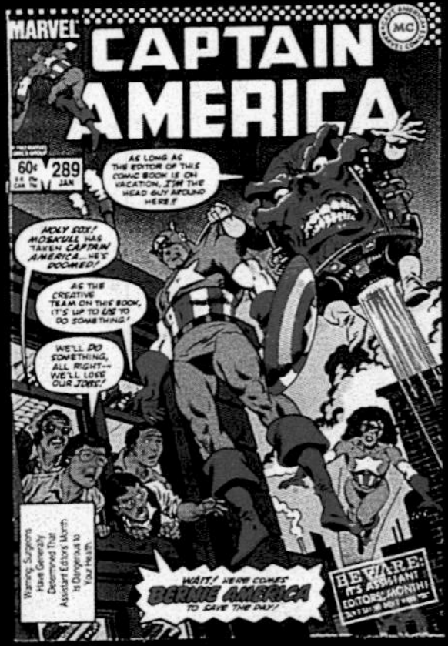
MARVEL
CAPTAIN AMERICA
60¢ 289 JAN
BEWARE

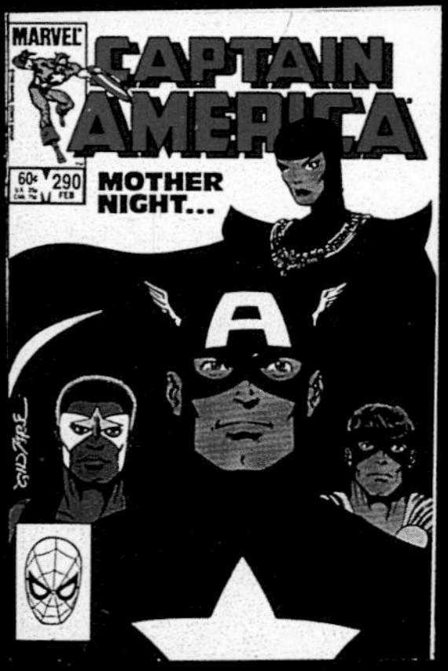
MARVEL
CAPTAIN AMERICA
60¢ 290 FEB
MOTHER NIGHT...

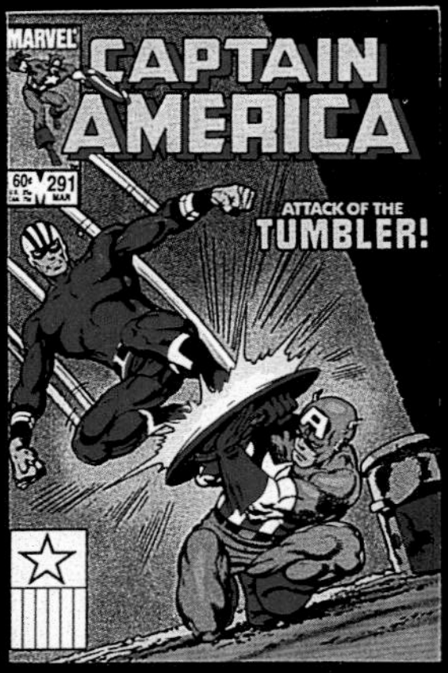
MARVEL
CAPTAIN AMERICA
60¢ 291 MAR
ATTACK OF THE TUMBLER!

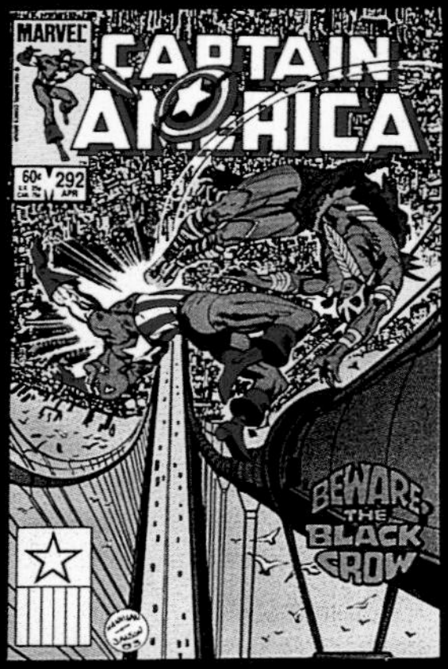
MARVEL
CAPTAIN AMERICA
60¢ 292 APR
BEWARE THE BLACK CROW

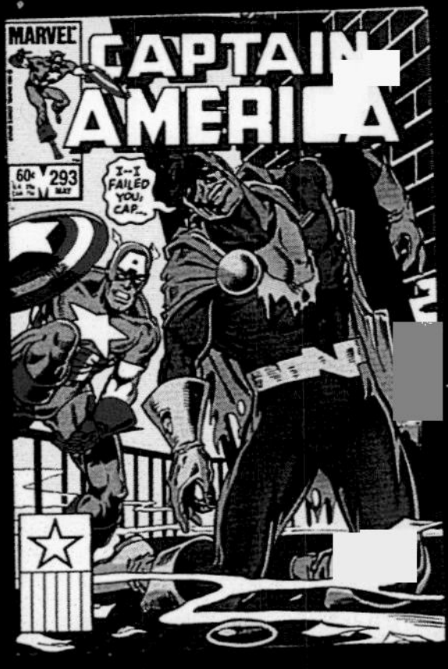
MARVEL
CAPTAIN AMERICA
60¢ 293 MAY

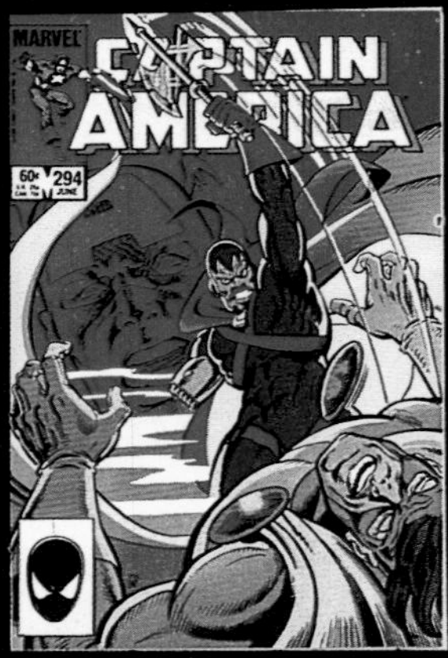
MARVEL
CAPTAIN AMERICA
60¢ 294 JUNE

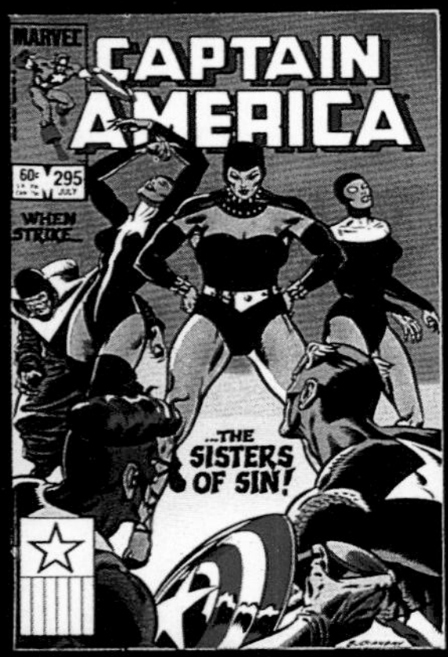
MARVEL
CAPTAIN AMERICA
60¢ 295 JULY
...THE SISTERS OF SIN!

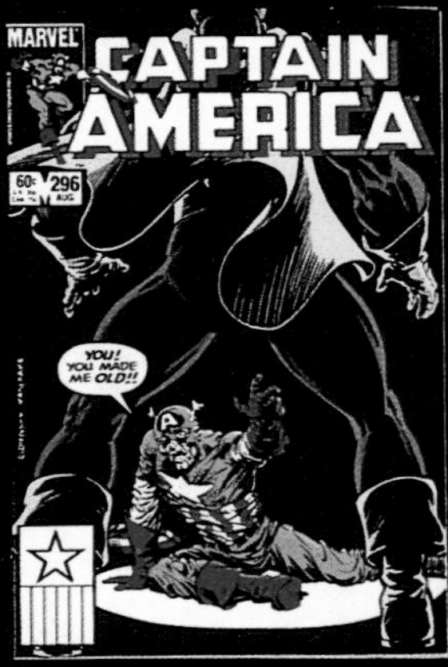
MARVEL
CAPTAIN AMERICA
60¢ 296 AUG
YOU! YOU MADE ME OLD!!

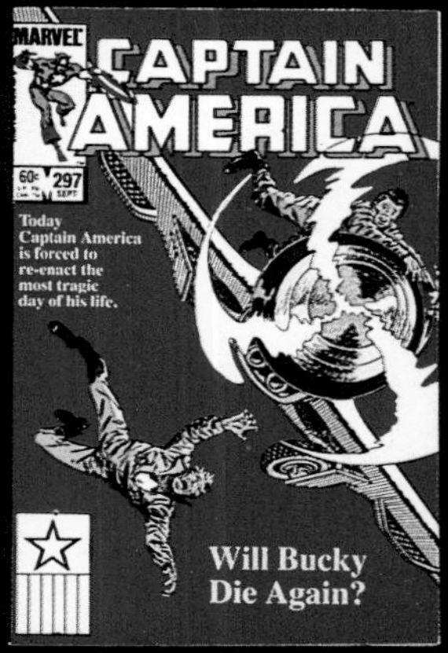
MARVEL
CAPTAIN AMERICA
60¢ 297 SEPT
Today Captain America is forced to re-enact the most tragic day of his life.
Will Bucky Die Again?

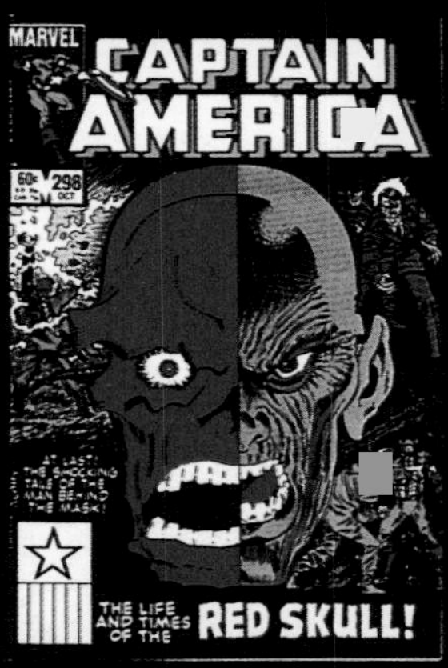
MARVEL
CAPTAIN AMERICA
60¢ 298 OCT
THE LIFE AND TIMES OF THE RED SKULL!

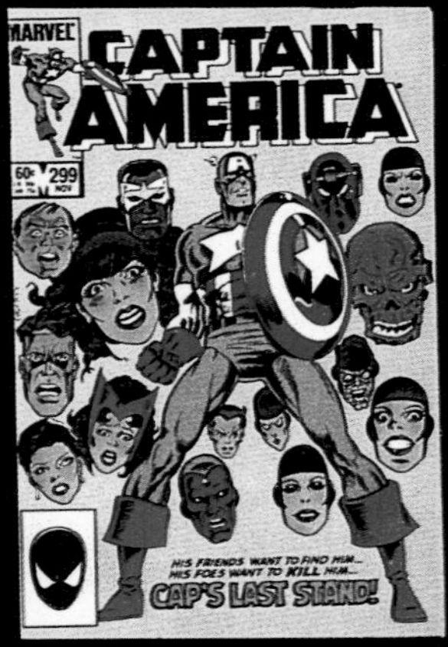
MARVEL
CAPTAIN AMERICA
60¢ 299 NOV
HIS FRIENDS WANT TO FIND HIM... HIS FOES WANT TO KILL HIM...
CAP'S LAST STAND!

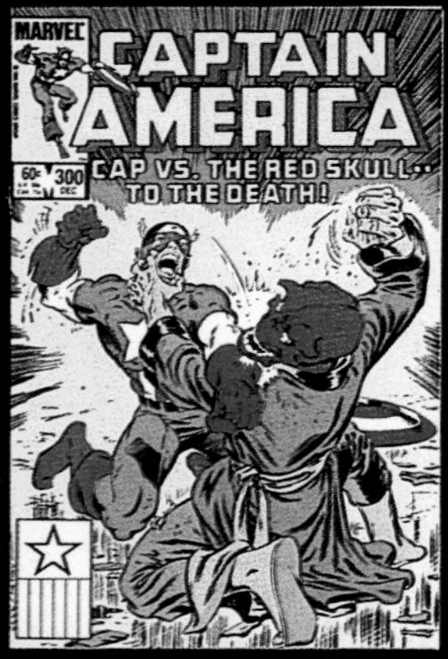
MARVEL
CAPTAIN AMERICA
60¢ 300 DEC
CAP VS. THE RED SKULL... TO THE DEATH!

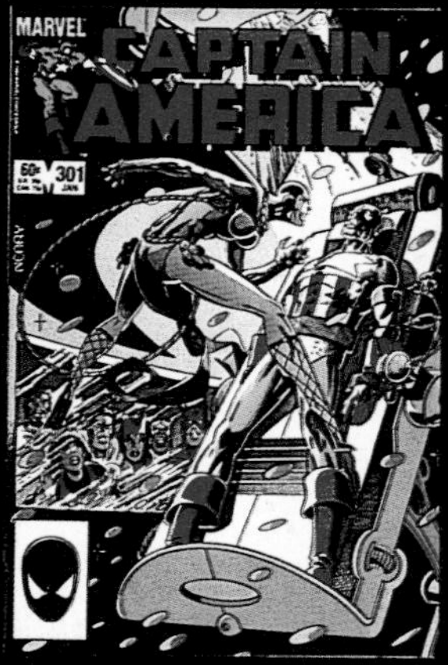
MARVEL
CAPTAIN AMERICA
60¢ 301 JAN

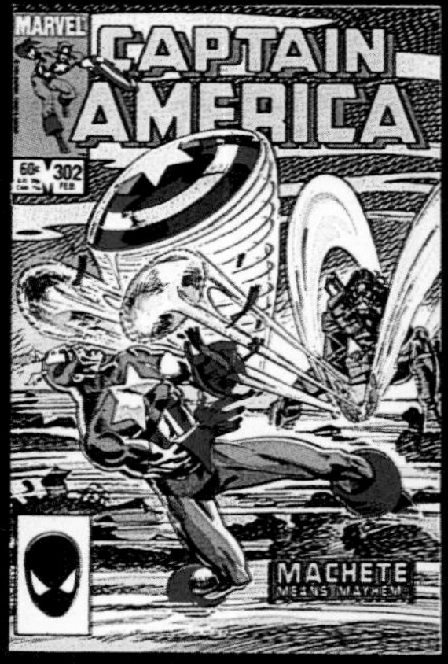
MARVEL
CAPTAIN AMERICA
60¢ 302 FEB
MACHETE MEANS MAYHEM

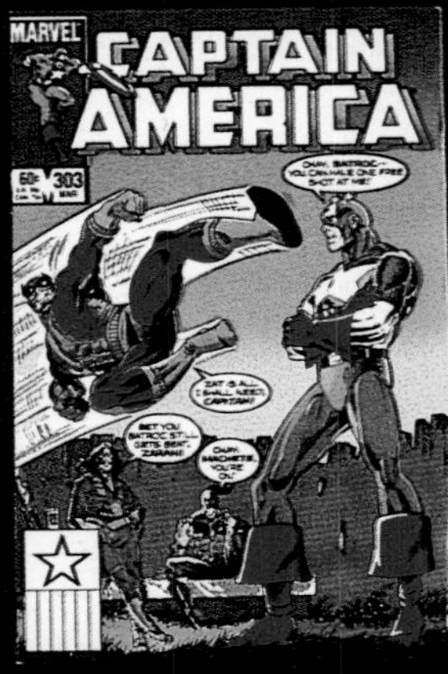
MARVEL
CAPTAIN AMERICA
60¢ 303 MAR

MARVEL
CAPTAIN AMERICA
65¢ 304

MARVEL
CAPTAIN AMERICA
65¢ 305
CAPTAIN BRITAIN!

MARVEL
CAPTAIN AMERICA
65¢ 306
MORDRED!

MARVEL
CAPTAIN AMERICA
65¢ 307
WHO AM I?
MADCAP!
THE INVADERS OF WORLD WAR II!

MARVEL
CAPTAIN AMERICA
65¢ 308
ARMADILLO!
HE'S NO LAUGHING MATTER

MARVEL
CAPTAIN AMERICA
65¢ 309
MADCAP

MARVEL
CAPTAIN AMERICA
65¢ 310
IN THE ARMS OF ANACONDA!

MARVEL
CAPTAIN AMERICA
65¢ 311

MARVEL
CAPTAIN AMERICA
65¢ 312

MARVEL
CAPTAIN AMERICA
65¢ 313
MODOK SCREAMS BLOODY MURDER!

MARVEL
CAPTAIN AMERICA
75¢ 314

MARVEL
CAPTAIN AMERICA
75¢ 315

MARVEL
CAPTAIN AMERICA
75¢ 316
ARMADILLO ATTACK--82 STORIES HIGH!
GUEST-STARRING HAWKEYE

MARVEL
CAPTAIN AMERICA
75¢ 317

CAPTAIN AMERICA
75¢ 318
BLUE STREAK
WAR ON WHEELS!

MARVEL
CAPTAIN AMERICA
75¢ 319
IF CAP CAN'T STOP SCOURGE EVERY SUPER-VILLAIN ON THIS COVER WILL DIE!

MARVEL
CAPTAIN AMERICA
75¢ 320
FACE TO FACE WITH SCOURGE!

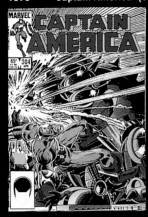

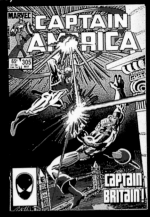

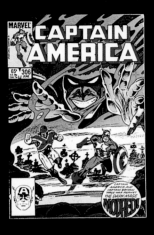

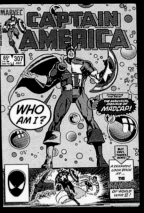

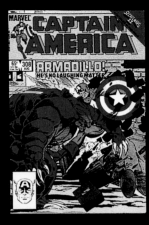

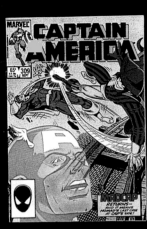

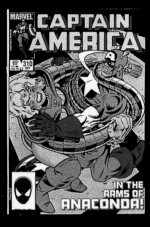

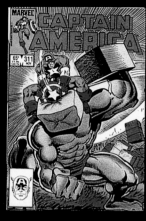

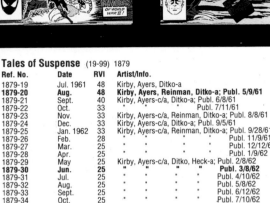

Tales of Suspense (19-99) 1879

Ref. No.	Date	RVI	Artist/Info.
1879-19	Jul. 1961	48	Kirby, Ayers, Ditko-a
1879-20	**Aug.**	**48**	**Kirby, Ayers, Reinman, Ditko-a; Publ. 5/9/61**
1879-21	Sept.	40	Kirby, Ayers-c/a, Ditko-a; Publ. 6/8/61
1879-22	Oct.	33	" " " Publ. 7/11/61
1879-23	Nov.	33	Kirby, Ayers-c/a, Reinman, Ditko-a; Publ. 8/8/61
1879-24	Dec.	33	Kirby, Ayers-c/a, Ditko-a; Publ. 9/5/61
1879-25	Jan. 1962	33	Kirby, Ayers-c/a, Reinman, Ditko-a; Publ. 9/28/61
1879-26	Feb.	28	" " " " Publ. 11/9/61
1879-27	Mar.	25	" " " " Publ. 12/12/61
1879-28	Apr.	25	" " " " Publ. 1/9/62
1879-29	May	25	Kirby, Ayers-c/a, Ditko, Heck-a; Publ. 2/8/62
1879-30	**Jun.**	**25**	**" " " " Publ. 3/8/62**
1879-31	Jul.	25	" " " " Publ. 4/10/62
1879-32	Aug.	25	" " " " Publ. 5/8/62
1879-33	Sept.	25	" " " " Publ. 6/12/62
1879-34	Oct.	25	" " " " Publ. 7/10/62
1879-35	Nov.	25	" " " " Publ. 8/9/62
1879-36	Dec.	25	Reinman, Ditko-a; Publ. 9/11/62
1879-37	Jan. 1963	25	Heck, Ditko-a; Publ. 10/7/62
1879-38	Feb.	25	Publ. 11/8/62
1879-39	Mar.	850	Kirby/Heck-c, Heck-a (Intro. Invincible Iron Man); Publ. 12/10/62
1879-40	**Apr.**	**370**	**Kirby, Heck-c/a; Publ. 1/10/63**
1879-41	May	200	Kirby/Roussos-c, Kirby/Ayers-a; Publ. 2/12/63
1879-42	Jun.	90	Kirby/Heck-c, Heck-a; Publ. 3/12/63
1879-43	Jul.	80	Kirby/Ayers-c, Kirby/Heck-a
1879-44	Aug.	80	Kirby/Ayers-c, Heck-a
1879-45	Sept.	80	Kirby/Heck-c, Heck-a
1879-46	Oct.	40	Kirby/Ayers-c, Heck-a
1879-47	Nov.	40	Kirby/Brodsky-c, Heck-a
1879-48	Dec.	57	Kirby/Brodsky-c, Ditko/Ayers-a (New Armor)
1879-49	Jan. 1964	34	Kirby/Brodsky-c, Ditko/Reinman-a
1879-50	**Feb.**	**21**	**Kirby/Roussos-c, Heck-a**
1879-51	Mar.	21	" " "
1879-52	Apr.	21	" " " (Intro. Black Widow) Publ. 1/10/64
1879-53	May	25	Kirby/Brodsky-c, Heck-a
1879-54	Jun.	42	Kirby/Stone-c, Heck-a
1879-55	Jul.	42	Kirby/Brodsky-c, Heck-a
1879-56	Aug.	42	Kirby/Ayers-c, Heck-a
1879-57	Sept.	46	Heck-c/a (Intro. Hawkeye); Publ. 6/9/64
1879-58	Oct.	50	Kirby/Stone-c, Heck/Ayers-a
1879-59	Nov.	71	Kirby/Ayers-c, Heck-a (Capt. America & Iron Man)
1879-60	**Dec.**	**21**	**Kirby/Stone-c, Heck/Ayers-a**
1879-61	Jan. 1965	21	" " " "
1879-62	Feb.	21	Kirby/Colletta-c, Heck/Ayers-a
1879-63	Mar.	45	" " " " (Origin)
1879-64	Apr.	40	Kirby/Stone-c, Heck/Stone-a
1879-65	May	40	Kirby/Stone-c, Heck/Demeo-a
1879-66	Jun.	40	Kirby/Giacoia-c, Heck/Demeo-a
1879-67	Jul.	13	Kirby/Esposito-c, Heck/Demeo-a
1879-68	Aug.	13	Kirby/Giacoia-c, Heck/Demeo-a
1879-69	Sept.	13	Kirby/Heck-c, Heck/Colletta-a
1879-70	**Oct.**	**13**	**Kirby/Sinnott-c, Heck/Demeo-a**
1879-71	Nov.	13	Kirby/Brodsky-c, Heck/W. Wood-a
1879-72	Dec.	12	Kirby/Heck-c, Heck/Demeo-a
1879-73	Jan. 1966	12	Colan/Abel-c, Austin/Michaels-a
1879-74	Feb.	12	Kirby/Broadsky-c, Austin/Michaels-a
1879-75	Mar.	12	Colan/Abel-c, Austin/Michaels-a
1879-76	Apr.	12	Kirby/Romita-c, Austin/Michaels-a
1879-77	May	12	Colan/Abel-c, Austin/Michaels-a
1879-78	Jun.	12	Kirby/Giacoia-c, Colan/Michaels-a
1879-79	Jul.	12	Colan/Abel-c/a
1879-80	**Aug.**	**12**	**Kirby/Heck-c, Colan/Michaels-a**
1879-81	Sept.	12	Colan/Abel-c, Colan/Michaels-a
1879-82	Oct.	12	Kirby/Giacoia-c, Colan/Giacoia-a
1879-83	Nov.	12	Colan/Giacoia-c, Colan/Michaels-a
1879-84	Dec.	12	Kirby/Giacoia-c, Colan/Giacoia-a
1879-85	Jan. 1967	12	Colan/Giacoia-c/a
1879-86	Feb.	12	Kirby/Giacoia-c, Colan/Giacoia-a
1879-87	Mar.	12	Colan/Giacoia-c/a
1879-88	Apr.	12	Kane-c, Colan/Giacoia-a
1879-89	May	12	Colan/Giacoia-c/a
1879-90	**Jun.**	**12**	**Kane/Sinnott-c, Colan/Giacoia-a**
1879-91	Jul.	12	Colan/Giacoia-c/a
1879-92	Aug.	12	Kirby/Giacoia-c, Colan, Kirby/Giacoia, Sinnott-a
1879-93	Sept.	12	Colan/Giacoia-c/a
1879-94	Oct.	12	Kirby/Sinnott-c, Colan, Kirby/Adkins, Sinnott-a
1879-95	Nov.	12	Colan/Giacoia-c/a, Kirby/Sinnott-a
1879-96	Dec.	12	Kirby/Giacoia-c/a, Kirby/Sinnott-a
1879-97	Jan. 1968	12	Colan/Giacoia-c/a, Kirby/Sinnott-a
1879-98	Feb.	12	Kirby/Shores-c, Kirby, Colan/Giacoia, Sinnott-a
1879-99	Mar.	12	Colan/Giacoia-c, Colan, Kirby/Craig, Shores-a

Continues as **Captain America** (100-Present) 1879

Ref. No.	Date	RVI	Artist/Info.
1879-100	**Apr. 1968**	**140**	**Kirby/Shores-c/a**
1879-101	May	40	" "
1879-102	Jun.	22	" "
1879-103	Jul.	19	" "
1879-104	Aug.	19	Kirby/Adkins-c/a
1879-105	Sept.	19	" "
1879-106	Oct.	19	Kirby/Giacoia-c/a
1879-107	Nov.	19	" "
1879-108	Dec.	19	Kirby/Shores-c/a
1879-109	Jan. 1969	21	" " (Origin)
1879-110	**Feb.**	**30**	**Steranko-c/a, Sinnott-a**
1879-111	Mar.	30	" "
1879-112	Apr.	10	Kirby/Giacoia-c, Kirby/Tuska-a
1879-113	May	30	Steranko-c/a, Palmer-a
1879-114	Jun.	7	Romita-c/a, Buscema-a
1879-115	Jul.	7	M. Severin/Giacoia-c, Buscema-a
1879-116	Aug.	7	Colan/Sinnott-c/a

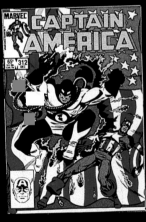

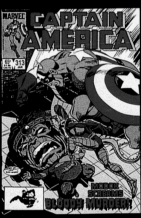

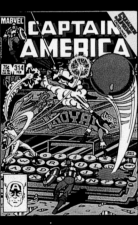

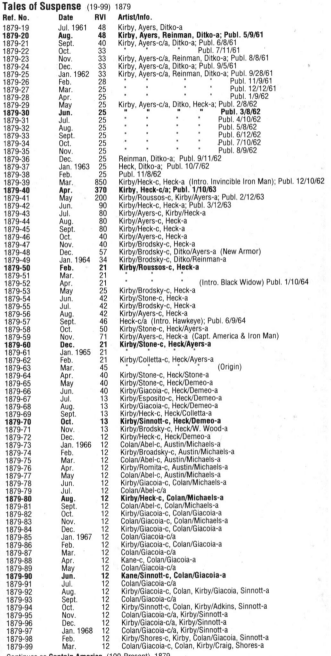

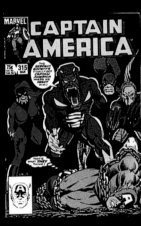

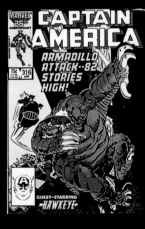

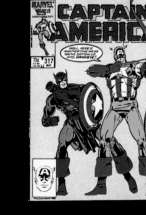

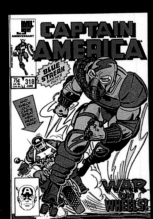

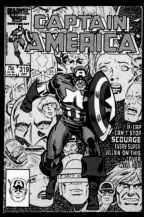

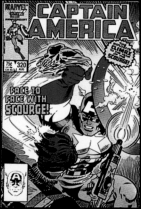

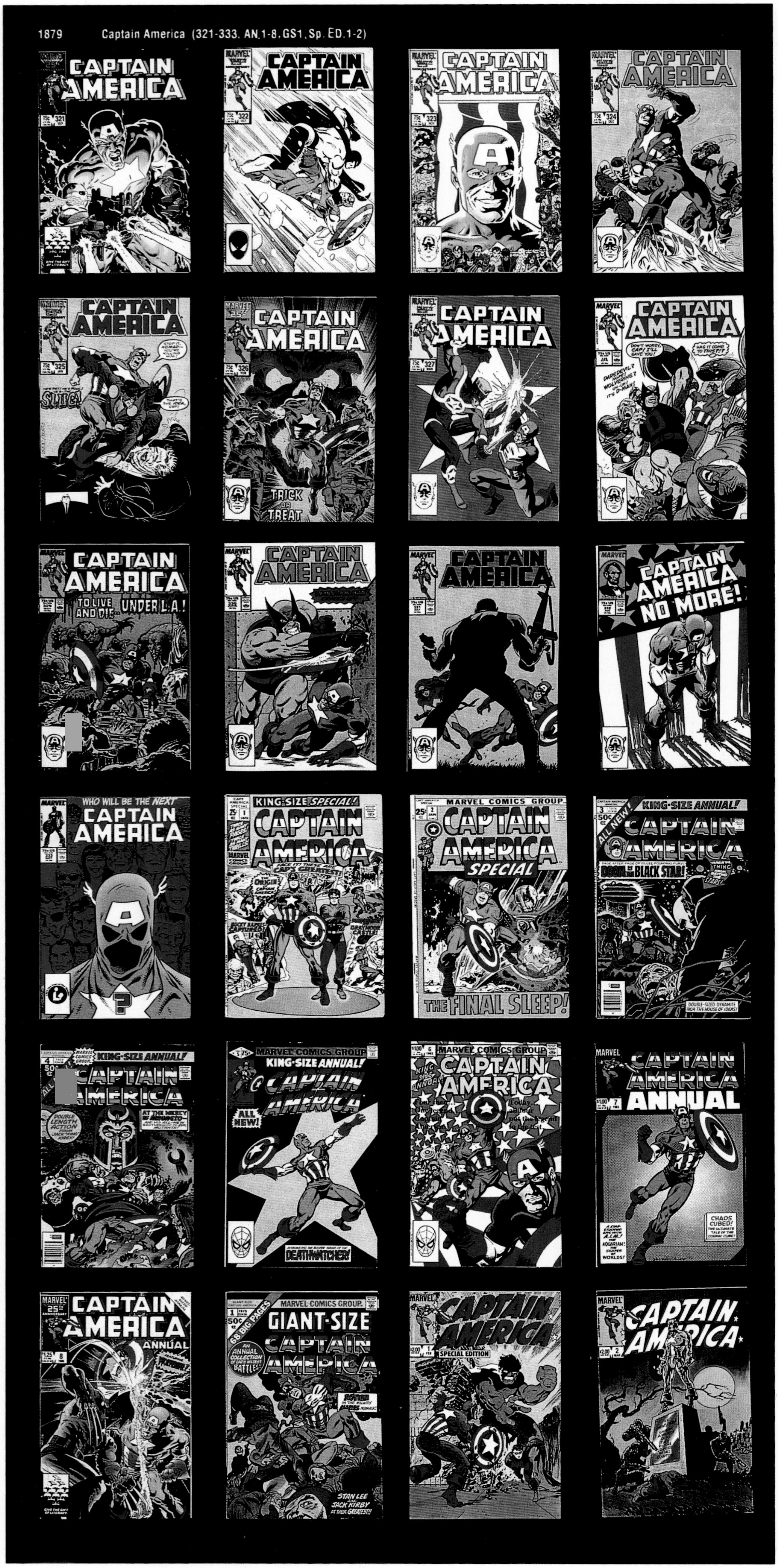
1879 Captain America (321-333, AN.1-8, GS1, Sp. ED.1-2)

Captain America (continued)

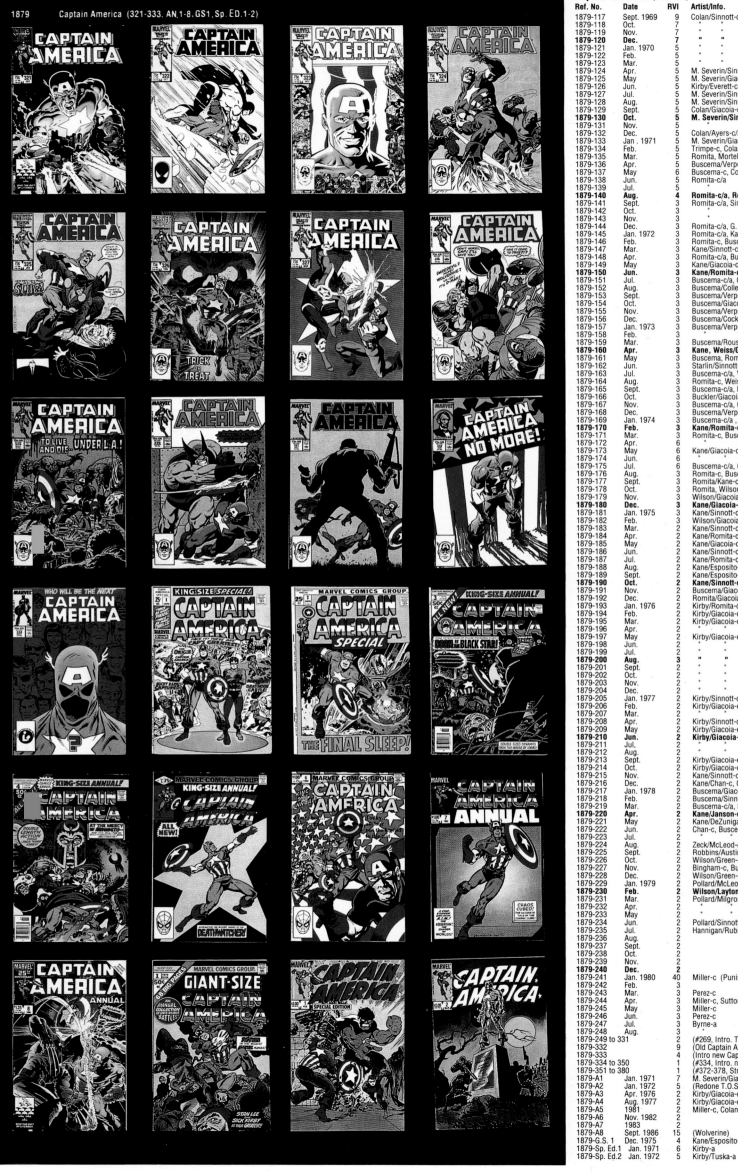

Ref. No.	Date	RVI	Artist/Info.
1879-117	Sept. 1969	9	Colan/Sinnott-c/a (Intro. the Falcon)
1879-118	Oct.	7	" "
1879-119	Nov.	7	" "
1879-120	**Dec.**	**7**	**" "**
1879-121	Jan. 1970	5	" "
1879-122	Feb.	5	" "
1879-123	Mar.	5	" "
1879-124	Apr.	5	M. Severin/Sinnott-c, Colan/Sinnott-a
1879-125	May	5	M. Severin/Giacoia-c, Colan/Giacoia-a
1879-126	Jun.	5	Kirby/Everett-c, Colan/Giacoia-a
1879-127	Jul.	5	M. Severin/Sinnott-c, Colan/Wood-a
1879-128	Aug.	5	M. Severin/Sinnott-c, Colan/Ayers-a
1879-129	Sept.	5	Colan/Giacoia-c, Colan/Ayers-a
1879-130	**Oct.**	**5**	**M. Severin/Sinnott-c, Colan/Ayers-a**
1879-131	Nov.	5	" " " "
1879-132	Dec.	5	Colan/Ayers-c/a
1879-133	Jan . 1971	5	M. Severin/Giacoia-c, Colan/Sinnott-a
1879-134	Feb.	5	Trimpe-c, Colan/Ayers-a
1879-135	Mar.	5	Romita, Mortellaro-c, Colan/Palmer-a
1879-136	Apr.	5	Buscema/Verpoorten-c, Colan/Everett-a
1879-137	May	6	Buscema-c, Colan/Everett-a
1879-138	Jun.	5	Romita-c/a
1879-139	Jul.	5	"
1879-140	**Aug.**	**4**	**Romita-c/a, Roussos-a**
1879-141	Sept.	3	Romita-c/a, Sinnott-a
1879-142	Oct.	3	" "
1879-143	Nov.	3	"
1879-144	Dec.	3	Romita-c/a, G. Morrow-a
1879-145	Jan. 1972	3	Romita-c/a, Kane-a
1879-146	Feb.	3	Romita-c, Buscema/Verpoorten-a
1879-147	Mar.	3	Kane/Sinnott-c, Buscema/Verpoorten-a
1879-148	Apr.	3	Romita-c/a, Buscema-a
1879-149	May	3	Kane/Giacoia-c, Buscema/Mooney-a
1879-150	**Jun.**	**3**	**Kane/Romita-c, Buscema/Verpoorten-a**
1879-151	Jul.	3	Buscema-c/a, Colletta-a
1879-152	Aug.	3	Buscema/Colletta-c, Buscema/Giacoia-a
1879-153	Sept.	3	Buscema/Verpoorten-c, Buscema/Mooney-a
1879-154	Oct.	3	Buscema/Giacoia-c, Buscema/Verpoorten-a
1879-155	Nov.	3	Buscema/Verpoorten-c, Buscema/McLaughlin-a
1879-156	Dec.	3	Buscema/Cockrum-c, Buscema/McLaughlin-a
1879-157	Jan. 1973	3	Buscema/Verpoorten-c/a (Intro. the Vipes)
1879-158	Feb.	3	" "
1879-159	Mar.	3	Buscema/Roussos-c, Buscema/Verpoorten-a
1879-160	**Apr.**	**3**	**Kane, Weiss/Giacoia-c, Buscema/McLaughlin-a**
1879-161	May	3	Buscema, Romita-c, Buscema/Verpoorten-a
1879-162	Jun.	3	Starlin/Sinnott-c, Buscema/Verpoorten-a
1879-163	Jul.	3	Buscema-c/a, Verpoorten, Mortellaro-a
1879-164	Aug.	3	Romita-c, Weiss-a (Intro. Nightshade)
1879-165	Sept.	3	Buscema-c/a, McLaughlin-a
1879-166	Oct.	3	Buckler/Giacoia-c, Buscema, McLaughlin-a
1879-167	Nov.	3	Buscema-c/a, Giacoia-a
1879-168	Dec.	3	Buscema/Verpoorten-c, Buscema/Tartaglione-a
1879-169	Jan. 1974	3	Buscema-c/a , McLaughlin-a
1879-170	**Feb.**	**3**	**Kane/Romita-c, Buscema/Colletta-a**
1879-171	Mar.	3	Romita-c, Buscema/Colletta-a
1879-172	Apr.	6	" " " (X-men)
1879-173	May	6	Kane/Giacoia-c, Buscema/Colletta-a "
1879-174	Jun.	6	" " " " "
1879-175	Jul.	6	Buscema-c/a, Colletta-a "
1879-176	Aug.	3	Romita-c, Buscema/Colletta-a
1879-177	Sept.	3	Romita/Kane-c, Buscema/Colletta-a
1879-178	Oct.	3	Romita, Wilson-c, Buscema/Colletta-a
1879-179	Nov.	3	Wilson/Giacoia-c, Buscema/Colletta-a
1879-180	**Dec.**	**3**	**Kane/Giacoia-c, Buscema/Colletta-a**
1879-181	Jan. 1975	3	Kane/Sinnott-c, Buscema/Colletta-a
1879-182	Feb.	3	Wilson/Giacoia-c, Robbins/Giella-a
1879-183	Mar.	2	Kane/Sinnott-c, Robbins/Giacoia-a
1879-184	Apr.	2	Kane/Romita-c, Trimpe/Giacoia-a
1879-185	May	2	Kane/Giacoia-c, Buscema/Robbins-a
1879-186	Jun.	2	Kane/Sinnott-c, Robbins/Esposito-a
1879-187	Jul.	2	Kane/Romita-c, Robbins/Chiaramonte-a
1879-188	Aug.	2	Kane/Esposito-c, Buscema, Colletta-a
1879-189	Sept.	2	Kane/Esposito-c, Robbins/Chiaramonte-a
1879-190	**Oct.**	**2**	**Kane/Sinnott-c, Robbins/Colletta-a**
1879-191	Nov.	2	Buscema/Giacoia-c, Robbins/D.B. Berry-a
1879-192	Dec.	2	Romita/Giacoia-c, Robbins/D.B. Berry-a
1879-193	Jan. 1976	2	Kirby/Romita-c, Kirby/Giacoia-a
1879-194	Feb.	2	Kirby/Giacoia-c/a
1879-195	Mar.	2	Kirby/Giacoia-c, Kirby/D.B. Berry-a
1879-196	Apr.	2	" " " "
1879-197	May	2	Kirby/Giacoia-c/a
1879-198	Jun.	2	" "
1879-199	Jul.	2	" "
1879-200	**Aug.**	**3**	**" " (Bicentennial issue)**
1879-201	Sept.	2	" "
1879-202	Oct.	2	" "
1879-203	Nov.	2	" "
1879-204	Dec.	2	" " (Intro. Agron)
1879-205	Jan. 1977	2	Kirby/Sinnott-c, Kirby/Verpoorten-a
1879-206	Feb.	2	Kirby/Giacoia-c/a
1879-207	Mar.	2	" "
1879-208	Apr.	2	Kirby/Sinnott-c, Kirby/Giacoia-a
1879-209	May	2	Kirby/Giacoia-c/a
1879-210	**Jun.**	**2**	**Kirby/Giacoia-c, Kirby/Royer-a**
1879-211	Jul.	2	" " " "
1879-212	Aug.	2	" " " "
1879-213	Sept.	2	Kirby/Giacoia-c, Kirby/Green-a
1879-214	Oct.	2	Kirby/Giacoia-c, Kirby/Royer-a
1879-215	Nov.	2	Kane/Sinnott-c, Tuska/Marcos-a
1879-216	Dec.	2	Kane/Chan-c, Cockrum/Giacoia-a
1879-217	Jan. 1978	2	Buscema/Giacoia-c, Buscema/Marcos-a
1879-218	Feb.	2	Buscema/Sinnott-c, Buscema/Esposito-a
1879-219	Mar.	2	Buscema-c/a, Sinnott-a
1879-220	**Apr.**	**2**	**Kane/Janson-c, Buscema, Esposito-a**
1879-221	May	2	Kane/DeZuniga-c, Buscema, Esposito-a
1879-222	Jun.	2	Chan-c, Buscema, Esposito-a
1879-223	Jul.	2	" " "
1879-224	Aug.	2	Zeck/McLeod-c, Zeck/Esposito-a
1879-225	Sept.	2	Robbins/Austin-c, Buscema/Esplosito-a
1879-226	Oct.	2	Wilson/Green-c, Buscema/Esposito-a
1879-227	Nov.	2	Bingham-c, Buscema/Esposito-a
1879-228	Dec.	2	Wilson/Green-c, Buscema/Esposito-a
1879-229	Jan. 1979	2	Pollard/McLeod-c, Buscema, Perlin-a
1879-230	**Feb.**	**2**	**Wilson/Layton-c, Buscema, Perlin-a**
1879-231	Mar.	2	Pollard/Milgrom-c, Buscema, Perlin-a
1879-232	Apr.	2	" " " "
1879-233	May	2	" " " "
1879-234	Jun.	2	Pollard/Sinnott-c, Buscema, Perlin-a
1879-235	Jul.	2	Hannigan/Rubinstein-c, Buscema, Miller-a
1879-236	Aug.	2	
1879-237	Sept.	2	
1879-238	Oct.	2	
1879-239	Nov.	2	
1879-240	**Dec.**	**2**	
1879-241	Jan. 1980	40	Miller-c (Punisher -app.)
1879-242	Feb.	3	
1879-243	Mar.	3	Perez-c
1879-244	Apr.	3	Miller-c, Sutton-a
1879-245	May	3	Miller-c
1879-246	Jun.	3	Perez-c
1879-247	Jul.	3	Byrne-a
1879-248	Aug.	3	"
1879-249 to 331		2	(#269, Intro. Team America)
1879-332		9	(Old Captain America is terminated)
1879-333		4	(Intro new Captain America)
1879-334 to 350		1	(#334, Intro. new Bucky)
1879-351 to 380		1	(#372-378, Streets of Poison)
1879-A1	Jan. 1971	7	M. Severin/Giacoia-c
1879-A2	Jan. 1972	5	(Redone T.O.S. #74 cover)
1879-A3	Apr. 1976	2	Kirby/Giacoia-c/a
1879-A4	Aug. 1977	2	Kirby/Giacoia-c, Kirby/Verpoorten-a
1879-A5	1981	2	Miller-c, Colan-a
1879-A6	Nov. 1982	2	
1879-A7	1983	2	
1879-A8	Sept. 1986	15	(Wolverine)
1879-G.S. 1	Dec. 1975	4	Kane/Esposito-c
1879-Sp. Ed.1	Jan. 1971	6	Kirby-a
1879-Sp. Ed.2	Jan. 1972	5	Kirby/Tuska-a

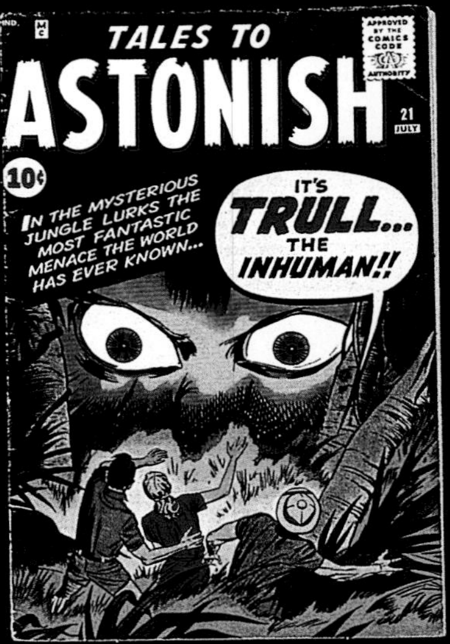
TALES TO ASTONISH
21 JULY
10¢
IN THE MYSTERIOUS JUNGLE LURKS THE MOST FANTASTIC MENACE THE WORLD HAS EVER KNOWN...
IT'S TRULL... THE INHUMAN!!

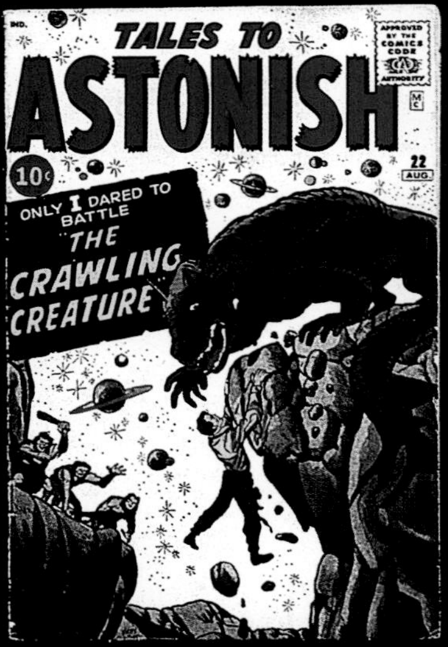
TALES TO ASTONISH
22 AUG.
10¢
ONLY I DARED TO BATTLE THE CRAWLING CREATURE

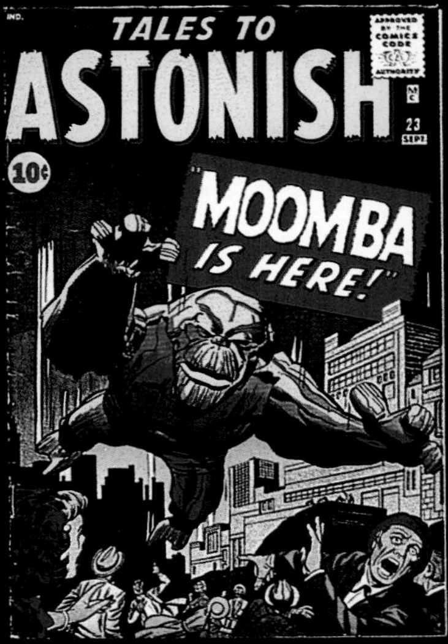
TALES TO ASTONISH
23 SEPT.
10¢
MOOMBA IS HERE!

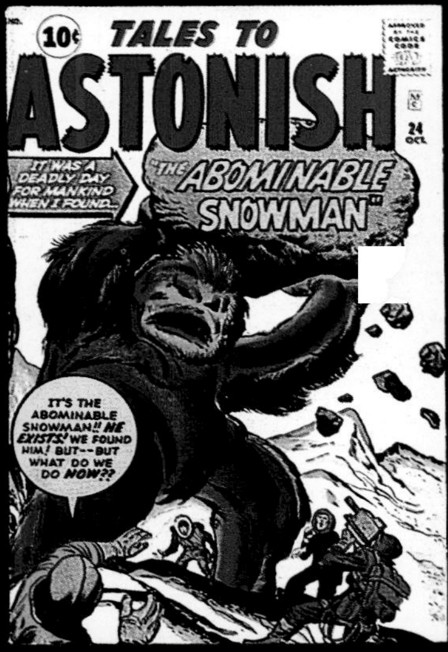
10¢ TALES TO ASTONISH
24 OCT.
IT WAS A DEADLY DAY FOR MANKIND WHEN I FOUND...
THE ABOMINABLE SNOWMAN
IT'S THE ABOMINABLE SNOWMAN!! HE EXISTS! WE FOUND HIM! BUT--BUT WHAT DO WE DO NOW??

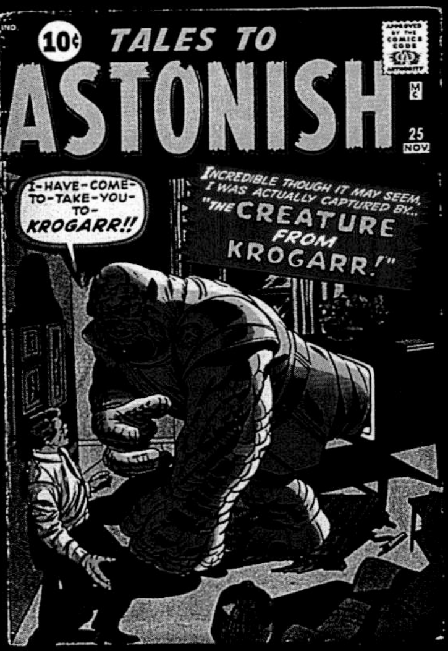
10¢ TALES TO ASTONISH
25 NOV
I-HAVE-COME-TO-TAKE-YOU-TO-KROGARR!!
INCREDIBLE THOUGH IT MAY SEEM, I WAS ACTUALLY CAPTURED BY "THE CREATURE FROM KROGARR!"

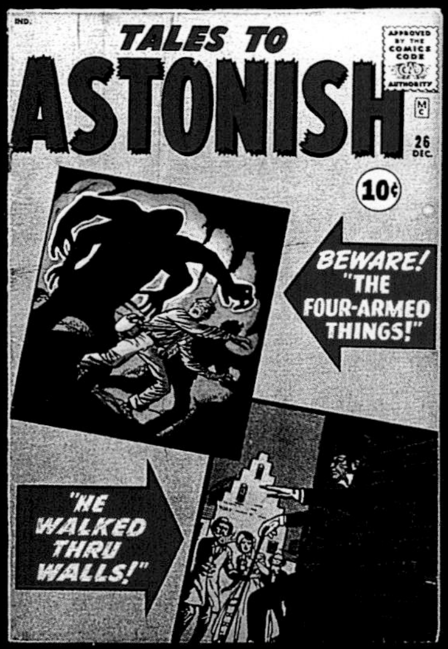
TALES TO ASTONISH
26 DEC.
10¢
BEWARE! "THE FOUR-ARMED THINGS!"
"HE WALKED THRU WALLS!"

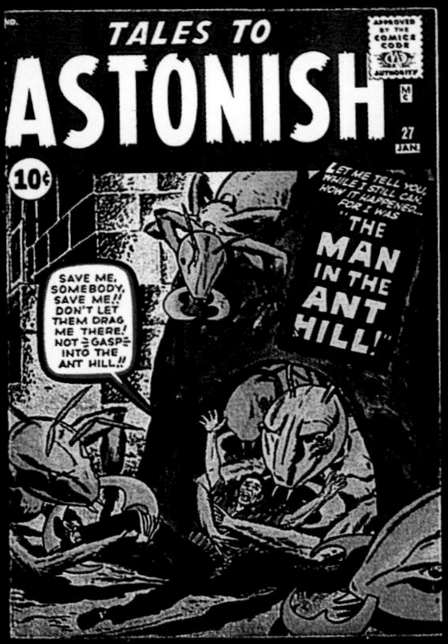
TALES TO ASTONISH
27 JAN
10¢
LET ME TELL YOU WHILE I STILL CAN HOW IT HAPPENED... FOR I WAS "THE MAN IN THE ANT HILL!"
SAVE ME, SOMEBODY, SAVE ME!! DON'T LET THEM DRAG ME THERE! NOT --GASP-- INTO THE ANT HILL!!

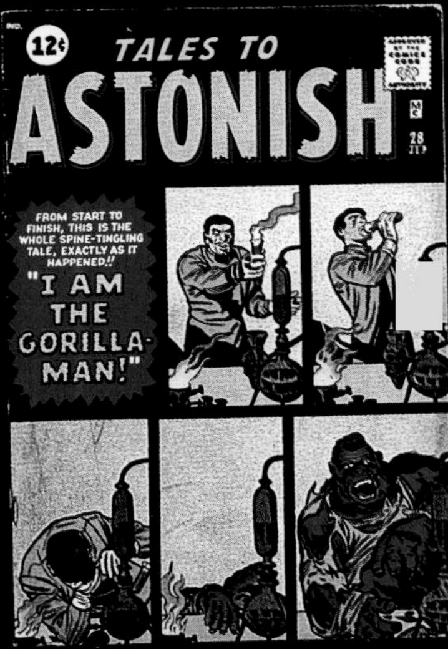
12¢ TALES TO ASTONISH
28 JLY
FROM START TO FINISH, THIS IS THE WHOLE SPINE-TINGLING TALE, EXACTLY AS IT HAPPENED!
"I AM THE GORILLA-MAN!"

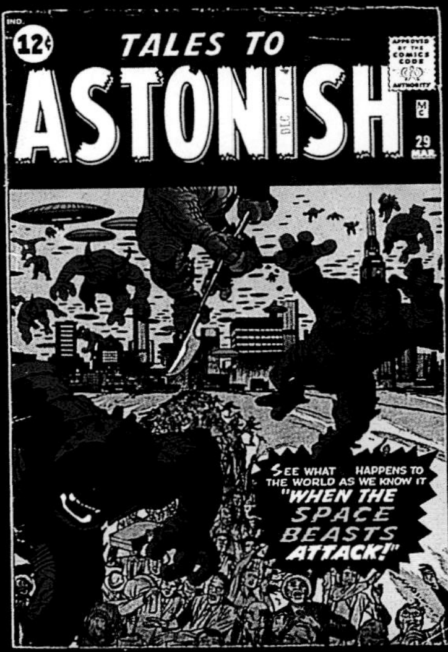
12¢ TALES TO ASTONISH
29 MAR.
SEE WHAT HAPPENS TO THE WORLD AS WE KNOW IT "WHEN THE SPACE BEASTS ATTACK!"

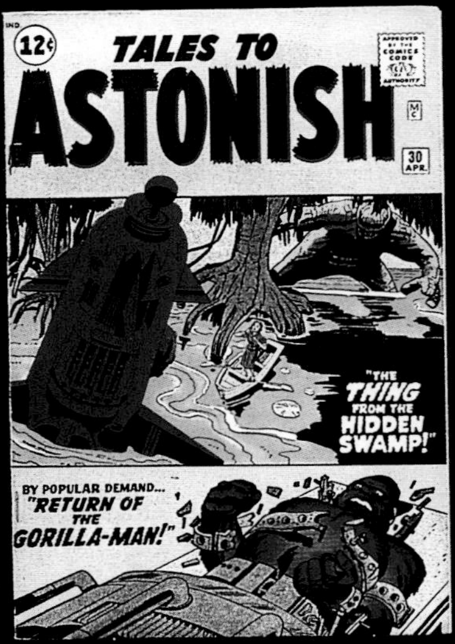
12¢ TALES TO ASTONISH
30 APR.
"THE THING FROM THE HIDDEN SWAMP!"
BY POPULAR DEMAND... "RETURN OF THE GORILLA-MAN!"

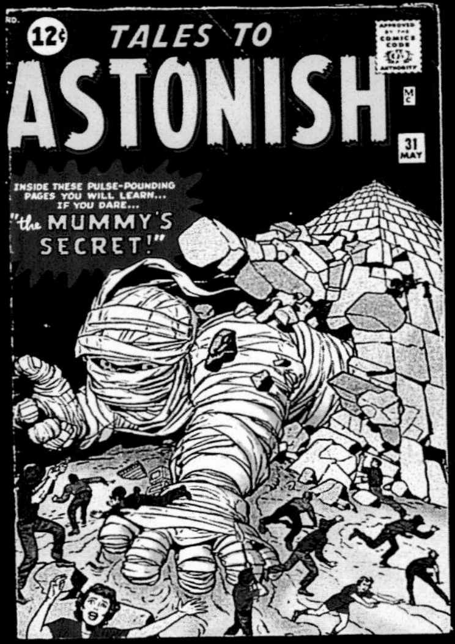
12¢ TALES TO ASTONISH
31 MAY
INSIDE THESE PULSE-POUNDING PAGES YOU WILL LEARN... IF YOU DARE... "the MUMMY'S SECRET!"

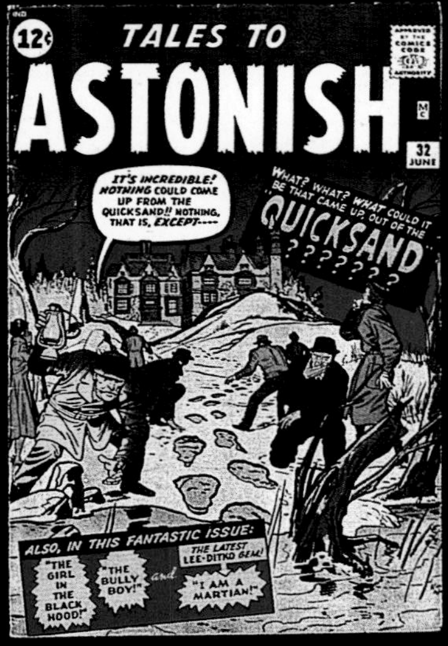
12¢ TALES TO ASTONISH
32 JUNE
IT'S INCREDIBLE! NOTHING COULD COME UP FROM THE QUICKSAND!! NOTHING, THAT IS, EXCEPT---
WHAT? WHAT? WHAT COULD IT BE THAT CAME UP OUT OF THE QUICKSAND ???????
ALSO, IN THIS FANTASTIC ISSUE:
"THE GIRL IN THE BLACK HOOD!"
"THE BULLY BOY!"
THE LATEST LEE-DITKO GEM! "I AM A MARTIAN!"

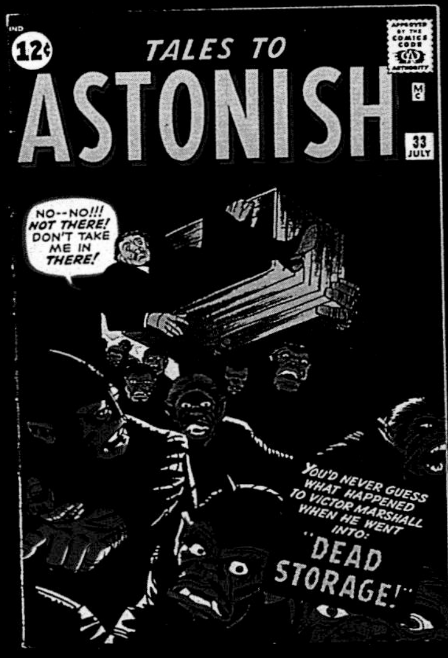
12¢ TALES TO ASTONISH
33 JULY
NO--NO!!! NOT THERE! DON'T TAKE ME IN THERE!
YOU'D NEVER GUESS WHAT HAPPENED TO VICTOR MARSHALL WHEN HE WENT INTO "DEAD STORAGE!"

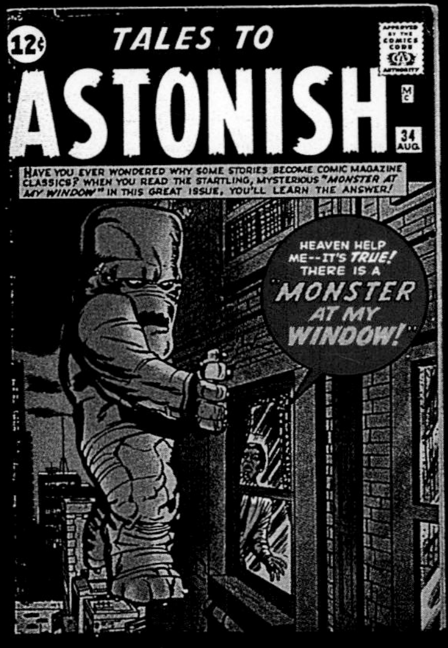
12¢ TALES TO ASTONISH
34 AUG.
HAVE YOU EVER WONDERED WHY SOME STORIES BECOME COMIC MAGAZINE CLASSICS? WHEN YOU READ THE STARTLING, MYSTERIOUS "MONSTER AT MY WINDOW" IN THIS GREAT ISSUE, YOU'LL LEARN THE ANSWER!
HEAVEN HELP ME--IT'S TRUE! THERE IS A MONSTER AT MY WINDOW!

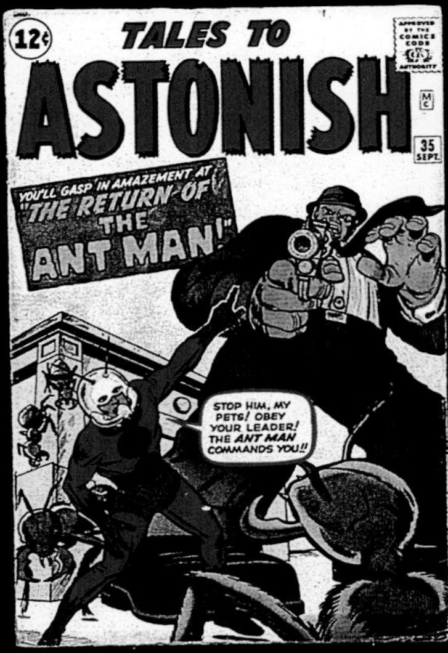
12¢ TALES TO ASTONISH
35 SEPT.
YOU'LL GASP IN AMAZEMENT AT "THE RETURN OF THE ANT MAN"
STOP HIM, MY PETS! OBEY YOUR LEADER! THE ANT MAN COMMANDS YOU!!

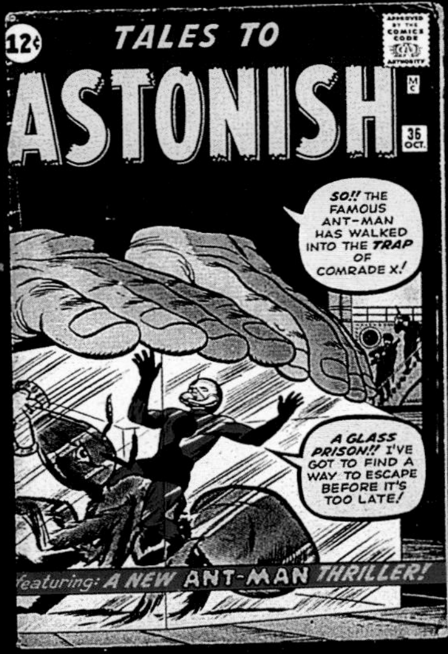
12¢ TALES TO ASTONISH
35 OCT.
SO!! THE FAMOUS ANT-MAN HAS WALKED INTO THE TRAP OF COMRADE X!
A GLASS PRISON!! I'VE GOT TO FIND A WAY TO ESCAPE BEFORE IT'S TOO LATE!
featuring: A NEW ANT-MAN THRILLER!

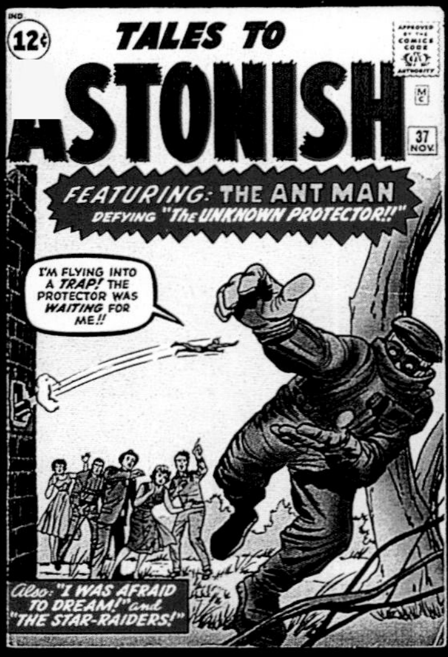
12¢
TALES TO ASTONISH
37 NOV
FEATURING: THE ANT MAN
DEFYING "The UNKNOWN PROTECTOR!!"
I'M FLYING INTO A TRAP! THE PROTECTOR WAS WAITING FOR ME!!
Also: "I WAS AFRAID TO DREAM!" and "THE STAR-RAIDERS!"

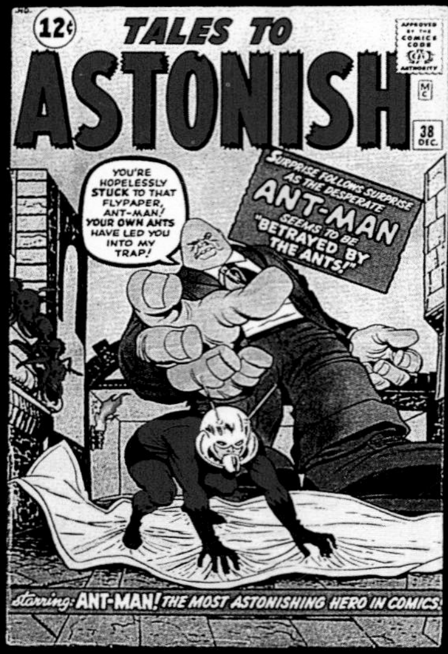
12¢
TALES TO ASTONISH
38 DEC.
YOU'RE HOPELESSLY STUCK TO THAT FLYPAPER, ANT-MAN! YOUR OWN ANTS HAVE LED YOU INTO MY TRAP!
SURPRISE FOLLOWS SURPRISE AS THE DESPERATE ANT-MAN SEEMS TO BE "BETRAYED BY THE ANTS!"
starring: ANT-MAN! THE MOST ASTONISHING HERO IN COMICS!

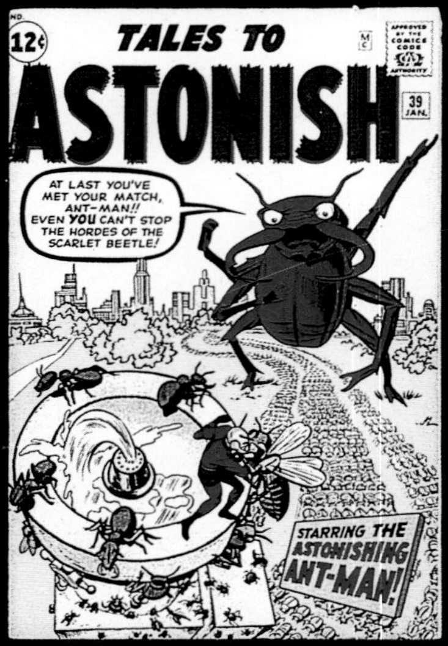
12¢
TALES TO ASTONISH
39 JAN.
AT LAST YOU'VE MET YOUR MATCH, ANT-MAN!! EVEN YOU CAN'T STOP THE HORDES OF THE SCARLET BEETLE!
STARRING THE ASTONISHING ANT-MAN!

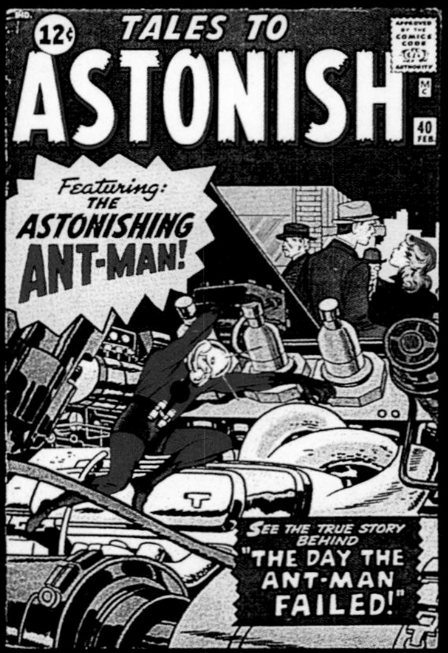
12¢
TALES TO ASTONISH
40 FEB.
Featuring: THE ASTONISHING ANT-MAN!
SEE THE TRUE STORY BEHIND "THE DAY THE ANT-MAN FAILED!"

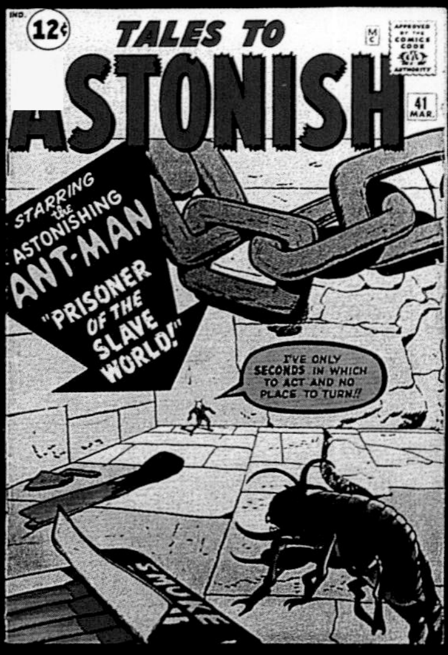
12¢
TALES TO ASTONISH
41 MAR.
STARRING the ASTONISHING ANT-MAN
"PRISONER OF THE SLAVE WORLD!"
I'VE ONLY SECONDS IN WHICH TO ACT AND NO PLACE TO TURN!!

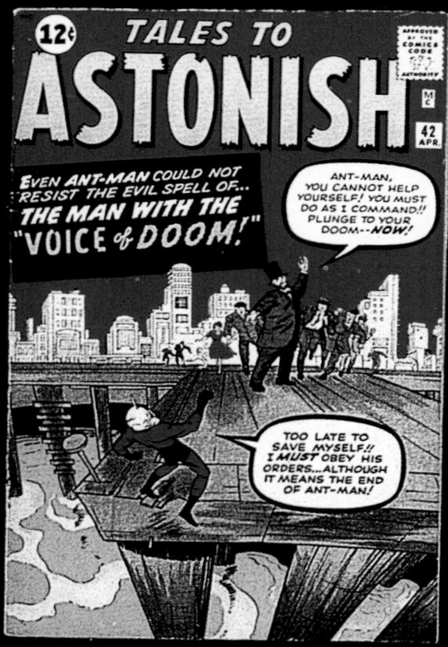
12¢
TALES TO ASTONISH
42 APR.
EVEN ANT-MAN COULD NOT RESIST THE EVIL SPELL OF... THE MAN WITH THE "VOICE of DOOM!"
ANT-MAN, YOU CANNOT HELP YOURSELF! YOU MUST DO AS I COMMAND! PLUNGE TO YOUR DOOM--NOW!
TOO LATE TO SAVE MYSELF!! I MUST OBEY HIS ORDERS...ALTHOUGH IT MEANS THE END OF ANT-MAN!

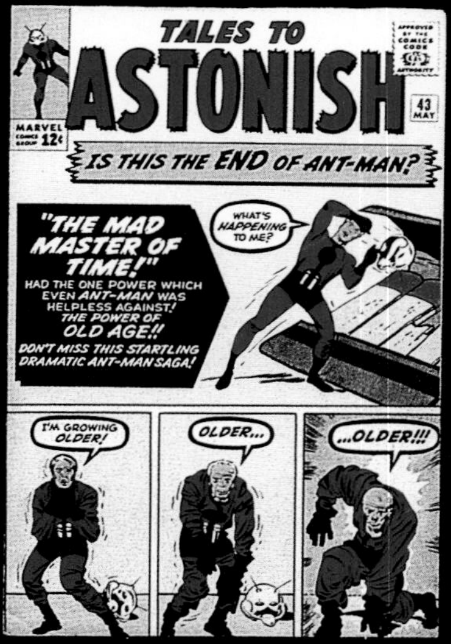
TALES TO ASTONISH
MARVEL COMICS GROUP 12¢
43 MAY
IS THIS THE END OF ANT-MAN?
"THE MAD MASTER OF TIME!" HAD THE ONE POWER WHICH EVEN ANT-MAN WAS HELPLESS AGAINST! THE POWER OF OLD AGE!!
DON'T MISS THIS STARTLING DRAMATIC ANT-MAN SAGA!
WHAT'S HAPPENING TO ME?
I'M GROWING OLDER!
OLDER...
...OLDER!!!

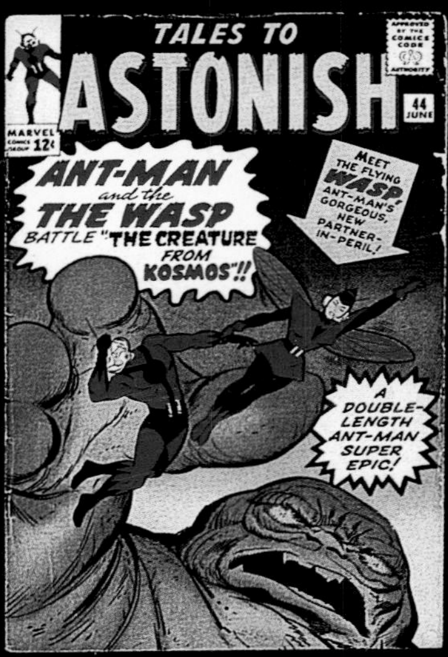
TALES TO ASTONISH
MARVEL COMICS GROUP 12¢
44 JUNE
ANT-MAN and the WASP BATTLE "THE CREATURE FROM KOSMOS"!!
MEET THE FLYING WASP, ANT-MAN'S GORGEOUS, NEW PARTNER-IN-PERIL!
A DOUBLE-LENGTH ANT-MAN SUPER EPIC!

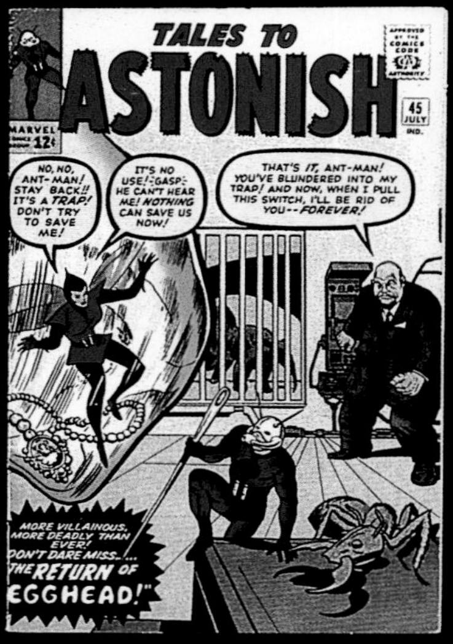
TALES TO ASTONISH
MARVEL COMICS GROUP 12¢
45 JULY
NO, NO, ANT-MAN! STAY BACK!! IT'S A TRAP! DON'T TRY TO SAVE ME!
IT'S NO USE! GASP! HE CAN'T HEAR ME! NOTHING CAN SAVE US NOW!
THAT'S IT, ANT-MAN! YOU'VE BLUNDERED INTO MY TRAP! AND NOW, WHEN I PULL THIS SWITCH, I'LL BE RID OF YOU--FOREVER!
MORE VILLAINOUS, MORE DEADLY THAN EVER! DON'T DARE MISS... THE RETURN OF EGGHEAD!

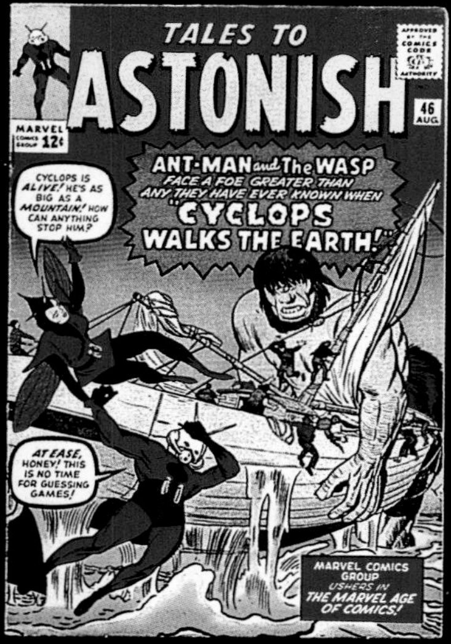
TALES TO ASTONISH
MARVEL COMICS GROUP 12¢
46 AUG.
ANT-MAN and The WASP FACE A FOE GREATER THAN ANY THEY HAVE EVER KNOWN WHEN "CYCLOPS WALKS THE EARTH!"
CYCLOPS IS ALIVE! HE'S AS BIG AS A MOUNTAIN! HOW CAN ANYTHING STOP HIM?
AT EASE, HONEY! THIS IS NO TIME FOR GUESSING GAMES!
MARVEL COMICS GROUP USHERS IN THE MARVEL AGE OF COMICS!

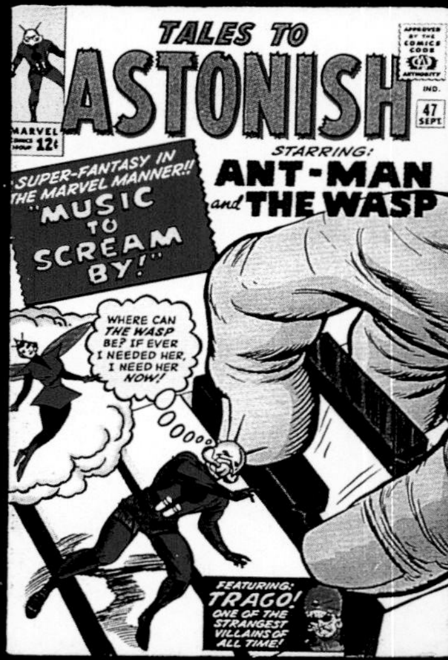
TALES TO ASTONISH
MARVEL COMICS GROUP 12¢
47 SEPT.
STARRING: ANT-MAN and THE WASP
SUPER-FANTASY IN THE MARVEL MANNER!! "MUSIC TO SCREAM BY!"
WHERE CAN THE WASP BE? IF EVER I NEEDED HER, I NEED HER NOW!
FEATURING: TRAGO! ONE OF THE STRANGEST VILLAINS OF ALL TIME!

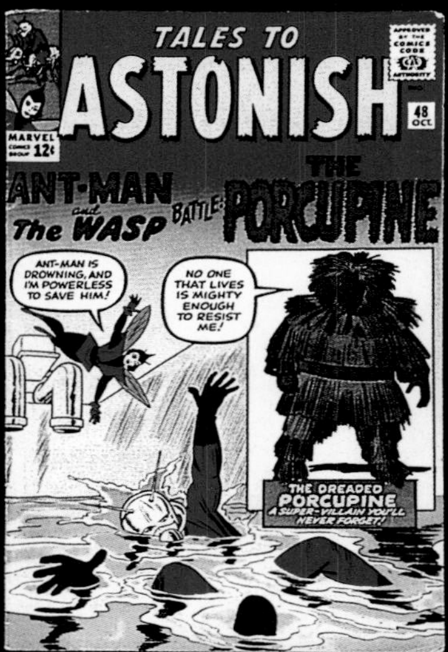
TALES TO ASTONISH
MARVEL COMICS GROUP 12¢
48 OCT.
ANT-MAN and The WASP BATTLE THE PORCUPINE
ANT-MAN IS DROWNING, AND I'M POWERLESS TO SAVE HIM!
NO ONE THAT LIVES IS MIGHTY ENOUGH TO RESIST ME!
THE DREADED PORCUPINE A SUPER-VILLAIN YOU'LL NEVER FORGET!

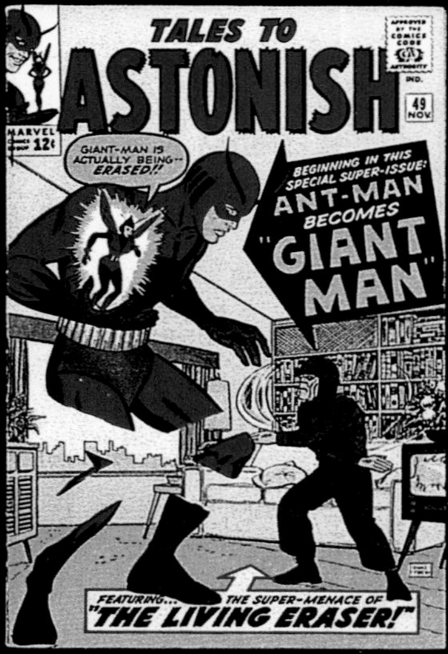
TALES TO ASTONISH
MARVEL COMICS GROUP 12¢
49 NOV
GIANT-MAN IS ACTUALLY BEING-- ERASED!!
BEGINNING IN THIS SPECIAL SUPER-ISSUE! ANT-MAN BECOMES "GIANT MAN"
FEATURING... THE SUPER-MENACE OF "THE LIVING ERASER!"

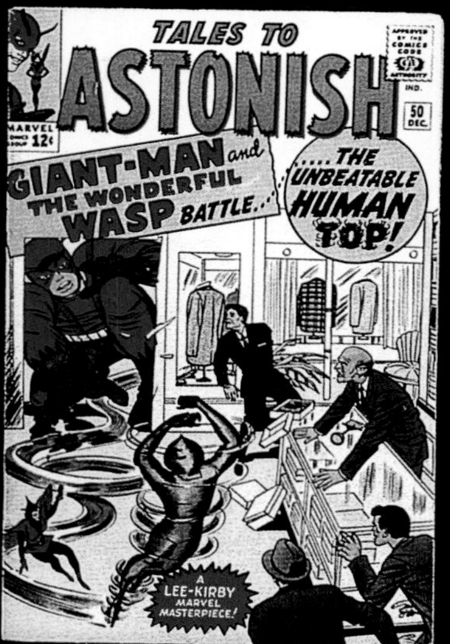
TALES TO ASTONISH
MARVEL COMICS GROUP 12¢
50 DEC.
GIANT-MAN and THE WONDERFUL WASP BATTLE... ...THE UNBEATABLE HUMAN TOP!
A LEE-KIRBY MARVEL MASTERPIECE!

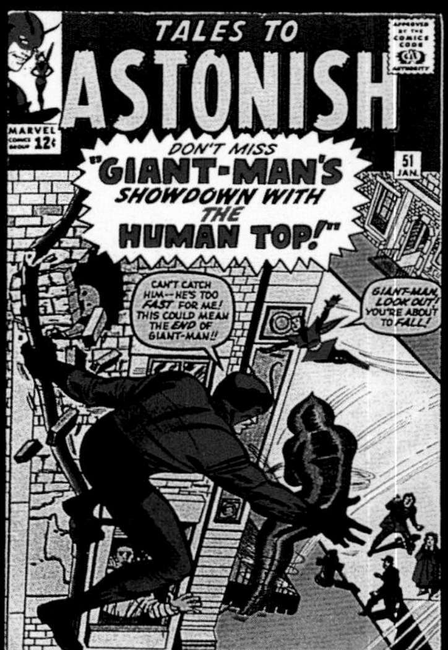
TALES TO ASTONISH
MARVEL COMICS GROUP 12¢
51 JAN.
DON'T MISS "GIANT-MAN'S SHOWDOWN WITH THE HUMAN TOP!"
CAN'T CATCH HIM--HE'S TOO FAST FOR ME! THIS COULD MEAN THE END OF GIANT-MAN!!
GIANT-MAN, LOOK OUT! YOU'RE ABOUT TO FALL!

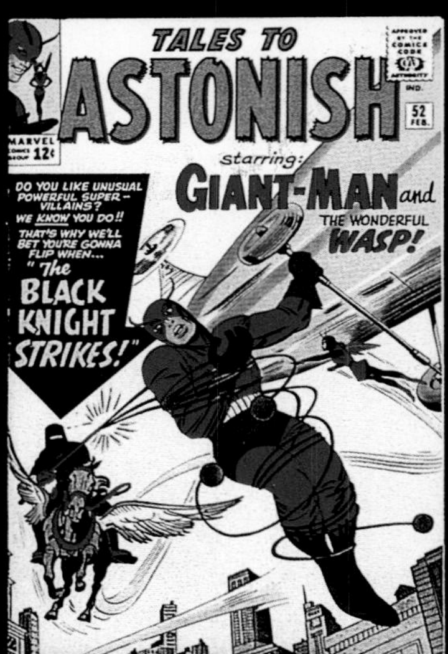
TALES TO ASTONISH
MARVEL COMICS GROUP 12¢
52 FEB.
starring: GIANT-MAN and THE WONDERFUL WASP!
DO YOU LIKE UNUSUAL POWERFUL SUPER-VILLAINS? WE KNOW YOU DO!! THAT'S WHY WE'LL BET YOU'RE GONNA FLIP WHEN... "The BLACK KNIGHT STRIKES!"

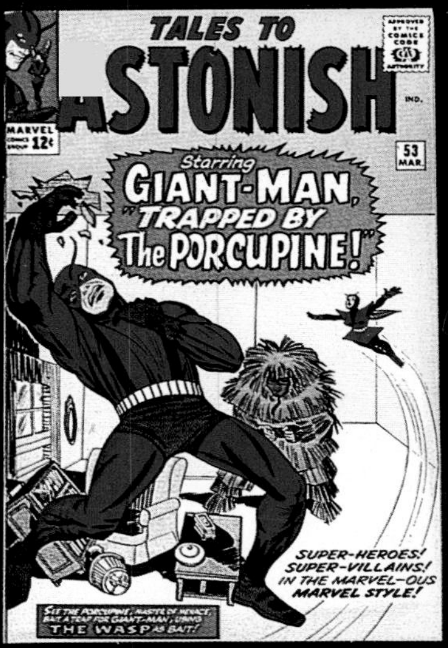
TALES TO
ASTONISH
53
MAR.
Starring
GIANT-MAN,
TRAPPED BY
The PORCUPINE!
SUPER-HEROES!
SUPER-VILLAINS!
IN THE MARVEL-OUS
MARVEL STYLE!

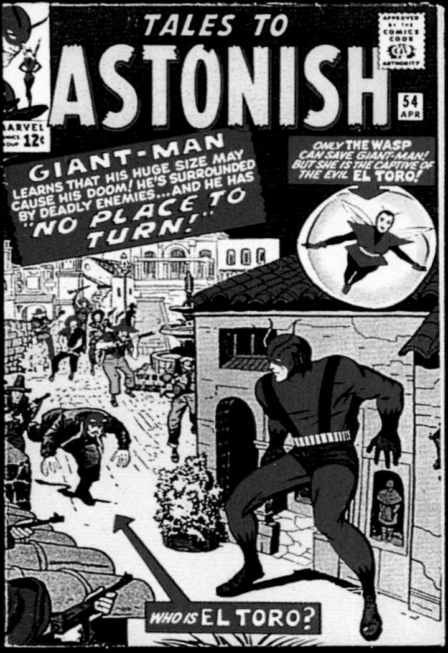
TALES TO
ASTONISH
54
APR
12¢
GIANT-MAN
LEARNS THAT HIS HUGE SIZE MAY CAUSE HIS DOOM! HE'S SURROUNDED BY DEADLY ENEMIES...AND HE HAS
"NO PLACE TO TURN!"
ONLY THE WASP CAN SAVE GIANT-MAN! BUT SHE IS THE CAPTIVE OF THE EVIL EL TORO!
WHO IS EL TORO?

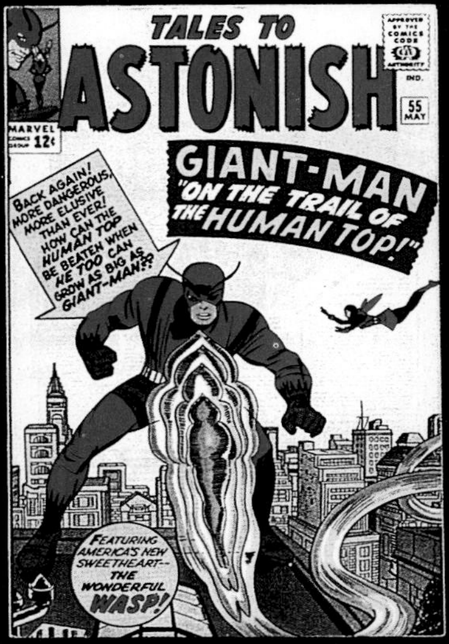
TALES TO
ASTONISH
55
MAY
12¢
GIANT-MAN
"ON THE TRAIL OF THE HUMAN TOP!"
BACK AGAIN! MORE DANGEROUS, MORE ELUSIVE THAN EVER! HOW CAN THE HUMAN TOP BE BEATEN WHEN HE TOO BIG AS GIANT-MAN?
FEATURING AMERICA'S NEW SWEETHEART--THE WONDERFUL WASP!

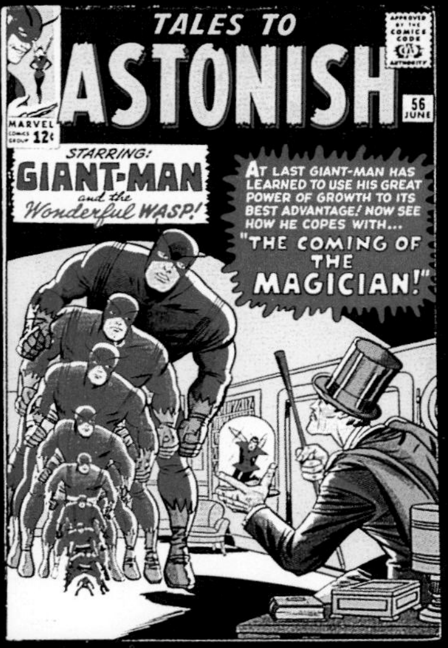
TALES TO
ASTONISH
56
JUNE
12¢
STARRING:
GIANT-MAN
and the Wonderful WASP!
AT LAST GIANT-MAN HAS LEARNED TO USE HIS GREAT POWER OF GROWTH TO ITS BEST ADVANTAGE! NOW SEE HOW HE COPES WITH...
"THE COMING OF THE MAGICIAN!"

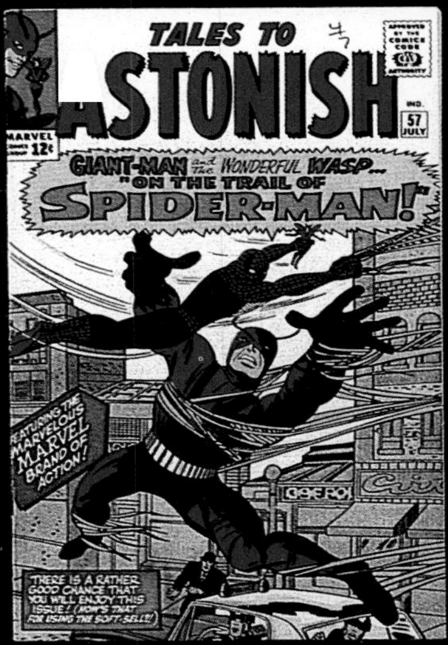
TALES TO
ASTONISH
57
JULY
12¢
GIANT-MAN and the WONDERFUL WASP...
"ON THE TRAIL OF SPIDER-MAN!"
FEATURING THE MARVELOUS MARVEL BRAND OF ACTION!

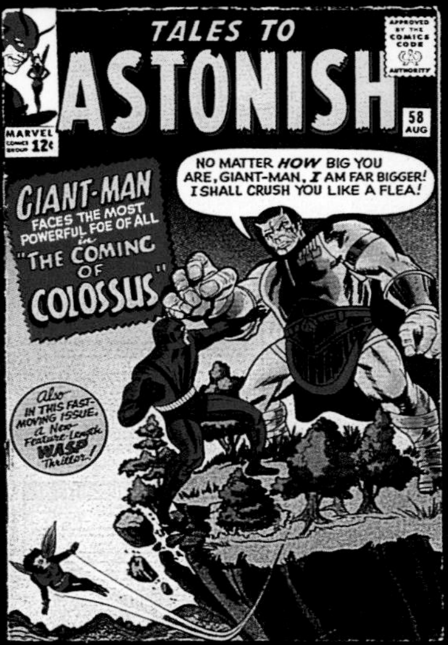
TALES TO
ASTONISH
58
AUG
12¢
NO MATTER HOW BIG YOU ARE, GIANT-MAN, I AM FAR BIGGER! I SHALL CRUSH YOU LIKE A FLEA!
GIANT-MAN
FACES THE MOST POWERFUL FOE OF ALL IN
"THE COMING OF COLOSSUS"

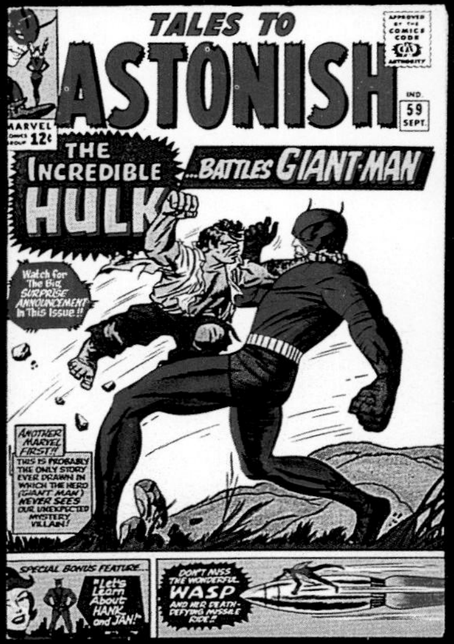
TALES TO
ASTONISH
59
SEPT
12¢
THE INCREDIBLE HULK
...BATTLES GIANT-MAN
SPECIAL BONUS FEATURE...
DON'T MISS THE WASP

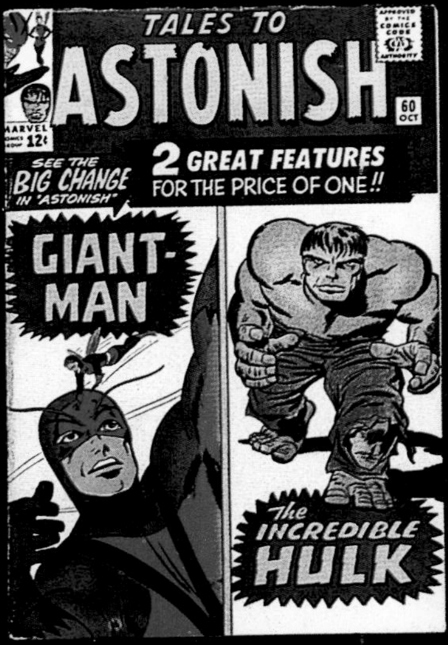
TALES TO
ASTONISH
60
OCT
12¢
SEE THE BIG CHANGE IN "ASTONISH"
2 GREAT FEATURES
FOR THE PRICE OF ONE!!
GIANT-MAN
The INCREDIBLE HULK

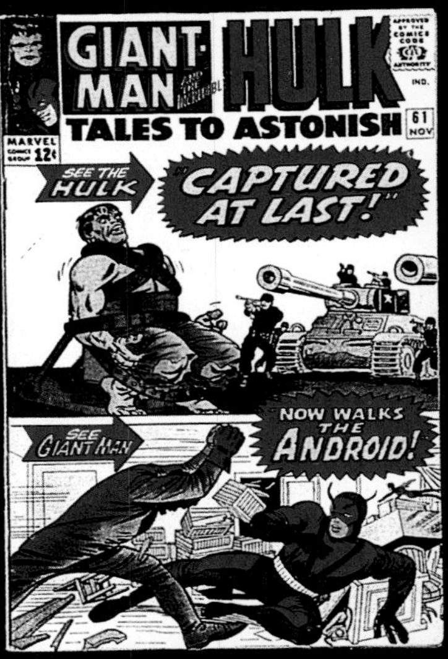
GIANT-MAN
HULK
TALES TO ASTONISH
61
NOV
12¢
SEE THE HULK
CAPTURED AT LAST!
SEE GIANT-MAN
NOW WALKS THE ANDROID!

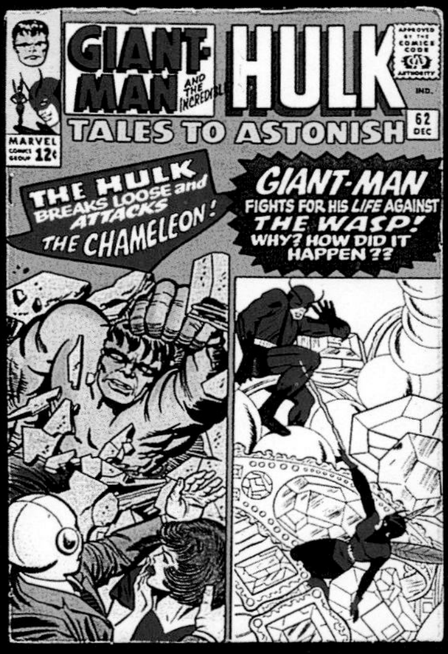
GIANT-MAN
HULK
TALES TO ASTONISH
62
DEC
12¢
THE HULK BREAKS LOOSE and ATTACKS THE CHAMELEON!
GIANT-MAN
FIGHTS FOR HIS LIFE AGAINST THE WASP! WHY? HOW DID IT HAPPEN??

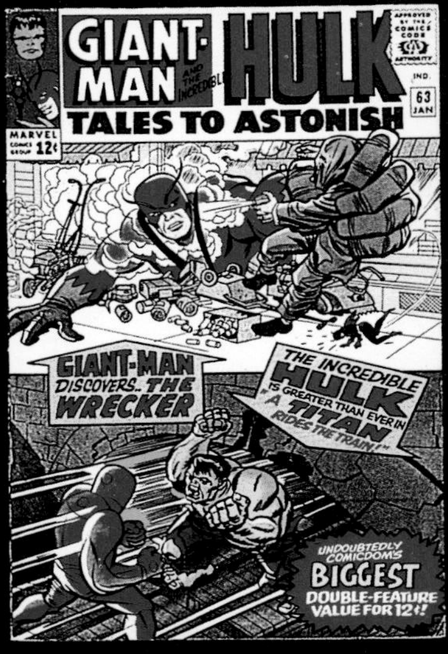
GIANT-MAN
HULK
TALES TO ASTONISH
63
JAN
12¢
GIANT-MAN DISCOVERS...THE WRECKER
THE INCREDIBLE HULK
UNDOUBTEDLY COMICDOM'S
BIGGEST
DOUBLE-FEATURE VALUE FOR 12¢!

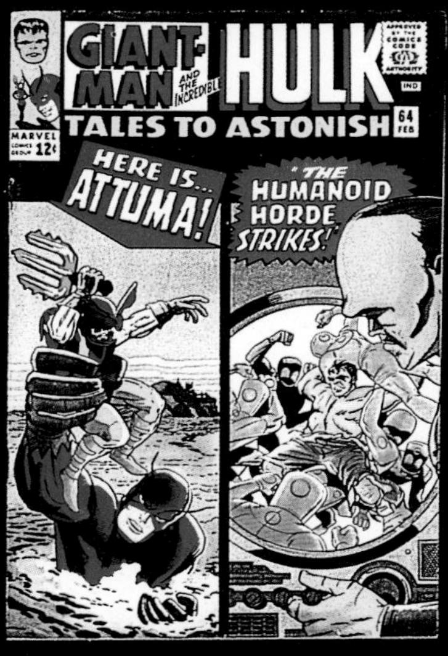
GIANT-MAN
HULK
TALES TO ASTONISH
64
FEB
12¢
HERE IS... ATTUMA!
"THE HUMANOID HORDE STRIKES!"

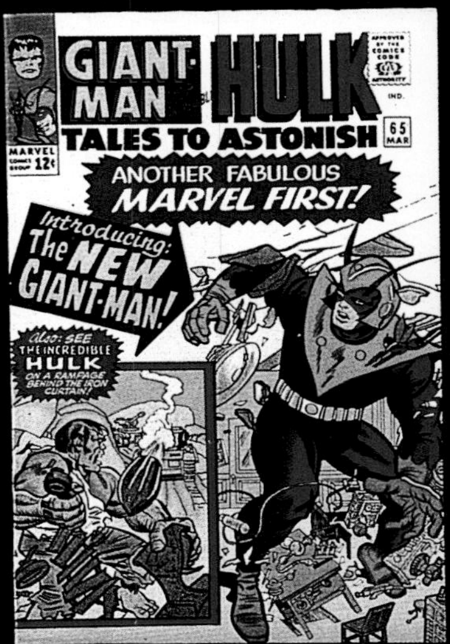
GIANT-MAN
HULK
TALES TO ASTONISH
65
MAR
12¢
ANOTHER FABULOUS
MARVEL FIRST!
Introducing: The NEW GIANT-MAN!
Also: SEE THE INCREDIBLE HULK

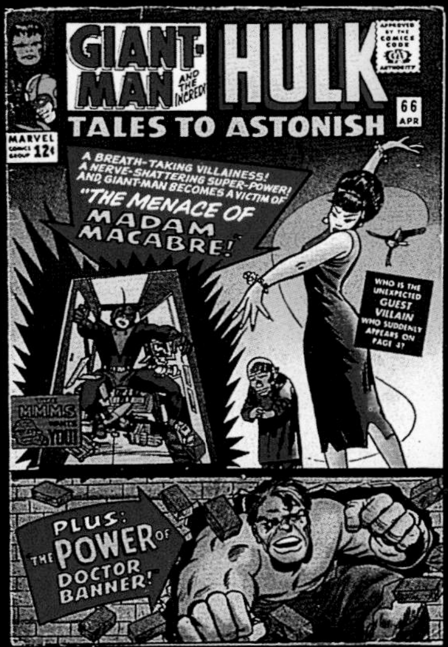
GIANT-MAN
HULK
TALES TO ASTONISH
66
APR
12¢
A BREATH-TAKING VILLAINESS! A NERVE-SHATTERING SUPER-POWER! AND GIANT-MAN BECOMES A VICTIM OF
"THE MENACE OF MADAM MACABRE!"
PLUS: THE POWER OF DOCTOR BANNER!

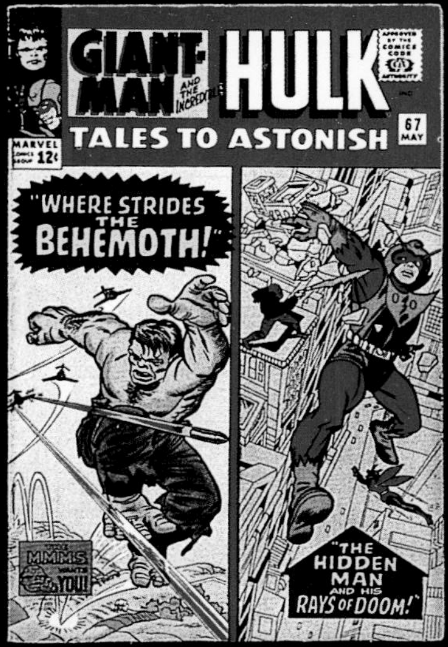
GIANT-MAN
HULK
TALES TO ASTONISH
67
MAY
12¢
"WHERE STRIDES THE BEHEMOTH!"
"THE HIDDEN MAN AND HIS RAYS OF DOOM!"

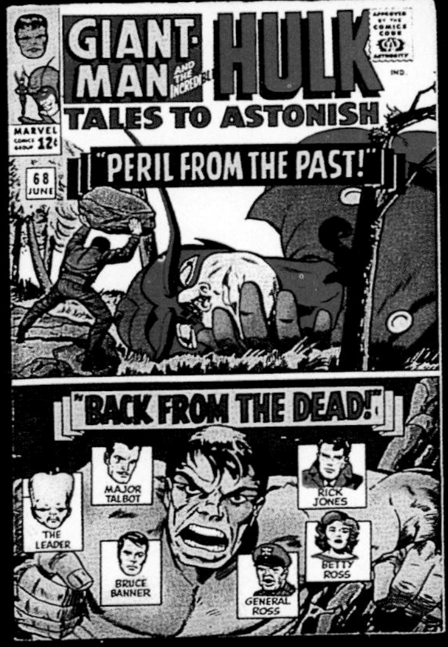
GIANT-MAN
HULK
TALES TO ASTONISH
68
JUNE
12¢
"PERIL FROM THE PAST!"
"BACK FROM THE DEAD!"
MAJOR TALBOT
RICK JONES
THE LEADER
BRUCE BANNER
BETTY ROSS
GENERAL ROSS

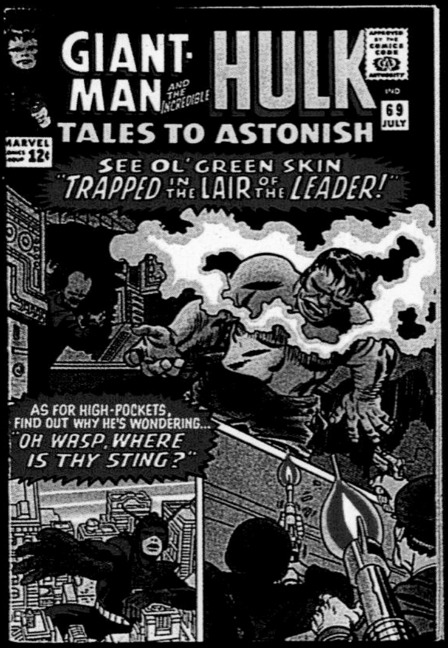
GIANT-MAN and the incredible HULK
TALES TO ASTONISH
69 JULY
SEE OL' GREEN SKIN TRAPPED IN THE LAIR OF THE LEADER!
AS FOR HIGH-POCKETS, FIND OUT WHY HE'S WONDERING... "OH WASP, WHERE IS THY STING?"

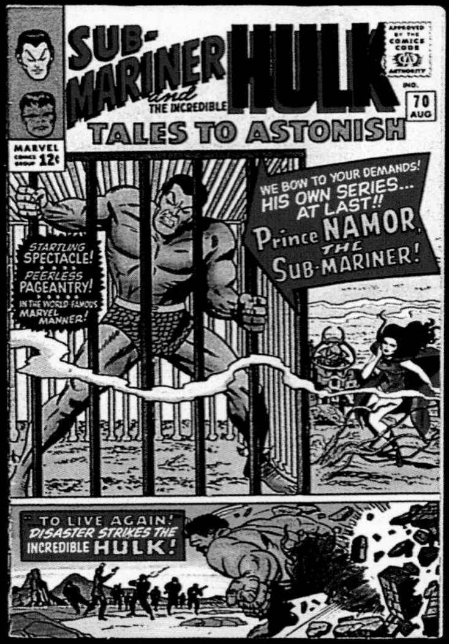
SUB-MARINER and the incredible HULK
TALES TO ASTONISH
70 AUG
WE BOW TO YOUR DEMANDS! HIS OWN SERIES... AT LAST!! Prince NAMOR, THE SUB-MARINER!
STARTLING SPECTACLE! PEERLESS PAGEANTRY!
"TO LIVE AGAIN!" DISASTER STRIKES THE INCREDIBLE HULK!

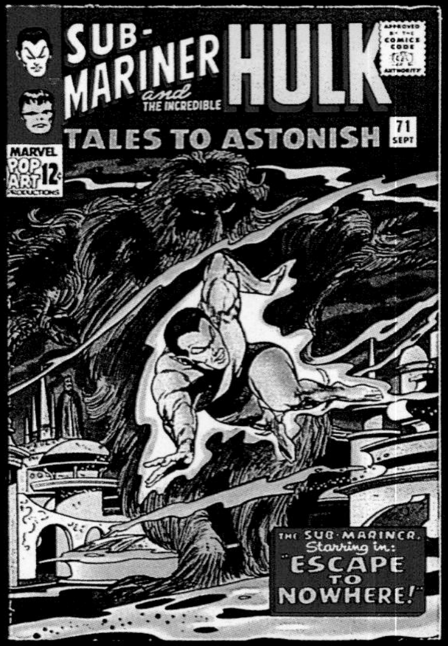
SUB-MARINER and the incredible HULK
TALES TO ASTONISH
71 SEPT
THE SUB-MARINER Starring in: ESCAPE TO NOWHERE!

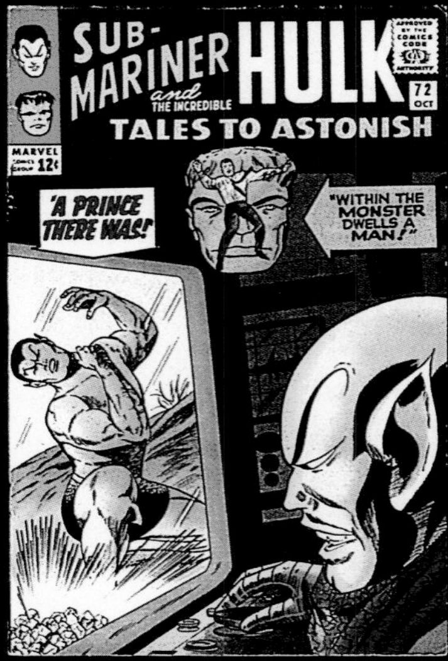
SUB-MARINER and the incredible HULK
TALES TO ASTONISH
72 OCT
"A PRINCE THERE WAS!"
"WITHIN THE MONSTER DWELLS A MAN!"

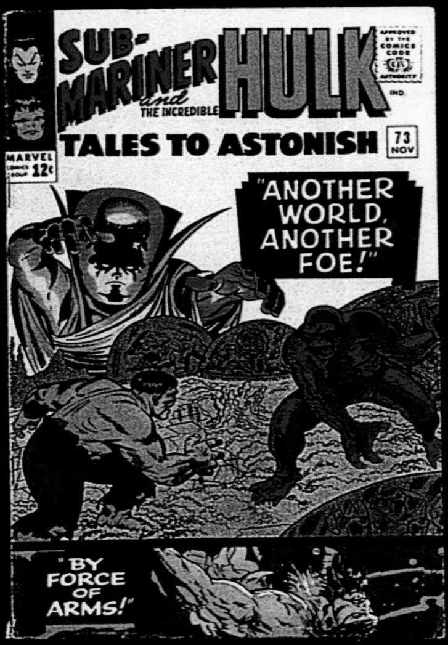
SUB-MARINER and the incredible HULK
TALES TO ASTONISH
73 NOV
"ANOTHER WORLD, ANOTHER FOE!"
"BY FORCE OF ARMS!"

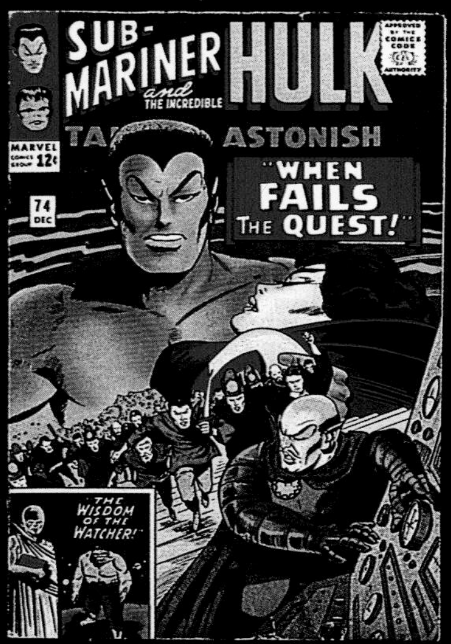
SUB-MARINER and the incredible HULK
74 DEC
"WHEN FAILS THE QUEST!"
"THE WISDOM OF THE WATCHER!"

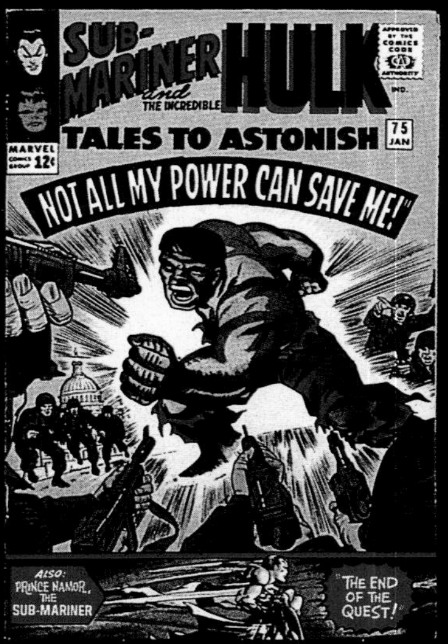
SUB-MARINER and the incredible HULK
TALES TO ASTONISH
75 JAN
NOT ALL MY POWER CAN SAVE ME!
ALSO: PRINCE NAMOR, THE SUB-MARINER
"THE END OF THE QUEST!"

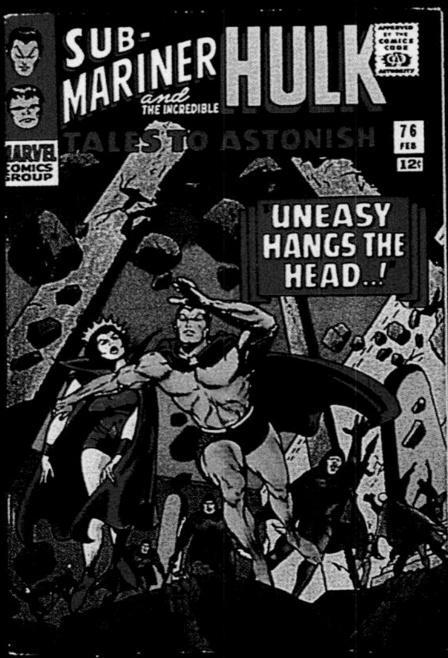
SUB-MARINER and the incredible HULK
76 FEB
12¢
UNEASY HANGS THE HEAD..!

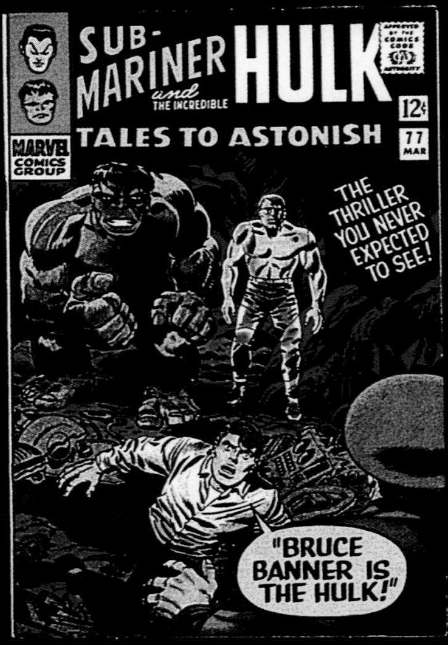
SUB-MARINER and the incredible HULK
TALES TO ASTONISH
77 MAR
12¢
THE THRILLER YOU NEVER EXPECTED TO SEE!
"BRUCE BANNER IS THE HULK!"

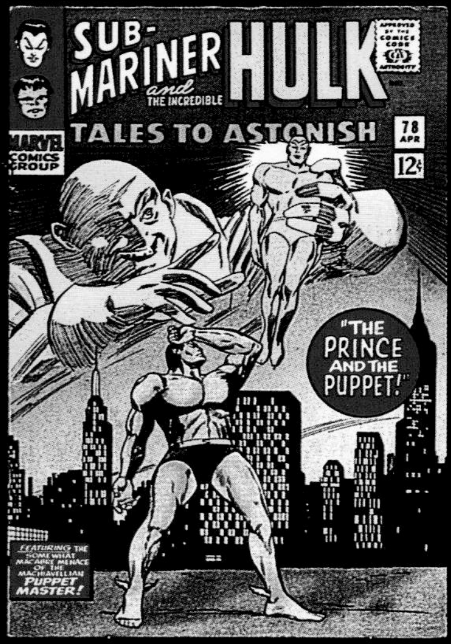
SUB-MARINER and the incredible HULK
TALES TO ASTONISH
78 APR
12¢
"THE PRINCE AND THE PUPPET!"
PUPPET MASTER!

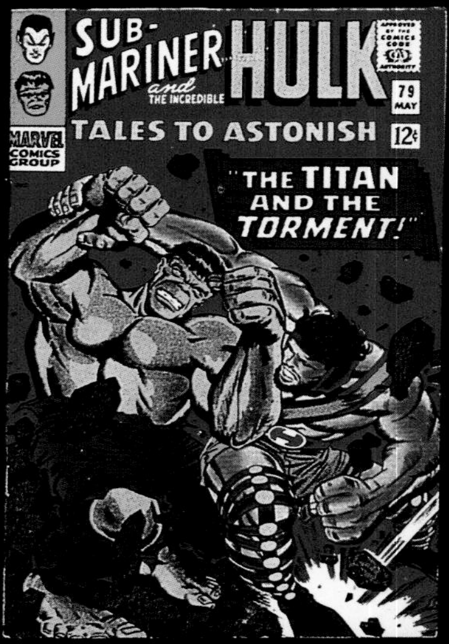
SUB-MARINER and the incredible HULK
TALES TO ASTONISH
79 MAY
12¢
"THE TITAN AND THE TORMENT!"

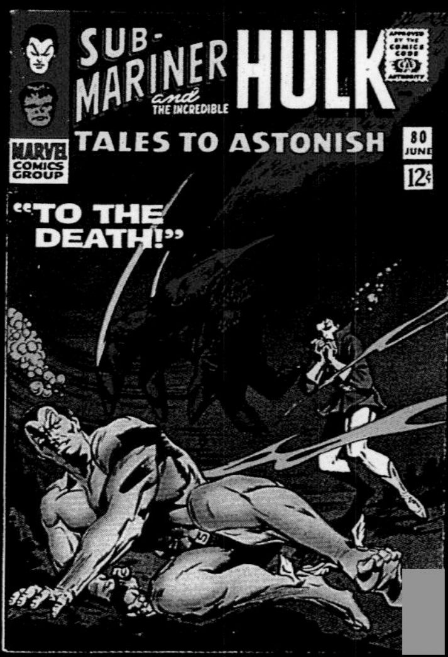
SUB-MARINER and the incredible HULK
TALES TO ASTONISH
80 JUNE
12¢
"TO THE DEATH!"

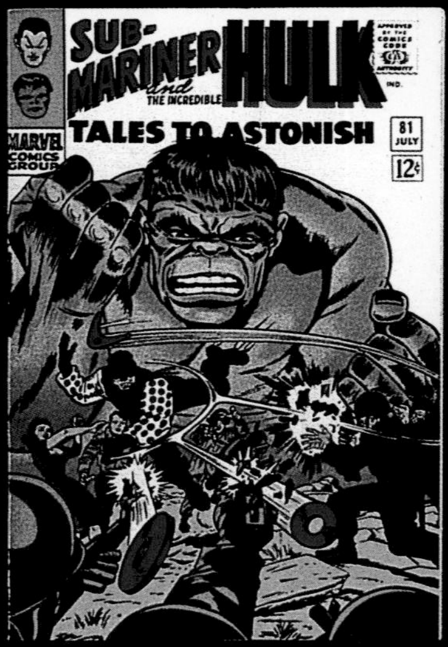
SUB-MARINER and the incredible HULK
TALES TO ASTONISH
81 JULY
12¢

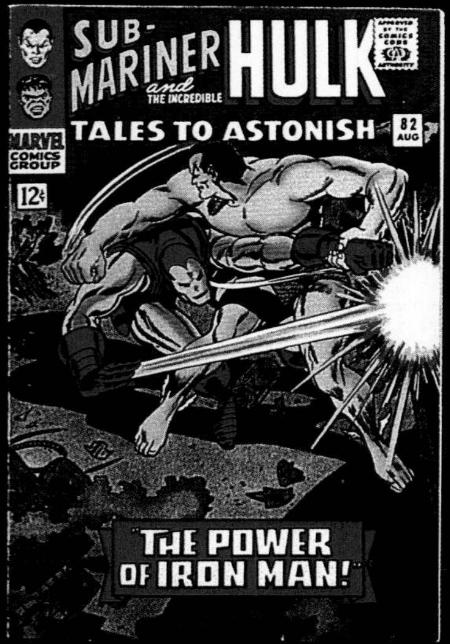
SUB-MARINER and the incredible HULK
TALES TO ASTONISH
82 AUG
12¢
THE POWER OF IRON MAN!

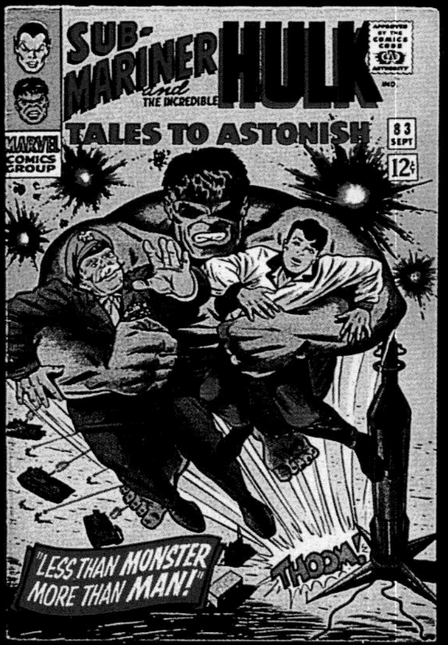
SUB-MARINER and the incredible HULK
TALES TO ASTONISH
83 SEPT
12¢
"LESS THAN MONSTER MORE THAN MAN!"
THOOM!

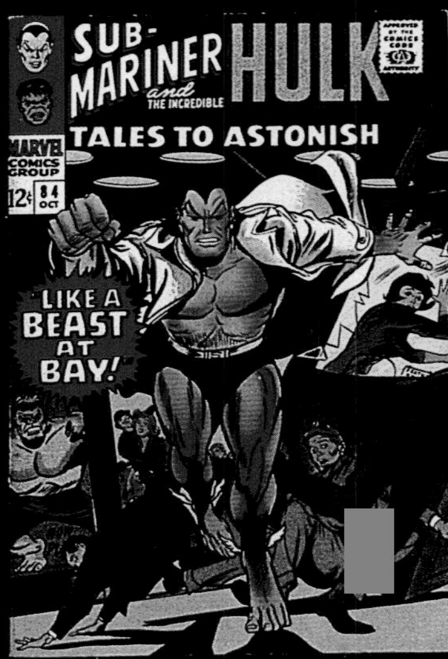
SUB-MARINER and the incredible HULK
TALES TO ASTONISH
12¢ 84 OCT
LIKE A BEAST AT BAY!

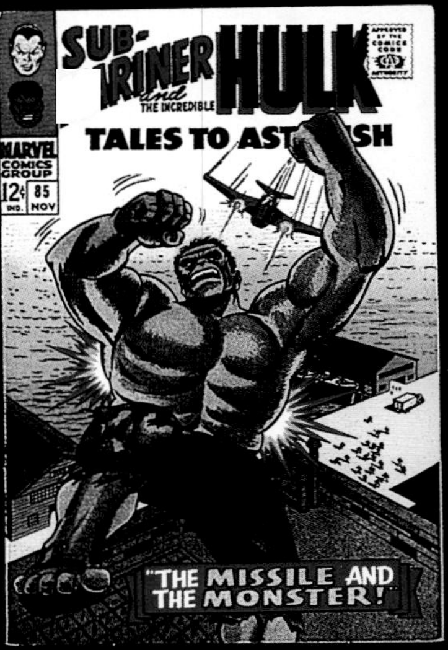
SUB-MARINER and THE INCREDIBLE HULK
TALES TO ASTONISH
"THE MISSILE AND THE MONSTER!"

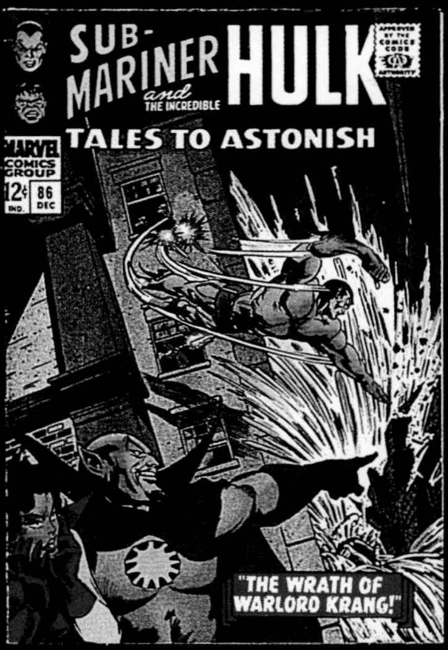
SUB-MARINER and THE INCREDIBLE HULK
TALES TO ASTONISH
"THE WRATH OF WARLORD KRANG!"

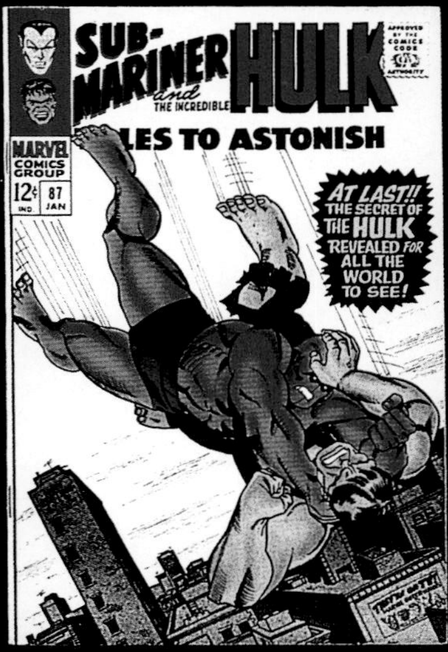
SUB-MARINER and THE INCREDIBLE HULK
TALES TO ASTONISH
AT LAST!! THE SECRET OF THE HULK REVEALED FOR ALL THE WORLD TO SEE!

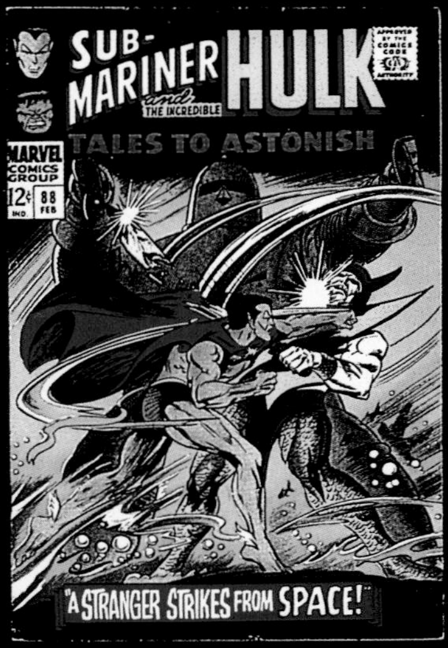
SUB-MARINER and THE INCREDIBLE HULK
TALES TO ASTONISH
"A STRANGER STRIKES FROM SPACE!"

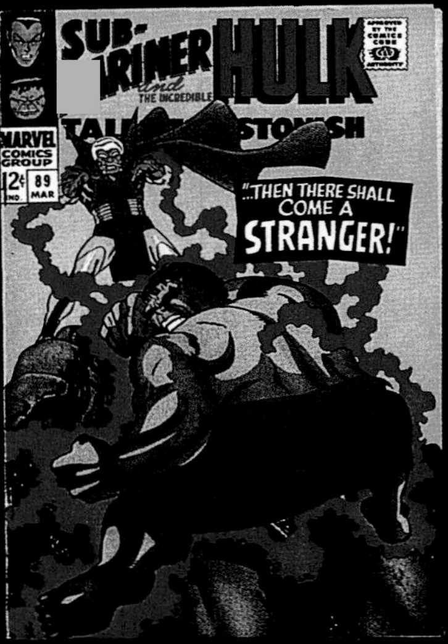
SUB-MARINER and THE INCREDIBLE HULK
"THEN THERE SHALL COME A STRANGER!"

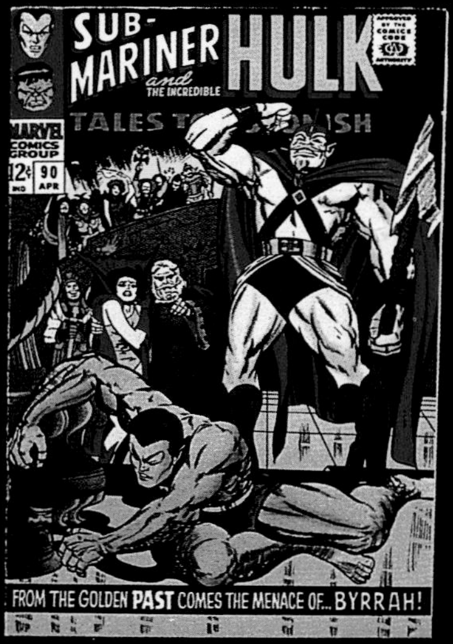
SUB-MARINER and THE INCREDIBLE HULK
FROM THE GOLDEN PAST COMES THE MENACE OF... BYRRAH!

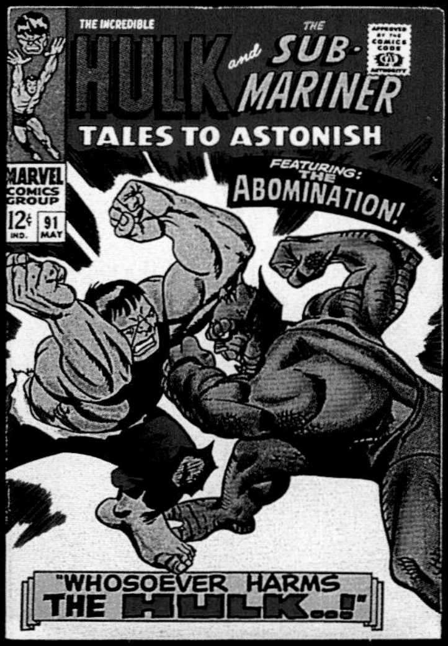
THE INCREDIBLE HULK and THE SUB-MARINER
TALES TO ASTONISH
FEATURING: THE ABOMINATION!
"WHOSOEVER HARMS THE HULK..!"

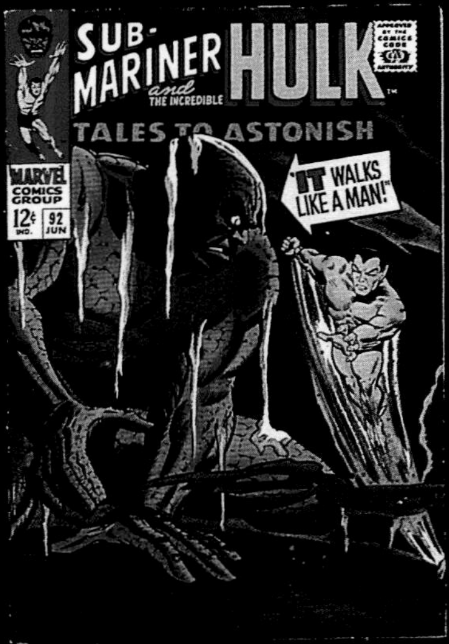
SUB-MARINER and THE INCREDIBLE HULK
TALES TO ASTONISH
"IT WALKS LIKE A MAN!"

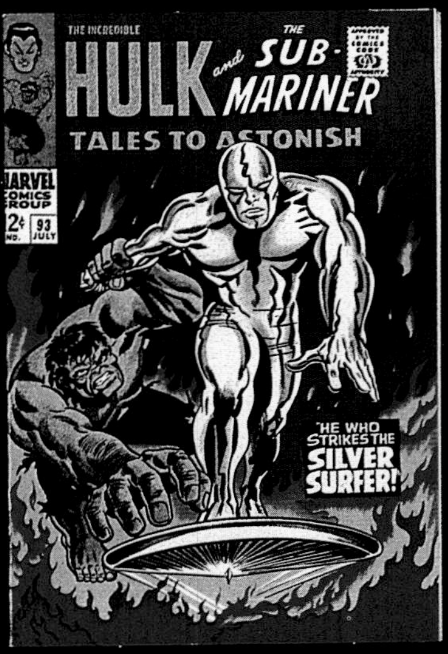
THE INCREDIBLE HULK and THE SUB-MARINER
TALES TO ASTONISH
"HE WHO STRIKES THE SILVER SURFER!"

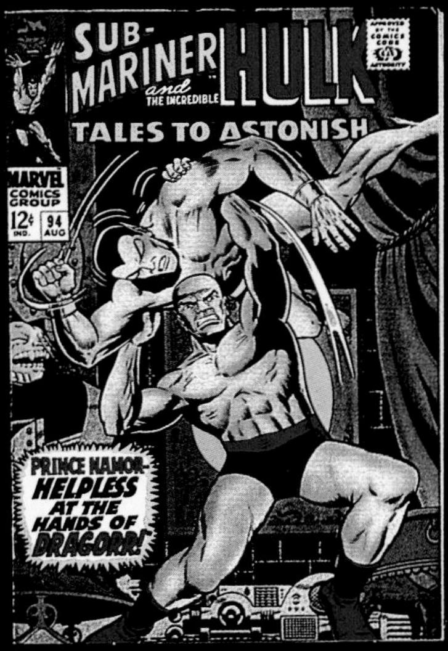
SUB-MARINER and THE INCREDIBLE HULK
TALES TO ASTONISH
PRINCE NAMOR HELPLESS AT THE HANDS OF DRAGORR!

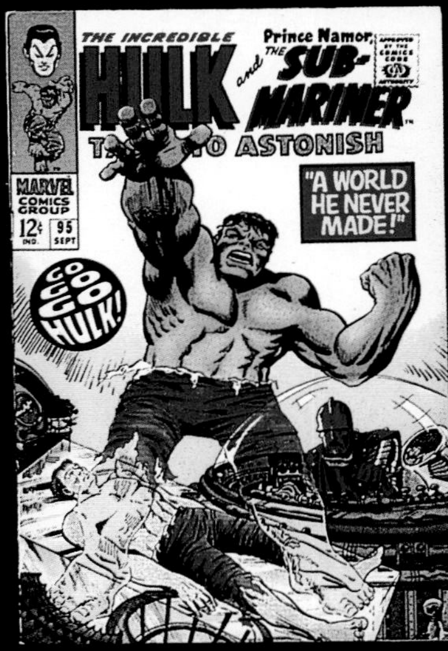
THE INCREDIBLE HULK and Prince Namor, THE SUB-MARINER
"A WORLD HE NEVER MADE!"

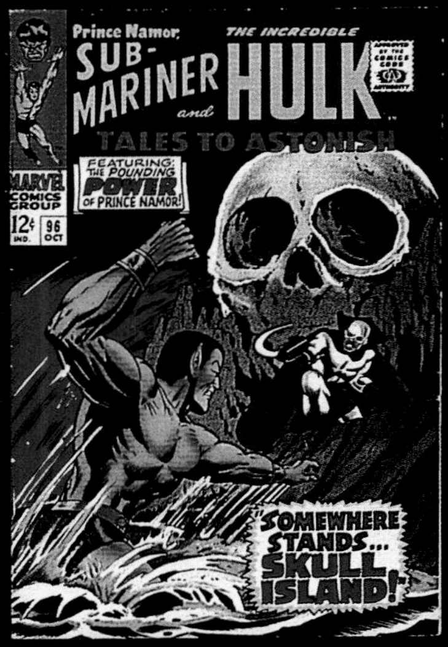
Prince Namor, SUB-MARINER and THE INCREDIBLE HULK
TALES TO ASTONISH
FEATURING: THE POUNDING POWER OF PRINCE NAMOR!
"SOMEWHERE STANDS... SKULL ISLAND!"

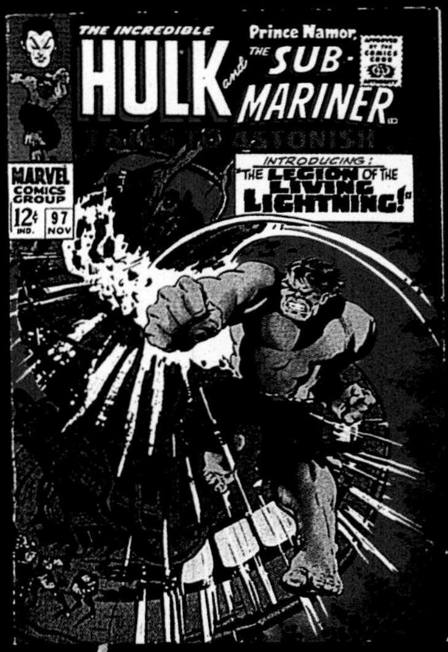
THE INCREDIBLE HULK and Prince Namor, THE SUB-MARINER
INTRODUCING: THE LEGION OF THE LIVING LIGHTNING!

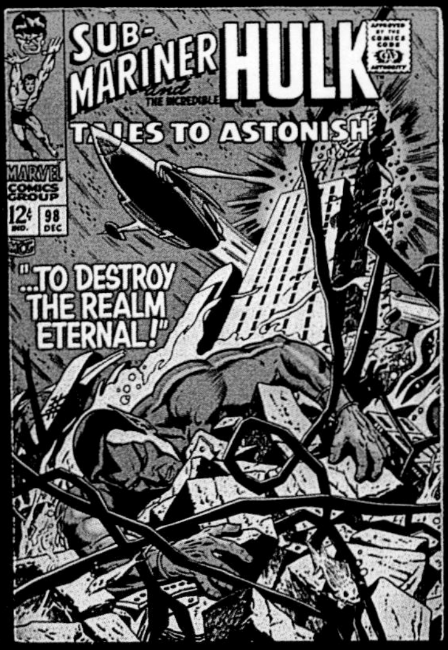
SUB-MARINER and THE INCREDIBLE HULK
TALES TO ASTONISH
"...TO DESTROY THE REALM ETERNAL!"

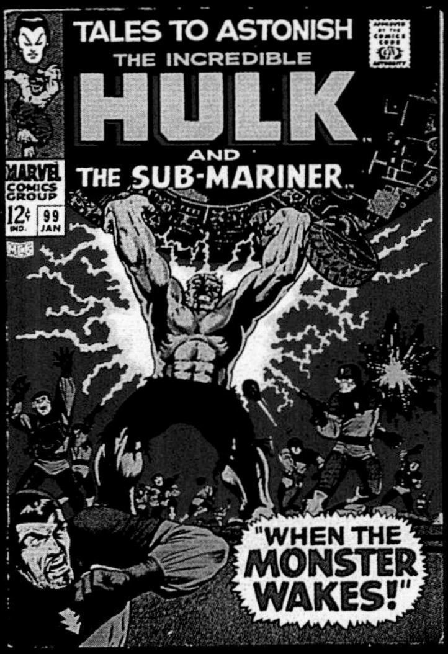
TALES TO ASTONISH
THE INCREDIBLE HULK AND THE SUB-MARINER
"WHEN THE MONSTER WAKES!"

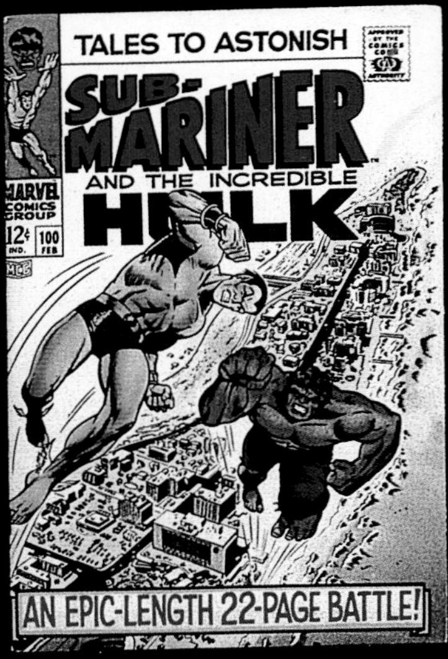
TALES TO ASTONISH
SUB-MARINER AND THE INCREDIBLE HULK
AN EPIC-LENGTH 22-PAGE BATTLE!

1884 Tales To Astonish (101) 1889.2 Tarzan (1-10)

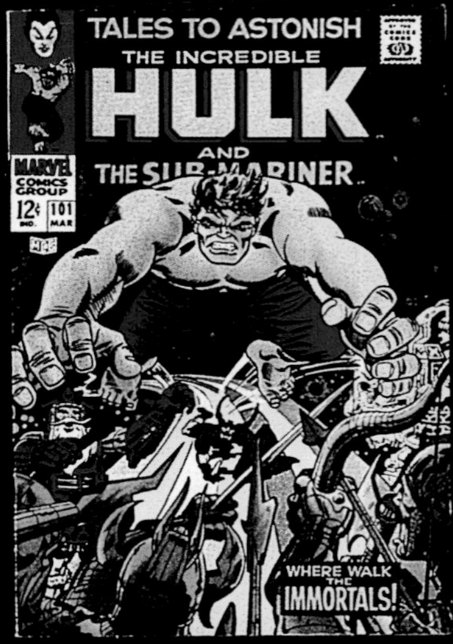
TALES TO ASTONISH
THE INCREDIBLE
HULK
AND
THE SUB-MARINER
12¢ 101
WHERE WALK THE IMMORTALS!

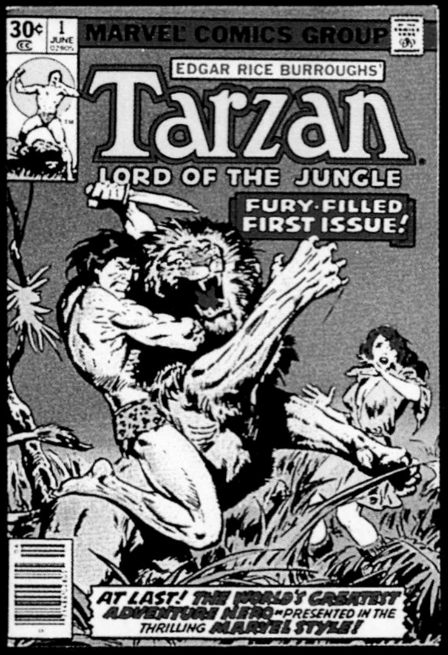
30¢ 1
MARVEL COMICS GROUP
EDGAR RICE BURROUGHS'
Tarzan
LORD OF THE JUNGLE
FURY-FILLED FIRST ISSUE!
AT LAST! THE WORLD'S GREATEST ADVENTURE HERO PRESENTED IN THE THRILLING MARVEL STYLE!

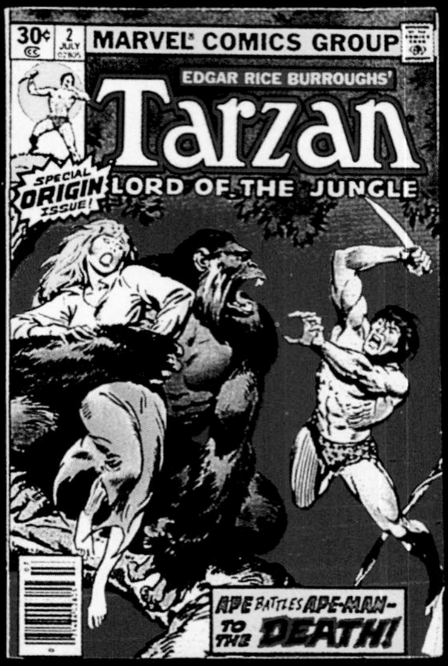
30¢ 2
MARVEL COMICS GROUP
EDGAR RICE BURROUGHS'
Tarzan
LORD OF THE JUNGLE
SPECIAL ORIGIN ISSUE!
APE BATTLES APE-MAN TO THE DEATH!

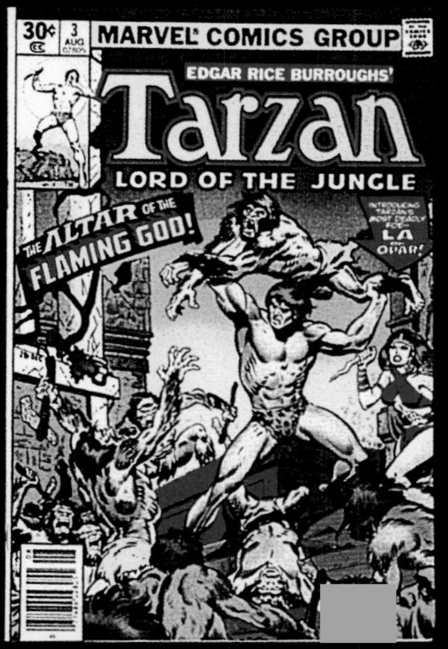
30¢ 3
MARVEL COMICS GROUP
EDGAR RICE BURROUGHS'
Tarzan
LORD OF THE JUNGLE
THE ALTAR OF THE FLAMING GOD!

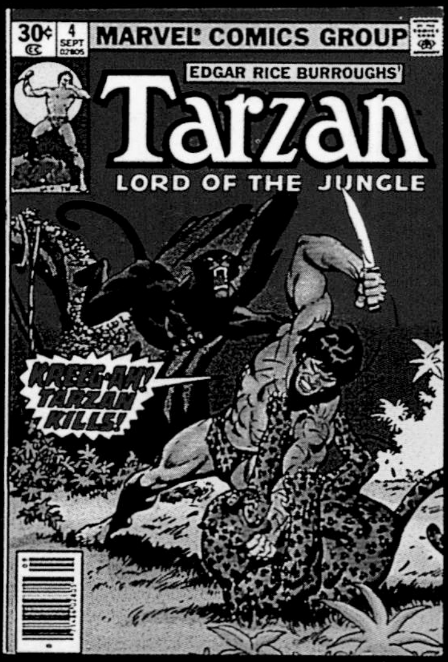
30¢ 4
MARVEL COMICS GROUP
EDGAR RICE BURROUGHS'
Tarzan
LORD OF THE JUNGLE
KREEG-AH! TARZAN KILLS!

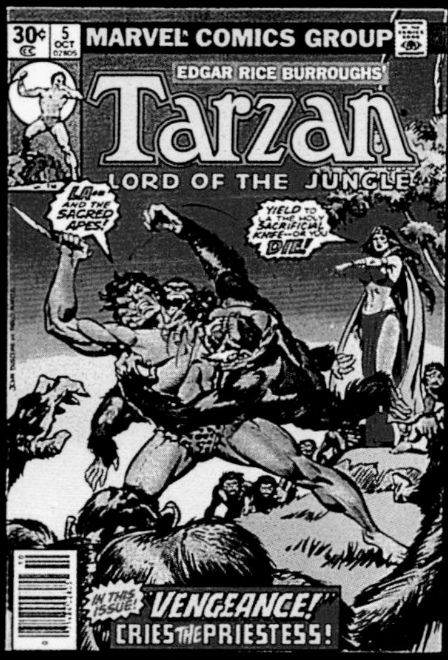
30¢ 5
MARVEL COMICS GROUP
EDGAR RICE BURROUGHS'
Tarzan
LORD OF THE JUNGLE
VENGEANCE! CRIES THE PRIESTESS!

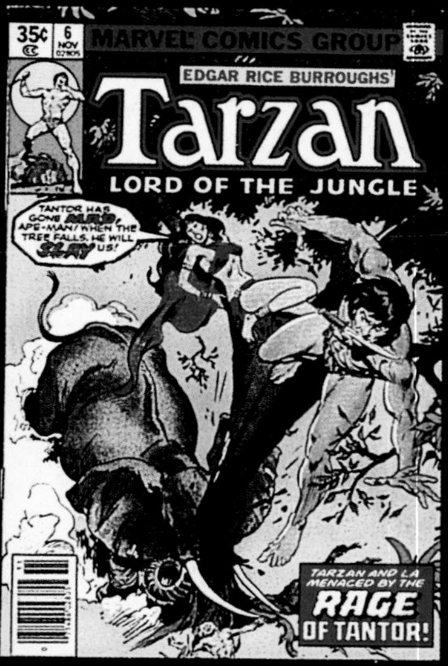
35¢ 6
MARVEL COMICS GROUP
EDGAR RICE BURROUGHS'
Tarzan
LORD OF THE JUNGLE
RAGE OF TANTOR!

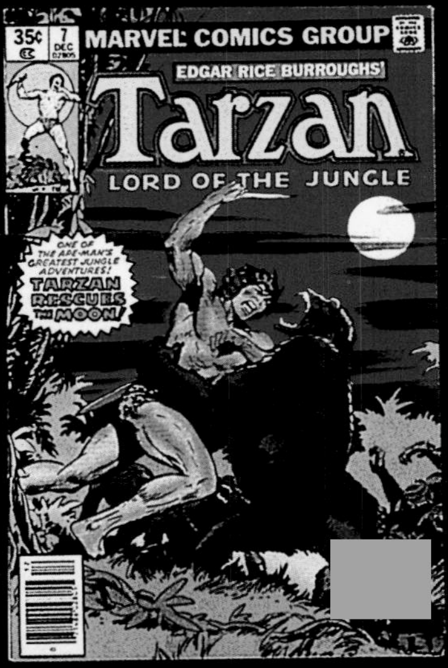
35¢ 7
MARVEL COMICS GROUP
EDGAR RICE BURROUGHS'
Tarzan
LORD OF THE JUNGLE
TARZAN RESCUES THE MOON!

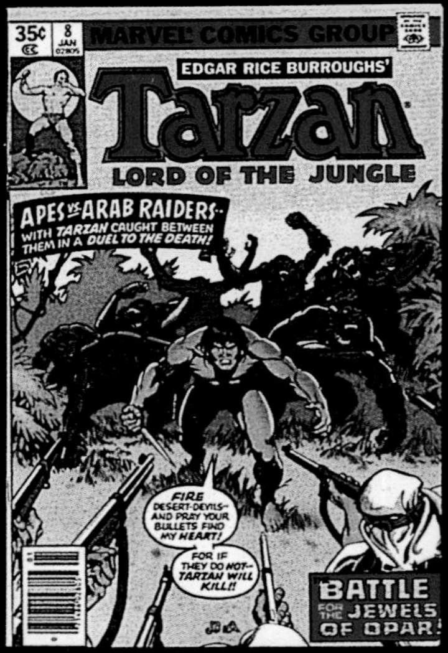
35¢ 8
MARVEL COMICS GROUP
EDGAR RICE BURROUGHS'
Tarzan
LORD OF THE JUNGLE
APES vs ARAB RAIDERS
BATTLE FOR THE JEWELS OF OPAR!

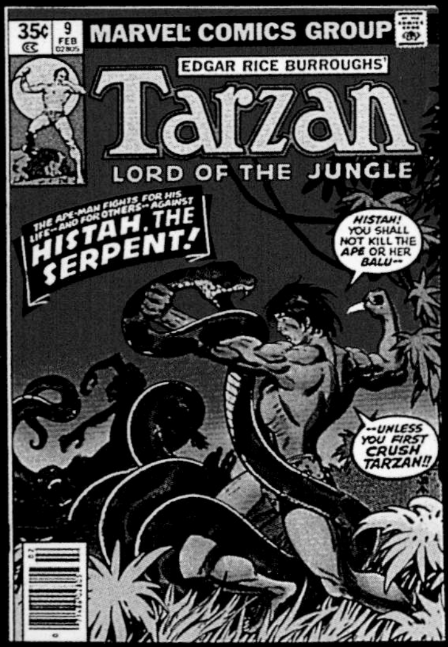
35¢ 9
MARVEL COMICS GROUP
EDGAR RICE BURROUGHS'
Tarzan
LORD OF THE JUNGLE
HISTAH, THE SERPENT!

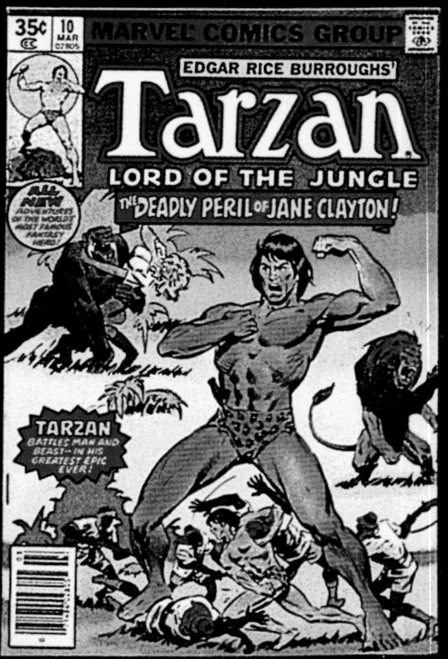
35¢ 10
MARVEL COMICS GROUP
EDGAR RICE BURROUGHS'
Tarzan
LORD OF THE JUNGLE
THE DEADLY PERIL OF JANE CLAYTON!
TARZAN

Tales to Astonish (21-101) 1884

Ref. No.	Date	RVI	Artist/Info.
1884-21	Jul. 1961	25	Kirby/Ayers/Ditko-a
1884-22	Aug.	25	Kirby/Ayers-c/a, Ditko-a
1884-23	Sept.	25	" " "
1884-24	Oct.	25	" " "
1884-25	Nov.	25	" " "
1884-26	Dec.	25	Kirby/Ayers-c/a, Ditko/Forgione-a
1884-27	Jan. 1962	675	Ditko/Dirby-a (Intro. the Antman) Publ. 9/28/61
1884-28	Feb.	20	Kirby/Ayers-c/a, Ditko-a; Publ. 11/9/61
1884-29	Mar.	20	Kirby/Ayers-c/a, Ditko-a; Publ. 12/5/61
1884-30	**Apr.**	**20**	**Kirby/Ayers-c/a, Ditko, Heck-a; Publ. 1/9/62**
1884-31	May	20	Kirby/Ayers-c/a, Ditko, Reinman-a; Publ. 2/1/62
1884-32	Jun.	20	Kirby/Ayers-c/a, Ditko-a; Publ. 3/8/62
1884-33	Jul.	20	Kirby/Ayers-c/a, Ditko, Heck-a; Publ. 4/3/62
1884-34	Aug.	20	Kirby/Ayers-c/a, Ditko, Heck-a; Publ. 5/8/62
1884-35	Sept.	450	Kirby/Ayers-c/a; Publ. 7/10/62 (2nd Antman in costume)
1884-36	Oct.	180	Kirby/Ayers-c/a
1884-37	Nov.	90	Kirby/Ayers-c/a, Ditko-a; Publ. 8/2/62
1884-38	Dec.	80	Kirby/Brodsky-c, Ditko, Ayers, Kirby-a; Publ. 9/11/62
1884-39	Jan. 1963	80	Kirby/Ayers-c/a, Ditko, Heck-a; Publ.10/2/62
1884-40	**Feb.**	**80**	**Kirby/Brodsky-c/a, Ditko, Heck-a; Publ. 11/8/62**
1884-41	Mar.	45	Kirby/Ayers-c, Heck, Sinnott, Dikto-a; Publ. 12/3/62
1884-42	Apr.	45	Kirby/Brodsky-c, Heck, Sinnott, Ditko-a; Publ. 1/10/63
1884-43	May	45	Kirby/Brodsky-c, Heck, Lieber, Ditko-a; Publ. 2/5/63
1884-44	Jun.	65	Kirby/Heck-c/a, Ditko-a (Intro. the Wasp)
1884-45	Jul.	35	Kirby/Ayers-c, Heck, Ditko, Reinman-a
1884-46	Aug.	35	" " " " "
1884-47	Sept.	35	Kirby/Ayers-c, Heck, Ditko, Lieber/Fox-a
1884-48	Oct.	35	Kirby/Brodsky-c, Heck, Ditko, Lieber/Fox-a
1884-49	Nov.	55	Heck-c/a, Kirby, Lieber/Roussos-a
1884-50	**Dec.**	**22**	**Kirby/Roussos-c, Kirby/Lieber, Fox-a; Publ. 9/3/63**
1884-51	Jan. 1964	22	Kirby/Roussos-c, Kirby, Lieber/Ayers, Fox-a
1884-52	Feb.	22	Kirby/Brodsky-c, Lieber/Ayers, Bell-a; Publ. 11/5/63
1884-53	Mar.	22	Kirby/Brodsky-c, Ayers, Lieber/Heck-a
1884-54	Apr.	22	Kirby/Ayers-c, Heck, Lieber/Reinman-a
1884-55	May	22	Kirby/Brodsky-c, Ayers, Lieber/Bell-a
1884-56	Jun.	22	Kirby/Brodsky-c, Ayers, Lieber/Reinman-a
1884-57	Jul.	34	Kirby/Brodsky-c (Spider-Man -app.)
1884-58	Aug.	22	Kirby/Brodsky-c, Ayers, Lieber/Reinman-a
1884-59	Sept.	33	Kirby/Brodsky-c, Ayers/Reinman-a
1884-60	**Oct.**	**55**	**Kirby/Brodsky-c, Ayers-a (Hulk series begins)**
1884-61	Nov.	15	Kirby/Roussos-c, Ditko/Bell-a
1884-62	Dec.	15	Kirby/Stone-c, Burgos, Ditko/Ayers, Bell-a
1884-63	Jan. 1965	15	Kirby/Stone-c, Burgos, Ditko/Stone, Bell-a
1884-64	Feb.	15	Kirby/Colletta-c, Burgos, Ditko/Reinman, Bell-a
1884-65	Mar.	15	Kirby/Stone-c, Powell, Ditko/Heck, Ayers-a
1884-66	Apr,	15	Powell/Giacoia-c, Kirby, Ditko-c, Colletta-a
1884-67	May	15	Kirby/Stone-c, Kirby, Powell, Ditko;Stone, Ray-a
1884-68	Jun.	15	Kirby/Colletta-c, Kirby, Powell/Demeo-a
1884-69	Jul.	15	Kirby/Brodsky-c, Kirby, Powell/Demeo-a
1884-70	**Aug.**	**30**	**Kirby/Esposito-c (Sub-Mariner and Hulk series begins)**
1884-71	Sept.	13	Colan/Colletta-c, Kirby/Demeo-a
1884-72	Oct.	13	Kirby/Colletta-c, Kirby, Austin/Colletta, Demeo-a
1884-73	Nov.	13	Kirby/Colletta-c, Kirby, Austin/Colletta, Powell-a
1884-74	Dec.	13	Colan, Powell/Colletta, Esposito-c, Kirby, Austin/Colletta, Powell-a
1884-75	Jan. 1966	13	Kirby/Colletta-c, Kirby, Austin/Colletta, Demeo-a
1884-76	Feb.	13	Colan/Colletta-c, Kirby, Austin/Colletta, Demeo-a
1884-77	Mar.	13	Romita/Esposito-c, Kirby, Austin/Colletta, Romita-a
1884-78	Apr.	13	Colan/Colletta-c, Kirby, Austin/Colletta, Everett-a
1884-79	May	13	Kirby/Everett-c, Kirby, Austin/Everett-a
1884-80	**Jun.**	**13**	**Colan/Everett-c, Kirby, Colan/Ayers, Everett-a**
1884-81	Jul.	13	Kirby/Everett-c, Kirby, Colan/Ayers, Everett-a
1884-82	Aug.	13	Colan/Ayers-c, Kirby, Colan/Ayers, Everett-a
1884-83	Sept.	13	Everett-c, Kirby/Ayers, Everett-a
1884-84	Oct.	13	Colan/Ayers-c/a
1884-85	Nov.	13	Everett-c, Colan, Buscema/Everett-a
1884-86	Dec.	13	Colan/Everett-c, Buscema, Grandenetti/Guerett-a
1884-87	Jan. 1967	13	Kane-c, Everett, Buscema/Demeo-a
1884-88	Feb.	13	Colan/Everett-c, Everett, Kane-a
1884-89	Mar.	13	Kane-c/a. Everett-a
1884-90	**Apr.**	**13**	**Kirby/Colletta-c, Kane, Everett-a; Publ. 1/10/67**
1884-91	May	13	Kane-c, Kane, Everett/Adkins-a
1884-92	Jun.	17	Adkins-c/a, M. Severin/Giacoia-a (Silver Surfer)
1884-93	Jul.	17	M. Severin/Giacoia-c/a, Adkins-a
1884-94	Aug.	15	Adkins-c, Everett, Severin/Trimpe-a
1884-95	Sept.	13	Severin/Trimpe-c, Everett, Severin/Trimpe, Colletta-a
1884-96	Oct.	13	Adkins-c, Everett, Severin/Trimpe, Colletta-a
1884-97	Nov.	13	Severin/Trimpe-c/a, Roth/Adkins-a
1884-98	Dec.	13	Adkins-c, Severin, Roth/Adkins, Trimpe-a
1884-99	Jan. 1968	13	Severin/Adkins-c/a, Tartaglione-a
1884-100	**Feb.**	**13**	**Severin/Adkins-c/a**
1884-101	Mar.	13	Kirby, Severin/Giacoia-c, Severin, Colan/Giacois-a

Tales to Astonish (2nd Series, 1-14) 1885

1885-1	Dec. 1979	1	Buscema-a	Sub-Mariner	Reprints
1885-2	Jan. 1980	1	"	"	"
1885-3	Feb.	1	"	"	"
1885-4	Mar.	1	"	"	"
1885-5	Apr.	1	"	"	"
1885-6	May	1	"	"	"
1885-7	Jun.	1	"	"	"
1885-8	Jul.	1	"	"	"
1885-9	Aug.	1	"	"	"
1885-10	**Sept.**	**1**	**"**	**"**	**"**
1885-11	Oct.	1	"	"	"
1885-12	Nov.	1	"	"	"
1885-13	Dec.	1	"	"	"
1885-14	Jan. 1981	1	"	"	"

Tarzan (1-29) 1889.2

1889.2-1	Jun. 1977	1	Buscema-c/a
1889.2-2	Jul.	1	" (Origin-Tarzan)
1889.2-3	Aug.	1	"
1889.2-4	Sept.	1	Buscema-c/a, DeZuniga-a
1889.2-5	Oct.	1	Buscema-c/a, DeZuniga-a

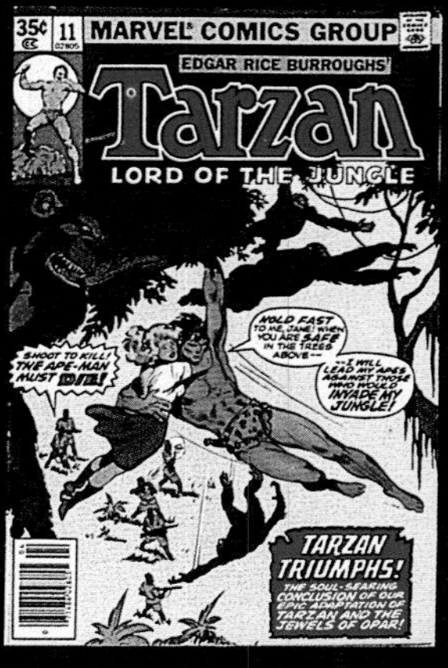
MARVEL COMICS GROUP
EDGAR RICE BURROUGHS'
Tarzan
LORD OF THE JUNGLE
TARZAN TRIUMPHS!

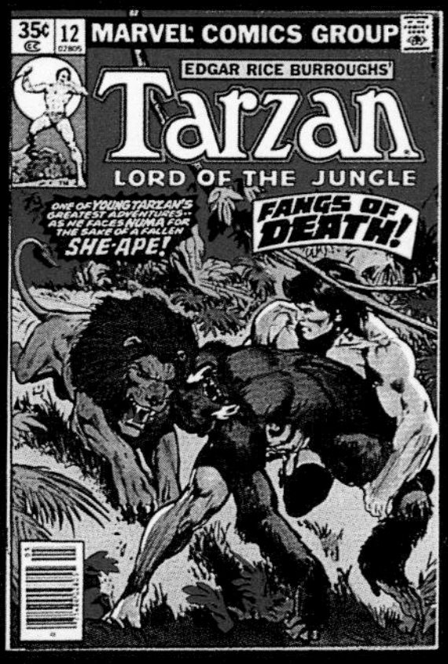
MARVEL COMICS GROUP
EDGAR RICE BURROUGHS'
Tarzan
LORD OF THE JUNGLE
FANGS OF DEATH!
SHE-APE!

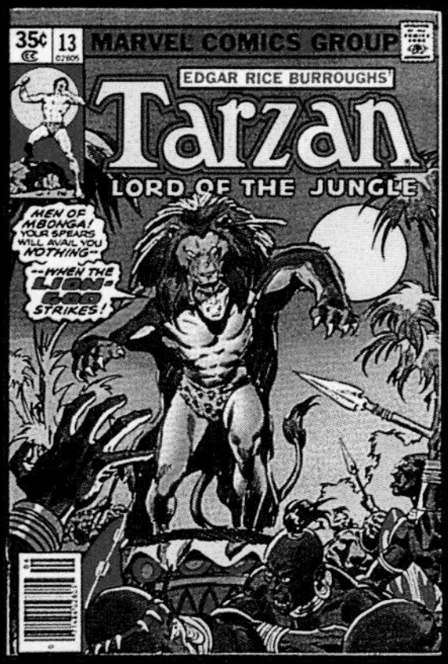
MARVEL COMICS GROUP
EDGAR RICE BURROUGHS'
Tarzan
LORD OF THE JUNGLE

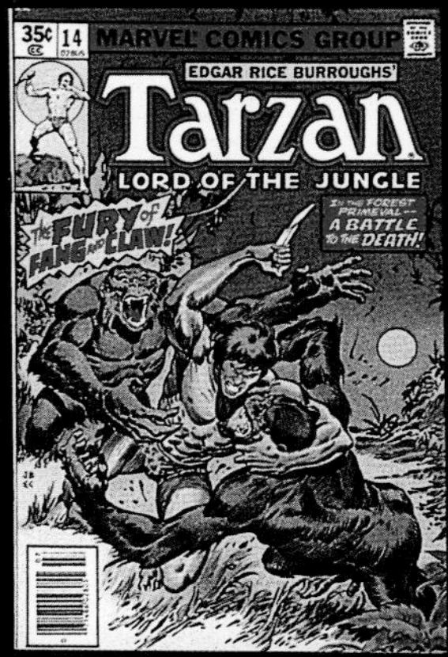
MARVEL COMICS GROUP
EDGAR RICE BURROUGHS'
Tarzan
LORD OF THE JUNGLE
A BATTLE TO THE DEATH!

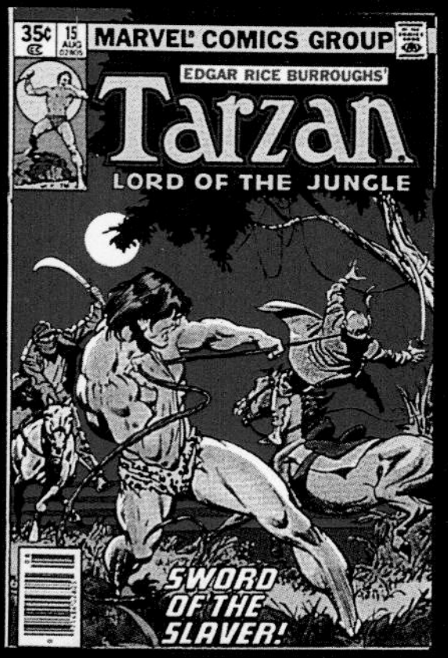
MARVEL COMICS GROUP
EDGAR RICE BURROUGHS'
Tarzan
LORD OF THE JUNGLE
SWORD OF THE SLAVER!

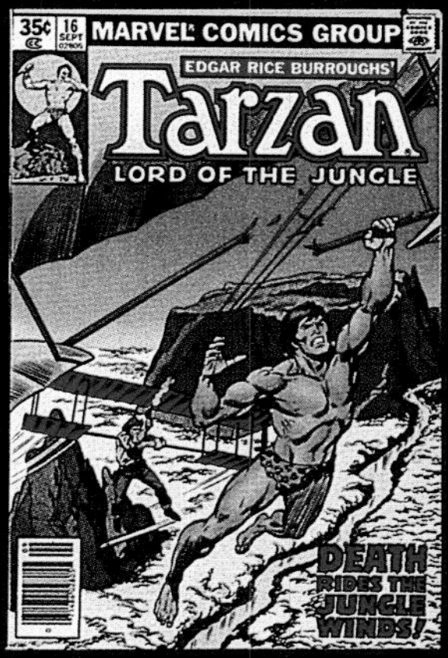
MARVEL COMICS GROUP
EDGAR RICE BURROUGHS'
Tarzan
LORD OF THE JUNGLE

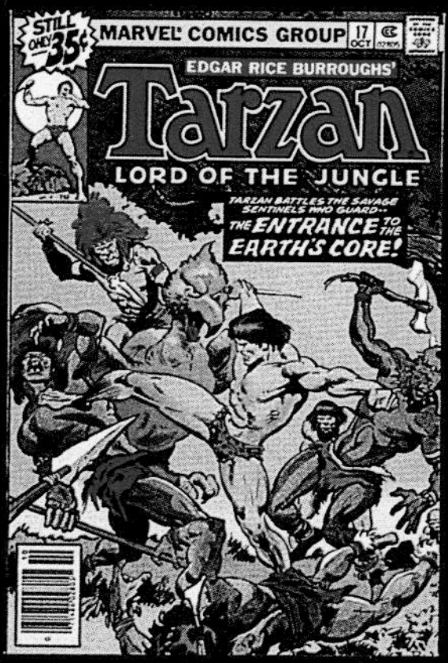
MARVEL COMICS GROUP
EDGAR RICE BURROUGHS'
Tarzan
LORD OF THE JUNGLE
THE ENTRANCE TO THE EARTH'S CORE!

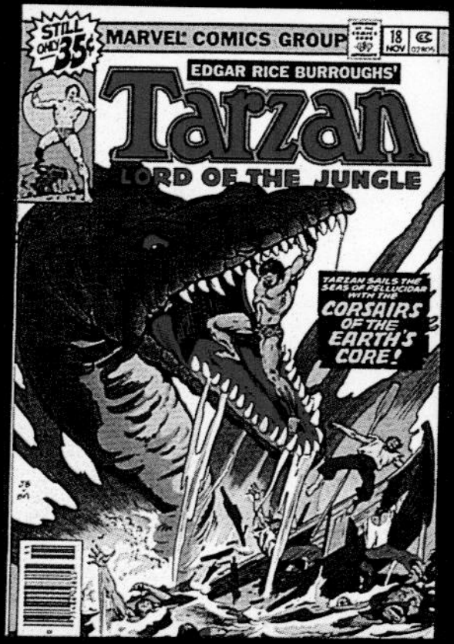
MARVEL COMICS GROUP
EDGAR RICE BURROUGHS'
Tarzan
LORD OF THE JUNGLE
CORSAIRS OF THE EARTH'S CORE!

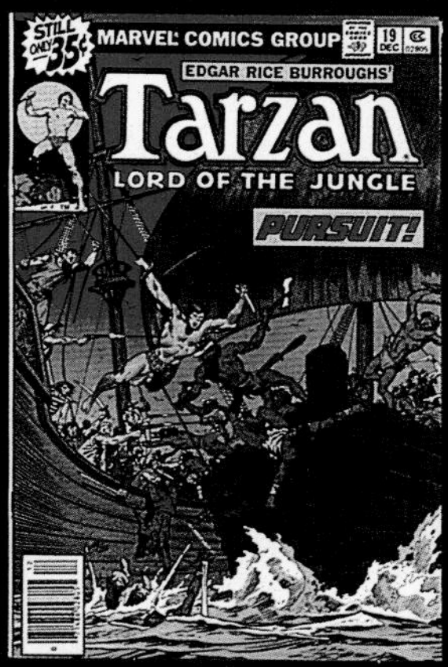
MARVEL COMICS GROUP
EDGAR RICE BURROUGHS'
Tarzan
LORD OF THE JUNGLE
PURSUIT!

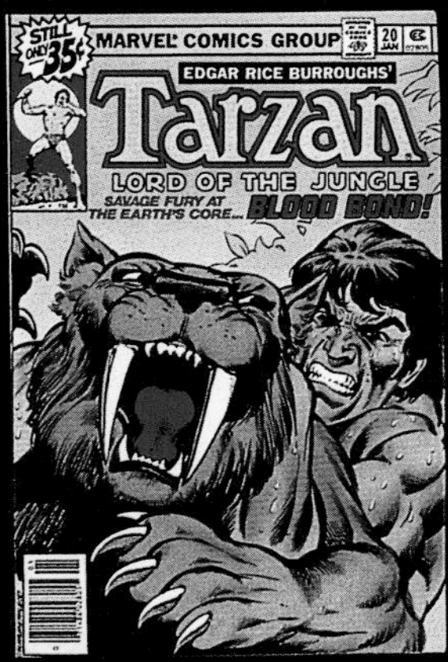
MARVEL COMICS GROUP
EDGAR RICE BURROUGHS'
Tarzan
LORD OF THE JUNGLE
BLOOD BOND!

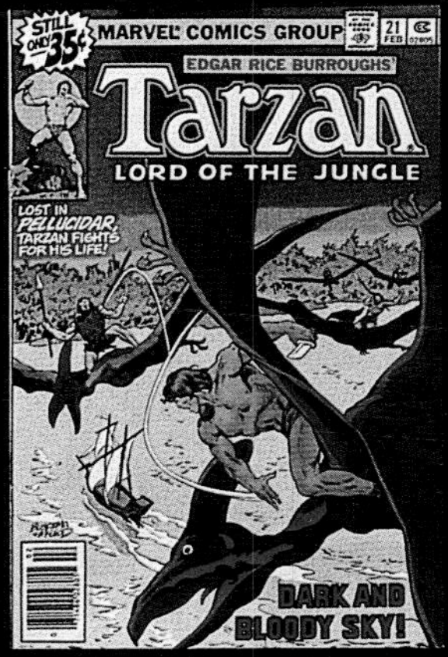
MARVEL COMICS GROUP
EDGAR RICE BURROUGHS'
Tarzan
LORD OF THE JUNGLE
LOST IN PELLUCIDAR, TARZAN FIGHTS FOR HIS LIFE!
DARK AND BLOODY SKY!

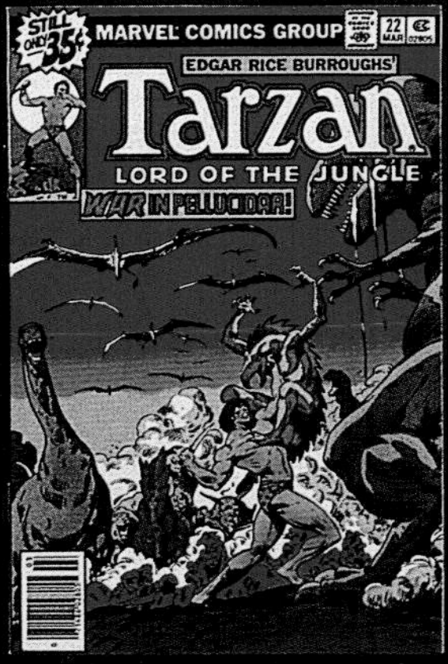
MARVEL COMICS GROUP
EDGAR RICE BURROUGHS'
Tarzan
LORD OF THE JUNGLE
WAR IN PELLUCIDAR!

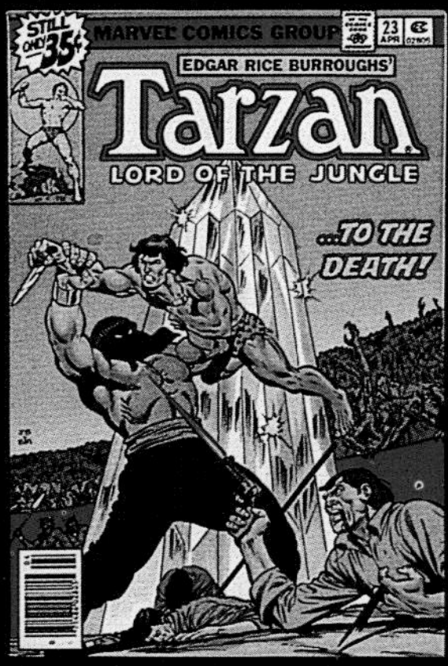
MARVEL COMICS GROUP
EDGAR RICE BURROUGHS'
Tarzan
LORD OF THE JUNGLE
...TO THE DEATH!

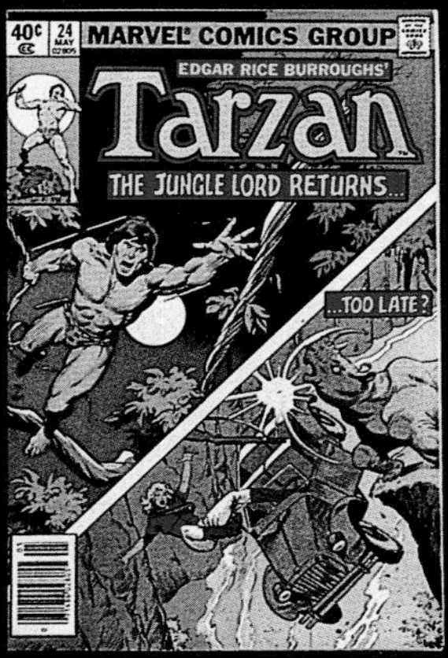
MARVEL COMICS GROUP
EDGAR RICE BURROUGHS'
Tarzan
THE JUNGLE LORD RETURNS...
...TOO LATE?

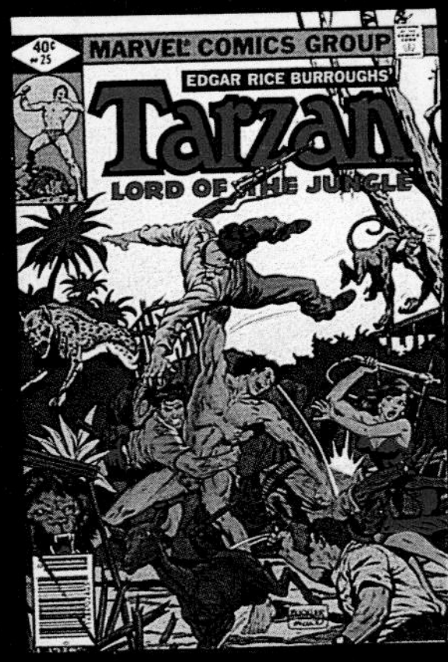
MARVEL COMICS GROUP
EDGAR RICE BURROUGHS'
Tarzan
LORD OF THE JUNGLE

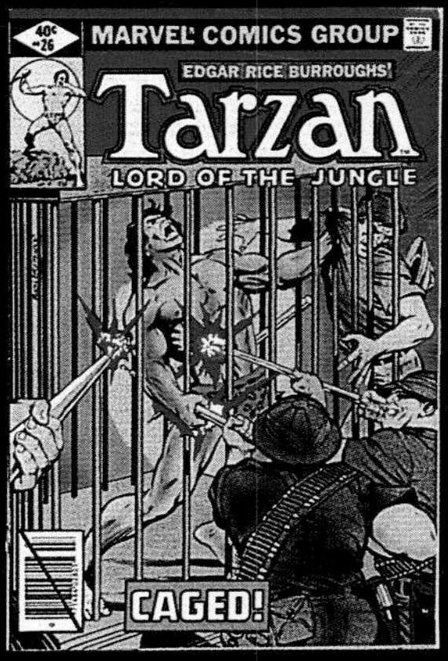
MARVEL COMICS GROUP
EDGAR RICE BURROUGHS'
Tarzan
LORD OF THE JUNGLE
CAGED!

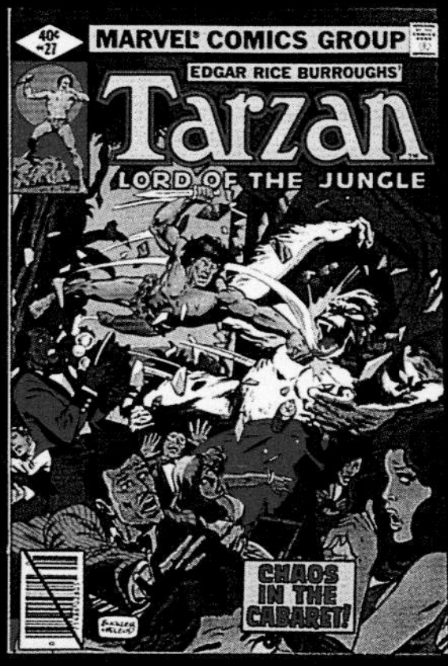
MARVEL COMICS GROUP
EDGAR RICE BURROUGHS'
Tarzan
LORD OF THE JUNGLE
CHAOS IN THE CABARET!

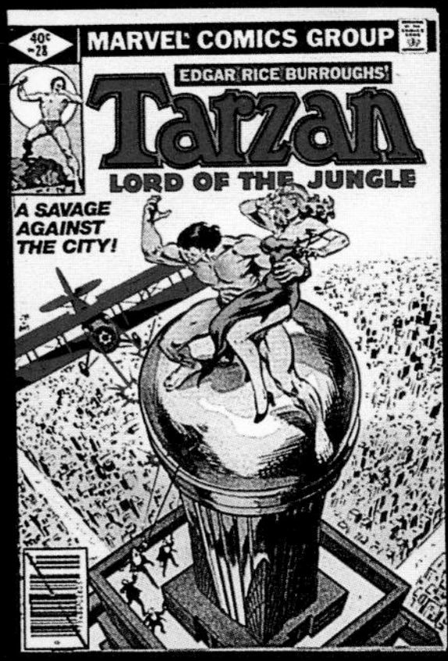
MARVEL COMICS GROUP
EDGAR RICE BURROUGHS'
Tarzan
LORD OF THE JUNGLE
A SAVAGE AGAINST THE CITY!

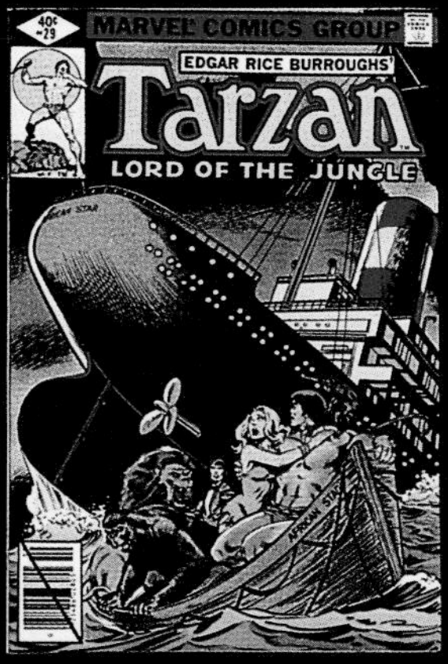
MARVEL COMICS GROUP
EDGAR RICE BURROUGHS'
Tarzan
LORD OF THE JUNGLE

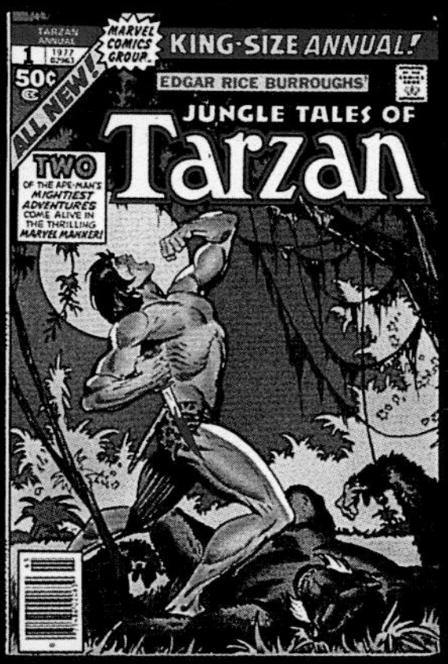
KING-SIZE ANNUAL!
EDGAR RICE BURROUGHS'
JUNGLE TALES OF
Tarzan
ALL NEW!

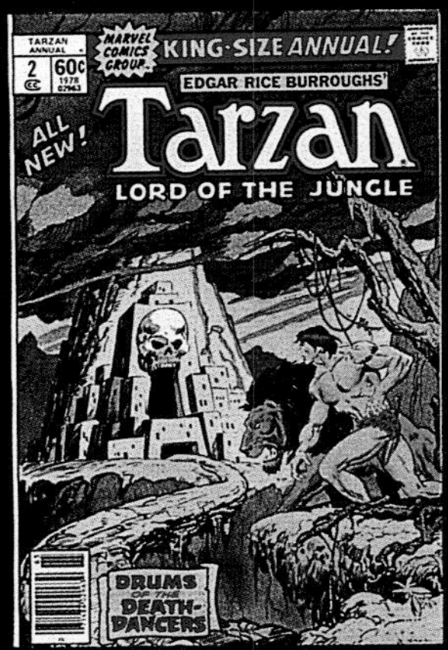
KING-SIZE ANNUAL!
EDGAR RICE BURROUGHS'
Tarzan
LORD OF THE JUNGLE
ALL NEW!
DRUMS OF THE DEATH-DANCERS

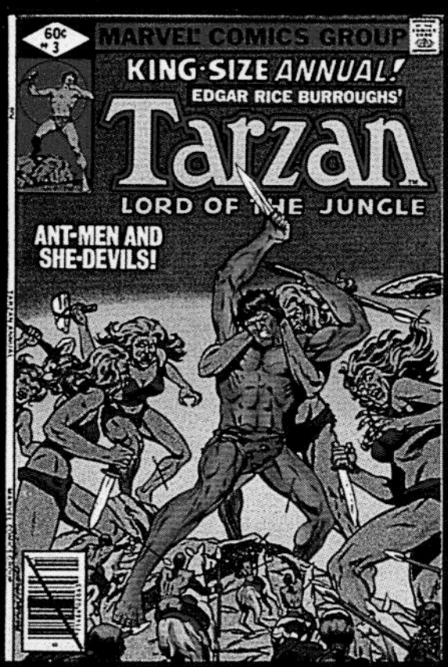
MARVEL COMICS GROUP
KING-SIZE ANNUAL!
EDGAR RICE BURROUGHS'
Tarzan
LORD OF THE JUNGLE
ANT-MEN AND SHE-DEVILS!

Tarzan (cont.)

Ref. No.	Date	RVI	Artist/Info.
1889.2-6	Nov.	1	Buscema-c/a, DeZuniga-a
1889.2-7	Dec.	1	" "
1889.2-8 to 29	Oct. 1979, (#29)	1	
1889.2-A1	Oct. 1977	1	Buscema-c/a, Gan-a
1889.2-A2	Nov. 1978	1	Hall-c, Buscema, Matera-a
1889.2-A3	Oct. 1979	1	Buckler/McLeod-c, Buscema, Villamonte-a

Tarzan of the Apes (1-2) 1889.6

Ref. No.	Date	RVI	Artist/Info.
1889.6-1	Jul. 1984	1	Spiegle-a
1889.6-2	Aug. 1984	1	"

Team America (1-12) 1890.4

Ref. No.	Date	RVI	Artist/Info.
1890.4-1	Jun. 1982	1	Layton-c, Vosburg/Colletta-a
1890.4-2	Jul.	1	Vosburg/Milgrom-c, Vosburg/Colletta-a
1890.4-3	Aug.	1	McDonnell/Colletta-a
1890.4-4	Sept.	1	" "
1890.4-5	Oct.	1	Kupperburg/Colletta-a
1890.4-6	Nov.	1	
1890.4-7	Dec.	1	
1890.4-8	Jan. 1983	1	
1890.4-9 to 12	May 1983	1	

1889.6 Tarzan of the Apes (1-2)

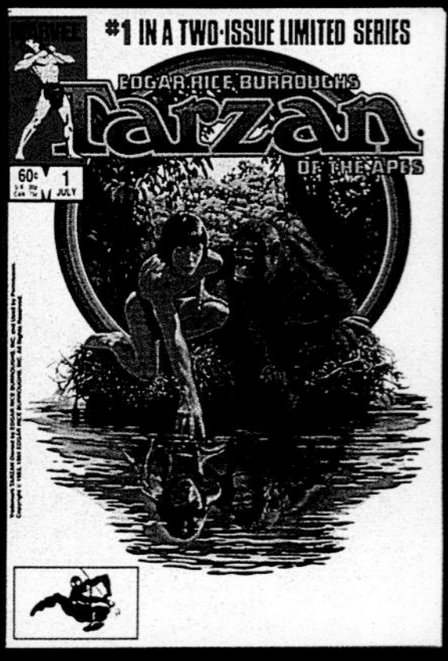
#1 IN A TWO-ISSUE LIMITED SERIES
EDGAR RICE BURROUGHS
TARZAN
OF THE APES

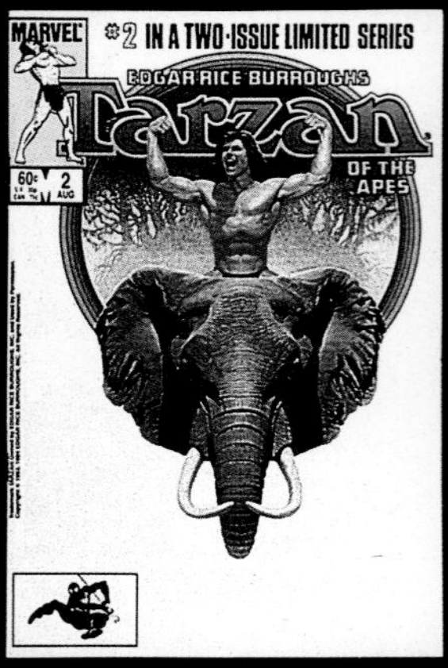
MARVEL
#2 IN A TWO-ISSUE LIMITED SERIES
EDGAR RICE BURROUGHS
TARZAN
OF THE APES

1890.4 Team America (1-10)

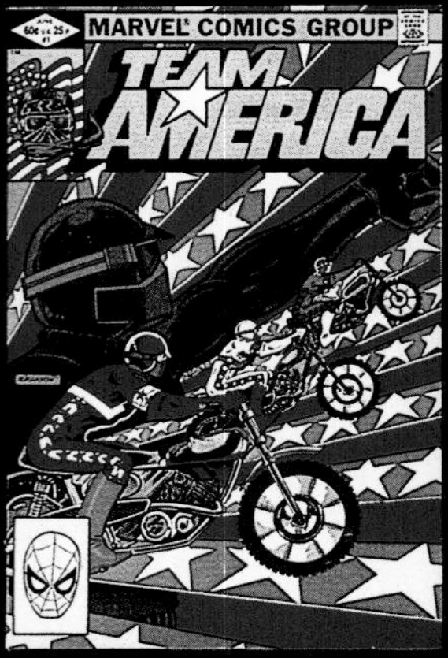
MARVEL COMICS GROUP
TEAM AMERICA

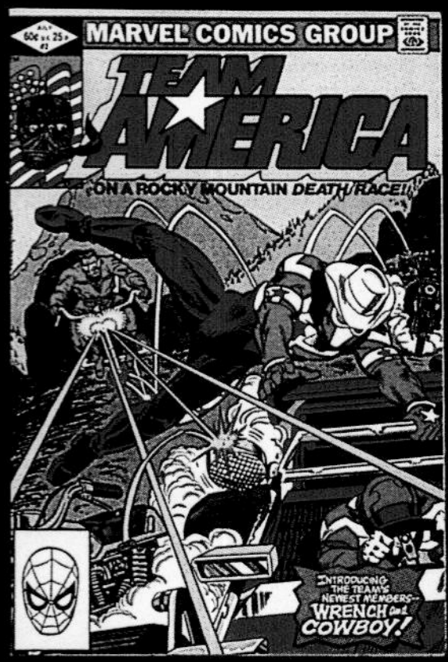
MARVEL COMICS GROUP
TEAM AMERICA
ON A ROCKY MOUNTAIN DEATH RACE!
WRENCH and COWBOY!

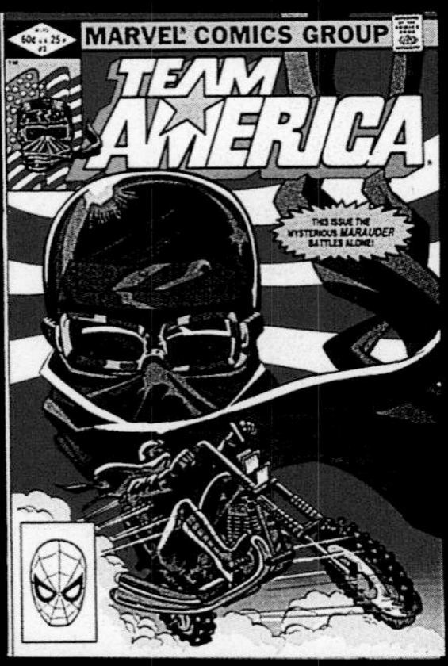
MARVEL COMICS GROUP
TEAM AMERICA

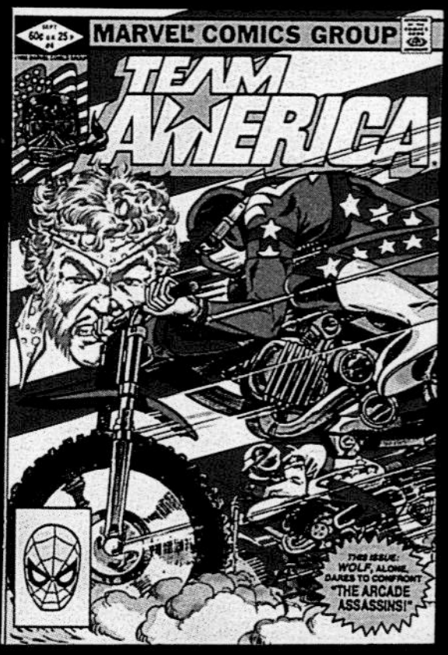
MARVEL COMICS GROUP
TEAM AMERICA

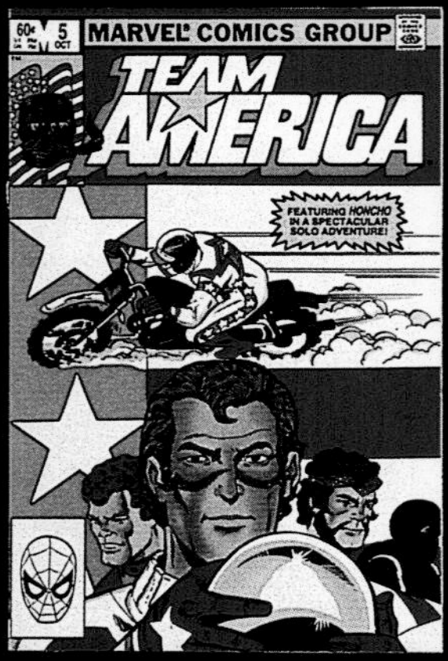
MARVEL COMICS GROUP
TEAM AMERICA

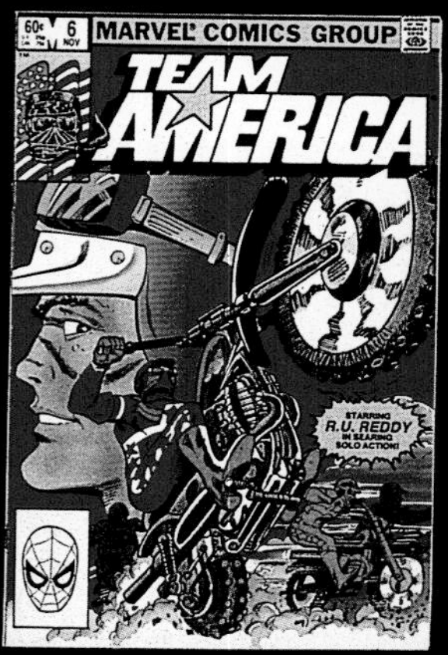
MARVEL COMICS GROUP
TEAM AMERICA
STARRING R.U. REDDY

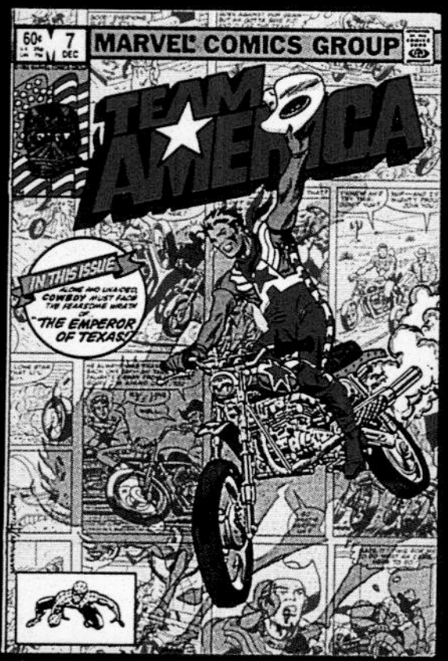
MARVEL COMICS GROUP
TEAM AMERICA
THE EMPEROR OF TEXAS!

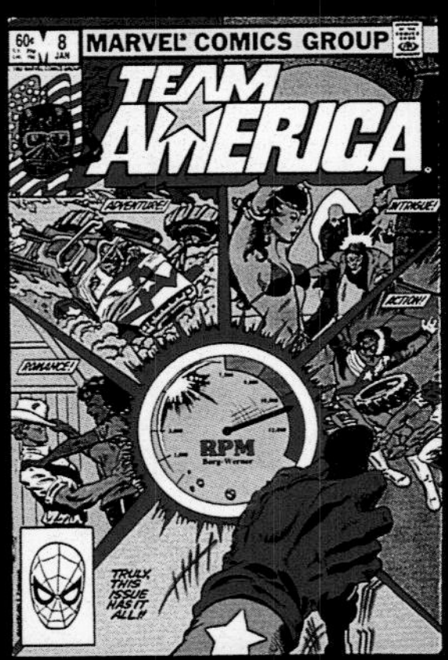
MARVEL COMICS GROUP
TEAM AMERICA
RPM

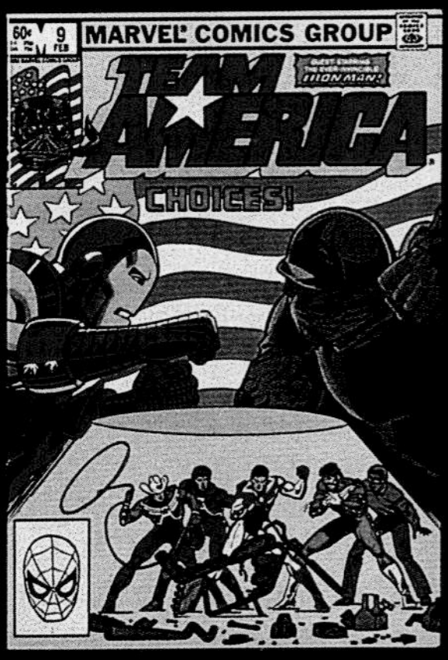
MARVEL COMICS GROUP
TEAM AMERICA
CHOICES!

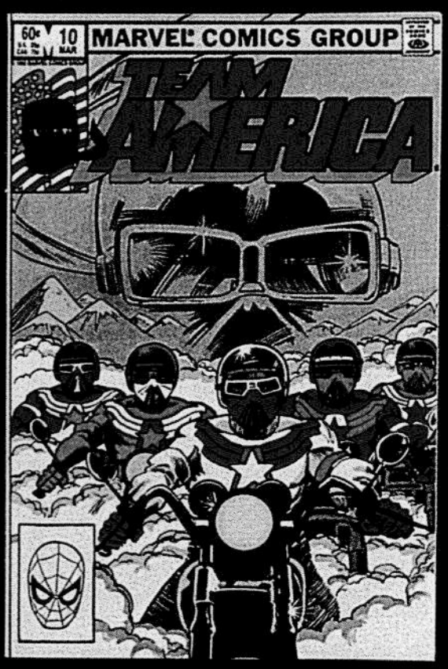
MARVEL COMICS GROUP
TEAM AMERICA

1923.3 The Thing (1-13)

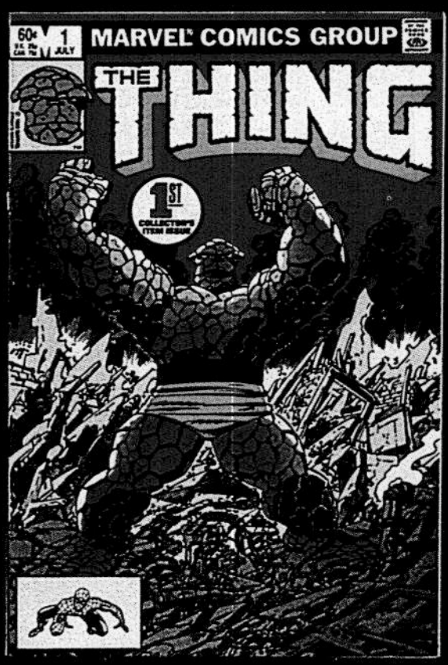
MARVEL COMICS GROUP
THE THING

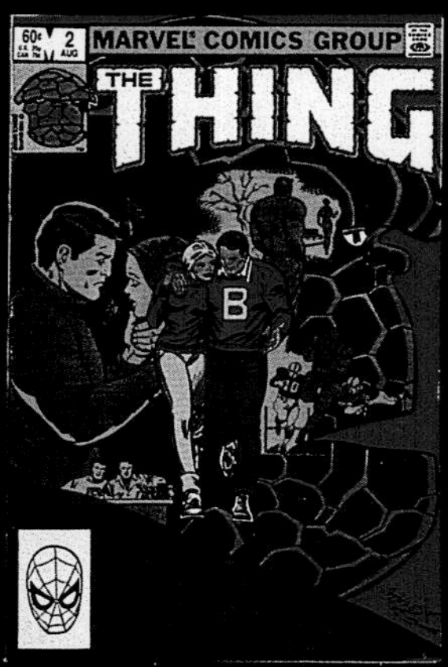
MARVEL COMICS GROUP
THE THING

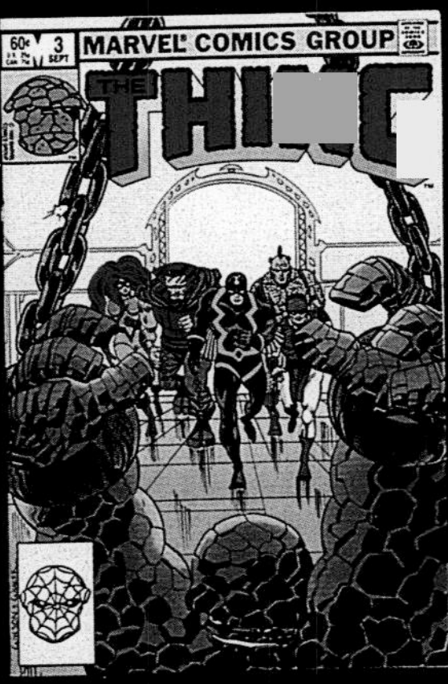
MARVEL COMICS GROUP

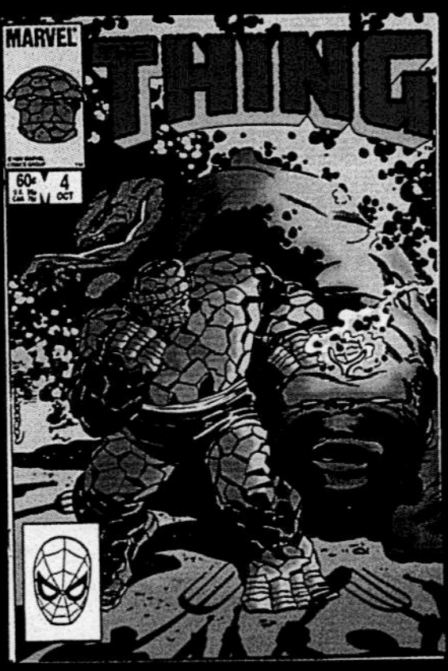
MARVEL
THING

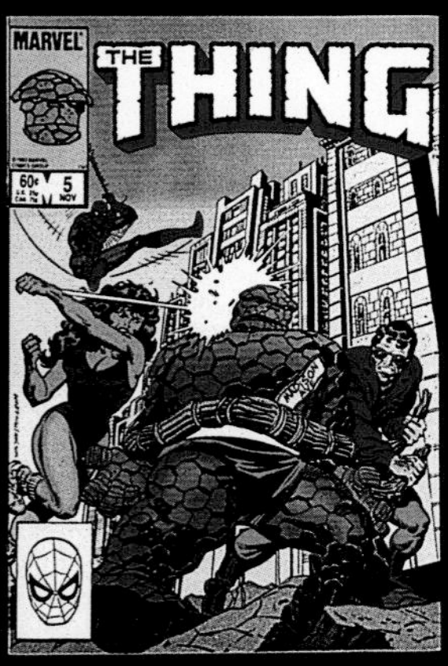
MARVEL
THE THING

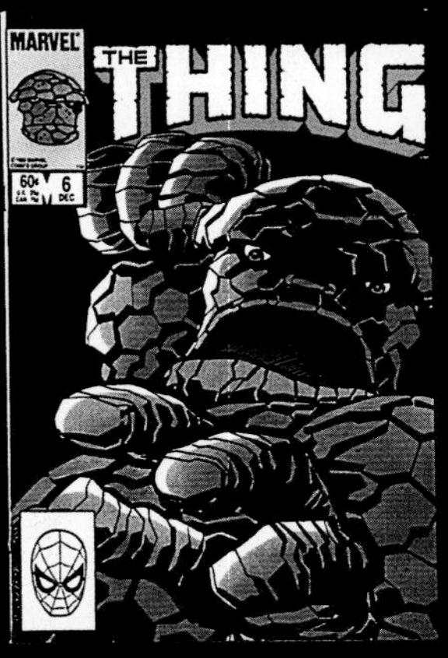
MARVEL
THE THING

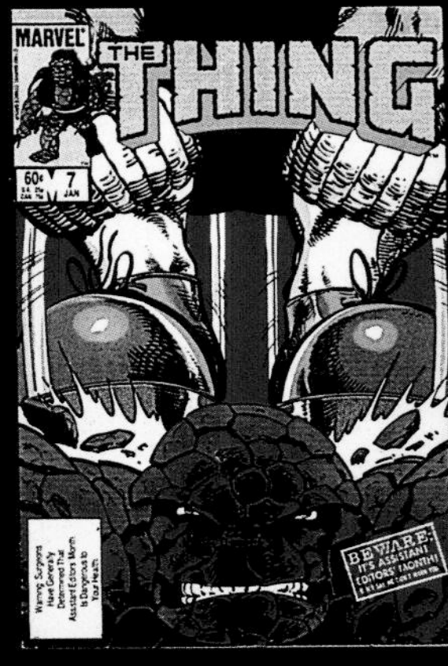
MARVEL
THE THING

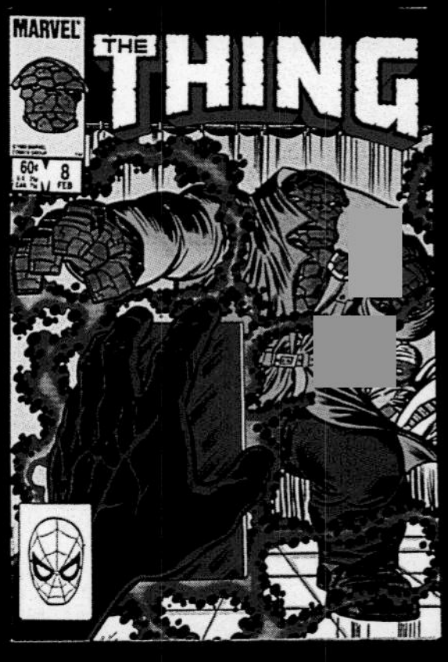
MARVEL
THE THING

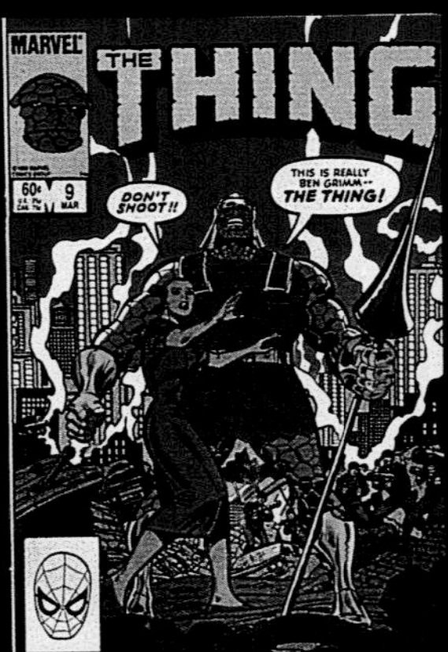
MARVEL
THE THING
DON'T SHOOT!!
THIS IS REALLY BEN GRIMM-- THE THING!

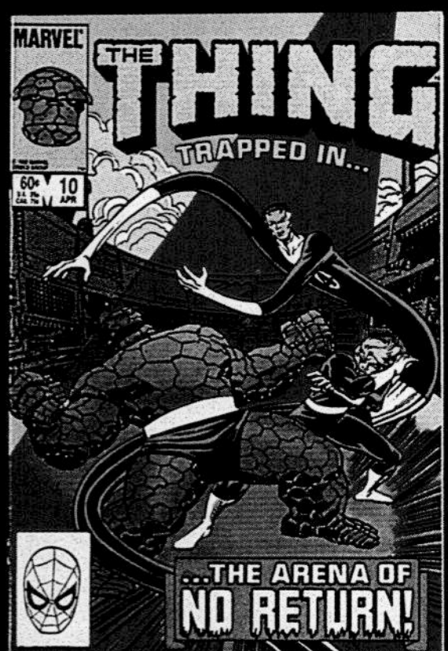
MARVEL
THE THING
TRAPPED IN...
...THE ARENA OF NO RETURN!

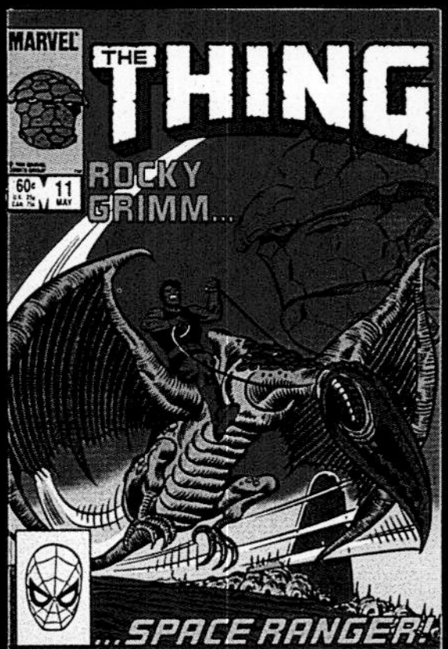
MARVEL
THE THING
ROCKY GRIMM...
...SPACE RANGER!

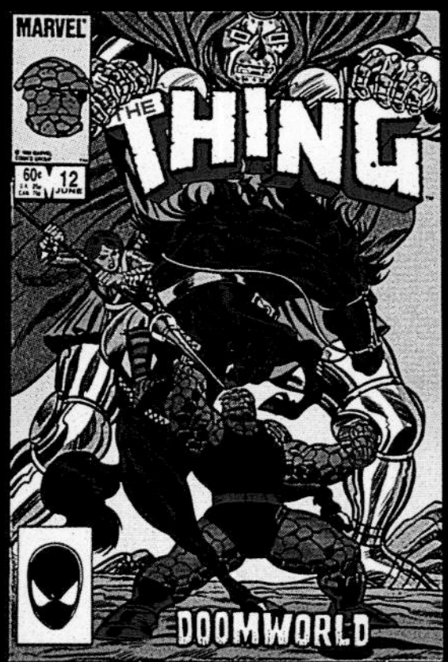
MARVEL
THE THING
DOOMWORLD

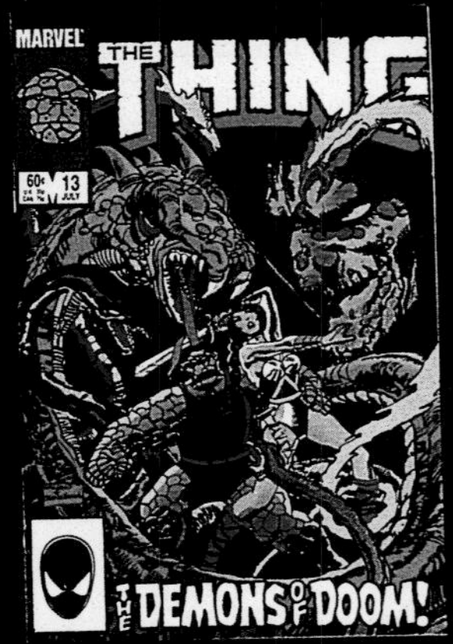
MARVEL
THE THING
THE DEMONS OF DOOM!

1923.3 The Thing (14-36)

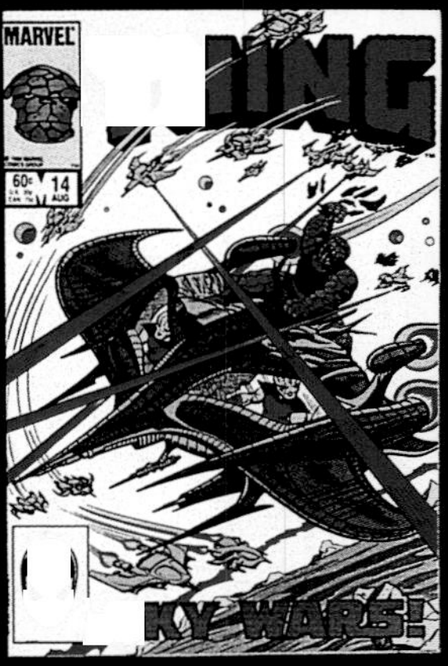
MARVEL
ING
60¢ 14 AUG
KY WARS!
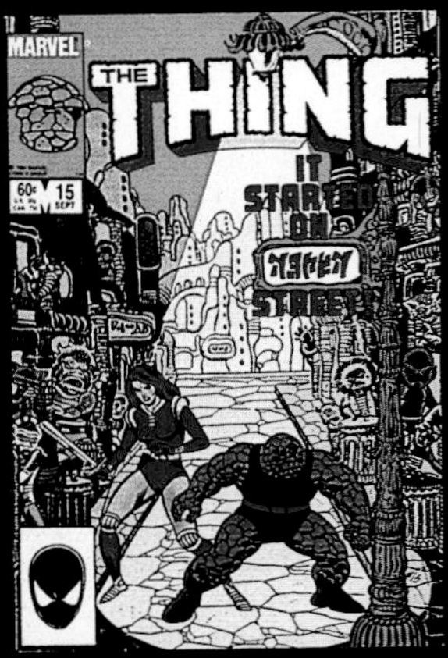
MARVEL
THE THING
60¢ 15 SEPT
IT STARTED ON
STREET!
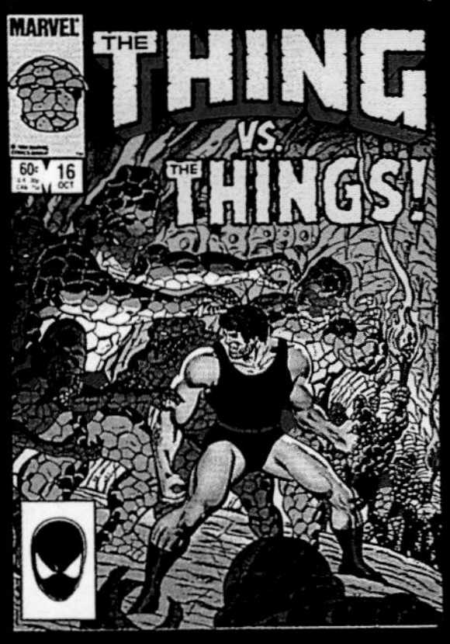
MARVEL
THE THING VS. THE THINGS!
60¢ 16 OCT
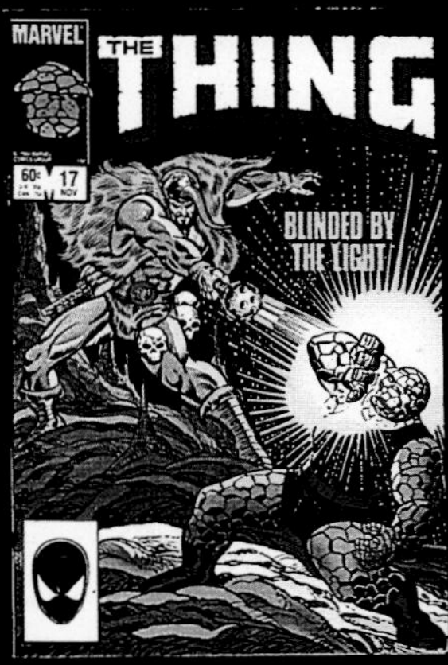
MARVEL
THE THING
60¢ 17 NOV
BLINDED BY THE LIGHT!
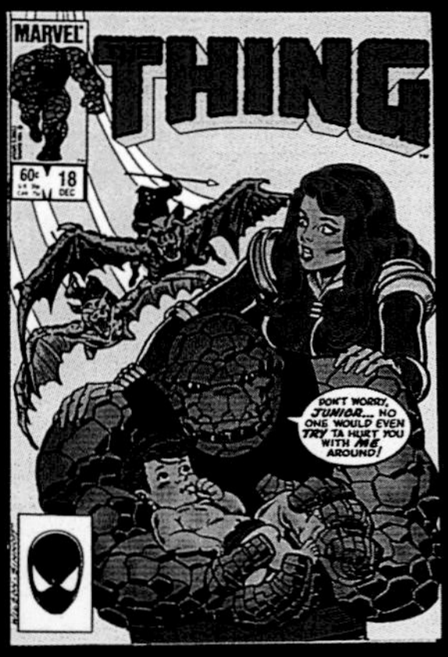
MARVEL
THING
60¢ 18 DEC
DON'T WORRY, JUNIOR... NO ONE WOULD EVEN TRY TA HURT YOU WITH ME AROUND!
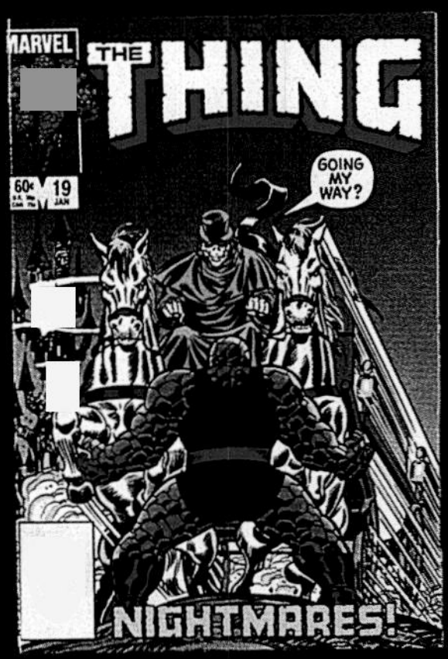
MARVEL
THE THING
60¢ 19 JAN
GOING MY WAY?
NIGHTMARES!
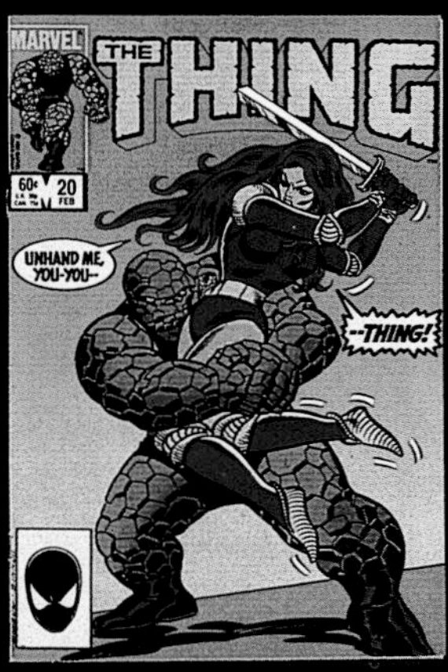
MARVEL
THE THING
60¢ 20 FEB
UNHAND ME, YOU-YOU--
--THING!
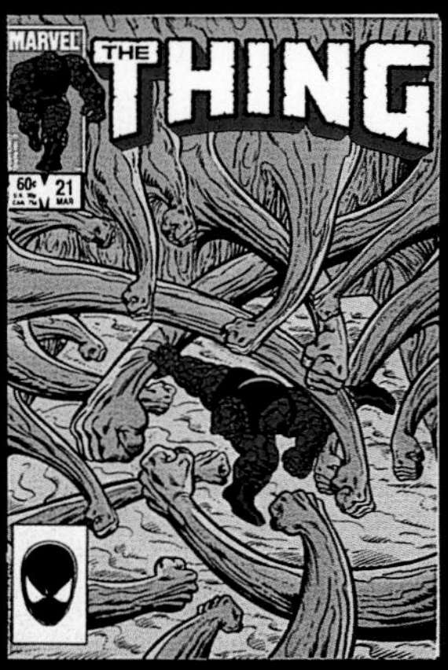
MARVEL
THE THING
60¢ 21 MAR
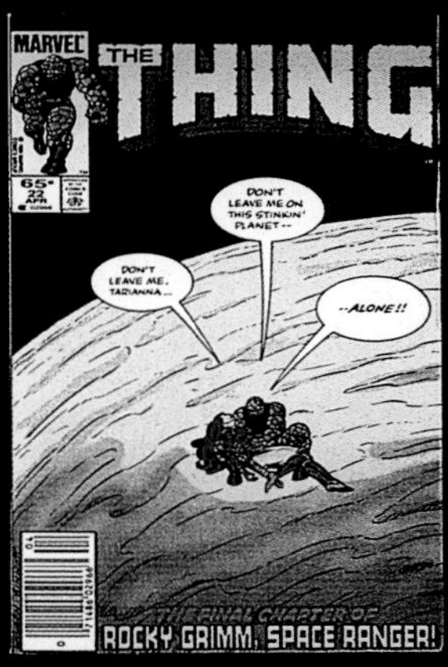
MARVEL
THE THING
65¢ 22 APR
DON'T LEAVE ME ON THIS STINKIN' PLANET--
DON'T LEAVE ME, TARIANNA--
--ALONE!!
ROCKY GRIMM, SPACE RANGER!
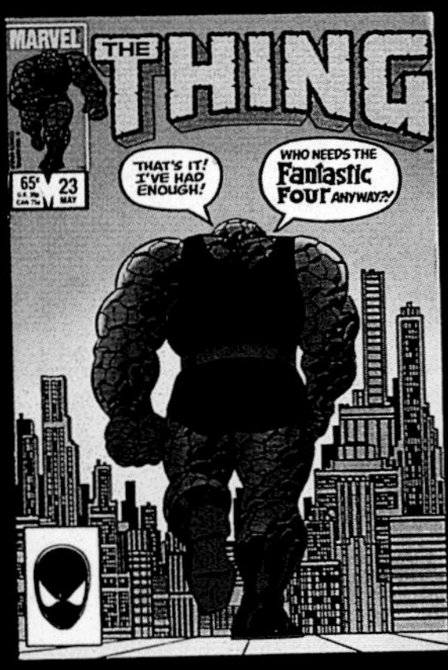
MARVEL
THE THING
65¢ 23 MAY
THAT'S IT! I'VE HAD ENOUGH!
WHO NEEDS THE Fantastic Four ANYWAY?!
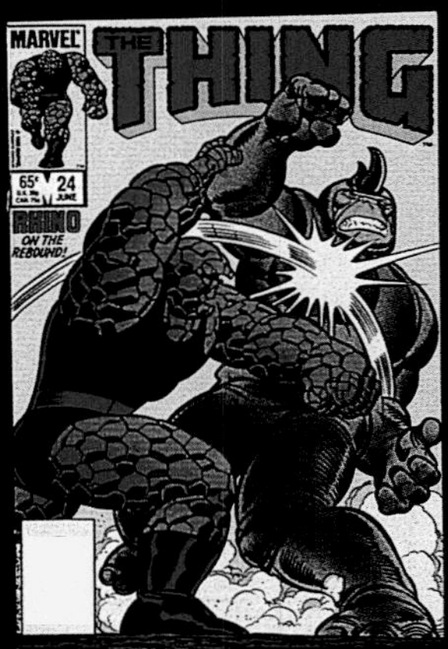
MARVEL
THE THING
65¢ 24 JUNE
RHINO ON THE REBOUND!
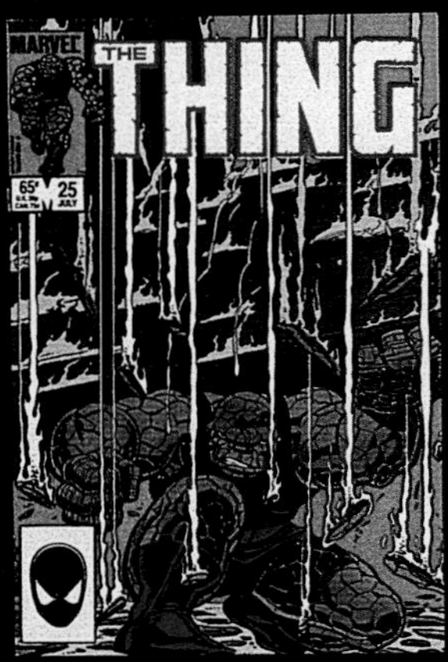
MARVEL
THE THING
65¢ 25 JULY
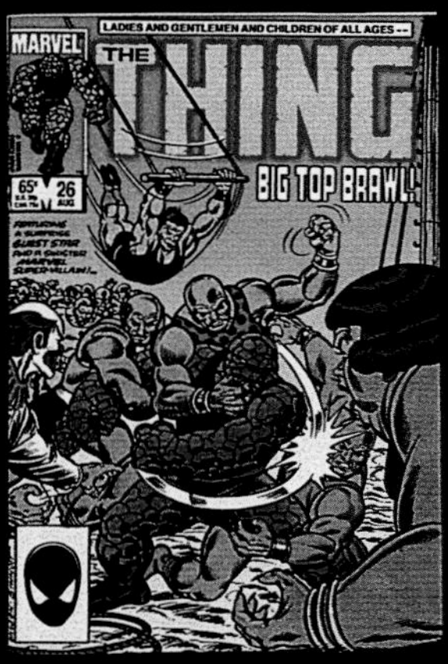
LADIES AND GENTLEMEN AND CHILDREN OF ALL AGES--
MARVEL
THE THING
65¢ 26 AUG
BIG TOP BRAWL!
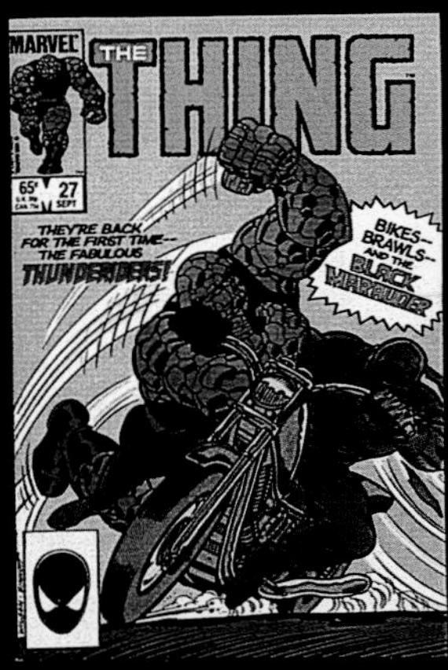
MARVEL
THE THING
65¢ 27 SEPT
THEY'RE BACK FOR THE FIRST TIME-- THE FABULOUS THUNDERIDERS!
BIKES-- BRAWLS-- AND THE BLACK WIDOW!
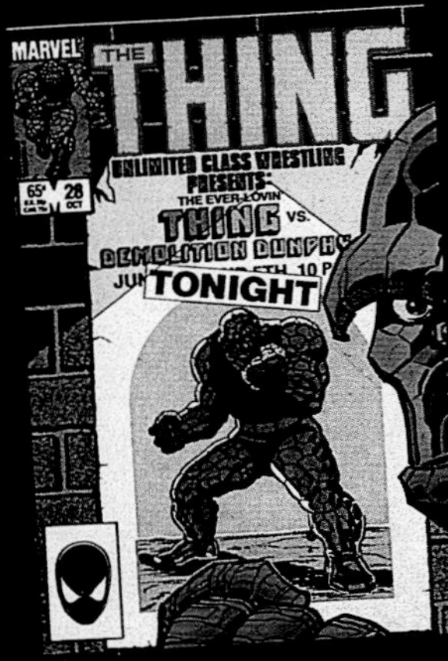
MARVEL
THE THING
65¢ 28 OCT
UNLIMITED CLASS WRESTLING PRESENTS--
THE EVER-LOVIN' THING VS.
TONIGHT
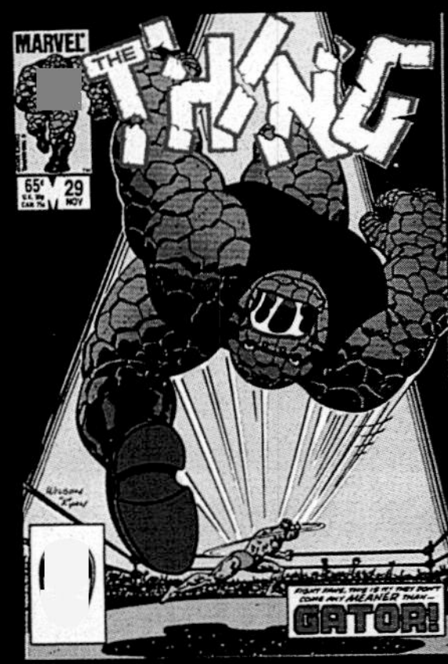
MARVEL
THE THING
65¢ 29 NOV
GATOR!
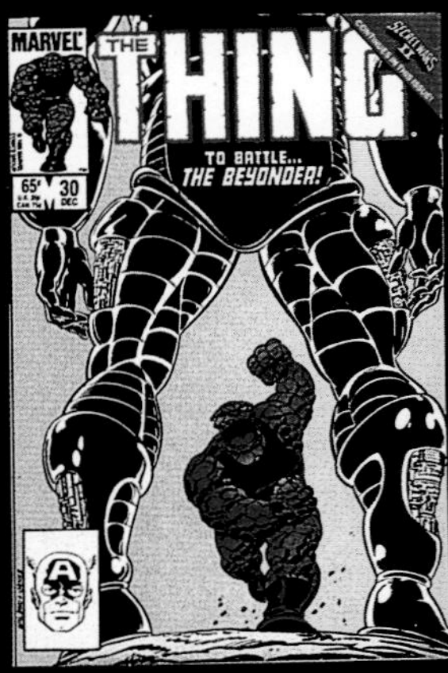
MARVEL
THE THING
65¢ 30 DEC
TO BATTLE... THE BEYONDER!
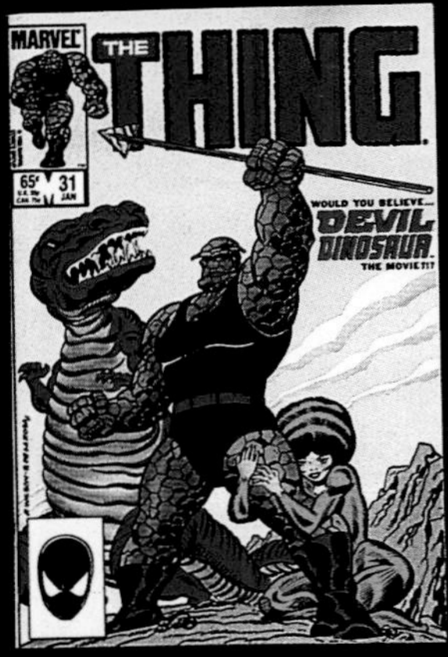
MARVEL
THE THING
65¢ 31 JAN
WOULD YOU BELIEVE... DEVIL DINOSAUR THE MOVIE!?!
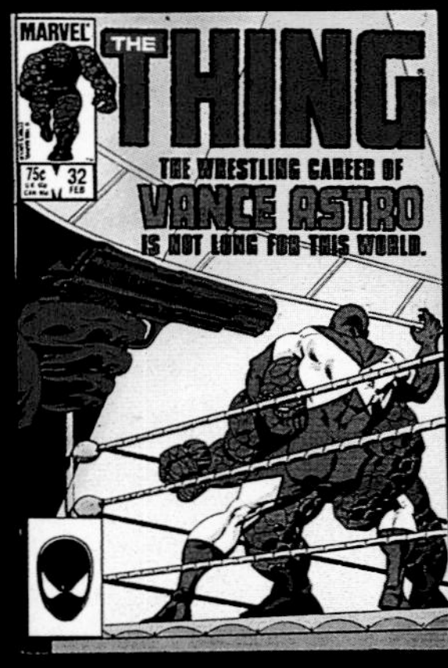
MARVEL
THE THING
75¢ 32 FEB
THE WRESTLING CAREER OF VANCE ASTRO IS NOT LONG FOR THIS WORLD.
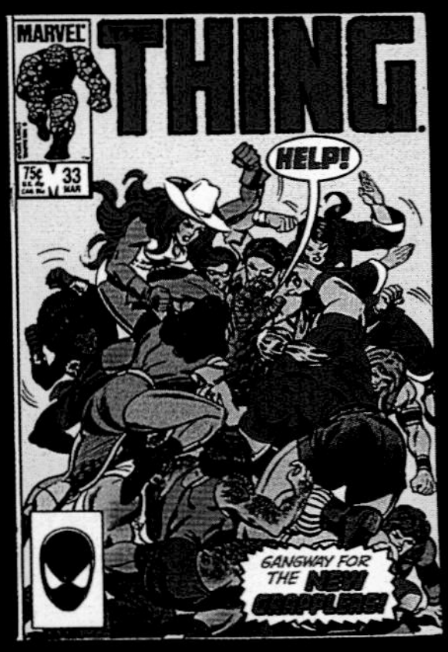
MARVEL
THING
75¢ 33 MAR
HELP!
GANGWAY FOR THE NEW GRAPPLERS!
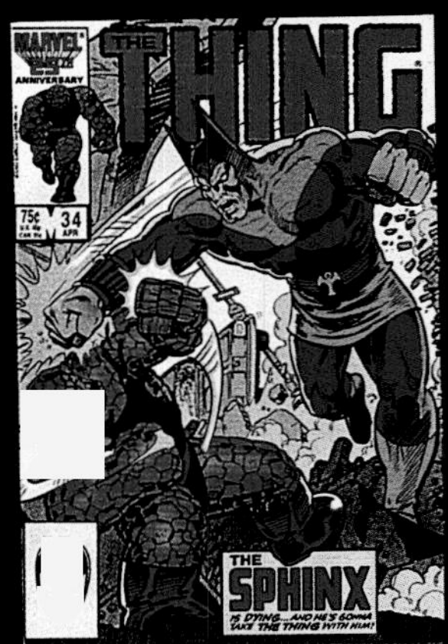
MARVEL
THING
75¢ 34 APR
THE SPHINX
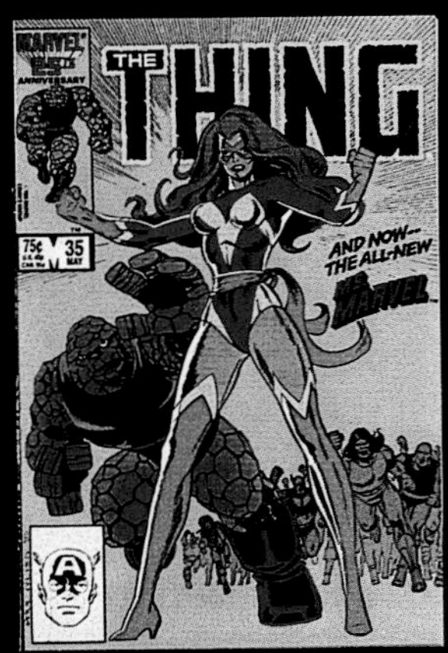
MARVEL
THE THING
75¢ 35 MAY
AND NOW-- THE ALL-NEW
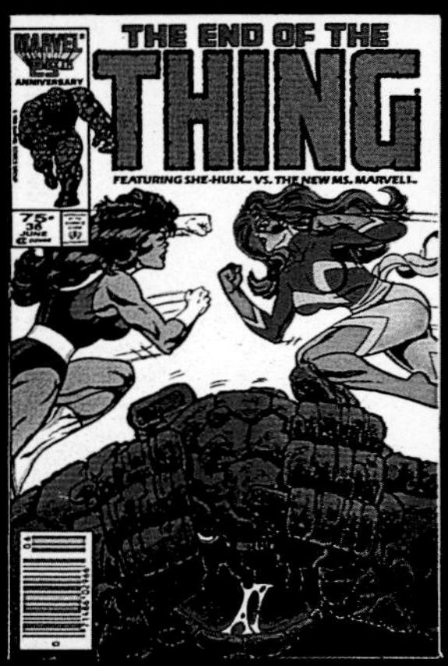
THE END OF THE THING
FEATURING SHE-HULK... VS. THE NEW MS. MARVEL!

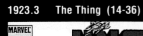

The Thing (1-36 1923.3

Ref. No.	Date	RVI	Artist/Info.
1923.3-1	Jul. 1983	1	Wilson/Sinnott-a
1923.3-2	Aug.	1	Wilson/Sinnot-c/a
1923.3-3	Sept.	1	Wilson/Wiacek-c, Wilson/Barta-a
1923.3-4	Oct.	1	Anderson-c, Wilson/Barta-a
1923.3-5	Nov.	1	Wilson/Milgrom-c, Wilson/Barta-a
1923.3-6	Dec.	1	Wilson/Anderson-c, Wilson/Barta-a
1923.3-7	Jan. 1984	1	Wilson/Barta-a
1923.3-8	Feb.	1	" "
1923.3-9	Mar.	1	Wilson/Sinnott-a
1923.3-10	**Apr.**	**1**	**Wilson/Barta-a**
1923.3-11	May	1	Wilson/Sinnott-a
1923.3-12	Jun.	1	Wilson/Sinnott-c/a
1923.3-13	Jul.	1	Wilson-c/a, Sinnott-a
1923.3-14	Aug.	1	Wilson/Mushynsky-c, Wilson/Sinnott-a
1923.3-15	Sept.	1	Wilson/Sinnott-a
1923.3-16	Oct.	1	(The Thing vs. Things)
1923.3-17	Nov.	1	
1923.3-18	Dec.	1	
1923.3-19	Jan. 1985	1	
1923.3-20	**Feb.**	**1**	
1923.3-21 to 36	Jun. 1986	1	

Tex Dawson, Gunslinger (1) 812.5

812.5-1	Jan. 1973	1	Steranko-c, Williamson-a

1955.3 Tomb of Dracula (1-16)

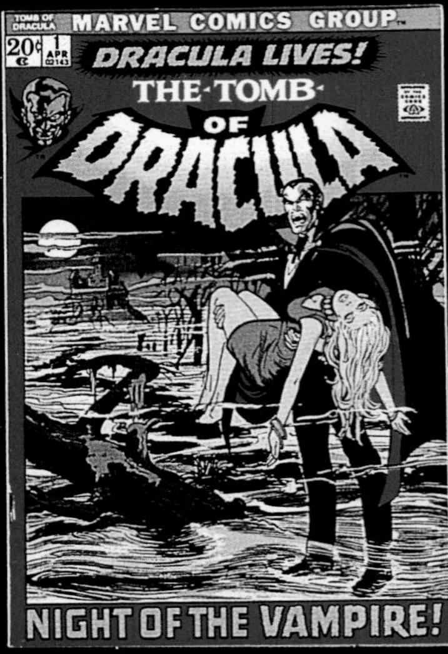
MARVEL COMICS GROUP
20¢ 1 APR
DRACULA LIVES!
THE TOMB OF DRACULA
NIGHT OF THE VAMPIRE!

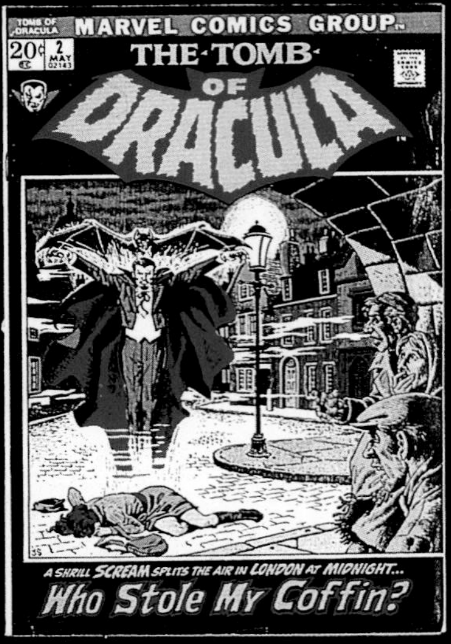
MARVEL COMICS GROUP
20¢ 2 MAY
THE TOMB OF DRACULA
A SHRILL SCREAM SPLITS THE AIR IN LONDON AT MIDNIGHT...
Who Stole My Coffin?

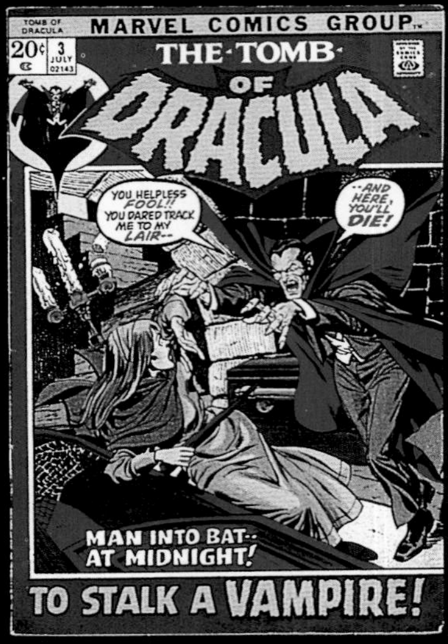
MARVEL COMICS GROUP
20¢ 3 JULY
THE TOMB OF DRACULA
YOU HELPLESS FOOL!! YOU DARED TRACK ME TO MY LAIR--
--AND HERE YOU'LL DIE!
MAN INTO BAT-- AT MIDNIGHT!
TO STALK A VAMPIRE!

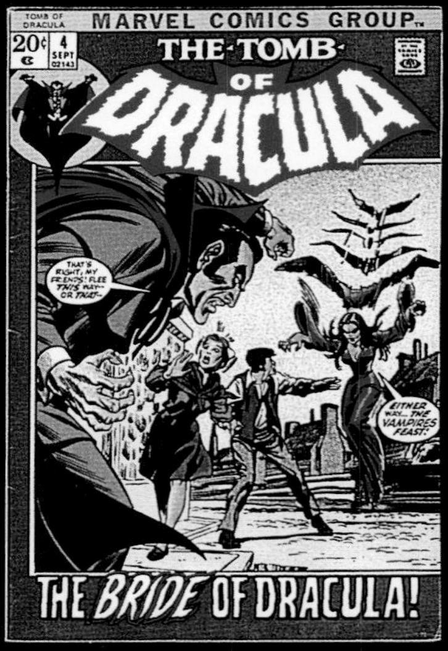
MARVEL COMICS GROUP
20¢ 4 SEPT
THE TOMB OF DRACULA
THE BRIDE OF DRACULA!

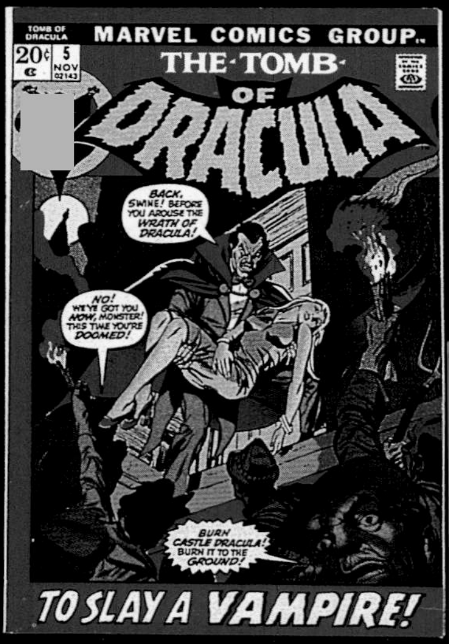
MARVEL COMICS GROUP
20¢ 5 NOV
THE TOMB OF DRACULA
BURN CASTLE DRACULA! BURN IT TO THE GROUND!
TO SLAY A VAMPIRE!

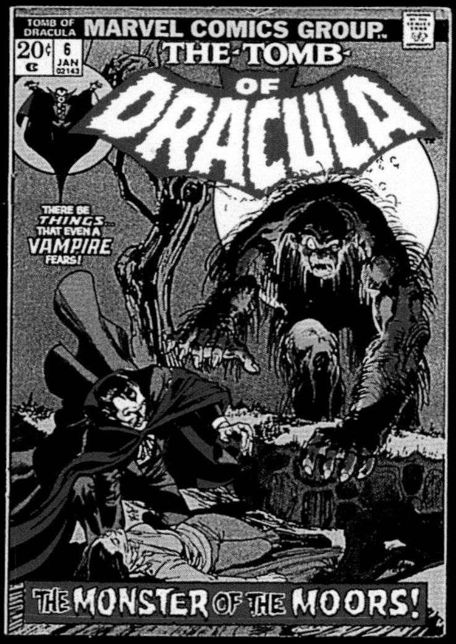
MARVEL COMICS GROUP
20¢ 6 JAN
THE TOMB OF DRACULA
THERE BE THINGS-- THAT EVEN A VAMPIRE FEARS!
THE MONSTER OF THE MOORS!

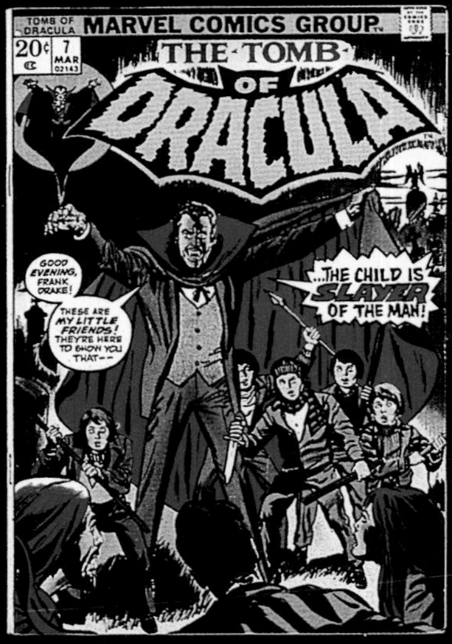
MARVEL COMICS GROUP
20¢ 7 MAR
THE TOMB OF DRACULA
GOOD EVENING, FRANK DRAKE!
...THE CHILD IS SLAYER OF THE MAN!

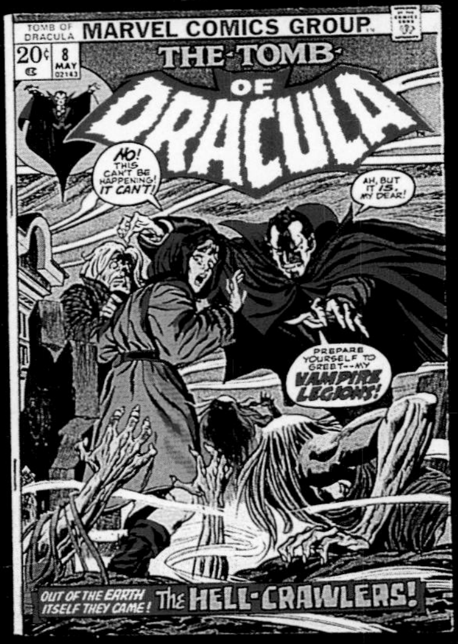
MARVEL COMICS GROUP
20¢ 8 MAY
THE TOMB OF DRACULA
OUT OF THE EARTH ITSELF THEY CAME! The HELL-CRAWLERS!

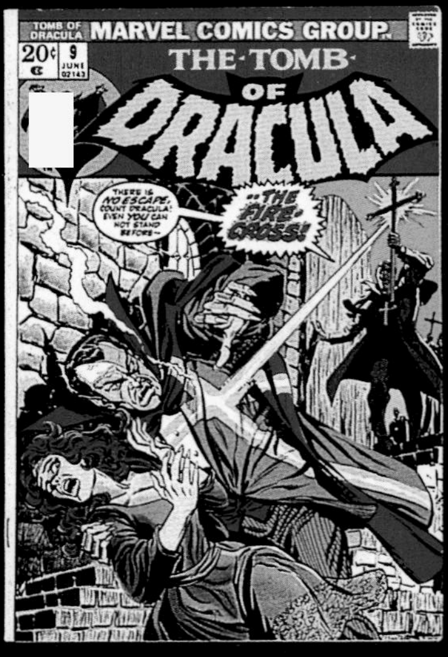
MARVEL COMICS GROUP
20¢ 9 JUNE
THE TOMB OF DRACULA

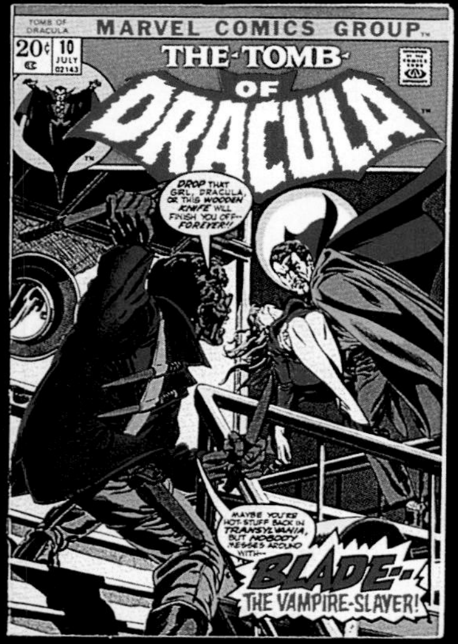
MARVEL COMICS GROUP
20¢ 10 JULY
THE TOMB OF DRACULA
BLADE-- THE VAMPIRE-SLAYER!

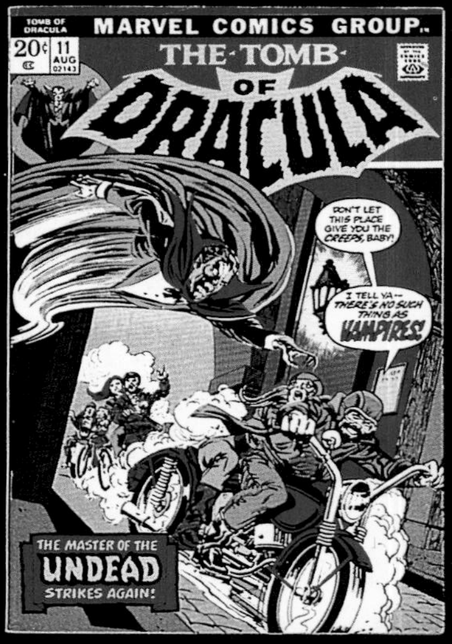
MARVEL COMICS GROUP
20¢ 11 AUG
THE TOMB OF DRACULA
THE MASTER OF THE UNDEAD STRIKES AGAIN!

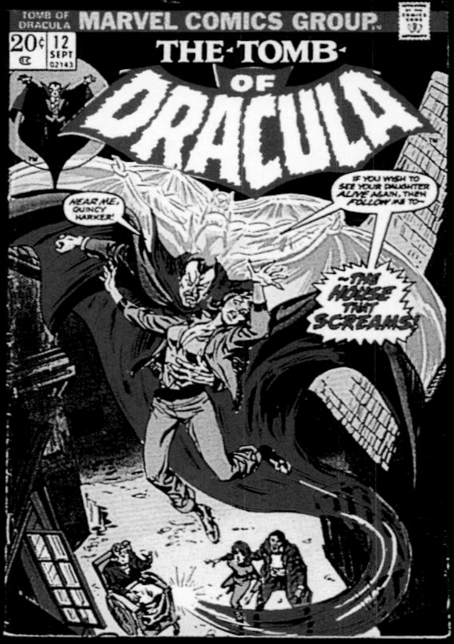
MARVEL COMICS GROUP
20¢ 12 SEPT
THE TOMB OF DRACULA

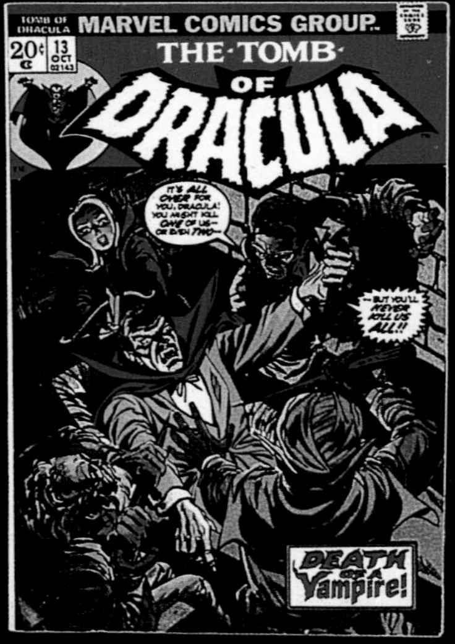
MARVEL COMICS GROUP
20¢ 13 OCT
THE TOMB OF DRACULA
DEATH of a Vampire!

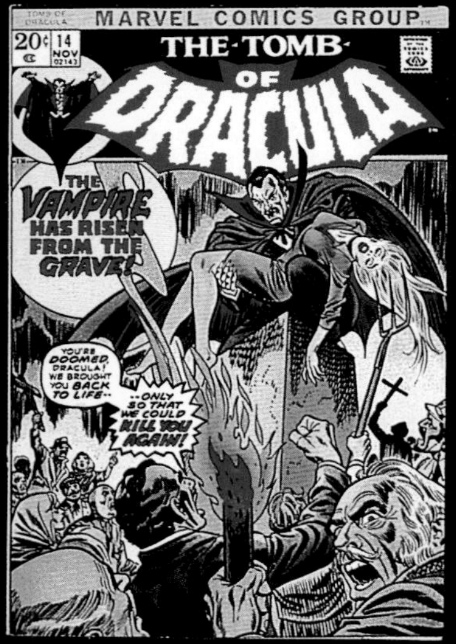
MARVEL COMICS GROUP
20¢ 14 NOV
THE TOMB OF DRACULA
THE VAMPIRE HAS RISEN FROM THE GRAVE!

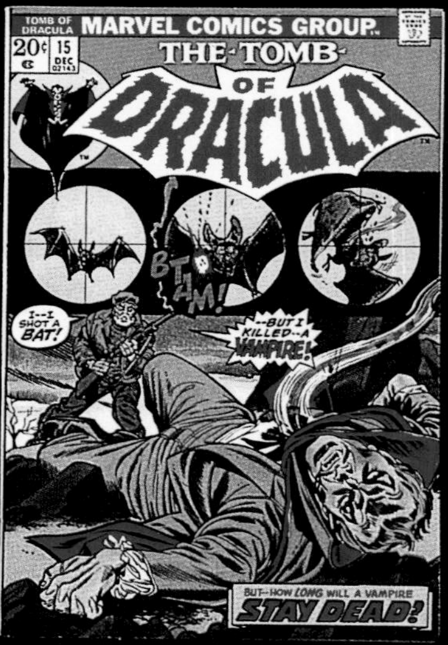
MARVEL COMICS GROUP
20¢ 15 DEC
THE TOMB OF DRACULA
BUT-- HOW LONG WILL A VAMPIRE STAY DEAD?

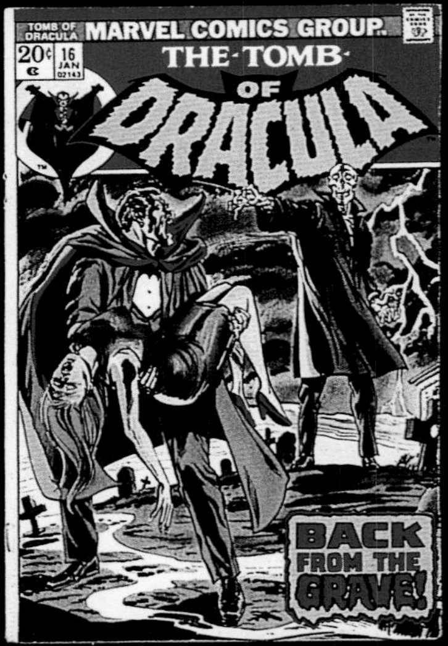
MARVEL COMICS GROUP
20¢ 16 JAN
THE TOMB OF DRACULA
BACK FROM THE GRAVE!

MARVEL COMICS GROUP
THE TOMB OF DRACULA
A VAMPIRE RIDES THIS TRAIN
MARVEL COMICS GROUP
THE TOMB OF DRACULA
MAN BY DAY-- WEREWOLF BY NIGHT!
TWO OF MARVEL'S MOST MACABRE SUPER-STARS IN A BATTLE OF THE MONSTERS!
MARVEL COMICS GROUP
THE TOMB OF DRACULA
SNOWBOUND in HELL!
MARVEL COMICS GROUP
THE TOMB OF DRACULA
WOODEN BULLETS!
MAN-HUNT FOR A VAMPIRE!
MARVEL COMICS GROUP
THE TOMB OF DRACULA
VAMPIRE BATTLES VAMPIRE
MARVEL COMICS GROUP
THE TOMB OF DRACULA
GORNA-- LORD OF THE LIVING LIGHTNING!
MARVEL COMICS GROUP
THE TOMB OF DRACULA
EXORCISM
SHADOW OVER HAUNTED CASTLE!
MARVEL COMICS GROUP
THE TOMB OF DRACULA
MARVEL COMICS GROUP
THE TOMB OF DRACULA
THEY, TOO, WILL BE VAMPIRES!
BLOOD-STALKERS OF COUNT DRACULA!
MARVEL COMICS GROUP
THE TOMB OF DRACULA
A VAMPIRE STALKS THE NIGHT!
SHOCK-ENDING
MARVEL COMICS GROUP
THE TOMB OF DRACULA
DEATH!
CITY IN FLAMES-- BENEATH THE HAND OF A VAMPIRE!
MARVEL COMICS GROUP
THE TOMB OF DRACULA
FIVE CAME TO KILL A VAMPIRE--
MARVEL COMICS GROUP
THE TOMB OF DRACULA
VAMPIRE GOES MAD!
MARVEL COMICS GROUP
THE TOMB OF DRACULA
ASSAULT ON A VAMPIRE!
BLADE!
MARVEL COMICS GROUP
THE TOMB OF DRACULA
CHILD OF BLOOD!
MARVEL COMICS GROUP
THE TOMB OF DRACULA
BATTLEGROUND OF BLOOD!
MARVEL COMICS GROUP
THE TOMB OF DRACULA
BLOOD ON MY HANDS!
MARVEL COMICS GROUP
THE TOMB OF DRACULA
BLOODY SHOWDOWN!
FULL-MOON THRILLER!
MARVEL COMICS GROUP
THE TOMB OF DRACULA
BROTHER VOODOO!
MARVEL COMICS GROUP
THE TOMB OF DRACULA
MARVEL COMICS GROUP
THE TOMB OF DRACULA
THE VAMPIRE WALKS AMONG US!
MARVEL COMICS GROUP
THE TOMB OF DRACULA
FEAR!
BLOODLUST FOR A DYING VAMPIRE!
MARVEL COMICS GROUP
THE TOMB OF DRACULA
LORD OF VAMPIRES
MARVEL COMICS GROUP
THE TOMB OF DRACULA
LORD OF VAMPIRES!
DRACULA IS TRULY DEAD!
THE TRIUMPH OF DR. SUN!
MARVEL COMICS GROUP
THE TOMB OF DRACULA
LORD OF VAMPIRES!
A HALLOWEEN HOLOCAUST!
DRACULA LIVES AGAIN!
BLADE
THE NUMBER 1 FEAR MAGAZINE!

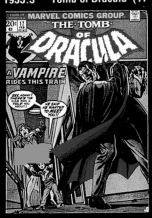

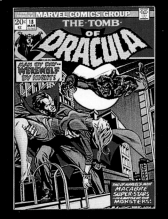

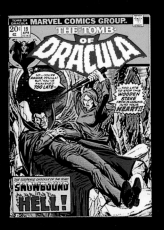

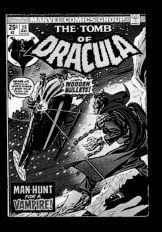

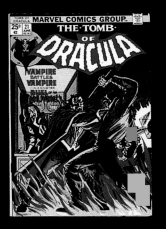

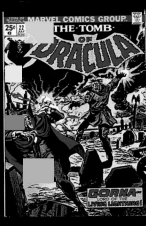

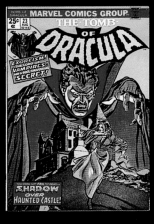

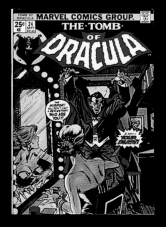

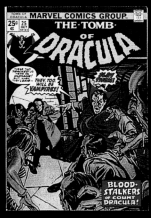

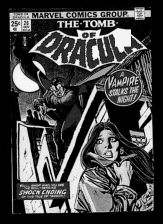

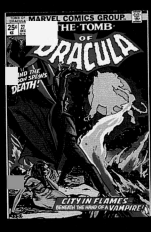

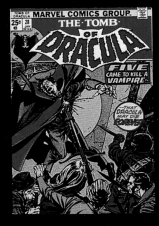

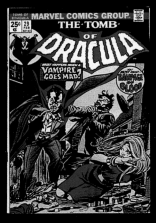

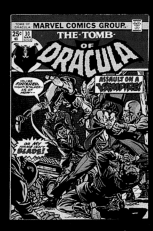

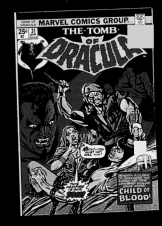

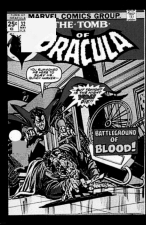

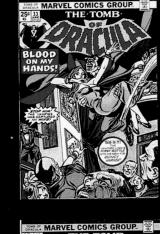

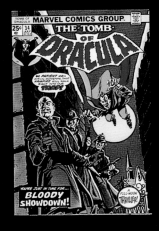

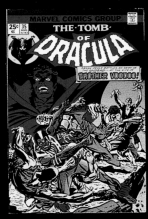

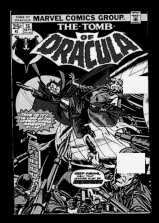

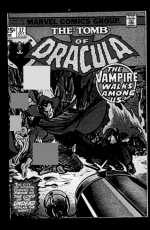

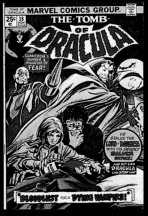

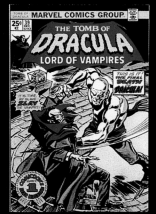

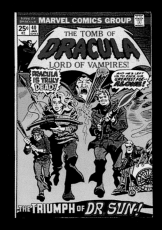

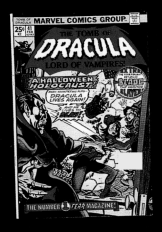

1955.3 Tomb of Dracula (42-70)

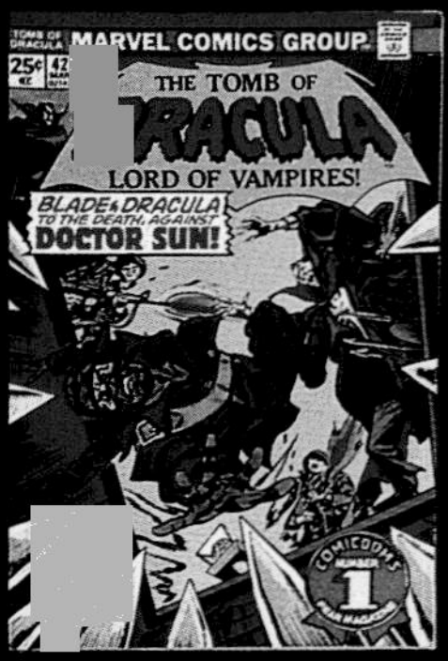
MARVEL COMICS GROUP
THE TOMB OF
DRACULA
LORD OF VAMPIRES!
BLADE & DRACULA
DOCTOR SUN!
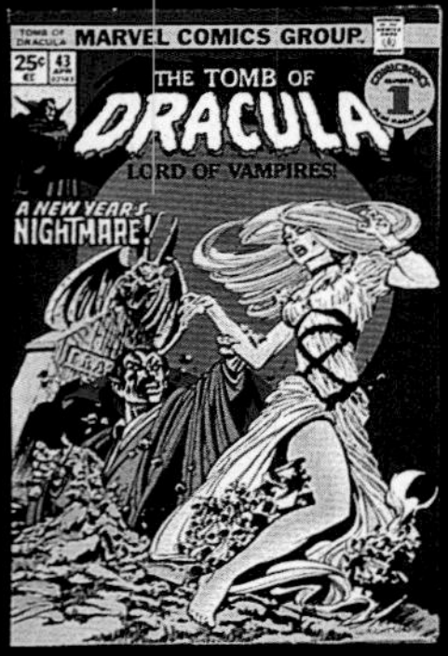
MARVEL COMICS GROUP
THE TOMB OF
DRACULA
LORD OF VAMPIRES!
A NEW YEAR'S NIGHTMARE!
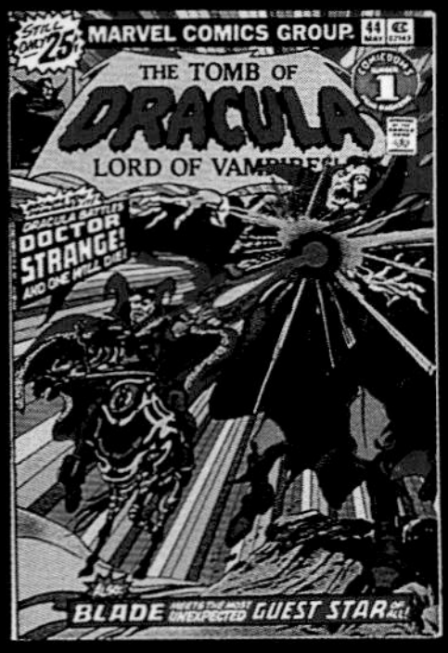
MARVEL COMICS GROUP
THE TOMB OF
DRACULA
LORD OF VAMPIRES!
DOCTOR STRANGE!
BLADE
GUEST STAR
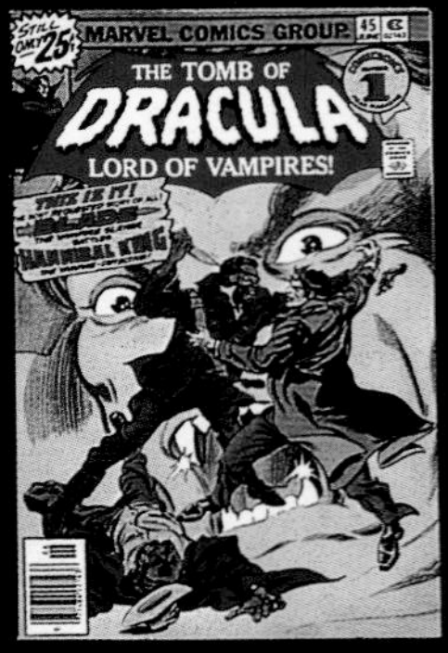
MARVEL COMICS GROUP
THE TOMB OF
DRACULA
LORD OF VAMPIRES!
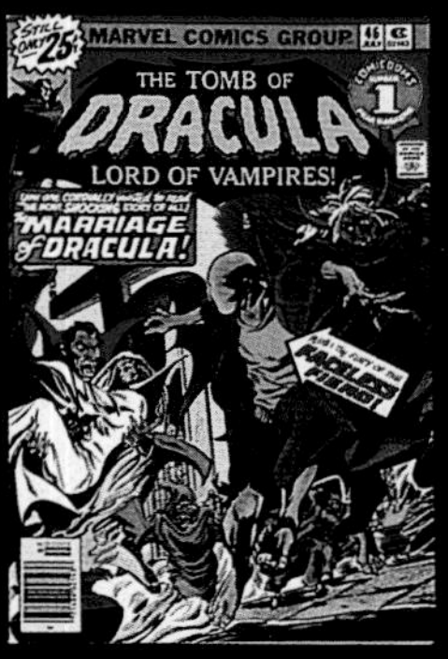
MARVEL COMICS GROUP
THE TOMB OF
DRACULA
LORD OF VAMPIRES!
MARRIAGE OF DRACULA!
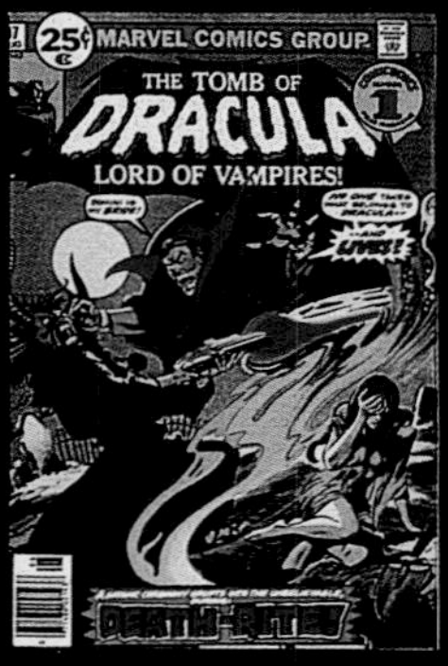
MARVEL COMICS GROUP
THE TOMB OF
DRACULA
LORD OF VAMPIRES!
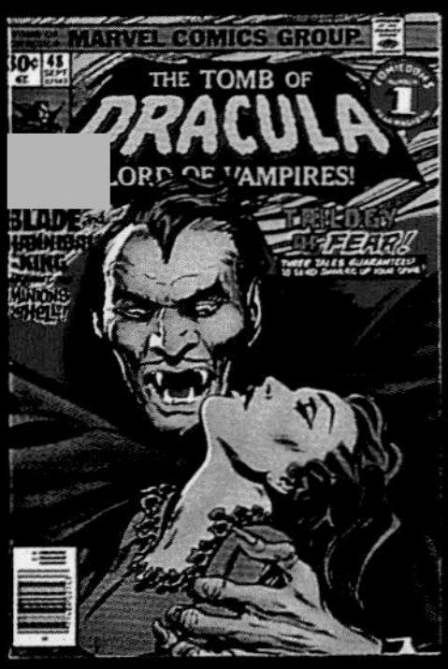
MARVEL COMICS GROUP
THE TOMB OF
DRACULA
LORD OF VAMPIRES!
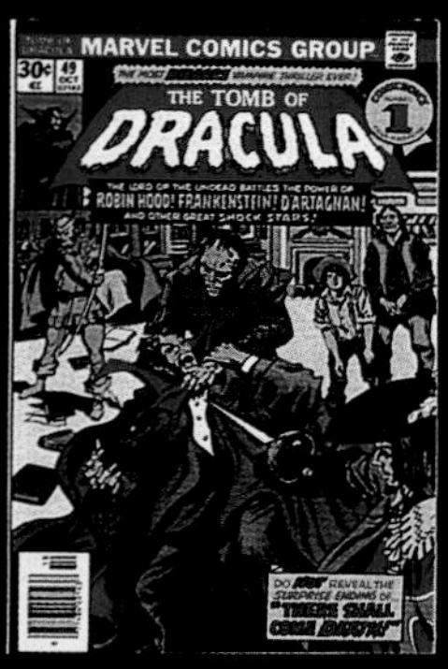
MARVEL COMICS GROUP
THE TOMB OF
DRACULA
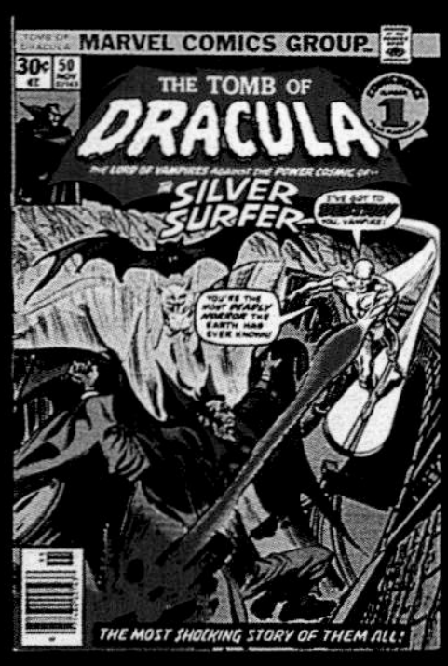
MARVEL COMICS GROUP
THE TOMB OF
DRACULA
SILVER SURFER
THE MOST SHOCKING STORY OF THEM ALL!
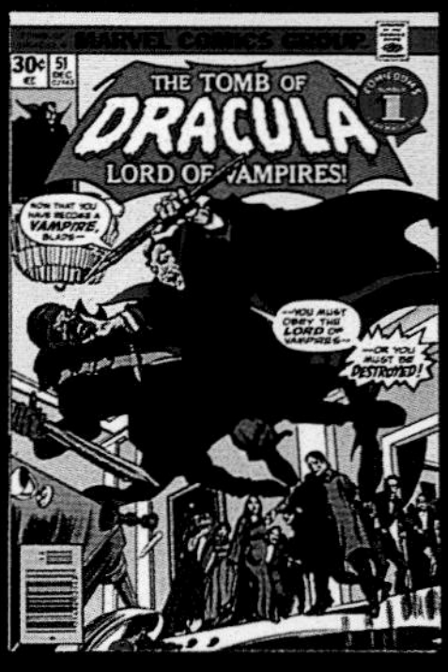
MARVEL COMICS GROUP
THE TOMB OF
DRACULA
LORD OF VAMPIRES!
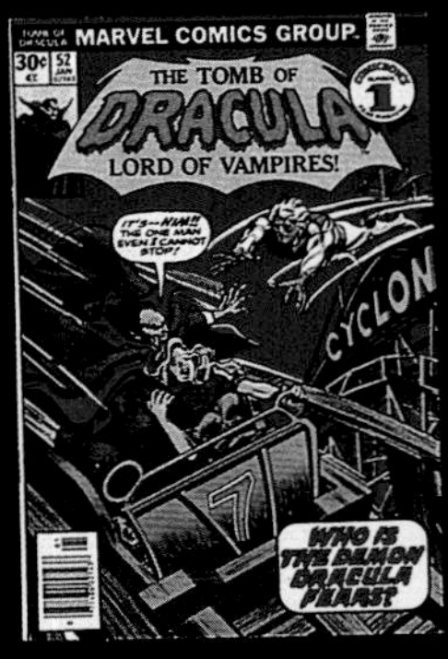
MARVEL COMICS GROUP
THE TOMB OF
DRACULA
LORD OF VAMPIRES!
CYCLON
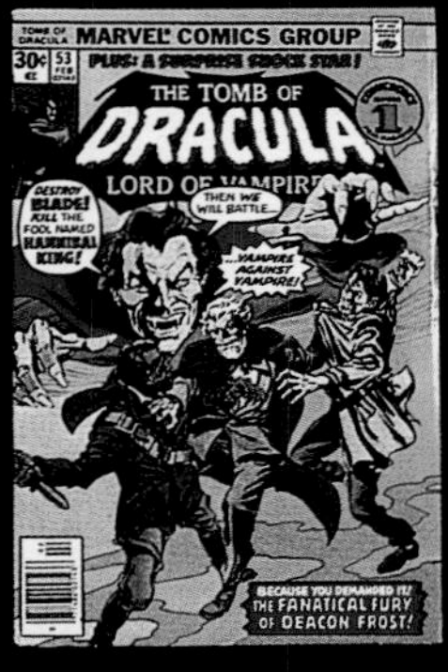
MARVEL COMICS GROUP
THE TOMB OF
DRACULA
LORD OF VAMPIRES!
THE FANATICAL FURY OF DEACON FROST!
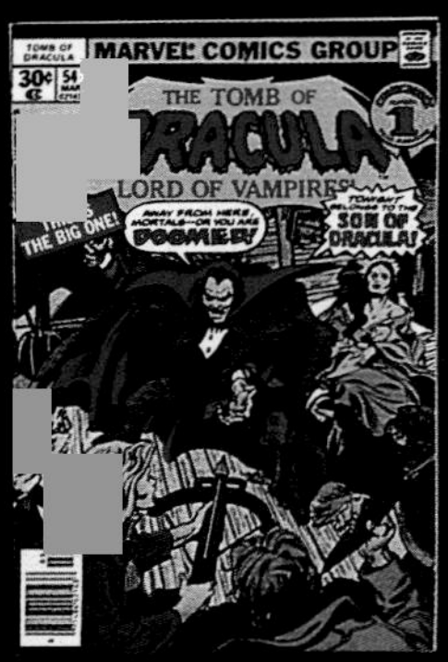
MARVEL COMICS GROUP
THE TOMB OF
DRACULA
LORD OF VAMPIRES!
THE BIG ONE!
SON OF DRACULA!
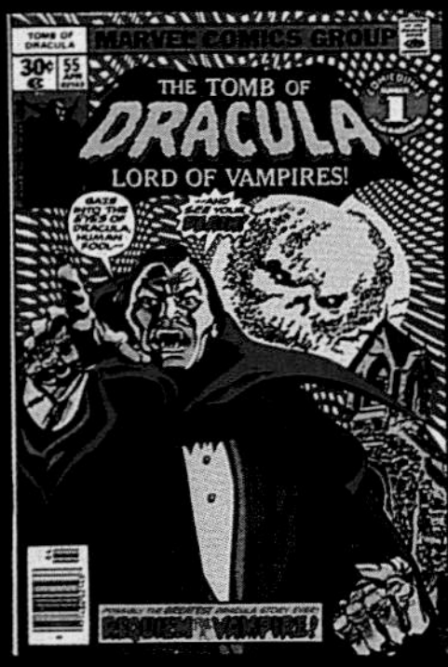
MARVEL COMICS GROUP
THE TOMB OF
DRACULA
LORD OF VAMPIRES!
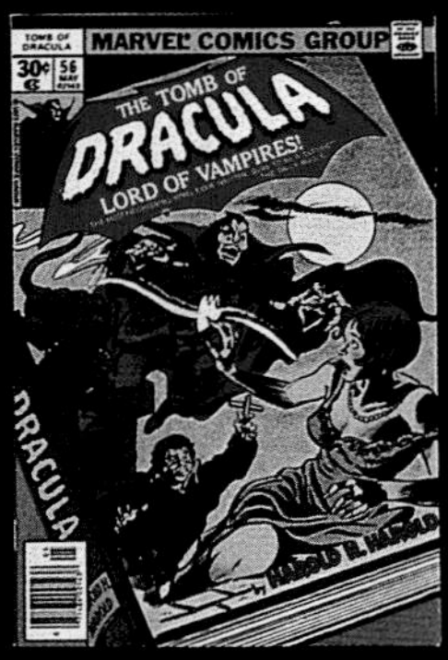
MARVEL COMICS GROUP
THE TOMB OF
DRACULA
LORD OF VAMPIRES!
DRACULA
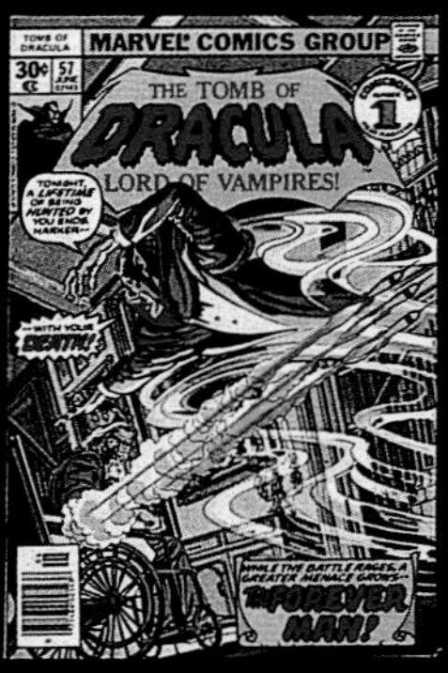
MARVEL COMICS GROUP
THE TOMB OF
DRACULA
LORD OF VAMPIRES!
THE FOREVER MAN!
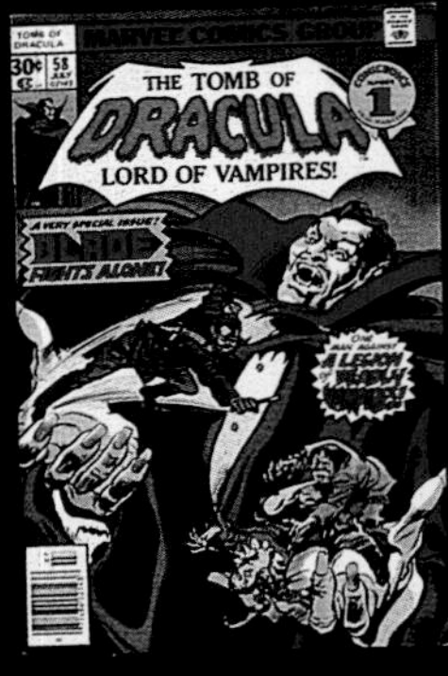
MARVEL COMICS GROUP
THE TOMB OF
DRACULA
LORD OF VAMPIRES!
BLADE
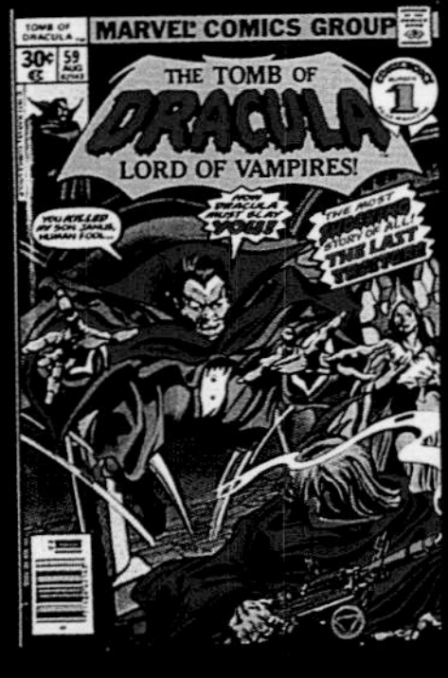
MARVEL COMICS GROUP
THE TOMB OF
DRACULA
LORD OF VAMPIRES!
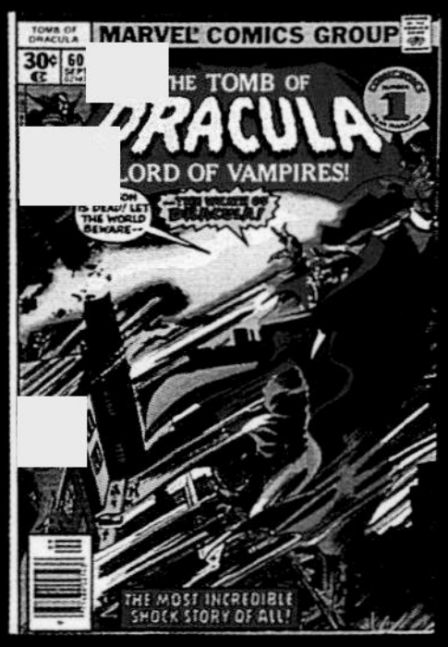
MARVEL COMICS GROUP
THE TOMB OF
DRACULA
LORD OF VAMPIRES!
THE MOST INCREDIBLE SHOCK STORY OF ALL!
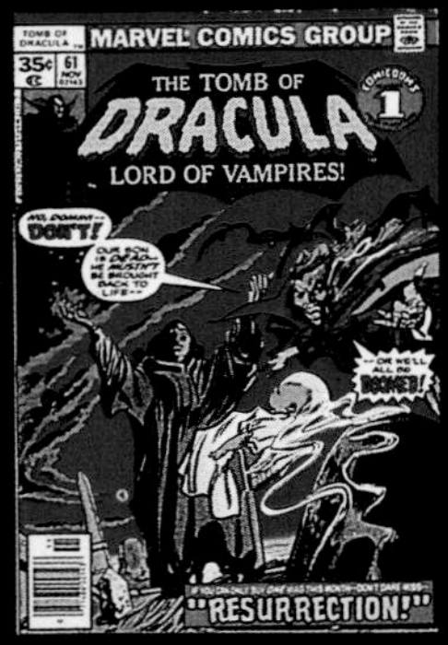
MARVEL COMICS GROUP
THE TOMB OF
DRACULA
LORD OF VAMPIRES!
RESURRECTION!
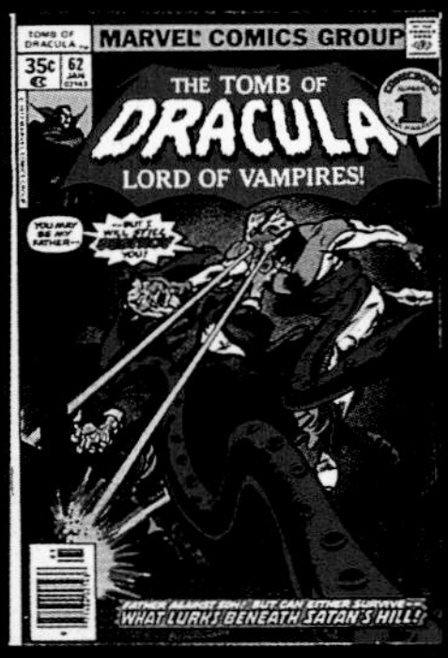
MARVEL COMICS GROUP
THE TOMB OF
DRACULA
LORD OF VAMPIRES!
WHAT LURKS BENEATH SATAN'S HILL?
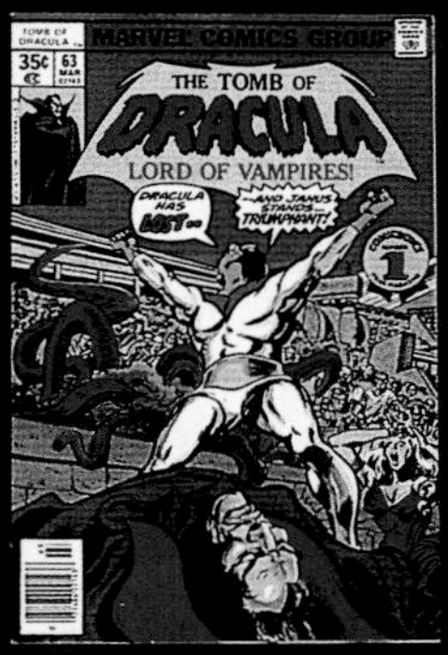
MARVEL COMICS GROUP
THE TOMB OF
DRACULA
LORD OF VAMPIRES!
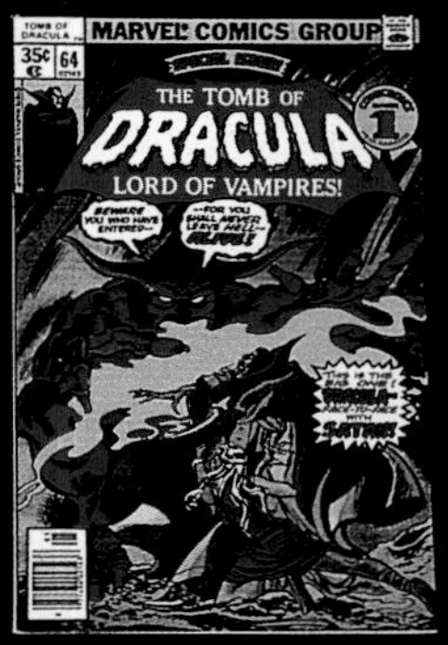
MARVEL COMICS GROUP
THE TOMB OF
DRACULA
LORD OF VAMPIRES!
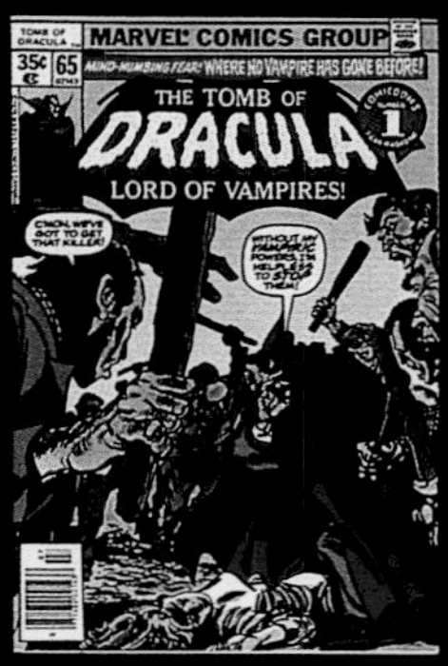
MARVEL COMICS GROUP
THE TOMB OF
DRACULA
LORD OF VAMPIRES!
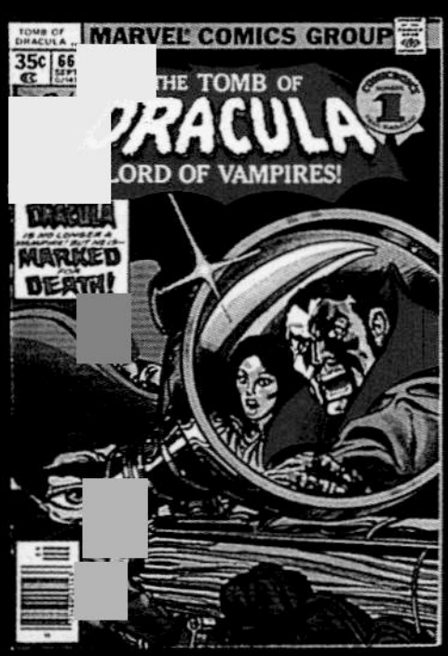
MARVEL COMICS GROUP
THE TOMB OF
DRACULA
LORD OF VAMPIRES!
MARKED FOR DEATH!
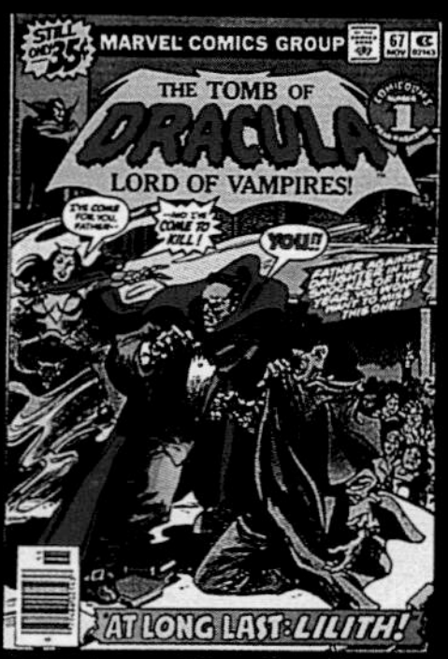
MARVEL COMICS GROUP
THE TOMB OF
DRACULA
LORD OF VAMPIRES!
AT LONG LAST: LILITH!
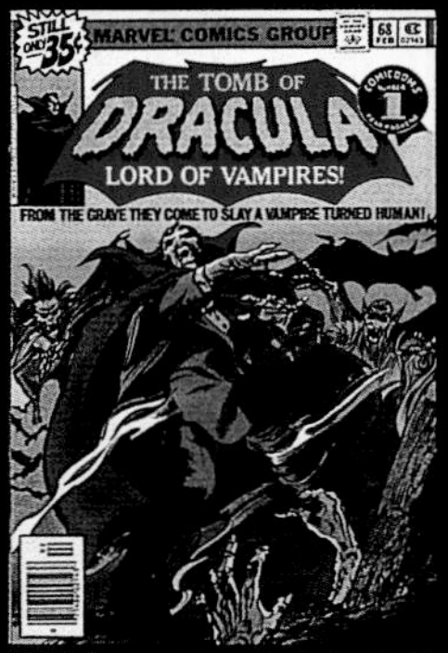
MARVEL COMICS GROUP
THE TOMB OF
DRACULA
LORD OF VAMPIRES!
FROM THE GRAVE THEY COME TO SLAY A VAMPIRE TURNED HUMAN!
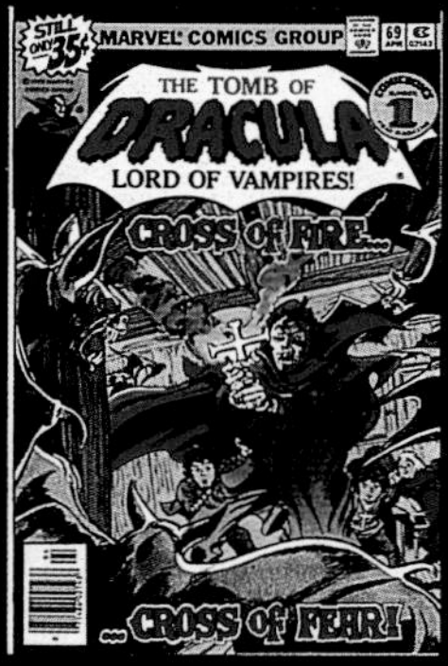
MARVEL COMICS GROUP
THE TOMB OF
DRACULA
LORD OF VAMPIRES!
CROSS OF FIRE
...CROSS OF FEAR!

1941.1 Time Bandits (1)

1941.3 Time Spirits (1-2)

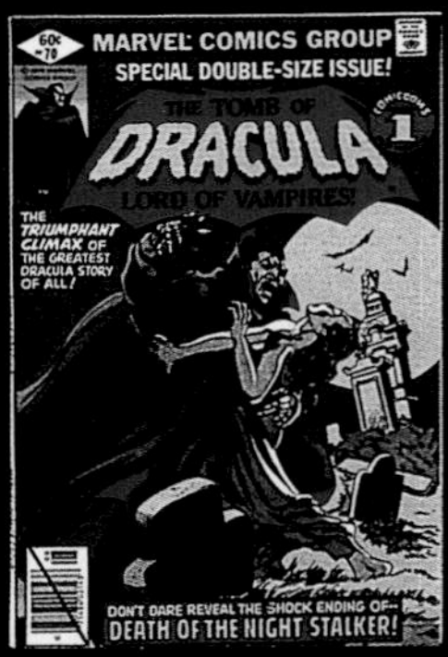
MARVEL COMICS GROUP
SPECIAL DOUBLE-SIZE ISSUE!
THE TOMB OF
DRACULA
LORD OF VAMPIRES!
THE TRIUMPHANT CLIMAX OF THE GREATEST DRACULA STORY OF ALL!
DON'T DARE REVEAL THE SHOCK ENDING OF
DEATH OF THE NIGHT STALKER!
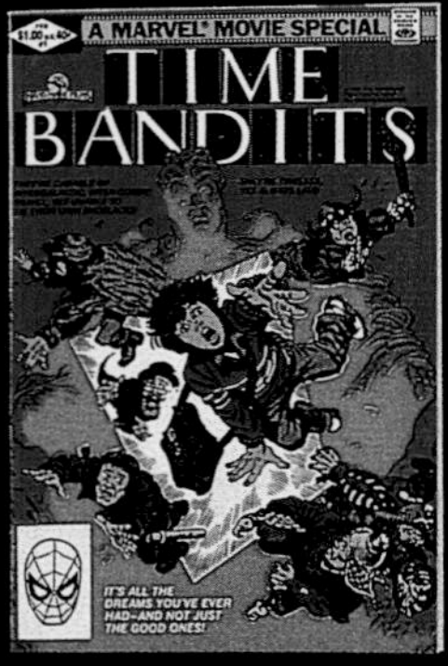
A MARVEL MOVIE SPECIAL
TIME
BANDITS
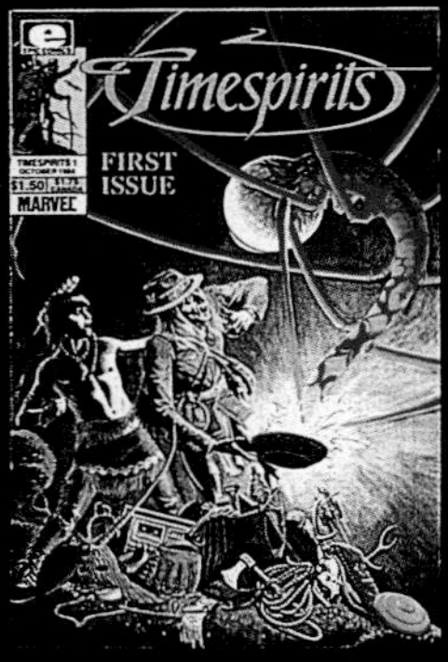
Timespirits
FIRST ISSUE
MARVEL
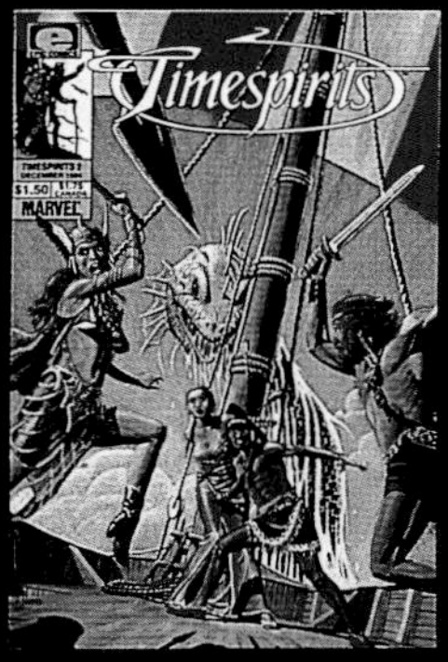
Timespirits
MARVEL

Tomb of Dracula (1-70) 1955.3

Ref. No.	Date	RVI	Artist/Info.
1955.3-1	Apr. 1972	10	Colan-a
1955.3-2	May	5	Colan/Colletta-a
1955.3-3	Jul.	5	Colan/Palmer-a
1955.3-4	Sept.	5	" "
1955.3-5	Nov.	4	" "
1955.3-6	Jan. 1973	4	" "
1955.3-7	Mar.	4	" "
1955.3-8	May	4	Colan/Chua-a
1955.3-9	Jun.	4	Colletta-a
1955.3-10	**Jul.**	**4**	**Colan/Abel-a (Intro. Blade the Vampire Slaye**
1955.3-11	Aug.	3	Colan/Abel-a
1955.3-12	Sept.	3	Brunner-c, Colan/Palmer-a
1955.3-13	Oct.	3	Colan/Palmer-a (Origin-Blade the Vampire Slay
1955.3-14	Nov.	3	" "
1955.3-15	Dec.	3	" "
1955.3-16	Jan. 1974	2	" "
1955.3-17	Feb.	2	" "
1955.3-18	Mar.	2	" "
1955.3-19	Apr.	2	" "
1955.3-20	**May**	**2**	**" "**
1955.3-21	Jun.	2	" "
1955.3-22	Jul.	2	" "
1955.3-23	Aug.	2	" "
1955.3-24	Sept.	2	" "
1955.3-25	Oct.	2	" "
1955.3-26	Nov.	2	" "
1955.3-27	Dec.	2	" "
1955.3-28	Jan. 1975	2	" "
1955.3-29	Feb.	2	" "
1955.3-30	**Mar.**	**2**	**" "**
1955.3-31	Apr.	1	" "
1955.3-32	May	1	" "
1955.3-33	Jun.	1	" "
1955.3-34	Jul.	1	" "
1955.3-35	Aug.	1	" "
1955.3-36	Sept.	1	" "
1955.3-37	Oct.	1	" "
1955.3-38 to 70	Aug. 1979, (#70)	1	" "

Time Bandits (1) 1941.1

1941.1-1	Feb. 1982	1	(Marvel Movie Special)

Time Spirits (1-8) 1941.3

1941.3-1	Jan. 1985	1
1941.3-2 to 8	Mar. 1986, (#8)	1

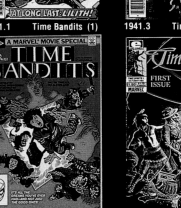

1983.5 Tower of Shadows (1-9)

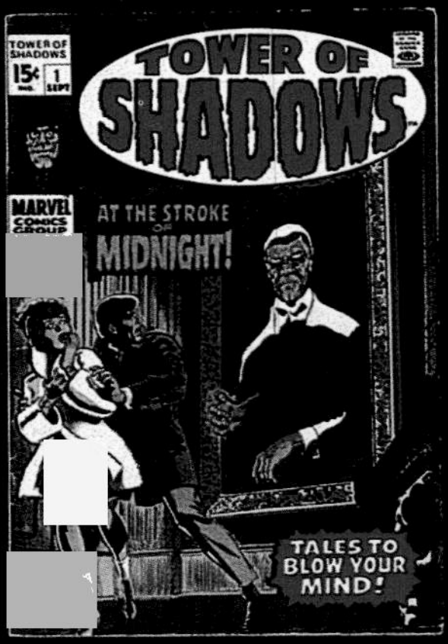
TOWER OF SHADOWS
AT THE STROKE OF MIDNIGHT!
TALES TO BLOW YOUR MIND!

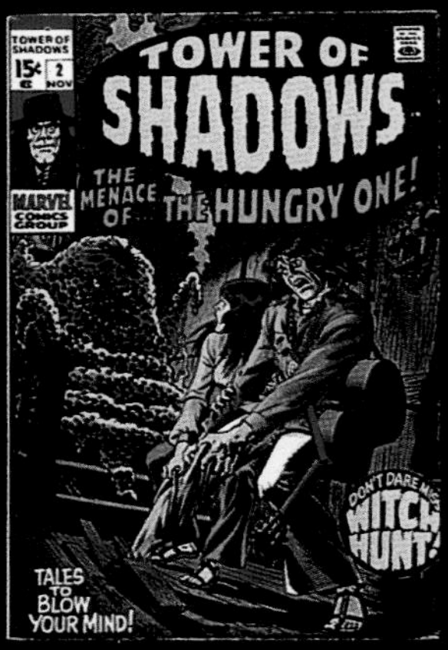
TOWER OF SHADOWS
THE MENACE OF... THE HUNGRY ONE!
DON'T DARE MISS WITCH HUNT!
TALES TO BLOW YOUR MIND!

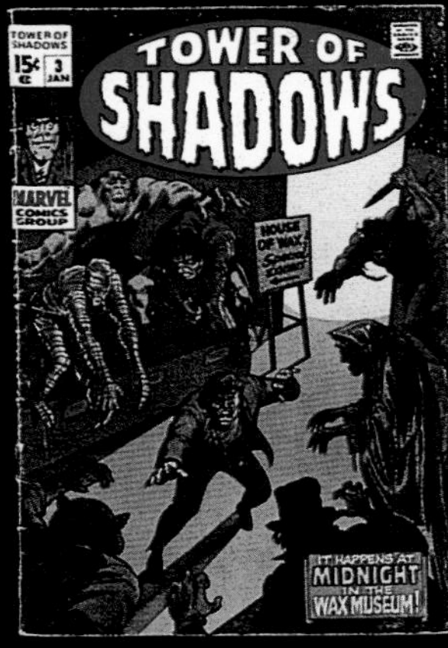
TOWER OF SHADOWS
IT HAPPENS AT MIDNIGHT IN THE WAX MUSEUM!

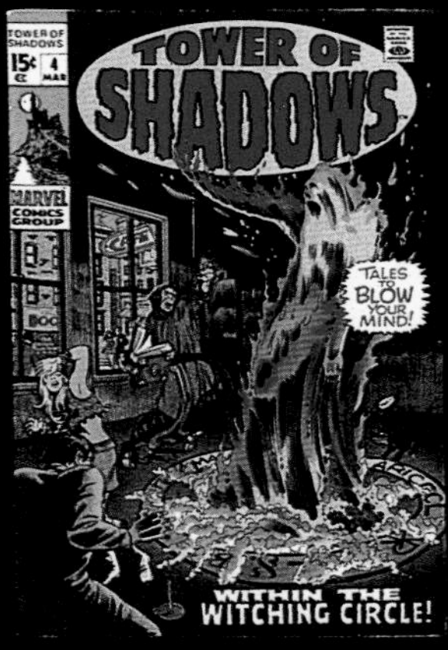
TOWER OF SHADOWS
TALES TO BLOW YOUR MIND!
WITHIN THE WITCHING CIRCLE!

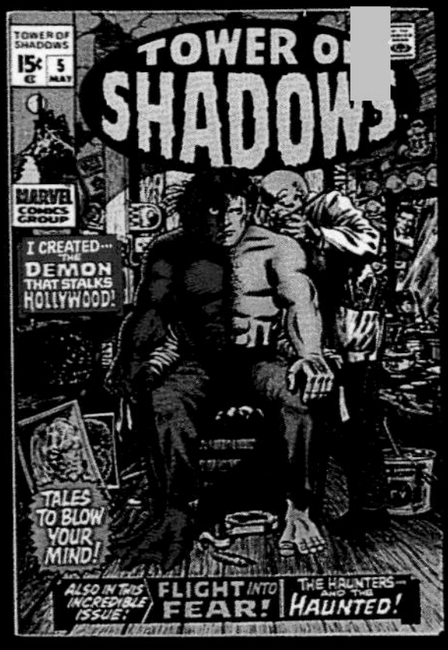
TOWER OF SHADOWS
I CREATED... THE DEMON THAT STALKS HOLLYWOOD!
TALES TO BLOW YOUR MIND!
FLIGHT INTO FEAR!
THE HAUNTERS AND THE HAUNTED!

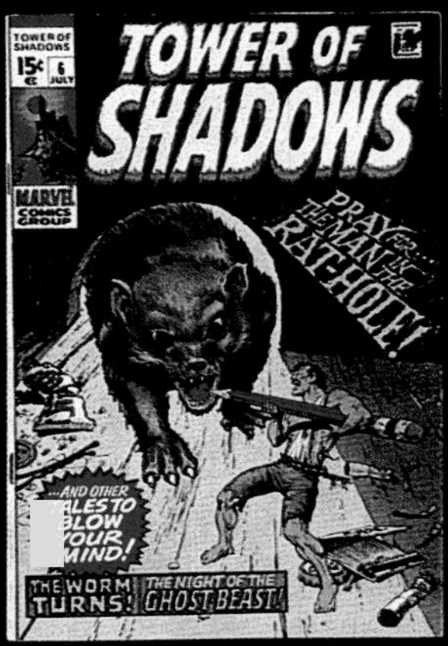
TOWER OF SHADOWS
PRAY FOR THE MAN IN THE RAT-HOLE!
THE WORM TURNS!
THE NIGHT OF THE GHOST BEAST!

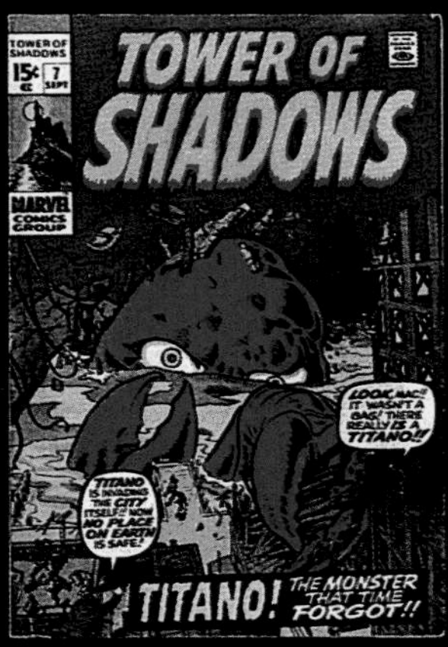
TOWER OF SHADOWS
TITANO!
THE MONSTER THAT TIME FORGOT!!

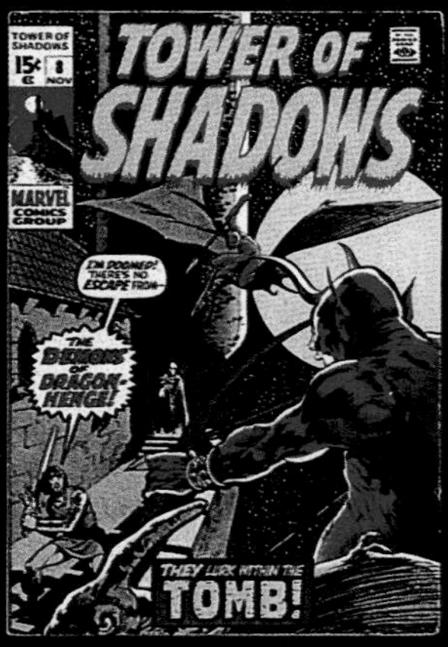
TOWER OF SHADOWS
THEY LURK WITHIN THE TOMB!

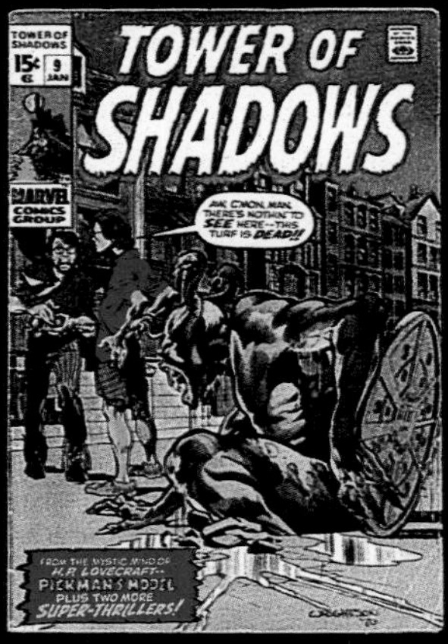
TOWER OF SHADOWS
PICKMAN'S MODEL
SUPER-THRILLERS!

1983.5 Creatures on the Loose (10-25)

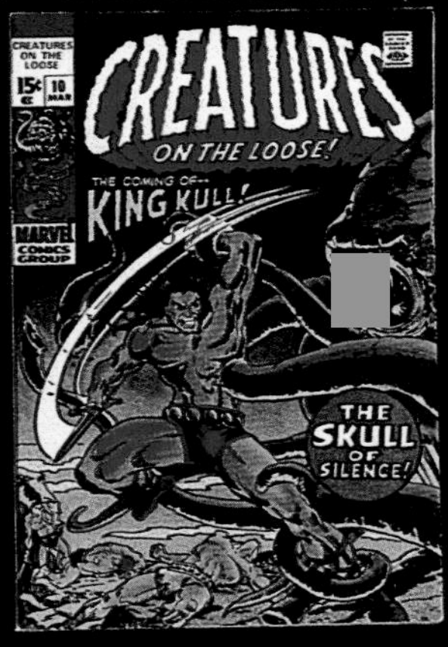
CREATURES ON THE LOOSE!
THE COMING OF... KING KULL!
THE SKULL OF SILENCE!

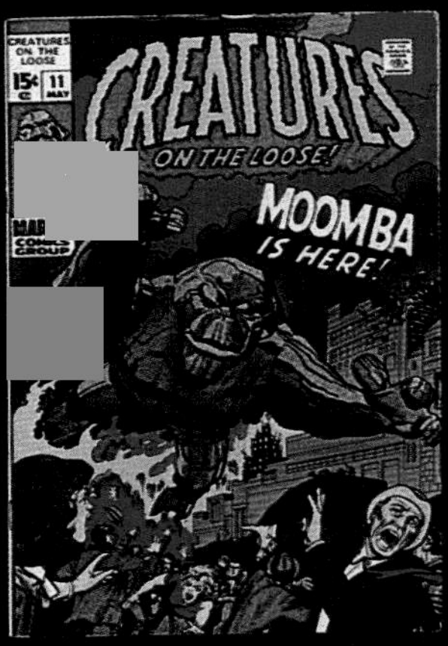
CREATURES ON THE LOOSE!
MOOMBA IS HERE!

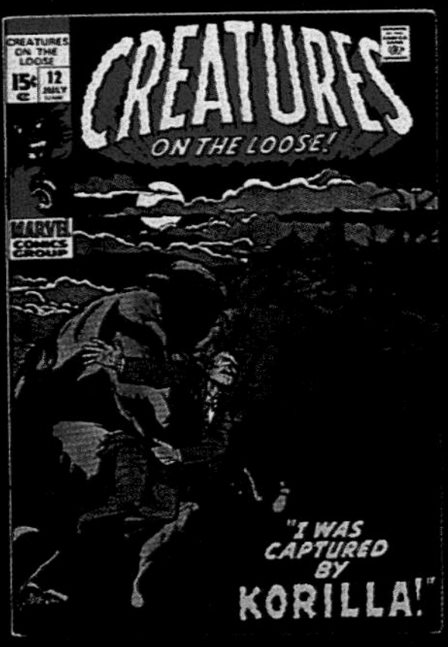
CREATURES ON THE LOOSE!
"I WAS CAPTURED BY KORILLA!"

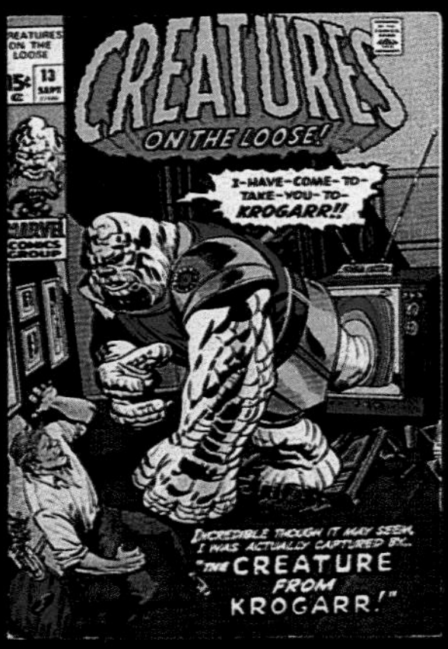
CREATURES ON THE LOOSE!
I-HAVE-COME-TO-TAKE-YOU-TO-KROGARR!!
"THE CREATURE FROM KROGARR!"

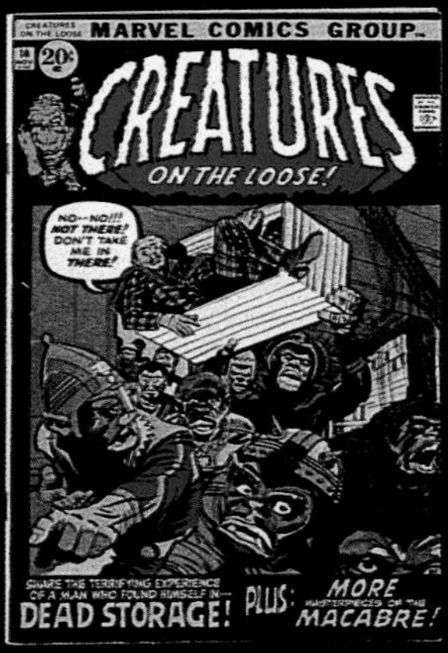
MARVEL COMICS GROUP
CREATURES ON THE LOOSE!
DEAD STORAGE!
PLUS: MORE MACABRE!

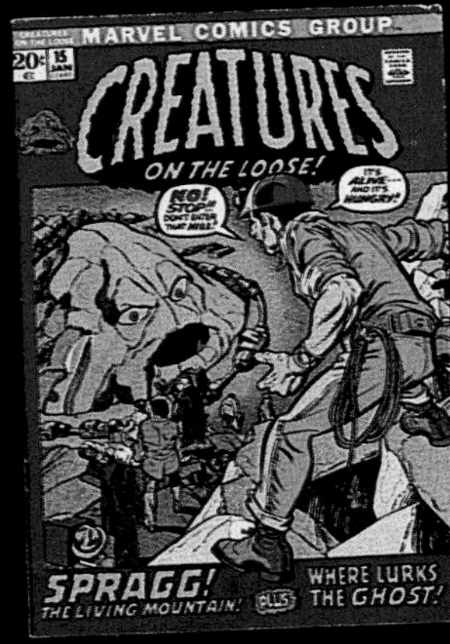
MARVEL COMICS GROUP
CREATURES ON THE LOOSE!
SPRAGG! THE LIVING MOUNTAIN!
PLUS WHERE LURKS THE GHOST!

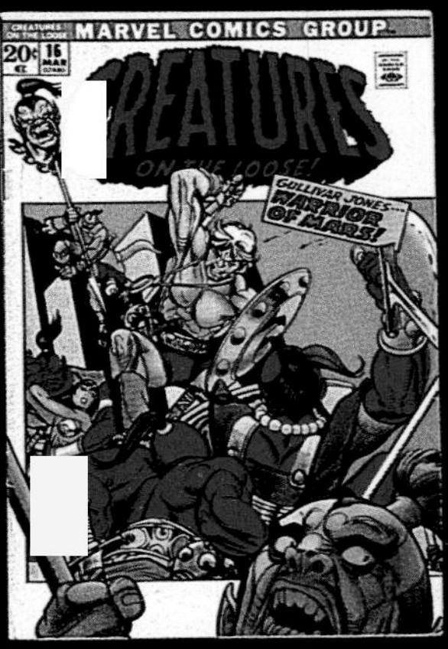
MARVEL COMICS GROUP
CREATURES

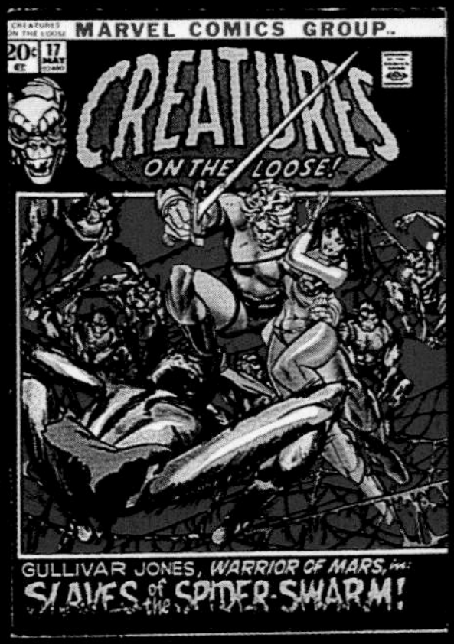
MARVEL COMICS GROUP
CREATURES ON THE LOOSE!
GULLIVAR JONES, WARRIOR OF MARS, in: SLAVES of the SPIDER-SWARM!

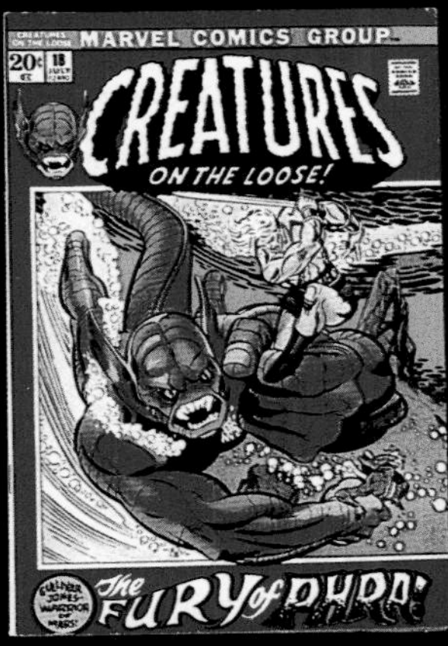
MARVEL COMICS GROUP
CREATURES ON THE LOOSE!
The FURY of PHRA!

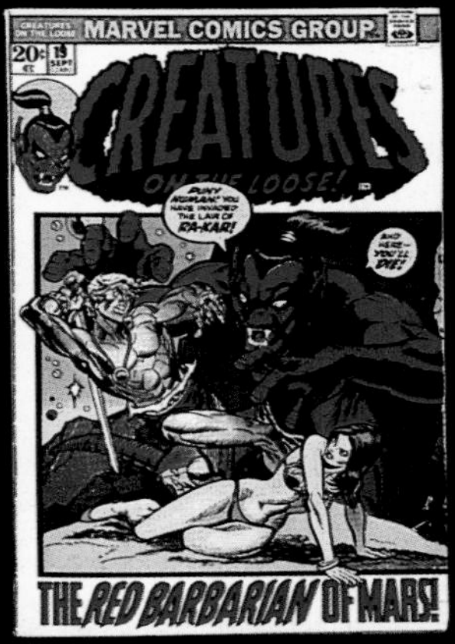
MARVEL COMICS GROUP
CREATURES
THE RED BARBARIAN OF MARS!

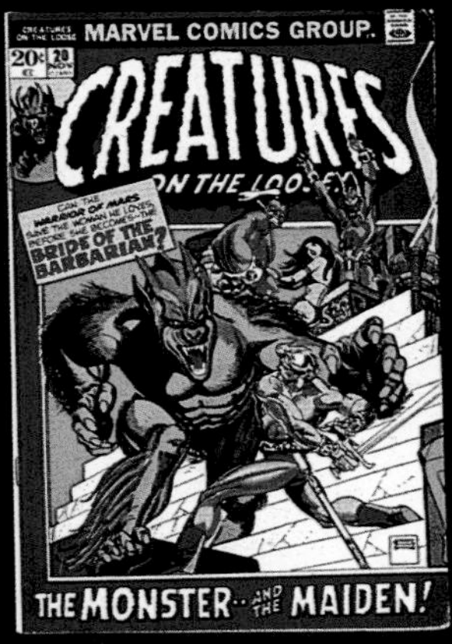
MARVEL COMICS GROUP
CREATURES
THE MONSTER AND THE MAIDEN!

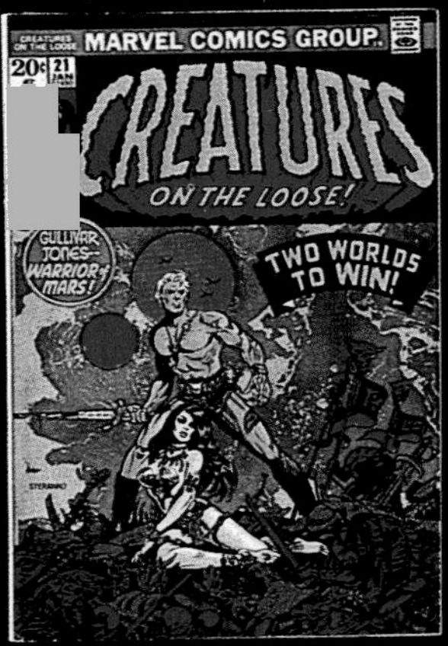
MARVEL COMICS GROUP
CREATURES ON THE LOOSE!
GULLIVAR JONES WARRIOR OF MARS!
TWO WORLDS TO WIN!

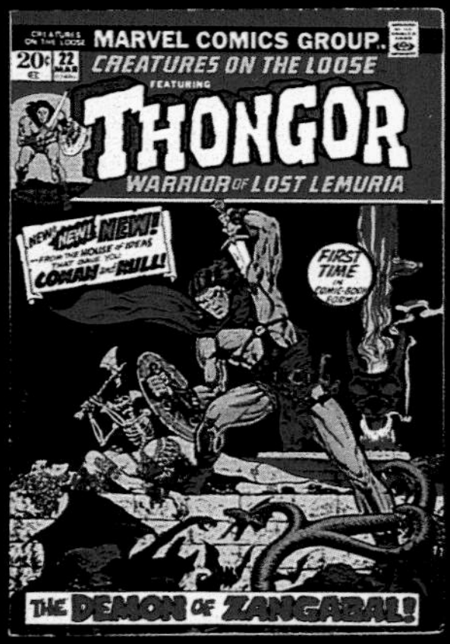
MARVEL COMICS GROUP
CREATURES ON THE LOOSE
THONGOR
WARRIOR OF LOST LEMURIA
FIRST TIME
THE DEMON OF ZANGABAL!

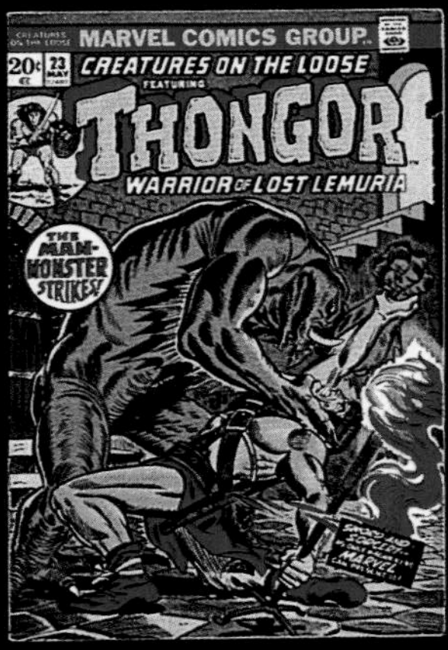
MARVEL COMICS GROUP
CREATURES ON THE LOOSE
THONGOR
WARRIOR OF LOST LEMURIA

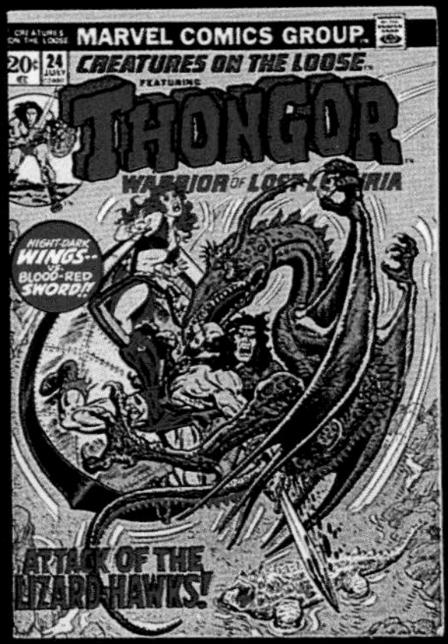
MARVEL COMICS GROUP
CREATURES ON THE LOOSE
THONGOR
ATTACK OF THE LIZARD-HAWKS!

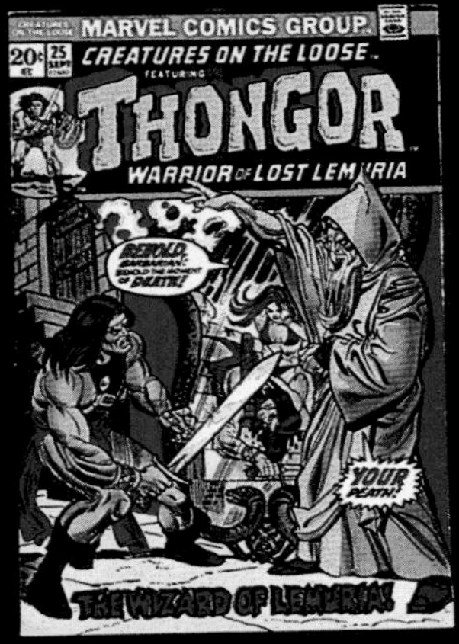
MARVEL COMICS GROUP
CREATURES ON THE LOOSE
THONGOR
WARRIOR OF LOST LEMURIA
THE WIZARD OF LEMURIA!

1983.5 Creatures on the Loose (26-37)

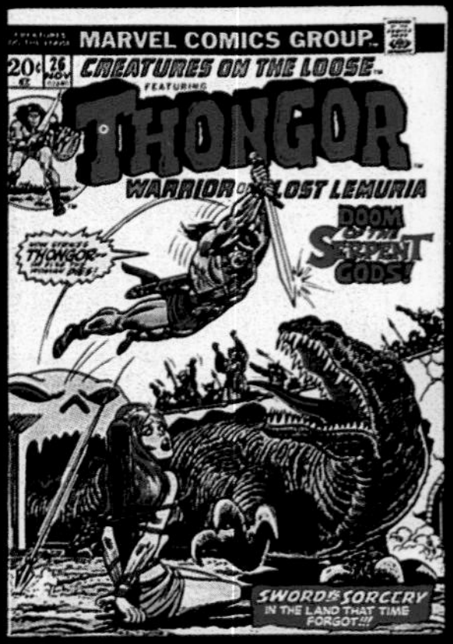
MARVEL COMICS GROUP
CREATURES ON THE LOOSE
THONGOR
WARRIOR OF LOST LEMURIA
SWORD & SORCERY IN THE LAND THAT TIME FORGOT!

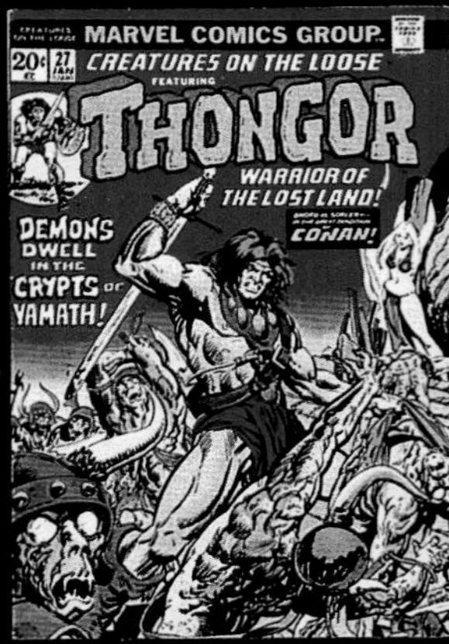
MARVEL COMICS GROUP
CREATURES ON THE LOOSE
THONGOR
WARRIOR OF THE LOST LAND!
DEMONS DWELL IN THE CRYPTS OF YAMATH!
CONAN!

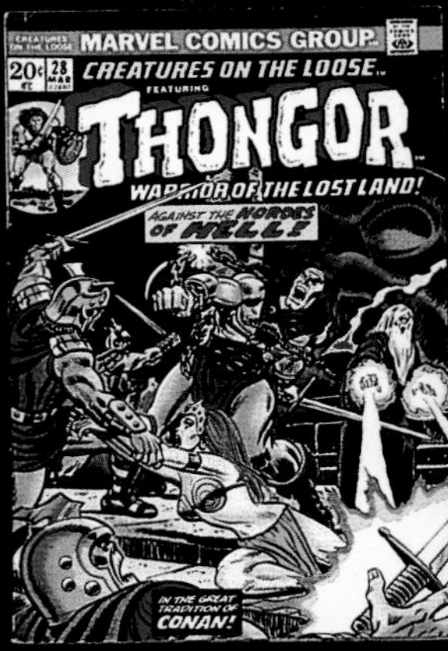
MARVEL COMICS GROUP
CREATURES ON THE LOOSE
THONGOR
WARRIOR OF THE LOST LAND!
CONAN!

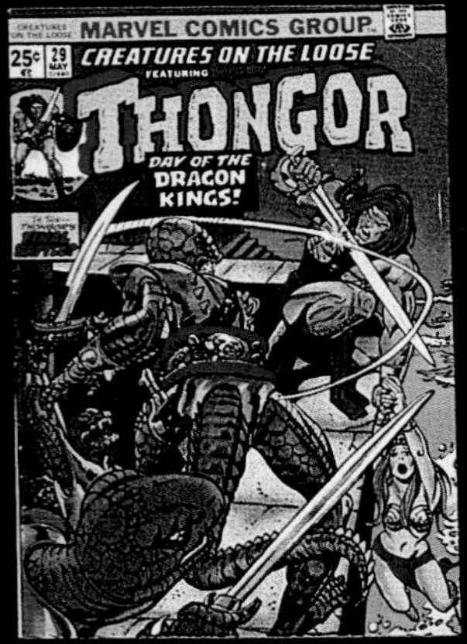
MARVEL COMICS GROUP
CREATURES ON THE LOOSE
THONGOR
DAY OF THE DRAGON KINGS!

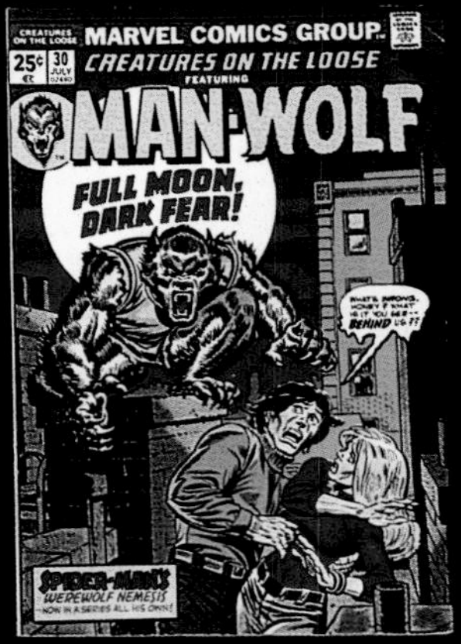
MARVEL COMICS GROUP
CREATURES ON THE LOOSE
MAN-WOLF
FULL MOON, DARK FEAR!

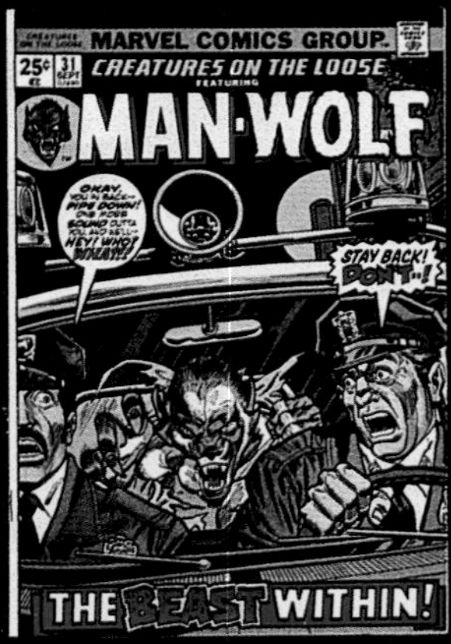
MARVEL COMICS GROUP
CREATURES ON THE LOOSE
MAN-WOLF
STAY BACK!
THE BEAST WITHIN!

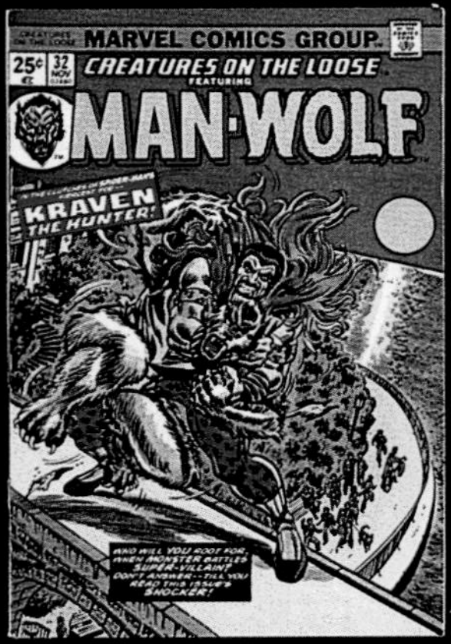
MARVEL COMICS GROUP
CREATURES ON THE LOOSE
MAN-WOLF
KRAVEN THE HUNTER!

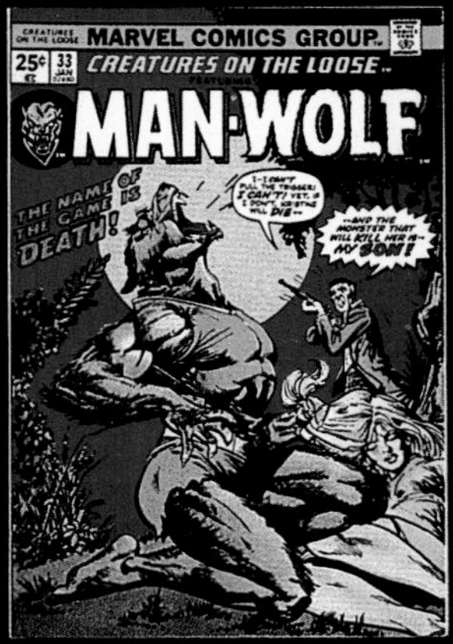
MARVEL COMICS GROUP
CREATURES ON THE LOOSE
MAN-WOLF
THE NAME OF THE GAME IS DEATH!

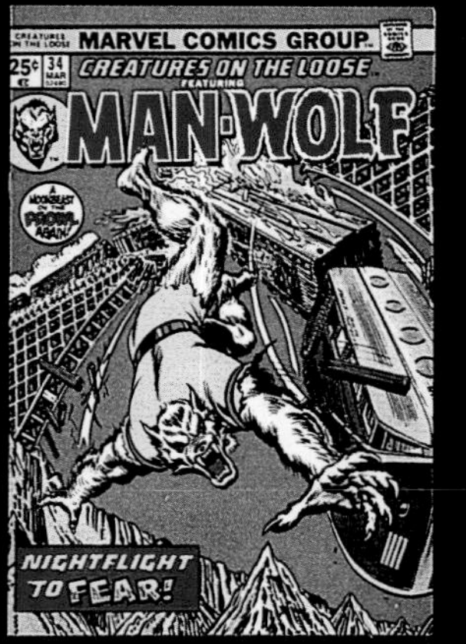
MARVEL COMICS GROUP
CREATURES ON THE LOOSE
MAN-WOLF
NIGHTFLIGHT TO FEAR!

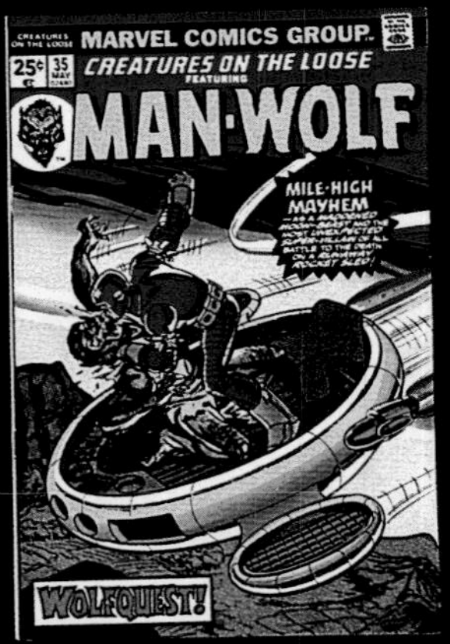
MARVEL COMICS GROUP
CREATURES ON THE LOOSE
MAN-WOLF
MILE-HIGH MAYHEM
WOLFQUEST!

1986.6 The Transformers (1-10)

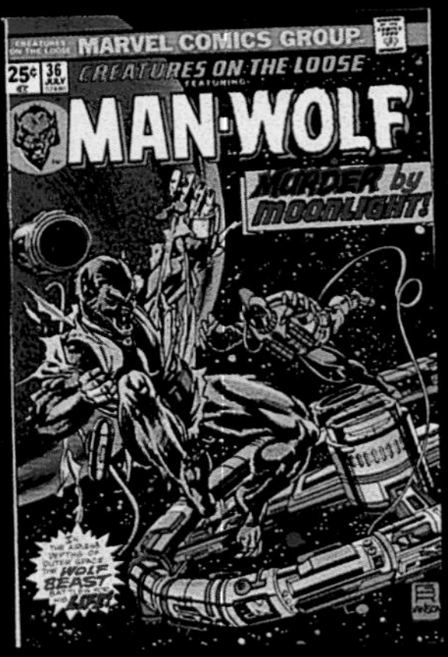
MARVEL COMICS GROUP
CREATURES ON THE LOOSE
MAN-WOLF
MURDER by MOONLIGHT!

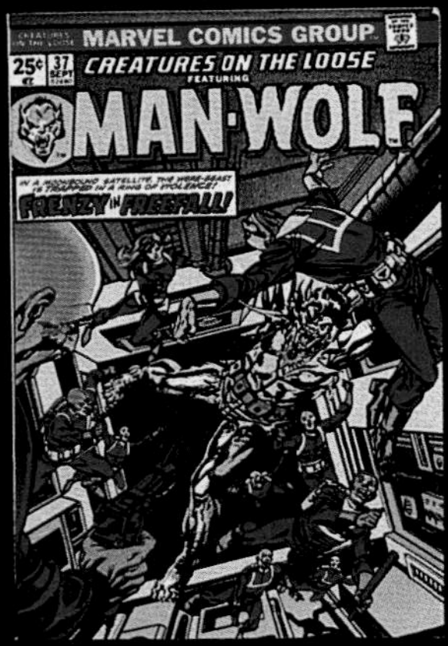
MARVEL COMICS GROUP
CREATURES ON THE LOOSE
MAN-WOLF

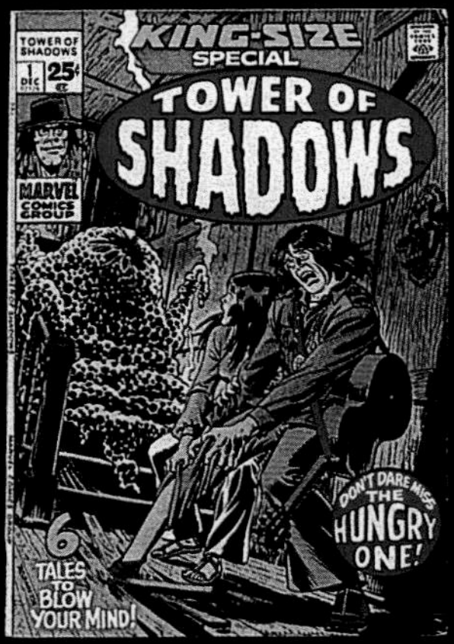
KING-SIZE SPECIAL
TOWER OF SHADOWS
DON'T DARE MISS THE HUNGRY ONE!
6 TALES TO BLOW YOUR MIND!

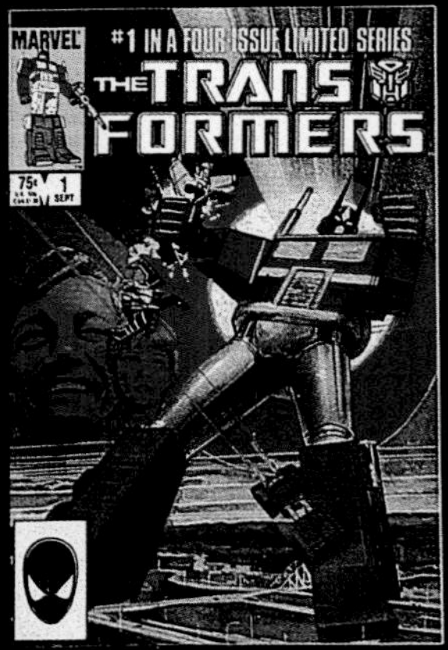
MARVEL
#1 IN A FOUR-ISSUE LIMITED SERIES
THE TRANS FORMERS

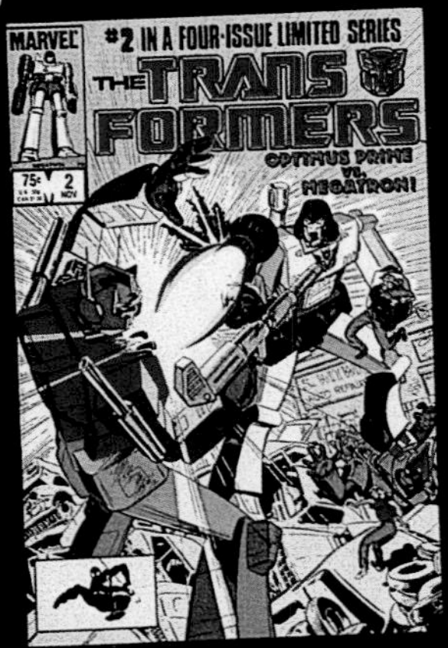
MARVEL
#2 IN A FOUR-ISSUE LIMITED SERIES
THE TRANS FORMERS

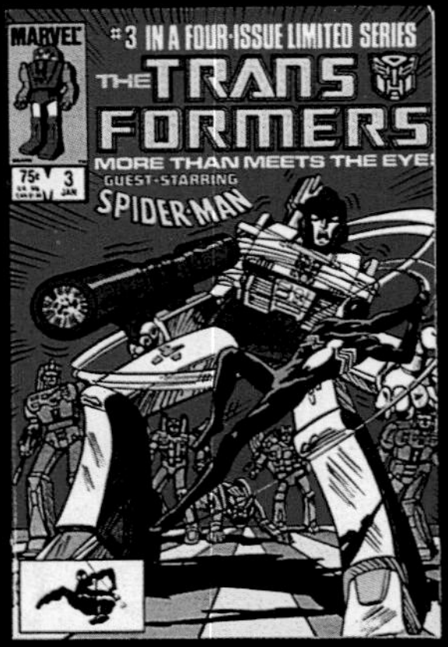
MARVEL
#3 IN A FOUR-ISSUE LIMITED SERIES
THE TRANS FORMERS
MORE THAN MEETS THE EYE!
GUEST-STARRING SPIDER-MAN

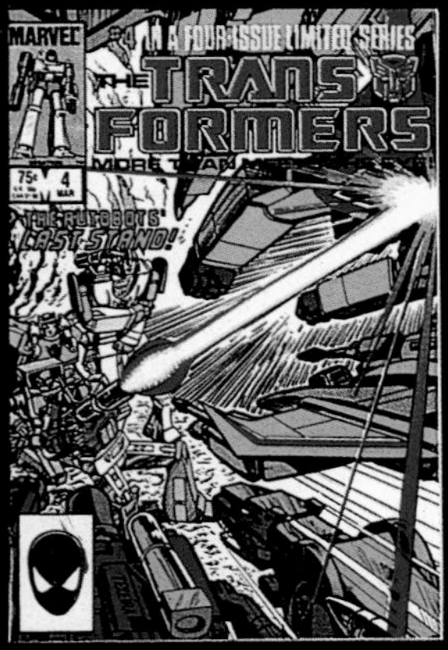
MARVEL
IN A FOUR-ISSUE LIMITED SERIES
THE TRANS FORMERS

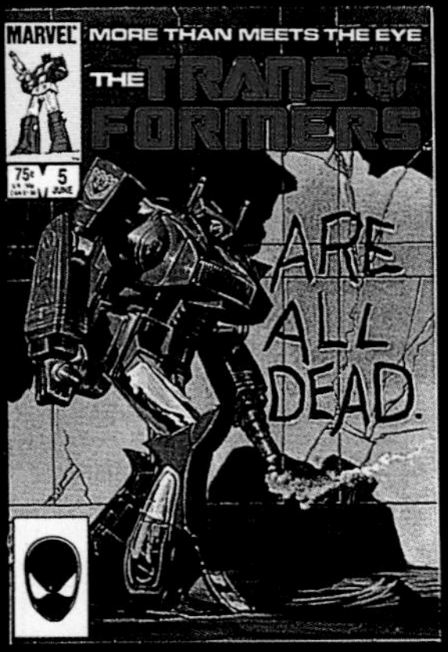
MARVEL
MORE THAN MEETS THE EYE
THE TRANS FORMERS
ARE ALL DEAD.

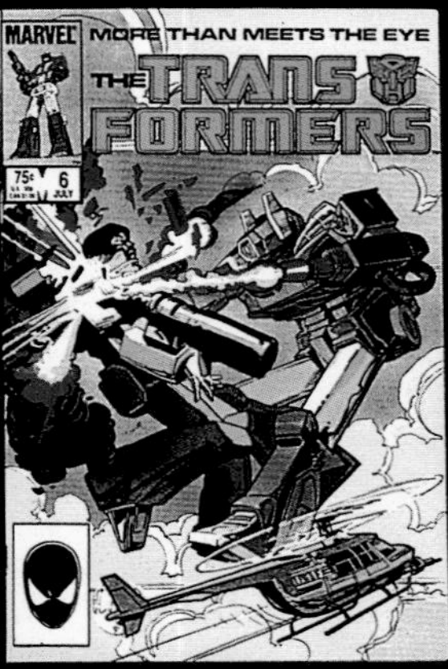
MARVEL
MORE THAN MEETS THE EYE
THE TRANS FORMERS

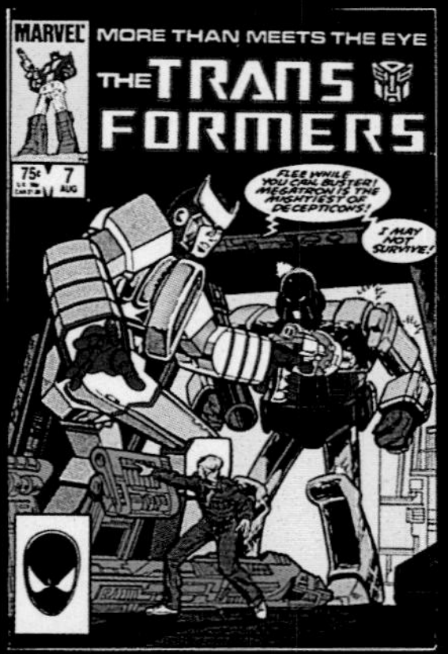
MARVEL
MORE THAN MEETS THE EYE
THE TRANS FORMERS

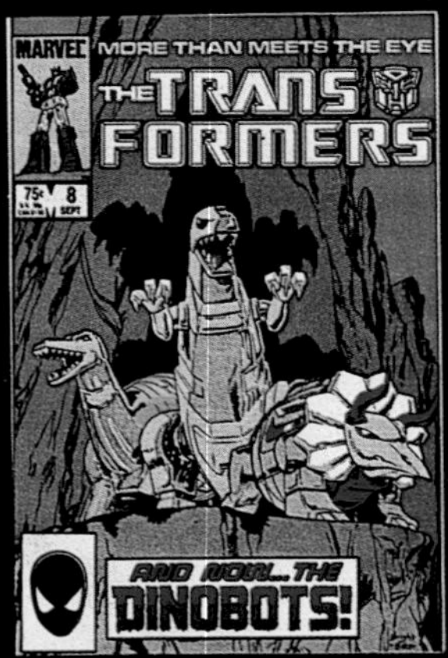
MARVEL
MORE THAN MEETS THE EYE
THE TRANS FORMERS
AND NOW... THE DINOBOTS!

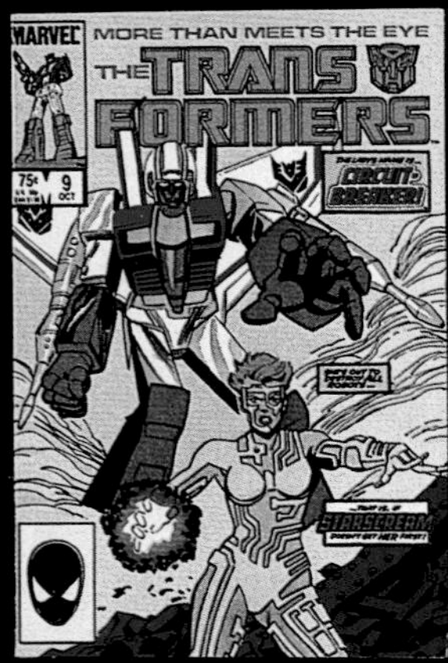
MARVEL
MORE THAN MEETS THE EYE
THE TRANS FORMERS

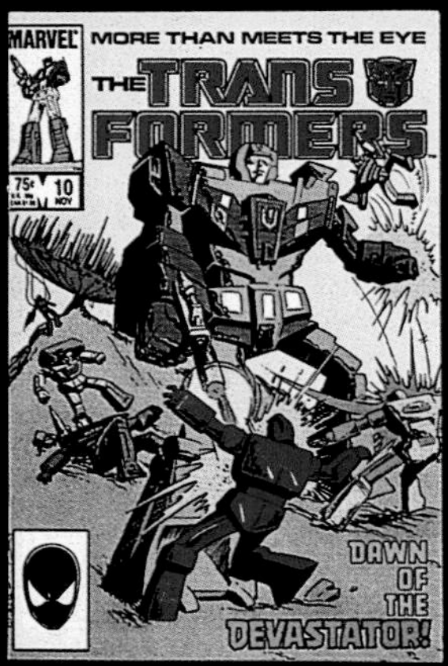
MARVEL
MORE THAN MEETS THE EYE
THE TRANS FORMERS
DAWN OF THE DEVASTATOR!

Tower of Shadows (1-9) 1983.5

Ref. No.	Date	RVI	Artist/Info.
1983.5-1	Sept. 1969	4	Romita-c, Steranko-a
1983.5-2	Nov.	2	Romita-c, Heck/Adkins-a
1983.5-3	Jan. 1970	3	Colan/Gaudioso-a
1983.5-4	Mar.	2	Heck-a
1983.5-5	May	3	Smith/Adkins-a
1983.5-6	Jul.	2	Ditko-a
1983.5-7	Sept.	3	Smith/Colletta-a
1983.5-8	Nov.	2	Wood-a
1983.5-9	Jan. 1971	2	Wrightson-c, Palmer-a
Continues as **Creatures on the Loose** (10-37)			
1983.5-10	**Mar.**	**10**	**Wrightson-a**
1983.5-11	May	1	Ayers-a
1983.5-12	Jul.	1	Kirby-a
1983.5-13	Sept.	1	Crandall-a
1983.5-14	Nov.	1	M. Severin-a
1983.5-15	Jan. 1972	1	Ditko-a
1983.5-16	Mar.	1	Kane/Everett-a
1983.5-17	May	1	Kane/Grainger-a
1983.5-18	Jul.	1	Andru, Grainger-a
1983.5-19	Sept.	1	Boring, Mooney, Kane-a
1983.5-20	**Nov.**	**1**	**Morrow-a**
1983.5-21	Jan. 1973	1	Steranko-c, Morrow-a
1983.5-22 to 37	Sept. 1975, (#37)	1	(#30, Manwolf begins)
1983.5-SP1	Dec. 1971	1	Adams-a

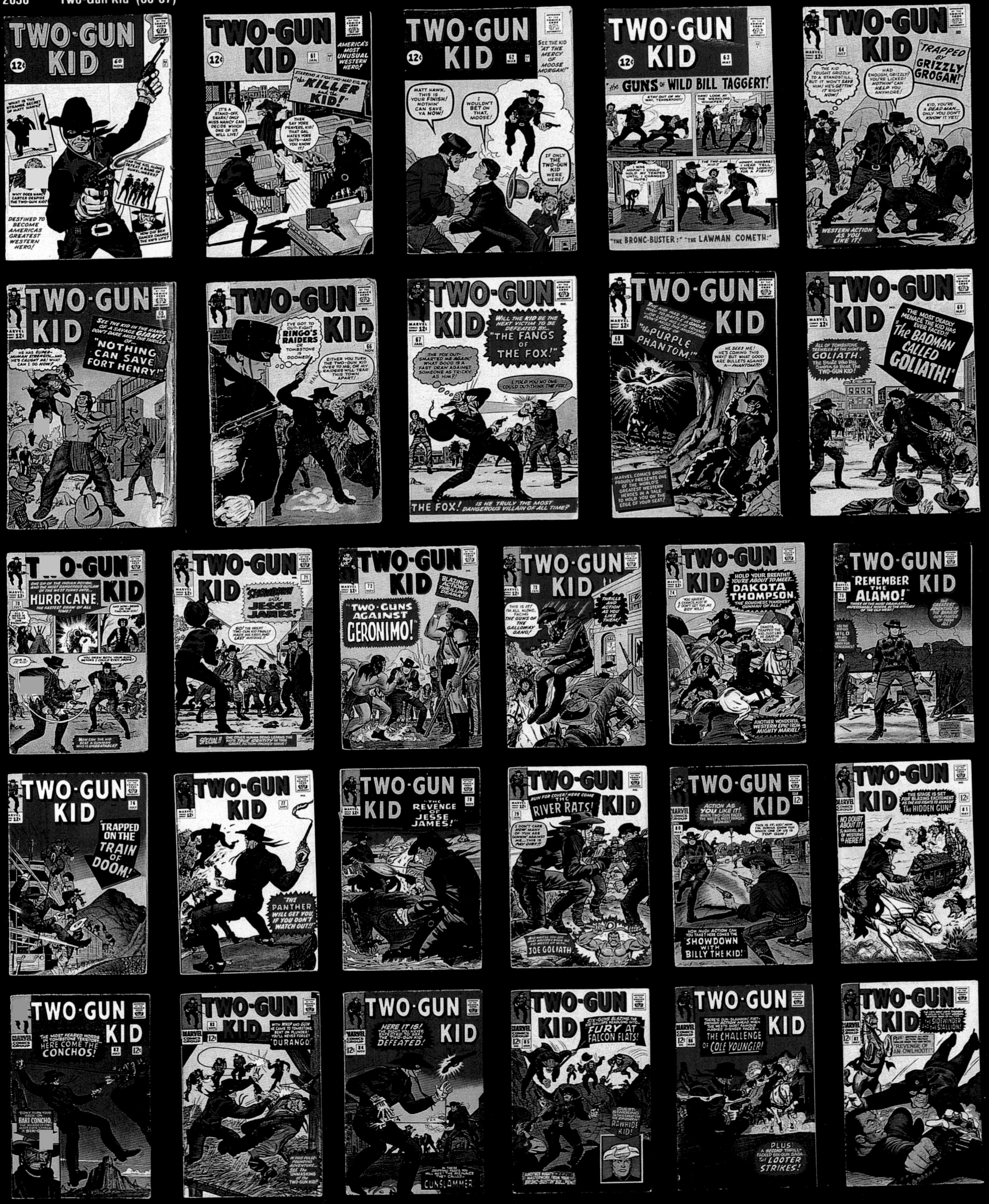

TWO-GUN KID
DESTINED TO BECOME AMERICA'S GREATEST WESTERN HERO!
AMERICA'S MOST UNUSUAL WESTERN HERO!
"the KILLER and the KID!"
SEE THE KID "AT THE MERCY OF MOOSE MORGAN!"
"the GUNS of WILD BILL TAGGERT!"
"THE BRONC-BUSTER!" "THE LAWMAN COMETH!"
"TRAPPED BY GRIZZLY GROGAN!"
WESTERN ACTION AS YOU LIKE IT!
"NOTHING CAN SAVE FORT HENRY!"
RINGO'S RAIDERS
"THE FANGS OF THE FOX!"
THE FOX! IS HE TRULY THE MOST DANGEROUS VILLAIN OF ALL TIME?
"the PURPLE PHANTOM!"
"The BADMAN CALLED GOLIATH!"
HURRICANE
JESSE JAMES!
"TWO-GUNS AGAINST GERONIMO!"
DAKOTA THOMPSON
ANOTHER WONDERFUL WESTERN EPIC FROM MIGHTY MARVEL!
"REMEMBER THE ALAMO!"
TRAPPED ON THE TRAIN OF DOOM!
"THE PANTHER WILL GET YOU IF YOU DON'T WATCH OUT!!"
"THE REVENGE OF JESSE JAMES!"
THE RIVER RATS!
JOE GOLIATH
SHOWDOWN WITH BILLY THE KID!
THE HIDDEN GUN!
HERE COME THE CONCHOS!
DURANGO!
HERE IT IS! DEFEATED!
GUNSLAMMER
FURY AT FALCON FLATS!
RAWHIDE KID!
THE CHALLENGE OF COLE YOUNGER!
THE LOOTER STRIKES!
"REVENGE OF AN OWLHOOT!"

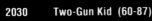

The Transformers (1-Present) 1986.6

Ref. No.	Date	RVI	Artist/Info.
1986.6-1	Sept. 1984	3	(Hasbro Toy adaptation)
1986.6-2	Nov.	2	Springer/DeMulder-a
1986.6-3	Jan. 1985	2	" "
1986.6-4 to 71		1	(#21, Intro. Aerialbots)

TV Stars (1-4) 2024.5

2024.5-1 to 4	Aug. 1978, (#1)	2	

Two Gun Kid (60-136) 2030

Ref. No.	Date	RVI	Artist/Info.
2030-60	Nov. 1962	8	Ayers-a (New Origin)
2030-61	Jan. 1963	4	Kirby/Ayers-a
2030-62	Mar.	4	Kirby, Hartley/Ayers-a
2030-63	May	2	Ayers, Reinman-a
2030-64	Jul.	2	Ayers, Reinman-a (Intro. Boom-Boom)
2030-65	Sept.	2	Ayers, Reinman-a
2030-66	Nov.	2	Ayers-a
2030-67	Jan. 1964	2	Ayers, Keller/Reinman-a
2030-68	Mar.	2	Ayers, Keller-a
2030-69	May	2	Ayers, Brodsky-a
2030-70	**Jul.**	**2**	**Ayers, Lieber-a**
2030-71	Sept.	2	Ayers, Lieber/Bell-a
2030-72 to 99	Nov. (#72)	2	Ayers, Lieber-a
2030-100		2	Whitney-a
2030-101		2	Whitney/Kirby-a (Origin retold)
2030-102 to 136	Apr. 1977, (#136)	1	

2030.2 2001: A Space Odyssey (1-10)

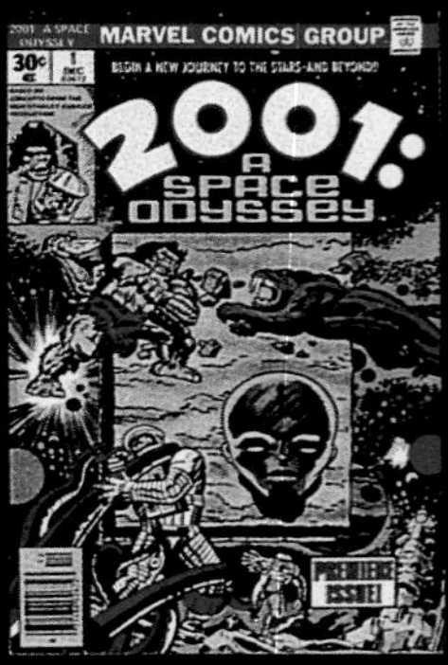
MARVEL COMICS GROUP
2001: A SPACE ODYSSEY
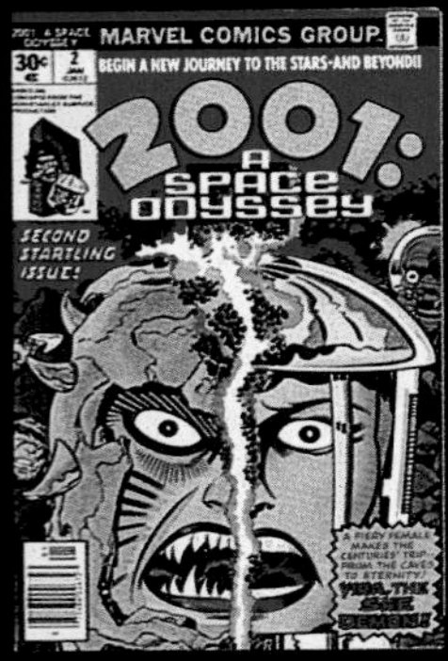
MARVEL COMICS GROUP
2001: A SPACE ODYSSEY
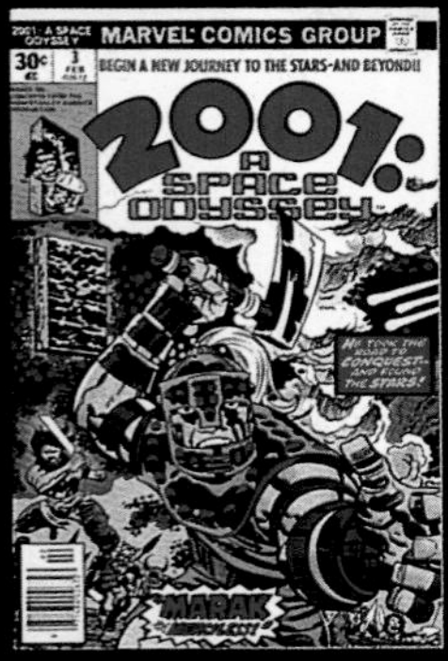
MARVEL COMICS GROUP
2001: A SPACE ODYSSEY
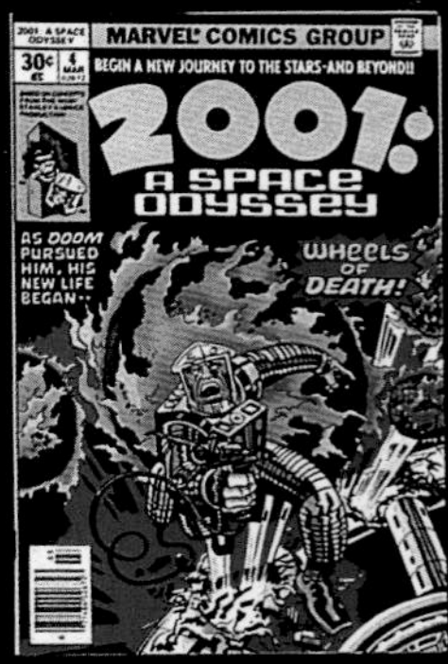
MARVEL COMICS GROUP
2001: A SPACE ODYSSEY
WHEELS OF DEATH!
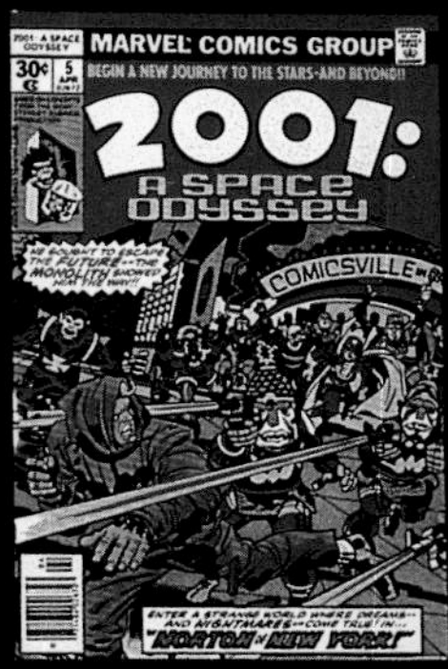
MARVEL COMICS GROUP
2001: A SPACE ODYSSEY
COMICSVILLE
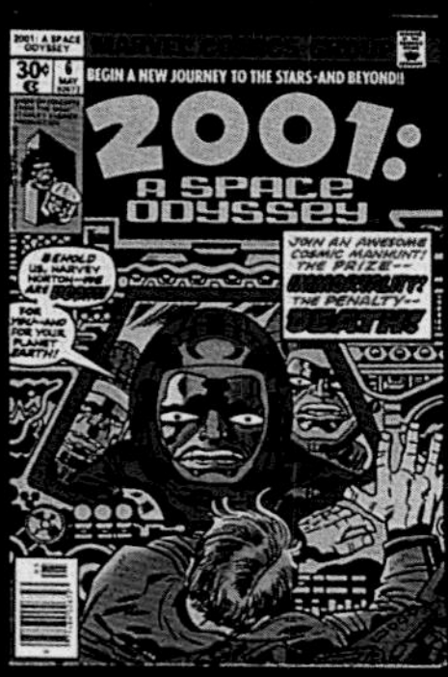
2001: A SPACE ODYSSEY
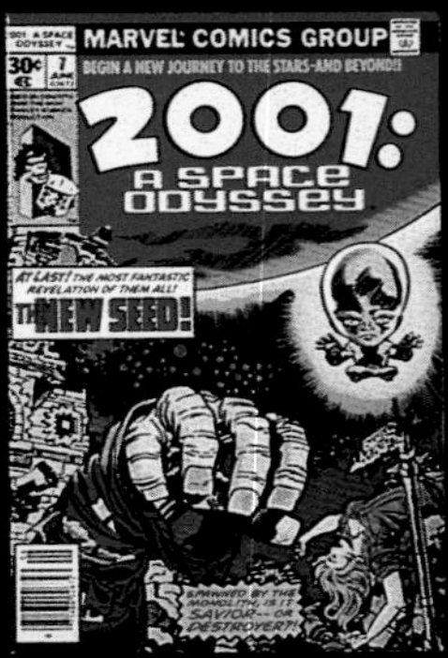
MARVEL COMICS GROUP
2001: A SPACE ODYSSEY
THE NEW SEED!
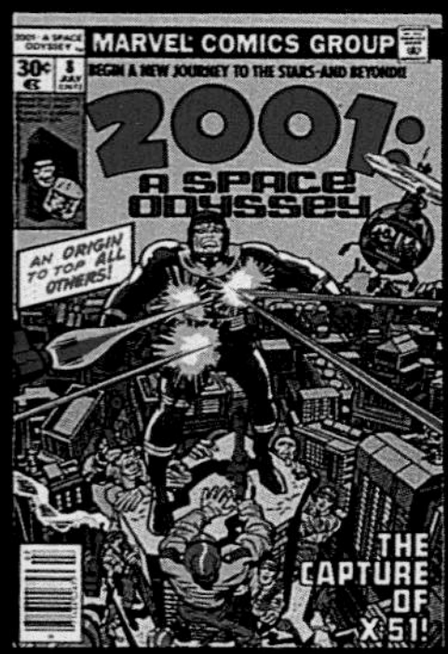
MARVEL COMICS GROUP
2001: A SPACE ODYSSEY
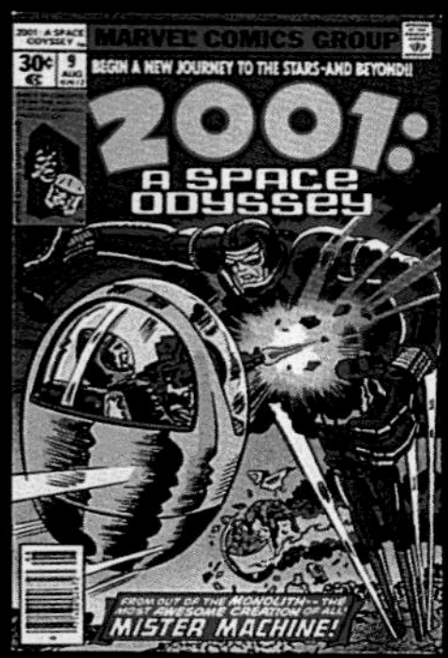
2001: A SPACE ODYSSEY
THE CAPTURE OF X-51!
MISTER MACHINE!
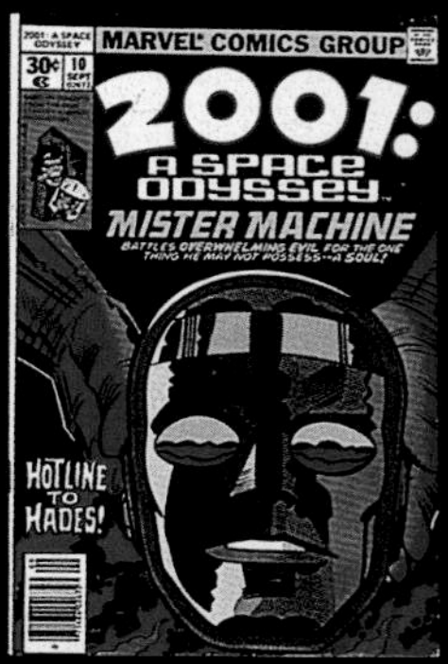
MARVEL COMICS GROUP
2001: A SPACE ODYSSEY
MISTER MACHINE
HOTLINE TO HADES!

2031.3 2010 (1-2)

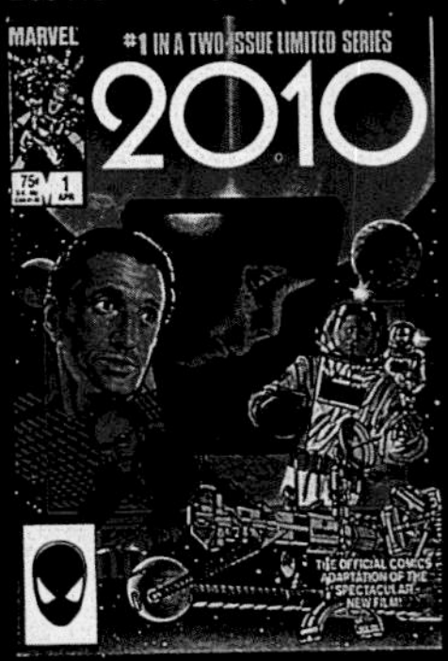
#1 IN A TWO-ISSUE LIMITED SERIES
2010
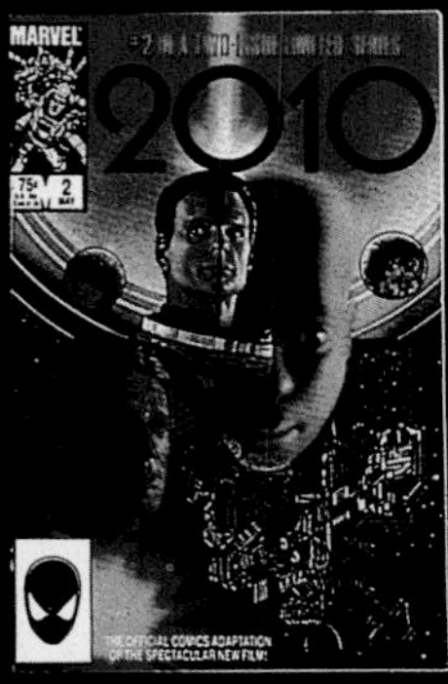
2010

2055.5 U.S. 1 (1-6)

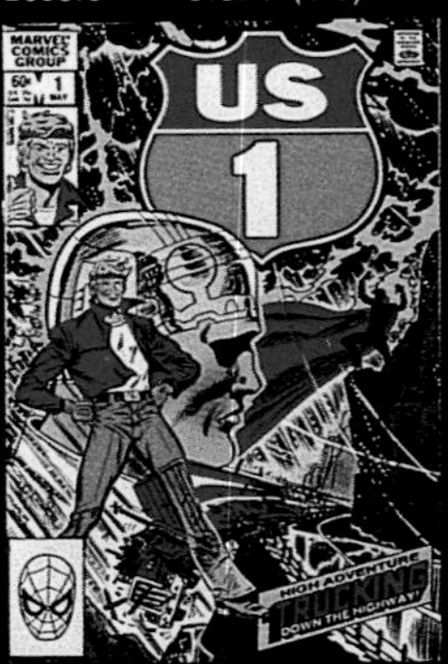
US 1
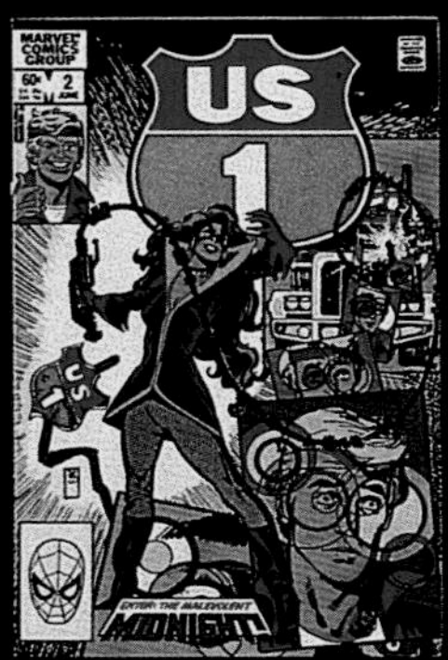
US 1
MIDNIGHT
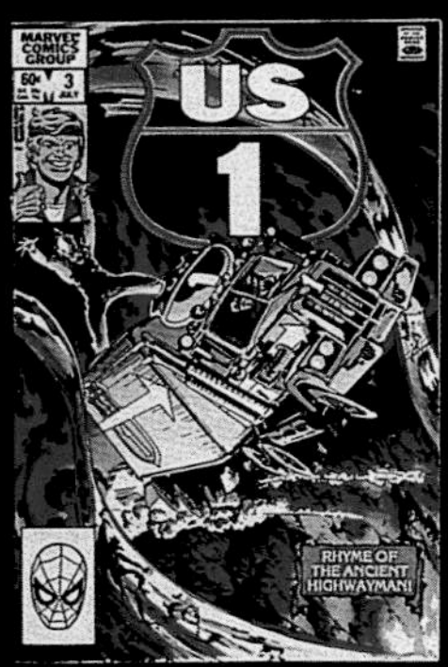
US 1
RHYME OF THE ANCIENT HIGHWAYMAN!
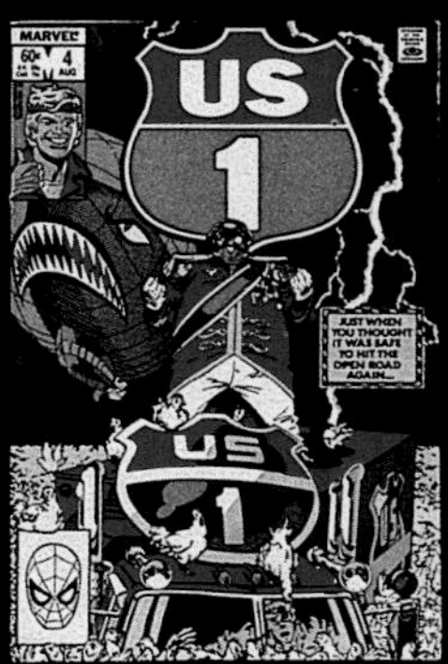
US 1
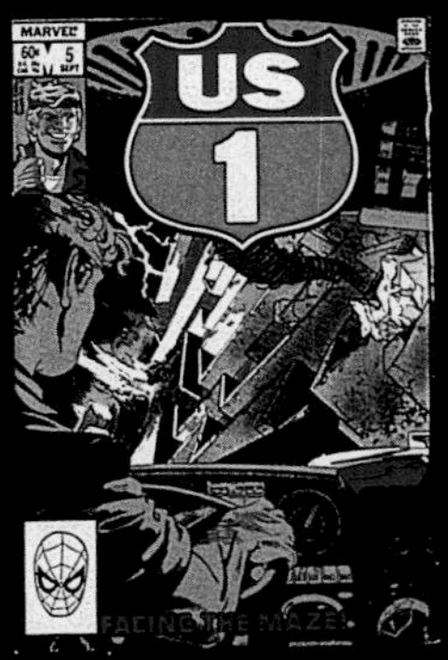
US 1
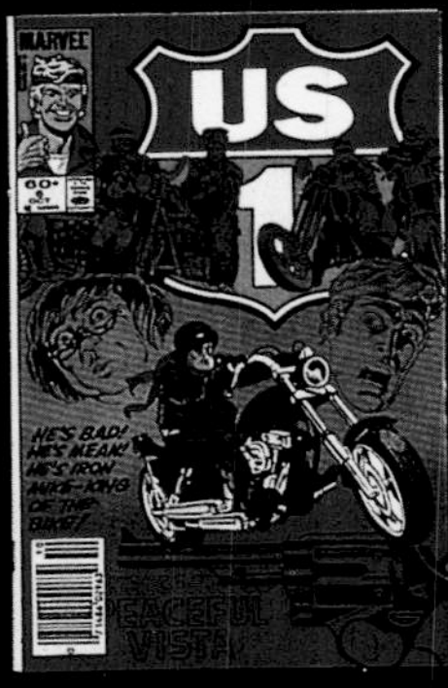
US 1

2032.2 Uncanny Tales (1-11)

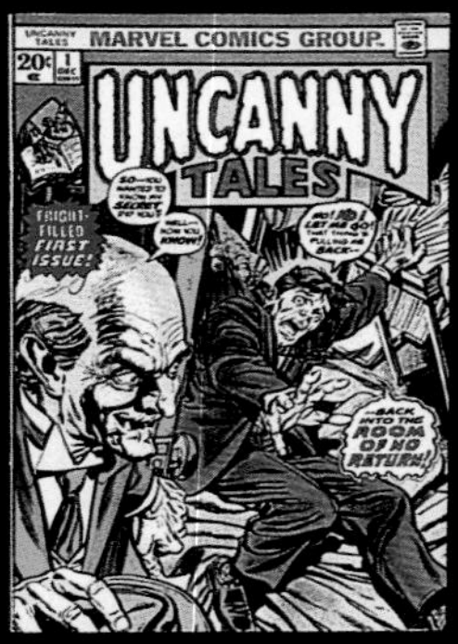
MARVEL COMICS GROUP
UNCANNY TALES
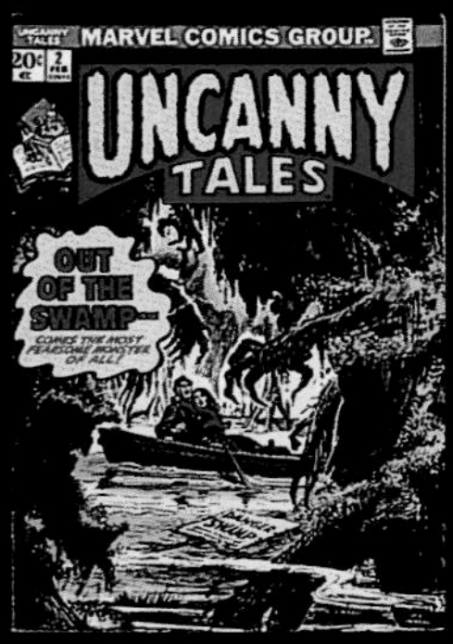
MARVEL COMICS GROUP
UNCANNY TALES
OUT OF THE SWAMP
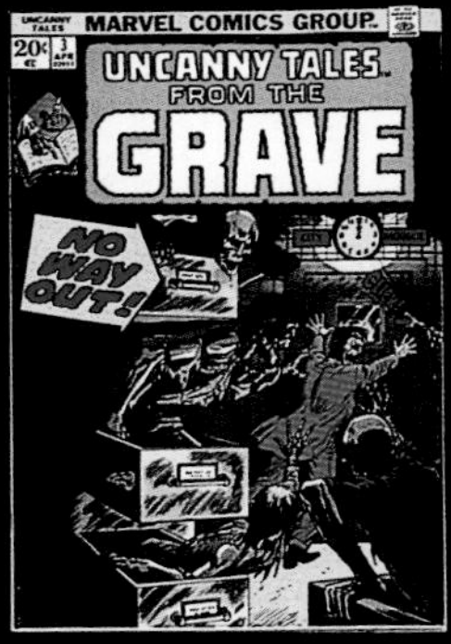
MARVEL COMICS GROUP
UNCANNY TALES FROM THE GRAVE
NO WAY OUT!
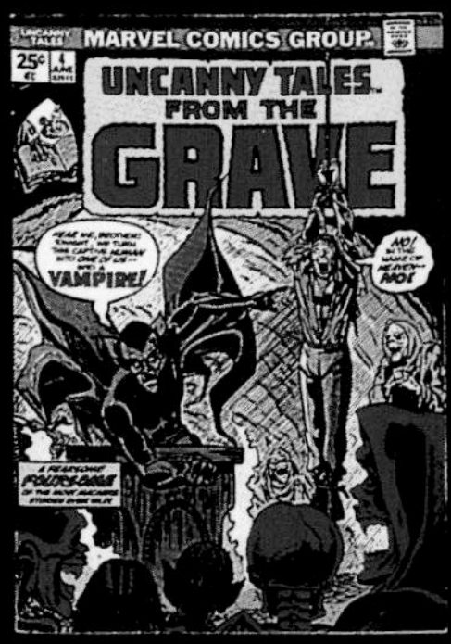
MARVEL COMICS GROUP
UNCANNY TALES FROM THE GRAVE
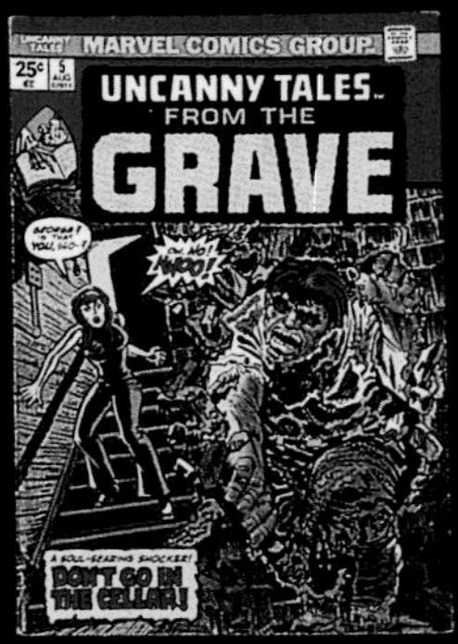
MARVEL COMICS GROUP
UNCANNY TALES FROM THE GRAVE
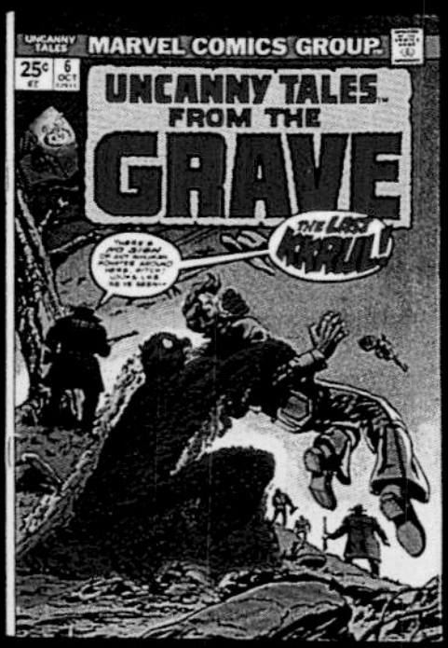
MARVEL COMICS GROUP
UNCANNY TALES FROM THE GRAVE
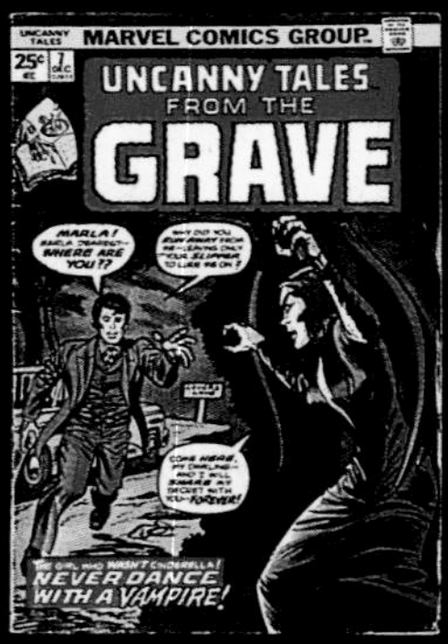
MARVEL COMICS GROUP
UNCANNY TALES FROM THE GRAVE
NEVER DANCE WITH A VAMPIRE!
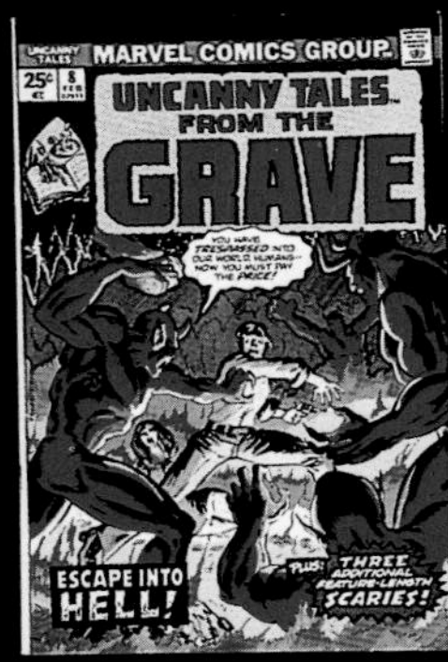
MARVEL COMICS GROUP
UNCANNY TALES FROM THE GRAVE
ESCAPE INTO HELL!
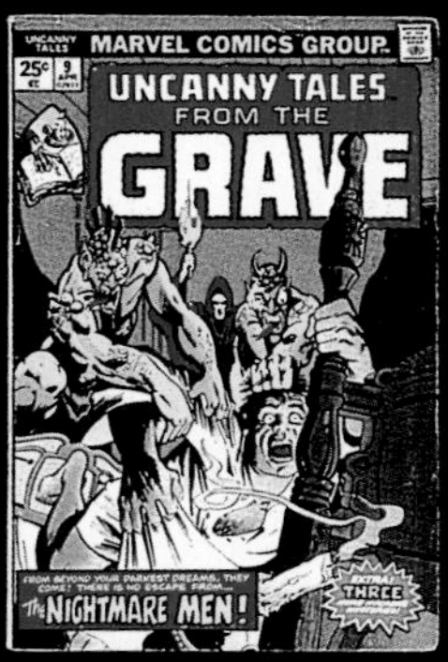
MARVEL COMICS GROUP
UNCANNY TALES FROM THE GRAVE
THE NIGHTMARE MEN!
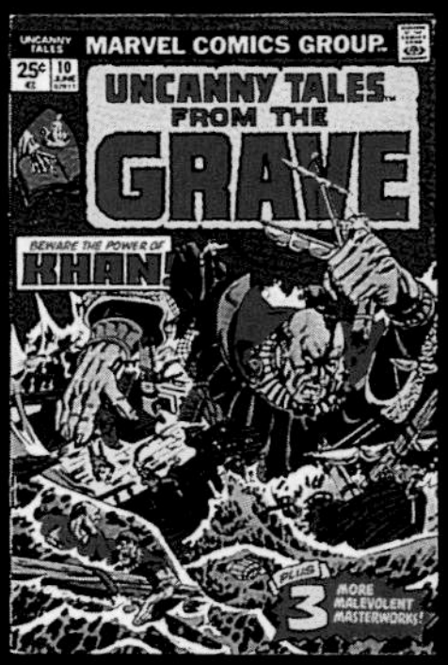
MARVEL COMICS GROUP
UNCANNY TALES FROM THE GRAVE
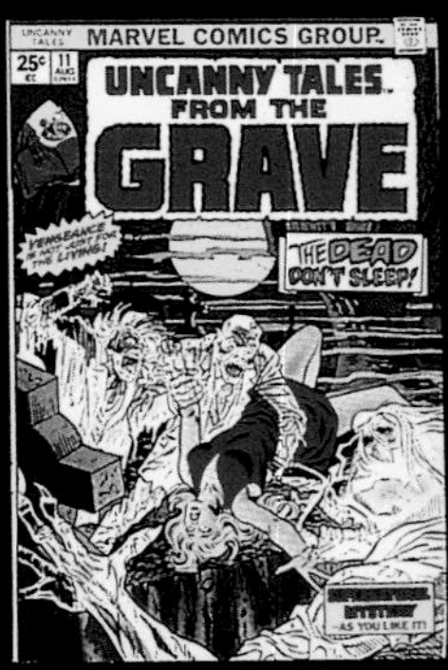
MARVEL COMICS GROUP
UNCANNY TALES FROM THE GRAVE
THE DEAD DON'T SLEEP!

2001: A Space Odyssey (1-10) 2030.2

Ref. No.	Date	RVI	Artist/Info.
2030.2-1	Dec. 1976	2	Kirby/Royer-a
2030.2-2	Jan. 1977	1	" "
2030.2-3	Feb.	1	" "
2030.2-4	Mar.	1	" "
2030.2-5	Apr.	1	" "
2030.2-6	May	1	" "
2030.2-7	Jun.	1	" "
2030.2-8	Jul.	1	" "
2030.2-9	Aug.	1	" "
2030.2-10	Sept.	1	" "

2010 (1-2) 2031.3

2031.2-1	Apr. 1985	1	Hama/Palmer-a
2031.2-2	May	1	" "

Uncanny Tales (1-12) 2032.2

2032.2-1	Dec. 1973	1	Crandall-a	Reprints
2032.2-2	Feb. 1974	1	Ayers, Gill, Carrobotta-a	"
2032.2-3	Apr.	1	DiPreta-a	"
2032.2-4	Jun.	1	Romita-a	"
2032.2-5	Aug.	1	Kane, Tuska-a	"
2032.2-6	Oct.	1	Romita, Keller-a	"
2032.2-7	Dec.	1	Heath, Ditko-a	"
2032.2-8	Feb. 1975	1	Jones/Janson-c, Ditko-a	"
2032.2-9	Apr.	1	Pakula, Benulis/Abel-a	"
2032.2-10	Jun.	1	Ditko, Reinman, Heck	"
2032.2-11	Aug.	1	Ditko, Forte, Heath-a	"
2032.2-12	Oct.	1	Ditko-a	"

The Uncanny X-Men at the State Fair of Texas (1) 2032.4

2032.4-1	1983	6

U.S. 1 (1-12) 2055.5

2055.5-1	May 1983	1	Milgrom-c, Trimpe-a
2055.5-2	Jun.	1	Timpe-a
2055.5-3	Jul.	1	Springer/Esposito-a
2055.5-4	Aug.	1	" "
2055.5-5	Sept.	1	" "
2055.5-6	Oct.	1	" "
2055.5-7 to 12	Oct. 1984 (#12)	1	" "

2061.5 Vault of Evil (1-23)

MARVEL COMICS GROUP
NO MAN ESCAPES ALIVE FROM THE...
VAULT OF EVIL
EERIE FIRST ISSUE!
COME MIDNIGHT-- COME MONSTER!
ANYTHING CAN HAPPEN IN... THE HOUR OF THE WITCH!
THE WOMAN WHO WASN'T!
FACE THAT FOLLOWS!
THE THING AT THE WINDOW!
THE VAMPIRE IS-- MY BROTHER!
GIANT KILLER!
SUPERNATURAL MYSTERY-- AS YOU LIKE IT!
THE LURKERS IN THE CAVES!
SHOCKERS
MIDNIGHT-IN THE HAUNTED MANSION!
NOT AS THE DEVIL!
SHOCKS! SUSPENSE! AND THE SUPER-NATURAL!
MIDNIGHT IN HAUNTED MANOR
DON'T SHAKE HANDS WITH THE DEVIL!
A GRAVE HONEYMOON!
GRAVE UNDERTAKING!
THAT'S RIDICULOUS!
DRUIDS DANCE AT DUSK!

MARVEL COMICS GROUP
NO MAN ESCAPES ALIVE FROM THE...
VAULT OF EVIL
BEWARE! YOU TOO CAN BECOME A VICTIM OF VALDOR!
FOUR FEAR-FRAUGHT TALES OF MADNESS
MURDER MIRROR ON THE WALL...

Vault of Evil (1-23) 2061.5

Ref. No.	Date	RVI	Artist/Info.
2061.5-1	Feb. 1973	1	Reprints
2061.5-2 to 23	Nov. 1975, (#23)	1	"

The Very Best of Dennis the Menace (1-3) 2065.3

2065.3-1 to 3	Apr. 1982, (#1)	1	Ketcham-c Reprints

Vision and the Scarlet Witch (1-4) 2073.5

2073.5-1	Nov., 1982	1	Leonardi/Akin, Garvey-a
2073.5-2	Dec.	1	" " "
2073.5-3	Jan. 1983	1	" " "
2073.5-4	Feb.	1	" " "

Vision and the Scarlet Witch V.2 (1-12) 2073.6

2073.6-1 to 12	Oct. 1985, (#1)	1	

Void Indigo (1-2) 2073.8

2073.8-1	Nov. 1984	1	
2073.8-2	Mar. 1985	1	

War is Hell (1-15) 2090.2

2090.2-1	Jan. 1973	1	Reprints
2090.2-2 to 15	Oct. 1975, (#15)	1	"

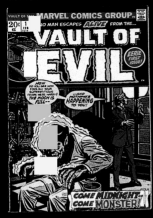

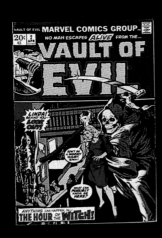

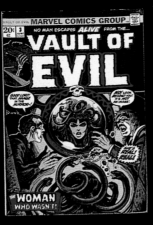

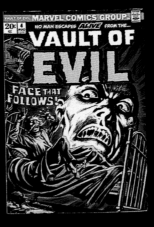

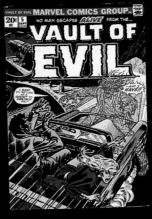

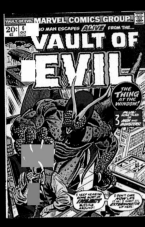

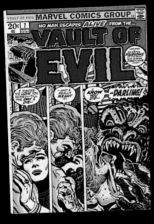

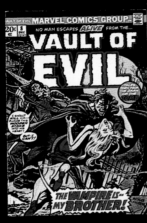

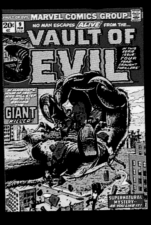

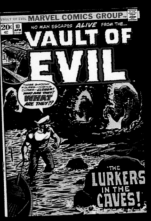

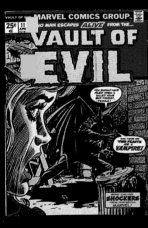

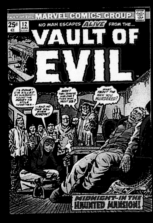

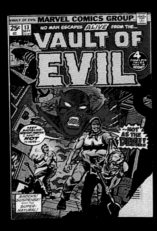

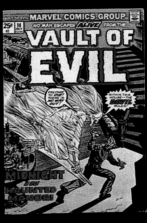

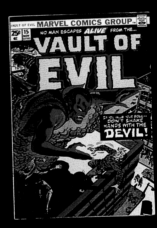

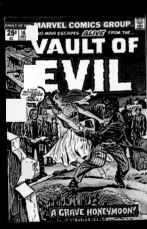

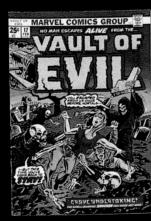

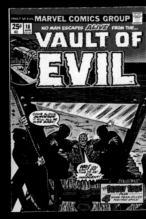

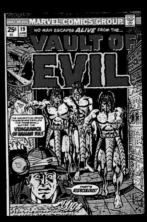

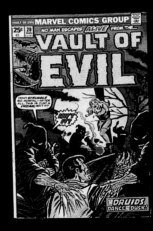

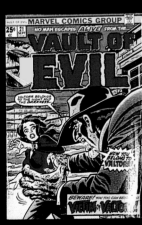

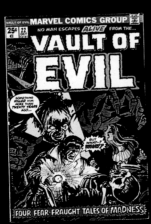

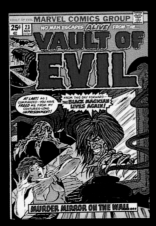

2073.5 Vision and the Scarlet Witch (1-4)

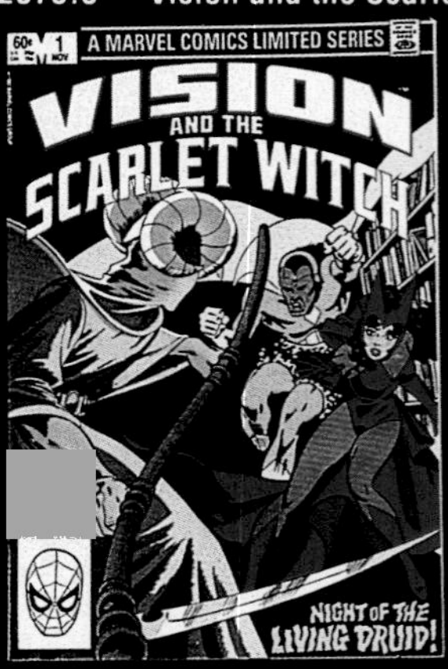
A MARVEL COMICS LIMITED SERIES
VISION AND THE SCARLET WITCH
NIGHT OF THE LIVING DRUID!
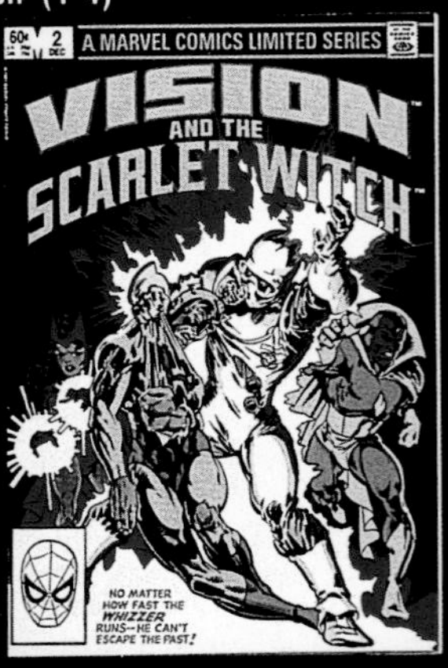
A MARVEL COMICS LIMITED SERIES
VISION AND THE SCARLET WITCH
NO MATTER HOW FAST THE WHIZZER RUNS--HE CAN'T ESCAPE THE PAST!
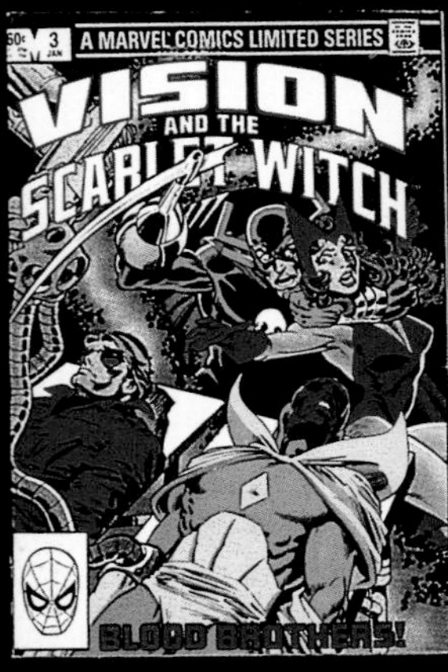
A MARVEL COMICS LIMITED SERIES
VISION AND THE SCARLET WITCH
BLOOD BROTHERS!
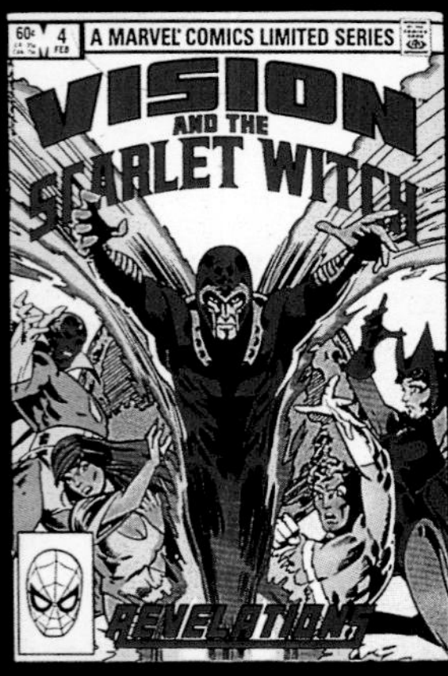
A MARVEL COMICS LIMITED SERIES
VISION AND THE SCARLET WITCH
REVELATION!
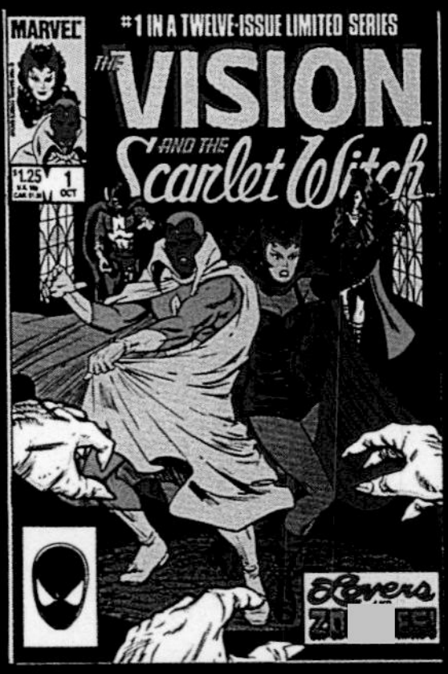
#1 IN A TWELVE-ISSUE LIMITED SERIES
THE VISION AND THE Scarlet Witch

2090.2 War is Hell (1-10)

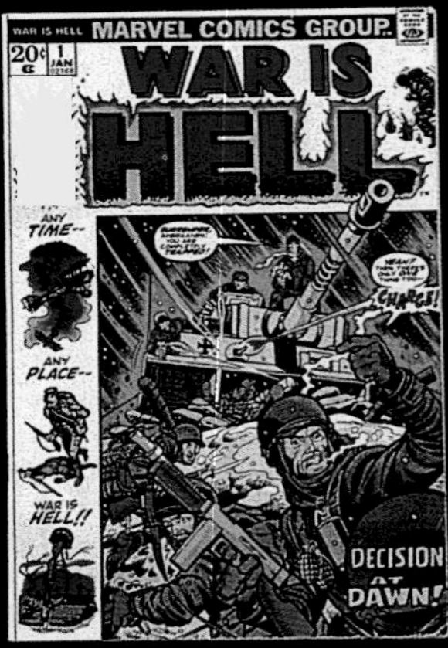
MARVEL COMICS GROUP
WAR IS HELL
ANY TIME--
ANY PLACE--
WAR IS HELL!!
DECISION AT DAWN!
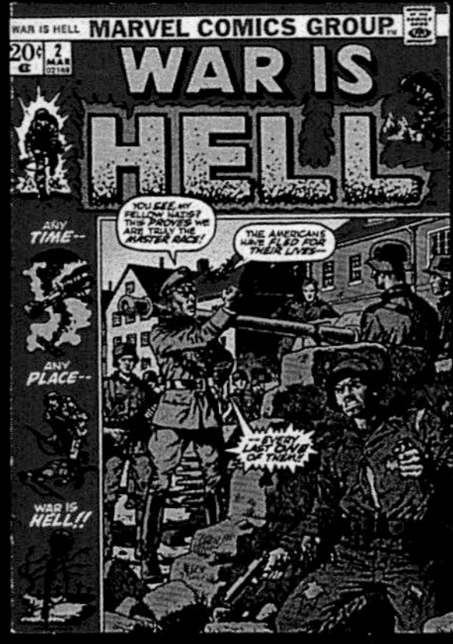
MARVEL COMICS GROUP
WAR IS HELL
ANY TIME--
ANY PLACE--
WAR IS HELL!!
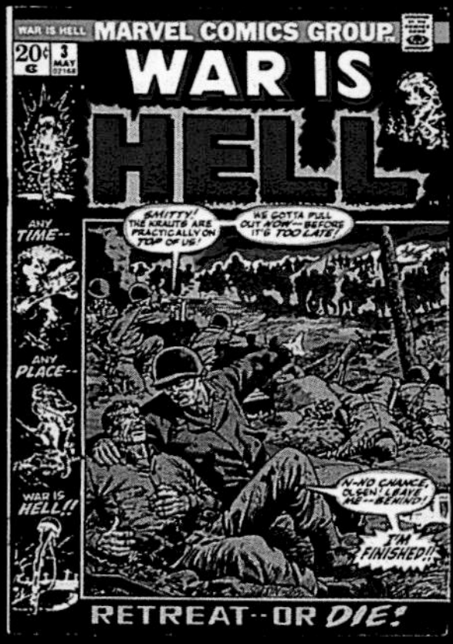
MARVEL COMICS GROUP
WAR IS HELL
ANY TIME--
ANY PLACE--
WAR IS HELL!!
RETREAT--OR DIE!
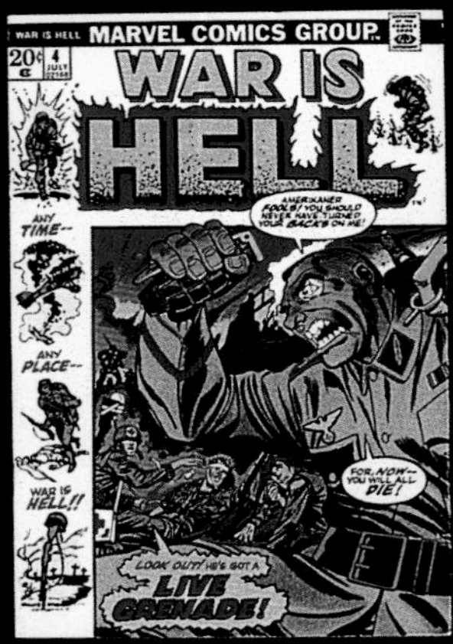
MARVEL COMICS GROUP
WAR IS HELL
ANY TIME--
ANY PLACE--
WAR IS HELL!!
LIVE GRENADE!
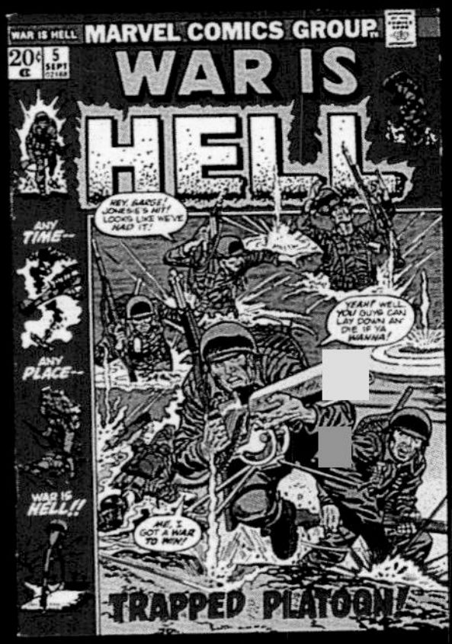
MARVEL COMICS GROUP
WAR IS HELL
ANY TIME--
ANY PLACE--
WAR IS HELL!!
TRAPPED PLATOON!
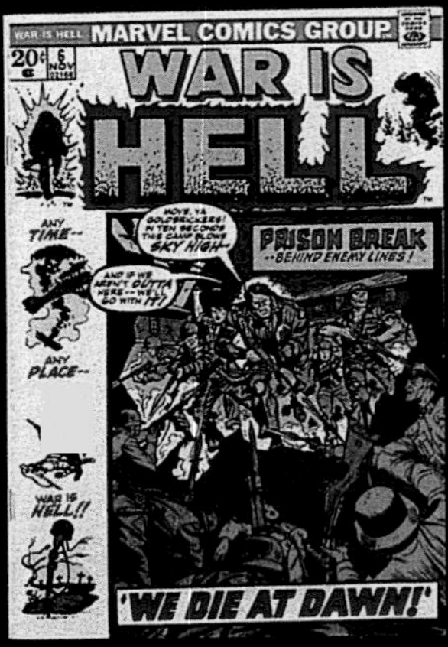
MARVEL COMICS GROUP
WAR IS HELL
PRISON BREAK --BEHIND ENEMY LINES!
ANY TIME--
ANY PLACE--
WAR IS HELL!!
'WE DIE AT DAWN!'
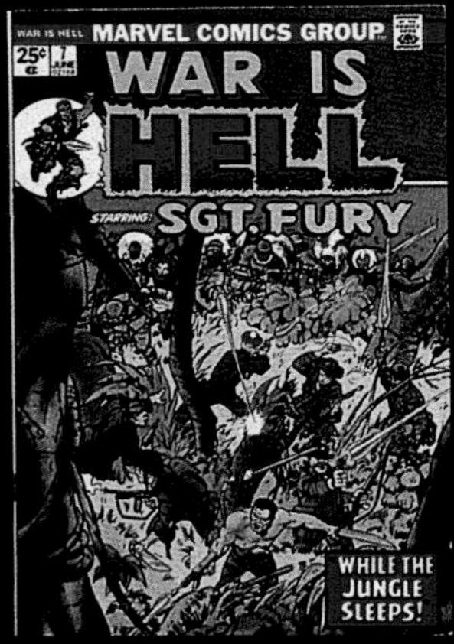
MARVEL COMICS GROUP
WAR IS HELL
STARRING SGT. FURY
WHILE THE JUNGLE SLEEPS!
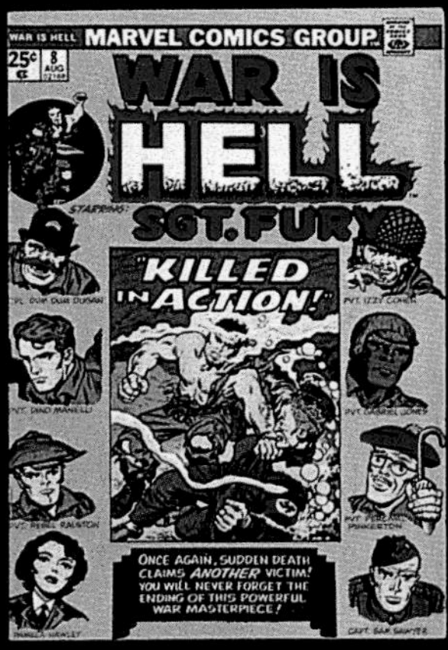
MARVEL COMICS GROUP
WAR IS HELL
STARRING SGT. FURY
KILLED IN ACTION!
ONCE AGAIN, SUDDEN DEATH CLAIMS ANOTHER VICTIM! YOU WILL NEVER FORGET THE ENDING OF THIS POWERFUL WAR MASTERPIECE!
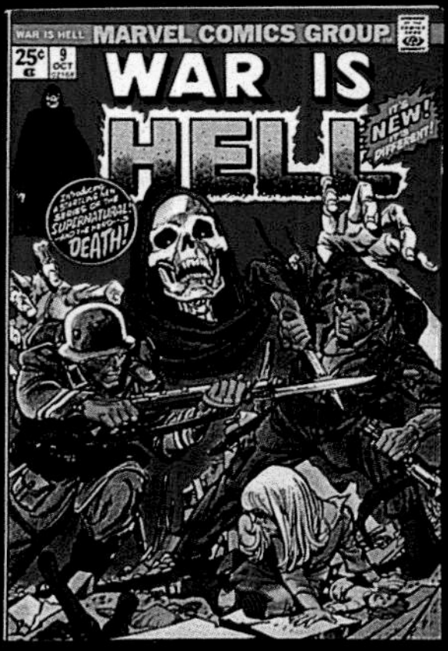
MARVEL COMICS GROUP
WAR IS HELL
DEATH!
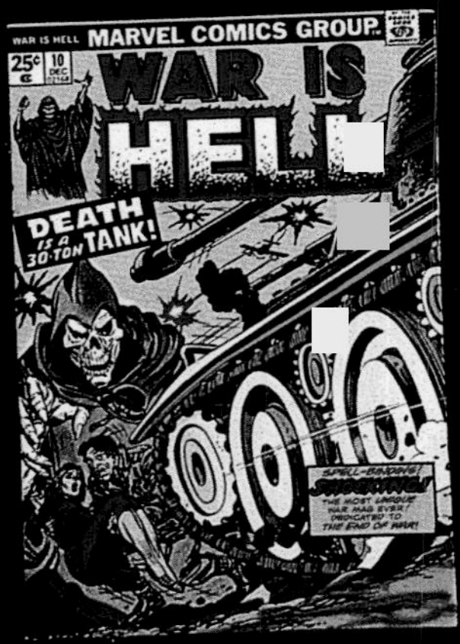
MARVEL COMICS GROUP
WAR IS HELL
DEATH IS A 30-TON TANK!

2090.3 Warlock (1-10)

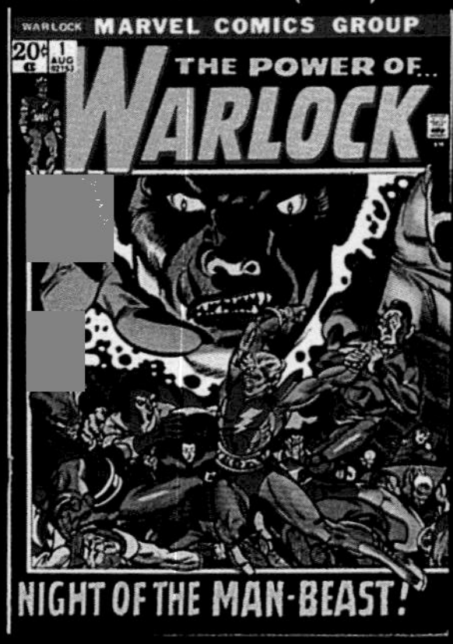
MARVEL COMICS GROUP
THE POWER OF... WARLOCK
NIGHT OF THE MAN-BEAST!
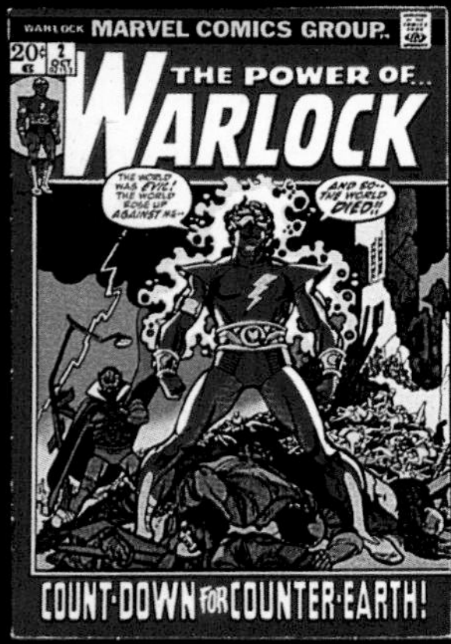
MARVEL COMICS GROUP
THE POWER OF... WARLOCK
COUNT-DOWN FOR COUNTER-EARTH!
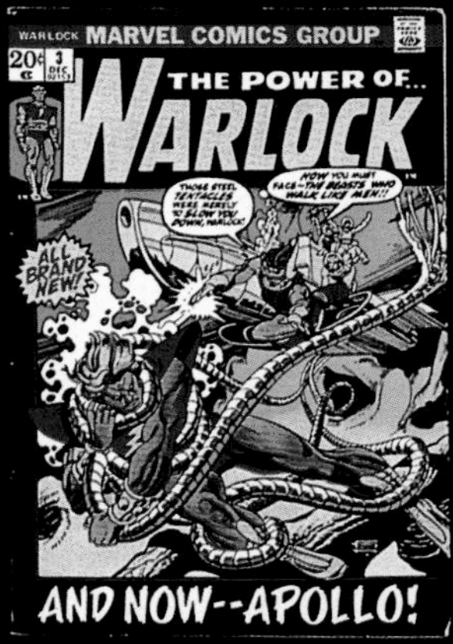
MARVEL COMICS GROUP
THE POWER OF... WARLOCK
AND NOW--APOLLO!
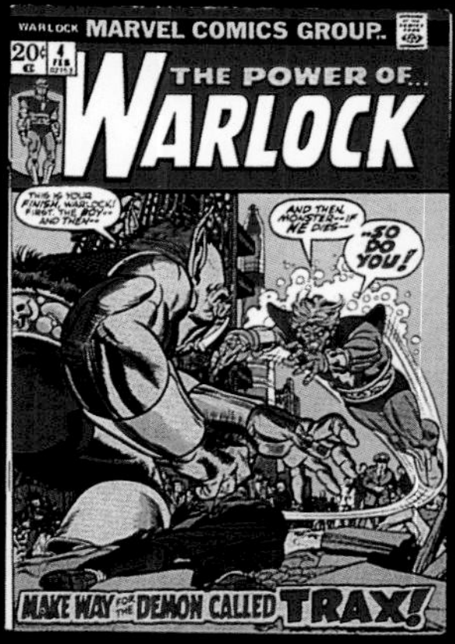
MARVEL COMICS GROUP
THE POWER OF... WARLOCK
SO DO YOU!
MAKE WAY FOR THE DEMON CALLED TRAX!
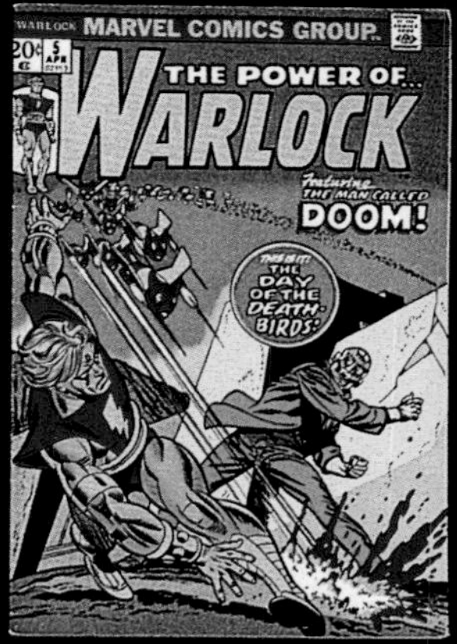
MARVEL COMICS GROUP
THE POWER OF... WARLOCK
DOOM!
THE DAY OF THE DEATH-BIRDS!
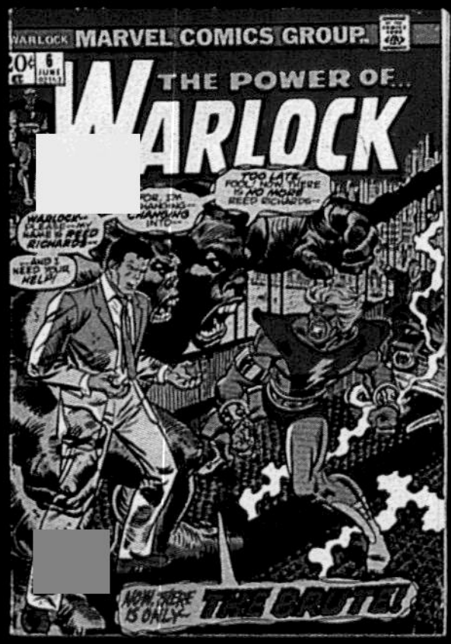
MARVEL COMICS GROUP
THE POWER OF... WARLOCK
THE BRUTE!
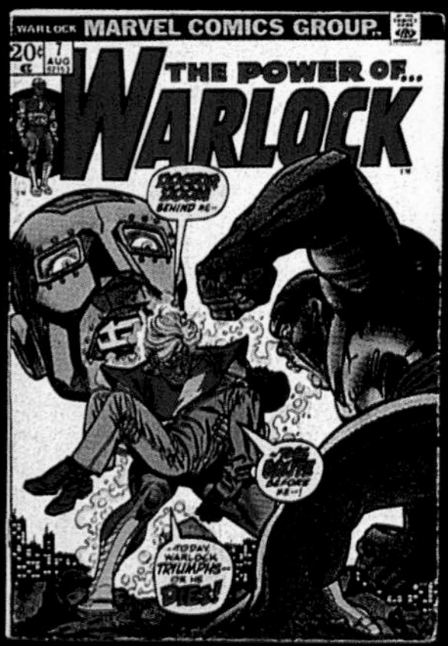
MARVEL COMICS GROUP
THE POWER OF... WARLOCK
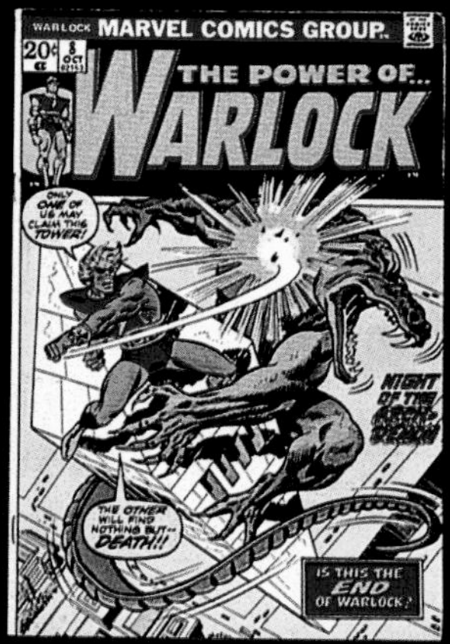
MARVEL COMICS GROUP
THE POWER OF... WARLOCK
IS THIS THE END OF WARLOCK?
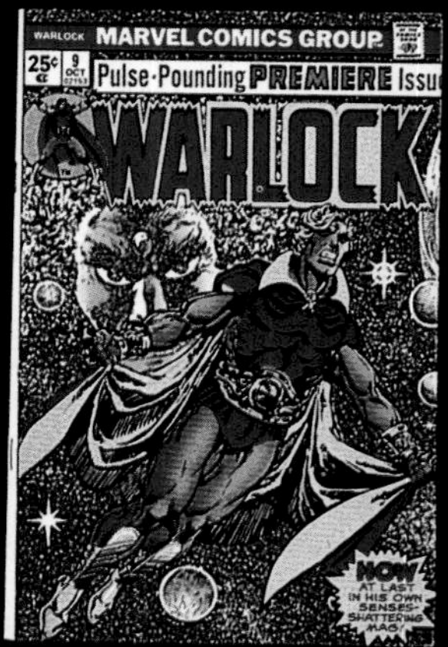
MARVEL COMICS GROUP
Pulse-Pounding PREMIERE Issue
WARLOCK
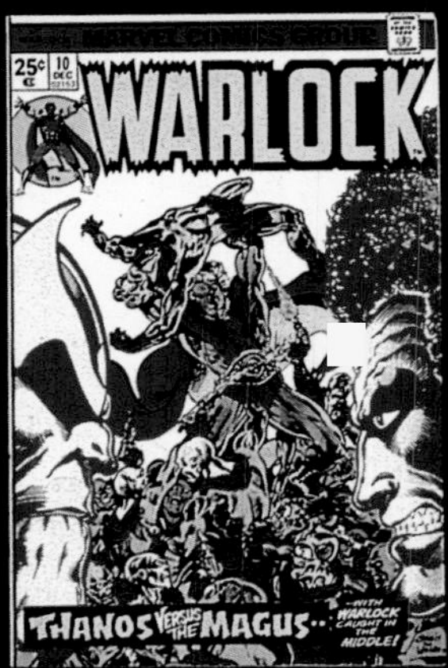
WARLOCK
THANOS VERSUS THE MAGUS

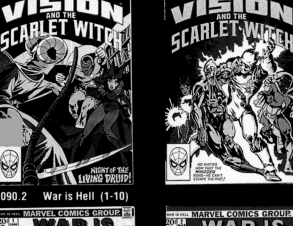

2090.3 Warlock (11-15)

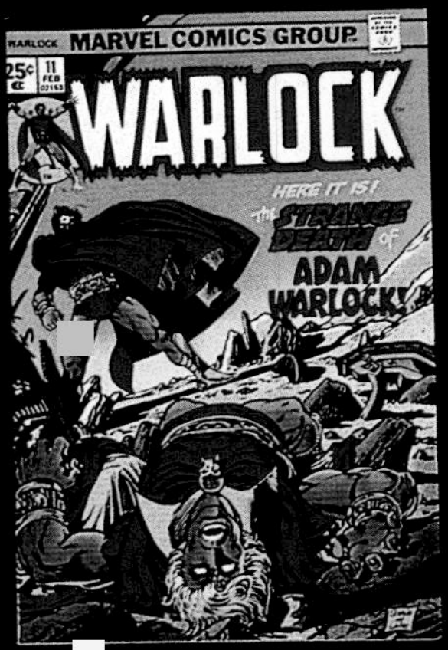
MARVEL COMICS GROUP
WARLOCK
HERE IT IS!
The STRANGE DEATH of ADAM WARLOCK!

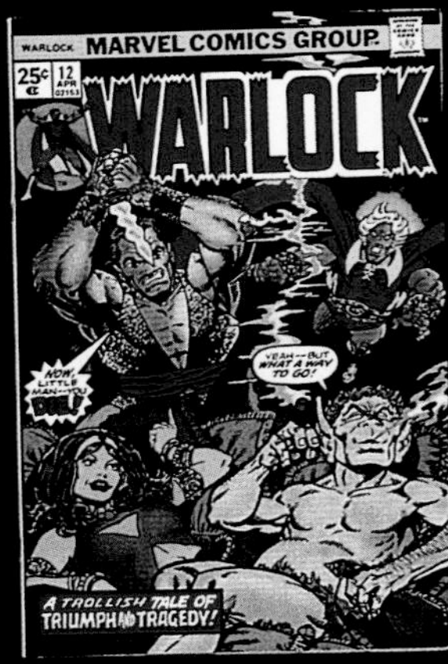
MARVEL COMICS GROUP
WARLOCK
A TROLLISH TALE OF TRIUMPH AND TRAGEDY!

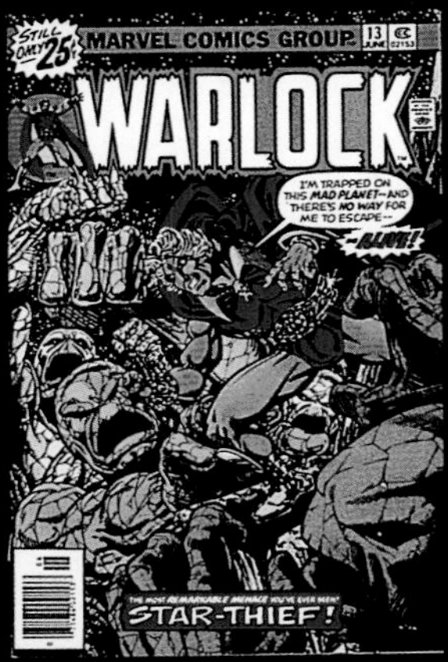
MARVEL COMICS GROUP
WARLOCK
I'M TRAPPED ON THIS MAD PLANET--AND THERE'S NO WAY FOR ME TO ESCAPE--
STAR-THIEF!

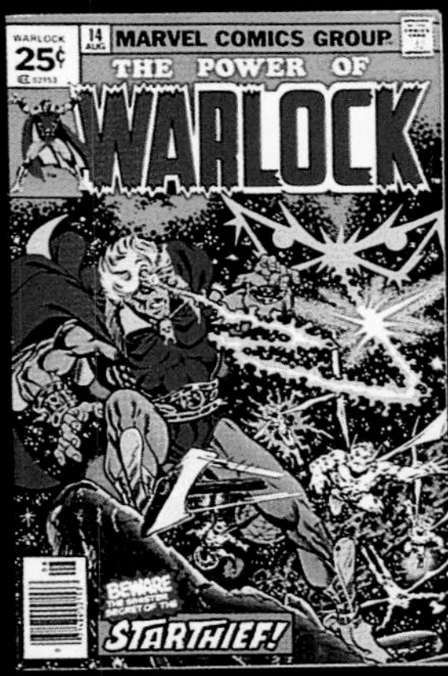
MARVEL COMICS GROUP
THE POWER OF
WARLOCK
STARTHIEF!

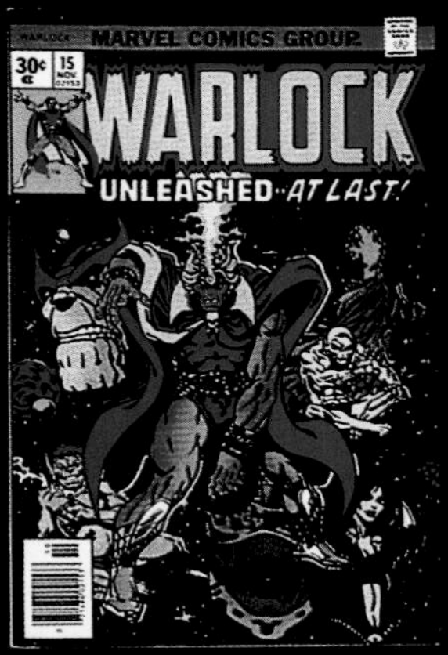
MARVEL COMICS GROUP
WARLOCK
UNLEASHED AT LAST!

2090 Warlock (1-5)

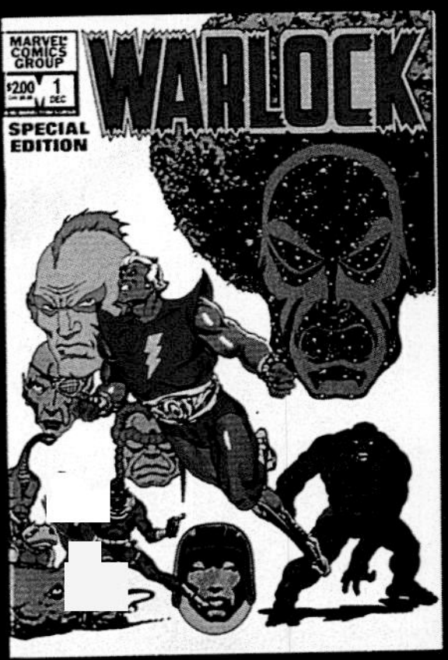
MARVEL COMICS GROUP
WARLOCK
SPECIAL EDITION

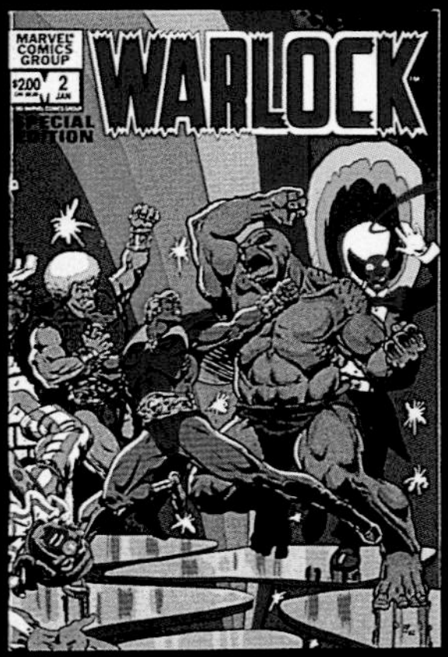
MARVEL COMICS GROUP
WARLOCK

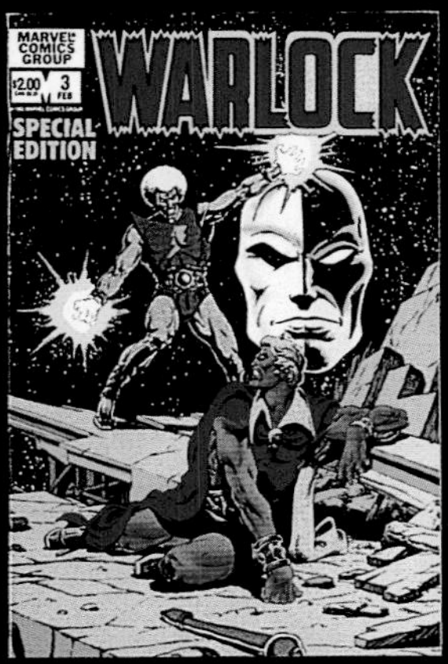
MARVEL COMICS GROUP
WARLOCK
SPECIAL EDITION

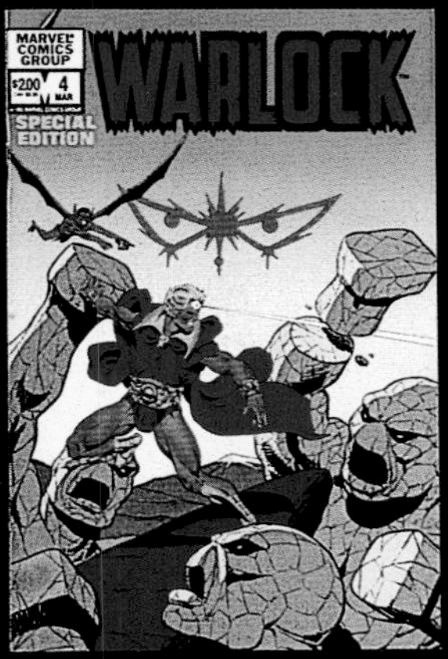
MARVEL COMICS GROUP
WARLOCK
SPECIAL EDITION

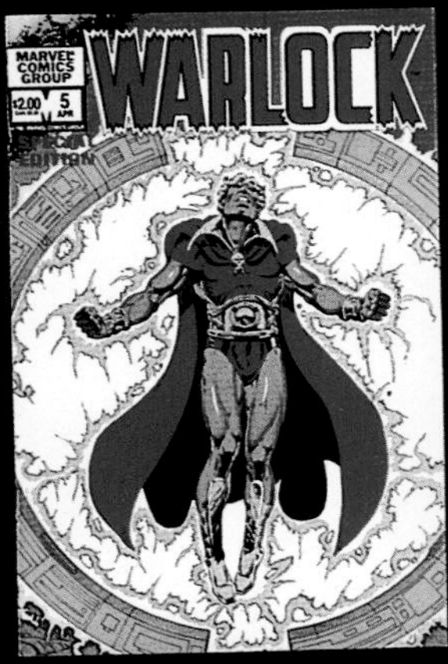
MARVEL COMICS GROUP
WARLOCK

2101.5 Web of Spider-Man (1-15)

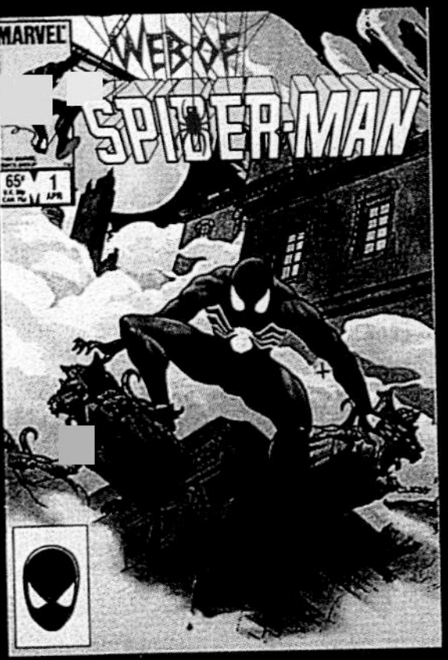
MARVEL
WEB OF
SPIDER-MAN

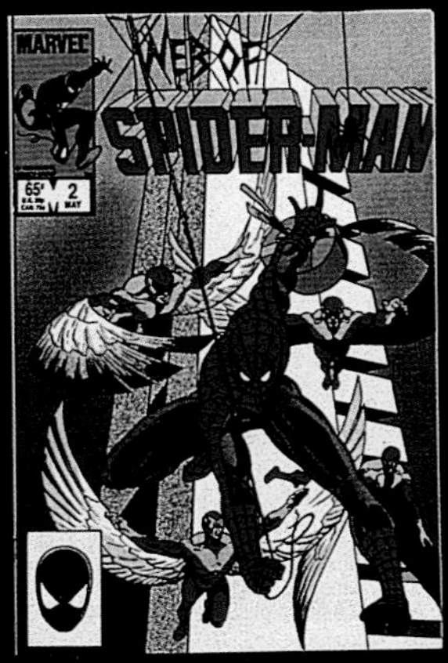
MARVEL
WEB OF
SPIDER-MAN

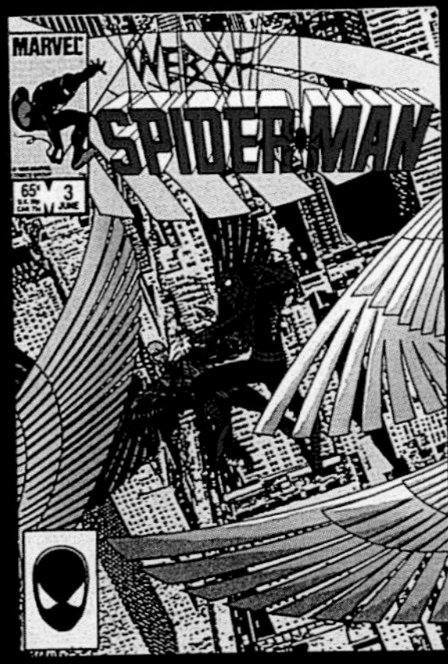
MARVEL
WEB OF
SPIDER-MAN

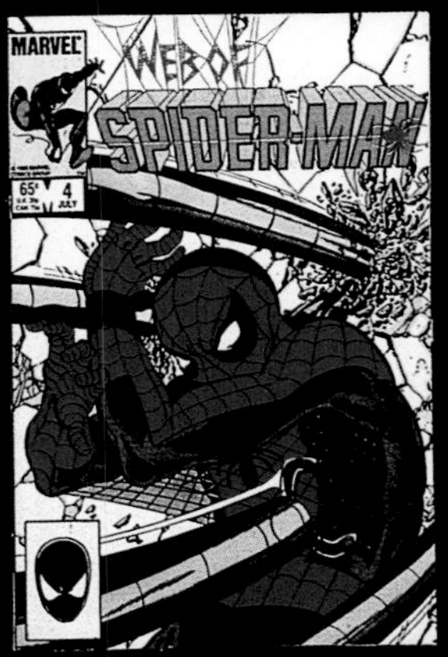
MARVEL
WEB OF
SPIDER-MAN

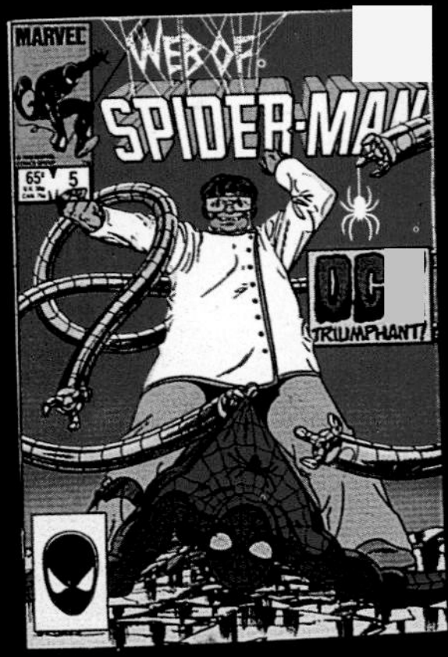
MARVEL
WEB OF
SPIDER-MAN
DOC
TRIUMPHANT!

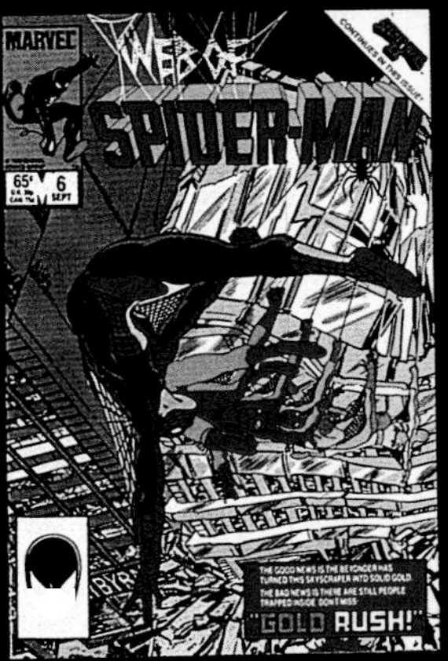
MARVEL
WEB OF
SPIDER-MAN
GOLD RUSH!

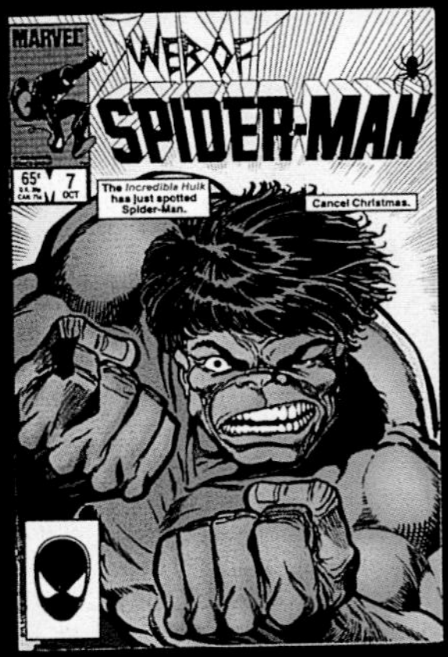
MARVEL
WEB OF
SPIDER-MAN
The Incredible Hulk has just spotted Spider-Man.
Cancel Christmas.

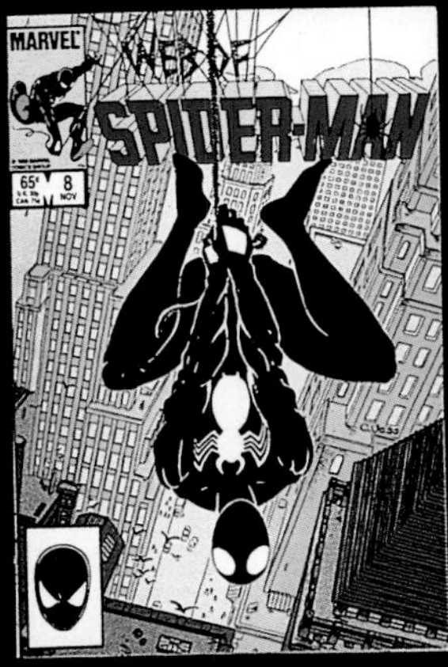
MARVEL
WEB OF
SPIDER-MAN

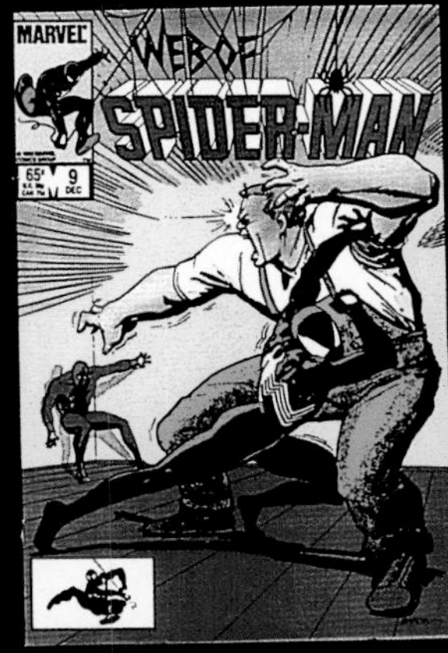
MARVEL
WEB OF
SPIDER-MAN

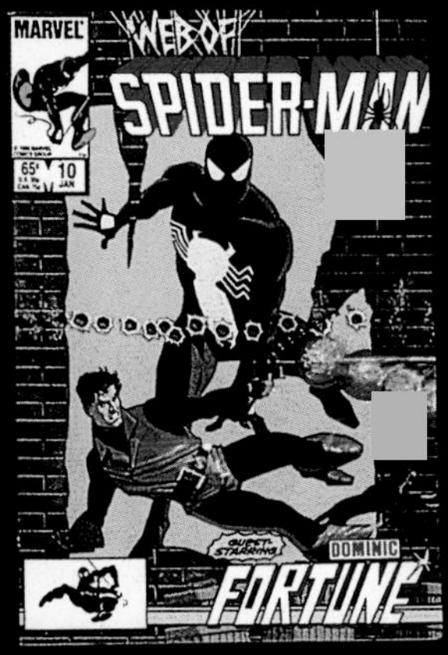
MARVEL
WEB OF
SPIDER-MAN
DOMINIC
FORTUNE

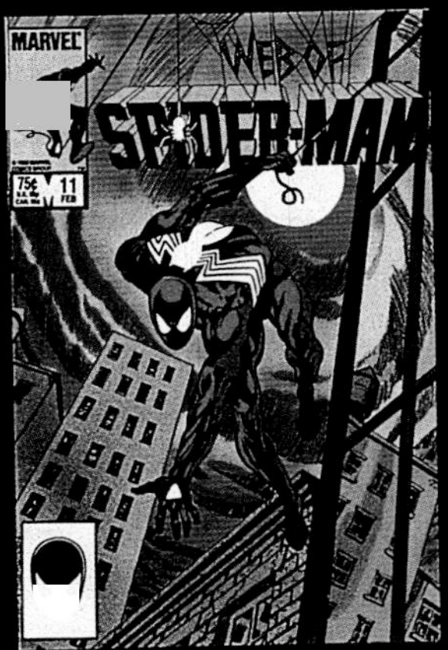
MARVEL
WEB OF
SPIDER-MAN

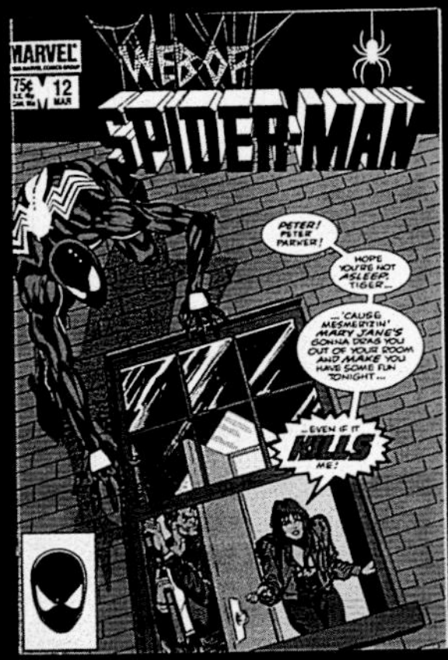
MARVEL
WEB OF
SPIDER-MAN
PETER! PETER PARKER!
KILLS

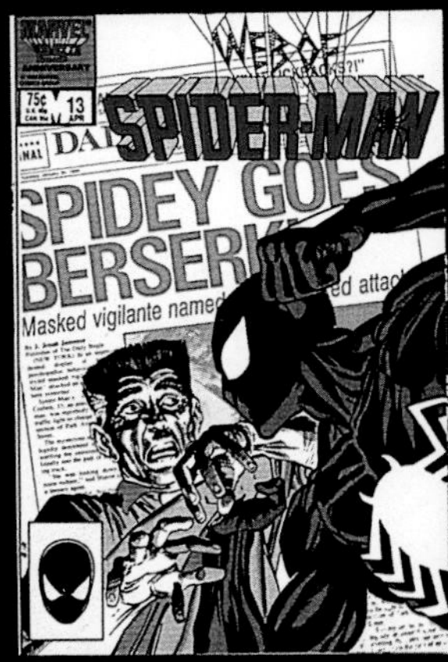
WEB OF
SPIDER-MAN
SPIDEY GOES BERSERK
Masked vigilante named

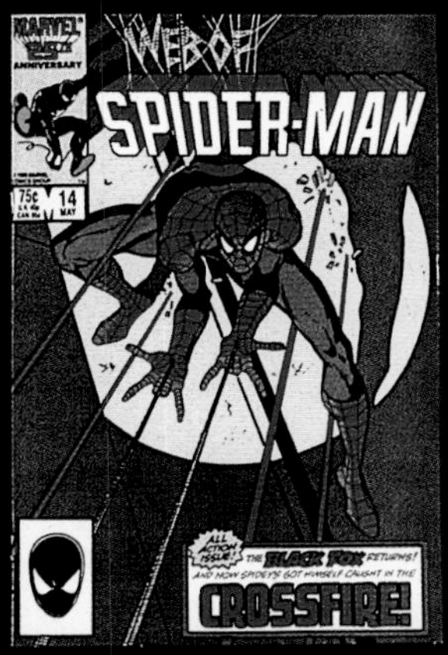
WEB OF
SPIDER-MAN
CROSSFIRE!

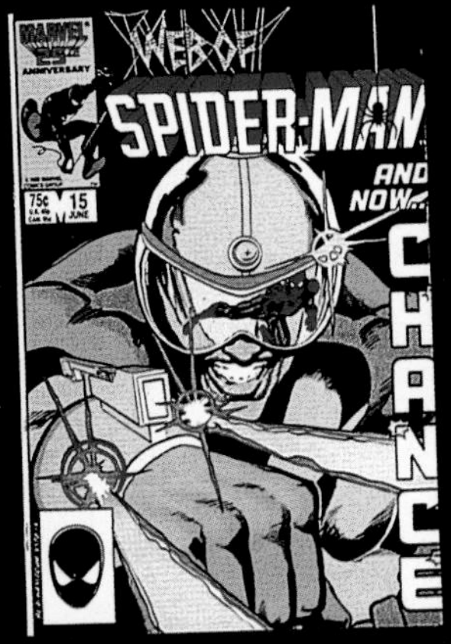
WEB OF
SPIDER-MAN
AND NOW
CHANCE

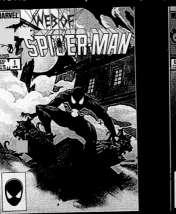

2116.3 Weird Wonder Tales (1-22)

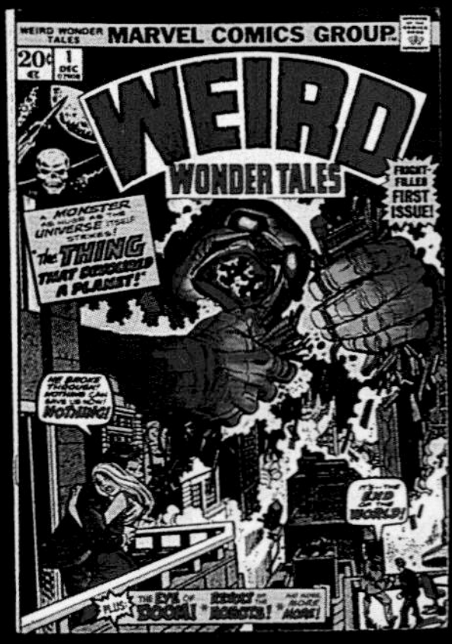
MARVEL COMICS GROUP
20¢ 1 DEC
WEIRD WONDER TALES
FRIGHT-FILLED FIRST ISSUE!
THE THING THAT ATE A PLANET!

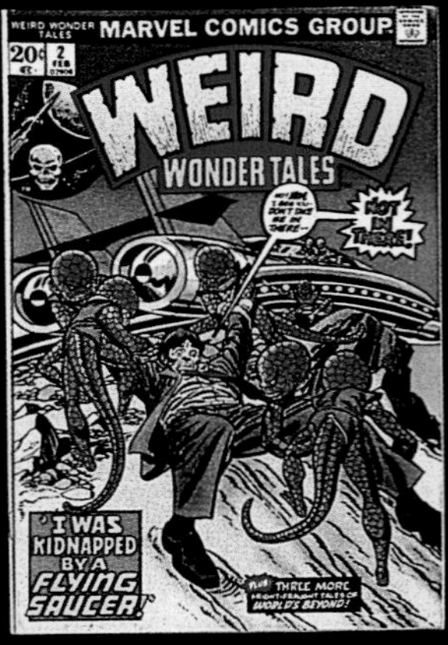
MARVEL COMICS GROUP
20¢ 2 FEB
WEIRD WONDER TALES
I WAS KIDNAPPED BY A FLYING SAUCER!

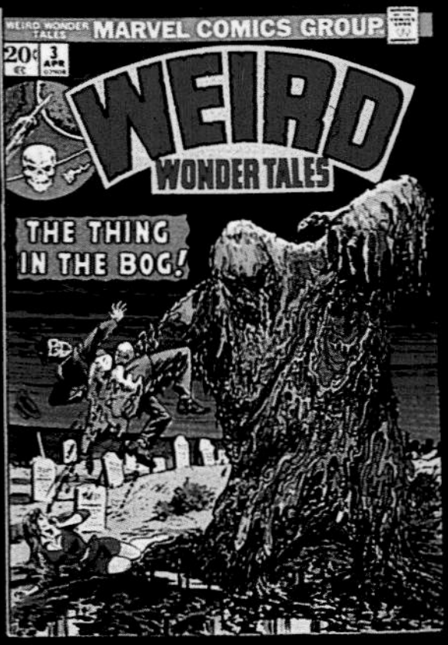
MARVEL COMICS GROUP
20¢ 3 APR
WEIRD WONDER TALES
THE THING IN THE BOG!

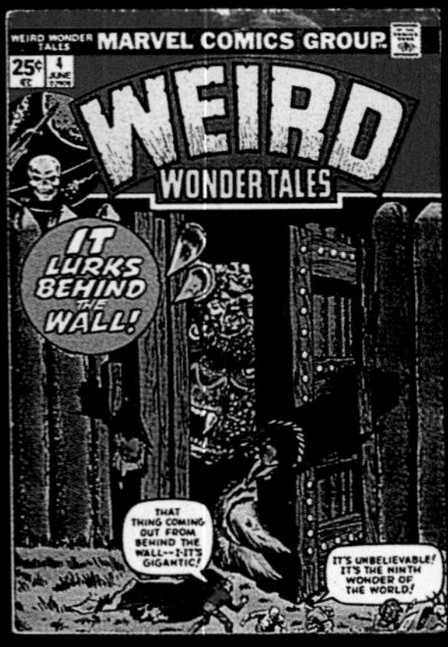
MARVEL COMICS GROUP
25¢ 4 JUNE
WEIRD WONDER TALES
IT LURKS BEHIND THE WALL!

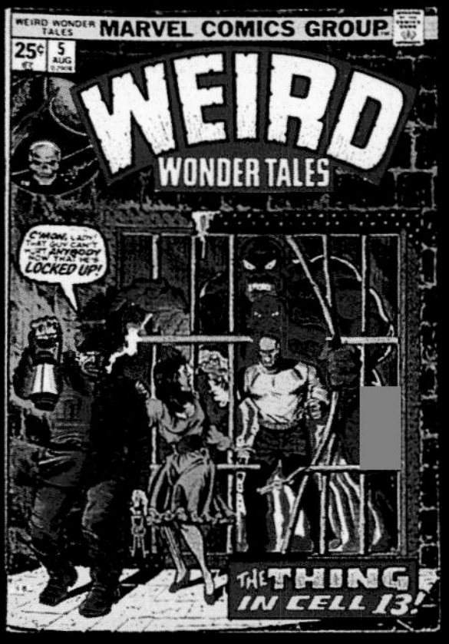
MARVEL COMICS GROUP
25¢ 5 AUG
WEIRD WONDER TALES
THE THING IN CELL 13!

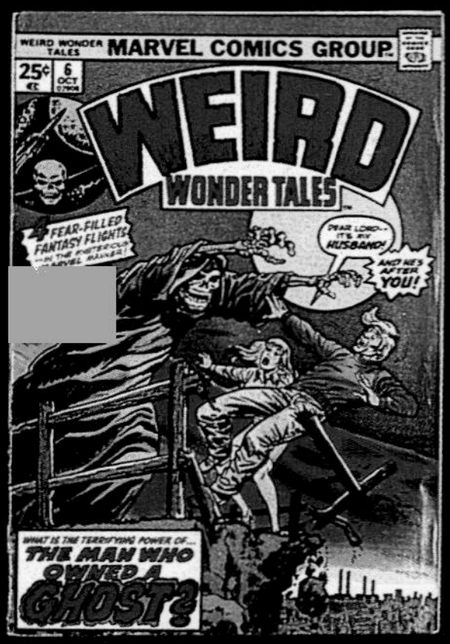
MARVEL COMICS GROUP
25¢ 6 OCT
WEIRD WONDER TALES
THE MAN WHO OWNED A GHOST!

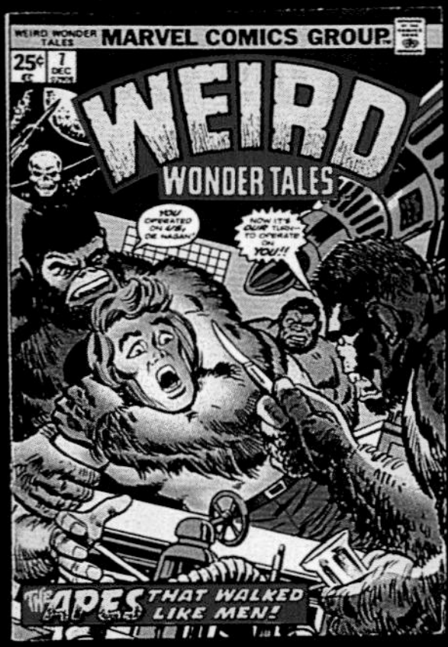
MARVEL COMICS GROUP
25¢ 7 DEC
WEIRD WONDER TALES
APES THAT WALKED LIKE MEN!

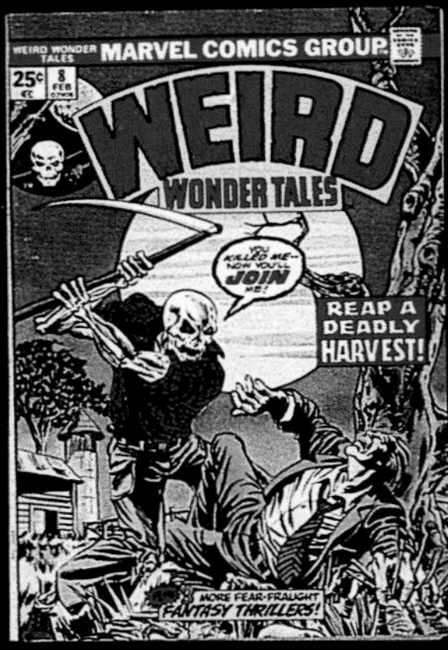
MARVEL COMICS GROUP
25¢ 8 FEB
WEIRD WONDER TALES
JOIN
REAP A DEADLY HARVEST!
MORE FEAR-FRAUGHT FANTASY THRILLERS!

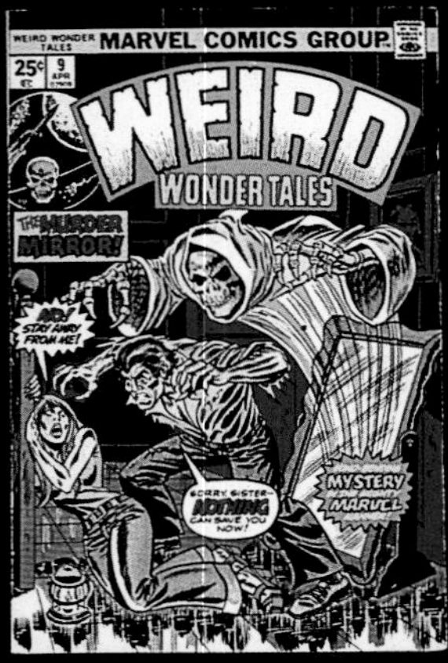
MARVEL COMICS GROUP
25¢ 9 APR
WEIRD WONDER TALES
MYSTERY MARVEL

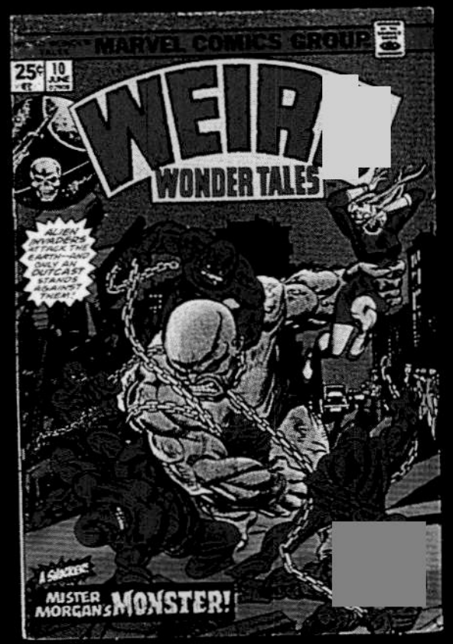
MARVEL COMICS GROUP
25¢ 10 JUNE
WEIRD WONDER TALES
MISTER MORGAN'S MONSTER!

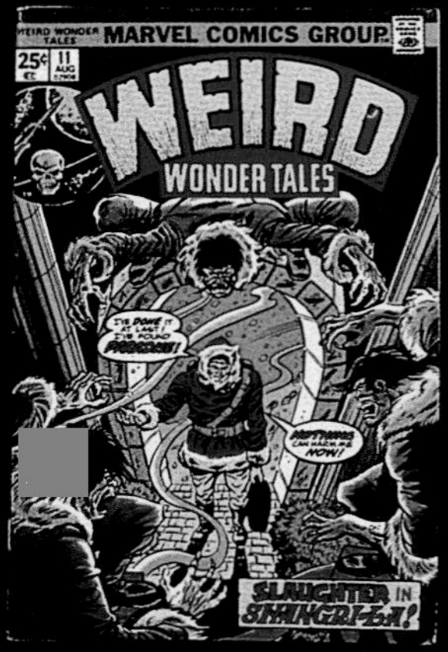
MARVEL COMICS GROUP
25¢ 11 AUG
WEIRD WONDER TALES
SLAUGHTER IN SHANGRI-LA!

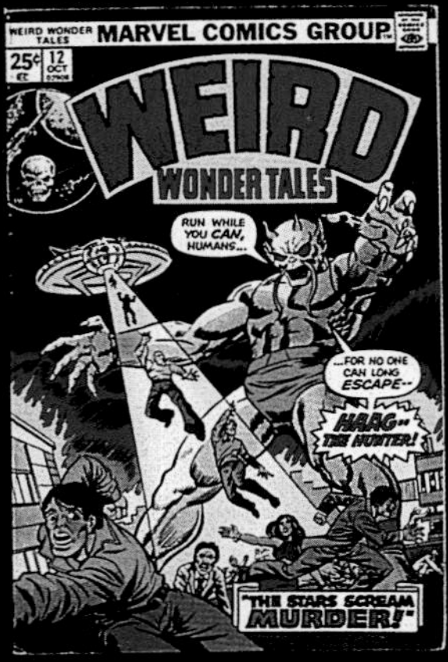
MARVEL COMICS GROUP
25¢ 12 OCT
WEIRD WONDER TALES
RUN WHILE YOU CAN, HUMANS...
...FOR NO ONE CAN LONG ESCAPE--
HARG THE HUNTER!
THE STARS SCREAM MURDER!

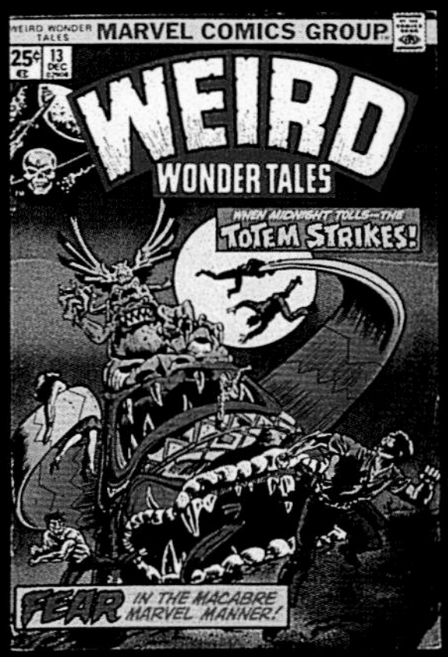
MARVEL COMICS GROUP
25¢ 13 DEC
WEIRD WONDER TALES
TOTEM STRIKES!
FEAR IN THE MACABRE MARVEL MANNER!

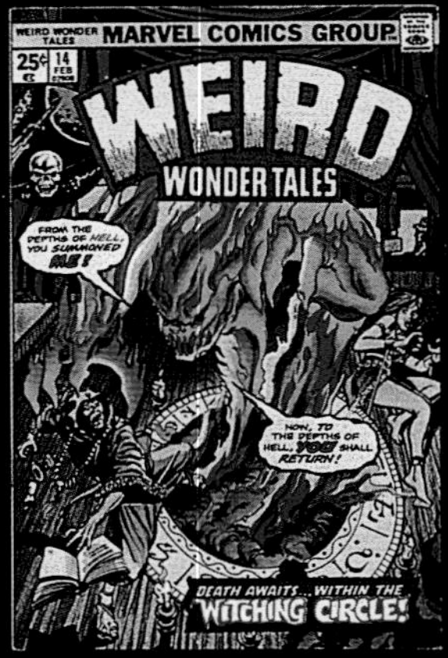
MARVEL COMICS GROUP
25¢ 14 FEB
WEIRD WONDER TALES
DEATH AWAITS... WITHIN THE WITCHING CIRCLE!

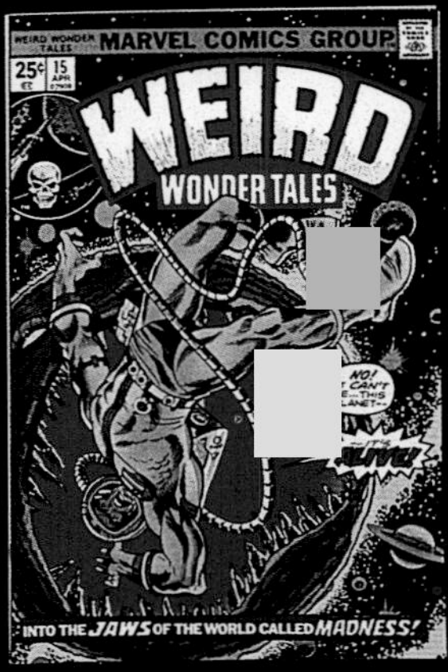
MARVEL COMICS GROUP
25¢ 15 APR
WEIRD WONDER TALES
INTO THE JAWS OF THE WORLD CALLED MADNESS!

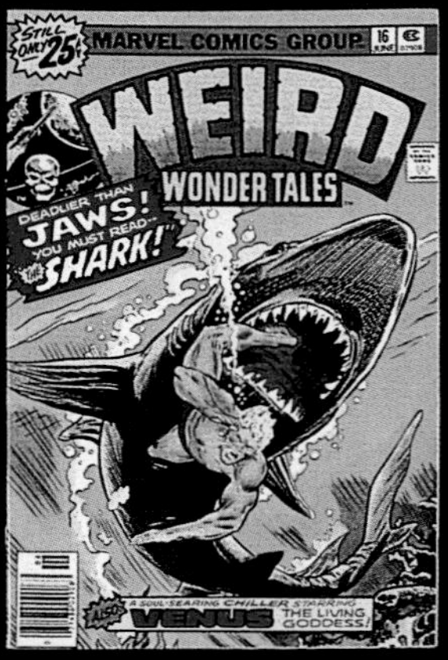
STILL ONLY 25¢
MARVEL COMICS GROUP
16 JUNE
WEIRD WONDER TALES
JAWS!
SHARK!
VENUS THE LIVING GODDESS!

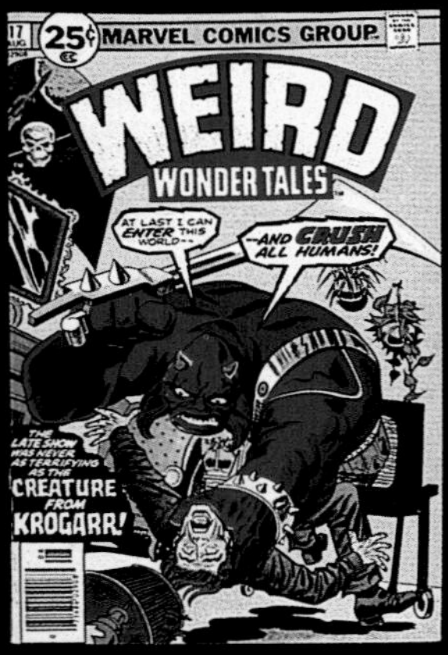
17 25¢
MARVEL COMICS GROUP
WEIRD WONDER TALES
--AND CRUSH ALL HUMANS!
CREATURE FROM KROGARR!

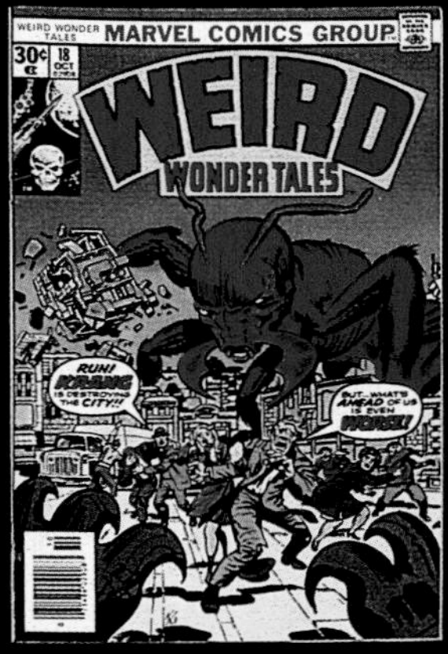
MARVEL COMICS GROUP
30¢ 18 OCT
WEIRD WONDER TALES

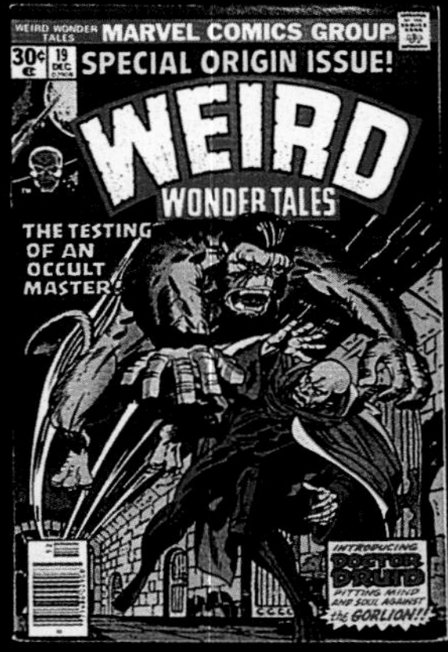
MARVEL COMICS GROUP
30¢ 19 DEC
SPECIAL ORIGIN ISSUE!
WEIRD WONDER TALES
THE TESTING OF AN OCCULT MASTER!

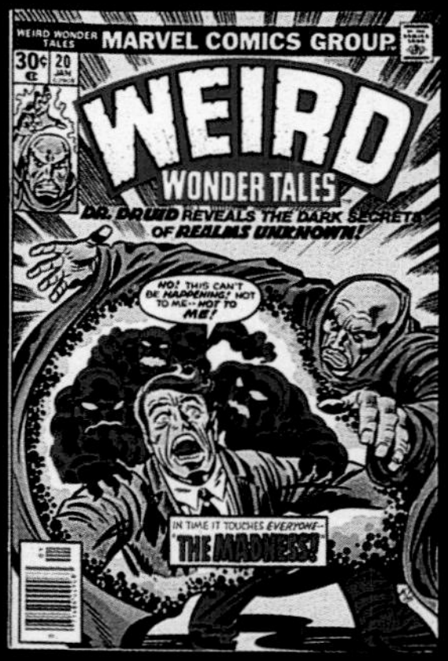
MARVEL COMICS GROUP
30¢ 20 JAN
WEIRD WONDER TALES
DR. DRUID REVEALS THE DARK SECRET OF REALMS UNKNOWN!
THE MADNESS!

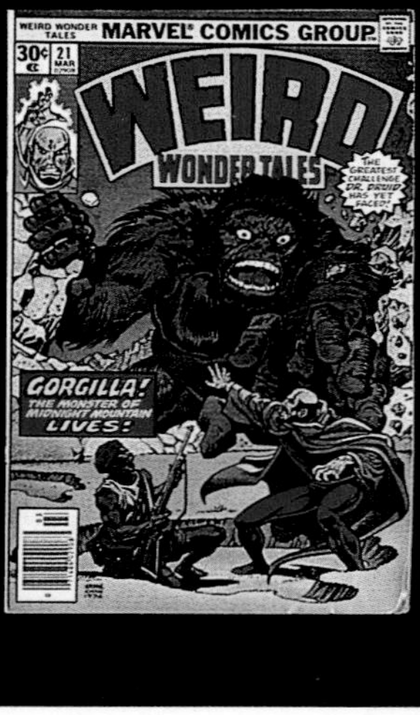
MARVEL COMICS GROUP
30¢ 21 MAR
WEIRD WONDER TALES
GORGILLA!

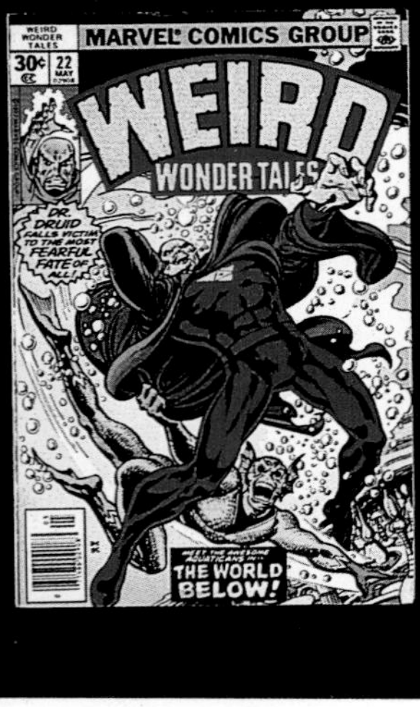
MARVEL COMICS GROUP
30¢ 22 MAY
WEIRD WONDER TALES
THE WORLD BELOW!

Warlock (1-15) 2090.3

Ref. No.	Date	RVI	Artist/Info.
2090.3-1	Aug. 1972	4	Kane/Sutton-c/a (Origin-Warlock)
2090.3-2	Oct.	2	Kane-c/a, Buscema, Sutton-a
2090.3-3	Dec. 2	2	Kane-c/a, Sutton-a
2090.3-4	Feb. 1973	2	Kane/Sinnott-c, Kane/Sutton-a
2090.3-5 to 15	Nov. 1976, (#15)	2	(9-15, Starlin-c/a) (all)

Warlock (1-6) 2090.4

2090.4-1	Dec. 1982	1	Starlin-c/a	Reprints
2090.4-2 to 6	May 1983, (#6)	1	"	"

The Web of Spider-Man (1-Present) 2101.5

2101.5-1	Apr. 1985	9	
2101.5-2	May	6	
2101.5-3	Jun.	4	
2101.5-4 to 28	Jul., (#4)	2	
2101.5-29		4	(Wolverine -app.)
2101.5-30 to 32		4	(#30, Origin-the Rose)
2101.5-33 to 70		1	(#44, Hulk -app.)
2101.5-A1	Sept. 1985	2	
2101.5-A2	Sept. 1986	3	Adams-a (New Mutants)

Weird Wonder Tales (1-22) 2116.3

2116.3-1	Dec. 1973	1	Woverton-a	Reprint
2116.3-2 to 22	May 1977, (#22)	1		Reprints

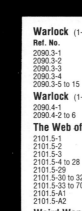

2119.2 Werewolf by Night (1-25)

MARVEL COMICS GROUP
NOW IN HIS OWN MAG!!
WEREWOLF BY NIGHT
FULL MOON RISE–WEREWOLF KILL!
MARVEL COMICS GROUP
WEREWOLF BY NIGHT
LIKE A WILD BEAST AT BAY!
MARVEL COMICS GROUP
WEREWOLF BY NIGHT
MYSTERY OF THE MAD MONK!
MARVEL COMICS GROUP
WEREWOLF BY NIGHT
THE DANGER GAME!
MARVEL COMICS GROUP
WEREWOLF BY NIGHT
A LIFE FOR A DEATH!
MARVEL COMICS GROUP
WEREWOLF BY NIGHT
WEREWOLF IN CAPTIVITY!
CARNIVAL OF FEAR!
MARVEL COMICS GROUP
WEREWOLF BY NIGHT
RITUAL OF BLOOD!
MARVEL COMICS GROUP
WEREWOLF BY NIGHT
KROGG! THE LURKER FROM BEYOND!
MARVEL COMICS GROUP
WEREWOLF BY NIGHT
MARVEL COMICS GROUP
WEREWOLF BY NIGHT
MARVEL COMICS GROUP
WEREWOLF BY NIGHT
FULL MOON FEAR MOON!
MARVEL COMICS GROUP
WEREWOLF BY NIGHT
CRY MONSTER
MARVEL COMICS GROUP
WEREWOLF BY NIGHT
TABOO!
MARVEL COMICS GROUP
WEREWOLF BY NIGHT
LO, THE MONSTER STRIKES!
MARVEL COMICS GROUP
WEREWOLF BY NIGHT WHEN DRACULA STRIKES!
MARVEL COMICS GROUP
WEREWOLF BY NIGHT
THE HUNCHBACK OF NOTRE DAME!
MARVEL COMICS GROUP
WEREWOLF BY NIGHT
BEHOLD BEHEMOTH!
MARVEL COMICS GROUP
WEREWOLF BY NIGHT
WAR OF THE WERE-WOLVES!
MARVEL COMICS GROUP
WEREWOLF BY NIGHT
WEREWOLF BATTLES VAMPIRES!
THE HAUNTING OF HOLLYWOOD HILLS!
MARVEL COMICS GROUP
WEREWOLF BY NIGHT
THE MONSTER BREAKS FREE!
MARVEL COMICS GROUP
WEREWOLF
"To Cure A Werewolf" ANOTHER MUST DIE!
MARVEL COMICS GROUP
WEREWOLF BY NIGHT
THE FACE OF THE FIEND!
MARVEL COMICS GROUP
WEREWOLF BY NIGHT
ARRRR
SILVER BULLET FOR A WEREWOLF!
MARVEL COMICS GROUP
WEREWOLF BY NIGHT
DEATH-BATTLE WITH... THE BRUTE!
MARVEL COMICS GROUP
WEREWOLF BY NIGHT
ECLIPSE OF EVIL!
SHOCKING MYSTERY SUPER-VILLAIN!

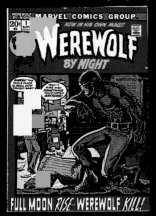

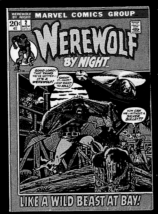

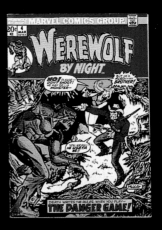

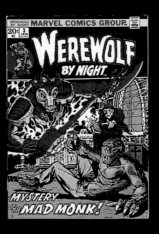

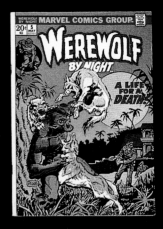

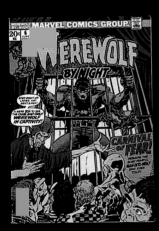

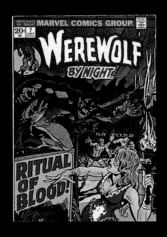

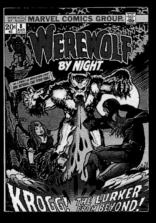

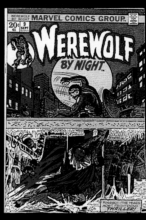

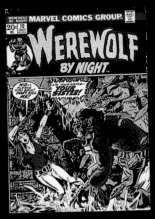

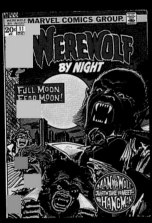

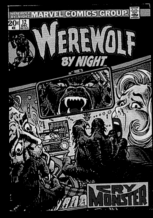

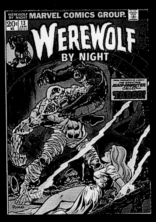

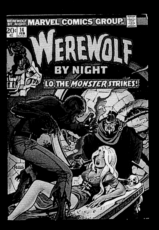

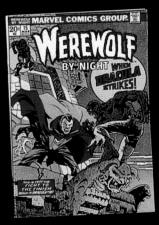

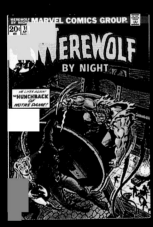

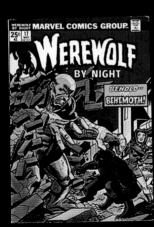

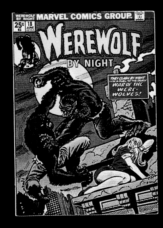

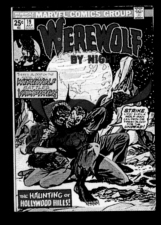

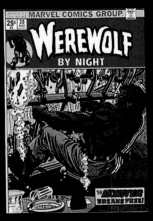

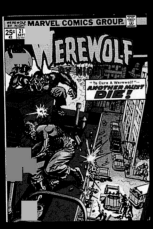

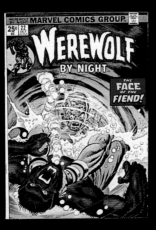

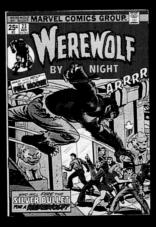

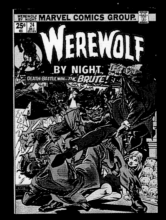

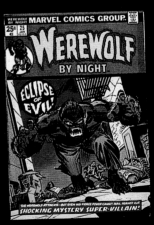

2119.2 Werewolf by Night (26-43, GS. 1-5)

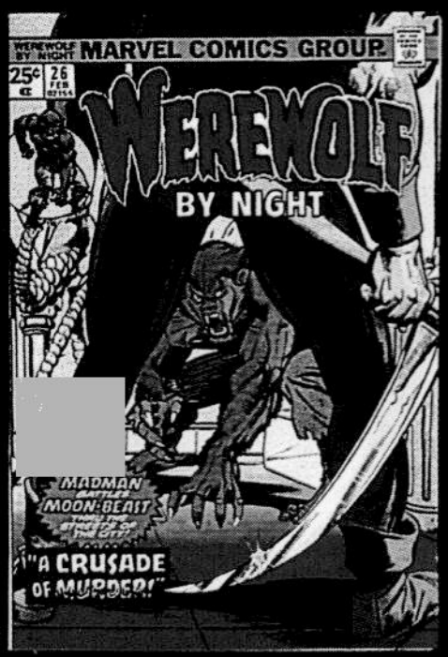
MARVEL COMICS GROUP
WEREWOLF BY NIGHT
A CRUSADE OF MURDER!
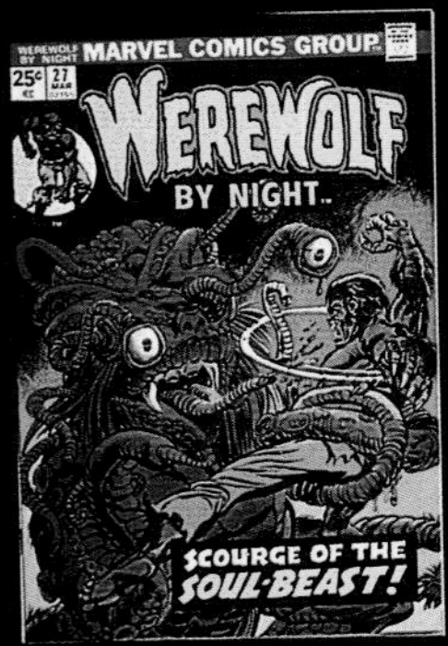
MARVEL COMICS GROUP
WEREWOLF BY NIGHT
SCOURGE OF THE SOUL-BEAST!
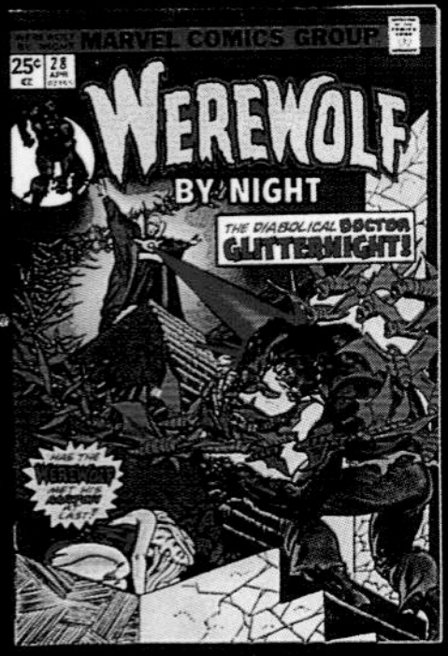
MARVEL COMICS GROUP
WEREWOLF BY NIGHT
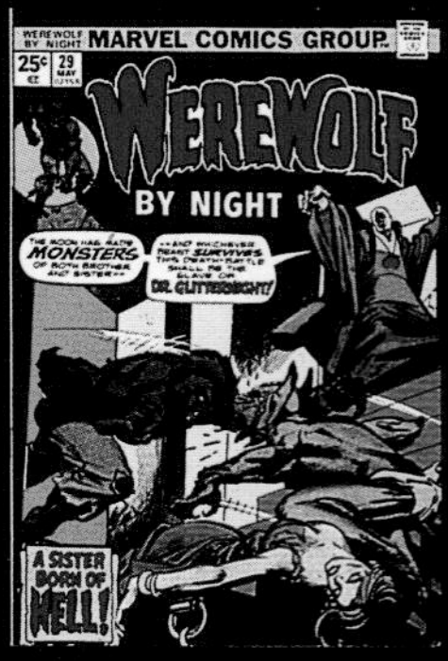
MARVEL COMICS GROUP
WEREWOLF BY NIGHT
A SISTER OF HELL!
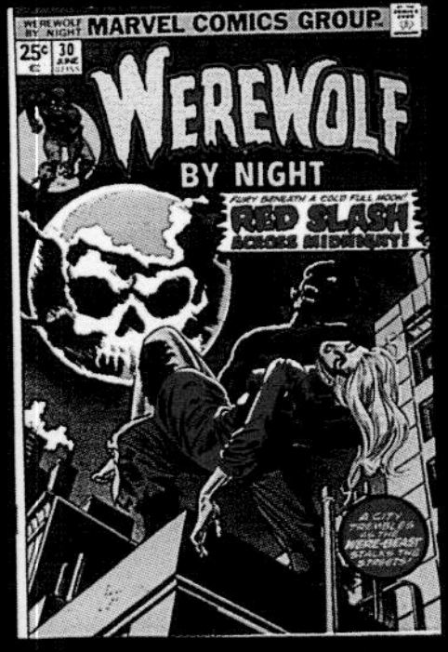
MARVEL COMICS GROUP
WEREWOLF BY NIGHT
RED SLASH
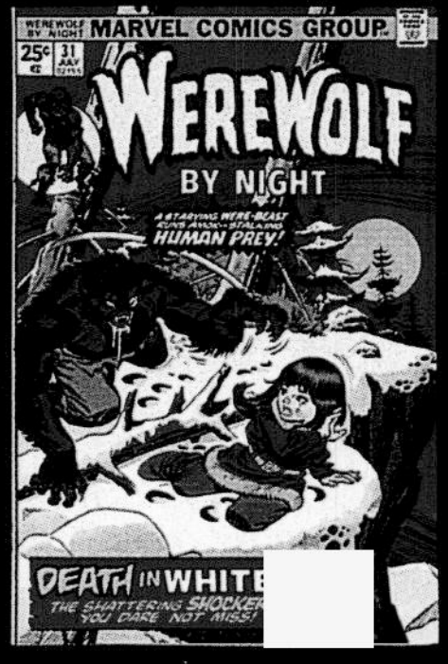
MARVEL COMICS GROUP
WEREWOLF BY NIGHT
HUMAN PREY!
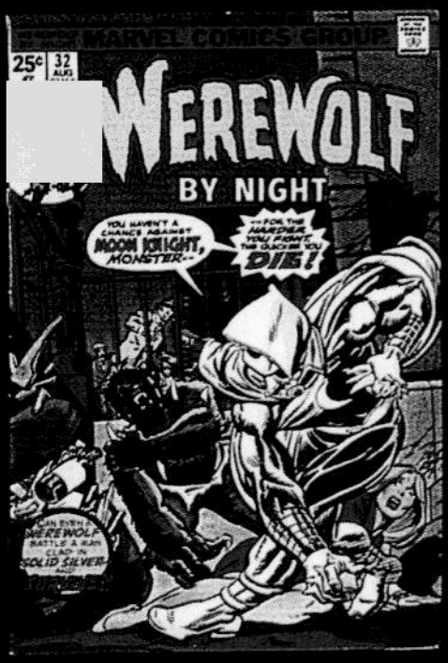
MARVEL COMICS GROUP
WEREWOLF BY NIGHT
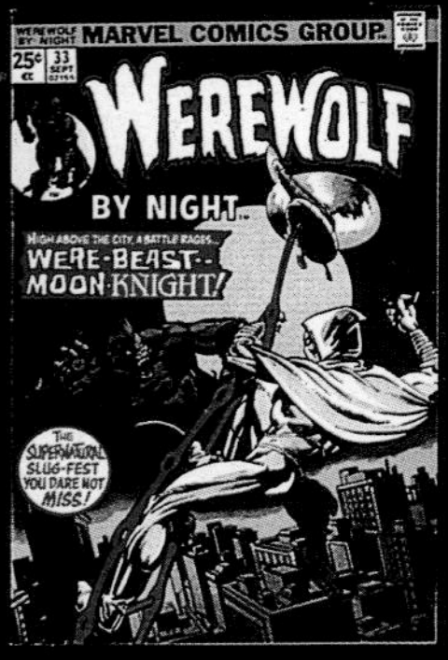
MARVEL COMICS GROUP
WEREWOLF BY NIGHT
WERE-BEAST -- MOON KNIGHT!
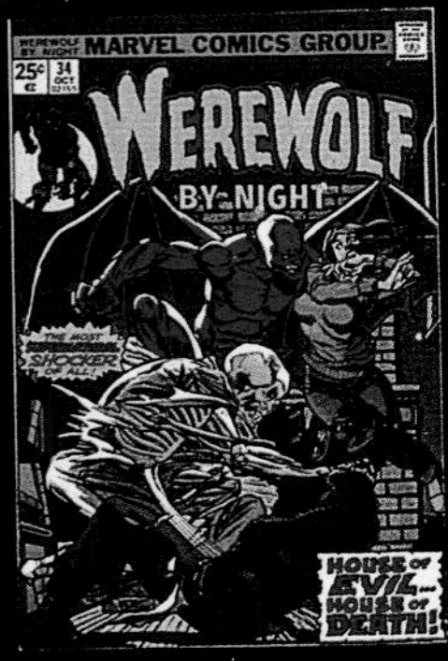
MARVEL COMICS GROUP
WEREWOLF BY NIGHT
HOUSE OF EVIL... HOUSE OF DEATH!
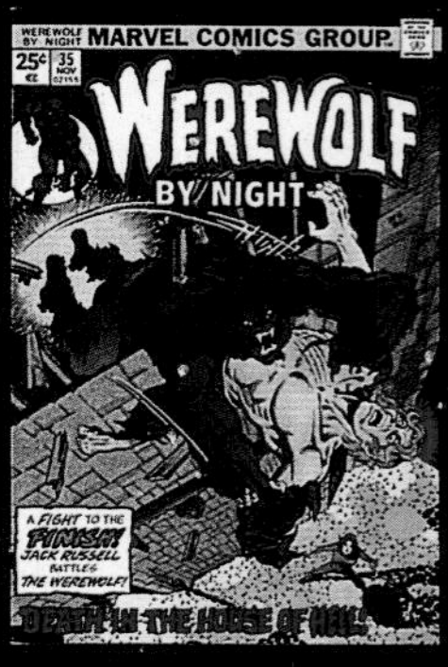
MARVEL COMICS GROUP
WEREWOLF BY NIGHT
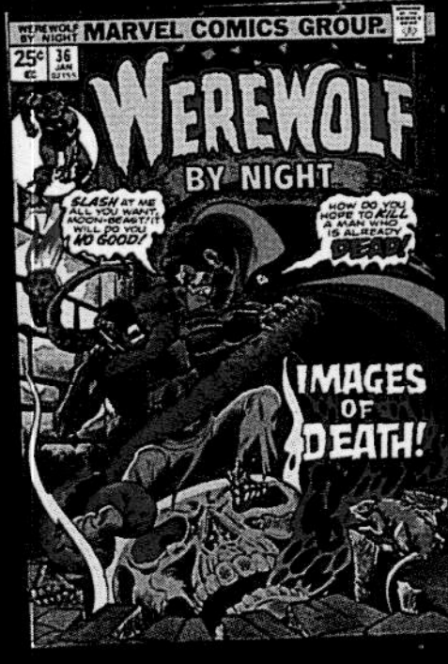
MARVEL COMICS GROUP
WEREWOLF BY NIGHT
IMAGES OF DEATH!
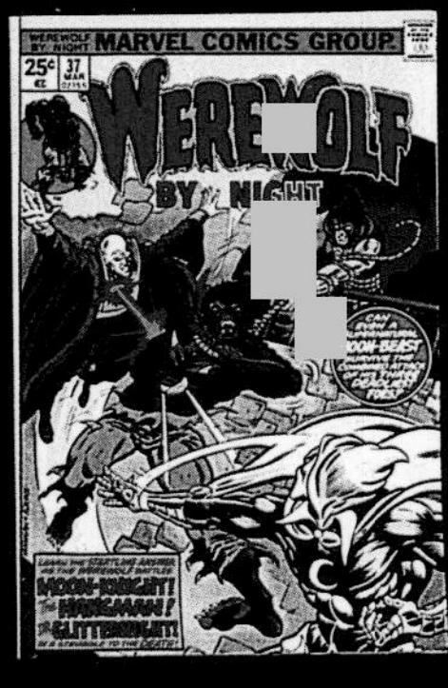
MARVEL COMICS GROUP
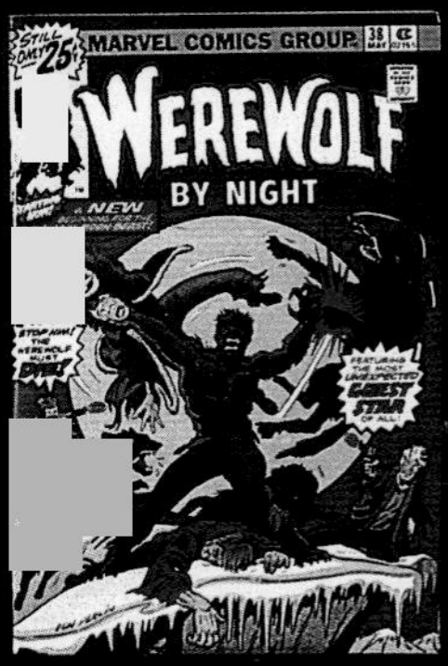
MARVEL COMICS GROUP
WEREWOLF BY NIGHT
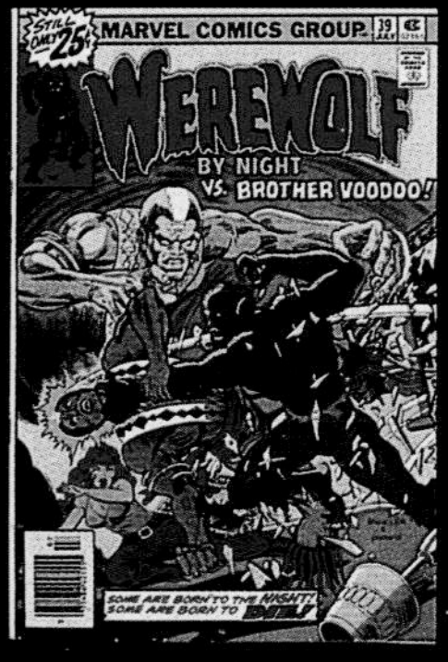
MARVEL COMICS GROUP
WEREWOLF BY NIGHT VS. BROTHER VOODOO!
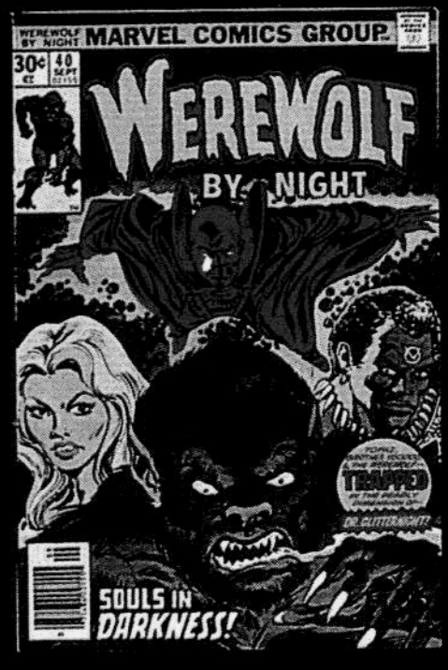
MARVEL COMICS GROUP
WEREWOLF BY NIGHT
SOULS IN DARKNESS!
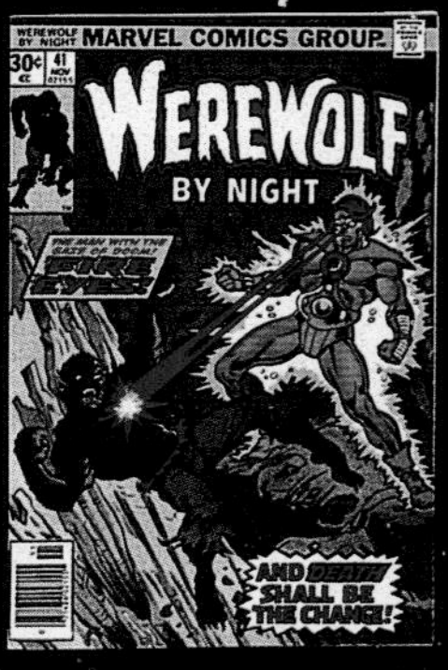
MARVEL COMICS GROUP
WEREWOLF BY NIGHT
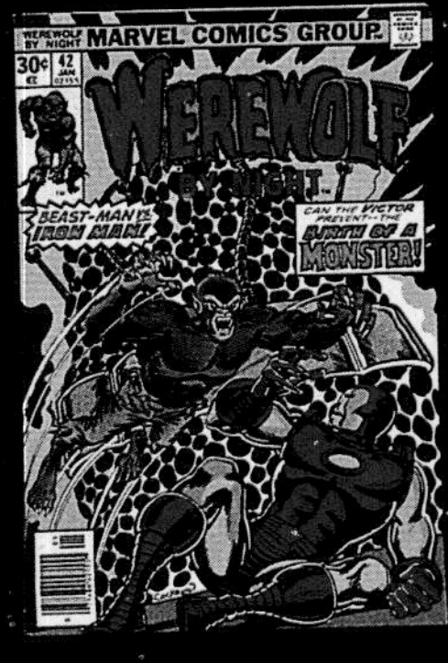
MARVEL COMICS GROUP
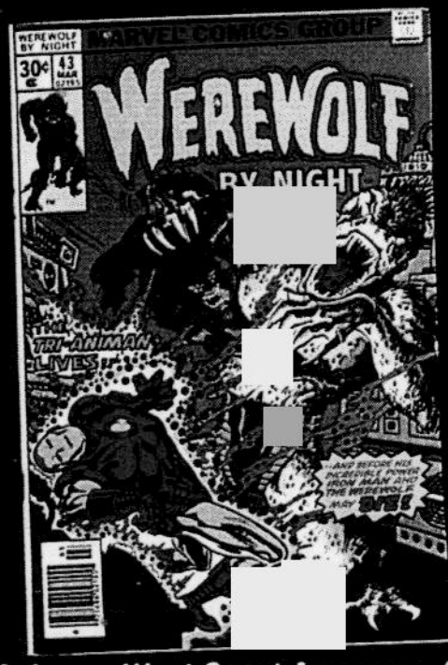
MARVEL COMICS GROUP
WEREWOLF

2119.4 West Coast Avengers (1-4)

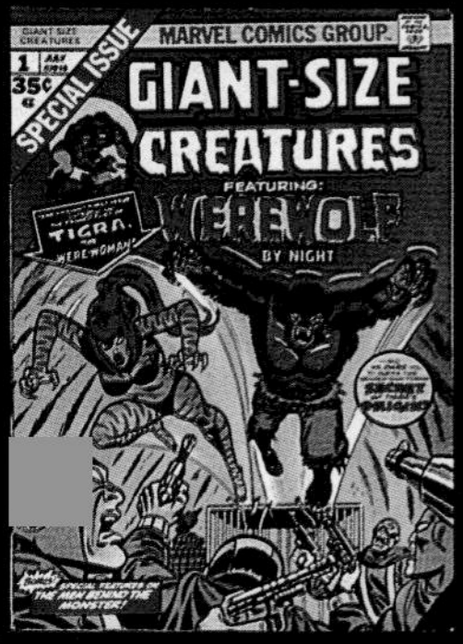
MARVEL COMICS GROUP
GIANT-SIZE CREATURES
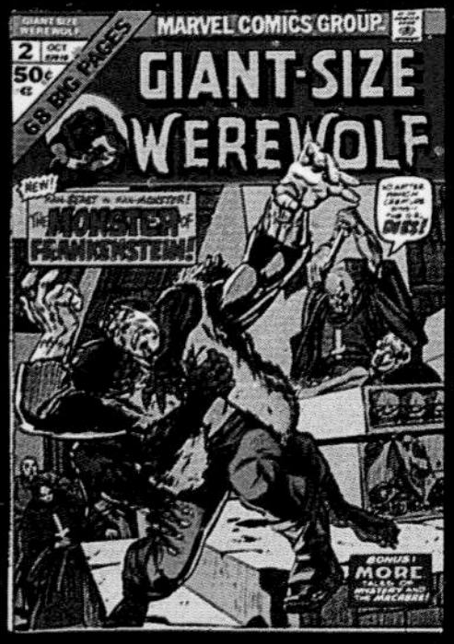
MARVEL COMICS GROUP
68 BIG PAGES
GIANT-SIZE WEREWOLF
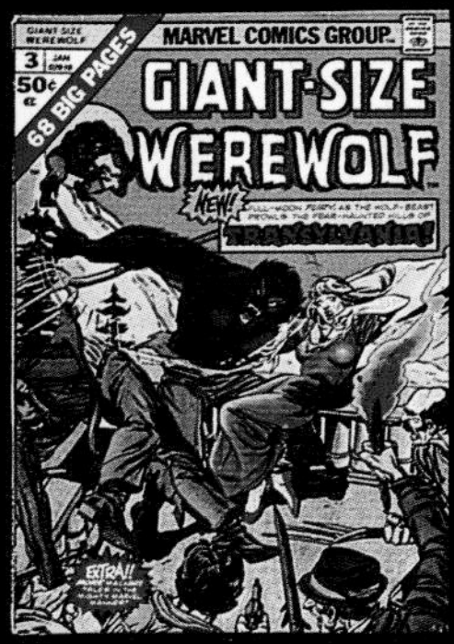
MARVEL COMICS GROUP
68 BIG PAGES
GIANT-SIZE WEREWOLF
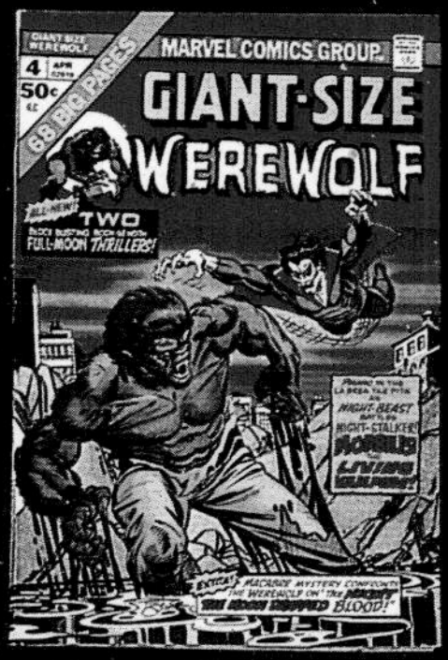
MARVEL COMICS GROUP
68 BIG PAGES
GIANT-SIZE WEREWOLF
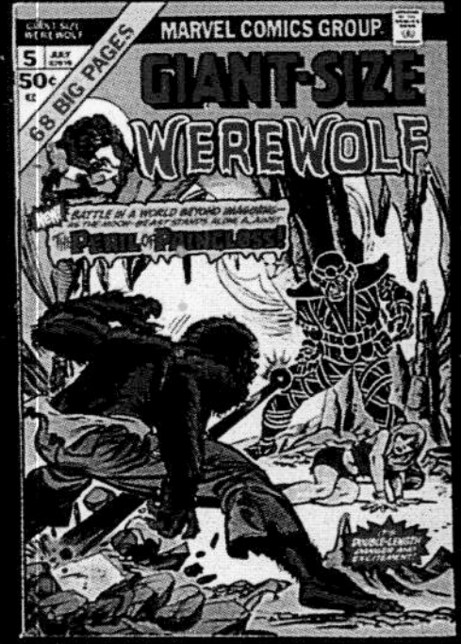
MARVEL COMICS GROUP
68 BIG PAGES
GIANT-SIZE WEREWOLF
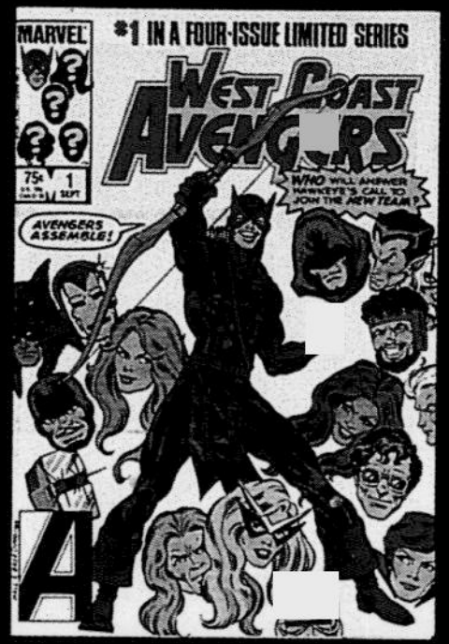
#1 IN A FOUR-ISSUE LIMITED SERIES
West Coast Avengers

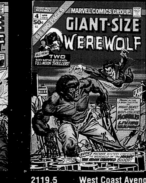

2119.5 West Coast Avengers (1-7)

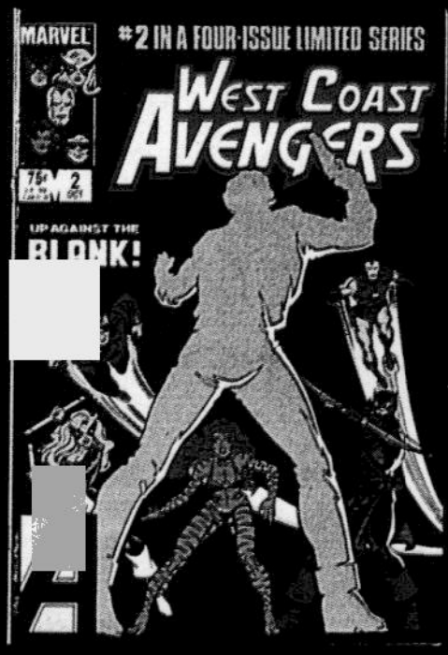
#2 IN A FOUR-ISSUE LIMITED SERIES
WEST COAST AVENGERS
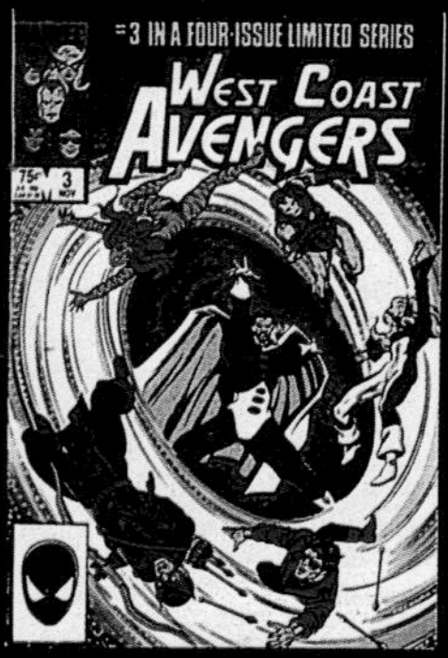
#3 IN A FOUR-ISSUE LIMITED SERIES
WEST COAST AVENGERS
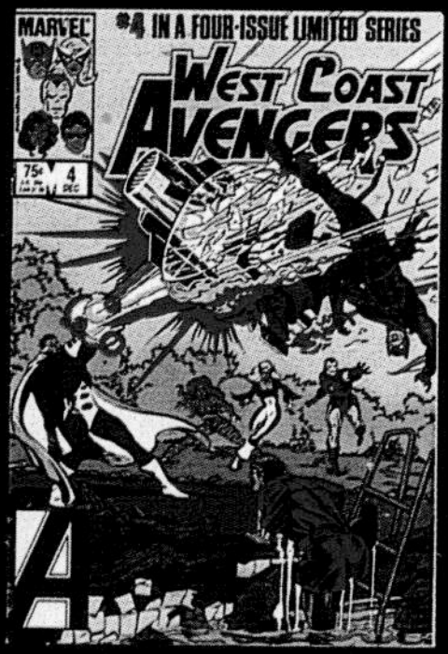
#4 IN A FOUR-ISSUE LIMITED SERIES
WEST COAST AVENGERS
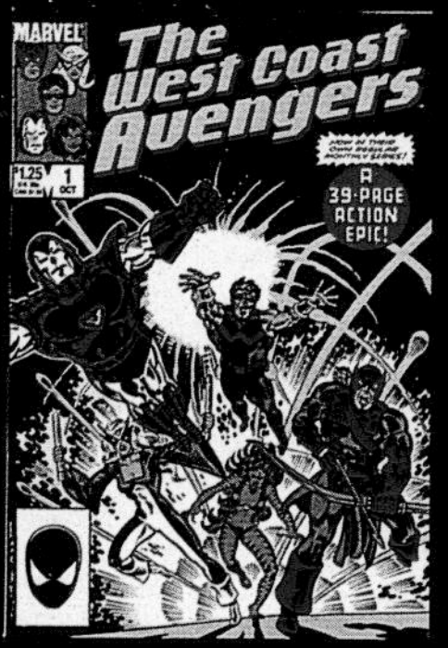
The West Coast Avengers
39-PAGE ACTION EPIC!
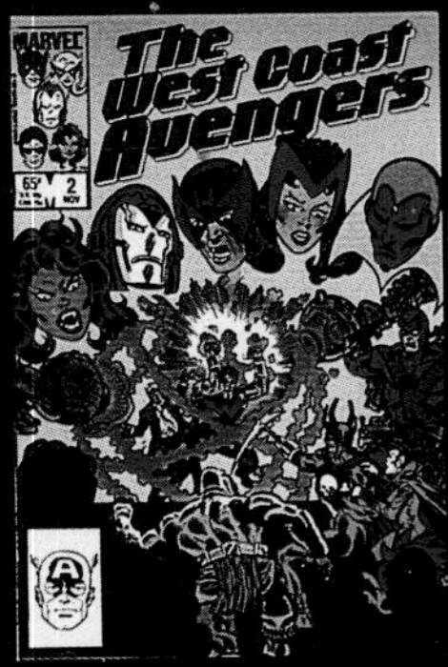
The West Coast Avengers
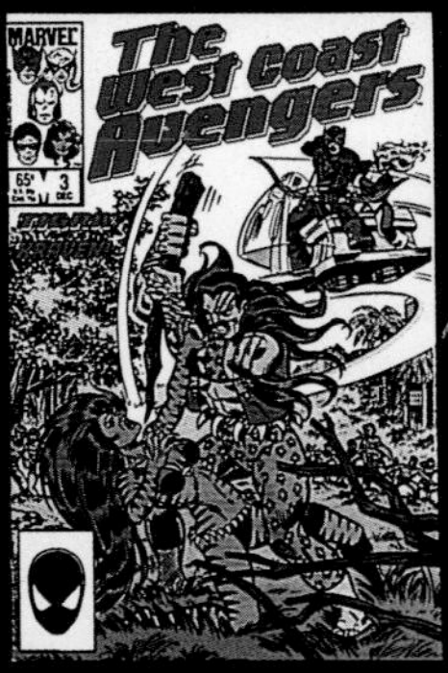
The West Coast Avengers
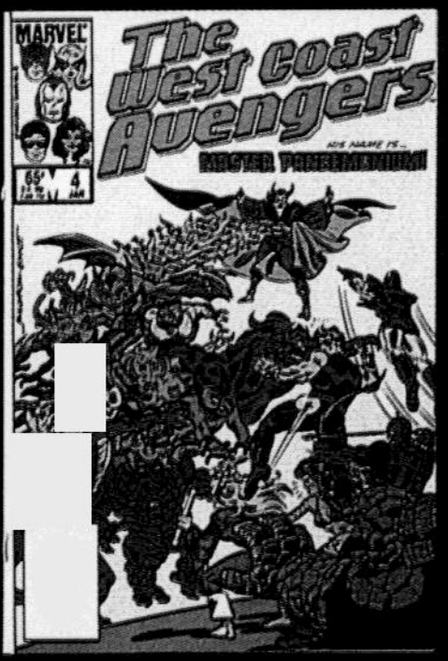
The West Coast Avengers
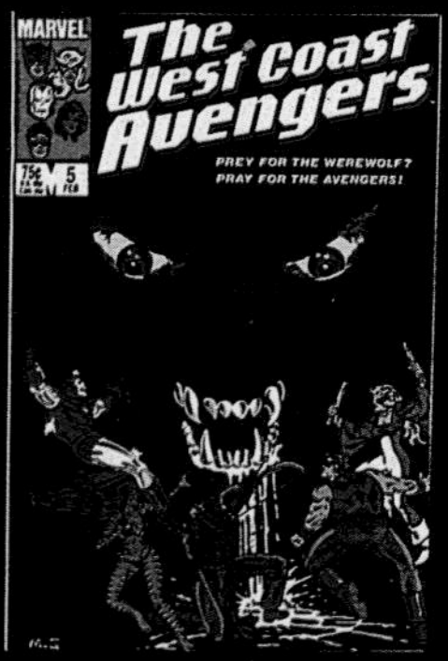
The West Coast Avengers
PREY FOR THE WEREWOLF?
PRAY FOR THE AVENGERS!
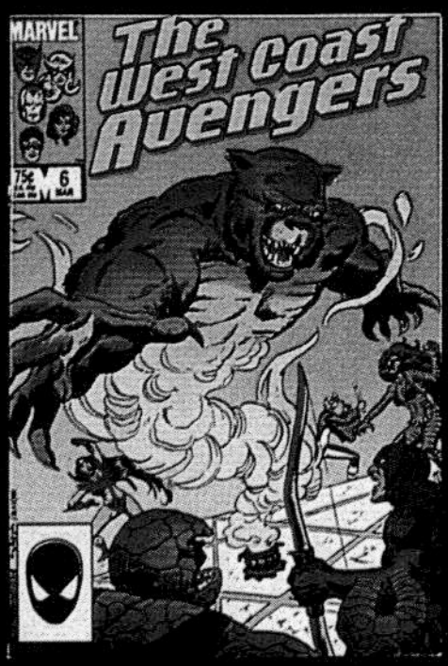
The West Coast Avengers
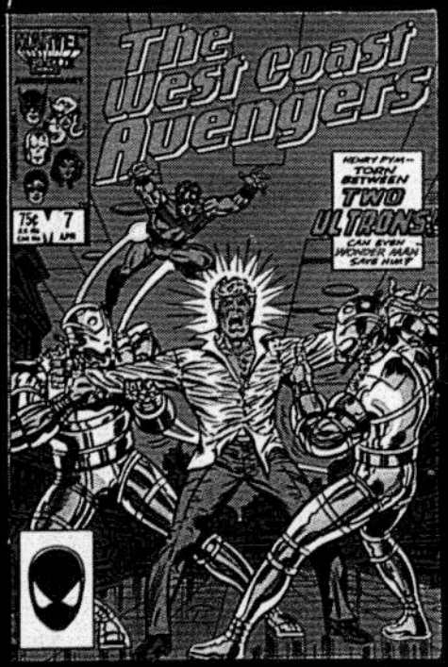
The West Coast Avengers

Werewolf by Night (1-43) 2119.2

Ref. No.	Date	RVI	Artist/Info.
2119.2-1	Sept. 1972	5	Ploog-c/a, Monte-a
2119.2-2 to 31		1	(#15, New origin-Werewolf)
2119.2-32	Aug. 1975	12	(Intro. and Origin-Moon Knight)
2119.2-33	Sept.	5	(Moon Knight -app.)
2119.2-34 to 36		1	
2119.2-37	Jan. 1976	4	Wrightson-c (Moon Knight -app.)
2119.2-38 to 43	Mar. 1977, (#43)	1	
2119.2-G.S. 2	Oct. 1974	1	Ditko-a (Frankenstein -app.) Reprints
2119.2-G.S. 3 to 5		1	Kane-c

West Coast Avengers (1-4) 2119.4

Ref. No.	Date	RVI	Artist/Info.
2119.4-1	Sept. 1984	8	(mini-series)
2119.4-2 to 4	Dec. 1984	3	

West Coast Avengers V.2 (1-47) 2119.5

Ref. No.	Date	RVI	Artist/Info.
2119.5-1	Oct. 1985	3	
2119.2-2 to 10		2	
2119.5-11 to 47	Aug. 1989, (#47)	1	(#46, Intro. Great Lakes Avengers)
2119.5-A1	Oct. 1986	1	
2119.5-A2 to A3	Oct. 1999 (#A3)	1	(Evolutionary War Gap)

2127.7 Western Gunfighters (1-26)

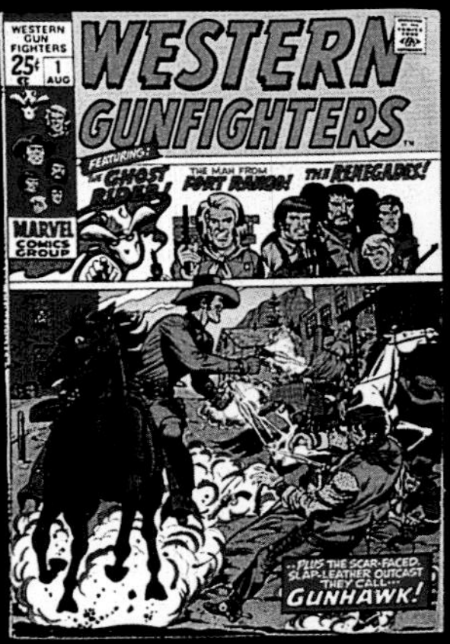
WESTERN GUNFIGHTERS
GUNHAWK!

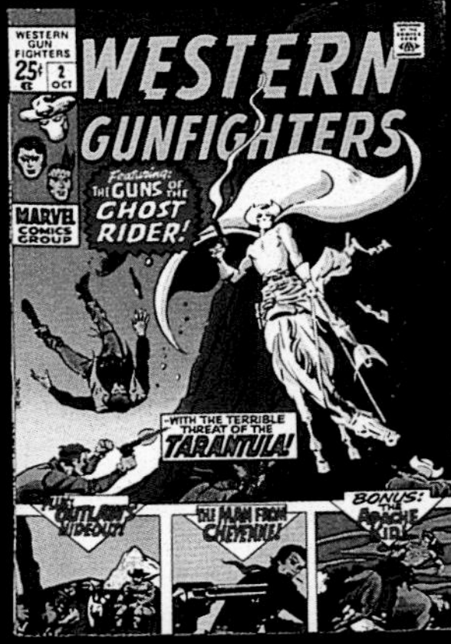
WESTERN GUNFIGHTERS
GHOST RIDER!
TARANTULA!

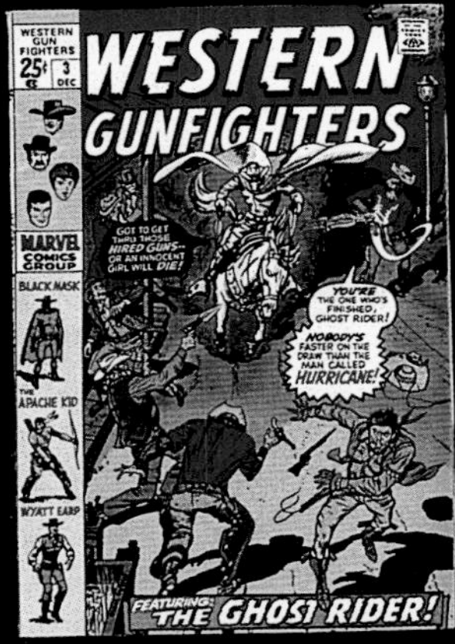
WESTERN GUNFIGHTERS
THE GHOST RIDER!

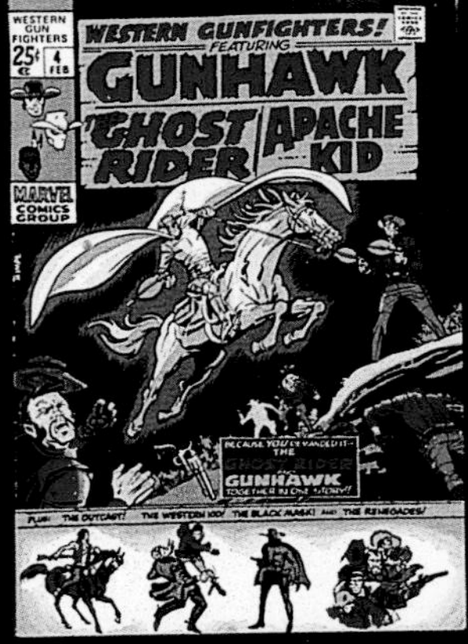
WESTERN GUNFIGHTERS!
GUNHAWK
GHOST RIDER
APACHE KID

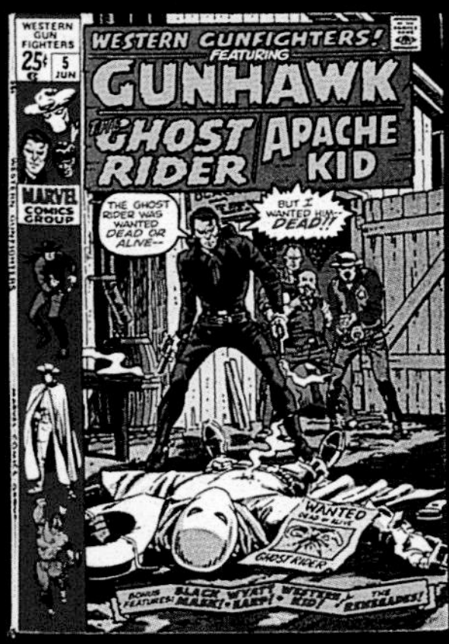
WESTERN GUNFIGHTERS!
GUNHAWK
GHOST RIDER
APACHE KID

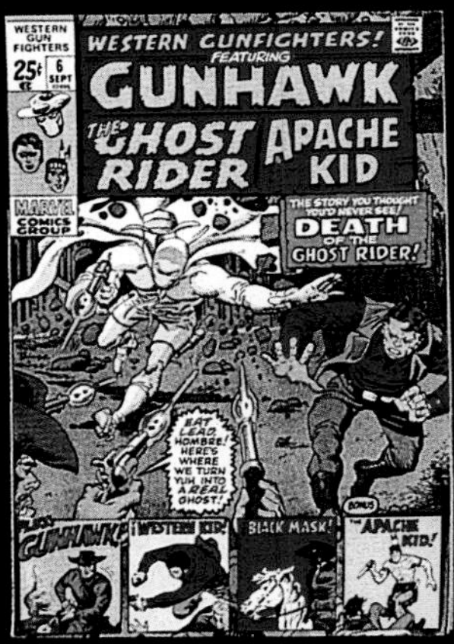
WESTERN GUNFIGHTERS!
GUNHAWK
GHOST RIDER
APACHE KID
DEATH

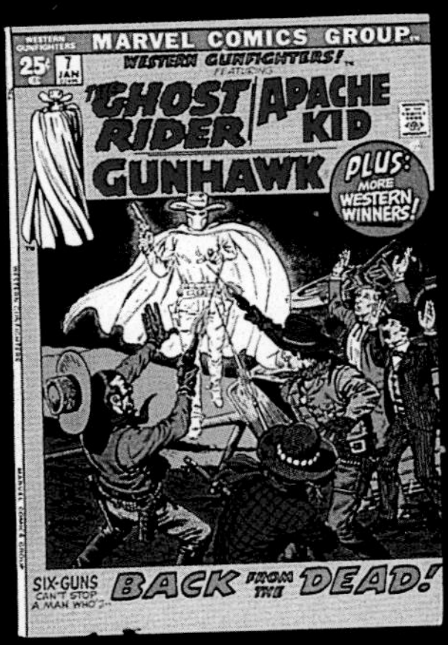
MARVEL COMICS GROUP
WESTERN GUNFIGHTERS!
GHOST RIDER
APACHE KID
GUNHAWK
BACK FROM THE DEAD!

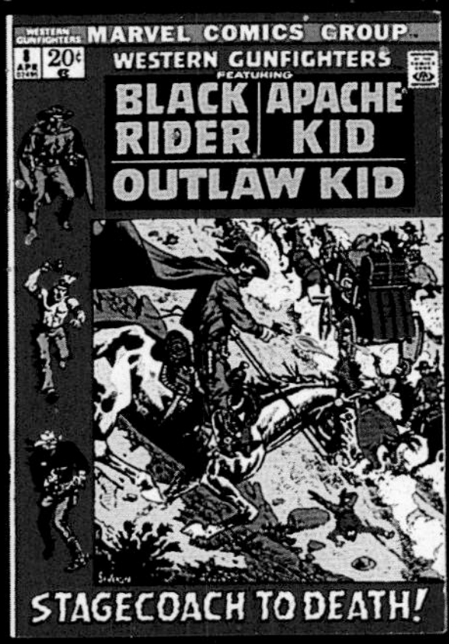
MARVEL COMICS GROUP
WESTERN GUNFIGHTERS
BLACK RIDER
APACHE KID
OUTLAW KID
STAGECOACH TO DEATH!

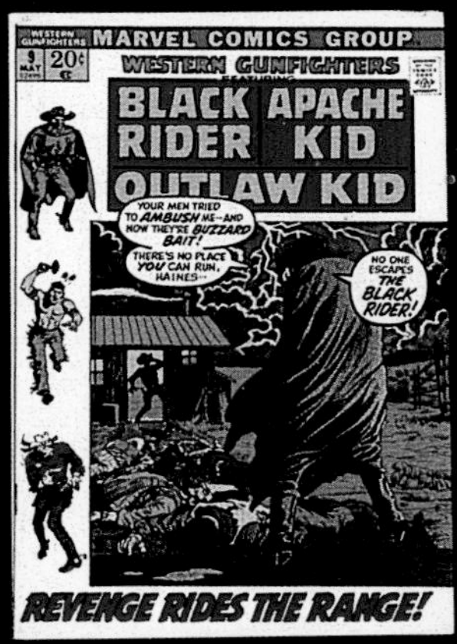
MARVEL COMICS GROUP
WESTERN GUNFIGHTERS
BLACK RIDER
APACHE KID
OUTLAW KID
REVENGE RIDES THE RANGE!

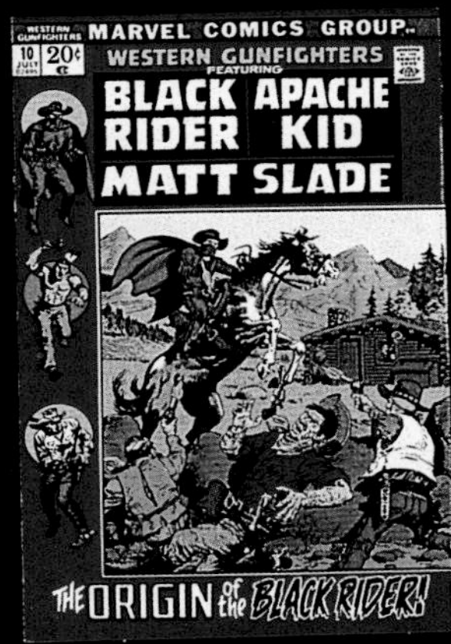
MARVEL COMICS GROUP
WESTERN GUNFIGHTERS
BLACK RIDER
APACHE KID
MATT SLADE
THE ORIGIN of the BLACK RIDER!

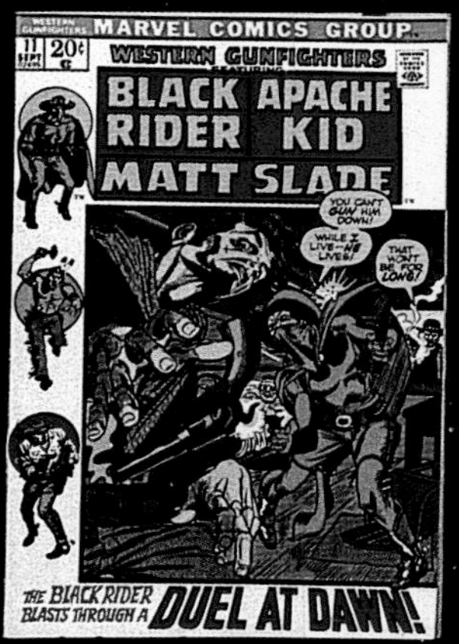
MARVEL COMICS GROUP
WESTERN GUNFIGHTERS
BLACK RIDER
APACHE KID
MATT SLADE
THE BLACK RIDER BLASTS THROUGH A DUEL AT DAWN!

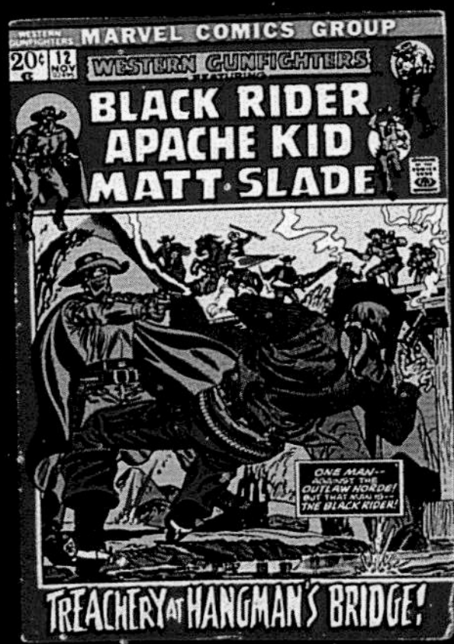
MARVEL COMICS GROUP
WESTERN GUNFIGHTERS
BLACK RIDER
APACHE KID
MATT SLADE
TREACHERY AT HANGMAN'S BRIDGE!

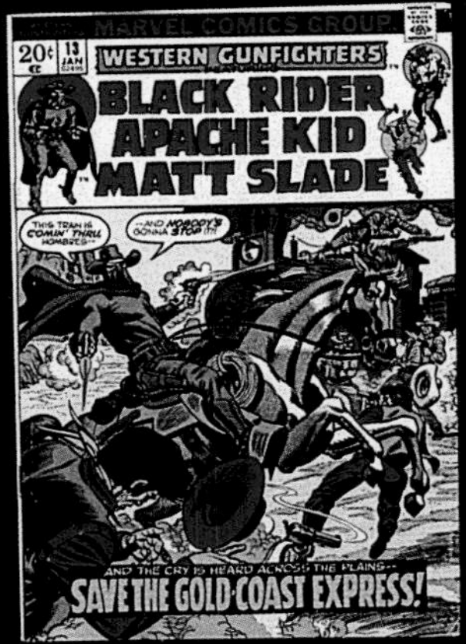
MARVEL COMICS GROUP
WESTERN GUNFIGHTERS
BLACK RIDER
APACHE KID
MATT SLADE
SAVE THE GOLD COAST EXPRESS!

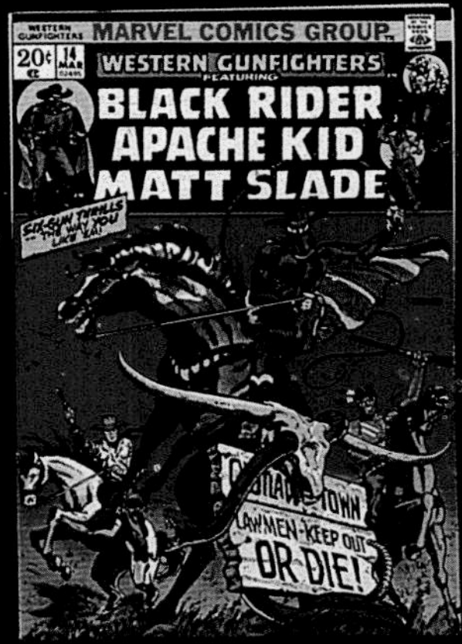
MARVEL COMICS GROUP
WESTERN GUNFIGHTERS
BLACK RIDER
APACHE KID
MATT SLADE
OR DIE!

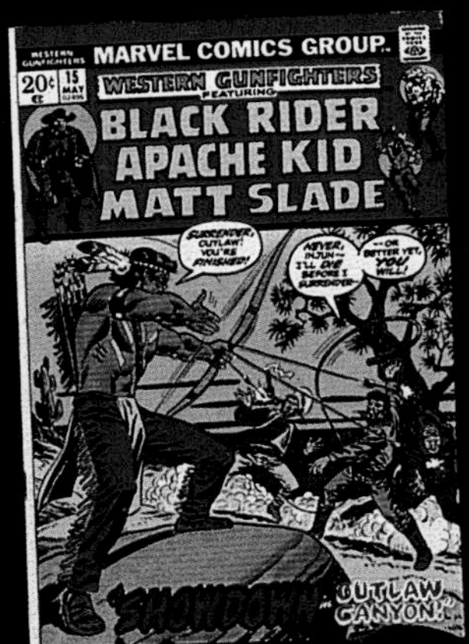
MARVEL COMICS GROUP
WESTERN GUNFIGHTERS
BLACK RIDER
APACHE KID
MATT SLADE
OUTLAW CANYON!

2136.5 Western Team-UP (1)

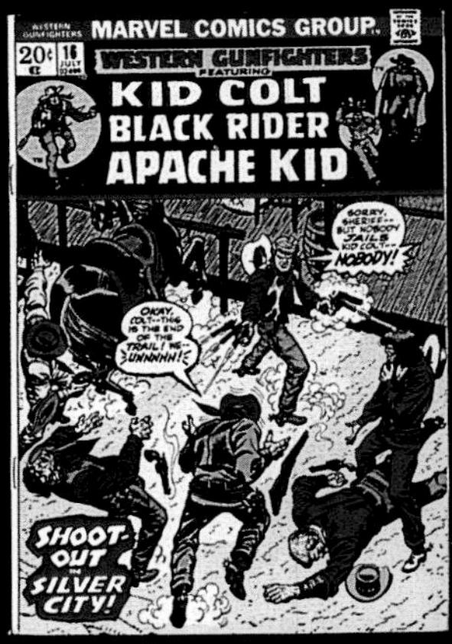
MARVEL COMICS GROUP
WESTERN GUNFIGHTERS
KID COLT
BLACK RIDER
APACHE KID
SHOOT-OUT AT SILVER CITY!

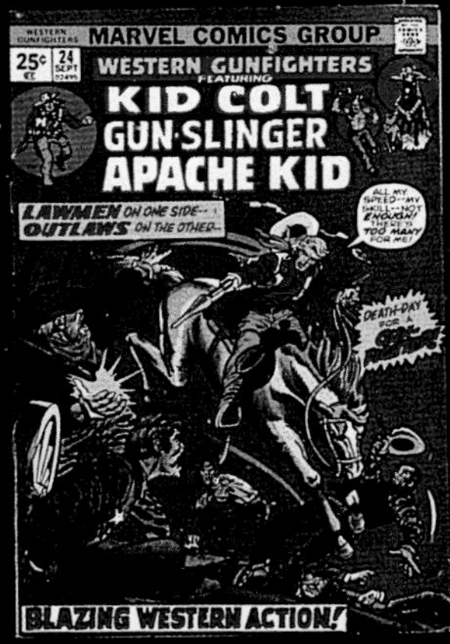
MARVEL COMICS GROUP
WESTERN GUNFIGHTERS
KID COLT
GUN-SLINGER
APACHE KID
BLAZING WESTERN ACTION!

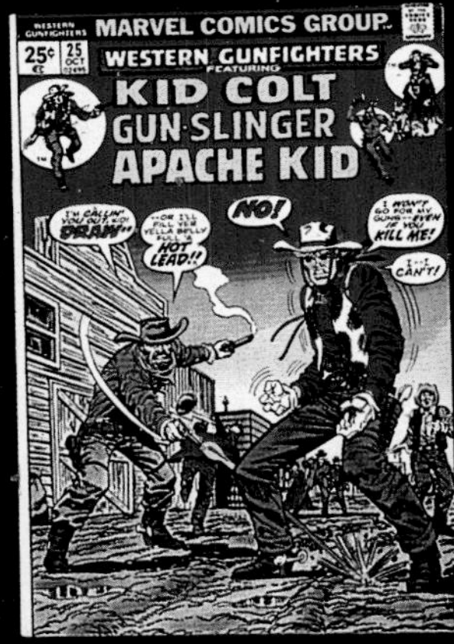
MARVEL COMICS GROUP
WESTERN GUNFIGHTERS
KID COLT
GUN-SLINGER
APACHE KID
NO!

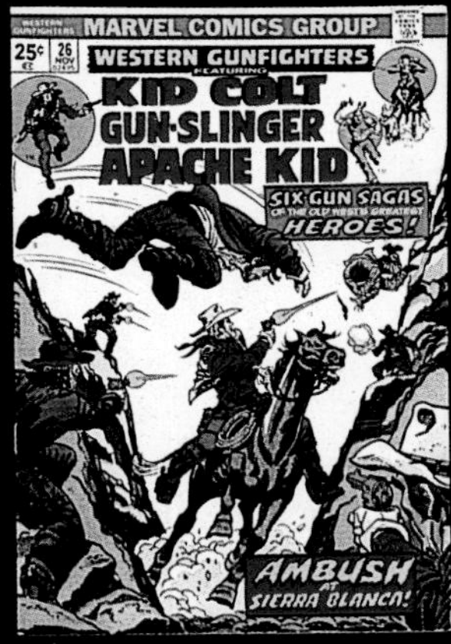
MARVEL COMICS GROUP
WESTERN GUNFIGHTERS
KID COLT
GUN-SLINGER
APACHE KID
SIX-GUN SAGAS HEROES!
AMBUSH AT SIERRA BLANCA!

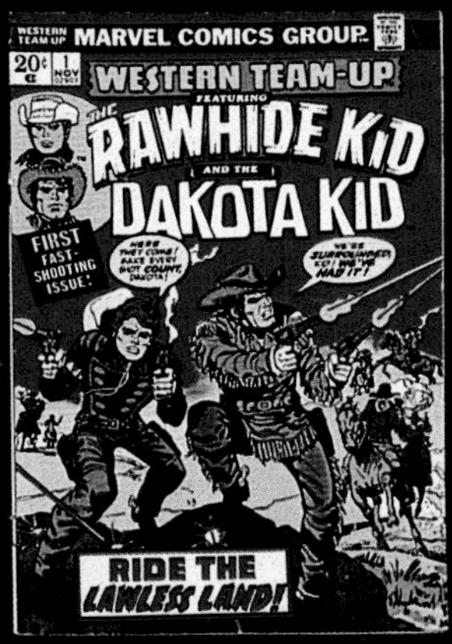
MARVEL COMICS GROUP
WESTERN TEAM-UP
RAWHIDE KID
DAKOTA KID
FIRST FAST SHOOTING ISSUE!
RIDE THE LAWLESS LAND!

2129.5 The Western Kid (1-3)

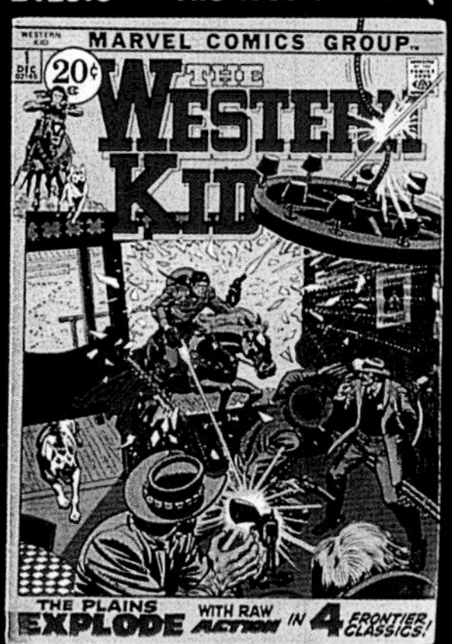
MARVEL COMICS GROUP
THE WESTERN KID
THE PLAINS EXPLODE WITH RAW ACTION IN 4 FRONTIER CLASSICS!

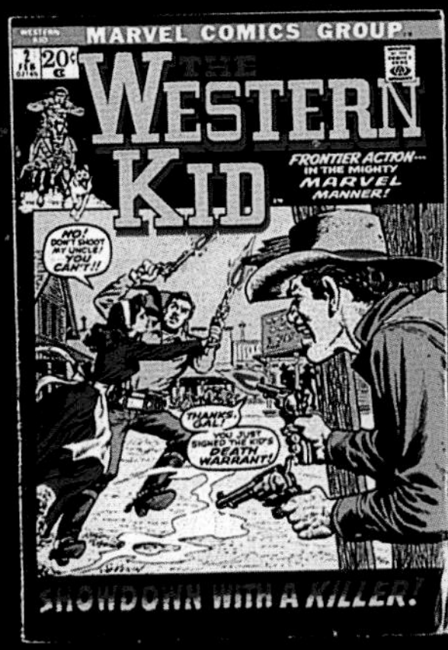
MARVEL COMICS GROUP
THE WESTERN KID
FRONTIER ACTION— IN THE MIGHTY MARVEL MANNER!
SHOWDOWN WITH A KILLER!

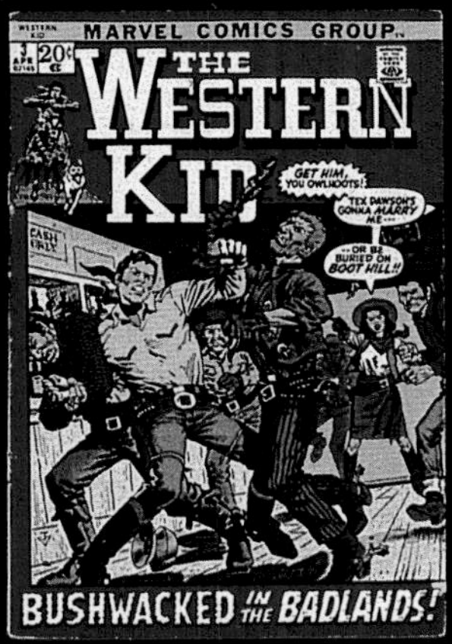
MARVEL COMICS GROUP
THE WESTERN KID
BUSHWACKED in the BADLANDS!

Western Gunfighters 2nd Series (1-33) 2127.7

Ref. No.	Date	RVI	Artist/Info.		
2127.7-1	Aug. 1970	2	Kirby, Roth/Buscema, Ayers-a (Intro. Ghost Rider)		
2127.7-2	Oct.	1	Trimpe-c, Ayers, Maneely-a (Origin-Nightwind)		
2127.7-3	Dec.	1	Ayers-c/a	Reprints	
2127.7-4	Feb. 1971	1	Trimpe-c, Ayers, Sutton-a		
2127.7-5	Jun.	1	Ayers/Giacoia-a	Reprints	
2127.7-6	Sept.	1	Trimpe-c, Ayers, Shores-a		
2127.7-7	Jan. 1972	1	Severin-c, Ayers/Shores-a (Origin Ghost Rider retold)		
2127.7-8	Apr.	1	Severin-c, Wildey-a	Reprints	
2127.7-9	May	1	Wildey-a	"	
2127.7-10	**Jul.**	**1**	**Severin-c, Kirby, Maneely-a (Origin Black Rider)**		
2127.7-11	Sept.	1	Kirby-a		
2127.7-12	Nov.	1	Maneely-a	Reprints	(Origin-Matt Slade)
2127.7-12	Jan. 1973	1	Reinman-a	"	
2127.7-14	Mar.	1	Steranko-c, McCarty-a	"	
2127.7-15	May	1		"	
2127.7-16 to 33	Nov. 1975, (#33)	1		"	

The Western Kid 2nd Series (1-5) 2129.5

Ref. No.	Date	RVI	Artist/Info.	
2129.5-1	Dec. 1971	1	Romita-c/a	Reprints
2129.5-2	Feb. 1972	1	Severin-c, Romita-a	"
2129.5-3	Apr.	1	Williamson, Romita-a	"
2129.5-4	Jun.	1	Everett-a	"
2129.5-5	Aug. 1972	1	Romita-a	"

Western Team-Up (1) 2136.5

Ref. No.	Date	RVI	Artist/Info.
2136.5-1	Nov. 1973	1	Lieber, Davis/Colletta-a (Origin/Intro. Dakota Kid) Reprint

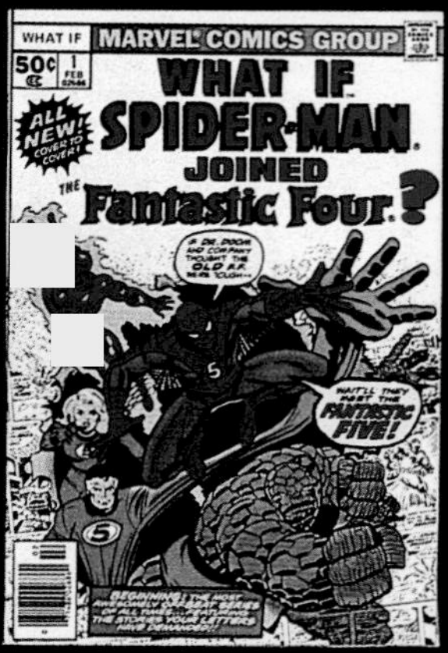
MARVEL COMICS GROUP
WHAT IF SPIDER-MAN JOINED THE Fantastic Four?

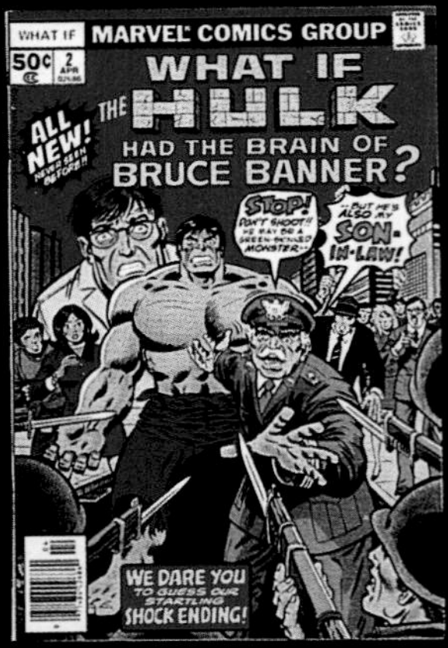
MARVEL COMICS GROUP
WHAT IF THE HULK HAD THE BRAIN OF BRUCE BANNER?
WE DARE YOU TO GUESS OUR STARTLING SHOCK ENDING!

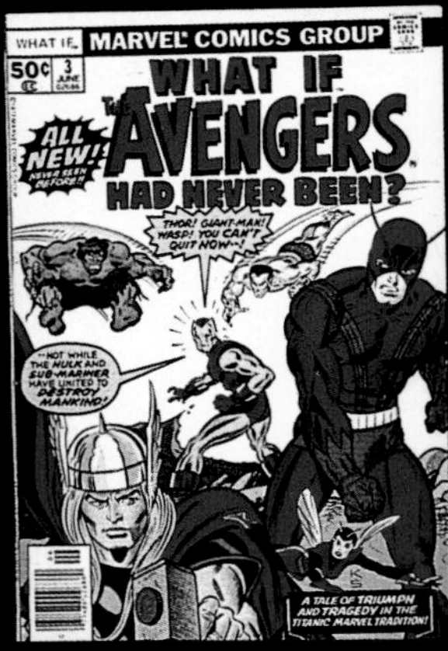
MARVEL COMICS GROUP
WHAT IF THE AVENGERS HAD NEVER BEEN?

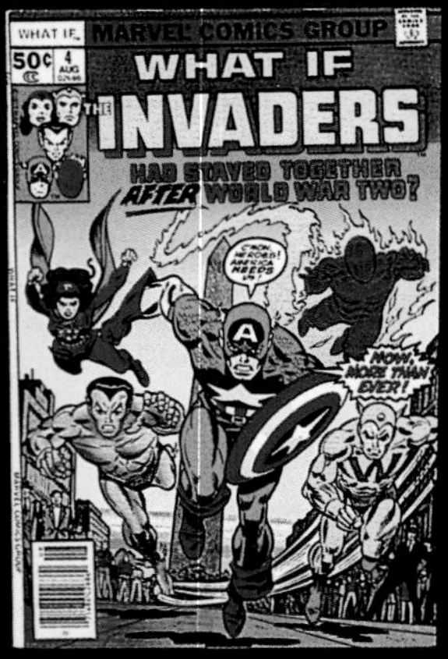
MARVEL COMICS GROUP
WHAT IF THE INVADERS HAD STAYED TOGETHER AFTER WORLD WAR TWO?

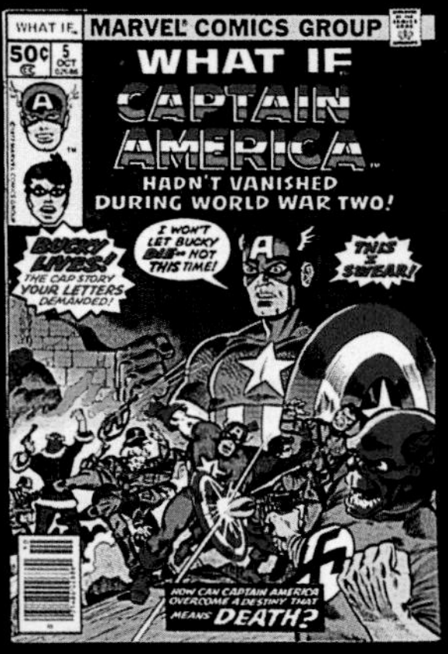
MARVEL COMICS GROUP
WHAT IF CAPTAIN AMERICA HADN'T VANISHED DURING WORLD WAR TWO!

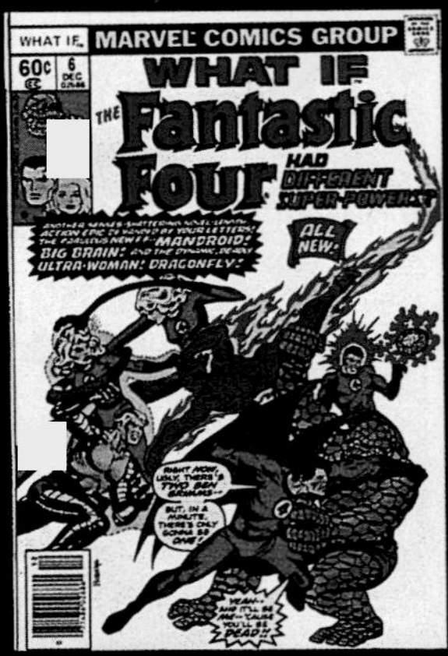
MARVEL COMICS GROUP
WHAT IF THE Fantastic Four HAD DIFFERENT SUPER-POWERS?

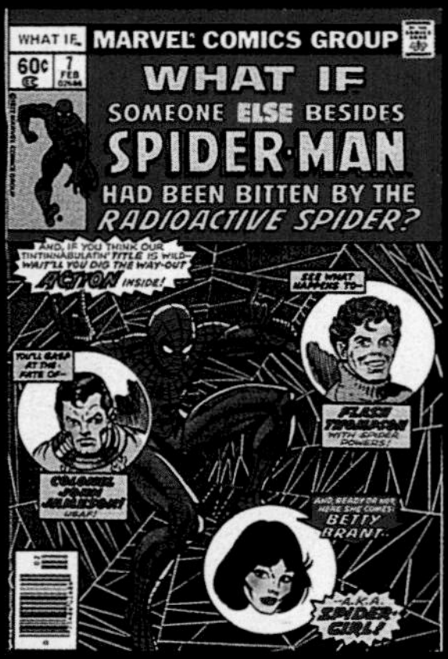
MARVEL COMICS GROUP
WHAT IF SOMEONE ELSE BESIDES SPIDER-MAN HAD BEEN BITTEN BY THE RADIOACTIVE SPIDER?

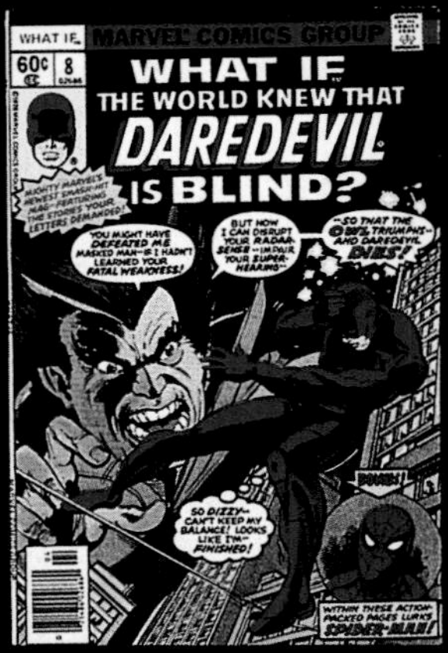
MARVEL COMICS GROUP
WHAT IF THE WORLD KNEW THAT DAREDEVIL IS BLIND?

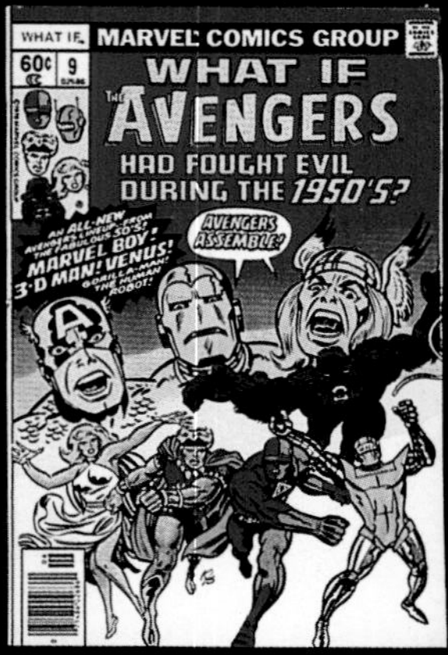
MARVEL COMICS GROUP
WHAT IF THE AVENGERS HAD FOUGHT EVIL DURING THE 1950'S?

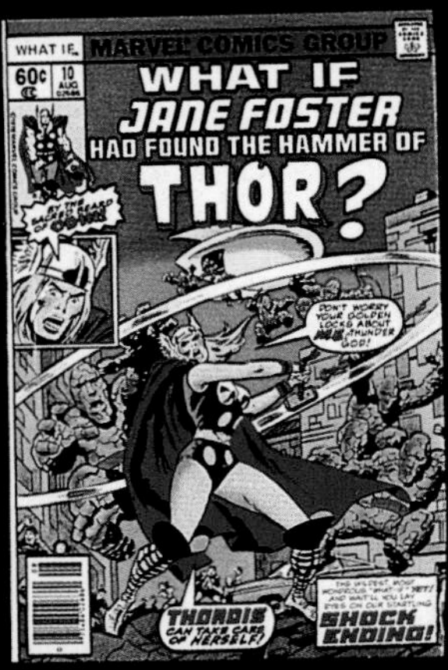
MARVEL COMICS GROUP
WHAT IF JANE FOSTER HAD FOUND THE HAMMER OF THOR?

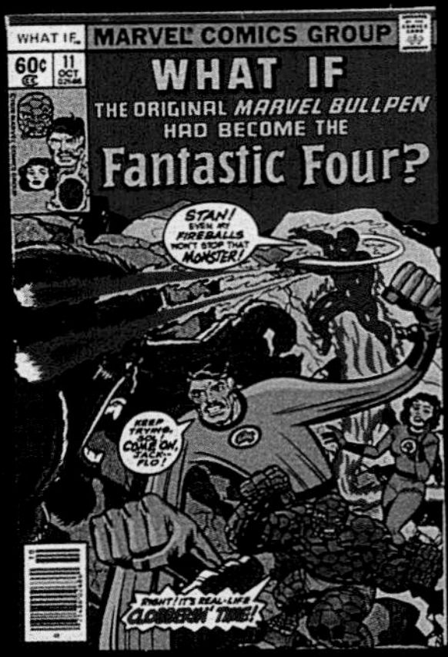
MARVEL COMICS GROUP
WHAT IF THE ORIGINAL MARVEL BULLPEN HAD BECOME THE Fantastic Four?

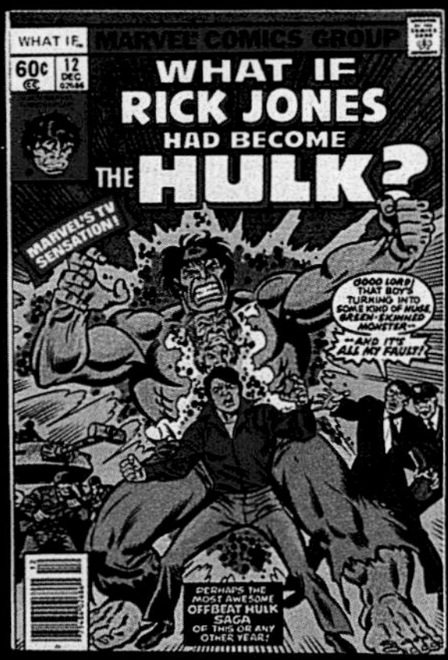
MARVEL COMICS GROUP
WHAT IF RICK JONES HAD BECOME THE HULK?

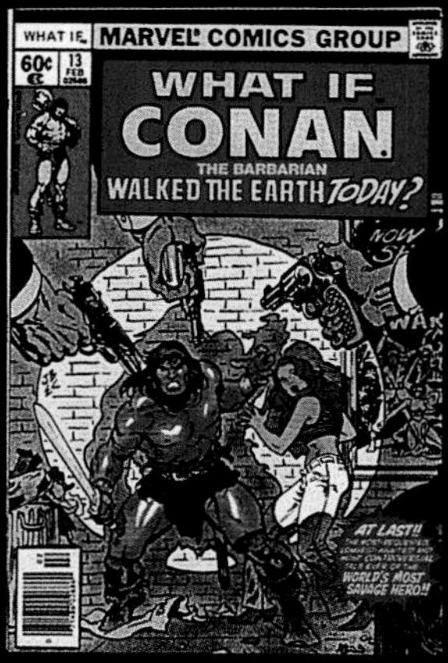
MARVEL COMICS GROUP
WHAT IF CONAN THE BARBARIAN WALKED THE EARTH TODAY?

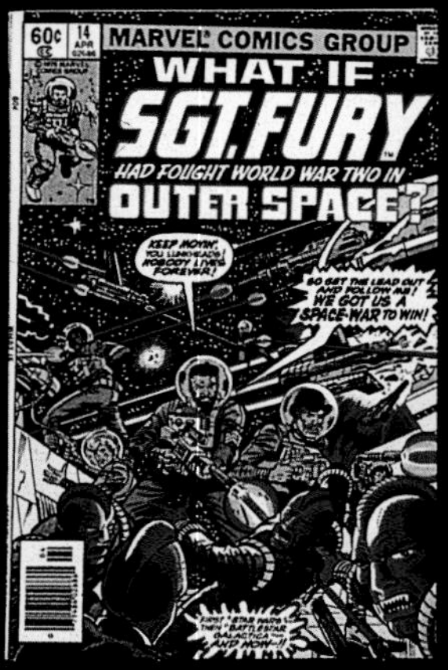
MARVEL COMICS GROUP
WHAT IF SGT. FURY HAD FOUGHT WORLD WAR TWO IN OUTER SPACE?

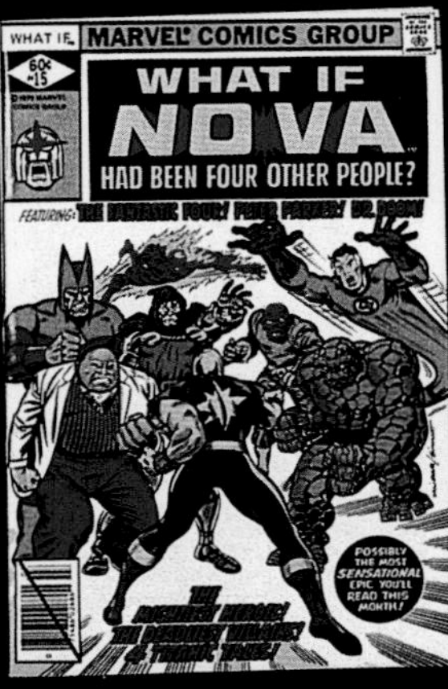
MARVEL COMICS GROUP
WHAT IF NOVA HAD BEEN FOUR OTHER PEOPLE?

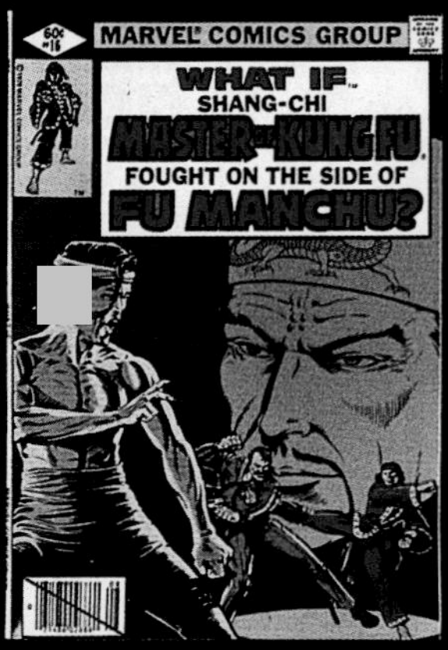
MARVEL COMICS GROUP
WHAT IF SHANG-CHI MASTER OF KUNG FU FOUGHT ON THE SIDE OF FU MANCHU?

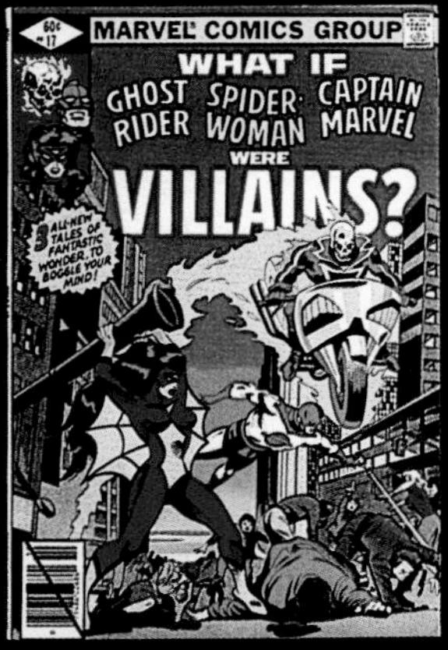
MARVEL COMICS GROUP
WHAT IF GHOST RIDER SPIDER-WOMAN CAPTAIN MARVEL WERE VILLAINS?

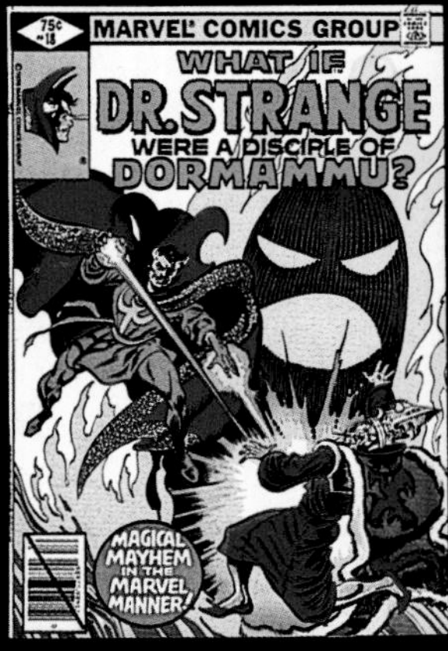
MARVEL COMICS GROUP
WHAT IF DR. STRANGE WERE A DISCIPLE OF DORMAMMU?
MAGICAL MAYHEM IN THE MARVEL MANNER!

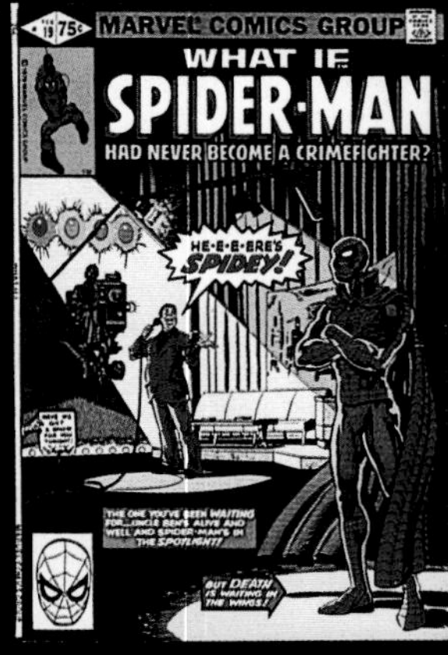
MARVEL COMICS GROUP
WHAT IF SPIDER-MAN HAD NEVER BECOME A CRIMEFIGHTER?

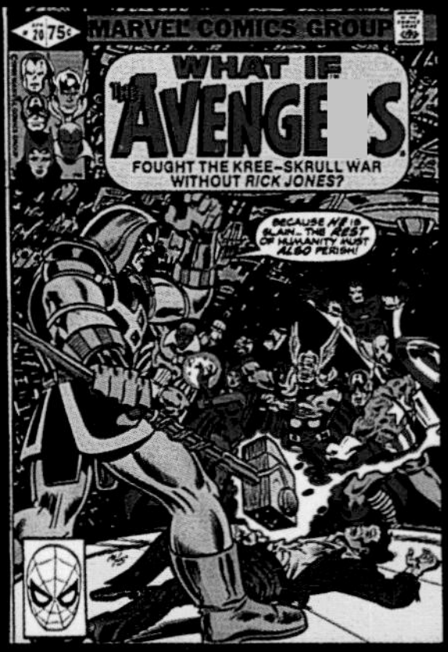
MARVEL COMICS GROUP
WHAT IF THE AVENGERS FOUGHT THE KREE-SKRULL WAR WITHOUT RICK JONES?

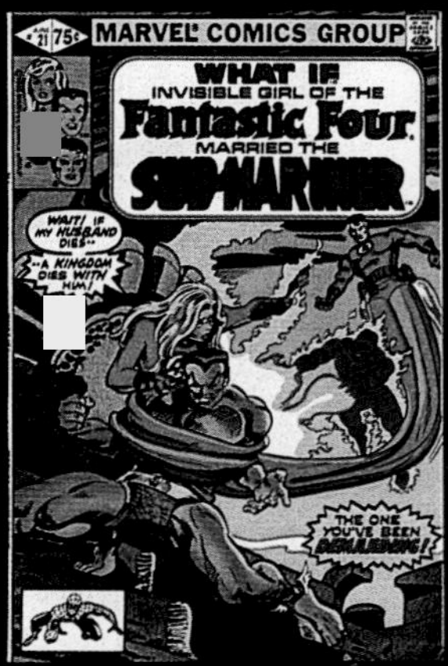
MARVEL COMICS GROUP
WHAT IF INVISIBLE GIRL OF THE Fantastic Four MARRIED THE SUB-MARINER

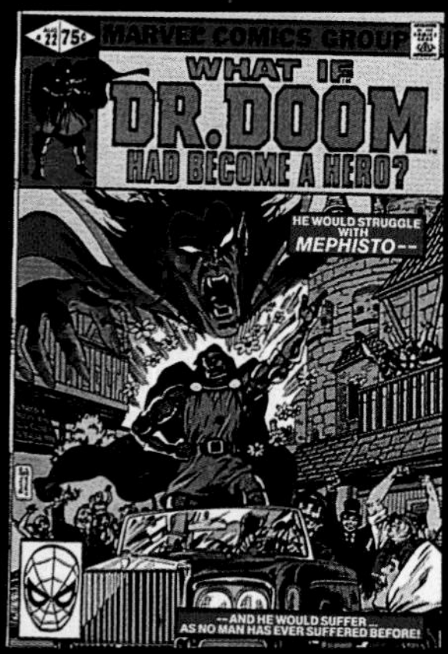
MARVEL COMICS GROUP
WHAT IF DR. DOOM HAD BECOME A HERO?
HE WOULD STRUGGLE WITH MEPHISTO--
--AND HE WOULD SUFFER AS NO MAN HAS EVER SUFFERED BEFORE!

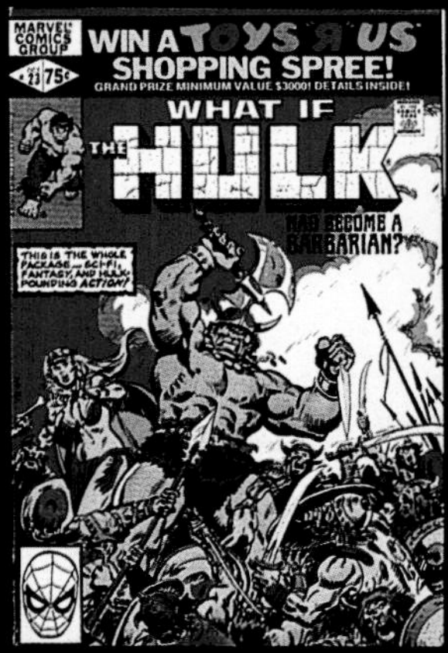
MARVEL COMICS GROUP
WIN A TOYS R US SHOPPING SPREE!
WHAT IF THE HULK HAD BECOME A BARBARIAN?

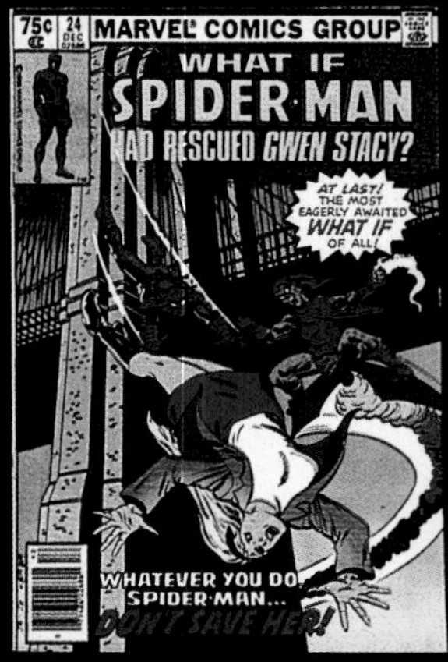
MARVEL COMICS GROUP
WHAT IF SPIDER-MAN HAD RESCUED GWEN STACY?
WHATEVER YOU DO SPIDER-MAN... DON'T SAVE HER!

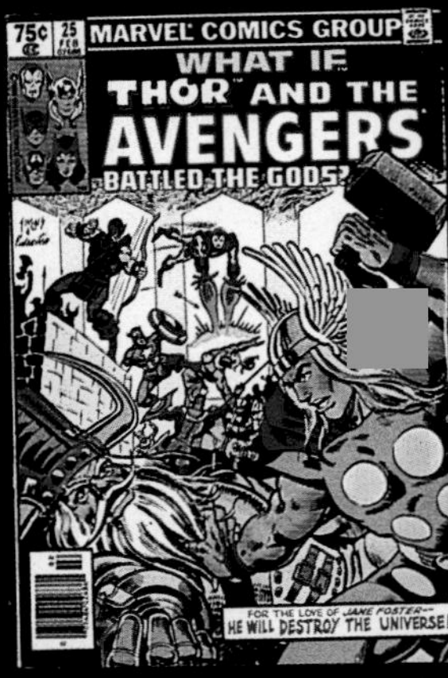
MARVEL COMICS GROUP
WHAT IF THOR AND THE AVENGERS BATTLED THE GODS?
FOR THE LOVE OF JANE FOSTER HE WILL DESTROY THE UNIVERSE!

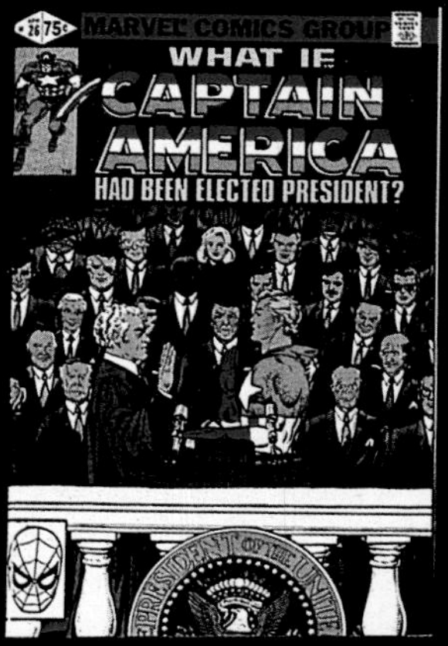
MARVEL COMICS GROUP
26 75¢
WHAT IF
CAPTAIN AMERICA
HAD BEEN ELECTED PRESIDENT?

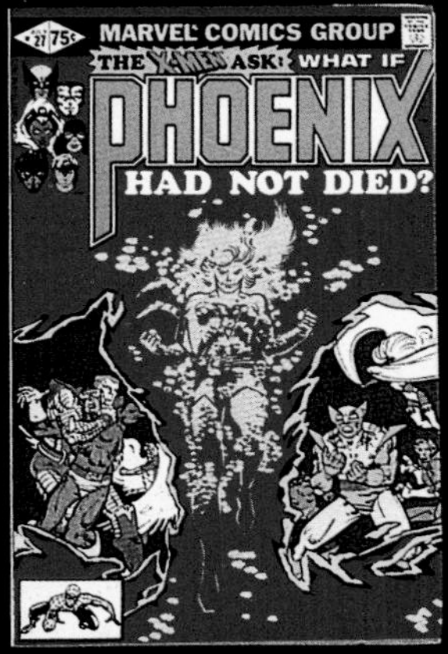
MARVEL COMICS GROUP
27 75¢
THE X-MEN ASK: WHAT IF
PHOENIX
HAD NOT DIED?

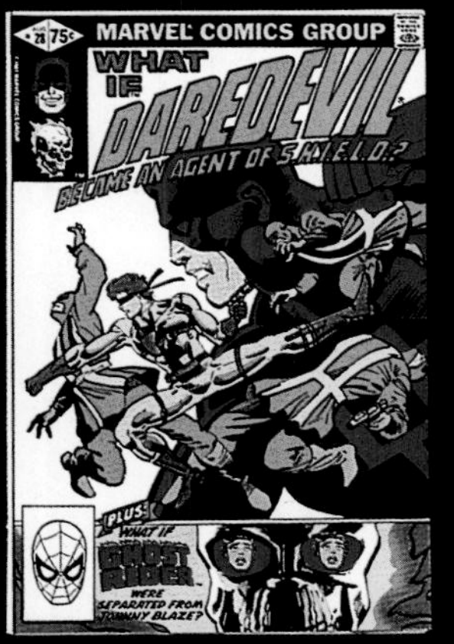
MARVEL COMICS GROUP
28 75¢
WHAT IF
DAREDEVIL
BECAME AN AGENT OF S.H.I.E.L.D.?

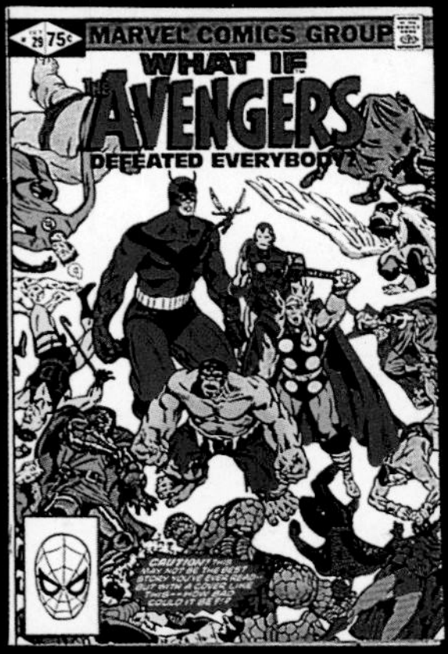
MARVEL COMICS GROUP
29 75¢
WHAT IF
AVENGERS
DEFEATED EVERYBODY

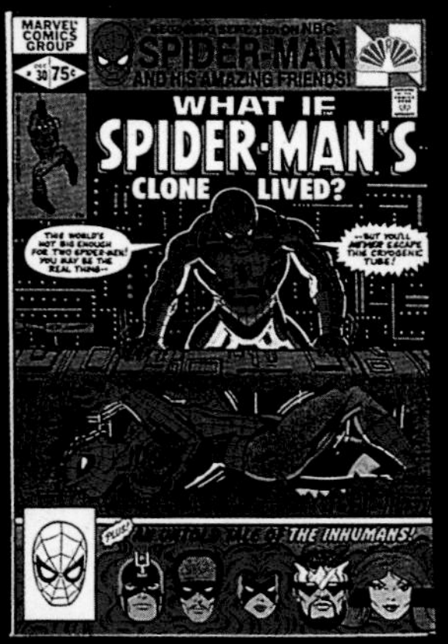
MARVEL COMICS GROUP
30 75¢
SPIDER-MAN
AND HIS AMAZING FRIENDS!
WHAT IF
SPIDER-MAN'S
CLONE LIVED?
THE INHUMANS!

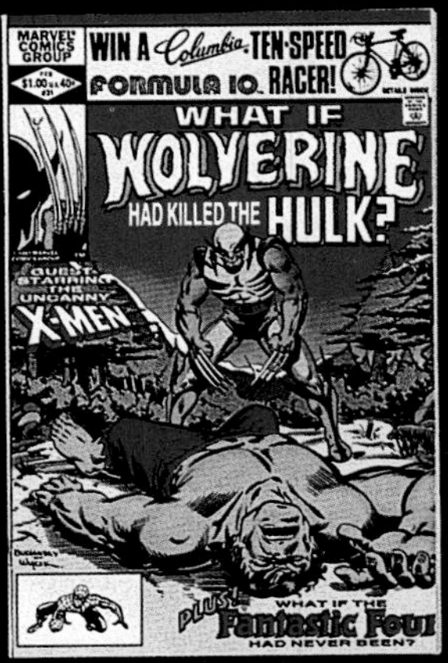
MARVEL COMICS GROUP
WIN A Columbia TEN-SPEED FORMULA 10 RACER!
WHAT IF
WOLVERINE
HAD KILLED THE HULK?
GUEST-STARRING THE UNCANNY X-MEN
PLUS: WHAT IF THE Fantastic Four HAD NEVER BEEN?

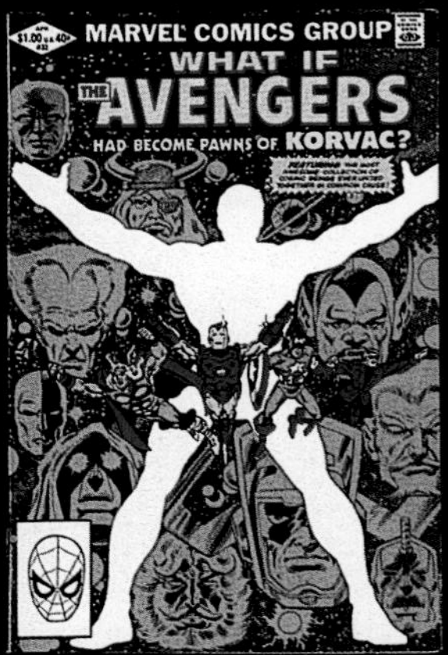
MARVEL COMICS GROUP
WHAT IF
THE AVENGERS
HAD BECOME PAWNS OF KORVAC?

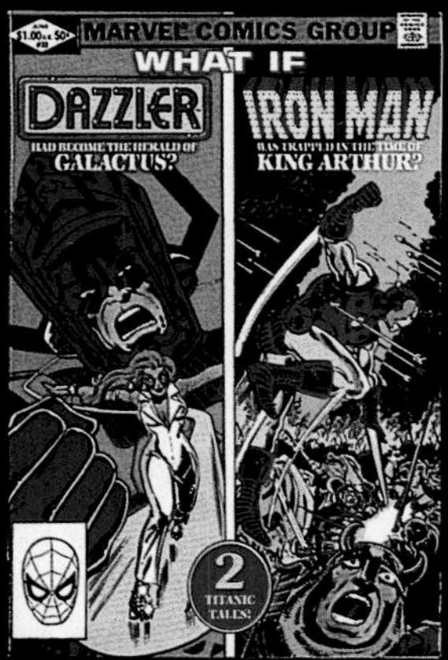
MARVEL COMICS GROUP
WHAT IF
DAZZLER
HAD BECOME THE HERALD OF GALACTUS?
IRON MAN
WAS TRAPPED IN THE TIME OF KING ARTHUR?
2 TITANIC TALES!

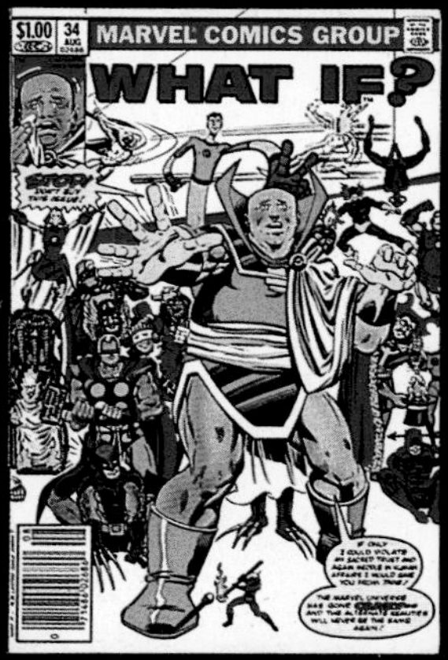
$1.00 34 AUG
MARVEL COMICS GROUP
WHAT IF?

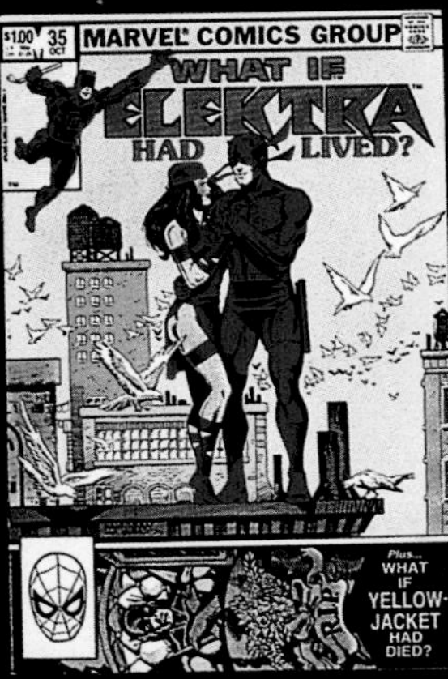
$1.00 35
MARVEL COMICS GROUP
WHAT IF
ELEKTRA
HAD LIVED?
Plus... WHAT IF YELLOW-JACKET HAD DIED?

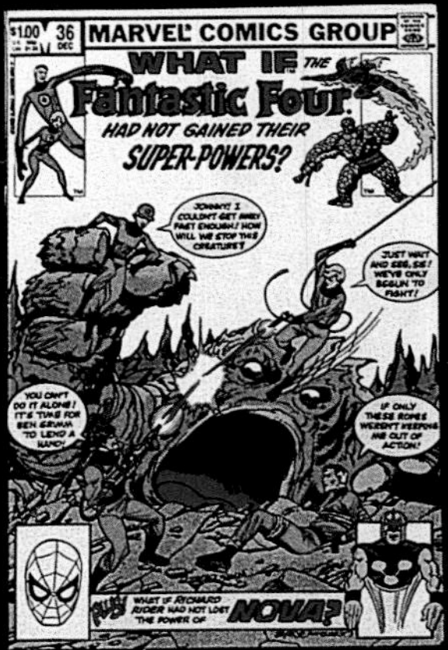
$1.00 36 DEC
MARVEL COMICS GROUP
WHAT IF THE
Fantastic Four
HAD NOT GAINED THEIR SUPER-POWERS?
NOVA?

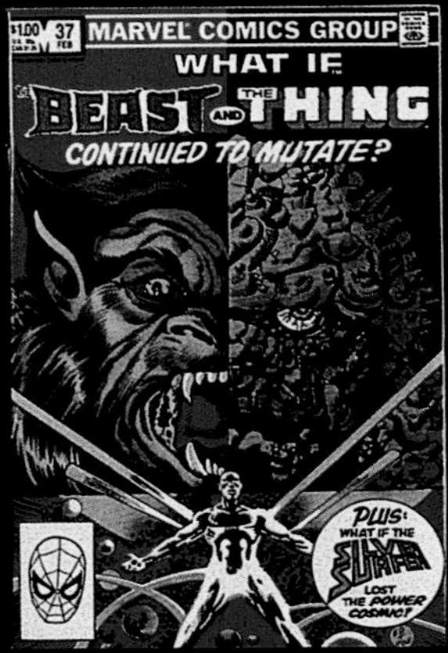
$1.00 37 FEB
MARVEL COMICS GROUP
WHAT IF
BEAST AND THING
CONTINUED TO MUTATE?
PLUS: WHAT IF THE SILVER SURFER LOST THE POWER COSMIC?

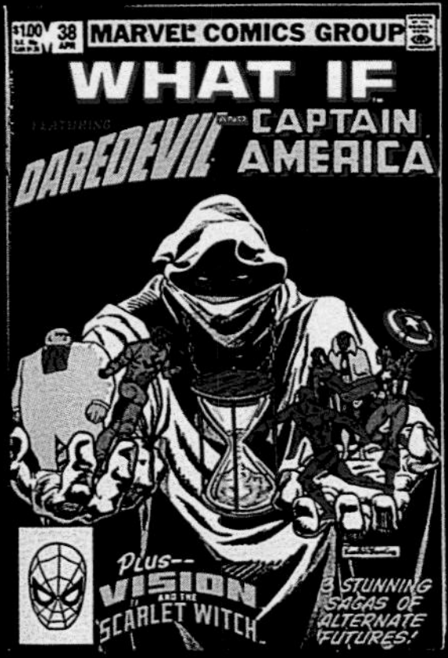
$1.00 38 APR
MARVEL COMICS GROUP
WHAT IF
DAREDEVIL AND CAPTAIN AMERICA
Plus-- VISION AND THE SCARLET WITCH
3 STUNNING SAGAS OF ALTERNATE FUTURES!

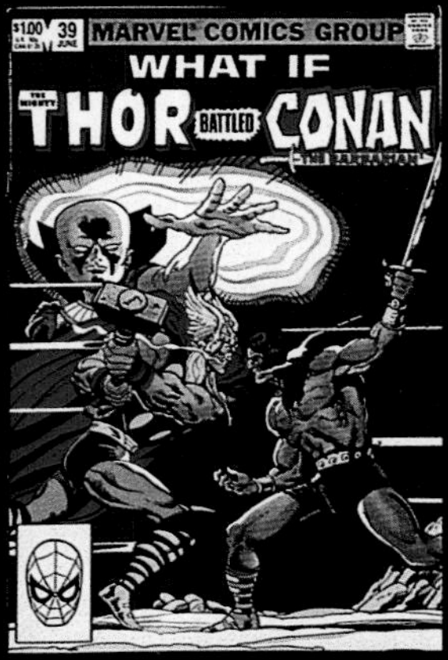
$1.00 39 JUNE
MARVEL COMICS GROUP
WHAT IF
THOR BATTLED CONAN
THE BARBARIAN

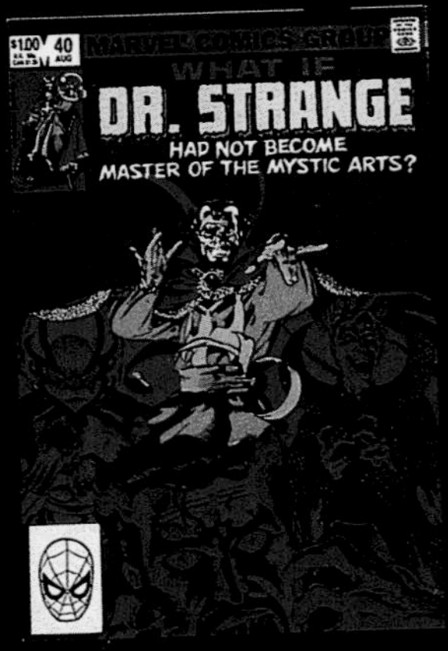
$1.00 40 AUG
MARVEL COMICS GROUP
WHAT IF
DR. STRANGE
HAD NOT BECOME MASTER OF THE MYSTIC ARTS?

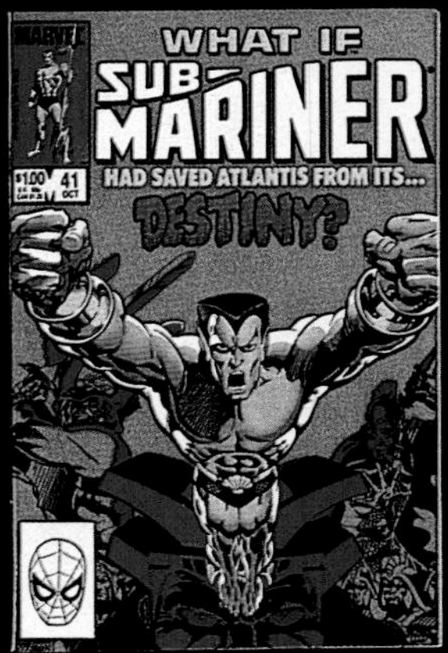
MARVEL
WHAT IF
SUB-MARINER
$1.00 41 OCT
HAD SAVED ATLANTIS FROM ITS...
DESTINY?

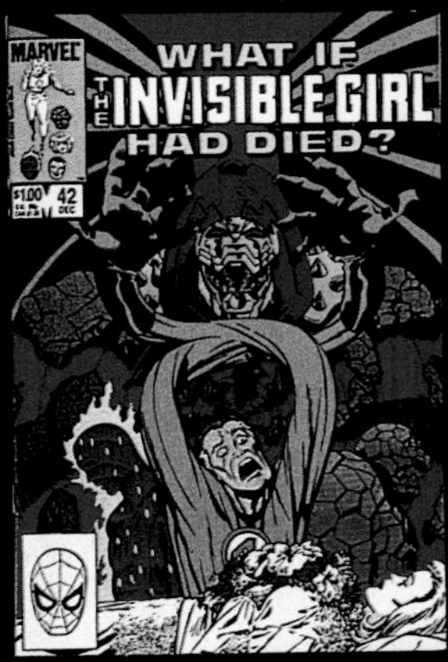
MARVEL
WHAT IF
THE INVISIBLE GIRL
HAD DIED?
$1.00 42 DEC

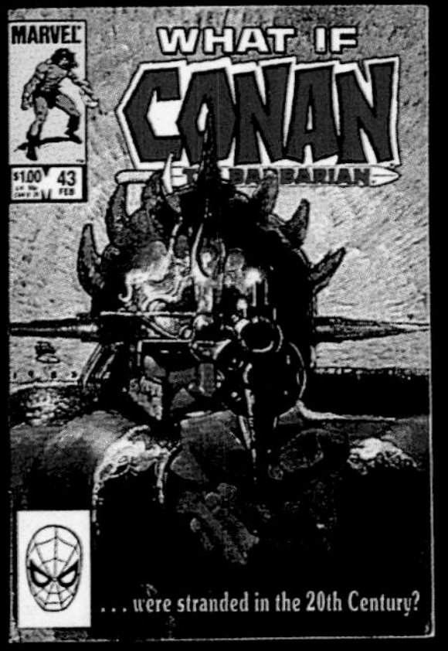
MARVEL
WHAT IF
CONAN
THE BARBARIAN
$1.00 43 FEB
... were stranded in the 20th Century?

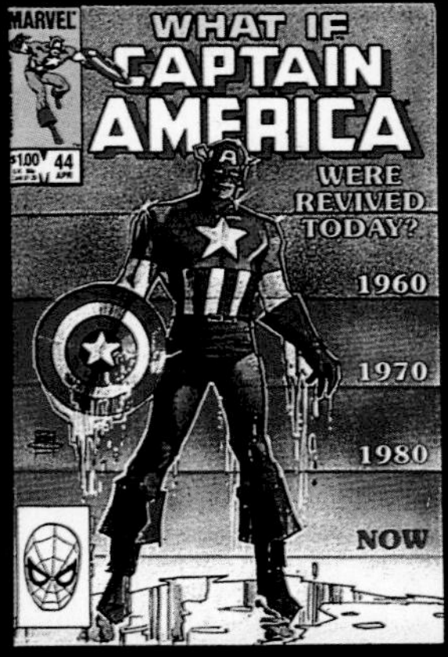
MARVEL
WHAT IF
CAPTAIN AMERICA
$1.00 44 APR
WERE REVIVED TODAY?
1960
1970
1980
NOW

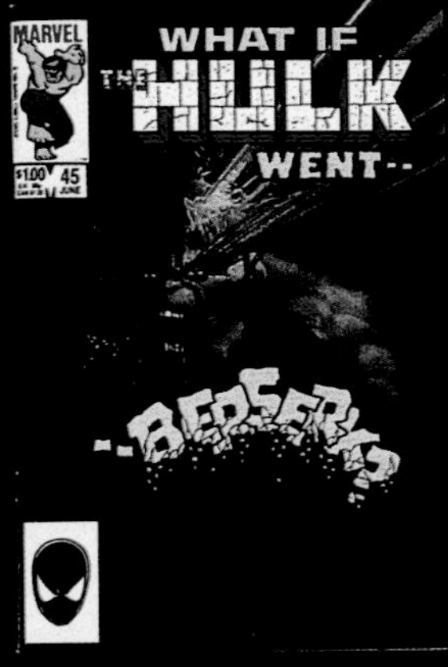
MARVEL
WHAT IF
THE HULK
$1.00 45 JUN
WENT--
--BERSERK?

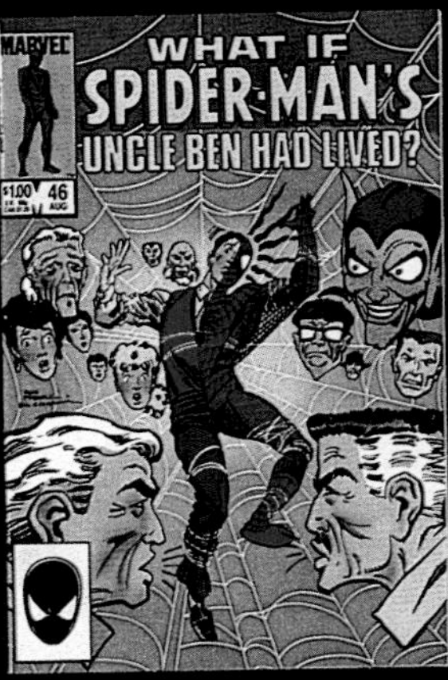
MARVEL
WHAT IF
SPIDER-MAN'S
UNCLE BEN HAD LIVED?
$1.00 46 AUG

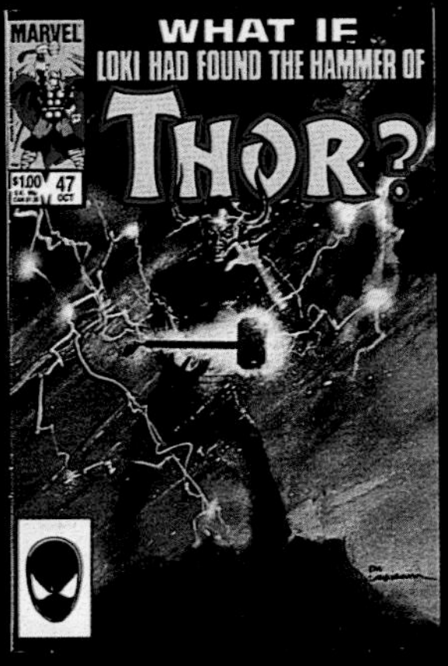
MARVEL
WHAT IF
LOKI HAD FOUND THE HAMMER OF
THOR?
$1.00 47 OCT

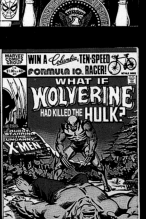

What IF...? (1-47) 2143

Ref. No.	Date	RVI	Artist/Info.
2143-1	Feb. 1977	9	Craig/Marcos-a (Origin Spiderman)
2143-2	Apr.	8	Trimpe/Sutton-a (Origin, Hulk)
2143-3	Jun.	3	Kane/Janson-a
2143-4	Aug.	3	Robbins/Springer-a
2143-5	Oct.	3	Hoberg/Sinnott-c, Tuska/Jones-a
2143-6	Dec.	3	Hoberg-c, Craig, Hoberg-a
2143-7	Feb. 1978	3	Hoberg/Grainger-a
2143-8	Apr.	2	Kupperberg, Mooney-a
2143-9	Jun.	2	Kupperberg, Black-a (Origin, Venus, Marvel Boy)
2143-10	**Aug.**	**2**	**Hoberg/Hunt-a**
2143-11	Oct.	2	Kirby/Sinnott-c, Kirby/Royer-a
2143-12	Dec.	2	Buscema/Black-a
2143-13	Feb. 1979	3	Buscema/Chan-c/a (Conan -app.)
2143-14	Apr.	2	Trimpe/Marcos-a
2143-15	Jul.	2	Buscema/Sinnott-a
2143-16	Aug.	2	Hoberg-c/a, Wray, Stevens-a
2143-17	Oct.	2	Infantino/Stone-a
2143-18	Dec.	2	Sutton/Patterson-a
2143-19	Feb. 1980	2	Broderick/Esposito-a
2143-20	**Apr.**	**2**	**Kupperberg/Patterson-a**
2143-21 to 26,29,30		2	(Origin-Dr. Doom)
2143-27	Jun. 1981	5	Miller-c/a (S-Men -app.)
2143-28	Aug.	4	Miller-c/a (Daredevil -app.)
2143-31	Feb. 1982	6	Miller-c/a (X-Men -app.)
2143-32 to 47	Oct. 1985, (#47)	1	(#37, Original X-Men -app.)
2143-SP1	Jun. 1988	1	Ditko-a

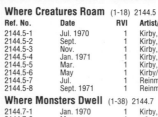

2144.5 Where Creatures Roam (1-8)

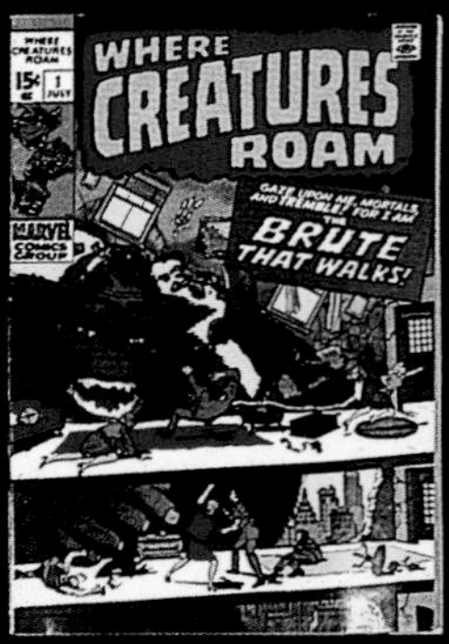
WHERE CREATURES ROAM
BRUTE THAT WALKS!

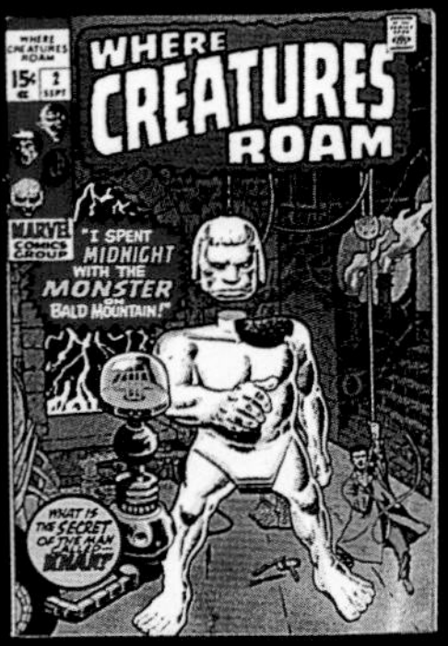
WHERE CREATURES ROAM
"I SPENT MIDNIGHT WITH THE MONSTER OF BALD MOUNTAIN!"

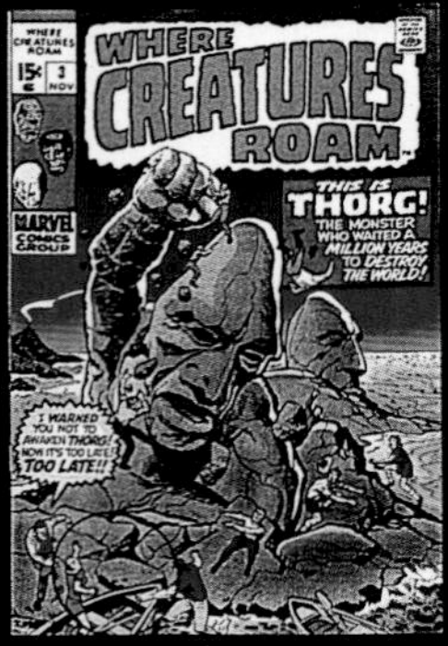
WHERE CREATURES ROAM
THIS IS THORG!

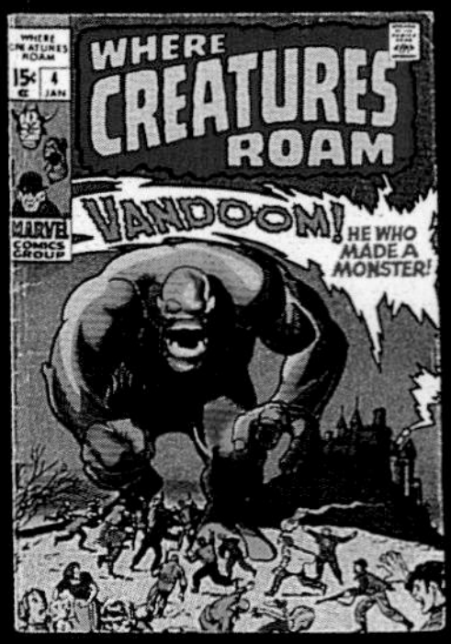
WHERE CREATURES ROAM
VANDOOM! HE WHO MADE A MONSTER!

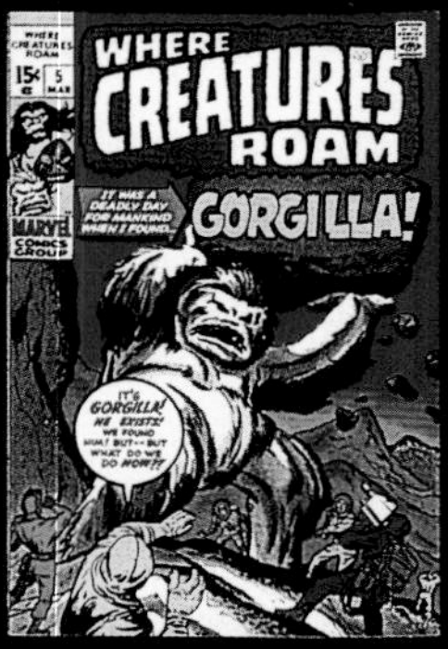
WHERE CREATURES ROAM
GORGILLA!

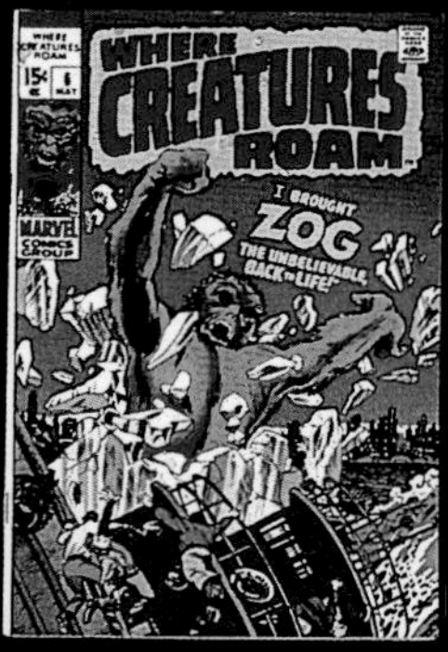
WHERE CREATURES ROAM
I BROUGHT ZOG THE UNBELIEVABLE BACK TO LIFE!

2144.7 Where Monsters Dwell (1-28)

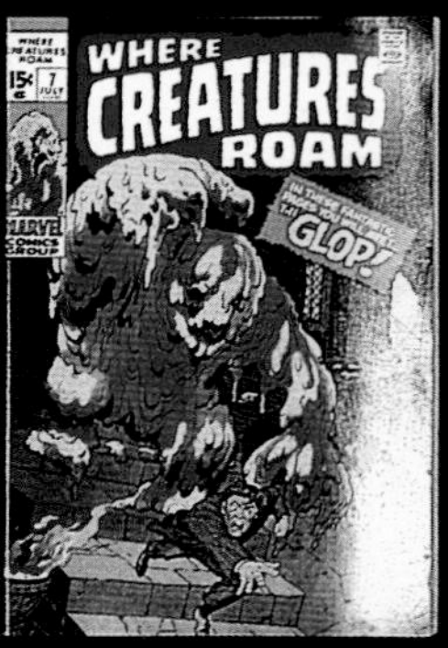
WHERE CREATURES ROAM
GLOP!

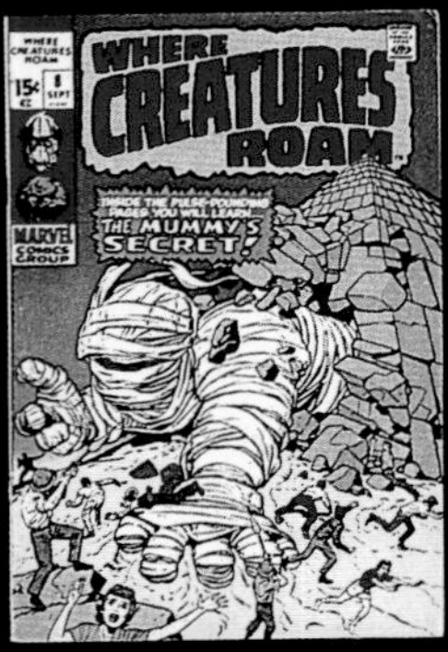
WHERE CREATURES ROAM
THE MUMMY'S SECRET

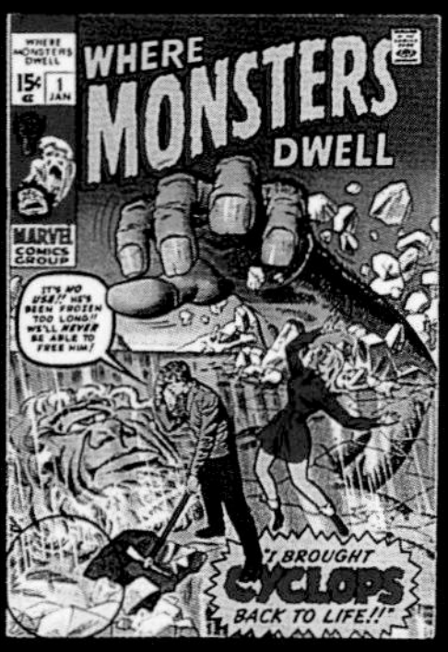
WHERE MONSTERS DWELL
I BROUGHT CYCLOPS BACK TO LIFE!!

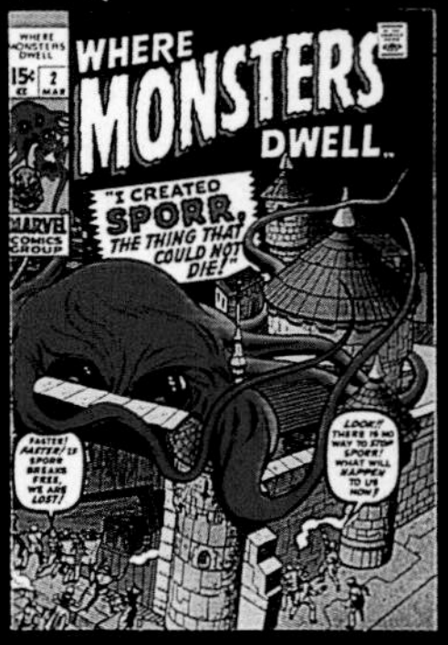
WHERE MONSTERS DWELL
"I CREATED SPORR, THE THING THAT COULD NOT DIE!"

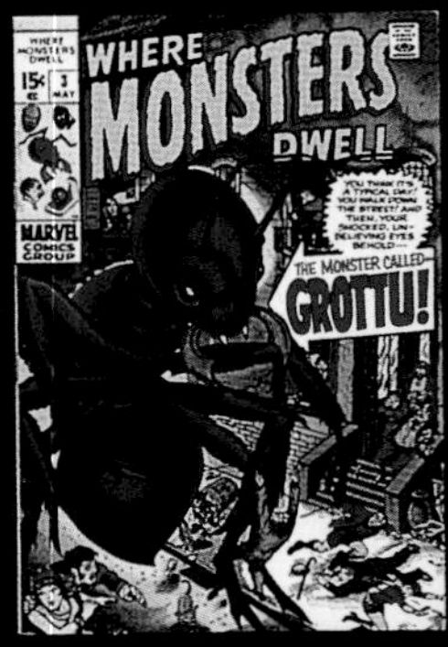
WHERE MONSTERS DWELL
THE MONSTER CALLED GROTTU!

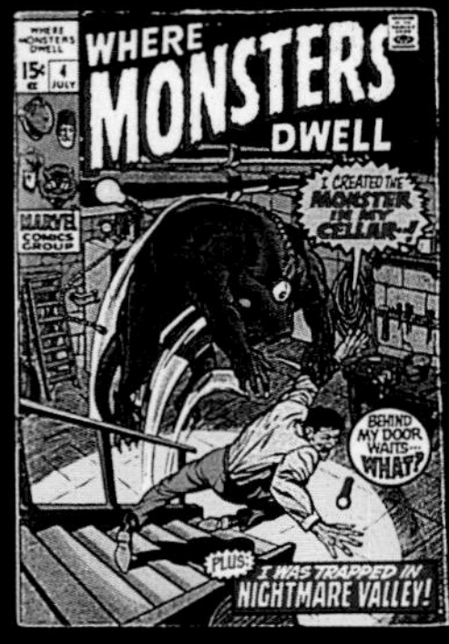
WHERE MONSTERS DWELL
I WAS TRAPPED IN NIGHTMARE VALLEY!

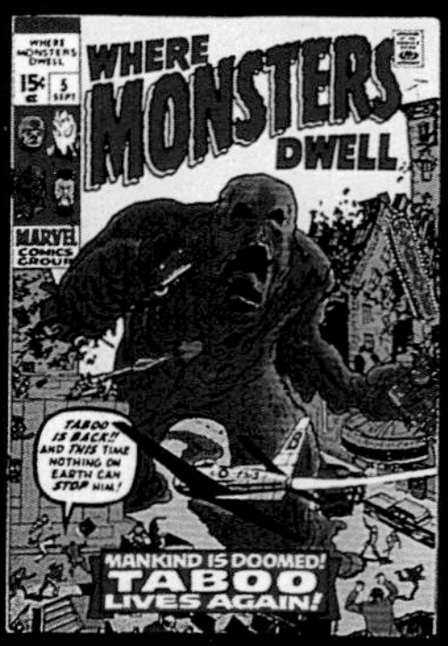
WHERE MONSTERS DWELL
MANKIND IS DOOMED! TABOO LIVES AGAIN!

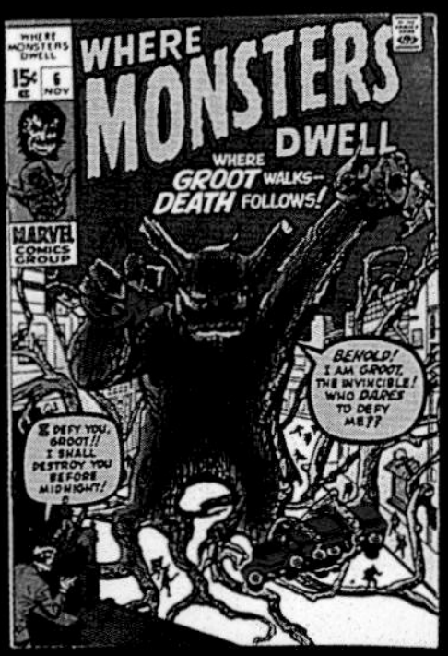
WHERE MONSTERS DWELL
WHERE GROOT WALKS-- DEATH FOLLOWS!

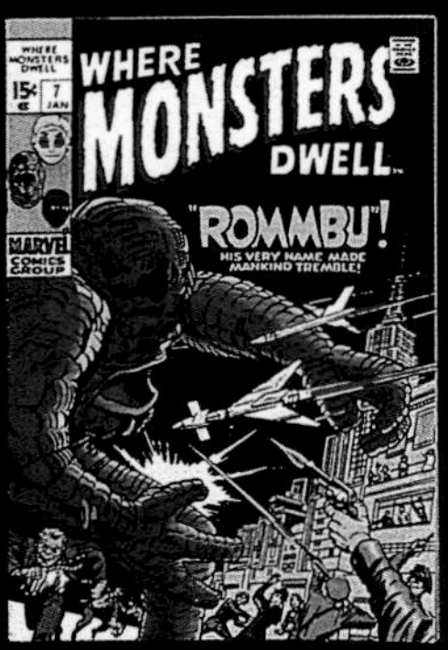
WHERE MONSTERS DWELL
"ROMMBU!" HIS VERY NAME MADE MANKIND TREMBLE!

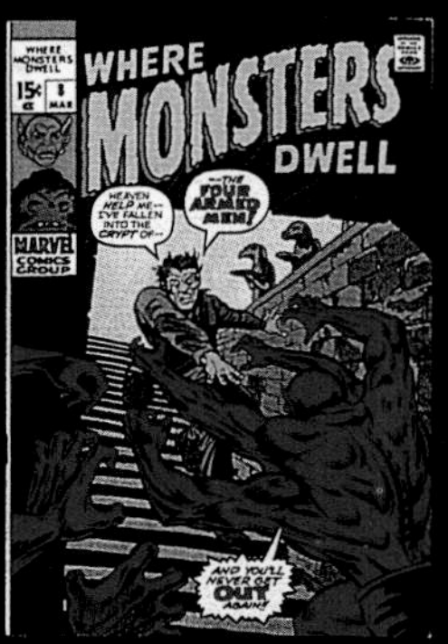
WHERE MONSTERS DWELL

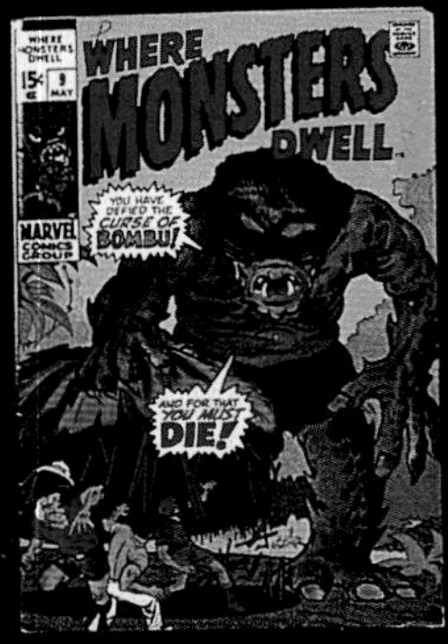
WHERE MONSTERS DWELL
DIE!

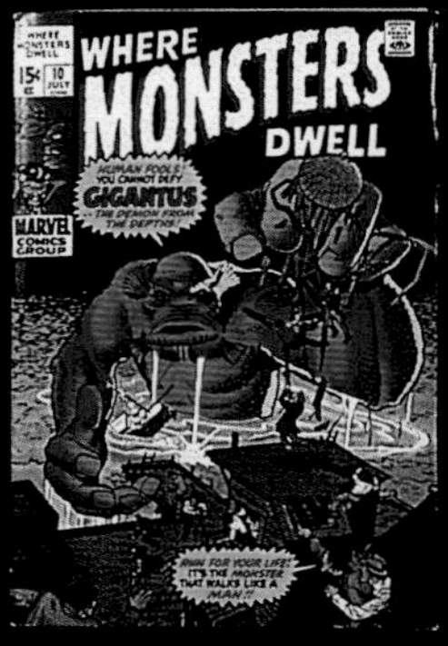
WHERE MONSTERS DWELL
GIGANTUS

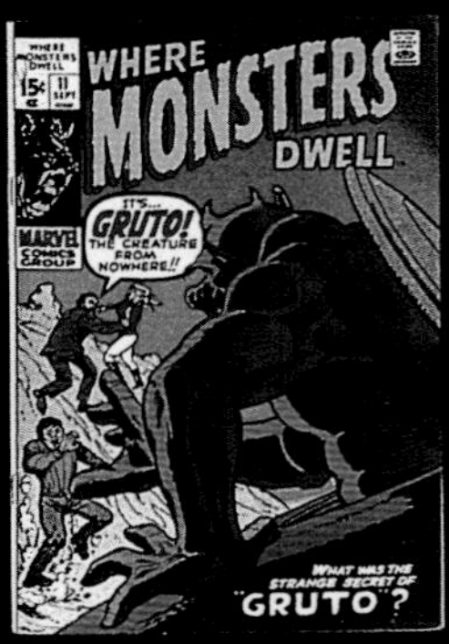
WHERE MONSTERS DWELL
GRUTO!
WHAT WAS THE STRANGE SECRET OF GRUTO?

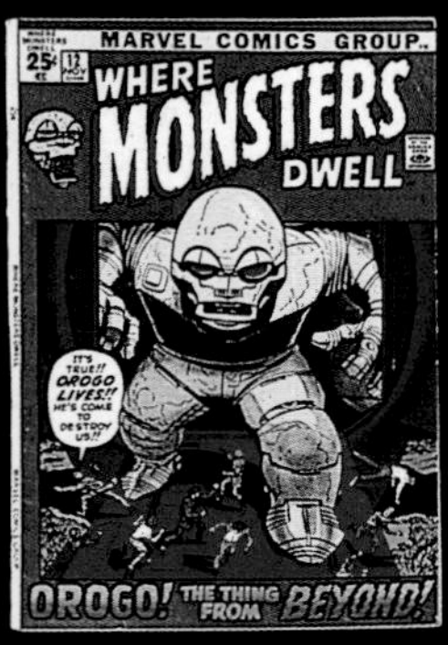
MARVEL COMICS GROUP
WHERE MONSTERS DWELL
OROGO! THE THING FROM BEYOND!

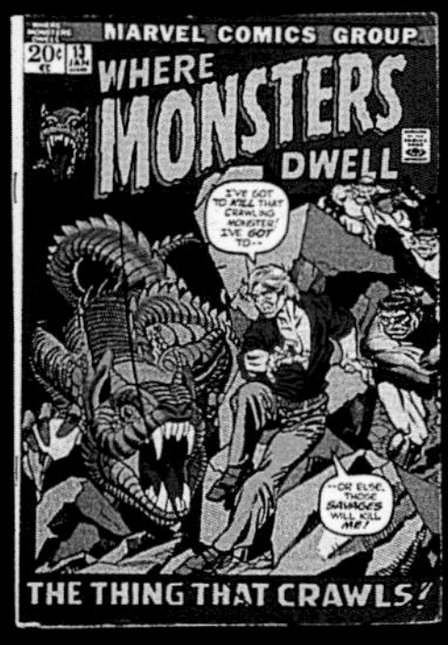
MARVEL COMICS GROUP
WHERE MONSTERS DWELL
THE THING THAT CRAWLS!

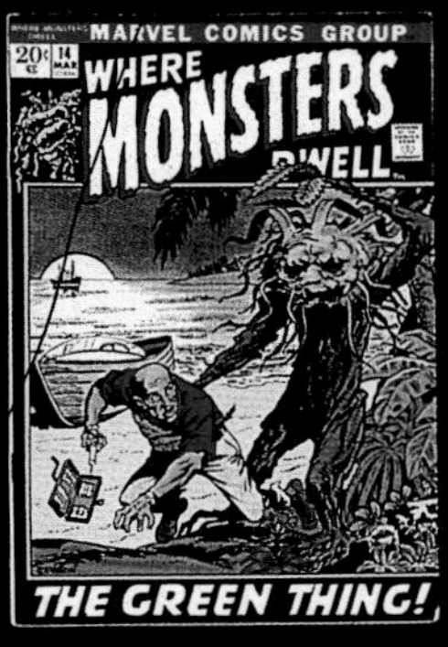
MARVEL COMICS GROUP
WHERE MONSTERS DWELL
THE GREEN THING!

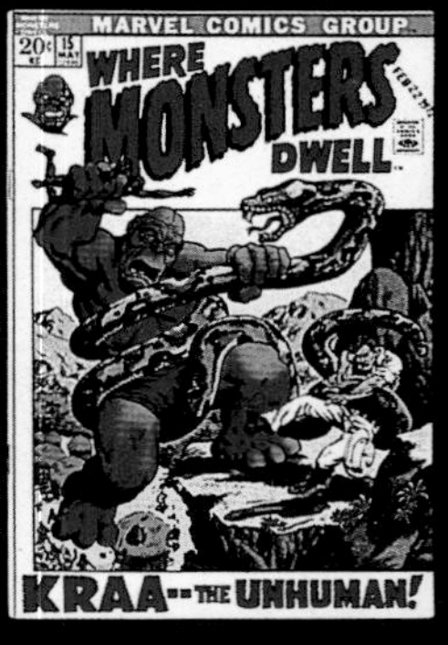
MARVEL COMICS GROUP
WHERE MONSTERS DWELL
KRAA--THE UNHUMAN!

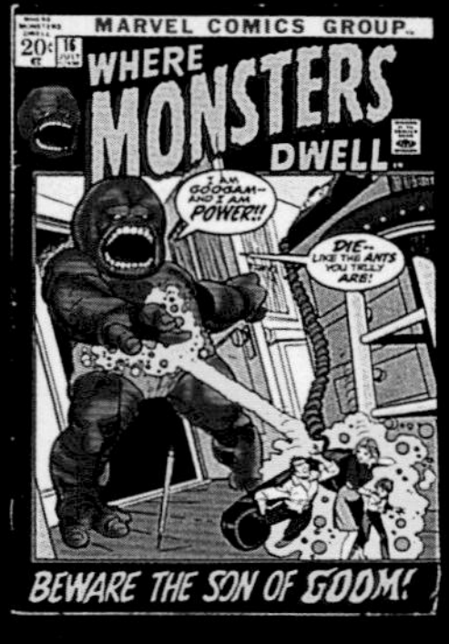
MARVEL COMICS GROUP
WHERE MONSTERS DWELL
BEWARE THE SON OF GOOM!

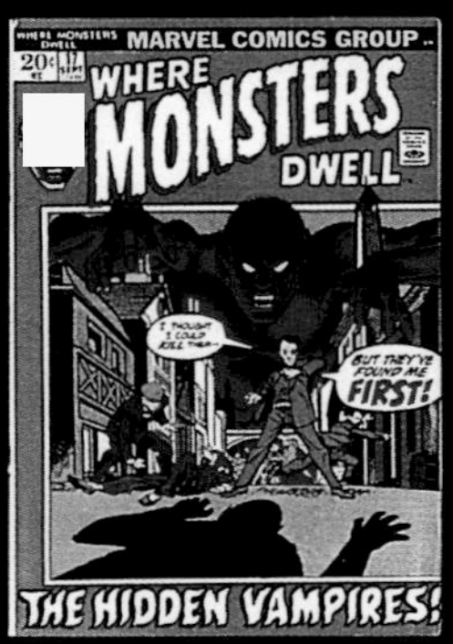
MARVEL COMICS GROUP
WHERE MONSTERS DWELL
THE HIDDEN VAMPIRES!

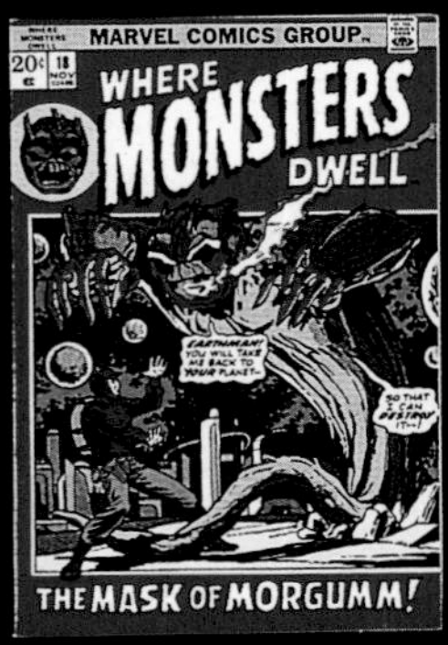
MARVEL COMICS GROUP
WHERE MONSTERS DWELL
THE MASK OF MORGUMM!

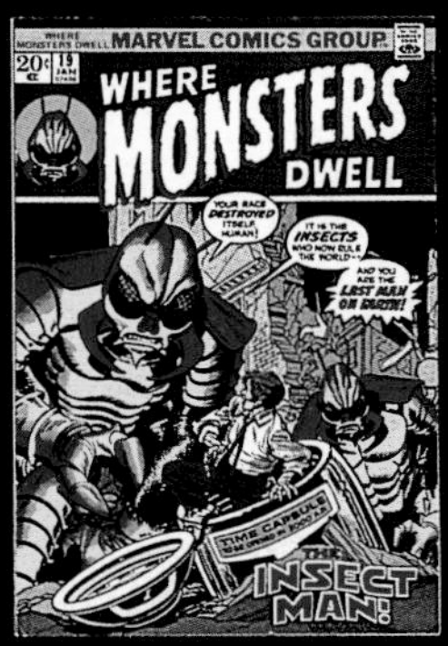
MARVEL COMICS GROUP
WHERE MONSTERS DWELL
THE INSECT MAN!

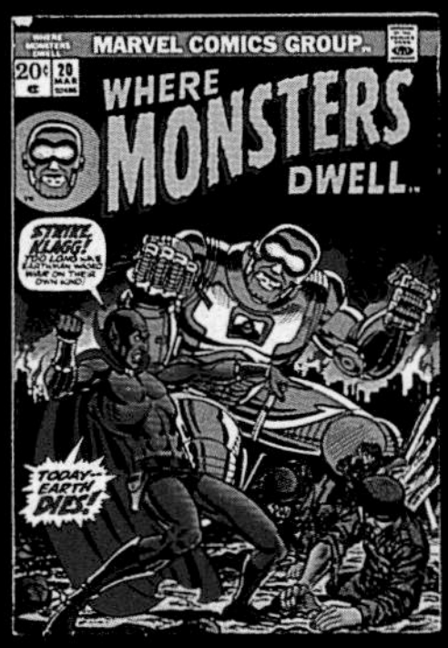
MARVEL COMICS GROUP
WHERE MONSTERS DWELL

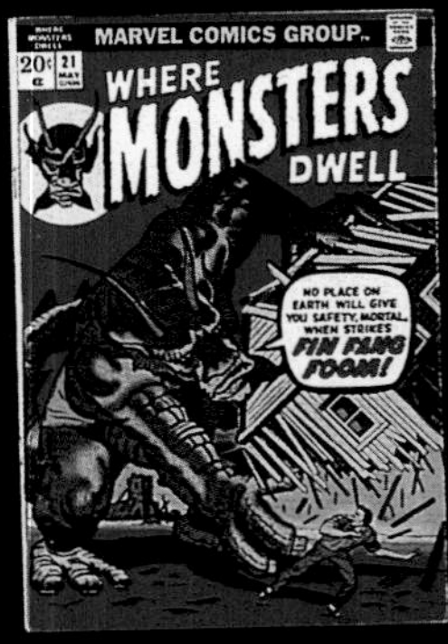
MARVEL COMICS GROUP
WHERE MONSTERS DWELL
FIN FANG FOOM!

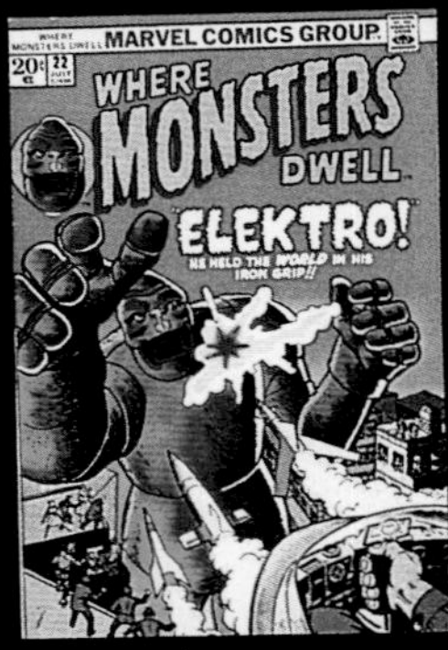
MARVEL COMICS GROUP
WHERE MONSTERS DWELL
ELEKTRO!

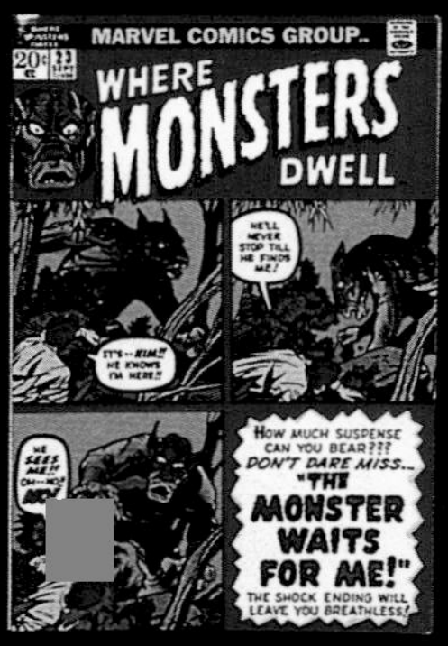
MARVEL COMICS GROUP
WHERE MONSTERS DWELL
"THE MONSTER WAITS FOR ME!"

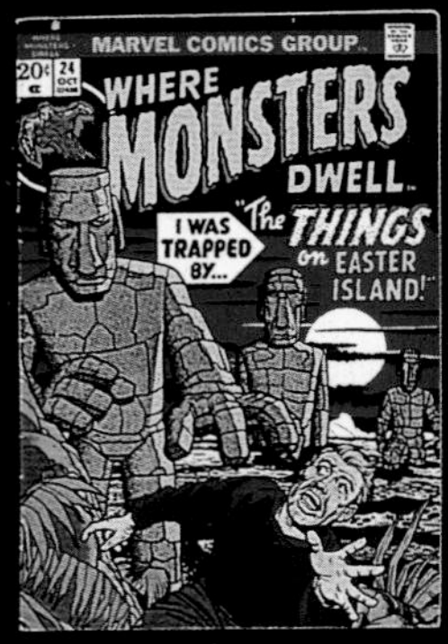
MARVEL COMICS GROUP
WHERE MONSTERS DWELL
I WAS TRAPPED BY...
"The THINGS on EASTER ISLAND!"

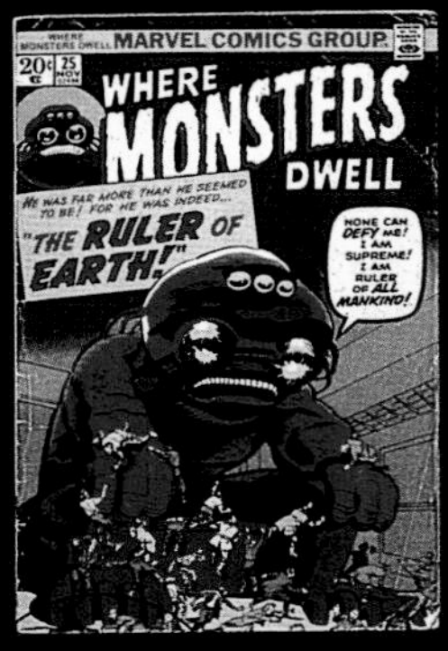
MARVEL COMICS GROUP
WHERE MONSTERS DWELL
"THE RULER OF EARTH!"

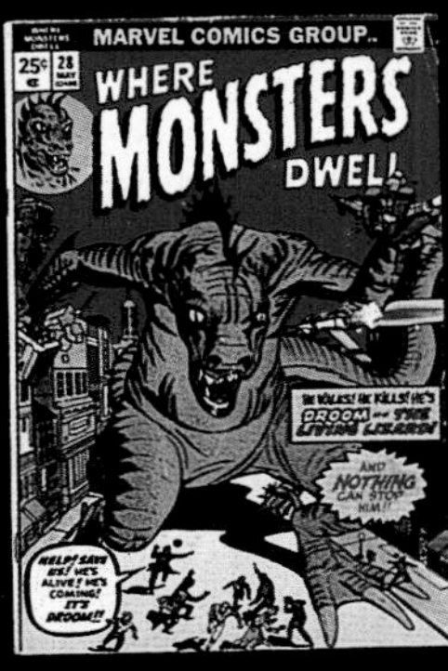
MARVEL COMICS GROUP
WHERE MONSTERS DWELL

Where Creatures Roam (1-18) 2144.5

Ref. No.	Date	RVI	Artist/Info.	
2144.5-1	Jul. 1970	1	Kirby, Ditko/Ayers-a	Reprints
2144.5-2	Sept.	1	Kirby, Ditko, Reinman-a	"
2144.5-3	Nov.	1	Kirby, Ditko/Ayers-a	"
2144.5-4	Jan. 1971	1	Kirby, Ditko-a	"
2144.5-5	Mar.	1	Kirby, Ditko-a	"
2144.5-6	May	1	Kirby/Ditko-a	"
2144.5-7	Jul.	1	Reinman, Ditko-a	"
2144.5-8	Sept. 1971	1	Reinman-a	"

Where Monsters Dwell (1-38) 2144.7

Ref. No.	Date	RVI	Artist/Info.	
2144.7-1	Jan. 1970	1	Kirby, Ditko/Ayers-a	Reprints
2144.7-2	Mar.	1	" " "	
2144.7-3	May	1	Kirby, Reinman/Ayers-a	"
2144.7-4	Jul.	1	Ditko/CSrandall-a	"
2144.7-5	Sept.	1	Ditko, Kirby/Ayers-a	"
2144.7-6	Nov.	1	Kirby, Ditko-a/Ayers-a	"
2144.7-7 to 38	Oct. 1975, (#38)	1		

2174 Wolverine (1-4)

2174.3 Wolverine (1-10)

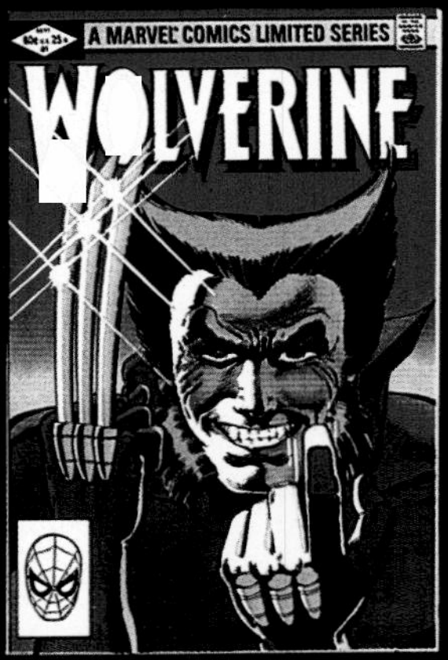
A MARVEL COMICS LIMITED SERIES
WOLVERINE

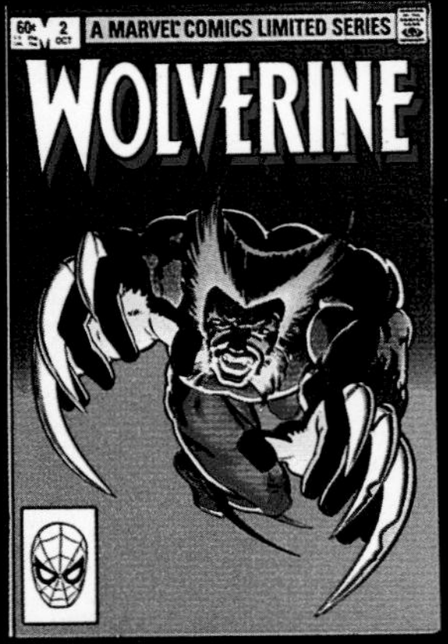
A MARVEL COMICS LIMITED SERIES
WOLVERINE

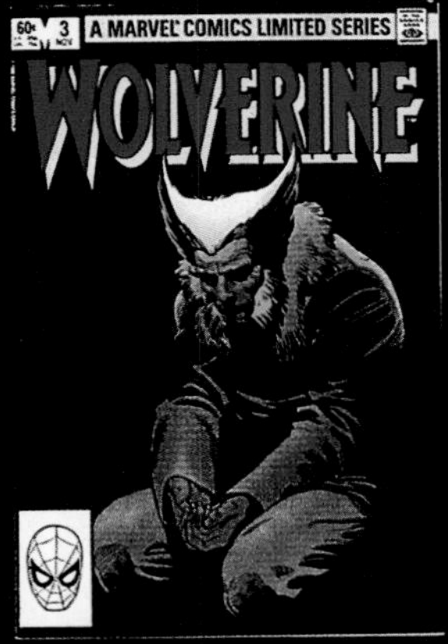
A MARVEL COMICS LIMITED SERIES
WOLVERINE

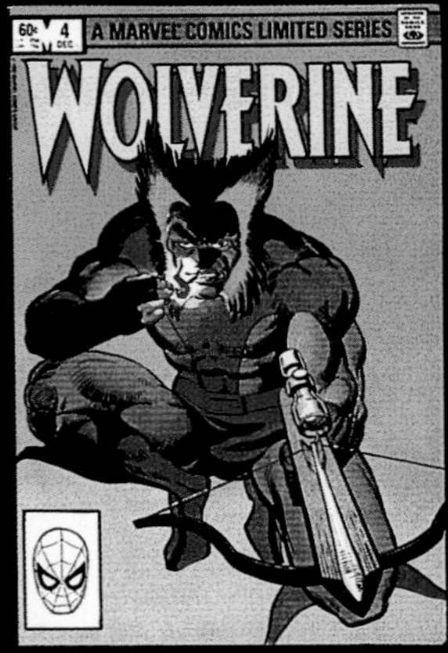
A MARVEL COMICS LIMITED SERIES
WOLVERINE

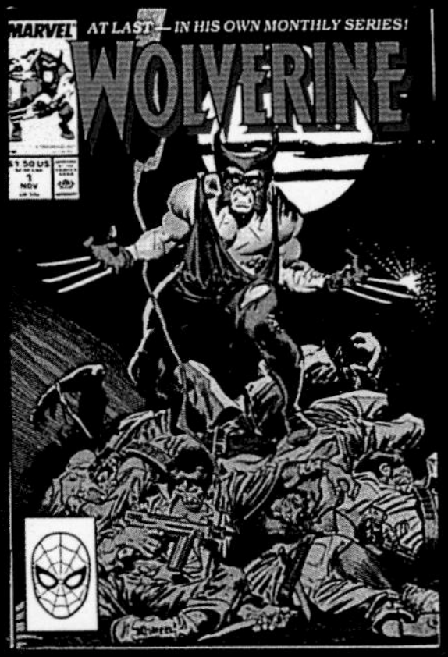
AT LAST—IN HIS OWN MONTHLY SERIES!
WOLVERINE

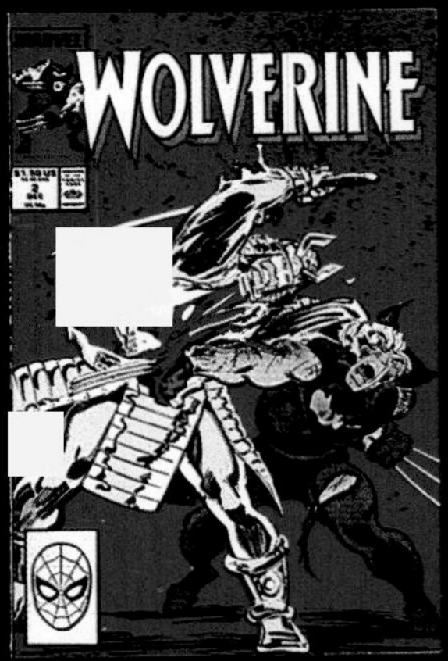
WOLVERINE

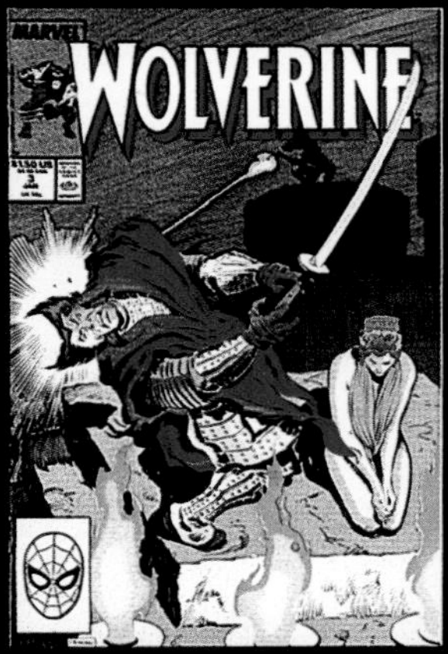
WOLVERINE

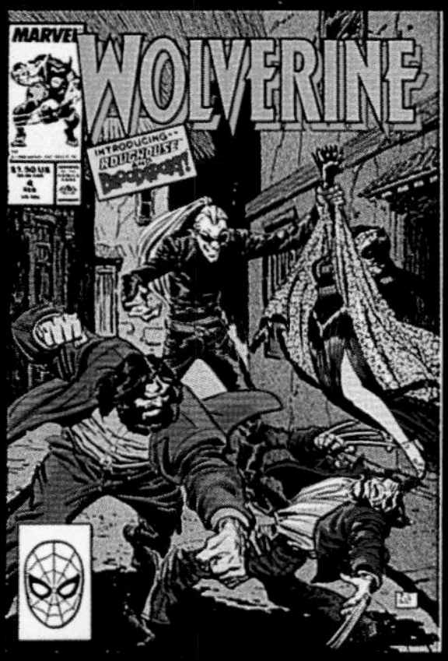
WOLVERINE

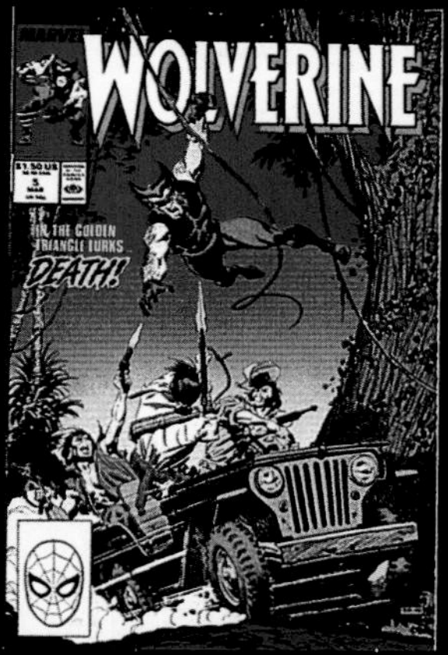
WOLVERINE

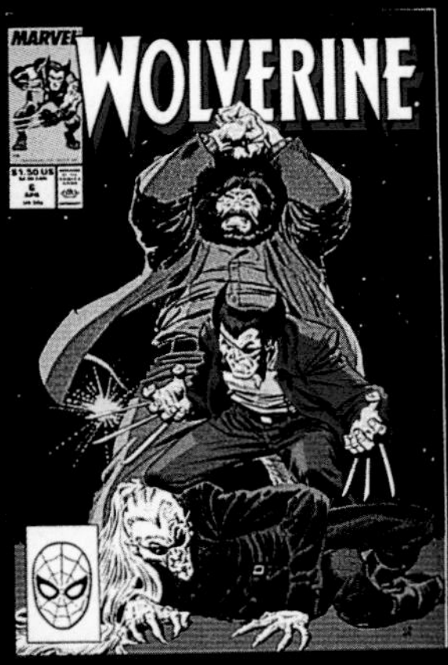
WOLVERINE

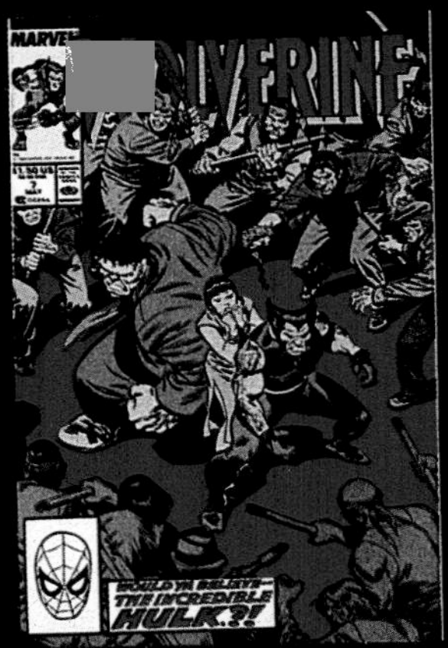

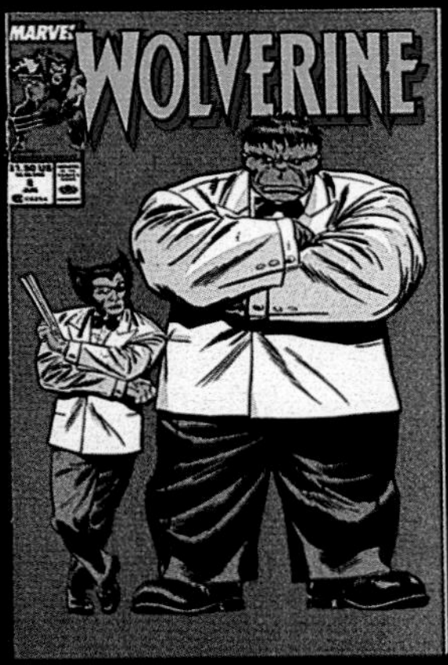
WOLVERINE

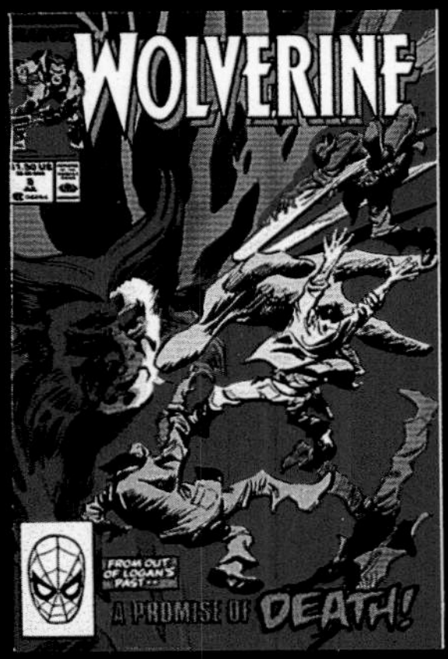
WOLVERINE
A PROMISE OF DEATH!

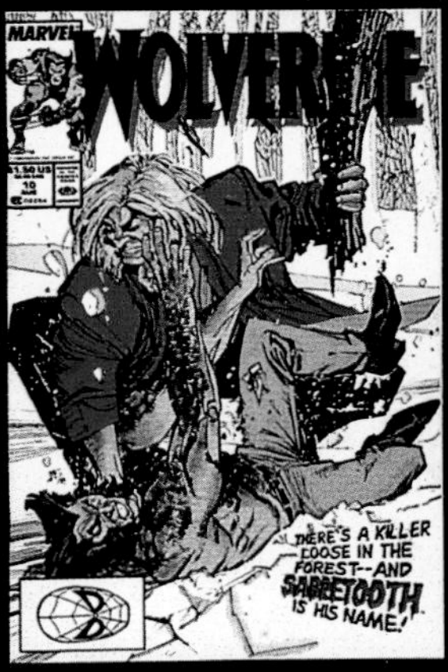
THERE'S A KILLER LOOSE IN THE FOREST—AND SABRETOOTH IS HIS NAME!

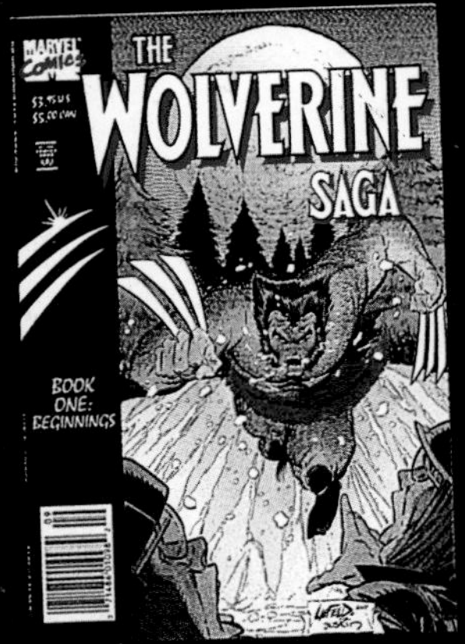
THE WOLVERINE SAGA
BOOK ONE: BEGINNINGS

2194.3 World's Unknown (1-8)

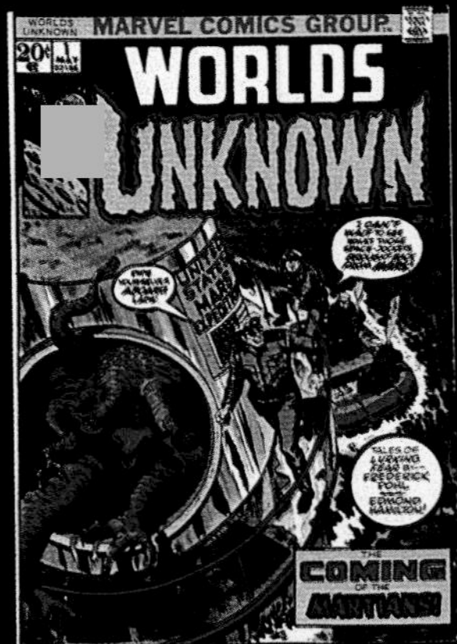
MARVEL COMICS GROUP
WORLDS UNKNOWN

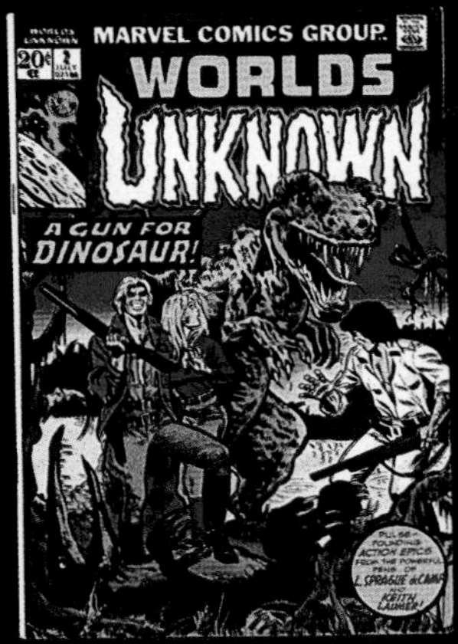
MARVEL COMICS GROUP
WORLDS UNKNOWN
A GUN FOR DINOSAUR!

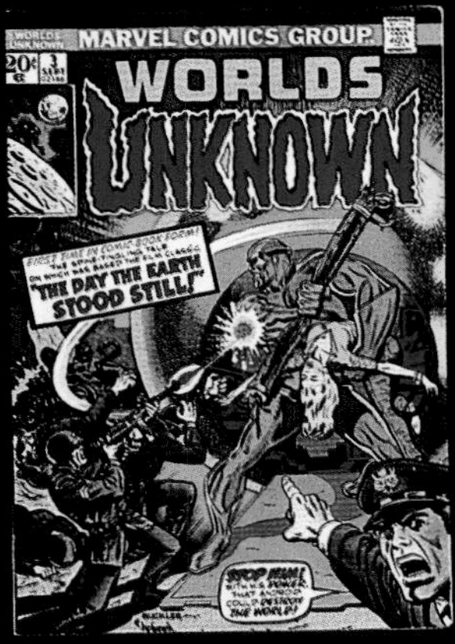
MARVEL COMICS GROUP
WORLDS UNKNOWN
"THE DAY THE EARTH STOOD STILL!"

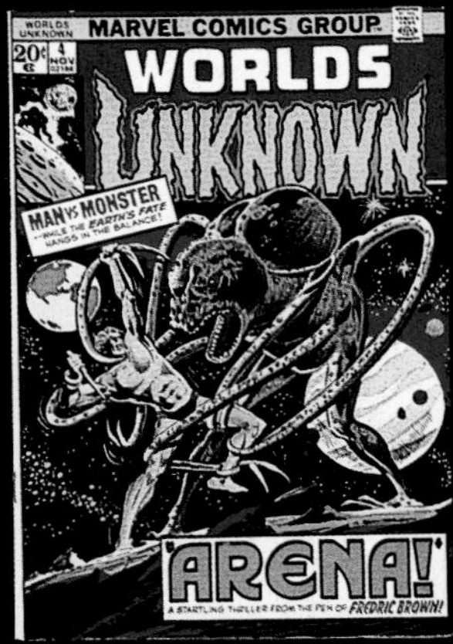
MARVEL COMICS GROUP
WORLDS UNKNOWN
MAN vs MONSTER
ARENA!
A STARTLING THRILLER FROM THE PEN OF FREDRIC BROWN!

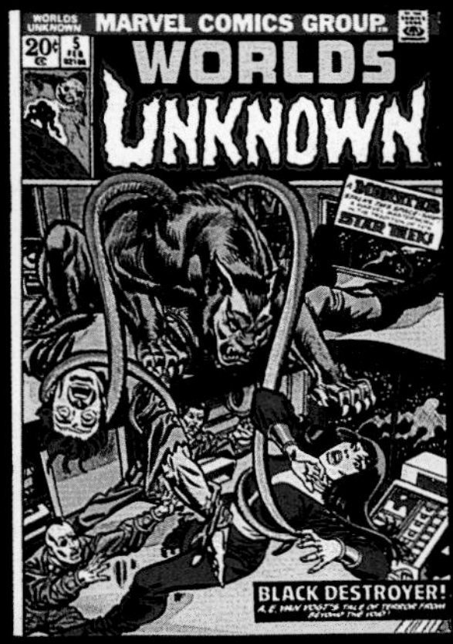
MARVEL COMICS GROUP
WORLDS UNKNOWN
BLACK DESTROYER!

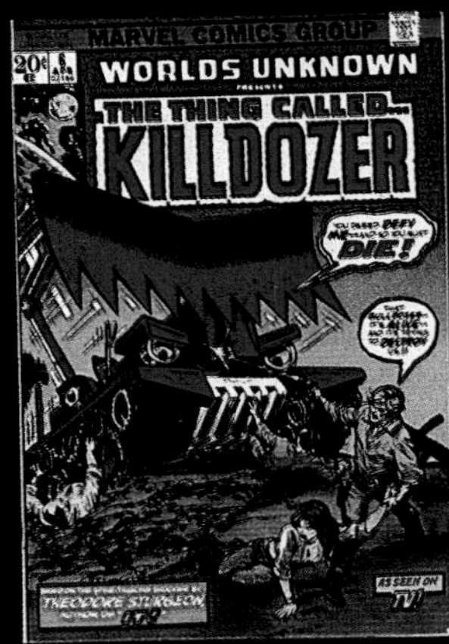
MARVEL COMICS GROUP
WORLDS UNKNOWN
THE THING CALLED... KILLDOZER

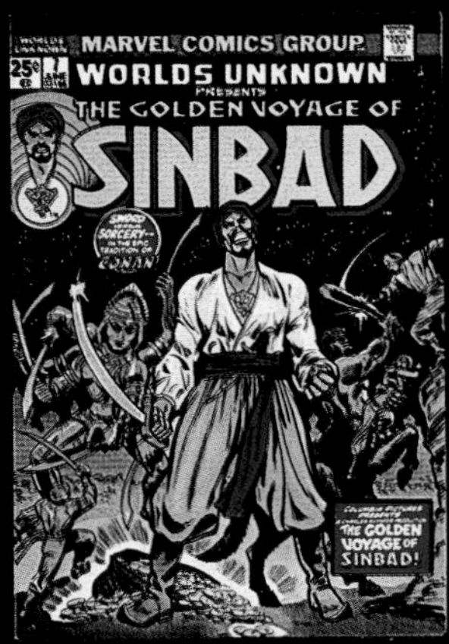
MARVEL COMICS GROUP
WORLDS UNKNOWN
THE GOLDEN VOYAGE OF SINBAD

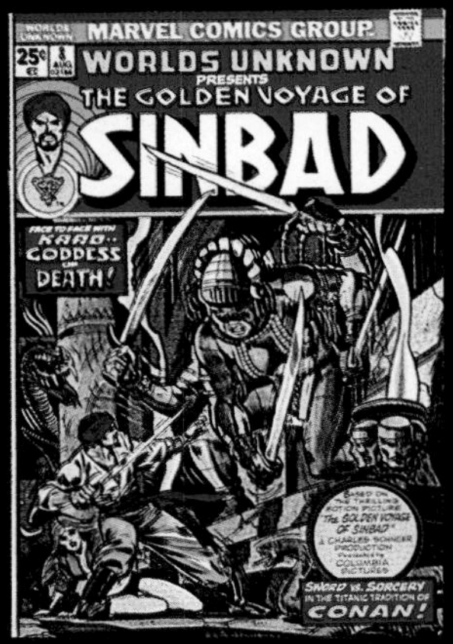
MARVEL COMICS GROUP
WORLDS UNKNOWN
THE GOLDEN VOYAGE OF SINBAD

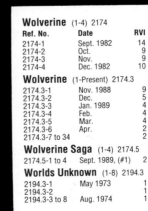

Wolverine (1-4) 2174

Ref. No.	Date	RVI	Artist/Info.
2174-1	Sept. 1982	14	Miller/Rubenstein-c/a
2174-2	Oct.	9	" "
2174-3	Nov.	9	" "
2174-4	Dec. 1982	10	" "

Wolverine (1-Present) 2174.3

2174.3-1	Nov. 1988	9	Buscema/Williamson-c/a
2174.3-2	Dec.	5	Buscema-c/a, Janson-a
2174.3-3	Jan. 1989	4	Buscema/Williamson-c/a
2174.3-4	Feb.	4	" "
2174.3-5	Mar.	4	" "
2174.3-6	Apr.	2	Buscema-c/a, Williamson-a
2174.3-7 to 34		2	(#17, Byrne art starts)

Wolverine Saga (1-4) 2174.5

2174.5-1 to 4	Sept. 1989, (#1)	2	Austin-a (The history of Wolverine)

Worlds Unknown (1-8) 2194.3

2194.3-1	May 1973	1	Torres, Reese-a Reprints
2194.3-2		1	Kane/Sutton-a
2194.3-3 to 8	Aug. 1974	1	

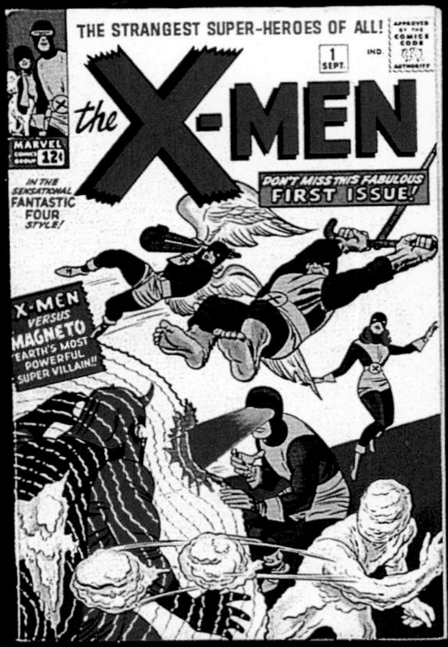
THE STRANGEST SUPER-HEROES OF ALL!
1 SEPT.
the X-MEN
MARVEL COMICS GROUP 12¢
IN THE SENSATIONAL FANTASTIC FOUR STYLE!
"DON'T MISS THIS FABULOUS FIRST ISSUE!"
X-MEN VERSUS MAGNETO EARTH'S MOST POWERFUL SUPER VILLAIN!

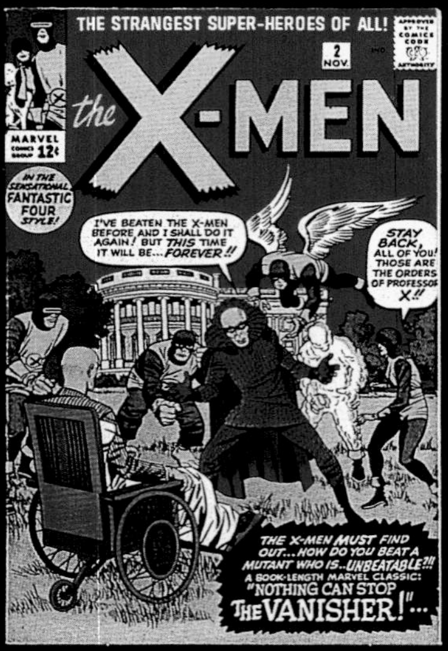
THE STRANGEST SUPER-HEROES OF ALL!
2 NOV
the X-MEN
MARVEL COMICS GROUP 12¢
IN THE SENSATIONAL FANTASTIC FOUR STYLE!
I'VE BEATEN THE X-MEN BEFORE AND I SHALL DO IT AGAIN! BUT THIS TIME IT WILL BE... FOREVER!!
STAY BACK, ALL OF YOU! THOSE ARE THE ORDERS OF PROFESSOR X!!
THE X-MEN MUST FIND OUT... HOW DO YOU BEAT A MUTANT WHO IS... UNBEATABLE?!! A BOOK-LENGTH MARVEL CLASSIC: "NOTHING CAN STOP THE VANISHER!"...

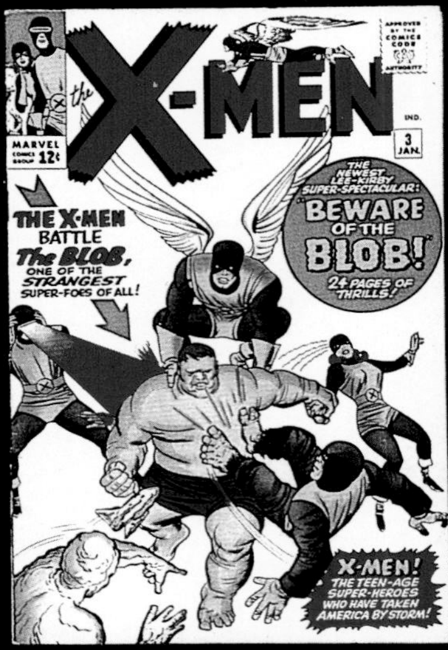
the X-MEN
3 JAN.
MARVEL COMICS GROUP 12¢
THE X-MEN BATTLE The BLOB, ONE OF THE STRANGEST SUPER-FOES OF ALL!
BEWARE OF THE BLOB!
24 PAGES OF THRILLS!
X-MEN! THE TEEN-AGE SUPER-HEROES WHO HAVE TAKEN AMERICA BY STORM!

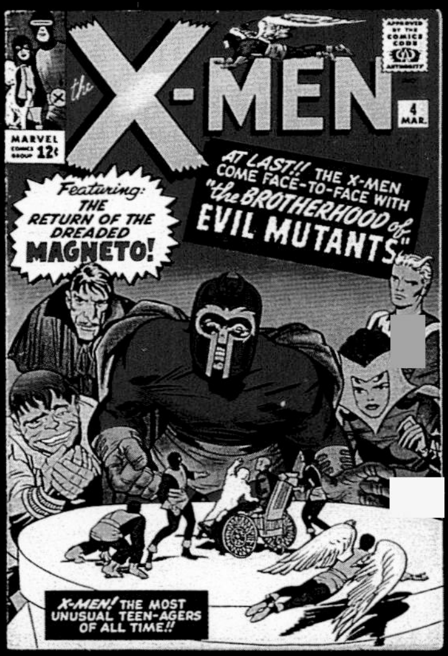
the X-MEN
4 MAR.
MARVEL COMICS GROUP 12¢
Featuring: THE RETURN OF THE DREADED MAGNETO!
AT LAST!! THE X-MEN COME FACE-TO-FACE WITH "the BROTHERHOOD of EVIL MUTANTS"
X-MEN! THE MOST UNUSUAL TEEN-AGERS OF ALL TIME!!

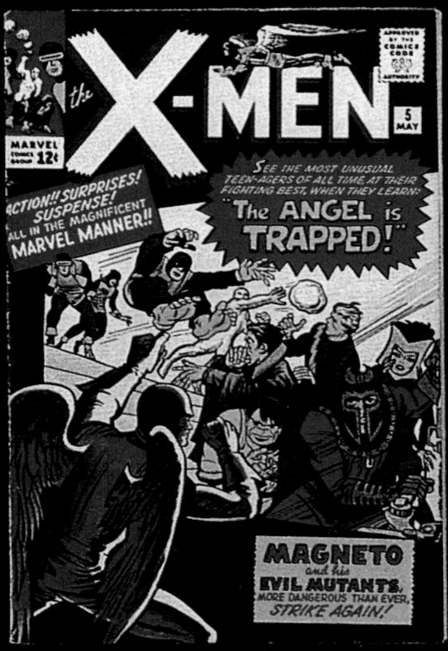
the X-MEN
5 MAY
MARVEL COMICS GROUP 12¢
ACTION!! SURPRISES! SUSPENSE! ALL IN THE MAGNIFICENT MARVEL MANNER!!
"The ANGEL is TRAPPED!"
MAGNETO and his EVIL MUTANTS, MORE DANGEROUS THAN EVER, STRIKE AGAIN!

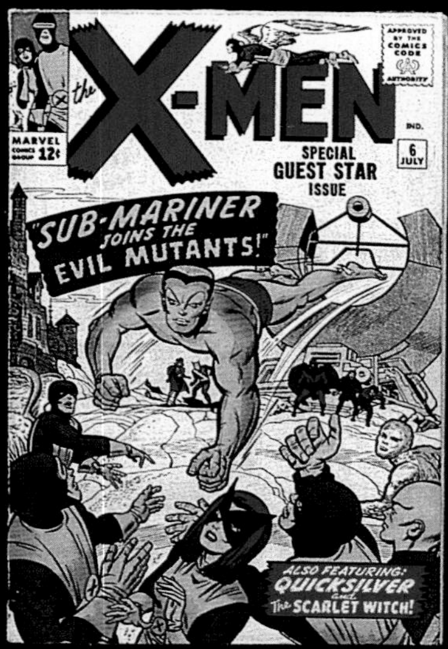
the X-MEN
6 JULY
MARVEL COMICS GROUP 12¢
SPECIAL GUEST STAR ISSUE
"SUB-MARINER joins the EVIL MUTANTS!"
ALSO FEATURING: QUICKSILVER and The SCARLET WITCH!

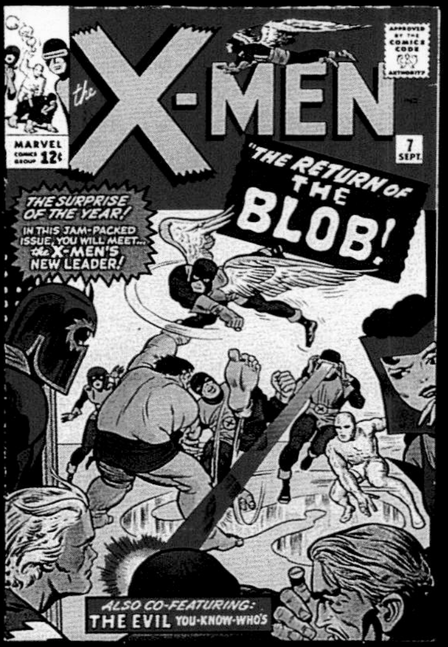
the X-MEN
7 SEPT.
MARVEL COMICS GROUP 12¢
THE SURPRISE OF THE YEAR! IN THIS JAM-PACKED ISSUE, YOU WILL MEET... the X-MEN'S NEW LEADER!
"THE RETURN OF THE BLOB!"
ALSO CO-FEATURING: THE EVIL YOU-KNOW-WHO'S

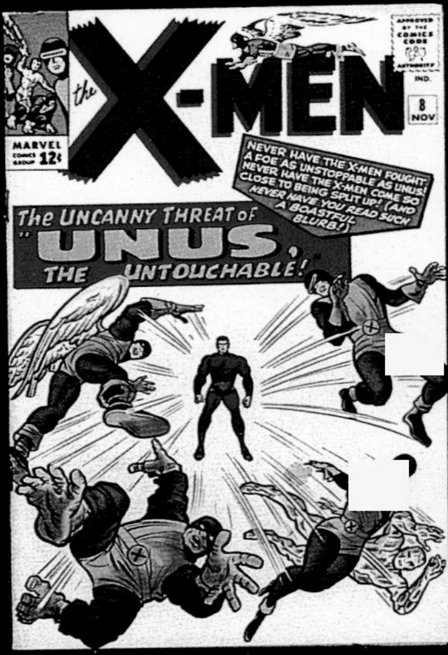
the X-MEN
8 NOV
MARVEL COMICS GROUP 12¢
The UNCANNY THREAT of "UNUS, THE UNTOUCHABLE!"

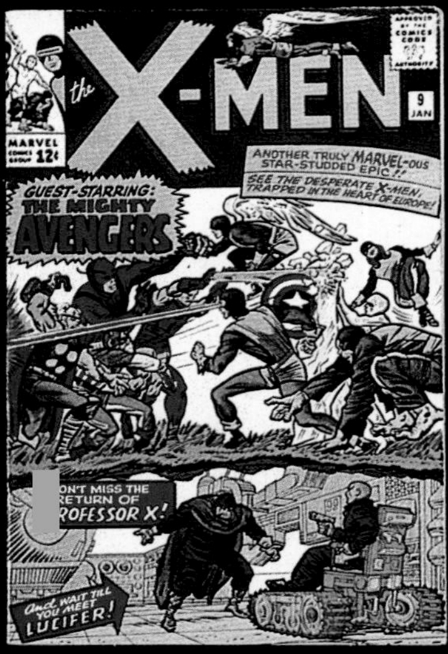
the X-MEN
9 JAN
MARVEL COMICS GROUP 12¢
GUEST-STARRING: THE MIGHTY AVENGERS
LUCIFER!

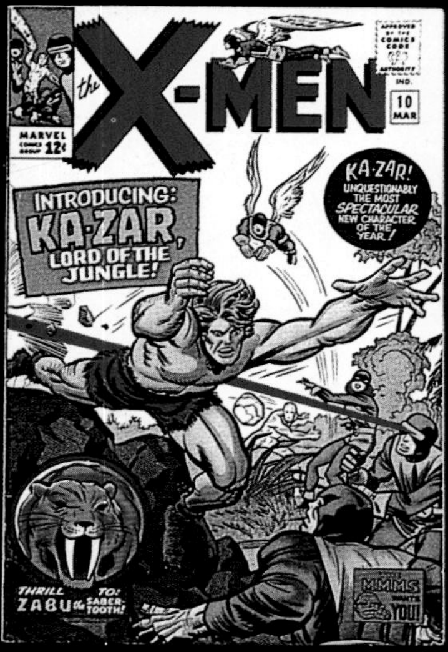
the X-MEN
10 MAR
MARVEL COMICS GROUP 12¢
INTRODUCING: KA-ZAR, LORD OF THE JUNGLE!
KA-ZAR! UNQUESTIONABLY THE MOST SPECTACULAR NEW CHARACTER OF THE YEAR!
THRILL TO ZABU the SABER-TOOTH!

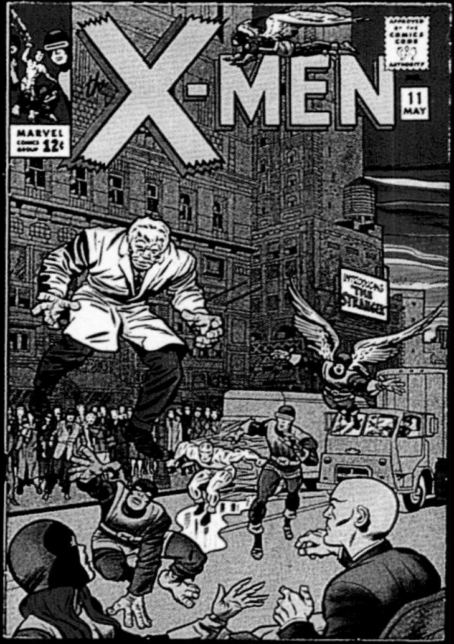
the X-MEN
11 MAY
MARVEL COMICS GROUP 12¢

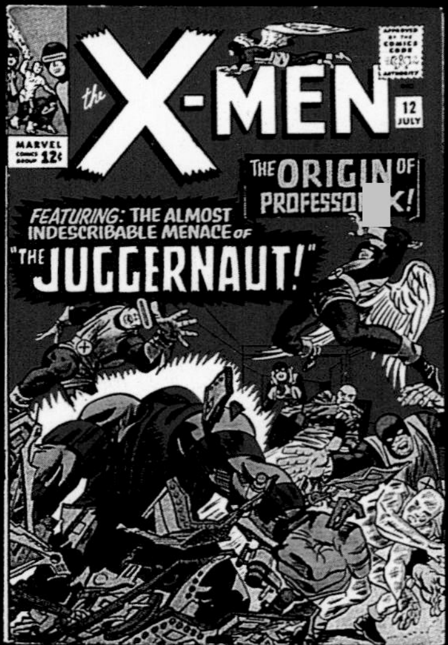
the X-MEN
12 JULY
MARVEL COMICS GROUP 12¢
FEATURING: THE ALMOST INDESCRIBABLE MENACE of "THE JUGGERNAUT!"

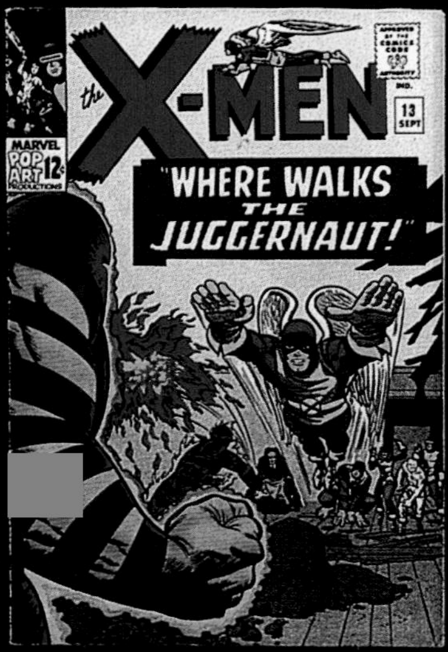
the X-MEN
13 SEPT
MARVEL POP ART PRODUCTIONS 12¢
"WHERE WALKS THE JUGGERNAUT!"

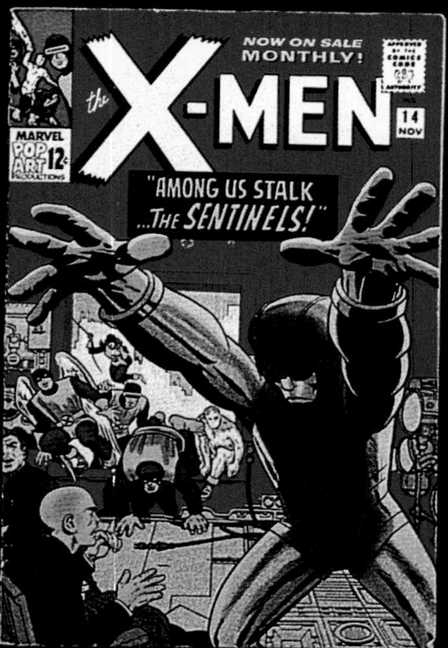
NOW ON SALE MONTHLY!
the X-MEN
14 NOV
MARVEL POP ART PRODUCTIONS 12¢
"AMONG US STALK ...The SENTINELS!"

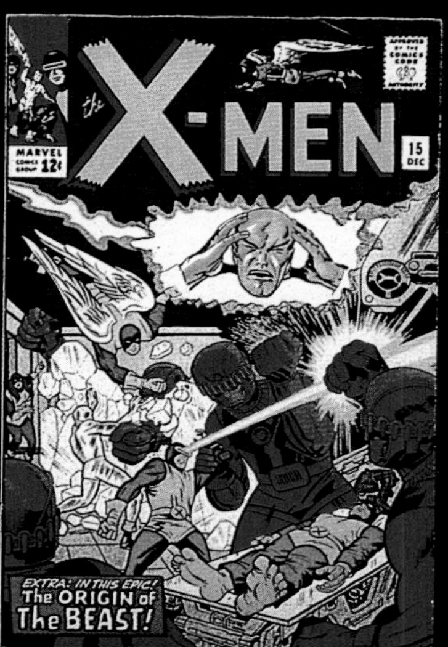
the X-MEN
15 DEC
MARVEL COMICS GROUP 12¢
EXTRA: IN THIS EPIC! The ORIGIN of The BEAST!

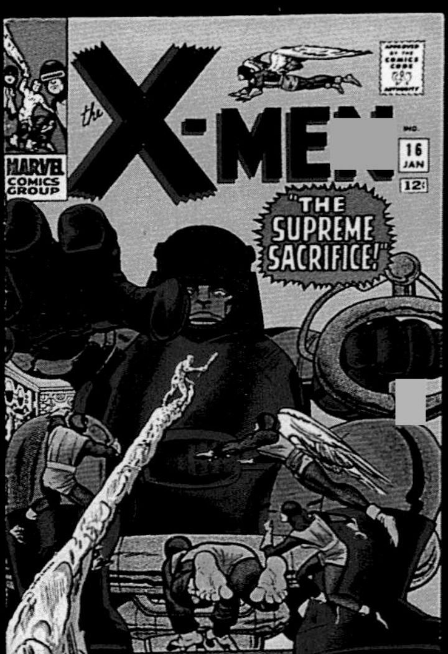
the X-MEN
16 JAN
MARVEL COMICS GROUP 12¢
"THE SUPREME SACRIFICE!"

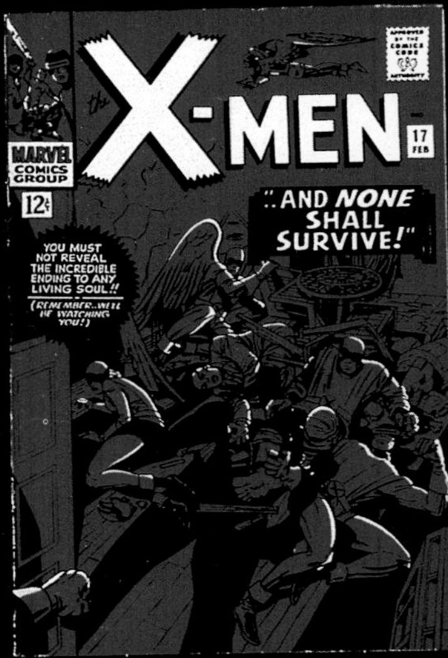
the X-MEN
17 FEB
MARVEL COMICS GROUP
12¢
"..AND NONE SHALL SURVIVE!"
YOU MUST NOT REVEAL THE INCREDIBLE ENDING TO ANY LIVING SOUL!!
(REMEMBER...WE'LL BE WATCHING YOU!)

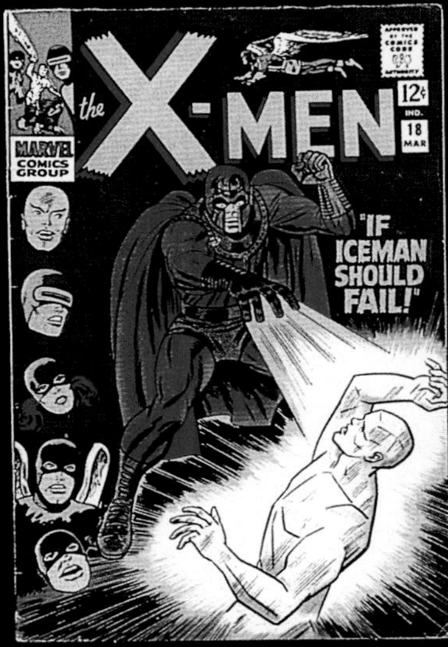
the X-MEN
12¢
18 MAR
MARVEL COMICS GROUP
"IF ICEMAN SHOULD FAIL!"

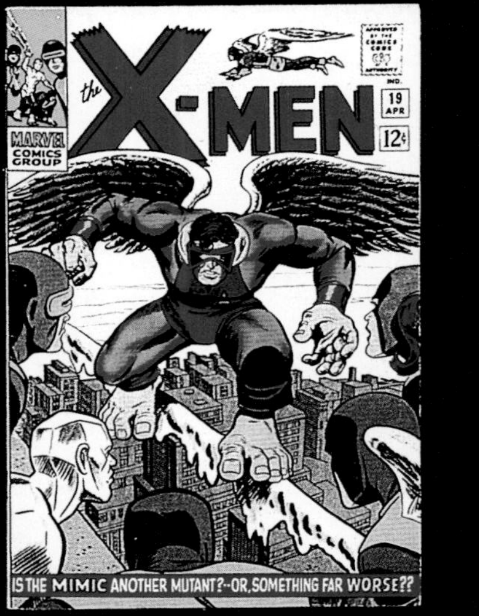
the X-MEN
19 APR
12¢
MARVEL COMICS GROUP
IS THE MIMIC ANOTHER MUTANT?--OR, SOMETHING FAR WORSE??

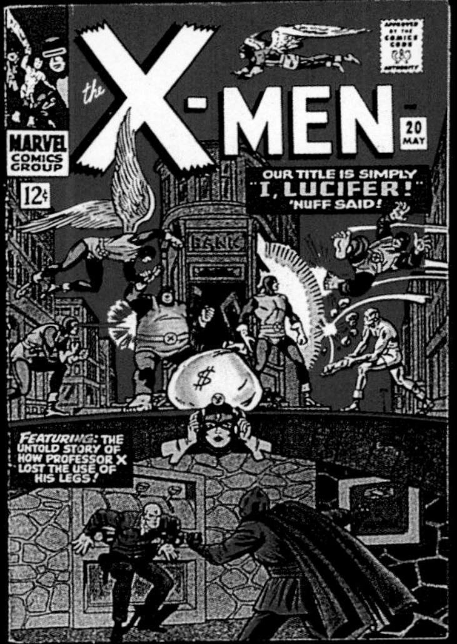
the X-MEN
20 MAY
MARVEL COMICS GROUP
12¢
OUR TITLE IS SIMPLY I, LUCIFER! 'NUFF SAID!
FEATURING: THE UNTOLD STORY OF HOW PROFESSOR X LOST THE USE OF HIS LEGS!

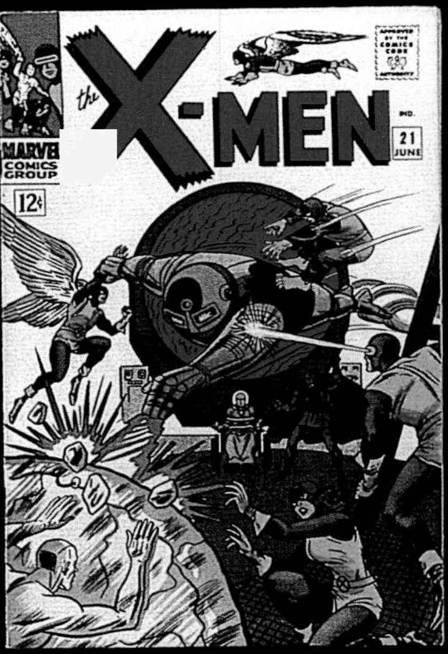
the X-MEN
21 JUNE
MARVEL COMICS GROUP
12¢

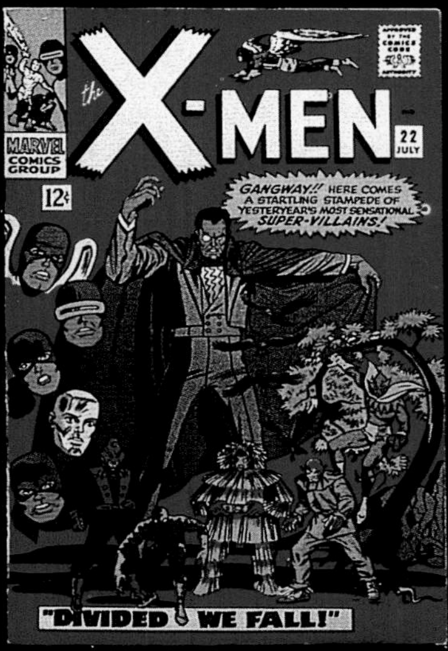
the X-MEN
22 JULY
MARVEL COMICS GROUP
12¢
GANGWAY!! HERE COMES A STARTLING STAMPEDE OF YESTERYEAR'S MOST SENSATIONAL SUPER-VILLAINS!
"DIVIDED WE FALL!"

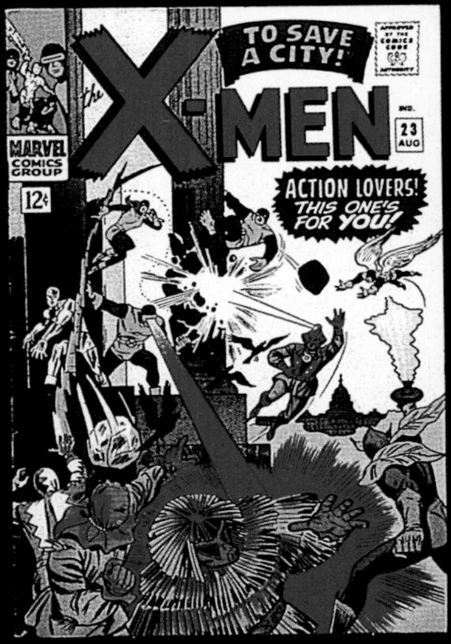
TO SAVE A CITY!
the X-MEN
23 AUG
MARVEL COMICS GROUP
12¢
ACTION LOVERS! THIS ONE'S FOR YOU!

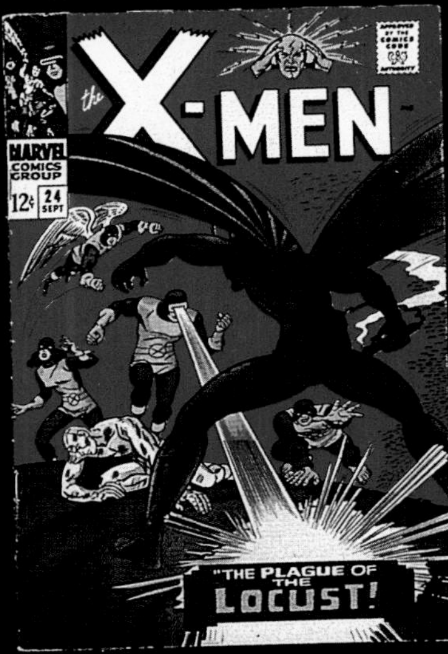
the X-MEN
MARVEL COMICS GROUP
12¢
24 SEPT
"THE PLAGUE OF THE LOCUST!"

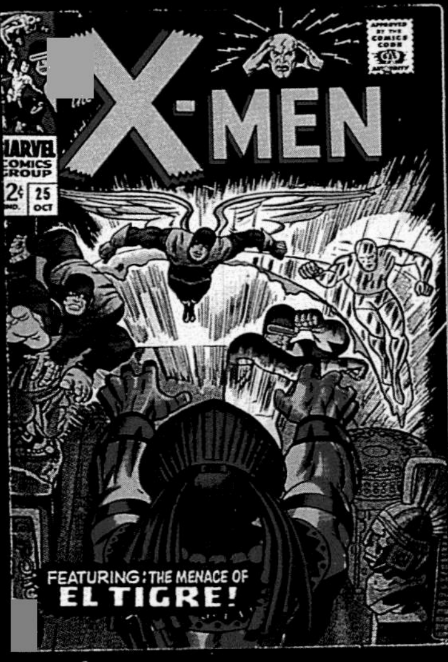
X-MEN
MARVEL COMICS GROUP
12¢
25 OCT
FEATURING: THE MENACE OF EL TIGRE!

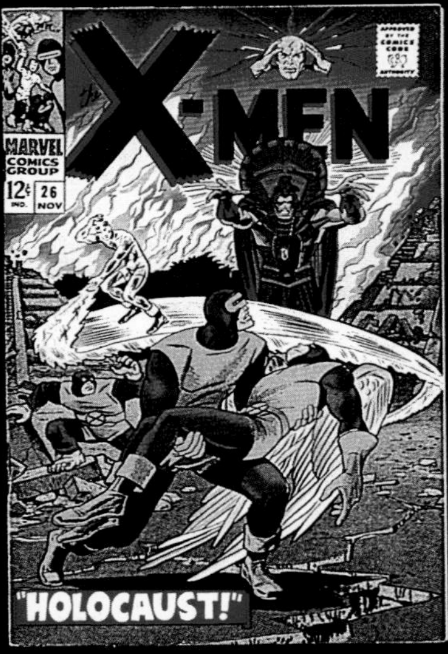
the X-MEN
MARVEL COMICS GROUP
12¢
26 NOV
"HOLOCAUST!"

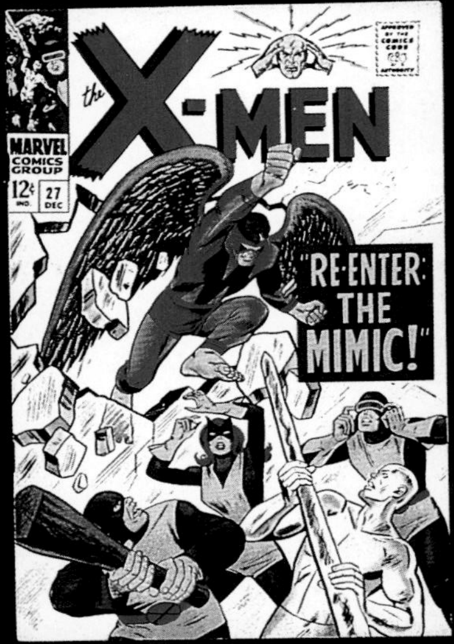
the X-MEN
MARVEL COMICS GROUP
12¢
27 DEC
"RE-ENTER: THE MIMIC!"

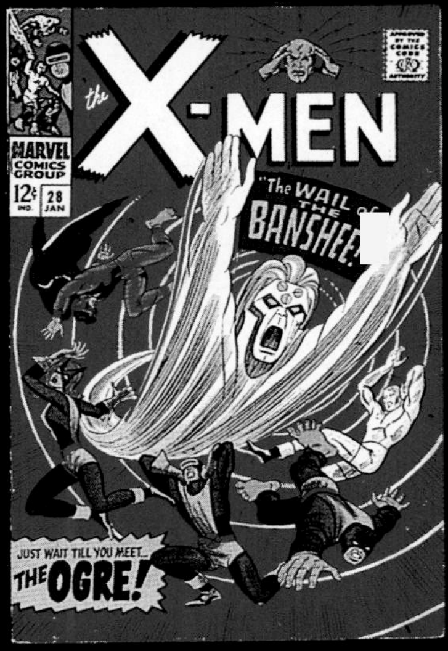
the X-MEN
MARVEL COMICS GROUP
12¢
28 JAN
"The WAIL of the BANSHEE!"
JUST WAIT TILL YOU MEET... THE OGRE!

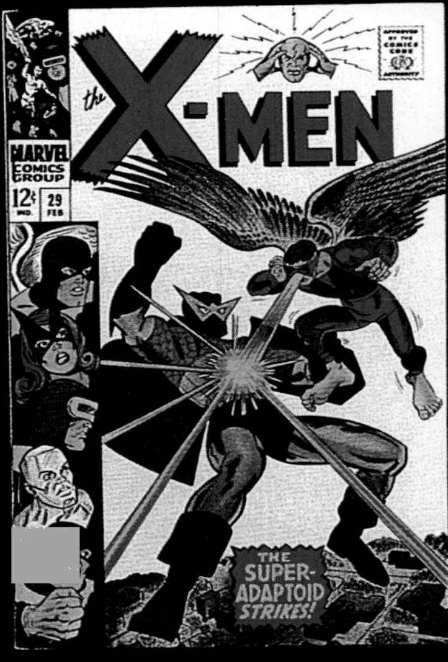
the X-MEN
MARVEL COMICS GROUP
12¢
29 FEB
THE SUPER-ADAPTOID STRIKES!

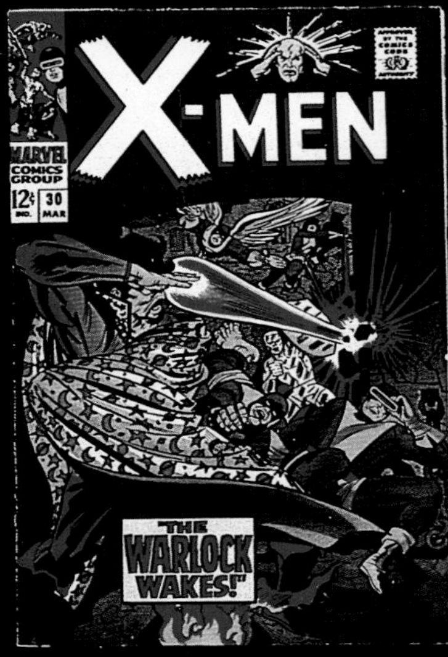
X-MEN
MARVEL COMICS GROUP
12¢
30 MAR
"THE WARLOCK WAKES!"

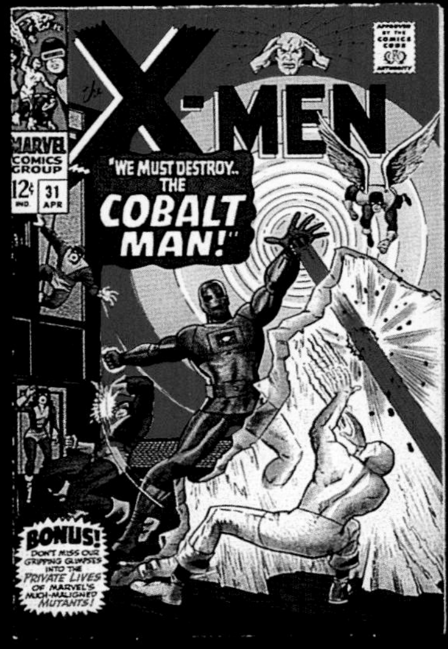
the X-MEN
MARVEL COMICS GROUP
12¢
31 APR
"WE MUST DESTROY... THE COBALT MAN!"
BONUS! DON'T MISS OUR GRIPPING GLIMPSE INTO THE PRIVATE LIVES OF MARVEL'S MUCH-MALIGNED MUTANTS!

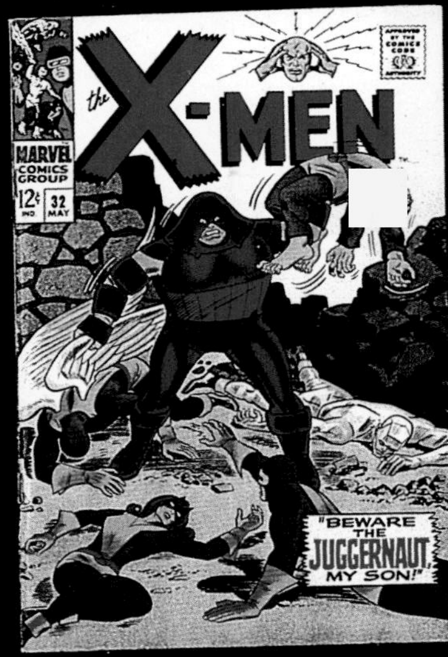
the X-MEN
MARVEL COMICS GROUP
12¢
32 MAY
"BEWARE THE JUGGERNAUT, MY SON!"

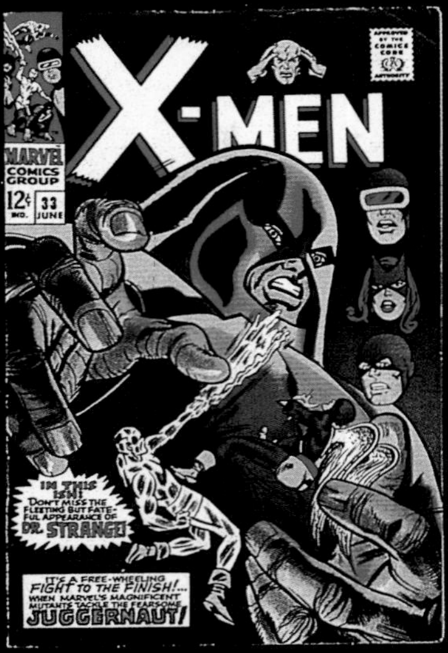
X-MEN
MARVEL COMICS GROUP 12¢ 33 JUNE
IN THIS ISH! DON'T MISS THE FLEETING BUT FATE-FUL APPEARANCE OF DR. STRANGE!
IT'S A FREE-WHEELING FIGHT TO THE FINISH!... WHEN MARVEL'S MAGNIFICENT MUTANTS TACKLE THE FEARSOME JUGGERNAUT!

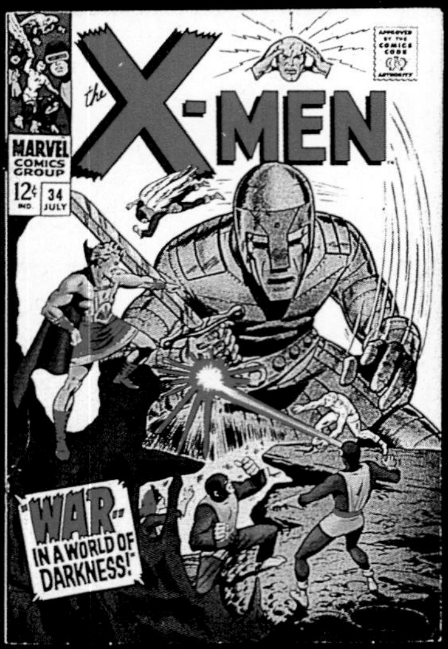
the X-MEN
MARVEL COMICS GROUP 12¢ 34 JULY
"WAR" IN A WORLD OF DARKNESS!

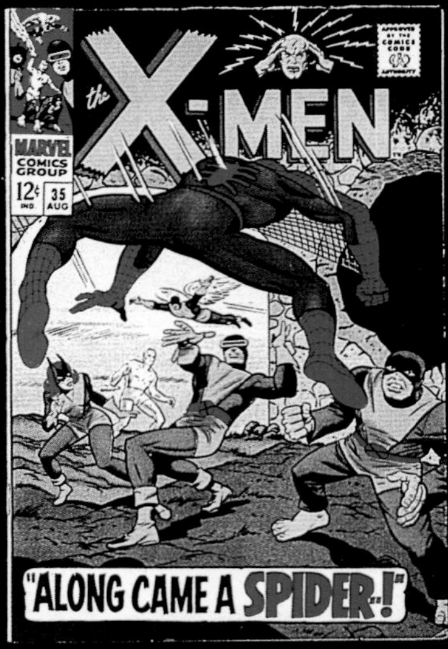
the X-MEN
MARVEL COMICS GROUP 12¢ 35 AUG
"ALONG CAME A SPIDER..!"

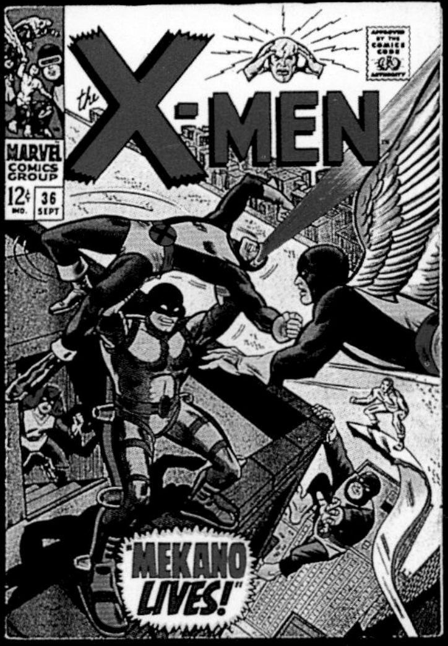
the X-MEN
MARVEL COMICS GROUP 12¢ 36 SEPT
"MEKANO LIVES!"

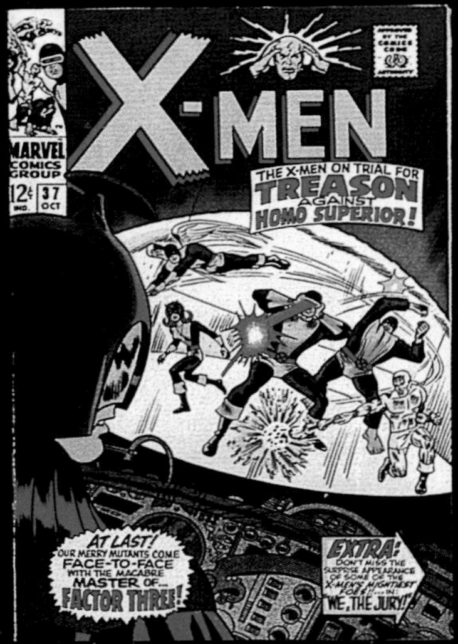
X-MEN
MARVEL COMICS GROUP 12¢ 37 OCT
THE X-MEN ON TRIAL FOR TREASON AGAINST HOMO SUPERIOR!
AT LAST! OUR MERRY MUTANTS COME FACE-TO-FACE WITH THE MACABRE MASTER OF... FACTOR THREE!
EXTRA: DON'T MISS THE SURPRISE APPEARANCE OF SOME OF THE X-MEN'S MIGHTIEST FOES!!... IN: "WE, THE JURY!"

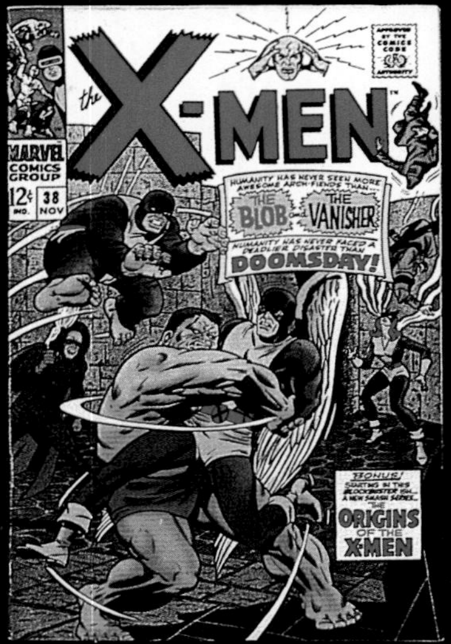
the X-MEN
MARVEL COMICS GROUP 12¢ 38 NOV
HUMANITY HAS NEVER SEEN MORE AWESOME ARCH-FIENDS THAN... THE BLOB and THE VANISHER
HUMANITY HAS NEVER FACED A DEADLIER DISASTER THAN DOOMSDAY!
BONUS! STARTING IN THIS BLOCKBUSTER ISH... A NEW SMASH SERIES... THE ORIGINS OF THE X-MEN

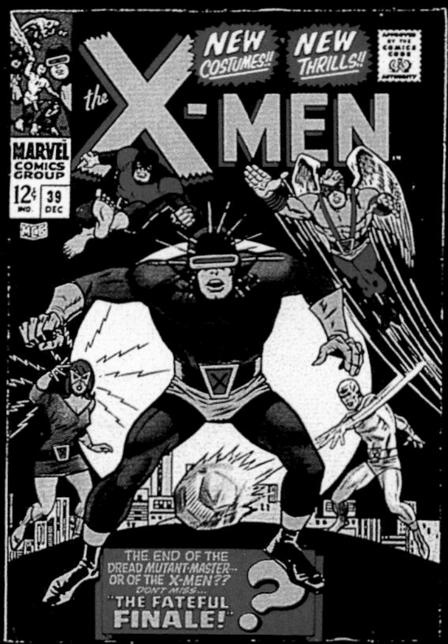
NEW COSTUMES!! NEW THRILLS!!
the X-MEN
MARVEL COMICS GROUP 12¢ 39 DEC
THE END OF THE DREAD MUTANT-MASTER-- OR OF THE X-MEN?? DON'T MISS... "THE FATEFUL FINALE!"?

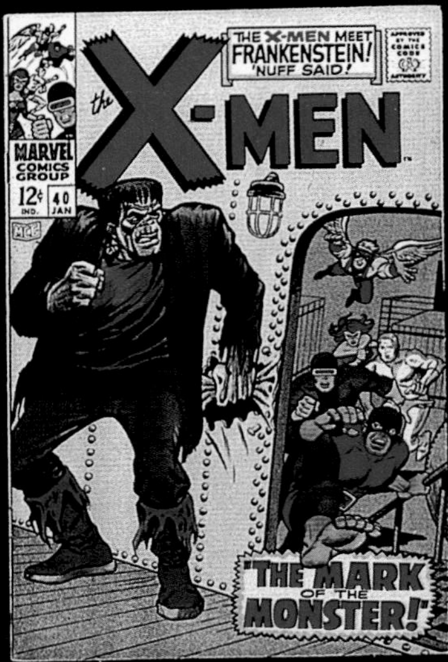
THE X-MEN MEET FRANKENSTEIN! 'NUFF SAID!
the X-MEN
MARVEL COMICS GROUP 12¢ 40 JAN
"THE MARK OF THE MONSTER!"

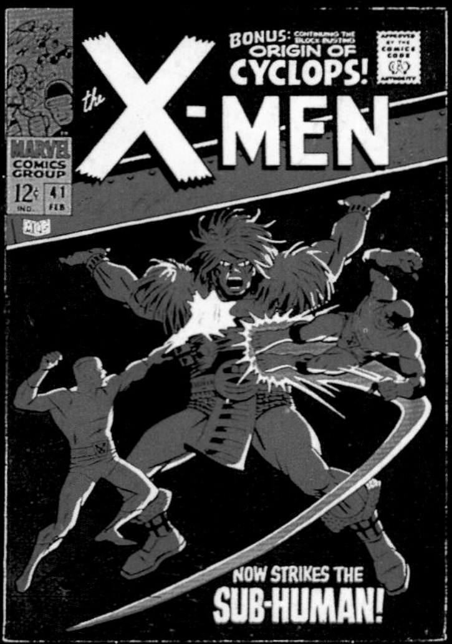
BONUS: CONTINUING THE BLOCK-BUSTING ORIGIN OF CYCLOPS!
the X-MEN
MARVEL COMICS GROUP 12¢ 41 FEB
NOW STRIKES THE SUB-HUMAN!

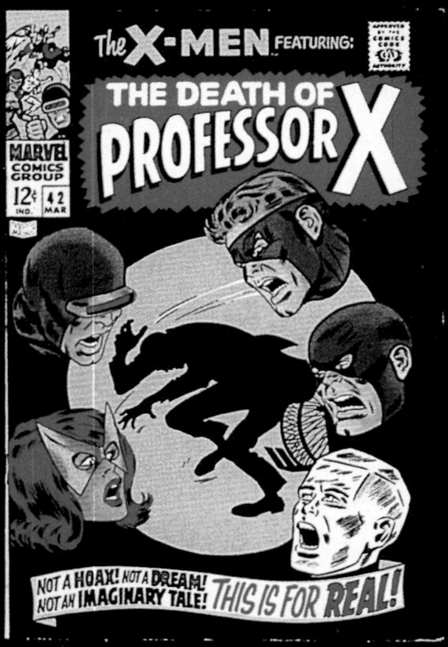
The X-MEN FEATURING:
THE DEATH OF PROFESSOR X
MARVEL COMICS GROUP 12¢ 42 MAR
NOT A HOAX! NOT A DREAM! NOT AN IMAGINARY TALE! THIS IS FOR REAL!

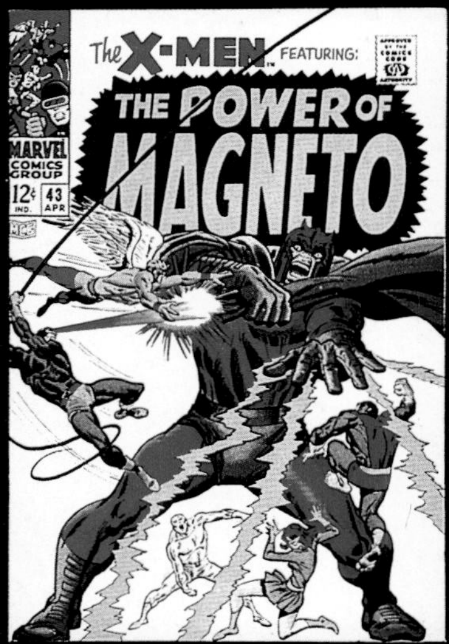
The X-MEN FEATURING:
THE POWER OF MAGNETO
MARVEL COMICS GROUP 12¢ 43 APR

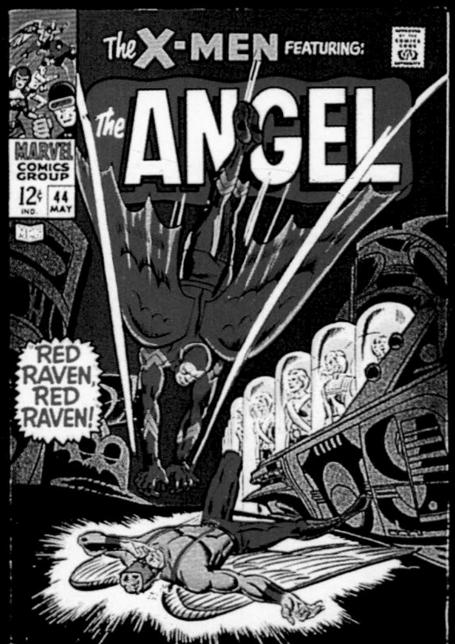
The X-MEN FEATURING:
The ANGEL
MARVEL COMICS GROUP 12¢ 44 MAY
RED RAVEN, RED RAVEN!

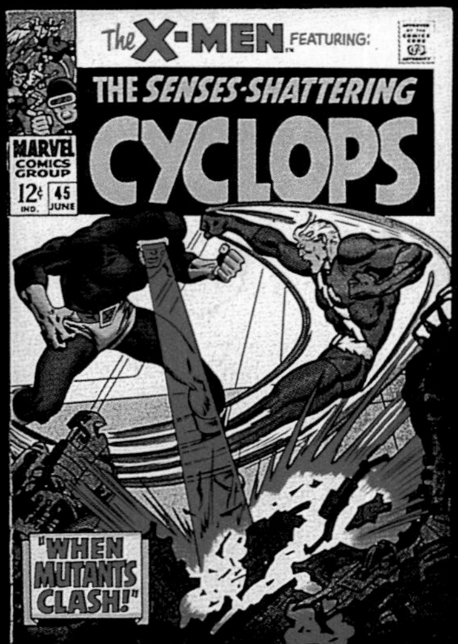
The X-MEN FEATURING:
THE SENSES-SHATTERING CYCLOPS
MARVEL COMICS GROUP 12¢ 45 JUNE
"WHEN MUTANTS CLASH!"

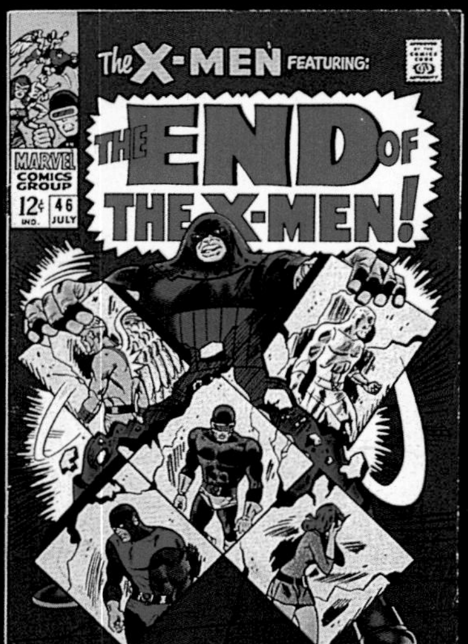
The X-MEN FEATURING:
THE END OF THE X-MEN!
MARVEL COMICS GROUP 12¢ 46 JULY

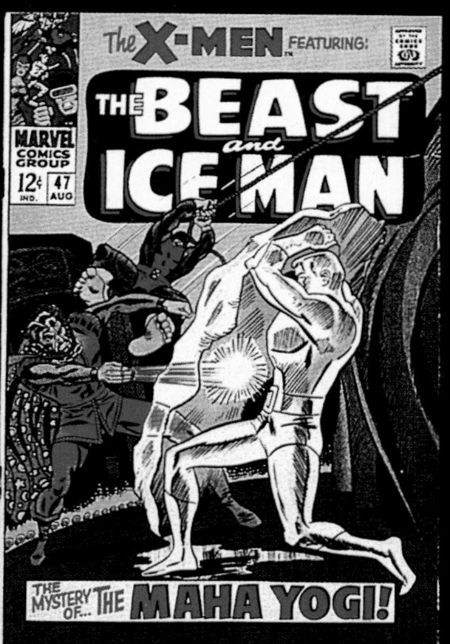
The X-MEN FEATURING:
THE BEAST and ICE MAN
MARVEL COMICS GROUP 12¢ 47 AUG
THE MYSTERY OF... THE MAHA YOGI!

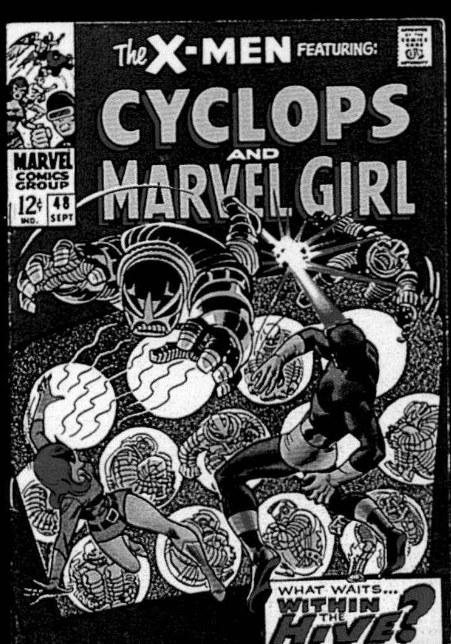
The X-MEN FEATURING:
CYCLOPS AND MARVEL GIRL
MARVEL COMICS GROUP 12¢ 48 SEPT
WHAT WAITS... WITHIN THE HIVE?

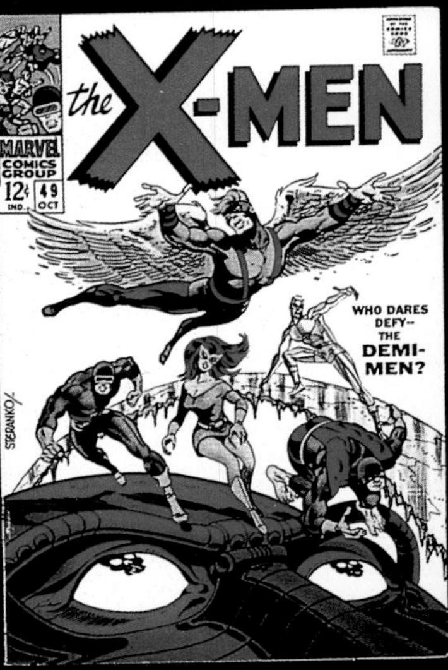
the X-MEN
MARVEL COMICS GROUP
12¢ 49 OCT
WHO DARES DEFY-- THE DEMI-MEN?
STERANKO

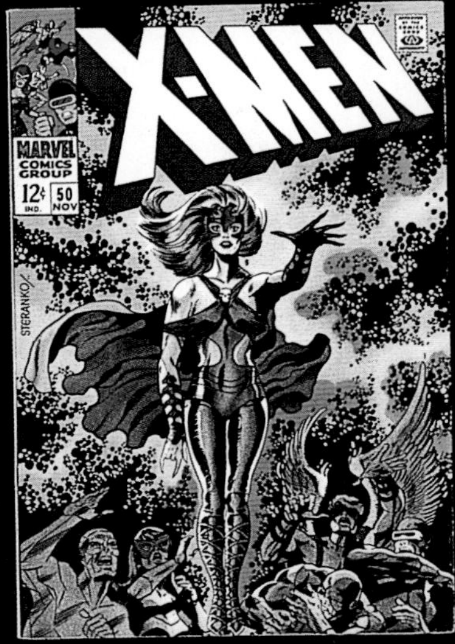
X-MEN
MARVEL COMICS GROUP
12¢ 50 NOV
STERANKO

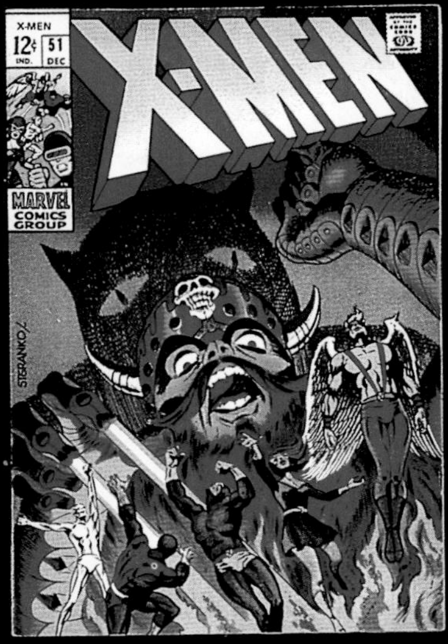
X-MEN
12¢ 51 DEC
X-MEN
MARVEL COMICS GROUP
STERANKO

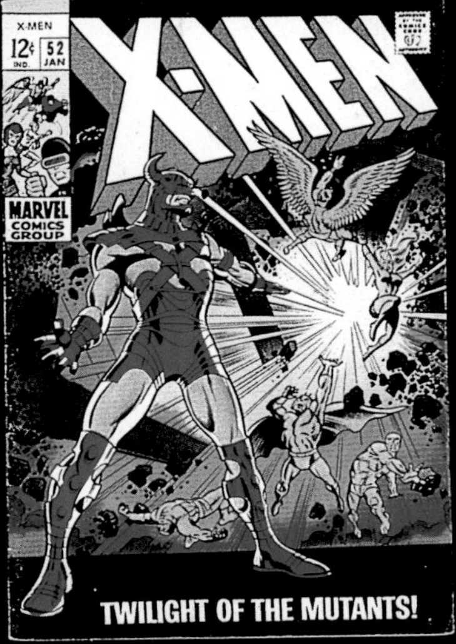
X-MEN
12¢ 52 JAN
X-MEN
MARVEL COMICS GROUP
TWILIGHT OF THE MUTANTS!

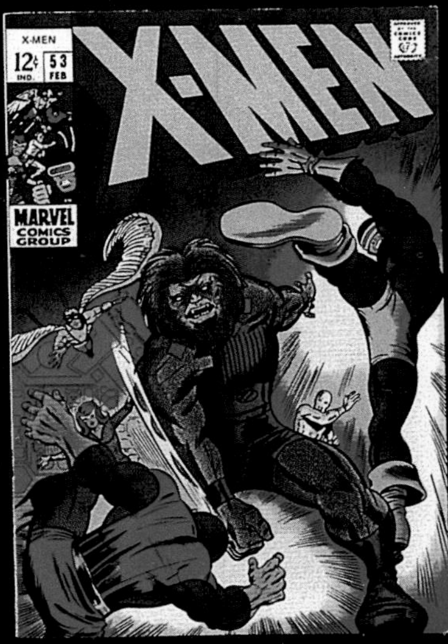
X-MEN
12¢ 53 FEB
X-MEN
MARVEL COMICS GROUP

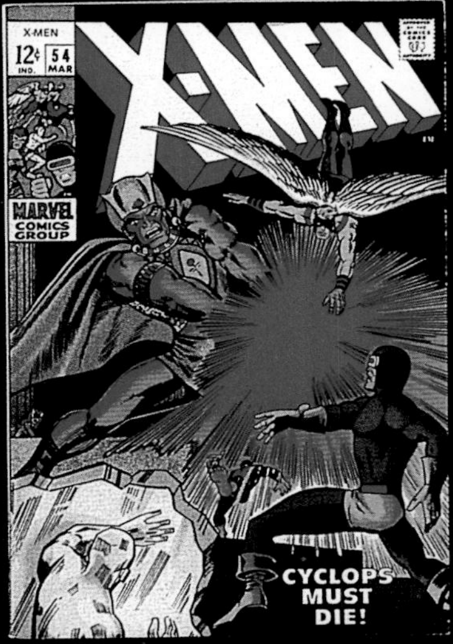
X-MEN
12¢ 54 MAR
X-MEN
MARVEL COMICS GROUP
CYCLOPS MUST DIE!

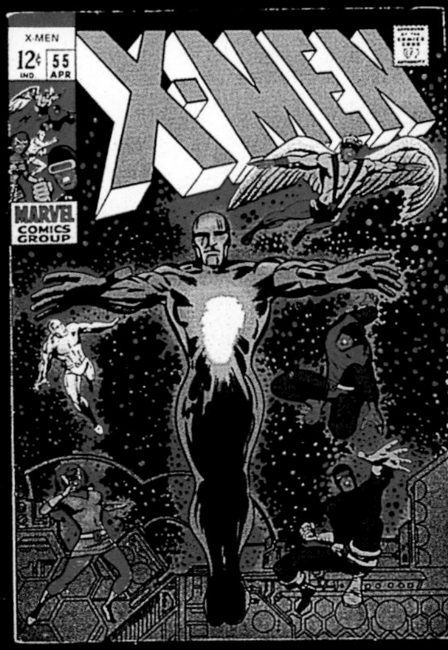
12¢ 55 APR
X-MEN
MARVEL COMICS GROUP

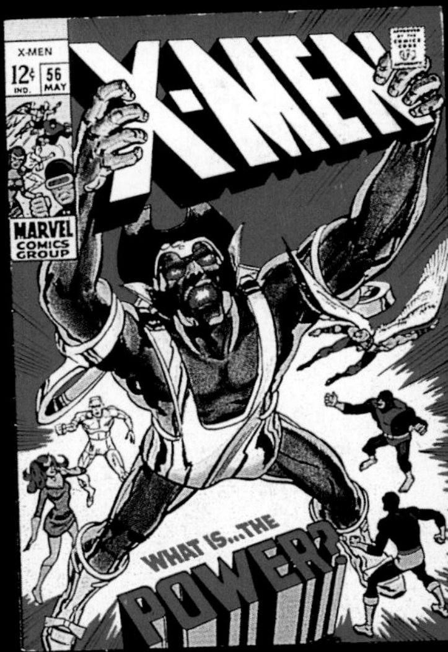
X-MEN
12¢ 56 MAY
X-MEN
MARVEL COMICS GROUP
WHAT IS...THE POWER?

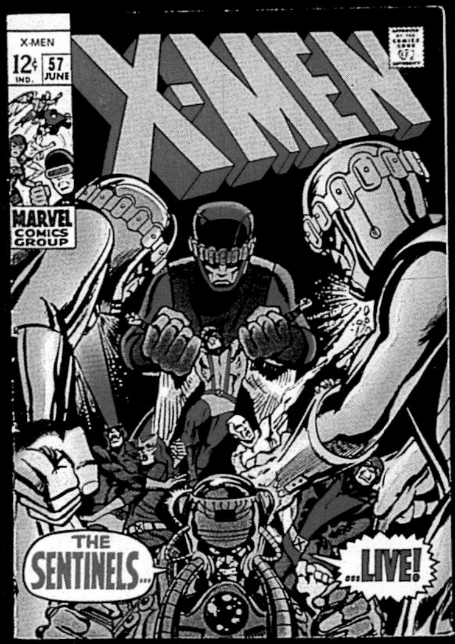
X-MEN
12¢ 57 JUNE
X-MEN
MARVEL COMICS GROUP
THE SENTINELS...
...LIVE!

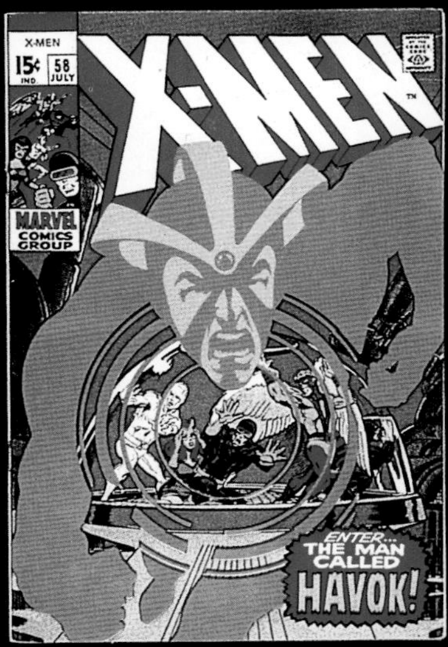
X-MEN
15¢ 58 JULY
X-MEN
MARVEL COMICS GROUP
ENTER... THE MAN CALLED HAVOK!

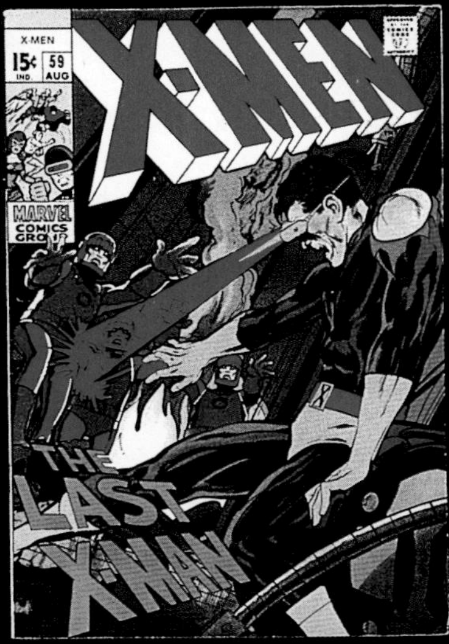
X-MEN
15¢ 59 AUG
X-MEN
MARVEL COMICS GROUP
THE LAST X-MAN

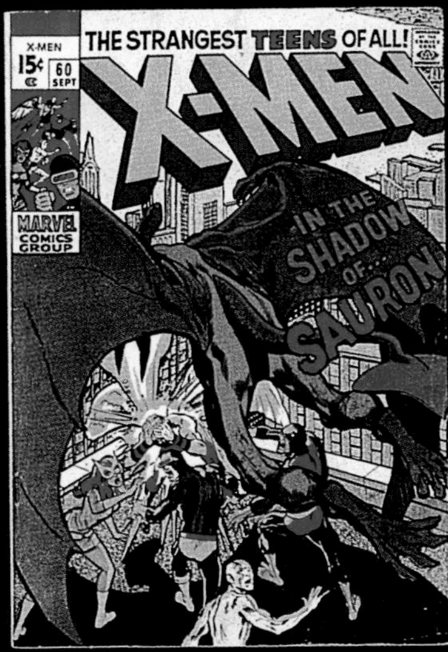
X-MEN
15¢ 60 SEPT
THE STRANGEST TEENS OF ALL!
X-MEN
MARVEL COMICS GROUP
IN THE SHADOW OF SAURON

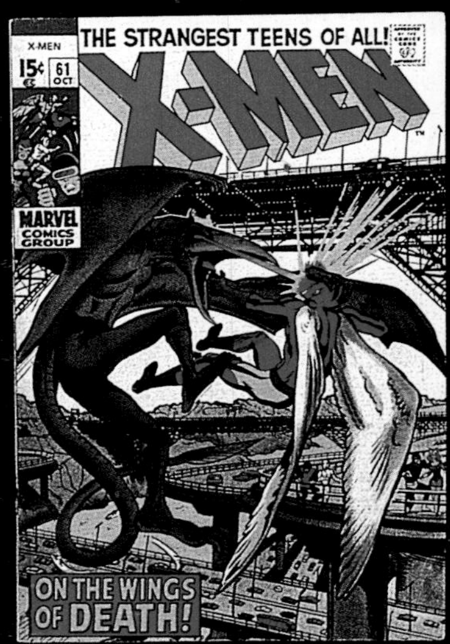
X-MEN
15¢ 61 OCT
THE STRANGEST TEENS OF ALL!
X-MEN
MARVEL COMICS GROUP
ON THE WINGS OF DEATH!

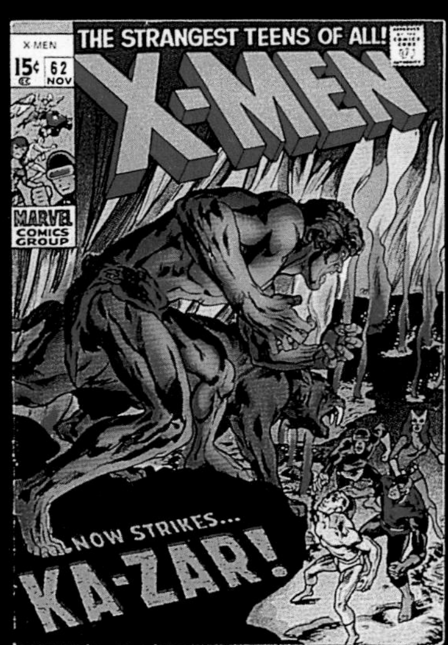
X-MEN
15¢ 62 NOV
THE STRANGEST TEENS OF ALL!
X-MEN
MARVEL COMICS GROUP
NOW STRIKES... KA-ZAR!

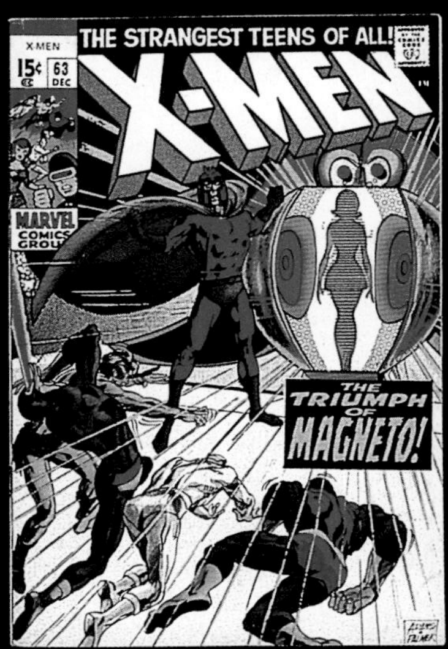
X-MEN
15¢ 63 DEC
THE STRANGEST TEENS OF ALL!
X-MEN
MARVEL COMICS GROUP
THE TRIUMPH OF MAGNETO!

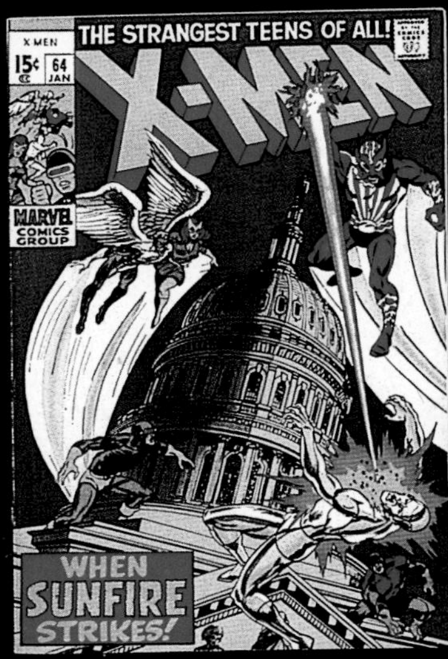
X-MEN
15¢ 64 JAN
THE STRANGEST TEENS OF ALL!
X-MEN
MARVEL COMICS GROUP
WHEN SUNFIRE STRIKES!

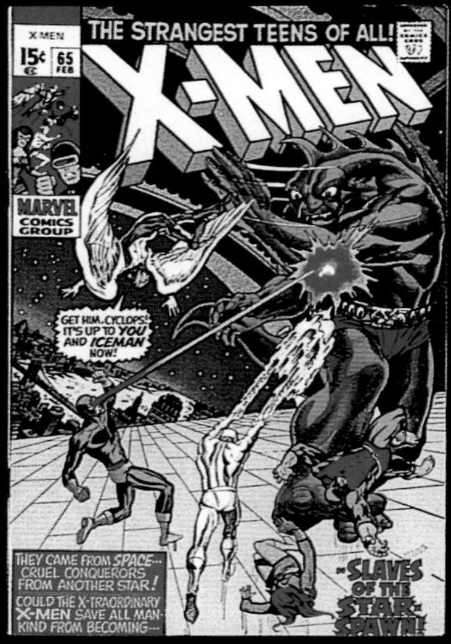
THE STRANGEST TEENS OF ALL!
X-MEN
MARVEL COMICS GROUP
GET HIM, CYCLOPS! IT'S UP TO YOU AND ICEMAN NOW!
THEY CAME FROM SPACE-- CRUEL CONQUERORS FROM ANOTHER STAR! COULD THE X-TRAORDINARY X-MEN SAVE ALL MAN KIND FROM BECOMING---
SLAVES OF THE STAR SPAWN!

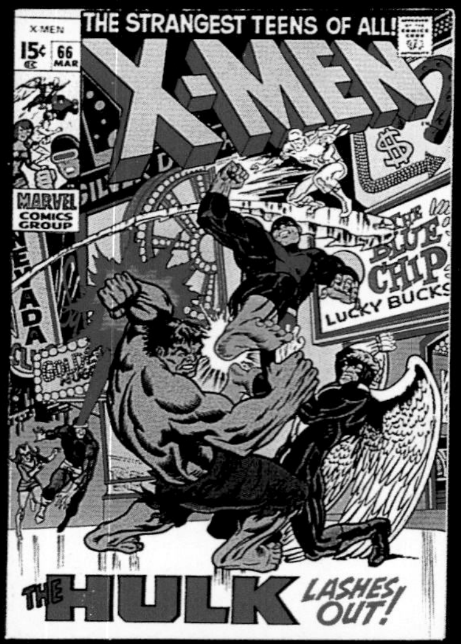
THE STRANGEST TEENS OF ALL!
X-MEN
MARVEL COMICS GROUP
LUCKY BUCKS
THE HULK LASHES OUT!

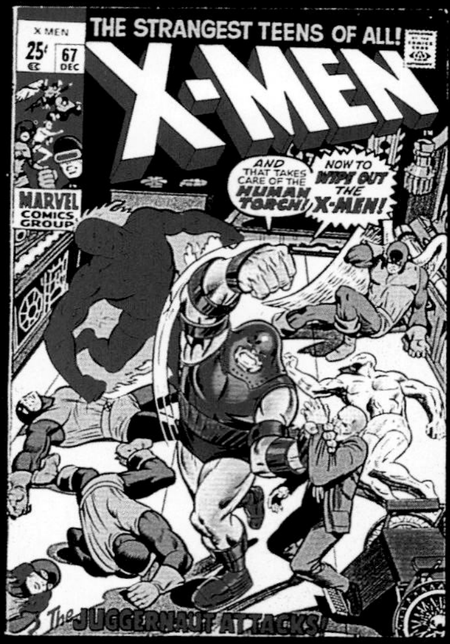
THE STRANGEST TEENS OF ALL!
X-MEN
MARVEL COMICS GROUP
AND THAT TAKES CARE OF THE HUMAN TORCH!
NOW TO WIPE OUT THE X-MEN!
THE JUGGERNAUT ATTACKS!

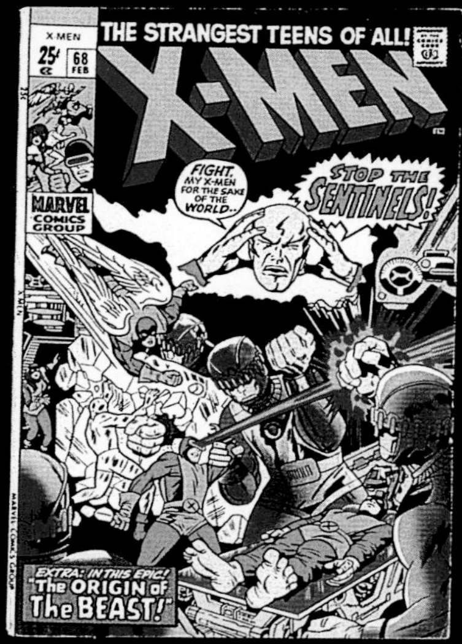
THE STRANGEST TEENS OF ALL!
X-MEN
MARVEL COMICS GROUP
FIGHT, MY X-MEN FOR THE SAKE OF THE WORLD--
STOP THE SENTINELS!
EXTRA: IN THIS EPIC! The ORIGIN of The BEAST!

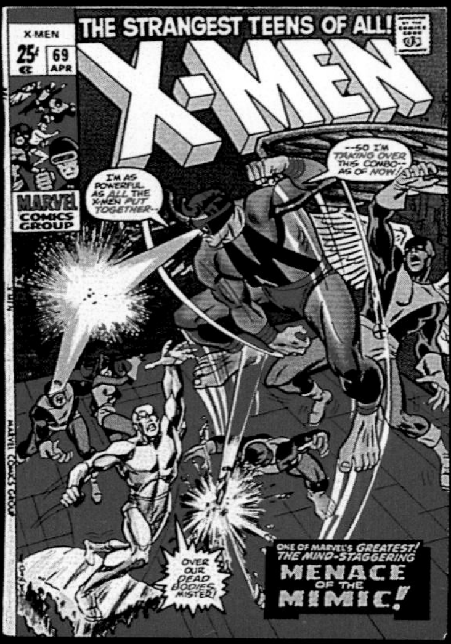
THE STRANGEST TEENS OF ALL!
X-MEN
MARVEL COMICS GROUP
I'M AS POWERFUL AS ALL THE X-MEN PUT TOGETHER--
--SO I'M TAKING OVER THIS COMBO-- AS OF NOW!
OVER OUR DEAD BODIES, MISTER!
ONE OF MARVEL'S GREATEST! THE MIND-STAGGERING MENACE OF THE MIMIC!

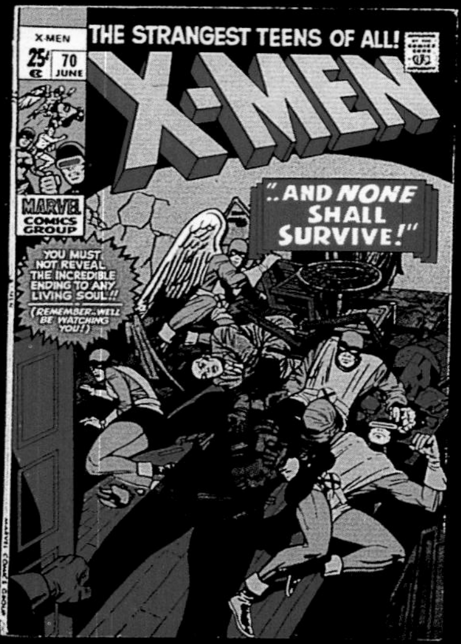
THE STRANGEST TEENS OF ALL!
X-MEN
MARVEL COMICS GROUP
"..AND NONE SHALL SURVIVE!"
YOU MUST NOT REVEAL THE INCREDIBLE ENDING TO ANY LIVING SOUL!
(REMEMBER..WE'LL BE WATCHING YOU!)

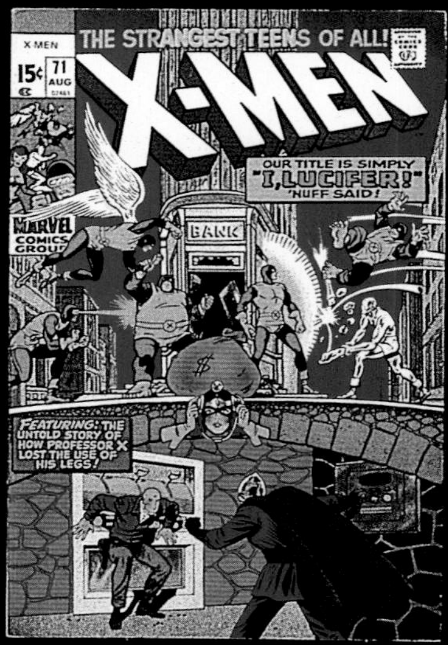
THE STRANGEST TEENS OF ALL!
X-MEN
MARVEL COMICS GROUP
OUR TITLE IS SIMPLY "I, LUCIFER!" 'NUFF SAID!
BANK
FEATURING: THE UNTOLD STORY OF HOW PROFESSOR X LOST THE USE OF HIS LEGS!

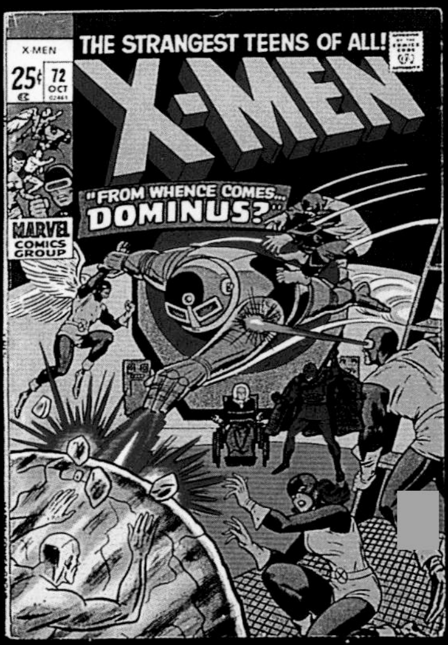
THE STRANGEST TEENS OF ALL!
X-MEN
MARVEL COMICS GROUP
"FROM WHENCE COMES... DOMINUS?"

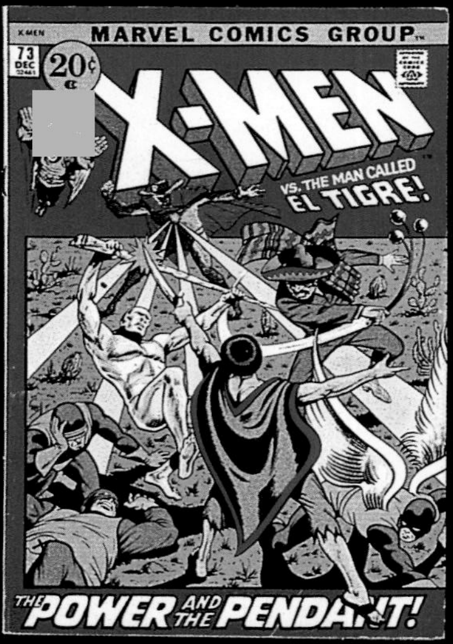
MARVEL COMICS GROUP
X-MEN
VS. THE MAN CALLED EL TIGRE!
THE POWER AND THE PENDANT!

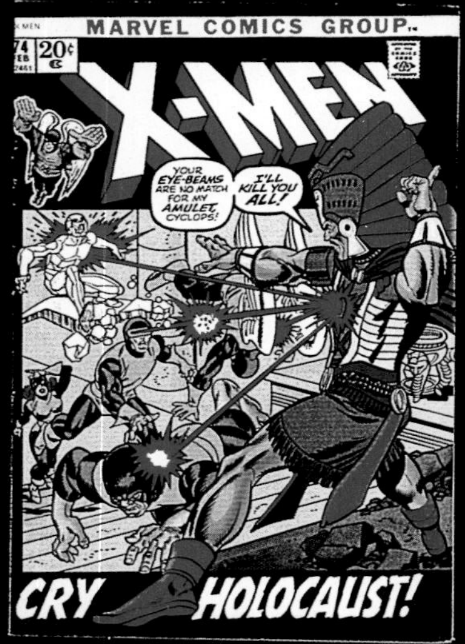
MARVEL COMICS GROUP
X-MEN
YOUR EYE-BEAMS ARE NO MATCH FOR MY AMULET, CYCLOPS!
I'LL KILL YOU ALL!
CRY HOLOCAUST!

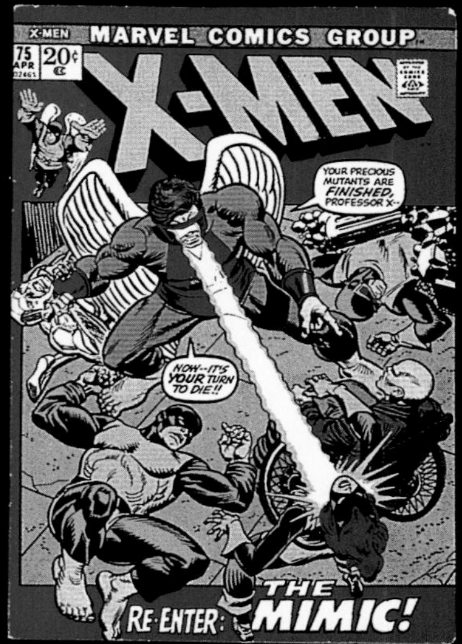
MARVEL COMICS GROUP
X-MEN
YOUR PRECIOUS MUTANTS ARE FINISHED, PROFESSOR X--
NOW--IT'S YOUR TURN TO DIE!!
RE-ENTER: THE MIMIC!

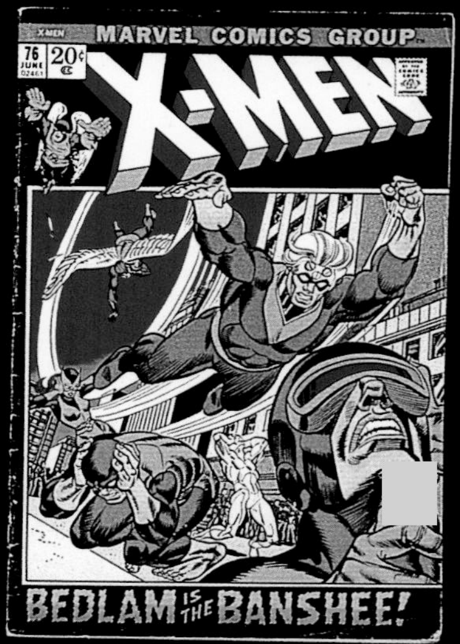
MARVEL COMICS GROUP
X-MEN
BEDLAM IS THE BANSHEE!

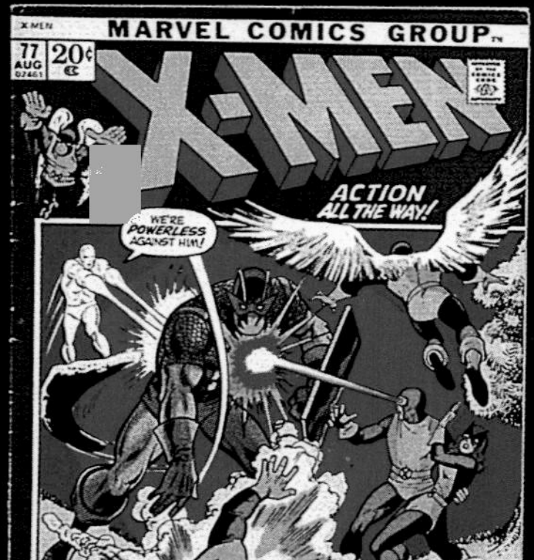
MARVEL COMICS GROUP
X-MEN
ACTION ALL THE WAY!
WE'RE POWERLESS AGAINST HIM!
THE WORLD'S STRANGEST TEENAGERS FINALLY MEET THEIR MATCH!
NOW STRIKES... THE SUPER-ADAPTOID!

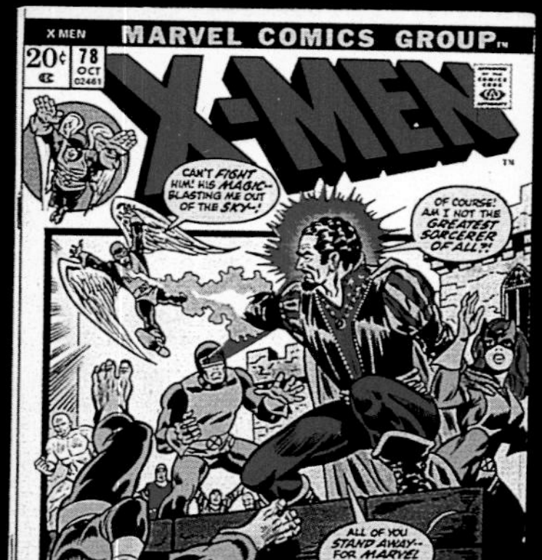
MARVEL COMICS GROUP
X-MEN
CAN'T FIGHT HIM! HIS MAGIC-- BLASTING ME OUT OF THE SKY--!
OF COURSE! AM I NOT THE GREATEST SORCERER OF ALL?
ALL OF YOU STAND AWAY-- FOR MARVEL GIRL IS MINE!
THE MENACE OF MERLIN!

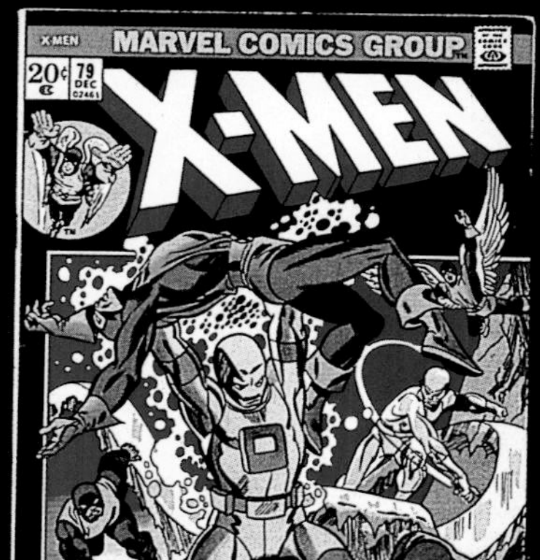
MARVEL COMICS GROUP
X-MEN
WHAT IS THE SECRET OF HIS POWER? WHY CAN NO ONE STOP--
THE COBALT MAN!

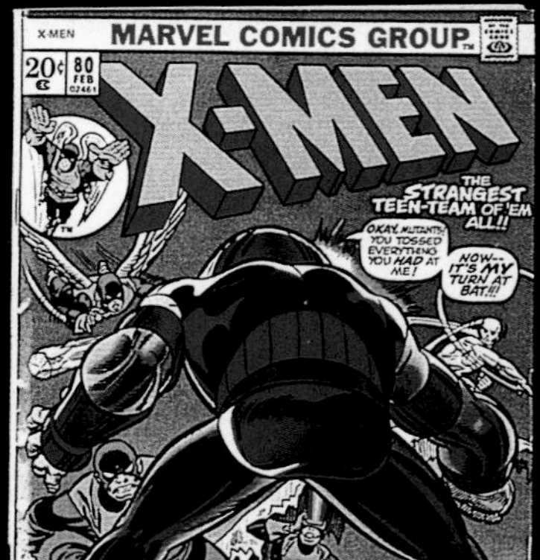
MARVEL COMICS GROUP
X-MEN
THE STRANGEST TEEN-TEAM OF 'EM ALL!
OKAY, MUTANTS-- YOU TOSSED EVERYTHING YOU HAD AT ME!
NOW-- IT'S MY TURN AT BAT!!
BEWARE...THE JUGGERNAUT!

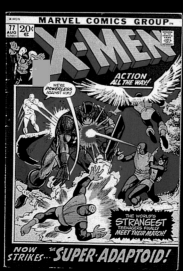

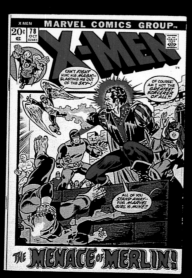

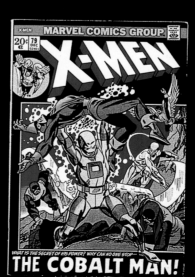

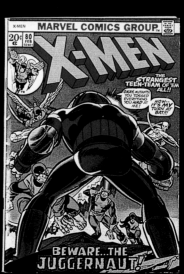

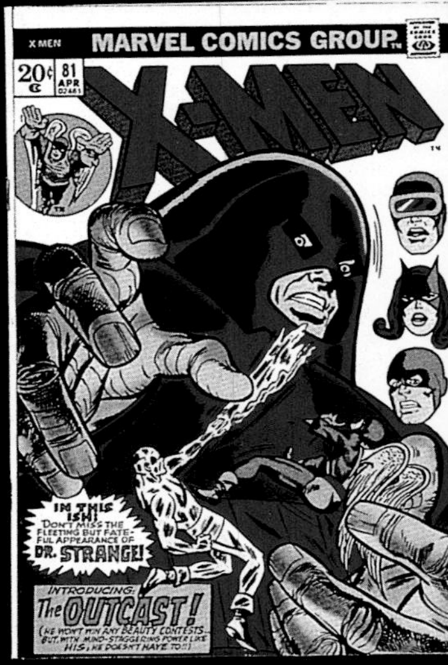
MARVEL COMICS GROUP
20¢ 81 APR
X-MEN
IN THIS ISH! DON'T MISS THE FLEETING BUT FATE-FUL APPEARANCE OF DR. STRANGE!
INTRODUCING: The OUTCAST!

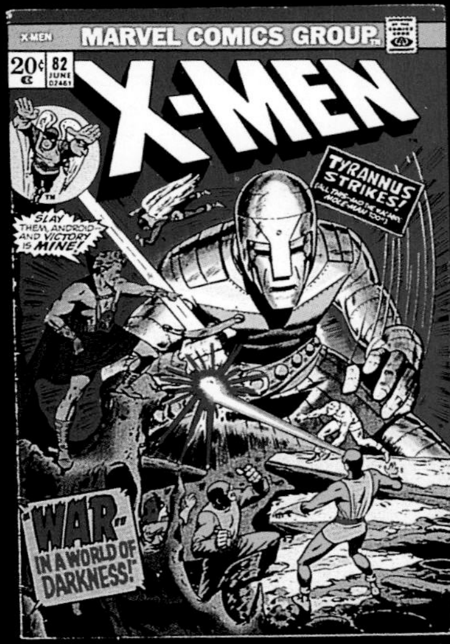
MARVEL COMICS GROUP
20¢ 82 JUNE
X-MEN
TYRANNUS STRIKES!
"WAR" IN A WORLD OF DARKNESS!

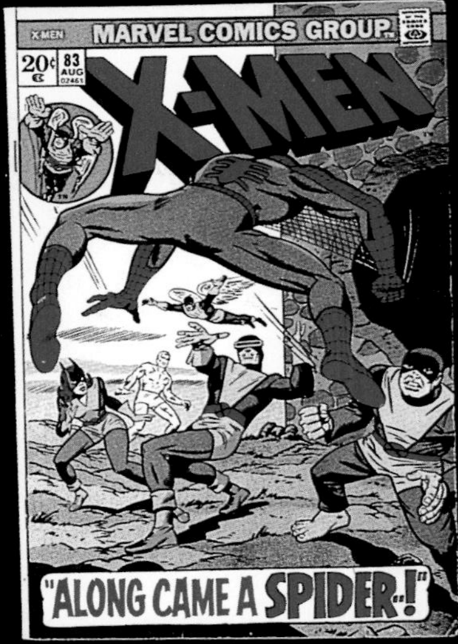
MARVEL COMICS GROUP
20¢ 83 AUG
X-MEN
"ALONG CAME A SPIDER!"

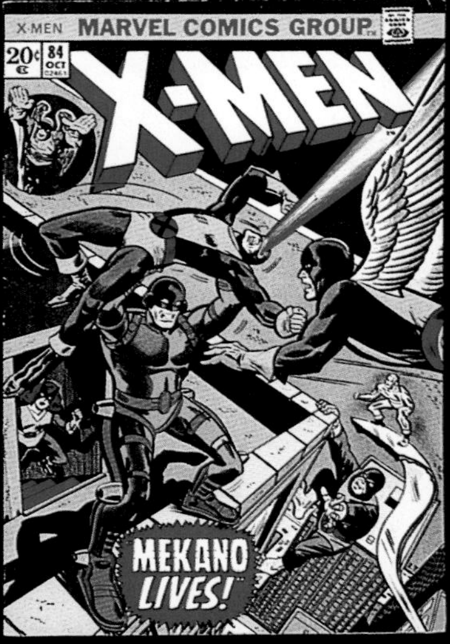
MARVEL COMICS GROUP
20¢ 84 OCT
X-MEN
MEKANO LIVES!

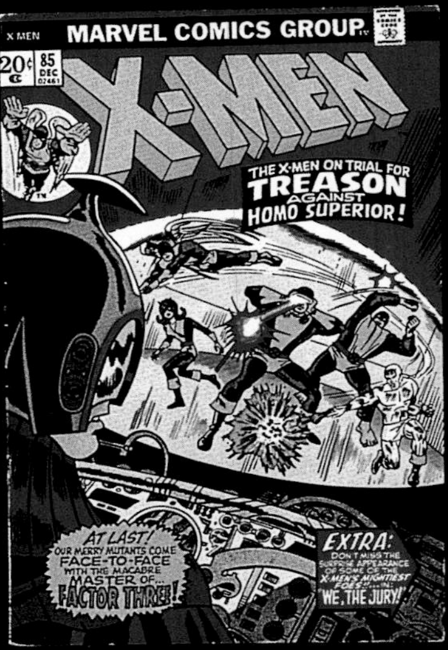
MARVEL COMICS GROUP
20¢ 85 DEC
X-MEN
THE X-MEN ON TRIAL FOR TREASON AGAINST HOMO SUPERIOR!
AT LAST! OUR MERRY MUTANTS COME FACE-TO-FACE WITH THE MACABRE MASTER OF FACTOR THREE!
EXTRA:
WE, THE JURY!

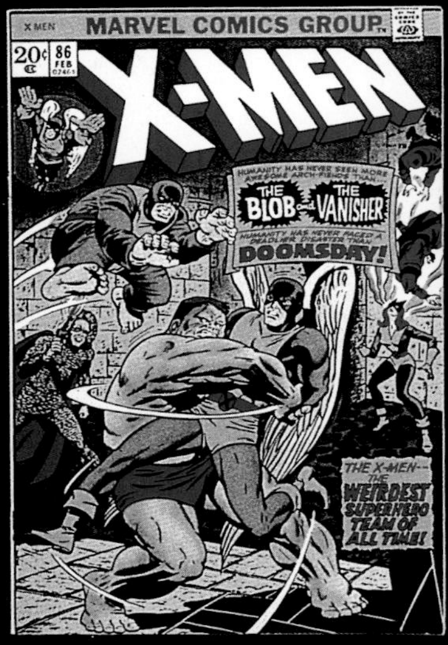
MARVEL COMICS GROUP
20¢ 86 FEB
X-MEN
THE BLOB AND THE VANISHER
DOOMSDAY!
THE X-MEN WEIRDEST SUPERHERO TEAM OF ALL TIME!

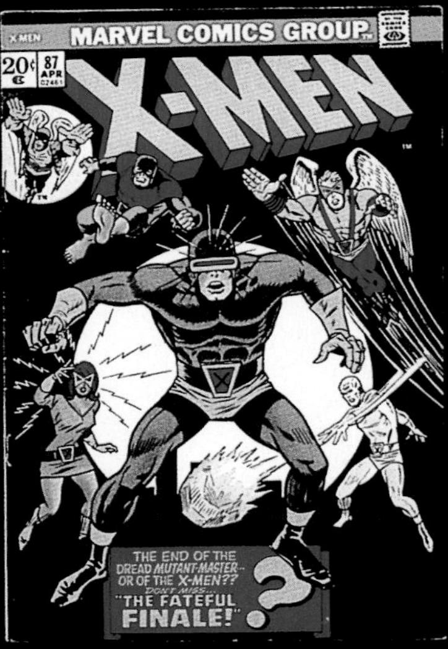
MARVEL COMICS GROUP
20¢ 87 APR
X-MEN
THE END OF THE DREAD MUTANT-MASTER OR OF THE X-MEN?? DON'T MISS "THE FATEFUL FINALE!"

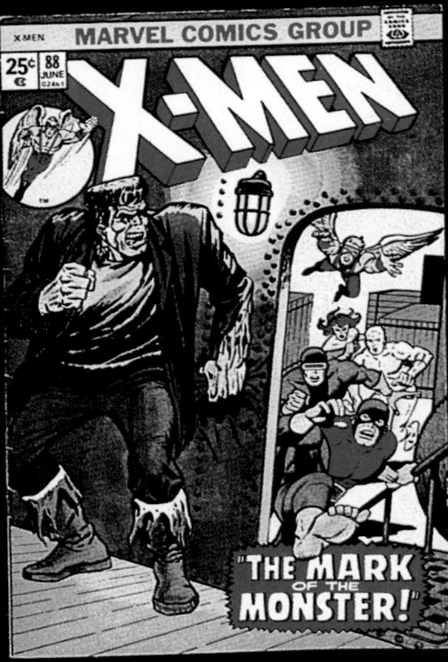
MARVEL COMICS GROUP
25¢ 88 JUNE
X-MEN
"THE MARK OF THE MONSTER!"

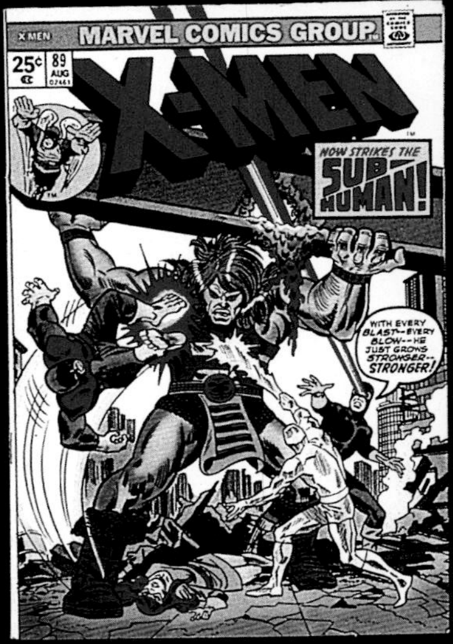
MARVEL COMICS GROUP
25¢ 89 AUG
X-MEN
NOW STRIKES THE SUB-HUMAN!
WITH EVERY BLAST—EVERY BLOW—HE JUST GROWS STRONGER—STRONGER!

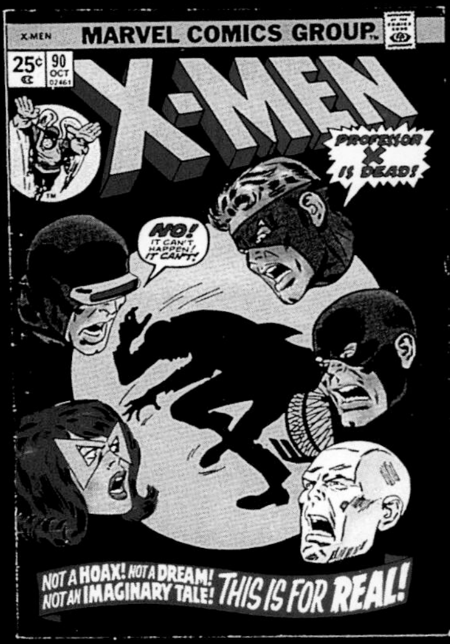
MARVEL COMICS GROUP
25¢ 90 OCT
X-MEN
PROFESSOR X IS DEAD!
NO! IT CAN'T HAPPEN! IT CAN'T!
NOT A HOAX! NOT A DREAM! NOT AN IMAGINARY TALE! THIS IS FOR REAL!

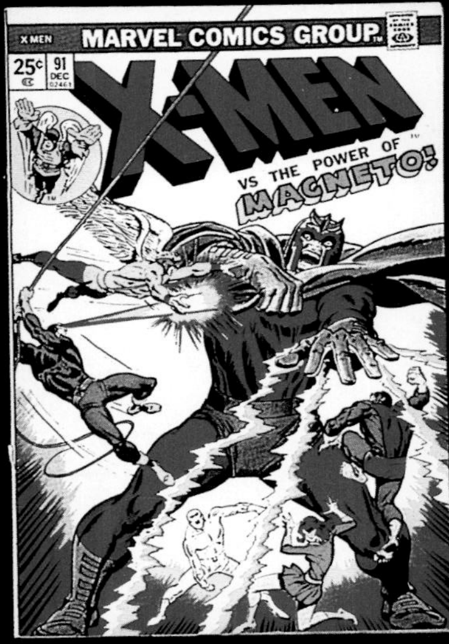
MARVEL COMICS GROUP
25¢ 91 DEC
X-MEN
VS THE POWER OF MAGNETO!

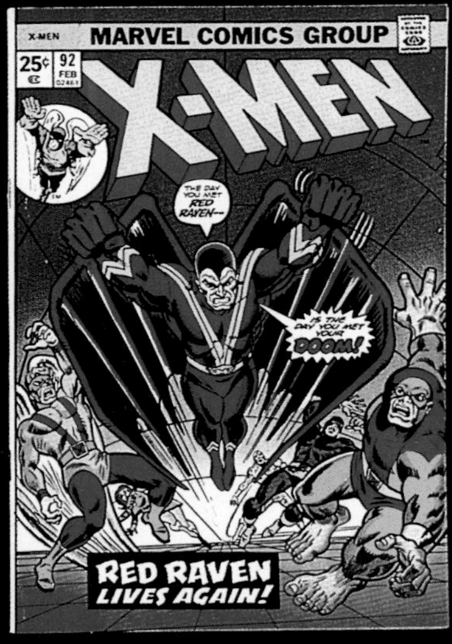
MARVEL COMICS GROUP
25¢ 92 FEB
X-MEN
THE DAY YOU MET RED RAVEN—
IS THE DAY YOU MET YOUR DOOM!
RED RAVEN LIVES AGAIN!

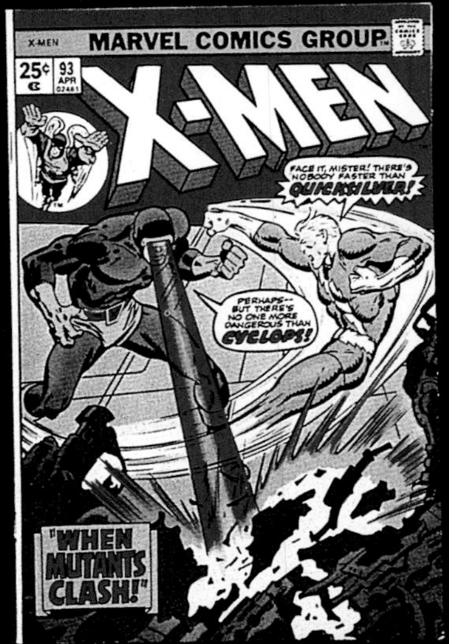
MARVEL COMICS GROUP
25¢ 93 APR
X-MEN
FACE IT, MISTER! THERE'S NOBODY FASTER THAN QUICKSILVER!
PERHAPS— BUT THERE'S NO ONE MORE DANGEROUS THAN CYCLOPS!
"WHEN MUTANTS CLASH!"

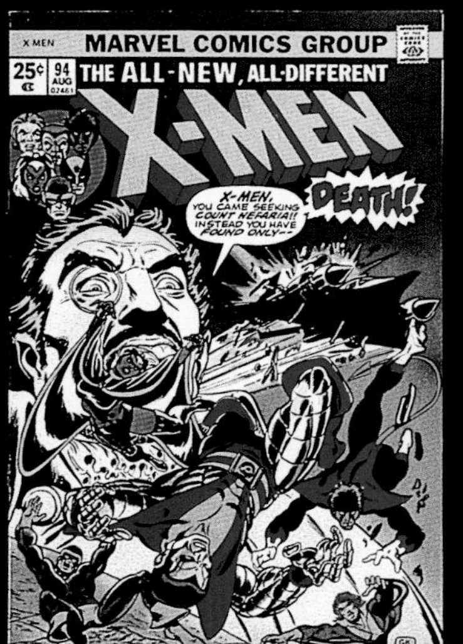
MARVEL COMICS GROUP
25¢ 94 AUG
THE ALL-NEW, ALL-DIFFERENT
X-MEN
X-MEN, YOU CAME SEEKING COUNT NEFARIA! INSTEAD YOU HAVE FOUND ONLY—
DEATH!

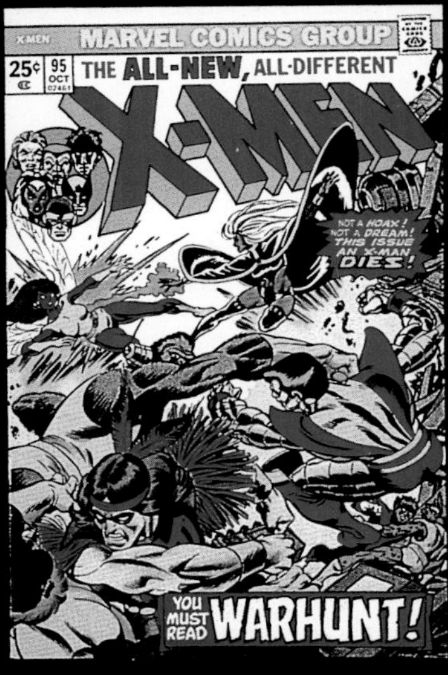
MARVEL COMICS GROUP
25¢ 95 OCT
THE ALL-NEW, ALL-DIFFERENT
X-MEN
NOT A HOAX! NOT A DREAM! THIS ISSUE AN X-MAN DIES!
YOU MUST READ WARHUNT!

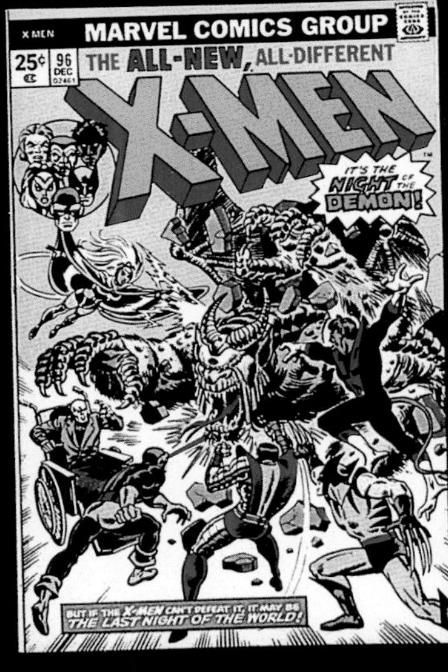
MARVEL COMICS GROUP
25¢ 96 DEC
THE ALL-NEW, ALL-DIFFERENT
X-MEN
IT'S THE NIGHT OF THE DEMON!
BUT IF THE X-MEN CAN'T DEFEAT IT, IT MAY BE THE LAST NIGHT OF THE WORLD!

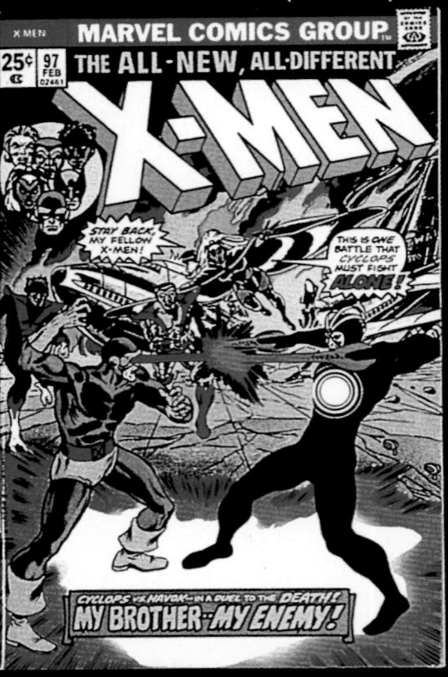
MARVEL COMICS GROUP
25¢ 97 FEB
THE ALL-NEW, ALL-DIFFERENT
X-MEN
STAY BACK, MY FELLOW X-MEN!
THIS IS ONE BATTLE THAT CYCLOPS MUST FIGHT ALONE!
CYCLOPS VS. HAVOK--IN A DUEL TO THE DEATH!
MY BROTHER--MY ENEMY!

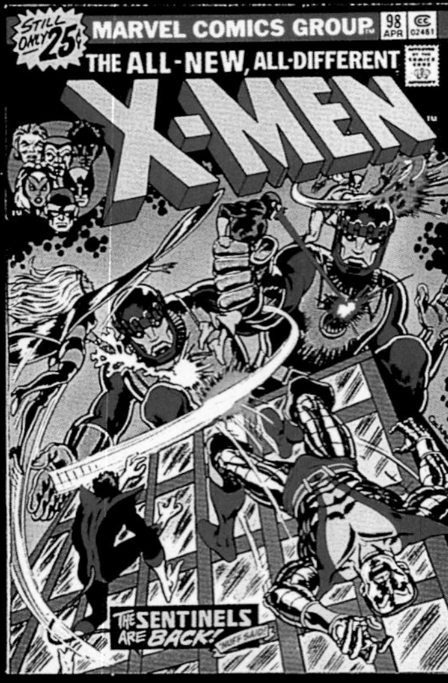
STILL ONLY 25¢
MARVEL COMICS GROUP
98 APR
THE ALL-NEW, ALL-DIFFERENT
X-MEN
THE SENTINELS ARE BACK!

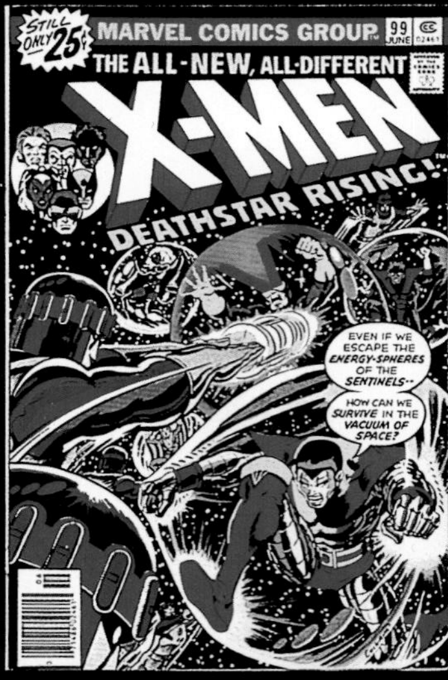
STILL ONLY 25¢
MARVEL COMICS GROUP
99 JUNE
THE ALL-NEW, ALL-DIFFERENT
X-MEN
DEATHSTAR RISING!
EVEN IF WE ESCAPE THE ENERGY-SPHERES OF THE SENTINELS--
HOW CAN WE SURVIVE IN THE VACUUM OF SPACE?

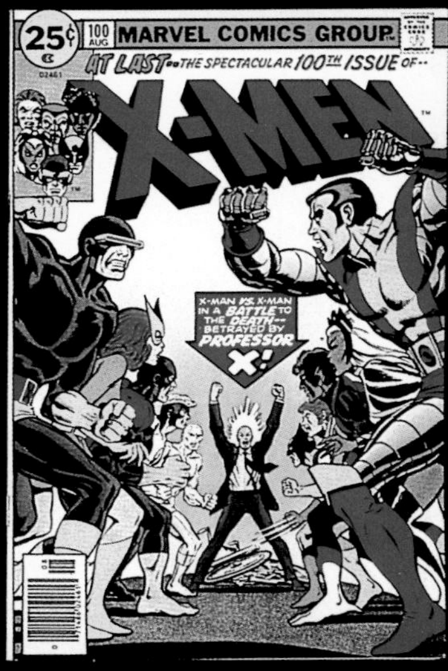
25¢ 100 AUG
MARVEL COMICS GROUP
AT LAST--THE SPECTACULAR 100TH ISSUE OF--
X-MEN
X-MAN VS. X-MAN IN A BATTLE TO THE DEATH-- BETRAYED BY PROFESSOR X!

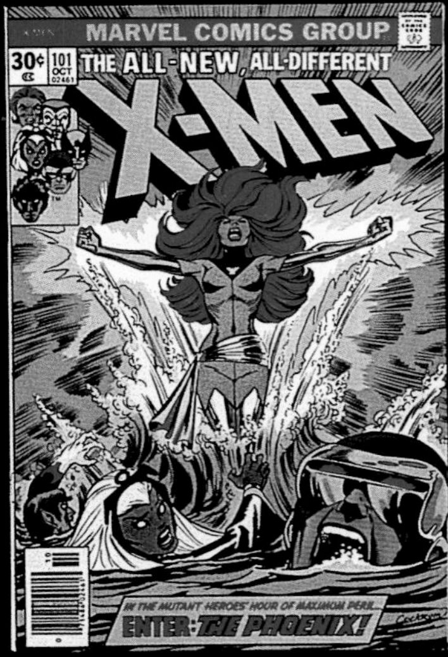
MARVEL COMICS GROUP
30¢ 101 OCT
THE ALL-NEW, ALL-DIFFERENT
X-MEN
IN THE MUTANT HEROES' HOUR OF MAXIMUM PERIL...
ENTER: THE PHOENIX!

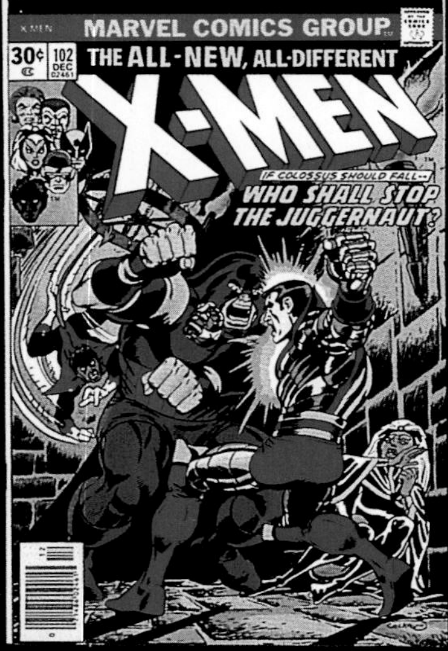
MARVEL COMICS GROUP
30¢ 102 DEC
THE ALL-NEW, ALL-DIFFERENT
X-MEN
IF COLOSSUS SHOULD FALL--
WHO SHALL STOP THE JUGGERNAUT?

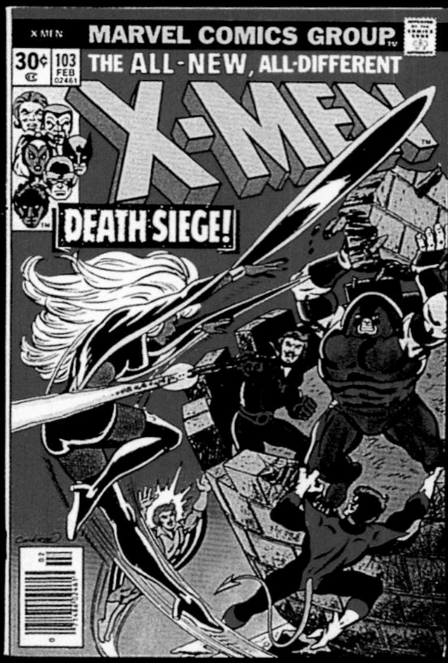
MARVEL COMICS GROUP
30¢ 103 FEB
THE ALL-NEW, ALL-DIFFERENT
X-MEN
DEATH SIEGE!

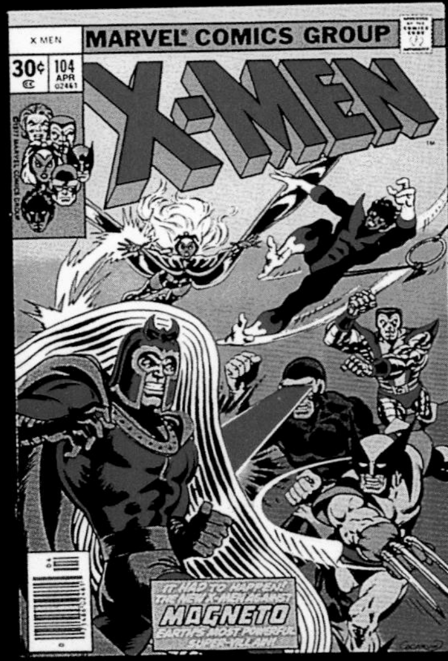
MARVEL COMICS GROUP
30¢ 104 APR
X-MEN
MAGNETO

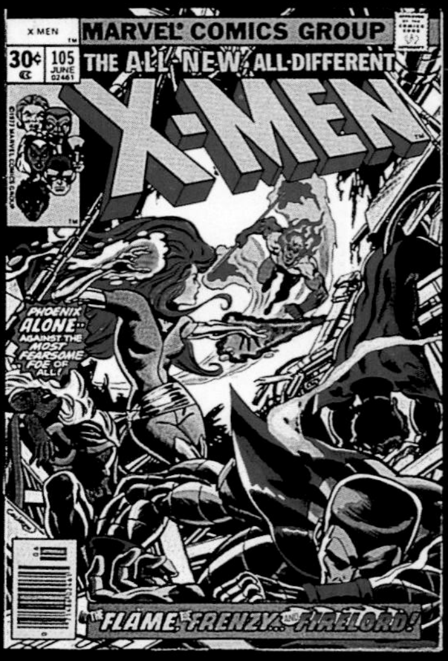
MARVEL COMICS GROUP
30¢ 105 JUNE
THE ALL-NEW, ALL-DIFFERENT
X-MEN
PHOENIX ALONE-- AGAINST THE MOST FEARSOME FOE OF ALL!
FLAME--FRENZY--FIRELORD!

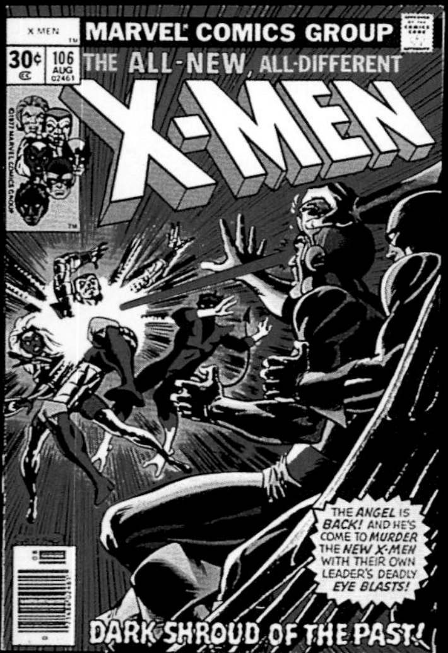
MARVEL COMICS GROUP
30¢ 106 AUG
THE ALL-NEW, ALL-DIFFERENT
X-MEN
THE ANGEL IS BACK! AND HE'S COME TO MURDER THE NEW X-MEN WITH THEIR OWN LEADER'S DEADLY EYE BLASTS!
DARK SHROUD OF THE PAST!

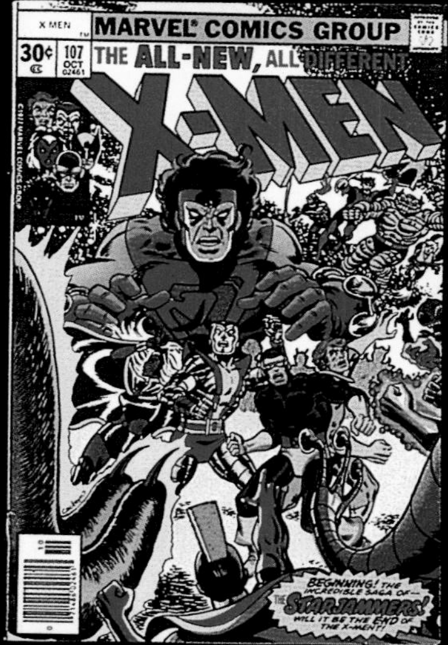
MARVEL COMICS GROUP
30¢ 107 OCT
THE ALL-NEW, ALL-DIFFERENT
X-MEN

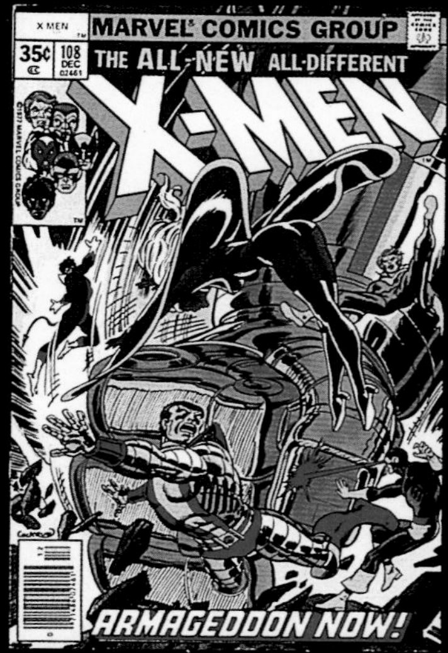
MARVEL COMICS GROUP
35¢ 108 DEC
THE ALL-NEW ALL-DIFFERENT
X-MEN
ARMAGEDDON NOW!

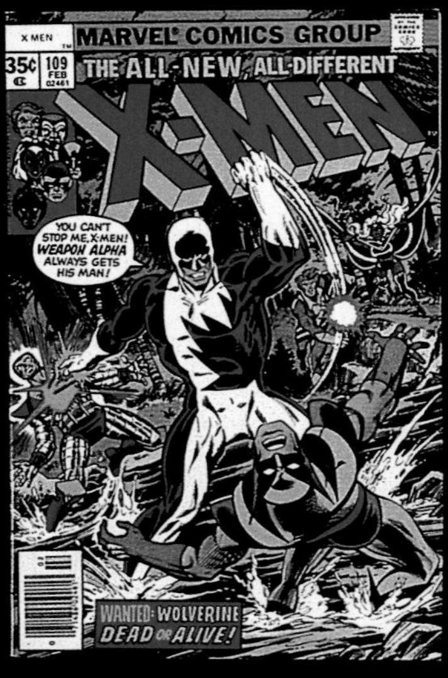
MARVEL COMICS GROUP
35¢ 109 FEB
THE ALL-NEW, ALL-DIFFERENT
X-MEN
YOU CAN'T STOP ME, X-MEN! WEAPON ALPHA ALWAYS GETS HIS MAN!
WANTED: WOLVERINE DEAD OR ALIVE!

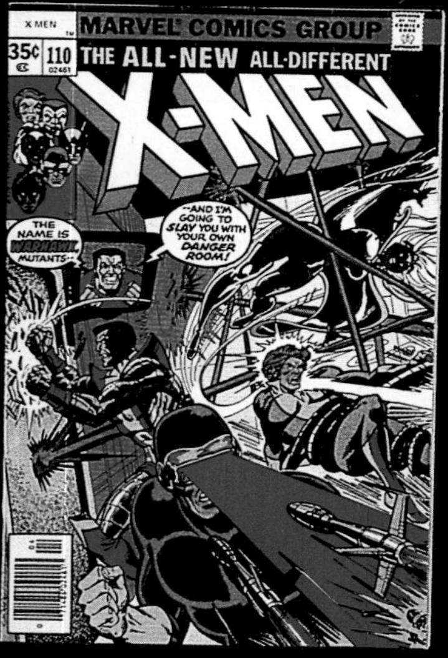
MARVEL COMICS GROUP
35¢ 110
THE ALL-NEW ALL-DIFFERENT
X-MEN
--AND I'M GOING TO SLAY YOU WITH YOUR OWN DANGER ROOM!

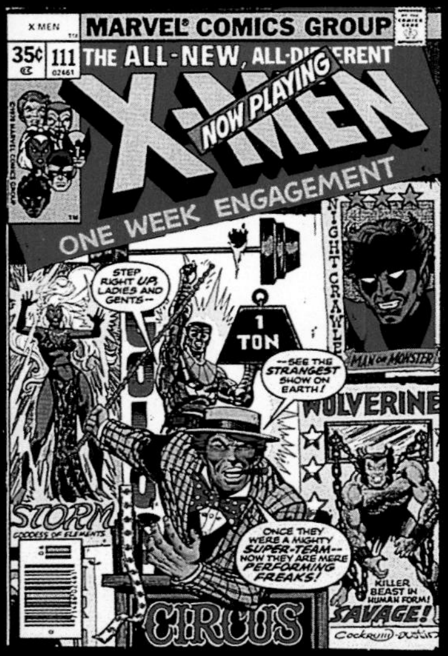
MARVEL COMICS GROUP
35¢ 111
THE ALL-NEW, ALL-DIFFERENT
X-MEN
NOW PLAYING
ONE WEEK ENGAGEMENT
STEP RIGHT UP, LADIES AND GENTS--
1 TON
--SEE THE STRANGEST SHOW ON EARTH!
WOLVERINE
STORM
ONCE THEY WERE A MIGHTY SUPER-TEAM-- NOW THEY ARE MERE PERFORMING FREAKS!
KILLER BEAST IN HUMAN FORM! SAVAGE!
CIRCUS

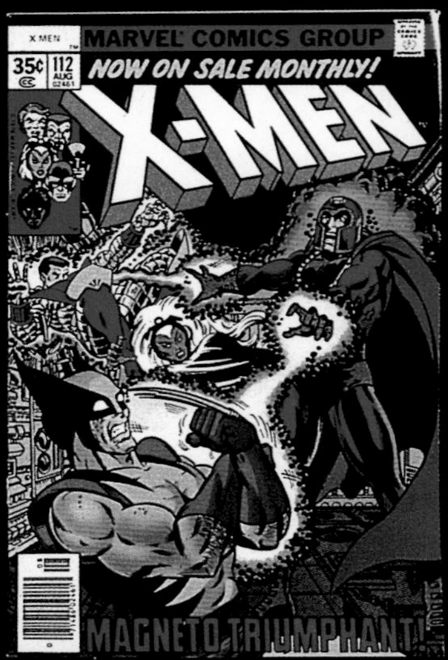
MARVEL COMICS GROUP
35¢ 112 AUG
NOW ON SALE MONTHLY!
X-MEN
MAGNETO TRIUMPHANT!

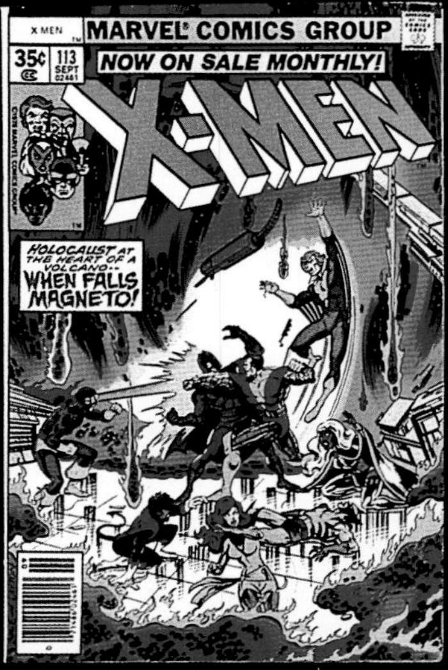
MARVEL COMICS GROUP
35¢ 113 SEPT
NOW ON SALE MONTHLY!
X-MEN
HOLOCAUST AT THE HEART OF A VOLCANO-- WHEN FALLS MAGNETO!

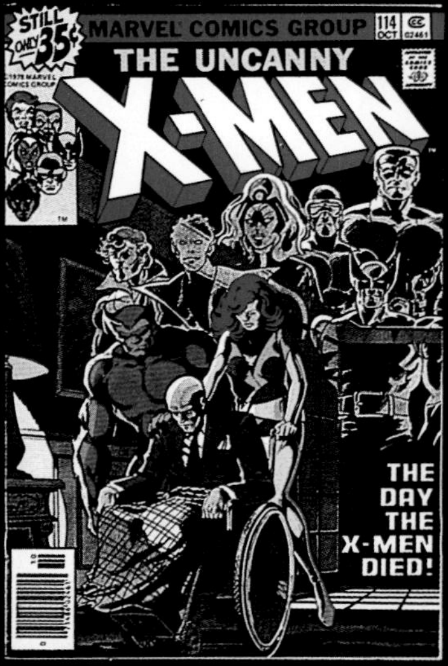
STILL ONLY 35¢
MARVEL COMICS GROUP 114 OCT
THE UNCANNY X-MEN
THE DAY THE X-MEN DIED!

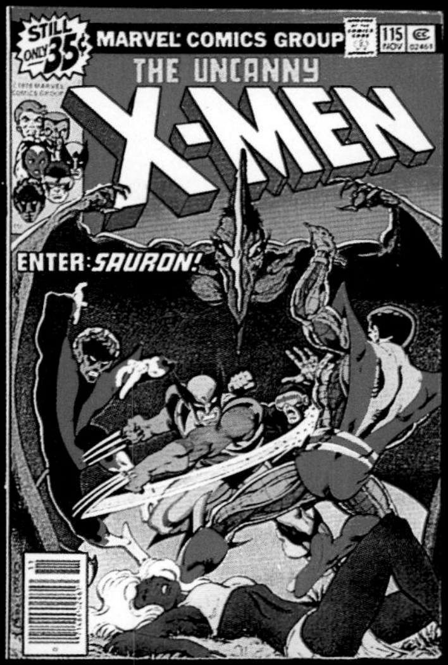
STILL ONLY 35¢
MARVEL COMICS GROUP 115 NOV
THE UNCANNY X-MEN
ENTER: SAURON!

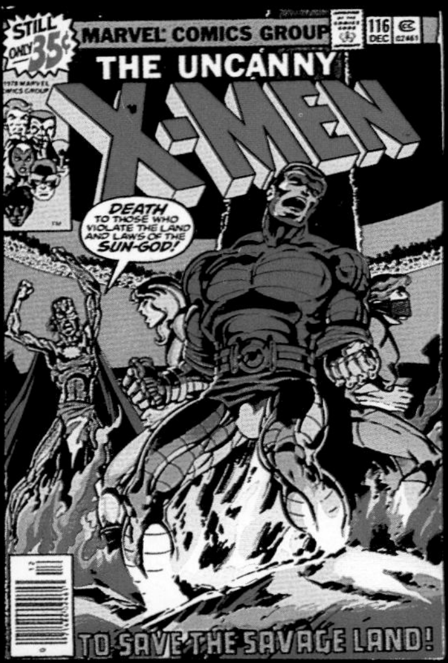
STILL ONLY 35¢
MARVEL COMICS GROUP 116 DEC
THE UNCANNY X-MEN
DEATH TO THOSE WHO VIOLATE THE LAND AND LAWS OF THE SUN-GOD!
TO SAVE THE SAVAGE LAND!

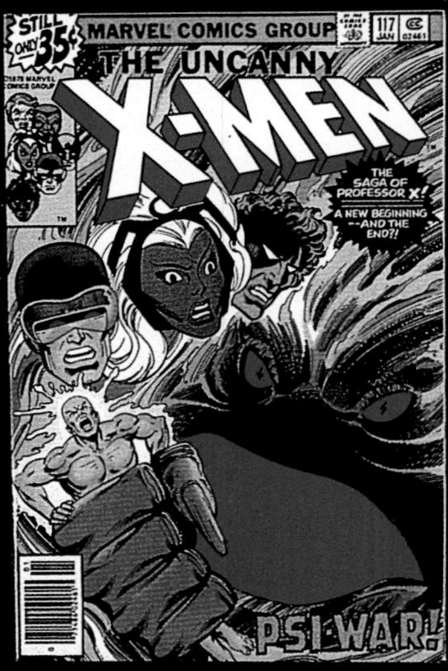
STILL ONLY 35¢
MARVEL COMICS GROUP 117 JAN
THE UNCANNY X-MEN
THE SAGA OF PROFESSOR X! A NEW BEGINNING --AND THE END?!
PSI-WAR!

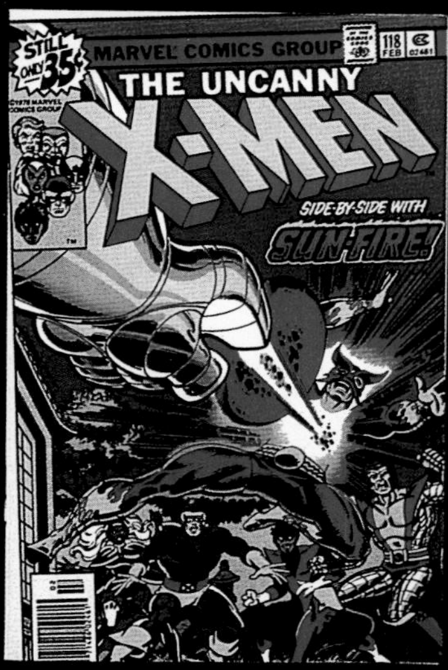
STILL ONLY 35¢
MARVEL COMICS GROUP 118 FEB
THE UNCANNY X-MEN
SIDE-BY-SIDE WITH SUN-FIRE!

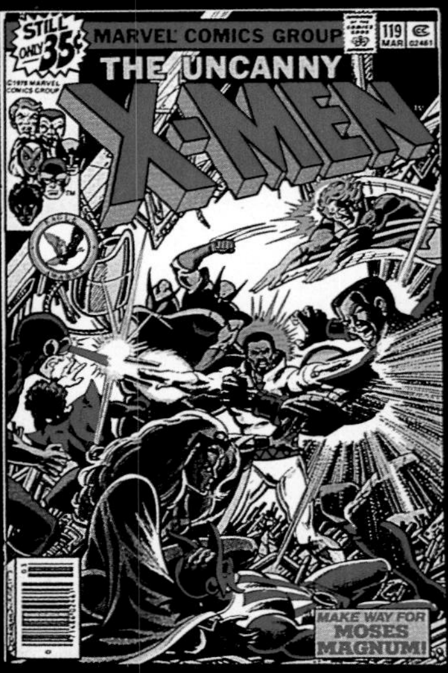
STILL ONLY 35¢
MARVEL COMICS GROUP 119 MAR
THE UNCANNY X-MEN
MAKE WAY FOR MOSES MAGNUM!

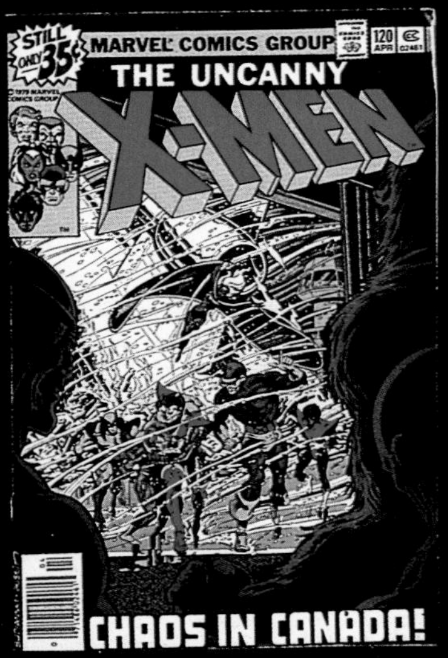
STILL ONLY 35¢
MARVEL COMICS GROUP 120 APR
THE UNCANNY X-MEN
CHAOS IN CANADA!

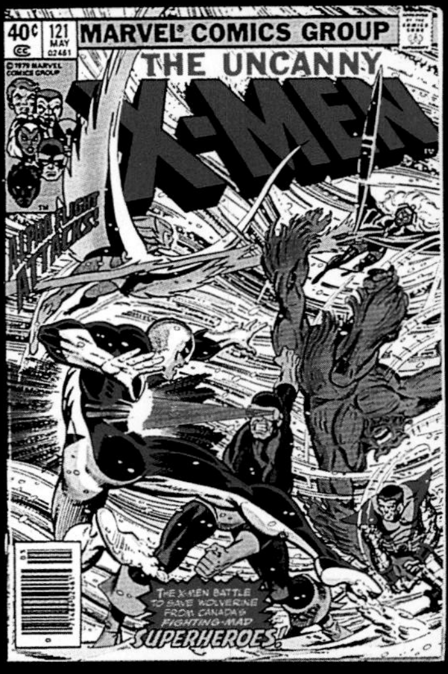
40¢ 121 MAY
MARVEL COMICS GROUP
THE UNCANNY X-MEN
SUPERHEROES!

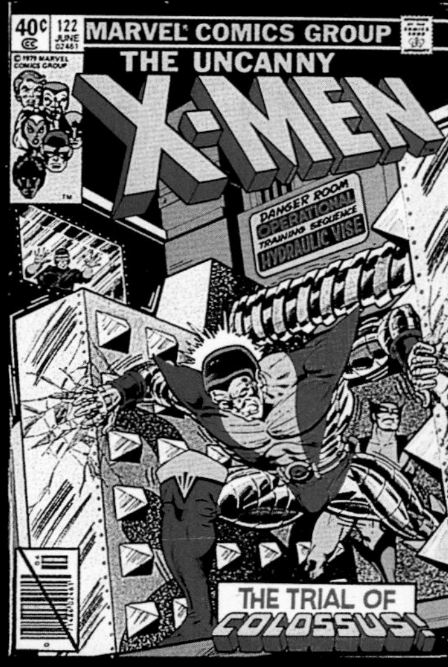
40¢ 122 JUNE
MARVEL COMICS GROUP
THE UNCANNY X-MEN
THE TRIAL OF COLOSSUS!

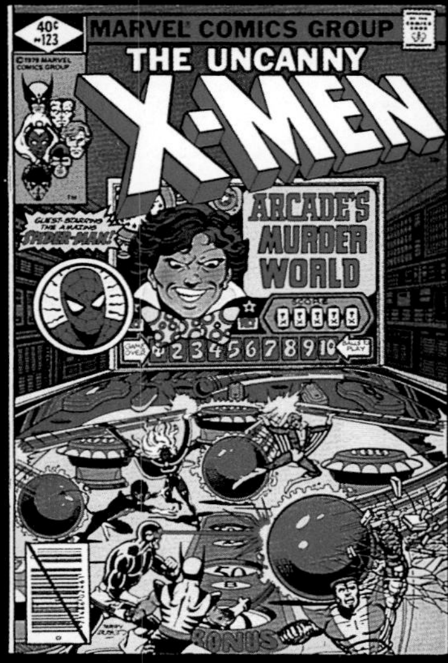
40¢ 123
MARVEL COMICS GROUP
THE UNCANNY X-MEN
ARCADE'S MURDER WORLD
2 3 4 5 6 7 8 9

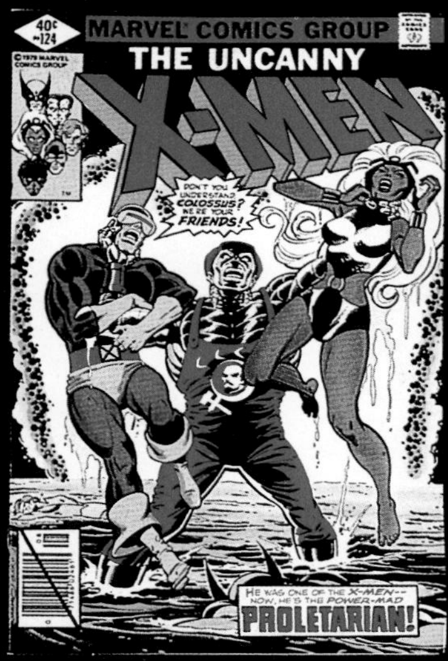
40¢ 124
MARVEL COMICS GROUP
THE UNCANNY X-MEN
DON'T YOU UNDERSTAND, COLOSSUS? THESE ARE YOUR FRIENDS!
HE WAS ONE OF THE X-MEN-- NOW, HE'S THE POWER-MAD PROLETARIAN!

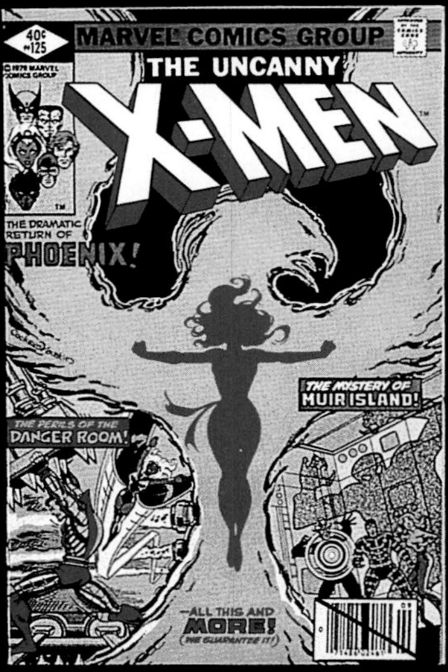
40¢ 125
MARVEL COMICS GROUP
THE UNCANNY X-MEN
THE DRAMATIC RETURN OF PHOENIX!
THE MYSTERY OF MUIR ISLAND!
DANGER ROOM!
--ALL THIS AND MORE!

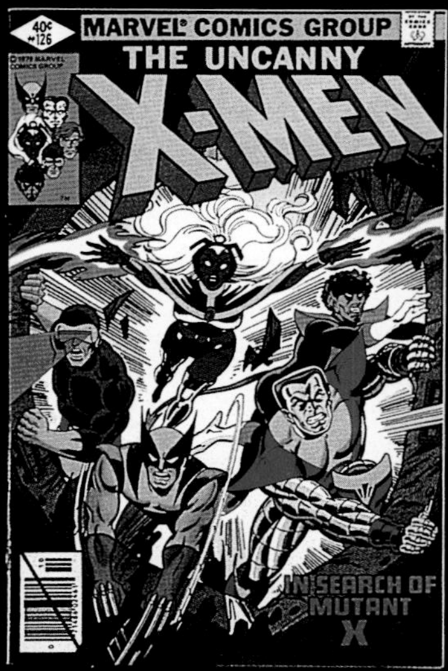
40¢ 126
MARVEL COMICS GROUP
THE UNCANNY X-MEN
IN SEARCH OF MUTANT X

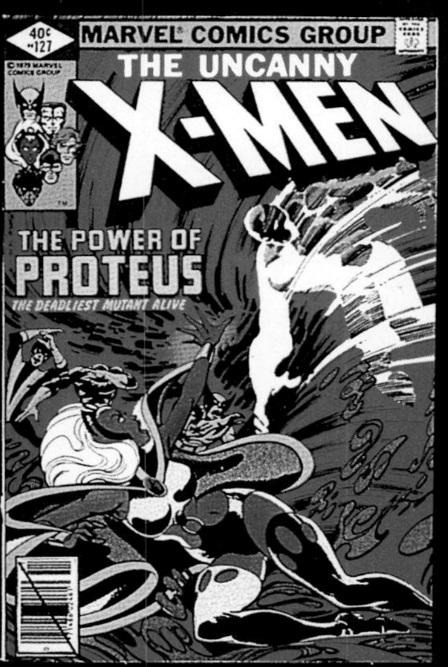
40¢ 127
MARVEL COMICS GROUP
THE UNCANNY X-MEN
THE POWER OF PROTEUS
THE DEADLIEST MUTANT ALIVE

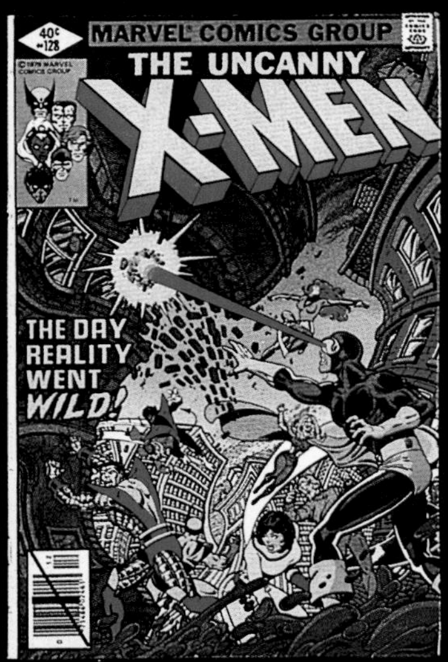
40¢ 128
MARVEL COMICS GROUP
THE UNCANNY X-MEN
THE DAY REALITY WENT WILD!

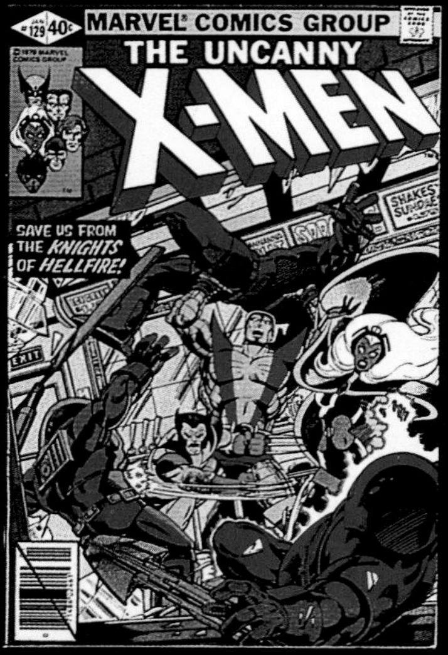
MARVEL COMICS GROUP
THE UNCANNY
X-MEN
SAVE US FROM THE KNIGHTS OF HELLFIRE!

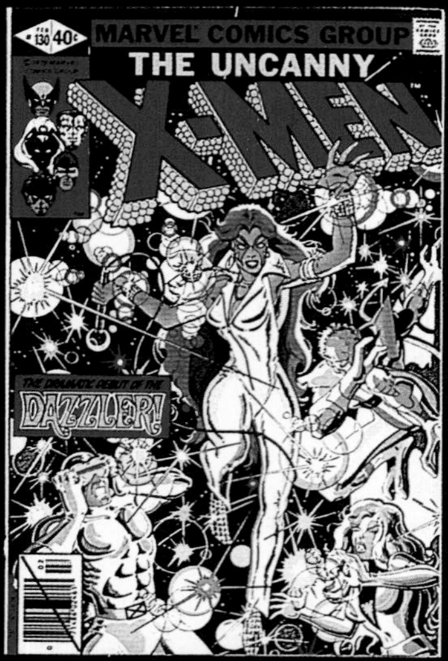
MARVEL COMICS GROUP
THE UNCANNY
X-MEN
THE DRAMATIC DEBUT OF THE DAZZLER!

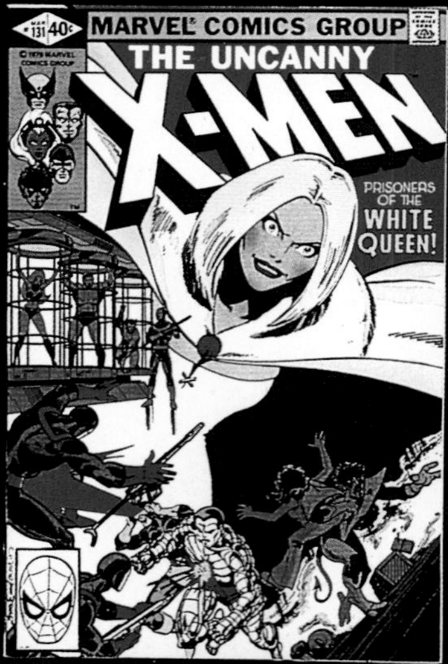
MARVEL COMICS GROUP
THE UNCANNY
X-MEN
PRISONERS OF THE WHITE QUEEN!

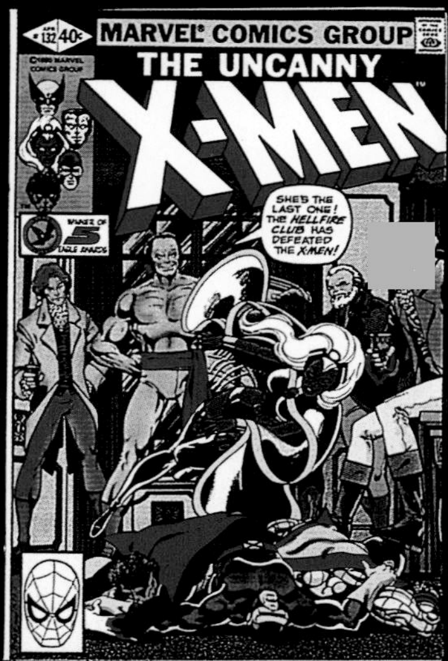
MARVEL COMICS GROUP
THE UNCANNY
X-MEN
SHE'S THE LAST ONE! THE HELLFIRE CLUB HAS DEFEATED THE X-MEN!

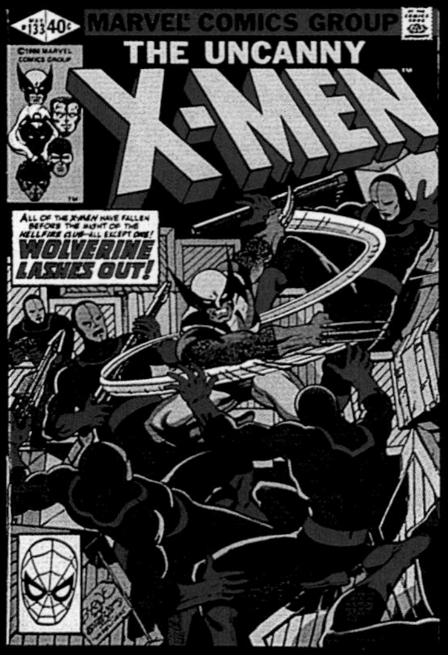
MARVEL COMICS GROUP
THE UNCANNY
X-MEN
ALL OF THE X-MEN HAVE FALLEN BEFORE THE MIGHT OF THE HELLFIRE CLUB--ALL EXCEPT ONE!
WOLVERINE LASHES OUT!

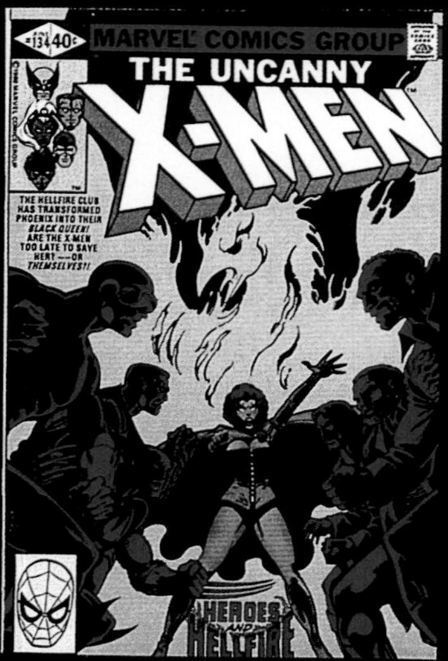
MARVEL COMICS GROUP
THE UNCANNY
X-MEN
THE HELLFIRE CLUB HAS TRANSFORMED PHOENIX INTO THEIR BLACK QUEEN! ARE THE X-MEN TOO LATE TO SAVE HER --OR THEMSELVES?!
HEROES AND HELLFIRE

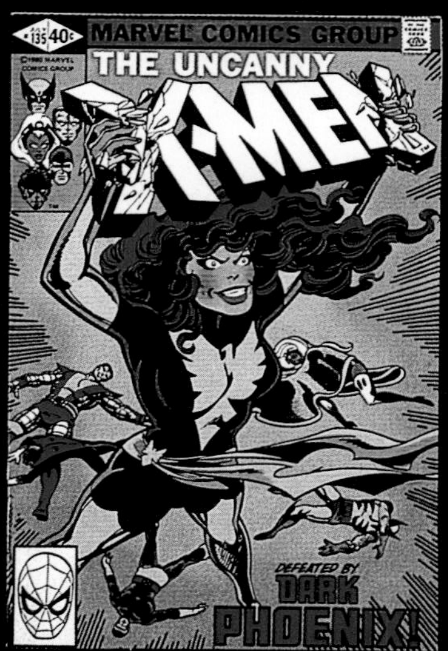
MARVEL COMICS GROUP
THE UNCANNY
X-MEN
DEFEATED BY DARK PHOENIX!

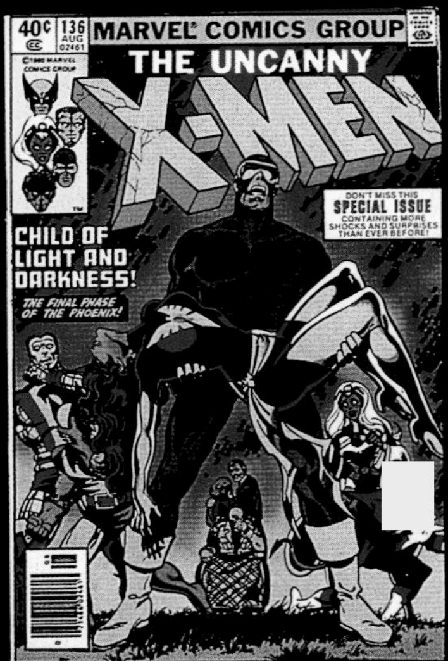
MARVEL COMICS GROUP
THE UNCANNY
X-MEN
DON'T MISS THIS SPECIAL ISSUE CONTAINING MORE SHOCKS AND SURPRISES THAN EVER BEFORE!
CHILD OF LIGHT AND DARKNESS!
THE FINAL PHASE OF THE PHOENIX!

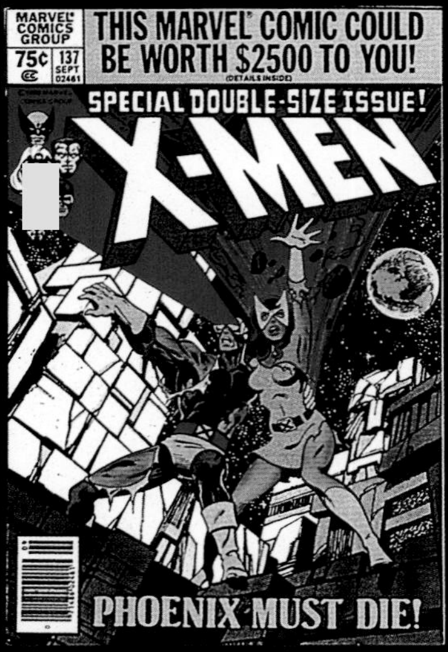
THIS MARVEL COMIC COULD BE WORTH $2500 TO YOU!
(DETAILS INSIDE)
SPECIAL DOUBLE-SIZE ISSUE!
X-MEN
PHOENIX MUST DIE!

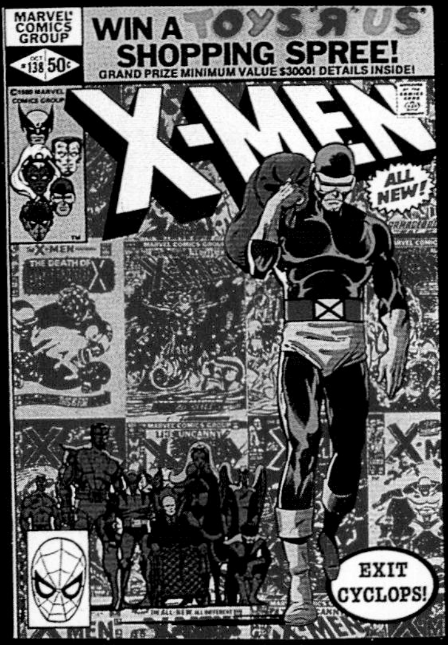
WIN A TOYS'R'US SHOPPING SPREE!
GRAND PRIZE MINIMUM VALUE $3000! DETAILS INSIDE!
X-MEN
ALL NEW!
EXIT CYCLOPS!

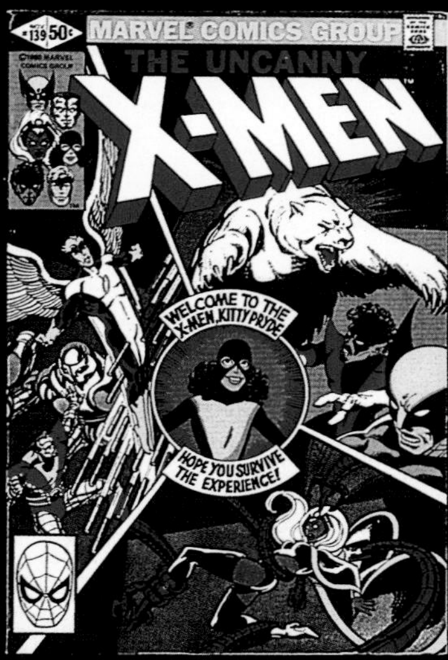
MARVEL COMICS GROUP
THE UNCANNY
X-MEN
WELCOME TO THE X-MEN, KITTY PRIDE
HOPE YOU SURVIVE THE EXPERIENCE!

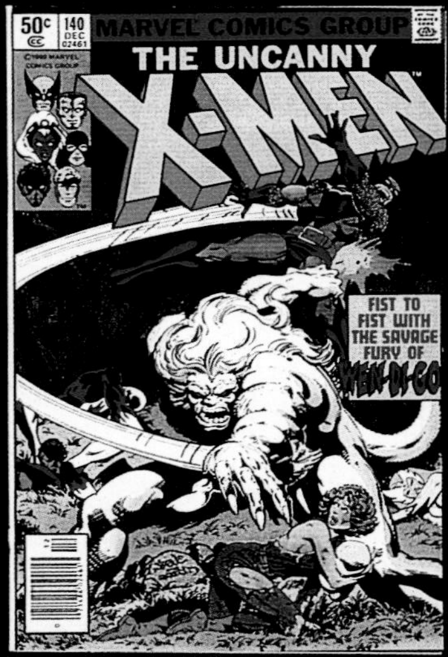
MARVEL COMICS GROUP
THE UNCANNY
X-MEN
FIST TO FIST WITH THE SAVAGE FURY OF MEN-DI-GO

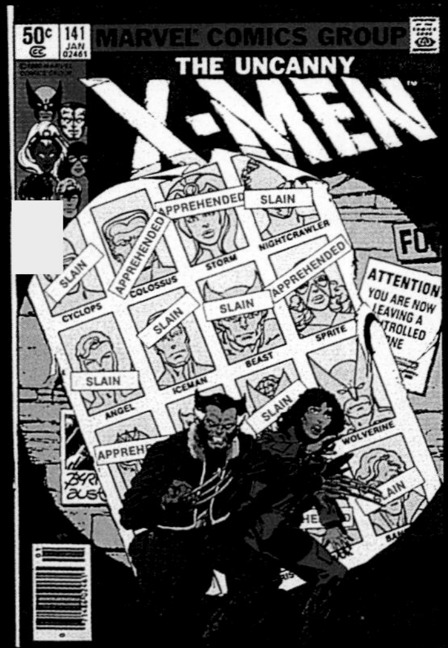
MARVEL COMICS GROUP
THE UNCANNY
X-MEN
APPREHENDED
SLAIN
STORM
NIGHTCRAWLER
CYCLOPS
COLOSSUS
ANGEL
BEAST
SPRITE
WOLVERINE
ATTENTION YOU ARE NOW LEAVING A ...TROLLED ZONE

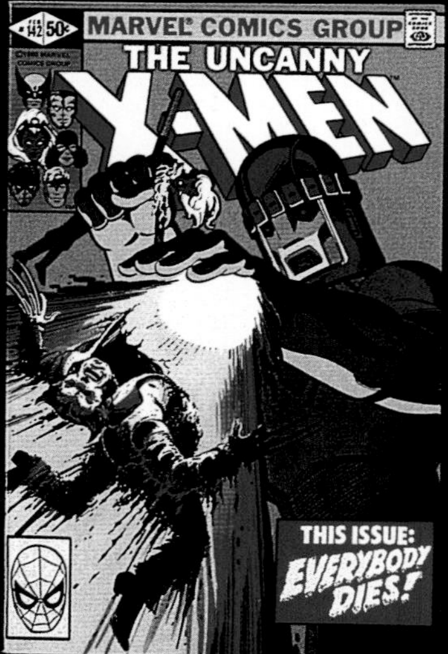
MARVEL COMICS GROUP
THE UNCANNY
X-MEN
THIS ISSUE: EVERYBODY DIES!

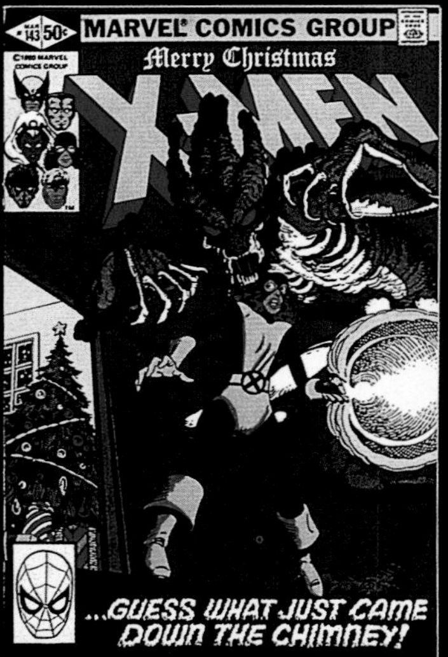
MARVEL COMICS GROUP
Merry Christmas
X-MEN
...GUESS WHAT JUST CAME DOWN THE CHIMNEY!

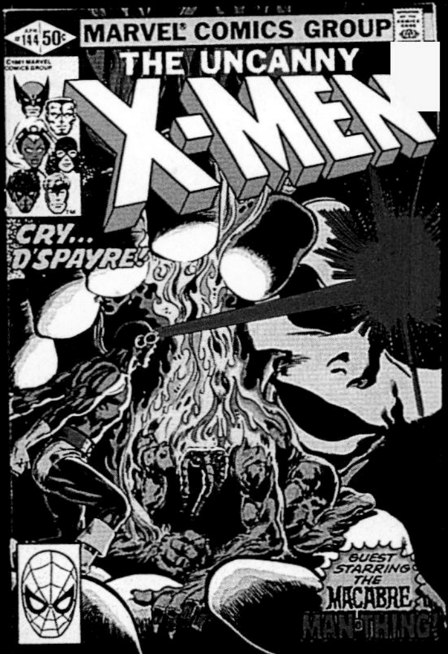
MARVEL COMICS GROUP
THE UNCANNY
X-MEN
GUEST STARRING THE MACABRE MAN-THING!

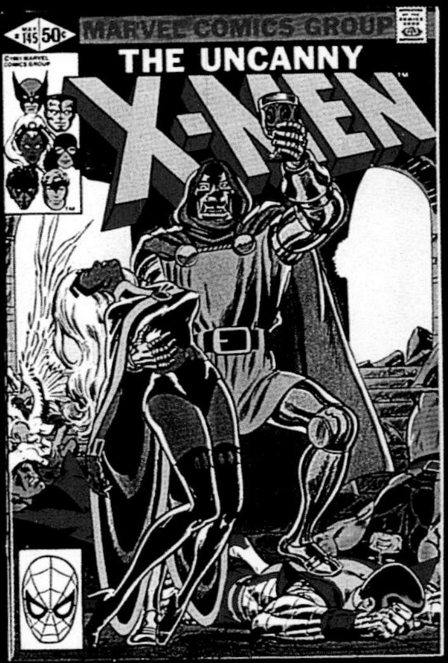
MARVEL COMICS GROUP
THE UNCANNY
X-MEN

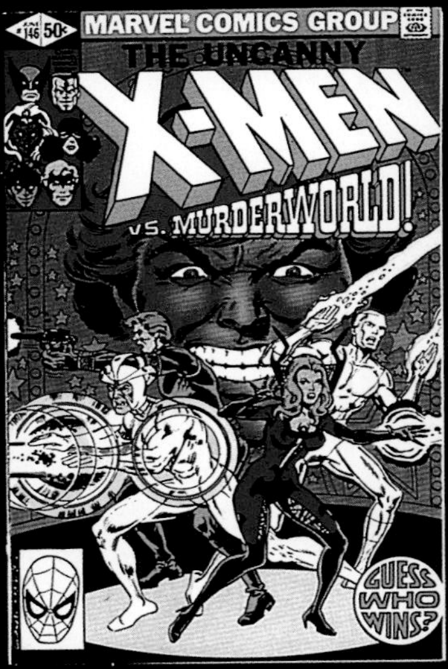
MARVEL COMICS GROUP
THE UNCANNY
X-MEN
VS. MURDERWORLD!
GUESS WHO WINS?

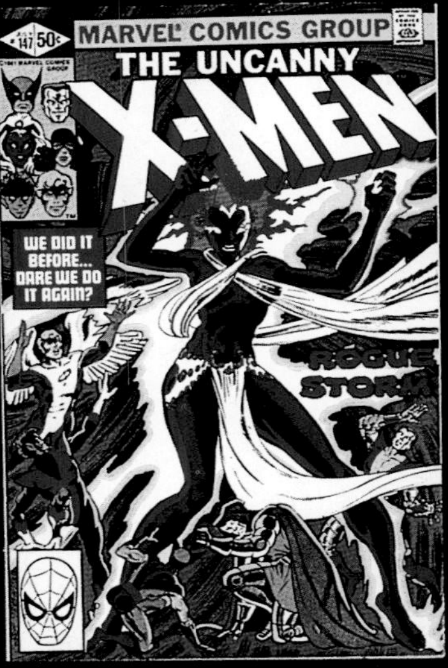
MARVEL COMICS GROUP
THE UNCANNY
X-MEN
WE DID IT BEFORE... DARE WE DO IT AGAIN?

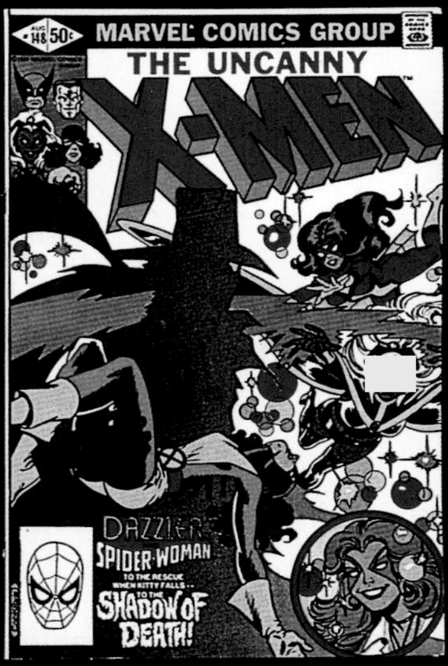
MARVEL COMICS GROUP
THE UNCANNY
X-MEN
DAZZLER
SPIDER-WOMAN
SHADOW OF DEATH!

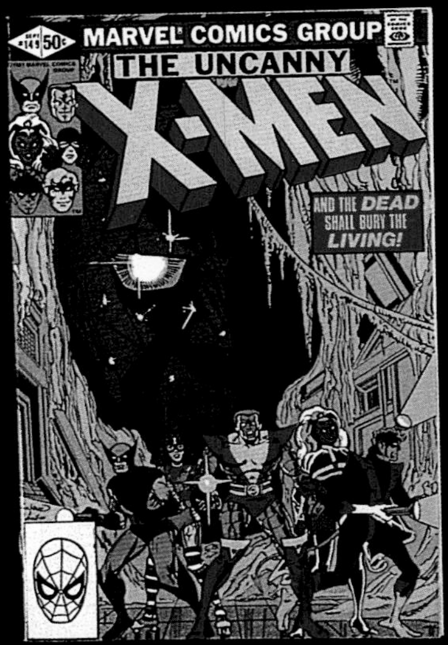
MARVEL COMICS GROUP
THE UNCANNY
X-MEN
AND THE DEAD SHALL BURY THE LIVING!

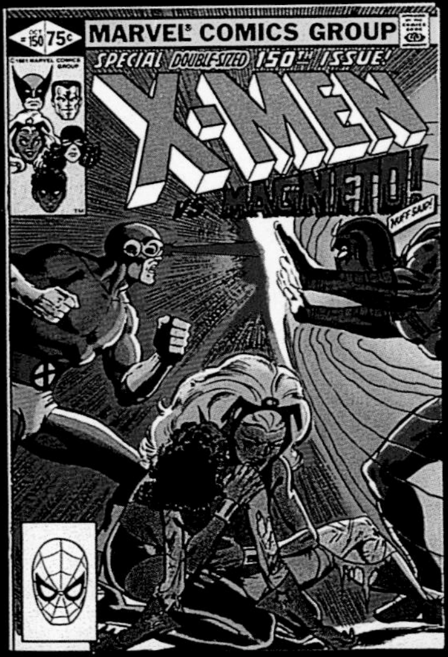
MARVEL COMICS GROUP
SPECIAL DOUBLE-SIZED 150TH ISSUE!
X-MEN
VS. MAGNETO!

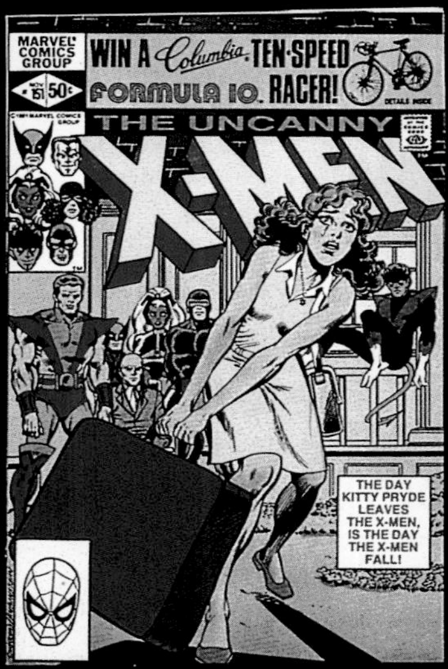
WIN A Columbia TEN-SPEED
FORMULA 10. RACER!
THE UNCANNY
X-MEN
THE DAY KITTY PRYDE LEAVES THE X-MEN, IS THE DAY THE X-MEN FALL!

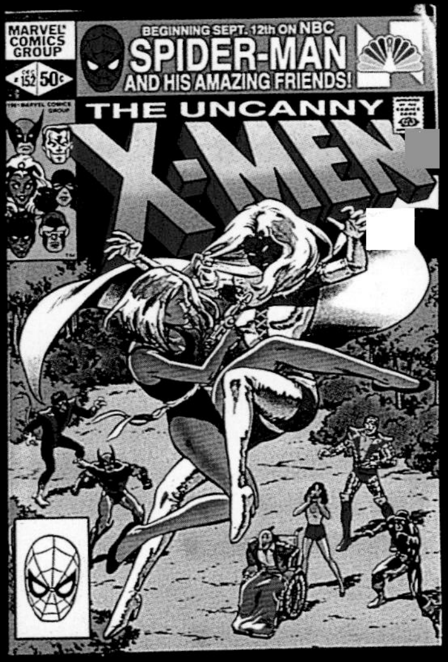
BEGINNING SEPT. 12th ON NBC
SPIDER-MAN
AND HIS AMAZING FRIENDS!
THE UNCANNY
X-MEN

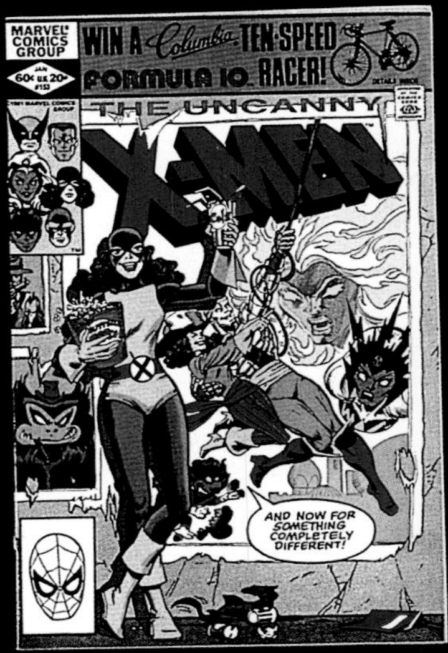
WIN A Columbia TEN-SPEED
FORMULA 10. RACER!
THE UNCANNY
X-MEN
AND NOW FOR SOMETHING COMPLETELY DIFFERENT!

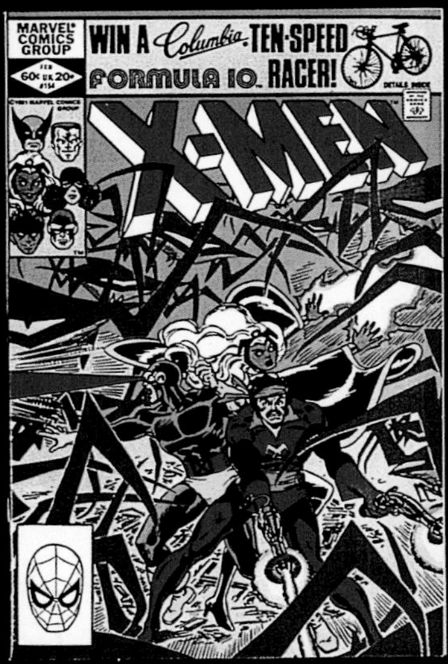
WIN A Columbia TEN-SPEED
FORMULA 10. RACER!
X-MEN

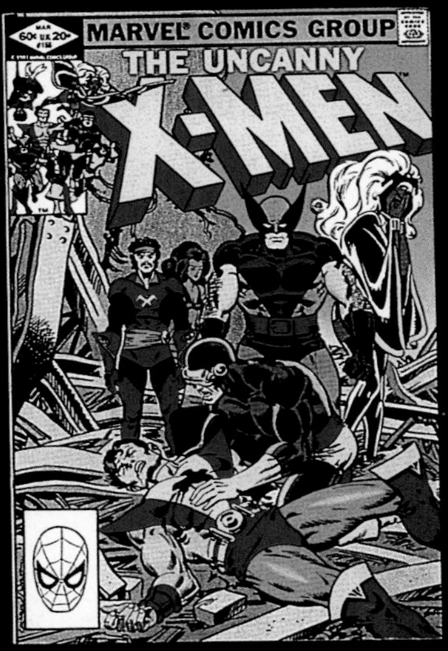
MARVEL COMICS GROUP
THE UNCANNY
X-MEN

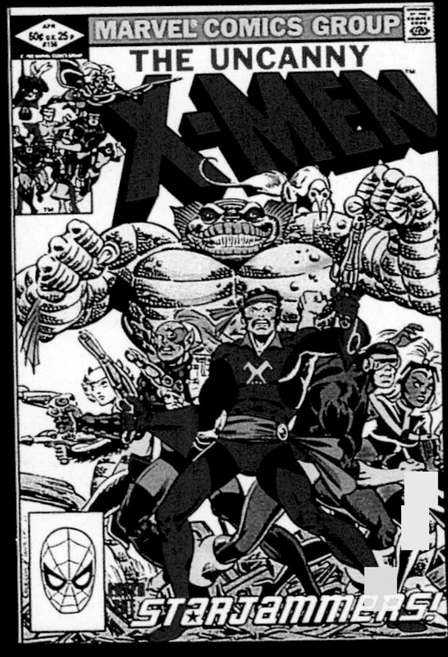
MARVEL COMICS GROUP
THE UNCANNY
X-MEN
STARJAMMERS!

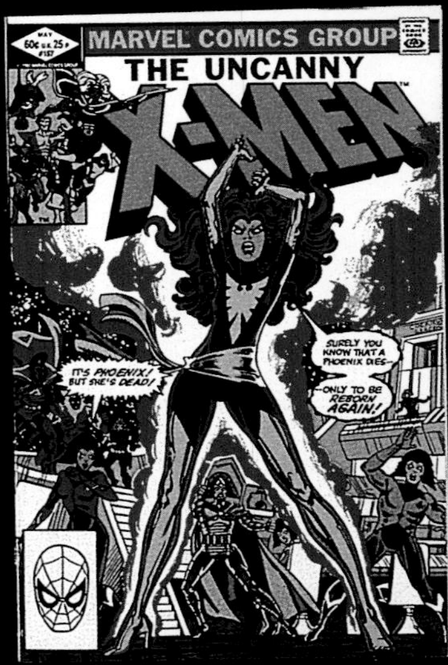
MARVEL COMICS GROUP
THE UNCANNY
X-MEN
IT'S PHOENIX! BUT SHE'S DEAD!
SURELY YOU KNOW THAT A PHOENIX DIES-
ONLY TO BE REBORN AGAIN!

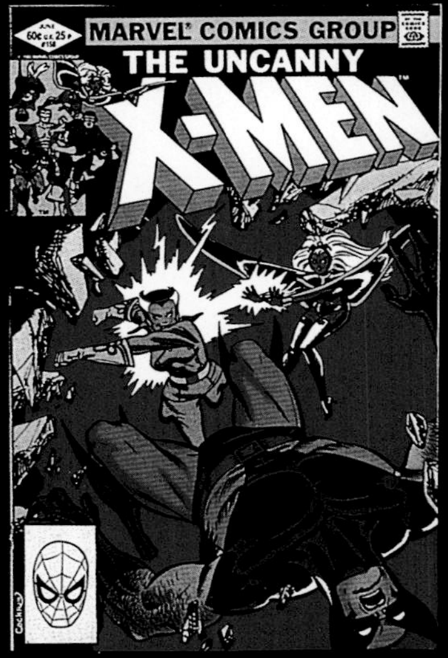
MARVEL COMICS GROUP
THE UNCANNY
X-MEN

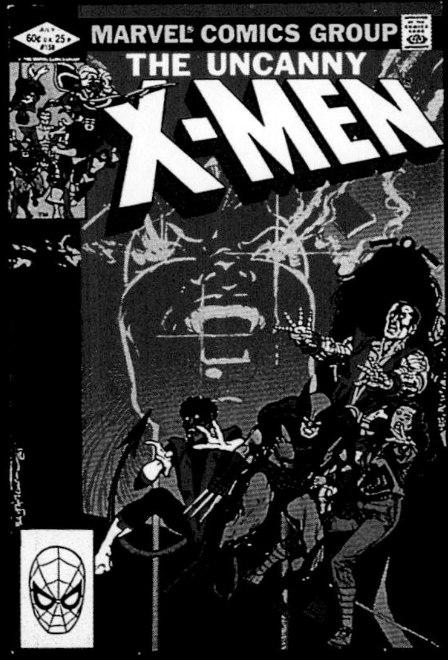
MARVEL COMICS GROUP
THE UNCANNY
X-MEN

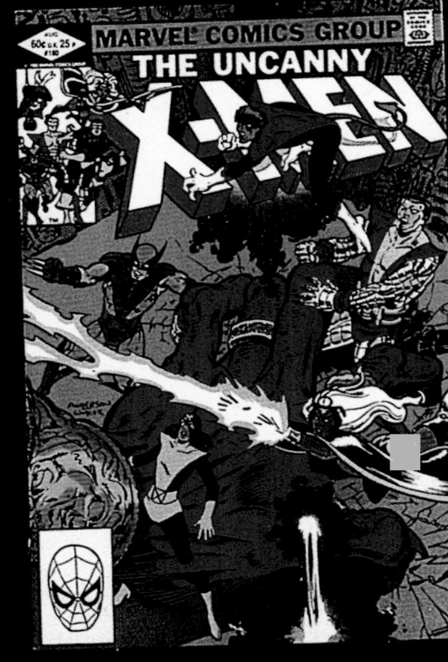
MARVEL COMICS GROUP
THE UNCANNY

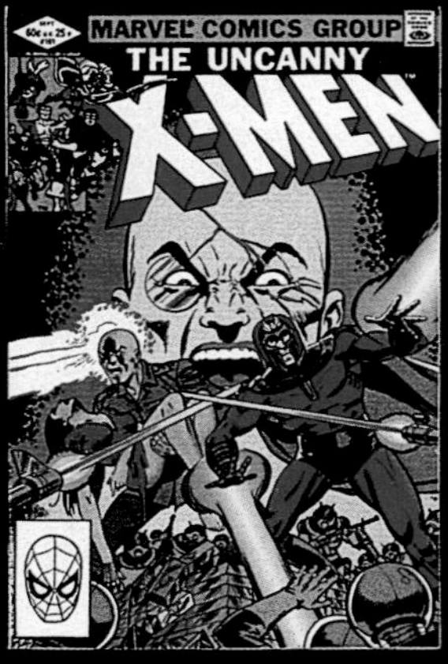
MARVEL COMICS GROUP
THE UNCANNY
X-MEN
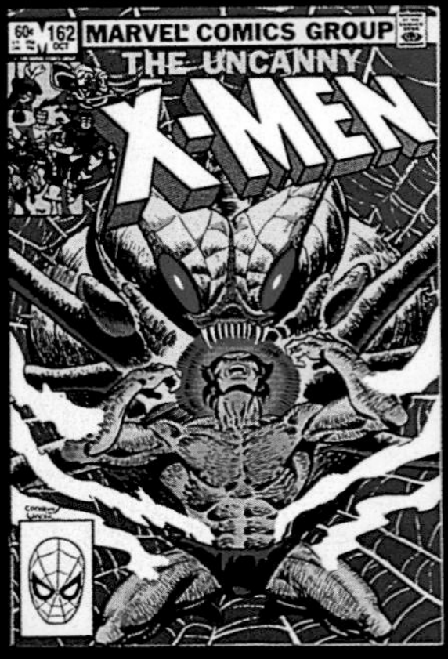
162
MARVEL COMICS GROUP
THE UNCANNY
X-MEN
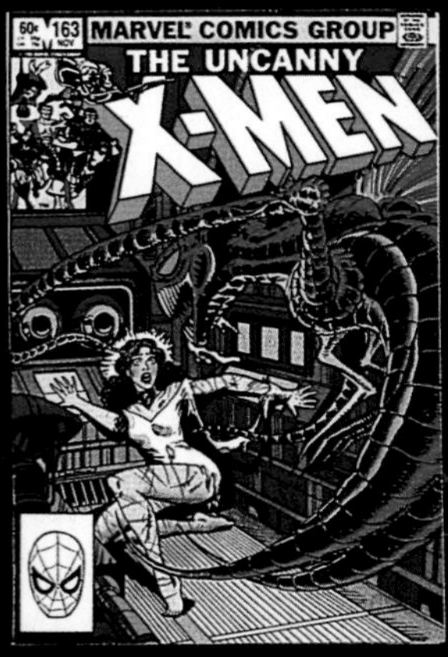
163
MARVEL COMICS GROUP
THE UNCANNY
X-MEN
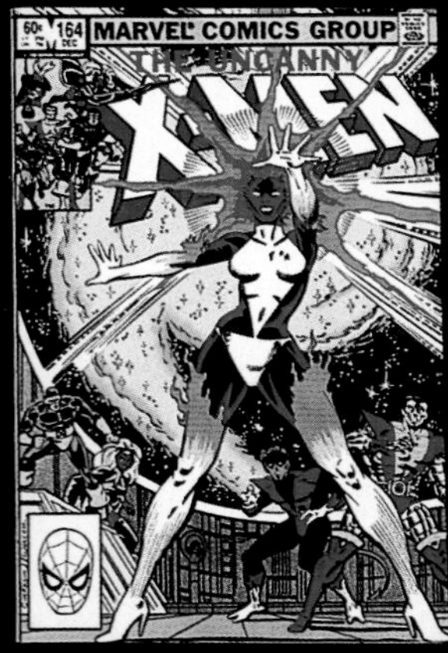
164
MARVEL COMICS GROUP
THE UNCANNY
X-MEN
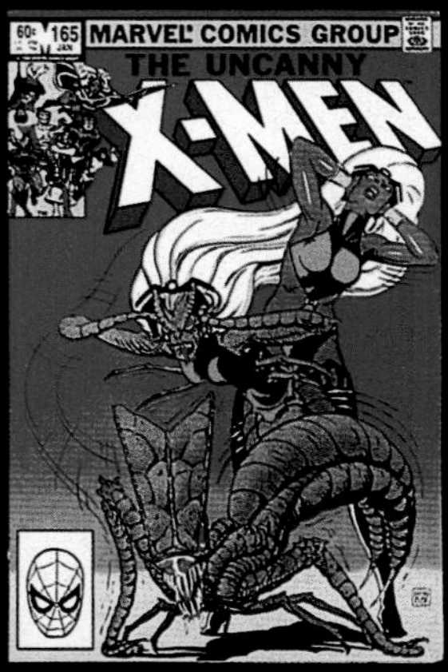
165
MARVEL COMICS GROUP
THE UNCANNY
X-MEN
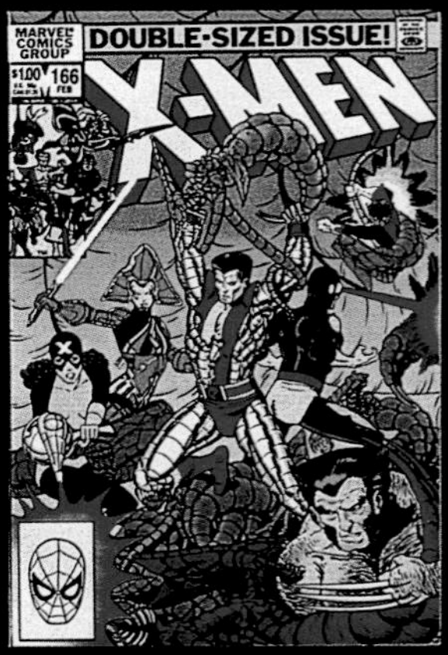
DOUBLE-SIZED ISSUE!
166
X-MEN
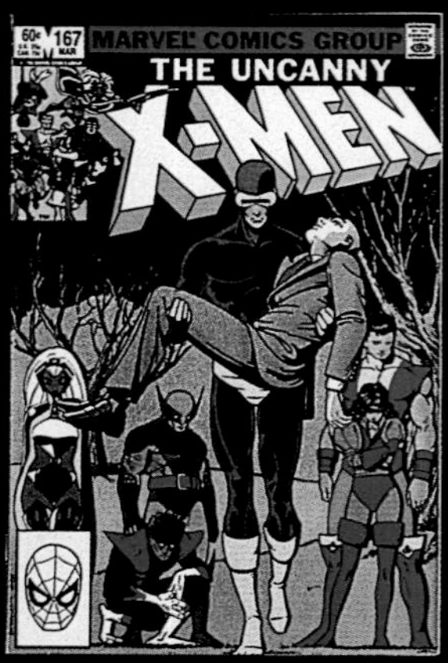
167
MARVEL COMICS GROUP
THE UNCANNY
X-MEN
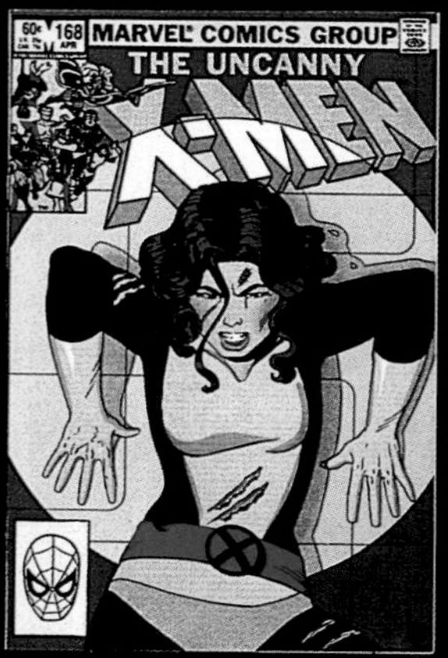
168
MARVEL COMICS GROUP
THE UNCANNY
X-MEN
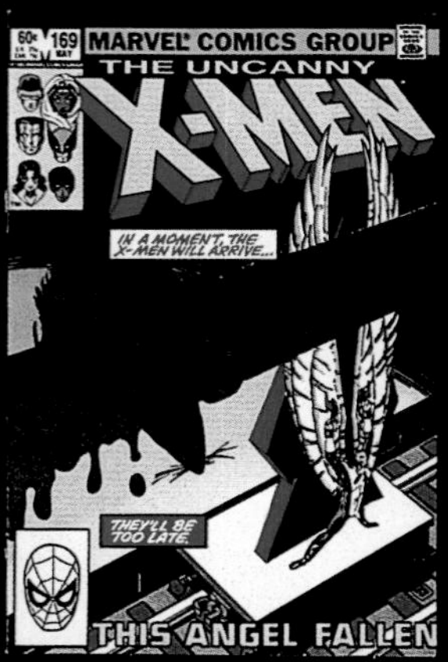
169
MARVEL COMICS GROUP
THE UNCANNY
X-MEN
IN A MOMENT, THE X-MEN WILL ARRIVE...
THEY'LL BE TOO LATE.
THIS ANGEL FALLEN
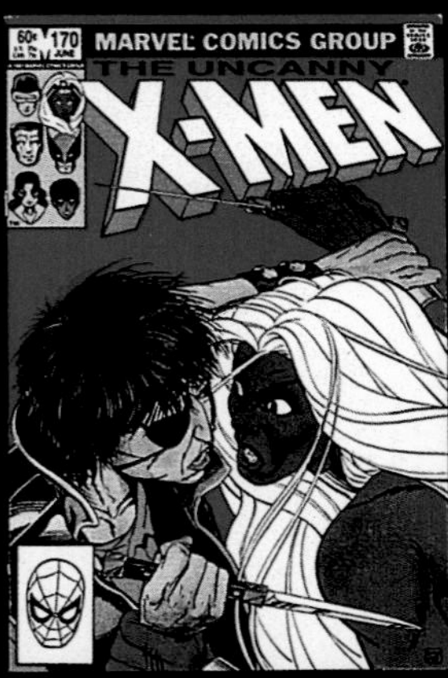
170
MARVEL COMICS GROUP
THE UNCANNY
X-MEN
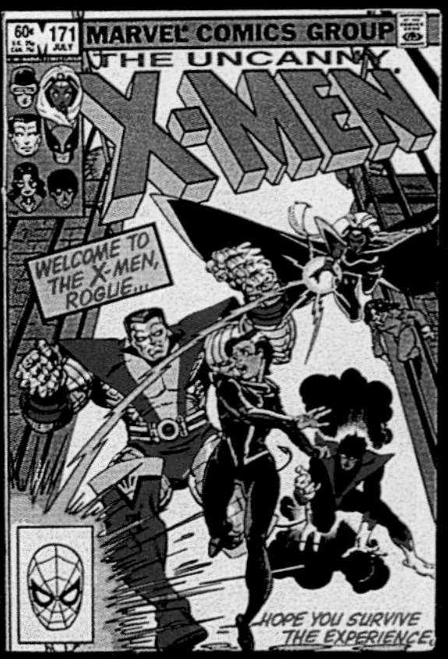
171
MARVEL COMICS GROUP
THE UNCANNY
X-MEN
WELCOME TO THE X-MEN, ROGUE...
HOPE YOU SURVIVE THE EXPERIENCE!
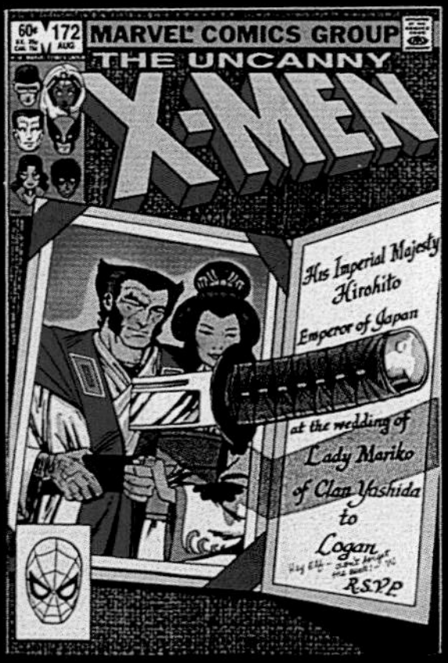
172
MARVEL COMICS GROUP
THE UNCANNY
X-MEN
His Imperial Majesty Hirohito Emperor of Japan
at the wedding of Lady Mariko of Clan Yashida to Logan
RSVP
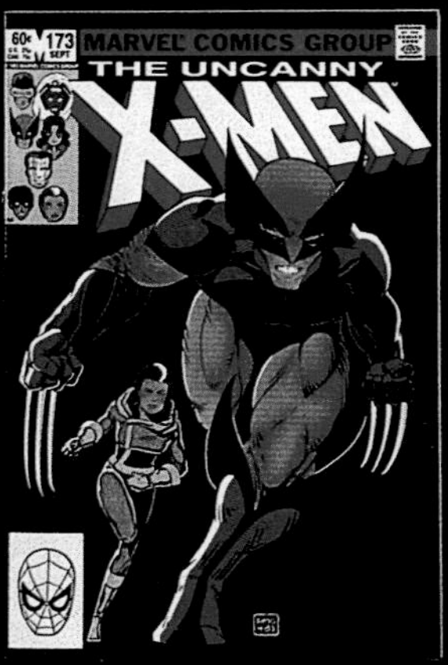
173
MARVEL COMICS GROUP
THE UNCANNY
X-MEN
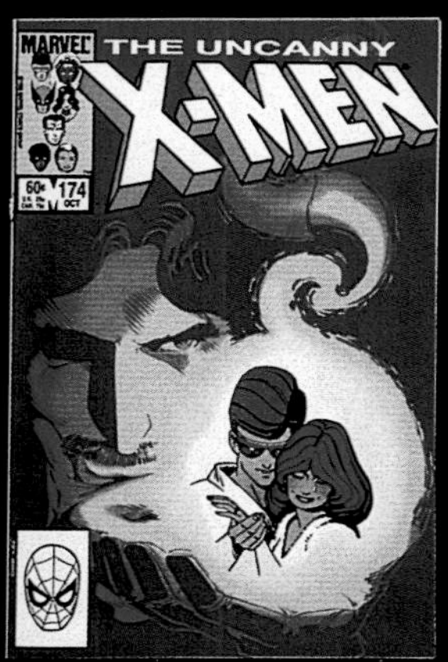
MARVEL
THE UNCANNY
X-MEN
174
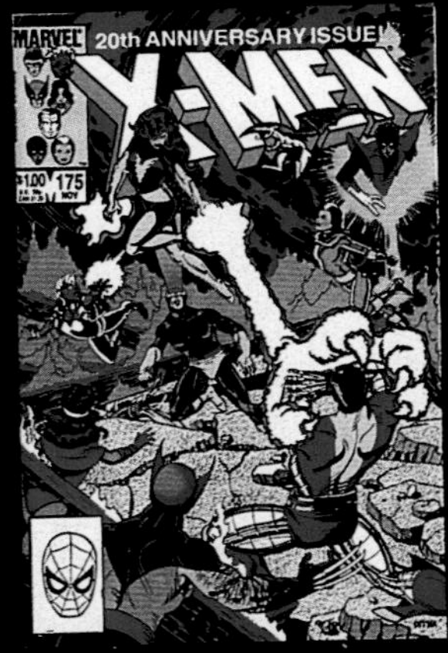
MARVEL
20th ANNIVERSARY ISSUE!
X-MEN
175
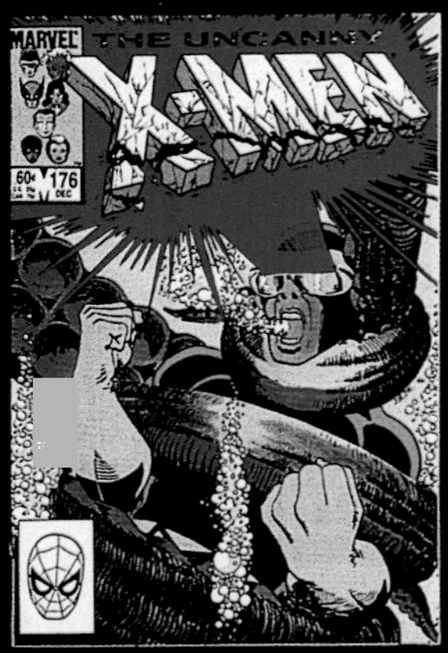
MARVEL
THE UNCANNY
X-MEN
176
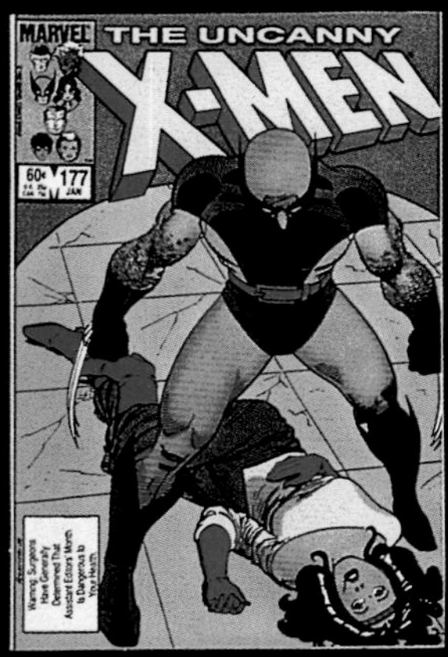
MARVEL
THE UNCANNY
X-MEN
177
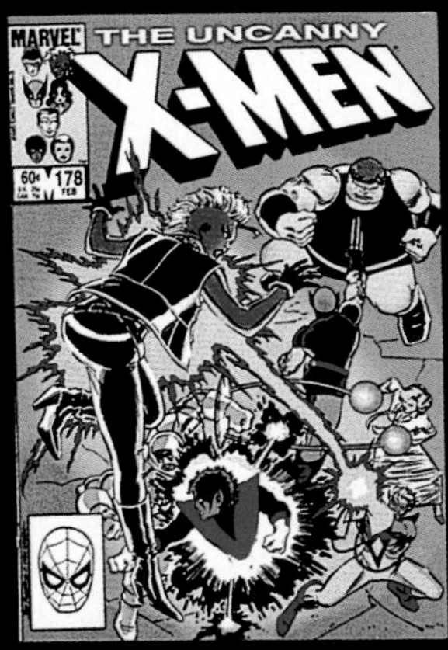
MARVEL
THE UNCANNY
X-MEN
178
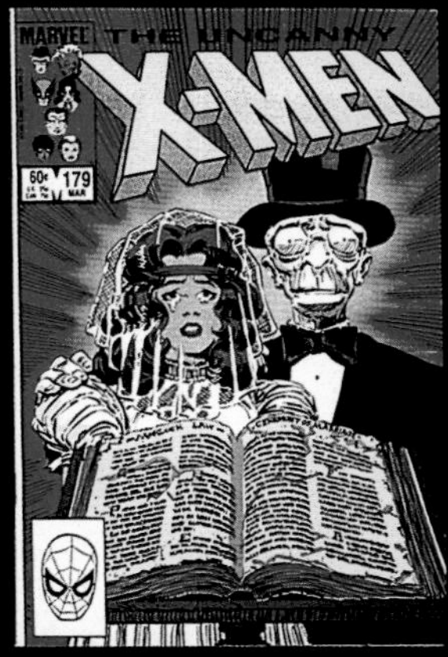
MARVEL
THE UNCANNY
X-MEN
179
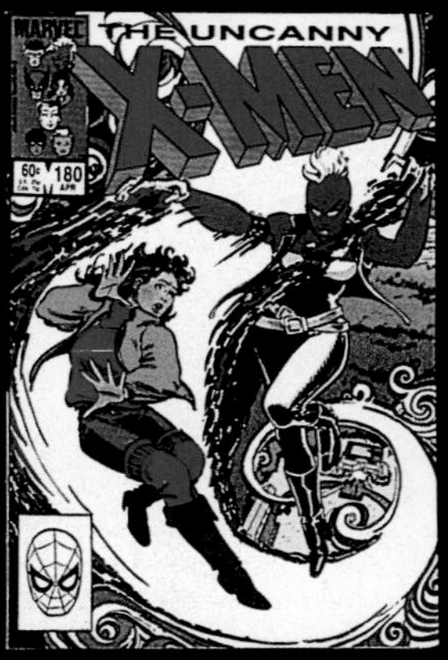
MARVEL
THE UNCANNY
X-MEN
180
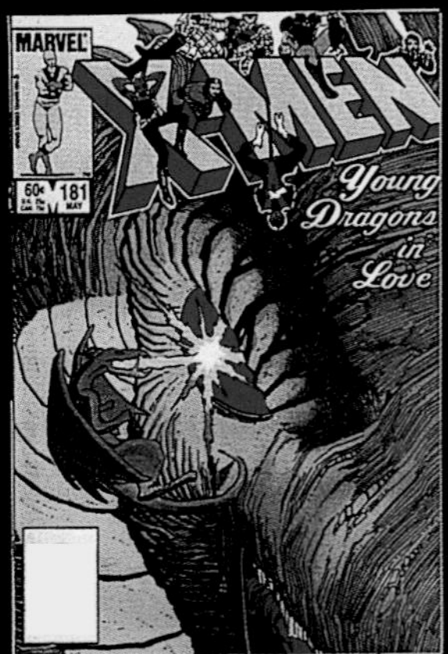
MARVEL
X-MEN
181
Young Dragons in Love
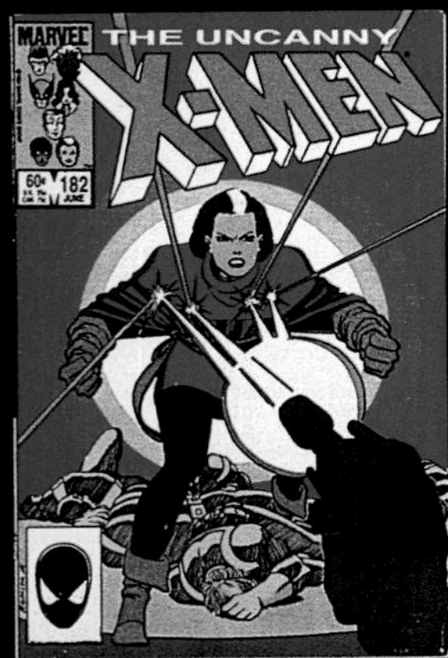
MARVEL
THE UNCANNY
X-MEN
182
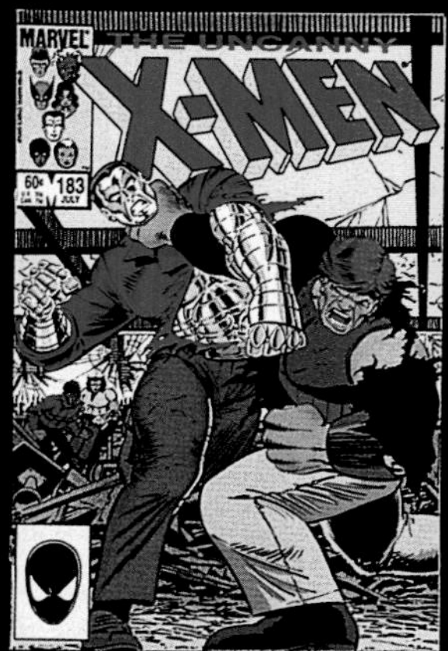
MARVEL
THE UNCANNY
X-MEN
183
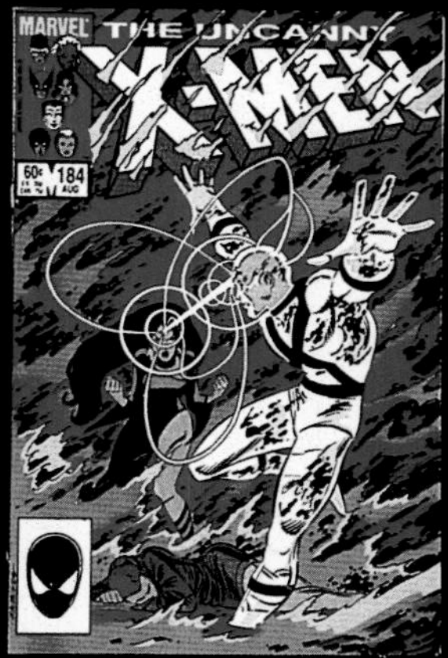
MARVEL
THE UNCANNY
X-MEN
184
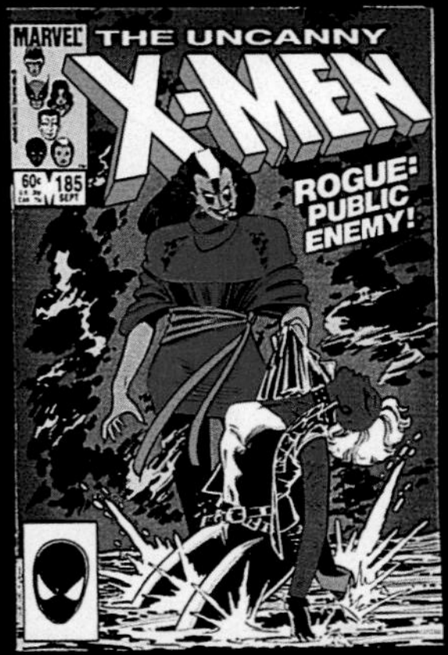
MARVEL
THE UNCANNY
X-MEN
185
ROGUE: PUBLIC ENEMY!

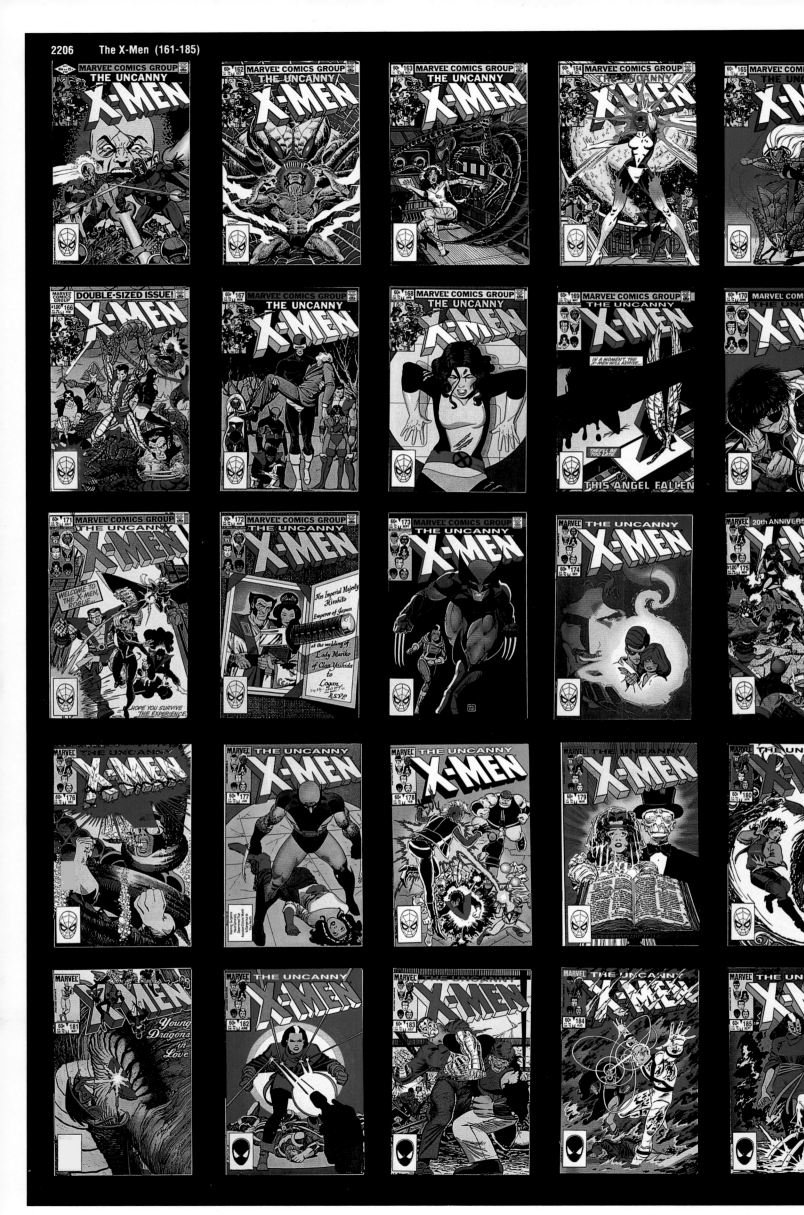

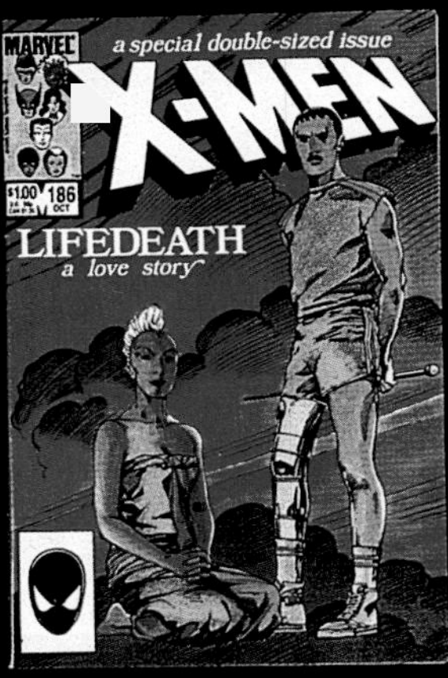
MARVEL
a special double-sized issue
X-MEN
186
LIFEDEATH
a love story

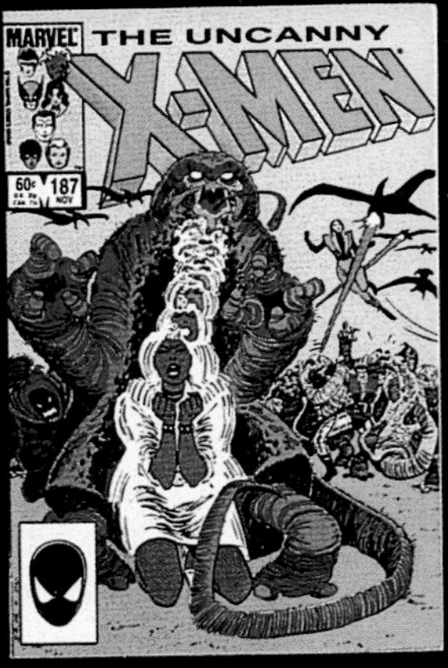
MARVEL
THE UNCANNY
X-MEN
187

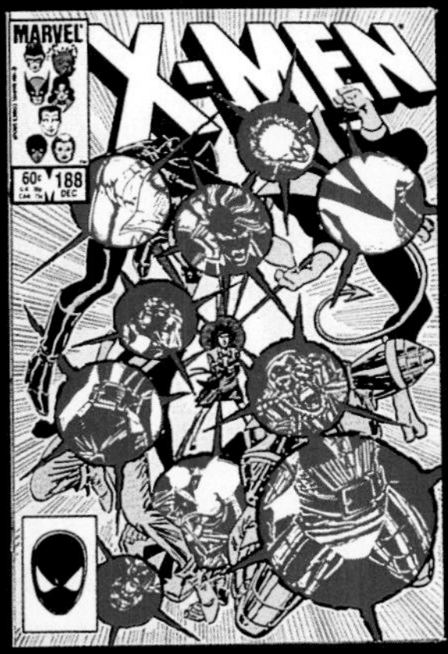
MARVEL
X-MEN
188

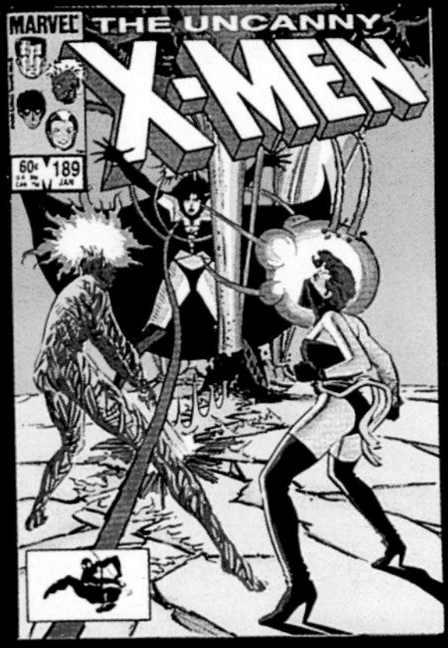
MARVEL
THE UNCANNY
X-MEN
189

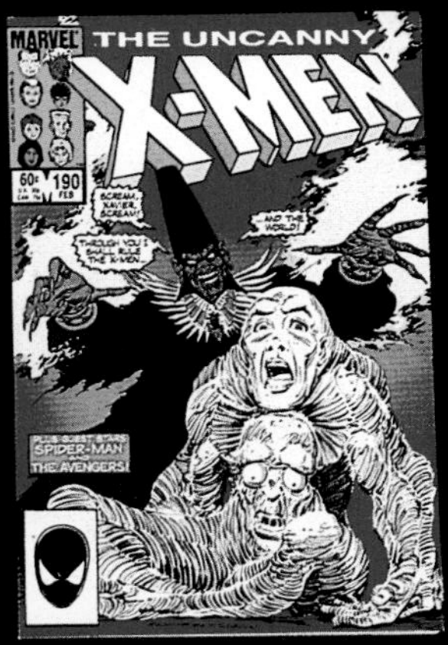
MARVEL
THE UNCANNY
X-MEN
190
SPIDER-MAN
THE AVENGERS!

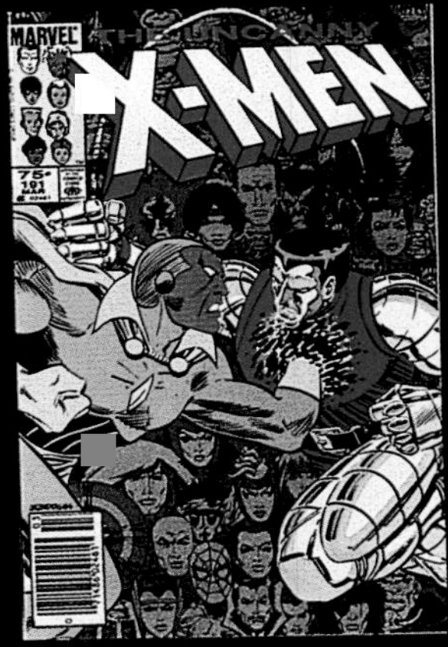
MARVEL
X-MEN
191

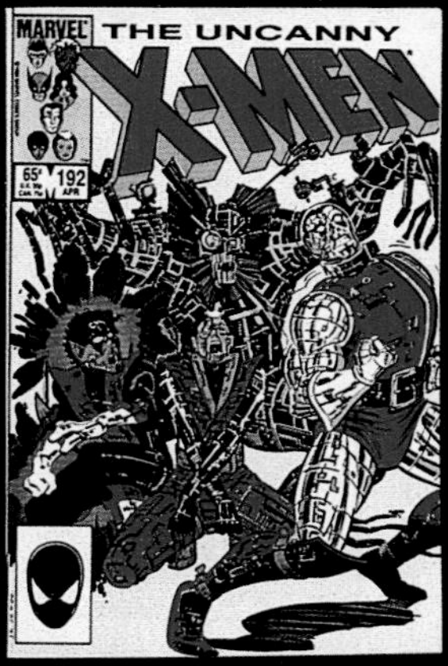
MARVEL
THE UNCANNY
X-MEN
192

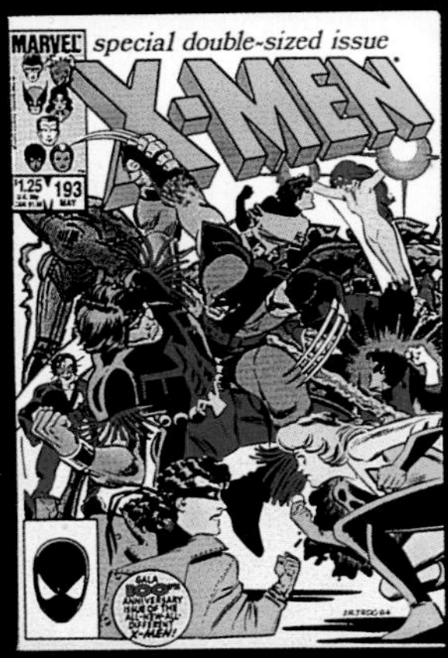
MARVEL
special double-sized issue
X-MEN
193

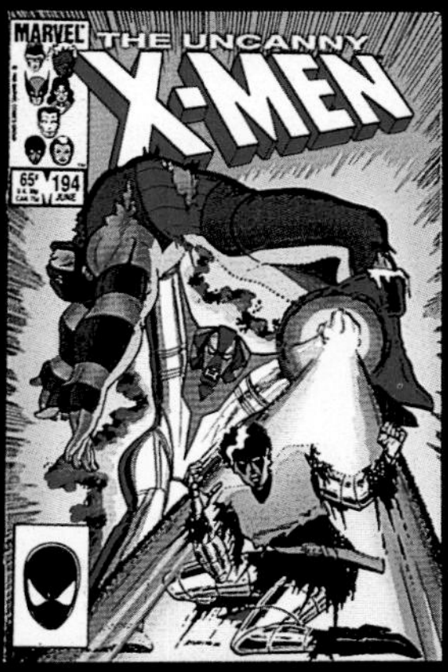
MARVEL
THE UNCANNY
X-MEN
194

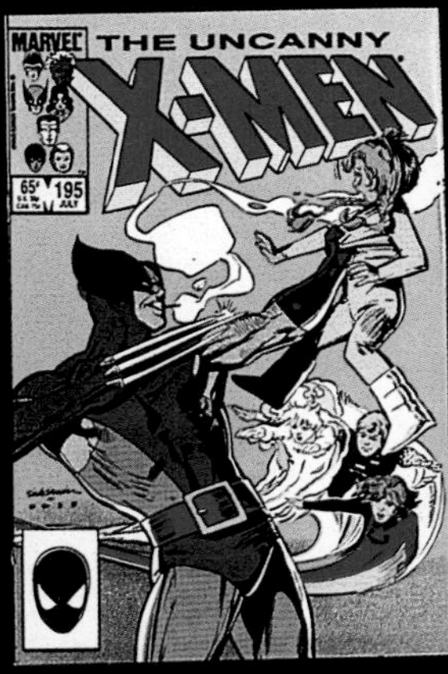
MARVEL
THE UNCANNY
X-MEN
195

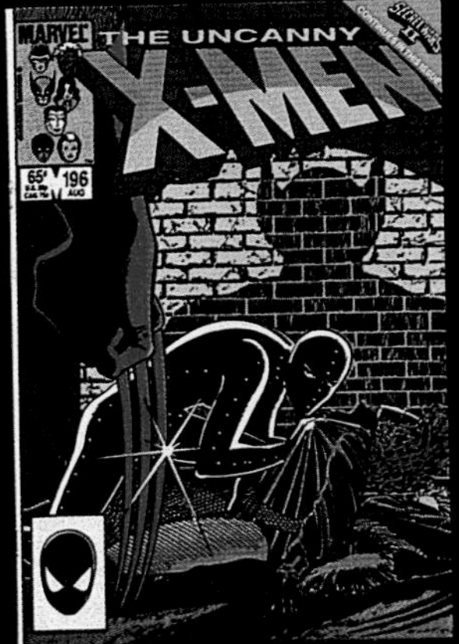
MARVEL
THE UNCANNY
X-MEN
196

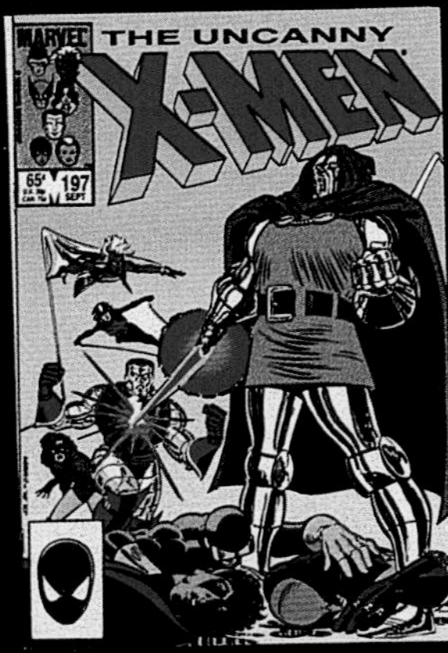
MARVEL
THE UNCANNY
X-MEN
197

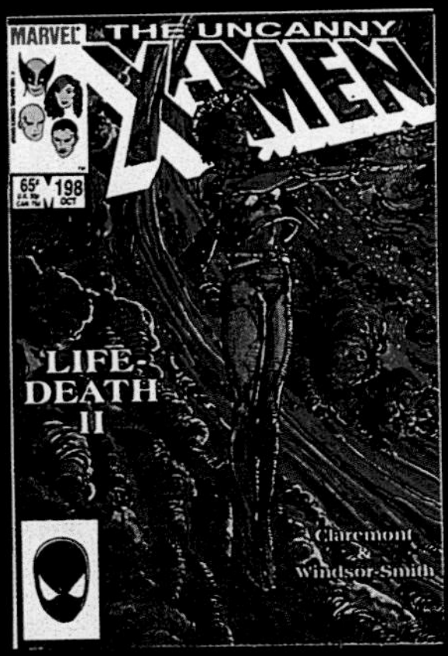
MARVEL
THE UNCANNY
X-MEN
198
LIFE-DEATH II
Claremont
&
Windsor-Smith

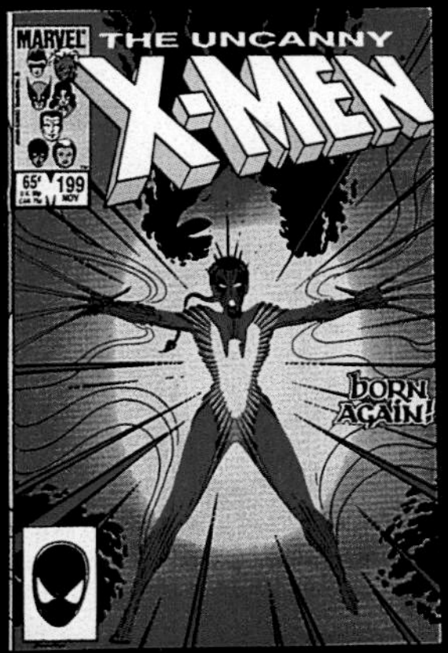
MARVEL
THE UNCANNY
X-MEN
199
BORN AGAIN!

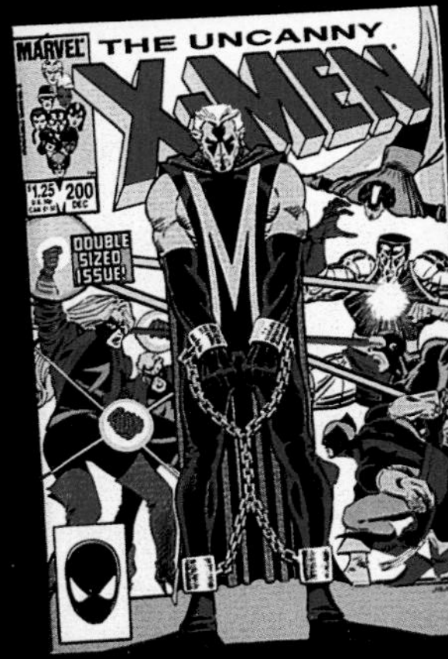
MARVEL
THE UNCANNY
X-MEN
200
DOUBLE SIZED ISSUE!

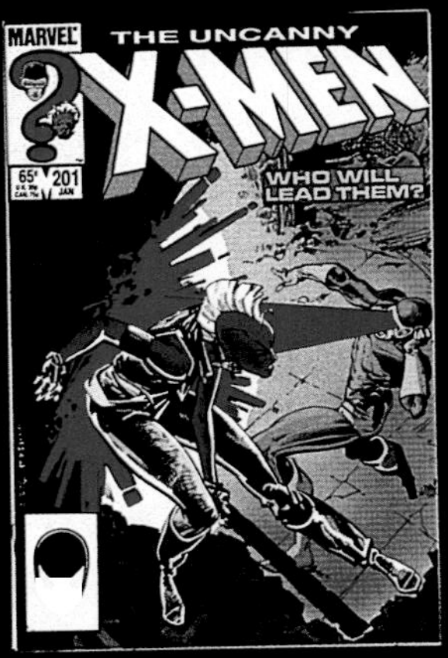
MARVEL
THE UNCANNY
X-MEN
201
WHO WILL LEAD THEM?

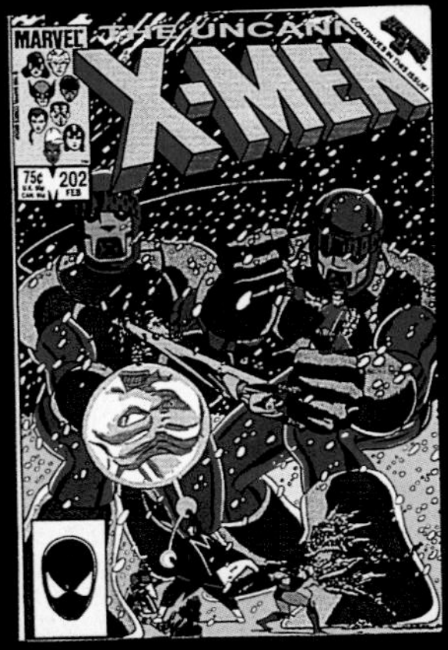
MARVEL
THE UNCANNY
X-MEN
202
PHOENIX VERSUS THE BEYONDER!

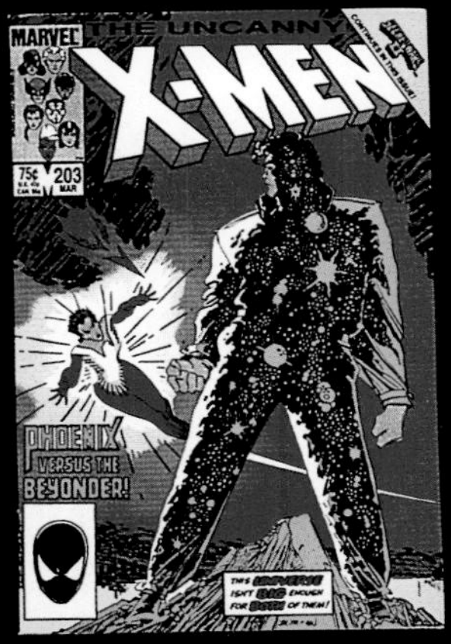
MARVEL
THE UNCANNY
X-MEN
203

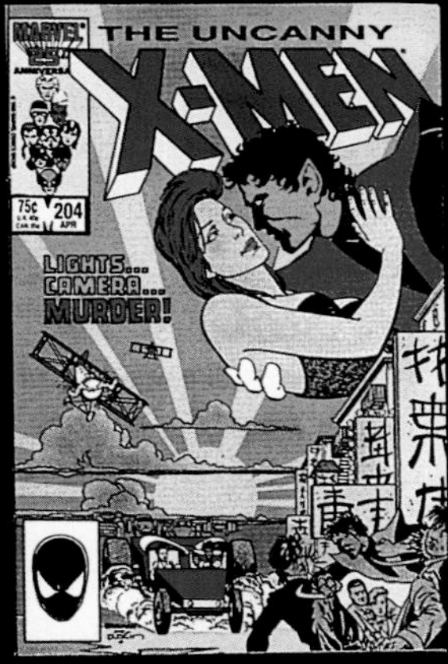
MARVEL
THE UNCANNY
X-MEN
204
LIGHTS... CAMERA... MURDER!

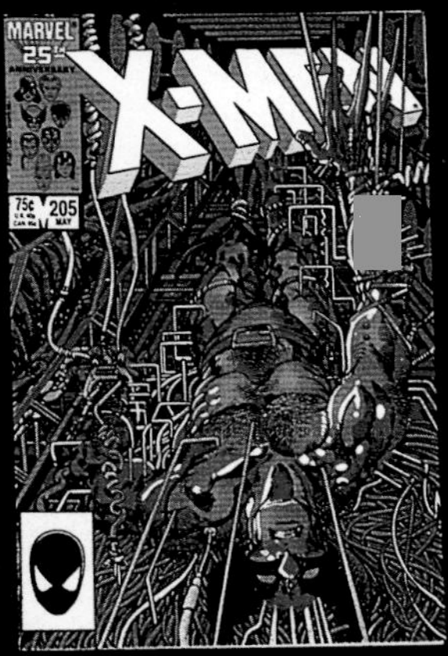
MARVEL
X-MEN
205

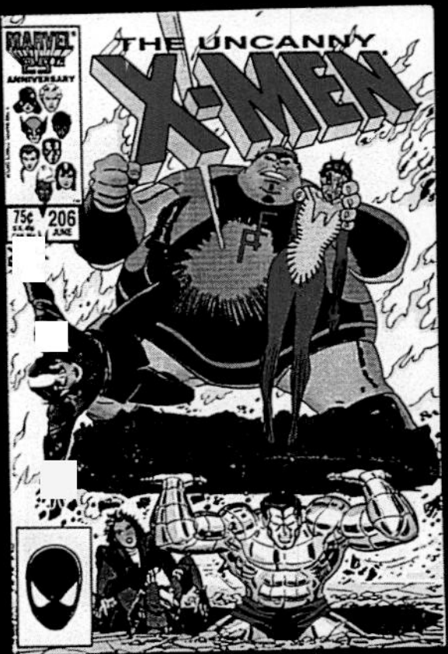
MARVEL
THE UNCANNY
X-MEN
206

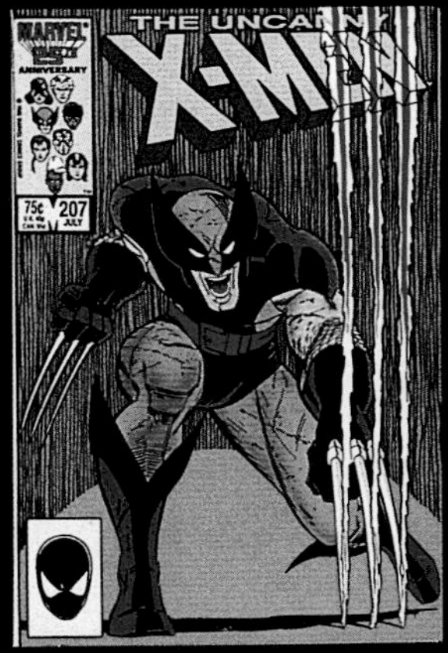
MARVEL
X-MEN
207

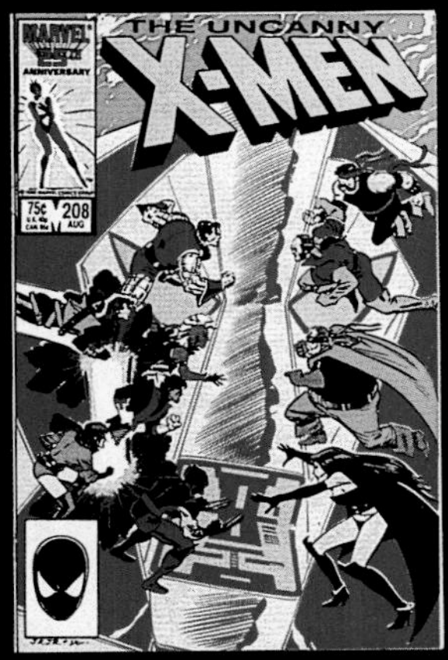
MARVEL
THE UNCANNY
X-MEN
208

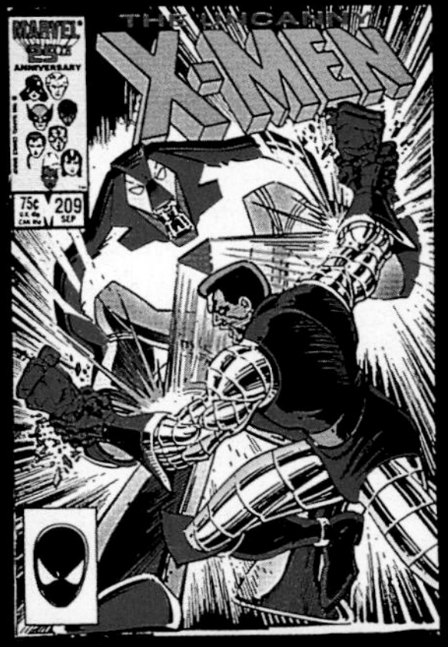
MARVEL
X-MEN
209

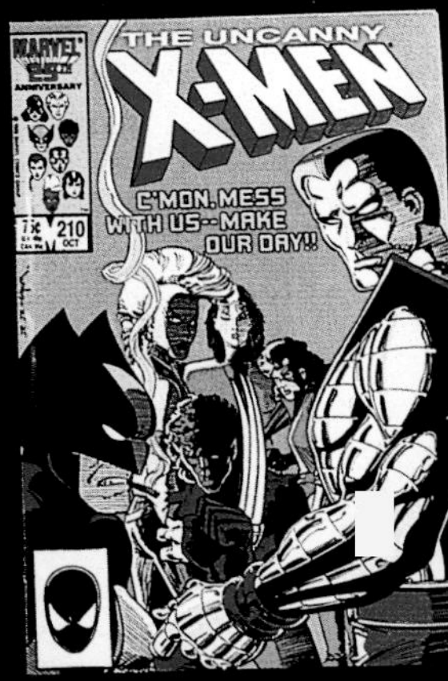
MARVEL
THE UNCANNY
X-MEN
210
C'MON, MESS WITH US-- MAKE OUR DAY!!

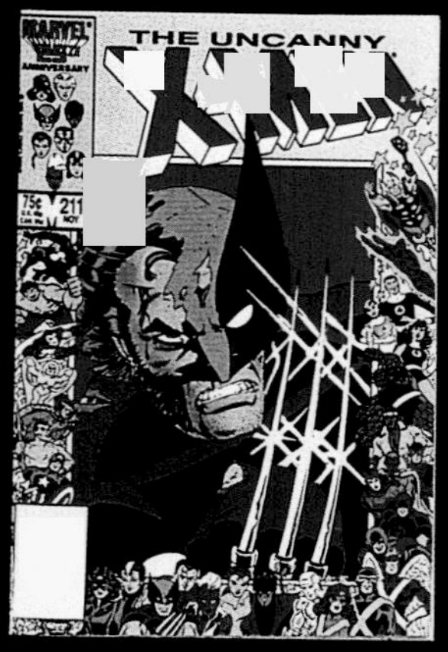
MARVEL
THE UNCANNY
75¢
211

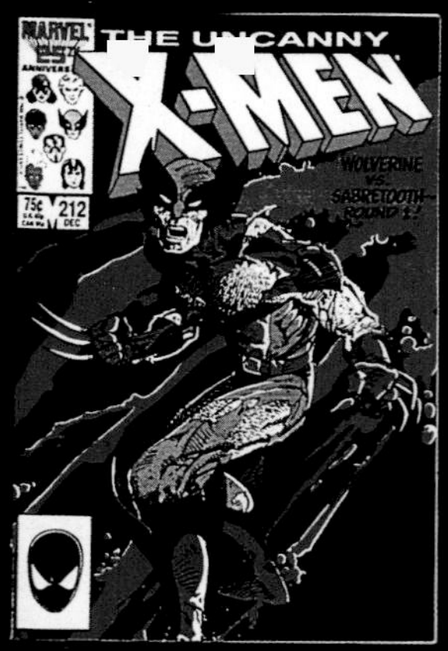
MARVEL
THE UNCANNY
X-MEN
75¢
212
DEC
WOLVERINE
vs.
SABRETOOTH
ROUND 2!

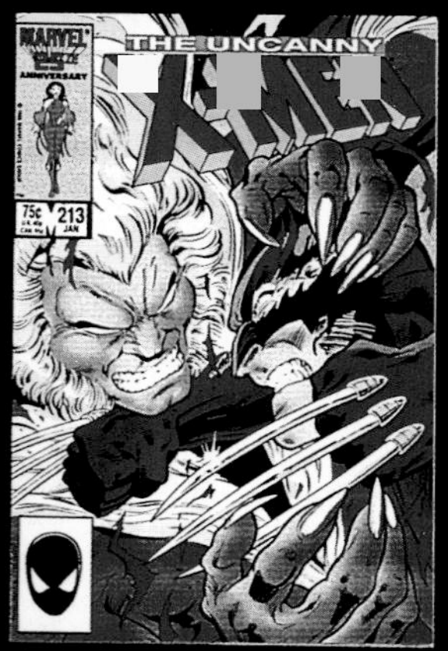
MARVEL
THE UNCANNY
75¢
213
JAN

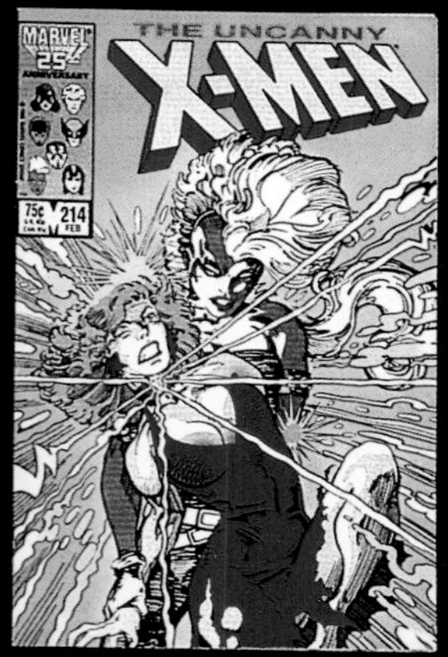
MARVEL
25
THE UNCANNY
X-MEN
75¢
214
FEB

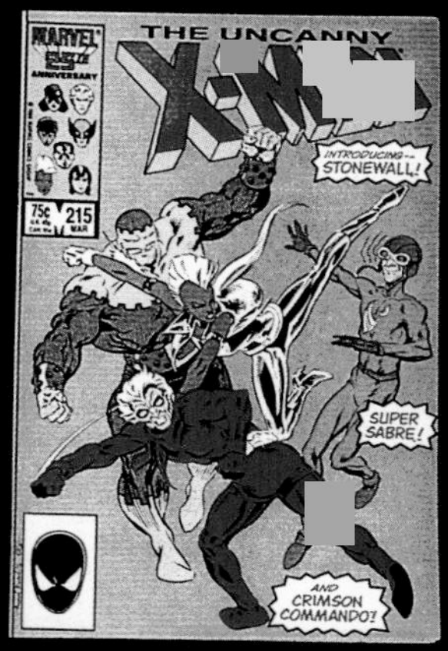
MARVEL
THE UNCANNY
75¢
215
MAR
INTRODUCING
STONEWALL!
SUPER SABRE!
AND CRIMSON COMMANDO!

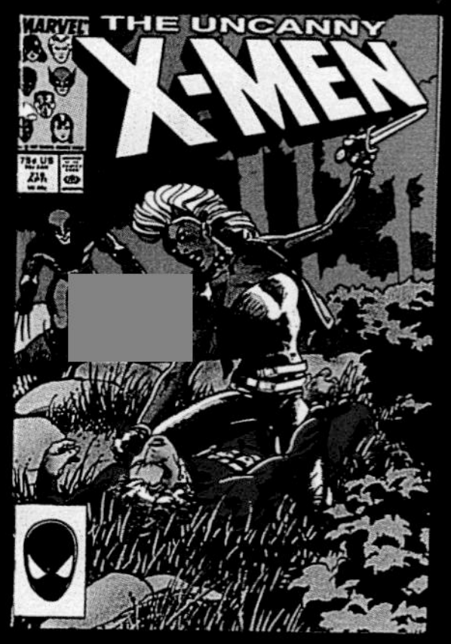
MARVEL
THE UNCANNY
X-MEN

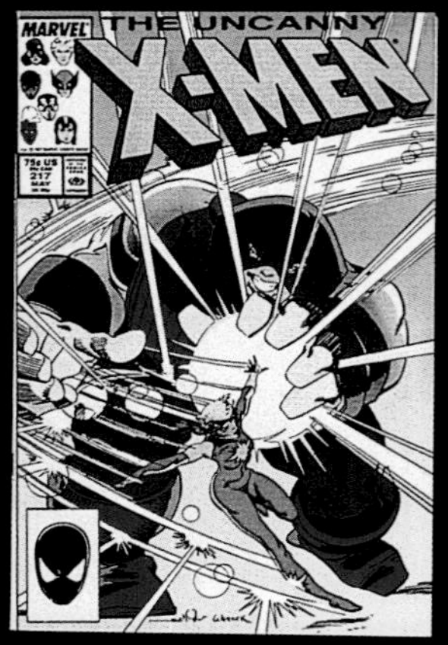
MARVEL
THE UNCANNY
X-MEN
75¢ US
217

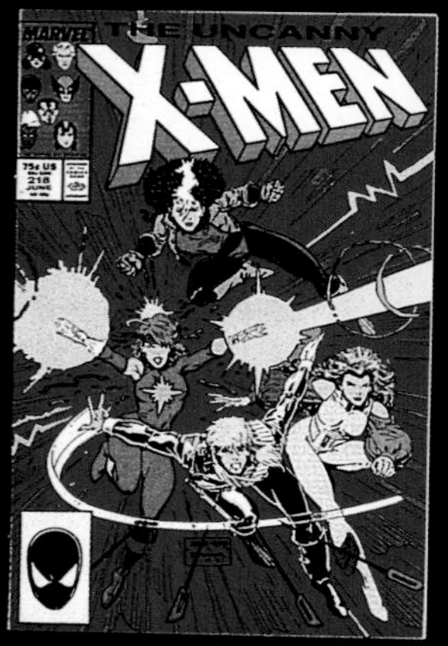
MARVEL
THE UNCANNY
X-MEN
75¢ US
218

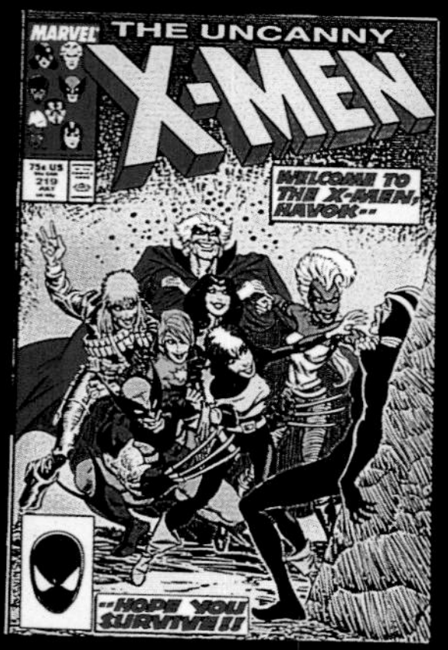
MARVEL
THE UNCANNY
X-MEN
75¢ US
219
WELCOME TO THE X-MEN, HAVOK--
--HOPE YOU SURVIVE!!

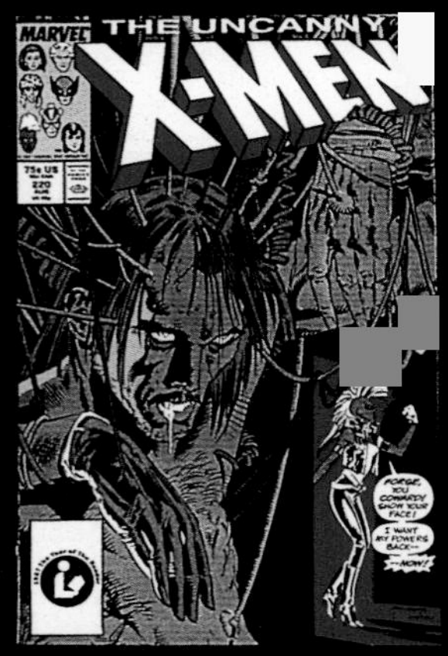
MARVEL
THE UNCANNY
X-MEN
75¢ US
220

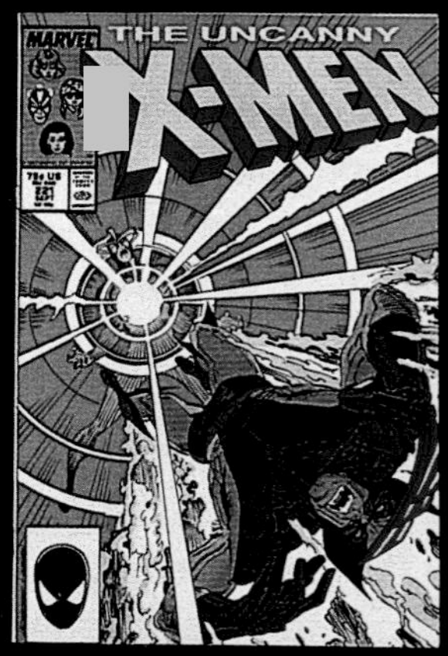
MARVEL
THE UNCANNY
X-MEN
75¢ US
221

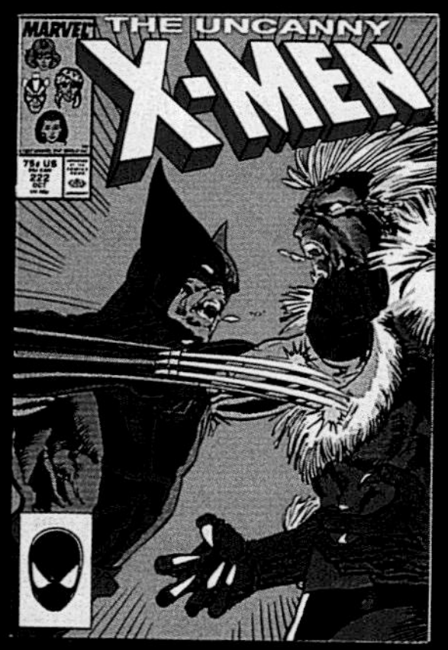
MARVEL
THE UNCANNY
X-MEN
75¢ US
222

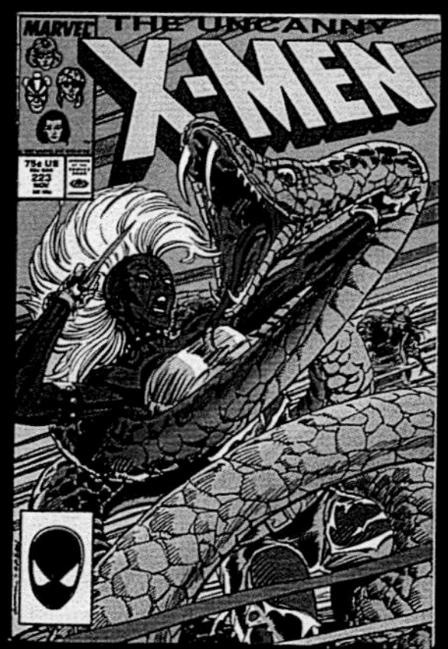
MARVEL
THE UNCANNY
X-MEN
75¢ US
223

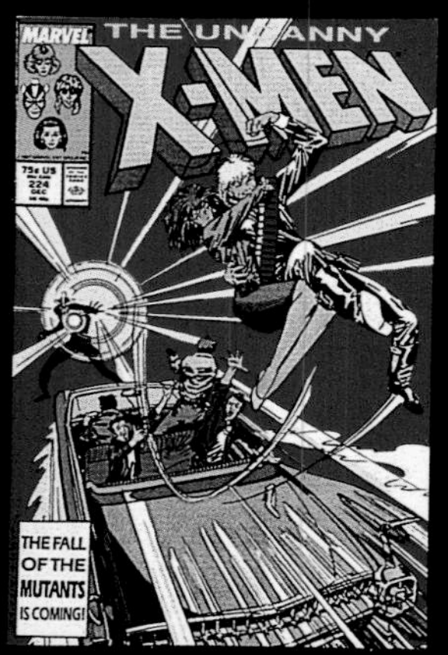
MARVEL
THE UNCANNY
X-MEN
75¢ US
224
THE FALL OF THE MUTANTS IS COMING!

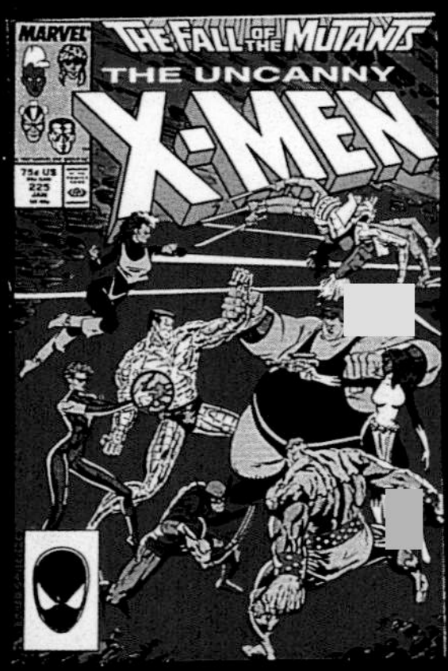
MARVEL
THE FALL OF THE MUTANTS
THE UNCANNY
X-MEN
75¢ US
225

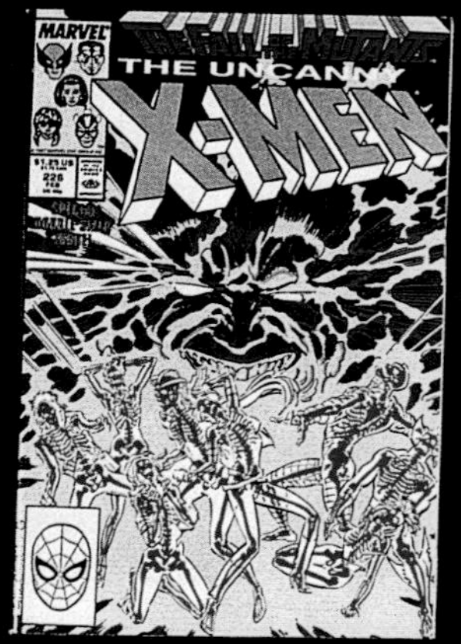
MARVEL
THE UNCANNY
X-MEN
$1.25 US
226

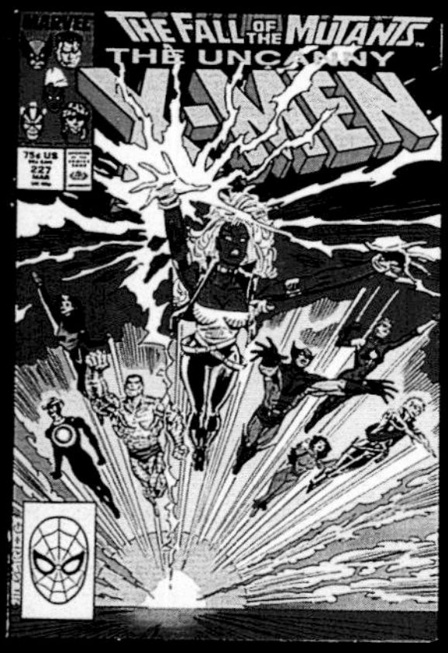
MARVEL
THE FALL OF THE MUTANTS
THE UNCANNY
X-MEN
75¢ US
227

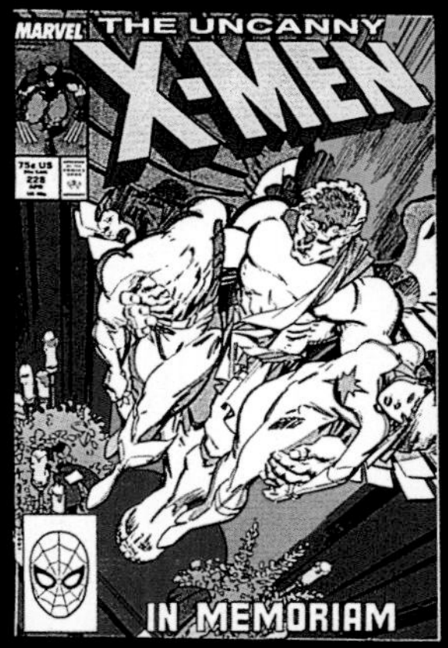
MARVEL
THE UNCANNY
X-MEN
75¢ US
228
IN MEMORIAM

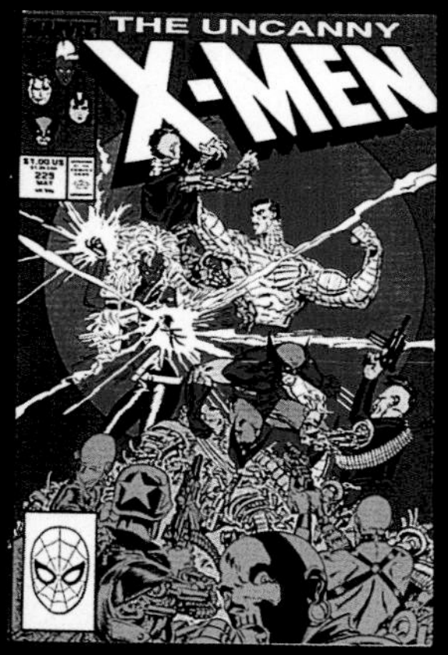
MARVEL
THE UNCANNY
X-MEN
$1.00 US
229

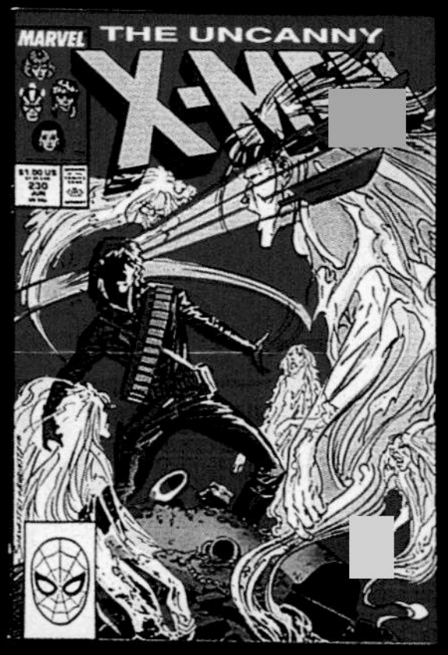
MARVEL
THE UNCANNY
X-MEN
$1.00 US
230

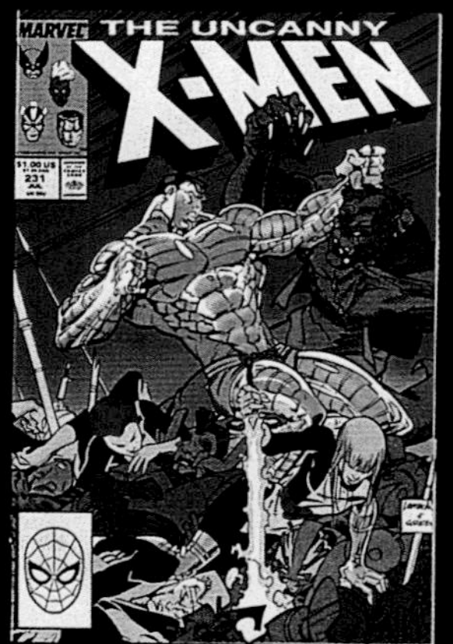
MARVEL
THE UNCANNY
X-MEN
$1.00 US
231

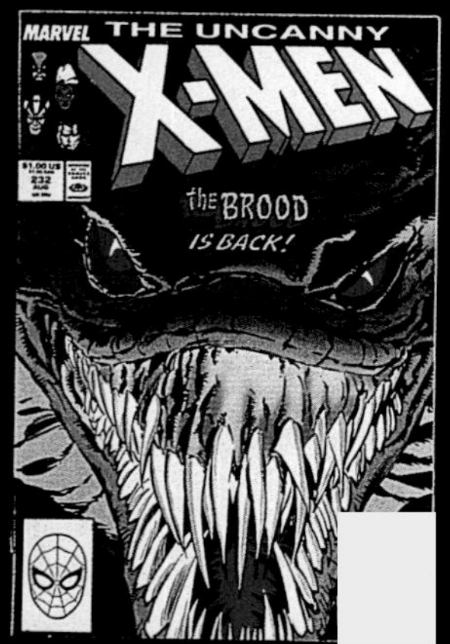
MARVEL
THE UNCANNY
X-MEN
$1.00 US
232
The BROOD IS BACK!

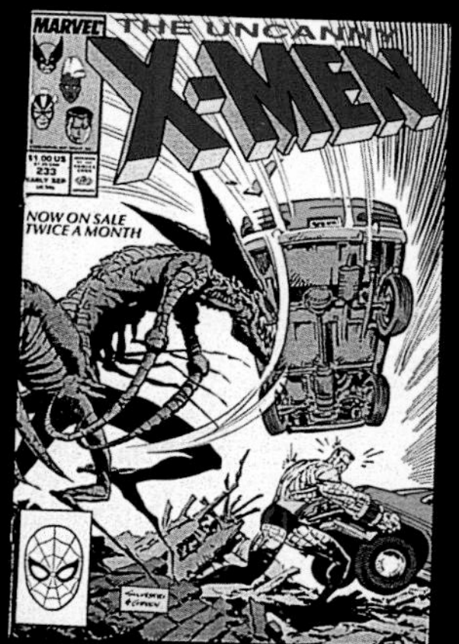
MARVEL
THE UNCANNY
X-MEN
$1.00 US
233
NOW ON SALE TWICE A MONTH

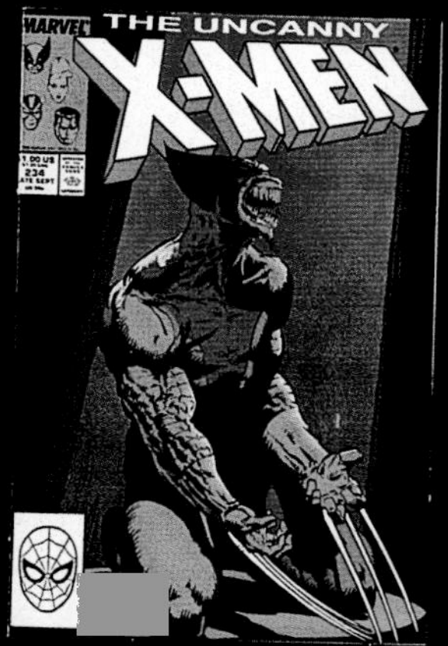
MARVEL
THE UNCANNY
X-MEN
$1.00 US
234

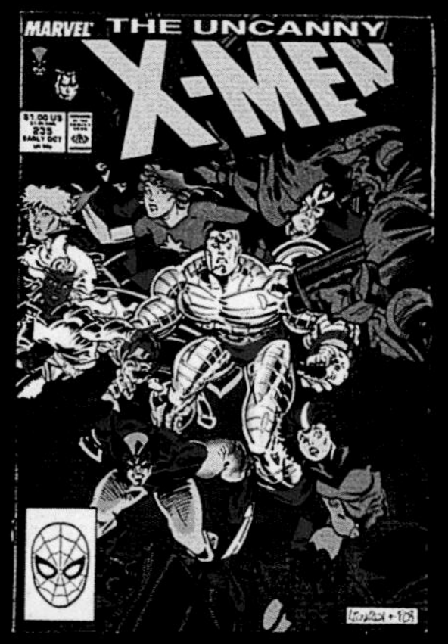
MARVEL
THE UNCANNY
X-MEN
$1.00 US
235

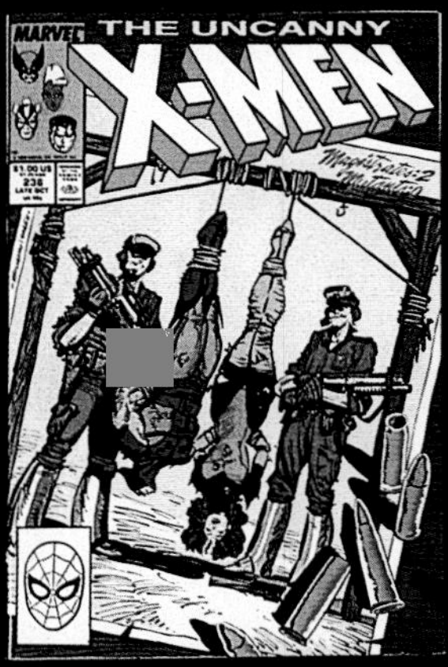
THE UNCANNY
X-MEN
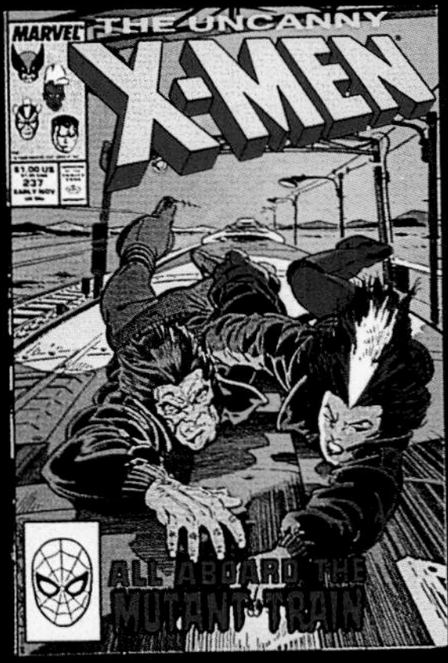
THE UNCANNY
X-MEN
ALL ABOARD THE MUTANT TRAIN
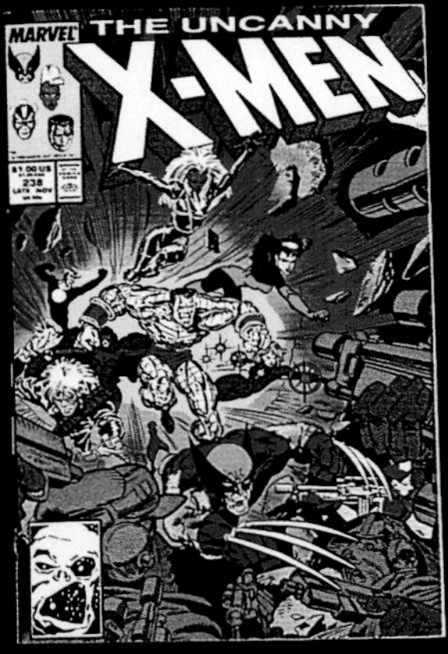
THE UNCANNY
X-MEN
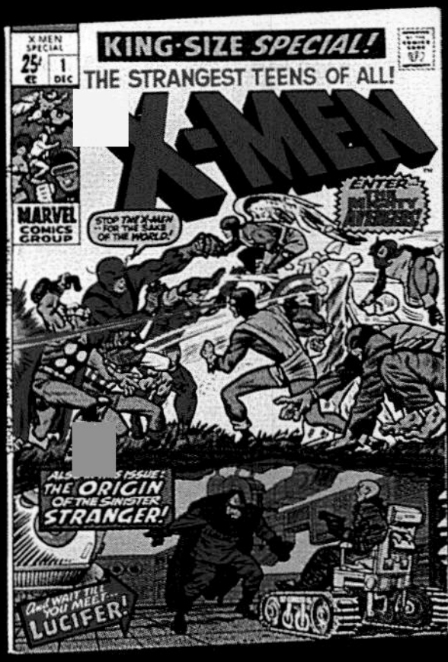
KING-SIZE SPECIAL!
THE STRANGEST TEENS OF ALL!
X-MEN
THE ORIGIN OF THE SINISTER STRANGER!
LUCIFER!
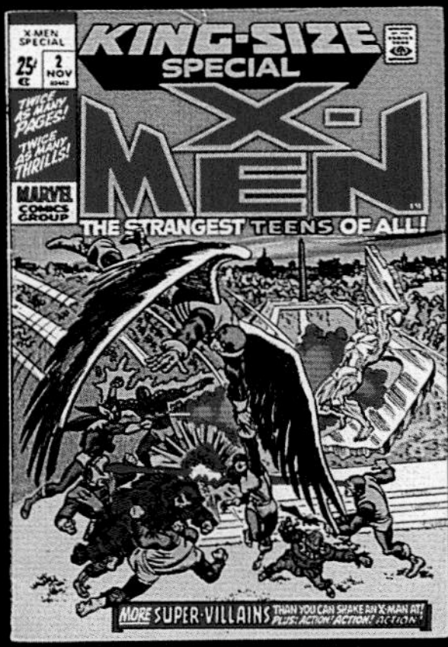
KING-SIZE SPECIAL
X-MEN
THE STRANGEST TEENS OF ALL!
MORE SUPER-VILLAINS
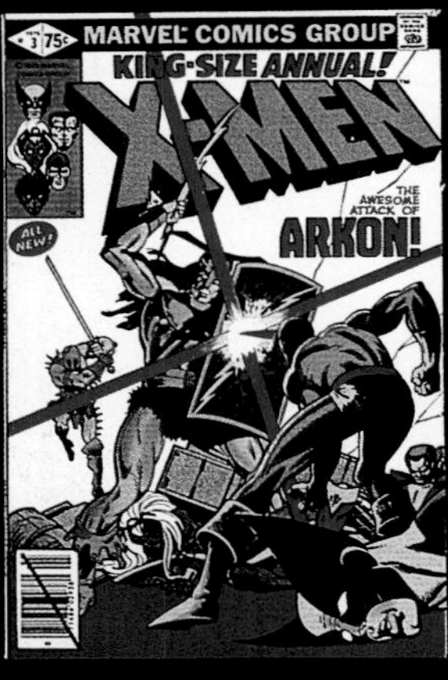
MARVEL COMICS GROUP
KING-SIZE ANNUAL!
X-MEN
THE AWESOME ATTACK OF ARKON!
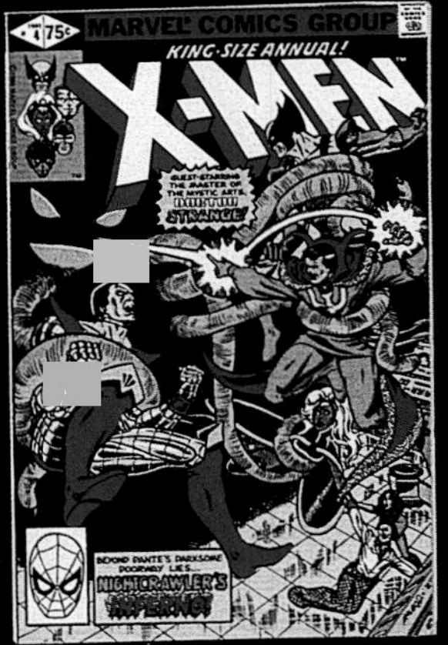
MARVEL COMICS GROUP
KING-SIZE ANNUAL!
X-MEN
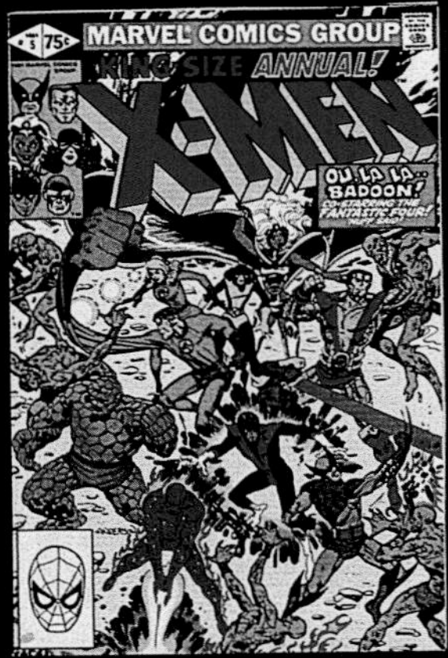
MARVEL COMICS GROUP
KING-SIZE ANNUAL!
X-MEN
OO LA LA! BADOON!
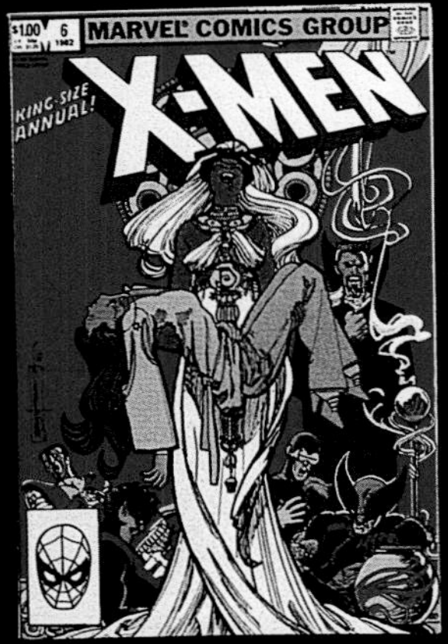
MARVEL COMICS GROUP
KING-SIZE ANNUAL!
X-MEN
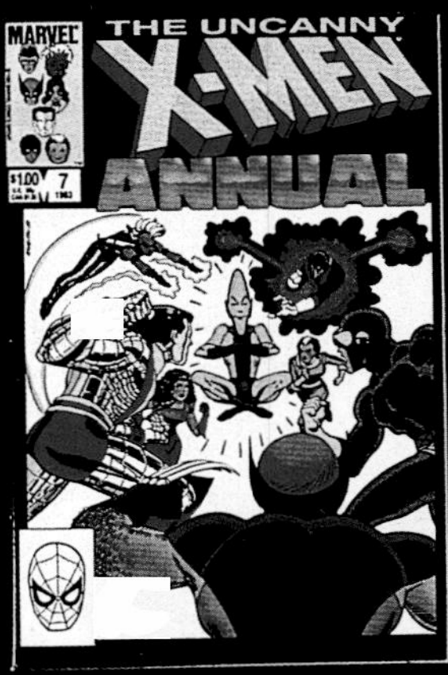
THE UNCANNY
X-MEN
ANNUAL
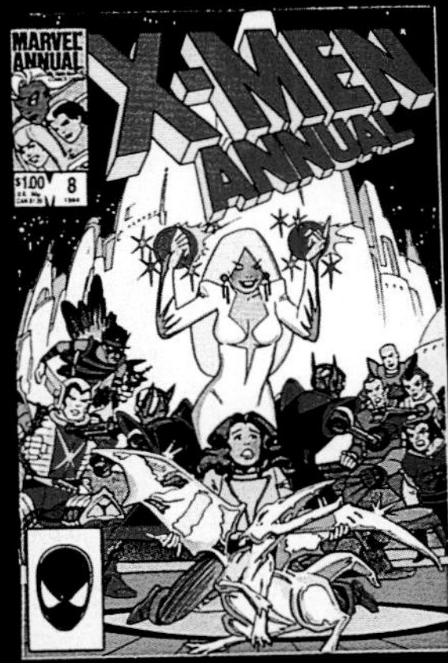
X-MEN
ANNUAL
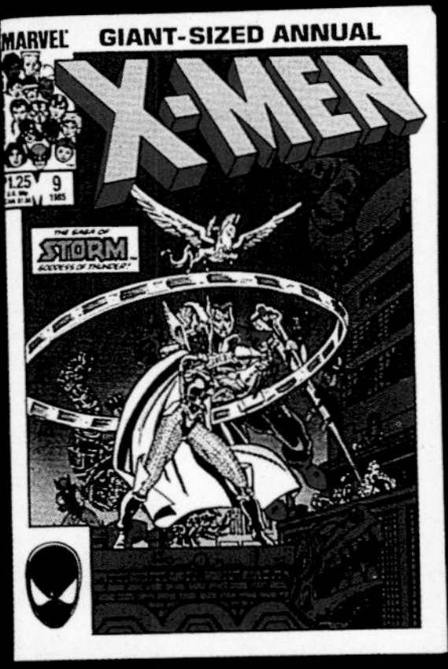
GIANT-SIZED ANNUAL
X-MEN
STORM
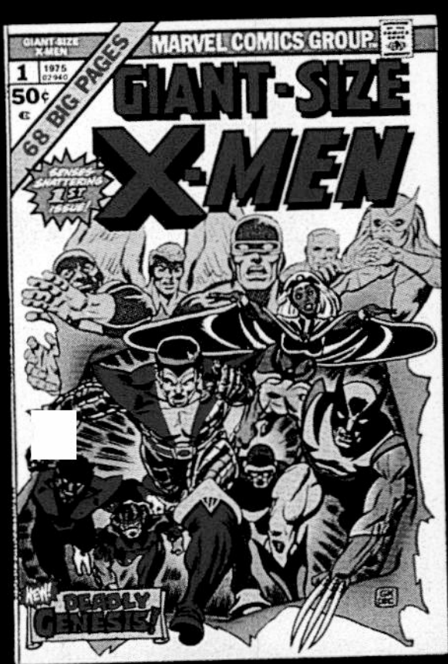
MARVEL COMICS GROUP
GIANT-SIZE
X-MEN
68 BIG PAGES
DEADLY GENESIS!
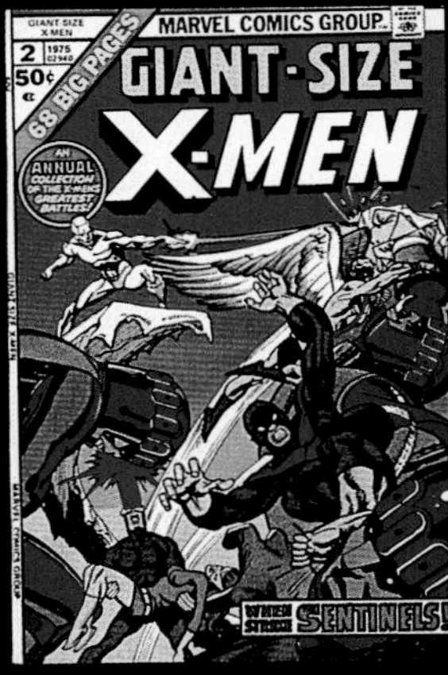
MARVEL COMICS GROUP
GIANT-SIZE
X-MEN
68 BIG PAGES
WHEN STRIKE THE SENTINELS!
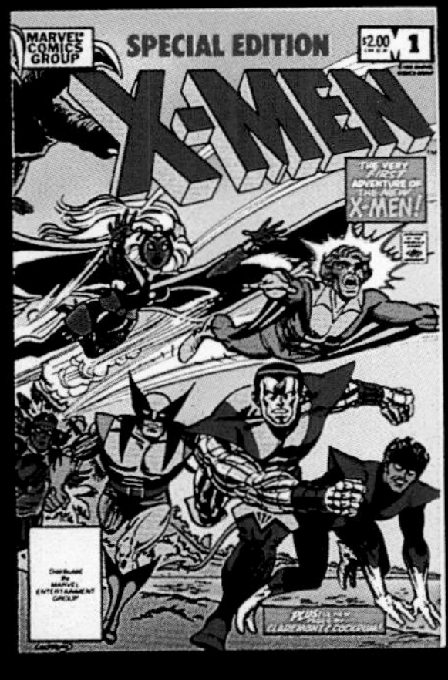
SPECIAL EDITION
X-MEN

The X-Men (1-Present) 2206

Ref. No.	Date	RVI	Artist/Info.
2206-1	Sept. 1963	935	Kirby/Brodsky-c, Kirby/Reinman-a; Publ. 7/2/63 (Origin X-Man)
2206-2	Nov.	340	Kirby/Reinman-c/a; Publ. 9/3/63 (1st Vanisher)
2206-3	Jan. 1964	165	Kirby/Brodsky-c, Kirby/Reinman-a; Publ. 11/5/63
2206-4	Mar.	145	Kirby/Reinman-c/a (Intro. Quicksilver); Publ. 1/3/64
2206-5	May	110	Kirby/Reinman-c/a; Publ. 3/3/64
2206-6	Jul.	80	Kirby/Stone-c/a; Publ. 5/5/64
2206-7	Sept.	75	Kirby/Stone-c/a; Publ. 7/2/64
2206-8	Nov.	71	Kirby/Stone-c/a; Publ. 9/1/64 (1st Unus)
2206-9	Jan. 1965	71	Kirby/Stone-c/a; Publ. 11/3/64
2206-10	**Mar.**	**71**	**Kirby/Stone-c/a (Intro. Ka-Zar and Zabu); Publ. 1/5/65**
2206-11	May	45	Kirby/Stone-c/a (Intro. the Stranger); Publ. 3/4/65
2206-12	Jul.	50	Kirby/Giacoia-c, Kirby, Toth-a (Origin Prof. X)
2206-13	Sept.	45	Kirby/Sinnott-c, Kirby, Gavin-a
2206-14	Nov.	45	Kirby/Wood-c, Kirby, Gavin-a (Origin-Angel); Publ. 9/2/65
2206-15	Dec.	45	Kirby/Ayers-c/a, Kirby-a (Origin-the Beast)
2206-16	Jan. 1966	45	" " "
2206-17	Feb.	35	" " "
2206-18	Mar.	35	Kirby/Ayers-c, Gavin/Ayers-a
2206-19	Apr.	35	" " " " (Intro. the Mimic); Publ. 2/3/66
2206-20	**May**	**35**	**" " " " (Origin-Prof. X)**
2206-21	Jun.	25	" " " "
2206-22	Jul.	25	" " " "
2206-23	Aug.	25	Roth/Ayers-c/a
2206-24	Sept.	25	Kirby/Ayers-c, Roth/Ayers-a
2206-25	Oct.	25	Kirby/Ayers-c, Roth/Ayers-a (Intro. El Tigre)
2206-26	Nov.	25	Roth/Ayers-c, Roth/Ayers-a
2206-27	Dec.	25	Roth/Brodsky-c, Roth/Ayers-a (Intro. the Defender)
2206-28	Jan. 1967	30	Roth/Tartaglione-c, Roth/Ayers-a (Intro. the Ogre, Banshee)
2206-29	Feb.	25	Roth/Tartaglione-c/a
2206-30	**Mar.**	**25**	**Kirby/Targaglione-c, Sparling/Tartaglione-a (Intro. the Warlock)**
2206-31	Apr.	20	Kirby/Adkins-c, Roth/Tartaglione-a (Intro. the Cobalt Man)
2206-32	May	18	Roth/Giacoia-c, Roth/Tartaglione-a
2206-33	Jun.	18	Kane/Tartaglione-c, Roth/Tartaglione-a (Dr. Strange -app.)
2206-34	Jul.	18	Adkins-c/a
2206-35	Aug.	25	Adkins-c/a, Roth-a (Intro. The Changeling; Spider-Man -app.)
2206-36	Sept.	15	Andru/Giacoia-c, Andru/Bell-a
2206-37	Oct.	15	Heck/Giacoia-c, Andru/Heck-a (Intro. Mutant Master)
2206-38	Nov.	15	Adkins-c, Heck/Bell-a (Origins of X-Men begin)
2206-39	Dec.	15	Tuska-c, Heck/Colletta-a
2206-40	**Jan. 1968**	**15**	**Tuska-c/a, Heck, Roth/Verpoorten-a**
2206-41	Feb.	15	" " " "
2206-42	Mar.	15	Buscema-a, Heck, Roth/Tuska, Trimpe-a
2206-43	Apr.	15	Buscema/Tartaglione-c, Tuska, Roth/Tartaglione, Verpoorten-a
2206-44	May	15	Heck/Tartaglione-c, Tuska, Roth/Tartaglione, Verpoorten-a
2206-45	Jun.	15	Buscema/Verpoorten-c, Tuska, Roth/Tartaglione, Verpoorten-a
2206-46	Jul.	15	" " " " " "
2206-47	Aug.	15	Heck/Giacoia-c, Heck, Roth/Tartaglione, Verpoorten-a
2206-48	Sept.	15	Romita/Giacoia-c, Heck, Roth/Verpoorten-a
2206-49	Oct.	15	Steranko-c, Heck, Roth/Verpoorten-a; Publ. 8/13/68
2206-50	**Nov.**	**18**	**Steranko-c/a, Roth/Tartaglione, Verpoorten-a**
2206-51	Dec.	18	Steranko-c/a, Roth/Tartaglione-a
2206-52	Jan. 1969	12	M. Severin/Sinnott-c, Heck, Roth/Tartaglione, Verpoorten-a
2206-53	Feb.	20	B. Smith/Esposito-c, Smith, Roth/M. Dee, Tartaglione-a
2206-54	Mar.	14	B. Smith/Colletta-c, Heck, Roth/Colletta-a (Origin-the Angel)
2206-55	Apr.	14	B. Smith/Colletta-c, Heck, Roth/Colletta, Grainger-a
2206-56	May	20	Adams-c/a, Roth/Palmer, Grainger-a
2206-57	Jun.	20	Adams-c/a, Roth/Palmer, Grainger-a
2206-58	Jul.	20	Adams-c/a, Palmer-a (Intro. Havok); Publ. 4/15/69
2206-59	Aug.	20	Adams-c/a, Palmer-a
2206-60	**Sept.**	**20**	**" "**
2206-61	Oct.	20	" "
2206-62	Nov.	20	" "
2206-63	Dec.	20	Adams/Palmer-c/a
2206-64	Jan. 1970	15	Heck/Palmer-c/a (Intro. and Origin-Sunfire); Publ. 10/21/69
2206-65	Feb.	20	M. Severin/Palmer-c, Adams/Palmer-a
2206-66	Mar.	12	M. Severin/Grainger-c, Buscema/Grainger-a
2206-67	Dec.	8	M. Severin/Sinnott-c Reprints X-Men 12, 13
2206-68	Feb. 1971	8	Cover of X-Men #15 redone " " 14, 15
2206-69	Apr.	8	Buscema-c " " 16, 19
2206-70	**Jun.**	**8**	**Cover of X-Men #17 redone " " 17, 18**
2206-71	Aug.	8	Cover of X-Men #20 redone " " 20
2206-72	Oct.	8	Cover of X-Men #21 redone " " 21, 24
2206-73	Dec.	8	Everett-c " " 25
2206-74	Feb. 1972	8	Kane/Giacoia-c " " 26
2206-75	Apr.	8	Kane/Romita-c " " 27
2206-76	Jun.	8	Kane/Sinnott-c " " 28
2206-77	Aug.	8	Tuska/Colletta-c " " 29
2206-78	Oct.	8	Tuska/Sinnott-c " " 30
2206-79	Dec.	8	Kane/Giacoia-c " " 31
2206-80	**Feb. 1973**	**8**	**" " " " 32**
2206-81	Apr.	8	Cover of X-Men #33 redone " " 33
2206-82	Jun.	8	Cover of X-Men #34 redone " " 34
2206-83	Aug.	8	Cover of X-Men #35 redone " " 35
2206-84	Oct.	8	Cover of X-Men #36 redone " " 36
2206-85	Dec.	8	Cover of X-Men #37 redone " " 37
2206-86	Feb. 1974	8	Cover of X-Men #38 redone " " 38
2206-87	Apr.	8	Cover of X-Men #39 redone " " 39
2206-88	Jun.	8	Cover of X-Men #40 redone " " 40 Venus #16
2206-89	Aug.	8	M. Severin/Giacoia-c " " 41
2206-90	**Oct.**	**8**	**Cover of X-Men #42 redone " " 42**
2206-91	Dec.	8	Cover of X-Men #43 redone " " 43
2206-92	Feb. 1975	8	Wildon/Esposito-c " " 44
2206-93	Apr.	8	Cover of X-Men #45 redone " " 45
2206-94	Aug.	95	Kane/Cockrum-c, Cockrum/McLeod-a (New X-Men begins)
2206-95	Oct.	32	Kane/Cockrum-c, Cockrum/Grainger-a
2206-96	Dec.	21	M. Severin/Buscema-c, Cockrum/Grainger-a
2206-97	Feb. 1976	21	Buckler/Cockrum-c, Cockrum/Grainger-a
2206-98	Apr.	21	Cockrum-c/a, Grainger-a (Wolverine -app. out of Costume)
2206-99	Jun.	21	Cockrum-c/a, Chiaramonte-a
2206-100	**Aug.**	**25**	**Cockrum-c/a**
2206-101	Oct.	21	Cockrum-c/a, Chiaramonte-a (Intro. the Phoenix)
2206-102	Dec.	14	Cockrum-c/a, Grainger-a (Origin-Storm)
2206-103	Feb.	10	Cockrum-c/a, Grainger-a
2206-104	Apr.	10	" "
2206-105	Jun.	10	Cockrum-c/a, Layton-a
2206-106	Aug.	10	Cockrum-c/a, Brown-a
2206-107	Oct.	10	Cockrum-c/a, Green-a (Intro. Gladiator)
2206-108	Dec.	25	Cockrum-c, Byrne/Austin-a (Origin-Cyclops, Havok)
2206-109	Feb. 1978	20	Cockrum/Austin-c, Byrne/Austin-a
2206-110	**Apr.**	**11**	**Cockrum/Austin-c, Cockrum, DeZuniga-a**
2206-111	Jun.	11	Cockrum/Austin-c, Byrne/Austin-a
2206-112	Aug.	9	Perez/Layton-c, Byrne/Austin-a
2206-113	Sept.	9	Byrne/Layton-c, Byrne/Austin-a
2206-114	Oct.	9	Byrne/Austin-c/a
2206-115	Nov.	9	Byrne/Austin-c/a ("The Uncanny X-Men")
2206-116	Dec.	9	Byrne/Austin-c/a
2206-117	Jan. 1979	9	Cockrum/Austin-c, Byrne/Austin-a
2206-118	Feb.	9	Cockrum/Austin-c, Byrne/Villamonte-a
2206-119	Mar.	9	Cockrum/Austin-c, Byrne/Austin-a
2206-120	**Apr.**	**25**	**Budianski/Austin-c, Byrne/Austin-a (Intro. Alpha Flight)**
2206-121	May	25	Cockrum/Austin-c, Byrne/Austin-a
2206-122	Jun.	9	Cockrum/Austin-c, Byrne/Austin-a (Origin-Colossus)
2206-123	Jul.	9	Austin-c, Byrne, Austin-a
2206-124	Aug.	9	Cockrum/Austin-c, Byrne/Austin-a
2206-125	Sept.	9	" " " "
2206-126	Oct.	9	" " " "
2206-127	Nov.	9	Byrne/Austin-c/a
2206-128	Dec.	9	Perez/Austin-c, Byrne/Austin-a
2206-129	Jan. 1980	9	Byrne/Austin-c/a (Intro. Kitty Pryde)
2206-130	**Feb.**	**10**	**Romita/Austin-c, Byrne/Austin-a (Intro. Dazzler)**
2206-131	Mar.	6	Byrne/Austin-c/a
2206-132	Apr.	6	Byrne/Austin-c/a
2206-133	May	6	" "
2206-134	Jun.	6	" "
2206-135	Jul.	6	" "
2206-136	Aug.	6	" "
2206-137	Sept.	10	" " (Double-size issue)
2206-138	Oct.	6	" "
2206-139 to 141	Jan. 1981, (#141)	11	(#140, Alpha Flight -app.)
2206-142 tp 171		4	(#165-175, P. Smith-a; Title change, Uncanny X-Men)
2206-172 to 209		2	(#175, 186, 193, 200 Double-size issues)
2206-210 to 213		9	(Mutant Massacre)
2206-214 to 224		1	
2206-225 to 227		4	(Mutants destroyed)
2206-228 to 258		1	(#253), New X-Men begin)
2206-SP1	Dec. 1970	15	Cover of X-Men #9 redone Reprints X-Men #9, 11
2206-SP2	Nov. 1971	10	M. Severin/Verpoorten-c Reprints #22, 23

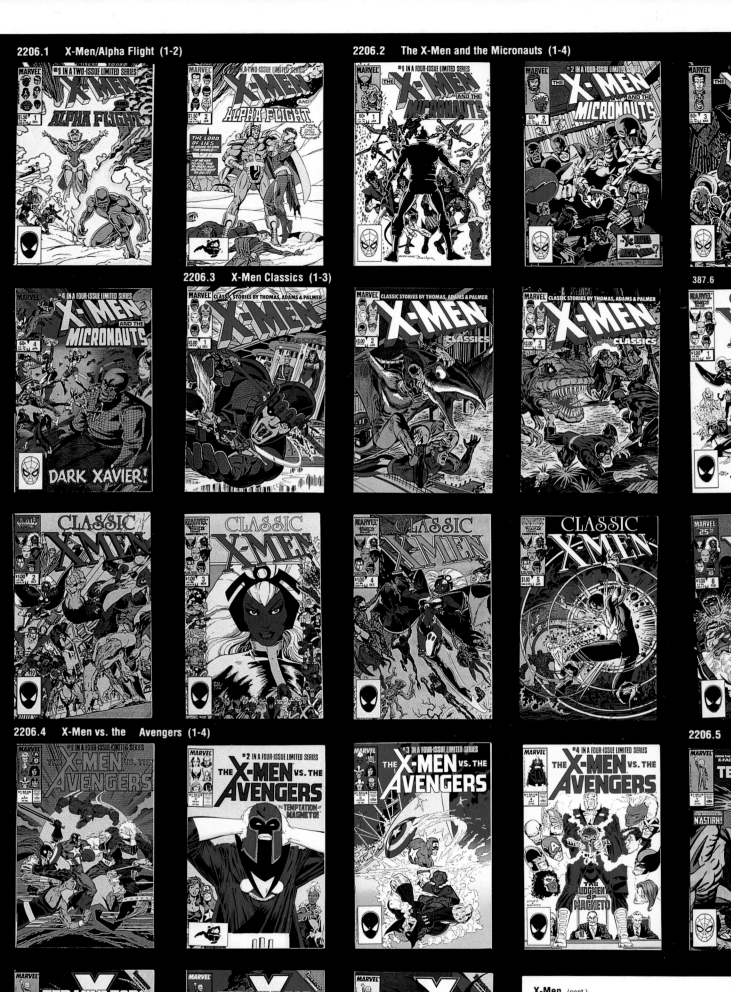

2206.1 X-Men/Alpha Flight (1-2)

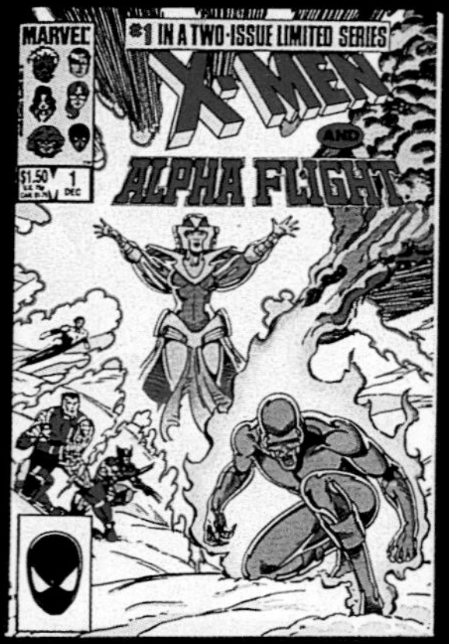
MARVEL
#1 IN A TWO-ISSUE LIMITED SERIES
X-MEN
AND
ALPHA FLIGHT

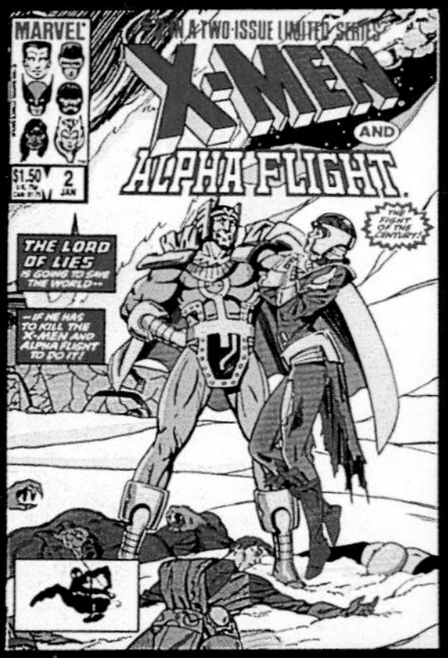
MARVEL
#2 IN A TWO-ISSUE LIMITED SERIES
X-MEN
AND
ALPHA FLIGHT
THE LORD OF LIES

2206.2 The X-Men and the Micronauts (1-4)

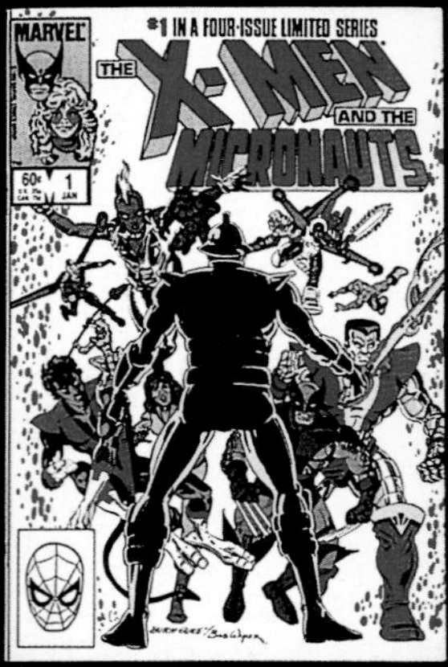
MARVEL
#1 IN A FOUR-ISSUE LIMITED SERIES
THE X-MEN
AND THE
MICRONAUTS

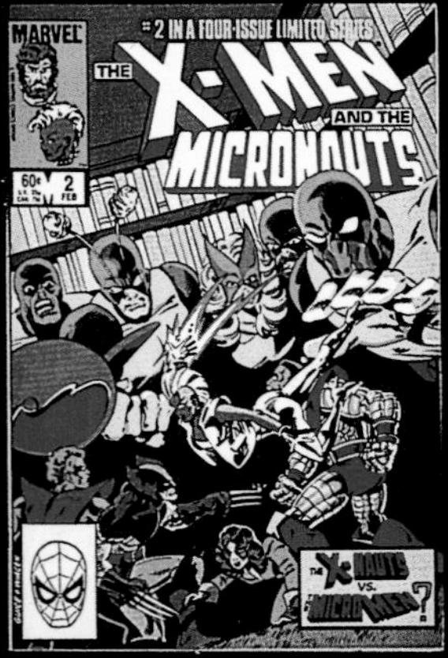
MARVEL
#2 IN A FOUR-ISSUE LIMITED SERIES
THE X-MEN
AND THE
MICRONAUTS

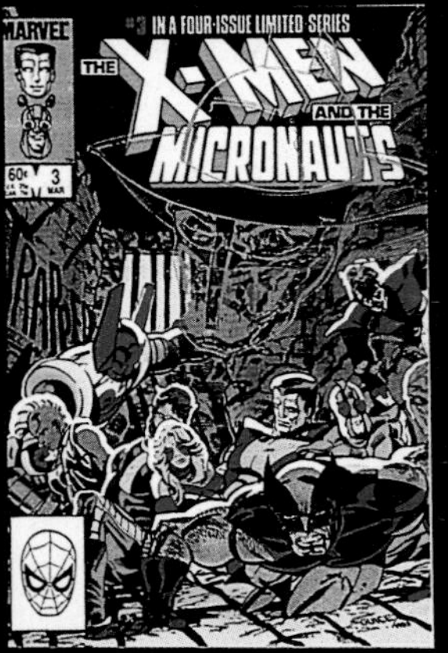
MARVEL
#3 IN A FOUR-ISSUE LIMITED SERIES
THE X-MEN
AND THE
MICRONAUTS

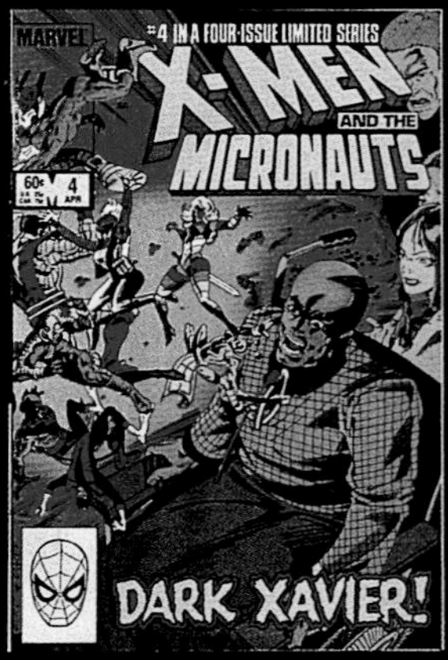
MARVEL
#4 IN A FOUR-ISSUE LIMITED SERIES
X-MEN
AND THE
MICRONAUTS
DARK XAVIER!

2206.3 X-Men Classics (1-3)

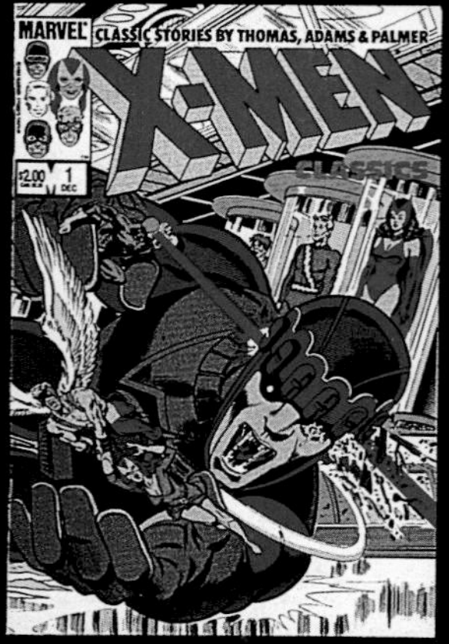
MARVEL
CLASSIC STORIES BY THOMAS, ADAMS & PALMER
X-MEN
CLASSICS

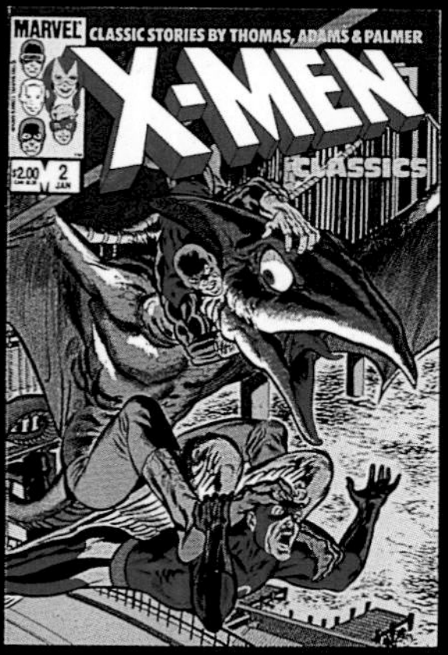
MARVEL
CLASSIC STORIES BY THOMAS, ADAMS & PALMER
X-MEN
CLASSICS

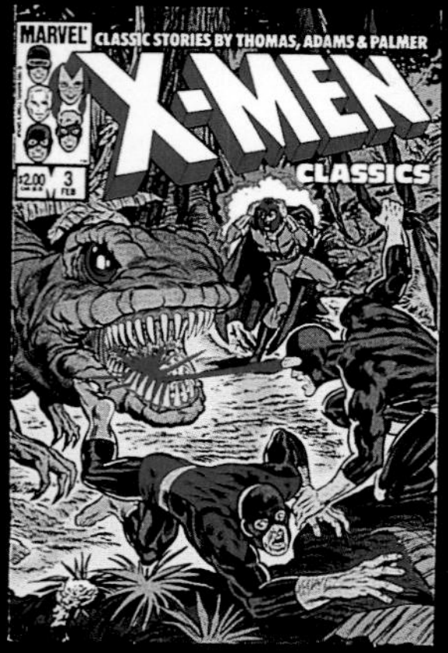
MARVEL
CLASSIC STORIES BY THOMAS, ADAMS & PALMER
X-MEN
CLASSICS

387.6 Classic X-Men (1-6)

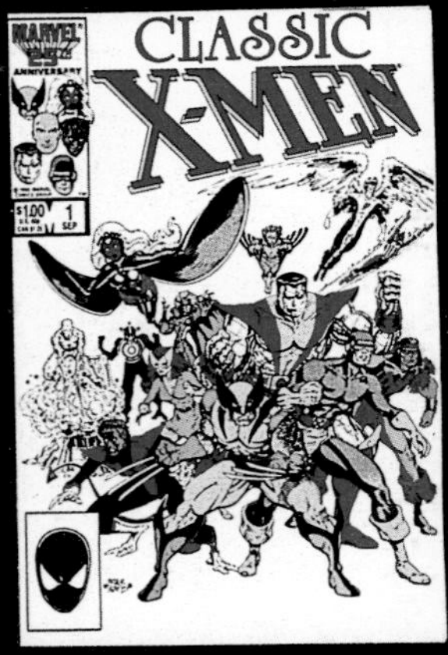
CLASSIC
X-MEN

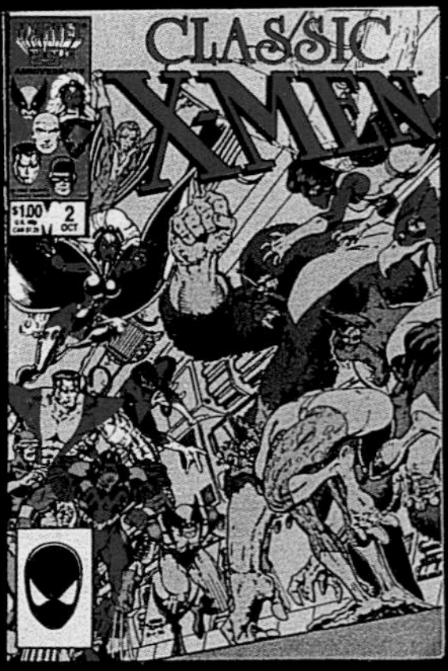
CLASSIC
X-MEN

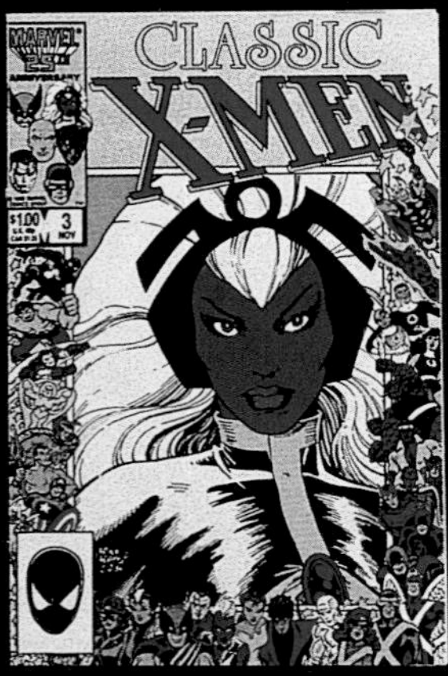
CLASSIC
X-MEN

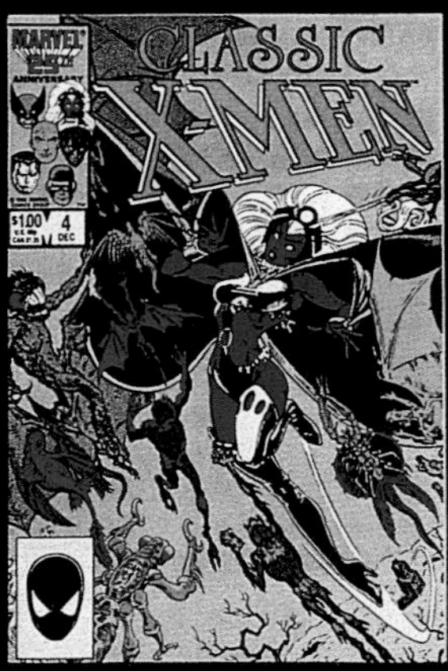
CLASSIC
X-MEN

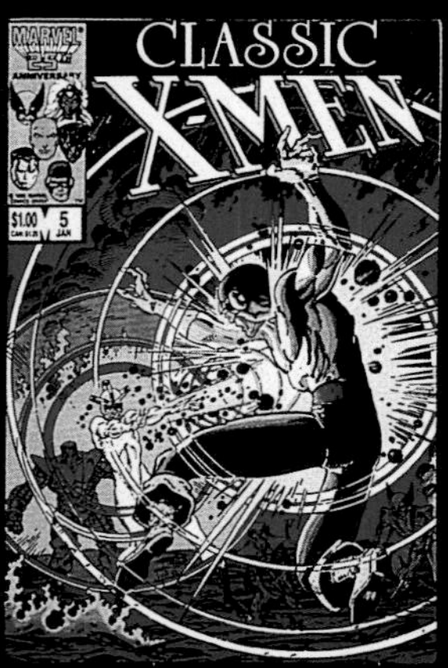
CLASSIC
X-MEN

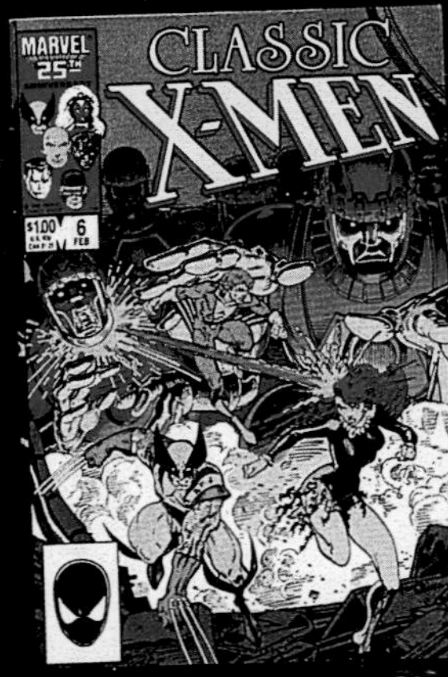
MARVEL
CLASSIC
X-MEN

2206.4 X-Men vs. the Avengers (1-4)

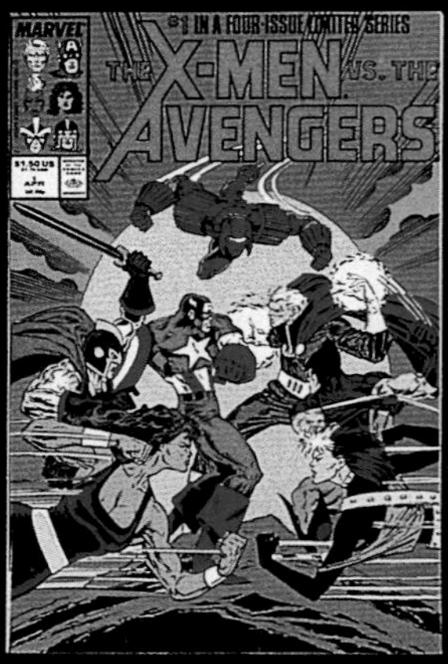
MARVEL
#1 IN A FOUR-ISSUE LIMITED SERIES
THE X-MEN VS. THE
AVENGERS

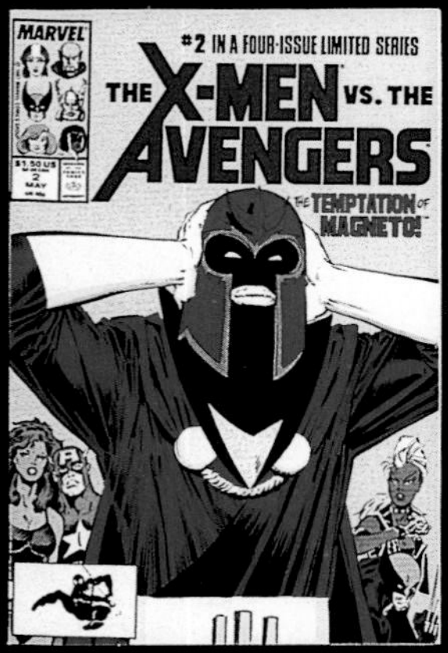
MARVEL
#2 IN A FOUR-ISSUE LIMITED SERIES
THE X-MEN VS. THE
AVENGERS
THE TEMPTATION OF MAGNETO!

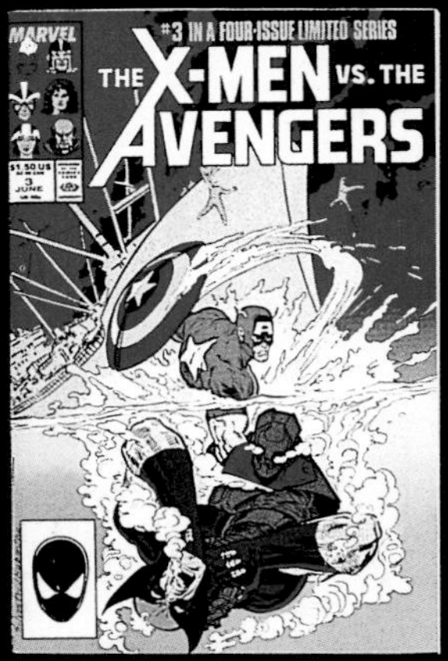
MARVEL
#3 IN A FOUR-ISSUE LIMITED SERIES
THE X-MEN VS. THE
AVENGERS

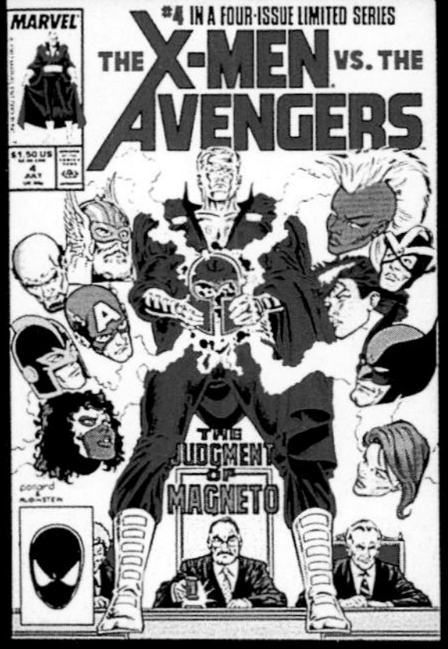
MARVEL
#4 IN A FOUR-ISSUE LIMITED SERIES
THE X-MEN VS. THE
AVENGERS
THE JUDGMENT OF MAGNETO

2206.5 X-Terminators (1-4)

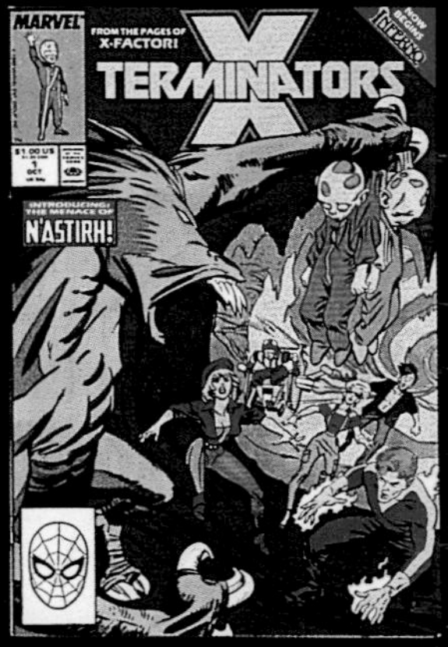
MARVEL
FROM THE PAGES OF X-FACTOR!
X
TERMINATORS
N'ASTIRH!

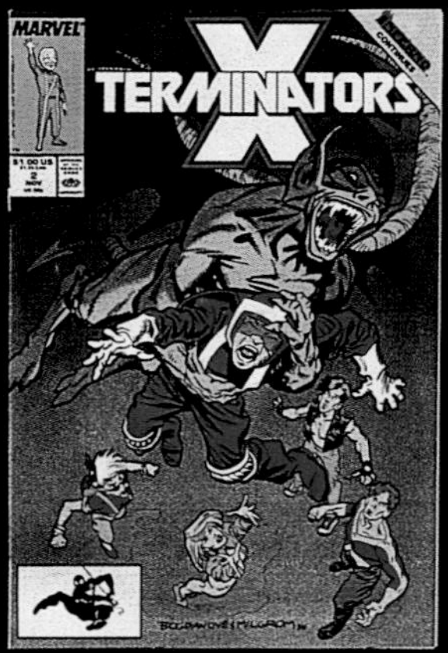
MARVEL
X
TERMINATORS

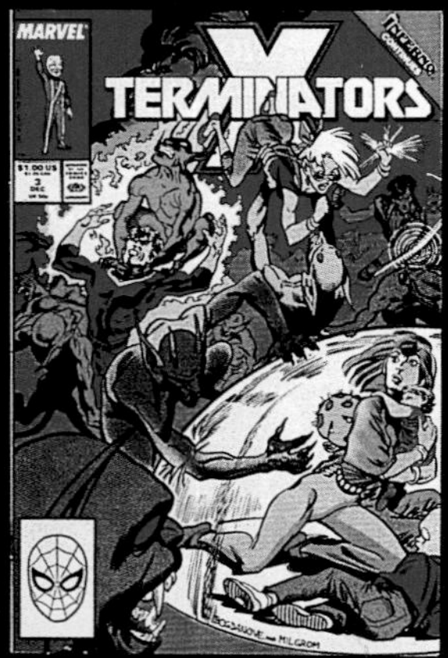
MARVEL
X
TERMINATORS

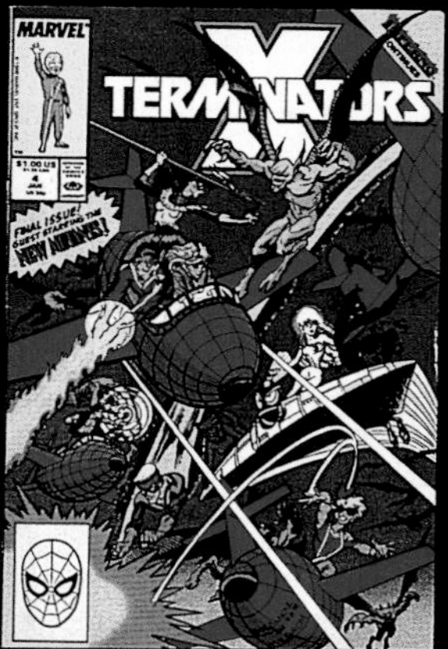
MARVEL
X
TERMINATORS

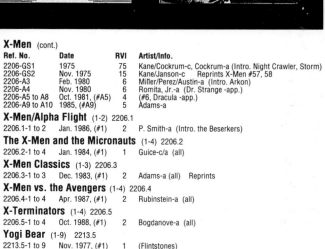

X-Men (cont.)

Ref. No.	Date	RVI	Artist/Info.
2206-GS1	1975	75	Kane/Cockrum-c, Cockrum-a (Intro. Night Crawler, Storm)
2206-GS2	Nov. 1975	15	Kane/Janson-c Reprints X-Men #57, 58
2206-A3	Feb. 1980	6	Miller/Perez/Austin-a (Intro. Arkon)
2206-A4	Nov. 1980	6	Romita, Jr.-a (Dr. Strange -app.)
2206-A5 to A8	Oct. 1981, (#A5)	4	(#6, Dracula -app.)
2206-A9 to A10	1985, (#A9)	5	Adams-a
X-Men/Alpha Flight (1-2) 2206.1			
2206.1-1 to 2	Jan. 1986, (#1)	2	P. Smith-a (Intro. the Beserkers)
The X-Men and the Micronauts (1-4) 2206.2			
2206.2-1 to 4	Jan. 1984, (#1)	1	Guice-c/a (all)
X-Men Classics (1-3) 2206.3			
2206.3-1 to 3	Dec. 1983, (#1)	2	Adams-a (all) Reprints
X-Men vs. the Avengers (1-4) 2206.4			
2206.4-1 to 4	Apr. 1987, (#1)	2	Rubinstein-a (all)
X-Terminators (1-4) 2206.5			
2206.5-1 to 4	Oct. 1988, (#1)	2	Bogdanove-a (all)
Yogi Bear (1-9) 2213.5			
2213.5-1 to 9	Nov. 1977, (#1)	1	(Flintstones)

Artist Index

The numbers listed in this index are Page Numbers where the artists names are written in the text of this book. The credited artists are pencillers and inkers. Regretably other contributors such as editors, authors, colorists, and letterers are not listed.

We always appreciate any additions or corrections regarding *any* artists during this time period.

Index

The numbers listed below are Page Numbers for the Marvel Title Runs actually illustrated. In some cases we alphabetically list other Marvel titles in text sections that are not illustrated.

In some cases Title runs are not in alphabetical order, but listed with companion runs, such as Captain America is illustrated together with Tales of Suspense.

For further information regarding the layout of Title runs, turn to the chapter entitled "Key".